THE LIBRARY

OF

LITERARY CRITICISM

OF

ENGLISH AND AMERICAN AUTHORS

VOLUME VIII
1891 - 1904

EDITED BY CHARLES WELLS MOULTON
ASSISTED BY A CORPS OF ABLE CONTRIBUTORS

GLOUCESTER, MASS.
PETER SMITH
1959

Copyright 1904
BY
THE MOULTON PUBLISHING COMPANY
Reprinted 1959
BY
PETER SMITH

To
William Isaac Fletcher, A. M.

INTRODUCTION.

AUTHORS AND AUTHORSHIP

The ink of the scholar is more sacred than the blood of the martyr.—MOHAMMED, 600? *Tribute to Reason.*

If I were a writer of books, I would compile a register, with a comment, of the various deaths of men; and it could not but be useful, for he who should teach men to die would at the same time teach them to live.—MONTAIGNE, MICHEL EYQUEM DE, 1571? *Essays, Book* I, *ch.* XIX.

He that commeth in print because he woulde be known, is like the foole that commeth into the Market because he woulde be seen.—LYLY, JOHN, 1579-80, *Euphues, The Anatomy of Wit, To the Gentlemen Readers.*

Write till your ink be dry; and with your tears
Moist it again; and frame some feeling line,
That may discover such integrity.
—SHAKESPEARE, WILLIAM, 1590-92, *Two Gentlemen of Verona, Act* III, *Sc.* 2.

Hoping that his name may deserve to appear not among the mercenary crew of false pretenders to learning, but the free and ingenious sort of such as evidently were born to study, and love learning for itself, not for lucre, or any other end than the service of God and truth, and perhaps that lasting fame and perpetuity of praise which God and good men have consented shall be the reward of those whose published labours advance the good of mankind.—MILTON, JOHN, 1644, *Areopagitica.*

A man starts upon a sudden, takes Pen, Ink and Paper, and without ever having had a thought of it before, resolves within himself he will write a Book; he has no Talent at Writing, but he wants fifty Guineas.—LA BRUYÈRE, JEAN DE, 1688, *The Characters or Manners of the Present Age, ch.* XV.

I profess writing news from the learned, as well as the busy world. As for my labours, which he is pleased to inquire after, if they can but wear one impertinence out of human life, destroy a single vice, or give a morning's cheerfulness to an honest mind, in short, if the world can be but one virtue the better, or in any degree less vicious, or receive from them the smallest addition to their innocent diversions, I shall not think my pains, or indeed my life, to have been spent in vain. —STEELE, SIR RICHARD, 1710, *The Tatler, No.* 89.

If writings are thus durable, and may pass from age to age through the whole course of time, how careful should an author be of committing anything to print that may corrupt posterity and poison the minds of men with vice and error! Writers of great talents who employed their parts in propagating immorality, and seasoning vicious sentiments with wit and humour, are to be looked upon as the pests of society, and the enemies of mankind. They leave books behind them (as it is said of those who die in distempers which breed an ill-will towards their own species) to scatter infection and destroy their posterity. They act the counterparts of a Confucius or a Socrates; and seem to have been sent into the world to deprave human nature and sink it into the condition of brutality.—ADDISON, JOSEPH, 1711, *The Spectator, No.* 166.

> Pride often guides the author's pen;
> Books as affected are as men;
> But he who studies nature's laws,
> From certain truth his maxims draws;
> And those, without our schools, suffice
> To make men moral, good and wise.

—GAY, JOHN, 1727-28, *The Shepherd and the Philosopher, Fables.*

An author! 'tis a venerable name!
How few deserve it, and what numbers claim!
Unbless'd with sense above their peers refined,
Who stand up dictators to mankind?
Nay, who dare shine, if not in virtue's cause?
That sole proprietor of just applause.
—YOUNG, EDWARD, 1730, *Two Epistles to Mr. Pope*.

If we look back into past times, we find innumerable names of authors once in high reputation, read perhaps by the beautiful, quoted by the witty, and commented on by the grave, but of whom we now know only that they existed. If we consider the distribution of literary fame in our own time, we shall find it a possession of very uncertain tenure; sometimes bestowed by a sudden caprice of the public, and again transferred to a new favorite, for no other reason than that he is new; sometimes refused to long labour and eminent desert, and sometimes granted to very slight pretensions; lost sometimes by security and negligence, and sometimes by too diligent endeavours, to retain it. A successful author is equally in danger of the diminution of his fame, whether he continues or ceases to write. The regard of the public is not to be kept but by tribute, and the remembrance of past service will quickly languish unless successive performances frequently revive it. Yet in every new attempt there is new hazard, and there are few who do not, at some unlucky time, injure their own characters by attempting to enlarge them. —JOHNSON, SAMUEL, 1750, *The Rambler*, No. 21.

Of all rewards, I grant, the most pleasing to a man of real merit is fame; but a polite age of all times is that in which scarcely any share of merit can acquire it. What numbers of fine writers in the latter empire of Rome, when refinement was carried to the highest pitch, have missed that fame and immortality which they had fondly arrogated to themselves! How many Greek authors, who wrote at the period when Constantinople was the refined mistress of the empire, now rest, either not printed, or not read, in the libraries of Europe! Those who came first, while either state as yet was barbarous, carried all the reputation away. Authors, as the age refined, became more numerous, and their numbers destroyed their fame. It is but natural, therefore, for the writer, when conscious that his works will not procure him fame hereafter, to endeavour to make them turn out to his temporal interest here. Whatever be the motives which induce men to write, whether avarice or fame, the country becomes most wise and happy in which they most serve for instructors.—GOLDSMITH, OLIVER, 1762, *A Citizen of the World*.

Writers, especially when they act in a body, and in one direction, have great influence on the public mind.—BURKE, EDMUND, 1790, *Reflections on the Revolution in France*.

Authors stand between the governors and the governed, and form the single organ of both. Those who govern a nation cannot at the same time enlighten the people, for the executive power is not empirical; and the governed cannot think, for they have no continuity of leisure.— DISRAELI, ISAAC, 1795–1818, *Literary Character of Men of Genius*, ch. xxv.

When, at the distance of more than half a century, Christianity was assaulted by a *Woolston*, a *Tindal*, and a *Morgan*, it was ably supported both by clergymen of the established church and writings among Protestant dissenters. The labours of a *Clarke* and a *Butler* were associated with those of a *Doddridge*, a *Leland*, and a *Lardner*, with such equal reputation and success as to make it evident that the intrinsic excellence of a religion needs not the aid of external appendages; but that, with or without a dowry, her charms are of sufficient power to fix and engage the heart.—HALL, ROBERT, 1800, *Modern Infidelity Considered, Preface*.

The society of dead authors has this advantage over that of the living: they never flatter us to our faces, nor slander us behind our backs, nor intrude upon our privacy, nor quit their shelves until we take them down. Besides, it is always easy to shut a book, but not quite so easy to get rid of a lettered coxcomb. Living authors, therefore, are usually bad companions: if they have not gained a character, they seek to do so by methods often ridiculous, always disgusting; and if they have established a character, they are silent, for fear of losing by their tongue what they have acquired by their pen: for many authors converse much more foolishly than Goldsmith who have never written half so well.—COLTON, CHARLES CALEB, 1820-22, *Lacon*.

But words are things, and a small drop of ink,
 Falling like dew, upon a thought produces
That which makes thousands, perhaps millions think.
—BYRON, LORD, 1821, *Don Juan, Canto* III, *st.* 88.

Just such is the feeling which a man of liberal education naturally entertains towards the great minds of former ages. The debt which he owes to them is incalculable. They have guided him to truth. They have filled his mind with noble and graceful images. They have stood by him in all vicissitudes, comforters in sorrow, nurses in sickness, companions in solitude. These friendships are exposed to no danger from the occurrences by which other attachments are weakened or dissolved. Time glides on; fortune is inconstant; tempers are soured; bonds which seemed indissoluble are daily sundered by interest, by emulation, or by caprice. But no such cause can affect the silent converse which we hold with the highest of human intellects. That placid intercourse is disturbed by no jealousies or resentments. These are the old friends who are never seen with new faces, who are the same in wealth and in poverty, in glory and in obscurity. With the dead there is no rivalry. In the dead there is no change. Plato is never sullen. Cervantes is never petulant. Demosthenes never comes unseasonably. Dante never stays too long. No difference of political opinion can alienate Cicero. No heresy can excite the horror of Bossuet. — MACAULAY, THOMAS BABINGTON, 1837, *Lord Bacon*.

Beneath the rule of men entirely great
The pen is mightier than the sword.
—LYTTON, SIR EDWARD LYTTON BULWER, 1838, *Richelieu, Act* II., *sc.* 2.

Write to the mind and heart, and let the ear
Glean after what it can.
—BAILEY, PHILIP JAMES, 1839, *Festus*.

Authors' lives in general are not uniform —they are strangely checquered by vicissitudes; and even were the outward circumstances uniform, the inward struggles must still be various.—LEWES, GEORGE HENRY, 1847, *The Spanish Drama, ch.* II.

Those works of fiction are worse than unprofitable that inculcate morality, with an exclusion of all reference to religious principle. This is obviously and notoriously the character of Miss Edgeworth's Moral Tales. And so entire and resolute is this exclusion, that it is maintained at the expense of what may be called poetical truth; it destroys, in many instances, the probability of the tale, and the naturalness of the characters. That Christianity does exist, every one must believe as an incontrovertible truth; nor can any one deny that, whether true or false, it does exercise—at least is supposed to exercise—an influence on the feelings and conduct of some of the believers in it. To represent, therefore, persons of various ages, sex, country, and station in life, as practising, on the most trying occasions, every kind of duty, and encountering every kind of danger, difficulty, and hardship, while none of them ever makes the least reference to a religious motive, is as decidedly at variance with reality—what is called in works of fiction *unnatural*—as it would be to represent Mahomet's enthusiastic followers as rushing into battle without any thought of his promised paradise. — WHATELY, RICHARD, 1856, *ed., Bacon's Essays.*

Unless a man can link his written thoughts with the everlasting wants of men, so that they shall draw from them as from wells, there is no more immortality to the thoughts and feelings of the soul than to the muscles and the bones.— BEECHER, HENRY WARD, 1858, *Oxford, Bodleian Library, Star Papers.*

Whatever an author puts between the two covers of his book is public property; whatever of himself he does not put there is his private property, as much as if he had never written a word.—DODGE, MARY ABIGAIL (GAIL HAMILTON), 1862, *Country Living and Country Thinking, Preface.*

The great and good do not die even in this world. Embalmed in books, their spirits walk abroad. The book is a living voice. It is an intellect to which one still listens.—SMILES, SAMUEL, 1871, *Character, ch.* x.

Nobody is interesting to all the world. An author who is spoken of as universally admired will find, if he is foolish enough to inquire, that there are not wanting intelligent persons who are indifferent to him, nor yet those who have a special emphatic dislike to him. If there were another Homer, there would be another Homeromastix. An author should know that the very characteristics which make him the object of admiration to many, and endear him to some among them, will render him an object of dislike to a certain number of individuals of equal, it may be of superior intelligence. Doubtless God never made a better berry than the strawberry, yet it is a poison to a considerable number of persons. There are those who dislike the fragrance of the water-lily, and those in whom the smell of a rose produces a series of those convulsions known as sneezes. He (or she) who ventures into authorship must expect to encounter occasional instances of just such antipathy, of which he and all that he does are the subjects. Let him take it patiently. What is thus out of accord with the temperament or the mood of his critic may not be blamable; nay, it may be excellent. But Zoilus does not like it or the writer,—the reason why he can not tell, perhaps, but he does not like either; and he is in his rights, and the author must sit still and let the critic play off his idiosyncrasies against his own.— HOLMES, OLIVER WENDELL, 1883, *An After-Breakfast Talk, Atlantic Monthly, vol* 51, *p.* 67.

It is almost superfluous to say that in the profession of literature the first requisite is ability to see, to feel, and to think, and a great part of this ability is education. Without education no one can expect to become a writer, and the more education the better, provided it be of the right sort. There are two objects to be attained by education. The first is knowledge, and the second is accuracy. Accuracy is the power of distinguishing the truth, and of expressing truth as it is. . . . The best school of writing is a newspaper office, with intelligence at the head. No other college is possible where the discipline of rhetoric, or taste, and of knowledge is so effectually applied. The first rule of good writing is to use always the simplest and plainest words. State the fact or express the point or principle which you desire to convey, so that every reader will understand it exactly as you intend it to be understood. Have only one idea in view at a time, and be sure that you have expressed it clearly and intelligently before you go to another. Above all, avoid affectation, and the worst affectation of all is the affectation of wit. The highest intellectual gift is the power to know the truth. Next to this is judgment; next, wit; and the greatest of all intellectual qualities is imagination. The writer who possesses imagination may become immortal.—DANA, CHARLES A., 1888, *Advice to Young Writers, The Writer, vol. 2, pp. 106, 107.*

It is by the number and charm of the individualities which it contains that the literature of any country gains distinction. We turn anywhither to know men. The best way to foster literature, if it may be fostered, is to cultivate the author himself —a plant of such delicate and precarious growth that special soils are needed to produce him in his full perfection. The conditions which foster individuality are those which foster simplicity, thought and action from self out, naturalness, and spontaneity. What are these conditions? In the first place, a certain helpful ignorance. It is best for the author to be born away from literary centers, or to be excluded from their ruling set if he be born in them. It is best that he start out with his thinking, not knowing how much has been thought and said about everything. A certain amount of ignorance will insure his sincerity, will increase his boldness and shelter his genuineness, which is his hope of power. Not ignorance of life, but life may be learned in any neighborhood;—not ignorance of the greater laws which govern human affairs, but they may be learned without a library of historians and commentators, by imaginative sens , by seeing better than by reading;—not ignorance of the infinitudes of human circumstance, but knowledge of these may come to a man without the intervention of universities;—not ignorance of one's self and of one's neighbor, but innocence of the sophistications of learning, its research without love, its knowledge without inspiration, its method without grace; freedom from its shame at trying to know many things as well as from its pride of trying to know but one thing; ignorance of that faith in small confounding facts which is contempt for large reassuring principles.—WILSON, WOODROW, 1891, *The Author Himself, Atlantic Monthly, vol. 68, p. 408.*

This sudden display of nervousness on the part of authors is perhaps partly due to their unreasonable confusion of the Reviewers with the Readers. The great mass of criticism is delivered *vivâ voce* and never appears in print at all. This spoken criticism is of far greater importance than printed criticism. It is repeated again and again, in all sorts of places, on hundreds of occasions, and cannot fail to make dints in people's minds, whereas the current printed criticism of the week runs lightly off the surface. "Press notices," as they are called, have no longer "boodle" in them, if I may use a word the genius of Mr. Stevenson has already consecrated for all delightful use. The pen may, in peaceful times, be mightier than the sword, but in this matter of criticism of our contemporaries the tongue is mightier than the pen. Authors should remember this. Mr. Buchanan's temper would be sweeter than it is had he done so. Few authors fare better in ordinary talk than Mr. Buchanan, to whom justice as a poet, a novelist, and a dramatist is always done. I presume from his stormy outcry that he is not a favourite with certain critics who publish, but what harm have they been able to do to him? You find him everywhere: in the cheerful playhouse, in the illustrated papers, on posters, in libraries. You can't have everybody on your side. Shakespeare had a contemporary who used to sneer at him in print.—BIRRELL, AUGUSTINE, 1892, *Authors and Critics, New Review, vol. 6, p. 99.*

An author, after all, is a man and, as all men ought to be, a work-man. His power comes to this, that he is man with a special capacity for exciting sympathy. That he should be a good work-man, therefore, goes without saying; and it follows that he should have a sense of responsibility in whatever department he undertakes; that he should not bestow his advice upon us without qualifying himself to be a competent adviser; nor write philosophical speculation without serious study of philosophy; nor, if possible, produce poetry or even fiction without filling his mind by observation or training it by sympathy with the great movements of thought which are shaping the world in which we live. It is a sort of paradox which can not be avoided, that we must warn a man that one condition of all good work is that it should be spontaneous and yet tell him that it should be directed to make men better and happier. It seems to be saying that the conscious pursuit of a given end would be inconsistent with the attainment of the end. Yet I believe that this is a paradox which can be achieved in practice, on the simple condition of a reasonable modesty. The author, that is, should not listen to those who would exaggerate the importance of his work. The world can get on very well without it; and even the greatest men are far more the product than the producers of the intellectual surroundings. The acceptance of that truth—I hold it to be a truth—will help to keep in check the exaggerated estimate of the importance of making a noise in the world which is our besetting sin, and help to make a regulating principle of what is a theoretical belief, that a man who is doing honestly good work in any department, whether under the eyes of a multitude or of a few, will be happiest if he can learn to take pleasure in doing it thoroughly rather than in advertising it widely. And, finally, with that conviction we shall be less liable to the common error of an author who grumbles at his want of success, and becomes morbid and irritable and inclined to lower his standard, when in reality he ought to remember that he is as unreasonable as a marksman who should complain of the target for keeping out of the line of fire. "It is my own fault" is often a bitter reflection, but a bitter may be a very wholesome tonic.—STEPHEN, SIR LESLIE, 1894, *The Duties of Authors, National Review*, vol. 23, p. 338.

Time was—and it is not so very long ago—that an author, when he sat down to write a book, felt as if he were approaching a devout task. He felt as if the pen were a sacred instrument: the book a gospel. He lived a sane life: that is, he feared God and slept eight hours every night,—and when a man does those two things he *is* sane and very far removed from pessimism.—BOK, EDWARD W., 1895, *The Modern Literary Kings, The Forum*, vol. 20, p. 334.

Every great writer is a friend of all the world, one whom we may come to know, who can aid us with solace and counsel and entertainment. In his books he has revealed himself, and in them we make his acquaintance. This is the purpose of serious reading. Not merely to be delighted with beauty of style; not merely to be informed and made wise; not merely to be encouraged and ennobled in spirit; but to receive an impetus in all these directions. Such is the object of culture. To know a good book is to know a good man. To be influenced by a trivial, or ignoble, or false book, is to associate with an unworthy companion, and to suffer the inevitable detriment. For the book, like the man, must be so true that it convinces our reason and satisfies our curiosity; it must be so beautiful that it fascinates and delights our taste; it must be so spirited and right-minded that it enlists our best sympathy and stirs our more humane emotions. A good book, like a good comrade, is one that leaves us happier or better off in any way for having known it. A bad book is one that leaves us the poorer, either by confusing our reason with what is not true, or by debasing our taste with what is ugly, or by offending our spirit with what is evil.—CARMAN, BLISS, 1903, *The Man Behind the Book, Literary World*, vol. 34, p. 31.

CONTENTS.

		PAGE.
AIRY, SIR GEORGE BIDDELL,	1801—1892	182
ARGYLL, DUKE OF,	1823—1900	433
ARNOLD, SIR EDWIN	1832—1904	501
BAILEY, PHILIP JAMES,	1816—1902	459
BANCROFT, GEORGE,	1800—1891	54
BESANT, SIR WALTER	1836—1901	449
BLACKIE, JOHN STUART,	1809—1895	304
BLACK, WILLIAM,	1841—1898	393
BLACKMORE, RICHARD DODDRIDGE,	1825—1900	430
BROOKS, PHILLIPS,	1835—1893	226
BUCHANAN, ROBERT,	1841—1901	445
BUNNER, HENRY CUYLER	1855—1896	359
CAMPBELL, GEORGE JOHN DOUGLAS,	1823—1900	433
CARROLL, LEWIS	1832—1898	396
CREIGHTON, MANDELL,	1843—1901	453
CURTIS, GEORGE WILLIAM,	1824—1892	184
DE VERE, AUBREY THOMAS,	1814—1902	462
DODGE, MARY ABIGAL,	1838—1896	360
DODGSON, CHARLES LUTWIGE,	1832—1898	396
DRUMMOND, HENRY,	1851—1897	362
DUMAURIER, GEORGE LOUIS PALMELLA BUSSON,	1834—1896	343
EDWARDS, AMELIA BLANDFORD,	1831—1892	174
EGGLESTON, EDWARD,	1837—1902	475
FIELD, EUGENE,	1850—1895	314
FISKE, JOHN,	1842—1901	455
FREEMAN, EDWARD AUGUSTUS,	1823—1892	153
FROUDE, JAMES ANTHONY,	1818—1894	254
GARDINER, SAMUEL RAWSON	1829—1902	465
GEORGE, HENRY	1839—1897	378
GLADSTONE, WILLIAM EWART,	1809—1898	383
HAMERTON, PHILIP GILBERT,	1834—1894	280
HAMILTON, GAIL,	1838—1896	360
HARTE, FRANCIS BRET,	1837—1902	466

CONTENTS

HENLEY, WILLIAM ERNEST	1849—1903	491
HOLMES, OLIVER WENDELL,	1809—1894	285
HUGHES, THOMAS,	1823—1896	346
HUTTON, RICHARD HOLT,	1826—1897	374
HUXLEY, THOMAS HENRY	1825—1896	320
INGELOW, JEAN,	1820—1897	376
INGERSOLL, ROBERT GREEN	1833—1899	401
JOWETT, BENJAMIN,	1817—1893	207
KEMBLE, FRANCES ANN,	1809—1893	213
KINGLAKE, ALEXANDER WILLIAM,	1809—1891	49
LECKY, WILLIAM EDWARD HARTPOLE,	1838—1903	437
LOCKER-LAMPSON, FREDERICK,	1821—1895	311
LOWELL, JAMES RUSSELL,	1819—1891	17
LYTTON, EDWARD ROBERT BULWER,	1831—1891	43
MANNING, HENRY EDWARD,	1807—1892	162
MARTINEAU, JAMES	1805—1900	425
MCCOSH, JAMES,	1811—1894	300
MELVILLE, HERMAN,	1819—1891	62
MEREDITH, OWEN,	1831—1891	43
MERIVALE, CHARLES,	1808—1893	217
MILLER, CINCINNATUS HINER,	1841—1903	498
MILLER, JOAQUIN,	1841—1903	498
MORRIS, WILLIAM,	1834—1896	329
MÜLLER, FRIEDRICH MAX,	1823—1900	435
NEWMAN, FRANCIS WILLIAM,	1805—1897	370
OLIPHANT, MARGARET O. W.,	1828—1897	366
OWEN, SIR RICHARD,	1804—1892	170
PALGRAVE, FRANCIS TURNER,	1824—1897	371
PARKMAN, FRANCIS,	1823—1893	218
PARSONS, THOMAS WILLIAM,	1819—1892	192
PATER, WALTER HORATIO	1838—1894	275
PATMORE, COVENTRY K. D.,	1823—1896	339
ROMANES, GEORGE JOHN,	1848—1894	283
ROSSETTI, CHRISTINA GEORGINA,	1830—1894	268
RUSKIN, JOHN,	1819—1900	404
SEELEY, SIR JOHN ROBERT,	1834—1895	307
SPENCER, HERBERT,	1820—1903	477
SPURGEON, CHARLES HADDON,	1834—1892	178
STANLEY, SIR HENRY MORTON,	1841—1904	506
STEPHEN, SIR LESLIE,	1832—1904	510
STEVENSON, ROBERT LOUIS,	1850—1894	234

STOCKTON, FRANCIS RICHARD,	. . .	1834—1902	472
STODDARD, RICHARD HENRY,	. . . .	1825—1903	494
STORY, WILLIAM WETMORE,	. . . .	1819—1895	318
STOWE, HARRIET ELIZABETH BEECHER,	.	1821—1896	349
STUBBS, WILLIAM, ...		1825—1901	451
SYMONDS, JOHN ADDINGTON,	. . . .	1840—1893	201
TENNYSON, ALFRED LORD, .	. . . .	1809—1892	64
TENNYSON, FREDERICK,	. . . . .	1807—1898	399
TYNDALL, JOHN		1820—1893	194
WARNER, CHARLES DUDLEY,	. . . .	1829—1900	440
WHITMAN, WALT, ...		1819—1892	129
WHITNEY, WILLIAM DWIGHT,	. . . .	1827—1894	302
WHITTIER, JOHN GREENLEAF, .	. . .	1807—1892	111

ENGRAVINGS.

	PAGE.
ARNOLD, SIR EDWIN, ...	405
Engraving from a Photogragh.	
BAILEY, PHILIP JAMES, ...	459
Engraving from a Plaster Bust by Alfred Toft.	
BANCROFT, GEORGE, ...	55
Engraved by T. Johnson, Drawn by J. W. Alexander.	
BESANT, SIR WALTER, ...	445
Engraving from a Photograph by Walery.	
BLACK, WILLIAM, ...	393
Engraving from a Photograph.	
BLACKIE, JOHN STUART, ...	393
Engraving from a Photograph by D. Macara.	
BROOKS, PHILLIPS, ...	17
Engraving from a Photograph by H. G. Smith.	
BUCHANAN, ROBERT, ...	445
Engraving from a Photograph by J. C. Armytage.	
CURTIS, GEORGE WILLIAM, ...	55
Engraving by W. G. Jackman, from a Photograph by Brady.	
DEVERE, AUBREY THOMAS, ...	459
Engraving from a copy by F. Hollyer.	
DU MAURIER, GEORGE, ...	329
Engraving from a Photograph.	
FREEMAN, EDWARD AUGUSTUS, ...	163
Engraving by Walker and Boutall, from a Photograph by Hills and Saunders.	
FROUDE, JAMES ANTHONY, ...	255
Engraving from an Etching by H. B. Hall.	
GEORGE, HENRY, ...	383
Engraving from a Photograph.	
GLADSTONE, WILLIAM EWART, ...	383
Engraving by Walker and Cockerell, from a Photograph by the London Stereoscopic Co.	
HAMERTON, PHILIP GILBERT, ...	255
Engraving from a Photograph by A. H. Palmer.	
HARTE, FRANCIS BRET, ...	285
Engraving by George E. Perine, from a Photograph by Sarony.	
HOLMES, OLIVER WENDELL, ...	285
Engraving by New York Photogravure Co., from a Photograph by Notman.	
HUXLEY, THOMAS HENRY, ...	321
Engraving by Swan Electric Engraving Co., from a Portrait by Hon. John Collier.	
KINGLAKE, ALEXANDER WILLIAM, ...	43
Engraving from a Photograph by Elliott and Fry.	
LOWELL, JAMES RUSSELL, ...	17
Engraving from a Photograph.	
LYTTON, EDWARD ROBERT BULWER EARL, ...	43
Engraving from a Photograph.	
MCCOSH, JAMES, ...	219
Engraving from a Photograph.	
MANNING, HENRY EDWARD, ...	163
Engraving from a Photograph by Elliott and Fry.	
MARTINEAU, JAMES	477
Engraving by Hollyer, from a Painting by Watts.	

ENGRAVINGS

		PAGE.
MORRIS, WILLIAM,		329

Engraving by Walker and Boutall, from a Photograph by F. Hollyer.

MÜLLER, FRIEDRICH MAX, ... 321
Engraving by Swan Electric Engraving Co., from a Photograph by London Stereoscopic Co.

PARKMAN, FRANCIS, ... 219
Engraving by J. J. Cade.

RUSKIN, JOHN, ... 405
Engraving from a Photograph, 1882.

SEELEY, SIR JOHN ROBERT, ... 65
Engraving by Walter L. Colls, from a Photograph by Elliott and Fry.

SPENCER, HERBERT, ... 477
Engraving by George E. Perine.

STEVENSON, ROBERT LOUIS, ... 235
Re-drawn by T. Blake Wirgman from a charcoal drawing by Mrs. Stevenson.

STOCKTON, FRANCIS RICHARD, ... 441
Engraving from a Photograph.

STODDARD, RICHARD HENRY, ... 129
Engraving by Kruell.

STOWE, HARRIET ELIZABETH BEECHER, ... 111
Engraving from the Original Painting by Chappel.

SYMONDS, JOHN ADDINGTON, ... 235
Engraving from a Photo-Etching by Walter L. Colls, 1886.

TENNYSON, ALFRED LORD, ... 65
Engraving by Walker and Boutall, from a Painting by G. F. Watts, R. A., 1859.

WARNER, CHARLES DUDLEY, ... 441
Engraving by Harley.

WHITMAN, WALT, ... 129
Engraving from a Pen-and-Ink sketch by Frank Fowler.

WHITTIER, JOHN GREENLEAF, ... 111
Engraving from an Etching.

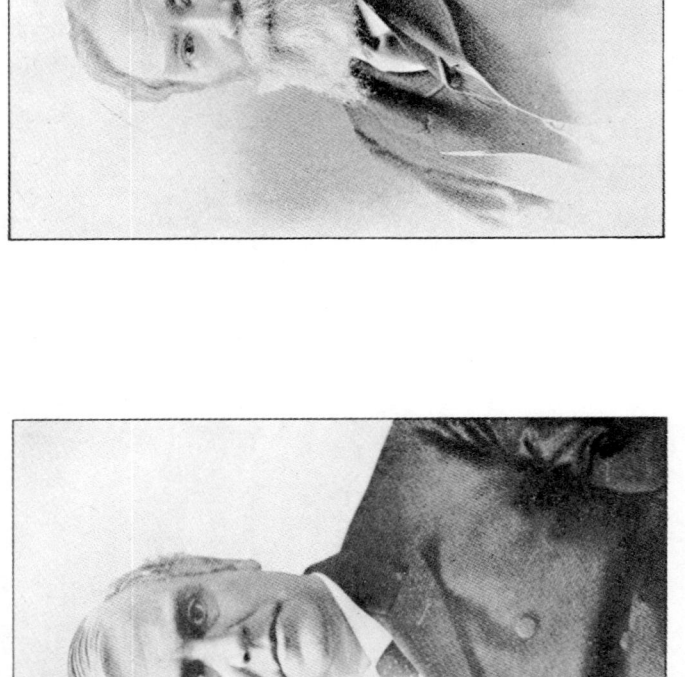

PHILLIPS BROOKS

Engraving from a Photograph by H. G. Smith.

JAMES RUSSELL LOWELL

Engraving from a Photograph.

The Library of Literary Criticism

of

English and American Authors

VOLUME VIII

James Russell Lowell
1819–1891

Born, at Cambridge, Mass., 22 Feb. 1819. Early education with tutor. To Harvard Univ., 1834; B. A., 1838; LL. B., 1840. Called to Bar, 1840. Soon devoted himself to literature. Married (i) Maria White, 26 Dec. 1844. Active in support of Abolition of Slavery. Contrib. "Biglow Papers" to "Boston Courier," 1846-48. Part editor of "The Pioneer," 1843. Corresponding editor of "National Anti-Slavery Standard," 1848. Contrib. to "Dial," "Democratic Rev.," "Mass. Quarterly Rev.;" to "Putnam's Monthly" from 1853. Visit to Europe, 1851–52. Wife died, 1853. Prof. of Mod. Languages, Harvard, Jan. 1855. Married (ii) Frances Dunlap, Sept. 1857. Edited "Atlantic Monthly" from 1857-62; part editor of "North American Rev.," 1863–72. Visit to Europe, 1872–75. Hon. D. C. L., Oxford, 18 June 1873. Hon. LL. D., Camb., 1874. U. S. A. Ambassador in Madrid, 1877–80; in London, 1880–85. Hon. LL. D., Edinburgh, 1884. Hon. LL. D., Harvard, St. Andrews, and Bologna. Returned to America, 1885. Died, 12 Aug. 1891. *Works:* "Class Poem," 1838; "A Year's Life," 1841; "Poems," 1844 (3rd edn. same year); "The Vision of Sir Launfal," 1845; "Conversations on Some of the Old Poets," 1845; "Reader! Walk up at Once! . . . A Fable for Critics" (anon.), 1848; "The Biglow Papers" (anon.), 1st series, 1848; 2nd series, 1867; "Poems" (2 vols.), 1849; "Poetical Works" (2 vols.), 1858; "Mason and Slidell," 1862; "Fireside Travels," 1864; "The President's Policy," 1864; "Ode recited at the Commemoration of the Living and Dead Soldiers of Harvard University," 1865; "Under the Willows," 1869 [1868]; "My Study Windows," 1870; "The Cathedral," 1870; "Among my Books," 1st series, 1870; 2nd series, 1876; "The Courtier," 1874; "Three Memorial Poems," 1876; "Favourite Poems," 1877; "A Moosehead Journal," 1877; "Works" (5 vols.), 1881; "Democracy, and Other Addresses," 1887; "Richard III. and the Primrose Criticism," 1887; "Heartsease and Rue," 1888; "Political Essays," 1888; "Address" [to American Mod. Language Soc.] 1890. *Posthumous:* "Last Literary Essays and Addresses," ed. by C. E. Norton, 1891; "The Old English Dramatists," 1892; "Letters," ed. by C. E. Norton, 1895 [1894]; "Last Poems," ed. by C. E. Norton, 1895. He *edited:* Keats' Poems, 1854; Shelley's Poems, 1875. *Collected Works:* in 10 vols., 1890–91.—SHARP, R. FARQUHARSON, 1897, *A Dictionary of English Authors,* p. 174.

PERSONAL

Among all the authors whose homes are noticed in this series, Lowell is the only one who has the fortune to reside in the house in which he was born. It is a happiness which few Americans of mature age can know. But Lowell has been peculiarly happy in his domestic relations; Nature has endowed him with a vigorous constitution and a healthy and happy temperament; and, but for the loss of his three children, the youngest of whom, his only boy, died recently in Rome, there would have been fewer shadows on his path than have fallen to the lot of most other poets. A nature like his can make its own sunshine, and find an oasis in every desert; yet it was a rare fortune that he found himself in such a home as his imagination would have created for him, if he had been cast homeless upon the world. He loves to throw a purple light over the familiar scene, and to invest it with a superfluousness of grateful gilding.—BRIGGS, CHARLES F., 1853-96, *Homes of American Authors*, ed., *Hubbard*, p. 140.

I have now been a week at Cambridge with the Lowells; they will have me stay, and I am quite willing to stay, because I am well off to my heart's content in this excellent and agreeable home. The house and a small quantity of land which surrounds it belong to the father of the poet, Dr. Lowell, a handsome old man, universally beloved and respected, and the oldest minister in Massachusetts. The whole family assembles every day for morning and evening prayers around the venerable old man, and he it is who blesses every meal. With him live his youngest son, the poet, and his wife; such a handsome and happy young couple as one can hardly imagine. He is full of life and youthful ardor; she, as gentle, as delicate, and as fair as a lily, and one of the most lovable women that I have seen in this country, because her beauty is full of soul and grace, as is everything which she does or says. The young couple belong to the class of those of whom one can be quite sure; one could not for an hour, nay, not for half an hour, be doubtful of them. She, like him, has a poetical tendency, and has also written, anonymously, some poems, remarkable for their deep and tender feeling, especially maternal, but her mind has more philosophical depth than his. Singularly enough, I did not discern in him that deeply earnest spirit which charmed me in many of his poems. He seems to me occasionally to be brilliant, witty, gay, especially in the evening, when he has what he calls his "evening fever," and his talk is then like an incessant play of fireworks. I find him very agreeable and amiable; he seems to have many friends, mostly young men. As one of his merits, I reckon his being so fascinated by his little wife, because I am so myself. There is a trace of beauty and taste in everything she touches, whether of mind or body; and above all, she beautifies life.—BREMER, FREDRIKA, 1853, *Homes in the New World*, p. 135.

In person Lowell is of medium height, rather slender, but sinewy and active. His movements are deliberate rather than impulsive, indicating what athletes call staying qualities. His hair at maturity was dark auburn or ruddy chestnut in color, and his full beard rather lighter and more glowing in tint. . . . Lowell's eyes in repose have clear blue and gray tones, with minute dark mottlings. In expression they are strongly indicative of his moods. When fixed upon study, or while listening to serious discourse, they are grave and penetrating; in ordinary conversation they are bright and cheery; in moments of excitement they have a wonderful lustre. Nothing could be finer than his facial expression while telling a story or tossing a repartee. The features are alive with intelligence; and eyes, looks, and voice appear to be working up dazzling effects in concert, like the finished artists of the Comédie Française.—UNDERWOOD, FRANCIS H., 1882, *James Russell Lowell, a Biographical Sketch*, p. 150.

There is a truly diverting *gaucherie*, an unsurpassable left-handness, in the compliments which a full five-sixths of Mr. Lowell's admirers in English society have been almost avowedly paying to him. They have most of them a certain acquaintance, not with his works—for in that respect a hackneyed gnome or two of Birdofredum Sawin's constitutes their whole equipment—but with the high estimation in which he is held by all competent English critics who really are familiar with Mr. Lowell's writings, serious as well as comic, prose as well as verse; and hearing him spoken of by these authorities with "for all the world, as much respect as if he were an Englishman," they ran at once into an excess of that sort of admiration which loses all its flattering quality in disclosing too large and obvious an admixture of surprise. The attitude of these foolish people towards this veteran man of letters, this highly-trained critic and most finished literary artist, would really almost remind one of the demeanor of some simple but unlettered father towards a clever son. —TRAILL, HENRY DUFF, 1885, *Mr. J. R. Lowell*, *Fortnightly Review*, vol. 44, p. 82.

Lowell has conferred such honors upon his country that all Americans will gladly unite in the "Well Done" that greets him, from every quarter, on his return to his home.—HAYES, RUTHERFORD B., 1885, *A Welcome to Lowell, Literary World, vol.* 16, *p.* 221.

I know of no instance, ancient or modern, of an equal combination of poetical power and eminence with the successful administration of high national and political trusts. He has delighted and honored us, and we honor ourselves in honoring him. —HOPKINS, MARK, 1885, *A Welcome to Lowell, Literary World, vol.* 16, *p.* 219.

As a conversationalist Mr. Lowell is unrivalled. His wit is apparently inexhaustible, and irradiates his whole conversation, as it does all his writing except his serious poetry. His "Fireside Travels" was pronounced by Bryant the wittiest book ever written; and it is not more witty than much of his conversation. The brilliancy of his conversation and the charm of his manners unite to make him one of the most fascinating companions in the world; and this charm is felt by all who come in contact with the man, and is not a thing reserved for his more favored companions. One who has witnessed an encounter of wit between Lowell and Dr. Holmes has witnessed one of the finest exhibitions of mental pyrotechnics of the day. His reading has been wide and varied, and he has all his resources at command. His observation of men and things has also been keen, and every variety of anecdote and illustration come forth from apparently inexhaustible sources as the needs of the moment demand.—GRISWOLD, HATTIE TYNG, 1886, *Home Life of Great Authors, p.* 270.

The attachment of its owner to these "paternal acres" is sufficient to explain why when others left Cambridge in summer—and then it is as quiet as Pisa—he still found it "good enough country" for him; but besides this affection for the soil, the landscape itself has a charm that would content a poet. To the rear of this room, or rather of its chimney, for there was no partition, was another, whose windows showed the grove and shrubbery at the back toward the hill; and this view was perhaps the more peaceful. Here in these two rooms were the usual furnishings of a scholar's study—tables and easy-chairs, pictures and pipes, the whole lending itself to an effect of lightness and simplicity, with the straw-matting islanded with books and (especially in the further room) strewn with scholar's litter, from the midst of which one day the poet, in search of "what might be there," drew from nearly under my feet the manuscript of Clough's "Amours de Voyage." The books filled the shelves upon the wall everywhere, and a library more distinctly gathered for the mere love of literature is not to be found. It is not large as libraries go—some four thousand volumes. To tell its treasures would be to catalogue the best works of man in many languages.—WOODBERRY, GEORGE EDWARD, 1886, *Authors at Home, James Russell Lowell at Elmwood, The Critic, vol.* 8, *p.* 151.

Lowell entered Harvard in his sixteenth year, and he has said of himself that he read everything except the text-books prescribed by the Faculty. He was graduated in the class of 1838, and then entered the Law School, intending, like Oliver Wendell Holmes, to become a lawyer. He even went so far as to open a law office in Boston, but it is more than suspected that one of his early attempts at fiction, bearing the title of "My First Client," referred to an entirely imaginary person. "The old melodious lays" were still more fascinating to him than the law-books bound up in yellow sheepskin, and his circumstances were so easy that he was not forced to continue work that was distasteful to him. He published a little book of verse, and when he was twenty-four he started a magazine; but, though neither the book nor the magazine met with success, he soon afterward proved that by the closing of the little office and Blackstone's "Commentaries," literature had gained more than law had lost.—RIDEING, WILLIAM H., 1887, *The Boyhood of Living Writers, p.* 160.

This singer whom we long have held so dear,
  Was Nature's darling, shapely, strong, and fair;
Of keenest wit, of judgment crystal-clear,
  Easy of converse, courteous, debonair.
. . . .
Peace to thy slumber in the forest shade,
  Poet and patriot, every gift was thine;
Thy name shall live while summers bloom and fade,
  And grateful Memory guard thy leafy shrine.
—HOLMES, OLIVER WENDELL, 1891, *James Russell Lowell, Before the Curfew.*

Of all the literary diplomats whom the United States have honored themselves by sending out to represent them, none has ever enjoyed a more brilliant reception. The services of the American minister were in constant demand upon occasions requiring literary or commemorative addresses. He responded with the best efforts of a singularly cultivated and astonishingly fertile mind; and America was proud of an envoy who with so much dignity and so obvious success represented not only her government, but the highest achievements of her civilization.—JAMESON, J. F., 1891, *Lowell and Public Affairs, Review of Reviews, American Ed., vol. 4, p.* 290.

So in her arms did Mother Nature fold
Her poet, whispering what of wild and sweet
Into his ear—the state-affairs of birds,
The lore of dawn and sunset, what the wind
Said in the tree-tops—fine, unfathomed things
Henceforth to turn to music in his brain;
A various music, now like notes of flutes,
And now like blasts of trumpets blown in wars.
Later he paced this leafy academe
A Student, drinking from Greek chalices
The ripened vintage of the antique world.
And here to him came love, and love's dear loss;
Here honors came, the deep applause of men
Touched to the heart by some swift-winged word
That from his own full heart took eager flight—
Some strain of piercing sweetness or rebuke,
For underneath his gentle nature flamed
A noble scorn for all ignoble deed,
Himself a bondman till all men were free.
—ALDRICH, THOMAS BAILEY, 1891, *Elmwood, Unguarded Gates and Other Poems, p.* 20.

In courage, in truthfulness, in everything he was the type of the Puritan idea in its most bracing expression, as Hawthorne (a man of rarer and finer genius) is a type of fervid Puritanism on its most unhealthy side. His courage, his honesty, his proud uncompromising independence, were all his own, but Puritanism fostered them. With all his love of England, America did not hold a more loyal son than he. In her glorious destiny he had a faith as strong as it was wise. Though for many years America has been peculiarly happy in the ministers she has sent to St. James's, never did she send a nobler son than Lowell, and never was he more loyal than at the very moment when he was saying those kind words about England which angered certain Americans whose loyalty to their country means "bumptiousness," or else a selfish hardening of the national conscience. Delightful as was personal intercourse with him, the charm was not quite undisturbed. Every now and then you felt yourself to be under the microscope of a Yankee naturalist. You felt that you were being examined, weighed, and classified for America, perhaps for Boston. It is this sagacity that gives life to his prose. What is called his wit is merely this almost preternatural sagacity in rapid movement. What is called his humour is this same sagacity at rest and in a meditative mood.—WATTS-DUNSTON, THEODORE, 1891, *James Russell Lowell, The Athenæum, No.* 3330, *pp.* 258, 259.

Lowell: the labours of your noble life,
Your state-craft, and your high poetic skill
Were aye a force that made for union, till
The peace now reigning hushed the ancient strife
Between the mighty land that gave you life,
And that whose kinship distance could not kill.
I think your death has drawn us nearer still!
Now with your praise our island home is rife,
While rings your continent with equal praise;
And here, as there, we sadly quote your lays.
And Lowell! I who knew you, also know
Some that you loved in England, who to-day
Not only share your countless readers' woe,
But mourn a dear old friend that's passed away.
—STEPHEN, JAMES KENNETH, 1891, *In Memoriam: J. R. Lowell, Lapsus Calami and Other Verses, p.* 183.

Many good Americans do we meet in letters and in the world, but Mr. Lowell was the flower of them all; in all that he did, wrote and said giving the world assurance of a man. Culture could not make him fanciful or unduly fastidious, nor the study of letters diminish his robust interest in and knowledge of public affairs. Yes, he was of the great race, was of mightier mould than the literary generations of today; had a genius at once sure, powerful, and kindly, without freak or paradox or doubt. Mr. Lowell's religious faith (if one may mention such matters) had a solidity and fervor which surprised some and might well convert others of a wavering temper. I know that I cannot praise him to the measures of his desert, nor bear adequate testimony to the qualities which we knew and admired and loved, and yet it is difficult to be silent in our regret *tam cari capitis.*—LANG, ANDREW, 1891, *At the Sign of the Ship, Longman's Magazine, vol.* 18, *p.* 666.

The biographers of James Russell Lowell are already pointing out that the main direction of his life was determined by a woman. So many men of genius have been shipwrecked in marriage that it is good to dwell on the signal cases of the contrary result. When Lowell first formed his attachment of Maria White, he was unquestionably at the parting of the ways. He came from college popular and brilliant indeed, perilously brilliant—with strong literary instincts, but morally immature. His suspension from college on the eve of graduation did not come, as is now charitably suggested, from irregularity in attendance on prayers, but from a more serious offense, indicating a more dangerous possibility. That he was saved from the reckless career of so many gifted men was partly due, of course, to his own better nature, but largely to that strongest influence which can be brought to bear on a young man of ardent impulses, a pure love towards a noble woman.—HIGGINSON, THOMAS WENTWORTH, 1891, *James Russell Lowell, Harper's Bazar*.

Fame, honour, fortune, crowned thee with its wreath;
Justly the world to thee adjudged its prize;
But simple, heedless of its flattering breath,
Thy path was onward with uplooking eyes,—
Onward through life, strong, earnest in the fight
For freedom, duty, justice, all things good,
Sowing brave words, high thoughts, for Truth, for Right,
And unseduced by all Life's siren brood.
—STORY, WILLIAM WETMORE, 1891, *To James Russell Lowell, Blackwood's Magazine, vol. 150, p. 589*.

God gave thee power to make such music as should soothe
Our wounded hearts, Melpomene;
Sing to us now, for, oh! we mourn, without regret or shame,
One most beloved.
Eternal sleep clasps our Quinctillus, whose like nor Honour,
Truth, Justice, nor Loyalty shall see again!
By good men wept, he died; Virgil, our friend is gone!
Yet all thy tears are vain—
Thou canst not call him back; nay, had thy lute
A subtler magic than the Thracian's harp
It could not summon from that Yonder Shore
The phantom that has crossed thereto.
Hard—hard is this!
And yet sweet Faith lightens the burthen of the cross
We elsewise could not bear.
—FIELD, EUGENE, 1891, *James Russell Lowell, Horace's Odes, I., p. 24*.

His heart was not with our monarchical traditions; it was always sternly Republican. Lowell in England was always looking longingly backward to the vast wooden mansion under the terrace of Mount Auburn where he was born and bred, and where the great writers of the world laid their hands upon his youth and dedicated it. It is much to be desired that the American Government, or the State of Massachusetts, may find some way of preserving Elmwood as it stands, or as it stood when I saw it six years ago, as national property. More, perhaps, than any other single building in America, it is a relic of the literary life, a solid piece of the intellectual history, of the country. Mr. Lowell, though ten years absent from Elmwood, was always thinking of it, and especially of the famous trees that deepen the seclusion of its lawns. I remember, when I first saw him, after a brief visit to America in 1885, he asked me immediately about the elms at Mount Auburn. "Did they send me a message?" he asked. Long may their venerable shadow be thrown across his household gods!—GOSSE, EDMUND, 1891, *James Russell Lowell, St. James's Gazette*.

I knew Mr. Lowell very well in the early years of the Civil War, when I lived near him in Cambridge. It was a rare delight to a young man to sit in this poet's disordered library and enjoy the sparkle of his rambling talk about books, and men, and courts (which he used to give forth without stint), meanwhile enjoying with him a long pipe-smoke. Mr. Lowell was at once genial and dignified. His greeting was cordial always, but it was one which forbade familiarity. His air was always one of distinction, and it needs not to be said that his talk was redolent of a rich and ripe scholarship, which was at once appreciative and critical. Nothing could be more infectious than was his enthusiasm for old writers; and especially, I think, he liked to set forth the literary virtues of the Elizabethan dramatists.—TOWLE, GEORGE MAKEPEACE, 1891, *Personal Tributes to Lowell, The Writer, vol. 5, p. 186*.

I think it will be generally conceded that, at the time of his death, Mr. Lowell occupied the position of the foremost American citizen. In public regard, at home and abroad, his name naturally headed the list of prominent Americans. Looked upon as a man of letters, as a representative of our country in foreign lands, or in any of the various positions in which he appeared before the public, there was no one to whom it was the custom to name James Russell Lowell as second. Without occupying the highest rank in any of his vocations, he stood in front of his fellow-citizens because he held so high a rank in so many of them.—STOCKTON, FRANK R., 1891, *Personal Tributes to Lowell, The Writer, vol. 5, p.* 187.

It may be professional prejudice, but as the whole color of his life was literary, so it seems to me that we may see in his high and happy fortune the most substantial honor gathered by the practice of letters from a world preoccupied with other things. It was in looking at him as a man of letters that one got closest to him, and some of his more fanatical friends are not to be deterred from regarding his career as in the last analysis a tribute to the dominion of style. This is the idea that his name most promptly evokes, to my sense; and though it was not by any means the only idea he cherished, the unity of his career is surely to be found in it. He carried style—the style of literature—into regions in which we rarely look for it; into politics, of all places in the world, into diplomacy, into stammering civic dinners and ponderous anniversaries, into letters and notes and telegrams, into every turn of the hour—absolutely into conversation, where indeed it freely disguised itself as intensely colloquial wit.— JAMES, HENRY, 1892, *James Russell Lowell, Atlantic Monthly, vol.* 69, *p.* 36.

With his lofty patriotism and his extraordinary public conscience, Lowell was distinctly the Independent in politics. He was an American and a Republican citizen. He acted with parties as every citizen must act if he acts at all. But the notion that a voter is a traitor to one party when he votes with another was as ludicrous to him as the assertion that it is treason to the White Star steamer to take passage in a Cunarder. When he would know his public duty, Lowell turned within, not without. He listened, not for the roar of the majority in the street, but for the still small voice in his own breast. For while the method of republican government is party, its basis is individual conscience and common-sense. This entire political independence Lowell always illustrated.—CURTIS, GEORGE WILLIAM, 1892, *James Russell Lowell, p.* 47.

In my Junior year, a lecture of Professor Norton's excited in me a wish to read Dante under Mr. Lowell. I did not know a word of Italian, though; and I was firmly resolved to waste no more time on elementary grammar. Without much hope of a favorable reception, then, I applied for admission to the course. Mr. Lowell received me in one of the small recitation-rooms in the upper story of University Hall. My first impression was that he was surprisingly hirsute, and a little eccentric in aspect. He wore a double-breasted sack-coat, by no means new. In his necktie, which was tied in a sailor-knot, was a pin—an article of adornment at that time recently condemned by an authority which some of us were then disposed to accept as gospel. On his desk lay a silk hat not lately brushed; and nobody, I then held, had any business to wear a silk hat unless he wore coat-tails, too. . . . His method of teaching was all his own. The class was small—not above ten or a dozen; and he generally began by making each student translate a few lines, interrupting now and then with suggestions of the poetic value of passages which were being rendered in a style too exasperatingly prosaic. Now and again, some word or some passage would suggest to him a line of thought—sometimes very earnest, sometimes paradoxically comical —that it would never have suggested to anyone else, and he would lean back in his chair, and talk away across country till he felt like stopping; or he would thrust his hands into the pockets of his rather shabby sack-coat, and pace the end of the room with his heavy laced boots, and look at nothing in particular, and discourse of things in general. We gave up note-books in a week. Our business was not to cram lifeless detail, but to absorb as much as we might of the spirit of his exuberant literary vitality. And through it all he was always a quiz; you never knew what he was going to do or to say next.—WENDELL, BARRETT, 1893, *Stelligeri and Other Essays Concerning America, p.* 205, 207.

He was full of life and animal spirits. The "Fables for Critics" published in 1848, affords ample illustration of the liveliness and sparkling spontaneity of his wits, as well as of his critical discrimination and the wide range of his reading. His spirits were constantly bubbling over in action as well as in writing. He enjoyed life thoroughly and in all its aspects. His bodily faculties were all at command, and served him well. He was no trained athlete, but he liked walking and swimming and skating, and could endure fatigue without harm. His eye was keen and true, his hand steady. He was a good shot, and he knew the excitement of the hunt, but he cared too much for the wild creatures to find great pleasure in killing them. To excel in everything he undertook was become a habit and an ambition with him. It was so in feats of bodily agility and strength. He liked to do whatever any one else could do. But he admired generously those who surpassed him. There was no jealousy in his nature. . . . Every pleasant quality that adds charm to social intercourse made Lowell among his intimates one of the most delightful of companions. His wit was as kindly as it was ready; his humour was always genial. . . . His tastes, his disposition, were aristocratic, but his principles, his faith, and his practice were thoroughly democratic. . . . His affections were singularly deep and steady. He had not only a tender but a very large heart. His love for his friends was such that at times if it did not blind it at least colored his judgment. He was sure to like what they did. He was to them all that a faithful and generous friend could be. His thoughtfulness for them, his readiness to take trouble for them and to put all his resources at their disposal, outwent the common rules and experience of friendship. . . . There was a vein of shyness in him which, associated with this self-distrust, made appearance before the public distasteful to him. It was not till late in life that the evidence of his success and effect as a public speaker became too clear to allow him any longer to question his abilities in this respect. During the twenty years of his professorship its duties never became easy to him. He fulfilled them with scrupulous fidelity, but the stated hours and seasons of work were irksome to him and averse from his natural inclinations.—NORTON, CHARLES ELIOT, 1893, *James Russell Lowell, Harper's Magazine*, vol. 86, pp. 849, 850, 851.

He had a power of enjoyment which was not Yankee, a power of enjoyment both mental and physical. He liked good food, drink, and tobacco, and was altogether very fond of the earth. He sometimes spoke of this quality and said that he had upon his ear a mark which is peculiar to the ear of the faun.—NADAL, EHRMAN SYME, 1893,

Some Impressions of Mr. Lowell, The *Critic*, vol. 22, p. 105.

A short walk under the arching elms of Brattle Street brings us to Elmwood, the lifelong home of Lowell. The house, erected by the last British lieutenant-governor of the province, is a plain, square structure of wood, three stories in height, and is surrounded by a park of simple and natural beauty, whose abundant growth of trees gives to some portions of the grounds the sombreness and apparent seclusion of a forest. A gigantic hedge of trees encloses the place like a leafy wall, excluding the vision of the world and harboring thousands of birds who tenant its shades. Some of the aquatic fowl of the vicinage are referred to in Longfellow's "Herons of Elmwood." In the old mansion, long the home of Elbridge Gerry, Lowell was born and grew to manhood, and to it he brought the bride of his youth, the lovely Maria White, herself the writer of some exquisite poems; here, a few years later, she died. . . . Here, where he wished to die, he died, and here his daughter preserves his former home and its contents unchanged since he was borne hence to his burial. Until the death of his father, Lowell's study was an upper front room at the left of the entrance. It is a plain, low-studded corner apartment, which the poet called "his garret," and where he slept as a boy. Its windows now look only onto the neighboring trees, but when autumn has shorn the boughs of their foliage the front window commands a wide level of the sluggish Charles and its bordering lowlands, while the side window overlooks the beautiful slopes of Mount Auburn, where Lowell now lies with his poet-wife and the children who went before. His study windows suggested the title of his most interesting volume of prose essays. In this upper chamber he wrote his "Conversations on the Poets," and the early poems which made his fame,—"Irene," "Prometheus," "Rhoecus," "Sir Launfal,"—which was composed in five days,—and the first series of that collection of grotesque drolleries, "The Biglow Papers." Here also he prepared his editorial contributions to the "Atlantic." His later study was on the lower floor, at the left of the ample hall which traverses the center of the house. It is a prim and delightful old-fashioned apartment, with low walls, a wide and cheerful fireplace, and pleasant windows which look out among the trees and lilacs upon a long reach of lawn. In this room the poet's best-beloved books, copiously annotated by his hand, remain upon his shelves; here we see his table, his accustomed chair, the desk upon which he wrote the "Commemoration Ode," "Under the Willows," and many famous poems, besides the volumes of prose essays.—WOLFE,THEODORE F.,1895,*Literary Shrines*, pp. 110, 111.

It was not long after his return from his position as minister to England; and, having made an appointment with him beforehand, I called on him in his home at Elmwood. He received me in his study, the large square room on the first floor, at the left of the entrance. Those who have seen him there will be familiar with the room, ideal in its arrangements, as the study of a poet. . . As I remember the way in which he received me, the quiet ease with which he made me perfectly at home, it may be proper for me to say a word concerning Lowell's general attitude toward the public. He was by birth and training an aristocrat in the best sense of that word. He never found it easy to make his life a common, to be freely entered and trodden down at random by all the world. He was not so easily accessible as Longfellow; he claimed that he had a right to his own time, his intimacies, and his friendships. But to those who knew him, to those to whom he opened his arms and his heart, he was the most delightful of companions. He has been severely criticised for the attitude of dignity and reserve which he took and maintained while he was our minister at the Court of St. James; and it is freely admitted that he was not one of those who liked to be slapped on the back by everybody, and that he was not willing to be made an errand boy or a London guide for wandering Americans. But no man who ever occupied a diplomatic position in Europe has ever stood more steadily for the essential principles of our republic, maintained more uncompromisingly the dignity of an American citizen, or reflected more credit on his country.—SAVAGE, MINOT J., 1895, *A Morning with Lowell, The Arena*, vol. 15, pp. 3, 4.

I remember when the papers announced that our plain Harvard professor had been appointed Minister to England we boys thought of the big shaggy dog that tagged him through the street, of the briar-wood pipe, and the dusty suit of gray, and we were struck dumb with amazement.—HUBBARD, ELBERT, 1896, *ed. Little Journeys to the Homes of American Authors*, p. 125.

He came to London the man he had been all his life long—a man of books and of literature, a thinker, a dreamer, a poet, almost a recluse. The world for which he most cared lay within the four walls of his library at Elmwood. He valued his friends—never was there a friend more loyal and stanch to his friends than Lowell; but, his friends excepted, men seemed to him more real or more near to him in their writings than in the flesh. With all his geniality he was extremely reserved with strangers or acquaintances in his own rank of life. He was an American with the culture of Europe, but with no great knowledge of the Europe of today outside of its literature and art. . . . For rank or for mere brilliancy of social position he never cared. He was supposed to care, or accused of caring, by those sour critics at home who find it agreeable to believe that an American of the Americans, as Lowell always was, is dazzled by the social splendors of London. But Lowell, always a student of human nature in books, now became a student of human nature in the flesh. He frankly avowed his astonishment at finding so many good specimens in regions hitherto unsuspected and unexplored. He saw that London society was, in truth, a kind of microcosm, or the whole world in little; a place where you had to make and keep your own footing. . . . His impatience of pretentious ignorance was, in truth, uncontrollable, and he became almost at once so great a figure in London that to him was tacitly accorded a license granted to none other. With this social supremacy his diplomatic quality had little or nothing to do. . . . The imagination cannot conceive of Lowell as a courtier. He had—which is a totally different matter—an admirable courtesy, whether to the Queen or to the flower-girl in the street of whom he bought roses for his button-hole and his friends. But to the Queen, as to everybody else, he would speak his mind. The freedom he used sometimes left courtiers aghast, but gave no offense to the Queen. It may have amazed her because of its originality; it certainly increased her respect and liking for the loyal gentleman who thought the ties of humanity universal. There was no fault of good-breeding in it; there was, no doubt, a certain indifference to court customs. A breath of fresh air swept through the presence-room when Mr. Lowell entered it. He was not afraid to be himself; to be simple, entertaining, literary even, or to pour out his stores of wit and learning where such gifts are unusual.— SMALLEY, GEORGE W., 1896, *Mr. Lowell in England, Harper's Magazine, vol. 92, pp. 488, 489, 490, 493.*

Mr. Lowell was singularly handsome in his young manhood. Paige painted him when he was a Titian young man with reddish beard and affluent curling hair, deep blue eyes, and a ruddy cheek. Afterwards, when he was Minister to England, I spoke to him of that portrait and those days. "You see," said he, "I didn't grow old handsomely." Nor did he. The trials of his life, and they were many, had marked his face and marred his coloring; but it made no difference how he looked, he was always the same delightful, witty, and distinguished man.—SHERWOOD, MARY E. W., 1897, *An Epistle to Posterity, p. 33.*

Soon after he was first married, Mrs. Lowell wrote to Mrs. Hawthorne, "I begin to fear we shall not have the satisfaction of being so *very* poor, after all." At times her fears were not realized, but they were the times when Lowell, in letters to his friends, could give the most amusing accounts of his condition. Once when he was in Europe he told his bankers to let him know when his money was spent, for then he meant to go home. He had no accounts of his own to tell him, and an error in the banker's accounts brought his visit prematurely to an end. But in later years the bankers made good this disappointment by a profitable investment of the sum which really had remained to his credit, and Lowell made the incident a text for a humourous denunciation of all accounts and figures. Humourous and enthusiastic, companionable and sympathetic, he was the best of friends, and the life of congenial assemblies.—HOWE, M. A. DEWOLFE, 1898, *American Bookmen, p. 261.*

My experience (that is, at Harvard), therefore, only permits me to speak of him as a professor in the recitation-room. In that relation his erudition, humor, and kindness made me, and I am sure all my associates, enjoy the hour with him as we did no other college exercise. I can sincerely say that it is one of my most highly cherished experiences. With us he was always conversational, and flattered us and gained us by an assumption that what interested him interested us. When now I take up my Dante, Mr. Lowell seems to be with me.—LINCOLN, ROBERT T., 1898–99, *Letter to Dr. Hale, James Russell Lowell and his Friends, ed. Hale, p. 142.*

Lowell first saw Maria White on the first of December, 1839. At the moment, I suppose, he did not know that it was preordained that they two should be one. Mr. Norton has hunted out an early letter of his which he wrote the day after that meeting: "I went up to Watertown on Saturday with W. A. White, and spent the Sabbath with him. . . . His sister is a very pleasant and pleasing young lady, and knows more poetry than any one I am acquainted with. I mean, she is able to repeat more. She is more familiar, however, with modern poets than with the pure wellsprings of English poesy." The truth is that their union was made in heaven, that it was a perfect marriage, that they belonged together and lived one life. She was exquisitely beautiful; her tastes and habits were perfectly simple; her education, as I look back on what I know of it, seems to me as perfect as any education can be.— HALE, EDWARD EVERETT, 1898–99, *James Russell Lowell and his Friends, p. 78.*

Mr. Lowell brought letters to my father, Don Pascual de Gayangos, a valued friend and correspondent of Prescott and Ticknor. We saw much of him. My father's fine library was a great resource to him, and hardly a day passed without one or more notes, or "notelets," passing between us. I am the happy possessor of one hundred and seventy-three of them, full of fun, and with comments on passing events and on the books which came to him from America and England. . . . He liked Spain, and looked with indulgence at our faults. The picturesqueness pleased him, and the tawny landscapes and the snow-covered mountains of Guadarrama were a delight to him. . . . He spoke much of the trees and birds that surrounded Elmwood, which were so dear to him and his wife. How thankful we must be that he closed his eyes in the home he loved so well!—DE RIAÑO, EMILIA GAYANGOS, 1900, *Mr. Lowell and his Spanish Friends, Century Magazine,* vol. 60, p. 292.

He was very sensitive to criticism, especially from those he valued through his head or heart. He would try to hide his hurt, and he would not let you speak of it, as though your sympathy unmanned him, but you could see that he suffered. This notably happened in my remembrance from a review in a journal which he greatly esteemed; and once when in a notice of my own I put one little thorny point among the flowers, he confessed a puncture from it. He praised the criticism heartily, but I knew that he winced under my recognition of the didactic quality which he had not quite guarded himself against in the poetry otherwise praised. He liked your liking, and he openly rejoiced in it; and I suppose he made himself believe that in trying his verse with his friends he was testing it; but I do not believe that he was, and I do not think that he ever corrected his judgment by theirs, however he suffered from it. . . . Any grossness of speech was inconceivable of him; now and then, but only very rarely, the human nature of some story "unmeet for ladies" was too much for his sense of humor, and overcame him with amusement which he was willing to impart, and did impart, but so that mainly the human nature of it reached you. In this he was like the other great Cambridge men, though he was opener than the others to contact with the commoner life. He keenly delighted in every native and novel turn of phrase, and he would not undervalue a vital word or notion picked up out of the road even if it had some mud sticking to it. He kept as close to the common life as a man of his patrician and cloistered habits could. . . . He did not care so much for popularity as for the praise of his friends. If he liked you he wished you not only to like what he wrote, but to say so. He was himself most cordial in his recognition of the things that pleased him. What happened to me from him, happened to others, and I am only describing his common habit when I say that nothing I did to his liking failed to bring me a spoken or oftener a written acknowledgment. This continued to the latest years of his life when the effort to give pleasure must have caused him a physical pang.—HOWELLS, WILLIAM DEAN, 1900, *A Personal Retrospect of James Russell Lowell, Scribner's Magazine,* vol. 28, pp. 368, 370, 371.

Holmes and Lowell were the antithesis of the New England intellect, and this more in their personality than in their writing. If Lowell could have acquired Holmes's respect for his work, he would have left a larger image in the American Walhalla; but he never gave care to the perfection of what he wrote, for his mind so teemed with material that the time to polish and review never came. Holmes, like a true artist, loved the *limae* labor. He was satisfied, it seemed to me, to do the work of one lifetime and then rest, while Lowell looked forward to a succession of lifetimes all full of work, and one can hardly conceive him as ever resting or caring to stop work. Lowell's was a generous, widely sympathizing nature, from which radiated love for humanity and the broadest and most catholic helpfulness for every one who asked for his help, with a special fund for his friends. Holmes drew a line around him, within which he shone like a winter sun, and outside of which his care did not extend. The one was best in what he did, the other in what he was. Holmes always seemed to me cynical to the general world; Lowell to have embodied the antique sentiment, "I am a man, and hold nothing human as indifferent to me." Both were adored by those around them, and the adoration kindled Holmes to a warmer reflection to the adorers; Lowell felt it as the earth feels sunshine, which sinks into the fertile soil and bears its fruit in a richer harvest.—STILLMAN, WILLIAM JAMES, 1901, *The Autobiography of a Journalist,* vol. I, p. 243.

The spring of 1891 came and Lowell had cheerful hope of further work. . . . But though he could go out but little, he had a pleasant glimpse of the world that lay about his house,—the earliest and the best known world to him. He had had a flat dish with stones in it conveniently placed in his garden, and connected it with his water pipe so that his little friends the thrushes, the orioles, and the squirrels might have free use of the modern improvements to which he was indifferent enough. Outside of his bedroom window a pair of gray squirrels had nested, and as he was imprisoned there by the illness which now closed in about him, he looked with kindly interest on their gambols in the tree-tops. His friends came as he could see them, and he entertained them with humorous diatribes on his gaoler gout. Now and then he could pencil a letter or note, sending a message perhaps to some equally bound sufferer, as when he commiserated his old friend Judge Hoar, shut up with an attack of inflammatory rheumatism, and whimsically cautioned him against mistaking it for the gout which he himself was enduring. A faint smile plays about these last expressions of his kindly nature, as he seems to wave the world aside that he may take his friends by the hand. Death found him cheerful, and he passed away in the middle of the bright summer.—SCUDDER, HORACE E., 1901, *James Russell Lowell, vol.* II, *pp.* 406, 407.

A FABLE FOR CRITICS
1848

Passed an hour or two with Lowell, who read to me his satire on American authors; full of fun, and with very true portraits, *as seen from that side.*—LONGFELLOW, HENRY WADSWORTH, 1848, *Journal, June* 15; *Life of Henry Wadsworth Longfellow, ed. Longfellow, vol.* II, *p.* 116.

No failure was ever more complete or more pitiable. By the publication of a book at once so ambitious and so feeble, so malevolent in design and so harmless in execution, a work so roughly and clumsily yet so weakly constructed, so very different in body and spirit from anything that he has written before, Mr. Lowell has committed an irrevocable *faux pas* and lowered himself at least fifty per cent in the literary public opinion.—POE, EDGAR ALLAN, 1849, *Lowell's "A Fable for Critics," Works ed. Stedman and Woodberry, vol.* VI, *p.* 249.

Common rumour attributes it to the same pen which wrote "The Biglow Papers," and if there was no other reason for this conjecture but the author's extraordinary command of Hudibrastic rhymes, and the easy flow of his versification, we should think it must be well founded. The "Fable," which, by the way, is no fable at all, is really a very pleasant and sparkling poem, abounding in flashes of brilliant satire, edged with wit enough to delight even its victims. It is far more spirited and entertaining than one would expect from the labored conceits of its title-page and preface, which, with their forced and concealed jingle, are but melancholy introductions for the lively and half-grotesque rhymes that follow. The framework of the poem is too slight to merit notice; the writer evidently began with some idea of a plot or an apologue, but soon tired of it, and throwing the reins upon the neck of his Pegasus, allowed the verse to "wander at its own sweet will." Goldsmith's "Retaliation" was certainly his model, and though he comes far short of that exquisite mixture of playful satire and discriminating portraiture of character, under which the good-nature of the kind-hearted poet appears so constantly that not one of his glittering shafts leaves a painful wound, he quite equals it in the easy flow of his rhymes, and surpasses it in wit and sauciness.— BOWEN, FRANCIS, 1849, *Humorous and Satirical Poetry, North American Review, vol.* 68, *p.* 191.

The whole, despite its rollicking style and its friendly tone, leaving upon the mind no impression that American literature in 1848 was hopelessly sentimental or likely to remain immature for too long a period. At any rate, there was enough of it to deserve the attention of a critic who knew when to denounce, when to correct, and when to praise, and who could prove, in a single work, the fallacy of the old idea that a critic is a broken-down creator.— RICHARDSON, CHARLES F., 1887, *American Literature,* 1607–1885, *vol.* I, *p.* 411.

I think that the "Fable for Critics," in which, with such keen intuition, he gave a critical estimate of the merits and defects of his most eminent fellow-countrymen, has been under-estimated rather than otherwise. It was marked not only by its sparkling and acute playfulness, and the clever oddity of rhymes in which even Browning has not surpassed him, but also by a very unusual power of seeing the real men through the glamour of temporary popularity and the cloud of passing dislike. —FARRAR, FREDERIC WILLIAM, 1891, *An English Estimate of Lowell, The Forum, vol.* 12, *p.* 147.

It is a proof of Lowell's excellence of judgment and of his independence of attitude, that the opinions he expressed about the leading American authors of that time coincide closely with that on which the best criticism is now agreed fifty years later. And the rattling lines of the poem are as readable now as when they were first written, with their scattering fire of verbal jokes, of ingenious rimes, and of personal witticisms. As the "Biglow Papers" is the firmest and the finest political satire yet written in the United States, so the "Fable for Critics" is the clearest and most truthful literary satire.—MATTHEWS, BRANDER, 1896, *An Introduction to the Study of American Literature*, p. 200.

BIGLOW PAPERS
1848–67

He is the Hudibras of America, and woe betide the unfortunate wight at whom he pokes his fun; for, while it is sport to him, it is death to the subject of his sarcasm.—BUNGAY, GEORGE W., 1854, *Off-Hand Takings, or Crayon Sketches*, p. 396.

Before I conclude them, may I ask you to give all our kindest regards to Lowell, and to express our admiration for the "Yankee Idyl." I am afraid of using too extravagant language if I say all I think about it. Was there ever anything more stinging, more concentrated, more vigorous, more just? He had condensed into those few pages the essence of a hundred diplomatic papers and historical disquisitions and Fourth of July orations. I was dining a day or two since with his friend Lytton (Bulwer's son, attaché here) and Julian Fane (Secretary of the embassy), both great admirers of him,—and especially of the "Biglow Papers,"—they begged me to send them the Mason and Slidell Idyl, but I wouldn't,—I don't think it is in English nature (although theirs is very cosmopolitan and liberal) to take such punishment and come up smiling. I would rather they got it in some other way, and then told me what they thought voluntarily. I have very pleasant relations with all the J. B.'s here.—MOTLEY, JOHN LOTHROP, 1862, *Letter to Holmes, Feb. 26*; *John Lothrop Motley by Oliver Wendell Holmes*, p. 116.

The "Biglow Papers" ended all question of Mr. Lowell's originality. They are a master-work, in which his ripe genius fastened the spirit of its region and period. Their strength lies in qualities which, as here combined were no man's save his own. . . . Never sprang the flower of art from a more unpromising soil; yet these are eclogues as true as those of Theocritus or Burns. Finally, they are not merely objective studies, but charged with the poet's own passion, and bearing the marks of the scholar's hand.—STEDMAN, EDMUND CLARENCE, 1882–85, *Poets of America*, p. 321.

It must be repeated, by way of emphasis, that, from the first fly-leaf to the colophon, this is the only complete and perfect piece of grotesque comedy in existence. In time, historical notes will be needed, as they are now for Hudibras. That the Yankee satire is to be enduring, there can be no doubt. Its total merits greatly outweigh those of Hudibras; it has far more humor, and more quotable lines; and it has a great advantage in its unique concomitants.—UNDERWOOD, FRANCIS H., 1882, *James Russell Lowell, a Biographical Sketch*, p. 48.

The popular instinct which has seized upon the "Biglow Papers," and will insist on regarding Mr. Lowell as the author of that comic masterpiece and of nothing else, is in one sense a sound one. For while it is just open to argument whether Mr. Lowell is an actual or an adopted son of the Muses, he is unquestionably a born humorist. He possesses a humour of thought which is at once broad and subtle; his humour of expression is his American birthright. The mere characterizations of the "Biglow Papers," have perhaps been overpraised, though Birdofredum Sawin certainly appears original and typical to an outsider, whatever may be said of Parson Homer Wilbur; but the graphic power of statement, the gnomic faculty of the sententious utterance, the extraordinary fluency and facility of the versification, make the book a perpetual delight.—TRAILL, HENRY DUFF, 1885, *Mr. J. R. Lowell, Fortnightly Review*, vol. 44, p. 86.

Among the books so received was a shilling paper-backed copy of James Russell Lowell's poems. It did not include the "Biglow Papers," but it contained most of his best poems, and among others it contained "Extreme Unction." It is only a short poem, eleven verses in all, but I think it made a deeper dint on my life than any other printed matter I ever read, before or since. A rich old man to whom the last sacraments of the Church are about to be administered repels the priest and dies in despair. It is very simple, and it seems strange that I, who was neither old, nor rich, nor at the point of death, should have been so affected by it. But the fact was so, nevertheless. I was in very ill-health at the time I read it, and was full of the enthusiasms of youth, intensified by a stimulating sense of ever-present duty derived from the Commonwealth.—STEAD, W. T., 1887, *Books which Have Influenced Me, p. 31.*

There are three books which I must needs name before I quite take leave of my readers, because they have, each in its own peculiar way, had a wholly incalculable influence upon my mind, and left upon me an impression so deep and lasting that I should find it impossible to exaggerate the effect produced. One of these books was Mr. Browning's "Paracelsus;" another, John Stuart Mills's book on "Liberty;" and the third, Mr. Lowell's "Biglow Papers." If I had the space at my disposal, I could easily show that the incongruity which may appear on the surface in bracketing these three books together is not really so great as it may seem at first sight. This only I know, that with the single exception of the Bible, there is no book in any language that during the last twenty years of my life, has been so much to me, has been so suggestive, so ever-present with me, so much quoted by me, so much "leaned upon," as the "Biglow Papers." Americans tell me that the book has almost "gone out." It may be so; but if it be so, I am at a loss to think what literary masterpiece in America can ever hope for imperishable fame.—JESSOPP, AUGUSTUS, 1888, *Books That Have Helped Me, p. 66.*

If I might venture a prediction as to Lowell's place among poets, it would be that his "Biglow" verses will outlive his finely-wrought and polished odes; precisely because the former is studded with such bits of homely wisdom as that which I disregard in offering the suggestion, viz.: "Don't never prophesy,—onless ye know." —ROCHE, JAMES JEFFREY, 1891, *Personal Tributes to Lowell, The Writer, vol. 5, p. 190.*

It was part of Mr. Lowell's art to contrast this rude working-Christian Biglow with the older-fashioned Puritan Parson Wilbur, still wedded to his creed and his books. . . . Clever as was the "swallertailed talk" of the parson, one is conscious that it is mere workmanship, and that at best it is but humorous translation artistically done. It is the rude dialect of Hosea that is alone real and vital. For this is not the "Yankee talk" of tradition, of the story books and the stage—tricks of pronunciation, illiterate spelling, and epithet—but the revelation of the character, faith, work, and even scenery of a people, in words more or less familiar, but always in startling and novel combination and figurative phrasing.—HARTE, BRET, 1891, *A Few Words About Mr. Lowell, New Review, vol. 5, p. 195.*

Our literature has no work more essentially American than "The Biglow Papers," not only in the dialect form, but in its dramatic portraiture of the popular conscience of New England, of Lincoln's "plain people" who have given the distinctive impulse to American civilization, and from whose virtues has largely sprung the American character. — CURTIS, GEORGE WILLIAM, 1891, *James Russell Lowell, Harper's Weekly.*

From purest wells of English undefiled
None deeper drank than he, the New World's child,
Who in the language of their farm-fields spoke
The wit and wisdom of New England folk,
Shaming a monstrous wrong. The world-wide laugh
Provoked thereby might well have shaken half
The walls of Slavery down ere yet the ball
And mine of battle overthrew them all.
—WHITTIER, JOHN GREENLEAF, 1891, *James Russell Lowell.*

"The Biglow Papers" have on their side some weighty considerations. They have immense animal spirits; I doubt if you will anywhere find verse of the kind, in writing which the poet has had more fun; and animal spirits is perhaps a quality to which posterity is partial, just as it is notoriously averse to the recondite and the abstruse. Moreover, these poems have the United States behind them. The country cannot afford to neglect them.— NADAL, EHRMAN SYME, 1893, *Some Impressions of Mr. Lowell, The Critic, vol. 22, p. 107.*

With pungent humor and in stanzas that had a sharp flavor of the soil, "Hosea Biglow" made fun of the attempts to rouse his fellow-citizens to military fervor. His stinging lines, which scorched themselves into the memory, were accompanied by the prose comments of "Parson Wilbur," who represented the other side of the New England character. While the clergyman was glad to air his culture and his classics, he served admirably to set off the simple frankness of the Yankee youth. That the lyrics of Hosea should linger in the ears of those who heard them, Lowell took care to give to each a swinging rhythm and often also a catching refrain. When at last the scattered "Biglow Papers" were collected into a volume in 1848, the author, just to show that the New England dialect was serviceable for other things than satire, added to the book a Yankee idyl, "The Courtin'," one of the most beautiful natural love episodes in all English poetry.—MATTHEWS, BRANDER, 1896, *An Introduction to the Study of American Literature*, p. 199.

Upon the humorous aspect of the "Biglow Papers" it is hardly necessary to dwell in the way of analysis or criticism. If the most casual reader does not appreciate this characteristic of Mr. Lowell's dialect poems no amount of explanation or suggestion could bring their shrewd hits down to the level of his comprehension. Attention may, however, be called to the fact that Lowell's humour as evinced in Hosea Biglow's sprightly poems or Parson Wilbur's laboriously learned introductions is always wholesome and never purposeless. Its prime object was not amusement, but the correction of social abuses and the abatement of political wrongs. . . . Because Mr. Lowell took such pains to make the dialect of Hosea Biglow and Birdofredum Sawin absolutely authentic, his "Biglow Papers," are sure of immortality on purely linguistic grounds. They faithfully represent a mode of speech which is too often outrageously caricatured. And their value in this direction is enhanced by the introduction to the Second Series, in which Mr. Lowell gives us a scholarly discussion of the English language in America, and the characteristics of American humour.—GILMORE, J. H., 1896, *The Biglow Papers, The Chautauquan*, vol. 23, pp. 19, 20.

"The Biglow Papers" are probably the only American political poems of any length destined to endure. Though the events, real and imaginary, which they recount are transient, the wit, philosophy, and poetry are perennial, and will in themselves keep alive in the popular mind certain episodes that would otherwise be preserved only in the memory of the historical student.—ONDERDONK, JAMES L., 1899–1901, *History of American Verse*, p. 285.

The Reverend Homer Wilbur is a semi-dramatic creation, yet much of Lowell's own genuine learning, his mastery of Latin good and bad, his reckless wit, and his wide knowledge of men, is accredited to the dim-eyed old parson. Indeed, after the humor of the verses has become largely obscured with the details of last century politics, part of this stilted prose may yet be treasured among the essayist's best utterances. But it would be difficult to name any canon of fairness in warfare which the young radical and man of genius observed scrupulously in this book.—LAWTON, WILLIAM CRANSTON, 1902, *Introduction to the Study of American Literature*, p. 233.

POETRY

Mr. Lowell, poetically speaking, is the child of his age, belonging to that class of poets in whom the imaginative and reflective element predominates over the passionate, and who are now occupying the highest place in the general favor. . . . Mr. Lowell has more of the "vision" than the "faculty divine." He has the eye and mind of a poet, but wants the plastic touch, which "turns to shape the forms of things unknown." His conceptions are superior to his power of execution. We are reminded, in reading his poetry, of the observation of a judicious critic in a sister art, that the picture would have been better painted if the painter had taken more pains. . . . Another conspicuous fault of Mr. Lowell's poetry is the perpetual presence of the daintinesses and prettinesses of expression. His thoughts are overdressed. He abounds with those affected turns, with which the poetry of Tennyson (which we suspect our friend has studied more than is good for him) is so besprinkled. He is too liberal in the use of the poetical vocabulary.—HILLARD, GEORGE STILLMAN, 1841, *Lowell's Poems, North American Review*, vol. 52, pp. 452, 454, 465.

Is entitled, in our opinion, to at least the second or third place among the poets of America. We say this on account of the vigor of his *imagination*—a faculty to be first considered in all criticisms upon poetry. In this respect he surpasses, we think, any of our writers (at least any of those who have put themselves prominently forth as poets) with the exception of Longfellow, and perhaps one other. His ear for rhythm, nevertheless, is imperfect, and he is very far from possessing the artistic ability of either Longfellow, Bryant, Halleck, Sprague, or Pierpont.—POE, EDGAR ALLAN, 1841, *A Chapter of*

Autography, Works ed. Stedman and Woodberry.

Sometimes, in hours of slumberous, melancholy musing, strange, sweet harmonies seem to pervade the air; impalpable forms, with garments trailing like shadows of summer clouds, glide above us; and wild and beautiful thoughts, ill-defined as the shapes we see, fill the mind. To echo these harmonies, to paint etherial forms, to embody in language these thoughts, would be as difficult as to bind the rainbows in the skies. Mr. Lowell is still a dreamer, and he strives in vain to make his readers partners in his dreamy, spiritual fancies. Yet he has written some true poetry, and as his later writings are his best, he may be classed among those who give promise of the highest excellence in the maturity of their power.—GRISWOLD, RUFUS WILMOT, 1842, *The Poets and Poetry of America*, p. 428.

There is Lowell, who's striving Parnassus to climb
With a whole bale of *isms* tied together with rhyme,
He might get on alone, spite of brambles and boulders,
But he can't with that bundle he has on his shoulders,
The top of the hill he will ne'er come nigh reaching;
Till he learns the distinction 'twixt singing and preaching
His lyre has some chords that would ring pretty well,
But he'd rather by half make a drum of the shell,
And rattle away till he's old as Methusalem,
At the head of a march to the last new Jerusalem.
—LOWELL, JAMES RUSSELL, 1848, *A Fable for Critics*.

We must declare it, though to the grief of some friends, and the disgust of more, is absolutely wanting in the true spirit and tone of poesy. His interest in the moral questions of the day has supplied the want of vitality in himself; his great facility at versification has enabled him to fill the ear with a copious stream of pleasant sound. But this verse is stereotyped; his thought sounds no depth, and posterity will not remember him.—OSSOLI, MARGARET FULLER, 1850, *American Literature; Art, Literature and the Drama*, p. 308.

Unites, in his most effective poems, the dreamy, suggestive character of the transcendental bards with the philosophic simplicity of Wordsworth.— TUCKERMAN, HENRY T., 1858, *A Sketch of American Literature*, p. 392.

Lowell seems to me the most perfect exponent in poetry, of the sense of national greatness, of any one that I know.— CHURCH, RICHARD WILLIAM, 1869, *To Asa Gray, April 5, Life and Letters of Dean Church*, ed. his Daughter, p. 219.

It is unquestionably superior to any other American poem ["Commemoration Ode"] which can be compared with it, and it seems to me to be the finest of its kind in the language. It is better than the "Ode on the Death of the Duke of Wellington," not because Lowell is a greater poet than Tennyson, but because it has a grander theme and was written a dozen years later, when "the last great Englishman" had been dwarfed by "the first American."— JOHNSON, ROSSITER, 1875, *Authors, Little Classics*, p. 163.

Mr. Lowell's ode ["Ode on the Fourth of July"] in your last Magazine seemed to me full of fine thought; but it wanted wings. I mean it kept too much to one Level, though a high Level, for Lyric Poetry, as Ode is supposed to be: both in respect to Thought, and Metre. Even Wordsworth (least musical of men) changed his Flight to better purpose in his Ode to Immortality. Perhaps, however, Mr. Lowell's subject did not require, or admit, such Alternations.— FITZGERALD, EDWARD, 1876, *Letters to Fanny Kemble*, Dec. 12, p. 115.

No one of our poets shows a richer or wider range of thought than Mr. Lowell: no one a greater variety of expression in verse. But whatever form his Muse may select, it is the individuality of an intellect rather than that of a literary artist which she represents. The reader is never beguiled by studied graces of rhythm; but, on the other hand, he is constantly refreshed and stimulated by sudden glimpses of heights and splendors of thought which seem to be revealed as much to the poet as to himself. Lowell rises with a swift wing, and can upbear himself, when he pleases, on a steady one; but his nature seems hostile to that quality which compels each conception to shape itself into clear symmetry, and which therefore limits the willful exercise of the imagination. He seems to write under a strong stress of natural inspiration, then to shrink from the cooler-blooded labor of revision and the adjustment of the rhythmical expression of the informing thought.

Hence he is frequently unequal, not alone in separate poems, but also in different portions of the same poem. This is much more evident, however, in his earlier than in his later verse. Such poems as "In the Twilight," "The Washers of the Shroud," "To the Muse," and the greater part of "Commemoration Ode" are alike perfect and noble.—TAYLOR, BAYARD, 1876–80, *Critical Essays and Literary Notes, p.* 299.

Or give me him, high culture's noble son,
The Scholar and the Poet both in one,
Whose verse of varied movement falls and swells
In melody like his cathedral bells:
Now full and grandly calm, now soft and tender,
Sparkling with wit, and bright with passion's splendor.
With him down Fancy's river let me sail,
And, with Sir Launfal, find the Holy Grail,
Or set myself some merry hours to spend
With quaint Hosea Biglow for my friend,
Or by the kitchen fire to sit in clover,
And do the blessed Courtin' ten times over!
—JOYCE, ROBERT DWYER, 1877, *Reflections, Scribner's Magazine, vol.* 14, *p.* 447.

Mirrored in the pages of James Russell Lowell, as the forests and headlands are mirrored in some far-stretching lake, are the deepest and strongest thoughts and emotions of the Transatlantic mind. Yet his name is, in the minds of many Englishmen, associated chiefly with one form of literary effort, and that not the highest, though in its way unsurpassed. . . . At the opening of his career a comparison was instituted between Mr. Lowell and his fellow-poet Whittier. But while both can touch a high note in the martial strains of freedom, and both possess descriptive power of no common order, here, it seems to us, the comparison ends. Lowell is an energetic genius, Whittier a contemplative; not that the former is devoid of the other's noble contemplative moods, but he is at his best as the poet of action. Even when dealing with pacific subjects there is an air of pugnacity about him. He is in the realm of poetry what Mr. Bright is in that of politics. For men of peace, both are the hardest hitters of all the public men of our time. Given the same conditions, and Mr. Lowell might have been the Bright of the American Senate.—SMITH, GEORGE BARNETT, 1885, *James Russell Lowell, Nineteenth Century, vol.* 17, *pp.* 988, 990.

We have in the new volume, "Heart-ease and Rue," all the virtues lying behind the prose—the sure touch of the critic; the shrewd cast of judgment which holds state affairs to the tests of conscience; satire, less in quantity. but equal in quality to his best; and wit flashing through satire, giving to it a kindlier glow.—MORSE, JAMES HERBERT, 1888, *Open Letters, Century Magazine, vol.* 36, *p.* 952.

Here's a poet's garden ground
Where no other flower is found
Save sweet heart's ease, bitter rue.
Idle thought, to part the two,
They have grown so one in one,
In this magic dew and sun!
From the rule the heart's-ease peers,
Laughs to lighten pains and fears,
While the plant of mournful grace
Shades the other's riant face.
Strive thou not to tear apart
These two congeners of the heart.

—THOMAS, EDITH M., 1888, *On Reading Lowell's "Hearts-Ease and Rue."*

Few indeed are poets of nature or the heart who can make obvious the ideal and universal. Lowell attempts to give us too much; the forty long stanzas of "An Indian Summer Reverie," full of apt illusions, we gladly exchange for the well-known June-lines of "The Vision of Sir Launfal." Seldom indeed can a singer succeed by the very opulence of suggestiveness, as in Shelley's "Cloud," which is itself dangerously near such repetition or confusion as one notes in Lowell's "To a Pine-Tree," which just escapes grandeur, but escapes it utterly. Few readers know what deep and rich philosophy, what fruits of thought and culture, are to be found in some of Lowell's work; for instance, in "Columbus," "Beaver Brook," "On a Portrait of Dante by Giotto," "Stanzas on Freedom," "The Ghost-Seer," "Prometheus," and a dozen others as good.—RICHARDSON, CHARLES F., 1888, *American Literature,* 1607-1885, *vol.* II, *p.* 193.

I do not forget Shelley or Keats or Tennyson; I greatly admire parts of Browning (though heartily sympathizing with Mr. Andrew Lang's clever skit on "Esoteric Browningism," which I wish he had extended to take in the Wordsworth cult); but on the whole I think that of all the poets of the Nineteenth Century we could least afford to lose Lowell. Perhaps, however, I am somewhat influenced by my feelings as an American; for exactly as Burns is distinctly Scotch, so Lowell at his best, the Lowell of the "Biglow Papers" and the "Commemoration Ode," is essentially and characteristically a national and American poet.—ROOSEVELT, THEODORE, 1889, *James Russell Lowell, The Critic, vol.* 9, *p.* 86.

It is no disparagement to so fine a poet as Mr. Lowell to remark that he has not published any exceptionally fine sonnet, though several that are much above the average level. The form does not suit him; and even at his best therein he rides his Pegasus somewhat cumbrously.—SHARP, WILLIAM, 1889, ed., *American Sonnets, Introductory Note, p.* xlviii.

In this, as in his life, he is versatile. He has sung on one clear harp to many tones. One cannot help thinking, sometimes, that the note had been clearer and sweeter if the tones had been fewer. For a large part of his verse strikes one not so much as the spontaneous burst of music that forces from the full-charged throat of the artist, as the dexterous imitative work of the clever artisan. The writing of most youthful poets is an echo, but much of Lowell's is not an echo, but the conscious, skillful fabrication of poetical commodities made to order in various styles. . . . The poet of "The Vision of Sir Launfal" struck a chord which is quivering round the world still. For if Lowell had some of the Yankee hard self-confidence, and his belief in material progress, he had not a little of the Yankee idealism.—LOW, SIDNEY, 1891, *Lowell and his Poetry, Fortnightly Review, vol.* 56, *pp.* 312, 319.

Almost the greatest and finest realist who ever wrought in verse.—HOWELLS, WILLIAM DEAN, 1891, *Criticism and Fiction.*

In his verse there was much poetry, though it was often in the rough. He was sometimes careless. He was sometimes so clever as to seem forced, and he was sometimes forced without being at all clever.—MABIE, HAMILTON W., 1892, *The Memorial Story of America, p.* 592.

I took back with me to New York a complete collection of Lowell's verse of which I had hitherto only seen portions, and studied it carefully. As I had always learned to read chronologically, I began with "A Year's Life" (1841), continued with "A Legend of Brittany" (1844), followed with "The Vision of Sir Launfal" (1848), and ended with "A Fable for Critics" (1848), and was thus able to trace the changes of his mind and work. I found in his first book a different theory than obtained among us, then, a more poetical theory, for if "Threnodia," "The Sirens," "The Beggar," and "Allegra," were not poems, they were nothing. I found in these poems, particularly in the first two, a lyrical quality which was as new in our verse as it was admirable; they sang themselves into life in jubilant melodies of their own making. I found another quality which was not so admirable, and which I wondered at in so poetical a poet,—the didactic quality. I could not understand why Lowell had cared to write "The Fatherland," "The Heritage," and the sonnets "On Reading Wordsworth's Sonnets in Defense of Capital Punishment," which were certainly not poems.—STODDARD, RICHARD HENRY, 1896, *James Russell Lowell, Lippincott's Magazine, vol.* 50, *p.* 538.

While Lowell is undoubtedly the greatest literary critic that America has thus far produced, it is as a poet that he has done his most permanent work. The best of his poems represent without question the highest and most sustained flights of the American Muse. Emerson alone among our poets is to be compared with him; and yet while Emerson occasionally touched the heights, it was but to fall ingloriously. The sustained excellence of "The Vision of Sir Launfal" and "The Commemoration Ode" is hard indeed to be equalled among the poets of the Victorian era.—PATTEE, FRED LEWIS, 1896, *A History of American Literature, p.* 292.

It is as a poet pre-eminently that we love and admire him. Perhaps to no other American is the name of poet more truly applicable. . . . Although a poet of Nature, he is still more the poet of Man; the weak and the oppressed found in him a courageous and impassioned spokesman; he feared no censure or scorn that his allegiance to the slave might bring him; he longed only to break his chains, and to help bring the happy day when each man should look upon his neighbor, whether of high or low degree, as his brother. He is even more deeply the poet of Love. His poems which have love for their theme are less numerous than the others, but they are quite as profound, and reach even more nearly to the core of the man's heart.

It was through this love, which so influenced and held his life, that he became the champion of the weak and downtrodden.— WILLARD, MABEL CALDWELL, 1896, *ed. Vision of Sir Launfal and Other Poems, Introduction, pp.* 4, 5.

Lowell's best poetic utterance is generally felt to mark our highest achievement in verse hitherto; but his poems are uneven, in the artistic sense often unfinished. Some of them, indeed, were prematurely printed before the vein of thought had worked itself out. It is not incredible, then, that the call of patriotism has indeed deprived us of our rarest poet's unuttered master-song.—LAWTON, WILLIAM CRANSTON, 1898, *The New England Poets, p.* 230.

The defects of Mr. Lowell's style need not concern us much. They consist chiefly, it may be assumed, in some cacophonious lines, which a slight revision would have remedied, occasionally confused metaphors, a self-confessed tendency to sermonize, and, more particularly in his prose, certain errors of taste, slovenly expressions, and carelessly formed sentences. These may be left to those critics who judge chiefly by faults. As our acknowledged foremost man of letters, he has raised the standard of Americanism, has advocated a loftier and more rational patriotism, has made political chicanery contemptible and ridiculous, and in his own career has shown that high intellectual attainments are not inconsistent with a lively interest in current political affairs. . . . If not absolutely great as an original or imaginative writer, he has honestly earned the distinction of being the greatest satiric poet in the English language since the days of Pope.—ONDERDONK, JAMES L., 1899-1901, *History of American Verse, pp.* 288, 289.

The fact would seem to be that Lowell's anti-slavery zeal, inspired by Maria White, not only saved him from going hopelessly wrong on the main question of his time, but made the poet in him more than he would otherwise have been; the operation in this case being partly matched in Whittier's. It is not only that the "Biglow Papers" were the best product of the younger, as the second series of them and the Commemoration Ode of the older man, but that they stirred a nature, not readily self-stirred, to an activity which did not stop with the immediate end.— CHADWICK, JOHN WHITE, 1901, *Scudder's Lowell, The Nation, vol.* 73, *p.* 417.

As a racy humorist and a brilliant wit using verse as an instrument of expression, he has no clear superior, probably no equal, so far at least as American readers are concerned, among writers who have employed the English language. As a satirist he has superiors, but scarcely as an inventor of *jeux d'esprit,* even if "The Unhappy Lot of Mr. Knott" stands as a still more unhappy example of the kind of noose into which such an inventor occasionally gets his neck. As a patriotic lyrist he has few equals and very few superiors in what is probably the highest function of such a poet—that of stimulating to a noble height the national instincts of his countrymen. But viewed in the light of cosmopolitanism, such lyrics are not supreme in their inspiration, and viewed in the light of technical criticism Lowell's odes are far from faultless. The rest of his poetry may fairly be said to gain on that of any of his American contemporaries save Poe, in more sensuous rhythm, in choicer diction, in a more refined and subtilized imagination, and in a deeper, a more brooding intelligence. But for some readers it lacks spontaneous passion from first to last, and in spite of many really admirable poems, some of which have been already named, it scarcely gives any form of asthetic or mental satisfaction that cannot be gained in larger measure from the work of some contemporary British poet. If this be true it is idle to expect Englishmen to value Lowell's work in the higher spheres of poetry to the same extent that they do the fresher, more original poetry of Poe and Whitman.—TRENT, WILLIAM P., 1903, *A History of American Literature, p.* 447.

LETTERS

All the drawbacks to Mr. Lowell's prose style, so laboriously dwelt upon by such critics as Wilkinson and Kirk, may be found in these letters; the long sentences, the mixed metaphors, the occasional bad taste, the sparkle of trivial puns, are here also. He who could write of Milton, in a printed essay, "A true Attic bee, he *made boot on every lip,*" and who would assert that no poet ever got much poetry out of a cataract except "Milton, and that was a cataract in his eye," would not be more guarded in his offhand letters; and what most proves him unconscious of these qualities is that he is sometimes most rollicking and nonsensical to some of the most dignified of his feminine correspondents. Indeed, that side of Lowell's nature, the pure bubble and ecstasy, the champagne quality, has never been so thoroughly exhibited as here; and the saying attributed to one of his Cambridge intimates, that "Lowell was always one bottle of champagne ahead of us all," is abundantly exemplified, in the figurative sense in which it was intended. His animal spirits were always too exuberant to make much demand upon any artificial exhilaration although the temporary impulse under which he followed his wife into the total-abstinence movements appears soon to have passed away. But it is a curious fact that, with all this insuperable vivacity there was for many years a certain cumbrousness in his written sentences, traceable, perhaps, to the old English writers whom he loved.—HIGGINSON, THOMAS WENTWORTH, 1893, *Lowell's Letters, The Nation*, vol. 57, p. 488.

There are those who do not rank Lowell high among the poets. There are those who do not think his prose is good. But the most captious of these will hardly question that as a letter-writer he is entirely satisfactory. We have here none of those essays or sermons which are often put off as letters on the reading world. Such are the letters of Goethe and Schiller to each other. They are magnificent, but they are not —letters. Emerson's letters to Carlyle had often five or six preliminary drafts. Carlyle's to Emerson had never one; and Lowell's, like Carlyle's, are profuse strains of unpremeditated artlessness. . . . He is more the poet in their literary form than he is anything else, and he is more the poet in the desires and aspirations they express than he is humorist, or scholar, or critic, or statesman, or reformer.—CHADWICK, JOHN WHITE, 1894, *Lowell in His Letters, The Forum*, vol. 17, pp. 115, 116.

Mr. Lowell's letters are not free from faults, but their faults spring from his conditions and temperament and not from proximity to a large and admiring audience. The letters are simple, frank, and often charmingly affectionate; they reveal the heart of the man, and perhaps their best service to us is the impression they convey that the man and his work were of a piece, and that the fine idealism of the poet was but the expression of what was most real and significant to the man. The self-consciousness of the young Lowell comes out very strongly if one reads his letters in connection with those of the young Walter Scott; but it was a self-consciousness inherited with the Puritan temperament rather than developed in the individual nature.—MABIE, HAMILTON WRIGHT, 1896, *My Study Fire, Second Series*, p. 81.

GENERAL

I am very glad to hear that James Lowell's work succeeds. . . . The specimen of the work you give—the prelude to it, if I remember right, struck me as very chaste and very beautiful. It had the freshness of a mind that drew from its own sources. I am tired, as well as yourself, of the endless imitations by American poets of the forms and figures, and topics of British poetry.—STORY, JOSEPH, 1841, *To W. W. Story, Feb. 9; Life and Letters*, ed. Story, vol. II, p. 366.

In Mr. Lowell's first volume, we thought we saw a tendency of this second-hand poetizing; a disposition to mimic the jingle of a man, who, with much genius and an exquisite ear for musical rhythm, has also a Titanian fondness for quaint and dainty expressions, affected turns, and mawkishly effeminate sentiment; and who would be the worst model, therefore, not only for a young poet to imitate, but even to read; so contagious are the vices of his manner. But the symptoms have, to a degree, passed off, or Mr. Lowell has nearly outgrown the disease with which his literary childhood was threatened, if not actually assailed. We recognize in his later productions a firmer intellect, a wider range of thought, a bolder tone of expression, and a versification greatly improved. We feel that he is now becoming master of his fine powers, and an artist in the execution of his conceptions. The character of his more elaborate productions is, in general, noble and elevated, though tinged somewhat with the vague speculations which pass current in some circles for philosophy. There is a similar vagueness in the expression of religious feeling; positive religious views, though not rejected, are kept far in the background. Many of the poems are devoted to the utterance of the sentiments of humanity; and here, though the feelings expressed are always amiable and tender, the youth and inexperience of the poet are clearly manifested. He is a dreamer, apparently, brooding over the wrongs which are endured in the present state of society, and rashly inferring that the existing institutions are bad, and should be overthrown. Such radical opinions are not perhaps directly uttered, but the general tone tends that way.—FELTON, CORNELIUS CONWAY, 1844, *Lowell's Poems, North American Review*, vol. 58, p. 286.

We take leave of Mr. Lowell with remarking, that his affected and hyperbolical praises heaped on the old English dramatists are as nauseous as any ignorant exaggeration can be, bombastically protruded on us at second-hand, from an article in an old number of the "Retrospective Review," from which most of the little he knows is taken, and in the taking, turned into most monstrous nonsense.— WILSON, JOHN, 1845, *Supplement to MacFlecnoe and the Dunciad, Blackwood's Magazine*.

He has a refined fancy and is graceful for an American critic, but the truth is, otherwise, that he knows nothing of English poetry or the next thing to nothing, and has merely had a dream of the early dramatists. The amount of his reading in that lirection is an article in the *Retrospective Review* which contains extracts; and he re-extracts the extracts, re-quotes the quotations, and, "a pede Herculem," from the foot infers the man, or rather from the sandal-string of the foot, infers and judges the soul of the man—it is comparative anatomy under the most speculative conditions. How a writer of his talents and pretensions could make up his mind to make up a book on such slight substratum, is a curious proof of the state of literature in America. Do you not think so? Why a lecturer on the English Dramatists for a "Young Ladies' Academy" here, in England, might take it to be necessary to have better information than he could gather from an odd volume of an old review! And then, Mr. Lowell's naïveté in showing his authority,—as if the Elizabethan poets lay mouldering in inaccessible manuscripts somewhere below the lowest deep of Shakespeare's grave,—is curious beyond the rest! Altogether, the fact is an epigram on the surface-literature of America.—BROWNING, ELIZABETH BARRETT, 1845, *To Robert Browning, Dec. 20; The Letters of Robert Browning and Elizabeth Barrett*, vol. I, p. 342.

Called attention to many beauties not usually commented on, which showed an intimate familiarity with them. He seems, however, to us to have hazarded some very questionable assertions. The consummate art of Pope's *Cœsura*, is sneered at as if it were a blemish, and called an "immitigable seesaw." He reproaches Queen Anne's reign for producing no better writer of English, than Swift—as if any age had produced a better. We are informed that Pope mixes water with the good old mother's milk of our tongue, rubs it down till there is no muscular expression left, and that a straightforward speech cannot be got out of him. It seems to us there is enough that is straightforward in "The Dunciad," and the "Prologue to the Satires," addressed to Arbuthnot, with its pungent characterization of Addison. . . . The "Conversations" purporting to be on Old Poets, one would have thought, that with Mr. Lowell's old love for them, he would have been able to keep among them. But so strong a hold upon him had his new love, Reform, taken, that he insists upon introducing her into all sorts of company.— THAYER, W. S., 1853, *Lowell the Poet, Putnam's Magazine*, vol. 1, pp. 552, 553.

Containing the deliberate words ["Among My Books"] of perhaps the best of living English critics—his final judgments on many of the great names of literature; judgments which are the result of long and wide study and reading, of marvellous acuteness of sight and delicacy of sympathy; containing a poet's opinion of our poets, a wit's opinion of our wits; in short, the careful opinions of a man of cultivated genius concerning other men of genius who are near and dear to all of us, but to all of us partly unintelligible without an interpreter—this book of Mr. Lowell's is one of the best gifts that for many years has come to the world of English literature. . . . There will not be two opinions among readers of the volume before us whether the finest piece of criticism in it is not the essay entitled "Shakespeare Once More;" and we doubt if the sincerest hater of the superlative would not be willing to admit that, on the whole, in virtue of its combined penetration and comprehensiveness, this is the best single essay that has yet been written on the poet and his works. —DENNETT, J. R., 1870, *Lowell's Essays, The Nation*, vol. 10, p. 258.

If you want delightful reading get Lowell's "My Study Windows," and read the essays called "My Garden Acquaintance" and "Winter."—ELIOT, GEORGE, 1871, *To Madame Bodichon, June 17; George Eliot's Life as related in her Letters and Journals*, ed. Cross, vol. III, p. 96.

It is not necessary to compare Lowell with the world's great authors; it is enough to say that his works deserve and will repay the study of the most thoughtful men. One cause that may repel the mere pleasure-loving reader is that the poet is more concerned for the full expression of his vigorous thought than for the melody of the resulting lines; and when the strong words of our language are borne on a torrent of feeling, they are sometimes like an ice-pack on one of our rivers at the breaking up of winter.—UNDERWOOD, FRANCIS H., 1872, *A Hand-Book of English Literature, American Authors*, p. 422.

Not prose, however, but verse is Mr. Lowell's true literary vernacular. He writes, as Milton wrote, with his left hand, in writing prose. But whether in prose or in verse, it is still almost solely by genius and acquirement quite apart from the long labor of art, and of course, therefore, apart from the exercised strength and skill of that discipline to art, which is the wages of long labor alone, that he produces his final results. He thus chooses his place in the Valhalla of letters among the many "inheritors of unfulfilled renown." It seems likely at least (but he is yet in his just mellowing prime, and Apollo avert the omen!) that his name is destined to be treasured in the history of American literature chiefly as a gracious tradition of personal character universally dear, of culture only second to the genius which it adorned, of fame constantly greater than the achievements to which it appealed. — WILKINSON, WILLIAM CLEAVER, 1872, *Scribner's Monthly*, vol. 4, p. 345.

With just a little less Ambition of fine, or smart writing, Lowell might almost do for many Books what Ste. Beuve has left undone. He has more Humour: but not nearly so much Delicacy of Perception, or Refinement of Style; in which Ste. Beuve seems to me at the head of all Critics. I should like to give him to you if you have him not.—FITZGERALD, EDWARD, 1876, *To Mrs. Cowell, Nov. 13; More Letters*, p. 185.

Lowell's scrutiny is sure, and his tests are apt and instant. He is a detective to be dreaded by pretenders. He wastes no reverence upon traditional errors, but no man is more impatient of sham-reform, less afraid of *odia*, whether theological, scientific, or æsthetic. As a comparative critic, there are few so well served by memory and reading.—STEDMAN, EDMUND CLARENCE, 1882–85, *Poets of America*, p. 334.

In Mr. Lowell's mind, the Conservative and Radical elements are mixed in truly statesmanlike proportions. Capable of that concentrated passion which did much towards sweeping slavery from his own land, and with a certain bitterness and scepticism towards established forms of religion, no one can fail to be reassured and won by the essential sobriety of his qualifying utterances.—HAWEIS, HUGH REGINALD, 1883, *American Humorists*, p. 84.

Lowell's address at Birmingham ["Democracy"] is full of good things, and the *Times* is loud in its praise. But here again I feel the want of body and current in the discourse as a whole, and am not satisfied with a host of shrewd and well-wrought and even brilliant sayings.—ARNOLD, MATTHEW, 1884, *To Charles Eliot Norton*, Oct. 8; *Letters ed. Russell*, vol. II, p. 313.

Men like Lowell the country can spare but for a season for a foreign field of labor; here, in our own great land, higher and nobler duties affecting the character of the nation crowd upon them with the surest promises of gladdening returns. If the great republic is bound, as Emerson taught, to exhibit in its life the beautiful as well as the true and the just, our ablest critic must strengthen the artist in resisting the tendency to substitute costly and often useless and trival details for the grandeur of simplicity.—BANCROFT, GEORGE, 1885, *A Welcome to Lowell, The Literary World*, vol. 16, p. 217.

It is a good sign for American literature that Lowell is warmly appreciated by all educated men and women of the country. The wonder is that he is not one of our most popular authors. He is in perfect sympathy with all shrewd and sensible people, whatever may be the degrees of their culture; and certainly none of the American writers of novels for the newspapers which circulate hundreds of thousands of copies weekly can compare with him in his appreciation of "the popular mind" and his command of the raciest English. At any farmer's fireside in the land he would be welcomed as a good "neighborly" man. Why is it that the circulation of his books is not commensurate with the extent of his literary reputation? It is hardly possible to take up a newspaper, whether published in New York or Nebraska, without finding an allusion to Lowell or a quotation from him; and to all appearance he is as popular as Whittier, or Bret Harte, or Artemus Ward, or Harriet Beecher Stowe. Still, his books are read mainly by what are called "cultivated" people. We are convinced that if the (so-called) "uncultivated" people only knew what delight they might find in Lowell's prose and verse, they would domesticate his books at once in their homes.—WHIPPLE, EDWIN PERCY, 1886–88, *Lowell as a Prose Writer, Outlooks on Society, Literature and Politics*, p. 312.

From my point of view no living American, in assuming to speak for American culture, has so thoroughly justified himself as has Mr. Lowell. While our novelists have been showing us how ill-bred and plebeian we are, and while our critics in general have been echoing Sainte-Beuve, or taking the pitch of their strain from London masters, there have been in his writings a vigor, a manliness and a patriotic independence, always pure, racy and refreshing, which have made us aware of our own value as the creators of a new civilization of which the old is not competent to judge. Wherever the most healthful and most fertilizing influence of American republicanism has gone, wherever the best essence of American aspiration has insinuated itself to liberalize human thought, or to give vigor to reforms, there have been felt the sincere force and the subtle earnestness of Mr. Lowell's words set in the phrasing of a master of style.—THOMPSON, MAURICE, 1889, *James Russell Lowell, The Critic*, vol. 9, p. 86.

We all know Mr. Lowell's brilliant quality as a poet, critic, scholar, and man of the world; but that in him which touches me most strongly belongs to his relations to his country—his keen and subtle yet kindly recognition of her virtues and her faults, and the sympathetic power with which in the day of her melancholy triumph, after the Civil War, he gave such noble expression to her self-devotion, sorrows, and hopes.—PARKMAN, FRANCIS, 1889, *James Russell Lowell, The Critic*, vol. 9, p. 87.

His critical essays are so perfect in their literary quality that one forgets that they are or are not criticism.—HARTE, BRET, 1891, *A Few Words About Mr. Lowell, New Review*, vol. 5, p. 200.

Excellence so high and so varied implies something more than versatility and cultivation. It implies a personality of remarkable originative power. For, after all, in literature it is personality that tells. Learning, culture, industry may make volumes, but they cannot make literature. The book is not immortal unless the man is in it, alive for evermore. Lowell's writing stands this test. However varied its themes, it is still the utterance of the always same voice, refined, imaginative, yet urgent and stimulating.—WINCHESTER, C. T., 1891, *Lowell as Man of Letters, Review of Reviews, American Ed.*, vol. 4, p. 291.

When James Russell Lowell died, on August 12th, the greatest of contemporary Americans passed away. He had no compeer since Emerson died; he has left no successor. On this side of the Atlantic there still linger veterans not unequal to him whom we have just lost. But neither on one side of the Atlantic nor on the other is there any poet left us whose verse is instinct with so much inspiration, or one who has in him so much of the seer of these latter days.—STEAD, WILLIAM THOMAS, 1891, *Lowell's Message and how it Helped Me, Review of Reviews, American Ed.*, vol. 4, p. 296.

When we ask ourselves what we have lost in Mr. Lowell—or rather, in happier and truer phrase, what we have gained permanently in spite of our present loss—we seem to answer, No one special book, whether of prose or verse; but an influence working sturdily and persistently in the direction of all that is most pure, most elevated, and most enthusiastic in the literary life. Few men have devoted their career to books with so little loss of manhood and citizenship as he. His tastes were distinguished; but they were wholesome and reasonable. He loved literature with passion; but he loved it wisely. As a poet, as an essayist, as a humorist, as a lecturer, as a critic, he was always in favor of what was sane. He was preserved from littleness and exaggeration by that saving grace of humor. He could even let himself go on an intellectual impulse, and swing back into perfect reasonableness on a quip or a fantastic phrase. He combined, and to a very rare degree, the broad view of the scholar-gentleman—which in less accomplished hands is thin—with the exactitude of the specialist—which in pedantic treatment is sterile and narrow. He despised the bitterness of the mere literary expert; and perhaps it will be found that his worst mistakes as a critic have been made when he hastily mistook the man of science for a dryasdust, and persuaded himself to smite him. Among Mr. Lowell's essays none is more unlucky than that on Chaucer when it attempts to crush the genuine learning of Prof. Skeat, none more charming when it illuminates the warm genius of the poet by the light of a nature almost as sweet and as serene as his In some respects the most academic man-of-letters whom America has produced, and recognized in that capacity by the universities of Europe, Mr. Lowell represented the older forms of learning, and was a little apt to look with contempt on the modern passion for an extreme subdivision of knowledge. He loved truth for its own sake, but he desired that it should have undergone preservation in "Fame's great antiseptic—style," before it was presented to him. — GOSSE, EDMUND, 1891, *James Russell Lowell*, St. James's Gazette, Aug. 12.

He holds so many rare elements in combination,—manhood, and patriotism, and spiritual insight underlying his love of nature, his wit, his tenderness, his subtle and passionate power of expression, his fine perception of the picturesque, and his exquisite rhymatic sense and facility. Both as a man of letters and as a poet, he is one of the few whom our American youth must always look up to and study with pride and reverence — an acknowledged standard American author.—LARCOM, LUCY, 1891, *Personal Tributes to Lowell, The Writer* vol. 5, p. 190.

He had so much wit that some critics have denied him imagination, but "Sir Launfal" is a work of imagination of a high order. He was the most thoughtful of our poets, the most scholarly of our critics, as learned as he was racy. No writer is more truly American and of the very soil, and no American writer had a larger appreciation of the life and literature of other nations. In the "Fable for Critics" he wrote one of our very best satires; in "The Unhappy Lot of Mr. Knott" he produced verbal play worthy of Hood; in the "Biglow Papers" there is no end of wit, humor, and biting satire, imagination and poetic feeling, racy rustic speech, combined with refinement and scholarship.—EGGLESTON, EDWARD, 1891, *Personal Tributes to Lowell, The Writer*, vol. 5, p. 187.

In him, as in so many other men, great and small, there was a certain dualism of nature and character. He, too, was of those who carry two heads under their hats, two men's hearts behind their waistcoats. Looking at him in the maturity of his years and experience those who knew him best recognised these diverse, but not warring, elements. He "beat his music out," from the clash and contact of the two influences. He was at once a Yankee and an European; a provincial and a cosmopolitan; a preacher and a poet; a vehement and even violent partisan and a critic of wide culture and large humanity; a citizen of Massachusetts and a citizen of the world. As Lowell grew older it was the wider element that waxed, the narrower and more limited that waned. But it was the latter that was the stronger and more characteristic during the years of his greatest activity and that inspired the larger part of the work by which he is likely to be permanently remembered. Literature will know him longest, not as the critic, or as the writer of elegies and lyrics and "odes," but as the poet who gave literary form and value to the indigenous humour, rhetoric, and satire of the farmers of New England.—LOW, SIDNEY, 1891, *Lowell and his Poetry, Fortnightly Review*, vol. 56, p. 310.

The fullness of this expression of a many-sided career is remarkable; but even more striking is the harmony of all these phases of life, one with another. There is no dividing line which sets off one part of his activity from its neighbor part; in his poetry there is politics, in his learning there is the vivifying touch of humor, in his reflection there is emotion, in the levels of his most familiar prose there is, at inconstant intervals, the sudden lift of a noble thought; and hence his works are at once too diverse and too similar—diverse in their matter and similar in the personality through which they are given out—to be easily summed or described by the methods of criticism. If there is a clue that may be used, it is to be sought in his individuality, in the fact that his ten talents have somehow been melted and fused into one, and that the greatest—the talent of being a man first and everything else afterwards.—WOODBERY, GEORGE EDWARD, 1891, *James Russell Lowell, Century Magazine, vol. 43, p. 113.*

He might have been greater, had he been in some respects less. He might have done more, had he not known so much. He would have attained to a more powerful originality, if it had not been a part of his training to be familiar with, and to be pervaded by, the best thoughts of many minds in many ages. His greatness in a single form of excellence would have been more unchallenged and permanent, but for his many claims to admiration.—FARRAR, FREDERIC WILLIAM, 1891, *An English Estimate of Lowell, The Forum, vol. 12, p. 143.*

Even so admirable, so sensible a writer as Mr. Lowell is apt to worry us with his Elizabethan profusion of imagery, epithet, and wit. "Something too much of this," we cry out before we are half-way through. —BIRRELL, AUGUSTINE, 1892, *Res Judicatæ, p. 301.*

Cultured America, we believe, has not yet fully made up her mind as to who is her best poet; but we imagine that she could have little hesitation in pointing to Mr. Lowell as her most brilliant "all-round" literary representative. Emerson's mission, on his visits to these shores, was philosophical rather than literary; Hawthorne's was mainly a mission of silence; and Dr. Holmes's, from all we could ever hear, a mission of dining. It is pre-eminently Mr. Lowell who comes to us as his Excellency the Ambassador of American literature to the court of Shakespeare. . . . Mr. Lowell's forte is profusion, and his foible prodigality. His good things lie about in all directions, so temptingly, so portably, like the diamonds in Sindbad's valley, that a reviewer, in his hurry to fill his pockets and retire on the proceeds to Balsora, is apt to forget the larger aspects of that earth and sky which encompass him. But it is a teeming earth, and a bracing sky. In his directness of speech and broad heartiness of manner, Mr. Lowell brings with him an air which, to use one of his own expressions, "blows the mind clear." It is delightfully fresh and tonic, with a certain saline shrewdness in it, reminding us that it has come across the ocean.—WATSON, WILLIAM, 1893, *Excursions in Criticism, pp. 89, 95.*

When we come to read Lowell's noble essay on Dante we are tempted to acknowledge in his paragraphs a certain colossal unity; at a little distance from the charm of the style we dare to speak of that unity as prolix; later, we begin to wonder whether there is any unity at all in a paragraph of, say, 2183 words. It is hard to make out Lowell's theory of the paragraph. Apparently he had a most elastic idea of the elasticity of that unit, and felt that if he looked to a proper alternation of emphasis by sentence-variation and kept up a general flow of coherence, his paragraphic duty was done. At any rate, it is easy to praise his emphasis, varied by 23 per cent of simple sentences and by skilful inversions that put the main idea first. And we may praise his coherence, depending as it does upon closeness of logical relation, and eschewing formal connectives.—LEWIS, EDWIN HERBERT, 1894, *The History of the English Paragraph, p. 158.*

Mr. Lowell's literary essays represent the highest order of criticism that has appeared in America. The two volumes of "Among My Books" and the collection called "My Study Windows" contain strong and original thought, unusual scholarship, and a poet's own power of feeling for poetry. Mr. Lowell was learned, and his learning did not dull him æsthetically, or blur his tact in distinguishing relative literary values. In criticism, as in his whole broad nature, he grew better as he grew old.—MCLAUGHLIN, EDWARD T., 1895, *Literary Criticism for Students, p. 173.*

Among men of letters Lowell is doubtless most typically American, though Curtis must find an eligible place in the list. Lowell was self-conscious, though the truest greatness is not; he was a trifle too "smart," besides, and there is no "smartness" in great literature. But both the self-consciousness and the smartness must be admitted to be American; and Lowell was so versatile, so urbane, of so large a spirit, and so admirable in the scope of his sympathies, that he must certainly go on the calendar.—WILSON, WOODROW, 1896, *Mere Literature and Other Essays, p.* 210.

Criticism which is the result of sympathetic relationship and consequent insight may serve to induce in a reader the right attitude toward a poet—the attitude demanded for the best response to him. Of such criticism James Russell Lowell's essay on Chaucer, contained in his "My Study Windows," affords a signal example. Every student of Chaucer should give a careful reading, should give several careful readings, to this essay.—CORSON, HIRAM, 1897, *Selections from Chaucer's Canterbury Tales, Introduction, p.* XXVII.

James Russell Lowell wears the title of a man of letters. He was a master of verse and a political disputant; he was to some extent a journalist, and in a high degree an orator; he administered learning in a great university; he was concerned, in his later years, with public affairs, and represented in two foreign countries the interests of the United States. Yet there is only one term to which, in an appreciation, we can without a sense of injustice give precedence over the others. He was the American of his time most saturated with literature and most directed to criticism; the American also whose character and endowment were such as to give this saturation and this direction—this intellectual experience, in short—most value. He added to the love of learning the love of expression; and his attachment to these things—to poetry, to history, to language, form, and style—was such as to make him, the greater part of his life, more than anything a man of study: but his temperament was proof against the dryness of the air of knowledge, and he remained to the end the least pale, the least passionless of scholars.—JAMES, HENRY, 1897, *Library of the World's Best Literature, ed. Warner, vol.* XVI, *p.* 9229.

Lowell is less remembered as a scholar than as an essayist, a poet, a critic, or, as what we may call for want of a better name, a man of letters. So far as concerns those best qualified to remember (namely, other scholars), he is as a scholar best remembered for the spirit, the impulse, the encouragement, which he gave scholarship rather than for any particular work. You will find little reference to learned works of his on Shakespeare or Chaucer. In fact, he wrote no learned works. . . . Lowell's scholarship was not the scholarship of today. He had but a dim conception of language as it exists at the universities today; or of literature, either, I had almost added. His ideas on language were, on the whole, such as he gained by reading the literature of any language in question for the moment. Further he had no especial care to go, so far as I can find out. As for the linguistic studies of his contemporary, Whitney, I presume that he regarded them as having especial connection with Sanskrit or Zend. . . . Before Lowell's death he had been felt generally and rightly to be the representative American man of letters of his day. As such he is still regarded, and in all probability time will never take from him the distinction of having been the successor in this respect of Washington Irving. Other reputations may change, but this one is likely to endure; for it is rather historical than critical. It is more a matter of fact than a question of taste.—HALE, EDWARD EVERETT, JR., 1899, *James Russell Lowell, pp.* 39, 41, 111.

His death took from us a man rich beyond all other Americans in poetic impulses, in width of training, in varied experience, and in readiness of wit; sometimes entangled and hampered by his own wealth; unequal in expression, yet rising on the greatest occasions to the highest art; blossoming early, yet maturing late; with a certain indolence of temperament, yet accomplishing all the results of strenuous labors; not always judicial in criticism, especially in early years, yet steadily expanding and deepening; retaining in age the hopes and sympathies of his youth; and dying, with singular good fortune, just after he had gathered into final shape the literary harvest of his life.—HIGGINSON, THOMAS WENTWORTH, 1899, *Old Cambridge, p.* 196.

It is as the poet of the American ideas, so nobly expressed in these early writings, and even more nobly in some of the later ones, that we cherish the memory of Lowell, and turn to him, rather than to any other, for cheer and consolation in such a time as our own, when the Idea upon which he had fixed his faith seems to have become submerged beneath a flood of corruption, self-seeking ambition, and the cynical disregard of our national obligations. It may be urged that the American Idea, as Lowell voiced it, was nothing more than the New England Idea, or the Puritan Idea, but we are of those who believe that the best expression thus far given to Americanism in its finer sense is the expression given it by the group of New England writers who for many years held the national conscience so largely in their keeping, and of whom Lowell was at once the raciest and the most deeply imbued with those moral principles which are the only real basis of our national greatness. And it is because in these dark recent days those principles seem to have lost their old-time hold upon our national life that we listen more yearningly than ever for some echo of the voice that thrilled with indignation in "The Biglow Papers" and with the pride of American manhood in the great ode consecrated to the sacred memory of Abraham Lincoln.—PAYNE, WILLIAM MORTON, 1901, *James Russell Lowell, The Dial, vol,* 31, *p.* 312.

How much of the allurement of the essay style did Lowell keep, however scholarlike his quest, in papers literary, historical, even philological! In a veritable essay-subject like "On a Certain Condescension in Foreigners," he displays himself as of the right line of descent from Montaigne; there is in him then all that unforced, winsome, intimate, yet ever restrained revelation of self which is the essayist's model, and despair. In the love letters of the Brownings may be found some strictures by both Robert and Elizabeth upon an early book of this great American's which must pain the admirer of the Brownings as well as of Lowell. It displays a curious insensitiveness to just this power of the Cambridge man which made him of so much more value to the world than if he had been a scholar and nothing more. One can hardly rise from anything like a complete examination of Lowell's prose without the regret that his fate did not lead him to cultivate more assiduously and single-eyed, this rare and precious gift for essay—a gift shared with very few fellow Americans.—BURTON, RICHARD, 1902, *Forces in Fiction and Other Essays, p.* 95.

Some of the strongest, most virile criticism ever produced was that of Hazlitt; but how few read Hazlitt now! In our own century Lowell reached the highest altitudes, but I cannot believe that his critical writings will be often read far down this century. Lowell's letters will outlive them all—those charming personal compositions, in which he put so much of learning, so much of wit and insight, so much even of life itself. In them we see a man deeply learned and widely cultured, but with all that a real, living, working man, now at his tasks, now at his play.—HALSEY, FRANCIS WHITING, 1902, *Our Literary Deluge and Some of its Deep Waters, p.* 53.

There can be little question that he is the most cultured writer, the most accomplished scholar, the most expert man of letters yet produced by America. He is also in all probability the most pregnant academic speaker, and although he is not the greatest American writer upon political subjects he is one of the wisest and most uplifting. . . . It seems certain that there is a wearying amount of corruscation in his essays, that they often contain poetical elements that might have been more serviceable if utilized in his verse, that they are far too frequently over-long, not to say sprawling in structure. On the other hand, they are so full of that indefinable something called flavour, they are so often illuminating, so packed with surprises and felicities of thought and imagination admirably expressed, that they may answer all challenges with something of the good-humoured sense of mastery their author was wont to display throughout his life.—TRENT, WILLIAM P., 1903, *A History of American Literature, pp.* 449, 450.

If his humour was his rarest, it was his most dangerous gift; so often did it tempt him to laugh out in some holy place. . . . What is most subjective in his verse, its keenest notes of joy and sorrow, draws us by a yet stronger cord. Less charming than Longfellow, less homely than Whittier, less artistic than Holmes, less grave than Bryant, less vivid than Emerson, less unique than Poe, his qualities, intellectual, moral, and æsthetic, in their assemblage and co-ordination assign him to a place among American men of letters which is only a little lower than that which is Emerson's, and his alone.—CHADWICK, JOHN WHITE, 1903, *Chambers's Cyclopædia of English Literature, ed. Patrick, vol.* III, *p.* 799.

ALEXANDER WILLIAM KINGLAKE

Engraving from a Photograph by Elliott & Fry.

EDWARD ROBERT BULWER LYTTON

Engraving from a Photograph.

Edward Robert Bulwer Earl Lytton
(Owen Meredith)
1831–1891

Born, in London, 8 Nov. 1831. To Harrow, June 1846. Removed after a short time; afterwards educated at Bonn. To Washington, as Sec. to Lord Dalling, Oct. 1849; Attaché to Embassy at Florence, Feb. 1852; at Paris, Aug. 1854; at the Hague, 1856; at St. Petersburg, April 1858; at Constantinople, June 1858; at Vienna, Jan. 1859; Second Sec., Vienna, Oct. 1862; Sec. of Legation at Copenhagen, Jan. 1863; at Athens, May 1864. Married Edith Villiers, 4 Oct. 1864. Sec. of Legation at Lisbon, April 1865; at Madrid, Feb. 1868; at Vienna, Sept. 1868; Sec. to Embassy at Paris, Oct. 1872. Succeeded to title of Baron Lytton at his father's death, Jan. 1873. British Ambassador at Lisbon, Dec. 1874. Viceroy of India, 1876–80. G. C. B., 1 Jan. 1876; G. C. S. I., 12 April 1876. Created Earl of Lytton, April 1880. British Ambassador at Paris, 1887–91. Privy Councillor, 29 June 1888. Died suddenly in Paris, 24 Nov. 1891. Buried at Knebworth. *Works:* "Clytemnestra" (under pseud.: "Owen Meredith"), 1855; "The Wanderer" (by "Owen Meredith"), 1859; "Lucile" (by "Owen Meredith"), 1860; "Tannhäuser" (with Julian Fane; under pseud. of "Neville Temple and Edward Trevor"), 1861; "Serbski Pesme" (by "Owen Meredith"), 1861; "The Ring of Amasis" (by "Owen Meredith"), 1863; "The Poetical Works of Owen Meredith" (2 vols.), 1867; "Chronicles and Characters," 1868 [1867]; "Orval," 1869; "Julian Fane," 1871; "Fables in Song," 1874; "Life, Letters, and Literary Remains of his father," 1883; "Glenaveril," 1885; "After Paradise," 1887. *Posthumous:* "Marah," ed. by Lady Lytton, 1892; "King Poppy," 1892 (priv. ptd., 1875). He *translated:* Edler's "Baldine," 1886.—SHARP, R. FARQUHARSON, 1897, *A Dictionary of English Authors, p. 177.*

PERSONAL

I haven't seen Owen Meredith, and don't feel the least curiosity about him.—ROSSETTI, DANTE GABRIEL, 1855, *Letters to William Allingham, p. 141.*

Among other persons there was Lytton, the son of Sir E. B. Lytton. I met him afterwards the same evening, and he made me a formal speech about the D. R., saying it was a great privilege to know the author, etc. He is a handsome young man, and very clever, having published some poems, which are good, under the *nom de plume* of "Owen Meredith."—MOTLEY, JOHN LOTHROP, 1858 *To his Wife, July* 4; *Correspondence, ed. Curtis, vol.* I., *p. 285.*

I think, for example, you speak rather too well of young Lytton, whom I regard both as an impostor and an Antinomian heretic.—LOWELL, JAMES RUSSELL, 1866, *Letter to E. C. Stedman, Letters, ed. Norton, vol.* I, *p. 365.*

My dear Lytton,—Lord Northbrook has resigned the Viceroyalty of India, for purely domestic reasons, and will return to England in the spring. If you be willing, I will submit your name to the Queen as his successor. The critical state of affairs in Central Asia demands a statesman, and I believe if you will accept this high post you will have an opportunity, not only of serving your country, but of obtaining an enduring fame.—DISRAELI, BENJAMIN (LORD BEACONSFIELD), 1875, *Letter to Lord Lytton, Nov. 23; Lord Lytton's Indian Administration, ed. Balfour, p. 2.*

As a diplomatist he occupied a great many posts and mastered a great many languages. He also acquired the highest art of which modern diplomacy is capable. He learned to cook. . . . Lord Lytton excels in so many arts that he is superlatively good in none. He is one of the most amiable, witty, and fair-minded of Englishmen. Had he been forced to make his own way, he might have been acclaimed as Lord Beaconsfield's successor. As it is, he does little to beseem the promise of his youth. His career has been purposeless, invertebrate.—SETON, R., 1881, *Lord Lytton, The Critic, vol.* 1, *p. 254.*

Lord Lytton inhabits at Paris the splendid mansion in the Faubourg Saint-Honoré, which once belonged to the beautiful Pauline Borghèse, sister of Napoleon I. Its spacious apartments and large garden running back to the Champs-Elysées are admirably adapted for fêtes, and if the Ambassador cannot repeat the gorgeous ceremonies he so well organized in the Orient, he will at least be able to dispense a hospitality worthy of the country he represents. He has brought back from the Indias a collection of curiosities that he has placed in the Ambassadorial palace, and as soon as the visitor puts foot in the large entry-way, he can, with a very slight stretch of the imagination believe that he has been transported to the Orient. Every room, besides, contains souvenirs of the most notable period of the Ambassador's official life. Socially speaking, Lord Lytton is well equipped for his high position. Of fine appearance, in the force of age and health, rich, surrounded by a charming family and counting among his friends all the members of the best French society, he will be able to do all that personal prestige can do to remove the prejudices existing between the two countries.— LELAND, FRANCIS, 1888, *The Earl of Lytton, The Epoch, Nov. 16.*

Lord Lytton's death came very suddenly, but it was perhaps a crowning mercy which spared him great suffering. Much is said of him in public, not entirely in accord with the opinion which prevailed in private life. I have heard him called a brilliant failure, which does not seem a kindly estimate. Brilliant he certainly was. Fail, in some high matters, he certainly did; but it was not a failure that destroyed the confidence of those who knew him. He knew how to win the confidence of Lord Beaconsfield and Lord Salisbury. When Lord Beaconsfield made him Viceroy of India, it was against the judgment of his party, and his Viceroyalty justified the hostility to his appointment. Lord Salisbury sent him as Ambassador to France, almost as great a post, and what he said of his nominee yesterday implies that he was satisfied with his work. Yet I fear the truth is that Lord Lytton's removal had been more than once very seriously discussed, if not determined. The English Ambassador was liked personally. He was not liked as an ambassador. He gave offence to the French sense of decorum by his Bohemian habits and his neglect of those conventionalities which are the most precious in French eyes. He held the Foreign Office in alarm. One of the most accomplished men in that office was sent over to keep things straight, and did keep them as straight as circumstances would allow; but as Lord Lytton left India after having embittered and endangered the relations of England with natives and neighbors, so he leaves France more jealous and hostile than he found her. India was his fault.

France is not; but viceroys and ambassadors are commonly judged by results. He had gifts of many kinds. He had literature, he had poetry, neither of the first order. He had delightful social qualities. He was one of those men whom Arnold used to call attaching. There was a touch of the feminine nature in him, and his caprices were innumerable. The French liked him because they knew he liked them, and for his fame as a writer and the son of a writer, which the English hardly understand. Perhaps to his own countrymen his title was more than his books or his father's books. When all is said, an amiable and gifted man, original, self-centred, free from Philistinism, free from cant, free from the commonplace, is gone.— SMALLEY, GEORGE W., 1891, *London Letter, New York Tribune.*

He, of all English poets, is the one who, since the days of Byron, has had the largest experience of life. . . . Now, whilst few of our modern poets have excelled him in devotion to his art, none have come near him in point of mundane experience. Let the reader consider his career, the outlines of which are known to everybody; and the fullness of what I mean will be apparent. . . . Few men have ever combined as he did mundane humour, fastidiousness, shrewdness, and *savoir faire*, with ultra-sensitive sympathy, and grave, meditative philosophy. In most men these latter qualities tend to withdraw them from life. In Lord Lytton their effect was different. They made his experiences richer and more vivid, fixing their colours in his imagination, and deepening their significance in his mind. No one who knew him well would fail to be struck with this. He had inherited from his father something of a taste in dress a little suggesting that of the traditional poet; but his whole bearing and manner showed, the first moment he spoke, the sanity, the suavity, and the polish of the complete man of the world. No one or suitable occasions could discuss literature and poetry with more enthusiasm, more judgment, more feeling, and more knowledge than he: but life at first hand he discussed with equal mastery, and in ordinary society he discussed little else.—MALLOCK, WILLIAM HURREL, 1892, *Poetry and Lord Lytton, Fortnightly Review, vol. 57, p. 805.*

Lytton's position among the public men

of his day was unique. It recalled the life of the Elizabethan noble, little concerned with the arts that influence deliberate assemblies, but leading alternately the lives of a scholar, a diplomatist, a magistrate, a courtier, and a man of letters. Had he but been a soldier too, the parallel would have been perfect. Few have touched life at so many points, have enjoyed such variety of interesting experiences, or have so profoundly fascinated their intimates, whether relatives, friends, or official colleagues. The antipathies he also provoked had seldom a deeper root than some unintentional slight or misinterpreted oddity on his part, or were affected for political purposes. The one serious fault of his public career was the unwise disregard of conventions, which passed for whimsical caprice, and, thus suggesting infirmity of judgment, injured the prestige on which the strongest must largely rely.—GARNETT, RICHARD, 1893, *Dictionary of National Biography*, vol. XXXIV, p. 391.

The Earl of Lytton was often cruelly misrepresented and misunderstood. I should like to give my humble testimony that, knowing him intimately for many years, having spent long hours in his society, having received from him many letters, having conversed with him on all conceivable topics, literary and religious, and having heard him in public as well as in private, he left on my mind the conviction that he was a man of brilliant ability, of generous instincts, of kindliest nature, and one whose sincere desire it was to do his duty faithfully and strenuously in the world.— FARRAR, FREDERIC WILLIAM, 1897, *Men I have Known*, p. 262.

LUCILE
1860

"Lucile," with all its lightness, remains his best poem, as well as the most popular; a really interesting, though sentimental, parlor-novel, written in fluent verse,—a kind of production exactly suited to his gift and limitations.—STEDMAN, EDMUND CLARENCE, 1875-87, *Victorian Poets*, p. 268.

"Lucile," in its day, was a literary sensation. It was given to the world at a time when the romantic fever was at its height, and when Englishwomen were sighing for a native school of fiction which should follow the footsteps of George Sand and Octave Feuillet. At what distance "Lucile" followed them has never been exactly determined. There appeared in a literary paper of the period a very circumstantial accusation that it was a close version, in plot, characters, and sometimes in language, of one of the earlier novels which the author of "Consuelo" had anonymously published. The charge was not pressed. It was rumoured that the new poet would make a terrible slaughter of his traducers after the manner of "English Bards and Scotch Reviewers," and he seems to have published a denial in some obscure publication. But there the matter dropped. It had little interest for Owen Meredith's readers, who for the most part were very young. It had no great interest for his critics, who discerned in him an extraordinary facility, an almost Byronic flow of fiction, and none of the marks of poetic greatness. His lines went cantering on their way unchecked.—SETON, R., 1881, *Lord Lytton, The Critic*, vol. 1, p. 254.

I, for one, should not think of expecting a serious critic to wax enthusiastic over "Lucile." As far as I am acquainted with the writings of Owen Meredith, everything he has done is well done. As the phrase is, it is good of its sort. But I do not think one can rate the "sort" in this case very highly. "Lucile" seems to stand mid-way between the vernal charm of "The Wanderer," and the rich autumn tints and autumn fruits to be met with in the riper writings of the Earl of Lytton. Like summer, "Lucile" is luscious, but its colour is uniform; it is neither blossom nor harvest. —AUSTIN, ALFRED, 1887, *Owen Meredith, Earl of Lytton, National Review*, vol. 8, p. 687.

Whatever rank as poetry we may assign to this work, there runs through it a complete but unconscious familiarity with life, which gives to every tone, sentiment, or epigram, a propriety, a precision, and point often absent in poems of a far more ambitious character. — MALLOCK, WILLIAM HURREL, 1892, *Poetry and Lord Lytton, Fortnightly Review*, vol. 57, p. 806.

FABLES IN SONG
1874

A form of literature so very innocent and primitive, looks a little over-written in Lord Lytton's conscious and highly-coloured style. It may be bad taste, but sometimes we should prefer a few sentences of plain prose narration, and a little Bewick by way of tail-piece. So that it is not among those fables that conform most nearly to the old model, but one had nearly said among those that most widely differ from it, that we find the most satisfactory examples of the author's manner. . . . And now for a last word, about the style. This is not easy to criticise. It is impossible to deny to it rapidity, spirit, and a full sound; the lines are never lame, and the sense is carried forward with an uninterrupted, impetuous rush. But it is not equal. After passages of really admirable versification, the author falls back upon a sort of loose, cavalry manner, not unlike the style of some of Mr. Browning's minor pieces, and almost inseparable from wordiness, and an easy acceptation of a somewhat cheap finish.—STEVENSON, ROBERT LOUIS, 1874, *Lord Lytton's Fables in Song, Fortnightly Review*, vol. 21, pp. 819, 822.

He has, to our thinking, achieved so much towards the resuscitation of a neglected phase of poetry, by bringing into play a curious and refined observation, a poet's insight into nature, large gifts of felicitous expression, cultivated to a degree very unusual in these rough and ready days, and withal a deep human tenderness struggling out of an external crust of cynicism, that it is worth while to examine the secret of his success, and to trace the causes of his adventuring a path over which he was not so sure of a literary public to follow him, as if he had chosen to lead off on a classical, romantic, or even homely track. These latter are to be gleaned from casual expressions in the course of his two volumes of "Fables in Song."—DAVIES, JAMES, 1874, *Fables in Song, Contemporary Review*, vol. 24, p. 94.

They are full of thought—sometimes overburdened with it; but they have a graceful facility of versification which entitles their author to rank with many of our cultivated poets.—SMITH, GEORGE BARNETT, 1875, *English Fugitive Poets, Poets and Novelists*, p. 421.

His "Fables in Song" are probably the portion of his compositions which will last the longest. Some of them are fine, visionary, and poetical, the "Blue Mountains" in particular, rising to our recollection as a charming rendering of the poetic wistfulness and strain towards a distant good, which recedes as the pilgrim advances, and is never fulfilled. These poems are of a higher class altogether than the volumes of verse produced by the elder Lord Lytton. —OLIPHANT, MARGARET O. W., 1892, *The Victorian Age of English Literature*, p. 454.

GLENAVERIL
1885

To judge from this first instalment, his lordship, though qualified to do good service as a pioneer, is too one-sided, and not quite powerful enough to show the very age and body of the time its form and pressure. But we must wait for the finished work. Thus far at least it is a very interesting production, full of life and character. The root-incident in the story, the starting-point of future complications, has never, so far as I know, appeared in such an exalted literary position before. It is one of the common-places of the circus-clown and the low comedian to jest about children getting mixed up in the washing, to the subsequent confusion of their respective identities. In Lord Lytton's story this accident happens to the infant sons of an English peer and a German Lutheran parson, and it has evidently given him no little trouble to tell with becoming dignity and delicacy how the mischance happened. A slight discrepancy between the first stanza and the seventeenth—a discrepancy which recalls the famous description of a battle-field as resounding with "the shrieks of the dying and the groans of the dead"—is indicative of the poet's difficulties, and probably means that he recast the opening more than once. It is not an easy matter to show in short compass the weaving of the knot of circumstances that brought such an extraordinary exchange of personalities within the range of possibility, and we read on for some time with a certain feeling of perplexity as to what the poet would be at. The meaning is conveyed with such indirectness that many readers are certain to miss it altogether; and it is not till we reach the thirty-seventh stanza that dim and wondering suspicion of the poet's daring humour changes into the full light of conviction. . . . In the third canto, *à propos* of young Lord Glenaveril's entrance into the House of Lords, he takes opportunity also for more personal criticism of his friends and opponents. This political episode will doubtless attract more general notice than any other portion of the present instalment of the poem. Looked at from a purely literary point of view, and without reference to their party spirit, these sketches must be pronounced to be the best of the kind that have been done in verse since the late Lord Lytton published "St. Stephen's." The son, however, is not quite equal to the father; the father was at least as brilliant, and his judgment was much more evenly balanced.—MINTO, WILLIAM, 1885, *Literature, The Academy, vol. 27, pp. 285, 286.*

In "Glenaveril" there is complete unity in the plot itself. Every book in every canto contributes to the solution of the main problem, which is always before the mind of the poet. Lord Lytton has rightly felt that it was incumbent on him to relieve the excessive strain on the reader's attention, and he has done this by the agreeable variety of his characters, and by the introduction of episodes of great beauty and animation, such as the legend of Marietta's Needle, and the Fable of King Usinara. The poem is also enlivened by sketches of social life in England, and with portraits of contemporary statesmen so admirably vivid that many readers must have wished that the poet had been tempted more frequently to stray from the severer lines he had prescribed for himself into the by-ways of satire and description. . . . There is plenty of variety, too, in the reflections and arguments interspersed through the narrative, and Lord Lytton's muse is never more felicitous than in political epigram. . . . Whatever may be the judgment of the critic on this poem, no one can rise from it without a sense of the extraordinary intellectual power that has been spent on its production. It is, as I have already said, a bold and original experiment in art. Lord Lytton has completely emerged from the semi-lyrical atmosphere of sentiment and reflection in which the poet has been long moving, and has once more carried metrical composition into the sphere of external *action*. In "Glenaveril" the plot is everything; the moral problem is solved by means of it; the characters owe their existence to it; the diction adapts itself to its requirements.—COURTHOPE, WILLIAM JOHN, 1886, *Glenaveril, National Review, vol. 6, pp. 854, 855.*

He himself, it seems, believed in the book; the more sacred band of his admirers believes in it; there are undoubtedly good things in it; and I recently found it easier to read it a second time than I did when it came out, to read it at first. But I am quite unable to regard it as anything on the whole but a huge and creditable mistake.—SAINTSBURY, GEORGE, 1896, *The Poetry of the Earl of Lytton, The Forum, vol. 22, p. 475.*

MARAH
1891

Is it because I am older and colder now, I wonder, that nothing in "Marah" moves me as did the linked sweetness and melancholy of those earlier strains? Or is it that William Morris has put me out of tune with Lord Lytton, as an hour under the white enchantment of the moon, among the wide spaces of the night, might unfit one for the electric lights of the ballroom?—MOULTON, LOUISE CHANDLER, 1892, *Three English Poets, The Arena, vol. 6, p. 48.*

The love portrayed in "Marah" is of the body rather than of the soul, it is founded on the "ruins of man's will," and its votaries are "zealous artisans," not artists. But, as of old, Lord Lytton's verses are fluent and musical. Mr. Wilfred Scawen Blunt has compared him to an improvisatore, and this volume contains the faults and merits peculiar to such a style, now free and vigorous, now tame and diffuse.—JOHNSON, REGINALD BRIMLEY, 1892, *Marah, The Academy, vol. 41, p. 416.*

"Marah" is the record of Lord Lytton's last deception in the world of sentiment, and it stands as such almost unique in English literature. Indeed, I know of nothing which can exactly be compared with it, for our passionate poets have seldom been long-lived, and Goethe's romance of old age has remained without an English imitator. On this account "Marah" will be found of supreme interest as well as inexpressibly touching by all who knew Lord Lytton either personally or as the young love-poet he was to readers in his days of "Owen Meredith."—BLUNT, WILFRED SCAWEN, 1892, *Lord Lytton's Rank in Literature, The Nineteenth Century, vol. 31, p. 571.*

GENERAL

Mr. Lytton has published an excess of lyrical pieces. He is, I should say, an intellectual poet with a dramatic tendency, not lyrical. The design of the "Chronicles and Characters" would argue for him the possession of a mind *contentus paucis lectoribus*, but there is still a slight *ad captandum* flavor in some of the minor poems and their metres which detracts from the merit of the volumes as a whole. He conceived possibly that variety and lightness were wanted to relieve the severe intellectual pressure. He might have trusted to his natural strength without any fears of the sort.—MEREDITH, GEORGE, 1868, *Mr. Robert Lytton's Poems, Fortnightly Review, vol. 9, p.* 661.

I have been reading Robert Lytton's "Chronicles and Characters." They belong to a generation in which there is a great deal of thinking for thinking's sake. They are not less than wonderful in the display of intellectual and imaginative power.—TAYLOR, SIR HENRY, 1869, *To Mrs. Edward Villiers, Jan.* 24; *Correspondence, ed. Dowden, p.* 287.

Lytton adds to an inherited talent for melodramatic tale-writing a poetical ear, good knowledge of effect, and a taste for social excitements. . . . Some of his early lyrics are tender, warm, and beautiful; but more are filled with hot-house passions,— with the radiance, not of stars, but of chandeliers and gas-lights.—STEDMAN, EDMUND CLARENCE, 1875-87, *Victorian Poets, p.* 268.

Mr. Disraeli gave the country another little surprise. He appointed Lord Lytton Viceroy of India. Lord Lytton had been previously known chiefly as the writer of pretty and sensuous verse, and the author of one or two showy and feeble novels. In literary capacity he was at least as much inferior to his father as his father was to Scott or Goethe.—MCCARTHY, JUSTIN,1879, *A History of our Own Times from the Accession of Queen Victoria to the Berlin Congress, ch.* LXIV.

There is much in this book that recalls the author's striking and beautiful "Fables in Song." It does not, I think, on the whole, maintain so high a level; but it has the same special merit, the same mixture of romantic thought with piercing *aperçus* from life and experience, reminding one of the finer work of the elder Lord Lytton, —the same defect, as I venture to think it, of mingling real poetry with a hard and gritty humor, a crackling of thorns under a pot.—MORSHEAD, E. D. A., 1887, *After Paradise, The Academy, vol.* 32, *p.* 195.

In Lord Lytton's case, I think, he has suffered doubly as a poet from his political attitude. He has incurred the resentment of the Liberal Press for being too strong a Tory, and at the same time his high public position has caused his political friends to treat his poetry as no more than that holiday flirtation with the Muse which statesmen are allowed. By neither side has he been treated according to his full literary deserts. Now, however, that the grave has closed over all contentious matters in his public career, I anticipate a wiser and less partial judgment of his poetic work. Each year as it goes by will withdraw him politically further from our gaze and bring him as a poet nearer to us. Then we may expect to see him take the high rank he deserves. My estimate of what this rank will be is that, as a lyric poet, the position given him will be next among his contemporaries after Tennyson, Swinburne, and Rossetti. He has neither Tennyson's full perfection of lyric style, nor Swinburne's wealth of musical rhetoric. Rossetti I personally should place before any of them as master of the purest English perhaps in our literature, but it is doubtful whether, his masterpieces being nearly all in sonnet form, the consensus of criticism will give him so high a place. Apart from these three I see no contemporary who is likely to be placed as Lytton's equal.—BLUNT, WILLIAM SCAWEN, 1892, *Lord Lytton's Rank in Literature, The Nineteenth Century, vol.* 31, *p.* 574.

Lord Lytton has been accused of borrowing too freely from other writers, and the accusation has not been invariably groundless. In writing "Lucile" he owed more to George Sand than one writer should owe to another, and his lines frequently recall the work of greater masters. A number of his lyrics are palpable imitations of Browning's. But they are to Browning's verse as the footlights are to sunlight and as rosewater is to wine. They breathe not of the open air but of the dress-circle and the boudoir. In occasionally echoing the rhythm and mimicking the sentiment of other men, Lord Lytton has done wanton injustice to his talents. He had more than culture and wit and knowledge of the world and the command of an easy and finished style. He was more than a lighthanded satirist and a masterly teller of a story. That he had a true vein of poetry, a strain and a message of his own, he has proved by the lofty imagery of his "Legends" and by more than one love-lyric where the language and the rhythm are unborrowed, and the thought and the passion are beautiful and moving and sincere.—WHYTE, WILLIAM, 1892, *The Poets and the Poetry of the Century, Kingsley to Thomson, ed. Miles*, p. 494.

All his books, from the early poems of Owen Meredith, to the posthumous volume, "Marah," were stamped with cleverness. They were rich in fancy: graceful, and sometimes almost perfect, in form; full of ease, eloquence, and charm. It would be difficult to say with precision what it was that they lacked; but something was absent from them, and perhaps it was that essential quality which Wordsworth defines as "the consecration and the poet's dream." Lord Lytton was himself apparently conscious of their insufficiency, for he flitted rapidly from one subject and one style to another, as though in quest of the unattained perfection; but it still remained unattained; and when "Marah," his last book, was found to be of the same character as its predecessors, Lord Lytton's place in literature seemed to have been finally determined.—COTTERELL, GEORGE, 1893, *King Poppy, The Academy*, vol. 43, p. 299.

Owen Meredith wrote lines which, if they had been written by Tennyson, would have been reckoned among his sweetest, but they were Owen Meredith and not Tennyson.—BENSON, ARTHUR CHRISTOPHER, 1894, *Essays*, p. 305.

The verse is often artificial and the sentiment false or strained.—ROBERTSON, J. LOGIE, 1894, *A History of English Literature*, p. 333.

"Genseric" is one of the, alas! too rare instances in which the poet did not write a line or a word too much, and which therefore shows what, with less fluency, his muse might have frequently given. The whole design to exhibit the ideals of the successive ages was too ambitious; and, except in the hands of an almost unimaginably supreme poet, would have required more knowledge than is easily compatible with poetical felicity, and more power of suppressing knowledge than the knower usually has. But as a series of frescoes,— as a sort of world-panorama dashed off freely and with mastery,—it has high value, and as a book to read—a quality of Lord Lytton's verse on which I always insist—it is extremely recommendable. . . . His distressing laxity in the matter of rhyme—which sometimes reminds one of, though it never equals, the enormities of Mrs. Browning—may have been partly caused and must certainly have been encouraged by his almost constant exile from his native country; for an ear so receptive as his could hardly fail to be affected by the daily hearing of Italian and French, German and Portuguese. But it must have been partly congenital, and partly due, like his companion laxities of metre, to a more general impatience—also congenital and increased by education and circumstance—of the labor of the file. And I do not know that either peccadillo has done him so much harm as his extreme facility and fluency.—SAINTSBURY, GEORGE, 1896, *The Poetry of the Earl of Lytton, The Forum*, vol. 22, pp. 473, 479.

Alexander William Kinglake
1809–1891

Born, at Tauton, 5 Aug. 1809. Early education at Eton. Matric. Trin. Coll., Cam., 1828; B. A., 1832; M. A., 1836. Student of Lincoln's Inn, 14 April 1832; called to Bar, 5 May 1837. Travelled in East, 1835. Contrib. to "Quarterly Rev.," Dec. 1844 and March 1845. To Algiers, 1845; accompanied St. Arnaud's forces. With English forces during Crimean War, 1854. M. P. for Bridgewater, 1857–69. Contrib. to "Blackwood's Mag.," Sept. 1872. Died, in London, 2 Jan. 1891. *Works:* "Eothen" (anon.), 1844; "Invasion of the Crimea," vols. i., ii., 1863; vols. iii., iv., 1868; vol. v., 1875; vol. vi., 1880; vols. vii., viii., 1887.—SHARP, R. FARQUHARSON, 1897, *A Dictionary of English Authors*, p. 156.

PERSONAL

There is nothing marquant in his appearance or conversation. He is blond of beard and visage, fortyish in years, with a good eye and a pleasant voice, like most Englishmen. He has thus far made no great figure in Parliament.—MOTLEY, JOHN LOTHROP, 1858, *To his Wife, July 26; Correspondence, ed. Curtis*, vol. I., p. 302.

When I first knew him he lived in Hyde Park Place, in rooms overlooking a churchyard. When he had first looked at them he said to the landlady, "I should not like to live here—I should be afraid of ghosts."

"Oh no, sir," she replied; "there is always a policeman round the corner." I really believe he took the rooms on the spur of his delight at this truly British answer. Gout was the first malady to attack him, and to wean him from his daily club. He had a fancy to try a lady doctor, and wrote to one to ask if gout was beyond her scope. She replied, "Dear Sir,—Gout is not beyond my scope, but men are." Then he called in Sir James Paget, because he had been very much struck with a portrait he had seen of him by Millais.—GREGORY, AUGUSTA, 1895, "*Eothen*" *and the Athenæum Club, Blackwood's Magazine, vol.* 158, *p.* 802.

On his shyness waited swiftly ensuing boredom; if his neighbour at table were garrulous or *banale*, his face at once betrayed conversational prostration; a lady who often watched him used to say that his pulse ought to be felt after the first course; and that if it showed languor he should be moved to the side of some other partner. "He had great charm," writes to me another old friend, "in a quiet winning way, but was 'dark' with rough and noisy people." So it came to pass that his manner was threefold; icy and repellent with those who set his nerves on edge; good-humoured, receptive, intermittently responsive in general and congenial company; while, at ease with friends trusted and beloved, the lines of the face became gracious, indulgent, affectionate, the *sourire des yeux* often inexpressibly winning and tender. . . . The chief characteristic of his wit was its unexpectedness; sometimes acrid, sometimes humorous, his sayings came forth, like Topham Beauclerk's in Dr. Johnson's day, like Talleyrand's in our own, poignant without effort. His calm, gentle voice, contrasted with his startling caustic utterance, reminded people of Prosper Mérimée: terse epigram, felicitous *apropos*, whimsical presentment of the topic under discussion, emitted in a low tone, and without the slightest change of muscle.—TUCKWELL, W., 1902, *A. W. Kinglake, A Biographical and Literary Study, pp.* 128, 129.

EOTHEN
1844

"Eothen" is written in almost a conversational style, but it is such conversation as a Pythagorean might have used after his probation of long silence:—the production of one more accustomed to intercourse with his own mind than with that of others. He deals more in ideas than opinions, and seems to speak as it were in a soliloquy, amusing and convincing *himself* with vivid pictures and well-formed thought. There is apparent in almost every page a puzzling contrast between a vivacity of expression and practiced wit that would argue a man of the world— and the bold originality, and daring indifference to the prejudices of society, which are seldom misinterpreted as indications of secluded habits. . . . This is a real book—not a *sham*. It displays a varied and comprehensive power of mind, and a genuine mastery over the first and strongest of modern languages. The author has caught the character and humour of the Eastern mind as completely as Anastasius; while in his gorgeous descriptions and power of sarcasm he rivals Vathek. His terseness, vigour, and bold imagery remind us of the brave old style of Fuller and of South, to which he adds a spirit, freshness, and delicacy all his own. —WARBURTON, ELIOT, 1844, *Eothen, Quarterly Review, vol.* 75, *pp.* 56, 86.

Do you know also "Eothen," a work of genius? . . . Do you know Leigh Hunt's exquisite essays called "The Indicator and Companion" &c., published by Moxon? I hold them at once in delight and reverence. —BROWNING, ELIZABETH BARRETT, 1844, *To Mrs. Martin, Nov.* 16; *Letters ed. Kenyon, vol.* I, *p.* 216.

Reading a brilliant book by a nameless man,—"Eothen, or Eastern Travel." Full of careless, easy, masterly sketches, biting satire, and proud superiority to common report. It is an intellectual egotism which he acknowledges and glories in. He has remarkably freed himself from religious prepossessions, and writes as he feels, not as he *ought* to feel, at Bethlehem and Jerusalem.—FOX, CAROLINE, 1845, *Memoirs of Old Friends, ed. Pym; Journal, June* 6, *p.* 220.

Dined with Kinglake, at the Athenæum, and talked to him about "Eothen." He wrote half of it in three weeks at Vevey, and the rest long afterwards.—DUFF, SIR MOUNTSTUART E. GRANT, 1863, *Notes from a Diary, vol.* I, *p.* 232.

The performance was wonderful; the promise a trifle dangerous.—QUILLER-COUCH, A. T., 1891, *Adventures in Criticism.*

This charming little work, spontaneous as it appears to be, as if it had flowed smoothly off the pen at once without a pause, was in reality recast more than once by the painfully conscientious author, before it was finally given to the world in 1844, some years after the actual journey. Few books have been more thoroughly appreciated by the reading public. The ground was still comparatively new, and the tale which was told with so much freshness and charm was still one of excitement and occasional danger. "Eothen" is indeed a perfect gem of literary art, with its blending of a refined and scholarly style with an almost familiar lightness of narrative, and the overflowing, but always delicate humour with which it is enlivened.—OLIPHANT, MARGARET O. W., 1892, *The Victorian Age of English Literature*, p. 546.

Once in my girlhood I, who seldom heard of books, and who grew up in a house without a Shakespeare, and in a province without a bookstall, caught the words of one friend to another, "What do you consider the most brilliant book of the last half-century?" And the answer that came was, "Eothen," and a sequel to the answer was a present to me of the copy of the book itself, with the frontispiece of impaled skeletons, afterwards brought up as evidence in the Bulgarian atrocity controversy. I took it to my heart at once, and there it has ever since remained. "Thank you so much for recommending me 'Eothen,'" a schoolboy friend wrote to me in after-days, "and please tell me of some more books like it." But he has grown to manhood, and the books, "like 'Eothen,'" have not yet appeared.—GREGORY, AUGUSTA, 1895, *"Eothen" and the Athenaeum Club, Blackwood's Magazine*, vol. 158, p. 800.

The popularity of "Eothen" is a paradox: it fascinates by violating all the rules which convention assigns to viatic narrative. It traverses the most affecting regions of the world, and describes no one of them: the Troad—and we get only his childish raptures over Pope's "Homer's Iliad;" Stamboul—and he recounts the murderous services rendered by the Golden Horn to the Assassin whose *serail*, palace, council chamber, it washes; Cairo—but the Plague shuts out all other thoughts; Jerusalem—but Pilgrims have vulgarized the Holy Sepulchre into a Bartholomew Fair. He gives us everywhere, not history, antiquities, geography, description, statistics, but only *Kinglake*, only his own sensations, thoughts, experiences. . . . To compare an idyll with an epic, it may be said, is like comparing a cameo with a Grecian temple; be it so; but the temple falls in ruins, the cameo is preserved in cabinets; and it is possible that a century hence the Crimean history will be forgotten, while "Eothen" is read and enjoyed.—TUCKWELL W., 1902, *A. W. Kinglake, A Biographical and Literary Study*, pp. 26, 86.

INVASION OF THE CRIMEA
1863–87

It is going to be a wonderful book, and will sell enormously, at least I think so. There is a sort of chorus in the style, which carries one along in a way to which I hardly know a parallel. There was a sort of dreaminess about "Eothen" which was exactly suited to the subject; but here, with all the flow of the language, there is a precision that makes one pause to think and feel that one is reading history. The book will give rise to much interpellation and much controversy, but this could not be otherwise if the history was to be worth anything. The scene in the drowsy Cabinet at Richmond made me shake with laughter, and it bears the stamp of truth. The survivors will be in a great state of mind about it, and if they deny the statement, will not be believed.—BLACKWOOD, JOHN, 1862, *Letter to A. W. Kinglake*, Oct. 19; *William Blackwood and his Sons*, ed. Mrs. Porter, vol. III, p. 90.

This history is the most remarkable book which has of late come before us; but it is also the book which most calls for exact and searching criticism. It has the freshness of an unwritten page of history, yet it awakens the remembrance of events which deeply stirred the heart of the nation. It records the greatest political transactions and the greatest military enterprise in which the men of our time have engaged. It exhibits the actors in these occurrences stripped of all disguise, for the author has not thought himself restrained by duty or discretion from dissecting to the quick the characters and motives of his own contemporaries. He has, therefore, thrown the passion of political life into this historical narrative, and he flavours it with the peremptory assertion, the biting sarcasm, the irritable sensitiveness, the lively retort of a man struggling to make a reputation in contentious debate. The result may be extremely flattering to Mr. Kinglake's literary pretensions. He has rendered the uninviting narrative of dead diplomatic negotiations attractive to fascination, by a vivid delineation of individual character and by a nice analysis of the wheelwork of affairs; and he has contrived to throw a romantic glow over the patrons and the clients for whose exaltation this history has, we presume, been chiefly written.—CLARENDON, GEORGE WILLIAM FREDERICK VILLIERS LORD, 1863, *The Invasion of the Crimea, Edinburgh Review*, vol. 117, p. 307.

I am sure you are right in your estimate of Kinglake's book. Such diatribes are no more history than the Balaclava charge was war. It was, however, his brief to make out the Crimean war a French intrigue, and he obeyed the old legal maxim in a different case—"Abuse the plaintiff's attorney."—LEVER, CHARLES, 1863, *Letter to Earl of Malmesbury*, Feb. 16; *Memoirs of an Ex-minister*, vol. II, p. 291.

The first two volumes of Mr. Kinglake's "Invasion of the Crimea" were certainly among the most successful and renowned English books of our time. Their style was one of the most renowned things about them, and yet how conspicuous a fault in Mr. Kinglake's style is this over-charge of which I have been speaking. Mr. James Gordon Bennett, of the "New York Herald" says, I believe, that the highest achievement of the human intellect is what he calls "a good editorial." This is not quite so; but, if it were so, on what a height would these two volumes by Mr. Kinglake stand! I have already spoken of the Attic and the Asiatic styles; besides these, there is the Corinthian style. That is the style for "a good editorial," and Mr. Kinglake has really reached perfection in it. It has not the warm glow, blithe movement, and soft pliancy of life, as the Attic style has; it has not the over-heavy richness and encumbered gait of the Asiatic style; it has glitter without warmth, rapidity without ease, effectiveness without charm. Its characteristic is, that it has no *soul;* all it exists for, is to get its ends, to make its points, to damage its adversaries, to be admired, to triumph. A style so bent on effect at the expense of soul, simplicity, and delicacy; a style so little studious of the charm of the great models; so far from classic truth and grace, must surely be said to have the note of provinciality. Yet Mr. Kinglake's talent is a really eminent one, and so in harmony with our intellectual habits and tendencies, that, to the great bulk of English people, the faults of his style seem its merits; all the more needful that criticism should not be dazzled by them.—ARNOLD, MATTHEW, 1865, *Literary Influence of Academies, Essays in Criticism, First Series*, p. 75.

Mr. Kinglake's still unfinished history of the Crimean War is full of brilliant description and of keen, penetrating thought. It shows many gleams of the poetic, and it has some of the brightest and bitterest satirical passages in the literature of our time. The chapters in which Mr. Kinglake goes out of his way to describe the career, the character, and the companions of the Emperor Napoleon III. cut like corrosive acid. Mr. Kinglake found his mind filled with detestation of Louis Napoleon and his companies. He invented for himself the theory that the Crimean War arose only out of Louis Napoleon's peculiar position, and his anxiety to become recognized among the great sovereigns of Europe. The invention of this theory gave him an excuse for lavishing so much labor of love and hate on chapters which must always remain a masterpiece of remorseless satire. They hardly pretend to be always just in their estimate of men, but no one rates them according to their justice or their injustice. They are read for their style, and nothing more. Perhaps it would not be altogether unjust to say much the same of the history as far as it has gone. It is brilliant; it is powerful; it is full of thrilling passages; but it remains after all the historical romance rather than history. Moreover, it is a good deal too long.—MCCARTHY, JUSTIN, 1880, *A History of Our Own Times from the Accession of Queen Victoria to the Berlin Congress*, vol. IV, ch. LXVII.

A work that has taken rank as one of the most important military histories in the English language. It is still incomplete, the last volume yet published bringing the history down only to the Battle of Inkermann; but enough has been published to establish its reputation. The author's style differs from that of Napier—perhaps the only other great military historian with whom he may properly be compared—in being less graceful, but more vigorous. While his descriptive powers are scarcely inferior, his political acumen is far greater, and his research into the complicated relations of the different nations at war far more subtle and successful. The presentation of the cause of the war, occupying more than three hundred pages of the first volume, is perhaps the most brilliant part of the history. The grasp and insight with which the author traced the impulses that finally led to the conflict are worthy of great admiration.—ADAMS, CHARLES KENDALL, 1882, *A Manual of Historical Literature*, p. 473.

The literary gifts of Kinglake, the historian of the Crimean war, would have amply sufficed to hand his book down to posterity. Unfortunately, the most brilliant parts are the least relevant, and the necessary is everywhere encumbered with the superfluous.—GARNETT, RICHARD, 1887, *The Reign of Queen Victoria*, ed. Ward, vol. II, p. 476.

The two first volumes appeared in 1863; the last was published but two years before he succumbed, in the first days of 1891, to a slow incurable disease. In all, the task had occupied thirty years. Long before these years ran out, the world had learnt to regard the Crimean struggle in something like its true perspective; but over Kinglake's mind it continued to loom in all its original proportions. To adapt a phrase of M. Jules Lemaître's, *"le monde a changé en trente ans: lui ne bouge; il ne lève plus de dessus son papier à copie sa face congestionnée."* And yet Kinglake was no cloistered scribe. Before his last illness he dined out frequently, and was placed by many among the first half-a-dozen talkers in London. His conversation, though delicate and finished, brimmed full of interest in life and affairs: but let him enter his study, and its walls became a hedge. Without, the world was moving: within, it was always 1854, until by slow toiling it turned into 1855. His style is hard, elaborate, polished to brilliance. Its difficult labour recalls Thucydides. In effect it charms at first by its accuracy and vividness; but with continuous perusal it begins to weigh upon the reader, who feels the strain, the unsparing effort that this glittering fabric must have cost the builder, and at length ceases to sympathise with the story and begins to sympathise with the author.—QUILLER-COUCH, A. T., 1891, *Adventures in Criticism*, p. 148.

The literary ability in any case is remarkable; the spirit of the writing is never quenched by the masses of diplomatic and military information; the occasional portraits of remarkable men are admirably incisive; the style is invariably polished to the last degree, and the narrative is as lucid as it is animated.—STEPHEN, LESLIE, 1892, *Dictionary of National Biography*, vol. XXXI, p. 172.

That this history shows no small literary faculties no competent judge can deny. The art of wordpainting—a dubious and dangerous art—is pushed to almost its furthest limits; the writer has a wonderful gift of combining the minutest and most numerous details into an orderly and intelligible whole; and the quality which the French untranslatably call *diable du corps*, or, as we more pedantically say, "dæmonic energy," is present everywhere. But the book is monstrously out of proportion,—a single battle has something like an entire volume, and the events of some two years occupy eight,—and, clear as the individual pictures are, the panorama is of such endless length that the minds's eye retains no proper notion of it. In the second place, the style, though brilliant, is hard and brassy, full of points that are more suitable to the platform or the newspaper than to the historic page,—not so much polished as varnished, and after a short time intolerably fatiguing. In the third,—and this is the gravest fault of all,—the author's private or patriotic likes or dislikes pervade the whole performance and reduce too much of it to a tissue of extravagant advocacy or depreciation, made more disgusting by the repetition of catch phrases and pet labels somewhat after the manner of Dickens.—SAINTSBURY, GEORGE, 1896, *A History of Nineteenth Century Literature*, p. 241.

We imagine there has been no such work about battles and fighting written by any layman.—OLIPHANT, MARGARET O. W., 1897, *William Blackwood and his Sons*, vol. II, p. 452.

"The Invasion of the Crimea" is open to several serious objections. It is far too long, and the style is florid, diffuse and highly mannered. Moreover, Kinglake is a most prejudiced historian. There is no mean in his judgment; he either can see no faults, or he can see nothing else. Raglan and St. Arnaud are examples of the two extremes. But frequently the historian supplies the corrective to his own judgment. If the battle of the Alma was won as Kinglake says it was, then it was won not by generalship but by hard fighting plus a lucky blunder on the part of the general. On the other hand, Kinglake sustains the interest with great skill, especially in the battle volumes. Long as are the accounts of the Alma and of Balaclava, they are perfectly clear, and the impression left is indelible.—WALKER, HUGH, 1897, *The Age of Tennyson*, p. 132.

In Kinglake, great merits as an historian are marred by serious blemishes. In the thoroughness with which he surveys everything within the field of his inquiry he falls no whit behind Professor Gardiner himself. Moreover, in all the qualities of life, motion, the play of changing colour, and the vivid dramatic realism of the pictures with which he fills the imagination, he is not unworthy even of Mr. Froude. But, on the other hand, not even Froude himself can outdo him in the spirit of the partisan. The special pleader stands revealed in every page of the history. Never was there a writer of stronger prejudices; never one that showed a more bitter animus towards the objects of his aversion. Thus the whole book is coloured by the writer's excessive dislike to Napoleon III.—GRAHAM, RICHARD D., 1897, *The Masters of Victorian Literature*, p. 225.

His "infirmities" as a writer, to which he makes almost touching allusion, are better characterized as extreme conscientiousness and honest endeavour to do full justice to his subject. Not only his own writing of the work, but the actual production of the book, were made more difficult by his extraordinary conscientious nature. Thus we find him objecting to the usual method of making stereotype plates from which to print. The word stereotype, it seems, had alarmed him with an irrevocable sound fatal to all alterations or corrections in which he largely indulged. He says in opposition to the stereotyping, "I am so constituted that it would be painful to me not to be able to satisfy the minds of one of my heroes who might write to me in anguish to explain that he is 'Captain Snook' and not 'Captain Cook,'" The foregoing conveys so much more than is expressed of the qualities which distinguish Kinglake, that it explains to a great extent why writing his History was such a lengthy process.—PORTER, MRS. MARY, 1898, *William Blackwood and his Sons*, vol. III, p. 117.

Kinglake's description of "Prince Louis Bonaparte," of his character, his accomplices, his policy, his crimes, is perhaps unequalled in historical literature; I know not where else to look for a vivisection so scientific and so merciless of a great potentate in the height of his power. With scrutiny polite, impartial, guarded, he lays bare the springs of a conscienceless nature and the secrets of a crime-driven career; while for the combination of precise simplicity with exhaustive synopsis, the masquerading of moral indignation in the guise of mocking laughter, the loathing of a gentleman for a scoundrel set to the measure not of indignation but of contempt, we must go back to the refined insolence, the ὕβρις πεπαιδευμένη, of Voltaire.—TUCKWELL, W., 1902, *A. W. Kinglake, A Biographical and Literary Study*, p. 81.

George Bancroft
1800–1891

Born at Worcester, Mass., Oct. 3, 1800: died at Washington, Jan. 17, 1891. An American historian, statesman, and diplomatist. He was graduated at Harvard College in 1817; studied at Göttingen; was tutor of Greek in Harvard; opened with Cogswell the Round Hill School at Northampton in 1823; was collector of the port of Boston 1838–41; was Democratic candidate for governor of Massachusetts in 1844; was secretary of the navy 1845–46 (established the Naval Academy at Annapolis), and was United States minister to Great Britain 1846–49, and minister to Berlin 1867–74. He wrote a "History of the United States" (10 vols.; vol. 1 published 1834; vol. 10, 1874; centenary edition, 6 vols. 1876); a "History of the Formation of the Constitution of the United States" (2 vols. 1882; revised edition of the entire history, 6 vols., 1883–84), etc.—SMITH, BENJAMIN E., ed., 1894–97, *The Century Cyclopedia of Names*, p. 115.

GEORGE BANCROFT

Engraving by T. Johnson. From a drawing by J. W. Alexander.

GEORGE WILLIAM CURTIS

Engraving by W. G. Jackman. From a Photograph by Brady.

PERSONAL

Not only has he obtained great celebrity as an essayist and historian, but the policy which he advocated while at the head of the Navy Department gave him the character of an accomplished statesman. While his views were sufficiently enlarged and liberal they received the approbation of one of the most ultra economists and reformers in the House of Representatives.*— CHASE, LUCIEN B., 1850, *History of the Polk Administration*, p. 25.

Mr. Bancroft's time is now divided between the city and the seaside. Early in the summer he repairs to Newport, and were the date of our book somewhat later, we might enrich our pages with an engraving of the house he is now building there. It will be a simple summer retreat, lying upon the seaward slope of the cliff. From his windows he will look down upon the ocean, and as he breathes its air, impart its freshness and vigor to his pages.— GREENE, GEORGE W., 1853-96, *Homes of American Authors*, ed. Hubbard, p. 388.

Bancroft's habits are essentially those of a student. He rises early, and his morning hours are devoted to literary labor. In the latter part of the day, if the weather is at all favorable, he takes a ride on horseback, and returns in time for dinner. The evening is devoted to the society of his friends, either in accepting invitations or in receptions in his own residence. Following the custom of his early friend Schleiermacher, he is at home on Sunday evening, and in the simplest and most unostentatious manner receives those who from personal friendship, or attracted by his reputation as a writer, fill his salons. While preparing a work on Private Libraries, I frequently saw Bancroft in his library, which occupies the entire third story of his residence. On such occasions he was always surrounded by papers and books, and deeply immersed in documentary examinations, historical composition, or the revisal of proofsheets. At this time he very rarely allows himself to be interrupted, and almost invariably declines to receive visitors until a later hour in the day.—WYNNE, JAMES, 1862, *George Bancroft, Harper's Magazine*, vol. 25, p. 54.

This very able and eloquent politician and historian received me with the utmost courtesy, and we frequently shared his

*Jame. J. McKay, of North Carolina.

hospitality in Eaton Square. Like all well-bred Americans, he was simple and unpretending in his manners; and, without affecting republican simplicity, his establishment was unostentatious, and made no attempt to vie with the magnificent display at the Russian and Prussian embassies. But nowhere in London at the time was the society more instructive, or the conversation on a higher strain in point of thought and expression. . . . His conversation was like his writings, judicious, sensible, and well-informed, with occasional flashes of genius, which struck you the more from the comparative sober tone of the ideas in which they were embedded.— ALISON, SIR ARCHIBALD, 1867-83, *Autobiography*, ed. Lady Alison, vol. II, p. 70.

Tall, spare, straight, incisive in speech and style, George Bancroft's appearance indicates deep thought and careful culture. He is a refined bookworm; a mingling of the Oxford professor, the ripe diplomatist, the seasoned man of the world. His tastes make him, in his eightieth year a genial philosopher, at peace with the world and himself. He is an early riser, and does his work generally before two o'clock in the afternoon, after which he rides and dines. In the evening he amuses himself among his friends, and is passionately fond of the opera.—FORNEY, JOHN W., 1881, *Anecdotes of Public Men*, vol. II, p. 35.

The prose-Homer of our Republic. Picture to yourself a venerable man, of medium height, slender figure, erect bearing; with lofty brow thinned, but not stripped, of its silvery locks; a full, snowy beard adding to his patriarchal appearance; bluish gray eyes, which neither use nor time has deprived of brightness; a large nose of Roman type, such as I have somewhere read or heard the first Napoleon regarded as the sign of latent force; "small white hands," which Ali Pasha assured Byron were the marks by which he recognized the poet to be "a man of birth;"—let your imagination combine these details, and you have a sketch for the historian's portrait. The frame is a medium-sized room of good, high pitch. In the centre is a rectangular table covered with books, pamphlets and other indications of a literary life. Shelving reaches to the ceiling, and every fraction of space is occupied by volumes of all sizes, from folio to duodecimo; a door on the left opens into a room which is also full to overflowing with the valuable collections of a lifetime; and further on is yet another apartment equally crowded with the historian's dumb servants, companions, and friends; while rooms and nooks elsewhere have yielded to Literature's rights of squatter sovereignty.—LOVEJOY, B. G., 1885, *Authors at Home, The Critic, vol. 6, p. 61.*

The figure which rises from behind the work-table, littered with reference-books and manuscripts, is full of dignity and impressiveness. The clear-cut features; the carefully trimmed hair and beard, revealing a massive and shapely head; the finely molded form and active movement, in no way suggest advanced years: even the expression of the eye and the lines of the forehead fail to reveal frailness or extreme old age. As has recently been said of his friend and contemporary Von Ranke, who was only five years his senior, he seems to have outgrown and conquered old age itself, and to have found a substitute for physical force in the continuous energy of faith and love, in an apparently inexhaustible and indomitable intellect. His stature, which is about that of the average man or somewhat less, has lost nothing under the burden of years, and he carries firm and erect the slight but close-knit chest and capacious head with which he had for so long pushed and wrought in the crises and struggles of the great world in which he lives. Nor is there a trace of lassitude in his manners.— SLOANE, WILLIAM M., 1887, *George Bancroft—in Society, in Politics, in Letters, Century Magazine, vol. 33, p. 473.*

Unlike most Newport "cottages," his house was within sight of the ocean; between it and the sea lay the garden, and the rose in Kenmure's cap in the Scottish ballad was not a characteristic more invariable than the same flower in Mr. Bancroft's hand or buttonhole. His form was familiar, too, on Bellevue Avenue, taking as regularly as any old-fashioned Englishman his daily horseback exercise. At the same time he was one of the few men who were capable, even in Newport, of doing daily the day's work; he rose fabulously early in the morning, and kept a secretary or two always employed. Since John Quincy Adams there has not been among us such an example of laborious, self-exacting, seemingly inexhaustible old age; and, unlike Adams, Mr. Bancroft kept his social side always fresh and active, and did not have, like the venerable ex-President, to force himself out in the evening in order "to learn the art of conversation." This combination, with his monumental literary work, will keep his memory secure. It will possibly outlive that of many men of greater inspiration, loftier aims, and sublimer qualities.—HIGGINSON, THOMAS WENTWORTH, 1891, *George Bancroft, The Nation, vol. 52, p. 66.*

Beginning early in life to make acquaintances we have found him associating in his student days with the principal scholars of Germany, France and Italy, and with such men of literary distinction as Goethe and Byron. From the time that he entered Polk's cabinet to the end of his life, he appears as the companion of the great men of the world. . . . We learn that, while in England, he used to have long conversations with Albert, the Prince Consort, in the German language, on literary and public questions. Later, in Germany, he enjoyed rare social distinction. He was intimate with Bismark, who welcomed him (a rare event in his intercourse with men) to familiar conversation in his own home. The emperor Wilhelm I. was strongly drawn towards him. So, too, was Friedrich; and the present emperor had a wreath placed upon the casket which contained his remains at the funeral services in Washington. For many years both in Washington and Newport, he has been the central figure in society. No man, American or foreigner, seemed to feel that he had seen either place if he had not been introduced to Mr. Bancroft, or at least seen him. Surely if the knowledge that he has performed a well-appreciated and great work and the undoubted assurance of being the cynosure of great men and of women of social eminence on both continents can make a man happy, Mr. Bancroft should have been happy. Whether he was so or not, he was one of the most successful of men, judging things from a worldly point of view. He had decided peculiarities in society; was regarded as artificial, and not only as playful but as frivolous. Still, in England, Germany and America his eccentricities were overlooked, for they were overshadowed by the conviction that he was distinguished by intellectuality and great attainments.—GREEN, SAMUEL

Sweet, 1891, *George Bancroft, Address Before the American Antiquarian Society,* p. 20.

It might be questioned if Mr. Bancroft's residence in Washington were a house with a library, or a library with a few rooms about it to live in. A large, high, square room, shelved from floor to ceiling, on the west side, may be called the main library. Every inch of the wall-space is occupied by books, and on many of the shelves are double rows. At the east side of the house is another room, not so large, but even more closely packed with books from top to bottom. Between these two is a smaller room, with a bookcase containing mostly English standard and dramatic authors, with between 2000 and 3000 historical pamphlets. In the third story, the east room is well filled with books. The hall of the second story is furnished with a case full of fine books, nor can any one get away from bookcases in the hall on the top floor. The reception room contains two well-filled oak bookcases.—Sabin, John F., 1891, *George Bancroft's Library, The Critic,* No. 415, p. 339.

George Bancroft presented the severest contrast that individual idiosyncrasy offers among literary men of the highest culture. Stern and inflexible in his records and speech when analyzing the events of the past and the character of the men who figured in them; serious and emphatic as if his historic pages were to be accepted without criticism as the *ipse dixit* of unquestioned authority from which no appeal was possible, the historian when he left his library to go into the world seemed to assume a new nature with his change of costume, and to enter the social circle with the playfulness of a school-boy released from the drudgery of study. It would be difficult to draw the line where natural pleasantry ended and the artificial began. "From grave to gay, from serious to severe," he passed so rapidly, that those who met Mr. Bancroft for the first time at some social assembly and had an opportunity of observing him could not well make out what sort of a character stood before them, or whether a sage of history, a profound philosopher, or a social punchinello was the most fitting term to apply to him. . . . Bancroft, the schoolmaster, the Unitarian preacher, the lecturer, the magazine writer, the politician—changing his party-colored coat with the facility of a harlequin—a member of the cabinet, secretary of the navy, minister at the court of St. James and at Berlin, and the historian of the United States, presented the same versatility of character while he excited universal respect for his intellectual qualities. In London he occasioned many amusing remarks in society, but his scholastic acquirements and diplomatic ability were justly acknowledged. His familiar acquaintance with German literature and the German language brought about a familiar friendship with the Prince Consort, with whom he held long conversations on politics, art, and letters in the prince's native tongue. The late Emperor of Germany, then Prince Royal of Prussia, in reply to the question how he liked our minister at Berlin, said to me, "Bancroft? I like him immensely. Such energy and investigation I have seldom seen. He is here, there, and everywhere. Really a remarkable man."—Tuckerman, Charles K., 1891, *An Hour With George Bancroft, Magazine of American History,* vol. 25, pp. 227, 229.

Then to know Mr. Bancroft and to have had the entrée to his always hospitable house was like going behind the scenes with the stage-manager after having been taken to the play. He knew everything and everybody; had a most exhaustive habit of reading, and sometimes asked me to come and hear the last chapter of his "History" as he read the MS. to his wife and a few friends.—Sherwood, Mary E. W., 1897, *An Epistle to Posterity,* p. 124.

HISTORY OF THE UNITED STATES
1834–84

We should be faithless to one of the first duties of a literary journal, did we not appropriate an ample portion of our pages to a notice of a volume like Mr. Bancroft's. A History of the United States, by an American writer, possesses a claim upon our attention of the strongest character. It would do so under any circumstances, but when we add that the work of Mr. Bancroft is one of the ablest of the class, which has for years appeared in the English language; that it compares advantageously with the standard British historians; that as far as it goes, it does such justice to its noble subject, as to supersede the necessity of any future work of the same kind; and if completed as commenced, will unquestionably forever be regarded, both as an American and as an English classic, our readers would justly think us unpardonable, if we failed to offer our humble tribute to its merit.—EVERETT, EDWARD, 1835, *Bancroft's History of the United States, North American Review*, vol. 40, p. 99.

The Americans have also a historian of promise. Mr. Bancroft's "History of the United States" is little more than begun, but the beginning is characterized by an impartial and benevolent spirit, and by the indications which it affords of the author's fidelity to democratic principles: the two primary requisites in a historian of the republic. The carrying on the work to a completion will be a task of great toil and anxiety, but it will be a most important benefit to society at large, if it fulfills its promise.—MARTINEAU, HARRIET, 1837, *Society in America*, vol. II, p. 212.

His Colonial History establishes his title to a place among the great historical writers of the age. The reader will find the pages of the present volume filled with matter not less interesting and important than the preceding. He will meet with the same brilliant and daring style, the same picturesque sketches of character and incident, the same acute reasoning and compass of erudition.—PRESCOTT, WILLIAM HICKLING, 1841, *Bancroft's United States, Biographical and Critical Miscellanies*, p. 337.

Bancroft is a philosophical historian; but no amount of philosophy has yet taught him to despise a minute accuracy in point of fact.—POE, EDGAR ALLAN, 1849, *A Chapter of Suggestions, Works*, ed. Stedman and Woodberry, vol. VIII, p. 342.

The adaptation of the subject to the author, and of the author to the subject, has been a singularly happy circumstance in Mr. Bancroft's literary career. Not that he would have failed of distinction in any department of intellectual effort, to which he might have devoted his energies. He possesses too choice and brilliant gifts of nature, not to have attained an enviable eminence. Uniting a remarkable versatility of thought with great activity of temperament, he has exhibited the qualities which insure the success of the poet, the orator, the elegant essayist, and the founder of philosophical systems. But in no other sphere than that with which his name has become identified, could he have found such scope for the exercise of his peculiar endowments. He was the first writer to conceive of the history of his country, as an integral unity; and in this conception he has opened "fresh fields and pastures new," converting the arid wastes of solitary and unrelated events into scenes of living and beautiful harmony.—RIPLEY, GEORGE, 1853, *Bancroft, Putnam's Magazine*, vol. 1, p. 300.

Bancroft is the "standard" American historian; the only one who has succeeded in attracting general attention, and in being accepted by all parties as an authority. He takes a philosophic view of events, and endeavors to show that the natural development of our government has been in accordance with the principles of the democratic party, as originated by Jefferson, and carried out by Jackson and his successors. He has been as fair as could be expected from a partisan who had his own theory of politics to establish. As a narrative, the work is clear and perspicuous; but the style, though carefully finished, is not indicative of genius. There are certain episodes, in which the desire for picturesque effect is quite evident; but the author is learned and laborious, rather than spirited and graphic. Perhaps it is too soon to expect a history of the United States that should unite accuracy in details with dramatic grouping, high moral views, and an imaginative style. The time may come for such a history; but Bancroft's differs as much from that ideal work as a topographical chart of Venice would differ from a painting by Turner of the domes of that sea-born city. It is not intended to depreciate the great merits of our historian; for it remains true that his is much the best thus far attempted, and no intelligent American can afford to leave it unread.—UNDERWOOD, FRANCIS H., 1872, *A Hand-Book of English Literature, American Authors*, p. 201.

Has natural qualifications, reinforced by wide reading, for the historian's works are exceptionally great. It has been charged by some English critics that his democratic prejudices are too manifest in his History; but this allegation has had little weight with those who are most competent to form a judgment in the case,—his own countrymen; and his judicial candor is generally reckoned among the most admirable components of his intellectual equipment. His style has received warm and universal praise; it is eminently scholarly, yet not pedantic, brilliant, yet not flashy, in narrative animated and picturesque, and in philosophical passages massive and majestic. This history is one of the proudest monuments of American scholarship.—CATHCART, GEORGE R., 1874, ed. *The Literary Reader*, p. 143.

The different volumes of his work are of various literary merit, but they are all stamped by the unmistakable impress of the historian's individuality. There is no dogmatism more exclusive than that of fixed ideas and ideals, and this dogmatism Mr. Bancroft exhibits throughout his history both in its declamatory and speculative form. Indeed, there are chapters in each of his volumes which, considered apart, might lead one to suppose that the work was misnamed, and that it should be entitled, "The Psychological Autobiography of George Bancroft, as Illustrated by Incidents and Characters in the Annals of the United States." Generally, however, his fault is not in suppressing or overlooking facts, but in disturbing the relations of facts,—substituting their relation to the peculiar intellectual and moral organization of the historian to their natural relations with each other. Still, he has written the most popular history of the United States (up to 1782) which has yet appeared and has made a very large addition to the materials on which it rests. Perhaps he would not have been so tireless in research had he not been so passionately earnest in speculation.—WHIPPLE, EDWIN PERCY, 1876-86, *American Literature and Other Papers*, ed. Whittier, p. 91.

The book is written for the most part in a vigorous style, somewhat defective, however, in elegance, and characterised by a certain monotony and want of ease which detracts from the pleasure of the reader.—NICHOL, JOHN, 1882-85, *American Literature*, p. 145.

The work has two striking peculiarities. The first is a certain stateliness of style, that is a little out of harmony with the easy methods of every-day life. The author's ideas are habitually clothed in court dress, and therefore often appear to be deficient in simplicity and energy. The other peculiarity is a more or less obvious tendency to discursiveness. There are several chapters that seem to have only a remote bearing on the subject in hand; and although they show great learning and ingenuity, they obstruct the general current of the narration. To many of those using the work, these discursions will doubtless appear necessary to the adequate presentation of the author's idea or argument, but to others they are likely to indicate a lack of harmonious construction. To these peculiarities different readers will attach different measures of importance; but they ought not to be regarded as detracting from the fundamental merit of the work. The table of contents, which is very complete, will enable every student to select such portions as he needs.—ADAMS, CHARLES KENDALL, 1882, *A Manual of Historical Literature*, p. 531.

This is the first of six volumes, into which the original twelve are to be cast. It is described as "an entirely new edition, partly rewritten and thoroughly revised." We, nevertheless, lay down the volume, after careful and extended examination, with a feeling of disappointment. That it is thoroughly revised, is not proven by the pencil marks in our copy indicating the errors. The work of recasting shows signs of haste. Omissions have been indiscriminately made, changes have been hastily effected, while it is evident that the distinguished author has failed, in more than one department, to read down carefully to the present date; nor can we tell, in some cases, where his questions end. This is the more to be regretted, as all foot-notes are swept away, rendering this "last revision" unserviceable to those who would inquire into the history of America.—DE COSTA, BENJAMIN FRANKLIN, 1883, *Literary Notices, Magazine of American History*, vol. 9, p. 300.

This work is universally recognized as one of the most important contributions to American history; prominent even among the works published in our language, and of no light standing in the literature of the world in our century. Few works have gone through so many editions, and fewer still have been translated into so many languages, and been published in so many different countries. The interest attaching to his theme, the ability and literary elegance with which he has written the history of the great republic, and the reputation and standing of the author, have all contributed to enhance its importance.—CLARKE, R. H.,

1883, *Bancroft's History of the United States*, Catholic World, vol. 37, p. 721.

Scarcely one who wished me good speed when I first essayed to trace the history of America remains to greet me with a welcome as I near the goal. Deeply grateful as I am for the friends who rise up to gladden my old age, their encouragement must renew the grief for those who have gone before me.—BANCROFT, GEORGE, 1884, *History of the United States*, p. 7.

His "History," which is universally regarded as a standard authority, has been translated into several European languages. It is, and will probably long continue, an authoritative work, both from its careful research and breadth of judgment. In parts, however, particularly in the account of the causes of the War of American Independence, it is decidedly one-sided, and should be read in conjunction with other authorities.—SMITH, GEORGE BARNETT, 1887, *Celebrities of the Century*, ed. Sanders, p. 91.

The work was successful from the beginning because it was done in a spirit so sincere and philosophical. It met with a reception which was most gratifying at home, and in Europe its popularity was remarkable. The first three volumes were translated into Danish, Italian, and German by translators who obtained the author's permission. It was done into French without his knowledge, and sent into the South American colonies to further the awakening spirit of Liberty. There was a Scotch edition in two volumes and an English one on which the author received copyright royalty until the courts decided that as an American he was not entitled to it.—SLOANE, WILLIAM M., 1887, *George Bancroft—in Society, in Politics, in Letters*, Century Magazine, vol. 33, p. 485.

George Bancroft has written a history of the United States which will no more become archaic than Macaulay or Grote. While one may now and then hear from the lips of the so-called "younger school of American historians" a criticism of George Bancroft, their carping is ungracious and gratuitous. Theirs has not been the art to equal him, nor will be. A literary life devoted to the mastery of one era of a nation's history is a worthy sight, good for the eyes, and arguing sanity of method and profundity of investigation. Whoever has read Bancroft can testify to his readableness, to his comprehensive knowledge, to his philosophical grasp, to his ability to make dead deeds vividly visible, and to his gift of interesting the reader in events and their philosophy. He has written a great history of the United States before the Constitution, so that no author has felt called on or equipped to reduplicate his task in the same detail and manner.—QUAYLE, WILLIAM A., 1890, *A Hero and Some Other Folks*, p. 251.

The labor which Mr. Bancroft performed in writing his history was enormous. The period embraced in his annals lacks but three years of three centuries. The vast material which he was obliged to gather was scattered through the archives and the libraries of America and Europe. The authorities which he was obliged to consult were numerous, prejudiced, contradictory, and, in many cases, obscure, unveracious and malignant. To collect, compare and sift this mass of material so as to winnow truth from error and secure accuracy in the relation of facts, even to the details and their coloring, and develop the narrative so lucidly that the reader may intelligently follow the changes of public affairs, and with every page be carried forward in the story of two hundred and ninety-seven years of diversified yet connected events, was a task which might well tax for half a century the abilities of the most accomplished and industrious historian. The arrangement of the work, in its chronological divisions and the orderly presentation of pivotal facts, greatly helps the reader to grasp the numberless details and to keep in mind both the contemporaneity of important incidents and personages and the epochal sequences of historical events.—DYER, OLIVER, 1891, *Life and Writings of George Bancroft*, p. 28.

Mr. Bancroft, as an historian, combined some of the greatest merits and some of the profoundest defects ever united in a single author. His merits are obvious enough. He has great enthusiasm for his subject. He is profoundly imbued with that democratic spirit without which the history of the United States cannot be justly written. He has the graphic quality so wanting in Hildreth and the saliency whose absence makes Prescott too smooth. He has a style essentially picturesque, whatever may be its faults. The reader is compelled to admit that his resources in the way of preparation are inexhaustible, and that his command of them is astounding. One must follow him minutely, for instance, through the history of the war for independence, to appreciate in full the consummate grasp of a mind which can deploy military events in a narrative as a general deploys brigades in a field. Add to this the capacity for occasional maxims to the highest degree profound and lucid, in the way of political philosophy, and you certainly combine in one man some of the greatest qualities of the historian.—HIGGINSON, THOMAS WENTWORTH, 1891, *George Bancroft, The Nation*, vol. 52, p. 66.

Although Bancroft did a great amount of work as a compiler of historical collections, as editor of many valuable works, and as orator of numberless important occasions, his fame rests almost wholly upon his one great history. The literary merits of the work are very moderate. While its style is clear and definite, it is often labored and diffuse; its author lacked the art of graphic narration so fully possessed by Prescott and Parkman; his pages are often "hard reading," but his scholarship, his analytical and critical powers, and his insistence upon perfect accuracy, more than compensate for the defects of his style. Taken for all in all, Bancroft is to be compared with no modern British historian save Froude, and with no American historian save Motley.—PATTEE, FRED LEWIS, 1896, *A History of American Literature*, p. 313.

He loved a good tale to his chapters—something to impress, and give emphasis; just as a coachman, proud of his conduct of a spirited team, loves to add *éclat* to his success by a good crack of his whip. Nor should we forget that 'tis the warmth of his democratic spirit which makes him boil over into his most exuberant utterances; and if he catch a rhetorical fall, it is oftenest from an over-eager step in his march to the music of American freedom. Of the larger and generally recognized qualities of Bancroft's history, of the wide and untiring research involved, of its painstaking, conscientious balancing of authorities, and of the earnest, unshrinking Americanism which warms it through and through, it is unnecessary to speak.—MITCHELL, DONALD G., 1899, *American Lands and Letters, Leather-Stocking to Poe's "Raven,"* p. 48.

He persevered in writing history all his life, and for all the diffuse floridity of his style, he is still a respectable authority.—WENDELL, BARRETT, 1900, *A Literary History of America*, p. 272.

A man of much learning and cultivation, Bancroft's extreme dependence upon rigid methods of work and recreation enabled posterity to chronicle a long list of achievements after his name; but not every man will write good history because he always takes a horseback ride at precisely three in the afternoon, though he may live to be ninety-one, as did Bancroft.—SWIFT, LINDSAY, 1900, *Our Literary Diplomats, The Book Buyer*, vol. 21, p. 38.

His work will always be indispensable, most of all to those future historians who seek to displace it.—LAWTON, WILLIAM CRANSTON, 1902, *Introduction to the Study of American Literature*, p. 259.

Remains to this day in the popular mind the representative historian of the country in spite of the fact that for all his length of years and his twelve massive volumes, he carried his narrative no farther than the adoption of the Constitution. It was Bancroft's "History of the United States" with which the unwary Robert Louis Stevenson purposed to regale and inform himself on his first journey to California. How many other foreigners and less excusable natives have floundered hopelessly amid Bancroft's rhetoric and philosophical speculations will never be known, but the number must be large, if the copies sold were read. Yet, as often happens, a good defence may be made for the gulling author and the gulled public. . . . Crude as were Bancroft's rhetoric and his philosophy, they were genuine and generous, and did not obscure his many merits as a narrator, an investigator, a collector of materials. Every student of the colonial and Revolutionary epochs owes him much, and a certain measure of his fame is secure. It would be a mistake, too, to suppose that he was incapable of filling the higher functions of the thoughtful historian. But that he could continue popular, except as a mere name, was impossible after the nation emerged from the callow stage. To consult him is often a necessity and sometimes a privilege; to read him is too frequently an infliction.—TRENT, WILLIAM P., 1903, *A History of American Literature*, pp. 541, 543.

Herman Melville
1819-1891

Born, in New York City, 1 Aug. 1819. Went to sea, 1836. Schoolmaster, 1837-40. To sea again Jan. 1841. Ran away from ship on Marquesas Islands, 1842. Rescued after four months' captivity among the Typees. For a short time clerk at Honolulu. Returned to Boston, 1844. Married Elizabeth Shaw, 4 Aug. 1847. Lived in New York, 1847-50; at Pittsfield, Mass., 1850-63. Visits to Europe, 1849 and 1856. Frequently lectured in America, 1857-60. Returned to New York, 1863. District Officer, New York Custom House, Dec., 1866-86. Died, in New York, 28 Sept. 1891. *Works:* "Typee," 1846; "Omoo," 1847; "Mardi," 1849; "Redburn," 1849; "White Jacket" 1850; "Moby Dick," 1851 (English edn., called: "The Whale," same year); "Pierre," 1852; "Israel Potter," 1855 (in 1865 edn. called: "The Refugee"); "Piazza Tales," 1856; "The Confidence Man," 1857; "Battle-Pieces," 1866; "Clarel," 1876; "John Marr and Other Sailors" (priv. ptd.), 1888; "Timoleon" (priv. ptd.), 1891.—SHARP, R. FARQUHARSON, 1897, *A Dictionary of English Authors*, p. 193.

PERSONAL

Duyckinck, of the *Literary World*, and Herman Melville are in Berkshire, and I expect them to call here this morning. I met Melville the other day, and liked him so much that I have asked him to spend a few days with me before leaving these parts.—HAWTHORNE, NATHANIEL, 1850, *Letter to Horatio Bridge, Personal Recollections of Nathaniel Hawthorne*, p. 123.

His extremely proud and sensitive nature and his studious habits led to the seclusion of his later years. . . . This seclusion endured to the end. He never denied himself to his friends; but he sought no one. I visited him repeatedly in New York, and had the most interesting talks with him. What stores of reading, what reaches of philosophy, were his! He took the attitude of absolute independence towards the world. He said, "My books will speak for themselves, and all the better if I avoid the rattling egotism by which so many win a certain vogue for a certain time." He missed immediate success; he won the distinction of a hermit. It may appear, in the end, that he was right. No other autobiographical books in our literature suggest more vividly than "Typee," "Omoo," "White Jacket," and "Moby Dick," the title of Goethe, "Truth and Beauty from my own life." "Typee," at least, is one of those books that the world cannot let die. —COAN, TITUS MUNSON, 1891, *Herman Melville, Literary World*, vol. 22, p. 493.

As Borrow possessed the secret of winning the confidence of the gipsies, so Melville, by the same talisman of utter simplicity and naturalness, was able to fraternise in perfect good fellowship with the so-called savages of the Pacific.—SALT, HENRY S., 1892, *"Marquesan Melville," Gentleman's Magazine*, vol. 272, p. 251.

GENERAL

We first examined its merits ["Omoo"] as a piece of description, then considered it more especially with reference to its spirit, in what it leaves us to infer of the writer's intercourse with the natives, and what he tells us of their religious condition. . . . "Omoo" is a book one may read once with interest and pleasure, but with a *perpetual recoil*. It is poetically written, but yet carelessly, and in a bad spirit.— PECK, G. W., 1847, *Omoo, American Review*, vol. 6, p. 45.

Mr. Melville lived for four months, absolutely like a primitive man, in Noukahiva, a Polynesian island, and it is his adventures while there that form the subject of his first books, the narratives of his actual voyages. . . . Unfortunately, Mr. Melville's style is so ornate, his Rubens-like tints are so vivid and warm, and he has so strong a predilection for dramatic effects, that one does not know exactly how much confidence to repose in his narrative. We do not take except *cum grano salis*, his florid descriptions.—CHASLES, PHILARÈTE, 1852, *Anglo-American Literature and Manners*, p. 118.

"Typee" told nothing. It had no antecedents. It might have been an animal, or it might have been a new game, or it might have been a treatise on magic. Did they open the book, and look over the chapters, they were not much wiser. Barbarous congregations of syllables, such as Kory-Kory, Nukuheva, Moa Artua, met their eyes. The end of it was, that the whole tribe of London and American critics had to sit down and read it all, before they dared speak of a book filled with such mysterious syllables. From reading they began to like it. There was a great deal of rich, rough talent about it. The scenes were fresh, and highly colored; the habits and manners described had the charm of novelty; and the style, though not the purest or most elegant, had a fine narrative facility about it, that rendered it very pleasurable reading. . . . "Typee," the first and most successful of Mr. Melville's books, commands attention for the clearness of its narrative, the novelty of its scenery, and the simplicity of its style, in which latter feature it is a wondrous contrast to "Mardi," "Moby Dick," and "Pierre."— O'BRIEN, FITZ-JAMES, 1853, *Our Young Authors, Putnam's Magazine*, vol. 1, pp. 155, 160.

Melville's own adventures had been those of a modern Captain John Smith in the Pacific islands and waters; so that the *pars magna fui* of his lively books gave them the needed fillip of personality, and duly magnified their elements of wonder. That brilliant power of delineation which, in Melville's conversation, so charmed his warm friends the Hawthornes, is apparently not heightened in his books, but would seem to be rather diminished by the exigencies of writing. But the personal narrative or fiction of "Typee," "Omoo," and "Moby Dick," with their adventurous rapidity of description of Pacific seas, ships, savages and whales, represented the restless facility which has always been an American trait, and which occasionally develops into some enduring literary success. —RICHARDSON, CHARLES F., 1888, *American Literature, 1607-1885*, vol. II, p. 404.

There was a wealth of imagination in the mind of Mr. Melville, but it was an untrained imagination, and a world of the stuff out of which poetry is made, but no poetry, which is creation and not chaos. He saw like a poet, felt like a poet, thought like a poet, but he never attained any proficiency in verse, which was not among his natural gifts. His vocabulary was large, fluent, eloquent, but it was excessive, inaccurate and unliterary. He wrote too easily, and at too great length, his pen sometimes running away with him, and from his readers. There were strange, dark, mysterious elements in his nature, as there were in Hawthorne's, but he never learned to control them, as Hawthorne did from the beginning, and never turned their possibilities into actualities.— STODDARD, RICHARD HENRY, 1891, *The Mail and Express*.

"Typee" and "Omoo," mistaken by the public for fiction, were, on the contrary, the most vivid truth expressed in the most telling and poetic manner. My father, the Rev. Titus Coan, went over Melville's ground in 1867, and while he has criticized the topography of "Typee" as being somewhat exaggerated in the mountain distances, a very natural mistake, he told me that the descriptions were admirably true and the characterizations faultless in the main. The book is a masterpiece, the outcome of an opportunity that will never be repeated. Melville was the first and only man ever made captive in a valley full of Polynesian cannibals, who had the genius to describe the situation, and who got away alive to write his book.—COAN, TITUS MUNSON, 1891, *Herman Melville, Literary World*, vol. 22, p. 493.

Melville's most artistic work is to be found in "Typee," the first blossom of his youthful genius. This idyl, which set all the world to talking, undoubtedly will hold a permanent position in American literature, and most people will wish to read its sequel, "Omoo." The character of "Fayaway" and, no less, William S. Mayo's "Kaloolah," the enchanting dreams of many a youthful heart, will retain their charm; and this in spite of endless variations by modern explorers in the same domain. . . . The events of the Civil War gave a strong lyrical movement to Melville's pen, which had rested for nearly ten years when the volume of "Battle-Pieces and Aspects of the War" appeared in 1866. Most of these poems originated, according to the author, "in an impulse imparted by the fall of Richmond," but they have as subjects all the chief incidents of the struggle. The best of them are "The Stone Fleet," "In the Prison Pen," "The College Colonel," "The March to the Sea," "Running the Batteries," and "Sheridan at Cedar Creek." Some of these had a wide circulation in the press, and were preserved in various anthologies. Mr. Stoddard has called "Sheridan" the "second best cavalry poem in the English language, the first being Browning's, 'How They Brought the Good News from Ghent to

Aix.'" There are in this poem lines as lofty in sentiment and expression as Bryant, or the author of "Lines on a Bust of Dante," or Mr. Stoddard himself could have written.—STEDMAN, ARTHUR, 1891, *Melville of Marquesas, Review of Reviews, American Ed., vol. 4, p. 429.*

In spite of all the obscurities and mannerisms which confessedly deform his later writings, it remains true that *naturalness* is, on the whole, Melville's prime characteristic, both in the tone and in the style of his productions. His narratives are as racy and vigorous as those of Defoe or Smollett or Marryat; his character-sketches are such as only a man of keen observation, and as keen a sense of humour, could have realised and depicted. His seamen and his sea captains all, his savages ashore and aboard, from the noble unsophisticated Mehevi in "Typee" to the semi-civilised comical Queequeg in "The Whale," are admirably vivid and impressive, and the reader who shall once have made their acquaintance will thenceforward in no wise be persuaded that they are not real and living personages. Moreover, there is a large-souled humanity in Melville— the direct outcome of his generous, emotional, yet uniformly sane temperament— which differentiates him entirely from the mere artist or *littérateur.*—SALT, HENRY S., 1892. *"Marquesan Melville," Gentleman's Magazine, vol. 272, p. 254.*

His masterpiece, "Moby Dick, or the White Whale." If it were not for its inordinate length, its frequently inartistic heaping up of details, and its obvious imitation of Carlylean tricks of style and construction, this narrative of tremendous power and wide knowledge might be perhaps pronounced the greatest sea story in literature. The breath of the sea is in it and much of the passion and charm of the most venturous callings plied upon the deep. It is a cool reader that does not become almost as eager as the terrible Captain Ahab in his demoniacal pursuit of Moby Dick, the invincible whale, a creation of the imagination not unworthy of a great poet.—TRENT, WILLIAM P., 1903, *A History of American Literature, p. 390.*

Alfred Lord Tennyson
1809–1892

Born, at Somersby, Lincs., 6 Aug. 1809. Educated at Louth Grammar School, till 1820; at home, 1820–28. Matric., Trin. Coll., Camb., 1828; Chancellor's English Prize Poem, 1829; left Cambridge, owing to death of his father, Feb. 1831. Lived at Somersby till 1835. Married Emily Sellwood, 13 June 1850. Poet Laureate, Nov. 1850. Settled at Farringford, I. of W., 1853. Hon. D. C. L., Oxford, 20 June 1855. Hon. Fellow Trin. Coll., Camb., May 1869. F. R. S. Play "Queen Mary," produced at Lyceum Theatre, 18 April 1876; "The Falcon," St. James's; "The Cup," Lyceum, 3 Jan. 1881; "The Promise of May," Globe, 11 Nov. 1882; "The Foresters," Daly's Theatre, New York, 17 March 1892; "Becket," Lyceum, 6 Feb. 1893. Created Baron Tennyson of Aldworth, Jan. 1884. Died, at Aldworth, 6 Oct. 1892. Buried in Westminster Abbey. *Works:* "Poems by Two Brothers" (anon.; with Charles and Frederick Tennyson), 1827; "Timbuctoo," 1829, "Poems, chiefly lyrical," 1830; "Poems," 1833 [1832]; "The Lover's Tale" (priv. ptd.), 1833; "Poems" (2 vols.), 1842; "The Princess," 1847; "In Memoriam" (anon.), 1850 (2nd edn. same year); "Poems" (6th edn.), 1850; "Poems" (7th edn.), 1851; "Ode on the Death of the Duke of Wellington," 1852; "Poems" (8th edn.), 1853; "The Charge of the Light Brigade" (priv. ptd.) [1855]; "Maud," 1855; "Enid and Nimuë" (priv. ptd.), 1857; "Idylls of the King" (4 pts.), 1859; "A Welcome" [to Princess of Wales], 1863; "Idylls of the Hearth," 1864 (another edn., same year, called: "Enoch Arden, etc."); "The Victim" (priv. ptd.), 1867; "Idylls of the King" (8 pts.), 1869; "The Holy Grail," 1870 [1869]; "The Windows," 1871, [1870] (priv. ptd., 1867); "Gareth and Lynette," 1872; "A Welcome" [to Duchess of Edinburgh], 1874; "The Lover's Tale" (priv. ptd.), 1875, "Queen Mary," 1875; "Harold," 1877 [1876]; "Ballads and other Poems," 1880; "The Promise of May," 1882; "Becket," 1884; "The Cup and The Falcon," 1884; "Tiresias," 1885; ' To H. R. H. Princess Beatrice" (priv. ptd.), 1885; "Poetical Works," 1886; "Locksley Hall Sixty Years After," 1887; "To Edward Lear," 1889; "Demeter," 1889; "The Foresters," 1892; "Idylls of the King" (12 pts.), 1892. *Posthumous:* "The Death of Œnone," 1892. *Collected Works:* 1894.—SHARP, R. FARQUHARSON, 1897, *A Dictionary of English Authors.*

ALFRED LORD TENNYSON

Engraving by Walker and Boutall. From Painting
by G. F. Watts, R. A., 1859.

SIR JOHN ROBERT SEELEY

Engraving by Walter L. Colls. From a
Photograph by Elliott & Fry.

PERSONAL

Mrs. Clarke, Miss James, the Messrs. M——, and Alfred Tennyson dined with us. I am always a little disappointed with the exterior of our great poet when I look at him, in spite of his eyes, which are very fine, but his head and face, striking and dignified as they are, are almost too ponderous and massive for beauty in so young a man; and every now and then there is a slightly sarcastic expression about his mouth that almost frightens me, in spite of his shy manner and habitual silence. But, after all, it is delightful to see and be with any one that one admires and loves for what he has done, as I do him.—KEMBLE, FRANCES ANN, 1832, *Records of a Girlhood, Journal, March* 16.

Long have I known thee as thou art in song,
And long enjoyed the perfume that exhales
From thy pure soul, and odour sweet entails
And permanence on thoughts that float along
The stream of life, to join the passive throng
Of shades and echoes that are Memory's being;
Hearing, we hear not, and we see not, seeing,
If Passion, Fancy, Faith, move not among
The never-present moments of reflection.
Long have I viewed thee in the crystal sphere
Of verse, that like the Beryl makes appear
Visions of hope, begot of recollection.
Knowing thee now, a real earth-treading man,
Not less I love thee and no more I can.
—COLERIDGE, HARTLEY, 1835, *Sonnet to Alfred Tennyson, After meeting him for the First time.*

Three of these autographs, which I send you to-day, are first-rate. A Yankee would almost give a dollar apiece for them. Entire characteristic letters from Pickwick, Lytton Bulwer, and Alfred Tennyson; the last the greatest genius of the three, though the vulgar public have not as yet recognized him for such. Get his poems if you can, and read the "Ulysses," "Dora," the "Vision of Sin," and you will find that we do not overrate him. Besides he is a very handsome man, and a noble-hearted one, with something of the gipsy in his appearance, which, for me, is perfectly charming. Babbie never saw him, unfortunately, or perhaps I should say fortunately, for she must have fallen in love with him on the spot, unless she be made absolutely of ice; and then men of genius have never anything to keep wives upon!—CARLYLE, JANE WELSH, 1843, *To Miss Helen Welsh, March; Letters and Memorials*, ed. Froude, vol. I, p 143.

Alfred is one of the few British or Foreign Figures (a not increasing number I think!) who are and remain beautiful to me;—a true human soul, or some authentic approximation thereto, to whom your own soul can say, Brother! . . . Being a man solitary and sad as certain men are, dwelling in an element of gloom,—carrying a bit of Chaos about him, in short, which he is manufacturing into Cosmos! . . . One of the finest-looking men in the world. A great shock of rough dusty-dark hair; bright-laughing hazel eyes; massive aquiline face, most massive yet most delicate; of sallow-brown complexion, almost Indian-looking; clothes cynically loose, free-and-easy;—smokes infinite tobacco. His voice is musical metallic,—fit for loud laughter and piercing wail, and all that may lie between; I do not meet, in these late decades, such company over a pipe!—CARLYLE, THOMAS, 1844, *Letter, Aug.* 5; *Correspondence of Carlyle and Emerson*, ed. Norton, vol. II, pp. 66, 67.

Avoiding general society, he would prefer to sit up all night talking with a friend, or else to sit "and think alone." Beyond a very small circle he is never to be met. There is nothing eventful in his biography, of a kind which would interest the public.—HORNE, RICHARD HENGIST, 1844, *A New Spirit of the Age*, p. 210.

I saw Tennyson, when I was in London, several times. *He is decidedly the first of our living poets*, and I hope will live to give the world still better things. You will be pleased to hear that he expressed in the strongest terms his gratitude to my writings. To this I was far from indifferent, though persuaded that he is not much in sympathy with what I should myself most value in my attempts, viz.: the spirituality with which I have endeavored to invest the material universe, and the moral relations under which I have wished to exhibit its most ordinary appearances. — WORDSWORTH, WILLIAM, 1845, *Letter to Henry Reed, July* 1; *Memoirs of William Wordsworth*, vol. II, p. 422.

I dined this day with Rogers. . . . We had an interesting party of eight. Moxon the publisher, Kenny, the dramatic poet . . . Spedding, Lushington, and Alfred Tennyson, three young men of eminent talent, belonging to literary Young England. Tennyson, being by far the most eminent of the young poets. . . . He is an admirer of Goethe, and I had a long *tête-à-tête* with him about the great poet. We waited for the eighth,—a lady, Hon. Mrs. Norton, who, Rogers said, was coming on purpose to see Tennyson. — ROBINSON, HENRY CRABB, 1845, *Letter to T. R., Jan.* 31; *Diary, Reminiscences and Correspondence.*

We have seen a good deal of Alfred Tennyson lately, and like him quite as well as the *man* as the poet. He is really a noble creature, with one of the purest, kindest spirits.—HOWITT, MARY, 1846, *Letter to Miss Mitford, Dec.* 16; *The Friendships of Mary Russell Mitford,* ed. *L'Estrange.*

Of the subsequent haunts of Alfred Tennyson we can give no very distinct account. . . . It is very possible you may come across him in a country inn, with a foot on each hob of the fireplace, a volume of Greek in one hand, his meerschaum in the other, so far advanced toward the seventh heaven that he would not thank you to call him back into this nether world. Wherever he is, however, in some still nook of enormous London, or the stiller one of some far-off sea-side hamlet, he is pondering a lay for eternity:—

"Losing his fire and active might
In a silent meditation,
Falling into a still delight
And luxury of contemplation."

That luxury shall, one day, be mine and yours, transferred to us in the shape of a third volume; so come away and don't disturb him. — HOWITT, WILLIAM, 1847, *Homes and Haunts of the Most Eminent British Poets,* vol. II, p. 532.

I saw Tennyson first at the house of Coventry Patmore, where we dined together. I was contented with him at once. He is tall and scholastic-looking, no dandy, but a great deal of plain strength about him, and, though cultivated, quite unaffected. Quiet, sluggish sense and thought; refined, as all English are, and good-humored. There is in him an air of general superiority. He lives with his college set, . . . and has the air of one who is accustomed to be petted and indulged by those he lives with. Take away Hawthorne's bashfulness, and let him talk easily and fast, and you would have a pretty good Tennyson. . . . Carlyle thinks him the best man in England to smoke a pipe with, and used to see him much; had a place in his little garden, on the wall, where Tennyson's pipe was laid up. — EMERSON, RALPH WALDO, 1848, *Journal; Ralph Waldo Emerson, a Memoir,* ed. *Cabot,* vol. II, pp. 540, 541.

I entreat you, Alfred Tennyson,
Come and share my haunch of venison.
I have too a bin of claret,
Good, but better when you share it.
Tho' 'tis only a small bin,
There's a stock of it within
And as sure as I'm a rhymer,
Half a butt of Rüdesheimer.
Come; among the sons of men is none
Welcomer than Alfred Tennyson!
—LANDOR, WALTER SAVAGE, 1853, *The Last Fruit of an Old Tree,* xii.

During two evenings when Tennyson was at their house in London, Mrs. Browning left T. with her husband and William and me (who were the fortunate remnant of the male party) to discuss the universe, and gave all her attention to some certainly not very exciting ladies in the next room. . . . I made a sketch of Tennyson reading, which I gave to Browning, and afterward duplicated it for Miss S. . . . He is quite as glorious in his way as Browning, and perhaps of the two even more impressive on the whole personally.—ROSSETTI, DANTE GABRIEL, 1856, *Letters to William Allingham,* p. 162.

I hardly think Tennyson has done well, as a poet, in fixing his house in such exceptional conditions. He lives, you know, about twenty miles from us along the coast. The country people are much amazed at his bad hat and unusual ways, and believe devoutly that he writes his poetry while mowing his lawn. However, they hold him in great respect, from a perception of the honor in which he is held by their "betters." Our housewife here is a friend of his servant, and she entertained us with an account of how said servant had lately been awed. Opening to a ring at the door, when the Tennysons were out, she saw a "tall, handsome gentleman" standing there who, on learning they were not at home turned to go. "What message shall I give?" quoth the maid. "Merely say Prince Albert called."—DOBELL, SYDNEY, 1857, *Letters.*

I spent two days with him in June, and you take my word for it he is a noble fellow, every inch of him. He is as tall as I am, with a head which Read capitally calls that of a dilapitated Jove, long black hair, splendid dark eyes, and a full mustache and beard. The portraits don't look a bit like him; they are handsomer, perhaps, but haven't half the splendid character of his face. We smoked many a pipe together, and talked of poetry, religion, politics, and geology. I thought he seemed gratified with his American fame; he certainly did not say an unkind word about us. He had read my oriental poems and liked them. He spoke particularly of their richness of imagery and conscientious finish. I need not tell you that his verdict is a valuable one to me. Our intercourse was most cordial and unrestrained, and he asked me, at parting, to be sure and visit him every time I came to England. His wife is one of the best women I ever met with, and his two little boys, Hallam and Lionel, are real cherubs of children.—TAYLOR, BAYARD, 1857, *To George H. Boker; Life and Letters, ed. Taylor and Scudder, vol. I, p. 334.*

A strange shaggy-looking man; his hair, moustache, and beard looked wild and neglected; these very much hid the character of the face. He was dressed in a loosely fitting morning coat, common grey flannel waistcoat and trousers, and a carelessly tied black silk neckerchief. His hair is black; I think the eyes too; they are keen and restless—nose aquiline—forehead high and broad—both face and head are fine and manly. His manner was kind and friendly from the first; there is a dry lurking humour in his style of talking.—DODGSON, CHARLES LUTWIDGE, 1857, *The Life and Letters of Lewis Carroll, ed. Collingwood, p. 69.*

Tennyson is the most picturesque figure, without affectation, that I ever saw; of middle size, rather slouching, dressed entirely in black, and with nothing white about him except the collar of his shirt, which, methought might have been whiter the day before. He had on a black wide-awake hat, with round crown and wide, irregular brim, beneath which came down his long black hair, looking terribly tangled; he had a long pointed beard, too, a little browner than the hair, and not so abundant as to encumber any of the expression of his face. His frock coat was buttoned up across the breast, though the afternoon was warm. His face was very dark, and not exactly a smooth face, but worn and expressing great sensitiveness, though not at that moment the pain and sorrow that is seen in his bust. His eyes were black; but I know little of them, as they did not rest on me, nor on anything but the pictures. He seemed as if he did not see the crowd, nor think of them, but as if he defended himself from them by ignoring them altogether; nor did anybody but myself cast a glance at him. . . . I heard his voice,—a bass voice, but not of a resounding depth,—a voice rather broken, as it were, and ragged about the edges, but pleasant to the ear. His manner, while conversing with these people, was not in the least that of an awkward man, unaccustomed to society; but he shook hands and parted with them, evidently as soon as he conveniently could, and shuffled away quicker than before. He betrayed his shy and secluded habits more in this than anything else that I observed; though, indeed, in his whole presence I was indescribably sensible of a morbid painfulness in him,—a something not to be meddled with. Very soon he left the saloon, shuffling along the floor with short, irregular steps,—a very queer gait, as if he were walking in slippers too loose for him. I had observed that he seemed to turn his feet slightly inward, after the fashion of Indians.—HAWTHORNE, NATHANIEL, 1857, *Nathaniel Hawthorne and His Wife, ed. Hawthorne, vol. II, pp. 143, 144.*

Tennyson is a grand specimen of a man, with a magnificent head set on his shoulders like the capital of a mighty pillar. His hair is long and wavy and covers a massive head. He wears a beard and moustache, which one begrudges as hiding so much of that firm, powerful, but finely chiselled mouth. His eyes are large and gray, and open wide when a subject interests him; they are well shaded by the noble brow, with its strong lines of thought and suffering. I can quite understand Samuel Laurence calling it the best balance of head he had ever seen. He is very brown after all the pedestrianizing along our south coast.—FOX, CAROLINE, 1860, *Memories of Old Friends, ed. Pym; Journal, Sept. 22, p. 351.*

I went to Tennyson's by one of his approaches, returned by another, and saw his house from top to bottom; and, having now seen all, I do think it is the most beautifully situated house I ever beheld (Rydal Mount would, no doubt, be excepted by those who love mountains better than I do). His park is scarcely less in extent than Lord Clarendon's, delightfully varied with grove and deep pasture; in one direction, the sea at a mile off, with cliff and promontory and jutting or detached masses of rock; in another, the crest of a down, covered with gorse bloom, rising at a distance and seen over a foreground of woodland; in a third, a wide plain, with the estuary of the Solent to bound it, and river craft coming and going. I saw the children again and liked them much. The younger is certainly good-looking; the other has pleasing manners, kindly and quiet, with an interested gaze. And in the midst of all this beauty and comfort stands Alfred Tennyson, grand, but very gloomy, whom it is a sadness to see, and one has to think of his works to believe that he can escape from himself and escape into regions of light and glory. . . . Alfred Tennyson came in the morning in an agreeable mood, though it *was* in the morning. His agreeable moods are generally in the evening. After I was in bed, Mrs. Cameron wrapped a shawl round her head and went down to the beach, and, finding a most magnificent state of things there, she sent for Alfred, who joined her, and whom she left to make the most of it. He seems to be independent of weather. Mrs. Cameron says that in one of the great storms of this year he walked all along the coast to the Needles, which is six miles off. With all his shattered nerves and uneasy gloom he seems to have some sorts of strength and hardihood. There is a great deal in him that is like ———. But his tenderness is more genuine, as well as his simplicity; and he has no hostilities and is never active as against people. He only grumbles.—TAYLOR, SIR HENRY, 1860, *Letter to Alice Taylor, Autobiography, vol.* II, *pp.* 157, 159.

Alfred talked very pleasantly that evening to Annie Thackeray and L—— S——. He spoke of Jane Austen, as James Spedding does, as next to Shakespeare! I can never imagine what they mean when they say such things. Alfred has grown, he says, much fonder of you since your two last visits here. He says he feels now he is beginning to know you and not to feel afraid of you, and that he is beginning to get over your extreme insolence to him when he was young and you in your meridian splendor and glory. So one reads your simplicity. He was very violent with the girls on the subject of the rage for autographs. He said he believed every crime and every vice in the world was connected with the passion for autographs and anecdotes and records; that the desiring anecdotes and acquaintance with the lives of great men was treating them like pigs, to be ripped open for the public; that he knew he himself should be ripped open like a pig; that he thanked God Almighty with his whole heart and soul that he knew nothing, and that the world knew nothing, of Shakespeare but his writings; and that he thanked God Almighty that he knew nothing of Jane Austen, and that there were no letters preserved either of Shakespeare's or of Jane Austen's; that they had not been ripped open like pigs.— CAMERON, MRS. CHARLES HAY, 1861, *Letter to Henry Taylor, Autobiography of Sir Henry Taylor, vol.* II, *p.* 160.

Evening at Farringford. Tennyson read "Boadicea" and "The Lincolnshire Farmer." The latter gains immensely by his giving the words their proper accent, and by the enormous sense of humor thrown into it by his voice and manner in reading it. I asked Tennyson which he preferred of the two poems, "Enoch Arden" and "Aylmer's Field." He replied "Enoch Arden," which he thought was very perfect, and a beautiful story. "Aylmer's Field" had given him more trouble than anything he ever did. At one time he had to put it aside altogether for six months; the story was so intractable, and it was so difficult to deal with modern manners and conversation. The Indian relative was introduced solely for the sake of the dagger, which was to be the instrument of the lover's suicide. —POLLOCK, SIR FREDERICK, 1864, *Personal Remembrances.*

As soon as my London engagements were satisfied, I came down here [Freshwater]. After half an hour's sail, quarter of an hour's drive brought me to this quiet and truly English little mansion. The lady of the house received me in the most gentle, gracious manner. She is of the genuine, sweet-blooded, sweet-voiced English style, dressed in black and white, loose-flowing. By this time it was five o'clock. The poet came down-stairs from a hot bath which he had just been taking, quite in an easy unaffected style; a certain slow heaviness of motion belongs essentially to his character, and contrasts strikingly with the alert quickness and sinew energy of Kingsley; head Jovian, eye dark, pale face, black flowing locks, like a Spanish ship-captain or a captain of Italian brigands,—something not at all common and not the least English. We dined, talked, and smoked together, and got on admirably. He reads Greek readily, and has been translating bits of

Homer lately in blank verse.—BLACKIE, JOHN STUART, 1864, *Letter, John Stuart Blackie, a Biography*, ed. Stoddard, vol. II, p. 9.

Soon after came coffee. Tennyson grew impatient, moved his great gaunt body about, and finally was left to smoke a pipe. It is hard to fix the difference between the two men, both with their strong provincial accent—Gladstone with his rich, flexible voice, Tennyson with his deep drawl rising into an impatient falsetto when put out; Gladstone arguing, Tennyson putting in a prejudice; Gladstone asserting rashly, Tennyson denying with a bald negative; Gladstone full of facts, Tennyson relying on impressions; both of them humorous; but the one polished and delicate in repartee, the other broad and coarse and grotesque. Gladstone's hands are white and not remarkable, Tennyson's are huge, unwieldy, fit for moulding clay or dough. Gladstone is in some sort a man of the world; Tennyson a child, and treated by Gladstone like a child.—SYMONDS, JOHN ADDINGTON, 1865–93, *Recollections of Lord Tennyson, Century Magazine*, vol. 46, p. 33.

At the Session of Poets held lately in London,
The Bard of Freshwater was voted the chair:
With his tress unbrush'd, and his shirt-collar undone,
He toll'd at his ease like a good-humor'd Bear;
"Come Boys!" he exclaimed, "we'll be merry together!"
And lit up his pipe with a smile on his cheek;
—While with eye, like a skipper's cock'd up at the weather,
Sat the Vice-chairman Browning thinking in Greek.
—BUCHANAN, ROBERT, (CALIBAN), 1866, *The Spectator, Sept. 15.*

Tennyson is remarkable for his plain, blunt way of talking, and utters his straightforward opinions in a simple deep voice somewhat surprising to those who know him by the superfine art indicated by his poems. He is especially addicted in his conversation to strong Saxon expressions, and is full of humorous anecdotes.—CONWAY, MONCURE DANIEL, 1870, *Southcoast Saunterings in England, Harper's Magazine*, vol. 40, p. 541.

Look at his photograph. Deep-browed, but not deep-lined; bald, but not grey; with a dark disappointment and little hopeful feeling on his face; with hair unkempt, heaped up in the carriage of his shoulders and with his figure covered with a tragic cloak, the Laureate is portrayed, gloomily peering from two ineffective and not very lustrous eyes, a man of sixty, looking more like a worn and a more feeling man of fifty. His skin is sallow, his whole physique not jovial nor red like Shakespeare and Dickens, but lachrymose, saturnine; lachrymose! and yet, as regards fame and reward, what a successful man he has been! At the age at which Shakespeare was holding horses, he was a pensionary of the Court. When he was very young the critics killed a far greater poet, John Keats, so that they might shower down repentant and self-recalcitrant praise on the successor. When he was but young, an old worn-out poet—a true prose man, but a poet still—contended for the Laureateship after years of toil and pen labor, but the young singer was crowned, and received the Laureate's wreath, the Laureate's fame and pension—the glory of which wreath was made purer and higher from that of his predecessor, Wordsworth. —FRISWELL, JAMES HAIN, 1870, *Modern Men of Letters Honestly Criticised*, p. 147.

It was during one of his rambles with Alexander Ireland through the Manchester Exhibition rooms that Hawthorne saw Tennyson wandering about. I have always thought it unfortunate that these two men of genius could not have been introduced on that occasion. Hawthorne was too shy to seek an introduction, and Tennyson was not aware that the American author was present. Hawthorne records in his journal that he gazed at Tennyson with all his eyes, "and rejoiced more in him than in all the other wonders of the Exhibition." When I afterwards told Tennyson that the author whose "Twice-Told-Tales" he happened to be then reading at Farringford had met him at Manchester, but did not make himself known, the Laureate said in his frank and hearty manner: "Why didn't he come up and let me shake hands with him? I am sure I should have been glad to meet a man like Hawthorne anywhere." . . . Once I remember Miss Mitford carried me on a pilgrimage to a grand old village church with a tower half covered with ivy. We came to it through laurel hedges, and passed on the way a magnificent cedar of Lebanon. It was a superb pile, rich in painted glass windows and carved oak ornaments. Here Miss Mitford ordered the man to stop, and, turning to me with great enthusiasm, said, "This is Shiplake Church where Alfred Tennyson was married!"—FIELDS, JAMES T., 1871, *Yesterdays With Authors, pp.* 81, 274.

DEDICATED TO
ALFRED TENNYSON
OF POETRY—ILLUSTRIOUS AND CONSUMMATE;
OF FRIENDSHIP—NOBLE AND SINCERE.
—BROWNING, ROBERT, 1872, *Selections from Poetical Works, Dedication.*

Tennyson receives from his publishers an annual income of about $20,000. In addition to this, the magazines are willing to pay fabulous prices for his poems. The verses beginning

"What does little birdie say
In her bed at peep of day?"

were bought by a periodical for $40 a line. The *Nineteenth Century* gave £300 for "The Ballad of the Revenge." Robert Bonner, of the *Ledger*, paid $5000 for "The May Queen." — WALSH, WILLIAM SHEPARD, 1882, *Author and Authorship, p.* 77.

After luncheon saw the great Poet Tennyson in dearest Albert's room for nearly an hour; and most interesting it was. He is grown very old, his eyesight much impaired. But he was very kind. Asked him to sit down. He talked of the many friends he had lost, and what it would be if he did not feel and know that there was another world, where there would be no partings; and then he spoke with horror of the unbelievers and philosophers who would make you believe there was no other world, no Immortality, who tried to explain all away in a miserable manner.—VICTORIA, QUEEN, 1883, *Private Journal, Aug.* 7.

Of course I have visited the great Tennyson at Farringford, and remember him showing me the tree overhanging his garden fence, which "Yankees" climb to have a look at him.—TUPPER, MARTIN FARQUHAR, 1886, *My Life as an Author, p.* 324.

Let me assume to pass verdict, or perhaps momentary judgment, for the United States on this poet—a removed and distant position giving some advantages over a high one. What is Tennyson's service to his race, times, and especially to America? First, I should say, his personal character. He is not to be mentioned as a rugged, evolutionary, aboriginal force—but (and a great lesson is in it) he has been consistent throughout with the native, personal, healthy, patriotic spinal element and promptings of himself. His moral line is local and conventional, but it is vital and genuine. He reflects the upper-crust of his time, its pale cast of thought—even its *ennui*. Then the simile of my friend John Burroughs is entirely true, "his glove is a glove of silk, but the hand is a hand of iron." He shows how one can be a royal laureate, quite elegant and "aristocratic," and a little queer and affected, and at the same time perfectly manly and natural. As to his non-democracy, it fits him well, and I like him the better for it. I guess we all like to have (I am sure I do) some one who presents those sides of a thought, or possibility, different from our own—different, and yet with a sort of home-likeness—a tartness and contradiction offsetting the theory as we view it, and construed from tastes and proclivities not at all our own.—WHITMAN, WALT, 1887, *A Word About Tennyson, The Critic, vol.* 10, *p.* 1.

I saw the poet to the best advantage under his own trees and walking over his own domain. He took delight in pointing out to me the finest and the rarest of his trees, and there were many beauties among them. I recalled my morning's visit to Whittier at Oak Knoll, in Danvers, a little more than a year ago. . . . In this garden of England, the Isle of Wight, where everything grows with such a lavish extravagance of greenness that it seems as if it must bankrupt the soil before autumn, I felt as if weary eyes and over-taxed brains might reach their happiest haven of rest.—HOLMES, OLIVER WENDELL, 1887-91, *Hundred Days in Europe.*

Everybody knows by photograph the manner of man he is,—surely a beautiful face, if ever the adjective could be applied to masculine features, and never more beautiful in any stage of life than now, when age has fixed all the finer features, and lent them a new dignity and majesty. Everybody is familiar with the broad forehead, the clear, deep eyes, the strongly cut nose, and finely chiselled lips, the long hair fringing those temples,—shrines of high thought,—and the genial, massive, and commanding aspect of the poet. Albeit past his eighty-second birthday, Lord Tennyson's figure is only weakened, not broken, by age. His hair preserves much of its old, dark color, and, excepting in places, is hardly more than "sable-silvered." His spirit is as alert, his glance as keen and alight, as ever. . . . On the left side of his neck there lodges a small brown birthmark, very characteristic, as if a drop of dark wine had dropped there, and had stained the skin. His hands are manly and powerful in outline, but delicate and finely formed as those of a poet should be.—ARNOLD, SIR EDWIN, 1891, *A Day with Lord Tennyson, The Forum, vol.* 12, *p.* 541.

An amusing story has been told regarding him at this stage of the movement on behalf of Tennyson. "Richard Milnes," said Carlyle one day, withdrawing his pipe from his mouth, as they were seated together in the little house in Cheyne Row, "when are you going to get that pension for Alfred Tennyson?" "My dear Carlyle," responded Milnes, "the thing is not so easy as you seem to suppose. What will my constituents say if I do get the pension for Tennyson? They know nothing about him or his poetry, and they will probably think he is some poor relation of my own, and that the whole affair is a job." Solemn and emphatic was Carlyle's response. "Richard Milnes, on the Day of Judgment, when the Lord asks you why you didn't get that pension for Alfred Tennyson, it will not do to lay the blame on your constituents; it is *you* that will be damned." — REID, T. WEMYSS, 1891, *The Life, Letters, and Friendships of Richard Monckton Milnes, First Lord Houghton, p.* 295.

Great man of song, whose glorious laurelled head
   Within the lap of death sleeps well at last,
Down the dark road, seeking the deathless dead,
   Thy faithful, fearless, shining soul hath passed.
Fame blows his silver trumpet o'er thy sleep,
   And Love stands broken by thy lonely lyre;
So pure the fire God gave this clay to keep,
   The clay must still seem holy for the fire.
—LEGALLIENNE, RICHARD, 1892, *Robert Louis Stevenson and Other Poems, p.* 12.

No one of those to whom his poetry has been among the greatest blessings of their lives (and such are to be numbered by thousands and tens of thousands) can have failed, though his eyes never beheld the poet, to love him as a dear friend unseen. But apart from personal loss, there still remains a meaning which we understand when we say that the English-speaking world, our English race, feels the poorer for this event. It dispirits and discourages us, because we feel that the last of a long line has departed, and we are anxious and uneasy as to the possibilities of the future.—AINGER, ALFRED, 1892, *The Death of Tennyson, Macmillan's Magazine, vol.* 67, *p.* 76.

Presently I heard a curiously marked and rather heavy footstep coming from an adjoining room, and Tennyson stood before me. I saw a tall man of curiously un-English aspect—as un-English as Lord Beaconsfield—carelessly dressed, almost slovenly, with a noble but somewhat narrow head, a domelike forehead, fine eyes and a tangled black beard streaked with gray. He advanced toward me, gave me his hand —which is, or was, a good deal for an Englishman—he sidled away to the high mantlepiece, leaned against it, and said, with the tone of a vexed schoolboy: "I am rather afraid of you Americans—your countrymen don't treat me very well. There was Bayard Taylor—" And he went on with a long complaint of a letter which had lately appeared, one which Taylor had not meant for publication, but which an injudicious friend had printed. Strange to say, the effect of his diatribe was not merely to amuse, but to put me entirely at my ease. I had no intention of writing anything about him personally—and have never before done so—and it was evident that with this assurance he would feel that he had said his worst, and would be kind and friendly thenceforward, as proved true. He took me to his study, showed me his favorite view, led me through the garden, and was as kind as possible.—HIGGINSON, THOMAS WENTWORTH, 1892, *A Morning with Tennyson, Harper's Bazar, Oct.* 22.

Few among the noteworthy personages of our time more assiduously shrank from the public gaze, or shunned with a more sensitive persistency the "fierce light" which, in this prying age, beats upon the domestic concerns of eminent men. His life was essentially one of retirement, yielding little to the "literary leeches" who swarm in these "days that deal in ana." Seldom, during a long life, to be met with in that vortex of wasted ambitions called "fashionable society"—rarely taking part in public affairs—avoiding with something of shyness all kinds of conventional ceremony and popular hero-worship, he "dwelt apart," in a very literal sense of the words, from the hubbub and turmoil of the great world, and in his country homes, in the company of a few chosen friends, secluded from the reach of the curious, led a life of studious contemplation, shaping into imperishable verse the strivings of the poet's soul. Although in later life the mellowing influences of age relaxed somewhat the austerity of his isolation and social reserve, he cherished for the most part an emphatic prejudice against, sometimes deepening into a great hatred of, the babbledom that dogs the heels of fame.—JENNINGS, HENRY J., 1892, *Lord Tennyson, p.* 1.

Tennyson once said that anybody could write a poem, but that very few people could read one. His own reading was unique and carefully adapted to his own poetry. In the last years of his life he appeared so old and so prophetic that he might have been Merlin himself. He looked simple, rustic, almost uncouth, but every inch of him a great man. The resemblance to Shakespeare was no fancy, although Shakespeare died before he was sixty. Tennyson thanked God that neither he nor anybody else knew anything about Shakespeare except his plays and his sonnets—that Shakespeare had never been "ripped up like a pig," a fate which it is rather to be hoped than expected that Tennyson will himself escape. Still, one likes to think of Shakespeare passing quiet years at Stratford-on-Avon, talking and drinking with his neighbours, guarding the fire within. Tennyson was a voracious consumer of books, especially of novels, with a wonderful memory for the classics, and for the great English poets. As an illustration of his delightful simplicity, it may be recorded that when the conversation turned upon the House of Lords, he suddenly exclaimed, "I was just going to say what I would do if I were a lord, and then I remembered I was one." He was eager for new facts, delighting in converse with travellers and men of science. Metaphysical speculation fascinated him, and, like Dr. Johnson, he looked in strange places for evidence of a future life. Even psychical reseach interested him, and it was, perhaps, with the same side of his mind that he cared for riddles. He enjoyed his port and his tobacco, as everybody knows.—PAUL, HERBERT, 1892, *Tennyson, New Review*, vol. 7, p. 531.

Tennyson's dislike to intrusions upon his solitude showed itself at times in an entire disregard of conventionalities. He allowed himself to indulge in what, in anybody else, would be called downright rudeness. One of his neighbours, with whom he was on good terms, once asked leave to bring to Aldworth a lady who was visiting him—a lady well known in society, as her husband is well known in a world much wider than society. She had, it was carefully explained, a great desire to see the poet, for whose writings her admiration was great. Tennyson assented with amiability, telling his friend to bring her to luncheon on a day named in the following week. When they arrived the poet had forgotten all about it, and, by ill-luck, was in one of his solitary moods. The lady was introduced, the poet bowed. Luncheon was announced and they went in; she sat next her host, who uttered not a word during the meal; at the end of which he rose and retired in silence to his own room. She left the house, to which she had made this pilgrimage in a spirit of hope and reverence, not having once heard so much as the sound of the poet's voice.— SMALLEY, GEORGE W., 1892, *Studies of Men,* p. 77.

Most of Tennyson's friends remember a small room high up at the top of the house [Farringford], formerly very bare except for books, afterwards made more comfortable, to which, when dinner was over, he retired, and, sometimes after half-an-hour's solitude, invited his friends to join him. We either smoked with him, or, if we did not smoke, we had the privilege of hearing him talk, and of talking with him. This was his temple, or it might be termed his den, where his poems and a few favourite books were kept. It was a sign of more intimate friendship to be allowed to visit him there. At such times, if he was not deterred by shyness, he said just what came into his head. But, in general he was very free and frank; he had nothing to conceal, and he felt so keenly, that if he had, he could not have concealed it. He used to utter strong thoughts in strong language, about recent discoveries in Science, about the politics of the day, about the deeper mysteries of human life. On a few topics he would discourse again and again with undiminished energy. There was, perhaps, no political matters in which he took so deep an interest as the defence of his country.—JOWETT, BENJAMIN, 1893, *Personal Recollections, A Memoir of Tennyson,* ed. Tennyson, vol. II, p. 461.

Tennyson's reading of his own poems was part of his poetry. It was illuminative and suggestive, the best of all commentaries. It

revealed the significance of his work, the conception which he had formed of the poet's mission and the poet's art, and the methods by which he accomplished certain results. Most of all it revealed the man himself behind the poems. A voice is a real thing. It has spirit and life in it. This was especially true of Tennyson's voice, which was, as Milton says of the angels,
Vital in every part.
To hear him was to know the man; to feel how genuine, how sympathetic, how strong he was. To hear him was to think of him, not as a classic on the shelves of a library, but as a living force in the living world. Thus the voice that fell upon the outward ear became the symbol of the spiritual voice with which he has moved the heart, and expressed the ideals, of the English race in this nineteenth century.—VAN DYKE, HENRY, 1893, *The Voice of Tennyson, Century Magazine, vol.* 45, *p.* 539.

The little affectations and insincerities of life so troubled him, and his natural shyness, increased by his disabling short sight, so fought with his innate courtesy to all, that general society was always an effort and a burden to him. His fame increased the trouble, and he often told me how he wished he could have had all the money which his books had made without the notoriety. Even a single stranger was, as such and at first, always a trial to him, and his instinctive desire was to hide as much of himself as possible from observation until he found his companion sympathetic. Then he expanded as a flower does in the sunshine, and he never hoarded or kept back any of the profuse riches and splendour of his mind. When Frederick Robertson of Brighton—the great preacher, who had written much and admirably about his poems, and for whom he had a high regard—first called upon him, "I felt," said Tennyson, "*as if he had come to pluck out the heart of my mystery—so I talked to him about nothing but beer.*" He could not help it; it was impossible for him to wear his heart upon his sleeve.—KNOWLES, JAMES, 1893, *Aspects of Tennyson, Nineteenth Century, vol.* 33, *p.* 165.

I have always thought that Tennyson's appearance was too emphatically that of a poet, especially in his photographs: the fine frenzy, the careless picturesqueness, were almost too much. He looked the part too well; but in reality there was a roughness and acrid gloom about the man which saved him from his over romantic appearance.—OLIPHANT, MARGARET O. W., 1894, *Autobiography, p.* 136.

IN LOVING MEMORY
OF
ALFRED LORD TENNYSON
WHOSE HAPPIEST DAYS WERE PASSED AT FARRINGFORD IN THIS PARISH.
BORN AUG. 6TH 1809
DIED OCT. 6TH 1892
BURIED IN WESTMINSTER ABBEY OCT. 12TH 1892

Speak, living Voice! with thee death is not death;
Thy life outlives the life of dust and breath.

ALSO IN LOVING MEMORY
OF HIS WIFE
EMILY LADY TENNYSON
BORN JULY 9TH 1813
DIED AUGUST 10TH 1896
"Dear, near and true, no truer Time himself
can prove you, tho' he make you evermore
dearer and nearer."

—INSCRIPTION ON TABLET, 1896, *Freshwater Church.*

When I first saw Lady Tennyson she was in the prime of life. Her two sons, boys of eight and ten years of age perhaps, were at her side. Farringford was at that time almost the same beautiful solitude the lovers had found it years before, when it was first their home. . . . I recall her figure at dinner as she sat in her soft white muslin dress, tied with blue, at that time hardly whiter than her face or bluer than her eyes, and how the boys stood sometimes one on either side of her in their black velvet dresses, like Millais' picture of the princes in the tower, and sometimes helped to serve the guests. By and by we adjourned to another room, where there was a fire and a shining dark table with fruit and wine after her own picturesque fashion, and where later the poet read to us, while she, being always delicate in health, took her accustomed couch. . . . After this the mists of time close over! I can recall her again in the gray dress and kerchief following our footsteps to the door. I can see her graceful movement of the head as she waved her adieux; I can see the poet's dusky figure standing by her side, and that is all. Sometimes she lives confusedly to the world of imagination as the Abbess of Almesbury; and sometimes, as one who knew her has said, she was like the first of the three queens, "the tallest of them all, and fairest," who bore away the body of

Arthur. She was no less than these, being a living inspiration at the heart of the poet's every-day life.—FIELDS, ANNIE, 1896, *Authors and Friends, pp.* 351, 353, 354.

Farringford he never forsook, though he added another home to it; and assuredly no poet has ever before called two such residences his own. Both of them were sweetened by the presence there, so graciously prolonged, of her to whom the lovers of Song owe so deep a debt of gratitude. The second home was as well chosen as the first. It lifted England's great poet to a height from which he could gaze on a large portion of that English land which he loved so well, see it basking in its most affluent summer beauty, and only bounded by "the inviolate sea." Year after year he trod its two stately terraces with men the most noted of their time, statesmen, warriors, men of letters, science and art, some of royal race, some famous in far lands, but none more welcome to him than the friends of his youth. Nearly all of those were taken from him by degrees; but many of them stand successively recorded in his verse. The days which I passed there yearly with him and his were the happiest days of each year. They will retain a happy place in my memory during whatever short period my life may last: and the sea-murmurs of Freshwater will blend with the sighing of the woods around Aldworth, for me, as for many more worthy, a music, if mournful, yet full of consolation.—DEVERE, AUBREY, 1897, *Alfred Lord Tennyson, a Memoir,* ed. Tennyson, vol. II, p. 208.

In many days at Farringford, on this and other later occasions, I came to know your father well, and long walks with him gave me much insight into his ways of thinking and feeling. His natural shyness seemed to have been afterwards considerably mitigated by periods of residence in London, but when I first knew him it was very apparent, and it was a good deal aggravated by his great short-sightedness. I well remember in one of our first walks his alarm at a flock of sheep which he took for tourists. There always seemed to me to be a strange and somewhat pathetic contrast between his character and his position. Nature evidently intended him for the life of the quietest and most secluded of country gentlemen, for a life spent among books and flowers and a few intimate friends, and very remote from the noise and controversies of the great world. Few men valued more highly domestic privacy. But a great gift had made his name a household word among the English race. True privacy, as he bitterly complained, became impossible to him, and troops of tourists, newspaper writers and interviewers were constantly occupied with his doings.— LECKY, WILLIAM EDWARD HARTPOLE, 1897, *Alfred Lord Tennyson, a Memoir,* ed. *Tennyson, vol.* II, p. 200.

A great man: strong and steady of purpose, in spite of surface fluctuation; self-withdrawn, yet social and benevolent; noble and rugged and human; a figure so veritably fine that the frankest detail of its human frailties could have injured it only for sentimentalists.—THOMPSON, FRANCIS, 1897, *The Life of Tennyson, New Review, vol.* 17, p. 548.

But if Freshwater has suffered somewhat since Tennyson went to live there, it is infinitely richer for the legacy he has left it. His memory exalts all that is permanent of its old beauty. The village has altered, but the beautiful swelling downs remain; the little sedge-embroidered Yar still makes seaward from Freshwater Gate, where the Channel spray mingles with its infant waters, to Yarmouth, by the Solent, as it did half a century of summers ago; and at Farringford, the poet's home, all remains as he left it. The personal memories which still linger in the neighborhood must die out one by one as the people of his time pass away; but meanwhile his portrait hangs in most of the old cottages, the village folk still have quaint personal recollections of the great man who moved among them wrapped in a sort of mystery, and a few of those who were privileged to be his intimate friends still reside in the neighborhood.—O'CONNOR, V. C. SCOTT, 1897, *Tennyson and his Friends at Freshwater, Century Magazine, vol.* 55, p. 242.

This garden is truly "a haunt of ancient peace." Left there alone with the bard for some time, I felt that I sat in the presence of one of the Kings of Men. His aged look impressed me. There was the keen eagle eye; and, although the glow of youth was gone, the strength of age was in its place. The lines of his face were like the furrows in the stem of a wrinkled oak-tree; but his whole bearing disclosed a latent strength and nobility; a reserve of power, combined with a most courteous grace of manner. I was also struck by the *négligé* air of the man, so different from that of Browning or Arnold or Lowell.—KNIGHT, WILLIAM, 1897, *A Reminiscence of Tennyson, Blackwood's Magazine, vol.* 162, *p.* 264.

His personality [1878] more than satisfied me, though I had been led to anticipate much from Mrs. Cameron's and Rejlander's artistic photographs. "The large dark eyes, generally dreamy, but with an occasional gleam of imaginative alertness," as De Vere describes them, still varied between haunting softness and eager brightness; "the great shock of rough dusky dark hair" that Carlyle wrote of in 1842 had been somewhat subdued, but far from subjugated by time; it revealed more of the poet's "high-built brow," but its raven hue was unimpaired. "The massive aquiline face" was still "most massive, yet most delicate," and still a healthy bronze. His gestures were free and spontaneous, his voice full and musical. It was impossible to believe he was in his seventieth year. His accent and speech both surprised me. I was quite prepared for the fastidious articulation and premeditated hesitation in the choice of words to which so many distinguished English University men are prone. There was a rich burr in his accent, Lincolnshire, I suppose, and a pungent directness in his utterance which were as refreshing as they were unlooked for. Then he evidently possessed the rare knack of getting the very best out of his fellow talkers at the same time that he gave them much more than he got for it. —GRAVES, ALFRED PERCIVAL, 1897, *Tennyson in Ireland, Cornhill Magazine, vol.* 76, *p.* 596.

He once very kindly offered to lend me his house in the Isle of Wight. "But mind," he said, "you will be watched from morning till evening." This was in fact his great grievance, that he could not go out without being stared at. Once taking a walk with me and my wife on the downs behind his house, he suddenly started, left us, and ran home, simply because he had descried two strangers coming toward us. I was told that he once complained to the Queen, and said that he could no longer stay in the Isle of Wight, on account of the tourists who came to stare at him. The Queen, with a kindly irony, remarked that she did not suffer much from that grievance, but Tennyson, not seeing what she meant, replied: "No madame, and if I could clap a sentinel wherever I liked, I should not be troubled either."—MÜLLER, FRIEDRICH MAX, 1898, *Auld Lang Syne, p.* 157.

Great as he was as a poet, Tennyson was greater still as a man and a Christian. What leader has made so profound an impression upon his fellows or won such tribute of praise from the great men of his time! . . . Precious as are his poems, Tennyson's character and career are treasures beyond all the achievement of his splendid intellect. Like his own King Arthur, he wore "the white flower of a blameless life."—HILLIS, NEWELL DWIGHT, 1899, *Great Books as Life Teachers, pp.* 156, 157.

It is to me a pleasure to recall the faces of distinguished people I have met at his house, but most of all to remember his own marked features and grand head. It has been called a "Rembrandt-like dome," and the poet himself once told me that the greatest compliment he ever had paid him was by two working men, masons, he thought, who passed him in a street, and he heard one say to the other, "There goes a Shakespeare-like fellow!" Nor can I ever forget the pleasant talks with his son Hallam, kindest and best of sons and most unselfish of men, nor the sweet charm of the poet's wife, always interesting, always full of affectionate kindness and wonderful feeling and good sense, a visit to whom lifted one up out of the ruts of this world on to a higher platform altogether. One felt that to her most fitly of all living people could Spenser's lines be applied:

"Whose sweet aspect both God and man doth move

In her unspotted pleasaunce to delight."
—RAWNSLEY, H. D., 1900, *Memories of the Tennysons, p.* 149.

Tennyson's face and demeanor, which have been preserved in the fine portraits of him by Watts and Millais, were so remarkable, that at the first sight one took the impression of unusual dignity and intellectual distinction. His voice, gesture, and bearing impersonated, so to speak, his character and reputation; his appearance fulfilled the common expectation (so often disappointed) of perceiving at once something singular and striking in the presence of a celebrity. Jowett wrote of him after his death that he was a magnificent man who stood before you in his native refinement and strength, and that the unconventionality of his manners was in keeping with the originality of his figure. He enjoyed his well-earned fame and the tokens of enthusiastic admiration that came to him from near and far; he listened to applause with straightforward complacency.—LYALL, SIR ALFRED, 1902, *Tennyson (English Men of Letters), p.* 190.

There was one salient characteristic of Tennyson that must have struck the most unobservant, and that was his direct honesty and simplicity in things small and great. On the pavement of the entrance-hall at Aldworth is the Welsh motto in encaustic tiles, "The Truth against the World." It was not idly placed there. Such was, indeed, the spirit that informed every act and utterance of the master of Aldworth. He hated shams of every sort; and that is, in great measure, as Mr. Knowles has observed, the key to his detestation of what we call "society." Its "small insincerities," without which it could not exist, repelled and disgusted him. He had a quick, almost an imperious way of flashing round on one with a sudden question, somewhat embarrassing to shy folk. A downright answer, or downright confession of ignorance, would win him to most delightful and instructive talk, but pinchbeck omniscience he would exploit relentlessly. As all lovers of his poetry know, that passion for truth and fidelity of detail underlies all his poetic art. . . . There was the rather unusual custom at Aldworth of every one's leaving the dinnertable, when the time came for the ladies to rise, and going into an adjoining room, where the men sat down at another table piled with fruit and flowers. On this second table, too, were placed crusty port, and Madeira that had doubled "the Cape" and here, as a special favor, and as being one of Charles Lamb's "blest tobacco boys," I was allowed a cigar. If the weather were at all cool, there was a bright fire of logs, and Tennyson, wearing his black velvet skullcap, as he always did indoors during the latter years of his life, sat at the board as supreme as "rare old Ben" at the "Devil in the Strand," or John Dryden at the "Rainbow," and poured forth such talk and reminiscences as I never expect to hear again.—MCCABE, W. GORDON, 1902, *Personal Recollections of Alfred Lord Tennyson, Century Magazine, vol.* 63, *pp.* 726, 731.

To the Max Müller house on High Street went, once for dinner, bed, and breakfast, during the Long Vacation, Mr. Tennyson. He seems to have been a little trying to his hostess, for he did not like the sauce on the salmon at dinner, and he said so frankly; while he declared, at breakfast, that "mutton chops were the staple of every bad inn in England." This was all very true, no doubt; but not altogether polite, even for a poet. He made himself agreeable in other respects, however, and, like almost all great men, he smoked a great deal!—HUTTON, LAURENCE, 1903, *Literary Landmarks of Oxford, p.* 152.

POEMS BY TWO BROTHERS
1826

A few years since, a volume of poems of the greatest promise, and indeed of very exquisite performance, was published by Alfred and Charles Tennyson; but their originality was defaced by strange and motley admixtures of the subtlety of Shelley, and a pseudo-simplicity contracted from Wordsworth. Great would have been the praise due to our critics, had they warmly welcomed all that was excellent in these poems, but kindly and leniently pointed out the blemishes that deteriorated from their effect. Instead of this, however, the blemishes were far more praised than the beauties; and the affectations themselves were quoted in all the journals as the most exquisite flowers of fanciful invention. We trust, however, that these young poets will be more wise than their judges. Streams purify themselves by running on,—especially those that come direct from Castaly.—LYTTON, SIR EDWARD LYTTON BULWER, 1838, *Present State of Poetry, p.* 344.

From Grantham, Eyre went to the grammar-school of Louth, in Lincolnshire, which Charles and Alfred Tennyson had left a year or two before. Their fame as poets was still traditionary in the school, and Edward Eyre seemed to feel a kind of noble envy, at once proud of the fact that two of "our boys" had actually published a volume of poems for which a bookseller gave them ten pounds, and grieved he could not emulate them.—HUME, HAMILTON, 1867, *Life of Edward John Eyre, p.* 11.

These *juvenilia* were written from the age of fifteen upwards. The copyright was sold for ten pounds to Messrs. Jackson, booksellers and printers, of Louth. Mr. Jackson, a member of the firm, died about three years ago, and his son-in-law now has the manuscript of the book. It was published in London by Simpkin and Marshall, who were then laying the foundation of their great connection. Eyre, afterwards so well known as Governor of Jamaica, went to the grammar school a year or two after the Tennysons had left, and found the boys very proud of school-fellows who had published a volume of poems. . . . It commands a price of about £5 in the book market.—NICOLL, WILLIAM ROBERTSON (WALTER E. WACE), 1881, *Alfred Tennyson, p. 7.*

TIMBUCTOO
1829

The splendid imaginative power that pervades it will be seen through all hindrances. I consider Tennyson as promising fair to be the greatest poet of our generation, perhaps of our century.—HALLAM, ARTHUR H. 1829, *Letter to W. E. Gladstone, Sep. 14; A Memoir of Tennyson, ed. Tennyson, vol.* I, p. 46.

What do you think of Tennyson's Prize Poem? If such an exercise had been sent up at Oxford, the author would have had a better chance of being rusticated—with the view of his passing a few months at a Lunatic Asylum—than of obtaining the prize. It is certainly a wonderful production; and if it had come out with Lord Byron's name, it would have been thought as fine as anything he ever wrote.—WORDSWORTH, CHARLES, 1829, *Letter to Christopher Wordsworth, Sept. 4; Annals of my Early Life, p. 73.*

Why Mr. Tennyson should have only retained one exquisite line in the whole of his prize poem "Timbuctoo"—a poem full of nature and sustained beauty—is to us as great a mystery as why Mr. Ruskin seems anxious to bury for ever in oblivion all his more important writings, which the world, however, will not willingly let die.—HAWEIS, HUGH REGINALD, 1882, *American Humorists, p. 68.*

POEMS
1830

Looked over both the Tennysons' poems at night; exquisite fellows. I know no two books of poetry which have given me so much pleasure as their works.—ALFORD, HENRY, 1830, *Journal, October 12.*

The features of original genius are clearly and strongly marked. The author imitates nobody; we recognize the spirit of his age, but not the individual form of this or that writer. His thoughts bear no more resemblance to Byron or Scott, Shelley or Coleridge, than to Homer or Calderon, Ferdúsí or Calidasa.—HALLAM, ARTHUR HENRY, 1831, *Englishman's Magazine, August.*

If our estimate of Mr. Tennyson be correct, he too is a poet; and many years hence may he read his juvenile description of that character with the proud consciousness that it has become the description and history of his own work.—BOWRING, SIR JOHN, 1831, *Westminster, Jan.*

It was not Elliott's billowy incursion of song that foretold the turn of the tide. A little ripple of poetry, edged with silver spray, went quivering up the sand. Some few eyes noticed it, and Triton out to seaward blew his triumphant conch. Enoch Wray was stalwart and real. The Claribels, and Adelines, and Sea Fairies of Mr. Tennyson's volume of 1830 seem a faint impalpable troop of poetic creatures; yet it was they and their successors who were destined to call back the singing-tide with insupportable advance upon our shores. Man does not live by bread alone. We are all conscious that we have received from Mr. Tennyson something which is real, substantial, and correspondent to our needs.—DOWDEN, EDWARD, 1877, *The French Revolution and Literature, Studies in Literature, p. 43.*

In his earliest volume indeed there was a preponderance of manner over matter; it was characterized by a certain dainty prettiness of style, that scarcely gave promise of the high spiritual vision and rich complexity of human insight to which he has since attained, though it did manifest a delicate feeling for Nature in association with human moods, an extraordinary subtle sensibility of all senses, and a luscious pictorial power. Not Endymion had been more luxuriant. All was steeped in golden languors. There were faults in plenty, and of course the critics, faithful to the instincts of their kind, were jubilant to nose them.—NOEL, RODEN, 1886, *Essays on Poetry and Poets, p. 225.*

POEMS
1832

Were we not afraid that our style might be thought too figurative, we should say that Alfred is a promising plant; and that the day may come when, beneath sun and shower, his genius may grow up and expand into a stately tree, embowering a solemn shade within its wide circumference, while the daylight lies gorgeously on its crest, seen from afar in glory—itself a grove. But that day will never come, if he hearken not to our advice, and, as far as his own nature will permit, regulate by it the movements of his genius. . . . At present he has small power over the common feelings and thoughts of men. His feebleness is distressing at all times when he makes an appeal to their ordinary sympathies. And the reason, that he fears to look such sympathies boldly in the face,—and will be metaphysical. . . . Mr. Tennyson should speak of the sea so as to rouse the souls of sailors, rather than the soles of tailors—the enthusiasm of the deck, rather than of the board. Unfortunately, he seems never to have seen a ship, or, if he did, to have forgotten it. The vessel in which the landlubbers were drifting, when the Sea-Fairies salute them with a song, must have been an old tub of a thing, unfit even for a transport. Such a jib! In the cut of her mains you smoke the old table-cloth. To be solemn—Alfred Tennyson is as poor on the sea as Barry Cornwall—and, of course, calls him a serpent. They both write like people who, on venturing upon the world of waters in a bathing-machine, would insure their lives by a cork-jacket. Barry swims on the surface of the Great Deep like a feather; Alfred dives less after the fashion of a duck than a bell; but the one sees few lights, the other few shadows, that are not seen just as well by an oyster-dredger. But the soul of the true sea-poet doth undergo a sea-change, soon as he sees the Blue Peter; and is off in the gig,

While bending back, away they pull,
With measured strokes most beautiful—
There goes the Commodore!

—WILSON, JOHN, 1832, *Tennyson's Poems*, *Blackwood's Magazine*, vol. 31, pp. 725, 731.

I have not read through all Mr. Tennyson's poems, which have been sent to me; but I think there are some things of a good deal of beauty in what I have seen. The misfortune is, that he has begun to write verses without very well understanding what metre is. Even if you write in a known and approved metre, the odds are, if you are not a metrist yourself, that you will not write harmonious verses; but to deal in new metres without considering what metre means and requires, is preposterous. What I would, with many wishes for success, prescribe to Tennyson,—indeed without it he can never be a poet in act—is to write for the next two or three years in none but one or two well-known and strictly defined metres; such as the heroic couplet, the octave stanza, or the octosyllabic measure of the "Allegro" and "Penseroso." He would, probably, thus get imbued with a sensation, if not a sense, of metre without knowing it, just as Eton boys get to write such good Latin verses by conning Ovid and Tibullus. As it is, I can scarcely scan some of his verses.—COLERIDGE, SAMUEL TAYLOR, 1833, *Table Talk*, *April 24, ed. Ashe*, p. 214.

This is, as some of his marginal notes intimate, Mr. Tennyson's second appearance. By some strange chance we have never seen his first publication, which, if it at all resembles its younger brother, must be by this time so popular that any notice of it on our part would seem idle and presumptuous; but we gladly seize this opportunity of repairing an unintentional neglect, and of introducing to the admiration of our more sequestered readers a new prodigy of genius —another and a brighter star of that galaxy or *milky way* of poetry of which the lamented Keats was the harbinger.— LOCKHART, JOHN GIBSON (?), 1833, *Poems by Alfred Tennyson*, *Quarterly Review*, vol. 49, p. 81.

He has lyrical ease and vigour, and is looked upon by sundry critics as the chief living hope of the Muse.—CUNNINGHAM, ALLAN, 1833, *Biographical and Critical History of the Literature of the Last Fifty Years.*

The greater part of these poems of Tennyson's which you have sent me we read together. The greater part of them are very beautiful. He seems to me to possess in a higher degree than any English poet, except, perhaps, Keats, the power of writing pictures. "The Miller's Daughter," "The Lady of Shalott," and even the shorter poems, "Mariana," "Eleänore," are full of exquisite form and color; if he had but the mechanical knowledge of the art, I am convinced he would have been a great painter. There are but one or two things in the volume which I don't like. "The little room with the two little white sofas," I hate, though I can fancy perfectly well both the room and his feeling about it; but that sort of thing does not make good poetry, and lends itself temptingly to the making of good burlesque.—KEMBLE,

FRANCES ANN, 1833, *Letter, Aug. 17; Records of a Girlhood*, p. 581.

These early editions are not in the Cambridge or Boston Libraries, and I have not been able to find them anywhere on this side of the Atlantic. An inquiry for them inserted in the *Literary World* proved as unavailing as the letters I had sent to friends in various parts of the country and in Canada. I did get track of the 1832 volume in several quarters; but all the "trails," when followed up, led to a single copy belonging to Ralph Waldo Emerson, which has recently disappeared from his library and cannot be traced. He lent it, fifty years ago, to many of his friends— among them, Mr. John S. Dwight, who reviewed it in the *Christian Examiner* in 1833, and Mrs. Hawthorne (then Miss Peabody), who made a drawing to illustrate "The Lady of Shalott."—ROLFE, WILLIAM J., 1885, *Select Poems of Alfred Lord Tennyson, Preface.*

LOTOS EATERS

The "Lotos eaters"—a kind of classical opium-eaters—are Ulysses and his crew. They land on the "charmed island," and eat of the "charmed root," and then they sing. . . . Our readers will, we think, agree that this is admirably characteristic, and that the singers of this song must have made pretty free with the intoxicating fruit. How they got home you must read in Homer:—Mr. Tennyson—himself, we presume, a dreamy lotus-eater, a delicious lotus-eater—leaves them in full song.— LOCKHART, J. G. (?), 1833, *Poems by Alfred Tennyson, Quarterly Review*, vol. 49, p. 92.

Full of Tennyson's excellences, no less than of early mannerisms since foregone,— while Gothic in some respects, is charged from beginning to end with the effects and very language of the Greek pastoral poets. As in "Œnone," there is no consecutive imitation of any one idyl; but the work is curiously filled out with passages borrowed here and there, as the growth of the poem recalled them at random to the author's mind. — STEDMAN, EDMUND CLARENCE, 1875-87, *Victorian Poets*, p. 214.

Contains passages not surpassed by the finest descriptions in the "Castle of Indolence." It is rich in striking and appropriate imagery, and is sung to a rhythm which is music itself.—CHAMBERS, ROBERT, 1876, *Cyclopædia of English Literature*, ed. Carruthers.

How perfectly in Tennyson's "Lotos Eaters" is the dreamy haze of the enchanted land he depicts reflected in the verse! How exquisitely do the refinement, the sentiment, the lazy skepticism of the age, find expression in his numbers! — MATHEWS, WILLIAM, 1881, *Literary Style*, p. 43.

The exquisite "Lotos-Eaters," with its wonderful melody, one of the most poetic poems Tennyson ever wrote, and one which, for suggestive beauty of thought as well as for rhythm, ranks among the masterpieces of the English language.—WALKER, HUGH, 1897, *The Age of Tennyson*, p. 40.

THE PALACE OF ART

A nobler allegory could not be conceived, or one more fitted to the age, and to the highest intellects of all ages. But it fails just where it ought to have been strongest; and what we have is a series of magnificent pictures in magnificent verse, followed, indeed, by a statement of the moral in very noble stanzas, but by no adequate dramatic presentation of the mode in which the great law of humanity works out its processes in the soul.—BRIMLEY, GEORGE, 1855-58, *Tennyson's Poems, Essays*, ed. Clark, p. 29.

Image comes on image, picture succeeds picture, each perfect, rich in color, clear in outline. When you first read the poem, every stanza startles you with a new and brilliant surprise. There is not a line which the most fastidious could wish away.— SHAIRP, JOHN CAMPBELL, 1881, *Aspects of Poetry*, p. 23.

The lesson conveyed in this poem is one of profound importance; and it may be taken as Tennyson's declaration of faith on the subject of art. The soul wholly intent on the artistic interpretation of life is made to realize that life is other than beauty and its enjoyment.—COOKE, GEORGE WILLIS, 1886, *Poets and Problems*, p. 146.

The "Palace of Art," first published in 1833, portrays in richly ornate allegory the mental and moral disasters that are apt to overtake the dilettante who isolates himself from his fellows in the pursuit of beauty. It seems almost a prophecy of what later befell Dante Gabriel Rossetti and a poetical diagnosis of his morbidness and maladies. It may justly be taken as expressing once for all Tennyson's unswerving conviction that an artist, in order both to preserve his normality and to give his art its widest scope and most vital power, must keep in close sympathy with the common life of his time.—GATES, LEWIS E., 1900, *Studies and Appreciations*, p. 60.

THE LOVER'S TALE
1833

Shortly after the publication of his second volume, Alfred Tennyson printed a poem called "The Lover's Tale:" this, however, he suppressed, contenting himself with giving a few copies away. It is decidedly unworthy his reputation.—POWELL, THOMAS, 1849, *The Living Authors of England*, p. 41.

It was written apparently in 1828, though not printed till five years later; but it doubtless received many after-touches and corrections during the interval. It must have been well known to Arthur Hallam, the period of whose friendship with Tennyson embraced precisely the years between the composition and the printing of it. . . . With all the blemishes arising from immaturity, "The Lover's Tale" is a work of indubitable genius and promise. In its wealth and exuberance of imagery, in the intensity of the speaker's emotion, as well as in those defects of which the author seems at a very early age to have become sensible, it reminds us forcibly of Robert Browning's first poem, "Pauline, a Fragment of a Confession," a blank-verse poem of about similar length, written at about the same age, and published, by a curious coincidence, in the same year.—SHEPHERD, RICHARD HERNE, 1879, *Tennysoniana*, Second Ed., pp. 48, 51.

Had it not been for this poem, the influence of Shelley over Tennyson would hardly have been traceable. It was soon to fade before the much more powerful influence of Keats, the one poet antecedent to Tennyson to whom he has at any time stood distinctly in the relation of a disciple. . . . In the poem, confused and overheated as its style may sometimes be, we have not only indubitable promise but valuable performance. It is still possible to turn with enthusiasm to this first serious production of the master and to hear in it, through all imitations, the melody of a new voice. It has been said to resemble Robert Browning's first poem, "Pauline, a Fragment of a Confession," which is in blank verse, of about similar length, written at about the same age, and published, by a curious coincidence, in the same year.—NICOLL, W. R.

(WALTER E. WACE), 1881, *Alfred Tennyson, his Life and Works*, p. 14.

As a storehouse of fine imagery, metaphor, and deftly moulded phrase, of blank verse also whose sonorous rhythm must surely be a fabric of adult architecture, the piece can hardly be surpassed; but the tale as tale lingers and lapses, over-weighed with the too gorgeous trappings under which it so laboriously moves.—NOEL, RODEN, 1886, *Essays on Poetry and Poets*, p. 226.

POEMS
1842

So Alfred is come out. I agree with you about the skipping-rope, &c. But the bald men of the Embassy would tell you otherwise. I should not wonder if the whole theory of the Embassy, perhaps the discovery of America itself, was involved in that very Poem. Lord Bacon's honesty may, I am sure, be found there. Alfred, whatever he may think, cannot trifle— many are the disputes we have had about his powers of badinage, compliment, waltzing, &c. His smile is rather a grim one. I am glad the book is come out, though I grieve for the insertion of these little things, on which reviewers and dull readers will fix; so that the right appreciation of the book will be retarded a dozen years.—FITZGERALD, EDWARD, 1842, *To W. F. Pollock*, May 22; *Letters and Literary Remains*, ed. Wright, vol. I, p. 95.

It would be far from our design to charge this great writer with want of feeling. A poet without feeling! Fire without warmth and a heart without pulsation! But it is clear that his feelings are always strictly watched by his meditative conscience too strictly, not for wisdom, but for rapture. . . . Even in these solemn elevations of soul he does not forget to impose a scheme of toils on human life. Among streams and rocks he begins with discourse of virtue; and when he has risen on the ladder of his vision to the stars, we still hear him singing from the solar way, that it is by temperance, soberness, and chastity of soul he has so climbed, and that the praise of this heroic discipline is his last message to mankind. . . . He has strangely wedded his philosophic lore to the sweetness of poetry. But the poetry would have streamed out in a freer gush, and flushed the heart with ampler joy, had the moral been less *obtruded* as its constant aim.—STERLING, JOHN, 1842,

Poems by Alfred Tennyson, Quarterly Review, vol. 70, pp. 415, 416.

The contents of these volumes are nearly equally divided between poems hitherto unpublished and a revised edition of the main part of those which Mr. Tennyson has already given to the public. The latter are considerably shortened, and many of them much altered, too much so, perhaps, for those who have already formed an affectionate familiarity with them, however much the general effect of the whole work may be improved by some concession to temporary criticism; at any rate Mr. Tennyson will not repent having given up any small peculiarities which stood in the way of his general acceptance as a great English poet.—MILNES, RICHARD MONCKTON (LORD HOUGHTON), 1842, *Tennyson's Poems, Westminster Review, vol. 38, p. 371.*

I have just been reading the new poems of Tennyson. Much has he thought, much suffered, since the first ecstasy of so fine an organization clothed all the world in rosy light. He has not suffered himself to become a mere intellectual voluptuary, nor the songster of fancy and passion, but has earnestly revolved the problems of life, and his conclusions are calmly noble. In these later verses is a still, deep sweetness; how different from the intoxicating, sensuous melody of his earlier cadence! I have loved him much this time, and take him to heart as a brother. One of his themes has long been my favorite — the last expedition of Ulysses—and his, like mine, is the Ulysses of the Odyssey, with his deep romance of wisdom, and not the worldling of the Iliad. How finely marked his slight description of himself and of Telemachus! In "Dora," "Locksley Hall," "The Two Voices," "Morte D' Arthur," I find my own life, much of it, written truly out.—OSSOLI, MARGARET FULLER, 1842, *Journal, Aug.; Memoirs, vol.* II, *p. 66.*

Tennyson's poems have been reprinted in Boston, and the reprint is a precise copy of the English edition in size, type, and paper, so that it is difficult to distinguish the two editions. It is reprinted for the benefit of the author, to whom the publisher hopes to remit some honorarium. Emerson and his followers are ardent admirers of Tennyson, and it is their enthusiastic unhesitating praise that induced a bookseller to undertake the reprint. There are some things in the second volume which I admire very much. "Locksley Hall" has some magnificent verses, and others hardly intelligible. "Godiva" is unequalled as a narrative in verse, and the little stories of Lady Clare and the Lord of Burleigh are told in beautiful measure. I am struck with the melody of his verse, its silver ring, and its high poetic fancy; but does it not want elevated thought and manliness? And yet, in its way, what can be more exquisite than Œnone making Mount Ida echo with her complaints? Was her story ever told in a sweeter strain in any language?—SUMNER, CHARLES, 1842, *Letter to Richard Monckton Milnes, Aug. 1; Life of Lord Houghton, ed. Reid, vol.* I, *p. 279.*

The decade during which Mr. Tennyson has remained silent has wrought a great improvement. The handling in his later pieces is much lighter and freer; the interest deeper and purer;—there is more humanity with less imagery and drapery; a closer adherence to truth; a greater reliance for effect upon the simplicity of nature. Moral and spiritual traits of character are more dwelt upon, in place of external scenery and circumstance. He addresses himself more to the heart, and less to the ear and eye.—SPEDDING, JAMES, 1843, *Tennyson's Poems, Edinburgh Review, vol. 77, p. 377.*

At the present day were this volume to be lost, we possibly should be deprived of a larger specific variety of Tennyson's most admired poems than is contained in any other of his successive ventures. It is an assortment of representative poems. To an art more restrained and natural we here find wedded a living soul. The poet has convictions: he is not a pupil, but a master, and reaches intellectual greatness.—STEDMAN, EDMUND CLARENCE, 1875-87, *Victorian Poets, p. 160.*

ULYSSES

Of the "Ulysses" we would say that the mild dignity and placid resolve—the steady wisdom after the storms of life, and with the prospect of future storms—the melancholy fortitude, yet kingly resignation to his destiny which gives him a restless passion for wandering—the unaffected and unostentatious modesty and self-conscious power—the long softened shadows of memory cast from the remote vistas of practical knowledge and experience, with a suffusing tone of ideality breathing over the whole, and giving a saddened charm even to the suggestion of a watery grave—all this, and much more, independent of the beautiful picturesqueness of the scenery, render the poem of "Ulysses" one of the most exquisite (as it has hitherto been one of the least noticed) poems in the language.—HORNE, RICHARD HENGIST, 1844, *A New Spirit of the Age*, p. 207.

For virile grandeur and astonishingly compact expression, there is no blank-verse poem, equally restricted as to length, that approaches the "Ulysses:" conception, imagery, and thought are royally imaginative, and the assured hand is Tennyson's throughout. —STEDMAN, EDMUND CLARENCE, 1875–87, *Victorian Poets*, p. 162.

One of the healthiest as well as most masterly of all Tennyson's poems.—BAYNE, PETER, 1879, *Lessons from my Masters*, p. 296.

LOCKSLEY HALL

Is not this a noble poem, a rich fruit of the imagination and the understanding, full of high and plain thoughts, of fancies crystallising into solid truth, and of truth breaking up into sparkling fancies? —MILNES, RICHARD MONCKTON (LORD HOUGHTON), 1842, *Tennyson's Poems, Westminster Review*, vol. 38, p. 377.

In saying that "Locksley Hall" has deservedly had so great an influence over the minds of the young, we shall, we are afraid, have offended some who are accustomed to consider that poem as Werterian and unhealthy. But, in reality, the spirit of the poem is simply anti-Werterian. It is man rising out of sickness into health,—not conquered by Werterism, but conquering his selfish sorrow, and the moral and intellectual paralysis which it produces, by faith and hope,—faith in the progress of science and civilization, hope in the final triumph of good.—KINGSLEY, CHARLES, 1850, *Tennyson, Miscellanies*, vol. I, p. 224.

Later still, in the 11th century, appeared Toghrai, who in his "Lameyyah," the title of his principal piece, entered the lists against Shanfarah, the most brilliant of pre-Islamitic poets, and, it seems, furnished our own Tennyson with the model of his "Locksley Hall."—PALGRAVE, WILLIAM GIFFORD, 1875, *Encyclopædia Britannica*, vol. II, p. 231.

To a large portion of the English-speaking race, perhaps to the larger portion of it, Tennyson is pre-eminently the poet of "Locksley Hall." There are others of his productions which commend themselves with far more effectiveness to minds of a certain order. There are others of them which will be conceded to display more varied if not greater power. But there is no other that has appealed to so wide a circle of sympathies, and, as a result, there is no other that has been so generally read and admired and quoted. Its popularity has never been fitful. The rank which it took at the very outset it has held since with not the slightest abatement.—LOUNSBURY, THOMAS R., 1889, *The Two Locksley Halls, Scribner's Magazine*, vol. 6, p. 250.

To praise the poem in detail would be impossible here, even if fifty years of praise had not made praise something like presumption. It will be enough to say that "Locksley Hall" is one of Tennyson's greatest successes; one of the most original, most fascinating, most popular short poems of our time.—LUCE, MORTON, 1895, *A Handbook to the Works of Alfred Lord Tennyson*, p. 164.

THE TWO VOICES

No argument was ever conducted in verse with more admirable power and clearness than that of the "Two Voices." The very poetry of it magnifies itself into a share of the demonstration: take away the poetry and the music, and you essentially diminish the logic.—HORNE, RICHARD HENGIST, 1844, *A New Spirit of the Age*, p. 208.

Perhaps, however, the crown of all Tennyson's verse is "The Two Voices." . . . In this poem there is no person who has passed through the searching, withering ordeal of religious doubts and fears as to the spiritual permanence of our existence—and who has not?—but will find in these simple stanzas the map and history of their own experience. The clearness, the graphic power, and logical force and acumen which distinguish this poem are of the highest order. There is nothing in the poems of Wordsworth which can surpass, if it can equal it.—HOWITT, WILLIAM, 1847, *Homes and Haunts of the most Eminent British Poets*, vol. II, p. 527.

Up at 6 A. M. and began the day by reading Tennyson. I am acquainted with no spirit so strong, pure, and beautiful. Every line sparkles with empyreal fire, so that it is difficult to make a selection. I will, however, notice "The Two Voices," simply because Tom [Hirst] has not placed upon it his prize mark. In this poem the tempter to despair is furnished with his best weapons, and foiled though armed *cap-a-pie*.—TYNDALL, JOHN, 1850, *Journal*, Oct. 20; *A Memoir of Tennyson*, ed. *Tennyson, vol.* II, p. 470.

It would be difficult to find another poem in which a conception so purely intellectual is clothed with such richness of imagination and imagery. — TANISH, EDWARD CAMPBELL, 1870, *A Study of the Works of Alfred Tennyson*, p. 129.

Tennyson, in "The Two Voices," has solved the problem by giving us in a philosophical poem sublime poetry. While sounding the deeps of personality, and showing the conflict of soul with direst doubt and tormenting fear, his music never falters, but flows on until it falls into peaceful triumph.—OATES, JAMES, 1895–98, *The Teaching of Tennyson*, p. 29.

THE PRINCESS
1847

I am considered a great heretic for abusing it; it seems to me a wretched waste of power at a time of life when a man ought to be doing his best; and I almost feel hopeless about Alfred now.—FITZGERALD, EDWARD, 1848, *To Frederic Tennyson, May 4; Letters and Literary Remains*, ed. *Wright*, vol. I, p. 188.

Fields came out in the afternoon, and brought me an English copy of Tennyson's new poem, "The Princess." F. read it in the evening. Strange enough! a university of women! A gentle satire, in the easiest and most flowing blank verse, with two delicious unrhymed songs, and many exquisite passages. I went to bed after it, with delightful music ringing in my ears; yet half disappointed in the poem, though not knowing why. There is a discordant note somewhere.—LONGFELLOW, HENRY WADSWORTH, 1848, *Journal*, Feb. 7; *Life of Henry Wadsworth Longfellow*, ed. *Longfellow, vol.* II, p. 109.

His "Princess," a gorgeous piece of writing, but to me new melancholy proof of the futility of what they call "Art." Alas! Alfred too, I fear, will prove one of the *sacrificed*, and in very deed it is pity.—CARLYLE, THOMAS, 1848, *Journal, Feb. 9; Thomas Carlyle, a History of his Life in London*, ed. *Froude, vol.* I, p. 360.

I had the misfortune to be deeply intoxicated yesterday—with Tennyson's new poem, "The Princess," which I shall bring to thee when I return home. I dare not keep it with me. For the future, for a long time at least, I dare not read Tennyson. His poetry would be the death of mine, and, indeed, a *pervadence* of his spirit would ruin me for the great purposes of life. His intense perception of beauty haunts me for days, and I cannot drive it from me.—TAYLOR, BAYARD, 1848, *To Mary Agnew, Feb. 13; Life and Letters* ed. *Taylor and Scudder*, vol. I, p. 119.

So vividly and clearly does the poet delineate the creatures of his fancy that we cannot help viewing them as actual existences. We find ourselves sympathizing with the Prince, and wishing him success in his arduous suit. We feel the rush of breathless expectation in the hot *mêlée* of the tourney. We wait anxiously the turn of fate beside the sick-bed of the wounded lover. We give him our heartiest congratulations on his eventual recovery and success. It is only when we set ourselves to criticising, that we are struck with the improbability of that which moved us, and become ashamed of our former feelings.— HADLEY, JAMES, 1849–73, *Tennyson's Princess, Essays Philological and Critical*, p. 316.

A medley of success, failure, and half-success—not even an attempt towards a whole.—GILFILLAN, GEORGE, 1849, *Second Gallery of Literary Portraits*, p. 206, note.

The poem being, as the title imports, a medley of jest and earnest, allows a metrical license, of which we are often tempted to wish that its author had not availed himself; yet the most unmetrical and apparently careless passages flow with a grace, a lightness, a colloquial ease and frolic which perhaps only heighten the effect of the serious parts, and serve as a foil to set off the unrivaled finish and melody of these latter. —KINGSLEY, CHARLES, 1850, *Tennyson, Miscellanies, vol.* I, p. 227.

In his "Princess," which he calls a "medley," the former half of which is sportive, and the plot almost too fantastic and impossible for criticism, while the latter portion seems too serious for a story so slight and flimsy, he has with exquisite taste disposed of the question which has its burlesque and comic as well as its tragic side, of woman's present place and future destinies. And if any one wishes to see this subject treated with a masterly and delicate hand, in protest alike against the theories that would make her as the man, which she could only be by becoming masculine, not manly, and those which would have her to remain the toy, or the slave, or the slight thing of sentimental and frivolous accomplishment which education has hitherto aimed at making her, I would recommend him to study the few last pages of "The Princess," where the poet brings the question back, as a poet should, to nature; develops the ideal out of the actual woman, and reads out of what she is, on the one hand, what her Creator intended her to be, and, on the other, what she never can nor ought to be.—ROBERTSON, FREDERICK WILLIAM, 1852, *The Influence of Poetry on the Working Classes, Lectures and Addresses,* p. 154.

We need hardly say that there are many graceful flights of fancy, many pleasing bits of description, many happy epithets, many fine thoughts, scattered over "The Princess;" but the prosaic so predominates over the poetic element, that it fairly passes our comprehension how it ever passed muster as a whole. Byron certainly contrived to mix up an extraordinary variety of heterogenous subjects in "Don Juan;" but "Don Juan" was composed in a mocking, laughing spirit: it runs over with wit and humor; and we should feel much obliged to any one who would point out either wit or humor in "The Princess."—HAYWARD, ABRAHAM, 1871, *Byron and Tennyson, Sketches of Eminent Statesmen and Writers,* p. 348.

Other works of our poet's are greater, but none is so fascinating as this romantic tale: English throughout, yet combining the England of Cœur de Lion with that of Victoria in one bewitching picture. . . . "The Princess" has a distinct purpose,—the illustration of woman's struggles, aspirations, and proper sphere; and the conclusion is one wherewith the instincts of cultured people are so thoroughly in accord, that some are used to answer, when asked to present their view of the "woman question," you will find it at the close of "The Princess."—STEDMAN, EDMUND CLARENCE, 1875-87, *Victorian Poets,* pp. 165, 166.

Perhaps ["Come down O Maid"] the most beautiful and splendid of all his shorter poems.—EDWARDS, AMELIA B., 1878, *A Poetry-Book, Modern Poets,* p. 321.

I may tell you that the songs were not an after-thought. Before the first edition came out I deliberated with myself whether I should put songs in between the separate divisions of the poem—again, I thought, the poem will explain itself, but the public did not see that the child, as you say, was the heroine of the piece, and at last I conquered my laziness and inserted them. . . . Your explanatory notes are very much to the purpose, and I do not object to your finding parallelisms. They must always recur. A man (a Chinese scholar) some time ago wrote to me saying that in an unknown, untranslated Chinese poem there were two whole lines of mine, almost word for word. Why not? are not human eyes all over the world looking at the same objects, and must there not consequently be coincidences of thought and impressions and expressions? It is scarcely possible for anyone to say or write anything in this late time of the world to which, in the rest of the literature of the world, a parallel could not somewhere be found. But when you say that this passage or that was suggested by Wordsworth or Shelley or another, I demur, and more, I wholly disagree.—TENNYSON, ALFRED, 1882, *Letter to S. E. Dawson, Nov. 21; A Study of "The Princess," Second Ed.,* pp. 8, 9.

"The Princess," with all her lovely court and glowing harmonies, was born in London, among the fogs and smuts of Lincoln's Inn, although, like all works of true art, this poem had grown by degrees in other times and places. The poet came and went, free, unshackled, meditating, inditing. One of my family remembers hearing Tennyson say that "Tears, idle Tears," was suggested by Tintern Abbey: who shall say by what mysterious wonder of beauty and regret, by what sense of the "transient with the abiding?" —RITCHIE, ANNE THACKERAY, 1883, *Alfred Tennyson, Harper's Magazine, vol.* 68, *p.* 31.

Tennyson's poem of "The Princess" has been and continues to be singularly underrated. Seldom, in the universal chorus of admiration, and even adulation, which for years his work has excited, do we meet with appreciation of this his longest continuous poem. A poem, moreover, published at the age when a writer usually produces his best work—equally removed from the exuberance of youth and the chill of age, and one which has been altered and retouched during five successive editions, until the utmost effort has been expended, and, in literary form at least, it stands out unsurpassed in perfect finish by anything in modern literature. In this respect, the "Princess" is to Tennyson's other works what the "Elegy" is to Gray's. In the adverse criticism it had called forth, we are reminded of Dr. Johnson's attack upon Milton's "Lycidas;" indeed, both the "Princess" and "Lycidas" have continuously, and with equal justice or injustice, been reproached for the same fault, that of incongruity of plan. . . . The poem of "The Princess," as a work of art, is the most complete and satisfying of all Tennyson's works. It possesses a play of fancy, of humor, of pathos, and of passion which give it variety; while the feeling of unity is unbroken throughout. It is full of passages of the rarest beauty and most exquisite workmanship. The songs it contains are unsurpassed in English literature. The diction is drawn from the treasure-house of old English poetry—from Chaucer, from Shakespeare and the poets of the Elizabethan age. The versification is remarkable for its variety; while the rhythm, in stateliness and expression, is modelled upon Milton. There are passages, which, in power over language to match sound with sense, are not excelled by anything in "Paradise Lost" for strength, or in Milton's minor poems for sweetness.—DAWSON, S. E., 1884, *A Study of the Princess, Second Ed., pp.* 1, 54.

Is like a piece of Renascence poetry born out of due time. It has the tone of the Elizabethans without their extravagances; though, we must add, without the cause of that extravagance— their Titanic force. It is bright, glowing, and most fascinating.— GALTON, ARTHUR, 1885, *Lord Tennyson, Urbana Scripta, p.* 55.

Through all emendations and additions, chiefly interesting to the bibliographer, the spirit and intention of the poem remain unchanged. While it served, on the one hand, as a piece to be staged with all the refinement of the poet's taste, backed by richly-coloured and harmonious scenery, it carried at its heart the poet's invariable creed. WAUGH, ARTHUR, 1892–96, *Alfred Lord Tennyson, a Study of his Life and Work.*

A more glorious-seeming but utterly impossible ideal would have won for him unstinted praise, but what was Tennyson if not a plain dealer? He abhorred woman's wrongs without subscribing fully to the modern programme of woman's rights. He had the candour to combat some of her claims and the courage to deny some of her pretensions. Less as a matter of principle than as a matter of propriety and expediency he showed where the impulsive Ida would fail. . . . When revised and re-written, and with the delicious lyrics interspersed, "The Princess" exhibited so much of the poet's power that, despite the pervading sense of disappointment, a future of great achievement was confidently predicted for its author.—WALTERS, J. CUMING, 1893, *Tennyson, Philosopher, Idealist, pp.* 66, 73.

"In Memoriam" is the most complete, most rounded to a polished sphere, of the larger poems of Tennyson; the "Idylls of the King" is the most ambitious; "Maud" is the loveliest, most rememberable; and "The Princess" is the most delightful. Holiday-hearted, amazingly varied, charming our leisured ease from page to page, it is a poem to read on a sunny day in one of those rare places in the world where "there is no clock in the forest," where the weight and worry of the past, the present, or the future, do not make us conscious of their care. There is no sorrow or sense of the sorrow of the world in it. The man who wrote it had reached maturity, but there is none of the heaviness of maturity in its light movement. It is really gay, as young as the Prince himself who is its hero; and the dreams and desires of youth flit and linger in it as summer bees around the honied flowers.—BROOKE, STOPFORD A., 1894, *Tennyson, his Art and Relation to Modern Life, p.* 145.

"The Princess" was both a history and a prophecy. While it lacked nothing of the lyric and picturesque qualities of the earlier poems, it contained the germs of that political and ethical philosphy which we now consider as the distinctive contribution of Tennyson to the thought of the century.— GEORGE, ANDREW J., 1896, *ed. The Princess, Preface, p.* viii.

To a few modern admirers, it is true, this work appeals as the poet's most satisfying product; but the most of us are content to see in it what Dr. Van Dyke has seen, "one of the minor poems of a major poet." It pleases us better than it pleased its earlier audience, not because we find in it so much more, but because we expect so much less, of the highest poetic value. If, as those first critics did, we attempt to square the poem with classic standards of narrative and dramatic excellence, or if, like certain later enthusiasts, we claim a place for it as a didactic masterpiece, we must find ourselves committed to the consideration of some difficult problems.—BOYNTON, HENRY W., 1896, ed., *The Princess, Introduction*, p. 13.

"The Princess" is undoubtedly Tennyson's greatest effort, if not exactly in comedy, in a vein verging towards the comic—a side of which he was not so well equipped for offence or defence as on the other. But it is a masterpiece. Exquisite as its author's verse always is, it was never more exquisite than here, whether in blank verse or in the (superadded) lyrics, while none of his deliberately arranged plays contains characters half so good as those of "The Princess" herself, of "Lady Blanche" and "Lady Psyche," of "Cyril," of the two "Kings," and even of one or two others. And that unequalled dream-faculty of his, which has been more than once glanced at, enabled him to carry off whatever was fantastical in the conception with almost unparalleled felicity.—SAINTSBURY, GEORGE, 1896, *A History of Nineteenth Century Literature*, p. 261.

The different motives in the poem are not harmonized into any unity of total effect. The pretty extravaganza which forms its central story makes no clear impression upon us. It is too strange to admit our belief; it is not strange enough to enthrall our wonder. It ought to be either more romantic or less so. The songs which fill the pauses of the story and many of the longer passages, if taken separately, are exquisitely beautiful or pathetic; but their effect as they stand in the poem is much diminished by the setting of purely fanciful or half-playful circumstance in which they are placed and by the obvious unreality of all the action. In a word, the whole is, as Tennyson called it, a Medley. There is a great deal of most charming poetry in "The Princess;" but "The Princess" is not a great poem.—WINCHESTER, CALEB THOMAS, 1899, *Some Principles of Literary Criticism*, p. 205.

IN MEMORIAM
1850

I know not how to express what I have felt. My first sentiment was surprise, for, though I now find that you had mentioned the intention to my daughter, Julia, she had never told me of the poems. I do not speak as another would to praise and admire; few of them indeed I have as yet been capable of reading, the grief they express is too much akin to that they revive. It is better than any monument which could be raised to the memory of my beloved son, it is a more lively and enduring testimony to his great virtues and talents that the world should know the friendship which existed between you, that posterity should associate his name with that of Alfred Tennyson.—HALLAM, HENRY, 1850, *Letter to Alfred Tennyson, A Memoir of Tennyson*, ed. Tennyson, vol. I, p. 327.

His poem I never did greatly affect: nor can I learn to do so: it is full of finest things, but it is monotonous, and has that air of being evolved by a Poetical Machine of the highest order. So it seems to be with him now, at least to me, the Impetus, the Lyrical œstrus, is gone.—FITZGERALD, EDWARD, 1850, *To Frederic Tennyson, Dec. 31; Letters, and Literary Remains*, ed. Wright, vol. I, p. 208.

Have you read Tennyson's "In Memoriam?" It is a wonderful little volume. Few —very few—words of such power have come out of the depths of this country's poetic heart. They might do much, one would think, to lay the dust in its highways and silence its market towns. But it will not be felt for a while, I suppose; and just now people are talking of the division of last Friday.—TAYLOR, SIR HENRY, 1850, *Letter to Miss Fenwick, July* 1; *Autobiography*, vol. II, p. 53.

In my opinion it is the first poem which this generation has yet produced. God bless him for the worthy consecration of a true friendship!—TAYLOR, BAYARD, 1850, *To George H. Boker, Dec.* 17; *Life and Letters*, ed. Taylor and Scudder, vol. I, p. 197.

I am thoroughly tired of Oxford, and hope I shall feel jollier again when we sit together on your tower and smoke a weed; but no "In Memoriam," rather something about airy, fairy Lilians and other sweet creatures without a soul. However, I do not mean to say that Tennyson's last poems are not very beautiful, yet I do not like those open graves of sorrow and despair, and wish our poets would imitate the good Christian fashion of covering them with flowers, or a stone with a short inscription on it.—MÜLLER, FRIEDRICH MAX, 1850, *To F. Palgrave, June* 18; *Life and Letters*, ed. his Wife, vol. I, p. 116.

I have just received your kind present of "In Memorian;" many thanks. What treasure it will be, if I can but think of it and feel about it as you do, and as Mr. T— does! You said, "The finest strain since Shakespeare;" and afterwards that you and Mr. T—agreed that it set the author above all modern poets, save only W. W. and J. T. C. My impression of the pieces you recited was that they expressed great *intensity* of feeling—but *all* that is in *such* poetry can not be perceived at first, especially from recitation. . . . But the poems, as a whole, are distinguished by a greater proportion of thought to sensuous imagery than his old ones; they recede from Keatsland into Petrarchdom, and now and then approach the confines of the Dantesean new hemisphere.—COLERIDGE, SARA, 1850, *Letter to Aubrey De Vere, Memoirs, p. 453, 455.*

I have read Tennyson's "In Memoriam," or rather part of it; I closed the book when I had got about halfway. It is beautiful; it is mournful; it is monotonous. Many of the feelings expressed bear, in their utterance, the stamp of truth; yet, if Arthur Hallam had been somewhat nearer Alfred Tennyson—his brother instead of his friend—I should have distrusted this rhymed, and measured, and printed monument of grief. What change the lapse of years may work I do not know; but it seems to me that bitter sorrow, while recent, does not flow out in verse.—BRONTË, CHARLOTTE, 1850, *Letter to Elizabeth Cleghorn Gaskell, May 27; Life of Charlotte Brontë by Mrs. Gaskell.*

There is no excessive or misplaced affection here; it is all founded in fact: while everywhere and throughout it all, affection —a love that is wonderful—meets us first and leaves us last, giving form and substance and grace, and the breath of life and love, to everything that the poet's thick-coming fancies so exquisitely frame. We can recall few poems approaching to it in this quality of sustained affection. The only English poems we can think of as of the same order, are Cowper's lines on seeing his mother's portrait:—

"O that these lips had language!"

Burns to "Mary in Heaven;" and two pieces of Vaughan—one beginning

"O thou know'st for whom I mourn;"

and the other—

"They are all gone into the world of light."

—BROWN, JOHN, 1851, *Arthur H. Hallam, Horæ Subsecivæ, vol.* I, *p.* 426.

In the series of monodies or meditations which compose it, and which follow in long series without weariness or sameness, the poet never moves away a step from the grave of his friend, but, while still circling round it, has always a new point of view. Strength of love, depth of grief, aching sense of loss, have driven him forth as it were on a quest of consolation, and he asks it of nature, thought, religion, in a hundred forms which a rich and varied imagination continually suggests, but all of them connected by one central point, the recollection of the dead.— GLADSTONE, WILLIAM EWART, 1859, *Tennyson, Gleanings of Past Years, vol.* II, *p.* 137.

He has written *the* poem of the hoping doubters, *the* poem of our age, the grand minor-organ-fugue of "In Memoriam." It is the cry of the bereaved Psyche into the dark infinite after the vanished Love. His friend is nowhere in his sight, and God is silent. Death, God's final compulsion to prayer, in its dread, its gloom, its utter stillness, its apparent nothingness, urges the cry. Moanings over the dead are mingled with profoundest questionings of philosophy, the signs of nature, and the story of Jesus, while now and then the star of the morning, bright Phosphor, flashes a few rays through the shifting cloudy dark. And if the sun has not arisen on the close of the book, yet the Aurora of the coming dawn gives light enough to make the onward journey possible and hopeful: who dares say that he walks in the full light? that the counsels of God are to him not a matter of faith, but of vision?—MACDONALD, GEORGE, 1868, *England's Antiphon, p.* 329.

Is cold, monotonous, and often too prettily arranged. He goes into mourning; but, like a correct gentleman, with bran new gloves, wipes away his tears with a cambric handkerchief, and displays throughout the religious service, which ends the ceremony, all the compunction of a respectful and well-trained layman.—TAINE, H. A., 1871, *History of English Literature, tr. Van Laun, vol.* II, *bk.* v, *ch.* vi, *par.* iv, *p.* 526.

His [M. Taine] impeachment of Lord Tennyson's great monumental poem as the cold and correct work of a "perfectly gentleman-like" mourner, who never can forget to behave himself respectably and carry his grief like a gentleman conscious of spectators, may be classed for perfection of infelicity with Jeffrey's selection of the finest lines in Wordsworth's finest ode for especially contemptuous assault on the simple charge of sheer nonsense.—SWINBURNE,

ALGERNON CHARLES, 1881, *Tennyson and Musset, Fortnightly Review,* vol. 35, p. 145; *Miscellanies,* p. 245.

The purport of some of the passages is so obscure, one might suspect that even the author himself could not exactly determine what he meant when he wrote them. He might possibly require the associations to recur which then affected him; just as Napoleon, when asked whether he would repeat a certain cavalry charge, if he had to fight the battle over again, replied, that he must be placed in the same circumstances to decide.—GATTY, ALFRED, 1881, *A Key to Tennyson's "In Memoriam," Introduction,* p. v.

The greatness of "In Memoriam" is the greatness of its delineation of faith and aspiration struggling under the chill shadow of profound doubt. Without its deep gloom, the gleams of light would lose all their special beauty, and any poem that could be less happily described as the reflection of confident optimism, I cannot even imagine. That a certain steady gain in the force of the brighter visions of the human heart, is perceptible towards the close of "In Memoriam," no one will deny, nor that the conclusion and the prelude may be regarded as the expression of triumphant faith; but even they are the expressions, not of faith unclouded but of faith that has attained a difficult triumph over grave misgivings, faith that no longer perhaps "faintly," but certainly not in any dogmatic or positive attitude of mind "trusts the larger hope."—HUTTON, RICHARD HOLT, 1881, *Tennyson's Poem on "Despair," Criticisms on Contemporary Thought and Thinkers,* vol. II, p. 199.

Has embalmed the memory of his friend in tears more precious than those which were shed by Moschus over the tomb of Bion. BATES, WILLIAM, 1883, *The Maclise Portrait Gallery,* p. 434.

A study of Tennyson's "In Memoriam," in order adequately to fulfil its object, must be as truly a study of the age as of the poem. For the poem stands inseparably related to what is deepest and most vital in the thought of its time; of an age whose devout minds are confessedly eager and earnest in the quest of eternal truth it is preëminently the poetical exponent. This is evident in the fact that ever since its first publication in 1850 it has been the treasure-house from which all reverent thinkers have drawn copiously not only for felicitous expression of truths not easily crystallized in words, but, what is more significant, often for the very spirit and mould of their deepest thoughts. —GENUNG, JOHN F., 1883, *Tennyson's In Memoriam, its Purpose and its Structure,* p. 1.

The "In Memoriam," may almost be said to be the poem of nineteenth century scepticism.—CORSON, HIRAM, 1886, *Introduction to the Study of Robert Browning's Poetry,* p. 23.

In several of the stanzas of this poem the third and fourth lines may change places without detriment to the sense. But if this change be made, the rhymes at the end of the first and fourth lines are brought nearer together, thus increasing the effect of rapidity as well as the emphasis at the end of the latter line. Moreover, all four lines are then heard at regular intervals, thus increasing also the effect of regularity. The consequence is, that the slow and therefore judicial, the unemphatic and therefore hesitating impression conveyed by the thought of the poem, as arranged in its present form, almost disappears, giving place to the easy and even flow of unwavering assurance.—RAYMOND, GEORGE LANSING, 1886, *Poetry as a Representative Art,* p. 122.

Though I have been familiar with the poem from boyhood, it is only in the last few years that the full import of that problem and of the noble solution offered by the poet has become clear to me. The work, as I now understand it, seems to me not only the greatest English poem of the century,— which I have always believed,—but one of the great world-poems, worthy to be placed on the same list with the "Oresteia," the "Divina Commedia," and "Faust." If my brief essay contribute to bring home this conviction to other persons, I shall feel that I have done them a service.—DAVIDSON, THOMAS, 1889, *Prolegomena to In Memoriam, Preface,* p. iii.

It is possible that "In Memoriam" is the greatest poetical work produced in England during the last half century; and, in the subject-matter of its thoughts, it rises to a height and penetrates to a depth which Dryden never approached. But even this great poem cannot be read from one end to another without an occasional stop to climb some poetical stile, or fathom some obscure riddle. And the effect of this is that our attention is concentrated upon the parts, until it becomes difficult to form a proper estimation of the whole. We do not conceal our opinion that this is a defect in art.—EVANS, JOHN AMPHLETT, 1890, *Dryden, Temple Bar, vol.* 88, *p.* 390.

"In Memoriam," viewed from the ground upon which we now stand, is a highly finished expression of the heart-hunger of a soul groping after the fulfilment of its desires and aspirations, searching into science and art, and challenging heaven and earth to yield up the secret of happiness and contentment, and in the primitive instincts of human nature together with the essential truths of the Christian religion—in these alone interpreted in the light of faith—discovering the meaning of life and answers to the questionings of doubt and materialism. In this fact lies the claim of the poem to rank with "Faust" and the "Divina Commedia," not indeed in degree of greatness and fulness of expression, but in kind. "In Memoriam" is also a world-poem.—AZARIAS, BROTHER, 1892, *Phases of Thought and Criticism*, p. 264.

The melodious languors of Tennyson's early poems soon gave way to the deep-centered activities of thought which were every-where rending men's lives apart, and the golden clime in which the poet was born was speedily vexed with the rolling cloud and tempest of the great upheaval. The "In Memoriam" is the nineteenth century's Book of Job, and is inseparably inwoven with the history of the century because it is woven out of the sentiment of the century.—DAWSON, WILLIAM J., 1892, *Quest and Vision*, p. 251.

Of "In Memoriam" it is no more than just to say that it is the best-loved and the most-quoted religious poem of the present age. It is a monumental work of true and noble art, in which the style is worthy of the substance, and the highest thoughts have fashioned for themselves a form of beauty and a voice of music.—VAN DYKE, HENRY, 1892, *Tennyson, The Critic, vol.* 21, *p.* 203.

Of necessity this poem is morbid, the product of a mind partly unbalanced by sorrow, and expressing his sorrow to the world as no writer had ever done before. It is the rule of originality that a writer must put something of himself in his work; but Tennyson turned himself spiritually inside out, so that people witness the contortions of his mind much as the accident to Alexis St. Martin a generation ago exposed his digestive organs and enabled curious doctors to note the hidden processes of digestion. It was a sight fit only for doctors to see. In Tennyson's case, too, there was much doubt at the last whether what was recorded was the normal process, unaffected by the exposure. The doctors generally agreed that the process of digestion was probably interfered with by exposing the digestive organs to unnatural conditions. Certainly thousands have borne as great sorrow as did Tennyson, and have come through suffering to greater strength and clearer faith than did the author of "In Memoriam."—FOWLER, WILLIAM J., 1892, *Whittier and Tennyson, The Arena, vol.* 7, *p.* 2.

"In Memoriam" is a typical product of his art, but it is even more representative of his attitude towards the problems and mysteries of human life; it is the poem which best reveals the secret of his largest popularity. It might have seemed hopeless to expect general favour for an elegy of such unprecedented length on a youth who had "miss'd the early wreath," leaving a memory cherished by a few friends, who alone could measure the unfulfilled promise. Never perhaps, has mastery of poetical resources won a more remarkable triumph than in Tennyson's treatment of this theme. —JEBB, RICHARD CLAVERHOUSE, 1894, *The English Poets, ed. Ward, vol.* IV, *p.* 760.

"In Memoriam" appeared in 1850. It is the central poem of the century, not only in date, but in scope and character. In its complexity and inwardness, its passion pulsing through every vein of thought, its faltering inconsistencies and slow approaches, it has caught the very movement of the age. In structure it is organic and vital. Supreme among elegies, it is more than an elegy: it is the epic of a soul, rendered not symbolically, as in the "Divine Comedy," but with a directness native to a scientific age. More than Clough's "Dipsychus" or Arnold's "Empedocles," the poem lays bare to us the interior life of the typical modern mind.—SCUDDER, VIDA D., 1895, *The Life of the Spirit in the Modern English Poets*, p. 282.

The broad treatment of the great theme of immortality in "In Memoriam," based as it was on profound knowledge and insight, has made the poem one of the most significant utterances of the century, while its deep and searching beauty has given it place among those few and famous poems of philosophic quality which are not only admired as classics, but loved as intimate confessions of the spirit.—MABIE, HAMILTON WRIGHT, 1897, *The Life of Tennyson, Atlantic Monthly*, vol. 80, p. 587.

I regard "In Memoriam" as the greatest poem of our century, both for substance and for form. It is the most representative poem of the age.—STRONG, AUGUSTUS HOPKINS, 1897, *The Great Poets and Their Theology*, p. 475.

Tennyson is probably the greatest poet of the Victorian era; without doubt "In Memoriam" is his greatest poem, "most weighted with thought, most varied in feeling" and most perfect in form.—KING, JOHN M., 1898, *A Critical Study of In Memoriam*, p. 13.

"In Memoriam" is the most expressive monument which has ever been erected to the memory of a man. It is also one of the most remarkable pieces of self-revelation which can be found in literature. So natural is it, however, and so true to the experience of man, that it will always be read while the English language is spoken. The time must come in the experience of almost every one who speaks our language when this poem becomes his chief counsellor and guide. It reveals to us the nature of our own experiences, and shows us the only path by which we may escape from the anguish of bereavement.—WARD, WILLIAM G., 1898, *Tennyson's Debt to Environment*, p. 35.

No books of consolation can console except by sympathy; and in "In Memoriam" sympathy and relief have been found, and will be found, by many. Another, we feel, has trodden our dark and stony path, has been shadowed by the shapes of dread which haunt our valley of tribulation: a mind almost infinitely greater than ours has been our fellow-sufferer. He has emerged from the darkness of the shadow of death into the light, whither, as it seems to us, we can scarcely hope to come. It is the sympathy and the example, I think, not the speculations, mystical or scientific, which make "In Memoriam," in more than name, a book of consolation: even in hours of the sharpest distress, when its technical beauties and wonderful pictures seem shadowy and unreal, like the yellow sunshine and the woods of that autumn day when a man learned that his friend was dead.—LANG, ANDREW, 1901, *Alfred Tennyson (Modern English Writers)*, p. 69.

To take the view taken here is not to bring a charge against Tennyson or to cast doubts on his originality. Indeed, to doubt his originality in the creation of poetic phrases would be to show the extreme of critical incapacity. It is quite possible to hold that in respect of thought and inventive imagination he was not among the most original of our poets; but if ever poet were a master of phrasing he was so, and the fact that he was so is quite unaffected by the further fact that he was sometimes unconsciously indebted to his predecessors.—BRADLEY, ANDREW CECIL, 1901, *A Contemporary of Tennyson's In Memoriam*, p. 75.

It resembles the "Divine Comedy" in that it takes us into the darkest regions, carries us through realms and times of self-conquest, and out again into a place of joy and gladness. We hear the sad dirge of the region of deepest sorrow: sorrow seems to petrify: the Old Yew becomes a symbol of a changelessness which knows no spring. . . . The poem is a tale of spiritual experience—the record of a soul's agony; in its earliest stages we might call it tragedy; but the glory of the close transforms it into comedy. It is dramatic, if by that we understand the story of the discipline and development of a man's character. It is a spiritual drama, the triumphant close of which is the victory of the man who emerges from his lower bondage into the glorious liberty of the children of God.—CARPENTER, WILLIAM BOYD, 1901, *The Religious Spirit in the Poets*, pp. 182, 185.

Its purely poetic merit is small, and it is easy to understand that a dirge in 129 stanzas cannot fail to weary us in the long run.—ENGEL, EDWARD, 1902, *A History of English Literature*, rev. Hamley Bent, p. 425.

ODE ON THE DEATH OF THE DUKE OF WELLINGTON
1852

Thanks, thanks! I have just returned from Reading and found your letter. In the all but universal depreciation of my ode by the Press, the prompt and hearty appreciation of it by a man as true as the Duke himself is doubly grateful.—TENNYSON, ALFRED LORD, 1852, *Letter to Henry Taylor*, Nov, 23; *A Memoir of Tennyson*, ed. Tennyson, vol. I, p. 362.

The hero of Waterloo ended his long life in 1852, and a nation was in mourning. Then, if ever, poets, whether laureled or leafless, were called to give eloquent utterance to the popular grief; and Tennyson, of all the poets, was looked to for its highest expression. The Threnode of the Laureate was forthcoming. The public was, as it had no right to be, disappointed. Tennyson's Muse was ever a wild and willful creature, defiant of rules, and daringly insubordinate to arbitrary forms. It could not, with the witling in the play, cap verses with any man. The moment its tasks were dictated and the form prescribed, that moment there was ground to expect the self-willed jade to play a jade's trick, and leave us with no decent results of inspiration. For odes and sonnets, and other such Procrustean moulds into which poetic thought is at times cast, Tennyson had neither gift, nor liking. When therefore, with the Duke's death, came a sudden demand upon his Muse, and that in shape so solemn as to forbid, as the poet conceived, any fanciful license of invention, the Pindaric form seemed inevitable; and that form rendered a fair exhibition of the poet's peculiar genius out of the question. Strapped up in prescription, and impelled to move by official impulse, his Pegasus was as awkward as a cart-horse. And yet men did him the justice to say that his failure out-topped the success of others.—HALPINE, C. D., 1858, *Daphnaides, Atlantic Monthly*, vol. 2, p. 463.

The greatest of the laureate poems is the "Ode on the Death of the Duke of Wellington." The writing of this was evidently no mere duty work; it was a labor of love, the poem being written very rapidly (it was published within a few days of the Duke's death), and having all the rush of genuine enthusiasm about it. Not many a hero has had his praises sung in a nobler ode.—TANISH, EDWARD CAMPBELL, 1870, *A Study of the Works of Alfred Tennyson*, p. 246.

Noble verse, perhaps the noblest he has ever written.—FRISWELL, JAMES HAIN, 1870, *Modern Men of Letters Honestly Criticised*, p. 154.

The "Dirge of Wellington" was a more magnificent monument than any or all of the histories that record that commander's life.—EMERSON, RALPH WALDO, 1875, ed. *Parnassus*, p. 10.

This noble poem, the first draught of which was written probably in some haste, and was originally published on the day of the Duke's funeral, has since been subjected to more than the usual amount of alteration. . . . In the "Ode on the Death of the Duke of Wellington" he has soared to lyric heights to which, perhaps, even Pindar never attained. The tolling of the Bell, the solemn and slow funeral march, the quick rush of battle, and the choral chant of the cathedral all succeed each other, and the verse sinks and swells, rises and falls to every alternation with equal power.—SHEPHERD, RICHARD HERNE, 1879, *Tennysoniana, Second Ed.*, pp. 113, 155.

One of the noblest elegiac odes in our language.—BALDWIN, JAMES, 1886, *Essential Studies in English and American Literature*, p. 334.

MAUD
1855

I am delighted with Tennyson's "Maud." In this poem how much higher and fresher is his laurel than the clipt and stunted ones of the old gardeners in the same garden! Poetry and philosophy have rarely met so cordially before. I wish he had not written the Wellington ode. He is indeed a true poet. What other could have written this verse, worth many whole volumes: "the breaking heart that will not break?" Infinite his tenderness, his thought, his imagination, the melody and softness as well as the strength and stateliness of his verse.—LANDOR, WALTER SAVAGE, 1855, *Letter, Aug., Life by Forster*.

Tennyson's "Maud," which I think wonderfully fine—the antiphonal voice to "In Memoriam." I tried to read it aloud, but broke down in the middle in a subdued passion of tears.—LOWELL, JAMES RUSSELL, 1855, *To C. E. Norton, Aug. 11; Letters*, ed. Norton, vol. I, p. 235.

I want to tell you how greatly I admire "Maud." No poem since Shakespeare seems to show equal power of the same kind, or equal knowledge of human nature. No modern poem contains more lines that ring in the ears of men. I do not know any verse out of Shakespeare in which the ecstasy of love soars to such a height.—JOWETT, BENJAMIN, 1855, *Letter to Tennyson, Dec.; A Memoir of Tennyson*, vol. I, p. 400.

If an unintelligible or even, for Mr. Tennyson, an inferior work, is still a work which no inferior man could have produced. — GLADSTONE, WILLIAM EWART,

1879, *Tennyson, Gleanings of Past Years,* vol. II, p. 147.

"Maud" is not a world-poem; it is not even a poem of great imaginative range or far-reaching power, but it finds the vulnerable points in modern civilisation, and has its place with those true works of art which will not leave us at rest with ourselves until we know our minds and sound the real depth of our feelings.—DIXON, WILLIAM MACNEILE, 1890, *A Tennyson Primer,* p. 89.

One does not truly enjoy the works of Tennyson who has no appreciation of their artistic beauty, and in a large part of "Maud" the art of the poet is as clearly manifested as in any of his other works. One who cannot take delight in the beauty of this poem can know nothing of the real charm of Tennyson. There are few English poets, perhaps few poets of any land, the music of whose songs is as perfect as that which is found in the verse of Tennyson, and in "Maud" the music is at its sweetest.—EVERETT, CHARLES CARROLL, 1893, *Tennyson and Browning as Spiritual Forces, New World,* vol. 2, p. 240.

He [Tennyson] held a volume of "Maud" in his hands, and was talking about it, as he loved to do: "I want to read this to you because I want you to feel what the poem means. It is dramatic; it is the story of a man who has a morbid nature, with a touch of inherited insanity, and very selfish. The poem is to show what love does for him. The war is only an episode. You must remember that it is not I myself speaking. It is this man with the strain of madness in his blood, and the memory of a great trouble and wrong that has put him out with the world."—VAN DYKE, HENRY, 1893, *The Voice of Tennyson, Century Magazine,* vol. 45, p. 539.

"Maud" seems to mark the central point in Tennyson's development: the period when a complete equilibrium between his plastic powers and his imagination—not so uniformly maintained in his earliest and latest years—had established itself. This was also the most passionate moment of his poetry; no landscape in our literature—perhaps in any literature—is so transfused and empurpled with love overmastering, whilst tinged with approaching madness.—PALGRAVE, FRANCIS TURNER, 1896, *Landscape in Poetry,* p. 289.

Its tone is somewhat jarring; its hero, always unsympathetic, at times almost declines into a mere sulky lout; and although it contains at least one unsurpassed utterance of passion, the passage beginning: "I have led her home, my love, my only friend," a lyric which would alone rank its singer among the great love poets of the world, the poem as a whole must be admitted to contain a larger alloy of rhetoric to a smaller amount of the pure gold of poetry than any other equal number of Tennysonian lines.—TRAILL, HENRY DUFF, 1897, *Social England,* vol. VI, p. 276.

Tennyson never wrote with greater force or with more perfect dramatic and lyric art, and his poem is as striking and effective today as at the time of its publication in 1855.—SHORTER, CLEMENT, 1897, *Victorian Literature,* p. 10.

"Maud," I fancy, will be remembered for the surpassing beauty of the love lyrics, and not from any lively interest in a hero who is not only morbid but silly.—STEPHEN, LESLIE, 1898, *Studies of a Biographer,* p. 237.

The poem in its development strikes all the lyrical chords, although it cannot be said that all of them are touched with equal skill. Probably the sustained and perfect execution of such a varied composition would be too arduous a task for any artist, since it is no easy matter to substitute, dramatically, different phases of passion in one person for different characters. Some considerable mental agility is needed to fall in with the rapid changes of mood and motive which succeed each other within the compass of a piece that is too short for the delineation of character: ranging from melodramic horror in the opening stanzas to passionate and joyous melodies in the middle part, sinking into a dolorous wail, rising into frenzy, and closing with the trumpet note of war.—LYALL, SIR ALFRED, 1902, *Tennyson (English Men of Letters),* p. 86.

IDYLLS OF THE KING
1859-92

The Duke of Argyll called, and left me the sheets of a forthcoming poem of Tennyson. I like it extremely;—notwithstanding some faults, extremely. The parting of Launcelot and Guinevere, her penitence, and Arthur's farewell, are all very affecting. I cried over some passages; but I am now ἀρτίδακρυς as Medea says.— MACAULAY,

THOMAS BABINGTON, 1859, *Journal, July* 11; *Life and Letters*, ed. *Trevelyan*, ch. xv.

Get from the publisher Tennyson's new poem, Four Idyls of the King. Eagerly devour the first of them, which is charming,—reminding one of Chaucer's "Griselda." . . . Finished the Four Idyls. The first and third could have come only from a great poet. The second and fourth do not seem to me so good.—LONGFELLOW, HENRY WADSWORTH, 1859, *Journal, June* 19, 20; *Life by Samuel Longfellow*, vol. II, p. 339.

Will you forgive me if I intrude upon your leisure with a request which I have thought some little time of making—viz., that you would be good enough to write your name in the accompanying volume of your "Idylls of the King?" You would thus add a peculiar interest to the book containing those beautiful songs, from the perusal of which I derived the greatest enjoyment. They quite rekindle the feeling with which the legends of King Arthur must have inspired the chivalry of old, while the graceful form in which they are presented blends those feelings with the softer tone of our present age.—Believe me, always, yours truly.—ALBERT, PRINCE, 1860, *Letter to Tennyson, May* 17.

"In Memoriam," "Maud," "The Miller's Daughter," and such like will always be my own pet rhymes, yet I am quite prepared to admit this to be as good as any, for its own peculiar audience. Treasures of wisdom there are in it; and word-painting such as never was yet for concentration, nevertheless it seems to me that so great power ought not to be spent on visions of things past but on the living. For one hearer capable of feeling the depth of this poem I believe ten would feel a depth quite as great if the stream flowed through things nearer the hearer.—RUSKIN, JOHN, 1860, *Letter to Tennyson, A Memoir of Tennyson*, ed. *his Son*, vol. I, p. 453.

By degrees we got to Guinevere, and he [Tennyson] spoke kindly of S. Hodges's picture of her at the Polytechnic, though he doubted if it told the story very distinctly. This lead to real talk of Arthur and "Idylls," and his firm belief in him as an historical personage, though old Speed's narrative has much that can be only traditional. He found great difficulty in reconstructing the character, in connecting modern with ancient feeling in representing the ideal king. I asked whether Vivien might not be the old Brittany fairy who wiled Merlin into her net, and not an actual woman. "But no," he said; "it is full of distinct personality, though I never expect women to like it." The river Camel he well believes in, particularly as he slipped his foot and fell in the other day, but found no Excalibur. Camel means simply winding, crooked, like the Cam at Cambridge. The Welsh claim Arthur as their own, but Tennyson gives all his votes to us. Some have urged him to continue the "Idylls," but he does not feel it expedient to take people's advice as an absolute law, but to wait for the vision.—FOX, CAROLINE, 1860, *Memoirs of Old Friends*, ed. *Pym*; *Journal, Sept.* 22, p. 350.

The crowning work of his genius, needs the rarest voices that have been attuned on the globe to read it, and set free the melody healthy and delicate as the echoes which his own Bugle Song describes:—

"O hark, O hear, how thin and clear,
 And thinner, clearer, farther going,
O sweet and far, from cliff and scar,
 The horns of Elfland faintly blowing."

So from souls on the western shore of the Atlantic, and from the borders of the Pacific, too, the echoes return of his genius.—KING, THOMAS STARR, 1861, *Substance and Show, and Other Lectures*, p. 386.

We read, at first, Tennyson's "Idylls," with profound recognition of the finely elaborated execution, and also the inward perfection of *vacancy*,—and, to say truth, with considerable impatience at being treated so very like infants, though the lollipops were so superlative. We gladly changed for one Emerson's "English Traits;" and read that, with increasing and ever increasing satisfaction every evening; blessing Heaven that there were still Books for grown-up people too!— CARLYLE, THOMAS, 1867, *To Emerson, Jan.* 27; *Correspondence of Carlyle and Emerson*, ed. *Norton*, vol. II, p. 339.

Then cried the King, and smote the oak,
"Love, Truth, and Beauty, one, but three,
This is the Artist's Trinity!"
And lo, 'twas Tennyson who spoke.
For this shall be through endless time
The burden of the golden rhyme
Of Tennyson, our Laureate.

—MONKHOUSE, WILLIAM COSMOS, 1869, *Recollections of Alfred Tennyson, A Day Dream.*

With admirable art, Tennyson has renewed the feelings and the language; this pliant soul takes all tones, in order to give itself all pleasures. This time he has become epic, antique, and ingenuous, like Homer, and like old *trouvères* of the *chansons de Geste*. It is pleasant to quit our learned civilization, to rise again to the primitive age and manners, to listen to the peaceful discourse which flows copiously and slowly, as a river on a smooth slope. The mark of the ancient epic is clearness and calm. The ideas were new-born; man was happy and in his infancy. He had not had time to refine, to cut down and adorn his thoughts; he showed them bare. He was not yet pricked by manifold lusts; he thought at leisure. Every idea interested him; he unfolded it curiously, and explained it. His speech never jerks; he goes step by step, from one object to another, and every object seems lovely to him; he pauses, observes, and takes pleasure in observing. This simplicity and peace are strange and charming; we abandon ourselves, it is well with us; we do not desire to go more quickly; we fancy we would gladly remain thus, and for ever.—TAINE, H. A., 1871, *History of English Literature*, tr. *Van Laun* vol. II, *bk*. v, *ch*. vi, *par*. v, *p*. 530.

There are very fine childish things in Tennyson's poem and fine manly things, too, as it seems to me, but I conceive the theory to be wrong. I have the same feeling (I am not wholly sure of its justice) that I have when I see these modern-mediæval pictures. I am defrauded; I do not see reality, but a masquerade. The costumes are all that is genuine, and the people inside them are shams—which, I take it, is just the reverse of what ought to be. One special criticism I should make on Tennyson's new Idyls, and that is that the similes are so often dragged in by the hair. They seem to be taken (*à la* Tom Moore) from note-books, and not suggested by the quickened sense of association in the glow of composition. Sometimes it almost seems as if the verses were made for the similes, instead of being the cresting of a wave that heightens as it rolls. This is analogous to the costume objection and springs perhaps from the same cause—the making of poetry with malice prepense. However, I am not going to forget the lovely things that Tennyson has written, and I think they give him rather hard measure now.—LOWELL, JAMES RUSSELL, 1872, *To C. E. Norton, Dec.* 4; *Letters, ed. Norton*, vol. II, *p*. 85.

We shall discern, as we proceed, more and more clearly, that these "Idylls" constitute essentially one long study of *failure*. They bring before us that sad doom of vanity, of disappointment, of blighted promises and withered prospects which, here as elsewhere, is seen to await many bright hopes and noble enthusiasms. And they show us the secret of this failure, the dread working of that mystery of iniquity which mars and ruins the fairest of prospects. The Evil comes first; but, following ever upon it, with slow and tardy, as it would appear, but certain and irresistible steps, we shall recognize the noiseless and stealthy tread of the avenging Nemesis of Retribution.—ELSDALE, HENRY, 1878, *Studies in the Idylls*, *p*. 9.

The real and radical flaw in the splendid structure of the "Idylls" is not to be found either in the antiquity of the fabulous groundwork or in the modern touches which certainly were not needed, and if needed would not have been adequate, to redeem any worthy recast of so noble an original from the charge of nothingness. The fallacy which obtrudes itself throughout, the false note which incessantly jars on the mind's ear, results from the incongruity of materials which are radically incapable of combination or coherence. Between the various Arthurs of different national legends there is little more in common than the name. It is essentially impossible to construct a human figure by the process of selection from the incompatible types of irreconcilable ideas. All that the utmost ingenuity of eclecticism can do has been demonstrated by Mr. Tennyson in his elaborate endeavor after the perfection of this process; and the result is to impress upon us a complete and irreversible conviction of its absolute hopelessness.—SWINBURNE, ALGERNON CHARLES, 1881, *Tennyson and Musset, Fortnightly Review*, vol. 35, *p*. 148; *Miscellanies*, *p*. 249.

In nothing has the revival of sound critical taste done better service than in recalling us to the Arthurian Cycle, the dayspring of our glorious literature. The closing books of Malory's Arthur certainly rank, both in conception and in form, with the best poetry of Europe; in quiet pathos and reserved strength they hold their own with the epics of any age. Beside this simple, manly type of the mediæval hero the figures in the "Idyls of the King" look like the dainty Perseus of Canova placed beside the heroic Theseus of Pheidias.—HARRISON, FREDERIC, 1886, *The Choice of Books*, p. 45, note.

Let it be admitted, too, that King Arthur, of the "Idyls" is like an Albert in blank verse, an Albert cursed with a Guinevere for a wife, and a Lancelot for friend. The "Idyls," with all their beauties, are full of a Victorian respectability, and love of talking with Vivien, about what is not so respectable. One wishes, at times, that the "Morte d'Arthur" had remained a lonely and flawless fragment, as noble as Homer, as polished as Sophocles. But then we must have missed with many other admirable things the "Last Battle in the West."—LANG, ANDREW, 1886, *The Independent*, October 28th.

His mannerism is great, but it is a noble and welcome mannerism. His very best work, to me, is contained in the books of "The Idyls of the King," all of them, and all that has grown out of them.—WHITMAN, WALT, 1887, *A Word About Tennyson, The Critic*, vol. 10, p. 1.

But fine as "The Idylls" are, they are not the poet's finest work, for the reason that they are not of the finest *genre*.—LE GALLIENNE, RICHARD, 1892, *Waugh's Tennyson, The Academy*, vol. 42, p. 428.

Of the "Idylls of the King" I ventured to say, ten years ago, that it was the finest piece of blank-verse since Milton; and it is certainly the only epic in our century which men have been willing to read.—VAN DYKE, HENRY, 1892, *Tennyson, The Critic*, vol. 21, p. 203.

The men and women in the "Idylls of the King" want life. The personal edges and angles have been worn away in order to establish the type. Enid, Tristram, Vivien, Arthur, even Lancelot who is the most living, are often like those photographs which are made by photographing the faces of a series of politicians or philosophers or artists one on the top of another. We get the general type—or they say we get it—but we do not get a man.—BROOKE, STOPFORD A., 1894, *Tennyson, his Art and Relation to Modern Life*, p. 76.

The very name, Merlin, is fascinating; his story is most romantic, and possesses strong human interest; yet it was left for Tennyson to discover its value. For centuries it lay in the quarry like a block of marble, hieroglyphs scrawled all over it by almanack makers, bits of it chipped off and carried away for doorsteps and pedestals, until the eye that could see beheld the immortal group in the forest of Broceliaunde, and liberated it from the tomb, where, like the enchanter himself, spell-bound it had slept for centuries. That Tennyson has told the story finally it would be unwise to assert. There is as yet no outstanding female embodiment of the "spirit that denies," and in Vivien is a possible she-Mephistopheles.—DAVIDSON, JOHN, 1895, *Sentences and Paragraphs*, p. 111.

The English poet whose work is most popular in our generation is Tennyson. The popular verdict would doubtless not hesitate to name as his most characteristic achievement "The Idylls of the King." This group of poems is the most extensive in mass and the most attractive in theme of all his works. Other poems of his have more depth and equal beauty, but they have not appealed so strongly to that innate fondness for a story which characterizes the general reader. Of "The Idylls of the King" all but one are based upon Malory's "Morte Darthur." The material is in some of the pieces treated very freely: "The Last Tournament," for example, is an expansion of a few hints suggested by Malory, but in many poems the borrowing extends to words and phrases, transferred with a slight change of order to the new setting. Tennyson does indeed transform the spirit of some of Malory's stories so that familiar acquaintances appear new and strange, but he retains enough of his original to indicate where he went for his inspiration.—MEAD, WILLIAM EDWARD, 1897, *Selections from Sir Thomas Malory's Morte Darthur, Introduction*, p. xlv.

Tennyson wished to introduce a character able to furnish a contrast to the erring Lancelot and noble Arthur, typifying the vulgar and superficial life of a gay court; such a personage he found in Gawain. Accordingly, he ventured to introduce the model of chivalry in the inconsistent role of a tale-bearer and newsmonger. Worse still, taking a suggestion from Dante, it pleased him to parody a scene in the English mediæval poem, where the king, before his final encounter with Mordred, is visited by the ghost of Gawain. The object of the apparition is to warn the king that the battle set for the morrow must be postponed, on penalty of ruin; in his advent, Arthur's nephew is surrounded by the blessed spirits of the lords and ladies, whom, in the course of his career as ally of the forsaken, he had been able to succor in time of need. The modern writer also brings on the scene the soul of the champion, but as a visitor from Hell rather than Paradise, blown forever "along a wandering wind," presenting himself for no useful purpose, but arriving only to take leave of his lord and announce his own destiny, a doom befitting one described as "light in life," and "light in death." Had he been acquainted with his great predecessor, Tennyson might have found that Wolfram, when desirous of comparing temporal and spiritual knighthood, chose Gawain as representative of the former, without for that reason finding it necessary to disparage his worth. Surely, in view of the wanton and unnecessary nature of the libel, the spirit is entitled to his remedy, and action for defamation of character should lie before the high court of criticism.—NEWELL, WILLIAM WELLS, 1898, *King Arthur and the Table Round*, vol. I, p. lvii.

Because they represent the maturity of his genius and the perfection of his art, his deepest convictions and his highest wisdom, the "Idylls" would seem to form the poem upon which his fame must ultimately rest. The works of Tennyson include more than three hundred quotations from the Bible, and are pervaded with a spirit so deeply devout that men have come to feel that he is essentially our religious poet, and that it is in the realm of religious thought that his genius has found its highest expression. If the "Paradise Lost" looks backward and shows how one sin sent one man into the wilderness; if the "Divine Comedy" looks forward and shows how sins may be punished and purged away, "The Idylls of the King" form a study of the present and offer an outlook upon the great epochs and teachers of the soul.—HILLIS, NEWELL DWIGHT, 1899, *Great Books as Life-Teachers*, p. 162.

The special service of Tennyson to romantic poetry lay in his being the first to give a worthy form to the great Arthurian saga; and the modern masterpiece of that poetry, all things considered, is his "Idylls of the King."—BEERS, HENRY A., 1901, *A History of English Romanticism in the Nineteenth Century*, p. 268.

ENOCH ARDEN
1864

The story of "Enoch Arden" as he has enhanced and presented it, is a rich and splendid composite of imagery and illustration. Yet how simple that story is in itself. A sailor who sells fish, breaks his leg, gets dismal, gives up selling fish, goes to sea, is wrecked on a desert island, stays there some years, on his return finds his wife married to a miller, speaks to a landlady on the subject and dies. Told in the pure and simple, the unadorned and classical style, this story would not have taken three pages, but Mr. Tennyson has been able to make it the principal —the largest tale in his new volume. He has done so only by giving to every event and incident in the volume an accompanying commentary. He tells a great deal about the torrid zone, which a rough sailor like Enoch Arden certainly would not have perceived; and he gives the fishing village, to which all the characters belong, a softness and a fascination which such villages scarcely possess in reality. . . . A dirty sailor who did *not* go home to his wife is not an agreeable being: a varnish must be put on him to make him shine. It is true that he acts rightly; that he is very good. But such is human nature that it finds a little tameness in mere morality. . . . The dismal act of a squalid man needed many condiments to make it pleasant, and therefore Mr. Tennyson was right to mix them subtly and to use them freely.—BAGEHOT, WALTER, 1864, *Wordsworth, Tennyson and Browning; Works, ed. Morgan*, vol. I, pp. 225, 236, 237.

Is in its author's purest idyllic style; noticeable for evenness of tone, clearness of diction, successful description of coast and ocean,—finally, for the loveliness and fidelity of its *genre* scenes.—STEDMAN, EDMUND CLARENCE, 1875–87, *Victorian Poets*, p. 181.

What if this earnest, smoothly-flowing narrative in verse shall more vitally than aught else in its author's rich bequest to the century transmit his name to far generations—and this despite the "jewels five-words-long" that dower "The Princess"—despite the noble harmonies of sound and sense that bear along the pageant chronicle of Arthur and his court? If "Enoch Arden" is destined thus to preserve its author's name as a household word, the reason is not far to seek. The poem is marvelously comprehensive. The essential whole of human life is in it. The stage is small, the *mise-en-scène* humble; but all the prime movers are present, and the drama is completely played.—THOMAS, EDITH M., 1887, *Enoch Arden, The Book Buyer, vol. 4, p.* 401.

In all the essential features of a moderately long poem, in design, construction, finish, and impression, "Enoch Arden" is excellent. It is probably more perfect than any other of Tennyson's poems of equal or greater length . . . and it is more perfect than many of his shorter poems. . . . Style, tone, atmosphere, feeling, humanity, all blend in one harmony of simplicity; there is also concentration of narrative, avoidance of sensation, repression of false sentiment.—LUCE, MORTON, 1895, *A Handbook to the Works of Alfred Lord Tennyson, pp.* 202, 207.

Whether "Enoch Arden" represented to its countrymen ornateness or simplicity, ethics or drama, to foreigners it represented a typical phase of English literature, and has been put down as the essentially English poem of Tennyson's collection.— CARY, ELISABETH L., 1898, *Tennyson, his Homes, his Friends and his Work, p.* 197.

Never for a moment in "Enoch Arden" is the reader brought into touch with real characters or with the real experiences of sailors. What the poem does is to put before the reader with exquisite deftness what such characters and such experiences become as they pass through the dreamy mind and before the visionary imagination of the poet who wrote the "Lady of Shalott" and "Tears, idle tears." The poem has none of the savour of fact. It is lyrically falsified from first to last—qualified into grace and music through the poet's refinement of temperament.—GATES, LEWIS E., 1900, *Studies and Appreciations, p.* 66.

LOCKSLEY HALL SIXTY YEARS AFTER
1886

It is a great poem, worthy of the maturity of a great poet; and, so far from suggesting to my mind any unpleasing sense of incongruity with the first part of "Locksley Hall," it enormously enhances the interest and spacious significance of that delightful work. In this respect it is a most felicitous exception to the generally unsatisfactory character of sequels, written in later life, by the authors of early masterpieces. Goethe's "Helena" has no vital connection with his "Faust." But the old lover of "Locksley Hall" is exactly what the young man must have become, without any change of character by force of time and experience, if he had grown with the growth of his age.— For that reason alone, the poem in its entirety has a peculiar historical importance as the impersonation of the emotional life of a whole generation. Its psychological portraiture is perfect—its workmanship exquisite—and its force and freshness of poetic fervour wonderful.—LYTTON, ROBERT BULWER LORD, 1886, *Letter to Mary Anderson, A Memoir of Tennyson, ed. Tennyson, vol.* II, *p.* 330.

For a writer who first published in the thirties to produce a great poem far on in the eighties is in itself a great achievement; but that this poem should be the continuation of one of the most popular poems of his youth is a still greater achievement. And it must be acknowledged the "Locksley Hall" of to-day is not inferior in workmanship to the poem of forty years ago. There is the same ringing rhythm, the same strength and swing, the same ease and variety that delighted our fathers.—BEECHING, H. C., 1887, *Locksley Hall Sixty Years After, The Academy, vol.* 31, *p.* 1.

The nation will observe with warm satisfaction that, although the new "Locksley Hall" is, as told by the Calendar, a work of Lord Tennyson's old age, yet is his poetic "eye not dim, nor his natural force abated." . . . Now that he gives us another "Locksley Hall," after "Sixty Years," the very last criticism that will be hazarded, or if hazarded will be accepted, on his work will be, that it betrays a want of tone and fibre. For my own part I have been not less impressed with the form, than with the substance. Limbs will grow stiff with age, but minds not always; we find here all undiminished that suppleness of the poet which enables him to conform without loss of freedom to the stringent laws of men and verse. Lord Tennyson retains his conspicuous mastery over the trochaic metre, and even the least favourable among the instantaneous, or "pistol-graph," criticisms demanded by the necessities of the daily press, stingily admits that the poem "here and there exhibits the inimitable touch."—GLADSTONE, WILLIAM EWART, 1887, *"Locksley Hall and the Jubilee," Nineteenth Century, vol.* 21, *p.* 1.

It is little to say of "Locksley Hall Sixty Years After" that English literature presents no similar instance of a work of anything like the same grade of intellectual achievement produced by a poet at the same period of life. No allowance has to be made for it on account of the age of its author. If it lack at times the gorgeousness of diction which characterized to so marked a degree the original creation it equals it in sustained power, and in energy of expression it occasionally leaves it behind.—LOUNSBURY, THOMAS R., 1889, *The Two Locksley Halls, Scribner's Magazine*, vol. 6, p. 255.

The poem had too much vigor, too much truth, to please the easy-going optimist. But Truth is the test by which all literature must be tried; and "Locksley Hall Sixty Years After" will be recognized, when the verdict of many more than another sixty years has been pronounced upon it, to be one of the clearest, most unsparing pictures of its age to be found in contemporary literature. And when that recognition ripens round it, Tennyson's sincerity will not be without its reward.—WAUGH, ARTHUR, 1892–96, *Alfred Lord Tennyson, a Study of his Life and Works*, p. 227.

In fact the second Locksley Hall is, despite a certain falling off of technical skill, still substantially the fulfillment of the first. Whatever unhealthiness exists in the latest poem, is in germ in the original one, and, on the whole, the new poem, notwithstanding a number of frantic opinions and of unpleasant lines, is healthier, more manly, more devout, and even more cheerful, in a deeper sense of the word cheerful, than was the first poem. Neither poem is truly sound. Both suffer from the same disease. Both illustrate Tennyson's characteristic weakness. But of the two the old man's poem, if artistically inferior, is ethically higher, and for this reason is far more satisfying.—ROYCE, JOSIAH, 1898, *Tennyson and Pessimism*, p. 77.

DRAMAS

Harold is no virgin, no confessor, no seer, no saint, but a loyal, plain, strong-thewed, truth-loving son of England, who can cherish a woman, and rule a people, and mightily wield a battle-axe. — DOWDEN, EDWARD, 1867, *Mr. Tennyson and Mr. Browning, Studies in Literature*, p. 197.

I cannot trust myself to say how greatly I admire the play ["Queen Mary"]. Beyond the immediate effect, you'll have hit a more fatal blow than a thousand pamphleteers and controversialists; besides this you have reclaimed one more section of English History from the wilderness and given it a form in which it will be fixed for ever. No one since Shakespeare has done that. When we were beginning to think that we were to have no more from you, you have given us the greatest of all your works.—FROUDE, JAMES ANTHONY, 1875, *Letter to Tennyson, May 7; A Memoir of Tennyson, ed. Tennyson*, vol. II, p. 180.

Has a fold of Shakespeare's mantle fallen upon Mr. Tennyson's shoulders? This is the question "Queen Mary" has started in the world of criticism. What seems clear is that the author would have spared his judges much expenditure of ink if, in place of calling his work a drama, he had given it the more flexible and less compromising title of dramatic poem. If by a drama is meant, as certain critics have defined it, a definite action with a beginning, a plot, and a denouement, "Queen Mary" hardly justifies its title. Strongly to desire marriage, to espouse an unamiable prince, to live very unhappily with him, to seek in the persecution of heretics an insufficient consolation, and to die in bed of a fever, constitute a variety of things, undoubtedly, and while they may be brought well together, the result is not, properly speaking, dramatic action. There is rich enough matter for romance; but tragedy is sought in vain in this succession of events. In all dramas it must be felt, however feebly, that there is a plot, a progression in interest; in one word, a crisis. There is nothing of the kind in "Queen Mary." Why the personages go and come, entering and departing, why they are there, even, and what they are doing, is a mystery. They are there by the poet's wish, that is all. A series of pictures are unfolded without other connection than that of chronological succession. — BOUCHER, LÉON, 1875, *Tennyson's Queen Mary*.

Mr. Tennyson may entertain himself by writing "Mary" and "Harold;" but they might as well have remained unwritten. They are too late. They are not good closetplays even, which I think Horne's tragedies are. — STODDARD, RICHARD HENRY, 1877, *Letters of Elizabeth Barrett Browning Addressed to R. H. Horne, Preface*, p. vii.

The play ["Becket"] is instinct with dramatic life, and is as various as Shakespeare, and (unlike Shakespeare) nowhere is there any fine writing thrust in because it is fine, and because the poet wanted to say the fine things which arose in his mind. Prophecy has been called "the most gratuitous form of error" by my better half, so I ought to be chary in prophecy; yet I have no hesitation in saying that whatever the critics of to-day may think or say, the critics of to-morrow will unanimously declare Alfred Tennyson to be a great dramatic genius. — LEWES, GEORGE HENRY, 1878, *On Reading the Drama in MS., New York Tribune.*

"Mary Tudor," considered as a poem, contains some passages as beautiful as any Tennyson ever penned; and a few which might well be omitted, as, for instance, the ridiculous song of the Milkmaid, which certain critics, ready to admire anything written by Tennyson, profess to consider "pretty and bucolic."—HAMILTON, WALTER, 1879, *The Poets Laureate of England,* p. 281.

One cannot imagine a more vivid ["Becket"], a more perfectly faithful picture than it gives both of Henry and of Thomas. Truth in history is naturally truth in poetry; but you have made the characters of the two men shine out in a way which, while it never deviates from the impression history gives of them, goes beyond and perfects history. This is eminently conspicuous in the way their relations to one another are traced; and in the delineation of the influence on Thomas of the conception of the Church, blending with his own haughty spirit and sanctifying it to his own conscience. There is not, it seems to me, anything in modern poetry which helps us to realize, as your drama does, the sort of power the Church exerted on her ministers: and this is the central fact of the earlier middle ages.—BRYCE, JAMES, 1884, *Letter to Tennyson; A Memoir of Tennyson,* ed. *Tennyson,* vol. II, p. 199.

The first actor of England, with matchless resources for theatrical presentation, was able more than once to make the performance of a play by Tennyson a notable and picturesque event, but nothing more; nor have those produced with equal care by others become any part of the stage repertory. There are charmingly poetic qualities in the minor pieces, and one of them," The Cup," is not without effects,—but even this will not hold the stage,—while "The Falcon" and "The Promise of May" are plainly amateurish. They contain lovely songs and trifles, but when a great master merges the poet in the playwright he must be judged accordingly. "Harold" and "Becket" are of a more imposing cast, and have significance as examples of what may—and of what may not—be effected by a strong artist in a department to which he is not led by compulsive instinct. Their ancestral themes are in every way worthy of an English poet. "Harold," in style and language, is much like the "Idylls of the King," nor does it greatly surpass them in dramatic quality, though a work cast in the standard five-act mold.—STEDMAN, EDMUND CLARENCE, 1887, *Twelve Years of British Song, Century Magazine,* vol. 34, p. 900.

Let me add my congratulations to the many on the success of "The Foresters." I cannot tell you how delighted I was when I felt and saw, from the first, the joy it was giving to our large audience. Its charm is felt by all. Let me thank you for myself for the honour of playing your "Maid Marion," which I have learned to love, for while I am playing the part I feel all its beauty and simplicity and sweetness, which make me feel for the time a happier and a better woman. I am indeed proud of its great success for your sake as well as my own.—REHAN, ADA, 1892, *Letter to Tennyson, A Memoir of Tennyson,* ed. *Tennyson,* vol. II, p. 396.

Tennyson, the dramatist, labours under the serious disadvantage that he has always to enter the lists against Tennyson the lyrist, Tennyson the elegist, Tennyson the idyllist. He is his own most formidable rival, and perhaps in this fact lies the explanation of that respectful coldness which on the whole has marked the reception of his dramas by both the critics and the public. Then, too—though no one could think of saying that Lord Tennyson had been positively infelicitous in his selection of dramatic subjects—there has yet always been some barrier to complete surrender of one's sympathies to his theme.—WATSON, WILLIAM, 1892, *The Foresters, The Academy,* vol. 41, p. 341.

GENERAL

He knows that "the poet's mind is holy ground;" he knows that the poet's portion is to be

"Dower'd with the hate of hate, the scorn of scorn,
The love of love;"

he has shown, in the lines from which we

quote, his own just conception of the grandeur of a poet's destiny; and we look to him for its fulfilment. . . . If our estimate of Mr. Tennyson be correct, he too is a poet; and many years hence may be read his juvenile description of that character with the proud consciousness that it has become the description and history of his own work.—MILL, JOHN STUART, 1831, *Tennyson's Poems, Westminster Review*, vol. 14, pp. 223, 224.

We all lounged on the beach most peacefully, John Sterling reading some of Tennyson to us, which displays a poetical fancy and intense sympathy with dreamy romance, and withal a pure pathos, drawn direct from the heart of Nature.—FOX, CAROLINE, 1841, *Memories of Old Friends*, ed. Pym; *Journal, Aug.* 30, p. 149.

The elegance, the wit, the subtlety of this writer, his fancy, his power of language, his metrical skill, his independence of any living masters, his peculiar topics, his taste for the costly and gorgeous. . . . Wants rude truth, however, he is too fine. . . . It is long since we have had as good a lyrist, it will be long before we have his superior. . . . The best songs in English poetry are by that heavy, hard, pedantic poet, Ben Jonson. Jonson is rude, and only on rare occasions gay. Tennyson is always fine, but Jonson's beauty is more graceful than Tennyson's. It is the natural, manly grace of a robust workman.—EMERSON, RALPH WALDO, 1843, *The Dial, April*.

So, Tennyson is "pretty," is he? Did I ever tell you that I heard a lady—a countess—by the order of St. Louis!—say, "The latter part of Homer is certainly very pretty?" These are your critics, O Israel!—BROWNING, ELIZABETH BARRETT, 1843, *Letters addressed to R. H. Horne*, p. 72.

I have been sauntering for some time reading Alfred Tennyson's poems and other light matters. Alfred's brother lent me his poems. Beautiful they are, certainly; strong and manly often, but oftener capricious, silly, and affected. Godiva was a most difficult affair, certainly, yet treated with that perfect grace and beauty.—AIRD, THOMAS, 1843, *Diary, April* 20.

The peculiarities of his style have attracted attention, and his writings have enough intrinsic merit, probably, to secure him a permanent place in the third or fourth rank of English contemporary poets.—GRISWOLD, RUFUS W., 1844, *The Poets and Poetry of England in the Nineteenth Century*.

Not mine, not mine (O muse forbid) the boon
Of borrow'd notes, tne mockbird's modish tune,
The jingling medley of purloined conceits,
Out-babying Wordsworth and out-glittering Keats;
Where all the airs of patchwork pastoral chime
To drown the ears in Tennysonian rhyme!
Let school-miss Alfred vent her chaste delight
On "darling little rooms so warm and light;"
Chant "I'm a-weary" in infectious strain;
And catch "the blue fly singing i' the pane;"
Though praised by critics and adored by Blues,
Though Peel with pudding plump the puling muse,
Though Theban taste the Saxon purse controlls,
And pensions Tennyson while starves a Knowles.
—LYTTON, SIR EDWARD BULWER, 1845, *The New Timon*.

Of all the successors of Shelley, he possesses the most sureness of insight. He has a subtle mind, of keen, passionless vision. His poetry is characterized by intellectual intensity as distinguished from the intensity of feeling. He watches his consciousness with a cautious and minute attention, to fix, and condense, and shape into form, the vague and mystical shadows of thought and feeling, which glide and flit across it. He listens to catch the lowest whisperings of the soul. His imagination broods over the spiritual and mystical elements of his being with the most concentrated power. His eye rests firmly on an object, until it changes from film into form. Some of his poems are forced into artistical shape, by the most patient and painful intellectual processes. His utmost strength is employed on those mysterious facts of consciousness, which form the staple of the dreams and reveries of others. His mind winds through the mystical labyrinths of thought and feeling, with every power awake, in action, and wrought up to the highest pitch of intensity. The most acute analysis is followed, step by step, by a suggestive imagination which converts refined abstractions into pictures, or makes them audible to the soul through the most cunning combinations of sound. Everything that is done is the result of labor. There is hardly a stanza in his writings but was introduced to serve some particular purpose, and could not be omitted without injury to the general effect. Everything has meaning. Every idea was won in a fair conflict with darkness, or dissonance, or gloom.—WHIPPLE, EDWIN P., 1845, *English Poets of the Nineteenth Century, Essays and Reviews*, vol. I.

The poems of Alfred Tennyson have certainly much of the beauty of a long-past time; but they have also a life so vivid, a truth so lucid, and a melody so inexhaustible, as to mark him the poet that cannot die.—MARTINEAU, HARRIET, 1849, *A History of the Thirty Years' Peace*, A. D. 1815–1846, vol. IV, p. 436.

In perfect sincerity I regard him as the noblest poet that ever lived. . . . I call him, and *think* him, the noblest of poets, *not* because the impressions he produces are, at *all* times, the most profound, *not* because the poetical excitement which he induces is, at *all* times, the most intense, but because it *is*, at all times, the most ethereal,—in other words, the most elevating and the most pure. No poet is so little of the earth, earthy.—POE, EDGAR ALLAN, 1850, *The Poetical Principle*, Works, ed. Stedman and Woodberry, vol. VI, p. 27.

His intellect at large, though good, is not, I think, great in proportion to the imaginative and poetical elements of it; and, therefore, I do not anticipate that he will take any such place in poetry as is filled by Coleridge or Wordsworth; but I think that his poetry will be felt to be admirable in its kind, and may well displace the poetry of sensibility and beauty which has gone before it in the present age.—TAYLOR, SIR HENRY, 1851, *To Sir Edmund Head, Nov. 16; Correspondence*, ed. Dowden, p. 194.

Tennyson belonged to a period in English annals somewhat later than the one with which we are now engaged; but the whirl of political events will not permit a recurrence to the inviting paths of poetry and literature—and he will, perhaps, not regret being placed beside his great compeers. He has opened a new vein in English poetry, and shown that real genius, even in the most advanced stages of society, can strike a fresh chord, and, departing from the hackneyed ways of imitation, charm the world by the conceptions of original thought. His imagination, wide and discursive as the dreams of fancy, wanders at will, not over the real so much as the ideal world. The grottos of the sea, the caves of the mermaid, the realms of heaven, are alternately the scenes of his song. His versification, wild as the song of the elfin king, is broken and irregular, but often inexpressibly charming. Sometimes, however, this tendency leads him into conceit; in the endeavor to be original, he becomes fantastic. There is a freshness and originality, however, about his conceptions, which contrast strangely with the practical and interested views which influenced the age in which he lived, and contributed not a little to their deserved success.—ALISON, SIR ARCHIBALD, 1853, *History of Europe*, 1815–1852, ch. v.

I have maintained in these Essays that a Theology which does not correspond to the deepest thoughts and feelings of human beings cannot be true Theology. Your writings have taught me to enter into many of those thoughts and feelings. Will you forgive me the presumption of offering you a book which, at least, acknowledges them and does them homage?—MAURICE, FREDERICK DENISON, 1853, *Theological Essays, Dedication*.

In consequence of this unselfishness and humility, Scott's enjoyment of Nature is incomparably greater than that of any other poet I know. All the rest carry their care to her, and begin maundering in her ears about their own affairs. Tennyson goes out on a furzy common, and sees it is calm autumn sunshine, but it gives him no pleasure. He only remembers that it is

"Dead calm in that noble breast
Which heaves but with the heaving deep."

He sees a thundercloud in the evening, and *would* have "doted and pored" on it, but cannot, for fear it should bring the ship bad weather.—RUSKIN, JOHN, 1856, *Modern Painters*, Part IV, ch. XV, par. XXXVIII.

Thy song can girdle hill and mead
  With choirs, more pure, more fair,
Their locks with wild flower dressed and weed,
  Than ever Hellas bare:
Theocritus, we cry, once more
Treads his beloved Trinacrian shore!
—DEVERE, AUBREY, 1856, *Ode, The Golden Mean*.

Tennyson, our present English King of Song, crowned as such not more by official nomination than by the general voice, has won to himself the personal attachment of his countrymen in a degree that has been rarely equalled in the history of literature. Among ourselves, Scott is the only other great writer who ever was held during his lifetime in anything like the same universal love and honor. The poetry of Tennyson has charmed all hearts by something more than its artistic qualities. It is as full of nobleness as of beauty. The laurel when he resigns it to another will again be acknowledged by all to be "greener from the brows of him that uttered nothing base." Everywhere his verse, whether tender or lofty, whether light-hearted or sad, breathes the kindest and manliest nature.— CRAIK, GEORGE L., 1862, *A Manual of English Literature*, p. 521.

There came a new poet who, to the science of rhythm, the resources of expression, the gift of epic narration, the deep feeling for nature, to all the caprices of a delightful fancy, to all the favorite ideas, noble or morbid, of modern thought, knew how to join the language of manly passion. Thus, as it were summing up in himself all his forerunners, he touched all hearts; he linked together all admirations; he has remained the true representative, the last expression and final, of the poetic period to which he belongs. Tennyson reigns to-day almost alone in increasing and uncontested glory.—SCHERER, EDMOND, 1863-91, *Taine's History of English Literature, Essays on English Literature*, tr. Saintsbury, p. 87.

I do not think Tennyson a great and powerful spirit in any line—as Goethe was in the line of modern thought, Wordsworth in that of contemplation, Byron even in that of passion; and unless a poet, especially a poet at this time of day, is that, my interest in him is only slight, and my conviction that he will not finally stand high is firm.—ARNOLD, MATTHEW, 1864, *To J. D. Campbell, Sep. 22; Letters*, ed. Russell, vol. I, p. 278.

Scarcely any other artist in verse of the same rank has ever lived on such scanty revenues of thought (both pure, and applied or mixed) as Tennyson. While it cannot be pretended that he is a great sculptor, he is certainly an exquisite carver of luxuries in ivory; but we must be content to admire the caskets, for there are no jewels inside. His meditation at the best is that of a good leading-article; he is a pensioner on the thought of his age. He is continually petty with that littleness of the second degree which makes a man brag aloud in avoiding some well-known littleness of the first degree. His nerves are so weak that any largish event—a Crimean War or a Volunteer movement—sets him off in hysterics. Nothing gives one a keener insight into the want of robustness in the educated English intellect of the age than the fact that nine-tenths of our best-known literary men look upon him as a profound philosopher. When wax-flowers are oracular oaks, Dodona may be discovered in the Isle of Wight, but hardly until then.—THOMSON, JAMES ("B. V."), 1864, *The Poems of William Blake, Biographical and Critical Studies*.

Alfred Tennyson never seems to have cared much for the Sonnet; at least, he has very rarely clothed his own thoughts in this form. One sonnet of his, of moderate merit, I can remember; another, found in the earlier editions of his Lyrical Poems, has dropt out of the later.—TRENCH, RICHARD CHENEVIX, 1867, *Afternoon Lectures on Literature and Art*, p. 163.

We have in the present day one grand master of blank verse, the Poet Laureate. But where would he have been if Milton had not gone before him; or if the verse amidst which he works like an informing spirit had not existed at all? No doubt he might have invented it himself; but how different would the result have been from the verse which he will now leave behind him to lie side by side for comparison with that of the master of the epic.—MACDONALD, GEORGE, 1864, *Shakespeare, The Imagination*, p. 94.

Mr. Tennyson is not a great poet, unquestionably not a poet of the first rank, all but unquestionably not a poet of the second rank, and probably—though no contemporary perhaps can settle that, not even at the head of poets of the third rank, among whom he must ultimately take his place.—AUSTIN, ALFRED, 1870, *The Poetry of the Period*, p. 4.

Tennyson is a born poet, that is, a builder of airy palaces and imaginary castles. But the individual passion and absorbing preoccupations which generally guide the hands of such men are wanting to him; he found in himself no plan of a new edifice; he has built after all the rest; he has simply chosen amongst all forms the most elegant, ornate, exquisite. Of their beauties he has taken but the flower. At most, now and then, he has here and there amused himself by designing some genuinely English and modern cottage. If in this choice of architecture adopted or restored, we look for a trace of him, we shall find it, here and there, in some more finely sculptured frieze, in some more delicate and graceful sculptured rosework; but we shall only find it marked and sensible in the purity and elevation of the moral emotion which we shall carry away with us when we quit his gallery of art. . . . Without being a pedant, he is moral; he may be read in the family circle by night; he does not rebel against society and life; he speaks of God and the soul, nobly, tenderly, without ecclesiastical prejudice; there is no need to reproach him like Lord Byron; he has no violent and abrupt words, excessive and scandalous sentiments; he will pervert nobody. We shall not be troubled when we close the book; we may listen when we quit him, without contrast, to the grave voice of the master of the house, who repeats the evening prayers before the kneeling servants. And yet, when we quit him, we keep a smile of pleasure on our lips. . . . The people who have listened to Tennyson are better than our aristocracy of townsfolk and bohemians; but I prefer Alfred de Musset to Tennyson.—TAINE, H. A., 1871, *History of English Literature, tr. Van Laun, vol. II, bk. v, ch. vi, p.* 534, 537, 541.

Tennyson, to be sure, has been childishly petulant; but what have these whippersnappers, who cry "Go up, baldhead," done that can be named with some things of his? He has been the greatest artist in words we have had since Gray—and remember how Gray holds his own with little fuel, but real fire. He had the secret of the inconsumable oil, and so, I fancy, has Tennyson.—LOWELL, JAMES RUSSELL, 1872, *To C. E. Norton, Dec. 4; Letters, ed. Norton, vol. II, p.* 86.

Tennyson (let me not blaspheme against the Gods!) is not a musical, tho' in other respects (particularly in that of phrasemaking) a very wonderful writer.—LANIER, SIDNEY, 1873, *To Paul Hamilton Hayne, May 26; Letters, p.* 236.

Tennyson's verse is apt to be too richly dressed, too perfumed. The clothing is costlier than the thoughts can pay for. Hence at every re-reading of him he parts with some of his strength, so that after three or four repetitions he has little left for you. . . . Tennyson's poetry has often been too much leaf and spray for the branches, and too much branch for the trunk, and too much trunk for the roots. There is not living stock enough of thought deeply set in emotion to keep the leaves ever fresh and fragrant.—CALVERT, GEORGE H., 1875, *Essays Æsthetical, pp.* 83, 84.

As for Tennyson, he has, it must be owned, never failed in anything, for he has been careful not to overweight himself. . . . His melody is stately and rich, but not overwhelming. He delights by grace, but never swells by passion. The light of consummate art gleams forth from all he does, ut his moments of high exaltation of soul are very rare.—SMITH, GEORGE BARNETT, 1875, *Poets and Novelists, p.* 65.

Tennyson, though an aristocratic poet, strikes his roots into the common soil; not into the uncultured to be sure; he demands the best tilth and a deep garden loam; but he is no hot-house plant, as Morris, and Rossetti, and Swinburne are. How easy is his touch, how broad and universal the elements with which he deals!—BURROUGHS, JOHN, 1876, *What makes the Poet? The Galaxy, vol.* 22, *p.* 56.

Not of the howling dervishes of song,
Who craze the brain with their delirious dance,
Art thou, O sweet historian of the heart!
Therefore to thee the laurel leaves belong,
To thee our love and our allegiance,
For thy allegiance to the poet's art.
—LONGFELLOW, HENRY WADSWORTH, 1877, *Wapentake to Alfred Tennyson.*

The milk and water of which his books are composed chiefly, make it almost impossible to discover what was the original nature of the materials he has boiled down in it.—MALLOCK, W. H., 1878, *Every Man his own Poet, or the inspired Singer's Recipe Book, p.* 11.

Tennyson possesses a consummate science of rhythm, the rarest resources of phrase, taste, grace, distinction, every sort of cleverness, of research, of refinement. He is the author of lyric pieces unequalled in any language, some of infinite delicacy, some of engrossing pathos, some quivering like the blast of a knightly horn. He lacks only one thing, one supreme gift, the pinion-stroke which sweeps Ganymede into the empyrean, and casts him panting at Jupiter's feet. He sins by his very elegance; he is too civilized, too polished. He has tried every style—grave, gay, and passionate—the idyl, the ode, and the elegy, mock-heroics, epics, drama. There is no style in which he has not had brilliant success, and yet it may be said that he has explored nothing thoroughly. There are ardors in passion, troubles in thought, bankruptcies of the ideal in life, which Tennyson's note is not equal to expressing. His poetry (whether as matter of inspiration or of determination

I do not know) keeps too strictly to the region of decencies and conventions.—SCHERER, EDMOND, 1880-91, *Wordsworth and Modern Poetry in England, Essays on English Literature,* tr. *Saintsbury,* p. 193.

I cannot say that Mr. Tennyson's lifelong tone about women and their shortcomings has ever commended itself to my poor mind as the note of a very pure or high one. . . . It may not be the highest imaginable sign of poetic power or native inspiration that a man should be able to grind a beauty out of a deformity or carve a defect into a perfection; but whatever may be the comparative worth of his peculiar faculty, no poet surely ever had it in a higher degree or cultivated it with more patient and strenuous industry than Mr. Tennyson. Idler men, or men less qualified and disposed to expend such length of time and energy of patience on the composition and modification, and rearrangement and re-scisson and reissue, of a single verse or copy of verses, can only look on at such a course of labor with amused or admiring astonishment, and a certain doubt whether the linnets, to whose method of singing Mr. Tennyson compares his own, do really go through the training of such a musical gymnasium before they come forth qualified to sing. But for one thing, and that a thing of great price, this hard-working poet had never any need to work hard. Whatever the early imperfection of his ear, no man was ever born with a truer and more perfect eye. During fifty years he has never given us a book without unquestionable evidence of this. Among his many claims and credentials as a poet, there is none more unimpeachable or more clear. Nor can any kind of study be more helpful or delightful to the naturally elect student of poetry than that which traces through the work of any poet the vein of colour or of sentiment derived from his earliest or deepest impressions of nature.—SWINBURNE, ALGERNON CHARLES, 1881, *Tennyson and Musset, Fortnightly Review, vol.* 35, pp. 149, 151, *Miscellanies,* p. 257.

Mr. Tennyson is, as all know, before all things an artist; and as such he has formed for himself a composite and richly-wrought style, into the elaborate texture of which many elements, fetched from many lands and from many things, have entered. His selective mind has taken now something from Milton, now something from Shakespeare, besides pathetic cadences from the old ballads, stately wisdom from Greek tragedians, epic tones from Homer. And not only from the remote past, but from the present; the latest science and philosophy both lend themselves to his thought, and add metaphor and variety to his language. It is this elaboration of style, this "subtle trail of association, this play of shooting colors," pervading the texture of his poetry which has made him be called the English Virgil. But if it were asked, which of his immediate predecessors most influenced his nascent powers, it would seem that, while his early lyrics recall the delicate grace of Coleridge, and some of his idyls the plainness of Wordsworth, while the subtle music of Shelley has fascinated his ear, yet, more than any other poet, Keats, with his rich sensuous coloring, is the master whose style he has caught and prolonged.—SHAIRP, JOHN CAMPBELL, 1881, *Aspects of Poetry,* p. 129.

To those who enquired with open minds it appeared that things which good and learned men were doubting about must be themselves doubtful. Thus all around us, the intellectual light-ships had broken from their moorings, and it was then a new and trying experience. The present generation which has grown up in the floating condition, which has got used to it and has learned to swim for itself, will never know what it was to find the lights all drifting, the compasses all awry, and nothing left to steer by except the stars. In this condition the best and bravest of my own contemporaries determined to have done with insincerity, to find ground under their feet, to let the uncertain remain uncertain, but to learn how much and what we could honestly regard as true, and believe that and live by it. Tennyson became the voice of this feeling in poetry; Carlyle in what was called prose, though prose it was not, but something by itself, with a form and melody of its own. Tennyson's poems, the group of poems which closed with "In Memoriam," become to many of us what the "Christian Year" was to orthodox Churchmen. We read them, and they become part of our minds, the expression in exquisite language of the feelings which were working in ourselves.—FROUDE, JAMES ANTHONY, 1884, *Thomas Carlyle, A History of his Life in London, vol.* I, p. 248.

Tennyson may, without extravagance, be

called the poet of women. His portrait gallery is second only to that of Shakespeare in extent and splendor. His canvas is not so distinct and vivid as that of the great master, but the coloring is rich, and the outlines are drawn with a graceful pencil. Has he not created for us "The lily maid of Astolat"—"Elaine the fair, Elaine the loveable," and Maud with her exquisite face? . . . and that peerless wonder in "The Princess," who may well be matched with Wordsworth's "perfect woman." . . . He has drawn for us also the "Airy fairy, Lilian," with her arch innocence and her simple tricksomeness, a creature who seems too dainty for the responsibilities of the wife and the mother; and the variable Madeline, with her many moods, each sweeter than the last, her "delicious spites and darling angers," and those lovely frowns and lovelier smiles which chase one another in quick succession, like bursts of sunshine and shadow over the bosom of the purple hills. Then we have the faintly smiling Adeline, "scarce of earth nor all divine," with more of imagination than her sportive sisters, and deeps of thought to be plumbed by no superficial observer. We seem to rise higher still, to approach a more elevated grade of womanhood in sweet pale Margaret, with her aspect of painful thought and the tearful power and pathos of her eloquent eyes.—ADAMS, W. H. DAVENPORT, 1884, *Woman's Work and Worth*, p. 125.

Certainly amongst his Peers there is no such Poet.—BIRRELL, AUGUSTINE, 1884, *Obiter Dicta*, p. 94.

When the history of the ideas of the nineteenth century comes to be written, it will be recognised that Tennyson contributed to form the national mind far more powerfully than any young men can now understand. —BESANT, SIR WALTER, 1887, *Books Which Have Influenced Me*, p. 23.

There were few of Tennyson's poems which I did not know by heart without any attempt to commit them to memory.— FARRAR, FREDERIC WILLIAM, 1887, *Books Which Have Influenced Me*, p. 87.

Like all young Englishmen thirty years ago who had any affinity for literature, I was a reader of Tennyson. He has had few warmer admirers than I have been, and I now appreciate better than ever the finish and the concentrated strength of his workmanship. But I am not aware that Tennyson has had any great influence upon me, as there is little in his art that is available as an example for a writer of prose, and the special qualities of his genius belong to himself alone.—HAMERTON, PHILIP GILBERT, 1887, *Books Which Have Influenced Me*, p. 55.

Tennyson has been to the last two generations of Englishmen the national teacher of poetry. He has tried many new measures; he has ventured on many new rhythms; and he has succeeded in them all. He is at home equally in the slowest, most tranquil, and most meditative of rhythms, and in the rapidest and most impulsive.—MEIKLEJOHN, J. M. D., 1887, *The English Language: Its Grammar, History and Literature*, p. 356.

Tennyson came just before I left college. Mr. Emerson, who was always kind to young people, brought one of the early copies from England and lent it freely. We used to copy the poems in manuscript and pass them from hand to hand. I used to say that I was the first person who ever quoted "Locksley Hall" in public address. I did so in a college part; and whether the brag is literally true or not, I know I must have been among the earliest.—HALE, EDWARD EVERETT, 1888, *Books That Helped Me*, p. 11.

Let us attempt to get rid of every bias, and, thinking as dispassionately as we can, we still seem to read the name of Tennyson in the golden book of English poetry. I cannot think that he will ever fall to a lower place, or be among those whom only curious students pore over, like Gower, Drayton, Donne, and the rest. Lovers of poetry will always read him as they will read Wordsworth, Keats, Milton, Coleridge, and Chaucer. Look his defects in the face, throw them into the balance, and how they disappear before his merits! He is the last and youngest of the mighty race, born, as it were, out of due time, late, and into a feebler generation. . . . He is with Milton for learning, with Keats for magic and vision, with Virgil for graceful recasting of ancient golden lines, and in even the latest volume of his long life, "we may tell from the straw," as Homer says, "what the grain has been."—LANG, ANDREW, 1889, *Letters on Literature*, pp. 4, 8.

Who represents the height of the Victorian period, brought poetic style again to the Miltonic or Virgilian point of finish. In him a just conception of the work as a whole, a consciousness of his aims and how to attain them, together with a high standard of verbal execution, are combined with richness of fancy and sensuous magnificence worthy of an Elizabethan poet in all his glory.—SYMONDS, JOHN ADDINGTON, 1890, *Essays Speculative and Suggestive, vol.* II, *p.* 262.

Here is no touch ["Vastness"] of ingenuity, no trace of "originality," no single sign of cleverness; the rhymes are merely inevitable—there is no visible transformation of metaphor in deference to their suggestions; nothing is antic, peculiar, superfluous; but here is epic unity and completeness, here is a sublimation of experience expressed by means of a sublimation of style. It is unique in English, and for all that one can see it is like to remain unique this good while yet. The impression you take is one of singular loftiness of purpose and a rare nobility of mind. Looking upon life and time and the spirit of man from the heights of his eighty years, it has been given to the Master Poet to behold much that is hid to them in the plain or on the slopes beneath him, and beholding it to frame and utter a message so lofty in style and in significance so potent that it sounds as of this world indeed but from the confines of experience, the farthest kingdoms of mortality.—HENLEY, WILLIAM ERNEST, 1890, *Views and Reviews, p.* 156.

The distance which separates the author of "In Memoriam" and the "Idylls of the King" from the author of the "Georgics" and the "Æneid," is almost as considerable as the distance which separates all other poets now living from the author of "In Memoriam." It measures indeed the difference between a great classic whose power and charm will be felt in all ages, and in all regions co-extensive with civilised humanity, and a poet who will be a classic intelligible to those only who speak his language and drink his thoughts. . . . It is well that we should not accustom ourselves to talk and judge loosely. It requires very little critical discernment to forsee that among the English poets of the present century the first place will ultimately be assigned to Wordsworth, the second to Byron, and the third to Shelley. Had the Poet Laureate fulfilled the promise of the *Morte d'Arthur* he might have stood beside his master, and England might have had her "Æneid." As it is, he will probably occupy the same relative position in English poetry as De Quincey occupies in English prose. Both are Classics—immortal Classics—but they are Classics in fragments.—COLLINS, JOHN CHURTON, 1891, *Illustrations of Tennyson, pp.* 177, 178.

We may examine the series of Tennyson's volumes with care, and scarcely discover a copy of verses in which he can be detected as directly urged to expression by the popular taste. This prime favourite of the educated masses never courted the public, nor strove to serve it. He wrote to please himself, to win the applause of the "little clan," and each round of salvos from the world outside seemed to startle him in his obstinate retirement. If it grew easier and easier for him to consent to please the masses, it was because he familiarised them more and more with his peculiar accent. He led literary taste, he did not dream of following it.—GOSSE, EDMUND, 1891, *The Influence of Democracy, Questions at Issue, p.* 40.

In regard of his poetical works, his fame already stands too high for panegyric; and times to come will surely confirm the contemporary verdict which places him in the front rank of English singers; side by side, indeed, with the greatest names. No man, with the exception of Shakespere, has wielded with greater vigor, grace, and variety that noblest metre of the English language, the blank verse, the use and value of which Lord Tennyson may almost be said to have revived. . . . Truly the echoes of Lord Tennyson's song will live forever and forever, and roll from soul to soul. I do not wonder at the serene self-possession, I had almost said the intellectual complacency, of the poet. He has achieved! Behind him lies the completed task of the spirit of the nineteenth century, especially in his own land, rendered articulate. Beyond all dispute he is the representative singer of the great reign of Victoria, having no doubt for worthy contemporaries, rather than rivals, such names as Browning, Swinburne, and those of one or two others; but by the sure judgment of posterity, as well as the reverence and estimation of his day, he reigns the laurelled king of English singers.—ARNOLD, SIR EDWIN, 1891, *A Day with Lord Tennyson, The Forum, vol.* 12, *pp.* 536, 545.

In spite of cliques and affectations which would exalt this or that minor favourite to a high place on Parnassus at our bard's expense, he is, and for sane and healthy criticism he will always remain, the prince of English Victorian singers. No petty detractions can make our Tennyson less than he is; no odious comparisons can mar his kingship. We may admit, indeed, the magic music of Swinburne's earlier voice, now, alas! grown hoarser; we may allow the broad human insight of Browning's dramatic genius, too often spoiled by the easy optimism of the well-fed, well-clad, middle-class Englishman; we may admire the even flow of Matthew Arnold's studied criticism of life, running calm and clear as his own beloved Isis by Godstow nunnery; but no rival can displace that many-sided Tennyson from his throne of song, or make him any less than our chief of poets. He has compassed the gamut of poesy in all its moods and passions. In this matter we need not wait for the judgment of posterity; for we *are* posterity: he has lived to hear after ages praise him.—ALLEN, GRANT, 1892, *Tennyson's Homes at Aldworth and Farringford, English Illustrated Magazine*, vol. 10, p. 150.

When that great shade into the silence vast
Through thinking silence passed;
When he, our century's soul and voice, was hushed,
We who,—appalled, bowed, crushed,—
Within the holy moonlight of his death
Waited the parting breath—
Ah, not in song
Might we our grief prolong.
Silence alone, O golden spirit fled!
Silence alone could mourn that silence dread.
—GILDER, RICHARD WATSON, 1892, *The Silence of Tennyson, The Critic*, vol. 21, p. 204.

'Tis o'er; he leaves the lonely road
  Whereon he fared so long;
The gentlest, brightest Knight of God,
  The Galahad of Song.
The only one of all our knights
  Who wore the snow-white mail,
And turned from strife and lewd delights,
  To seek the Holy Grail.
His path was not where factions cry,
  Or where the fretful moan;
Where life runs stillest he passed by,
  In maiden thought alone.
Calm were the ways his white steed trod,
  Calm were the heavens and air;
Where'er he rode and sang of God
  The world grew very fair.
—BUCHANAN, ROBERT, 1892, *The Galahad of Song*.

Akin to this clear-cut form was the accuracy and minuteness of observation which made him so successful a painter of domesticated Nature. His achievements in this direction may have been over-estimated. He is not immaculate; the songster nightingale is always with him, the female, not the male, as it is in Nature: he was probably misled by the myth of Philomela. But the minuteness and independence of his powers of observation are acknowledged on all hands, and go naturally with the clear vision of the artist in words. Yet here again the result is to impair the true poetic effect, except of course in the purely landscape poems, where this power gave him an advantage over every predecessor in that *genre* of poetry.—JACOBS, JOSEPH, 1892, *Alfred Tennyson, Literary Studies*, p. 159.

Thy place is with the Immortals. Who shall guage
Thy rank among thy peers of world-wide song?
Others, it may be, touched a note more strong,
Scaled loftier heights, or glowed with fiercer rage;
But who like thee could slay our modern Doubt?
Or soothe the sufferers with a tenderer heart?
Or dress gray legends with such perfect grace?
Or nerve life's world-worn pilgrims for their part?
Who, since our English tongue first grew, has stirred
More souls to noble effort by his word?
More reverent who of Man, of God, of Truth?
More piteous of the sore-tried strength of Youth?
Thy chaste, white Muse, loathing the Pagan rout,
Would drive with stripes the goatish Satyr out.
Thy love of Righteousness preserved thee pure.
Thy lucid genius scorned to lurk obscure,
And all thy jewelled Art and native Grace
Were consecrate to God and to the Race.
—MORRIS, SIR LEWIS, 1892, *Alfred Lord Tennyson, Oct. 6*.

All ages thou hast honored with thine art,
And ages yet unborn thou wilt be part
Of all songs pure and true!
Thine now the universal homage due
From Old and New World—aye, and still the New!
— RILEY, JAMES WHITCOMB, 1892, *Tennyson: England, Oct. 5*.

Not England's pride alone, this Lord of Song!
  We—heirs to Shakespeare's and to Milton's speech—
Claim heritage from Tennyson's proud years:
  To us his spacious, splendid lines belong—
We, too, repeat his praises, each to each —
  We share his glory, and we share your tears.
—MOULTON, LOUISE CHANDLER, 1892, *From Over the Seas*.

Tennyson need not fear comparison with the scholarly poets who preceded him. Jonson and Milton were very learned men. Dryden was a good scholar, and may be thought to have achieved, at least once, when he translated the Twenty-ninth Ode of the third book of Horace, the feat of surpassing his own author. Samuel Johnson, a real poet at his best, knew Juvenal as well as Tennyson knew Lucretius. But not one of them, not even rare Ben himself, was more thoroughly imbued with the spirit of classical antiquity than the author of the "Lotos Eaters." Milton is sometimes the servant rather than the master of his learning. He was not unfrequently, if one may say so without irreverence, the worse for Latin. Tennyson was the better for everything he read.—PAUL, HERBERT, 1893, *The Classical Poems of Tennyson, Men and Letters*, p. 21.

I will remind the reader that for any estimation of Tennyson's final opinions, the later poems are, of course, the most significant. In his last years there was inequality of poetic merit,—an inequality which admitted nevertheless of more than one masterpiece;—but there was no decline in intellectual grasp and power. Nay, I think that all will some day recognise that there was even a lifelong gain in wisdom; a lifelong maintenance of that position, in sympathy with and yet in advance of his time, which was first manifest when "In Memoriam"—now so intelligible and so orthodox—perplexed as well as charmed the reading public of its earlier day.— MYERS, FREDERIC W. H., 1893, *Modern Poets and the Meaning of Life, Nineteenth Century*, vol. 33, p. 108.

Tennyson kicks the beam weighed against any of his robust predecessors. By a sort of eclectic selection he seems to have resumed in himself many of the qualities of his immediate masters, but always with a loss of their primal vigor and freshness. Compared with Keats he is Praxiteles after Pheidias; compared with Wordsworth he is a chanter in a cathedral choir beside a Druid of the dawn.—MOORE, CHARLES LEONARD, 1893, *The Future of Poetry, The Forum*, vol. 14, p. 774.

When he separated himself from men he did not banish himself from their interests. It was an isolation for the purposes of his craft; it was not an alienation from thoughts and movements of his day. He still kept a keen eye and ready heart for the stirring interests of his time. You have only to recall how he sang, in his earliest songs warning men not to fall into subjection to the tyranny of the past. He was no vassal of the past, but the child of his age, and as a child of his age his face was set forward. As a child of his age he ripened with ripening thoughts of the men and women round about him; he realized that whatever the lavish inheritance of the past was, the future was before us, and in reverent mindfulness of it we must do our present work.— CARPENTER, WILLIAM BOYD, 1893, *The Message of Tennyson, A Sermon in Westminster Abbey, April* 30, p. 17.

Tennyson was not persecuted. He was not (and more honour to him for his clearness) even misunderstood. I have never met with the contention that he stood an inch ahead of the thought of his time. As for seeing through death and life and his own soul, and having the marvel of the everlasting will spread before him like an open scroll,—well, to begin with, I doubt if these things ever happened to any man. Heaven surely has been, and is, more reticent than the verse implies. But if they ever happened, Tennyson most certainly was not the man they happened to.— QUILLER-COUCH, A. T., 1894, *Adventures in Criticism*, p. 251.

The pre-Raphaelites have for twenty years exercised a great influence on the rising generation of English poets. All the hysterical and degenerate have sung with Rossetti of "damozels" and of the Virgin Mary, have with Swinburne eulogized unnatural license, crime, hell, and the devil. They have, with Morris, mangled language in bardic strains, and in the manner of the "Canterbury Tales;" and if the whole of English poetry is not to-day unmitigatedly pre-Raphaelite, it is due merely to the fortunate accident that, contemporaneously with the pre-Raphaelites, so sound a poet as Tennyson has lived and worked. The official honours bestowed on him as Poet Laureate, his unexampled success among readers, pointed him out to a part at least of the petty strugglers and aspirants as worthy of imitation, and so it comes about that among the chorus of the lily-bearing mystics there are also heard other street-singers who follow the poet of the "Idylls of the King."—NORDAU, MAX, 1895, *Degeneration*, p. 99.

His poetry, with its clearness of conception and noble simplicity of expression, its discernment of the beautiful and its power of revealing and shaping it with mingled strength and harmony, has become an integral part of the literature of the world, and so long as purity and loftiness of thought expressed in perfect form have power to charm, will remain a possession for ever.—ROWE, F. J., AND WEBB, W. T., 1895, *ed. Lancelot and Elaine, General Introduction, p.* xxviii.

In the case of no English poet is it more important and interesting than in the case of Tennyson, considering the excellence of his own work in the first place, and altogether unparalleled extent of his influence in the second, to trace the nature and character of his poetical quality.—SAINTSBURY, GEORGE, 1896, *A History of Nineteenth Century Literature, p.* 256.

Tennyson's chief claim to fame is that, coming after so many poets who had worked in the same field, the field of nature, he is still himself—not Wordsworth, nor Shelley, nor another. To this he attained mainly by two things—brevity and precision, but mainly by precision.—SPENDER, HAROLD, 1897, *Tennyson: a Study of Poetic Workmanship, Fortnightly Review, vol.* 68, *p.* 783.

More than any other poet Tennyson has accepted the verdicts of modern science. Not in any just sense a scientist himself, he was, nevertheless, an observer of nature and a student of the teachings of the scientists. These teachings, with a fulness and clearness never before known in poetry, he gave to mankind in a literary form.—BROWN, CALVIN S., 1897, *ed. Enoch Arden and the Two Locksley Halls, Preface, p.* vi.

A poet who is, as I think, *the* English poet of this age of ours: the poet who will, in the event, hold much the same predominant position in English literature of the nineteenth century as Pope holds in English literature of the eighteenth century. There are perhaps only two poets who could dispute that position with Tennyson—Wordsworth and Browning. . . . There is not a poem of Tennyson's—or there is hardly one —which is not the outcome of prolonged meditation and prolonged labour: the result of the supreme art which veils itself in the achievement. His work is classical in the best sense of the word: classical in its "happy coalescence of matter and style." If you take up Pope's "Essay on Criticism" —and I know of no more valuable aid to judgment on the subject with which it deals —and test Tennyson's work by the rules and precepts so admirably given there, you will find they bear the test singularly well. . . . I find Tennyson peculiarly and completely English in his cast of thought. He is distinguished, in the highest degree, by what I regard as the dominant English characteristic—reverence for duty as the supreme law of life: the subordination of all the ideals to the moral ideal.—LILLY, W. S., 1897, *The Mission of Tennyson, Fortnightly Review, vol.* 67, *pp.* 239, 240, 248.

He was not only keenly sensitive to criticism, but he was also keenly critical of himself. It is doubtful if any poet of the time has had a sounder judgment of the quality of his own verse. His ear had acquired extraordinary sensitiveness; his feeling for words was quite as delicate as his sense of sound; and this instinctive perception of the musical qualities in sounds and words had been trained with the highest intelligence and the utmost patience. If to natural aptitude and trained skill there are added great power of expression and depth and volume of thought, it is evident that all the elements of the true poet were present. Poe had a magical command of sounds; Tennyson had the same magic with a far wider knowledge of the potencies and mysteries of words. No detail escaped him; nothing was insignificant in that perfection of expression toward which he consciously and unweariedly pressed. His artistic instinct is seen in nothing more clearly than in his passion to match his thought with the words which were elected from all eternity to express it. If he did not always feel the inevitableness of every word in a perfect style, as Flaubert felt it and worked for it with a kind of heart-breaking passion, he was alive to that subtle adjustment of sound to sense which makes a true style in its entirety as resonant of the deepest thought of a writer as Westminster is resonant of every note of its organ.—MABIE, HAMILTON WRIGHT, 1897, *The Life of Tennyson, Atlantic Monthly, vol.* 80, *p.* 583.

The man whom the English have been extolling, while their French neighbours have been picking his great rival to pieces, was obviously a noble and conscientious artist in verse, a poet fully impressed with the sacred nature of his calling, a critic of remarkably acute powers, a widely read and observant student of nature and of men, an intensely spiritual seeker after God, a loyal patriot and friend—in short, an ideal character of a high and attractive type. Such was the man—except perhaps in his rôle of critic—that had stood out behind the Poems; such is the man that stands out behind the Biography. But neither the poetry nor the memoir proves Tennyson to have been the profound seer that Mr. Gladstone and other contemporaries have thought him, nor does either source of information disprove the charge that he was morbidly sensitive, and hence unable to give full expression to the lyric passion that was a fundamental constituent of his nature. . . . If, however, Tennyson's longer poems are to be forgotten save for selected passages, and if his reputation is to rest on the shorter poems in his early manner and on the tradition of his artistic command of rhythm and diction; if, furthermore, the world that is now sated with composite art renews its youth through some stirring crisis, and once more demands passion as a primary element of literature, will the bard of Aldworth and Farringford hold his own against the poet of the streets of Paris? Surely he will in spite of all that may be said about the suppression of his passion and about the deficiencies of his longer poems. Should the world come once more to demand passion, it will be Byron that will eclipse Tennyson, not Alfred de Musset, whose star will nevertheless rise splendidly in the poetic heavens.—TRENT, W. P., 1898, *Tennyson and Musset Once More, The Bookman, vol. 7, pp. 108, 113.*

The emancipation of woman had made but little progress in Tennyson's day. He may not have contributed much to this end, but his ideas were certainly in advance of prevailing opinion. There is one respect, however, in which his view of womankind never can be excelled; that is, his reverential regard for her, and the ennobling and glorifying enthusiasm with which he treats the mutual love of man and woman. This is only what we should expect, when we remember his affection for his mother and for his wife, as well as all the story of his relations to his family.—WARD, WILLIAM G., 1898, *Tennyson's Debt to Environment, p. 52*

Tennyson was profoundly in touch with his age. There were not many men who understood it better than he. He had his finger on its pulse, and his ear upon its breast; so that he heard its very heart beat. He was acquainted with its problems, and he knew also the tremendous issues involved in the attitude of his age toward them.—SNEATH, E. HERSHEY, 1900, *The Mind of Tennyson, p. 21.*

You can get the poetry of the Alhambra only by moonlight; and to a mind so wholly poetic as Tennyson's it seemed possible to get the poetry of conduct only by seeing it in the moonlight of departed years. To-day is matter-of-fact in dress and design; mediævalism was fanciful, picturesque, romantic. Chivalry was the poetry of the Christ in civilization; and the knight warring to recover the tomb of God was the poem among soldiers, and in entire consonance with his nature, Tennyson's poetic genius flits back into the poetic days, as I have seen birds flit back into a forest. In Tennyson's poetry two things are clear. They are mediæval in location; they are modern in temper. Their geography is yesterday, their spirit is to-day; and so we have the questions and thoughts of our era as themes for Tennyson's voice and lute. His treatment is ancient: his theme is recent. He has given diagnosis and alleviation of present sickness, but hides face and voice behind morion and shield.—QUAYLE, WILLIAM A., 1900, *A Hero and Some Other Folks, p. 204.*

Why is it that the "Idylls of the King" and the "In Memoriam" contain so many passages that the world will quite willingly let die? If the chief thing in poetry were the style, one part of these poems would be as good as another, for the style is uniform throughout. The answer, in all such cases, is that "soul is form and doth the body make." What is wanting in the weak places of these great poems is the soul, the poetic vision and enthusiasm, the absence of which no style can compensate.—BEECHING, H. C., 1901, *Expression in Poetry, p. 33.*

Tennyson lived in the time of a conflict more crucial and frightful than any European struggle, the conflict between the apparent artificiality of morals and the apparent immorality of science. A ship more symbolic and menacing than any foreign three-decker hove in sight in that time— the great, gory pirate-ship of Nature, challenging all the civilisations of the world. And his supreme honour is this, that he behaved like his own imaginary snubnosed rogue. His honour is that in that hour he

JOHN GREENLEAF WHITTIER

Engraving from an Etching.

HARRIET BEECHER STOWE

Engraving from an Original Portrait by Chappel.

despised the flowers and embroideries of Keats as the counter-jumper might despise his tapes and cottons. He was by nature a hedonistic and pastoral poet, but he leapt from his poetic counter and till and struck, were it but with his gimcrack mandolin, home.—CHESTERTON, G. K.,1902, *Tennyson, The Bookman, vol.* 16, *p.* 350.

Tennyson's keen and abiding interest in religious and ethical problems is shown throughout his work; his fervid patriotism was conspicuous at all times, and he took his side unhesitatingly in the great political issues of the day.— BROTHERTON, MARY, 1903, *Chambers's Encyclopædia of English Literature, ed. Patrick, vol.* III, *p.* 542.

John Greenleaf Whittier
1807–1892

1807, December 17—John Greenleaf Whittier was born at Haverhill, Massachusetts. 1815, December 7—Elizabeth Whittier was born. 1826, June 8—Whittier's first published poem, "The Exile's Departure," appeared in Newburyport *Free Press.* 1827, May 1—Entered Haverhill Academy, where he spent two terms of six months each. 1828–29—Spent the winter in Boston, editing the *American Manufacturer.* 1830—Began editing the Haverhill *Gazette.* Went to Hartford to edit the *New England Review.* 1831—Published his first book, "Legends of New England." 1832—Published "Moll Pitcher." 1833—Published "Justice and Expediency." November. Went to Philadelphia as delegate to National Anti-slavery Society. December. One of the committee to draft the "Declaration of Sentiments." 1835—Elected Representative of Haverhill in State Legislature. Stoned by mob in Concord, New Hampshire. 1836—Again assumed editorial charge of the Haverhill *Gazette.* Sold the Haverhill farm, and removed to Amesbury. Published "Mogg Megone." 1837—Isaac Knapp, of Boston, published first edition of Whittier's poems, entitled "Poems written during the Progress of the Abolition Question in the United States, between the Years 1830 and 1838." 1838—Became editor of the *Pennsylvania Freeman* of Philadelphia. May 17. Pennsylvania Hall, in which was Whittier's office, burned by mob. 1840—February. Severed his connection with the *Freeman,* and returned to Amesbury. 1843—Published "Lays of my Home, and Other Poems." 1844—Went to Lowell for six months to edit the *Middlesex Standard.* 1845—Published "The Stranger in Lowell." 1847—Began writing for the Washington *National Era.* 1849—Published "Voices of Freedom." 1850—Published "Songs of Labour." 1854—Published "Maud Muller" in the *Era.* 1857—Whittier's mother died. Contributed poem entitled "The Gift of Tritemius" to the initial number of the *Atlantic Monthly.* Ticknor & Fields published complete edition of Whittier's poems, known as "Blue and Gold Edition." 1858—Published "Telling the Bees" in the *Atlantic.* Elected Overseer of Harvard College. 1860—Published "Home Ballads, and Other Poems." Member of the electoral college. Received the degree of M. A. from Harvard. 1863—Published "In War Time, and Other Poems." 1864—Elizabeth Whittier died. 1866—Published "Snow-Bound" and prose works in two volumes. Received degree of LL. D. from Brown University. 1867—Published "The Tent on the Beach." 1868—Published "Among the Hills, and Other Poems." 1870—Published "Miriam, and Other Poems." 1874—Published "Mabel Martin." 1876—Removed to Oak Knoll, Danvers. Wrote the Centennial Hymn for the Exposition at Philadelphia. 1877—December 17. Dinner, in honour of Whittier, given by Houghton, Mifflin & Co. to the contributors to the *Atlantic Monthly.* 1881—Published "The King's Missive, and Other Poems." 1886—Published "St. Gregory's Guest, and Other Poems." 1888—Riverside Edition of Whittier's writings was published. 1892—Published "At Sundown." September 7. John Greenleaf Whittier died at Hampton Falls, New Hampshire.—BURTON, RICHARD, 1901, *John Greenleaf Whittier (Beacon Biographies), p.* xi.

PERSONAL

He has a good exterior, a figure slender and tall, a beautiful head with refined features, black eyes full of fire, dark complexion, a fine smile, and lively but very nervous manner. Both soul and spirit have overstrained the nervous cords and wasted the body. He belongs to those natures who would advance with firmness and joy to martyrdom in a good cause, and yet who are never comfortable in society, and who look as if they would run out of the door every moment. He lives with his mother and sister in a country-house to which I have promised to go. I feel that I should enjoy myself with Whittier, and could make him feel at ease with me. I know from my own experience what this nervous bashfulness, caused by the over-exertion of the brain, requires, and how persons who suffer therefrom ought to be met and treated.—BREMER, FREDERIKA, 1853, *Homes of the New World.*

I knew quite well that I was in the presence of one of the purest-minded and most gifted men in America; a man whose name and fame are world-wide, and "as familiar as household words;" a man whose mighty thoughts are winged with words of fire; but he is so unassuming, so accessible, so frank, and so well "posted up" on all matters of news, that, whatever subject is broached, one feels at home in the presence of a *friend*, while conversing with him. This eminent poet of the slave is forty years of age. His temperament is nervous-bilious; he is tall, slender, and straight as an Indian; has a superb head; his brow looks like a white cloud, under his raven hair; eyes large, black as sloes, and glowing with expression. He belongs to the society of Friends, and in matters of dress and address, he is of "the strictest sort." Should a stranger meet him in the street, with his collarless coat and broad-brimmed hat, he would not discover anything remarkable in his appearance, certainly would not dream that he had seen the Elliott of America. But, let him uncover that head, and see those star-like eyes flashing under such a magnificent forehead, and he would know, at a glance, that a great heart, a great soul, and a great intellect, must light up such a radiant frontispiece.—BUNGAY, GEORGE W., 1854, *Crayon Sketches, or Off-Hand Takings.*

Some blamed him, some believed him good,—
  The truth lay doubtless 'twixt the two,—
He reconciled as best he could
  Old faith and fancies new.

In him the grave and playful mixed,
  And wisdom held with folly truce,
And Nature compromised betwixt
  Good fellow and recluse.

He loved his friends, forgave his foe;
  And, if his words were harsh at times,
He spared his fellow-men,—his blows
  Fell only on their crimes.
—WHITTIER, JOHN GREENLEAF, 1857, *My Namesake.*

Before his human heart we bend,
  Far nobler than his noblest song.
—LARCOM, LUCY, 1877, *Whittier, Poetical Works*, p. 254.

O thou, whose daily life anticipates
  The life to come, and in whose thought and word
The spiritual world preponderates,
  Hermit of Amesbury! thou too hast heard
Voices and melodies from beyond the gates,
  And speakest only when thy soul is stirred!
—LONGFELLOW, HENRY WADSWORTH, 1877, *The Three Silences of Molinos.*

The faith that lifts, the courage that sustains,
  These thou wert sent to teach:
Hot blood of battle, beating in thy veins,
  Is turned to gentle speech.
Not less, but more, than others hast thou striven;
  Thy victories remain;
The scars of ancient hate, long since forgiven,
  Have lost their power to pain.
Apostle pure of Freedom and of Right,
  Thou had'st thy one reward:
Thy prayers were heard, and flashed upon thy sight
  The Coming of the Lord!
Now, sheathed in myrtle of thy tender songs,
  Slumbers the blade of truth;
But Age's wisdom, crowning thee, prolongs
  The eager hope of Youth!
—TAYLOR, BAYARD, 1877, *A Friend's Greeting, Poetical Works, Household Ed.*, p. 321.

From this far realm of pines I waft thee now
  A brother's greeting, Poet, tried and true;
So thick the laurels on thy reverend brow,
  We scarce can see the white locks glimmering through!
O pure of thought! Earnest in heart as pen,
  The tests of time have left thee undefiled;
And o'er the snows of threescore years and ten
  Shines the unsullied aureole of a child.
—HAYNE, PAUL HAMILTON, 1877, *To the Poet Whittier on his 70th Birthday.*

I should be glad to celebrate in verse the seventieth return of John Greenleaf Whittier's birthday; but I find I must content myself with humble prose. . . . I rejoice at the dispensation which has so long spared to the world a poet whose life is as beautiful as his verse, who has occupied himself only with noble themes and treated them nobly and grandly, and whose songs in the evening of life are as sweet and thrilling as those of his vigorous meridian. If the prayers of those who delight in his poems shall be heard, that life will be prolonged in all its serenity for the sake of a world which is the better of his having lived.—BRYANT, WILLIAM CULLEN, 1877, *Letter on Whittier's Seventieth Birthday.*

Peaceful by birthright as a virgin lake,
The lily's anchorage, which no eyes behold
Save those of stars, yet for thy brother's sake
That lay in bonds, thou blewst a blast as bold
As that wherewith the heart of Roland brake,
Far heard across the New World and the Old.
—LOWELL, JAMES RUSSELL, 1882, *To Whittier on his Seventy-fifth Birthday, Heartease and Rue,* p. 43.

Whittier has never forgotten his connection with the gentle craft in early life; nor has he been ashamed to own fellowship with its humble but worthy members. What he thinks of the craft itself, and of the spirit of the men who have followed it, may be learned from his lines addressed to shoemakers in the "Songs of Labor," published in 1850.—WINKS, WILLIAM EDWARD, 1882, *Lives of Illustrious Shoemakers,* p. 279.

Of Mr. Whittier's social side less has been written than of the reformatory and literary. He is generally spoken of as a shy man, avoiding all society. If by society we mean large parties, dinners, and receptions, the general idea is a true one. But I think that no one enjoys the society of a few friends better than this accredited society hater; and with these, his humor, and sometimes keen wit, finds ready play. No one relishes a good story more, nor can relate one with better grace. The sense of the ludicrous is very vivid, and the absurdities of life and its situations strike him never more forcibly than when they involve himself. Thus in the many instances where the celebrity hunter, the autograph tramp, has ferreted him out, some point of the ludicrous in the experience has lighted up, and made a little comedy of what would otherwise have been an unmitigated bore.—PERRY, NORA, 1883, *A Personal Sketch of Whittier, John Greenleaf Whittier, a Biography by Francis H. Underwood,* p. 386.

Recurring once more to the matter of character, it must be said that few men have presented such a tempting and such a baffling study. While he is neither "odd" nor "eccentric" (in usual parlance), his personality is marked, and there is a strongly individual flavor in all his utterances. Many great writers adopt the state of kings, and their only sincere worshippers are those who adore from a distance. Goethe came to be more royal than the Grand Duke whom he served. In the case of Whittier, with his perception of the beautiful, his devotion to right, his hatred of falsity and oppression, there are found many endearing human traits—generous sympathy, a well-spring of humor, a relish for native wit and for quaint phases of character. He is utterly free from the vanity, envy, and jealousy which belittle so many writers. Some imperfection clings to all souls, but few have been observed in our time so well poised, so pure, and so stainless as his.—UNDERWOOD, FRANCIS H., 1883, *John Greenleaf Whittier, a Biography,* p. 375.

Dear Angel: Is it your birthday? Thank Heaven you were born! Thank Heaven a thousand times more that you will never die, for a kingdom of heaven is within you. Sweetheart, I am going to Newburyport this week, but I don't believe you will be in Amesbury so soon. Early next week I am going to Salem, and thence I will run up and sit with you for an hour or two "between meals"—I shall not come to stay—but just tell you how lovely you are, and how blessed the ground on which you stand, and a few little newsy things like that. And if you don't want me, why, I will run away and come again—but I will write you beforehand of the exact day. Will this suit you? Tell a lie for once, and say yes,—there's the dearest of dears. Always *truly,* whatever else I am.—DODGE, MARY A. (GAIL HAMILTON), 1884, *To Whittier, Dec. 17; Life in Letters,* ed. Dodge, vol. II, p. 855.

Through all thy life the foe of every wrong,
Strong of heart to labour, high of soul to pray,
Guide to recall when errant footsteps stray;
What blessed memories round thy dear name throng!
—MOULTON, LOUISE CHANDLER, 1887, *To John Greenleaf Whittier on his Eightieth Birthday.*

I doubt if any boy ever rose to intellectual eminence who had fewer opportunities for education than Whittier. He had no such pasturage to browse on as is open to every reader, who, by simply reaching them out, can lay his hands on the treasures of English literature. He had to borrow books wherever they could be found among his neighbors who were willing to lend, and he thought nothing of walking several miles for one volume. The only instruction he received was at the district school, which was open a few weeks in midwinter, and at the Haverhill Academy, which he attended two terms of six months each, paying for his tuition by work done in his spare hours. A feeble spirit would have languished under such disadvantages, and how he would have bewailed them after outliving them! But Whittier scarcely refers to them, and, instead of begging for pity, he takes them as part of the common lot, and seems to remember only what was beautiful and good.—RIDEING, WILLIAM H., 1887, *The Boyhood of Living Authors*, p. 112.

The poet's dwelling in Amesbury is exceedingly simple and exquisitely neat, the exterior of a pale cream color, with many trees and shrubs about it, while, within, one room opens into another till you reach the study that should be haunted by the echoes of all sweet sounds, for here have been written the most of those verses full of the fitful music,

Of winds that out of dreamland blew.

Here, in the proper season, the flames of a cheerful fire dance upon the brass andirons of the open hearth, in the centre of a wall lined with books; water-colors by Harry Fenn and Lucy Larcom and Celia Thaxter, together with interesting prints, hang on the other walls, rivaled, it may be, by the window that looks down a sunny little orchard, and by the glass-topped door through which you see the green dome of Powow Hill. What worthies have been entertained in this enticing place? Garrison, and Phillips, and Higginson, and Wasson, and Emerson, and Fields, and Bayard Taylor, and Alice and Phœbe Cary, and Gail Hamilton, and Anna Dickinson, are only a few of the names that one first remembers, to say nothing of countless sweet souls, unknown to any other roll of fame than heaven's, who have found the atmosphere there kindred to their own.—SPOFFORD, HARRIET PRESCOTT, 1888, *John Greenleaf Whittier, Authors at Home*, ed. Gilder, p. 350.

Best loved and saintliest of our singing train,
  Earth's noblest tributes to thy name belong.
A lifelong record closed without a stain,
  A blameless memory shrined in deathless song.
Lift from its quarried ledge a flawless stone;
  Smooth the green turf and bid the tablet rise,

And on its snow-white surface carve alone
  These words,—he needs no more,—HERE WHITTIER LIES.
—HOLMES, OLIVER WENDELL, 1892, *In Memory of John Greenleaf Whittier, Poetical Works*, Cambridge Ed., p. 297.

The house where Mr. Whittier was a guest was ornamented indeed; for a more genial, suggestive, inspiring friend, or one with a more distinct personality, has rarely given the blessing and benediction of his presence to any home, and the family fortunate enough to have him with them at the fireside, counted themselves especially favored and enriched. He was unique in his absolute simplicity and truthfulness—the simplicity and truthfulness of clear conviction and sturdy strength, and of a nature that in its tenderness and justice seemed to reflect the very heart of God. Mr. Whittier was responsive to every appeal, whether of joy or sorrow, as his hearty laugh, his "smartly smitten knee," at some amusing story, or his burst of righteous indignation, at a tale of injustice and wrong, plainly showed. As intense in nature as he was sagacious, though ordinarily shy and cautious and reserved, he could, under favorable conditions, blossom into rare graciousness and sympathy of speech and manner. Those who have sat with him of an evening, in a quiet firelit room, will never forget his charming vivacity and pleasant confidences, alternating with dreamy silence and repose.—CLAFLIN, MARY B., 1893, *Personal Recollections of John G. Whittier*, p. 7.

His friends were to Whittier, more than to most men, an unfailing source of daily happiness and gratitude. With the advance of years, and the death of his unmarried sister, his friends became all in all to him. They were his mother, his sister, and his brother; but in a certain sense they were always friends of the imagination. He saw some of them only at rare intervals, and sustained his relations with them chiefly in his hurried correspondence. He never suffered himself to complain of what they were not; but what they were, in loyalty to chosen aims, and in their affection for him, was an unending source of pleasure. With the shortcomings of others he dealt gently, having too many shortcomings of his own, as he was accustomed to say, with true humility. He did not, however, look upon the failings of his friends with indifferent eyes. "How strange it is!" he once said. "We see those whom we love going to the very verge of the precipice of self-destruction, yet it is not in our power to hold them back!" A life of invalidism made consecutive labor of any kind an impossibility. For years he was only able to write for half an hour or less, without stopping to rest, and these precious moments were devoted to some poem or other work for the press, which was almost his only source of income. His letters suffered, from a literary point of view; but they were none the less delightful to his friends; to the world of literature they are perhaps less important than those of most men who have achieved a high place.—FIELDS, MRS. JAMES T., 1893, *Whittier, Notes of his Life and of his Friendships*, p. 3.

Mr. Whittier's remains were interred in the village cemetery, in the section reserved for the Society of Friends. His lot is surrounded by a well-kept arbor vitæ hedge. At the corner where his brother is buried is a tall cedar, and at the foot of his own grave is another symmetrical tree of the same kind. Between him and his brother lie their father and mother, their two sisters, their aunt Mercy and uncle Moses. These comprise the whole family commemorated in the poem "Snow-Bound." Plain marble tablets, all exactly alike, mark these graves, and the poet's tombstone, afterward erected, is of the same simple pattern. The cemetery is upon an eminence overlooking the valley of the Powow in which nestles the thriving village of Amesbury; and the broad waters of the noble Merrimac, here a tidal stream, are close at hand, with the hills of old Newbury beyond. It is a spot midway between his birthplace and the place where he died,—a fit resting-place for him whose verse has celebrated every phase of the scenery it overlooks. Hither for all time will come those who love the memory and admire the genius of the prophet of freedom, the poet of New England life.—PICKARD, SAMUEL T., 1894, *Life and Letters of John Greenleaf Whittier*, vol. II, p. 771.

Seldom have I known any one who better relished jokes and humorous anecdotes than Mr. Whittier; and he told them with that peculiar zest and sparkle which so delights the hearer. Both in letters and conversation, he would often use a term or tone with most amusing effect. . . . Mr. Whittier was himself notably fearless and self-reliant, in regard to his literary opnions, as well as all others. He was not afraid of being the first to commend what he liked, and did not wait to hear what others thought, before venturing on its praise. Best of all, he stood by what he said, and was as ready to write it as to speak it, ever willing that whatever he spoke should be used in printed criticism.— BATES, CHARLOTTE FISKE, 1894, *Whittier Desultoria, The Cosmopolitan*, vol. 16, pp. 303, 306.

In his old age he enjoyed the celebrity of his more vigorous years as if it had been the fame of a constant friend; but I think he enjoyed still more the consciousness of having succeeded in living through life as he intended to do in the beginning.— STEARNS, FRANK PRESTON, 1895, *Sketches from Concord and Appledore*, p. 276.

He was full of frolic, in a gentle way; no one of the world's people ever had a keener sense of humor. From every interview with him one carried away a good story, or a sense of having had a good time; he never darkened the day, or shadowed the heart. He inspirited. He invigorated. "I like," he wrote to a friend, "the wise, Chinese proverb: 'You cannot prevent the birds of sadness from flying over your head, but you may prevent them from stopping to build their nests in your hair.'" —WARD, ELIZABETH STUART PHELPS, 1896, *Chapters from a Life*, p. 160.

The life of Whittier, no less than his inspiring lines, bears a message of deep import to present-day civilization. In the fever and intoxication of modern existence, rife, too, as it is, with artificiality and duplicity, he maintained a lofty serenity of soul and in his simplicity, naturalness, and candor proved the falsity of the teachings of certain modern sophists, who claim that the Christ-life cannot be lived in the environment of modern times. He, more than any of the illustrious singers who were his contemporaries, preserved from youth to silver age the soul of a child. Many men who in their higher and truer moments have given the world noble and elevating thoughts, have themselves signally failed to live up to their fine teachings and, in unguarded moments and hours of temptation, have so fallen that the recollection of their shortcomings rests like a sable cloud over their noble utterances. Not so with Whittier; his life was exceptionally pure, and while I imagine no man ever reaches at all times his ideals, our Quaker poet, in a greater degree than most of us, maintained that serenity of soul, that purity of thought and kindliness of nature, which reflect the divine side of man.—FLOWER, B. O., 1896, *Whittier: Prophet, Seer and Man*, p. iii.

From our upper piazza [about 1846] we had a fine view of Boston harbor. Sitting there late one moonlight night, admiring the outlines of Bunker Hill Monument and the weird effect of the sails and masts of the vessels lying in the harbor, we naturally passed from the romance of our surroundings to those of our lives. I have often noticed that the most reserved people are apt to grow confidential at such an hour. It was under such circumstances that the good poet opened to me a deeply interesting page of his life, a sad romance of love and disappointment, that may not yet be told, as some who were interested in the events are still among the living.—STANTON, ELIZABETH CADY, 1898, *Eighty Years and More*, p. 141.

Mr. Whittier himself appeared, with all that report had ever told of gentle sweetness and dignified cordial courtesy. He was then seventy-seven years old, and, although he spoke of age and feebleness, he showed few signs of either; he was, in fact, to live eight years more. Perhaps because the room was low, he seemed surprisingly tall; he must, in fact, have been a little less than six feet high. The peculiarity of his face rested in the extraordinary large and luminous black eyes, set in black eyebrows, and fringed with thick black eyelashes curiously curved inwards. This bar of vivid black across the countenance was startlingly contrasted with the bushy snow-white beard and hair, offering a sort of contradiction which was surprisingly and presently pleasing. He was careful to keep on my right side, I noticed, being presumably deaf in the right ear; even if this were the case, which he concealed, his hearing continued to be markedly quick in a man of his years.—GOSSE, EDMUND, 1899, *A Visit to Whittier, The Bookman*, vol. 8, p. 459.

There was no literary man of his time who worked under such a lifelong embargo in respect to health as Whittier. He once said, "I inherited from my parents a nervous headache, and on account of it have never been able to do all I wished to do." Whittier's early trouble was regarded by physicians as a disease of the heart, and he was told that he must carefully avoid excitement. With care, as one of them assured him, he might live to be fifty years old. His headaches always pursued him, and he could not read continuously for half an hour without severe pain. At public dinners and receptions he was obliged to stipulate that he should be allowed to slip out when he felt fatigue coming on. It showed great strength of will surely for one man, combining the functions of author, politician, and general reformer, under such disadvantages, to outlive his fellow chiefs, carry so many points for which he had toiled, and leave behind him seven volumes of his collected works. The most successful of these, "Snow-bound," was written to beguile the weariness of a sick-chamber.—HIGGINSON, THOMAS WENTWORTH, 1902, *John Greenleaf Whittier (English Men of Letters)*, p.171.

Whittier received me very kindly, but was reluctant in giving his consent for sittings. My idea of Whittier had been formed by an engraving from a daguerreotype in a volume of his poetry. In this the face was closely shaven—a face large and rugged, with a strong chin, and a large mouth kindly in expression. I now found him with a full beard, excepting the upper lip, making the mouth seem small, and giving him a general look of commonplaceness and lack of character. . . . I never found in Whittier that ruggedness which I had imagined, but soon grew to like him very much, and the sittings became most enjoyable.—EATON, WYATT, 1902, *Recollections of American Poets, Century Magazine*, vol. 64, p. 846.

The pleasant little town of Burlington, N. J., in which I spent my earliest ministry, was the headquarters of orthodox Quakers. I was thrown much into the society of their most eminent people, and very delightful society I found it. The wittiest quaker in the town was my neighbor, William J. Allinson, the editor of the "Friends Review," and an intimate friend of John G. Whittier. One afternoon he ran over to my room, and said: "Friend Theodore, John G. Whittier is at my house, and wants to see thee; he leaves early in the morning."

I hastened across the street, and, in the modest parlor of Friend Allinson, I saw, standing before the fire, a tall, slender man in Quaker dress, with a very lofty brow, and the finest eye I have ever seen in any American, unless it were the deep ox-like eye of Abraham Lincoln. We had a pleasant chat about the anti-slavery, temperance and other moral reforms; and I went home with something of the feeling that Walter Scott says he had after seeing "Rabbie Burns." Whittier was a retiring, home-keeping man. He never crossed the ocean and seldom went even outside of his native home in Massachusetts.—CUYLER, THEODORE L., 1902, *Recollections of a Long Life.*

VOICES OF FREEDOM
1846

These "Voices of Freedom" are not bad reading at the present day. They are of that strenuous quality, that the light of battle brings to view a finer print, which lay unseen between the lines. They are themselves battles, and stir the blood like the blast of a trumpet. What a beat in them of fiery pulses! What a heat, as of molten metal, or coal-mines burning underground! What anger! What desire! And yet we have in vain searched these poems to find one trace of base wrath, or of any degenerate and selfish passion. He is angry, and sins not. The sun goes down and again rises upon his wrath; and neither sets nor rises upon aught freer from meanness and egotism.—WASSON, DAVID ATWOOD, 1864, *Whittier, Atlantic Monthly,* vol. 13, p. 334.

They are earnestly written, but as the events which suggested them were of a temporary character, one has to stimulate an interest to read them now, and this not so much because the vexed question which so fiercely agitated the poet is happily an obsolete one, as because in grasping with it he forgot to be a poet.—STODDARD, RICHARD HENRY, 1879, *John Greenleaf Whittier, Scribner's Monthly,* vol. 181, p. 574.

If the conservative is still unable to appreciate the merits of the "Voices," the anti-slavery man who bore his part in the long and often desperate conflict is perhaps equally disqualified to form an impartial opinion. We may say once more that in his mind and memory the "Voices" are associated with all his toils and his triumphs; they represent his inmost feelings at the time when they were profoundly moved. They accord with his deepest convictions of right and duty; and their high, solemn phrases seem to come with a divine authority. For an abolitionist to assume a critical attitude in regard to the "Voices" would be as hard as for a Hebrew to find fault with "The horse and his rider" or "By the rivers of Babylon."—UNDERWOOD, FRANCIS H., 1883, *John Greenleaf Whittier, a Biography,* p. 155.

Some of his verse, as a pattern for verse hereafter, is not what it might have been if he had consecrated himself to poetry as an art; but it is memorably connected with historic times, and his rudest shafts of song were shot true and far and tipped with flame. This should make it clear to foreigners why we entertain for him a measure of the feeling with which Hungarians speak of Petöfi, and Russians of Turgénieff. His songs touched the hearts of the people.—STEDMAN, EDMUND CLARENCE, 1885, *Poets of America,* p. 105.

A large proportion of the "Voices of Freedom" may be mere improvisations, uttered, hardly to be said composed, on the spur of the occasion, with the passionate purpose of immediately reaching the hearts of his readers, with neither time nor care for consideration of artistic perfectness. The impulse which gave birth to them was, indeed, patriotic rather than poetic: so, however good the declamatory verse, it was often to be classed as rhetoric rather than poetry. But after any deduction on such ground there is enough, even in these first outbursts, and leaving aside what he did when he reached his full stature, to show the true and gifted poet, sure to find at last, in his own country, but compeers and no superiors. — LINTON, WILLIAM JAMES, 1893, *Life of John Greenleaf Whittier (Great Writers),* p. 166.

SNOW-BOUND
1866

It is true to Nature and in local coloring, pure in sentiment, quietly deep in feeling, and full of those simple touches which show the poetic eye and the trained hand. Here is a New England interior glorified with something of that inward light which is apt to be rather warmer in the poet than the Quaker, but which, blending the qualities of both in Mr. Whittier, produces that kind of spiritual picturesqueness which gives so peculiar a charm to his verse. There is in this poem a warmth of affectionate memory and religious faith as touching as it is uncommon, and which would be altogether delightful if it did not remind us that the poet was growing old. . . . We have before had occasion to protest against Mr. Whittier's carelessness in accents and rhymes, as in pronouncing "ly' ceum," and joining in unhallowed matrimony such sounds as *awn* and *orn*, *ents* and *ence*. We would not have the Muse emulate the unidiomatic preciseness of a Normal schoolmistress, but we cannot help thinking that, if Mr. Whittier writes thus on principle, as we begin to suspect, he errs in forgetting that thought so refined as his can be fitly matched only with an equal refinement of expression, and loses something of its charm when cheated of it.—LOWELL, JAMES RUSSELL, 1866, *Whittier's Snow-Bound, North American Review*, vol. 102, pp. 631, 632.

"Snow-Bound" is the most faithful picture of our Northern winter that has yet been put into poetry.—BURROUGHS, JOHN, 1879, *Nature and the Poets, Scribner's Monthly*, vol. 19, p. 291.

In the poem of "Snow-Bound" there are lines on the death of the poet's sister which have nothing superior to them in beauty and pathos in our language. I have read them often with always increasing admiration. I have suffered from the loss of those near and dear to me, and I can apply the lines to my own case and feel as if they were written for me.—BRIGHT, JOHN, 1884, *Letters; Life and Letters of John Greenleaf Whittier*, ed. Pickard, vol. II, p. 704.

Years ago, when "Snow-Bound" was published, I was surprised at the warmth of its reception. I must have underrated it in every way. It did not interest one not long escaped from bounds, to whom the poetry of action then was all in all. And in truth such poetry, conceived and executed in the spirit of art, is of the higher grade. But I now can see my mistake, a purely subjective one, and do justice to "Snow-Bound" as a model of its class. Burroughs well avows it to be the "most faithful picture of our northern winter that has yet been put into poetry." If his discussion had not been restricted to "Nature and the Poets," he perhaps would have added that this pastoral gives, and once for all, an ideal reproduction of the inner life of an old-fashioned American rustic home; not a peasant home,—far above that in refinement and potentialities, —but equally simple, frugal, and devout; a home of which no other land has furnished the coadequate type.—STEDMAN, EDMUND CLARENCE, 1885, *Poets of America*, p. 117.

Of "Snow-Bound,"—that matchless, inimitable, victoriously original blending of real and ideal,—what can be said, except that it is the truest idyl of home and homeborn joys and memories penned in English speech during the century that has elapsed since Goldsmith sang of sweet Auburn. . . . "Snow-Bound" fairly entitles this author of so many rude and jarring notes to a place as a literary artist by the side of Goldsmith,—I was about to say by the side of Gray. Inferior to Goldsmith in humor and to Gray in classic conciseness, he equals them both in pathos, he equals them both in tender grace, and he far surpasses them in depth of feeling and spontaneity. I find in "Snow-Bound" more marks of the abiding classic than in any other American poem. It bears the test of quotation; it bears the test of repeated perusal; it appeals alike to the simplest and to the most fastidious.—ANDERSON, MELVILLE B., 1888, *Whittier, The Dial*, vol. 9, pp. 195, 196.

It is not without perfect justice that "Snow-Bound" takes rank with "The Cotter's Saturday Night" and "The Deserted Village;" it belongs to this group as a faithful picture of humble life. It is perfect in its conception and complete in its execution; it is the New England home, entire, with its characteristic scene, its incidents of household life, its Christian virtues. Perhaps many of us look back to it as Horace did to the Sabine farm; but there are more who can still remember it as a reality, and to them this winter idyl is the poetry of their own lives. It is, in a peculiar sense, the one poem of New England,—so completely indigenous that the soil has fairly created it, so genuine as to be better than history. It is by virtue of this poem that Whittier must be most highly rated, because he is here most impersonal, and has succeeded in expressing the common life with most directness.—WOODBERRY, GEORGE EDWARD, 1892, *John Greenleaf Whittier, Atlantic Monthly*, vol. 70, p. 646.

"Snow-Bound," simple and radiant as it is with human life, is also the reflection of a mind equally at home in spiritual realities. It may be said to sum up Whittier's personal experience and faith, and yet so absolutely free is it from egotism that it has taken its place as the representative poem of New England country life, quite as surely as Burns' "The Cotter's Saturday Night" expresses one large phase of Scottish life.—SCUDDER, HORACE E., 1894, *The Complete Poetical Works of John Greenleaf Whittier, Cambridge Ed.*, Biographical Sketch, p. XVII.

"Snow-Bound," which was printed a year after the close of the war, and written during the summer following the downfall of the Confederacy, is expressive of his essential qualities. The position usually awarded it as his master-work rests on solid ground. Whittier was a New Englander in blood and bone. "Snow-Bound" is a representative poem of New England, describing in a series of etched scenes the typical life of a country household—in a setting of external nature that is deliciously recognisable to any son of New England. The poem is also intensely autobiographical. It commemorates the family group that was wont to gather before the big fireplace in the old kitchen of the Haverhill farm-house; and the members of that circle are seen through the pensive half-light of memory, touched with the glamour of the years, yet the more distinctly drawn (there is a Dutch-like fidelity of drawing) because in place of photography the idealism of art produces veritable portraiture. It is all so clearly, so lovingly visualised and felt. . . . Its charm is that of a homely *genre* piece by a Low Country painter. Perhaps such poetry does not thrill one with a passionate sense of beauty, but it has a household virtue.—BURTON, RICHARD, 1901, *John Greenleaf Whittier (Beacon Biographies)*, pp. 87, 89.

The gem of the group, indeed the most artistic, sustained, and in many ways the most important of Whittier's poems, is the admirable idyll of New England rural life in winter, the several times mentioned "Snow-Bound." It is not always safe to pay attention to comparisons of American literary productions with those of British writers, but it is entirely safe to say that the comparison so often instituted between Whittier's best poem and Burns's "Cotter's Saturday Night" is not only warranted, but not altogether in favour of the greater poet. Whittier's description in octosyllabics of the snow-beset farmhouse and of the cheerful glow of cottage hearth and rural hearts is not marked by great imaginative power or by conspicuous charm of style; but it is marked to a notable extent by the charm of faithfulness of description as well as by that of sincerity of feeling. The lines that are devoted to the memory of his dead kinsfolk are not often surpassed in tenderness, and the portraits given are so clear that one regrets that Whittier did not oftener try his hand at idyllic and sustained narrative verse.— TRENT, WILLIAM P., 1903, *A History of American Literature*, p. 417.

GENERAL

The author of the following graphic sketch, which would do credit to riper years, is a youth of only sixteen years, who we think bids fair to prove another Bernard Barton, of whose persuasion he is. His poetry bears the stamp of true poetic genius, which, if carefully cultivated, will rank him among the bards of his country. —GARRISON, WILLIAM LLOYD, 1826, *Free Press*, June 22.

Editor of the *American Manufacturer*, a newspaper of Boston. He is one of the most youthful of our poets, but his verses show a more than common maturity of power.—KETTELL, SAMUEL, 1829, *Specimens of American Poetry, vol.* III, p. 373.

Is placed by his particular admirers in the very front rank of American poets. We are not disposed, however, to agree with their decision in every respect. Mr. Whittier is a fine versifier, so far as strength is regarded independently of modulation. His subjects, too, are usually chosen with the view of affording scope to a certain *vivida vis* of expression which seems to be his forte; but in taste, and especially in *imagination*, which Coleridge has justly styled the *soul* of all poetry, he is ever remarkably deficient. His themes are *never* to our liking.—POE, EDGAR ALLAN, 1841, *A Chapter on Autography, Works*, ed. Stedman and Woodberry, *vol.* IX, p. 244.

A common thought comes from the pen "rammed with life." He seems, in some of his lyrics, to pour out his blood with his lines. There is a rush of passion in his verse which sweeps everything along with it. His fancy and imagination can hardly keep pace with their fiery companion. His vehement sensibility will not allow the inventive faculties fully to complete what they may have commenced. The stormy qualities of his mind, acting at the suggestions of conscience, produce a kind of military morality which uses all the deadly arms of verbal warfare. When well intrenched in abstract right, he always assumes a hostile attitude towards the champions or exponents of abstract wrong. He aims to give his song "a rude martial tone, —a blow in every thought." His invective is merciless and undistinguishable; he almost screams with rage and indignation. Occasionally, the extreme bitterness and fierceness of his declamation degenerate into mere shrewishness and scolding.—WHIPPLE, EDWIN PERCY, 1844, *Poets and Poetry of America, Essays and Reviews*, vol. I.

Although boldness and energy are Whittier's leading characteristics, his works are not without passages scarcely less distinguished for tenderness and grace. In his later poems his style is more subdued and correct, though it is divested of none of his peculiar freshness. . . . Whittier may reasonably be styled a national poet. His works breathe affection for and faith in our republican polity and unshackled religion, but an affection and faith that do not blind him to our weakness or wickedness. He dares to "tell the world it lies." He is of that class of authors whom we most need in America to build up a literature that shall elevate with itself the national feeling and character.—GRISWOLD, RUFUS WILMOT, 1847, *Poets and Poetry of America, Second Ed.*, p. 363.

There was ne'er a man born who had more
  of the swing
Of the true lyric bard and all that kind of thing;
And his failures arise (though perhaps he don't
  know it,)
From the very same cause that has made him a
  poet,—
A fervor of mind which knows no separation
'Twixt simple excitement and pure inspiration.
. . . .
Then his grammar's not always correct, nor his
  rhymes,
And he's prone to repeat his own lyrics sometimes,
Not his best, though, for those are struck off at
  white-heats,
When the heart in his breast like a trip-hammer beats,

And can ne'er be repeated again any more
Than they could have been carefully plotted
  before.
—LOWELL, JAMES RUSSELL, 1848, *A Fable for Critics*.

To the descriptive talent as related to natural scenery, which we have noted as the gift of our best poets, John Greenleaf Whittier unites the enthusiasm of the reformer and the sympathies of the patriot. There are a prophetic anathema and a bard-like invocation in some of his pieces. He is a true son of New England, and beneath the calm, fraternal bearing of the Quaker, nurses the imaginative ardor of a devotee both of nature and humanity.—TUCKERMAN, HENRY T., 1852, *A Sketch of American Literature*.

We are not sure but that we like Whittier's prose better than his poetry.—PEABODY, ANDREW P., 1854, *Critical Notices, North American Review*, vol. 79, p. 539.

In considering Whittier's merits as an author, it is quite manifest that we should mention, first, his intensity,—that vivid force of thought and expression which distinguishes his writings. His verses sometimes bear marks of extreme haste, but the imperfections which would result from this cause are in a great measure obviated by the strength and simplicity of his conceptions. He begins to write with so clear an apprehension of what he intends to say, that in many cases his poems come out at first heat with a roundness and perfection which would lead one to suppose that they had passed through the fires of revision. But at times this vehemence is overdone, and needs a restraint which longer consideration would have supplied. This vividness, which Whittier possesses in a greater degree than any other living author with whom we are acquainted, is in part a natural peculiarity of his mind, and in part arises from the urgent circumstances under which he wrote. . . . Like every other true lyric poet, Whittier does not lack his multitude of friendly critics who advise him to concentrate his efforts upon some great work, instead of dissipating his energy upon what they consider mere ephemerals,—to devote himself to some gigantic undertaking, which shall loom up like the Pyramids to tell posterity his fame. But in our opinion the author has unwittingly best consulted his genius and reputation in the course which he has adopted.

His shortest productions are his happiest. There is no doubt that the writing of long poems is sanctioned by many eminent examples; but they are the least read of an author's works and are known to most people only by certain favorite extracts.— —THAYER, W. S., 1854, *John G. Whittier and his Writings, North American Review,* vol. 79, pp. 42, 43.

His writings are characterized by earnestness of tone, high moral purpose, and energy of expression. His spirit is that of a sincere and fearless reformer; and his fervid appeals are the true utterance of a brave and loving heart. . . . He describes natural scenery correctly and beautifully, and a vein of genuine tenderness runs through his nature. — HILLARD, GEORGE STILLMAN, 1856, *A First-Class Reader*, p. 488. .

The most intensely national of American bards. . . . The march of the verse ["Cassandra Southcote"] has something that reminds us of the rhythm of Mr. Macaulay's fine classical ballads, something which is resemblance, not imitation; while in the tone of mind of the author, his earnestness, his eloquence, his pathos, there is much that resembles the constant force and occasional beauty of Ebenezer Elliott. While equally earnest, however, and equally eloquent, there is in Mr. Whittier not only a more sustained, but a higher tone than that of the Corn-law rhymer.— MITFORD, MARY RUSSELL, 1857, *Recollections of a Literary Life*, pp. 334, 335.

He is as genuine, as wholesome and real as sweet-flag and clover. Even when he utters pure sentiment, as in that perfect lyric, "My Psalm," or in the intrepid, exquisite humility—healthful and sound as the odor of new-mown hay or balsam-firs— of "Andrew Rykman's Prayer," he maintains the same attitude of realism. He states God and inward experience as he would state sunshine and the growth of grass. This, with the devout depth of his nature, makes the rare beauty of his hymns and poems of piety and trust. He does not try to *make* the facts by stating them; he does not try to embellish them; he only seeks to utter, to state them; and even in his most perfect verse they are not half so melodious as they were in his soul. . . . It is, however, in his ballads that Whittier exhibits, not perhaps, a higher, yet a rarer, power than elsewhere,—a power, in truth, which is very rare indeed. —WASSON, DAVID ATWOOD, 1864, *Whittier, Atlantic Monthly*, vol. 13, pp. 337, 338.

Of all our American poets, John G. Whittier has from first to last done most for the abolition of slavery. All my antislavery brethren, I doubt not, will unite with me to crown him our laureate. . . . All his antislavery poetry helped mightily to keep us alive to our high duties, and fired us with holy resolution. Let our laureate's verses still be said and sung throughout the land, for if the portents of the day be true, our conflict with the enemies of liberty, the oppressors of humanity, is not yet ended.—MAY, SAMUEL J., 1869? *Some Recollections of our Antislavery Conflict*, pp. 263, 266.

He has everywhere devoted himself to the cause of truth and justice. No poet has spoken with more tenderness for humanity, or waged war more constantly and more defiantly with error and oppression. His intense hatred of wrong, and inexhaustible sympathy for struggling manhood, are always expressed with remarkable force and beauty in his prose and poetry.—HUNT, EPHRAIM, 1870, *Literature of the English Language*, p. 67.

No American poet, it may be said, is so free as Mr. Whittier from obligations to English writers; his poems show no evidence of appropriation, or even of a study of masterpieces so assiduous and appreciative as almost inevitably to entail a general resemblance. He is eminently original, and eminently American. One principal charm of his poetry consists in its catholicity; he sings not of himself, but for humanity, and his voice is heeded as if it bore a special call to all who heard it. The moral tone of his writings is uncompromisingly high; his highest inspiration is found in the thought of elevating or helping his fellow man, or widening the bounds of his freedom. The sentiment of Mr. Whittier's verse is generally elevated, and is expressed with mingled tenderness and dignity. His style lacks elegance, and is sometimes marred by positive faults; but these are more than balanced by the vigor of his lyrics and the intensity of his didactic passages.—CATHCART, GEORGE R., 1874, ed. *Literary Reader*, p. 214.

We have no American ballad-writer— that is, writer of ballads founded on our native history and tradition—who can be compared with him, either in the range or skillful treatment of his material.—TAYLOR, BAYARD, 1876, *Three Old and Three New Poets, International Review, vol.* 3, *p.* 405.

John G. Whittier, the poet of New England: his genius drew its nourishment from her soil; his pages are the mirror of her outward nature, and the strong utterance of her inward life.—PARKMAN, FRANCIS, 1877, *On Whitter's Seventieth Birthday.*

He is the true poet whose *life* is a poem, and our friend has received grace of the Father to live such a life. His life has been a consecration, his songs an inspiration, to all that is highest and best. It has been his chief glory, not that he could speak inspired words, but that he spoke them for the despised, the helpless, and the dumb; for those too ignorant to honor, too poor to reward him. Grace was given him to know his Lord in the lowest disguise, even that of the poor hunted slave, and to follow him in heart into prison and unto death. He had words of pity for all—words of severity for none but the cruel and hard-hearted. Though the land beyond this world be more beautiful and more worthy of him, let us pray the Father to spare him to us yet more years, and to fill those years with blessing.—STOWE, HARRIET BEECHER, 1877, *On Whittier's Seventieth Birthday.*

Or, snow-bound, let me, lingering, cheer the mind
In happy converse with companions kind,
And with them watch the pearly wonders gleam
O'er forest, plain, rough glen and gelid stream,
Or frosty magic on the panes assume
New forms of light, transcending summer's bloom.
And, if I had them not, then let me ride
With Skipper Ireson, feathered, tarred, and dyed,
Through Marblehead, with rope-coils round my wrists,
And hear the yells, and feel the fishwives' fists
Till I repent me, and roll back the wain
Of truant thought to nature's joys again!
—JOYCE, ROBERT DWYER, 1877, *Reflections, Scribner's Monthly, vol.* 14, *p.* 448.

They who love their country will thank him for the verses, sometimes pathetic, sometimes stirring, which helped to redeem that country from a great sin and shame; they who rejoice in natural beauty will thank him that he has delightfully opened their eyes to the varied charms of the rough New England landscape, by highway, river, mountain, and seashore; they who love God will thank him from their hearts for the tenderness and simple trust with which he has sung of the Infinite Goodness.—ELIOT, CHARLES W., 1877, *On Whittier's Seventieth Birthday.*

Whittier certainly has no fear of trivial and commonplace subjects, but in his treatment of them he rarely, if ever, rises above the level of the verse-maker. It was the opinion of Keats that a long poem is the test of invention; and if we accept this as a canon of criticism, we shall want no other evidence of Whittier's poverty of imagination. All his pieces are short, though few readers, we suppose, have ever wished them longer. He cannot give sprightliness or variety to his verse, which like a sluggish stream creeps languidly along. There is no freshness about him, none of the breeziness of nature, none of its joyousness, exuberance, and exultant strength. In his youth, even, he had all the stiffness and slowness of age with its want of graceful motion. . . . We willingly bear testimony to the moral tone and purity which pervade Whittier's verse. There is nothing to offend the most delicate ear; nothing to bring a blush to a virgin's cheek. He lacks the power to portray passion, and was not tempted into doubtful paths. He delights in pictures of home, with its innocent joys and quiet happiness; sings of friendship and the endearing ties that bind the parent to the child; or, if he attunes his harp to love, he does it in numbers so sadly sweet that we only remember that the fickle god has wreathed his bowers with cypress boughs and made his best interpreter a sigh. . . In Whittier's verse we often catch the unmistakable accent of genuine feeling, and his best lyrics are so artless and simple that they almost disarm criticism.—SPALDING, JOHN LANCASTER, 1877, *John Greenleaf Whittier, Catholic World, vol.* 24, *pp.* 437, 442, 444.

Fresh as on breezy seas the ascendant day,
And bright as on thick dew its radiant trace;
Pure as the smile on some babe's dreaming face,
Hopeful as meadows at the breath of May,
One loftiest aim his melodies obey,
  Like dawnward larks in roseate deeps of space—
  While that large reverent love for all his race
Makes him a man in manhood's lordlier way!
His words like pearls are luminous yet strong;

His duteous thought ennobles while it calms;
We seem to have felt the falling, in his song,
Of benedictions and of sacred balms;
To have seen the aureoled angels group and throng
In heavenly valleylands, by shining palms!
—FAWCETT, EDGAR, 1878, *Whittier, Fantasy and Passion, p.* 183.

Whittier has been characterized as the poet of freedom and humanity, and richly he deserves the compliment. During the antislavery discussions, his poetry, in its defiant and spirited tone, exerted great influence; and during the Civil War his soul-stirring strains sounded through the land, animating the friends of the nation.—PATTON, J. H., 1879, *Brooke's English Literature (Primer), Appendix, p.* 177.

Mr. Whittier is one of the few American poets who have succeeded in obtaining the suffrages of the reading public and of the literary class. Men of letters respect his work for its sincerity, simplicity, and downright manliness, and average readers of poetry respect it because they can understand it. . . . I do not rank him high as an artist, though he has art enough to answer his purposes generally. Poetry seems never to have been a pursuit with him, but a charge which was entrusted to him, and which he was to deliver when the spirit moved him, well or ill, as it happened, but honestly, earnestfully and prayerfully. — STODDARD, RICHARD HENRY, 1879, *John Greenleaf Whittier, Scribner's Monthly, vol.* 18, *pp.* 581, 583.

"Notwithstanding their many common points of harmony, Whittier's sympathies —though fine and noble—find a less pleasing and less noble form of expression than Bryant's. He habitually, and Bryant never or rarely, subordinates the poet to the man; and he obtrudes his own peculiar notions or opinions, on subjects religious, political, social, and philanthropic, upon his poetical utterances, and makes them important or ruling factors in some of his finest poems. It is also to be said that he differs from Bryant, very delightfully too sometimes, in making his poems vehicles for illustrating the familiar speech and lives and feelings of the men and women belonging to those simple-hearted folk in the lower and middle walks of life, whom President Lincoln was used to call "plain people." In these last, Whittier best displays his powers and diffuses his bosky sweetness; but in the class first named a rigid austerity dominates, and poetry is only a garb contrived to cloak the writer's ethics."—DESHLER, CHARLES D., 1879, *Afternoons with the Poets, p.* 293.

His poems are among the greatest favorites of the American people, and are admired wherever the English language is used.—SCHAFF, PHILIP, AND GILMAN, ARTHUR, 1880, ed. *Library of Religious Poetry, p.* 187.

In Whittier, with his special themes— (his outcropping love of heroism and war, for all his Quakerdom, his verses at times like the measured step of Cromwell's old veterans)—in Whittier lives the zeal, the moral energy, that founded New England— the splendid rectitude and ardour of Luther, Milton, George Fox—I must not, dare not, say the wilfulness and narrowness— though doubtless the world needs now, and always will need, almost above all, just such narrowness and wilfulness.—WHITMAN, WALT, 1881, *Specimen Days, April* 16, *p.* 181.

After Lowell, John Greenleaf Whittier is the political lyrist, *par excellence,* of America. . . . Whittier's later verse, rapid as a torrent, is apt to overflow its banks. He seldom knows when to stop, and, ringing endless changes on a few ideas, has never sufficiently discerned the difference between nouns and adjectives.— NICHOL, JOHN, 1882–85, *American Literature, p.* 240.

"The Eternal Goodness" is another poem which is worth a crowd of sermons which are spoken from the pulpits of our sects and churches, which I do not wish to undervalue. It is a great gift to mankind when a poet is raised up among us who devotes his great powers to the sublime purpose of spreading among men principles of mercy and justice and freedom. This our friend Whittier has done in a degree unsurpassed by any other poet who has spoken to the world in our noble tongue.— BRIGHT, JOHN, 1884, *Letter; Life and Letters of John Greenleaf Whittier, ed. Pickard, vol.* II, *p.* 705.

Although not claiming it as a superior distinction, yet, to our mind, Mr. Whittier is perhaps the most peculiarly American poet of any that our country has produced. The woods and water-fowls of Bryant belong as much to one land as to another;

and all the rest of our singers—Emerson, Longfellow, Lowell, and their brethren—with the single exception of Joaquin Miller, might as well have been born in the land of Shakespeare and Milton and Byron as in their own. But Whittier is entirely the poet of his own soil. . . . Thousands of his countrymen have lived their boyhood over again with him in the "Barefoot Boy."—SPOFFORD, HARRIET PRESCOTT, 1884, *The Quaker Poet, Harper's Magazine, vol. 68, p. 179.*

The associations of Whittier's poetry are almost everywhere to be found in the country in which he lives. The Merrimack, which clasps many historic towns in its arm, on its bending way to the sea, is his river of song. Marblehead, perhaps the quaintest town in America, with its sea-worn rocks, and its lighthouses flaming at evening above the silvery lagoons of the ocean, is the scene of Skipper Ireson's punishment. Newburyport, where Whitefield's coffin may still be seen,—
"Under the church on Federal Street,"
is the scene of "The Preacher." The curving beaches that sweep away from the old coast-towns of Gloucester, Ipswich, and Marblehead, are accurately described in "The Tent on the Beach," and in other poems. "The Shoemakers," "The Huskers," "The Drovers," and "The Fishermen," are subjects of poems that but picture familiar scenes in Amesbury, and in the neighboring towns. . . . His poems are among the æsthetic treasures of every intelligent family, as far as the English language is spoken. They are recited in every school, and quoted from many a platform and pulpit. Their influences range widely, and always for good.—BUTTERWORTH, HEZEKIAH, 1885, *The Home of J. G. Whittier; Some Noted Princes, Authors and Statesmen of Our Time*, ed. Parton, pp. 322, 323.

The Hermit of Amesbury, the Woodthrush of Essex, the Martial Quaker, the Poet of Freedom, the Poet of the Moral Sentiment—such are some of the titles bestowed upon Whittier by his admirers. Let us call him the Preacher-Poet, for he has written scarcely a poem or an essay that does not breathe a moral sentiment or a religious aspiration. — KENNEDY, W. SLOANE, 1886, *John Greenleaf Whittier, his Life, Genius, and Writings*, p. 9.

The faults of Whittier's early poetry may be summed up in the lack of the Hellenic element, the want of artistic taste. The void was never entirely filled, so enduring was the influence of his early training and of the Abolitionist movement. But in his later and more literary poetry the blemishes are less conspicuous. As his mental horizon widens, the grey atmosphere of his Quaker youth grows brighter. . . . His descriptive poetry is never cold. He paints in fresh bright colours, transfers the living scene to his page, and, without pausing to analyse or philosophise, gives us pictures of Nature at first hand. His poetry is fresh and simple; but it is not deep. He is a genuine story-teller. The want of depth here becomes a positive advantage. He never mars the vivid directness of his narrative by the intrusion of his own personality. Mystic beauty, dreamy grace, rounded art, lofty imagination are not his gifts. He would not, if he could, soar into the unreal world of Shelley. "Snowbound" is on the whole, his most finished production. In it his pictures stand out with sharply defined outline against the snow; his background gives emphasis and expression to every feature which he describes.—PROTHERO, R. E., 1886, *John Greenleaf Whittier, Longman's Magazine, vol. 9, pp. 188, 189.*

It was a lucky day for American verse when Whittier made the study which led up to his Legendary Poems; for, although these early poems are probably less read today than his later work, an original bent of mind was cultivated, and the American flavor of all his later work was assured by this study. The Indian and colonial names and events entered into his stock as a poet, and enriched his verse long after he had ceased to use the material as subject-matter. There came a time, perhaps, when he grew tired of the Indian legend, grew broader in his poetical range.
Leaving the land of hackmatack and pine,
For Tuscan valleys glad with olive and with vine;
but the best is always the native home flavor such as one perceives in "The Maids of Attitash," "Rivermouth Rocks," "Amy Wentworth," "Maud Muller," "Telling the Bees," "The Witch's Daughter," and "My Playmate." The graces of his verse appeared more and more persuasively when the War was coming to an end, and the young soldiers were dragging their

battered cannon home. There were many young Quakers among the soldiers, who had forgotten the drab and donned the blue. Whittier could not handle the guns; but he sounded the bugle, and none louder than he sang the *jubilate* of victory. Much of his broader verse has appeared since the War, and it is as grave, tender, and melodious as art, in long wedlock with genius, can make. There is a rich home quality that will endear verse and man to our American youth and manhood,—and there exists no man for whom we may more justly twine the garland which his brother poet Lowell bespoke for him nearly fifty years ago:—

A wreath, twine a wreath for the loyal and true Who, for the sake of the many, dared stand with the few.

—MORSE, JAMES HERBERT, 1887, *John Greenleaf Whittier, The Critic, vol.* 11, *p.* 308.

His verse is diffuse and of irregular merit; from it there might be drawn an instructive glossary of mispronunciations and excruciating rhymes; and it contains a large percentage of those "occasional" poems which would be a literary pest were they not so promptly and efficaciously covered by the recurrent tides of time. Yet Whittier, without being able to avail himself of the spoils of classical culture, and with all the disadvantages incident to the calling of the political poet, has succeeded by the strength of his conviction,—a conviction affecting, as well as relying upon, the spontaneous grace of a natural melodist. Sometimes his lame muse of language "goes halting along where he bids her go free;" but at other times thought and form unite in unstudied beauty. Not one of the chief American poets, in the strictest use of the adjective, Whittier has slowly reached, in a green old age, a recognised fame which the cold classicist in verse, or the restless sensationalist, might well envy.—RICHARDSON, CHARLES F., 1888, *American Literature*, 1607–1885, *vol.* II, *p.* 174.

Whose Quaker righteousness, like the oratory of John Bright, often glows with such splendid indignation, because he hates cruelty and oppression with a hatred commensurate with the depth of his love for all that is tender and true.—FARRAR, FREDERIC WILLIAM, 1891, *An English Estimate of Lowell, The Forum, vol.* 12, *p.* 142.

The pieces which make up the volume of "Voices of Freedom," published in 1849, were written during the years from 1833 to 1848. There, and elsewhere, he made visible the wrongs of the slave, and helped to arouse the moral sentiment which should abolish those wrongs. Whether in this Whittier kept within the legitimate functions of the poet need not be discussed here. It may be that the poet, like the critic, should refuse "to lend himself to the point of view of the practical man." Probably Whittier's best poetry is to be found elsewhere than in his slave pieces. Be this as it may, he served humanity more and poetry not less than do those writers who pass as poets, whose poetry springs from no depth of character or earnestness of purpose, but is for the most part a chronicle of bar-parlor amours and the equally unedifying reflections of the next morning, given in the shape of sonnet, triolet, or rhymed epigram. Not the slave alone, but the victim of any form of oppression, had a claim on Whittier's sympathy. . . . Quick as Whittier was to see and sympathise with those who were wronged, he was far from being a melancholy or despairing poet. He had faith that there was an overruling providence which could and would evolve good even out of seeming evil. . . . His tone, generally, is energetic and hopeful. It is distinctly less melancholy than that of Longfellow. Which of these was the greater poet is a point upon which opinions may differ. Longfellow, however, had the advantage in graceful and befitting phrase. —LEWIN, WALTER, 1892, *Whittier and Curtis, The Academy, vol.* 42, *p.* 237.

The free flow of his thought, the simplicity of his structure, the willingness not to select with too nice a sense, but to tell the whole, all helped to that frankness of the man which is the great charm of his works, taken together, and assisted him in making his expression of old New England life complete. No man could have written "Snow-Bound" who remembered Theocritus. In Whittier, Nature reminds us, as she is wont to do from time to time, that the die which she casts exceeds the diploma of the schools. Art may lift an inferior talent to higher estimation, but genius makes a very little art go a long way. This was Whittier's case. The poetic spark was inborn in him, living in his life; and when academic criticism has said its last word, he remains a poet, removed by a broad and not doubtful line from all stringers of couplets and filers of verses. . . . In the war time, he rose, under the stress of the great struggle, to finer poetic work; the softer feelings of pity, together with a solemn religious trust, made the verses of those battle-summers different in quality from those of the literary conflict of the earlier years. He never surpassed, on the lower level of rhetoric, the lines which bade farewell to Webster's greatness, nor did he ever equal in intensity those rallying-cries of defiance to the South, in which the free spirit of the North seemed to speak before its time. — WOODBERRY, GEORGE EDWARD, 1892, *John Greenleaf Whittier, Atlantic Monthly, vol.* 70, *pp.* 643, 645.

New Englander of New Englanders is the Quaker poet of Massachusetts, John Greenleaf Whittier. Although not a Puritan, he is the most typical of the New England poets. His early life was that of a farmer's boy, and his poems are full of farm scenes and homestead incidents. His "Snow Bound" pictures the cheer within and the cold without of a New England winter. He makes graphic the sturdy qualities of the old New England settlers. The reminiscences of his early days, picturing, as they do, a stalwart human nature, confirm the conscience of his readers against present temptations. His rhymes are often faulty, his metre sometimes rough, his spirit too surcharged with local feeling to be called national, his verse falls just short of inspiration, but what he has added to the moral worth of American letters is invaluable. He has given to American poetry a dignity of its own—the dignity of unaffected but undaunted manhood.— MABIE, HAMILTON W., 1892, *The Memorial Story of America, p.* 591.

Taken for all in all, Whittier, "our bard and prophet best-loved," that purely American minstrel, so virginal and so impassioned, at once the man of peace and the poet militant, is the Sir Galahad of American song. He has read the hearts of his own people, and chanted their emotions, and powerfully affected their convictions. His lyrics of freedom and reform, in his own justified language, were "words wrung from the nation's heart, forged at white heat."—STEDMAN, EDMUND CLARENCE, 1892, *The Nature and Elements of Poetry: Century Magazine, vol.* 44, *p.* 861.

Even the lightest touch of Whittier's fancy bears the earnest purpose of a master-workman. All of Whittier's work is characterized by intense earnestness, and this atones, in the eyes of the masses for defects which critics note.—FOWLER, WILLIAM J., 1892, *Whittier and Tennyson, The Arena, vol.* 7, *p.* 1.

All through Whittier's writings the spirit of trust in a beneficent order of things and a loving superintendence of the universe shows itself, ever hopeful, ever cheerful, always looking forward to a happier, brighter era when the Kingdom of Heaven shall be established. . . . I was first drawn to him by his strong human sympathies. In the great struggle with slavery, I found my slower sensibilities kindled by his burning enthusiasm; but more than all, I was attracted by that larger faith which is shared by the Brotherhood of Singers with whom he was enrolled.— HOLMES, OLIVER WENDELL, 1892, *Memorial Service, The Critic, vol.* 21, *pp.* 221, 222.

If Spenser was responsible for the magnificent poetry of Keats, Burns was Whittier's literary godfather. An itinerant pedlar, a Scotchman, and himself a bit of a poet, bartered a copy of the Ayrshire ploughman's works, together with a miscellaneous lot of fancy articles, to the Whittier family, and the young John Greenleaf dated his earliest inspiration from that fortunate purchase. . . . Some of Whittier's short pieces remind us of the "Twice-told Tales;" they are vignettes in verse. "Andrew Rykman's Prayer" and "The Two Rabbis" are an illustration of this similarity, but the poet has rarely attained the poetic excellence of the prose writer's exquisite allegory, "The Great Stone Face." We must not claim for Whittier even the slight measure of intellectuality which constitutes the baggage of most poets of his eminence; he was unintellectual in his spontaneity, unintellectual in his mode of looking at life and its appanage of triumphs and pain, unintellectual even in his literary style, which rarely presents any technical subtleties. He was certainly well acquainted with foreign masterpieces, as his poems are full of quotations and allusions to extraneous topics; but he had not the vivid assimilative power which renders the poet compatriot for the time being with the poets of all time. It is surely the strong accent of sincerity running through Whittier's poetry which has brought him so prominently to the fore, for high-class magazine poetry at the present day is often superior as regards literary excellence.—NEGREPONTE, MARY, 1893, *John Greenleaf Whittier, Westminster Review, vol.* 139, *pp.* 7, 10.

But this is not the place for political speculation. I have tried to show Whittier as he was, extenuating nothing nor setting down aught in malice. Above most men, he was one who can stand the test. His faults are patent. One cannot read him long without forgetting them in admiration of his nobly simple merits. Before considering his work in detail, I suggested that his chance of survival is better than that of any other contemporary American man of letters. Our consideration of his work has perhaps shown why. In the first place, he has recorded in a way as yet unapproached the homely beauties of New England Nature. In the second, he accepted with all his heart the traditional democratic principles of equality and freedom which have always animated the people of New England. These principles he uttered in words whose simplicity goes straight to the hearts of the whole American people. Whether these principles be true or false is no concern of ours here. If our republic is to live, they are the principles which must prevail. And in the verses of Whittier they are preserved to guide posterity, in the words of one who was incapable of falsehood.—WENDELL, BARRETT, 1893, *Stelligeri and Other Essays Concerning America, p.* 200.

Mr. Whittier was himself notably fearless and self-reliant, in regard to his literary opinions, as well as all others. He was not afraid of being the first to commend what he liked, and did not wait to hear what others thought, before venturing on its praise. Best of all, he stood by what he said, and was as ready to write it as to speak it, ever willing that whatever he spoke should be used in printed criticism.— BATES, CHARLOTTE FISKE, 1894, *Whittier Desultoria, The Cosmopolitan, vol.* 16, *p.* 306.

The necessity laid on him as a poet was accepted by Whittier with the glad and solemn earnestness of a prophet, and for sixty years he was more influential as a teacher of religion than any other man in America. Believing as ne did in God and human nature he was a foredoomed emancipator. Whether the slave was black or white, whether the tyrant was an evil law or a superstition that held men captive in the service of an infinite hate, Whittier never ceased to proclaim liberty to the captives and the opening of the prison to them that were bound. And he had the felicity, rare in the experience of prophets, of living to see his message heeded both by the state and the church. . . . Dreamer and mystic as he was, he was also a New England Puritan, and he served his turn at "the Crank" with a Puritan's grim devotion to duty. "His rustic reed of song," made into a weapon, had a point that pierced through body and soul of many a champion who managed to parry the blows of Garrison's bludgeon. In such poems as "The Pastoral Letters," "Moloch in State Street," and "Official Piety," he turned his crank and used his weapons in a way that gave to both church and state a bitter foretaste of the judgment which was to come, which was to prove the rustic "dreamer" a better Christian and a truer statesman than any of those who were then misguiding the people of the land. . . . . He had no hesitation about mixing religion with politics, and he believed in democracy because it made it possible for the religion of the whole nation, and of every man in it, to find expression in the laws and the life of the people. More than any other of our poets, Whittier was the singer and the prophet of the common people.—SAVAGE, W. H., 1894; *Whittier's Religion, The Arena, vol.* 10, *pp.* 153, 154, 156, 166.

The deep spiritual insight, the celestial music, and the brooding tenderness of Whittier have always taken me more than his fierier appeals and his civic virtues, though I do not underrate the value of these in his verse.—HOWELLS, WILLIAM DEAN, 1895, *My Literary Passions, p.* 238.

[Anonymous.] Narrative of James Williams, an American Slave; who was for Several Years a Driver on a Cotton Plantation in Alabama. Portrait. 16mo. New York, 1838. . . . A copy of this work has recently been sold by Messrs. Bangs & Co., New York, for $111, and in connection therewith a statement is repeated, which was advanced in 1895, to the effect that Whittier's connection with the

Narrative was never made public. This view is not supported by the fact that the Proceedings of the American Anti-Slavery Society, Third Decade, 1864 (which appears in its chronological arrangement in the present list), contains a catalogue of anti-slavery publications, 1750-1863, where the Narrative is described as "drawn up by J. G. Whittier;" and considering Whittier's devotion to, and labors in, the anti-slavery cause, the appearance of his name on the original board cover of the little volume would scarcely seem in keeping with the theory of rigid secrecy.—FOLEY, P. K., 1897, *American Authors, 1795-1895, p.* 312.

Whittier, perhaps less graceful than Longfellow, will influence men longer, for his content of thought is more weighty, and the emotions called out by a great struggle of principle pulsate in his verse.—JOHNSON, CHARLES F., 1898, *Elements of Literary Criticism, p.* 126.

One could almost wish "Barbara Frietchie" and "Maud Muller"—like tunes that lose their charm from too much repetition—less familiar. But "Snowbound," —which many agree upon as Whittier's masterpiece,—"In School Days," "Ichabod," "My Psalm," and the dozen on dozens of other poems which other tastes will elect, could ill be spared from the pages of our literature; nay, the best of them could not be spared at all. When Whittier fails of his best, his artistic faults are not far to seek. Still farther from the beaten way of books, however, are his sweetness and purity of spiritual sense, his faithfulness to simple and true standards of living, and his hatred of wrong, however strongly entrenched. In such qualities as these he and his work make their quiet claim to abiding remembrance.—HOWE, M. A. DE WOLFE, 1898, *American Bookmen, p.* 252.

It was printed in the office of the "Hartford Review," of which Whittier was then editor, and contains eleven poems and seven prose sketches. Only two of the poems, one of them with a new title, and none of the prose pieces were included in the last edition of his collected works prepared shortly before his death. In later life whenever he could obtain a copy of his first book he destroyed it. He is said on one occasion to have paid $5 for a copy which he afterwards burned. He probably thought that a high price, but it is worth much more now. Mr. Bierstadt's copy brought $41 and Mr. Roos's copy $31, both in the original boards, uncut, and Mr. Foote's copy, levant morocco uncut, bound by Matthews and with four lines in the author's autograph, was sold in 1894 for $40.—LIVINGSTON, L. S., 1898, *The First Books of Some American Authors, The Bookman, vol.* 8, *p.* 42.

Mr. Whittier was composing verses all his life, and the difference of quality between those he wrote at twenty and at eighty is remarkably small. He was a poet in the lifetime of Gifford and Crabbe, and he was still a poet when Mr. Rudyard Kipling was already famous. During this vast period of time his style changed very little; it had its ups and downs, its laxities and then its felicities, but it bore very little relation to passing conditions. There rose up beside it Tennyson and Browning, Rossetti and Swinburne, but none of these affected Whittier. His genius, or talent, or knack—whichever we choose to call it—was an absolutely local and native thing. . . . . None but a very hasty reader will fail to recognise Whittier's lasting place in the history of literature. He is not rich, nor sonorous, nor a splendid artist; he is even rather rarely exquisite; but he has an individuality of his own that is of durable importance. He is filled with moral enthusiasm as a trumpet is filled with the breath of him who blows it. His Quaker quietism concentrates itself until it breaks into a real passion-storm of humanity, and when Whittier is roused he sings with the thrilling sweetness of a woodthrush.—GOSSE, EDMUND, 1899, *A Visit to Whittier, The Bookman, vol.* 8, *pp.* 461, 462.

The secret of Whittier's influence may be the best explained, perhaps, by one word, —sympathy. "Pure and unspotted from the world" as he was, so strong were his sympathies for humanity that it is not in normal human nature to resist the charm of his simplicity, charity, and courage; his loyalty to truth, honor, and conscience; his contempt for sham, tyranny, and hypocrisy. Denied scholastic training, he was recognized by the people as one who had risen from their own ranks, who had passed through their own experiences of life, and was in full sympathy with their own aims and purposes. It was not because he was intensely religious, for moral and didactic poets in this age rarely excite the enthusiasm of their readers. It was not because

RICHARD HENRY STODDARD

Engraving by Kruell. From a Photograph.

WALT WHITMAN

Engraving from a Pen-and-Ink Sketch by Frank Fowler.

he was the poet of a section, for the whole nation now approves him as its interpreter. It was not because he was an ardent reformer, for reformers as such seldom ingratiate themselves in the love of their own contemporaries. It was not alone because he sang of freedom, goodness, and love of home. Other American singers had been doing the same thing for a century before his death. In all he wrote there was that broadly sympathetic spirit which went straight to the hearts of his readers.—ONDERDONK, JAMES L., 1899-1901, *History of American Verse, p.* 191.

No one can dwell much on Whittier without recognising him as the distinctively American poet of familiar life. More than any other he reaches the actual existence of the people, up to the time of his death. He could say of himself what Lowell said dramatically only, "We draw our lineage from the oppressed." Compared with him Longfellow, Holmes, and even Lowell, seem the poets of a class; Whittier alone is near the people; setting apart Emerson, who inhabited a world of his own, "so near and yet so far." His whole position was indeed characteristic of American society; had he lived in England, he would always have been at his highest, in the position of some Corn-Law Rhymer, some Poet of the People; or at best, in the often degrading position of his favorite Burns himself, whereas in his own country this external difference was practically forgotten. Having gone thus far in fitting out this modest poet, nature gave to him, more directly than to either of the others, the lyric gift—a naturalness of song and flow, increasing with years and reaching where neither of the others attained. A few of Longfellow's poems have this, but Whittier it pervades; and beginning like Burns, with the very simplest form, the verse of four short lines, he gradually trained himself, like Burns, to more varied or at least to statelier measures.—HIGGINSON, THOMAS WENTWORTH, 1902, *John Greenleaf Whittier (English Men of Letters), p.* 151.

He interprets as no other of our poets the innermost feelings of religious faith and trust. In all hymn books, of whatever creed, he is represented. In conscious mental weakness, in physical agony, under the shadow of death and deadly doubt, his words come to the lips as inevitably as David's sweetest psalms. His "Burying Ground" is less lonely than Bryant's "Crowded Street." Even Tennyson's "Crossing the Bar," Browning's "Prospice," or Stevenson's cheeriest note of them all, the "Requiem," is not more inspiriting, as we face in thought the last great earthly change, than "My Psalm" or "The Eternal Goodness." If Whittier's music, his thought, his fancy, was essentially commonplace, as older critics insist, so much the more marvelous is its infinite helpfulness to millions of men and women.—LAWTON, WILLIAM CRANSTON, 1902, *Introduction to the Study of American Literature, p.* 184.

Walt Whitman
1819-1892

Born, at West Hills, near Huntington, Suffolk County, New York, 31 May, 1819. At school at Brooklyn, 1824-28. Lawyer's clerk in Brooklyn, 1830-32. Worked as printer in Brooklyn, 1834-37. Schoolmaster on Long Island, 1837-38. Founded and edited a weekly newspaper, 1839-40. Returned to Brooklyn, 1840; worked as printer till 1848. On staff of New Orleans "Daily Crescent," 1848. Edited Brooklyn "Daily Eagle," 1848-49. At Brooklyn working as housebuilder and agent, 1850-62; during this period contrib. to various periodicals, and published "The Freeman." At Washington, 1862-73. Nurse and surgeons' assistant during war, 1862-66. Held clerkships in Indian Office of Interior Dept., in Office of Solicitor to Treasury, and in Attorney-General's Office, 1865-73. Settled at Camden, New Jersey, summer of 1873. Died there, 26 March 1892. Buried at Harleigh Cemetery, Camden. *Works:* "Leaves of Grass," 1855; "Drum Taps," 1865; "Sequel to Drum Taps," 1866; "Memoranda during the War," 1867; "Democratic Vistas," 1871; "After All, not to Create only," 1871; "Passage to India," 1871; "As a Strong Bird on Pinions Free," 1872; "Two Rivulets," 1876; "Complete Works, revised to 1877" (2 vols.), 1878; "Specimen Days and Collect," 1882-83; "November Boughs," 1888; "Good-bye, my Fancy," 1891; "Autobiographia," 1892; "Complete Prose Works," 1892.—SHARP, R. FARQUHARSON, 1897, *A Dictionary of English Authors, p.* 299.

PERSONAL

Walt the satyr, the Bacchus, the very god Pan. We sat with him for two hours, and much to our delight; he promising to call on us at the International at ten in the morning to-morrow, and there have the rest of it.—ALCOTT, AMOS BRONSON, 1856, *Letter, Nov. 9; Familiar Letters of Henry David Thoreau*, ed. Sanborn, p. 349.

At my third knock a fine-looking old lady opened the door just enough to eye me carefully, and ask what I wanted. It struck me, after a little, that his mother—for so she declared herself—was apprehensive that an agent of the police might be after her son, on account of his audacious book. At last, however, she pointed to an open common with a central hill, and told me I should find her son there. The day was excessively hot, the thermometer at nearly 100, and the sun blazed down as only on sandy Long Island can the sun blaze. The common had not a single tree or shelter, and it seemed to me that only a very devout fire-worshipper indeed could be found there on such a day. No human being could I see at first in any direction; but just as I was about to return I saw stretched upon his back, and gazing up straight at the terrible sun, the man I was seeking. With his grey clothing, his blue-grey shirt, his iron-grey hair, his swart sun-burnt face and bare neck, he lay upon the brown-and-white grass—for the sun had burnt away its greenness—and was so like the earth upon which he rested, that he seemed almost enough a part of it for one to pass by without recognition. I approached him, gave my name and reason for searching him out, and asked him if he did not find the sun rather hot. "Not at all too hot," was his reply; and he confided to me that this was one of his favourite places and attitudes for composing "poems." He then walked with me to his home, and took me along its narrow ways to his room. A small room of about fifteen square feet, with a single window looking out on the barren solitudes of the island; a small cot, a wash-stand with a little looking-glass hung over it, from a tack in the wall, a pine table with pen, ink, and paper on it; an old-line-engraving, representing Bacchus, hung on the wall, and opposite a similar one of Silenus; these constituted the visible environment of Walt Whitman. There was not, apparently, a single book in the room. In reply to my expression of a desire to see his books, he declared that he had very few. I found, upon further enquiry, that he had received only such a good English education as every American lad may receive from the public schools, and that he now had access to the libraries of some of his friends. The books he seemed to know and love best were the Bible, Homer, and Shakespeare: these he owned, and probably had in his pockets whilst we were talking. He had two studies where he read; one was the top of an omnibus, and the other a small mass of sand, then entirely uninhabited, far out in the ocean, called Coney Island. Many days had he passed on that island, as completely alone as Crusoe.—CONWAY, MONCURE DANIEL, 1866, *Walt Whitman, Fortnightly Review*, vol. 6, p. 542.

Here is Walt Whitman—a man who has lived a brave, simple, clean, grand, manly life, irradiated with all good works and offices to his country and his fellow-men—intellectual service to the doctrines of liberty and democracy, personal service to slaves, prisoners, the erring, the sick, the outcast, the poor, the wounded and dying soldiers of the land. He has written a book, welcomed, as you know, by noble scholars on both sides of the Atlantic; and this, for ten years, has made every squirt and scoundrel on the press fancy he had a right to insult him. Witness the recent editorial in the Chicago *Republican*. Witness the newspapers and literary journals since 1856, spotted with squibs, pasquinades, sneers, lampoons, ferocious abuse, libels. The lying jabber of the boys, drunkards and libidinous persons privileged to control many of the public prints, has passed as evidence as to his character; the ridiculous opinions of callow brains, the refraction of filthy hearts, have been received as true interpretations of his volume. All this is notorious. You know it, I suppose, as well as I. And finally after the years of defamation, calumny, private affronts, public contumely, my pamphlet refers to—after the social isolation, the poverty, the adversity which an evil reputation thus manufactured for a man and following him into every detail of his life must involve—Mr. James Harlan, Secretary of the Interior, lifting the charge of autorial obscenity into the most signal consequence, puts on the top-stone of outrage by expelling him from

office with this brand upon his name.—
O'CONNOR, WILLIAM DOUGLAS, 1866, "*The Good Gray Poet,*" *Supplemental; In Re Walt Whitman,* ed. *Traubel, Bucke, and Harned,* p. 154.

The spirit that was in him has come forth most eloquently in his actions. Many who have only read his poetry have been tempted to set him down as an ass, or even as a charlatan; but I never met any one who had known him personally who did not profess a solid affection and respect for the man's character.—STEVENSON, ROBERT LOUIS, 1882, *Familiar Studies of Men and Books,* p. 116.

When I shook hands with him there, at the door of his little house in Camden, I scarcely realised the great privilege that had been given to me—that of seeing face to face the wisest and noblest, the most truly great, of all modern literary men. I hope yet, if I am spared, to look upon him again, for well I know that the earth holds no such another nature. Nor do I write this with the wild hero-worship of a boy, but as the calm, deliberate judgment of a man who is far beyond all literary predilections or passions. In Walt Whitman I see more than a mere maker of poems, I see a personality worthy to rank even above that of Socrates, akin even, though lower and far distant, to that of Him who is considered, and rightly, the first of men. I know that if that other were here, his reception in New England might be very much the same. I know, too, that in some day not so remote, humanity will wonder that men could dwell side by side with this colossus, and not realize his proportions.—BUCHANAN, ROBERT, 1886, *A Look Round Literature,* p. 345.

In the works of Bryant, Longfellow, Whittier, and other eminent American poets, it will, I believe, be difficult to point out a single example of lusty self-appreciation. Walt Whitman does not hesitate to take a reader into his personal confidence, though he may sometimes make the reader blush and wish the poet had been more reticent.—MORRILL, JUSTIN S., 1887, *Self-Consciousness of Noted Persons,* p. 43.

It is not a little difficult to write an article about Walt Whitman's *home,* for it was humorously said by himself, not long ago, that he had all his life possessed a home only in the sense that a ship possesses one. . . . Of late years the poet, who was sixty-nine years old on the last day of May, 1888, has been in a state of half-paralysis. He gets out of door regularly in fair weather, much enjoys the Delaware River, is a great frequenter of the Camden and Philadelphia Ferry, and may occasionally be seen sauntering along Chestnut or Market Streets in the latter city. He has a curious sort of public sociability, talking with black and white, high and low, male and female, old and young, of all grades. He gives a word or two of friendly recognition, or a nod or smile, to each. Yet he is by no means a marked talker or logician anywhere. I know an old book-stand man who always speaks of him as Socrates. But in one respect the likeness is entirely deficient. Whitman never argues, disputes, or holds or invites a cross-questioning bout with any human being. Through his paralysis, poverty, the embezzlement of book-agents (1874-1876), the incredible slanders and misconstructions that have followed him through life, and the quite complete failure of his book from a wordly and financial point of view, his splendid fund of personal equanimity and good spirits has remained inexhaustible, and is to-day, amid bodily helplessness and a most meagre income, more vigorous and radiant than ever.— SELWYN, GEORGE, 1888, *Authors at Home,* ed. *Gilder,* pp. 335, 341.

Here health we pledge you in one draught of song,
Caught in this rhymer's cup from earth's delight,
Where English fields are green the whole year long,
The wine of might,
That the new-come Spring distils, most sweet and strong,
In the viewless air's alembic, wrought too fine for sight.
Good health! we pledge, that care may lightly sleep,
And pain of age be gone for this one day,
As of this loving cup you take, and, drinking deep,
Grow glad at heart straightway
To feel once more the kindly heat of the sun
Creative in you, as when in youth it shone,
And pulsing brainward with the rhythmic wealth
Of all the summer whose high minstrelsy
Shall soon crown field and tree,
And call back age to youth again, and pain to perfect health.

—RHYS, ERNEST, 1889-94, *To Walt Whitman on his Seventieth Birthday, A London Rose and Other Rhymes.*

Good-bye, Walt!
Good-bye, from all you loved of earth—
Rock, tree, dumb creature, man and woman—
To you, their comrade human.
　　The last assault
Ends now; and now in some great world has
　　birth
A minstrel, whose strong soul finds broader
　　wings,
　　More brave imaginings.
Stars crown the hilltop where your dust shall
　　lie,
　　Even as we say good-bye,
　　　　Good-bye, old Walt!
—STEDMAN, EDMUND CLARENCE, 1892, *W. W.*, *March* 30,

My first meeting with Walt Whitman occurred when I was a boy and had occasion to ask for a certain residence in his street. I did not know who or what he was, but on his answering my question I was so struck with the quality of his voice, which was musical and resonant, that I took the earliest opportunity to make enquiry as to the new-comer, and received the information that it was a man named Walt Whitman, who had written what some people called poetry and others nonsense. Had the present city directory of the town been in existence, I could have found it authoritatively stated that the gentleman was "Walt Whitman, *poet*." My first visit to him occurred some years later, in the little house on Mickle Street which has been the scene of the closing years of his life. When I entered the room the poet was sitting in his great chair by the window, in front of him a table heaped up at least to the height of four feet with books of all sorts, old and new, gift-editions from men famous in letters, and cheap second-hand purchases; the floor was knee-deep in newspapers, manuscript, and books, among the last a well-thumbed Latin Lexicon. . . . The most interesting talk that I ever had with Walt Whitman was on one winter afternoon some five years ago, when I dropped in and found the poet ready and eager "to gossip in the early candle-light of old age." His theme was himself and his book, and he told the story not at all to me, as it seemed, but as though he were taking a backward glance o'er travelled roads, alone. The starting-point was an answer to the question,— "Mr. Whitman, how did you come to write poetry?" And in his reply he said that at the time when he was a carpenter-builder in Brooklyn he would buy a bit of property in the suburbs, erect a little house upon it with his own hands, sell the place at an average profit of about two hundred dollars, and, taking the money thus earned, go down to Long Island and lie out on the rocks, reading, dreaming, and watching the ships. . . . Whitman seemed to have the keenest enjoyment of bright colors. On one Sunday afternoon while entertaining some half-dozen callers he halted the general talk to call attention to the bright red dress of a little girl whom he spied out of his window. "How that color brightens up the whole street!" he said. And on another occasion, when he had driven out to a horse race (his first appearance at a race-track), he told me he lost all interest in the sporting event to sit in admiration of a clump of green trees that outlined themselves against a white fence. "Isn't that beautiful?" he said. "How the white back-ground sets off the many shades of the green leaves!" One of the most satisfying qualities that Whitman possessed, as a man, was the dignified, unruffled demeanor that he never lost, whether he was hobnobbing with a deck-hand or a 'bus-driver or entertaining some guest who was a celebrity in two continents.—GARRISON, WILLIAM H., 1892, *Walt Whitman*, *Lippincott's Magazine*, vol. 49, pp. 623, 624.

I saw Whitman in war times and later with an experience akin to that of some Athenian who had known Socrates, and perhaps followed the grand pug-nosed old loafer from place to place to hear him talk. If ever the loafer come to his own, and we amend our Christian legends, Saint Socrates will be his patron. Even as I had fancied the shaggy-browed Socrates floating about Athens, the eyes of the police upon him with their own thoughts as to his means of support, there was the suggestion of a parallel in Whitman. He had a conspicuous, massive figure, invariably in frowsy picturesque raiment. You ran against him in out of the way places—riding on the front of horse cars in conversation with the driver, giving pennies to ragged groups of negro children; sailing down Pennsylvania avenue, with that wonderful hat, that collar that was never buttoned, like some old three-decker of ninety-four, or trailing out toward the camps in suburban Washington with packages under his arms or in his coat pockets, presumably for the hospital. There was something of a rude, enviable splendor in his superb, rugged health,—the body dominant with wholesome conditions; something also of the Horace Greeley in this personality—the same shambling, go-as-you-please gait, Whitman rather the sturdier of the two; nothing of the inspired childhood; phenomenal touch of genius, as in the famous journalist. You were apt to find him silent, civil, not communicative, but cordial when you could reach him.— YOUNG, JOHN RUSSELL, 1892–1901, *Men and Memories*, ed. Young, p. 78.

Serene, vast head, with silver cloud of hair,
Lined on the purple dusk of death
A stern medallion, velvet set—
Old Norseman throned, not chained upon thy chair,
Thy grasp of hand, thy hearty breath
Of welcome thrills me yet
As when I faced thee there.
—GARLAND, HAMLIN, 1893, *Walt Whitman, In Re Walt Whitman*, ed. Traubel, Bucke, and Harned, p. 328.

In his book he despised riches, in his actual life he probably never gave up one day to the pursuit of them. In his book the ideal man gives alms to everyone that asks; in actual life the man, Walt Whitman, gave his days and nights, his labor, his love and sympathy, his time and strength, and at last his splendid health, to those who needed help and a friend. The ideal man in "Leaves of Grass" is a lover of his kind in a new and higher sense, affection, devotion, faith, pride, all the lofty passions, are in him developed to an unprecedented degree. Those who know the actual flesh and blood Walt Whitman can bear witness that the living man fell not an iota short of his pen and ink prototype.—BUCKE, RICHARD MAURICE, 1893, *The Man Walt Whitman, In Re Walt Whitman*, ed. Traubel, Bucke, and Harned, p. 68.

His Quaker ancestry, in my judgment, dominated all other elements in his character. He was from early childhood of a quiet, thoughtful and kindly disposition, full of calm seriousness and powerful faith. . . . If to have Christlike qualities is to be a Christian, then it would be difficult to select a more perfect example than Walt Whitman. His gentleness, unselfishness, charity and lovingness for every living creature were so thoroughly natural and spontaneous, that those who knew him personally fully realize how perfectly he has placed a man in his book.—HARNED,

THOMAS B., 1893, *The Poet of Immortality, In Re Walt Whitman*, ed. Traubel, Bucke, and Harned, p. 353.

No one was ever more generous and frank of nature, more ready to accept differences of opinion, more tolerant of criticism. At the same time he displayed a desire to diffuse his doctrines, an eagerness to be acknowledged in his life time. He craved for responsive affection in the audience to whom he appealed, and regarded his literary teaching in the light of a cause. He acted like one who did not trust to the certainty of the eventual success of genius. He collected and distributed trifling panegyrics of himself, culled from the holes and corners of American journalism. He showed small sense of proportion in criticism, and seemed to value people by the amount of personal zeal they displayed in the propagation of his views.—SYMONDS, JOHN ADDINGTON, 1893, *Walt Whitman, a Study*, p. 3.

I liked the man much, a fine-natured, good-hearted, big fellow, who must have been handsome in young days (as indeed an early portrait shows him).—LINTON, WILLIAM JAMES, 1894, *Threescore and Ten Years, 1820 to 1890*, p. 217.

Whitman's magnetic quality was peculiar. I never knew a person to meet him for the first time who did not come under its spell; most people going away in such a curious state of exaltation and excitement as to produce a certain wakefulness, the general feeling not wearing off for a fortnight.—KENNEDY, WILLIAM SLOANE, 1896, *Reminiscences of Walt Whitman*, p. 109.

It was a poet's life from first to last,— free, unhampered, unworldly, unconventional, picturesque, simple, untouched by the craze of money-getting, unselfish, devoted to others, and was on the whole, joyfully and contentedly lived. It was a pleased and interested saunter through the world, —no hurry, no fever, no strife; hence no bitterness, no depletion, no wasted energies. A farm boy, then a school-teacher, then a printer, editor, writer, traveler, mechanic, nurse in the army hospitals, and lastly government clerk; large and picturesque of figure, slow of movement; tolerant, passive, receptive, and democratic,—of the people; in all his tastes and attractions, always aiming to walk abreast with the great laws and forces, and to live thoroughly in the free, nonchalant spirit of his own day and land.—BURROUGHS, JOHN 1896, *Whitman, a Study, p.* 23.

Walt Whitman was at this time fifty-eight, but he looked seventy. His beard and hair were snow-white, his complexion a fine colour, and unwrinkled. He had still, though stricken in 1873 by paralysis, a most majestic presence. He was over six feet, but he walked lame, dragging the left leg, and leaning heavily on a stick. He was dressed always in a complete suit of gray clothes with a large and spotless white linen collar, his flowing white beard filling in the gap at his strong sunburnt throat. He possessed a full-toned, rather high, baritone voice, a little harsh and lacking in the finer modulations for sustained recitation; having an excellent memory, he declaimed many scenes from Shakespeare, poems by Tennyson, and occasionally his own. The "Mystic Trumpeter" was a favorite with him, because he had often recited to his soldiers in the hospitals the opening lines.—GILCHRIST, GRACE, 1898, *Chats with Walt Whitman, Temple Bar*, vol. 113, p. 201.

LEAVES OF GRASS
1855

I am not blind to the worth of the wonderful gift of "Leaves of Grass." I find it the most extraordinary piece of wit and wisdom that America has yet contributed. I am very happy in reading it, as great power makes us happy. It meets the demand I am always making of what seems the sterile and stingy Nature, as if too much handiwoi k or too much lymph in the temperament were making our Western wits fat and mean. I give you joy of your free and brave thought. I have great joy in it. I find incomparable things, said incomparably well, as they must be. I find the courage of treatment which so delights us, and which large perception only can inspire. I greet you at the beginning of a great career, which yet must have had a long foreground somewhere, for such a start. I rubbed my eyes a little, to see if this sunbeam were no illusion; but the solid sense of the book is a sober certainty. It has the best merits—namely, of fortifying and encouraging.—EMERSON, RALPH WALDO, 1855, *Letter to Whitman, July* 21.

How I loathe "Wishi-washi,"—of course without reading it. I have not been so happy in loathing anything for a long while—except, I think, "Leaves of Grass," by that Orson of yours. I should like just to have the writing of a valentine to him in one of the reviews.—ROSSETTI, DANTE GABRIEL, 1856, *Letters to William Allingham, ed. Hill*, p. 181

I've read "Leaves of Grass," and found it rather pleasant, but little new or original; the portrait the best thing. Of course, to call it poetry, in any sense, would be mere abuse of language.—ALLINGHAM, WILLIAM, 1857, *Letter to W. M. Rossetti, April* 10; *Letters of Dante Gabriel Rossetti to William Allingham, ed. Hill*, p. 185.

The plainness of speech in "Leaves of Grass" is indeed biblical; there is, too, a startling priapism running through it; nay, squeamish readers must needs hold their noses, for the writer does not hesitate to bring the slop-bucket into the drawing-room to show that the chemic laws work therein also; yet from its first sentence, "I celebrate myself," there starts forth an endless procession of the forms and symbols of life—now funeral, now carnival, or again a masquerade of nations, cities, epochs, or the elements, natural and human —fascinating the eye with wonder or dread. To these terrible eyes Maya surrenders; faces, forms, skeletons, are unsheated. Here are the autographs of New York, and of the prairies, savannahs, Ohio, Mississippi, and all powers, good and evil. There is much that is repulsive to the ordinary mind in these things and in the poems that really express them; but as huge reptiles help to fashion the pedestal of man, as artists find in griffins and crouching animal forms the fundamental vitality upon which the statue or pillar may repose one might not unreasonably find in the wild and grotesque forms of Walt Whitman's chants, so instinct with life, the true basis of any shaft, not the duplicate of any raised elsewhere, that American thought is to raise.—CONWAY, MONCURE DANIEL, 1866, *Walt Whitman, Fortnightly Review,* vol. 6, p. 539.

I read through the three volumes on Sunday: and upon a sober comparison I think Walt Whitman's "Leaves of Grass" worth at least a million of "Among My Books" and "Atalanta in Calydon." In the two latter I could not find anything which has not been much better said before; but "Leaves of Grass" was a real refreshment to me—like rude salt spray in your face—in spite of its enormous fundamental error that a thing is good because it is natural, and in spite of the world-wide difference between my own conceptions of art and its author's.—LANIER, SIDNEY, 1878, *To Bayard Taylor, Feb. 3; Letters, p. 208.*

In two things he fairly did take the initiative, and might, like a wise advocate, rest his case upon them. He essayed, without reserve or sophistry, the full presentment of the natural man. He devoted his song to the future of his own country, accepting and outvying the loudest peak-and-prairie brag, and pledging These States to work out a perfect democracy and the salvation of the world.—STEDMAN, EDMUND CLARENCE, 1880, *Walt Whitman, Scribner's Monthly, vol. 21, p. 60.*

They have neither rhyme nor metre, neither form nor melody. His poetry, although well received in England, has but few admirers in America, and has been very justly characterized as "mere dirty rubbish, full of blatancy and obscenity."—BALDWIN, JAMES, 1882, *English Literature and Literary Criticism, Poetry, p. 559.*

I come next to Whitman's "Leaves of Grass," a book of singular service, a book which tumbled the world upside down for me, blew into space a thousand cobwebs of genteel and ethical illusions, and, having thus shaken my tabernacle of lies, set me back again upon a strong foundation of all the original and manly virtues. But it is, once more, only a book for those who have the gift of reading.—STEVENSON, ROBERT LOUIS, 1887, *Books Which Have Influenced Me, p. 7.*

In "Leaves of Grass" Whitman has bodied forth a biography of the human soul; of his own ostensibly, of all souls really, for the experience of the individual is simply the experience of the race in miniature. "Leaves of Grass" is a record of the soul's voyage through life; a gathering of experience, of joy and sorrow, of feeling, emotion and thought. This gives to the book its power and charm, and also, in some aspects and to some persons, makes it repellent. . . . I do not advise any one to read "Leaves of Grass" except as a whole. It would not be understood. Passages are easy to find which, when detached, seem foolish or offensive but in their proper place contribute to the harmony of the structure. When one of the editions was in preparation a friend of Whitman urged him to omit certain passages, saying, "What in the world do you want to put in that stuff for that nobody can read?" Whitman replied, "Well, John, if you need to ask that question it is evident, at any rate, that the book was not written for you;" a fitting answer to other objectors. . . . Tested by scholastic rules, I suppose "Leaves of Grass" would not be called poetry at all. It does not obey the laws of prosody, yet musicians have affirmed that it does obey the laws of music. When, however, the key of the meaning is found, the propriety of the form is felt; it almost seems as though no other form would have served. A comparison between "Leaves of Grass" and the finest of Whitman's prose, shows that the former stands upon a level altogether higher than the latter. Here, as in all works of true power, the thought has created its own befitting form.—LEWIN, WALTER, 1887, *Leaves of Grass, Murray's Magazine, vol. 2, pp. 327, 335, 336.*

I have thought of him as a bard devoted by the gods to America as those of old were to Britain. His mission has seemed to me to be the rendering into the early speech of his race what things it is meet should be kept for the future races to know —to know truly, not historically—about the young America. As we know the thought and life of early England through its druids and bards, so I suppose it is intended that Walt Whitman shall be the recorder of our early nationality. Future scholars or patriots in the time when America has grown old in word and deed, and no longer wears the freshness of youth, will go to his book for refreshment, and drink from it promise of the future, because the past has been true and unaffected. Other books there are, certainly, which will help to form the foundation of a great national literature; but none so smack of the very soil, none grow out of it as do "Leaves of Grass."—MORRIS, HARRISON S., 1888, *The Poetry of Walt Whitman, The American, July 7.*

I had my choice when I commenc'd. I bid neither for soft eulogies, big money returns, nor the approbation of existing schools and conventions. As fulfill'd, or partially fulfill'd, the best comfort of the whole business (after a small band of the dearest friends and upholders ever vouchsafed to minor cause — doubtless all the more faithful and uncompromising—this little phalanx!—for being so few) is that, unstopp'd and unwarp'd by any influence outside the soul within me, I have had my say entirely on my own way, and put it unerringly on record—the value thereof to be decided by time. . . . "Leaves of Grass" indeed (I cannot too often reiterate) has mainly been the outcropping of my own emotional and other personal nature—an attempt from first to last, to put a Person, a human being (myself, in the latter half of the Nineteenth Century, in America), freely, fully and truly on record. I could not find any similar personal record in current literature that satisfied me. But it is not on "Leaves of Grass" distinctively as literature, or a specimen thereof, that I feel to dwell, or advance claims. No one will get at my verses who insists upon viewing them as a literary performance, or as aiming mainly toward art or æstheticism.— —WHITMAN, WALT, 1888, *November Boughs, pp.* 6, 18.

"Leaves of Grass" started in almost universal displeasure. It shocked literary and sex traditions. Two things, at least, in its own plane and theory, were necessary to its life. It needed to reflect the broadening spirit of our new age and new land. The rhyme, the convention, the formal measure, insisted upon by old literary codes, were unequal to the current conditions. Whitman made his own vehicle. His book was to get as close to nature as her reserves would permit. The natural was to reflect the healthy and the abiding. Sex, under this treatment, must reclaim its heritage. No middle-age monastic contempt could longer be visited upon motherhood, the body, or any corporeal functions. To dare so dire a thraldom, to strike so near the throne, seemed to be to dare everything. No antisubjectivist could delight in "Leaves of Grass," for that one volume uncurtains the frankest confession of life found in annal or story. Who touches this, the author himself teaches, touches not art nor intellect, but a man. Yet there was no sign, as in Amiel, of the disease of introspection. The whole work precipitates the manliest salutations. "Leaves of Grass" has passed through about ten editions.—TRAUBEL, HORACE L., 1891, *Walt Whitman: Poet and Philosopher and Man, Lippincott's Magazine, vol.* 47, *p.* 387.

The reader may scan page after page without perceiving an image boldly and clearly drawn. If obscurity is a virtue, much of this author's work has merit; but he does not fulfil the requirements of the literary artist. In style, not only is he open to criticism, but in thought as well. In his "Children of Adam," he gives utterance to ideas that verge on indecency. He protects himself, of course, by the time-worn adage, "Evil to him who evil thinks;" but purity of thought and expression is a boasted characteristic of American scholars. No author is justified in using words and expressions that would create a vulgar thought in the minds of even the outcast from society. . . Though open to criticism, based possibly upon differences of opinion, "Leaves of Grass" is the life work of an American patriot who had the genius to conceive the necessities of our literature and the hardihood to attempt a great original poem. The first edition was a thin volume. Then, during the civil war, the author spent three years as an army nurse, gaining experience preparatory to new literary ventures. From time to time during his after life, appeared additions and annexes until the entire work forms a good-sized volume.—BOUGHTON, WILLIS, 1892, *Walt Whitman, The Arena, vol.* 6, *pp.* 478, 479.

There is in "Leaves of Grass" a freshness almost physical, and from one end to the other the reader breathes that odor of open air and earth, wholesome and refreshing, such as overtakes and invigorates one who has long been shut within the walls of the city and at last goes forth into the ample fields.—SARRAZIN, GABRIEL, 1893, *Walt Whitman, tr. from the French by Harrison S. Morris, In Re Walt Whitman, ed. Traubel, Bucke, and Harned, p.* 178.

Everyone who so far has ventured on the reading of "Leaves of Grass" has had the following experiences: After the perusal of the first few pages it has seemed to him that the book must have been the work of a madman. Soon, however, he has been suddenly arrested by an original thought which has revealed to him the meaning of what he has so far read, and has irresistibly urged him to read further. He has found himself, then, in the condition of the magician's pupil in Goethe's ballad, who is unable to free himself from the spirits which he has called up. . . . The reading of "Leaves of Grass" may be compared to the ascent of a mountain, where every laborious step is rewarded with new and fascinating views. The summit, however, of this spirit-mountain has never yet been reached, as is confessed readily by his most ardent worshippers and most industrious readers, who comfort themselves with the thought that as they have already conquered so many difficulties, the remaining secrets will be yet unveiled to them.—KNORTZ, KARL, 1893, *Walt Whitman, tr. from the German by Forman and Bucke, In Re Walt Whitman,* ed. *Traubel, Bucke, and Harned, pp.* 219, 220.

Looked at as a whole, "Leaves of Grass" is mystical, joyous, full of the power to impart courage and moral strength. It resembles the Iliad or the Nibelungen Lied in being a growth, not a make, a true epos, not an epopee. It is perhaps the only great epos in the world in which some individual woman is not the prime and the centre around which all revolves. Yet it honors woman more than all the others . . . Shallow students of Whitman never get hold of this cardinal premise at all, but serenely criticise him for not attaining what he avowed at the start he did not intend to do.—KENNEDY, WILLIAM SLOANE, 1896, *Reminiscences of Walt Whitman, pp.* 99, 103.

In 1860 a much enlarged edition was printed at Boston in which the most objectionable verses were grouped under the grotesque title, "Enfans d'Adam." It was at this juncture that Emerson took his famous walk with Whitman and calmly expostulated with him in regard to his over-frank treatment of sexual matters. Whitman listened in silence, years later confessed that the arguments were unanswerable, but was more convinced than ever that he must let his verses stand. What Emerson could not do with Whitman it is not likely that any reader or critic will be able to do with Whitman's disciples. The "Children of Adam" poems need, therefore, no discussion here. It should be remarked, however, that the time for upbraiding the author—if such a time ever existed—has long since passed. No careful student of Whitman's life and works can now fail to perceive that he was thoroughly sincere in believing that his frank speaking was demanded in the interest of the highest morality. It was a part of his message, and it is permissible to maintain that his most questionable poems can have done few people harm, and must have done something towards shaking the hold of prudery and cant. It is equally permissible to maintain that his concrete presentation of this portion of his message was, to say the least, singularly open to misconstruction.— TRENT, WILLIAM P., 1903, *A History of American Literature, p.* 484.

GENERAL

It has been a melancholy task to read this book; ["Drum-Taps"] and it is a still more melancholy one to write about it. Perhaps since the day of Mr. Tupper's "Philosophy" there has been no more difficult reading of the poetic sort. . . . Mr. Whitman prides himself especially on the substance—the life—of his poetry. It may be rough, it may be grim, it may be clumsy—such we take to be the author's argument— but it is sincere, it is sublime, it appeals to the soul of man, it is the voice of a people. He tells us, in the lines quoted, that the words of his book are nothing. To our perception they are everything, and very little at that. A great deal of verse that is nothing but words has, during the war, been sympathetically sighed over and cut out of newspaper corners, because it has possessed a certain simple melody. But Mr. Whitman's verse, we are confident, would have failed even of this triumph, for the simple reason that no triumph, however small, is won but through the exercise of art, and that this volume is an offence against art. It is not enough to be grim and rough and careless; common sense is also necessary, for it is by common sense that we are judged. There exists in even the commonest minds, in literary matters, a certain precise instinct of conservatism, which is very shrewd in detecting wanton eccentricities. To this instinct Mr. Whitman's attitude seems monstrous. It is monstrous because it pretends to persuade the soul while it slights the intellect; because it pretends to gratify the feelings while it outrages the taste. The point is that it does this *on theory,* wilfully, consciously, arrogantly. It is the little nursery game of "open your mouth and shut your eyes." Our hearts are often touched through a compromise with the artistic sense, but never in direct violation of it.— JAMES, HENRY, 1865, *Mr. Walt Whitman, The Nation, vol.* 1, *pp.* 625, 626.

That glorious man Whitman will one day be known as one of the greatest sons of Earth, a few steps below Shakespeare on the throne of immortality.—ROSSETTI,

WILLIAM MICHAEL, 1869, *Letter to Mrs. Gilchrist*.

I think it was very manly and kind of you to put the whole of Walt Whitman's poems into my hands; and that I have no other friend who would have judged them and me so wisely and generously. I had not dreamed that words could cease to be words, and become electric streams like these. I do assure you that, strong as I am, I feel sometimes as if I had not bodily strength to read many of these poems. In the series headed "Calamus," for instance, in some of the "Songs of Parting," the "Voice out of the Sea," the poem beginning "Tears, Tears," etc., there is such a weight of emotion, such a tension of the heart, that mine refuses to beat under it—stands quite still—and I am obliged to lay the book down for a while. Or again, in the piece called "Walt Whitman," and one or two others of that type, I am as one hurried through stormy sea, over high mountains, dazed with sunlight, stunned with a crowd and tumult of faces and voices, till I am breathless, bewildered, half dead. Then come parts and whole poems in which there is such calm wisdom and strength of thought, such a cheerful breadth of sunshine, that the soul bathes in them renewed and strengthened. Living impulses flow out of these that make me exult in life, yet look longingly towards "the superb vistas of Death." Those who admire this poem, and don't care for that, and talk of formlessness, absence of meter, etc., are quite as far from any genuine recognition of Walt Whitman as his bitter detractors.—GILCHRIST, ANNE, 1869, *Letter to W. M. Rossetti*, July 11; in *Re Walt Whitman*, ed. Traubel, Bucke and Harned, p. 42.

Pupils who are accustomed to associate the idea of poetry with regular classic measure in rhyme, or in ten-syllabled blank verse, or elastic hexameters, will commence these short and simple prose sentences with surprise, and will wonder how any number of them can form a poem. But let them read aloud, with minds in sympathy with the picture as it is displayed, and they will find by nature's unmistakable responses that the author is a poet, and possesses the poet's incommunicable power to touch the heart. This power is the inheritance into which the poet is born, and as Webster said of eloquence, labor and learning will toil for it in vain.—UNDERWOOD, F. H., 1872, *English Literature, American Authors*, p. 461.

Whitman is unceasingly gay, and fresh and racy. He speaks of common things, and men, and the common sights of everyday life, and yet he is always artistic. The things he observes are significant and such as arrest the eye and the mind, and make a deep mark in the memory. He expresses more than happiness, he expresses exultation. The two hemispheres of the soul he describes as love and dilatation, or pride:—

I was Manhattanese, friendly, and proud.

And so he often uses the word arrogant in a good sense. His poems teem with such words as superb, perfect, gigantic, divine. At his touch the dry bones of our meagre humanity are transformed, and man starts forth like a god, in body and in soul superhuman. . . . No English poet except perhaps Shelley was so well acquainted with all that could be learned from books. But they give expression to their learning in widely different ways. Shelley's knowledge did not appear in his poetry, it went to feed his idealism and egotism. Whitman's appears as a natural growth. He alludes to the solar system and the formation of the earth, and to what he has learned from travellers and ethnologists, as he alludes to the apple-blossom or any other common thing. No poet ever assimilated his knowledge so well as Whitman or so vitalised it with his own large and joyous life. . . . He is the noblest literary product of modern times, and his influence is invigorating and refining beyond expression. —CLIVE, ARTHUR, 1875, *Walt Whitman, the Poet of Joy, Gentleman's Magazine*, N. S., vol. 15, pp. 706, 710, 716.

"The Leaves of Grass" is redeemed by few grand descriptive passages from absolute barbarism both of manner and matter. It is a glorification of nature in her most unabashed forms, an audacious protest against all that civilization has done to raise men above the savage state. The "Drum Taps," a set of generally vigorous pictures of the war, are less objectionable; the dirge on Lincoln in particular has many qualities of a noble elegy,—the imagery is rich though sometimes fantastic, and there is here and there a wild music in the composition,—but it is still defaced by pedantic words and unjustifiable, because unnecessary, novelties of phrase.—NICHOL, JOHN, 1875, *American Literature, Encyclopædia Britannica*, vol. I, p. 643.

If I ever saw anything in print that

deserved to be characterized as atrociously bad, it is the poetry of Walt Whitman; and the three critics of repute, Dr. Dowden, Mr. W. Rossetti, and Mr. Buchanan, who have praised his performances, appear to me to be playing off on the public a well-intentioned, probably good-humoured, but really cruel hoax. . . . He is in no sense a superlatively able man, and it was beyond his powers to make for himself a legitimate poetical reputation. No man of high capacity could be so tumid and tautological as he—could talk, for instance, of the "fluid wet" of the sea; or speak of the aroma of his armpits, or make the crass and vile mistake of bringing into light what nature veils, and confounding liberty with dissolute anarchy. The poet of democracy he is not; but his books may serve to buoy, for the democracy of America, those shallows and sunken rocks on which, if it is cast, it must inevitably, amid the hootings of mankind, be wrecked. Always, unless he chooses to contradict himself for the sake of paradox, his political doctrine is the consecration of mutinous independence and rabid egotism and impudent conceit. In his ideal city "the men and women think lightly of the laws." His advice is to resist much and to obey little. This is the political philosophy of Bedlam, unchained in these ages chiefly through the influence of Rousseau, which has blasted the hopes of freedom wherever it has had the chance, and which must be chained up again with ineffable contempt if the self-government of nations is to mean anything else than the death and putrescence of civilization. Incapable of true poetical originality, Whitman had the cleverness to invent a literary trick, and the shrewdness to stick to it. As a Yankee phenomenon, to be good-humouredly laughed at, and to receive that moderate pecuniary remuneration which nature allows to vivacious quacks, he would have been in his place; but when influential critics introduce him to the English public as a great poet, the thing becomes too serious for a joke.—BAYNE, PETER, 1875, *Walt Whitman's Poems, Contemporary Review,* vol. 27, pp. 49, 68.

We are rather vexed, now it is too late, that I did not carry out a sort of incipient intention to expunge a motto from Walt Whitman which I inserted in Book IV. Of course the whole is irrevocable by this time; but I should have otherwise thought it worth while to have a new page, not because the motto itself is objectionable to me—it was one of the finer things which has clung to me from among his writings—but because, since I quote so few poets, my selection of a motto from Walt Whitman might be taken as a sign of a special admiration, which I am very far from feeling. —ELIOT, GEORGE, 1876, *To John Blackwood, April 18; George Eliot's Life as related in her Letters and Journals,* ed. Cross, vol. III, p. 200.

Wordsworth speaks of Chatterton as "the marvellous boy;" Walt Whitman, in his first "Leaves of Grass," might have been styled the marvellous "b'hoy." Walt protested against all convention, even all forms of conventional verse; he seemed to start up from the ground, an earth-born son of the soil, and put to all cultivated people the startling question, "What do you think of Me?" They generally thought highly of him as an original. Nothing is more acceptable to minds jaded with reading works of culture than the sudden appearance of a strong, rough book, expressing the habits, ideas, and ideals of the uncultivated; but, unfortunately, Whitman declined to listen to the suggestion that his daring disregard of convention should have one exception, and that he must modify his frank expression of the relations of the sexes. The author refused, and the completed edition of the "Leaves of Grass" fell dead from the press. Since that period he has undergone new experiences; his latest books are not open to objections urged against his earliest; but still the "Leaves of Grass," if thoroughly cleaned, would even now be considered his ablest and most original work.—WHIPPLE, EDWIN PERCY, 1876-86, *American Literature and Other Papers,* ed. Whittier, p. 113.

As everything that he has written is easily included in one medium-sized volume, it must be supposed that this increasing audience is not due to freshness of matter brought before the public at frequent intervals, but to the something inherent and of value in the old. But, with this increase, the audience is even now but a limited one. It is a minority, and a small minority; yet it has in its range some of the distinguished names of the century. Emerson is one of them, though perhaps Emerson may be reckoned as one of the earlier heralds of enthusiasm, whose glow and fervor faltered a little in the heat of the day, which later made the atmosphere about Mr. Whitman something of a trial-test to his admirers. But it is certainly enough to know that Mr. Emerson at once, after reading the first issue of "Leaves of Grass," wrote to Mr. Whitman, expressing in the strongest terms his approbation and admiration of the book. Then later we come to such adherents as Rossetti, Swinburne, Buchanan, Dowden, and our own O'Connor, and John Burroughs, author of that delightful book, "Winter Sunshine." Thoreau, too, "that austere spirit," testifies in his last volume to his great esteem for Whitman, and, greater than all, Thomas Carlyle, that fiery router and detester of shams, considers Walt Whitman "a man furnished for the highest of all enterprises—that of being the poet of his age." . . . I cannot call myself an ardent admirer of Mr. Whitman's poems, but I am confident that, though my individual taste may not be pleased by the poet's *method*, his *purpose* is noble. And I do not see how an unprejudiced critic can fail to perceive something, at least, of this good intention.—PERRY, NORA, 1876, *A Few Words about Walt Whitman, Appleton's Journal, vol.* 15, *pp.* 531, 532.

The real American poet is Walt Whitman—a man enormously greater than Longfellow or any other of his poetic compatriots.—ROSSETTI, WILLIAM MICHAEL, 1878, *Lives of Famous Poets*, p. 391.

These are quite glorious things you have sent me. Who is Walt (Walter?) Whitman, and is much of him like this?—RUSKIN, JOHN, 1879, *Letter to William Harrison Riley, In Re Walt Whitman*, ed. Traubel, Bucke, and Harned, p. 352.

No one more conspicuously shines by difference. Others are more widely read, but who else has been so widely talked of, and who has held even a few readers with so absolute a sway? Whatever we may think of his chantings, the time has gone by when it was possible to ignore him; whatever his ground may be, he has set his feet squarely and audaciously upon it, and is no light weight. Endeavor, then, to judge him on his merits, for he will and must be judged. . . . The fault was not that he discussed matters which others timidly evade, but that he did not do it in a clean way,—that he was too anatomical and malodorous withal; furthermore, that in this department he showed excessive interest, and applied its imagery to other departments, as if with a special purpose to lug it in. His pictures sometimes were so realistic, his speech so free, as to excite the hue and cry of indecent exposure; the display of things natural, indeed, but which we think it unnatural to exhibit on the highway, or in the sitting-room, or anywhere except their wonted places of consignment. . . . As an assimilating poet of nature he has positive genius, and seems to me to present his strongest claims. Who else, in fact, has so true a hand or eye for the details, the sweep and color, of American landscape? Like others, he confronts those superb physical aspects of the New World which have controlled our poetry and painting, and deferred the growth of a figure-school, but in this conflict with nature he is not overcome; if not the master, he is the joyous brother-in-arms. He has heard the message of the pushing, wind-swept sea, along Paumanok's shore; he knows the yellow, waning moon and the rising stars,—the sunset, with its cloudbar of gold above the horizon,—the birds that sing by night or day, bush and brier, and every shining or swooning flower, the peaks, the prairie, the mighty, conscious river, the dear common grass that children fetch with full hands. Little escapes him, not even "the mossy scabs of the worm fence, and heap'd stones, mullen and poke-weed;" but his details are massed, blended,—the wind saturates and the light of the American skies transfigures them. Not that to me, recalling the penetrative glance of Emerson, the wood and way-side craft that Lowell carried lightly as a sprig of fir, and recalling other things of others, does Whitman seem our "only" poet of nature; but that here he is on his own ground, and with no man his leader.—STEDMAN, EDMUND CLARENCE, 1880, *Walt Whitman, Scribner's Monthly, vol.* 21, *pp.* 47, 54, 59.

While I differ from him utterly as to every principle of artistic procedure; while he seems to me the most stupendously mistaken man in all history as to what constitutes true democracy, and the true advance of art and man; while I am immeasurably shocked at the sweeping invasions of those reserves which depend on the very personality I have so much insisted upon, and which the whole consensus of the ages has considered more and more sacred with every year of growth in delicacy; yet, after all these prodigious allowances, I owe some keen delights to a certain combination of bigness and naïveté which make some of Whitman's passages so strong and taking, and indeed, on the one occasion when Whitman has abandoned his theory of formlessness and written in form he has made "My Captain, O my Captain" surely one of the most tender and beautiful poems in any language. . . . Professing to be a mudsill and glorying in it, chanting democracy and shirt-sleeves and equal rights, declaring that he is nothing if not one of the people, nevertheless the people, the democracy, will yet have nothing to do with him, and it is safe to say that his sole audience has lain among such representatives of the highest culture as Emerson and the English *illuminated*. The truth is, that if closely examined, Whitman, instead of being a true democrat, is simply the most incorrigible of aristocrats masquing in a peasant's costume, and his poetry, instead of being the natural outcome of a fresh young democracy, is a product which would be impossible except in a highly civilized society.—LANIER, SIDNEY, 1881, *The English Novel, pp.* 45, 47.

He is perhaps of all writers the most repellent to the reader who glances at him superficially. In the first place he is indecent, and that too not accidentally but on principle. Whatever may be thought of his morality, and that I hold to be essentially sound and healthy, it cannot be denied that in one section of his work, and occasionally throughout the poems and prose, he outrages every ordinary rule of decency. There is nothing impure in this kind of exposure; it has indeed the direct antithesis of prurient suggestion, and the intention of it is unquestionably honest, but from an artistic point of view it is the gravest of faults, it is essentially and irredeemably ugly, and repulsive. . . . He stands convicted of ἀπειροκλία, if of nothing worse. Akin to this first instance of defect in artistic preception is a second—his use, namely, of words which are either not English, or essentially vulgar; and to this must be added a not unfrequent neglect of syntax, which, together with looseness in the application of some words, makes him at times vague or unintelligible. Occasionally there occur words or expressions which, though not ordinarily found in literature, have a native force which justifies them; but generally it is the case that for the French word or for the vulgarism savouring either of the gutter on the one hand or of the Yankee penny-a-liner on the other might be substituted a good English word equally expressive.—MACAULAY, G. C., 1882, *Walt Whitman, Nineteenth Century, vol.* 12, *p.* 905.

The acrid taste is no more than a pleasant sharpness now and again; and in the main these "Notes of a Half-Paralytic" are sweet and sane and nourishing, more, perhaps, than their writer knows or can know. No diary of an invalid is wholesomer reading than this; never a groan or a growl, never a word of complaint; but every bright hour, every breeze of health, every delight in flower and bird and stream and star, and in the kind voice or hand of a friend, remembered and recorded. Always, in this invalid's diary, the pure, fresh air, and the sky overhead; never the blinds drawn down, the table crowded with medicine bottles, and the foot of the spiritual medicine-man upon the threshold. . . . Connected with the notes of convalescence in this volume are Whitman's previously published memoranda of the war; and the national frenzy and agony (with underlying sanity and strength) of the one period goes well with the tender calm and restorative happiness of the other. His lecture on Lincoln, a record of his visits to Emerson and Longfellow, a reminiscence and a criticism, severe, yet sympathetic, of Edgar Poe, will interest readers who care to see great or distinguished persons through a poet's eyes.—DOWDEN, EDWARD, 1882,*Specimen Days and Collect, The Academy, vol.* 22, *pp.* 357, 358.

Whether he may greatly influence the future or not, he is a notable symptom of the present. As a sign of the times, it would be hard to find his parallel. I should hazard a large wager, for instance, that he was not unacquainted with the works of Herbert Spencer; and yet where, in all the history books, shall we lay our hands on two more incongruous contemporaries? Mr. Spencer so decorous—I had almost said, so dandy—in dissent; and Whitman, like a large shaggy dog, just unchained, scouring the beaches of the world and baying at the moon. And when was an echo more curiously like a satire, than when Mr. Spencer found his Synthetic Philosophy reverberated from the other shores of the Atlantic in the "barbaric yawp" of Whitman?

—STEVENSON, ROBERT LOUIS, 1882, *Familiar Studies of Men and Books, p.* 92.

Mr. Whitman, indeed, appears not to be content with the abrogation of all conventional notions of poetry and artificial contrivances for constructing and testing it. Not only are rhymes avoided by him and even measures shunned—spondees, dactyls, trochees, iambics, anapests, odes, ballads, and sonnets, kicked into chaos together, as frippery suited only to poets who lull their readers with "piano tunes,"—but he overrides and crushes out with remorseless effort even those innocently recurring cadences and natural rhythms which are so often the involuntary accompaniment of the expression of impassioned thought. He thus succeeds not only in avoiding all semblance of piano tunes or any other musical thing, but in producing singularly harsh and disagreeable prose. Whatever may be Mr. Whitman's powers of imagination and description, his lack of a sense of poetic fitness, his failure to understand the business of a poet, is certainly astounding.—BROWNE, FRANCIS FISHER, 1882, *Briefs on New Books, The Dial, vol.* 2, *p.* 218.

He stands there in his stricken old age, contemplating with serene, nay, with still glowing eyes, the vast growth of his beloved nation, refusing to despair over its diseases, looking steadfastly to a golden age beyond; the most significant living figure in American literature. . . . Looking round on contemporary poetry, English and French, one is led to suspect that much of it will go the way of last generation's theology, and that poets who have spun their philosophies and gospels into vast webs of verse, "laying great bases for eternity," will be found in a century or so to have spent much labour in vain. But the poetry of Whitman, ill-smelted as so much of it is, cataloguial as is so much of his transcription from life, and lacking as his song so often is in music, somehow does not seem thus marked for doom even in respect of his didacticism. And the reason would seem to be not merely that his message is the intense expression of his deepest passion, but that the passion is the very flower of the life of the race thus far, and carries in it the seeds of things to come. He cannot soon be left behind—he has gone so far before.—ROBERTSON, JOHN, 1884, *Walt Whitman, Poet, Democrat, pp.* 50, 52.

I feel no hesitation in saying that the spirit of Mr. Whitman's poetry is the contrary of the democratic spirit, because it is deficient in clearness, in consistency, in art, and in common sense. At first blush there may seem to be a kinship of liberty; but the liberty of democracy is the highest evolutionary step in the struggle for the rights of man, while the liberty of Walt Whitman's poetry is license of thought and anarchy of expression. Most people take pride in conquering the thoughts which he takes a riotous glee in giving vent to.—KENNEDY, WALKER, 1884, *Walt Whitman, North American Review, vol.* 138, *p.* 600.

His strong individuality, wilfulness, audacity, with his scorn of convention and rote, have unquestionably carried him far outside the regular metes and bounds. No wonder there are some who refuse to consider his "Leaves" as "literature." It is perhaps only because he was brought up a printer, and worked during his early years as newspaper and magazine writer, that he has put his expression in typographical from, and made a regular book of it, with lines, leaves and binding.—SELWYN, GEORGE, 1885, *Walt Whitman at Camden, The Critic, vol.* 6, *p.* 98.

I had never shared in the general vituperation which greeted "Leaves of Grass" when it appeared in an English dress, under the auspices of Dante Gabriel Rossetti, much as there was repulsive even in that expurgated edition. There seemed to me flashes of genius and clear insight which no age, least of all our own, can afford to despise. The man who wrote "Whispers of Heavenly Death" could not be a mere licentious charlatan. The revolt of Whitman against rhyme is like the revolt of Wagner against stereotyped melody, and in his way he seemed to me to be in search of a freer and more adequate method for conveying the intimate and rapid interior changes of the soul. Over and above this Whitman's wild stanzas, with their lists of carpenters' tools and "barbaric yawps," their delight in the smoke and roar of cities, as well as in the solitudes of woods and the silence of mountains and seas of prairies—seemed to me to breathe something distinctive, national, American—with all his confusion of mind. I could hardly read his superb prose description of the Federal battlefields—and those matchless pages on the assassination of President Lincoln (of which he was an eye-witness), without feeling that Whitman was no figurehead—one more monkey, in fact—but a large and living soul, with a certain width of aboriginal sympathy, too rare in these days of jejune thought and palsied heart.— HAWEIS, HUGH REGINALD, 1886, *The Pall Mall Gazette.*

When I think of that gray head, gently bowing before the contempt of the literary class in America, when I think that Boston crowns Emerson and turns aside from the spirit potent enough to create a hundred Emersons and leave strength sufficient for the making of the whole Bostonian cosmogony, from Lowell upwards, I for a moment lose patience with a mighty nation; but only for a moment: the voice of my gentle master sounds in my ear, and I am reminded that if he is great and good, it is because he represents the greatness and goodness of a free and noble people.—BUCHANAN, ROBERT, 1886, *A Look Round Literature.*

There is one American poet whose faults of art and judgment are on a scale commensurate with his original genius. I mean Walt Whitman, whose speech is often as drearily prosaic as the wide sands and mud-flats of the sea which he so loves, when they are left bare by the tide; but after one is fairly embarked on the ocean of his more rhythmic lines, their long swing —their multitudinous rise, and fall—have the same strange, irregular harmony that one feels in the curve and motion of the billows. . . . Whitman, like Browning, has invaded and annexed a new province, although one that is less habitable. But he is always, and above everything, meditative, moralizing, introspective; seeing all other objects and persons in himself, and himself in all other persons and objects.— LATHROP, GEORGE PARSONS, 1886, *Representative Poems of Living Poets,* ed. *Gilder, Introduction,* p. xxii.

The term *poet* does not fully describe Walt Whitman: the word *prophet* would come nearer; but that might be misunderstood. Schopenhauer has been well described as "the great prophet of the world's despair." Walt Whitman may be termed conversely the great prophet of the world's hope. . . . He sounds all the chords of human feeling with the depth and urgency of one who has suffered, in his own person and by sympathy, all woes and agonies, but whose spirit is too great to be turned by any suffering from the clear faith that "*all is* well."—FORMAN, H. BUXTON, 1887, *Celebrities of the Century,* ed *Sanders,* p. 1047.

To the better qualities discernible in the voluminous and incoherent effusions of Walt Whitman it should not be difficult for any reader not unduly exasperated by the rabid idiocy of the Whitmaniacs to do full and ample justice: for these qualities are no less simple and obvious than laudable and valuable. A just enthusiasm, a genuine passion of patriotic and imaginative sympathy, a sincere though limited and distorted love of nature, an eager and earnest faith in freedom and in loyalty—in the loyalty that can only be born of liberty; a really manful and a nobly rational tone of mind with regard to the crowning questions of duty and of death; these excellent qualities of emotion and reflection find here and there a not inadequate expression in a style of rhetoric not always flatulent or inharmonious. . . . Assuredly I never have meant to imply what most assuredly I never have said—that I regarded Mr. Whitman as a poet or a thinker in the proper sense; the sense in which the one term is applicable to Coleridge or to Shelley, the other to Bacon or to Mill. Whoever may have abdicated his natural right, as a being not born without a sense of music or a sense of reason, to protest against the judgment which discerns in "Childe Harold" or in "Drum-Taps" a masterpiece of imagination and expression, of intelligence or of song, I never have abdicated mine. The highest literary quality discoverable in either book is rhetoric: and very excellent rhetoric in either case it sometimes is; what it is at other times I see no present necessity to say. . . . If any thing can justify the serious and deliberate display of merely physical emotion in literature or in art, it must be one of two things: intense depth of feeling expressed with inspired perfection of simplicity, with divine sublimity of fascination, as by Sappho; or transcendant supremacy of actual and irresistible beauty in such revelation of naked nature as was possible to Titian. But Mr. Whitman's Eve is a drunken apple-woman, indecently sprawling in the slush and garbage of the gutter amid the rotten refuse of her overturned fruit-stall; but Mr. Whitman's Venus is a Hottentot wench under the influence of cantharides and adulterated rum. Cotytto herself would repudiate the ministration of such priestesses as these. But what then, if anything, is it that a rational creature who has studied and understood the work of any poet, great or small, from Homer down to Moschus, from Lucretius down to Martial, from Dante down to Metastasio, from Villon down to Voltaire, from Shakespeare down to Byron, can find to applaud, to approve, or to condone in the work of Mr. Whitman? To this very reasonable and inevitable question the answer is not far to seek. I have myself repeatedly pointed out—it may be (I have often been told so) with too unqualified sympathy and too uncritical enthusiasm— the qualities which give a certain touch of greatness to his work, the sources of inspiration which infuse into its chaotic jargon some passing or seeming notes of cosmic beauty, and diversify with something of occasional harmony the strident and barren discord of its jarring and erring atoms. His sympathies, I repeat, are usually generous, his views of life are occassionally just, and his views of death are invariably noble. . . . As a poet, no amount of improvement that self-knowledge and self-culture might have brought to bear upon such exceptionally raw material could ever have raised him higher than a station to which his homely and manly patriotism would be the best claim that could be preferred for him, a seat beside such writers as Ebenezer Elliott—or possibly a little higher, on such an elevation as might be occupied by a poet whom careful training had reared and matured into a rather inferior kind of Southey.—SWINBURNE, ALGERNON CHARLES, 1887, *Whitmania, Fortnightly Review, vol.* 48, *pp.* 170, 171, 175, 176.

Bold innovator in the realm of thought;
Strong-sinewed Titan fighting for the right,
And wresting from the panoplies of night
The glories that the patient stars have caught
From an evanished sun; brave teacher, taught
By Nature's lips to see with Nature's sight,
And so to shed day's fair, unsullied light
Upon the work thy ruggedhandshavewrought,
Thou stand'st serene upon thy mountain crag,
Unmindful of the shallow hum which fills
The valleys with derision. Thou canst wait,
And, waiting, find thine own, when prescient Fate
Shall grant thee justice, and unfurl the flag
Of Innocency on a thousand hills.
—WILLIAMS, FRANCIS HOWARD, 1887, *To Walt Whitman, Lippincott's Magazine, Jan.*

To endorse, in any valid sense, much of the tenor of modern opinion as to the poetic merit of the school of Whitman, is altogether impossible, though the oracle at Delphi order it.—HUNT, THEODORE W., 1887, *Representative English Prose and Prose Writers, p.* 295.

In absolute ability he is about equal to Taylor, Stoddard, Stedman, or Aldrich; but by minimizing the spiritual and the artistic, and magnifying the physical and the crudely spontaneous, he has attracted an attention among critics in America, England, and the Continental nations greater, for the moment, than that bestowed upon any contemporary singer of his nation, and fairly rivalling the international adulation of his exact opposite, Poe. To him the ideal is little and the immediately actual is much; love is merely a taurine or passerine passion; and to-day is a thing more important than all the past. His courage is unquestionable; his vigor is abounding; and therefore, by the very paradox of his extravagant demands, he has impressed some and interested more, and has induced a limited but affectionate and exceedingly vociferous coterie to attempt, for his sake, to revise the entire canon of the world's art.—RICHARDSON, CHARLES F., 1888, *American Literature,* 1607–1885, *vol.* II, *p.* 269.

Whitman is a force in modern poetry. He has sought to give new and striking expression to what is distinctive in American life, by breaking with the accepted laws of poetic form. With his profound humanity, his breadth, strength, and insight, I believe that he has proved himself a great poet,—but this in spite of, and not by means of, his contempt of form.— ROBERTS, CHARLES G. D., 1888, *ed. Poems of Wild Life, p.* 238, *note.*

Walt Whitman, stricken in years and health, but as serene as of yore, still alert to all the infinite possibilities of his own soul and of mankind in general, still oblivious of the irredeemable commonplace of so much of his barbaric chant.—SHARP, WILLIAM, 1889, *ed. American Sonnets, Introductory Note, p.* xxiv.

Yes, Walt Whitman has appeared. He has his place upon the stage. The drama is not ended. His voice is still heard. He is the poet of Democracy—of all people. He is the poet of the body and soul. He has sounded the note of individuality. He has given the pass-word primeval. He is the Poet of Humanity—of Intellectual Hospitality. He has voiced the aspirations of America—and, above all, he is the poet of Love and Death.—INGERSOLL, ROBERT G., 1890, *Liberty in Literature, In Re Walt Whitman*, ed. Traubel, Bucke, and Harned, p. 281.

Thy soul hath revelled in the forests green;
  The solemn purple plains;
The immense far range of hills whose summits hoar
Mix with the eternal blue; the ceaseless roar
  Of rivers swollen by Titanic rains:
Somewhat thy soul hath gathered of the might
Of thine America; by day, by night,
  Watching, thy gaze hath won
A measured glimpse of what man's eyes shall see;
While Europe's slaves to kings have bent the knee
Thou, yokeless, hast been vassal of the sun:
Thou, scaling thought's untrodden mountain-sides,
Hast felt the heart of Freedom like a bride's
  Against thine own heart beat;
While the old world struggled, cramped by prison-bars,
Thou, seeking Freedom's palace lit by stars,
  Didst pass the heights where storms and the eagles meet.

—BARLOW, GEORGE, 1890, *Walt Whitman, From Dawn to Sunset*.

Whitman offers enormous difficulties to the critic who wishes to deal fairly with him. The grotesqueness of his language and the uncouth structure of his sentences render it almost impossible to do justice to the breadth of his thought and the sublimity of his imagination. He ought to be taken in large draughts, to be lived with in long solitudes. His peculiar mode of utterance suffers cruelly by quotation. Yet it is needful to extract his very words, in order to escape from the vagueness of a summary.... Whitman expels miracles from the region of mysticism, only to find a deeper mysticism in the world of which he forms a part, and miracles in commonplace occurrences. He dethrones the gods of old pantheons, because he sees God everywhere around him. He discrowns the heroes of myth and romance; but greets their like again among his living comrades.—SYMONDS, JOHN ADDINGTON, 1890, *Essays Speculative and Suggestive*, vol. II, pp. 47, 50.

The large number of persons who are blinded to Whitman's genius by the incidental nakedness of his writing would do well to ponder Mr. Ellis's most apposite contrast in this particular of Whitman with Swift. Swift regarded men and women not only as beasts, but as lower than other beasts, on account of the grotesque hypocrisy which leads them to muffle up their beasthood under decorous names; and this mask his dire indignation and misapplied sincerity impelled him ruthlessly to strip off. There is all the legacy of mediaeval body-hatred in the portrait of the Yahoo; and Swift is a Christian *manqué*. Whitman is a pagan, and takes his nudity as sanely as he does everything else. Neither writer is likely to hurt any healthy grown person; it is the thin and eager minds, the erotic mystics, who really have the "seminal principle in their brains," not these burly and virile spirits. Where many of Whitman's poems fall short is, in one word, in *Art*. That is a sufficiently fatal shortcoming, and one which avenges itself speedily by the extinction of the peccant work. Whitman's capacity for inspiration, for prophecy, and for hope is very far ahead of his literary sense; he wrestles with difficulties of expression and construction, and constantly succumbs before them. Now and then he conquers; and an immortal flower of verse is born like

"Warble me now for joy of lilac-time,"

or like "Captain! my Captain!" Some, therefore, of the poetry, or rhythmic prose, which contains certain of Whitman's farthest reaching thought, is artistically faulty; and Mr. Ellis, as befits his somewhat doctrinal purpose, puts aside the question of Whitman's poetic accomplishment, and is engrossed rather with enquiring what creed he can extract from him.—ELTON, OLIVER, 1890, *The Academy*, vol. 37, p. 231.

There is much imperfection in his work. In fact, but little is perfect. Let us say it while there is yet opportunity. A time will come when Walt Whitman—the so long ignored (except by a few among whom were those who scorned, insulted, persecuted him), afterwards the butt of the irrepressible witling:—nay, perhaps the day is coming fast when it will be heresy, presumption, folly, to suggest that this Walt Whitman is not perfect and complete. ... We wear the very garb of philosophers after reading Spencer, we are more vigorous after Carlyle, more healthy in reading Walt Whitman.—LYNCH, ARTHUR, 1891, *Modern Authors.*

Walt Whitman, notwithstanding his many great and glaring faults, is perhaps the most interesting living personality in American literature. His works have attracted the favourable attention of some of our most distinguished critics, and aroused the wrath of many others, not less distinguished, both in the country of his birth and in England. . . . It is extremely doubtful whether the name of poet can with propriety be applied to Whitman, since his works lack one of the first and most essential qualities of poetry —concrete and artistic expression. He is undoubtedly a great and original genius; and would have been a very great poet had he possessed this indispensable faculty. . . . The "Song of the Broad Axe," and "Salut au Monde," are two of his longest poems. The first is a chant of Democracy and Labour, of a very vigorous character, suited to its subject; of the other, we may say that it almost justifies its name. Both are thoroughly characteristic examples of their author's best use of his peculiar style. Whitman wrote two funeral hymns on the death of Lincoln. One of these entitled, "O Captain! my Captain!" is the only instance in which he attempts regular artistic structure. It is a really beautiful poem, and is entitled to quotation in its entirety, showing as it does the great results which he might have achieved with a proper and persevering cultivation of poetic form.—CURTIS, WILLIAM O'LEARY, 1891, *Whitman's Defects and Beauties, The Month,* vol. 71, pp. 527, 531.

His words are perpetual warnings to all sects and syndicates, to all leagues and orders which bind men's minds or muscles to the bidding of another, which make them slaves in thought or in action; and a warning against that worse and commoner bondage to one's own self, to imbibed traditions, to cultivated fears, to accepted and self-forged shackles. He who would gain true freedom, who would feel soul and body stinging with a new, and electric life, the life of one's self, let him patiently, persistently seek the meaning of that legacy of verse left with us by him whom now we consign to the clasp of the tomb.—BRINTON, DANIEL G., 1892, *At the Graveside of Walt Whitman, In Re Walt Whitman,* ed. Traubel, Bucke, and Harned, p. 443.

There were quite special reasons wny it would have been fortunate had Walt Whitman been persuaded to visit London. For there is no doubt whatever that, whether or not endowed with any kind of literary genius—poetic genius no one now dreams of crediting him with—he was very richly endowed with the genius of a magnetic personality, which enables a few rare individuals throughout the entire animal kingdom to create a following by means of shear unintelligibility and muddleheadedness. . . . When, not so many years ago, I was attacked, perhaps I might say abused, by the young gentlemen—bards for the most part—who "did" the literature in a little group of newspapers, on the ground that I was a "reactionary poet"—that is to say an anti-Whitmanite who had corrupted a certain set of great poets, including Dante Rossetti, inoculating them with my reactionary views— the gravest charge against me was that I had christened Whitman the "Jack Bunsby of Parnassus." Well, there is no doubt that I did give him that name, but not as a poet, as a naturalist; now that he is dead, and now that I know what a fine and manly soul it was that expressed itself with so much incoherence, I regret that I should ever have given him such a name. . . . Of course, if Whitman really has a message for humanity we will listen to him in whatsoever jargon he may deliver it. But what is his message? No Capt. Cuttle has ever formulated this. At one moment this teaching is that of an intense individualism, at the next that of a kind of democratic Socialism, at the next it is Carlylean. It is extremely easy to disguise puzzle-headedness the moment that you pass away from prose statement. As to benevolence, comradeship, some of the countrymen of Shakespeare, of Sterne, of Burns, of Ebenezer Elliott, of Dickens, seem really to think that Whitman invented these qualities, or, at least, gave first expression to them. As to his amazing indecency, that may be forgiven. It has done no harm. It is merely the attempt of a journalist to play the "tan-faced man"— to play "the noble savage" by fouling with excrement the doorstep of Civilization. —WATTS, THEODORE, 1892, *Walt Whitman, The Athenæum,* No. 3362, pp. 436, 437.

He had absorbed divine influences from past thinkers, but he had no sense of the laws of style, or, indeed, the sense that there were any laws. Hence, the sometimes—one might be induced to say, the frequent—formless lines, and the attempts to produce effects which no great artist would have employed. The poet was unable, through lack of literary culture, to clothe his novel and often glowing conceptions in any ideal poetic form. Rather he flings his ideas at us in a heap, leaving it to us to arrange them in order in our minds. His results, therefore, fail to satisfy many not unsympathetic readers.—CLARKE, WILLIAM, 1892, *Walt Whitman*, p. 50.

To him the dirtiest puddle reflects the beauty of the skies. We have heard of a child who wept on being told that a flower she admired was nothing but a weed. To Whitman there are no weeds in the world. With the child's simple eye to nature he takes them all for plants of precious growth, bearing each one of them, buried deep, perhaps, within its calyx, the seed of perfection. And in this he is not like the child, that his trust can be destroyed by the first rude unthinking hand. With authority, as if he spoke for God, he gives his imperious verdict on behalf of what the world despises, and pronounces it also to be good. He rejects nothing, he despises nothing: "Good or bad, I never question you, I love all—I do not condemn anything." For the poet, as in one of his softly rounded, tenderly suggestive phrases he asserts, "judges not as the judge judges, but as the sun falling round a helpless thing;" or else, as in this case, like the young child who has no standard but its own clinging nature to measure people by. To his pure, spiritualised vision "objects gross and the unseen soul are one." No head to him but wears its "nimbus of gold-coloured light." He takes everyone, the meanest and most worthless, by the hand, and whispers to him or her that he understands and loves what none others have understood or loved; that the true being, soul and body (he will never separate them), stands revealed in its glory and perfection to him, unhidden by the most repulsive exterior; that at the worst, though premature death should have already fallen, the means will be provided that it may "pick its way." . . . What might shock and disgust if it came from any one else only startles us with its note of strangeness from him. His coarseness is as the coarseness of the earth, which, with "disdainful innocence," takes all for clean. . . . As we study him his utterances take on power and beauty. His character seems to gather cohesion and to expand; so that whereas, in our first perusal of him, when we came across some passage of exquisite beauty or on some announcement of matured wisdom, we were startled almost as if a very child amid its careless babblings had uttered words of inspiration, we end by acknowledging in him both the giant and the child, a man,

full-statured in magnificence.

—ROOSE, PAULINE W., 1892, *A Child-Poet: Walt Whitman, Gentleman's Magazine, N.S. vol.* 48, *pp.* 479, 480.

Their author is virile, but not always rational. Too often he opens his eyes wide with amazement at mere matters of quantity and magnitude. He makes extravagant claims for his extravagant muse. He does not appreciate delicate effects and nice distinctions of thought. He has something of mob violence about him, but also much mob power and vehemence. He is the pioneer and extreme of his class, but certain of his traits appear, scattered and incidental, in the work of some of our recent novelists and critics.—MABIE, HAMILTON W., 1892, *The Memorial Story of America*, p. 589.

What is he? What is his class? Is he the Homer of America? What will he be to posterity? If answers to these questions were obtained from the knowing ones in the world of letters, the result would show some interesting contrasts. Only a few people deny that there are some good and strong things in Whitman. But most people agree that these grains of wheat are hidden under a wilderness of—chaff, our figure requires; but it is a heavier rubbish than that. Even judging him through his devoted little band of adherents, the result of his great theory of "formlessness" is notably against him, for the poem which they admire most and point to before all others is the fine one, "O Captain, my Captain;" and—it is most significant—this comes nearer to conventional form than anything else in Whitman's whole collection. . . . If Whitman reminds us, in his use of the fag ends of foreign tongues, of a cosmopolitan hotel waiter, it is also true that in the midst of his queer phraseology he sometimes stumbles on a felicity of expression that is Homeric in its simplicity, its strength, and its grandeur. This is the most unexplainable thing about the man: he can be grand and grandisse in the same line. Genius and fatuity go hand in hand throughout his writings.—LANIER, C. D., 1892, *Walt Whitman, The Chautauquan, vol.* 15, *pp.* 311, 312, 313.

The general characteristic of the outward form of Whitman's poems, and the only quality of accepted poetical form which they possess, is a rhythm at once majestic and subtle, completely separating them from verse as well as from prose, yet defying analysis. Considering his poetry, however, not merely in its formal aspect, but regarding it as an undivided whole in which matter and form are organically one, regarding it as the single and sincere expression of the mind of a poet who says what he thinks in his own best natural way, we shall find that Whitman's most general characteristics are a sustained and magnetic power, and a deep spiritual insight. He writes with the force of the primeval poets, as well befits one who is indeed a solitary singer in the morning of the new day of men and women which has succeeded to that of lords and ladies, kings and hierarchs. In him the world, retaining the wisdom of ages, renews its youth. Confronting history, science, philosophy, he cheerfully accepts and absorbs them, and goes on singing with the joyful freshness that springs from perfect faith. In complete rapport with modern life, he is the poet of the great movements in which that life is expressing itself. He does not merely go to science for new metaphors, but he takes up the inanimate mechanism of science itself and breathes into it the breath of life.—GAY, WILLIAM, 1893, *Walt Whitman the Poet of Democracy, p.* 45.

Walt Whitman's verses are arbitrarily divided into very different lengths. Sometimes it is undeniable that the rhythmic swing does not strike the ear at all, at others every line is marked by a rapid certainty and majestic force which can only be compared with the heaving breast of the ocean or the course of wind over the prairies. German, as well as Scandinavian, literature can certainly show poems in rhythmic prose, but the most casual comparison will establish the radical difference between them and those of Walt Whitman. The only thing which approximately reminds us of the American poet's mode of expression is the peculiar accent which is here and there discovered in our translation of the Old Testament or in one or two of H. Wergeland's unrhymed poems. . . . Whitman is a democratic poet, who has become the spokesman of a democratic people. The breadth of the continent is illustrated in his poems.—SCHMIDT, RUDOLF, 1893, *Walt Whitman the Poet of American Democracy, tr. from the Danish by Bain, and Bucke, In Re Walt Whitman, ed. Traubel, Bucke, and Harned, pp.* 231, 240.

There are many things in Whitman's works which should assure him special consideration in Germany. He is the greatest poetic representative of that which is usually considered a prime focal point in German philosophy. In the philosophy of the modern world there are apparently only two principal currents—the one starting from England, the other from Germany. . . . Walt Whitman is essentially and in the first place a poet, not a philosopher; but that he has occupied himself with philosophic questions, and in a philosophic manner, will be clear to every reader. And in this respect he stands in a special relationship to his age, in which thought has achieved an unexampled influence over action.—ROLLESTON, T. W., 1893, *Walt Whitman, tr. from the German by Forman, and Bucke, In Re Walt Whitman, ed. Traubel, Bucke, and Harned, pp.* 286, 289.

Walt Whitman pleases one reader and repels ten thousand. . . . You know at a glance that Walt Whitman's sincerity is a matter of his own manufacture; it is an assumption that has grown into his tissues and become indurated.—THOMPSON, MAURICE, 1893, *The Ethics of Literary Art, p.* 70.

In this same period, there is a single figure who seems steadily and constantly to face not what is now past, but what is now present or to come. Though his right to respect is questioned oftenest of all, we cannot fairly pass Walt Whitman without mention. He lacks, of course, to a grotesque degree, artistic form; but that very lack is characteristic. Artistic form, as we have seen, is often the final stamp that marks human expression as a thing of the past. Whitman remarkably illustrates this principle: he lacks form chiefly because he is stammeringly overpowered by his bewildering vision of what he believes to be the future. He is uncouth, inarticulate, whatever you please that is least orthodox; yet, after all, he can make you feel for the moment how even the ferry-boats plying from New York to Brooklyn are fragments of God's eternities.—WENDELL, BARRETT, 1893, *Stelligeri and Other Essays Concerning America*, p. 142.

Walt Whitman's figure is surely one of the most commanding in American literature, yet its full stature will never be realized by the cultivated public at large, so long as the fanatical devotees of the poet's memory continue to lavish their extravagant encomiums upon his faults and his virtues alike.—PAYNE, WILLIAM MORTON, 1893, *Whitmaniana, The Dial, vol.* 15, *p.* 390.

I had on this occasion [1875] a long and interesting discussion with Mr. Tennyson relative to Walt Whitman, and involving the principles or nature of poetry. According to the poet-laureate, poetry, as he understood it, consisted of elevated or refined, or at least superior thought, expressed in melodious form, and in this latter it seemed to him (for it was very modestly expressed) that Whitman was wanting.—LELAND, CHARLES GODFREY, 1893, *Memoirs*, p. 395.

The most original and national of American poets; originator of a unique style, which is neither prose nor verse, yet is not wanting in a wild kind of rhythm, and is often highly poetical.—ROBERTSON J. LOGIE, 1894, *A History of English Literature*, p. 336.

If he reads "Walt Whitman" carefully, a reader of middle life will probably come to the conclusion that the best way to classify the wholly anomalous and irregular writer who produced it is to place him by himself as a maker of poems in solution. I am inclined to admit that in Walt Whitman we have just missed receiving from the New World one of the greatest of modern poets, but that we have missed it must at the same time be acknowledged. To be a poet it is not necessary to be a consistent and original thinker, with an elaborately-balanced system of ethics. The absence of intellectual quality, the superabundance of the emotional, the objective, the pictorial, are no reasons for undervaluing Whitman's imagination. But there is one condition which distinguishes art from mere amorphous expression; that condition is the result of a process through which the vague and engaging observations of Whitman never passed. He felt acutely and accurately, his imagination was purged of external impurities, he lay spread abroad in a condition of literary solution. But there he remained, an expanse of crystallisable substances, waiting for the structural change that never came; rich above almost all his coevals in the properties of poetry, and yet, for want of a definite shape and fixity, doomed to sit for ever apart from the company of the Poets.—GOSSE, EDMUND, 1894, *A Note on Walt Whitman, New Review, vol.* 10, *p.* 456.

Whitman has a rhythm which is all his own, as much as the waves and the surf-beat belong to the sea. Some of his work is exquisite in its word-music and grand as the roll of breakers. Some of his passages need not fear comparison with the finest in the Old Testament. Still I cannot think he will have many followers or imitators.—SAVAGE, MINOT J., 1894, *The Religion of Walt Whitman's Poems, The Arena, vol.* 10, *p.* 449.

For the magnitude of his vision Whitman owes much to Homer, to Shakespeare, and to the Book of Job. He was also largely influenced by Emerson's essays, whose independence and exaggeration he has imitated. The most important source for his genius is his observation of American barbarism, as he terms it. He embodies his sense of this in vivid imagery; imagining frequently and boldly that America and himself possess the same traits,—pride, carelessness, and generous receptivity. . . . Whitman had a mind of great power,—so far he ought to have the homage that he has received at home as well as from abroad. Still we may be not less firm in believing, on account of his disregard of the broad canons of literary form, and still more of the ideas, that praise of him should be moderate, although, with less disdain of literary form he would certainly have been a much larger and more important figure in American literature than he can now be considered.—SIMONDS, ARTHUR B., 1894, *American Song, pp.* 107, 109.

One of the deities to whom the degenerate and hysterical of both hemispheres have for some time been raising altars. Lombroso ranks him expressly among "mad geniuses." Mad Whitman was without doubt. But a genius? That would be difficult to prove. He was a vagabond, a reprobate rake, and his poems contain outbursts of erotomania so artlessly shameless that their parallel in literature could hardly be found with the author's name attached. For his fame he has to thank just those bestially sensual pieces which first drew to him the attention of all the pruriency of America. He is morally insane, and incapable of distinguishing between good and evil, virtue and crime. "This is the deepest theory of susceptibility," he says in one place, "without preference or exclusion; the negro with the woolly head, the bandit of the highroad, the invalid, the ignorant—none are denied." And in another place he explains he "loves the murderer and the thief, the pious and good, with equal love." An American driveller, W. D. O'Connor, has called him on this account "The good gray Poet." We know, however, that this "goodness," which is in reality moral obtuseness and morbid sentimentality, frequently accompanies degeneration, and appears, even in the cruellest assassins, for example, in Ravachol. . . . In his patriotic poems he is a sycophant of the corrupt American vote-buying, official-bribing, power-abusing, dollar-democracy, and a cringer of the most arrogant Yankee conceit. His war-poems—the much renowned "Drum Taps"—are chiefly remarkable for swaggering bombast and stilted patter.—NORDAU, MAX, 1895, *Degeneration, pp.* 230, 231.

Whitman brings the warmth of the sun to the buds of the heart so that they may open and bring forth form, color, perfume. He becomes for them aliment and dew; so these buds become blossoms, fruits, tall branches, and stately trees that cast refreshing shadows. There are men who are to other men as the shadow of a mighty rock in a weary land—such is Walt Whitman.—HUBBARD, ELBERT, 1896, *Little Journeys to the Homes of American Authors, p.* 195.

Opinion will doubtless long be divided about the value of his work. He said he was "willing to wait to be understood by the growth of the taste" of himself. That this taste is growing, that the new generations are coming more and more into his atmosphere, that the mountain is less and less forbidding, and looms up more and more as we get further from it, is obvious enough. That he will ever be in any sense a popular poet is in the highest degree improbable: but that he will kindle enthusiasm in successive minds; that he will be an enormous feeder to the coming poetic genius of his country; that he will enlarge criticism, and make it easy for every succeeding poet to be himself and to be American; and finally that he will take his place among the few major poets of the race, I have not the least doubt.—BURROUGHS, JOHN, 1897, *Library of the World's Best Literature, ed. Warner, vol.* XXVII, *p.* 15891.

Walt Whitman was unable or unwilling to master the art of writing, and consequently his works, though abounding in lines and phrases of the highest excellence in form as well as in substance, are so uneven and unfinished that he cannot be called a great writer, and can hardly be expected to endure. But he was a man of great democratic ideas. He is the only author yet produced in this country or in any other, who has perceived what democracy really means, and who has appreciated the beauty and the heroism which are found in the daily lives of the common people. Millet troubled himself not at all about political theories or forms of government, but his whole life was devoted to the representation upon canvas of those same qualities of every-day beauty and heroism which were the delight and the study of Walt Whitman. An appropriate line from Whitman's prose or verse could easily be found to put beneath every one of Millet's pictures.—MERWIN, HENRY CHILDS, 1897, *Men and Letters, Atlantic Monthly, vol.* 79, *p.* 719.

It is a curious phase of Whitman's greatness—this intense personal following. There has been nothing like it in the history of letters. Johnson had only one Boswell. No man, apparently, could come near Whitman without being swayed from his own orbit. John Burroughs appears to be almost the only man who, knowing him very well, is able to stand up straight after it. . . . "I am not a Comtist nor a Buddhist nor a Whitmanite," a friend writes me. Is the shade of ridicule towards the last class a figment of the fancy? A Whitmanite, it is to be feared, no matter how dignified his bearing, is never taken quite seriously. Perhaps it is the "ite," the remnant of the prejudice that hovers in the minds of men over the Hittites, Kenites, Perizzites, Jebusites. Perhaps it is phonetic. While Whitman lived he was never, in spite of the well-intentioned efforts of his friends, a ridiculous figure. The robustness and breeziness of the man put sentimentality where it belonged, and turned childish adulation into decent praise. Even the charity that his admirers brought upon him he accepted with sturdy good humour—and opened a bank-account. But now that Whitman is dead, all this is changed. Now that the head is gone, the decapitated body waves wild members, and calls it eulogy. First there was "In Re," a volume that some of us who admire Whitman's genius cannot even yet open without qualms; and then "Whitman the Man," and then "The Pete Letters," and now, worse and most persistent of all, this Whitman journal. Is it any wonder that Whitman had the foresight to enter protest:

"I call the world to distrust the accounts of my friends, but listen to my enemies, as I myself do.
I charge you forever reject those who would expound me, for I cannot expound myself,
I charge that there be no theory or school founded out of me,
I charge you to leave all free, as I have left all free."
—PERRY, JENNETTE BARBOUR, 1898, *Whitmania, The Critic, vol. 32, pp. 137, 138.*

Walt Whitman has given utterance to the soul of the tramp. . . . In Whitman's works the elemental parts of a man's mind and the fragments of imperfect education may be seen merging together, floating and sinking in a sea of insensate egotism and rhapsody, repellent, divine, disgusting, extraordinary. . . . The attraction exercised by his writings is due to their flashes of reality. Of course the man was a poseur, a most horrid mountebank and ego-maniac. His tawdry scraps of misused idea, of literary smartness, of dog-eared and greasy reminiscence, repel us. The world of men remained for him as his audience, and he did to civilized society the continuous compliment of an insane self-consciousness in its presence. . . . It is doubtful whether a man ever enjoyed life more intensely than Walt Whitman, or expressed the physical joy of mere living more completely. He is robust, all tingling with health and the sensations of health. All that is best in his poetry is the expression of bodily well-being.
—CHAPMAN, JOHN JAY, 1898, *Emerson and Other Essays, pp. 119, 121, 125.*

Instead of defining Walt Whitman as an "American Bookman," one might with greater justice describe him and his "Leaves of Grass"—for they are virtually one, as an American Book and a Man. It is merely a distinction of syllables, yet it has an important significance.—HOWE, M. A. DE-WOLFE, 1898, *American Bookmen, p. 222.*

The essential fault of Whitman's poetry was well pointed out by a man of more heroic nature and higher genius, Lanier, who defined him as a dandy. Of all our poets, he is really the least simple, the most meretricious; and this is the reason why the honest consciousness of the classes which he most celebrates,—the drover, the teamster, the soldier,—has never been reached by his songs. He talks of labor as one who has never really labored; his "Drum-Taps" proceed from one who has never personally responded to the tap of the drum. This is his fatal and insurmountable defect; and it is because his own countrymen instinctively recognize this, and foreigners do not, that his following has always been larger abroad than at home. But it is also true that he has, in a fragmentary and disappointing way, some of the very highest ingredients of a poet's nature: a keen eye, a ready sympathy, a strong touch, a vivid but not shaping imagination. In his cyclopædia of epithets, in his accumulated directory of details, in his sandy wastes of iteration, there are many scattered particles of gold—never sifted out by him, not always abundant enough to pay for the sifting, yet unmistakable gold. He has something of the turgid wealth, the self-conscious and mouthing amplitude of Victor Hugo, and much of his broad, vague, indolent desire for the welfare of the whole human race; but he has none of Hugo's structural power, his dramatic or melo-dramatic instinct, and his occasionally terse and brilliant condensation. It is not likely that he will ever have that place in the future which is claimed for him by his English admirers or even by the more cautious indorsement of Mr. Stedman; for, setting aside all other grounds of criticism, he has phrase, but not form—and without form there is no immortality.—HIGGINSON, THOMAS WENTWORTH, 1899, *Contemporaries, p. 83.*

To none ought Whitman's faults and flaws be more obvious than to those who love him. His rejection by the world in general is not to be construed necessarily as a sign manual of martyred genius. It was not the inspired side of Whitman that wrought his ruin as a universal propagandist. Indeed, to accept him without reservation, to refuse to see egregious absurdities of style and frequent incoherence of idea in his writings, to deny that read in part, the poet may exert an influence contrary to the one he coveted, is to display a wilfulness or ill-balanced judgment only equaled by Whitman's adversaries, who recognize none of the compensating virtues of his works. Walt Whitman's poetry is, in other words, an extraordinary literary landscape, which offers a scale of altitude ranging from sea level banalities to Alpine peaks of real greatness of prospect. Although the annunciator of a new heaven and earth, he was at times capable of uttering the veriest commonplaces of the uninspired. It is unfortunately the fantastic yeoman side of Whitman, which has struck the majority of readers and repelled them from the innumerable beauties of phrase and thought that lie hidden elsewhere in his pages. And frankly speaking, the bowlders in the path of ordinary appreciation are not easily surmounted: they represent perhaps the most flagrant departures literature has ever known. It is therefore thoroughly irrational of his followers to express surprise that proselytism is not more promptly accomplished.—VALENTINE, EDWARD A. UFFINGTON, 1899, *The Poet of Manhood, Conservative Review,* vol. 1, *p.* 140.

Like all our great poets Whitman uses mostly vigorous Anglo-Saxon words, but he does not eschew Latin derivatives, and with strange effect he uses constantly words frankly foreign or else manufactured for the occasion. Here are a few of these of which he is very fond: "ostent," "imperturbe," "debouch," "melange," "ensemble," "eleves,"mafemme," "allons," "cadaver." These are introduced without warning into beautiful lines which their presence completely spoils, and are only surpassed by the use of such *de trop* expressions as "shoulder your duds," "sour dead," "boss," &c. All this betrays what Holmes would call a blind spot in Whitman's brain and makes him produce what offends us as much as a glaring poster on some noble *façade.* This blind spot is also responsible for the vicious way in which the poet exaggerates his style, for the strangeness of some of his themes, for the improprieties of which he is guilty. Another grave defect is his sheer lack of humour, which in a poet of his kind is somewhat fatal. . . . It is no small claim he has upon greatness, that while democracy is tending here to throw off the ancient faiths, or there to preserve merely the cant catchwords of piety, he, the poet of democracy, preached that brotherly love and religion must go hand in hand with it. And conjointly with these he adds two truths, the greatness of the soul and the hope of immortality.—MACCULLOCH, J. A., 1899, *Walt Whitman: The Poet of Brotherhood, Westminister Review,* vol. 152, *pp.* 552, 553.

It was the singularity of his literary form —the challenge it threw to the conventions of verse and of language—that first gave Whitman notoriety: but this notoriety has become fame, because those incapacities and solecisms which glare at us from his pages are only the obverse of a profound inspiration and of a genuine courage. Even the idiosyncrasies of his style have a side which is not mere perversity or affectation; the order of his words, the procession of his images, reproduce the method of a rich, spontaneous, absolutely lazy fancy.—SANTAYANA, GEORGE, 1900, *Interpretations of Poetry and Religion, p.* 177.

Whitman's later work, and especially his prose, often expresses in inspiring fashion the exultant vigor, the generous humanity, of our national life. But to the masses he was unintelligible, while to most of the critical few his own defiant scorn for conventions, still more his utter lack of deeper insight or artistic charm, have made him— uninteresting.—LAWTON, WILLIAM CRANSTON, 1902, *Introduction to the Study of American Literature, p.* 249.

What Whitman's ultimate rank among writers will be is a matter upon which no living man is warranted to speak with confidence. The more we study him the more we perceive the impossibility of criticising him adequately. From an apparently hopeless jungle of jargon we pass without warning into a passage marked by superb rhythm, almost infallible diction, and at least vivid imagination. From a "barbaric yawp" of seemingly idiotic chauvinism we pass to a profoundly moving exposition of the dangers, material and spiritual, confronting American democracy. If we think that we can put a finger upon this or that defect of the poet and his work, straightway we discover a poem or a passage that necessitates a modification of opinion. In a word, Whitman seems not only a far better man and truer poet than his censors are willing to admit, but too large a man and poet for adequate comprehension at present. He may turn out to be a mouse in the telescope rather than an elephant in the moon, but who shall take to pieces the instrument through which we view the literary heavens when the instrument is nothing more nor less than—Time?—TRENT, WILLIAM P., 1903, *A History of American Literature.*

Edward Augustus Freeman
1823—1892

Born, at Harborne, Staffordshire, 2 Aug. 1823. Educated at school at Northampton, 1831-37; at Cheam, 1837-39; with private tutor, 1840-41. Verses pubd. in "Cromer Telegraph," 1834. Matric. Trinity Coll., Oxford, as scholar, 7 June 1841; B. A., 10 May 1845; M. A., 14 Jan. 1848; Fellow, May 1845 to April 1847; Reader in Rhetoric, 1846. Married Eleanor Gutch, 13 April 1847. Settled at Oaklands, Gloucestershire, 1849; removed to Lanrumney, Cardiff, 1855. Contrib. to "British Quarterly Rev.," 1851-81; to "North Brit. Rev.," 1854-66; to "Edin. Rev.," 1856-65; to "National Rev.," 1858-64; to "Fortnightly Rev.," 1865-89; to "Macmillan's Mag.," 1870-92; to "Contemp. Rev.," 1877-91, etc., etc. Hon. D. C. L., Oxford, 22 June 1870. Rede Lecturer, Camb., 1872. Hon. Mem. Hist. Soc. of Massachusetts, 1873. Hon. LL. D., Camb., 1874. Knight Commander of Greek Order of Redeemer, 1875. Corresp. Mem. of Imp. Acad. of Science, St. Petersburg, 1876. Hon. Fellow Trin. Coll., Oxford, 1880. Mem. of Royal Commission on Ecclesiastical Courts, 1881. Regius Prof. of Modern Hist., and fellow of Oriel Coll., Oxford, 1884. Hon. LL. D., Edinburgh, 17 April 1884. Ill health from 1886. Died, at Alicante, 16 March 1892. Buried in Protestant Cemetery there. *Works:* "Principles of Church Restoration," 1846; "Thoughts on the Study of History," 1849; "History of Architecture," 1849; "Notes on the Architectural Antiquities of . . . Gower," 1850; An "Essay on . . . Window Tracery in England," 1850; "Remarks on the Architecture of Llandaff Cathedral," 1850; "Poems," (with G. W. Cox), 1850; "The preservation and restoration of Ancient Monuments," 1852; "Suggestions with regard to certain proposed alterations in the Universities" (with F. H. Dickinson), 1854; "The History and Conquests of the Saracens," 1856; "The History and Antiquities of St. David's (with W. B. Jones), 1856; "Ancient Greece and Mediæval Italy," 1857; "History of Federal Government," vol. i. (no more pubd.), 1863; "Leominster Priory Church" (with G. F. Townsend), [1863]; "The History of the Norman Conquest of England" (6 vols.), 1867-79; "Old English History for Children," 1869; "History of the Cathedral Church of Wells,"1870; "Historical Essays" (4 series), 1871-92; "General Sketch of European History," 1872; "The Growth of the English Constitution," 1872; "The Unity of History," 1872; "Comparative Politics," 1874; "Disestablishment and Disendowment," 1874; "History of Europe," 1876; "Historical and Architectural Sketches," 1876; "The Turks in Europe," 1877; "The Ottoman Power in Europe," 1877; "How the Study of History is let and hindered," 1879; "A Short History of the Norman Conquest," 1880; "The Historical Geography of Europe," 1881; "Sketches from the Subject and Neighbour Lands of Venice," 1881; "An Introduction to American International History," 1882; "The Reign of William Rufus," 1882; "Lectures to American Audiences," 1882; "English Towns and Districts," 1883; Letterpress to "Cathedral Cities: Ely and Norwich," 1883; "Some Impressions of the United States," 1883; "The Office of the Historical Professor," 1884; "Greater Greece and Greater Britain," 1886; "The Methods of Historical Study," 1886; "The Chief Periods of European History," 1886; "Exeter," 1887; "Four Oxford Lectures," 1888; "William the Conqueror," 1888; "Sketches from French Travel," 1891; "The History of Sicily," (4 vols.), 1891-94; "Sicily: Phœnician, Greek and Roman," 1892. *Posthumous:* "Studies of Travel" (papers from "Sat. Rev.," "Pall Mall Gaz.," and "Guardian," ed. by F. Freeman), 1893. He *edited:* "Historical Course for Schools," 1872; etc., "Historic Towns" (with W. Hunt), 1887 [1886], etc. *Life:* "Life and Letters," by W. R. W. Stephens, 1895.
—SHARP, R. FARQUHARSON, 1897, *A Dictionary of English Authors, p.* 103.

PERSONAL

I am so delighted with your kind remembrance of me in your pretty letter, that I must write a line to tell you how much I continue to love you. I have sent you a few little tracts of my own writing, as I thought you would think them the better for that. I hope you continue fond of reading, and that you will make a wise choice in your books, on which your future character will much depend. You will therefore take the advice of the wise and the good, till you attain an age when you may be able to chuse for yourself. The Bible must have the pre-eminence of all other books. History opens a vast field to a youthful reader. But always inquire the character of the author. Poetry and polite literature must be deferred till the proper age.—MORE, HANNAH, 1832, *Letter to Mr. Freeman, Life and Letters of Edward A. Freeman, ed. Stephens, vol.* I, *p.* 6.

If I have not succeeded in showing that Mr. Freeman in bringing his charges against me has been more rash in his own statements, more mistaken in his facts, more unfair in his inferences, than he has shown me to be, nothing that I can add will be of the least avail. Mr. Freeman talks of an "incurable twist." To me it seems that there is an "incurable twist" in Mr. Freeman whenever he has to speak of myself, and that where every object appears to him distorted the cause is in the eye which sees and not in the thing which is seen. If I were to argue from his own language as he has argued from mine, I should suppose him influenced by "fanatical hatred" of me. Here, so far as there is any personal controversy between myself and Mr. Freeman, the matter must end. His friend the Saturday Reviewer has pursued me for twenty years, secure in his coat of darkness, with every species of unfounded insinuation. He has himself appeared at last on the field in his own person, and I have desired him to take back his imputations. For the future he will take his own course; I shall not be a party in any further controversy with him. No one is more conscious than I am of the faults of my literary work. No one is less anxious to defend them. But, after thirty years of severe and I believe honest labour, I will not suffer a picture to be drawn of me in such colours as Mr. Freeman has been pleased to use without entering my own protest with such emphasis as I can command.—FROUDE, JAMES ANTHONY, 1879, *A Few Words on Mr. Freeman, Nineteenth Century, vol.* 5, *p.* 637.

In a room of small size, before a strictly University audience, without a sheet of paper between him and his hearers, with no lyceum-apparatus save a pointer and one or two outline-maps, prepared for the illustration of special matters, Mr. Freeman in plain English,—vigorous, and eloquent—set forth "the Eternal Eastern Question" in the light of past Politics and present History. He spoke of the Roman Power in the East; the Saracens and the Slavs; the final Division of the East and the West; the Turks, Franks, and Venetians; the Ottomans and the Beginnings of Deliverance. Probably no such telling, inspiring course was anywhere given by the English historian in his American tour.—ADAMS, HERBERT B., 1882, *Mr. Freeman's Visit to Baltimore, Johns Hopkins' University Studies, vol.* I, *p.* 10.

I belong to no profession; I can hardly be said to belong to any class. But I have points of contact with several classes. At once a Professor in Oxford and a justice of the peace in Somerset, I do not feel that I am exactly a country gentleman; still less do I feel that I am exactly an Oxford don; I suppose I am not a "literary man," because I have never lived by writing; I suppose I am not a political character, because I have never sat in Parliament. But I feel that I have enough in common with all these classes and with other classes as well to understand all of them, without exactly belonging to any of them.—FREEMAN, EDWARD A., 1892, *A Review of My Opinions, The Forum, vol.* 13, *p.* 154.

Piae memoriae
EDWARDI AUGUSTI FREEMAN
qui
Origines Angliae
Normannorum dicionem
Fata Siciliae
Literis illustravit perpetuis,
Ac studio impulsus loca pernoscendi,
Hispanico in itinere,
Morte correptus inopina,
Hic inter Lucentinos occubuit.
Die xvi. Martii
Anno salutis MDCCCXCII.
Requiescat in pace.

—EVANS, A. J. 1892, *Inscription on Tomb, Protestant Cemetery at Alicante.*

The first time I saw Freeman was at Cambridge (the English Cambridge), on a fine day of May in 1872. He had come to deliver the Rede Lecture before the University, on "The Unity of History;" and as I had always had from my earliest days a passion for seeing any celebrated man, I made my way into the Senate House, where the great man was welcomed by a crowd of black-gowned university men and by a considerable gathering of the ladies who grace Cambridge with their presence in what has been conventionally termed the "merry month of May." I was particularly struck with Freeman's massive head, leonine aspect, and deep, full voice, which resounded in sonorous periods through that ugly, pseudoclassic building. I afterwards saw him, when the lecture was over, walking through the courts of St. John's College with his friend Professor Babington, the venerable Professor of Botany, and was irreverently amused at the shortness of the historian's legs, which rendered his walking not very unlike the waddling of a duck, while he was pointing all the time at the red brick gables of one of the older courts and probably gesticulating on architecture.—CLARKE, WILLIAM, 1892, *Edward Augustus Freeman, New England Magazine, vol. 12, p. 607.*

To the faithful student of his works the tidings of Freeman's death must have come like the news of the loss of a personal friend. To those who enjoyed his friendship even in a slight way the sense of loss was keen, for he was a very lovable man. Some people, indeed, seemed to think of him as a gruff and growling pedant, ever on the lookout for some culprit to chastise; but, while not without some basis, this notion is far from the truth.—FISKE, JOHN, 1892, *A Century of Science and Other Essays, p. 281.*

Rough as he could be with others—too rough, in truth—he was never rough with his trusted friends, and would bear from them criticisms and corrections which a less generous nature would have deeply resented. He might blurt out a loud "What d'ye mean?" accompanied with a fierce look, and would contest the point vehemently; but he was always amenable to reason, and gave in when he was shown to be in the wrong. But towards those who professed a knowledge, which he saw to be merely superficial and destitute of that groundwork of painstaking accuracy which characterises all his work,—"impostors" as he called them,—he sometimes manifested an intolerance which was not always kept within the bounds of courtesy and was painful to his victims and distressing to others. . . . Freeman was the most industrious and painstaking worker that I ever knew. I am certain that he never knew what it was to be idle. From early morning till the afternoon meal, and then again, after a period of exercise and relaxation and the society of his family, deep into the night, he was always either writing or gathering material for his writings. He had a happy power of snatching ten minutes' sleep, which rested his sorely taxed brain, and from which he woke "like a giant refreshed with wine," ready for fresh labours.—VENABLES, EDMUND, 1892, *Reminiscences of E. A. Freeman, Fortnightly Review, vol. 57, pp. 742, 745.*

Mr. Freeman was "a character." With a heart that bled for rabbits and partridges, he reveled in trampling, armed with heavy boots of accurate citations, on the intellectual toes of other historians. About their feelings he "took no keep," yet who so touchy as Mr. Freeman if you trifled gaily round any little error of his own? Nationalities (invariably "oppressed"), the English, the Germans, architecture, Charlemagne, the Burgundies, the Holy Roman Empire, —how much he told us about these things, with what laudable iteration! Mr. Freeman was always effervescent, and if any one whispered the word "urbanity," he marked him not. Great must have been his joy when Mr. Froude ventured light-heartedly into his territory, and ran up his famous score of blunders over "Sainte-Ampulle," "Saint-Croix," les écrouelles, and other mysteries. In his letters we hear the old voice, rating, humorous, not really unfriendly. He reminds one, by his ways and his kind of usefulness, of the elephant: he moved mountains of erudition, he went fast and trampled his foes, he was kind to children, devotedly loyal to his friends, and, had he owned the gift of compression, he would have held a higher place than the high place he holds among historians.— LANG, ANDREW, 1895, *The Month in England, The Cosmopolitan, vol. 19, p. 694.*

His intense dislike of unreality and pretence extended even to theatrical performances, and he could sympathize with the saying of good old Mrs. Blower in "St. Ronan's Well," "in my mind, Dr. Cacklehen, it's a mere blasphemy for folk to gar themselves look otherwise than their Maker made them." The occasional roughness and rudeness also of his manner, although sometimes the effect of shyness and mere awkwardness in the presence of strangers, was in the main due to that abhorrence of seeming to be what he was not, which made it impossible for him to acquiesce in conventional insincerities. For the same reason he was unable to write or speak politely of any one who pretended to more knowledge than he really had, or who enjoyed a reputation for learning which was undeserved. Nay more, he considered it to be a positive duty to expose such persons. . . He entertained no ill-will whatever towards literary or political opponents. . . . . The number of hours which he spent in reading and writing is carefully noted each day in his journal. Eleven is the maximum number recorded; but the average seems to have been about 7½. In his most vigorous days he used to begin work, in the summer, about 6 a. m., breakfasted at 8 or 8.30, and after a short walk in the garden worked on to the dinner hour, which for many years varied from 2 to 4 according to the length of the days. After dinner he went for a walk or ride, and wrote letters after his return till supper time, and then worked again from 10 or 11 to 12. In winter, dinner was commonly at 1.30, but at Oxford, and for some years before, he conformed to the practice of late dinners, and as his health became uncertain his hours of work were necessarily less regular.—STEPHENS, WILLIAM R. W., 1895, ed. *The Life and Letters of Edward A. Freeman, vol.* II, *pp.* 464, 471.

Edward Augustus Freeman was loved by many friends, and we see here how well he deserved their love; to them he was tender, affectionate and playful, with a somewhat elephantine playfulness. He said he was shy, but shyness veiled itself under an abrupt brutality of manner; he meant to be courteous, except to a fool, but then he unfortunately counted as fools most of those who did not know something of, and were not interested in, his special subjects; he once wrote, "I have always thought that the hardest precept—or rather implied precept—in the New Testament, is that which bids us to suffer fools gladly." His rudeness was startling; he loved his fellow-creatures, but with some exceptions, and towards these exceptions he used ferocious expressions; though he would have shrunk from the practices his words implied. . . He stood for parliament twice without success, and indeed was never likely to succeed in any country constituency; for though he became a Justice of the Peace, and took his part in county meetings, he was far from being a typical squire. The tenderness he showed for enslaved races he extended to hunted animals; he detested field sports of all kinds, and engaged in a rough and tumble contest with Anthony Trollope, in which it is difficult to say who hit the hardest; while both were unsubdued. But unprejudiced lookers-on must admit that Freeman had the best of the logical argument, even if illogical natures might sometimes sanction their following the hounds. With this exception, and this was of a public nature, Freeman was, as a rule, happy in his correspondents.—PAUL, C. KEGAN, 1895, *Edward A. Freeman, The Month, vol.* 84, *pp.* 337, 343.

He was a man of tremendous mental energy, and he was an advanced reformer in the truest sense of the word. Every cause which concerned the welfare of humanity had his strenuous support. There was a common impression among the general public that Professor Freeman was a man of rough, arrogant and overbearing manners. The writer of this History can only say that he never found anything rough, arrogant, or overbearing in Professor Freeman's demeanour. Freeman was thought by some people to be a man who had little regard for the growth of his country's empire, but as a matter of fact he had a regard above all other political desires for the reputation and the honour of his country. . . . He allowed no opinion to be with him a fetish, and, on the other hand, he recognized every opinion as a possible working instrument. He was emphatically a strong man, and his name will probably grow steadily with the growth of historical literature.—McCARTHY, JUSTIN, 1897, *A History of Our Own Times from* 1880 *to the Diamond Jubilee, p.* 323.

Much has been heard about Mr. Freeman's want of sympathy with modern Oxford, much that is mistaken and untrue. It is true that he loved most the Oxford of his young days, the Oxford of the Movement by which he was so profoundly influenced, the Oxford of the friends and fellow-scholars of his youth. But with no one were young students more thoroughly at home, from no one did they receive more keen sympathy, more generous recognition, or more friendly help. He did not like a mere smattering of literary chatter; he did not like to be called a pedant; but he knew, if any man did, what literature was and what was knowledge. He was eager to welcome good work in every field, however far it might be from his own. It is true that Mr. Freeman was distinctly a conservative in academic matters, but it is quite a mistake to think that he was out of sympathy with modern Oxford. No man was more keenly alive to the good work of the younger generation. Certainly no man was more popular among the younger dons. A few, in Oxford and outside, snarled at him, as they snarl still, but they were very few who did not recognize the greatness of his character as well as of his powers. It is not too much to say of those who had been brought into at all near relations with him that they learnt not only to respect but to love him. He was—all came to recognize it—not only a distinguished historian, but, in the fullest sense of the words, a good man. He leaves behind him a memory of unswerving devotion to the ideal of learning—which no man placed higher than he. His remembrance should be an inspiration to every man who studies history in Oxford.—HUTTON, W. H., 1897, *Freeman's Sketches of Travel in Normandy and Maine*, Preface, p. xiv.

Though his temper was impatient, and he was apt to be rude to people who were distasteful to him, he was truly kind, generous-hearted, and loveable. Unsparing in his condemnation of false pretenders to learning, he would cheerfully interrupt his own work to enlighten the ignorance of an honest student. All cruelty to man or beast aroused his fiercest indignation, all suffering drew forth his pity, and he was liberal in his gifts. He was eminently truthful and expressed his thoughts and feelings without reserve. No more affectionate or constant friend ever lived. . . . His memory was excellent, his intellect clear, and his mind orderly and logical. His industry was amazing, he worked methodically and with an eager desire to get at the truth, and he loved his work with an intensity which rendered him limited in intellectual sympathy.—HUNT, WILLIAM, 1901, *Dictionary of National Biography*, Supplement, vol. II, p. 250.

As an undergraduate he was slight in figure, retired in manner, and very shy and silent in the presence of strangers. The entries in his Journal, which he began to keep in Oxford, show that it was his habit to attend chapel twice a day; that almost invariably he went to hear the University sermon at St. Mary's; and that not infrequently he attended the celebration of Holy Communion in that church. Sometimes he read all night, until two o'clock in the morning; at other times he rose early, even at four o'clock in the winter months; now and then he would fall asleep in his study chair, wake up again to read until four or five, go to bed and sleep, until the hour of morning chapel. In 1845 he wrote to his affianced wife; "after the requisite cursing and swearing—the former as usual directed against his Holiness—I knelt down before the President, and was admitted a Probationary Fellow of the noble Society (Trinity). Since then I have been chiefly engaged in investigating a great problem, as to wherein the duties of a Probationary Fellow consist; for, as far as I have yet done, my chief business is reading newspapers in the Common Room, and drinking ale out of a silver tankard instead of a crockery-ware mug." His Fellowship was vacated by his marriage. His figure at this time, we are told, was still slight; and his old habit of skipping in his walk was not overcome. He had also, it seems, an odd way of flapping the sleeves of his Scholar's gown like wings, which earned for him the nickname, among his fellow Fellows, of "The Bantam Cock."—HUTTON, LAURENCE, 1903, *Literary Landmarks of Oxford*, p. 234.

HISTORY OF THE NORMAN CONQUEST IN ENGLAND
1867-79

Mr. Freeman's prejudices, strong as they may be, are an essential part of the man, and his book would be tame without them. His patriotic enthusiasm for his Saxon ancestors, who were presumably the ancestors of New England as well, is an element of the book which has positive value, if only because it is a healthy reaction against the old tendency to consider everything good in civilization as due to Rome and Greece, to Cicero, to Homer, and to Justinian. Even if it were not so, enthusiasm such as his would still make a dull subject amusing. . . . Most of Mr. Freeman's critics had long ago pointed out the unquestionable fact that the patriotic object at which he aims would be much more effectually reached if he would consent to put ever so slight a curb upon the really rampant vivacity of his enthusiasm, and moderate his pace a little, merely to keep his breathless followers in sight. It seemed reasonable to turn to the page which contains the well-known character of Alfred, in the hope that the opinions expressed there might have been somewhat affected by criticism. But the sentence still stands:—"Alfred . . . is the most perfect character in history." . . . It is not from any wish to contradict this statement that one ventures to question its propriety. Mr. Freeman is as safe as though he made the same assertion about Alfred's progenitor Adam, or his other famous ancestor Woden. But although few English scholars will care to enter the lists in order to prove from the scanty pages of Asser and the Chronicle that Alfred was not the most perfect character in history, many will smile at what they will call the vivacity of Mr. Freeman's hobby, and will wonder that authors of his eminence should not know their art better than to undertake to browbeat their readers by sheer dogmatism.—ADAMS, H., 1874, *Freeman's History of the Norman Conquest, North American Review*, vol. 118, pp. 177, 178.

Mr. Freeman's "History of the Norman Conquest" may be ranked among the great works of the present century.—CHAMBERS, ROBERT, 1876, *Cyclopædia of English Literature*, ed. Carruthers.

One of the greatest monuments of English historical scholarship. It not only surpasses in importance every former work on the period, but for the purposes of the general student is of greater value than all former works combined. . . . The style of the author is remarkable for its perspicuity, and his learning is everywhere obvious. While he is the advocate of a particular theory, he furnishes the means by which those who differ from his conclusions may determine on what basis their own views rest. He is a firm believer in the continuity of the Saxon, or, as he prefers to call it, the English, element, maintaining that the Norman Conquest, instead of overthrowing the Saxon civilization, only modified it somewhat, and that its essential characteristics have continued to be predominant throughout the whole history of England.—ADAMS, CHARLES KENDALL, 1882, *A Manual of Historical Literature*, p. 445.

His "History of the Norman Conquest" with the companion work on William Rufus, is the most characteristic and influential production of his school. It is, moreover, the work of a real historian, not of a mere historical critic, one endowed with a sense of art and symmetry, and able to paint a battle or a man. Its defects are those incident to the author's position as a pioneer in this field of history. He is compelled to argue while he narrates, and half his book reads like a commentary on the other half.—GARNETT, RICHARD, 1887, *The Reign of Queen Victoria*, ed. Ward, vol. II, p. 475.

Mr. Freeman may have admired Macaulay greatly, but he has certainly not caught his style. Freeman is always clear, but he is often clumsy, and he repeats himself so often as to become rather tedious. His manner of compiling a historical work like the "Norman Conquest" can scarcely be commended, as any one will say who has waded through those bulky tomes. There are notes, scores of pages long, which ought to have been incorporated into the text, so that over and over again the reader has to turn back in a state of mental confusion. The whole work, too, might have been considerably abridged with advantage.—CLARKE, WILLIAM, 1892, *Edward Augustus Freeman, New England Magazine*, vol. 12, p. 612.

Upon this subject he had thought and studied for nearly twenty years, or ever since the time when he was publishing works on architecture. As one turns the leaves of these stout volumes, each of seven or eight hundred pages, crowded with minute and accurate erudition, one marvels that the author could carry along so many researches and of such exhaustive character at the same time. Alike in Greek, in German, and in English History, along with abundant generalizations, often highly original and suggestive, we find investigations of obscure points in which every item of evidence is weighed as in an apothecary's scale, and in all these directions Mr. Freeman was working at once.—FISKE, JOHN, 1893, *Edward Augustus Freeman, Atlantic Monthly* vol. 71, p. 102.

GENERAL

It is Mr. Freeman's great merit to rely on the power of argument in an age which delights in sentiment. It is also his great merit that he scarcely ever writes on any subject to which he has not devoted careful study; but neither of these virtues would have enabled him to fight the successful battles which he has fought against all historical wrong-doers, down from the heinous criminals who think Charlemagne was a Frenchman to the petty offenders who persist in using the term "Anglo-Saxon," unless he had possessed another peculiar quality. This quality is a faculty for repetition. Men of equal ability with Mr. Freeman, when once they have propounded their doctrines to an unheeding world, often feel it an absolutely unbearable task to repeat what they have already said until they have attracted the attention of what Austin calls "the vast confederacy of fools." . . . Mr. Freeman, in short, is a man who wields a sort of intellectual hammer, and who (as children say) "hammers and hammers and hammers" until he has forced his point upon even the most unwilling hearers.—DICEY, A. V., 1871, *Two Historical Essayists, The Nation*, vol. 13, p. 403.

Among eminent English Radicals, Freeman, the historian, occupies a unique place. He goes forward by going backward. He is a Radical because he is a Conservative. He is a Democrat because he is a student of antiquity. . . . His politics and his religion like Gladstone's inspire all his writings. . . . His mind is a peculiarly English mind, strong in facts and shrewd in inferences, but weak and timid in the application of first principles.—DAVIDSON, J. MORRISON, 1880, *Eminent Radicals In and Out of Parliament*, pp. 251, 254, 255.

One cannot but think that, like all ardent reformers, he has pushed his theory to an extreme.—ALLEN, W. F., 1880, *Freeman's Historical Essays, The Nation*, vol. 30, p. 331.

For myself, I may at once say frankly that my study of the works of the Regius Professor, so far as it has yet proceeded, has led me to question more and more, in the first place his supposed pre-eminent accuracy, and in the second, the soundness of his judgment, that quality so essential to the historian, when the truth has to be discovered from various, if not conflicting authorities. In the present article I have only space to adduce some instances on the matter of *accuracy*, the other question being, obviously, far too wide for such treatment. And I wish it clearly to be understood that I do not seek in any way to disparage Mr. Freeman's true achievements, or to deny that his work on this period may have surpassed that of any predecessor. Into that question I do not enter. The power and vigour of Mr. Freeman's style, his attractive enthusiasm for his great subject, may be left to speak for themselves. I merely seek to expose that "mischievous superstition," as I have termed it, that his "accuracy" may be implicitly relied on, a superstition which is based on his formidable array of foot-notes and quotations from original authorities, and on his own criticisms of the efforts of others, and which has led the critics of our leading reviews to pronounce that the work he has done "need never to be done again."—ROUND, J. H., 1886, *Is Mr. Freeman Accurate? The Antiquary*, vol. 13, p. 240.

From the very beginning Freeman's historical studies were characterized on the one hand by philosophical breadth of view, and on the other hand by extreme accuracy of statement, and such loving minuteness of detail as is apt to mark the local antiquary whose life has been spent in studying only one thing. It was to the combination of these two characteristics that the pre-eminent greatness of his historical work was due.—FISKE, JOHN, 1892, *A Century of Science and Other Essays*, p. 266.

To have produced as much as he has done, on so many and diverse subjects—in books, lectures, magazines, and weekly Reviews—would have been a marvel of literary industry, even if it had come partly from the brains and partly from the pens of others. But Mr. Freeman never spared himself the labour of ascertaining his facts, of thinking out his conclusions, and of writing with his own hand. The next century will be better able to assign him his place among great historians. The present generation are indebted to him, more than to any other man, for the revival of history as a serious study in this country. Apart from the example of his own unwearied activity, we owe to him at least two doctrines of supreme importance: the continuity of man's doings in Europe from the earliest times to the present day, and the value of geography and archæology as handmaids to the historian. Mr. Freeman had, indeed, the defects of his qualities, upon which this is not the occasion to dwell. If he was unrelenting in controversy where he thought that truth was at stake, he was also one of the staunchest of friends and most kind-hearted of men. Alike by his patriotic ambition for the future of Greater England, and by his sympathy with down-trodden nationalities, he represented in politics the nobler tendencies of the day. Never seeking popularity, and owing nothing to patronage, he preserved his independence as a public teacher, and reflected honour upon the profession of letters.—COTTON, J. S., 1892, *E. A. Freeman, The Academy, vol.* 41, *p.* 301.

Severe as is the unflinching correctness of Mr. Freeman, he is not above the human weakness of picturesque writing. The "Norman Conquest" and the "Reign of William Rufus" would live by their literary power, if there was no more truth in them than in the leasings of Hector Boece, that most delightful of imaginative chroniclers. We bear Mr. Freeman grudge for introducing into the harmless English language various loathly distortions of familiar names, such as Eadwine and Ecghberht, which belong to no language known in the nineteenth century, and for whose accuracy if accurate these relics of barbarism be, the inveterate angliciser of every French name he uses can advance no defence. But he does not always write in early Gothic dialects, and the value of his historical writings cannot be disputed.—OLIPHANT, MARGARET O. W., 1892, *The Victorian Age of English Literature, p.* 545.

The late professor rarely wrote anything which did not bear the mark of his masculine and independent mind, but it does not follow that everything he wrote is worth preserving in a permanent form. . . . With all the force of genuine conviction and all the courage which untiring industry, a powerful memory, and wide interest could give him, he put into practice his theory that history should be studied and taught as a whole. It may probably be said, without much fear of contradiction, that no historian of the century, except Leopold von Ranke, has so clearly grasped or so consistently maintained this doctrine.—PROTHERO, G. W., 1893, *Historical Essays, English Historical Review, vol.* 8, *p.* 384.

To Mr. Freeman "Truth" was the one object of historical study, and he would never have borne a grudge against those who pointed out his own mistakes. His only antagonism was towards the arrogance of ignorance that tried to pass itself off for knowledge.—ARCHER, T. A., 1893, *Mr. Freeman and "The Quarterly Review," Contemporary Review, vol.* 63, *p.* 354.

No one who has studied Mr. Freeman's writings, or who has followed the story of his life, more especially in his correspondence, can fail to perceive that his merits as an historian depended upon certain moral qualities almost as much as upon his intellectual gifts. Devotion to truth, which counts no pains too great to ascertain it, courage in speaking it at all hazards, a deep sense of duty, and that power of appreciating whatever is truly noble in human character and action, which comes from keeping a high moral standard steadily in view—these qualities, which were most conspicuous in him, are indeed essential elements in the character of a really great historian.—STEPHENS, WILLIAM R. W., 1895, *ed. The Life and Letters of Edward A. Freeman, vol.* III, *p.* 462.

Freeman was pre-eminently an historical geographer. His published work in this field will probably long remain the best in the English world. . . . His writings upon English history are all based upon exact local studies of English topography. He extended his local observations to Normandy, France, Italy, Dalmatia, Greece, Sicily, and Spain. From first to last he was under the same irresistible impulse to see with his own eyes places of historical interest and to describe them minutely for the benefit of his countrymen.—ADAMS, HERBERT B., 1895, *Freeman the Scholar and Professor, Yale Review, vol.* 4, *pp.* 232, 238.

Mr. Freeman was a student of untiring energy, and will always deserve honourable memory as the first historian who recognised and utilised the value of architecture in supplying historical documents and illustrations. His style was at times picturesque but too diffuse, and disfigured by a habit of allusion as teasing as Macaulay's antithesis or Kinglake's stock phrases. That he was apt to pronounce very strong opinions on almost any question with which he dealt, was perhaps a less drawback to his excellence as a historian than the violently controversial tone in which he was wont to deal with those who happened to hold opinions different from his own. Putting defects of manner aside, there is no question that, for his own special period of English history (the eleventh and twelfth centuries), Mr. Freeman did more than any man had done before him, and as much as any man has done for any other period; while in relation to his further subjects of study, his work, though less trustworthy, is full of stimulus and information.—SAINTSBURY, GEORGE, 1896, *A History of Nineteenth Century Literature,* p. 245.

His style has been called "architectural;" but the epithet is hardly just, for it shows little of the inspiration which his deep study of architecture might have given. His work is rather strong conscientious masonry, without that harmony of line and disposition of parts which reveal the mind of the artist. His natural emphasis of manner gives to certain themes a polemical, sometimes eloquent expression. He is fond of the trick of repetition, especially in those passages which were written to be spoken, and, when once he is satisfied as to his facts, defends his view with the pertinacity of an advocate. In this way he weakens the judicial value of his work, which the reader, impressed by the learned investigation of fact and argument, is ready to assume. What of fervour he denies himself in description, he makes good in polemic. It is there he is at his best: in strictly historical narrative he is unequal and irritatingly slow, but in the swing of political passion he may be impressive. His literary art is at the highest when it approaches the grandiloquent: he fails when he attempts a light and vivacious manner. His humour is ponderous and provokes a smile by reason of its ingenious pedantry.—SMITH, G. GREGORY, 1896, *English Prose,* ed. Craik, vol. V, p. 724.

It must be confessed that great as Mr. Freeman's authority is as an historian, his manner is often most unattractive; and that profound as is the respect paid him by the student of history called to work within the same fields, he is but little known or appreciated by the general reader. None the less will his name be handed down as that of one of the most industrious, widely learned, and reliable historians of this or any period. He grasped, as few have done, the conception of history as a unity that can only be properly studied when realised as a whole.—GRAHAM, RICHARD D., 1897, *The Masters of Victorian Literature,* p. 215.

No historian has had a keener grasp of hard, solid facts, or is more able to make common-sense deductions from them.— SHORTER, CLEMENT K., 1897, *Victorian Literature,* p. 82.

It is said that Froude worked up his authorities, inflamed his imagination, and then, with scarcely a note to help his memory, covered his canvas with a flowing brush. Freeman, on the other hand, is never out of sight of his authorities, and in many instances, through pages and pages, his volumes are simply a cento of paraphrases from the original chroniclers. He gained freshness, and, when his text was trustworthy, an extreme exactitude; but he missed the charm of the fluid oratory of narrative, the flushed and glowing improvisation of Froude. In consequence, the style of Freeman varies so extremely that it is difficult to offer any general criticism of it. In certain portions of the "Harold," for instance, it reaches the very nadir of dreariness; while his famous "night which was to usher in the ever-memorable morn of Saint Calixtus" suggests how finely he might have persuaded himself to see and to describe. The cardinal gift of Freeman, however, was certainly not his painstaking treatment of documents, but the remarkable breadth of his historical view.—GOSSE, EDMUND, 1897, *A Short History of Modern English Literature,* p. 375.

His supreme merit as historian is to have insisted in season and out of season on the "Unity of History." But his own practice did not altogether do justice to his great theory. Those who do not know his occasional essays and voluminous notes and articles might imagine that he confined himself to the grand struggle between English Danes and Normans. And it must be admitted that, with all his passion for having the whole of history read together as one continuous biography of Man, he speaks at times as if Gauls, the Latin races altogether, and modern men in general, were a poor and degenerate race, whose scuffles and vagaries need not detain "a serious historian" bent on attaining to the highest truth. . . . Freeman was a politician, as was his master Thomas Arnold, as was Macaulay, as was Gibbon, as were De Commines and Machiavelli. Freeman was a politician; and for all his vast learning and patient collation of every written authority, he looked at men and events with a political eye and with a grasp of a practical politician. It is unfortunately true that Freeman as a politician had many of the defects of that quality. He had prejudices—some really furious prejudices; he had race antipathies, religious odium, loathing of particular schools of thought, of nations, and writers. All this deeply discredited his impartiality as a general authority on universal history—a pretention indeed which he would have been the first to disclaim. It made several of his judgments unsound and some of them laughably unfair. His contemptuous ignoring of almost every deed, man, or movement in any member of the Latin races, later at least than the fifteenth century, his hatred of all Buonapartes (*sic*), his contempt for the eighteenth century and all its work in Europe, his loathing of Turks and all things Turkish—these things detract from his standing as a great historian, but happily they did not seriously affect his principal tasks. . . . If Freeman were not a philosophic historian, not even a great historian at all, he was a consummate master of historical research, and a noble inspirer of historical enthusiasm.—HARRISON, FREDERIC, 1898, *Historical Method of Prof. Freeman, Nineteenth Century*, vol. 44, pp. 791, 799, 805.

Freeman felt himself to be a man of learning rather than an author and his style is in keeping with this. There are few passages in his works that are valuable as being artistic; but among them his account of the day of the battle of Hastings (Oct. 14, 1066), and the night which followed it must be so regarded.—ENGEL, EDWARD, 1902, *A History of English Literature*, rev. Hamley Bent, p. 469.

Industry came naturally to Freeman, because he was fond of his own studies and did not think of his work as task work. The joy in reading and writing about bygone times sprang from the intensity with which he realised them. He had no geographical imagination, finding no more pleasure in books of travel than in dramatic poetry. But he loved to dwell in the past, and seemed to see and feel and make himself a part of the events he described. Next to their worth as statements of carefully investigated facts, the chief merit of his books lies in the sense of reality which fills them. The politics of Corinth or Sicyon, the contest of William the Red with St. Anselm, interested him as keenly as a general election in which he was himself a candidate. Looking upon current events with an historian's eye, he was fond, on the other hand, of illustrating features of Roman history from incidents he had witnessed when taking part in local government as a magistrate; and in describing the relations of Hermocrates and Athenagoras at Syracuse he drew upon observations which he had made in watching the discussions of the Hebdomadal Council at Oxford. This power of realising the politics of ancient or mediæval times was especially useful to him as a writer, because without it his minuteness might have verged on prolixity, seeing that he cared exclusively for the political part of history. It was one of the points in which he rose superior to most of those German students with whom it is natural to compare him. Many of them have equalled him in industry and diligence; some have surpassed him in the ingenuity which they bring to bear upon obscure problems; but few of them have shown the same gift for understanding what the political life of remote times really was.—BRYCE, JAMES, 1903, *Studies in Contemporary Biography*, p. 282.

Henry Edward Manning
1807–1892

Born 15th July 1808 [1807] at Totteridge, Hertfordshire, from Harrow passed in 1827 to Balliol College, Oxford, and, after taking a classical first in 1830, was in 1832 elected a fellow of Merton. An eloquent preacher and a High Churchman, but not a contributor to the "Tracts for the Times," in 1833 he became rector of Woollavington and Graffhan, Sussex, and in 1840 Archdeacon of Chichester. In 1833 he had married Caroline Sargent, a lady whose sisters married Samuel and Henry Wilberforce; she died in 1837. On 6th April 1851, deeply moved by the "Gorham Judgment" he joined the Church of Rome. He studied two years in Rome, in 1857 founded the congregation of the Oblates of St. Charles Borromeo at Bayswater, London; and in 1865 succeeded Cardinal Wiseman as Archbishop of Westminster. At the Œcumenical Council of 1870, Manning was one of the most zealous supporters of the infallibility dogma; and, named cardinal in 1875, he continued a leader of the Ultramontanes. He was a member of the Royal Commissions on the Housing of the Poor (1885) and on Education (1886), and took a prominent part in temperance and benevolent movements. Before his secession he published several volumes of powerful sermons; amongst his later writings are discussions of the temporal power,

EDWARD AUGUSTUS FREEMAN

*Engraving by Walker & Boutall. From a
Photograph by Hills & Saunders.*

HENRY EDWARD MANNING

Engraving from a Photograph by Elliott & Fry.

infallibility, the Vatican Council, Ultramontanism, "The Four Great Evils of the Day" (1871), "Internal Mission of the Holy Ghost" (1875), "The Catholic Church and Modern Society" (1880), "Eternal Priesthood" (1883), "Characteristics" (1885), and "Towards Evening" (1889). He died 14th Jan. 1892, and was buried at Kensal Green. See "Life" by E. S. Purcell (2 vols. 1896).—PATRICK, AND GROOME, eds.; 1897, *Chambers's Biographical Dictionary*, p. 626.

PERSONAL

He is a tall thin personage, some sixty-two years of age. His face is bloodless—pale as a ghost, one might say. He is so thin as to look almost cadaverous. The outlines of the face are handsome and dignified. There is much of courtly grace and refinement about the bearing and gestures of this pale, weak, and wasted man. He wears a long robe of violet silk, with some kind of dark cape or collar, and has a massive gold chain round his neck, holding attached to it a great gold cross. There is a certain nervous quivering about his eyes and lips, but otherwise he is perfectly collected and master of the occasion. His voice is thin, but wonderfully clear and penetrating. It is heard all through this great hall—a moment ago so noisy, now so silent. The words fall with a slow, quiet force, like drops of water. Whatever your opinion may be, you cannot choose but listen.— MCCARTHY, JUSTIN, 1872, *Archbishop Manning, Modern Leaders*, p. 176.

No other great man is more accessible than the Cardinal. Through no rooms are ushered men of more various opinions than through these great halls, Italian in their spaciousness, all English in their chilliness. And yet a certain dignity and grandeur seem to haunt them and surround also their spare, even emaciated tenant.—PAUL, C. KEGAN, 1883, *Cardinal Manning, Century Magazine*, vol. 26, p. 130.

He is a man of dignified and graceful manners, with what I should call, though I hardly know on what grounds, a mediæval countenance, austere but gentle, and some qualities which have deservedly given him a personal influence, as well as an ecclesiastical pre-eminence, in the church to which he was converted, though there is one party in it to which he is anything but acceptable. Indeed, it has been said by a cynical member of that church that the greatest misfortune it has suffered in this century was the death of *Mrs*. Manning.—TAYLOR, SIR HENRY, 1885, *Autobiography*, vol. I, p. 198.

Before Mr. Gladstone paid much attention to the Debating Society, the leader of our house was Manning (the present Cardinal and Archbishop). Besides possessing great natural talents, he was, I think, having been at first intended for a different career, rather older than his average contemporaries. He would always have been in the ascendent, but his greater maturity, as might have been expected, increased that ascendency. He possessed a fine presence, and his delivery was effective. These qualities, joined to an impressive and somewhat imposing manner, enabled him to speak as one having authority, and drew into his orbit a certain number of satellites who revolved round him, and looked up to him, with as much reverence as if he had been the actual Pope, instead of only an embryo Cardinal. Their innocent adulation led him into his most obvious weakness, an assumption of omniscience which now and then overshot itself.—DOYLE, SIR FRANCIS HASTINGS, 1887, *Reminiscences and Opinions*, p. 105.

In the pulpit, his spare figure and keen face seem all aglow with the fire of his words —perfectly simple words, but showing wonderful knowledge and mastery of human nature. When he drives home a sentence, he has an expressive habit of clinching the rail of the pulpit with both hands, throwing himself back at arm's-length as he throws his words forward, which is as affective as it is peculiar. Since his entrance into the Roman Catholic Church in 1851, he has published more than thirty volumes and pamphlets, beginning with "The Grounds of Faith," mostly in defence of the Church, and he has also been prominent and efficient in the many movements for temperance reform and the uplifting of the people in the metropolis.—BOWKER, RICHARD ROGERS, 1888, *London as a Literary Centre, Harper's Magazine*, vol. 76, p. 836.

I was with him at Oxford; and I hope I may still reckon him as a friend, though on one subject, and that a momentous one, we are, alas, and ever must be, far apart. We have met but once since his secession to Rome; but that was enough to show that our affection for each other had not died out.—OXENDEN, ASHTON, 1891, *The History of my Life.*

Ecce sacerdos magnus,—that is the conclusion to which from every point we come when we review the various aspects of Manning's life and work. Whatever we find, either to praise or perhaps to blame, it is always the characteristic of a great and good priest. Those to whom the idea of the Catholic priesthood is altogether unwelcome, and who regard it as the very incarnation of evil on this earth, can hardly be expected therefore to admire a man who was always and before all things a priest.—HUTTON, ARTHUR WOLLASTON, 1892, *Cardinal Manning (English Leaders of Religion),* p. 258.

A noble figure was his on the platform, and in the pulpit; but where he was at his best and greatest was in his own armchair. . . . What his own life of devotion was, that he wished the lives of all his clergy to be. Beautiful and inspiring were the addresses he gave them—then was a time when his Master's name was on his lips at every breath, as it was always in his heart. Between no man's words and acts was there ever so complete a parity. He denied himself the indulgences he ceded to others. The cigarette, which has penetrated everywhere, even into a convent during a "ladies' retreat," got no entrance into the Archbishop's House. The cigar was a waste and indulgence beyond words; and though he had been at athlete at Harrow he did not like his clergy to care for sports. "I do not like a priest to run after a piece of leather," he said, with characteristic summariness of thought and speech, when he heard of a clerical football player. Yet he took a five-bar gate when he went to Ushaw College in the sixties. . . . His manners with ladies were always charming; and his bow, when he took off the hat of more than Quaker brim, was a homage the most gracious ever made. It was not often that he permitted himself a mere compliment; when he did so it was only because a neat phrase carried him away. . . . The most humble of men, he was not without an imperiousness all his own, which well became him. . . . In his own outwardly way he loved the world and all the people in it. He did not want to die; but none was ever so submissive to the summons. "When you hear I have taken to my bed, you can order my coffin," he said to me; "in that I shall be like Lord Beaconsfield." Wearily and reluctantly he climbed the stone stairs for the last time, just after signing a business letter to the Vatican in the Italian. He had economised time at Balliol by learning while he shaved. He had borne the burden of a long day; and he leaves a memory that must illustrate those who come after him in the work which remains for them to do.—MEYNELL, WILFRID, 1892, *Reminiscences of Cardinal Manning, Contemporary Review,* vol. 61, pp. 172, 174, 177, 183.

People who only saw the Cardinal at a distance, especially when they were so violently anti-Papist as not to be able to discern the man on account of his vestments, have often marvelled and have been dismayed at the enthusiastic love and admiration I have always been proud to profess for Cardinal Manning. If they only knew what the man was to those who knew him they would never even so much as think of his clothes. Human hearts all aglow with love and sympathy are not so plentiful in this world that we can afford to pass them by because they beat behind a Roman cassock. . . . I never knew a man so weighted with grave affairs of church who always found time to write his own letters and to see his visitors. I have been at the palace as early as ten'clock in the morning and as late as nine o'clock at night. I never found him hurried or flurried or driven for time. Over and over again, when, after talking for an hour or an hour and a half, I rose to go he would insist upon my sitting down again. "I have not said my say yet," he would say. And so the conversation would begin again. He was always fresh, always interested about everything, and always eager to hear the latest news. He listened to everything, and enriched everything from his inexhaustible store of anecdote and incident. What a memory he had! He seemed to have heard everything and, until the last few months, to have forgotten nothing. As a gossip, in the highest sense of that much-abused word, I never knew his equal. He was never dull, never prosy, never at a loss for a humorous story or an apt retort. Catholic friends tell me that the Cardinal could pose magnificently as the prince of the Church. To me he never "put on side" in any shape or form. He was as simple as General Gordon, as healthy as a schoolboy, and as fond of fun and as merry as any man I ever met.—STEAD, W. T., 1892, *Cardinal Manning, Review of Reviews, vol.* 5, *p.* 183.

I remember, on the first vacation from Oxford that I spent at Chichester, seeing the Archdeacon for the first time—his grand head, bald even then, his dignified figure in his long white surplice, occupying the Archdeacon's stall in the Cathedral. His face was to me some first dim revelation of the meaning of the *supernatural in man.* I have never forgotten it, I see him as vividly now in my mind's eye as when I first beheld him.—LOCKHART, WILLIAM, 1892, *Some Personal Reminiscences of Cardinal Manning when Archdeacon of Chichester, Dublin Review, vol.* 110, *p.* 372.

No man was ever wittier than Manning's brother-in-law, Bishop Wilberforce; no man less humorous. Manning had no wit, but a vast deal of humour. And it was his peculiar genius that, while he noted the way of the world with ready observation and dexterous look, marking its amusements, follies, sins, together with all that is great and good in it, he never laid aside his religious character, because in that was his life. Upon various sides of his nature he resembled both his friends, Lord Beaconsfield and Mr. Gladstone: he was both subtle and sincere. . . . He was the indefatigable official, the untiring ruler of a great diocese, the unfailing friend of all philanthropic and national movements: he had relations with the world upon all sides, and was well in touch with his contemporaries. But the man himself remained unknown, save to his immediate friends; no one could anywhere read the story of his soul. No poems, no sermons, no personal revelations, full of yearning and affection, and sorrow and faith, gave him a place in the hearts of strangers; instead, they only knew a few hard, external facts, nothing intimate, nothing spiritual, nothing "psychological." And so, Manning was the organiser, the man of practical policy, the ecclesiastic of administrative genius; the world almost forgot the man in the archbishop.—JOHNSON, LIONEL, 1893, *Cardinal Manning, The Academy, vol.* 44, *p.* 223.

When a young lady had the audacity to tell him, "But, your Eminence, I *like* going to balls," his characteristic answer was, "*Better not, my child.*" His whole leaning was toward counsels of perfection, and he died when he did because he absolutely refused to take stimulants lest his tempted children should thereby feel themselves ever so slightly loosened from their pledge; and for these and other most unpopular causes he "bore the reproach" with a certain pathetic severity. And little by little, year by year, the ascetic old man, who went about on ordinary occasions like "a shabby curate," won upon his own recalcitrant people, and upon the outer English world. They came to understand his point of view, which was that if a man saw a good thing he was to strive after it utterly regardless of human respect; and if he saw a bad thing he was to fling himself against it; and if he was clear about a text of Scripture it was to be obeyed in all its length and breadth. His natural fastidiousness never stopped him for an instant. To the repentant woman he simply said, "Go and sin no more;" the drunken man he took literally into Archbishop's House and set him on his feet again.—BELLOC, BESSIE RAYNER, 1894, *In a Walled Garden, p.* 217.

All England paid not only a tribute of respect on the day of his Funeral, but grieved, it is not too much to say, almost with one heart at the passing-away of Cardinal Manning. His fellow-countrymen recognised with one accord that England had lost in him one of the greatest and noblest of its sons. The world was all the poorer by the death of a large-hearted philanthropist, a friend of the oppressed, a father of the poor. The Church, too, and not in England only, was all the poorer by the loss of one of her most faithful sons and servants; an unflinching champion of her rights, temporal and spiritual; a holy and ascetic prelate, inspired in word and deed by faith, spiritual fervour, and the love for souls. English life, already dull enough, was all the duller by the passing-away from the stage which he had so long and so gracefully filled of a unique and picturesque personality.—PURCELL, EDMUND SHERIDAN, 1895, *Life of Cardinal Manning, vol.* II, *p.* 817.

From the time that Manning became an Archdeacon he never lost sight of the possibility of a Bishopric. He was quite in earnest about renouncing the world, but the world for some time liked him all the better for the elegant unearthliness of his aspect. He was knowing in horseflesh and he told good stories, and his health required him to spend his winters with his half-sister in

Cadogan-place. Meanwhile his views were becoming more advanced; he was moving by a route of his own in the same direction as the Tractarians. He was an ally rather than a disciple. He was beginning to find that the witness of the undivided Church covered much that would have shocked the Reformers. But like Rose, and unlike the Tractarians, he had a high and hopeful opinion of the Church of England as a working institution.—SIMCOX, G. A., 1896, *Life of Cardinal Manning, The Academy*, vol. 49, p. 150.

His intentions were often excellent; but he never got anything quite right. He wanted to help on the cause of temperance; but it may be doubted how far he did it any good by his well-meant exaggerations. He plunged into the furious controversies connected with the dock strike, without having taken the trouble to acquaint himself with the position of the dock proprietors, whom he believed to be rolling in riches when they were very much more than half ruined. He always took a superficially kind, gushing view of things, and his public utterances about social matters, as recorded by his biographer, are melancholy enough.—DUFF, SIR MOUNTSTUART E. GRANT, 1896, *Out of the Past*, p. 143.

That which struck one most on first getting to know Cardinal Manning well, some ten years ago, when serving with him, for nearly three years, on the Royal Commission on Education, and on further acquaintance also, was, I think, his extraordinary charm of manner and fascination of personality. He had the art, very rare, unfortunately—possessed to a marked degree by the late Lord Houghton—of taking the trouble and having the power of quickly putting at their ease men far younger than himself. His sense of humour was high, his own humour dry and expressive; his conversation vivacious and entertaining. His stately bearing, his beautifully cut features, his extraordinary ascetic look, his prominent forehead, his lustrous, deep-set eyes, his tightly-shut mouth, his dress, his age, his record, made a combination which was at once picturesque, strikingly interesting, and remarkably impressive. . . . On my first visits, I was conducted no further, by the old butler who was then alive, than to the inner of the two reception rooms. Almost immediately the Cardinal would appear from the side door leading from his private room; his beretta in his hand, his crimson skull cap on his head, a gold cross on his breast; his Cardinal's dress, effective and becoming, but untidy, even at times almost ragged, a button here or there undone or gone. Then, in the sparsely, almost meanly furnished but well-warmed room, seated each on one side of the fire or the fireplace, we would discuss the rights and wrongs of a labour dispute, and the ethics of the labour question; or, if his mood were different, the problems of life, or some more trivial and topical subject—religion or theology, never. . . . Then, as our intimacy grew, I was admitted, when I went alone, to the inner sanctum; where, screened off from the draught, he sat in the middle of the room opposite the fire in an easy chair. On each hand of him an enormous, untidy, and ever-rising heap of books, pamphlets, magazines, papers and letters, apparently in inextricable confusion; but from which he always seemed able to unearth any particular paper or book of which he spoke, or to which he wished to refer. His abstemiousness was remarkable; and his ascetic-looking and emaciated features were witness to the fact. . . . He wrote a beautiful, fine, small, distinct hand. . . . To me he had a sort of personal magnetism; a personal magnetism that I have only myself experienced with reference to one other man—Parnell. —BUXTON, SYDNEY. 1896, *Cardinal Manning—A Reminiscence, Fortnightly Review*, vol. 59, pp. 576, 593, 594.

Cardinal Manning was not only one of the noblest minds I have ever met, but one of the most patient and forgiving, through the restraint he knew how to put upon his natural feelings. He was also one of the most tender-hearted and charitable of men. I will also add that I always found him to be one of the most generous and forbearing. Though I was in most complete sympathy with him in most matters, there were others on which we took totally different views; and he would characterise these differences in his own playfully caustic way, as was his wont; but he bore them without any interruption of friendship. He was always to me as a father. — VAUGHAN, HERBERT CARDINAL, 1896, *The Life of Cardinal Manning, Nineteenth Century*, vol. 39, p. 252.

I have tried to tell the story of his life: that long effort in the direction of truth, that heroic sacrifice of all that is dear to man, that passion for certitude which cast him at the feet of the infallible Church and, in that Church, at the feet of the Vicar of Jesus Christ, the incorruptible guardian of the deposit of faith. I have tried to tell also of that noble attempt to bring mankind to the Church, and to give to the Church consciousness of its mission of enfranchisement, of consolation and of salvation for society as well as for the individual. In the presence of that grand figure, made up of austerity and love, of asceticism and of charity, in the presence of the memory of that man who loved power, but only to devote it to the noblest of uses, the word that involuntarily rises to the lips to sum up all that history is that Scripture: *Ecce sacerdos magnus;* his was truly the soul of a priest.— DePressensé, Francis, 1897, *Purcell's "Manning" Refuted,* tr. Furey.

It seemed to me as if a great cause, rather than any individual man, was that which drew out the strongest ardours of Manning's nature. He might easily have preferred the interests of a great friend to his own; but he would certainly have preferred that of a great cause to that of either self or friend. His human affections concentrated themselves on a few, while to the many beyond these he gave respect rather than admiration and a helpful and benevolent regard rather than ardent sympathies. The intensity of his nature, however, could not be doubted by any one who had seen him in church at prayer. His stillness was one that seemed as if it could not have been shaken if the church had caught fire.—DeVere, Aubrey, 1897, *Recollections,* p. 290.

Cardinal Manning, then, was, before and beyond all things, an ecclesiastical statesman—and an ecclesiastical statesman of a high order: a Churchman cast in the heroic mould of St. Gregory VII. And William of Malmesbury's description of the Pontiff applies equally well to the Cardinal:—"Vir apud Deum felicis gratiæ et apud homines austeritatis fortassis nimiæ." He was essentially a man of action; and it was in matters of ecclesiastical polity that his great gifts found their proper sphere: his imperious will, his clear intellect, his strong purpose. . . . He had the defects of his qualities—his great qualities. But I do not understand how any man who had the privilege of intercourse with him could doubt his faith unfeigned, his deep devotion, his spotless integrity, his indomitable courage, his singleness of aim, his entire dedication of himself to the cause which he, in his inmost soul, believed to be the only cause worth living for. "The purity of his heart, the sanctity of his motives, no man knowing him can question," Archdeacon Hare bore witness when lamenting his secession. This testimony is true.—Lilly, W. S., 1898, *Mr. Wilfrid Ward's "Cardinal Wiseman," Fortnightly Review,* vol. 69, pp. 306, 307.

GENERAL

Archbishop Manning's pastoral letter to his clergy on the first council, "The Vatican and its Definitions," to which are appended the two constitutions the council adopted— the one the "Constitutio de Fide Catholica," and the other the "Constitutio Dogmatica Prima de Ecclesia"—the case of Honorius, and the Letter of the German bishops on the council, though containing little that is new to our readers, is a volume which is highly valuable in itself, and most convenient to every Catholic who would know the real character of the council and what is the purport of its definitions. Few members of the council were more assiduous in their attendance on its sessions or took a more active part in its deliberations than the illustrious Archbishop of Westminster, and no one can give a more trustworthy account of its dispositions or of its acts. . . . The character of the book and of the documents it contains renders any attempt by us either to review it or to explain it alike unnecessary and impertinent. The pastoral is addressed officially by the Archbishop to his clergy.—Brownson, O. A., 1871, *The Church Accredits Herself, Catholic World,* vol. 13, p. 145.

The literary works of Henry Edward, Cardinal of Westminster, constitute a longer list than people outside the Catholic Church might be inclined to suppose, although any visitor to London who remembers his brilliant and interesting dark face, will readily accord to him a place among the intellectual men of the day. The Cardinal's book on "The Internal Mission of the Holy Ghost" contains a generous share of reason and truth, and will strike all its readers as an enlightened and intellectual production. Its style is sweet and easy to follow, and its divisions are interesting and apposite.— Anagnos, Julia R., 1883, *Cardinal Manning, Unitarian Review,* vol. 20, p. 38.

The publication during his lifetime of the

history of his Anglican days was laid aside at the Cardinal's wish. Up to the time of his serious illness in the winter of '88-9 the Cardinal was, I may say, eager for its publication. Afterwards his mind changed on the subject, caused in part no doubt, by the depression due to his illness; in part, to that nervous apprehension, which was one of the most characteristic elements in the Cardinal's mind, of the results of any work or action appertaining to things Catholic, in which he had not a guiding or controlling hand. Love of power has often been attributed to the Cardinal. "His finger is in every man's pie." And so it was; not from love of power; but from an intense fear that others would make a mess of it. No Catholic movement, ecclesiastical or lay; no work, secular or religious, he was firmly persuaded in his own mind, would be safe or free from blunders or bungling, unless it were in his own hands. Conscious of his own capacity and skill, he mistrusted, perhaps somewhat overmuch, the capacity or skill of others. Hence, perhaps not unnaturally, the unpopularity, limited indeed to the more active-minded among the clergy and laity, which attached itself to the Cardinal in the earlier days of his ecclesiastical rule.—PURCELL, EDMUND SHERIDAN, 1892, *Episodes in the Life of Cardinal Manning in his Anglican Days, Dublin Review, vol.* 110, *p.* 384.

It is more uncertain, though, whether Manning "made a mark on the religious history of his country greater, perhaps, than that made by Newman." Manning was more prominent, he made a greater show; but, perhaps, not a greater mark, perhaps not a religious mark at all. It is too soon to judge of these things, or of these men; all we can say is that, without Newman, Manning would have had much less to work upon, and much more to contend against. . . . We have heard much lately of Manning's victories, and little of his failures; perhaps the most conspicuous and disastrous of all his failures was the Catholic University of Kensington. He failed to provide the Catholic youth with a university of their own; he employed all his influence to thwart Newman's wiser conception, that all that is best in Oxford might be made their own, to the great advantage of Oxford and of themselves. It might be truer to say in conclusion, that Manning's "mark" is not so clear in religion as in philanthropy. It was when he put aside his Catholicism, and met his countrymen upon the common ground of good works, that he had most influence. There we are all proud of him; there we can admire him without reserve. But to see him a Radical in London, and a reactionary in Rome, is almost as distressing as to see Mr. Stead teaching the Pope how to be infallible. It is true that Roman Catholicism increased enormously in London under Manning's rule; but before we can decide the question of Manning's influence in religion, we must ascertain what proportion that increase bears to the general increase of the people at large, of the other dissenting bodies, and of the Church of England.—GALTON, ARTHUR, 1892, *Cardinal Manning, The Academy, vol.* 41, *p.* 535.

A man and his style are inseparable; and Manning wrote always with a certain stately beauty, a grave and chastened simplicity, measured and academic. But he had no modern ingenuities. In these days, Addison and the Augustan writers seem deplorably uningenious: they never tortured a thought into contortions; they were simple and unashamed. Manning was no more afraid of a truism than Sophocles or Horace; truisms are probably the truest truths, the best attested in the world. But the word indicates our longing for some new thing; and he who will invert a truism into a paradox passes for the happiest and most refreshing of wits.—JOHNSON, LIONEL, 1893, *Cardinal Manning, The Academy, vol.* 44, *p.* 224.

He was not, like Newman, a blend of high and distinguished poetic imagination, dialectical acumen, and historical learning. He was not carried away by the rush of the Oxford Movement; he had always lived well outside it. He was not influenced by intimate friends; he hardly seems to have had the genius of intimate friendship. Nor was he deceived by his own rhetoric or that of others; no man had more distrust of rhetoric and rhetoricians. His own speeches, sermons, and writings were cold, austere, correct, and methodical. It was not poetry then that led Manning to Rome, nor art, nor erudition, nor the spirit of romance, nor friendship, nor self-deluding eloquence, nor was it love of the past.—HOLLAND, BERNARD, 1896. *The Conversion of Manning, National Review, vol.* 27, *pp.* 111, 114.

It is no disparagement to Leo XIII to say that had Manning become Pope his reign would have been only a degree less brilliant than Leo's own. At the death of Pius IX he was the idol of the English-speaking Catholic world and its only real representative in Rome. Moreover, Manning had outgrown his diocese and his nation, and even the Sacred College, even Leo XIII in the first days of his pontificate, could not compare with Manning in world-wide fame. He had become the world's Cardinal. It crowded his doors, bringing every cause and every theory that man's restless brain can invent, for approval and blessing. His delight was to be with the children of men, and their delight was to be with him; and prudence of the clerical sort stood mourning in the street while the motley procession went in and out of the Cardinal's doors, undisturbed, unchecked, until that day when it followed him weeping to his grave. Let us stop here. This is the Manning the world knew: the gracious, noble, exalted figure, whose native dignity the world's honors could never obscure, and to whom a world turned with confidence and love.— SMITH, JOHN TALBOT, 1896, *Cardinal Manning and his Biographer, The Forum*, vol. 22, p. 105.

Manning was a vigorous administrator, a man of policies and methods, who was determined to have work done in his own way; but he was not always as careful as he ought to have been about the means he used. His early inclination to politics was a real expression of nature, for his aptitudes were for the service of the State rather than the Church, and he loved and served the Church as if it were a State. He had the ambition that place satisfied, and that could not be happy without place; power he loved more than fame, and if he sometimes gained it by ignoble arts, he yet used it for more noble ends. He was a man success improved; and when the temptations which appealed to his lower instincts were removed, he showed in his age some of those finer qualities of nature and character which we miss in his strong and aggressive manhood.— FAIRBAIRN, A. M., 1896, *Cardinal Manning and the Catholic Revival, Contemporary Review*, vol. 69, pp. 309, 325.

Great as Manning undoubtedly was, it may be doubted whether, when the great historian of the future enumerates the leaders of thought and men of action of the nineteenth century, Manning will be found among them. His indecision, his dislike of facing a danger boldly, betray a mind that would stoop to almost any shift rather than lose the good opinion of those who looked up to him. His was a character that lacked generosity.—WILBERFORCE, REGINALD G., 1896, *Cardinal Manning's Memory, Nineteenth Century*, vol. 39 p. 898.

Nothing will ever persuade me that Cardinal Manning intended his diaries, of which he said, "No eye but yours has ever seen this," to be printed in full and sold to the public within four years of his death. They contain matters too sacred, too secret, too personal. That Cardinal Manning intended his diaries to be read by his biographer—such parts as he had not erased—as a guide to accurate judgment in estimating motives, and to enable him to see the inner life of the man whose public life especially he was to portray, is no doubt true. But that he ever intended his spiritual struggles and confessions, the record of his own impressions, criticisms, and judgments on men and measures, many of them still in the process of solution, together with private and personal letters and notes dealing with the faults, real or imaginary, of others, and with matters the most contentious, to be gathered together and launched back on to the stormy sea he has left behind, the moment he had himself set foot upon the eternal shore, is simply inconceivable.... Those who knew the Cardinal well, knew that he had two moods of character. One of great caution and self-restraint when he spoke or wrote for the public. Measure and prudence were then dictated by a high sense of responsibility. Another, of singular freedom and playfulness of speech, when he thoroughly unbent with those whom he trusted in private. Hyperbole, epigram, paradox, lightened with a vein of humour, of sympathy, or of indignation, according to the subject of the moment, entered not only into his daily conversation, but into many a note and record of impressions, jotted down in the last years of his life. These notes, I know with certainty, were never intended for publication any more than private letters dealing with men's characters. — VAUGHAN, HERBERT CARDINAL, 1896, *The Life of Cardinal Manning, Nineteenth Century*, vol. 39, pp. 249, 250.

Intelligent, skilful, versatile he was in the highest degree; cultivated, too, with a knowledge of all that a highly educated man ought to know; dexterous rather than forcible in theological controversy; an admirable rhetorician, handling language with something of that kind of art which Roman ecclesiastics most cultivate, and in their possession of which the leading Tractarians showed their affinity to Rome, an exact precision of phrase and a subtle delicacy of suggestion. Newman had it in the fullest measure. Dean Church had it, with less brilliancy than Newman, but with no less grace and dignity. Manning equalled neither of these, but we catch in him the echo. He wrote abundantly and on many subjects, always with cleverness and with the air of one who claimed to belong to the *âmes d'élite*, yet his style never attained the higher kind of literary merit. There was no imaginative richness about it, neither were there the weight and penetration that come from sustained and vigorous thinking. Similarly, with a certain parade of references to history, and to out-of-the-way writers, he gave scant evidence of solid learning. He was an accomplished disputant in the sense of knowing thoroughly the more obvious weaknesses of the Protestant (and especially of the Anglican) position, and of being able to contrast them effectively with the external completeness and formal symmetry of the Roman system. But he never struck out a new or illuminative thought; and he seldom ventured to face—one could indeed sometimes mark him seeking to elude—a real difficulty.—BRYCE, JAMES, 1903, *Studies in Contemporary Biography*, p. 252.

Sir Richard Owen
1804–1892

Zoologist, born at Lancaster, July 20th, 1804, studied medicine at Edinburgh and at St. Bartholomew's; became curator in the museum of the Royal College of Surgeons, where he produced a marvelous series of descriptive catalogues; and in 1834–55 he lectured as professor of Comparative Anatomy, for two years at Bartholomew's, and afterwards at the College of Surgeons. Meanwhile he helped to give new life to the Zoological Society of London, and was a commissioner of health (1843–46), and for the Great Exhibition of 1851. In 1856 he became superintendent of the natural history department of the British Museum, but continued to teach at the Royal Institution and elsewhere. F. R. S. (1834), president of the British Association (1857), Associate of the French Institute (1859), C. B. (1873), K. C. B. (1883), recipient of many scientific medals, degrees, and honorary titles from many nations, he gained the immortality of a true worker, and died 18th December 1892. Owen's anatomical and palæontological researches number towards four hundred, and concern almost every class of animals from sponge to man. He greatly advanced morphological inquiry by his clear distinction between *analogy and homology*, and by his concrete studies of the nature of limbs, on the composition of the skull and on other problems of vertebrate morphology; while his essay on "Parthenogenesis" was a pioneer work. A pre-Darwinian, he maintained a cautious attitude to detailed evolutionist theories. See "Life" by his Grandson (1894).—PATRICK, AND GROOME, eds., 1897, *Chambers's Biographical Dictionary*, p. 712.

PERSONAL

The day before yesterday, in the evening, I had fallen asleep on the sofa; a loud doorknock woke me; in the twilight, the tea standing on the table, a man entered in white trousers, whom Helen (not the servant) named—Œdipus knows what! some mere mumble. In my dim condition I took him for Mackintosh: "he was empowered to call on me by Miss Fox, of Falmouth." He got seated; disclosed himself as a man of huge, coarse head, with projecting brow and chin, like a cheese in the *last* quarter, with a pair of large protrusive glittering eyes, which he did not direct to me or to anybody, but sate staring into the blue vague. There he sate and talked in a copious but altogether vague way, like a man lecturing, like a man hurried, embarrassed, and not knowing well what to do. I thought with myself, "Good heavens! can this be some vagrant Yankee, lion-hunting insipidity, biped perhaps escaped from Bedlam, coming in upon me by stealth?" He talked a minute longer. He proved to be Owen, the geological anatomist, a man of real faculty, whom I had wished to see. My recognition of him issued in peals of laughter, and I got two hours of excellent talk out of him—a man of real ability, who could tell me innumerable things. — CARLYLE, THOMAS, 1842, *Letter to His Wife, Aug. 20; Thomas Carlyle, a History of His Life in London,* ed. Froude, vol. I, p. 232.

A seafaring man brought a piece of bone, about three or four inches in length,—as he said, from New Zealand,—and offered it for sale at one or two museums, and, amongst others, at the College of Surgeons. We shall not here detain the reader by telling all that happened. These things are often brought with intent to deceive and with false allegations. Most of those to whom the bone was submitted dismissed it as worthless, or manifested their incredulity; among other guesses, some insinuated that they had seen bones very like it at the London Tavern, regarding it, in fact, as part of an old marrow-bone, to which it bore, on a superficial view, some resemblance. At length it was brought to Professor Owen, who, having looked at it carefully, thought it right to investigate it more narrowly; and, after much consideration, he ventured to pronounce his opinion. This opinion from almost anybody else would have been, perhaps, only laughed at; for, in the first place, he said that the bone (big enough, as we have seen, to suggest that it belonged to an ox) had belonged to a bird; but, before people had had time to recover from their surprise or other sensation created by this announcement, they were greeted by another assertion yet more startling,—namely, that it had been a bird without wings. Now, we happen to know a good deal of this story, and that the incredulity and doubt with which the opinion was received was too great for a time even for the authority of Professor Owen entirely to dispel. But mark the truthfulness of a real science! contemplate the exquisite beauty and accuracy of relation in nature! By-and-bye, a whole skeleton was brought over to this country,—when the opinion of the Professor was converted into an established fact.—MACILWAIN, GEORGE, 1853, *Memoirs of John Abernethy,* ch. xxix.

I cannot but think, that this arrangement would be beneficial in the highest degree to the Museum. I am sure that it would be popular. I must add that I am extremely desirous that something should be done for Owen. I hardly know him to speak to. His pursuits are not mine. But his fame is spread over Europe. He is an honor to our country, and it is painful to me to think that a man of his merit should be approaching old age amidst anxieties and distresses. He told me that eight hundred a year without a house in the Museum, would be opulence to him. He did not, he said, even wish for more. His seems to me to be a case for public patronage. Such patronage is not needed by eminent literary men or artists. A poet, a novelist, an historian, a painter, a sculptor, who stood in his own line as high as Owen stands among men of science, could never be in want except by his own fault. But the greatest natural philosopher may starve, while his countrymen are boasting of his discoveries, and while foreign Academies are begging for the honor of being allowed to add his name to their list.—MACAULAY, THOMAS BABINGTON, 1856, *To Lord Lansdowne, Feb.; Life and Letters,* ed. Trevelyan, ch. xiv.

I never heard so thoroughly eloquent a lecture as that of yesterday; and I can assure you that I have not in the course of my life been more gratified than by the proofs which Owen gave of his admirable qualifications for carrying out those higher behests which, as a Trustee of the British Museum, it has been my pride to have so warmly assisted in promoting. It is the first time I have had the pleasure of seeing our British Cuvier in his true place, and not the less delighted to listen to his fervid and convincing defense of the principle laid down by his great precursor. Every one was charmed, and he will have done more (as I felt convinced) to render our institution favorably known than by any other possible event.—MURCHISON, SIR RODERICK, 1857, *Letter, Feb. 27th; Life of Richard Owen,* ed. Owen, vol. II, p. 61.

Professor Owen, whom I like most hugely —we met him, if you remember, at the Bates's at Sheen—a tall, thin, cadaverous, lantern-jawed, bright-eyed, long-chinned, bald-headed, old man, full of talk on his own subject of the animal creation, a great friend and admirer of Agassiz—an immense man, I humbly think, and ever ready to be pumped on scientific matters.—MOTLEY, JOHN LOTHROP, 1867, *Letter to his Wife, Sept. 6; Correspondence,* ed. Curtis, vol. II.

One useful and rare quality he, like the late historian Green, possessed in an eminent degree. His innate modesty, or his art concealed by art, enabled him, when speaking upon his own subjects, so to let himself down to the level of ordinary listeners that they not only felt quite at their ease with him, but fancied for the moment that they were experts like himself.—TOLLEMACHE, LIONEL A., 1893, *Sir Richard Owen and Old-World Memories, National Review,* vol. 21, p. 616.

A keen chess-player himself, Sir Richard was always ready for a game in the evenings, and until very recent years played exceedingly well. His chief relaxation, however, was music, of which he had always been passionately fond. He was never tired of listening to his favorite compositions, although as he grew older his taste in music became much narrower, and he could only listen with pleasure to the music admitted to be "classical" in his younger days. Wagner, Grieg, and more modern composers were to his mind "tolerable and not to be endured." The keys of his little old-fashioned piano had been touched by many of his musical friends—Moscheles, John Ella, and Hallé, and had served many a time to accompany Jenny Lind and his own famous 'cello by Forster. The love of his home and of his beautiful garden only grew stronger with his declining years. Every day he would go round his garden—no small distance—supported by his favorite curiously-carved stick; then he would generally make his way to an extraordinary specimen of a garden-seat, made out of the vertebra of a whale, which he himself had put up. There are many such curiosities to be seen in that picturesque piece of ground.—OWEN, SIR RICHARD, 1894, *The Life of Richard Owen,* vol. II, p. 260.

Despite the prodigious amount of work that Owen did in his special subjects, he found time for many other occupations or relaxations. He was a great reader of poetry and romance, and, being gifted with a wonderful memory, could repeat by heart, even in his old age, page after page of Milton and other favourite authors. For music he had a positive passion; in the busiest period of his life he might constantly be seen at public concerts, listening with rapt attention, and in his earlier days was himself no mean vocalist, and acquired considerable proficiency in playing the violoncello and flute. . . . Owen's was a very remarkable personality, both physically and mentally. He was tall and ungainly in figure, with massive head, lofty forehead, curiously round, prominent and expressive eyes, high cheek bones, large mouth and projecting chin, long, lank, dark hair, and during the greater part of his life, smooth-shaven face, and very florid complexion. Though in his general intercourse with others usually possessed of much of the ceremonial courtesy of the old school, and when in congenial society a delightful companion, owing to his unfailing flow of anecdote, considerable sense of humour, and strongly developed faculty of imagination, he was not only an extremely adroit controversialist, but no man could say harder things of an adversary or rival. Unfortunately, he grew so addicted to acrimonious controversy that many who followed kindred pursuits held somewhat aloof from him, and in later life his position among scientific men was one of comparative isolation.—FLOWER, SIR WILLIAM H., 1895, *Dictionary of National Biography,* vol. XLII, p. 443.

From the very outset of his career he came in contact with distinguished personages, and, winning his way rapidly among them, the circle of his friendly and familiar acquaintance widened, until seemingly it embraced every notable character from the heads of the Royal House down through the various ranks of inherent and acquired nobility. He bore himself through it all with the quiet, simple grace of one born to the purple, or, better still, of one unconscious of worldly honors and successes, intent solely upon the accomplishment of the work he was given to do.—HUBBARD, SARA A., 1895, *The Lives of Two English Naturalists, The Dial,* vol. 18, p. 171.

Owen I saw frequently, and, though my scientific education was, and is, superficial, he interested me greatly; for he had, like Agassiz, the gift of making his knowledge accessible to those who only understood the philosophy and not the facts of science, and I knew enough of the former to profit by his knowledge. Then he was a warm friend of Agassiz, and we used to talk of his theories and studies, of which I knew more than of any other scientific subject.—STILLMAN, WILLIAM JAMES, 1901, *The Autobiography of a Journalist,* vol. I, p. 304.

GENERAL

It would not be fair to Blumenbach and Cuvier to compare this work with theirs, for science advances with such rapid strides, that they have become antiquated. . . . In the present day there is no work with which to compare Owen's "Lectures," except the classical work of Siebold. Owen has the superiority of philosophical grasp, which gives life and purpose to otherwise dry details. Vast as his knowledge is, careful as his mind is, Owen of course is not infallible. Probably no man has dissected so many animals, and to such purpose; yet it is certain that his industry has not carried the scalpel into every corner of every organism described by him. . . . In short, the work is not unapproachable from the trenches of criticism; but whatever lynx-eyed eagerness may discover in it, he is a bold man who will look down upon it from the height of *his* mole-hill. We cannot here attempt a detailed criticism of such a work, but we may earn the gratitude of philosophic readers by directing their attention to it.— LEWES, GEORGE HENRY, 1856, *Professor Owen and the Science of Life, Fraser's Magazine, vol.* 53, *pp.* 81, 82.

The ablest comparative anatomist of his time, Owen ranks with Darwin and Lyell as one of the greatest naturalists that England has yet produced. . . . Richard Owen was a giant, both in stature and in intellect, and the best monument that can be raised to his memory already exists in the Palæontological Galleries of the British Museum. Label after label calls to mind that Owen first studied and described the remains exhibited, and though he was not free from the errors of the early investigators, and was very jealous of his contemporaries, his triumphs will linger in our memories longer than his weaknesses or mistakes. Few students realise the magnitude of Owen's work, and it is only those who search in many fields that can comprehend the genius of the man who has now passed to his rest.— SHERBORN, G. DAVIES, 1893, *Owen, Natural Science, vol.* 2, *pp.* 16, 17.

It is now more than sixty years since the Zoological Society published the earliest of those anatomical papers on the Anthropoid Apes, among the later of which was the first thorough and detailed description of the skulls of the Chimpanzee and Gorilla. These together with the skilful restorations of the extinct birds of New Zealand and many other anatomical papers well-known to zoologists, will cause the name of Owen long to live in the grateful memory of all men who have the cause of Natural Science at heart. It seems, indeed, that the fame of our veteran Comparative Anatomist is likely rather to augment than decline. As time goes on and the disputes which formerly arose about the precise definition of "corpus callosum," and the presence of the "hippocampus minor" fade from memory, the many merits of the greatest English Zoologist of the first half of the nineteenth century will, we think, be more and more generally recognised. The esteem in which he has continued to be held during recent years is clearly shown by the award to him by the Council of the Linnean Society of their first Zoological Medal.—MIVART, ST. GEORGE, 1893, *Sir Richard Owen's Hypotheses, Natural Science, vol.* 2, *p.* 18.

Owen's archetypal theory may be said to have died with him. It was little more than a quasi-theological adaptation of Platonism; and it affords a striking confirmation of Comte's hypothesis that every science, between its early and its final condition, has to pass through a chrysalis stage—an unsightly and impotent stage of metaphysical abstractions. But in such a mind as Owen's, even if errors crop up, a fine quality of wheat is sure to be mingled with the tares. Indeed, he seems to have been among the first to anticipate a modification of Darwinism which is now coming to the front.—TOLLEMACHE, LIONEL A., 1893, *Sir Richard Owen and Old-World Memories, National Review, vol.* 21, *p.* 608.

Obvious as are the merits of Owen's anatomical and palæontological work to every expert, it is necessary to be an expert to discern them; and endless pages of analysis of his memoirs would not have made the general reader any wiser than he was at first. On the other hand, the nature of the broad problems of the "Archetype" and of "Parthenogenesis" may easily be stated in such a way as to be generally intelligible; while from Goethe to Zola, poets and novelists have made them interesting to the public. I have, therefore, permitted myself to dwell upon these topics at some length; but the reader must bear in mind that, whatever view is taken of Sir Richard Owen's speculations on these subjects, his claims to a high place among those who have made great and permanently valuable contributions to knowledge remain unassailable.— HUXLEY, THOMAS HENRY, 1894, *Owen's Position in the History of Anatomical Science, The Life of Richard Owen, ed. Owen, vol.* II, *p.* 332.

So far as the permanent forces of civilization are concerned, he was one of the leading Englishmen of the middle part of this century.... The memoir upon the Pearly Nautilus gave Owen a world-wide reputation, and from this time forward he worked over the broad field of living and extinct fishes, reptiles, birds, and mammals with marvellous rapidity and accuracy, producing from fifteen to thirty memoirs or papers annually until he was over eighty.... Owen laid the foundation of our modern work upon the fossil reptilia, especially the dinosaurs, and monographed the marsupials of Australia. From New Zealand he procured and finally restored the giant bird Dinornis, and one of his triumphs was the restoration of the great South American sloth, Mylodon. He was also an enthusiastic student of the microscope, discovering and tracing the life-history of the trichina as the cause of trichinosis, studying and speculating upon the phenomena of parthenogenesis, and being elected the first President of the Royal Microscopical Society. It is safe to say that no living naturalist is covering one-fourth the ground represented by these researches. We can hardly overestimate Owen's public services in spreading natural science through his facts and imparting his own enthusiasm.—OSBORN, H. F., 1895, *Richard Owen and the Evolution Movement, The Nation*, vol. 61, p. 66.

At a public dinner given in June, 1838, on behalf of the Actors' Benevolent Fund, it happened that the attention of the chairman, Lord Glengall, was called to one of the guests whom he did not know. On asking "Who's that?" he received for answer, "Oh, nobody in particular—only the first anatomist of the age!" The person so distinguished was Robert Owen, at that time not quite thirty-four years old. Somewhat later we find him described by Carlyle as a "tall man with great glittering eyes:" one of the few who was "neither a fool nor a humbug." In 1859 a brother of Mr. John Blackwood, the publisher, meeting Owen accidentally speaks of him as "a deuced clever-looking fellow, with a pair of eyes in his head!" and suspects that he may be the then unrevealed author of the "Scenes of Clerical Life"—a somewhat less extravagant supposition than that which had ascribed the "Vestiges" to Thackeray. On the continent his fame stood not less high than in England. Humboldt salutes in him "le plus grand anatomiste du siècle."... Owen seems to have enjoyed a celebrity which extended far beyond the scientific world, and which before the advent of Darwin surpassed that of every other English scientist.—BENN, ALFRED W., 1895, *The Life of Richard Owen, The Academy*, vol. 47, p. 73.

Acknowledged to be the greatest anatomist of the century, he was also a man of wide and generous culture, as might be expected of the friend and associate of the greatest thinkers, poets, novelists, musicians, and statesmen of the time. He was never a convert to Darwinism. He was not convinced that the origin of species by natural selection had been made out; and he deprecated the materialistic trend of this theory, clinging to the last to the belief in an immaterial spirit, and the hope of continuing in a future life the researches intermitted here.—GRAHAM, RICHARD D., 1897, *The Masters of Victorian Literature*, p. 469.

Amelia Blandford Edwards
1831–1892

Born, 1831. Began to contribute to periodicals, 1853. Hon. Sec. and Vice-Pres. of Egypt Exploration Fund. Hon. L. H. D. Degree, Columbia Coll., New York, 1887. Lectured in United States, 1889–90. Died, 15 April 1892. *Works:* "My Brother's Wife," 1855; "A Summary of English History," 1856; "The Ladder of Life," 1857; "The Young Marquis" [1857]; "Hand and Glove," 1858; "The History of France," 1858; Letterpress to "The Photographical Historical Portrait Gallery," 1860; "Sights and Stories," 1862; "The Story of Cervantes," 1863 [1862]; "Barbara's History," 1864 [1863]; "Ballads," 1865; "Miss Carew," 1865; "Half a Million of Money," 1865; Poems in "Home Thoughts and Home Scenes," 1865; "Debenham's Vow," 1870; "Untrodden Peaks," 1873; "In the Days of my Youth," 1873; "Monsieur Maurice," 1873; "A Thousand Miles up the Nile," 1877 [1876]; "A Poetry-Book of Elder Poets," 1879; "A Poetry-Book of Modern Poets," 1879; "Lord Brackenbury," 1880; "Pharaohs, Fellahs and Explorers," 1891.—She *translated:* Loviot's "A Lady's Captivity among the Chinese Pirates," [1858]; Maspero's "Egyptian Archæology," 1887.—SHARP, R. FARQUHARSON, 1897, *A Dictionary of English Authors, p.* 91.

PERSONAL

Summer or winter, in rain or sun or snow, Miss Edwards does her half-mile before and half-mile after breakfast, previous to beginning work, touching an index dial at the bottom of the path to make sure of her record. When tired at her desk she also takes a few turns. After luncheon, in the afternoon, a carriage drive of a couple of hours and an incidental walk give further recreation, and at dinner-time she repeats the morning walk. Otherwise than this she works all the time, forenoon, afternoon, and evening, giving to the cause of the Egyptian Exploration Fund, of which she is the founder and one of the honorary secretaries, in the writing of letters and articles, time and work worth some hundreds of pounds a year. In starting a novel, which she never expects to complete under two years, Miss Edwards maps out an elaborate plot, chapter by chapter, most conscientiously. Then she begins to write, and writes something entirely different. A new plot is evolved out of the *débris* of the old in a few brief memoranda, and this serves. She never describes scenery nor buildings which she has not seen and studied, though her interiors are furnished by the imagination to suit the situation. Thus a special visit to Cheshire laid the ground for "Lord Brackenbury," and some of the illustrations for it were redrawn from her own sketches. . . . Miss Edwards, with her strong, keen, fine face, is a fitting type for the woman scholar, a scholar made by hard study, but a writer born, since she wrote her first novel "before she could write," when four years old, printing the letters and making pictures; printed a long poem at eleven; and at twelve wrote an elaborate historical novel, which was published serially in a London penny weekly.—BOWKER, RICHARD ROGERS, 1888, *London as a Literary Centre, Harper's Magazine*, vol. 77, pp. 23, 24.

As a woman she is simple and earnest in her manner; free from anything like affectation, cordial and kind, and entertaining to the point of fascination. All this she carries into her lectures, and a fresh charm is given by her voice, which is music itself. It is not hard, nor is it pitched high, but it is beautifully clear, and has a carrying quality, which makes it possible for every one in her audience to hear distinctly any word she utters. She speaks with deliberation, but without the suggestion of slowness. . . . In personal appearance Miss Edwards is a tall, fine-looking woman, with silvery hair brushed straight back from her forehead, kindly gray eyes, a fresh complexion, and a clear-cut, very expressive mouth. She has a most genial, winning, and cordial manner, and is a charming conversationalist.—WHITE, SALLIE JOY, 1890, *Amelia B. Edwards, New England Magazine*, N. S., vol. 2, pp. 196, 198.

With regard to "my manners and customs" and the course of my daily life, there is little or nothing to tell, I am essentially a worker, and a hard worker, and this I have been since my early girlhood. When I am asked what are my working hours, I reply: —"All the time when I am not either sitting at meals, taking exercise, or sleeping;" and this is literally true. I live with the pen in my hand, not only from morning till night, but sometimes from night till morning. I have, in fact, been a night bird ever since I came out of the school-room, when I habitually sat up reading till long past midnight. Later on, when I adopted literature as a profession, I still found that "To steal a few hours from the night" was to ensure the quietest time, and the pleasantest, for pen and brain work; and, for at least the last twenty-five years, I have rarely put out my lamp before two or three in the morning. Occasionally, when work presses and a manuscript has to be despatched by the earliest morning mail, I remain at my desk the whole night through; and I can with certainty say that the last chapter of every book I have ever written has been finished at early morning. In summer-time, it is certainly delightful to draw up the blinds and complete in sunlight a task begun when the lamps were lighted in the evening.— EDWARDS, AMELIA B., 1891, *My Home Life, The Arena*, vol. 4, p. 309.

So long as she lived Miss Edwards devoted herself to the work of the Egypt Exploration Fund, abandoning all her other literary interests. As it was her contagious enthusiasm that originally brought the members together, so it was her genius for organization that smoothed over difficulties and insured success. With her own hand she wrote innumerable letters, acknowledging receipt of subscriptions, and labelled the objects presented to museums. During this period she regularly contributed articles on Egyptological subjects to the "Times" and the "Academy," as well as to other journals at home and abroad.—COTTON, J. S., 1901, *Dictionary of National Biography, Supplement*, vol. II, p. 177.

GENERAL

"A Thousand Miles up the Nile" is far from being a mere book of travel, though it is enlivened with the incidental narratives and picturesque descriptions customary in such a volume. . . . The style of the whole book is marked by precision and sustained vigour. . . . All the attractive and popular qualities which I have enumerated are placed by the author at the service of a strong and ardent passion for Egyptian archæology. . . . It is this enthusiasm for old Egypt, running, powerful and deep, throughout the volume, as an undercurrent to its many other interests, that gives its real charm to the work.—SYMONDS, JOHN ADDINGTON, 1877, *A Thousand Miles up the Nile, The Academy*, vol. 11, p. 65.

The name of Amelia B. Edwards is one that is familiar as an admirable writer of fiction; it also represents a lady with whom I can boast of an acquaintance, though some years have passed since we met. I have derived so much pleasure from that lady's books that I should be ungrateful if I did not place the writer prominently among the "people I have known." . . . I venture to recommend Miss Edwards' novel called "Barbara's History" to any one who doubts the authoress's right to be placed very high in the ranks of novelists. A reading of that book will dispel any such doubts. —FRITH, W. P., 1888, *My Autobiography and Reminiscences*, vol. II, p. 305.

On Feb. 13 Mr. Lowell added to his formal signature these words: "Dear Dr. Winslow: I have great pleasure in signing the above document." What he signed reads: "The proposed visit of Miss Amelia B. Edwards to the United States to see our Country and to lecture upon subjects in which she is an acknowledged authority, if carried into effect, will be an event of special interest to the intelligent and cultivated people of our land. She may be assured of a hearty welcome, and her lectures cannot fail to prove of rare profit and pleasure to her audiences." . . . I am sure that Miss Edwards will now yield to the desire of her heart to see a people that she loves so well as the Americans. I imagine she will come when next the maples are all aglow, which will recall to her "the after-glow on the Nile," and so be ready to begin to lecture on Egypt in November. Already some of our choicest rostrums, in institutes and universities have been placed at her disposal. I note that the English and Scotch press refer, in most appreciative terms, to her lectures in great cities and university centres, before crowded and enthusiastic audiences. . . . We shall be glad, too, to hear Miss Edwards on fiction, music and art (apart from Egypt), in which she is a foremost critic of the day.—WINSLOW, WILLIAM C., 1889, *Miss Edwards' Visit to America, The Critic*, vol. 11, p. 107.

No other novel ["Barbara's History"] has ever been to me quite what this was. "Charles Auchester" and a sweet English story, "St. Olave's," came the nearest to sharing my regard with it, but, much as I liked these books, they were not the first in my regard. That place of honor was given to "Barbara's History." . . . It is in her works of travels that Miss Edwards is at her best. She brings such a spirit of enthusiastic enjoyment to this work that she fascinates her readers and holds them spellbound by the beauty of her description and the rich results of her research. Many of her books are illustrated by herself, and a story told of her when she was a girl of fourteen is of decided interest, as showing the many-sidedness of her genius. At this time she sent a short story to *The Omnibus*, a periodical edited by the celebrated caricaturist, the late George Cruikshank. On the back of her manuscript she had drawn caricatures of her principal characters, which showed a cleverness that so delighted the great humorist that he called at once to see his unknown contributor. Fancy his surprise on being presented to a child. Recovering from his astonishment he offered to train her in his special work, but she declined his offer. Later on, for her own satisfaction, and as a recreation from her literary work, she studied art under the best masters. The advantage of this training she has reaped in being able to make her own illustrations for her books.—WHITE, SALLIE JOY, 1890, *Amelia B. Edwards, New England Magazine, N. S.*, vol. 2, pp. 194, 196.

I shall not attempt to write a biography of the eminent English woman who has just passed away, but must limit myself to an endeavour to record her services to learning. Therefore I pass by the early musical training of Miss Edwards, her skill as a landscape artist, and the long series of novels which gave her a name before Egyptology made her famous. I begin with the year 1883, when at the age of fifty-two she began her life's work, and joined Sir Erasmus Wilson in founding the Egypt Exploration Fund. This great enterprise, with which her name is by desert indissolubly linked, was the outcome of Mariette's so-called "archæological will." It took shape after a visit to Egypt described in "A Thousand Miles up the Nile," which excited in a highly-imaginative mind an undying interest in the monuments. . . . To Miss Edwards is due the success of the Fund. On her fell the duty of maintaining the subscriptions to the Fund in England, and of corresponding with the explorers and editing the Memoirs—a labour on which she spared no pains, and made many lasting friends and not a single enemy. This was not due to diplomacy, but to a keen sympathy with the workers, and a full appreciation of their hardships.—POOLE, REGINALD STUART, 1892, *Amelia B. Edwards*, The Academy, vol. 41, pp. 397, 398.

Her work in the field of fiction has stood the test of time, her merits as an Egyptologist are now universally acknowledged—it is pleasant to know that the cordial recognition of the "Athenæum" a few weeks ago was one of the last things read to her. . . . Although English literature was from childhood to middle life her absorbing study and pursuit, music in early years had taken such hold of her that at one time it seemed as if Amelia B. Edwards would rather distinguish herself in that field than authorship. . . . For drawing also she possessed marked talent, though I am unaware that she ever received a drawing lesson in her life. Indeed, excepting in the matter of music, few distinguished persons have been less indebted to teachers; she always said that she could teach herself anything better than others could teach her, and as an Egyptologist she was entirely self-taught. . . . A happy chance led her into the field of her latest and most brilliant successes. It was quite by accident that she visited Egypt some years since, the results of her journey being now well before the world. No need here to dwell on her exertions as honorary secretary of the Egypt Exploration Fund, or her numerous contributions to Egyptian archæology. As was lately pointed out in the columns of the "Athenæum," she is the first lady who has attained distinction as an Egyptologist.— BETHAM-EDWARDS, M., 1892, *Miss A. B. Edwards*, The Athenæum, No. 3365, pp. 534, 535.

Miss Edwards knew Egypt personally, and its history completely; she mastered the literature of research and exploration, and caught the freshest news of every discovery; she was profoundly interested in whatever cast light on philological and ethnical questions, or that related to the arts or sciences of contemporaneous nations, and withal she had a fair or respectable knowledge of the hieroglyphic text. Her talents, tastes, previous training, studies in her adopted profession, eminently qualified her for the post of honorary secretary of the society which she, with Sir E. Wilson and Prof. R. Stuart Poole founded in 1883. Nay, was she not born to be an Egyptologist? . . . Miss Edwards was the best delineator that Old Egypt has ever had. "The Saturday Review" thinks "no other writer did so much to render Egypt popular. . . . Hers was pre-eminently the rôle of interpreter" (April 23). Her lectures to American audiences, in their substance and expressions, most happily establish my claim. . . . Miss Edwards's genius belongs to the objective rather than the subjective school; and she assiduously cultivated her powers and tastes in the direction of objects rather than subjects of thought, or, if the latter, from without rather than within. She splendidly illustrated what it is to see and think through the eye rather than through pure reason. I do not know indeed that she ever read Plato, Aristotle, Descartes, and Hamilton; and although she could aptly quote "The immortal Dogberry" and other Shakespearean characters, yet I think she enjoyed the wit more than the human philosophy of Shakespeare. She was searching, investigating, logical for a woman in her deductions (witness her treatment of the Ka question), but she lacked at least in her novels, that imperial philosophic element, that *subjective* insight and genius of creation which permeates and sways the "Daniel Derondas" that are given the world. "Lord Brackenbury," so full of life, light, color, and abounding in suggestions to the imagination and eye, typifies, I think, the objective novel as distinctively as "Middlemarch" represents the subjective novel of our day. This may explain why some people fail to appreciate Miss Edwards's novels who praise her as an archaeologist.—WINSLOW, WILLIAM COPLEY, 1892, *The Queen of Egyptology, The American Antiquarian*, vol. 14, *pp.* 306, 312.

In "Barbara's History," in "Lord Brackenbury," and in other stories by Miss Edwards, there are beautiful and graphic descriptions of foreign scenery, and we meet plenty of foreign people; but we feel that the latter are described by an English woman who has taken an immense amount of pains to make herself acquainted with their ways and their speech—they somewhat lack spontaneity. In the two novels named there are chapters so full of local history and association that one thinks it might be well to have the books for companions when visiting the places described; they are full of talent—in some places near akin to genius.—MACQUOID, KATHARINE SARAH, 1897, *Women Novelists of Queen Victoria's Reign*, p. 262.

Charles Haddon Spurgeon
1834–1892

Born at Kelvedon, Essex, June 19, 1834: died at Mentone, France, Jan. 31, 1892. An English Baptist preacher. He was educated at Colchester and Maidstone, and became usher in a private school at Cambridge. In 1851 he became pastor of the Baptist church at Waterbeach, five miles from Cambridge, while retaining his place as usher. He accepted a call to the pastorate of the New Park Street Baptist Church in Southwark, London, in 1853, removing with his congregation in 1861 to a new edifice, the Tabernacle, in Newington, London. He was also the founder of a pastors' college, schools, almshouses, and an orphanage; and edited a monthly magazine, "The Sword and the Trowel." Among his works are "The Treasury of David: Exposition of the Book of Psalms" (1870–85), "Feathers for Arrows, or Illustrations for Preachers and Teachers" (1870), "Lectures to my Students" (1875–77), "Commenting and Commentaries: together with a Catalogue of Biblical Commentaries and Expositions" (1876), "John Ploughman's Pictures: More of his Plain Talk" (1880), and many volumes of sermons.—SMITH, BENJAMIN E., *ed.* 1894–97, *The Century Cyclopedia of Names*, p. 952.

PERSONAL

Spurgeon's lecture was well worth hearing, though, from William's getting us places of honour on the bench close behind Spurgeon, we did not see or hear him to such advantage as the less favoured public in the body of the hall. It was a study in the way of speaking and management of the voice; though his voice is not beautiful as some people call it, nor is his pronunciation quite pure. Still, it is a most striking performance, and reminded me very much of Bright's. Occasionally there were bits in which he showed unction and real feeling; sometimes he was the mere dissenting Philistine; but he kept up one's interest and attention for more than an hour and a half, and that is the great thing. I am very glad I have heard him.—ARNOLD, MATTHEW, 1866, *To his Mother*, Nov. 9; *Letters ed., Russell*, vol. I, p. 398.

Take him all in all there is no figure since old Simeon's comparable to Spurgeon as a great middle-class orator, and even Rowland Hill's and Simeon's piety and pulpit power rolled together would hardly amount to one Spurgeon! Indeed no one since the world began has ever accomplished the feat habitually performed by Spurgeon without apparent effort—I mean the feat of attracting and retaining a congregation of 6,000 persons twice every Sunday for over thirty years. His simple and unaffected egotism—like that of Oliver Wendell Holmes—had something very frank and winning about it. The head was perhaps deficient in a sense of proportion, but then the heart was so good. He was perfectly unconscious of any inconsistency. No one disliked the Pope's arrogant assumptions more than Spurgeon, but as a dogmatic teacher the Pope would have to climb down before the great Baptist—and certainly no Pope ever had a more perfect belief in his own infallibility.—HAWEIS, HUGH REGINALD, 1892, *The Late Mr. Spurgeon, English Illustrated Magazine*, vol. 9, p. 503.

Time did not wear out his reputation; the light shone to the last. He had talent, but he had qualities without which talent is of little avail: he had what athletes would call staying power. He passed through the ordeal of the *furore* of early fame. A lighter character and a less stable soul might have been ruined by the popularity which met him on the threshold of his manhood. The prosperity of fools destroys them; but Mr. Spurgeon had the instinct of a strong nature. He knew that no man can produce great effects without hard work. He had won a reputation: he did more, he did the much harder thing, he maintained it.—CARPENTER, WILLIAM BOYD, 1892, *Mr. Spurgeon, Contemporary Review, vol.* 61, *p.* 307.

His success has been accounted for in some degree by natural causes. He certainly had not such attractions as Rowland Hill, in high social connection, imposing presence, and university prestige. At first he had to encounter hostile criticisms, lampoons, caricatures, and malicious inventions. His voice was certainly a great power; so clear, strong, incisive, penetrating without effort the remotest corner of the largest building. His style was attractive—so lucid, yet so strong in its Saxon simplicity, that the best-cultured could not but admire it, while "the common people heard him gladly." He was easy and natural in his manner; never toiling as he spoke and never fatiguing those who listened. He never hesitated for a word or retracted an utterance. . . . He never *tried* to be witty. It grew out of his subject.—HALL, NEWMAN, 1892, *Charles Haddon Spurgeon, Good Words, vol.* 33, *p.* 233.

Spurgeon had no creative genius; he has contributed nothing to religion or to ethics, nothing doctrinal or vital or formative. Creeds and dogmas are what they were before his voice was heard. But he has contributed Spurgeon, and it will be many a generation before the echo of those tones which filled the Tabernacle Sunday after Sunday has ceased to vibrate in men's memories.—SMALLEY, GEORGE W., 1892, *Studies of Men, p.* 61.

He was a strict vegetarian, and drank only water at his meals. His one cigar per diem he smoked, to use his own words, "to the glory of God." He spent not one shilling of his salary upon himself. Of the £1,500 received in this way, £1,000 were devoted to his orphanage or clerical college, and £500 as salary to his assistant clergyman. He supported his family, so he told me, from the proceeds of his dairy farm and from the sale of his books.—TUCKERMAN, CHARLES K., 1895, *Personal Recollections of Notable People, vol.* II, *p.* 349, *note*.

I was taken to the chapel and placed not far from the attraction of the day; a short, stout figure, with no personal advantage except the starlike eyes of genius. A hymn was given out, that is read, two lines at a time, or rather "entunéd (Chaucer) through the nose," to be repeated in song. I felt sorry for the preacher, who bore the not too harmonious result with such sweet patience. The hymns were the only set form of words admitted in worship; even the Lord's prayer was unheard. Presently Mr. Spurgeon filled the pulpit and his petition went up, drawing the souls of others into a clearer light than our common earthly day. Then he rose to his feet: the "weak bodily presence" became fraught with a passion and intensity that might have been Edmund Kean's; with a grace in every varying attitude that no sculptor could correct: as he spoke, he became illuminated, eyes, smile, motion, he rose upon you like an indescribable source of light. Setting his Bible on end, he would lean with one arm laid firm above it, or raise heavenward both expressive hands with a perfection of curves and an harmonious turn of the head that passed the most accomplished art. It was unlike any preacher I had ever seen or heard. He was master of all the secrets of speech and motion. He possessed to the uttermost that gift of action so rare in the English-speaking race, and added to it the power, still rarer, of eloquent repose. His voice, like all his talents, was held under a tight rein, or let go, at his absolute will. Never was a syllable dropped too low to penetrate to the most distant corner of space beneath him. It was like a clear peal of musical bells, endless in natural variety. Natural it was, colloquial mostly; but rising and falling at need to every tone of human emotion.—GOWING, EMILIA AYLMER, 1895, *Spurgeon, Belgravia, vol.* 86, *p.* 261.

It became the fashion to hear Mr. Spurgeon, and not to have heard him argued one's self out of the movement of public life. Great statesmen and Parliamentary orators rushed to listen to him, and public opinion, of course, became greatly divided as to his eloquence. People ran into wild extremes about him. Some insisted that he was the greatest pulpit orator who had ever been heard in England, or, indeed, anywhere else. Others as stoutly argued that he was nothing but a windbag and a loud voiced charlatan. On one point all had to agree—that Spurgeon had a magnificent voice, a fine dramatic gesticulation, and a style which rose from conversational simplicity to an impassioned and thrilling rhetoric. He had come into the pulpit determined to be heard—determined to be heard because, as he said himself, he had a message to deliver, and deliver it he would. He knew perfectly well the importance of getting himself talked about as soon as possible. He once told a friend that he was determined to attract attention, and that if there were no other way of securing his object he would have worn a soldier's red coat when he got into the pulpit. This, it should be understood, was not in the least because Spurgeon cared for notoriety for its own sake. He had no personal desire to be known by the public. It was because notoriety, even through eccentricity, was of value to him as a means of attracting an audience. All sorts of ridiculous anecdotes, most of them absolutely without foundation, were commonly told of the efforts he made to startle his audiences into attention. He very soon found that he needed nothing but his own eloquence to gather a crowd around him wherever he went.—MCCARTHY, JUSTIN, 1897, *A History of Our own Times from* 1880 *to the Diamond Jubilee*, p. 320.

Mr. Spurgeon was a very quick reader, but the rapidity of his glance at the page did not interfere with the completeness of his acquaintance of its contents. He could read from cover to cover of a large octavo or folio volume in the course of a very short space of time, and he would thus become perfectly familiar with all that it contained. . . . At the time of Mr. Spurgeon's homegoing, he possessed at least 12,000 volumes. The number would have been far larger if he had not given so generously to the libraries of the Pastors' College and many of the ministers trained within its walls, and if he had not also, from his abundant stores, so freely enriched other friends.—SPURGEON, MRS. CHARLES HADDON, 1900, *C. H. Spurgeon's Autobiography Compiled from his Diary, Letters and Records*, vol. IV, pp. 273, 287.

GENERAL

In freshness and vigor of thought, in simplicity and purity of language, in grasp of gospel truth, and in tact and force in its presentation, he is perhaps without a peer in the pulpit.—HOLME, STANFORD, 1879, *Christian Herald, Jan*.

You might search the whole world and find no one whose mind was more thoroughly under the domination of theological ideas than Spurgeon's. To a Positivist the reverend gentleman must appear like a survival not of the fittest, but of the unfittest—a painful anachronism to remind good Positivists and advanced thinkers generally of the lowly estate from which they have emerged. Not even reached the metaphysical stage; and yet Mr. Spurgeon has thousands and thousands of excellent men and women who hang on his every word, spoken and written, as if it were the very bread of life.—DAVIDSON, J. MORRISON, 1880, *Eminent Radicals In and Out of Parliament*, p. 179.

Mr. Spurgeon's chief work as a humourist is "John Ploughman's Talk." This proved such a success as a serial that it was afterwards issued as a book, and the fact that 370,000 have been sold of it proves it to be worth reading. This book was followed by "John Ploughman's Pictures," of which 130,000 have been issued. If wit be employed merely to gladden sad lives, or to impart velocity to truth, it is not misemployed, for with many people life is terribly dreary and crushing; but when humour is so directed as to make evil absurd and good attractive, it is indeed well employed, and is indeed a moral force of the utmost importance. Of course, like anger, it must be well under control, just as the same fire prepares our food when kept within the kitchen grate, that would be fearful if it were in our pocket. Mr. Spurgeon's wit is of the kitchen-range order, that is, it is ready to burn up rubbish and make food more palatable and nourishing; it is, indeed, part of his original endowment, and one element of his success.—ELLIS, JAMES J., 1892, *Charles Haddon Spurgeon (Lives that Speak)*, pp. 160.

It is true that Mr. Spurgeon wrote books. His "John Ploughman's Talk" has had a circulation of more than half a million. His "Treasury of David" has sold by thousands. We admit it; but it is not as an author that Mr. Spurgeon will be remembered; his works are not in the true sense ventures in literature. They are rather chips from his workshop; and in his workshop not books but sermons were made. These were his true work; the others were but groupings of accumulated material. He was not tempted, as others have been, into really new ventures. Preaching was his trade; and he kept to it. *Hoc unum*—this one thing he did—whatever he wrote he threw it off in the course of, and not in addition to, his main and much-loved work of preaching. To this, and not to authorship, he devoted his life. . . . If we were to class Mr. Spurgeon we must place him among the men of action; he belongs more to the type of Luther than to that of Erasmus or Fenelon. He belongs to the class which produces strong leaders rather than strong thinkers—men of action, not men of contemplation.—CARPENTER, WILLIAM BOYD, 1892, *Mr. Spurgeon, Contemporary Review, vol.* 61, *p.p* 308, 311.

Of all his writings, "John Ploughman's Talk" and "John Ploughman's Pictures" achieved by far the greatest success, and for the same reason, because they were packed full of pithy, racy sayings. The circulation of his sermons was world-wide. It is interesting to know that his uncompromising denunciation of slavery before the outbreak of the great rebellion destroyed at a stroke the circulation of his sermons in the United States. That denunciation practically cost him in hard cash $3,000 a year, which was the annual profit derived from the sale of his sermons across the Atlantic. A selection of his sermons was translated into Russian, and issued with the imprimatur of the Russian ecclesiastical authorities for use by the orthodox clergy. They could not do better than use them, but the majority never preach at all. To read one of Spurgeon's sermons is one of the unfailing resources in many a chapel when the supply fails to arrive, and many a time his sermons are laid under contribution, even by the Lord Mayors of London, without always due recognition of the source from which the pulpit thunder was borrowed.—STEAD, W. T., 1892, *Three Eminent Englishmen, Review of Reviews, vol,* 5, *p.* 180.

Perhaps you will allow me to say a word or two about his power as a writer,—his power to express himself in writing. In this democratic age, when sympathy with the masses is on everyone's lips, it often seems to me wonderful that the power of communicating with the multitude is so rare. We have scores of ministers who are ambitious of writing for the world of the cultivated; but a book frankly and successfully addressing the average man, in language which he can understand, is one of the rarest products of the press. It really requires very exceptional power. It requires knowledge of human nature, and knowledge of life. It requires common sense; it requires wit and humor; and it requires command of simple and powerful Saxon. Whatever the requirements may be, Mr. Spurgeon had them in an unexampled degree. To find his match in this respect, you have, I think, in England, to go back to John Bunyan.—STALKER, JAMES, 1894, *At the Unveiling of the C. H. Spurgeon Memorial, June 20th; C. H. Spurgeon's Autobiography, ed. His Wife, vol.* IV, *p.* 277.

The productions of no other preacher's heart and brain ever kept a great printing and publishing firm constantly engaged with the issue of his works alone. I have been through the publisher's store rooms; these contain many *tons* of Mr. Spurgeon's works, which are in constant demand. "John Ploughman's Pictures" has reached its 140th thousand; and "John Ploughman" is now in its 400th thousand. For a shilling book, dealing with moral and religious matters, this sale is, I believe, absolutely unprecedented. The choice volumes "Morning by Morning" and "Evening by Evening" have enjoyed a sale of over two hundred and ten thousand. These have been amongst the most useful *sermon saplings* many a preacher has possessed; thousands of sermons have been delivered which were suggested by these charmingly gracious chapters; while of the yearly volumes the Chairman of the London Congregational Union for 1895 said: *"No preacher's library was complete without them."* . . . The four volumes of Mr. Spurgeon's "Sermon Notes," containing in all two hundred and sixty-four outlines of sermons, from which he preached, are by far the most helpful books to preachers in sermon-making which he has published. With each skeleton are given extracts from some of the best authors; and illustrations also, which bear directly on the subject in hand, so that if the preacher feels he would rather treat his subject in his own way—and all surely ought to feel this—he has nevertheless many practical suggestions he may very justly appropriate both for exposition and adornment.—WILLIAMS, W., 1895, *Personal Reminiscences of Charles Haddon Spurgeon, pp.* 287, 288.

Charles H. Spurgeon contributed little or nothing to the theological thought of his age; for, intellectually, he lived in the thought-atmosphere of the seventeenth century. But he contributed a great deal to the ethical and spiritual life of his age; for, ethically and spiritually, he lived in the London of the last half of the nineteenth century. He was ambitious, but his ambition was pure and ennobling. "I would rather," he said, "be the means of saving a soul from death than be the greatest orator on earth." That was the secret of his unoratorical oratory. "I would rather bring the poorest woman in the world to the feet of Jesus than I would be made Archbishop of Canterbury." That was the secret which made his church the centre of activities greater, probably, than those of any single cathedral in Great Britain. He lived in the perpetual consciousness of God, a consciousness which pervaded his preaching not more distinctly than it did his personal and daily life. . . . He had a remarkable power of insight, which enabled him to read the men with whom he dealt in personal and pastoral relations—an insight which amounted almost to genius, and gave him a skill which was better than tact —which is, indeed, the best form of tact. His sense of humor saved him from the follies in which pietism sometimes involves men who have no such sense, and carried him through difficulties in which so energetic and strong-willed a man would have been plunged had he not been well supplied with that lubricating oil. . . . I heard Spurgeon in his own Tabernacle. The congregation was a depressing, not an inspiring one. The music was heavy and uninteresting. The sermon was at no point what could be called eloquent. The text was an enigmatical passage from Isaiah. But the impression I shall carry with me to my dying day was that of a man who had found life made real, noble, joyous, by his living faith in a living Christ, and who longed to impart to others the life which Christ had imparted to him.—ABBOTT, LYMAN, 1898, *Charles H. Spurgeon: a Personal Study, The Outlook*, vol. 59, pp. 627, 628.

Spurgeon was a prolific author, writing with the directness and earnestness that distinguished him as a speaker.—BUCKLAND, A. R., 1898, *Dictionary of National Biography*, vol. LIII, p. 434.

Perhaps, among all Mr. Spurgeon's published works, the one that gives the best idea of his familiarity with the whole range of expository literature, is his unpretentious half-crown volume, issued under the unattractive title, "Commenting and Commentaries." The book has long since been accepted as a most reliable standard of appeal, and its commendations and valuations are frequently quoted in catalogues of theological works. — SPURGEON, MRS. CHARLES HADDON, 1900, *C. H. Spurgeon's Autobiography Compiled from his Diary, Letters and Records*, vol. IV, p. 269.

Sir George Biddell Airy
1801–1892

A celebrated English astronomer; born at Alnwick, Northumberland, July 27, 1801; died Jan. 4, 1892. Soon after graduation from Trinity College, Cambridge, he was appointed professor of astronomy and director of the observatory. Here he introduced improvements and inventions that led to his selection as director of the Greenwich Observatory. It was due to his efforts that the observations taken at Greenwich from 1750 to 1830 were compiled. Among his works are: "Reductions of Observations of the Moon" (1837); "Sound and Atmospheric Vibrations" (1871); "Treatise on Magnetism" (1871).— WARNER, CHARLES DUDLEY, ed. 1897, *Library of the World's Best Literature*, vol. XXIX, p. 8.

PERSONAL

Were it not that you are now so happy with them, I should regret that you were not here during the last few days, to have met Professor Airy. He would have interested you much. To myself his visit gave more pleasure than I had anticipated: he likes the mountains of Cumberland, which he has already visited five times, and hopes to visit five times more. But, on the whole, his mind appeared to me an instance, painful to contemplate, of the usurpation of the understanding over the reason, too general in modern English Science.—HAMILTON, SIR W. R., 1831, *To Viscount Adare, Aug. 23; Life, ed. Graves*, vol. I.

Airy alone has gain'd that double prize
Which forc'd musicians to divide the crown:
His works have rais'd a mortal to the skies,
His marriage vows have drawn an angel down.
—SMITH, SYDNEY, 1831? *On Professor Airy, the Astronomer, and his Beautiful Wife.*

A lover of Nature and a close observer of her ways, as well as in the forest walk as in the vault of heaven, Mr. Airy has roamed among the beautiful scenery of the Lake region until he is as good a mountain guide as can be found. He has strolled beside Grasmere and ascended Helvellyn. He knows the height of the mountain peaks, the shingles that lie on their sides, the flowers that grow in the valleys, the mines beneath the surface.—MITCHELL, MARIA, 1857, *Journal; Life, Letters, and Journals*, ed. Kendall, p. 97.

A hardy little figure, of edacious energetic physiognomy, eyes hard, if strong, not fine; seemed three or four years younger than I; and to be, in secret, serenely, not insolently, enjoying his glory, which I made him right welcome to do, on those terms.—CARLYLE, THOMAS, 1866, *Edward Irving, Reminiscences*, ed. Norton, vol. II.

Sir George was one of those calm, self-reliant men who seldom give any outward evidence of the remarkable strength of character they possess. His sense of duty and rectitude overruled all selfish considerations. He once refused to recommend a relative for an official post, for which he was admirably fitted, solely because he was his relative; and when Palmerston offered to confer upon the retired astronomer a royal pension, he declined it, and begged that the money might be settled upon his wife. Even an increase of salary offered by the Government was refused by him until just before his resignation of the post, when he accepted the augmentation, in order that his successor might receive a salary more in accordance with the value of the services rendered.—TUCKERMAN, CHARLES K., 1895, *Personal Recollections of Notable People*, vol. II, p. 4.

One of his most interesting researches in these early days is on the subject of Astigmatism, which defect he had discovered in his own eyes. His investigations led him to suggest a means of correcting this defect by using a pair of spectacles with lenses so shaped as to counteract the derangement which the astigmatic eye impressed upon the rays of light. His researches on this subject were of a very complete character, and the principles he laid down are to the present day practically employed by oculists in the treatment of this malformation. —BALL, SIR ROBERT S., 1895, *Great Astronomers*, p. 290.

He was of medium stature, and not powerfully built. . . . The ruling feature of his character was order. From the time he went up to Cambridge to the end of his life his system of order was strictly maintained. —AIRY, WILFRID, 1896, ed., *Autobiography of Sir George Biddell Airy*.

GENERAL

Prof. Airy, of Cambridge, the first of living mathematicians and astronomers,—the first of this country, at least.—PEEL, SIR ROBERT, 1835, *Letters to Robert Southey, April 14; Southey's Life and Correspondence*, ed. C. C. Southey, ch. xxxvi.

Every year Sir George publishes a report on the work done in the Royal Observatory; these reports form a series which will be of the greatest use for the writer of the history of astronomy and science in general in the nineteenth century. Since the year 1833 the incessant activity of Sir George Airy had been directed to an undertaking, proposed to astronomers by Bessel, in the preface of his "Tabulæ Regiomontanæ," viz., the reduction of the Greenwich lunar and planetary observations since 1750. This most arduous task was completed in the year 1848; and we may say that our present tables of the motions of the moon and the planets rest, for the greatest part, on those bulky volumes, containing these reductions. . . . Only very briefly can I mention his very useful experiments on iron-built ships, for the purpose of discovering a correction for the deviation of the compass, which resulted in a system of mechanical corrections, universally adopted; his researches on the density of the earth by observations in the Harton Colliery; his extensive aid to Government in recovering the lost standard for measures; in fixing the breadth of railways; in introducing a new system for the sale of gas, &c. All these transactions have proved Sir George Airy "the thorough man of business." Indeed, the promptness of his correspondence and his kindness in answering every scientific enquiry in the most minute manner, is most remarkable and seldom to be met with in so profound a philosopher. . . . Sir George Airy has, of course, deservedly received the recognition of his country and the scientific world in general.—WINNECKE, A., 1878, *Sir George Biddell Airy, Nature*, vol. 18, p. 690.

His work in many branches of science was highly valuable, but it would be hardly possible to treat his scientific labours from the point of view of literature. His best known works, the treatises on "Errors of Observation," on "Sound," and on "Magnetism." Sir George was one of the last survivors of the great band of *savants* who shed lustre upon the earlier years of the present reign.—OLIPHANT, M. O. W., 1892, *The Victorian Age of English Literature*, p. 390.

The amount of his labours almost exceeds belief. On the literary side alone they have rarely been equalled.—CLERKE, MISS A. M., 1901, *Dictionary of National Biography, Supplement*, vol. I, p. 25.

George William Curtis
1824-1892

Born at Providence, R. I., Feb. 24, 1824: died on Staten Island, N. Y., Aug. 31, 1892. A noted American journalist, orator, publicist, and author. He lived in the community at Brook Farm, remaining there 18 months; traveled abroad 1846-50; on his return in the latter year became connected with the New York "Tribune;" was connected with "Putnam's Monthly" 1852-57; and became editor of the "Easy Chair" (Harper's Magazine) in 1854, and in 1863 of "Harper's Weekly" (founded 1857). He was an influential advocate of civil-service reform. In 1871 he was appointed by Grant, one of the commissioners to draw up rules for the regulation of the civil-service, but resigned on account of differences with the President. He was president of the New York State Civil Service League in 1880, and of the National Civil Service Reform League from its foundation until his death. He wrote "Nile Notes of a Howadji" (1851), "Howadji in Syria" (1852), "Lotus Eating" (1852), "Potiphar Papers" (1853), "Prue and I" (1856), "Trumps" (1862), "From the Easy Chair" (1891), "Washington Irving" (1891).—SMITH, BENJAMIN E., *ed.*, 1894-97, *The Century Clycopedia of Names*, p. 298.

PERSONAL

In 1856, he took a very active part in the "Fremont campaign," speaking constantly through the summer, with great effect. Those who had the good fortune to hear any of these addresses will not soon forget them, uniting as they did the soundest argument to a chaste and brilliant oratory.—CLEVELAND, CHARLES D., 1859, *A Compendium of American Literature*, p. 758.

Mr. Curtis is as agreeable in private as he is pleasing in public. He is natural, gentle, manly, refined, simple and unpretending, and quiet. I liked him very much. There is a certain lacadaisicalness in his published portrait which is not seen in his face.—DODGE, MARY ABBY (GAIL HAMILTON), 1865, *Letter, Nov. 27; Gail Hamilton's Life in Letters*, ed., Dodge, vol. I, p. 528.

Curtis, skilled equally with voice and pen
To stir the hearts or mould the minds of men,—
That voice whose music, for I've heard you sing
Sweet as Casella, can with passion ring,
That pen whose rapid ease ne'er trips with haste,
Nor scrapes nor sputters, pointed with good taste,
First Steele's, then Goldsmith's, next it came to you,
Whom Thackeray rated best of all our crew,—
Had letters kept you, every wreath were yours;
Had the World tempted, all its chariest doors
Had swung on flattered hinges to admit
Such high-bred manners, such good-natured wit;
At courts, in senates, who so fit to serve?
And both invited, but you would not swerve,
All meaner prizes waiving that you might
In civic duty spend your heat and light,
Unpaid, untrammelled, with a sweet disdain
Refusing posts men grovel to attain.
Good Man all own you; what is left me, then,
To heighten praise with but Good Citizen?
—LOWELL, JAMES RUSSELL, 1874, *To George William Curtis, Heartsease and Rue*, p. 49.

Mr. Curtis long since gained national reputation as a lecturer. His first venture in that line was "Contemporary Art in Europe," in 1851; then he fairly got under way with "The Age of Steam," and soon became one of that remarkable group, including Starr King, Phillips and Beecher, who built up the lyceum into an important institution, and went all over the country lecturing. Mr. Curtis gave lectures every winter until 1872. I remember his saying, some time before that, "I have to write and deliver at least one sermon a year;" and indeed they *were* sermons, of the most eloquent kind, rife with noble incitements to duty, patriotism, lofty thought, ideal conduct. . . . Twenty years a lecturer, without rest; twenty-one years a political editor; thirty-two years the suave and genial occupant of the "Easy Chair;" always steadfast to the highest, and ignoring unworthy slurs;—may we not say reasonably that he has "staying power?" One source of it is to be found in the serene cheer of his family life in that Staten Island cottage to which he clings so closely.— LATHROP, GEORGE PARSONS, 1884, *Authors at Home, The Critic, vol. 5, pp. 265, 266.*

At supper it was whispered that George W. Curtis would sing at the Eyrie, upon which several young men volunteered to assist with the dishes. My services were also cordially accepted. . . . And now we ascended the winding, moonlit path to the Eyrie, where Curtis was already singing. We went up the steps of the building cautiously, lest a note of the melody which floated through the open French windows should be lost to us. Entering the large parlor, we found not only the chairs and sofas occupied, but the floor well covered with seated listeners. I did not at first recognize the operatic air, so admirably modified and retarded it was, and its former rapid words replaced by a sad and touching theme, which called for noble endurance in one borne down by suffering. The accompaniment consisted of simple cords and arpeggios, a very plain and sufficient background. Curtis, though not yet twenty—not nineteen, if I remember rightly—had a grave and mature appearance. He was full of poetic sensibility, and his pure, rich voice had that sympathetic quality that penetrates to the heart. . . . Curtis was not ever guilty of singing a comic song. It would indeed have been most inappropriate to our intensely earnest mood. Often his brother would join him in a duet with his agreeable tenor. Low praises and half-spoken thanks were murmured as the grave and gracious young friend, at the expiration of an hour, swung around on the piano-stool and attempted to make his exit.—KIRBY, GEORGIANA BRUCE, 1887, *Years of Experience: an Autobiographical Narrative.*

That which always struck me as his strongest mental characteristic was his common sense. His judgment was almost unerring, and his tact was marvelous. His mind seemed never closed to a new suggestion. If it had force, he recognized it immediately; if not, he put it aside with such gentle but conclusive refutation that its author was almost glad not to have it accepted. High as was the standard of his own thinking and living, he was of all men the least censorious. Easily superior in mental gifts and accomplishments in that personal attractiveness which is the genius of character, he never showed that he was conscious of it. His associates in the League felt that he was the natural leader; but among them, while most effectively leading, he seemed to be only the most hearty and generous of comrades.—ROGERS, SHERMAN S., 1893, *George William Curtis and Civil Service Reform, Atlantic Monthly, vol. 71, p. 23.*

The art in which Curtis excelled all his contemporaries of the last thirty years was the art of oratory. Many other authors wrote better in verse, and some others wrote as well in prose. Hawthorne, Motley, Lowell, Whipple, Giles, Mitchell, Warner, and Stedman were masters of style. But in the felicity of speech Curtis was supreme above all other men of his generation. My reference is from the period from 1860 to 1890. Oratory as it existed in America in the previous epoch has no living representative. Curtis was the last orator of the great school of Everett, Sumner, and Wendell Phillips. His model—in so far as he had a model—was Sumner, and the style of Sumner was based on Burke. But Curtis had heard more magical voices than those—for he had heard Daniel Webster and Rufus Choate; and although he was averse to their politics, he could profit by their example.—WINTER, WILLIAM, 1893, *George William Curtis, a Eulogy, p. 45.*

A few feared lest the adulations heaped upon him should seduce him from the student's smoky lamp to Paphian bowers lit by gilded chandeliers and eyes more bright than jewels; but they knew little of his native good sense, his strong self-respect and his broad sympathies, which would have saved him at any time from scorching his wings in any false glare, however flattering or seductive. He got out of society, as out of everything else, whatever he thought to be good, and the rest he let go to the ash-barrel. . . . A harder-working literary man I never knew; he was incessantly busy; a constant, careful, and wide reader; yet never missing a great meeting or a great address or a grand night at the theatre. From our little conclaves at No. 10 Park Place, where, I fear, we remorselessly slaughtered the hopes of many a bright spirit (chiefly female), he was seldom absent, and when he came he took his full share of the routine—unless Irving, Bryant, Lowell, Thackeray, or Longfellow sauntered in, and "that day we worked no more."—GODWIN, PARKE, 1893, *Address Before the Century Club, Dec. 17*.

In him, as Jacobi or Novalis said of Luther, body and soul were not divided. The whole man was made at one cast. The graces of his person corresponded to the graces of his mind; the beauty of his character found a fitting symbol in the beauty of his face, the expressive mouth, the eyes that grew less mournful as he found his proper place among the helpers of his kind. But if we could forget these things, we could not forget the tenderness with which he used to go away from us, or let us go from him: "Good-bye!" and then again, and with a lingering emphasis that made the word as kind as a caress, "Good-bye!" We seem to hear it now from far away.—CHADWICK, JOHN WHITE, 1893, *Recollections of George William Curtis, Harper's Magazine*, vol. 86, p. 476.

Adjoining is the old "wash-room," where some who have since become famous in literature or politics pounded the soiled linen in a hogshead with a heavy wooden pestle; and just without is the turf-carpeted yard where the dignified and handsome Hawthorne, the brilliant Charles A. Dana (who certainly was the most popular member of the community), and the genial Curtis were sometimes seen hanging the moist garments upon the lines, a truly edifying spectacle for gods and men. It was from Curtis's pockets that the clothes-pins sometimes dropped during the evening dances.—WOLFE, THEODORE F., 1895, *Literary Shrines*, p. 149.

He was not the greatest of those who, in this New World, have used the platform as a vantage-ground of leadership. He had not the organ-tones of Webster, nor the incisive style and matchless vocal skill of Phillips, nor the compass of Beecher; but in that fine harmony of theme, treatment, style, and personality which make the speech literature, he surpassed them all. Less effective for the moment than Phillips, his art has a finer fibre and a more enduring charm. When he spoke, it seemed as if one were present at the creation of a piece of literature. He saw his theme in such large relations, he touched it with a hand so true and so delicate, he phrased his thought with such lucid and winning refinement and skill, his bearing, enunciation, voice, and gesture were so harmonious, that what he said and his manner of saying it seemed all of a piece, and the product was a beautiful bit of art,—something incapable of entire preservation, and yet possessing the quality of the things that endure. The enchantments of speech were his beyond any man of his generation, and he gave them a grace of manner which deepened and expanded their charm.—MABIE, HAMILTON WRIGHT, 1896, *My Study Fire, Second Series*, p. 97.

The two years spent at Brook Farm formed an important episode in the life of George William Curtis. It is evident that he did not surrender himself to the associationist idea, even when he was a boarder at Brook Farm and a member of its school. He loved the men and women who were at the head of the community; he found the life attractive and genial, the atmosphere was conducive to his intellectual and spiritual development; but he did not surrender himself to the idea that the world can be reformed in that manner. In a degree he was a curious looker-on; and in a still larger way he was a sympathetic, but not convinced, friend and well-wisher. If not a member, he retained throughout life his interest in this experiment, and remembered with delight the years he spent there. He more than once spoke in enthusiastic terms of Brook Farm, and gave its theories and its practice a sympathetic interpretation. In one of his "Easy Chair" essays of 1869 he described the best side of its life.—COOKE, GEORGE WILLIS, 1898, ed., *Early Letters of George William Curtis to John S. Dwight*, p. 5.

George William Curtis has filled, as no other American man of letters of this generation, the ideal of clear intellect, pure taste, moral purpose, chivalry of feeling, and personal refinement and grace. The grace and culture he possessed were as natural as his courtesy and his faith in mankind. They were ingrained as part of his being, wrought into every strain and making the strands of his every-day life. From the moment of his entrance into public life as a speaker, now nearly fifty years ago, he entirely satisfied the higher conception of purity, dignity, and sweetness. He was a lecturer of beautiful presence and was superbly artificial, yet this artificiality was natural. His hair and beard were a beautiful silver-gray, his face was pale, his manner studied, his voice cultivated. It was as enjoyable to hear him as to listen to an opera, and was a lesson in grand manners and elocution. His voice, like his manners and appearance on the platform, was ideal—clear, bell-like, silvery. He could be heard in the largest of halls without apparently any special effort. It was a delight to listen; every syllable was distinct, yet there was no strain. The enunciation was perfect. The matter of his speeches was like the sound, perfect in sense, clear in meaning, as graceful as the speaking, and always carrying the sense of conviction to the hearers.—POND, JAMES BURTON, 1900, *Eccentricities of Genius*, p. 341.

EDITOR

They handle ["Easy Chair"] with admirable taste and breeding, topics of society, literature, and the every-day popular life, with an unfailing honor for elegance, good manners, and hearty sense. There is nowhere else in our journalism so much truth so amiably yet so clearly spoken, and one does not mind that these papers are a little mannered, they are essentially so well-mannered. It is that part of morality to be distinguished as civilization or civility in its wide significance which Mr. Curtis chiefly teaches from his Easy-Chair; and he does it with an art that never lapses or fatigues. There must be not only brains and heart in those little papers, but a constant charm of style which shall take the reader in spite of the narrowness of their limitations.—HOWELLS, WILLIAM DEAN, 1868, *George William Curtis, North American Review*, vol. 107, p. 108.

He won, and has kept the enthusiastic personal support and admiration of his audience, as no other editor has succeeded in doing, with the single exception of Horace Greeley. The relations between Mr. Curtis and his readers are, in fact, almost personal in their nature, and he has never seriously entertained proposals, however brilliant and tempting, that would interrupt those relations. Thus, although he could serve as a Regent of the University, and as non-resident Professor at Cornell University for four years, he declined, in 1869, upon the death of Mr. Henry J. Raymond, who had previously asked him to become assistant editor, an invitation to the chief editorship of the New York "Times."—CONANT, S. S., 1883, *George William Curtis, Century Magazine*, vol. 25, p. 581.

How many thousands gladly recall what a privilege and delight it has been for many years to have this commentator visit them every month, to tell them what to admire and what to impugn, and to inspire them as they sat in their own easy-chairs with kindlier feelings towards their fellows, to dissipate the blues of business or public affairs, and to send them to bed with buoyant hopes for the morrow! . . . You may say, perhaps, that any editor of a periodical can play this showman's part. Oh, yes; but not with the inexhaustible variety of matter, the inimitable grace of manner, of Curtis. His superiority was shown when, called away altogether, the whole literary world asked, "And who can take his place?" and the whole literary world answered, "No one." Well might that world feel kindly towards him, for in all those forty years he had made and left no rankling wound.—GODWIN, PARKE, 1893, *Address Before the Century Club*, Dec. 17.

He brought to the discussion of the public affairs of the hour a wealth of knowledge, historical, contemporary, practical, and a thoroughness of reflection, which are unusual even with writers of the most deliberate and elaborate kind. One has but to read his orations to find the evidence of these qualities, and of the skill with which he could marshal a long array of facts in support of a logical conclusion. In "Harper's Weekly" he gave us the fruit of these capacities, but rarely any sign of them in exercise. The simplest-minded reader could feel the force of his reasoning; only the more highly trained could understand from what deep and widely-fed sources that force was supplied.—CARY, EDWARD, 1894, *George William Curtis (American Men of Letters)*, p. 175.

From his Easy Chair in "Harper's Magazine," for thirty-five years, he preached social and political righteousness, with a genial grace, a sparkle of wit, and a wide-ranging culture, which raise many of these utterances almost to the level of permanent literature.—LAWTON, WILLIAM CRANSTON, 1902, *Introduction to the Study of American Literature*, p. 322.

HOWADJI PAPERS
1851-52

In the evening no visitors, and we sailed up the "palmy Nile," with the poetic Howadji, in the Ibis. A fascinating book. He has caught the true spirit of the East, and there is a golden glow on his pages, as if he dipped his pencil in the sun. — LONGFELLOW, HENRY WADSWORTH, 1851, *Journal*, March 30; *Life, ed., Longfellow, vol.* II, *p.* 192.

Mr. Curtis was twenty-seven when he published the "Nile Notes," and the book was doubtless the fruit of yet earlier years. It suggests this in style and manner; in its redundant hues and tones, in its wonderful use of words, which so often degenerates into play with words. It is prose measured so deliberately that you continually feel its pulsation, and often find it too much for the nerves of middle life. The prodigious excess of alliteration is perhaps not so much to blame, for that is the instinct of our tongue; still its absence is to be noted with relief in the author's very next book, "Howadji in Syria," where the whole atmosphere seems cooler and sharper. The feeling is much the same, but the soul of youth has wreaked itself upon the mystic grandeur and melancholy of Egypt, and has finally indulged that riot of expression which leaves a gifted man's thought clearer for a whole lifetime.—HOWELLS, WILLIAM DEAN, 1868, *George William Curtis, North American Review, vol.* 107, *p.* 105.

Curtis seems to me to have been, in an important sense, born an orator. Even the words of these first pages read as if they had been thought aloud, as if their cadence had been realized to the ear in the sound of his own rare voice. Often they come to the mind like the singing of the solitary and unconscious singer. His passionate and constant delight in music shaped his phrases and marshaled his sentences. There are plentiful instances of excess in this indulgence in the oriental books, before his taste had been trained and his judgment enlightened, but the excess is incidental—accidental even—and the sense remains to the reader of a pure, sincere and constant joy in the music of his own expression.—CARY, EDWARD, 1894, *George William Curtis (American Men of Letters), p.* 72.

Delicate humor, quaint fancy, and rare refinement breathe from every page. These rare qualities, mingled with his description and adventures, combine to make the "Howadji" volumes the most charming of their kind in our literature.—PATTEE, FRED LEWIS, 1896, *A History of American Literature, p.* 237.

POTIPHAR PAPERS
1853

They should never have been united under one name, for they do not form a whole. There is sometimes infirmity as well as sketchiness of handling in the same paper; though this does not make such bad effect as the fact that some of the people not only change their aspects but their characters in the different papers, while they keep their names. In one, Paul Potiphar is said to have a library of book-backs; in another we are asked to believe that he reads and enjoys Thackeray. Moreover, there is on the part of the author too much attitude, too much self-defence, too much consciousness; and a man who has very good eyes of his own will insist, at times, upon looking at New York society through Mr. Thackeray's spectacles, and talking of Major Dobbin, and Becky Sharpe, and the Pendennises. It is only the spectacles, however; neither the voice nor the manner is Thackeray's, while the feeling is quite different from his.—HOWELLS, WILLIAM DEAN, 1868, *George William Curtis, North American Review, vol.* 107, *p.* 109.

They had great vogue, and greatly helped the young magazine, while they brought to their writer much notoriety and some fame. As was natural they made "hard feelings" among those who were, or thought they were, satirized in these pages; but on the whole they were greatly enjoyed, and their healthy purpose was recognized. Taken up now after forty years, a reader must be well through middle age to recognize their substantial basis of fact, and, so far as they survive, it is as satire on the one hand and a picture of the author's mind on the other, rather than as a description of society. Yet a description of society they really were, with a sadly substantial basis of fact. Mr. Curtis's own letters and those of his contemporaries, and the recollections of men who moved in the same circles, are not lacking in evidence that the brush was not very heavily overloaded.—CARY, EDWARD, 1894, *George William Curtis (American Men of Letters), p.* 92.

PRUE AND I
1856

"Putnam's Monthly" was established in the same year, and Mr. Curtis was one of the original editors. For this magazine he wrote a number of sketches and essays, some of which were afterwards published with the title "Prue and I." In this work Mr. Curtis is seen at his best, in our judgment. A pretty rill of a story runs through it like a musical little brook through a romantic valley. The pervading sentiment is tender and pure. The lovely young matron, "Prue," is the sharer in the thoughts and the reminiscences of the story-teller, as well as in his affection and measureless content. The style is as unpretentious and as lovely as the story. If it were more musical its melody would glide into verse. The sketches are full of the best fruits of reading and travel, and preserve for us those picturesque associations of the old world for which we look in the note-books of tourists in vain.—UNDERWOOD, FRANCIS H., 1872, *A Hand-Book of English Literature, American Authors*, p. 505.

More truly of the Irving type, with a Brook Farm fervor added, was the distinguished editor, lecturer, and patriot, George William Curtis. That shining soul, "loyal to whatever is generous and humane, full of sweet hope, and faith, and devotion," is radiant still in the jewel lights of "Prue and I."—BATES, KATHERINE LEE, 1897, *American Literature*, p. 292.

"Prue and I" was a series of papers written, as Curtis's letters show, in odd moments and with great rapidity, to meet the exigencies of the magazine. But the papers survive as an example of the pure literary work of the author. The opulence and extravagance of the "Howadji" books disappear; but the rich imagination, and sportive fancy, the warm and life giving sentiment, the broad philosophy, are expressed in a style of singular beauty, flexibility, and strength.—CARY, EDWARD, 1897, *Library of the World's Best Literature*, ed. Warner, vol. VII, p. 4223.

GENERAL

It is no purpose of ours to fix Mr. Curtis's rank in our literature, and we do not mean to measure his powers or his performance in classing him with Irving and Longfellow in literary refinement of tone, and a predominant grace of execution. He is bound to both by many ties of mental sympathy; though not right New-Englander nor right New-Yorker, he has the spirit of either civilization in him, like his native city of Providence. He has for the Old World the New-World love of both Irving and Longfellow, but he enjoys it more critically than either, and will commonly be found making a lesson of it, one way or other. He has not Irving's archaic spirit; and his writings, though they have dealt so much with the today which has now become yesterday, have a greater affinity with Longfellow's. In most things, however, and in essentials, he is alone; and he has so characteristic a vein that it could hardly ever be taken for another's, or not known for his. In all his books he is utterly free from provincialism and vulgarity of thought or feeling: he has neither American nor European narrowness. He has none of the frenzied or bad intention which is so common in our present literary art, and which comes chiefly from ignorance of life and the world. The effects he seeks are to be achieved only through his reader's refinement or innate fineness.—HOWELLS, WILLIAM DEAN, 1868, *George William Curtis, North American Review*, vol. 107, p. 116.

I might call him the Bayard of our political struggles, the Sydney of our literature, so much has his most disinterested and gracious nature been employed in his public and literary work, so courageous his action, so stainless his record. Called from epicurean experience of a social favorite and of a literary gourmand, his daintiness has become delicacy, his sensuousness moral suavity. If, fresh from the enervating Orient, he wrote with the tepid lassitude of a fibreless and springless nature, and, so to speak, spilt his mind in memories of the exhausted East, at twenty-eight he wrote the "Potiphar Papers." His mind had regained its tone; fibre, purpose, and skill were in his work. At twenty-six a sensuous sentimentalist, at twenty-eight a social satirist, then a moralist. To-day a journalist, that is to say preacher, politician, and essayist, but in each character alike serene and thoughtful. At first he was superfine; superfine in his reading, superfine in his expression, superfine in his experience. But he seems to have been touched by the serious and penetrating genius of Thackeray. The phrase-maker formed under Emerson and English poetry disappeared; in place of that exquisite writer, a clear-eyed, delicate, and decided man looked and reflected upon the comedy of actual life, instead of brooding over nature and recalling the felicities of poets. His literary work in his new phase was admirably done; with good sense, with humour, with dramatic life. — BENSON, EUGENE, 1869, *New York Journalists, The Galaxy, vol.* 7, *p.* 328.

His tone is not only manly, but gentlemanly; his persuasiveness is an important element of his influence; and no reformer has equalled him in the art of insinuating sound principles into prejudiced intellects by putting them in the guise of pleasantries. He can on occasion send forth sentences of ringing invective; but in the Easy Chair he generally prefers the attitude of urbanity which the title of his department suggests. His style, in addition to its other merits, is rhythmical; so that his thoughts slide, as it were, into the reader's mind in a strain of music. Not the least remarkable of his characteristics is the undiminished vigor and elasticity of his intelligence, in spite of the incessant draughts he has for years been making upon it.—WHIPPLE, EDWIN PERCY, 1876–86, *American Literature and Other Papers, ed. Whittier, p.* 89.

Broader than Dr. Holland in his range, less devoted to the work of lay-preaching, and of higher literary ability than either Holland or Mitchell, is George William Curtis. In him, more than in any American writer of his time, is represented, *mutatis mutandis*, the temper of Addison and Irving as well as some of their methods. Addison has not been repeated, nor have his times; but if Addison had been a modern American, perhaps he might, like Curtis, have written for many a year graceful and finished little essays for the closing pages of successive numbers of *Harper's Magazine*, or more frequent editorials for a weekly newspaper. . . . But for Curtis the essayist one may make high claims, with confidence. If, as I have intimated, he is not, more than any living writer, the successor or representative of the spirit of Addison, Lamb, Irving, I know not whose name could more fitly be mentioned. He resembles Addison rather than Lamb or Irving. If his humor, wisdom, broad culture, catholic temper, and attractive style are not well known to future readers, it will be due to the changed place of the periodical press in the last part of the nineteenth century, as compared with its place seventy-five or a hundred and seventy-five years ago. — RICHARDSON, CHARLES F., 1887, *American Literature,* 1607–1885, *vol.* I, *pp.* 381, 383.

When we review such a career as that which in all that was earthly has just closed, the considerate ask: "What has he left?" It is a question not difficult to answer; the readiest reply is that he has made the world better for having been a part of its experience; he put more into the common stock of our truest wealth than he took out of it; he made that rarest of all gifts to his time, the gift of a noble nature nobly dedicated to the highest tasks. When there shall be gathered into more accessible form the political wisdom which he had for forty years contributed to a better knowledge of the people, and that store of gentle satire and sweet persuasion, which he spoke as he sat in the Easy Chair, shall have become a part of our literature, then we will find ourselves wondering at the fertility of resource, the lightness of a strong touch, the varied culture which our friend possessed.—SLICER, THOMAS R., 1892, *George William Curtis, an Address Delivered Sept.* 11.

He is the direct descendant of Addison, whose style is overrated, of Steele, whose morality is humorous, of Goldsmith, whose writing was angelic, and of Irving, whose taste was pretty. Mr. Curtis recalls all of these, yet he is like none of them. Humorous as they are and charming, he is somewhat sturdier, of a more robust fibre, with a stronger respect for plain living and high thinking, with a firmer grasp on the duties of life.—MATTHEWS, BRANDER, 1892, *Concerning Certain American Essayists, The Cosmopolitan, vol.* 13, *p.* 86.

It is no disparagement of his contemporaries to say that, of living American men of letters, Mr. George William Curtis stands easily at the head. There are few, if any, English writers on either side of the Atlantic who, in the regions of pure literature, are entitled to rank with him. . . . A man of letters, the master of a style second only to Hawthorne, a scholar and thinker. He has been before the public as a writer of books for more than forty years; and, although we suppose he is not without honour now among his countrymen, yet Mr. Charles F. Richardson, who undertook to produce a history of American literature up to date, hardly names him, while in an American

"Synopsis," where the merit of authors is distinguished by style of type, Mr. Curtis ranks in the same class as Mr. Henry James and Mr. Whipple.—LEWIN, WALTER, 1892, *From the Easy Chair, The Academy*, vol. 41, p. 441.

When his prototype, Sir Philip Sidney, on that fatal September morning, three hundred and seven years ago, set forth for the field of battle at Zutphen, he met a fellow-soldier riding in light armor, and thereupon he cast away a portion of his own mail—and in so doing, as the event proved, he cast away his life—in order that he might be no better protected than his friend. In like manner Curtis would have no advantage for himself, nor even the semblance of advantage, that was not shared by others. He could not—with his superlative moral fervor—dedicate himself exclusively to letters, while there was so much wrong in the world that clamored for him to do his part in setting it right. He believed that his direct, practical labor was essential and would avail, and he was eager to bestow it. Men of strong imagination begin life with illimitable ideals, with vast illusions, with ardent and generous faith. They are invariably disappointed, and they are usually embittered. Curtis was controlled less by his imagination than by his moral sense. He had ideals, but they were based on reason. However much he may have loved to muse and dream, he saw the world as a fact and not as a fancy. He was often saddened by the spectacle of human littleness, but, broadly and generally, he was not disappointed in mankind, and he never became embittered.—WINTER, WILLIAM, 1893, *George William Curtis, a Eulogy*.

It is a charming book ["Lotus Eating"]; so charming that to stay at home and read it would perhaps give more pleasure than those famous places now afford. Doctor Channing thought it not presumptuous to hope that something corresponding to our earthly joys of air and light would be permitted us in another life and in this particular Curtis must have sympathized with him. He had the art of husbanding these joys and of so making his words express them that those days of long ago still shed their beauty on our hearts. In these studies there was a good deal of comparative scenery; the writer was so drenched in mists of Alpine heights and falling water, and in the associations of an older civilization. The "emotion recollected in tranquility" was often keener than any which the immediate object could excite. But more important than the description of each lovely scene was the eye for social manners and the stroke that gave their hollowness and insincerity, their meanness and vulgarity, a shameful perpetuity upon the vivid page. . . . The scholar, the writer, the humorist, the orator, the patriot, the reformer, the man, "whose every word and thought was a good deed."—CHADWICK, JOHN WHITE, 1893, *George William Curtis*, pp. 21, 76.

Curtis represents, no doubt, what may prove to be a transitory phase of American literature. Even now, in the latest as well as in the earliest essays in this delightful volume, there is a flavour as of something that is passing away. The leisureliness, the dignity, the marked and sometimes almost elaborate courtesy of manner, the style in which the absence of all impatience is only one mark of its invariable distinction—are those of to-day? The style flows on with the smoothness of the Concord River itself, but without its shallows or sluggishness. There are flowers upon its surface, and it mirrors the heavens above. —SMALLEY, GEORGE W., 1895, *Studies of Men*, p. 391.

The kind of training which Curtis secured at Brook Farm and Concord better fitted him for such a career as his than he could have obtained at any college of his day. It brought him into actual contact with life, made him self-reliant, and increased his knowledge of men and the world. It brought him into sympathy with some of the ablest men of our century, so that he learned of them what no book could give. He received from them the enthusiasms which youth needs, and which are the manure of all its after-crop of ideas and achievements. He fertilized his mind at the very sources of culture; and the whole of his mind, instead of some part of it, was affected by the process of enrichment. He became strong in body, mind, conscience, imagination, by his first-hand study of life and men, by his open-air sympathy with nature, and by his daily intercourse with men of toil and of affairs. His whole after-career found its incentive and its meaning in these years of unique preparation.— COOKE, GEORGE WILLIS, 1898, *George William Curtis at Concord, Harper's Magazine*, vol. 96, p. 149.

Thomas William Parsons
1819-1892

A poet of Boston who for some years practiced his profession of dentistry there. The quality of his writing is uneven, but in such poems as the "Lines on the Bust of Dante," and "When Francesca Sings," he is at his best. His work includes a much-admired though incomplete translation in English verse of "Dante's Divina Commedia," of which an edition was issued in 1893, with introduction by C. E. Norton, and memorial sketch by Miss Guiney; "Ghetto di Roma;" "The Magnolia;" "The Old Home at Sudbury;" "The Shadow of the Obelisk, and other Poems" (1893).—ADAMS, OSCAR FAY, 1897, *A Dictionary of American Authors*, p. 286.

PERSONAL

Friend who hast gone, and dost enrich to-day
New England brightly building far away,
And crown her liberal walk
With company more choice, and sweeter talk,
Look not on Fame, but Peace; and in a bower
Receive at last her fulness and her power:
Nor wholly, pure of heart!
Forget thy few, who would be where thou art.
—GUINEY, LOUISE IMOGEN, 1893, *T. W. P., 1819-1892, A Roadside Harp.*

During the last twenty-five or thirty years a tall, slight figure, somewhat bent of late, with Dantean eyebrows overhanging eyes of a singularly penetrative sweetness when they looked at you, was a frequent figure on the streets of Boston. Here and there it encountered a friendly glance of recognition, but to the hurrying throng in the city of his birth Thomas William Parsons was virtually a stranger. The passers-by, brushing against him, were unconscious that that shy man with the inward-looking eyes was a poet of rare gifts, who, however lacking in variousness, occasionally managed in his own direct artesian way to pierce as deep as any of his great contemporaries, excepting, possibly, Emerson. . . . He was a man of great simplicity and alert sympathies; a charming companion, when he was out of his cloud, and even when in his cloud, a most courteous dreamer. That he sometimes dropped his reserve with me, in his enthusiasm over some question of literature or art, is now among my cherished memories. — ALDRICH, THOMAS BAILEY, 1894, *A Portrait of Thomas William Parsons, Century Magazine*, vol. 26, pp. 323, 324.

Dr. Parsons was emphatically a man of moods. He could be merry with the meriest and jolly with the jolliest, changing suddenly
From grave to gay, from lively to severe.
He had the keenest sense of the ludicrous; nothing escaped his observing eyes or his subtle irony. . . . What delightful recollections come to me of hours spent in the charming home in Scituate where was dispensed a genuine hospitality! The latch-string was always out for friends. One often met there uniquely interesting guests, and days passed in such delightsome company were red-letter days indeed. In the unconventional atmosphere of that home, so invigorating to breathe, reigned wit and jollity. These golden days were enlivened by sparkling repartee, the impromptu rhyme, merry games, songs written by Dr. Parsons, delightfully sung by his niece Francesca. In that never-to-be-forgotten home "plain living and high thinking" were exemplified.—PORTER, MARIA S., 1901, *Thomas William Parsons, Century Magazine*, vol. 40, p. 937.

GENERAL

His poems stand out in relief from the mass of American versification, by the ripe accomplishments of mind they show, by the artistic atmosphere they breathe, and by the rare combination in them of fulness of matter with finish of form. The strength of his thought, the genuineness of his humor, the delicate sureness of his touch, the profound tenderness of his feeling, the completeness of his artistic skill, the perfect vitality of his work, now appreciated by one and another, soon by more and more, will finally enroll him among the select classics of his land; destined to be honored ages after the mediocrities who at first surpassed them in fame have been forgotten. . . . He is never flat, never stilted, never verbose, never bombastic, never affected. He is one of the truest of the humorists who have set pen to paper in this country. Nothing ridiculous escapes his keen and competent eye; and he portrays it with a smiling ease, a sound judgment, and a polished brevity, comparable with those of the best workmen in this department. Those who would rather laugh in their minds than by explosions of the organs of cachinnation, will search far

before they can find a more delightfully enjoyable satire than the "Saratoga Eclogue."
—ALGER, WILLIAM ROUNSEVILLE, 1869, *American Poets: T. W. Parsons, Christian Examiner, vol.* 86, *pp.* 76, 83.

Parsons' briefer poems often are models, but occasionally show a trace of that stiffness which too little employment gives even the hand of daintier sense. "Lines on a Bust of Dante," in structure, diction, loftiness of thought, is the peer of any modern lyric in our tongue. Inversion, the vice of stilted poets, becomes with him an excellence, and old forms and accents are rehandled and charged with life anew. It is to be regretted that Dr. Parsons has not used his gift more freely. He has been a poet for poets, rather than for the people; but many types are required to fill out the hemicycle of a nation's literature.—STEDMAN, EDMUND CLARENCE, 1885, *Poets of America, p.* 54.

"O Time! whose verdicts mock our own,
  The only righteous judge art thou."

This judge, in a generation, has not established Dr. Parsons' reputation on any other basis than that on which may stand a minor poet of thought and grace; nor will Parsons sing for a larger future. To-day his books hold forth some few finely-wrought verses, enriched by culture, adorned by the touch of beauty, and occasionally illumined by the light of the land of Dante's vision, described by Dr. Parsons in his "Paradisi Gloria:"

"There is a city builded by no hand,
  And unapproachable by sea or shore,
  And unassailable by any band
Of storming soldiery forever more."

—RICHARDSON, CHARLES F., 1888, *American Literature*, 1607–1885, *vol.* II, *p.* 242.

His characteristic at his best is great sensibility of impression, great control and discipline of expression. He is one of those who speak from the stress of emotion—as few men do, as few women can—without any explosion of sensation. However you feel his genius, you must feel first its highbred, forerunning condition of art. He is not reticent, but his saving accent makes you think him so. His themes are often such as would seem to evade and decline adequate language, and he can always present them with masterful delicacy and terseness. Upon him, who is akin to no one else,

"The marks have sunk of Dante's mind."

It is not in vain that for nearly fifty years he has had great companionship, paying for it his magnificent coin of interpretation to the English world. What he has won thereby is not an actual gain, but the precious vivifying and clarifying of his poetic gift. In his thrusting, lance-like humor, his high-handed individuality, his genuine pathos, his secure scholarship, his literary equipment, his scorn of pomp and artifice, his large, patient note of patriotism and brotherliness, his irresistible reverence of what is reverend, and antagonism of the world's paltry aims; above all, in his conception and treatment of religion and of love, Dr. Parsons is markedly Dante's man. . . . Artistic governance is the sign-manual of Dr. Parsons' rapt verse, which, never tame nor timid, has a restrained and tempered glow of Phaethon holding his horses in. His "Paradisi Gloria" has caught all the beams of the Christian heaven, and prisons them as in an opal.— GUINEY, LOUISE IMOGEN, 1889, *"The Poet" of the Wayside Inn, Catholic World, vol.* 49, *pp.* 12, 13.

Parsons was probably Gray's inferior in point of taste, for otherwise we can hardly understand how he could put forth in the same volume, and sometimes in the same poem, such inequalities as he permitted himself. Yet it must be said, as an offset to this, that he seldom made himself responsible for a poem by publishing it. He occasionally had verses in the magazines, and even, if the whim took him, in the newspapers; but only twice in his life did he bring the question of his critical judgment fairly within the scope of comment by issuing a volume to the public. The first of these volumes, which contains the famous "Lines on a Bust of Dante," may perhaps rely upon the youth of its author as an explanation of its unevenness. The other, "Circum Præcordia," published in the year of his death, and consisting of a versification of the collects of the Church together with a few original poems of a religious character, is of even and sustained excellence, though rising to the level of his best work only in the concluding poem, "Paradisi Gloria." Mrs. Parsons had several other volumes printed for private circulation only, but of these the author frequently knew nothing until the bound copies were placed in his hands. What he would himself now select to give to the world no one can tell; possibly as carefully edited a volume as even that of Gray. Such a volume would, I believe, be one of the treasures of American verse,—a book that lovers of poetry would carry with them as they would similar thin volumes of Herrick, Marvell, Collins, or Landor. The lyrics addressed to Francesca are true Herrick for grace and daintiness, and there is nothing in Landor finer than such passages. — HOVEY, RICHARD, 1893, *Thomas William Parsons, Atlantic Monthly, vol. 71, p. 265.*

Dr. Parsons had much in common with Landor, outside of the Englishman's fine moroseness. Each possessed that delicate precision of touch which, to the observing, betrays the steel gauntlet under the velvet glove. Both were scholars, both loved Italy, and both wrote marvelously finished verse, which poets praised, and the public neglected to read. Dr. Parsons's lighter lyrics have a grace and distinction which make it difficult to explain why they failed to win wide liking. That his more serious work failed to do so is explicable. Such austere poetry as the stanzas "On a Bust of Dante," for instance, is not to the taste of the mass of readers: but such poetry, once created, becomes a part of the material world; it instantly takes to itself the permanency of mountains, prairies, and rivers; it seems always to have existed. . . . The study of the great Florentine and his period was a life-long pursuit of Dr. Parsons. His translation of "The Divine Comedy," so far as he carried it, for it was left like "the unfinished window in Aladdin's tower," places him in the first rank of Dante's disciples. He brought to this labor of love something of his master's own passion. Whether or not the translation is literal in detail, Dr. Parsons's fragmentary versions have a spell beyond that of all other metrical versions, in being poems in themselves. —ALDRICH, THOMAS BAILEY, 1894, *A Portrait of Thomas William Parsons, Century Magazine, vol. 26, pp. 323, 324.*

He occupies in American literature a place somewhat analogous to that held in English literature by Gray and Collins, having written only a few poems, but those of surpassing excellence.—PATTEE, FRED LEWIS, 1896, *A History of American Literature, p. 301.*

He did not write much, but nearly all is precious for its justness of thought and feeling, its classic finish, artistic restraint, and terse strength, without frigidity, and its occasional quiet pleasantry and Attic wit.— BRONSON, WALTER C., 1899, *A Short History of American Literature, p. 176.*

The charm of his writings is in their chaste and earnest diction, in the highest form of art. He was never a poet of the people, though no collection of American poetry seems complete without his "Lines on a Bust of Dante." His verse is strong and clear, and in its sincere, devout spirit seems like an earnest protest against many of the tendencies in modern life and thought. An elaborate edition of his translation of the "Inferno" was published in 1867. It naturally challenged comparison with that of Longfellow, appearing in the same year. While not so faithful as that of the elder poet, its very freedom enables the translator the better to preserve the spirit of the original. For the general reader rather than the student it must be admitted to be the more readable of the two. —ONDERDONK, JAMES L., 1899–1901, *History of American Verse, p. 232.*

After all, the touch of genius to be found in Dr. Parsons is probably not shown concretely by his translation or by his own poems, but rather by his capacity to give himself up so completely and so beautifully to his pursuit of a noble ideal. For it is surely a noble ideal to steep one's self in a poem and a poet so noble as the "Divine Comedy" and Dante, not merely for self-gratification and elevation, but in order that one's fellow-countrymen may be allowed to share in one's joy and profit.— TRENT, WILLIAM P., 1903, *A History of American Literature p. 460.*

John Tyndall
1820–1893

Born, at Leiglinbridge, near Carlow, Ireland, 21 Aug. 1820. Early education at village school. On Irish Ordnance Survey, 1839–44. Held post as engineer, 1844–47. Assistant Master at Queenwood Coll., Hamps., 1847. Studied in Germany, 1848–51. F. R. S., 1853. Prof. of Nat. Philos., Royal Institution, 1853; Resident Director, 1867–87.

Examiner to Council of Military Education, 1855. First visit to Switzerland, with Prof. Huxley, to study glaciers, 1856. Rumford Medal, Royal Society, 1864. Hon. LL. D., Camb., 1865. Hon LL. D., Edinburgh, 1866. Lectured in U. S. A., 1872. Hon. D. C. L., Oxford, 18 June 1873. Pres. British Association, 1874. Married Hon. Louisa Hamilton, 29 Feb. 1876. Pres. of Birmingham and Midland Institute, 1877. For some years Scientific Adviser to Board of Trade; resigned, 1883. F. G. S. Died, at Haslemere, 4 Dec. 1893. *Works:* "The Glaciers of the Alps," 1860; "Mountaineering in 1861," 1862; "Heat considered as a Mode of Motion," 1863; "On Radiation," 1865; "Sound," 1867; "Faraday as a Discoverer," 1868; "Natural Philosophy in Easy Lessons" [1869]; "Notes of a Course of Nine Lectures on Light," 1869; "Researches on Diamagnetism," 1870; "Notes of a Course of Seven Lectures on Electrical Phenomena," 1870; "On the Scientific use of the Imagination," 1870; "Hours of Exercise in the Alps," 1871; "Fragments of Science for Unscientific People" (2 vols.), 1871; "Contributions to Molecular Physics," 1872; "The Forms of Water," 1873; "Principal Forbes and his Biographers," 1873; "Six Lectures on Light," 1873; "Address delivered before the British Association," 1874; "On the Transmission of Sound by the Atmosphere," 1874; "Lessons in Electricity," 1876; "Fermentation," 1877; "The Sabbath," 1880; "Essays on the Floating Matter of the Air," 1881; "Free Molecules and Radiant Heat," 1882; "Perverted Politics" (from "St. James's Gaz."), 1887; "Mr. Gladstone and Home Rule," 1887; "New Fragments," 1892 [1891].—SHARP, R. FARQUHARSON, 1897, *A Dictionary of English Authors, p. 287.*

PERSONAL

I should have liked to have seen your handwriting this morning, though none the less obliged to Mr. Tyndall, who makes the best of your having had a bad night. What a dear, warm-hearted darling he is! I should like to kiss him!—CARLYLE, JANE WELSH, 1866, *To Thomas Carlyle, March 30; Letters and Memorials, ed. Froude, vol.* II, *p.* 372.

The other thing was a lecture of Tyndall's at the Royal Institution. It was said not to be one of his best; but his experiments were curious, and neat, and uniformly successful. But all the time I could not help a kind of sense of the insolence of the man, such as he appeared to be, claiming to bring all truth within what he called science. There was hardheadedness, originality, and sometimes a touch of imagination. But there seemed to be also a hard and hopeless onesidedness, as if nothing in the world would open his eyes to the whole domain of soul and spirit close about him, and without which he would not be talking or devising wonderful experiments.—CHURCH, RICHARD WILLIAM, 1868, *To Rev. J. B. Mozley, Feb.* 11; *Life and Letters of Dean Church, ed. his Daughter, p.* 215.

From climbing we drifted off to books and literature, especially in America. I found my companion singularly well informed in our literature, and especially enthusiastic about Ralph Waldo Emerson, whom he pronounced with some energy by far the greatest mind in our literary annals. Such an admiration, coming from a professor of physical science, sounded a little surprising. It has been amply explained, however, by later utterances of Tyndall, which have made plain to us that along with his study of material forces, he has always maintained a lively and sympathetic interest in the subtler refinements of imaginative or metaphysical thought, and that side by side with his scientific formulæ has always lain, half hidden, a spring of fresh poetic feeling and appreciation which has, in an unevident way, permeated and adorned all his severer labors.—CARROLL, CHARLES, 1873, *A Tramp with Tyndall, Scribner's Monthly, vol.* 5, *p.* 187.

Tyndall is here: last night he sat out with a lot of us, as we took our post-prandial coffee and what not. He talked well, and seemed to enjoy it. I like what I have seen of him. He is quite unaffected, so much so as not to mind flinging out, every now and then, dashes of real Hibernian rhetoric.—BROWN, THOMAS EDWARD, 1881, *To G. H. Wollaston, July* 5; *Letters, ed. Irwin, vol.* I, *p.* 95.

Tyndall had a harsh voice, but he made it do its work. He spoke clearly. His sentences had a beginning, a middle, and an end. He was a born rhetorician and— what is perhaps more—a trained rhetorician. Of course he was not English; he was

Irish, or at most Anglo-Irish; his ancestors having migrated two centuries ago from Gloucestershire to Ireland. But he and his forbears had during these two hundred years breathed the air of Ireland, and had become in many respects altogether Irish. You would never be in doubt when you heard Tyndall speak among what people his youth had been spent and his accent acquired.—SMALLEY, GEORGE W., 1893, *Studies of Men, p.* 169.

Professor Tyndall was one of the earliest, if not the earliest, of the great Alpine climbers. What will the Aletsch glacier hereafter be to those of us who have enjoyed the homely hospitality of Alp Lusgen—what will it be without Professor Tyndall? He was the most conspicuous man of science of his time; but it is as a mountaineer that he will be most widely and affectionately remembered. A week on the Bel Alp, with Tyndall as guide, philosopher, and friend, was an era in a life. He was familiar with all the secrets of the wonder-world that lies above the snow-line, and he had a rare power, which he freely and graciously exercised, of imparting them to others. Those summer nights, when, from the terrace in front of his chalet, we heard the thundercloud break over Italy, and saw the lightning play round Monte Rosa, are not to be forgotten. It pleases me to think that he was able the autumn of his death to revisit altitudes which he loved so well,—to pass, indeed, almost without a pause, from the august company of the "silent summits" to "the infinite azure" beyond.—SKELTON, JOHN, 1893-95, *Mainly about Tyndall, The Table Talk of Shirley, p.* 100.

Though it is scarcely needful to say anything about his sincerity, yet it cannot properly be passed over, since it was a leading trait in his nature. It has been conspicuous to all, alike in his acts and in his words. . . . In him there was no spirit of compromise. It never occurred to him to ask what it was politic to say, but simply to ask what was true. The like has of late years been shown in his utterances concerning political matters—shown, it may be, with too great an outspokenness. This outspokenness was displayed, also, in private, and sometimes perhaps too much displayed, but everyone must have the defects of his qualities, and where absolute sincerity exists, it is certain now and then to cause an expression of a feeling or opinion not adequately restrained. But the contrast in genuineness between him and the average citizen was very conspicuous. . . . In addition to generosity under its ordinary form, which Professor Tyndall displayed in unusual degree, he displayed it under a less common form. He was ready to take much trouble to help friends. I have had personal experience of this. Though he had always in hand some investigation of great interest to him, and though, as I have heard him say, when he had bent his mind to a subject he could not with any facility break off and resume it again, yet, when I have sought his scientific aid—information or critical opinion—I never found the slightest reluctance to give me his undivided attention. Much more markedly, however, was this kind of generosity shown in another direction. Many men, while they are eager for appreciation, manifest little or no appreciation of others, and still less go out of their way to express it. With Tyndall it was not thus: he was eager to recognise achievement.—SPENCER, HERBERT, 1894, *The Late Professor Tyndall, Fortnightly Review, vol.* 61, *pp.* 146, 147.

Before one knew him well, it seemed possible to give an exhaustive definition of him in a string of epigrammatic antitheses, such as those in which the older historians delight to sum up the character of a king or leading statesman. Impulsive vehemence was associated with a singular power of self-control and a deep-seated reserve, not easily penetrated. Free-handed generosity lay side by side with much tenacity of insistence on any right, small or great; intense self-respect and a somewhat stern independence, with a sympathetic geniality of manner, especially towards children, with whom Tyndall was always a great favorite. Flights of imaginative rhetoric which amused (and sometimes amazed) more phlegmatic people, proceeded from a singularly clear and hard-headed reasoner over-scrupulous, if that may be, about keeping within the strictest limits of logical demonstration; and sincere to the core. A bright and even playful companion, Tyndall had little of that quick appreciation of the humorous side of things in general, and of one's self in particular, which is as oil to the waves of life, and is a chief component of the worthier kind of tact; indeed, the best reward of the utterer of a small witticism, or play upon words, in his presence, was the blank, if benevolent, perplexity with which he received it.—HUXLEY, THOMAS HENRY, 1894, *Professsor Tyndall, Nineteenth Century, vol.* 35, *p.* 2.

As a matter of fact John Tyndall himself was a thorough-going Celt in physique and in temperament. He had the iron constitution, the wiry strength, and the reckless love of danger and adventure, the fervid imagination, the fiery zeal, the abundant eloquence, the somewhat flowery rhetoric, the tenderness of heart, the munificent generosity, which distinguish the character of his Celtic countrymen. Even the obstinate determination with which in later life he opposed, tooth and nail, the claim of his nation to national self-government was itself thoroughly Irish. — ALLEN, GRANT, 1894, *Professor John Tyndall ; a Character Sketch, Review of Reviews, vol.* 9, *p.* 174.

Tyndall was a personality of exceeding interest. He exercised an often magical charm upon those with whom he was closely associated, but when his opposition was aroused he showed himself a keen controversalist.—RAYLEIGH, LORD, 1895, *The Scientific Work of Tyndall, Popular Science Monthly, vol.* 46, *p.* 658.

GENERAL

Tyndall is a man of great ability and earnestness. He has done, perhaps, more practical work in science than Huxley has; he has written more; he sometimes writes more eloquently. But he wants, to my thinking, that pure and colorless impartiality of inquiry and judgment which is Huxley's distinguishing characteristic. There is a certain coarseness of materialism about Tyndall; there is a vehement and almost an arrogant aggressiveness in him which must interfere with the clearness of his views. He assails the orthodox with the temper of a Hot Gospeller. Perhaps his Irish nature is partly accountable for this warm and eager combativeness: perhaps his having sat so devotedly at the feet of his friend, the great apostle of force, Thomas Carlyle, may help to explain the unsparing vigor of his controversial style. However that may be, Tyndall is assuredly one of the most impatient of sages, one of the most intolerant of philosophers.—MCCARTHY, JUSTIN, 1872, *Science and Orthodoxy in England, Modern Leaders, p.* 239.

Because Tyndall is great in experimental science, many are apt to accept his cosmological conclusions. Because he is a great observer in natural history, his metaphysical theories are supposed to be supported by observation, and to rest on experience. Professor Tyndall's own address terminates, not in science, but nescience. It treats of a realm of atoms and molecules whose existence science has never demonstrated, and attributes to them potencies which science has never verified. It is a system, not made necessary by the stringent constraint of facts, but avowedly constructed in order to avoid the belief in an intelligent Creator, and a universe marked by the presence of design. His theory, he admits, no less than that of Darwin, was not constructed in the pure interests of truth for its own sake. There was another purpose in both—to get rid of a theology of final causes, of a theology which conceives of God as a human artificer. He wished to exclude religion from the field of cosmogony, and forbid it to intrude on the region of knowledge. . . . Professor Tyndall accepts religious faith as an important element of human nature, but considers it as confined to the sentiments, and as not based in knowledge.—CLARKE, JAMES FREEMAN, 1874, *A propos of Tyndall, The Galaxy, vol.* 18, *p.* 836.

As a metaphysician he is a fatalistic evolutionist with a dash of imaginative optimism. As a theologian he is a sentimental atheist or an imaginative agnostic. In each of these several capacities he dexterously shifts from one phase to the other of his sensitive many-sidedness of opinion and phraseology, according to the varying needs and aspects of his argument and his audience. . . . As we have read the occasional addresses of Professor Tyndall with unabated interest, and noticed that they have usually represented the results of the meditations of his summer holidays, we have learned to conceive of them as the romantic essays of an imagination surcharged with the ferment of philosophical speculations, and kindled to a midsummer excitement by the glow of his inward fervor.—PORTER, NOAH, 1878–82, *Professor Tyndall's Last Deliverance, Science and Sentiment, p.* 220.

What we and the public have to do with are not Dr. Tyndall's moods of mind, nor his personal creed, but his treatment of grave questions in the name of science. This treatment has appeared, in our judgment, open to grave comment. It has meddled with much that lay outside his province, and upon which science, following its only true methods, can never be able to pronounce,—suggesting what it has not proved, and leading, without excuse, the thoughts of his hearers toward absurd negations or equally absurd imaginations, —hanging out, in short, old rags of Democritism as if they were new flags of scientific triumph. — TULLOCH, JOHN, 1884, *Modern Scientific Materialism, Modern Theories in Philosophy and Religion*, p. 166.

The position of Professor Tyndall in the world of science is somewhat unique. He is one of our most popular teachers of physical science; he is one of our most successful experimentalists; and he is one of our most attractive writers. By his discoveries he has largely extended our knowledge of the laws of Nature; by his teachings and writings he has probably done more than any other man in England to kindle a love of science among the masses; and by his life he has set an example to students of science which cannot be too widely known or appreciated. There are men who have made greater and more useful discoveries in science, but few have made more interesting discoveries. There are men whose achievements have been more highly esteemed by the devotees of pure science, but rarely has a scientific man been more popular outside the scientific world. There are men whose culture has been broader and deeper, but who have nevertheless lacked his facility of exposition and gracefulness of diction. The goddess of Science, which ofttimes was presented to the public with the repulsive severity of a skeleton, he has clothed with flesh and blood, making her countenance appear radiant with the glow of poesy, and susceptible even to a touch of human sympathy.—JEANS, WILLIAM T., 1887, *Lives of the Electricians*, p. 1.

He was a first-rate man of science. He stood next after Huxley, who stood next after Darwin, in the Darwinian trilogy.— SMALLEY, GEORGE W., 1893, *Studies of Men*, p. 167.

Among those of Tyndall's books which have a place in literature as well as in science, "Heat considered as a Mode of Motion" is doubtless the most eminent. At the time when it was published, in 1863, the doctrines of the correlation of forces and the conservation of energy were still among the novelties, and the researches of Joule, Helmholtz, and Mayer, which had done so much to establish them, were not generally understood. Tyndall's book came in the nick of time; it was a masterpiece of scientific exposition such as had not been seen for many a day; and it did more than any other book to make men familiar with those all-pervading physical truths that lie at the bottom of evolution. This book, moreover, showed Tyndall not only as a master in physical investigation, but as an eminent literary artist and one of the best writers of English prose that our age has seen.— FISKE, JOHN, 1893–1902, *John Tyndall, Essays, Historical and Literary*, vol. II, p. 245.

As a writer he had a singularly charming style; and it is not unlikely that his gift of grace and clearness has really been an injury to his scientific reputation. In this and other respects his fortune has not been unlike that of his friend Prof. Huxley. Their talent for happy exposition has caused them to be looked upon by many rather as great expounders than as great investigators and discoverers in science. But those who are familiar with their writings are aware that this view is a mistaken one, and that while none of their contemporaries have surpassed them in industrious experiment and research, few have equalled them in the value of their contributions to scientific progress. To attempt even to enumerate the most striking results of Tyndall's studies relating to magnetism and electricity, to radiant heat, to light and sound, to the properties of water and air, to glacial formations, and indeed to almost every branch of physics, would extend this sketch beyond its reasonable limits. . . . As a controversialist, his powers of argument, his learning and his courtesy to opponents were well displayed in the long discussion evoked by his noted Belfast address. An often-quoted expression in his address brought against him the imputation of materialism—an imputation which, in the sense implied by his assailants, was undeserved.—HALE, HORATIO, 1893, *John Tyndall, The Critic*, vol. 23, p. 389.

With the death of Professor Tyndall has passed away the second of the men whose names are associated as the three English men of science of the Victorian era. His claim to be included in this trio does not rest on his being the deepest thinker, the most accurate and ingenious experimentalist, or the most original investigator in the branch of science upon which he was engaged. If it did so, he might have to yield his place to another, for Lord Kelvin is probably as much his superior as a physicist, as Browning is thought by many to have surpassed Tennyson as a poet. Nevertheless, in both cases, the lesser man may be the more typical of and more influential on the age in which he lived. Though Tyndall's work must be ranked far below that of Darwin, he was far more the representative man of the two, owing to his brilliant versatility, restless energy, his combination of the culture of the literary student with the insight of the scientist and the power of the man of action, his breadth of sympathy and the apostolic zeal with which he fought for a sounder and more scientific system of education.—GREGORY, JOHN WALTER, 1894, *Tyndall, Natural Science, vol. 4, p. 10.*

I need not dwell on the more conspicuous of Professor Tyndall's intellectual traits, for these are familiar to multitudes of readers. His copiousness of illustration, his closeness of reasoning, and his lucidity of statement, have been sufficiently emphasised by others. Here I will remark only on certain powers of thought, not quite so obvious, which have much to do with his successes. Of these the chief is "the scientific use of the imagination." He has himself insisted upon the need for this, and his own career exemplifies it. . . . Professor Tyndall's thoughts were not limited to physics and allied sciences, but passed into psychology; and though this was not one of his topics, it was a subject of interest to him. Led as he was to make excursions into the science of mind, he was led also into that indeterminate region through which this science passes into the science of being; if we can call that a science of which the issue is nescience. He was much more conscious than physicists usually are, that every physical inquiry, pursued to the end, brings us down to metaphysics, and leaves us face to face with an insoluble problem.— SPENCER, HERBERT, 1894, *The Late Professor Tyndall, Fortnightly Review, vol. 61, pp. 141, 143.*

He has written in a style informed with much literary grace, on heat, sound, and kindred subjects, and has done more, perhaps, than any other writer to popularize science throughout the English-speaking world.—ROBERTSON, J. LOGIE, 1894, *A History of English Literature, p. 380.*

It was at the Royal Institution that Tyndall became really a power in the land. Endowed with a marvelous gift of clear presentation, and with a rare faculty for holding the interest of an audience, he was soon recognised above all things as the popular exponent of physical science. When one comes to ask, "What one great work did Tyndall perform in life?" it would be difficult for any man to give a definite answer. He advanced many branches of science in certain directions; but, for the most part, those directions had been amply indicated beforehand by others. His observations on glaciers took up the varied threads of Agassiz, Forbes and Faraday: his researches on heat were in the direct line of Count Rumford and Joule and Melloni. It is the same throughout. We cannot say of him that he gave us any one great conception, like natural selection or the conservation of energy; any one great discovery, like spectrum analysis or the meteoric nature of comets; any one great invention, like the telephone or the phonograph. But his personality and his influence were pervasive and important; his powers of exposition were in every way remarkable; and his investigations, though never quite reaching the first rank in value, stood very high, indeed, in the forefront of the second. . . . No man had ever a profounder conception of the ultimate atom, its nature and its powers, its sympathies and antipathies, its forces and its energies. Few men have looked deeper behind the world of sense and illusion into the impalpable verities which constitute the universe.—ALLEN, GRANT, 1894, *Professor John Tyndall: a Character Sketch, Review of Reviews, vol. 9, pp. 175, 178.*

Between a great man recognised by his generation, and a man made great by his reputation, there is need of careful discrimination. I fancy that Darwin and Tyndall may serve as contrasting types. . . . Tyndall's actual scientific work has left little impression upon science. He has founded no school; he has stimulated no large bulk of original research. Yet his actual publications were voluminous: besides the well-known volumes that have delighted so many readers—as for instance, the volumes on "Heat as a Mode of Motion," or the "Researches on Diamagnetism and Magne-crystallic Action," or the later volumes dealing with germs. He contributed largely to technical memoirs. Thus in the "Royal Society Catalogue of Scientific Papers" up to 1863, there are 72 articles under his name; in the later catalogue, complete up to 1873, there are 40 more, and after that date there are at least 30 more as yet uncatalogued. A close inspection of these shows that his original researches were confined chiefly to three subjects: Diamagnetism, Heat, the Action of Ice, and the Influence of Dust Particles in the Air and in other Gases. But in all these he was completing the work and developing the ideas of other men—notably Faraday, Knoblauch, and Pasteur. . . . He had all the instincts of the intelligent amateur joined with an intellectual vigour and a herculean capacity for work. Keen, alert, and discriminating in his survey of contemporary work in all branches of science, he was ready at any moment to anticipate the importance of discoveries, and by his own work to help largely in their development. No doubt his position as a lecturer at the Royal Institution accentuated this bent of his talent: his business was to cater for the public, and to bring to their notice the newest scientific goods from France and Germany. A scientific eclecticism was unavoidable, and he fulfilled the duties of his post to admiration. But his greatness did not depend on his original research, and Physics and Biology were little advanced by his work.—MITCHELL, P. CHALMERS, 1894, *Professor Tyndall, New Review*, vol. 10, pp. 77, 78.

It was his power as a scientific expositor that gave Prof. Tyndall his worldwide reputation, and it is on this that his fame chiefly rests. His ability to present even abstruse subjects to a popular audience was unexcelled. The vividness of his imagination, which enabled him to form clear mental pictures of the phenomena he sought to explain, and his aptness in illustration led him to translate abstract ideas in their concrete equivalents. . . . It was these rare gifts as an interpreter of science which first drew the attention of American readers to Prof. Tyndall, and which finally led to his visit to this country in 1872. Many now living will recall that event and the impulse given to American science by the brilliant course of lectures which he delivered in our chief Atlantic cities. — YOUMANS, ELIZA ANN, 1894, *Tyndall and his American Visit, Popular Science Monthly*, vol. 44, pp. 503, 504.

It is an easy thing to remand Professor Tyndall, without more ado, to the camp of materialists, and thereby attach to his name the opprobrium which falls upon all those who hold that grosser form of materialism which Carlyle characterizes as the "philosophy of mud." There are materialists and materialists. Professor Tyndall must be carefully distinguished from the spirit-blind devotees of matter, who stoutly insist that the manifold problems of being and destiny find a ready solution in the properties of matter and the law of the conservation of energy. He differs radically at this point, from the rank and file of pure materialists. To overlook the difference between them prevents an honest and just estimate of the man, as a scientist and a philosopher. . . . At the outermost rim of his scientific investigation, Professor Tyndall acknowledges ever a bourne of mystery beyond. Towards this he looks with interest and with reverence. There is no indifference in his attitude towards the great unknown—and no conceit. You may call the position in reference to the world of the unseen, and its mysteries, as that of an agnostic; but here also his agnosticism must be distinguished from many who thus style their philosophy or rather lack of philosophy. With him, knowledge is either observed fact, or induced law through verified experiments. All else he has been accustomed to regard as lying beyond his ken. . . . In his "Hours of Exercise in the Alps," his love of nature, again and again, breaks into apostrophe. His admiration is akin to reverence. His communion with nature is not that of a materialist; it is that of the humble child of nature.—HIBBEN, JOHN GRIER, 1894, *Professor Tyndall as a Materialist, North American Review*, vol. 158, pp. 122, 123, 124.

He had the German training, and he combined the German thoroughness with the English instinct for systematic and perspicuous presentation. Great as was his service in the character of an investigator, he did a still greater service to his countrymen in the character of an expositor. What Professor Huxley did for the new biology created by Darwin, was done by Professor Tyndall for the new physics created by Joule and Faraday and Maxwell.—PAYNE, WILLIAM MORTON, 1895, *Little Leaders*, p. 247.

The value of his contributions to science,

especially on such subjects as light, heat, and sound, secured for him a European reputation, which he brilliantly sustained. To the gift of clear exposition, Professor Tyndall united eloquence, imagination, and a feeling for poetry. When the matter was one of purely scientific exposition, these qualities were wont to lend a peculiar charm to his deliverances.—GRAHAM, RICHARD D., 1897, *The Masters of Victorian Literature, p.* 468.

Conciliated critical opinion by the courage with which he insisted on the value of the imagination in the pursuit of scientific inquiry. He had remarkable rhetorical gifts, and in his early publications on mountain structure he cultivated a highly coloured style, influenced by Ruskin, and even by Tennyson. Perhaps the best-written of his philosophical treatises is the "Forms of Water" (1872), where his tendency to polychromatic rodomontade is kept in some check.—GOSSE, EDMUND, 1897, *A Short History of Modern English Literature, p.* 378.

The man who has done the most to popularise natural science in England is John Tyndall. . . On January 21st, 1870, Tyndall delivered a lecture, at the Royal Institution, on "Dust and Disease," and gave the results of some investigations of his own on floating organic matter in the air. Examination of air before and after being subjected to a very high temperature showed that a large proportion of the dust it contained was organic matter, since it disappeared on being burnt. In the course of the lecture Tyndall propounded a germ theory of diseases, saying that as surely as a pig comes from a pig, or a grape from a grape, so surely does the typhoid virus, or seed, when scattered about among people, give rise to typhoid fever, scarlatina virus to scarlatina, and small-pox virus to small-pox; and that the virus was carried about by the floating organic matter in the air. Many eminent men were present at the lecture, and those of the medical profession received his views with disfavour, going so far as to ridicule the germ theory. The accuracy of the germ theory has since, however, been proved over and over again. The discovery of the way in which diseases are spread has been of incalculable benefit to mankind, by showing that if the sanitary arrangements of a district are perfect, and all diseased organic matter carried away without access to the atmosphere, the risk of infection is reduced to a minimum. It was as a popular lecturer that Tyndall excelled. The reason of his success in lecturing to the "unscientific" may be found in his aptitude for imparting his knowledge in the simplest language, and in exciting the interest of an audience by homely illustrations. He has probably done more than any other man of science to raise the standard of education amongst the uneducated classes. — RHODES, W. G., 1897, *Social England, ed. Traill, vol.* VI, *pp.* 348, 349.

John Addington Symonds
1840–1893

Born, at Bristol, 5 Oct. 1840. At Harrow School, May 1854 to 1858. Matric., Balliol Coll., Oxford, 28 May 1858; Exhibitioner, 1859–62; Newdigate Prize, 1860; B. A., 1862; Fellow of Magdalen Coll., 1862–64; English Essay Prize 1863; M. A. 1865. Student of Lincoln's Inn, 1862. Married Janet Catherine North, 10 Nov. 1864. Settled in London. Frequent visits to Continent. Removed to Clifton, Nov. 1868. Removed to Davos Platz, Switzerland, for health, 1876. Resided there for greater part of each year, till his death. Died, in Rome, 19 April 1893. *Works:* "The Escorial," 1860; "The Renaissance," 1863; "An Introduction to the Study of Dante," 1872; "The Renaissance of Modern Europe," 1872; "Studies of the Greek Poets," 1st series, 1873; 2nd series, 1876; "Sketches in Italy and Greece," 1874; "The Renaissance in Italy" (5 pts.), 1875–86; ("The Age of the Despots," 1875; "The Revival of Learning," 1877; "The Fine Arts," 1877; "Italian Literature," 2 vols., 1881; "The Catholic Reaction," 2 vols., 1886); "Many Moods," 1878; "Shelley: a Biography," 1878; "Sketches and Studies in Italy," 1879; "New and Old," 1880; "Animi Figura," 1882; "Italian Byways," 1883; "Shakspere's Predecessors in the English Drama," 1884; "Vagabunduli Libellus," 1884; "Sir Philip Sidney," 1886; "Ben Jonson," 1886; "Essays" (2 vols.), 1890; "Our Life in the Swiss Highlands" (with his daughter Margaret), 1892; "Life of Michelangelo Buonarroti" (2 vols.), 1893, [1892]; "In the Key of Blue," 1893; "Walt Whitman," 1893. *Posthumous:*

"Blank Verse," 1894; "Giovanni Boccaccio as Man and Author," 1895 [1894]. He *translated:* "The Sonnets of Michelangelo Buonarroti and Tommaso Campanella," 1878; "Wine, Women and Song," 1884; "Life of Benvenuto Cellini," 1887; "Memoirs of Count Carlo Gozzi," 1890. He *edited:* J. A. Symonds (the elder)'s "Miscellanies," 1871; J. Conington's "Miscellaneous Writings," 1872; "Selected Works of Ben Jonson," 1886 and *contributed introductions* to: Sir T. Browne's "Religio Medici," 1886; "The Best Plays of Christopher Marlowe," 1887; "The Best Plays of Thomas Heywood," 1888; "The Best Plays of Webster and Tourneur," 1888; J. Van der Straet's "Dante" 1892. *Life:* by Horatio F. Brown, 1895.—SHARP, R. FARQUHARSON, 1897, *A Dictionary of English Authors, p.* 273.

PERSONAL

I believe that, psychologically, Symonds was constructed thus: a highly analytical and sceptical intellect, with which was connected a profound sense of the one ultimate positive fact knowable to him—himself; a rich, sensuous, artistic temperament, with which was united a natural vein of sweetness and affection: an uncompromising addiction to truth, a passion for the absolute, a dislike of compromises, of middle terms, of the *à peu près* . . . . "Theological" his temperament certainly was not. He had arrived early at the conviction that the "theos" about whom the current "logos" was engaged must be a "theos" apprehended, if not created, by the human intellect, therefore not the universal, all-embracing "theos" for whom he was in search. . . . If the honest, courageous recognition of the Self confronted with God, the soul with the universe, the struggle to comprehend and be comprehended, is religious, then Symonds was pre-eminently a religious man. . . . It is no ignoble melancholy which overshadowed so large a part of Symond's life. The passionate desire to reach God, to understand what we are, and why we are here, meeting with an equally powerful devotion to truth in its purest, simplest form, an equally potent resolve to accept no theory that is not absolute, final, larger than ourselves, inevitably produced a spiritual conflict, to witness which may make us sad, but can hardly fail to raise both respect and love for the soul which was its battle-field. It is possible that many who met Symonds did not surmise behind the brilliant, audacious exterior, underlying the witty conversation, and the keen enjoyment of life and movement about him, this central core of spiritual pain. — BROWN, HORATIO, 1894, *John Addington Symonds, a Biography, Preface, vol.* I, *p.* XII, XIII.

Symonds was one of the most lovable of men: brave in his outlook, courageous in the face of adverse and often disastrous circumstances, youthfully enthusiastic and enthusiastically youthful, generous, a nature of sweet human sunshine. Even casual acquaintances were wont to admit the charm of his personality, the grace and distinction of his conversation, the alertness of his spirit, his swift responsiveness and sympathy. He was a scholar in the best sense of the word: a man of catholic culture. There has, in our time, been no mind more sensitive to beauty, and that not only in one or even in two, but in all the arts—in nature to an exceptional degree, and in human life and human nature to a degree still rarer. In a word, Symonds was in several essential respects fitted to be a great writer, and certainly a great critic. He had a warm heart, an eager brain, an exquisite sensibility: his critical insight was often extraordinarily keen: and with an innate capacity for severe analysis he combined a trained synthetical faculty, which made him, potentially, one of the surest and brightest beacons in contemporary literature.—SHARP, WILLIAM, 1895, *John Addington Symonds, The Academy, vol.* 47, *p.* 95.

Notwithstanding his habitual association with men of the highest culture, no trait in his character was more marked than his readiness to fraternize with peasants and artisans. He always made a point of providing relief for others, when possible, from his own earnings as a man of letters, leaving his fortune intact for his family. . . . There are two men in Symonds whom it is hard to reconcile. His friends and intimates unanimously describe him as one endowed with an ardour and energy amounting to impetuosity, and their testimony is fully borne out by what is known of his taste for mountain-climbing and bodily exercise, his quick decision in trying circumstances, his ability in managing the affairs of the community to which he devoted himself, and the amount and facility of his literary productions. The evidence of his own memoirs and letters, on the other hand, would stamp him as one given up to morbid introspection, and disabled by physical and spiritual maladies from accomplishing anything. The former is the juster view.—GARNETT, RICHARD, 1898, *Dictionary of National Biography*, vol. XLV, pp. 274, 275.

GENERAL

The student of the transitional period, extending from the thirteenth to the end of the sixteenth century, should apply himself to these "Renaissance in Italy" portly volumes with diligence. Though the author's method is dignified and even severe, his style is graceful and at times brilliant. . . . As a whole, these works are among the most valuable of the many recent contributions to our knowledge of Italy.—ADAMS, CHARLES KENDALL, 1882, *A Manual of Historical Literature*, pp. 226, 227.

He has written a large number of sonnets, and one of his latest books—"Vagabunduli Libellus"—consists of poems in this form only. His sonnets are unequal, owing partly to his fondness for writing sonnet-sequences—a great mistake in nine cases out of ten. That Mr. Symonds is a true poet, a poet of generally high standing, no one will be prepared to deny after perusal of his verse. The author of that eminently critical, fascinating, picturesquely yet learnedly and carefully written *magnum opus*, "The History of the Renaissance in Italy," has so great a power over words that his natural tendency, even in verse, is to let himself be carried away by them. Some of his later sonnets are very markedly of Shakespearian inspiration.—SHARP, WILLIAM, 1886, *Sonnets of this Century*, p. 322, note.

Between the æsthetic epicure or exquisite literary voluptuary like Mr. Pater, and the purely intellectual connoisseur of men and books and epochs, like Mr. Leslie Stephen, Mr. Symonds occupies a place perhaps scarcely so well defined as theirs, but not less necessary to be filled; and he fills it worthily, by virtue of the trained judgment and varied erudition which he always has at command.—WATSON, WILLIAM, 1890, *Essays Speculative and Suggestive, The Academy*, vol. 38, p. 167.

I like the adjectives which Mr. Symonds has chosen to describe the essays contained in his recently published volumes. "Speculative and Suggestive." They are eminently that; and they are eminently welcome just because they are that. In his Preface Mr. Symonds tells us that his surmises and suggestions are advanced in no dogmatic spirit. Perhaps their great merit is—to borrow a phrase from Kant—that they are admirably fitted to arouse readers out of dogmatic slumber. They are admirably fitted to make people think, or—which is the next best thing—to think of thinking. It is impossible for any moderately intelligent and cultivated reader to open these volumes anywhere, and not to find his intellect more or less stimulated. Whether Mr. Symonds is discoursing of "The Principles of Criticism," or of "The provinces of the Several Arts," of "Landscape," or of "Nature Myths and Allegories," of "The Pathos of the Rose in Poetry," or of "Realism and Idealism," he is always fertile in ideas and helpful to reflection. Always, moreover, whether we agree or differ with the views which he expresses, he wins our admiration by the soundness of his scholarship, the breadth of his culture, the opulence of his imagination, the fascination of his style. . . . Every page of his writings exhibits him as an accomplished master of style. In the "Notes" which he prints, in the present volumes, he discourses of the art which he so admirably exercises; tracing its history; formulating its laws; and illustrating its applications. I incline to think that Mr. Symonds has never given the world anything better than these "Notes" replete as they are with varied learning, judicious criticism, pregnant suggestion. Specially felicitous is the second part of them, in which he deals with "National Style."—LILLY, W. S., 1890, *Mr. Symonds's Essays Speculative and Suggestive, Nineteenth Century*, vol. 28, pp. 244, 246.

These volumes of essays differ from the ordinary collection of miscellanies by men of letters. Some of the papers are old, some are new, and they deal with many topics; but they are so arranged as to constitute a continuous and for the most part analytical criticism of the art of expression, principally in literature, but also in architecture, sculpture, painting, and music. They comprise, moreover, the fruits of many years of experience in a wide range of scholarly interests, and sum up the reflections of their author on the whole mass of his intellectual acquirements. . . . The larger part of Mr. Symonds's conclusions is consistent with other hypotheses than that form of pantheism which he regards as the logical conclusion of the evolutionist, and which he puts in the forefront of his work as its determining idea. . . . The metaphysical weakness of these volumes, which has been self-exposed, cannot but obstruct the reader's sense of their many excellences in the department of literary criticism. It is, nevertheless, easy to disengage the really solid and valuable matter, which constitutes four-fifths of the work at least, from the vague and hybrid speculation which impairs it as a whole, and which is mainly of interest as an example of the working of an eclectic and assimilative mind amid the confusions of modern thought. As a critic of literature the author brings no inconsiderable matter of his own wide gathering, for he has been a student of culture all his life, and speaks from a various experience.—WOODBERRY, GEORGE EDWARD, 1890, *Symonds's Essays, The Nation*, vol. 51, pp. 173, 175.

It would seem impossible that anything new could be said about Style; yet here are four essays ["Essays"] on that subject richly repaying the closest attention. There is perhaps no other English critic whose appreciation of style is at once so wide in range, so just, and so penetrative.—MEAD, MARIAN, 1891, *Essays from Higher Altitudes, The Dial*, vol. 12, p. 178.

Mr. Symonds has the happy faculty of adorning whatever he touches, and the gates leading into Greek, Italian, and French fields, fast-locked to so many critical writers of the present day, open at his command.—WAY, W. IRVING, 1893, *In the Key of Blue, The Dial*, vol. 14, p. 181.

His magnum opus is, of course, his "Renaissance in Italy," which appeared in no less than seven volumes between 1875 and 1886. But with all its learning, its insight, and its eloquence, this somehow fails to reach the standard of an ideal history. It is rather a series of aperçus than a continuous narrative. So, again, with his recent "Life of Michelangelo." Despite the labour expended upon it, and the brilliance of the style, we seem to feel that the final word has not been spoken: that the author did not lose himself in his subject. The shorter biographies of "Shelley," "Sir Philip Sidney," and "Ben Jonson" are adequate to the series to which they belong, but not otherwise notable. The four or five volumes of verse show a graceful fancy and a competent technique; but their matter is chiefly of interest as revealing the emotions of the author. The two collections of "Sketches in Italy" together with "Italian Byways," contain admirable descriptions of scenery, illuminated by historical associations and by sympathy with the realities of modern life. The two early books, "Introduction to the Study of Dante," and "Studies of the Greek Poets"—both of which are immediately to appear in new editions—are excellently adapted to their purpose, of stimulating knowledge of classical masterpieces by criticism that is both scholarly and popular.—COTTON, J.S., 1893, *John Addington Symonds, The Academy*, vol. 43, p. 371.

Of the sonnet form he was a master, and the poems have that beauty of natural description with which most people are more familiar in his prose. . . . I consider the poetry of Symonds to have been quite unjustly underrated; but it is almost impossible, if a man has established a reputation in prose, to get a hearing for him in verse, the absurdity of which let Milton, Dryden, Cowper, Gray, Byron, Shelley, and Arnold prove. I shall say without reserve how highly I have always esteemed my friend's poetry. . . . Symonds' earlier volumes of poetry were not equal to the two last. They were, indeed, full of fire, colour and light; they contained gorgeous description, and occasionally tender sentiment; but as a rule, they were, perhaps, too much the books of a man of the study, verses that might have been derived from those of others, almost too facile, and fluent in their phraseology and versification. Yet they contained a few most notable poems, such as "Callicrates, a tale of Thermopylæ," "In the Syracusan Stone Quarries," "Le jeune homme caressant sa chimère," and "The Valley of Vain Desires." In the subject of comradeship, as also in that of flesh wrestling with spirit, Symonds ever found a real personal inspiration. . . . Of his prose writings I have little space to speak;

they are better known than his poetry, very voluminous, and cover an extraordinarily large field. He was a discriminating, but very catholic and generous critic who enjoyed the beautiful wherever he found it, and whose taste led him rather to appreciate the good points than to gloat over his own "fine taste," as evinced in the ready detection of defects; even the more or less conventional and unindividual verse of a minor poet he could say a gracious word for, if it were nicely put together. His long histories of the "Renaissance in Italy," his "Life of Michael Angelo," and his "Predecessors of Shakespeare" are monuments of erudition and industry, containing much that is of permanent value to the student, as well as many brilliant pages. Perhaps he was at his best in the short study or essay, in that unique kind of essay particularly which he made his own, combining the narration of some historical event or moving episode of private life characteristic of its epoch, with the described environment of natural scenery in the midst of which it occurred, all being portrayed by the loving and graphic pen of a poet, who was a master of language and of picturesque style. His translations from Benvenuto Cellini and Carlo Gozzi could not be bettered.—NOEL, RODEN, 1893; *John Addington Symonds, Gentleman's Magazine*, vol. 275, pp. 309, 310.

There is no corner of history on which the human spirit has left its impress that is not eloquent to him, and to which he is without some answering sympathy. His is the insatiable curiosity to experience the best that has been thought and done in the world, but the artist's rather than the mere scholar's: the passionate inquisitiveness of the Renaissance, when the mere acquisition of learning was tinged with romance. And, consequently, whatever subject he writes upon, we feel a confidence that he treats it with a full knowledge of all its relations, its antecedents, and all its various conditions. Culture has done its perfect work, and endowed him with its greatest gift—the sense of proportion.—LE GALLIENNE, RICHARD, 1893, *In the Key of Blue and Other Prose Essays by John Addington Symonds, The Academy*, vol. 43, p. 213.

Symonds cannot be said to have reached the rank of poet, to which he aspired, if we confine poetry to the art of versifying; but of the higher mission of poetry, the imparting of form and beauty and human interest to the crude materials and fragments of knowledge, whether of history, science or art, which lacked these in their isolation, few modern writers afford so happy an example. As a verse writer his achievements are indeed far from inconsiderable. His fine sense of form and melody enabled him to present with a large measure of their original beauty the voluminous extracts from classical and Italian poets which his works contain. He has been the chief interpreter to English readers of the Sonnets of Michel Angelo, and in treating these he reveals his own susceptibility to the magic spell of that most subtle and most powerful of all poetic forms.—SEWALL, FRANK, 1894, *John Addington Symonds, The New World*, vol. 3, p. 716.

Our only objection to Mr. Symonds's treatment here ["Art Essays"] is that he does not sufficiently distinguish between the ostensible "subject" of a work of art and its true theme or motive and assumes them to be one. This is not necessarily the case, and is often the reverse of true, and this is why the believers in art for art's sake and the believers in a meaning to be expressed in the language of art misunderstand each other so constantly.—Cox, KENYON, 1894, *Symonds's Art Essays, The Nation*, vol. 58, p. 88.

There is much in this volume ["Shakespeare's Predecessors"] which will, we fear, be of ill precedent in the future. What we expected, and what we felt we had a right to expect, in so ambitious a work, were some indications of the *meditatio et labor in posterum valescentes*, something that smacked, as the ancient critics would put it, of the file and the lamp. What we found was, we regret to say, every indication of precipitous haste, a style which where it differs from the style of extemporary journalism differs for the worse—florid, yet commonplace; full of impurities; inordinately, nay, incredibly diffuse and pleonastic; a narrative clogged with endless repetitions; without symmetry, without proportion.—COLLINS, JOHN CHURTON, 1895, *Essays and Studies*, p. 93.

Mr. Symonds was all his days "in trouble about his style," as some other men are about their souls. He examined it as regularly and as severely as a devotee examines his conscience. He confessed its sins to himself and refused them absolution. In short he was almost to the hour of his death in travail with artistic perfection without, in his own opinion, having "the strength to bring forth;" and it may therefore soothe his departed spirit if it can still be touched by mortal things, to know that he has at least left behind him a portrait of himself which comes as near to perfection as literary skill, analytic subtlety, and the invaluable quality of an utterly fearless egotism can succeed in raising it. . . . Partly in the autobiographic memoir which he has left behind him, and partly in his carefully composed correspondence during his later years with his literary friends in England, Mr. Symonds bequeathed materials for a history of his inner life, as minute as Amiel's, without his tediousness, and as outspoken as Marie Bashkirtseff's, without that young woman's continual and comically obvious sacrifices of truth to theatrical effect. A comparison of the book with Rousseau's "Confessions" might be misunderstood. Mr. Symonds had none of Rousseau's sins to confess, and certainly none of his morbid propensity to the invention of sins for the purpose of confessing them. It is not to moral but to physical weaknesses that I refer: but I doubt whether anyone since the "self-torturing sophist" has ever made such full and unreserved disclosures on these delicate matters as Mr. Symonds.—TRAILL, H. D., 1895, *The Life of Mr. J. A. Symonds, Nineteenth Century, vol. 37, p. 342.*

One subject Mr. Symonds made his own, and by his work done upon that subject he will be chiefly remembered. The Italian Renaissance has had historians of more minutely accurate scholarship, and its separate phases have perhaps found occasional treatment subtler and more profound than it was in his power to give them. But the period as a whole, its political and domestic life, its literature and art, received at his hands a treatment that lacks neither grasp nor sympathy, that is distinctly the best and most attractive in English literature.—PAYNE, WILLIAM MORTON, 1895, *Little Leaders, p. 234.*

Symonds was certainly far more widely and profoundly versed in Greek poetry than any Englishman who in our day has analysed it for the general reader. And it is plain that no scholar of his eminence has been master of a style so fascinating and eloquent. He has the art of making the Greek poets live to our eyes as if we saw in pictures the scenes they sing. A fine example of this power is in the admirable essay on Pindar in the first series, when he describes the festival of Olympia as Pindar saw it. . . . Whenever Symonds is deeply stirred with the nobler types of Greek poetry, this dithyrambic mood comes on him, and he gives full voice to the god within. . . . In all these seven volumes ["Renaissance in Italy"] there is hardly one word about the *science* of the Renascence. Now, the revival for the modern world of physical science from the state to which Science had been carried by Hippocrates, Aristotle, Archimedes, and Hipparchus in the ancient world was one of the greatest services of the Renascence—one of the greatest services ever conferred on mankind. And in this work Italy held a foremost part, if she did not absolutely lead the way. . . . A whole chapter might have been bestowed on Leonardo as a man of science, and another on Galileo, whose physical discoveries began in the sixteenth century. And a few pages might have been saved for Christopher Columbus. And it is the more melancholy that the great work out of which these names are omitted has room for elaborate disquisitions on the *Rifacimento* of Orlando, and a perfect Newgate Calendar of Princes and Princesses, Borgias, Cencis, Orsinis, and Accorambonis. Symonds has given us some brilliant analyses of the Literature and Art of Italy during three centuries of the Renascence. But he has not given us its full meaning and value in science, in philosophy, or in history, for he has somewhat misunderstood both the Middle Ages which created the Renascence and the Revolution which it created in turn, nor has he fully grasped the relations of the Renascence to both.—HARRISON, FREDERIC, 1896, *John Addington Symonds, The Nineteenth Century, vol. 39, pp. 982, 983, 988.*

Both in prose essays (which he wrote in great numbers, chiefly on Greek or Renaissance subjects) and in verse (where he was not so successful as in prose) Mr. Symonds was one of the most characteristic and copious members of the rather foolishly named "æsthetic" school of the last third of the century, the school which, originally deriving more or less from Mr. Ruskin, more and more rejected the ethical side of his teaching. . . . But for the redundance above mentioned, which is all pervading with him both in thought and style, and which once suggested to a not unfriendly critic the remark that he should like to "squeeze him like a sponge," Symonds would probably or rather certainly occupy a much higher place than he has held or ever will hold. For his appreciation both of books and of nature was intense, and his faculty of description abundant. But the *ventosa et enormis loquacitas* of his style was everywhere, so that even selection would be hard put to it to present him really at his best.—SAINTSBURY, GEORGE, 1896, *A History of Nineteenth Century Literature*, pp. 401, 402.

The perusal of Mr. Symonds's letters is not a pleasurable occupation. They are too intense to be restful reading. But to possess ourselves of the *essence* of that life in his works is a pleasure which no scholar has given us in a greater degree. He has, with subtle and fluent eloquence, presented every phase, responded to every wave of thought and feeling in that capricious moment of world-development. On the other hand, Mr. Symonds was guilty of certain weaknesses which generally evidence themselves in all intense natures. He went to extremes not only in his measure of people and events, but in his literary expression. The element of partisanship was too strong. A judge may not indulge in enthusiasms. He possessed, in a superlative degree, the one thing which Miss Martineau accused Macaulay of lacking. "Thomas Macaulay wanted heart: this was one deficiency which lowered all his other gifts," she wrote upon the statesman's death. The result in the latter's case was a shell-like brilliancy, while Symond's warm-hearted enthusiasm produced a richness of tone which made him generous oftentimes when he should have been critical.—WENDELL, WINIFRED LEE, 1901, *John Addington Symonds, The Book Buyer*, vol 22, p. 44.

Benjamin Jowett
1817–1893

Born, at Camberwell, 15 April 1817. At St. Paul's School, 16 June 1829 to 1836. Scholar, Balliol Coll., Oxford, Dec. 1835 to 1839; matric., 30 Nov., 1836; Hertford Scholar, 1837; Fellow, Balliol Coll., 1838–70; Tutor, 1843–70. B. A., 1839; Latin Essay Prize, 1841; M. A., 1842. M. A., Durham, 1842. Ordained Deacon, 1842;. Priest, 1845; Mem. of Commission on I. C. S. Exams., 1853. Regius Prof. of Greek, Oxford, 1855–93. Master of Balliol Coll., 1870–93. Hon. Doc. Leyden Univ., Feb. 1875. Vice-Chancellor of Oxford Univ., 1882–86. Hon. LL. D., Edinburgh, 1884; Hon. LL. D., Dublin, 1886; Hon. LL. D., Cambridge, 1890. Died, at Oxford, 1 Oct. 1893. *Works:* "De Etruscorum Cultu," 1841; Edition of "Epistles to Galatians, Thessalonians and Romans" (2 vols.), 1855; "On the Interpretation of Scripture," in "Essays and Reviews," 1860; Translation of Plato's Dialogues (4 vols.) 1871; "Lord Lytton," 1873; Translation of Thucydides (2 vols.), 1881; Translation of the "Politics" of Aristotle (2 vols.), 1885. *Posthumous:* "College Sermons," ed. by Hon. W. H. Fremantle, 1895. *Life:* by E. Abbott and L. Campbell, 1897.—SHARP, R. FARQUHARSON, 1897, *A Dictionary of English Authors*, p. 153.

PERSONAL

This morning the sermon was preached by Jowett (not of South Quay, but) of Balliol College. This man has the reputation of being an infidel, simply because he has a profound contempt for show, and humbug, and external rites. His sermon was beautiful, and seemed to me to indicate a heart sincerely interested in the subject. He is a pale, boyish, almost effeminate-looking man, something like little Deemster Drinkwater.—BROWN, THOMAS EDWARD, 1851,

To his Mother, Jan. 26; Letters, ed., Irwin, vol. I, p. 57.

Jowett, as you say, believes very firmly in an ordering God, a moral, personal, lawgiving God. He does so because he cannot help it, because it has been too deeply stereotyped in his nature to be effaced, because when questioning and parting with all else, he has never stirred this, because, perhaps, he belongs to the generation of Newman and not to its successor, because he is an ordained priest, because, again I say, he cannot help it.—SYMONDS, JOHN ADDINGTON, 1867, *Life by Brown*, vol. II, p. 113.

For a man who had a great and a deserved renown as a talker, Dr. Jowett was often singularly silent. He was silent unless the company pleased him, and unless the topic pleased him. Some of those who saw him but seldom, and then not in favourable circumstances, have called him rude. He never was rude, or never consciously so, but he had no doubt a certain intellectual arrogance which, though it was entirely intellectual, expressed itself at times in a way which gave offence. He had fits of apparent abstraction. When they seemed to be deepest, they were broken by a remark which indicated that nothing of what had been said had escaped him, and that nothing had pleased him. These hard sayings were delivered with a gentleness of demeanour which added to the sting. Woe to the man who talked on a subject he did not understand, if he talked pretentiously. For pretence and for the insincerity of character which it implies, Jowett had no mercy.—SMALLEY, GEORGE W., 1893, *Studies of Men*, p. 155.

Of the average academic or collegiate one is inclined to think that, in Rossetti's accurate phrase, "he dies not—never having lived—but ceases": of Mr. Jowett it is almost impossible at first to think as dead. I, at any rate, never found it harder, if so hard, to realize the death of any one. There was about him a simple and spontaneous force of fresh and various vitality, of happy and natural and wellnigh sleepless energy, which seemed not so much to defy extinction as to deride it. "He laboured, so must we," says Ben Jonson of Plato in a noble little book which I had the pleasure of introducing to Mr. Jowett's appreciative acquaintance; and assuredly no man lived closer up to that standard of active and studious life than the translator of Plato. But this living energy, this natal force of will and action, was coloured and suffused and transfigured by so rare a quality of goodness, of kindness, of simple and noble amiability, that the intellectual side of his nature is neither the first nor the last side on which the loving and mourning memory of any one ever admitted to his friendship can feel inclined or will be expected to dwell.—SWINBURNE, ALGERNON CHARLES, 1893, *Recollections of Professor Jowett, Studies in Prose and Poetry*, p. 42.

Jowett's person was, like his mind, dainty. An irreverent writer once spoke of his face as of the tombstone-cherub order; and the phrase was descriptive. But cherubs too frequently have something gross in their chubbiness; and everything about the Master was delicate and fine. Perhaps it was his appearance which helped to create the affection which mingled with our awe and respect; he was the *Doctor Seraphicus* of the College. Yet we trembled when we had to go and see him, even at a breakfast party, to say nothing of less agreeable occasions. In his clear little staccato voice he could say such biting things. . . . Yet he could be very kind to the obscure. Meeting a young graduate making a living by "coaching" or private tuition, he asked him how he was getting on. He was told that there had been few pupils that term, and that the coach had been obliged to give up his hope of going to Germany in the vacation. A few days later the coach was sent for and given an envelope with the words: "I hope you will go to Germany; goodbye." Four years later the Master had quite forgotten he had ever drawn that check.—ASHLEY, W. J., 1893, *The Master of Balliol, The Nation*, vol. 57, p. 266.

It was impossible to be in Jowett's company—even if, as sometimes happened, he did not open his mouth—without recognising that he was a remarkable man. That noble forehead with its nimbus of silver hair, that mild eye and cherubic countenance, that beautiful softness of hand, that small rotund figure clad in old-fashioned garb, that venerable bearing—all combined to make up a picture which no painter has adequately reproduced. Add the thin, small voice, the deliberate intonations that could be either bitter or sweet, the abrupt questionings that sometimes quivered like a dart, the intervals of silence that were yet more formidable, the wise maxims that come only from age and experience; and some part of the secret of Jowett's charm will be understood. No Oxford don had a wider circle of acquaintance in the outer world; none knew intimately so many generations of undergraduates. He possessed, in supreme measure, that power, invaluable to statesmen and generals, of penetrating the character of others at a glance. Of his exceeding kindness to individuals, and of his munificence when such was needed, it is not necessary to speak. His college stood to him in the place of a wife, and he took a paternal interest in the careers of its sons.—COTTON, J. S., 1893, *Professor Jowett, The Academy, vol.* 44, *p.* 294.

I have not unfrequently heard him preach. When I was Headmaster of Marlborough College, I asked him to come down and preach to the boys, which he readily did, and was my guest. Since then I have heard him in Balliol College and in Westminster Abbey. His sermons had all the unusual characteristics of his individuality. There was a charm about them which it was wholly impossible to explain. Just as his face was pleasing, and must once have been almost beautiful, so his style was attractive. It was exquisitely simple and lucid, and there was not a fault to find with it, unless it were that it was wholly devoid of humour, of eloquence, and of passion. But it gave the sense of continual self-repression.—FARRAR, FREDERIC WILLIAM, 1893, *Benjamin Jowett, Review of Reviews, vol.* 8, *p.* 669.

The high-water mark of his religion may be indicated by saying that, like most religious philosophers of our day, but more than most of them, he cherished an ennobling aspiration which, superficially at least, is more Platonic than Christian. He was one of those happily constituted persons who keep alive the hope which is born of an ardent wish, and is its own and only justification—the hope that there is an Ideal World in which Absolute Goodness, of which the highest earthly goodness is but a feeble and transient reflection, has its habitation in perfect fulness and for ever.— TOLLEMACHE, LIONEL A., 1895, *Benjamin Jowett, Master of Balliol, p.* 140.

There were so many Jowetts! That is what, looking back, strikes one first of all. There was the Jowett, for instance, who was the pioneer of a religious movement; there was Jowett, philosopher, teacher, scholar; there was Jowett, the cordial and skilful host, entertaining at his house, year by year, the men and women of most note in contemporary England; there was the Jowett of legendary fame—the Jowett who, by some caprice of the public, has been popularized in the general mind as the true Master of Balliol—a Jowett unsympathetic and cold, deliberately causing discomfort to shy undergraduates, habitually embarrassing his guests with intentional silences, dealing in sharp speeches, of which the unkindliness dominated the wit—the Jowett, in fact, of the innumerable anecdotes which have gathered round his name, and of which the portrait, so often and so persistently presented does not strike his friends so much in the light of a caricature —since a caricature should be, at the least, an easily recognisable exaggeration of truth—as in that of a Jowett-myth, with regard to which they hesitate between laughter and anger. And besides all these Jowetts, each in his measure familiar to the general public, there was another Jowett less well known—the Jowett with which this paper is alone concerned—the Jowett of his Friends, the kindly, intimate, and affectionate companion; the shrewd yet indulgent observer, ready at all times to impart to those of less experience the results of his observations upon human life, the steadfast, just, and wide-minded counselor. — TAYLOR, I. A., 1895, *The Master of Balliol, Longman's Magazine, vol.* 26, *p.* 78.

He had a marvellous genius for friendship and could love a score as few men can love anyone. The close of his life was shadowed by their departure. Stanley, Lord Iddesleigh, Matthew Arnold, Robert Browning, Lord Sherbrooke, Alfred Tennyson, were gone, and it was time for an old man to

"Wrap the drapery of his couch
About him and lie down to pleasant dreams."

At Hedley Park, on a visit to dear friends, the not unwelcome summons came.— RICHARDS, C. A. L., 1897, *The Late Master of Balliol, The Dial, vol.* 23, *p.* 11.

Though Jowett was audacious, he was never indiscreet. If he did a bold thing— and he did many—it was not by impulse or by accident, but of set purpose; and he was too wise ever to explain it or to apologise for it, being well content to leave it to be justified or condemned by the results. His correspondence and memoranda are peculiarly instructive, and open up unexpected glimpses into the beliefs and ideals that were the springs of his action. The mind revealed in his letters and note-books is so pure, the aims so high and generous, the life so unselfish, the spirit so silent as to its own sorrows while so tender and sympathetic to those of others, that even the men who were most alien from his creed and his policy may well feel compelled to respect the man.—FAIRBAIRN, A. M., 1897, *Oxford and Jowett, Contemporary Review, vol.* 71, *p.* 829.

He did more than any other man of his time to raise the ideal of University teaching and of the relation of teacher and pupil. But when we try to explain the secret of his influence, it is not easy to say anything definite. In truth, an original personality like Jowett is very difficult to describe. . . He was primarily a man of very sensitive temper, with the strong desire that usually goes with such a temper for the sympathy of others. At the same time, he was naturally shy, reserved, and unwilling, or even unable, to disclose himself unless he was sure of a response; and the effect of his manner, therefore, was at first somewhat chilling, especially to those who had any kindred tendency to reserve.—CAIRD, EDWARD, 1898, *Professor Jowett, International Journal of Ethics, vol.* 8, *p.* 41.

Those who remember him, as the Master, will be amused at the pictures of him, as a Freshman, which his biographers preserve. He entered Balliol in a round jacket, and with a turned down collar, we are told. His appearance was juvenile in the extreme; and Hobhouse alluded to his pretty, girlish looks, his quiet voice, and his gentle, shy manner. Even in later life he was spoken of as "a middle-aged cherub" and as "a little downy owl." But there was a good deal that was manly, and very manly, behind it all.—HUTTON, LAURENCE, 1903, *Literary Landmarks of Oxford, p.* 45.

GENERAL

It is true that Jowett ever preached "plain living and high thinking;" but he presented them not so much as their own reward, or as the necessary conditions of learning, but as the means to worldly success. Balliol men have been better than their instruction; but who shall estimate how much the university has lost in exact scholarship and in original research? The same practical and commonsense side of Jowett's nature was shown in his contributions to literature. Though Professor of Greek for nearly forty years, he did not conceive it his duty to represent the highest standard of Hellenic philology. The science of palæography, the fine art of emendation, the discoveries of modern archæology, were to him alike unknown and indifferent. Practically he gave no public lectures (though he did not exclude members of other colleges from his private teaching), nor did he ever edit an ancient text. But what was within his power and suited his tastes, that he did to a marvel. His translation of the whole of Plato, with introductions to the several dialogues, has already become a sort of English classic. . . . The translation itself is a *tour de force.* All the artifices of rhetoric—the breaking up of sentences, the changing of the order of words, the use of conjunctions—are intentionally employed, in order to imitate faithfully not only the thought but also the style of the original, and yet read as idiomatic English. It may be that the study of Greek will ere long become rare in England, even at the universities. If that time should arrive, Jowett's "Plato" will at any rate permit our grandchildren to appreciate the supremest effort of imaginative prose, without the drudgery of learning the Greek grammar.—COTTON, J. S., 1893, *Professor Jowett, The Academy, vol.* 44, *p.* 294.

If it be asked whether Dr. Jowett was a writer whose works will live, we answer that of his sermons not half a dozen have found their way into print; that his original contributions to literature were very few in number, and were never collected; that his edition of St. Paul's Epistle to the Romans and Galatians—original as it was and sometimes suggestive—was marred by many inaccuracies, and must be regarded as an incursion into a domain of theological literature for which Dr. Jowett was not well adapted. . . . Dr. Jowett's most permanent contributions to English literature were the translations of Thucydides, of Aristotle's Politics, and above all, of Plato's Dialogues. All three in their original form—especially the first and the last—were disfigured by inaccuracies. But these are removed in the later editions, and no living scholar has done anything like so much as Dr. Jowett to make the thoughts of the greatest Greeks familiar to our generation. The translation of the whole of Plato could not be accomplished without consummate diligence, and the late Master of Balliol performed his task in such a manner as renders it little likely that his work will soon be superseded.—FARRAR, FREDERIC WILLIAM, 1893, *Benjamin Jowett, D. D., Master of Balliol, Review of Reviews,* vol. 8, pp. 667, 668.

Because the work of his life was mainly if not wholly devoted to Oxford it does not follow that it would be a mistake to assume —as certain of his official mourners or admirers might induce their hearers or readers to assume—that apart from Oxford he was not, and that his only claim to remembrance and reverence is the fact that he put new blood into the veins of an old university. He would have been a noticeable man if he had known no language but the English of which he was so pure and refined a master; and if he had never put pen to paper he would have left his mark upon the minds and the memories of younger men as certainly and as durably as he did.—SWINBURNE, ALGERNON CHARLES, 1893, *Recollections of Professor Jowett, Nineteenth Century,* vol. 34, pp. 912, 916.

He wrote well, but with much less distinction and elegance than Pattison, nor had he by any means the same taste for literature and erudition in it. But, as an influence on the class of persons from whom men of letters are drawn, no one has exceeded him in his day.—SAINTSBURY, GEORGE, 1896, *A History of Nineteenth Century Literature,* p. 374.

He had his weakness, like Johnson; but we feel in his case, as in Johnson's, that the core of the man's nature was sweet, sound, and masculine. This is part of the explanation of a problem which, I must confess, has often appeared to me as to others, to be rather enigmatic. What was the secret and the real nature of Jowett's remarkable influence? . . . Jowett was a man of wide philosophical culture. He was prominent in Oxford society during some remarkable intellectual changes. He lived there for some fifty-seven years. As an undergraduate he was a looker-on at the singular and slightly absurd phenomenon called the Oxford Movement, and keenly interested in the contest finally brought to a head by his friend W. G. Ward. Soon afterwards he was a leading tutor, at a time when the most vigorous youths at Oxford were inclining rather in the direction of J. S. Mill, and some of them becoming disciples of Comte. His edition of St. Paul's Epistles made him an arch heretic in the eyes of the High Church party, and his simultaneous appointment to the Greek Professorship gave the chance, of which its members were foolish enough to avail themselves, of putting him in the position of a martyr of free thought. His share in the "Essays and Reviews" (1860) made him a representative man in a wider sphere. Though we have now got to the stage of affecting astonishment at the sensation produced by the avowal of admitted truths in that work, nobody who remembers the time can doubt that it marked the appearance of a very important development of religious and philosophical thought. The controversy raised by "Essays and Reviews" even distracted men for a time from the far more important issues raised by the publication of Darwin's "Origin of Species." . . . Jowett was a man of mark and intellectual authority at a time when vital questions were being eagerly agitated and the most various conclusions reached. . . . Is any phase of speculation marked by Jowett's personal stamp? That is the question which one naturally asks about a man who is a well-known writer upon philosophy, and one can hardly deny that the answer must be unequivocally in the negative.—STEPHEN, LESLIE, 1897, *Jowett's Life, National Review,* vol. 29, pp. 443, 445, 446.

Of Jowett as one of the greatest masters of English prose nothing need here be said in addition to the expression of Pater's unqualified admiration in his letter written less than three months before his lamented death, describing Jowett's fame among the youth of Oxford, and the impression produced when he taught the University for nothing. "Such fame," writes Pater, "rested on his great originality as a writer and thinker. He seemed to have taken the measure not merely of all opinions, but of all possible ones, and *to have put the last refinements on literary expression.* The charm of that was enhanced by a certain mystery about his own philosophical and other opinions." Mr. Abbott gives some of Jowett's counsels of perfection in the writing of English which are worth their weight in gold. Jowett's Plato undoubtedly exhibits his style at its best, and with the original conception of this work is connected one of the greatest intellectual benefits conferred by Jowett upon Oxford. We mean the prominent place first assigned by him in the "Humanities" course to the "Republic" of Plato—a place which it still occupies unchallenged. . . . The reforms of his Oxford vice-chancellorship alone entitle him to rank very high among the great administrators of these days, and he has earned the fame of the second founder of the modern Balliol College.—DYER, L., 1897, *Benjamin Jowett, The Nation*, vol. 64, p. 419.

His theological writings first attracted to him the notice of the world at large; his translations have opened the treasures of Greek thought to thousands who could profit by them, and to whom they would otherwise have remained sealed. . . . Jowett was not a great classical scholar, in either the German or the English sense of the word. In the field of university politics, moreover, he does not seem to have initiated any one movement of the first importance. But as Master he was a great and brilliant success, and in the college and through the college he exercised enormous influence.—ASHLEY, W. J., 1897, *Jowett and the University Ideal, Atlantic Monthly*, vol. 80, p. 96.

He contributed more to form the mind and character of his age than many men who occupied more conspicuous positions. He fought a battle that was the more splendidly successful that it was so long without the outward signs and spoils of victory. It was not that he had transcendent gifts in any one direction; nay, in most respects he could be easily surpassed. As a scholar he had superiors both in his own and in the sister university; as a philosophical thinker he was eclipsed by some even of his own disciples; as a theologian he early fell out of the race, and though to the last wistfully anxious to take up the running, grew progressively unfit to do it; as an administrator of the university he had the defects of a man whose ends and means were too much his own to be easily adjusted to the temper and ways of an assembly which can only be deliberative by being critical. But when every deduction has been made, it will remain true that the late Master of Balliol was the most potent academic personality which Oxford, at least, has known in this century. To have been this was to be a person whose memory, especially as regards the elements and secrets of power, ought not to be willingly let die. . . . He was an educator rather than a scholar, and a man of letters rather than a man of learning. He is distinguished at once by the comparative feebleness of his scientific interest and the intensity of his interest in persons. He was an enthusiast for the creation of the best men for the service of the church and State; and he believed that there was no place for their creation equal to a well-equipped, well-governed, and well-disciplined college, where the most cultured minds of the present introduced the learners to the classical literatures of the past. And he lived to make the college he ruled what he conceived a college ought to be. It was a noble ambition nobly carried out.—FAIRBAIRN, A. M., 1897, *Oxford and Jowett, Contemporary Review*, vol. 71, pp. 830, 851.

Jowett was one of the few men who leave upon us the distinct stamp of an individual force without any weakening of the outline by the intrusion of what is conventional and commonplace. His intellectual and moral originality, his single-minded devotion to public ends,—above all, to the well-being of the University and the College over which he presided,—his integrity and consistency with himself, his great powers of working and getting others to work for the objects he sought, his wonderful memory for the characters and circumstances of his old pupils and his steadfast interest in their welfare—these with all the individual traits of severity and gentleness, of earnestness and humor, which characterized him, indelibly impressed the image of his personality upon all with whom he was brought into near relations. Perhaps not the least remarkable of his gifts, and that which prevented him from being ever less than himself, was his courage. Few men had a better claim to have inscribed on their graves the epitaph which the Regent Morton pronounced upon John Knox: "Here lies one who never feared the face of mortal man." —CAIRD, EDWARD, 1898, *Professor Jowett, International Journal of Ethics*, vol. 8, p. 46.

He was an eminently pregnant and suggestive thinker and writer, warmly attached to what he regarded as the central truths of religion.—PATRICK, DAVID, ed., 1903, *Chambers's Cyclopædia of English Literature*, vol. III, pp. 454, 455.

Frances Ann Kemble
1809–1893

Born, in London, 27 Nov. 1809. First appearance at Covent Garden Theatre, 5 Oct. 1829; acted there till 1832. Tragedy, "Francis I.," produced at Covent Garden, 15 March 1832. Acted with her father in America, 1832–34. Married Pierce Butler, 7 Jan. 1834. Separated from him, 1846. Visit to England, 1847; acted in Manchester and London. Acted in America, autumn 1847 to spring 1848. Obtained divorce from husband, 1848. First Public Reading in London, April 1848; in Philadelphia, Oct. 1849. Resumed maiden name. Lived at Lenox, Mass., 1849–68; lived near New York, 1868–69. Gave public Readings in America, 1856–60, 1866–68. In Europe, 1869–73. In America, 1873–77. Returned to London, 1877. Died there, 15 Jan. 1893. *Works:* "Francis the First," 1832; "Journal of F. A. Butler," 1835; "The Star of Seville," 1837; "Poems," 1844; "A Year of Consolation," 1847; "Plays," 1863; "Journal of a Residence on a Georgian Plantation," 1863; "Poems," 1866 [1865]; "Records of a Girlhood," 1878; "Records of Later Life" (3 vols.), 1882; "Notes upon some of Shakespeare's Plays," 1882; "Poems," 1883; "Far Away and Long Ago," 1889; "Further Records" (2 vols.), 1890.—SHARP, R. FARQUHARSON, 1897, *A Dictionary of English Authors,* p. 155.

PERSONAL

In those days Mrs. Kemble had certain dresses which she wore in rotation whatever the occasion might be. If the black gown chanced to fall upon a gala day she wore it, if the pale silk gown fell upon a working day she wore it; and I can still hear an American girl exclaiming with dismay as the delicate folds of a white silk embroidered with flowers went sweeping over the anemones in the Pamphili Gardens. Another vivid impression I have is of an evening visit Mrs Kemble paid Mrs. Browning in the quiet little room in the Bocca di Leone, only lit by a couple of tapers and by the faint glow of the fire. I looked from one to the other: Mrs. Browning welcoming her guest, dim in her dusky gown unrelieved; Mrs. Kemble upright, and magnificent, robed on this occasion like some Roman empress in stately crimson edged with gold. It happened to be the red dress day, and she wore it. . . . Mrs. Kemble once asked me suddenly what colour her eyes were, and confused and unready I answered "light eyes." At this moment indeed they looked like amber, not unlike the eyes of some of those captive birds one sees in their cages sitting alone in the midst of crowds. Mrs. Kemble laughed at my answer. "Light eyes! Where are your own? Do you know that I have been celebrated for my dark eyes?" she said; and then I looked again and they were dark and brilliant, and looking at me with a half-amused, half-reproachful earnestness.—
RITCHIE, ANNE THACKERAY, 1893, *Chapters from some Unwritten Memoirs, Macmillan's Magazine,* vol. 68, pp. 191, 192.

It is vain to talk of Mrs. Kemble at all if we are to lack assurance in saying, for those who had not the privilege of knowing her as well as for those who had, that she was one of the rarest of women. To insist upon her accomplishments is to do injustice to that human largeness which was the greatest of them all, the one by which those who admired her most knew her best. One of the forms, for instance, taken by the loyalty she so abundantly inspired was an ineradicable faith in her being one of the first and most original of talkers. To that the remembering listener turns as, on the whole, in our bridled race, the fullest measure and the brightest proof. Her talk was everything, everything that she was or that her interlocutor could happen to want; though indeed it was often something that he couldn't possibly have happened to expect. . . . The finest comedy of all, perhaps, was that of her own generous whimsicalities. She was superbly willing to amuse, and on any terms; and her temper could do it as well as her wit. If either of these had failed her eccentricities were always there. She had, indeed, so much finer a sense of comedy than anyone else that she herself knew best, as well as recked least, how she might exhilarate. I remember that at the play she often said: "Yes, they're funny; but they don't begin to know how funny they might be!" . . . If she had not lived by rule (on her showing), she would have lived infallibly by riot. Her rules and her riots, her reservations and her concessions, all her luxuriant theory and all her extravagant practice; her drollery that mocked at her melancholy; her imagination that mocked at her drollery; and her wonderful manners, all her own, that mocked a little at everything: these were part of the constant freshness which made those who loved her love her so much.—JAMES, HENRY, 1893, *Frances Anne Kemble, Temple Bar, vol.* 97, *pp.* 521, 522.

Of personal beauty, so important a desideratum in the career of an actress, she could scarcely claim a share. The majestic dignity of form and beauty of feature which distinguished Mrs. Siddons had not descended to her. A little woman, inclined to a stoutness too great for her height, her hopes of beauty were destroyed early in her girlhood by an attack of small-pox, which, as she herself records, "rendered my complexion thick and muddy and my features heavy and coarse, leaving me so moderate a share of good looks as quite to warrant my mother's satisfaction in saying when I went on the stage, 'Well, my dear, they can't say we have brought you out to exhibit your beauty.' Plain I undoubtedly was, but I by no means always looked so: and so great was the variation in my appearance at different times, that my comical friend, Mrs. Fitzhugh, once exclaimed, 'Fanny Kemble, you are the ugliest and the handsomest woman in London!' " The justice of this somewhat paradoxical pronouncement was in great measure borne out by the fact, that in Fanny Kemble there was visible a certain grace of deportment and bearing, which, innate and hereditary as it was, she shared in some degree with the greater members of her family, while her countenance was both expressive and pleasing.—MACMAHON, ELLA, 1893, "*Fanny Kemble,*" *Belgravia, vol.* 80, *p.* 373.

ACTOR AND READER

We are just now in the full flush of excitement about Fanny Kemble. She is a most captivating creature, steeped to the very lips in genius. You will not see her till the middle of April. Do not, if you can bear unmixed tragedy, do not fail to see her Belvidera. I have never seen any woman on the stage to be compared with her, nor even an actor that delighted me so much. She is most effective in a true woman's character, fearful, tender, and true. On the stage she is beautiful, far more than beautiful; her face is the mirror of her soul. I have been to see her: she is a quiet gentlewoman in her deportment.—SEDGWICK, CATHARINE M., 1833, *To Mrs. Frank Channing, Feb.* 12; *Life and Letters, ed. Dewey, p.* 230.

I heard Mrs. Butler read on Monday the "Merchant of Venice," and to-day "Much Ado about Nothing." It is wonderful what an effect she produces; it is like seeing the *whole* play admirably acted, and delightful to hear the beautiful poetry, which is usually so murdered on the stage, spoken by her melodious voice, and with her subtle expression.—GREVILLE, HENRY, 1848, *Leaves from his Diary, p.* 254.

O precious evenings! all too swiftly sped!
Leaving us heirs to amplest heritages
Of all the best thoughts of the greatest sages,
And giving tongues unto the silent dead!
How our hearts glowed and trembled as she read,
Interpreting by tones the wondrous pages
Of the great poet who foreruns the ages,
Anticipating all that shall be said!
O happy Reader! having for thy text
The magic book, whose Sibylline leaves have caught
The rarest essence of all human thought!
O happy Poet! by no critic vext!
How must thy listening spirit now rejoice
To be interpreted by such a voice!
—LONGFELLOW, HENRY WADSWORTH, 1849, *On Mrs. Kemble's Reading from Shakespere.*

Mrs. Kemble lacked the stature and perfect symmetry of Mrs. Siddons, but she had the noble head, the effulgent eyes, the sensitive mouth and flexible nostrils, the musical voice, the dignified and graceful gestures, which distinguished her aunt; and, in addition, the sense of humor, the mobile temperament quick as flame, the poetic sensibility, which characterized her mother. . . . So endowed, she soared at once to heights reached by others only after years of toil, substituting feeling for simulation, spontaneous action for studied gesture and movements, the intuition of poetic and dramatic genius for the training of talent; and this abandonment of herself to inspiration, "letting her heart go, while she kept her head," gave a vividness and pathos to her personations never equaled on the English stage in our day.—LEE, HENRY, 1893, *Frances Anne Kemble, Atlantic Monthly, vol.* 71, *p.* 662.

No public reader in this country has been so successful. None is so gratefully remembered. Charles Dickens, though reading scenes drawn, possibly, from the experience of his own life, was not worthy to be named beside her. To many, her readings are the memory of a life-time. In various cities, with intense delight I heard her read "Romeo and Juliet," "Twelfth Night," "Richard III.," "A Midsummer-Night's Dream" and "King Lear." Would that I could have heard her in her favorite, "The Tempest!" In every reading she captivated her audience. Her simplicity was charming. Sitting alone, behind the reading desk, she began invariably with the unpretentious words, "I have the honor to read—;" and for two hours or more, with rare exceptions, she held the fixed attention of her audience. Though masculine in her appearance and intellect, she had a feminine appreciation of the fitness of things. Her dress was appropriate and very suggestive. For "Romeo and Juliet" there was the moonlight gleam and shadow of white satin; for "Midsummer-Night's Dream," velvet of a mossy green; in "King Lear," the sombre richness of black velvet; in "King Richard the Third," black velvet, her breast crossed by a broad, blue ribbon. There seemed to be no end to the variety of her characterizations. You could see the personages in her face and hear them in her voice. Her energy seemed inexhaustible. Her voice had a remarkable compass and power. It took on, at will, the strident roughness of a tavern brawler, or the velvet softness of Juliet's tone or the delicate purity of Titania's. Few actors could express such a range of passion as she did in "Lear," or such sustained vigor, with no trace of rant as did she in "King Richard the Third." . . . I doubt if, as a dramatic reader, we shall ever listen to her like again. —UPSON, ANSON J., 1893, *Frances Kemble in America, The Critic, vol. 22, p. 152.*

POEMS

Her dramas, "Francis the First" and the "Star of Seville," were written when she was very young, and do not retain possession of the stage, though superior to many pieces which in this respect have been more fortunate. The volume of her shorter poems published in Philadelphia in 1844 entitles her to be ranked with the first class of living English poetesses. Their general tone is melancholy and desponding; but they are vigorous in thought and execution, and free from the sickly sentiment and puerile expression for which so much of the verse of the day is chiefly distinguished. She has written besides the works mentioned "A Journal," which was published on her return from this country to London. It is a clever, gossiping book, with such absurdities of opinion as might have been expected from a commentator on national character of her age and position: very amusing and very harmless. — GRISWOLD, RUFUS WILMOT, 1844, *The Poets and Poetry of England in the Nineteenth Century, p. 437.*

More than once we have had occasion to express admiration of Mrs. Butler's various and vigorous ability; but we own that the present volume, though including no piece of considerable length or in any ambitious form, has raised our estimate of her as a poetess. She has never before written so simply or so strongly. Never before has she dealt so boldly with the realities of life, and yet never before in our judgment did she display an equal richness of imaginative power. It is very rarely that a woman's poetry—real poetry—does not betray its source in her personal experiences and emotions. With whatever art she may endeavor to envelop it, the self peeps through wherever the inspiration reaches its height. But here there is no attempt at concealment. It is impossible not to feel that we have before us the fragments of an autobiography in verse. . . . It is a long time since we have met with any love-verses equal to these. We pity the oldest who does not feel young again as he reads.— LOCKHART, JOHN GIBSON, 1845, *Poems by Frances Anne Butler (late Fanny Kemble), Quarterly Review, vol. 75, pp. 325, 329.*

I believe that in the course of a few years, when time shall have sobered down the perhaps too-vividly painted lines of her mental character and shall have corrected her hasty estimates of the world and of humanity, Mrs. Butler will rank with the foremost poets of our land.—ROWTON, FREDERIC, 1848, *The Female Poets of Great Britain, p. 477.*

Her versification is very bold and vigorous, and her rhythm is often melodious beyond any other writer of equal strength. Her sonnets, especially when she forgets herself, are among the finest in our language and it is easy to see that, if a more apprehensive future uplifted her thoughts, those of a personal character would be closely allied to some of Milton's. As it is, she is nobly disdainful of all mawkishness or artificial conceit. She dashes at her main idea with an honest earnestness which one can scarcely help believing is a principal trait of her character.—BETHUNE, GEORGE WASHINGTON, 1848, *British Female Poets.*

Her poems are marked by thought, by fancy, and by great love of nature and art. She has written in many metres and almost always with a sense of distinction and of ease. Her sonnets are very finished—some of them, indeed, will compare with the most successful of those written by any, say the half-dozen or so who stand supreme in this department of poetry. Much of her work is autobiographical and bears the impress of her changeful life.—JAPP, ALEXANDER H., 1892, *The Poets and the Poetry of the Century, Joanna Baillie to Mathilde Blind,* ed. *Miles,* p. 255.

GENERAL

The whole intention of this is to express my deep regret at having, in a late letter, used such undue harshness in speaking of the lady best known to us as Fanny Kemble. I formed a hasty judgment of her character and talents, from reading a criticism on her "Journal in America," in which all the most repulsive points of her writings are brought out in full array, without producing one instance of good feeling or good taste, or of any strong indication of good principle, that so frequently occur in her Journal. All this penitence of mine has been produced merely by reading half of the first volume; yet I hope it is a repentance not to be repented of. But, lest you think me too amiable in my penitence, as I was too severe in my censure, I must add that I still think it a very injudicious publication. I am willing to allow the errors are all upon the surface, and accompanied with many compensating qualities. The Journal was well enough to write, but by no means to publish without much pruning and softening.—GRANT, ANNE, 1835, *Letters, June* 24; *Memoir and Correspondence,* ed. *Grant, vol.* III, *p.* 262.

Read Mrs. Butler's Diary ["Journal"]: it is much better than the reviews and papers will allow it to be: what is called vulgarity is useful and natural contempt for the exclusive and superfine.—SMITH, SYDNEY, 1835, *Letters to Sir Wilmot Horton.*

The great merit of the work ["A Year of Consolation"] consists in the admirable descriptions of scenery and nature which it contains. Her sense of beauty—of the beauty of color especially—is very keen; and in conveying impressions to her reader she uses language with uncommon skill. A single expression, or even word, dashed with an apparently careless hand upon the canvas, produces a fine effect.—HILLARD, GEORGE STILLMAN, 1853, *Six Months in Italy.*

Her various books, springing in every case but two or three straight from the real, from experience, personal and natural, humorous and eloquent, interesting as her character and life were interesting, have all her irrepressible spirit, or if the word be admissible, her spiritedness. The term is not a critical one, but the geniality (in the German sense) of her temperament makes everything she wrote what is called good reading. She wrote exactly as she talked, observing, asserting, complaining, confiding, contradicting, crying out and bounding off, always effectually communicating. Last not least, she uttered with her pen as well as with her lips the most agreeable, uncontemporary, self-respecting English, as idiomatic as possible and just as little common.—JAMES, HENRY, 1893, *Frances Anne Kemble, Temple Bar, vol.* 97, *p.* 517.

When we review Fanny Kemble's achievements, her acting, her reading, her writing, her personal influence, we must accord her genius. As to her writings, her Journal is sometimes saucy, as written by a young girl who had gone forth from home for the first time, but how graphic her pictures of places and people, how sparkling with wit and full of feeling, with a sad undertone, for an early disappointment had already shaded her young days; her Poems, written for the most part after joy and hope had vanished, so charged with anguish; her Year of Consolation, breathing the atmosphere of Italy, and imparting the refreshment and fitful happiness she enjoyed; her Residence on a Georgian Plantation, as pathetic and cruel as Uncle Tom's Cabin, and fateful to her, haunted by the sin of such possession; her Notes upon some of Shakespeare's plays and upon the stage, so discriminating, especially her remarks upon the Dramatic and Theatrical. But the most valuable of all her writings are the Records of her Girlhood and of her Later Life; for these, beginning with a reminiscence of her earliest years, are soon succeeded by what is much more reliable, a record, not reverting to, but running along with, her life from day to day, incidentally revealed by letters to her dearest friend, communicating events and outpouring her inmost thoughts and feelings. — LEE, HENRY, 1893, *Frances Anne Kemble, Atlantic Monthly, vol.* 71, *p.* 670.

Mrs. Kemble's vivid impress upon society and the stage during the century just gone out does not need recall. Englishwoman to the heart's core, her lot was cast in America at a period when its crudities overwhelmed her sensitive spirit with distaste. Her journal of "Life on a Georgian Plantation" dropped vitriol upon the then festering sore of the slave question in the South. But her two volumes of reminiscences of her own life are among the most readable and agreeable of their class. She won fame upon the stage in England and America, returning to it after an interval of married life. Her charm as a reader of Shakespeare's plays is recalled with enthusiasm by those fortunate enough to have heard her. When she died several years ago in London, that bounding vitality and originality of hers, cloaked and masked in the lendings of old age and feebleness, must have seemed to lookers-on but another part she had assumed, to be cast aside at the curtain's call with a mock at the apparent submission of her powers to decay.— HARRISON, CONSTANCE CARY, 1900, *Fanny Kemble, The Critic, vol.* 37, *p.* 520.

Charles Merivale
1808–1893

Born, in London, 8 March 1808. At Harrow, Jan. 1818 to Dec. 1824; at Haileybury College, 1825–26. Intention of entering H. E. I. C.'s service given up. Scholar, St. John's Coll., Camb., 1826; Browne Medalist, 1829; B. A., 1830; M. A., 1833; B. D., 1840; D. D., 1870. Fellow, St. John's Coll., 1833–48; Hon. Fellow, 1874. Ordained Deacon, 1833; Priest, 1834. Select Preacher, Camb., 1838. Whitehall Preacher, 1840. Rector of Lawford, 1848–70. Married Judith Mary Sophia Frere, 2 July 1850. Hulsean Lecturer, Camb., 1862. Chaplain to Speaker, 1863–69. Boyle Lecturer, 1864–65. Hon. D. C. L., Oxford, 13 June 1866. Dean of Ely, 1869. D. D., Durham, 1883. Hon. LL. D., Edinburgh, 1884. Died, at Ely, 27 Dec. 1893. *Works:* "The Church of England a Faithful Witness," 1839; "Sermons Preached in the Chapel Royal, Whitehall," 1841; "History of the Romans under the Empire" (7 vols.), 1850–62; "The Fall of the Roman Republic," 1853; "Open Fellowships," 1858; "The Conversion of the Roman Empire," 1864; "The Conversion of the Northern Nations," 1866 [1865]; "The Contrast between Pagan and Christian Society," 1872; "General History of Rome," 1875; "Four Lectures on Some Epochs of Early Church History," 1879; "Herman Merivale, C. B., [1884]. [Also several separate sermons]. He *translated:* Keats' "Hyperion" (into Latin), 1863; Homer's "Iliad," 1869; and *edited:* Sallust's "Catilina et Jugurtha," 1852; translation of Abeken's "Account of the Life and Letters of Cicero," 1854.—SHARP, R. FARQUHARSON, 1897, *A Dictionary of English Authors, p.* 194.

PERSONAL

Merivale is married! to a daughter of George Frere's, a lawyer in London. I have not heard of M. since this fatal event: but I stayed two days with him, in his Essex parsonage just before it. He is grown very fat—an Archdeacon, if ever there were one —and tries to screw himself down to village teaching, etc. He does all he can, I dare say: but what use is an historical Fellow of a college in a Country parish? It is all against the grain with him, and with his people.—FITZGERALD, EDWARD, 1850, *To F. Tennyson, Aug.* 15; *More Letters, p.* 25.

It is worthy of note that when Charles Merivale was but six years old he took delight in playing with his brother Herman, aged seven, a game which they called "Roman history." It was played in Queen's Square, the northern end of which they named "Italy," and the northeast corner "Rome." The trundling of hoops was a leading feature of the game, the career of each consul being typified by the course which the player's hoop chanced to take. "The straight line of public virtue was the narrow path of the kerbstone, and few magistrates kept it to the end." In his school days at Harrow the future historian of the Roman Empire committed to memory, for his own amusement, all but a few hundred lines of Lucan's "Pharsalia," when his sudden removal to Haileybury interrupted the task. That largeness of view and generosity of sentiment which characterize Merivale's writings may, it seems not improbably, be largely owing to the variety of scene and of personal intercourse which he enjoyed in his youth.—BICKNELL, PERCY FAVOR, 1900, *Dean Merivale, The Dial*, vol. 28, p. 150.

GENERAL

Mr. Merivale has told this part of the Roman story in a way that leaves little to be desired. His work is not a compilation, but an original history, the fruit of careful and prolonged investigation. If it does not possess the splendor of Gibbon, or the vigorous grasp of Arnold, it is yet admirable as a work of art, and worthy to hold a place between these two great masters, and to form with them the continuous story of Roman affairs.—HART, JOHN S., 1872, *A Manual of English Literature*, p. 567.

Is a scholarly, calm, and unprejudiced representation of the period of Roman history which lies between the establishment of the first Triumvirate and the last of the Cæsars. This work is written with great care, and exhibits marked opulence of scholarship and thorough comprehension of the subject. The author is a profound rather than brilliant historian, and is especially to be praised for his accuracy and fulness.—CATHCART, GEORGE R., 1874, *ed. The Literary Reader*, p. 222.

Its worst defect is that the author is not quite equal to his subject. Merivale was a respectable historian, but the successful treatment of the Romans under the Empire demanded a great one.—WALKER, HUGH, 1897, *The Age of Tennyson*, p. 127.

Francis Parkman
1823–1893

Born at Boston, Sept. 16, 1823; died at Jamaica Plain, near Boston, Nov. 8, 1893. An American historian. He graduated at Harvard in 1844, and began the study of law, but ultimately abandoned this study in order to devote himself to literature. He was professor of horticulture in the agricultural School of Harvard 1871–72. His historical works include "Conspiracy of Pontiac" (1851), "Pioneers of France in the New World" (1865), "Jesuits in North America" (1867), "Discovery of the Great West" (1869), "The Old Régime in Canada" (1874), "Count Frontenac and New France under Louis XIV." (1877), "Montcalm and Wolfe" (1884), "A Half Century of Conflict" (1892). He wrote also "The California and Oregon Trail" (1849), "Vassall Morton," a novel (1856), and "Historic Handbook of the Northern Tour" (1885).—SMITH, BENJAMIN E., *ed.* 1894–97, *The Century Cyclopedia of Names*, p. 782.

PERSONAL

There is no mistaking the energy that lights up his eye or the determination which is impressed upon his mouth, while the underlying delicacy of his nature is reflected in the general expression of his countenance. Mr. Parkman's experience has been such as to develop qualities which are rare among literary men, for he has united the untiring application of the closet student with a devotion to nature in her wildest aspects and amid her most savage votaries. A natural taste for adventure aided this phase of his development, but its inciting cause was a literary conscientiousness which made him resolve to brave dangers, hardships, and privations in the accomplishment of his purpose. —YOUNG, ALEXANDER, 1890, *The Book Buyer*, p. 421.

At the very outset Parkman was beset with conditions which threatened to leave him a hopeless invalid. The physicians assured him that he would die, but he told them that he should not die; they told him that mental work would be fatal, but with all respect to their diagnosis, he refused to follow their advice. While his brain was in such a condition that he could not use it at all, his eyes gave out, and for three years he was obliged to suspend all intellectual work and live the quietest of lives. But nothing could quench his intellectual vitality, and with every physical trial his spirit rose above the enfeebled body and controlled it to his will.—WARD, JULIUS H., 1893, *Francis Parkman and his Work, The Forum*, vol. 16, p. 421.

In personal appearance Mr. Parkman was distinctly noticeable. He was about five feet eleven in height, square-shouldered and firm-set. He had a strong, clear-cut face, always closely shaved, with a chin and jaw of marked vigor of outline. His forehead was rugged and broad; the whole carriage and expression was that of a

JAMES McCOSH

Engraving from a Photograph.

FRANCIS PARKMAN

Engraving by J. J. Cade.

modest but resolute man, capable, spite of whatever drawbacks and infirmities, of hard work and the persistent prosecution of difficult undertakings. His physical suffering and disability never seemed to abate his powers of research or mar the sweetness of his temper. He belonged, like Lowell, to a generation of Boston littérateurs who never forgot that they were gentlemen as well as literary men, and upheld under all circumstances the tradition of personal dignity which came down from an earlier generation. He was a rather shy-mannered man, yet in no sense a recluse; fond of boating, horseback riding, and not averse to genial society, as his six years' presidency of St. Botolph's Club in Boston bears witness. His increasing infirmities of late years more and more withdrew him from the social life of that city, but nobody who ever saw him in the serene simplicity of his own home will readily forget the charm of that gracious and patient presence.—WALKER, J. L., 1893, *Francis Parkman, The Nation, vol.* 57, *p.* 367.

Many of other circles in life, who met him then and there [St. Botolph's Club], for the first and only time, were surprised to find him in appearance, when approaching threescore, not an invalid bent with years and sufferings, delicate, with pallid face furrowed with wrinkles, but decidedly elastic in step, fresh and handsome in appearance, with an impressive aspect of well-preserved and even healthful maturity. His height could scarcely have been an inch under six feet; his whole frame was compacted and even sturdy looking; his hair, though tinged with gray, was abundant, and his head and full neck were firmly set upon broad and capable shoulders. He showed a high forehead, a face closely shaven, which exposed strong and resolute features, a chin and mouth bespeaking firmness and persistency, at the same time that his beaming eyes, of a soft brown color, were full of kindly and even tender expression. In his whole demeanor he showed dignity and an innate gentility happily combined. — SCHOULER, JAMES, 1894, *Francis Parkman, Harvard Graduates' Magazine, vol.* 2, *p.* 315.

Parkman's physical organism was strangely compounded of strength and weakness. It lacked that equilibrium of forces which secures health and makes consecutive labor possible. His eyes failed him in college, and ever afterwards refused their usual service; his brain was affected by some disorder that limited, and often entirely prevented intellectual activity; in short, he had to endure a great deal of pain and suffering nearly all his life. In the intimate question of the body's relation to mental action, it must be noted that his senses were not highly developed; he was more or less insensible to delicate impressions from sound, color, odors, taste, and touch. His physical organism thus imposed on him many limitations, although it gave him the advantages of exceptional energy, a great love of activity, and a very tenacious vitality and power of endurance. The mental make-up of the man corresponded with his physical development, his character being marked by a few simple and elementary powers rather than by delicacy, subtlety, and variety of sensibilities and emotions. His entire personality was moulded by the master quality of manliness. Impetuosity, courage, honesty, energy, reserve, a practical turn of mind, and an iron will were his chief forces. A lack of certain elements of spirituality constituted his chief defect.— FARNHAM, CHARLES HAIGHT, 1900, *A Life of Francis Parkman, p.* 8.

There is perhaps no American author whose character and career so test the skill of the biographer as do Francis Parkman's.—HIGGINSON, THOMAS WENTWORTH, 1900, *Life of Francis Parkman, The Nation, vol.* 71, *p.* 368.

I made Parkman's acquaintance in 1863 at the house of Mr. Charles Eliot Norton, in Cambridge, and my later intercourse with him was, if not frequent, continuous. I never went to Boston without spending some hours in his company, either at Milton or at his house in Chestnut street. There were few subjects of the day on which I did not become intimately acquainted with his views, and I can safely say that he impressed me, of all the men I have ever known, as the most of an American. His tastes were singularly American, as a traveler and an explorer. He cared little for the works of man, either here or in Europe, but a great deal for those of nature, and had certain fixed views concerning American politics and society. Our last interview was about a year before his death, and he then had nothing to alter or retract of the things I had heard from him when we first met. To sum up, he had, in the rarest degree, that virtue which the Romans called "constantia," and placed so high among the qualities of character.... Parkman often reminded me of Walter Scott. His mental make-up was very much the same; he had the same deep and abiding love of his native land, of "the brown heath and shaggy woods," in which his boyhood had been passed, and the same reverence for the America of his ancestors that Scott felt for the Borderland.—GODKIN, E. L., 1900, *Francis Parkman, The Nation, vol. 71, p. 441.*

That Parkman lived to see his life work completed, and the story of France and England in the New World told in full in nine portly volumes, the last of which appeared only a year or so before his death, at the age of seventy, was an end that could have been foreseen only by the eye of faith, when the demon of nervous disorder marked him out as its victim. And not only did he accomplish this major task, but four other books stand to his credit, and a long tale of newspaper and magazine articles. And he was a successful horticulturist besides, and for years an efficient member of the governing body of Harvard University. Such a record for a man who spent three quarters of his time, for forty years, in sitting on his mind, so to speak, to keep it quiet, is a record that shames those who possess sound minds in sound bodies, yet accomplish nothing beyond their routine tasks. With his bad knee, bad eyes and execrable nerves, Parkman was dowered with a fine mind, a retentive memory, and a force of will seldom matched in history.—GILDER, JOSEPH B., 1901, *An Heroic Man-of-Letters, The Critic, vol. 38, p. 416.*

GENERAL

There, sir, is not there a list of faults for you? Yes, more than all your critics in the reviews, I suppose, have found with you. But if I did not respect you and think you capable of better things than you have done yet ["Conspiracy of Pontiac"], I should not go to the trouble of pointing out all these faults. You seem to have chosen literature for your profession, and history for your special department thereof, and I do so love to see literary conscientiousness applied to explain the meaning of human history and convey its lesson to mankind, that I have taken the pains to point out particular things in which your book might have been made better. You have already received so much commendation that it is not necessary I should go into the pleasanter business of telling you how many things I like in the book.—PARKER, THEODORE, 1851, *Letter to Francis Parkman, Dec. 22; A Life of Francis Parkman by Farnham, p. 377.*

It is now nearly twenty-five years since "The Conspiracy of Pontiac" was first published; "The Pioneers of France in the New World" followed fifteen years later; in 1867 "The Jesuits in North America" appeared; in 1869 "The Discovery of the Great West;" and now in 1874 we have "Canada under the Old Régime," in furtherance of the author's design to present an unbroken series of historical narratives of France and England in North America. This design, though fully formed before the publication of "The Conspiracy of Pontiac," began to be realized in "The Pioneers of France in the New World," which should be read first in the series of narratives by such as still have before them the great pleasure of reading the entire work.... From first to last the author is more and more fortunate in fulfilling his purpose of giving a full view of the French dominion in North America. One moral is traced from beginning to end,—that spiritual and political despotism is so bad for men that no zeal, or self-devotion, or heroism can overcome its evil effects; one lesson enforces itself throughout,—that the state which persistently meddles with the religious, domestic, and commercial affairs of its people, dooms itself to extinction.... It is in Mr. Parkman's last volume that these facts, tacitly or explicitly presented in all his books on Canada, are most vividly stated; and we do not know where else one should find any part of the past more thoroughly restored in history. In all this fullness of striking and significant detail, one is never conscious of the literary attitude, and of the literary intent to amuse and impress; Mr. Parkman soberly and simply portrays the conditions of that strange colony of priests, lawyers, and soldiers, without artificial grouping, and reserves his own sense of the artistic charm which the reader will be sure to feel in the work.—HOWELLS, WILLIAM DEAN, 1874,

Mr. Parkman's Histories, Atlantic Monthly, vol. 34, pp. 602, 603.

The various histories of Francis Parkman—"The Conspiracy of Pontiac," "The Pioneers of France in the New World," "The Jesuits in North America," "The Discovery of the Great West"—exhibit a singular combination of the talents of the historian with those of the novelist. The materials he has laboriously gathered are disposed in their just relations by a sound understanding, while they are vivified by a realizing mind. The result is a series of narratives in which accuracy in the slightest details is found compatible with the most glowing exercise of historical imagination, and the use of a style singularly rapid, energetic, and picturesque. — WHIPPLE, EDWIN PERCY, 1876-86, *American Literature and Other Papers*, ed. *Whittier*, p. 93.

Whatever works upon Canada may have been printed, there have been none worthy of the subject until the appearance of the series by Francis Parkman. His volumes are the result of nearly forty years' labour, and have been written after careful examination of authorities and study of contemporary history. He has prepared himself by going over the immense field, and becoming familiar with the topography of all important cities, of towns and battle fields. Further, he has seen the native Indian at home, untouched by civilization, has learned his language, and studied his habits as a hunter and as a warrior. He has also spent much time in Canada, not only with men of letters versed in its history, but with the *habitants* and other rural people. It is seldom that a writer has come to his task with such thorough preparation, and it is still rarer to find a man so prepared with the taste and skill of a practiced writer, and able to make sober history as attractive as romance. . . Comment upon the separate volumes would lead us too far. It is enough to indicate their quality, and the importance of the subject for all readers of English. It may be added that the thoroughness with which Parkman has done his work renders it quite unlikely that any later historian will supplant him. His works have a solid foundation, and will endure, something which cannot be said with certainty of some of the most brilliant histories written in the United States.—UNDERWOOD, FRANCIS H., 1888,

Francis Parkman, Contemporary Review, vol. 53, pp. 644, 659.

Many pages of Mr. Parkman's histories are taken up with the quarrels of Canadian governors, the intrigues of Jesuit priests and petty Indian wars; but when the history of the French in North America is viewed in the broad way. . . we see how important these small matters are to the understanding of the large problem. However petty the events described, no dull pages are to be found in Mr. Parkman's books, nor pages that have no meaning with reference to the larger bearings of his subject. Each book prepares for those which succeed it, and helps to a full appreciation of the fin' l struggle. The minuteness of detail is possible because the seventeenth century was an age of memoirs and much writing of every kind; but we cannot regret this when it enables us to penetrate so completely into a form of life that has passed away forever, but which has left many traces of itself behind. . . . Mr. Parkman's literary style is well adapted to his subject, for no tame or merely fine style could have done justice to the people and the events he has had to describe. He is fond of adventure, by nature he is a lover of the woods and wild sport, an enthusiast by temperament, nervous and energetic in every fibre of his being, and thoroughly capable of appreciating such men as Champlain, La Salle, Frontenac, Pontiac, and the life which they represent. His style is that which is natural to such a man,—thrilling, dramatic, picturesque, and at times even fervid. It is a natural style, well fitting the man and his character, and it is admirably adapted to the kind of story he had to tell. . . . However graphic and picturesque is Mr. Parkman's style, he is thoroughly accurate throughout his books. . . . It may be said of Mr. Parkman, that he is an artist in history, concealing his art by simplicity and fidelity, but using it with great skill to entertain, impress, and convince his reader.—COOKE, GEORGE WILLIS, 1889, *Francis Parkman, New England Magazine*, N. S., vol. 1, pp. 259, 260, 261.

The volumes composed under the pressure of these calamities need no indulgence from the critic. It may also be said that they need no praise, so widely spread and so permanent has been their fame. The first of the series, though published only twenty-seven years ago, has already long passed its twentieth edition. Others are approaching it. The series has shown a continuous improvement, and especially in thoroughness and fulness of research. . . . It will be seen how wide is the range of interest covered by these volumes. They are not simply a history of a great attempt to create, under the forms of absolute monarchy, feudalism, and Catholicism, a centralized and military power. Nor are they simply a history of the effects of that power to overbalance and check the system of free, Protestant and English colonies, unorganized and discordant indeed, but strong with the strength of popular institutions, of love of freedom, and of habits of individual initiative. This alone would be sufficient to make the tale bright and commanding. But we have also the adventures of explorers and traders, the achievements of missionaries, the heroism of martyrs, the wild life of the Indian tribes, the scenery of the forest, the events of war, the brilliant picture of French aristocracy transferred, for purposes of war or government or devotion, to the wilds of America; and it cannot be said that the writer has proved unequal to the adequate treatment of a single one of these so varied elements of interest.—JAMESON, JOHN FRANKLIN, 1891, *The History of Historical Writing in America, pp.* 128, 131.

These seven works in nine volumes, to which must be added in their proper place, the two volumes of "Pontiac's Conspiracy," constitute Mr. Parkman's contribution to American history; and a magnificent contribution it has been. For originality of investigation, fidelity of statement, fairness of treatment of conflicting interests, and for chaste excellence of literary style, these volumes are unsurpassed, nay, unequalled, by those of any other writer of American annals. Some of the most vivid and beautiful passages of nature description anywhere to be found illuminate Mr. Parkman's pages. Mr. Parkman had a magnificent opportunity, but no advantage of subject or material could have availed but for the rich personal endowment he brought to his work: his poet's eye, his tireless industry, his scrupulous honesty, his absolute sincerity and sanity of mind and heart.—WALKER, J. L., 1893, *Francis Parkman, The Nation, vol.* 57, *p.* 367.

It is the crowning merit of his work that it will stand. Born and bred a Unitarian, and not in any sense accepting the religious faith which dominated French civilization, he treated the Jesuits and the old régime in Canada with such fairness that his statements, at times severe and revealing things that it was not pleasant to mention, compel the acceptance of what he wrote as the truth. A higher compliment to his fairness as a historian could not be paid. He was just and fair to all parties, and he had the courage to state the truth so that it must be accepted. This veracity and fidelity have been so distinct a feature of his historical writing that his volumes have been accepted without dispute as an authority for the period which they cover. Their statements have borne the brunt of attack, and though the narratives have been in some cases subjected to the fierce light of criticism for nearly half a century, when the series was completed in 1892, there was but little for the historian to revise in the text of the earlier work.—WARD, JULIUS H., 1893, *Francis Parkman and his Work, The Forum, vol.* 18, *p.* 425.

As the wand of Scott revealed unsuspected depths of human interest in Border castle and Highland glen, so it seems that North America was but awaiting the magician's touch that should invest its rivers and hillsides with memories of great days gone by. Parkman's sweep has been a wide one, and many are the spots that his wand has touched, from the cliffs of the Saguenay to the Texas coast, and from Acadia to the western slopes of the Rocky Mountains.—FISKE, JOHN, 1894, *Francis Parkman, Atlantic Monthly, vol.* 73, *p.* 666.

Mr. Parkman's peculiar merits as a historian we have already indicated,—thoroughness of preparation, a painstaking accuracy, justness in balancing authorities, scholarly tastes and comprehension, and the constant disposition to be truthful and impartial, to which were added skill and an artistic grace and dignity in composition. His style was crystal-clear and melodious as a mountain-brook, which flows obedient to easy impulse, setting off the charms of natural scenery by its own exquisite naturalness. The aroma of the woods and of woodland life is in all his books, among which, perhaps, "The Conspiracy of Pontiac" will remain the favorite. Here and constantly in dealing with the Indian, with the primeval American landscape and its primeval inhabitants, his touch is masterly and unapproachable; and so, too, in describing the sympathetic contact of France with a race which British interference doomed to destruction. French explorers, French missionaries and warriors, stand out lifelike from these interesting narratives, since he wrote to interest and not merely to instruct. Generalization and the broader historical lessons are to be found rather in the pages of his preface, as Mr. Parkman wrote, than in the narratives themselves, most of his later subjects being, in fact, extended ones for the compass of the book. . . . But in these preliminary, or rather final, deductions may be found pregnant passages of force and eloquence.—SCHOULER, JAMES, 1894, *Francis Parkman, Harvard Graduates' Magazine,* vol. 2, p. 313.

Francis Parkman is the first historian who has seriously undertaken the story of the great fight for America between the Saxon and the Gaul, and to him every Saxon, and indeed every Gaul, owes a great debt. Indeed the Frenchman owes perhaps the greater one, for it is amid the French camps and forts and villages that Mr. Parkman chiefly leads us. And if he has to close his long work with the downfall of New France, he leaves us with a respect for the gallantry of our vanquished foe that should satisfy the most exacting even of Frenchmen. Apart from the literary and historical merit of these volumes there is another reason that will help to secure them undisputed position as the classics of this period. Two of the types which figure conspicuously in these wars, the Indian and the backwoodsman, are upon the verge of extinction. To the next generation they will be but legends. Mr. Parkman came in time to study them, to live among them, and to know them as they were in his younger days, shifted westward it is true, but not materially altered from their ancestors who butchered one another on the banks of the Ohio a hundred years before.—BRADLEY, A. E., 1894, *Francis Parkman and his Work, Macmillan's Magazine,* vol. 69, p. 420.

Parkman had already published his "Pontiac," and had lapsed into a condition of body that made it seem as if his genius were to be permanently eclipsed by his infirmities, when a still more brilliant opening of a career was signalized by the appearance of "The Rise of the Dutch Republic." Ten years were to pass before Parkman could produce the first of that series of books with which his name is indissolubly connected, and by which he has made the story of the rise and decline of the French rule in North America entirely his own. By this time, Motley, in his "United Netherlands," had rounded the measure of his fame, and Prescott and Sparks had left us. . . . The rising historian was now in his forty-third year, but his mind had been drilled under such exactions and had been forced to such restraints as few men had ever encountered. Remembering this, we can better understand the remarkable repression of superfluities in the treatment of his themes. He was too genuine to be an imitator, but the eclectic instinct had become strongly developed by his being obliged to hold in his memory what had been read to him. . . . Parkman has been said to represent in the highest degree the picturesque element in the schools of history. It is an element which is better calculated than any other to engage attention and secure fame. It is also an element that naturally flourishes with the graceful aids of a brilliant style. But it is a characteristic that is apt to make us forget the consummate research which, in the case of Parkman, accompanied it. He is certainly less demonstrative of his material than is now the fashion; but while, in this suppression, he sometimes disappoints the students who would track his movements, there is no question that he has gained in popular regard.— WINSOR, JUSTIN, 1894, *Francis Parkman, Atlantic Monthly,* vol. 73, pp. 662, 663.

There, in Parkman's volumes, is told vividly, strongly, and truthfully, the history of the great struggle between France and England for the mastery of the North American continent, one of the most important events of modern times. This is not the place to give any critical estimate of Mr. Parkman's work. It is enough to say that it stands in the front rank. It is a great contribution to history, and a still greater gift to the literature of this country. All Americans certainly should read the volumes in which Parkman has told that wonderful story of hardship and adventure, of fighting and of statesmanship, which gave this great continent to the English race and the English speech.—LODGE,

HENRY CABOT, 1895, *Hero Tales from American History*, p. 170.

Much as has been said, and deservedly said, of Mr. Parkman's industry in research, even more may be said, and with no less justice, of his brilliancy of style. Perhaps "brilliant" is not the happiest epithet one could choose, for it may convey to some an implication that the style is unfavorable to strict veracity. . . . If Mr. Parkman had been a novelist he would be classed as a realist, for he has carried the realistic method into history as no other man of our time has done it. Picturesqueness is a striking feature of his style; his descriptions do not impress one as beautiful, though they are that, but as vivid, and, above all, as truthful. This is precisely what they are. The historian has made his sketch on the spot and from nature, precisely as a painter would do it, and with the same fidelity to detail that a painter would study. A similar method and effect are discernible in all his descriptions of character. Not only are the great personages in his pages—Pontiac and La Salle, Montcalm and Wolfe—drawn with wonderful clearness and actually made to live and move before us, but most of the men who receive more than a passing mention are sketched with equal fidelity and effectiveness.—VEDDER, HENRY C., 1895, *American Writers of To-Day*, p. 35, 36.

While Parkman can never take rank with the great narrative and critical historians like Froude and Motley, he has one advantage over all other historians of the century,—his work can never be done again.—PATTEE, FRED LEWIS, 1896, *A History of American Literature*, p. 322.

Though the "Conspiracy of Pontiac" is Parkman's first contribution to the history of the Indians and half-breeds of the West, the series proper, which deals with the wars of the English and French and red men, and treats of France and England in North America, begins with "The Pioneers of France in the New World." "Pontiac," which came first, may be read as a sequel to the collection. To the preparation of his histories, which are marked by an eloquent and graceful style and strict faithfulness to facts, Parkman devoted an industry, care and thoroughness which leave unquestioned the statements put forward. We know of the vastness of his task, and the difficulties under which he worked for many years. He neglected nothing. He visited all the scenes which his luminous pen so admirably describes, not once or twice, but many times. The archives of France, England, Russia, and Canada yielded their treasures to him. Every known letter, journal, report and despatch which bore, even in the remotest way, upon his subject were copied and sent to him, until at the end of his work he found himself possessed of no fewer than 3,400 manuscript pages, which he had bound in several large volumes.—STEWART, GEORGE, 1899, *The Work of Francis Parkman*, New England Magazine, N. S., vol. 20, p. 705.

Parkman's works prove to possess great philosophic interest. With full sympathy for both sides, with untiring industry in the accumulation of material, with good sense so judicial as to forbid him the vagaries of preconception, and with a literary sensitiveness which made his style—at first marked by the floridity fashionable in 1850—finally a model of sound prose, he set forth the struggles which decided the political futures of America. Moved to this task by an impulse rather romantic than scientific, to be sure, gifted with a singularly vivid imagination, too careful a scholar to risk undue generalisation, and throughout life so hampered by illness that he could very rarely permit himself prolonged mental effort, Parkman sometimes appears chiefly a writer of romantic narrative. As you grow familiar with his work, however, you feel it so true that you can infuse it with philosophy for yourself. It is hardly too much to say that his writings afford as sound a basis for historic philosophising as does great fiction for philosophising about human nature.—WENDELL, BARRETT, 1900, *A Literary History of America*, p. 274.

Of "Vassal Morton" it is sufficient to say that its chief importance to-day lies in its reflection of Parkman's character. In parts it is a thinly disguised self-portrait. Parkman mentions in several of his prefaces his disabilities in a purely objective way, just as he recorded the other conditions of his work. In the narratives there is, however, no odor of the sick-room, no feebleness; the artist's all-embracing memory and constructive imagination transport him to the woods, and the strain of the effort is betrayed only by a certain tenseness of style. But in "Vassal Morton" he let himself out, and under the mask of Morton's agony in his dungeon, his own sufferings are revealed. The novel is full of sharply drawn portraits, vivid descriptions of nature and life-like pictures of manners. It is a little melodramatic in plot, rather too brilliant in conversation, and unreal at critical junctures, but it is interesting, and hardly deserved oblivion. Parkman did not include it in his works, and is said not to have liked to hear it mentioned. One cannot help feeling that as he attained distinction he felt a certain shame at having betrayed his feelings even in that indirect fashion and recovered his consistency of stoicism by ignoring this single lapse.—BOURNE, EDWARD GAYLORD, 1901, *Essays in Historical Criticism*, p. 283.

Francis Parkman is hailed by general consent of critics and the reading public as our greatest historian, as one of our four or five supreme literary artists.—LAWTON, WILLIAM CRANSTON, 1902, *Introduction to the Study of American Literature*, p. 264.

Parkman, Bancroft, Prescott, Motley, Irving: these are the historians of past generations in this country whose writings may be said to remain potent still. Various have been their fortunes. Motley and Irving have been the most popular, but Bancroft won the earliest and highest fame. Parkman rose to his eminence slowly; indeed, he scarcely came into his own until old age had gathered round him, but chief among them all stands Parkman now. Bancroft seems already to have been threatened with being superseded, or at least with remaining no longer essential. Among all the historians who have written in English, where, in fact, save to Gibbon, shall we look for a superior to Parkman, in originality of research, accuracy of statement, and charm of style? Surely not to Macaulay, with his brilliant fragment steeped in partisanship; not to Hume, with his chronic indifference to facts; not to Green; not to Stubbs; nor to Freeman or Froude. . . . His books are unrivalled among histories as books of the finest romance. The events he chronicled happened on frontiers; often at mere trading posts; sometimes on the shores of lakes, where no one dwelt except savages; again in the dense forest, as at Great Meadows, where Washington won his spurs as a soldier, and where, in the death of Jumonville, was fired the shot which, as Parkman says, "set the world on fire." No volumes have been written by any historian which Americans ought to read with more absorbing interest, or with minds more completely charmed. It is not merely the theme which produces all this; not the savage martyrdom of Father Jogues, not the tales Bressani told, not the expedition of Pepperell, not Wolfe, wishing rather than to win the morrow's battle that he might have been the author of Gray's "Elegy"—that memorable scene on that momentous night before he scaled the heights of Quebec to win a renown that surely ought to last as well as Gray's. Parkman's style accounts measurably for the charm of all his books. While he has the restraint that befits the man of learning, he has elevation of style and picturesqueness. In the student and man of letters we see the accomplished artist. Something of graceful dignity always abides with him, and at times superb grandeur is there. Many pitfalls of style into which Gibbon fell and for which the world has held Gibbon blameful, Parkman escaped. If he be not our hero among men of letters, where shall we find a better name to fill that place?—HALSEY, FRANCIS WHITING, 1902, *Our Literary Deluge and Some of its Deep Waters*, pp. 172, 174.

Parkman's style was chastened with practice until it became in its blending of charm and power and flexibility almost unrivalled among the American authors of his epoch.—TRENT, WILLIAM P., 1903, *A History of American Literature*, p. 555.

Parkman's style of writing changed with the ripening of the man. From the outset his observation was fresh and vivid. But otherwise his early style, influenced perhaps by the prevailing standards of the time, was often florid, the images formal, and the illustrations commonplace. His power of more spontaneous expression developed slowly, in part, it may be, because of his illness. He was seldom able to read more than five minutes without rest, or to listen to reading more than twenty; and the limitations of safety which his nervous condition placed upon his efforts at composition were not less cramping. Still, there is no sign of physical weakness in his manner of writing, not even the tenseness which intermittent dictation might be expected to produce.

His style seems rather to reflect the increasing moral strength with which he adhered to the purpose of his youth. Losing nothing of its vividness, it becomes fluent and direct, an adequate medium for the expression of his strong narrative impulse.—HULL, CHARLES H., 1904, *Chambers's Cyclopædia of English Literature*.

Phillips Brooks
1835-1893

1835, December 15,—Phillips Brooks was born at 56 High St., Boston. 1842-46,—Attended Adams School, Boston. 1846-51,—Attended Boston Latin School. 1851,—Entered Harvard College. 1855,—Graduated at Harvard College. 1855-56,—Taught at Boston Latin School. 1856,—Entered Alexandria (Va.) Theological Seminary. 1859, —Graduated at Alexandria. July 1,—Ordained deacon. Became rector of the Church of the Advent, Philadelphia. 1860, May 27,—Ordained priest. 1862,—Became rector of the Church of the Holy Trinity, Philadelphia. 1863, November 26,—Delivered "The Mercies of Reoccupation: A Thanksgiving Sermon," Holy Trinity Church, Philadelphia. 1865, April 23,—Delivered "The Life and Death of Abraham Lincoln:" Sermon at Holy Trinity Church, Philadelphia. August,—First journey abroad. 1869, November 7,—Became rector of Trinity Church, Boston. 1870, June-September,—Visited the Tyrol and Switzerland. Elected overseer of Harvard College. 1872, June-September,—Visited Norway, Sweden, Finland, Russia, and Germany. November 10,—Old Trinity Church, Boston, destroyed by fire. 1873, Present Trinity Church, Boston, begun. 1874, —Spent the summer in Europe. 1876,—Re-elected overseer of Harvard College. 1877, February 11,—Historical sermon, dedication of Trinity Church, Boston. Delivered and published "Lectures on Preaching." Received Degree of S. T. D., Harvard College. Summer in Europe. 1878,—Published "Sermons." 1879,—Delivered and Published "The Influence of Jesus" (Bohlen Lectures). 1880,—Spent the summer in Great Britain and France. 1882,—Invited to Plummer Professorship, Harvard College. Published "The Candle of the Lord, and Other Sermons." June,—Set out on journey to England, France, Italy, Germany, Austria, India, and Spain. 1883,—Elected to third term as overseer of Harvard College. Published "Sermons preached in English Churches." 1885, April 23,—Delivered Address at celebration of two hundred and fiftieth anniversary of the foundation of the Public Latin School, Boston. May-September,—Travelled in England, Germany, Italy, and France. 1886,—Elected assistant bishop of Pennsylvania. Declined. May-June,—Made a journey to California, Yosemite, and Vancouver's Island. Became one of the Board of University Preachers, Harvard College, holding the post till 1891. November,—Delivered the sermon at the two hundred and fiftieth anniversary of the foundation of Harvard College. December 15,—Delivered Address at two hundredth commemoration of the foundation of King's Chapel, Boston. 1887,—Published "Twenty Sermons" (Fourth Series). Delivered and published "Tolerance." Spent the summer in England, and attended the Queen's Jubilee. 1889, June-September,—Made a journey to Japan. 1890,—Delivered Noonday Lenten lectures to business men in Trinity Church, New York. Spent the summer in Switzerland and England. Published "The Light of the World, and Other Sermons." 1891, April 30,—Elected bishop of Massachusetts. October 14,—Consecrated bishop of Massachusetts. 1892,—Delivered Noonday Lenten lecture to business men in St. Paul's Church, Boston. June-September,—Made a journey to England, France, Tyrol, and Switzerland. December 21,—Delivered address at annual celebration of the New England Society, Brooklyn, N. Y. 1893, January 23,—Phillips Brooks died. "Sermons" (Sixth Series), published. 1894,—"Letters of Travel," published. 1895,—"Sermons for the Principal Festivals and Fasts of the Church Year," (Seventh Series), published. 1896,—"New Starts in Life, and Other Sermons" (Eighth Series), published. 1899,—Phillips Brooks House, Harvard College completed.—HOWE, M. A. DEWOLFE, 1899, *Phillips Brooks, Chronology*.

PERSONAL

I have just heard the most remarkable sermon I ever heard in my life—I use the word in no American sense—from Mr. Phillips Brooks, an Episcopal clergyman here: equal to the best of Frederick Robertson's sermons, with a vigour and force of thought which he has not always. I have never heard preaching like it, and you know how slow I am to praise preachers. So much thought and life combined—such a reach of mind, and such a depth of insight and soul. I was electrified. I could have got up and shouted. I shook hands with the preacher afterwards, who asked me to preach in the afternoon for him; but I would not do this, remembering your caution.— TULLOCH, JOHN, 1874, *Letter to his Wife, April 26; A Memoir*, ed. *Mrs. Oliphant, p.* 292.

Phillips Brooks as we behold him moving amongst us to-day, is a representative man in many of the elements that constitute humanity. He is physically well endowed. Tall, and well proportioned, head and shoulders above other men, chest broad and deep, face full-orbed, beaming with health and sympathetic kindness, forehead wide, and deep, large, dark eyes, flashing gleams of intelligence and good nature. The contour of the face is very mobile, since its muscles of expression are flexible and spontaneously adapt the face to express the emotion that is welling up from the heart. His step is firm, carriage of body erect, head thrown well backward denoting vitality. Over six feet in height, his entire bodily make-up constitutes him a physical king of men. The qualities of mind and heart are not less marked, and are even more potential in rendering him successful as a preacher.... On listening for the first time to the enunciation of his discourses, no one would fail to be struck with the wonderful rapidity with which he delivers his words, and would probably be at a loss to discover the cause. Brooks possesses many of the natural gifts of a great orator. His temperament is a harmonious blending of the vital, mental, and motive systems. Such a combination is highly oratorical, possessing many excellent qualities. Some have complained that it was hard to follow Dr. Brooks' discourse because he spoke so rapidly, not knowing that such rapidity was the effect mainly of his excessive vitality.—HYDE, THOMAS ALEXANDER, 1890, *The Rev. Phillips Brooks, The Arena*, vol. 1, pp. 721, 724.

What amount of preparation he may have given to his discourses I do not know. But there was no sign of art about them, no touch of self-consciousness. He spoke to his audience as a man might speak to his friend, pouring forth with swift, yet quiet and seldom impassioned earnestness the thoughts and feelings of a singularly pure and lofty spirit. The listeners never thought of style or manner, but only of the substance of the thoughts. They were entranced and carried out of themselves by the strength and sweetness and beauty of the aspects of religious truth and its helpfulness to weak human nature which he presented. Dr. Brooks was the best because the most edifying of preachers. . . . There was a wealth of keen observation, fine reflection, and insight both subtle and imaginative, all touched with a warmth and tenderness which seemed to transfuse and irradiate the thought itself. In this blending of perfect simplicity of treatment with singular fertility and elevation of thought, no other among the famous preachers of the generation that is now vanishing approached him.—BRYCE, JAMES, 1893, *The Westminster Gazette, Feb.* 6.

Great bishop, greater preacher, greatest man,
Thy manhood far out-towered all church, all
   creed,
And made thee servant of all human need.
Beyond one thought of blessing or of ban,
Save of thy Master, whose great lesson ran,
"The great are they who serve." So now, indeed,
All churches are one church in loving heed
Of thy great life wrought on thy Master's plan!
As we stand in the shadow of thy death,
How petty all the poor distinctions seem,
That would fence off the human and divine!
Large was the utterance of thy living breath;
Large as God's love thy human hope and dream
And now humanity's hushed love is thine!
—SAVAGE, MINOT JUDSON, 1893, *Phillips Brooks.*

The intellect of Phillips Brooks was as striking as the man himself. There was in it a platonic subtlety, sweep, and penetration, a native capacity for the highest speculations,—a capacity that did not always become apparent, because he passed at once, like a flash of lightning to the substance of things, and because he believed that the forms of the understanding, into which the highest in man throws its findings, are at best only inadequate symbols. He could not endure the men who say that nothing can be known, nor could he abide those who say that everything can be known.... There was in his mind a Hindu swiftness, mobility, penetrativeness, and mysticism.... Had he chosen, he could have been one of the subtlest metaphysicians, or one of the most successful analysts of the human heart, throwing upon his screen the disentangled and accurately classified contents of the soul. But he chose, as indispensable for his calling, to let the artist in him prevail, to do all his thinking through the forms of the imagination, and to give truth a body corresponding, as far as possible, to its own ineffable beauty. Thus it happens that the sermons with the noblest form, with the greatest completeness, and the finest artistic quality have come from his mind. — GORDON, GEORGE A., 1893, *Phillips Brooks, a Memorial Sermon*.

I cannot follow into detail that power of personal contact and assistance to which allusion has been made incidentally. It is written in the consciousness of thousands of men and women who delight to think of Phillips Brooks as their friend, just as the summer's sunbeams lie in the ruddy fruit of harvest. It was a power which shared in the growth and development of his life, it was one which he loved to exercise, and yet which with the most delicate taste he carefully guarded from the danger of undue familiarity and of false expression of friendship. It came from and ever fastened itself more deeply in the conviction of the divine life that belonged to all men.—BROOKS, ARTHUR, 1893, *Phillips Brooks*, p. 35.

I cannot but think that if he had not accepted the call to the Bishopric of Massachusetts he might have lived for many a long and happy year. Assuredly it was not ambition which led him to desire such empty shadows as precedence and a title. I knew him too well to suppose that he would care a broken straw for such gilt fragments of potsherd, such dust in the midnight, as the worldly adjuncts of an inch-high distinction. His heart was too large for so small an ambition. Had he chosen to answer the world according to its idols, to trim his sails to the veering breezes of ecclesiastical opinion, to suppress or tamper with his cherished convictions, and, as Tennyson says, "to creep and crawl in the hedgebottoms," he, with his rich gifts, might easily have been a Bishop thirty years ago. In ability and every commanding quality he towered head and shoulders above the whole body of American ecclesiastics, only one or two of whom are known outside their own parishes or dioceses. Probably no severer lot could have befallen him than to be made Bishop. For he was a man who had lived a very happy life, and although he was in no sense of the word indolent, he managed to escape the entanglements of work which so disastrously crowd the lives of too many of us, not only with harassing labors, but also with endless worry, fussy littlenesses and an infinite deal of nothing. Wisely and rightly he left a margin to his life and did not crowd its pages to the very edge. He enjoyed his quiet smoke and hour of social geniality in the evenings. . . . I have known many men—even not a few clergymen—of higher genius, of far wider learning, of far more brilliant gifts. But I never met any man, or any ecclesiastic, half so natural, so manly, so large-hearted, so intensely Catholic in the only real sense, so loyally true in his friendships, so absolutely unselfish, so modest, so unartificial, so self-forgetful. He is gone and I for one never hope to look upon his like again.—FARRAR, FREDERIC WILLIAM, 1893, *Phillips Brooks, Review of Reviews*, vol. 7, pp. 173, 177.

He was a preacher easily and first; nor, to my mind, since Frederick Robertson died thirty-six years ago in Brighton, England, has there been his equal as a preacher across the water. Genius of insight, wonderful power of expression, soul-compelling love—all these elements of power were richly his.—RAINSFORD, WILLIAM STEPHEN, 1893, *Bishop Brooks, The Critic*, vol. 22, p. 69.

I have never known any great man—and I think I never knew a greater than he in certain lines of greatness—who had in him, in the first place, the simplicity of a child, and, in the next place, the humility of a saint, and, in the third place, absolute impersonality, in spite of the fact that it was the personal element in him which gave him his marvellous influence. He was supremely above all petty and little things, utterly unmoved by the adulation that was poured out upon him, and lived a life upon the highest possible level of true spirituality. His own unusual purity of nature gave him a thoroughly optimistic view of humanity, which sometimes he seemed to push almost to a denial of the need of grace; and I think he had so little consciousness of sin himself that he left it out too much in dealing with the provisions which are made for its recovery. The atmosphere in which he lived made a sort of glamour through which he looked at other men; and, as one compares him with the great American preachers, one is struck with the entire absence of any factitious elements of influence; indeed, I think the power of his preaching was shown in nothing so much as in the fact that it overcame certain real deficiencies—I mean his great rapidity of speech and consequent indistinctness of utterance.—DOANE, WILLIAM CROSWELL, 1893, *Bishop Brooks, The Critic*, vol. 22, p. 69.

One who, while wonderfully beautiful and grand in his own sublime and solitary self in communion with things above, yet was the embodiment of human sympathy, who lived not only for the life of mankind, but in and by that life also, drawing his own ever-fresh life from it, reflecting its joys and sorrows in his own clear depths, and bringing each part of it closer to every other by his many-sidedness and breadth which touched and watered all.—BROOKS, JOHN COTTON, 1894, ed. *Essays and Addresses Religious, Literary and Social, Preface.*

In conversation he was one of the merriest of entertainers. Sometimes I used to think him almost too ready to let the occasion float away in jest, while I, like so many others, whould have chosen to sound with him some theme of height or depth; but of course one can readily understand how weary his nerve might have become of the seriousness of life, and how much it needed "the light touch."—PHELPS, ELIZABETH STUART, 1896, *Chapters from a Life*, p. 186.

As an extemporaneous speaker he was simply matchless. I heard him twice during the war, at public meetings where he was unexpectedly called upon. The effect was such as I have never seen before in any assembly of men. . . . When Brooks came to Philadelphia he had been long away from the conventional, either in the Divinity School or in his little up-town church. At first he remonstrated with our efforts to make him see the need for much that he found irksome and destructive of time. He soon yielded, and became in the end careful as to ordinary social rules and duties. He was subject to rare moods of utter silence. I have seen him sit through a dinner party and hardly utter a word; usually he was an easy and animated guest. He did not much affect the clerical style or ways, and on our long canoe journeys the guides were three weeks before they found out that he was a clergyman. . . . I have known a number of the men we call great,—poets, statesmen, soldiers,—but Phillips was the only one I ever knew who seemed to me entirely great. I have seen him in many of the varied relations of life, and always he left with me a sense of the competent largeness of his nature.—MITCHELL, S. WEIR, 1900, *An Appreciation of Phillips Brooks, Life and Letters of Phillips Brooks*, ed Allen, vol. I, pt. II, pp. 634, 635.

Those who enjoyed his hospitality know how rich and abounding it was, what power of welcome he could offer. His letters already given show how he was constantly beseeching his friends for visits, or the short notes he was constantly writing: "Come, won't you? The years are not so many as they were." . . . It was very impressive, impressive beyond measure, to be with him on Sunday and watch him as he prepared himself to preach at the afternoon service. There was no appearance of nervous anxiety, no exigency in the manner, but a calmness and serenity that went deeper than words can describe, his face aglow with spiritual beauty. He would answer questions with a gentle refinement and sweetness of tone, but beneath the appearance there was the intense concentration of the whole man upon some theme he was inwardly revolving, to whose power he seemed to be submitting himself.—ALLEN, ALEXANDER V. G., 1901, *Life and Letters of Phillips Brooks*, vol. III, p. 348.

The affection of Phillips Brooks for his university was continuous and unbounded, and remains a happy reminiscence for those who witnessed his devotion. . . . His conduct of morning prayers can never be forgotten by those who had the privilege of worshiping with him. He was not infrequently in the pulpit before any of the congregation had arrived, as though he could hardly wait to begin the service. As a rule the first words of his prayer were those of some short collect in the prayer-book, uttered with great rapidity and as though to touch the note of his desire; but after a few sentences his mind, as it were, took wings, and soared away into the region of free prayer, with a fulness, liberty and delight, of amazing richness and power. I have always believed that these unstudied petitions, uttered thus for the sake of young men in the confidential intimacy of college life, disclosed more than any other expression of his mind the interior greatness, sanity, range and elevation of his spiritual life.—PEABODY, FRANCIS G., 1903, *Influence at Harvard, Phillips Brooks as His Friends Knew Him, pp. 61, 62.*

GENERAL

Of the style of Mr. Brooks, as seen in these Sermons and Lectures, one can scarcely say too much in praise. His command of the English language is remarkable. Over it his sway is regal. His diction, largely made up of Anglo-Saxon words, is copious and varied, and admirably adapted to the pulpit. He seems never at a loss for the right words with which to set forth a thought, and sometimes does not hesitate to make use of such obsolete and unauthorized words as monotonize, personalness, purposeful, richen, and the like, if he thinks they will best serve his purpose. . . . Especially in the use of appropriate illustrations we regard Mr. Brooks as well-nigh unsurpassed. Having an affluent imagination, exquisite taste, and a vivid perception of the manifold relations and correspondences of religious truth to man and to nature, he draws from them with remarkable skill, fresh, varied, and apt illustrations with which to make clear, adorn, and enforce Divine truth. But though he has such regal command of appropriate illustrations, he rarely uses them when not needed. He does not overload his sermons with them.—FISK, FRANKLIN W., 1880, *Phillips Brooks as a Preacher, both in Theory and in Practice, The New Englander, vol. 39, p. 333.*

His illustrations are sometimes over bold; occasionally newly coined words and multiplied adjectives suggest haste; for the preacher is after deeper things than style; he has no time for polish and erasures. Sometimes the preacher is caught and held in the interest of his own thought and imagination; he gives his fancy and sagacity too full play; he talks about the truth too elaborately; he overloads with words and imagery; he does not seem to move as directly as he might; but the work is interesting; the attention is more than held, it is enslaved. Some shrewd remark, some flash of quiet humor, a delightful or suggestive figure snatched from the hillsides of New England, often betokens his heritage; and then an aphorism, a fresh statement of old truth or a side remark throws a flash of light up some path of thought which we fain would follow.—LAWRENCE, WILLIAM, 1891, *Phillips Brooks, Andover Review, vol. 19, p. 190.*

It is very noticeable in him that, whether writing or speaking, he never seems satisfied till the note struck is the *octave*-note—that view of the matter in hand which is the *highest* his thought and life have yielded him—and every subject he handles he seeks to lead up and attach to the loftiest he knows: he is never willing to rest till he has reached that theme. A loyal knight, ever alert to duty. Dr. Lyman Abbott has recently remarked of him that he always *preaches:* any of his after-dinner speeches he might use the next Sunday in his pulpit. Not only is he complex, and instead of coming down to his readers, invites them to come up to him: he is never afraid of giving full measure, heaped up and running over.—DUNBAR, NEWELL, 1891, *Phillips Brooks, Bishop of Massachusetts, p. 68.*

The subjects of his sermons are greatly diversified, and their treatment is so rich and varied that the thought and illustrations captivate the listener or reader, apart from the purpose of the preacher, and yet the central purpose is always the same. He grasps each one's points of contact with life and brings him to a personal conception of what it is to be a disciple of Christ. I have never heard him preach a sermon and I have never read a discourse of his where this highest and supreme claim was sacrificed to moral and spiritual entertainment. The very structure of his sermons bears witness to his vitalizing process. Master as he is of literary form and concise expression and the graces of style, he is never able to stop long enough to dally with his gifts. They are consecrated to a purpose, and his aim is so high and earnest that they are mainly used to help him to fulfill the great aim of his preaching. The only volume of his discourses in which this literary gift is allowed any freedom is that which contains his sermons preached in English churches, and even here it finds somewhat scant expression. The same characteristic is found in Robertson's sermons and in Cardinal Newman's.—WARD, JULIUS H., 1892, *Bishop Brooks, Andover Review, vol. 17. p. 447.*

In his sermons there is almost a total lack of discursiveness. At the beginning of each there may be a few words of introduction, simply to make a connection between the mind of the hearer and the special theme to be considered; but after this, the special theme is never for a moment lost from the mind. You may open one of his volumes anywhere, and a very few words will make clear what the subject is that the sermon before you presents. Even the sermons of Robertson, which Phillips Brooks rightly exalted as at least among the best of our modern world, have often a discursiveness, a temporary absorption in details, of which the sermons of Phillips Brooks show little trace. There are not many popular preachers from whose sermons the hearer would carry away fewer special impressions. He did not deal in epigrams; thus there were few separate sayings to be recalled. He was a perfect master of words, but never their servant. Each word filled its place as perfectly as if it stood in some finished poem, but no one was allowed to claim undue preëminence. — EVERETT, CHARLES CARROLL, 1893, *Phillips Brooks, Harvard Graduates' Magazine*, vol. 1, p. 340.

Vast and unparalleled in volume was the language of his discourse. Sometimes it resembled a coast tide washing over the land to make islets of meadows and lakes of creeks. The feeling swelled out of proportion beyond the thought, and when it subsided left, like the ark of Ararat, but the remnant of a few clear-cut and indispensable though precious periods on the printed page. In the perusal he is less impressive than Channing, while Taylor in letters has no mark. — BARTOL, CYRUS AUGUSTUS, 1893, *The Boston Pulpit, New World*, vol. 2, p. 480.

No one is less open than he to the charge of formalism, yet no one has made a more earnest plea for the due observance of Lent than that which is chosen for the Ash-Wednesday Reading in this book. It is no narrow asceticism to which he invites us, but a "more abundant life," not of the flesh but of the spirit, to be lived in loving dependence upon the Saviour, in loving commemoration of the suffering and death which He endured in order that all who believe in Him might have life.—JAY, W. M. L., 1897, ed. *The More Abundant Life, Preface*, p. iii.

There is reason to believe that Phillips Brooks might have been a great poet, if he had not preferred to be a great preacher. We all know and love the Bethlehem hymn; but there were other poems. But more important than the writing of poetry is the poetical insight. The poet is the man who sees the soul of things; the secrets of being. The philosopher is supposed to do the same thing; and the psychologist is supposed to do this thing as applied to man. Phillips Brooks had the power of seeing the essence of things. And this power was joined to the element of poetical expression. What fine, carefully adjusted metaphors! What suggestion of beauty! What glimpses of the divine! What happy choice of phrase and word!—THWING, CHARLES F., 1899, *The Inner Life of Phillips Brooks, The Chautauquan*, vol. 30, p. 302.

He was the ideal minister of the American gospel, for he gathered into himself the best elements of American manhood, he had the deepest faith in American institutions, he had the energy, the large vision, the persistent hope of the young nation dealing with its problems of government, education, and character. And he was peculiarly the preacher of a gospel. Many of the American clergy have written books on various subjects, been influential in the affairs of state, been professors and heads of colleges, and through these various channels have affected American life, but the power of Phillips Brooks was the power of he preacher, the man who chose to reach the people through the spoken word; and throwing his whole personality into his thought and its expression, he gave them the truth which he had to bring. Instead of writing books on literary subjects, he wrote sermons which in themselves are literature.— ADDISON, DANIEL DULANY, 1900, *The Clergy in American Life and Letters*, p. 341.

The last commanding spiritual teacher of New England chanced to be of another faith, but what made Phillips Brooks such a power in Boston was the same kind of personality which half a century before him had generally distinguished the Unitarian clergy. Whoever knew the great bishop personally can hardly have failed to observe the trait which was at once his strongest and his weakest: his instinctive nature was so good that he never quite realised the badness and the uncleanness which beset the lives of common men with temptation. In him, just as in the fathers of Unitarianism, the national inexperience of America permitted almost unrestrained the development of a moral purity which to those who possess it makes the grim philosophy of damnation seem an ill-conceived nursery tale.—WENDELL, BARRETT, 1900, *A Literary History of America*, p. 287.

The "Lectures on Preaching" possess a further literary charm because they connect the pulpit with life, and with the highest, richest manifestations of life. The book took its place as an important contribution to literature, apart from its value as a treatise on homiletics. It abounds with literary allusions and illustrations new and effective, showing at once the scholar and the man widely read in the world's best books. The work that he had done in the Virginia seminary, as seen in the note-books that he had kept, is constantly reappearing. The movement is rapid, there is no lingering by the way; every page is full of condensed purpose. There is nothing artificial, no posing for effect; but plainness and great directness of speech, perfect naturalness and simplicity. The book captivates the reader, simply for this reason alone,—the transparency of the soul of its writer, between whom and the reader there intervenes no barrier. And further it is redolent with happiness and hope for the world, as if at last the new day had dawned for humanity, and mankind might enter on its heritage, long promised and seen from afar, but now ready to be ushered in. It set the standard high, yet it did not discourage; it rather stimulated, begetting an enthusiasm which overrode all obstacles.—ALLEN, ALEXANDER V. G., 1901, *Life and Letters of Phillips Brooks*, vol. II, p. 303.

No one can deny Phillips Brooks's greatness in almost every field of human endeavour which his life permitted him to enter upon; but we do not remember him, . . . as a great writer, as a deep thinker, as a man of varied and profound learning, as an investigator, or a philosopher, though he was in some measure all of these things; nor do we even think of him so much as a preacher—though perhaps that is hardly a fair statement—but we do remember him above all as a *Personality!*—BRADY, CYRUS TOWNSEND, 1901, *Phillips Brooks, The Book Buyer*, vol. 22, p. 121.

While we may believe his genius capable of many things which it left unattempted, we must see that its special province was to take great truths out of the rubbish heap of dead phrases, revitalize and freshly illustrate them, and cause them mightily to prevail over the hearts and lives of men. There was power for men to live by, if it could only get at them, in the old theology that in this period of the New Reformation was everywhere finding restatement and elucidation. What had grown obscure and was in danger of becoming obsolete, what had been familiar in words and was in danger of passing into the realm of cant, what was really new in its form and was in peril of becoming a heresy by standing alone, Phillips Brooks seized with a certain swift and fine apprehension and redeemed for the service of life. That was his peculiar province in which he stood peerless, the application of truth to common living, bringing Jesus Christ, with all the glow of divine light upon His face, down among everyday men and things.—RICHARDS, C. A. L., 1901, *The Life of Phillips Brooks, The Dial*, vol. 30, p. 135.

Phillips Brooks was pre-eminently a sane man—rational, calm, self-controlled, with wise practical judgment, which, so far as we know, was never obscured by his enthusiasms. His emotional and visionary temperament he appears to have inherited from his mother; his practical, worldly-wise judgment from his father. The first made him a great preacher, the second made him a wise bishop; the combination made him a teacher able both to inspire with divine ideals and to guide in life with practical counsels. . . . We regard Phillips Brooks as probably the greatest preacher of the century. He was not comparable as an orator to Henry Ward Beecher, nor as a reformer to John B. Gough, nor as a theologian to Horace Bushnell or Elisha Mulford; but as a preacher he was without a peer. If by preacher we mean the herald and minister of a divine life, if by prophet we mean one who speaks for Another, if by apostle we mean one who is sent forth by Another to bear witness to his presence, Phillips Brooks was pre-eminently a preacher, a prophet, an apostle.—ABBOTT, LYMAN, 1901, *The Making of a Great Preacher, The Outlook*, vol. 67, pp. 718, 720.

It should be said that there is much more theological clearness in his addresses to his theological club, the Clericus, and in his letters and journals, than in his sermons. This was because his ideal sermon excluded the concrete and everything that could not be expressed in terms of poetry and the imagination. Even civil service reform he must treat as imaged forth in Hebrew politics, and so obscure it to a degree that made the sermon far less practically effective than it might otherwise have been. The conservatism of his theological temper brings out his liberality into strong relief. This was a grief to his friends of the more churchly kind; but Phillips Brooks was not churchly. If there was one thing that he cordially disliked, in any form, it was clericalism. The clericals will be sorely displeased with many of his references, in the freedom of his correspondence, to their works and ways. They will be shocked at the specific levity with which he treats his episcopal clothes, and the ecclesiastical minutiæ to which he is expected to conform. — CHADWICK, JOHN WHITE, 1901, *Phillips Brooks, The Nation, vol. 72, p. 160.*

The persuasive, benignant influence of Phillips Brooks, not limited to any religious, sectional, or even national line, was in a degree oratorical. His published essays, both purely religious and relatively secular, are exquisitely literary, often highly poetic in quality. They are full of vitality and force, even for those men who cannot supply from memory the monumental presence, the impetuous rushing tones, of the great preacher. In his optimism, his humanism, his patriotic and philanthropic zeal, Bishop Brooks was a true successor of Channing. Both have relatively humble places in our literature, yet their influence is felt constantly in the air we breathe. That is merely saying that literature, or any fine art, is but a partial expression of life.— LAWTON, WILLIAM CRANSTON, 1902, *Introduction to the Study of American Literature, p. 274.*

He was, undoubtedly, the greatest American preacher of his generation. Beecher and Moody may have aroused more immediate popular interest; but the great literature that has grown up about Phillips Brooks, the unprecedented circulation of his printed sermons, as well as the immediate response of the thronging congregations that hung upon his words, give ample testimony to his wide-spread influence and fame. The secret of his power was in his vital sympathy, his large humanity. . . . I do not think that it can be truly said that Phillips Brooks added anything of permanent value to the substance of systematic divinity.—ELIOT, SAMUEL A., 1903, *Pioneers of Religious Liberty in America, p. 369, 373.*

Phillips Brooks, like most men of genius, was essentially a lonely man. Without the intimacy of the marriage relation, habitually reticent about his own thoughts and feelings, a Puritan by inheritance and by inclination, he needed some form of self-expression and found it, especially in his younger years, in poetry. The mood, the hour of vision, the stress of feeling, called for some outlet and found it in the measured words that sung themselves in his mind. He was a stronger and a happier man, more cheerful and more helpful, because he could give utterance in forms of beauty to the burning thought. With few exceptions, all the verse which has been given to the public falls under one or the other of these conditions. It was written as an exercise in words, or it was the natural expression and relief of intense feeling or vivid impression. This personal factor explains his success as a hymn writer. . . . It is because Phillips Brooks was so great a man, powerful in intellect, large in view and intense in feeling, that the public has taken for its own a portion of his work in verse. He might have given us still more which the world would have remembered gratefully, but it would have been at the expense of his true message to the world, which he delivered from the pulpit, and this would have been too large a price to pay. As they now are, even the poems which his biographer has shared with us show that they were thrown off at a white heat of feeling and never received that careful revision which often makes the difference between failure and success.— RANKIN, ISAAC OGDEN, 1903, *As a Poet, Phillips Brooks as His Friends Knew Him, pp. 30, 31.*

Phillips Brooks was a prophet of God, a preacher of Christ to men. He is claimed, and by right, as the spiritual guide of people of all churches and of no church. His message and influence passed over all denominational boundaries. Thousands outside of his own church looked to him as their religious interpreter and pastor, and he gratefully accepted the fact. He had, as we have seen, very little interest in efforts for Christian unity by adjustments or ecclesiastical treaties and alliances. His whole temper and his faith in the reality of spiritual powers compelled him to emphasize the unity of the spirit. . . . He was at home in his church. He was perfectly conscious that he could be at home in no other. His whole temperament, his grasp of the historic significance of the Church, his conceptions of the Christian life and religious culture, his sense of proportion and of spiritual unity, his love of order, his conservative instincts, his artistic and poetic temperament, were satisfied in the Episcopal Church.—LAWRENCE, WILLIAM, 1903, *Phillips Brooks, a Study*, p. 41, 44.

As a religious teacher, what shall we say of him? There is no system of doctrine, there are few attempts to set forth Christian truth in philosophical form. In his Lectures on Preaching, in his Essay on Tolerance, and in his Bohlen Lectures on "The Influence of Jesus," as well as in his sermons, there are many implications, but the fashioning of dogmatic formulas was not his work. For this reason, some have declared that he was no theologian, but that is a superficial judgment. You might as well say that the elm is no builder because it does not furnish you, before it goes to work, a front and side elevation, and architect's drawings. Brooks was a teacher whose business it was to organize doctrine into life. He thought, profoundly, upon all the themes with which the theologian deals, but he gave you the results of his thinking, not its processes. It was not the chemist's method, but the artist's, that he employed. But just as Michelangelo was a great anatomist, so was Phillips Brooks a great theological thinker. — GLADDEN, WASHINGTON, 1903, *Phillips Brooks: An Estimation, North American Review, vol.* 176, p. 279.

Robert Louis Stevenson
1850–1894.

Born, in Edinburgh, 13 Nov. 1850. Educated at Private schools, and at Edinburgh University. Originally intended for profession of Engineer. Gave it up, and studied Law; was called to Scottish Bar. Owing to ill-health, did not practise. Travelled on Continent, and in America. Married Mrs. Fanny Van de Grift Osbourne, 1880. Settled in Samoa, Oct. 1880. Died there, 8 Dec. 1894. Buried there. *Works:* "The Pentland Rising" (anon.), 1866; "The Charity Bazaar" (anon.) [1868]; "An Inland Voyage," 1878; "Edinburgh," 1879 [1878]; "Travels with a Donkey in the Cevennes," 1879; "Virginibus Puerisque," 1881; "Not I, and other poems" (priv. ptd.), 1881; "Familiar Studies of Men and Books," 1882; "New Arabian Nights," 1882; "Treasure Island," 1883; "The Silverado Squatters," 1883; "A Child's Garden of Verses," 1885 (2nd edn. same year); "Prince Otto," 1885; "The Dynamiter" (with his wife), 1885; "The Strange Case of Dr. Jekyll and Mr. Hyde," 1886; "Kidnapped," 1886; "Ticonderoga" (priv. ptd.), 1887; "The Merry Men," 1887; "Underwood's" 1887; "Memories and Portraits," 1887; "The Black Arrow," 1888; "The Wrong Box" (with L. Osbourne), 1889; "The Master of Ballantrae," 1889; "Ballads," 1890; "Father Damien," 1890; "The Wrecker" (with L. Osbourne) [1892]; "Three Plays" (with W. E. Henley), 1892; "Across the Plains," 1892;" A Footnote to History," 1892; "Catriona," 1893; "Island Nights' Entertainment," 1893; "The Ebb-Tide" (with L. Osbourne), 1894; "Macaire" (with W. E. Henley), 1895. *Posthumous:* "Vailima Letters," ed. by Sidney Colvin, 1895; "Songs of Travel, and other verses," ed. by Sidney Colvin, 1896; "Weir of Hermiston," ed by Sidney Colvin, 1896; "St. Ives" (unfinished; completed by A. T. Quiller-Couch), 1897. *Collected Works:* ed by Sidney Colvin, 1894, etc.—SHARP, R. FARQUHARSON, 1897, *A Dictionary of English Authors, p.* 269.

PERSONAL

Thin-legged, thin-chested, slight unspeakably,
Neat-footed and weak-fingered: in his face—
Lean, large-boned, curved of beak, and touched with race,
Bold-lipped, rich-tinted, mutable as the sea,
The brown eyes radiant with vivacity—
There shines a brilliant and romantic grace,
A spirit intense and rare, with trace on trace
Of passion, impudence, and energy.
Valiant in velvet, light in ragged luck,
Most vain, most generous, sternly critical,
Buffoon and poet, lover and sensualist:
A deal of Ariel, just a streak of Puck,
Much Antony, of Hamlet most of all,
And something of the Shorter-Catechist.
—HENLEY, WILLIAM ERNEST, 1888, *In Hospital, a Book of Verses*, p. 41.

I have been writing to Louis's dictation the story of "Anne de St. Ives," a young Frenchman in the time of Napoleon. Some days we have worked from eight o'clock until four, and that is not counting

JOHN ADDINGTON SYMONDS

From Photo-Etching by Walter L. Colls, 1886.

ROBERT LOUIS STEVENSON

Redrawn by T. Blake Wirgman. From a Charcoal Drawing by Mrs. Stevenson.

the hours Louis writes and makes notes in the early morning by lamplight. He dictates with great earnestness, and when particularly interested unconsciously acts the part of his characters. When he came to the description of the supper Anne has with Flora and Ronald, he bowed as he dictated the hero's speeches and twirled his mustache. When he described the interview between the old lady and the drover, he spoke in a high voice for the one, and a deep growl for the other, and all in broad Scotch even to "cōma" (comma). When Louis was writing "Ballantrae" my mother says he once came into her room to look in the glass, as he wished to describe a certain haughty, disagreeable expression of his hero's. He told her he actually expected to see the master's clean-shaven face and powdered head, and was quite disconcerted at beholding only his own reflection.—STRONG, ISOBEL, 1892–1902, *Memories of Vailima*, p. 8.

Our children and grandchildren shall rejoice in his books; but we of this generation possessed in the living man something that they will not know. So long as he lived, though it were far from Britain—though we had never spoken to him and he, perhaps, had barely heard our names—we always wrote our best for Stevenson. To him each writer amongst us—small or more than small—had been proud to have carried his best. That best might be poor enough. So long as it was not slipshod, Stevenson could forgive. While he lived, he moved men to put their utmost even into writings that quite certainly would never meet his eye. Surely another age will wonder over this curiosity of letters—that for five years the needle of literary endeavour in Great Britain has quivered towards a little island in the South Pacific, as to its magnetic pole.—QUILLER-COUCH, A. T., 1894, *Adventures in Criticism*, p. 184.

Stevenson's early school days do not bulk largely in the "Memories." In fact he was not much at school. His father had a terror of education (so called), and often plumed himself on having been the author of Louis' success in life, by keeping him as much as possible from pedagogic influence. That the paternal efforts met with filial support, Stevenson's own confession assures us. "All through my boyhood and youth," he writes, "I was known and pointed out for the pattern of an idler;" and this was highly probable, for his industry was by no means the sort to be recognised in scholastic high places. He was a day pupil first at Henderson's, Inverleith Row, and then, for a year, at the Edinburgh Academy. While at the latter he edited a MS school magazine, called the "Sunbeam." A water-color sketch by him in connection with this is still extant. . . . But, ere long, memory is busy again with the old haunts. Edinburgh University, in all innocence, inscribes a new classic on her roll. In the self-likeness he has left us of this period, he is a "lean, ugly, idle, unpopular student." He takes care here, too, that his education shall not be interfered with, by acting upon "an extensive and highly rational system of truancy." In the intervals, however, of his serious work—scribbling in penny version books, noting down features and scenes, and commemorating halting stanzas —his professors get some of his attention. But even then it is more as men than teachers. He could have written much better papers on themselves than on their subjects. Indeed he has done so.—ARMOUR, MARGARET, 1895, *The Home and Early Haunts of Robert Louis Stevenson*, pp. 22, 63, 72.

We first knew Louis Stevenson when his schooldays and teens were past, and he was facing what he called "the equinoctial gales of youth," and beginning to put his self-taught art of writing into print. . . . He would frequently drop in to dinner with us, and of an evening he had the run of our smoking-room. After 10 P. M., when a stern old servant went to bed, the "open sesame" to our door was a rattle on the letter-box. He liked this admittance by secret sign, and we liked to hear his special rat-a-tat, for we knew we would then enjoy an hour or two of talk which, he said, "is the harmonious speech of two or more, and is by far the most accessible of pleasures." He always adhered to the same dress for all entertainments, a shabby, short, velveteen jacket, a loose, Byronic, collared shirt (for a brief space he adopted black flannel ones), and meagre, shabby-looking trousers. His straight hair he wore long, and he looked like an unsuccessful artist, or a poorly-clad but eager student. He was then fragile in figure and, to use a Scottish expression, *shilpit* looking. There is no English equivalent for *shilpit*, being lean, starving, ill-thriven, in one. His dark, bright eyes were his most noticeable and attractive feature;—wide apart, almost Japanese in their shape, and above them a fine brow. He was pale and sallow, and there was a foreign, almost gipsy look about him, despite his long-headed Scotch ancestry.—SIMPSON, EVA BLANTYRE, 1895, *Some Edinburgh Notes; Class-Book, Essays; pp.* 196, 197.

> Her breast is old, it will not rise,
> Her tearless sobs in anguish choke,
> God put His finger on her eyes,
> And then it was her tears that spoke.
> "I've ha'en o' brawer sons a flow,
> My Walter mair renown could win,
> And he that followed at the plough,
> But Louis was my Benjamin!
> Ye sons wha do your little best,
> Ye writing Scots, put by the pen,
> He's deid, the ane abune the rest,
> I winna look at write again!
> . . . .
> And when he had to cross the sea,
> He wouldna lat his een grow dim,
> He bravely dree'd his weird for me,
> I tried to do the same for him.
> Ahint his face his pain was sair,
> Ahint hers grat his waefu' mither
> We kent that we should meet nae mair,
> The ane saw easy thro' the ither."
> . . . .
> A star that shot across the night
> Struck fire on Pala's mourning head,
> And left for aye a steadfast light,
> By which the mother guards her dead.
> The lad was mine! Erect she stands,
> No more by vain regrets oppress't,
> Once more her eyes are clear; her hands
> Are proudly crossed upon her breast.

—BARRIE, JAMES MATTHEW, 1895; *Scotland's Lament, McClure's Magazine, vol.* 4, *p.* 286.

Perhaps no one was ever quicker to make deep friends when the true metal was found, or surer to grapple them "with hooks of steel." A witty, ever-ready talker, a charmingly responsive listener, he was the best of company, even when he was in his bed-prison. His eager vivacity seemed to show no abatement save in the total eclipses of health.—LANIER, CHARLES D., 1895, *Robert Louis Stevenson, Review of Reviews, American Ed., vol.* 2, *p.* 185.

Mr. Stevenson, when I first saw him in his room in the Occidental Hotel in San Francisco, was sitting up in bed, not rightly able to speak for the cold that oppressed him, haggard from the illness that was sapping him, thin, pale, and wan. The first sight was something more than of a man with the blankets and counterpanes hunched up about him; it was an impression of flowing black hair, keen eyes, and a wonderful interlacing of taper fingers. At this time he was so hoarse that his voice had none of the charm which was really one of the most marked attributes of the man. More pleasant days, and strength growing in the nervous hope that the South Sea might indeed yield him what was nowhere else for him on earth, gave chances to hear that voice as it really was—gentle, deep, sympathetic. But those fingers—long, sinewy, sinuous, never resting, but rubbing each the other as if there was a mania of the nerves in their tips.—CHURCHILL, WILLIAM, 1895, *Stevenson in the South Sea, McClure's Magazine, vol.* 4, *p.* 279.

It has often been asked what gave Mr. Stevenson his standing in Samoa; what it was that made this English man of letters such a power in the land of his adoption. It must be remembered that to the Samoan mind he was inordinately rich, and many of them believe in the bottom of their hearts that the story of the bottle-imp was no fiction, but a tangible fact. Mr. Stevenson was a resident, a considerable land-owner, a man like themselves, with taro-swamps, banana plantations, and a Samoan "aiga" or family. He was no official with a hired house, here to-day with specious good-will on his lips, and empty promises, but off to-morrow in the mail steamer to that vague region called "papa lagi" "or the white country." He knew Samoan etiquette, and was familiar with the baser as well as the better side of the native character; he was cautiously generous after the fashion of the country, and neither excited covetousness by undue prodigality nor failed to respond in a befitting way for favors received.—OSBOURNE, LLOYD, 1895, *Mr. Stevenson's Home Life at Vailima, Scribner's Magazine, vol.* 18, *p.* 462.

I came home dazzled with my new friend, saying as Constance does of Arthur, "Was ever such a gracious creature born?" That impression of ineffable mental charm was formed at the first moment of acquaintance, [about 1877] and it never lessened or became modified. Stevenson's rapidity in the sympathetic interchange of ideas was, doubtless, the source of it. He has been described as an "egotist" but I challenge the description. If ever there was an altruist, it was Louis Stevenson; he seemed to feign an interest in himself merely to stimulate you to be liberal in your confidences. Those who have written about him from later impressions than these of which I speak seem to me to give insufficient prominence to the gaiety of Stevenson. It was his cardinal quality in those early days. A childlike mirth leaped and danced in him; he seemed to skip the hills of life. He was simply bubbling with quips and jests; his inherent earnestness or passion about abstract things was incessantly relieved by jocosity; and when he had built one of his intellectual castles in the sand, a wave of humor was certain to sweep in and destroy it. I cannot, for the life of me, recall any of his jokes; and written down in cold blood, they might not be funny if I did. They were not wit so much as humanity, the many-sided-outlook upon life. I am anxious that his laughter-loving mood should not be forgotten, because later on it was partly, but I think never wholly, quenched by ill health, responsibility, and the advance of years. He was often, in the old days, excessively and delightfully silly—silly with the silliness of an inspired school-boy; and I am afraid that our laughter sometimes sounded ill in the ears of age.—GOSSE, EDMUND, 1895, *Personal Memories of Robert Louis Stevenson, Century Magazine, vol.* 50, *p.* 448.

I never had heard of his existence till, in 1873, I think, I was at Mentone, in the interests of my health. Here I met Mr. Sidney Colvin, now of the British Musuem, and, with Mr. Colvin, Stevenson. He looked as, in my eyes, he always did look, more like a lass than a lad, with a rather long, smooth oval face, brown hair worn at greater length than is common, large lucid eyes, but whether blue or brown I cannot remember, if brown, certainly light brown. On appealing to the authority of a lady, I learn that brown *was* the hue. His color was a trifle hectic, as is not unusual at Mentone, but he seemed, under his big blue cloak, to be of slender, yet agile frame. He was like nobody else whom I ever met. There was a sort of uncommon celerity in changing expression, in thought and speech. I shall not deny that my first impression was not wholly favorable. "Here," I thought, "is one of your æsthetic young men, though a very clever one." What the talk was about I do not remember; probably of books. Mr. Stevenson afterwards told me that I had spoken of Monsieur Paul de St. Victor, as a fine writer, but added that "he was not a British sportsman." Mr. Stevenson himself, to my surprise, was unable to walk beyond a very short distance, and, as it soon appeared, he thought his thread of life was nearly spun. He had just written his essay, "Ordered South," the first of his published works, for his "Pentland Rising" pamphlet was unknown, a boy's performance. On reading "Ordered South," I saw, at once, that here was a new writer, a writer indeed; one who could do what none of us, *nous autres*, could rival, or approach. I was instantly "sealed of the Tribe of Louis," an admirer, a devotee, a fanatic, if you please. . . . I have known no man in whom the pre-eminently manly virtues of kindness, courage, sympathy, generosity, helpfulness, were more beautifully conspicuous than in Mr. Stevenson, none so much loved—it is not too strong a word—by so many and such various people. He was as unique in character as in literary genius.—LANG, ANDREW, 1895, *Recollections of Robert Louis Stevenson, North American Review, vol.* 160, *pp.* 186, 194.

Son of a race nomadic, finding still
Its home in regions furthest from its home,
Ranging untired the borders of the world,
And resting but to roam;
Loved of his land, and making all his boast
The birthright of the blood from which he came,
Heir to those lights that guard the Scottish coast,
And caring only for a filial fame;
Proud, if a poet, he was Scotsman most,
And bore a Scottish name.
—LEGALLIENNE, RICHARD, 1895, *Robert Louis Stevenson, an Elegy, p.* 1.

No man could have a more definite personality than Louis Stevenson's; none could more surely awaken immediate interest or exert a more instant charm, or could seem more convincingly to guarantee that the charm and interest would perennially flourish and increase. There is one kind of success which Stevenson rarely can have known—the slow subdual of indifference; and one kind of disappointment which he seldom can have felt—the pause of the foot of friendliness on the threshold of love. . . . I find myself repeating the one word "eager." There is none which better befits Stevenson's appearance and manner and talk. His mind seemed to quiver with perpetual hope of something that would give it a new idea to feed upon, a new fact to file away, a new experience to be tested and savored. I could read this attitude even in the quick cordiality of his greeting. The welcome was not for me, as myself, but for the new person — for the new human being, who, possessing ears and a tongue, might possibly contribute some item to the harvest of the day.—VAN RENSSELAER, M. G., 1896, *Robert Louis Stevenson and his Writings, Century Magazine*, vol. 51, p. 124, 125.

A face of youth mature: a mouth of tender,
Sad human sympathy yet something stoic
In clasp of lip; wide eyes of calmest splendor,
And brow serenely ample and heroic;—
The features—all —lit with a soul ideal.
—RILEY, JAMES WHITCOMB, 1897, *On a Youthful Portrait of Robert Louis Stevenson, Scribner's Magazine*, vol. 22, p. 770.

Life for those who remained in the Samoan home became an impossible thing without him, and so Mrs. Stevenson, with her son and daughter, by-and-bye left Vailima, and the home of so much happiness is now falling into ruin, the cleared ground lapsing back to the bush. And perhaps it is best so; without him Vailima is like a body without a soul; and he who so dearly loved nature would hardly have regretted that the place he loved should return to the mother heart of the earth and become once more a solitude—a green place of birds and trees.—BLACK, MARGARET MOYES, 1898, *Robert Louis Stevenson (Famous Scots Series)*, p. 148.

These to his memory: may the age arriving,
        As ours recall
That bravest heart, that gay and gallant striving,
        That laurelled pall,
Blithe and rare spirit! We who later linger
        By blacker seas
Sigh for the touch of-the magician's finger,
        His golden keys!
—DOBSON, AUSTIN, 1901, *In Memoriam, Eclectic Magazine*, vol. 137, p. 89.

Stevenson calls himself "ugly" in his student days, but I think that is a term that never at any time fitted him. Certainly to him as a boy about fourteen (with the creed which he propounded to me, that at sixteen one was a man) it would not apply. In body Stevenson was assuredly badly set up. His limbs were long and lean and spidery, and his chest flat, so as almost to suggest some malnutrition, such sharp angles and corners did his joints make under his clothes. But in his face this was belied. His brow was oval and full, over soft brown eyes, that seemed already to have drunk the sunlight under southern vines. The whole face had a tendency to an oval Madonna-like type. But about the mouth and in the mirthful, mocking light of the eyes, there lingered ever a ready Autolycus roguery, that rather suggested the sly god Hermes masquerading as a mortal. Yet the eyes were always genial, however gaily the lights danced in them; but about the mouth there was something tricksy and mocking, as of a spirit that had already peeped behind the scenes of Life's pageant and more than guessed its unrealities.—BAILDON, H. BELLYSE, 1901, *Robert Louis Stevenson, a Life Study in Criticism*, pp. 20, 21.

For me there were two Stevensons; the Stevenson who went to America in '87; and the Stevenson who never came back. The first I knew, and loved; the other I lost touch with, and, though I admired him, did not greatly esteem. My relation to him was that of a man with a grievance; and for that reason, perhaps—that reason and others—I am by no means disposed to take all Mr. Balfour says for Gospel, nor willing to forget, on the showing of what is after all an official statement, the knowledge gained in an absolute intimacy of give-and-take which lasted for thirteen years, and includes so many of the circumstances of those thirteen years, that, as I believe, none living now can pretend to speak of them with any such authority as mine. . . . Mr. Balfour does me the honour of quoting the sonnet into which I crammed my impressions of my companion and friend; and, since he has done so, I may as well own that "the Shorter Catechist" of the last verse was an afterthought. In those days he was in abeyance, to say the least; and if, even then, *il allait poindre à l'horizon* (as the composition, in secret and as if ashamed, of "Lay Morals" persuades me to believe he did), I, at any rate, was too short-sighted to suspect his whereabouts. When I realized it, I completed my sonnet; but this was not till year's had come and gone, and the Shorter Catechist, already detested by more than one, was fully revealed to me. I will say at once that I do not love the Shorter Catechist, in anybody, and that I loved him less in Stevenson than anywhere that I have ever found him. . . . At bottom Stevenson was an excellent fellow. But he was of his essence what the French call *personnel*. He was, that is, incessantly and passionately interested in Stevenson. He could not be in the same room with a mirror but he must invite its confidences every time he passed it; to him there was nothing obvious in time and eternity, and the smallest of his discoveries, his most trivial apprehensions, were all by way of being revelations, and as revelations must be thrust upon the world; he was never so much in earnest, never so well pleased (this were he happy or wretched), never so irresistible, as when he wrote about himself. . . . In print Stevenson was now and then witty enough for seven; but in talk his way was, not Congreve's but, Harry Fielding's. No; he was certainly not a wit, in the sense that Congreve was a wit.—HENLEY, WILLIAM ERNEST, 1901, *R. L. S. Pall Mall Magazine, vol.* 25, *pp.* 506, 508, 511.

Considering his fragility, his muscular strength was considerable, and his constitution clearly had great powers of resistance. Perhaps what helped him as much as anything was the faculty he had under ordinary circumstances of going to sleep at a moment's notice. Thus, if he anticipated fatigue in the evening, he would take a quarter of an hour's sound sleep in the course of the afternoon. His speech was distinctly marked with a Scottish intonation, that seemed to every one both pleasing and appropriate, and this, when he chose, he could broaden to the widest limits of the vernacular. His voice was always of a surprising strength and resonance, even when phthisis had laid its hand most heavily upon him. It was the one gift he really possessed for the stage, and in reading aloud he was unsurpassed. In his full rich tones there was a sympathetic quality that seemed to play directly on the heart-strings like the notes of a violin. . . . His hearing was singularly acute, although the appreciation of the exact pitch of musical notes was wanting. But between delicate shades of pronunciation he could discriminate with a great precision.—BALFOUR, GRAHAM, 1901, *The Life of Robert Louis Stevenson, vol.* II, *pp.* 191, 192.

My *credo* as to "R. L. S." is brief; that Stevenson was one of the bravest, sweetest, and most winsome of men, an artist in every nerve, and a writer of infinite charm; but that, being human, indeed in its merits and defects poignantly human, he had a more or less distracting swarm of minor inconsistencies and flaws habitually in evidence about the honey of his brilliant mind and his good and sane heart. It is not to be supposed that anything recently written could hurt the good fame of R. L. S. We have his works, his letters, the record of worthy deeds and of a brave and loyal life. He had hardly a friend who did not love the man more than his writings, for all their winsomeness, their art, their power at times, their perpetual atmosphere of youth, of life. If there are people who "call off" because of some hard-hitting, it is not R. L. S. who is the loser. The more he stands revealed in his weakness as well as in his strength, in his failures as in his achievements, in his vices as in his virtues, the more lovable and, in the end, the more admirable does he appear.—SHARP, WILLIAM, 1902, *In Stevenson's Country, Harper's Magazine, vol.* 105, *p.* 497.

I have visited him in a lonely lodging—it was previous to his happy marriage—and found him submerged in billows of bedclothes; about him floated the scattered volumes of a complete set of Thoreau; he was preparing an essay on that worthy, and he looked at the moment like a half-drowned man—yet he was not cast down. His work, an endless task, was better than a straw to him. It was to become his life-preserver and to prolong his years. I feel convinced that without it he must have surrendered long before he did. I found Stevenson a man of frailest physique, though most unaccountably tenacious of life; a man whose pen was indefatigable, whose brain was never at rest; who as far as I am able to judge, looked upon everybody and everything from a supremely intellectual point of view. His was a superior organisation that seems never to have been tainted by things common or unclean; one more likely to be revolted than appealed to by carnality in any form. A man unfleshly to the verge of emaciation, and, in this connection, I am not unmindful of a market in fleshpots not beneath the consideration of sanctimonious speculators; but here was a man whose sympathies were literary and artistic; whose intimacies were born and bred above the ears.—STODDARD, CHARLES WARREN, 1903, *Exits and Entrances*, p. 16.

TREASURE ISLAND
1883

To whom we could almost have raised a statue in the market-place for having written "Treasure Island."—BIRRELL, AUGUSTINE, 1887, *Obiter Dicta, Second Series*, p. 217.

The best boys' story since Marryatt, and one of a literary excellence to which Marryatt could make no pretensions.—SAINTSBURY, GEORGE, 1896, *A History of Nineteenth Century Literature*, p. 339.

"Treasure Island" is a piece of astounding ingenuity, in which the manner is taken from "Robinson Crusoe," and the plot belongs to the era of the detective story.—CHAPMAN, JOHN JAY, 1898, *Emerson and Other Essays*, p. 229.

"Treasure Island" is, properly speaking, a boy's book, but, like "Robinson Crusoe" (the only book with which it ought to be compared, though "Reuben Davidger" runs it close), children of a larger growth are fascinated by it. There is not a dull page in it, and every incident seems to be, in turn, more effective than the other. We hurry through it, eager to be in at the death; we feel, at the end, as if we had been among the pirates and endured many a strange adventure; and then we read it again, rolling it, like a sweet morsel, under the tongue.—MACCULLOCH, J. A., 1898, *R. L. Stevenson, Westminster Review*, vol. 149, p. 642.

KIDNAPPED
1886

"Kidnapped" is the outstanding boy's book of its generation.—BARRIE, JAMES MATTHEW, 1889, *An Edinburgh Eleven*, p. 120.

The whole of "Kidnapped" is written with so much salt and piquancy, such happy invention, and fullest measure of the author's spirit of dexterity and finish, of his power of humorously graphic portraiture, as to make it stand out preeminent even among Mr. Stevenson's own works.—NEWTON-ROBINSON, JANETTA, 1893, *Some Aspects of the Work of Mr. Robert Louis Stevenson, Westminster Review*, vol. 139, p. 603.

It may be said of "Kidnapped' that there is absolutely no love-interest, and we have been so starved of the feminine element that the good-natured lass at Limekilns, who so pluckily saves the pair of fugitives, quite takes our eye, so that we feel it quite ungallant of Stevenson when he, so to speak, slams the door of his tale in her face the moment his Dioscuri have no further use for her. To some extent friendship takes the place of love in the story, and the humours of the two friends towards each other are the only substitute we have for the lovers' differences and misunderstandings of the more ordinary plot. Later on we shall meet David in love, and a pretty bad job he would have made of it, left to himself.—BAILDON, H. BELLYSE, 1901, *Robert Louis Stevenson, a Life Study in Criticism*, pp. 137, 138.

THE STRANGE CASE OF DR. JEKYLL AND MR. HYDE
1886

I doubt whether any one has the right so to scrutinise "The abysmal deeps of personality." You see I have been reading Dr. Jekyll. At least I think he ought to bring more of distinct belief in the resources of human nature, more faith, more sympathy with our frailty, into the matter than you have done. The art is burning and intense. The Peau de Chagrin disappears, and Poe's work is water. . . . Louis, how had you the "ilia dura, ferro et ære triplici duriora," to write Dr. Jekyll? I know now what was meant when you were called a sprite. . . . The suicide end of Dr. Jekyll is too commonplace. Dr. Jekyll ought to have given Mr. Hyde up to justice. This would have vindicated the sense of human dignity which is so horribly outraged in your book. —SYMONDS, JOHN ADDINGTON, 1886, *Letter to Stevenson, March 1; Life ed. Brown*, vol. II, pp. 256, 257.

The subject is one which has haunted literature and men's minds for ages; and perhaps Mr. Stevenson, by transferring the ghost to a living and comfortable *bourgeois*, may have done something to allay its wanderings. It seems, however, as if the possibilities of the theme would have admitted of a treatment a trifle finer and more subtle than he has chosen to give it. It may be misreading the intention of the book, with its hint of unfathomed depths in the soul, to suggest that the evil of Mr. Hyde is hardly that which would belong to Dr. Jekyll; but its effect as a tale of situation and moral would scarcely have been marred if the link of connection between the two characters had been a little more delicate, and the individuality of each more carefully worked out. As it is, its gruesomeness has just a touch of the perfunctory: it does not thrill with so poetic a terror as that stirred by the inimitable one-legged sailor in "Treasure Island," or by the ghastliness of Thrawn Janet.—KIRK, SOPHIA, 1887, *Mr. Stevenson as a Story-teller, Atlantic Monthly*, vol. 60, p. 753.

"Dr. Jekyll and Mr. Hyde" was the flashing inspiration of a dream, worked out, however, not in a flash, but in patient toil.—BOWKER, RICHARD ROGERS, 1888, *London as a Literary Centre, Harper's Magazine*, vol. 77, p. 15.

If "The Pavilion of the Links" has claims to be considered a masterpiece, and may confidently hope to stand the merciless test of time, the same must also be conceded to "Dr. Jekyll." In fact, of the two, "Dr. Jekyll," though slightly inferior as a work of art, has the greater certainty of longevity. The allegory within it would lengthen its days, even should new methods and changes of taste take the charm from the story. As long as man remains a dual being, as long as he is in danger of being conquered by his worse self, and, with every defeat, finds it the more difficult to make a stand, so long "Dr. Jekyll" will have a personal and most vital meaning to every poor, struggling human being. *Mutato nomine de te fabula narratur*, so craftily is the parable worked out that it never obtrudes itself upon the reader or clogs the action of the splendid story. It is only on looking back, after he has closed the book, that he sees how close is the analogy and how direct the application.—DOYLE, CONAN, 1890, *Mr. Stevenson's Methods in Fiction, National Review*, vol. 14, p. 647.

A bit of criticism may be permitted, in which most readers will agree. On the morning of March 12, the record of the time bears: "Read a most powerful and extraordinary story by R. L. Stevenson: 'Dr. Jekyll and Mr. Hyde.'" In the few days which followed, I read the story seven times over, with as much care as when of old preparing for an examination: watching every clause of every sentence, and its bearing. The story deserves to be studied in that way. And its moral is most awful: but irresistibly true.—BOYD, ANDREW K. H., 1892, *Twenty-five Years of St. Andrews*, vol. II, p. 246.

Only a Scotsman could have written the "Strange Case of Dr. Jekyll and Mr. Hyde," as only a New Englander could have written the "Scarlet Letter." There is an inheritance from the Covenanters and a memory of the Shorter Catechism in Stevenson's bending and twisting the dark problems of our common humanity to serve as the core of his tales.—MATTHEWS, BRANDER, 1894–96, *Aspects of Fiction*, p. 137.

Even in so fine a story as "Dr. Jekyll and Mr. Hyde," the reader is unjustifiably cheated into attempting a natural solution of apparently inexplicable phenomena. The supernatural solution, when it comes, is no solution; there are a hundred ways of explaining the impossible by the impossible.—RALEIGH, WALTER, 1894, *The English Novel*, p. 224.

What piece of prose fiction is less likely to be forgotten? To begin with, the central idea, strange as it is, at once comes home to everybody. . . . This is the only case where Mr. Stevenson, working by himself, has used a mystery; and most skilfully it is used in the opening chapters to stimulate curiosity. . . . In the third part, when the mystery has been solved, nothing but consummate art could have saved the interest from collapsing. But Jekyll's own written statement gives the crowning emotion when it recites the drama that passed in the study behind the locked door; the appalling conflict between the two personages in the same outwardly changing breast. Other writers have approached the same idea. Gautier, for instance, has a curious story of a gentleman who gets translated into another man's body to court the other's wife; but Mr. Stevenson has everything to gain by the comparison.—GWYNN, STEPHEN, 1894, *Mr. Robert Louis Stevenson, Fortnightly Review*, vol. 62, p. 787.

Mr. Stevenson was in town, now and again, at the old Savile Club which had the tiniest and blackest of smoking rooms.

Here, or somewhere, he spoke to me of an idea of a tale, a Man who was Two Men. I said "William Wilson!" and declared that it would never do. But his "Brownies," in a vision of the night, showed him the central scene, and he wrote "Jekyll and Hyde." My "friend of these days and of all days," Mr. Charles Longman, sent me the manuscript. In a very common-place London drawing-room, at 10:30 P. M., I began to read it. Arriving at the place where Utterson, the lawyer, and the butler wait outside the Doctor's room, I threw down the MS. and fled in a hurry. I had no taste for solitude any more. The story won its great success, partly by dint of the moral (whatever that may be), more by its terrible lucid visionary power. I remember Mr. Stevenson telling me, at this time, that he was doing some "regular crawlers," for this purist had a boyish habit of slang, and I *think* it was he who called Julius Cæsar "the howlingest cheese who ever lived." One of the "crawlers" was "Thrawn Janet;" after "Wandering Willie's Tale" (but certainly *after* it), to my taste, it seems the most wonderful story of the "supernatural" in our language.—LANG, ANDREW, 1895, *Recollections of Robert Louis Stevenson, North American Review, vol.* 160, p. 188.

A subject much in his thoughts at this time was the duality of man's nature and the alternation of good and evil; and he was for a long while casting about for a story to embody this central idea. Out of this frame of mind had come the sombre imagination of "Markheim," but that was not what he required. The true story still delayed, till suddenly one night he had a dream. He awoke and found himself in possession of two, or rather three, of the scenes in "The Strange Case of Dr. Jekyll and Mr. Hyde." Its waking existence, however, was by no means without incident. He dreamed these scenes in considerable detail, including the circumstance of the transforming powders, and so vivid was the impression that he wrote the story off at a red heat, but just as it had presented itself to him in his sleep.—BALFOUR, GRAHAM, 1901, *The Life of Robert Louis Stevenson, vol.* II, p. 15.

In his journey to the Cevennes he reflects that every one of us travels about with a donkey. In his "Strange Case of Dr. Jekyll and Mr. Hyde," the donkey becomes a devil. Every Jekyll is haunted by his Hyde. Somebody said that "The Strange Case of Dr. Jekyll and Mr. Hyde" showed Stevenson as Poe, with the addition of a moral sense. Critics may differ as to the exact literary value of the famous little book, but as an expression of Stevenson's deepest thought about life it will retain its interest. He was not content to dwell in a world where the lines are drawn clear, where the sheep are separated from the goats. He would have a foot in both worlds, content to dwell neither wholly with the sheep nor wholly with the goats. No doubt his ruling interest was in ethical problems, and he could be stern in his moral judgments, as, for example, in his discussion of the character of Burns.—NICOLL, W. ROBERTSON, 1901, *Robert Louis Stevenson (The Bookman Biographies),* p. 1.

MASTER OF BALLANTRAE
1889

In his latest romance "The Master of Ballantrae" Stevenson seems to have touched high-water mark. I am tempted to go beyond this and say that no modern work of fiction in the English Language rises higher in the scale of literary merit than this.—BROOKS, NOAH, 1889, *The Book Buyer,* p. 440.

If a strong story, strongly told, full of human interest, and absolutely original in its situations, makes a masterpiece, then this may lay claim to the title.—DOYLE, CONAN, 1890, *Mr. Stevenson's Methods in Fiction, National Review, vol.* 14, p. 646.

"The Master of Ballantrae" is stamped with a magnificent unity of conception, but the story illuminates that conception by a series of scattered episodes. That lurid embodiment of fascinating evil, part vampire, part Mephistopheles, whose grand manner and heroic abilities might have made him a great and good man but for the "malady of not wanting," is the light and meaning of the whole book. Innocent and benevolent lives are thrown in his way that he may mock or distort or shatter them. Stevenson never came nearer than in this character to the sublime of power.—RALEIGH, WALTER, 1895, *Robert Louis Stevenson,* p. 56.

There is a scene in "The Master of Ballantrae" which, powerful as it is, has never, I confess, been a favourite of mine, because the story is so utterly repulsive from the beginning to the end—the conflict of a scoundrel against a maniac narrated by a coward. But in "The Master of Ballantrae" there is a scene which we see before us vividly as I see your faces now, where the old steward comes out with a silver candle in each hand glaring into the still and silent night, ushering the brothers to their death struggle like a landlord handing out illustrious guests to their apartments. He walks through the night, and he holds the lights while they fight, and you next see the dead body, or seemingly dead body, of the elder lying with the wax candles flickering on each side in the silent night, and when again the steward returns, the body is gone, one wax candle has fallen down, the other is upright, still flickering over the bloodshed. Can you not all see it as you read it in the page of Stevenson? To me there seems nothing more vivid in all history.—ROSEBERY, ARCHIBALD PHILIP PRIMROSE LORD, 1896, *Appreciations and Addresses*, ed. Geake, p. 96.

"The Master of Ballantrae," a weird and striking tale of the times of "the forty-five," is extraordinarily graphic both in its descriptions of places and of people. The gloomy house of Durrisdeer, with its stately panelled hall, the fine grounds so carefully laid out, the thick shrubberies, the spot where the duel was fought on the hard, frozen ground by the light of the flickering candles in the tall silver candlesticks, the wave-beaten point where the smuggling luggers land goods and passengers, and finally the awful journey through the uncleared woods of America, make a fit seting, in our memories, for the splendidly drawn pictures of the three Duries, the old father, the unappreciated Henry, the mocking master, their faithful land-steward, Mackellar, and the more shadowy personalities of the Frenchman, the lady, and the children. The tale is one of unrelieved horror, but it is a masterpiece nevertheless, and it has had a very large sale.—BLACK, MARGARET MOYES, 1898, *Robert Louis Stevenson (Famous Scots Series)*, p. 124.

POEMS

His art has a stronger hold on nature. Were he only the bright and clever man of talent, who does the bright and clever thing that a man may do with his talent, it would be easy enough to dismiss him with a hatful of thanks and compliments. But we who have read the half dozen books which he has given us must see clearly that we have to deal, not with talent, but with that strange and precious thing which we call genius. If he does no more than he has done—and he gives every sign and promise of doing more—Robert Louis Stevenson is one of these men whom we have to label with the name of genius. And the mission of genius, however it reveal itself, is sad at bottom. There is much in this book ["A Child's Garden of Verses"] that we may teach to the children, at our side; there is much that we may smile over, remembering the childhood from which we grew; but there is also something there that hints of the stifled-childhood in us that never grew up; some thing that touches us with a deep, half-understood, wholly unspeakable grief.— BUNNER, HENRY CUYLER, 1885, *The Stevenson's Child's Garden of Verses, The Book Buyer*, vol. 2, p. 104.

There is in these poems ["Underwoods"] little or nothing either of that originality or of that satisfying beauty which conjointly characterise Mr. Stevenson's best prose.— SHARP, WILLIAM, 1887, *The Academy*, vol. 32, p. 213.

Now, as a minor but genuine example of poetic art, not alone for art's sake, but for dear nature's sake,—in the light of whose maternal smile all art must thrive and blossom if at all,—take "A Child's Garden of Verses" by Stevenson. This is a real addition to the lore for children, and to that for man, to whom the child is father. The flowers of this little garden spring from the surplusage of a genius that creates nothing void of charm and originality. Thanks, then, for the fresh, pure touch, for the revelation of childhood with its vision of the lands of Nod and Counterpane, and of those next-door Foreign Lands spied from cherry-tree top, and beyond the trellised wall.—STEDMAN, EDMUND CLARENCE, 1887, *Victorian Poets*, p. 468.

It would be arrogant in the extreme to decide whether or no Mr. R. L. Stevenson's poems will be read in the future. They are, however, so full of character, so redolent of his own fascinating temperament, that it is not too bold to suppose that so long as his prose is appreciated those who love that will turn to this. There have been prose writers whose verse has not lacked accomplishment or merit, but has been so far from interpreting their prose that it rather disturbed its effect and weakened its influence.—GOSSE, EDMUND, 1887, *Mr. R. L. Stevenson as a Poet, Questions at Issue,* p. 253.

The volume ["A Child's Garden of Verses"] is a wonder, for the extraordinary vividness with which it reproduces early impressions; a child might have written it if a child could see childhood from the outside, for it would seem that only a child is really near enough to the nursery-floor. And what is peculiar to Mr. Stevenson is that it is his own childhood he appears to delight in, and not the personal presence of little darlings. Oddly enough, there is no strong implication that he is fond of babies; he does'nt speak as a parent, or an uncle, or an educator—he speaks as a contemporary absorbed in his own game.—JAMES, HENRY, 1888, *Robert Louis Stevenson, Century Magazine,* vol. 35, p. 871.

Fascinating as his verses are, artless in the perfection of art, they take no reader a step forward. The children of whom he sings so sweetly are cherubs without souls.—BARRIE, JAMES MATTHEW, 1889, *An Edinburgh Eleven,* p. 124.

His "Child's Garden of Verses" is delightful. It is fresh, new, unconventional, unexpected; it has grace and it has charm; but despite all these qualities we receive it rather as the play of a prose writer than as the work of a poet. And so with his new book of ballads. They are dramatic, picturesque, vigorous. They are as direct and lusty as anyone could wish, but they are not convincingly poetic. They are not inevitable enough, as Wordsworth would say. They are rather the recreation of one of the cleverest literary artificers of modern times, than the work of a poet who sings in numbers because his speech is naturally rhythmic. Mr. Stevenson wrote these ballads because he wanted to write them, not because he could not help it.—MATTHEWS, BRANDER, 1891, *On Certain Recent Volumes of Verse, The Cosmopolitan,* vol. 10, p. 636.

In these ballads there are infelicities of expression and defects of style which it is hard to believe that the author of "Kidnapped" could have allowed to remain in any work of his, whether in prose or verse, except by way of a joke.—MONKHOUSE, COSMO, 1891, *Ballads, The Academy,* vol. 39, p. 108.

The gallant muse of Mr. Stevenson has already played many parts in literature. Even here, in the course of a page or two, we have had occasion to refer to the author of "Treasure Island" as a writer of nursery, and of dialect poetry. His best verse, his most distinctive metrical compositions, must be classed under yet another heading. His Polynesian "Ballads" are too long to be quoted here in full, and they do not lend themselves to the extract. But, in spite of one noticeable and regrettable falling away, it is in these ballads that the author's finest and most characteristic poetry is to be found.—DOUGLAS, SIR GEORGE, 1893, *ed. Contemporary Scottish Verse, Introductory Note,* p. xiv.

In spite of that unique achievement "A Child's Garden of Verses," at the time of its publication the only collection of poems in the tongue properly to be called child poetry in contradistinction from poetry about children for the delectation of older folk,—the critic might well have hesitated to award to Stevenson the proud names of singer and maker. But with the appearance of the final edition of his metrical work, permitting for the first time an opinion based upon a complete survey, such reserve becomes unnecessary. The forty additional pieces of the final edition chiefly constitute the ground for the consideration of Stevenson as a verse-writer of individuality and fine accomplishment. They show his genius at its ripest, and are as interesting for their mastery of the art of verse as they are moving in the imaginative revelation of his deepest nature. For strength and beauty we should, on the whole, point to them as the Scotchman's most authentic gift to poetry.—BURTON, RICHARD, 1898, *Literary Likings,* p. 24.

The celebrated "Child's Garden of Verses," as decisive and important a success in its own field of literature as "Treasure Island" had been two years before. The field was in this case almost wholly new; the "Child's Garden" may be said not only to have founded a new school, but to have opened up a new side of life, and to be a substantial contribution towards the theory of human development and the science of psychology.—MACKAIL, J. W., 1904, *Chambers's Cyclopædia of English Literature,* ed. Patrick, vol. III, p. 700.

LETTERS

Such as they remain, then, these letters will be found a varied record, perfectly frank and familiar, of the writer's everyday moods, thoughts, and doings during his Samoan exile. They tell, with the zest and often in the language of a man who remained to the last a boy in spirit, of the pleasures and troubles of a planter founding his home in the virgin soil of a tropical island; the pleasures of an invalid beginning after many years to resume habits of outdoor life and exercise; the toils and satisfactions, failures and successes, of a creative artist whose invention was as fertile as his standards were high and his industry unflinching. These divers characters have probably never been so united in any man before. Something also they tell of the inward movements and affections of one of the bravest and tenderest of human hearts.—COLVIN, SIDNEY, 1895, *ed.*, *Vailima Letters, Editorial Note*, p. 19.

It is when we hold in our hands in bound volumes the Letters of one we have seen in the body and whose books and papers as they fell from him were always, in whatever mood they found us, sources of pleasure and delight, that we feel in all its sharpness the sting of death. Then we realize how the end has indeed come and that we have before us the last effort of a master of expression to express himself. . . . The reader of these Letters, if he will but ruminate a little over them and not be in too great a hurry to return them to the Lending Library from whence cometh his Literature, will find, scattered up and down them, food for his fancy and matter for his thought. He will be able to compare the rough core with the finished ornament, the thought as it struck the brain and as it is to be found recorded in one or another of the writer's books or papers. This is always an interesting parallelism. One strange feeling he had evidently great possession of Stevenson, a romantic attachment to the memory of Robert Fergusson, the ill-fated forerunner in modern Scottish song of Robert Burns. . . . How in time to come Stevenson's Letters may chance to compare with Pliny's or with Cicero's, with Cowper's or with Lamb's, I am at no pains to inquire. To thousands of living men and women Stevenson was a friend and an ally, and they it is at all events who have the *first* reading of his letters.—BIRRELL, AUGUSTINE, 1900, *Robert Louis Stevenson's Letters, Contemporary Review*, vol. 77, pp. 50, 58, 60.

The letters are not quite perfect letters, but that was hardly to be looked for in the case of a writer whose special gift lay in the painful and slowly-rewarded search for the perfect word, a labour no one would undergo in writing to his friends. But for us, at this moment, there are few, if any, more readable letters in the language. They are full to the very brim of life, of humour, of strangeness, of wisdom, goodness, bookknowledge, breadth of human sympathy—in one word, of Robert Louis Stevenson. . . . They show us that the delightfulness of the man's nature, as we saw him in the Essays, or "The Inland Voyage," was not the mere pose or trick of a clever man of letters, but was the very fact and essence of him as he lived and spoke. And we grow prouder of him too. For we see that when he comes to be given his definite place in the great company into which all who can judge in these matters saw from the first that he would be called, it will be, not at all among the greatest, no doubt, but among the very best that he will be found. No man among them all—not Scott himself—was more beautifully free from the common faults of the man whose chief business is writing. These letters show him to us snow-pure from any stain of envy, jealousy, or suspicion. He is liberal to profusion in his encouragement of young rivals; he is humble almost to excess when he thinks of his great predecessors.—BAILEY, J. C., 1900, *Stevenson's Letters, Fortnightly Review*, vol. 73, pp. 91, 92.

We are sorry, we repeat, that these letters have been given to the world. So far as Stevenson's reputation is concerned they can only detract from it. When they illustrate him on his best side they merely emphasise what his works illustrate so abundantly that further illustration is a mere work of supererogation. When they present him, as for the most part they do, in dishabille, they exhibit him very greatly to his disadvantage. If Professor Colvin had printed about one-third of them, and retained his excellent elucidatory introductions, which form practically a biography of Stevenson, he would have produced a work for which all admirers of that most pleasing writer would have thanked him. As it is, he has been guilty, in our opinion, of a grave error of judgment.—COLLINS, JOHN CHURTON, 1901, *R. L. Stevenson's Letters, Ephemera Critica*, p. 171.

In the "Letters" no man using English speech has chattered more unreservedly, and with more essential charm; it is the undress of literature that always instinctively stops this side of etiquette, of decency. The Stevenson epistles drive us on a stillhunt outside of the mother-tongue for their equal, with little prospect of quarry save within French borders.—BURTON, RICHARD 1902, *Forces in Fiction and Other Essays*, p. 98.

GENERAL

I wonder how many people there are in England who know that Robert Louis Stevenson is, in his own way (and he is wise enough to write simply in his own way), one of the most perfect writers living, one of the very few who may yet do something that will become classical?—HAMERTON, PHILIP GILBERT, 1878, *The Academy*, vol. 13, p. 547.

He is a critic in method and intelligence, and an advocate in manner and temperament; and he makes you glad or sorry as —with his reflections and conclusions— he has made himself before you. If his criticism were less acute and methodical than it is, the accent and the terms in which it is conveyed would sometimes get it mistaken for an outcome of mere æsthetic emotion. As it is, the critic is equally apparent in it with the man; you can see that the strong feeling has come of clear thinking, and what is purely intellectual is rendered doubly potent and persuasive by the human sentiment with which it is associated. It is possible that this fact will ultimately militate against the success of Mr. Stevenson's "Studies" as criticism; for criticism—a science disguised as Art—is held to be incapable of passion. I cannot but think, however, that it will always count for a great deal in their favour as literature, and that meanwhile it clothes them with uncommon interest and attraction.—HENLEY, WILLIAM ERNEST, 1882, *Familiar Studies of Men and Books, The Academy*, vol. 21, p. 224.

The quality by which Mr. Stevenson is chiefly distinguished, and which differentiates his writing from the story-writing of the period, is imagination—the power of creating characters which are as real as creatures of flesh and blood, and of devising and shaping events which are as inevitable as fate. Beyond all the writers of his time, he is remarkable for clearness and accuracy of vision; he seems to see, and we believe he *does* see, all that he describes, and he makes all his readers see likewise. How he accomplishes this last feat, which is a very uncommon one, we have never been able to discover, for on returning to a scene or a chapter which has impressed us deeply, which has sent the blood tingling through our veins, or has darkened our souls with foreboding, we have always failed to detect the secret of his power. It can hardly be in his language which is always of the simplest, nor in the feeling that he depicts, which is always natural, and often common; but it is there all the same.—STODDARD, RICHARD HENRY, 1887, *The Mail and Express*.

Mr. Stevenson delights in a style, and his own has nothing accidental or diffident; it is eminently conscious of its responsibilities and meets them with a kind of gallantry—as if language were a pretty woman and a person who proposes to handle it had, of necessity, to be something of a Don Juan. This element of the gallant is a noticeable part of his nature, and it is rather odd that, at the same time, a striking feature of the nature should be an absence of care for things feminine. His books are for the most part books without women, and it is not women who fall most in love with them. But Mr. Stevenson does not need, as we may say, a petticoat to enflame him; a happy collocation of words will serve the purpose, or a singular image, or the bright eye of a passing conceit, and he will carry off a pretty paradox without so much as a scuffle.—JAMES, HENRY, 1888, *Robert Louis Stevenson, Century Magazine*, vol. 35, p. 870.

Truly in his power to "harrow up the soul, freeze the young blood," etc., Stevenson is unsurpassed by modern writers. We feel our flesh creep upon our bones as we sit absorbed in some of his weird and witchlike tales. Then, though we may be ashamed to confess it, we seem to lose our years, and shrink into an eager, uninitiated boy once more, as we huddle over "Treasure Island" or "Kidnapped," "The New Arabian Nights" or "The Black Arrow," letting the hour-hand on the clock creep on to midnight unheeded; we may protest that it is the sheerest juvenile nonsense in the world, but none the less are we held by a spell; there are no pauses, no tame meanderings, when we might break away and be gone; but the racy narrator hurries us on over adventurous by-ways, twisting and turning, bursting upon new surprises, dashing into dangerous pit-falls, until breathless, we come plump into an unwelcome *Finis*, and close the book perforce.—FALCONER, W. L., 1888, *Robert Louis Stevenson, The Critic*, vol. 13, p. 323.

I look forward to the work of Robert Louis Stevenson with more eagerness than to that of any other author of today. I rejoice in the exquisite quality of his style; I am the captive of his intimate and enchanting verse; in his literary essays I find an unfailing delight; and as for his stories, which he and I both like, I do not mean that he shall ever write one which I do not read.—MOULTON, LOUISE CHANDLER, 1888, *Literary Letters*.

In depicting the characters of others who stood about him in his boyhood he not only succeeds in making them lifelike, but he lends his own appreciation to our eyes, and we see them by the help of his memories and associations. They are Scotchmen of the type known to the world. . . . He has many admirable sentences struck clear with the die of the workman who knows the craft in its intellectual laws as well as in its mechanical execution, by his mind as well as his hand.—WOODBERRY, GEORGE EDWARD, 1888, *Mr. Robert Louis Stevenson's Collected Papers, The Nation*, vol. 46, p. 34.

Where is the man among us who could write another "Virginibus Puerisque," the most delightful volume for the hammock ever sung in prose? . . . He has attained a popularity such as is, as a rule, only accorded to classic authors or to charlatans. For this he has America to thank rather than Britain, for the Americans buy his books, the only honor a writer's admirers are slow to pay him. Mr. Stevenson's reputation in the United States is creditable to that country, which has given him a position here in which only a few saw him when he left. Unfortunately, with popularity has come publicity. All day the reporters sit on his garden wall.—BARRIE, JAMES MATTHEW, 1889, *An Edinburgh Eleven*, p. 120, 121.

Yet there is one thing lacking in Stevenson's style. It is not distinctive, not characteristic; it does not reveal the man, but rather hides him. The motley of Lamb, the homespun of Swift, the imperial purple of De Quincey, clothe them in shining garments which sit easily upon them. Stevenson's, with all its beauty, is a misfit style. It is measured for the Apollo Belvidere, not for him. We feel, somehow, that he is in disguise, that his livery is a stolen one. There is an element, too, of the fictitious in his humor, his wit, his morality, his philosophy—as of something assumed rather than innate. We yield him an admiration which, after all, we do not quite believe in. We can not away with a lurking doubt. Is this Moses, or a false priest who performs similar marvels? Is it miracle or sleight of hand?—WALSH, WILLIAM S., 1889, *In the Library, The Cosmopolitan*, vol. 7, p. 526.

He can claim to have mastered the whole gamut of fiction. His short stories are good, and his long ones are good. On the whole, however, the short ones are the more characteristic, and the more certain to retain their position in English literature. The shorter effort suits his genius. With some choice authors, as with some rare vintages, a sip gives the real flavour better than a draught. It is eminently so with Mr. Stevenson. His novels have all conspicuous virtues, but they have usually some flaw, some drawback, which may weaken their permanent value. In the tales, or at least in the best of the tales, the virtues are as conspicuous as ever, but the flaws have disappeared. The merits of his short stories are more readily assessed too as his serious rivals in that field are few indeed, Poe, Nathaniel Hawthorne, Stevenson: those are the three, put them in what order you will, who are the greatest exponents of the short story in our language. —DOYLE, CONAN, 1890, *Mr. Stevenson's Methods in Fiction, National Review*, vol. 14, p. 649.

It is as a writer of romances that Mr. Stevenson is most widely read and popular, and as an essayist that his intimates know and love him, for his books for boys are among the best that have ever been written and his essays are the most fascinating that have appeared in England since the time of Lamb. Not the finest critical essays, be it understood, but the most delightful of the discursive, fanciful, frankly egotistical description, dealing with human relations, with sentiment, conduct, or mental experience, with the essence of literature rather than its accidents or objective manifestations. . . . Mr. Stevenson's quality is not so much style in the classical sense, as that of Milton or Gibbon, or even of Addison, but he has an exquisite ear for prose rhythms, and an absurd felicity of expression which leaves us in doubt whether to laugh or to cry aloud with pleasure. His power is that of the striking and picturesque use of words, of lucid exposition, of coloured and graphic narration, and his pages have a quality like velvet—a delicate pile or bloom, soft and buoyant, yet lustrous and full of intricate light and shade. His sentences make their way into the mind with a courtly, considerate tactfulness, and linger pleasantly in the memory, while he relates, argues, illustrates his meaning, or repeats himself with a difference until he is sure of being fully understood, writing with an evident and infectious delight in words, and rejoicing in the alertness and agility of his brain.—NEWTON-ROBINSON, JANETTA, 1893, *Some Aspects of the Work of Mr. Robert Louis Stevenson, Westminster Review*, vol. 139, pp. 601, 605.

For ease there has been nothing like Stevenson's style since Lamb, while for vivacity and vividness there is nothing like it elsewhere in English prose. The richer rhythms he perhaps lacks, and his tone has possibly at times a touch of affectation. But no more subtle instrument of human thought has ever been wielded more gracefully outside the shores of France.—JACOBS, JOSEPH, 1894, *Robert Louis Stevenson, Literary Studies*, p. 176.

When he writes of himself, how supremely excellent is the reading. It is good even when he does it intentionally, as in "Portraits and Memories." It is better still when he sings it, as in his "Child's Garden." He is irresistible to every lonely child who reads and thrills, and reads again to find his past recovered for him with effortless ease. It is a book never long out of my hands, for only in it and in my dreams when I am touched with fever, do I grasp the long, long thoughts of a lonely child and a hill-wandering boy—thoughts I never told to any; yet which Mr. Stevenson tells over again to me as if he read them off a printed page.—CROCKETT, SAMUEL RUTHERFORD, 1895, *Mr. Stevenson's Books, McClure's Magazine*, vol. 4, p. 289.

It was difficult to name a living artist in words that could be compared with him who reminded us at every turn of Charles Lamb and William Hazlitt. There are certain writers who compel words to serve them and never travel without an imperial body guard; but words waited on Stevenson like "humble servitors," and he went where he pleased in his simplicity because every one flew to anticipate his wishes. His style had the thread of gold, and he was the perfect type of the man of letters—a humorist whose great joy in the beautiful was annealed to a fine purity by his Scottish faith; whose kinship was not with Boccaccio and Rabelais, but with Dante and Spenser. His was the magical touch that no man can explain or acquire; it belongs to those only who have drunk at the Pierian spring.—WATSON, JOHN (IAN MACLAREN), 1895, *In Memoriam, R. L. S., McClure's Magazine*, vol. 4, p. 292.

He fashioned his life after his own heart, like the artist he was. In the game against Fate, he made the very utmost of the cards he held, playing so skillfully as to score even with the weak suit of bodily health. Within its limits, his life was a masterpiece. . . . He never wrote anything more consummate in their kind than the "New Arabian Nights;" yet one is glad to think that these exercises in blood-curdling humour came at the beginning of his career as a story-teller, and the Dutch scenes of "Catriona" near the close. In "Treasure Island," masterpiece though it be, he is still imitating, parodying, pouring his genius into a ready made form. In "Kidnapped" he breaks away, half unwittingly perhaps, from the boy's-book convention. "The Master of Ballantrae" is an independent, self-sufficing romance, no more imitative than "The Bride of Lammermoor" or "Esmond;" and "Catriona," imperfect though it be in structure, carries the boy's book projected in "Kidnapped" into the higher region of serious character-study and exquisite emotion. Not even Catriona—that pearl of maidenhood, whom Viola and Perdita would hail as their very sister—not even Catriona has succeeded in dissipating the illusion that Robert Louis Stevenson could not draw a woman. . . . For my own part, I believe that Stevenson's greatness in prose has unduly overshadowed the rare and quite individual charm of his verse. It is true that verse was not his predestinate medium, that he wrote it rather as a man of consummate literary accomplishment than as a born poet, who "did but sing because he must." But on the other hand, he never wrote save from a genuine poetic impulse; he never lashed himself into a metric frenzy merely because it was his trade. Therefore all his verse is alive with spontaneous feeling, and so unfailing was his mastery of words, that he succeeded in striking a clear, true note that was all his own. In his lighter rhymes, both in the "Child's Garden" and "Underwoods," there is a cool, fresh, limpid grace, in which I, for one, never fail to find pleasure and refreshment; and his blank verse, if it lacked freedom and variety of accent, attained a singular dignity, as of exquisite carving in alabaster.—ARCHER, WILLIAM, 1895, *In Memoriam, New Review*, vol. 12, pp. 89, 94, 95.

Virgil of prose! far distant is the day
When at the mention of your heartfelt name
Shall shake the head, and men, oblivious, say:
"We know him not, this master, nor his fame."
Not for so swift forgetfulness you wrought,
Day upon day, with rapt fastidious pen,
Turning, like precious stones, with anxious thought,
This word and that again and yet again,
Seeking to match its meaning with the world;
Nor to the morning stars gave ears attent,
That you, indeed, might ever dare to be
With other praise than immortality
Unworthily content.
—LE GALLIENNE, RICHARD, 1895, *Robert Louis Stevenson, an Elegy*.

We are told by those who are always critics and always objectors—and nothing in this world was ever done by critics and objectors—we are told by them that, after all, the works of Robert Louis Stevenson are his best memorials. In one sense that is undoubtedly true. No man of ancient or modern times since the beginning of the world has ever left behind him so splendid a collection of his works as has Robert Louis Stevenson—I mean not merely of what they contain, but the outward and visible form of them.—ROSEBERY, ARCHIBALD PHILIP PRIMROSE LORD, 1896, *Appreciations and Addresses*, ed. Geake, p. 98.

Commonplace morality and conventional expression are impossible to him, his questing avidity could never be harnessed in the shafts of everyday purpose. In an age of journalism, of barren repetition and fruitless expatiation, it is high praise to give even to a great prose-writer to say of him that he never proses. This praise is due to Stevenson; his chisel, which rang in the workshops of many masters, was always wielded under the direction of a marvellously quick eye, by a hand that gathered strength and confidence every year. He has left no slovenly work, none that has not an inimitable distinction, and the charm of expression that belongs only to a rare spirit. If the question be raised of his eventual place in the great hierarchy of English writers, it is enough to say that the tribunal that shall try his claims is not yet in session; when the time comes he will be summoned to the bar, not with the array of contemporaries whose names a foolish public linked to his, but with the chief prose-writers of the century, few of whom can face the trial with less to extenuate and less to conceal.—RALEIGH, WALTER, 1896, *English Prose*, ed. Craik, vol. v, p. 763.

Adopting to the full, and something more than the full, the modern doctrine of the all-importance of art, of manner, of style in literature, Mr. Stevenson early made the most elaborate studies in imitative composition. There is no doubt that he at last succeeded in acquiring a style which was quite his own; but it was complained and with justice, that even to the last he never attained complete ease in this style; that its mannerism was not only excessive but bore, as even excessive mannerism by no means always does, the marks of distinct and obvious effort. This was perhaps most notable in his essays, which were further marred by the fact that much of them was occupied by criticism, for which, though his taste was original and delicate, Stevenson's knowledge was not quite solid enough, and his range of sympathies a little deficient in width. In his stories, on the other hand, the devil's advocate detected certain weak points, the chief of them being an incapacity to finish, and either a distaste or incapacity for introducing women. This last charge was finally refuted by "Catriona," not merely in the heroine, but in the much more charming and lifelike figure of Barbara Grant; but the other was something of a true bill to the last. It was Stevenson's weakness (as by the way it was also Scott's) to huddle up his stories rather than to wind them off to an orderly conclusion. But against this allowance—a just but an ample one—for defects, must be set to Stevenson's credit such a combination of literary and storytelling charm as perhaps no writer except Mérimée has ever equalled; while, if the literary side of him had not the golden perfection, the accomplished ease of the Frenchman, his romance has a more genial, a fresher, a more natural quality.—SAINTSBURY, GEORGE, 1896, *A History of Nineteenth Century Literature*, p. 340.

Perfect accord between sense and sound, perfect beauty of sound, and a perfect avoidance of palpable artifice—these, with freshness and a very masculine vigor, are the qualities of Stevenson's prose style.— VAN RENSSELAER, M. G., 1896, *Robert Louis Stevenson and his Writings, Century Magazine*, vol. 51, p. 127.

Gold-belted sailors, bristling buccaneers,
The flashing soldier, and the high, slim dame,
These were the Shapes that all around him came,—
That we let go with tears.
His was the unstinted English of the Scot,
Clear, nimble, with the scriptural tang of Knox
Thrust through it like the far, strict scent of box,
To keep it unforgot.
No frugal Realist, but quick to laugh,
To see appealing things in all he knew,
He plucked the sun-sweet corn his fathers grew,
And would have naught of chaff.
—REESE, LIZETTE WOODWORTH, 1896, *Robert Louis Stevenson, A Quiet Road*.

The place that Stevenson will take in literature is surely not to be made evident so long as the glamour of his personality remains over those who were his contemporaries. And with his personality so fully interwoven with his works, it seems hard to believe that the glamour can soon fade away. It is easy to imagine that, like Charles Lamb, he can never become wholly a "figure in literature," but will remain vividly present to many generations of readers as a gifted child of genius who is to be fervently loved.—BRIDGES, ROBERT, 1897, *Library of the World's Best Literature*, ed. Warner, vol. XXIV, p. 13935.

It is the holiday mood of life that Stevenson expresses, and no one has ever expressed it with a happier abandonment to the charm of natural things. In its exquisite exaggeration, it is the optimism of the invalid, due to his painful consciousness that health, and the delights of health, are what really matter in life. . . . In the phrase of Beddoes, Stevenson was "tired of being merely human." Thus there are no women in his books, no lovers; only the lure of hidden treasures and the passion of adventure. It was for the accidents and curiosities of life that he cared, for life as a strange picture, for its fortunate confusions, its whimsical distresses, its unlikely strokes of luck, its cruelties, sometimes, and the touch of madness that comes into it at moments. For reality, for the endeavor to see things as they are, to represent them as they are, he had an impatient disregard. These matters did not interest him.—SYMONS, ARTHUR, 1897, *Studies in Two Literatures*, pp. 242, 244.

His plays—written in collaboration with Mr. W. E. Henley—had a power of their own, and one of them, "Beau Austin," although not accepted by the public is probably the greatest contribution to the drama of the era.—SHORTER, CLEMENT, 1897, *Victorian Literature*, p. 59.

It would be hard to choose among Stevenson's books; his exquisite mastery of form, and of all that form can do, no less than his gay and gallant heart, is in them all.—HAWKINS, ANTHONY HOPE, 1897, *My Favorite Novelist and his Best Book, Munsey's Magazine*, vol. 18, p. 351.

Of all the writers of English fiction of the younger generation, the impression of the highest genius was probably conveyed by Robert Louis Stevenson—an impression which his many admirers hold, notwithstanding the conviction that nothing he has ever done, however exquisite, has quite realized all his possibilities. It is indeed singularly to Stevenson's credit that no achievement in literature to which he might have risen, however high, would have been altogether a surprise to anyone acquainted with his work. For all have admitted in him a rare distinction of style, the qualities of a fine imagination, humour and pathos in a high degree, the fancy of the poet, and the sympathy, both wise and tender, of the genial lover of his kind.—GRAHAM, RICHARD D., 1897, *The Masters of Victorian Literature*, p. 127.

The romantic movement in fiction, except in so far as it is mere reaction from pessimistic realism, is again a sign of reviving strength. And it is a fortunate circumstance for the future of literature that its leader and foremost representative should have possessed the distinguished literary gift of Robert Louis Stevenson, a writer whose exquisitely finished style, while for the reader it suffers somewhat from its evidences of too conscious art, affords for that very reason an all the more inspiring and serviceable model to the student. His influence is largely traceable in all the lighter literature of the imagination of the present day, and, due allowance being made for the dangers which beset all young writers still in the imitative stage, it has been on the whole, an influence for good.—TRAILL, HENRY DUFF, 1897, *Social England*, vol. VI, p. 518.

Writing was to him an art, and almost everything that he has written has a little the air of being a *tour de force*. Stevenson's books and essays were generally brilliant imitations of established things, done somewhat in the spirit of an expert in billiards. In short, Stevenson is the most extraordinary mimic that has ever appeared in literature.—CHAPMAN, JOHN JAY, 1898, *Emerson and Other Essays*, p. 220.

Robert Louis Stevenson was the literary man pure and simple, in the sense that Hazlitt, or Leigh Hunt, or Matthew Arnold was, and this is his most honourable distinction. . . . Like those of the Wizard of the North, his writings are for the most part intensely Scottish. . . . In his criticisms, Stevenson, because he knew himself so well, at once seems to see with the eyes of his author and to know his mind. What fine discrimination in his essay on that enigma of seventeenth-century character, Samuel Pepys. What anatomising and analysis of François Villon, blackguard and poet! It is doubtful if any of the host of writers who have blamed or excused Robert Burns has arrived more nearly at the truth than this keen critic in his famous essay on the "Old Hawk." Yet he neither weeps nor grows abusive. He is sane, truthful, judicious. . . . In his short stories Stevenson seems to occupy a middle place between Hawthorne and Poe. He is neither so moonstruck an idealist as the former, nor so ghastly a realist as the latter. If he does terrify us now and then, the feeling is mixed with delight and wonder at his marvelous skill, his absolute precision in his epithets and phrases, his consummate artistic power.—MACCULLOCH, J. A., 1898, *R. L. Stevenson, Westminster Review*, vol. 149, pp. 631, 640, 644.

To attain the mastery of an elastic and harmonious English prose, in which trite and inanimate elements should have no place, and which should be supple to all uses and alive in all its joints and members, was an aim which he pursued with ungrudging, even with heroic, toil. Not always, especially not at the beginning, but in by far the greater part of his mature work, the effect of labour and fastidious selection is lost in the felicity of the result. Energy of vision goes hand in hand with magic of presentment, and both words and things acquire new meaning and a new vitality under his touch. Next to finish and brilliancy of execution, the most remarkable quality of his work is its variety. Without being the inventor of any new form or mode of literary art (unless, indeed, the verses of the "Child's Garden" are to be accounted such), he handled with success and freshness nearly all the old forms—the moral, critical, and personal essay, travels sentimental and other, romances and short tales both historical and modern, parables and tales of mystery, boys' stories of adventure, drama, memoir, lyrical and meditative verse both English and Scottish. To some of these forms he gave quite a new life: through all alike he expressed vividly his own extremely personal way of seeing and being, his peculiar sense of nature and of romance.—COLVIN, SIDNEY, 1898, *Dictionary of National Biography*, vol. LIV., p. 253.

Of course one has to agree that writing was to Stevenson an art, and also that, as Mr. Chapman acutely says, everything "he has written has a little the air of a *tour de force*." But it is to be noted that nothing of his has this air so much when it is taken by itself as when it is taken in connection with other pieces of his work. In comparing "Treasure Island" with "The English Admirals," or "The New Arabian Nights" with "The Beach at Falesa," one cannot help seeing that sustained efforts in styles so different involve a strain even upon the highest literary skill. One may even be in doubt, in the presence of so many styles assumed with so much skill, what was really the writer's own bent. Now we have the utmost sophistication, in which the style is a tissue, a panoply, of allusions, and now a "naked and open daylight," in which the reader is not aware of style, and there is no explicit reminder that the writer has ever read anything. This versatility is bewildering, but Mr. Chapman is the only reader of Stevenson I know of who has found it irritating. . . . Is there a more transparent medium than the atmosphere through which we see the scenes and figures of his "picture-making romance?" The fight in the heather in "Kidnapped," the trial in "David Balfour," the duel in the dark in "The Master of Ballantrae"—who but Mr. Chapman fails to number these among the great achievements of modern fiction?—SCHUYLER, MONTGOMERY, 1899, *The Canonization of Stevenson, Century Magazine, vol. 58, pp. 479, 480.*

Stevenson, who, brilliant though he was, had neither the accumulated resourses of Scott, nor so luxuriant a fancy, collected his materials with immense pains, sifted them laboriously, and when he came to use them never rested till he had everything in its proper place, and displayed to the best possible advantage. His jewels are none of them rough diamonds. Every gem is cut, polished to the highest point, and set in gold of rare and cunning workmanship. But, conscious though he was, in every fibre, of his own art, he was far too shrewd not to acknowledge that it was beyond his power to reach the lofty eminence occupied by Scott, and that he could never have created the Baron of Bradwardine, or the Antiquary, or Jeanie Deans, nor woven together such a masterpiece as the plot of "Guy Mannering." He spoke of Scott as "out and away the King of romantics," who shared with Balzac and Thackeray in "Vanity Fair" "the real creator's brush." . . . There can be little doubt that what he wrote will stand the test of time, and that hereafter he will hold a place in the goodly fellowship of the immortals, but no man knew better than Stevenson that, far above them all, Scott moves himself along the higher ridges of the mountain-tops, unapproachable.—OMOND, G. W. T., 1900, *Notes on the Art of Robert Louis Stevenson, North American Review, vol. 171, pp. 357, 358.*

The time has hardly come to assign Stevenson his position in English literature. It is not easy to separate his personality from his books; perhaps it will never be quite possible to separate them. The generation of critics who knew and loved him—and could not help infusing the rapture of love into their appreciations—must pass away before he can be judged in cold blood. . . . . Like all men who are egotists, but whose egoism, owing to the sweetness of their nature, is never repellant, he was his own best critic. He says, not once but a thousand times, that the view of life which dominated him was the romantic-comic. Holding this view he could not help becoming the perpetuator of the traditions of Scott and Dumas. . . . Two generations of novelists have not produced a more effective short story than "The Pavilion on the Links." As a Scottish poet, as an English critic, as a cosmopolitan moralist, Stevenson was confessedly the "sedulous ape" of Fergusson, of Hazlitt, of Montaigne, but not the equal of any one of the three, except in finish of style.—WALLACE, WILLIAM, 1900, *The Life and Limitations of Stevenson, Scottish Review, vol. 35, pp. 33.*

Stevenson is open to a particularly subtle, a particularly effective and a particularly unjust disparagement. The advantage of great men like Blake or Browning or Walt Whitman is that they did not observe the niceties of technical literature. The far greater disadvantage of Stevenson is that he did. Because he had a conscience about small matters in art, he is conceived not to have had an imagination about big ones. It is assumed by some that he must have been a bad architect, and the only reason that they can assign is that he was a good workman. The mistake which has given rise to this conception is one that has much to answer for in numerous departments of modern art, literature, religion, philosophy, and politics. The supreme and splendid characteristic of Stevenson, was his levity; and his levity was the flower of a hundred grave philosophies. . . . He had what may be a perfect mental athleticism, which enabled him to leap from crag to crag, and to trust himself anywhere and upon any question. His splendid quality as an essayist and controversialist was that he could always recover his weapon. He was not like the average swashbuckler of the current parties, tugged at the tail of his own sword.—CHESTERTON, G. K., 1901,

Robert Louis Stevenson (The Bookman Biographies), pp. 10, 11.

His was the royal wholeness of a nature moving all together, without apology or evil discount. He had not to think of self but to be; not to cipher out an attitude to life but to live; not even to appoint himself a missionary of the doctrine of happiness to other men, like those actors who posture and snigger in order to raise a laugh, but simply to be happy and make that happiness, with its solid glow of heat, its own excuse for being. Such happiness is contagious; it needs no bolstering of propaganda; it awakens echoes, it calls out responsive cheer by its mere self-evidencing wholesomeness. This happiness in Stevenson was more than temperamental; it had based itself in the wise and penetrative spirit. Nor was it any shallow evasion of the deeps of life; it was at polar remove from the mere physical well-being of a gourmand, or the glee of an empty-headed dancer. It had made itself good against too much ill health for that; and underlying it were centuries of digested thought and doctrine. An efflorescence, a fruitage, it truly was, culminating from profound strains of vital meditation; it was, in a word, Stevenson's religion, and when we consider all that went to the shaping of it, a religion fair and sufficient.—GENUNG, JOHN FRANKLIN, 1901, *Stevenson's Attitude to Life*, p. 28.

What, precisely, was Mr. Henley's share in the plays done jointly by Robert Louis Stevenson and himself? . . . Take "Macaire" first, "A Melodramatic Farce" it is called though it is rather a farce suddenly transformed, at last, into a melodrama. Stevenson, single-handed, was prolific of both these forms in his books. As examples of his farce we have the immortal "New Arabian Nights;" of his melodrama, "The Pavilion on the Links," "Dr. Jekyll and Mr. Hyde" and the greater part of every romance that he wrote. Therefore there is no reason why he should not have alone conceived the plot of "Macaire." There is (I forestall, unscientifically, the proper working of the process) very good reason to suppose that Mr. Henley did not conceive the plots of the plays written with Stevenson, inasmuch as he has never by himself shown any tendency to story-telling. . . . The choice of Macaire as protagonist is, surely, his also. Not only was Macaire among the figures enumerated by him as being in Skelt's repertory, but the whole conception of Macaire—its difference from the traditional conception—is essentially Stevensonian. This eloquently philosophic scoundrel, this tatterdemalion with transcendental schemes for subjugating his fellows, is too like Stevenson's Villon and Stevenson's Dynamiter not to have sprung fully equipped from Stevenson's own brain. His companion, too, Bertrand—how could one attribute him to anyone but that writer who always so persistently revelled and excelled in delineating a timid nature thrown into perilous affairs? The passion of fear was the one passion that Stevenson never could keep out of anything he wrote.— BEERBOHM, MAX, 1901, *A Puzzle in Literary Drama, Saturday Review*, vol. 91, p. 600.

Stevenson, by whatever means, acquired not only a delicate style, but a style of his own. If it sometimes reminds one of models, it does not suggest that he is speaking in a feigned voice. I think, indeed, that this precocious preoccupation with style suggests the excess of self-consciousness which was his most obvious weakness; a daintiness which does not allow us to forget the presence of the artist. But Stevenson did not yield to other temptations which beset the lover of exquisite form. He was no "æsthete" in the sense which conveys a reproach. He did not sympathise with the doctrine that an artist should wrap up himself in luxurious hedonism and cultivate indifference to active life. He was too much of a boy. A true boy cannot be "æsthetic." He had "day-dreams," but they were of piracy; tacit aspirations towards stirring adventure and active heroism. His dreams were of a future waking.—STEPHEN, LESLIE, 1902, *Studies of a Biographer, Second Series*, vol. IV., p. 215.

Stevenson has already taken his place as an entertaining novelist of the second or third class, and his singularly lovable personality is not now mistaken for literary genius by any great number of persons.— PAYNE, WILLIAM MORTON, 1902, *Editorial Echoes*, p. 61.

The title of this paper may seem to some not a particularly hopeful one. Stevenson, the romancist, we all know and rejoice in. Stevenson, the moral philosopher, to say the least of it, does not sound promising. So little are we apt to find of moral theory in the books we love best that we should be sorry to be set to seek even for morals. His best characters have few enough of the copy-book virtues; his worst are as bad as they are made; yet we find something admirable in them all.—MUIRHEAD, J. H., 1902, *Robert Louis Stevenson's Philosophy and Life*, p. 37.

Stevenson's romanticism shows itself most interestingly in a spirit of artistic enterprise and adventure. His novels and tales are more various and daring in their method and technique than those of any of his predecessors; and on the whole his artistic experiments justify themselves. In firmness and clearness of structure, in novelty and variety of method, methods of description and narrative, and in surface brilliancy of style, he marks the extraordinary technical advance which the novel has made since the days of Scott. For another reason, also, Stevenson's name may fittingly stand at the end of a chapter on the English novel. He represents in a sense the return of the century upon itself.—MOODY, WILLIAM VAUGHN, AND LOVETT, ROBERT MORSS, 1902, *A History of English Literature*, p. 383.

Stevenson with all his genius, made the mistake of approaching the theatre as a toy to be played with. The facts of the case were against him, for the theatre is not a toy; and, facts being stubborn things, he ran his head against them in vain. Had he only studied the conditions, or, in other words got into a proper relation to the facts, with what joy should we have acclaimed him among the masters of the modern stage!—PINERO, ARTHUR WING, 1903, *Robert Louis Stevenson the Dramatist, The Critic*, vol. 42, p. 353.

James Anthony Froude
1818–1894.

Born, at Dartington, Devon, 23 April 1818. At Westminster School, 1830–33. Matric. Oriel Coll., Oxford, 10 Dec. 1835. B. A., 28 April 1842; Chancellor's Eng. Essay Prize, 1842; Fellow of Exeter Coll., 1842–49; M. A., 2 March 1843. Ordained Deacon, 1844. Contrib. to "Westminster Rev." Rector of St. Andrews Univ., and Hon. LL.D., 23 March 1869. For some time editor of "Fraser's Mag." Resigned Deaconship, under Clerical Disabilities Act, 21 Sept. 1872. Lectured in U. S. A., 1872. On political mission to Cape of Good Hope, Dec. 1874 to March 1875. Travelled in Australia, 1885; and in West Indies. Regius Prof. of Modern Hist. Oxford, 1892. Died 20 Oct. 1894. *Works:* "Shadows of the Clouds" (under pseud: "Zeta"), 1847; "A Sermon . . . on the death of the Rev. G. M. Coleridge," 1847; "The Nemesis of Faith," 1849 (2nd edn. same year); "The Book of Job" (from "Westm. Rev."), 1854; "Suggestions on the best means of teaching English History," 1855; "History of England" (12 vols.), 1856–70; "Short Studies on Great Subjects" (2 vols.), 1867; second ser., 1871; third ser., 1877; fourth ser., 1883; "Inaugural Address" at St. Andrews, 1869; "The Cat's Pilgrimage," 1870; "Calvinism," 1871; "The English in Ireland in the Eighteenth Century" (3 vols.), 1872–74; "Cæsar," 1879; "Bunyan," 1880; "Two Lectures on South Africa," 1880; "Thomas Carlyle: history of the first forty years of his life" (2 vols.), 1882; "Luther," 1883; "Thomas Carlyle: history of his life in London" (2 vols.), 1884; "Oceana," 1886; "The English in the West Indies," 1888 (2nd edn. same year); "Liberty and Property" [1888]; "The Two Chiefs of Dunboy," 1889; "Lord Beaconsfield," 1890; "The Divorce of Catharine of Arragon," 1891; "The Spanish Story of the Armada," 1892 (2nd edn. same year); "Life and Letters of Erasmus," 1894 (2nd edn. same year). *Posthumous:* "English Seamen in the Sixteenth Century," 1895; "Lectures on the Council of Trent," 1896 (2nd edn. same year). He *edited:* "The Pilgrim," by W. Thomas, 1861; Carlyle's "Reminiscences," 1881–82; J. W. Carlyle's "Letters and Memorials," 1883.—SHARP, R. FARQUHARSON, 1897, *A Dictionary of English Authors*, p. 104.

PERSONAL

Mr. Froude to me is simply the writer of certain books. Whatever I have said about him has arisen naturally from his writings. I believe those writings to be, in more ways than one, misleading and dangerous, and I have spoken accordingly. But of Mr. Froude, apart from his writings, I know nothing, except one or two facts which are known to everyone. Mr. Froude thinks that

PHILIP GILBERT HAMERTON

Engraving from a Photograph by Mr. A. H. Palmer.

JAMES ANTHONY FROUDE

From an Etching by H. B. Hall, 1878.

I feel for him "personal dislike," if not "fanatical hatred." Such a feeling, in any strictly personal sense, is impossible on my part. I never saw Mr. Froude; I never had any dealings with him, except that I think he and I once, long ago, exchanged a pair of very formal letters; he has never done me personally either good or harm. The only things that I have said that could be twisted into an "invective" or "aspersions" on his personal character are two. I charged him with "fanatical hatred towards the English Church, at all times and in all characters;" I do not think that these words were too strong. Mr. Froude's habitual way of speaking of the English Church and its ministers in all ages is a way of speaking which I should be sorry to use of Buddhist Lamas or of Mussulman Mollahs. I said, what is certainly true, that I know nothing to be compared to Mr. Froude's ecclesiastical bitterness. I said that I guessed that such "a degree of hatred must be peculiar to those who have entered her ministry and forsaken it, perhaps peculiar to the one man who first wrote 'Lives of the Saints,' and then 'Shadows of the Clouds.'" The reference is to publicly known facts in Mr. Froude's life—facts which seem to me to have had their effect on his writings. . . . He plainly believes himself to be an injured innocent, as he plainly believes himself to be an accurate historian. The truth is that, in controversy just as in history, Mr. Froude is pursued by his usual ill-luck —by that hard destiny which makes it impossible for him accurately to report anything. His controversial case against me now, just like his St. Alban's Annals, or his Life of Thomas, is made up of misconceptions and misquotations of every kind.— FREEMAN, EDWARD A., 1879, *Last Words on Mr. Froude, Contemporary Review*, vol. 35, pp. 217, 218.

I do not think that a single being in Oriel interfered in the slightest degree with Anthony Froude's religious convictions while he was there. For the time I was at college with him I had relations with him as *Censor Theologicus* in which capacity I might be supposed at liberty to make any demands on Anthony's faith or submission. But all I had to do was to look over his sermon notes, and satisfy myself as well as I could that he had been at one of the university sermons, and had given some attention to it. In this capacity I can answer for it that nothing remarkable passed between me and Anthony, unless it be that Anthony, having once hurt his knee, begged leave to analyse any sermon I might name instead of walking to St. Mary's.—MOZLEY, THOMAS, 1882, *Reminiscences Chiefly of Oriel College and the Oxford Movement*, vol. II, p. 34.

My Dear Old Man,—Yes, old we are, but there are few old men who have made such a good fight for it as you have. After all, from the first day of our life, our life is but a constant fight with death. . . . However, there are few men who, after that alloted time, could walk the hours that you could, and now produce another book as you have. I was so pleased to get it, and I am beginning to read it. Many thanks for it. . . . I hope you will go on fighting. I do the same, though one feels that, after all, the best of life is gone, and there is little left worth fighting for. Still Aunt Eh seems very happy on her small allowance of vitality.— MÜLLER, FRIEDRICH MAX, 1894, *To J. A. Froude, Oct. 3; Life and Letters*, ed. his Wife, vol. II, p. 337.

Froude was something more than the most accomplished prose writer of his time. He was a man of the world, who lived a full and various life. There was no trace of the bookworm on him, nothing of that awkwardness which the mere student often betrays in the company of his fellow-men and of women. . . . He liked out-doors, loved nature, loved certain out-door sports, and practised them. When he chose he could be a man of affairs, and had a practical business-like sagacity which did not fail him when the occasion arose. — SMALLEY, G. W., 1894, *Studies of Men*, pp. 299, 300.

Mr. Froude's death is a personal infliction upon the Old World and the New. He had many friends, and not a few enemies, in both hemispheres. He was a strenuous man who enjoyed himself in many ways, and could adapt himself to a great variety of circumstances. With sorrow he was indeed well acquainted—he knew what it was to be both bitterly disappointed and cruelly wounded. He carried about with him in all his wanderings much sad human experience; his philosophy of life was more sombre than sweet. I do not think anybody who knew him would have described him as a happy man. But for all that he managed to enjoy himself heartily enough.—BIRRELL, AUGUSTINE, 1895–1901, *James Anthony Froude, Essays and Addresses*, p. 161.

Had Arthur Stanley lived, a corner would have been found for Anthony Froude within the walls of the Abbey; but probably it is better as it is. The son of Devon will sleep the sounder "upon the beached verge of the salt flood," within hearing of the surf that beats upon Bolt Head and the Start.—SKELTON, JOHN, 1895, *Reminiscences of James Anthony Froude, Blackwood's Magazine, vol. 157, p. 63.*

I was ushered into the drawing-room, where were two young ladies, the daughters of Mr. Froude. The room struck me as very quaint and pretty, antique and tasteful. I was cordially welcomed, and was just enjoying a cup of tea when Mr. Froude came into the room. A fine man, above the ordinary height, and with a certain stateliness of aspect, younger-looking than I had expected. He must have beeen about seventy; well-knit, but slender; a fine head and brow, with abundant grey, not white, hair; handsome eyes, brown and well opened, with a certain scrutiny or watchfulness in their regard—eyes which look you well and searchingly in the face, but where you might come to see now and then a dreamy and far-off softness, telling of thoughts far from present surroundings and present companionship. The eyes did not reassure me at that first interview, though they attracted me strangely. The upper part of the face undeniably handsome and striking, but on the mouth sat a mocking bitterness, or—so it seemed to me—a sense of having weighed all things, all persons, all books, all creeds, and all the world has to give, and having found everything wanting in some essential point; a bitterness, hardly a joylessness, but an absence of sunshine in the lower part of the face. A smile without much geniality, with rather a mocking causticity, sometimes seen; and the facial lines are austere, self-contained, and marked. Laughter without mirth—I would not like to say without kindness—but Froude's kindness always appeared to me in much quieter demonstrations. His manners struck me as particularly fine and courteous but if one was of a timid nature, one need only look in his face and *fear*.—IRELAND, MRS. ALEXANDER, 1895, *Recollections of James Anthony Froude, Contemporary Review, vol. 67, p. 17.*

Of the group, James Anthony Froude was the oldest, and he was at Oxford just at the time when the Tractarian Movement was exciting all generous minds. Greatly under the influence of Newman in the forties, Froude took orders, and was closely connected with the High Church party. With this group Freeman also, though less prominently, was and remained allied, and his anger was excited when Froude, instead of following Newman to Rome, or staying with the agitated Anglican remnant, announced his entire defection from the religious system by the publication of the "Nemesis of Faith" in 1849. From this time forth the indignation of Freeman was concentrated and implacable, and lasted without intermission for more than forty years. The duel between these men was a matter of such constant puplic entertainment that it claims mention in a history, and distinctly moulded the work of both these interesting artists.—GOSSE, EDMUND, 1897, *A Short History of Modern English Literature, p. 373.*

My first recollections of Mr. Froude carry me back to some of the earlier years of my literary work in London. He used to attend occasionally at the meetings of the Newspaper Press Fund Committee, where his handsome, thoughtful face, his retiring ways, and his grave meditative demeanour reminded me somehow—I cannot tell why—of Nathaniel Hawthorne, as I had known him years before in Liverpool. But Froude had really none of Nathaniel Hawthorne's shyness and love for habitual silence. His manner when he got into conversation was always bright and genial, often became even careless and joyous, and presented a curious contrast with the gravity and stillness of his habitual demeanour.—McCARTHY, JUSTIN, 1899, *Reminiscences, vol. II, p. 101.*

My friendship with Froude lasted as long as he lived. He was a warm and sincere friend, always ready with word or deed to help one who needed it, and one of the men for whom I retain the warmest feeling of all I knew at this epoch of my life.—STILLMAN, WILLIAM JAMES, 1901, *The Autobiography of a Journalist, vol. II, p. 486.*

That he could be very charming in personal intercourse, and that he was cordially beloved by men who knew him most intimately, is nearly all that I can say. I may add, however, one remark: Froude impressed casual observers as somehow enigmatic. He was reticent to the outer circle at least, and incurred the usual penalty. Men who are shy and sensitive are often misjudged by their neighbours: they are supposed to be supercilious because they shrink from irritating topics, and cynical because they keep their enthusiasm for the few really sympathetic hearers. I have heard Froude accused of Jesuitism, of insinuating opinons which he would shrink from openly expressing, and even of a malicious misrepresentation of the man whom he chose as his prophet. I believe such a view to be entirely mistaken.—STEPHEN, LESLIE, 1901, *James Anthony Froude, National Review*, vol. 36, p. 671.

THE NEMESIS OF FAITH
1849

S. Sutton came in, and we had a talk about Anthony Froude's astonishing book, "The Nemesis of Faith," which has made an ugly stir, and has been publicly burned at Oxford, and so on. I guess it is a legitimate outcome of the Oxford party's own dealings; for I remember how a few years since he was warmly associated with them, soon afterwards employed in writing some of the lives of the saints, then by degrees growing disgusted at the falseness of their *modus operandi*. All this must have given what was good and Truth-seeking in him a terrible shake, and now comes out this "Nemesis," which is a wild protest against all authority, Divine and human.—Fox, CAROLINE, 1849, *Memories of Old Friends*, ed. Pym; *Journal*, March 21, p. 256.

In "Nemesis of Faith" he controverted, under the form of a novelette, the inspiration of the Bible and revealed religion. In these Darwinian days such a work would produce little sensation. In those days of lingering orthodoxy, and coming from a clerical pen, it produced a marked sensation, not, we may suppose, greatly to the dissatisfaction of the writer, since spiritual agony of a very serious kind is not apt to vent itself in novelettes. The "Nemesis of Faith" and the pair of novelettes entitled "Shadows of the Clouds" are beautifully written, though rather lachrymose, and, taken together with Froude's later tale, "The Two Chiefs of Dunboy," and with the powers of delineating character, emotion, and action displayed in his histories, seem to show he would have been very great as a writer of fiction.—SMITH, GOLDWIN, 1894, *Froude, North American Review*, vol. 159, p. 678.

A book ["Nemesis of Faith"] which at present would call forth no remark, no controversy, was discussed in all the newspapers, and raised a storm all over England. Bishops shook their heads, nay even their fists, at the young heretic, and even those among his contemporaries at Oxford who ought to have sympathized with him, and were in fact quite as unorthodox as he was, did not dare to stand up for him or lend him a helping hand. Stanley alone never said an unkind word of him. The worst was that Froude not only lost his fellowship, but when he had accepted the Headmastership of a college far away in Tasmania, his antagonists did not rest till his appointment had been cancelled. Froude unfortunately was poor, and his father, a venerable and well-to-do Archdeacon, was so displeased with his son that he stopped the allowance which he had formerly made him. It seems almost as if the poverty of a victim gave increased zest and enjoyment to his pursuers. Froude had to sell his books one by one, and was trying hard to support himself by his pen. This was then not so easy a matter as it is now. At that very time, however, I received a cheque for £200 from an unknown hand, with a request that I would hand it to Froude to show him that he had friends and sympathisers who would not forsake him. It was not till many years later that I discovered the donor, and Froude was then able to return him the money which at the time had saved him from drowning.— MÜLLER, FRIEDRICH MAX, 1898, *Auld Lang Syne*, p. 89.

HISTORY OF ENGLAND
1856–70

You are really unjust to Froude. Even if his idea of Henry VIII is mistaken, his picture of English life is not affected by that. There are chapters in his work that are really masterly—the Irish rebellion, the Charterhouse Monks; and he has described the secret workings of the Reformation among the common people with genuine feeling and sympathy. Froude's idea of Henry VIII seems to me too problematical. But at all events Henry was one of the most popular kings, and has his admirers not only in Froude but in his people, and in such historians as Sharon Turner, and such philosophers as Carlyle. I have a great affection for Froude, for I know him with all his faults, and know that he prays and works. Kingsley is a more brilliant nature, but his relation to Froude has never been that of a teacher; on the contrary, that of an admirer.—MÜLLER, FRIEDRICH MAX, 1857, *To Chevalier Bunsen, May* 1; *Life and Letters,* ed. *his Wife, vol.* I, *p.* 205.

I am in Froude's eleventh volume, which you cannot lay down when you have once taken it up. It is only disagreeable to find Elizabeth growing more and more odious at every page of her history.—THIRLWALL, CONNOP, 1869, *Letters to a Friend,* ed. *Stanley, p.* 208.

He has imagination; he has that sympathetic and dramatic instinct which enables a man to enter into the emotions and motives, the likings and dislikings of the people of a past age. His style is penetrating and thrilling; his language often rises to the dignity of a poetic eloquence. The figures he conjures up are always the semblances of real men and women. They are never wax-work, or lay figures, or skeletons clothed in words, or purple rags of description stuffed out with straw into an awkward likeness to the human form. The one distinct impression we carry away from Froude's history is that of the living reality of his figures. . . . What is there in literature more powerful, more picturesque, more complete and dramatic than Froude's portrait of Mary Queen of Scots? It stands out and glows and darkens with all the glare and gloom of a living form, that now appears in sun and now in shadow. It is almost as perfect and as impressive as any Titian. But can any reasonable person doubt that the picture on the whole is a dramatic and not an historical study?—MCCARTHY, JUSTIN, 1872, *Mr. James Anthony Froude, Modern Leaders, pp.* 230, 231.

Since the appearance of Macaulay's great work no volumes on English history have awakened so great a popular interest as these. The period of the Reformation in England is not only of great political importance, but is filled with such incidents as encourage a spirited narration. The characteristics of the period, therefore, in the hands of a literary artist of Mr. Froude's skill could not fail to result in the production of a work of great popularity. The author's style is remarkable for its perspicuity, his narrative is vivacious, his theories are ingenious, and his sympathies are intense. In consequence of these peculiarities, the pages of the work often have more of the characteristics of an essay than of a history, and the author appears to write as an advocate rather than a judge. While these features increase the spirit of the narration, they detract from the value of the work as an authority. . . . Numerous errors have been brought to light by the vigorous criticisms to which Mr. Froude's work has been subjected. But the principal fault of the history is not in its errors in matters of detail so much as in its constant tendency to one-sidedness. The likes and dislikes of the author are too intense to allow him ever to be strictly judicial. Hence, while this history never fails to interest, it always leaves the impression that there is still something of importance to be said in reply.—ADAMS, CHARLES KENDALL, 1882, *A Manual of Historical Literature, pp.* 449, 450.

I think our friend Mr. Froude, whose history we all read, is a little unfair toward Queen Bess, as he was a little over-fair, and white-wash-i-ly disposed in the case of Henry VIII.: both tendencies being attributable to a mania this shrewd historian has—for unripping and oversetting established forms of belief. I think that he not only bears with a greedy zeal upon her too commonly manifest selfishness and heartlessness, but that he enjoys putting little vicious dabs of bad color upon her picture—as when he says, "she spat, and swore like a trooper." Indeed it would seem that this clever biographer had carried a good deal of his fondness for "Vicious dabs" in portraiture into his more recent *post-mortem* exhibits; as if it were his duty and pleasure to hang out all sorts of soiled linen, in his office of Clean Scrubber. Yet, I wish to speak with all respect of the distinguished historian—whose vigor is conspicuous—whose industry is remarkable, whose crisp sentences are delightful, but whose accuracy is not of the surest; and whose conscience does, I think, sometimes go lame—under strain of his high, rhetorical canter.—MITCHELL, DONALD G., 1889, *English Lands, Letters, and Kings, From Celt to Tudor, p.* 207.

A very remarkable book, perhaps since Macaulay's time the most excellently written historical work that has been added to English literature. Mr. Froude is a strong partisan—probably his work would not be nearly as interesting if he were not so—and he had collected much new and valuable matter from the archives of Simancas. The bias, however, of his writing is perhaps almost too strong, and it is difficult to thoroughly appreciate his work unless one entirely agrees with him. It had been our lot to enter deeply into a small incident contained in the extensive scope of his "History;" we afterwards read his account of the same episode founded undoubtedly upon the original papers we had been studying, and we were lost in wonder at the extraordinary art with which he had developed the dry bones of a little considered incident into a very picturesque passage, and the strange bent of mind which had obscured all but one side of the story of this inconsiderable event. But as we have often repeated, facts really depend on the way they are looked at, and Mr. Froude has unquestionably made admirable use of his materials in forming so eminently readable a history.—OLIPHANT, MARGARET O. W., 1892, *The Victorian Age of English Literature*, p. 543.

In spite of their literary merits, which are unquestionably great, the volumes comprising the reign of Henry VIII. must, as a history, be laid aside. The subject, so full of tragic and criminal interest, still waits for an historian. When he comes we wish him Froude's narrative and pictorial power combined with the strict adherence to fact and a sound sense of justice. . . . Froude has also, it must be said, given way to prejudice—perhaps it would be fairer as well as kinder to say, to the influence of his creative imagination—in the case of Mary, Queen of Scots. He has dressed her up as an incarnation of guile and falsehood. . . . The ruthlessness of his antipathy to the Queen of Scots is shown in the execution scene, where he tells us, and with evident gusto, that as the headsman held up the head the wig fell off and showed that the enchantress was an old woman made up to look young and wore false hair. That scene, however, and, in a different way, the defeat of the Armada, are masterpieces of description. The gifts of pictorial and narrative power, of skill in painting character, of clear, eloquent, and graceful language, Froude had to a degree which places him in the first rank of literary artists. That which he had not in so abundant a measure was the gift of truth. Happily for him, nine readers out of ten would care more for the gifts of which he had the most than for the gift of which he had the least.—SMITH, GOLDWIN, 1894, *Froude, North American Review*, vol. 159, pp. 687, 688.

If the average reader were asked to name Froude's special quality, he would probably reply that he is uniformly interesting. With some confidence one may hazard the guess that the twelve volumes of the "History of England" have been read from cover to cover by more persons than any other consecutive English work of equal length written during the last half-century.—DODDS, JAMES MILLER, 1896, *English Prose*, ed. Craik, vol. v, p. 638.

The critics were divided. Froude was a man who usually either carried his readers wholly with him or alienated them. Those who loved clear, vigorous, pointed English, keen intelligence and life-like portraiture, were delighted with the book. Students, familiar with the original documents and able to criticise details, regarded it with very different eyes. Both sides were right in their principal assertions, and both were prone to forget that there was another aspect of the case. On the one hand, it has been established beyond the reach of reasonable dispute that Froude was habitually and grossly inaccurate. It is indeed doubtful whether any other historian, with any title to be considered great, can be charged with so many grave errors. Froude is inaccurate first of all in his facts. He does not take the trouble to verify, he misquotes, he is not careful to weigh evidence. But moreover, he is inaccurate in what may be called his colour. He paints his picture in the light of his own emotions and prejudices, he is rather the impassioned advocate than the calm judge. He would not only have acknowledged this, but he would have defended himself; and there is something to be said for his view. . . . A history is a piece of literature as well as a record of facts; and as literature Froude's work stands very high. In the first place, it is great in style. Not that his English is of the kind that calls attention to itself. It is seldom magnificent, but it is always adequate, and the reader never feels himself jarred by want of taste or befogged by obscurity either of thought or expression.—WALKER, HUGH, 1897, *The Age of Tennyson*, pp. 128, 130.

History, indeed, has never enlisted a more brilliant pen, and whatever may be thought regarding Froude's merits as a working historian, no one will dispute the high distinction of his style, or his supreme excellence in the region of historic art. It is true that nothing like the popularity of Macaulay has fallen to his lot, nor can we wonder. Nevertheless, not even in Macaulay's hands has the drama of history been more vividly portrayed, or its characters and events been made to appeal more strongly to the imagination of the reader. Froude's colours glow upon the canvas with an extraordinary brilliancy, and in spite of protests, burn themselves into the memory, so that the historic figures already imprinted there insensibly take tone from the stronger portraits which he has placed beside them.—GRAHAM, RICHARD D., 1897, *The Masters of Victorian Literature, p. 207.*

As a writer of English prose he had few equals in the nineteenth century; and the ease and gracefulness of his style, his faculty for dramatic presentation, and command of the art of picturesque description have secured for his "History" a permanent place in English prose literature. On the other hand, while appealing to the prejudices of a large class of readers and to the æsthetic sense of all, he has failed to convince students of the fidelity of his pictures or the truth of his conclusions. Indeed, Froude himself hardly seems to have regarded truth as attainable in history.—POLLARD, A. F., 1901, *Dictionary of National Biography, Supplement, vol.* II, *p. 261.*

THOMAS CARLYLE
1882-84

We have vainly striven to fashion some conceivable hypothesis why Mr. Froude has not done what any one else would have done. He had here the most valuable materials for the biography of the man he wished to commemorate; he is endowed by nature with all the powers needed for a worthy commemoration; and he has so used these materials, that when the biography comes, all his great literary power will hardly prevent his work from falling flat. He has acted like the discoverer of a gold mine, who should cart away tons of the earth in which the ore is embedded before beginning to separate any. He has given wanton and reckless pain, has hurt tender recollections and sacred feelings, and he has bereaved us all of a noble ideal that was most dear and precious; but we must remember that he has not yielded to any comprehensible temptation in doing so; on the contrary, he has made the task he has yet to fulfill less interesting, both to himself and his readers. It is not as in the publication of a book to which these Reminiscences have been compared—the Greville Memoirs. They, at least, were a contribution, of a certain kind, to literature; it never occurred to the reader that any other use could be made of them than giving them with more or less revision to the public. . . . We write thus with no intention of sarcasm, but in a real desire to discover that an eminent historian has not acted with reckless cruelty in giving this book to the world. If he really knew what he was doing, it was an act of literary cruelty in some respects without a parallel.—WEDGWOOD, JULIA, 1881, *Mr. Froude as a Biographer, Contemporary Review, vol.* 39, *p. 825.*

I humbly think his "Reminiscences" as given to the world by his executor, Mr. Froude, is a very unsatisfactory book, and does not show the sunny side of his character—that society would have lost very little if it had been suppressed; indeed, the writer himself seems haunted by a suspicion that it would have been "so best." It inculcates no sentiment akin to religion, impresses no feeling of loyalty, and if any of the virtues are advocated it is so rather in the manner of a lawyer who finds a few words concerning them in his brief. His domestic relations, I have reason to know, were not healthful, and his frequent allusions to his wife, whom he here calls his "darling," and concerning whom he writes much, but says little, I fear are to be regarded rather as a confession that requires absolution than the outpouring of a loving soul that perpetually mourns separation, while not a solitary word occurs to intimate the hope of a reunion hereafter. If "truth will be cheaply bought at any price," so well; but I greatly fear the book teaches more of what should be avoided than of what it would be wise to imitate and copy. —HALL, SAMUEL CARTER, 1883, *Retrospect of a Long Life, p. 366.*

I am in the midst of Froude—two new volumes of Carlyle. Very interesting I find them, and him more problematic than ever, but fine on the whole. A kind of sentimental Ajax furens. I don't think that sincerity towards his hero justifies Froude in printing Carlyle's diatribes (result of dyspepsia mainly)—about Gladstone, for example. In a world where there is so much unavoidable pain, why add to the avoidable? Gladstone won't mind, but his wife and daughters?—LOWELL, JAMES RUSSELL, 1884, *To Thomas Hughes, Oct.* 20; *Letters, ed. Norton, vol.* II, *p.* 282.

What a strange, wild production is poor Carlyle's "Remains," and yet what a genius he was! (A book called "Obiter Dicta" is worth reading about *him* and others). What amused me most was that Froude tells us he came in his last days to think Athanasius was quite right about the "Ομοουσία," and that Christianity would have become a myth without it. Froude I consider his *bête noire*, delighting to drag out all his coarsest dicta.—LAKE, WILLIAM CHARLES, 1885, *Letter to Dean Merivale, Jan.* 17; *Memorials, ed. his Widow, p.* 269.

Jeremy Bentham, in the interest of mankind and to the furtherance of science, left his body to be dealt with by the surgeons, and then to be preserved to the gaze of the world in the museum of University College. Thomas Carlyle has chosen to leave his life and his home, his aches and his sores, his grumblings and his washing-bills, to the impartial verdict of posterity. In Mr. Froude he has found a trustee who is ready to carry out his wishes without flinching. The Shakespearean wealth of imagery that Carlyle carried about with him into every detail of the supper-table or the wardrobe, the scrupulosity of the disciple, and his abundant power as a colourist, have contrived to present a series of pictures which, to those not accustomed to the methods of psychological portrait painting, may give the effect of a caricature. It is as if the living body of Thomas Carlyle were subjected to the resources of modern science, and the untrained public were called in to stand at the instruments. The microphone is used to enlarge his speech. The grunt or the pshaw that escapes the best of us at times is heard, by Mr. Froude's scientific appliances, as the roaring of a wounded buffalo. The old man's laugh, which in life was so cheery, comes up to us as out of a phonograph, harsh as the mockery of the devils that Dante heard in Malebolge. The oxyhydrogen microscope is applied to the pimples on his chin, or the warts on his thumb, and they loom to us as big as wens or cancers. The electric light is thrown upon the bared nerve; the photograph reveals the excoriations or callosities of every inch of skin. Poor Swift suffered something of the kind, and Rousseau; and one cannot but regret that, to a brain so far more sane, to a nature so far more robust than theirs, it has been needful to apply a somewhat similar resource.—HARRISON, FREDERIC, 1885, *The Choice of Books and Other Literary Pieces, p.* 177.

Hardly had the sods begun to join themselves over the grave in the Ecclefechan burying-ground when there came forth, under Mr. Froude's editorship, hurriedly printed and full of the most slovenly press-errors, those two volumes of Carlyle's own "Reminiscences," consisting of papers selected from his manuscripts, which are certainly among the most interesting things Carlyle ever wrote, and would have been received as such with delight by all the world, had it not been for unexpected portions and particles of their contents the publication of which acted in many quarters like the opening of a bag of wasps. . . . It is these nine volumes of Carlyle Reminiscence and Biography, edited or written by Mr. Froude, that have done the mischief, if mischief it be. The Carlyle of the present day for all the world is not that ideal sage and patriarch of letters that went to his grave in peaceful dignity and amid universal honours four years ago, but is Mr. Froude's Carlyle, the Carlyle of those nine volumes. . . . Wherever Mr. Froude himself becomes the narrator or commentator, his mood is too uniformly like that of a man driving a hearse. The contrast in this respect between what is from his own pen and much of the documentary material he digests and edits is very remarkable. There is gloom enough, seriousness enough, in the matter of the documents; but they are not all gloomy or serious. They abound with the picturesque, the comic, the startlingly grotesque, or the quaintly pleasant; some of them actually swim in humour, or sparkle with wit. These Mr. Froude faithfully prints, and perhaps relishes; but they do not seem to have any influence on his own gait or countenance in his office of biographer. This is unfortunate. No mind not profoundly in earnest itself could understand Carlyle or represent him properly to others; but, if ever there was a life that required also some considerable amount of humour in the bystander for correct apprehension and interpretation of its singularities it was Carlyle's.—MASSON, DAVID, 1885, *Carlyle Personally and in his Writings, pp.* 7, 8, 17.

On December 23, 1880, Froude informed

me that he had begun to print Carlyle's "Reminiscences." He had allowed me to read the earlier sketches some years previously, and I had been delighted by their idiomatic force and freshness. The pictures of the old homely Scottish life were, it seemed to me, racy of the soil. Now he asked me to revise them as they went through the press, with reference more particularly to various Scotch names and idioms in the early sheets. "I therefore venture to hope that you will look through the pages, and mark anything that seems doubtful to you." This I did, aided by Dr. John Brown. Only the proofs of the Scotch section of the book were corrected by me: had I seen the others I might possibly have suggested the omission of one or two passages; but surely the "ootbrak" of outraged decorum which followed the publication was out of all proportion to the offence,—if offence there was.—SKELTON, JOHN, 1895, *Reminiscences of James Anthony Froude, Blackwood's Magazine, vol.* 157, p. 42.

The biography throughout shows that he was even keenly sensible to Carlyle's arrogance, and yet felt it as a valuable support. Carlyle might be rough, but he could sweep away any misgivings with delightful positiveness. When Froude became aware of the revelations in Mrs. Carlyle's journal he could feel, even more keenly than most people, the painful side. But then they illustrated just his masterful temper, which, if sometimes startling, was yet so comfortable a support to a weaker brother. . . . He went on to read earlier letters with the preconception and, according to the best authority to misrepresent the whole story materially, and to Carlyle's disadvantage. Such a faculty for misrepresentation is too often shown in his history, and the fact shows that he might yield to it without any bad intention. In truth, he seems to have expected that his readers would be as ready as himself to condone Carlyle's faults of temper, and regard his posthumous confession as so "supremely honourable" as to be an ample atonement for the offence. He, unluckily, succeeded in exaggerating the faults, without carrying his readers along with him in the implied apology. They did not appreciate the charm, which to him was so obvious, of the despotic side of Carlyle's character. That was the real difficulty. Froude was, I believe, as loyal to his master's memory as he had been affectionate to him in life. The loyalty did not prevent him from facing the shades as well as the lights, and he was quite right in his desire to delineate both in his portrait. What he did not see was that the merit which, for him, altogether overbalanced the faults, was not a merit at all for the outside world.— STEPHEN, LESLIE, 1901, *James Anthony Froude, National Review, vol.* 36, *p.* 683.

GENERAL

The Robert-Houdin of modern English writers, and author of that popular serial novel grimly entitled "The History of England," appears to be only at home in an element of paradox, and in the clever accomplishments of some literary *tour de force*. "Calvinism· An Address delivered at St. Andrews, March 17, 1871, by James Anthony Froude, M. A." is his latest performance. Always liberal in his assumption of premises, no one need be surprised that the author should claim Calvinism to have been "accepted for two centuries in all Protestant countries as the final account of the relations between man and his Maker," and should represent that "the Catholics whom it overthrew" assail it, etc. . . . Mr. Froude does not appear by his writings to have an unvarying standard of morality. Apparently incapable of judging actions as they are, he measures them by his personal like or dislike of the actors. Always the advocate, never the philosophical historian, he presents but one side of a case. Certain personages in history are with him always right, certain others are always wrong. Even the crimes of the former are meritorious, or, at worse, indifferent, while the indifferent sayings and doings of the latter are sins of deepest dye. We may see this tendency exemplified in the address before us which seeks to make Calvinism lovely. The author says, in plain terms, that it was not more criminal in a Calvinist to burn a witch than for any other person to invite a spirit-rapper to dinner. Of course he expresses the opinion euphuistically and in mellifluous phrase, but, nevertheless, he does express it.—MELINE, J. G., 1871, *Mr. Froude and Calvinism, Catholic World, vol.* 13, *pp.* 541, 544.

It is a startling and incongruous conjunction in the theological sphere. The men are both unusually distinguished in their respective ages, both are stars, and stars of the first magnitude, but they move in diametrically opposite spheres—wide as the poles asunder. East and west, north and south, do not indicate a more thorough and irreconcilable anthithesis than "The Nemesis of Faith" and Calvin's "Institutes of the Christian Religion." One is forced to cast about, to discover, if it be possible, what could have attracted or entrapped a man so unequivocally pronounced elsewhere, into a flagrant self-contradiction. Had the northern air, the keen religious atmosphere, surcharged with Calvinism, which envelops, not St. Andrews alone, but Scotland in its entire length and breath, touched and turned the brain of the athletic doubter? Be it as it may, here is *pro tanto* an avowed vindication and glorification of Calvin and Calvinism by one who is deemed to stand at the extreme opposite pole from both. —YOUNG, JOHN, 1873, *Froude and Calvin, Contemporary Review*, vol. 21, p. 431.

It is a melancholy essay ["Progress"], for its tone is that of profound skepticism as to certain influences and means of progress upon which we in this country most rely. With the illustrative arguments of Mr. Froude's essay I do not purpose specially to meddle; I recall it to the attention of the reader as a representative type of skepticism regarding progress which is somewhat common among intellectual men, and is not confined to England. . . . If Mr. Froude's essay is anything but an exhibition of the scholarly weapons of criticism, it is the expression of a profound disbelief in the intellectual education of the masses of the people. . . . Mr. Froude runs lightly over a list of subjects upon which the believer in progress relies for his belief, and then says of them that the world calls this progress, he calls it only change.— WARNER, CHARLES DUDLEY, 1874, *Thoughts Suggested by Mr. Froude's "Progress," Scribner's Monthly*, vol. 7, pp. 351, 355.

Some of his dramatic passages are equal to any in our historical literature.—CATHCART, GEORGE R., 1874, ed. *The Literary Reader*, p. 317.

Mr. Froude ranks among historical writers. His attractive style, his vivid imagination, his warm partisanship are admitted; his historical accuracy has been questioned. Meline, in defending Mary, Queen of Scots, against Froude, obtained from the State Paper Office documents cited by this English writer, and proved, as English judges mildly expressed it, that Mr. Froude did not seem to know the value of quotation marks; in fact, that he garbled documents by suppressing passages and making paragraphs read on consecutively which in the original had no relation to each other. Of our present position Mr. Froude speaks vaguely. But as a prophet he is sublime. Historian he may not be; philosophical observer of the present he may not be; but as a prophet he surpasses all we have hitherto read. He foresees the future with unerring eye. What we American Catholics will do under any possible contingency, at any period of time, is as clear to him as noonday. Starting with the absurd theory that we Catholics are opposed to the Constitution, and with the false assertion that our Church had condemned it, he cries like some tragic ranter on a provincial stage: "Give them the power and the Constitution will be gone." . . . From the specimen afforded, we must decline to consider Mr. Froude as an historian, at least where American topics are concerned, and we submit the question, with all deference, to the various historical societies from Maine to California, convinced that they will decide as we have.—SHEA, J. G., 1880, *Is Froude a Historian? American Catholic Quarterly Review*, vol. 5, pp. 114, 136, 137.

Had Mr. Froude's articles on "Romanism and the Irish Race in the United States" appeared anonymously, they would have been allowed to pass by unheeded, as a very ordinary contribution to anti-Catholic sensational literature. Our ears are so familiar with the outcries and screams of the alarmist that we do not take the trouble to stop to ask him for the grounds of his terror.—SPALDING, JOHN LANCASTER, 1880, *Mr. Froude's Historical Method, North American Review*, vol. 130, p. 280.

Mr. Froude is probably the most popular historian since Macaulay, although his popularity is far indeed from that of Macaulay. He is widely read where Mr. Freeman would seem intolerably learned and pedantic, and Mr. Lecky too philosophic to be lively. His books have been the subject of the keenest controversy. His picture of Henry VIII. set all the world wondering. It set an example and became a precedent. It founded a new school in history and biography—what we may call the paradoxical school; the school which sets itself to discover that some great man had all the qualities for which the world had never before given him credit, and none of those which it had always been content to recognize as his undoubted possession. The virtues of the misprized Tiberius; the purity and meekness of Lucrezia Borgia; the disinterestedness and forbearance of Charles of Burgundy: these and other such historical discoveries naturally followed Mr. Froude's illustration of the domestic virtues, the exalted chastity, and the merciful disposition of Henry VIII. Mr. Froude has, however, qualities which raise him high above the level of the ordinary paradoxical historian. He has a genuine creative power. We may refuse to believe that his Henry VIII. is the Henry of history, but we cannot deny that Mr. Froude makes us see his Henry as vividly as if he stood in life before us. A dangerous gift for an historian; but it helps to make a great literary man. Mr. Froude may claim to be regarded as a great literary man, measured by the standard of our time. He has imagination; he has that sympathetic and dramatic instinct which enables a man to enter into the emotions and motives, the likings and dislikings, of people of a past age. His style is penetrating and thrilling; his language often rises to the dignity of a poetic eloquence. The figures he conjures up are always the resemblance of real men and women. They are never waxwork, or lay-figures, or skeletons clothed in words, or purple rags of description stuffed out with straw into an awkward likeness of the human form. The one distinct impression we carry away from Mr. Froude's history is that of the living reality of his figures.—MCCARTHY, JUSTIN, 1880, *A History of Our Own Times from the Accession of Queen Victoria to the Berlin Congress*, vol. IV, ch. LXVII.

Though this volume ["Cæsar"] bears a modest title, it is one of great popular interest. Few persons at all interested in ancient history will find themselves willing, after getting a taste of the book, to put it down until they have completed it. It would be easy for a severe critic to point out faults in the work. But its faults are not those of a dangerous kind. It is at least something to have written a book on a great subject which many people will be interested in reading. The author's point of view is essentially the same as Mommsen's. He believes that the nation was in a hopeless state of demoralization, and that, if recovery was possible, it was possible only through the efforts of Julius Cæsar. He is more temperate in his condemnation of Cicero, but the facts he presents are much more effective than Mommsen's harsh words. In the opinion of Froude, "Nature half made a great man and left him incomplete." With "magnificent talents, high aspirations, and a true desire to do right," Cicero united "an infirmity of will, a passion, a cunning, a vanity, and an absence of manliness and veracity." On the whole, the picture of Cicero is probably one of the best ever drawn in few words.—ADAMS, CHARLES KENDALL, 1882, *A Manual of Historical Literature*, p. 132.

He certainly derived much of his style from Newman, for it is hard to say whom else he could have derived it from. It is far more imaginative and poetic; far more capable of carrying the reader away, and placing him in a new and unexpected position, than the style of any one else about him.—MOZLEY, THOMAS, 1882, *Reminiscences Chiefly of Oriel College and the Oxford Movement*, vol. II, p. 30.

Consider the great will-power Mr. James Anthony Froude has brought to bear upon the distortion of history. Note the facility with which he ignores the virtues of Mary Stuart; see the perfections he finds in Queen Elizabeth; and there is that "great blot of blood and grease on the history of England," Henry VIII.; Mr. Froude can't perceive it; it is to his mind an unsullied page, and Henry VIII. a humane ruler and a profound statesman. In like spirit can Mr. Froude read a quotation until it begins to tell against his preconceived notion, drop out words that damage the view he would hold, garble sentences to suit his purposes, and play such pranks with quotation-marks as to make him the laughing-stock of all conscientious historians.—MULLANY, PATRICK FRANCIS (BROTHER AZARIAS), 1889, *Books and Reading*, p. 29.

There is probably no finer example of the right use of the historic imagination. There is certainly none which has put the pedants more completely to shame.—SMALLEY, GEORGE W., 1894, *Studies of Men, p. 290.*

Whatever people may think of Froude as an historian, no one can resist the charm of his style. It is a feminine rather than a masculine style, and challenges no comparison with that of Tacitus, Gibbon, or even Macaulay. But in its way it is perfection. It is singular that nobody seems to have noted its source. It was formed in the school of John Henry Newman, and recalls that of the master in its ease, grace, limpid clearness, and persuasiveness. Even Newman's mannerisms and artifices recur. . . . It is pretty apparent, when he touches on general history, that he had not much prepared himself by the study of it for dealing with a particular period. If he had, he could scarcely have failed to know what a debasement of the currency was, or taken it for a loan from the mint. Hence he misses his historical bearings. . . . Daring and startling paradox will always amuse and excite, though perhaps there is no easier method of counterfeiting genius. But, taken seriously, Froude's apologies for the crimes, brutalities, perfidies, and hypocrisies of Henry VIII. can awaken but one feeling in any man of sound understanding and unperverted heart.—SMITH, GOLDWIN, 1894, *Froude, North American Review, vol. 159, pp. 677, 680, 681.*

Near the close of 1863 I was invited by Froude to visit him, in consequence of an article of mine sent, by Carlyle's suggestion, to *Fraser* ("The Transcendentalist of Concord"), and for eighteen years I enjoyed his friendship. I continued writing for *Fraser* so long as he was its editor. His characteristic liberality was a good deal pressed by my articles during the civil war in America and the period of reconstruction. He was not quite a captive of Carlyle on the negro question; he regarded slavery as an evil, but he had the instinctive dislike of a philosophical historian to revolutionary or militant methods of reform. At the time, many of his views on American questions appeared to me merely academic, but I have since often had to reflect on the greater foresight with which he apprehended some of the sequelæ of a reform secured, however, inevitably, by force. Moreover, Froude was able to quote some of the most eminent abolitionists in America against the policy of "coercing the South," such sentiments having been freely uttered before the attack on Fort Sumter. —CONWAY, MONCURE DANIEL, 1894, *Working with Froude on Fraser's Magazine, The Nation, vol. 59, p. 378.*

Froude wrote history as he conceived it with a power rarely equalled. His pages pulse with life. But though he drew from sources of the highest value, many of them never before utilized, he lacked a sound critical method of dealing with them. In this respect his later volumes show a marked improvement over the earlier ones. Unbiased perception seems at times to have been simply beyond his powers; the facts of his own narrative he often saw as no one else saw them. Objective description he professed to aim at, but rarely attained for he approached his material too much in the spirit of an artist. In his pictures the shadows are too deep and the lights are too richly glowing. A sentimentalist by nature, he was deficient in sobriety and poise of judgment, and he lacked the patience for accuracy in details. He had little interest in modern social or political science, and to the reader of the present day one of the most serious deficiencies of his work is its failure to give adequate attention to the constitutional and economic aspects of the period. —BOURNE, EDWARD GAYLORD, 1894-1901, *Essays in Historical Criticism, p. 296.*

Which for scholarly finish ranks with the inimitable "Eothen" of Kinglake. In "Oceana," Mr. Froude as a man of letters is seen at his best; and at his best Mr. Froude had few rivals. No other writer of our day, not Cardinal Newman himself, had, as I think, such an easy mastery of our mother tongue,—in no other writer were masculine vigour and feminine delicacy so blended in the expression of what may be called, intellectual emotion. The thought was personal; the personality was unique. From the purely literary point of view "Oceana" is indeed a masterpiece. Froude complained in it, as he complained in his letters (as we have seen), of being an old man: but there is no trace of age in the book.—SKELTON, JOHN, 1895, *Reminiscences of James Anthony Froude, Blackwood's Magazine, vol. 157, p. 57.*

With all his faults thick as autumn leaves upon him, Froude was a great writer well equipped to play a great part. It may be his fate to stand corrected, just as it is

Freeman's fate to be superseded, but he will long continue to be read—who can doubt it?—not merely for the vivacity of his too often misleading descriptions and for the masculine vigour of his style, but for the interest of his peculiar point of view, the piquancy of his philosophy, the humour of his commentary, for his quick insight into certain phases of faith and shades of character. . . . The first thing that must strike the mind of anyone who looks at Froude's writings as a whole is their amazing sameness of object, or, at all events, point of view. It is always the same nail he is hammering on the head. It reminds one of Pope's ruling passion. It crops up everywhere and at all time, firing his zeal wherever he is. What is that object? Why, to counteract what he calls "the Counter-Reformation"; to denounce monkery; to unfrock priests by stripping them of all sacramental pretensions; to topple over everything standing between man and the Force which called him into being; to preach good works and plain homespun morality.— BIRRELL, AUGUSTINE, 1895-1901, *James Anthony Froude, Essays and Addresses*, pp. 164, 165.

One of the greatest historians of the century, except for one curious and unfortunate defect, and (without any drawback) one of the greatest writers of English prose during that century, was James Anthony Froude. . . . I have sometimes doubted whether Mr. Froude at his best has any superior among the prose writers of the last half of this century. His is not a catching style; and in particular it does not perhaps impress itself on green tastes. It has neither the popular and slightly brusque appeal of Macaulay or Kinglake, nor the unique magnificence of Mr. Ruskin, not the fretted and iridescent delicacy of some other writers. It must be frankly confessed that, the bulk of his work being very great and his industry not being untiring, it is unequal, and sometimes not above (it is never below) good journey-work. But at its best it is of a simply wonderful attraction—simply in the pure sense, for it is never very ornate, and does not proceed in point of "tricks" much beyond the best varieties of the latest Georgian form. That strange quality of "liveliness" which has been noticed in reference to its author's view of history, animates it throughout. It is never flat; never merely popular; never merely scholarly; never merely "precious" and eccentric. And at its very best it is excelled by no style in this century, and approached by few in this or any other, as a perfect harmony of unpretentious music, adjusted to the matter that it conveys, and lingering on the ear that it reaches.—SAINTSBURY, GEORGE, 1896, *A History of Nineteenth Century Literature*, p. 246, 251.

Froude cannot be called a master of style in the sense in which Gibbon, or Newman, or Macaulay deserves the name. There are few pages in his writings of which we could say with certainty, were they shown to us for the first time, that Froude, and Froude alone, could have written them. There are many passages, on the other hand, especially in his earlier works, which reveal the disciple. . . . His vivid imagination enabled him to bring not only scenes, but characters and motives, before the reader, in the most effective, sometimes in the most dramatic form; and it may be noted that more than any other recent English writer he affects that familiar, but dangerous, companion of our youth, the *oratio obliqua*.—DODDS, JAMES MILLER, 1896, *English Prose ed. Craik, vol.* V, *pp.* 638, 639.

Froude stands before the English-reading public prominent in three characteristics: First, as a technical prose artist, in which regard he is entitled to be classed with Ruskin, Newman, and Pater; less enthusiastic and elaborately ornamental than the first, less musically and delicately fallacious than the second, and less self-conscious and phrase-caressing than the third, but carrying a solider burden of thought than all three. Second, as a historian of the modern school, which aims by reading the original records to produce an independent view of historical periods. Third, as the most clear-sighted and broad-minded of those whose position near the centre of the Oxford movement and intimacy with the principal actors gave them an insight into its inner nature.—JOHNSON, CHARLES FREDERICK, 1897, *Library of the World's Best Literature, vol.* XL, *p.* 6060.

I take it that he may properly be ranked among the greatest masters of word-painting in the English language. There are passages in his writings—for example, his account of the judicial murder of Sir

Thomas More, or of the destruction of the French and Spanish floating batteries before Gibraltar—which have seldom been surpassed in splendour of diction and dramatic power. But here all the praise that can be honestly bestowed upon him ends. He was incapable of critically investigating facts. Nay, he was incapable, congenitally incapable, I believe, even of correctly stating them. A less judicial mind probably never existed. There is hardly a page of his which is not deformed by passion, prejudice, and paradox. He is everywhere an advocate, and an utterly unscrupulous advocate. . . . It has happened to me, in the course of my poor historical studies, to go over much of the ground trodden by Mr. Froude. And the conclusion to which I was long ago led is that it is never safe to accept any statement upon Mr. Froude's mere word.— LILLY, WILLIAM SAMUEL, 1897, *Essays and Speeches*, pp. 212, 213.

Froude's style as a writer is much in his favor. It is not so impressive as Carlyle's, nor so pleasant-flavored as Thackeray's; neither does it have the splendor of Burke and Bacon; but for clear crystalline English there is hardly its superior in the present century. Froude is sometimes slightly melodramatic in feeling, but the purity of his language is beyond dispute. It would seem as if he wished to place his case before the world in the plainest possible manner, considering good sense the finest ornament of speech. His writing can be read with great rapidity and yet be perfectly intelligible.—STEARNS, FRANK PRESTON, 1897, *Modern English Prose Writers*, p. 115.

A history wherein the pursuit of trivial facts is carried to confusion, and where the sense of faithful proportion is ruined by antiquarian curiosity, is little more than a comic photograph as taken in a distorted lens. The details may be accurate, curious, and inexhaustible; but the general effect is that of preposterous inversion. We learn nothing by the process. We are wearied and puzzled. From these things— the Seven Deadly Sins of the Learned— James Anthony Froude was conspicuously free. He never (or hardly ever) wearies us or puzzles us. As a master of clear, vivid, epical narration he stands above all his contemporaries. He claims our interest, brings us face to face with living men and women, leaves on our memory a definite stamp that does not fade, gives our brain much to ponder, to question, to investigate for ourselves. The result is that he is read, attacked, admired, condemned. But he is not put upon the shelf, and he will not be put upon the shelf. He is a popular writer of history, in the teeth of all his critics, and in spite of all his shortcomings—fierce as are the one, and grave as are the other. He is read, and no doubt deserves to be read, as Livy, Froissart, and Voltaire are read, for the sake of his graphic power in narration; which gives him more readers than Freeman, and more public influence than Stubbs or Gneist. . . . Froude is of course of the followers of Herodotus and Livy in the past and Voltaire and Robertson in the modern world, not of Thucydides and Tacitus, of Gibbon and Macaulay. He has neither the philosophy nor the genius of these ancient historians, nor the marvellous reading and portentous memory of our own historians. But in narration he is equal to the best; and where there is no ambiguity in the facts, and no cause to defend, he has reached a very high point.— HARRISON, FREDERIC, 1898, *The Historical Method of J. A. Froude*, Nineteenth Century, vol. 44, pp. 375, 379.

If I call Froude a poet it is because, as I explained before, I do not consider rhyme as essential to poetry. But for really poetical power, for power of description, of making the facts of history alive, of laying bare the deepest thoughts of men and the most mysterious feelings of women, there was no poet or historian of our age who came near him.—MÜLLER, FRIEDRICH MAX, 1898, *Auld Lang Syne*, p. 88.

To call Mr. Froude insincere in the ordinary sense of that word would be misleading. He was seldom conscious of anything but perfect sincerity. And yet the perfect sincerity which alone makes written words perennially valuable was never quite reached by him. Byron too, as Carlyle remarked, in the essay on Burns, hated insincerity, heartily detested it, and declared formal war against it in words. Yet he also never quite reached sincerity. "So difficult is it even for the strongest to make this primary attainment, which might seem the simplest of all: *to read its own consciousness without mistakes*, without errors involuntary or wilful!" Whether Mr. Froude had force of character and intellect enough to have reached perfect sincerity under other circumstances is perhaps doubtful. But his early trainings made it doubly difficult. The habits of make-believe and loose readiness to believe whatever he wished to believe, which he had learned perhaps in boyhood, and afterwards in part at least from his clerical associates, could not be laid aside like a garment, could not, indeed, be laid aside without a far harder struggle than Mr. Froude felt called upon to make. He was in haste to write, and to win success in his writing—what is called success.—WILSON, DAVID, 1898, *Mr. Froude and Carlyle*, p. 80.

That Froude suffered from constitutional inaccuracy, made strange blunders even in copying a plain document, and often used his authorities in an arbitrary and desultory fashion, seems, however, to be admitted. Yet, if I want to know something of the Elizabethan period I can nowhere find so vivid and interesting a narrative. It is true that Froude's interest in history was to some extent an afterthought, that he took it up mainly to illustrate certain principles and confined his attention to the topics directly relevant to his purpose. One cannot feel that he has become a contemporary of Elizabeth as Macaulay had made himself a contemporary of Queen Anne, but rather that his excursions into topics outside of the main stream of political events had been incidentally suggested in the course of his reading.—STEPHEN, LESLIE, 1901, *James Anthony Froude, National Review*, vol. 36, pp.672, 673.

Like his master, Carlyle, Froude holds a place apart among the historical writers of his age: both the one and the other (due proportion guarded) are in the first place and pre-eminently, prophets and men of letters rather than historical specialists. In choosing to write history. both were primarily determined not by the simple scientific desire of ascertaining what had actually happened in the past, but by the consideration that historical narrative was a suitable vehicle for the expression of their individual views regarding man's life and destiny. In the case of Froude the distinction is forced upon us at once by the character of his work as a whole, and by the special gifts and temperament of which it is the expression. He belongs to a different order of spirits from Hallam or Macaulay or Freeman; and it is as a literary artist and a teacher of complex and illusive nature that he presents himself equally in his writings and in his mental history.—BROWNE, P. HUME, 1903, *Chambers's Cyclopædia of English Literature*, ed. Patrick, vol. III, p. 500.

Christina Georgina Rossetti
1830–1894

Born in London, 1830; died London, 1894. Daughter of Gabriel Rossetti, an Italian political exile and distinguished student of Dante, and sister of Dante Gabriel Rossetti. In the front rank of modern women poets. Her later work is devotional in sentiment and consists chiefly of poetical commentaries on religious subjects. Collective editions of her poems have been published in England and America. Author of "Goblin Market and Other Poems," 1862; "The Prince's Progress and Other Poems," 1866; "Sing-Song, a Nursery Rhyme-book," 1872; "Annus Domini, a Collect for Each Day of the Year," 1874; "A Pageant and Other Poems," 1881; "Letter and Spirit, Notes on the Commandments," 1883; "Time Flies, a Reading Diary," 1885.—STEDMAN, EDMUND CLARENCE, ed. 1895, *A Victorian Anthology*, p. 702.

PERSONAL

One of the saintliest of women, as well as one of our finest poets. . . . In some ways she reminded me of Mrs. Craik, the author of John Halifax, Gentleman; that is, in the Quaker-like simplicity of her dress, and the extreme and almost demure plainness of the material, with, in her mien, something of that serene passivity which has always a charm of its own. She was so pale as to suggest anæmia, though there was a bright and alert look in her large and expressive azure-gray eyes, a color which often deepened to a dark, shadowy, velvety gray; and though many lines were imprinted on her features, the contours were smooth and young. Her hair, once a rich brown, now looked dark, and was thickly threaded with solitary white hairs rather than sheaves of gray. She was about the medium height of women, though at the time I thought her considerably shorter. . . . The circumstance that a clergyman came regularly to talk and pray with her—to be, in fact, her confessor—is no doubt responsible for the assertion sometimes made that, in later life, she was a Roman Catholic. This was not so. From her girlhood to her death she was strictly a member of the Anglican Church.—SHARP, WILLIAM, 1895, *Some Reminiscences of Christina Rossetti, Atlantic Monthly, vol.* 75, *pp.* 736, 742, 745.

A soul more sweet than the morning of newborn May
Has passed with the year that has passed from the world away.
A song more sweet than the morning's firstborn song
Again will hymn not among us a new year's day.
Not here, not here shall the carol of joy grown strong
Ring rapture now, and uplift us, a spell-struck throng,
From dream to vision of life that the soul may see
By death's grace only, if death do its trust no wrong.
. . . .
And now, more high than the vision of souls may climb,
The soul whose song was as music of stars that chime,
Clothed round with life as of dawn and the mounting sun,
Sings, and we know not here of the song sublime.
No word is ours of it now that the songs are done
Whence here we drank of delight as in freedom won,
In deep deliverance given from the bonds we bore
There is none to sing as she sang upon earth, not one.
—SWINBURNE, ALGERNON CHARLES, 1895, *A New Year's Eve, Nineteenth Century, vol.* 37, *p.* 367.

Throughout all her life, indeed, she was the most notable example that our time has produced of the masterful power of man's spiritual nature when at its highest to conquer in its warfare with earthly conditions, as her brother Gabriel's life was the most notable example of the struggle of the spiritual nature with the bodily when the two are equally equipped. It is the conviction of one whose high privilege it was to know her in many a passage of sorrow and trial that of all the poets who have lived and died within our time, Christina Rossetti must have had the noblest soul. . . . In worldly matters her generosity may be described as boundless; but perhaps it is not difficult for a poet to be generous in a worldly sense—to be free in parting with that which can be precious only to common-place souls. What, however, is not so easy is for one holding such strong religious convictions as Miss Rossetti held to cherish such generous thoughts and feelings as were hers about those to whom her shibboleths meant nothing. This was what made her life so beautiful and such a blessing to all. The indurating effects of a selfish religiosity never withered her soul nor narrowed it. With her, indeed, religion was very love—A largeness universal like the sun.
—WATTS-DUNTON, THEODORE, 1895, *Christina Georgina Rossetti, The Athenæum, No.* 3506, *p.* 16.

It was little for her to die,
For her to whom breath was prayer,
For her who had long put by
Earth-desire;
Who had knelt in the Holy Place
And had drunk the incense-air,
Till her soul to seek God's face
Leapt like fire.
—BATES, KATHARINE LEE, 1895, *The Passing of Christina Rossetti, The Dial, vol.* 18, *p.* 135.

Christina's habits of composing were eminently of the spontaneous kind. I question her having ever once deliberated with herself whether or not she would write something or other, and then, after thinking out a subject, having proceeded to treat it in regular spells of work. Instead of this, something impelled her feelings, or "came into her head," and her hand obeyed the dictation. I suppose she scribbled the lines off rapidly enough, and afterwards took whatever amount of pains she deemed requisite for keeping them right in form and expression—for she was quite conscious that a poem demands to be good in execution, as well as genuine in impulse; but (strange as it seems to say so of a sister who, up to the year 1876, was almost constantly in the same house with me) I cannot remember ever seeing her in the act of composition (I take no count here of the *boutsrimés* sonnets of 1848). She consulted nobody, and solicited no advice; though it is true that with regard to her published volumes—or at any rate the first two of them—my brother volunteered to point out what seemed well adapted for insertion, and what the reverse, and he found her a very willing recipient of his monitions.—ROSSETTI, WILLIAM MICHAEL, 1895, *ed.*

New Poems by Christina Rossetti, Preface, p. xii.

Christina Rossetti comes to us as one of those splendid stars that are so far away they are seen only at rare intervals. She never posed as a "literary person"—reading her productions at four-o'clocks and winning high praise from the unbonneted, and the discerning society editor. She never even sought a publisher. Her first volume of verses was issued by her grandfather Polidori unknown to her—printed by his own labor when she was seventeen and presented to her. What a surprise it must have been to this gentle girl to have one of her own books placed in her hands! There seems to have been an almost holy love in this proud man's heart for his granddaughter. His love was blind, or nearsighted at least, as love is apt to be (and I am glad!) for some of the poems in this little volume are sorry stuff. Later, her brothers issued her work and found market for it; and once we find Dante Gabriel almost quarrelling with that worthy Manxman, Hall Caine, because the Manxman was compiling a volume of the best English sonnets and threatening to leave Christina Rossetti out.—HUBBARD, ELBERT, 1897, *Little Journeys to the Homes of Famous Women*, p. 167.

Of Christina I saw a good deal, for the hospitality of the Rossetti family was informal and cordial. She was then in excellent health, and, though she was never what would be, by the generality of tastes, considered a beautiful woman, there was a noble serenity and dignity of expression in her face which was, as is often said of women of the higher type of character, "better than beauty," and in which one saw the spiritual exaltation that, without the least trace of the *dévote*, dominated in her and made her, before all other women of whom I know anything, the poetess of the divine life. The faith in the divine flamed out in her with a mild radiance which had in it no earthly warmth. She attracted me very strongly, but I should as soon have thought of falling in love with the Madonna del Gran Duca as with her. Being myself in the regions of dogmatic faith, I was in a position to judge sympathetically her religion, and though we differed in tenets as far as two sincere believers in Christianity could, I found in our discussions of the dogmas a broad and affectionate charity in her towards all differences from the ideal of credence she had formed for herself. I do not remember ever meeting any one who held such exalted and unquestioning faith in the true spiritual life as was hers. From my mother, who was in most respects the most purely spiritual woman I have ever known, Christina differed by this serenity, which in my mother was often disturbed by the doubts that had their seeds in the old and superstitious Calvinism mingled with the ground of her creed, and from which she never could liberate herself. Christina believed in God, in Heaven, in the eternal life, with an unfaltering constancy and fullness which left no questionings except, it might be, concerning her fulfillment of her religious obligations.—STILLMAN, WILLIAM JAMES, 1901, *The Autobiography of a Journalist*, vol. I, p. 299.

GENERAL

Any American reader who for the last two or three years has occasionally seen and admired the stray poems attributed to Miss Rossetti, being asked to describe them by one word, would have pronounced them Pre-Raphaelite. They were certainly most picturesque poetry; it was her practice to dwell elaborately upon details; oftenest her theme was nature; when they were devotional, her pieces were full of that phase of religious feeling which contemplates, not without sentimentality, God made man, which, we may almost say, agonizes at the feet of a Saviour who suffers and yearns, who is bleeding and aching with fleshy wounds. To have attributed to Pre-Raphaelitism such qualities as these would, perhaps, have been to give it a definition rude or incorrect. But whether right or wrong as regards the sister art, it was not a mistake to fix upon these as the distinguishing features of Miss Rossetti's poetry, and if with these we name a pervading sensuousness, we have the list of its essential characteristics complete. . . . Miss Rossetti's merit, though unique, will never be of the supreme order.—DENNETT, J. R., 1866, *Miss Rossetti's Poems, The Nation*, vol. 3, p. 47.

The first cursory impression of this book would be, we think, that its cardinal axiom was "Poetry is versified plaintiveness." The amount of melancholy is simply overwhelming. There is a forty-twilight power of sombreness everywhere. . . . These verses may be as well as she can do. They contain poetical passages of merit and promise, but they show also a defectiveness of versification, a falseness of ear, and occasionally a degree of affectation and triviality that, we can only hope, are not characteristic. To borrow a little of the style and technology of a sister branch of thought, the case, as now presented, can be accounted for as in essence a simple attack of the old and well-known endemic, *cacoethes scribendi*. Probably it befell her at the usual early age. Only instead of the run of gushing girls, we have Dante Gabriel Rossetti's sister, Jean Ingelow's intimate friend and a young lady of intelligence and education, constantly in contact with real literary society, and—what is thoroughly evident in this book—read in our best poets. Add all these complicating symptoms, and is there not a something plausible about the diagnosis? We do not say, observe, and we do not mean to say, that this is Miss Rossetti's case; only all she has done so far seems explicable on this hypothesis. For ourselves, we lean to the view that she will do more. We judge hers a strong, sensuous, impulsive, earnest, inconsiderate nature, that sympathizes well, feels finely, keeps true to itself at bottom, but does not pause to make sure that others must, as well as may, enter into the spirit that underlies her utterances, and so buries her meaning sometimes beyond Champollion's own powers of deciphering.—RUDD, F. A. 1867, *Christina G. Rossetti, Catholic World*, vol. 4, pp. 839, 846.

There are reasons for not subscribing to the claim more than once put forward in Miss Rossetti's behalf to take rank beside the great Mrs. Browning. The calibre of mind required for the production of such works as "Casa Guidi Windows," "Mother and Poet," "Sonnets from the Portuguese," &c. (not to name "Aurora Leigh," the sacred dramas, and the incomparable second translation of the "Prometheus,") is bigger than the calibre of mind demanded for the creation of such poems as "Goblin Market," "The Prince's Progress," and many of the smaller and more perfectly gem-like poems of Miss Rossetti. Nor can I see that the *powers* of expression exhibited by Mrs. Browning were less superior to those shown as yet by Miss Rossetti than her exhibited powers of idealisation were:— simply, Miss Rossetti has betrayed a *keener sense of the necessity* of execution than Mrs. Browning did; not a greater *executive ability*, not even as great an executive ability, for the intuitive manipulation of Mrs. Browning is, in numerous cases, not short of perfection.—FORMAN, H. BUXTON, 1871, *Our Living Poets*, p. 235.

She is a woman of genius, whose songs, hymns, ballads, and various lyrical pieces are studied and original. I do not greatly admire her longer poems, which are more fantastic than imaginative; but elsewhere she is a poet of a profound and serious cast, whose lips part with the breathing of a fervid spirit within.—STEDMAN, EDMUND CLARENCE, 1875-87, *Victorian Poets*, p. 280.

If you should happen to see Christina Rossetti, please to give my kind regards to her. I saw a little poem of hers, some two or three years ago, which uttered, as it were, a cry out of my own heart—to be delivered from "Self." It was the whole cry of an earnest soul embodied in a few words; a wonderful little outburst of prayer.— HOWITT, MARY, 1879, *Letter to Mrs. Alfred Watts*, Nov. 29; *Autobiography*, ed. her Daughter, vol. II, p. 301.

Several of Miss Rossetti's more ambitious pieces of verse unmistakably betray a southern cast of imagination, and the pictorial element in her poems is so strong, and of such a kind, that Dante Rossetti could have found twenty or thirty congenial themes in them for his pencil. But while, of the spiritual and artistic elements in his nature, Rossetti gave most freedom to the latter element, in Miss Rossetti the spiritual predominates. And anyone who has happened to see Rossetti's portrait of his sister and mother, can easily interpret the poetess's face by her works, and discern how much of her corresponds, in form and fibre to an Italian type that is centuries old. The minds of brother and sister seem to have been made out of some specially wistful "divine dream-element." — ROBERTSON, ERIC S., 1883, *English Poetesses*, p. 340.

Poverty of ideas cannot be imputed to Christina Rossetti, but the bulk of her poetry, rich as it is in music and colour, is fitter for the cloister than the hearth. In "Goblin Market," however, she was able to clothe her mystic thought in an objective shape, and, while displaying all her wonted lyrical charm, to give an insight into natures beyond the confines of humanity, a power also evinced in Cardinal

Newman's nearly contemporary "Dream of Gerontius."—GARNETT, RICHARD, 1887, *The Reign of Queen Victoria*, ed. Ward, vol. II, p. 487.

Here, in four hundred and fifty clearly printed pages, we have the exquisite product of a life which cannot yet have left off singing, poems of as fair an art, lyrics of as fresh a note, dreams of as strange a phantasy, as ever made blessed the English tongue. To say that Miss Rossetti is the greatest English poet among women is to pay regard to a distinction which, in questions of art, is purely arbitrary—a distinction which has given us the foolish word "poetess," a standing witness in our language to the national obtuseness. How little must the artistic constitution—the third sex—be understood among a people with such a word in their dictionary. How inorganic such distinctions are, of course, needs no illustration, though, if such were necessary, Miss Christina Rossetti's genius would form an admirable text; for, to my mind, she is, in right of its rarest quality, our one imaginative descendant of the magician of "Kubla Khan." No English poet till the appearance of "Goblin Market" ever again found the hidden door to Xanadhu save she. . . . Sometimes in her best poems we come across a word insensitive or out of colour. This, obviously, cannot be from lack of the power of art, it can only be because her exercise of the power is mainly unconscious. We find the same flaws in the early work of Keats; but he, on the other hand, soon learnt to train his song by a mature study of style. I should say, however, that Miss Rossetti has never done this; and so great is her instinctive power of art that she has really been able to afford the neglect, her poetry retaining thereby a charming *naiveté* which by a self-conscious culture might have been lost to us.—LE GALLIENNE, RICHARD, 1891, *The Academy*, vol. 39, pp. 130, 131.

Her customary music is sad, often poignantly sad. Her lyrics have that *desiderium*, that obstinate longing for something lost out of life, which Shelley's have, although her Christian faith gives her regret a more resigned and sedate character than his possesses. In the extremely rare gift of song-writing Miss Rossetti has been singularly successful. Of the poets of our time she stands next to Lord Tennyson in this branch of the art, in the spontaneous and complete quality of her *Lieder*, and in her propriety for the purpose of being sung. . . . Her music is very delicate, and it is no small praise to her that she it is who, of living verse-writers, has left the strongest mark on the metrical nature of that miraculous artificer of verse, Mr. Swinburne. In his "Poems and Ballads," as other critics have long ago pointed out, as was shown when that volume first appeared, several of Miss Rossetti's discoveries were transferred to his more scientific and elaborate system of harmonies, and adapted to more brilliant effects. . . . From the first a large section of Miss Rossetti's work has been occupied with sacred and devotional themes. Through this most rare and difficult department of the art, which so few essay without breaking on the Scylla of doctrine on the one hand, or being whirled in the Charybdis of commonplace dullness on the other, she has steered with extraordinary success. Her sacred poems are truly sacred, and yet not unpoetical. As a religious poet of our time she has no rival but Cardinal Newman, and it could only be schismatic prejudice or absence of critical faculty which should deny her a place, as a poet, higher than that of our exquisite master of prose. To find her exact parallel it is at once her strength and her snare that we must go back to the middle of the seventeenth century. She is the sister of George Herbert; she is of the family of Crashaw, of Vaughan, of Wither.—GOSSE, EDMUND, 1893, *Christina Rossetti, Century Magazine,* vol. 46, pp. 216, 217.

Miss Rossetti's gifts, unfairly, as I think, obscured for some time by the marvellous genius of her brother, have none the less won recognition in the hearts of many men. Her poetry has always been reticent and unassuming, but always stamped with a rare distinction, a perfection of form, and an elevation of spirit which are as welcome as flowers in May. It is with a pride of possession that one puts her new volume upon the shelf, to return to again and again for refreshment of the appropriate mood.— CHAMBERS, EDMUND K., 1894, *Verses, The Academy*, vol. 45, p. 162.

All who have human hearts confess her to be a sad and a sweet poet, all who have a sense of poetry know how rare was the quality of poetry in her—how spiritual and how sensuous—somewhat thin, somewhat dispread in her laxer writing, but perfectly strong, perfectly impassioned in her best. To the name of poet her right is so sure that proof of it is to be found everywhere in her "unconsidered ways," and always irrefutable. . . . We are not to reverence the versification of Christina Rossetti as we have learnt to reverence that of a great and classic master. She proves herself an artist, a possessor of the weighty matters of the law of art, despite the characteristic carelessness with which she played by ear. That thought so moving, feeling so urgent, as the thought and feeling of her "Convent Threshold" are communicated, are uttered alive, proves her an artist.—MEYNELL, ALICE, 1895, *Christina Rossetti, New Review*, vol. 12, pp. 201, 203.

Of all the great themes with which Miss Rossetti deals, she is, above all writers, the singer of Death. Whether as the eternal home-coming, or the quiet relief after the intolerable restlessness of the world, or as the deep reality in which the fretful vanities of life are merged, it is always in view, as the dark majestic portal to which the weary road winds at last.—BENSON, ARTHUR CHRISTOPHER, 1895, *Essays*, p. 288.

Miss Rossetti's verses sometimes suggest those of other poets, but we always feel that her art is distinctly her own. . . . Miss Rossetti's genius was too original to be chargeable with anything more than that assimilation of spiritual influence from which no poet can hope wholly to escape, and which links together in one golden chain the poetic tradition of the ages. If in most of the provinces of the lyric realm Miss Rossetti's verse challenges comparison with that of our greater singers, it is in the religious province that the challenge is most imperative and her mastery most manifest. —PAYNE, WILLIAM MORTON, 1895, *Little Leaders*, pp. 242, 243.

Miss Rossetti is perhaps best known to the outside world as the author of "Goblin Market," "The Prince's Progress," a selection of sonnets and of a series of sacred and devotional pieces. I can never forget the day I first opened a volume of her poems; I could neither relinquish the book nor yet satisfactorily account to myself for the fascination it exercised upon me. Many of the thoughts struck me as new, and all were of a unique setting. . . . Miss Rossetti's ear was close to nature; she listened for its simple voices, and uttered the sounds just as she heard them. Her Nature poetry is thus saturated with the greenness and freshness of spring, or bright with the glamour of summer. There is nothing strained or affected about it; it is as natural as Nature herself. By virtue of this spontaneous natural flow it is the true *Fountain Arethuse:* there has been nothing like it since Herrick. . . . The keynote of much of Miss Rossetti's word-music is its æsthetic mysticism and rich melancholy. . . . Countless passages in these poems illustrate that pure, warm ecstasy of early Italian colouring which Rossetti's brush has immortalised for us. . . . But it is specially in the "Prince's Progress" that Miss Rossetti's subtle and mysterious art finds its most perfect expression. . . . Miss Rossetti . . . though rarely posing as teacher, philosopher, or moralist, is yet always a consummate artist; open her pages where we will, me must needs light upon beauty. Mrs. Browning was never restrained by any apprehension of treating a subject inartistically. Whatever she felt or thought was expressed, small matter how. Sometimes it came in a never-to-be-forgotten word-music, but just as often in prose that passed for the poetry it should have been. Miss Rossetti, on the contrary, treated everything as only an artist could treat it.— LAW, ALICE, 1895, *The Poetry of Christina G. Rossetti, Westminister Review*, vol. 143, pp. 444, 446, 447, 452.

Miss Rossetti, in her sacred poems, brings together all the elements of art's excellence and of a Christian faith. Their chief note, their unique interest and delight, is a tenderness in them, a tremulous and wistful beauty of adoration, rising and passing, at times, into something like a very joyous adoration of friend by friend. . . . The severer poems of Miss Rossetti, solemn with the solemnity of the "Four Last Things" are no less alien from the average English attitude. . . . Some of her poems are awful with the awfulness of the "De-Profundis" or the "Dies Irae." In her three hundred sacred poems we find all possible tones of feeling and thought. There are poems with a homely, carolling air about them, in their grace and sweetness, as though they were (*slava reverentia*) the nursery songs of Heaven. There are poems, metrically and imaginatively marvellous, surging and sweeping forward with a splendour of movement to their victorious, their exultant close, as though they were the national hymns of Heaven. There are poems, as I have said, which are the very dirges and burdens of earth: in Crashaw's phrase, they are a "pathetical descant upon the plain song of *Stabat Mater Dolorosa:*" they hold the austere and solemnising sorrow of the world. . . . I have dwelled upon this side of Miss Rossetti's incomparable work, because in these "New Poems" the divine are by far the finest and the most welcome. . . . Her sonnets have, far beyond most, that singleness of a dominant emotion, piercingly felt and craving expression, joined to a rich magnificence of strict rhythm, which is the sonnet's perfect praise. —JOHNSON, LIONEL, 1896, *Miss Rossetti and Mrs. Alexander, The Academy, vol.* 50, *pp.* 59, 60.

There are those who seriously maintain Miss Rossetti's claim to the highest rank among English poetesses, urging that she excels Mrs. Browning, her only possible competitor, in freedom from blemishes of form and from the liability to fall into silliness and maudlin gush, at least as much as she falls short of her in variety and in power of shaping a poem of considerable bulk. But without attempting a too rigid classification we may certainly say that Miss Rossetti has no superior among Englishwomen who have had the gift of poetry.—SAINTSBURY, GEORGE, 1896, *A History of Nineteenth Century Literature, p.* 293.

Most of Miss Rossetti's later work is intensely devotional in its character, and reveals a nature strung to an almost saintlike ecstacy. Moreover, the spiritual fervour of these poems is no mere artistic mood assumed in sympathy with the forms of mediæval devotion as in her brother's case, but the genuine outcome of a personality steeped in the true spirit of passionate worship. But while their fervour is almost ascetic in its religious intensity, there is no trace of feebleness in them. They are strong both in intellectual and in artistic qualities. In expression they are finished and exquisite as in thought they are noble and elevating.—GRAHAM, RICHARD D., 1897, *The Masters of Victorian Literature, p.* 352.

Christina had the faculty of seizing beautiful moments, exalted feelings, sublime emotions and working them up into limpid song that comes echoing to us as from across soft seas. In all of her lines there is a half sobbing undertone—the sweet minor chord that is ever present in the songs of the Choir Invisible, whose music is the gladness as well as the sadness of the world.—HUBBARD, ELBERT, 1897, *Little Journeys to the Homes of Famous Women, p.* 168.

By the death of Christina Rossetti, literature, and not English literature alone, has lost the one great modern poetess. . . . In Miss Rossetti we have a poet among poets, and in Miss Rossetti alone. Content to be merely a woman, wise in limiting herself within somewhat narrow bounds, she possessed, in union with a profoundly emotional nature, a power of artistic self-restraint which no other woman who has written in verse, except the supreme Sappho, has ever shown; and it is through this mastery over her own nature, this economy of her own resources, that she takes rank among poets rather than among poetesses. . . . A power of seeing finely beyond the scope of ordinary vision; that, in a few words, is the note of Miss Rossetti's genius, and it brings with it a subtle and as if instinctive power of expressing subtle and yet as if instinctive conceptions; always clearly, always simply, with a singular and often startling homeliness, which is the sincerity of a style that seems to be innocently unaware of its own beauty. This power is shown in every division of her poetry; in the peculiar witchery of the poems dealing with the supernatural, in the exaltation of the poems of devotion, in the lyrical quality of the songs of children, birds, and corn, in the special variety and the special excellence of the poems of passion and meditation. The union of homely yet always select literalness of treatment with mystical visionariness, or visionariness which is sometimes mystical, constitutes the peculiar quality of her poetry.—SYMONS, ARTHUR, 1897, *Studies in Two Literatures, pp.* 135, 139.

Whether we look to the quality or to the quantity of her poetry of devotion—was pre-eminent among the illustrious English poets who have enriched the literature of Christian teaching by their genius. As long as Christianity remains the most vital force in the lives of millions of English-speaking people, the memory of that poet of their faith who gave them such a poem as "Passing away, saith the world, passing away," or "Paradise," with its exquisite last stanza the very quintessence of Christian expectation— who gave them that beautiful hymn, part of which, beginning "The Porter watches at the gate," was sung so fittingly at her funeral service—who gave them the perfect lines, beginning "Thy lovely saints do bring Thee love"—will be cherished and honoured.—BELL, MACKENZIE, 1898, *Christina Rossetti, a Biographical and Critical Study, p.* 338.

Walter Horatio Pater
1839-1894

Born, in London, 4 Aug. 1839. Early education at a school at Enfield. At King's School, Canterbury, 1853-58. Matric. Queen's Coll., Oxford, 11 June 1858; B. A., 1862; Fellow of Brasenose Coll., 1864; M. A., 1865; Junior Dean, 1866; Tutor, 1867-83; Dean, 1871; Lecturer, 1873. Contrib. to "Westminster Rev.," "Fortnightly Rev.," etc., from 1866. Died, at Oxford, 30 July 1894. Buried in St. Giles's Cemetery, Oxford. *Works:* "Studies in the History of the Renaissance," 1873; "Marius the Epicurean," 1885; "Imaginary Portraits," 1887; "Appreciations," 1889; "Plato and Platonism," 1893; "The Child in the House," 1894. *Posthumous:* "Greek Studies," ed. by C. L. Shadwell, 1895; "Miscellaneous Studies," ed. by C. L. Shadwell, 1895; "Gaston de Latour," ed. by C. L. Shadwell, 1896; "Essays from the 'Guardian' " (priv. ptd.), 1897.—SHARP, R. FARQUHARSON, 1897, *A Dictionary of English Authors, p.* 223.

PERSONAL

When I had known him first he was a pagan, without any guide but that of the personal conscience; years brought gradually with them a greater and greater longing for the supporting solace of a creed. His talk, his habits, became more and more theological, and it is my private conviction that, had he lived a few years longer, he would have taken orders and a small college living in the country. Report, which found so much to misrepresent in a life so orderly and simple, has erred even to the place and occasion of his death. He was taken ill with rheumatic fever in the month of June of this year, being, as he remained to the end, not in college, but with his sisters in their house in St. Giles. He was recovering, and was well enough to be busy upon a study on "Pascal," which he has left nearly completed, when, in consequence of writing too close to an open window, pleurisy set in and greatly reduced his strength. Again he seemed convalescent, and had left his room, without illeffect, on July 29, when, repeating the experiment next day, the action of the heart failed, and he died, on the staircase of his house, in the arms of his sister, at ten o'clock on the morning of Monday, July 30, 1894. Had he lived five days longer, he would have completed his fifty-fifth year. He was buried, in the presence of many of his oldest friends, in the beautiful cemetery of St. Giles at Oxford.— GOSSE, EDMUND, 1894, *Walter Pater: a Portrait, Contemporary Review, vol.* 66, *p.* 805.

From the first, I never took Walter Pater for an Englishman. In appearance, in manner, he suggested the Fleming or the Hollander; in the mien and carriage of his mind, so to say, he was a Frenchman of that old northern type which had its meditative and quiet extreme in Maurice de Guérin, and its intensely actual extreme in Guy de Maupassant. Neither mentally nor physically could I discern anything British in him, save in his appreciations; and he had traits which affiliated him to those old Huguenot bearers of his name who no doubt had a strong Flemish strain in their French blood.— SHARP, WILLIAM, 1894, *Some Personal Reminiscences of Walter Pater, Atlantic Monthly, vol.* 74, *p.* 803.

I do not remember to have heard that the prospective author of "Marius" was ever a candidate for a scholarship at his college and mine; his life, in those days, [1861] was tranquil, his manner shy, even to silence, his habits were severely reserved, yet he was not unpopular even with those who knew least of him; for an innate grace of manner never failed him, and he had the instinctive courtesy of a natural gentleman. His reputation was above his known achievements, but he was the subject of rumours, complimentary alike to his modesty and his abilities, crediting him while yet a boy with the authorship of papers crowned with honours of print; and from the first had been marked out by his singularly shrewd college tutor as the sure winner of a fellowship in the fulness of time. —ESCOTT, T. H. S., 1894, *Some Oxford Memories of the Præ-Æsthetic Age, National Review, vol.* 24, *p.* 235.

For many years, however, Pater's real home in Oxford was in his rooms at Brasenose. He is described as disliking the society of strangers; as hating all unnecessary noise and all extravagance of any kind; as loving to surround himself with beautiful things, caring nothing for their association or for their money-value, only for their beauty. He is said to have been simple in manner, and to have had a sense of fun, which was as playful as that of a child. These Brasenose rooms of Pater's are still remembered as being "No. Seven Staircase, Room Three." They look out onto Radcliffe Square, with slight views of All Souls and St. Mary's. They are more cheerful than are Heber's rooms: and Pater could almost have swung a kitten, if it were a small kitten, between his bed, his window, and his door.—HUTTON, LAURENCE, 1903, *Literary Landmarks of Oxford*, p. 57.

His life was self-contained, subjective, stationary; it was a life of academic amenity, singularly devoid of the "rubs, doublings, and wrenches" which afford the biographer his best, most picturesque opportunity. The annals of it are short, and, if confined to external happenings, simple. But the interpretation of them is a more difficult affair. If we can capture some clews and hints of character, however diffused and indirect, if we can partially apprehend a fugitive and recondite but strangely effective literary personality, we shall be fortunate.—GREENSLET, FERRIS, 1903, *Walter Pater (Contemporary Men of Letters)*, p. 4.

MARIUS THE EPICUREAN
1885

"Marius" I have not read. I suppose I must. But I shrink from approaching Pater's style, which has a peculiarly disagreeable effect upon my nerves—like the presence of a civet cat. Still, I believe I must read it.—SYMONDS, JOHN ADDINGTON, 1885, *Letter to Henry Sidgwick, April 5; Life*, ed. Brown, vol. II, p. 246.

While it is entirely free from anything like a sensational element, it is replete with matter that will never cease to appeal to serious and cultivated minds. As a piece of composition, it has the grace of style, the clear-cut precision, the high-bred tone, the exquisite flavour and solidity, that make literature enduring. It is the work of a scholar, but of a scholar breathing our modern air while charged with the free spirit of antiquity; of clear vision and profound experience, and the gift of delineating with fascinating art both the inner life and the outward world. . . . Only one familiar with the profound influences that shape and color human life, and who at the same time is furnished with the lore and saturated with the spirit of antiquity, could produce a picture so vital and faithful and instructive as this. . . . Nothing can be more graceful and charming than the way the story of Cupid and Psyche is told, and the use that is made of it in tracing the influences that wrought upon the plastic life of young Marius. A chapter that shows the fine dialectic power of the author is a dialogue between the sceptical poet Lucian and a gifted youth who had accepted the Stoical Philosophy as the true doctrine.—POWERS, HORATIO N., 1885, *Marius the Epicurean, The Dial*, vol. 6, pp. 90, 91.

"Marius the Epicurean" was the result of twelve years' work, and is undoubtedly the writer's most strenuous and beautiful book. One of the century's masterpieces, one feels, as one turns over its felicitous pages, or lingers over some phrase of matchless magic and music. It is certainly unique in the literature of England, being our only philosophical romance. A novel it is not, in the real sense of the word; there is little incident, and it deals with subjects which are not for fiction. It is a philosophical treatise with a setting of romance. Here Marius is created that the author may show us, in the analysis of his character, a development of theories which had evidently taken place in his own mind. By using the third person the author is given a freer hand. And in addition the book is certainly more forcible than it would have been if merely cast in the form of an essay. The hero Marius is sufficiently real to make us keenly interested in the history of his mind—those of us, that is to say, who care for analysis at all.—ADDLESHAW, STANLEY, 1897, *Walter Pater, Gentleman's Magazine*, vol. 282, p. 232.

Perhaps the most poetic book of the latter part of the century. — JOHNSON, CHARLES F., 1898, *Elements of Literary Criticism*, p. 44.

GENERAL

A style like Mr. Pater's ought to be taken in thankfulness, without too much questioning, and only a prayer for more of the same kind. For what richness it has, and what sweetness always! Every word has its meaning with him, and its value. . . . If I have said half of what I feel, I have shown those who would care for Mr. Pater's writing that they would care for it very much indeed. It is easy to praise it vaguely, but nothing can render its infinite grace and indescribable charm. You must go to the books themselves. . . . Mr. Pater has not dramatic power, the power of presenting characters. Neither is he a writer to go to for intellectual or moral support. Certain people might find these in him; but most of us would not. Nor is he an artist of the highest order, in spite of his style; he has not the broad, swift, unerring touch of the great masters.—BRADFORD, GAMALIEL, JR., 1888, *Walter Pater, Andover Review*, vol. 10, pp. 149, 154, 155.

Mr. Pater's criticism, in my opinion, suffers from the same defect as Lamb's—excess of sympathy. In his fine perception of the motives of his authors, and in his delicate description of their styles, his "Appreciations" are all that can be desired; but he seems to me to flinch from the severe application of critical law. He exhibits invariably the taste of a refined literary epicure. But the taste of an epicure is not always that of a judge.—COURTHOPE, WILLIAM JOHN, 1890, *Appreciations, Nineteenth Century*, vol. 27, p. 662.

Perhaps no prose writer of to-day has a more sensitive imagination or a more chaste and musical style than Walter Pater.—BAINTON, GEORGE, 1890, *The Art of Authorship*, p. 292.

> The freshness of the light, its secrecy,
> Spices, or honey from sweet-smelling bower,
> The harmony of lines, love's trembling hour
> Struck on thee with a new felicity.

—FIELD, MICHAEL, 1894, *Walter Pater, July* 30; *The Academy*.

Aside from "Marius the Epicurean," there is a radical mistake on the part of those who affirm that Pater is, after all, but a subtle and seductive writer on art; meaning the arts of painting and sculpture. It is true that, from his first able essay, that on Winckelmann, to those on The School of Giorgione and the Marbles of Ægina he is the profoundest, and generally the most trustworthy of art critics; but—and again, apart from the creative quality informing each of these essays, making them not only interpretations, but works of art—he is, of course, much more than this. His volume of studies of contemporary poetry and prose, and kindred themes, is alone sufficient to base an enduring reputation upon.—SHARP, WILLIAM, 1894, *Some Personal Reminiscences of Walter Pater, Atlantic Monthly*, vol. 74, p. 812.

The fame of Walter Pater will not be wrecked on the holiday of an editor or the indolence of a reporter. It is grounded on the respect which has not yet failed to follow pure and distinguished excellence in the art of writing. . . . I have known writers of every degree, but never one to whom the act of composition was such a travail and an agony as it was to Pater. . . . The sentences of the Oxford critic are often too long, and they are sometimes brokenbacked with having had to bear too heavy a burden of allusion and illustration. His style, however, was his peculiarity. It had beautiful qualities, if we have to confess that it had the faults of those qualities. It was highly individual; it cannot be said that he owed it to any other writer, or that at any period of his thirty years of literary labour he faltered or swerved from his own path. He was to a high degree self-centered.—GOSSE, EDMUND, 1894, *Walter Pater, a Portrait, Contemporary Review*, vol. 66, pp. 795, 806, 807.

There is not one page in Mr. Pater's writings on which the most trivial carelessness can be detected. Think what the reader may of the beauty, or the power, or of lack of them, in this sentence or in that, he recognises the predetermination, which sets each word in its place, precisely as he finds it. Raphael, true scholar that he was, seems always, writes Mr. Pater, to be saying "I am utterly purposed that I will not offend." It is equally so with himself. But there must always be a class of readers to whom the acts of "recollection" and of "attention," in the spiritual sense, necessary for the enjoyment of his work, are a bodily distress; and in this, as in much else, he resembles the laborious and enduring Flaubert. . . . He stands quite alone. We sometimes hear of his "school," but it does not exist: it is a genius, as was Lamb's, unique. His *Renaissance* studies have induced a certain revival of interest in certain somewhat novel aspects of early France and later Italy: writers have written about certain kinds of theme, because of his writing. But none have caught his tones, their peculiar felicity and proper charm.—JOHNSON, LIONEL, 1894, *The Work of Mr. Pater, Fortnightly Review*, vol. 62, pp. 353, 359.

In Ruskin, Newman, and certain other writers, there is to be noted a decided reaction toward the long sentence. This movement reaches in Mr. Walter Pater perhaps the limit at which the paragraph and the long period can be reconciled. Mr. Pater is conscious of the tendency of his style towards complexity and minute qualification, and he therefore conscientiously keeps to the unity of the paragraph. What is even more noticeable, he uses a large percentage of appositional clauses and phrases that, while they have partly the effect of parentheses, yet avoid the multiplication of predications and connectives. It is a weighty style, a correct style, a beautiful style in its fitting of word to notion; but it has a wholly different order of procedure from that introduced by Macaulay. The coherence, always present, but seen by the reader at some expense to his attention, depends equally upon order of words and upon connectives; very little indeed upon parallel structure.—LEWIS, EDWIN HERBERT, 1894, *The History of the English Paragraph*, p. 165.

Persons only superficially acquainted, or by hearsay, with his writings, are apt to sum up his merits as a writer by saying that he was a master, or a consummate master of style; but those who have really studied what he wrote do not need to be told that his distinction does not lie in his literary grace alone, his fastidious choice of language, his power of word-painting, but in the depth and seriousness of his studies. That the amount he has produced, in a literary life of thirty years, is not greater, is one proof among many of the spirit in which he worked. His genius was "an infinite capacity for taking pains." That delicacy of insight, that gift of penetrating into the heart of things, that subtleness of interpretation, which with him seems an instinct, is the outcome of hard, patient, conscientious study. If he had chosen, he might, without difficulty, have produced a far greater body of work of less value; and from a worldly point of view, he would have been wise.—SHADWELL, CHARLES L., 1894, ed. *Greek Studies*, Preface, p. viii.

This ["Greek Studies"] is the final gift of one who gave but sparingly, yet whose rare good fortune it was to increase the conscious joy of living. Echoes of that finely tempered and restrained content which succeeded the rapturous license of youth, and which reached its highest spiritual development in "Marius the Epicurean," relieve and lighten the more somber pages of his later studies. If he turns now and again to the "worship of sorrow," even among the happy Greeks; if he dwells unsparingly upon the vengeful grief of Demeter, or the mysterious suffering of Dionysus (a subject which, in "Imaginary Portraits," has awakened his subtlest powers of imagination), his true charm and helpfulness lie still in his recognition of beauty as a factor in life, and in his delicate philosophy of "happy moments," by which we snatch, even amid sordid and fretful cares, some portion of serenity and delight. No writer of modern times has surpassed Mr. Pater in sympathetic appreciation of classic literature and art.—REPPLIER, AGNES, 1895, *Greek Studies by Walter Pater, The Cosmopolitan*, vol. 19, p. 116.

Mr. Pater's reputation extended but slowly. There must have been many readers of Mr. Mallock's "New Republic" twenty years ago who wondered somewhat at that singular and disagreeable Mr. Rose. Who was it that could be put in along with Matthew Arnold and John Ruskin? At that time Mr. Pater was generally known only by his studies in "The Renaissance." To-day it is not so unnatural to think of him as one of the chief critics of art and literature of our day. His seven volumes are well-known, and he is well or ill thought of by many. . . . A style Mr. Pater certainly had, although there exists no very valuable characterization of it. "Long-drawn music" it is called by one, and "whipt cream" by another; but more definite views are somewhat to seek. It is an interesting style, however, and one which rather challenges a man to define it. One thing obvious enough is that in the course of the thirty years in which his work was published, his style underwent a great change. Certain enduring qualities his writing always possessed,—it was always scholarly, always harmonious, always subtle, and there were also certain constant minor habits,—but in his later years his style had undergone so great a change that many admirers of "The Renaissance" must have been out of patience with "Plato and Platonism."—HALE, EDWARD E., JR., 1895,

Walter Pater's Last Volume, The Dial, vol. 19, p. 279.

No writer since the revolutionary movement in English prose at the beginning of this century, not even Landor, has paid such extraordinary and successful attention to the architecture of the sentence. As against the snipsnap shortness of some writers, the lawless length of others, and the formlessness of a third class, his best sentences are arranged with an almost mathematical precision of clause-building, while their rhythm, though musical, is rarely poetic. Yet it must be acknowledged that this elaborate construction never became a perfectly learnt art with him; and that his sentences in his later work were sometimes apt to waver and wander. Still, on the whole, Mr. Pater, as an exponent in prose of the tendencies of which in verse Rossetti and Mr. Swinburne have been the chief masters, deserves a rank which it is impossible for any careful and impartial critic to ignore or to refuse. Few writers are fortunate in their imitators, and he has been especially unfortunate. His theories sometimes, his style often, have been the victims of a following not seldom silly, and not very seldom disgusting. But it would be unjust to charge this on the author himself. In himself, though owing a little, and not always happily, to Matthew Arnold and more to Newman, he is an extremely careful and on the whole a distinctly original producer of literature, who has chosen to make literature itself the main subject of his production, and has enforced views distinct in kind in a manner still more distinct.—SAINTSBURY, GEORGE, 1896, *English Prose*, ed. Craik, vol. v, p. 748.

A Keats in prose was this Walter Pater; endowed with the same genius for rendering sensations in words vivid as colour, definite as marble, he was yet a Greek in body as well as in spirit—a Keats with health, maturity, and a placid indifference to passion. Thanks to a rare conjunction of physical serenity and intensely delicate sensibilities, he brought æsthetic hedonism to its perfect type. . . . Pater's style has little of the charm of personality—that constant presence behind the words of a smiling face or the gleam of ardent eyes. This is the charm of Heine or Renan or Robert Louis Stevenson. Pater's work delights us with a series of beautiful pictures; the charm is in the words themselves; it is, so to speak, objective. This is due to the absence of emotion, rhythm, eloquence. It is the art of a painter—the patient and flawless rendering of sensations, of colours and forms, and of fleeting, delicate impressions. It is a style made up of words and phrases that are truly magical in their power to evoke images, to convey "with a single touch," as he says of Cornelius Fronto, "the sense of colours, textures, incidents." And these wonderful phrases are curiously heaped together into sentences whose construction is frequently hideous. But what phrases!—JACOBUS, RUSSELL P., 1896, *The Blessedness of Egoism*, Fortnightly Review, vol. 65, p. 384.

In those pages there are, it is true, occasional lapses from a perfectly sound method; there is at times a loss of simplicity, a cloying sweetness in the style of this accomplished writer. There are, however, the perils of a very sensitive temperament, an intense feeling for beauty, and a certain seclusion from the affairs of life. That which characterises Mr. Pater at all times is his power of putting himself amid conditions that are not only extinct, but obscure and elusive; of winding himself back, as it were, into the primitive Greek consciousness and recovering for the moment the world as the Greeks saw, or, rather, felt it.—MABIE, HAMILTON WRIGHT, 1896, *Books and Culture*, p. 100.

Of the critics who have written during the last sixty years, Mr. Pater is probably the most remarkable. His work is always weighted with thought, and his thought is always fused with imagination. He unites, in a singular degree of intensity, the two crucial qualities of the critic; on the one hand a sense of form and colour and artistic utterance; on the other hand a speculative instinct which pierces behind these to the various types of idea and mood and character that underlie them. He is equally alive to subtle resemblances and to subtle differences; and art is to him not merely an intellectual enjoyment, but something which is to be taken into the spirit of a man and to become part of his life. . . . With wider knowledge and a clearer consciousness of the deeper issues involved, he may be said to have taken up the work of Lamb and to have carried it forward in a spirit which those who best love Lamb will be the most ready to admire.—VAUGHAN, C. E., 1897, *English Literary Criticism*, p. 210.

The book of "Studies in the Renaissance," even with the rest of Pater to choose from, seems to me sometimes to be the most beautiful book of prose in our literature. Nothing in it is left to inspiration: but it is all inspired. Here is a writer who, like Baudelaire, would better nature; and in this goldsmith's work of his prose he too has "rêve le miracle d'une prose poétique, musicale sans rhythme et sans rime." An almost oppressive quiet, a quiet which seems to exhale an atmosphere heavy with the odour of tropical flowers, broods over these pages; a subdued light shadows them.—SYMONS, ARTHUR, 1897, *Studies in Two Literatures*, p. 172.

Of Pater's style much has been said in praise and detraction. It expresses his hunger for perfection in its extreme polish, its elaborate form, its verbal nicety. But it is never spontaneous, and its art is sometimes artifice. Its merits are perhaps too evident to make of it a great style. Yet it will always witness to the value of patience and of conscientiousness in the handling of words: furthermore, it is an effective key to the otherwise shadowy personality of Pater; to the complex nature, tinged with morbidness, in which end-of-the-century passions broke in upon classic, perhaps pseudo-classic calm.—SHOLL, ANNA MCCLURE, 1897, *Library of The World's Best Literature*, ed. Warner, vol. XIX, p. 11160.

Pater was, indeed, pre-eminently a scholarly writer. This does not mean that he was quite a purist. He was not above coining a form if it served his turn, and for certain French words and relative constructions he had a fondness hardly warranted under the self-denying ordinance of the purist. But he was a scholarly writer in his use of the rich resources of the English tongue. He plays deftly, for example, with the archaic, radical meaning of words like *express, entertain*, or *mortified*, never using the inherent, hidden meaning so crassly as to perturb the untutored reader, yet always with a retrospective, pictorial turn which delights the scholar. Like all good writers he was exquisitely sensitive to the expressive shading and colour of language. With him, as with Marius, "his general sense of a fitness and beauty in words became effective in daintily pliant sentences, with all sorts of felicitous linking of figure to abstraction." This linking of figure to abstraction is, perhaps, the most salient feature of Pater's style.—GREENSLET, FERRIS, 1903, *Walter Pater (Contemporary Men of Letters)*, p. 92.

Philip Gilbert Hamerton
1834–1894

An English writer on art, painter, and etcher. He was the son of a solicitor, and was born at Laneside, near Shaw, Lancashire. His mother died when he was an infant, and his father, who was an inebriate, died ten years later. For these and other reasons Hamerton's boyhood was lonely. He gave up in displeasure his preparation for Oxford, turned to poetry and art, and began writing for the reviews. He traveled in Wales, visited France, and in 1857 began his periodic encampments on an island in Loch Awe in the Scotch Highlands, described in "A Painter's Camp in the Highlands and Thoughts About Art" (1862). This notable work was followed by the more technical "Etching and Etchers" (1868); "Contemporary French Painters" (1868); and "Painting in France After the Decline of Classicism" (1869). In 1869 he founded the *Portfolio*, an excellent art magazine, which he edited till his death. Among his other numerous writings are "The Intellectual Life" (1873); "Life of Turner" (1879); "The Graphic Arts" (1882); "Human Intercourse" (1884); "Landscape" (1885); and "French and English" (1889). Hamerton, who had married a French woman, passed his later years in France, and died at Boulogne-sur-Seine. Like Ruskin, Hamerton was an art interpreter to his generation, the medium between the artist and the public. For this he was eminently suited because of the catholicity of his taste, and his agreeable style. Consult "Philip Gilbert Hamerton: An Autobiography and a Memoir by His Wife" (London, 1896).—GILMAN, PECK, AND COLBY, eds., 1903, *New International Encyclopædia*, vol. IX, p. 25.

PERSONAL

In person, Mr. Hamerton is well formed and athletic, with a noble head. regular features, a very fine eye, and a superb beard, which is worn full. Like George Macdonald, he has the American type of face, rather than the English.—POWERS, HORATIO N., 1873, *Philip Gilbert Hamerton, Old and New*, vol. 8, p. 202.

The notion of being a dead man is not entirely displeasing to me. If the dead are defenceless, they have this compensating advantage, that nobody can inflict upon them any sensible injury; and in beginning a book which is not to see the light until I am lying comfortably in my grave, with six feet of earth above me to deaden the noises of the upper world, I feel quite a new kind of security, and write with a more complete freedom from anxiety about the quality of the work than has been usual at the beginning of other manuscripts.—HAMERTON, PHILIP GILBERT, 1894, *An Autobiography, 1834–1858*, ed. *his Wife*, p. 2.

Throughout his life he made rules to bind his dreamy fancy to active study and production; they were frequently altered, according to the state of his health and the nature of his work at the time; but he felt the necessity of self-imposed laws to govern and regulate his strong inclination towards reflection and reading. . . . His love of sailing must have been closely connected with the inclination to a restful, peaceful, dreamy state, for although fond of all kinds of boating, he greatly preferred a sailing-boat to any other, and never wished to possess a steamer, or cared much to make use of one. Still, he took great pleasure in some forms of physical exercise: he could use an oar beautifully; he was a capital horseman, having been used to ride from the age of six, and retained a firm seat to the last; he readily undertook pedestrian excursions and the ascent of mountains.—HAMERTON, MRS. PHILIP GILBERT, 1896, *Philip Gilbert Hamerton, an Autobiography and a Memoir*, pp. 224, 225.

GENERAL

Ruskin is superb in his combinations; Hamerton exact in his method, and careful to protect his rear. Therefore the most *useful* books that could be placed in the hands of the American Art public at present are Hamerton's "Painter's Camp" and "Thoughts about Art." . . . Mr. Hamerton's first volume, entitled "A Painter's Camp in the Highland," we regret to say, is not a felicitous introduction to the valuable "Thoughts about Art," which give the title to the second. It is unpleasantly inlaid with egotism and enamelled with self-consciousness. Mr. Hamerton's critics cannot withhold attention from so prominent a feature of his book. The obtrusiveness of his personality invites attention. He seems not to have learned the art of existing fully in his work, without dreaming to speak of himself. True, any account of a painter's camp necessarily solicits much consideration of its occupant; but it does not follow that we should be bored with trivial details, and anecdotes simply flattering to the personal appearance of the painter. . . . The personality revealed in Mr. Hamerton's "Painter's Camp" is very English; and when we have said this, we have said all. But let no one be deterred from making the acquaintance of Mr. Hamerton even in his "Painter's Camp;" for he is young, he is hearty, he is interesting, and he is manly. We know of no books which are the result of more faithful study and practical consideration of the painter's function, and which, at the same time, are so free from technical jargon. Mr. Hamerton is preëminently a useful writer on Art; he is certainly accurate and comprehensive.—BENSON, EUGENE, 1865, *A New Art Critic, Atlantic Monthly*, vol. 16, pp. 325, 326.

It is not my purpose to discuss his literary performances; and yet this brief sketch would lack an essential feature, without an assertion of their great utility, as well as their graphic force and beauty. You are not merely stimulated by his thought, but are helped in the field of art, just where you need assistance. His style has the prime excellence of pleasing while it instructs. Instead of astonishing and bewildering you with a maze of splendid works, or a cloud of such pictures as Ruskin sometimes puts before you, he gives you the clear-cut conception which throbs with vitality. You feel that you are in the leadership of a guide who knows his ground, and exactly what he is about.—POWERS, HORATIO N., 1873, *Philip Gilbert Hamerton, Old and New*, vol. 8, p. 202.

Once his back is turned we find it difficult to tell what he did say or what he did not say and yet this man may have been more useful to us than the teacher every one of whose items of information could be duly registered in a copybook. This, to my mind, is the case with all essayists of the class to which Mr. Hamerton belongs; and it is most of all the case when, as with the book under review, the subject is as vast and vague as the treatment is unsystematic. . . .

It would be satisfactory could one undo the binding of this rather overpowering treatise, not merely in order to tear up a large number of quite unnecessary pages, but also in order to place some of the really valuable contents in the hands of one set of people, and another portion in the hands of another set of people. There is a large class of intelligent, but not intellectual, persons to whom the careful perusal of the two admirable chapters, "Why we are apparently getting less religious" and "Why we are really getting less religious," would be of the greatest practical use, by showing them the time, feeling, and effort daily wasted by a timid or hypocritical clinging to effete standards. And there is, on the other hand, a large class also of persons more intellectual (I mean more conversant with books and theories) than intelligent, to whom it would do a world of good, freeing them from a certain frumpish and goody-goody middle class philistinism extremely common in literary people, to meditate over the chapters in which Mr. Hamerton expounds the infinitely greater variety of æsthetic, imaginative, and psychological impressions obtainable by and among the richer and more socially conspicuous members of society.—LEE, VERNON, 1884, *Human Intercourse*, *The Academy*, vol. 26, p. 315.

Few artists are more expert than Mr. Hamerton in the art of etching, and his various works on and in connection with this art have made for him a high reputation.—PARKES, KINETON, 1892, ed. *The Painter-Poets*, p. 248, note.

Was one of the most sagacious and best informed of art writers, a critic whose elasticity and range of mind, whose breadth of mental vision, whose possession, too, of literary taste and of historical knowledge, placed him—it is scarcely necessary to say it—in a category altogether distinct from, and above, that of the fluent scribbler who has no knowledge, and of the blameless but bigoted sectarian painter who, if he writes, writes with no literary talent, and with no range of even artistic vision beyond the walls of his own studio. Sympathetic and careful, flexible and amply instructed, Mr. Hamerton touched no subject on which he was not heard with profit. . . . Of the other works associated with Mr. Hamerton's name, the very large volume on "Landscape"—at once pictorial and literary—and the substantial tome which goes under the title of "The Graphic Arts" are probably the two principal. To the second that I have mentioned I should give the higher place. Nowhere else is there afforded such admirable opportunity of weighing the claims of one artistic method or medium against the claims of another—not so much their actual degrees of merit (a matter practically impossible to gauge and idle to discourse about) as their individual characteristics, and their relative appropriateness for a particular labour. But by much that has not been mentioned in the few preceding lines, as well as by the books here briefly described, did Mr. Hamerton establish his claim to be esteemed as one of the most agreeable and serviceable contributors to the art literature of the time.— WEDMORE, F., 1894, *Fine Art*, *The Academy*, vol. 46, p. 381.

Anyone who is familiar with his style will be prepared for the pleasure that he will find in this volume. The great charm of this author's writings is the agreeable personal note that runs through everything that he has published. He is always frank, and he is nowhere more so than in the story of his life. He gives as his principal reason for writing an autobiography that he is the only person in the world who knows enough about his personal history to give a truthful account of it, and because he dreaded the possibility of falling into the hands of some writer who might attempt to write his biography with inadequate materials.— GILDER, J. L., 1896, *A Book and its Story*, *The Critic*, vol. 29, p. 408.

Hamerton confined himself to the critics' true rôle of interpreter of the artist to the public, and for this office he had many qualifications besides the essential one of considerable practical knowledge of art. Even his limitations and defects were in a manner part of his effectiveness. Take, for instance, his style. It is a model of simplicity and lucidity, and has a certain elegance and charm. So clear is it that its possessor complains somewhere that it prevented his having any reputation in England for profundity, it being an English idea that a clear writer is a shallow one. It is without passion, or warmth of coloring, or brilliancy of fancy, as cold as it is clear— the style of a well educated, gentlemanly person, not that of a poet or a rhapsodist. It can hardly be doubted that this is the style best calculated to carry conviction to the people for whom he wrote.—Cox, KENYON, 1896, *Philip Gilbert Hamerton, The Nation*, vol. 63, p. 440.

He was probably as far from being a genius as an able and versatile man with his mind set on high ideals can well be. Nowhere in his work does it seem that he saw human life, external nature, spiritual or physical matters, with other eyes than those of the everyday Englishman. . . . He failed to explain rightly in his printed works that the language of the fine arts is wholly different from the language of literature, nor did he ever endeavor to make it clear to the English-speaking public which he addressed—and which of all modern societies of European origin, has the least knowledge of its own in these matters of fine art—that it is necessary to approach the work of art from the entirely non-literary standpoint occupied by the artist in order to understand it aright. It may be that he did not see his way to explain this without throwing his public entirely off the track and ceasing to keep it interested. It is certain that he knew how to keep it interested, and that, for his works in many volumes, some half dozen of which are large and costly, he retained an audience which constantly increased in magnitude until the close of his career. It is true, also, that no word of all the immense amount of printed discussion on art which he has left will tend to the confusion or the misleading of any one. It is probable that Hamerton had no more sense of humor than Wordsworth, nor, in spite of the apparent suggestions to the contrary which occur in Mrs. Hamerton's "Memoir," that he had much power of enthusiasm.—STURGIS, RUSSELL, 1896, *Notes of a Useful Life, The Book Buyer*, vol. 13, pp. 960, 962.

His death was sudden. . . . He left an autobiography brought down to the date of his marriage. It was completed and published in 1897 by his widow, better qualified than himself to render justice to the many admirable traits of a sterling character somewhat deficient in superficial attractiveness, and less likely to bring into relief, as he has done, the foibles hardly to be escaped by one doubly prone to sensitiveness as author and artist. Much, however, that seems vanity is merely lack of a sense of humour. The writer's undoubting conviction that whatever interests him must interest others burdens his page with superfluous detail.—GARNETT, RICHARD, 1901, *Dictionary of National Biography, Supplement*, vol. II, p. 381.

George John Romanes
1848–1894

Man of science; was born at Kingston, Canada West, 1848, but came with his parents to England at an early age: B. A. Gonville and Caius College, Cambridge, 1870; honorary fellow, 1872; Burney prizeman, 1873; formed friendship with Darwin; studied physiology at University College, London, 1874–6; engaged in researches on medusæ and echinoderms; F. R. S., 1879; made investigation respecting mental faculties of animals in relation to those of man, 1881–3; held professorship at Edinburgh, 1886–90; Fullerian professor of physiology at Royal Institution, 1888–91; expounded in paper contributed to Linnean Society, 1886, theory of physiological isolation, dealing with the possible evolution of a distinct species from an isolated group of an original species; zoological secretary of Linnean Society; incorporated M. A. Oxford; founded Romanes lecture at Oxford, 1891; Hon. LL. D. Aberdeen, 1882. His publications include "Candid Examination of Theism," 1878, "Animal Intelligence," 1881, "Mental Evolution in Animals," 1883, "Mental Evolution in Man," 1888, and "Darwin and after Darwin," 1892.—HUGHES, C. E. 1903, *Dictionary of National Biography, Index and Epitome*, p. 1126.

PERSONAL

He was one of the men whom the age specially requires for the investigation and solution of its especial difficulties, and for the concilation and harmony of interests between which a factitious rivalry has been created.—GLADSTONE, WILLIAM EWART, 1894, *To Mrs. Romanes, June; Life and Letters of George John Romanes*, ed. his Wife, p. 386.

The strength and simplicity and patience of his character appeared in nothing else more remarkably, more happily, than in his undiscouraged grasp of those unseen realities which invade this world in the name and power of the world to come. The love of precision and completeness never dulled his care for the things that he could neither define, nor label, nor arrange; in their fragmentariness he treasured them, in their reserve he trusted them, waiting faithfully to see what they might have to show him. And they did not fail him. — PAGET, FRANCIS, 1894, *The Guardian, June* 6.

Looking back over these two years of illness, it is impossible not to be struck by the calmness and fortitude with which that illness was met. There were, as has been said, moments of terrible depression and of disappointment and of grief. It was not easy for him to give up ambition, to leave so many projects unfulfilled, so much work undone. But to him this illness grew to be a mount of purification.

Ove l'umano spirito si purga,
E di salire al ciel diventa degno.

More and more there grew on him a deepening sense of the goodness of God. No one had ever suffered more from the Eclipse of Faith, no one had ever been more honest in dealing with himself and with his difficulties. The change that came over his mental attitude may seem almost incredible to those who knew him only as a scientific man; it does not seem so to the few who knew anything of his inner life. To them the impression given is, not of an enemy changed into a friend, of antagonism altered into submission; rather is it of one who for long has been bearing a heavy burden upon his shoulders bravely and patiently, and who at last has had it lifted from him, and lifted so gradually that he could not tell the exact moment when he found it gone, and himself standing, like the Pilgrim of never to be forgotten story, at the foot of the Cross, with Three Shining Ones coming to greet him. It was recovery, to some extent discovery, which befell him, but there was no change of purpose, no sudden intellectual or moral conversion.—ROMANES, MRS. GEORGE JOHN, 1895-97, *The Life and Letters of George John Romanes,* ed. his *Wife,* p. 382.

For some time before his death Romanes suffered from a disease —a condition of the arteries resulting in apoplexy—the gravity of which he fully realised, facing the inevitable event with admirable fortitude. . . . Romanes was through the greater part of his career an ardent sportsman, and frequently visited Scotland to indulge his sporting tastes. In private life he was a genial and delightful companion, and to those who knew him intimately a warm and staunch friend.—MORGAN, C. LLOYD, 1897, *Dictionary of National Biography,* vol. XLIX, p. 180.

GENERAL

We hail, then, with much pleasure and very sincere satisfaction, the publication by Mr. Romanes of his recent work on human mental evolution. In him we have at last a Darwinian who, with great patience and thoroughness, applies himself to meet directly and point-blank the most formidable arguments of the anti-Darwinian school, as well as to put forward persuasively the most recent hypotheses on his side. Mr. Romanes is exceptionally well qualified— amongst the disciples of Mr. Darwin—to assume the task he has assumed. For a long time past he has made this question his own, and has devoted his energies to the task of showing that there is (as Mr. Darwin declared) no difference of kind, but only one of degree, between the highest human intellect and the psychical faculties of the lowest animals. Mr. Romanes has become the representative of Mr. Darwin on this special and most important field of inquiry, and he has accumulated, in defence of the position he has taken up, an enormous mass of facts and anecdotes, which he regards as offering decisive evidence in his favour. His new book on this subject is written with great clearness and ability, and though it is, of course, possible that other advocates might have avoided this or that erroneous inference and mistaken assertion (as we deem them) of Mr. Romanes, we are convinced that no one could, on the whole, have made out a better case for his side than he has done; no other naturalist could, we are persuaded, have done more, or done better, to sustain Mr. Darwin's great thesis.— MIVART, ST. GEORGE, 1889, *The Origin of Human Reason,* p. 2.

He had a keen love of public discussion and a native skill in dialect, which may sometimes have led him to seek too eagerly an argumentative triumph. But his writings bear evidence of the most extensive knowledge and of a conscientious examination of all sources of information, combined with independence of judgment and much subtlety of analysis. . . . Whilst it would be premature to claim for Romanes the merit of a great discoverer or originator in

OLIVER WENDELL HOLMES

Engraving by New York Photogravure Co.
From a Photograph by Notman.

FRANCIS BRET HARTE

Engraving by George E. Perine. Photograph by Sarony.

psychology or in the philosophy of evolution, it is nevertheless true that by his keen criticism, careful mastery of details, and great literary fertility, he has exercised a most important influence—stimulating the thought and research of others by his example and enthusiasm, and by those contests in the arena of the "reviews" with Wallace, Spencer, and Weismann, which have made his name so widely known. It is not generally known, though a fact, that Romanes produced, in addition to his numerous scientific writings, a considerable volume of verse, which was printed for private distribution, as well as occasional poems. These poems deal with philosophic and emotional subjects, and are often of greaty beauty.—LANKESTER, E. RAY, 1894, *George John Romanes, Nature,* vol. 50, pp. 108, 109.

His investigations were by no means confined to observations and experiments upon the lower forms of sea-life, but they concerned also the signs and symptoms of mental evolution among animals in general. . . . In the year 1885, Lord Rosebery founded a professorship at Edinburgh for the special behoof of Mr. Romanes, who delivered there his lectures on the "Philosophy of Natural History." The same matter, or practically the same, was incorporated in the more extensive course which Mr. Romanes gave when appointed, in 1888, Fullerian Professor of Physiology at the Royal Institution in London. These lectures were published under the title of "Before and After Darwin," and should be distinguished at least chronologically from Mr. Romanes's "Darwin and After Darwin," published in 1892. . . . Not the least interesting among the traits of this strictly scientific scholar was the poetic temperament which found private expression in verses known to his friends. The wideness of his view of life is further exemplified in the active sympathy given by him to the movement in favor of opening galleries, museums, and libraries on Sunday. While in London he gave many Sunday lectures, and thus contributed by efforts of his own toward the practice of the sort of Sunday observance in which he believed. Such a man was not in his element where controversy was at its height, but still he had a fair share even of that.—DYER, L., 1894, *The Late G. J. Romanes, The Nation,* vol. 58, p. 424.

There was something very winning and attractive about Romanes. But the deepest thing in him was his love of truth, and his honest, fearless, unselfish pursuit of it. Quite early in his career he had signalised his abandonment of the Christian faith by the publication of a work entitled "A Candid Examination of Theism." Towards the close of his brief life he returned to the faith of his earlier years. This was made known by the fine "Life" of Romanes by his widow, and still more emphatically by his own notes published by Canon Gore after his death, under the title, "Thoughts on Religion."—GRAHAM, RICHARD D., 1897, *The Masters of Victorian Literature,* p. 472.

Oliver Wendell Holmes
1809–1894

Born, at Cambridge, Mass., 29 Aug. 1809. At schools at Cambridge and Andover, 1819–25. To Harvard University, summer of 1825; B. A., 1829. First poems appeared in the Harvard "Collegian," 1830. Studied medicine in Paris, 1833–35. M. D., Cambridge, Mass., 1836. Prof. of Anatomy and Physiology, Dartmouth Coll., 1838–40. Married Amelia Lee Jackson, 15 June 1840. Prof. of Anatomy, Harvard Univ., 1847–82; Professor Emeritus, 1882. Gave up medical practice, 1849. Contributor to "Atlantic Monthly" from 1857. Edited "The Atlantic Almanack" with D. G. Mitchell, 1867. Hon. LL. D., Harvard, 1886. Visit to Europe, 1886. Hon. LL. D., Cambridge, 1886; Hon. D. C. L., Oxford, 1886; Hon. LL. D., Edinburgh, 1886. Died, in Boston, Mass., 7 Oct. 1894. Buried there. *Works:* "Poems," 1836; "Boylston Prize Dissertations," 1838; "Lectures on Homœopathy," 1842; "Terpsichore," 1843; "Urania," 1846; "An Introductory Lecture," 1847; "Astræa," 1850; "The Benefactors of the Medical School of Harvard," 1850; "Oration" [before New England Soc.], 1855; "The Autocrat of the Breakfast Table," 1858; "The Professor at the Breakfast Table," 1860; "Currents and Counter-Currents in Medical Science," 1861; "Songs in Many Keys," 1861; "Elsie Venner," 1861; "Border Lines in some provinces of Medical Science," 1862; "Oration" [on Independence Day], 1863;

"Soundings from the 'Atlantic,'" 1866; "The Guardian Angel" 1867; "Wit and Humor," 1867, "Mechanism in Thought and Morals," 1870 (2nd edn., "with Notes and Afterthoughts," same year); "The Poet at the Breakfast Table," 1872; "The Claims of Dentistry," 1872; "Songs of Many Seasons," 1875; "The Story of Iris," 1877; "John Lothrop Motley," 1878; "The School-Boy," 1879; "The Iron Gate," 1881; "Pages from an Old Volume of Life," 1883; "Medical Essays," 1883; "Grandmother's Story, and other poems," 1883; "Ralph Waldo Emerson," 1885; "A Mortal Antipathy," 1885; "The Last Leaf," 1886; "Our Hundred Days in Europe," 1887; "Before the Curfew," 1888; "Over the Teacups," 1891 [1890]. *Collected Works:* in 13 vols., 1891. *Life:* by J. T. Morse, 1896.— SHARP, R. FARQUHARSON, 1897, *A Dictionary of English Writers*, p. 134.

PERSONAL

His chirography is remarkably fine, and a quick fancy might easily detect, in its graceful yet picturesque quaintness, an analogy with the vivid drollery of his style.—POE, EDGAR ALLAN, 1842, *A Chapter on Autography; Works*, ed. Stedman and Woodberry, vol. IX, p. 255.

The Boston *literati* have come and gone. I sat beside Longfellow at dinner, and had some very pleasant conversation with him. But O. W. Holmes was the great talker, and kept asking questions constantly about Scotland, how Burns could come out of its Calvinistic atmosphere, &c.—a little dapper man, hard and brusque, and more inquisitive than pleasant, but very bright and intelligent, he and Longfellow more ignorant of Scotland and Scotch modes of thought than I had imagined possible.— TULLOCH, JOHN, 1874, *Letter to his Wife, April 24; A Memoir of the Life of John Tulloch*, ed. Oliphant, p. 291.

Holmes has encountered no adverse fates, nor has he passed through those vicissitudes that try the souls of some men. Nature gave him a good outfit, and fortune has favored him at every step of his career. His has been an active life, devoted to earnest study and the pursuit of high ideals; it has been rewarded by ample contemporary honor, and, above all, blest with domestic happiness and with love of friends. Not until the silver cord is loosed, and the golden bowl is broken, can the curtain be lifted from the serene beauty of the poet's home.—UNDERWOOD, FRANCIS H., 1879, *Oliver Wendell Holmes, Scribner's Monthly*, vol. 18, p. 127.

As a boy he had tendencies towards flutes and flageolets; he was the possessor of a gun, and a pistol, in the barrel of which he hid his surreptitious cigars. At this distance of time he might confess to being one of the "gunners" who shot "Deacon Peleg's tame wild-goose." Full of animal spirits and vivacity, he had little natural inclination for the ministry. Even if his home had not been visited by sad and wailing ministers, who twitted him with his blessings as a Christian child till he wished he was a Moor. . . . He loves horses—saw Plenipotentiary in 1834 and Ormonde in 1886 win the Derby—and prefers a racer to a trotter. A "proud pedestrian," an oarsman, and, like Bernard Langdon, a boxer, familiar in his youth with the pets of the fancy and the heroes of the prize-ring, he despises the dandified languor of many of his countrymen. Aristocrat, athlete, conservative, insisting on the importance of neat dress and good manners, excelling in the patrician talent of "vers de société," and preferring the straight-backed metre of Dryden and Pope to the nimbler measures of modern verse, he seems to belong rather to the Old than the New World. — PROTHERO, ROWLAND EDMUND, 1886, *Oliver Wendell Holmes, Longman's Magazine*, vol. 8, pp. 303, 305.

Holmes's devotion to the two Muses of science and letters was uniform and untiring, as it was also to the two literary forms of verse and prose. But although a man of letters, like the other eminent men of letters in New England he had no trace of the Bohemian.—CURTIS, GEORGE WILLIAM, 1891, *Oliver Wendell Holmes, Harper's Magazine*, vol. 83, p. 281.

On every page of the "Autocrat" the author stands out, and everywhere with a smile on his face and an outstretched hand. He was so sympathetic that the relation of author to reader became surprisingly intimate, and the wish to verify the impression was universal. It sometimes happens that there is a disappointment. In Holmes there was none. His readers found him more delightful than his books. Those who knew him only by hearsay used to declare that they must read what so charming a man had written, and some of them did. He was looked upon as a kind of social phenomenon; this youthful and cheerful activity in a man nearing the eighties. To a phenomenon of another kind, also nearing the eighties, London had long been used. But Mr. Gladstone impressed people by his commanding qualities and his tremendous energy, while Holmes enchanted them. It was the difference between the whirlwind and the vernal breeze, or between the torrent and the brook which sparkles and flows serenely on between smiling banks.—SMALLEY, GEORGE W., 1894, *Studies of Men, p.* 319.

It is a significant fact that the great group of poets of which Oliver Wendell Holmes was the last were all Unitarians —Bryant, Emerson, Lowell, Longfellow, Whittier, Holmes, all Unitarians. . . . Two or three days before his death it is said that, anticipating the fact that he must go before long, and having in mind, as his son easily understood him, the funeral service in King's Chapel, which has always been his ecclesiastical home, he said to his son, Judge Holmes, "Well, Wendell, what is it— King's Chapel?" "Oh, yes, father," said he. "All right; then I am satisfied. That is all I am going to say about it." And that was all he did say, except what he has left on record for us all. . . . A student of science, a careful student of the human body, he lost his faith in the old, the cruel and the unjust as it seemed to him; but he did not, like many an anatomist, come to the conclusion that the flesh and the bones were all. Holmes never lost his faith in the Father, never lost his faith in the soul, never lost his burning belief in the future—a magnificent future for the poorest and the meanest of us all. . . . If you wish to find out his main religious ideas, read all of the poems called "Wind-clouds and Stardrifts."—SAVAGE, MINOT JUDSON, 1895, *The Religion of Holmes' Poems, The Arena, vol.* 11, *pp.* 41, 43, 45.

His knowledge of anatomy was that of the scholar, rather than that of the practitioner. He delighted in the old anatomists, and cared little for the new. He maintained that human anatomy is much the same study that it was in the days of Vesalius and Fallopius. He actually button-held book agents, little accustomed to be pressed to stay, in order to put them to shame by the superiority of the illustrations in his old anatomies. It pleased him to discuss whether we should say the Gasserian or the Casserian ganglion. His books were very dear to him. He had said more than once that a twig from one of his nerves ran to everyone of them. Literature was his career. That early attack of poisoning from type was fatal to his eminence in any other. Though I fear many will disagree with me, I venture to say, that while he would have been a great anatomist had he made it his life's work, he could never have been a great teacher of anatomy. Successful teaching of concrete facts requires a smack of the drill-master, which was foreign to his gentle nature. The very methods which did so much to make his lectures popular and charming, at times irritated the more earnest students, hungry for knowledge.—DWIGHT, THOMAS, 1895, *Reminiscences of Dr. Holmes as Professor of Anatomy, Scribner's Magazine, vol.* 17, *p.* 127.

With Dr. Holmes sunshine and gaiety came into the room. It was not a determination to be cheerful or witty or profound; but it was a natural expression, like that of a child, sometimes overclouded and sometimes purely gay, but always as open as a child to the influences around him, and ready for "a good time." His power of self-excitement seemed inexhaustible. Given a dinner-table, with light and color, and somebody occasionally to throw the ball, his spirits would rise and coruscate astonishingly. He was not unaware if men whom he considered his superiors were present; he was sure to make them understand that he meant to sit at their feet and listen to them, even if his own excitement ran away with him. "I've talked too much," he often said, with a feeling of sincere penitence, as he rose from the table. "I wanted to hear what our guest had to say." But the wise guest, seizing the opportunity, usually led Dr. Holmes on until he forgot that he was not listening and replying.—FIELDS, ANNIE, 1895, *Oliver Wendell Holmes, Century Magazine. vol.* 49, *p.* 505.

Death drew near to Dr. Holmes with steps so slow, so gently graded, that the approach was hardly perceptible. Body and mind could be seen to be losing something in vigor, if one measured by intervals of months, but hardly by shorter periods. He was out of doors, taking his usual walks, a few days before the end came; he was up and about the house actually to the last day, and he died in his chair,—painlessly, as so humane a man well deserved to make his escape out of life,—on October 7, 1894. Two days later he was buried from King's Chapel.—MORSE, JOHN T., JR., 1896, *Life and Letters of Oliver Wendell Holmes, vol.* II, *p.* 92.

Doctor Holmes was decidedly the most brilliant converser whom I have ever met. —PHELPS, ELIZABETH STUART, 1896, *Chapters from a Life, p.* 166.

In this pleasant study he lived among the books, which seemed to multiply from case to case and shelf to shelf, and climb from floor to ceiling. Everything was in exquisite order, and the desk where he wrote was as scrupulously neat as if the slovenly disarray of most authors' desks were impossible to him. He had a number of ingenious little contrivances for helping his work, which he liked to show you; for a time a revolving book-case at the corner of his desk seemed to be his pet; and after that came his fountain-pen, which he used with due observance of its fountain principle, though he was tolerant of me when I said I always dipped mine in the inkstand; it was a merit in his eyes to use a fountain-pen in any wise. After you had gone over these objects with him, and perhaps taken a peep at something he was examining through his microscope, he sat down at one corner of his hearth, and invited you to an easy-chair at the other. His talk was always considerate of your wish to be heard, but the person who wished to talk when he could listen to Dr. Holmes was his own victim, and always the loser. . . . He had, indeed, few or none of the infirmities of age that made themselves painfully or inconveniently evident. He carried his slight figure erect, and until his latest years his step was quick and sure. . . . If you met him in the street, you encountered a spare, carefully dressed old gentleman, with a clean-shaven face and a friendly smile, qualified by the involuntary frown of his thick, senile brows; well coated, lustrously shod, well gloved, in a silk hat, latterly wound with a mourning-weed. Sometimes he did not know you when he knew you quite well, and at such times I think it was kind to spare his years the fatigue of recalling your identity; at any rate, I am glad of the times when I did so. In society he had the same vagueness, the same dimness; but after the moment he needed to make sure of you, he was as vivid as ever in his life. He made me think of a bed of embers on which the ashes have thinly gathered, and which, when these are breathed away, sparkles and tinkles keenly up with all the freshness of a newly kindled fire.—HOWELLS, WILLIAM DEAN, 1897, *Oliver Wendell Holmes, Harper's Magazine, vol.* 94, *pp.* 129, 131.

He was intensely proud of his Boston, and was yet to show by the literary uses to which he put it how the local might be extended into the universal. For himself, he declared in later life that he would rest upon having said, "Boston is the hub of the universe." And this Boston which he knew came to know him well as a delightful wit and talker, a curious student of himself—so frank that he could write, "I have always considered my face a convenience rather than an ornament,"—a shrewd observer of men, and the local laureate of civic, social, and academic "occasions." Nothing that he has left shows more clearly than the "Poems of the Class of '29" the strength of the social instinct and the nature of his social gift.—HOWE, M. A. DEWOLFE, 1898, *American Bookman, p.* 275.

He had no marked development of systematic memory, but his accumulation of odds and ends of knowledge was unsurpassed, and this is what a talker, or indeed a literary man as such, chiefly needs. His ready wit supplied the rest. It is to be noticed also that he had an arsenal of his own in a scientific direction from which he could draw weapons not accessible to others. . . . It might, doubtless, be said that Dr. Holmes was always conventional, though never in any sense a fop or an exquisite—to revert to the phrase of that day. With an unconcealed preference for what is called the best society, he yet had, in his early medical practice, the advantage enjoyed by all of that profession, in alternating between the houses of rich and poor, and learning that they are composed mentally, as physically, of much the same material. . . . Perhaps, indeed, Holmes's talk was not to be seen at best advantage in his pet clubs where he sat as undisputed autocrat, while in the more familiar intercourse of common life his conversational fertility can hardly be exaggerated, and was, perhaps, never surpassed even by Sydney Smith. There was certainly no one in his day with whom it was so impossible to spend five minutes without bringing away something worth recalling. — HIGGINSON, THOMAS WENTWORTH, 1899, *Old Cambridge, pp.* 88, 92, 105.

He loved his Cambridge friends serenely, Lowell, Agassiz, and Wyman, I think, above others; but he enjoyed himself most of all, and Boston more than any other thing on earth. He was lifted above ennui and discontent by a most happy satisfaction with the rounded world of his own individuality and belongings. Of the three men whom I have personally known in the world who seemed most satisfied with what fate and fortune had made them,—viz., Gladstone, Professor Freeman, and Holmes, —I think Holmes enjoyed himself the most. There was a tinge of Dandyism in the doctor; not enough to be considered a weakness, but enough to show that he enjoyed his personal appearance and was content with what he had become, and this in so delightful a way that one accepted him at once at his own terms. The Doctor stood for Boston as Lowell for Cambridge, the archetype of the Hub. Nobody represented it as he did.—STILLMAN, WILLIAM JAMES, 1901, *Autobiography of a Journalist, vol.* I, *p.* 242.

My week's experience with Holmes would lead me to say that the charm of his wit was that it came from a man of seriousness, and of his seriousness that it came from a man of wit.—EATON, WYATT, 1902, *Recollections of American Poets, Century Magazine, vol.* 64, *p.* 450.

I never heard Holmes converse when he did not converse well. . . . With one of the kindest hearts, open to friends, and often sympathizingly helpful to strangers, he yet cherished a sort of Brahminical exclusiveness; something in the earlier Autocrat papers even made you feel that he was at times too complacently conscious of a superior caste and culture.—TROWBRIDGE, JOHN TOWNSEND, 1903, *My Own Story, pp.* 405, 406.

POETRY

Mr. Holmes does not write in this mezzotinto style; he reminds us more of the clear strong lines of the ancient engravers. His manner is entirely his own, manly and unaffected; generally easy and playful, and sinking at times into "a most humorous sadness."—PALFREY, JOHN GORHAM, 1837, *Holmes's Poems, North American Review, vol.* 44, *p.* 276.

As a poet he has won an enduring reputation. He possesses a rich vein of humor, with learning and originality, and great skill as an artist.—GRISWOLD, RUFUS WILMOT, 1842–46, *The Poets and Poetry of America, p.* 341.

To write good comic verse is a different thing from writing good comic poetry. A jest or a sharp saying may be easily made to rhyme; but to blend ludicrous ideas with fancy and imagination, and display in their conception and expression the same poetic qualities usually exercised in serious composition, is a rare distinction. Among American poets, we know of no one who excels Holmes in this difficult branch of the art. Many of his pleasant lyrics seem not so much the offspring of wit, as of fancy and sentiment turned in a humorous direction. His manner of satirizing the foibles, follies, vanities, and affectations of conventional life is altogether peculiar and original. . . . Holmes is also a poet of sentiment and passion. . . . Those who know him only as a comic lyrist, as the libellous laureate of chirping folly and presumptuous egotism, would be surprised at the clear sweetness and skylark thrill of his serious and sentimental compositions.—WHIPPLE, EDWIN PERCY, 1844, *Poets and Poetry of America, Essays and Reviews, vol.* I, *pp.* 64, 65.

Though he has published very little, he is one of the most popular of American poets, and the corollary from our theorem is, that he deserves all his reputation. Some may object, that much of his popularity is to be ascribed to the exuberance of his wit, in which he easily surpasses all his contemporaries excepting Hood. . . "Urania"—a title which for some inexplicable reason he has chosen to annex to this later publication—has some striking faults; but it has also characteristic passages enough to support our high estimate of the writer's powers. It is a mere medley of bright thoughts and laughing satire, with here and there a momentary expression of deep feeling, which betrays a spirit that may be touched to nobler issues. The poet glances about like a butterfly from one topic to another, hardly resting on any one long enough to obtain more than a sip of its honey. The versification is uniformly flowing and harmonious, and the lines are never bolstered out with feeble or unmeaning expressions.—BOWEN, FRANCIS, 1847, *Holmes's Urania, North American Review, vol.* 64, *pp.* 212, 213.

You went crazy last year over Bulwer's New Timon:
Why, if B., to the day of his dying, should rhyme on,
Heaping verses on verses, and tomes upon tomes,
He could ne'er reach the best point and vigour of Holmes.
His are just the fine hands, too, to weave you a lyric
Full of fancy, fun, feeling, or spiced with satiric,
In so kindly a measure, that nobody knows
What to do but e'en join in the laugh, friends and foes.
—LOWELL, JAMES RUSSELL, 1848, *A Fable for Critics.*

Of all this flight of genuine poets, I hardly know any one so original as Dr. Holmes. For him we can find no living prototype; to track his footsteps, we must travel back as far as Pope or Dryden; and to my mind it would be well if some of our bards would take the same journey—provided always, it produced the same result. Lofty, poignant, graceful, grand, high of thought and clear of word, we could fancy ourselves reading some pungent page of "Absalom and Achitophel," or of the "Moral Epistles," if it were not for the pervading nationality, which, excepting Whittier, American poets have generally wanted, and for that true reflection of the manners and follies of the age, without which satire would fail alike of its purpose and its name. . . . He excels in singing his own charming songs, and speaks as well as he writes.—MITFORD, MARY RUSSELL, 1851, *Recollections of a Literary Life,* pp. 399, 410.

The most concise, apt, and effective poet of the school of Pope this country has produced is Oliver Wendell Holmes. . . . His best lines are a series of rhymed pictures, witticisms, or sentiments, let off with the precision and brilliancy of the scintillations that sometimes illuminate the northern horizon. The significant terms, the perfect construction, and acute choice of syllables and emphasis, render some passages of Holmes absolute models of versification, especially in the heroic measure. Besides these artistic merits, his poetry abounds with fine satire, beautiful delineations of nature, and amusing caricatures of manners. The long poems are metrical essays more pointed, musical, and judicious, as well as witty, than any that have appeared, of the same species, since the "Essay on Man" and the "Dunciad."—TUCKERMAN, HENRY T., 1852, *A Sketch of American Literature.*

His longest productions are occasional poems which have been recited before literary societies and received with very great favour. His style is brilliant, sparkling, and terse; and many of his heroic stanzas remind us of the point and condensation of Pope. In his shorter poems, he is sometimes grave and sometimes gay. When in the former mood, he charms us by his truth and manliness of feeling, and his sweetness of sentiment; when in the latter, he delights us with the glance and play of the wildest wit and the richest humour. Everything that he writes is carefully finished, and rests on a basis of sound sense and shrewd observation.—HILLARD, GEORGE STILLMAN, 1856, *A First Class Reader.*

The poems of Holmes are not only of lasting weight and worth, they are also extensively known and enjoyed; they win general favor by their manly vigor, cultivated thoughtfulness, deep pathos, sparkling humor, graphic precision of language, and ringing melody of rhythm. Not to name other pieces of different sorts, his "Many-Chambered Nautilus" is as perfect a poem in its kind as exists in literature. Embalmed afresh in the delighted memory of successive generations, it will be oblivion proof.—ALGER, WILLIAM ROUNSEVILLE, 1869, *American Poets: T. W. Parsons, Christian Examiner,* vol. 86, p. 75.

We learned in our childhood the charm of his page,
And his verse does not show yet one sign of old age;
Though our own heads may whiten, he makes us feel young
With his songs, through all seasons so cheerily sung.
—LARCOM, LUCY, 1879, *Holmes, Poetical Works,* p. 255.

The dew of youth so fills his late-sprung flowers,
And day-break glory haunts his evening's hours.
Ah, such a life prefigures its own moral:
That first "Last Leaf" is now a leaf of laurel,
Which—smiling not, but trembling at the touch—
Youth gives back to the hand that gave so much.
—LATHROP, GEORGE PARSONS, 1879, *Youth to the Poet, Scribner's Monthly,* vol. 19, p. 740.

When violets fade the roses blow;
  When laughter dies the passions wake:
His royal song that slept below,
  Like Arthur's sword beneath the lake,
Long since has flashed its fiery glow
  O'er all we know.
—WINTER, WILLIAM, 1879, *Oliver Wendell Holmes: or The Chieftain, Wanderers, p.* 149.

To criticise a complete collection of Dr. Holmes's poetry at this late date would be a somewhat invidious duty, for the public has long since passed its own judgment. Many of his pieces, especially his sparkling *vers de société*, are literally "household words" to every reader and reciter of the English language. "The Last Leaf," "My Aunt," "The Comet," "The Treadmill Song," "The Stethoscope Song," "The Mysterious Visitor," and a long list of other pieces are as well known as the best of Hood's humorous verse. Of course these are not Dr. Holmes's best productions, but they are the most popular. Far better, and yet not nearly so widely known, because they only appeal to a more limited class, are those naive and sweet lines entitled "The Last Reader." . - . The chief drawback to Dr. Holmes's poetry, not to his popularity, is the excessive number of pieces he has thrown off about events of temporary interest, in this respect his many years of labour being against him. The reader can relish one or two brightly worded "occasional" pieces on the anniversary of a national event, but the most catholic appetite is cloyed by an accumulation of fifty years' industrious manufacture of odes, lyrics, and ballads on the reception of Grand Dukes and Banquets to Foreign Ambassadors. Still it must be confessed that all these fugitive pieces are so neatly rhymed, so appropriate to the events they commemorate, and so besprinkled with pretty conceits that were one called upon to exclude the less worthy, it would be difficult to know where to commence the work of excision. . . . The general reader, of course, admires Dr. Holmes for his humor and satire and not for his sentiment; and it must be confessed that in these popular forms of verse he is nearly unique. His satire is always tempered with kindness, is never personal nor spiteful, and probably never annoyed a single person—in that respect being almost unparalleled in the history of satiric verse.—INGRAM, JOHN H., 1882, *The Poetical Works of Oliver Wendell Holmes, The Academy, vol.* 21, *p.* 4.

I shall never be able to regard Holmes as first and foremost a Poet, although a vein of poetry and admirable sentiment runs through all his prose. I shall say he is first Essayist, and Poet afterwards; and this because he is never "rapt," never quite caught up into Heavens inaccessible to ordinary fancy and baffling to common intelligence. He is, indeed, full of intuition, but far too reflective ever to be quite inspired. The "Metrical Essay" and "Astræa" resound with high strains, and his longer poems contain bright bursts of patriotism and noble religious utterances, as well as those sudden transitions to satire and almost low comedy.—HAWEIS, HUGH REGINALD, 1883, *American Humorists, p.* 41.

These occasional poems, like the lyrics destined for longer life, are eminently free from imitativeness. The emancipation of American letters from foreign fashions—not necessarily from foreign thought—owes much to Doctor Holmes' sturdy and successful, because natural, display of independent genius. The "cleverness" of this characteristic writer, not less than his deeper pathos and humor, has played its part in the intellectual movement of his time; it has made it easier for everybody to follow his own bent and say his own say. Holmes' occasional poems have simply amused hundreds of delighted hearers, most of whom have hardly stopped, at the moment, to think of any higher result; but sooner or later they reflect that here is more than an individual neatness, here an alertness and daring felicity that have in them something national.—RICHARDSON, CHARLES F., 1888, *American Literature, 1607–1885, vol.* II, *p.* 213.

Climbing the path that leads back nevermore
We heard behind his footsteps and his cheer;
Now, face to face, we greet him standing here
Upon the lonely summit of Fourscore!
Welcome to us, o'er whom the lengthened
    day
Is closing and the shadows colder grow,
His genial presence, like an afterglow,
Following the one just vanishing away.
Long be it ere the table shall be set
For the last breakfast of the Autocrat,
And love repeat with smiles and tears thereat
His own sweet songs that time shall not forget.
Waiting with him the call to come up higher,
Life is not less, the heavens are only nigher.
—WHITTIER, JOHN GREENLEAF, 1889, *Oliver Wendell Holmes on his Eightieth Birthday.*

It is retrospective and contemplative, but it is also full of the buoyancy of youth, of the consciousness of poetic skill, and of blithe anticipation. Its tender reminiscence and occasional fond elegiac strain are but clouds of the morning. Its literary form is exquisite, and its general impression is that of bright, elastic, confident power. It was by no means, however, a first work, nor was the poet unknown in his own home. But the "Metrical Essay" introduced him to a larger public, while the fugitive pieces already known were the assurance that the more important poem was not a happy chance, but the development of a quality already proved. — CURTIS, GEORGE WILLIAM, 1891, *Oliver Wendell Holmes, Harper's Magazine, vol.* 83, *p.* 277.

As a poet—and in the final settlement the poet will outweigh the writer of prose—Holmes preserved for us the spirit of the classical age at a time when romanticism was in full cry. . . . We have no other so expert in personal and occasional verse, no other who could so distill the very quintessence of Yankee humor, or of the other and finer qualities of the New England intellect, into the most limpid of song. And when he was entirely serious, how exquisite was his touch, how pure his pathos, how clear his ethical sense! "Let The Voiceless," "Under the Violets," and "The Chambered Nautilus" bear witness.—PAYNE, WILLIAM MORTON, 1895, *Little Leaders, p.* 268.

His first appearace by himself in book form and the first book to have his name on the title page was the "Poems" of 1836, issued while he was trying half-heartedly, and not very successfully, to build up a medical practice in Boston. In this volume, the stirring lyric, "Old Ironsides" was incorporated in "Poetry, a Metrical Essay." "Old Ironsides" originally appeared in the *Boston Daily Advertiser*, and was afterwards printed as a handbill and distributed in the streets of Washington. No copy of this separate issue seems to have survived. This poem has been the most widely read of his early productions, and was, perhaps, the real means of preventing the demolition of the U. S. frigate "Constitution."—LIVINGSTON, LUTHER S., 1898, *First Books of Some American Authors, The Bookman, vol.* 8, *p.* 142.

In one field Dr. Holmes was chief without a second among American poets—the poetry of festival and compliment. Who could so graciously welcome a coming, speed a parting guest? Who hide so tenderly with laurel the whitening temples of his friends? For poetry of this kind he had a wonderful facility, and what was so largely impromptu might well lack something of abiding charm. It was enough that it touched some memorable occasion with a momentary gleam of tenderness and beauty. It was at the annual meetings of his college class that he exercised this gift with the most daring playfulness.—CHADWICK, JOHN WHITE, 1904, *Chambers's Cyclopædia of English Literature, ed. Patrick, vol.* III, *p.* 789.

BREAKFAST TABLE SERIES

The "Autocrat" is as genial and gentle, and, withal, as philosophical, an essayist as any of modern times. Hazlitt, saturnine and cynical, would yet have loved this writer. Charles Lamb would have opened his heart to one who resembles him so much in many excellent points. Leigh Hunt, we dare say, has been much delighted with him. Thomas Hood, the great humanitarian, would have relished his fine catholic spirit. Dickens, no doubt, has read him more than once, admiring his command of our common language,—the "well of English undefiled,"—and, above all, the pervading tone of practical philosophy. The "Autocrat," however, is somewhat more than an essayist: he is contemplative, discursive, poetical, thoughtful, philosophical, amusing, imaginative, tender,—never didactic. This is the secret of his marked success: he interests variously-constituted minds and various moods of mind. It needed not the introduction of lyrical pieces (which we are glad to have) to show that the "Autocrat" is essentially a poet. Of all who would have most enjoyed him we may foremost name Professor Wilson, who would have welcomed him to a seat "above the salt" at the far-famed "Noctes Ambrosianæ," placing him next to William Maginn, the wayward "O'Doherty" of Blackwood's Magazine.—MACKENZIE, R. SHELTON, 1858, *A Critical Dictionary of English Literature, ed. Allibone, vol.* I, *p.* 870.

I value the "Autocrat of the Breakfast Table" more highly than all the writings of Shelley put together.—BOYD, ANDREW K. H., 1862, *Leisure Hours in Town, p.* 85.

I would not say that the "Autocrat" **is** as well worth re-reading as the "Essays" of

Emerson; but I do not hesitate to say to the hard-working average American, whether a toiler with hands or brains, that for healthful relaxation of spirit, for getting the kinks and stiffness out of the brain, there is nothing better than the pages of Holmes. While one is amused, one is also all the while coming across passages full of food for reflection worthy of Bacon, advice that would be the making of a man if followed, tender lessons in charity, deep openings into human nature and everywhere a profound sense of law and its operation. . . . "The Autocrat," "The Professor" and "Elsie Venner" are a series of clinics. The patient is not often in bed, but he is undergoing pathological examination; and a good part of the interest in these books lies in the fact that whatever is seen and said comes from a keen-eyed physician. — MUNGER, THEODORE THORNTON, 1895, *Oliver Wendell Holmes, New World*, vol. 4, pp. 38, 41.

It ["Poet at the Breakfast Table"] was by no means the popular success that we had hoped; not because the author had not a thousand new things to say, or failed to say them with the gust and freshness of his immortal youth, but because it was not well to disturb a form associated in the public mind with an achievement which had become classic. It is of the "Autocrat of the Breakfast Table" that people think, when they think of the peculiar species of dramatic essays which the author invented, and they think also of the "Professor at the Breakfast Table," because he followed so soon; but the "Poet at the Breakfast Table" came so long after, that his advent alienated rather than conciliated liking. Very likely, if the Poet had come first he would have had no second place in the affections of his readers, for his talk was full of delightful matter; and at least one of the poems which graced each instalment was one of the finest and greatest that Dr. Holmes ever wrote. I mean "Homesick in Heaven," which seems to me not only what I have said, but one of the most important, the most profoundly pathetic in the language. Indeed, I do not know any other that in the same direction goes so far with suggestion so penetrating.—HOWELLS, WILLIAM DEAN, 1897,*Oliver Wendell Holmes, Harper's Magazine*, vol. 94, p. 127.

The "Autocrat" might suggest a series of riddles or problems for some future examiner in English literature. Why is controversy like the Hydrostatic Paradox? Why is a poem like a meerschaum? What is the very obvious resemblance between the pupil of the eye and the mind of a bigot? In what respects may truths be properly compared to dice and lies to marbles? Why should a trustworthy friend be like a cheap watch? How does the proper treatment for Guinea-worm illustrate the best mode of treating habitual drunkards? The answers to these and many equally ingenious parallels illustrate Holmes's power of procuring analogies; and show, too, how his talent had been polished in the conversational arena. . . . The instrument upon which Holmes had performed, the circle of congenial friends, was, of course, far more responsive.—STEPHEN, LESLIE, 1898, *Studies of a Biographer*, vol. II, pp. 181, 182.

NOVELS

I was in some anxiety before I began ["Elsie Venner"] because I knew that you had never written a novel before, and I felt somehow as if you had announced yourself to come out as Hamlet, or to walk over Niagara on a tight rope, or to do, in short, some of those things by which men achieve fame, but to which they are apt to have apprenticed themselves in their tender epochs. . . . You have been perfectly successful: I assure you that the interest is undying throughout the book—that the characters are sharply and vigorously drawn and colored—that the scenery is fresh, picturesque, and poetical, and the dialogue, particularly when it is earnest and thoughtful, is suggestive, imaginative, and stimulating in the highest degree. As to the mother-thought of the book, it is to me original, poetical, and striking.—MOTLEY, JOHN LOTHROP, 1861, *To Oliver Wendell Holmes, April* 19; *Correspondence, ed. Curtis*, vol. I, p. 368.

It follows almost necessarily from the choice of his subject ["Elsie Venner"], that Mr. Holmes is carried into a world of stage effects, with "striking" scenes and out-of-the-way characters; though, to do him justice, he has done his utmost, by artistic treatment, to subdue the melodramatic element in them. Who, indeed, would care for a rattlesnake that didn't bite? Who would care for a quasi-rattlesnake who could not act out her savagery? In what familiar association could she be exhibited but with persons having some kind of affinity to herself? . . . I do not quarrel with Mr. Holmes for his choice of subject; still, notwithstanding the delicacy of hand with which he has treated it, one cannot but regret that he should have chosen one which cannot be fully canvassed in general society. Nor has he lessened the regret by his choice of scenery. There is something repulsive to the English mind in the picture of the relation between a young and handsome male teacher and a number of nearly full-grown schoolgirls. However skilfully handled, such a picture is always sensuous, must often border almost on the prurient. As a warning to ourselves, indeed, against the encouragement of the practice from which it is taken, the picture may be a wholesome one. If such be the effect of it, with a pure and high-minded "young Brahmin" like Bernard Langdon for central figure, what would be the reality, with a coarser but weaker type of man in his place?—LUDLOW, JAMES MEEKER, 1861, *Elsie Venner and Silas Marner, Macmillan's Magazine*, vol. 4, pp. 307, 308.

Dr. Holmes's three novels, "Elsie Venner," "The Guardian Angel," and "A Mortal Antipathy" (his latest production), are not only delightful reading, but afford palpable evidence of what their author might have, yet has not, done. It is indeed surprising that a writer capable of weaving tales thus brimful of human interest, and of portraying with such consummate skill the most idiosyncratic aspects of American life, should have been content, as it were, to sample the rich mine lying open at his feet, instead of exploring it fully—impossible, after reading "Elsie Venner," to doubt that Dr. Holmes could have been (had he but wished it) *the* American novelist of the century. Hawthorne, unsurpassed as an artist and psychologist, was hardly the man to treat that every-day existence from which his dreamy soul recoiled. Mr. Howells, at the present day, is somewhat lacking in vigour and in breadth. But Dr. Oliver Wendell Holmes possesses in the highest degree the power of depicting character; this is, among his various literary gifts, the most genuine and the foremost.—DELILLE, EDWARD, 1886, *Oliver Wendell Holmes, Fortnightly Review*, vol. 46, p. 241.

The novel of "Elsie Venner" is a strong and interesting book. The story holds us fast, and the study of a strange and morbid state of mind has the fascination given to the snakes themselves. Such a book would have made the fame and fortune of a lesser man. But as lasting literature in the highest sense, it falls behind the "Autocrat."—LODGE, HENRY CABOT, 1894, *Two Great Authors, North American Review*, vol. 159, p. 675.

The critics—the trained professional ones I mean—have dealt severely with the book. They admit that it abounds in brilliant passages, and that it is generously impregnated with New Englandism; they can hardly deny that local color was never shed upon paper with more truth and skill than in the description of the party at "the elegant residence of our distinguished fellow-citizen, Colonel Sprowle." But having said these things, some go on to say that the book has too much monologue by the author—though in this Holmes sinned in the good company of Thackeray; and so good a critic as George William Curtis wrote "This colloquial habit is very winning, when governed by natural delicacy and an exquisite literary instinct." Others think that the characters are not real and lifelike, and that the incidents are but indifferent inventions. The crowning objection, taken by all alike, is, that it is that hybrid creation condemned by the inexorable canons of literature, a novel with a purpose. Whether these canons are dogmas of truths, it is probable that a novel written for a purpose will rarely survive the elimination of the purpose from popular interest, either by its achievement or defeat. Certain it is, however, that whether Elsie Venner was or was not justly entitled to popularity, she enjoyed it, and for many years was widely read, and eagerly discussed, nor is it yet time to be composing an epitaph for her tombstone.—MORSE, JOHN T., JR., 1896, *Life and Letters of Oliver Wendell Holmes*, vol. I, p. 256.

His novels all belonged to an order of romance which was as distinctly his own as the form of dramatized essay which he invented in the Autocrat. If he did not think poorly of them, he certainly did not think too proudly, and I heard him quote with relish the phrase of a lady who had spoken of them to him as his "medicated novels."—HOWELLS, WILLIAM DEAN, 1897, *Oliver Wendell Holmes, Harper's Magazine*, vol. 94, p. 125.

That provoking book, "Elsie Venner." I call it "provoking" merely because it will not square nicely with any orthodox canons of criticism. In the first place it has an air of being didactic, or is a book with a tendency, or, in the old-fashioned phrase, is a novel with a purpose. . . . Holmes, it must be remarked, did not suppose that he was proving anything in "Elsie Venner;" he recognised the truth of the axiom propounded in the "Rose and the Ring" that blank verse is not argument; and the imaginary behaviour of an impossible being cannot possibly lead to any conclusion. When we meet a woman who is half a woman and half snake it will be time to settle the moral code for judging her. Holmes, in fact, says in his preface that he only took an imaginary case in order to call attention to the same difficulty in the common course of things. To that I can see no objection.—STEPHEN, LESLIE, 1898, *Studies of a Biographer*, vol. II, p. 173.

"Elsie Venner," achieved a permanent fame both as a picture of New England life and as a scientific study.—HIGGINSON, THOMAS WENTWORTH, 1899, *Old Cambridge*, p. 98.

GENERAL

We have always contended that in the satirical, humorous and burlesque, Holmes has hardly a superior among the highest of his fellow-bards in America. And we quite agree with him, in his argument for the hyperbolical, that a tendency of the mind which has been shown in all ages and forms, and has its foundation in nature, cannot justly be condemned by any reasonable critic, and least of all by the same judges who would write treatises upon the sculptured satyrs and painted arabesques of antiquity, which are only hyperbole in stone and colors. . . . What we especially admire in the writings of Holmes is the *picturesqueness* of his descriptions, and his inimitable ease and grace of rhythm. In this he is *facile princeps.*—WHITTIER, JOHN GREENLEAF, 1845, *Editor's Table, The Knickerbocker,* vol. 26, p. 570.

His sense of the ludicrous is not keener than his sense of the beautiful; his wit and humor are but the sportive exercise of a fancy and imagination which he has abundantly exercised on serious topics; and the extensive learning and acute logic of the man of science are none the less solid in substance because in expression they are accompanied by a throng of images and illustrations which endow erudition with life, and give a charm to the most closely linked chain of reasoning. The first thing which strikes a reader of Holmes is the vigor and elasticity of his nature. He is incapable of weakness. He is fresh and manly even when he securely treads the scarcely marked line which separates sentiment from sentimentality. This prevailing vigor proceeds from a strength of individuality which is often pushed to dogmatic self-assertion. It is felt as much in his airy, fleering mockeries of folly and pretension, as in his almost Juvenalian invectives against baseness and fraud—in the pleasant way in which he stretches a coxcomb on the rack of wit, as in the energy with which he grapples an opponent in the tussle of argumentation. He never seems to imagine that he can be inferior to the thinker whose position he assails, any more than to the noodle whose nonsense he jeers at.—WHIPPLE, EDWIN PERCY, 1876–86, *American Literature and Other Papers,* ed. *Whittier,* p. 76.

Sweet Horace of our modern land and tongue,
Who paintest mankind's thoughts as they arise,
With kindly pencil dipped in rainbow dyes;
Whose genial verse this glad conclusion shows:
The sum of human joys outweighs the woes!
—JOYCE, ROBERT DWYER, 1877, *Reflections, Scribner's Magazine,* vol. 14, p. 446.

It is no easy task to characterize with nice discrimination a writer so versatile, and in some respects so nearly unique. If he exhibits some single intellectual traits which in themselves are rare, it is likewise true that the combination which he exhibits is very rare indeed. First of all, he thinks clearly. One finds nowhere in his volumes crude and half-formed thoughts. He writes as clearly as he thinks. His sentences come from his pen clean-cut. The language of his prose is pure, classical English; affluent, in the sense that it apparently never fails to come spontaneously at need, and in the fittest form; but not exuberant, to the obscuring of the thought. His style is simple, direct, forcible; not ambitiously elaborate nor fastidiously finished to excess. In his professional and literary addresses there is a compactness and polished vigor in his sentences, an effectiveness and point, which remind one of the pungency of Junius. To these characteristics Dr. Holmes adds a wonderful wit and humor in rare conjunction.—PALMER, RAY, 1880, *Oliver Wendell Holmes, International Review,* vol. 8, p. 503.

Master alike in speech and song
Of fame's great antiseptic—Style,
You with the classic few belong
Who tempered wisdom with a smile.
Outlive us all! Who else like you
Could sift the seedcorn from our chaff,
And make us with the pen we knew
Deathless at least in epitaph?
—LOWELL, JAMES RUSSELL, 1884, *To Holmes on his Birthday, Heartsease and Rue*, p. 25.

If it seems wonderful that living almost exclusively in one locality Dr. Holmes should have succeeded as few have succeeded in dealing with the mysteries of universal human nature, still more wonderful is it, perhaps, that dealing very largely with the foibles and follies of human nature, nothing that he has ever written has given offence. True, this is partly owing to his intense unwillingness to hurt the feelings of any human being. No fame for saying brilliant things that came to this gentlest of Autocrats and most genial of gentlemen, tinged with a possibility that any one had winced under his pen, would seem to him of any value, or give him any pleasure. But, as a matter of fact, no bore ever read anything Dr. Holmes has cleverly written about bores with the painful consciousness, "Alas I was that bore!" We may take to ourselves a good deal that he says, but never with a sense of shame or humiliation. On the contrary, we laugh the most sincerely of any one, and say "Of course! that is exactly it! Why, I have done that thing myself a thousand times!" And so the genial, keen-eyed master of human nature writes with impunity how difficult he finds it to love his neighbor properly till he gets away from him, and tells us how he hates to have his best friend hunt him up in the cars and sit down beside him, and explains that, though a radical, he finds he enjoys the society of those who believe more than he does better than that of those who believe less; and neighbor and best friend, radical and conservative, laugh alike and alike enjoy the joke, each only remembering how *he* finds it hard to love *his* neighbor and how *he* hates to talk in the cars.—ROLLINS, ALICE WELLINGTON, 1885, *Authors at Home, Dr. Oliver Wendell Holmes in Beacon Street, The Critic*, vol. 6, p. 13.

As a poet his equipment is greater than his achievement. . . . Had he not been the Scherzerade of American feasts he might have written more poetry as immortal as the "Chambered Nautilus," or more ballads having the ring of—
Come hither, God-be-glorified.
. . . . But it is as "the Autocrat" that his name will live. Out of the medley of bright thoughts and quaint satire shine gleams of deeper feeling and sparks of brilliant fancy. His extraordinary alertness of mind enables him to expound his subject by a variety of ingenious images, to decorate it with novel suggestions, and throw upon it many charming side-lights. His humour is in America almost peculiar to himself. Puritanism checked the outlet of merriment, enforced the duty of resisting ridiculous ideas, determined the demure, covert drollery which characterizes the national humour.—PROTHERO, ROWLAND EDMUND, 1886, *Oliver Wendell Holmes, Longman's Magazine*, vol. 8, pp. 305, 306.

At once so quaint and so excellent, from whom the most exigent must no longer demand rivalries of past achievement.—SHARP, WILLIAM, 1889, ed., *American Sonnets, Introductory Note*, p. xxiv.

The indexes to the several volumes of his collected works are in themselves a curious monument of the very wide range of his fun and of his speculation. I suppose this is, perhaps, the feature of these essays which has given them the most popularity. Take such a series of nine successive entries as this:
"Agassiz,
"Age, softening effects of,
"A good time coming,
"Air-pump, animal under,
"Alps, effect of looking at,
"American, the Englishman re-enforced,
"Analogies, power of seeing,
"Anatomist's hymn,
"Anglo-Saxons die out in America, Dr. Knox thinks."
Take down any other book you choose from the shelf, and look at ten entries in the index, and you will see that they have nothing like this range. It speaks, in the first place, of a matchless memory. I do not know what machinery he had for making note of what he read. I do know that he was fond of good books of reference, and had a remarkable collection of them. But behind any machinery there was the certainty, or something which approached certainty, that his memory would serve him, and that it would bring up what he wanted from his very wide range of reading at the right time and place, and would so

bring it up that he could rely upon it.—HALE, EDWARD EVERETT, 1894, *Oliver Wendell Holmes, Review of Reviews*, vol. 10, p. 498.

His fame, of course, was won as a man of letters, not as a man of science, and it is as a man of letters that the world at large looks upon him. . . . Dr. Holmes is perhaps most often thought of as the poet of occasion, and certainly no one has ever surpassed him in this field. . . . Dr. Holmes had one personal quality which ought not to be passed over without mention anywhere or at any time. He was a thorough American and always a patriot, always national and independent, and never colonial or subservient to foreign opinion. In the war of the rebellion no one was a stronger upholder of the national cause than he. In his earliest verse we catch constantly the flutter of the flag, and in his war poems we feel the rush and life of the great uprising which saved the nation. He was in the best sense a citizen of the world, of broad and catholic sympathies. But he was first and before that an American and a citizen of the United States, and this fact is at once proof and reason that he was able to do work which has carried delight to many people of many tongues, and which has won him a high and lasting place in the great literature of the English-speaking people.—LODGE, HENRY CABOT, 1894, *Two Great Authors, North American Review*, vol. 159, pp. 671, 673, 677.

An attempt—not particularly happy—has been made to "place" Dr. Holmes by linking his genius with that of Charles Lamb. The resemblance between them, if any, is quite superficial, but their difference is marked. As Mr. George William Curtis said of Dr. Holmes's early poems, so we might say of Lamb's most characteristic work: "The high spirits of a frolicsome fancy effervesce and sparkle;" but, while Lamb was essentially whimsical and often capricious, Dr. Holmes, even in his most daring moods, was wary. He was exceedingly sensitive on the subject of his good breeding, and felt he could not afford to forget his manners. If bold, he was not too bold; judicious always, without being false. He was much bound by social usage—a Boston man, having the fear of eminently respectable Boston always before his eyes—and it would have horrified him to have been responsible for those little outrages on the conventionalities in which Lamb took an exquisite delight. Moreover, Lamb's taste was more literary than that of Dr. Holmes, and not in the least scientific; and his touch, like Irving's, was more delicate. It is, in truth, difficult to classify Dr. Holmes at all. He was somewhat of a man apart. He followed no model, and has had no successful imitators.—LEWIN, WALTER, 1894, *Oliver Wendell Holmes, The Academy*, vol. 46, p. 279.

From the day when I read the first page of Dr. Holmes's work until now, he has seemed to me to carry to every mind and mood a sense of his benevolent presence like nothing else so much as the call of a kind physician to the bedside of a child. In the constellation of American literary masters his light is the kindliest of all. It shone and must shine on through the generations as it shone from the first, with the soft, unvarying glow of a perfect human affection. We might reasonably fancy him beginning the utterances of a life beyond this in those words in which, with such sweet and playful pretense of austerity so many years ago, he began the "Autocrat"—"I was just going to say when I was interrupted."—CABLE, GEORGE WASHINGTON, 1894, *Personal Tributes to Dr. Holmes, The Writer*, vol. 7, p. 162.

His work was the sunlight of American literature.—STANTON, FRANK L., 1894, *Personal Tributes to Dr. Holmes, The Writer*, vol. 7, p. 163.

He was to me the prince of our humorists, the gentlest of our satirists, the gladdest of our singers. It is only the clay that has returned to its own. *He* lives with us and our children and children's children so long as time shall last.—KING, CHARLES, 1894, *Personal Tributes to Dr. Holmes, The Writer*, vol. 7, p. 163.

Oliver Wendell Holmes loved all the world, and all the world loved him. I am sure that I voice the sentiment of the South in saying that he appealed to its people with a personality more vivid than any other writer of New England.—PECK, SAMUEL MINTURN, 1894, *Personal Tributes to Dr. Holmes, The Writer*, vol. 7, p. 163.

The essayist rises higher than the poet—witty, tender; wise in human frailty, but never bitter. — GARLAND, HAMLIN, 1894, *Personal Tributes to Dr. Holmes, The Writer*, vol. 7, p. 167.

As a writer of verse, he is scarcely entitled to a place among the immortals. But as Oliver Wendell Holmes, the genial Autocrat, the novelist, the fanciful and versatile poet, the wit, the wag, the royal companion, *i. e.*, in the totality of what he was, he seems to be safe from oblivion for some centuries to come.—BOYESEN, HJALMAR HJORTH, 1894, *Personal Tributes to Dr. Holmes, The Writer, vol. 7, p. 162.*

This concentration of his power and his affection has had its effect on Dr. Holmes's literary fame. He is another witness, if one were needed, to the truth that identification with a locality is a surer passport to immortality than cosmopolitism. The local is a good starting-point from which to essay the universal. Thoreau perhaps affected a scorn of the world outside of Concord, but he helped make the little village a temple, and his statue is in one of the niches. Holmes, staying in Boston, has brought the world to his door, and a society which is already historic will preserve him in its amber. It is the power to transmute the near and tangible into something of value the world over which is the mark of genius, and Holmes had his philosopher's stone.—SCUDDER, HORACE E., 1894, *Dr. Holmes, Atlantic Monthly, vol. 74, p. 832.*

His writings are really, if we judge them by a rigid standard, what the Abbé Coyot calls "bagatelles morales"—delicious fancies, full of intelligence and grace, neatly turned, always well-bred, instinct with vitality, reasonable, moderate, harmonious. That the author of "The Chambered Nautilus" should come to be named with Emerson, the novelist of "Elsie Venner" with Hawthorne, the "Autocrat of the Breakfast Table" with the author of "My Study Windows"—and in the history of literature Holmes will stand as an equal among these men—is another proof of that fact which in early youth we are so unwilling to learn, that more goes to a great reputation as a writer than merely writing pre-eminently well. Character, attitude, physical health, the condition of the times in Boston, all combined with the genuine art and indisputable talent of Dr. Holmes to make him the illustrious figure that he is and will remain. Few men under the age of fifty can possess a clear recollection of what Dr. Holmes was at the height of his powers. Perhaps no man of modern times has given his contemporaries a more extraordinary impression of wit in conversation.—GOSSE, EDMUND, 1894, *St. James's Gazette.*

No one in America has done so much as he to cheer us with sweet, guileless laughter. . . . Whittier did much more than Holmes to soften the Puritan theology, but Holmes did vastly more than Whittier to soften the Puritan temper of the community. And here was his most characteristic work. He was neither stoic nor ascetic; neither indifferent to life's sweet and pleasant things, nor, while hankering for their possession, did he repress his noble rage and freeze the genial currents of his soul.—CHADWICK, JOHN WHITE, 1894, *Oliver Wendell Holmes, The Forum, vol. 18, pp. 285, 287.*

While the personality of Dr. Holmes is full of interest, and while he is an author worthy of high commemoration, we cannot separate him from the group whose writings almost constituted the literature of America. Bryant, Emerson, Longfellow, Whittier, Lowell, Holmes. . . . The last of the group is Holmes, not so great as those named, but worthy to be classed with them. . . . It is not simply as a writer of verse that he is to be considered, but also as a novelist, an essayist, a biographer, a lecturer and a man of science. I shall not attempt any analysis of his works or of his genius. There is nothing hidden about him to be brought out; there is no subtlety that requires explication; there are scarcely two opinions as to the place to be assigned him as a writer or as a man. He was the most open and undisguised of men. Every sentence is full of self-revelation. He prattles on in his pages like a child, taking for granted that what the reader wants is to hear him talk; and in fact the reader wants nothing else, for it is as delightful talk as was ever put on paper. He wrote for more than sixty years, but at eighty he was as young as at twenty. . . . It is not probable that Holmes will ever be ranked among the great men of the world, but he has this rare distinction: he was a man of science and also a man of sentiment; the law of science and the law of poetry were both imprinted on him, and he wrote under their combined influence. Hence, there is a certain authoritative character in whatever he says; his sentiment is backed up by science, and his wisdom rests on facts. It is this that makes his opinions so valuable. As a poet simply, a long immortality cannot be expected for him—except for the fact that the writer of a good hymn stands the best chance for remembrance of all who ever speak in this world;—but it is probable that he will grow in critical estimate as a thoughtful observer of men and things, his genius embalming his wisdom.—MUNGER, THEODORE THORNTON, 1895, *Oliver Wendell Holmes, New World, vol. 4, pp.* 33, 34, 36, 38.

His works are not voluminous; and, though he had published some of his best verses before he was thirty, he was nearly fifty before he began the series of essays which really made him famous. Few popular authors have had a narrower escape from obscurity. He would, in any case, have been remembered in his own circle as a brilliant talker, and there would have been some curiosity as to the writer of the "Last Leaf" and two or three other poems. But had it not been for the judicious impulse given by his friend Lowell which induced him to make his appearance as the "autocrat," his reputation would have resembled that of Wolfe, of "not a drum was beat" celebrity. Who, it would have been asked, was the author of the few lines which we all know by heart? and we should have turned up the article devoted to him in a biographical dictionary. But he would not have revealed himself with that curious completeness upon which all his critics have remarked. . . . But I need not try to expound what every one perceives who has read his poems, such especially as the famous "Last Leaf" and "Dorothy Q." and the "Chambered Nautilus." The last of these, I humbly confess, does not quite touch me as it should, because it seems too ingenious. . . . He is one of the writers who is destined to live long—longer, it may be, than some of greater intellectual force and higher imagination, because he succeeds so admirably in flavouring the milk of human kindness with an element which is not acid and yet gets rid of the mawkishness which sometimes makes good morality terribly insipid.—STEPHEN, LESLIE, 1896, *Oliver Wendell Holmes, National Review, vol.* 27, *pp.* 629, 640, 641.

As a writer Dr. Holmes always reminded me of certain of our bird songsters, like the brown thrasher or the cat-bird, whose performance always seems to imply a spectator and to challenge his admiration. The vivacious doctor always seemed to write with his eye upon his reader, and to calculate in advance upon his surprise and pleasure. If the world finally neglects his work, it will probably be because it lacks the deep seriousness of the enduring productions.— BURROUGHS, JOHN, 1897, *On the Re-reading of Books, Century Magazine, vol.* 55, *p.* 147.

The open secret in Boston that Dr. Holmes was its author soon became open everywhere; and particularly when the second series, "The Professor at the Breakfast Table," dealing somewhat more freely with religious beliefs, began to appear, the name of Holmes associated itself in many minds with everything that was dangerous and iconoclastic. The mildness to modern ears of many of the passages that seemed most shocking forty years ago is more eloquent than any words could be about general tempering of religious beliefs in which Dr. Holmes was undoubtedly one of the strongest influences.—HOWE, M. A. DEWOLFE, 1898, *American Bookman, p.* 284.

Like Molière, Holmes took his own property, no matter in whose hands he found it, even if in the possession of writers so diverse as Jonathan Swift and John Quincy Adams. They were his own materials that he found, and he made right royal use of them. He was the social, as Emerson was the intellectual reactionist against the puritan asceticism of their forefathers. He delighted in warmth and light and geniality. He believed in throwing open the windows of the soul and making the spiritual "living temple" radiant with the rays of truth and beauty. His songs were, therefore, of the sunshine—of the sunshine and sometimes scorched, as when he satirized "The Moral Bully" —but oftener inspired cheer, hope, and good-will. If it be true that "a good wit will make use of anything; it will turn diseases to a commodity," the wit of Dr. Holmes is among the best. For if it has not turned moral and physical diseases to a "commodity" it has at least done a great deal toward counteracting their effects. "Be cheerful" is one of his prescriptions for inducing longevity. This cheerful nature of his poetry and philosophy has lulled to serenity many a careworn spirit and made easier and lighter many of the burdens of life. — ONDERDONK, JAMES L., 1899–1901, *History of American Verse, p.* 275.

Dr. Holmes never affiliated at all with the Transcendentalists. He had ridiculed Emerson's "Sphinx" in unmistakable fashion, in verse. He shrank from radical reform, feeling the full force of that tradition, convention, social usage, to which Emerson was so calmly indifferent. He was as little an idealist as any true poet can be. Instead of solitude and contemplation, he loved above all things congenial society, discussion, conversation. Of course, such a man's view of Emerson was an outside one after all, yet it is accurate, vivid, even sympathetic in tone.—LAWTON, WILLIAM CRANSTON, 1902, *Introduction to the Study of American Literature*, p. 221.

After all that may be said, criticism remains a matter largely of individual opinion. That opinion may not necessarily be founded in prejudice, neither for nor against the work in hand; but it very commonly results from an individual notion of what literature is or ought to be. Even with the highest order of minds, we often see what this means when we find well-endowed men who acknowledge an indifference to writers on whom time has set its fixed seal. This was curiously illustrated many years ago, when Oliver Wendell Holmes undertook to write a life of Emerson. Dr. Holmes was probably the least fitted of his contemporaries to write about Emerson. His intellectual obtuseness with respect to Emerson produced painful results.—HALSEY, FRANCIS WHITING, 1902, *Our Literary Deluge and Some of its Deep Waters*, p. 52.

No study of American humor can omit his name. His fun was that of the fine gentleman and appealed equally to the head and the heart. He had wit, that intellectual quality which sees incongruities and expresses them in such apt terms of language that a keen, mental delight follows; but quite as truly, he had that atmospheric quality of humor which rests upon kindliness, exhibits temperament, and is so close akin to pathos that often the two blend, as does an April day of sun and shower. In the second book of the Autocrat series, wherein the Professor is the speaker, the Story of Iris, embedded like a precious stone in the lighter satire of the book, is a tenderly pathetic love-romance and a fine example of the underlying emotional seriousness of the author, as many of his passages which grapple with some serious topic of the day are of his equally serious intellectual position. Dr. Holmes's greatest ambition was to be a poet. Yet his achievements in prose, on the whole, outweigh what he did in verse, familiar and well loved as are certain of his lyrics. He will be longest remembered as an essayist.—BURTON, RICHARD, 1903, *Literary Leaders of America*, p. 211.

He enriched our literature with a new form of essay as distinctly individual as Montaigne's or Charles Lamb's. In metrical composition his work is voluminous and varied, much of it ephemeral, but all of it lucid and musical; and he has left a few lyrics that take high rank— one of them almost the highest—as pure poetry. A characteristic note is a certain playful tenderness; and I think his Muse charms us most when she appears, like the bride in the ballad,—

"With a smile on her lips and a tear in her eye,"—

when the verses are dewy and tremulous with a feeling which the wit irradiates and sets off, yet seems half designed to conceal.

"Of sweet singers the most sane,
Of keen wits the most humane."

—TROWBRIDGE, JOHN TOWNSEND, 1903, *My Own Story*, p. 417.

His constant urbanity, his rarely flagging humour, his unfailing felicity as the spokesman of a friendly gathering, have not been questioned, and his supremacy as conductor of imaginary table talk is generally allowed; but the infrequency of his rises to "higher moods," the monotony of his measures and to a certain extent of his subjects, the fact that popular taste in the matter of humour is liable to undergo rapid changes, the further fact that much of his work is so local as to be provincial in the extreme, have suggested to his more critical admirers doubts with regard to the permanence of a very large part of his poetry and prose.—TRENT, WILLIAM P., 1903, *A History of American Literature*, p. 419.

James McCosh
1811–1894

A prominent Scottish-American theologian; born in Carskeoch, Ayrshire, Scotland, April 1, 1811; died in Princeton, N. J., in 1894. He came to America in 1865, was president of Princeton College (1868–88), and was one of the foremost men of his day in university life. His principal works include: "Christianity and Positivism" (1871); "A

Reply to Prof. Tyndall's Belfast Address" (1875); "The Development Hypothesis" (1876); "The Emotions" (1880); "Herbert Spencer's Philosophy as Culminating in his Ethics" (1885).—WARNER, CHARLES DUDLEY, ed. 1897, *Library of the World's Best Literature, Biographical Dictionary*, vol. XXIX, p. 358.

PERSONAL

The personality of Dr. McCosh is thoroughly Scotch, and his address very impressive—not to say aggressive. With a massive but spare frame, which, when his mind is roused, abandons its scholarly stoop and towers above expectation, is combined an unusual nervous force which often manifests itself in vigorous gestures. His head and brow are even more expressive of power; even to the usual observer the broad forehead and keen eyes bring into prominence his well-known capacity for an impetuous, unyielding, intellectual onset. But in repose the philosopher and the divine stand revealed in the bowed and meditative attitude which is customary, and in the wrapt, abstracted expression of the features, and in the contemplative poise of the head so familiar to all who have paused to observe him in his daily walks. . . . There is no need to fill in the outlines of the familiar picture. Its colors, like those of the old masters, mellow and soften with age. But it will be somber and dusky enough to some of us when we make our annual pilgrimage and miss the familiar form of the master from among his colleagues and his boys. We will forget his austerity in the faithfulness with which he reproved the *vitium regere non posse impetum*. Our awe will melt with affection, and our respect for his wisdom and knowledge will awaken memories both lasting and beneficent.—VAN CLEVE, JOHN, 1887, *James McCosh, President of Princeton College*, Century Magazine, vol. 33, p. 647.

Young to the end, through sympathy with youth,
Gray man of learning! champion of truth!
Direct in rugged speech, alert in mind,
He felt his kinship with all human kind,
And never feared to trace development
Of high from low—assured and full content
That man paid homage to the Mind above
Uplifted by the "Royal Law of Love."
The laws of nature that he loved to trace
Have worked, at last, to veil from us his face;
The dear old elms and ivy-covered walls
Will miss his presence, and the stately halls
His trumpet-voice; while in their joys
Sorrow will shadow those he called "my boys."
—BRIDGES, ROBERT, 1895, *Life of James McCosh by Sloane*, p. 267.

Dr. McCosh was one of the organizers of the Free Church, and he regarded this as the greatest event of his life. Perhaps his most distinguishing characteristic was an absolute devotion to truth. In its service he was utterly unselfish, and the straightforward way in which he describes his labours in aid of the new movement is very impressive. . . . A very striking trait was his open-mindedness. He always turned his face toward the light, kept watch of the signs of the times, and was ready to take up his stakes and set them further along. There was a vein of sentiment in his nature, and his sighs over a young man hardened in vice were those of a father, and tears of joy sprang unbidden to his eyes on the return of a prodigal.—CLARKE, GRACE JULIAN, 1896, *A Scottish Philosopher and American College President*, The Dial, vol. 21, p. 115.

To have seen a century rise and wane; to have spent threescore years of active, influential life in its very noon; to have moulded in some degree the thought of two generations in three lands; to have shared in Scotland's latest struggle for religious liberty; to have wrought in the great enterprise of Ireland's intellectual emancipation; to have led a powerful educational movement in America, and to have regenerated one of her most ancient universities,—these are the titles of James McCosh to public distinction. He was a philosopher, but no dreamer; a scholar, but no recluse; a preacher, but no idealogue; a teacher, but no martinet; he was a thinker, public leader, and a practical man of affairs.—SLOANE, WILLIAM MILLIGAN, 1897, *The Life of James McCosh*, p. 1.

GENERAL

Though in many respects original, ["Intuitions of the Mind"] professing to follow no school, and in reality independent in its spirit of all authority but that of the religious truths in behalf of which it is written, this work is nevertheless substantially a development from the Scottish school. . . . It is to be regretted that the author does not give us a more explicit account of what he means by such expressions as "primitive particular convictions carrying necessity with them, and a consequent universality in their very nature." In all the definitions of necessity with which we are acquainted, we have nowhere found it extended beyond the facts and the logical consequences of the facts in which it is supposed to exist primitively. That the universal does not follow logically from the particular or from any number of particulars, is what the author strenuously maintains.—WRIGHT, C., 1865, *McCosh on Intuitions, The Nation, vol.* 1, *p.* 627.

His life work as a teacher and writer began when in his forty-first year he accepted the chair of Logic and Metaphysics in Queen's College, Belfast. From that time forward his contributions to philosophical and religious literature have not ceased to grow in number and importance, and his seventy-fifth year finds his mind and pen in constant activity. The work which spread his fame most widely and put him among the leaders of the Intuitional School was written at Belfast. In the "Intuitions of the Mind Inductively Investigated" the author is at his best both as a thinker and a writer. His reasoning is vigorous and his logic unassailable, if his premises be once granted; while his style is direct, easy, and elegant and, without being florid, adorned and enlivened by abundant metaphor and illustration.—VAN CLEVE, JOHN, 1887, *James McCosh, President of Princeton College, Century Magazine, vol.* 11, *p.* 648.

A chapter on Dr. McCosh's travels in Germany ["Autobiography"] is surprising from a certain feebleness of stroke when he is writing of Humboldt, Bunsen, and others famous in the walks of science and theology. His own account of his philosophical career is extremely slight, as if his mind had lost its grip on the studies which had formerly engrossed it.—CHADWICK, J. W., 1896, *The Life of Dr. McCosh, The Nation, vol.* 63, *p.* 276.

McCosh is said to have been an effective lecturer and preacher, and his simplicity and perspicuity of style render this extremely probable. His philosophy, however, had never an appreciable influence of English thought. To the defects of the Scottish school he was by no means blind, but his early training had included no systematic study of transcendentalism, and a visit to Germany in 1858 led to no result. It may even be doubted whether he had apprehended the earlier forms of idealism. At any rate his polemical works evince no adequate appreciation of the positions which he attacked, and his own "intuitional" theory is a mere *ignoratio elenchi*.—RIGG, J. M., 1901, *Dictionary of National Biography, Supplement, vol.* III, *p.* 118.

William Dwight Whitney
1827–1894

An American professor, eminent as a philologist and editor, born in Northampton, Mass. Feb. 9, 1827; died at New Haven, Conn., June 7, 1894. He graduated at Williams College, 1845; spent some years abroad in study; in 1854 was made professor of Sanskrit at Yale, in 1870 of comparative philology, holding both positions till death. His writings are authority on all philological questions, and his rank as a Sanskrit scholar is of the first order. From 1849 he was a member of the American Oriental Society, and its president from 1884. His contributions to the North American Review, the New Englander, and other periodicals were numerous and varied. His earliest work was the preparation, in company with Rudolph Roth, of Tübingen, of an edition of the Atharva Veda Sanhita (Berlin, 1856). Among his other works are: "Language and the Study of Language" (1867); "On Material and Form in Language" (1872); "Darwinism and Language (1847); "Logical Consistency in Views of Language" (1880); "Mixture in Language" (1881); "The Study of Hindu Grammar and the Study of Sanskrit" (1884); "The Upanishads and their Latest Translation" (1886). He has also written: "Compendious German Grammar" (1869); "German Reader in Prose and Verse" (1870); "Essentials of English Grammar" (1877); "Sanskrit Grammar" (1877); and "Practical French Grammar" (1886). Professor Whitney was the superintending editor of the "Century Dictionary" (1889–91), and assisted in the preparation of "Webster's Dictionary" (1864).—WARNER, CHARLES DUDLEY, *ed.* 1897, *Library of the World's Best Literature, Biographical Dictionary, vol.* XXIX, *p.* 572.

PERSONAL

Mr. Whitney was no recluse, nor a typical professor in manner. He attracted men to him and enjoyed being with them. He was not at all emotional, however, and cared little for general society. . . . Like

Aristotle's "magnanimous man," he gave little heed to praise or blame—not being elated or cast down by either. He loved learning for its own sake and not for its reward of fame.— SEYMOUR, THOMAS DAY, 1894, *William Dwight Whitney, American Journal of Philology, vol.* 15, *p.* 294.

The prince of American scholars.—HATFIELD, JAMES TAFT, 1894, *William Dwight Whitney, The Dial, vol.* 16, *p.* 353.

GENERAL

First published ["Oriental and Linguistic Studies"] in the "Journal of the American Oriental Society" and our heavy reviews, they are now collected for us, and thousands who had never seen them will read them gladly. . . . Thoroughness is his most marked characteristic. Then there are few books of such depth and compass as his, expressed with as much simplicity. And compression never fails. In a wonderfully small space we get a sufficient body of facts for a general understanding of the history of Vedic study, of the Vedas themselves, and their relations to modern mind and life. Now and then the author rises with his thought to rhythm and eloquence. The essay on the Avesta has the same merits. . . . In two articles on Max Müller's "Lectures on Language," (in which Professor Whitney is very exacting), and in those which follow, . . . Professor Whitney sets forth his views of the nature of language against Müller, Bleek, Schleicher, and Steinthal. . . . When we read Professor Whitney's statements of his own views, we assent; but when we read his assaults on others, we often dissent. The fact seems to be that this region of language is under the concurrent jurisdiction of the will and the unconscious involuntary activities; so that those who would exclude the will from it, and those who would make the will sole cause in it, alike err. — MARCH, FRANCIS ANDREW, 1872, *The Nation, vol.* 16, *p.* 96.

The philological views with which Professor Whitney is identified are presented ["Life and Growth of Language"] in a clear and compendious shape, with no mass of details and side-issues to distract or seduce the reader.—SAYCE, A. H., 1875, *The Life and Growth of Language, The Academy, vol.* 8, *p.* 310.

In this country he is known chiefly as a comparative philologist, and a writer upon the problems of linguistic science. But his reputation as a scholar rests rather upon his work in Sanskrit. His grammar of the Vedic dialect is an enduring monument of labour, accuracy and scholarship. . . . Prof. Whitney was lacking in imagination; but he had a clear and logical mind, and did not shrink from carrying out the premises he adopted to their logical conclusions. He was the opponent of all theories which made language an organic product: it was to him merely a human "institution."— SAYCE, A. H., 1894, *The Academy, vol.* 45, *pp.* 499, 500.

Perhaps Mr. Whitney's most important service to Sanskrit philology was the preparation of his "Sanskrit Grammar, including both the classical language and older dialects, of Veda and Brahmana." . . . No one has done so much as Mr. Whitney to teach sound views of linguistic science. Although the writer of this sketch has not ventured to include a detailed discussion of his views, perhaps mention may be made fitly of two points in which he was in advance of his contemporaries: he was among the very first to call attention to *analogy* as a force in the growth of language, and the first (after Latham in 1851) to doubt the then generally accepted view that Asia was the original home of the Indo-Europeans. —SEYMOUR, THOMAS DAY, 1894, *William Dwight Whitney, American Journal of Philology, vol.* 15, *pp.* 287, 290.

His lectures on "Language and the Science of Language," originally given before the popular audiences of the Smithsonian and Lowell Institutes, were published in 1867, and at once attracted the attention of the learned world, remaining to the present time an authoritative statement of the mission and methods of philological research. Somewhat discursive in treatment, they are supplemented by his later essays, particularly his chapter on the Science of Language in the article "Philology" in the ninth edition of the Encyclopædia Britannica, which is of particular interest for its putting of his standpoint regarding the ultimate beginnings of human speech, which, according to Whitney, have their origin in man's practical necessity for a means of communication, and not in any natural existence of names corresponding to certain conceptions. — HATFIELD, JAMES TAFT, 1894, *William Dwight Whitney, The Dial, vol.* 16, *p.* 354.

In the encyclopædias, Whitney is catalogued as a famous Indianist, and so indeed he was. But it was not because he was an Indianist that he was famous. Had he devoted his life to the physical or natural sciences, he would doubtless have attained to equal, if not greater eminence. Truly, it is not the *what*, but the *how!* . . . His distinguishing qualities, as reflected in his work, are everywhere so palpable that it is not hard to describe them. Perhaps the most striking and pervading one is that which Professor Lounsbury calls his "thorough intellectual sanity." . . . Breadth and thoroughness are ever at war with each other in men, for that men are finite. The gift of both in large measure and at once,—this marks the man of genius. That the gift was Whitney's is clear to any one who considers the versatility of his mind, the variousness of his work, and the quality of his results. . . . Of all his technical works, his Sanskrit Grammar, with its elaborate supplement, The Roots, Verb-forms, and Primary Derivatives of the Sanskrit Language, forms the crowning achievement. Here he casts off the bonds of tradition wherever they might hamper his free scientific procedure, and approaches the phenomena of language in essentially the same spirit and attitude of mind as that in which Darwin or Helmholtz grappled the problem of their sciences. . . . If I may cite my own words used on a former occasion, Whitney's life-work shows three important lines of activity,—the elaboration of strictly technical works, the preparation of educational treatises, and the popular exposition of scientific questions.—LANMAN, CHARLES ROCKWELL, 1895, *William Dwight Whitney, Atlantic Monthly, vol.* 75, *pp.* 399, 402, 403, 406.

John Stuart Blackie
1809–1895

A Scottish author; born in Glasgow in July 1809; died in Edinburgh, March 2, 1895. He received his education in Edinburgh, Göttingen, Berlin, and Rome; was professor of Greek in Edinburgh University from 1852 till 1882, and continued to write and lecture till his death. He was one of the most important men of his day; promoted educational reform, and championed Scottish nationality. He advocated preserving the Gaelic language, and by his own efforts founded a Celtic chair in Edinburgh University. His books include translations from Greek and German; moral and religious and other philosophy; "Lays of the Highlands and Islands" (1872); "Self-Culture" (1874); "Language and Literature of the Scottish Highlands" (1875); "Altavona; Fact and Fiction from my Life in the Highlands" (1882); "Wisdom of Goethe" (1883); "Life of Burns" (1888); and "Essays on Subjects of Moral and Social Interest" (1890).—WARNER, CHARLES DUDLEY, *ed*, 1897, *Library of the World's Best Literature, Biographical Dictionary, vol.* XXIX, *p.* 61.

PERSONAL

Thou brave old Scot! And art thou gone?
How much of light with thee's departed!
Philosopher, yet full of fun,
Great humorist, yet human-hearted;
A Caledonian, yet not dour.
A scholar, yet not dry-as-dusty,
A pietist, yet never sour!
O stout and tender, true and trusty,
Octogenarian optimist,
The world for thee seemed aye more sunny;
We loved thee better for each twist
Which streaked a soul as sweet as honey.
We shall not see *thy* like again!
We've fallen on times most queer and quacky
And oft shall miss the healthy brain
And manly heart of brave old Blackie.
—PUNCH, MARCH 9th, 1895.

The influence of Blackie was for me a sunrise of the soul in admiration, wonder, sympathy, esteem, and love, and its colours were never fresher or brighter than at this hour.—BAYNE, PETER, 1895, *Letter, Professor Blackie, his Sayings and Doings, ed. Kennedy, p.* 68.

There was a notebook which appeared year after year in the class. It contained the Professor's jokes of a former session, carefully classified by an admiring student. It was handed down from one year's men to the next; and thus, if Blackie began to make a joke about haggis, the possessor of the book had only swiftly to turn to the H's, find out what the joke was, and send it along the class quicker than the Professor could speak it.—BARRIE, JAMES MATTHEW, 1895, *Reminiscences of Prof. Blackie, British Weekly.*

The Professor welcomes all [at breakfast] with a few kind words, and, after grace in

Greek, recommends his guests, as a rule of their lives, to read, as he does, a chapter of the Septuagint every morning on rising. At these repasts the rule is that every one shall express his ideas and wants, as far as possible, in the speech of Xenophon. All the guests are somewhat sheepish and shy; but the Professor, aided by the tact of Mrs. Blackie, will occasionally elicit a shrewd remark. Raw, red-haired Donald Macleod, from the Isle of Skye, who lives all the week on herring, oatmeal, and potatoes, being importuned, will treat the company to a Gaelic song; and then the Professor will launch out on the importance of this tongue for philological and other purposes. Then some remark will make him revert to his past career, and he will inflame the peripatetic ambition of his audience by referring to his wanderings all over Europe in search of truth and beauty, or he will recount how he met that doughty champion of Chartism, Ernest Jones, on the platform of the Music Hall to hold public appeal to reason on the merits of Democracy. Then, to vary the entertainment, the Professor will sing one of his own songs. Then all rising will join in pealing forth "Gaudeamus Igitur," and file out, filled in body and in mind, to woo digestion on the shores of the Forth or the slopes of Arthur's Seat.—
Lowe, Charles, 1895, *Reminiscences of Professor Blackie, The World.*

It was about twelve years ago that I first met Professor Blackie at the house of a mutual friend in London. We were having five-o'clock tea, when, to my astonishment, an elderly gentleman, with long white hair, handsome features, attired in a kind of blue-grey dressing-gown, with a straw helmet on his head, rushed in amongst us, humming a tune. His appearance was so eccentric that I was surprised when told that this was the famous Professor Blackie. I suppose that I stared rather rudely at his straw helmet, for he fixed his blue eyes upon me, and twirling a big walking-stick, suddenly exclaimed, "Ah, lassie, you are wondering why I have this headgear on. It is to protect my eyes from the fierce rays of the sun. I have been prowling about, basking in his warm rays." . . . He seemed unable to keep still, paced to and fro like a restless spirit, with a cup of tea in one hand, and the inevitable stick in the other, reciting a poem of Burns'. I remember it was all so very Scotch that I could hardly understand a word of it. . . . A year or so after this visit Professor Blackie came to my studio in Cranley Gardens, and at my request gave me a sitting for a pastel sketch. He jumped on the dais or throne with the alacrity of a schoolboy—I drew him in profile—but it was impossible for him to keep still. Every feature moved, forehead, eyes, nose, and as for his mouth, it was never shut. When he was not gossiping, he was either singing or reciting passages in Greek, from his beloved Homer, or in German, from Goethe or Heine. He was a picturesque old man, and of a most mercurial temperament. I never met any one so restless, exuberant, almost gushing, and yet he struck me as being sincere, and most loyal to his many friends. — Corkran, Henriette, 1895, *Recollections of Three Great Men, Temple Bar, vol.* 105, *pp.* 520, 521.

My introduction to Blackie was away back in those mid-century days. I came from Germany after the session had opened, and applied for admission to his class, but asked for a short respite for the payment of my fee. This he readily granted, filled up my ticket and stuck it into the looking-glass in his retiring-room. Some weeks after, I followed him into his room to pay my debt. He looked over his list and assured me I had payed. I assured him to the contrary, and he protested, till I pointed out my ticket on his mantlepiece. Then, in the exuberance of his pleasure, he literally danced about the room, his gown streaming behind him, and explained that as he had settled his accounts for the year with Mrs. Blackie, here was a clear ten guineas of pocket money to spend as he might think best. Our weekly treat was the hour he devoted to reading us selections from his translation of Homer—a treat only excelled by Aytoun's recitations of Scottish Ballads, in his lectures on that subject. . . . While inspiring us with his likes and dislikes, no professor had his class under more perfect control. A look or a gesture sufficed to arrest the slightest approach to unruliness, which was only too prevalent in other classes.—Douglas, J., 1895, *The Late Professor Blackie, The Nation, vol.* 60, *p.* 256.

We all know that the public seldom notice minute distinctions, and there are innumerable eyes that would never observe the difference between Blackie and Blaikie. . . . Of course our letters were continually going to the wrong house. Usually a glance showed the mistake. . . . He liked enjoyment and relaxation, like the theatre, and thought it wholesome. Strict Sabbatarianism seemed an unwholesome cramping of the soul. And sometimes he talked as if we Puritans disliked brightness and cheerfulness, and thought that if men were to be good they must be always grave and self-repressed. . . . Professor Blackie frequently stayed at my house when lecturing in Glasgow. He was always at his best when one had him alone.—BLAIKIE, W. G., 1895, *Professor Blackie and his "Doppel-Gänger," Good Words*, vol. 36, pp. 297, 298, 300, 301.

Blackie at home and Blackie abroad differed considerably. He was a compound of two individualities both wholesome and good, but not the same in manifestation. At home he was gentle, considerate, methodical, serious; only at table relaxing into discursive talk and occasional explosiveness. His domestic pleasantries were tranquil, and took the form of genial banter and of equally genial irony. . . . A student reading with the book in his left hand was called to order and bidden hold it in the other. He coloured and continued to read as before. The Professor was annoyed, and reprimanded him sharply. The class hissed at this, and the student held up the stump which was all that remained of his right arm. Then Blackie stepped down from his desk, and taking the young fellow in his arms, begged his pardon with tears in his eyes, and turning to the rest, he said, "I am glad that I have gentlemen to teach," and went back to his desk in an outburst of applause. The men loved him, and if the more riotous spirits took advantage of his sympathetic boyishness, and sometimes turned order into rout, even the most ungovernable amongst them acknowledged at heart his patience and tolerance and indomitable pluck and manliness.—STODDART, ANNA M. 1895, *John Stuart Blackie, A Biography*, pp. 218, 223.

GENERAL

His mind is of a quick, bold cast, and he has, at all times, the fearless courage of his convictions, in consequence of which virtue, he has become the most widely quoted of platform speakers. He can never possibly be dull or uninteresting in a book, or in debate, as he unites, in high perfection, the two popular qualities of humour and animation. As a poet, he is distinguished for sense, enthusiasm, and melody.—MURDOCH, ALEXANDER G., 1883, ed. *The Scottish Poets Recent and Living*, p. 60.

It is to his short lyrics, his light, rollicking lays, that his popularity with his countrymen has been mainly due. *La rime n'est pas riche*, it may be said, and assuredly the author has been all too lax and copious a versifier. And it may be that his countless deliverances on religion, and science, and politics, and Scottish music, and manners—and who can say what besides?—have not invariably deepened the wisdom of nations. One may wish the writer had been less boisterously patriotic, less aggressively voluble, less inconsistently cocksure. One may wish that he had worked more in the spirit of an artist. But his hearty, bracing songs, so vigorous and unforced, so rich in jollity and sympathy with youth, so full of hearty love of the bens and braes and sea-lochs of the North, are unquestionably a possession which has enheartened and enlivened not a few. And of the works of how many cautious thinkers and laborious lyric artists can as much be said? After all there are moods in which rollicking, careless stanzas, merrily jingled, lusty in sentiment, and breathing of hill and sea, are more welcome than verses deeper in import and fastidiously chiselled, which fail, however, to exhilarate and arouse.—WHYTE, WALTER, 1892, *The Poets and the Poetry of the Century, Frederick Tennyson to A. H. Clough*, ed. *Miles*, p. 215.

Verse, if one may hazard a guess, has been with him rather a relaxation than a pursuit; but, whether in verse or prose, everything that he does is essentially *sui generis*. And, in Scotland at least, his appeal seldom fails of a response.—DOUGLAS, SIR GEORGE, 1893, ed., *Contemporary Scottish Verse, Introductory Note*, p. xviii.

The Professor wrote much in many metres. His pen dropped into verse as naturally as his voice into song; and as he "piped more for pleasure than for fame" he disdained the chipping and changing and trimming and polishing carried on in some poetical workshops. Naturally, therefore, some of his verse lacks "distinction," and is deprived of its power over the imagination by the occasional cropping up of a phrase prosaic to the verge of commonplace. . . . This book ["Self-Culture"] has run through twenty-four editions, not to speak of a shorthand version, in this country. . . . It has been translated into French, German, Italian, Greek,—in fact almost every European language and I believe several others. The book was written as a holiday amusement in a summer month, and the Professor at first meant it for a trio of lectures to his students in Edinburgh.—KENNEDY, HOWARD ANGUS, 1896, *Professor Blackie, his Sayings and Doings*, p. 272.

The plain fact is—and it may as well be said firmly—that Blackie was not a great original poet. There was a certain marching music about his verses, as though they had been improvised to the tread of his own martial stride, and he had also a "fowth o' rhymes" at his command; yet his poems were lacking in either that concentrated fervour or that highly refined polish which ought to mark the work of a successful and popular poet. Even in his later days, when some passing event incited him to send a sonnet, or a poem that defied classification, to the *Scotsman*, it was painfully evident that he was not even a passable rhymster. Crude, unformed, rugged lines were strung together by him and pitchforked at the public, as though anything that bore the name of Blackie was good enough for the "Bœotian herd." It is a notable fact that great translators (with few exceptions) have never been great original poets; and Blackie was no exception. . . . It was neither by his "Æschylus" nor his "Homer," laborious as these were, that Blackie became known to a very wide circle of readers. His little volume entitled "Self-Culture," published first in 1873, and since re-issued almost annually, did more to bring him face to face with the great world that lies outside the Universities than his most scholastic works.—MILLAR, A. H., 1896, *John Stuart Blackie, Scottish Review*, vol. 27, pp. 29, 31.

His "Songs of Religion and Life" give him claims to a place in any volume devoted to the sacred poetry of his time.— MILES, ALFRED H., 1897, *The Poets and the Poetry of the Century, Sacred, Moral, and Religious Verse*, p. 257.

Sir John Robert Seeley
1834–1895

Born, in London, 10 Sept. 1834. Early education at a school at Stanmore, and at City of London School. Matric., Christ's Coll., Camb., as Scholar, 1852; B. A., 1857; M. A., 1860. Fellow of Christ's Coll., July 1858 to 1869. Assistant Master, City of London School, 1860–63. Prof. of Latin, University Coll., London, 1863–69. Prof. of Modern Hist., Camb., Oct. 1869. Married Mary Agnes Phillott, 1869. Professorial Fellow, Caius Coll., Camb., Oct. 1882. K. C. M. G., 1894. Died at Cambridge, 13 Jan. 1895. *Works*: "Three Essays on . . . King Lear" (by Seeley, W. Young, and E. A. Hart), 1851; "David and Samuel" (under pseud. "John Robertson"), 1859; "The Greatest of all the Plantagenets" (anon.), 1860 (new edn., called: "The Life and Reign of Edward I., 1872); "Classical Studies as an introduction to the Moral Sciences" 1864 [1863]; "Ecce Homo" (anon.), 1866 (5 edn. same year); "An English Primer" (with E. A. Abbott), 1869; "Roman Imperialism," 1869; "Lectures and Essays," 1870; "English Lessons for English People" (with E. A. Abbott), 1871; "Life and Times of Stein," (3 vols.), 1878; "Natural Religion," anon., 1882, (2nd edn. same year); "The Expansion of England," 1883; "Short History of Napoleon the First," 1886; "Greater Greece and Greater Britain," 1887; "Goethe: reviewed after sixty years," 1894. *Posthumous*: "The Growth of British Policy," ed. by G. W. Prothero (2 vols.), 1895; "Introduction to Political Science," ed. by H. Sidgwick, 1896. He *edited*: "The Student's Guide to the University of Cambridge," 1863; Livy, bk. i., 1871.—SHARP, R. FARQUHARSON, 1897, *A Dictionary of English Writers*, p. 251.

PERSONAL

If Seeley's style was highly artistic, it was also highly artificial. The effects were consummate, but they were all carefully planned. His voice was never strong, but it was clear, and he managed it with the utmost ability, using all the delicate shades of emphasis. The lucidity of his arrangement seemed almost to communicate itself to his reading, and to find physical expression, as it were, in his modes of speech. His old pupils will recollect also with what infinite skill he utilised a slight cough, in order to point a sentence or emphasise a phrase. His use of quotations was masterly and suggestive in the highest degree.—TANNER,

J. R., 1895, *John Robert Seeley, English Historical Review*, vol. 10, p. 509.

He did not avoid society, but he was no great lover of it. Not a voluble talker, he yet conversed readily with intimate friends or on topics in which he took interest. On such occasions his conversation was infallibly brilliant and epigrammatic, and abounding in apt and humorous illustration. When deeply interested, whether in conversation or on the platform, there shone forth a fire of enthusiasm, generally kept under close restraint or concealed in later years by a somewhat lethargic exterior. In University affairs of the ordinary kind he took little part; the routine of academic business, of syndicates, examinations and college meetings, was distasteful to him. As a young man he used to play racquets and cricket, and in his vacations he sometimes went on walking tours, in the Welsh mountains and Switzerland. But he had no natural fondness for athletic exercises: in later life his only form of physical recreation was a walk, and a solitary walk, he complained, afforded but little rest, for his mind was working all the time. It was his misfortune that he never acquired the art of lying fallow.—PROTHERO, G. W., 1895, ed. *The Growth of British Policy, Memoir*, p. 21.

ECCE HOMO
1865

Have been reading lately "Ecce Homo," a book neither quite orthodox nor critical, but with many good points of reflection: a touch of a dry Robertson, and of my own sermons. It seems working up rather than down. Most of the orthodox journals most flattering to it, especially the *Guardian*, though similar but more ecclesiastical things said by me had been treated with offensive bitterness by them. The *Quarterly Review* falls on the book in its accustomed style, and with far more consistency, though less civility, than the complimentary critics.—WILLIAMS, ROWLAND, 1866, *Journal-Notes*, May 27; *Life and Letters*, ed. his Wife, vol. II, p. 250.

The book was published anonymously and was extraordinarily successful, something as "Robert Elsmere" has been, with a similar cause. It was full of eloquence and preached with much fervour the "Enthusiasm of Humanity" as a substitute for that love of God and of man which is the inspiration of Christianity. We believe that it has fallen almost completely into oblivion, and that few, at least of the younger readers of the day, would recognise the "Enthusiasm of Humanity" even as a name.—OLIPHANT, MARGARET O. W., 1892, *The Victorian Age of English Literature*, p. 353.

"Ecce Homo" was, above all, an historian's conception of Jesus. In fact, it was Seeley's answer to Gibbon's problem in the celebrated fifteenth chapter. Gibbon wished to explain the remarkable spread and success of the early Church; Seeley tried to trace it back to the personal influence of the Founder. In doing this he had naturally to lay stress on Jesus's personal influence as man upon men, and thereby raised the ire of the Evangelicals. Curiously enough, it was on the historical side of his work that Seeley was most wanting. He failed to show from the Gospel records that the conscious aim of Jesus's life was the formation of a Society of Humanity. He could find no text for his refrain "L'Église, c'est moi." Yet his insistence on the social side of Jesus's work has done more for Christian union than any theological utterance of the past third of a century.—JACOBS, JOSEPH, 1895, *Sir John R. Seeley, The Athenæum*, No. 3508, p. 86.

That book marks the appearance of the plain lay judgment upon a sphere which had been long monopolised either by the disciples of a pious ecclesiastical tradition, or by professed biblical scholars. It was inspired by a moral rather than by a strictly scientific interest. . . . It was a book which at any rate was not professedly unorthodox, and yet it invited the orthodox for a moment to discard the associations of divinity, and to concentrate their gaze upon the spectacle of a perfect human life passed upon earth. And it raised questions which had not been so clearly put before, precisely because those, for whom they were most interesting, had never considered them from an exclusively human standpoint, and they were fundamental questions.—FISHER, HERBERT A. L., 1896, *Sir John Seeley, Fortnightly Review*, vol. 66, p. 185.

LIFE AND TIMES OF STEIN
1878

Unquestionably one of the most important contributions to the history of Germany ever placed before English readers. It is founded upon a long and arduous study of original materials, and it is a substantial contribution to the knowledge of the world. . . . The work has to do with the whole range of activity during the long period under review, and perhaps its most striking characteristic is that the author never for a moment allows himself to become the victim either of a prejudice or an enthusiasm. It may, perhaps, be said that the work lacks spirit; but it is so eminently judicial in tone that even when reason for a position taken is not given, the reader does not doubt that a good reason exists.—ADAMS, CHARLES KENDALL, 1882, *A Manual of Historical Literature*, p. 256.

If his biography of Stein fails to attract, it is mainly because Stein is not an attractive personality. The best parts of the book are where he is not dealing with Stein at all, but with some great movement of European feeling, like the national protest of Spain. What lends the book, however, an almost epic note, is the *rôle* played by Napoleon as the Satan of the action. This he also treated separately in his monograph on the great *condottiere*, as he regarded him. —JACOBS, JOSEPH, 1895, *Sir John R. Seeley, The Athenæum*, No. 3508, p. 86.

Seeley for the first time explained the Germany of the Napoleonic period to Englishmen. . . . The "Life and Times of Stein" is the only book of Seeley's which lacks unity. But what it lacks in unity it gains in interest and in instructiveness. Who would willingly miss the vigorous sketches of Dalberg and Humboldt, and Niebuhr and Scharnhorst? They are essential to the real understanding of the period. And there is another feature in the book which adds to its value. The German history is constantly illustrated by the better-known history of England and of France, the author is always careful to guard us against such misconceptions as may naturally arise in English minds. When he is describing Stein's municipal reforms he warns us against misinterpreting the spirit of the law. It was indeed a measure of self-government; but the people were not allowed but commanded to govern. The book appears to me to be in many ways a model of the way in which foreign history should be written for English readers; and to confirm a thesis, for which may be said, that the best history of any land is generally the work of a foreigner. —FISHER, HERBERT A. L., 1896, *Sir John Seeley, Fortnightly Review*, vol. 66, p. 193.

NATURAL RELIGION
1882

"Natural Religion" is not (it may be said at once) a book which attempts to deal with the speculative points at issue among the schools or the churches. Still less does it profess to cast any fresh light on the old problems of *whence* and *whither*, or to supply to morality that independent standing-point for which she still is vainly feeling in the void. The task which it attempts is a lesser one, but great nevertheless, and within the power of man. It is to prove to the earnest, but divergent, schools of modern thought, to the artist, the Positivist, the man of science, the orthodox Christian, that their agreement lies deeper than their differences, that the enemy of all is the same; that for the most part they are but looking at different sides of the shield, whether they worship the Unity of the Universe by the cold silver light of His power and reality, or in the golden radiance of His love. And thus the author claims for all forms of enthusiastic admiration of truth, beauty, goodness, the title of religion, which he deems theirs by right both of logic and of history. . . . Whether we call our author's utterances by the name of religion or philosophy, they contain, at any rate, sublime ideas, vast generalizations, far-reaching hopes. As a mere model of simple and noble style this work is likely to be widely studied and to be remembered long.—MYERS, FREDERIC W. H., 1882, *A New Eirenicon, Fortnightly Review*, vol. 38, pp. 596, 605.

"Natural Religion" cannot yet claim to be classical work, but this at any rate can be said of it,—that the appreciation of it is likely to furnish a decisive test, by which an interest in religion itself may be distinguished from an interest in some particular set of religious or anti-religious ideas. No one who has the cause of religion at heart, no one who, however orthodox or however unorthodox he may be, believes religion to be the best thing in the world, will fail to be affected by it or to learn something from it. . . . The greatest service that the remarkable book before us will render to those who honestly and patiently study it, comes from the fact that in it, perhaps for the first time in England, the question is raised and answered in a way that must compel attention:—Granting the infinite value of religion, what kind of religion is possible apart from certain beliefs, apart from all "supernaturalism?" It is a question that concerns every one interested in religion, and not those alone who are compelled to reject a part or the whole of the received theology.—BRADLEY, ANDREW CECIL, 1883, *Some Points in "Natural Religion," Macmillan's Magazine, vol.* 47, *pp.* 144, 146.

In "Natural Religion" we have the philosophy of Goethe subordinated to the strong practical interests of the English historian. . . . Seeley's special form of culture was history, and I doubt whether any English historian has cast so many valuable historical truths into a portable form.—FISHER, HERBERT A. L., 1896, *Sir John Seeley, Fortnightly Review, vol.* 66, *pp.* 188, 189.

GENERAL

Everyone who has read "Ecce Homo" with any degree of care must have felt that the author was a man capable of strong, close, consecutive thinking, however much they may have disapproved of his standpoint or disagreed with his conclusions. And the continued demand for the book—it has already gone through sixteen editions— would *a priori* be sufficient evidence, were other proof wanting, that a fresh work coming from the same author would be certain to bring with it the weight of authority for many, the expectation of originality for others, and the hope of novelty for not a few. "Natural Religion" quickly reached a second edition, and the authorised publication of a private letter from the author in *The Spectator* not long since, as well as frequent allusions to it, show that the interest in the book is not ephemeral.—LAMBERT, AGNES, 1884, *False Coin, Nineteenth Century, vol.* 15, *p.* 949.

Seeley's light was a dry one, I have said, but it was pure and steady, and illumined every branch of thought on which he turned it. There are those who prefer this species of illumination to the more iridescent glare and more fantastic shadows cast by the *jeu follet* of imagination. Truth has its triumphs no less than Fancy, and of these were Seeley's. The votaries of Veracity need, above all things, restraint and repression; Imagination must be their servant, not their master. Throughout Seeley's work, so original in so many directions, one feels that he never brought out all that was in him. Of Gray—another Cambridge man, and Seeley's predecessor in his chair— it was said that he never spoke out. May we not say of Seeley that he never let himself go? Yet in this restraint and repression Seeley was English of the English. I have called his a Cambridge mind. Should I not supplement this by saying that the Cambridge mind, in all its strength, with all its limitations, is the characteristic English mind?—JACOBS, JOSEPH, 1895, *Sir John R. Seeley, Literary Studies, p.* 195.

One very important aspect of Seeley's work has been left untouched—his work as one of the most stimulating and inspiring of Cambridge teachers. . . . The posthumous work on "The Growth of British Policy," still in the press, is based on forty manuscript volumes of extracts copied from the Record office and other sources. Critics who read his finished work, and talk of "hasty generalisation," fail to appreciate the laborious process by which the finished work was produced. This habit of thoroughness Seeley communicated insensibly to his pupils. He never preached it to them, but it soon came to influence unconsciously the standard of criticism which they were accustomed to apply to what they wrote for him. . . . It will be doubted by some whether Seeley's view of history is one that can be maintained in the present imperfect state of human knowledge. His critics may be disposed to regard his use of the terminology of science as somewhat misleading; they may urge that the concessions made to them are so great as to involve a practical surrender of the whole position; the fact remains that for five-and-twenty years an acute subtle thinker invested this view with an irresistible fascination. And there can be no doubt that for the purposes of education it possessed great practical value.— TANNER, J. R., 1895, *John Robert Seeley, English Historical Review, vol.* 10, *pp.* 507, 508, 514.

What was most remarkable in his teaching of history was its suggestive and stimulative character, and the constancy of its scientific aim. The facts which Seeley mentioned in his lectures were, as a rule, well known; it was the use he made of them that was new. Historical details were worth nothing to him but as a basis for generalisation; the idea to which they pointed was everything. In dealing with history he always kept a definite end in view—the solution of some problem, the establishment of some principle, which would arrest the attention of the student, and might be of use to the statesman. History pure and simple, that is narrative without generalisation, had no interest for him: it appeared trivial, unworthy of serious attention. With this habit of mind, it was inevitable that his conclusions should sometimes appear disputable, but in any case they were thoughtful, bold and original. Except perhaps in his "Life of Stein," he added little to the sum of historical knowledge, if by that is meant the knowledge of historical events. But he pointed out a further aim, to which the mere acquisition of knowledge is subsidiary. Taking facts as established, he insisted on thinking about them, and on deducing from them the main lines of historical and political evolution.—PROTHERO, G. W., 1895, *ed. The Growth of British Policy, Memoir, p.* 19.

In the line of great English teachers Sir John Seeley will assuredly hold a most honourable place. I question whether we fully appreciate either the amount or the value of his influence and instruction. And yet even from an external point of view there is something extraordinary in his literary career. Twice he took the English reading world by storm, once by a book on religion, and again by a book on politics; and each book, in its own sphere, may be held to mark an epoch in the popular education of the Anglo-Saxon race. . . . He always treated large themes, and he treated them with enthusiasm, and with power and with originality. He was all his life a professed teacher, with a creed of his own to impart, and he gloried in the office. Few men have devoted to the cause of national education a purpose so widely conceived, so seriously and nobly sustained. He had the opportunity of giving oral instruction, and he must have been an ideal lecturer, with that refined and concentrated ardour glowing through those lucid, those severe, those cogent demonstrations. He had, too, one of the essential talents of a teacher, the gift of saying common things in a memorable way; and even when he issues upon a familiar conclusion, the route by which the conclusion is reached is so new, so full of fresh incident, of surprising turns, of enchanting glimpses into the animating landscape of possibility, that we are easily tempted to forget that we knew anything about it before.—FISHER, H. A. L., 1896, *Sir John Seeley, Fortnightly Review, vol.* 66, *p.* 183.

In the space of thirty years German critical ideas have made great progress in England, and nowadays it is hard to understand how such a moderate book as "Ecce Homo" could have caused such deep offence, even to ignorant pietists. . . . Yet "Ecce Homo" left one side of the question unanswered, and many looked forward to the promised sequel. But it did not appear for sixteen years, and dealt with different problems. I have heard admirers of "Ecce Homo" speak disparagingly of "Natural Religion," as though the writer's religious faith or literary power had receded in the interval. But though it appeals less to ordinary minds, it is in no way inferior to its more exoteric forerunner. The distinctively Christian enthusiasm of his earlier years is supplemented by another view of life, principally derived from the study of Goethe's writings. . . . His knowledge of modern literature was enormous. Not only the well-kept high-roads, but even the moon-lit by-paths in the forests of German thought, had become familiar ground to him. French and Italian writers always occupied his attention. No one knew the English classics better. — TODHUNTER, MAURICE, 1896, *Sir John Seeley, Westminster Review, vol.* 145, *pp.* 503, 504, 508.

Frederick Locker-Lampson
1821–1895.

Born (Frederick Locker), at Greenwich Hospital, 1821. Educated at various private schools, 1829-36. Clerk in colonial broker's in London, Sept. 1837 to Dec. 1838. Visit to Continent, 1840. Clerk at Somerset House, March 1841. Transferred to Admiralty, Nov. 1842. Married (i.) Lady Charlotte Bruce, 4 July 1849. Contrib. to "Cornhill Mag." from 1860. Wife died, 26 April 1872. Married (ii.) Hannah Jane Lampson, 6 July 1874. Took additional surname of Lampson on death of wife's father, 1890. Died, at Rowfant, 30 May 1895. *Works:* "London Lyrics," 1857; "Lyra Elegantiarum," 1867 (first edn. suppressed; revised edn. same year). *Posthumous:* "My Confidences," ed. by A. Birrell, 1896.—SHARP, R. FARQUHARSON, 1897, *A Dictionary of English Writers, p.* 171.

PERSONAL

In life as in literature he has both humor and good humor. Although satiric by nature, he is thoroughly sympathetic and generous. Well-to-do in the world, he has been able to indulge his liking for the little things in art which make life worth living. His collections of china, of drawings, of engravings, are all excellent; and his literary curiosities, first editions of great books and precious autographs of great men, make a poor American wickedly envious. He is a connoisseur of the best type, never buying trash or bargain-hunting, knowing what he wants, and why he wants it, and what it is worth; and his treasures are freely opened to any literary brother who is seeking after truth.—MATTHEWS, BRANDER, 1883, *Frederick Locker, Century Magazine, vol.* 23, *p.* 597.

As a diplomat, his knowledge of men and of society, his judgment, his *finesse*, his unerring tact and taste, and his fine presence and charm of personality, would have made him a marked man. But his dislike to everything which tended to disturb the level of things, and his habitual "backwardness," added, one is bound to confess, to constitutional indolence and love of ease, made him shrink from the excitement and distraction of public life, as he shrank from challenging that serious recognition as a poet—apart from his reputation as a writer of light verse—to which he had it in his power to make good his claim.—KERNAHAN, COULSON, 1895, *Frederick Locker-Lampson, Nineteenth Century, vol.* 38, *p.* 634.

A personality which combined in an extraordinary degree an enchantingly gentle bearing, a kindness of heart that defies description, a keen perception, and (though in undertones) a rare incisiveness of speech. For his friends—and he had friends everywhere and in all ranks of life—there was nothing he would not do.—BIRRELL, AUGUSTINE, 1896, *Frederick Locker, Scribner's Magazine, vol.* 19, *p.* 42.

Mr. Frederic Locker-Lampson always struck me as a droll figure. He posed as a friend to men of letters, and subscribed, I believe, to the Literary Fund; yet he held up his head as if his sole *status* had been his ancient descent and his territorial importance, whereas in reality his main title to notice was what he did in *vers de société*—some very clever and pretty things, but assuredly no poetry.—HAZLITT, W. CAREW, 1897, *Four Generations of a Literary Family, vol.* II, *p.* 293.

GENERAL

Mr. Frederick Locker is happily exempted from the possibility of undergoing the post-mortem examination to which we have been able to subject his illustrious predecessors, and at our hands at least he is equally safe from vivisection. In predicating of him that he is no spectator *ab extra* of the social life which he has depicted in his "London Lyrics," we affirm nothing that they will not abundantly warrant. We are delighted to welcome this charming volume in an improved edition. In returning afresh to it, after a study of Prior and Praed, we have been forcibly struck by the superior healthiness of the atmosphere pervading it. This impression may be heightened by a natural association of ideas. All three are more or less poets of the city; but whereas with his forerunners we are mewed within walls, Mr. Locker invites us out of doors.... Studies, minute but delicate, drawn from every rank of society and every period of life, appeal to differing tastes. While in the choice of subjects he has nearly as much variety as Prior, and more than Praed, though he has written far less than either, the uniformity of his mode of handling is the test of his sincerity. None of the sharpness of contrast between gravity and gaiety, such as we remark in Prior, no sudden revulsions of sentiment, such as Praed exhibits, will be found in these poems. A subtle intermixture of seriousness and irony, of humour and pathos, is their prevailing characteristic.... Mr. Locker seems most deservedly characterized by two epithets which no one dreams of applying to Prior, and we think must be denied to Praed—earnest and tender.... Mr. Locker has a fine ear for rhythm and rhyme, and his employment of assonance and alliteration is judiciously subdued. With the efforts of Mr. Morris and Mr. Swinburne to obtain variety—the one by means of false accentuations, the other by experiments which vie with the "Peter Piper" of our childhood—he has no sympathy.—HEWLETT, HENRY G., 1872, *Poets of Society, Contemporary Review, vol.* 20, *pp.* 259, 260, 267.

Mr. Locker is not quite so elegant, perhaps, as his forerunner Praed; but he is more sprightly and humourous. Liveliness, and what we should call the humour of surprise, are two of his distinguishing features.

... Mr. Locker's talent is in harmony with the spirit of the time. He lives so in the age and belongs so much to what is best in its society that he may fairly be remembered and quoted hereafter as a representative of the period. His earnestness and sincerity are very marked characteristics, and the genuineness of his song will provide against its extinction. His fancy is chaste and selective, his wit delicate, his style polished and graceful, and it is possible that some of his light fabrics may outlive more stately and solid edifices.—SMITH, GEORGE BARNETT, 1875, *English Fugitive Poets, Poets and Novelists, pp.* 408, 417.

> I meet thee not by yonder lea,
>   Where fruited fields are waving;
> But Mincing Lane and Battersea
> Have meanings fresh and sweet to thee,
>   Thou poet of the paving!
> A grass blade from the gardener's plot,
>   A crannied wall-flower peeping,
> Are more to thee than meadows shot
> With daisies white and clover spot,
>   And wild brooks in their leaping.

—HAYWARD, EDWARD F., 1886, *To Frederick Locker, Century Magazine,* vol. 31, p. 964.

Mr. Locker is the du Maurier of song, and his "London Lyrics" are as entertaining and as instructive to the student of Victorian manners as Mr. du Maurier's "Pictures of English Society." Mr. Locker has succeeded Praed as the laureate of the world, and he ignores the flesh, and is ignorant of the devil, just like Praed, and just like society itself. But it seems to me that Mr. Locker's range is wider than Praed's, whose success lay almost altogether in his songs of society; Praed was out of place when he ventured far from Mayfair and beyond the sound of St. George's in Hanover Square; while Mr. Locker's Pegasus pauses at the mouth of Cite Fadette as gracefully as it treads the gravel of Rotten Row. The later poet has wider sympathies than the elder, who, indeed, may be said to have but one note.—MATTHEWS, BRANDER, 1888, *Pen and Ink,* p. 95.

As you turn his pages you feel as freshly as ever his sweet, old-world elegance, the courtly amiability, the mannerly restraint, the measured and accomplished ease. True, they are colourless, and in these days we are deboshed with colour; but then they are so luminously limpid and serene, they are so sprightly and graceful and gay! In the gallantry they affect there is a something at once exquisite and paternal.— HENLEY, WILLIAM ERNEST, 1890, *Views and Reviews,* p. 116.

In Mr. Locker's work, the graceful nothings of the drawing-room are so dexterously set to music, that we are hardly aware that conversation has passed into song, while remaining conversation. And whenever he essays to sing, he seems to me to have the true lyrical note. . . . Though Mr. Locker had his literary limitations— though his work was not marked by dramatic or creative power, any more than by originality of thought—the grace of "style" dignifies everything to which he put his hand. It is apparent even in the books which he edited, as well as in the books which he wrote. . . . Humour—keen, kindly, and playful—was of the very framework of his being. It was humour which made his sight so clear, his judgments so generous; and humour was the secret alike of his light-heartedness and of his occasional tender melancholy. . . . That the excellence of technique and of taste, and the ease, grace, and restraint which are never absent from Mr. Locker's work, entitle him to rank among the best writers of Occasional Verse, few will deny. As compared with his contemporaries, it will generally be conceded that he shares with Mr. Austin Dobson the highest place. Mr. Lang, Mr. Gosse, and Mr. Henley have written occasional poems which may challenge comparison with the best; but when the—it is to be hoped, far distant—time comes to draw the final line under the list of their works, and to add up the column, they will be judged by another standard than as writers of *vers de société.* Between Mr. Dobson and Mr. Locker, then, the honours may be equally divided, and between these brothers in friendship, as in song, no comparison of merits need be instituted.— KERNAHAN, COULSON, 1895, *Frederick Locker-Lampson, Nineteenth Century,* vol. 38, *pp.* 635, 640, 641, 642.

"My Confidences" is, indeed, a book wherein an affluent humour, now sportive, now gravely tender, blends with a shrewd, kindly wisdom, and a keen though unenvenomed wit, to form a style of unique idiosyncratic charm. Its pages brim and run over with delicious laughter—a laughter none the less sweet because of its occasional neighbourhood to tears. In his "Lyrics" Frederick Locker had revealed himself as the poet of society, singing the hearts of London folk out to their face; here, as in "Patchwork," he shows at once as the humorist who, with a stroke of his wizard's rod, turns to favour and to prettiness the dull follies and ugly foibles of his fellow-men, and as the steadfast lover and bold, persuasive advocate of all that is true, honest, pure, lovely, and of good report. . . . Locker's faculty of observation was keen; he had a devouring eye. Moreover— and the like is true of all humorists—its activity does not seem to have been checked by any tenderness which he might happen to feel for the object of his study. Flaws, foibles and frailties, in one and all alike, were scrutinised by him with strictness and registered with fidelity. Not a little in these "Confidences" reminds us of the uncompromising touches in Charles Lamb's portrayal of his brother John, or of Edward Fitzgerald's speculations as to what feature in his "mother's fine face betrayed what was not so good in her character."—HUTCHINSON, THOMAS, 1896, *My Confidences*, The Academy, vol. 49, p. 337.

He would not do anything bad, and apparently he did not feel inclined to do anything good. And as this is a century when almost everybody must still be doing, and taking the chance of goodness and badness, such an exception to the rule should meet with honour.—SAINTSBURY, GEORGE, 1896, *A History of Nineteenth Century Literature*, p. 310.

He was a great student of verse. There was hardly a stanza of any English poet, unless, indeed, it was Spenser, for whom he had no great affection, which he had not pondered over and duly considered as does a lawyer his cases. He delighted in a successful verse, and grieved over any lapse from the path of metrical virtue, over any ill-sounding rhyme or unhappy expression. —BIRRELL, AUGUSTINE, 1896, *Frederick Locker*, Scribner's Magazine, vol. 19, p. 43.

The verse of Frederick Locker-Lampson is of the kind which the French call *vers de société*, and which may be seen in all its English varieties in his "Lyra Elegantiarum." He belongs to the seventeenth-century school of light and airy singers, of which Carew, Suckling, Lovelace, Herrick, and Sedley were masters, and which in the days of Queen Anne was conducted by such modish, jaunty ushers as Pope and Prior. But he belongs to it in its nineteenth-century conditions, which, in common with Hood, Praed, and Thackeray, he has bettered and enlarged with his finer taste, purer sentiment, and more genuine feeling. His "London Lyrics" are the perfection of humorous-pathetic poetry. — STODDARD, ELIZABETH, 1897, *Library of the World's Best Literature*, ed. Warner, vol. XVI, p. 9114.

As a poet he belonged to the school of Prior, Praed, and Hood, and he greatly admired the metrical dexterity of Barham. His chief endeavour, he said, was to avoid flatness and tedium, to cultivate directness and simplicity both in language and idea, and to preserve individuality without oddity or affectation. In this he achieved success. His work is always neat and clear; restrained in its art, and refined in its tone; while to a wit which rivals Praed's, and a lightness worthy of Prior, he not unfrequently joins a touch of pathos which recalls the voice of Hood. His work mellowed as he grew older, and departed further from his first models—those rhymes *galamment composées* which had been his youthful ambition; but the majority of his pieces, at all times, by their distinctive character and personal note, rise far above the level of the mere *vers d'occasion* or *vers de société* with which it was once the practice to class them.—DOBSON, AUSTIN, 1901, *Frederick Locker-Lampson, Dictionary of National Biography, Supplement*, ed. Sidney Lee, vol. III, p. 106.

Eugene Field
1850–1895.

An American poet and humorous journalist; born at St. Louis, Mo., Sept. 2, 1850; died Nov. 4, 1895. His latter years were spent in Chicago. By his poems and tales in the press he won a high reputation in the West, which before his death had become national. His poems for children are admirable in their simplicity and in their sympathetic insight into the child's world of thought and feeling. His complete works comprise: "Love Songs of Childhood"; "A Little Book of Western Verse"; "A Second Book of Verse"; "The Holy Cross, and Other Tales"; "The Love Affairs of a Biblomaniac." He made, in collaboration with his brother Roswell Martin Field, some good translations from Horace—"Echoes from the Sabine Farm."—WARNER, CHARLES DUDLEY, ed. 1897, *Library of the World's Best Literature, Biographical Dictionary*, vol. xxix, p. 187.

PERSONAL

A tall, thin-haired man with a New England face of the Scotch type, rugged, smoothly shaven, and generally very solemn—suspiciously solemn in expression. His infrequent smile curled his wide, expressive mouth in fantastic grimaces which seemed not to affect the steady gravity of the blue-gray eyes. . . . His voice was deep but rather dry in quality.—GARLAND, HAMLIN, 1893, *Real Conversations*, *McClure's Magazine*, vol. 1, p. 195.

Clever, witty, and beautiful as were the poems and stories of Eugene Field, he was himself far more lovable than them all. My own acquaintance with Mr. Field was confined to one meeting, but I shall never forget that, or rather I shall never forget *him*. He came into the room, a long, lank, loose-jointed figure, looking far more like a man of business than a creator of fancies. At first his thin, cadaverous face seemed to me as one of the ugliest I had ever seen; a few moments later, when he had begun to talk freely, I thought it was one of the most attractive. He had been visiting in the afternoon one of the big book-stores of New York, and he spoke with enthusiasm of the rare volumes he had seen there and had longed to possess, but was too poor to buy. Then when his work was mentioned he spoke of that with a freedom from affectation, an absolute unconsciousness, that was most charming. On this occasion I had the good fortune to hear him recite, and I can say in all sincerity that I have never heard any one else recite so well. He possessed the qualities of the greatest of all actors, the actor who knows how to appeal to the heart by simple, direct, and wholly natural methods.—BARRY, JOHN D., 1895, *Literary World*, vol. 26, p. 420.

Of recent years Mr. Field rarely went to the office of the Chicago *News*, the paper for which during the last ten years he had written a daily column under the title of "Sharps and Flats," but did most of his work at his home in Buena Park, which he called the Sabine Farm. Here he began his day about nine o'clock, by having breakfast served to him in bed, after which he glanced through the papers, and then settled himself to his writing, with feet high on the table, and his pages before him laid neatly on a piece of plate glass. He wrote with a fine-pointed pen, and had by him several different colored inks, with which he would illuminate his capitals and embellish his manuscript. The first thing he did was his "Sharps and Flats" column, which occupied three or four hours, the task being usually finished by one o'clock. His other work he did in the afternoons and evenings, writing at odd hours, sometimes in the garden if the weather was pleasant. He was much interrupted by friends dropping in to see him; but, however busy, he welcomed whoever came, and would turn aside good-naturedly from his manuscript to entertain a visitor or to hear a story of misfortune. After dinner he retired to his "den" to read; for he read constantly, whatever the distractions about him, and was much given to reading in bed. Of all his visitors the most constant and appreciative were children. These he never sent away without some bright word, and he rarely sent them away at all.—MOFFETT, CLEVELAND, 1895, *Eugene Field and his Child Friends*, *McClure's Magazine*, vol. 6, p. 138.

The determination to found a story or a series of sketches on the delights, adventures, and misadventures connected with bibliomania did not come impulsively to my brother. For many years, in short during the greater part of nearly a quarter of a century of journalistic work, he had celebrated in prose and verse, and always in his happiest and most delightful vein, the pleasures of book-hunting. Himself an indefatigable collector of books, the possessor of a library containing volumes obtained only at the cost of a great personal sacrifice, he was in the most active sympathy with the disease called bibliomania, and knew, as few comparatively poor men have known, the half-pathetic, half humorous side of that incurable mental infirmity.—FIELD, ROSWELL MARTIN, 1895, *The Love Affairs of a Bibliomaniac*, Introduction, p. v.

There were many Eugene Fields. Like the Apostle, he was all things to all men and much to many. . . . He was a terror to politicians, a Homer to the children, and different to, as well as from, everybody. He bore unique relations to each of his

friends and acquaintances, as many of them have eloquently and affectionately testified.
. . . Possessed of a sonorous bass voice, an unconventional manner, and much magnetism, he easily made himself the centre of any group in which he chanced to mingle. He constantly attracted people who were as far removed as possible, seemingly, from any interest in the work in which he was engaged; then his missionary labors began; and in a few weeks, under the stimulating guidance of their poetic friend, his new acquaintances would be collecting books and rapidly developing into gentle bibliomaniacs. In this conversion of an indifferent soul into an enthusiastic worshipper at the shrine of literature, Eugene Field rejoiced. His devotion to his friends was beautiful. . . . Except at those infrequent times when he permitted his face to take a serious cast, the Eugene Field whom I knew had little or nothing morose about him, little or nothing that was not of the brightest, sunniest character. He had a wonderfully keen appreciation of the humorous and the ridiculous, and a facility for turning a proposition from grave to gay and from gay to grave as unusual as it was diverting.—WILSON, FRANCIS, 1898, *The Eugene Field I Knew, pp.* 1, 2, 4.

With his wonderful brain and all his charm of manner, it was, after all, his great-heartedness that won for him the love of the world. He loved humanity and drank in the sunshine and beauties of nature until there blossomed therefrom the beautiful flower of his verse, and his scarcely less poetic prose. The parent stalk is dead, but the scattered leaves forever shall shed abroad their sweet perfume; and the children for all time to come will bless the sweet spirit that gave them so much joy.—BELOW, IDA COMSTOCK, 1898, *Eugene Field in his Home, p.* 88.

Reserved in some ways, yet reckless, with the buoyancy of temperament which comes from a keen sense of humor, he was, at the same time, a man of judgment and keen perception, though not among the pence-getters. I presume Tom Hood was somewhat like him. He was watchful, though, in the midst of his buoyancy, and shrewd and careful and energetic in working for his friends or for what he considered right. There were tossing whitecaps on the river and ten thousand laughing ripples, but, underneath, the current was strong and swift and its course was well defined. One of the greatest among American writers was Eugene Field, but he was not greater in what he wrote than he was in his own personality—something exquisite and noble.—WATERLOO, STANLEY, 1898, *Eugene Field in his Home by Ida Comstock Below, Introduction, p.*xii.

Eugene Field's study of the pleasure of others was something he never allowed to show on the surface of his words or acts. Whenever he made one of a group in conversation he seemed to do just so much of the talking as suited his caprice and no more; yet by and by you would notice that he never monopolized the conversation and that it was mainly through his impulse that it kept passing around the circle. He did not send out his heart to persons or things; he took them into it as wholly without effort or show of goodness as the clover takes the bee. . . . Of course, this mere memorandum is no portrait. It is but the vehicle for a few impressions of one who knew Eugene Field not nearly so long or so well as did many others, but amply long and well enough to testify to the sweetness and strength of a character and life comparatively unfettered by that mechanical order which to persons of less native sweetness or strength—to the most of us, indeed —is as indispensable as rails and couplings to a moving train. It took but a short while and no special generosity of mind for anyone to see that traits which would have set radically wrong the clock-work lives of commoner men were but the shadows and shadow-play of the gifts that made him a boon to the world; and that it was to their own and the world's advantage that his most familiar friends took him as fortune gave him and wore him close to their hearts as something that did infinitely better things than keep time.—CABLE, GEORGE W., 1898, *The Eugene Field Book, ed. Burt and Cable, Introduction, pp.* xv, xx.

"In wit a man, in simplicity a child," nothing gloomy, narrow, or pharisaical entered into the composition of Eugene Field. Like Jack Montesquieu Bellew, the editor of the Cork Chronicle, "his finances, alas! were always miserably low." This followed from his learning how to spend money freely before he was forced to earn it laboriously. He scattered his patrimony gaily and then when the last inherited cent was gone, turned with equal gayety to earning, not only enough to support himself, but the wife and family that, with the royal reckless prodigality of genius, he provided himself with at the very outset of his career. ... With Eugene Field the man was always a bundle of delightful surprises, an ever unconventional personality of which only the merest suggestion is given in his works.—THOMPSON, SLASON, 1901, *Eugene Field, a Study in Heredity and Contradictions*, vol. I, pp. 10, 12.

GENERAL

With gentlest tears, no less than jubilee
Of blithest joy, we heard him and still hear
Him singing on, with full voice, pure and clear,
Uplifted as some classic melody
In sweetest legends of old minstrelsy;
Or swarming elfinlike upon the ear,
His airy notes make all the atmosphere
One blur of bird and bee and lullaby.
—RILEY, JAMES WHITCOMB, 1895, *Eugene Field*.

The humanity of Mr. Field has brought him safely through waters where many another vessel has gone to pieces. The dialect story or poem, if it be more than mere curiosity or a scientific disclosure of an out-of-the-way phase of life, must reveal some trait that touches the universal heart. Mr. Field has fairly done this in his best efforts of the kind, although he would doubtless have agreed with the critic who classed the dialect effusions among writings of his that he estimated at the lowest rate. ... The poetry of Eugene Field contains his truest contribution to the thought and art of his day; whether we consider his disclosures of the pleasures and weaknesses of the bibliophile, in which he was so immersed and which he knew so well, or whether we read his renderings of Horace into a modernity at times perhaps somewhat too insistent, we touch the truest chord of the poet's nature; and when we come to his songs of the intimate life of home and childhood, we are aware of a gift unique and tender. Whatever technical deficiencies we may find, or however a false note in some of the best known of these verses may offend our ear, we are quick to overlook it in the simplicity and genuineness of the feeling.—BLOCK, LOUIS J., 1896, *Eugene Field, The Dial*, vol. 20, p. 334.

He [James Whitcomb Riley] is a sympathetic singer of childhood, although he falls short here of Eugene Field. This sweet-souled lyrist, a native of St. Louis and in his later life a resident of Chicago, left in the ten volumes of his collected works nothing so dear to West and East as the simple stanza of "Little Boy Blue."—BATES, KATHARINE LEE, 1897, *American Literature*, p. 204.

It is in my own schoolroom and among my own pupils that the most genuine realization of Eugene Field's genius has come to me. The child, when left to his own inner leadings, his opinions not constrained, speaks out with great courage; his criticism has the delicacy of the downy bloom of his own cheek. His velvet voice lingers over the lines most exquisite in finish, like his own feelings, and "from these presents" I know that the child, the perfection of creation, has found his own poet, his own interpreter. A roguish brownie of eight years, as full of play as the day is long, finds leisure in some way, to learn "Wynken, Blynken, and Nod," and begs to recite it, and all the other brownies listen with eyes sparkling. A more serious child presents "The Wanderer" or "Christmas Treasures" or "Pitty-Pat and Tippy-Toes" and every rosy face becomes thoughtful. What a world of little people was left unrepresented in the realms of poetry until Eugene Field came in!—BURT, MARY E., 1898, ed. *The Eugene Field Book, Preface*, p. viii.

Everything Field wrote in prose or verse reflects his contempt for earth's mighty and his sympathy for earth's million mites. His art, like that of his favorite author and prototype, Father Prout, was "to magnify what is little and fling a dash of the sublime into a two-penny post communication." Sense of earthly grandeur he had little or none. Sense of the minor sympathies of life—those minor sympathies that are common to all and finally swell into the major song of life—of this sense he was compact. It was the meat and marrow of his life and mind, of his song and story. With unerring instinct Field, in his study of humanity, went to the one school where the emotions, wishes, and passions of mankind are to be seen unobscured by the veil of consciousness. He was forever scanning whatever lies hidden within the folds of the heart of childhood. He knew children through and through because he studied them from themselves and not from books. He associated with them on terms of the most intimate comradeship and wormed his way into their confidence with assiduous sympathy. Thus he became possessed of the inmost secrets of their childish joys and griefs and so became a literary philosopher of childhood.—THOMPSON, SLASON, 1901, *Eugene Field, a Study in Heredity and Contradictions, vol.* I, *p.* 10.

Eccentric, prodigal, uneven in quality to the last degree, the work of Field, in prose and verse, bears the unmistakable stamp of his unique and powerful genius. Especially, whether in dialect, mock archaic, or straightforward English, Field utters the very heart's secrets of boyhood as not even Riley or Louis Stevenson can do. "Wynken, Blynken, and Nod" became long ago a kindergarten classic. His echoes of Horace are not mere irreverent travesties, but seize the very essence of the thought, and render it in the most startlingly up-to-date English, spiced both with current slang and with Field's own invented idioms. He was really a learned man in many lines rarely, if ever, united before. He was not a cynic, though he never lost the opportunity for mockery, banter, and jest.—LAWTON, WILLIAM CRANSTON, 1902, *Introduction to the Study of American Literature, p.* 331.

William Wetmore Story
1819–1895.

Sculptor, was born in Salem, Mass., Feb. 12, 1819, and was graduated at Harvard in 1838. He was the son of the renowned jurist, Joseph Story. Law first claimed the son's attention also; he was admitted to the bar, and became known as the author of treatises on the "Law of Contracts" (1844) and "Law of Sales" (1847), and other legal tomes. But he also contributed to various periodicals, delivered poems on several occasions, in 1847 brought out his first volume of poems, and in 1851 published "The Life and Letters of Joseph Story" (2 vols.). The direction in which his tastes lay had already been indicated in some of his writings, and in 1848 he went to Italy, where he devoted himself chiefly to art. He has modelled portrait-statues of his father, Edward Everett, and George Peabody; busts of Theodore Parker, Josiah Quincy, and James Russell Lowell; and a number of ideal works, among them Sappho, Saul, Cleopatra, Delilah, Helen, Jerusalem in her Desolation, Semiramis, Judith, Sardanapalus, and Thetis and Achilles. Some critics have seen talent rather than genius in these thoughtful, carefully executed works, but though not strikingly original, they are noble and pure in sentiment, the products of a highly cultivated mind. In Europe he has been regarded by many as the foremost among American sculptors. As an author he is almost equally well known, and has published "Roba di Roma," sketches of Italian life, "Proportions of the Human Figure," and various volumes of poems, including "Graffiti d' Italia" and "The Roman Lawyer in Jerusalem."—WEITENKAMPF, FRANK, 1889, *Supplement to Encyclopædia Britannica, Ninth Ed., ed. Crosby, vol.* IV, *p.* 605.

PERSONAL

The man was wiser, better than his books. One of the elect whom fate had fitted to his surroundings, he put to flight the old idea that to follow art aright one must forsake father and mother and cleave only unto her. He loved "dear Nature" and, leaning on her breast, he dreamed dreams and saw visions. In cool, shadowy places, with sense attuned to finest harmonies, he had ears to hear the grass grow, the trees stretch their limbs, the calling voices of naiads haunting the oaks, or to interpret far-off music, the messages of the winds and the waterfalls.—WALLACE, SUSAN E., 1896–98, *Along the Bosphorus and Other Sketches, p.* 246.

Mrs. Story was a power in Rome, and for thirty years made her house a charming rendezvous for her country people. She had the gift of exclusiveness, so that it was never (as the houses of hospitable entertainers on the Continent are apt to be) abused or made common. One met the best people from every country there. Mr. Story was so exceptionally delightful and so renowned as an artist that everybody wanted to see him. He needed a wife with just such social gifts as she had. His studio on certain days could be visited, but of course every one was taught to respect his hours of work.—SHERWOOD, MARY E. W., 1897, *An Epistle to Posterity, p.* 242.

Story had above all, among his many gifts, the right sensibility, given his New England origin; the latter had left him plenty to learn, to taste, to feel and assimilate, but it had not formed him, fortunately, without a universal curiosity, a large appetite for life or a talent that yearned for exercise. Nothing, indeed, seems to me to have been more marked for envy than the particular shade of preparation . . . . involved in his natural conditions. . . . The best elements of the New England race, of its old life and its old attitude, had produced and nourished him, and it is quite, for our imagination, as if he had thus been engendered and constituted to the particular end of happily reacting from them. There are reactions that are charming, adequate, finely expressive; there are others that are excessive, extravagant, treacherous. Story's was not of the violent sort, of the sort that makes a lurid picture for biography or drama; but it was conscious and intelligent, arriving at the pleasure and escaping the pain, a revolution without a betrayal.—JAMES, HENRY, 1903, *William Wetmore Story and his Friends, vol.* I, *pp.* 13, 14.

GENERAL

His dramatic studies, of which "A Roman Lawyer in Jerusalem," "A Jewish Rabbi in Rome," and the repulsive strong "Cleopatra" are the chief, display a philosophic strength or a passionate fire rare indeed in a division of literature to which other Americans have made but feeble additions. Method and result occasionally suggest Browning, but only because the scenes and the historic thought of Italy seem naturally to have affected two minds in somewhat similar ways. A few of Story's delicate and muse-born lyrics, such as "In the Moonlight," "In the Rain," "Love and Death," and "In the Garden," are of the poet's own land—not merely Italy's but Ariel's and Endymion's. Yet, notwithstanding the manlier tone of "Io Victis" (the thought of which Holmes better sang in "The Voiceless"), and "After Many Days," Story's sweetly verbose melancholy becomes monotonous, as in all other followers of Heine save Longfellow.—RICHARDSON, CHARLES F., 1888, *American Literature,* 1607–1885, *vol.* II, *p.* 241.

"Conversations in a Studio" is not an era-maker in any sense. It purports to be the record of a series of long rambling conversations in the intervals of work, between one Mallet, who discourses, and one Belton who questions and mildly disagrees. Mallet is immediately recognizable as the author himself, and Belton is an imaginary foil invented by Mr. Story to keep himself going. But the illusion of argument is not well sustained, and if there is any disagreement in these pages it is an unrecorded one between Mr. Story and his reader. Simplicity is alike the characteristic of epigram and platitude, and both express some fundamental truth in a condensed form; but an epigram expresses truth which has been felt and not expressed,—a platitude expresses again what has been said and resaid until the world is weary. Mr. Story has always noted that line which divides the one from the other. It may be invidious to complain that he has not thundered out what he thinks in a great world-message, like the *ipse dixit* of Sartor; but it seems hardly necessary to make a book to tell us that "Shelley had a delicate and refined nature," and that Burns's "Farewell to Nancy" is "charming." It cannot be denied that Mr. Story's pen is an eminently facile one, and that he has succeeded in filling two volumes with opinions scarcely more valuable than these, and that his observations on art and literature are at times gracefully stated and nearly always amusing.—DE KOVEN, ANNA FARWELL, 1890, "*Conversations in a Studio,*" *The Dial, vol.* 10, *pp.* 330.

Those who have known that the hand which chiselled the "Cleopatra" of the 1862 Exhibition, and wrote "Roba di Roma," has also been for some years past contributing poems to sundry magazines, must have read those poems with considerable interest as they appeared from time to time; and whoever read Mr. Story's "Primitive Christian in Rome," published in *The Fortnightly Review* for December, 1866, must have been struck at once with the ability of that poem as a product of the psychological method employed by Browning. So able was that piece that it was evident 'that the author was no novice, though it was just as evident that he was not a poet of the *first* water. The poem lacked music more than anything else; but even in that it was not glaringly deficient; and, at the same time, it was so well thought out, the historic situation as well as the attitude of the speaker's mind were so well rounded off to an issue, that it was impossible not to be interested to know what hoard of such wares the author was saving up. . . . Not imitative of Browning in matters of detail, Mr. Story has yet, in the best of his poems, clearly assimilated the method of this most original and powerful of contemporary poets, and, I should say, he has consciously and studiously assimilated it—a thing which is the more to his credit, looking at the difficulty of working in that method as compared with many others.—FORMAN, H. BUXTON, 1896, *Graffiti d'Italia, Fortnightly Review*, vol. 11, pp. 118, 119.

His verse is easy, elevated and correct, but it is the verse of a sculptor with whom form is everything. It must be admitted, too, that while there is nothing in his mature verse to betray his nationality, save the occasional appearance of so-called Americanisms in his diction, he has not been without his obligation to American literature, as reflected in certain echoes of Longfellow and Holmes. Story's intellectual powers, however, were of too high an order to rest at imitation. His narratives and dialogues hold a place entirely their own in our literature. The vein of melancholy which Hawthorne was surprised to observe among Story's personal traits runs through the artist's narratives and lyrics. This tone of sadness leaves an impression of "beauty akin to pain" impossible to resist, but utterly different from the Byronic despair which afflicted the songsters of Story's youth. He is a master of expression, though his facile command of language occasionally leads to an infringement of the rule which he so felicitously announced in his "Couplets."—ONDERDONK, JAMES L., 1899-1901, *History of American Verse*, p. 231.

Thomas Henry Huxley
1825–1896

Born, at Ealing, 4 May 1825. At school there. Studied medicine at Charing Cross Hospital. M. B., London, 1845. Assistant-surgeon to H. M. S. "Victory," 1846; to H. M. S. "Rattlesnake," 1847–50. F. R. S., 1851; Medal, 1852. Prof. of Nat. Hist. at Royal School of Mines, 1854; Fullerian Prof. to Royal Institution, 1854; Examiner to London Univ., 1854. Croonian Lecturer to Royal Soc., 1858. Prof. of Comparative Anatomy to Royal Coll. of Surgeons, 1863–70. Hon. LL. D., Edinburgh, 1866. Pres. Geological Soc., 1869. Edited "Journal of the Ethnological Soc." (with G. Busk and Sir J. Lubbock), 1869–70. Pres. Ethnological Soc., 1870. Pres. British Association, 1870. Memb. of London School Board, 1870–72. Lord Rector of Aberdeen Univ., 1872–74. Sec. of Royal Soc., 1873. Wollaston Medal, Geol. Soc., 1876. Hon. LL. D., Dublin, 1878; Hon. LL. D., Cambridge, 1879; Hon. Ph. D., Breslau; Hon. M. D., Würzburg. Corresponding member of many foreign scientific bodies. Member of various scientific and educational commissions. Knight of Pole Star of Sweden. Fellow of Eton Coll., 13 May 1879, afterwards Governor. Memb. of Senate of London Univ., 29 Aug. 1883. Inspector of Salmon Fisheries, 1881–1885. Rede Lecturer, Camb., June 1883. Pres. Royal Soc., July 1883–1885. F. R. C. S., 1884. Hon. D. C. L., Oxford, 17 June 1885. Trustee of British Museum, 29 Feb. 1888. Privy Councillor, Aug. 1892. Romanes Lecturer, Oxford, May 1893. Frequent contributor to periodicals. Died, 29 June 1895. *Works:* "On the Educational Value of the Natural History Sciences," 1854; "The Oceanic Hydrozoa," 1859; "Evidence as to Man's Place in Nature," 1863; "On our Knowledge of the Causes of the Phenomena of Organic Nature," 1863; "Lectures on the Elements of Comparative Anatomy," 1864; "An Elementary Atlas of Comparative Osteology," 1864; "Catalogue of the . . . Fossils in the Museum of Practical Geology (with R. Etheridge), 1865; "Palæontologia Indica: Vertebrate Fossils," 1866; "Lessons in Elementary Physiology," 1866; "An Introduction to the Classification of Animals," 1869; "Protoplasm: the Physical Basis of Life," 1869; "Lay Sermons, Addresses, and Reviews," 1870 ("Essays," selected from preceding, 1871); "A Manual of the Anatomy of Vertebrated Animals," 1871; "On Yeast," 1872; "Critiques and Addresses," 1873; "A Course of Practical Instruction in Elementary Biology" (with H. N. Martin), 1875; "A Manual of the Anatomy of Invertebrated Animals," 1877; "American Addresses," 1877; "Physiography," 1877; "Hume," 1879; "Science Primers: Introductory," 1880; "The Crayfish," 1880; "Science and Culture," 1881; "Inaugural Address to Fishery Congress," 1883; "Essays upon some Controverted Questions," 1892; "Evolution and Ethics," 1893; "Collected Essays" (9 vols.), 1893-94. He *translated:* Koelliker's "Manual of Human Histology" (with G. Busk), 1853-54; Von Siebold's "On Tape and Cystic Worms," 1857; *edited:* Prescott's

THOMAS HENRY HUXLEY

Engraving by Swan Electric Engraving Co.   From
a Painting by Hon. John Collier

FREDERICH MAX MÜLLER

Engraving by Swan Electric Engraving Co.   From
a Photograph by London Stereoscopic Co.

"Strong Drink and Tobacco Smoke," 1869; "Science Primers" (with Prof. Roscoe and B. Stewart), 1872, etc.; and contributed prefatory notes to various scientific publications. —SHARP, R. FARQUHARSON, 1897, *A Dictionary of English Authors*, p. 143.

PERSONAL

Science seems to me to teach in the highest and strongest manner the great truth which is embodied in the Christian conception of entire surrender to the will of God. Sit down before fact as a little-child, be prepared to give up every preconceived notion, follow humbly wherever and whatever abysses nature leads, or you shall learn nothing. I have only begun to learn content and peace of mind since I have resolved at all risks to do this. —HUXLEY, THOMAS HENRY, 1860, *Letter to Charles Kingsley, Sept. 20; Life and Letters*, ed. Huxley, vol. I, p. 235.

To me his whole nature, intellectual and moral, presented a singular unity; both elements appeared to be in perfect harmony with each other, and the distinctive note of both was the combination of strength and simplicity. From this source was derived the manly dignity of his bearing, the uncompromising directness of his thought, and the enviable lucidity of his style. No subtle analysis is needed to explain his character, the beauty of which consisted in being completely natural.—BRODRICK, GEORGE C., 1895, *Professor Huxley, Fortnightly Review*, vol. 64, p. 310.

As I recall the hours spent with him, first of all the memory of his charming personality presents itself, and in this respect, no man I have ever met surpassed him. To go further and name his chief characteristics, I should place his ability, his honesty, and his courage, next in order. His marvelous ability no one will question. One qualified to judge has said, that, in his intellectual grasp, Huxley was the greatest man of the century. His honesty, in the broadest sense of the word, was the dominant feature of the man. His love of truth for its own sake, wherever it might lead him, was one of the strongest elements in his character, and this resulted not only in his well-known intellectual honesty, but also in his hatred of the opposite, wherever found. His courage, especially the courage of his convictions, is known to all, and has borne good fruits. Every man of science to-day is indebted to Huxley for no small part of the intellectual freedom he enjoys.—MARSH, O. C., 1895, *Thomas Henry Huxley, American Journal of Science*, vol. 150, p. 183.

On the platform Mr. Huxley was a commanding figure. He had in him the gift of oratory, had he cared to cultivate it. . . . I used always to admire the simple and business-like way in which Huxley made his entry on great occasions. He hated anything like display, and would have none of it. . . . The square forehead, the square jaw, the tense lines of the mouth, the deep flashing dark eyes, the impression of something more than strength he gave you, an impression of sincerity, of solid force, of immovability, yet of the gentleness arising from the serene consciousness of his strength. . . . The hair swept carelessly away from the broad forehead and grew rather long behind, yet the length did not suggest, as it often does, effeminacy. He was masculine in everything—look, gesture, speech.—SMALLEY, GEORGE W., 1895, *Mr. Huxley, Scribner's Magazine*, vol. 18, pp. 520, 521.

I shall best describe the impression Huxley made on me by contrasting it with the general idea which I, in common no doubt with many another, had formed of him. He always wrote, as Darwin has said, with his pen dipped in *aqua fortis*, and one naturally conceived of him as a combative and even as an aggressive man. Moreover the layman's idea of the professional man of science generally includes something of the pedantic. One anticipates that his conversation, however instructive, will deal largely with every technical subject in very technical language. Again, the tone of some of the essays to which I have referred was unquestionably Voltairian. All the greater was my surprise to find the three elements of pugilist, pedant, and scoffer not only not prominent, but conspicuous by their absence. In their place was a personality of singular charm. External gifts of manner and presence, and powers of general conversation which would have ensured popularity to any mere man of the world, were combined with those higher endowments—including great breadth of culture as well as the acquirements of a distinguished specialist—to which no mere man of the world could aspire. . . . His appearance is well known. Above the middle height, the white hair without parting brushed straight back, the lips firm and slightly compressed; a very mobile expression; and I would add (what the current photographs do not represent), eyes full of fire, rather deep-set beneath bushy eyebrows, and a look of keenest interest in all around him, often of great wistfulness. Both in his manner and in his appearance there was marked distinction and dignity. The general impression left by his face was certainly one of intellectual force and activity rather than of scorn. His conversation was singularly finished and (if I may so express it) cleancut; never long winded or prosy; enlivened by vivid illustrations.—WARD, WILFRED, 1896, *Thomas Henry Huxley, Nineteenth Century, vol.* 40, p. 276.

It was on the 22d of February, 1859, that I was introduced to him in the Palæontological and Mineral Gallery of the British Museum in Great Russell Street, by the then keeper of that department. . . . Huxley was then in his thirty-fourth year. He had a well-knit, strong frame, rather tall than short, with deep-set dark eyes, bright and full of expression. His hair was black and rather long, and he wore whiskers, his chin and upper lip being shorn. His manner was dignified with a slight reserve, yet, withal, kindly, even at this first interview. . . . Two characteristics specially struck me. The first was remarkable mobility of his countenance—the way in which his face would "light up," and the rapid changes of expression it could assume as the character of the conversation changed. The second was the frankness and fulness with which his judgments about certain problems were expressed.—MIVART, ST. GEORGE, 1897, *Some Reminiscences of Thomas Henry Huxley, Nineteenth Century, vol.* 42, p. 988.

Like the old Greek sage and statesman, my father might have declared that old age found him ever learning. Not indeed with the fiery earnestness of his young days of stress and storm; but with the steady advance of a practised worker who cannot be unoccupied. History and philosophy, especially biblical criticism, composed his chief reading in these [1892] later years. Fortune had ceased her buffets; broken health was restored; and from his resting-place among his books and his plants he watched keenly the struggle which had now passed into other hands, still ready to strike a blow if need be, or even, on rare occasions, to return to the fighting line, as when he became a leader in the movement for London University reform. His days at Eastbourne, then, were full of occupation, if not the occupation of former days. The day began as early; he never relaxed from the rule of an eight o'clock breakfast. Then a pipe and an hour and a half of letter-writing or working at an essay. Then a short expedition around the garden. . . . Then would follow another spell of work till near one o'clock; the weather might tempt him out again before lunch; but afterwards he was certain to be out for an hour or two from half-past two. However hard it blew, and Eastbourne is seldom still, the tiled walk along the seawall always offered the possibility of a constitutional. But the high expanse of the Downs was his favourite walk. . . . After his walk, a cup of tea was followed by more reading or writing till seven; after dinner another pipe, and then he would return to my mother in the drawing-room, and settle down in his particular arm-chair, with some tough volume of history or theology to read, every now and again scoring a passage for future reference, or jotting a brief note on the margin. At ten he would migrate to the study for a final smoke before going to bed.—HUXLEY, LEONARD, 1900, ed. *Life and Letters of Thomas Henry Huxley, vol.* II, pp. 468, 469.

It is not only because we, many of us, loved him as a friend, not only because we all of us recognize him as a great naturalist, but also because he was a great example to us all, a man who did his best to benefit the people, that we are here to do honor to his memory to-day.—AVEBURY, LORD, 1900, *Huxley Memorial Lecture, Anthropological Institute,* Nov. 13; *Popular Science Monthly, vol.* 58, p. 359.

Huxley was of middle stature and rather slender build. His face, as Professor Ray Lankester described it, was "grave, black-browed, and fiercely earnest." His hair, plentiful and worn rather long, was black until in old age it became silvery white. He wore short side whiskers, but shaved the rest of his face, leaving fully exposed an obstinate chin, and mobile lips, grim and resolute in repose, but capable of relaxation into a smile of almost feminine charm.

He was a very hard worker and took little exercise. Professor Howes describes a typical day as occupied by lecture and laboratory work at the College of Science until his hurried luncheon; then a cab-drive to the Home Office for his work as Inspector of Fisheries; then a cab home for an hour's work before dinner, and the evening after dinner spent in literary work or scientific reading. While at work, his whole attention was engrossed, and he disliked being disturbed. . . . He was devoted to music, regarding it as one of the highest of the æsthetic pleasures. . . . He had a hot temper, and did not readily brook opposition, especially when that seemed to him to be the result of stupidity or of prejudice rather than of reason, and his own reason was of a very clear, decided, and exact order.—MITCHELL, P. CHALMERS, 1900, *Thomas Henry Huxley (Leaders in Science), pp.* 278, 279.

Huxley was above all things a man absolutely simple and natural; he never posed, was never starched, or prim, or on his good behavior; and he was nothing if not playful. . . . If absolute loyalty to truth, involving complete self-abnegation in the face of the evidence, be the ideal aim of the scientific inquirer, there have been few men in whom that ideal has been so perfectly realized as in Huxley. If ever he were tempted by some fancied charm of speculation to swerve a hair's breadth from the strict line of fact, the temptation was promptly slaughtered and made no sign. For intellectual integrity he was a spotless Sir Galahad. I believe there was nothing in life which he dreaded so much as the sin of allowing his reason to be hoodwinked by personal predilections, or whatever Francis Bacon would have called "idols of the cave."—FISKE, JOHN, 1901, *Reminiscences of Huxley, Atlantic Monthly, vol.* 87, *pp.* 275, 280.

As a lecturer he was simply perfect: clear, incisive, illuminating, admirably adapting his words to the calibre of his audience. If he and I had sparring matches in the press or face to face, it was only an incident which I shared in common with others of every school and of any opinion. Huxley was a born controversialist,—"a first-class fighting man,"—whether the subject was science, theology, or metaphysics, and his skill as a debater has no doubt given a somewhat artificial rank to his purely scientific work. Personally, as his letters and the memoir by his son would show, he was a brilliant companion, and if the objects of his attacks were seldom delighted with his vivacity, his many friends and the bystanders greatly enjoyed it. He would fly at a Positivist with even more zest than at a bishop; nor did he always observe the rule laid down by Justice Stephen, one of his colleagues in the Metaphysical Society, that "dog should not bite dog!" Huxley was always ready to go for mastiff, bulldog, or terrier. He was proud of having added the term Agnostic to the language of philosophy; and he never seemed to learn that no mere negative could be a title worthy of a serious philosopher.—HARRISON, FREDERIC, 1901, *George Washington and other American Addresses, p.* 204.

In spite of the immense amount of work he contrived to perform, Huxley never enjoyed robust health after the accidental poisoning already mentioned. Fresh air and some daily exercise were necessary in order to ward off digestive difficulties, accompanied by lassitude and depression of a severe kind; but fresh air and exercise are the most difficult of all things for a busy man in London to obtain. The evil effects of a sedentary life had shown themselves at the very beginning of his work in London, and they increased year by year. At the end of 1871 he was forced to take a long holiday; but this produced only a temporary improvement, and finally symptoms of cardiac mischief became too evident to be neglected. For this reason he gave up his public work in 1885, and in 1890 he finally left London, living thenceforward at Eastbourne.—WELDON, W. F. R., 1901, *Dictionary of National Biography, Supplement, vol.* III, *p.* 30.

Beyond all doubt he never had any organic disease; the supposed dilation of the heart was even laughed at by Sir Henry Thompson a few years before his death. And yet from the age of fourteen he was a great sufferer. . . . Huxley's eye-strain symptoms correspond in a general way to those of others but with the inevitable differences and peculiarities of all biologic phenomena. We must remember that his extraordinary energy of mind and body gave him noteworthy powers of resistance and recuperation. This demonstrates all the more convincingly the single nature and cause of his sufferings. The immediate cessation of the effects of eyestrain when he walked from ten to sixteen miles a day, or climbed mountains, or tramped the moors, shows at once the natural ruggedness and health of all his organs, and the single cause of his ill-health.—GOULD, GEORGE M., 1902, *Biographical Clinics*, pp. 114, 119.

Darwin realized to the full the essential strength of Mr. Huxley's nature; he knew, as all the world now knows, the delicate sense of honour of his friend, and he was ever inclined to lean on his guidance in practical matters, as on an elder brother.—DARWIN, FRANCIS, 1903, ed. *More Letters of Charles Darwin*, vol. I, p. 71.

GENERAL

No man is more disliked and dreaded by the orthodox than Thomas Huxley. . . . It would be wrong to regard Huxley merely as a scientific man. He is likewise a literary man, a writer. What he writes would be worth reading for its style and its expression alone, were it of no scientific authority; whereas we all know perfectly well that scientific men generally are read only for the sake of what they teach, and not at all because of their manner of teaching it. Huxley is a fascinating writer, and has a happy way of pressing continually into the service of strictly scientific exposition illustrations caught from literature and art—even from popular and light literature.—MCCARTHY, JUSTIN, 1872, *Science and Orthodoxy in England, Modern Leaders*, pp. 237, 238.

Huxley's works on the comparative anatomy of the Vertebrata are the only ones which can be compared with the otherwise incomparable investigations of Carl Gegenbaur. These two enquiries exhibit, particularly in their peculiar scientific development, many points of relationship. . . . More important than any of the individual discoveries which are contained in Huxley's numerous less and greater researches on the most widely different animals are the profound and truly philosophical conceptions which have guided him in his inquiries, have always enabled him to distinguish the essential from the unessential, and to value special empirical facts chiefly as a means of arriving at general ideas. Those views of the two germinal layers of animals which were published as early as 1849 belong to the most important generalisations of comparative anatomy. . . . His treatment of the celebrated vertebral theory of the skull, in which he first opened out the right track, following which Carl Gegenbaur has recently solved in so brilliant a manner this important problem, and above all his exposition of the Theory of Descent and its consequences, belong to this class. After Charles Darwin had, in 1859, reconstructed this most important biological theory, and by his epoch-making theory of Natural Selection placed it on an entirely new foundation, Huxley was the first who extended it to man, and in 1863, in his celebrated three Lectures on "Man's Place in Nature," admirably worked out its most important developments.—HAECKEL, ERNST, 1874, *Scientific Worthies, Nature*, vol. 9, p. 258.

Whenever Professor Huxley enters on the defence of his science, as distinguished from the exposition of it, there are traces in his language of the *gaudium certaminis* which has found expression in so many hard-fought fields in his own country, and which has made him perhaps the most formidable antagonist, in so far as dialectics go, that the transcendental philosophers have ever encountered. He is, *par excellence*, a fighting man, but certainly his pugnacity diminishes neither his worth nor his capacity.—GODKIN, E. L., 1876, *Professor Huxley's Lectures, The Nation*, vol. 23, p. 193.

Huxley is an able, well-read, industrious, and conscientious biologist, and has a boldness of utterance and an instinct in favor of fair dealing and equal rights, along with a genuine hatred of humbug and superstition. If his argument for evolution is inconclusive, the fault is in the theory rather than in its advocate, who has given the best possible presentation of it in the space at his command, and on the line of argument which he adopted.—DAWSON, J. W., 1877, *Professor Huxley in New York, International Review*, vol. 4, p. 50.

Professor Huxley has now, in this work on Hume, given his own philosophy, which is substantially that of Hume and James Mill, with some not very valuable suggestions from Bain, and a criticism now and then derived from Descartes and Kant, of whose profounder principles he has in the meanwhile no appreciation. It is expounded in the form of an epitome of the system of the Scottish sceptic with constantly interspersed criticisms of his own.

His style is not that usually supposed to be philosophic; it is not calm or serene or dignified; but it clearly expresses his meaning, and it is graphic, living, and leaping. He shows everywhere great acuteness, and the shrewdness of one who is not to be taken in by show and pretension, or awed by authority. No man is quicker in starting an objection, which, however, may be of a surface character, and not penetrating into the heart of the subject. I can not discover in his speculations the calmness of one who is waiting for light, or the comprehension of one who goes round the object examined and views it on all sides.—Mc-COSH, JAMES, 1879, *Agnosticism as Developed in Huxley's Hume, Popular Science Monthly, vol.* 15, *p.* 478.

Professor Huxley is always an interesting writer, whatever may be his theme. He never fails to be clear and forcible, and he is usually both vivacious and amusing. It is true, his positiveness makes him defiant and contemptuous of men and opinions of whom and of which he has very little knowledge, and ought to say little or nothing. . . . Professor Huxley may not inaptly be styled the William Cobbett of our current philosophical radicalism. He is like Cobbett in acuteness, directess, humor, and earthliness. He is like Cobbett in the clearness, directness, and vigor of his style. Above all, he is like Cobbett in being never weary of "having a fling at the parsons." . . . We appreciate and enjoy Professor Huxley's acuteness and wit, without a thought of whom or what he strikes; but we cannot enjoy his superficial ignorance or shallow appreciation of considerations to which men of the highest rank in the world of thought have attached supreme importance. — PORTER, NOAH, 1879-81, *Professor Huxley's Exposition of Hume's Philosophy, Science and Sentiment, pp.* 293, 329.

The eye is as clear for seeing and the arm as strong for hitting as they have always been, and on every page ["Science and Culture"] we meet with new instances of that same versatility of learning, force of thought, and brilliancy of style which, while producing so wide an influence on the science and philosophy of our time, have justly placed this distinguished leader of both in a class *sui generis* as an expositor.— ROMANES, GEORGE J., 1882, *Professor Huxley's Essays, Nature, vol.* 25, *p.* 333.

On the subject of natural law, especially in its relation to ethics, I owe more to Professor Huxley than to any one else. He has been the first to state with perfect clearness the true relation of man to nature, and though his statement of the case is neither devotional nor enthusiastic it disengages us from what is untenable in natural religion and sets human ethics on a higher plane. I value especially his Romanes Lecture of 1893.—HAMERTON, PHILIP GILBERT, 1894, *The Chief Influences on my Career, The Forum, vol.* 18, *p.* 424.

Writes in a manner rather awkward and clumsy ["Science and Christian Tradition"]; he jokes a great deal, but "wi' deeficulty," and, much as he writes about demonology, I see in him no signs of a technical acquaintance with the subject, or of wide reading in a theme which, as Littré says, has been most sketchily treated.— LANG, ANDREW, 1894, *The Month in England, The Cosmopolitan, vol.* 17, *p.* 504.

Professor Huxley loved to throw down the glove to those who seemed to him to bar the way against the exploring genius of a very daring nature. But, none the less, he had that in him which often spurred him on to renounce his own most cherished canons of judgment and most approved repudiations of faith. Before that unseen player, whom he recognized as so utterly unknown and unknowable that he contrasted him almost scornfully with the God of Christian creeds, he sometimes invited us all to bow our heads in acts of true adoration. And so long as he could combine his love of Christ with some sort of defiance of conventional Christianity, he did not hesitate to prostrate himself before the Being whose normal nature subdued him into a feeling of awe for which he could find no adequate utterance, and in the presence of which, physical wonders lost their impressiveness, and the ethics of tribunal evolution, to which he subscribed, found themselves so utterly bereft of all sublimity, that they seemed the pallid ghosts of the vision and the thought of Christ.—HUTTON, RICHARD H., 1895, *Professor Huxley, The Forum, vol.* 20, *p.* 32.

I entertain the most sincere admiration for Professor Huxley. I admire him as a passed-master of his craft; as a man in the foremost ranks of science; as a consummate reasoner; as an indefatigable worker and a fearless controversialist. Few things have given me greater pleasure than the reading of his "Essays on Controverted Questions." As an evolutionist and agnostic I find myself in harmony with his teaching. In a word, I may venture to call myself a humble disciple of Professor Huxley.—GREENWOOD, GEORGE G., 1895, *Professor Huxley on Hume and Berkeley, Westminster Review*, vol. 144, p. 1.

His eagerness to penetrate the deeper mysteries may perhaps have sometimes led him astray; while his superficial acquaintance with some subjects on which he professed to make authoritative statements, exposed him to the severe criticism which he occasionally merited and received from Owen and other contemporaries. But his influence on progress cannot be measured solely by his own writings. He inspired many younger workers, by his personal example and advice, to follow the same line of research; and he left the Geological Survey well equipped with an accomplished naturalist, who has worthily followed in his footsteps.—WOODWARD, A. SMITH, 1895, *Huxley: As Palæontologist and Geologist, Natural Science*, vol. 7, p. 128.

Like other great biologists whose career was opened by an exploring expedition, Huxley had an early view of the varieties of mankind which turned his mind with keen interest to Anthropology. The time when his influence was rising to its full height in the scientific world, was in England full of difficulty as well as promise to the systematic study of man, and at this critical period he was able to render services not to be forgotten. . . . It need hardly be said that Huxley, a scientific fighter if there ever was one, was in his element in resisting any attempt to overbear the new Anthropology by philosophical declamation or claim of authority.—TYLOR, E. B., 1895, *Professor Huxley as Anthropologist, Fortnightly Review*, vol. 64, pp. 311, 312.

There has not been by any means a unanimous expression among liberal people of admiration for Huxley. He trod on the theoretical toes of various schools of freethinkers; he repudiated the materialistic as well as the Christian flag, the atheistic along with the theistic; he would not join the Liberationists to disestablish the Church, and he held ideas of the parental functions of the State, which, while they offended the anti-vaccinationists and individualists, fell short of the friendship of socialists. Myself a personal-liberty man, I dissent strongly from some of his sociology. But what of that? All of these differentiations represent the man. That was Huxley. Had he been able to work in any harness, or bear any label, he would have been another man; and though the favored clan might have rejoiced in a powerful chief, the empire of thought would never have known its unique figure, its finest free lance. You who see, or think you see, faults in a great man, remember the profound truth of Shakespeare: "Best men are moulded out of faults."—CONWAY, MONCURE DANIEL, 1895, *Huxley, Open Court*, vol. 9, p. 4712.

The history of scientific progress has been marked by a few periods of intellectual fermentation when great bounds have been taken forward and a complete revolution ensued. Very few have been such, but in one the name of Huxley must be ever conspicuous. It was as a lieutenant of the organizer of that revolution that he appeared, but unquestionably without him it would have been long delayed, and it was through his brilliant powers of exposition that the peoples of the English-speaking lineage soon learned to understand, to some extent, what evolution was and, learning, to accept it.—GILL, THEODORE, 1896, *Huxley and his Work, Smithsonian Report*, 1895, Pt. I, p. 759.

A great number of brilliant essays and lectures were composed by him on different parts of what may be called the debatable land between science, philosophy, and theology. And one of his most characteristic and masterly single studies was a little book on Hume, contributed to the series of "English Men of Letters" in 1879. This varied, copious, and brilliant polemic may or may not have been open in substance to the charge which the bolder and more thorough-going defenders of orthodoxy brought against it, that it committed the logical error of demanding submission on the part of supernaturalism to laws and limits to which, by its very essence, supernaturalism disclaimed allegiance. But the form of it was excellent. Mr. Huxley had read much, and had borrowed weapons and armour from more than one Schoolman and Father as well as from purely profane authors. He had an admirable style, free alike from the great faults of his contemporaries, "preciousness" and slipshodness, and a knack of crisp but not too mannered phrase recalling that of Swift or, still more, of Bentley.—SAINTSBURY, GEORGE, 1896, *A History of Nineteenth Century Literature,* p. 416.

It is of the utmost interest to trace the influence of Darwin upon Huxley, his great General in the numerous controversial battles which had to be fought before the new views were to secure a fair hearing and, at length, complete success. Now that we are quietly enjoying the fruit of his many victories, we are apt to forget how much we owe to Huxley, not only for evolution, but for that perfect freedom in the expression of thought and opinion which we enjoy. For Huxley fought on wider issues than those raised by evolution, wide as these are; and with a success so great that it is inconceivable that any new and equally illuminating thought which the future may hold in store for us, will meet with a reception like that accorded to the "Origin of Species."—POULTON, EDWARD B., 1896, *Charles Darwin and the Theory of Natural Selection,* p. 119.

Professor Huxley's Romanes Lecture on "Evolution and Ethics" deservedly attracted a large amount of attention on its appearance. That attention was due not only to the importance of the subject handled and the reputation of the lecturer, but quite as much to the breadth and scope of the treatment, to the nobility of tone and the deep human feeling which characterised a singularly impressible utterance. Popular interest was also excited by the nature of the conclusion reached, which in the mouth of the pioneer and prophet of evolution, had the air of being something like a palinode. Criticisms of the lecture appeared at the time by Mr. Leslie Stephen in the "Contemporary Review," and by Mr. Herbert Spencer in a letter to the "Athenæum;" and many discussions appeared in theological quarters. But the subject as a whole was perhaps dismissed from public attention before its significance had been exhausted, or indeed properly grasped. Professor Huxley's argument and the criticisms it called forth illuminate most instructively some deep-seated ambiguities of philosophical terminology, and at the same time bring into sharp relief the fundamental difference of standpoint which divides philosophical thinkers. The questions at issue, moreover, are not merely speculative, already they cast their shadow upon literature and life.—SETH, ANDREW, 1897, *Man's Place in the Cosmos,* p. 1.

Huxley produced so great an effect on the world as an expositor of the ways and needs of science in general, and of the claims of Darwinism in particular, that some, dwelling on this are apt to overlook the immense value of his direct original contributions to exact science. The present volume and its successors will, we trust, serve to take away all excuse for such a mistaken view of Huxley's place in the history of biological science. They show that quite beyond and apart from the influence exerted by his popular writings, the progress of biology during the present century was largely due to labours of his of which the general public knew nothing, and that he was in some respects the most original and most fertile in discovery of all his fellow-workers in the same branch of science. —FOSTER, MICHAEL, AND LANKESTER, E. RAY, 1898, ed. *The Scientific Memoirs of Thomas Henry Huxley, Preface,* vol. I, p. 6.

Huxley's lifelong devotion to the task of teaching the right method of using our reason in the search for truth has been so fruitful that the success or failure of his attempts to teach the application of this method to specific problems is a matter of very subordinate importance. As he was not only a man and a citizen, but, above all, a naturalist, peculiar interest attaches to his utterances on the problems of biology, although his various essays on this subject differ so much in perspective that their effect upon many thoughtful readers has proved to be practically equivalent to inconsistency. It is easy to show that, in this case, as in others, the responsibility rests with the reader and not with the author.—BROOKS, WILLIAM KEITH, 1899, *The Foundation of Zoölogy,* pp. 30, 35.

Probably the most influential disciple and exponent of the theory of descent was the great English zoologist, Thomas Huxley. . . . Huxley's palæontological works, like those of Gaudry and Cope, are mostly devoted to the vertebrate animals, and are distinguished by his remarkable acuteness of observation and his genius for inductive combination. His determination of the genealogy of the horse, his elucidation of the genetic relations of birds and reptiles, his memoir on Crossopterygia, are among the classical productions of palæontological and zoological science.—VON ZITTEL, KARL ALFRED, 1899-1901, *History of Geology and Palæontology to the End of the Nineteenth Century,* tr. *Ogilvie-Gordon, p.* 381.

Huxley's resolution to be strictly logical and to be clear before anything only forces him to exert his powers of vivifying the subject by happy illustration or humorous side-lights, or sometimes by outbursts of hearty pugnacity, and now and then by the eloquent passages, the more effective because under strict control, which reveal his profound sense of the vast importance of the questions at issue. He had one disadvantage as compared with Swift. If Swift wanted a fact, he had not many scruples about inventing it, whereas Huxley's most prominent intellectual quality was his fidelity to fact, or to what he was firmly convinced to be fact. . . . He was not an indiscriminate philanthropist; he hated a rogue and did not love a fool; and he held that both genera were pretty numerous. But he was a most heartily loyal citizen; doing manfully the duties which came his way and declining no fair demand upon his co-operation. . . . Men of science have their weaknesses and temptations. They are not always more free than their literary brethren from petty jealousies and unworthy lust for notoriety. Huxley's life shows an admirable superiority to such weaknesses. His battles, numerous as they were, never led to the petty squabbles which disfigure some scientific lives. Nobody was ever a more loyal friend.—STEPHEN, LESLIE, 1900, *Thomas Henry Huxley, Nineteenth Century, vol.* 48, *pp.* 908, 916, 917.

Huxley's work has been incorporated in the very body of science. A large number of later investigators have advanced upon the lines he laid down; and just as the superstructures of a great building conceal the foundations, so later anatomical work, although it has only amplified and extended Huxley's discoveries, has made them seem less striking to the modern reader. The present writer, for instance, learned all he knows of anatomy in the last ten years, and until he turned to it for the purpose of this volume he had never referred to Huxley's original paper. When he did so, he found from beginning to end nothing that was new to him, nothing that was strange: all the ideas in the memoir had passed into the currency of knowledge and he had been taught them as fundamental facts. It was only when he turned to the text-books of anatomy and natural history current in Huxley's time that he was able to realise how the conclusions of the young ship-surgeon struck the Fellows and President of the Royal Society as luminous and revolutionary ideas. . . . Huxley was a wide and omnivorous reader, and so had an unusually large fund of words at his disposal. His writings abound with quotations and allusions taken from the best English authors, and he had a profound and practical belief in the advantage to be gained from the reading of English. . . . Huxley's style was a style of ideas and not of words and sentences. The more closely you analyse his pages the more certainly you find that the secret of the effect produced on you lies in the gradual development of the precise and logical ideas he wished to convey, in the brilliant accumulation of argument upon argument, in the logical subordination of details to the whole, in fact, in the arts of the convinced, positive, and logical thinker.—MITCHELL, P. CHALMERS, 1900, *Thomas Henry Huxley (Leaders in Science), pp.* 34, 214, 216.

Approaching what we may term the problem of Huxley by the way of such an account of his work as Mr. Mitchell has set forth, the reader will find his way to the true value of the letters which give an inner view of a wonderfully active and efficient life. Probably no other man of action, so far as his intimate relations are concerned, has ever been more faithfully portrayed or would leave a nobler impression of his essential quality. After reading this evidently incomplete collection of hastily written letters, none of them bearing the least sign that they were meant for more than the moment's use, the reader will find that he has been in the presence of a singularly strong personality. He is likely to feel that the man who wrote them was in his nature a true builder; one of those who send their influence far. Those who knew Huxley and watched his activities could not help seeing past the commonplace effects with which his endless controversies surrounded him, that he was one of the larger figures of his century.—SHALER, N. S., 1901, *Huxley's Life and Letters, The Critic, vol.* 38, *p.* 253.

To regard Huxley as a compound of

WILLIAM MORRIS

Engraving by Walker & Boutall. From a Photograph by F. Hollyer.

GEORGE DU MAURIER

Engraving from a Photograph.

Boanerges and Iconoclast is to show entire misapprehension of the aims which inspired his labours. In Biology his discovery of the structor of the Medusæ laid the foundations of modern zoology; his theory of the origin of the skull gave a firm basis to vertebrate morphology; and his luminous exposition of the pedigree of man imported order where confusion had reigned. In the more important matter of Education he formulated principles whose adoption would bring out the best that is in every scholar, and inspire him with love of whatever "is of good report;" while his invention of the laboratory system of zoological teaching has been adopted with the best results in every school and university of repute.—CLODD, EDWARD, 1902, *Thomas Henry Huxley, p.* 245.

In many minds the name of Huxley has for its most prominent association *controversialism;* and though his constructive work was far more important, there is no denying that he spent no small part of his time and energy in fighting, and that he thoroughly enjoyed it. He was the champion of the scientific point of view, as contrasted with the metaphysical or the thelogical; he looked forward to the time when the scientific interpretation "will organize itself into a coherent system, embracing human life and the world as one harmonious whole," but we misunderstand his controversialism if we forget the motive that prompted it—"the fanaticism of veracity." Whether we consider his famous duel with Bishop Wilberforce at the British Association meeting in 1860, or his criticism of Owen, or his battles with the bishops and Mr. Gladstone, or any other of the many controversies, we cannot but feel that they express no merely polemical spirit but that of an earnest truth-seeker who hit hard out of conviction, who never sought to destroy without also replacing. Huxley's style is especially distinguished by lucidity, accuracy, and force; and no small part of the wide extension of scientific interest has been due to its charm.— THOMSON, J. ARTHUR, 1903, *Chambers's Cyclopædia of English Literature, ed. Patrick, vol.* III, *p.* 617.

—— ——

William Morris
1834–1896

Born, at Walthamstow, 24 March, 1834. At Marlborough Coll., Feb. 1848 to Dec. 1851. Matric. Exeter Coll., Oxford, 2 June 1852; B. A., 1856; M. A., 1875; Hon. Fellow, 1882. Founded "Oxford and Cambridge Mag.," 1856. For some time after leaving Oxford studied painting and architecture. Married Jane Burden, 26 April 1859. Started manufactory of artistic house decorations and implements, 1863. Lectured on art in Birmingham, London and Nottingham, 1878-81. Contrib. to various periodicals. In later years, active in support of Socialist doctrines. Started Kelmscott Press, 1891. Died, in London, 3 Oct. 1896. *Works* (exclusive of various broadsides and single sheets printed for distribution): "Sir Galahad," 1858; "The Defence of Guenevere," 1858; "The Life and Death of Jason," 1867; "The Earthly Paradise" (3 vols.), 1868 [1868-70]; "Love is Enough," 1873 [1872]; "The Two Sides of The River, etc." (priv. ptd.), 1876; "The Story of Sigurd the Volsung," 1877 [1876]; "The Decorative Arts," [1878]; "Hopes and Fears for Art," 1882; "Art and Socialism," 1884; "Textile Fabrics," 1884; "A Summary of the Principles of Socialism" (with H. M. Hyndman), 1884; "For Whom shall we Vote?" (anon.), [1884]; "Chants for Socialists," 1885; "Useful Work v. Useless Toil," 1885; "The Manifesto of the Socialist League," 1885; "A Short Account of the Commune of Paris" (with E. B. Bax), 1886; "The God of the Poor" [1886]; "The Labour Question from the Socialist Standpoint," 1886; "The Aims of Art," 1887; "Alfred Linnell," 1887; "The Tables Turned," 1887; "A Dream of John Ball," 1888; "True and False Society," 1888; "Signs of Change," 1888; "A Tale of the House of the Wolfings," 1889; "The Roots of the Mountains," 1890 [1889]; "Monopoly," 1890; "News from Nowhere," 1891 [1890]; "Poems by the Way," 1891; "The Story of the Glittering Plain," 1891; "A King's Lesson," 1891; "Under an Elm Tree," 1891; "The Socialist Ideal of Art," 1891; "Addresses" [at Birmingham Art Gallery], 1891; "The Reward of Labour" [1892]; "Gothic Architecture," 1893; "Socialism (with E. B. Bax), 1893; "The Wood beyond the World," 1894; "Letters on Socialism" (priv. ptd.), 1894; "Concerning Westminster Abbey" (anon.), [1894]; "Child Christopher," 1895,

"The Well at the World's End," 1896; "The Water of the Wondrous Isles," 1897. He *translated:* "Grettis Saga" (with M. E. Magnusson), 1869; "Völsunga Saga" (with M. E. Magnusson), 1870; "Three Northern Love-Stories" (with M. E. Magnusson), 1875; Virgil's "Æneid," 1876 [1875]; Homer's "Odyssey," 1887; "The Saga Library" (with M. E. Magnusson; 5 vols.), 1891-95; "The Order of Chivalry," 1892-93; "Of the Friendship of Amis and Amile," 1894; "The Tale of Beowulf" (with A. J. Wyatt), 1895; "Old French Romances," 1896; and *edited:* "Arts and Crafts Essays," 1893. *Collected Works:* "Poetical Works," 1896.—SHARP, R. FARQUHARSON, 1897, *A Dictionary of English Writers,* p. 205.

PERSONAL

You would think him one of the finest little fellows alive—with a touch of the incoherent, but a real man. . . . Morris means to be an architect, and to that end has set about becoming a painter, at which he is making progress. In all illumination and work of that kind he is quite unrivalled by anything modern that I know—Ruskin says, better than anything ancient.—ROSSETTI, DANTE GABRIEL, 1856, *Letters to William Allingham,* p. 193.

In making the personal acquaintance of one whose artistic work is familiar and admirable to us, the main interest must ever be to trace the subtle, elusive connection between the man and his creation. In the case of Mr. Morris, at first sight, nothing can be more contradictory than the "dreamer of dreams born out of his due time," and the practical business man and eager student of social questions who successfully directs the Surrey factory and the London shop. Little insight is required, however, soon to find beneath this thoroughly healthy exterior the most impersonal and objective English poet of our generation. The conspicuous feature of his conversation and character is the total absence of egoism, and we search in vain through his voluminous writings for that morbid habit of introspection which gives the keynote to nineteenth-century literature.—LAZARUS, EMMA, 1886, *A Day in Surrey with William Morris, Century Magazine,* vol. 32, p. 394.

Morris's figure is the most picturesque in prosaic England. A stout, sturdy, stalwart man, with ruddy face, who looks frankly out upon the world with bright blue eyes. His grand, massive head is covered with a shock of gray hair, tumbled about in wild disorder, while upper lip (which is short) and chin are covered with gray mustache and beard. He is always clad in the same fashion when I see him; a black slouch hat, black sack coat, and a most picturesque blue shirt with collar to match. In winter time he envelopes himself in a thick, dark Inverness cape. A lady informed me that the poet had taken her in to dinner at a party in irreproachable evening dress; but I have never seen him in that conventional garb, and have no wish to. Many years ago he sat accidentally upon his silk hat and crushed it; he has never worn one since. His subsequent career may be said to have consisted, metaphorically speaking, in the crushing of silk hats generally, as well as all other symbols of our artificial society. Not even Shelley or Whitman is a more unconventional figure than is Morris. His very aspect is a perpetual challenge to all that is smug and respectable and genteel.—CLARKE, WILLIAM, 1891, *William Morris, Poet, Artist, Socialist, Ed. Lee, Introduction,* p. 4.

William Morris came, too—he who divides his time, now, between writing poems that will live, and planning decorations for houses for other people to live in —and with him came his wife, whose beauty he sang and Rossetti painted, till she became part of the literary history of the Victorian epoch. She was "divinely tall," this "daughter of the gods," and by many accounted the most "divinely fair" woman of her time. She is a striking figure yet, with her remarkable height and her equally remarkable grace, her deep eyes, her heavy, dark hair, and her full, sensitive red lips.— MOULTON, LOUISE CHANDLER, 1894, *Arthur O'Shaughnessy, His Life and His Work, with Selections from his Poems,* p. 16.

A skald, a viking indeed, was William Morris. I have never met any man who gave an impression of more exhaustless vitality. There never was a man who lived a fuller life; he was the very incarnation of ceaseless mental and bodily energy. . . . In his personality and views, Morris might be spoken of as Shelley translated into a viking. He was like Trelawney in one thing—that his appearance suggested to the stranger the mien and manner of a sea-captain. When people who knew nothing of the poet save as the author of "The Earthly Paradise" had their attention directed to him, they could hardly believe that, in the robust, square-set, ruddy-faced, blue-eyed, pilot-coated, blue-shirted, sea-captain-looking man, they beheld "the idle dreamer of an empty day."—SHARP, WILLIAM, 1896, *William Morris: the Man and his Work, Atlantic Monthly, vol.* 78, *pp.* 768, 772.

Few men seemed to drink so full a measure of life as William Morris, and, indeed, he frankly admitted in his last days that he *had* enjoyed his life. I have heard him say that he only knew what it was to be alive. . . . William Morris was a singularly sane and what is called a "level-headed" man. He had the vehemence, on occasion, of a strong nature and powerful physique. He cared greatly for his convictions. Art and life were real to him, and his love of beauty was a passion. His artistic and poetic vision was clear and intense—all the more so, perhaps, for being exclusive on some points. The directness of his nature, as of his speech, might have seemed singularly unmodern to some who prefer to wrap their meaning with many envelopes. He might occasionally have seemed brusque, and even rough; but so does the north wind when it encounters obstacles.—CRANE, WALTER, 1897, *William Morris, Scribner's Magazine, vol.* 22, *pp.* 88, 98.

William Morris deserves high praise for his attempts to put typography back in its proper field. He seems to have been the first of moderns to see that typography was a manly art that could stand on its own legs without crutches lent by sister arts, and that it should be treated and clothed in manly fashion. . . . About the mechanical merit of his work there can be no difference of opinion. For an amateur in difficult trades, his workmanship is surprising, if not unexampled. A prominent American typefounder, who has closely scrutinized his cuts of type, testifies that he has successfully passed the pitfalls that beset all tyros, and has made types that in lining, fitting, and adjustment show the skill of the expert. A printer of the old school may dislike many of his mannerisms of composition and make-up, but he will cheerfully admit that his types and decorations and initials are in admirable accord; that the evenness of color he maintains on his rough paper is remarkable, and that his registry of black with red is unexceptionable. No one can examine a book made by Morris without the conviction that it shows the hand of a master.—DEVINNE, THEODORE, L., 1897, *The Printing of William Morris, The Book Buyer, vol.*13, *pp.* 920, 921.

No man on earth dies before his day; and least of all can the departure be called premature of a man whose life had been so crowded in activity and so rich in achievement. To one judging by the work done in it, his working day was longer and ampler than often falls to the lot of our brief and pitiable human race. But the specific reasons why that life was not protected beyond its sixty-third year are not difficult to assign. On the paternal side of his family there was a marked neurotic and gouty tendency. Himself of powerful physique, deep-chested sound-lunged, big-hearted, he yet carried in him that family weakness, which was developed under the pressure of an immensely busy life. On a constitution made sensitive by gout, the exposure of the years of the Socialist crusade, when he had perpetually spoken in the open air in all weathers, and in the worse than open air of indoor meetings, and had often neglected or foregone proper food and rest, told with fatal effect. "I have no hesitation," his family doctor writes to me, "in saying that he died a victim to his enthusiasm for spreading the principles of Socialism." Yet this was only the special form that, in those years, his unceasing and prodigious activity had taken: and these words may be enlarged or supplemented by those of an eminent member of the same profession: "I consider the case is this: the disease is simply being William Morris, and having done more work than most ten men." . . . With all the patience and conciliatoriness of his later years, he remained absolutely unshaken in his loyalty to his old opinions and to his old associates.—MACKAIL, J. W., 1899, *The Life of William Morris, vol.* II, *pp.* 335, 336.

One piece of William Morris furniture has become decidedly popular in America, and that is the "Morris Chair." The first chair of this pattern was made entirely by the hands of the master. Unlike most chairs and all church pews, it was built by a man who understood anatomy. It was also strong, durable, ornamental, and by a simple device the back could be adjusted so as to fit a man's every mood. There has been a sad degeneracy among William Morris chairs; still, good ones can be obtained, nearly as excellent as the one in which I rested at Kelmscott House—broad, deep, massive, upholstered with curled hair, and covered with leather that would delight a bookbinder. Such a chair can be used a generation and then passed on to the heirs. —HUBBARD, ELBERT, 1899, *Little Journeys to the Homes of English Authors*, p. 17.

So died a knight of the beautiful, without fear and without reproach. In the service of beauty he did the work of seven men, or at least kinds of work enough to make so many men distinguished. His career was a most important factor in the mediæval renascence, and knowledge of it is necessary not only to an understanding of English civilization but of the nineteenth century as well.—WHITE, GREENOUGH, 1899, *A Study in Biography, Conservative Review*, vol. 2, p. 358.

The least sympathetic of his audience could hardly see him on the platform and not be impressed by his wonderful personality; he looked the man he was, powerfully built, thickset, stalwart and sturdy, without any swagger, but with the air of a conqueror as he stood up to speak; an open face of fresh complexion, unshaven and rather rugged beard; his hair, grizzled and curly, upstanding like a mane from his broad forehead in a way that gave him the look of a lion; good grey eyes which could twinkle with merriment, light up with enthusiasm, or flash with indignation; a voice that deepened as he spoke; action and speech so sudden, it seemed it must be spontaneous.—DAY, LEWIS F., 1899, *The Art of William Morris*, p. 8.

The divorce of brain and hand, wrought by the present social order—ever more passionate grew his sense of the injustice, chaos and misery this was breeding in the industrial world. The nightmare of it invaded his very sleep, distressed and tormented him at his daily work and finally drove him out as a socialist agitator, to harangue radical gatherings, to face mobs, to spend wrangling nights in vain struggles to harmonize the individualistic and anti-social tempers of the socialistic bodies with which he allied himself. He stood on call to go anywhere and address any meeting before which he could say a word in behalf of the sacred cause. He was ready for revolution, ready to see the whole present social or anti-social, order, go down in ruin, that something better might emerge from the wreck. Here alone, to his mind, lay the possibility of the coming of any kingdom of heaven on earth, and for this he was eager to shed his life's blood. Poetry, architecture, culture, his interest in these he flung to the winds as child's play till the new order of things should be ushered in. Caste would be abolished and all would be a common band of toilers for common ends. Then first would the real reign of art and beauty begin, and each one's daily life, through the marriage of brain and hand, become an espousal of joy. And so the Viking of a man, the craftsman prophet of the new dispensation, wore out his last remnants of ebbing strength in the rapt pursuit of this vision.—TIFFANY, FRANCIS, 1900, *William Morris, Craftsman and Socialist, New World*, vol. 9, p. 114.

The Golden Rule was always in his mind as he built up in his imagination his Paradise on earth. He possessed the optimism of the kind-hearted, the faith in his fellow men that made him sure of their right acting could they only start afresh with a field clear of injury and abuse. He never dreamed in all his dreaming that these would again grow up and destroy the beautiful fabric of his new society, so bright and unspotted in his mind. . . . His Socialism, from one point of view, was certainly a tremendous failure, but no other side of his life visible to the public at large showed so plainly his moral virtues, his generosity, his sincerity, his power of self-sacrifice, his effort toward self-control. — CARY, ELISABETH LUTHER, 1902, *William Morris, Poet, Craftsman, Socialist*, pp. 188, 190.

THE LIFE AND DEATH OF JASON
1867

It should now be clear, or never, that in this poem a new thing of great price has been cast into the English treasure-house. Nor is the cutting and setting of the jewel unworthy of it; art and instinct have wrought hand in hand to its perfection. Other and various fields await the workman who has here approved himself a master, acceptable into the guild of great poets on a footing of his own to be shared or disputed by no other.—SWINBURNE, ALGERNON CHARLES, 1867, *Morris's "Life* and Death of Jason," *Fortnightly Review*, vol. 8, p. 28.

He has foraged in a treasure-house; he has visited the ancient world, and come back with a massive cup of living Greek wine. His project was no light task, but he has honorably fulfilled it. He has enriched the language with a narrative poem which we are sure that the public will not suffer to fall into the ranks of honored but uncherished works,—objects of vague and sapient reference,—but will continue to read and to enjoy. In spite of its length, the interest of the story never flags, and as a work of art it never ceases to be pure. To the jaded intellects of the present moment, distracted with the strife of creeds and the conflict of theories, it opens a glimpse into a world where they will be called upon neither to choose, to criticise, nor to believe, but simply to feel, to look, and to listen.—JAMES, HENRY, 1867, *Morris's Life and Death of Jason, North American Review*, vol. 105, p. 692.

No narrative poem comparable with this in scope of design or in power of execution has been produced in our generation. By this work Mr. Morris wins a secure place among the chief English poets of the age. The production of such a poem is not only proof of a rare individual genius, but the sign of the abiding vigor and freshness of our literature.—NORTON, CHARLES ELIOT, 1867, *The Life and Death of Jason, The Nation*, vol. 5, p. 146.

After seven years of silence "The Life and Death of Jason" was a surprise, and was welcomed as the sustained performance of a true poet. It is a narrative poem, of epic proportions, all story and action, composed in the rhymed pentameter, strongly and sweetly carried from the first book to the last of seventeen. In this production, as in all the works of Morris,—in some respects the most notable raconteur since the time of his avowed master, Geoffrey Chaucer,—the statement is newly illustrated, that imaginative poets do not invent their own legends, but are wise in taking them from those historic treasuries of fact and fiction, the outlines of which await only a masterhand to invest them with living beauty. . . . The poem is fresh and stirring, and the style befits the theme, though not free from harshness and careless rhymes.— STEDMAN, EDMUND CLARENCE, 1875-87, *Victorian Poets*, pp. 370, 371.

THE EARTHLY PARADISE
1868-70

In this important work Morris reaches the height of his success as a relator. . . . "The Earthly Paradise" has the universe of fiction for a field, and reclothes the choicest and most famous legends of Asia and Europe with the delicate fabric of his verse. — STEDMAN, EDMUND CLARENCE, 1875-87, *Victorian Poets*, p. 372.

Thy luckless wanderers, Poet, sought a land
  Of timeless ease, where aye the fields are green,—
Where flowers know not the touch of winter's hand,
And hills and valleys glow in changeless sheen,—
  Where Age can never come, and Love is queen.
World-worn we too seek peace and sun-lit skies,
And find—thy book an Earthly Paradise.
—HOWE, M. A. DE WOLFE, 1888, *To William Morris, The Critic*, Aug. 11.

That huge decorative poem in which slim maidens and green-clad men, and waters wan, and flowering appletrees, and rich palaces are all mingled as on some long ancient tapestry, shaken a little by the wind of death. They are not living and breathing people, these persons of the fables; they are but shadows, beautiful and faint, and their poem is fit reading for sleepy summer afternoons. — LANG, ANDREW, 1889, *Letters on Literature*, p. 17.

The rich and fluent verse, with its simple, direct, Old World diction; the distinct vision, the romantic charm, the sense of external beauty everywhere, with a touch of wistfulness. The voice was the voice of a poet, but the eye was the eye of an artist and a craftsman.—CRANE, WALTER, 1897, *William Morris, Scribner's Magazine*, vol. 22, p. 89.

Through all the great lengths of these poems, the verse flows sweetly, with many restful modulations. There is no stress of emotion, no harrowing anguish of circumstance, no rugged, harsh outlines of character. All seems remote. The voices come to us softened by distance, the men and women are seen as through a refining medium. The peace and glamour of an ideal world wrap us in their gloomy haze. A gentle sadness runs through all these poems, and is, indeed, characteristic of this writer's work throughout. The wine of life ran full enough within the veins of the poet himself, but he gives us no sound of human laughter in his verse. The absence, if not the defect, of humour is everywhere apparent. But no less apparent is the absence of any sympathetic recognition of the serious tragedy of nineteenth century life.— GRAHAM, RICHARD R., 1897, *The Masters of Victorian Literature*, p. 368.

"The Earthly Paradise" is the work of a born teller of stories for the story's sake; and it is to be enjoyed very simply, with the same child-likeness of interest which went to its making.—MOODY, WILLIAM VAUGHN, AND LOVETT, ROBERT MORSS, 1902, *A History of English Literature*, p. 348.

It contains much that is beautiful but nothing original. Of all the Romanticists Morris most lacked spontaneity and initiation.—ENGEL, EDWARD, 1902, *A History of English Literature*, rev. Hamley Bent, p. 433.

THE STORY OF SIGURD THE VOLSUNG
1877

In "The Story of Sigurd," which remains his masterpiece of sustained power, he goes sheer through civilization, and finds an ampler beauty shadowed under the dusk of the Gods. He gets a larger style, a style more rooted in the earth, more vivid with the impulse of nature; and the beauty of his writing is now a grave beauty, from which all mere prettiness is clean consumed away. And now, at last, he touches the heart; for he sings of the passions of men, of the fierceness of love and hate, of the music of swords in the day of battle. And still, more than ever, he is the poet of beauty; for he has realized that in beauty there is something more elemental than smiling lips, or the soft dropping of tears.— SYMONS, ARTHUR, 1896, *Morris as Poet, Saturday Review*, vol. 82, p. 388.

The one English poet of the 19th century who might have given us a well-rounded Arthurian epic wrote only four short poems based on Arthurian material. William Morris as a young man was attracted by the Arthurian story, and, if Tennyson had not early occupied the field, might have been led to produce a long Arthurian poem. A less consummate master of technique than Tennyson, Morris had nevertheless an ease of movement and a power of conception hardly equalled by the older poet. The "Idyls" are exquisite, but they lack the vigor and the onward sweep of a great epic. We could well spare some of the tales in "The Earthly Paradise" for an Arthurian poem worthy to stand beside "Sigurd the Volsung."—MEAD, WILLIAM EDWARD, 1897, *Selections from Sir Thomas Malory's Morte Darthur, Introduction*, p. xlvi.

Here not only does he fill a large canvas with an art higher and subtler than that shown in "Jason," or even in "The Earthly Paradise," but he betrays a profound concern in the destinies of the race, such as we do not exact from the mere story-teller. Love and adventure he had already treated in a manner approaching perfection; and a sympathetic intelligence of all beautiful legends breathes throughout his works; but Sigurd is something more than a lover and a warrior: he is at once heroic and tragic; and he is surrounded by characters heroic and tragic. In his mythic person large spiritual questions are suggested; he is the typical saviour as conceived by the Northern race; and this side of the conception is more emphatic and unmistakable in the modern work than in the Völsunga Saga, which is the basis of this great poem. . . . Let it be clearly understood that "Sigurd the Volsung" is no mere rythmic and metrical triumph, though in those matters its merits are, as has been said, of a superb kind. In the much higher qualities, which derive from knowledge of life, feeling for natural myth, epic action and tragic intensity combined, this epic in anapæstic couplets which rounds the second period, stands among the foremost poems not only of this century but of our literature.— FORMAN, H. BUXTON, 1897, *The Books of William Morris Described*, pp. 8, 9.

GENERAL

Morris's facility at poetising puts one in a rage. He has been writing at all for little more than a year, I believe, and has already poetry enough for a big book.— ROSSETTI, DANTE GABRIEL, 1856, *Letters to William Allingham*, p. 192.

I saw Morris's poetry in manuscript. Surely 19-20ths of them are of the most obscure, watery, mystical, affected stuff possible. The man who brought the manuscript (himself well known as a poet) said that "one of the poems which described a picture of Rossetti was a very fine poem; that the picture was not understandable, and the poem made it no clearer, but that it was a fine poem, nevertheless."—PARKER JOHN, 1860, *Letter to "Shirley."*

Even to the most cheerful minds, a pensive sentiment lingers about the autumnal days, and this is the prevailing sentiment of the works which Mr. Morris has written. True sorrow is sharply bitter; but there is a mood of mind which is sorrowful in form, and yet in substance is hardly so. It is the mood of the man who recognises the tragic conditions and limitations of human life, but who recognises them as inevitable, universal, not to be subdued nor escaped from, but to be accepted and made the best of. This is the key-note of "Jason" and "The Earthly Paradise." . . . I have spoken highly of Mr. Morris's Greek stories; yet it is impossible not to feel that, exquisite though they are, they lie in many respects *apart* from us; that there is a fancifulness even in their sorrow (sorrow being, as Arthur Hallam once said, the deepest thing in our nature) which prevents them from appealing to our profoundest sympathies. In his Scandinavian, on the other hand, we feel that we are dealing with our own ancestors, and that there is to us a root of reality even in their most grotesque superstitions.—SKELTON, JOHN, 1869, *William Morris and Matthew Arnold, Fraser's Magazine, vol.* 79, *pp.* 230, 235.

"Love is Enough," Mr. Morris's latest poem, will not rank, we think, among his highest efforts. The adaptation to modern taste of a mediæval "Morality" has been an experiment of which the result does not tempt us to desire a repetition. The dramatic form lacks its *raison d'être* when there is no action to support, and an abstract personage such as Love is apt to talk too metaphysically to be readily intelligible to a concrete audience. The sing-song monotony of the dactylic measure, and the cloying alliteration of the language combine to produce an effect of weakness which is increased rather than diminished by the prevailing tone of the poem.—HEWLETT, HENRY G., 1875, *The Poems of Mr. Morris, Contemporary Review, vol.* 25, *p.* 122.

Mr. William Morris is, in his own way, a true poet, and except, perhaps, one or two faults which might be justified as beauties, his work is so nearly perfect in its kind that one is sometimes tempted to ask the idle question, Why is he excellent in this kind only? It is true that men are not as coins, dead metal. They have within themselves a constant power of development; but it is best spent in the constant bettering of their own form of work. . . . Mr. William Morris may be said to be the painter's poet. Every book of his includes a gallery of pictures upon classical and mediæval subjects, various in detail but all full of charm.—MORLEY, HENRY, 1877, *Recent Literature, Nineteenth Century, vol.* 2, *p.* 704.

Nothing can be more beautiful, tender, and melancholy than some of his sweet, pathetic stories. Mr. Morris has been compared to Chaucer, but he is at the best a Chaucer without strength and without humor. He has such story-teller's power as one might suppose suited to absorb the evening hours of some lady of mediæval days. She would have loved Mr. Morris's beautiful tales of love and truth and constancy and separation, tales which, to quote the poet's own words, "would make her sweet eyes wet, at least sometimes, at least when heaven and earth on some fair eve had grown too fair for mirth." But the broad strength of Chaucer, the animal spirits, the ringing laughter, the occasional fierceness of emotion, the pain, and the passion are not to be found in Mr. Morris's exquisite and gentle verse.—MCCARTHY, JUSTIN, 1880, *A History of Our Own Times from the Accession of Queen Victoria to the Berlin Congress, vol.* IV. *ch.* lxvii.

To indicate briefly some points of contrast—how does the spire of hope spring and upbound into the infinite in Chaucer; while, on the other hand, how blank, worldbound, and wearying is the stone *façade* of hopelessness which rears itself uncompromisingly behind the gayest pictures of William Morris! Chaucer is eager, expectant. To-day is *so* beautiful, perhaps to-morrow will be more beautiful: life is young, who knows?—he seems to cry, with splendid immeasurable confidence in the reserved powers of nature and of man. But Morris does not hope: there is, there will be, nothing new under the sun. To-morrow? that may not come; if it does, it will be merely to-day revamped; therefore let us amuse ourselves with the daintiest that art and culture can give: this is his essential utterance. . . . Morris too has his sensuous element, but it is utterly unlike Chaucer's; it is *dilettante,* it is amateur sensualism; it is not strong, though sometimes excessive, and it is nervously afraid of that satiety which is at once its chief temptation and its most awful doom.—LANIER, SIDNEY,

1880, *Music and Poetry, Chaucer and Shakspere*, pp. 198, 200.

William Morris has a sunny slope of Parnassus all to himself.—BIRRELL, AUGUSTINE, 1884, *Obiter Dicta*, p. 94.

In whom Chaucer and Keats seemed to have revived so long as he was contented to remain "the idle singer of an empty day," but whose recent espousal of the Socialist cause proves at least that this position is not easily tenable in an age like ours.—GARNETT, RICHARD, 1887, *The Reign of Queen Victoria*, ed. Ward, vol. II, p. 487.

Clearness, strength, music, picturesqueness, and easy flow, are the chief characteristics of Morris' style. . . . His pictorial power—the power of bringing a person or a scene fully and adequately before one's eyes by the aid of words alone—is as great as that of Chaucer. . . . Morris' stores of language are as rich as Spenser's; and he has much the same copious and musical flow of poetic words and phrases.—MEIKLEJOHN, J. M. D., 1887, *The English Language: Its Grammar, History and Literature*, p. 360, 361.

In which of his many spheres of activity Mr. Morris has exercised the widest influence it would be hard to say; but it is as the sturdy Socialist lecturer who may be seen any Sunday during the summer months haranguing a crowd in one or another of the open spaces of London, that he is dearest to the "Common People" of the great metropolis. But his work is of far more than mere local interest: wherever his earnest zeal for human well-being becomes known, there he is sure to have many ardent admirers. . . . Morris is too often regarded by the unthinking as a reactionist—one who would turn back the wheels of progress—and yet such a conception can only be founded on a gross misunderstanding of the whole trend of his work.—LEE, FRANCIS WATTS, 1891, ed. *William Morris, Poet, Artist, Socialist, Introduction*, pp. vii, viii.

Among all the Utopian or ideal pictures of a reformed world, drawn for our contemplation by enthusiasts, this book ["News from Nowhere"] by Mr. William Morris has a singular charm. It cannot, indeed, rank with the great schemes of Plato, More, and Bacon: it has far less perfection of workmanship, less completeness of design, less dignity of tone.—JOHNSON, LIONEL, 1891, *News from Nowhere*, The Academy, vol. 39, p. 483.

It is not often that three volumes by well-known poets are issued almost simultaneously, as has lately been the case, when new books by William Morris, Lord Lytton (Owen Meredith), and Sir Edwin Arnold appeared within a few days of each other. Of these three singers there can be no question as to which is the poet *par excellence*. The high gods gave their royal largesse to William Morris at his birth; and though he may choose to be decorator, printer, or socialist, he cannot resign his divine inheritance—he must be always and above all a poet. What is the spell that from first to last makes one his captive?—how impossible it would be to put it into words! It is something remote from the present world; for when he writes of social problems and the clamorous issues of the time, he ceases for the nonce to be a poet, and we are no longer his thralls. But when he returns to his true *métier*, he carries us with him, and bears us on to regions east of the sun and west of the moon—to the dreams and the visions of long ago.—MOULTON, LOUISE CHANDLER, 1892, *Three English Poets*, The Arena, vol. 6, p. 46.

We have in Mr. Morris what we have not had since Chaucer, and what no other nation has had since a time older than Chaucer's, a real *trouvère* of the first class—a person of inexhaustible fertility and power in weaving the verse and the prose of romance, and with a purely lyrical gift which even Chaucer did not often show. It is the quality of poetry in him much more than the particular forms or the agreeable volume in which it manifests itself that has always attracted me, and attracts me now as much as ever to this very remarkable writer.—SAINTSBURY, GEORGE, 1894, *Two Corrected Impressions*, The Critic, vol. 25, p. 103.

William Morris is intellectually far more healthy than Rossetti and Swinburne. His deviations from mental equilibrium betray themselves, not through mysticism, but through a want of individuality, and an overweening tendency to imitation. His affectation consists in mediævalism. . . . Morris pursuades himself that he is a wandering minstrel of the thirteenth or fourteenth century, and takes much trouble to look at things in such a way, and express them in such language, as would have befitted a real contemporary of Chaucer. Beyond this poetical ventriloquism, so to speak, with which he seeks so to alter the sound of his voice that it may appear to come from far away to our ear, there are not many features of degeneracy in him to notice.—NORDAU, MAX, 1895, *Degeneration*, pp. 98, 99.

Despite the marvelous charm of the old stories and the grace of the telling, it is difficult to linger long in the world of Morris the poet. An intense narrowness has invaded his conception of life. One woman forever wanders through his varied climes, and we weary soon of clinging draperies, gray eyes and tender feet. One young hero, superb, but if the truth be told, monotonous, beholds the maiden, loves, loses, wins, or dies. Delight in the deed is feeble in all the poets of art, and the blows that ring through the poems of Morris sound hollow and false. If the motif of action is unused, the range of feeling even is narrowed. Emotion reduces itself to two phases or indeed to one; a solitary natural passion, death-haunted to the end. Of the subtleties of the inner life, he gives no hint. The whole world of experience so intimately known to Rossetti, the world where the soul meets or seeks the Eternal, is closed to him. In the first pre-Raphaelites religious passion was welded in strange and enthralling unison with the passion for earthly beauty. In Morris it has vanished. —SCUDDER, VIDA D., 1895, *The Life of the Spirit in the Modern English Poets*, p. 276.

Morris was conspicuous, with many of the best artists contemporary with him, for the success with which he reverted to earlier methods of design; but in his genius for fine craftsmanship he was alone; a unique figure of our time. . . . Certainly, the mere craft of printing has rarely been practiced with finer results; in material and workmanship, the paper and press-work of his books are equal to the best that have been produced. The decorative beauty and richness of Morris's work is so generally acknowledged, that these traits of fine craftsmanship are apt to be overlooked and forgotten; yet, perhaps in these very qualities of good workmanship, unique in our time, the peculiar value of Morris's work will finally be found to consist.— HORNE, HERBERT P., 1896, *William Morris as Printer*, The Saturday Review, vol. 82, p. 439.

It is Malory ["The Well at the World's End"], enriched and chastened by the thought and learning of six centuries, this story of Ralph and his Quest of the Well at the World's End. It is Malory, with the glow of the dawn of the Twentieth Century warming his tapestries and beaten metal. It is Malory, but instead of the mystic Grail, the search for long life and the beauty of strength. . . . Save that its spirit is living, the story does not seem to be coherently symbolical. Such analysis as a transient reviewer may give discovers no clue to a coherent construction. Life is too short for many admirable things—for chess, and the unravelling of the "Faerie Queen" and of such riddles as this. Ever and again the tale is certainly shot and enriched with allegory. But as we try to follow these glittering strands, they spread, twist, vanish, one after the other, in the texture of some purely decorative incident. . . . All the workmanship of the book is stout oaken stuff that must needs endure and preserve the memory of one of the stoutest, cleanest lives that has been lived in these latter days.—WELLS, H. G., 1896, *The Well at the World's End*, Saturday Review, vol. 82, pp. 414, 415.

To read "Love is Enough," or "The Earthly Paradise," or "The Life and Death of Jason," is like taking opium One abandons oneself to it, and is borne on clouds as in a gondola of the air. Never was one so gently carried along, so imperceptibly, and with so luxurious a motion. There is not even enough sharpness of interest, or novelty in the progression, to jar one on the way.—SYMONS, ARTHUR, 1896, *Morris as Poet*, Saturday Review, vol. 82, p. 388.

In his poetry Morris has always shown a delight in physical existence such as Achilles or Hector would have at once appreciated. He drew his inspiration not only from early Greece, but from the wild, free life depicted in the Scandinavian sagas. . . . "The Story of Sigurd the Volsung" manifests an intense concern for man's physical and intellectual well-being in this world. "In The Pilgrims of Hope" he embodied his political convictions and social aspirations. His writings in *The Commonwealth* may be regarded as the gospel of English Socialism. . . . As poetry the "Chants for Socialists" seem as if they had been written by a different hand from that which wrote "The Earthly Paradise" and "The Defense of Guinevere;" but who can deny the noble humanitarianism that inspires these simple "chants?"—HANNIGAN, D. F., 1897, *William Morris, Poet and Revolutionist, Westminster Review,* vol. 147, pp. 118, 119.

It is interesting also to notice that while some poets are thus able to recollect their emotion and improve by revision the expression of it, others totally lack this power. A striking instance was William Morris.—BEECHING, H. C., 1901, *Expression in Poetry,* p. 48.

Of all this group, the one most thoroughly steeped in mediævalism—to repeat his own description of himself—was William Morris. He was the English equivalent of Gautier's *homme moyen âge*; and it was his endeavour, in letters and art, to pick up and continue the mediæval tradition, interrupted by four hundred years of modern civilization. The sixteenth and seventeenth centuries did not attract him; and as for the eighteenth, it simply did not exist for him. The ugliness of modern life, with its factories and railroads, its unpicturesque poverty and selfish commercialism, was hateful to him as it was to Ruskin—his teacher. He loved to imagine the face of England as it was in the time of Chaucer—his master.—BEERS, HENRY A., 1901, *A History of English Romanticism in the Ninteeenth Century,* p. 316.

On the whole, I consider Morris to have been the largest all-round man of the group, not merely on account of the diversity of his faculties, for he had in his composition a measure, greater or less, of most of the gifts which go to make up the intellectual man and artist, but because he had, in addition to those, a largeness and nobility of nature, a magnanimity and generosity, which rarely enter into the character of the artist; and perhaps the reason why his gifts were not more highly developed was that his estimation of them was so modest. His facility in versification led him to diffuseness in his poems, and the modest estimation in which he held his work, when done, was a discouragement to the "limæ labor" so necessary to perfection. He told me that he had written eight hundred lines of one of his tales in one night, but at the same time he regretted that he could not invent a plot, though the exquisite manner in which he carried out the old plots which have been the common property of poets since poetry existed in the form of tales is honor enough.—STILLMAN, WILLIAM JAMES, 1901, *The Autobiography of a Journalist,* vol. II, p. 481.

Pure beauty may indeed be taken as the note of all the poetry that William Morris has left for the enrichment of our literature. "Full of soft music and familiar olden charm," to use Mr. Stedman's felicitous phrase, it has the power to lull the senses into forgetfulness of this modern workaday world, to restore the soul with draughts from the wellsprings of life, to bring back the wonder of childhood, the glory and the dream that we may perhaps have thought to be vanished beyond recall. It is poetry to read in the long summer days when we seek rest from strenuous endeavor; it is poetry for the beguilement of all weariness, and for the refreshment of our faith in the simple virtues and the unsophisticated life; it is poetry that brings a wholesome and healing ministry akin to that of Nature herself; it is poetry that leaves the recollection unsullied by any suggestion of impurity and unhaunted by any spectre of doubt. Like Lethe, it has the gift of oblivion for those who seek the embrace of its waters; but, unlike the dark-flowing stream of the underworld, its surface is rippled by the breezes of earth, its banks are overarched by living foliage, and its waves mirror the glad sunlight.—PAYNE, WILLIAM MORTON, 1902, *Editorial Echoes,* p. 257.

He represents not only that rapacious hunger for beauty which has now for the first time become a serious problem in the healthy life of humanity, but he represents also that honourable instinct for finding beauty in common necessities of workmanship, which gives it a stronger and more bony structure. The time has passed when William Morris was conceived to be irrelevant to be described as a designer of wall-papers. . . . The limitations of William Morris, whatever they were, were not the limitations of common decoration. It is true that all his work, even his literary work, was in some sense decorative, had in some degree the qualities of a splendid wall-paper. His characters, his stories, his religious and political views, had, in the most emphatic sense, length and breadth without thickness.—CHESTERTON, G. K., 1903, *Varied Types,* pp. 15, 16.

I do not think it was accident, so subtle are the threads that lead the soul, that made William Morris, who seems to me the one perfectly happy and fortunate poet of modern times, celebrate the Green Tree and the goddess Habundia, and wells and enchanted waters in so many books. . . . When William Morris describes a house of any kind, and makes his description poetical, it is always, I think, some house that he would have liked to have lived in, and I remember him saying about the time when he was writing of that great house of the Wolfings, "I decorate modern houses for people, but the house that would please me would be some great room where one talked to one's friends in one corner and ate in another and slept in another and worked in another." Indeed all he writes seems to me like the make-believe of a child who is remaking the world, not always in the same way, but always after its own heart; and so unlike all other modern writers he makes his poetry out of unending pictures of a happiness that is often what a child might imagine, and always a happiness that sets mind and body at ease. . . . His art was not more essentially religious than Rossetti's art, but it was different, for Rossetti, drünken with natural beauty, saw the supernatural beauty, the impossible beauty, in his frenzy, while he being less intense and more tranquil would show us a beauty that would wither if it did not set us at peace with natural things, and if we did not believe that it existed always a little and would some day exist in its fulness. He may not have been, indeed he was not, among the very greatest of the poets, but he was among the greatest of those who prepare the last reconciliation when the Cross shall blossom with roses.—YEATS, WILLIAM BUTLER, 1903, *Ideas of Good and Evil*, pp. 72, 82, 89.

Coventry Kearsey Deighton Patmore
1823–1896.

Born, at Woodford, Essex, 23 July, 1823. Educated privately. First poems written about 1839. For some time engaged in scientific studies. Assistant Librarian, British Museum, 1846-65. Married (i) Emily Augusta Andrews, 11 Sept. 1847; settled in Hampstead. Wife died, 5 July 1862. Married (ii) Mary Byles, 1865; settled in Sussex. After death of second wife, removed to Hastings. Removed to Lymington, 1891. Died there, 26 Nov. 1896. Buried there. *Works:* "Poems," 1844; "Tamerton Church Tower," 1853; "The Angel in the House" (anon.; 2 pts. "The Betrothal," "The Espousals"), 1854-56; "Faithful for Ever," 1860; "The Victories of Love," 1863; "Odes" (anon.; priv. ptd.), [1868]; "The Unknown Eros" (anon.), 1877; "Florilegium Amantis" (selected poems), ed. by R. Garnett [1879]; "Poems" (4 vols.) [1879]; "How I Managed and Improved my Estate" (anon.) 1886; "Poems" (2 vols.), 1887; "Principle in Art," 1889; "Religio Poetæ," 1893; "The Rod, the Root, and the Flower," 1895. He *translated:* St. Bernard "On the Love of God" (with M. C. Patmore), 1891; and *edited:* "The Children's Garland from the Best Poets," 1862 [1861]; "Bryan Waller Procter; an autobiographical fragment," 1877.—SHARP, R. FARQUHARSON, 1897, *A Dictionary of English Authors*, p. 223.

PERSONAL

He is a man of much more youthful aspect than I had expected, . . . a slender person to be an Englishman, though not remarkably so had he been an American; with an intelligent, pleasant, and sensitive face,—a man very evidently of refined feelings and cultivated mind. . . . He is very simple and agreeable in his manners; a little shy, yet perfectly frank, and easy to meet on real grounds.— HAWTHORNE, NATHANIEL, 1858, *English Note-Books, vol.* II, *p.* 367.

In March, 1847, her relatives left the south of London for Hampstead, and shortly afterwards Emily became engaged to Coventry Patmore. They were married on the 11th of September, 1847, in the parish church of St. John's, Hampstead, and spent their honeymoon, some of the incidents of which are described in "The Angel in the House," at Hastings. . . . The beauty of her life and the charm which her refined and intellectual nature gave to the simplest domestic details converted many to a belief in that higher standard of home, which is now often taken for granted. She was the bright, poetical, artistic wife, who dressed gracefully and rejoiced in her good looks because they made others happy. At the same time she was the practical wife, who strove to keep a bright heart without overstepping her income, and who understood something of cooking and needlework. Her artistic perception kept her from believing that nothing could be beautiful unless it was costly, and her good sense preserved her from the folly of expecting to satisfy a healthy appetite from an empty blue china dish. Her influence for good went far beyond her own little family circle. She was always teaching by example, and there are many now reaping the advantage of those silent lessons.—NICOLL, W ROBERTSON, AND WISE, THOMAS J., 1896, *Literary Ancedotes of the Nineteenth Century, vol.* II, *pp.* 380, 384.

When I came, a mere lad, to work in the Library of the British Museum, I was introduced to all my colleagues with one, doubtless accidental, exception. I was some time before finding out who the tall, spare, silent man was who, alone of the assistants, sat in the King's Library; who, though perfectly urbane when he did converse, seemed rather among than of the rest of the staff, and who appeared to be usually entrusted with some exceptional task, now cataloguing a mighty collection of sermons from the King's Library gallery, now the pamphlets of the French Revolution. . . . His composition was rapid. I have frequently seen twenty or more lines which he had written, he said, in the last half-hour, and re-fashioning were rarely needful, though he was an unwearied corrector in minor details. . . . Patmore did not go much into society. I have heard him speak, however, of meetings with Carlyle and Ruskin, Browning and Palgrave. The three latter were numbered among his friends, and he was at one time intimate with Tennyson, the MS. of whose "In Memoriam" he rescued from the kitchen of a lodging-house.—GARNETT, RICHARD, 1896, *Saturday Review, vol.* 82, *pp.* 582, 583.

He was so very loyal to his restricted friendships, that a fresh incongruity is to be traced in the notorious fact that he had sacrificed more illustrious friends on the altar of caprice than any other man in England. He had been intimate with Carlyle, Tennyson, Browning, Rossetti, Millais, and Mr. Ruskin, yet each of the intimacies closed early, and each was broken off by Patmore.—GOSSE, EDMUND, 1897, *Coventry Patmore, Contemporary Review, vol.* 71, *p.* 201.

THE ANGEL IN THE HOUSE
1854–56

Of course it is very good indeed, yet will one ever want to read it again? The best passages I can recollect now are the ones about "coming where women are," for the simile of the frozen ship—and the part concerning the "brute of a husband." From what I hear, I should judge that, in spite of idiots in the *Athenæum* and elsewhere, the book will be of use to its author's reputation—a resolute poet, whom I saw a little while back, and who means to make his book bigger than the "Divina Comedia," he tells me.—ROSSETTI, DANTE GABRIEL, 1855, *Letters to William Allingham, p.* 99.

The volume published last year, with the title of "The Angel in the House, Part I.," inspired us with the hope that a poet of no ordinary promise was about to lay down the leading lines of this great subject, in a composition half narrative and half reflective, which should at least show, as in a chart, what its rich capabilities were, and give some indication of the treasures that future workers in the same mine have gathered in, one by one. But two Parts have been already published, and he has only got as far as the threshold of his subject; while the age is no longer able to bear poems of epic length, even with, and much less without, epic action. He has encumbered himself besides with the most awkward plan that the brain of poet ever conceived.—BRIMLEY, GEORGE, 1856-58, *The Angel in the House, Essays, ed. Clark, p.* 234.

The gentle reader we apprise, That this new Angel in the House contains a tale not very wise, About a person and a spouse. The author, gentle as a lamb, Has managèd his rhymes to fit, And haply fancies he has writ Another "In Memoriam." How his intended gathered flowers, And took her tea and after sung, Is told in style somewhat like ours, For delectation of the young. But, reader, lest you say we quiz The poet's record of his she, Some little pictures you shall see, Not in our language, but in his. . . . Fear not this saline, Cousin Fred; He gives no tragic mischief birth; There are no tears for you to shed, Unless they may be tears of mirth. From ball to bed, from field to farm, The tale flows nicely purling on; With much conceit there is no harm, In the love-legend here begun. The rest will come another day, If public sympathy allows; And this is all we have to

say, About the "Angel in the House."—
CHORLEY, HENRY FOTHERGILL, 1856, *The Athenæum*, Jan. 20.

It is a most beautiful and original poem,—a poem for happy married people to read together, and to understand by the light of their own past and present life; but I doubt whether the generality of English people are capable of appreciating it.—HAWTHORNE, NATHANIEL, 1858, *English Note-Books*, vol. II, p. 368.

It is curious that this enthusiastic singer of domestic life should himself be one of the last writers with whom we can feel thoroughly at home; but assuredly the most sensible impression we have derived from every reperusal of the "Angel in the House" has been one of astonishment at the amount of beauty which the last reading had left for us to discover.—GARNETT, RICHARD, 1861, *Poetry, Prose, and Mr. Patmore*, *Macmillan's Magazine*, vol. 3, p. 125.

The more essential passages of Mr. Coventry Patmore's . . . "The Angel in the House"—are classic, and very high in that noble rank. He plays with this power of his art in the brief metre, the symmetrical stanza, and the colloquial phrase. He has here accepted the dailiest things and made them spirit and fire. There has been something said against these colloquialisms; and indeed they would not be tolerable in hands less austere and sweet. The newest Philistine, who is afraid of the reproach of Philistinism, who denies Philistinism in the name of a Philistine, and ultimately receives a Philistine's reward, has been known to make light of some of Mr. Patmore's couplets, which he finds too "domestic." But such "domestic" couplets as those in "Olympus," for instance, are a smiling defiance of Philistinism. So are the brilliant stanzas, made of life, sense, and spirit, in which the very accessories,—the spoilt accessories—of a modern English wedding are rendered grave and blithe, and the bridegroom is restored to the dignity of the sun.—MEYNELL, ALICE, 1896, *ed. The Poetry of Pathos and Delight, Introductory Note*, p. viii.

That the general reading public should have been captivated by the unexceptionable sentiments, the conventional piety, the idealisation of that pure home-life which the Englishman likes to believe can only be found in his own country, and by the facile gracefulness of diction which adorns many of the stanzas of the "Angel," was natural enough. But that poets like Tennyson and Browning, thinkers like Ruskin and Carlyle, should have accepted the work as a serious contribution to English poetry, will remain—like *Blackwood's* attitude towards Keats—one of the incomprehensible mysteries of criticism.—CRAWFORD, VIRGINIA M., 1901, *Coventry Patmore, Fortnightly Review*, vol. 75, p. 305.

GENERAL

Your pages abound with unmistakable testimonials of no common genius;—not one which does not proclaim the mind and heart of a Poet.—I honestly, and without compliment, think the promise you hold out to us—is perfectly startling, both from the luxuriance of your fancy, and the subtle and reflective inclinations of your intellect. It rests with yourself alone to fulfill that promise,—for no less honestly, I may say, tho' with respect, that I doubt if very large and material alterations in the faculty we call taste, are not essentially necessary to secure you the wide Audience and the permanent Fame which must root themselves in the universal sympathies, and the household affections of men.—LYTTON, SIR EDWARD LYTTON BULWER, 1844, *Letter to Coventry Patmore*, July 27; *Memoirs and Correspondence of Coventry Patmore*, ed. *Champneys*, vol. I, p. 54.

I wrote to Patmore after reading his book "Faithful Forever," which he sent me, saying all that I (most sincerely) admired in it, but perhaps leaving some things unsaid; for what can it avail to say some things to a man after his third volume? "Of love which never finds its published close, what sequel?" And how many?—ROSSETTI, DANTE GABRIEL, 1860, *Letters to William Allingham*, p. 236.

A carpet-knight in poetry, as the younger Trollope latterly is in prose, he merely photographs life, and often in its poor and commonplace forms. He thus falls short of that aristocracy of art which by instinct selects an elevated theme. It is better to beautify life, though by an illusive reflection in a Claude Lorraine mirror, than to repeat its every wrinkle in a sixpenny looking-glass.—STEDMAN, EDMUND CLARENCE, 1875-87, *Victorian Poets*, p. 266.

Neither "The Angel in the House" nor the "Odes" are quite satisfactory as wholes; the foundations of the former are sandy, its view of domestic relations is open to grave exception, and it remains incomplete because it could not be completed. The "Odes" are enveloped in a cloud of mysticism. But these imperfections are more than redeemed by exquisite and surprising beauties of detail; and if the writer had possessed a more equable and symmetrical genius, he would hardly have exhibited the depth of insight, the energy of thought, or the intensity of descriptive power in which, among his contemporaries, he is rivalled only by Browning.—GARNETT, RICHARD, 1896, *Recollections of Coventry Patmore, The Saturday Review*, vol. 82, p. 583.

His most constant theme is woman and love in their purer existence: woman, intelligent, winning, worshipping, comforting, confiding; love, in its power of enchantment, elusive, pervasive and controlling. What in all his word-pictures would place Patmore's woman for a moment with Longfellow's Evangeline, for poetic charm of surroundings, for pathetic interest of situation, for delicious home qualities; or with the women of our own reverential Whittier, for tenderness, constancy, wholesome sweetness; or with Tennyson's, for play of emotions, exquisite purity of mood, elegance and grace of womanhood? Of the women of Browning, Patmore knew nothing; he never saw them so as to know them. To pass from subject matter, our poet reminds us of Wordsworth in ground treatment of theme; but there the resemblance ends.—MORSE, JAMES HERBERT, 1896, *Coventry Patmore, The Critic*, vol. 29, p. 365.

The "Sponsa Dei," this vanished masterpiece, was not very long, but polished and modulated to the highest degree of perfection. No existing specimen of Patmore's prose seems to me so delicate, or penetrated by quite so high a charm of style, as this lost book was. I think that, on successive occasions, I had read it all, much of it more than once, and I suppose that half a dozen other intimate friends may have seen it. The subject of it was certainly surprising. It was not more nor less than an interpretation of the love between the soul and God by an analogy of the love between a woman and a man; it was, indeed, a transcendental treatise on divine desire seen through the veil of human desire. The purity and crystalline passion of the writer carried him safely over the most astounding difficulties, but perhaps, on the whole, he was right in considering that it should not be thrown to the vulgar. Yet the scruple which destroyed it was simply deplorable; the burning of "Sponsa Dei" involved a distinct loss to literature.— GOSSE, EDMUND, 1897, *Coventry Patmore, Contemporary Review*, vol. 71, p. 198.

He probably looked forward with the same keen assurance to the verdict of posterity as did Southey; and posterity is all but certain will be as ruthless in the one case as in the other.—SHORTER, CLEMENT, 1897, *Victorian Literature*, p. 32.

We have never met with anything in literature more full of a pathetic *desiderium* than the poem called "Departure," more instinct with tenderness and compassion for the heart of childhood than the "Toys." These things will live.—TOVEY, DUNCAN C., 1897, *Reviews and Essays in English Literature*, p. 167.

The Laureate of Home and the Domestic Affections.—GRAHAM, RICHARD D., 1897, *The Masters of Victorian Literature*, p. 408.

Whether the nerve of the mass of mankind is open to conviction by the lovely austerity of Mr. Patmore's music is at least doubtful. For a minority of mankind the music of no poet touches the nerve more exquisitely. By some not insensitive to the best in modern poetry, the odes of Mr. Coventry Patmore would be accepted as the most exacting of all tests of a delicate apprehension. The eye falling upon the pages of "The Unknown Eros" perceives the absence of the ordinary elements of lyrical effect—of the stanzaic structure with its obvious correspondence of verse and regular return of rhyme. Instead of the ordinary lyric form which is a multiplicity of similar parts, Mr. Patmore's odes develop a real complexity of speech. The page presents a broken flow of apparently discrepant lines, varying in length from one and two beats to as many as five and seven. But the ear soon divines that there is a celestial music most cunningly involved by this apparently capricious method of composition. . . . To those who had grotesquely misconceived the author of "The Angel in the House" as a domestic sentimentalist, "The Unknown Eros" revealed a personality among the most vivid and virile of our literature. The odes suggest an intellect trenchant and delicate; an emotion wide and sensitive as the sea.—GARVIN, LOUIS, 1897, *Coventry Patmore, The Praise of the*

Odes, Fortnightly Review, vol. 67, pp. 213, 217.

All his studies, his introspection, his reading of the Fathers of the early church like St. Augustine, his dabbling in physical science, his explorations into what he calls "that inexhaustible poetic mine of psychology"—all these are used but to sound his three mysteries, the three *motifs* of all his music: God, Woman, Love. Throughout the procedure his intentions are as limpid as crystal. . . . If in verse execution and technique Patmore be defective, his vitality is so imperious that we yield out of sheer weakness to his mannerisms.—O'KEEFFE, HENRY E., 1899, *Coventry Patmore, The Catholic World*, vol. 69, pp. 652, 653.

To me at least it always seemed that Patmore had obtained a far deeper insight into the feminine soul than is given to any but a very few men; nor do I think that this is more largely due to his natural qualifications for his task than to the privilege of a specially close union, both of heart and mind, with a wife of unusual power and delicacy of feeling. It was in fact the combination of original interest and discernment with exceptional advantages of circumstance that served to raise him above most of those masculine writers who have had similar aims. Scarcely ever can a poet have owed to his wife so large a debt.—CHAMPNEYS, BASIL, 1900, *Memoirs and Correspondence of Coventry Patmore*, vol. I, p. 119.

George Louis Palmella Busson Du Maurier
1834–1896.

The famous delineator of English society in *Punch*, and in later years a novelist; born in Paris, March 6, 1834; died in London, Oct. 8, 1896. In his childhood his parents settled in London. He began in 1850 to study art in London, Paris, Antwerp; returning to London, he was employed on the illustrated periodicals, and from 1864 to his death was of the regular staff of *Punch*. He wrote and illustrated three stories; "Peter Ibbetson" (1891); "Trilby" (1894); "The Martian" (1897.)—WARNER, CHARLES DUDLEY, ed. 1897, *Library of the World's Best Literature, Biographical Dictionary*, vol. XXIX, p. 155.

PERSONAL

It was here that I first saw Du Maurier, a quiet man of no great stature, who at the first sight of him impresses one as a man who has suffered greatly, haunted by some evil dream or disturbing apprehension. His welcome is gentle and kindly, but he does not smile, even when he is saying a clever and smile-provoking thing. "You must smoke. One smokes here. It is a studio." Those were amongst the first words that Du Maurier said, and there was hospitality in them and the freemasonry of letters. . . . He reminds one as to physique, and in certain manifestations of a very nervous temperament, of another giant worker, whose name is Emile Zola. But he is altogether original and himself, a strong and striking individuality, a man altogether deserving of his past and present good fortune.—SHERARD, ROBERT H., 1895, *The Author of "Trilby," Human Documents*, pp. 180, 188.

That novel ["Trilby"], has been dramatized and played with great success, a son of the author being in the cast. That son recalls some interesting reminiscences of his father. He says: "Father never thought that 'Trilby' would be a success as a play when he was first told that it was going to be dramatized. However, he said he didn't care what was done with it, so long as he was not obliged to see it. He always hated the theater, anyway, and never went unless he had to, for the sake of some one else. But he rather changed his mind later about 'Trilby.' That is, he thought it was awfully clever to be able to make a play out of it at all, and was quite pleased at the way in which several of the scenes were reproduced. He went to the dress rehearsal, and several times after that. . . . He had not the slightest idea of fashion, or what was the correct thing in dress. People supposed that he noticed those things, of course, and girls used to come to call upon my mother and sisters got up beautifully, and expecting that father would want to put them into his drawings, or would at least get some ideas from them. But, dear me, he hadn't the least notion of what they had on! My sisters looked to it that he got the right things in his pictures. He would come home sometimes and sketch something which had attracted him in a passer-by on the street. Often it would be some impossibly queer arrangement, and my sisters would protest: 'Why, father, you mustn't use that in 'Punch.' Nobody wears those things now; they're dreadfully old-fashioned,' and he would give in immediately to what he recognized as their superior judgment."—JOHNSON, FLORENCE K., 1896, *Appleton'*, *Annual Cyclopædia*, vol. XXXVI, p. 250.

No artist of du Maurier's generation was more justly loved by his personal friends or had made a larger circle of unknown friends by the pleasure he had afforded every week for more than thirty years. And it is not unfair to du Maurier's undeniable literary gift to predict that on his long and remarkable connection with satiric art in the pages of "Punch" his fame will ultimately rest. A recognized lover and follower of Thackeray, he resembled that eminent master more nearly when he used the pencil than when he used the pen. —AINGER, ALFRED, 1901, *Dictionary of National Biography, Supplement*, vol. II, p. 166.

PETER IBBETSON
1891

The romance of "Peter Ibbetson," despite its one annoying lapse into slang just where the language should have been of the simplest and tersest, despite, too, a certain tendency to wander, is a great work—one that seizes the reader firmly and touches the best in him.—SCULL, W. DELAPLAINE, 1892, *George Du Maurier Romanticist, Magazine of Art*, vol. 15, p. 229.

It is graceful, gentle, enchanting in its unsubstantiality. It is indeed a book to be loved by those who like it at all—a book for the few, therefore, rather than the many—a book to be passed over carelessly by those who do not feel its charm—a book to be treasured by those who have delighted in it.—MATTHEWS, BRANDER, 1892, *Recent British Fiction, The Cosmopolitan*, vol. 13, p. 159.

Like the work of most amateur authors it is clumsy in its construction, and is in no sense a novel. Had the chapters been written as impressions—mere reminiscences of the artist's youth—with his own illustrations, they would have been far better in a literary sense. The story is a sort of elegant "Alice in Wonderland," but it entirely lacks the wit that made the latter a classic, nor has it even the humor the author afterward developed in "Trilby." One does not wonder that the story was not a marked success, though the illustrations were fully appreciated.—KNAUFFT, ERNEST, 1896, *George Du Maurier, Review of Reviews*, vol. 14, p. 574.

TRILBY
1894

I read "Trilby" in *Harper* as it came out. It simply astonished me. Whole pages of it were delicious, the very *medulla* of the *sweeter* Thackeray. But one misses the bitter-sweet. Still it is much to give the Thackerayan honey alone; for "Trilby" is a veritable honeysuckle, if ever there was. As a *tour-de-force* I imagine nothing has been written for many years that comes near it. And weren't the pictures good? And after "Peter Ibbetson," with both text and illustrations so disappointing. I see some reviews are calling upon Du Maurier to advance and challenge the higher issues. But surely that is unfair. He has done admirably, and I don't think he is ever likely to do better. His work is an extraordinary felicitous product, an *acme*, I should call it, or high-water mark for him. Apparently it has been written with the greatest care. Isn't that the very condition of its excellence? Let him lash himself for some mighty effort, and ten-to-one we shall see a dismal failure.—BROWN, THOMAS EDWARD, 1894, *To. S. T. Irwin, Nov. 21; Letters*, vol. II, p. 70.

The whole of Mr. du Maurier's *dramatis personæ* have taken such a firm hold of the little imagination I possess that it has become a question of my escape, not of theirs. I should have liked to be a kind of Niebuhr to them, from *Dudor, Zouzou*, and *Gecko* up to *Little Billee* and *Trilby O'Ferrall*, for in some shape or other I have known the counterparts of nearly all, living and breathing in the atmosphere in which they breathed, and in their habit as they lived. As it is, *Trilby* must come first; for I have known, perhaps, a half-dozen Trilbys, all differing in accidentals from each other and from our heroine, but alike in essentials. It proves to me that Mr. du Maurier went to work in the right way in delineating a human type instead of creating a more or less phenomenal human being. Astonishing though it may seem to those who are not familiar with the inner life of the French artists' models,—I have no knowledge of the English, and am not aware that they exist as a class,—the susceptibility of a great many of them to hypnotic influence, especially among the female members, is an ascertained fact. What *Svengali* did in such terrible earnestness and with such terrible results to poor *Trilby* is done out of sheer fun almost every day by the pupils at the "Beaux Arts," at private drawing-schools, and the *académies libres*.—VANDAM, ALBERT D., 1895, *The Trail of "Trilby," The Forum*, vol. 20, pp. 432, 435, 436.

"*Pauvre* Trilby!" Still the Philistine
Assails Bohemia's sweetest queen,
While stands apart the Pharisee
In "smug respectability."
" 'Tis shocking," writes the *Friend of Youth*,
"To thus display 'the naked truth,'
And wrong in such alluring dyes
A fallen creature to disguise."
A Scholar says, "It moves the heart,
But, if it's 'proper,' is it art?"
While every paragraphing prude
Sneers at "these studies from the lewd,"
Finds not a charm the book reveal,
And Trilby but "a new Camille."
Materfamilias warns young men
To shun the studio's naughty den;
While *Pedagogue* the book would ban
Because it's so "American,"
Saying, "It's *morals* I endure;
It is its *English* that's impure."
"Here dangerous fascinations lurk,"
Writes one who longs to love the work.
"It's gnosticism up to date,"
A Theologue is proud to state;
And all the pack in fullest roar
Its "ethical defect" deplore.

. . . .

Chère Trilby! 'twas consummate art
That gave the world your golden heart;
While purists prate of right or wrong,
Flower in the field of books, "*Je prong!*"
Let me among your lovers be!
"*Voilà l'espayce d'hom ker jer swee!*"
—CHURCH, EDWARD A., 1895, *The Altogether, Literary World*, vol. 26, p. 40.

✢he book is so untrue to life, its spirit and sentiment are so sentimental and false, that its popularity is a serious comment upon public taste. Such reading unfits one for real life, and leaves one cold in real sympathy.—HUSBAND, MARY GILLILAND, 1896, *Trilby, Westminster Review*, vol. 146, p. 457.

Without question, the play that has made of late the most noise, the wheels of whose chariot have raised a dust that threatens to smother all other drama, is "Trilby." It was my fortune to be in the United States when the taste for "Trilby" became a passion, when the passion grew into a mania, and the mania deepened into a madness. In the mælstrom of Chicago, as in the calm of Philadelphia, men added to their labour or their repose the worship of "Trilby." The languor of Southern cities quickened, the energy of New England cities intensified with the stimulus of Trilby O'Ferrall's name. Never in our time has a book been so suddenly exalted into a Bible. It flowed in a ceaseless stream over the counters of every bookshop on the American continent. It was discussed in the dialect of every state in the Union. Clergy of all denominations preached upon it from their pulpits. Impassioned admirers—for the most part women—formed societies, and debated over the moralities and the possibilities of the Altogether. The enthusiasm of the inhabitants of Abdera for the "Eros king of gods and men" of Euripides was but a joke to the enthusiasm of solid America for George du Maurier's novel. Finally, somebody made a play of it, and fanned an adoration that had not yet begun to flag, higher and higher above the fever line of the human thermometer. The delight of the Republic became a delirium when "Trilby" took incarnation in the body of Miss Virginia Harned. . . . "Trilby" is a very creditable piece of work of its kind and class.—MCCARTHY, JUSTIN HUNTLY, 1896, *Pages on Plays, Gentleman's Magazine*, vol. 280, pp. 207, 208.

His new rôle of popular novelist, or rather of propagator of microbes.—ZANGWILL, ISAAC, 1896, *The Newer Men, The Cosmopolitan*, vol. 20, p. 447.

As to "Trilby," it is *sui generis*. Two thirds of the story were charming, but the last third of it was impossible—I mean as to what would probably have grown out of such a character. I do not object to the hypnotism; I like the mystical very much; what I do object to is making church and state and society bow down to *Trilby*, and making her die in the odor of sanctity! She was simple, honest, and natural, but nothing of that would have happened. Till it came to that "Trilby" was my favorite novel, as "Peter Ibbetson" was before it.—HOWELLS, WILLIAM DEAN, 1897, *My Favorite Novelist, Munsey's Magazine*, vol. 17, p. 21.

The intrusion of the supernatural into the commonplace as in modern spiritualism is very bad art. The first part of the story of "Trilby" is admirable, worthy of Thackeray at his best. But the supernatural element, the hypnotic possession of the heroine by an evil nature, which might have harmonized with some tale of mediæval artist life, is entirely out of keeping with the realistic presentation of Paris thirty years ago.—JOHNSON, CHARLES F., 1898, *Elements of Literary Criticism*, p. 45.

GENERAL

Du Maurier possesses in perfection the genuine artist's perception of the snobbish. We have said, however, that the morality, so to speak, of his drawings, was a subordinate question; what we wished to insist upon is their completeness, their grace, their beauty, their rare pictorial character. It is an accident that the author of such things should not have been a painter—that he has not been an ornament of the English school. Indeed, with the restrictions to which he has so well accommodated himself, he *is* such an ornament. No English artistic work in these latter years has, in our opinion, been more exquisite in quality.—JAMES, HENRY, 1883, *Du Maurier and London Society*, Century Magazine, vol. 26, p. 65.

Dying at what is now considered to be but the approach of old age, Mr. du Maurier yet leaves behind him the record of a volume of work, more remarkable perhaps for continuity, good quality, and general serviceableness to the purposes for which it was designed, than for sustained freshness.—WEDMORE, F., 1896, *George Du Maurier, The Academy*, vol. 50, p. 290.

Du Maurier had indeed many sides to his talent, which a too exclusive devotion to the humours of society hindered him from cultivating. Especially may this be said of his real gift for poetry, which he wrote with equal skill in French and English. His ear for the harmonies of English verse had been trained on the best models, as the few specimens scattered through his writings abundantly prove. Although an imitator of no man, his "Vers de Société" —for he did not aim at more ambitious heights—show the mingled grace, humour, and tenderness of Oliver Wendell Holmes. —AINGER, ALFRED, 1901, *Dictionary of National Biography, Supplement*, vol. II, p. 166.

Thomas Hughes
1823–1856

Born, at Uffington, Berks, 20 Oct. 1823. At school at Twyford, 1830-33; at Rugby, 1833-41; Matric. Oriel Coll., Oxford, 2 Dec. 1841; B. A., 1845. Student of Lincoln's Inn, 21 Jan. 1845; removed to Inner Temple, 18 Jan. 1848; called to Bar there, 28 Jan. 1848. Married Anne Frances Ford, 17 Aug. 1847. F. S. A., 22 March, 1849; resigned 1854. M. P. for Lambeth, 1865-68; for Frome, 1868-74. Q. C., 23 June, 1869. Bencher of Lincoln's Inn, 31 May, 1870. Visit to U. S. A., 1870. Founded Colony of Rugby, Tennessee, 1880. Judge of County Court Circuit No. 9, July 1882. Died, at Brighton, 22 March 1896. *Works:* "History of the Working Tailors' Association, 34, Great Castle Street" (under initial: H.), [1850]; "A Lecture on the Slop System," 1852; "Tom Brown's School Days" (anon.) 1857; "The Scouring of the White Horse" (anon.), 1859 [1858]; "Account of the Lock-out of Engineers," 1860; "Tom Brown at Oxford," 1861; "Religio Laici," 1861 (another edn., called "A Layman's Faith," 1868); "The Cause of Freedom," 1863; "Alfred the Great," 1869; "Memoir of a Brother," 2nd edn., 1873; "Lecture on the History and Objects of Co-operation," 1878; "The Old Church: What shall we do with it?" 1878; "The Manliness of Christ," 1879; "Rugby, Tennessee," 1881; "A Memoir of Daniel Macmillan," 1882; "Address . . on the occasion of . . a testimonial, etc.," 1885; "James Fraser, second Bishop of Manchester," 1887; "Co-operative Production" [1887]; "David Livingstone," 1889; "Vacation Rambles" (from "Spectator"), 1895. He *edited:* Whitmore's "Gilbert Marlowe," 1859; Lowell's "Biglow Papers," 1859; the Comte de Paris' "Trade Unions of England," 1869; Philpot's "Guide Book to the Canadian Dominion," 1871; Maurice's "The Friendship of Books," 1874; Kingsley's "Alton Locke," 1876; "A Manual for Co-operators" (with E. V. Neale) 1881; "Gone to Texas," 1884; Lowell's "Poetical Works," 1891; Marriott's "Charles Kingsley," 1892.— SHARP, R. FARQUHARSON, 1897, *A Dictionary of English Writers*, p. 141.

PERSONAL

Hughes is an excellent fellow, very plain, unsophisticated and jolly, of course full of talent. He is not a professional author, but a working barrister. His wife is a pretty and pleasing person, and they live in a pretty cottage near Wimbledon Common.—MOTLEY, JOHN LOTHROP, 1858, *To his Wife, July 4; Correspondence, ed. Curtis, vol.* I, *p.* 285.

If it is proved that Hughes must lose his reputation at the Bar by taking the course which helped to win Jeffrey and Brougham much of theirs, do not let him enter upon it. If the Review interferes in the least with his practice, he must hold to his first vows and break the latter. But I think, and shall continue to think, that he is almost an ideal editor, because he is an honest free man, tied to no notions and theories about books, able to judge what is worthy to go forth whether he agrees with it or not; one who will fearlessly admonish a contributor, and never dictate or be squeamish. He will of course not review the current literature. Many can be got to do that. He will speak what he knows and nothing else. He says he wishes to preach, and he ought to have a pulpit if one can be found for him.—MAURICE, FREDERICK DENISON, 1858, *Letter to Charles Kingsley, May* 27; *Life, ed. Maurice, vol.* I, *p.* 323.

He is universally esteemed for the nobleness of his nature, for his robust intellect, and his liberal culture. His own manly traits are fully evident in the tone of his delightful books.—UNDERWOOD, FRANCIS H., 1871, *A Hand-Book of English Literature, British Authors, p.* 575.

It would be hard to find a finer type of English character than Thomas Hughes. His faults were only those of temperament and intellect. He was hasty; he was oversanguine. He might let fly a hard word; he was incapable of harbouring an evil thought or feeling. He was often taken in by rogues; with anything savouring to him of dishonesty he never made terms. No one who had any genuineness in him could know him without loving him. And to how many, who never saw the man in the flesh, has he made himself beloved through his books? Surely there were never any written through which the author revealed himself so utterly, without anything of conscious self-portraiture.—LUDLOW, J. M., 1896, *Thomas Hughes and Septimus Hansard, Economic Review, vol.* 6, *p.* 312.

In the House of Commons the line he took was definitely that of a reformer, and especially of a friend of the working classes; a trades union bill he introduced was read a second time on 7 July, 1869, but made no further progress. He was not a very successful speaker, and, though greatly liked and respected, he would not have been able to reach the front rank in politics. When Gladstone went over to home rule for Ireland, Hughes's opposition to that policy was touched with indignation, and he became a vehement liberal unionist. In 1869 he was chairman of the first co-operative congress, and spoke against the tendency to shelve "productive" co-operation, which he never ceased to denounce.—DAVIES, J. LLEWELYN, 1901, *Dictionary of National Biography, Supplement, vol.* III, *p.* 9.

TOM BROWN
1857–61

I have often been minded to write to you about "Tom Brown," so here goes. I have puffed it everywhere I went, but I soon found how true the adage is that good wine needs no bush, for every one had read it already, and from every one, from the fine lady on the throne, to the red-coat on his cock-horse, and the school-boy on his forrum (as our Irish brethren call it), I have but one word, and that is, that it is the jolliest book they ever read. Among a knot of red-coats at the cover-side, some very fast fellow said, "If I had such a book in my boyhood, I should have been a better man now!" and more than one capped his sentiment frankly. Now isn't it a comfort to your old bones to have written such a book, and a comfort to see that fellows are in a humour to take it in?—KINGSLEY, CHARLES, 1857, *To Mr. Hughes; Charles Kingsley, his Letters and Memories of his Life, ed. his Wife, vol.* II, *p.* 26.

Just behind me is the portrait of some fine oaks painted for me by an artist friend of mine. He wanted a human figure as a standard of size, and so put me in as I lay in the shade reading. So long as the canvas lasts I shall lie there with the book in my hand, and the book is "Tom Brown." A man cannot read a book out of doors that he does not love. Q. E. D.—LOWELL, JAMES RUSSELL, 1859, *To Thomas Hughes, Sept.* 13; *Letters, ed. Norton, vol.* I, *p.* 297.

Though his one remarkable book can scarcely be called a novel, the name of Mr. Thomas Hughes, now Judge Hughes, whose "Tom Brown" was the beginning of that interest of the general public in public schools which has never flagged since then, and which made the remarkable reign of

Dr. Arnold at Rugby, and his ideal of the English Schoolboy better known than the more legitimate medium of biography and descriptive history could ever have made it. "Tom Brown at Oxford" was not equally successful, but the introduction of the ideal young man of Victorian romance, the fine athlete, moderately good scholar, and honest, frank, muscular, and humble-minded gentleman, of whom we have seen so many specimens, is due to Judge Hughes more than to any other. If circumstances have occurred since to make us a little tired of that good fellow, and disposed to think his patronage of the poorer classes somewhat artificial, it is not Judge Hughes' fault.—OLIPHANT, MARGARET O. W., 1892, *The Victorian Age of English Literature*, p. 493.

All peoples who can read English, and some who cannot, have fallen under the spell of "Tom Brown's School Days,"—generally in those plastic years of the early teens when the deepest and most lasting impressions may result from such winning sermons as Judge Hughes cunningly worked into that classic. Robinson Crusoe and "Tom Brown" are our boy epics. Critics who can be suspected of no envy have found that Mr. Hughes' masterpiece was "thin," that its humor was false, that its style was naught, that the standards of boy-excellence were beefy and unfeeling; but after forty years, the story of Rugby life still furnishes the one pre-eminent example of the schoolboy in fiction. It has even been translated into French—how the pupils of a *lycée* can understand it, much less like it, is a mystery; and if any final evidence is needed of its triumphant and irresistible veracity, one need only add that the English boys of the rival public schools admit its sovereignty.—LANIER, CHARLES D., 1896, *Thomas Hughes and "Tom Brown," Review of Reviews*, vol. 13, p. 567.

*On one such occasion the talk fell on children's books, and Hughes said that he had often thought that good might be done by a real novel for boys—not didactic, like "Sandford and Merton"—written in a right spirit, but distinctly aiming at being interesting. I agreed with him. He then went on to say that he had tried his hand on the thing, but did not know whether it was worth publishing. Sometimes he thought it was, and sometimes that it wasn't. Would I mind looking at what he had written? I said that I should be very glad; and either that night or the next, I forget now which, he put into my hands a portion of "Tom Brown." I read it, I own, with amazement. God forgive me, but, notwithstanding his tract, his various articles in the "Christian Socialist" and "Journal of Association," his "Lecture on the Slop System," I had in nowise realized his literary power. I found, now, that I was reading a work of absorbing interest, which would place its writer on the front rank in contemporary literature. As I handed it back to him, I said, "Tom, this *must* be published." He left it, within the next day or two, with Alexander Macmillan, who, after writing to me on the subject, gave him a favorable answer. . . . "Tom Brown's School Days" came out in April, 1857. No author's name was on the title-page; it had to fight its way by its own merits. To these some of the critics were simply blind, treating the volume as a mere child's book. But in three months a second edition had to be issued (July), a third two months later (September), others in the following and next following months, making five in nine months; and the number of editions since then is almost beyond reckoning.—LUDLOW, J. M., 1896, *Thomas Hughes and Septimus Hansard, Economic Review*, vol. 6. pp. 306, 307.

This book is Hughes's chief title to distinction. His object in writing it was to do good. He had no literary ambition, and no friend of his had ever thought of him as an author. "Tom Brown's School Days" is a piece of life, simply and modestly presented, with a rare humour playing all over it, and penetrated by the best sort of English religious feeling. And the life was that which is peculiarly delightful to the whole English-speaking race—that of rural sport and the public school. The picture was none the less welcome, and is none the less interesting now, because there was a good deal that was beginning to pass away in the life that it depicts. The book was written expressly for boys, and it would be difficult to measure the good influence which it has exerted upon innumerable boys by its power to enter into their ways and prejudices, and to appeal to their better instincts; but it has commended itself to readers of all ages, classes, and characters. The author was naturally induced to go on writing, and his subsequent books, such as "The Scouring of the White Horse" (1859) and "Tom Brown at Oxford" (1861) are not without the qualities of which the "School Days" had given evidence; but it was the conjunction of the subject and the author's gifts that made the first book unique.—DAVIES, J. LLEWELYN, 1901, *Dictionary of National Biography, Supplement*, vol. III, p. 8.

Harriet Elizabeth Beecher Stowe
1812–1896

Born [Harriet Elizabeth Beecher], at Litchfield, Conn., 14 June, 1812. At school kept by her sister at Hartford, as scholar and teacher, 1824-32. Removed, with her father, to Cincinnati, 1832. Married to Rev. Calvin Ellis Stowe, Jan. 1836. Contrib. "Uncle Tom's Cabin," as serial, to "National Era," 1851-52. Removed to Andover, where her husband was Prof. of Sacred Lit., 1852. Visits to Europe, 1853, 56, 59. Removed to Hartford, 1864. Part-editor of "Hearth and Home," 1868. Contrib. paper on "Lady Byron" to "Atlantic Monthly," Sept. 1869. Husband died there, 22 Aug. 1886. Failing health in later years. Died, at Hartford, Conn., 1 July 1896. *Works:* "Uncle Tom's Cabin," (from "National Era"), 1852; "A Key to Uncle Tom's Cabin," 1853; "A Peep into Uncle Tom's Cabin; for Children," 1853; "Sunny Memories of Foreign Lands" (2 vols.), 1854; "Geography for My Children," 1855; "The Christian Slave; a drama" (dramatised from "Uncle Tom's Cabin"), 1855; "Dred," 1856 (another edn., called "Nina Gordon," 1866); "Our Charley," 1858; "The Minister's Wooing," 1859; "The Pearl of Orr's Island," 1862; "Reply on Behalf of the Women of America," 1863; "The Ravages of a Carpet," 1864; "House and Home Papers" (under pseud. "Christopher Crowfield"), 1864; "Religious Poems," 1865; "Stories about our Dogs," 1865; "Little Foxes," 1865; "Queer Little People," 1867; "Daisy's First Winter," 1867; "The Chimney Corner" (under pseud. "Christopher Crowfield"), 1868; "Men of Our Times," 1868; "The American Woman's Home" (with C. E. Beecher), 1869; "Old Town Folks," 1869; "Lady Byron Vindicated," 1869; "Little Pussy Willow," 1870; "Pink and White Tyranny," 1871; "Sam Lawson's Fireside Stories," 1871; "My Wife and I," 1872; "Palmetto Leaves," 1873; Betty's Bright Idea," 1875; "We and our Neighbours," 1875; "Footsteps of the Master," 1876; "Bible Heroines," 1878; "Poganuc People," 1878; "A Dog's Mission," 1881. *Life:* [to the year 1888] by her son, C. E. Stowe, 1889.—SHARP, R. FARQUHARSON, 1897, *A Dictionary of English Authors*, p. 270.

PERSONAL

Mrs. Stowe has arrived in London. She is come with husband, brothers, sister-in-law, and nephew. She is a simple, kindly creature, with a face which becomes beautiful from expression.—HOWITT, MARY, 1853, *Letter to William Howitt, May 8; Autobiography*, ed. her Daughter, vol. II, p. 100.

If we could have been biassed at all, it would have been rather against, than in favour of, a writer who had been over-persuaded by her friends to come to this country, for the purpose of making a sort of public appearance, at the moment that admiration of her work was at fever height. Nothing could palliate such an indiscretion on the part of this lady's advisers, in the eyes of a fastidious Englishman, but the belief that she was a simple-minded enthusiastic crusader against American slavery, considering that the totally unexpected celebrity of her work had afforded her an opportunity of accelerating a European movement, in a holy cause, by her personal presence. Criticism, however, ought not to be influenced by petty disturbing forces like these, nor will ours.—WARREN, SAMUEL, 1853, *Uncle Tom's Cabin, Blackwood's Magazine*, vol. 74, p. 394.

Mrs. Beecher Stowe is now in Scotland, and has been staying at Dunrobin, where she made herself popular by her pleasing, gentle, and unaffected manners.—GREVILLE, HENRY, 1856, *Leaves from His Diary, Second Series*, p. 384.

I went to a reception given to her at Willis's Rooms, when she seemed to me a weird, uncanny creature, more French than English, and her husband a remarkably fine specimen of the Anglo-Saxon race, and no improvement upon it.—MOZLEY, THOMAS, 1882, *Reminiscences Chiefly of Oriel College and the Oxford Movement*, vol. II, p. 396.

It is difficult to realize, as one is shown

memorials of this kind, that the fragile, gentle-voiced little lady, who stands by explaining them, is herself the heroine in chief of the sublime conflict they recall. For a more unpretending person every way, or one seeming to be more unconscious of gifts and works of genius, or of a great part acted in life, it is not possible to imagine. In her quiet home, attended by her daughters, surrounded by respect and affection, filled with the divine calm of the Christian faith, in perfect charity with all mankind, the most celebrated of American women is passing the tranquil evening of her days. She will often be found seated at the piano, her hand straying over its keys—that hand that has been clothed with such mighty power—singing softly to herself those hymns of Gospel hope which have been dear to her heart through all her earthly pilgrimage, alike in cloud and in sunshine. Of late she has almost wholly laid her pen aside; though just now she is engaged with her son's assistance, in preparing for publication a brief memoir of her honored husband, who passed away a few months since.—TWICHELL, JOSEPH H., 1886, *Authors at Home, The Critic, vol. 9, p. 302.*

A little woman entered, seventy-five years old, decidedly undersize, and weighing less than a hundred pounds. She was very simply attired in a dress of black and white check, with linen collar and small brooch, her hair which had once been brown, hung fluffily upon a broad brow and was bound by a black ribbon in front and gathered in a low knot behind. Her nose is long and straight, eyes dimmed by years, mouth large and with long, Beecher lip, full of the pathos of humanity's mystical estate. This is what time has left of the immortal Harriet Beecher Stowe. She greeted us with cordial hand and voice and smile.—WILLARD, FRANCES E., 1887, *Harriet Beecher Stowe at Home, The Chautauquan, vol. 8, p. 288.*

When Mrs. Beecher Stowe visited London soon after the great success of "Uncle Tom's Cabin," I was taken to an afternoon reception given in her honor. I am ashamed to say I forget the name of her host, but I have an impression that he was a dissenting minister of some celebrity. It was certainly in the early "fifties," I think in 1852 or 1853; and perhaps few authors ever received more genuine homage, during a brief stay in England, than did the little woman on the sofa to whom we were in turn introduced. I did not actually hear the words from her lips, but they were buzzed about the room as having just been uttered by her, that she "felt like a child who had set fire to a packet of gunpowder." Notwithstanding the strong Yankee twang of her dialect, there was a very charming simplicity of manner about Mrs. Beecher Stowe. She did not ignore the fact that she had done an important piece of work in the world, but showed neither mock humility nor self-laudation on the subject. I suppose she was under forty years of age at the time of which I am speaking, but her skin looked dry and withered as if by a settled tan. Her countenance was distinctly intelligent, yet I can fancy certain commonplace people ranking her as one of themselves, and rather wondering how she could have written such a book. I mean those people who seem to fancy that authors are always attired in their "foolscap uniform," much as little children imagine that kings and queens always wear crowns. But more expressive, to my mind, than her countenance, were Mrs. Stowe's hands, which, for the most part, lay very quietly in her lap. I noticed there was no wedding-ring. Small, brown, and thin, the gnarling of the joints revealed the energy of character that usually accompanies such hands. Though by no means so "spirit small" as Mrs. Browning's hands, they had something of the same character.—CROSLAND, MRS. NEWTON (CAMILLA TOULMIN), 1893, *Landmarks of a Literary Life, p. 213.*

The last time that I saw Mrs. Stowe was on the occasion of her seventieth birthday; when, at the country-seat of Governor and Mrs. Claflin, in Newtonville, Messrs. Houghton and Mifflin, her publishers, tendered her a reception—I think she called it a birthday party. . . . Mrs. Stowe's appearance that day—one of her last, I think, in public—was a memorable one. Her dignity, her repose, a certain dreaminess and aloofness of manner characteristic of her, blended gently with her look of peace and unmistakable happiness. Crowded with honors as her life had been, I have fancied that this, among her latest, in her quiet years, and so full of the tenderness of personal friendship, had especial meanings to her, and gave her deep pleasure.—PHELPS, ELIZABETH STUART, 1896, *Reminiscences of*

Harriet Beecher Stowe, McClure's Magazine, vol. 7, pp. 3, 6.

Mrs. Stowe's face, like those of all her mother's children, showed the delicate refinement of the Foote mask, overlaid by the stronger and more sanguine Beecher integument. Her curling, crispy hair, more or less freeing itself from the velvet bands with which she was accustomed to confine it, gave an informal grace to her head. Her eyes, whether twinkling with merriment or subdued to thoughtfulness, were always kind and pleasant. Her slender frame, with something of the "scholar's stoop" of the shoulders (although so faithful a mother and housekeeper might claim other reasons besides study, for that), was neatly but not stylishly dressed. Her manner was very self-possessed, gentle, considerate; without the graces of one habituated to society, she was most evidently a gentlewoman, born and bred.—HOWARD, JOHN R., 1896, *Harriet Beecher Stowe, The Outlook, vol. 54, p. 138.*

It appeared to those who listened most frequently to her conversation that a large part of the charm of her tales was often lost in the writing down; yet with all her unusual powers she was an excellent listener herself. Her natural modesty was such that she took keen pleasure in gathering fresh thought and inspiration from the conversation of others. Nor did the universal homage she received from high and low leave any unworthy impression upon her self-esteem. She was grateful and pleased and humble, and the only visible effect produced upon her was the heightened pleasure she received from the opportunities of knowing men and women who excited her love and admiration. Her name was a kind of sacred talisman, especially in New and Old England. It was a banner which had led men to battle against slavery. Therefore it was often a cause of surprise and social embarrassment when the bearer of this name proved to be sometimes too modest, and sometimes too absent-minded to remember that anything was expected of her on great occasions, or anything arranged for her special entertainment.—FIELDS, ANNIE, 1897, *Life and Letters of Harriet Beecher Stowe, p. 376.*

UNCLE TOM'S CABIN
1852

You must feel and know what deep impression "Uncle Tom's Cabin" has made upon every heart that can feel for the dignity of human existence; so I, with my miserable English, would not even try to say a word about the great excellency of that most beautiful book, but I *must* thank you for the great joy I have felt over that book. . . . I have the feeling about "Uncle Tom's Cabin" that great changes will take place by and by from the impression people receive out of it, and that the writer of that book can "fall asleep" to-day or to-morrow with the bright sweet conscience of having been a strong, powerful means, in the Creator's hand, of operating essential good in one of the most important questions for the welfare of our black *brethren.*— GOLDSCHMIDT, JENNY (NÉE LIND), 1852, *Letter to Mrs. Stowe, May 23.*

My dear Sir,—I have to offer you my thanks for sending me a very remarkable book, "Uncle Tom's Cabin," which followed on the receipt of your letter of the 25th of April last. The book horrifies and haunts me; and I cannot help writing to you somewhat at large upon it. . . . Many readers and reviewers will, I have no doubt, at once explain the book to themselves, and make their minds, comparatively speaking, easy upon it, by saying that it contains gross exaggerations, and that it gives no fair account of slavery in America. I am, unfortunately, but too well acquainted with the records of slavery in most parts of the New World, and under nations differing very much from one another, for me to be able to comfort myself in this way. In truth, unless by some special Providence, planters were imbued with angelic nature, of which there is at present no evidence before us, I cannot see how the state of things can be much otherwise than as it is described to be in this fearful book, which seems to have set all America again thinking about slavery. . . . I have now said all that I have to say, and more than I ought to ask you to read, about "Uncle Tom's Cabin." If I had the honor of any acquaintance with the authoress, I would send through you my best regards and most earnest expressions of encouragement to her. She is evidently a noble woman and an excellent writer. And her book is one of those which insist upon being read when once begun.—HELPS, SIR ARTHUR, 1852, *Uncle Tom's Cabin, Fraser's Magazine, vol. 46, pp. 237, 244.*

Mrs. Stowe is all instinct: it is the very reason that she appears to some not to have talent. Has she not talent? What is talent? Nothing, doubtless, compared to genius; but has she genius? I cannot say that she has talent, as one understands it in the world of letters; but she has genius, as humanity feels the need of genius,—the genius of goodness, not of the man of letters, but of the saint. Yes, a saint! Thrice holy the soul which thus loves, blesses, and consoles the martyrs. Pure, penetrating, and profound the spirit which thus fathoms the recesses of the human soul. Noble, generous, and great the heart which embraces in her pity, in her love, an entire race, trodden down in blood and mire under the whip of ruffians and the maledictions of the impious.—SAND, GEORGE, 1852, *Review of Uncle Tom's Cabin, December* 17.

The enthusiastic reception of Mrs. Stowe's novel is the result of various causes. One is the merit of the book itself. It is, unquestionably, a work of genius. It has defects of conception and style, exhibits a want of artistic skill, is often tame and inadequate in description, and is tinctured with methodistic cant; but, with all its blemishes,—thought, imagination, feeling, high moral and religious sentiment, and dramatic power shine in every page. It has the capital excellence of exciting the interest of the reader; this never stops or falters from the beginning to the end. The characters are drawn with spirit and truth. FISHER, S. G., 1853, *Uncle Tom's Cabin, North American Review, vol.* 77, *p.* 466.

"Uncle Tom's Cabin" is a remarkable book, unquestionably; and, upon the whole, we are not surprised at its prodigious success, even as a mere literary performance; but whether, after all, it will have any direct effect upon the dreadful INSTITUTION at which it is aimed, may be regarded as problematical. Of one thing we are persuaded—that its author, as she has displayed in this work undoubted genius, in some respects of a higher order than any American predecessor or contemporary, is also a woman of unaffected and profound piety, and an ardent friend of the unhappy black. Every word in her pages issues glistening and warm from the mint of woman's love and sympathy, refined and purified by Christianity. We never saw in any other work, so many and such sudden irresistible appeals to the reader's heart—appeals which, moreover, only a wife and a mother could make. One's heart throbs, and one's eyes are suffused with tears without a moment's notice, and without anything like effort or preparation on the writer's part. We are, on the contrary, soothed in our spontaneous emotion by a conviction of the writer's utter artlessness; and when once a gifted woman has satisfied her most captious reader that such is the case, she thenceforth leads him on, with an air of loving and tender triumph, a willing captive to the last. There are, indeed, scenes and touches in this book which no living writer, that we know of, can surpass, and perhaps none even equal.—WARREN, SAMUEL, 1853, *Uncle Tom's Cabin, Blackwood's Magazine, vol.* 74, *p.* 395.

Tell her I can send her nothing *half so good*, if I were to lay out pounds instead of pence. I have never read anything which has made such a profound impression on me. I should like to know, when you write again, what you think of this wonderful, human-hearted, and deeply Christian book. It is not a *religious novel*, but a religious book in the sense in which our life should be religious.—GREENWELL, DORA, 1854, *Letter, Memoirs, ed. Dorling, p.* 33.

The humor, the pathos, the keen observation, the power of characterization, displayed in the novel, were all penetrated by an imagination quickened into activity by a deep and humane religious sentiment.—WHIPPLE, EDWIN PERCY, 1876–86, *American Literature and Other Papers, ed. Whittier, p.* 123.

Thrice welcome from the Land of Flowers
And golden-fruited orange bowers
To this sweet, green-turfed June of ours!
To her who, in our evil time,
Dragged into light the nation's crime
With strength beyond the strength of men,
And, mightier than their swords, her pen!
To her who world-wide entrance gave
To the log-cabin of the slave;
Made all his wrongs and sorrows known,
And all earth's languages his own,—
North, South, and East and West, made all
The common air electrical,
Until the o'ercharged bolts of heaven
Blazed down, and every chain was riven!
—WHITTIER, JOHN GREENLEAF, 1882, *A Greeting, Read at Harriet Beecher Stowe's Seventieth Anniversasy, June* 14.

The fact was a terrible blow had just fallen on English literature. This was a funeral feast over scores of promising works, born to die at once, some indeed never to be heard of, so I have been told, but to pass straight from the press to the vat. It was the year of "Uncle Tom's Cabin." All the 'ologies, all the arts and sciences, histories, travels, fictions, facts, light literature, heavy literature, everything that man can read, perished in that fatal blight. Mrs. Beecher Stowe had found the Garden of Eden before her, but she left a wilderness behind.—MOZLEY, THOMAS, 1882, *Reminiscences Chiefly of Oriel College and the Oxford Movement, vol.* II, *p.* 395.

She was in the forefront of the broadest Puritanic movement—the anti-slavery reform. She developed amid the finest culture, and ripened in mind when the times were ripest for action. These were her opportunities. Her gifts from nature were of the Walter Scott pattern. Her mind was masculine in its perception of humor, in its broad, healthy common sense. She absorbed, like Scott, everything that goes to the fullest expression of human action—incident, gesture, dialect, feature, tone, inflection—both the peculiar and the general. She could generalize and individualize—her individuals being both types and distinct personages—warm, full-blooded, alive all over, and characteristic. She had such a large intellectual endowment that she could give a fair fund of mind to each of her creations; such a wealth of humor and *bonhomie* that she could warm the coldest blood; such a wide possibility of the sinner and saint in her nature that she could endow a double-headed procession to march with Eva heavenward, or with Legree in the other direction. In "Uncle Tom's Cabin" she was lavish. This book contains her whole range of characters, and everything combined to make it her great work.—MORSE, JAMES HERBERT, 1883, *The Native Element in American Fiction, Century Magazine, vol.* 26, *p.* 297.

The author of "Uncle Tom's Cabin" had the wisdom—not possessed by the pessimistic or self-blinded delineators of later woes in Russia—to brighten her pages by touches of humor and kindly humanity, and to obey the canons of the novelist's art as well as those of the moralist's conscience. Thereby her force was quadrupled, for literature both popularizes and perpetuates morality, while morality without art is fatal to literature. The book remains a vivid panorama of people and scene in a bygone time, now remanded by final war to a past that must ever be historic and can never be repeated.—RICHARDSON, CHARLES F., 1888, *American Literature*, 1607–1885, *vol.* II, *p.* 411.

"Uncle Tom's Cabin" was published in book form in March, 1852. The despondency and uncertainty of the author as to whether any one would read her book, was soon dispelled. Ten thousand copies were sold in a few days, and over three hundred thousand within a year. Eight powerful presses running day and night for months were barely able to keep pace with the demand for it. It was read everywhere, by all classes of people. Talk of it filled the atmosphere. Heated discussions occasioned by it resounded in cottage, farm-house, business offices, and palatial residences all over the land. . . . Echoes of its clarion tones came back to its author in her quiet home in Brunswick, returning as they had struck the world, with clashing dissonance or loud alarum, or low, sweet tones of feeling. Letters, letters of all sizes, colors, directions, and kinds of chirography, astonished the postmaster at Brunswick by their countless numbers, and the author began to feel the nation's pulse. Friends applauded, remonstrated, or vociferously deprecated her course. Literary associates praised the *technique* of the story, but thought the subject ill-chosen. Abolitionists wrote with irrepressible enthusiasm, and praised God that she had been raised up to do this thing. Politicians angrily expressed their amazement that her husband should permit her to commit this incendiarism, which might burst into a conflagration that would dissolve the national Union. Slaveholders heaped reproaches and contumely upon her, and badly spelled productions, evincing cowardly ruffianism, were taken with tongs by her husband and dropped almost unread into the fire.—MCCRAY, FLORINE THAYER, 1890, *Uncle Tom's Cabin and Mrs. Stowe, Magazine of American History, vol.* 23, *p.* 16.

Even the careless reader today will see that the story straggles not a little and lacks firm structure; it bears evidence that it was written from week to week, without a settled plan, and that it grew on the author's hands almost in spite of herself. As Mrs. Stowe told the publisher, "the story made itself, and that she could not stop till it was done." The tale was nearly half told before the need for "comedy relief," as the playmakers phrase it, led to the introduction of Topsy, perhaps the most popular figure in the book; and it was drawing to its close before we were made acquainted with Cassy, perhaps the most picturesque character in the story and certainly not the least true. The intensity of the author's feeling was so keen, her knowledge of her subject was so wide, her unconscious and intuitive impulse was so vigorous, that she shaped her story so as best to accomplish its purpose, building better than she knew and doing more than she dared to hope.—MATTHEWS, BRANDER, 1892, *American Fiction Again, The Cosmopolitan*, vol. 12, p. 637.

Mrs. Stowe's experiences were exceptional, her achievements conspicuous. The ethical was dominant in her career—the world of spirits, ideas, ideals, and aspirations was the world of her chief interest. In the making of her mightiest book she regarded herself as a medium—in the noble sense of that much misused word. "Are you not thankful, Mrs. Stowe," said a neighbor of late, "that you wrote 'Uncle Tom's Cabin?'" With a flash of the old fire she replied, "I did not write that book: God put a pen into my hand; he wrote it."—BURTON, RICHARD, 1896, *The Author of "Uncle Tom's Cabin," Century Magazine*, vol. 52, p. 704.

It was plain that no immediate literary success, tried by the ordinary standards, was ever greater than this. If now the question be asked, how far "Uncle Tom's Cabin" has vindicated its claim to be one of the great and permanent works of literature, it can only be replied that it is too soon to judge, but that the probabilities now seem rather against such a destiny. It had, like Cooper's novels, the immense advantage of introducing to the reading world a race of human beings practically new to literature, and it had, beyond the writings of Cooper, the advantage of a distinctly evangelical flavor, such as had of itself secured a great success for the novels of the Warner sisters, now almost forgotten. Finally, it roused the world's resentment against a mighty wrong. All these things together could not sufficiently explain the success of the book, but they helped to explain it. . . . "Uncle Tom's Cabin" implied a marked literary ability in its author. Characterization, grouping, incident, all were good; but, in view of the favourable conditions offered by the subject and the occasion, it is not necessary to account for its success by calling it a work of pure genius, nor is it likely that this will be the judgment of future criticism. The simple fact that the same publishers issued soon after a story of the most mediocre quality, called "The Lamplighter," which, without any special interest of theme, yet made a tour through Europe and was abundantly translated, seems to imply that there may have been something favorable in the conditions of the times.—HIGGINSON, THOMAS WENTWORTH, 1896, *Harriet Beecher Stowe, The Nation*, vol. 63, p. 25.

Until after the war we had no real novels in this country, except "Uncle Tom's Cabin." That is one of the great novels of the world, and of all time. Even the fact that slavery was done away with does not matter; the interest in "Uncle Tom's Cabin" never will pass, because the book is really as well as ideally true to human nature, and nobly true. It is the only great novel of ours before the war that I can think of.—HOWELLS, WILLIAM DEAN, 1897, *My Favorite Novelist, Munsey's Magazine*, vol. 17, p. 22.

Say what we will, we can only let it stand in our serene Walhalla side by side with mighty master-pieces, a stranger withal, a Topsy among the gods, an Uncle Tom that had to be let in. There it stands. No one shall move it thence—an inspired crime, a blundering apocalypse. However inferior in many respects to her other work Mrs. Stowe's "Uncle Tom's Cabin" may be, it is impossible to consider anything that she ever did—perhaps her ever doing anything,—except through this great tidal experience which swept her personality out into the full current of its power. Uncle Tom meant in Mrs. Stowe's art what the Civil War meant in the life of every soldier who fought in it. No thought that he could ever think, nothing that he could refrain from doing, would be the same as it otherwise would have been, without those three immortal years with shot and shell and passion, day and night, and with Death for a comrade. All that is masterful in the painting of pictures, in the crises of life, the composing of symphonies, the writing of books, would seem to be the infinite coming back of some Moment we never forget. It is decreed that this moment shall be God to us. "Uncle Tom's Cabin" was Mrs. Stowe's Moment. . . . The success of Uncle Tom was based upon the moments in which she was a genius and an artist both.—LEE, GERALD STANLEY, 1897, *Harriet Beecher Stowe, The Critic, vol.* 30, *pp.* 282, 283.

I believe that Uncle Tom and Eva are as imperishable as Hector and Andromache. As long as human error and atonement are intelligible subjects of tragedy, as long as men need to be reminded that the innocent must suffer for the guilty, as long as tyrants torture and helpless creatures cringe, so long this dramatic romance will retain its power.—LAWTON, WILLIAM CRANSTON, 1902, *Introduction to the Study of American Literature, p.* 193.

Forgetting alike her false step in the Byron matter, her volumes of travels, her religious verses, her sketches, her juvenile fiction, and even most of her better novels, the great world appears to have decided to remember Mrs. Stowe as the woman that wrote "Uncle Tom's Cabin." In this case, as in so many others, the decision of the world seems to be the safest one for criticism to adopt. Mrs. Stowe lives as the writer of one great book. She had the faculty of giving a fair amount of life to some characters; of sketching others very effectively, even if she frequently lapsed into carricature, of telling an interesting story. Her descriptive powers were good, her command of pathos and humour was very considerable, her intellectual ability was respectable, and with regard to slavery and theology more than respectable, her womanliness lent charm and dignity to many of her pages, her style improved with practice and was at least fairly adequate to her purposes; yet we have but to set Mrs. Stowe beside Jane Austen, George Eliot, and George Sand to be convinced that she was not an eminent author. Her art was not sufficiently sure, her intellect not sufficiently strong and deep, her power not sufficiently affluent. These deficiencies of the writer are plainly visible in her single masterpiece, but "Uncle Tom's Cabin" is alive with emotion, and the book that is alive with emotion after the lapse of fifty years is a great book. The critic of to-day cannot do better than to imitate George Sand when she reviewed the story on its first appearance—Waive its faults and affirm its almost unrivalled emotional sincerity and strength.—TRENT, WILLIAM P., 1903, *A History of American Literature, p.* 508.

Even more remarkable than the external fortunes of the book is the author's lack of intellectual and moral preparation for it and pre-engagement with it. Her first knowledge of slavery on its own ground was in 1833, when she visited a Kentucky plantation, which became Colonel Shelby's in the book. She saw something of pro-slavery riots in Cincinnati, and something of runaway slaves, only the Ohio's width intervening between Cincinnati and slave territory. Once she had a slave girl as a servant in her house, and when the manhounds were on the girl's track Mrs. Stowe's husband and brother spirited her away towards Canada, so furnishing Mrs. Stowe with one of her strong incidents. Had her own scent upon the trail of slavery been keen, her opportunities for intimate knowledge of it would have been adequate to her demands. But living for eighteen years next door to slavery, and, as it were, in the first station of the "underground railroad," she does not appear to have had any deep interest in the matter during those years. She probably sympathised with her father when, at the dictation of the slave holding interests, he silenced the discussion of slavery in his school and forced the withdrawal of the anti-slavery students. She disliked the abolitionists and was still a "colonisationist" when she wrote "Uncle Tom's Cabin." Apparently she waited, as did many others, for the operation of the Fugitive Slave Law (1850) to wake her sleeping heart, and it was first through another's eyes that she saw the horror of the situation. Her brother Edward's wife in Boston had a close view of the slave captures and renditions, and she wrote to Mrs. Stowe commanding her to "write something that would make this whole nation feel what an accursed thing slavery is." Mrs. Stowe read the letter in her little Brunswick parlour, and then crushing it in her hand, as if it were the monster, said, erecting her tired body, "I *will* write something. I *will*, if I live." No vow was ever kept more sacredly. Once launched upon the tide of her story, she was swept along with passionate sympathy. Much of it was written in the small hours of night, after the baking, mending, child-nursing, house painting, and other drudgery of the day. The book written in this fashion had the defects of its qualities. The plot was loose and rambling; the style had ailing spots; the knowledge of Southern life and character and situation had its defective side. But the author had the divine gift of imagination, and her book was all alive. Every character had reality; so had the scenery of the book; so had its main effect. It did not exaggerate the horrors of slavery. It confessed the better side.—CHADWICK, JOHN WHITE, 1903, *Chambers's Cyclopædia of English Literature*, ed. Patrick, vol. III, p. 809.

DRED
1856

I wish I were within reach of you to read "Dred" to you: not that it is so good as "Uncle Tom"—that, indeed, was impossible, for she could never write her first book again; but I think the comic part of this last one admirable.—KEMBLE, FRANCES ANN, 1856, *Letter to Henry Greville, Leaves from his Diary, Second Series*, p. 396.

She has lately published a new book called "Dred," which contains some fine things, but is not likely, from its exaggeration, to advance the cause she has so much at heart, and which just now appears to be anything but in the ascendant in the United States.—GREVILLE, HENRY, 1856, *Leaves from his Diary, Second Series*, p. 384.

"Dred," intended by the writer to be in some sort a complement to the earlier novel, appeared in 1856, and one hundred thousand copies were sold in England within four weeks. Harriet Martineau thought it superior to "Uncle Tom," and the work certainly contains some vivid scenes, and, moreover, has the merit of depicting the normal social conditions of the South during slavery days.—BURTON, RICHARD, 1896, *The Author of "Uncle Tom's Cabin," Century Magazine*, vol. 52, p. 704.

It was less an inspiration than its predecessor, and more a deliberate construction; and was judged to be inferior in power. Yet it was a very strong book, both in human interest and in effective attack upon the slave system. In logical sequence to the simple story of the earlier book, it went on to portray the treatment of slavery on its own ground by the church, the law, and the would-be reformer. It showed how its essential evils were supported by statute and by judicial interpretation. It pictured the ways of the clerical politician. It depicted the attempt of a high-minded slaveholder to elevate his servants and purify the system, and his defeat by mob violence and by statute law. These were trenchant attacks on the system they were aimed at. But the more abiding charm of the book is in its life-like picturing of men and women; and especially in "life among the lowly." Best of all, perhaps, are "Old Tiff," a counterpart of the "Uncle Remus" whom the present generation knows and loves; and Milly, the slave "mammy,"—the type which of all the negroes Mrs. Stowe portrays best, and perhaps the finest type of character which slavery produced.—MERRIAM, GEORGE S., 1897, *Library of the World's Best Literature*, ed. Warner, vol. XXIV. p. 14069.

THE MINISTER'S WOOING
1859

Marked a new era in American novel-writing. Here we had the genuine novel,—no mere romance, or allegory, or evolution from the inner consciousness, but a work saturated with American life,—not local, but spanning the whole arch of the States.—MORSE, JAMES HERBERT, 1883, *The Native Element in American Fiction, Century Magazine*, vol. 26, p. 296.

She was the first to break the spell of a theology which had wrought terrible mischief with sensitive minds and which is to-day responsible for the indifference of multitudes. . . . Contained the keynote of the later Andover movement and led the way to the larger hope. If this is the significance of this book to-day, it is to be valued also as a delineation of New England society at the beginning of this century. It is refreshing to read it in comparison with the highly-seasoned fiction of the hour. It holds and entertains the reader by its truth to life, and yet the sensational features of the modern story are entirely wanting. In the character of Candace Mrs. Stowe gives her solution of a religious problem, and in the person of Mrs. Marvyn one sees what the effect of the teaching of eternal punishment was upon a sensitive and devout mind. This novel shows a conscious effort on the part of Mrs. Stowe to write up to the level of her great reputation. She would have been more than human had she not betrayed this weakness, and it is the only one of her later writings in which it appears.—WARD, JULIUS H., 1896, *Harriet Beecher Stowe, The Forum*, vol. 21, p. 732.

The most artistic and complete of all her

books.—HOWARD, JOHN R., 1896, *Harriet Beecher Stowe, The Outlook, vol. 54, p. 319.*

Late in 1858 began in *The Atlantic Monthly* her widely liked and good novel of colonial life, "The Minister's Wooing." Lowell, then editing the magazine, prophesied that her fame would chiefly rest upon the new story, and other readers agreed with him. It is almost needless to remark that, if this ever happens, Mrs. Stowe's fame will have shrunk to such small dimensions that it will make little difference what it rests on.—TRENT, WILLIAM P., 1903, *A History of American Literature, p. 505.*

LADY BYRON VINDICATED
1869

Forty years after his death his wife produces notes she had taken nearly half a century past, accusing her liege lord of a heinous offence. Mrs. Beecher Stowe, a New England Puritan of the deepest dye, is called into council, and these two pious and remorseless saints, after conferring, condemn the Poet, and the stern Yankee lady puts on the black cap and passes sentence of death on the memory of a great man, without counsel being fee'd, or witnesses summoned on either side, and when all implicated are mouldering in their graves. If men's characters are to be thus summarily impugned and condemned, who is safe amongst the dead from being dragged from his grave and trailed in the mud as Cromwell was.—TRELAWNY, EDWARD JOHN, 1858-78, *Records of Shelley, Byron and the Author, p. 46.*

What grounds had she to publish to the world such a tale of impurity, from which even as a woman she was doubly bound to hold aloof? She desired, she says, to meet the accusations against Lady Byron contained in the book of the Countess Guiccioli, which she characterises as "the mistress *versus* the wife." But surely this was the business of the family or of their solicitors,—it was clearly not her affair; not to mention that the imputations of the Countess Guiccioli do not go beyond what had been said again and again before her, and said with justice against Lady Byron. It causes no pain to the pious soul of Mrs. Stowe to heap accusations on the dead, who cannot defend themselves; she appears to think that the end justifies the means, and that the godly are exempt from the application of the ordinary standards of morality. She might, no doubt, have considered herself absolved from any feelings of respect to the memory of Byron; for he of course, before and after his death, was considered by the pious world as proscribed and outlawed. But her feelings as a woman should have restrained her from branding with such infamy the memory of Mrs. Leigh, especially as some of Mrs. Leigh's children are still living. That from her religious point of view she should be ready to impute to Byron every possible deed of infamy, is conceivable; but what could entitle her to hold Mrs. Leigh capable of such an enormity? Where in Mrs. Leigh's life and character could she find any ground for such an accusation? Here, too, Mrs. Stowe betrays an utter want of the discrimination requisite for the sifting and weighing of evidence.— ELZE, KARL, 1870-72, *Lord Byron, p. 167.*

In the "Byron Controversy," many who agree with Dr. Holmes that Mrs. Stowe had made good her accusation, will equally agree with George Eliot that the advantage to Lady Byron's character from Mrs. Stowe's disclosure was no sufficient compensation for the harm it did to the community, by fixing its attention on a matter so intolerably vile.—CHADWICK, JOHN WHITE, 1890, *Mrs. Stowe, The Nation, vol. 50, p. 36.*

She startled the repose of society by publishing in the *Atlantic Monthly* what she conceived to be the true story of Lord Byron's quarrel with his wife, afterwards amplified and published as "Lady Byron Vindicated." It was a revelation so utterly ghastly that it aroused a large part of her readers against it; and as it was incapable of further proof—resting entirely upon verbal statements of Lady Byron—it never succeeded in establishing itself in the public mind. That Mrs. Stowe fully believed her own theory as to Lord Byron is unquestionable, but the motive of the exposure still remains unexplained. Had Lord Byron been a falsely canonized saint, there might have been some possible object in unveiling his sins; but as he occupied no moral eminence, it was not worth while to disgust the public in order to settle the mere question of more or less, and as Lady Byron had died in the odor of sanctity, there seemed no reason for vindicating her from the charge of a too zealous and exacting virtue. In the long run the publication neither helped Lady Byron's reputation nor hurt that of the poet, and it gave temporary stimulus to the sale of his works, which were steadily losing their influence.—HIGGINSON, THOMAS WENTWORTH, 1896, *Harriet Beecher Stowe, The Nation*, vol. 63, p. 25.

GENERAL

Her book, though it is called a novel, is better to be described as a series of pictures of life as seen from the kitchen, and best-room, and barnyard, and meadow, and wood-lot of a Massachusetts parsonage of the pre-locomotive days. So far as it is a novel, "Oldtown Folks" cannot be said to call for remark except from those whose duty it may be to point out defects of literary workmanship. Such persons will discover matter for fault-finding throughout the book. There is none of Mrs. Stowe's books that we know in which she has not failed as completely in the creation of character as she has succeeded decidedly in depicting typical Massachusetts men and women who—embodied in this and that individual person—have been under her observation ever since she began to observe, and whom she puts before us as she has seen the outside of them, and not as she has tried to imagine them. . . . Nothing could be much better in its way than Mrs. Stowe's picture of the village do-nothing Sam Lawson—whose do-nothingness is perhaps a little too much insisted upon—a being with whom every observer who knows New England villages is perfectly familiar in one or another incarnation of him, and whose traits lie upon the surface crying to be drawn. But no 'prentice hand could do much worse work than Mrs. Stowe's picture of Horace Holyoke. The entirely needless mistake is made, too, of putting the whole story into the mouth of this person, who has a deal too much to do to look like a man in his own place in the story without having it imposed on him to think and talk like a man about men's and women's acts and thoughts and feelings.—DENNETT, J. R., 1869, *Mrs. Stowe's "Oldtown Folks," The Nation*, vol. 8, p. 437.

A special influence may be attributed to this single marked manifestation of force, to this imposing popular triumph. In the face of the fact that the one American book which had stormed Europe was the work of a woman, the old tone of patronage became ridiculous, the old sense of ordained and inevitable weakness on the part of the "female writer" became obsolete. Women henceforth, whatever their personal feelings in regard to the much discussed book, were enabled, consciously or unconsciously, to hold the pen more firmly, to move it more freely.—CONE, HELEN GRAY, 1890, *Woman in American Literature, Century Magazine* vol. 40, p. 926.

Mr. James Russell Lowell considered Mrs. Stowe a woman of genius; at any rate she was the possessor of high talent, even if a certain lack of clearness of mental perception, which caused her judgment to be sometimes faulty, makes us hesitate to apply to her the word genius. She was an emotional rather than an inspired woman. If we compare her with country-women of her own, we find she had neither the large mental grasp of Margaret Fuller nor the spiritual height and breadth of Louisa Alcott. Yet, within her narrower sphere, she was admirable—an earnest, brave, and pious woman. If she erred in judgment, assuredly she was never false to the highest truth she knew. . . . Other works followed from Mrs. Stowe's pen, only less powerful than "Uncle Tom's Cabin" for the special end she had in view, and superior to it as contributions to literature. In her time she was the victim of extravagant praise and of equally extravagant censure; and it speaks well for the steadfastness of her character that neither one nor the other spoiled her in the least. From first to last there is the same cheerful outlook upon life, the same fidelity to duty, and the same simplicity.—LEWIN, WALTER, 1890, *Life of Harriet Beecher Stowe, The Academy*, vol. 37, pp. 162, 163.

The greatest of American women.—PHELPS, ELIZABETH STUART, 1896, *Chapters from a Life*, p. 131.

No woman in history has ever gone on living her life as Harriet Beecher did, recklessly individual, provincial, shut out from the metropolis of art and letters, criticized by inferiors or not at all—only to be suddenly, by a single story, confronted with the whole human race, an audience no mortal has had before or since. This concentration of praise and obloquy was as if the whole universe of the human spirit had opened itself with a flash and arched itself over this hidden life, and almost cosmic criticism—all for one little woman writing across a cradle in a New England town.—LEE, GERALD STANLEY, 1897, *Harriet Beecher Stowe, The Critic*, vol. 30, p. 282.

Henry Cuyler Bunner
1855–1896

An American poet and story-writer; born in Oswego, N. Y., Aug. 3, 1855; died in Nutley, N. J., May 11, 1896. He became a journalist in 1873, and was editor of *Puck* from shortly after its start till his death. Author of "A Woman of Honor" (New York, 1883); "Airs from Arcady and Elsewhere" (1884); "The Midge" (1886); "The Story of a New York House" (1887); "Zadoc Pine and Other Stories" (1891); "Short Sixes" (1891); "The Runaway Browns" (1892); "Jersey Street and Jersey Lane" (1896); and "In Partnership," with Brander Matthews (1883). Also a play, "The Tower of Babel," (1883); and uncollected magazine articles.—WARNER, CHARLES DUDLEY, ed. 1897, *Library of the World's Best Literature, Biographical Dictionary*, vol. XXIX, p. 83.

PERSONAL

We had lived in the same house for a while; we had collaborated more than once; we had talked over our plans together; we had criticised each other's writings; we had revised each other's proof-sheets; and there was between us never any misunderstanding or doubt, nor any word of disagreement. I never went to Bunner for counsel or for aid that I did not get it, freely and sympathetically given, and always exactly what I needed. Sympathy was indeed the keynote of Bunner's character, and cheery helpfulness was a chief of his characteristics. To me the companionship was of inestimable benefit; and it is bitter to face a future when I can no more hope for his hearty greeting, for the welcoming glance of his eager eye, for the solid grip of his hand and for the unfailing stimulus and solace of his conversation.—MATTHEWS, BRANDER, 1896, *H. C. Bunner, Scribner's Monthly*, vol. 20, p. 287.

He read me in advance all the poems, afterward collected together as the "Airs from Arcady." We talked for hours over "Love in Old Cloathes," the best, perhaps, of his tales, and a little bit of work which cost him infinite care, and thought, and labour. . . . He was very quick of insight, and remarkably ready of utterances and expression, even in verse. . . . He was very strong in his likes and in his dislikes—often without good reason. And I like to think now that, when we came to know each other, he always liked me, whatever his reason may have been. A more disinterestedly loyal man to his friends I never met, and no man more devotedly attached to his own family. He was always sympathetic, always ready to help, always full of encouragement, never sparing of his words of praise for the work of others. His laugh was hearty and contagious, and how quick was his appreciation of everything that was good all the world who reads can tell. He was an excellent listener, and he was an admirable talker upon all sorts of subjects, grave and gay. He had an unusual knowledge of books and of their contents, particularly of the works of the poets, ancient and modern. He quoted readily, correctly, appropriately, and at length; and if one wanted to remember a line or a sonnet of any of the half-forgotten men of the period of the very beginning of English verse, Bunner could always say where it was, whose it was.—HUTTON, LAURENCE, 1896, *Henry Cuyler Bunner, The Bookman*, vol. 3, pp. 399, 400.

GENERAL

It has some real stuff in it "[Airs from Arcady]" and woven, too, with no creak of machinery.—LOWELL, JAMES RUSSELL, 1885, *To R. W. Gilder*, Nov. 9; *Letters*, ed. Norton, vol. II, p. 301.

It has always seemed to me that Bunner was one of the great parodists of the nineteenth century. Not Smith's "Rejected Addresses," not Thackeray's "Prize Novelists," not Mr. Bret Harte's "Condensed Novels," not Bayard Taylor's "Diversions of the Echo Club," shows a sharper understanding of the essentials of another author's art or a swifter faculty for reproducing them, than Bunner revealed in these V. Hugo Dusenberry papers, or in his "Home, Sweet Home, with Variations" (now included in his "Airs from Arcady"). There are two kinds of parody, as we all know. One is a mere imitation of the external form, and is commonly inexpensive and tiresome. The other is rarer and calls for an evocation of the internal spirit; and it was in the accomplishment of this that Bunner excelled. . . . To Bunner verse was perhaps the most natural form of expression; and it is as a poet that he is most likely to linger in men's memories.—MATTHEWS, BRANDER, 1896–1901, *The His-*

torical *Novel and Other Essays,* pp. 175, 188.

The charm that the late Henry Cuyler Bunner exercised as a writer of fiction was due not only to the fact that he was a natural story-teller, and that, having this talent, he cultivated it, but also to the fact that he was of an intensely sensitive and sympathetic nature, and had, besides, the indispensable sense of humor. . . . The necessities of his place made him a political writer, but his enthusiasm, his patriotism, his hatred of shams, together with his literary training, made him a political writer of high rank. The paper naturally responded to the strong convictions and individuality of its editor, and its development from a mere free-lance in journalism into a powerful organ with a settled, definite policy, was a necessary consequence. To make the fine, violin-like tones of his "comments" heard through all the trumpet-blast of Keppler's cartoons, was no easy task, yet Bunner accomplished it. It was also necessary for him to write so as to attract and to hold the attention of the man who bought a funny paper because he wanted to laugh. . . . He determined to give to the English reading world some of the best of Maupassant's stories that were translatable and had not already been translated; and the result was "Made in France." These were not translations, however, but transformations. While the French originals were recognizable by those who knew Maupassant, the stories were still Bunner, and this in spite of the fact that Bunner was undoubtedly the best parodist in the English language.—PAINE, H. G., 1896, *H. C. Bunner, The Critic,* vol. 28, p. 363.

Mr. Bunner's legacy to American poetry is very small in bulk, but most excellent in quality. He had a rare gift of humour, a quick ear for rhyme and rhythm, a fortunate choice of epithet and figure, and, best of all, he knew his own capabilities and did not attempt to go beyond them. It is easy to trace the influence of three other poets in his work—Herrick, Aldrich and Dobson; but it is to be said that, wherever the influence of any one of them is traceable, the poem is not unworthy of its master and always it must be owned that

"He held his pen in trust
To Art, not serving shame or lust."

—SHERMAN, FRANK DEMPSTER, 1896, *The Poet, The Critic,* vol. 28, p. 364.

Mary Abigail Dodge
Gail Hamilton
1833–1896

An American journalist and author; born in Hamilton, Mass., in 1833; died there, Aug. 17, 1896. For several years she was instructor in the High School at Hartford, Conn. From 1865 to 1867 she was one of the editors of *Our Young Folks.* Besides numerous contributions to current literature, she has written under the pseudonym of "Gail Hamilton:" "Gala Days" (1863); "Woman's Wrongs" (1868); "The Battle of the Books" (1870); "Woman's Worth and Worthlessness" (1871); "The Insuppressible Book" (1885); "A New Atmosphere;" "Red-Letter Days;" "Country Living and Country Thinking;" "A Washington Bible Class;" "Twelve Miles from a Lemon;" and "Biography of James G. Blaine."—WARNER, CHARLES DUDLEY, ed. 1897, *Library of the World's Best Literature, Biographical Dictionary,* vol. XXXI, p. 148.

PERSONAL

Gail Hamilton's home at Hamilton was a big roomy house standing well back from the main road, nearly a mile below the Hamilton and Wenham railway station. . . There has been a very generally received impression that her name was Mary Abigail Dodge, and that she took the last part of her middle name and the name of her native town for a *nom de plume;* but I have the authority of her sister for saying that this is incorrect, and that the name "Abigail," so persistently hurled at her sister, was always distasteful to her. In her home and among her townspeople she was "Miss Abby." The familiar name indicates something of the affection which all who knew her at all well came to have for her —an affection which had its origin in, and was fostered by, her unfailing desire to help others.—THRASHER, MAX BENNETT, 1896, *The Last Year of Gail Hamilton's Life, The Arena,* vol. 17, pp. 114, 115.

Her circumstances were easy, and she

found a great deal of pleasure in life with her work, her friends, and her frequent visits in the houses of her publishers, of Hawthorne, Mrs. Stowe, Mr. Whittier, Mr. Storrs, and others. She was radiant with youth and health and spirit and happiness, helping every one, making the world glad about her, and herself the pride and joy of a large and adoring family circle. Wherever she came the wind and the sunshine seemed to come in with her, so bright and breezy was her presence, with a thought, an opinion, an epigram, for everything, and sparkling with sweet and wholesome wit, fearlessly frank and tenderly kind. While her stricture was unsparing, her praise was equally so. Her spirit was something not to be daunted, and she was intrepid in maintaining her cause and fighting for faith or friend. But her magnanimity was as great as her courage. She was generosity itself, giving her personal care, her interest, her money in large sums, herself. . . . She dressed her part well, too, in simplest garb upon the street or in the galleries of Congress; but she was resplendent at home in her white silks, her gown of silver brocade, her pale peach satin, or whatever the occasion demanded. In summer she swung in her hammock at home in Hamilton, and wandered over her hills as if she had never known any other life. Although not beautiful, she was yet attractive, of about the medium height, and with a good figure. Her skin very fair and blooming, her mouth sweet, her teeth fine, her forehead white, her nose well cut, her bright brown hair curling naturally. She had great beauty of expression, and her smile was enchanting.—SPOFFORD, HARRIET PRESCOTT, 1896-1901, *Gail Hamilton's Life in Letters*, ed. Dodge, *Biographical Sketch*, vol. I, pp. XI, XII.

Through her whole life, Miss M. A. Dodge insisted upon the separation of her private personality from that involved in her authorship and public writings. Letters sent to "Miss Abigail Dodge" she refused to answer. She always felt it a burden upon her to have the two sides of her life brought together, and believed that her power would have been magnified greatly if her pen-name had remained a secret. Yet she took the frankest pleasure in the measure of fame her published work brought her, and these letters reveal a desire for praise and appreciation which is almost childlike. In the face of this fact, the good taste of such an exposure as is here made ["Letters"] of her inmost heart is questionable; nor has the editor showed the highest qualities of her office in making her selections. . . . In spite of everything, there was little that Gail Hamilton did during her public life which was not interesting, and her writings, whether in public prints or to private persons, have the charm of a fascinating and always intelligent personality. She had a clever knack of hitting off the characterisitcs of those with whom she was brought into contact.—RICE, WALLACE, 1901, *Leaves from a Busy Life, The Dial*, vol. 31, pp. 178, 179.

GENERAL

It was good in thee to send me thy new book. I had read most of it before in the "Independent." But a second perusal in fair type has been none the less satisfactory. It is one of thy very ablest books—shorn of some of the redundant wealth of diction which some reviewers complained of in thy first publications, but lacking none of their vigor and life and insight. I quarreled with thee often as I read, but, after all, laid the book down with a most profound respect for the wise little woman who wrote it. I shall not put my quarrels on paper, but when a kind Providence gives me an opportunity I shall "withstand thee to thy face." I will simply say that my old bachelor reverence for woman has been somewhat disturbed by thy revelations. I am not going to condemn her because thee turn State's evidence against her. Voter, or non-voter, I have faith in her.—WHITTIER, JOHN GREENLEAF, 1872, *To Gail Hamilton, March 1; Life and Letters*, ed. Pickard, vol. II, p. 577.

Miss Mary A. Dodge (Gail Hamilton) might be styled an essayist, but that would be but a vague term to denote a writer who takes up all classes of subjects, is tart, tender, shrewish, pathetic, monitory, objurgatory, tolerant, prejudiced, didactic, and dramatic by turns, but always writing with so much point, vigor, and freshness that we can only classify her among "readable" authors.—WHIPPLE, EDWIN PERCY, 1876-86, *American Literature and Other Papers*, ed. Whittier, p. 136.

All direct aims at the acquisition of a style, for the style's sake, are always, in some sense or another, failures. We beg the lady's pardon for mentioning it, but

Gail Hamilton's incisive, brusque, and forceful style—sometimes saucy, always clear, though often redundant, and strong beyond the average feminine quality—has done, without any premeditated guilt, a great deal of harm to the lower grade of literary women in America. The weaker woman, undertaking to speak through such a style, is simply and insipidly pert. She lacks the strong common sense and the height and breadth of imagination of her model, and so appears as ridiculous as if she were to "assist" at a New York party in an old dress of Queen Elizabeth or the soldier clothes of Jeanne d'Arc.—HOLLAND, JOSIAH. GILBERT, 1876, *Every-Day Topics, First Series*, p. 22.

Her earlier books had an immediate success and a wide circulation. Her later writings, though much more able, were on heavier themes and had not so great popularity.—JOHNSON, FLORENCE K., 1896, *Appleton's Annual Cyclopædia*, vol. XXXVI, p. 248.

Henry Drummond
1851–1897

A Scotch geologist and religious writer; born at Stirling, 1851; died at Tunbridge Wells, England, March 11, 1897. He studied theology at Edinburgh University, but did not adopt the clerical profession. In 1877 he was appointed professor of natural science in the Free Church College, Glasgow. "Natural Law in the Spiritual World" (1883), and its successor "The Ascent of Man," applications of modern scientific methods to the immaterial universe, have made his popular fame. He traveled in Central Africa (1883-84) studying its botany and geology, and later wrote the highly interesting and instructive volume on "Tropical Africa" (1888). Other semi-religious writings of his are: "Pax Vobiscum" (1890); "The Greatest Thing in the World" (1890); "The Programme of Christianity" (1892).—WARNER, CHARLES DUDLEY, ed. 1897, *Library of World's Best Literature, Biographical Dictionary*, vol. XXIX, p. 153.

PERSONAL

Tall and somewhat slim, as I have said, dressed and bearing himself like a perfect gentleman; a head finely molded, a forehead of unusual breadth and height, eyes of magnetic power with light-points of sparkling brilliance; hair, mustache, and side-whiskers of delicate texture and fair of hue—such was my first physiognomic impression of Professor Drummond. . . . Few popular writers have so rare a gift of self-repression; fewer still can rely with such perfect confidence on the internal evidences of authorship.—SHELLEY, H. C., 1894, *Professor Henry Drummond, The Outlook*, vol. 49, p. 1093.

Drummond was a good talker; but what was more striking than his talk was his capacity for listening. There was a genuine modesty in him which made it easy for him to assume the attitude of a learner, even toward those whose knowledge gave them less right to speak than himself. He stooped to learn where another would have exalted himself to teach. Often it would happen that a theological discussion would go on for an hour or two in which Drummond took no part. He would lie back in an easy-chair listening in perfect silence. Then at the end he would ask a quiet question, or make an epigrammatic remark, which was more luminous than all our talk.—ROSS, D. M., 1897, *Professor Henry Drummond, McClure's Magazine*, vol. 9, p. 764.

What impressed me that pleasant evening in the days of long ago I can now identify. It was the lad's distinction, an inherent quality of appearance and manner of character and soul which marked him and made him solitary. . . . Upon a platform of evangelists, or sitting among divinity students in a dingy classroom, or cabined in the wooden respectability of an ecclesiastical court, or standing in a crowd of passengers at a railway station, he suggested golden embroidery upon hodden gray. . . . Drummond was a handsome man, such as you could not match in ten days' journey, with delicately cut features, rich auburn hair, and a certain carriage of nobility, but the distinction and commanding feature of his face was his eye. No photograph could do it justice, and very often photographs have done it injustice, by giving the idea of staringness. His eye was not bold or fierce; it was tender and merciful. But it had a power and hold which were little else than irresistible and almost supernatural. When you talked with Drummond he did not look at you and out of the window alternately, as is the usual manner, he never moved his eyes and gradually their penetrating gaze seemed to reach and encompass your soul. It was as Plato imagined it would be in the judgment; one soul was in contact with another —nothing between.—WATSON, JOHN, 1897, *Henry Drummond, North American Review, vol. 164, p. 515.*

His presence was bright and exhilarating as sunshine. An even happiness and disengagement from all selfish care were his characteristics. Sometimes one thought that with his brilliant gifts, his great opportunities, his rare success, it was easy for him to be happy; but his prolonged and painful illness has shown us that his happiness was far more surely founded. Penetrate as deeply as you might into his nature, and scrutinise it as keenly, you never met anything to disappoint, anything to incline you to suspend your judgment or modify your verdict that here you had a man as nearly perfect as you had ever known anyone to be. To see him in unguarded moments was only to see new evidence of the absolute purity and nobility of his nature, to see him in trying circumstances was only to have his serenity and soundness of spirit thrown into stronger relief.—DODS, MARCUS, 1897, *Memorial Sermon, Free North Church, Sterling, p. 227.*

Not four years have passed by since Professor Drummond visited the colleges of this New World. Those whose good fortune it was to hear Mr. Drummond will recall the patrician face and form, the finely cut features, the countenance suffused with solar light, the great, rich, wonderful soul throbbing and blushing behind its defenses of flesh and cuticle. He seemed what the lower class men in his university called him, *the Prince.*—HILLIS, NEWELL DWIGHT, 1899, *Great Books as Life-Teachers, p. 211.*

Perhaps the most conspicuous service which Henry Drummond rendered to his generation was to show them a Christianity which was perfectly natural. You met him somewhere, a graceful, well-dressed gentleman, tall and lithe, with a swing in his walk and a brightness on his face, who seemed to carry no cares and to know neither presumption nor timidity. You spoke, and found him keen for any of a hundred interests. He fished, he shot, he skated as few can, he played cricket; he would go any distance to see a fire or a football match. He had a new story, a new puzzle, or a new joke every time he met you. . . . If you were alone with him, he was sure to find out what interested you, and listen by the hour. The keen brown eyes got at your heart, and you felt you could speak your best to them. Sometimes you would remember that he was Drummond the evangelist, Drummond the author of books which measured their circulation by scores of thousands. Yet there was no assumption of superiority nor any ambition to gain influence—nothing but the interest of one healthy human being in another.—SMITH, GEORGE ADAM, 1899, *Henry Drummond as his Friends Knew Him, McClure's Magazine, vol. 12, p. 550.*

Out of doors, salmon-fishing, deer-stalking, and, when he got the chance, the pursuit of "big game," all had considerable fascination for him. Salmon-fishing was once characterised by him as his besetting sin, and he missed few opportunities of indulging in it, either in our Scottish Highlands, or in Canada and the Wild West. He was also a very good skater. Rambling too, as might have been expected in one of his scientific turns of mind, had great attractions for him. As an onlooker, he retained a well-informed interest in and knowledge of cricket and foot-ball, and was frequently to be seen on the grand stand at International matches.—LENNOX, CUTHBERT, 1901, *The Practical Life Work of Henry Drummond, p. 218.*

The fibre of his nature was vigorous; it was the virility of his manhood which, combined with his freedom from religious professionalism and the fascination of his personality, made him pre-eminently a preacher to young men. He knew men and boys thoroughly and was at home with them; there is a noticeable absence of references to women in the biographical sketches which have appeared. His supreme interest was in young men, and he became pre-eminently a teacher of youth. Like all men of contagious enthusiasm and captivating vitality, he had high spirits and a great appetite for fun. The boy was immortal in him; that abiding presence of the spirit of youth which is the witness of the creative mood. To the end of his life humor and gayety were matched in him with charming urbanity and unfailing courtesy.—MABIE, HAMILTON W., 1901, *The Practical Life Work of Henry Drummond*, ed. Lennox, Introduction, p. xx.

NATURAL LAW IN THE SPIRITUAL WORLD
1883

Have you seen a book by a certain Professor Henry Drummond, called "Natural Law in the Spiritual World," which has had an astonishing success over here? The best public, perhaps, does not much care for it; but the second best, all the religious world, and even the more serious portion of the aristocratical world, have accepted the book as a godsend, and are saying to themselves that here at last is safety and scientific shelter for the orthodox supernaturalism which seemed menaced with total defeat. I should like much to know what you think of the book, though I can hardly imagine its suiting any public but that very peculiar and indirect-thinking public which we have in England. What is certain is, that the author of the book has a genuine love of religion and a genuine religious experience; and this gives his book a certain value, though his readers, in general, imagine its value to be quite of another kind.—ARNOLD, MATTHEW, 1885, *To M. Fontanès, July* 18; *Letters*, ed. Russell, vol. II, p. 327.

It is evident that it is simply our old friend, the "Shorter Catechism," in a scientific dress. In other words, it is the world of Calvinistic Christianity—of the peculiar system of theology which turns on the ideas of original sin, fall, redemption, regeneration, election and pre-destination. —LAING, S., 1888, *Modern Science and Modern Thought*, Sixth Ed., p. 348.

The genesis of "Natural Law in the Spiritual World" indicates the secret of its success. It is not a contribution to philosophy; it was not conceived in a philosophic spirit. It is not an attempt to reconcile Science and Religion, and it is not written with a dogmatic purpose to defend the latter from attack by the former. It is a statement of religious truth by a man schooled in scientific methods, but animated by the religious spirit. . . . It was no sooner published than it began to create a great excitement. Some scientists, of course, sneered at its science; some religionists assailed its religion; some philosophers measured it as a contribution to philosophy and criticised its fundamental postulate. . . . Men who had been revolted from religion by the patois in which it had been clothed were attracted to it when they found it disrobed of the patois expressed in terms with which they were familiar and which they could understand. Regeneration became Biogenesis; Depravity became Degeneration; Sanctification became Growth, and so throughout. "Natural Law in the Spiritual World" affords a splendid illustration of how a minister possessing the spirit of Christ may impart it to new auditors and in new circles if he will not foolishly confuse life with the phrases with which he is familiar and insist that men can accept the one only in case they will use the other.—ABBOTT, LYMAN, 1899, *Henry Drummond: Evangelist—Professor—Author, The Outlook*, vol. 61, pp. 214, 215.

THE ASCENT OF MAN
1894

In his book, "The Ascent of Man," the extraordinary attitude taken by him, and the stupendous self-satisfaction of his "find," affect the reader with the same feeling as would the immensity of an ocean of froth—the infinitude of a universe of cloud. In his preface he strikes the key-note, of which the whole book is simply a variation in different movements; and the key-note is—no one before Professor Henry Drummond discovered the law of altruism as a natural condition of moral and social evolution, as a governing factor in the conduct of man to man. Where others have been content to regard it as a modifying and progressive influence, sweetening the acerbities and softening the severities of that earlier condition wherein the struggle for life was the absolute necessity, if racial and individual life were to survive at all, he has found it as the supreme motive force from the beginning. And this is the first sound given by the tinkling cymbal he calls his philosophy. . . . We take exception to the unscientific and more than sickly tone of Professor Drummond's eulogium on the Love which he asserts rules creation from the protoplastic base to the summit of human society at the end of the nineteenth century. . . . That he has succeeded in his aim is proved by the enormous success of his book—mere hash of other men's labour as it is—a plagiarism from first to last. It is a thing of this kind which makes one despair of one's generation. . . . Whatever is true is borrowed; whatever is false, strained, and inconclusive, is his own. His sin is the sin of plagiarism, with the additional offence of distortion in the lifting.—LINTON, E. LYNN, 1894, *Professor Henry Drummond's Discovery, Fortnightly Review*, vol. 62, pp. 451, 456, 457.

The work is much the most important he has left us.—NICOLL, W. ROBERTSON, 1897, *Henry Drummond, Contemporary Review*, vol. 71, pp. 508, 509.

The great contribution which this volume makes to the doctrine of evolution is the emphasis which it puts upon the Struggle for Others as a necessary accompaniment to the Struggle for Existence in the process of development. It is a scientific representation of the law of love. Scientists have criticised this volume because of its prose-poetry; but Tyndall has shown that imagination has rendered an inestimable service in the discoveries of science, and Henry Drummond has simply proved that it may be equally useful in the exposition of science. But the theme of the book is not fully worked out, and carries man's religious development scarcely farther than Le Conte had carried it in his "Evolution in its Relation to Religious Thought."—ABBOTT, LYMAN, 1899, *Henry Drummond: Evangelist—Professor—Author, The Outlook*, vol. 61, p. 215.

The book did not please the orthodox party so well as the "Natural Law," and it met with much scientific opposition, but, at the same time, it made a host of friends. It certainly did something to correct the exaggeration of natural selection as a selfish and brutal struggle for existence, though it was less original in this respect than Drummond seemed to think, and it is true that he confounded the struggle of species, of which "the struggle for others" is a part, with that of individuals.—CHADWICK, JOHN WHITE, 1899, *Henry Drummond, The Nation*, vol. 68, p. 32.

"The Ascent of Man" was Drummond's greatest piece of work. It had not a circulation that compared either with that of the earlier book, although this is no inexplicable fact, or of those marvellous addresses on Love, Peace, The Programme of Christianity, The City without a Church, and The Changed Life, that carried his name into thousands of widely separated homes. The mission of "The Ascent of Man" was different,—a mission that is yet not perfectly fulfilled. Critics pointed out slight errors of fact in the text, but they are insignificant beside the mistaken judgment involved in the title of the book, which seemed to challenge an altogether insupportable but utterly unintentional comparison with the better-known Darwinian volume. Drummond himself had said in the Preface to the work, "It is a History, not an Argument."—SIMPSON, JAMES Y., 1901, *Henry Drummond (Famous Scots Series)*, p. 143.

GENERAL

Wherein lies the secret of Professor Drummond's success? To answer this question satisfactorily would require much more time and space than can be given to it in the present article; we would simply state our belief that the secret of Professor Drummond's success lies in the kind of Christianity which he preaches. . . . What the college student of the present time asks for, and must have, is a Christianity which appeals not only to his emotions and sentiment, but also to his sound common sense and enlightened reason. It was such Christianity as this which was preached by Professor Henry Drummond. Liberal in his views, in the truest and best sense of the word, he set before his hearers a Christianity which was at once pure, simple, and manly. To their proper place within the walls of theological seminaries he relegated the discussion of dogmas and creeds, and left in their place a faith which was human as well as divine. . . . The Christianity inculcated by Professor Drummond does not ask that we frown on the beauties of art in all its varied forms, nor does it consider amusement, either in-door or out-door, to be the play-things of the devil. On the other hand, we are entreated to bring our Christianity into everything, whether it be business or pleasure, and in this manner elevate and ennoble all that we do. . . . So much for "Athletic Christianity" and the work of the "noble Scotchman" among the college students of America.—FROST, T. GOLD, 1888, *Professor Drummond and Athletic Christianity in our American Colleges, Andover Review*, vol. 10, pp. 507, 508, 509.

Professor Drummond's influence on his contemporaries is not to be measured by the sale of his books, great as that has been. It may be doubted whether any living novelist has had so many readers, and perhaps no living writer has been so eagerly followed and so keenly discussed on the Continent and in America. . . . Professor Drummond had the widest vogue from Norway to Germany. There was a time when scarcely a week passed in Germany without the publication of a book or pamphlet in which his views were canvassed. In Scandinavia, perhaps, no other living Englishman was so widely known. In every part of America his books had an extraordinary circulation. This influence reached all classes. It was strong among scientific men, whatever may be said to the contrary. Among such men as Von Moltke, Mr. Arthur Balfour, and others belonging to the governing class, it was stronger still. It penetrated to every section of the Christian Church, and far beyond these limits. Still, when this is said, it remains true that his deepest influence was personal and hidden.—NICOLL, W. ROBERTSON, 1897, *Henry Drummond, Contemporary Review, vol. 71, p. 499*.

If Martin Luther and Bishop Butler came at a strategic hour, it was the good fortune of Professor Drummond to speak at one of those psychological moments when the world, eager and expectant, waited for some prophet of reconciliation. Not an intellectual giant himself, it was given him to usher in an era of friendship between giants hitherto at enmity. He taught the world that it was possible to be a rigid scientist and also a sweet-hearted Christian. With him character was a thousand times more than culture, and Christ's words about the soul were infinitely more important than man's words about sticks, stones, and stars.—HILLIS, NEWELL DWIGHT, 1899, *Great Books as Life-Teachers, p. 226*.

It is possible to imagine that the truth in "Natural Law in the Spiritual World" may so become part of universal experience that the volume will drop out of sight,—some books are forgotten because they succeed; it is easy to fancy that fuller appreciation of the relations between scientific and religious thought will make the thesis of "The Ascent of Man" a commonplace, and to read the book a work of supererogation; but so long as boys are keen to play straight in the game of life, so long will this allegory live for their encouragement and their love. . . . In Drummond's mind there was no sharp demarcation of things as secular and sacred. Life itself was too divine in its opportunities to suffer such cleavage.—SIMPSON, JAMES Y., 1901, *Henry Drummond (Famous Scots Series), pp. 27, 157*.

Margaret Oliphant Wilson Oliphant
1828–1897

Novelist, born in 1828 at Wallyford, near Musselburgh. In 1849 her "Passages in the Life of Mrs. Margaret Maitland" instantly won approval. This was followed by "Caleb Field" (1850), "Merkland" (1850), "Adam Graeme" (1852), "Katie Stewart" (1852), "Harry Muir" (1853), "Magdalen Hepburn" (1854), "The Quiet Heart" (1854), "Lilliesleaf" (1855), "Zaidee" (1855). It was by the "Chronicles of Carlingford" (first in "Blackwood's," 1861-64) that her reputation as a novelist was secured. In the first of them, "The Doctor's Family," Little Netty is an original creation; the next, "Salem Chapel," indicates a wider and more vigorous grasp. Mrs. Oliphant settled at Windsor. Other works are "Agnes" (1865), "Madonna Mary" (1866), "The Minister's Wife" (1869), "Ombra" (1872), "A Rose in June" (1874), "Phœbe Junior" (1876), "Within the Precincts" (1879), "In Trust" (1882), "The Ladies Lindores" (1883), "The Wizard's Son" (1884), "Madam" (1885), and "Kirsteen" (1890). Contributions to general literature have been "Life of Edward Irving" (1862); "Historical Sketches of the Reign of George II." (1869); "St. Francis of Assisi" (1871); "Montalembert" (1872); "Makers of Florence" (1876); "Dress" (1878); "Literary History of England, 1790-1825" (1882); "A Little Pilgrim: in the Unseen" (1882); "Makers of Venice" (1888); "Dante" and "Cervantes" in the "Foreign Classics" series (edited by her); "Memoir of Tulloch" (1888); "Royal Edinburgh" (1890); "Life of Laurence Oliphant" (1891); "Makers of Rome" (1894); "Reign of Queen Anne" (1895); "Jeanne d' Arc" (1896); "Child's History of Scotland" (1896); and "William Blackwood & Sons" (1897). Mrs. Oliphant, who received a pension in 1868, died at Wimbleton, 25th June, 1897.—PATRICK AND GROOME, eds., 1897,*Chambers's Biographical Dictionary, p. 704*.

PERSONAL

I have seen that most eminent woman much, through more than thirty years: I never once, nor for one moment, saw her fall short of the beautiful ideal of genius, sweetness, and goodness, which all who knew her link with her name. For many a day, one could not make out when it was she wrote. But this year, in an afternoon, one sometimes saw the sheet of paper lying on a table near her, covered with the minute handwriting. It was felt as presumptuous to talk to her of her work. But when, now and then, one ventured, there was the unaffectedness, there was the frankness, which characterise all she says and does. The hearty good wish of the smallest may somewhat help the biggest: and in the record of that evening, which never mortal saw save its writer, there stands the warm *God bless her.*—BOYD, ANDREW K. H., 1892, *Twenty-Five Years of St. Andrews, vol.* II, *p.* 316.

When one turns over the pages and pages of letters all addressed to this one correspondent, all either suggesting subjects for her pen or accepting her own selections, the question arises: When did she find time to get through the mass of work they represent? Even the inmates of her own home would find it difficult to explain how it was accomplished. Marvellous industry was a feature in her character, but even that estimable trait is sometimes found to be useless when mental exertion has to be called upon as well. With Mrs. Oliphant perhaps the secret was to be found in the fact of her being able to concentrate her thoughts quickly on the matter that had to be attended to, and her ability to do her work at any time. She worked early and she worked late, and yet there was no time in the day when she could not be seen. She may be said to have been always working, yet her work was never obtruded. In her own home the kindest and most attentive of hostesses, she always had time to take part in anything that was going on. To a stranger who saw her leaning back in her chair, her hands occupied with some needle-work, she would seem one of the most leisured of women, no hurry in her speech nor in her movements, only now and then a swift glance from her dark eyes would tell she was quickly turning over in her mind all that was passing. When she was writing at Strathtyrum we can recall many instances of her charming adaptability to the ways of the house. A guest for whom naturally host and hostess would have wished to make hours and arrangements suit, she would have nothing altered. Down in the morning in time for the golfers' early breakfast, she would wait about and see them off, and talk and work with the ladies of the party, and then quietly steal away to her room to do a good morning's work—a contrast to the solemn fuss that usually prevails when the ladies of a country house-party announce that they have "letters to write." The time she perhaps did the greater part of her writing was during the hours which most of us consecrate to slumber, and in the quiet hush of the night I believe some of her best work was done.—PORTER, MRS. GERALD, 1898, *William Blackwood and his Sons, vol.* III, *p.* 350.

For more than a generation Mrs. Oliphant produced novel after novel, and essay after essay, not to mention many books of a more ambitious and serious nature. Her readers have been limited to no one nationality, no hemisphere, no zone. That her books have given delight to many thousands need not be said. None of them great books—among them all (and they number perhaps a hundred) not one that will penetrate far into the new century—there is scarcely one that has not been read with pleasure, not to say with profit. She produced them so rapidly that the public long since marvelled until marvelling from exhaustion ceased.—HALSEY, FRANCIS WHITING, 1902, *Our Literary Deluge and some of its Deep Waters, p.* 128.

GENERAL

Nothing half so true ["Margaret Maitland"] or so touching (in the delineation of Scottish character) has appeared since Galt published his "Annals of the Parish"—and this is purer and deeper than Galt, and even more absolutely and simply true. It would have been better though and made a stronger impression if it had copied Galt's brevity, and is sensibly injured by the indifferent matter which has been admitted to bring it up to the standard of three volumes.—JEFFREY, FRANCIS, 1850, *Mrs. Oliphant's Autobiography and Letters.*

To me she is charming. To read her is like being with a delightful woman—a woman of powerful intellect, which she veils perhaps from the eyes of many readers, though not from mine, by her thoroughly feminine tact. And then her style seems to me so perfect. I wish, in token of my admiration, you would send her a copy of my new volume.—KINGLAKE, ALEXANDER WILLIAM, 1874, *Letter to John Blackwood*, William Blackwood and his Sons, ed. Mrs. Porter, vol. III, p. 114.

Mrs. Oliphant has recently given to the world the memoirs of Mr. Laurence Oliphant. Of her capabilities to do justice to that portion of his career which represents his social, diplomatic and literary success, there is no question. But she confesses herself "bewildered" and "ignorant" in dealing with that mystical side which—from her point of view—was so potent in upsetting that otherwise brilliant career. On the worldly side of Mr. Oliphant's nature his biographer is ably eloquent; but the spiritual side is to her a closed book. It is to be deplored, however, that what she is unable to understand of it, she should have employed her powers as a mistress of fiction to supply. By calling in the aid of the stage villain to serve as a foil to her hero she has developed a romance rather than a biography.—PHILLIPS, JANET (BERYL), 1891, *Mr. Harris and Mr. Oliphant*, National Review, vol. 17, p. 681.

To me, her fertility is miraculous; and the high standard steadily maintained through all. Surely she is the most remarkable woman now living: and she has written as good material as any woman ever wrote. I know you think of George Eliot. Mrs. Oliphant, writing ten times as much, has written as excellent thought as ever came from that pen. She has done enough to make half-a-dozen reputations. Her two stories, "A Rose in June," and "Madam," hardly noted among so many, would have set a novelist in the highest place. And her Lives of Edward Irving, and of Tulloch, would set her high among biographers. In quite another walk, think of Florence, Venice, and Edinburgh. Then, as time goes on, her writing grows ever fresher and brighter.—BOYD, ANDREW K. H., 1892, *Twenty-Five Years of St. Andrews*, vol. I, p. 66.

It is, of course, as a novelist that Mrs. Oliphant did her work and earned her reputation. When one begins to specify particular books, it is easy to see that Mrs. Oliphant never wrote anything conspicuously above or conspicuously below her standard. In our judgment—a judgment which it must be confessed fluctuates on this point—"Phœbe Junior" is on the whole the best and most perfect of Mrs. Oliphant's works. . . . She was truly religious, but shrank from the more intimate expressions of religious feeling. Perhaps her heart never opened itself so fully as in that beautiful book, "The Beleaguered City," a book which had several companions not unworthy to stand beside it. . . . Mrs. Oliphant's articles did not meet with unmixed approval, and on various occasions we have ourselves challenged them. She had eyes like a hawk. She could say more easily than most people the things that stab and blister. She was often merciless, and sometimes she was unfair. She fiercely resented popularities that were undeserved. She could not abide mawkish sentiment. She had educated herself into the true aristocrat's view of life, and had a genuine contempt for the Philistine. It need not be wondered if she was sometimes cruel, but we have often been surprised that her hard experience never seemed to school her into charity and restraint. To the last she was as fierce, as uncontrolled, as bitter as ever when her temper was touched. . . . Much of her critical writing has been collected in books, the best of these being undoubtedly "Historical Sketches of The Reign of George III." [?] In this occurs, perhaps, the finest thing she ever wrote—the noble panegyric of "Clarissa Harlowe."—NICOLL, W. ROBERTSON, 1897, *Mrs. Oliphant*, The Bookman, vol. 5, pp. 485, 486.

The author of the "Chronicles of Carlingford" has been a classic since the 'sixties. From the time that those famous sketches of society appeared in *Blackwood's* her position in our foremost rank of novelists has been assured, and she has maintained it in an unbroken series of novels through all the ensuing years; in thirty-five years more than sixty important novels have come from her pen—a most wonderful record in point of fertility and industry, but still more so if we consider the quality and characteristics of the work.—SLATER, GERTRUDE, 1897, *Mrs. Oliphant as a Realist*, Westminster Review, vol. 148, p. 682.

There have been, perhaps there are (and she herself would have been the first to say it with full belief), greater novelists, but who has ever achieved the same variety of literary work with anything like the same level of excellence? A great deal of her very best remains at present anonymous—biographical and critical papers, and others dealing with an extraordinary variety of subjects. But merely to divide her books into classes gives some little idea of the range of her powers. Her novels, long and short, can hardly number much less than a hundred, but these for a long time back were by no means her works of predilection; they were necessary pot-boilers, and in the three last sad years all fiction had been heavy labour to her. . . . Then come the brilliant papers on the reign of George II., collected some years ago; and those of the reign of Queen Anne, the laborious, but not entirely successful "Literary History of England" and "A Child's History of Scotland." The "Makers of Florence" began a fresh series in 1876; it was followed at intervals by the "Makers of Venice," "Rome" and "Jerusalem," each of these books involving immense labour, and all, except "Rome," having its materials carefully collected on the spot. The typography of Rome she knew well; every aspect of it had been engraved on her memory with the pencil of sorrow. Finally, there remains one of the most wonderful set of writings in our language—that which began very simply and sweetly with "A Little Pilgrim," and went on through various "Stories of the Seen and the Unseen," reaching a strange poetic power and beauty in "A Beleaguered City," and finding, to those who were near enough to her life to guess the thoughts with which it was written, a most fitting end in "The Land of Suspense."—COGHILL, ANNIE L., 1897, Mrs. Oliphant, Fortnightly Review, vol. 68, p. 280.

Mrs. Oliphant will probably be thought to have touched the height of her creative and dramatic power in the "Chronicles of Carlingford," stories of the quiet, decorous, and yet concentrated life of an old-fashioned English provincial town, in several of which the same characters reappear. In their manner of treatment, midway between the demure conventionalism and half-unconscious drolleries of Miss Austen and the labored intellectuality and excessive research of the more imposing George Eliot, they seem to me among the soundest, sweetest, fairest fruits we have of the unforced feminine intelligence.—PRESTON, HARRIET WATERS, 1897, Men and Letters, Atlantic Monthly, vol. 80, p. 425.

Notwithstanding Mrs. Oliphant's advanced years and multiplied sorrows, her wonderful vitality to the last gave little sign of decay, and she continued to the day of her death to be one of the ornaments of a profession which she had adorned for nearly fifty years.—GRAHAM, RICHARD D., 1897, The Masters of Victorian Literature, p. 99.

We may perhaps be fairly asked for a general estimate of Mrs. Oliphant's character and place in literature. As to the first, her books, her autobiography, and her letters leave on our minds the impression of a very noble character, who to a certain extent missed her path in life, and sacrificed her obvious and most beneficial destiny to an exaggerated idea of duty to kinsfolk little worthy of such devotion. As to the second, we should, in respect of the best of her work, which was very great in mass, place her exactly where she obviously placed herself—that is, next after George Eliot of the feminine writers of the second half of the century. She had not the almost Shakespearean power of Miss Evans, but she is the superior of any other competitor, even of Charlotte Brontë, whose range was much more limited, and who, if she probed deeper, did not make her figures so exquisitely lifelike.—TOWNSEND, MEREDITH, 1899, Mrs. Oliphant, Cornhill Magazine, vol. 79, p. 779.

Most distinguished novelists who have not completely attained the highest rank, have written themselves, so to speak, into form, passing through a period of apprenticeship before reaching a level which they long retained, and ending by writing themselves out. Mrs. Oliphant's literary history is different. Totally inexperienced in composition, she began by a book which she never very greatly surpassed, and the end of her career found her almost as fresh as at the beginning. It seemed a natural criticism that she should have devoted herself to some concentrated effort of mind which would have placed herself in the front rank; but the probability is that she made the best possible use of her powers. Her great gifts—invention, humour, pathos, the power of bringing persons and scenes vividly before the eye—could hardly have been augmented by any amount of study, and no study could have given her the incommunicable something that stamps the great author. She resembled the George Sand of George Sand's later period in her

Francis William Newman
1805-1897

Scholar and man of letters; brother of John Henry Newman; B. A. Worcester College, Oxford, 1826; fellow of Balliol College, Oxford, 1826-30; classical tutor at Bristol College (unsectarian), 1834; professor of classical literature, Manchester New College, 1840, and of Latin, University College, London, 1846-69; principal of University Hall, London, 1848; acquired repute by his writings on religion, among the most important of which were "History of Hebrew Monarchy," 1847, "The Soul," 1849, and "Phases of Faith" (an autobiographical account of his religious changes, which excited much controversy), 1850; joined British and Foreign Unitarian Association, 1876, and was vice-president, 1879; took keen interest in political questions bearing on social problems; published numerous educational, political, social, and religious works and phamphlets.—HUGHES, C. E., 1903, *Dictionary of National Biography, Index and Epitome*, p. 940.

PERSONAL

Francis Newman, then and still an ardently inquiring soul, of fine University and other attainments, of sharp-cutting, restlessly advancing intellect, and the mildest pious enthusiasm; whose worth since better known to all the world, Sterling highly estimated;—and indeed practically testified the same; having by will appointed him, some years hence, guardian to his eldest son; which pious function Mr. Newman now successfully discharges.—CARLYLE, THOMAS, 1851, *Life of John Sterling*, Pt. III, ch. I.

Francis Newman has not the qualities that a leader wants, to be successful. He is not robust enough. He is too sensitive.—CHADWICK, JOHN WHITE, 1866, *Francis William Newman, Christian Examiner*, vol. 80, p. 358.

Like his brother, he is a poor public speaker. At his very best he is the professor talking to his class, not the orator addressing a crowd. His manner is singularly constrained, ineffective, and even awkward; his voice is thin and weak. . . . He is feeble, ineffective, and often even commonplace. Nature has denied to him the faculty of adequately expressing himself in spoken words. He is almost as much out of his element when addressing a public meeting as he would be if he were singing in an opera. Few Englishmen living can claim to be the intellectual superiors of Francis Newman; but you would never know Francis Newman by hearing him speak on a platform.—MCCARTHY, JUSTIN, 1872, *Par Nobile Fratrum—The Two Newmans, Modern Leaders*, p. 172.

Another good man on the popular side was Francis William Newman, the brother of the Cardinal, not a man of the same high genius, but a man of culture and fine thought, with excellent sympathies and intentions, but, as it seemed to me, hesitating in action and always appearing to doubt if his accepted course had been really right in politics. He, I used to think, ought to have stooped under the yoke of the Roman Church, and John Henry to have stood upright as a leader of progress, which he might have been.—LINTON, WILLIAM JAMES, 1894, *Threescore and Ten Years, 1820 to 1890, Recollections*, p. 159.

As professor of Latin literature his methods were in marked contrast to those of Henry Malden, the professor of Greek; he succeeded in awaking interest in his subject rather than in promoting depth of study; his prelections, always without notes, were bright and vivid. He introduced the Italian mode of pronouncing Latin.—GORDON, ALEXANDER, 1901, *Dictionary of National Biography, Supplement*, vol. III, p. 222.

GENERAL

Now I have read "The Soul," and shall bless you for it, with thanks I cannot speak, so long as I have a Soul that lives. Nothing that I have ever read—unless some scattered thoughts of Pascal's—has come so close to me, and so strengthened a deep but too shrinking faith. . . . Your book is not one that I can criticise, and where I cannot heartily assent I feel more inclined to doubt myself than it. The chief thing that affects me with a certain obscure dissatisfaction is your sharp distinction between the several powers of human nature and your absolute isolation of the *Soul* as the region of exclusive communication with God.—MARTINEAU, JAMES, 1850, *To. F. W. Newman, Feb.* 1; *Life and Letters,* ed. Drummond, vol II, p. 317.

No work contributed more than Mr. Newman's "Phases of Faith," to force upon me the conviction that little progress can be hoped either for religious science or charitable feeling till the question of Biblical authority shall have been placed upon a sounder footing, and viewed in a very different light.—GREG, WILLIAM RATHBONE, 1851, *The Creed of Christendon, p.* 64.

Professor Newman's reputation as a linguist was already made when he began to translate Greek and Latin Poetry. If his translations add nothing to that reputation, surely they can take nothing away. They belong to the domain of taste, and not to that of scholarship. His "Odes of Horace," which are translated into meters partially akin to those of the original, have been well received. Not so his traaslation of the "Iliad" into a compromise between the ballad measure and a peculiar metre of his own. The result is neither poetry nor prose. And this result is one which human nature never can endure.—CHADWICK, JOHN WHITE, 1866, *Francis William Newman, The Christian Examiner,* vol. 80, p. 342.

There is a turn or twist of some kind in his nature and intellect which always seems to mar his best efforts at practical accomplishment. Even his purely literary and scholastic productions are marked by the same fatal characteristic. All the outfit, all the materials are there in surprising profusion. There is the culture, there is the intellect, the patience, the sincerity. But the result is not in proportion to the value of the materials. The blending is not complete, is not effectual. Something has always intervened or been wanting. Francis Newman has never done and probably never will do anything equal to his strength and his capacity.—MCCARTHY, JUSTIN, 1872, *Par Nobile Fratrum—The Two Newmans, Modern Leaders, p.* 173.

Poor Mr. Francis Newman must be aged now and rather weary of the world and explanations of the world. He can hardly be expected to take in much novelty. I have a sort of affectionate sadness in thinking of the interest which, in far-off days, I felt in his "Soul" and "Phases of Faith," and of the awe I had of him as a lecturer on mathematics at the Ladies' College. How much work has he done in the world which has left no deep, conspicuous mark, but has probably entered beneficially into many lives.—ELIOT, GEORGE, 1874, *To Miss Sara Hennell, March* 27; *George Eliot's Life as related in her Letters and Journals,* ed. Cross, vol. III, p. 165.

Prof. Newman's diction, polished *ad unguem,* is the very acme of simplicity and clearness; but how the colorless diamond blade flashes as he brandishes it on the battlefield of controversy. Ask the ghost of poor Kingsley [?], if you doubt its edge. —MATHEWS, WILLIAM, 1881, *Literary Style,* p. 25.

Francis Turner Palgrave
1824–1897

Born, at Great Yarmouth, Norfolk, 28 Sept. 1824. At Charterhouse, 1838-43. Matric., Balliol Coll., Oxford, 1 Dec. 1842; Scholar, 1842-47; Fellow of Exeter Coll., 1847-62; B. A., 1851; M. A., 1856. Vice-Principal of Training Coll. for Schoolmasters, Kneller Hall, 1850-55. Assistant-Sec., Education Dept., Privy Council, 1855. Private Sec. to Earl Granville, 1858-64; Hon. LL.D., Edinburgh, 23 April, 1878. Prof. of Poetry at Oxford, 1885-95. *Works:* "Preciosa" (anon.), 1852; "Idyls and Songs," 1854; "The Works of Alfred de Musset" [a review], 1855; "The Passionate Pilgrim" (under pseud. "Henry J. Thurstan") 1858; "The Golden Treasury" 1861; "Descriptive Hand-Book to the Fine Art Collection of the International Exhibition," 1862; "Essays on Art," 1866; "Hymns," 1867; "The Five Days' Entertainments at Wentworth Grange," 1868; Text to "Gems of English Art," 1869; "Lyrical Poems," 1871; "A Lyme Garland" [1874]; "The Children's Treasury of English Song," 1875; "The Visions of England" (2 parts), 1880-81; "The Life of . . . Jesus Christ, illustrated from the Italian Painters," 1885; "Ode for the 21st of June," 1887; "The Treasury of Sacred Song," 1889; "Amenophis, and other Poems," 1892; "Prothalamion," 1893; "Golden Treasury: book second," 1896; "Landscape in Poetry," 1897. He has *edited:* Clough's "Poems," 1862; Vols. 3, 4, of Sir F. Palgrave's "History of Normandy," 1864; "Selected Poems of Wordsworth," 1865; "Songs and Sonnets of Shakespeare," 1865; "Scott's Poems," (with memoir), 1866; "Chrysomela, from Herrick," 1877; Keats' "Poems," 1884; Tennyson's "Lyrical Poems," selected, 1885; J. C. Shairp's "Glen Desseray," 1888.—SHARP, R. FARQUHARSON, 1897, *A Dictionary of English Authors, p.* 221.

PERSONAL

One had but to touch on any subject in the history of English literature, or to ask him a question, and there was always an abundance of most valuable information to be got from him. I owe him a great deal, particularly in my early Oxford days. For it was he who revised my first attempts at writing in English, and gave me good advice for the rest of my journey, more particularly as to what to avoid.—MÜLLER, F. MAX, 1898, *Auld Lang Syne, p.* 144.

Palgrave was one of those men whose distinction and influence consist less in creative power than in that appreciation of the best things which is the highest kind of criticism, and in the habit of living, in all matters of both art and life, at the highest standard. This quality, which is what is meant by the classical spirit, he possessed to a degree always rare, and perhaps more rare than ever in the present age. Beyond this, but not connected with it, were qualities which only survive in the memory of his friends—childlike transparency of character, affectionateness, and quick human sympathy.—MACKAIL, J. W., 1901, *Dictionary of National Biography, Supplement,* vol. III, *p.* 244.

GENERAL

He trains and curbs his own Pegasus with as much anxiety or more than he shows in selecting perfect gems for his Golden Treasury, or in applying rules of art in his Essays. . . . The poem of "Alcestis" is one of the best examples of Mr. Palgrave's classical taste. . . . Neither Euripides nor Sophocles would have cared to throw their treatment of Alcestis into a mould which was difficult for their countrymen to appreciate, and if they had done so, the sense of effort would have taught them and their audience that they were following an unnatural process. And so with Mr. Palgrave and with all the other poets, great and small, who have imitated the Greeks; as studies, their work is no doubt not only valuable, but necessary to high excellence; as poems, one might almost say that the greater the success the greater is the failure; the closer the copy the more obvious is the *tour de force.* Study of Greek art is therefore only the stepping-stone to success, and Mr. Palgrave, after showing, as in his "Alcestis," how careful his study had been, was yet to find his natural vein and to prove the quality of his genius. That this is refined is obvious enough. That it is generous in its sympathies, is evident.—ADAMS, H., 1875, *Palgrave's Poems, North American Review, vol.* 120, *pp.* 439, 440.

He may be said to represent the latest attitude of the meditative poets, and in this closely resembles Arnold, of whom I have already spoken as the most conspicuous and able modern leader of their school. Indeed, there is scarcely a criticism which I have made upon the one that will not apply to the other. Palgrave, with less objective taste and rhythmical skill than are displayed in Arnold's larger poems, is in his lyrics equally searching and philosophical, and occasionally shows evidence of a musical and more natural ear.—STEDMAN, EDMUND CLARENCE, 1875-87, *Victorian Poets, p.* 245.

He is masculine, dignified, large, lucid. There is a studious simplicity, a singular fitness, both in his phraseology and his style. He is never carried away by his subject, and his critical faculties always seem to reign supreme. And yet he knows well the value of feeling in poetry. Of childhood, girlhood, and womanhood, of Love Mr. Palgrave sings with rare delicacy and originality. His verse is characterised by graceful and dignified simplicity, but there is no lack of fire and vigour when the subject calls for them.—GIBBS, H. J., 1892, *The Poets and the Poetry of the Century, Kingsley to Thomson, ed. Miles, p.* 244.

Mr. Palgrave has little care for technique: his rhymes are hackneyed; he uses loose stanza-forms, in which the first and third lines are unrhymed: always the thought is more to him than its metrical setting. And it is in the region of thought that Mr. Palgrave's strength is to be found. He is at home with the problems that lie on the borderland of religion and philosophy, the problems of doubt and faith and hope, of world-weariness and world-despair. In such poems as "On Lyme Beach," "Quatuor Novissima," "At Ephesus," the influence of Matthew Arnold, with his music of mournful speculation, is plainly apparent. Only it is always with a difference: Mr. Palgrave's tendency is to acceptance, not rejection; he questions, but it is to emphasise his final reliance upon the orthodox answer. . . . His hymns have not indeed the delicate beauty of Miss Rossetti's religious lyrics: yet there are several that for dignity and simplicity of phrase are far beyond compare with the doggerel that mostly fills our hymn books.—CHAMBERS, EDMUND K., 1893, *Amenophis and Other Poems, Sacred and Secular, The Academy*, vol. 43, pp. 29, 30.

Mr. Palgrave must have felt that he could count upon a large circle of readers who thought as he himself thought, not with regard to the merits of this or that poem, of this or that school, of this or that author, but with regard to the vastly wider questions concerning the qualities that belong to and distinguish the best poetry. There is no note of uncertainty in Mr. Palgrave's voice. His is no mere effort to satisfy the prevailing fancy of his own generation, but a challenge to all generations to come; he has, in effect, made definite pronouncement and proclamation upon every English lyric. Bold as he was sagacious, Mr. Palgrave has achieved unique success, and the respect as well as the gratitude of all lovers of poetry has long been freely rendered him.—DIXON, W. MACNEILE, 1895, *Finality in Literary Judgment, The Westminster Review*, vol. 143, p. 402.

There is no arguing on matters of taste, and exception might easily be taken sometimes to Palgrave's judgment as a compiler and sometimes to his dicta as a critic. But this at least must be conceded by everybody, that in the best and most comprehensive sense of the term he was a man of classical temper, taste and culture, and that he had all the insight and discernment, all the instincts and sympathies, which are the result of such qualifications. . . . As a scholar, Palgrave was rather elegant than profound or exact, and to judge from a series of lectures delivered by him as Professor of Poetry at Oxford, on "Landscape in Classical Poetry," and afterwards published in a work which was reviewed in these columns, his acquaintance with the Greek and Roman poets was, if sympathetic, somewhat superficial. — COLLINS, JOHN CHURTON, 1897, *An Appreciation of Professor Palgrave, The Saturday Review*, vol. 84, p. 487.

Francis Turner Palgrave was preëminent in two offices: he was a perfect critic, and a perfect friend. The fairest and most famous English spirits of his time, "all the clear-ranged unnumbered heads," moved in accord with his, and their names star the pages of his biography. . . . His elegantly strenuous mental life, best surveyed in Miss Gwenllian Palgrave's volume, leaves us an equally divided legacy of original verse, and of English verse edited by him. His own poetry is full of feeling and of high-mindedness; it has a certain clean strength, a music, a wide survey, even where it lacks the extreme of craftsmanship. Of these sweet, wise, and most useful books, four in number, it seems hard to say: "these have their time to pass." But to say so is only to anticipate the verdict of posterity. The name Palgrave will not suffer: it is an immortal name. It will come to mean one glorious service, one gift exquisitely and easily given. Anthologies come, and anthologies go, but only the Greek Garland and England's Helicon, and with them, the first series of "The Golden Treasury" stand bright as the sun.—GUINEY, LOUISE IMOGEN, 1899, *The Golden Treasurer, Conservative Review*, vol. 2, pp. 44, 45.

During annual holidays spent with Tennyson in England or abroad, the scheme and contents of the "Golden Treasury" were now being evolved. It was published in 1861, and obtained an immediate and decisive success which has continued for forty years. The enterprise was one often attempted before, and often renewed since; but it at once blotted out all its predecessors, and retains its primacy among the large and yearly increasing ranks of similar or cognate volumes towards which it has given the first stimulus. In itself it is, like all anthologies, open to criticism both for its inclusions and its omissions. In later editions some of these criticisms were admitted and met by Palgrave himself. But it remains one of those rare instances in which critical work has a substantive imaginative value, and entitles its author to a rank among creative artists.—MACKAIL, J. W., 1901, *Dictionary of National Biography, Supplement, vol.* III, *p.* 243.

Palgrave has the unique distinction of having acquired, merely by compiling an anthology, a degree of literary reputation such as comes only to authors who write very successful books. Palgrave, indeed, is known where many authors, properly to be called successful, are not known. His modest volume, "The Golden Treasury of the Best Songs and Lyrics in the English Language," was published nearly forty years ago. Such has been its repute that not to know it is to argue one's self strangely unfamiliar with the books of the generations now past. Not only has the book gone through edition after edition, but it has given its name to one of the most successful series of books of our generation. There can be no doubt that the success of that series in very considerable degree was indebted to the name it bore and the distinguished company its volumes kept.—HALSEY, FRANCIS WHITING, 1902, *Our Literary Deluge and Some of its Deep Waters, p.* 74.

Richard Holt Hutton
1826–1897

Theologian, journalist, and man of letters; educated at University College school and University College, London; B. A., 1845; M. A., 1849; studied at Heidelberg and Berlin; prepared for Unitarian ministry at Manchester New College, 1847; principal of University Hall, London; edited Unitarian magazine, "The Inquirer," 1851-3; studied at Lincoln's Inn; joint-editor with Walter Bagehot of "National Review," 1855-64; professor of mathematics at Bedford College, London, 1856-65; assistant-editor of the "Economist," 1858-60; joint-editor and part-proprietor of the "Spectator," 1861-97; definitively abandoned Unitarianism and accepted principles of English church. His publications include "Essays on some Modern Guides of English Thought," 1887, and "Criticisms on Contemporary Thought and Thinkers," 1894.—HUGHES, C. E., 1903, *Dictionary of National Biography, Index and Epitome, p.* 667.

PERSONAL

For the last twenty years and more of Hutton's life, reports, sometimes made with the utmost precision, were current that he had become or was about to become a convert to Rome. More than once I put the question to him; I have had his answers *viva voce* and in writing. They satisfied me that he had no intention of taking any such step, that he had never got further than this—that Rome was better than unbelief—and so far most of us are ready to go. But the reports never surprised me. Hutton's hero, so to speak, was John Henry Newman. There was much in the Roman system that he admired. He was ready to do more than justice to its practical working. . . . He was an Anglican communicant to the very last. I feel sure that it would have been impossible for him to make such a surrender of his intellectual liberty as accession to the Roman communion would have implied.—CHURCH, ALFRED, 1900, *Richard Holt Hutton, The Critic, vol.* 37, *p.* 273.

GENERAL

His theological writings are not of a generally "popular" kind, being too much out of the beaten track of the routine controversies that impose on so many would-be theological readers. It is needless to say that he has no anxiety to be regarded as "orthodox;" but it may not be equally superfluous to observe that he is no less free from the converse ambition to be a proficient in heresy—an ambition which, consciously or unconsciously, bewitches and distorts the mind of many an active and generous theologian at the present time. Mr. Hutton's imagination is wholly undisturbed by the phantoms of orthodoxy and heresy in any way; all he cares for is to discover truth, and he is equally ready to hold it in a "minority of one" or in the fulness of social sympathy. . . . Mr. Hutton's contributions to the *National Review,* scarcely amount to one-half of his best productions, but they include the maturest of his longer Essays, and except for the absence of political, humorous, and satirical papers, give a very fair representation of his mind as a whole.—COLLET, S. D., 1871, *Mr. Richard H. Hutton as Critic and Theologian, Contemporary Review*, vol. 16, pp. 635, 636.

I have closed Mr. R. H. Hutton's book of Essays on "Guides of English Thought in Matters of Faith," with a yet stronger sense of the interest of the intellectual converse between the critic and the subjects of his criticism, than of Mr. Hutton's own conclusions, valuable though they are. Mr. Hutton's own attitude presents two different sides, each very strongly marked. On the one hand there is a very subtle and searching critical power. This satisfies in his purely literary work Goethe's test of true criticism—a quick eye for and appreciation of the *beauties* of his author. Again and again a passage in George Eliot or Matthew Arnold, which had left its mark on the reader, he could not quite tell why, is reproduced by Mr. Hutton, and the complex source of our admiration faithfully delineated by him, whether it be a striking contrast, or fine insight into the inmost recesses of character, or the touching of some of the deepest chords of human feeling, or the purely artistic presentation of a scene of human life. Mr. Hutton's critical power, when he touches the deeper aspects of religious thought, is also very acute, if not quite so remarkable. . . . Mr. Hutton's choice of spiritual diet may be somewhat Spartan, and unsuited to weak digestions; but it is invigorating and sustaining to those who are equal to it.—WARD, WILFRID, 1888, *Mr. R. H. Hutton as a Religious Thinker, Dublin Review*, vol. 103, pp. 1, 21.

The very fact that the objective does not count for much with Mr. Hutton in making his estimates of events, men, and books, and that he resolutely disregards it, adds to his subjective strength. He cares only for the heart of a matter and goes as straight to it as he can. And I doubt whether any public writer of the present generation or of its predecessor—Mr. Hutton recalls Mr. William Rathbone Greg and Mr. Walter Bagehot and Mr. John Morley rather than the hierophants of the New Journalism—has on the spur of the moment said so many true and sagacious things with so much point. This is all the more notable that he certainly does not strain after literary effect in any of its modern forms. He never struggles to be epigrammatic. He is no devotee of the modern cult of the snippet; on the contrary his sentences—here again he resembles Mr. Gladstone—are often long and involved. But his resolute and transparent modesty, and his obvious aversion to the character of *poseur*, lend emphasis to that beauty of sanity which is the outstanding feature of his judgments.—WALLACE, WILLIAM, 1894, *A Journalist in Literature, Scottish Review*, vol. 24, p. 163.

He is not to be measured merely by the work, important as it is, which bears his own name. He is also the head of what may fairly be called a school. Consciously or unconsciously, he has influenced that majority, at least, of the numerous writers who must have collaborated in the weekly literary articles of the *Spectator*. This is the first point to be insisted upon in an appreciation of Mr. Hutton as a critic. We must put to his credit, not only all that is of merit in his writings, but that personal power which he has wielded over others. . . . We find that the most prominent features of Mr. Hutton's criticism are variety of interest and a sympathy, comprehensive indeed, but not entirely catholic. The unifying principle is given by theology, and theology determines likewise the limits of the sympathy.—WALKER, HUGH, 1896, *Living Critics, The Bookman*, vol. 2, pp. 498, 499.

No one—not even the writer of the *Pall Mall Gazette*, who encloses Richard Hutton's audience within the walls of a Rectory garden—will deny that he abjured, throughout his career, that alliance with scorn which ordinarily supplies journalism with its most pungent condiments. Nothing that he has written is bitter, or stinging, or pregnant with *innuendo*. Think of all that he cut off in that renunciation! Remove ill-nature, and how much of what the world counts wit would remain? Perhaps the best, but how vastly reduced in amount! That removal, at all events, would blunt no single sentence due to his pen; no criticism from him ever wounded a tender memory, or impoverished the springs of creative power in a single mind. Could the same be said of any other journalist of his time? . . . He is admitted by respectful but decided opponents to have been a force on the side of our national union, a tribute to his political weight which could be given to no other spiritual teacher of this century.

Few indeed are the leaders of thought who turn, as he did, both to the heights of eternal principles, and to the valleys of concrete application. — WEDGWOOD, JULIA, 1897, *Richard Holt Hutton, Contemporary Review,* vol. 72, pp. 457, 468.

One of the ablest essayists, as well as one of the best men who has lived in our times. —DUFF, SIR MOUNTSTUART GRANT, 1900, *The National Review,* vol. 34, p. 532.

In the "Spectator" Hutton found a pulpit from which he could speak on subjects nearest his heart, as well as on books and events of the day. In theological questions he first made his mark as the champion of Christianity against agnostic and rationalistic teachers. For this task Hutton was qualified by the breadth of his mind, the accuracy of his understanding, and his profound knowledge of current religious thought. Pre-eminently catholic in spirit he was removed from lesser party differences, and was able to comprehend and reconcile many positions which to smaller men seemed hopelessly antagonistic. While it would be idle to regard him as standing in the first rank of theologians, it may be questioned whether any of his contemporaries influenced public opinion more widely. This influence was exercised both through the "Spectator" and by means of the vast correspondence he kept up with private persons on matters of religious controversy.— LEE, SIDNEY, 1901, *ed. Dictionary of National Biography, Supplement,* vol. III, p. 21.

Jean Ingelow
1820–1897

Born, at Boston, Lincs., 1820. Active literary life. Died, in Kensington, 20 July 1897. *Works:* "A Rhyming Chronicle" (anon), 1850; "Allerton and Dreux" (anon.), 2 vols.), 1851; "Tales of Orris" [1860]; "Poems," 1863 (4th edn. same year); "Studies for Stories, from Girls' Lives" (anon.), 1864; "Stories told to a Child" (anon.), 1865; "Home Thoughts and Home Scenes," (anon.), 1865; "Little Rie and the Rosebuds" (anon.), 1867; "The Suspicious Jackdaw" (anon.), 1867; "The Grandmother's Shoe" (anon.), 1867; "The Golden Opportunity" (anon.), 1867; "Deborah's Book" (anon.), 1867; "A Story of Doom," 1867; "The Moorish Gold" (anon.), 1867; "The Minnows with Silver Tails" (anon.), 1867; "The Wild-Duck Shooter" (anon.), 1867; "A Sister's Bye-Hours" (anon.), 1868; "Mopsa the Fairy," 1869; "The Little Wonder-Horn," 1872; "Off the Skelligs" (4 vols.), 1872; "Fated to be Free," 1875; "Poems," second series, 1876; "Poems" (collected; 2 vols.), 1879; "Sarah de Berenger," 1879; "Don John," 1881; "The High Tide on the Coast of Lincolnshire, 1571," 1883; "Poems," third series, 1885; "John Jerome," 1886; "Lyrical and other poems" (selected), 1886; "The Little Wonder-Box," 1887; "Very Young; and, Quite Another Story," 1890.—SHARP, R. FARQUHARSON, 1897, *A Dictionary of English Authors,* p. 145.

GENERAL

Many thanks for your kind note. I have just returned to town, and found the "Rhyming Chronicle." Your Cousin must be worth knowing: there are some very charming things in her book, at least it seems so to me, tho' I do not pique myself on being much of a critic at first sight, and I really have only skimmed a few pages. Yet I think I may venture to pronounce that she need not be ashamed of publishing them. Certain things I saw which I count abominations, tho' I myself in younger days have been guilty of the same, and so was Keats. I would sooner lose a pretty thought than enshrine it in such rhymes as "Eudora" "before her," "vista" "sister." She will get to hate them herself as she grows older, and it would be a pity that she should let her book go forth with these cockneyisms. If the book were not so good I should not care for these specks, but the critics will pounce upon them, and excite a prejudice. I declare I should like to know her.—TENNYSON, ALFRED LORD, 1849, *Letter to Miss Holloway; A Memoir,* ed. *Tennyson,* vol. I, p. 286.

Miss Ingelow—although she knows the niceties of language, the horrors, for example, that Herman Melville tells us enshroud the word "white"—possesses no such drowning surge of splendor, such weltering wealth of words, as Mr. Swinburne has; but her pictures rise from a gray-toned ground into warm and perfect tints of beauty; she wastes no thought on alliteration, and does not deal with the uproarious emotions. Her finest passages wait upon the intellect, and when she addresses the heart, it is through her tenderness and pathos. We might adduce page after page in witness of this were it not obvious to every reader. . . . Without having so large a nature as Mrs. Browning, she is her equal in many special powers, sometimes, as in her various melody of rhyme, surpassing her, and failing only in that ability which Mrs. Browning held of inspiring her admirers with passionate personal devotion. It has been the habit to class Jean Ingelow with Miss Rossetti and a host of minor singers, but she rises as much above them as some wave that shoots its shaft of spray into the sunlight rises above the level ocean. . . . The "Story of Doom" is one of the most magnificent things that have been given to this generation.—SPOFFORD, HARRIET PRESCOTT, 1867, *Jean Ingelow's New Volume*, The Galaxy, vol. 4, pp. 570, 573.

As the voice of Mrs. Browning grew silent, the songs of Miss Ingelow began, and had instant and merited popularity. They sprung up suddenly and tunefully as skylarks from the daisy-spangled, hawthorn-bordered meadows of old England, with a blitheness long unknown, and in their idyllic under-flights moved with the tenderest currents of human life. Miss Ingelow may be termed an idyllic lyrist, her lyrical pieces having always much idyllic beauty, and being more original than her recent ambitious efforts in blank verse. Her faults are those common to her sex,—too rapid composition, and a diffuseness that already has lessened her reputation—STEDMAN, EDMUND CLARENCE, 1875-87, *Victorian Poets*, p. 280.

In poems of direct narrative or of simple reflection or description, Miss Ingelow has always had her pen well in hand; and all her best work belongs to one of these classes. From the first, however, she has displayed an unfortunate taste for a kind of poem made up of a skeleton of narrative, the structure of which is all but concealed by a body of description of reflection. When I say unfortunate, I use the word with a distinct personal reference, for as we all know some of the finest poems in the English language may be thus described; but the form does not suit Miss Ingelow, because in leaving the narrative, and then working back to it, she is tempted to the besetting sin of all "natural" poets—the sin of diffuse and formless expatiation.— NOBLE, JAMES ASHCROFT, 1885, *Poems*, The Academy, vol. 27, p. 397.

It is the best told of all Miss Ingelow's tales,—the most direct and dramatic and symmetrical; and, in short, Don John is, to our mind, an exceedingly beautiful little story; a finished and charming specimen of that minor English fiction which is often as good, from a literary point of view, as the best produced elsewhere.—PRESTON, HARRIET WATERS, 1885, *Miss Ingelow and Mrs. Walford*, Atlantic Monthly, vol. 56, p. 238.

Among the small group of eminent English women-poets that the present century has produced, Jean Ingelow holds a conspicuous place. She is greater than Felicia Hemans or Letitia Landon, for she avoids sentimentality—the characteristic weakness of both these poets. It is true that she does not possess in an equal degree with Elizabeth Barrett Browning that breadth of thought, that strength of passion—that imaginative fervour, and that vigour of execution—which give to the latter the first place among English women-poets, nor has she that peculiarly exalted spirituality tinctured with asceticism which distinguishes the best work of Christina Rossetti. Nevertheless her poems exhibit high qualities of their own. . . . Jean Ingelow's verse is always distinguished by graceful fancy, and often by imagination of the more lofty kind. Though it cannot be said that her range is wide, her pictures within this range are vivid, and her verse displays a tender womanliness, a reverent simplicity of religious faith, and a deep touch of sympathy with the pain inherent in human life which are very fascinating.—BELL, MACKENZIE, 1892, *The Poets and the Poetry of the Century, Joanna Baillie to Mathilde Blind*, ed. Miles, p. 385.

Jean Ingelow survived, as did Eliza Cook, to see her verse well-nigh forgotten, and yet it is stated that two hundred thousand copies of her poems have been sold in America alone.—SHORTER, CLEMENT, 1897, *Victorian Literature*, p. 29.

Her work, though in date it belongs mainly to the years between 1860 and 1870, is typically Early Victorian. She is a Mrs. Hemans who has read Tennyson, an L. E. L. who has read Mrs. Browning. Like those writers, she is definitely a poetess, not a poet. In this at the outset, we see her complete distinction from her less popular

contemporary, Christina Rossetti, who is a poet among poets, womanly but not feminine. It is because she is rather feminine than womanly—feminine in the broadest and most honourable sense certainly—that Jean Ingelow has always appealed so widely to women and to that part of the reading public whose judgment in literature is similar to the literary judgment of women.
. . . In her realism, as in her emotion, she still always generalizes; her very descriptions, so true in outline, of English scenes and landscapes, are for the most part lacking in precision; she is vague even among flowers, to which she refers not without a certain felicity; the exact word rarely comes, flashing the exact image. She seems, indeed, almost to seek the ready-made in language, as a visible sign of that spontaneity which she is feminine enough to think the origin and not the result of the "art which conceals art." Thus she writes in a favorite poem, of raindrops in "genial showers," of trees "wherewith the dell was decked;" she begins a stanza, "While swam the unshed tear." Certainly she has the virtues of the improvisatore; but at what a cost!—SYMONS, ARTHUR, 1897, *Jean Ingelow, The Saturday Review*, vol. 84, p. 80.

There was a great charm for readers in general in the directness and simplicity of her style. Ordinary themes were dealt with in simple Saxon language, yet with a sufficient freightage of thought. When she touched the cords either of some gentle familiar emotion or of some strong passion, it was in a manner convincing and agreeable to the great majority of readers. Her absolute sincerity was beyond all question. But the qualities of a higher gift were there also—imagination, earnestness of feeling, the power to realise the varying moods and aspects of nature, and—her most distinctive quality—an unfailing lyrical gift of exceptional sweetness and melody. Such qualities were more than sufficient to counterbalance her chief fault—an occasional diffuseness.—GRAHAM, RICHARD D., 1897, *The Masters of Victorian Literature*, p. 357.

Not to read Jean Ingelow is to miss something from our store, a small quantity it may be, a few grains of gold sifted from a sandheap, but genuine gold for all that. And what are they? First a poem without blemish, of complete and sustained art within its limits, of poignant pathos, of dramatic intensity, of perfect tunefulness, I mean of course, "The High Tide on the Coast of Lincolnshire;" then two or three songs of a quality rare amongst modern song-writers, showing a complete understanding of the limits and nature of the medium chosen not often found; and many fragments to be gleaned from many pages, flashes of vivid impressionism, the heart of a summer day, the vision of colour, the sound of the tide on the shore, poetic and melodious to a haunting degree, by no means to be spared from our anthology.—BIRCHENOUGH, MABEL C., 1899, *Jean Ingelow, Fortnightly Review*, vol. 71, p. 487.

Her verse is mainly characterised by lyrical charm, graceful fancy, pathos, close and accurate observation of nature, and sympathy with the common interests of life. The language is invariably clear and simple. She is particularly successful in handling anapæstic measures. Her poetry is very popular in America, where some 200,000 copies of her various works have been sold. As a novelist she does not rank so high.—LEE, ELIZABETH, 1901, *Dictionary of National Biography, Supplement*, vol. III, p. 31.

Henry George
1839–1897

An American political economist; born in Philadelphia, Sept. 2, 1839; died in New York, Oct. 29, 1897. "His Progress and Poverty" was published in 1879. Mr. George removed to New York in 1880. The following year "The Irish Land Question" was given to the world. In 1886 he was candidate of the United Labor Party for mayor of New York. He subsequently founded the *Standard*, a weekly newspaper. "Social Problems" appeared in 1884, and "Protection or Free Trade" in 1886. "The Perplexed Philosopher," etc., followed. Posthumous work on political economy is announced for publication in 1898. He was candidate for Mayor of Greater New York at the time of his death.—WARNER, CHARLES DUDLEY, ed. 1897, *Library of the World's Best Literature, Biographical Dictionary*, vol. XXIX, p. 213.

PERSONAL

I noticed his large head and bright eyes, and at once compared them with a picture of Henry Clay that had been familiar to me from childhood, and thought the head before me was the finer of the two. . . . In the new building of the *Post* he had two editorial rooms, one of them an inner office, where he was supposed to withdraw from visitors. But at that time and always Henry George was the most social of men; he loved to know people, not to hear himself talk, but to listen to others, to learn from their daily experience, to argue with them when questions for argument were brought up, so that very seldom did he shut himself in the inner office, but wrote at the desk in the reception-room. In those days he wrote always with pen and ink on long narrow slips of paper, and almost invariably under greatest pressure. It was not until after the publication of "Progress and Poverty," and indeed not for several years after moving to New York, that he used the typewriter for composition. . . . Ever and always Henry George maintained his sense of humor, and the recollection of that fact is more keen to his friends to-day in that he did not write humorous articles. He certainly could have done so, for his conversation was punctured with wit and pervaded by a most refined humor.—McLEAN, MRS. C. F., 1889, *Henry George: a Study from Life, The Arena*, vol. 20, pp. 297, 299, 308.

Few can speak of Henry George's personal charm of character and disposition with more confidence than I can. He and his family were the guests of my wife and myself for several weeks when he visited England for the first time. He was then at the height of his reputation. I have never seen or read of a man so little affected by sudden and astounding success. From first to last he remained the simple, unaffected, genuine good fellow which in himself he really was. In my own controversies with him, first in the "Nineteenth Century" and afterwards on the platform of St. James's Hall, he exhibited the same charming temper that he did in private life. . . . Do what you would, to the Single Tax he returned and to the Single Tax he devoted himself. Beyond that and Free-trade he would not budge. His enthusiasm would not permit him to see the force of reason; his anxiety to be practical confined his mind to a single idea. That his work was done cannot be disputed. He stirred up thought by propagating error with as much success as any man that ever lived.—HYNDMAN, H. M., 1897, *Henry George, Saturday Review*, vol. 84, pp. 485, 486.

I know of no American whose career, unfavored by accident or the help of others, is so impressive. . . . The Henry George of the past decade is the Henry George of New York. The diminutive figure—he is under five and a half feet and of less weight and smaller girth than many a boy of sixteen—is familiar to the people of Fort Hamilton, where he lives and has taken his walks, constitutionals without distinction, and heedless in the choice of roadway or sidewalk, ambles for fresh air and thought that excluded observation of external things. The fine head, the graying-reddish beard, the blue eyes looking absently out from under the thickest of brows and through large spectacles, the soft hat set on any way —when these have appeared at the door of an editorial-room to inquire for a friend or bring an article, the stranger journalist, unaware of the visitor's identity, has mistaken him for a colporteur, a retired schoolmaster, an unrecognized poet, or anything meek and unworldly.—McEWEN, ARTHUR, 1897, *Henry George: a Character Sketch, Review of Reviews*, vol. 16, pp. 548, 549.

PROGRESS AND POVERTY
1879

A noteworthy book that bears the traces of a master's hand—which for freshness of thought, the steady march of its logic, wealth of illustration, strong grasp of economic abstractions, and facile handling of facts, no student of social problems can afford to pass by.—BARROWS, CHARLES H., 1879, *Literary World*, vol. 10, p. 122.

It is possible to affirm without hesitation that the appearance of that one book formed a noteworthy epoch in the history of economic thought both in England and America. It is not simply that the treatise itself was an eloquent, impassioned plea for the confiscation of rent for the public good as a means of abolishing economic social evils, but rather that the march of industrial forces had opened a way for the operation of ideas new and strange to the great masses. . . . Henry George has rendered two distinct services to the cause of socialism. First, in the no-rent theory, or in other words, the confiscation of rent *pro bono publico*, he has furnished a rallying point for all discontented laborers; second, his book has served as an entering wedge for other still more radical and far-reaching measures. It is written in an easily understood, and even brilliant style, is published in cheap form, both in England and America, and in each country has attained a circulation, which for economic work is without parallel. Tens of thousands of laborers have read "Progress and Poverty," who never before looked between the two covers of an economic book, and its conclusions are widely accepted articles in the workingman's creed.—ELY, RICHARD T., 1885, *Henry George and the Beginnings of Revolutionary Socialism in the United States, Johns Hopkins University Studies in Historical and Political Science, vol. 3, pp. 16, 18.*

So superb a work, so persuasively constructed, and so full of great, needed truth, that he has almost overwhelmed the very elect with one of the most glaring and disjointed non-sequiturs that ever broke itself in two with its own logic.—CLARK, EDWARD GORDON, 1887, *Henry George's Land Tax, North American Review, vol. 144, p. 109.*

With the exception of "The Wealth of Nations," perhaps no book on political economy has been more widely read than Mr. George's "Progress and Poverty." In fact, it is really the first book on economics that was ever read to any considerable extent by the working classes. Nor is the reason for this difficult to understand. Unlike the ordinary treatises on political economy, Mr. George's book is to the laborer the unmistakable voice of a friend. He cannot read a single chapter of it without feeling that whether Mr. George is right or wrong, in him the laborers have a friend in court. "Progress and Poverty" is as much a special effort to present their interests as the political economy of the Manchester school has been to present that of their masters. This feature, together with Mr. George's fascinating style of writing, has made "Progress and Poverty" a most powerful means of directing public attention to the social problem. In this sense Mr. George may be said to have done an important work. But if "Progress and Poverty" is to be considered in the sense of a contribution to sound economic literature we shall be compelled to form a very different estimate of its value. . . . A little examination, however, will serve to show that Mr. George's economic reasoning is no better than his facts. As to his theory of rent Mr. George is orthodox, and accepts Ricardo without question or qualification.—GUNTON, GEORGE, 1887, *Henry George's Economic Heresies, The Forum, vol. 3, pp. 15, 21.*

The reader of "Progress and Poverty" is struck with the fact that the book contains no statements derived from painstaking inquiries into the statistics of land values and rents. The book is eloquent and effective, its author evidently an earnest and disinterested philantropist. But his theories all relate to numbers of population, rates of wages, prices of food, amounts of rent, and the ratios of these numbers to one another. These are not *a priori* questions, but matters of statistics. There is not only no investigation of statistics in "Progress and Poverty," but there is not even an attempt to make definite estimates, although there are occasional references to isolated data. If it should be found that the total ground-rent is an insignificant item compared with the total income of the nation, it would be necessary to conclude that Mr. George is mistaken in supposing that private property in land exercises a power to rob capital and labor. And such, indeed, must be our conclusion in whatever way we approach the study of the actual statistics.—HARRIS, WILLIAM TORREY, 1887, *Henry George's Mistake About Land, The Forum, vol. 3, p. 435.*

That it should be necessary, at this time of day, to set forth such elementary truths as these may well seem strange; but no one who consults that interesting museum of political delusions, "Progress and Poverty," some of the treasures of which I have already brought to light, will doubt the fact, if he bestows proper attention upon the first book of that widely-read work. . . . The doctrine respecting the relation of capital and wages, which is thus opposed in "Progress and Poverty," is that illustrated in the foregoing pages; the truth of which, I conceive, must be plain to anyone who has apprehended the very simple arguments by which I have endeavoured to demonstrate it. One conclusion or the other must be hopelessly wrong; and, even at the cost of going once more over some of the ground traversed in this and my last paper, I propose to show that the error lies with "Progress and Poverty;" in which work, so far as political science is concerned, the poverty is, to my eye, much more apparent than the progress.—HUXLEY, THOMAS HENRY, 1890, *Capital—The Mother of Labour, The Nineteenth Century*, vol. 27, p. 523.

GENERAL

I have spoken to —— about your works, which he expects to print in full. I am anxious to have you popularized as fully as may be, for I know you must exert a powerful and beneficial effect upon thought. To get it into the head of the average man that his race and his creed are not everything is to melt away bigotry and prejudice and admit larger and nobler views.— MÜLLER, FRIEDRICH MAX, 1883, *To Henry George, August 21; Life and Letters*, ed. his Wife, vol. II, p. 152.

Never, perhaps, have communistic theories assumed a form more curious, or lent themselves to more fruitful processes of analysis, than in the writings of Mr. Henry George. These writings now include a volume on "Social Problems," published recently. It represents the same ideas as those which inspire the work on "Progress and Poverty." They are often expressed in almost the same words, but they exhibit some development and applications which are of high interest and importance. . . . Everything in America is on a gigantic scale, even its forms of villainy, and the villainy advocated by Mr. George is an illustration of this as striking as the Mammoth Caves of Kentucky, or the frauds of the celebrated "Tammany Ring" in New York. The world has never seen such a Preacher of Unrighteousness as Mr. Henry George. For he goes to the roots of things, and shows us how unfounded are the rules of probity, and what mere senseless superstitions are the obligations which have been only too long acknowledged.— ARGYLL, DUKE OF, 1884, *The Prophet of San Francisco, Nineteenth Century*, vol. 15, pp. 540, 548.

The treatment is more popular ["Social Problems"] than in "Progress and Poverty;" it is less laboured and controversial, and, it must be said, less sophistical. The book is marked by the same eloquence, the same sympathy with the claims of labour, and the same wide and often true insight into the great industrial movements of our time. In these qualities, and not in his theory of the land, lies the strength of Mr. George.—KIRKUP, T., 1884, *Social Problems, The Academy*, vol. 25, p. 87.

Mr. George's great merit is as an alarmbell; for men must be awakened before they can see or think or act, however little they may approve the music after thought and action are at once in full play. He tells us little that is really new; but his old things, right or wrong, have taken the voice of the times and will have their audience.— BABCOCK, W. H., 1887, *The George Movement and Property, Lippincott's Magazine*, vol. 39, p. 133.

Since the mistakes of Moses were so triumphantly demolished by Col. Ingersoll, his example has been followed by numerous writers, who, possibly because they concluded that the Mosiac field has been sufficiently occupied, have devoted themselves to an equally triumphant demonstration of the mistakes of Henry George. Space could not be afforded for even an abstract of these brilliant productions. Crushed by the Duke of Argyll, refuted by Mr. Mallock, extinguished by Mayor Hewitt, undermined by Mr. Edward Atkinson, exploded by Mr. Harris, excommunicated by archbishops, consigned to eternal damnation by countless doctors of divinity, put outside the pale of the Constitution by numberless legal pundits, waved out of existence by a million Podsnaps, and finally annihilated by Mr. George Gunton, still Henry George's theories seem to have a miraculous faculty of rising from the dead. For it is certain that his general doctrines are more widely believed in to-day than ever before; while the one practical measure which he advocates for present and immediate enactment is accepted by a vast number of intelligent men on both sides of the Atlantic. —SHEARMAN, THOMAS G., 1889, *Henry George's Mistakes, The Forum*, vol. 8, p. 40.

Henry George, the prophet of an industrial millennium, could claim all the signs of a fate-favored avatar. He was thoroughly in earnest; he had the courage and the eloquence of an enthusiastic belief in the earth-redeeming tendency of his gospel, and that gospel appealed strongly to the hopes of toil-burdened millions, the pariahs and step-children of modern civilization. . . . Like Voltaire, Henry George died amid a blaze of triumphs that probably shortened his life by several years, but the work of that life sufficed to insure the progress of his propaganda.—OSWALD, FELIX L., 1889, *Henry George an Apostle of Reform, The Chautauquan, vol.* 26, *pp.* 416, 422.

No doubt it is easy to impute excessive influence to the mouthpiece of a rising popular sentiment. George, like other prophets, co-operated with the "spirit of the age." But after this just allowance has been made, Henry George may be considered to have exercised a more directly powerful formative and educative influence over English radicalism of the last fifteen years than any other man.—HOBSON, J. A., 1897, *The Influence of Henry George in England, Fortnightly Review, vol.* 68, *p.* 844.

Henry George is the natural reasoner. He starts with the world of natural things and man. He moves from the simple to the complex, naturally. He appeals to the common sense of his readers. He is not engaged in showing his learning, his orthodoxy; he is seeking the simple solution which lies at the bottom of the problem. He wishes to enlighten, to convince, to do justice, and so a mighty power goes out from his writings. His aim is truth; his standard, justice. . . . I seem to hear his voice once more and see his face glow and lighten as in the days when his presence on the platform was a menace to every wrong, a terror to every tyranny, and the hope of every robbed and cheated man who faced him. He made the world better. He fought unremittingly till his slight material self gave way. Now here are his books— including the last and greatest of them all. They and the men he inspired must carry forward his work.—GARLAND, HAMLIN, 1898, *Henry George's Last Book, McClure's Magazine, vol.* 10, *p.* 486.

He labored in an humble way at the printer's case, after the example set by Jesus Christ at his carpenter's bench. Presently a stress of hard times forced him to seek another field. He who so long had been thinking, thinking, thinking, was too humble to believe himself a prophet. He took up the pen by compulsion. He wielded it slowly and awkwardly. The eagle that was to soar to the highest empyrean had been forced to try his wings. He scarcely knew what they were, or what flight meant. With each stroke confidence grew. Presently he no longer sank. He could hold himself on the plain. Then he began to rise, to soar. Henry George the thinker came East and gave his first book to the world—which received it, as it has been the custom of the world to receive all great messages, including that of Christ himself, first in contemptuous silence and later on with ignominy.. . . . The man who, living, was great before the Almighty God, became great before the peoples when dead. —WALKER, JOHN BRISBEN, 1898, *Men and Events: Henry George and Charles A. Dana, The Cosmopolitan, vol.* 24, *pp.* 200, 203.

I have been acquainted with Henry George since the appearance of his "Social Problems." I read them, and was struck by the correctness of his main idea, and by the unique clearness and power of his argument, which is unlike anything in scientific literature, and especially by the Christian spirit, which also stands alone in the literature of science, which pervades the book. After reading it I turned to his previous work, "Progress and Poverty," and with a heightened appreciation of its author's activity.—TOLSTOI, LEO, 1898, *Count Tolstoi on the Doctrine of Henry George, Review of Reviews, vol.* 17, *p.* 73.

For at least fifteen or sixteen years Henry George stood in the full glare of world-wide publicity, as a writer and speaker on some of the most controversial topics of our time. The book by which he became famous, "Progress and Poverty," created as great a stir amongst social reformers as did the "Origin of Species" amongst scientists. Some of the most robust and active intellects in England, such as Huxley, Harrison, and the ubiquitous Duke of Argyll, thought him a foeman worthy of their steel, and for a season at least his theory of landreform became the universal theme of discussion amongst political clubs and debating societies throughout the land. . . . Probably no man, working, as George did, single-handed, has in such a short space of time ever left so deep an impression upon the current thought and the legislative tendencies of the age in which he lived. . . . It was George who saw the land question in its true vital relation to the other burning questions which to-day agitate civilised society. It is his crowning merit that certain germs of doctrine, which but for him would have remained germs, have by his

WILLIAM EWART GLADSTONE

Engraving by Walker and Cockerell. From a
Photograph by the London Stereoscopic Co.

HENRY GEORGE

Engraving from a Photograph.

pen and tongue been ripened into vigorous life, and made part and parcel of the educated public opinion of our time.—SCANLON, THOMAS, 1901, *Henry George's Biography, Westminster Review*, vol. 156, pp. 197, 201.

William Ewart Gladstone
1809-1898

Born, in Liverpool, 29 Dec. 1809. At Eton, 1821-27; Matric. Ch. Ch., Oxford, 23 Jan. 1828. Student, 1829-39; B. A., 1832; M. A., 1834; Hon. Student, 1867; Hon. D. C. L., 5 July 1848; Hon. Fellow All Souls' Coll., 1858. M. P. for Newark, 1832-45. Student at Lincoln's Inn, 25 Jan. 1833. Junior Lord of Treasury, Dec. 1834; Under Sec. for Colonies, Jan. to April, 1835. Married Catherine Glynne, 25 July 1839. Privy Councillor, 1841. Vice-President of Board of Trade, Sept. 1841 to May 1843; President, May 1843 to Feb. 1845. Master of Mint, Sept. 1841 to Feb. 1845. Sec. of State for Colonies, Dec. 1845 to July 1846. M. P. for Oxford Univ., 1847 ; re-elected, 1852-65. Chancellor of Exchequer, Dec. 1852 to Feb. 1855. Lord High Commissioner to Ionian Islands, winter 1858-59. Chancellor of Exchequer, June 1859 to July 1866. Lord Rector Edinburgh Univ., 1859-65. M. P. for South Lancashire, 1865-68; for Greenwich, 1868-74; re-elected 1874-80. Premier and First Lord of Treasury, Dec. 1868 to Feb. 1874; Chancellor of Exchequer, Aug. 1873 to Feb. 1874. Resigned Leadership of Liberal Party, Jan. 1875. Visit to Ireland, Oct. to Nov. 1877; received Freedom of City of Dublin. Lord Rector of Glasgow Univ., Nov. 1877. M. P. for Midlothian, 1880. Premier and Chancellor of Exchequer, April 1880 to Dec. 1882; Premier and First Lord of Treasury, Dec. 1882 to June 1885. Premier and Lord Privy Seal, Feb. to July, 1886. Premier, First Lord of Treasury and Lord Privy Seal, Aug. 1892 to March 1894. Romanes Lecturer, Oxford, Oct. 1892. Freedom of City of Liverpool, 3 Dec. 1894. Retired from public life, March 1894. *Works:* [exclusive of political speeches, addresses, and pamphlets]: "The State in its relations with the Church," 1838; "Church Principles considered in their results," 1840; "Manual of Prayers from the Liturgy," 1845; "On the place of Homer in Classical Education," 1857; "Studies on Homer and the Homeric Age," (3 vols.), 1858; " 'Ecce Homo,'" 1868; "A Chapter of Autobiography," 1868; "Juventus Mundi," 1869; "The Vatican Decrees," 1874; "Vaticanism," 1875; "Rome and the Newest Fashions in Religion" (a reprint of the two preceding, with " Speeches of the Pope"), 1875; "The Church of England and Ritualism," (from "Contemporary Rev."), 1876; "Homeric Synchronism," 1876; "Homer," 1878; "Gleanings of Past Years," (7 vols.), 1879; "Landmarks of Homeric Study," 1890; "The Impregnable Rock of Holy Scripture," (from "Good Words") 1890; "An Introduction to the People's Bible History," 1895; "Studies Subsidiary to the Works of Bishop Butler," 1896; " On the Condition of Man in a Future Life" pt. I., 1896. He has *translated:* Farini's " The Roman State from 1815 to 1850," 1851; the "Odes" of Horace, 1894; and *edited:* Bishop Butler's "Works," 1896.—SHARP, R. FARQUHARSON, 1897, *A Dictionary of English Authors*, p. 113.

PERSONAL

I was out all yesterday evening with Gladstone, who is one of the cleverest and most sensible people I ever met with.—MILNES-GASKELL, JAMES, 1826, *Letters, June 30*.

William Gladstone is at home now, and last Tuesday I and one of the other boys were invited to breakfast with him; so we went, had breakfast in grand style, went into the garden and devoured strawberries. which were there in great abundance, unchained the great Newfoundland, and swam him in the pond; we walked about the garden, went into the house and saw beautiful pictures of Shakespeare's plays, and came away at twelve o'clock. It was very good fun, and I don't think I was very shy, for I talked to William Gladstone almost all the time about all sorts of things. He is so very good-natured, and I like him very much. He talked a great deal about Eton, and said that it was a very good place for those who liked boating and Latin verses. I think from what he said, I might get to like it. . . . He was very good-natured to us all the time, and lent me books to read when we went away.—STANLEY, ARTHUR PENRHYN, 1828, *Letter, June 26; Life and Correspondence of Stanley*, ed. Prothero and Bradley, vol. I, p. 22.

The man that *took* me most was the

youngest Gladstone of Liverpool—I am sure, a very superior person.—MILNES. RICHARD MONCKTON, 1829, *Letters, Dec. 5*.

A young man of unblemished character, and of distinguished parliamentary talents, the rising hope of those stern and unbending Tories, who follow, reluctantly and mutinously, a leader, whose experience and eloquence are indispensable to them, but whose cautious temper and moderate opinions they abhor. It would not be at all strange if Mr. Gladstone were one of the most unpopular men in England. But we believe that we do him no more than justice when we say, that his abilities and his demeanour have obtained for him the respect and good will of all parties.—MACAULAY, THOMAS BABINGTON, 1839, *Church and State, Edinburgh Review*, vol. 69, p. 231.

He has a face like a lion's; his head is small above it, though the forehead is broad and massive—something like Trajan's in its proportion to the features. Character, far more than intellect, strikes me in his physiognomy, and there is a remarkable duplicity of expression—iron, vice-like resolution combined with a subtle, mobile ingenuousness.—SYMONDS, JOHN ADDINGTON, 1865-93, *Recollections of Lord Tennyson, Century Magazine*, vol. 46, p. 32.

Gladstone, *en route* homewards, called on Monday, and sate a long time talking, principally waiting for Madame Bunsen, his old friend, whom it was his one chance of seeing, as he had to leave for Paris the next day. Talk copious, ingenious, but of no worth or sincerity—pictures, literature, finance, prosperities, greatness of outlook for Italy, &c.—a man ponderous, copious, of evident faculty, but all gone irrecoverably into House of Commons shape—man once of some wisdom or possibility of it, but now possessed by the Prince, or many Princes, of the Power of the Air. Tragic to me rather, and far from enviable; from whom one felt oneself divided by abysmal chasms and immeasurabilities. He went next morning; but it seems, by the journals, will find his M. Fould, &c., suddenly thrown out by some jerk of their inscrutable Copper Captain, and unable to do the honors of Paris in the way they wished.— CARLYLE, THOMAS, 1867, *Journal, Jan. 23; Carlyle's Life in London*, ed. Froude, vol. II, p. 285.

Mr. Gladstone's nature is essentially moral; the categories to which he refers all things are those of good and evil. And his extreme seriousness, though it excludes extravagance, does not exclude enthusiasm. Mr. Gladstone brings the fervor of faith into every cause that he espouses. He is also essentially a believer; he has the noble sides of the character—its sincerity, its straight-forwardness, its ardor. He has also its defects; his gravity lacks humor, his solidity becomes stiffness, his intelligence— gifted as it is with the most varied aptitudes, served by prodigious activity and capacity for work, able to descend from the general direction of an empire to the technical details of a bill or the complicated schedules of a budget—his intelligence has more breadth than suppleness. His reasonings are abstract because he occupies himself rather with principles than with facts; his judgments absolute because he takes every truth at the same valuation—that of an article of religion.—SCHERER, EDMOND, 1880-91, *Endymion, Essays on English Literature*, tr. Saintsbury, p. 246.

My father and I met the Gladstones at Chester. Thence to Barrow we had a triumphal progress, crowds shouting "Gladstone" at every station. At Barrow we embarked on a tug for the "Pembroke Castle," and left our native land in a tumult of acclaim! Thousands of people lining the shore, and cheering for "Gladstone" and "Tennyson." . . . It seemed to me that, in the conversations between my father and Gladstone, my father was logical and brilliant in his talk, made his points clearly, and every word and phrase of his, as in his poems and plays, bore directly on the subject under discussion; that Gladstone took longer to go from point to point, and wrapt up his argument in analogies which he thoroughly thrashed out before he returned to his thesis. What struck me most in Gladstone's expression of his thoughts was his eagerness, and mastery of words, coupled with a self-control and a gentle persuasiveness; and a certain persistence in dwelling on those topics which he had himself started for discussion. Yet, like my father, he was always most anxious to learn from anyone whom he thought better informed than himself on the matter in hand. . . . Both men were as jovial together as boys out for a holiday.—TENNYSON, HALLAM, 1883, *Diary Sept. 8; Life of Tennyson*, vol. II, p. 278, 281.

His features are almost as familiar to me as my own, for a photograph of him in his library has long stood on my revolving bookcase, with a large lens before it.—HOLMES, OLIVER WENDELL, 1887, *Our Hundred Days in Europe*, p. 43.

I do not believe I ever saw a more magnificent human face than that of Mr. Gladstone after he had grown old. Of course, the eyes were always superb. Many a stranger, looking at Gladstone for the first time, saw the eyes, and only the eyes, and could think for the moment of nothing else. Age never dimmed the fire of those eyes.—MCCARTHY, JUSTIN, 1897, *The Story of Gladstone's Life*, p. 31.

For my part I am disposed to fix upon the Bradlaugh debates as the epoch upon which the future historian will dwell with fullest appreciation. There were connected with it circumstances almost terrible in their intensity and pathos. Mr. Gladstone's speeches, his writings—as finally illustrated in that noble document, his last will and testament—and above all, his daily life, testified to his devotional habits of mind, the spirituality of his character.—LUCY, HENRY W., 1898, *Mr. Gladstone as an Orator, The Life of William Ewart Gladstone*, ed. Reid, vol. II, p. 510.

Mr. Gladstone was a man of prayer. Through and through Mr. Gladstone was intensely religious. His mind was capacious, his learning was large, his eloquence was unsurpassed; yet he would never have been the man he was but for his steadfast and glowing faith in God.—PARKER, JOSEPH, 1899, *A Preacher's Life*, p. 298.

Standing upon the summit of the Alpine mountain, the traveler looks into sunny Italy or the German forest, toward the vineyard of France or the far-off plains of Austria. And Mr. Gladstone stands forth like some sun-crowned mountain-peak, supremely great in every side of his character and career. He was a scholar, and with Homer lingered long before the gates of Troy, or with Pericles and Plato sauntered through the groves of Athens. He was an author, and the mere titles of his speeches and books fill twenty pages in the catalogue of libraries. He was an orator, and his eloquence was such that oft it seemed to his rapt listeners as if Apollo had come again—the music of the morning breathing from his lips. He was a statesman, and the reforms he proposed and the laws he created are milestones measuring the progress of the English people. Above all, he was a Christian gentleman, for religion goes with the name of Gladstone as poetry with the name of Burns or Browning, as war with Wellington or Washington.—HILLIS, NEWELL DWIGHT, 1899, *Great Books as Life-Teachers*, p. 311.

Mr. Gladstone's liberality, little heard of, while never exceeding the bounds of his income, was very great, and was curiously accompanied by his love of small economies—his determination to have the proper discount taken off the price of his second-hand books, his horror of a wasted half-sheet of note-paper, which almost equalled his detestation of a wasted minute; for his arrangement of every hour of the day, and for the occupation of that hour, was extraordinary. There was never in his busy life an idle dawdle by the fire after luncheon, or a doze over a novel before dinner. Sauntering, as Lord Rosebery said, was an impossibility to him—mentally or physically; a walk meant four miles an hour sharp, and I remember his regretting the day when he could only go up the Duke of York's steps two at a time. When about to travel he would carefully pack his own despatch-box, so that the book or paper he was reading was uppermost and ready at a moment's notice to his hand.—WEST, SIR ALGERNON, 1899, *Recollections, vol.* II, p. 36.

I have often heard Gladstone both in Parliament and on the platform; but I doubt if he quite equalled Bright in majestic imagery as an orator, or, in convincing logic and unanswerable facts, quite equalled Richard Cobden. Gladstone, of course, was immensely superior to both of them in range of experience, in constructive power, and in the management of men. As I frequently met Mr. Gladstone in society, both in and out of office, and at times have stayed for days with him in a country house, I had abundant opportunity to observe his extraordinary versatility and the range of his reading, the rapidity with which he was wont to master intricate detail, his consummate command of every resource, and his beautiful courtesy of nature and considerate forbearance with all men. If I were asked to pick out the three personal characteristics in which Mr. Gladstone surpassed all the eminent men of his time, I should choose the following out of his great union of diverse qualities. With a fiery spirit at bottom and a singularly masterful nature, he had a strange power of curbing himself at need and keeping a cool head in the exuberance of his own oratory. Next, it was almost impossible to find any topic or incident into which he could not fling himself with interest and master it with rapidity. Lastly, of all men involved in a multitude of distracting cares, he had the most marvellous faculty of keeping his mind concentrated on the immediate point in hand. — HARRISON, FREDERIC, 1901, *George Washington and other American Addresses*, p. 196.

At Cortina, too, I saw again Gladstone. . . . The old man was full of physical and mental energy, and we had several moderate climbs in the mountains of the vicinity. . . . Gladstone was a good walker, and talked by the way,—which not all good walkers can do,—but I do not remember his ever talking of himself; and in this he was like Ruskin,—he assumed himself as an element in the situation, and thought no more about it; never in our conversations obtruding his views as of more importance than the conversation demanded, and never opinionated, not even dogmatic, but always inquiring, and more desirous of hearing of the things that had interested him than of expressing his own views about them.—STILLMAN, WILLIAM JAMES, 1901, *The Autobiography of a Journalist*, vol. II, p. 628.

Gladstone, though not tall, was above the middle height, broad-shouldered, but otherwise slight in figure, and muscular, with no superfluous flesh. He was gifted with an abundance of physical strength, and enjoyed throughout his life remarkably good health. His hair, in his youth and the prime of his manhood, was black. His complexion was pale, almost pallid, and an artist compared it with alabaster. His eyes were large, lustrous, and piercing; not quite black, but resembling agate in colour. His face, always handsome, acquired in old age an expression of singular dignity, majesty, and power. His voice, naturally musical and melodious, gained by practice an almost unexampled range of compass and variety. Scarcely any building was too large for it to fill, and at a meeting in the open air it could be heard by many thousands with perfect ease. Yet he could modulate it at will, and even sink it to a whisper without ceasing to be audible. There were traces in its tone of his Lancashire origin, especially in the pronunciation of the word "sir," which he had so often to employ. But its marvellous richness always fell pleasantly on the ear. His manners were courteous, even ceremonious, and to women habitually deferential. He was a great stickler for social precedence, and would not go out of the room before a peer of his own creation. Bishops, and, indeed, all clergymen, he treated with peculiar respect. His temper, though quick, and, as he said himself, "vulnerable," was in private life almost invariably under perfect control.—PAUL, HERBERT WOODFIELD, 1901, *The Life of William Ewart Gladstone*, p. 321.

Gladstone's rooms were on Canterbury Quadrangle. If his life in those rooms had been less studious and more playful, if he had stolen knockers and frozen out Dons, instead of devoting himself to the classics and to winning a Double First, he might have proved a more amusing figure in these records; but he would hardly have proved so useful and so distinguished a figure in the history of his country and of the world. —HUTTON, LAURENCE, 1903, *Literary Landmarks of Oxford*, p. 79.

ORATORY

Saturday, October 27. "Whether the deposition of Richard II. was justifiable or not." Jelf opened: not a good speech. Doyle spoke *extempore*, made several mistakes, which were corrected by Jelf. Gladstone spoke well. The Whigs were regularly floored; only four Whigs to eleven Tories, but they very nearly kept up with them in coughing and Hear, hears. Adjourned to Monday, after 4. *Monday, 29.*— Gladstone finished his speech, and ended with a great deal of flattery of Doyle, saying that he was sure he would have courage enough to own that he was wrong. It succeeded. Doyle rose amidst reiterated cheers to own that he was convinced by the arguments of the other side. He had determined before to answer them and cut up Gladstone. *December 1.* — Debate, "Whether the Peerage Bill of 1719 was calculated to be beneficial or not." Thanks voted to Doyle and Gladstone; the latter spoke very well: will be a great loss to the Society.—COWPER, WILLIAM (LORD MOUNT-TEMPLE), 1827, *Diary.*

The debate had been opened, and Gladstone soon rose, the person I had mainly come to hear. He spoke about three quarters of an hour, and was much cheered. His manner is perfectly natural, almost conversational, and he never hesitates for the right word, or fails to have the most lucid and becoming arrangement of his argument. If anything, he lacked force. But his manner was so gentlemanlike, and so thoroughly appropriate to a great deliberative body, that I could not help sighing to think we have so little like it in our legislatures.—TICKNOR, GEORGE, 1857, *Letter to Mrs. Ticknor, July 24; Life, Letters and Journals, vol.* II, *p.* 378.

Mr. Gladstone does not possess the physical attributes of the popular orator. He has rather a recluse-like air; and, like his rival, Disraeli, seems to be possessed by an abstraction of thought from which he with difficulty rouses himself. His voice is clear and musical, but wanting in tone and volume: it sounds somewhat like a voice clearly heard afar off. His countenance is that of a student,—pale and intellectual; his eye is of remarkable depth, and might almost be described as fascinating. Like Disraeli, he wants dignity of gait, and slouches somewhat. But in the House of Commons, personal short-comings such as these are thought lightly of.— SMILES, SAMUEL, 1860, *Brief Biographies, p.* 254.

It is needless to say that Mr. Gladstone is a great orator. Oratory is one of the pursuits as to which there is no error: the criterion is ready. Did the audience feel? Were they excited? Did they cheer? These questions, and others such as these, can be answered without a mistake. A man who can move the House of Commons—still, after many changes, the most severe audience in the world—must be a great orator; the most sincere admirers and the most eager depreciators of Mr. Gladstone are agreed on this point, and it is almost the only point on which they are agreed.—BAGEHOT, WALTER, 1860, *Mr. Gladstone, Works, ed. Morgan, vol.* III, *p.* 95.

A sophistical rhetorician, inebriated with the exuberance of his own verbosity, and gifted with an egotistical imagination that can at all times command an interminable and inconsistent series of arguments to malign an opponent and to glorify himself. —DISRAELI, BENJAMIN (LORD BEACONSFIELD), 1878, *Banquet at Duke of Wellington's Riding School, July* 28.

His choice of language was unbounded. It has been said of Lord Holland and his illustrious son, Charles James Fox, that from the very wealth of their vocabulary there arose a tendency to hesitation. But the wealth of the vocabulary which was at Mr. Gladstone's command never produced that effect. His flow of words was not that of the mountain-stream, which comes tumbling down helter-skelter. It was that of the river with an immense volume of water, whose downward course is as regular as it is stately. He never gabbled. He never drawled. . . . He was a living thesaurus or "Gradus," containing synonym after synonym, and it was this extraordinary wealth of words which laid him open to the charge, not without reason, of being verbose. Mr. Gladstone's sentences were often very long, and one sometimes wondered how he would ever extricate himself from the maze of words. But there was nothing faulty in the construction of a sentence. There were parentheses, and occasionally even parentheses within parentheses; but no sentence was ever ungrammatical or unfinished.—HAMILTON, SIR EDWARD W., 1898, *Mr. Gladstone: a Monograph, pp.* 3, 4.

We have the memory of a matchless individuality, an oratory which has never been surpassed in our time, never perhaps been equalled in all its forms and varieties, and which, perhaps, will stand unrivalled in the history of eloquence since the great Athenian models existed. — ROSEBERY, ARCHIBALD PHILIP PRIMROSE LORD, 1898, *Appreciations and Addresses, p.* 118.

Few men have had so many faces, and the wonderful play of his features contributed very largely to the effectiveness of his speaking. It was a countenance eminently fitted to express enthusiasm, pathos, profound melancholy, commanding power and lofty disdain; there were moments when it could take an expression of intense cunning, and it often darkened into a scowl of passionate anger. In repose it did not seem to me good. With its tightly compressed lips and fierce, abstracted gaze it seemed to express not only extreme determination, but also great vindictiveness, a quality, indeed, by no means wanting in his nature, though it was, I think, more frequently directed against classes or parties than against individuals. He had a wonderful eye—a bird-of-prey eye—fierce, luminous and restless. "When he differed from you," a great friend and admirer of his once said to me, "there were moments when he would give you a glance as if he would stab you to the heart." There was something, indeed, in his eye in which more than one experienced judge saw dangerous symptoms of possible insanity.—LECKY, WILLIAM EDWARD HARTPOLE, 1899, *Democracy and Liberty, New Ed., Introduction*.

If Mr. Gladstone be judged by the impression he made on his own time, his place will be high in the front rank. His speeches were neither so concisely telling as Mr. Bright's nor so finished in diction; but no other man among his contemporaries— neither Lord Derby nor Mr. Lowe, nor Lord Beaconsfield, nor Lord Cairns, nor Bishop Wilberforce, nor Bishop Magee—taken all around, could be ranked beside him. And he rose superior to Mr. Bright himself in readiness, in variety of knowledge, in persuasive ingenuity. Mr. Bright spoke seldom and required time for preparation. Admirable in the breadth and force with which he set forth his own position, or denounced that of his adversaries, he was not equally qualified for instructing nor equally apt at persuading. Mr. Gladstone could both instruct and persuade, could stimulate his friends and demolish his opponents, and could do all these things at an hour's notice, so vast and well ordered was the arsenal of his mind. Pitt was superb in an expository or argumental speech, but his stately periods lacked variety. Fox, incomparable in reply, was hesitating and confused when he had to state his case in cold blood. Mr. Gladstone showed as much fire in winding up a debate as skill in opening it. His oratory had, indeed, two faults. It wanted concentration, and it wanted definition. There were too many words, and the conclusion was sometimes left vague because the arguments had been too nicely balanced.—BRYCE, JAMES, 1903, *Studies in Contemporary Biography*, p. 428.

STATESMAN

There is but one statesman of the present day in whom I feel entire confidence, and with whom I cordially agree, and that statesman is Mr. Gladstone. I look upon him as the representative of the party, scarcely developed as yet, though secretly forming and strengthening, which will stand by all that is dear and sacred in my estimation, in the struggle which I believe will come ere *very* long between good and evil, order and disorder, the Church and the world, and I see a very small band collecting round him, and ready to fight manfully under his leading.—NORTHCOTE, SIR STAFFORD, 1842, *Letters*.

I write to you from a feeling of anxiety. You will see what is being said here by public men who speak on your question, and most of all, and *worst of all*, by your old acquaintance and friend Mr. Gladstone. He has made a vile speech at Newcastle, full of insulting pity for the North, and of praise and support for the South. He is unstable as water in some things. He is for union and freedom in Italy, and for disunion and bondage in America. A handful of Italians in prison in Naples, without formal trial, shocked his soul so much that he wrote a pamphlet, and has made many speeches upon it; but he has no word of sympathy or of hope for the four millions of the bondsmen of the South! I have known for months past that he talked of a European remonstrance, or mediation, or recognition, or some mischief of that kind; but I did not expect that he would step out openly as the defender and eulogist of Jeff. Davis and his fellow-conspirators against God and man. He *has* spoken, as you will see by the time you receive this; and what he has said will encourage the friends of the South here to increased exertions to promote something hostile to your government and people.— BRIGHT, JOHN, 1862, *Letter to Sumner*, Oct. 10; *Memoir and Letters of Charles Sumner*, ed. Pierce, vol. iv, p. 157.

British statesmen, forgetting for the moment moral distinctions, forgetting God who will not be forgotten, gravely announce that our cause must fail. . . . Opinions are allies more potent than subsidies. . . . Nothing is more clear than that whoever assumes to play prophet becomes pledged in character and pretension to sustain his prophecy.—SUMNER, CHARLES, 1863, *Address in New York*, Sept. 10; *Works*, vol. VII, pp. 351, 352.

If he was famous for the splendor of his eloquence, for his unaffected piety, and for his blameless life, he was celebrated far and wide for a more than common liveliness of conscience. He had once imagined it to be his duty to quit a Government, and to burst through strong ties of friendship and gratitude, by reason of a thin shade of difference on the subject of white or brown sugar. It was believed that, if he were to commit even a little sin, or to imagine an evil thought, he would instantly arraign himself before the dread tribunal which awaited him within his own bosom; and that, his intellect being subtle and microscopic, and delighting in casuistry and exaggeration, he would be likely to give his soul a very harsh trial, and treat himself as a great criminal for faults too minute to be visible to the naked eyes of laymen. His friends lived in dread of his virtues as tending to make him whimsical and unstable, and the practical politicians, perceiving that he was not to be depended upon for party purposes, and was bent upon none but lofty objects, used to look upon him as dangerous—used to call him behind his back a good man—a good man in the worst sense of the term.—KINGLAKE, ALEXANDER WILLIAM, 1863, *The Invasion of the Crimea*.

Although the Prime Minister of England is always writing letters and making speeches, he seems ever to send forth an "uncertain sound." If a member of Parliament announces himself a republican, Mr. Gladstone takes the earliest opportunity of describing him as a "fellow-worker" in public life. If an inconsiderate multitude calls for the abolition or reform of the House of Lords, Mr. Gladstone says that is no easy task, and that he must think once or twice, or perhaps even thrice, before he can undertake it. If your neighbor, the member for Bradford, Mr. Miall, brings forward a motion in the House of Commons for the severance of Church and state, Mr. Gladstone assures Mr. Miall with the utmost courtesy that he believes the opinion of the House of Commons is against him; but that if Mr. Miall wishes to influence the House of Commons he must address the public out of doors.—DISRAELI, BENJAMIN, (LORD BEACONSFIELD), 1872, *Speech at Manchester, April 3*.

I sometimes think that great men are like great mountains, and that we do not appreciate their magnitude while we are still close to them. You have to go to a distance to see which peak it is that towers above its fellows; and it may be that we shall have to put between us and Mr. Gladstone a space of time before we shall know how much greater he has been than any of his competitors for fame and power. I am certain that justice will be done to him in the future, and I am not less certain that there will be a signal condemnation of the men who, moved by the motives of party spite, in their eagerness for office, have not hesitated to load with insult and indignity the greatest statesman of our times; we have not allowed even his age which should have commanded their reverence, or his experience which entitles him to their respect, or his high personal character or his long services to his Queen and to his country, to shield him from the vulgar affronts and the lying accusations of which he has nightly been made the subject in the House of Commons. He, with his great magnanimity, can afford to forget and forgive these things. Those whom he has served so long it behooves to remember them, to resent them, and to punish them.—CHAMBERLAIN, JOHN, 1885, *Speech at Birmingham*.

The elections are raging still, and I find myself quoted on both sides. I made an epigram (extempore) one day on the G. O. M., and repeated it to Lord Acton.

His greatness not so much in Genius lies
As in adroitness, when occasions rise,
Lifelong convictions to extemporize.

This morning I find the last lines quoted by Auberon Herbert in a letter to the *Times*, but luckily without my name. It is a warning.—LOWELL, JAMES RUSSELL, 1886, *To Mrs. Edward Burnett, July 7; Letters, ed. Norton, vol.* II, *p. 315*.

Mr. Gladstone was always great enough to meet the buffetings of adverse fortune with a calm heart and a smiling countenance. . . . As one looks back now upon the character of the greatest Parliamentarian the House of Commons has ever known, the features which seem to stand out in the strongest relief are his undying enthusiasm, his indomitable courage in conflict, whether the tide was with him or against him, his intensely religious spirit, and that all-pervading faith in and love of his fellow-creatures which, more perhaps than any other quality, made him the master of so many hearts and the victor in so many fights.—REID, SIR WEMYSS, 1898, *The Life of William Ewart Gladstone, Introduction, vol.* I, *pp. 51, 52*.

A good, great, learned, eloquent statesman, William Ewart Gladstone towers in moral grandeur above his fellows like a mountain peak above the foothills, and the far-surrounding plain.—JOY, JAMES RICHARD, 1902, *Ten Englishmen of the Nineteenth Century, p. 165*.

CHURCH AND STATE
1838

Inscribed to the University of Oxford; tried, and not found wanting, through the vicissitudes of a thousand years; in the belief that she is providentially designed to be a fountain of blessings, spiritual, social, and intellectual to this and to other countries, to the present and future times; and in the hope that the temper of these pages may be found not alien from her own.— GLADSTONE, WILLIAM EWART, 1838, *The State Considered in its Relations with the Church, Dedication.*

She is a noble vessel, freighted with the riches of a true wisdom, directed by a spirit of pure and fervent piety, furnished out with knowledge and a practical experience. May God's blessing be with her, and may she so sail upon the troubled and uncertain sea of men's opinions, that through her we may in some degree be brought on our voyage towards "the haven where we would be."—HOPE-SCOTT, J. R., 1838, *Memoirs*, vol. I, pp. 165.

Gladstone's book has disappointed me more than I like to confess, but he seems to be an excellent and really wise man.— MAURICE, FREDERICK DENISON, 1838, *Life*, vol. I, p. 257.

I quite agree with you in my admiration of its spirit throughout; I also like the substance of about half of it; the rest of course appears to be erroneous. But it must be good to have a public man writing on such a subject, and it delights me to have a good protest against that wretched doctrine of Warburton's, that the State has only to look after body and goods.— ARNOLD, THOMAS, 1838, *Stanley's Life of Dr. Arnold*, vol. II, p. 144.

Mr. Gladstone seems to us to be, in many respects, exceedingly well qualified for philosophical investigation. His mind is of large grasp; nor is he deficient in dialectical skill. But he does not give his intellect fair play. There is no want of light, but a great want of what Bacon would have called dry light. Whatever Mr. Gladstone sees is refracted and distorted by a false medium of passions and prejudices. His style bears a remarkable analogy to his mode of thinking, and indeed exercises great influence on his mode of thinking. His rhetoric, though often good of its kind, darkens and perplexes the logic which it should illustrate. Half his acuteness and diligence, with a barren imagination and a scanty vocabulary, would have saved him from almost all his mistakes. He has one gift most dangerous to a speculator,—a vast command of a kind of language, grave and majestic, but of vague and uncertain import, — of a kind of language which affects us much in the same way in which the lofty diction of the chorus of Clouds affected the simple-hearted Athenian.—MACAULAY, THOMAS BABINGTON, 1839, *Church and State, Edinburgh Review*, vol. 69, p. 233.

One day in the year 1839 a party of guests were assembled at Sir Robert Peel's house at Drayton Manor, when a servant brought into the room a new book which had just been received. The great statesman took it up, turned over its pages for a few moments with a somewhat contemptuous air, and then flung it into the fire, saying as he did so, "Confound that young fellow; if he goes on writing stuff of this sort he'll ruin his future. Why can't he stick to politics?" The book in question was called "The State considered in its Relations with the Church," and the "young fellow" who roused the irritation of Sir Robert Peel, was the eminent man whose name I have placed at the head of this chapter. This little anecdote, which I repeat on the authority of an eye-witness of the scene, is worth recalling, because it shows that just forty years ago Mr. Gladstone's illustrious political friend and patron was making the same complaint regarding him as that which one hears to-day from many of his professed admirers.— REID, T. WEMYSS, 1880, *Politicians of To-Day*, vol. I, p. 73.

The Treatise on State and Church, on which Gladstone exhibits so much learning, to me is heavy, vague, hazy, and hard to read. The subject, however, has but little interest to an American, and is doubtless much more highly appreciated by English students, especially those of the great Universities whom it more directly concerns. It is the argument of a young Oxford scholar for the maintenance of a Church establishment; is full of ecclesiastical lore, assuming that one of the chief ends of government is the propagation of religious truth,—a ground utterly untenable according to the universal opinion of people in this country, whether churchmen or laymen, Catholic or Protestant, Conservative or

Liberal.—LORD, JOHN, 1891, *Beacon Lights of History*, vol. VI, p. 566.

It created a great sensation at the time, all the greater because Macaulay attacked it in one of his famous essays. Except as an illustration of Mr. Gladstone's intellectual development and his way of thinking on religious questions, a way which has never since materially altered, the book has little interest for the world just now. It effected nothing in the progress of human thought; it neither advanced nor retarded anything; but it gives us in the cleverest style an understanding of Mr. Gladstone's peculiar views. . . . The book and its whole history are interesting if only as an illustration of Mr. Gladstone's insatiable ardor for intellectual work of various kinds. He was always looking out for new and different fields of labor. Goethe was not content to be a poet and a novelist, but he must also be a naturalist and a pioneer of the theory of evolution. Gladstone was not content with being an orator and a statesman, he must also be a theologian, a reverent critic of Homer and Dante, and a translator of Horace.—MCCARTHY, JUSTIN, 1897, *The Story of Gladstone's Life*, pp. 65, 76.

STUDIES ON HOMER

I am reading, too, Gladstone's "Homer," it is very direct and plain-sailing, and in that respect is an agreeable contrast to German annotation. The working out of his theory about Danaans, Achæans, Argives, and Hellenes was to me satisfactory; but at the end he goes off all at once out of his depth into general ethnology. Gladstone's uncompromising belief in Homer and the heroes, as real people, gives the book a solidity and substance which is acceptable. — CLOUGH, ARTHUR HUGH, 1858, *Letter to Charles Eliot Norton. May 17; Prose Remains*, p. 243.

Gladstone has lately published a marvellous book on Homer, in three thick volumes. There is a volume on the mythology, in which he traces a large part of the Greek mythology to traditions from the patriarchs, to whom he moreover assumes that Christianity was in some way revealed by anticipation. Hence he finds the doctrine of the Trinity in Homer, and holds that Latona is compounded of Eve and the Virgin Mary. It seems to me a *réchauffée* of old Jacob Bryant.—LEWIS, SIR GEORGE CORNEWALL, 1858, *Letter to Sir Edward Walker Head, May* 3; *Letters to Various Friends*, ed. Lewis, p. 333.

These three volumes of Mr. Gladstone's form a great, but a very unequal work. They would be a worthy fruit of a life spent in learned retirement. As the work of one of our first orators and statesmen, they are altogether wonderful. . . . Perhaps his familiarity with the purest and most ennobling source of inspiration may have had some effect in adorning Mr. Gladstone's political oratory with more than one of its noblest features. He is not unlike the Achilleus of his own story. . . . What strikes one more than anything throughout Mr. Gladstone's volumes is the intense earnestness, the loftiness of moral purpose, which breathes in every page. He has not taken up Homer as a plaything, nor even as a mere literary enjoyment. To him the study of the Prince of Poets is clearly a means by which himself and other men may be made wiser and better. . . . Not the least, to our mind, of Mr. Gladstone's services to Homer is his defence of the ninth book of the Iliad. In his section "Aoidos" he has thoroughly overthrown Mr. Grote's idea of an Achilleid developed into an Iliad; and he has fully vindicated the plot of the poem in its received form. . . . The freshest and most genial tribute to ancient literature which has been paid even by an age rich in such offerings.—FREEMAN, EDWARD A., 1858-73, *Mr. Gladstone's Homer and the Homeric Age, Historical Essays, Second Series*, pp. 52, 53, 91, 92.

I looked at Gladstone's book "Homeric Synchronism"—it is very disapointing. So great a man, so imperfect a scholar! He has no idea how shaky the ground is on which he takes his stand. The reading of those ethnic names in the hieroglyphic inscriptions varies with every year and with every scholar. I do not blame them—their studies are and must be tentative, and they are working in the right direction. But the use which Gladstone makes of their labours is to me really painful, all the more so, because it is cleverly done, and I believe bona fide.—MÜLLER, FRIEDRICH MAX, 1871, *To Rev. G. Cox; Life and Letters*, ed. his Wife, vol. I, p. 441.

One would suppose, in looking over these volumes, [On Homer] that the distinguished premier had abandoned the arts of statesmanship for the vocation of a professor of Greek. From the beginning to the end of these three huge octavos, the author's familiarity with the minute details of Greek learning is curiously obvious. To the historical student the third volume is the only one to be of special interest. Of this volume the first chapter, that on the Politics of the Homeric Age, will amply reward the student's examination. In other respects the work is chiefly technical.—ADAMS, CHARLES KENDALL, 1882, *A Manual of Historical Literature*, p. 105.

GENERAL

Had he been a writer and nothing else, he would have been famous and powerful by his pen. He might, however, have failed to secure a place in the front rank. His style was forcible, copious, rich with various knowledge, warm with the ardor of his nature. But it had three serious defects. It was diffuse, apt to pursue a topic into detail when these might have been left to the reader's own reflection. It was redundant, employing more words than were needed to convey the substance. It was unchastened, indulging too freely in tropes and metaphors, in quotations and adapted phrases even when the quotation added nothing to the sense, but was due merely to some association in his own mind. Thus it seldom reached a high level of purity and grace, and though one might excuse its faults as natural to the work of a swift and busy man, they were sufficient to prevent readers from deriving much pleasure from the mere form and dress of his thoughts.—BRYCE, JAMES, 1898, *William Ewart Gladstone*, p. 82.

Mr. Gladstone hurriedly passed Mr. Disraeli on the stairs of the House of Commons. The observant Jew said under his breath, referring to Mr. Gladstone in his rush to the House, "Ardent creature!" That was the man in two words! That was the man both as a politician and as a scholar. When I read his Homer I feel that he longs to be in the House of Commons, and that his Homeric work is merely recreative and interstitial. . . . Mr. Gladstone does, indeed, acknowledge in the third volume and last page of his Homer that "to pass from the study of Homer to the ordinary business of the world is to step out of a palace of enchantment into the cold grey light of a Polar day." No doubt of it; yet it would be a larger and better defended palace than any that has yet been built that would keep Mr. Gladstone out of the "cold grey light" of the House of Commons I do not wonder at his partiality for Homer, because Homer was the poet of action Where so much is said about battles and races, cities and politics, Mr. Gladstone was sure to be at home. I have read all his criticism, and I have been amazed at the number and variety of his allusions and quotations within the whole range of classical learning; yet I never could get away from the impression that he was very anxious to see how things were going on at the House, and that he would have no hesitation, had circumstances suggested or permitted it, to make an election speech on the steepest slopes of Olympus.—PARKER, JOSEPH, 1899, *A Preacher's Life*, pp. 290, 291.

It is characteristic of Gladstone's mental energy and versatility that on the very day of his retirement he completed his translation of Horace's "Odes." Among the many attempts to perform an apparently impossible task, Gladstone's holds a high place. It is scholarly, lucid, and dignified. If it wants the lightness and ease which are part of Horace's inimitable charm it shows a perfect appreciation of an author whose ideas, tastes, and thoughts were removed by an infinite distance from those of the translator.—PAUL, HERBERT, 1901, *Dictionary of National Biography, Supplement*, vol. II, p. 322.

What were his achievements? He covered the whole field; nothing was too great, nothing too small for him. He was a financial Nasmyth Hammer, which, with equal facility and equal precision, could revolutionize a Tariff or modify the duty on Dice. His wonderful genius enabled him to make Finance popular; to be understanded of the People. He taught the Country to appreciate its importance. His work was based on the solid rock of a substantial annual Surplus, and on the less easily secured foundation of strict Economy. The Customs Tariff was completely and finally purged. The remaining duties on food were repealed. Commercial relations with other countries were extended. The last remaining Excise duties, other than those on Intoxicants, were abolished.—BUXTON, SYDNEY, 1901, *Mr. Gladstone as Chancellor of the Exchequer*, p. 167.

When all is said, however, Mr. Gladstone's place is not in literary or critical history, but elsewhere. His style is sometimes called Johnsonian, but surely without good

JOHN STUART BLACKIE

Engraving from a Photograph by D. Macara.

WILLIAM BLACK

Engraving from a Photograph.

ground. Johnson was not involved, and he was clear, and neither of these things can always be said of Mr. Gladstone. Some critic charged him in 1840 with "prolix clearness." The old charge, says Mr. Gladstone upon this, was "obscure compression. I do not doubt that both may be true, and the former may have been the result of a well-meant effort to escape from the latter." He was fond of abstract words, or the nearer to abstract the better, and the more general the better. One effect of this was undoubtedly to give an indirect, almost a shifty, air that exasperated plain people. Why does he beat about the bush they asked; why cannot he say what he means? . . . His critical essays on Tennyson and Macaulay are excellent. They are acute, discriminating, generous. His estimate of Macaulay, apart from a piece of polemical church history at the end, is perhaps the best we have.—MORLEY, JOHN, 1903, *The Life of William Ewart Gladstone, vol.* III, *p.* 546.

William Black
1841–1898

Born, at Glasgow, 15 Nov. 1841. Educated at private schools. Studied at Glasgow School of Art. Contrib. to "Glasgow Weekly Citizen." First married, 1862. To London, 1864. Joined staff of "Morning Star," 1865. War correspondent during Austro-Prussian War, 1866. For a time Assistant Editor of "Daily News." *Works:* "James Merle," 1862; "Love or Marriage?" 1868; "In Silk Attire," 1869; "Kilmeny," 1870; "Mr. Pisistratus Brown, M. P., in the Highlands" (from "Daily News," anon.), 1871; "The Monarch of Mincing Lane," 1871; "A Daughter of Heth" (anon.), 1871; "Strange Adventures of a Phaeton," 1872; "Princess of Thule," 1873; "Maid of Killeena" 1874; "Three Feathers," 1875; "Madcap Violet," 1876; "Lady Silverdale's Sweetheart," 1876; "Green Pastures and Piccadilly," 1877; "Macleod of Dare," 1878; "Goldsmith," 1879; "White Wings," 1880; "Sunrise," 1880; "The Beautiful Wretch: The Four Macnicols: The Pupil of Aurelius," 1881 ("The Four Macnicols" separately, 1882); "Adventures in Thule," 1883; "Yolande," 1883; "Shandon Bells," 1883; "Judith Shakespeare" 1884; "White Heather," 1885; "Wise Women of Inverness," 1885; "Sabrina Zembra," 1887; "Strange Adventures of a House-Boat," 1888; "In Far Lochaber," 1888; "Nanciebel," 1889; "The Penance of John Logan," 1889; "The New Prince Fortunatus," 1890; "Donald Ross of Heimra," 1891; "Stand Fast, Craig-Royston," 1891; "Wolfenberg," 1892; "The Magic Ink," 1892; "The Handsome Humes," 1893; "Highland Cousins," 1894; "Briseis," 1896.—SHARP, R. FARQUHARSON, 1897, *A Dictionary of English Authors, p.* 25.

PERSONAL

Have always found him the same pleasant, sympathetic companion, the same thoughtful, unostentatious, quick-witted gentleman. Tightly built, lithe of limb, strong in the arm, capable of great physical endurance, the novelist is nevertheless below the medium height. Short black hair, thick brown moustache, a dark hazel eye, a firm mouth, a square forehead, Black gives you the idea of compact strength—a small parcel, so to speak, well packed. You might sooner take him for an artillery officer who had seen service, a yachtsman, or a man who spent most of his life in outdoor sports and pastimes, than set him down as an author, and particularly as a novelist. Black might pass for a member of any profession except the clerical, or for an ordinary gentleman of the time, until you came to know him well enough to talk to him familiarly, and then you would find as you always do in men who have made a mark on the current history of the times, in whatever direction, something extraordinary in his talk and in his appearance. You would first be impressed with the bead-like brightness of his eye, and its steadfastness; and then you would probably be struck with the fact, if you were travelling with him, that every bit of natural phenomena going on around him is an object of constant interest to him; that he knows the names of the birds you see and their habits; if you are at a sea-port, that he knows every class of craft, and the name of every rope in its rigging; if you are talking of art, or literature, or politics, that he has strong, well-formed opinions, and that he is perfectly frank and open in expressing them and, moreover, that if you do not want to talk, he can be silent as an oyster.

—HATTON, JOSEPH, 1882, *William Black at Home, Harper's Magazine, vol.* 66, *p.* 15.

He had no ambition whatever to shine in Society. His books, everyone knows, were greatly admired by Queen Victoria; and there were many inducements to him to seek for a welcome in the very highest circle of English life. But Black had no social ambition of that kind to trouble his mind, and would not have crossed the street for the sake of having his name chronicled in the pages of a Society newspaper.... Black was not a great talker, although he could always say good things, and he loved to keep the talk going. Indeed, he impressed strangers by his habitual quietness and reserve; he did not care in the least to be lionised, and people who came obviously with the intention of transacting a literary conversation with him were apt to set him down as naturally shy and silent.... One thing I believe William Black could not do: he could not make a speech.... He was a thoroughly modest worker; he did his very best, and he did it in his own way; but he was a keen observer of everything, even of his own work, and he was too conscientious an artist to indulge in self-conceit. Some of his literary friends used to say that he had a very easy time of it, for during a great part of his successful years it was his custom to write but two hours a day, and that not by any means on every day in the week. But then Black was working hard at his books before he put a pen to paper. He thought out his scenes and his characters, and their meetings and their talk (he had seldom much of a story to trouble himself with); he thought them out in the streets, in hansom cabs, on the deck of his yacht, in long walks by the sea; and when he sat down to his desk he had only, as he told me himself more than once, to copy out what was already written down in his mind.—MCCARTHY, JUSTIN, 1898, *William Black, The Academy, vol.* 55, *p*: 482.

> We fain would let thy memory dwell
> Where rush the tidewaves of the sea,
> Where storms will moan or calms will tell
> To all the world our love for thee,
> Whom all men loved in this old land,
> And all men loved across the sea,
> We well may clasp our brethren's hand,
> And light the Beacon light for thee.

—CAMPBELL, ARCHIBALD, 1899, *To William Black, Eclectic Magazine, vol.* 133, *p.* 914.

GENERAL

A novel ["Madcap Violet"] which ought to be buoyant enough to float down the stream of time. . . . Mr. Black has had the courage—it needed a great deal—to recognise that our forefathers always took for granted in all their dealings—that there are "unlucky" men and women, marked by fate with almost visible sign. "Madcap Violet" is the story of two of these, on whom presses a wilful destiny, not born from any ancient curse or sin, but merely from the caprice of fate. It is impossible that the tale should be so pleasing as some of its predecessors, and it will always be a question whether the slight details of commonplace life, and the everyday topics introduced, heighten tragic effect by force of contrast; or, on the other hand, give an air of triviality to a story in which the awful stress of an inexplicable will in the world works so powerfully.—LANG, ANDREW, 1877, *Three New Novels, Fortnightly Review, vol.* 27, *p.* 88, 92.

Mr. William Black is the head of a school of fiction which he himself called into existence. Scottish scenery and Scottish character, alternating with certain phases of London life, are the field in which he works, and in which he has no rival. He has not as yet shown himself great in passion or pathos. The deeper emotions of the human heart, the sterner phases of human life, he has apparently not often cared to touch. But in his own province, somewhat narrow though that be, his art approaches to perfection. He can paint not merely scenery, but even atmosphere, with a delicacy and strength of touch which in themselves constitute an art.—MCCARTHY, JUSTIN, 1880, *A History of Our Own Times from the Accession of Queen Victoria to the Berlin Congress, vol.* iv, *ch.* LXVII.

In Mr. William Black's beautiful story of "A Daughter of Heth" there is nothing that might not have happened precisely as he relates it.—LEWIS, WALTER, 1889, *The Abuse of Fiction, The Forum, vol.* 7, *p.* 662.

Mr. William Black, who has filled the islands and rocks of the Western Highlands with many new friends and acquaintances since the time when the "Princess of Thule" came among us with all the glory of the sunsets about her, and who has made all that beautiful but stormy region his own—not to speak of the milder landscape which he embodies in a "Daughter of Heth," and the abundant sketches of English scenery, as well as the men and women of all nations whom he has added to our acquaintance, and the shoals of salmon glittering in silver and gold in whom he has compelled us to take a sometimes excited interest.—OLIPHANT, MARGARET O. W., 1892, *The Victorian Age of English Literature, p. 497.*

The novelist gives us some very charming pictures ["Judith Shakespeare"] of the Warwickshire landscape, and he has made Miss Judith Shakespeare very arch and engaging; but it was perilous ground for any novelist to venture upon; and I think the author felt it, and has shown a timidity and doubt that have hampered him; I do not recognize in it the breezy freedom that belonged to his treatment of things among the Hebrides.—MITCHELL, DONALD G., 1895, *English Lands, Letters and Kings, From Elizabeth to Anne, p. 33.*

No one has furnished healthier and purer entertainment, especially to the young of the present generation. It may be, as has been said, that interest in these novels is now on the wane; if so, it is probably because their subjects lie so much in the domestic sphere, and pander so little to an unhealthy craving for excitement. Manlier men and sweeter women we could not wish to meet, nor could we reasonably desire to have them set before us with a more charming and exquisite art. Of tragic passion, and even of pathos in its intenser forms, there is but little in these pages. Even such humour as they show most frequently takes the form of genial pleasantry. The thought, moreover, is a trifle commonplace, while of the dark problems with which it seems so much the business of the modern novel to perplex and make miserable the muchenduring average reader, there is absolutely nothing. Instead of this we have a well-constructed, well-told tale, over which plays a pleasant ripple of thought, suffused with a sentiment that is always generous and healthy, like the breezes that blow over the Scottish moors and lochs this author loves so well. No doubt these tales are open to the charge of sameness. The landscapes, and even the characters and situations, we have seen before, and we may have even caught the trick of them. But if we miss the robustness, the various energy and depth of a more virile genius, it is but right to consider the simple unalloyed pleasure obtained at so little cost of pain which these works have afforded, and conceive that probably to give such pleasure was the soul aim and ambition of the author.—GRAHAM, RICHARD D., 1897, *The Masters of Victorian Literature, p. 117.*

His third book ["Daughter of Heth"] and his best. It is true a note of plaintiveness was sounded so often in this otherwise delightful story that we wearied a little from time to time, and wished Coquette would pluck up her spirits, or that Lord Earlshope would emigrate to Borneo; but then we could always turn for distraction to the "third volume of Josephus," hollowed out to hold white mice: or we could watch the Whaup and his fellow-conspirators dipping their good little brother, Wattie, into the burn until he consented to "say a sweer," and this "vision of sin" confronted us through a great many melancholy chapters. . . . "A Princess of Thule," and Mr. Black's literary reputation reached its zenith, both in England and in the United States. The novelty, not of the theme, but of the setting, the wild, sweet vision of that far northern land cradled in waves, swathed in mists, rocked by the voice of the tempest, touched all hearts with a sentiment that was half pleasure and half pain. There are books which bring to the tired dweller in towns some gleam of nature's face, some fresh keen wind from the Hebrides, some gentle breath from the Adriatic, some fleeting dream of sea and sky, valley or moor or mountain peak; and, reading of them, one sickens of brick walls and the city's hateful din. Such a book was "A Princess of Thule."—REPPLIER, AGNES, 1899, *The Novels of William Black, The Critic, vol. 34, pp. 146, 147.*

The author's first real triumph was won by "A Daughter of Heth" (1871). Here he was most fortunate in his subject, depicting the domestication of a lively French woman in a Scotch puritan family. "The Strange Adventures of a Phaeton" (1872) was even more successful, and introduced what became Black's special characteristic—so through a combination of scenes of actual experience in travel and sport with fictitious adventures that the reader sometimes hardly knew whether he was reading a book of travel or a novel. In 1874 "A Princess of Thule" thoroughly confirmed his reputation. Both in this book and in "Madcap Violet" (1876), as previously in "A Daughter of Heth," the delineation of female character was an especial charm. The certainty of meeting with an agreeable woman, and of details of travel and sport which, if not perfectly legitimate in their place, were sure to be entertaining, continued to maintain his popularity to the end of an active career, although he never regained the level of the best work of his middle period.—GARNETT, RICHARD, 1901, *Dictionary of National Biography, Supplement, vol.* I, *p.* 203.

There was a moment when William Black might have been recognized as the leading writer of English fiction, unless we are to count some novelists of finer skill and greater force in the American condition of English fiction. But unhappily for his supremacy the vaster and deeper and fresher naturalism of Mr. Thomas Hardy began to make itself known, and William Black's chance was gone. . . . No writers could be more opposite in their realism than the novelist whom I have just named, and Black. Both are poets, and both are apt to seek in nature the charm they make us feel, but the final sense of the mystery and loveliness imparted by Mr. Hardy is of something which his heroine confers upon her circumstances, and in Black's fiction it seems something which she derives from it. I am now thinking chiefly of such a girl as Gertrude White in "Macleod of Dare," who is as dependent upon society for means of self-expression as any heroine I know, and yet is as genuine a personality as may be met in fiction.—HOWELLS, WILLIAM DEAN, 1901, *Heroines of Fiction, vol.* II, *p.* 215.

It is related that Carlyle once said to Black, in the course of a conversation: "Ay, ay, ye ken our Scotland weel, but tell me, mon, when are ye gaun to do some wark?" Souls of the strenuous sort, who expect novelists to deal with the serious problems of society, and who insist upon the ethical motive, if not upon the didactical method, will not find their account in the novels of William Black, unless they think of him solely as the author of "Sunrise." Such souls have their Mr. Meredith and their Mr. Hardy and their Mrs. Humphry Ward, and we do not deny them the right to their point of view. But when they go out of the way to institute invidious comparisons between the novelists they happen to like and such accomplished craftsmen of a different sort as Mr. Black and Mr. Blackmore, we feel bound to protest. The novelist now under connsideration did not have the genius of Mr. George Meredith, for example, but he cultivated a saner method, and the talent that expresses itself by the methods of sanity is not unworthy of being ranked, in the total estimate, upon a level with the genius that expresses itself by, let us say,—that we may avoid the harsher term so obviously suggested,—the methods of perversity. Those *intellectuels*, in the name of whatever uncouth or morbid form of art they may make their plea, are not to be allowed the final word when it comes to an appraisal of so graceful and abundantly endowed a writer as was William Black. He is likely always to be reckoned as one of the five or six best English novelists of his time.—PAYNE, WILLIAM MORTON, 1902, *Editorial Echoes, p.* 267.

Charles Lutwige Dodgson
Lewis Carroll
1832–1898

Born 1832. Matric, Ch. Ch. Oxford, 23 May 1850; Student, 1852-70; B. A., 1854; M. A., 1857. Ordained Deacon, 1861. Mathematical Lecturer, Ch. Ch., 1855-81. *Works:* "A Syllabus of Plane Algebraical Geometry," 1860; "The Formulæ of Plane Trigonometry," 1861; "A Guide to the Mathematical Student," 1864; "Alice's Adventures in Wonderland" (under pseud. "Lewis Carroll"), 1866; [1865]; "An Elementary Treatise on Determinants," 1867; "The Fifth Book of Euclid treated Algebraically," 1868; "Phantasmagoria" (by "Lewis Carroll"), 1869; "Songs from 'Alice's Adventures in Wonderland,'" 1870; "Through the Looking-Glass" (by "Lewis Carroll"), 1871; "Facts, Figures and Fancies, (reprint of part of Phantasmagoria), 1871; "Euclid, Bk.V., proved Algebraically," 1874; "The Hunting of the Snark" (by "Lewis Carroll"), 1876; "Euclid and his Modern Rivals," 1879; "Doublets" (by "Lewis Carroll"), 1879; "Rhyme and

Reason" (by "Lewis Carroll"), 1883; "Lawn Tennis Tournaments," 1883; "The Principles of Parliamentary Representation," 1884; "A Tangled Tale" (by "Lewis Carroll"), 1885; "Alice's Adventures Underground: a facsimile of the original MS.," 1886; "The Game of Logic" (by "Lewis Carroll"), 1887; "Curiosa Mathematica," pt. i., 1888; "Sylvie and Bruno" (by "Lewis Carroll"), 1889; "The Nursery 'Alice,' " 1890; "Sylvie and Bruno concluded" (by "Lewis Carroll"), 1893; "Symbolic Logic," pt. i., 1896; He has edited: Euclid, Bks. i, ii, 1882.—SHARP, R. FARQUHARSON, 1897, *A Dictionary of English Authors*, p. 83.

PERSONAL

It would be futile to attempt even a bare list of the children whom he loved, and who loved him; during forty years of his life he was constantly adding to their number. Some remained friends for life, but in a large proportion of cases the friendship ended with the end of childhood. . . . These friendships usually began all very much in the same way. A chance meeting on the seashore, in the street, at some friend's house, led to conversation; then followed a call on the parents, and after that all sorts of kindnesses on Lewis Carroll's part, presents of books, invitations to stay with him at Oxford, or at Eastbourne, visits with him in the theatre. For the amusement of his little guests he kept a large assortment of musical-boxes, and an organette which had to be fed with paper tunes. On one occasion he ordered about twelve dozen of these tunes "on approval," and asked one of the other dons, who was considered a judge of music, to come in and hear them played over. In addition to these attractions there were clock-work bears, mice, and frogs, and games and puzzles in infinite variety. . . . It was only to those who had but few personal dealings with him that he seemed stiff and "donnish;" to his more intimate acquaintances, who really understood him, each little eccentricity of manner or of habits was a delightful addition to his charming and interesting personality. He very seldom sat down to write, preferring to stand while thus engaged. When making tea for his friends, he used, in order, I suppose, to expedite the process, to walk up and down the room waving the teapot around, and telling meanwhile those delightful anecdotes of which he had an inexhaustible supply. . . . At meals he was very abstemious always, while he took nothing in the middle of the day except a glass of wine and a biscuit. Under these circumstances it is not very surprising that the healthy appetites of his little friends filled him with wonder, and even with alarm.—COLLINGWOOD, STUART DODGSON, 1898, *The Life and Letters of Lewis Carroll*, pp. 367, 369, 389.

To have ever known such a man as he was is an inestimable boon. To have been with him for so long as a child, to have known so intimately the man who above all others had understood childhood, is indeed a memory on which to look back with thanksgiving and with tears. . . . He was afflicted with what I believe is known as "Housemaid's Knee," and this made his movements singularly jerky and abrupt. Then again he found it impossible to avoid stammering in his speech. He would, when engaged in an animated conversation with a friend, talk quickly and well for a few minutes, and then suddenly and without any very apparent cause would begin to stutter so much, that it was often difficult to understand him. He was very conscious of this impediment, and he tried hard to cure himself. For several years he read a scene from some play of Shakespeare's every day aloud, but despite this he was never quite able to cure himself of the habit. Many people would have found this a great hindrance to the affairs of ordinary life, and would have felt it deeply. Lewis Carroll was different. His mind and life were so simple and open that there was no room in them for self-consciousness, and I have often heard him jest at his own misfortune, with a comic wonder at it. The personal characteristic that you would notice most on meeting Lewis Carroll was his extreme shyness. With children, of course, he was not nearly so reserved, but in the society of people of maturer age he was almost old-maidishly prim in his manner. When he knew a child well this reserve would vanish completely, but it needed only a slightly disconcerting incident to bring the cloak of shyness about him once more, and close the lips that just before had been talking so delightfully.—BOWMAN, ISA, 1900, *The Story of Lewis Carroll*, pp. 3, 10.

To Dodgson's shyness may partially be attributed the circumstance that his friendships were carried on more by letter than by personal intercourse; and it may account to some extent for the fact that his most cherished intimates were little girls, in entertaining whom he was tireless. There is also no doubt that the dictates of a conscience which was perhaps over exacting for daily life were obeyed too closely for him to be companionable to ordinary adult persons. He made, however, acquaintance with eminent men—among them Ruskin, Tennyson, Millais, and Rossetti—of who he has left valuable photographs, amateur photography having been successfully practiced by him almost from boyhood.—LUCAS, E. V., 1901, *Dictionary of National Biography*, Supplement, vol. II, p. 142.

He must have been, if all the stories still told about him are true, one of the most eccentric of Eccentrics. He did not care for young men, it seems, but he liked young women, who all liked him; and Oxford is now full of women, mature and immature, who adore the gentle memory of the creator of "Alice." One of them, still a young woman, who was but a baby when "Wonderland" was originally visited, says of him that, "he was a man whom one had to read backward." He had to be looked at "As Through a Looking Glass." She describes him as moody, and as a man of strong dislikes. But he liked her; and, hand in hand on the roofs of the College, she, as a child, and he used to wander, he always amiable and full of queer conceits of speech and of imagination.—HUTTON, LAURENCE, 1903, *Literary Landmarks of Oxford*, p. 77.

ALICE'S ADVENTURES IN WONDERLAND
1866

Mr. Dodgson's specialty, as all the world knows, was mathematics; his passion,—children. He wasted no time on "grown-ups" that could be given to the little ones—girls, I should add, for he paid little attention to mere boys! "Alice in Wonderland," as all the world also knows, originated in a series of stories told to his particular pet child, Alice Liddell (Mrs. Reginald Hargreaves), and her two younger sisters. . . . We have Dr. George Macdonald to thank for the Lewis Carroll books. Their author had no idea of publishing them, but his friend, Dr. Macdonald, who had read them, persuaded him to submit them to a publisher. . . . To the surprise of author and publisher, two thousand copies of the book were sold at once, and "Alice" increased the bank account of her creator for many years.—GILDER, J. L., 1899, *The Creator of Wonderland, The Critic*, vol. 34, pp. 138, 139.

It is now more than thirty years ago since "Alice's Adventures in Wonderland" was first published. The book at once met with wide-spread appreciation. Some years later, a companion volume, entitled, "Through the Looking Glass," made its appearance, and soon became equally popular. How many editions of these inimitable books have since been reprinted, we know not; yet we may surely take it for granted that, since their publication, few children, amongst those who are fortunate enough to enjoy the privilege of having children's books, have been brought up in ignorance of these "classics of the nursery." But the two "Alices" are not merely "classics of the nursery," they are something more. How many older children—"children of an uncertain age," as their author naïvely calls them in his preface to "The Nursery Alice"—have delighted in their pages and laughed over their droll humor! There is, indeed, much in that humor which appeals only to such "older children;" and no books written for children within recent years, have enjoyed such a marvellous popularity, or have been so extensively quoted in all sorts of connection as the "Alices."—AIKMAN, C. M., 1899, *Lewis Carroll, The New Century Review, The Living Age*, vol. 220, p. 427.

"Lewis Carroll" may be numbered with those writers of our day who have added a new note to literature; therefore his books have that in them which is likely to win them readers for many years to come. "Alice in Wonderland" may well prove to be one of the world's books whose freshness time cannot stale.—JOHNSON, E. G., 1899, *Lewis Carroll of Wonderland, The Dial*, vol. 26, p. 192.

"Alice's Adventures in Wonderland" is a play in which the subordinate actors are quite as excellent in their way as the leading character. They are differentiated from each other by a variation in their personalities, rather than by an inequality in their ability to entertain. Creatures are they of a vagrant fancy, which, like a rushing mountain stream, ofttimes reflects distorted images, but is ever pure, with the sunlight glancing from its bosom. But, like the rapid-flowing brook, there are placid pools in its course, and in one crystal, reposeful spot is the face of Alice. "Alice's Adventures in Wonderland" is a book which appeals alike to young and old. It is an object-lesson that tends to make us realize the truth of the adage, "Men are but boys grown tall."—NEWELL, PETER, 1901, *Alice's Adventures in Wonderland, Harper's Magazine, vol.* 103, *p.* 716.

GENERAL

Equal to the author of "Fly Leaves" in fame, but diverse in his peculiar genius, stands the immortal "Lewis Carroll," the inventor of what may be called the modern domestic humour, the creator of that fascinating dreamland through which, veiled in a sunny mist of ethereal mirth, the daily round of life, its peaceful joys, its inanities, its fuss, friction and augmentation pass before our eyes in admired disorder. "Father William," "The Walrus and the Carpenter" and "Jabberwocky" would, it is needless to say, have been more remarkable by their absence from our collection than anything which could have taken their place.—POWELL, G. H., 1894, *ed. Musa Jocosa, p.* 18.

"Sylvie and Bruno" was issued in 1889, and its sequel "Sylvie and Bruno Concluded" followed four years later. In this work, Mr. Collingwood says, are embodied the ideals and sentiments most dear to the author. It is didactic in aim, written with a definite purpose of turning its writer's influence to account in enforcing neglected truths; but it falls short of the fresh and spontaneous "Alice" books as a work of art—considerably short of them, we think.—JOHNSON, E. G., 1899, *Lewis Carroll of Wonderland, The Dial, vol.* 26, *p.* 192.

What more healthy influence can be at work in the world than that which inclines busy, careworn men to identify themselves with an eternal youth? Genial, kindhearted, loving Lewis Carroll! What better tribute can be paid to his excellence than to say that it was his mission in life not only to popularize purity in child literature, but to incite an emulation in other writers, productive of results the extent of the beneficent effects of which it is impossible to estimate.—NEWELL, PETER, 1901, *Alice's Adventures in Wonderland, Harper's Magazine, vol.* 103, *p.* 716.

Although like Lear's in some respects, Lewis Carroll's nonsense is perhaps of a more refined type. There is less of the grotesque and more poetic imagery. But though Carroll was more of a poet than Lear, both had the true sense of nonsense. Both assumed the most absurd conditions and proceeded to detail their consequences with a simple seriousness that convulses appreciative readers, and we find ourselves uncertain whether it is the manner or the matter that is more amusing. Lewis Carroll was a man of intellect and education; his funniest sayings are often based on profound knowledge or deep thought. Like Lear, he never spoiled his quaint fancies by over-exaggerating their quaintness or their fancifulness, and his ridiculous plots are as carefully conceived, constructed, and elaborated as though they embodied the soundest facts. No funny detail is ever allowed to become *too* funny; and it is in this judicious economy of extravagance that his genius is shown.— WELLS, CAROLYN, 1902, *ed., A Nonsense Anthology, Introduction, p.* XXVII.

Frederick Tennyson

1807-1898

Born, at Louth, 5 June 1807. Early education at Louth Grammar School. At Eaton, 1820-27. Matric. Trin. Coll., Camb., 1829; B. A., 1832. Browne Medallist (for Greek Ode), Camb. After leaving Cambridge lived abroad for some years. Married Maria Giuliotti, 1839. Settled in Florence. Removed to Jersey, 1859, *Works*: "Poems by Two Brothers" (anon,; with Alfred and Charles Tennyson), 1827; "The Isles of Greece," 1890; "Daphne," 1891; "Poems of the Day and Year," 1895. He has *edited:* H. Melville's "Veritas," 1874. — SHARP, R. FARQUHARSON, 1897, *A Dictionary of English Authors, p.* 278.

GENERAL

The fluency and freshness of Mr. Tennyson never fail him ["Isles of Greece"]: his heroines and heroes live, to him, in a land of eternal summer, amid immortal memories, and with a dim hope clinging to them that death may not be the end that it appears. The "intersection" of several stories in this book, and the amazing fertility of the poet's vocabulary, combine to make the poem somewhat unmanageably long. It contains, I compute, between twelve and thirteen thousand lines; and there is not really poetic material in it, corresponding to this bulk. There is no growth, no concentration of interest in it; "linked sweetness long drawn out" defines it exactly. . . . The personality of Sappho as here depicted seems to me to be just such a shock to all previous notions of her as would be received by a person who, looking for a draught of fiery wine, quaffed by mistake a sort of drench of pure but tepid water. The perverted passions and sexless frenzy of Lesbos have been, rightly or wrongly, presented to us in English; whatever could be done in that way has been done, and with genius. No one will blame Mr. Tennyson for taking a more reticent line, and showing us a Sappho clothed and in her right mind. But all tradition, all poetic probability, is violated by making the one poetess who spoke the language of passion with fierce and absolute simplicity use the language of sermons on these subjects.—MORSHEAD, E. D. A., 1890, *The Isles of Greece, The Academy, vol. 38, p. 385.*

"Daphne and Other Poems," though not openly confessing itself a continuation, has so much in common with its predecessor in spirit, construction, and cadence, that the critic finds himself half-unconsciously repeating the opinions which he formed last autumn. . . . His Greek subjects are treated in a diffuse way, unrecognisable in his early work, and hardly to be expected from a scholar-poet. Herein is the radical difference between him and the singer of the "Lotos Eaters" or the author of "Empedocles." There is no restraint, and consequently little artistic coherence; the tears of Niobe are an overflowing stream of introspective grief, and the miles in Atlantis are wearily long. The reader's attention is taxed over-much, to the hurt of many fine passages of emotion and natural description which lie embedded in the verse. Mr. Tennyson has kinship rather with Wordsworth in his longer poems, where the "poetry" is strewn like oases in a weary land of philosophical theory.— SMITH, G. GREGORY, 1891, *Daphne and Other Poems, The Academy, vol. 40, p. 352.*

If criticisms might be made on the tendency here and there to dwell on the same note through too wide a sweep of verse, and to put into the mouth of Sappho and the rest too spiritualized sentiments, and thoughts which are too modern and involved, this, in our idea, is amply compensated by the unexpected fecilities of metre and phrase, and the quick, penetrating glances into the secrets and springs of life that lie beyond the material and sensible. To lovers of poetry this work, indeed, only requires to be made known to ensure its wide acceptance, as something approaching to the adequate expression of a genius which has been only too reserved and carefu not to weaken its claims by too frequent appeals to the public.—JAPP, ALEX. H., 1892, *The Poets and the Poetry of the Century, Frederick Tennyson to Arthur Hugh Clough, ed. Miles, p. 5.*

Here was a man of noble nature, imaginatively gifted, a poet who deserved a wider hearing. But he was indifferent to form. Poetry with him was but a side task. He had not Alfred's passion for artistic excellence. There is usually no greatness without hard striving. He is to be classed with the singers of talent, but not of genius. Probably none of Frederick Tennyson's books would have been published, but for the urgent solicitations of friends. It was chiefly through Hallam Tennyson's influence that the later volumes were printed. His "Days and Hours" contained sixty-six short pieces, most of them characterized by luxuriant fancy and chaste diction. But the fatal defect of redundancy is found on almost every page. . . . Evidently, his main strength was put on his Greek studies, of which he was always fond. The first instalment of "The Isles of Greece"—namely, "Sappho and Alcæus"—appeared in 1890; the second, "Daphne," in 1891. Properly speaking, they constitute one poem, for there is a thread of connection running through the stories of Sappho, Alcæus, Daphne, Pygmalion, Ariadne, Niobe, and other legendary characters of antiquity. The tales are wrought out with the epic fulness of the olden days, not suited to this hurrying age of ours which has no time to muse and dream. Life is too short to give more than an occasional half-hour to the old mythologies, however charming the fancies of the poet may be. . . . Here is the classical spirit, but not the classical restraint.—PARSONS, EUGENE, 1898, *Frederick Tennyson, The Critic, vol. 32, p. 185.*

Frederick Tennyson is practically without a style; he is, indeed, too simple, too genuine, to affect or to exaggerate. The antipodes of Browning, whose art he, naturally, as we have seen, could not accept, he recalls, in his directness and sincerity, our own Longfellow. But he is no imitator. Thus he does not—as it might be expected that he would do—take color from his greater brother. Throughout his poems there is scarcely a reminder of the conceptions, or of the diction, of the late Laureate. In one respect the difference between them is especially marked,— the poetry of Frederick is not characterized by the sage generalizations which are found in Alfred Tennyson's lines, the wise sayings that lend themselves to quotation. At the same time, to continue the comparison, Frederick Tennyson's verse is more equable and unflawed in its literary excellence than is that of Alfred. . . . His true distinction, and in this he is hardly less than his brother, is picture-painting,—delineation of what is grand and lovely in nature, reflection of what is noble and beautiful in humanity. . . . His is a softly glowing fire,—a lambent flame that illumines without consuming. The peculiar virtue and significance of the poetry of Frederick Tennyson may be said to be that it is the product of a cultured, virile English intellect and imagination, vivified and ripened by the sunshine and the genius of Italy and Greece. It is this rare fusion that has made the poet.—WINTHROP, W., 1898, *Frederick Tennyson and his Poetry, Poet-Lore, vol. 10, pp. 274, 275.*

Frederick Tennyson was from the first overshadowed by the greater genius of his brother Alfred. His lyric gift was considerable, his poetic workmanship choice and fine, and the atmosphere of his poetry always noble. But he has remained almost unknown to the modern student of poetry, and a selection of four lyrics in Palgrave's second "Golden Treasury" has probably for the first time made Frederick Tennyson something more than a name to the readers of 1898. The poet was for some years under the influence of Swedenborg and other mystical religionists, but returned in his last years to the more simple Christian faith of his childhood.—AINGER, ALFRED, 1898, *Dictionary of National Biography, vol.* LVI, *p.* 75.

Robert Green Ingersoll
1833-1899

An American lawyer and infidel writer and lecturer. He was born at Dresden, N. Y., August 11, 1833, the youngest of the five children of a Congregational minister of liberal views. The family removed to Illinois in 1845, and there Robert studied law, and was admitted to the bar, and entered politics as a Democrat. In 1857 he made his residence in Peoria, where he soon became recognized as an able lawyer, chiefly employed in railroad litigation. In 1860 he was nominated for Congress, but was defeated. In 1862 he went to the war as colonel of the Eleventh Illinois Cavalry, and was taken prisoner, but exchanged. He returned to citizenship a Republican in politics, and was appointed Attorney-General of Illinois in 1868. In 1876, at the Republican Presidential Convention at Cincinnati, he delivered a fervid and vigorous speech in favor of the candidacy of James G. Blaine, which won for him a national reputation, and from this time he was recognized as one of the foremost orators of the country. He soon after entered the lecture field, where the matter as well as the manner of his discourse excited public attention. He developed the views of a pronounced opponent to Christianity, and, adopting religious topics as his subjects attacked the Bible, the personal nature of the Deity, and the existence of a hell, with all the force of which he was capable, and with the advantage of splendid rhetorical powers. In matter his orations were much dependent upon Thomas Paine. Colonel Ingersoll was president of several railroad companies and counsel for large corporations. He died suddenly at Dobbs Ferry, N. Y., July 21, 1899. His published works include: "The Gods, and Other Lectures" (1876); "Some Mistakes of Moses" (1879); "Great Speeches" (1887); "Prose Poems" (1884). His complete works were published in New York, 1900, 12 vols. Consult the biographical sketch by Handford (Chicago, 1899).—GILMAN, PECK, AND COLBY, eds. 1903, *The New International Encyclopædia, vol.* X, *p.* 17.

PERSONAL

It is a dozen years since I first saw Ingersoll in a court room in Washington, and by his invitation spent an evening under his roof. . . . He was a man of generous instincts, who, if he did not quite come up to the Gospel rule to love all men, at least came half way; he loved his friends and hated his enemies. When he came to New York to live, our acquaintance was renewed; and I was a frequent visitor at his house, where I was made to feel at home. . . . There as no one whom he loved to talk about so much as Abraham Lincoln, whom he had known in his early manhood, when they were both at the bar in Illinois. . . . In all the years that I have known Ingersoll, *I never saw him in a hurry.* The crowd might rush by, but he never quickened his pace, but walked slowly as if in deep thought. When I met him in Broadway he was always ready to stop under an awning, or by a friendly door, and discuss the questions of the day. If all the wisdom that was exchanged between us had been preserved, possibly some might have been wiser, but alas, it has been blown away like the autumn leaves! The two gods that Americans worship are time and money. Ingersoll cared for neither. Money had no attractions for him except for the use he could make of it. . . . Though Robert Ingersoll was a captivating talker, he was far more than that; he was one of the greatest orators that our country ever produced. It was not by the fireside, but on the platform, facing thousands of men, that he showed all his power. . . . His intonations were varied, now soft and gentle, as if he were in conversation, with many a bit of pleasantry; then, straightening himself up to his full height, he gave such a burst that the thousands who heard him trembled at the thunder of his voice. Such rhetorical effects are like great symphonies, which ring through the arches of cathedrals, or rather like the sound of distant thunder, coming nearer and nearer till there is one last tremendous peal, that rolls majestically away. The tradition of such marvellous eloquence will live as long as this generation.—FIELD, HENRY M., 1899, *The Influence of Ingersoll, North American Review, vol. 169, pp. 322, 323, 325.*

Col. Robert G. Ingersoll was without doubt one of the greatest popular orators of the age. He never received the full credit due to his great success as an orator during his lifetime, as his vehement assaults on the Christian religion aroused so many and such powerful enmities. But without regarding his creed, judging him solely by his power as an orator, no nation can to-day produce his equal. There was poetry, wit, humor, sarcasm, and tenderest pathos in nearly every lecture he delivered, whether on religion or politics.—POND, J. B., 1900, *Eccentricities of Genius, p. 27.*

GENERAL

Mr. Ingersoll is not, as some have estimated him, the most formidable enemy that Christianity has encountered since the time of Julian the Apostate. But he stands at the head of living infidels, "by merit raised to that bad eminence." His mental organization has the peculiar defects which fit him for such a place. He is all imagination and no discretion. He rises sometimes into a region of wild poetry, where he can color everything to suit himself. His motto well expresses the character of his argumentation—"mountains are as unstable as clouds:" a fancy is as good as a fact, and a high-sounding period is rather better than a logical demonstration. His inordinate self-confidence makes him at once ferocious and fearless. He was a practical politician before he "took the stump" against Christianity, and at all times he has proved his capacity to "split the ears of the groundlings," and make the unskillful laugh.—BLACK, JEREMIAH S., 1881, *The Christian Religion, Answer to Ingersoll, Essays and Speeches, ed. Black, p. 78.*

To the orthodox, Mr. Ingersoll is the sum of all wickedness and depravity. They can see nothing good either in him or his purposes. His very name is a synonym of whatever is blasphemous and profane. . . . His style is vigorous, aggressive and powerful, abounding in epigrams, sparkling with wit, and not unfrequently bursting into sentences which, if they do not rise to the dignity of true eloquence, are at least full of pathos and power. If his speeches lack the eloquence and refinement that form so marked a feature of the oratory of Mr. Wendell Phillips, or the solid and substantial merit that belongs to all the utterances of Mr. Beecher and Robert Collyer, the deficiency, so far as the popular judgment is concerned, is perhaps more than compensated by peculiarities which distinguish him from all other orators of the age. His vivid imagination, his pungent wit, his terrible and withering sarcasm, his power of quick and telling repartee, his skill in turning even the most solemn and sacred subjects into ridicule, and, above all, his utter fearlessness, amounting at times even to recklessness of expression, are all characteristically his own. These qualities, aided by a fine manly presence and a countenance indicative of a general satisfaction with the part he has played in life, together with a vigorous and impressive delivery, make him what is very rare at this day—a great popular orator.—MYALL, WILLIAM, 1882, *Mr. Ingersoll as a Reformer, International Review*, vol. 12, pp. 225, 229.

Colonel Ingersoll certainly made no promise and entered into no pledge that he would respect Mr. Gladstone's theories or be guided by his rules. He presented himself in his own person, with his known peculiarities of warfare, with his avowed disregard for the opinion of decorous Christian disputants. His raillery, his scorn, his ridicule, his humour, have never bowed in homage before Christian revelation, never quailed before the most solemn theme, never suffered bit or bridle to restrain them before any antagonist. . . . Colonel Ingersoll utters many noble sentiments in eloquent speech, but it is no disrespect to say that he did not first discover them. If I mistake not, every one of them comes down in a straight line of descent from that Magna Charta of human fraternity, the prayer which first taught that men were brothers and that forgiveness of offenses was a virtue.—COUDERT, FREDERICK R., 1888, *The Combat for the Faith: The Combatants, North American Review*, vol. 147, pp. 31, 36.

It may be said, and should be said, that Mr. Ingersoll's life work has been to destroy degrading shams and superstitions. In this iconoclastic crusade he has kindled the fierce furies of bigots and won the implacable hatred of hypocrites, and he would long since have worn the jeweled crown of martyrdom, except for the enlightening influence of Truth. . . . I am tempted to turn to his published utterances and select gems of thought which everywhere abound, with which to embellish this imperfect tribute to his well-earned fame and to show the "mighty wrongs" he has assailed and the "petty perfidies" he has overcome. . . . To see Mr. Ingersoll on the rostrum when his aroused genius "courts the sunbeam's fire," when he wears his dagger in his mouth and the enemies of Liberty and Truth fall before him like shanties in the pathway of a cyclone, is to behold a revelation of power which bewilders the senses and in the presence of which exaggeration has no mission.— DEBS, EUGENE V., 1893, *Robert G. Ingersoll, The American Journal of Politics*, vol. 2, pp. 199, 200.

He had a strong constitution and good digestion, and was without nerves except on the field of battle. His career as a soldier was very short; while his career as an anti-Christian lecturer was too long for the good of his own soul, and for the faith of the many half-educated people who listened to his speeches or read them in print, laughed at his jokes, and took his caricatures of Christian doctrines for solid arguments against them. . . . He had a tenth-rate intellect, much inferior to that of Tom Paine or of Voltaire, whom he affected to imitate. Ingersoll had some wit, a talent for turning pretty sentimental phrases, and for caricature. He had something of the caricaturist of the Nast and Keppler order, who by a stroke of the brush could change a smiling into a crying face, a pretty into a hideous countenance. That's all. Nothing that he ever wrote or said will live a decade.—BRANN, HENRY A., 1899, *Robert Ingersoll, Catholic World*, vol. 69, pp. 787, 790.

For all his attacks on the faith of the people Colonel Ingersoll was a sort of a popular idol, and deserved to be. He had the full courage of his convictions and the faculty of indignation at what he believed to be wrong. It was a sight to see the delight with which a mighty audience of negroes in Cooper Institute listened to his eulogy on Frederick Douglass, peppered though it was with sarcasm on the Christian faith, in which most of them were believers. He had full command of the best treasures of oratory, whether passion, or wit, or imagination, or elocution, or gesture. A lecture of his was an intellectual treat for those who most opposed his views. . . . It is true that he declared himself an agnostic as to the existence of God. But he was no atheist. There might be a God, he said, only he did not find the sure evidence of a God or of a future life. He wished he might believe. What he actually disbelieved in was a God who damned people for sinning in conditions they could not help, who damned non-elect or unbaptized infants. To be sure, this damnable doctrine was once in the creeds and in our common Christian faith, but it was given up early in this century. . . . His appeals for freedom, for honesty, and his personal examples in favor of what is beautiful in domestic life have, I believe, of more permanent influence than his sometimes violent attacks on popular faith. Those who have heard him will remember longest his exquisite oratory, and will give him credit for the courage and the loyalty to truth which he possessed.—WARD, WILLIAM HAYES, 1899, *Colonel Ingersoll, Review of Reviews, vol.* 20, *pp.* 319, 320.

For more than twenty years the name of Robert Ingersoll has been known to all his countrymen. On the day when, in the Republican Convention of 1876, he rose to urge the nomination of Mr. Blaine for the Presidency of the United States, his reputation ceased to be a merely local one, and in a short half-hour had become distinctly national. . . . Colonel Ingersoll delivered his attacks on Christianity before audiences made up in part, at least, of intelligent, serious-minded, influential men and women. The political partisan had won a hearing for the professional atheist. It is, indeed, as a professional atheist that Colonel Ingersoll is destined to be now remembered. . . . Colonel Ingersoll was in no respect a thinker. He had received a good professional training; he had read a reasonable amount of standard literature; and he possessed the oratorical temperament, with a liberal fund of wit and racy humour. But that was all. He had none of the scholar's thoroughness and the scholar's sobriety of thought. His controversial addresses when stripped of all their rhetoric, their pungent phraseology and their often rather unsavory jokes exhibit absolutely nothing that had not been advanced a hundred years before Colonel Ingersoll was born. His criticisms on the Bible were mainly taken from the writings of Thomas Paine; his "arguments" against the truth of revelation have been the common property of infidels for centuries. He added nothing whatsoever to the literature of the subject, nor to the strength of the agnostic position. All that can be styled his own is to be found in the bits of declamation, the flights of rhetoric, the neatness of expression and also in the gibes and jeers, the ludicrous similes, the irreverent stories and the pointed jests with which the old material was seasoned and made for the moment to appear original and startling.— PECK, HARRY THURSTON, 1899, *Robert G. Ingersoll, The Bookman, vol.* 10. *pp.* 24, 26, 27.

John Ruskin

1819—1900

Born in London, 8 Feb. 1819. Privately educated. Matric. Ch. Ch., Oxford, 20 Oct. 1836; went into residence, 14 Jan. 1837; Newdigate Prize Poem, 1839; B. A., May 1842; M. A, 28 Oct. 1843; Hon. Student, Ch. Ch., 1867; Hon. Fellow, Corpus Christi Coll., 1871; Slade Prof. of Fine Art, 1869-79 and 1883-85. Contrib. to various periodicals, from 1834. Rede Lecturer, Camb., 1867; Hon. LL. D., Camb., 15 May 1867. Endowed School of Drawing in Taylorian Museum, Oxford, 1871. *Works:* "Salsette and Elephanta" (Newdigate Prize Poem), 1839; "Modern Painters," vol. i. (anon.) 1843; vol. ii. (anon.) 1846; vols. iii., iv., 1856; vol. v., 1860; "The Seven Lamps of Architecture," 1849; "Poems" (under initials: J. R.), 1850; "The King of the Golden River" (anon.), 1851; "The Stones of Venice, vol. i., 1851; vols. ii., iii., 1853; abridged edn. of whole, 1879; "Examples of the Architecture of Venice," 1851; "Notes on the Construction of Sheepfolds," 1851; "Pre-Raphaelitism," 1851; "The National Gallery" (from the "Times," anon.), 1852; "Giotto and his Works in Padua" (3 pts.), 1854-60; "Lecturers on Architecture and Painting," 1854; "Letters to the 'Times' on the principal Pre-Raphaelite Pictures in the Exhibition," 1854; "The Opening of the Crystal Palace," 1854; "Notes on . . . the Royal Academy," no. i., 1855; no. ii., 1856; no. iii., 1857; no. iv., 1858; no. v., 1859; "The Harbours of England," 1856; "Notes on the Turner Gallery at Marlborough House," 1857; "Catalogue of the Turner Sketches

JOHN RUSKIN

Engraving from a Photograph, 1882.

SIR EDWIN ARNOLD

Engraving from a Photograph.

in the National Gallery," pt. i., 1857 (enlarged edn. same year); "Catalogue of the Sketches and Drawings by J. M. W. Turner . . . at Marlborough House," 1857 (enlarged edn., 1858); "The Elements of Drawing," 1857; "The Political Economy of Art," 1857; "Inaugural Address at the Cambridge School of Art," 1858; "The Oxford Museum" (with H. W. Acland), 1859; "The Two Paths," 1859; "The Unity of Art" (priv. ptd.), 1859; "The Elements of Perspective," 1859; "Selections" from his works, 1861; "Unto this Last," 1862; "Sesame and Lilies," 1865; "An Enquiry into some of the Conditions at present affecting the Study of Architecture in our Schools," 1865; "The Ethics of the Dust," 1866; "The Crown of Wild Olive," 1866; "Time and Tide by Weare and Tyne," 1867; "First Notes on the General Principles of Employment for the Destitute and Criminal Classes" (priv. ptd.), 1868; "Leoni" (under initials: J. R.), 1868; "The Queen of the Air," 1869; "Samuel Prout" (priv. ptd.), 1870; "The Future of England" [1870]; "Verona and its Rivers," 1870; "Lectures on Art," 1870; "Catalogue of Examples . . . in the University Galleries," 1870; "Works" (11 vols.), 1871-83; "Fors Clavigera" (8 vols.), 1871-84; ["Index" to preceding, 1887]; "Munera Pulveris," 1872; "Aratra Pentelici," 1872; "The Relation between Michael Angelo and Tintoret," 1872; "The Eagle's Nest," 1872, "The Sepulchral Monuments of Italy," 1872; "Instructions in Elementary Drawing" (priv. ptd.), 1872; "Instructions in the Preliminary Exercises," 1873; "Love's Meinie," 1873; "The Nature and Authority of Miracle" (priv. ptd.), 1873; "Val d'Arno," 1874; "Frondes Agrestes" (selected from "Modern Painters"), 1875; "Notes on Some of the Principal Pictures in the . . . Royal Academy," 1875; "Proserpina" (10 pts.), 1875-86; "Deucalion" (8 pts.), 1875-83; "Mornings in Florence" (8 pts.), 1875-77; "Ariadne Fiorentina," 1876; Letters to the "Times," (anon.), 1876; "Letter to Young Girls" [1876]; "St. Mark's Rest," 1877-84; "Guide to the Principal Pictures in the Academy of Fine Arts at Venice," 1877; "Yewdale and its Streamlets," 1877; "The Laws of Fésole" (4 pts.), 1877-79; "Abstract of the Objects . . . of St. George's Guild" [1878]; "Notes by Mr. Ruskin on his Collection of Drawings by the late J. M. W. Turner," 1878; "Letters to the Clergy" (priv. ptd.), 1879; "Circular respecting . . . St. Mark's," 1879-80; "Elements of English Prosody," 1880; "Notes . . . on S. Prout and W. Hunt," 1880; "Arrows of the Chase" (2 vols.), 1880; "The Lord's Prayer and the Church," 1880; "Our Fathers have told us," 1880-85; "General Statement explaining the . . . St. George's Guild," 1882; "The Art of England," 1883-84; "Cœli Enarrant" (selected from "Modern Painters"), 1884; "Catalogue of Selected Examples of Native Silica in the British Museum," 1884; "The Pleasures of England," 1884; "In Montibus Sanctis" (selected from "Modern Painters"), 1884; "The Storm-cloud of the Nineteenth Century," 1884; "On the Old Road" (2 vols.), 1885; "Præterita" (3 vols.), 1885-88; "Notes on the Principal Pictures of Sir. J. E. Millais," 1886; "Dilecta" (2 pts.), 1886-87; "Hortus Inclusus," 1887; "Poems," 1891; "Gold" (priv. ptd.), 1891; "Letters . . . to various Correspondents" (priv. ptd.), 1892; "Stray Letters to a London Bibliophile" (priv. ptd.), 1892; "The Poetry of Architecture," 1893 [1892]; "Three Letters and an Essay on Literature," 1893; "Letters to W. Ward" (priv. ptd.), 1893; "Letters addressed to a College Friend," 1894; "Letters . . . to Earnest Chesneau" (priv. ptd.), 1894; "Letter on Art and Literature" (ed. by T. J. Wise; priv. ptd.), 1894; "Verona, and other Lectures," 1894; "Letters to . . . Rev. J. P. Faunthorpe" (ed. by T. J. Wise; priv. ptd.), 1895, etc.; "Studies in Both Arts," 1895. He has *edited:* A. C. Owen's "The Art Schools of Mediæval Christendom," 1876; "Bibliotheca Pastorum," vols. i., ii., 1876-77; vol. iv., 1885; F. Alexander's "The Story of Ida," 1883; F. Alexander's "Roadside Songs of Tuscany," 1884-85; "Dame Wiggans of Lee," 1885; "Ulric the Farm Servant," 1886; F. Alexander's "Christ's Folk in the Appennine;" and has contributed prefatory letters or introductions to various works.—SHARP, R. FARQUHARSON, 1897, *A Dictionary of English Authors*, p. 242.

PERSONAL

I am very self-indulgent, very proud, very obstinate, and *very* resentful; on the other side, I am very upright—nearly as just as I suppose it is possible for man to be in this world—exceedingly fond of making people happy, and devoutly reverent to all true mental or moral power. I never betrayed a trust—never wilfully did an unkind thing—and never, in little or large matters, depreciated another that I might raise myself. I believe I once had affections as warm as most people; but partly from evil chance, and partly from foolish misplacing of them, they have got tumbled down and broken to pieces. It is a very great, in the long-run the greatest, misfortune of my life that, on the whole, my relations, cousins and so forth, are persons with whom I can have no sympathy, and that circumstances have always somehow or other kept me out of the way of the people of whom I could have made friends. So thât I have no friendships, and no loves.—RUSKIN, JOHN, 1855, *Letter to Dante Rossetti, April; Ruskin, Rossetti, Pre Raphaelitism, ed. Rossetti, p. 71.*

Froude, however, was there, and Browning, and Ruskin; the latter and I had some talk, but I should never like him.—ARNOLD, MATTHEW, 1863, *To his Mother, June 16; Letters, ed. Russell, vol.* I, *p.* 228.

Few authors have put themselves more completely into their writings than Ruskin has done. His own personal history and opinions, his manner of life, the inmost soul of the man, are revealed to the attentive reader of his books, as in the case of almost no other author. He is sympathetic and confidential, touched with egotism, and always open and responsive to whatever influences life may bring to him. Ruskin has the strong and insistent personality of genius, and he will not dress, live, or think in the manner of other men. He has given little heed to the conventional beliefs of his time in art, morals, or religion, preferring to follow his own convictions of truth and duty. His personality is impressed on his every word and act, and stands forth as a magnetic and commanding presence above all his works of every kind.—COOKE, GEORGE WILLIS, 1886, *Poets and Problems, p.* 194.

Professor Ruskin is emotional and nervous in manner, his large eye at times soft and genial and again quizzing and mischievous in its glance, the mouth thin and severe, chin retreating, and forehead prominent. He has an iron-grey beard, wears old-fashioned coats, sky-blue neckcloths, and gold spectacles; is rather *petit*, about five feet five in height; his pronunciation as broad as Dundee Scotch, and at times "as indistinct as Belgravia Cockney." He is one of the most popular lecturers in England, and his influence over the students at Oxford is said to have been such that, at one time, he purposely avoided (in a measure) their society that it might not be thought that he was doing an injustice to his fellow-professors.—KENNEDY, WILLIAM SLOANE, 1886, *ed. Art, a Ruskin Anthology.*

Those who see him now find a strange appearing man, close upon seventy, with a rather sad face, somewhat "out of drawing," a large, expressive mouth, and faraway eyes of light grayish-blue, wonderfully charming when he will, and a fascinating though dictorial talker, identifiable always by a particular blue neckcloth, curiously associated with his personality in the eyes of his friends, the like of which he has worn from time immemorial. The fortune left him by his father was largely spent upon his St. George's Guild and its Museum at Sheffield, and for other public purposes, but his books, which he now sells through his own book-seller, at a price intended to require readers to know the worth of what they are purchasing, happily assure him a large and sufficient income for the rest of his days.—BOWKER, RICHARD ROGERS, 1888, *London as a Literary Centre, Harper's Magazine, vol.* 76, *p.* 831.

Mr. Ruskin's first professional lecture at Oxford, it may be interesting to say, was announced for the theatre in the Museum, but so great was the crowd that the Professor and his audience adjourned to the large Sheldonian Theatre. This, however, was an exception, and the usual lecture-room was in the Museum. The crowd was always very great, and it was necessary to be outside the doors an hour beforehand to secure a good seat.—COOK, EDWARD T., 1890, *Studies in Ruskin, p.* 47.

Ruskin seemed less picturesque as a young man than in his later days. Perhaps gray waving hair may be more becoming than darker locks, but the speaking, earnest eyes must have been the same, as well as the tones of that delightful voice, with its slightly foreign pronunciation of the *r*, which seemed so familiar again when it welcomed us to Coniston long, long years after. Meeting thus after fifteen years, I was struck by the change for the better in him; by the bright, radiant, sylvan look which a man gains by living among woods and hills and pure breezes. . . . He, the master of Brantwood, came, as I remember, dressed with some ceremony, meeting us with a certain old-fashioned courtesy and manner; but he spoke with his heart, of which the fashion doesn't change happily from one year to another; and as he stood in his tall hat and frock-coat upon the green, the clouds and drifts came blowing up from every quarter of heaven, and I can almost see him stamp his foot upon the sward, while he spoke with emphasis and remembrance of something which was then in both our minds.—RITCHIE, ANNE THACKERAY, 1890, *John Ruskin, an Essay*, Harper's Magazine, vol. 80, p. 579.

As I recall my first welcome, I recall too the face and figure of the man who tendered it. But it was the manner that first attracted and arrested attention. In no other man have I seen sweetness, gentleness, genial frankness, and sympathetic cordiality so perfectly allied with virility and activity of mind. His look inspired confidence, just as his hand-grip awoke friendship—a magic quality, it has often been remarked, that he shares in equal degree with his political *bête noire*, Mr. Gladstone. His smile is sweet and tender, and his whole bearing instinct with kindness, courtesy, and good-fellowship. But it is his eyes that pin you—bright, clear, frank blue eyes that look you through and through, and make you wonder—eyes so pure and truthful that they seem to disarm at once all disingenuousness, but keenly intelligent, notwithstanding, and full of fun; the eyes, in short, that the novelists tell us "dance" upon occasion. Their strong blue—of the intensity of an Italian sky—for all that in these latest years they are to be seen through the screen of the bushy, overhanging eyebrows, is echoed in the satin stock-tie, of the same hue which he has worn for half a century or more. . . . Nothing could be more vivacious than his conversation, partly through his enormous range of information and experience, partly through his command of language and expression, and partly, too, through his keen and rapid intelligence and striking originality of thought.—SPIELMANN, MARION H., 1894, *John Ruskin at Home*, McClure's Magazine, vol. 2, pp. 316, 317.

A man of the noblest nature. I knew from W. B. Scott, very friendly with him until differing views of artistic teaching (at the Workingmen's College and elsewhere) sundered them, of his great life and generosities. Scott, no doubt, was right on the Art question.—LINTON, WILLIAM JAMES, 1894, *Threescore and Ten Years*, p. 166.

His voice was always most winning, and his language simply perfect. He was one of the few Englishmen I knew who, instead of tumbling out their sentences like so many portmanteaux, bags, rugs, and hat-boxes from an open railway van, seemed to take a real delight in building up their sentences, even in familiar conversation, so as to make each deliverance a work of art.—MÜLLER, F. MAX, 1898, *Auld Lang Syne*, p. 147.

I can scarcely imagine that Ruskin ever resembled the old sentimental portrait, with its smooth regularity of feature and softly flowing hair, from which my mental picture of him had been derived. Doubtless the first actual sight of a man whom one has dreamed about for years always dissipates something of the glamour with which fancy has surrounded him. But I am glad to record that the real Ruskin, though widely divergent from his poetic presentment, at once approved himself to me a much more congruous and satisfactory apparition. The disappointment, so far as any was felt, pertained to his size. I have called him slight; he was distinctly short as well, wholly lacking the suave majesty of proportions implied, if not depicted, in the early prints. Not that one could by any means have thought him undignified; but his dignity was no affair of material bulk or imposing manner; it was the worthier dignity of intense earnestness and imperious sincerity. The man's insistent genuineness would have made any conventional grace or elegance seem affectation and artificiality. Rugged and angular, he still was never awkward. The eager swiftness and vitality of his intellect precluded that. It could not happen to him to be, as Emerson bitingly says, "awkward for want of thought, the inspiration not reaching the extremities." His face was small, in spite of the largeness of his features; the hair a somewhat tumbled shock of reddish brown, broadly streaked, like the straggling beard and whiskers, with gray. In his costume, simple enough beneath his professor's gown, there was a suggestion of originality and picturesqueness, chiefly due, I think, to the broad necktie of bright blue satin which he habitually wore.—BRUCE, JAMES MANNING, 1898, *Ruskin as an Oxford Lecturer, Century Magazine, vol.* 55, *p.* 590.

His manner of speech had a peculiar power of appeal in it. Its tone and timbre were full of feeling. It was the speech of one who sang rather than spoke to us. His message was rhythmic and musical. His peculiar dwelling on the roll of the *r* in such a word as "entirely" was never to be forgotten. His manner changed with his feeling, and was swift or slow as suited his subject. He used his hands to emphasize what he said—hands so delicate, so full of expression; hands he used to clap with pleasure, or fold together almost as in prayer. He won all our hearts, not only by his unconventionality and undonnish ways, but because he took such infinite pains for us; and of all men I ever met he was the best listener. . . . People asked me what he looked like. His notable personal features were his delicate aquiline nose, his sensitive mouth, his tender blue eyes, his abundance of straight yellow-brown hair. Below the average height and somewhat hollow-chested, he made up for a certain unrobustness of appearance by his habit of dressing in the thick gray-brown laxey cloth, as seen in that best of photographs by Barraud. The sky-blue tie, except when he mourned for his mother, was always part of his dress, and a long, delicate gold chain for his watch hung loosely round his neck and fell about his waistcoat.—RAWNSLEY, H. D., 1900, *John Ruskin, The Outlook, vol.* 64, *pp.* 514, 515.

Ruskin's later years were over-shadowed by a dark cloud. Repeated attacks of illness, and continuous overwork, brought on a disease of the brain, which made him sometimes, for months at a time, violently insane. The cloud passed by, and the evening of his life was quiet and serene, but his life's work was done. On the roll of England's great men we find few who have been so much revered and loved, by that large mass of people whom we call the laboring classes, as was Mr. Ruskin.—WARD, MAY ALDEN, 1900, *Prophets of the Nineteenth Century, p.* 130.

Ruskin's was an opulent nature, with material in it to have made three men, as men go. He had in him, indeed, much of the spirit of the knight of chivalry, as well as of the monk or the preacher. Truth was his mistress: he was ready with immediate battle for her against all comers or for whomsoever he saw oppressed. He was sensitive as well as pugnacious; but his own sensitiveness did not teach him indulgence for the sensitiveness of an opponent; so he was continually making enemies of those with whom he had no personal quarrel, and unexpectedly offending all but the closest of his friends. That Whistler, for being called in print a coxcomb flinging a pot of paint in the public's face, should sue him seemed to surprise him. He called Gladstone an old windbag, and notes, as if it were unexpected, that after this Miss Gladstone would not look at him.—LONGFELLOW, WILLIAM P. P., 1900, *John Ruskin, The Forum, vol.* 29, *p.* 310.

His most compelling claim on our attention is the assurance his life affords us of a perfect *bona fides*, of an unselfish motive in all he said and did. No man, surely, could be less led by personal profit. His lavish generosity dissipated before his death nearly the whole of the £200,000 inherited from his father; a circumstance in itself sufficient, with many folk, to wreck his reputation for sanity. Thus £17,000 were disbursed at once to relatives who, he thought, had been neglected in the will; £5,000 went to endow the drawing-school at Oxford, in addition to the valuable drawings placed in the school; £7,000 went to the St. George's Fund; £15,000 to set up a relative in business; and so on. Of his preference of duty before inclination there are many instances; but the best is that crusade of social and industrial reform which withdrew him for long periods from his beloved field of art, plunged him into endless controversy, and brought so much gloom and bitterness into a naturally sunny spirit.—BOND, R. WARWICK, 1900, *Ruskin, Man and Prophet, Contemporary Review, vol.* 78, *p.* 126.

More princely hospitality than his no man ever received, or more kindly companionship; but, as might have been expected, we agreed neither in temperament nor in method, if indeed the mainly self-taught way in which I worked and thought could be called method. . . . Ruskin had dragged me from my old methods, and given me none to replace them. I lost my faith in myself, and in him as a guide to art, and we separated definitely, years later, on a personal question in which he utterly misunderstood me; but, apart from questions of art, he always remains to me one of the largest and noblest of all the men I have known, liberal and generous beyond limit, with a fineness of sympathy in certain directions and delicacy of organization quite womanly. Nothing could shake my admiration for his moral character or abate my reverence for him as a humanist. That art should have been anything more than a side interest with him, and that he should have thrown the whole energy of his most energetic nature into the reforming of it, was a misfortune to him and to the world, but especially to me.—STILLMAN, WILLIAM JAMES, 1901, *The Autobiography of a Journalist*, vol. I, pp. 308, 320.

Ruskin's own bedroom was entirely hung with the choice specimens of Turner's drawings, which were so rapturously described in his various books. His own library had a case of exquisite illuminated manuscripts, some rare printed books, some manuscript originals of Scott's romances, written with the master's own hand in quarto pages at a furious pace, legible and very little disfigured by erasers; a few smaller pieces of Prout, Hunt, and Burne-Jones; and cases of rare specimens of minerals and precious stones. Until you had closely looked at all these things—the choice remains that had been saved out of the splendid collections of paintings, engravings, specimens, and works of art which he had lavished on public museums and libraries—but for these things, you would not immediately perceive that you were in anything but the ordinary comfortable home of a retired professional gentleman. Here, for twenty years, after life's fitful fever, John Ruskin sought peace.—HARRISON, FREDERIC, 1902, *John Ruskin (English Men of Letters)*, p. 159.

MODERN PAINTERS
1843-60

If we examine how far, in Mr. Ruskin's writings, desire for display has superseded the love of truth, the task is entered on, not because it is agreeable, but because it is seasonable. After having made a fame, by hanging on to the skirts of a famous artist—after deluding those craving for novelty into the belief that a dashing style must imply precious discoveries—after having met the humour of the time, by preaching the religion of architecture with a freedom in the use of sacred names and sacred things from which a more reverential man would have shrunk—after having served as an eloquent though too flattering guide to the treasures of Venice, —after having enriched the citizens of this Scottish metropolis with receipts how to amend the architecture of our city by patching Paladin squares, streets, and crescents with Gothic windows, balconies, and pinnacles—after having lectured to decorators on the beauty and virtue of painting illegible letters on signboards and shop-fronts—the wisdom of Mr. Ruskin has of late begun to cry in the streets. He attempts to erect the most extravagant paradoxes into new canons of taste; and the virulence of his personalities is only exceeded by the eccentricity of his judgment. He now periodically enters the exhibition-room as an overseer, summoning gallery-loungers to stand and deliver their sympathies,—calling on bad painters to tremble,—and assailing those whom he dislikes with menaces and insults. . . . Rarely has vanity, so overweening in stature, so unblushing in front, so magisterial in language, risen up between a writer and his public. . . . We have already bestowed upon this volume more space than its merits deserve, but its gross and glaring extravagances and defects constitute a strong claim to notice. It is the worst book of a bad series of books, mischievous to art, mischievous to literature, but mischievous most of all to those young and eager minds, animated by the love of art and of literature, which may mistake this declamatory trash for substantial or stimulating food.—CHORLEY, HENRY FOTHERGILL, 1856, *Ruskinism*, *Edinburgh Review*, vol. 103, pp. 536, 537, 557.

Before I had begun to paint either of these pictures an event of no little importance occurred to me; a fellow-student, one Telfer spoke to me of Ruskin's "Modern Painters," and ended by lending it for a few days. Up to that time I thought that the world regarded art as a sort of vagabondish cleverness; that it was almost a disgrace to have a passion for art in modern times, and that it was useless to hope that modern intellect would profess its enthusiasm for it. I name this with full knowledge that it reveals a one-sided acquaintance with the society of the day. To get through the book I had to sit up most of the night more than once, and I returned it before I had got half the good there was in it; but, of all readers, none so strongly as myself could have felt that it was written expressly for him. When it had gone, the echo of its words stayed with me and pealed a further meaning and value in their inspiration whenever my more solemn feelings were touched in any way.—HUNT, WILLIAM HOLMAN, 1886, *The Pre-Raphaelite Brotherhood, Contemporary Review, vol. 49, p. 478*.

I was profoundly moved by the second volume of Ruskin's "Modern Painters."—FARRAR, FREDERIC WILLIAM, 1887, *Books Which Have Influenced Me, p. 87*.

If young Americans and young Englishmen do not read Ruskin's "Modern Painters" now, they ought to read it and if they cannot read all the volumes, let them at least read that most precious and incomparable second volume, which constitutes the third part of the work, and deals with the imaginative and theoretic faculties. What I owe to John Ruskin's writings I shall never be able to set down in black and white. The only harm that I think they ever did me was, that coming upon me, as they did for the first time, when I was deep in my mediæval researches, they occasioned me an impatient distaste for any book written in a slip-slop style; and, whereas I formerly never cared much *how* an author told his story, provided he had a story to tell, I found myself suddenly growing over-fastidious as to the manner of a writer, and I became more and more exacting as to the form, and less curious as to the matter, of a book than I had been.—JESSOPP, AUGUSTUS, 1888, *Books That Have Helped Me, p. 65*.

It was calculated that the money-value of the new "Modern Painters" was nearly £20,000, and the weight over six tons! A portion of this was described as a special edition of 450 copies only, every one of which had been subscribed for, at ten guineas—and already the price had mounted to fourteen guineas. It was said that the author would receive for the whole edition some £6,000!—FITZGERALD, PERCY, 1890, *Mr. Ruskin, Artist and Publisher, Gentleman's Magazine, vol. 268, p. 147*.

It was nearly twenty years before the five volumes of the work were completed, and during that time Mr. Ruskin's views had broadened and changed, so that there is something of contradiction in the volumes; but it to-day stands as his most forceful work. Philosophical it is not, because lacking in system; scientific it is not, because lacking in fundamental principles. The logic of it is often weak, the positiveness of statement often annoying, the digressions and side issues often wearisome; yet with all this it contains some of his keenest observations on nature, his most suggestive conceits, and his most brilliant prose passages. It made something of a sensation, and Mr. Ruskin came into prominence at once.—VAN DYKE, JOHN C., 1897, *Library of the World's Best Literature, ed. Warner, vol. XXI, p. 12510*.

All Ruskin is in the "Modern Painters," which, as everyone knows, was a most eloquent and fervid glorification of landscape and of the superior way in which it had been painted by certain English painters of the present era, notably Turner—*mirabile dictu*, who systematically violated every article of the Ruskin creed —compared with its insufficient treatment by the old masters. Five volumes of this surprising work appeared in quick succession, and they revolutionized English feeling on the subject with which they dealt. It may be safely asserted that no writer ever "made" a man as Ruskin did Turner. Plato did less for Socrates. From that time on every work of the new author was greeted with applause and read with avidity.—BROWNELL, W. C., 1900, *John Ruskin, Scribner's Monthly, vol. 27, p. 502*.

THE STONES OF VENICE
1851–53

Here are bold and effective architectural scenes, set off with colour and conceived in a true Venetian spirit. Here, too, we find a perfect embodiment of the theory which he has unfolded when expounding the charm of Prout.—FITZGERALD, PERCY, 1890, *Mr. Ruskin, Artist and Publisher, Gentleman's Magazine, vol. 268, p. 128*.

His monumental architectural work, "The Stones of Venice," has probably done more than any other book to awaken admiration for the beauty of the enchanting city of the sea. In an earlier essay,

"The Seven Lamps of Architecture," he had already formulated what he regarded as the fundamental principles of architectural design. . . . "The Stones of Venice" abounds in misconceptions and mistaken affirmations; but these are largely due to the state of ideas and understanding in respect to mediæval architecture half a century ago. I have said that Ruskin's interest in architecture was primarily pictorial. I do not, however, mean that he was wholly wanting in apprehension of its structural basis. To a limited extent he felt this strongly. He has, in many parts of the work, shown a just, and even an acute, sense of the elementary structural principles of ordinary wall, column, and arch construction. But beyond this he has hardly understood the more important types of mediæval building on their structural side.—MOORE, CHARLES H., 1900, *John Ruskin as an Art Critic*, Atlantic Monthly, vol. 86, pp. 444, 445.

In "The Stones of Venice," he arraigned the modern system of industry for this tendency [to dehumanize men], in words as trenchant as any he has ever written. Indeed the germ of all his teaching as a social reformer is found in that chapter on The Nature of Gothic.—GLADDEN, WASHINGTON, 1903, *Witnesses of the Light, p. 265.*

SESAME AND LILIES
1865

The present work consists of two lectures which are more immediately devoted to personal education, and particularly to the proper use of books. It seems to Mr. Ruskin, as it seems to every thinker of our time, that the desire for amusement is becoming the controlling desire of the people, especially of the upper classes; that the disregardful spirit which, as we all know, the present generation shows toward art, it shows also in a less but in an increasing degree toward literature, and indeed toward every manifestation of intellectual and moral life; and that the persistent rejection of thought, and of subjects of occupation requiring thought, is fast depriving people of the power of thought. The truth of these propositions he endeavors to establish, and the right way to deal with the evil is what his lectures are intended to suggest. . . . The union of imagination and thought is the most remarkable feature of the volume before us.—STURGIS, RUSSELL, JR., 1866, *Sesame and Lilies, North American Review*, vol. 102, p. 307.

Perhaps the most popular of Mr. Ruskin's works. . . . The substance of the first lecture may be described in the words of Bacon's aphorism, "Knowledge is Power." Its purport is to show, besides, that companionship with the royal leaders of thought, hence the title, "King's Treasuries," is the most enobling condition of humanity. Rules are laid down accordingly for a careful selection of books, and the manner of reading them. If we cannot quite reach Mr. Ruskin's own standard of minute analysis in reading, or his curious trick of nice discernment for the multifarious shades of meaning in every single word, and even syllable, of the books of great authors, we can at least see here the practical tendency of the specialist combined with both elevation and catholicity of thought. . . . And it is the absence of this higher sense, as distinguished from common sense, which no doubt prevents the best ideas from gaining currency among the literary mob, and which renders the works of Mr. Ruskin himself caviare to the mixed multitude of general readers.—KAUFMANN, M., 1894, *Mr. Ruskin as a Practical Teacher, Scottish Review*, vol. 24, p. 41.

"Sesame and Lilies" is written in a style of wonderful strength and richness. It affords perhaps the best example of its author's mastery over the manifold chords of prose expression.—MOODY, WILLIAM VAUGHN, AND LOVETT, ROBERT MORSS, 1902, *A History of English Literature, p. 339.*

FORS CLAVIGERA
1871-84.

It is not surprising that these "Letters" have had but little sale hitherto, and for yet another reason than their cost, their inaccessibility, and their plain-speaking; namely, that their author will not consent in any way to advertise them. . . . Let us turn at once to his definitely constructive effort in criticism, which has occupied the letters of the last four years, as the destructive criticism occupied the first three; and, also, to the great scheme of his life, now beginning to be made real in lands, and houses, and labourers, the establishment of St. George's Guild, or St. George's Company, as he called it at first and until last August. For all these letters were written with this practical object in view. . . . We may close his letters, I hope, with this clear perception: that after setting aside all of Mr. Ruskin's "peculiar theories," the thing that he is doing is what all great reformers have actually done, and will continue to do; namely, he is striving to persuade men that honest living is still possible in the world, and to help them toward it. . . . And upon those superior persons who tell us, in scorn, that they have "given Ruskin up," we must pass, I think, the sentence of the Vulgate upon people who "speak evil of the things they understand not:" *In corruptione sua peribunt.*— COAN, TITUS MUNSON, 1878, *Ruskin's "Fors Clavigera," Appleton's Journal*, vol. 20, pp. 58, 61, 65.

"Fors Clavigera" is at once the wittiest, the charmingest, and the most painfully cynical of Ruskin's works. No one can understand him who does not read it; and no one but will regret the necessity of having to read certain parts. The work is the autobiography of a soul, a journal of the daily thoughts of one possessing the clear courage to reveal both the good and the bad side of his nature. What pretty little trifles he writes down! If he alights on the recipe for a rich and savory Yorkshire Goose Pie, straightway he imparts it to his readers, consults with his cook, and announces his intention instantly to build the out-of-door brown-bread oven indispensable for the delicate incrustation of the dish. He spills his match-box while dressing, and we learn that just two hundred and sixty-six wax matches were picked up by him, one by one. . . . One object kept continually in view is the discussion of the prospects of St. George's Guild, and the publication of portions of the correspondence of its master with those interested in his plans; so that "Fors" may be regarded as the official journal of the Guild, and, in a vague and unintended way, a sort of proselyting medium for the propagation of its principles. . . . Certainly never before was there a title so loaded with meaning. And the fact that its inventor is still finding out new ones for it indicates his wisdom in choosing two words from the most elastic vocabulary in literature to cover a collection of writings classifiable only in the vaguest way as writings chiefly on social and political topics.—KENNEDY, WILLIAM SLOANE, 1885, *Ruskin's "Fors Clavigera," Literary World*, vol. 16, p. 289.

If we fairly judge the whole series of Letters in "Fors" and seek to understand their purport, we shall find a perfectly definite scheme of ideas and a real working aim. With a mysterious belief in the creation of all Nature and living creatures by a loving and Almighty God, whose eye watches the fall of every sparrow and the opening of every leaf, mixed with an equally active belief in the polytheistic, or fetichist, sanctity of natural things as objects of worship in themselves, Ruskin has brought himself to regard the disfigurement of natural things and the slaughter of gentle creatures as desecration and sacrilege, almost as a Hindoo regards the slaughter of a Brahminee cow, or a Greek would regard the pollution of a Fountain of the Nymphs.—HARRISON, FREDERIC, 1902, *John Ruskin (English Men of Letters)*, p. 194.

PRÆTERITA
1885-88

As one reads "Præterita" it seems as if John Ruskin wrote his history not with ink, but painted it down with light and color; he brings the very atmosphere of his life and its phases before us with such an instantaneous mastery as few besides have ever reached—the life within and the sight without, the sweet eternal horizons (even though they be but Norwood hills and ridges), the living and delightful figures in the foreground. Its author has chosen to christen the story "Præterita," but was ever a book less belonging to the past and more entirely present to our mood than this one? Not Goethe's own autobiography, not even Carlyle's passionate reminiscences, come up to it in vividness. There are so few words, such limpid images are brought flashing before us, that one almost asks, "Is it a book or is it something out of our own secret consciousness that we *remember* as we read?" Are we not actually living in its pages, in the dawning light of that austere yet glorious childhood?—RITCHIE, ANNE THACKERAY, 1890, *John Ruskin: An Essay, Harper's Magazine*, vol. 80, p. 585.

One of the most charming examples of the most charming kind of literature. No autobiographer surpasses him in freshness and fulness of memory, nor in the power of giving interest to the apparently commonplace. There is an even remarkable absence of striking incident, but somehow or other the story fascinates, and in the last resort, no doubt on account of the unconscious revelation of character. One point is the way in which a singular originality of mind manages to work out a channel for itself, though hedged in by the prejudices of a sufficiently narrow-minded class and an almost overstrained deference to his elders and his spiritual guides. But it is enough to say here that the book should be acceptable even to those to whom his social and artistic dogmas have ceased to have much significance. — STEPHEN, LESLIE, 1900, *John Ruskin, National Review, vol.* 35, *p.* 255.

Is certainly the most charming thing that he ever gave to the world, and is one of the most pathetic and exquisite *Confessions* in the language. After the great cerebral disturbance of 1884 and his final retirement from Oxford, his friend, Professor Eliot Norton, suggested that he should occupy his mind with jotting down reminiscences of his own life, at least, down to the crisis of 1875; and this he began to do at intervals of restored activity. These, with the fragments called *Dilecta*, are now collected in three volumes, and were composed at odd times down to as late as 1889, in Ruskin's seventy-first year— HARRISON, FREDERIC, 1902, *John Ruskin (English Men of Letters), p.* 197.

GENERAL

I don't know whether you look out for Ruskin's books whenever they appear. His little book on the "Political Economy of Art" contains some magnificent passages, mixed up with stupendous specimens of arrogant absurdity on some economical points. But I venerate him as one of the greatest teachers of the day. The grand doctrines of truth and sincerity in art, and the nobleness and solemnity of our human life, which he teaches with the inspiration of a Hebrew prophet, must be stirring up young minds in a promising way. The last two volumes of "Modern Painters" contain, I think, some of the finest writing of the age. He is strongly akin to the sublimest part of Wordsworth —whom, by-the-bye, we are reading with fresh admiration for his beauties and tolerance for his faults.—ELIOT, GEORGE, 1858, *To Miss Sara Hennell, Jan.* 17;
George Eliot's Life as related in her Letters and Journals, ed. Cross, vol. II, *p.* 5.

May I get Ruskin's late volumes of "Modern Painters," from Mr. Langford? I have got the "Life of Turner," but I believe the last of these volumes is much occupied with that strange, shabby divinity. I suppose it does not much matter in choosing a god what sort of creature it is you choose, as persistent worship seems always to gain a certain amount of credit for the object of it.—OLIPHANT, MARGARET O. W., 1861, *To Mr. Blackwood, Nov.* 4; *Autobiography and Letters, ed. Mrs. Coghill, p.* 180.

Mr. Ruskin's power of analysis and habit of subtile and close reasoning are, therefore, more important tools to him as a critic, than even his acquired knowledge of art and literature. But his peculiar gift, which marks him out among men of almost or quite equal intellectual power, is the force of imagination, which is so evident and remarkable in all his reasoning.— STURGIS, RUSSELL, JR., 1866, *Sesame and Lilies, North American Review, vol.* 102, *p.* 307.

When he says that poetry not first-rate adds altogether to human weariness, in a most uncomfortable manner, I may imagine that I catch the tones of a famous voice, whose natural accent is a Scottish one—a voice which belongs not so much to Mr. Ruskin as to an elder if not a better dogmatizer. I may think that even if Mr. Ruskin be the appointed heir of our well-known Chelsea Elijah, it might have been more discreet to wait, before wrapping himself in the familiar mantle, until the prophet in possesion had let it drop.— DOYLE, SIR FRANCIS HASTINGS, 1868, *Lectures Delivered Before the University of Oxford, p.* 17.

Of all men he should be the last to object to criticism, for his own sword seldom seeks the scabbard. And on the whole, though he professes with a certain archness a desire for peace, nothing gives him so much pleasure, or brings out his intellect so well, as war, when it is on a subject with which he is acquainted. He will run on, giving birth to paradox after paradox in an apparently gloomy manner, choosing for very wilfulness the obscurity of the Pythoness, as long as his listeners sit rapt and receptive at his feet. But the moment one of them, seeing that the paradoxes are becoming intolerable, starts up and meets them with a blunt contradiction, and declares war, Mr. Ruskin becomes radiant with good humour, his intellect becomes incisive, and he rushes to the fight with joy. Nothing is worse for him than worship; and if he had had less of it, he would have done the State more service. Half of his morbid and hopeless writing comes directly of this—that he has not been of late sufficiently excited by respectful opposition to feel happy. . . . His theories may, many of them, be absurd, but we may well put up with the absurdity of some for the sake of the excellence of others, more especially for the sake of the careful work which hangs on to them and can be considered apart from them. We should be dismayed to lose the most original man in England.—BROOKE, STOPFORD A., 1870, *Ruskin's Lectures on Art, Macmillan's Magazine, vol. 22, pp. 423, 433.*

For myself I doubt whether Mr. Ruskin has any great qualities but his eloquence, and his true, honest love of Nature. As a man to stand up before a society of which one part was fashionably languid and the other part only too busy and greedy, and preach to it of Nature's immortal beauty and of the true way to do her reverence, I think Ruskin had and has a place almost worthy the dignity of a prophet. I think, too, that he has the capacity to fill the place, to fulfill its every duty. Surely this ought to be enough for the work and for the praise of any man. But the womanish restlessness of Ruskin's temperament, combined with the extraordinary self-sufficiency which contributed so much to his success when he was master of a subject, sent him perpetually intruding into fields where he was unfit to labor, and enterprises which he had no capacity to conduct. No man has ever contradicted himself so often, recklessly, so complacently, as Mr. Ruskin has done. . . . When all his errors and paradoxes and contradictions shall have been utterly forgotten, this his great praise will remain: No man since Wordsworth's brightest days ever did half so much to teach his countrymen, and those who speak his language, how to appreciate and honor that silent Nature which "never did betray the heart that loved her."—MCCARTHY, JUSTIN, 1872, *John Ruskin, Modern Leaders, p. 191.*

Take a man of unusual if not morbid sensibility, and place him in the midst of the jostling, struggling, unsavoury, and unreasonable crowd; suppose him to have a love of all natural and artistic beauty, which is outraged at every moment by the prevailing ugliness; a sincere hatred for all the meanness and imposture too characteristic of modern life; a determination to see things for himself, which involves an antipathy to all the established commonplaces of contented respectability; an eloquence and imaginative force which transfuses his prose with poetry, though his mind is too discursive to express itself in the poetical form; and a keen logical faculty, hampered by a constitutional irritability which prevents his teaching from taking a systematic form; let him give free vent to all the annoyance and the indignation naturally produced by his position, and you will have a general impression of Mr. Ruskin's later writings. . . . Mr. Ruskin, as I have said, is at war with modern society. He sometimes expresses himself in language which, but for his own assurances to the contrary, might be taken for the utterance of furious passion rather than calm reflection. —STEPHEN, LESLIE, 1874, *Mr. Ruskin's Recent Writings, Fraser's Magazine, vol. 89, pp. 689, 690.*

I cannot forget how much I owe you and how much our age has owed you; and what we owe to those who have taught us is a debt that we never can repay, a claim that never grows stale. There are so few whose lips have been touched as it were with sacred fire, having eyes that see behind the veil, and whose ears can hear the voices to which the rest are deaf; and when the utterances of such do seem to us to wander—I will almost say to mislead— it is better to keep silence even from good words. Yet when I find you publishing to the world things about those whom I honour, very contrary as I think to the fact, I will ask you to consider your judgment again. You can yet stir men of the finer fibre, and your words from time to time make us all pause and think, as men pause when violet flashes of lightning glance across the sky. Genius, like nobility, has its duties. But to me all blackening of the human race, all outbursts against the generation and its hopes are profoundly painful, born, I should say, of unnatural self-musing and self-torture, sad as those fulminous imprecations on mankind, when Lear bows his head to the storm.—HARRISON, FREDERIC, 1876, *The Choice of Books and Other Literary Pieces,* p. 121.

There is not, there never can be, a test of sincerity but the plain one of doing; and Mr. Ruskin, though he has been crying passionately that the axe is laid at the root of the tree, seems to turn, almost with scorn at his own ineffectual words, to take up the axe himself, striking a blow with a force which is rather nervous than muscular. The eloquence of this writer, and the almost painful precision of his style,— by which he is constantly trying to make his words carry more freight than they ever bore,—his zeal, and the largeness of his intellectual sympathy, carry the reader over many doubtful stretches of logic, and make the entire scheme of St. George's Company assume an ideal perfectness of proportion and a grace of being which fill the eye as a poetic structure. . . . The ideal St. George pins the dragon with his lance, but Mr. Ruskin's St. George sometimes appears to be armed with a fork, vainly endeavoring to expel, not a dragon, but Nature herself.—SCUDDER, HORACE E., 1878, *St. George's Company, Atlantic Monthly,* vol. 42, pp. 47, 48.

What greater sarcasm can Mr. Ruskin pass upon himself than that he preaches to young men what he cannot perform! Why, unsatisfied with his own conscious power, should he choose to become the type of incompetence by talking for forty years of what he has never done! Let him resign his present professorship, to fill the chair of Ethics at the university. As master of English literature, he has a right to his laurels, while, as the populariser of pictures he remains the Peter Parley of painting.—WHISTLER, J. M'NEILL, 1878, *The Gentle Art of Making Enemies,* p. 34.

I spoke of Mr. Ruskin in my lecture at the Royal Institution as the prophet of a new religion, and this is true in a wider sense than I at the time intended; he is not only its prophet but its high-priest. He has the genuine priestly intolerance of independent judgment; partial admission of his doctrine he will not endure; you must accept it in its entirety, or you are of the enemy; he allows of no independence of opinion gained from experience. That anything should be generally accepted that he has not propounded or asserted to be true is in his eyes the unpardonable sin. Hence the comparison between Michelangelo and Tintoret; Mr. Ruskin *invented* Tintoret in his "Modern Painters," whereas Michelangelo and Raphael are accepted masters about whom others have ventured to write; and one is irresistibly tempted to believe that for this reason they are disparaged to Tintoret's advantage.— POYNTER, EDWARD J., 1879, *Ten Lectures on Art,* p. 222.

Sparkling bits of aphoristic wit and wisdom are scattered in profusion over these letters ["Arrows of the Chase"], even those of which the main tenor is paradoxical or unpractical. Without attempting to deny that many of the social and economical opinions and proposals here put forward are of this unpractical character, I think the reader will nevertheless feel himself stirred and animated in a way which more sober and well-considered suggestions never move him. Mr. Ruskin does not feel more keenly than the rest of us those evils which spoil and darken the wholesomeness and beauty of modern life. . . . Discussion or argument is not forwarded by such downright denunciation of existing evil as is here found. But we are quickened and invigorated for the struggle in which we are all engaged with the misery of the world, and the sluggish and the selfish may be reached by Mr. Ruskin's random arrows where homilies and exhortations are all in vain.—PATTISON, MARK, 1880, *The Academy,* vol. 19, p. 110.

There are many curious points of parallelism between the careers of Carlyle and Ruskin, particularly in their attitude towards public affairs and political economy. . . . Mr. Ruskin's impatience with political economy is to be traced partly to the same source with Carlyle's— the feeling that a science which professes to be based on general, ascertained laws regulating man's action implies a curtailment of man's free agency, and seems in so far an impious and immoral science. In Mr. Ruskin's case, however, this seems to be complicated with an æsthetic feeling that in an ideal state of society, which his conversation leads him to believe once existed on earth, exchanges, rents, profits, etc., were governed not by economic but by moral laws; so that political economy represents a real moral decline, the disappearance of primitive Arcadian simplicity and fair-dealing. . . . Mr. Ruskin has unquestionably greatly weakened his influence even as an art-critic by his extraordinary excursions during the last ten or fifteen years into non-æsthetic fields. Nobody who feels the force and beauty and moral elevation of much of his writing can help regretting that the fatal gift of expression should have misled him into attempting to deal with subjects with which he is totally unfamiliar.—SEDGWICK, ARTHUR GEORGE, 1881, *Ruskin's Arrows of the Chase, The Nation, vol.* 33, *p.* 221.

Admiration ought ungrudgingly to be bestowed on one who has done good service as an art critic and as a contributor to English literature. The sympathy, moreover, which, denied to those who are in advance of their age, is naturally accorded to the archaic type of mind, is enhanced by the attractiveness of a personality whose idealism is as lofty as that of Mr. Ruskin. But we maintain that there is a further sentiment which contributed to the applause which Mr. Ruskin's audiences bestowed upon him. Speaking generally, "broadly and comfortably," as he would say, Mr. Ruskin is not a representative man, yet he represents a certain spirit of Philistinism (for it merits this name), which is far from being unpopular, and which shows itself in opposition to scientific culture. He is the spokesman of that mental attitude which misinterprets the province of science and affects to misunderstand the plainest utterances of the physicist. . . . We recommend those who sympathise with Mr. Ruskin to study some of those little books which are beginning to be the delight of our children. Such readers may never attain the scientific spirit, yet they may possibly catch a few chords of that great song in which there is complete harmony between the Universe of Nature and that of poetic and artistic sentiment, whose faint beginnings will alone be heard in this plague-stricken century. . . . His English is often delicious, always in his most dyspeptic diatribes amusing. And we can all appreciate his concluding advice that we should "bring back our own cheerfulness and our own honesty; and cease from the troubling of our own passions," and (not least we think of all) "the insolence of our own lips."

A good recipe: add a dash of humility and of respect for the opinions of wiser men;—and all may yet be well, even though our return to the paths of rectitude should fail to dissolve the "mangey" clouds, and quench the fevered wind of a storm-harried and woe-worn era.—LEY, W. CLEMENT, 1884, *Mr. Ruskin's Bogies, Nature, vol.* 29, *pp.* 353, 354.

In busying himself with his autobiography, Mr. Ruskin is not hampered with considerations of chronology. He notes events as they occur to him, with small deference to order and succession. This irregularity is but another grace adorning the narrative. The privilege is so precious of viewing the inner experience of a beloved author, uncovered by himself with the *naïveté* of a child, that any waywardness or eccentricity in the proceeding forms a part of its charm. There are repetitions in the story, but none too many. Ruskin never tells a story twice in the same language, and there is always a new and wonderful word-painting when he puts the particles of speech together to convey a favorite idea. . . . Not more remarkable has been Ruskin's literary career than the formative period of his life. The account of it is strange and instructive. How much of the brilliant talent and the strong self-poised character which have made him a power for good in the world, is to be referred to the singular manner of his education?—HUBBARD, SARA A., 1886, *The Autobiography of John Ruskin, The Dial, vol.* 7, *pp.* 82, 86.

Probably the reading public has long ceased to expect anything but fresh outbursts of whim and caprice from Ruskin. Carlyle said of him, in 1872, that if he could hold out for another fifteen years or so, he might produce, even in this way, a great effect. But the prophecy has not turned out a true one. "A weak man," as the sage of Chelsea felt compelled to call him in the same breath in which he ventured the above prediction, will never produce a great effect, give him any length of time. And Ruskin seems fast weakening any impression his earlier works may have made. He has degenerated into a common scold. The public laughs at him, and when the public laughs at a man's rage, his day is about over. He affects one, in his later utterances, as a tipsy Carlyle. He provokes our mirth and pity instead of convincing us in our own hearts of sin and folly, as Carlyle did. Never a man of such genius with so little commonsense. If ever a writer could be likened to a "dim comet wagging its useless tail of phosphorescent nothing across the steadfast stars," the description may be applied to Ruskin in his late verdict upon Gibbon and Darwin. —BURROUGHS, JOHN, 1886, *Ruskin's Judgment of Gibbon and Darwin, The Critic, May* 1.

On the part of this tender and beautiful writer, whose courageous protest against greed and all sorts of moral uncomeliness has brought strength to so many souls, and whose exquisite style is the delight of so many readers, we find the most violent aversion to physical science.— NETTLESHIP, HENRY, 1886, *Natural Science and Literature, Lectures and Essays, Second Series, p.* 240.

Ruskin had a powerful influence upon me at one time, though I was interested in art and studied it in various ways before reading him. His influence was agreeable whilst it lasted, and charmed me by authorising my boyish love of nature, but on the side of art it was very harmful by turning aside my attention from what is really essential in art to kinds of truth which are not essential, and have never been considered to be so by the great artists. Mr. Ruskin's substitution of topography for beauty and character as the aim of the modern landscape painter was at one time most prejudicial to me, and the more so that I had naturally an intense affection for certain favourite places. In the way of literary style, I am not aware that Mr. Ruskin ever did me either good or harm. Every author should express himself in his own way, and as it is right for Mr. Ruskin to utter his thoughts in an ornate style, so it is right for me to use a simple one.—HAMERTON, PHILIP GILBERT, 1887, *Books Which Have Influenced Me, p.* 58.

A glowing eloquence, a splendid and full-flowing music, wealth of phrase, aptness of epithet, opulence of ideas—all these qualities characterize the prose style of Mr. Ruskin. His similes are daring, but always true. . . . His power of painting in words is incomparably greater than that of any other English author; he almost infuses colour into his words and phrases, so full are they of pictorial power. —MEIKLEJOHN, J. M. D., 1887, *The English Language: Its Grammar, History and Literature, p.* 363, 364.

One very great writer, Ruskin, developing hints already given by Shelley and De Quincey, showed what criticism may be when united with a poetical temperament. The appreciation of his æsthetic teaching belongs to another department of his work; but literature no less than art responded to his passionate demand for absolute veracity and his assertion of the substantial oneness of utility and beauty. The most vital portion of this teaching was adopted from Carlyle, but the unequalled splendor of Ruskin's diction recommended him to many whom Carlyle repelled.—GARNETT, RICHARD, 1887, *The Reign of Queen Victoria, ed. Ward, vol.* II, *p.* 467.

Ruskin is always wandering and digressive, imaginative, and capricious in style and thought. He is generally egotistical, sometimes ill-tempered, occasionally even childish and absurd. Many of his earlier sentences were penned in prejudice and ignorance; some of his last, in senile irritation at the world in which he writes; and, having said all this once, his critic should forever and finally dismiss it from the question. . . . Insensibly, inevitably, we recur to Ruskin as a moralist; and it is perhaps in this capacity that posterity will chiefly take him.—STIMSON, F. J., 1888, *Ruskin as a Political Economist, Quarterly Journal of Economics, vol.* 2, *pp.* 414, 442.

In those days all young men who were interested in literature read "Blackwood's Magazine," with a unanimity such as the present age will hardly understand, unless, indeed, they learn to read the "Forum" in the same way. In "Blackwood" we began to find careful criticisms of the English Art Exhibitions, by "A Graduate of Oxford." There did not, at first, seem much hope of interest in articles describing pictures which we have not seen and were not likely to see, but we found these articles worth reading. After the first there was no question with us whether we should read another. Such was the introduction of my generation to John Ruskin. When he revealed his name to the outer world by the first volume of "Modern Painters," the book made a revolution even in the habits of life of intelligent young people. It taught them to watch the clouds, the shapes of trees, their habits of growth, even, as they had not done, and gave to them a new and higher enjoyment of natural beauty. The new generation of to-day does not read these books of Ruskin, can hardly be made to read them. That is their affair more than it is mine. But the real reason why they do not read them is that they have been already trained in a habit of enjoying nature, and the open. This was largely, as I believe, created by these very books, so that they do not need them as we did. The young artists of our time would look in a very cavalier way on much of Ruskin's instruction. But nine in ten of them would, perhaps, not be artists, had he not led the English-speaking race out of doors, in a sympathy with landscape painting and the work of true art, which has led to the new enthusiasm of our own time for the arts of design.—HALE, EDWARD EVERETT, 1888, *Books that Have Helped Me, p. 11.*

His mistakes in art are in some measure due to his fundamental mistake of measuring it by its moral powers and influence, and the roots of the error are so deeply involved in his character and mental development that it can never be uprooted. It is difficult for me (perhaps for any of his contemporaries) to judge him as a whole because, besides being his contemporary and a sufferer by what I now perceive to be the fatal error of his system, I was for so many years his close personal friend, and because, while I do not argue with his tenets and am obliged by my own sense of right to combat many of his teachings, I still retain the personal affection for him of those years which are dear to memory, and reverence the man as I know him; and because I most desire that he should be judged rightly,—as a man who for moral greatness has few equals in his day, and who deserves an honor and distinction which he has not received, and in a selfish and sordid world will not receive, but which I believe time will give him,— that of being one who gave his whole life and substance to the furtherance of what he believed to be the true happiness and elevation of his fellow-men. Even were he the sound art critic so many people take him to be, his real nature rises above the office as much as humanity rises above art. When we wish to compare him with men of his kind, it must be with Plato or Savonarola rather than with Hazlitt or Hamerton.—STILLMAN, WILLIAM JAMES, 1888, *John Ruskin, Century Magazine, vol. 35, p. 364.*

The cardinal doctrine which runs through all his teaching can be stated in a line. It is that men—men and not the works of men, men and not materials, or machines, or gold, or even pictures, or statues, or public buildings—should be the prime objects of our care, and reverence, and love. Hence it is that, as a writer on art he necessarily becomes a moralist, since he must needs inquire from what human faculties does this work of art arise, and to what human faculties does it appeal. Hence it is that in the decline of architecture or painting he reads the degradation of national character. Hence it is that the life of the workman appears to him to be of higher importance than the quantity of work which he turns out. Hence is it that he has opposed himself to the orthodox political economy, with a sense that man, and the life and soul of man, cannot be legitimately set aside while we consider apart from these laws of wealth or of so-called utility. No other truth can be quite so important for our own age, or for any age, as the truth preached so unceasingly and so impressively by Mr. Ruskin.—DOWDEN, EDWARD, 1888, *Victorian Literature, Transcripts and Studies, p. 233.*

His books, so cleverly written, so intensely earnest, were a revelation to his day and generation, but they no longer evoke the enthusiasm that greeted their first appearance. Not that we cannot still find much to learn from Ruskin. He has nurtured his own mind upon high thought, and he would have all other minds equally nurtured. He holds up noble ideals of life. He would see men and women harboring elevating thoughts, pure of heart, honest in their convictions, unselfish in their pursuits, each extending a helping hand, each living for the highest and best. And these are lessons for all ages. He hates sham with the honest soul of Dr. Johnson; he scorns the worship of getting-on to the exclusion of the free exercise of the higher faculties with the unfettered soul of Epictetus; he loves the Gothic past, and he finds little in our modern world to love outside of Turner's pictures and Walter Scott's novels. All else in modern life is censurable. He quarrels with our railroads, and our smoking manufactures, and our modern methods of money-getting. Pages of his books are as charming as ever grew under the driving pen, but his digressions are more than his subjects. He lacks ballast.—MULLANY, PATRICK FRANCIS (BROTHER AZARIAS), 1889, *Books and Reading*, p. 32.

In the field of practical ethics and politics Ruskin's preaching propensities find a more suitable and just scope than in the more theoretical spheres of his literary activity. And his great literary power of diction has enabled him to give new form and emphasis to principles that have almost been adopted by us as moral commonplaces, however little they may have been acted upon, and do show in glaring light the contradiction which obtains between the higher moral and religious tenets and the ordinary working traditions of modern society. He has thus become one of the foremost writers on what might be called practical sociology or economic ethics. . . . He passes judgment not only upon all forms of art, but upon the works of great and sober men of science, on the problems of these departments of science themselves, whether it be the works of an Agassiz or of a Darwin, the purport of whose work he had never trained himself to realize. Such exaggerations may, alas, from a literary point of view appear to be innocent, but in their effect they certainly are not. He will, for instance, in "Præterita" II., page 298, tell us, with the emphatic terms of a convinced authority, speaking of Sidney Smith's "Elementary Sketches on Moral Philosophy," that "they contain in the simplest terms every final truth which any rational mortal needs to learn on this subject." We must ask what right his reading of that vast subject called philosophy has given him to pass judgment in any way upon it. And so, in almost every chapter of all his books, we cannot help feeling that this is a positive blemish, the influence of which cannot be good; and we turn with pure gratitude to his descriptive passages, where there is no scope for this intellectual vice, and where the good that is in him has brought forth fruit that will be the delight and profit of all the ages in which the English language is read.—WALDSTEIN, CHARLES, 1889, *The Work of John Ruskin*, Harper's Magazine, vol. 78, pp. 406, 418.

Mr. Ruskin never forgets himself and never can endure to be in the background. Not in any of his writings is he "the man behind the book;" he is always the man in the book, and about whom the book is, in greater part, written. A man of magnificent generosity "ever avaricious of giving," no one supposes for a moment that he ever gave anything in order that the gift might be talked about. It is not the less true that there does not abide in him that self-abnegation which after he had done good would make him blush to find it fame. He would not be happy if he were not talked about. With this consuming desire to be noticed, Mr. Ruskin's salvation lies in the nobleness of his sentiment, which leads him to desire to be noticed for noble things.—LEWIN, WALTER, 1891, *Cook's "Studies in Ruskin,"* The Academy, vol. 39, p. 177.

Mr. Ruskin laid no claim to any inspiration for himself; he was content to glorify the work of others. When he gave up versifying it was not because he had failed in it; though he has often laughed at some of his less original and more openly derivative juvenile verses, and regretted the haste which led him into their premature publication. He has warned young people against rushing into verse, just as he has warned them against setting themselves up for artists, before they really understand and appreciate the masterpieces of acknowledged genius. But his self-denial has had its reward. In extolling the water-colour and oil painting of Turner and Tintoret he became a painter in words no less renowned than they. In expounding Dante and Chaucer, Shakespeare and Spenser, he has given us prose poems, if I may be allowed the expression, which pedestal him in the "house of Fame" hardly lower than the highest of them. In his case, indeed, the saying is fulfilled, "whosoever will be great among you, let him be your minister, and whosoever will be chief among you, let him be your servant."—COLLINGWOOD, W. G., 1892, *The Poets and the Poetry of the Century, Tennyson to Clough*, ed. Miles, p. 587.

I have never been a Ruskinite, though I have always thought that nobody in our time has touched Mr. Ruskin at his very best as an artist in the *flamboyant* variety of English prose; and I have never been an anti-Ruskinite, though I know perfectly well what the anti-Ruskinites mean by their fault-finding, and even to a certain extent agree with it. When Mr. Ruskin began, as above remarked, to cry in the wilderness, it must be admitted by everyone who gives himself the trouble to know, that he had a very great and terrible wilderness to cry in. . . . He had perfect leisure, a considerable fortune, a wonderful literary faculty, an intense love for art. He was gifted by nature with what is the most fortunate gift for a man of genius, the most unfortunate for another, an entire freedom from the malady of self-criticism. It has never during his long career ever troubled Mr. Ruskin to bethink himself whether he knew what he was talking about, whether he was or was not talking nonsense, whether he was or was not contradicting flatly something that he had said before. These are the requisites of a prophet in these modern times; and Mr. Ruskin had them. . . . To sum up the impression side of the matter—when I was young, Mr. Ruskin's crotchets used to irritate me more than they ought: they now irritate me hardly at all, and only bore me a little. But I think I like his beauties more than ever; and I am disposed to think, also, that he has brought more folk to art than he has ever bitten with his own heresies about it. And these are, after all, harmless heresies enough; and not more dangerous, while they are much less disgusting, than the exaggerations on the other side.—SAINTSBURY, GEORGE, 1894, *Two Corrected Impressions, Mr. William Morris—Mr. Ruskin, The Critic*, vol. 25, pp. 115, 117.

Ruskin early began to boast of his analytic powers, and not without reason. His works are divided and subdivided with great elaboration, the later ones more intelligently but less elaborately than the earlier. He usually employs the words *paragraph* and *section* synonymously, preferring, however, the former term. The section-mark § he often places before divisions that he calls paragraphs. He is fond of compound paragraphs, numbering the main paragraph and indicating by indentation the subdivisions. In his first edition of collected works he divided the text into "paragraphs," numbering these consecutively through the volumes. The paragraphs, even of the "Modern Painters," are almost never heterogeneous, although Ruskin's later changes in these early works result in breaking up a few of the sections. In the "Modern Painters" the sections are longer than in the "Sesame and Lilies" and later works. The sequence of Ruskin's early work is marred by dislocations rather than by digressions. Many paragraphs in the "Modern Painters" would be bettered much by mere re-arrangement of the sentences or groups of sentences.—LEWIS, EDWIN HERBERT, 1894, *The History of the English Paragraph*, p. 159.

Ruskin is one of the most turbid and fallacious minds, and one of the most powerful masters of style, of the present century. To the service of the most wildly eccentric thoughts he brings the acerbity of a bigot and the deep sentiment of Morel's "emotionalists." His mental temperament is that of the first Spanish Grand Inquisitors. He is a Torquemada of æsthetics. He would liefest burn alive the critic who disagrees with him, or the dull Philistine who passes by works of art without a feeling of devout awe. Since, however, stakes do not stand within his reach, he can at least rave and rage in word, and annihilate the heretic figuratively by abuse and cursing. To his ungovernable irascibility he unites great knowledge of all the minutiæ in the history of art. If he writes of the shapes of clouds he reproduces the clouds in seventy or eighty existing pictures, scattered amongst all the collections of Europe. And be it noted that he did this in the forties, when photographs of the masterpieces of art, which render the comparative study of them to-day so convenient, were yet unknown.—NORDAU, MAX, 1895, *Degeneration*, p. 77.

In Ruskin's poetry there is much less of himself than young writers of capacity usually contrive to put into their early work. The great prose stylist, as he himself long ago confessed, made a false start when he donned the Byronic collar and set off to climb Parnassus.—DAVIDSON, JOHN, 1895, *Sentences and Paragraphs*, p. 27.

Painter in words, on whose resplendent page,
Caught from the palette of the seven-hued bow,
The colors of our English Turner glow,—
Silver of silent stars, the storm's red rage,
The spray of mountain streams, rocks gray
  with age,
Gold of Athena, white of Alpine snow,

Cool green of forests, blue of lakes below,
And sunset-crimsoned skies,—O seer and sage,
Crowned with wild olive, fine of sense and sight,
In thy prophetic voice, through work, trade, strife,
The stones cry out: "By truth the nations live,
And by injustice die. Be thy weights right,
Thy measures true. These be the lamps that give
The way of beauty and the path of life."
—BOWKER, RICHARD ROGERS, 1897, *Ruskin, Century Magazine, vol. 54, p.* 715.

The prose of essay and criticism which had sought, perhaps, an excess of point, precision, and emphasis under the long-continuing and only now declining domination of Macaulay has—thanks in part to the unparalleled power and fascination of John Ruskin, the happily still living successor to the tradition of Landor, De Quincey, and the other early nineteenth-century masters of the rhetorical and "impassioned" prose style—acquired a colour and flexibility, and an adequacy of response to emotional and æsthetic needs, in which for more than a generation it had been lacking.—TRAILL, HENRY DUFF, 1897, *Social England, vol.* VI., *p.* 519.

The happy life being that in which illusion is most prevalent, and Mr. Ruskin's enthusiasm having fired more minds to the instinctive quest of beauty than that of any other man who ever lived, we are guilty of no exaggeration if we hail him as one of the first of benefactors. Yet his intellectual nature was from the start imperfect, his sympathies always violent and paradoxical; there were whole areas of life from which he was excluded; and nothing but the splendour and fulness of his golden trumpets concealed the fact that some important instruments were lacking to his orchestra. It is as a purely descriptive writer that he has always been seen at his best, and here he is distinguished from exotic rivals—at home he has had none—by the vivid moral excitement that dances, an incessant sheet-lightning, over the background of each gorgeous passage. In this effect of the metaphysical temperament, Mr. Ruskin is sharply differentiated from Continental masters of description and art initiation—from Fromentin, for instance, with whom he may be instructively contrasted.—GOSSE, EDMUND, 1897, *A Short History of Modern English Literature, p.* 357.

No master of impassioned prose has endowed his writings with more perspicuity of meaning and more force of utterance, or used a fuller liberty of reiteration in placing his chief thoughts before the reading public. And yet these very qualities of brilliance and amplitude have helped to hide from many the supreme value of Mr. Ruskin's criticism of life, especially in reference to social reform, by giving too great emphasis and attractiveness to unrelated individual thoughts, set in single jewelled sentences, or in purple patches, and by thus concealing the consistency of thought and feeling which underlay and gave intellectual unity and order to his work.—HOBSON, J. A., 1898, *John Ruskin, Social Reformer, p.* v.

Among the heroic souls who have sought to recover the lost paradise and recapture the glory of an undefiled and blessed world stands John Ruskin, oft an apostle of gentle words that heal like medicines, and sometimes a prophet of Elijah-like sternness and grandeur, consuming man's sins with words of flame. . . . Full fifty years have passed since this glorious youth entered the arena, his face glowing with hope, the heroic flame of the martyrs burning within his breast, his message a plea for a return to the simplicities of virtue. During all these years he has been pouring forth prose of a purity and beauty that have never been surpassed. Over against the brocaded pages of Gibbon and the pomposity of Dr. Johnson's style stands Ruskin's prose, every page embodied simplicity, every sentence clear as a cube of solid sunshine. Effects that Keats produced only through the music and magic of verse, John Ruskin has easily achieved through the plainness of prose. What Leigh Hunt said of Shelley we may say of Ruskin—he needs only the green sod beneath his feet to make him a kind of human lark, pouring forth songs of unearthly sweetness.— HILLIS, NEWELL DWIGHT, 1899, *Great Books as Life-Teachers, p.* 39.

He is by turns reactionary and progressive, simple and shrewd, a mystic and a man of practical affairs. He has bewildered men by the very brilliance of his versatility. No sooner has the world owned him as the prince of art-critics than he sets up as the exponent of a new political economy. He will show us how to weave cloth honestly as well as to draw truly; how to build character, as a matter of greater import even than the building of a Venice; and he who is an authority on Botticelli must needs also be an authority on drains. He links together in the strangest fashion the remotest things—philosophy and agriculture, theology and sanitation, the manner of a man's life and the quality of his pictures. It is this very variety and exuberance of mind which has kept the estimate of his genius low among his countrymen.—DAWSON, W. J., 1899, *The Makers of Modern Prose*, p. 237.

The remedy of the bad Art of the day must begin in the healing of the national life. "Have you seen Keble Chapel, Mr. Ruskin?" we innocently ask him. "No!" "Are you going to see it?" "No! If it is new, it is hideous. Or if it is beautiful, it ought not to be. We don't deserve it. You clergy ought not to have any beautiful churches. You ought to be out in the wilderness with St. John the Baptist. When you have converted England, it will be time to think whether we may have any beautiful things again." That was his verdict. It was no day for Art, while our filthy cities cried to Heaven against us. So he preached with ever intenser vehemence and skill, giving precision and reality and exquisite utterance to that which had been, in Carlyle, but as a thunderous roar. To this teaching, he gave close study and thought; and ever he perfected, for its expression, his amazing skill over language. His style freed itself from the overloaded consciousness of its earlier forms; and, without losing any of its beauty, became more concise, well-grit, muscular.—HOLLAND, SCOTT, 1900, *The Dead Ruskin, Letters to M. G. & H. G. by John Ruskin*, p. 139.

Since Tennyson died no greater loss has been sustained by English literature in the memory of the present generation than that of John Ruskin. Of all men who have dominated the Art-world of Britain during the nineteenth century, Ruskin is beyond all question and beyond all comparison the greatest, and, by universal admission the most individual and most interesting. What his exact position as a critic and preacher of Art may be, what his rank of scientist or a leader of thought, I make no pretence here of determining. But, by common consent, he has been the most distinguished figure in the arena of Art-philosophy for half-a-century and more, the philanthropist-militant *par excellence*. He is the man who has admittedly moulded the taste of the public to a preponderating extent in matters æsthetic, and, apart from his labours outside the pale of Art, has exerted an influence so powerful that he has given a direction to the practice of painting and architecture that may still be traced in some of the happiest productions of the day. His death has given reason for mourning to many; no one has more eloquently, more passionately, pleaded the cause of the poor than Ruskin—no one (except perhaps it be Mr. Gladstone, his political *bête noire*) could boast so vast a number of friends amongst the great mass of the public.—SPIELMANN, MARION H., 1900, *John Ruskin*, p. 15.

Ruskin's diction is noble in vigour and high in vitality in this work of impassioned intellect, "Fors Clavigera." Not here does he force with difficulty the tired and inelastic common speech to explain his untired mind, as in some pages of "Modern Painters;" not here are perorations of eloquence over-rich; not here constructions after Hooker, nor signs of Gibbon. All the diction is fused in the fiery life, and the lesser beauties of eloquence are far transcended. During the publication of these letters the world told him, now that he could express himself but could not think, and now that he was effeminate. But he was giving to that world the words of a martyr of thought, and the martyr was a man.—MEYNELL, ALICE, 1900, *John Ruskin (Modern English Writers)*, p. 272.

Though there is much that is true and useful in "Modern Painters" and "Stones of Venice," there is also much that is old fashioned, and the newest notions on the technique and ideals of art are not to be found there. But if it is acknowledged that Ruskin wrote the "Elements of Drawing," "Lectures on Art," and "Aratra Pentilici," I cannot conceive that Ruskin's theories generally should be spoken of in the tone in which we might speak of crinolines. Nay, not only do I not think them stale, but I should be extremely curious to know what code of art-criticism —whether in England, France, Germany, or Italy—has more clearly understood and defined, or more eloquently set forth the *newest* tendencies of contemporary art. . . . Where is the art-critic who has more clearly set forth the principle of the division of colour than the author of the "Elements of Drawing," published in 1856? . . . I do not believe that, before Ruskin, any art-critic ever troubled himself, as he has done, about the relation of art to life; and no man since has spoken of it with greater eloquence. . . . Whether we consider the most recent innovations in the technique of painting: the *subdivision of colours;* or the latest movement in decorative art: *the collaboration or identity of the artist and the craftsman;* or the aim of contemporary criticism to delimit *the social function of art,* we perceive that it was Ruskin who traced the first outlines of each, and that his thoughts have not lost their inspiration. It was at the lamp now burnt out in the seclusion of Brantwood that the torches were lighted which at this day illuminate the world.—SIZERANNE, ROBERT DE LA, 1900, *Is Ruskin out of Date? Magazine of Art, vol.* 24, *pp.* 258, 259, 263, 265.

His long and laborious work has no *authority* with artists. Nor, indeed, even with some of those whom he has most prominently caressed and encouraged. At the bottom of what Mr. Ruskin did was the main trouble of teaching not art, but Mr. Ruskin; a perfectly fair thing, as a practical teaching, if Mr. Ruskin had been a practical artist.—LA FARGE, JOHN, 1900, *Ruskin, Art and Truth, International Monthly, vol.* 2, *p.* 513.

As Carlyle said long ago, "everything not made of asbestos is going to be burned." There is, even in a purely literary sense, exceedingly little "asbestos" to be found in the sum of Mr. Ruskin's works. It is not, indeed, hazardous to venture the prophecy that posterity will find his writings lacking in form as to style, and lacking in substance as to matter. He was to an extraordinary degreee a pure sentimentalist, and there are many signs that the day of pure sentimentalists is over. He was not, in fact, of his own time. He not only revolutionized the state of feeling in regard to fine art in England, did wonders both for the awakening of the humdrum, the matter-of-fact, and the Philistine element of English society to the vital truth and real beauty of art, and against the conventionality heretofore accepted as artistic beauty and truth—he made a very deep moral impression upon many serious minds, who still regard him (such is the chaotic condition of our culture) as an evangelist rather than as a mere writer upon fine art. . . . It is because his great defect is excess of emotion, and because emotion in one way or another is nearly his only source of strength, and because poetical form is almost sure to counteract excess, that English literature has perhaps lost from Mr. Ruskin's exclusive devotion to prose. To the preponderance of his emotional over his intellectual side, at all events, are justly attributable the two great defects which imperil his position as an English classic, namely, the lack of substance in his matter and the lack of form in his style. —BROWNELL, W. C., 1900, *John Ruskin, Scribner's Magazine, vol.* 27, *pp.* 503, 505.

At his first lecture we are told that undergraduates climbed into the crowded room through the windows and sat on the cupboards. The popularity and the bold excursions of the lecturer, whose comprehensive view of Art enabled him to treat of everything under the sun without digressing from his subject, even excited the alarm of the University authorities. It is a striking testimony to his power that they actually put pressure on him to postpone a lecture in which it was anticipated that he would attack vivisection. He resigned his post on this question, but his name has always remained one to conjure with, and the cheap editions of recent years have carried his influence wide over the English-speaking world. His complete works are about to be translated into French. In spite of attacks of mental disease, of his occasional violence, prejudice, and injustice, of hostile criticism, and of the grave aloofness maintained by some cooler heads and keener intellects, there is probably no Englishman in the last thirty years, not Matthew Arnold, not Tennyson, no! not Mr. Gladstone himself, whose works have excited so much attention, or round whose person has gathered a more genuine affection and respect.—BOND, R. WARWICK, 1900, *Ruskin, Man and Prophet, Contemporary Review, vol.* 78, *p.* 121.

The name of John Ruskin recalls phases of intellectual activity so diverse, even so heterogeneous, that many of those who pronounce it with a common admiration may be said to be thinking of different men. To express any judgment as to the relative merits of these men—to decide between the claims of the art-critic and the social reformer on the gratitude of their kind—may be rather to communicate information about oneself than to contribute towards a judgment of one in whom, through all these varied aspects of his personality, we must reverence lofty ideals, untiring industry, and disinterested devotion to his fellow men. The opinion here avowed, that the earliest phase of his genius was its brightest, may be partly due to the fact that the glow of its emergency blends with that of a far-off youth. When Ruskin speaks of Nature and Art, he seems to me inspired. When he turns to finance, to politics, to the social arrangement and legislative enactments of mankind, I can recognize neither sober judgment nor profound conviction.—WEDGWOOD, JULIA, 1900, *John Ruskin, Contemporary Review, vol. 77, p. 334.*

The dictatorship of taste which Arnold held in matters of literature, was held in matters of art by John Ruskin who also broadened his criticism, as did Arnold, into the region of social and moral ideals. His nature was a more ardent one than Arnold's and his crusade against bad art, as well as against social and moral falsehood, partook of the Hebraic intensity of Carlyle, whose disciple, indeed, he acknowledged himself to be.—MOODY, WILLIAM VAUGHN, AND LOVETT, ROBERT MORSS, 1902, *A History of English Literature, p. 336.*

There is no Englishman of his intellectual and moral stature left alive; his peers have all gone before him, and the last of the great spirits who shaped for the Victorian age its ethical and æsthetical ideals has been gathered to his rest.—PAYNE, WILLIAM MORTON, 1902, *Editorial Echoes, p. 223.*

Of the two, Ruskin's is the more sunny, more hopeful nature; unlike Carlyle, he takes no pleasure in censuring or condemning: he points out what is better, and the path leading to it. Nor is he so obstinate or opinionated as his great contemporary and friend, Carlyle; in later editions of his work, we find Ruskin readily and ingenuously admitting errors he had discovered. His style is a charming mixture of sublimity, enthusiasm, and sound English common sense. There is no book of his, even of those which appear to be written in the most technical style (such, for instance, as his work on thunderclouds in painting) which the reader can peruse without deep interest. And even when Ruskin's views are diametrically opposed to the so called spirit of the times (as, especially, in his hatred of machine labor), they are founded on noble and very justifiable grounds.—ENGEL, EDWARD, 1902, *A History of English Literature, rev. Hamley Bent, p. 481.*

Great in himself, and greater because he changed the minds of many. But for Ruskin, much of Carlyle's teaching would never have reached people, who, in their turn again, have been allowed to reach yet others. Even if we leave Art, Nature, and the philosophy of Science aside, the man who wrote "Unto this Last" remains a great force, which, thank God, is not yet expended.—WYNDHAM, GEORGE, 1903, *Letters to M. G. and H. G. by John Ruskin, Preface, p. XI.*

His genius was indeed intellectually far remote from that of Dante, but morally of a type closely akin. There was a similar mingling in both sternness and of tenderness, of self-confidence and of humility; but the resemblances only accentuate the essential differences in their respective natures. The one was self-contained, concentrated, and supported by a steadfast religious faith; the other unrestrained, diffused, and lacking the support of fixed religious convictions. Dante won his way to Paradise: Ruskin did not even attain to the Earthly Paradise upon the summit of the Mount of Purgatory. But Ruskin's unequalled observation of the aspects of nature deepened his appreciation of the truth and power of Dante's descriptions of the scenery alike of the actual and of the imagined world; his fancy was stimulated by the mystic symbolism of the "Divine Comedy" and his poetic sensibilities were quickened into poetic sympathies by the spirit with which the poem is inspired. Ruskin was also qualified by experience as well as by genius, beyond most other men to interpret the "Divine Comedy;" yet in spite of the lessons of life and the teachings of Dante himself, he did not learn to control the waywardness of his temperament, or to balance and correct the force of immediate impressions by recollection or comparison.—NORTON, CHARLES ELIOT, 1903, *Comments of John Ruskin on the Divina Commedia, ed. Huntington, Introduction, p. X.*

James Martineau
1805–1900

Theologian, was born at Norwich, 21st April 1805. He was educated at the grammar-school there and under Dr. Lant Carpenter at Bristol, and had been a Unitarian minister at Dublin and Liverpool, when in 1841 he was appointed professor of Mental and Moral Philosophy at Manchester New College. He removed to London when that institution was transferred thither in 1857, becoming also a pastor in Little Portland Street Chapel. He was principal of the college 1868-85. As one of the profoundest thinkers and most effective writers of his day, he has received degrees from Harvard, Leyden, and Edinburgh; and on his 90th birthday (1895) was presented with an address from a very wide circle of disciples and admirers. His works include "The Rationale of Religious Inquiry" (1836), "Hymns for the Christian Church and Home" (1840), "Endeavours After the Christian Life" (1843-47), "Miscellanies" (1852), "Studies of Christianity" (1858), "Hymns of Praise and Prayer" (1874), "Hours of Thought on Sacred Things" (1876-80), "A Study of Spinoza" (1882), "Types of Ethical Theory" (1885), "A Study of Religion" (1888), "The Seat of Authority in Religion" (1890), and "Studies, Reviews, and Addresses" (1891).—PATRICK, AND GROOME, eds., 1897, *Chambers's Biographical Dictionary, p.* 637.

PERSONAL

One of the handsomest men I ever saw. He cannot be more than thirty, or if he is he has kept his dark hair remarkably. He has large, bluish-gray eyes, and is tall and elegant in manner.—MITCHELL, MARIA, 1857, *Diary, Aug.* 4; *Life, Letters, and Journals,* ed. Kendall, *p.* 86.

Well does the writer remember, though it is forty-five years ago, how the circular staircase of the somewhat conspicuous pulpit was quietly ascended by a tall man, thin, but of vigorous and muscular frame, with dark hair, pale but not delicate complexion, a countenance full in repose of thought, and in animation of intelligence and enthusiasm, features belonging to no regular type or order of beauty, and yet leaving the impression of a very high kind of beauty, and a voice so sweet, and clear, and strong, without being in the least degree loud, that it covered all the inspiration of music without any of its art or intention. When this young man, with the background of his honour and courage, rose to speak of the inspiration that was not in the letter but in the soul, and (for that time of day) boldly distinguished between the inspiration of Old Testament books and Old Testament heroes, he completed the conquest of his hearers.—WICKSTEED, CHARLES, 1877, *National Portrait Gallery, Pt.* 78, *p.* 139.

The Rev. James Martineau was not handsome, but what a splendid fellow he was! Benevolently ugly, if ugly at all, with his rough-cut features, wild upstanding black hair, low broad forehead, and swarthy complexion. I loved that man, I studied with him for a year or two, and whatever of good is in me I date to that time, and for it honour him. He taught me to think; I followed his flowing periods, flowery eloquence, and close reasoning with an appreciation, veneration and attention I never have felt for man since; for he fascinated my expanding intellect, because he had not only a great brain, but a great *heart.* I have lived a useless lifetime since then, but at least I have never forgotten that prince among men.—GRUNDY, FRANCIS H., 1879, *Pictures of the Past, p.* 45.

TO JAMES MARTINEAU, D.D., LL.D. We desire to express to you on your eighty-third birthday the feelings of reverence and affection which are entertained towards you, not only by your own Communion, but by members of other Christian Churches who are acquainted with your character and writings. We thank you for the help which you have given to those who seek to combine the love of truth with the Christian life; we recognize the great services which you have rendered to the study of Philosophy and Religion; and we congratulate you on having completed recently two great and important works, at an age when most men, if their days are prolonged, find it necessary to rest from their labours. You have taught your generation that, both in politics and religion, there are truths above party, independent of contemporary opinion, and which cannot be overthrown, for their foundations are in the heart of man; you have shown that there may be an inward unity transcending the divisions of the

Christian world, and that the charity and sympathy of Christians are not to be limited to those who bear the name of Christ; you have sought to harmonize the laws of the spiritual with those of the natural world, and to give to each their due place in human life; you have preached a Christianity of the spirit, and not of the letter, which is inseparable from mortality; you have spoken to us of a hope beyond this world; you have given rest to the minds of many. We admire the simple record of a long life passed in the strenuous fulfillment of duty, in preaching, in teaching the young of both sexes, in writing books of permanent value, a life which has never been distracted by controversy, and in which personal interest and ambitions have never been allowed to have a place. In addressing you we are reminded of the words of Scripture, "His eye was not dim, nor his natural force abated," and we wish you yet a few more years both of energetic thought and work, and of honoured rest.

Tennyson.
B. Jowett, Balliol College, Oxford.
Dr. E. Zeller, Prof. Phil., Berlin.
J. R. Seeley.
Edwin Arnold.
Theodore Martin.
Lady Martin.
Elgin.
Lewis Morris.
E. Renan.
Leonard Courtney, M. P.
Robert Browning.
G. G. Bradley, Dean of Westminster.
F. Max Müller.
J. R. Lowell.
W. E. H. Lecky.
Francis Wm. Newman.
Anna Swanwick.
J. H. Stirling.
Andrew Clark, Bart.
Stopford A. Brooke.
Roden Noel.
John Lubbock, Bart., Etc.

—1888, *Birthday Address.*

In his figure Dr. Martineau was tall and spare. Of adipose tissue he had no superfluity. One meeting him in later years observed a slight stoop, though it seemed rather the stoop of the scholar than of the octogenarian. His features were thin, his complexion delicate. His eyes, which were "changeful blue," were not particularly noticeable until he became animated; and then his very soul seemed shining through them. His head was not much beyond the average in size, but compact, and perfect in its poise. His perceptive organs were large; his hair, always remarkable for its abundance, in later years was bleached almost to whiteness. . . . His personal habits were always natural and healthful. So far from being self-indulgent, his general conduct was mildly suggestive of asceticism. . . . He had not artificial appetites: tobacco he never used; without being pledged to total abstinence, his use of wines and liquors was almost wholly medicinal. His only intemperance was intemperate work, if that can be called intemperate which, though vast in amount, he sustained to extreme age unfalteringly. All his pleasures were of the rational and ennobling sort. Good art afforded him agreeable diversion; he enjoyed music and sought its solace; he delighted in conversation with the wise and good. His home was the magnet of his heart; and in the shelter of its domesticities was his rest, his solace, his joy.—JACKSON, A. W., 1900, *James Martineau, pp.* 135, 136.

He was a charming talker, with the vein of humor which seems always to belong to greatness. He would tell a Scotch ghost story in such a way as to make your flesh crawl, and you wanted him to do nothing but tell ghost stories from that moment. And so of whatever subject happened to take his attention at that moment. He was not in the least a dictator in conversation; and whether you met him at the hospitable round tea-table of his own house or at a formal dinner-party, there was, in all the courtly elegance of what people call an old-fashioned manner, the cordiality and sympathy and interest which not only made you feel completely at ease, but made you wish that the evening might never be done. He was an aristocrat through and through. That is to say, though on principle and theoretically democratic, he sympathized in the old-fashioned way of handling the outside of things, and did not care who knew that he did.—HALE, EDWARD EVERETT, 1900, *James Martineau, The Outlook, vol.* 64, *p.* 262.

Whatever favourable conception I had previously formed of the personality of the man was fully satisfied by the reality that met me in Dr. Martineau—this alike as to the public and as to the private impression which he made. Nothing could well surpass the mingled dignity and urbanity with which, on that public occasion, he had borne himself as teacher to the audience that hung docile and eager on his lips. And now in the private interview that I was enjoying, the same gracious and winning qualities were manifest. . . . Dr. Martineau had every appearance of being in the enjoyment of a serene old age, in the full exercise of all his mental powers. He was evidently surrounded in his home, as he was surrounded in public, by a meet and beautiful reverence, well won by a prolonged pure life of strenuous and fruitful activity directed toward high ends. I shall have to confess that I did not at the moment of my interview with him know so fully as I afterward came to know, how well qualified he was, as master of style himself, to pronounce an authoritative opinion on a point of style.—WILKINSON, WILLIAM C., 1901, *An Hour With James Martineau, The Bookman*, vol. 13, pp. 428, 429.

And now the evening shadows were plainly lengthening. The erect figure was slightly stooped and shrunk; the mass of dark hair had become silvered, and, though still wonderfully abundant, was thinner than in former days; the step was less elastic, and the movements slower, although up to quite recent years he had been able to climb his favourite mountains. The expression had lost something of its ancient strength, but perhaps, in compensation, the innate sweetness and gentleness of his character were more clearly discernible. The memory began gradually to fail, and he would sometimes repeat the same thoughts in conversation after a short interval. But he still spent the mornings sitting upright at his desk, reading or writing, clad in a long dressing-gown, and scorning during the early hours the luxury of an easy-chair, which he reserved for any casual visitor. Visitors, however, were not always admitted; for sometimes now he fell asleep in his study, and, if suddenly wakened, felt a little confused. But when he was able to see a friend for a short time, he received him with all the old warmth of affection, and conversed freely on congenial topics. The grey heads of much younger men brought home to him the consciousness of his own great age. He would refer with some amusement to the superannuation of his own son Russell, who was compelled to retire on his pension from the British Museum at the age of sixty-five.—DRUMMOND, JAMES, 1902, ed. *The Life and Letters of James Martineau*, vol. II, p. 203.

GENERAL

Though we are inclined to controvert some of Mr. Martineau's positions, in the spirit of frank discussion which pervades his book, we must acknowledge the uncommon pleasure we have taken in its perusal, and the admiration we feel for the independence, manliness, and wisdom, with which it is written. . . . The last lecture discusses the "Influence of Christianity on Morality and Civilization." This topic is more in accordance with the genius of the author, if we may venture to express the opinion, than those which had been previously considered. He treats it with the hand of a master and in the course of his argument, presents some specimens of eloquent prose composition which it would be difficult to match in any theological writings of the present day. . . . No one can peruse his book without feeling that he is brought into fraternal communion with a sincere and earnest mind. Every page bears the marks of an honest love of truth, a hearty attachment to her for the sake of her own exceeding beauty and intrinsic worth. He writes like a man who cherishes an unquenchable faith in the exalted destiny of humanity, and who cannot fear that it will ever be injured by the boldest exercise of its divine powers. —RIPLEY, GEORGE, 1836, *Martineau's Rationale of Religious Enquiry, Christian Examiner*, vol. 21, pp. 228, 237, 240.

We read Mr. Martineau's "Rationale of Religious Inquiry" soon after it came out, about ten years ago, but were not much interested in it. Afterwards, hearing it spoken of as one of the most remarkable works of the age, we supposed that we must have done it great injustice, and therefore took it up again, but with the same result as before. It did not fulfil the expectations to which the title naturally gave rise. It is not sufficiently comprehensive and complete for a philosophical treatise, and is altogether too loose in its style, arrangement, and definitions. It seemed to us the hasty work of a very able man, and, while the actual performance left us disappointed, it left us also with high expectations of what the author might still do. The public evidently do not agree with us, for a third edition has been called for in England; and there is perhaps no living Unitarian preacher, except Dr. Dewey, whose works are uniformly received with so much favor as Mr. Martineau's. . . . He who can write in this manner ["Endeavour after the Christian Life"], must be a master of our English style, and have at the same time a brilliant, elevated, far-reaching, and vigorous mind. The style, however, though more natural than that of the volume which precedes it, is not well sustained, and is often hard and forced, nor is the thought always consistent with itself. But such flashes of light, such gleams and intervals of clear and holy faith, such moments even as are here revealed of religious elevation and repose, are enough to stamp the volume as an uncommon one, and to mark it out for high uses among men.—MONSON, J. H., 1848, *Martineau's Discourses, Christian Examiner*, vol. 44, pp. 113, 124.

No one, we think, who has faithfully read Mr. Martineau's "Discourses and Reviews," with an eye capable of catching the system of thought of whose outline and spirit they are hints and gleams, will hesitate to say that, in all the essentials of a commanding liberal theologian and scholar, he is our foremost man. . . . It would be commonplace to speak of Mr. Martineau's eminence as a theological critic. The faculty of philosophical penetration by which he strikes through all subordinate detail or development to the principles that animate and characterize a system or a school, and the concise vigor with which he tests their soundness or disease, give his principal essays permanent value in the higher departments of spiritual science. While a quick and generous sympathy with all healthy religious thought, even when cast in uncongenial forms, makes him one of the most valuable interpreters, as well as appraisers, amid the Babel confusion of our ecclesiastical literature.—KING, THOMAS STARR, 1857, *James Martineau, Christian Examiner*, vol. 63, pp. 96, 98.

Spencer and Martineau are alike in roominess of mind, as well as in the critical and systematic distribution of their knowledge; yet they are of antagonistic schools, and have several attributes strikingly unlike. Martineau is an ethical and religious philosopher, but with an immense command of the resources, and an unprejudiced attitude towards the processes, of physical science. Spencer is a philosophical scientist, not without a fair acquaintance with the scholastic discipline and a strong sense of that mystery which is so impressive and attractive to the artistic mind. Martineau is a poetic metaphysician, whose spacious intellect, stored with exact information and teeming with reflective activities, is surrounded with vivid wonder, and vibrates with trustful and affectionate aspiration.—ALGER, WILLIAM ROUNSEVILLE, 1868, *Emerson, Spencer, and Martineau, Christian Examiner*, vol. 84, p. 264.

In a literary point of view, the book ["Types of Ethical Theory"] plainly suffers from its origin in the author's lectures. It suffers yet more, artistically, from the author's naturally genial and infinitely diffuse flow of learned discourse. His estate is wide, full of winding roads, of pleasant views, of gardens and of thickets. He has certain fine outlooks, certain especially beautiful meadow-lands and mountain summits that he wants you to see. So he takes you to them: but first, by the way, numberless paths open, and must be followed here and there, to show you whither they lead. At last the heights are reached and the views seen; but then you must be taken home again by another road, through more groves and thickets. When you are done you know not exactly why just this route has been followed; and your guide, confident that you have been at all events well instructed, refuses to give you further explanation, save that he has willed it so, and likes that road best himself.—ROYCE, J., 1885, *Martineau's Types of Ethical Theory, The Nation*, vol. 41, pp. 304.

Dr. Martineau, the champion of intuitive ideas, of the innate moral sense, of the freedom of the will, of everything antagonistic to the reigning views, familiar throughout a long life with all "types of ethical theory," mustered and judged them all in the book thus entitled: a work unapproached by any contemporary in austere yet seductive beauty of language and sentiment.—GARNETT, RICHARD, 1887, *The Reign of Queen Victoria*, ed. Ward, vol. II, p. 472.

The general impression that we carry away from this book ["Types of Ethical Theory"] is, that his is an ascetic delineation of duty. The theory that virtue is generated by happiness is one at variance with his character. But in spite of the sympathetic Stoicism of many, very many passages to be found in his work, and without openly and avowedly surrendering the belief in the innateness of moral ideas, he yet "after all" seems to recognize legitimate functions for pleasure and pain in ethical problems.—HERTZ, JOSEPH H., 1894, *The Ethical System of James Martineau*, p. 81.

The strength of the strong man is seen not merely in the load he carries, but also in the manner in which he carries it. A massive erudition may suggest an "ass of Parnassus," an often useful, but a relatively ignoble animal, which of all things Dr. Martineau was not. For, secondly, while it is given the mere scholar to think as learner, it was given Dr. Martineau to learn as thinker: this power of acquisition was associated with a more characteristic power of reflection. Hence his learning, however rapidly gained, was scarcely less rapidly taken into the mould of his thought. Here we probably meet the supreme proof of a great scholar, in that a rapidly gained knowledge may be at once transformed from pabulum into light. Compare Dr. Martineau, for instance, with Theodore Parker, who as confidently as the youthful Bacon might have taken all knowledge for his province, but who failed in the test here provided. He acquired with a readiness scarcely less wonderful than the miracles he repudiated; but he did not assimilate so readily, and something like intellectual congestion was the consequence. Of this nothing in Dr. Martineau. A new truth gained meant at once new lustre to his torch.—JACKSON, A. W., 1900, *James Martineau, North American Review*, vol. 171, p. 553.

One of the most striking things about his contributions to English thought was their style, which contrasted so favourably with the cacophonies of the Neo-Hegelians. Only Mill can vie with him as a stylist among the professed philosophers, and even Mill he surpassed in grace if not in lucidity. It has been plausibly argued that this combination of clearness and elegance in Martineau's style was due to his Huguenot descent, and he was only rivalled in this regard by Newman, himself derived from the same stock. The style certainly reflected the man in Martineau's case. The beauty of order, the nobility of tone, the chastened enthusiasm, the austerity of truth with the charm of sincerity, shone out both in the man and his books.—JACOBS, JOSEPH, 1900, *Dr. James Martineau, The Athenæum*, No. 3769, p. 84.

The victory which the ideas of God, and the Soul, and immortality are now beginning to secure over their enemies is largely due to Martineau's stern and quiet leadership, under the banners of the intellect and the conscience, of the soldiers of religion. He taught, strictly within the realms of philosophy and criticism, that all science begins and ends in God; and all ethics begin and end in God; and that without the postulate of the soul in man akin to God and going to Him, science and ethics have no secure foundation. No other man has done this needful work so firmly or so clearly as he has done. Even the Church of England, with its cry "Can any good thing come out of the Unitarian Village," has been goaded into dim confessions of his use. On the whole, I have no doubt that the battle is practically won against the forces of godless science and godless ethics, and that Martineau has been the best builder, among many others, of a religion, bound up with Jesus Christ, rooted in the confession of the Fatherhood of God, which is agreeable to reason, and in full accordance with the ethical progress of man in history.— BROOKE, STOPFORD A., 1900, *Memorial Address, Meeting at the National Conference at Leicester, Eng.*

The mind of Dr. Martineau was as lithe and strong as his body. As his body delighted in feats of strength, especially as these were connected with the climbing of his favorite hills, so did his mind rejoice in the pleasure of the athlete. He loved to climb the heights of thought. He gloried in the measurement of strength with strength, in the encounter of mind with mind. Here, too, he was fitted by nature and training to mingle with the best. He took his place with the great thinkers of the world, as one who could at least comprehend them and converse with them on an equal plane, even if he had not their power of original constructive thought. To the development of body and mind was added the graces of the spirit. His religious nature was tender and devout. His spiritual life was as humble as his intellectual was exalted. More to him than his theology was his religion.—EVERETT, CHARLES C., 1900, *James Martineau, Atlantic Monthly*, vol. 86, p. 319.

But when these deficiencies are noted and allowed for, the student of the philosophy of religion will still feel that in Martineau we have one of the great masters of the subject, one of the men who have made contributions of permanent value to its literature in Great Britain. . . . If to these excellences we add the extraordinary profusion of delicate analysis of experience, of expressions of original thought and profound personal feeling, given to us in nervous, lucid, and most richly varied English, we can see that Martineau has secured one of the places of highest honour in the literature of our English Theism, and has given us many thoughts of the kind which raise the whole level of man's religious meditations.—CALDECOTT, ALFRED, 1901, *The Philosophy of Religion in England and America, pp.* 482, 483.

I owe much to Unitarian thinkers, and feel it a privilege to have been under Unitarian influences, and to serve the group of Churches called by this name; but none the less do I believe that there is a serious weakness in the current Unitarian presentation of religion, which may be detected in Dr. Martineau's writings whenever he is on the line of Ethical Deism. . . . Dr. Martineau, seeking for the Seat of Authority, makes no appeal to the history of mankind, or to the past or present experience of our race.—MELLONE, SYDNEY HERBERT, 1902, *Leaders of Religious Thought in the Nineteenth Century, pp.* 135, 136.

James Martineau ranks pre-eminently amongst philosophical thinkers of the nineteenth century as the apostle of Christian Theism. This school of ethical and religious thought approximates to the Theism of Theodore Parker, Francis William Newman, and Frances Power Cobbe, but differs from it somewhat in its estimate of the character and mission of Jesus of Nazareth. Dr. Martineau was not the founder of any philosophical system, although Christian Theism doubtless owes more to him than to anyone else. From first to last he was a diligent student and seeker. Singularly open for the reception of new ideas, he sought for them and received them from many antagonistic sources, both ancient and modern. An acute reasoner and critic, he was not readily misled into mistaking superficial suggestions for substantial truth, and the sifting process which he applied to the theories and conclusions of others gave to the world some admirable expositions of philosophical doctrines far removed from his own, and also served to build up, step by step, that conception of a spiritual philosophy on the lines of Theism—organized and consistent, but not amounting to a system—which is associated with his name. . . . His literary style was dignified, yet markedly simple in structure, and often highly poetical. He had a moderate gift of humor, and sarcasm was a weapon which he used sparingly but with effect. He had the faculty of lucid exposition in a high degree. —LEWIN, WALTER, 1903, *Chambers's Cyclopædia of English Literature, ed.* Patrick, *vol.* III, *pp.* 391, 392.

Richard Doddridge Blackmore

1825–1900

Novelist and barrister; educated at Blundell's school, Tiverton, and Exeter College, Oxford; M. A., 1852; engaged as private tutor; called to bar at Middle Temple, 1852; practised as conveyancer; classical master at Wellesley House school, Twickenham Common, 1853; published "Poems by Melanter," 1853, and, later, "Epullia," and other volumes of verse, including "The Farm and Fruit of Old," 1862; established himself, *c.*, 1858, at Gomer House, Teddington, where he remained till death; produced "Clara Vaughan," 1864, "Cradock Nowell," 1866, "Lorna Doone," 1869, and twelve other novels.—HUGHES, C. E., 1903, *Dictionary of National Biography, Index and Epitome, p.* 109.

PERSONAL

Presently the master appeared, my letter unread, save the name, in his hand. He looked me straight in the eye, gave me a warm, hearty grasp of the hand, bade me welcome, and asked me to be seated and to excuse him, while he read the letter. During the reading I took my never-to-be-forgotten mental photograph. I had seen just one engraving of his face. Now I know it was a poor one. The face before me is much finer in line and more spiritual. The head is well modelled; long thin hair almost white was combed from one side over the ivory top, though now in artistic disorder, for Mr. Blackmore had just come in from the garden where he had been superintending the planting of some bulbs for next spring's growing. His face is clean shaven, but the beard is allowed to make a silvery fringe above the long-pointed rolling collar, which is very becomingly unbuttoned at the throat. I was just thinking how my friends in America would like such a picture as a frontispiece for "Lorna" or "The Maid of Sker," when Mr. Blackmore looked up with a kindly smile.—BAILEY, HENRY TURNER, 1898, *Two Glimpses of Blackmore, The Critic, vol.* 36, *p.* 220.

I knew Mr. Blackmore intimately during the last ten years of his life, and to know him in that sense was to love him. Genius apart, he was a delightful man—perhaps all the more so because he did not wear his heart upon his sleeve. His outlook on life was singularly independent, his speech was kindly, picturesque and shrewd. His gift of humour flashed forth on the least provocation, and played around almost every subject which arose in the give-and-take of after-dinner talk. He was an uncompromising Conservative in the social even more than in the political sense. . . . His closing years were spent in strict seclusion. He led the intellectual life, sat lightly on the verdict of the crowd, minded his own business, and cultivated horticulture and the philosophic mood. Although his fame was world-wide, he was not known even by sight to the majority of the worthy inhabitants of Teddington, and as years went on he more and more hugged his own seclusion, much to the chagrin of Villadom. . . . Blackmore was by no means easy of access, a circumstance that was due in part to his own proud shyness. Few great writers were more kind, however, to younger men, especially novelists, and I could give instances of this, but to do so would be to violate the confidences of intimate unguarded talk.—REID, STUART J., 1900, *Mr. Blackmore, Cornhill Magazine, vol.* 81, *pp.* 533, 534, 535.

A strong, calm, steadfast, single-hearted soul,
Sincere as Truth, and tender like a maid,
He lived as one whom nothing could persuade
From reticence and manly self-control,
Insight, and humour, and the rhythmic roll
Of antique lore, his fertile fancies sway'd.
And with their various eloquence array'd
His sterling English, pure and clean and whole.
Fair Nature mourns him now, as well she may
So apt a pupil and so close a friend;
But what of us, who through his lifelong day
Knew him at home, and loved him to the end?
One thing we know; that Love's transcendent name
Is link'd with his, and with his honour'd fame.
—MUMBY, ARTHUR, 1900, *Richard Doddridge Blackmore, The Athenæum No.* 3771, *p.* 146.

LORNA DOONE
1869

Mr. Blackmore's "Lorna Doone" seems to us, on the whole, the best novel of the second class produced in England in our time. That is to say, we rank it distinctly below the great novels of Dickens and Thackeray and Charlotte Brontë and George Eliot, but above any novel produced by any writer short of these, and above the inferior works of these great artists themselves.—MCCARTHY, JUSTIN, 1880, *A History of Our Own Times from the Accession of Queen Victoria to the Berlin Congress, vol.* IV, *ch.* LXVII.

The assumed narrator of the tale is great, strong, modest, God-fearing, clumsy, romantic, poetic, John Ridd himself. He so tells the story of his whole life that the reader feels as if he were listening to a human voice, brought down by phonographic miracle from the seventeenth century, and now uttered audibly in the nineteenth. We see the sights, we hear the sounds, we feel the pains and pleasures of the past. It is a grand achievement of genius to make the life of those old days and nights real and living, so that the observer loses the thought of art, and fancies he is looking at breathing nature.—KIRKLAND, JOSEPH, 1889, *Lorna Doone, The Book Buyer, vol.* 6, *p.* 431.

"Lorna Doone," his masterpiece, has many fine qualities of genius. It describes with extraordinary fidelity and minuteness of detail the borderland between Devon and Somerset; and no one who has read this book can ever forget its powerful description of the great snowstorm. Local character and dialect Mr. Blackmore is able to give with a much nearer approach to accuracy than even Mr. Hardy can lay claim to. Poetic feeling and the glamour of romance hang around this picture of England as it was two hundred years ago. The brave and nobly-born but bloody Doones of Bagworthy Forest, the redoubtable, and, in contrast with them, even respectable highwaymen, Tom Faggus, and John Ridd himself, the hero of the story, such a delightful mixture of honest simplicity, native shrewdness, Herculean strength, and almost womanly gentleness—to say nothing of such charming female characters as Lorna and Ruth—go to make up a work which after Scott it would be hard to beat among the historical romances of English Literature.—GRAHAM, RICHARD

D., 1897, *The Masters of Victorian Literature, p.* 97.

Whatever else one may say of Mr. Blackmore's most widely known novel, none can deny that it possesses atmosphere. The style may be over-strenuous and artificial, the characters and episodes of the story may speedily be forgotten, but there will always remain some impression of the wonderful picture of Exmoor as Blackmore conceived it to be in the days of the second Charles and the second James.—MAURICE, ARTHUR BARTLETT, 1901, *R. D. Blackmore's Country, The Bookman, vol.* 14, *p.* 29.

There are other stories of his which are not without charming qualities, but on this romance alone he has put the stamp of beauty and individuality. "Lorna Doone" cannot be regarded as a great story; it is, rather, a lovable story—one of those pieces of art that live by reason of their close touch upon the most intimate and tender of human relations; a story which, upon analysis, reveals serious faults of construction and defects of style, but which nobody is willing to analyze. It is too long; it drags in places; the manner, under the guise of great simplicity, is sometimes artificial; and yet it captivates, and its charm is likely to abide.—MABIE, HAMILTON WRIGHT, 1903, *Backgrounds of Literature, p.* 183.

GENERAL

A style racy and quaint, without excessive affectation; a good old-fashioned scholarship; a perpetual fount of humour; a store of English patriotism, sense, and sanity—these are some of the good things which Mr. Blackmore always gives us, but which he seems (we do not know whether it is by contrast or not) to give us in "Perlycross" to an extent surpassing most of his later gifts. . . . A certain complication too, and in-and-outness of sub-plots and minor interests, which is not uncommon with Mr. Blackmore, may offend those who like either a very simple and straightforward story or else one the ravelments of which are unravelled in a strictly mathematical and orderly fashion. But these are mere technical objections; the merits of the book for reading are as indisputable as ever, more so indeed, as we have hinted, than those of some of its immediate predecessors. The author's gift, not merely of creating a character or two, but of filling a whole village and almost a whole district with live people, has seldom been better shown. . . . And it is a proof of Mr. Blackmore's strength that one has some difficulty in deciding whether his most elaborate or his slightest sketches are the best. . . . The story of "Perlycross" is too complicated and the characters too numerous for it to be possible to do anything like justice in such a notice as this. But what we have said of it is equivalent to saying that the intending reader need fear no mistake in it, seeing that he is in the hands of a master.—SAINTSBURY, GEORGE, 1894, *Perlycross, The Academy, vol.* 46, *pp.* 299, 300.

It is common report that "The Maid of Sker," and not "Lorna Doone," was of all his novels the late Mr. Blackmore's favourite, and many have been puzzled by his preference. There was much, however, to account for it in the circumstances under which the novel was written, though perhaps it was more especially due to the pride which Mr. Blackmore felt in the drawing of one of the chief characters. . . . I have lived for several years past just two miles away from the "vast lonely house" of Sker and in the very parish of Newton Nottage where Davy Llewellyn schemed and preached; and my love for the book, which began in the old novel-room of the Oxford Union some twenty-five years ago, has of late been ever deepened and widened, till it is no longer to me a subject of wonder that Mr. Blackmore set "The Maid of Sker" on the highest pinnacle of his esteem. . . . It cannot be said the "The Maid of Sker" is popular in the parish of Newton Nottage. There are two small circulating libraries at Porthcawl, but neither of them contains it, though "Lorna Doone" and "Alice Lorraine" are there, and we boast our acquaintance with the novels of popular authors which it is fashionable to read.—NEWELL, E. J., 1900, *Mr. Blackmore and "The Maid of Sker," Macmillan's Magazine, vol.* 82, *pp.* 98, 101.

Absolutely without fear, Blackmore answered to none but his own ideal, and no critic ever handled his work with such severity as he did himself. His humor kept him sound on all self-estimates; his modesty alone led him to rate himself too low. His work will surely endure. . . . Full of the very sap and scent of country life are all his stories, and long before the advent of Richard Jefferies, you shall find Blackmore noting the details of rural scenery through the procession of the seasons and setting them forth, as only an artist can, in their due relation to the mass of mountains, to the volume of rivers, to the life of men and women. Indeed, while to appreciate the greatest in Blackmore one need only to be a student of our common nature, there is another quality in which he stands absolutely alone; and for understanding his achievement in this sort, a man must know the country and know it well. The love and appreciation of green growing things is a fruitful secret of his inspiration. His harvests of the years are painted in such mellow colors as only autumn knows, and his fruit pieces have not been equalled in the language.—PHILLPOTTS, EDEN, 1901, *Richard Doddridge Blackmore, The Literary Year Book.*

His first novel, "Clara Vaughan," appeared in 1864, when he had entered his fortieth year, and it marked the beginning of his renown. In spite of the dramatic situations of the book and the remarkable powers of observation which it revealed, "Clara Vaughan" was regarded as a curiously unequal sensational story, dealing with the unravelling of crime, and yet lit up by exquisite transcripts from nature. . . .

"Cradock Nowell" was described by its author as a tale of the New Forest. It was the only book in which he laid himself open to a charge of a parade of classical scholarship. It gave him a vogue with people who, as a rule, care little for fiction, but its allusions proved caviare to the general, and taxed the patience of the circulating libraries. Cradock Nowell, notwithstanding this, is one of the best of Blackmore's heroes, and in Amy Rosedew he gave the world one of the most bewitching of heroines. It was in 1869, with his third attempt in fiction, that Blackmore rose suddenly to the front rank of English novelists with the publication of "Lorna Doone." Some of the critical journals, he used to say, damned the book at the outset with faint praise; but it eventually took the great reading world by storm, for Lorna herself was resistless in her beauty and grace, and John Ridd was made to tell his own story with manly simplicity and dramatic force. The novel of manners was in ascendency when "Lorna Doone" appeared, and Blackmore was the pioneer of the new romantic movement, which, allying itself more or less closely with historical research, has since won a veritable triumph.—REID, STUART J., 1901, *Dictionary of National Biography, Supplement, vol.* I, *p.* 208.

George John Douglas Campbell
Duke of Argyll
1823–1900

Succeeded his brother, John Henry (*b.* 1821), as Marquis of Lorne, 1837; published writings relating to the struggle in church of Scotland, 1842–8; succeeded to dukedom, 1847; F. R. S., 1851; chancellor of St. Andrews University, 1851; lord rector of Glasgow University, 1854; president of Royal Society of Edinburgh, 1861; prominent in politics as a whig; privy seal, 1853–5, 1859–60, and 1860–6; postmaster-general, 1855–8 and 1860; secretary of state for India, 1868–74, and adopted foreign policy of friendship to neighbouring states, and financial policy of "decentralisation;" opposed tory government's policy in Eastern question, and in Afghanistan, 1877–80; privy seal, 1880–1; opposed home rule, 1886 and 1893; K. T., 1856; D. C. L. Oxford, 1870; K. G., 1883. A follower of the cataclysmal school in geology, and never in agreement with the younger evolutional school, he yet exerted a useful influence on scientific progress. He published works on science, religion, and politics.—HUGHES, C. E., 1903, *Dictionary of National Biography, Index and Epitome, p.* 195.

PERSONAL

The Duke of Argyll has a strikingly interesting and intellectual face. He has long red hair, which he dashes from off his high white forehead in a most effective manner, while he speaks.—LEVERT, OCTAVIA WALTON, 1853, *Souvenirs of Travel, vol.* I, *p.* 24.

He never grew to be popular in the House of Lords, and I believe is not popular anywhere. His style is far too self-assured and pedantic, his faith in his own superiority to everybody else is too evident, to allow of his having many enthusiastic admirers. Moreover, though the Duke of Argyll has shown himself a much sounder and better man than most people at first believed him to be, he is far indeed from holding the place which his manner would seem to claim as a right. He never could be in politics more than a second-class man; and he is not even a remarkably good second-class man. Every commendation that is given him must be qualified. He has written one or two remarkable books—for a duke. He has been a very liberal politician—for a duke. He is a good speaker—for one who never had any oratorical gift. Of all the noblemen who have been put into high office during my time, merely because they were noblemen, he is, I think, on the whole, the ablest and the best. . . . When the Duke of Argyll is not vehement he is rather an uninteresting speaker. He is fluent, but formal and pedantic, and his speeches are not brightened by fancy or humor. As an after-dinner speaker he is especially ineffective. To be heard to advantage, he should be taken either in the sudden heat of some parliamentary contest, or else when addressing from the lecturer's platform some scientific or philosophical society. In political life he has "given his measure," and I think we may safely assume that he will never be a great statesman.—MCCARTHY, JUSTIN, 1874, *The Duke of Argyll, The Galaxy*, vol. 17, pp. 10, 11.

O Patriot Statesman, be thou wise to know
The limits of resistance, and the bounds
Determining concession; still be bold
Not only to slight praise but suffer scorn;
And be thy heart a fortress to maintain
The day against the moment, and the year
Against the day; thy voice, a music heard
Thro' all the yells and counter-yells of feud
And faction, and thy will, a power to make
This ever-changing world of circumstance,
In changing, chime with never-changing Law.
—TENNYSON, ALFRED LORD, 1885, *Tiresias and Other Poems*.

GENERAL

As a speaker the Duke of Argyll has many imperfections; he talks with a pedantic positiveness which has been compared to the harangues of a school-master. His very virtues of enthusiasm and earnestness often carry him away, and losing control of himself, he not infrequently exposes himself to the telling attacks of Lords Derby and Cairns. Sometimes he is passionate, and transcends the rules of parliamentary law; he attacks his opponents fiercely and sometimes recklessly; he has neither the patience, nor the craft, nor the fertility of forensic resources, to fit him for the position of party leadership. . . . Although not an orator he is a fluent speaker; has confidence in himself, and says always what he means without apparent difficulty. He is probably destined to rank no higher in the national councils than the position he has already attained; but by his earnest liberalism he has already a reputation if less brilliant, at least no less honorable, than that of any of that long succession of Argylls who have for so many centuries illustrated the history of Britain. In his leisure hours, he has composed and (recently) published a very highly regarded philosophical treatise on "The Reign of Law;" and perhaps his best claim to fame rests in the literary works which he has from time to time given to the world, and which have, far better than his parliamentary career, done justice to mental accomplishments which, even had he been untitled and obscure, would certainly have given him no mean position in the literary annals of his generation.—TOWLE, G. M., 1869, *The Radical Duke, Putman's Magazine*, vol. 14, p. 573.

"The Reign of Law" is like everything else the Duke of Argyll does. It is far above average work. It would be sure to be read with attention even if it were not written by a duke. But it is not one of the books that force themselves upon the public. It is one of the books that, although good enough in themselves and worthy of careful reading when once they are found out, stand in need of some external impulse to push them into notice.—MCCARTHY, JUSTIN, 1874, *The Duke of Argyll, The Galaxy*, vol. 17, p. 12.

The Duke has laid his contemporaries and those who shall come after under an obligation it would be difficult to estimate. "The Reign of Law" was published opportunely. Physical science had achieved great triumphs both as science and as subservient to the practical purposes of life. In view of this, not her special devotees alone, but all right-thinking men were exultant. . . . While, therefore, we have a very high estimate of both the ability and value of "The Reign of Law," and of each of the papers on the "Unity of Nature," we yet feel that in their total effect they do not present truly the relation of personality to Natural Law.—HOPKINS, MARK, 1882, *Personality and Law—The Duke of Argyll, Princeton Review*, N. S., vol. 10, pp. 180, 199.

Though the Duke of Argyll can hardly be ranked as a man of science, he undoubtedly exerted a useful influence on the scientific progress of his day. His frequent controversies on scientific questions roused a wide-spread interest in these subjects, and thus helped to further the advance of the departments which he subjected to criticism. It is perhaps too soon to judge finally of the value of this criticism. There can be no doubt, however, that it was in itself stimulating, even to those who were opposed to it. A prominent public man, immersed in politics and full of the cares of a great estate, who finds his recreation in scientific inquiry, must be counted among the beneficient influences of his time. The duke began his writings on scientific subjects in 1850, and continued them almost to the end of his life.—GEIKIE, SIR ARCHIBALD, 1901, *Dictionary of National Biography, Supplement, vol.* I, *p.* 391.

Friedrich Max Müller
1823–1900

Philologist, was born 6th December 1823, at Dessau, where his father, Wilhelm Müller (1794-1827), lyric poet, was ducal librarian. He studied at Dessau, Leipzig, and Berlin, devoting himself to Sanskrit; and his translation of the "Hitopadesa" appeared in 1844. In Paris he began (1845), at the instigation of Burnouf, to prepare an edition of the Rig-Veda, coming to England in 1846 to examine the MSS. in the East India House and the Bodleian; and the East India Company commissioned him (1847) to edit it at their expense (6 vols. 1849-74; new ed. 1890). For a time Taylorian professor of Modern Languages at Oxford, he was in 1866 appointed professor there of Comparative Philology, a study he did more than any one else to promote in England. He has published "The Languages of the Seat of War in the East" (1854), "Comparative Mythology" (1856), "History of Sanskrit Literature" (1859), "Science of Language" (1861-63), "Science of Religion" (1870), "Chips from a German Workshop" (1868-75), "Origin and Growth of Religion" (Hibbert Lectures, 1878), "Biographical Essays" (1883), "The Science of Thought" (1887), "Biographies of Words" (1888), "Natural, Physical, Anthropological, and Psychical Religion" (Glasgow Gifford Lectures, pub. 1889-93), "Vedanta Philosophy" (1894), and "Science of Mythology" (1897). A German novel, "Deutsche Liebe," is by him. He is editor of "Sacred Books of the East." A foreign member of the French Institute, knight of the Ordre pour le Mérite, commander of the Legion of Honour (1896), &c., he is LL.D. of Cambridge, Dublin, Edinburgh, and Bologna, and in 1896 was made a P. C. See his "Literary Recollections."—PATRICK, AND GROOME, *eds*, 1897, *Chambers's Biographical Dictionary, p.* 645.

PERSONAL

His marriage to Miss Grenfell, by which he became connected with the families of Charles Kingsley and of Froude, served only to widen and render more intimate the circle of literary and professional friends which has been so characteristic of Müller's life from the first. In Leipzig, Hermann, Haupt, and Brockhaus; in Berlin, Alexander von Humboldt and Boeckh; in Paris, Burnouf; in England, Thackeray, Tennyson, Browning, Arnold, Clough, Jowett, Ruskin,—and indeed almost every one of prominence in scientific and literary affairs,—have been his friends or have been helpful to his fame. This argues exceptional gifts of heart and person, as well as of intellect. His strong and beautiful face, now crowned with a wealth of snowy hair, shines with eager intelligence and the sweetness of thorough kindliness.—STIMSON, HENRY A., 1897, *Library of the World's Best Literature, ed. Warner, vol.* XVIII, *p.* 10428.

I can imagine a stranger on first seeing him, especially if in university or court dress, associating some *hauteur* with his erect mien, his handsome, courtly look, and a certain military air characteristic of most high-born Germans. He was a very peculiar man: his virility was expressed in his ruddy face and sparkling eye, and some ancestral huntsman survived in him to such an extent that when on a walk with a friend he would at times unconsciously point his cane as if it were a spear, levelling it to his eye. The cane was pointed at nothing, unless at some point emphasized in discussion, wherein sweetness of speech was always his enforcement. Max Müller was a man even of humility; he listened to the humblest person addressing him with a strict attentiveness; he looked up to some who were really his inferiors. For his great contemporaries his love and reverence was boundless.—CONWAY, MONCURE D., 1900, *Memories of Max Müller, North American Review*, vol. 171, p. 889.

To the unlearned world at large he was the personification of philological scholarship—which he knew how to render accessible to his public in inimitably simple and charming style. There was no domain of philosophy, mythology or religion that he left untouched or unmodified by his comprehensive researches, and the science of language, which is the greatest scholastic glory of the German nation, would appear, judging from his books alone, to have received in him its final incarnation and Messianic fulfillment. There was no national or international dispute of modern times, ever so remotely connected with philological questions, but his ready pen was seen swinging in the thick of the combat, and his Sanskirt roots made to bear the burden of a people's destiny. He was the recipient of more academic honors, orders, titles, royal and imperial favors, perhaps, than any other scholar since Humboldt, and he bore the greatness that was thrust upon him with the grace and dignity of a born aristocrat. Many were the pummelings he received from the hands of his less favored but more plodding colleagues; yet their buffets of ink but served to throw his Titanic figure into greater relief, and to afford him an opportunity by his delicate, insidious irony to endear himself still more to his beloved public. Apart from his great and sound contributions to the cause of learning and thought, which none will deny, Max Müller's indisputably greatest service was to have made knowledge agreeable—nay, even fashionable—and his proudest boast was that when delivering his lectures on the Science of Language at the Royal Institution, Albermarle Street was thronged with the crested carriages of the great, and that not only "the keen dark eyes of Faraday," "the massive face of the Bishop of St. David's," but even the countenances of royalty shone out upon him from his audiences.—MCCORMACK, T. J., 1900, *Open Court*.

Being a passionate smoker, he, on his part, could not pardon me, in a jocose manner, for being, and always having been, strongly averse to the *stink-giftige Rauchkraut*, as tobacco has been called by counterblast men. He often forgot this peculiarity of mine, and again offered me cigars. . . . In society, among friends, he easily unbent, comporting himself with as much pleasant joviality as simplicity; a true sign of real intellectual greatness. At table, where he showed himself a connoisseur of good wine, he was easily disposed to humorous remarks; sometimes with a dash of sarcasm of the milder kind. All possible things in science and politics were discussed on the Welsh Island and in Oxford, from questions of ethnology, of language, of history and literature to German affairs and the condition of Turkey, where his son at that time occupied a post in the Embassy. . . . Max Müller was not cut out for a politician. It is a pity that the cloud of obloquy which thus suddenly overshadowed his name should have dimmed the lustre of his renown near the very end of his laborious life.—BLIND, KARL, 1901, *Max Müller, The Westminster Review*, vol. 155, pp. 535, 540.

Blessings to you! I was in the holy city of Benares when I received the mournful news of the departure of your beloved husband, the illustrious scholar, from this plane of action to another life in the evolution of existence. So useful a life, indefatigable in the search after truth, one meets only after long intervals. Personally your late husband was kindness personified, and he aided my labours in the cause of eternal truth. When I was yet in my teens I was brought under the influence of his writings, and I have been a reader of his works since 1883. In obedience to nature's law, the physical body of the illustrious individuality known as Professor Max Müller has ceased to exist, but his name will continue to exist in influencing future generations. I now offer the deepest sympathy of all Buddhists in your bereavement; and I repeat the noble Words of our Lord Buddha, which he uttered 2,489 years ago: "Do not grieve at my passing away, since it is natural to die."— DHARMAPÂLA, ANAGARIKA, 1901, *To Mrs. Max Müller, Nov. 29; Life and Letters of Friedrich Max Müller*, ed. Mrs. Müller, vol. II, p. 448.

It may be mentioned here that Max Müller's library, consisting of about 13,000 volumes, besides eighty-one valuable Sanskrit MSS., and several finely illustrated books, was, in accordance with his wish, sold *en bloc*, and bought by a rich Japanese nobleman, Baron Iwasaki, at the instance of Professor Takakuse, and presented to the University of Tokio, where a hall, to be called the "Max Müller Library" is being erected to contain it. Nothing could be more in accordance with his own wishes.—MÜLLER, MRS. FRIEDRICH MAX, 1902, *Life and Letters of Friedrich Max Müller, vol.* II, *p.* 462.

GENERAL

The giant in the old story, when he was shown the champion seven feet high, swaddled in baby clothes, went off in dismay at the assurance that a father of proportionate bigness was expected home presently. This is something like the effect that the present volumes ["Chips from a German Workshop"], title and contents taken together, may produce upon many readers. They are full of condensed matter of so high a quality that the remark comes naturally, "if these are the chips, what must the block be?" The editing of the Rig-Veda has been Max Müller's twenty years' labour. And an estimate of the difficulty and importance of this colossal task is perhaps not unfairly given by inspecting the incidental work which has grown up around it. . . . Treating of ancient religion, philosophy, mythology, and culture in general, their central point is still the Veda, and the records of the early Aryan race as connected with it. The course of this great people can now be traced onward to the highest civilization of our own times. . . . No doubt many who open these volumes well remember their first reading of the essay on Comparative Mythology when it appeared ten years and more ago in the "Oxford Essays," and gave them their first glimpse of the beautiful theory of mythologic development which the Sanskirtists were then just beginning to establish in some settled form. . . . When we come to discuss Comparative Mythology, we find the argument in a very different state. It is true that no one, however prejudiced, could have read Max Müller's "Oxford Essay" without admitting that its views have an element of truth in them, but the question is not yet nearly settled how far the new ground is safe. English readers who compare, for instance, the books of Mr. Cox and Mr. Kelley, will be apt to think that, while such disagreement even on vital points is possible, they had better not pin their faith to any exponent.—TYLOR, E. B., 1868, *Chips from a German Workshop, Fortnightly Review, vol.* 9, *pp.* 225, 226.

We may regret that the work (a collection of essays and reviews printed at intervals since 1853) should at once attract us by the writer's marvellous extent of knowledge, keen insight, and reverential sympathy, and disappoint us by the fragmentary form, and often tantalizing brevity of the articles. As a rule, such collections need a careful sifting and revision, and the absence of such a process is sure to lead sometimes to a needless repetition, cometimes to seeming inconsistency. In the first volume of these essays, *e. g.*, the religious statistics of mankind are given no less than three times (pp. 23, 160, 215), and the elementary facts connected with the mythology of the Vedas meet us again, until they become as familiar friends. But when we recollect what has been the writer's main employment, that these "Chips of a German Workshop" represent the leisure half-hours of one whose day-work has been to edit and translate the Vedas, we can but look on them with ever-increasing admiration. As "the gleaning of the grapes of Ephraim" was to "the vintage of Abiezer," so are these "Chips" to the whole stock-in-trade of many a timber firm enjoying a high reputation in England, France or Germany.—PLUMPTRE, EDWARD HAYES, 1868, *Max Müller on the Science of Religion, Contemporary Review, vol.* 7, *p.* 71.

No one living probably is better qualified than Prof. Müller for the task which he has here undertaken. His speciality, the study of the Veda, sets him in the very heart of the myths and creeds and rites of the Indo-European peoples, and hardly any one has studied them more deeply, or in a more original spirit, than he. The circle of Vedic divinities and their Greek correspondents are his most engrossing theme; but he is hardly less full upon the subject of the Zend-Avesta; while the monotheism of the Semites, the dry utilitarian precepts of Confucius, the dizzying doctrines of Buddhism, and the simple beliefs of half-civilized American aborigines, receive also not a little of his attention. Such trustworthy and comprehensive information, so attractively presented within so brief compass, is not elsewhere to be found by the student of the general religious history of mankind. . . . The manner and style of these essays of Müller, as of his larger and more serious works heretofore published are worthy of high praise. No English author in this department has a greater power as a writer of English than he; none writes with more fervid thought or more genuinely eloquent expression. Of course, the essays are not of entirely equal merit in these respects; and it should be especially noted that one who commences his persual of the work with the first essay in the first volume, the author's lecture at Leeds on the Veda, will gain a too unfavorable idea of the whole, of which it is the heaviest and least attractive portion, though replete with valuable information.—WHITNEY, WILLIAM DWIGHT, 1869, *Müller's Chips from a German Workshop, North American Review*, vol. 109, pp. 544, 551.

Mere "chips" though they be, fragmentary essays like these contain much of the most vital discussion of the day. . . . That stage in language which he calls the mythological is of the first importance in the history of language, and was indispensable to the formation of mythology—of much, too, which is not mythology. The recognition and illustration of this stage, and of its bearing on the development of myths, is one of the author's great services to scholarship and thought; but it will not explain everything that we call mythology. It appears to us, therefore, that Professor Müller nowhere shows sufficient appreciation of the part which the religious sense must have had in the creation of mythology—nowhere recognizes that earnest faith in the dæmonic powers of nature which lay at the bottom of the ancient polytheism. Even in the fine passage in the first essay, in which he treats of the personification of abstract nouns and the powers of nature, it seems to us that he inverts the true process, and looks to language for an explanation, rather than to the instructive beliefs of the human mind.—ALLEN, W. F., 1869, *Max Müller's "Chips," The Nation*, vol. 8, p. 317.

His position, indeed, has been one that would have been apt to turn a much stronger head. Early making England his home, he brought to the students of that country a realizing sense that there was something in language beside the writing of Greek and Latin verses. It was to them the revelation of a new religion. It was not that others had not before entertained and expressed the same ideas. He was the first to make them attractive and operative, —the first who united knowledge of the subject with the power of popular exposition,—who possessed the faculty of clothing the driest details with the freshness and interest of living reality. The apostle of a new faith, he became identified in that country with the faith itself; an attack upon him was looked upon as an attack upon it. It would certainly have been strange, if the adulation of which he has been made the object, the indisposition to doubt, or the inability to contradict his most questionable utterances had not made him self-confident and careless. Secure in the ignorant and unsuspecting devotion of the English public, he felt himself for a long time under no necessity of taking any apparent notice of the severe sifting which his views were receiving in other quarters, though the bitterness of his late expression shows how deeply the hostile criticism must have rankled.—LOUNSBURY, THOMAS R., 1876, *Müller's Chips from a German Workshop, North American Review*, vol. 123, p. 208.

Another eminent philologist, entering the discussion now rife upon the relations of English writing and English speech, had given his adhesion to the scheme for a thorough change in the writing of the English language. Max Müller, in a paper on "Spelling," recently published in the "Fortnightly Review," puts forth views upon the subject than which none could be more radical, and which, if put in act and force, would not so much reform our present spelling as uproot it, overturn it, and sweep it away. His argument, like all his writings, commands admiration by its ability, its candor, its good faith, and its common sense. The very extremity of the change which he favors is a claim upon the respect even of those who cannot agree with him; for it shows the sincerity of the man and the logical clearness of his mind.—WHITE, RICHARD GRANT, 1877, *A Word with Max Müller, The Galaxy*, vol. 22, p. 75.

The name of Professor Max Müller is now by common consent enrolled with the names of famous Englishmen. Max Müller has adopted England as his home, and England has quietly annexed his reputation. He has approached the history of man's development, by the study of man's speech.

He has opened a new and most important road for the student. In his hands philology ceases to be a dry science of words, and becomes quickened into a living teacher of history. Max Müller has contributed to various departments of thought, and has proved himself a charming writer, who can invest even the least attractive subject with an absorbing interest.—MCCARTHY, JUSTIN, 1880, *A History of Our Own Times from the Accession of Queen Victoria to the Berlin Congress, vol. IV, ch.* LXVII.

Although he has excited strong opposition, standing almost alone among academic men, his influence has been second to that of few. The number of sermons that have been constructed from his "Chips from a German Workshop" would be almost beyond estimate—and so much the better. Thus his ideas and rare information have been scattered broadcast over the Anglo-Saxon world. He has been looked upon as a dangerous Radical by some, and by others he has been considered the enemy of progress; but he has held his course consistently to his own thought and belief, for forty years, without swerving from the ideal of high-minded scholarship, which he set for himself in the beginning.— STEARNS, FRANK PRESTON, 1897, *Modern English Prose Writers, p.* 307.

To do precise justice to Max Müller as a scholar is not easy. His genial manner as a lecturer, his clear style as a writer made for him a host of devout admirers forty years ago amongst the thoughtful public of this country, while in India his name for a long term of years has been one to conjure with, and some of his quite recent essays show a sympathy and just appreciation of native character from which most Anglo-Indians may learn something. Consequently, although he himself derided "Mezzofantiasis," many of the admiring public credited him with linguistic gifts far surpassing those of the great cardinal, and some of the notices in the daily papers this week have shown that the idea survives among journalists. On the other hand, the severe condemnation which he received from equals in his own kindred lines of research is hard to explain away. Even if one grants that his attitude towards fellow-scholars left something at times to be desired, Orientalists at least know that one can hardly brush aside the views of men like Böhtlingk or of Whitney (each of whom devoted a separate work to detailed refutation of Müller's statements) as mere diatribes of disappointed rivals. Something, no doubt, was due to the unprogressive nature of his scholarship. This may be seen in observing his attitude, uncompromising to the last, towards the anthropological school in their contribution to Vedic interpretation. Contrast this with a recent dictum of Professor Oldenberg, his friend and coadjutor in Vedic translations, who has characterized this contribution as "eine Entdeckung höchster Bedeutung." So, too, in the realms of thought and mind most specialists consider that he overrated the influence of language. One of his greatest merits was the clear, lucid, captivating style in which he clothed his thoughts. He could make a dull subject interesting where many of his detractors only made an interesting subject dull.— BENDALL, CECIL, 1900, *The Right Hon. F. Max Müller, The Athenæum, No.* 3810, *p.* 580.

Müller's fame waned before his death, and for the last ten years no critic has been too humble to speak of him lightly in his capacity of linguist and mythologist. But the master of a generation ago cannot be dismissed without the meed of praise due to his ability and to the work actually accomplished by him. It is true that he was at his best as an interpreter. His unrivalled style, his enthusiasm, his eloquence in a domain distinguished for arid research, made him and his field known to those who would otherwise have had no interest in the line which he represented. . . . In a word, Müller, even as a middle-man between the inner shrine and the outer world, deserved well of two generations. In his matured strength he was an inspiration, and he always aided his chosen science by his poetic insight and suggestiveness, even when the cause for which he fought was wrong. Regarded solely from the material side, the benefit he conferred upon Sanskrit studies in winning means for others as well as for himself to prosecute their labors, is not a small item in the score of good he must have entered to his credit.—HOPKINS, W., 1900, *Max Müller, The Nation, vol.* 71, *p.* 343.

He had, above all, the gift of contagion, of personal and moral magnetism, which came not only from his faith in his subject, but far more from the warmth and fervor of his imagination, from the riches of a profoundly poetical nature. There is something in this peroration which recalls the moral earnestness and elevation of Gladstone, and establishes another link between these two great minds. . . . By his studies in the "Veda," the "Avesta," the Pali and Sanskrit texts of Buddhism, Max Müller was well qualified to penetrate the dark places of Oriental thought; his philosophical sense, always keen, had been whetted by his work on Kant's great critique. His long years of research into the relationships and growth of language had trained him to see the same mind working throughout all history, the same human heart clothing in words its hopes, its fears, its aspirations. He was profoundly convinced of the brotherhood of all the races of man—a kinship, not of animals, but of living souls. We can see in all this the preparation for his third and greatest undertaking —a task so great that many years have yet to run before its fruits are fully ripe; before the minds of the majority are ripe enough to comprehend its purpose.— JOHNSTON, CHARLES, 1900, *An Estimate of Max Müller, Review of Reviews*, vol. 22, p. 705.

In all his writings Max Müller never lost sight of the religious bearing of the subject which he treated or of the importance of the studies in which he was interested for the history of the religious thought of the world. Not only was the study of comparative religion enriched by his hand, but philosophers also owe him a debt because of his accomplishment of the difficult task of translating Kant's "Critique of Pure Reason." Those who are acquainted with Kant's metaphysical thought, best know the problem which was implied in rendering the German into the English. And one further contribution in the philosophical line must be recorded. Almost his last piece of work was "The Six Systems of Indian Philosophy," published in 1898-99. In this solid volume of over six hundred pages he has given the best general presentation that we have, as yet, of the whole system of Indian speculative thought.— JACKSON, A. V. WILLIAMS, 1901, *Max Müller and his Work, The Forum*, vol. 30, p. 626.

Max Müller was far from being a philologist and a student of comparative religion in the sense in which Renan was both, and his intellectual armor was doubtless vulnerable at many points; nevertheless, it is unquestionably true that he accomplished much work of solid value, and deserved well of science for his services. That science, especially as represented by the younger school of men trained at the German universities, has done him something less than justice, is a fact that must be admitted by the impartial observer. If he failed in accuracy of knowledge, if he could not overcome certain intellectual prejudices, if he did not keep abreast of the scholarship of his time, his was still a larger personality than that of many a critic who assailed him, and who, without one-tenth of his actual accomplishment, affected to hold his authority beneath serious consideration.—PAYNE, WILLIAM MORTON, 1902, *Editorial Echoes*, p. 245.

There was Max Müller's book, which no dry-as-dust Orientalist wrote. A strong souled, sound-minded, eminently human man shone forth in delightful reminiscences of a boyhood spent in Germany, a manhood in Oxford, recollections of Goethe and Lowell, of Tennyson and Gladstone, of Pusey and Oliver Wendell Holmes.—HALSEY, FRANCIS WHITING, 1902, *Our Literary Deluge and Some of its Deep Waters*, p. 190.

Charles Dudley Warner
1829–1900

An American author, born in Plainfield, Mass. He graduated at Hamilton College, N. Y., in 1851. After spending a short time in surveying on the Missouri frontier (1853), he returned to the East (1854) to take up the study of law. He graduated at the Law School of the University of Pennsylvania in 1856, when he removed to Hartford. Here he became assistant editor and later editor-in-chief of the Hartford *Press*, and in 1867 co-editor of the Hartford *Courant*, with which he was connected till his death. In 1884 he took charge of the department of *Harper's Magazine* called "The Editor's Drawer," and in 1892 succeeded W. D. Howells in "The Editor's Study," of the same periodical. He made several visits to Europe and the East as correspondent of American newspapers and traveled extensively in the United States and Mexico, contributing papers of descriptive

FRANCIS RICHARD STOCKTON

Engraving from a Photograph.

CHARLES DUDLEY WARNER

Engraving by Harley. From a Photograph.

and social life to *Harper's Magazine*. His separately published work began in 1870 with "My Summer in a Garden," a volume of genial sketches, and was afterwards varied and extended. Among his best known books are: "Saunterings" (1872); "Backlog Studies" (1872); "Baddeck, and That sort of Thing" (1874); "Mummies and Moslems" (1876); "In the Levant" (1877); "Being a Boy" (1877); "Washington Irving" (1881); "Captain John Smith" (1881); "A Roundabout Journey" (1883); "Their Pilgrimage" (1887); "On Horseback" (1888); "Studies in the South and West, with Comments on Canada" (1889); "A Little Journey in the World" (1889), a novel; "Our Italy" (1891); "As We Were Saying" (1894); and "The Golden House" (1895), a novel. He was also editor of the "American Men of Letters" (1881), a series of biographies, and of the "Library of the World's Best Literature" (1896-97). In conjunction with S. L. Clemens ("Mark Twain") he wrote "The Gilded Age" (1873).—GILMAN, PECK, AND COLBY, *eds*, 1904, *The New International Encyclopædia, vol.* XVII, *p.* 511.

PERSONAL

Warner is rather tall and slender, with keen blue eyes under gold-rimmed glasses, a fair and transparent complexion, wholly white hair, and beard, a prominent nose, a high, retreating forehead, and a look of refinement, dignity, and good-humour. He appears nervous and delicate, but by no means weak or effeminate. In fact, he is athletic, and keeps himself in training. His manners are cordial and prepossessing, and his solid qualities and perfect tact have secured for him fast friends. . . . His house is modest, but one of the most attractive in a city of beautiful dwellings. It is in the western suburb, near a pleasant piece of woods and a wild glen that is a surprise and a delight in the border of a city.—UNDERWOOD, FRANCIS H., 1889, *Charles Dudley Warner, Good Words, vol.* 30, *p.* 195.

In appearance Mr. Warner is tall and erect in form, with a strong countenance, indicative of thought and refinement. When at his work, he wears a black velveteen jacket. His pedestrian powers are good, and in the summer he takes long tramps, accompanied by one or two friends; the Adirondack region being a favorite resort. As an angler, he is patient and expert. All the walls in his house are covered with brown wrapping-paper, or paper such as is used to put down under carpets. There are different shades of the paper, to be sure, and the frieze in each room is of some bright color, which relieves the monotony. An unnoticed, plain wall surface Mr. Warner considers the best background for pictures. —WESTCHESTER, DAVID, 1889, *Charles Dudley Warner at Home, The Author, vol.* 1, *p.* 37.

But after all, delightful as a glimpse of his house is, it is Mr. Warner himself who is of the most importance to those who have admired for years the sanity and delicacy of his genial humor. Looking at the tall, spare, athletic figure of Mr. Warner as he moves about his study, the visitor finds it hard to realize that he lacks just one year of three-score and ten. It is true that his hair and beard are white, but his dark eye is as keen and his voice as buoyant as of a man twenty years younger. One secret, he thinks, of his activity has been his habit of seeking at intervals a complete rest from routine. Thus after a protracted period of editorial and literary work he will take a year off for a visit to Europe and Egypt, or three months for California or Mexico. Only a man, of course, who has succeeded could afford to do this. But Mr. Warner, by filling an editorial chair as a vocation, has been able to pursue literature as an avocation. His advice to all young writers, he tells me, is to follow somewhat the same course—to engage in a definite occupation that will provide a sure income. In this way it is possible for any one to pursue his literary ideals without regard to their money value.—REED, HÉLEN LEAH, 1898, *Authors at Home, New York Times Saturday Review, Sept.* 24.

As a man Mr. Warner was a typical American of the older stock, full of shrewd common-sense, of kindly feeling and of healthy optimism. Bred up in the country, he retained to the last a little touch of rustic simplicity and quaintness, which imparted something exceedingly agreeable to his manner, and it was seen also in the unaffected love of nature, which, with his humour, won for him his earliest success. He was interested in many things. He liked his library and the company of his books. It was a pleasure to him to write, and this is, perhaps, the secret why his own particular public found always in his books something that it was a pleasure for them to read. He was interested also in the happenings of the larger world, that lay beyond his library. He showed himself an earnest advocate of social and political reforms. He both wrote and spoke in behalf of a more humane and a more efficient prison system. He was, in short, a useful, liberal-minded citizen with a genuine sense of civic duty and responsibility.—PECK, HARRY THURSTON, 1900, *A Note on Charles Dudley Warner, The Bookman*, vol. 12, p. 369.

He had the air of a man who had been accustomed to the best society among books and men. His sanity and poise reflected a wide contact with the world; he was tolerant of everything except vulgarity, sham, and cheapness. His ease of manner suggested liberal opportunities and an ample background of social and intellectual life. His humor was the free play of a nature which felt itself at home in the world and qualified to compare varying standards of action, diverse ideals of manners and types of character.—MABIE, HAMILTON WRIGHT, 1900, *Charles Dudley Warner, The Bookman*, vol. 37, p. 549.

Amongst my fellow-students at De Ruyter was Charles Dudley Warner, with whom I contracted a friendship which survives in activity, though our paths in life have been since widely separated. I recall him as a sensitive, poetical boy,—almost girlish in his delicacy of temperament,—and showing the fine *esprit* which has made him one of the first of our humorists. His "Being a Boy" is a delightful and faithful record of the existence of a genuine New England boy, which will remain to future generations as a paleontological record when the race of them is extinct, if indeed it be not so already.—STILLMAN, WILLIAM JAMES, 1901, *The Autobiography of a Journalist*, vol. I, p. 60.

I have heard of an Irishman who, being asked to give his recollections of one with whom he had long been intimate, declined to do so, for the reason, he said, that the best of them he had forgotten. I can, at this moment, well understand what he meant. For more than thirty years Charles Dudley Warner was my neighbor and friend. The humour, softly radiant, refined, winsome, dewy, mixed with wisdom, that was so distinct a feature of his mind and utterance, was memorably to me one of the refreshments that went with his dear company for all that time. But though the impression of it vividly remains, and cannot but be abiding, in trying to convey that impression, far fewer things to the purpose than I should have expected return to me in shape to tell. This is, doubtless, in great measure due to the fact I have already noted, that the stamp of humor peculiar to him was eminently such as to elude description. His beloved shade haunts the places long gladdened by his presence, the echo of his voice seems there to linger in kindly benediction, the unfailing delight yielded by the affluent felicities of his discourse comes fondly back to memory; but the words in which they were clothed are mostly escaped and gone.— TWICHELL, JOSEPH H., 1903, *Qualities of Warner's Humor, Century Magazine*, vol. 65, p. 380.

GENERAL

Our prose-poet here ["Back Log Studies"] takes hold of morals, sentiment, and modes, with a dainty lightness of touch— again conveying an impression that he is not putting forth all his strength—confining himself by certain limits, yet within those bounds giving us delightful and satisfactory work, of the class which Mr. Higginson aptly designates as literature of the Meditative School. . . . As a piece of literary workmanship, "Back Log Studies" is an advance upon his earlier productions. Much of it is cast in the form of dialogue, but the characteristic monologues which frequently occur are the portions wherein Mr. Warner is wholly at ease, and exhibit his most attractive delicacy of thought and style. . . . An extended notice of Mr. Warner's writings does not come within our present limits, otherwise some of the foregoing remarks might be illustrated most agreeably by extracts from his earlier and later works. I should like to quote his anathema of the gas-log fire—a fraud, which no one can poke, and before which no cat would condescend to lie down—a "centre of untruthfulness," demoralizing the life of an entire family. I should like to transfer this picture of King Jehoiakim sitting by the hearth-stone, reading the Memphis *Palimpsest*, or the contributions of Sappho and Anacreon to the *Attic Quarterly*. In his graver passages the language is pure, without extravagance—held in with a sort of dry restraint, betokening the genuine Yankee aversion to outspoken sentiment—a disdain of any thing like "gush." Half-ashamed of the happiest descriptions in the story of his Northern tour, he relieves them with a light mirth and is almost Hudibrastic in comparing the slow rising of the sun to that of the sluggish ferryman at Canso. But these matters are in every reader's memory. He has been chided for occasional slips of language, and his merrier work has been too seriously taken as a gauge of his prevailing motives or cast of thought. The arduous requirements of his profession should be kept in mind. — STEDMAN, EDMUND C., 1874, *Charles Dudley Warner, Appleton's Journal*, vol. 2, p. 803.

"My Summer in a Garden" was simply a series of papers reprinted from the Hartford *Courant*. They retained, even in book form, an unmistakable newspaper flavor. Yet they had a freshness that delighted every one, a charming out-door atmosphere, and much delicate and quiet humor. On the other hand, their literary quality was alloyed by some cheap puns and short-lived poetical allusions; and these gave the impression that the author, even at forty-two years of age, did not fully discern his own highest vein, or—which is more probable—that he did not fully trust his public, and would not risk himself on his best work alone. . . . It is undeniable that up to this time, Mr. Warner's works, with all their uncommon charm, yet suggest the suspicion of a certain thinness of material. He may possess greater resources than he has yet shown, deeper motives, higher originality, firmer convictions. This is the problem which his admirers are waiting to see him solve. Until its solution, he is in the position of the American troops at Bunker Hill; victory within his grasp, if only the ammunition holds out; and a highly creditable service, even if the supply should fail.—HIGGINSON, THOMAS WENTWORTH, 1874, *Charles Dudley Warner, Scribner's Monthly*, vol. 7, p. 333, 334.

Warner, like Howells, is an author whose humor is intermixed with his sentiment, understanding and fancy. In "My Summer in a Garden," "Back-Log Studies," and other volumes he exhibits a reflective intellect under the guise of a comically sedate humor. Trifles are exalted into importance by the incessant play of his meditative facetiousness.— WHIPPLE, EDWIN PERCY, 1876-86, *American Literature and Other Papers*, ed. *Whittier*, p. 117.

After graduating at college, he engaged for awhile in railroad surveying in the West; then studied, and for a short time practised, law; but finally, at the call of his friend Hawley, came to Hartford and settled down to the work of an editor, devoting his whole strength to it, with marked success from the outset, and so continued for the years before, during and after the War, supposing that as a journalist he had found his place and his career. His editorial work, however, was such as to give him a distinctly literary reputation; and a share of it was literary in form and motive. People used to preserve his Christmas stories and letters of travel in their Scrap-books. The chapters of "My Summer in a Garden" were originally a series of articles written for his paper, without a thought of further publication. It was in response to numerous suggestions coming to him from various quarters that they were made into a book. The extraordinary favor with which the little volume was received was a surprise to Mr. Warner, who insisted that there was nothing in it better than he had been accustomed to write. He was much disposed to view the hit he had made as an accident, and to doubt if it would lead to anything further in the line of authorship. But he was mistaken. The purveyors of literature were after him at once. That was in 1870. Since then his published works have grown to a considerable list, and there is time, if fortunately his life is spared, for a good many more.—TWICHELL, JOSEPH H., 1885, *Authors at Home, The Critic*, vol, 6, p. 121.

Warner is chiefly, one might almost say always, the essayist. His humor is not wit; he pleases by the diffused light which illuminates his writings on various themes, not by any startling or sensational effect. American humor, as displayed in his masterpiece, "My Summer in a Garden," is shown in its better estate. Warner's intellectual kinship is with Irving, Curtis, and Holmes, not with Artemus Ward or Mark Twain,—though he wrote a book in collaboration with the last-named popular writer. Truth and wholesomeness, a genuine local flavor without coarseness, and a power to amuse without conspicuous effort,—these qualities one finds in his graceful papers. Delicacy of touch, as seen in his work, is after all the prevalent characteristic of the really representative American humorous essayists, the men who, like Warner, have actually contributed to literature. Those in search of rude and clownish "merriment," may not appreciate the fact at the present time, but the future may be trusted to emphasize the truth of the statement.—RICHARDSON, CHARLES F., 1887, *American Literature, 1607–1885, vol.* I, *p.* 396.

"Back Log Studies" is a maturer and more substantial book than its predecessor, full of wise and witty observation, and delightful in its quiet, mellow tone. There is no effort to shine by laboured antithesis in style, but only a bright and playful fancy, a suggestion of quaint images, and the warmth of a genial and generous nature; in short, that rare quality or assemblage of qualities never yet defined, Humour. The wit which glitters at the expense of another, and exults in sardonic laughter, may touch the intellect, but not the heart. There are brilliant jokers whose want of human feeling gives to their points a malignity that shocks us. Far different is the effect of the obtrusive and kindly humour of Warner. He never poses, nor cackles over his jokes. His sentences have a buoyant swell like the waves of a summer sea, inspiring and restful. Modest to a fault, and sparing of words, he merely suggests a pleasantry, but never pursues it. His books leave with the reader the enduring impression of a wholly lovable man. . . . "My Winter on the Nile" is a book with vivid colour movement, and is full of brilliant bits of description; but its successive scenes are rather overloaded so as to produce after a while the effect of repetition; and the author's pleasantry too often takes the form of Yankee colloquialisms, which impair the literary quality. To be easy in narration and never trivial or profuse is a most difficult art. The Nile book has a great store of information from latest Egyptologists; the scenery is done in a masterly way; the people we meet are real flesh and blood; and all the incidents of the voyage are as vivid as the pictures in one's own memory. These are great and positive merits. If the author had made the book for the English-speaking world and not specially for the American people, and had somewhat shortened the occasional descriptions which have a family likeness, he would have made a masterpiece like "Eothen." As it is, it is one of the very best accounts of Egypt ever written.—UNDERWOOD, FRANCIS H., 1889, *Warner, Good Words, vol.* 30, *pp.* 193, 194.

He sustains the impact of the world with a humorous smile; he sees everything, but sees it in an entertaining light; he is tranquil and observant where another would be bewildered and fractious. Whether digging and planting in his garden, or contemplating the majesty of the Sphinx at Memphis, he is always true to himself—an American of Americans, and therefore free from prejudices and provincialisms, but redolent of the native flavor, unterrified by conventions and pretences, yet reverent always in the presence of what deserves reverence; testing all things with the talisman of simple common-sense, which counteracts false enchantments and restores objects to their real shapes. To look upon the world independently and, as it were, primitively, and to report the unhackneyed and untraditional truth about it, is a rare and precious faculty; it is of the essence of the best type of American humor, which is Warner's. He makes himself impersonal by identifying himself with his own reader; it is as if the reader were writing the book, or the writer reading it.—HAWTHORNE, JULIAN, AND LEMMON, LEONARD, 1891, *American Literature, p.* 304.

His pungent and witty, yet wise and kindly essays revealed to us a truly French perception of beauty of form, and a new virtuosity in literary color. His early work was interpenetrated with mellow sympathy for all the pure outgoings of youth. No one has caught the American boy and girl better; no one has shown more dramatic instinct in setting a scene or in letting a story tell itself in a dry, clever, bantering, paradoxical tone which wins a smile that seldom degenerates into a laugh.—WELLS, BENJAMIN W., 1897, *Contemporary American Essayists, The Forum, vol.* 23, *p.* 490.

He was an eager traveller and a born observer; and he came at a time when Americans were going out of themselves to see the world and to understand their own places in it. Mr. Warner's roots were deep in the soil of the New World, and he carried a very independent mind abroad; but he had a tolerant temper, the tastes and charity of a man of the world, and the receptivity of nature which loves excellence and is quick to recognize it wherever it discloses its presence. From all taint of that narrow Americanism which has its roots in local ignorance Mr. Warner was absolutely free; there was no touch of provincialism in him. He

SIR WALTER BESANT

Engraving from a Photograph by Walery

ROBERT BUCHANAN

Engraving by J. C. Armytage. From a Photograph

believed in having the best, and if the best could not be had at home he believed in importing it free of duty. He believed in and loved his country, but he was as free to speak of its faults as Lowell. Patriotism is to be measured in the long run by a man's willingness to offend his countrymen for the sake of his country.—MABIE, HAMILTON WRIGHT, 1900, *Charles Dudley Warner, The Bookman*, vol. 37, p. 548.

Mr. Warner was by no means a man of the boldest creative imagination. He was not a poet at all. The form of the novel he deliberately adopted, quite late in his career, expressly to criticise most effectively certain dangerous phases of metropolitan life. There is something of the clever amateur in his rather transparent plots, as in Dr. Holmes's; but his shrewd observation, and his genial philosophy of life, make his three stories valuable, chiefly as realistic studies by a keen yet kindly critic.—LAWTON, WILLIAM CRANSTON, 1902, *Introduction to the Study of American Literature*, p. 324.

Robert Buchanan
1841-1901

Author, dramatist, and publisher of his own writings; born, Caverswall, Staffordshire, 18 Aug. 1841; only son of Robert Buchanan, socialist, missionary, and journalist, and Margaret Williams, of Stoke-upon-Trent. edu.: Glasgow Academy and High School; Glasgow University. Came to London from Scotland in 1860, and has since then been journalist, novelist, and dramatist; passing part of the time in Scotland and Ireland; visited America in 1880. *Publications:* Poems, including "London Poems," 1866; "Book of Orm," 1868; "Collected Poetical Works," 1880; "The Wandering Jew," 1890; published anonymously, "St. Abe·and His Seven Wives," "White Rose and Red;" first novel, "The Shadow of the Sword," published about 1874; from 1880 onward has produced many popular plays; became his own publisher in 1896, issuing "The Devil's Case" and other works.—SLADEN, DOUGLAS, ed, 1898, *Who's Who*, p. 244.

PERSONAL

A man of passionately cherished ideals, most of which were utterly opposed to the practice of his day; a man who, while he lived, must freely speak whatever truth he saw, at whatever cost to the feelings or interests of individuals; he was incapable of the least personal malice towards an opponent. His relations with Rossetti furnish an illustrative case. . . . The student of Buchanan who would thoroughly understand his work and more especially his critical work, literary or social—must be careful to keep in mind one pregnant fact regarding him. He was the descendant of a long line of Calvinistic Puritans, and, although half an Englishman by the maternal side, and bred, to his tenth year, south of the Border, he was, in many respects, a thorough-going Scotsman. The Celtic ichor accounted for much of his utterances as a writer, and much of his conduct as a man.—MURRAY, HENRY, 1901, *Robert Buchanan, A Critical Appreciation and Other Essays*, pp. 3, 9.

During the earlier days of the return of the malady I was in London again and saw a great deal of him, was witness to his having become subject to illusions, and heard his declarations that he was beset by enemies and that he continually heard them in an adjoining room conspiring to attack him, and he attributed the savage criticism of Buchanan on his volume of poems to his being in the conspiracy to ruin him. The attack of Buchanan had a most disastrous effect on his mind. It was the first time that Rossetti had experienced the brutalities of criticism, and his sensitiveness was excessive. No reassurance had any effect; he had heard, he declared, the voices of those who had combined to ruin his reputation discussing the measures they were going to take, and it was evident that it had become a mania closely resembling insanity. Buchanan's criticism had a rancor and breadth of personality in it which had no excuse; it was a savage, wanton attack on the poet which he felt not only as a poet and artist but as personal; for, to Rossetti, the two were silver and golden sides of the shield. Though the morbid state was there, I think that the article of Buchanan had more to do with the intensification of the mania of persecution than anything else that occurred. And at that time he had not yet contracted the habit of taking chloral.—STILLMAN,

WILLIAM JAMES, 1901, *The Autobiography of a Journalist*, vol. II, p. 474.

POETRY

Robert Buchanan seems to me a man of genius. Whatever deductions may have to be made; whatever faults and shortcomings may limit his reputation and lower his rank, there will not long be a doubt that he deserves to rank among the poets—a small class in every age. . . . When I have said that the poems need severe revision, and especially need to have at least two-thirds of the references to honey blotted out, I have said all that is necessary in the way of general fault-finding. The other shortcomings and errors are mainly such as may fairly be set down to the writer's youth, or to the natural limitations of his genius. He has no tricks to be warned against. He has nothing to unlearn, though much, of course, to learn. Such as he is, I believe him to be a genuine poet, who may one day become a distinguished poet. Even if his stature never enlarges, his place among the pastoral poets will be undisputed.—LEWES, GEORGE HENRY, 1865, *Robert Buchanan, Fortnightly Review*, vol. 1, pp. 446, 458.

He seems to us one of the few young singers of the day who is really a poet, and who has a future before him.—STODDARD, RICHARD HENRY, 1866, *Buchanan's Poems, The Nation*, vol. 2, p. 24.

Refined critics certainly objected in the first instance to Mr. Buchanan's choice of vulgar everyday subjects. But now they have been driven out of this position, and the new ground taken up against him by a certain school is that he has treated these subjects unpoetically. It is difficult to answer this except by saying that he *hasn't* —"Meg Blane" being one of the finest poems of the kind in the language—though occasionally, no doubt, he may be open to the charge. In the "Poems and Ballads of Life" the treatment is indeed somewhat slight; but if it were not so, dramatic propriety would be violated, because the poet's method is usually to relate his story through a third person who is in the same rather humble class of life as those whose fortunes he narrates. Now in a poem like "Widow Mysie," I think it may be conceded there *is* a certain commonness, even vulgarity of flavour, chiefly because the heroine is a commonplace person in commonplace circumstances; and while there is no tragic intensity in these, the humour is not subtle enough to redeem the superficial vulgarity of the subject. For poetry, surely the level of these lines, which give the keynote of the whole, is low:—

Tam Love, a man prepared for friend or foe,
Whiskered, well-featured, tight from top to toe.

But on the whole, Mr. Buchanan in his narrative poems probably makes his people talk more *naturally* than any other verse-writer of the day. . . . I believe Mr. Buchanan to have given adequate expression in imaginative rhythmical form to some of the deepest special perceptions and ideal aims of the time, I believe him to be one of our foremost living poets, and destined to become (directly or indirectly) one of our most influential.—NOEL, RODEN, 1875, *Robert Buchanan's Poetry, Gentleman's Magazine*, N. S., vol. 15, pp. 556, 571.

By "Meg Blane," our author not only sustained his previous claim to the attention of the public, but deepened his hold as the translator of the tragic elements of modern existence into the common language of humanity. There is a strange mingling of weirdness and reality about the ballad which is both fascinating and appalling. Edgar Allan Poe has given us a thrilling picture of despair in the form of a monologue, and though we are bound to admit that on the score of musical effect the American poet has the advantage, yet there are other points in which the verdict must be decidedly in favour of the English one. . . . All the qualities which are admirable in poetic art find a lodgment to a greater or less degree in "The Book of Orm." It has simplicity, grandeur; beauty, sublimity; sweetness, pathos. The word-painting—to adopt a phrase for which we have no special liking, but which is very expressive—is wonderful; whilst we witness also a felicitous handling of all kinds of rhythm and rhyme. . . . Besides Tennyson and Browning, there is no other person except Mr. Buchanan whose work we could consider it ["White Rose and Red"] to be, and there are insuperable aspects which would immediately forbid us associating the authorship with the Poet Laureate, or the writer of "Pippa Passes."—SMITH, GEORGE BARNETT, 1875, *Robert Buchanan, Poets and Novelists*, pp. 333, 349, 358.

Mr. Robert Buchanan at one time gave promise of taking a high rank among modern poets. Assuredly he has not fulfilled all the hopes of his first days, but he must always stand well among the singers who only claim to form the second order of the poets of our time.—MCCARTHY, JUSTIN, 1880, *A History of Our Own Times from the Accession of Queen Victoria to the Berlin Congress*, vol. IV, ch. LXVII.

At least fifteen years ago I read with sympathy Mr. Buchanan's "North Coast." His other poems I do not know. Of that I retain a distinct impression. It contained true, and even strong, poetry. This impression was confirmed by the two novels I have read. In spite of some opinions I ought to respect, in spite of such a concentration in his writings of all that is, to me personally, so repellent, I have always maintained—twice in these columns—that Mr. Buchanan does possess that mental fire we call genius—a power of grandiose conception, and a rich breadth and sweep in his dramatic delineation of human passions. But he is seldom, if ever, himself.—PURCELL, E., 1886, *The Earthquake, The Academy*, vol. 29, p. 35.

As an abstract record of the spiritual vicissitudes of the unrestful, enquiring human soul it has genuine interest; but probably there will be some, at any rate, among Mr. Buchanan's admirers (among whom the present writer includes himself) who will agree with me in finding that, unlike most epics, "The City of Dream" cannot be satisfactorily read in parts. Its impressiveness is the result of ordered narrative and of culminating interest. . . . Regarded in its literary aspect, "The City of Dream" seems to me a poem which, while full of fine lines and beautiful passages, is no advance upon the author's previous work. Personally, I find the "Book of Orm"—with all its incompleteness and faults of excessive mysticism—superior; and "Balder the Beautiful" has more of the white-heat glow of genuine poetry, while its purely lyrical portions are unmistakably finer than the rhymed interludes in the blank verse of "The City of Dream."—SHARP, WILLIAM, 1888, *The City of Dream, The Academy*, vol. 33, p. 231.

I confess that I am and always have been one of those lovers of poetry—be the number large or small—who have an undoubting faith in Mr. Buchanan's genius. Occasionally I have regretted to see him waste his powers on work and on interests that were beneath them; though in saying this I do not refer to his romances or to his chief plays, and it is needless to particularise further. Of this I am sure, that if he will let politicians and all the other quarrelsome people fight out their differences for themselves, and will devote his powers to creative work, he may take a foremost place among living men of letters.—COTTERELL, GEORGE, 1891, *The Outcast, The Academy*, vol. 40, p. 375.

To compare him with Chaucer would be absurd extravagance; but it is not extravagant to say that since Chaucer we have had no poet who can be more emphatically described as a poet of flesh and blood. . . . For reasons too obvious to need statement the making of ballads—without the final "e"—is rapidly becoming a lost art, but Mr. Buchanan is one of the very few surviving inheritors of the old tradition. "The Ballad of Judas Iscariot," one of its author's most arresting performances, has the directness, simplicity, and glamour of the ancient work, but the intellectual or spiritual conception which dominates it belongs to our own day, and therefore with all its power and beauty it is hardly so representative as are some of Mr. Buchanan's other achievements in this manner.— NOBLE, JAMES ASHCROFT, 1892, *The Sonnet in England and Other Essays*, pp. 163, 169.

Mr. Buchanan tells us that he conceived the scheme of his poem twenty years ago. Had he published it then, one would have had less cause to question its relevancy. As it is, it must be pronounced an anachronistic performance. Many of us who have thought and wrestled with thought have as boys or striplings, written in prose or in verse violent attacks upon Christianity. But for a man to wait until he has reached middle age, and then, after being for years a kind of household god among the devout, to spring upon them a long-cherished but carefully concealed attack upon all they hold dear, may be "smart;" though it is hardly considerate. . . . Mr. Buchanan has a loud voice and a heavy tread: that is his manner. It is unfortunate, but he cannot help it. A man who has been persistently ostracised has no need, he may think, to be too particular. In any case that person is noble indeed, who, painted black, does not end in becoming what he is painted. The author of "The Wandering

Jew" is not the man, we may be sure, to show everybody his hand.—LITTLE, JAMES STANLEY, 1893, *The Wandering Jew, The Academy, vol.* 43, *p.* 192.

Mr. Buchanan, if we mistake not, is a poet who, notwithstanding inequalities, has scarcely any superiors among English poets now living. . . . We see unmistakably a richly endowed poet ["London Poems"], full of imagination, dramatic insight, humour, pathos, and an abundance of sympathy with the unintelligible anguish of life that so often meets us in the lowest human forms. Here was no playing with the gossamer hues of air-spun fancies. There is a terrible earnestness in these poems; and if at times we are tempted to revolt against the plainness with which the almost hopeless enigmas of life are set forth, we find comfort in the representation, again and again repeated, that after all the bad is not altogether bad, and that there is a saving leaven in human nature even at its worst.— GRAHAM, RICHARD D., 1897, *The Masters of Victorian Literature, pp.* 373, 374.

GENERAL

It is not necessary that we should here detail the successive volumes of poetry, criticism, and fiction, which have from year to year flowed from his fertile and brilliant pen. It is sufficient to say, that he is, beyond comparison, the foremost living Scottish poet, and has permanently enriched English literature with some of the noblest poems of the present century. He possesses in affluence, dramatic insight, imagination, humour, and pathos, and is, perhaps, the most variously-gifted, as he is certainly the most illustrious of living literary Scotsmen.—MURDOCH, ALEXANDER G., 1883, *ed. The Scottish Poets Recent and Living, p.* 352.

I find Mr. Buchanan's volume of essays fresh, vigorous, original, and full of suggestion, admirable and varied in substance, strenuous and powerful in style. The book gives abundant proof that Mr. Buchanan is an excellent critic when not too strongly under the influence of personal feeling. His knowledge of literature is broad and intimate, his insight is keen and deep, and his sympathies are catholic. As a critic of poetry he finds room enough in the world for the poetry of enchanted symbolism, and for the poetry of kicking up one's heels and rolling with the milkmaids in the hay. Æschylus and Victor Hugo, Goethe and Walt Whitman, Burns and Rossetti, Shelley and the author of the burlesque on the "Wicked World," have all their points of appeal for him. Nevertheless, his opinions are clear and his aim is distinct. He is a Philistine, and he knows that the name of Philistine is only the name in modern parlance which it is possible for him to bear.— CAINE, HALL, 1887, *A Look Round Literature, The Academy, vol.* 31, *p.* 140.

A little more than a year after the publication of the "Poems," an unimportant scribbler, whose name does not deserve to be dignified by mention, obtained access to the pages of a leading review, and published over a pseudonymous signature an article entitled "The Fleshy School of Poetry." This article was a direct attack upon Rossetti's poems, and fairly reeked with what Swinburne calls a "rancid morality."—PAYNE, WILLIAM MORTON, 1897, *Library of the World's Best Literature, ed. Warner, vol.* XXI, *p.* 12413.

Robert Buchanan was a soldier of fortune, who fought under any leader or against any cause so long as there was heavy fighting to be done. After a battle or two, he left the camp and enlisted elsewhere, usually with the enemy. He was, or aimed at being, a poet, a critic, a novelist, a playwright; he was above all a controversialist; he also tried being his own publisher. As a poet he wrote ballads, lyrics, epics, dramas, was realist and transcendentalist; was idyllic, tragic, pathetic, comic, religious, objective, subjective, descriptive, reflective, narrative, polemic, and journalistic. He wrote rhetorical and "Christian" romances before Mr. Hall Caine; his plays were done entirely for the market, some of them in collaboration with Mr. G. R. Sims; his criticism was all a kind of fighting journalism. . . . With infinite poetic ambition, he had a certain prose force, which gave his verse, at times, the vehemence of telling oratory. He attempted in verse many things which were not worth attempting and some which were. In all he aimed at effect, sometimes getting it. He was indifferent to the quality of the effect, so long as the effect was there, and the mere fact of his aiming at it disqualified him, at his best, from a place among genuine, that is to say disinterested artists.—SYMONS, ARTHUR, 1901, *Robert Buchanan, Saturday Review, vol.* 91, *p.* 764.

Sir Walter Besant
1836-1901

English essayist and novelist, died in London, June 9, 1901. He was born at Portsmouth, England, August 14, 1836, and was educated at King's College, and at Christ's College, Cambridge, graduating from the latter in 1859. Appointed senior professor at the College of Mauritius, French Island of Mauritius, East Africa, in 1861, Mr. Besant remained there for six years. Ill health necessitated his return to England, where he devoted his energy to writing, and in 1868 his first book, "Studies in Early French Poetry," appeared. From this time to 1874 he was a frequent contributor to various newspapers and periodicals, forming (1871) a literary partnership with James Rice, which was one of the happiest known to letters. This alliance remained unbroken until Rice died in 1882, and among the books that resulted may be mentioned "The Golden Butterfly" (1876), "Ready Money Mortiboy" (1872), and "The Seamy Side" (1881). Thereafter Mr. Besant devoted himself principally to writing novels, among which are "All Sorts and Conditions of Men" (1882), which is perhaps the best known, and practically started the social movement resulting in the building of the People's Palace in London; "Dorothy Forster" (1896), "The City of Refuge" (1896), and "The Orange Girl" (1898). Of his essays the most notable are, "The French Humorists," "Rabelais," and lives of "Coligny," "Whittington," "Edward Palmer," and "Richard Jefferies" (1892), "South London" (1898), and "East London" (1900). . . . Sir Walter founded in 1884 the Society of Authors, an organization designed to secure for authors, especially the young and inexperienced, fair treatment at the hands of the publishers. He was knighted in 1895.—COLBY, FRANK MOORE, ed. 1902, *The International Year Book for 1901, p.* 110.

PERSONAL

Urbanity—that, to put it in one word, is the first characteristic which comes into one's mind when one thinks of Walter Besant. He is always the same: calm, cultured, polished. A "traveled" gentleman, a man who has seen many countries and many peoples, a university man and a scholar, he never fails to impress those who meet him with a sense of his innate kindliness of heart and of his cultivated charm. Nobody who wanted help—and deserved it—ever approached the author of "All Sorts and Conditions of Men" in vain. . . . Mr. Besant's feelings towards Woman amount almost to reverence. She is either a goddess—a superior being who must be placed upon a pedestal, and to whom man must perpetually offer up incense and bring gifts—or she is the sweet sharer of his domestic joys, in which case she has to sit at home by the fireside while Man goes out cheerfully to work and fight, bringing home his spoils and his golden guineas to throw them in her lap. These have been his views from youth up; you may feel them, expressed or implied, in any one of his books. Woman is divine, and Woman must reign.—UNDERHILL, JOHN, 1893, *Mr. Walter Besant: a Character Sketch, Review of Reviews, vol.* 8, *pp.* 436, 437.

I am very sorry for Sir Walter Besant. He has always had a place in my heart with the other Knights of fame—the good souls who mean so well, yet who are always on the side of the loaves and fishes and the big battalions. I am quite sure that he hates cruelty and wrong just as much as I do, and is incapable of a brutal thought or deed. But the mischief is that his very amiability leads him astray. I blame him not for loving and defending his fellow craftsmen; for kindling with indignation when he witnesses what he considers "a venomous attack" on a noble reputation. I am quite sure, indeed, that he would defend even the malefactor Buchanan, if he thought him subjected to cruelty and cowardly maltreatment. But alas, although he is kindly, he is not wise.—BUCHANAN, ROBERT, 1900, *The Ethics of Criticism, Contemporary Review, vol.* 77, *p.* 229.

Sir Walter Besant was a short, stout, thick-set man. His hair was iron-gray, he wore a full beard and had a ruddy face. His large, clear eyes looked at you through gold-rimmed spectacles. His manner was simple and sincere; his words were direct and to the point. He was a type of the John Bull whom we all love. . . . Sir Walter, keen on any subject, was the keenest of all the diners on the subject of America. He had been there, had known many Americans, had anyway and always been an enthusiast in promoting the friendship between England and America, and especially had he shown it in using his very exceptional and accurate knowledge of the conditions obtaining in the book-markets of London and New York to bring about international copyright—perhaps not so much for its own sake as to emphasize the solidarity of the traditions of English and American literature. On the very day of his death, indeed, he was to have presided at the Atlantic Union's banquet; he was one of the organizers of the Union. He was at once the most English and the least insular of Englishmen.—BALDWIN, ELBERT F., 1901, *The Founder of the People's Palace, The Outlook, vol.* 68, *p.* 571.

A quality of Sir Walter Besant's autobiography must be touched upon—its modesty. It will only be touched upon, for to thrust praise upon one who shrank so from praise is somewhat of an outrage. The modesty in his autobiography is a fault that he would never have corrected, and throughout his record of his life he studiously underrates himself, hardly at any time assuming credit for aught but industry. . . . He never revised the manuscript as a whole, an important fact, because it was his habit to make considerable corrections in all his written work. Yet it is certain that he intended his autobiograpy to be published. For my own part, though I am sure that he would have improved the autobiography in certain directions if he could have followed the promptings of second thoughts, I am equally sure that the work as it stands must have a useful, nay, a noble influence. A scholar who was never a pedant, a beautiful dreamer who was a practical teacher, a modest and sincere man speaks in its pages, and teaches with conviction a brave scheme of life.— SPRIGGE, S. SQUIRE, 1902, *Autobiography of Sir Walter Besant, A Prefatory Note, pp.* XXIII, XXVII.

GENERAL

I am more deeply interested than I can tell you in "All Sorts and Conditions of Men." It is the first by Besant that I have read. It affects me like the perfected fruit of some glorious tree which my dear husband and I had a dim dream of planting more than thirty years ago, and which we did, in our ignorance and incapacity, attempt to plant in soil not properly prepared and far too early in the season. I cannot tell you, dear Nannie, how it has recalled the hopes and dreams of a time which, by the overruling providence of God, was so disastrous to us. It is a beautiful essay on the dignity of labour.—HOWITT, MARY, 1866, *Letter to Miss Leigh Smith, Aug.* 11; *Autobiography, ed. her Daughter, vol.* II, *p.* 338.

Mr. Besant so genial, so friendly, with so persuasive and humorous a vein of whim. . . . The impersonation of good nature.—STEVENSON, ROBERT LOUIS, 1881, *A Humble Remonstrance, Memories and Portraits, p.* 344.

It is not the intention of this article to offer a literary criticism on Mr. Besant's novels. But it seems hard to ignore the graceful handling of both plot and local character in "All in a Garden Fair," the wit and sarcasm of "The Seamy Side," the ingenious weaving of an impossible situation in "All Sorts and Conditions of Men" and in the "Children of Gibeon," and above all the telling dramatic character of special scenes in each and all. But many readers seek for much more than mere amusement in these pages, and the founding of the People's Palace is a brilliant proof not only of Mr. Besant's resources in the way of suggestion, but also of the prompt readiness of the wealthier classes to forward any scheme that offers a fair hope of giving comfort and relief to the working people. The most satisfactory feature in Mr. Besant's treatment of the methods by which such help can be extended lies in the fact that all the plans which he puts forward have already been tested and tried in various places.— WORTLEY-STUART, JANE, 1887, *The East End as Represented by Mr. Besant, Nineteenth Century, vol.* 22, *p.* 362.

One of the few real novelists we have left.— ASHBY-STERRY, J., 1890, *English Notes, The Book Buyer, p.* 373.

A book ["Dorothy Forster"], which, according to many, is the best thing of its kind that has appeared in this country since the publication of "Esmond" in 1852. It deals with the history of the unfortunate Earl of Derwentwater—he who led the brief but romantic Northumbrian rebellion in 1715. Mr. Besant mastered first of all the history of that rebellion. Then he studied carefully from printed books and from manuscript records the story of the family concerning which he had decided to write. Next he made four journeys to Northumberland, walked from end to end of the county, and saw every thing there is to be seen in it. All this had to be done before he could put pen to paper, so to speak.—UNDERHILL, JOHN, 1893, *Mr. Walter Besant: A Character Sketch, Review of Reviews, vol. 8, p. 433.*

He appeals to a larger body of readers than either Meredith or Hardy, his subjects and his treatment alike commending themselves to the general taste. No one knows better the art of handling delicate subjects without offence. His tales, moreover, require just that amount of thought that yields enjoyment—they never spoil pleasure by a sense of effort. They show a knowledge of life and character that may not be so subtle and intuitive as that of the novelists just referred to, but it is considerable, and gives the impression of having been gleaned from an intimate personal acquaintance with human nature under various conditions and in various social spheres. His plots are ingenious, and are enlivened by an abundance of incident and adventure. The characters are sharply outlined and well sustained. He has a pleasant humour, and a style that never tortures by its complexity of affectations. To all these qualities of the successful novelist, Besant unites the heart of the philanthropist and social reformer, and an attitude, generous and hopeful even towards life in its baser and less attractive forms.—GRAHAM, RICHARD D., 1897, *The Masters of Victorian Literature, p. 113.*

Rarely have a novelist's books better reflected a novelist's personality. Despite some later ventures which do not rise in point of charm to his earlier romances, despite apparent over-attention paid to certain phases of thought—as to the subject of heredity, for instance, in "The Changeling" or in "The Fourth Generation"—despite the desire that he might write less prodigiously and not spread out his stories thinly; despite the wish that he might return to the peculiar vividness and vivacity of "The Children of Gibeon," for example, the world's verdict will probably be that Sir Walter Besant never wrote an unwholesome or an unentertaining book. . . . Sir Walter Besant's transcripts of life meant entire justice to all classes—high and low, rich and poor. In his passion for humanizing society, paupers and princes were ever alike to him, for he was one of the few Londoners equally at home in the East End and the West End. He knew as much about the anarchist holding Sunday afternoon meetings at Victoria Park and the riff-raff who gathered to listen as he did about the Earl of Rosebery at Berkeley Square— and that was a great deal.—BALDWIN, ELBERT F., 1901, *The Founder of the People's Palace, The Outlook, vol. 68, p. 572.*

Sir Walter Besant was a clear-headed man who delighted in thinking out mental and social problems for himself, and detested anything that savoured of the incomprehensible. In more than one of his novels an important situation is the exposure of the vain pretension of one of the characters to extraordinary powers—powers of supernatural achievement, powers of discrimination or criticism of higher and more delicate character than those granted to ordinary mortals. He was ready to allow that we now see only through a glass darkly; but he was not ready to allow that any form of ordination would make one man see further than another, nor to believe that ceremonial might help insight by helping faith. Feeling deeply as he did the mystery of immortality, he resented any assumption on the part of a class of ability to see further into the mystery than other persons. Sir Walter Besant was, it must always be remembered, a scholar—and so successful a scholar that although in his modest record of his achievements he makes light of what he did as a young man, it is quite clear that he was from childhood an intellectual leader. His natural place was at the head.—SPRIGGE, S. SQUIRE, 1902, *Autobiography of Sir Walter Besant, A Prefatory Note, p. XII.*

William Stubbs
1825–1901

Bishop of Oxford. Born at Knaresborough, 21st June 1825, the son of a solicitor, he was educated first at Ripon Grammar School, whence he passed to Christ Church, Oxford, where in 1848 he graduated with a classical first-class. He was immediately elected to a fellowship at Trinity College, and took orders and became vicar of Navestock, Essex, in 1850. He was librarian to Archbishop Longley at Lambeth Palace from 1862 to 1868;

and in 1866 was appointed Regius Professor of Modern History at Oxford. This he retained until 1884, when he was made Bishop of Chester. In 1889 he was translated to the See of Oxford. Thus during the best years of his life his official duties were fortunately not so heavy as to hinder his historical work. In 1858 he published "Registrum Sacrum Anglicanum," an attempt to exhibit the course of Episcopal succession in England; and in 1863 he issued a translation of Mosheim's "Institutes of Ecclesiastical History," thoroughly revised and modernised. The two works, however, which gave Bishop Stubbs his distinctive reputation for historical acumen, impartiality, and erudition, are—"Select Charters and other illustrations of English Constitutional History" from the earliest period to the reign of Edward I. (1870); and the "Constitutional History of England in its origin and Development" down to the accession of the House of Tudor (1874-1878). He also wrote "The Early Plantagenets," in Longman's Epochs of Modern History (1876), and in 1886 published "Seventeen Lectures" on the study of Mediæval and Modern History. He edited numerous volumes of chronicles, &c., for the Rolls Series.—GILBERT, HENRY, 1902, *The Literary Year-Book*, p. 76.

PERSONAL

Bishop Stubbs's character was essentially of an English type; in its logic, its absence of extreme partisanship, and its balanced judgment. His love of humour was not the least attribute of this native distinction; many of his dry or merely funny sayings gave him more credit as a man than conventional minds were willing to allow to a bishop.—GILBERT, HENRY, 1902, *The Literary Year-Book*, p. 77.

GENERAL

This is ["Constitutional History of England"] incomparably superior to all other general authorities on the period of which it treats. . . . With this spirit of sober earnestness, the author has brought to his work unrivalled familiarity with the original sources of information, untiring industry, coolness of judgment, and keenness of discrimination. Every student of English constitutional history should make this his text-book and his chief authority. By some students it may be deemed dry; but all such should remember that nine-tenths of all fruitful work is drudgery; and, if they find it impossible to take an interest in this work, they may as well abandon all hope of acquiring any comprehensive knowledge of the subject.—ADAMS, CHARLES KENDALL, 1882, *A Manual of Historical Literature*, p. 477.

Dr. Stubbs stands by universal recognition at the head of English historical scholars. There is hardly an aspect of English mediæval history on which he has not thrown new light, while in constitutional and ecclesiastical history his work is quite unique. He unites to colossal learning and unwearied research a thoroughness and patience surpassing that of the German scholar, and historical power and insight of the highest kind. In matters of fact he is the most accurate and trustworthy of all historians, and it has been said that he never makes a mistake. His judgment is invariably sober and impartial, and his only object is to find out the truth. His strong ecclesiastical and political sympathies only serve to make more real and vivid to him the continuity of Church and Constitution. As a writer he is always strong and clear.—SANDERS, LLOYD C., ed., 1887, *Celebrities of the Century*, p. 962.

Shares with Professor Freeman the distinction of being the most learned, painstaking, and reliable of the historians of the earlier periods of British history, and follows the same methods of historical research and composition.—GRAHAM, RICHARD D., 1897, *The Masters of Victorian Literature*, p. 217.

Probably no one man has done so much to throw light on the obscure by-ways of history.—SHORTER, CLEMENT, 1897, *Victorian Literature*, p. 79.

No other Englishman has so completely displayed to the world the whole business of the historian from the winning of the raw material to the narrating and generalising. We are taken behind the scenes and shown the ropes and pulleys; we are taken into the laboratory and shown the unanalysed stuff, the retorts and test tubes; or rather we are allowed to see the organic growth of history in an historian's mind and are encouraged to use the microscope. This "practical demonstration," if we may so call it, of the historian's art and science from the preliminary hunt for manuscripts, through the work of collation and filiation and minute criticism, onward to the perfected tale, the eloquence and the reflections, has been of incalculable benefit to the cause of history in England and far more effective than any abstract discourse on methodology could be. In this respect we must look to the very greatest among the Germans to find the peer of Dr. Stubbs, and we must remember that a Mommsen's productive days are cut short by a bishopric.—MAITLAND, F. W., 1901, *William Stubbs, Bishop of Oxford, English Historical Review, vol.* 16,*p.* 419.

Perhaps no Englishman of learning, certainly no English historian, has left behind him so large a number of works of the highest excellence. . . . No one who knew anything of the Bishop's work doubted that one of his characteristic excellences was due to the fact that he was a theologian as well as a historian. Much that has been dark to other writers on mediæval history was clear to him because he knew the theology of the Fathers and the philosophy of the schoolmen as well as the chronicles of the monks and the laws of the kings. The extraordinary width of his reading in ancient and modern literature was another special feature which gave distinction to his work. It gave, too, it may be added, inimitable humor to his lectures. . . . William Stubbs was a great historian in the widest sense. Men in high place know too that he was a wise and great man. And those who have worked under him, as historian or as Bishop, remember, most of all, the generosity, the sincerity, the beauty, of his character.—HUTTON, W. H., 1901, *William Stubbs Bishop of Oxford, Literature.*

Perhaps constitutional history does not lend itself either to humor or to eloquence. At any rate, Stubbs was more eminent as a historian than as a man of letters. For evidence of his ability to write with vigour and point the reader must go either to his little book on the Early Plantagenets, his only contribution to the innumerable manuals which have been produced in such profusion by later historians, or preferably to the Prefaces in the Rolls Series. Since Stubbs's death these Prefaces have been collected and re-published in a separate volume, and they will probably prove more attractive to the general reader than the "Constitutional History," which is too solid and substantial for the ordinary appetite.—DODGE, RICHARD, 1903, *Chambers's Cyclopædia of English Literature,* ed. Patrick, *vol.* III, *p.* 629.

Mandell Creighton
1843–1901

Bishop of London; fellow of Merton College, Oxford, 1866; B. A., 1867; tutor; held living of Embleton, Northumberland, 1875-84; rural dean of Alnwick, 1879; took prominent part in organising new diocese of Newcastle, 1881, was examining chaplain to Bishop Wilberforce, 1882; honorary canon of Newcastle, 1883; published, 1882, the first two volumes of his "History of the Papacy" (vols. iii. and iv., appearing in 1887, vol. v., 1894); honorary D.D., Cambridge; first Dixie professor of ecclesiastical history, and fellow of Emanuel College, Cambridge, 1884; first editor of "English Historical Review," 1886-91; canon of Worcester, 1885; canon of Windsor, 1890; bishop of Peterborough, 1891; represented English church at coronation of Emperor Nicholas II. at Moscow, 1896; first president of Church Historical Society, 1894-1901; Hulsean lecturer, 1893-4, and Rede lecturer, 1895, at Cambridge; Romanes lecturer at Oxford, 1896; bishop of London, 1897; opposed the extravagances of some of the ritualistic clergy; D. D. Oxford and Cambridge; Hon. LL.D. Glasgow and Harvard; Hon. D.C.L. Oxford and Durham; Hon. Litt. D. Durham. His works include "The Age of Elizabeth," 1876; "Cardinal Wolsey," 1888; "Queen Elizabeth," 1896; and numerous sermons, lectures, and historical and other writings. He contributed several memoirs to the "Dictionary of National Biography."—HUGHES, C. E., 1903, *Dictionary of National Biography, Index and Epitome, p.* 296.

PERSONAL

As a preacher, Creighton improved after he became a bishop. In earlier days, he had been dull and dry in the pulpit; of all exercises of his talent, I used to think this the one in which he shone the least. But he was an interesting lecturer, an uncertain although occasionally felicitous orator, and an unrivaled after-dinner speaker. . . . On all ceremonial and professional occasions Creighton rose to the event. He could so hold himself as to be the most dignified figure in England. . . . He was noticeably tall, lean, square-shouldered. All through his youth and early middle age his frame was sinewy, like that of a man accustomed to athletic exercises, although he played no games. His head was held erect, the cold blue-gray eyes ever on the alert. His hair was red, and he wore a bushy beard, which was lately beginning to turn grizzled. The clearness of his pink complexion and the fineness and smoothness of his skin were noticeable quite late on in his life. The most remarkable feature of his face, without doubt, was his curious mouth, sensitive and mobile, yet constantly closing with a snap in the act of will. Nothing was more notable and pleasing than the way in which his severe, keen face, braced by the aquiline nose to a disciplinarian austerity, lightened up and softened with this incessantly recurrent smile. — GOSSE, EDMUND, 1901, *Mandell Creighton Bishop of London, Atlantic Monthly, vol.* 87, *p.* 688.

There was something singularly attractive and also singularly Christian in the kindness which underlay Dr. Creighton's superficial irony and cynicism. His pecuniary generosity, perhaps the cheapest form of the virtue, is known to have been great. His hospitality was unbounded, and seemed to be part of his nature. There was nothing of the recluse in him. He really and truly loved all sorts and conditions of men. He also, I fancy, felt that most of them had rather a dull time, and he was the more determined that they should not be dull when they were with him. He and Mrs. Creighton adopted the pleasant theory that Fulham was a country-house, to which Londoners might be asked from Saturday till Monday. To his friends the Bishop was more than kind; he was sympathetic, warm-hearted, and affectionate. And he was always the same. Whatever worries he might have in his diocese, he did not inflict them, or the depression they must have caused, upon his guests. . . . He was the best practical Christian I have ever known.—PAUL, HERBERT, 1901, *The Late Bishop of London, Nineteenth Century, vol.* 50, *p.* 113.

In person Creighton was tall, spare, and upright; and his lithe and wiry figure showed great capacity for enduring fatigue. His features were regular and finely cut; his hands long and well-shaped, and he wore a long beard. Extremely scrupulous about his dress and personal appearance, he was not averse to a certain degree of external magnificence on proper occasions, and generally wore his mitre as bishop. Hospitably inclined, with a large circle of friends, he was always accessible, and never appeared hurried or preoccupied. His conversation was sparkling and witty, and he had a large fund of humorous anecdote. A certain love of paradox, a shrewdness which some mistook for cynicism, a notable lack of unction, and occasional lapses into flippancy as a protest against cant or a refuge from boredom, sometimes conveyed a wrong impression, concealing the natural kindliness, the wide sympathy, the deep inner seriousness of a man who was more highly appreciated the more fully he was known. His domestic life was of the happiest, and he left a family of three sons and four daughters.—PROTHERO, G. W., 1901, *Dictionary of National Biography, Supplement, vol.* II, *p.* 86.

GENERAL

Dr. Creighton was among the ablest and most learned historians of the century. The work which he did before he became a bishop—I mean his "History of the Papacy during the Reformation"—will long outlast the fruits of his episcopal labours, important as they were.—PAUL, HERBERT, 1901, *The Late Bishop of London, Nineteenth Century, vol.* 50, *p.* 103.

Though devoid of the pictorial power of Macaulay and the majesty of Gibbon, his narrative is more picturesque and animated than that of the unimpassioned Ranke; and he fully recognises the existence of general laws controlling individual action, while his good sense shows him that the action is more ascertained than the law. He thus avoids the besetting sins of some modern schools of history, the substitution of mere disquisition for narrative, and the ambitious reconstruction after merely subjective data. Nor did he belong to the more serviceable if less speciously gifted class of writers who imagine themselves to be writing history while they are merely purveying its materials. He aimed and he attained to present a faithful picture of the age he delineated; but this was a picture not from the point of view of the dramatist, or the observer of manners, or the sympathiser with the general condition of the people, but from that of the statesman: and perhaps no reflection upon his History has so frequently visited the minds of those personally acquainted with him as one upon the part he might himself have performed had his lot been cast in an age when the ecclesiastical profession was rather a help than a hindrance to effective participation in public affairs. . . . We may well claim for the Bishop that he has, beyond all the historians of his day, exemplified the virtue of impartiality.—GARNETT, RICHARD, 1901, *Mandell Creighton Bishop of London, English Historical Review, vol. 16, pp.* 211, 214.

Bishop Creighton owed his great reputation to his versatility. . . . Some of the writings and addresses of Bishop Creighton have been published since his death. Their strength lies in their humanity; their influence is likely to be such as to keep in mind the career of a man who did more to reconcile the differences which separate the intellectual from the clerical classes than any prelate or writer of his time.—GILBERT, HENRY, 1902, *The Literary Year-Book, p.* 66.

John Fiske
1842–1901

American historian, was Professor of American History at Washington University, St. Louis, at the time of his death. He had early been impressed by the theories and writings of Herbert Spencer and Charles Darwin, and his earliest works were able attempts to reconcile their doctrines with Christianity and to apply the results of evolution to the teaching of history, a philosophical method which he believed justified itself by reason of its reference to ultimate and universal principles. Most of Professor Fiske's later works had reference chiefly to American History. Those of his books which were also published in England are as follows—"Myths and Myth-Makers" (1873); "Outlines of Cosmic Philosophy" (1874); "The Unseen World" (1876); "Darwinism" (1879); "Man's Destiny Viewed in the Light of his Origin;" "Excursions of an Evolutionist" (1884); "The Idea of God as Affected by Modern Knowledge" (1885); American Political Ideas from the Standpoint of Universal History" (1885); "A Critical Period of American History, 1783-89" (1888); "The Beginnings of New England" (1889); "Civil Government in the United States with Reference to its Origins" (1890); "The American Revolution" (1891); "The Discovery of America" (1892); "School History of the United States" (1894); "Life and Letters of Edward L. Youmans" (1894); . . . "Old Virginia and her Neighbors" (1897); "Through Nature to God;" "Dutch and Quaker Colonies in America" (1899); "The Mississippi Valley in the Civil War;" and "A Century of Science, and other Essays" (1900).—GILBERT, HENRY, 1902, *The Literary Year-Book, p.* 67.

PERSONAL

Nothing could be simpler or more sincerely kind than this big-brained man's reception of a visitor. He tells you how he selected his ground a score of years ago; how he added to it to prevent some too-neighborly house from rising; how a family of crows has for years maintained a home in the trees yonder unterrified by the building operations that have gone on in Berkeley Place, a charming little no-thoroughfare that runs by one side of his estate; how the other birds come and go, and what vines thrive best along the piazza. Then you perhaps take a quick, mental photograph of the man. He is big and tall and burly. His head is large, and his florid face is fittingly girt with a full brown beard, slightly touched with gray, rather long and rather careless. The whole make-up suggests the Norseman. But the calm and deliberate speech betrays the philosopher, the man who will not deliver an opinion in a rush. "I hate to go off half-cocked," was the very characteristic remark in the course of some conversation on the Philippine question. . . . Prof. Fiske's library and working place is . . . a large, high and raftered room, elegantly sombre in design and finish. Its pictures and ornaments are of dignity and value. Thousands of books line its walls from end to end and from floor to ceiling. Ponderous tomes are scattered about on tables and revolving cases, and everything has the air of research. Over the ample fireplace—a practical one, where big logs glow in Winter—is this motto, which has no idle meaning here: Disce ut semper victurus; vive ut cras moriturus. The historian's writing place is an excellent example of household evolution. It is in a large square bay window, originally thrown out from the library as a means of observation and rest. But finding the light in the main room not exactly satisfactory, Prof. Fiske bethought himself of the aforesaid nook and moved all his literary paraphernalia into it with most excellent results. With great windows on three sides, the light is perfect, and in Summer a fine breeze is always wafted through.—QUINT, WILDER D., 1898, *Authors at Home, New York Times Saturday Review*, Oct. 15.

Mr. Fiske did not commonly write out and read his historical lectures; he spoke without notes, his diction bubbling like an overflowing spring. Whatever the critical effect of silent and satisfied hearers, there is no additional stimulus in a course of lectures ten times delivered; while travel, interruption of the normal course of life, the physical demands of lectures often an hour and a half long, the effort to meet new people and places, was a heavy drain and a withdrawal of a part of Mr. Fiske's possibilities as a literary man. His vital forces were lower, his year's product was less, his prospect of long life was reduced. The criticism is that of one who wishes that John Fiske had been physically able to write more or rather to write less hastily. On the other hand, the lectures were of great consequence as an intellectual force in the community; and as a means of spreading abroad sound ideas on American history. Thousands of hearers caught the inspiration which few men can put into a printed page; throughout the land people took a more rational view of our history, because John Fiske was a lecturer. His hearers became his readers; his readers wished to hear their favorite author. No American historian has ever had such personal relations with the public; he was the last of the race of lyceum speakers who for two generations helped to make the public sentiment of America; he had no rival, he leaves no successor.—HART, ALBERT BUSHNELL, 1901, *The Historical Service of John Fiske, International Monthly*, vol. 4, p. 561.

Nearly half a century ago, in a small New England town, lived a small boy, not yet into his "teens," who wished a certain lexicon, supposed to be necessary only to boys much his senior in years and in experience, and which he could not afford to buy. The sympathetic vendor of second-hand books to whom he appealed, impressed by the unexpected desire of so immature-looking a student, sold the volume on the instalment plan, the boy collecting old bones in the streets and disposing of them to a dealer in such things for a cent or two a pound, until the necessary amount, only a dollar or two, was raised, and the account settled. The title of the work was Liddell and Scott's "Greek-English Lexicon" and the boy, a good many years later, told the story in Oxford once to one of its compilers, who said that he considered it the most touching compliment which he and his co-laborer had ever received. The book—well thumbed by more than one generation of young students—is still carefully preserved and cherished in a private library in Cambridge, Massachusetts; and the name of the boy was John Fiske.—HUTTON, LAURENCE, 1903, *Literary Landmarks of Oxford*, p. 76.

GENERAL

The book ["Myths and Myth-Makers"] in itself is not an uninteresting one. It is chockfull of mythical stories, or folk-lore, or whatever people may please to call what in our younger days we should have comprised under the one delicious head of fairy-tales. To be sure, the stories were all told before and by somebody else; but then, Mr. Fiske gives everybody due credit, and confines his own portion of the work to a running commentary with an undercurrent of foot-notes, and all sorts of quotations, from the Rig-Veda down to Jack and Jill. We cannot in justice say that Mr. Fiske's portion is as interesting as the myths themselves, though partaking considerably of their character. . . . Mr. Fiske seems to think that he has struck a new vein, and opened up to the world a golden ore long hidden. His theory is as old as any other; and he has only given us a poor rehash of what much cleverer men than he have oversurfeited us with ages ago. Before attempting to handle the subjects he has touched upon, it would be advisable to go to school again, and he might thus be saved a lamentable display of childish ignorance on points known to all the world, save apparently to Mr. Fiske.—HASSARD, J. R. G., 1873, *Myths and Myth-Mongers, Catholic World*, vol. 17, pp. 209, 216.

There is also one work of such pretension that it should not be omitted here, namely, "Outlines of Cosmic Philosophy, based on the Doctrine of Evolution," by John Fiske. It is mainly a lucid exposition of the philosophy of Herbert Spencer, with the addition of original and critical matter. The breadth and strength of understanding, the fulness of information, the command of expression, in this book are worthy of all commendation. The curious thing in it is that the author thinks that a new religion is to be established on the co-ordination of the sciences; and of this religion, whose God is the "Unknowable," he is a pious believer.—WHIPPLE, EDWIN PERCY, 1876-86, *American Literature and Other Papers*, ed. *Whittier*, p. 137.

Mr. Fiske is an able advocate. His thought and his method of presentation are in harmony with those of Mr. Spencer. He states the positions of the philosophy clearly, combines them well, enforces them vigorously with new and old material. It may be rightly claimed that he does something more than this, and occasionally makes a fresh and cardinal point. We do think, however, that he has a little of the zeal of a proselyte, that he bandies too freely about the adjectives *metaphysical* and *theological*, in the restricted and abusive meaning they have acquired in a limited school, and that there is an assumption, unintended perhaps, but none the less real, of superiority in his philosophical attitude, that can hardly receive a milder epithet than offensive.—BASCOM, JOHN, 1876, *The Synthetic or Cosmic Philosophy*, *Bibliotheca Sacra*, vol. 33, p. 619.

The work before us ["Excursions of an Evolutionist"], as its title indicates, is a collection of disconnected essays on a great variety of subjects, but all treated from the standpoint of evolution. It is truly a series of gems strung on this thread. The book is certainly one of the most fascinating imaginable. . . . The first two essays give an admirable and, on the whole, a reliable résumé of the history of primeval man in Europe. Some of the statements are indeed a little more positive than the facts warrant, but perhaps the essays are all the more readable on that account. . . . The book certainly deserves all the commendation we have given or can give it. It is admirable in its spirit and in its style. Yet some slight blemishes are detectable. . . . Some scientific statements are made with more positiveness than are warranted by the facts, and some supposed facts are too easily accepted when they fit in with cherished views.—LE CONTE, JOSEPH, 1884, *Excursions of an Evolutionist*, *Overland Monthly, N. S.*, vol. 3, pp. 329, 331.

If Mr. Fiske must bear the reproach of being a literary historian it is not because he is defective in thoroughness of method or in knowledge of his field, but because he fails to give his narrative the dryness of the documents out of which history is reconstructed. He cannot avoid being interesting and clear; he writes of the past as if it had once been alive, instead of peopled with phantoms and abstractions.—MABIE, HAMILTON WRIGHT, 1892, *A Year's Literary Production*, *The Forum*, vol. 12, p. 802.

Among the most interesting books of the past year is Mr. John Fiske's "Discovery of America." It is a history of that fascinating kind which tells us, to be sure, little that was not known beforehand; but it shows us, so simply that we hardly realize we are being taught, where each scattered bit of knowledge belongs. Careful students of one period or another may find in Mr. Fiske's work errors of detail: to write so comprehensive a book without minor errors were almost to transcend human frailty. But no one, I think, can read the book without a fresh and a lasting appreciation of that great process of human development whose most significant moment we celebrate today. —WENDELL, BARRETT, 1892-93, *Stelligeri and Other Essays Concerning America*, p. 23.

The current criticism of Mr. Fiske that he lacked original power, that he was primarily an assimilator and expositor, is in the main probably true, but both Darwin and Spencer have left it upon record that he was an expositor of the very highest order. Both give him cordial credit for something more than this. . . . He was among the first to understand the bearing of the new thought upon the whole of life. He was almost without a peer in restating the great problems with clear and penetrating power. Neither is it to be gainsaid that his interpretation of evolution, as the years passed, took on an even higher and more spiritual note. His learning was not more astonishing than were his sympathy and imagination. These qualities have rightly endeared him to one of the most splendid audiences that any American man of letters has yet won. . . . Extraordinary range of admirable scholarship, versatility, commanding power of clear and simple expression in narrative, together with exhaustless good-will toward all his fellows and the whole of life,—these were the gifts of this man of letters whom one does not know quite how to name. Philosopher? lecturer? religious teacher? historian? To many thousands he has become at the same time each and all.—BROOKS, JOHN GRAHAM, 1901, *John Fiske, Review of Reviews*, vol. 24, pp. 175, 176, 178.

Mr. Fiske was much more widely known through his historical work, which was the chief subject of his lectures, than through his scientific work. The latter was, however, extremely important. I am not competent to say how far it had original value, that is, how far it really threw new light on the very difficult and complex questions with which it dealt. But undoubtedly Mr. Fiske contributed, and largely, to the spread among us of those scientific truths which are included in the general term of "evolution," and to the very great change in the mental attitude of thinking men which those truths demand.—CARY, EDWARD, 1901, *John Fiske, The Book Buyer*, vol. 23, p. 15.

John Fiske's mind was powerful, but not originating. He knew what true learning was, and where it was; and it was his delight and highest function to go into the workshops of the great laborers in philosophy and in history, and come out to tell the world what they were doing. He was essentially a lecturer.

"Child of an age that lectures, not creates," said Lowell of himself, ruefully. But lecturing may be made so much of a fine art that it may almost be said to be itself creative. It was so in Fiske's hands. For mastery of his subject without dullness, for lucidity and charm and fresh enthusiasm, we probably have never had his like—at least, in the abstruser philosophical and historical subjects which it was his joy to expound and illuminate. . . . His forte was, as we have said, lecturing. After hearing him you would not say, as Lowell said was your impression after hearing Emerson lecture, that "something beautiful had passed that way;" but you would say that such an expository gift, such lucidity combined with such learning, marked their possessor out as a prince of his art.—OGDEN, R., 1901, *John Fiske, Popularizer, The Nation*, vol. 73, pp. 26, 27.

In wealth and diversity of learning he stood unrivalled, and, thanks to a pellucid and limpid style, he was able to give the public the benefit of his vast knowledge in a highly attractive form. In these respects he was a type that America produces but sparingly, and which seems rather characteristic of English civilization. In breadth of mental activity in combination with a fine style, he reminds us forcibly of Lecky, of Goldwin Smith, of John Morley, and of many other prominent Englishmen. . . . Though a man of brilliant talents, of vast learning, Fiske's name will never stand conspicuous in the list of American philosophers and historians.—BEER, GEORGE L., 1901, *John Fiske, The Critic*, vol. 39, p. 117.

When we speak of "John Fiske's historical service" we necessarily mean his formal pre-constitutional history in nine volumes, which alone entitles him to the name of historian. The first exception to that work must be the haphazard method. Having written four of his volumes irregularly, he could not later arrange his scheme so as to include all that he would have treated; for instance the "neglected half-century" from 1700 to 1750 is still neglected. Some repetitions are also inevitable; the Andros episode is cut into two halves, though it had a grim unity. On the other hand, there is some gain in treating the three groups of colonies throughout as separate entities. HART, ALBERT BUSHNELL, 1901, *The Historical Service of John Fiske, International Monthly*, vol. 4, p. 566.

Nothing else in the domain of American history is so much needed to-day as a true and reasonably full account of the youthful years of the city of Manhattan. This is what we hoped that Mr. Fiske would write. He has never been one of those thorough investigators of fundamental data and ideas whose conclusions are accepted by historical scholars, even when unfamiliar and unwelcome. But the great popular vogue of his books has been based upon a belief that facts so well presented, with such clarity of statement and such attractiveness of style, must have been well considered. He has shown less narrowness of vision in dealing with New England than some of her other sons. And the knowledge that his new book ["History of New York"] was to form part of a comprehensive history of the antecedents and the formation of the Republic, supported the

PHILIP JAMES BAILEY

Engraving from the Plaster Bust by Alfred Toft.

AUBREY DE VERE

Engraving from a Copy by F. Hollyer.

belief that it would be sympathetically approached and carefully prepared. But these expectations have been disappointed. . . . Evidently, he did not study those sources of knowledge which have not yet been incorporated into easily accessible books; and on scores of pages he shows that he was very careless even in the use of the narratives and documents that he did consult. His mistakes in matters of fact are frequent and sometimes very grave. Some of them are simple repetitions of current errors. Others are resurrections of errors long ago buried under a convincing weight of evidence. And others again are novelties. Moreover, although Mr. Fiske's formally pronounced estimate of the significance of the tale he has to tell is more justly sympathetic than that of many writers on American history, it is but slenderly supported by the specific judgments and passing comments that one finds in the course of his narrative.—VAN RENSSELAER, MRS. SCHUYLER, 1901, *Mr. Fiske and the History of New York, North American Review, vol.* 173, *pp.* 171, 172.

Some books are said to smell of the lamp; these books smack of the platform, and the flavor is excellent. We do not know anything in historical literature quite parallel in this respect to Mr. Fiske's American histories. . . . Like Thackeray, Mr. Fiske talks to his readers and tells rather than writes his story. It is partly for this reason that his volumes are such fascinating material for reading aloud. . . . It is not, however, as a discoverer but as an interpreter that John Fiske is pre-eminent. His sympathies are unconcealedly and unreservedly democratic. His statement that Jefferson "was in his way a much more profound thinker than Hamilton, though he had not such a constructive genius as the latter," sufficiently indicates his political point of view. The reader who compares Mr. Fiske's account of the preliminary events which led up to the American Revolution with that furnished by Goldwin Smith in his "History of the United States," or the portraits of Samuel Adams furnished by the two historians, will perhaps, think as we do, that Mr. Fiske overestimates the selfrestraint of the New England colonists, if he does not overstate the wrongs which they suffered. . . . As a reader of men Mr. Fiske appears to us to be unsurpassed. He neither deifies George Washington nor vilifies Benedict Arnold. In all his portrayal of men he is himself intensely human.— ABBOTT, LYMAN, 1901, *John Fiske's Histories, The Outlook, vol.* 69, *pp.* 709, 710.

Such an unwearying and wise absorber, recaster, and expounder we shall not soon see again. His earlier and later philosophic studies certainly helped to give his books on American history the broad perspective of Von Ranke's school. But the chief task of the historian, begun somewhat late, doubtless remains a large and tantalizing fragment.—LAWTON, WILLIAM CRANSTON, 1902, *Introduction to the Study of American Literature, p.* 262.

Philip James Bailey
1816–1902

Born at Nottingham, 22 April 1816. Educated at schools in Nottingham. To Glasgow University, 1831. Student at Lincoln's Inn, 26 April 1834; called to Bar, 7 May 1840. "Festus" written, 1836-39. Twice married. *Works:* "Festus" (anon.), 1839; "The Angel World," 1850; "The Mystic," 1855; "The Age," 1858; "The Universal Hymn," 1867; "The International Policy of the Great Powers," 1861.—SHARP, R FARQUHARSON, 1897, *A Dictionary of English Authors, p.* 14.

PERSONAL

A dark, handsome, rather picturesque-looking man, with a grey beard, and dark hair, a little dimmed with grey. He is of quiet and very agreeable deportment, and I liked him and believed in him. . . . There is sadness glooming out of him, but no unkindness nor asperity.—HAWTHORNE, NATHANIEL, 1856, *English Note-Books, vol.* II, *p.* 92.

Whether working at the University or elsewhere his studies were determinately, although tacitly directed towards the one object of his life, the development of his faculties as a poet. Habitual converse with speculations moral and metaphysical, embracing the whole orbit of mental philosophy, ancient and modern, both when at college and many years subsequently,— indeed throughout his life,—became with him an all-absorbing passion; and this blending with an impressionable nature, and a retiring and contemplative disposition, imparted no doubt ultimately that tinge of transcendentalism to his poetry which, sobered by those serious associations to which he had from his earliest years been accustomed at home, forms one of its chief and especial charms in the estimation of the most thoughtful of his admirers.—BROWN, J. HENRY, 1892, *The Poets and the Poetry of the Century, Tennyson to Clough*, ed. *Miles*, p. 467.

He was never in close touch with literary circles, though about 1870 he was sometimes present at Westland Marston's symposia, where Rossetti, Swinburne, "Orion" Horne, and other celebrities were wont to meet. He was sweet, gentle, and rather timid in nature. Superbly handsome in physique and countenance, he rivalled Tennyson in the art of looking like a poet.—DOUGLAS, JAMES, 1903, *Chambers's Cyclopædia of English Literature*, ed. *Patrick*, vol. III, p. 507.

FESTUS
1839

To most readers, the poem would appear a monstrous compound of blasphemy and licentiousness. Though evincing power, and variety of power, it excites the most wonder from its disregard of all the moral, religious and artistical associations of others. Pantheism and fatalism, in their most objectionable forms, are inculcated as absolute truth. The two flaming ideas in his mind, are God and Lucifer. . . . Doctrines of the most monstrous import, and doctrines of the utmost purity and holiness, so follow each other that the author evidently sees no discord in their connection. He can delineate the passion of love with great refinement, without seeming to distinguish it from the most unhallowed lust. If he be not mad, it is certain that all the rest of the world are. To accept the poem of "Festus" as the product of a sane mind, would be to declare other literature superficial, and P. J. Bailey the most miraculously gifted of all created men. Its madness is not altogether fine madness, but half comes from Parnassus and the rest from Bedlam. It is the madness of a mind unable accurately to distinguish the moral and intellectual differences of things.—WHIPPLE, EDWIN PERCY, 1845, *The Poets and the Poetry of England, American Review*, vol. 2, p. 55.

Like most philosophical poems, as they are called, "Festus" is neither good science nor good poetry, but an indescribable medley, which, so far as we know, has never been appropriately named. The book contains neither prose nor verse—neither fact nor imagination; is made up neither of persons nor of propositions; instead of life-like characters and passions, we have a long, tedious masquerade of abstract ideas; and, generally, the only hint vouchsafed of a change of speakers, is in the names prefixed to the speeches. Lucifer, it is true, preaches some very strange doctrine; but not stranger than the hero, Festus. They seem, indeed, but duplicates of the same idea—twin apostles, giving a biform development of the same theory; and, for aught we can see, the discourses of both might as well have come from the same person. On the whole, they are a little the oddest man and devil we have ever encountered. . . . The book is not only without the moral elements of a poem on a sacred subject, but is without the literary elements of a *poem* on any subject. . . . His style has neither the rhythm of verse nor of prose; nay, it has not the *rhythm* of anything, unless of chaos or bedlam. We should suppose he had cultivated his musical ear in filing and rasping cast-iron plates. We had not imagined that such a crude, awkward, bungling, uncouth, grotesque piece of versification could be wrought out of the English language. . . . Theologically speaking, the book is in no wise a development of an idea or principle into a coherent, original system, but an eclecticism of whatever is most absurd and offensive in several systems: Calvinism, Fatalism, Universalism, Swedenborgianism, Pantheism, and Rationalism. Our author, as he informs us in the person of Festus, is "an ominist and believer in all religions."—HUDSON, HENRY N., 1847, *Festus, American Review*, vol. 5, pp. 45, 57, 134, 137.

A poem of which the brave and earnest corn-law rhymer, Elliott, could say, "it contains poetry enough to set up fifty poets," must be an extraordinary work; and the author is certainly a most remarkable man, if at the age of twenty-three he has actually won the high position which a critic, not prone to overpraise, has assigned to him, in saying, that "Wordsworth excepted, who belongs to the past generation, there are but two living poets in England, Taylor and Tennyson, who can be named *near* him." . . . We are willing for our own part to confess, here in the outset, that taking "Festus" for all in all, we regard it as unsurpassed, perhaps unequalled by any creation of genius in the light literature of our age. This is a strong statement, but it is calmly made; and a thorough acquaintance with the book will, we are confident, establish the correctness of this judgment. . . . The first, superficial, outside impression of Festus Bailey, for the author and the book are wholly one, is of his extremely quick sensibility and of his prodigal expenditure of life. The creature is all nerve; he feels with agonizing intensity both pleasure and pain, and seems to be consuming, to use his own image,

"Like a bright wheel, which burns itself away,
Benighting even night with its grim limbs."—

No poem of any time or language has manifested greater keenness of sensation.— CHANNING, W. H., 1845, *Festus, Christian Examiner*, vol. 39, pp. 365, 366.

We have made repeated attempts, but we cannot get through this poem. It beats us. We must want the Festus sense. Some of our best friends, with whom we generally agree on such matters, are distressed for us, and repeat long passages with great energy and apparent intelligence and satisfaction. Meanwhile, having read the six pages of public opinion at the end of the third and people's edition, we take it for granted that it is a great performance, that, to use one of the author's own words, there is a mighty "somethingness" about it—and we can entirely acquiesce in the quotation from "The Sunday Times," that they "read it with astonishment, and closed it with bewilderment." It would appear from these opinions, which from their intensity, variety, and number, (upwards of 50,) are to us very surprising signs of the times, that Mr. Bailey has not so much improved on, as happily superseded the authors of the Books of Job and Ecclesiastes, of the Divine Comedy, of Paradise Lost and Regained, of Dr. Faustus, of Hamlet, of Faust, of Don Juan, The Course of Time, St. Leon, of the Jolly Beggars, and the Loves of the Angels. He is more sublime and simple than Job. More royally witty and wise, more to the point than Solomon. More picturesque, more intense, more pathetic than Dante. More Miltonic (we have no other word) than Milton. More dreadful, more curiously blasphemous, more sonorous than Marlowe. More worldly-wise and clever, and intellectually *svelt* than Goethe. More passionate, more eloquent, more impudent than Byron. More orthodox, more edifying, more precocious than Pollok. More absorptive and inveterate than Godwin, and more hearty, more tender, more of manhood all compact than Burns. More gay than Moore. More μυζιανους than Shakespeare. It may be so. We have made repeated and determined incursions in various directions into its substance, but have always come out greatly scorched and stunned and affronted. Never before did we come across such an amount of energetic and tremendous words, going "sounding on their dim and perilous way," like a cataract—not flowing like a stream, nor leaping like a clear waterfall, but always among breakers—roaring and tearing and tempesting—a sort of transcendental din; and then what power of energizing and speaking, and philosophizing and preaching, and laughing and joking *in vacuo*.—BROWN, JOHN, 1849, *Vaughan's Poems, etc., North British Review*, vol. 11, p. 60, note.

As a poet in actual achievement, I can have no hesitation in placing him far above either Browning or Stirling. His Festus is in many respects a very remarkable production—remarkable alike for its poetic power, and its utter neglect of all the requirements of poetic art. . . . Yet with all these excesses and defects, we are made to feel that Festus is the work of a poet. . . . In The Angel World, we have the youthful poet more sobered down; and the consequent result has been one not exactly to be wished—its beauties and its defects are each alike less prominent.—MOIR, D. M., 1851-52, *Sketches of Poetical Literature of the Past Half-Century*.

He was known a few years since as the author of "Festus," the rhapsodies and religiosities of which were so greedily absorbed by the spongy brains of his admirers.—DUYCKINCK, E. A., 1854, *Edward Young, North American Review*, vol. 79, p. 272, note.

Was "Faust" emasculated, trimmed and scented and sent forth on a harmless round among the circulating libraries, forty years ago.—SANBORN, F. B., 1885, *Life and Genius of Goethe*, p. 184.

I see that Mr. Bartlett, in his "Dictionary of Quotations," preserves three from Bailey's "Festus," a book much in vogue in my early days, from which we remembered many passages. This shows that the book is now not wholly forgotten. But I suppose it would be safe to say that not ten copies have been sold in ten years.—HALE, EDWARD EVERETT, 1888, *Books That Have Helped Me*, p. 12.

The attraction which it manifestly holds for certain classes of readers is no doubt due to the blending of poetical elements that often attain to a high degree of beauty and imaginative force with theological and philosophical speculation concerning the profoundest questions of life, death, and immortality. A glowing fervour of spiritual passion, an exuberant wealth of imagery, and a magnificent sweep of diction are all strikingly present in this poem, but these are mixed with so much extravagance, unevenness, and mere frothy declamation, and are, moreover, so wanting in human interest and spontaneity as to justify the censure implied in the name "Spasmodic" which has been affixed to Bailey and the younger poets whom he is supposed to have influenced by his example.—GRAHAM, RICHARD D., 1897, *The Masters of Victorian Literature*, p. 339.

"Festus" is not profound philosophy, and still less is it true poetry. The thought when probed is commonplace. A vigorous expression here and there is hardly enough to redeem the weak echoes of Goethe and Byron. Frequently the verse is distinguishable from prose only by the manner of printing. "Swearers and swaggerers jeer at my name" is supposed to be an iambic line. We are told that a thing is our "soul-blood" and our "soul-bones;" and we hear of "marmoreal floods" that "spread their couch of perdurable snow." Yet this passes for poetry, and "Festus" has gone through many editions in this country, and still more in America. The aberration of taste is not quite as great as that which raised Martin Farquhar Tupper and his "Proverbial Philosophy" to the highest popularity, but it is similar in kind. —WALKER, HUGH, 1897, *The Age of Tennyson*, p. 64.

So far as it appears, there was nothing but irresistible vocation and a selective use of the most sympathetic models which led Bailey back to what had so long and so completely been neglected in English poetry, the record of the subtler action of the mind. In the midst of a fashion for scrupulous common sense, and "the equipoise of reason," here was a young man of twenty who, without any sort of impetus from without, and in defiance of current criticism, devoted himself to the employment of clothing philosophic speculation with almost reckless imagery. . . . The "Festus" of 1901 is a very different affair from the volume of the same name of 1839. In the first place, it is very unlike it in size, since it contains about forty thousand verses, while the original edition has something less than ten thousand. . . . The effect made upon his own generation was not made by the huge and very unwieldy book, which one now buys as "Festus" in the shops, but by a poem which was already lengthy, yet perfectly within the bounds of easy reading. It seems essential, if we are to gauge that effect, to turn back to the first edition. This was a large octavo, with no name on the title-page, but with a symbolic back presenting a malignant snake flung downwards through the inane by the rays that dart from a triangle of light, a very proper preparation for the redundant and arcane invocations of the text within the covers.—GOSSE, EDMUND, 1902, *Philip James Bailey, The Critic*, vol. 41, pp. 459, 460.

Aubrey Thomas De Vere
1814–1902

An Irish poet, from the death of Tennyson the dean of English verse, died in London, January 21, 1902. Born at Curragh Chase, Ireland, January 10, 1814, he was educated at Trinity College, Dublin, subsequently passed some time at Rydal Mount, and in 1842 published his first volume, "The Waldenses, or the Fall of Rora: A Lyrical Tale;" In the year following, his "Search After Proserpine" brought him into favorable prominence as a maker of graceful verse. Other poetical works are: "Irish Odes" (1869), "The Legends of St. Patrick" (1872), "Legends of the Saxon Saints" (1879), "St. Peter's Chains" (1888), and the dramas "Alexander the Great" (1874), and "St. Thomas of Canterbury" (1876).

PERSONAL

I am sorry to learn that in all these years you have had no better specimen of London at Ballyshannon than Aubrey de Vere, who is surely one of the wateriest of the well-meaning. — ROSSETTI, DANTE GABRIEL, 1860, *Letters to William Allingham*, p. 245.

The writer of these lines had the rare pleasure, by kind invitation, of spending some hours at Curragh Chase, in July, 1888. . . . This is a magnificent old estate—an ideal home for a poet and lover of nature. It contains some two thousand acres of field and forest, "upland, glade and glen." The grand old mansion stands upon a moderate elevation, overlooking a most beautiful little lake. Across the lake, upon a high crag is planted a large pillar in the form of an Irish cross, around the base of which are inscribed the names of those of the family who have passed away. A belt of timber surrounds the whole tract. How much of this had been planted one could hardly determine—the arrangement was so natural and so beautiful; but I have seldom seen such grand old elms, oaks, lindens and beeches, and they were almost everywhere interspersed with evergreens and thickets of shrubbery. The beeches—both the common and the red varieties—grow in wonderful perfection, with wide-spreading limbs, forming perfect pyramids to the height of 60 to 80 feet. When we were there they were so loaded with nuts that the lower branches often rested upon the ground. I did not wonder that the poet was proud of his trees.—ALDRICH, CHARLES, 1889, *Aubrey De Vere, The Magazine of Poetry*, vol. 7, p. 406.

The friend of Cardinals Manning and Newman, the disciple of Wordsworth, the associate of most of the well-known men of the century which has almost reached its end, he is a connecting link of the present with the past, one of the solitary survivors—does he find it, one wonders, a little lonely? —of the notable group of world-wide reputation which counted among its members such men as Tennyson, Southey, Sir William Hamilton, Lord Houghton, Henry Taylor, Landor, Coventry Patmore, and many others.—TAYLOR, I. A., 1898, *The Recollections of Aubrey de Vere, Catholic World*, vol. 66, p. 621.

GENERAL

Welcome! who last hast climbed the cloven hill
Forsaken by its Muses and their God!
Show us the way; we miss it, young and old.
Roses that cannot clasp their languid leaves,
Puffy and odourless and overblown,
Encumber all our walks of poetry;
The satin slipper and the mirror boot
Delight in pressing them; but who hath trackt
A Grace's naked foot amid them all?
Or who hath seen (ah! how few care to see!)
The close-bound tresses and the robe succinct?
Thou hast; and she hath placed her palm in thine.
Walk ye together in our fields and groves.
—LANDOR, WALTER SAVAGE, 1848, *To Aubrey De Vere, The Last Fruit off an Old Tree*, VI.

He is not the most poetical poet of this century; but of the poetical poets he is by far the most intellectual, next after, if after, Coleridge and Wordsworth. If the justness of his intellect were equal to its range of power, few among the poets would be greater than he.—TAYLOR, SIR HENRY, 1864, *Autobiography*, vol. II, p. 143.

In point of language, our author inherits an Irishman's full measure of vocabulary. Through a most varied series of metres, his verse is full of ease, fluency, and grace. In rhythm he rises to the rank of an artist. He has passed the first degree—that baccalaureateship of verse-making whose diploma is perfect smoothness and melody; where Tom Moore took a double first, and beyond which so few ever attain. He is one of the *maestri*, like Tennyson and Swinburne, who know the uses of a discord, and can handle diminished sevenths. His lines are full of subtle shadings, and curious sub-felicities of diction, that not everyone feels, and few save the devotees to metre (such as we own ourselves to be) pause to analyze and admire. His taste, too, is fastidiously unerring; there is never a swerve beyond the cobweb boundaries of the line of beauty. Sometimes he misses the exact word he wants, but he never halts for want of a good one. The only deficiency arises from his temperament.— RUDD, F. A., 1866, *Aubrey De Vere, Catholic World*, vol. 4, p. 74.

The most marvellous character in human history, is the one of all others whom Mr. de Vere, with a courage which, if not justified by the result, can only be looked upon as either rashness or folly, has undertaken to set living and real before us, speaking the speech, thinking the thoughts, scheming the schemes, dreaming the dream of Alexander. Greatness thus becomes one of the necessary standards by which we must judge Mr. de Vere's work. . . . The action of the piece is rapid; the characters, small and great, rounded and full; the scenes most varied and dramatically set. The clew to the play we take to be that old whisper which first allured our parents from the allegiance, and tempts forever the race of man: *Ye shall be as gods.*—MCCARTHY, JUSTIN, 1875, *Swinburne and De Vere, Catholic World*, vol. 20, pp. 353, 358.

As a rule Mr. Aubrey de Vere prefers the high places of the intellect to these lower literary levels, and is more uniformly philosophical than we expect any man to be who writes "chiefly on poetry." . . . Mr. Aubrey de Vere's style, though fluent, correct, and dignified, is lacking in that grip which is given by the living expression of the vividly conceived thought in the apt word that such a thought always brings with it. It is expatiatory, and gives us no sense of inevitableness. The writer himself wisely remarks that "energetic truth forbids diffuseness, for it is through brief select expression that thoughts disclose their character. Clearness and intensity are thus found together, and to write with these is to write with force." This is well put; but if we apply these words to Mr. Aubrey de Vere's own style, we are compelled to draw the inference that his realisation of the truth he has to expound is very insufficiently "energetic," for he is frequently diffuse, hardly ever intense, and not always even clear. . . . I must not be understood to say that Mr. Aubrey de Vere is ever obscure with that purely literary obscurity which makes any single sentence at all difficult to understand. The want of clearness inheres not in parts, but in the whole; and it evidently comes from the lack of that energetic dealing with truth which he so rightly admires.—NOBLE, JAMES ASHCROFT, 1888, *Essays Chiefly on Poetry, The Academy*, vol. 33, p. 35.

He is acknowledged by the most careful and best equipped critics to be, in certain departments of poetry, unequalled. If he were not so Christian, I should, nevertheless, proclaim him as a poet who deserves to rank beside Tennyson. But as he is, above all, Christian, I am very happy in pointing out to you, among a race of literary neo-pagans, the one poet who is great as a poet, true as a man, magnificent in his adherence to Divine Truth. . . . Aubrey de Vere's "Saint Thomas of Canterbury" has a foil in "Becket" which, by contrast, makes it glow and seem more full of lustre and color, as a diamond of flawless purity when put in a circle of brilliants. It is hard to account for the blindness of the poet of the "Idyls of the King" in venturing to attempt a work that had already been perfectly done. Aubrey de Vere's place as a great dramatic poet was settled when "Alexander the Great" appeared. "Saint Thomas of Canterbury" was not needed to teach the world what he could do. But he has given it out of the abundance of his heart; and we Catholics who have the key of faith with which to unlock its mysteries, which are unknown to a poet of even Tennyson's insight, may thank God that he has raised up a seer at once strong, pure, true to his ideals both in religion and art, more than worthy to wear the mantle that fell from the shoulders of Wordsworth, and with much of the divine fire that made Shakepeare an arbiter of English thought and speech.—EGAN, MAURICE FRANCIS, 1889, *Lectures on English Literature*, p. 131.

Much of Mr. de Vere's finest verse is cast in a meditative and serious mould, and is occasionally mystical. Hence probably it is that his poems have not been popular in the strict sense, though they have never lacked warm admirers. At his best he shows a distinct command over poetic methods. As a sonneteer he is especially successful; indeed, it is, perhaps, as a writer of sonnets that he, like his father, is most widely known. In reality, however, there is more variety in his poetry than is supposed by readers only partially acquainted with his work. Many of his idylls prove conclusively that he has caught the true feeling for the old Greek mythology which distinguishes some of the most splendid work of the great poets of our time.—BELL, MACKENZIE, 1892, *The Poets and the Poetry of the Century, Tennyson to Clough*, ed. Miles, p. 416.

No other poem of mine was written more intensely, I may say more painfully, from my heart than "Inisfail." Some of its English readers were displeased at Irish history being thus interpreted, though one of them, I remember, exclaimed on reading it, "Either this is the true meaning of Irish history or else it never had a meaning." If those who were displeased imagined that the book was one likely to excite Irish political passions they must have been very simple. The book was addressed not to the many, but to the thoughtful and the few, and at least as much to English statesmen as to Irish patriots.—DE VERE, AUBREY, 1897, *Recollections*, p. 355.

Reverence and awe—essential characteristics of the devotional spirit—are strongly marked in Mr. de Vere's religious verse; and short as some of his religious poems are, they seem to reproduce the very atmosphere of devotion from which they evidently sprung.—MILES, ALFRED H., 1897, *The Poets and the Poetry of the Century, Sacred, Moral and Religious Verse*, p. 479.

De Vere's poetry moves on a high plane of ethical contemplation, and is brightened by a rich imagination; but he lacked the lyrical gift, and his best work is to be praised chiefly as possessing a grave austerity of thought and a stately dignity in its diction.—FALKINER, C. LITTON, 1903, *Chambers's Cyclopædia of English Literature*, ed. Patrick, vol. III, p. 581.

Samuel Rawson Gardiner
1829–1902

Born at Ropley, near Alresford, 4th March 1829, was our most eminent historian of later days. Educated at Winchester, he proceeded to Oxford in 1847, gaining a first class *in Lit. Hum.* in 1851. Moving to London, he began in 1855 the work that was to be his life's labour, namely, the history of England from 1603 to 1660. By 1863 he had published two volumes, being for the period from the accession of James I. to the year 1616. At the same time that he was studying and reading, he was earning his livelihood; and in spite of the absolute indifference of the public, and the failure of any adequate return for his books, he continued publishing further parts of the history until, in 1883, some public recognition was made in a demand for a second edition of the work already completed. This was published in ten volumes under the title of "A History of England from the Accession of James I. to the Outbreak of the Civil War," 1603-1642. Meanwhile he had written many school books of history, besides filling several posts as lecturer or examiner. Among the text-books mentioned are "The Thirty Years' War" (1874); "The First Two Stuarts" (1876); "An Outline of English History" (1881-83); and "A Student's History of England" (1891). In 1894 he declined the Regius professorship of Modern History at Oxford, offered to him by Lord Rosebery, for he was determined not to be deflected from his life's work. At intervals from 1886 until 1901 he issued further parts of his history, bringing up the period treated to 1656. He at last decided to complete the work to the death of the Protector, not to the Restoration, as originally intended. But death did not suffer the crowning volume to be added. . . . Besides the work above mentioned, Dr. Gardiner edited many collections of papers for the Camden Society, the Scottish History Society, and the Navy Records Society. For eleven years also, from 1890 to 1901, he was editor of the "English Historical Review."—GILBERT, HENRY, 1903, *The Literary Year-Book*, pp. 60, 61.

GENERAL

Mr. Gardiner's one defect is that he is more successful in laying bare the springs of action than portraying the actors.—GARNETT, RICHARD, 1887, *The Reign of Queen Victoria*, ed. Ward, vol. II, p. 476.

Has by his last work, published a few months ago, completed his laborious undertaking of giving a complete history of England during the seventeenth century. It is undoubtedly the most painstaking and we should say the most carefully accurate historical work that we have known; that it is not as interesting as some brilliant works that have been written with all the ardour of a partisan, is perhaps as much a praise as a censure. Human nature instinctively recoils from the even level of unbiased accuracy, but as a work of reference Professor Gardiner's history will probably remain without a rival.—OLIPHANT, MARGARET O. W., 1892, *The Victorian Age of English Literature*, p. 544.

Those who value the teaching of the past

owe a deep debt to the luminous and judicial work of Leopold von Ranke. Beside that great and honoured name students of the Stewart age will gratefully place that of Samuel Rawson Gardiner. It is impossible for any one who works at this very difficult and complicated period adequately to acknowledge the enormous obligation under which he stands to Mr. Gardiner's knowledge and patience and fairness. It is not the least of his services to the cause of truth that he has done more than any other living writer to enable men to critically examine and justly estimate the career of Laud.—HUTTON, WILLIAM HOLDEN, 1895, *William Laud (Leaders of Religion), Preface, p.* VI.

Is the greatest living authority on the period of English history between the death of Elizabeth and the Restoration. . . . The writer is careful to dissociate himself from the methods of Macaulay and Forster, who, he says, look at the events and the men embraced within their narrative through the political feelings and prepossessions proper to our own time. Professor Gardiner's desire is to judge them as from their own standpoint, and if possible to see these times and events as they appeared to the main actors in them. It must be admitted that although dealing with the most exciting period of English history, his narrative wants fire. Interesting it could not fail to be, considering the nature of the subject. But, rightly or wrongly, the graces of style that lend such a charm to the pages of Macaulay and Froude are not to be found here. In plain, often prosaic fashion, the narrative goes on, but we have at least the satisfaction of knowing that the truth, as far as that can be ascertained, has been placed before us with absolute fidelity. For the first time we feel competent to pass a final judgment upon the many actors in our great English historical epic.—GRAHAM, RICHARD D., 1897, *The Masters of Victorian Literature, pp.* 221, 222.

The greatness of Gardiner's work does not proceed from his power as a thinker or from his skill as a literary artist; it was by his passion for truth and accuracy, his candour and breadth of sympathy, his unwearying industry, that he achieved a work which must ever hold its place among the chief historical productions in English literature. In the same sense in which the expression is now employed, Gardiner was not, and did not desire to be, a "scientific historian." He did not conceive it to be the duty of the historian to efface himself in the presentation of his materials, nor to eschew all expression of his own opinion on the events and actions he has to narrate. Everywhere he frankly pronounces his judgements, whether of condemnation or approval; and in so doing he held that he was discharging not the least important function of the historian. In his conception, if history was not directly didactic, the writing of it is a vain labour; and the true scientific historian is he who most conscientiously seeks to ascertain and present the lessons which the past has to offer.—BROWN, P. HUME, 1903, *Chambers's Cyclopædia of English Literature*, ed. Patrick, *vol.* III, *p.* 631.

Francis Bret Harte
1839–1902

Born at Albany, New York, 25th August 1839. His father, a professor, dying early, Bret Harte was left to make his own way in life. He began his experiences in the rough romance of the Californian gold mines; later he took part in the Indian wars, turned to newspaper writing, shouldered his gun in the Civil War, and in 1864 became secretary of a branch of the U. S. Mint at San Francisco. In 1868 the "Overland Monthly" was started, and Bret Harte was given the editorship. In the second number of this appeared the short story that made Harte's name known the world over. "The Luck of Roaring Camp" was too human a narrative for many minds, but the stronger natures turned to the writer as to a kinsman. After this his work looked for everywhere. He was working in New York from 1870 to 1878; was U. S. Consul at Crefeld, Germany, from 1878 to 1880, then at Glasgow, Scotland, in the same capacity till 1885, when he definitely took to residence in London. As a whole his work is strong within certain limits, which, laid down in his first two or three tales, he never broke through. He lacked in too great a measure "general ideas;" his imagination could never get far from reality, so that the greater powers of the creative artist were to him impossible of achievement, yet this does not depreciate his great attainments. "The Outcast of Poker Flat," "The Luck of Roaring Camp," and many of his poems are hewed out of the very living heart of humanity, and will live while romance lives. Of his later prose works the more important are as follows: "Echoes of the Foothills" (1874); "Tales of the Argonauts" (1875); "Thankful Blossom" (1877); "The Twins of Table Mountain" (1879); "Maruja" (1885); "Snowbound at Eagle's'" (1886); "A Phyllis of the Sierras" (1888); "Mr. Jack Hamlin's Mediation" (1899); "Under the Redwoods" (1901).—GILBERT, HENRY, 1903, *The Literary Year-Book*, p. 62.

PERSONAL

A great reception—about 100 New York notables. I think I was most interested in Bret Harte. Tell Baynes I met him, and had a long talk with him,—a very gentlemanly quiet fellow.—TULLOCH, JOHN, 1874, *Letter, April 22; A Memoir*, ed. Oliphant, p. 289.

At the desk, surrounded by an incalculable visitation of Christmas cards, sits Bret Harte, the Bret Harte of actuality, a gentleman as far removed from the Bret Harte of popular fancy as is the St. James Club from Mount Shasta, or a Savoy Hotel supper from the cinder cuisine of a mining camp in the glorious days of '49. Instead of being, as the reader usually conceives, one of the long-bearded, loose-jointed heroes of his Western Walhalla, he is a polished gentleman of medium height, with a curling gray mustache. In lieu of the recklessness of Western methods in dress, his attire exhibits a nicety of detail which, in a man whose dignity and sincerity were less impressive, would seem foppish. This quality, like his handwriting and other characteristic trifles, perceptibly assists one in grasping the main elements of a personality which is as harmonious as it is peculiar, and as unconventional as it is sensitive to fine shades, of whatever kind they may be. Over his cigar, with a gentle play of humor and a variety of unconscious gestures which are always graceful and never twice the same, he touches upon this very subject—the impressions made upon him by his first sight of gold-hunting in California, and the eye and mind which he brought to bear upon the novel scene.—DAM, HENRY J. W., 1894, *A Morning With Bret Harte, Human Documents*, p. 165.

He was a slender, rather handsome young man with very black hair, and looked as Dickens did at his age. He was pathetically pleased to get rid of California, which he hated. He admired some wild daisies which decorated Mrs. Peterson's always beautiful table, and showed them to his wife. He gave me such an idea of the dreariness, absence of color, and degradation of a mining camp that I never read one of his immortal stories that I do not seem to taste that dust-laden air. I had the pleasure during ten years to assist at lionizing this great genius, and he was so natural, simple, and charming that he became a familiar figure in my family. I met him in London at the height of his foreign fame, in 1884. White-haired and ruddy-faced, he had become a typical John Bull.—SHERWOOD, MARY E. W., 1897, *An Epistle to Posterity*, p. 192.

Harte always manifested in his work that fastidiousness in choice of words which has characterized him ever since. It was humorously complained of him that he filled the newspaper-office waste-baskets with his rejected manuscripts and produced next to nothing for the printer. Once, assigned to the task of writing an obituary article that was not to exceed "two stickfuls" in length, he actually filled a wastebasket with fragments of "copy" which he tore up before he produced the requisite amount of matter. . . . In conversation among his fellows, Bret Harte was always one of the most delightful of talkers. I use here the past tense, for I do not know what a long residence in foreign parts may have done for our old friend. But with us in California he was a charming companion, with a perpetual flow of gentle humor and good spirits that fascinated his associates. Conversation in which he had part was never dull, and many a sparkling "feast of reason and flow of soul" can they recall who were comrades of the poet and story-teller in those far-off days.—BROOKS, NOAH, 1899, *Bret Harte in California, Century Magazine*, vol. 58, pp. 447, 451.

One feature that could not fail to strike Bret Harte's associates was his strong attachment to the land of his birth. Throughout his long exile his love for and loyalty towards his fatherland never wavered. America was always *"my* country" with him; and I remember how he flushed with almost boyish pleasure when, in driving through some casual rural festivities, his quick eye noted a stray American flag among the display of bunting. At the time when there was some foolish talk of war between Britain and America, he, while deploring even the suggestion of such a catastrophe, earnestly avowed his intention of instantly returning to his own country should hostilities break out.—BOYD, MARY STUART, 1902, *Some Letters of Bret Harte, Harper's Magazine*, vol. 105, p. 773.

GENERAL

Bret Harte's genius is not unlike Rembrandt's, so far as it is a matter of art. Take Miggles—Miggles telling her story at the feet of the paralytic Jim—take the description of his old face, with its solemn eyes; take the alternate gloom and light that hides or illuminates the group in Miggles' cabin; and then consider the gleam and grace with which the portrait of that racy and heroic boy-woman is placed before you. Does it not touch your sense of the picturesque and is it not unexpected, and startling, and admirable, like a sketch of Rembrandt? But for the pathos, but for the "tears that rise in the heart and gather to the eyes," where shall we find any homely art to be compared with that? Beauty in painting or sculpture may so touch a man. It did so touch Heine, at the feet of the Venus of Milo. It may be pathetic to us, as in Da Vinci's wonderful heads. But no great plastic artist, no mere pictorial talent, is potent over the sources of our tears, as is the unheralded story-writer from the Western shores. In this he employs a means beyond the reach of Holbein or Hogarth. . . . Bret Harte has deepened and broadened our literary and moral sympathies; he has broken the sway of the artificial and conventional; he has substituted actualities for idealities—but actualities that manifest the grandeur of self-sacrifice, the beauty of love, the power of childhood, and the ascendancy of nature.—GODWIN, PARKE, 1870, *Editorial Notes, Putnam's Magazine*, vol. 16, pp. 110, 111.

In the region of pure poetry, he has given us some things we would not willingly part with: two or three clearly-outlined, fresh-tinted descriptive pieces,—such as "Madroño," and "Grizzly;" and a few poems of tender sentiment,—"Dickens in Camp," "The Pen of Starr King," and the pensive, charming little reverie "To a Seabird." But his best success as a poet has been, thus far, in that borderland between prose and poetry which combines the choicest features of both kingdoms. . . . Although by no means destitute of imagination, Mr. Harte belongs to the realistic rather than the ideal school of writers; his greatest success has been in describing what he sees and knows, and his most striking characters are evidently drawn from life: "Oakhurst," "Jack Hamlin," "Tennessee's Partner," "Miggles," "M'liss," are all as clear and finished as photographs; and even many of his minor characters, such as "Yuba Bill," "Sandy Morton," "David Fagg," and "McSnagley," have all the faithfulness of portraits.—FORMAN, EMILY S., 1871, *Old and New*, vol. 4, pp. 714, 715.

Where our author really deserves hearty praise is in his "Poems in Dialect." They are less often poems, strictly so-called, than humorous character-pieces illustrative of the wild life and the strange personages of the early Californian days. In some of these pieces—as in that which treats of the "heathen Chinee;" and of the sudden revulsion of feeling in the breast of Mr. Nye when he finds that the Chinee who was to be cheated is not altogether guileless, but can himself violate the moral law with a skill, effect, and sinfulness sickening to Mr. Nye's Caucasian moral sense; and of the instant discovery and assertion by Mr. Nye of the politico-economical truth that "we are ruined by Chinee cheap labor;" and of the promptness and thoroughness with which he vindicates the moral and the economical law—in this and some of the other pieces, Mr. Harte not only jumps luckily with the popular thought and feeling of the moment, but proves himself a satirist with a keen eye, and a humorist with a light and sure hand, and a fine power of expression.—DENNETT, J. R., 1871, *Bret Harte's Poems, The Nation*, vol. 12, p. 43.

Nevertheless he remains what he is—the Californian and the gold-digger. But the gold for which he has dug, and which he found, is not the gold in the bed of rivers,—not the gold in the veins of mountains; it is the gold of love, of goodness, of fidelity, of humanity, which even in rude and wild hearts,—even under the rubbish of vices and sins,—remains forever uneradicated from the human heart. That he there searched for this gold,—that he found it there and triumphantly exhibited it to the world,—that is his greatness and his merit. That it is which drew hearts to him wherever the language of Shakespeare, of Milton and Byron is spoken. And that it is which has made me, the old German poet, the translator of the young American colleague; and which has led me today to reach to him warmly and cordially my hand across the sea. Good luck, Bret Harte! Good luck, my golddigger!—FREILIGRATH, FERDINAND, 1872, *Harte's Prose Tales, Preface.*

What Harte's repute and standing are in his own land need not now be told. Few writers of modern times have been more discussed; it were better if his critics had always been generous as well as just. But it would not be fair to close this little sketch without noting the fact that most of his works have found eager readers in other lands. English editions of his stories are popular and widely circulated. In Germany, the genial old poet, Ferdinand Freiligrath, has translated a volume of Harte's prose tales, to which is prefixed a charming preface by the translator. . . . Th. Bentzon has charmingly introduced some of Harte's California sketches to the French world of readers, and, in an article in the *Revue des Deux Mondes*, she has given at great length a critical analysis of the powers and genius of our favorite story-teller. Our French and German friends alike wrestle with the difficulties of the untranslatable; but, *malgré* their failure to master the dialect of the gold-digger, they reproduce admirably the delicate finish and felicitous manipulation of the author. Thus his genius has found expression in many languages, and the gentle, loving spirit which animates his works lives and walks in other lands beyond the sea.—BROOKS, NOAH, 1873, *Bret Harte, Scribner's Monthly, vol. 6, p.* 161.

This is only equalled by the "Heathen Chinee." This poet humorist of the Sierras, producing the Patois of the miner and the hunter of the Pacific slope, and drawing an economical lesson out of the game of euchre by the aid of Ah Sin, the pensive and child-like Celestial, has in it all the facetiousness of Dickens and of his Sairy Gamp in Truthful James, all the mischievous deviltry which Bill Nye could furnish, and all the roistering rowdyism of a scene in "Harry Lorrequer." Besides, it has in it a moral which an Oriental story-teller would envy. It brings together the Orient and Occident of cunning fun. Withal, it has the element of exaggeration, without which no American humor seems to be possible.—COX, SAMUEL SULLIVAN, 1875, *American Humor, Harper's Magazine, vol.* 50, *p.* 848.

His subtility of ethical insight, his depth of sentiment, his power of solid characterization, and his pathetic and tragic force are as evident as his broad perception of the ludicrous side of things. In his California stories, as in some of his poems, he detects "the soul of goodness in things evil," and represents the exact circumstances in which ruffians and profligates are compelled to feel that they have human hearts and spiritual natures. He is original not only in the ordinary sense of the word, but in the sense of discovering a new domain of literature, and of colonizing it by the creations of his own brain. Perhaps the immense popularity of some of his humorous poems, such as "The Heathen Chinee," has not been favorable to a full recognition of his graver qualities of heart and imagination.—WHIPPLE, EDWIN PERCY, 1876–86, *American Literature and Other Papers,* ed. *Whittier, p.*116.

The scene and society of this continent have found perhaps in the works of no writer of the land such graphic expression as in those of Bret Harte. It is true that Mr. Harte's books describe the life of a remote region and of a rude frontier people. But that life was an extravaganza of the traits of our whole democratic society. It is the scenery and the society of the country, then, which are expressed in Mr. Harte's books. Mr. Harte is a bad critic of his own writings; his humor is often feeble; he is very melodramatic; he writes an ill-conditioned style; he applies the phrases of the magazine to thoughts good enough to be well expressed. But he is a writer of marked genius, and has produced works which are as certain as any of his time and country to be read in the future. The only parts of Mr. Harte's poetry which are of value are the dialect poems, and those other poems, not in dialect, which yet preserve the spirit of the dialect poems.

The rest of his verse has not much merit. . . . The gifts of Bret Harte are vivid imagination, color, dramatic dialogue, power to attract and power to entertain, a good sense of nature, a lively and daring humor, and considerable keenness of perception. His power of dialogue is surpassed by no living writer. The similitude of the talk of his characters to real speech is apparent in all his books. A few words sketch for us Miggles as his vivid fancy sees her, and then she sits down and talks exactly as such a woman would talk.—NADAL, EHRMAN SYME, 1877, *Bret Harte, North American Review*, vol. 124, pp. 81, 85.

Mr. Harte's fame in this quarter rests chiefly upon his California poems. They make but a small volume, covering about one-third of the complete edition of his poetical works. They are notably narrow in scope, but they bear witness beyond all question to the originality of his powers. They are the unique product on which his genius has stamped the spirit of the period and place that gave them birth. Their power lies in qualities which, as here grouped, were entirely new with him. They echo the opinions of an acute—and in some cases slightly snobbish—thinker with regard to social solecisms; they are satires that cut at the way in which public opinion was molded by the ignorant, the vulgar, and the shoddy. The criticism was just, but often—as on the Chinese question—it was not the popular view, and required some decision to advance it. Again, these dialect poems are the best metrical exposition of western character in its actions, speech, deportment, and odd mingling of crudeness and wickedness, with the real virtues of delicacy and honor. Never was there a more unpromising poetical field; but these pastorals are as true to California as the "Biglow Papers" are to Yankee life and manners. . . . His American poetry will always be overshadowed by his Californian verse; but he has shown himself quite equal to delighting us all in English of perfect saneness and sobriety. His earlier work—the Spanish legends and the war lyrics—are noticeable for their taste and vigor. He has a free hand as a poet. Satire, dialect verse and humor, seem to flow from him as naturally as his most delicate fancies. He seldom becomes subjective; it is not consistent with his mental equipment; and he does not always make truth the object of his serious verse.—CHENEY, WARREN, 1883, *Francis Bret Harte, Overland Monthly*, N. S., vol. 1., pp. 71, 74.

It will be remembered how like a conquering hero Bret Harte came from California in the summer of 1871. An enterprising firm in Boston had caught the gleam of a new light, a new Dickens in verse and story, and with the most magnificent offers they tempted him East. His coming was like a royal progress. Almost without a hint from these enterprising wise men of the East, all flocked to welcome the new star. And the star was wonderfully luminous, equally brilliant in prose and verse. It flashed from a region little known, and yet peculiarly fascinating to the sober people of the eastern sea-board.—MORSE, JAMES HERBERT, 1883, *The Native Element in American Fiction, Century Magazine*, vol. 26, p. 363.

That the public is always on the alert for what is both good and novel was illustrated by Bret Harte's leap into favor with his portraitures of a new and scenic world. His prose idyls of the camp and coast, even more than his ballads, were the vouchers of a poet; familiar as the verse at once became, it is far less creative than the stories. The serious portion of it, excepting a few dialect pieces,—"Jim," "In the Tunnel," etc.,—is much like the verse of Longfellow, Whittier, and Taylor; the humorous poems, though never wanting in some touch of nature, are apt to be what we do not recognize as American. But of either class it may be said that it is, like the rhyming of his master, Thackeray, the overflow of a rare genius, whose work must be counted among the treasures of the language. Mr. Harte may be termed the founder, and thus far has been the most brilliant exemplar, of our transcontinental school.—STEDMAN, EDMUND CLARENCE, 1885, *Poets of America*, p. 451.

Of contemporary Americans, if I may be frank, I prefer the verse of Mr. Bret Harte, verse with so many tunes and turns, as comic as the "Heathen Chinee," as tender as the lay of the ship with its crew of children that slipped its moorings in the fog. To me it seems that Mr. Bret Harte's poems have never (at least in this country) been sufficiently esteemed.—LANG, ANDREW, 1889, *Letters on Literature*, p. 155.

Bret Harte plays always one tune, although he pitches it in many keys, and good as it is, it is perhaps becoming a little wearisome. He expounds an important half-truth which has been too much neglected: that as being is greater than seeming, appearances are often deceitful; under the most repellent exterior a soul of goodness may exist. But if we study him over much, we may become victims of the delusion that any person whose dress and manners are respectable, is, to say the least, a suspicious character, while drunken and profane ruffians are the saints of the earth.—LEWIN, WALTER, 1889, *The Abuse of Fiction, The Forum*, vol. 7, p. 670.

His own style, as finally formed, leaves little to be desired; it is clear, flexible, virile, laconic and withal graceful. Its full meaning is given to every word, and occasionally, like all original masters of prose, he imparts into a familiar word a racier significance than it had possessed before. His genius is nowhere more unmistakable than in the handling of his stories, which is terse to the point of severity, yet wholly adequate; everything necessary to the matter in hand is told, but with an economy of word and phrase that betokens a powerful and radical conception. Nothing in his plots or characters is conventional; they are aspects of genuine life, selected and seen with surpassing skill and insight.—HAWTHORNE, JULIAN, AND LEMMON, LEONARD, 1891, *American History*, p. 245.

Bret Harte was not yet thirty when "The Luck" captured and comforted the hungry heart of Roaring Camp, and that Camp the heart of all the world. Yet his success never once agitated him. He did not value "The Heathen Chinee," and seemed to deplore the emotional interest it excited; I believe he sought consolation in the knowledge that rash enthusiasm is necessarily ephemeral. His reputation was founded upon a basis of solid worth; even the sensational success of " The Heathen Chinee" could not endanger it. Its establishment was sudden, one might almost say instantaneous; for parallels, I recall at this moment "Waverley" and "The Pickwick Papers." . . . The greatest successes have ever been, and most likely will ever be where the scene is laid on California soil, and the characters are Californians of the pioneer and early native types. . . . Of American authors, Bret Harte and Mark Twain have traveled farthest, and are likely to tarry longest. Whom would you substitute for these?—STODDARD, CHARLES WARREN, 1896, *Early Recollections of Bret Harte, Atlantic Monthly*, vol. 78, pp. 677, 678.

During the earlier period of his literary career, when his message to the world was as yet untold and burning within him, Harte as often expressed himself in poetry as in prose, and indeed his first prose sketches in their intensity, their conception, and workmanship are very near to poetry. His poems were innovations as truly original in conception and execution as they were in subject and theme. They are mostly monologues written in the dialect of the mines, full of slang and exclamation. There is little variety. A few stock characters and a few incidents are used over and over again. The wit is sometimes forced and the humor overdrawn. But nevertheless there is in them the indefinable charm of genius. Here and there are lyrics that, judged by any standard, are faultless gems.—PATEE, FRED LEWIS, 1896, *A History of American Literature*, p. 397.

Bret Harte got his California and his Californians by unconscious absorption, and put both of them into his tales alive. But when he came from the Pacific to the Atlantic and tried to do Newport life from study—conscious observation—his failure was absolutely monumental.—CLEMENS, SAMUEL LANGHORNE (MARK TWAIN), 1897, *What Paul Bourget Thinks of Us, How to Tell a Story and Other Essays*, p. 187.

Much objection has been raised to some of Bret Harte's stories on the ground of their supposed immoral tendency. It must be admitted by his most ardent admirers that he decidedly prefers as heroes and heroines of his tales people of shady antecedents,— social outcasts preferred, but anybody who is in the habit of daily shattering a few of the commandments will answer his purpose. . . . The real objection to Bret Harte's stories does not rest on moral, but on artistic grounds. The trouble with his villains is not that they are too bad, but that they are not bad enough,—that is to say, they are not real. Such villains never were on sea or land outside of his stories, unless we except the Bowery stage in the melodrama of "ye olden time." There is a glare of the footlights, an atmosphere of the theatre, about too many of these tales,— not the best of them, for the best work of Mr. Harte is free from this defect, and ranks among the choicest in recent American literature.—VEDDER, HENRY C., 1897, *American Writers of To-Day, pp.* 225, 227.

In the case of the more objective heroines of such a writer as Bret Harte, one recalls out of the whole number of his more conventionalized types, his Miggles, who belongs rather with the edifying Magdalenes of the mining communities than with the sinuous and ophidian group of his politer ladies, too recognizably descended from the heroines of Charles Reade. Neither sort forms the forte of a writer who stamped his peculiar literary personality upon the fancy of his generation so vigorously, and who still keeps so large a public faithful to him. He is at his strongest with his men.—HOWELLS, WILLIAM DEAN, 1901, *Heroines of Fiction, vol.* II, p. 226.

Over thirty years ago Bret Harte's "Luck of Roaring Camp," and other sketches of California miners, gamblers, stage robbers, of the motley, lawless life generally in the gulches and gold fields, were welcomed with general delight, very like the later reception of Kipling's first stories. While his years have more than doubled, Mr. Harte, through one decade spent in the Eastern states and more than one in England, has worked the same vein. Readers he must still find, in other lands at least; but his very name is now hardly familiar to our boys' ears. His verse, serious or comic, is still less remembered to-day, and yet "Ah Sin" is probably the last example of a poem that set our whole people laughing. It perceptibly affected public opinion on a burning question, that of the Chinese Exclusion Bill. There is no dangerous immorality in Mr. Harte's stories. But they pall upon us at last, because, after the novelty wears off, their melodramatic unreality forces itself even upon the most boyish mind.—LAWTON, WILLIAM CRANSTON, 1902, *Introduction to the Study of American Literature*, p. 333.

There are more than nine hundred and ninety-nine excellent reasons which we could all have for admiring the work of Bret Harte. But one supreme reason stands out in a certain general superiority to them all—a reason which may be stated in three propositions, united in a common conclusion: first, that he was a genuine American; second, that he was a genuine humorist; and, third, that he was not an American humorist. Bret Harte had his own peculiar humor, but it had nothing in particular to do with American humor. American humor has its own peculiar excellence, but it has nothing in particular to do with Bret Harte. American humor is purely exaggerated; Bret Harte's humor was sympathetic and analytical.—CHESTERTON, G. K., 1902, *American Humor and Bret Harte, The Critic, vol.* 41, p. 170.

Francis Richard Stockton
1834–1902

Born Philadelphia, April 5, 1834; graduate Philadelphia High School; journalist on Philadelphia and New York newspapers; began career as author (under name of Frank R. Stockton) by contributions to magazines; joined staff of Scribner's Monthly, and later was asst. editor St. Nicholas. *Author* (juvenile books): "Roundabout Rambles;" "Tales Out of School;" "A Jolly Fellowship;" "Captain Chap;" " The Story of Viteau;" "Ting-A-Ling Stories;" "What Might Have Been Expected;" "The Floating Prince Kobel Land;" "The Bee Man of Orn;" "The Clocks of Rondaine;" "Personally Conducted;" "Stories of New Jersey;" "Buccaneers and Pirates of Our Coast." Novels and Stories: "The Lady or the Tiger;" "The Young Master of Hyson Hall;" "The Late Mrs. Null;" "The Great War Syndicate;" "The Hundredth Man;" "Stories of Three Burglars;" "A Chosen Few;" "Adventures of Captain Horn;" "Mrs. Cliff's Yacht;" "The Great Stone of Sardis;" "The Girl at Cobhurst;" "Rudder Grange;" "The Rudder Grangers Abroad;" "Pomona's Travels;" "The Casting Away of Mrs. Lecks and Mrs. Aleshine;" "Christmas Wreck and Other Stories;" "The Dusantes" (sequel to Mrs. Lecks & Aleshine); "Amos Kilbright;" "Ardis Claverden;" "The Merry Chanter;" "The House of Martha;" "The Watchmaker's Wife;" "A Story Teller's Pack;" "The Associate Hermits;" "The Vizier of the Two-Horned Alexander;" "Afield and Afloat;" "Bicycle of Cathay."—LEONARD, JOHN W., ed., 1901, *Who's Who in America*, p. 1901.

PERSONAL

Mr. Stockton's habit of dictating was acquired when his days were given to editing. Then it rested him to be able to register his ideas without the intervention of a pen. Now, he would find it difficult to write freely in any other way. With the regularity of the clock he begins his morning's work at ten. If he is drawing on his store-house of finished stories he dictates for two hours and a half, seldom longer. But if he is composing ne gives his thoughts entirely to himself, with the same regularity as to time, and perhaps for many days together. Few changes, and these only verbal, are made in the first written draft; and while he always seeks to find the word of all words that would lend felicity and vigor to a phrase, he never polishes. Once penned, a story is seldom kept over night, but is at once sent to its destination. In the afternoon he goes forth for recreation and acquaintance with the world that he paints. He studies character everywhere, and in an imaginative way is as much given to models as any graphic artist.—BUEL, CLARENCE CLOUGH, 1886, *The Author of "The Lady, or the Tiger," Century Magazine, vol.* 32, *p.* 411.

We see a quiet, mild-manered man, slight of figure, vibrant of voice, strong yet mobile of face, with hair and mustache of iron-gray, and with large, dark, luminous eyes that behold everything about them,—responsive eyes that dance with merriment or deepen with feeling. This study, in which so much of his literary work has been done, is of all places the one most meet for a chat with the author concerning his books. It is a spacious, cheerful, pleasantly furnished apartment, with panelled ceiling, and with windows that look out upon an entrancing landscape of green and golden fields and farther forest-clad hills. . . . The usual disorder of manuscripts, papers, and books is conspicuously absent, and we look in vain for some justification of the averment of a visitor that, while the touch of the lady is seen in the other apartments, the tiger evidently holds undisputed sway in the study: except for an array of unanswered letters upon the desk, this room is as orderly as any other in that well-ordered house. . . In this room he is, when at home, regularly engaged for about three hours of each morning. Seated in the easiest of easy chairs, or more often reclined in a hammock swung across a portion of the apartment, he dictates the first draft of his matchless stories, which usually—even to the conversations and the minutest details—have been constructed in his mind perhaps months before a word of them is written.—WOLFE, THEODORE F., 1899, *Where Stockton Wrote his Stories, Lippincotts Magazine, vol.* 64, *pp.* 370, 371.

GENERAL

It is scarcely four years since Frank R. Stockton broached the enigma of "The Lady, or the Tiger?" and ceasing to be only "a rising young man," realized the complete success which he is now enjoying at the age of fifty-two. As he himself says, his career is an instance of "protracted youth." Before he was twenty he had made up his mind to be an author, and during nearly thirty years of sporadic literary work his nimbus, like the northern lights, had flickered a little this side or that, or momentarily shown a spectacular glow. It was entirely visible to many when the "Rudder Grange" sketches appeared in a hap-hazard, transient way. But not until the little conundrum of three magazine pages had set everybody talking did he become a celebrity. . . . He is never loath to explain that from the first adventure of the fairy Ting-a-ling, through "The Floating Prince" series, and down to the recent story of "The Griffin and the Minor Canon," all of his marvelous tales were written for grown people. But when editors of "grownup" magazines have objected to his "machinery," he has been compelled to carry them to the children, who, to be sure, carry them direct to the grown people. In large part the humor of his fairy stories depends upon their travesty of the traditions of fairy literature; something that only the adult or maturing mind can fully enjoy; but with the humor, there is always a story of incident which satisfies a child's love of adventure and of the marvelous. . . . Must stand ["Rudder Grange"] as a master-piece of fanciful, refined comicality, profound enough in its way to entitle the author to a seat in the American Academy. Nearly all of its incidents and characters are real. But who else would have seen fun and philosophy in them and touched them with the same life-giving art? Surely in its quiet, wholesome, fireside humor this book is inimitable. . . . Of "The Late Mrs. Null," everybody has just made an opinion or is forming one. It has been praised with the criticism that it is too clever and running over with prodigality of invention and surprises of situation. . . . Though "The Late Mrs. Null" is a little uneven in texture, as might be expected of a first novel from a hand long practiced in the form of the short story, we may still think it the author's deepest and broadest work. It certainly proves that he is perfectly at home in the region of novels, and it is no secret that his studio is now set with large canvasses.—BUELL, CLARENCE CLOUGH, 1886, *The Author of "The Lady, or The Tiger," Century Magazine, vol.* 32, *pp.* 405, 410, 411, 412.

A delightful piece of delicate and humorous extravaganza, with a quality so distinctive and yet so difficult to characterize that this very difficulty bears witness to its originality.—MABIE, HAMILTON WRIGHT, 1892, *A Year's Literary Production, The Forum, vol.* 12, *p.* 801.

From one point of view Mr. Stockton may almost be said to have no style. There is nothing, one means, in the mere turn of his sentences, in his method of expression, that can be seized upon as characteristic, and laid away in memory as a sort of trademark by which the author's other work may be tested, judged and identified. It is very plain, simple, flowing English, this style of Stockton's, the sort of writing that appears to the inexperienced the easiest thing in the world to do—until they have tried. The art that conceals art, until it can pass for nature itself,—that, we are continually told, is the highest type, and the secret of that Mr. Stockton has somehow caught. . . . He has made for himself a place unique and unapproachable in the regard of those who love good literature. Original to the verge of eccentricity, he provokes no comparisons with any writer.—VEDDER, HENRY C., 1895, *American Writers of To-Day, pp.* 293, 299.

He is of the few, of the little group sparely increased by the fastidious ages, whom we call masters. It is not my business to declare whether Mr. Stockton is one of these: I willingly leave that to the infant epoch, which is still too young to know if it be the Twentieth Century or not; but I am sure that his literary personality was as charming to me when I read a story of his last night as it was when I first made his acquaintance in fiction thirty years ago. . . . He has not changed, and I think he has been as good in some of the achievements least acclaimed, as in those which have spread his fame the widest, like "The Lady or the Tiger," and "Negative Gravity," although I will not allow that any man likes these more than I. The means in all have been the same: the quiet confidence that every intelligent person enjoys an absurdity reduced from the most logical argument; and prefers the wildest capers of the fancy performed with a countenance of the gravest sobriety. . . . I am not going to let the reader suppose that I think all Mr. Stockton's work equally good, and so leave him to plume himself upon an apparent critical superiority. In fact, I have never been quite able to satisfy myself that among Mr. Stockton's novels which I liked best there were any that I liked so well as his short stories. I have had my doubts whether he really has the long breath. But some of the novels—they are really romances in the truest meaning of the word—are so good that they have given me doubts of my doubts. When I think of "The Adventures of Captain Horn" and "The Merry Chanter," I am not at all satisfied with my misgivings, and I am inclined to think it would be well for any doubter to read the romances in this new Shenandoah Edition again.—HOWELLS, WILLIAM DEAN, 1900, *Mr. Stockton and all his Works, The Book Buyer, vol.* 20, *p.* 20.

His ship of fancy flew the flag
Of goodly mirth and banter.
No sounder sail e'er breasted gale
Than owned our *Merry Chanter*.
Its hold was stored with priceless freight,
Pure humor, fun capricious;
Beneath the cheer there lurked no sneer,
Cold, cynical, malicious.
It spurned the bitter tang of brine,
It plumbed no depths of trouble;
It rode the sea as light and free
As it had been a bubble.
Its course was ever clear and true,
Its steersman loved bold faring.
Where is one now to point a prow
With such delightful daring?

—LIPPMANN, JULIE M., 1902, *To Our "Merry Chanter," Century Magazine, vol.* 64, *p.* 422.

The most elaborately and solemnly absurd of all our humorists. Everything his characters perpetuate is copiously justified, even urged plausibly upon us as obviously the only thing to do; and while we are vaguely aware that in our own world these people would all be labeled idiots, under his kindlier sky they invariably come to fortune, fame, and happy wedlock. His sea tales strike a more novel vein than Cooper's. In one child's story, "Old Pipes and the Hamadryad," he tosses us, with a gentle grin, an exquisite, genuine mock-Hellenic myth. So it is possible our mirth is bought, in the case of Stockton, at the price of a poet's birthright.—LAWTON, WILLIAM CRANSTON, 1902, *Introduction to the Study of American Literature*, p. 346.

Was a novelist who had to work and wait for many years before popularity came to him. Not that his work was of that extraordinary kind that does not lend itself to being easily labelled and assimilated by careless critics, but the public did not easily take to his quiet humour. . . . In 1879, on the publication of "Rudder Grange," a world-wide fame was his reward. He never greatly varied from the level he had first attained; he helped to amuse people, but his whimsicality played on the surface of men and things, and therefore lacks to many minds the arrestive air of the best writings.—GILBERT, HENRY, 1903, *The Literary Year-Book*, p. 66.

Edward Eggleston
1837–1902

Author; born Vevay, Ind., Dec. 10, 1837; educated in country and village schools in Ind. and at boarding school in Amelia Co., Va. (hon. degrees A.M., S.T.D., L.H.D.); married 2d, Sept. 14, 1891, Frances E. Goode. Entered M.E. ministry, 1857, traveling circuit in Southeast Ind., and later for 9 yrs. in Minn.; asso. editor *Little Corporal*, Chicago 1866-7; chief editor *National Sunday School Teacher*, 1867-70; editor *Independent*, New York, 1870-2; *Hearth and Home*, New York, 1871-2; pastor Ch. of Christian Endeavor, Brooklyn, 1874-9; since then retired from ministry and devoted to literature; pres. Am. Hist. Soc.; mem. Century Club, Authors Club. *Author:* "Mr. Blake's Walking Stick," 1870; "The Hoosier Schoolmaster," 1871; "The End of the World," 1872; "The Mystery of Metropolisville," 1873 "The Circuit Rider," 1874; "The Schoolmaster's Stories," 1874; "Roxy," 1878; "The Hoosier School-Boy," 1883; "Queer Stories," 1884; "The Graysons," 1888; "History of the United States and Its People, for the Use of Schools," 1888; "Household History of the United States and Its People," 1888; "First Book in American History," 1889; "The Faith Doctor," 1891; "Duffels," 1893; "Stories of Great Americans for Little Americans;" "Stories of American Life and Adventure;" "The Beginners of a Nation," 1896; "The Transit of Civilization from England to America," 1900. *Editor:* "Christ in Art," 1874; "Christ in Literature," 1875.—LEONARD, JOHN W., ed., 1901, *Who's Who in America*, p. 342.

PERSONAL

He was a sickly boy, never able to endure the confinement of the schoolroom. One year he spent in quest of health among his father's relatives in Virginia, and while there enjoyed such facilities of instruction as the sons of Southern planters were able to get in their native State; but all his knowledge of "schools and schoolmasters" was gained in a little more than two years. Apart from this he is wholly self-educated. A little Latin, less Greek, more Italian and Spanish, and of French a plenty, he has acquired without a teacher; the rest of his education has come through a wide reading of English literature.—GLADDEN, WASHINGTON, 1873, *Scribner's Monthly*, vol. 6, p. 561.

I first got acquainted with Dr. Eggleston through his novels "The Circuit Rider" and "Roxy," and being then in the novel-reading phase of intellectual development, I of course believed them unrivalled in contemporary literature, as they fairly are of their kind. My enthusiasm lasted till I heard him preach from the pulpit, and straightway my admiration for the writer was lost in astonishment at the preacher. Never had I heard such sermons; and I still believe I never have. But upon closer acquaintance my astonishment at the preacher was swallowed up in wonder at the conversational powers of my new friend. Never had I heard such a talker—never have I heard such a one. But the best unveiling was the last, when I discovered under all these multifarious aspects the characteristics and attributes of a born philanthropist. Hitherto I had known only the writer, the preacher, and the talker; now I began to know the man. . . . Fortunately a splendid physique defeats the ill-effects that would seem inevitable. And indeed every literary man should possess the nerves of a farmer and the physique of a prize-fighter as a natural basis of success. Dr. Eggleston is a good sailor and an expert climber, and with these accomplishments, and a perpetually cheerful humor, he manages to keep his body in trim. . . . Everybody knows something of his personal appearance, if not by sight, then by report—the great bulk of frame, the large leonine head, now slightly grizzled, the deep, sharp, kindly eyes, the movements deliberate but not slow; and more, perhaps, of his conversation—precise, rapid, multifarious, swarming with ideas and the suggestions of things which the rapidity of his utterance prevents him from elaborating—original, opulent of forms, rich in quotation and allusion. And then the laugh—vast, inspiriting, uplifting.—AURINGER, OBADIAH CYRUS, 1887, *Dr. Edward Eggleston at Lake George, The Critic*, vol. 11, p. 112.

GENERAL

Its author has made for himself an opportunity to do for some of the more obvious phases of Western life what such books as "Locke Amsden, the Yankee Schoolmaster," and scores of others of various merit have done for the life of New England. The band of thieves such as still here and there infest the Western country, keeping grand juries in awe, electing or killing sheriffs, and necessitating or instigating lynch-law executions; the "protracted meeting;" the spelling school in the evening; the "rough and tumble" fights; the brutality and sodden vulgarity of the ruder part of the community; the jumble of religious sects—something of these things which all once were of the West, if not precisely the West itself, is, on the whole, not ill sketched by Mr. Eggleston, and as these things are rapidly passing away, and are not finding too many or too clever observers, it is well that a man like Mr. Eggleston, with a fair share of literary skill, has taken occasion to sketch them.—DENNETT, J. R., 1872, *The Hoosier Schoolmaster, The Nation*, vol. 14, p. 45.

Dr. Eggleston is a close and sympathetic student of human nature, and his characters and the incidents of his stories are drawn from the life. We can scarcely point to any truer work in American fiction than some of the character-drawing in his first two stories. He has given us, thus far, chiefly *genre* pictures; but art of this sort requires as fine a pencil and as large a sympathy as that of a more pretentious nature. As contributions to the history of civilization in America, these stories are also valuable. In "The Hoosier Schoolmaster," Dr. Eggleston has given us as faithful a picture of life in Southern Indiana, twenty-five years ago, as Bret Harte has given us of "The Argonauts of '49," or as Scott has given us, in "Ivanhoe," of life in England after the Norman conquest. The life thus described is, like that described by Bret Harte, only one episode in this great epic of our civilization; and the description of it is only one study for the complete picture of our national life; but it is of immense value for all that to all who want to know what manner of nation this has been and is to be. The chief defect of these stories is in the plot. In this respect they are no more faulty than some of the stories of George MacDonald, yet those who read novels for the action rather than the philosophy, may have cause of complaint against them.—GLADDEN, WASHINGTON, 1873, *Edward Eggleston, Scribner's Monthly*, vol. 6, p. 563.

The starting-point of novel-writing with me was the accidental production of a little newspaper story, dashed off in ten weeks, amid pressing editorial duties, and with no thought of making a book. The "Hoosier Schoolmaster," faulty and unfinished as it is, first won public attention for me, and now, after sixteen years, the exasperating public still buys thousands of copies of it annually, preferring it to the most careful work I can do. I am often asked in regard to the immediate impetus to the writing of this story. . . . I had just finished reading Taine's "Art in the Netherlands." Applying his maxim, that an artist ought to paint what he has seen; I tried my hand on the dialect and other traits of the more illiterate people of Southern Indiana.—EGGLESTON, EDWARD, 1888, *Books that Have Helped Me*, p. 55.

JAMES MARTINEAU

Engraving by Hollyer. From a Painting by Watts.

HERBERT SPENCER

Engraving by George E. Perine.

All men have marked, along life's mountain tops
How broad and varied was his soul's domain
With earnest crags, the fruitful, fair champaign,
And hollows brimmed with sunshine, cloistered copse;
But few how high, by what sky-reaching props
That realm was lifted heavenward o'er the plain,
Or known how native to his ear that strain
Hymming the Highest through a thousand stops.
Not his the travel of some pilgrim wight
Who buys with pain a space whereon to spread
His narrow death-couch upon sacred sod;
Familiar there, he has but said good-night,
And drawn around the curtain of his bed,
And laid him down upon the breast of God.
—AURINGER, OBADIAH CYRUS, 1902, *Edward Eggleston, The Critic, vol.* 41, *p.* 332.

Herbert Spencer
1820–1903

Born, at Derby, 27 April 1820. Privately educated. Civil Engineer, 1837-46. Subeditor of "The Economist," 1848-53. Contrib. to various reviews. Life mainly devoted to philosophical studies since 1855; occupied on his "Synthetic Philosophy" since 1860. Visit to U. S. A., 1882. Declined all academical distinctions. *Works:* "Social Statics," 1851 [1850]; "A Theory of Population" (from "Westminster Rev."), 1852; "Over-Legislation," 1854; "Railway Morals and Railway Policy," 1855; "The Principles of Psychology," 1855 (enlarged edn., 2 vols. 1870-72); "Essays . . . from the Quarterly Reviews," series. I., 1858; series II., 1863; series III., 1874; library edn. (3 vols.), 1891; "Education," 1861; "First Principles," 1862; "The Principles of Biology," (2 vols.), 1864-67; "The Classification of the Sciences," 1864; "The Study of Sociology," 1873; "The Principles of Sociology," (3 vols.), 1876-96; "The Man versus the State," 1884; "The Factors of Organic Evolution," 1887; "The Principles of Ethics," [including "The Data of Ethics," 1879, and "Justice," 1891] (2 vols.), 1892-93; "The Inadequacy of Natural Selection" (from "Contemp. Rev.") [1893]; "A Rejoinder to Prof. Weismann" (from "Contemp. Rev.") [1893]; "Weismannism Once More" (from "Contemp. Rev."), 1894; "Against the Metric System" (from the "Times"), 1896; "Various Fragments" [1852-1896], 1897. He has *edited:* "Descriptive Sociology" (8 pts.), 1873-81.—SHARP, R. FARQUHARSON, 1897, *A Dictionary of English Authors, p.* 265.

PERSONAL

Herbert Spencer's article on the "Genesis of Science" is a good one. He will stand in the Biographical Dictionaries of 1954 as "Spencer, Herbert, an original and profound philosophical writer, especially known by his great work . . . which gives a new impulse to psychology, and has mainly contributed to the present advanced position of that science, compared with that which it had attained in the middle of the last century. The life of this philosopher like that of the great Kant, offers little material for the narrator."—ELIOT, GEORGE, 1854, *To Miss Sara Hennell, July* 10; *George Eliot's Life as related in her Letters and Journals, ed. Cross, vol.* I, *p.* 234.

Walked along the Thames towards Kew to meet Herbert Spencer, who was to spend the day with us, and we chatted with him on matters personal and philosophical. I owe him a debt of gratitude. My acquaintance with him was the brightest ray in a very dreary, *wasted* period of my life. I had given up all ambition whatever, lived from hand to mouth, and thought the evil of each day sufficient. The stimulus of his intellect, especially during our long walks, roused my energy once more and revived my dormant love of science. His intense theorizing tendency was contagious, and it was only the stimulus of a *theory* which could then have induced me to work. I owe Spencer another and a deeper debt. It was through him that I learned to know Marian—to know her was to love her—and since then my life has been a new birth. To her I owe all my prosperity and all my happiness. God bless her!—LEWES, GEORGE HENRY, 1859, *Journal, Jan.* 28; *George Eliot's Life as related in her Letters and Journals, ed. Cross, vol.* II, *p.* 55.

It is, I suppose, no new or unseemly revelation to say that Spencer has lived for the most part a life of poverty as well as of seclusion. He is a sensitive, silent, self-reliant man, endowed with a pure passion for knowledge, and the quickest, keenest love of justice and right. There is something indeed quite Quixotic, in the better sense, about the utterly disinterested and self-forgetting eagerness with which

Herbert Spencer will set himself to see right done, even in the most trivial of cases. Little, commonplace, trifling instances of unfairness or injustice, such as most of us may observe every day, and which even the most benevolent of us will think himself warranted in passing by, on his way to his own work, without interference, will summon into activity—into positively unresting eagerness—all the sympathies and energies of Herbert Spencer, nor will the great student of life's ultimate principles return to his own high pursuits until he has obtained for the poor sempstress restitution of the over-fare exacted by the extortionate omnibus-conductor, or seen that the policeman on duty is not too rough in his treatment of the little captured pickpocket. As one man has an unappeasable passion for pictures, and another for horses, so Herbert Spencer has a passion for justice.—McCarthy, Justin, 1872, *Science and Orthodoxy in England, Modern Leaders, p.* 241.

A quiet, modest, unassuming gentleman, with no assumption of greatness, with no air of pretence, with not the slightest approach to an appearance of patronage toward those who may be considered as less noted or great than himself, has been for the last two or three months seeking rest and refreshment here in America. Heard in public but once, seen in private only by a few, the country has still felt that a great man was here, a man like to those whom Emerson refers when he says, "A great man is himself an occasion."—Savage, Minot J., 1883, *Herbert Spencer in America, Knowledge, vol.* 3, *p.* 97.

Mr. Spencer is a bachelor. Evidently he has had no time to get married. He was not, however, a recluse, till obliged to be by the exigencies of his work and the necessity of caring for his health. In 1879 I missed the pleasure of meeting him at a dinner party, because, as he wrote, he had engaged to take two ladies to the opera that evening. Observe that he took *two* ladies; he knew how to protect himself; it is a mistake to suppose that philosophers are never practical. He has always entered into social life as much as he could without interfering with his work, and he has been a welcome and an agreeable guest in many households.—Thompson, Daniel Greenleaf, 1888, *Herbert Spencer, Evolution, p.* 7.

Herbert Spencer, after his visit to America, was my fellow-voyager to England. I had pleasant talks with him, rather from him, when he was well enough to be on deck. He appeared to me a very full man, full of knowledge and sure of it, and not anxious for more from me, even if I had had it at his command, but I had not even on wood-engraving.— Linton, William James, 1894, *Threescore and Ten Years,* 1820 to 1890, *p.* 204.

The philosopher, whose life-work we have endeavoured to depict in this little volume, is still with us. He is now well advanced in years and in failing health; but his mind is amazingly fresh, as his last book brilliantly proved. In power of expression, dialectical skill, and wealth of illustration it need fear no comparison with any of his former writings. We cannot conclude this little work better than by expressing the hope that the "Grand Old Man" of philosophy may still and for long continue to regale us from the treasure of his knowledge, and by offering our sincerest congratulations upon the fact that, amid difficulties which would soon have warned off less stout hearts and finally crushed less mighty minds, he has at last reached the goal which he set himself in his youth.—Von Gaupp, Otto, 1897, *Herbert Spencer.*

Whatever the future has in store for philosophy, one prediction may confidently be made, that humanity will owe to Herbert Spencer an everlasting debt of gratitude. Forty years ago he set himself a colossal task. He resolved to give to the world a new system of philosophy. Ill-health dogged the footsteps of the philosopher all through the long spell of years, and at times it seemed as if the Synthetic Philosophy would be left an unfinished monument of splendid audacity. Handicapped by ill-health, uncheered by popular sympathy, unrewarded by the reading public, Herbert Spencer went his lonely way with a courage akin to heroism. Now he sees his task completed. Only those who have been privileged with Mr. Spencer's friendship fully know the difficulties with which he had to battle, and can estimate the victory he has won. Many thinkers in the flush of opening manhood have conceived great systems of thought, and entered upon far-reaching projects. But too often the glow of intellectual enthusiasm has died away in presence of the daily drudgery of lonely toil. Even those who get beyond the Coleridgean stage of weaving philosophic dreams, find their ideal receding as they get tangled in the pleasures, anxieties, and ambitions of Vanity Fair. Herbert Spencer has refused to soil his robes in Vanity Fair. He has treated the baubles of the passing hour with philosophic indifference. Into old age he has carried the intellectual vigor of youth, and the mellow wisdom of ripe manhood. He has never wavered in his devotion to the great interpretative and constructive ideas with which his name is associated; and thus the reader has the rare pleasure of studying a system of thought which, from start to finish, breathes the spirit of continuity. There are no gaps to fill in; the various volumes hang on "First Principles" like golden beads upon a golden string. Herbert Spencer may rest from his labors with the proud consciousness that with his own right hand he has carved his path from obscurity to a philosophic throne. He now stands among the sceptred immortals.—MACPHERSON, HECTOR, 1900, *Spencer and Spencerism*, p. 232.

Mr. Spencer's life for some fifty years has been a model of single-minded devotion to a great philosophic career. His resolute purpose to live his own life without hindrance from society, or distractions, or pursuit of fortune, fame, or rank; his unbending consistency and assertion of right and justice; his fervid enthusiasm for the cause of Peace, Industry, and Civilisation, form a spotless record in English letters.—HARRISON, FREDERIC, 1901, *George Washington and Other American Addresses*, p. 203.

All who have the privilege of knowing him are aware of his wonderful courtesy and modesty, allied to intellectual integrity. Many members of the Athenæum Club have the pleasantest recollections of the veteran philosopher, his genial ways, his clear-sighted talk, his fair mindedness and his urbanity. In appearance he might be taken for a septuagenarian rather than an octogenerian. He still reads his correspondence without eyeglasses, and his hearing powers are above the average.—MICHAUD, GUSTAVE, 1901, *Herbert Spencer; The Man and the Philosopher*, *The Bookman*, vol. 14, p. 159.

GENERAL

The title of this book ["First Principles"] gives an inadequate notion of the importance of the subjects with which it deals, and of the reach and subtlety of thought which characterize it. Though some of the generalizations appear to me rather premature, no well-instructed and disciplined intellect can consider them without admiration of the remarkable powers displayed by their author.—BUCKLE, HENRY THOMAS, 1862-66, *History of Civilization in England*, vol. III, p. 364, note.

Mr. Spencer is one of the small number of persons who by the solidity and encyclopedic character of their knowledge, and their power of co-ordination and concatenation, may claim to be peers of M. Comte, and entitled to a vote in the estimate of him.—MILL, JOHN STUART, 1865, *The Positive Philosophy of Auguste Comte*, p. 39.

The views he has very vigorously propounded are shared by a number of distinguished scientific men; and not a few of the unscientific believe that in them is shadowed forth the education of the future. It is perhaps to be regretted that Mr. Spencer has not kept the tone of one who investigates the truth in a subject of great difficulty, but lays about him right and left, after the manner of a spirited controversialist. This, no doubt, makes his book much more entertaining reading than such treatises usually are, but, on the other hand, it has the disadvantage of arousing the antagonism of those whom he would most wish to influence. . . . Mr. Spencer differs very widely from the great body of our schoolmasters. I have ventured in turn to differ on some points from Mr. Spencer; but I am none the less conscious that he has written not only one of the most readable, but also one of the most important books on education in the English language.—QUICK, ROBERT HERBERT, 1868, *Essays on Educational Reformers*, pp. 224, 254.

For the past ten years I have been very carefully observing the point now in question; and my conclusion is, that it is not the "experts" who do the scoffing at Mr. Spencer, but almost without exception the literary *dilettanti* who have never received the special scientific training without which Mr. Spencer's works cannot possibly be understood or appreciated. Hitherto Mr. Spencer's reputation has been mainly a reputation with special investigators—such as Messrs. Hooker, Tyndall, and Huxley

—and of this reputation the "general public" has within the last five or six years, caught the echo. As for the "general public" having *any* opinion of its own about the merits of the "First Principles" or the "Psychology," I imagine it is about as well qualified to have an opinion about Schrauf's "Physikalische Studien" or Schleicher's "Vergleichende Grammatik."— FISKE, JOHN, 1869, *Herbert Spencer and the Experts, The Nation, vol.* 8, *p.* 434.

Among Philosophers, as among scientific men, there are original and independent minds, of an order above those who explain, comment upon, and develop truths already discovered or foreseen, and make them known to all. These original minds are, so to speak, creators, who are felt, on approaching them, to be like men of another race, in power, depth, and unity of thought. Whether their discoveries remain permanent acquisitions, or whether they only give a new aspect to insoluble problems, they are recognized in the sovereign fashion which is due to them; they cannot touch any question without setting their mark upon it. Mr. Herbert Spencer appears to us to be a man of this order. One of his countrymen, who is well entitled to be critical, Mr. Stuart Mill, unhesitatingly places him among the greatest of the philosophers, and says that the variety and depth of his encyclopedic knowledge would permit him to treat, as equal, with the founder of the positivist school himself; that he is not a disciple, but a master.— RIBOT, THÉODULE, 1874, *English Psychology, p.* 124.

There are, as we have seen, some errors and inaccuracies of detail and some very important "beggings" of the main question as to the distinction between thought and feeling. Together with these defects there are also certain failures of analysis, resulting in a confusion of thought and a mode of treatment tending, by implication, to prejudice readers who are not on their guard, against truths which are not directly attacked or even explicitly referred to.— WARD, W. G., 1874, *Examination of Mr. Herbert Spencer's Psychology, Dublin Review, vol.* 75, *p.* 496.

There have been but few advocates of any system better fitted to enlarge, harmonize, compact, and present a philosophy than is Mr. Spencer. His powers of analysis and synthesis are extraordinary, and his style is clear, full, and plausible in the extreme. The breadth of the topics discussed, and his fulness of knowledge in each, enable him to frame an argument captivating in matter, and impressing the mind with more than its real strength. The scope and vigor of Mr. Spencer's discrimination and combining powers are something to be proud of, and to be rejoiced in, on the part of all who heartily entertain the themes presented. His candor also is very noteworthy; the candor of a mind too much occupied with its own conclusions, too sure of their value and too able to confirm them by material taken from many diverse systems, to feel any strong temptation to leave its primary constructive labor and enter on an aggresive, destructive one. He pulls down only as he is in search of space or material for a new edifice.—BASCOM, JOHN, 1876, *The Synthetic or Cosmic Philosophy, Bibliotheca Sacra, vol.* 33, *p.* 618.

A spacious-brained arch-enemy of lies,
For years he has followed, with sure pace and fleet,
The stainless robe and radiant-sandalled feet
That truth makes vaguely visible as she flies.
For years he has searched, with undiscouraged eyes,
Deep at the roots of life, eager to meet
One law beneath whose sovereignty complete
Each vast and fateful century dawns or dies.
His intellect is a palace, on whose walls
Great rich historic frescoes may be seen,
And where, in matron dignity of mien,
Meeting perpetually amid its halls
Messages from victorious generals,
Calm Science walks, like some majestic queen!
—FAWCETT, EDGAR, 1878, *Herbert Spencer, Fantasy and Passion, p.* 189.

Mr. Herbert Spencer begins his lately published "Data of Ethics" by remarking that among the correlatives which imply one another in thought is the idea of part and whole; and he gives various illustrations to show that no correct conception of a part can be obtained without some understanding of the whole to which it belongs. . . . Mr. Spencer might have taken the work he was writing as a good exemplification of this principle; for it is part of a systematic body of thought, and is only to be fully understood in connection with it. Moreover, the entire system has been given out in detached fragments, which were only partially intelligible in the absence of the whole that did not yet exist. This protracted and piecemeal mode of publication has not only favored misconception on the part of the fair-minded, but it has offered advantages to ill-disposed critics which they have not been slow to use in producing erroneous impressions upon the public mind regarding the character of Spencer's work. . . . That Mr. Spencer is in the strictest sense the creator of his own work is not open to doubt, nor has there been any intelligent question about it. That which characterizes his system of thought, its wealth of facts, its searching analysis, its synthetic grasp, its logical unity, and its noble beneficence of application—stamps it also as the product of a single, original, and independent mind.—YOUMANS, EDWARD LIVINGSTON, 1879, *Spencer's Evolution Philosophy, North American Review*, vol. 129, pp. 389, 403.

Mr. Herbert Spencer may be said to have taken the sphere of the naturalist and the spheres of the metaphysician and the psychologist, and drawn a circle around, embracing and unfolding them all, and adopting them as his province. If Mr. Darwin's attempt to map out the process by which vegetable and animal life are gradually constructed was an ambitious effort, the task which Mr. Herbert Spencer undertook was of still more vast and venturous scope. . . . His views of education and of civic government seem occasionally to degenerate almost to the degree of crotchets. His style is not fascinating. It is clear, strong, and simple, but it has little literary beauty, and borrows little from illustration of any kind. Mr. Spencer himself utterly undervalues what he regards as superfluous words. Attractiveness of style is part of the instrumentality by which a great writer or speaker accomplishes his ends. If a man would convince, he must not disdain the arts by which people can be induced to listen. Much of Mr. Spencer's greatest work had long been little better than a calling aloud to solitude for the lack of the attractiveness of style which he despises, but which Plato or Aristotle would not have despised. Mr. Spencer, however, rather prides himself on not caring much about the Greeks and their literature. A great thinker he undoubtedly is—one of the greatest thinkers of modern times; perhaps a man to be classed among the the few great and original philosophers of all time. It is only of late years that his fame has begun to spread among his own countrymen. Gradually it has become known to the English public in general that there was among them a great lonely thinker, surveying the problems of mind and matter as from some high, serene watchtower. His words were well known among reading people in the United States long before they had ceased to be the exclusive property of a very select few in England.—MCCARTHY, JUSTIN, 1880, *A History of Our Own Times from the Accession of Queen Victoria to the Berlin Congress*, vol. IV, ch. LXVII.

Mr. Spencer's strength lies in his familiarity with the conceptions of physical science. He astonishes his readers through the apparently encyclopedic comprehensiveness of his scientific information. This qualifies him to take up and repeat with an effort of imposing authority the parable of his British predecessors, to the general effect that such conceptions and such information constitute the impassable limit of all possible human knowledge. His weakness is in his deficient knowledge and grasp of philosophic ideas. I find no evidence that the history of philosophic thought is much better than a sealed book for Mr. Spencer.— MORRIS, GEORGE S., 1880, *British Thought and Thinkers*, p. 340.

Many persons will have welcomed with great interest Mr. Herbert Spencer's recent work on "The Data of Ethics." He is the recognized exponent of a principle which has of late been asserting a claim to be paramount in all domains of human thought and life. He has projected a comprehensive system of philosophy, embracing the whole sphere of existence—inanimate, animate, and human—founded upon the hypothesis of Evolution.—WARE, HENRY, 1880, *Mr. Spencer's Data of Ethics, Contemporary Review*, vol. 38, p. 254.

In criticism of the earlier portion of "The Data of Ethics," it seems to me that Mr. Spencer's own theory fails to account for the facts which he himself recognizes as coming within the moral sphere; and, on the other hand, that he does not accurately represent the intuitional theory, and consequently his criticism of it is altogether wide of the mark.—CALDERWOOD, H., 1880, *Herbert Spencer on the Data of Ethics, Contemporary Review*, vol. 37, p. 76.

Mr. Herbert Spencer's Philosophy has at least one conspicuous merit—it can claim to be the most comprehensive, or rather ambitious, of English Philosophies. It is in its psychology distinctively English and empirical; but in its spirit and endeavour, distinctively encyclopædic and transcendental.—FAIRBAIRN, A. M., 1881, *Mr. Herbert Spencer's Philosophy, The Contemporary Review, vol. 40, p. 74.*

I began to read Mr. Spencer's works more than twenty years ago. They have been meat and bread to me. They have helped me through a great many difficulties. I desire to own my obligation personally to him, and to say that if I had the fortune of a millionaire, and I should pour all my gold at his feet, it would be no sort of compensation compared to that which I believe I owe him.—BEECHER, HENRY WARD, 1882, *Herbert Spencer on the Americans and the Americans on Herbert Spencer, p. 66.*

I can see no boundaries to the scope of the philosophy of evolution. That philosophy is sure to embrace all the interests of man on this earth. It will be one of its crowning triumphs to bring light and order into the social problems which are of universal bearing on all mankind. Mr. Spencer is breaking the path for us into this domain. We stand eager to follow him into it, and we look upon his work on sociology as a grand step in the history of science. When, therefore, we express our earnest hope that Mr. Spencer may have health and strength to bring his work to a speedy conclusion, we not only express our personal respect and good-will for himself, but also our sympathy with what, I doubt not, is the warmest wish of his own heart, and our appreciation of his great services to true science and to the welfare of mankind. —SUMNER, WILLIAM GRAHAM, 1882, *Herbert Spencer on the Americans and the Americans on Herbert Spencer, p. 39.*

Mainly a systematizer and organizer of ideas—a sort of intellectual clearing-house on a scale befitting the nineteenth century. BURROUGHS, JOHN, 1883, *Carlyle, Century Magazine, vol. 26, p. 530.*

This man, to whom we have been so ready to listen, has during the last quarter of a century wrought a work that, I think I may say, without exaggeration, has no parallel in the history of human thought. He has so wrought himself into the very fibre, the warp and woof of this modern world, that I can say of him, what can be said of no other man living, and what has never been said of any man who has ever lived; he has made himself so vital a part of science, of philosophy, of education, of the science of government, of sociology, of ethics, of religion — he has so mastered and entered into the possession of all these great realms of human thought and human life, which in their totality almost make up what is meant by life itself, that to-day no serious and intelligent thinker can discuss any important question pertaining to any one of these departments without being compelled to reckon with Herbert Spencer.—SAVAGE, MINOT J., 1883, *Herbert Spencer in America, Knowledge, vol. 3, p. 97.*

A biologist must, I fancy, rise from a review of Mr. Spencer's work with very mingled feelings of approbation and disappointment. There is wonder at the comprehensive grasp of thought which seizes building material for its argument from so many fields of knowledge. There is admiration for his genius in classifying phenomena and for the polemic power with which his generalizations are stated. But it would probably be safe to say that, had not the "Origin of Species" been written, the hypothesis presented in the "Principles of Biology" would still be regarded as but a "philosophical phantasy." For the biologist, the facts presented are too general, too little specific, to prove their case. There is in Mr. Spencer (as it appears to me) too marked that theological tendency, which he himself so well condemns to confound belief with evidence, and mistake the desire for a truth as a proof of the truth itself. There is too rapid a hurrying on toward the fruit of his thought without sufficiently binding together the thought itself with a tissue of facts.—SEWELL, HENRY, 1886, *Herbert Spencer as a Biologist, p. 12.*

Close upon the back of my discovery of Whitman, I came under the influence of Herbert Spencer. No more persuasive rabbi exists, and few better. How much of his vast structure will bear the touch of time, how much is clay and how much brass, it were too curious to inquire. But his words, if dry, are always manly and honest; there dwells in his pages a spirit of highly abstract joy, plucked naked like an algebraic symbol, but still joyful; and the reader will find there a *caput-mortuum* of piety, with little indeed of its loveliness, but with most of its essentials; and these two qualities make him as wholesome, as his intellectual vigour makes him a bracing, writer. I should be much of a hound if I lost my gratitude to Herbert Spencer.—STEVENSON, ROBERT LOUIS, 1887, *Books which Have Influenced Me, p.* 8.

In any list of living Englishmen eminently distinguished for the originality and importance of their books, Mr. Spencer cannot fail to be ranked high. Yet, as every student of his later work knows, he has stated in the preface of one of those bold and inexpensive volumes in which he enshrines his thought, that the sale of his books does not cover the cost of their publication. This is the case of a man famous, it is not too much to say, in every civilized country on the globe. In pure literature there is probably no second existing instance so flagrant as this.—GOSSE, EDMUND, 1889, *Making a Name in Literature, The Forum, vol.* 8, *p.* 190.

Mr. Spencer's little book, "The Man versus the State," is the most conspicuous work of recent years in defence of "individualism" and in opposition to the growing tendency of State intervention in matters which the older English economists and Radical politicians held to be best left to private enterprise and unchecked competition. From its very nature it demands and challenges critical examination. Mr. Spencer's conception of what the State is appears to me to involve grave philosophical errors, and to be inconsistent with principles which he himself has done more than any one else to popularise. . . . No one who has any interest in philosophy can refuse admiration to an Englishman who has given the energies of his life to philosophical studies, who believes that philosophy must be systematic, and who, although acting up to this belief, has made his countrymen read his books. But there are some things that demand more respect than distinguished persons—philosophy itself, and the growing sense of a common and public responsibility to diminish the misery of human life.—RITCHIE, DAVID G., 1891, *The Principles of State Interference, pp.* 3, 4.

So large is the field over which Mr. Spencer's writings have ranged, so many are the special branches of knowledge he has laid under contribution, so difficult to the ordinary mind are the abstractions in which he has dealt and the terminology in which they are couched, that this great reputation is with the large majority of the intelligent men who accept it more as a matter of faith than of reason. But this rather adds to than detracts from the popular estimate; for what to us is vague often seems on that account the greater, and what we have no means of measuring, all the more profound. Nor does Mr. Spencer's standing as one of the greatest, to many the very greatest, of philosophers, lack substantial basis in the opinions of those deemed competent to gauge intellectual power.—GEORGE, HENRY, 1892, *A Perplexed Philosopher, Introduction, p.* 3.

This volume "Social Statics," contained an extremely fresh and original treatment of social problems; was startling in many of its ideas, and extremely radical in its whole tone and tendencies. It is natural, therefore, that it should have made no small stir in the thinking world, though of course it never applied to a very large body of readers. That which it did for him personally was to bring him rather prominently into public notice, and to introduce him to a select circle of advanced thinkers, who were not slow to recognize the exceptional strength and independence of his mind.—HUDSON, WILLIAM HENRY, 1892, *Herbert Spencer: A Biographical Sketch, The Arena, vol.* 5, *p.* 281.

Who knows the influence Gall exerted, directly or indirectly, on Mr. Herbert Spencer? It seems to me impossible for any man, however great his genius, to write a work like the "Principles of Psychology," without relying at least to some extent on the legacies of the past. True, Mr. Spencer made no mention of Gall's name; but he does not on any occasion give references to or make quotations from authors who have preceded him.—HOLLÄNDER, BERNARD, 1893, *Herbert Spencer as a Phrenologist, Westminster Review, vol.* 139, *p.* 148.

It is incredible that the great saint of the new departure in Judaism should be traduced by the great saint of modern evolution, when they ought to be brothers in unity. In point of real character I do not know that there is anything to choose. In certain very trying circumstances Mr. Spencer has shown himself a perfect Christian, and if I knew as much about him as I do about Saint Paul I dare say I should find him just as good—not so fiery in temperament, not so impetuous in style, not so irresistible in his current of thought or action (suppose the enthusiasm of investigation necessitates an entirely different mental constitution from the enthusiasm of humanity)—but just as single-hearted, just as truth-seeking in regard to the action of structure on function, as was Paul over the action of Jewish law on Gentiles. But that which befalleth the sons of men befalleth also philosophers, even one thing befalleth them—the necessity of knowing what they are talking about. I abate no whit of positiveness regarding Mr. Spencer's orthodoxy as soon as Mr Spencer thinks it worth his while to learn what orthodoxy is, or to render the Bible as accurately as he renders a bird track. But, until that happy hour arrives, so often as the ever-recurring question thunders down from the Spirit of Truth, Who is this that darkeneth counsel by words without knowledge? Thousands of his most ardent disciples will rise and answer, shame-faced, but unwavering, "Herbert Spencer, God bless him!"—DODGE, MARY ABIGAIL (GAIL HAMILTON), 1893, *A Bible Lesson for Mr. Herbert Spencer, North American Review, vol.* 156, *p.* 97.

Spencer's averages are interesting as belonging to a scientific manner,—the manner, moreover, of the author to whom is due the theory that economy of attention is the governing principle of style. We find the discourse carefully analyzed into short paragraphs. These are mostly loose in structure, a definite conclusion being offered in the first sentence and defended in those following. Evidently Spencer's theory of periodic structure as the more economical, stops short of the paragraph. It is interesting, again, to note that, while Spencer's sentences rather favor the periodic type, they are not long; like the short paragraphs, they are for the untechnical reader, if not for the popular one. The variability in sentence-length is quite as great as could be expected from a style appealing so little to the emotions: the percentage of sentences of less than 15 words is 17 per cent. The coherence and sequence of Mr. Spencer's prose are philosophical and correct. The use of connectives is less than might be supposed.— LEWIS, EDWIN HERBERT, 1894, *The History of the English Paragraph, p.* 162.

It is probably accurate to describe Mr. Spencer as an empiricist; though he has added to the accustomed first principles of empiricism certain doctrines of his own which, while they do not strengthen his system, make it somewhat difficult to classify.

BALFOUR, ARTHUR JAMES, 1894, *The Foundations of Belief, p.* 124.

Like some mighty architect, thy mind
Works up the rock those lesser builders frame,
With conscious end and purpose clear defined,
In arch and column, toward a single aim,
Till joining part to part thy broader soul
Rears high a stately fane, a grand harmonious whole.
—ALLEN, GRANT, 1894, *To Herbert Spencer, The Lower Slopes, p.* 46.

Mr. Spencer seeks to shake himself free of the charge of being opposed to religion because he affirms "that out of the depths of unfathomable mystery there *may*. . . . emerge the certitudes of religion." But those familiar, as we are, with Mr. Spencer's system will understand what that "may" is worth. We are reminded by it of the proverb which declares there *may* be such things as volant, nonruminating artiodactyles, but at the same time declares them to be "very unlikely birds."—MIVART, ST. GEORGE, 1895, *Spencer Versus Balfour, Nineteenth Century, vol.* 38, *p.* 277.

We rightly make much of a man like Nansen who has braved the dangers and solitudes of the frozen North in eager search for the physical Pole; but we are apt to overlook the no less heroic qualities, and the far more tremendous labours, of such a man as Spencer, who gives forty years of his life to prodigious researches and the most arduous speculations in search of what may be called the Polar thought of the Universe—the grand conception that will explain the progress of all matter, and life, and human institutions from the beginning until now. No less than this is what Spencer sought to do. Darwin applied the doctrine of Evolution to the development of Organic Life only; and by his vast accumulations and admirable ordering of biological facts has undoubtedly done more than any other man to place it almost beyond dispute. But Spencer went far beyond that. He showed how Evolution might account not only for the development of animal and plant life on the globe, but also from the genesis of worlds, the slow upbuilding of the earth into its present form, the grouping of human beings into races and nations, and the rise and expansion of language and of law, of philosophy and of government, of morality and of religion, and of all social institutions from their crude germ in the rudimentary ideas of the untutored ages to their full flower and fruit in the marvellous civilizations of the nineteenth century. Truly a sublime and comprehensive theory, which, even more completely than Darwin's seems to realize once again the cosmical grandeur of the Newtonian Conception of a unity of power and of law binding together all things within the universe.—GRAHAM, RICHARD D., 1897, *The Masters of Victorian Literature*, p. 487.

Many years have now passed away since Herbert Spencer claimed the whole domain of knowledge as his own, and undertook to revise, in accordance with the latest lights, the whole sphere of philosophy. What must have seemed intolerable presumption in 1860 became in 1896 a completed task. In universality of knowledge he rivals Aristotle and Bacon at a time when the sphere of learning is immensely larger than in their epochs.—SHORTER, CLEMENT, 1897, *Victorian Literature*, p. 146.

For Germany, Herbert Spencer, until the beginning of the 'eighties, did not exist, and one is scarcely liable to err by assuming that even at the present day Mr. Spencer, for many German *savants* and philosophers, is not much more than a name, a fact so much more astounding as Spencer, contrary to all other English philosophers, has that in the whole character of his philosophy which makes it akin to German thought. He in no way shares the instinctive aversion of his countrymen to the deductive treatment, but everywhere insists on a close union (*innige Verknüpfung*) of the inductive and deductive methods; and again, unlike his countrymen, he sees in the analysis, not the aim and end of Philosophy, but merely a labour preparatory to the completion of her great task which lies in the synthesis, *i. e.*, in the binding and welding together of the analytically ascertained truths and facts into one harmonious *Weltanschauung*.—VON GAUPP, OTTO, 1897, *Herbert Spencer*.

"The Synthetic Philosophy," just completed, is distinguished for the vastness of its design, the accomplishment of which gives Mr. Spencer a place among the few encyclopædic thinkers of the world. His philosophy is interesting also because it concentrates and reflects the spirit of the time. No other thinker has so strenuously laboured to gather together all the accumulations of modern knowledge and to unite them under general conceptions. The alliance between the Spencerian philosophy and physical science is unusually close; and Mr. Spencer in his illustrations shows an all-embracing range of knowledge, which becomes minute in those branches of science bearing directly upon the phenomena of life. The future only can determine the exact value of this knowledge, for there are grave differences of opinion between Mr. Spencer and some of the leading biologists, like Weismann; but it may at least be said of him that he is the first philosopher since Bacon ("who wrote on science like a Lord Chancellor"), or at latest Leibnitz, who has met men of science on something like equal terms within the domain of science. Mr. Spencer's unique interest is that he has attempted an exhaustive survey of all the facts relating to the development of life and of society. He does not go beyond that, to the origin of all things; for it is one of his cardinal principles that behind the Knowable there is dimly visible a something not only unknown but unknowable.—WALKER, HUGH, 1897, *The Age of Tennyson*, p. 170.

The strength of Mr. Spencer's writings lies first in the absolute perfection of his logic; to use a mechanical analogy, they are as it were the outpourings of a perfect logical machine, whose levers and cranks are so adjusted as to work without the possibility of error; a loom in which no strand of weft or woof has ever become entangled, and from which the finest cloth is drawn without spot or blemish. Deduction, Induction, and Verification are so perfectly blended that in this nineteenth century it seems impossible to conceive their higher development. The constituent parts of this logical method which usually excite the greatest wonder and surprise are the brilliant and unsurpassed power of generalization, which is ever present, and which unites in one whole, subjects which at first appear to be as far removed as the antipodes upon our globe. This of course implies the knowledge of an immense range of subjects; and any one reading through, say only one volume such as "First Principles," may easily count up more than the metaphorical "speaking acquaintance" with over thirty clearly and well defined sciences, commencing with Anatomy at one end of the alphabet, and ending with Zoölogy at the other. How accurate this knowledge is may be seen by the currency his writings have amongst men of pure science,—meaning by this term, specialists in the smaller departments and branches of human understanding. — COLLINS, F. HOWARD, 1897, *Library of the World's Best Literature,* ed. Warner, vol. XXIII, p. 13726.

My criticism of Mr. Herbert Spencer implies no disrespect to himself, no want of appreciation of the great work he has performed, his vast knowledge, his active, comprehensive, and acute intellect, and his heroic devotion to the cause of scientific truth. If he would only incorporate systematically into his sociological system those "views" and "conceptions" which he declares he himself holds, but which are not incorporated with that system at present, his teachings would constitute the strongest of authorities for those truths of practical sociology which it has been my own endeavour to elucidate.—MALLOCK, W. H., 1898, *Mr. Herbert Spencer in Self-Defense, Nineteenth Century,* vol. 44, p. 327.

If Comte tells us, "Be parts; be mere parts, living for the sake of the whole," Spencer thinks such advice the very worst possible. Each for himself; fair-play all round; justice the supreme consideration, politically and socially; the occasional surrender of individual rights purely a personal matter, with which public action and public opinion dare not interfere—such is Mr. Spencer's social programme. It is the antithesis of Comte's. Where Comte says, "Yes," Spencer says "No," very nearly all the way through. We take it therefore, that, beyond serving to explain his views lucidly and add a grace to them, the doctrine of the social organism does nothing for Mr. Spencer.—MACKINTOSH, ROBERT, 1899, *From Comte to Benjamin Kidd,* p. 102.

In the cause of truth Mr. Spencer worked for twenty-four years without fee or reward. His solitary intellectual labours were utterly ignored by the public, and, in spite of that, he laboriously and heroically toiled up the steep ascent of philosophy. In this there is a grandeur quite Miltonic. In the midst of the general neglect Mr. Spencer had the sympathy of a number of philosophic thinkers who knew his real worth. A number of American admirers, hearing of his determination to stop the series, forwarded to Mr. Spencer through Mr. Youmans, his devoted adherent and friend, a purse of money and a gold watch. The money, with characteristic highmindedness, he accepted as a public trust for public ends.—MACPHERSON, HECTOR, 1900, *Herbert Spencer; The Man and his Work,* p. 61.

All that is best in the thought of our own age has been summoned to his aid by Mr. Spencer. His generalisations have been based upon the widest possible induction from particulars. He has only refrained from further verification of his theories when he realised that for all practical purposes the proofs already furnished were sufficient. "The Synthetic Philosophy," with which his name shall ever be associated—in other words, the system in which the great doctrine of Evolution is applied to the "whole" of the universe of life and thought, and not merely, as in the Darwinian theory, to a section of it—seeks to supply an explanation of much that has been esteemed "unknowable," by applying the same rigorously scientific methods to the problems of "Life and Mind" as have been employed in science.—SMEATON, OLIPHANT, 1900, *Hector Macpherson on Herbert Spencer, Westminster Review,* vol. 154, p. 59.

If asked to select the one book among the many he has written by which Mr. Spencer has done most for the world I would unhesitatingly say it is his "First Principles;" all the more because it contains, along with his most characteristic teaching, the largest residuum of disputable propositions. I cannot here discuss its prevailing merits, or its place in the treasure-house of English philosophical literature, and I have expressed elsewhere my dissent from much that it contains. But, while even a casual reader is struck by its width and depth—while there may be some elements in his remarkable synthesis left out—no ingenuous student can peruse and re-peruse that volume without finding himself a debtor to the man who wrote it. Idealist and Realist, Monist and Dualist, every thinker of the century must own the debt—however he may construe it.—MICHAUD, GUSTAVE, 1901, *Herbert Spencer; the Man and the Philosopher, The Bookman,* vol. 14, p. 159.

His chief work, "A System of Synthetic Philosophy" (in ten volumes) embraces all the branches of philosophical knowledge, and, particularly in the sections "Principles of Sociology" (a word coined by Spencer) and "Principles of Ethics," is the most valuable production of English philosophy that has appeared since Bacon's days.—ENGEL, EDWARD, 1902, *A History of English Literature*, rev. Hamley Bent, p. 471.

Let me here end in hearty sympathy with the distinguished thinker whom I have so long been criticising, and wish him all success in his crusade against the follies of the fashionable world. I fear, however, that he will not persuade any large part of that world to follow him through the two volumes of "The Principles of Ethics."— SIDGWICK, HENRY, 1902, *Lectures on the Ethics of T. H. Green, Mr. Herbert Spencer, and J. Martineau*, ed. Jones, p. 312.

The works of Herbert Spencer exhibit the latest form of the positive philosophy, and foreshadow its future development. Reverent and bold, reverent for truth, though not for the forms of truth, and not for much that we hold true, — bold in the destruction of error, though without that joy in destruction which often claims the name of boldness,—these works are interesting in themselves and in their relation to the earnest thought of the time. They seem at the first sight to form the turning-point in the positive philosophy; but closer examination shows us that it is only a new and marked stage in a regular growth. — EVERETT, CHARLES CARROLL, 1902, *Immortality and Other Essays*, p. 207.

There are blanks in his exegesis which working biologists, for example, are apt to accentuate; and to the purely reasoning mind he often seems, particularly in his "Data of Ethics," to have somehow let slip from his hands the lines that, held strictly, would have enabled him every instant to test his results by first principles, and thus save himself much that seems fruitless and ineffectual thinking. His aim indeed often appears to have escaped him; he substitutes immediate for ultimate causation, and the splendid chain of his reasoning, which every lucid sentence slowly forges out, is often broken by a link of base metal. In the main, nevertheless, his work is of the highest and finest quality and power. Its results have permeated throughout the world; it has changed the mental outlooks of all modern men; and made even the simplest realise that the future of society lies in the hands of science.—GILBERT, HENRY, 1904, *The Literary Year-Book*, p. 63.

William Edward Hartpole Lecky
1838–1903

Born in 1838 near Dublin, was educated at Trinity College, where he graduated B.A. in 1859 and M.A. in 1863. He was always prominently studious and something of a recluse. In 1865 appeared "The History of the Rise and Influence of Rationalism in Europe," and "The History of European Morals" was published in 1869. Both books established his reputation as a historian of wide research, lucid style, and scientific selection of facts. Yet it must be confessed that the impression given by both works is of a writer whose views lacked depth or a sense of philosophic comparison. "The History of England in the XVIIIth Century," published in 1878-90, was a work with claims to higher distinction. A volume of "Poems" appeared in 1891; "Democracy and Liberty" in 1896; and the "Map of Life" in 1899.—GILBERT, HENRY, 1904, *The Literary Year-Book*, p. 55.

PERSONAL

The House holds no man to-day who is worthier to sit in the seat that Gibbon occupied a century and a quarter ago than Mr. W. E. H. Lecky. It is only as historians, however, that the two can be compared. No contrast could be greater than that between the chronicler of the "Decline and Fall" and the author of "England in the Eighteenth Century," as respects the outward man. It is the contrast between the Epicurean and the Stoic, between the England of Horace Walpole and the England of Herbert Spencer. The two seem somehow to be incommensurable with the incommensurability of the Indulgent Uncle and the Maiden Aunt. Eminent respectability and a considerable consciousness of it is writ large on every feature of Mr. Lecky's rugged face. As he sits in his place, softly stroking his silk hat while the debate drags its slow length along, the onlooker feels a comfortable assurance that the British Matron can never withhold her taxes as America was fain to do on the ground of lack of representation. There is something almost lugubrious in the regard which Mr. Lecky seems to cast on men and

events. He instinctively reminds us of one of his own frequent verses, which sums up life's tragedy in the apostrophe:
"How hard to die, how blessed to be dead!"
—CHAPMAN, EDWARD MORTIMER, 1900, *American History and English Historians*, New England Magazine, N. S. vol. 22, p. 148.

It is a rare thing for a stenographer to make a correct report of what the member representing Trinity University really said on a subject before the House, for Mr. Lecky could not be called an orator, nor, as Cicero once said of a certain speaker, was his speech *dulciora melle*. His strength lay in his profound and practical thought, and in his variegated language, which was rich in both beauty and vigor, but it flowed right on from beginning to end, without pause or break, and nothing but a phonograph could reproduce it with literary justice. . . . As he sat in the chair chatting so pleasantly, I hardly realized his stature, until he rose to invite me into the dining room, where Mrs. Lecky and three other ladies, one a visitor from Holland, were standing. Then I saw that he was over six feet high, large-shouldered, but spare rather than portly, with a high forehead, his hair brushed back, a blond in appearance, and in the full power of intellectual manhood, being then in his fifty-fourth year. Mr. Lecky's marriage was a very happy one, and my first impressions of Mrs. Lecky confirmed the pleasant reports I had heard about her as the intellectual companion of her husband. I can honestly say that the toothsome delights of the dainty and satisfying luncheon, and the tasteful equipment and service of the table, gave me a high idea also of her domestic abilities, while as a talker she was delightful.—GRIFFIS, WILLIAM ELLIOT, 1903, *William E. H. Lecky*, The Outlook, vol. 75, pp. 489, 491.

GENERAL

He has prepared himself for its ["Rationalism in Europe"] production by an unusual amount of well-directed reading; he has chosen his facts and quotations with much judgment; and he gives proof of those important moral qualifications—impartiality, seriousness, and modesty. This praise is chiefly applicable to the long chapter on the history of magic and witchcraft, which opens the work, and to the two chapters on the antecedents and history of persecution, which occur, the one at the end of the first volume, the other at the beginning of the second. In these chapters Mr. Lecky has a narrower and better-traced path before him than in other portions of his work; he is more occupied with presenting a particular class of facts in their historical sequence, and in their relation to certain grand tide-marks of opinion, than with disquisition; and his writing is freer than elsewhere from an apparent confusedness of thought and an exuberance of approximate phrases, which can be serviceable in no other way than as diluents needful for the sort of reader we have just described.—ELIOT, GEORGE, 1865, *The Influence of Rationalism: Lecky's History*, Essays, p. 202.

A book of much reading and candour, but which does not reach my ideal standard of either. It is an old commonplace, unfortunately too true, that theologians and apologists colour and soften; but I must add that the propensity is not a bit less apparent in philosophical historians, though they are often just as well intentioned.—CHURCH, RICHARD WILLIAM, 1869, *To Asa Gray, April 5; Life and Letters of Dean Church*, ed. his Daughter, p. 219.

Mr. Lecky has probably more of the philosophic mind than any of his contemporaries. He has treated history on a large scale and in the philosophical spirit. He has taken a wide and liberal survey of the progress of thought and of morals as a whole, and then has brought the knowledge and observation thus acquired to the practical purpose of illustrating certain passages of history and periods of human development. His "History of England in the Eighteenth Century" is not more remarkable thus far for the closeness and fulness of its details than for its breadth of view and its calmness of judgment. Mr. Lecky is always the historian, and never the partisan. His works grow on the reader. They do not turn upon him all at once a sudden glare like the flash of a revolving light, but they fill the mind gradually with a sense of their justice, their philosophic thought, and the clear calmness of their historical observation.—MCCARTHY, JUSTIN, 1880, *A History of Our Own Times from the Accession of Queen Victoria to the Berlin Congress*, vol. iv, ch. LXVII.

A work ["European Morals"] abounding in important facts and suggestive thought. To all but students in philosophy the first chapter, "The Natural History of Morals," is likely to be found somewhat tedious, though it has great intrinsic merits. One of the most valuable chapters is the fourth—that on the period from Constantine to Charlemagne—in which, however, the weaknesses of the various monastic orders, are probably given a somewhat undue prominence. The second volume concludes with a valuable but rather depressing chapter on the position of woman. The work is very scholarly, and may be read with profit by every student. It is, however, subject to one criticism. In dealing with the ecclesiastical phases of the period, the author cannot resist the temptation to indulge in innuendoes and sarcasm. A little less contempt or pity for the religious zeal of the early monks, and a somewhat larger allowance for the turbulence of the times, would have improved the work. . . . A very able and interesting historical study ["Rationalism in Europe"]. It is an effort to trace the historical development of that method of reasoning which, since the Reformation, has been steadily gaining an ascendency in Europe. . . . The work abounds in facts and discussions of extreme interest. The author's style is always attractive. His learning is extensive, though he seems not to have made much use of the numerous German authorities on the subject. His sympathies are obviously rationalistic, though he usually succeeds in maintaining a moderate and judicious spirit.—ADAMS, CHARLES KENDALL, 1882, *A Manual of Historical Literature*, pp. 170, 213, 214.

It is a strange thing that so able a prose writer as Mr. Lecky should, when unfortunately laid low through an attack of versifying fever, contentedly abuse common sense, and even good grammar. In his profoundly interesting and valuable philosophical and historical works, he writes with vigour, lucidity, and a native directness which is often of singular charm; with serene judgment and logical foresight, he marshals his words and phrases with all the wise economy and tactical skill of a veteran. . . . Mr. Lecky's mistake has been in making public that which should have been reserved for a private circle. When he appears as a poet he must be judged accordingly, and without respect to his high achievement in other departments of letters. It would be insincere for the present writer to say that he finds anywhere in Mr. Lecky's verse that particular magic which is the outcome of the transforming imagination—in a word, that essential breath of poetic life without which all is vanity.—SHARP, WILLIAM, 1891, *Poems, The Academy*, vol. 40, p. 449.

We find in Mr. Lecky a historical writer whose works are among the most interesting and significant literary products of his time. His place is neither with the annalists nor with the political historians, but with those for whom the philosophy of history has had a perennial fascination. And while it is pre-eminently with such literary historians as Macaulay and Froude and Green,—in so far as he has written to the end of being read, in a style which has merits of its own comparing favorably with theirs,—he is widely separated from these respectively: with less continuity than Macaulay, far less dramatic energy than Froude, and nothing of Green's architectonic faculty. But few historians have excelled his diligence or carefulness, or chosen greater themes, or handled them with a more evident desire to bring the truth of history to bear upon our personal and social life.—CHADWICK, JOHN WHITE, 1897, *Library of the World's Best Literature*, ed. Warner, vol. XV, p. 8934.

"Liberty and Democracy" is a Book of Lamentations over the decadence of "the old belief, or prejudice, or superstition, that the administration of government ought to be chiefly intrusted to gentlemen," and by the last word the author means the land aristocracy, for the "doctrine that the men to whom the land belonged were the men who ought to govern it" appears to him fundamental. . . . It assumes, what seems to Mr. Lecky too plain to require argument, that the right of property in land is superior to the right of property in anything else. While he might not admit this, the distinction which is always present in his mind rests upon the fact that the right of property in land runs back to the gentlemanly art of conquest, and takes its starting-point from the sword, while the rights of property in nearly all other things rest upon so humble and servile a thing as labor, and start from the right of every man to himself and to the work of his own hands. . . . Indeed, we do not need to go back of this century, or outside of "Liberty and Democracy," to see what government was when it was carried on by gentlemen. Mr. Lecky quotes Paley's statement that "about one-half of the House of Commons obtain their seats in that assembly by the election of the people, the other half by purchase or by nomination of single proprietors of great estates." . . . Mr. Lecky's conception of the purposes of our political activity are as inadequate as his ideas about our political methods are erroneous. Nothing could be more superficial than the remarks of this historian and philosopher that there is "no country in the world in which the motives that inspire them (political contests) are purely or more abjectly sordid" than in the United States.—POWERS, FRED PERRY, 1897, *Government by "Gentlemen," Lippincott's Magazine*, vol. 60, pp. 670, 674, 675.

It is an attempt ["Map of Life"] made by a man of eminence, to impress once more upon the world the importance of testing the conduct of life by the standard of philosophic common sense. His book is easy to read; it is interesting in itself; it is still more interesting as a sketch (and a perfectly truthful sketch) of the view of the world taken by a man of letters who, though a student, has mixed with society, and, though devoted to the study of history, has always shown a keen interest in public life. But, after all, the main interest of the book, to a thoughtful reader, will be found to lie in its suggesting the question: How far does the improvement of society arise from adherence to the maxims of common sense; or how far is it due, in the main, to those bursts of feeling or enthusiasm which, at particular eras, lift sometimes individuals and sometimes whole societies above the level of their ordinary every-day existence? . . . It is impossible to deny that the precepts it contains are sound, and the reflections which it suggests are true. Open it anywhere at chance and you will find something which it is just as well should be said about some topic of practical importance.—DICEY, A. V., 1900, *Lecky's Map of Life, The Nation*, vol. 70, p. 187.

He has brought to it an erudition that renews the surprise which the world of scholars felt when, as a young man of seven and twenty, he published his "History of the Rise and Influence of the Spirit of Rationalism in Europe." Any one who has investigated the wealth of his footnotes and followed some of them into the by-paths of curious literature, must bear glad witness to the keenness of his historic sense. His manifest purpose to be fair is worthy of all praise. Between the lines of his work we can seem to read something of his desire to cultivate an attitude of detachment and to regard his material as objectively as Maupassant or Henry James regards the material of fiction. It would probably be unjust to say that he has formed himself upon German models; but his kinship with the academic German is manifest enough, and it was a part of the eternal fitness of things that Dr. Jolowicz should translate all his principal works and that the "History of European Morals" should become a textbook in German Universities.—CHAPMAN, EDWARD MORTIMER, 1900, *American History and English Historians, New England Magazine*, N. S., vol. 22, p. 149.

Mr. Lecky was a moralist in the eighteenth-century sense. In the turmoil of our rapidly shifting civilization, he was distinctly the enlightened man. He attained as early as his undergraduate years at Dublin that serenity and impartiality of spirit which the Encyclopedists regarded as the most desirable possession, but hardly achieved. In other respects, also, he was of the eighteenth century. Before that appalling mass of evidence which crushes the generalizing spirit back to the journeyman work of heaping up facts, he remained unruffled. As a young man he undertook "A History of European Morals" with the cheerful curiosity of Bayle compiling a Universal Dictionary. This poised and indomitable spirit, which he maintained in the face of constant invalidism, brings him perhaps nearer to Spencer than to any man of his time. It certainly removes him as far from the class of documented athletes of Freeman's kind as it does from the eloquent special pleaders of the Gibbon-Macaulay-Carlyle dispensation. In the fearless mind which he brought to the great task of interpreting history through philosophy, Mr. Lecky distinctly recalls Hume, Montesquieu, Adam Smith, Voltaire. His superiority in method and his essentially modern quality lay in a truer sense of the difficulties that invested his problems. To read his books is to be instructed in the complexity of historical causes. One feels that he has moved more cautiously and patiently among his facts than those soaring minds who were his constant admiration and study.—MATHER, F. J., JR., 1903, *A Philosophical Historian, The Nation,* vol. 77, p. 337.

It is probable that as the historian of "European Morals from Augustus to Charlemagne" Mr. Lecky anchored his fame to the ages. There was another fresh and delightful surprise to the whole world when his brace of portly volumes appeared in 1869. The book showed the same philosophic grasp and the ease of an intellectual giant in handling mighty material. Quickly translated into German, it has become a text-book in the universities of the Fatherland. I remember delightful days in far-off Japan, when, fresh from the press, his book on the "History of European Morals" reached me, carried over the mountains by Japanese runners. I read it amid the autumn glories and beautiful scenery of Echizen and the Japanese Mont Blanc in Kaga. Besides digesting the rich food of thought, I could not but liken the style to that of autumn ripeness and mellowness, and the legitimate rhetorical decoration seemed as brilliant as that of the gold and colors on a Kaga vase. With thousands of Americans, I own in Lecky a true intellectual teacher.—GRIFFIS, WILLIAM ELLIOT, 1903, *William E. H. Lecky, The Outlook,* vol. 75, p. 490.

William Ernest Henley
1849–1903

Born in Gloucester, 23 Aug. 1849; married Anna, daughter of Edward Boyle, Edinburgh, 1878. Educ.: the Crypt Grammar School, Gloucester; LL.D. St. Andrews. Editor in London, 1877-78; the "Magazine of Art," 1882-86; the "Scots"—afterwards the "National Observer," 1888-93; "The New Review," 1893-98; "The Tudor Translations" (North, Florio, Shelton, Holland, Urquhart, Berners, and others), etc. *Publications:* "Book of Verses," 1888, 4th ed. 1893; "Memorial Catalogue of the French and Dutch Loan Collection," 1888; "Views and Reviews, I. Literature," 1890; "Song of the Sword," 1892; 2nd ed. 1893; "The Centenary Burns" (with T. F. Henderson: Terminal Essay by W. E. H., published separately, 1898), I.–IV. 1896-97; the "Works of Lord Byron," Vol. I. 1897, etc.; "English Lyrics," 1897; "Poems," 1898; "The Poetry of Wilfrid Blunt" (with George Wyndham); "London Types" (with W. Nicholson), 1898; "For England's Sake," 1900; "Shakespeare, The Edinburgh Folio," 1901; "Hawthorn and Lavender, and other verses," 1901; "Views and Reviews, II. Painting and Scripture," 1901. "Deacon Brodie," "Beau Austin," "Admiral Guinea," "Macaire" (plays, with R. L. Stevenson).—ANONYMOUS, 1903, *Who's Who,* p. 638.

PERSONAL

Hail and farewell! Through gold of sunset glowing,
Brave as of old your ship puts forth to sea;
We stand upon the shore to watch your going,
Dreaming of years long gone, of years to be.
The ship sails forth, but not for our remembrance,
We who were once of your ship's company:
Master of many a strong and splendid semblance,
Where shall we find another like to thee?
Your ship sets sail. Whate'er the end restore you,
Or Golden Isles, or Night without a star,
Never, Great-Heart, has braver barque before you
Or sailed, or fought, or crossed the soundless bar.
—WATSON, ROSAMUND MARRIOTT, 1903, *The Lost Leader, The Athenæum, No.* 3951, p. 92.

Henley was built on a scale designed for exercise and a vigorous life. Unkindly fate chained him to his desk and his crutch. His broad face shining like John Silver's, bearded like the pard, he was a modern representative of the Viking—in design. Nature unhappily marred what she should have made to the design. His nature was simply composite. He breathed fire with all the fury of his baresark ancestors one moment, and he was capable of weeping like a child at the next. This feminine or emotional trait entered into that strange and virile nature. It is nine years since his child died, and it was evident to all his friends that from the date of the loss he began to die.—WATSON, HENRY BRERETON MARRIOTT, 1903, *William Ernest Henley, The Athenæum, No.* 3951, p. 93.

In the days of my early acquaintance with Henley, some fourteen or fifteen years ago, I could never look at him without wondering why none of his artist friends had taken him for a model of Pan. They say he was like Johnson, and like Heine; and he had something of both. But to me he was the startling image of Pan come on earth and clothed—the great God Pan, down in the reeds by the river, with halting foot and flaming shaggy hair, and arms and shoulders huge and threatening, like those of some Faun or Satyr of the ancient woods, and the brow and eyes of the Olympians. Well-nigh captive to his chair, with the crutch never far from his elbow, dragging himself when he moved, with slow effort, he yet seemed instinct with the life of the germinating elemental earth, when gods and men were vital with the force that throbbed in breast and flower and wandering breeze. The large heart, and the large frame, the broad tolerant smile, the inexhaustible interest in nature and mankind, the brave, unquenchable cheerfulness under affliction and adversities, the frank appreciation and apology for the animal side of things, all helped to maintain the impression of a kind of Pagan strength and simplicity.—Low, SIDNEY, 1903, *William Ernest Henley, Cornhill Magazine, vol.* 88, *pp.* 411.

How, as the hair greyed and whitened, the shining soul in the face crowned and glorified all! In the clear eyes were friendly looks and laughter, the lips gave kindly advice with smiling humour, and encouraging words that half deprecated his own criticism; or he talked of his contemporaries, friends and enemies, showering out generous words of praise, or emitting the bullet-like phrase of contempt, or the nickname that transfixed some weakness or vanity in the person mentioned. His faculty of criticism, indeed, was one of the finest gifts with which his multiplex nature was endowed; but, as with all expressions of his mind, it was of an intensely individual character, his definition was perfect, within the limits of his view, and every phrase helped to chisel out the clear-cut cameos of description, passion, or emotion. This intense faculty of seeing was part of the "hard, gem-like" flame with which life seemed to burn within his crippled body, and explains the limitless self-belief, the sacrifice of all to his view of the truth, and the indifference to conventions and received creeds that all his life procured him the atmosphere of a fighter.—GILBERT, HENRY, 1904, *The Literary Year-Book, p.* 53.

GENERAL

There is something revolutionary about all Mr. Henley's work; but it is in his poetry that the stirrings of a new element have worked to most effectual issues. This new volume of poems, by its very existence, is a vigorous challenge, a notable manifesto, on behalf of a somewhat new art—the art of modernity in poetry. Based on the same principles as "A Book of Verses," it develops those principles yet further, and, in the "London Voluntaries" particularly, and in such poems as the second, twenty-second and twenty-fourth of the "Rhymes and Rhythms," succeeds to a remarkable degree in working out a really modern art of verse. . . . The style of the "Hospital Sonnets" is founded on the style of "Modern Love;" both from the rhymed and unrhymed poems in irregular metres, it is evident that Mr. Henley has learnt something from the odes of the "Unknown Eros;" there are touches of Walt Whitman, some of the notes of Heine; there is, too, something of the exquisitely disarticulated style of Verlaine. But with all this assimilation of influences that are in the air, Mr. Henley has developed for himself a style that becomes in the highest degree personal, and one realises behind it a most vigorous, distinct, and interesting personality. . . . The very subject, to begin with, was a discovery. Here is poetry made out of personal sensations, poetry which is half physiological, poetry which is pathology—and yet essentially poetry.—SYMONS, ARTHUR, 1892, *Mr. Henley's Poetry, Fortnightly Review, vol.* 58, *pp.* 183, 185, 186.

We may deny to Mr. Henley certain faculties, as, for instance, a very liberal faculty for romance, such as was given to the gifted being whom he most resembles at his best—Heinrich Heine,—but we must credit him with a fascinating lyrical grace. . . . Mr. Henley's poems, as his prose, bear the mark of concentration, precision, and the power of rejection,—which is perhaps the greatest quality an artist can have: in it is the root of the whole matter. Mr. Henley's canvas is always small. In this regard he compares with some of his contemporaries and ancestors in poetry as Meissonier does with De Neuville. There is no plethora of expression or sentiment in the work of the New School; no cantos or multiplied stanzas; no languor nor linked sweetness; no attempt to "thrill the girls with dandy pathos." Mr. Henley's lyrics, full of delightful freshness and sprightliness and sentiment, have the quality of the perfect miniature. One feels that his words are etched out of the thought for their own sake as well as the thought's sake, and that he will sacrifice neither for the girls nor the dandy pathos. Through Mr. Henley's poetry there runs one note piped in many keys. He sings the gospel of conflict—of war; but he sings it without whining.—PARKER, GILBERT, 1893, *"The New Poetry" and Mr. W. E. Henley, Lippincott's Magazine, vol.* 52, *pp.* 110, 114.

It is as a poet he has the highest claim upon us now, and as a poet he will take rank hereafter; yet he has certainly made a deeper mark upon his generation as a critic than any of his contemporaries. Mr. Lang, who once reigned paramount, has long since discarded his influence, and there is none left to dispute Mr. Henley's royalty. . . . I am not here dealing with him as a poet, but merely as a critic of literature. As such, it is not too much to say that his authority has slowly undermined the prestige of the middle Victorian ideals. In a sense he is the foundation of a new period. That these words are none too extravagant is proved by his present position as the arbiter of a distinct school of fiction. For one who is no novelist himself this is a considerable performance. . . . By a number of young writers he is regarded with the affection and reverence that a high priest might claim. . . . Mr. Henley's critical insight recalls the flare of an electric light. There are queer patches of blackness outside of the path of the illumination, passages of darkness along the angles; but within these confines the white light cuts its way rudely, sharply, and with pitiless severity. Along the sphere of the irradiation the white flare is merciless in its scrutiny; every fault and flaw is picked out as by magic, every virtue is assigned its value. For sheer illumination of insight within these broad boundaries Mr. Henley, so far as I know, has no peer alive. —WATSON, HENRY BRERETON MARRIOTT, 1895, *Literary Critics, The Bookman, vol.* 2, *pp.* 186, 187, 188.

Mr. Henley, in his verse, is two things: a painter-etcher and a pure lyrist. In the former capacity his touch is too stern, too precise, and of too condensed significance to allure the popular eye, which prefers a smoother surface, a more luscious tone. As a lyrist, again, Mr. Henley, though a master-rhymer when he pleases, is apt to renounce the aid of rhyme and strict melodic form. Now the triangle, though we may not realise it, is one of the most popular instruments in the band, and not to be lightly dispensed with. Moreover, though Mr. Henley does not, if I may put it so, deliberately intellectualise, a somewhat aggressive personal philosophy runs through his lyrics—a grim stoicism, with an inclination to envisage life in its grotesquer aspects.—ARCHER, WILLIAM, 1898, *Mr. Henley's Poems, The Academy, vol.* 53, *p.* 249.

If his leading trait is a rugged strength and faithfulness to the thing seen or known, such as looks from his bust by Rodin, he has also the capacity for sudden intimacies of beauty or feeling which is the birthright of strength. Not much more gravely and poignantly tender has been written than the rhymeless lyric, "When you wake in your crib," while the minor lyrics cover a very various range of quality. From the direct truth of "In Hospital" to the gates of romance in the later book, you have measured a compass very unique, and this romance is drawn from the stony ground of London. Perhaps, indeed, it is as the poet of London that he will best be remembered.—THOMPSON, FRANCIS, 1903, *W. E. Henley, The Academy and Literature, vol.* 65, *p.* 64.

He was a strong, honest, full-blooded man, a good lover and a good hater, and singer of the best English lyrics during half a generation.—BOYNTON, HENRY WALCOTT, 1903, *W. E. Henley and Journalism, Atlantic Monthly, vol.* 92, *p.* 418.

He seemed incapable of what an eighteenth century critic would have called a sustained flight; and he was apparently destitute of any real constructive or creative power. He never wrote a story, or a narrative poem, or anything in prose which was beyond the limits of a short essay; and if in his three plays he was able to "stay" over a somewhat longer course, it was only with the assistance of Stevenson, who no doubt was responsible for the constructional and dramatic part of the work, such as it is. Henley was the painter of miniatures, the maker of cameos. There are some rough, and even brutal, passages in his poems; but his art, taken as a whole, was delicate, precise, and finished. When he set to work, the violence that one noticed in his talk, the over-emphasis of his intellectual temper, died away; in his best passages he has the subtle restraint, the economy of material, and the careful manipulation, of the artist-workman. He will live through his lyric passages, and his vignettes, in prose and verse. No man of our time has expressed a mood of the emotions with more absolute appropriateness and verbal harmony, and that is lyric poetry in its essence.—LOW, SIDNEY, 1903, *William Ernest Henley, Cornhill Magazine*, vol. 88, p. 420.

He saw shrewdly, felt keenly, and blessed or banned with a zest that stimulated whether it convinced or not. His views, whether one accepted or rejected them, were at least wholly his own. In that sense they were original, and in another sense they were original also, for they were not shared by the average reader or critic. His criticisms, and the criticisms he inspired were apt to be of the "slashing" sort. He wielded, not the finely tempered, needle-pointed rapier of the duellist, but a well-ground axe, that sometimes turned in his hand, and came down headforemost with the blunt force of a navvy's hammer. In considering the ferocity of much of the criticism that he wrote himself, or impelled the young men gathered about him to write, due allowance must be made—and some of his victims made it—for the galling physical disabilities under which he laboured. . . . How long he will be remembered by the outer world, no one can guess. It is only as a poet that his reputation can last; and his present reputation is wholly disproportionate to his popularity. But the man who wrote "A Book of Verses," "London Voluntaries," and, only this year, that buoyant and imaginative glorification of the Mercédes motorcar, "A Song of Speed" needs no brand to proclaim him a true bard. His style, always vivid and picturesque, was preeminently "of the man himself."—BLACKSHAW, RANDALL, 1903, *William Ernest Henley, The Critic*, vol 43, pp. 262, 263.

Life touched his mind at every point, yet though it was in general transmuted into merely literary and poetic values, the keenness and the poignancy of his expression have given a richness to English literature that, surely, will never be tarnished by time. He had his weakness and lackings; he was something of a Pagan; he had nothing to teach except how to be a good Englishman, to be honest, and speak the truth; he had no deep religious convictions to express, for at the best Deity was to him merely an asset of literary capital to be used for the most telling effect. In the intense zestfulness of his life things appealed to him as much from their emotional as from their brutal or even obscene aspect; but ever he loved tender beauty, and saw wistfulness in the dearest things, and with his poet's vision found loveliness in the darkest corners of his beloved London as on the flashing downs beneath an April sky. At the last his manner of pride and aggressiveness was but the expression of the sanity and truth that were the texture of his life as they are of all his work.—GILBERT, HENRY, 1904, *The Literary Year-Book*, p. 54.

Richard Henry Stoddard
1825–1903

Poet, born Hingham, Mass., July 2, 1825; worked as iron moulder in youth; soon began to contribute to papers; held a position in custom house, 1853-70; confidential clerk to Gen. McClellan, 1870-3; city librarian, New York, 1874-5; literary reviewer New York *World*, 1860-70; of New York *Mail and Express* since 1880. *Author:* "Poems;" "Adventures in Fairy Land;" "Life of Humboldt;" "Songs of Summer;" "The King's Bell;" "The Book of the East;" "Abraham Lincoln, A Horatian Ode;" "Putnam the Brave;" "A Century After;" "Life of Washington Irving;" "The Lion's Cub and Other Verse;" "Under the Evening Lamp;" etc. *Edited* the Bric-a-Brac Series; married Elizabeth D. Barstow, 1852.—LEONARD, JOHN W., ed., 1901, *Who's Who in America*, p. 1902.

PERSONAL

A personal description of Mr. Stoddard should be unnecessary. At this late day few of his readers can be unfamiliar with his face. It has been engraved more than once, and printed not only with his collected poems but in magazines of wider circulation than the books of any living

American poet. It is not likely to disappoint the admirer of his work, for it is a poet's face, as well as a handsome one. The clear-cut, regular features are almost feminine in their delicacy; but in the dark eyes, now somewhat dimmed though full of thought and feeling, there is a look that counteracts any impression of effeminacy due to the refinement of the features, or the melodious softness of the voice. The hair and beard of snowy whiteness make a harmonious setting for the poet's ruddy countenance. Though slightly bowed, as he steps forward to meet you (with left hand advanced) Mr. Stoddard still impresses you as a man of more than middle height. His cordial though undemonstrative greeting puts the stranger at his ease at once; for his manner is as gentle as his speech is frank.—GILDER, JOSEPH B., 1888, *Authors at Home, The Critic, Aug. 18, p. 74.*

Books—always books—are piled around; some musty, and all old;
Tall, solemn folios, such as Lamb declared he loved to hold;
Large paper copies with their virgin margins white and wide,
And presentation volumes with the author's comps. inside;
I break the tenth commandment with a wild impassioned cry:
Oh, how came Stoddard by these things? Why Stoddard, and not I?
From yonder wall looks Thackeray upon his poet friend,
And underneath the genial face appear the lines he penned;
And here, gadzooks, ben honge ye prynte of marvaillous renowne
Yt shameth Chaucer's gallaunt knyghtes in Canterbury towne;
And still more books and pictures. I'm dazed, bewildered, vexed;
Since I've broke the tenth commandment, why not break the eighth one next?
And, furthermore, in confidence inviolate be it said,
Friend Stoddard owns a lock of hair that grew on Milton's head;
Now I have Gladstone axes and a lot of curious things,
Such as pimply Dresden teacups and old German wedding-rings;
But nothing like that saintly lock have I on wall or shelf,
And, being somewhat short of hair, I should like that lock myself.
But Stoddard has a soothing way, as though he grieved to see
Invidious torments prey upon a nice young chap like me.

He waves me to an easy chair and hands me out a weed
And pumps me full of that advice he seems to know I need;
So sweet the tap of his philosophy and knowledge flows
That I can't help wishing that I knew a half what Stoddard knows.
—FIELD, EUGENE, 1895, *The Stoddards, Songs and Other Verses.*

The life and work of Mr. Stoddard are a saddening instance of the short-sightedness of mankind, of the imperfection of our present social order, of the way in which a man may be compelled to waste endowments of a high order, that he may wring from a niggard world a bare subsistence. . . . If, as Seneca thinks, the gods are well pleased when they see great men contending with adversity, Mr. Stoddard must have afforded the gods much delight, for his life has been one struggle with adverse fortune. . . . It would not be easy to name the other American author who has done so much hard work for so insignificant pay. Mr. Stoddard has been all his life a most laborious man, working harder than any mechanic in town and receiving wages but little better than those of a clever mechanic. Most of this labor has been mere hack work. One says this in no disparagement of Mr. Stoddard, or of the usefulness of what he has done, but in hot indignation of soul that Pegasus should thus be put in the plough. . . . Mr. Stoddard has not complained; he has borne his burden as a brave man should, cheerfully, nobly, but the iron must have entered into his soul.—VEDDER, HENRY C., 1895, *American Writers of To-Day, pp. 275, 276, 280, 281.*

The dinner had been announced for eight o'clock, but an hour was passed in the reception given to the poet before the guests sat at the tables. Mr. Stoddard, bowed and feeble, made a very touching figure as he received the congratulations of his friends, whom he tried to recognize as they thronged around him by the sound of their voices, for his sight was too dim to enable him to distinguish their features. His wits, however, were alert enough; and it was delightful to hear his replies to the sallies of some of his old comrades, and to observe how cleverly he managed conversation with those he had met long before, and whose feelings he could not hurt by betraying forgetfulness of the acquaintance they claimed with him.—BARRY, JOHN D., 1897, *The Stoddard Banquet, Literary World*, vol. 28, p. 104.

Stoddard's story of his boyhood is a painful one. His was that greatest of all possible misfortunes, a mother whom he could not respect or love. She subjected him to work for which he had no aptitude or sufficient strength, culminating in an iron-foundry from his eighteenth year till his twenty-first. If he had not been born a poet, he would not have been made one by these hard conditions. The wonder is that they did not kill at once the poet and the boy.—CHADWICK, JOHN WHITE, 1903, *Recollections, The Nation*, vol. 77, p. 469.

It is not given to every man to live such a life as that which closed when Richard Henry Stoddard passed away in May of the present year. To say nothing of having the poetic gift, few indeed have the stamina, the energy, the divine enthusiasm which carry them over the stony places and enable them to win an honorable and permanent place in the guild of poets. To few has been granted the privilege of knowing, and knowing intimately, so many of the men who made our literature during three score of years. He knew Bryant, Halleck, Willis, Poe, and nearly all of the famous New England group; he was the intimate friend of Bayard Taylor, George Boker, and Buchanan Read; he was the friend and counsellor of a host of younger writers, such as Stedman and Howells.—NORTHUP, CLARK SUTHERLAND, 1903, *Recollections of a Notable Literary Life, The Dial*, vol. 35, p. 299.

In the last ten years it has been my privilege to see much of Richard Henry Stoddard. To one who belonged to a younger generation it was the opening of a volume of literary history to enter that second-floor study where nearly all the poet's time was passed. There he sat at his desk, with Thackeray's portrait and verses on the wall above, laboriously writing, with the strongest lights and glasses aiding his failing eyesight, or more often seated at the corner of the hearth, with books heaped on the floor about him, he dropped the volume in his hands to give the visitor a greeting which rarely lacked a note of cheeriness even in his darker hours. Books lined the walls. There were rare editions, autograph copies, all manner of literary treasures which have been made known through his magnificent gift to the Authors' Club. There were rare manuscripts and letters also; Petrarch, Poe, Tennyson, Browning, as the case might be, and despite the apparent disorder, Mr. Stoddard's persistent memory usually held all their stories and their resting-place as well. In these surroundings there was abundant invitation to reminiscence and comment. A box behind his chair contains letters from Poe, and perhaps the box was opened, and the opening meant a vivid story of his meetings with Poe, and descriptions, told with dry chuckles, of certain curious members of the Poe environment.—HITCHCOCK, RIPLEY, 1903, *Richard Henry Stoddard, The Lamp*, vol. 26, p. 404.

GENERAL

"The King's Bell," exquisite for the limpid flow of its verse and the sweetly melancholy tone of its thought, together with other poems by Richard Henry Stoddard, have not received their due meed of praise.—WHIPPLE, EDWIN PERCY, 1876-86, *American Literature and Other Papers*, ed. *Whittier*, p. 130.

The peculiar traits of Stoddard's genius are distinct through all the changing forms and preparing studies that taught him the mastery of his art. At the first, as at the last, his thought is clear, virile and single, and uttered in words of force and simplicity. There is not in all his work a hazy conception nor a wavering line. There are in it combinations purely original, and sentences cut like gems. Its sincerity bespeaks freedom from conceit and strained effects—its direct purpose compels it into Saxon syllables and lucid phrase. The outline of his subjects is firm, positive as a swift-drawn circle, bounding the parts in proportioned concord. . . . Until the history of our country has grown so old that its earliest records have lost all distinctness, we may believe that Stoddard's name will remain written in them as that of one of the few poets—less than a score would round the tale—whose genius illustrated the first century of its national literature.—MCDONOUGH, A. R., 1880, *Richard Henry Stoddard, Scribner's Monthly*, vol. 20, pp. 689, 694.

Last of all poets should we call Mr. Stoddard a preacher, and he would smile if we called him a moralist; but his narrative poems are saturated with elevated moral sentiment, derive indeed their power from it; though it is the *beauty* of virtue with which he, as a poet, is primarily concerned. . . . His rank among the singers, not as regards popularity, but as regards the beauty and permanence of his work, is not to be a low one; he can not, I think, be placed among the poets of the third or of the second rank in our generation.—COAN, TITUS MUNSON, 1880, *Mr. Stoddard's Poems, Appleton's Journal, vol.* 24, *pp.* 232, 235.

The characteristics of Stoddard's verse are affluence, sincere feeling, strength, a manner unmistakably his own, very delicate fancy, and, above all, an imagination at times exceeded by that of no other American poet. This last quality pervades his ambitious pieces, and at times breaks out suddenly in the minor verse through which he is best known. The exigencies of his profession have too constantly drawn upon his resources; the bulk of his miscellaneous verse is large, and to this is somewhat due its unevenness. No poet is more unequal; few have more plainly failed now and then. On the other hand, few have reached a higher tone, and a selection could be made from his poems upon which to base a lasting reputation. "The Fisher and Charon," "The Dead Master," and the "Hymn to the Sea," are noble pieces of English blank verse, the secret of whose measure is given only to the elect; one is impressed by the art, the thought, the imagination, which sustain these poems, and the Shakespeare and Lincoln odes. Stoddard's abundant songs and lyrics are always on the wing and known at first sight,—a skylark brood whose notes are rich with feeling.—STEDMAN, EDMUND CLARENCE, 1885, *Poets of America, p.* 58.

Stoddard is the exponent of retrospective sorrow and a gentle melancholy. Sombre themes generally suit him best; and yet, even in his mourning over "The Flight of Youth," there is a note of warm, quick feeling, which proves that the heart of youth is with him still and takes wing only in his verse.—LATHROP, GEORGE PARSONS, 1886, *Representative Poems of Living Poets, ed. Gilder, Introduction, p.* XXI.

The gap between his best and worst is sadly wide. But his five hundred pages of collected poems are full-freighted with the *opima spolia* of observation, reflection, fancy, imagination. Let him who fears that American materialism can silence the chant of the soul and the carol of nature turn to Stoddard and find sufficient answer in him alone. . . . I remember, as of yesterday, the fresh open-air delight, the seeming presence of bird, breeze, and flower, with which in boyhood I read Stoddard's "Songs of Summer;" and as I return to them I find indeed that their season "never dies," for it is the eternal summer of song. —RICHARDSON, CHARLES F., 1888, *American Literature,* 1607-1885, *vol.* II, *pp.* 251, 252.

I know of no other English-speaking poet of the day who can turn a song so gracefully and easily as Mr. Stoddard can. Certain of his lyrics are, to my mind, unsurpassed for haunting charm of cadence. He has also written several odes of admirable nobility and stateliness.—ROBERTS, CHARLES G. D., 1888, *ed. Poems of Wild Life, p.* 237, *note.*

In Stoddard the critic and the creator are united. Probably no living man rivals him in knowledge of ancient and modern poetry; and this knowledge does not lie inert in his memory, but is incorporate in his thought, rendering his naturally sound and wholesome taste next to infallible in questions of literary judgment. He has applied this taste to his own verse, leaving little for other critics of it to do. If anything, he has been too remorseless; sometimes nothing but the naked conception seems to be left. Yet in his severity he never forgets beauty; he both remembers it and understands it, as his "Hymn to the Beautiful" sufficiently testifies. He finds it everywhere, and his words are transfigured with its spirit.—HAWTHORNE, JULIAN, AND LEMMON, LEONARD, 1891, *American Literature, p.* 272.

Stoddard I believe to be the highest poetic genius now living in America, his work always good, always of the very highest character.— LINTON, WILLIAM JAMES, 1894, *Threescore and Ten Years,* 1820 *to* 1890.

Whatever poets may have strongly influenced Mr. Stoddard in his earlier years, no one poet dominated him. His was a catholic taste, a universal worship of the beautiful, and he could appreciate what was good or great in every English poet. As his mind matured, these suggestions of other poets disappear from his verse, and his style becomes more distinctive, more individual. The passion for beauty, however, does not become weaker. In the "Songs of Summer," published during the flower of his young manhood, there is almost a tropical luxuriance of feeling and a prodigality of fancy not always matched by felicity of expression.—VEDDER, HENRY C., 1895, *American Writers of To-Day*, p. 283.

Stoddard belongs to the purely imaginative school. He has a passionate love of the beautiful that reminds one of his early master, Keats. His poems are spontaneous and impassioned, yet in them all there is not a single inartistic or faulty line. Like Poe and Aldrich, he has pruned his work with remorseless care. He has the rare gift of being able to apply his broad critical powers to his own work as if it were the production of another, and he has not hesitated many times to reject that which a less conscientious poet would have left unquestioned.—PATTEE, FRED LEWIS, 1896, *A History of American Literature*, p. 363.

Although the lingering glow of Keats and of Tennyson, whom the young workman loved, may be discerned here and there, as in the graceful minstrelsy of "The King's Bell," and the liquid measures of the "Hymn to the Beautiful," Stoddard's verse has taken on more and more a frank, half-homely quality, suggestive of the plain American manhood it embodies. How truly this manhood, for all its quiet self-control, thrills with the poet's passion, is proved by such a noble lyric as "Adsum." Yet the white-haired minstrel, whom New York delights to honor, does not forget, in his "golden flush of sunset," the fearless flame of dawn.—BATES, KATHARINE LEE, 1897, *American Literature*, p. 196.

As a writer of odes, Mr. Stoddard stands second only to Lowell in American literature. They all show the lofty tone, the energetic, virile style, the melodious cadences echoing and re-echoing the thought, and the glowing imagination of which he early gave such proof in his "Carmen Naturæ." It is the music of these and some of his shorter lyrics that gives significance to the word "song" in the general sense of poetry. Stoddard is a "singer" in the true meaning of the term.—ONDERDONK, JAMES L., 1899-1901, *History of American Verse*, pp. 260, 261.

We have no truer poet than Mr. Stoddard to-day, none older or better known, none who more than he has "learned in suffering what he taught in song." It is meet that we should remember him, and pay tribute now and then to the beauty of his work and to the manliness of his life.—GILDER, JOSEPH B., 1900, *Mr. Stoddard at Seventy-five*, The Critic, vol. 37, p. 215.

Like every sturdy, uncompromising individuality, Mr. Stoddard roused antagonisms, sometimes by the spoken, sometimes by the written word. His standards were high for letters and for men, and he hated smug literary affectation, or moral cowardice, with all the force of a singularly vigorous nature. If he was frank in denouncing shams, however, he was equally prompt to point out promise or performance, and all that he said was sure to be infused with a spirit due to long and reverent association with the masters of English letters. But these imperfect notes are not intended to touch the poet's purely literary side save as this is inevitable in the case of one whose love of letters was his life.—HITCHCOCK, RIPLEY, 1903, *Richard Henry Stoddard*, The Lamp, vol. 26, p. 408.

Cincinnatus Hiner Miller
Joaquin Miller
1841–1903

Born in Wabash Dist., Ind., Nov. 10, 1841; removed with parents to Ore., 1850; mined in Calif.; returned to Ore., 1860; studied law; express messenger in Idaho, 1861; edited, 1863, the Eugene (Ore.) *Democratic Register*, a weekly, which was suppressed on charges of disloyalty; practiced law Cañon City, Ore., 1863-6; co. judge Grant Co., Ore., 1866-70; went to London and published his first book of poems, which met with a favorable reception; several yrs. in newspaper life at Washington; since 1887 has been resident of Oakland; corr. New York *Journal* in Klondike, 1897-8. *Author:* "Songs of the Sierras;" "Pacific Palms;" "Songs of the Sunland;" "The Ship of the Desert;" "Life Among the Modocs;" "First Families of the Sierras;" "The One Fair Woman;" "The Danites in the Sierras;" "Shadows of Shasta;" "Memorie and Rime;" "Baroness of New York;" "Songs of Far-Away Lands;" "The Destruction of Gotham;" "The Building of the City Beautiful, a Poetic Romance;" "49: or, the Gold-Seekers of the Sierras;" "The Life of Christ;" "Chants for the Boer," 1900. *Plays:* "The Danites;" "The Silent Man;" "'49;" "Tally-Ho;" etc.—LEONARD, JOHN W., ed., 1901, *Who's Who in America*, p. 780.

PERSONAL

The latest chapter in the life of the Poet of the Sierras is only a little less bizarre than those that have preceded it. On his few acres of rough land he has built three small structures of an architectural style that is all their own. One is his bedroom and workshop—the two terms are nearly synonymous, for most of his literary work is done in bed; one is his kitchen and diningroom; and the third is the dwelling of his aged mother. On a tree at the entrance to the eccentric genius's domain there is posted, or recently was posted, a characteristic notice: "To Gentlemen: These grounds are for my own private use, where I desire absolute quiet and seclusion. (Verbum sap.) To Hoodlums, Thieves, and Housebreakers: I am stocking these grounds with imported birds, I want to preserve the native ones. Now, as you have no business here except to destroy, you will be treated as thieves and burglars if found on these grounds. Any one shooting at this notice or shooting in this direction will be effectually fired at in return." It is said that the gun which hangs where Mr. Miller can reach it, to enforce the order in case of need, has never been taken down. . . . As in London, he electrified society in Washington by the eccentric costume he affected —flowing hair beneath a wide brimmed Mexican sombrero, a red bandanna protruding from his vest, and the extremities of his nether integuments tucked inside a pair of cowboy's boots. Literary genius is appreciated at the national capital, and Miller received a good deal of attention, but his taste in dress is said to have caused some annoying mistakes on the part of footmen who failed to distinguish him from the genus tramp. Miller was christened Cincinnatus Hiner—which latter name has frequently been given, in more poetic form, as Heine. But these baptismal appellations he long ago discarded for the picturesque Spanish "Joaquin" with which all his literary work has been signed.—CLARKE, HENRY V., 1893, *The Poet of the Sierras, Munsey's Magazine*, vol. 9, pp. 308, 309.

He is a brilliant conversationalist with a limitless fund of anecdote. His accent is singularly pure, his voice full and pleasant; and as he discusses some congenial theme his thoughts rove from early pioneer days when as a boy in the diggers' camp he cooked their unvaried fare of salt pork and boiled beans, allotted to each man his share of the gold dust, and in his spare hours wrote and cultivated that divine faculty that later brought him fame. His appearance is striking and his face beams with intelligence. He usually wears long boots into the tops of which his trousers are tucked. His hair, streaked here and there with silver, hangs almost to his shoulders, and is inclined to curl as is also his beard.— GREGORY-FLESHER, HELEN E., 1895, *A Day with Joaquin Miller, The Arena*, vol. 12, p. 88.

GENERAL

Excitement and ambition may be called the twin geniuses of Mr. Miller's poetical character. Everything is to him both vital and suggestive; and some curious specimens might be culled of the fervid interfusion of external nature and the human soul in his descriptive passages. The great factors of the natural world—the sea, the mountains, the sun, moon, and stars — become personalities, animated with an intense life and a dominant possession. . . . At times he runs riot in overcharged fancies, which, in "Ina" especially, recall something of the manner of Alexander Smith, whether in characterizing the objects of nature, or in the frenzied aspirations of the human spirit. It should be understood, however, that the only poet to whom he bears a considerable or essential analogy is Byron. . . . He is a poet, and an admirable poet. His first works prove it to demonstration, and superabundantly; and no doubt his future writings will reinforce the proof with some added maturity and charm. He is not the sort of man to be abashed or hurt by criticism. . . . America may be proud of him.—ROSSETTI, WILLIAM MICHAEL, 1871, *A New American Poet, The Academy, Eclectic Magazine*, vol. 77, p. 243.

The poet himself is as typical of our country as are his poems; for from his preface we learn to identify him with the "rough edges of the frontier," and a region "walled from the world by seas on one hand and the Sierra Nevada Mountains in savage grandeur on the other," where, as he says, the city of Mexico was his Mecca; while there is something peculiarly characteristic in the audacity that took him to the world's capital to confront the world's criticism with his book. We cannot deny that these poems exhibit some crudities. There are repetitions of the same thought and phrase, and those blemishes which proceed from ignorance of the established canons of verse; but less could hardly be expected from a man not yet thirty, whose whole life had been spent among the rude scenes of which he writes, while even these blemishes are gilded by his genius. . . . There are indications of dramatic force in "Ina;" but it is far less apparent there than in the Arizonian poem, which, in spite of its narrative form and lyric loveliness, gives a projection and an action to its characters as lively as that of a bas-relief.—SPOFFORD, HARRIET PRESCOTT, 1871, *Joaquin Miller's Poems, Old and New*, vol. 4, pp. 372, 373.

The best poem in Mr. Miller's small volume ["Songs of the Sierras"] is the first one, which bears the title of "Arizonian." . . . We cannot say as much for the rest of the volume. Bitterly bad, indeed, is what it is necessary to call it if one would be accurately descriptive, for the other poems have all the faults of "Arizonian," and none, or next to none, of its merits, and have besides abundant faults of their own; and are not only, as poems, sad affairs, but, as giving distinct and strong indications of the moral notions and the taste and the power of thought which Mr. Miller brings to his works—as revealing his admirations and his aspirations, they should be sufficiently discouraging to his friends. Unless, indeed, Mr. Miller is very young; and has a long time to live.—DENNETT, J. R., 1871, *Miller's "Songs of the Sierras," The Nation*, vol. 13, p. 196.

Joaquin Miller has not grown under the influence of culture and civilization and longer practice in writing into the poet it was hoped he would become. The "Songs of Italy" have the same spontaneous vigor, the same vividness and originality of imagery, the same lack of proportion, of taste and thought, the same excellences and defects, as the "Songs of the Sierras," although their distribution is perhaps more even.—WOODBERRY, GEORGE E., 1878, *Recent Poetry, The Nation*, vol. 27, p. 336.

Joaquin Miller is, first of all, a poet, if one may judge from the relative merits of his verse and prose,—the latter of which does not show his spirit and invention at their best. The "Songs of the Sierras," as a first book, was no ordinary production. Its metrical romances, notwithstanding obvious crudities and affectations, gave a pleasurable thrill to the reader. Here was something like the Byronic imagination, set aglow by the freedom and splendor of the Western ranges, or by turns creating with at least a sensuous *vraisemblance* an ideal of the tropics which so many Northern minstrels have dreamed of and sung. Miller still has years before him, and often lyrics from his pen suggest that, if he would add a reasonable modicum of purpose to his sense of the beautiful, the world would profit by the result.—STEDMAN, EDMUND CLARENCE, 1885, *Poets of America*, p. 452.

The genius of Miller is peculiarly fitted to bring this kind of verse to perfection. By nature, by temperament, he belongs to a self-conscious and long-established society. He is continually analysing himself in others. He is always holding himself sufficiently apart from his surroundings to be able to analyse their savour to the full. At the same time, his intense human sympathy keeps him in touch with the subject of his observation; and a childhood spent in his wild Oregon home, the associations of his youth and early manhood among the turbulent pioneers and miners of the Pacific coast, have so indelibly impressed his genius, that the master-passions alone, and those social problems only that are of universal import, concern him when his singing robes are on. There is thus a primitive sincerity in his expression, and in his situations a perennial interest. His passion is manly, fervent, wholesome; and the frankness of it particularly refreshing in these indifferent days. He is a lover of sonorous rhythms, and betrays here and there in his lines the enthralling cadences of Swinburne. But in spite of such surface resemblances, he is fundamentally as original as fresh inspiration, novel material, and a strongly individualised genius might be expected to make him.—ROBERTS, CHARLES G. D., 1888, ed. *Poems of Wild Life, Introduction*, p. xiii.

Miller is the Sierra minstrel, who, on the basis of a natural aptitude fortified by an enthusiastic study of Byron and Swinburne, easily sings of the romantic experiences of a rich *terra incognita*, where the dash and fire of personal life stand forth against the background of snowy mountain,—"lonely as God and white as a winter moon,"—darksome gulch or tropical river. His poems, however, are but essays in song, perishable utterances of a freedom that must more slowly take to itself the lessons of lasting art.—RICHARDSON, CHARLES F., 1888, *American Literature*, 1607-1885, vol. II, p. 232.

"The City Beautiful" will gain for Mr. Miller a new circle of readers, and it will endear him to many fine souls who are hungering and thirsting for a higher, truer, and more ideal civilization.—FLOWER, B. O., 1893, *A New Social Vision, The Arena*, vol. 9, pp. 553, 560.

One thing should have saved the British critic from this mistake of his,—the lack of artistic merit in this first book ["Songs of the Sierras"] of Mr. Miller's. Whatever merits it may be allowed to contain, the merit of good workmanship is certainly absent. The instructed reader should have perceived at once that if here was a poet born, here was not a poet made. The critic might have perceived also, what is certainly there,—evidence that this was a poet who had an innate faculty of expression, that might be improved by practice and polished by the learning and following of rules, but not without attractiveness in its natural wildness. What is bad in this book is bad without disguise, so fatuously bad that one never ceases wondering how an author capable of such stuff could ever do anything good. Yet the good, in turn, is so strong and so beautiful as to make the reader temporarily insensible to irregularities and inequalities of style, as well as to gross defects of taste. — VEDDER, HENRY C., 1895, *American Writers of To-Day*, p. 307.

Waiving for the moment his claims as a poet, Mr. Miller wins his first claim to our attention by his power to hold it. Most books of poems can be laid aside without any overwhelming reluctance on the part of the reader. But with these poems— especially "The Isles of the Amazons" and "Songs of the Sun Land"—it is not so. Indeed, one old gentleman I know nearly finished the entire volume at one sitting— a feat requiring several hours. What the secret of the poet's charm is, it would perhaps be hard to say. If we could have but one word to describe it, we should say that *freshness* defines the alluring quality of his style. Read only a few pages and you will feel assured that Pan sent a wood-nymph to the poet's christening, presenting him with a secret pass into Nature's inner council chambers. Few, if any, other writers, make us feel so much out-of-doors. We hear so plainly in all his poems the tidal beat of the ocean, the roar of geysers and rivers and the rustling whispers of forests, with never a suggestion of secondhand messages from Nature.—SHERMAN, ELLEN BURNS, 1896, *Joaquin Miller, The Critic*, vol. 29, p. 19.

He is, despite grievous errors as man and author, a real poet, perhaps the boldest, freest voice of the far West. In a severely winnowed yet copious selection he will live as one of our most original singers.—LAWTON, WILLIAM CRANSTON, 1902, *Introduction to the Study of American Literature*, p. 334.

Sir Edwin Arnold
1832-1904

Born 10 June 1832. At King's School, Rochester, 1845-50. At King's Coll., London, 1850-51. Scholarship at University Coll., Oxford, 1851; Newdigate Prize Poem, 1852. B. A., 1854; M.A., 1856. To King Edward's School, Birmingham, as Assistant Master, 1854. Principal of Govt. Sanscrit Coll. at Poona, and Fellow of Bombay University, 1857. Joined staff of "Daily Telegraph," 1861. F. R. G. S., Jan. 1875 to May 1887. C. S. I., 1 Jan. 1877. Siamese Order of White Elephant (on publication of "The Light of Asia"), 1879. Second Class of Imperial Order of Medjidieh, 1876; Imperial Order of Osmanieh, 1886. K. C. I. E., 1888. Japanese Imperial Order of Rising Sun, 1892. Pres. of Birmingham and Midland Institute for 1893. Mem. Royal Asiatic Soc. *Works:* "The Feast of Belshazzar," 1852; "Poems, Narrative and Lyrical," 1853; "Griselda," 1856; "The Wreck of the Northern Belle," 1857; "Education in India," 1860; "The Marquis of Dalhousie's Administration," 1862; "The Poets of Greece," 1869; "Simple Transliteral Grammar of the Turkish Language," 1877; "The Light of Asia," 1879; "Indian Poetry" (in "Trübner's Oriental Series"), 1881; "Pearls of the Faith," 1883; "The Secret of Death," 1885; "India Revisited" (from "Daily Telegraph"), 1886; "Lotus and Jewel," 1887; "Poems, National and Non-Oriental" (selected), 1888; "With Sa'di in the Garden," 1888; "In my Lady's Praise," 1889; "The Light of the World," 1891; "Seas and Lands" (from "Daily Telegraph"), 1891; "Japonica" (from "Scribner's Magazine"), 1892; [1891]; "Potiphar's Wife," 1892; "Adzuma, 1893; "Wandering Words," 1894; "The Tenth Muse," 1895; "East and West," 1896; "Victoria, Queen and Empress" (from "Daily Telegraph"), 1896. He has *translated:* "The Book of Good Counsel" from "Hitopadesa," 1861: "Political Poems by Victor Hugo and Garibaldi" (under initials: E. A.), 1868; "Hero and Leander," from Musæus [1873]; "The Indian Song of Songs," from "Jayadeva," 1875; "Indian Idylls," from the "Mahâbhârata," 1883; "The Song Celestial," from the "Mahâbhârata," 1885; "The Chaurapanchâsika," 1896.—SHARP, R. FARQUHARSON, 1897, *A Dictionary of English Authors, p. 8.*

PERSONAL

I have seldom seen a look even of surprise on the mobile face of this delightful optimist; never in my life one of anger. Few of us who study character have met a man of genius with such an enviable disposition, such courtesy and grace of manner, or one gifted with such an incessantly sunny nature. Most of us have our dark hours of depression. We are changeable, moodish, sometimes roaring with laughter, often down in the dumps, but never for one instant have I seen a dark cloud overshadow Edwin Arnold's bright and attractive countenance. One of the best talkers I have ever met. . . . A man of Sir Edwin Arnold's temperament can never grow old. He has, and ever must have, a young heart.—SCOTT, CLEMENT, 1894, *A Happy Hour with Sir Edwin Arnold, The English Illustrated Magazine, vol. 12, pp. 119, 123.*

As he appeared to American audiences, Sir Edwin Arnold was of large frame and good stature, with an open face, strong features, expansive brow, and a broad, full, and well-rounded head, thickly covered with iron gray hair. His complexion was fair, his eyes blue, mild, and courteous in expression. His general air was one of kindness and good breeding. He was in personal manner quite free from self-consciousness, and on the platform was always absorbed in his task and by his audience. His speaking voice was melodious, excellent in compass and timbre. It was, in fact, among the very best for use and wear that the lecture audiences had heard during twenty years. He has shown himself the respect of securing a careful training for his voice, and he knows how to take care of it. It has much of the highbred gentleness in it that made George William Curtis so great a favorite. In personal speech his English intonation was apparent, but when he read, it seemed as though the language lifted him above all such peculiarities. The modulation was perfect, and was indeed sometimes thrilling. He is one of the few poets that can both read and declaim their own poems. I was constantly reminded of Stanley's expression that if Arnold had not been a great writer and poet, he would most assuredly have been a great actor, for at fitting times the delivery became animated and dramatic.—POND, JAMES BURTON, 1900, *Eccentricities of Genius, p. 380.*

Just at this moment from the parlor I heard the flutter of a silk dress, and a beautiful Japanese vision entered the room, and Sir Edwin Arnold arose and said, "Colonel, allow me to introduce Lady Arnold." The fair Japanese lady was slender and statuesque; she had the bright eyes that lend brightness and never know shadow. Her knowledge of the English language was almost perfect, and she impressed me as a woman possessing a great, tender, loving heart, giving her all and asking no idolatrous homage. Her delight is in serving and willingly, more than willingly, for without thought she breaks the vase of precious ointment and wipes the feet of her beloved with the hair of her head. Sir Edwin Arnold is of medium height, straight as an arrow, and dressed in a gray suit. His eyes are gray, and his conversation gives you the impression, as Emerson says, "A man for whom no surprises await." His rooms were filled with bric-a-brac, and many articles of rare beauty and exquisite taste, brought from India, Egypt, South Africa, America, and Japan, for he has roamed with willing feet over many lands. Many years he was Professor in an institution of learning at Poona, India.—SCOVEL, JAMES MATLACK, 1902, *Sir Edwin Arnold, Poet, At Home, Overland Monthly, N. S. vol. 39, p. 660.*

THE LIGHT OF ASIA
1879

As to this great faith of Asia, a generation ago, Mr. Arnold tells us, little or nothing was known about it in Europe. This Poem, it may be hoped, will make it more widely known to English readers than anything else which has been written about it. For it is a work of great beauty. It tells a story of intense interest, which never flags for a moment; its descriptions are drawn by the hand of a master with the eye of a poet and the familiarity of an expert with the objects described; its tone is so lofty that there is nothing with which to compare it but the New Testament; it is full of variety, now picturesque, now pathetic, now rising into the noblest realms of thought and aspiration; it finds language penetrating, fluent, elevated, impassioned, musical always, to clothe its varied thoughts and sentiments. Nor is this surprising when we remember that the religion which is its inspiration is that of so many millions and so many ages, finding expression in the language of a scholar and a poet.—HOLMES, OLIVER WENDELL, 1879, *The Light of Asia, International Review*, vol. 7, p. 347.

Mr. Arnold's poem is in many ways the most "important" that has been published in English for some time. In both theme and treatment it is as ambitious as it is possible to be without pretentiousness; it is interesting enough to secure the popular favor which will miss its finer points, and as an intellectual performance its merit is unmistakable enough to secure the instant recognition of reflective criticism. It has, it may be said, a prodigious advantage in its theme. It might be called the gospel of Buddha in verse according to Edwin Arnold, and the gospel of Buddha is, as every one knows, a very attractive thing. . . . In fine, we question if this poem would ever have been written if Mr. Arnold and his ancestors had never read the New Testament, by which we by no means intend to deny the parallelisms so often drawn between Buddha and Jesus, of course, but only to intimate the sense of its unworthiness as a natural reproduction of the life, character, and philosophy of Buddha with which this poem leaves one. On the one hand, therefore, Mr. Arnold stimulates small confidence as a synoptic evangelist, and on the other it is not wholly due to him that we have in his "Light of Asia" a noble and touching story, which can only be compared with that of the New Testament, as it is so often observed, and any passable presentation of which would have attractions that few narratives possess. Mr. Arnold's presentation of it is much more than passable, but we shall not venture to call it poetic. Parts of it appear poetic, such as the lyric in the third book, and some of the sermon of Buddha before the king in book eight, though this is sorely weighted with its philosophy, which last is far too simple in essence to be paraded with pomp as a discovery.—BROWNELL, W. C., 1879, *Recent Poetry, The Nation*, vol. 29, pp. 314, 315.

In the "Light of Asia" we find a life of the true sort. It is a life of Buddha by a hero-worshipper who is not ashamed to own his devotion. He has chosen his hero well, we must think. If only for the extent and duration of his influence, the founder of the great faith of Asia which has seen four-and-twenty centuries roll by, and still holds the hearts of a third of mankind, must claim the reverence which belongs to a masterpiece of religious insight. . . . It matters little to us that the story mounts back to times when it is hard to look for authentic records, that priestly tradition has overlaid the tale with many corruptions and inventions, and that the "Light of Asia" is a restoration, so to say, of the original story, and, like all restorations, but in a peculiarly high degree, is subject to the distortions and misconceptions of the restorer. . . . It would be a useless sort of flattery to tell Mr. Arnold that he has written one of the world's great epics; for he shows too much poetical feeling not to be aware of his shortcomings. It cannot be denied that there is too large a proportion of halting lines, that he allows too often a false accent, and that he will write the same name (Himalâya, for instance) in several ways to fit the exigencies of his five feet. A much more serious fault is his fondness for queer words and odd constructions, which give the poem an air of affectation which can only mar its effect.—LANE-POOLE, STANLEY, 1880, *The Light of Asia, Macmillan's Magazine*, vol. 41, pp. 496, 498.

I have been reading a most melancholy, but in parts beautiful book, Edwin Arnold's poetisation of Buddhism, "The Light of Asia." But what a Light.—CHURCH,

RICHARD WILLIAM, 1889, *To his Daughter, Life and Letters of Dean Church*, ed. his Daughter, p. 411.

The world was ready for "The Light of Asia" when it appeared. It might not have been ready for it twenty years before, and it may outgrow it before another twenty years is past. Meantime, Sir Edwin occupies a place among the poets of England, and deservedly so, for admitting the obvious faults of its careless and hasty writing, and granting Buddhism as popularly interpreted, particularly in New England, to be as great a fad as the Faith Cure, "The Light of Asia" is a production that will preserve the name of its author.—STODDARD, RICHARD HENRY, 1890. *The Book Buyer*, p. 493.

THE LIGHT OF THE WORLD
1891

What might be expected from the nature of his studies, and the ethical cast of his sympathies. It contains the poetical qualities that distinguished "The Light of Asia;" is rapid in its movement, picturesque in its treatment, reverent in intention, and is likely to interest a larger class of readers than he has ever had before—an emotional class, which, admiring rather than criticising, will give him a high place among sacred English poets.—STODDARD, RICHARD HENRY, 1890, *The Book Buyer*, p. 493.

It is no disparagement of Sir Edwin Arnold to say that he has failed where none of his contemporaries could well have succeeded. I have endeavoured to measure his work by the great standards of poetic aim—such an attempt challenges no less a consideration. Sir Edwin Arnold would ask no less—but, judged by the smaller ideal of mere literary workmanship, there is, within the broad failure, much of charming and strenuous success, many vivid pictures, beautiful lines, and strongly expressed thought.—LE GALLIENNE, RICHARD, 1891, *The Light of the World, The Academy*, vol. 39, p. 295.

In "The Light of the World" Sir Edwin Arnold essays the profoundly difficult task of telling anew the story of Christ. Though not without occasional beauty, the poem is far from being successful, and exhibits in a marked degree many of its author's most characteristic faults.—BELL, MACKENZIE, 1892, *The Poets and the Poetry of the Century, Kingsley to Thomson*, ed. Miles, p. 534.

GENERAL

There is little that need be said in praise of this wonderful Oriental love-song, after such passages as these. Whether one reads it for its poetry alone, or, as some are said to read the love-songs of Solomon, to discover figurative meanings underneath the poetry, there is an abundant reward for the perusal. Its passion is genuine and deep—like that of the love-songs of Burns; and its music is in many places exquisite and haunting. Mr. Arnold's warm admiration of Radha, will be little wondered at by those to whom this embodiment of this lovely being in the colder form and more sombre colorings of English verse shall suggest the free and luxurious charm which she must have owned in her native garb.—BROWNE, F. F., 1880, *The Indian "Song of Songs," The Dial*, vol. 1, p. 134.

The Sanskrit scholar who takes up the translations which Mr. Edwin Arnold has made from the Mahâbhârata will first ask himself how far the Anglicised version corresponds with the phraseology of the original; but the literary critic who cannot claim acquaintance with the prodigious poem that epitomises the antique Hindu world will first ask himself how far the net result of the translation as he finds it is an addition to the store of English poetry. . . . In any case, Mr. Arnold's book is rightly named; and, when we bring it to that first test to which we think it fairly liable, we have no difficulty in saying that it is a valuable addition to the store of English poetry. . . . We cannot better describe these legends than to say they are works of fancy and understanding. There is elation and grandeur in them here and there, but the great body of them do not rise above the level of ordinary common-sense, rendered beautiful by gleams of that faculty—fancy—which finds parallels of imagery and antithesis of phrase. . . . It was Milton's rule of poetry that it should be simple, sensuous, and impassioned. The first two of these conditions Mr. Arnold's "Idylls" fulfil, but they fall short of the last.—CAINE, HALL, 1883, *Literature, The Academy*, vol. 24, p. 357.

The artistic value of these "Idylls" is of a high order. Mr. Arnold assures us that "the Sanskrit verse is ofttimes as musical and highly wrought as Homer's own Greek." His translation makes good the statement. The reader easily forgets that he is reading a translation. Mr. Arnold's muse strings her own lyre. Poetic inspiration rings through every line. The themes are simple; but the artistic treatment lends them a weight and gives them a rounded finish rarely held by poems of greater pretensions.—HIRSCH, EMIL G., 1883, *Edwin Arnold's New Indian Poems, The Dial, vol. 4, p.* 158.

During the latest quarter of a busy life he has gained a respectful hearing in his own country and something like fame in America. He is not a creative poet, yet the success of his Asiatic legends is due to more than an attractive dressing-up of the commonplace. He has zest, learning, industry, and an instinct for color and picturesqueness strengthened through absorption of the oriental poetry, by turns fanciful and sublime. Above all, he shows the advantage of new ground, or of ground newly surveyed, and an interest in his subject which is contagious. There is a man behind his cantos, and a man clever enough to move in the latest direction of our unsettled taste and thought.—STEDMAN, EDMUND CLARENCE, 1887, *Twelve Years of British Song, Century Magazine, vol.* 34, *p.* 907.

It is scarcely possible to open Sir Edwin Arnold's version of Sa'Di' without finding something that one would like to quote. . . . The perusal of them has something of the effect of a change of climate. We open the book, and forthwith leave behind our modern practical life, to find ourselves in a spiritual region of yearning, an ecstacy, and high-strung devotion. We close in, and come back to our work-a-day world with a feeling as if we had been breathing a softer and purer air.—HUNTER, W. W., 1889, *With Sa' Di' in the Garden, The Academy, vol.* 35, *p.* 68.

He cannot of course be placed—he would not, I am sure, dream of any claim to be placed—on the same line with the two great poets whom this era has produced—Lord Tennyson and Mr. Browning. In any attempt to rank the poets of this generation a line must be drawn between their names and that of any of their contemporaries. . . . Nor again can Sir Edwin Arnold match the exquisite felicities of diction, the consummate taste and classical refinement of Mr. Matthew Arnold; nor is he gifted with the rich vocabulary and lyric frenzy—what De-Quincey might have called the "jewelly hæmorrhage" of words and metaphors— which are to be found in the best work of Mr. Swinburne. But he has little to fear from comparison with any other poet of our time, and the intrinsic merit of his poems will secure them a permanent place in English literature.—FARRAR, FREDERIC WILLIAM, 1891, *The Light of the World, Longman's Magazine, vol.* 17, *pp.* 495, 496.

Does not the frank story of the fair Asenath ["Potiphar's Wife"], the wife of Potiphar, belong to "the locked bookcase?" Surely no French novel was ever more "realistic."—MOULTON, LOUISE CHANDLER, 1892, *Three English Poets, The Arena, vol.* 6, *p.* 50.

The popularity of Sir Edwin Arnold's poetry is curiously characteristic of the British temper. His two pseudo-epical productions, "The Light of Asia" and "The Light of the World," have found a joyous acceptance in every middle-class household. There is sufficient reason for this: the literary sensibilities of the great middle-class are but coarse; monotonous rhythm and poverty of imagination jar not upon them at all; the exaggeration of ineffective epithet and the constant strain after cheap sensuousness give them mild but unfeigned pleasure. Then, again, Sir Edwin Arnold, is always intelligible; not, indeed, through any crystal limpidity of phrase, but because his thought never goes deep enough to be obscure, or to call for answering subtleties of intellectual activity on the part of the reader. And, lastly, he has drawn his materials from the only subjects perennially interesting to the middle-class, the mysteries of religion; that is to say, he has uniformly degraded high themes by tawdry treatment, and presented ideal figures in a lurid and distressing light. —CHAMBERS, EDMUND KERCHEVER, 1892, *Potiphar's Wife and Other Poems, The Academy, vol.* 41. *p.* 391.

Give me red loamy poppy-lands this summer night,
Let Lethe's stream flow soft 'twixt banks of moon-drenched rue.
Let me not waken in that paradise of light
Where sleeps the bulbul with a waft of song— and you.
But let me dream and through the silvery pleasuance roam,
Where lemon-grass grows spear-like and the blue doves coo.
There may I pluck white lotus from the whiter foam,
And on the rippled shores find peace and love— and you.

Go with me, find with me the sun-bird's glowing nest,
Hid 'neath a musky branch of amaranth and dew.
Shake not the leafage dense, but let us love and rest.
I love your lute when silent, and your lips—and you.
So will we dream within the cloistered green and gold,
Where sapphired wings are folded all the warm night through.
And when we wake enclasped in new love ne'er grown old,
I will content my love with rest and morning—and with you.
—GUNSAULUS, FRANK W., 1895, *After Reading Sir Edwin Arnold's Verses; Songs of Night and Day.*

Sir Henry Morton Stanley
1841–1904

A celebrated explorer and author; born in Denbigh, Wales, in 1840; and now living in London. Originally named John Rowlands, he was adopted at 15 by a New Orleans merchant, whose name he took. He served in both the Confederate and Union armies in the Civil War; was a newspaper correspondent in Turkey and Abyssinia in 1868; and started on the search for Dr. Livingston in October 1869, returning in July 1872. He made an exploration of Equatorial Africa 1874–78; founded the Congo Free State 1879–84; and headed a successful expedition for the relief of Emin Pasha in 1887–90. He has been a member of Parliament since 1896. His works include: "Coomassie and Magdala" (1872); "How I found Livingston" (1872); "Through the Dark Continent" (1879); "The Congo and the founding of its Free State" (1885); and "In Darkest Africa," the title best known to general readers in America.—WARNER, CHARLES DUDLEY, ed. 1897, *Library of the World's Best Literature, Biographical Dictionary*, vol. XXIX, p. 503.

PERSONAL

The last time I saw him was four or five years ago in London, on his return from one of his extraordinary expeditions. He had been to Africa for good King Leopold of Belgium, and was living modestly in a suite of rooms in Sackville street, London. I had not then met him since his first lecturing tour in the United States, when he was in his prime—young, vigorous, and handsome. The change in his appearance was startling. The rich black hair had become tawny and tow-colored; the bright, fresh, clear complexion had become sallow and the skin was pitted almost as if from smallpox. I was so startled by the change that I could not resist asking what had produced the marvellous transformations. . . . And how he had grown intellectually in the years that had elapsed! I was amazed at his power of description when he began to tell me of some of the scenes and incidents of his then last expedition. I was charmed to find him unspoiled by success: as natural and unaffected as the first time I met him after his search for Livingston.—CONNERY, THOMAS B., 1891, *Reminiscences of Two Modern Heroes, The Cosmopolitan*, vol. 11, p. 156.

A man who fills every room he enters with his knowledge, energy, and force of character, yet so quiet in manner that you might overlook him if you did not notice the head, cast in a mould which would turn out cannon-balls, and with eyes that burnt their way through everything.—SMALLEY, GEORGE W., 1895, *Mr. Huxley, Scribner's Magazine*, vol. 18, p. 519.

His manners always seemed to me—even when being lionized in social circles—to be distinctly modest and unassuming, and his conversation was extremely interesting. He was original in many of his ways, and especially so in his neglect of the conventionalism of dress. At an evening party at Versailles, given expressly for his honour, he appeared in a white flannel suit, whether in ignorance of the requirements of the occasion, or in wilful defiance of them, it is difficult to say.—TUCKERMAN, CHARLES K., 1895, *Personal Recollections of Notable People*, vol. II, p. 153.

Leaving Archdeacon Farrar I went to No. 2 Richmond Terrace and called upon Henry M. Stanley. His home is on a quiet little street just off the bank of the Thames and not more than one hundred steps from the entrance to the House of Commons. It is a little stone house with an English basement and the words "Knock and ring" on the lintels of its door. As you enter the wide hall you find yourself in a very museum. The walls are covered with curios from every part of the world and rare articles from Africa interspersed with photographs of Stanley's friends in Europe and America. As I looked at these the great explorer entered and led me into his library. This was a large square room looking out upon the Terrace; the walls were covered with books and the desks in the center were littered with manuscripts.—CARPENTER, FRANK G., 1896, *Fireside Talks with Great Men, The Chautauquan,* vol. 23, p. 444.

Henry M. Stanley was never fond of company. He appreciates friends, and those who know him intimately are very fond of him. He is generally cautious and sparing of words, especially when strangers are about. Receptions and dinners worry him, as he cannot bear being on exhibition under showers of forced compliments. His manners and habits are those of a gentleman. He shows great fondness for children, especially young lads, who often approach him for his autograph. He will enter into conversation with them and question them as to their purposes in life, advising them as to the importance of honesty and character as essential to success in life, and generally concluding with some incident in his experience that is sure to make a lasting impression. . . . Stanley is one of the best-read men I have ever met. He is familiar with the histories of all civilized and uncivilized peoples. As a journalist he is appreciated by reporters and interviewers more highly than any man I ever knew except Mr. Beecher. Never did he refuse to see a representative of the press who sent up his card. If busy, he would say: "Please make my compliments to the gentleman and say that as soon as I am disengaged I will be pleased to see him."—POND, JAMES BURTON, 1900, *Eccentricities of Genius,* pp. 279, 280.

EXPLORER

I was particularly struck when I first found myself face to face with Mr. Stanley, under his palaver shed at Msuwa, with his healthy, robust appearance. I was expecting to see a man prematurely old, worn out and enfeebled by the innumerable attacks of African fever he has sustained, and the accumulated effects of the hardships of nineteen years off and on, of African exploit. His hair and mustache were gray, it is true, but apart from that, he did not look older to me than his nine and forty years. He is a man slightly below medium height, but weighs much more than one would be likely at first sight to guess. His normal weight is about a hundred and seventy-five pounds. He looks like a hard, stocky man of the Phil Sheridan or Stonewall Jackson type, and struck one, on first appearance, as being good yet for two or three more such expeditions as the relief and rescue of Emin Pasha. He nevertheless suffered much on the expedition.—THOMAS, STEVENS, 1890, *Scouting for Stanley in East Africa.*

A born leader of men, white or black, with reserve power for the greatest emergencies, unhampered by scruples as to its exercise while the need lasts, self-reliant, of almost super human endurance, and with the experience of many African campaigns behind him, it is not strange that he lived a life apart, bore his own responsibilities, and made his own decisions, sometimes without the sympathy of his subordinate officers, whom, notwithstanding his high praise of them, he could not always take into his unlimited confidence.—NORTON, MINERVA B., 1890, *Stanley and his Work in Africa, The Dial,* vol. 11, p. 235.

The expedition for the rescue of Emin Pasha must always remain, so far as Mr. Stanley is concerned, one of the greatest feats of courage and endurance in the annals of adventure. No criticism of its objects or methods can dim its luster as an example of what fortitude can accomplish in the teeth of difficulties of nearly every description. It would be no small thing to make one's way across Africa on foot, without other concern than one's own capacity for supporting physical suffering and fatigue. But Mr. Stanley crossed Africa on foot at the head of a column of unwilling, half-hearted, uncivilized followers, for whom he had to supply all the necessary experience and forethought about food, and clothing, and arms, and ammunition, and health. He was the one man in his party who never could afford to be sick, or sorrowful, or discouraged, or doubtful. . . . He had to flog or hang his own men to maintain discipline. He had to shoot the inhabitants and to pillage and burn their village in order to protect himself against treachery and to supply himself with provisions. As I have said, when he was fairly launched on his march, self-preservation became his first law; but the question still remains to be answered, Who sent him on his march? From whom did he get authority to begin the series of military operations that ended in depositing Emin Pasha at Zanzibar? Under whose order did he enlist troops, and exercise among the Africans the power of a general in the field? If his commission was what it ought to have been, he was really entitled under it to shoot and hang the white men of his command as well as the black ones.—GODKIN, EDWIN LAWRENCE, 1890, *Was the Emin Expedition Piratical? The Forum, vol.* 10, *pp.* 633, 639.

Crowned with highest honors from all the powers of Europe, no tribute, as Stanley has said, gave such gratification as that from the United States, which, proud of the achievements of its great citizen, extended to him the unprecedented honors of its official, well-considered, and merited commendation, wherein, under date of February 7, 1878, it was "*Resolved*, by the Senate and House of Representatives in Congress assembled, That, regarding with just pride, the achievements of their countryman, Henry M. Stanley, the distinguished explorer of Central Africa, the thanks of the people of the United States are eminently due and are hereby tendered him as a tribute to his extraordinary patience, prudence, fortitude, enterprise, courage, and capacity in solving by his researches many of the most important geographical problems of our age and globe, problems of a continental scope, involving the progress of our kind in commerce, science, and civilization."—GREELY, ADOLPHUS WASHINGTON, 1893, *Explorers and Travellers* (*Men of Achievement*), *p.* 373.

The broad features of Stanley's work show that it had humanitarian and economic as well as geographical value. He was the first to give us an approximately accurate idea of the form and size of Victoria Nyanza, the second largest of freshwater lakes; he revealed the Congo Basin, of which we had no conception, as surpassed in size and in water tribute to the sea only by the Amazon system; he threaded the gloomy and almost inpenetrable mazes of the forest belt, larger than most of our States; he made over four hundred treaties with native chiefs who learned to know him as a man who kept his word, and the relations of friendship and confidence which he established paved the way for the teacher, the merchant, and the colonial governments of Europe; he studied the peoples and the economic resources from sea to sea through tropical Africa and incessantly proclaimed that these peoples were capable of development, and that these resources were worth the world's seeking; he called for missionary volunteers to go to Uganda, where to-day there are ninety thousand professing Christians, three hundred and twenty churches, and fifty thousand persons able to read; he preached the gospel of humanity to the natives, used fire-arms against them, alas! but only on the comparatively few occasions when the existence of his expedition was at stake; and in his dealings with them he set an example of patience, mercy, and justice that has not always been emulated. For over twenty years, he saw the African movement impelled, not only by his own hands, but also by ceaseless reënforcement of strong men and mighty influences, and he lived fourteen years longer to see white agents of the leading European nations firmly established in nearly every nook and corner of the continent.—ADAMS, CYRUS C., 1904, *What Stanley Lived to see Accomplished in Africa, American Monthly Review of Reviews, vol.* 29, *p.* 673.

GENERAL

Whatever may be the value of Mr. Henry M. Stanley's late discoveries in Central Africa, the indomitable courage and energy with which he has, under the most untoward circumstances, pursued his explorations in that far-off region must command general admiration and respect. If his book entitled "Through the Dark Continent," lately published in London, shows that he has not yet succeeded in revealing the grand secret of the Nile sources, it goes to prove that he has at least contributed largely towards narrowing the problems down to comparatively circumscribed limits, and added many striking facts to the common stock of geographical knowledge. By the aid of the camera he has enriched his book with a number of interesting pictures, which are particularly valuable because of their being faithful illustrations of the beautiful scenery of Central Africa, and of the manners prevailing among her savage tribes. . . . An introductory chapter is given, covering almost everything worthy of notice which historians and travelers have said of the Nile Country, from the time of Herodotus down to that of Stanley himself. In fact, nearly everything on the subject that may be met with in any respectable cyclopædia is given; and if he has omitted the pretty story about the Nile related by the Registrar of Minerva's treasury in Egypt to the father of history, he may be pardoned on the score of desiring to economize space. — MILLEN, F. F., 1878, *Mr. Stanley as an Explorer, International Review, vol.* 5, *pp.* 678, 679.

It was in that part of the hotel farthest removed from the street that Mr. Stanley took up his abode. Here he had a fine suite of rooms on the ground floor, very handsomely furnished in the oriental style. A large, lofty reception room and an equally large and handsome dining-room. In these he received some of the most important or most persistent of his many callers; but as a rule he shut himself up in his bedroom, and there he wrote from early morning till late at night, and woe betide anyone who ventured unasked into this sanctum. He very rarely went out, even for a stroll round the garden. His whole heart and soul were centered on his work. He had set himself a certain task, and he had determined to complete it to the exclusion of every other object in life. He said of himself, "I have so many pages to write, I know that if I do not complete this work by a certain time, when other and imperative duties are imposed upon me, I shall never complete it at all. When my work is accomplished, then I will talk with you, laugh with you, and play with you, or ride with you to your heart's content; but let me alone now, for Heaven's sake." Nothing worried him more than a tap at the door while he was writing; he sometimes glared even upon me like a tiger ready to spring, although I was of necessity a frequent and privileged intruder, and always with a view to forwarding the work in hand. He was a perfect terror to his courier and black boy. When his courier knocked tremblingly at his door, he would cry out, "Am I a prisoner in my own house?" "I've brought you this telegram, sir." "Well, I detest telegrams; why do you persist in bringing them?"—MARSTON, EDWARD, 1890, *How Stanley Wrote his Book, Scribner's Magazine, vol.* 8, *p.* 211.

There are few of us who are acquainted with his earlier books, and who have cared to follow intelligently not only what they say, but what they imply, who feel inclined to sanction. . . . Mr. Stanley's habitual conduct towards the natives with whom he came in contact; and there is perhaps no modest or honourable Englishman who has not felt a touch of shame in reading these narratives at the boastfulness and arrogance of the writer, and at the peculiarly unpleasant mixture of journalistic exaggeration, unscrupulous dealing, and religious sentiment which characterise Mr. Stanley's actions as they are depicted in Mr. Stanley's own words. . . . Mr. Stanley is not only an explorer, with a sword in his hand and a Bible in his jack-boot, as we are sometimes inclined to fancy in reading his highly spiced narratives, he is an ambitious, wary, and long-headed man of the world; a keen weapon in the hands of a king desirous of territory, or a commercial company eager for wealth.—QUILTER, HARRY, 1890, *Mr. H. M. Stanley: As Leader and Comrade, Universal Review, vol.* 8, *pp.* 314, 331.

"In Darkest Africa" is a narrative on whose current the reader is borne from the hour of setting forth to that of returning, without a break in the fascination of the story and its setting. The contributions which it brings to science are not inconsiderable. . . . For brilliant description and tragic interest, Mr. Stanley's pages are unsurpassed.—NORTON, MINERVA B., 1890, *Stanley and his work in Africa, The Dial, vol.* 11, *p.* 235.

An author may have a great name and yet fail to write a successful book. Stanley afterward published a volume called "Through South Africa." His fame had in no wise grown dim, and the land in which he won it was again his theme; but his book awakened no interest whatever. Three weeks after its publication his own American publishers had not heard of it, and no American edition has ever been brought out. The secret of this indifference lay in the fact that Stanley recorded no great achievement. His book comprised merely a series of newspaper letters from a region fast passing into the list of well-ordered and prosperous States. It was cast aside, while James Bryce's weighty book on the same subject, issued at the same time, aroused wide interest, bearing as it did to South Africa the relation which his "American Commonwealth" bears to the United States. Stanley's book was a commonplace traveller's chronicle, for which its author had created no public waiting to receive it.— HALSEY, FRANCIS WHITING, 1902, *Our Literary Deluge and some of its Deep Waters, p.* 21.

Sir Leslie Stephen
1832–1904

Born, in Kensington, 28 Nov. 1832. Early education at Eton and at King's Coll., London. Matric., Trin. Hall, Camb., 1851; B. A., 1854; M.A., 1857; Fellow Trin. Hall, 1855. Left Cambridge and settled in London, 1864. Married (i). Harriet Marion Thackeray, 1864; she died, 1875. Editor of "Cornhill Mag.," 1871–82. Married (ii.) Julia Prinsep Duckworth, 1878. Editor of "Dict. of Nat. Biog.," 1882–91. Clark Lecturer in English Literature, Camb., 1883–84. LL.D., Camb. Hon. Fellow Trin. Hall., Camb. Pres. of Ethical Society. *Works:* "Sketches from Cambridge" (anon.), 1865; "The Times on the American War" (under initials: "L. S."), 1865; "The Play-Ground of Europe," 1871; "Essays on Freethinking," 1873; "Hours in a Library" (3 vols), 1874–79; "History of English Thought in the Eighteenth Century" (2 vols), 1876; "Samuel Johnson," 1878; "Alexander Pope," 1880; "The Science of Ethics," 1882; "Swift," 1882; "Life of Henry Fawcett," 1885; "What is Materialism?" 1886; "An Agnostic's Apology," 1893; "The Life of Sir James Fitz-James Stephen," 1895; "Social Rights and Duties" (2 vols.), 1896. He has *translated:* Berlepsch's "The Alps," 1861; and *edited:* W. K. Clifford's "Lectures and Essays" (with Sir F. Pollock), 1879; Fielding's Works, 1882; Richardson's Works 1883; "Dictionary of National Biography," vols. i.–xxvi., 1885–91.—SHARP, R. FARQUHARSON, 1897, *A Dictionary of English Authors*, p. 269.

PERSONAL

He is by no means the traditional Englishman in appearance, being tall and rather thin; and his manner is that of a gentle and refined scholar. Without being a fluent speaker he is never at a loss for an appropriate expression, and he has a vein of pleasant humor which enlivens his speech and conversation.—YOUNG, ALEXANDER, 1890, *The Critic*.

Among all the coronation honors, none has been greeted with such universal and unfeigned satisfaction as the knighthood conferred upon Leslie Stephen. . . . Sir Leslie Stephen's most obvious claim to honor is that he is a most eminent "man of letters," and that men of letters, in the sense in which that term used to be used, are rare in modern England.—DICEY, A. V. 1902, *Sir Leslie Stephen, K. C. B., The Nation*, vol. 75, p. 49.

As, on Wednesday, February 24 last, in the sombre chapel at Hudson, the coffin stood on the bier in its violet covering before the portal of the crematorium, the profound silence was charged deep with a thousand memories to the friends who were gathered for the last time around him. There were men and women who had grown to old age in close touch with him—who had worked with him, worked for him, enjoyed life with him, who had loved him, whom he had loved—men who had served the State, or served the people, who had governed provinces, formed schools, written their names in the roll of statesmanship, literature, and science for the best part of two generations. Stephen's last book, composed, we might say, on his very death-couch, appeared to the public almost on the day of his funeral. He died literally in harness, as the Roman emperor said a general should die, erect and in his armor. But the inner memory of Leslie Stephen will remain for us, his coevals as a stalwart of the mid-Victorian age.—HARRISON, FREDERIC, 1904, *Sir Leslie Stephen, In Memoriam, Cornhill Magazine*.

GENERAL

Have I read your book? ["Hours in a Library"]. I wish you had read it so carefully, for then I should not have a string of *errata* to send you for your next edition.—LOWELL, JAMES RUSSELL, 1876, *To Leslie Stephen, May 15; Letters, ed. Norton*, vol. II, p. 165.

On looking back over Mr. Stephen's book a single feeling of admiration possesses me for the width of his knowledge, the vigour of his style, and the versatility of mind which has enabled him to do justice to so many subjects.—MORISON, JAMES COTTER, 1877, *Leslie Stephen's History of English Thought, Macmillan's Magazine*, vol. 35. p. 336.

Mr. Stephen is a bracing writer. His criticisms are no sickly fruit of fond compliance with his authors. By no means are they this, but hence their charm. There is much pestilent trash now being talked about "Ministry of Books," and the "Sublimity of Art," and I know not what other fine phrases. It almost amounts to a religious service conducted before an altar of first editions. Mr. Stephen takes no part in such silly rites. He remains outside with a pail of cold water.—BIRRELL, AUGUSTINE, 1894, *Essays about Men, Women and Books*, p. 192.

When, a hundred years hence, some one sets himself to write the history of English critical literature in the nineteenth century, he will probably regard Mr. Leslie Stephen as a transition figure, and see in his work a bridge spanning the gulf between two important and sharply differentiated schools. There are certain years during which Lord Macaulay and Mr. Walter Pater were contemporaries; but to pass from the pure literary essays of the former to those of the latter is like passing from one age into another. . . . There is no doubt that, in the main, Mr. Leslie Stephen's critical work has more in common with the Edinburgh than with the Oxford school. It is, to use words which are in some danger of becoming terms of literary slang, "judicial" rather than "æsthetic;" its conclusions are based rather on general principles than on particular sensibilities or preferences; it strives after impersonal estimates rather than personal appreciations. Nevertheless there is, in addition to all this, a constant admission, explicit or implicit, of the fact that even the critic cannot jump off his own shadow, and that, though he must appeal to the common reason, his appeal must in the nature of things be made on behalf of some individual approval or disapproval which it is his business to justify. . . . Mr. Leslie Stephen's style is the style which his substance makes inevitable. The manner of the seer or the rhetorician would indeed be an ill-fitting vesture for the thought of a shrewd, humorous observer who knows how to admire wisely, how to condemn sanely, but who, neither in eulogy nor condemnation, will allow himself the perilous luxury of excitement.—NOBLE, JAMES ASHCROFT, 1896, *Living Critics, The Bookman*, vol. 2, pp. 399, 401.

Mr. Stephen's criticism is of a peculiar, personal kind, and it is marked, above all, by an extreme sincerity, which has moulded his style, not inelegantly, into simply the most direct of possible vessels for pouring fact and opinion from the mind to the paper. Among other qualities he has an intellectual mastery over fact, precisely such as he demands, in one of the pages before us, from the ideal biographer, whom he contrasts, very happily, with the "dry antiquary," to whom "any and every fact is of the same importance." And, through this peculiar mastery, he has the gift of always being interesting, no matter what he is writing about; for in the first place, he never allows fact to stray from its logical place in an argument or an analysis, and, secondly, he humanises speculation while he intellectualises fact.—SYMONS, ARTHUR, 1898, *Mr. Leslie Stephen as a Critic, Saturday Review*, vol. 86, p. 113.

Granted the moral judgment — given a soul devoted to the social weal—Mr. Stephen offers vigorous and pointed encouragement, and dissuades one from being argued out of obedience to conscience. But, if the moral judgment be disputed, and if any soul prefers his own private weal, Mr. Stephen gives no help. To call selfish men "idiots" merely because they distinguish *meum* from *tuum* is not helpful. Tastes differ—that is the last word on these questions, if we adopt Mr. Stephen's premises.— MACKINTOSH, ROBERT, 1899, *From Comte to Benjamin Kidd*, p. 113.

His intense and thoroughgoing desire to arrive at true conclusions on the fundamental principles of morality gives a speculative interest to the pictures and analysis of character which belong to biography of the best kind. His immense knowledge of the actual lives of men guards him against that abstract, and therefore unreal, way of looking at things which is the special weakness of systematic thinkers; it supplies indeed, a good deal of that sort of knowledge which some writers have gained from large acquaintance with affairs or from mixing with the world, and is often lacking in teachers who have studied books more than men. John Mill, for one, would assuredly have gained a good deal from that wide knowledge of the lives and feelings of men who have lived and played their part in the world, which gives a tone of reality to even the most abstract of Stephen's speculative works. It is this quality, at any rate, combined with his subtle and playful humor, that makes Sir Leslie Stephen a moralist in the sense in which our grandfathers applied the word to Dr. Johnson.—DICEY, A. V., 1902, *Sir Leslie Stephen, K. C. B., The Nation*, vol. 75, p. 50.

The most personal and characteristic trait in all these collected essays is the continual play of a kind of ironical casuistry. On every page we see a keen and brilliant intellect seeking to ease the burden of the mystery, or of sad conviction, by the exercise of witty logic. . . . For all his ironical casuistry and mocking wit, it is always these deeper and more permanent emotions of human nature which warm and vitalize Sir Leslie Stephen's writing. His cool, familiar manner, so express and admirable, tells of turbulence subdued; and reveals rather than hides the mellow soundness of the writer. He is the chief biographical craftsman of English Literature, and the "Dictionary of National Biography" is a practical achievement which must have brought its first editor a fuller joy "than the conquest of Persia to the Macedonian." . . . The things that are eternally worth while, are seen for what they are.—GREENSLET, F., 1903, *The Studies of a Biographer, Atlantic Monthly*, vol. 92, pp. 137, 138.

A book such as this ["An Agnostic's Apology and Other Essays"] is bound to be difficult reading even for a fairly trained mind and despite its author's avoidance of intricate sentences and technical phraseology. Sir Leslie's "Apology" is hard reading, because it is close reasoning, and the reader who perseveres intelligently to the end of it cannot possibly be the kind of reader for whom any intelligent person should be rash enough to offer himself as a guardian. Then again, if, as Sir Leslie says, "A religion is the synthesis of a philosophy and a poetry," it is fairly clear that a number of persons capable of following the line of argument presented in this book, so far as it is philosophical, will be either repelled or disappointed by the fact that the poetical element of religion receives scarcely a word of attention. Hence the comparatively small number of readers capable of being radically affected by Sir Leslie's arguments is, I should say, at least cut in half.—TRENT, WILLIAM PETERFIELD, 1904, *Leslie Stephen's Agnosticism, The Bookman*, vol. 19, p. 70.

It remains to say that in the "Hours in a Library" and "Studies of a Biographer" we have Sir Leslie's sunnier side, in which many have delighted who have sometimes shivered in that clear cold air which blows from off the coasts of his more continental works and from his heights of passionate reality. Here, too, he can be the acute dialectician, but is oftener the delightful humorist, the brilliant satirist, the master of vivid characterization, the writer whose style is always clear and strong, often genial, and habitually abounding in felicity and charm. How many books and authors have we enjoyed more perfectly when walking in his steps! It is a great and lofty work that he has done for us, and it has qualities that will ensure for it some permanent and grateful recognition in a world where nothing but the best lasts very long.—CHADWICK, JOHN WHITE, 1904, *Sir Leslie Stephen, The Critic*, vol. 44, p. 311.

When that noble body of scholarly and cheerful pedestrians, the Sunday Tramps, were on the march, with Leslie Stephen to lead them, there was a conversation which would have made the presence of a shorthand writer a benefaction to the country. A pause to it came at the examination of the leader's watch and Ordnance map under the western sun, and word was given for the strike across country to catch the tail of a train offering dinner in London, at the cost of a run through hedges, over ditches and fallows, past proclamations against trespassers, under suspicion of being taken for more serious depredators in flight. The chief of the tramps had a wonderfully calculating eye in the observation of distances and the nature of the land, as he proved by his discovery of untried passes in the higher Alps, and he had no mercy for pursy followers. I have often said of this life-long student and philosophical head, that he had in him the making of a great military captain. He would not have been opposed to the profession of arms if he had been captured early for the Service, notwithstanding his abomination of bloodshed. He had a high, calm courage, was unperturbed in a dubious position, and would confidently take the way out of it which he considered to be the better. . . . His work in literature will be reviewed by his lieutenant of Tramps, one of the ablest of our writers. The memory of it remains with us as being the profoundest and the most sober criticism we have had in our time. The only sting in it was an inoffensive humorous irony that now and then stole out for a roll over, like a furry cub, or the occasional ripple on a lake in grey weather. We have nothing left that is like it.—MEREDITH, GEORGE, 1904, *Sir Leslie Stephen, Author, April*.

The Library of Literary Criticism
of English and American Authors

INDEXES:

VOLUMES I-VIII.

INDEX TO AUTHORS   -   -   PAGE 515

INDEX TO CRITICISMS   -   -   PAGE 541

GENERAL INDEX TO AUTHORS.

Vols. I to VIII.

	Born.	Died.	Vol.	Page.
Abbot, George,	1562	1633	I.	725
Adams, Hannah,	1755	1832	V	124
*Adams, John,	1735	1826	V	50
*Adams, John Quincy,	1767	1848	V	514
Adams, Samuel,	1722	1803	IV	440
Adams, Sarah Flower,	1805	1848	V	529
*Addison, Joseph,	1672	1719	II	632
Ælfric,	955?	1025?	I	45
Agassiz, Jean Louis Rodolphe,	1807	1873	VI	719
Aguilar, Grace,	1816	1847	V	504
Ainsworth, William Harrison,	1805	1882	VII	485
Airy, Sir George Biddell,	1801	1892	VIII	182
Akenside, Mark,	1721	1770	III	540
Alcott, Amos Bronson,	1799	1888	VII	662
Alcott, Louisa May,	1833	1888	VII	665
Alcuin,	c. 735	804	I	32
Aldhelm,	c. 640	709	I	24
*Alexander, Sir William,	1567?	1640	II	34
Alford, Henry,	1810	1871	VI	635
*Alfred the Great,	849	901	I	36
Alison, Archibald,	1757	1839	V	341
Alison, Sir Archibald,	1792	1867	VI	519
Allingham, William,	1824	1889	VII	734
Allston, Washington,	1779	1843	V	418
Ames, Fisher,	1758	1808	IV	527
Amory, Thomas,	1691?	1788	IV	47
Andrews, Lancelot,	1555	1626	I	635
Anselm,	1033	1109	I	49
Anstey, Christopher,	1724	1805	IV	479
*Arbuthnot, John,	1667	1735	III	81
Argyll, Duke of,	1823	1900	VIII	433
*Armstrong, John,	1709	1779	III	697
*Arnold, Sir Edwin,	1832	1904	VIII	501
*Arnold, Matthew,	1822	1888	VII	627
*Arnold, Thomas,	1795	1842	V	376
Ascham, Roger,	1515	1568	I	288
Asgill, John,	1359	1738	III	97

Those marked * are accompanied by engraved portrait.

		Born. Died.	Vol.	Page.
Ashmole, Elias,		1617—1692	II	436
Asser,		— 910?	I	41
*Atterbury, Francis,		1662—1732	III	63
Aubrey, John,		1626—1697	II	451
Audubon, John James,		1780—1851	V	695
Aungerville, Richard,		1287—1345	I	88
*Austen, Jane,		1775—1817	IV	612
Ayton, Sir Robert,		1570—1638	I	768
Aytoun, William Edmondstoune,		1813—1865	VI	444
Bacon, Delia,		1811—1859	VI	202
*Bacon, Francis,		1561—1626	I	638
Bacon, Roger,		1214—1292	I	77
Bage, Robert,		1728—1801	IV	418
Bagehot, Walter,		1826—1877	VII	96
Baillie, Joanna,		1762—1851	V	689
*Bailey, Philip James,		1816—1902	VIII	459
Baker, Sir Richard,		1568—1645	II	93
Bale, John,		1495—1563	I	285
*Bancroft, George,		1800—1891	VIII	54
Banim, John,		1798—1842	V	389
Barbauld, Anna Lætitia,		1743—1825	V	22
Barbour, John,		1316?-1395	I	113
Barclay, Alexander,		1475?-1552	I	264
Barclay, John,		1582—1621	I	618
Barclay, Robert,		1648—1690	II	411
Barham, Richard Harris,		1788—1845	V	474
*Barlow, Joel,		1754—1812	IV	573
Barnard, Lady Anne,		1750—1825	V	28
Barnes, Barnabe,		1569—1609	I	439
Barnes, Joshua,		1654—1712	II	571
Barnes, William,		1810—1886	VII	584
*Barrow, Isaac,		1630—1677	II	310
Barry, Girald de,	c.	1147—1220	I	67
Barton, Bernard,		1784—1849	V	594
Basse, William,		1583?-1653?	II	130
Baxter, Richard,		1615—1691	II	423
Bayly, Thomas Haynes,		1797—1839	V	339
*Beaconsfield, Earl of,		1804—1881	VII	276
*Beattie, James,		1735—1803	IV	428
*Beaumont, Francis,		1584—1616	I	586
Beaumont, Sir John,		1583—1627	I	679
Beaumont, Joseph,		1616—1699	II	461
Beaumont and Fletcher,			I	578
*Beckford, William,		1759—1844	V	446
Beddoes, Thomas Lovell,		1803—1849	V	584
Bede,	c.	673— 735	I	25
*Beecher, Henry Ward,		1813—1887	VII	599

GENERAL INDEX TO AUTHORS 517

	Born.	Died.	Vol.	Page.
BEECHER, LYMAN,	1775	—1863	VI	339
BEHN, APHRA,	1640	—1689	II	407
BENTHAM, JEREMY,	1748	—1832	V	162
*BENTLEY, RICHARD,	1662	—1742	III	109
BENTON, THOMAS HART,	1782	—1858	VI	86
BEOWULF,			I	17
BERKELEY, GEORGE,	1685	—1753	III	318
BERNERS, JULIANA,	c. 1388	—c. 1461	I	191
BERNERS, LORD,	1467	—1533	I	228
*BESANT, SIR WALTER,	1838	—1901	VIII	449
BIRCH, THOMAS,	1705	—1766	III	499
BLACK, JOSEPH,	1728	—1799	IV	344
BLACK, WILLIAM,	1841	—1898	VIII	393
*BLACKIE, JOHN STUART,	1809	—1895	VIII	304
BLACKLOCK, THOMAS,	1721	—1791	IV	129
BLACKMORE, RICHARD DODDRIDGE,	1825	—1900	VIII	430
BLACKMORE, SIR RICHARD,	1650?	–1729	II	746
BLACKSTONE, SIR WILLIAM,	1723	—1780	III	702
BLAIR, HUGH,	1718	—1800	IV	403
BLAIR, ROBERT,	1699	—1746	III	241
*BLAKE, WILLIAM,	1757	—1827	V	56
BLAMIRE, SUSANNA,	1747	—1794	IV	204
BLANCHARD, SAMUEL LAMAN,	1804	—1845	V	480
BLESSINGTON, MARGUERITE COUNTESS OF,	1789	—1849	V	589
BLIND HARRY,	fl. 1460	—1492	I	201
BLOOMFIELD, ROBERT,	1766	—1823	IV	723
BOECE, HECTOR,	1465?	–1536	I	242
BOKER, GEORGE HENRY,	1823	—1890	VII	764
BOLINGBROKE, VISCOUNT,	1678	—1751	III	282
BORROW, GEORGE HENRY,	1803	—1881	VII	306
BOSWELL, JAMES,	1740	—1795	IV	209
BOUCICAULT, DION,	1822	—1890	VII	762
BOURCHIER, JOHN,	1467	—1533	I	228
BOWLES, WILLIAM LISLE,	1762	—1850	V	658
BOWRING, SIR JOHN,	1792	—1872	VI	663
*BOYLE, ROBERT,	1627	—1691	II	416
BRADFORD, WILLIAM,	1590	—1657	II	157
BRADSTREET, ANNE,	1612	—1672	II	228
BRAINARD, JOHN GARDINER CALKINS,	1796	—1828	V	84
BRETON, NICHOLAS,	1545?	—1626?	I	678
BREWSTER, SIR DAVID,	1781	—1868	VI	546
*BRIGHT, JOHN,	1811	—1889	VII	720
BRONTË, ANNE,	1820	—1849	V	599
*BRONTË, CHARLOTTE,	1816	—1855	VI	17
BRONTË, EMILY,	1818	—1848	V	521
BROOKE, ARTHUR,		—1563	I	284
BROOKE, HENRY,	1703?	–1783	III	713

	Born.	Died.	Vol.	Page.
Brooke, Lord,	1554	—1628	I	689
*Brooks, Phillips,	1835	—1893	VIII	226
Broome, William,	1689	—1745	III	238
*Brougham, Henry Lord,	1779	—1868	VI	522
*Brown, Charles Brockden,	1771	—1810	IV	552
Brown, John,	1810	—1882	VII	477
Brown, Thomas,	1663	—1704	II	540
Brown, Thomas,	1778	—1820	IV	657
Browne, Charles Farrar,	1834	—1867	VI	501
Browne, Sir Thomas,	1605	—1682	II	339
Browne, William,	1591	—1643?	II	72
*Browning, Elizabeth Barrett,	1806?	—1861	VI	228
*Browning, Robert,	1812	—1889	VII	677
Brownson, Orestes Augustus,	1803	—1876	VII	72
Bruce, James,	1730	—1794	IV	205
Brunne, Robert de,	1260	—1340	I	87
*Bryant, William Cullen,	1794	—1878	VII	109
Brydges, Sir Samuel Egerton,	1762	—1837	V	320
Buchanan, George,	1506	—1582	I	313
*Buchanan, Robert,	1841	—1901	VIII	445
Buckingham, Duke of,	1628	—1687	II	375
Buckland, Francis Trevelyan,	1826	—1880	VII	210
Buckle, Henry Thomas,	1821	—1862	VI	278
Budgell, Eustace,	1686	—1737	III	91
Bull, George,	1634	—1710	II	564
Bunner, Henry Cuyler,	1855	—1896	VIII	359
Bunyan, John,	1628	—1688	II	388
*Burke, Edmund,	1729	—1797	IV	287
*Burnet, Gilbert,	1643	—1715	II	590
Burnet, Thomas,	1635?	—1715	II	596
Burnett, James,	1714	—1799	IV	346
Burney, Charles,	1726	—1814	IV	587
Burney, Frances,	1752	—1840	V	343
*Burns, Robert,	1759	—1796	IV	221
Burton, John Hill,	1809	—1881	VII	315
Burton, Sir Richard Francis,	1821	—1890	VII	757
Burton, Robert,	1577	—1640	II	37
Bushnell, Horace,	1802	—1876	VII	69
*Butler, Joseph,	1692	—1752	III	306
Butler, Samuel,	1612	—1680	II	329
*Byron, George Gordon Lord,	1788	—1824	IV	731
Byrom, John,	1692	—1763	III	468
Cædmon,		c. 680	I	21
Calhoun, John Caldwell,	1782	—1850	V	674
Calverley, Charles Stuart,	1831	—1884	VII	541
Cambrensis Giraldus,	c. 1147	—1220	I	67
Camden William,	1551	—1623	I	620

GENERAL INDEX TO AUTHORS 519

	Born.	Died.	Vol.	Page.
Campbell, George John Douglas,	1823	1900	VIII	433
Campbell, John Lord,	1779	1861	VI	257
*Campbell, Thomas,	1777	1844	V	433
Canning, George,	1770	1827	V	64
Capgrave, John,	1393	1464	I	192
Carew, Thomas,	1589?	1639?	II	20
Carey, Henry,		—1743	III	137
Carleton, William,	1794	1869	VI	547
*Carlyle, Thomas	1795	1881	VII	229
Carroll, Lewis,	1832	1898	VIII	396
Carte, Thomas,	1686	1754	III	337
Carter, Elizabeth,	1717	1806	IV	491
Cartwright, Thomas,	1535?	1603	I	416
Cartwright, William,	1611	1643	II	70
Cary, Alice,	1820	1871	VI	637
Cary, Henry Francis,	1772	1844	V	455
Cary, Phœbe,	1824	1871	VI	640
Cavendish, George,	1500	1561?	I	282
Cavendish, Margaret,	1624	1673	II	230
Caxton, William,	1422?	1492	I	197
Centlivre, Susannah,	1667?	1723	II	682
Challoner, Richard,	1691	1781	III	710
Chalmers, George,	1742	1825	V	29
*Chalmers, Thomas,	1780	1847	V	489
Chamberlayne, William,	1619	1689	II	406
Chambers, Robert,	1802	1871	VI	618
Channing, William Ellery,	1780	1842	V	365
Chapman, George,	1559?	1634	I	727
Chapone, Hester,	1727	1801	IV	417
Chatham, Earl of,	1708	1778	III	678
Chatterton, Thomas,	1752	1770	III	527
*Chaucer, Geoffrey,	1340?	1400	I	124
Cheke, Sir John,	1514	1557	I	277
Chesterfield, Lord,	1694	1773	III	598
Chettle, Henry,	1540?	1607?	I	429
Child, Lydia Maria,	1802	1880	VII	218
Chillingworth, William,	1602	1644	II	84
Choate, Rufus,	1799	1859	VI	195
Church, Richard William,	1815	1889	VII	728
*Churchill, Charles,	1731	1764	III	475
Churchyard, Thomas,	1520?	1604	I	417
Cibber, Colley,	1671	1757	III	369
Cibber, Theophilus,	1703	1758	III	395
Clare, John,	1793	1864	VI	396
Clarendon, Earl of,	1609	1674	II	299
Clarke, Adam,	1762?	1832	V	184
Clarke, James Freeman,	1810	1888	VII	672

	Born.	Died.	Vol.	Page.
CLARKE, SAMUEL,	1671	1729	II	747
CLAY, HENRY,	1777	1852	V	730
*CLEVELAND, JOHN,	1613	1658	II	158
CLIVE, CAROLINE,	1801	1873	VI	739
CLOUGH, ARTHUR HUGH,	1819	1861	VI	248
COBBETT, WILLIAM,	1762	1835	V	269
*COBDEN, RICHARD,	1804	1865	VI	439
COCKBURN, CATHERINE,	1679	1749	III	275
COKE, SIR EDWARD,	1552	1634	I	739
COLENSO, JOHN WILLIAM,	1814	1883	VII	522
COLERIDGE, HARTLEY,	1796	1849	V	572
*COLERIDGE, SAMUEL TAYLOR,	1772	1834	V	205
COLERIDGE, SARA,	1802	1852	V	733
COLET, JOHN,	1466	1519	I	210
COLLIER, JEREMY,	1650	1726	II	698
COLLINS, MORTIMER,	1827	1876	VII	81
COLLINS, WILLIAM,	1721	1759	III	414
COLLINS, WILLIAM WILKIE,	1824	1889	VII	725
COLMAN, GEORGE (THE ELDER)	1732	1794	IV	200
COLMAN, GEORGE (THE YOUNGER),	1762	1836	V	315
COMBE, GEORGE,	1788	1858	VI	88
*CONGREVE, WILLIAM,	1670	1729	II	733
CONSTABLE, HENRY,	1562	1613	I	444
CONYBEARE, JOHN,	1692	1755	III	365
COOPER, ANTHONY ASHLEY,	1671	1713	II	576
*COOPER, JAMES FENIMORE,	1789	1851	V	679
CORBET, RICHARD,	1582	1635	I	743
CORNWALL, BARRY,	1787	1874	VI	744
COTTON, CHARLES,	1630	1687	II	370
COTTON, SIR ROBERT,	1570	1631	I	709
COVERDALE, MILES,	1488	1568	I	291
COWLEY, ABRAHAM,	1618	1667	II	193
*COWPER, WILLIAM,	1731	1800	IV	370
CRABBE, GEORGE,	1754	1832	V	170
CRAIK, DINAH MARIA MULOCK,	1826	1887	VII	623
*CRANMER, THOMAS,	1489	1555	I	270
CRASHAW, RICHARD,	1613?	1649	II	110
CREIGHTON, MANDELL,	1843	1901	VIII	453
CROKER, JOHN WILSON,	1780	1857	VI	71
CROLY, GEORGE,	1780	1860	VI	224
CROSS, MARY ANN,	1819	1880	VII	170
CRUDEN, ALEXANDER,	1701	1770	III	545
CUDWORTH, RALPH,	1617	1688	II	384
CUMBERLAND, RICHARD,	1631	1718	II	623
*CUMBERLAND, RICHARD,	1732	1811	IV	558
CUNNINGHAM, ALLAN,	1784	1842	V	382
*CURTIS, GEORGE WILLIAM,	1824	1892	VIII	184

GENERAL INDEX TO AUTHORS 521

	Born. Died.	Vol.	Page.
Cynewulf,	c. 8th Century?	I	30
Dalrymple, Sir David,	1726—1792	IV	145
Dana, Richard Henry,	1787—1879	VII	152
Dana, Richard Henry, Jr.,	1815—1882	VII	499
Daniel, Samuel,	1562—1619	I	611
D'Arblay, Madame,	1752—1840	V	343
Darwin, Charles Robert,	1809—1882	VII	415
*Darwin, Erasmus,	1731—1802	IV	420
D'Avenant, Sir William,	1606—1668	II	216
Davidson, Lucretia Maria,	1808—1825	V	26
Davies, Sir John,	1569—1626	I	632
Davy, Sir Humphry,	1778—1829	V	90
Day, Thomas,	1748—1789	IV	49
De Bury, Richard,	1287—1345	I	88
*Defoe, Daniel,	1661?-1731	III	23
Dekker, Thomas,	1570?-1641?	II	55
De Morgan, Augustus,	1806—1871	VI	632
Denham, Sir John,	1615—1668	II	220
Dennis, John,	1657—1734	III	75
De Quincey, Thomas,	1785—1859	VI	115
*De Vere, Aubrey Thomas,	1814—1902	VIII	462
Dewey, Orville,	1794—1882	VII	495
Dibdin, Charles,	1745—1814	IV	585
Dibdin, Thomas Frognall,	1776—1847	V	506
*Dickens, Charles,	1812—1870	VI	550
Digby, Sir Kenelm,	1603—1665	II	181
Dillon, Wentworth,	1633?-1684	II	360
*Disraeli, Benjamin,	1804—1881	VII	276
*Disraeli, Isaac,	1766—1848	V	510
Dobell, Sydney Thompson,	1824—1874	VI	758
Dodd, William,	1729—1777	III	675
Doddridge, Philip,	1702—1751	III	299
Dodge, Mary Abigal,	1838—1896	VIII	360
Dodgson, Charles Lutwige,	1832—1898	VIII	396
Dodington, George Bubb,	1691—1762	III	458
Dodsley, Robert,	1703—1764	III	482
Dodwell, Henry,	1641—1711	II	565
*Donne, John,	1573—1631	I	710
Dorset, Earl of,	1536—1608	I	431
Dorset, Earl of,	1638—1706	II	552
Douglas, Gawin,	1474?-1522	I	212
Doyle, Sir Francis Hastings Charles,	1810—1888	VII	649
Drake, Joseph Rodman,	1795—1820	IV	659
Draper, John William,	1811—1882	VII	502
Drayton, Michael,	1563—1631	I	701
Drummond, Henry,	1851—1897	VIII	362
Drummond, William,	1585—1649	II	100

GENERAL INDEX TO AUTHORS

	Born.	Died.	Vol.	Page.
*Dryden, John,	1631	—1700	II	462
*Du Maurier, George,	1834	—1896	VIII	343
Dunbar, William,	1465	—1530	I	224
Duns Scotus,	1265?	–1308?	I	85
Dunstan,	925—	988	I	43
D'Urfey, Thomas,	1653	—1723	II	686
Dwight, Timothy,	1752	—1817	IV	625
Dyer, Sir Edward,	1540?	-1607	I	427
Dyer, John,	1700?	-1758	III	398
Eadmer,	1060?	-1124?	I	52
Earle, John,	1601?	-1665	II	183
Echard, Laurence,	1670?	-1730	III	22
*Edgeworth, Maria,	1767	—1849	V	561
Edwards, Amelia Blandford,	1831	—1892	VIII	174
*Edwards, Jonathan,	1703	—1757	III	380
Edwards, Richard,	1523?	-1566	I	287
Eggleston, Edward,	1837	—1902	VIII	475
*Eliot, George,	1819	—1880	VII	170
Eliot, John,	1604	—1690	II	412
Elliott, Ebenezer,	1781	—1849	V	579
Ellwood, Thomas,	1639	—1713	II	575
Elyot, Sir Thomas,	1490?	-1546	I	253
*Emerson, Ralph Waldo,	1803	—1882	VII	342
Erceldoune, Thomas of,	c. 1225	—c. 1300	I	83
Erigena, John Scotus,	fl.	850	I	34
Erskine, Thomas,	1750	—1823	IV	728
Etheredge, Sir George,	1635?	—1691?	II	413
Evans, Marian,	1819	—1880	VII	170
*Evelyn, John,	1620	—1706	II	546
*Everett, Edward,	1794	—1865	VI	421
Faber, Frederick William,	1814	—1863	VI	332
Fabyan, Robert,	c. 1456	—1512	I	206
Fairfax, Edward,	c. 1580	—1635	I	742
Falconer, William,	1732	—1769	III	524
Fanshawe, Sir Richard,	1608	—1666	II	184
*Faraday, Michael,	1791	—1867	VI	511
Farmer, Richard,	1735	—1797	IV	340
Farquhar, George,	1678	—1707	II	554
Fawcett, Henry,	1833	—1884	VII	548
Feltham, Owen,	1602?	-1677?	II	309
Fenton, Elijah,	1683	—1730	III	20
Ferguson, Adam,	1723	—1816	IV	609
*Ferguson, James,	1710	—1776	III	668
Fergusson, Robert,	1750	—1774	III	639
Ferrier, James Frederick,	1808	—1864	VI	410
Ferrier, Susan Edmonstone,	1782	—1854	V	763
Field, Eugene,	1850	—1895	VIII	314

GENERAL INDEX TO AUTHORS 523

	Born.	Died.	Vol.	Page.
FIELDING, HENRY,	1707	—1754	III	338
FIELDING, SARAH,	1710	—1768	III	518
FIELDS, JAMES THOMAS,	1816	—1881	VII	339
FINCH, ANNE,		1720	II	668
FINLAY, GEORGE,	1799	—1875	VII	48
FISHER, JOHN,	1459?	—1535	I	230
FISKE, JOHN,	1842	—1901	VIII	455
*FITZGERALD, EDWARD,	1809	—1883	VII	514
FLAMSTEED, JOHN,	1646	—1719	II	662
FLETCHER, ANDREW,	1655	—1716	II	610
FLETCHER, GILES,	1588?	—1623	I	623
*FLETCHER, JOHN,	1579	—1625	I	628
FLETCHER, PHINEAS,	1582	—1650	II	115
FOOTE, SAMUEL,	1720	—1777	III	671
FORD, JOHN,		fl. 1639	II	25
FORSTER, JOHN,	1812	—1876	VII	64
FORTESCUE, SIR JOHN,	1394?	—1476?	I	194
FOSTER, JOHN,	1770	—1843	V	424
*FOX, CHARLES JAMES,	1749	—1806	IV	498
FOX, GEORGE,	1624	—1691	II	420
*FOXE, JOHN,	1516	—1587	I	334
FRANCIS, SIR PHILIP,	1740	—1818	IV	637
*FRANKLIN, BENJAMIN,	1706	—1790	IV	79
*FREEMAN, EDWARD AUGUSTUS,	1823	—1892	VIII	153
FRENEAU, PHILIP,	1752	—1832	V	186
FRERE, JOHN HOOKHAM,	1769	—1846	V	485
*FROUDE, JAMES ANTHONY,	1818	—1894	VIII	254
*FULLER, SARAH MARGARET,	1810	—1850	V	663
FULLER, THOMAS,	1608	—1661	II	168
FULLERTON, GEORGIANA CHARLOTTE LADY,	1812	—1885	VII	566
GALT, JOHN,	1779	—1839	V	334
GARDINER, SAMUEL RAWSON,	1829	—1902	VIII	465
*GARRICK, DAVID,	1717	—1779	III	693
*GARRISON, WILLIAM LLOYD,	1805	—1879	VII	157
*GARTH, SIR SAMUEL,	1661	—1719	II	664
GASCOIGNE, GEORGE,	1530	—1577	I	307
GASKELL, ELIZABETH CLEGHORN,	1810	—1865	VI	427
GAUDEN, JOHN,	1605	—1662	II	176
*GAY, JOHN,	1685	—1732	III	52
GEOFFREY OF MONMOUTH,	c. 1100	—1154	I	55
*GEORGE, HENRY,	1839	—1897	VIII	378
*GIBBON, EDWARD,	1737	—1794	IV	172
GIFFORD, WILLIAM,	1756	—1826	V	31
GILFILLAN, GEORGE,	1813	—1878	VII	150
GIRALDUS CAMBRENSIS,	c. 1147	—1220	I	67
*GLADSTONE, WILLIAM EWART,	1809	—1898	VIII	383
GLOUCESTER, ROBERT OF,	fl. 1260	—1300	I	81

GENERAL INDEX TO AUTHORS

	Born.	Died.	Vol.	Page.
Glover, Richard,	1712	1785	IV	17
*Godwin, Mary Wollstonecraft,	1759	1797	IV	326
*Godwin, William,	1756	1836	V	292
*Goldsmith, Oliver,	1728	1774	III	613
Gore, Catherine Grace,	1799	1861	VI	262
Gower, John,	1325?	1408	I	172
Graham, James,	1612	1650	II	121
Grahame, James,	1765	1811	IV	566
Grainger, James,	1721?	1766	III	498
Granger, James,	1723	1776	III	670
Grant, Anne,	1755	1838	V	328
Granville, George,	1667	1735	III	87
Gray, Asa,	1810	1888	VII	669
Gray, David,	1838	1861	VI	260
*Gray, Thomas,	1716	1771	III	553
*Greeley, Horace,	1811	1872	VI	666
*Green, John Richard,	1837	1883	VII	504
Green, Matthew,	1696	1737	III	94
Greene, Robert,	1560	1592	I	339
Greg, William Rathbone,	1809	1881	VII	320
Greville, Sir Fulke,	1554	1628	I	689
Griffin, Gerald,	1803	1840	V	351
Grimoald, Nicholas,	1519	1562	I	283
Griswold, Rufus Wilmot,	1815	1857	VI	76
Grosseteste, Robert,	c. 1175	1253	I	72
*Grote, George,	1794	1871	VI	606
Guildford, Nicholas of,	fl. 1250		I	76
Guthrie, Thomas,	1803	1873	VI	735
Habington, William,	1605	1654	II	134
Hailes, Lord	1726	1792	IV	145
Hakluyt, Richard,	1552?	1616	I	445
Hale, Sir Matthew,	1609	1676	II	305
Hales, Alexander,	?	1245	I	71
Hales, John,	1584	1656	II	149
Haliburton, William Chandler,	1796	1865	VI	455
Halifax, Earl of,	1661	1715	II	586
Halifax, Marquis of,	1633	1695	II	448
Hall, Basil,	1788	1844	V	456
Hall, Edward,	1499?	1547	I	259
Hall, Joseph,	1574	1656	II	143
*Hall, Robert,	1764	1831	V	108
Hallam, Arthur Henry,	1811	1833	V	197
*Hallam, Henry,	1777	1859	VI	173
Halleck, Fitz-Greene,	1790	1867	VI	493
Halley, Edmund	1656	1742	III	107
*Hamerton, Philip Gilbert,	1834	1894	VIII	280
*Hamilton, Alexander,	1757	1804	IV	456

GENERAL INDEX TO AUTHORS 525

	Born. Died.	Vol.	Page.
HAMILTON, GAIL,	1838—1896	VIII	360
HAMILTON, THOMAS,	1789—1842	V	394
HAMILTON, WILLIAM,	1704—1754	III	335
HAMILTON, SIR WILLIAM,	1788—1856	VI	50
HAMPOLE, RICHARD ROLLE OF,	c. 1290—1349	I	91
HARDING, JOHN,	c. 1378—1465?	I	193
HARE, JULIUS CHARLES,	1795—1855	VI	49
HARRINGTON, JAMES,	1611—1677	II	307
HARRINGTON, SIR JOHN,	1561—1612	I	440
HARRIS, JAMES,	1709—1780	III	709
*HARTE, FRANCIS BRET,	1837—1902	VIII	466
*HARTLEY, DAVID,	1705—1757	III	376
HARVEY, GABRIEL,	1545?-1630	I	695
HARVEY, WILLIAM,	1578—1657	II	155
HAVERGAL, FRANCES RIDLEY,	1836—1879	VII	166
HAWES, STEPHEN,	1476?-1523?	I	216
HAWKESWORTH, JOHN,	1715?-1773	III	608
HAWKINS, SIR JOHN,	1719—1789	IV	50
*HAWTHORNE, NATHANIEL,	1804—1864	VI	341
HAYLEY, WILLIAM,	1745—1820	IV	651
*HAYNE, PAUL HAMILTON,	1831—1886	VII	590
HAZLITT, WILLIAM,	1778—1830	V	97
HEARNE, THOMAS,	1678—1735	III	88
HEBER, REGINALD,	1783—1826	V	36
HELPS, SIR ARTHUR,	1813—1875	VII	38
*HEMANS, FELICIA DOROTHEA,	1793—1835	V	254
HENLEY, WILLIAM ERNEST,	1849—1903	VIII	491
HENRY OF HUNTINGDON,	c. 1084—1155	I	58
HENRY THE MINSTREL,	fl. 1460—1492	I	201
HENRY, MATTHEW,	1662—1714	II	584
HENRY, PATRICK,	1736—1799	IV	349
HENRY, ROBERT,	1718—1790	IV	106
HENRYSON, ROBERT,	1430?-1506?	I	207
HERBERT, EDWARD LORD,	1583—1648	II	95
HERBERT, GEORGE,	1593—1633	I	720
HERSCHEL, SIR JOHN FREDERICK WILLIAM,	1792—1871	VI	623
HERRICK, ROBERT,	1591—1674	II	233
HERVEY, JAMES,	1714—1758	III	396
HERVEY, JOHN LORD,	1696—1743	III	127
HEYLIN, PETER,	1600—1662	II	174
HEYWOOD, JOHN,	1497?-1575?	I	304
HEYWOOD, THOMAS,	1575?-1650?	II	122
HICKS, GEORGE,	1642—1715	II	598
HILDRETH, RICHARD,	1807—1865	VI	453
HILL, AARON,	1685—1750	III	276
HILL, JOHN,	1716?-1775	III	644
HILLHOUSE, JAMES ABRAHAM,	1789—1841	V	363

	Born.	Died.	Vol.	Page.
HOADLY, BENJAMIN,	1676	1761	III	422
*HOBBES, THOMAS,	1588	1679	II	320
HOGG, JAMES,	1770	1835	V	262
HOLCROFT, THOMAS,	1745	1809	IV	544
HOLINSHED, RAPHAEL,		1580	I	311
*HOLLAND, JOSIAH GILBERT,	1819	1881	VII	333
*HOLMES, OLIVER WENDELL,	1809	1894	VIII	285
HOME, HENRY,	1696	1782	III	711
HOME, JOHN,	1722	1808	IV	512
HONE, WILLIAM,	1780	1842	V	391
*HOOD, THOMAS,	1799	1845	V	458
HOOK, THEODORE EDWARD,	1788	1841	V	355
HOOKER, RICHARD,	1553	1600	I	402
HOPKINS, MARK,	1802	1887	VII	613
HOPKINS, SAMUEL,	1721	1803	IV	437
HOPKINSON, FRANCIS,	1737	1791	IV	131
HORNE, GEORGE,	1730	1792	IV	143
HORNE, JOHN,	1736	1812	IV	569
HORNE, RICHARD HENGIST,	1803	1884	VII	544
HORNER, FRANCIS,	1778	1817	IV	628
HORSLEY, SAMUEL,	1733	1806	IV	494
HOUGHTON, LORD,	1809	1885	VII	559
HOVEDEN, ROGER DE,	fl. c. 1200		I	63
HOWARD, HENRY,	1516?	1547	I	255
HOWE, JOHN,	1630	1705	II	544
HOWELL, JAMES,	1594?	1666	II	186
HUGHES, JOHN,	1677	1720	II	667
HUGHES, THOMAS,	1823	1896	VIII	346
*HUME, DAVID,	1711	1776	III	646
*HUNT, JAMES HENRY LEIGH,	1784	1859	VI	153
HUNTER, JOHN,	1728	1793	IV	164
HUNTINGDON, HENRY ON,	c. 1084	1155	I	58
HURD, RICHARD,	1720	1808	IV	516
HUTCHESON, FRANCIS,	1694	1746	III	244
HUTCHINSON, THOMAS,	1711	1780	III	706
HUTTON, JAMES,	1726	1797	IV	337
HUTTON, RICHARD HOLT,	1826	1897	VIII	374
*HUXLEY, THOMAS HENRY,	1825	1896	VIII	320
*HYDE, EDWARD,	1609	1674	II	299
INCHBALD, MRS. ELIZABETH,	1753	1821	IV	686
INGELOW, JEAN,	1820	1897	VIII	376
INGERSOLL, ROBERT GREEN,	1833	1899	VIII	401
IRELAND, WILLIAM HENRY,	1777	1835	V	289
IRVING, EDWARD,	1792	1834	V	245
*IRVING, WASHINGTON,	1783	1859	VI	132
JACKSON, HELEN HUNT,	1831	1885	VII	571
JAMES I., OF SCOTLAND,	1394	1437	I	179

	Born.	Died.	Vol.	Page.
James, George Payne Rainsford,	1801	1860	VI	216
*Jameson, Anna,	1794	1860	VI	212
Jay, John,	1745	1829	V	94
Jefferies, Richard,	1848	1887	VII	618
*Jefferson, Thomas,	1743	1826	V	40
*Jeffrey, Francis Lord,	1773	1850	V	647
Jenyns, Soame,	1704	1787	IV	30
Jerrold, Douglas William,	1803	1857	VI	66
Jevons, William Stanley,	1835	1882	VII	491
Jewell, John,	1522	1571	I	293
John of Salisbury,	1120?	1182?	I	59
*Johnson, Samuel,	1709	1784	III	720
Johnston, Arthur,	1587	1641	II	54
Johnstone, Charles,	1719?	1800?	IV	413
Jones, Sir William,	1746	1794	IV	197
*Jonson, Ben,	1573?	1637	I	745
Jortin, John,	1698	1770	III	551
*Jowett, Benjamin,	1817	1893	VIII	207
Junius,			IV	638
Kames, Henry Home Lord,	1696	1782	III	711
Kane, Elisha Kent,	1820	1857	VI	80
*Keats, John,	1795	1821	IV	662
*Keble, John,	1792	1866	VI	457
Kelly, Hugh,	1739	1777	III	677
Kemble, Frances Ann,	1809	1893	VIII	213
Ken, Thomas,	1637	1711	II	566
Kennedy, John Pendleton,	1795	1870	VI	604
Kenrick, William,	1725?	1779	III	701
Kent, James,	1763	1847	V	500
King, Henry,	1592	1669	II	222
King, Thomas Starr,	1824	1864	VI	408
*Kinglake, Alexander William,	1809	1891	VIII	49
*Kingsley, Charles,	1819	1875	VII	17
Kingsley, Henry,	1830	1876	VII	79
Knight, Charles,	1791	1873	VI	741
Knowles, James Sheridan,	1784	1862	VI	285
*Knox, John,	1505	1572	I	295
Knox, William,	1789	1825	V	30
Kyd, Thomas,	1557?	1595?	I	358
Lamb, Lady Caroline,	1785	1828	V	81
*Lamb, Charles,	1775	1834	V	228
Lamb, Mary Ann,	1764	1847	V	507
*Landon, Letitia Elizabeth,	1802	1838	V	322
*Landor, Walter Savage,	1775	1864	VI	371
Lane, Edward William,	1801	1876	VII	83
Lanfranc,	1005?	1089	I	47
Langhorne, John,	1735	1779	III	700

	Born. Died.	Vol.	Page.
LANGLAND, WILLIAM,	c. 1322—1400?	I	116
LANIER, SIDNEY,	1842—1881	VII	325
LANSDOWNE, LORD,	1667—1735	III	87
LARDNER, NATHANIEL,	1684—1768	III	522
LATIMER, HUGH,	1485?-1555	I	267
LAUD, WILLIAM,	1573—1645	II	88
LAW, WILLIAM,	1686—1761	III	425
LAWRENCE, GEORGE ALFRED,	1827—1876	VII	84
LAYAMON,	fl. c. 1200	I	64
LAZARUS, EMMA,	1849—1887	VII	610
LECKY, WILLIAM EDWARD HARTPOLE,	1838—1903	VIII	487
LEE, NATHANIEL,	1653—1692	II	430
LEIGHTON, ROBERT,	1611—1684	II	358
LELAND, JOHN,	1506?-1552	I	262
LELAND, JOHN,	1691—1766	III	500
LENNOX, CHARLOTTE,	1720—1804	IV	469
LESLIE, CHARLES,	1650—1722	II	679
LESLIE, SIR JOHN,	1766—1832	V	189
L'ESTRANGE, SIR ROGER,	1616—1704	II	537
*LEVER, CHARLES JAMES,	1806—1872	VI	650
LEWES, GEORGE HENRY,	1817—1878	VII	137
LEWES, MRS. GEORGE HENRY,	1819—1880	VII	170
LEWIS, SIR GEORGE CORNEWALL,	1806—1863	VI	335
*LEWIS, MATTHEW GREGORY,	1775—1818	IV	631
LIDDON, HENRY PARRY,	1829—1890	VII	761
LILLO, GEORGE,	1693—1739	III	99
LINCOLN, ABRAHAM,	1809—1865	VI	411
LITTLETON, SIR THOMAS,	1402—1481	I	196
LIVINGSTON, WILLIAM,	1723—1790	IV	108
LIVINGSTONE, DAVID,	1813—1873	VI	726
*LOCKE, JOHN,	1632—1704	II	518
LOCKER-LAMPSON, FREDERICK,	1821—1895	VIII	311
LOCKHART, JOHN GIBSON,	1794—1854	V	753
LODGE, THOMAS,	1558?-1625	I	624
LOGAN, JOHN,	1748—1788	IV	43
*LONGFELLOW, HENRY WADSWORTH,	1807—1882	VII	381
LOVELACE, RICHARD,	1618—1658	II	160
LOVER, SAMUEL,	1797—1868	VI	542
*LOWELL, JAMES RUSSELL,	1819—1891	VIII	17
LOWTH, ROBERT,	1710—1787	IV	28
LOWTH, WILLIAM,	1660—1732	III	62
LYDGATE, JOHN,	1370?-1451?	I	183
*LYELL, SIR CHARLES,	1797—1875	VII	33
LYLY, JOHN,	1554?-1606	I	420
LYNDSAY, SIR DAVID,	1490?-1555	I	273
LYTE, HENRY FRANCIS,	1793—1847	V	499
LYTTLETON, GEORGE LORD,	1709—1773	III	610

	BORN.	DIED.	VOL.	PAGE.
*LYTTON, SIR EDWARD GEORGE BULWER,	1803	—1873	VI	678
*LYTTON, EDWARD ROBERT BULWER,	1831	—1891	VIII	43
MACAULAY, CATHERINE (NEE GRAHAM),	1731	—1791	IV	133
*MACAULAY, THOMAS BABINGTON LORD,	1800	—1859	VI	90
MACKAY, CHARLES,	1814	—1889	VII	764
MACKENZIE, SIR GEORGE,	1636	—1691	II	428
MACKENZIE, HENRY,	1745	—1831	V	112
MACKINTOSH, SIR JAMES,	1765	—1832	V	177
MACKLIN, CHARLES,	1699?	—1797	IV	342
MACKNIGHT, JAMES,	1721	—1800	IV	407
MACLEAN, MRS. GEORGE,	1802	—1838	V	322
MACLEOD, NORMAN,	1812	—1872	VI	660
MACPHERSON, JAMES,	1736	—1796	IV	270
MADISON, JAMES,	1751	—1836	V	311
MAGINN, WILLIAM,	1793	—1842	V	385
MAHON, LORD,	1805	—1875	VII	46
MAHONY, FRANCIS,	1805	—1866	VI	483
*MAINE, SIR HENRY JAMES SUMNER,	1822	—1888	VII	651
MAITLAND, SIR RICHARD,	1496	—1586	I	333
MALLET, DAVID,	1705?	—1765	III	494
MALMESBURY, WILLIAM OF,	c. 1095	—1143	I	53
*MALONE, EDMOND,	1741	—1812	IV	577
MALORY, SIR THOMAS,	1430?	—1496 ?	I	203
MALTHUS, THOMAS ROBERT,	1765	—1834	V	249
MANDEVILLE, BERNARD,	1670?	—1733	III	68
MANDEVILLE, SIR JOHN,	1300?	—1372?	I	94
MANGAN, JAMES CLARENCE,	1803	—1849	V	600
MANLEY, MARY DE LA RIVIERE,	1672?	—1724	II	693
MANN, HORACE,	1796	—1859	VI	199
*MANNING, HENRY EDWARD,	1807	—1892	VIII	162
MANNYNG, ROBERT,	1260	—1340	I	87
MANSEL, HENRY LONGUEVILLE,	1820	—1871	VI	626
MANSFIELD, LORD,	1705	—1793	IV	169
MAP, WALTER,	c. 1140	—1210?	I	61
MARLOWE, CHRISTOPHER,	1564	—1593	I	346
*MARRYAT, FREDERICK,	1792	—1848	V	530
*MARSH, GEORGE PERKINS,	1801	—1882	VII	492
MARSHALL, JOHN,	1755	—1835	V	281
MARSTON, JOHN,	1575?	—1634	I	735
MARSTON, PHILIP BOURKE,	1852	—1887	VII	626
*MARTINEAU, HARRIET,	1802	—1876	VII	54
*MARTINEAU, JAMES,	1805	—1900	VIII	425
*MARVELL, ANDREW,	1621	—1678	II	313
*MASON, WILLIAM,	1724	—1797	IV	323
MASSINGER, PHILIP,	1583	—1640	II	41
MATHER, COTTON,	1663	—1728	II	727
MATHER, INCREASE,	1639	—1723	II	689

	Born.	Died.	Vol.	Page.
MATHIAS, THOMAS JAMES,	1754?-	1835	V	287
MATURIN, CHARLES ROBERT,	1782—	1824	IV	766
*MAURICE, JOHN FREDERICK DENISON,	1805—	1872	VI	643
MAXWELL, JAMES CLERK,	1831—	1879	VII	168
MAY, THOMAS,	1595—	1650	II	118
MCCARTHY, DENNIS FLORENCE,	1820—	1882	VII	489
MCCOSH, JAMES,	1811—	1894	VIII	300
MELCOMBE, LORD,	1691—	1762	III	458
MELVILLE, HERMAN,	1819—	1891	VIII	62
*MEREDITH, OWEN,	1831—	1891	VIII	43
MERIVALE, CHARLES,	1808—	1893	VIII	217
MICKLE, WILLIAM JULIUS,	1735—	1788	IV	40
MIDDLETON, CONYERS,	1683—	1750	III	279
MIDDLETON, THOMAS,	1570?-	1627	I	680
MILL, JAMES,	1773—	1836	V	304
MILL, JOHN STUART,	1806—	1873	VI	701
MILLER, CINCINNATUS HINER,	1841—	1903	VIII	498
MILLER, HUGH,	1802—	1856	VI	62
MILLER, JOAQUIN,	1841—	1903	VIII	498
*MILMAN, HENRY HART,	1791—	1868	VI	533
*MILNES, RICHARD MONCKTON,	1809—	1885	VII	559
*MILTON, JOHN,	1608—	1674	II	242
MINOT, LAWRENCE,	1300?-	1352?	I	93
*MITFORD, MARY RUSSELL,	1787—	1855	VI	40
MITFORD, WILLIAM,	1744—	1827	V	69
MOIR, DAVID MACBETH,	1798—	1851	V	704
MONBODDO, LORD,	1714—	1799	IV	346
MONMOUTH, GEOFFREY OF,	c. 1100—	1154	I	55
MONROE, JAMES,	1758—	1831	V	122
MONTAGU, CHARLES,	1661—	1715	II	586
MONTAGU, ELIZABETH,	1720—	1800	IV	398
*MONTAGU, LADY MARY WORTLEY,	1689—	1762	III	459
MONTGOMERY, JAMES,	1771—	1854	V	765
MONTGOMERY, ROBERT,	1807—	1855	VI	46
MONTROSE, MARQUIS OF,	1612—	1650	II	121
MOORE, EDWARD,	1712—	1757	III	375
MOORE, JOHN,	1729—	1802	IV	426
*MOORE, THOMAS,	1779—	1852	V	705
*MORE, HANNAH,	1745—	1833	V	190
*MORE, HENRY,	1614—	1687	II	372
*MORE, SIR THOMAS,	1478—	1535	I	232
*MORGAN, SYDNEY OWENSON LADY,	1783?-	1859	VI	192
MORRIS, GEORGE POPE,	1802—	1864	VI	400
*MORRIS, WILLIAM,	1834—	1896	VIII	329
MOTHERWELL, WILLIAM,	1797—	1835	V	276
*MOTLEY, JOHN LOTHROP,	1814—	1877	VII	85
MOZLEY, JAMES BOWLING,	1813—	1878	VII	147

GENERAL INDEX TO AUTHORS

	Born. Died.	Vol.	Page
Mulgrave Earl of,	1648—1721	II	670
*Müller, Friedrich Max,	1823—1900	VIII	435
Munday, Anthony,	1553—1633	I	726
Murchison, Sir Roderick Impey,	1792—1871	VI	629
Murphy, Arthur,	1730—1805	IV	481
Murray, Lindley,	1745—1826	V	54
Murray, William,	1705—1793	IV	169
Nabbes, Thomas,	1600?-1645?	II	94
Nairne, Baroness,	1766—1845	V	476
Napier, Sir John,	1550—1617	I	588
Napier, Gen. Sir William Francis Patrick,	1785—1860	VI	220
Nashe, Thomas,	1567—1600?	I	411
Neal, Daniel,	1678—1743	III	140
Neal, John,	1793—1876	VII	76
Newcastle, Duchess of,	1624—1673	II	230
Newman, Francis William,	1805—1897	VIII	370
*Newman, John Henry,	1801—1890	VII	738
*Newton, Sir Isaac,	1642—1727	II	711
Nicholas of Guilford,	fl. 1250	I	76
Norris, John,	1657—1711	II	570
North, Christopher,	1785—1854	V	744
North, Roger,	1653—1734	III	79
*Norton, Caroline Elizabeth Sheridan,	1808—1877	VII	101
Norton, Thomas,	1532—1584	I	318
Occam, William of,	1270—1347	I	90
Occleve, Thomas,	c. 1370—1454	I	187
Ockley, Simon,	1678—1720	II	669
O'Keeffe, John,	1747—1833	V	196
Oldham, John,	1653—1683	II	349
Oldmixon, John,	1673—1742	III	124
Oldys, William,	1696—1761	III	456
Oliphant, Carolina,	1766—1845	V	476
Oliphant, Laurence,	1829—1888	VII	654
Oliphant, Margaret O. W.,	1828—1897	VIII	366
Opie, Amelia,	1769—1853	V	741
O'Reilly, John Boyle,	1844—1890	VII	767
Orford, Earl of,	1717—1797	IV	309
Orme, Robert,	1728—1801	IV	414
Ormin,	fl. c. 1200—1240	I	70
Osgood, Frances Sargent,	1812—1850	V	677
O'Shaughnessy, Arthur William Edgar	1844—1881	VII	322
Ossoli, Marchioness,	1810—1850	V	663
Otis, James,	1725—1783	III	716
Otway, Thomas,	1652—1685	II	361
Overbury, Sir Thomas,	1581—1613	I	441
Owen, John,	1616—1683	II	351

	Born.	Died.	Vol.	Page.
OWEN, SIR RICHARD,	1804	1892	VIII	170
OWEN, ROBERT,	1771	1858	VI	83
PAINE, THOMAS,	1737	1809	IV	529
*PALEY, WILLIAM,	1743	1805	IV	470
PALFREY, JOHN GORHAM,	1796	1881	VII	337
PALGRAVE, SIR FRANCIS,	1788	1861	VI	265
PALGRAVE, FRANCIS TURNER,	1824	1897	VIII	371
PARIS, MATTHEW,	?	1259?	I	74
PARK, MUNGO,	1771	1806?	IV	483
PARKMAN, FRANCIS,	1823	1893	VIII	218
*PARKER, THEODORE,	1810	1860	VI	205
PARKER, MATTHEW,	1504	1575	I	303
PARNELL, THOMAS,	1679	1718	II	614
*PARR, SAMUEL,	1747	1825	V	17
PARSONS, THOMAS WILLIAM,	1819	1892	VIII	192
PATER, WALTER HORATIO,	1838	1894	VIII	275
PATMORE, COVENTRY K. D.,	1823	1896	VIII	339
PATTISON, MARK,	1813	1884	VII	538
PAULDING, JAMES KIRKE,	1779	1860	VI	226
PAYNE, JOHN HOWARD,	1792	1852	V	735
PEACOCK, THOMAS LOVE,	1785	1866	VI	472
PEARSON, JOHN,	1613	1686	II	368
PECOCK, REGINALD,	1395?	1460?	I	188
PEELE, GEORGE,	1558?	1597?	I	363
PENN, WILLIAM,	1644	1718	II	625
PEPYS, SAMUEL,	1633	1703	II	512
PERCIVAL, JAMES GATES,	1795	1856	VI	58
PERCY, THOMAS,	1729	1811	IV	562
PHILIPS, AMBROSE,	1675?	1749	III	272
PHILIPS, JOHN,	1676	1708	II	562
*PHILIPS, KATHERINE,	1631	1664	II	179
*PHILLIPS, WENDELL,	1811	1884	VII	552
PIERPONT, JOHN,	1785	1866	VI	480
PINDAR, PETER,	1738	1819	IV	647
PINKNEY, EDWARD COATE,	1802	1828	V	85
PIOZZI, HESTER LYNCH,	1740	1821	IV	684
PITT, CHRISTOPHER,	1699	1748	III	254
PITT, WILLIAM,	1708	1778	III	678
*PITT, WILLIAM,	1759	1806	IV	507
PLANCHÉ, JAMES ROBINSON,	1796	1880	VII	216
*POE, EDGAR ALLAN,	1809	1849	V	534
*POLE, REGINALD,	1500	1558	I	279
POLLOK, ROBERT,	1798	1827	V	72
POMFRET, JOHN,	1667	1702	II	510
POOR, RICHARD,	?	1237	I	69
*POPE, ALEXANDER,	1688	1744	III	144
*PORSON, RICHARD,	1759	1808	IV	520

GENERAL INDEX TO AUTHORS 533

	Born.	Died.	Vol.	Page.
Porter, Jane,	1776	1850	V	673
Praed, Winthrop Mackworth,	1802	1839	V	330
Prentice, George Denison,	1802	1870	VI	601
*Prescott, William Hickling,	1796	1859	VI	181
Price, Richard,	1723	1791	IV	135
Prideaux, Humphrey,	1648	1724	II	697
*Priestley, Joseph,	1733	1804	IV	444
Prince, Thomas,	1681	1758	III	400
Prior, Matthew,	1664	1721	II	672
Procter, Adelaide Anne,	1825	1864	VI	393
Procter, Bryan Waller,	1787	1874	VI	744
Proctor, Richard Anthony,	1837	1888	VII	659
Proute, Father,	1805	1866	VI	483
Prynne, William,	1600	1669	II	223
Purchas, Samuel,	1575?	1628	I	693
*Pusey, Edward Bouverie,	1800	1882	VII	466
Puttenham, George,	1530?	1600?	I	401
Pye, Henry James,	1745	1813	IV	580
*Quarles, Francis,	1592	1644	II	77
Quincy, Josiah,	1772	1864	VI	404
Radcliffe, Ann Ward,	1764	1823	IV	717
*Raleigh, Sir Walter,	1552	1618	I	590
*Ramsay, Allan,	1686	1758	III	402
Randolph, Thomas,	1605	1635	I	744
Ray, John,	1628	1705	II	541
Read, Thomas Buchanan,	1822	1872	VI	676
Reade, Charles,	1814	1884	VII	526
Reeve, Clara,	1729	1807	IV	511
Reid, Thomas,	1710	1796	IV	282
*Reynolds, Sir Joshua,	1723	1792	IV	137
Rhymer, Thomas the,	c. 1225	c. 1300	I	83
Ricardo, David,	1772	1823	IV	725
Richardson, Samuel,	1689	1761	III	431
*Ridley, Nicholas,	1500?	1555	I	266
Ripley, George,	1802	1880	VII	223
Ritson, Joseph,	1752	1803	IV	435
Robert of Gloucester,	fl. 1260	1300	I	81
Robertson, Frederick William,	1816	1853	V	737
*Robertson, William,	1721	1793	IV	154
Robinson, Mary,	1758	1800	IV	411
Rochester, Earl of,	1647	1680	II	335
Roe, Edward Payson,	1838	1888	VII	674
*Rogers, Samuel,	1763	1855	VI	31
Rolle, Richard, of Hampole,	c. 1290	1349	I	91
Romanes, George John,	1848	1894	VIII	283
Romilly, Sir Samuel,	1757	1818	IV	634
Roscoe, William,	1753	1831	V	116

	Born.	Died.	Vol.	Page.
Roscommon, Earl of,	1633?	–1684	II	360
Ross, Alexander,	1699	–1784	III	718
Rossetti, Christina Georgina,	1830	–1894	VIII	268
*Rossetti, Gabriel Charles Dante,	1828	–1882	VII	434
Rowe, Elizabeth,	1674	–1737	III	96
Rowe, Nicholas,	1674	–1718	II	618
Rowley, William,	1585?	–1642?	II	68
Rumford, Count,	1753	–1814	IV	589
*Ruskin, John,	1819	–1900	VIII	404
*Russell, John Lord,	1792	–1878	VII	143
Rutherford, Samuel,	1600	–1661	II	166
Ryan, Abram Joseph,	1839	–1886	VII	598
Rymer, Thomas,	1641	–1713	II	582
Sacheverell, Henry,	1674?	–1724	II	695
Sackville, Charles,	1638	–1706	II	552
*Sackville, Thomas,	1536	–1608	I	431
Sadler, Michael Thomas,	1780	–1835	V	286
*Saint-John, Henry,	1678	–1751	III	282
Sale, George,	1697?	–1736	III	90
Salisbury, John of,	1120?	–1182?	I	59
Sanderson, Robert,	1587	–1663	II	178
*Sandys, George,	1578	–1644	II	80
Savage, Richard,	1690?	–1743	III	131
Savile, George,	1633	–1695	II	448
Savile, Sir Henry,	1549	–1622	I	619
Saxe, John Godfrey,	1816	–1887	VII	616
Saxon Chronicle,	45	–1154	I	57
Schoolcraft, Henry Rowe,	1793	–1864	VI	402
Scott, Alexander,	1525?	–1584?	I	319
Scott, Michael,	1180?	–1235	I	68
Scott, Michael,	1789	–1835	V	278
*Scott, Sir Walter,	1771	–1832	V	125
Scotus, Duns,	1265?	–1308?	I	85
Secker, Thomas,	1693	–1768	III	521
Sedgwick, Catharine Maria,	1789	–1867	VI	505
Sedley, Sir Charles,	1639?	–1701	II	508
*Seeley, Sir John Robert,	1834	–1895	VIII	307
*Selden, John,	1584	–1654	II	137
Settle, Elkanah,	1648	–1724	II	690
Sewall, Samuel,	1652	–1730	III	17
Seward, Anna,	1747	–1809	IV	541
Seward, William Henry,	1801	–1872	VI	672
Shadwell, Thomas,	1642?	–1692	II	433
Shaftesbury, Earl of,	1671	–1713	II	576
Shairp, John Campbell,	1819	–1885	VII	568
*Shakespeare, William,	1564	–1616	I	447
Sheffield, John,	1648	–1721	II	670

	Born.	Died.	Vol.	Page.
Shelley, Mary Wollstonecraft,	1791	1851	V	700
*Shelley, Percy Bysshe,	1792	1822	IV	689
Shenstone, William,	1714	1763	III	471
*Sheridan, Richard Brinsley,	1751	1816	IV	593
Sheridan, Thomas,	1719	1788	IV	46
Sherlock, Thomas,	1678	1761	III	454
Sherlock, William,	1641?	1707	II	561
Shirley, James,	1596	1666	II	189
Sidney, Algernon,	1622	1683	II	353
*Sidney, Sir Philip,	1554	1586	I	320
Sigourney, Lydia Huntley,	1791	1865	VI	450
Silliman, Benjamin,	1779	1864	VI	406
Simms, William Gilmore,	1806	1870	VI	596
Skelton, John,	c. 1460	1529?	I	219
Smart, Christopher,	1722	1771	III	591
Smith, Adam,	1723	1790	IV	53
Smith, Alexander,	1830	1867	VI	515
Smith, Charlotte,	1749	1806	IV	496
Smith, Horace,	1779	1849	V	597
Smith, James,	1775	1839	V	337
Smith, John,	1579	1631	I	698
Smith, Sydney,	1771	1845	V	466
Smollett, Tobias George,	1721	1771	III	573
Somers, John Lord,	1651	1716	II	612
Somerville, Mary,	1780	1872	VI	657
Somerville, William,	1675	1742	III	125
Sotheby, William,	1757	1833	V	204
South, Robert,	1634	1716	II	606
Southerne, Thomas,	1660	1746	III	239
Southey, Caroline Anne Bowles,	1787	1854	V	762
*Southey, Robert,	1774	1843	V	395
Southwell, Robert,	1561?	1595	I	360
Sparks, Jared,	1789	1866	VI	476
Speed, John,	1552?	1629	I	694
Spedding, James,	1808	1881	VII	317
Spelman, Sir Henry,	1564?	1641	II	53
Spence, Joseph,	1699	1768	III	519
*Spencer, Herbert,	1820	1903	VIII	477
*Spenser, Edmund,	1552	1599	I	368
Spotiswood, John,	1565	1639	II	24
Sprague, Charles,	1791	1875	VII	52
*Sprat, Thomas,	1635	1713	II	572
Spurgeon, Charles Haddon,	1834	1892	VIII	178
Stanhope, Philip Dormer,	1694	1773	III	598
Stanhope, Philip Henry Earl,	1805	1875	VII	46
*Stanley, Arthur Penrhyn,	1815	1881	VII	296
Stanley, Sir Henry Morton,	1841	1904	VIII	506

	Born.	Died.	Vol.	Page.
*Steele, Sir Richard,	1672	1729	II	751
Steevens, George,	1736	1800	IV	408
Stephen, Sir Leslie,	1832	1904	VIII	510
Sterling, John,	1806	1844	V	451
*Sterne, Laurence,	1713	1768	III	501
Sternhold, Thomas,	c. 1500	1549	I	261
Stevenson, John Hall,	1718	1785	IV	24
*Stevenson, Robert Louis,	1850	1894	VIII	234
Stewart, Dugald,	1753	1828	V	76
Still, John,	1543?	1608	I	429
Stillingfleet, Edward,	1635	1699	II	453
Stirling, Earl of,	1567?	1640	II	34
Stirling-Maxwell, Lady,	1808	1877	VII	101
*Stockton, Francis Richard,	1834	1902	VIII	472
*Stoddard, Richard Henry,	1825	1903	VIII	494
Story, Joseph,	1779	1845	V	482
Story, William Wetmore,	1819	1895	VIII	318
*Stowe, Harriet Elizabeth Beecher,	1821	1896	VIII	349
Stowe, John,	1525?	1605	I	419
Strickland, Agnes,	1796	1874	VI	766
Strype, John,	1643	1737	III	93
Stuart, Gilbert,	1742	1786	IV	27
Stubbs, William,	1825	1901	VIII	451
*Suckling, Sir John,	1609	1642	II	62
*Sumner, Charles,	1811	1874	VI	750
*Surrey, Earl of,	1516?	1547	I	255
*Swift, Jonathan,	1667	1745	III	196
Sylvester, Joshua,	1563	1618	I	608
*Symonds, John Addington,	1840	1893	VIII	201
Talfourd, Sir Thomas Noon,	1795	1854	V	759
Tannahill, Robert,	1774	1810	IV	547
Tate, Nahum,	1652	1715	II	588
*Taylor, Bayard,	1825	1878	VII	128
Taylor, Brook,	1685	1731	III	51
*Taylor, Sir Henry,	1800	1886	VII	579
*Taylor, Jeremy,	1613	1667	II	203
Taylor, John,	1580	1654	II	132
Taylor, Thomas,	1758	1835	V	290
Taylor, Tom,	1817	1880	VII	213
Taylor, William,	1765	1836	V	318
*Temple, Sir William,	1628	1699	II	455
Tennant, William,	1784	1848	V	527
*Tennyson, Alfred Lord,	1809	1892	VIII	64
Tennyson, Frederick,	1807	1898	VIII	399
*Thackeray, William Makepeace,	1811	1863	VI	290
Theobald, Lewis,	1688	1744	III	140
Thirwall, Connop,	1797	1875	VII	42

GENERAL INDEX TO AUTHORS

	Born.	Died.	Vol.	Page.
Thomas the Rhymer,	c. 1225	–c. 1300	I	83
Thompson, Sir Benjamin,	1753	–1814	IV	589
Thompson, William,	1712?	–1766?	III	500
*Thomson, James,	1700	–1748	III	254
Thomson, James,	1834	–1882	VII	473
*Thoreau, Henry David,	1817	–1862	VI	267
Thrale, Mrs. Hester Lynch,	1740	–1821	IV	684
Tickell, Thomas,	1686	–1740	III	103
*Ticknor, George,	1791	–1871	VI	614
Tighe, Mary,	1772	–1810	IV	550
*Tillotson, John Robert,	1630	–1694	II	437
Timrod, Henry,	1829	–1867	VI	508
Tindal, Matthew,	1653?	–1733	III	72
Titcomb, Timothy,	1819	–1881	VII	333
Toland, John,	1670	–1722	II	681
Tooke, John Horne,	1736	–1812	IV	569
Toplady, Augustus Montague,	1740	–1778	III	681
Tourneur, Cyril,	1575?	–1626?	I	687
Trench, Richard Chenevix,	1807	–1886	VII	588
Trollope, Anthony,	1815	–1882	VII	456
Trollope, Frances Milton,	1780	–1863	VI	329
Trumbull, John,	1750	–1831	V	119
Tucker, Abraham,	1705	–1774	III	643
Tucker, Josiah,	1712	–1799	IV	369
Tuckerman, Henry Theodore,	1813	–1871	VI	641
Tupper, Martin Farquhar,	1810	–1889	VII	731
Turberville, George,	1540?	–1610?	I	438
Turner, Charles Tennyson,	1808	–1879	VII	161
Turner, Sharon,	1768	–1847	V	498
Tusser, Thomas,	1524?	–1580	I	310
*Tyndale, William,	c. 1484	–1536	I	244
Tyndall, John,	1820	–1893	VIII	194
Tyrwhitt, Thomas,	1730	–1786	IV	24
Udall, Nicholas,	c. 1506	–c. 1557	I	278
Urquhart, Sir Thomas,	1611	–1660	II	163
Usher, James,	1580	–1656	II	152
Vanbrugh, Sir John,	1664	–1726	II	702
Vaughan, Henry,	1622	–1695	II	441
Vaux, Thomas Lord,	1510	–1557	I	276
Very, Jones,	1813	–1880	VII	226
Villiers, George,	1628	–1687	II	375
Wace, Robert,	c. 1124	–1184	I	60
Wakefield, Gilbert,	1756	–1801	IV	415
*Walpole, Horace,	1717	–1797	IV	309
Waller, Edmund,	1606	–1687	II	378
Wallis, John,	1616	–1703	II	517
Walsh, William,	1663	–1708	II	560

	Born.	Died.	Vol.	Page.
*Walton, Isaac,	1593	—1683	II	345
*Warburton, William,	1698	—1779	III	682
Ward, Artemus,	1834	—1867	VI	501
Ward, Nathaniel,	1578	—1652	II	129
Ward, William George,	1812	—1882	VII	481
Ware, Henry, Jr.,	1794	—1843	V	431
*Warner, Charles Dudley,	1829	—1900	VIII	440
Warner, William,	1558?	-1609	I	436
*Warren, Samuel,	1807	—1877	VII	106
Warton, Joseph,	1722	—1800	IV	395
Warton, Thomas,	1728	—1790	IV	71
*Washington, George,	1732	—1799	IV	353
Waterland, Daniel,	1683	—1740	III	102
Watson, Thomas,	1557?	-1592	I	337
*Watts, Isaac,	1674	—1748	III	248
Wayland, Francis,	1796	—1865	VI	447
*Webster, Daniel,	1782	—1852	V	719
Webster, John,	fl.	1620	I	670
Webster, Noah,	1758	—1843	V	427
Wells, Charles Jeremiah,	1800	—1879	VII	164
*Wesley, Charles,	1707	—1788	IV	34
*Wesley, John,	1703	—1791	IV	110
Wesley, Samuel,	1662	—1735	III	86
West, Gilbert,	1703	—1756	III	368
Whately, Richard,	1787	—1863	VI	323
Whetstone, George,	1544?	-1587?	I	334
Whewell, William,	1794	—1866	VI	466
Whipple, Edwin Percy,	1819	—1886	VII	594
Whiston, William,	1667	—1752	III	304
White, Gilbert,	1720	—1793	IV	147
White, Henry Kirke,	1785	—1806	IV	487
White, Joseph Blanco,	1775	—1841	V	359
White, Richard Grant,	1822	—1885	VII	576
Whitefield, George,	1714	—1770	III	546
Whitehead, William,	1715	—1785	IV	21
*Whitman, Walt,	1819	—1892	VIII	129
Whitney, William Dwight,	1827	—1894	VIII	302
*Whittier, John Greenleaf,	1807	—1892	VIII	111
Wilberforce, Samuel,	1805	—1873	VI	731
*Wilberforce, William,	1759	—1833	V	199
Wilde, Richard Henry,	1789	—1847	V	503
Wilkes, John,	1727	—1797	IV	332
Wilkie, William,	1721	—1772	III	595
Wilkins, John,	1614	—1672	II	226
Wilkinson, Sir John Gardner,	1797	—1875	VII	50
William of Malmesbury,	c. 1095	—1143	I	53
Williams, Sir Charles Hanbury,	1708	—1759	III	411

	Born.	Died.	Vol.	Page.
WILLIAMS, HELEN MARIA,	1762	—1827	V	74
WILLIAMS, ROGER,	1604?	—1683	II	356
*WILLIS, NATHANIEL PARKER,	1806	—1867	VI	485
WILMOT, JOHN,	1647	—1680	II	335
WILSON, ALEXANDER,	1766	—1813	IV	581
WILSON, ARTHUR,	1596	—1652	II	128
*WILSON, JOHN,	1785	—1854	V	744
WILSON, SIR THOMAS,	1525?	-1581	I	312
WILSON, THOMAS,	1663	—1755	III	366
WINCHILSEA, COUNTESS OF,		1720	II	668
WINTHROP, JOHN,	1588	—1649	II	107
WINTHROP, THEODORE,	1828	—1861	VI	266
*WISEMAN, NICHOLAS PATRICK,	1802	—1865	VI	434
WITHER, GEORGE,	1588	—1667	II	212
*WOLCOT, JOHN,	1738	—1819	IV	647
WOLFE, CHARLES,	1791	—1823	IV	722
WOLLSTONECRAFT, MARY,	1759	—1797	IV	326
WOOD, ANTHONY,	1632	—1695	II	446
WOOLMAN, JOHN,	1720	—1772	III	596
WOOLSEY, THEODORE DWIGHT,	1805	—1889	VII	736
WOOLSTON, THOMAS,	1670	—1733	III	73
*WORDSWORTH, WILLIAM,	1770	—1850	V	605
*WOTTON, SIR HENRY,	1568	—1639	II	17
WOTTON, WILLIAM,	1666	—1726	II	709
*WYATT, SIR THOMAS,	1503	—1542	I	249
*WYCHERLEY, WILLIAM,	1640?	-1715	II	599
*WYCLIF, JOHN,	1324?	-1384	I	99
WYNTOUN, ANDREW,	1395?	-1420	I	177
YOUNG, ARTHUR,	1741	—1820	IV	654
*YOUNG, EDWARD,	1683	—1765	III	484
*YOUNG, THOMAS,	1773	—1829	V	86

GENERAL INDEX TO CRITICISMS.

Vols. I to VIII.

Author of Criticisms; Author Treated; Volume and Page.

ABBEY, CHARLES J.,
    Brooke, Henry...III, 714 715
  Butler, Joseph...........III, 313
  Carter, Elizabeth.........IV, 493
  Clarke, Samuel...........II, 750
  Conybeare, John.........III, 366
  Hoadley, Benjamin......III, 423
  Law, William............III, 429
  Secker, Thomas..........III, 521
  Sherlock, Thomas........III, 454
  Toplady, Augustus M....III, 681
  Wilson, Thomas.........III, 367
ABBEY, HENRY,
  Byron,George Gordon Lord.IV, 765
ABBOT, CHARLES (Lord Colchester),
  Fox, Charles James.......IV, 502
ABBOT, GEORGE (Archbishop of Canterbury),
  Sackville, Thomas..........I, 431
ABBOTT, EDWIN ABBOTT,
  Bacon, Francis........I, 647, 669
  Newman, John Henry ....
    .... VII, 742, 749, 754
  Pope, Alexander..........III, 191
ABBOTT, FRANCIS M.,
  Rumford, Count..........IV, 592
ABBOTT, LYMAN,
  Beecher,Henry Ward.VII, 600, 609
  Brooks, Phillips........VIII, 232
  Browning, Robert.......VII, 718
  Drummond, Henry..VIII, 364, 365
  Fiske, John...........VIII, 459
  Spurgeon, Charles Haddon....
    .... VIII, 181
ABERNETHY, JOHN,
  Hunter, John.............IV, 166
ACKERSON, DAVID,
  Washington, George.......IV, 358
ADAMS, ABIGAIL,
  Adams, John..............V, 50
ADAMS, CHARLES,
  Irving, Washington....VI, 139, 142
ADAMS, CHARLES FRANCIS,
  Adams, John..........V, 51, 53
  Adams, John Quincy..V, 517, 519
  Hamilton, Alexander .....IV, 463
  Junius....................IV, 645
  Madison, James...........V, 314
  Seward, William Henry.....VI, 674
  Stanhope, Philip Dormer...III, 601
  Walpole, Horace...........IV, 319
ADAMS, CHARLES FRANCIS, JR.,
  Sewall, Samuel...........III, 18
ADAMS, CHARLES KENDALL,
  Adams, John Quincy.......V, 520

Adams, Samuel............IV, 440
Alison,Sir Archibald......VI, 521
Arnold, Thomas.........V, 381, 382
Bacon, Francis.............I, 656
Bagehot, Walter.........VII, 99
Bancroft, George........VIII, 59
Beecher, Lyman..........VI, 339
Benton, Thomas Hart.....VI, 87
Blair, Robert............III, 241
Brougham, Henry Lord....VI, 532
Brownson, Orestes Augustus'.
  .... VII, 75
Buckle, Henry Thomas....VI, 283
Burke, Edmund.......IV, 296, 301
Burton, John Hill........VII, 316
Carlyle, Thomas......VII, 248, 256
Carte, Thomas...........III, 337
Clarke, James Freeman....VII, 673
Coverdale, Miles............I, 291
Draper, John William.....VII, 503
Evelyn, John..............II, 549
Fabyan, Robert............I, 207
Farmer, Richard..........IV, 340
Finlay, George........VII, 48, 50
Fletcher, Phineas..........II, 115
Forster, John............VII, 67
Freeman, Edward Augustus
  .... VIII, 158
Froude, James Anthony......
  ....VIII, 258, 264
Gibbon, Edward..... IV, 188
Gladstone,William Ewart.VIII, 391
Greeley, Horace...........VI, 671
Green, John Richard..VII, 508, 509
Grote, George............VI, 611
Hallam, Henry...VI, 175, 176, 177
Herbert, Edward Lord.....II, 95
Hildreth, Richard.........VI, 453
History,..................VI, 9
Hume, David............III, 659
Hunter, John .... IV, 164
Irving, Washington...VI, 146, 148
Kennedy, John Pendleton .VI, 604
Kinglake, Alexander William
  .... VIII, 52
Kingsley, Charles........VII, 31
Knight, Charles ....VI, 743
Lane, Edward William ...VII, 84
Lardner, Nathaniel........III, 522
Lecky, William E. H....VIII, 488
Lewis, Sir George Cornewall VI, 338
Macaulay, Thomas Babington
  Lord ....VI, 108
Mackintosh, Sir James.....V, 183
Maine, Sir Henry James Sumner ....VII, 652

Marshall, John ....V, 285
Martineau, Harriet ......VII, 63
Maurice, John Frederick Denison ....VI, 648
Mill, James ....V, 307
Milman, Henry Hart..VI, 535, 538
Mitford, William ....V, 71
More, Sir Thomas..........I, 240
Motley, John Lothrop...VII, 90, 92
Palfrey, John Gorham....VII, 338
Prescott, William Hickling
  ....VI, 185, 188
Robertson, William.......IV, 159
Schoolcraft, Henry Rowe..VI, 404
Sedgwick, Catharine Maria.VI, 505
Seeley, Sir John Robert..VIII, 308
Simms, William Gilmore...VI, 599
Speed. John ....I, 694
Stanley, Arthur Penhryn......
  ....VII, 302, 304
Strickland, Agnes.........VI, 768
Stubbs, William........VIII, 452
Symonds, John Addington
  .... VIII, 203
Taylor, Brook ....III, 51
Thirlwall, Connop ....VII, 43
Ticknor, George . .:.......VI, 617
Trollope, Anthony.......VII, 460
Turner, Sharon ....V. 498
Warton, Thomas,.........IV, 74
Whewell, William ....VI, 471
Wilkison, Sir John Gardner VII, 52
ADAMS, CYRUS C.,
  Park, Mungo ....IV, 483
  Stanley. Sir Henry Morton
  .... VIII, 508
ADAMS, D. C. O.,
  Bede ....I, 26
ADAMS, EDWARD W.,
  Burton, Robert ....II, 40
ADAMS, FRANCIS,
  Shelley, Percy Bysshe.....IV, 698
ADAMS, GEORGE BURTON,
  Bacon Roger ....I, 81
ADAMS, H.,
  Palgrave, Francis Turner VIII, 372
  Ticknor, George ....VI, 614
ADAMS, HENRY,
  Jefferson, Thomas ....V, 44
ADAMS, HERBERT B.,
  Freeman, Edward Augustus
  ....VIII, 154, 160
  Sparks, Jared ....VI, 479
ADAMS, JOHN,
  Adams, John Quincy.......V, 515
  Franklin, Benjamin.....IV, 81, 84

INDEX TO CRITICISMS

	Vol. and Page
Hamilton, Alexander	IV, 458
Hopkinson, Francis	IV, 131
Hutchinson, Thomas	III, 706
Mather, Cotton,	II, 731
Monroe, James	V, 122
Otis, James	III, 716
Trumbull, John	V, 120
Washington, George	IV, 355
Webster, Daniel	V, 724

ADAMS, JOHN QUINCY,
Bacon, Francis	I, 652
Byron, George Gordon Lord	IV, 757
Emerson, Ralph Waldo	VII, 344
Halleck, Fitz-Greene	VI, 498
Hamilton, Alexander	IV, 462
Horsley, Samuel	IV, 495
Jefferson, Thomas	IV, 41, 48
Literature	I, 7
Lytton, Sir Edward George Bulwer,	VI, 685
Madison, James	V, 312
Wolcot, John	IV, 650

ADAMS, MRS. M. L.,
Scott, Sir Walter	V, 145

ADAMS, OSCAR FAY,
Austen, Jane	IV, 613, 618
Bradford, William	II, 157
Bradstreet, Anne	II, 228
Brainard, John Gardiner Calkins	V, 84
Defoe, Daniel	III, 38
Eliot, John	II, 412
Freneau, Philip	V, 186
Hopkins, Samuel	IV, 437
Hutchinson, Thomas	III, 706
Livingston, William	IV, 108
Mather, Cotton,	II, 727
Neal, John	VII, 76
Palfrey, John Gorham	III, 337
Parsons, Thomas William	VIII, 192
Prince, Thomas	III, 400
Sprague, Charles	VII, 52
Trumbull, John	V, 119
Tuckerman, Henry Theodore	VI, 641
Ware, Henry, Jr.	V, 431
Williams, Roger	II, 356

ADAMS, SAMUEL,
Paine, Thomas	IV, 539

ADAMS, SARAH FLOWER,
Browning, Elizabeth Barrett	VI, 235

ADAMS, W. DAVENPORT,
Aubrey, John	II, 451
Barnes, Barnabe	I, 439
Blackmore, Sir Richard	II, 746, 747
Boece, Hector	I, 242
Chettle, Henry	I, 429
Cibber, Theophilus	III, 395
Greene, Robert	I, 339
Henry of Huntingdon	I, 58
Junius	IV, 638
Manley, Mrs. Mary de la Riviere	II, 693
Minot, Lawrence	I, 93
Norris, John	II, 570
Parker, Matthew	I, 303
Steele, Sir Richard	II, 766
Usher, James	II, 152
Villiers, George	II, 375
Whetstone, George	I, 334

ADAMS, W. H. DAVENPORT,
Defoe, Daniel	III, 26
Fenton, Elijah	III, 21
Green, Matthew	III, 95
Poe, Edgar Allan	V, 552
Prideaux, Humphrey	II, 697
Prior, Matthew	II, 678
Saint-John, Henry	III, 297
Savage, Richard	III, 135
Tennyson, Alfred Lord	VIII, 104
Trollope, Frances Milton	VI, 331

ADAMSON, ROBERT,
Bacon, Roger	I, 80
Berkeley, George	III, 333
Brown, Thomas	IV, 658
Butler, Joseph	III, 307, 312
Hales, Alexander	I, 72

ADDISON, DANIEL DULANEY,
Beecher, Henry Ward	VII, 610
Brooks, Phillips	VIII, 231
Bushnell, Horace	VII, 72

ADDISON, JOSEPH,
Authors and Authorship	VIII, 5
Bacon, Francis	I, 641, 664
Baker, Sir Richard	II, 93
Blackmore, Sir Richard	II, 746
Brown, Thomas	II, 540
Butler, Samuel	II, 330
Chaucer, Geoffrey	I, 155
Clarke, Samuel	II, 748
Congreve, William	II, 740
Cowley, Abraham	II, 198
Critic, The	II, 5
Denham, Sir John	II, 221
Dillon, Wentworth	II, 360
Dryden, John	II, 490
D'Urfey, Thomas	II, 686
Etheredge, Sir George	II, 431
History	VI, 6
Knowledge	V, 6
Lee, Nathaniel	II, 431
Mandeville, Sir John	I, 95
Milton, John	II, 257, 284
Montagu, Charles	II, 587
More, Sir Thomas	I, 234
Philips, Ambrose	III, 274
Pope, Alexander	III, 158, 181
Shakespeare, William	I, 519, 551
Somers, John Lord	II, 613, 614
Spenser, Edmund	I, 379
Swift, Jonathan	III, 228
Waller, Edmund	II, 380

ADDLESHAW, PERCY.
Burton, Sir Richard Francis	VII, 759

ADDLESHAW, STANLEY.
Pater, Walter Horatio	VIII, 276

ADLER, CYRUS.
Borrow, George Henry	VII, 314

ADLER, FELIX.
Longfellow, Henry Wadsworth	VII, 408

ADOLPHUS, JOHN.
Franklin, Benjamin	IV, 95

ÆLFRIC.
Ælfric	I, 46

AGASSIZ, ELIZABETH CARY.
Agassiz, Louis Jean Rudolph	VI, 720

AGASSIZ, LOUIS.
Darwin, Charles Robert	VII, 427

	Vol. and Page
Gray, Asa	VII, 670
Miller, Hugh	VI, 64

AGNEW, MARY COURTENAY.
Campbell, Thomas	V, 438
Canning, George	V, 66
Southey, Robert	V, 402
Taylor, Sir Henry	VII, 582
Wotton, Sir Henry	II, 18

AIKMAN, C. M.
Dodgson, Charles Lutwige	VIII, 398

AINGER, ALFRED.
Bowles, William Lisle	V, 660
Brown, John	VII, 480
Du Maurier, George	VIII, 344, 346
Elyot, Sir Thomas	I, 254
Hood, Thomas	V, 464
Lamb, Charles	V, 238, 242
Tennyson, Alfred Lord	VIII, 71
Tennyson, Frederick	VIII, 401
Turner, Charles Tennyson	VII, 164

AIRD, THOMAS.
Moir, David Macbeth	V, 704, 705
Tennyson, Alfred Lord	VIII, 100
Wilson, John	V, 746

AIRY, OSMUND.
Burnet, Gilbert	II, 592, 594
North, Roger	III, 79
Pepys, Samuel	II, 515

AIKIN, BERKELEY (FANNY AIKIN KORTRIGHT).
Hawthorne, Nathaniel	VI, 353

AIKIN, JOHN.
Armstrong, John	III, 698
Goldsmith, Oliver	III, 630
Green, Matthew	III, 94, 94
Pope, Alexander	III, 168, 175
Selden, John	II, 138, 139
Somerville, William	III, 126
Thomson, James	III, 258

AIKIN, LUCY.
Addison, Joseph	II, 641
Bacon, Francis	I, 642, 652
Barbauld, Anna Lætitia	V, 24
Brougham, Henry Lord	VI, 523
Carlyle, Thomas	VII, 246
D'Avenant, Sir William	II, 217
Gauden, John	II, 177
Martineau, Harriet	VII, 55, 60
Milman, Henry Hart	VI, 537
Prescott, William Hickling	VI, 183
Raleigh, Sir Walter	I, 594
Selden, John	II, 142
Steele, Sir Richard	II, 753
Strickland, Agnes	VI, 767

AIRY, WILFRID.
Airy, Sir George Biddell	VIII, 183

AITKEN, GEORGE A.
Addison, Joseph	II, 645
Arbuthnot, John	III, 83, 84
Defoe, Daniel	III, 31, 27, 42, 50
Farquhar, George	II, 559
Gay, John	III, 56
Oldmixon, John	III, 125
Parnell, Thomas	II, 615, 617
Philips, John	II, 564
Prior, Matthew	II, 676
Ross, Alexander	III, 719
Shadwell, Thomas	II, 435
Shenstone, William	III, 474
Steele, Sir Richard	II, 754, 756, 758, **761**

INDEX TO CRITICISMS 543

	Vol. and Page
Swift, Jonathan	III, 223
Tickell, Thomas	III, 107
Wycherley, William	II, 602, 603 606

A. KEMPIS, THOMAS.
Knowledge ....V, 5

AKENSIDE, MARK.
Chaucer, Geoffrey ....I, 157
Hoadley, Benjamin ....III, 422

ALAND, JOHN FORTESCUE.
Fortescue, Sir John ....I, 194

ALBEE, ERNEST.
Cumberland, Richard .....II, 625
Hume, David ....III, 665

ALBEE, JOHN.
Emerson, Ralph Waldo ...... VII, 354, 380
Keats, John..............IV, 669

ALBERT, PRINCE.
Tennyson, Alfred Lord ...VIII, 93

ALBRIZZI, COUNTESS.
Bryon, George Gordon Lord... IV, 736

ALCOTT, AMOS BRONSON.
Beecher, Henry Ward .. .VII, 604
Berkeley, George ....III, 332
Carlyle, Thomas......... VII, 264
Coleridge, Samuel Taylor ...V, 225
Cowley, Abraham ....II, 201
Emerson, Ralph Waldo... VII, 364
Fuller, Sarah Margaret ..... V, 668
Hawthorne, Nathaniel .... VII, 345
Herrick, Robert........... II. 238
Landor, Walter Savage..... VI. 389
Phillips, Wendell .... VII, 555
Selden, John ....II, 141
Thoreau, Henry David .... VI, 272
Webster, Daniel.......... V, 720
Whitman, Walt .... VIII, 130

ALCOTT, LOUISA MAY.
Emerson, Ralph Waldo... VII, 350
Thoreau, Henry David .... VI, 268

ALCUIN.
Alcuin ....I, 32

ALDEN, HENRY MILLS.
DeQuincey, Thomas ...... VI, 126
Fields, James Thomas.... VII, 340

ALDEN, WILLIAM L.
Hawthorne, Nathaniel .... VI, 360

ALDRICH, CHARLES.
DeVere, Aubrey........ VIII, 463

ALDRICH, THOMAS BAILEY.
Arnold, Matthew..........VII, 641
Emerson, Ralph Waldo... VII, 371
Herrick, Robert...II, 235, 237, 241
Longfellow, Henry Wadsworth .... VII, 411
Lowell, James Russell....VIII, 20
Parsons, Thomas William..... .... VIII, 192, 194
Philips, Wendell.........VII, 554
Poe, Edgar Allan..........V, 557
Poets and Poetry......... IV, 9
Shakespeare, William ....I, 452
Taylor, Bayard...........VII, 129

ALEXANDER, ARCHIBALD.
Berkeley George .....III, 325, 334
Henry, Matthew .... III, 585
Henry Patrick .... IV, 351

ALEXANDER, JAMES.
Dickens Charles .... VI 581

	Vol. and Page
Whatley, Richard	VI, 326

ALEXANDER, JAMES W.
Adams, John Quincy....... V, 515
Brainard, John Gardiner Calkins......................V, 84
Dewey, Orville...........VII, 498
Dickens, Charles..........VI, 572
Doddridge, Philip.....III, 301, 303
Edwards, Jonathan.......III, 383
Gibbon, Edward..........IV, 192
Guthrie, Thomas ....VII, 736
Hopkins, Mark..........VII, 614
Irving, Washington.........VI, 145
Milman, Henry Hart.......VI, 537
Sigourney, Lydia Huntley...VI, 451
Webster, Noah..............V, 430
Whitefield, George........III, 550

ALEXANDER, WILLIAM.
Arnold, Matthew..........VII, 637

ALEXANDER, WILLIAM JOHN.
Browning, Robert ....VII, 709

ALEXANDER, WILLIAM LINDSAY.
Arnold, Thomas...........V, 378
Chalmers, Thomas..........V, 490
Channing, William Ellery....V. 373

ALFIERI, VITTORI.
Washington, George.......IV, 355

ALFORD, HENRY.
Shakespeare, William ....I, 558
Tennyson, Alfred Lord .. VIII, 77
Wordsworth, William ...... V, 632

ALFORD, MRS. HENRY.
Alford, Henry............ VI, 636

ALFRED, KING.
Alfred the Great ....I, 39

ALFRIC.
Alcuin ....I, 32

ALGER, WILLIAM ROUNSEVILLE.
Holmes, Oliver Wendell . VIII, 290
Martineau, James........VII, 428
Parsons, Thomas William VIII, 192
Thoreau, Henry David .... VI, 269

ALISON, SIR ARCHIBALD.
Alison, Archibald.......... V, 341
Alison, Sir Archibald...... VII, 519
Aytoun, William Edmondstoune ....VI, 445
Bancroft, George ......VIII, 55
Brougham, Henry Lord....VI, 527
Burns, Robert............IV, 253
Byron, George Gordon Lord.IV, 740
Campbell, Thomas..........V, 437
Cobden, Richard..........VI, 440
Croly, George............VI, 225
Disraeli, Benjamin........VII, 292
Edgeworth, Maria ....V, 563
Franklin, Benjamin........IV, 86
Gibbon, Edward..........IV, 182
Grote, George............VII 609
Hallam, Henry............VI, 178
Hazlitt, William...........V, 103
Hemans, Felicia Dorothea... ....V, 256, 260
Hume David ....III. 657
James, George Paine Rainsford ....VI, 219
Jeffrey, Francis Lord........V, 654
Knowles James Sheridan...VI, 288
Landon Letitia Elizabeth....V 328

	Vol. and Page
Lockhart, John Gibson..V, 756, 757
Lytton, Sir Edward George Bulwer................VI, 688, 688

Macaulay, Thomas Babington
Lord................VI, 99, 102
Mackintosh, Sir James.......V, 182
Malthus, Thomas Robert.....V, 252
Mitford, William............V, 71
Milnes, Richard Monckton.VII, 563
Moore, Thomas.........V, 708, 710
Napier, Gen. Sir Wm. Francis
Patrick..................VI, 222
Norton, Caroline E. S..VII, 102, 105
Paley, William ....IV, 475, 476
Palgrave, Sir Francis.......VI, 265
Prescott, William Hickling..VI, 189
Reid, Thomas.............IV, 284
Robertson, William....IV, 159, 163
Rogers, Samuel............VI, 39
Scott, Sir Walter........V, 132, 158
Smith, Adam..............IV, 70
Smith, Sydney.............V, 468
Southey, Robert............V, 405
Stanhope, Philip Henry Earl.. ....VII, 47
Stewart, Dugald............V, 80
Strickland, Agnes.....VI, 767, 768
Tennyson, Alfred Lord....VIII, 101
Turner, Sharon.............V,499
Warren, Samuel..........VII, 108
Wilson, John............V, 747, 751
Wordsworth, William.......V, 636

ALLAN, GEORGE.
Scott, Sir Walter........V, 149, 155

ALLBUT, ROBERT.
Dickens, Charles..........VI, 559

ALLEN, ALEXANDER V. G.
Brooks, Phillips......VIII, 229, 232
Bushnell, Horace.........VII, 71
Edwards, Jonathan......... ....III, 388, 388, 393
Hopkins, Samuel..........IV, 440
Maurice, John Frederick Denison.................. VI, 650
Stanley, Arthur Penrhyn...VII, 305
Wyclif, John.................I, 112

ALLEN, CHARLES.
Shakespeare, William.......I, 547

ALLEN, F. STURGES.
Littleton, Sir Thomas........I, 196

ALLEN, GRANT.
Agassiz, Louis Jean Rudolph .
......................VI, 721
Browning, Robert........VII, 702
Cynewulf ....I, 30
Darwin, Charles Robert...... ....VII, 419, 425, 426
Darwin, Erasmus.........IV, 425
Eliot, George............VII, 195
Green, John Richard......VII. 510
Lyell, Sir Charles.........VI, 38
Malthus, Thomas Robert....V, 253
Poets and Poetry.........IV, 9
Proctor, Richard Anthony.... ....VII, 659, 661
Spencer, Herbert........VIII 484
Tennyson, Alfred Lord...VIII, 106
Tyndall, John.......VIII, 197, 199

ALLEN, JOHN.
Stowe John. 1,420
Turner Sharon .... V, 498

INDEX TO CRITICISMS

ALLEN, JOSEPH HENRY.
  Channing, William Ellery....V, 374
  Lardner, Nathaniel.......III, 523
ALLEN, STEPHEN M.
  Webster, Daniel............V, 723
ALLEN, WALTER.
  Bushnell, Horace.........VII, 72
ALLEN, W. F.
  Freeman, Edward Augustus..
    ....VIII, 159
  Müller, Friedrich Max...VIII, 438
ALLIBONE, S. AUSTIN.
  Andrews, Lancelot..........I, 636
  Ashmole, Elias............II, 436
  Atterbury, Francis.......III, 67
  Bentley, Richard.........III, 114
  Barclay, John..............I, 618
  Barclay, Robert...........II, 411
  Barnes, Joshua............II, 572
  Beaumon', Sir John.........I, 679
  Beaumont, Joseph.........II, 461
  Berners, Juliana............I, 191
  Blair, Robert.............III, 242
  Boyle, Robert.............II, 419
  Bradstreet, Anne..........II, 229
  Bryant, William Cullen....VII, 122
  Burney, Frances............V, 350
  Burnet, Thomas...........II, 597
  Carte, Thomas............III, 338
  Cartwright, William........II, 71
  Cavendish, Margaret.......II, 230
  Chaucer, Geoffrey...........I, 162
  Cibber, Colley............III, 375
  Cleveland, John...........II, 158
  Cockburn, Catherine......III, 275
  Conybeare, John..........III, 365
  Cruden, Alexander........III, 546
  Cumberland, Richard......II, 624
  Disraeli, Benjamin.......VII, 292
  Drake, Joseph Rodman....IV, 659
  Earle, John...............II, 183
  Edwards, Richard...........I, 287
  Falconer, William........III, 526
  Ferguson, James..........III, 668
  Geoffrey of Monmouth.......I, 55
  Gilfillan, George.........VII, 151
  Gore, Catherine Grace.....VI, 264
  Granville, George.........III, 87
  Harrington, James........II, 308
  Harvey, Gabriel............I, 695
  Hawkesworth, John......III, 608
  Henry, Robert............IV, 108
  Hill, Aaron..............III, 276
  Hill, John...............III, 646
  Hopkinson, Francis.......IV, 131
  Horner, Francis..........IV, 631
  Jortin, John.............III, 552
  Kelly, Hugh..............III, 677
  Kenrick, William.........III, 701
  King, Henry...............II, 222
  Knight, Charles...........VI, 743
  Leland, John...............I, 263
  Logan, John...............IV, 43
  Longfellow, Henry Wadsworth
    ....VII, 404
  Mason, William...........IV, 323
  Middleton, Conyers.......III, 281
  Monroe, James............V, 122
  Munday, Anthony...........I, 726
  Nabbes, Thomas...........II, 94
  Neal, John................VII, 78

  Ockley, Simon.............II, 669
  O'Keeffe, John.............V, 196
  Oldys, William...........III, 456
  Pomfret, John............II, 510
  Robinson, Mary...........IV, 411
  Sadler, Michael Thomas.....V, 286
  Sale, George.............III, 90
  Smith, John................I, 698
  Somerville, William......III, 125
  Southerne, Thomas........III, 239
  Thomson, William.........III, 50
  Thrwhitt, Thomas.........IV, 26
  Tighe, Mary..............IV, 550
  Ward, Nathaniel..........II, 129
  Wilkie, William..........III, 595
  Williams, Sir Charles Hanbury.
    ....III, 411
  Wilson, Sir Thomas.........I, 312
  Woolman, John...........III, 596
  Wordsworth, William......V, 614
  Wotton, William..........II, 709
ALLINGHAM, WILLIAM.
  Clough, Arthur Hugh..VI 249, 259
  Milnes, Richard Monckton..VII, 560
  Whitman, Walt..........VIII, 134
ALSOP, ANTHONY.
  Bentley, Richard.........III,120
ALSOP, RICHARD.
  Washington, George.......IV, 357
ALZOG, JOHN.
  Erigena, John Scotus........I, 34
  Wyclif, John...............I, 106
ALVIELLA, COUNT GOBLET.
  Parker, Theodore..........VI, 211
AMES, FISHER.
  Hamilton, Alexander......IV, 457
  Madison, James............V, 311
  Washington, George.......IV, 356
AMES, MARY, CLEMMER.
  Cary, Alice..............VI, 639
  Cary, Phœbe..........VI, 640, 641
  Greeley, Horace..........VI, 668
AMES, NATHANIEL.
  Adams, John................V, 50
AMORY, THOMAS.
  Swift, Jonathan..........III, 198
AMPÉRE, J. J.
  Byron, George Gordon Lord.IV, 750
ANAGNOS, JULIA R.
  Manning, Henry Edward..VIII, 167
ANDERDON, J. L.
  Ken, Thomas..............II, 568
ANDERSON, HANS CHRISTIAN.
  Blessington, Countess of,.....V, 592
  Dickens, Charles......VI, 553, 572
  Scott, Sir Walter..........V, 142
ANDERSON, CHRISTOPHER.
  Tyndale, William...........I, 244
ANDERSON, EDWARD PLAYFAIR.
  Dana, Richard Henry, Jr...VII, 501
  Oliphant, Laurence...VII, 656, 657
ANDERSON, JAMES.
  Bradstreet, Anne..........II, 229
ANDERSON, JOHN P.
  Bunyan, John............II, 397
ANDERSON, MARY (MADAME DE NAVARRO).
  Browning, Robert.........VII, 682
ANDERSON, MELVILLE B.
  Addison, Joseph..........II, 656

  FitzGerald, Edward.......VII, 521
  Landor, Walter Savage....VI, 386
  Pattison, Mark..........VII, 541
  Whittier, John Greenleaf..VIII, 118
ANDERSON, ROBERT.
  Blacklock Thomas........IV, 130
  Garth, Sir Samuel.........II, 665
  Moore, John..............IV, 427
  Smart, Christopher....III, 594, 595
  Smollett, Tobias George.....
    ....III, 574, 578
ANDERSON, W.
  Bunyan, John.............II, 404
ANDERSON, WILLIAM.
  Grant, Anne...............V, 329
  Hemans, Felicia Dorothea...V, 260
  More, Hannah..............V, 195
ANDREWS, I. W.
  Hopkins, Mark...........VII, 613
ANDREWS, WILLIAM.
  Doyle, Sir Francis Hastings
    Charles...............VII, 650
  Gibbon, Edward...........IV, 191
ANDREWS, WILLIAM P.
  Very, Jones...............VI, 227
ANGELL, JAMES BURRILL.
  Shairp, John Campbell....VII, 570
  Wayland, Francis.........VI, 448
ANGELLIER, AUGUSTE.
  Burns, Robert............IV, 234
ANGUS, JOSEPH.
  Amory, Thomas...........IV, 48
  Bacon, Francis.............I, 661
  Bloomfield, Robert.......IV, 723
  Chamberlaye, William....II, 406
  Clarke, Samuel...........II, 749
  Henry, Matthew..........II, 585
  Henry, Robert............IV, 108
  John of Salisbury...........I, 60
  Mandeville, Bernard......III, 69
  Owen, John...............II, 352
  Quarles, Francis...........II, 78
  Saxon Chronicle............I, 57
  Southwell, Robert.........I, 362
  White, Henry Kirke......IV, 489
ANGUS, J. KEITH.
  Oliphant, Laurence.......VII, 658
ANNE, QUEEN OF DENMARK.
  Raleigh, Sir Walter........I, 591
ANTHONY, HENRY B.
  Sumner, Charles..........VI, 754
ANTON, P.
  Havergal, Frances Ridley..VII, 167
APJOHN, LEWIS.
  Bright, John.............VII, 724
APPLETON, THOMAS GOLD.
  Johnson, Samuel.........III, 730
  Shelley, Percy Bysshe......IV, 690
ARAGO, FRANÇOIS.
  Young, Thomas.............V, 87
  Addison, Joseph..........II, 653
ARBER, EDWARD.
  Howell, James............II, 186
  More, Sir Thomas..........I, 237
  Puttenham, George........I, 402
  Wyatt, Sir Thomas..........I, 253
  Selden, John.............II, 141
  Smith, John................I, 699
  Villiers, George..........II, 377
ARBUCKLE, JOHN.
  Lamb, Charles............V, 241

INDEX TO CRITICISMS

Vol. and Page
ARBUTHNOT, JOHN.
Arbuthnot, John......III, 81, 83
Bentley, Richard..........III, 110
D'Urfey, Thomas..........II, 686
Gay, John................III, 59
Tickell, Thomas..........III, 104
Prior, Matthew............II, 673
Swift, Jonathan..........III, 219
ARCHER, FRANK.
Browning, Robert.........VII, 692
Goldsmith, Oliver.........III, 633
Reade, Charles..........VII, 537
ARCHER, THOMAS.
Hunt, James Henry Leigh....
..................VI, 164 171
Lamb, Charles............V, 237
Moore, Thomas............V, 718
ARCHER, T. A.
Freeman, Edward Augustus..
......................VIII, 160
ARCHER, WILLIAM.
Henley, William Ernest...VIII, 493
Lewes, George Henry......VII, 143
Macklin, Charles..........IV, 344
Stevenson, Robert Louis..VIII, 248
ARGYLL, DUKE OF.
Darwin, Charles Robert.....VII, 430
George, Henry............VIII, 381
ARMOUR, MARGARET.
Stevenson, Robert Louis.VIII, 235
ARMSTRONG, JOHN.
Thomson, James..........III, 255
ARMSTRONG, RICHARD A.
Butler, Joseph............III, 318
Clough, Arthur Hugh......VI, 250
ARMSTRONG, SIR WALTER.
Reynolds, Sir Joshua.......IV, 143
ARNOLD, A. S.
Carlyle, Thomas..........VII, 270
ARNOLD, SIR EDWIN.
Arnold, Matthew..........VII, 629
Chaucer, Geoffrey..........I, 162
Knowledge................V, 10
Procter, Adelaide Anne....VI, 394
Reade, Charles..........VII, 531
Shakespeare, William......I, 562
Tennyson, Alfred Lord.....
....................VIII, 70, 106
ARNOLD, FREDERICK.
Macaulay, Thomas Babington
Lord....................VI, 106
ARNOLD, FREDERICK.
Robertson, Frederick William
........................V, 738
ARNOLD, MATTHEW.
Addison, Joseph...........II, 657
Beecher, Henry Ward......VII, 600
Brontë, Emily.............V, 521
Burke, Edmund...........IV, 305
Burns, Robert..........IV, 246, 260
Butler, Joseph........III, 309, 312
Byron, George Gordon Lord...
..............IV, 740, 749, 761
Carlyle, Thomas......VII, 258, 267
Chapman, George...........I, 730
Chaucer, Geoffrey..........I, 165
Clough, Arthur Hugh....VI, 248, 249
Colenso, John William.VII, 524, 524
Coleridge, Samuel Taylor.....V, 225
Cowper William...........IV, 381
Critic, The...............II, 7

Vol. and Page
Dickens, Charles..........VI, 573
Drummond, Henry.......VIII, 364
Emerson, Ralph Waldo......
..................VII, 357, 370
Gray, Thomas....III, 559, 562, 569
Junius...................IV, 645
Keats, John.........IV, 669, 677
Kinglake, Alexander William..
........................VIII, 52
Lewes, George Henry......VII, 142
Longfellow, Henry Wadsworth
..................VII, 392, 404
Lowell, James Russell......VIII, 37
Lytton, Sir Edward George
Bulwer.........VI, 681, 692
Macauley, Thomas Babington
Lord................VI, 99, 102
Macpherson, James........IV, 277
Marsh, George Perkins......VII, 492
Martineau, Harriet........VII, 57
Milnes, Richard Monckton..VII, 560
Milton, John.....II, 248, 263, 295
Montgomery, James.........V,768
Newton. Sir Isaac..........II, 725
Pope, Alexander..........III, 166
Robertson, Frederick William.
........................V, 739
Ruskin, John............VIII. 406
Scott, Sir Walter..........V, 136
Shakespeare, William...I, 561, 569
Shelley, Percy Bysshe..IV, 696, 713
Smith, Alexander.........VI, 517
Spenser, Edmund...........I, 397
Spurgeon, Charles Haddon.
........................VIII, 178
Stanley, Arthur Penrhyn.....
..................VII, 298, 302
Tennyson, Alfred Lord....VIII, 102
Whately, Richard..........VI, 324
Wilson, Thomas..........III, 367
Wordsworth, William........
..................V, 623, 635. 639
ARNOLD, THOMAS.
Addison, Joseph...........II. 650
Akenside Mark...........III. 543
Arnold, Matthew..........VII. 628
Bacon, Francis............I, 655
Beattie, James............IV, 432
Beaumont and Fletcher......I, 583
Bentley, Richard..........III, 116
Beowulf..................I, 20
Bunyan, John............II, 394
Burton, Robert............II, 39
Camden, William..........I, 622
Campbell, Thomas.........V, 438
Centlivre, Susannah.......II, 684
Cleveland, John...........II, 159
Clough, Arthur Hugh......VI, 250
Coleridge, Samuel Taylor.......V, 222
Collins, William...........III, 420
Cowper, William..........IV, 390
Drayton, Michael.......I, 702, 703
Dyer, John..............III, 399
Falconer, William..........III, 526
Ferguson, Adam..........IV, 611
Fielding, Henry..........III, 347
Gladstone, William Ewart VIII, 390
Glover, Richard..........IV, 19
Hobbes, Thomas..........II. 327
Holinshed, Raphael........I, 311
Hughes, John ....II, 668

Vol and Page
Hume, David.............III. 657
Law, William............III. 429
Milton, John ....II. 277
Napier, Gen. Sir Wm. Francis
Patrick.................VI. 222
Pearson, John.............II. 369
Philips, John.............II. 564
Pollok, Robert.............V. 73
Pope, Alexander...........III. 178
Porson, Richard..........IV. 525
Quarles, Francis...........II 79
Raleigh, Sir Walter..........I 600
Robertson. William ......IV. 161
Savage, Richard..........III 135
Shakespeare, William ....I. 522
Shenstone, William.........III 474
Sheridan. Richard Brinsley....
..................IV. 601. 607
Southerne, Thomas........III. 241
Southwell, Robert..........I. 362
Surrey, Earl of............I. 258
Thirlwall. Connop........VII 43
Whately, Richard.....VI. 323 327
Wordsworth, William.......V. 609
Young, Edward. ....III 489
ARNOLD, MRS THOMAS.
Wordsworth, William.......V. 609
ARNOLD, WILLIAM T.
Browne, William............II 73
Browning, Elizabeth Barrett..
..................VI. 241. 246
Habington, William......II. 134 137
Wither, George.............II 215
ARTHUR, CHESTER A.
Washington, George........IV 363
ASCHAM, ROGER.
Ascham, Roger............II 290
Chaucer, Geoffrey......I, 153. 153
Malory, Sir Thomas ....I. 203
Wyatt, Sir Thomas.........I. 250
ASHBY-STERRY. JOSEPH.
Besant, Sir Walter........VIII 450
Collins, William Wilkie......VII 726
Dryden, John.............II. 468
Lever, Charles James........VI 655
Pope, Alexander..........III. 192
ASHE, T.
Herrick, Robert........... II. 236
ASHLEY, W. J.
Jowett, Benjamin....VIII, 208, 212
Ricardo, David..........IV, 727
ASHWELL. A. R.
Wilberforce. Samuel........VI, 733
ASHLAND, R. BROOK.
Manley, Mrs. Mary de la Riviere
........................II, 693
ASQUITH, HERBERT HENRY.
FitzGerald, Edward........VII. 518
ASSER.
Alfred The Great..........I. 36
ASTOR, JOHN JACOB.
Halleck, Fitz-Greene........VI. 494
ATHERTON, GERTRUDE FRANKLIN.
Hamilton, Alexander........IV, 462
ATKINSON, W.
Wayland, Francis.........VI. 448
ATKINSON, WILLIAM P.
Buckle, Henry Thomas....VI. 285
Disraeli, Benjamin........VII 293
Trollope, Anthony........VII 460

INDEX TO CRITICISMS

ATTENBOROUGH, JOHN MAX,
Parr, Samuel .... V, 19, 21
ATTERBURY, FRANCIS,
Bentley, Richard .... III, 117, 120
Swift, Jonathan .... III, 213
ATTERBURY, LEWIS,
Atterbury, Francis .... III, 64
AUBREY, JOHN,
Abbot, George .... I, 725
Andrews, Lancelot .... I, 635
Ashmole, Elias .... II, 436
Aubrey, John .... II, 451
Ayton, Sir Robert .... I, 768
Bacon, Francis .... I, 641
Bacon, Roger .... I, 78
Barclay, Robert .... II, 411
Barrow, Isaac .... II, 310
Beaumont and Fletcher .... I, 578
Boyle, Robert .... II, 416
Butler, Samuel .... II, 329
Camden, William .... I, 621
Cartwright, William .... II, 70
Chaucer, Geoffrey .... I, 125
Chillingworth, William ..... II, 85
Cleveland, John .... II, 159
Corbet, Richard .... I. 743
Cowley, Abraham .... II, 194
D'Avenant, Sir William ......
.... II, 216
Denham, Sir John ...... II, 220, 220
Digby, Sir Kenelm .... II, 181
Dyer, Sir Edward .... I, 428
Fletcher, John .... I, 628
Fuller, Thomas .... II, 168
Greville, Sir Fulke .... I, 690
Hales, John .... II, 149
Hall, Joseph .... II, 147
Halley, Edmund .... III, 107
Harvey, William .... II, 155
Harrington, James ..... II, 307, 307
Herbert, Edward Lord ...... II, 95
Herbert, George .... I, 720
Hobbes, Thomas .... II, 320, 323
Hyde, Edward, Earl of Clarendon .... II, 301
Jonson, Ben .... I, 746
Lovelace, Richard .... II, 160
Mandeville, Sir John .... I, 95
Marvell, Andrew .... II, 314
Massinger, Philip .... II, 41
May, Thomas .... II, 118
Milton, John .... II, 243
Penn, William .... II, 626
Phillips, Katherine .... II, 179
Prynne, William .... II, 223
Raleigh, Sir Walter ..... I, 593, 601
Sanderson, Robert .... II, 178
Sandys, George .... II, 80, 82
Selden, John .... II, 137
Shadwell, Thomas .... II, 434
Shakespeare, William ... I, 499, 550
Sidney, Sir Philip .... I, 322
Spelman, Sir Henry .... II, 53
Spenser, Edmund .... I, 370
Suckling, Sir John .... II, 62
Taylor, John .... II, 132
Vaughn, Henry .... II, 441
Waller Edmund .... II, 378
Wilkins, John .... II, 227
Wither, George .... II, 212
Wood, Anthony .... II, 447

AUBREY, W. H. S.,
Fielding, Henry .... III, 354
Foote, Samuel .... III, 674
Gibbon, Edward .... IV, 190
Oldmixon, John .... III, 125
Paris, Matthew .... I, 76
Smollett, Tobias George ......
.... III, 582, 585
Swift, Jonathan .... III, 223
, William of Malmesbury ......
.... I, 54
Young, Edward .... III, 490
AUDLEY, SIR THOMAS,
Fisher, John .... I, 230
AUDUBON, JOHN JAMES,
Wilson, Alexander .... IV, 582
AUDUBON, MRS. JOHN J.,
Audubon, John James .... V, 697
AUERBACH, BERTHOLD,
Taylor, Bayard .... VII, 128
AULD, WILLIAM,
Burns, Robert .... IV, 237
AURINGER, OBEDIAH CYRUS,
Eggleston, Edward ....
.... VIII, 475, 477
AUSTEN, JANE,
Austen, Jane .... IV, 612
Scott, Sir Walter .... V, 147
AUSTIN, ALFRED,
Alfred the Great , ... I, 39
Arnold, Matthew ..... VII, 630, 638
Burns, Robert .... IV, 267
Dickens, Charles ...... VI, 554, 584
Disraeli, Benjamin .... VII, 279
Eliot, George .... VII, 173
Lytton, Edward Robert Bulwer
.... VIII, 45
Poets and Poetry .... IV, 10
Procter, Adelaide Anne .... VI, 395
Shelley, Percy Bysshe ..... IV, 695
Tennyson, Alfred Lord ... VIII, 102
AUSTIN, GEORGE LOWELL,
Longfellow, Henry Wadsworth
.... VII, 387, 394, 397
Phillips, Wendell .... VII, 553
AUSTIN, HENRY,
Timrod, Henry .... VI, 509,510
AUSTIN, J. T.,
Lytton, Sir Edward George Bulwer .... VI, 686
AUSTIN, L. F.,
Cibber, Theophilus .... III, 395
AUSTIN, MARY S.,
Freneau, Philip .... V. 186
AUSTIN, SARAH.,
Smith, Sydney .... V. 468
AUSTIN, WILLIAM STANTON, JR., AND RALPH J.,
Pye, Henry James .... IV, 580
AVEBURY, LORD,
Huxley, Thomas Henry ... VIII, 322
AVELING, EDWARD AND ELEANOR MARY,
Shelley, Percy Bysshe ..... IV, 711
AVERY, BENJAMIN P.,
Clare, John .... VI, 399
AXON, WILLIAM E. A.,
Ainsworth, William Harrison
.... VII, 488
AYRE, WILLIAM,
Pope, Alexander .... III, 170

AYTOUN, WILLIAM EDMONDSTOUNE,
Cunningham, Allan .... V, 384
Hogg, James ...... V, 262, 264, 267

BABCOCK, W. H.,
George, Henry ...... VIII, 381
BABINGTON, CHURCHILL,
Peacock, Reginald .... I, 189
BACKUS, TRUMAN J.,
Berners, Lord .... I, 229
Burnet, Thomas .... II, 597
BACON, DELIA,
Shakespeare, William .... I, 543
BACON, FRANCIS LORD,
Bacon, Francis ...... I, 638, 639, 653
Books .... III, 5
History .... VI, 5
Knowledge .... V, 5
Poets and Poetry .... IV, 5
BACON, LEONARD,
Hopkins, Samuel .... IV, 438
Williams, Roger .... II, 356
BACON, R. H.,
Gilfillan, George .... VII, 151
BACON, THEODORE,
Bacon, Delia .... VI, 203
BADEAU, ADAM,
Disraeli, Benjamin .... VII, 280
BAGEHOT, WALTER,
Brougham, Henry Lord VI, 529,531
Browning, Robert .... VII, 700
Burke, Edmund .... IV, 304
Butler, Joseph .... III, 307, 313
Canning, George .... V. 67
Clough, Arthur Hugh ...... VI, 252
Cobden, Richard .... VI, 442
Coleridge, Hartley ...... V, 576, 577
Cowper, William .... IV, 388
Cudworth, Ralph .... II, 386
Dickens, Charles .... VI, 583
Disraeli, Benjamin .... VII, 284
Eliot, George .... VII, 199
Gibbon, Edward ...... IV, 186, 192
Gladstone, William Ewart VIII, 387
Gray, Thomas .... III, 568
Hazlitt, William .... V, 104
Horner, Francis .... IV, 630
Hume, David .... III, 666
Jeffrey, Francis Lord .... V, 654
Keble, John .... VI, 463
Lewis, Sir George Cornewall ...
.... VI, 335, 338
Malthus, Thomas Robert ...... V, 251
Mill, James .... V, 310
Mill, John Stuart ..... VI, 707, 714
Milton, John .... II, 291
Montagu, Lady Mary Wortley.
.... III 464, 466
Newman, John Henry ..... VII, 750
Newton, Sir Isaac .... II, 725
Pitt, William .... IV, 509
Pope, Alexander .... III, 153, 189
Saint-John, Henry .... III, 288
Scott, Sir Walter .... V, 142
Shelley, Percy Bysshe ...... IV, 708
Smith, Sydney .... V, 471
Southey, Robert .... V, 415
Stanhope, Philip Henry Earl.
.... VII, 46, 47
Sterne, Laurence .III, 510, 511. 514

INDEX TO CRITICISMS 547

Vol. and Page
Tennyson Alfred Lord.....VIII, 96
Thackeray, William Makepeace.
........................VI, 314
Wordsworth, William ....V, 626
BAILDON, H. BELLYSE.
Stevenson, Robert Louis......
..................VIII, 238, 240
BAILEY, BENJAMIN.
Keats, John..............IV, 664
BAILEY, JOHN BURN.
Amory, Thomas........IV, 47, 48
Somerville, Mary............VI, 658
BAILEY, J. C.
Cowper, William...........IV, 393
Gibbon, Edward............IV, 177
Stevenson, Robert Louis..VIII, 245
BAILEY, HENRY TURNER,
Blackmore, Richard D.....VIII, 430
BAILEY, PHILIP JAMES,
Authors and Authorship...VIII, 7
Knowledge ....V, 8
Poets and Poetry...........IV, 8
BAILLIE, JOANNA,
Knowledge ....V, 7
Scott, Sir Walter...........V, 138
BAILLY, JEAN SYLVAIN,
Bacon, Francis.............I, 658
BAILY, FRANCIS,
Flamsteed, John............II, 663
BAIN, ALEXANDER,
Bacon Francis.............I, 668
Bentham, Jeremy..........V, 164
Brougham, Henry Lord.....VI, 528
Burns, Robert.............IV, 264
Cumberland, Richard........II, 624
Grote, George.........VI, 608, 610
Hume, David..............III, 663
Junius ....IV, 647
Locke, John...............II, 528
Macaulay, Thomas Babington
Lord.....................VI, 113
Mandeville, Bernard........III, 70
Mill, James....V, 306, 307, 309, 311
Mill, John Stuart ......V, 705, 716
Smith, Adam..............IV, 59
BAINTON, GEORGE,
Collins, William Wilkie......VII, 727
Pater, Walter Horatio....VIII, 277
BAKER, ADALLA L,
Cary, Phœbe..............VI, 641
BAKER, DAVID ERSKINE,
Savage, Richard............III, 132
BAKER, ERNEST A.,
Disraeli, Benjamin..........VII, 288
BAKER, GEORGE E.,
Seward, William Henry.......VI, 673
BAKER, HENRY BARTON,
Barbauld, Anna Lætitia........V, 25
Cibber, Colley.............III, 373
Colman, George...........V, 317
Foote, Samuel............III, 674
Hook, Theodore Edward.....V, 358
Montagu, Lady Mary Wortley.
........................III, 465
Robinson, Henry..........IV, 412
Sheridan, Richard Brinsley.IV, 601
Wilkes, John..............IV, 334
BAKER, SIR RICHARD,
Donne, John...............I, 711
BAKER, SAMUEL W.,
Livingstone, David..........VI, 731

Vol. and Page
BALDWIN, A. C.,
Barlow, Joel...........IV, 575, 576
BALDWIN, CHARLES SEARS,
DeQuincey, Thomas.........VI, 130
BALDWIN, ELBERT F.,
Beasant, Sir Walter..VIII, 449, 451
BALDWIN, H.,
Butler, Samuel.............II, 331
BALDWIN, JAMES,
Barham, Richard Harris....V, 475
Barlow, Joel...............IV, 575
Berners, Lord..............I, 229
Boswell, James............IV, 218
Draper, John William.......VII, 503
Eadmer....................I, 52
Ellwood, Thomas..........II, 575
Fielding, Sarah............III, 518
Glover, Richard............IV, 18
Hawthorne, Nathaniel......VI, 354
Holland, Josiah Gilbert....VII, 336
Lytton, Sir Edward George Bul-
wer....................VI, 689
Park, Mungo..............IV, 486
Poe, Edgar Allan...........V, 547
Porter, Jane...............V, 674
Tennyson, Alfred Lord...VIII, 91
Webster, Daniel...........V, 729
Webster, John.............I, 677
Whitman, Walt...........VIII, 135
Wilkie, William...........III, 596
BALDWIN, J. M.,
Hildreth, Richard..........VI, 454
Wayland, Francis..........VI, 447
BALDWIN, LOAMMI,
Rumford, Count...........IV, 590
BALE, JOHN,
Cranmer, Thomas...........I, 270
Leland, John...............I, 262
Mandeville, Sir John..........I, 95
Pole, Reginald.............I, 280
BALFOUR, ARTHUR JAMES,
Berkeley, George.III, 322, 324, 334
Cobden, Richard...........VI, 543
Spencer, Herbert.........VIII, 484
BALFOUR, CLARA LUCAS,
Barbauld, Anna Lætitia......V, 25
BALFOUR, GRAHAM,
Stevenson, Robert Louis....
..................VIII, 239, 242
BALL, SIR ROBERT S.,
Airy, Sir George Biddell...VIII, 183
Halley, Edmund......III, 108, 109
Herschel, Sir John Frederick
William................VI, 624
Newton, Sir Isaac........II, 720, 726
BALLANTINE, WILLIAM,
Planché, James Robinson...VII, 215
Talfourd, Sir Thomas Noon...V, 760
BALLANTYNE, JAMES,
Edgeworth, Maria...........V, 568
BALLANTYNE, JOHN,
Defoe, Daniel...........III, 24, 33
BALLOU, MATURIN M.,
Bacon, Francis.............I, 648
Combe, George.............VI, 89
Maturin, Charles Robert....IV, 767
Porson, Richard............IV, 526
BALMANNO, MARY,
Lamb, Charles.............V, 233
BANCROFT, AARON,
Washington, George........IV, 357

Vol. and Page
BANCROFT, FREDERIC,
Seward, William Henry.......VI, 675
Sumner, Charles............VI, 755
BANCROFT, GEORGE,
Bancroft, George..........VIII, 60
Berkeley, George...........III, 322
Edwards, Jonathan.........III, 390
Emerson, Ralph Waldo......
..................VII, 350, 358
Everett, Edward......VI, 423, 426
Franklin, Benjamin.....IV, 87, 87
Hakluyt, Richard...........I, 446
Hamilton, Alexander........IV, 459
Hutchinson, Thomas.......III, 708
Hemans, Felicia Dorothea... V, 258
Irving, Washington.........VI, 147
Jefferson, Thomas..........V, 47
Lincoln, Abraham..........VI, 413
Lowell, James Russell......VIII, 37
Marshall, John.............V, 285
Mather, Cotton............II, 728
Penn, William.............II, 630
Prescott, William Hickling...
....................VI, 182, 190
Raleigh, Sir Walter..........I, 594
Smith, John................I, 698
Stanhope, Philip Henry Earl.
........................VII, 47
Taylor, Bayard.............VII, 132
Williams, Roger.............II, 356
BANCROFT, SIR SQUIRE BAN-
CROFT,
Sheridan, Richard Brinsley..IV, 602
BANCROFT, THOMAS,
Shakespeare, William.........I, 549
Shirley, James..............II, 190
BANFIELD, FRANK,
Wesley, John..........IV, 110, 117
BANNATYNE, RICHARD,
Knox, John................I, 295
BARBAULD, ANNA LÆTITIA,
Addison, Joseph.......II, 655, 658
Akenside, Mark............III, 543
Burney, Frances............V, 343
Burns, Robert..............IV, 249
Byron, George Gordon Lord.
..................IV, 749, 756
Fielding, Henry............III, 351
Johnson, Samuel..........III, 754
Montagu, Elizabeth........IV, 402
Priestley, Joseph.......IV, 447, 452
Richardson, Samuel
..................III, 433, 435, 439
BARCLAY, ALEXANDER,
Literature..................I, 7
Skelton, John..............I, 219
BARHAM, RICHARD HARRIS,
Scott, Sir Walter...........V, 149
BARHAM, R. H. DALTON,
Barham, Richard Harris........V, 474
Hook,Theodore Edward.V, 356, 358
Smith, James............V., 338
BARKER, C.
Defoe, Daniel.............III, 45
BARKER, EDMUND HENRY,
Jones, Sir William..........IV, 198
BARKER, G. F. RUSSELL,
Burnett, James............IV, 347
Carter, Elizabeth..........IV, 493
Clive, Caroline.............VI, 741
Echard, Laurence..........III, 22

INDEX TO CRITICISMS

	Vol. and Page
Frere, John Hookham	V, 488
Hawkesworth, John	III, 610
Hervey. John Lord	III, 129, 131
Hill, John	III, 645
Holcroft, Thomas	IV, 545
Horner. Francis	IV, 631
Lamb, Lady Caroline	V, 82
Langhorne, John	III, 701
Lewis, Sir George Cornewall	VI, 338
Lyttleton, George Lord	III, 611
Pitt, William	III, 680
BARKER, H. BARTON,	
Colman, George	IV 203
BARKER, MRS ,	
Swift, Jonathan	III, 212
BARKER, WILLIAM,	
Chaucer, Geoffrey	I,·135
BARKSTEAD, WILLIAM,	
Shakespeare, William	I, 454
BARLOW, GEORGE,	
Marston, Philip Bourke	VII, 627
Whitman, Walt	VIII, 145
BARLOW, JOEL,	
Paine, Thomas	IV, 532
BARNARD, ANNE LADY,	
Hume, David	III, 650
BARNARD, AND GUYOT,	
Brougham, Henry Lord	VI, 522
Canning, George	V, 64
Kent, James	V, 500
King, Thomas Starr	VI, 408
Leighton, Robert	II, 358
Pitt, William	IV, 507
Usher, James	II, 152
BARNES, ALBERT,	
Johnson, Samuel	III, 741
Marshall, John	V, 284
Miller, Hugh	VI, 64
Paley, William	IV, 476
Whewell, William	VI, 471
BARNFIELD, RICHARD,	
Daniel, Samuel	I, 613
Drayton, Michael	I, 706
Shakespeare, William	I, 456
Sidney, Sir Philip	I, 321
Spenser, Edmund	I, 378, 392
Watson, Thomas	I, 337
BARON, JOHN,	
Hunter, John	IV, 164
BARON, R.,	
Jonson, Ben	I, 757
BARRETT, LAWRENCE.	
Boker, George Henry	VII, 766
Browning, Robert	VII, 691, 708
BARRIE. JAMES MATTHEW,	
Knowledge	V, 10
Stevenson, Robert Louis	VIII, 236, 240, 244, 247
Thackeray, William Makepeace	VI, 319
BARRINGTON, SIR JONAH,	
Edgeworth, Maria	V, 565
Morgan, Sydney Owenson Lady	VI, 194
BARROW, JOHN,	
Raleigh, Sir Walter	I, 603
BARROWS. CHARLES H.,	
George, Henry	VIII, 379
BARROWS. JOHN HENRY,	
Beecher, Henry Ward.	VII, 601, 608

	Vol. and Page
BARRY, JOHN D.,	
Field, Eugene	VIII, 315
Stoddard, Richard Henry.	VIII, 495
BARRY, WILLIAM,	
Newman, John Henry	VII, 745, 750, 755
BARTLETT, DAVID W.,	
Greeley, Horace	VI, 670
BARTLETT, THOMAS,	
Butler, Joseph	III, 307
BARTOL, CYRUS AUGUSTUS,	
Beecher, Henry Ward.	VII, 601, 608
Brooks, Phillips	VIII, 231
Bushnell, Horace	VII, 70, 71
Emerson, Ralph Waldo	VII, 349, 373
Knowledge	V, 9
Whipple, Edwin Percy	VII, 595
BARTON, BERNARD,	
Bloomfield, Robert	IV, 724
Cunningham, Allan	V, 383
Montgomery, Robert	VI, 48
Tupper, Martin Farquhar	VII, 732
BARTON, LUCY,	
Barton, Bernard	V, 596
BASCOM. JOHN,	
Akenside Mark	III, 545
Burns, Robert	IV, 259
Carlyle, Thomas	VII, 270
Chaucer, Geoffrey	I, 145
Collins, William	III, 420
Cowper, William	IV, 389
Dryden, John	II, 503
Edwards, Jonathan	III, 387
Emerson, Ralph Waldo	VII, 374
Fiske, John	VIII, 457
Hamilton Sir William	VI 56
Hooker, Richard	I, 408
Johnson, Samuel	III, 760
Knowledge	V, 9
Mandeville, Sir John	I, 96
Milton, John	II, 293
Paley, William	IV, 474
Percy, Thomas	IV, 564
Reid, Thomas	IV, 286
Scott, Sir Walter	V, 160
Shakespeare, William	I, 568
Shelley, Percy Bysshe	IV, 713
Spencer, Herbert	VIII, 480
Steele, Sir Richard	II, 764
Wordsworth, William	V, 643
BASKERVILLE, WILLIAM MALONE.	
Lanier, Sidney	VII, 326, 330
BASSE, WILLIAM.	
Shakespeare, William	I, 448
BASTARD, THOMAS,	
Barnes, Barnabe	I, 439
BATCHELOR, GEORGE,	
Very, Jones	VII, 227
BATE, PERCY H.,	
Rossetti, Gabriel Charles Dante	VII, 443
BATES, ARLO,	
Arnold, Matthew	VII, 646
Blake William	V, 64
Browning, Robert	VII, 706
Chaucer, Geoffrey	I, 171
Emerson, Ralph Waldo	VII, 377
Hawthorne, Nathaniel	VI, 355
Keats, John	IV, 683

	Vol. and Page
O'Reilly, John Boyle	VII, 767
Spenser, Edmund	I, 400
Steele, Sir Richard	II, 768
BATES, CHARLOTTE FISKE,	
Whittier, John Greenleaf	VIII, 115, 127
BATES, KATHARINE LEE	
Alcott. Louisa May	VII, 668
Brown, Charles Brockder	IV, 554
Bryant, William Cullen	VII, 127
Cary, Phœbe	VI, 641
Curtis, George William	VIII, 189
Davidson, Lucretia Maria	V, 28
Emerson, Ralph Waldo	VII, 377
Field, Eugene	VIII, 317
Franklin, Benjamin	IV, 92, 105
Freneau, Philip	V, 188
Fuller, Sarah Margaret	V, 673
Hawthorne, Nathaniel	VI, 361
Hayne, Paul Hamilton	VII, 594
Jackson, Helen Hunt	VII, 576
Lanier, Sidney	VII, 330
Lincoln, Abraham	VI, 421
Longfellow, Henry Wadsworth	VII, 414
Marshall, John	V, 286
Mather, Cotton	II, 732
Mather, Increase	II, 600
Motley, John Lothrop	VII, 96
Paulding, James Kirke	VI, 228
Poe, Edgar Allan	V, 549
Poets and Poetry	IV, 10
Prescott, William Hickling	VI, 191
Rossetti, Christina Georgina	VIII, 269
Sedgwick, Catharine Maria	VI, 508
Sewall, Samuel	III, 18
Simms, William Gilmore	VI, 600
Stoddard, Richard Henry.	VII, 498
Timrod, Henry	VI, 510
Ward, Nathaniel	II, 130
Washington, George	IV, 369
Webster, Daniel	V, 727
Willis, Nathaniel Parker	VII, 492
Woolman, John	III, 597
BATES, WILLIAM.	
Ainsworth, William Harrison.	VII, 486
Brown, Thomas	II, 541
Brydges, Sir Samuel Egerton.	V, 321
Campbell, Thomas	V, 438
Cunningham, Allan	V, 384
Disraeli, Isaac	V, 512
Hook, Theodore Edward	V, 357
Lamb, Charles	V, 237
Lockhart, John Gibson	V, 758
Maginn, William	V, 386
Moore, Thomas	V, 717
Rogers, Samuel	VI, 35
Smith, James	V, 339
Tennyson, Alfred Lord	VIII, 88
BATHURST, LORD,	
Atterbury, Francis	III, 64
BAUDOIN, J.,	
Sidney, Sir Philip	I, 324
BAX, ERNEST BELFORT,	
Jevons, William Stanley	VII, 491
Mill, John Stuart	VII, 709
Smith, Adam	IV, 67
BAXTER, RICHARD,	
Baxter, Richard	II, 423

INDEX TO CRITICISMS 549

	Vol. and Page
Books	III, 5
Cowley, Abraham	II, 198
Davies, Sir John	I, 632
Greville, Sir Fulke	I, 690
Hale, Sir Matthew	II, 306
Herbert, George	I 722
History	VI 5
Philips Katherine	II, 180
Selden, John	II, 138
Villiers, George	II, 376
Wither, George	II, 213

BAYLY, ADA ELLEN (EDNA LYALL).
  Gaskell, Elizabeth Cleghorn......VI, 429, 433

BAYNE, PETER.
Arnold, Matthew	VII, 634
Blackie, John Stuart	VIII, 304
Brontë, Charlotte	VI, 29, 29
Browning, Elizabeth Barrett	VI, 237
Burns, Robert	IV, 261
Coleridge, Samuel Taylor	V, 224
Dickens, Charles	VI, 583
Henry the Minstrel	I, 202
Hyde, Edward, Earl of Clarendon	II, 301, 304
Kingsley, Charles	VII, 25, 30
Lytton, Sir Edward George Bulwer	VI, 697
Miller, Hugh	VI, 62, 64
Milton, John	II, 248, 252, 265
Tennyson, Alfred Lord	VIII, 82
Thackeray, William Makepeace	VI, 313
Whitman, Walt	VIII, 138

BAYNE, RONALD.
Feltham, Owen	II, 310
Havergal, Frances Ridley	VII, 167

BAYNE, THOMAS.
Alison, Sir Archibald	VI, 520
Campbell, Thomas	V, 441
Douglas, Gawin,	I, 215
Dunbar, William	I, 226
Grahame, James	IV, 568
Gray, David	V, 262
Hamilton, Thomas	V, 395
Hamilton, William	III, 337
Henryson, Robert	I, 209
Hogg, James	V, 268
Knox, William	V, 30
Mickle, William Julius	IV, 41
Motherwell, William	V, 277
Oliphant, Carolina	V, 479
Pollok, Robert	V, 73
Ramsay, Allan	III, 409
Rossetti, Gabriel Charles Dante	VII, 452
Shairp, John Campbell	VII, 570
Smith, Alexander	VI, 519
Tannahill, Robert	IV, 550
Turner, Charles Tennyson	VII, 162
Wilkie, William	III, 595, 596

BAYNE, WILLIAM.
Darwin, Erasmus	IV, 423
Hill, Aron	III, 278
Thomson, James	III, 257, 261, 263, 264, 265
Wordsworth, William	V, 624

BAYNES, THOMAS SPENCER.
  Beddoes, Thomas Lovell......V, 587

	Vol. and Page
Brydges, Sir Samuel Egerton	V, 320
Burton, Robert	II, 37
Carlyle, Thomas	VII, 236
Carter, Elizabeth	IV, 491
Clarke, Adam	V, 184
Grahame, James	IV, 566
Hayley, William	IV, 651
Henry, Robert	IV, 106
Holcroft, Thomas	IV, 544
Howe, John	II, 546
Jortin, John	III, 551
Moore, John	IV, 427
Orme, Robert	IV, 414
Shakespeare, William	I, 452
Shelley, Percy Bysshe	IV, 709
Thomas of Erceldoune	I, 83

BEALE, DOROTHEA,
  Browning, Robert......VII, 692

BEARD, THOMAS,
  Marlowe, Christopher......I, 346

BEATTIE, JAMES,
Addison, Joseph	II, 643
Arbuthnot, John	III, 84
Beattie, James	IV, 431
Berkeley, George	III, 329
Blackmore, Sir Richard	II, 747
Blair, Hugh	IV, 404
Burke, Edmund	IV, 299
Churchill, Charles	III, 476
Defoe, Daniel	III, 33
Dryden, John	II, 487, 497
Fielding, Henry	III, 356
Gibbon, Edward	IV, 180
Gray, Thomas	III, 553, 563
Hobbes, Thomas	III, 323
Johnson, Samuel	III, 743
Johnston, Arthur	II, 54
Locke, John	II, 532
Milton, John	II, 259
Montagu, Elizabeth	IV, 399
Pope, Alexander	III, 178, 183
Quarles, Francis	II, 78
Ramsay, Allan	III, 405
Reid, Thomas	IV, 283
Saint-John, Henry	III, 286
Spenser, Edmund	I, 394
Warton, Thomas	IV, 76
Young, Edward	III, 492

BEATTIE, WILLIAM,
Akenside, Mark	III, 543
Campbell, Thomas	V, 435
Fielding, Henry	III, 345
History	VI, 6
Spenser, Edmund	I, 393

BEAUMONT, SIR JOHN,
  Beaumont, Francis......I, 586
  Jonson, Ben......I, 759

BECKER, BERNARD HENRY,
  Caxton, William......I, 198
  Mandeville, Sir John......I, 96

BECKET, ANDREW,
  Warburton, William......III, 691

BECKET, THOMAS,
  Macpherson, James......IV, 273

BECON, THOMAS,
  Latimer, Hugh......I, 267

BEDE,
  Bede......I, 26
  Cædmon......I, 21

BEDDOES, THOMAS,
  Gray, Thomas......III, 564

	Vol. and Page
BEDDOES, THOMAS LOVELL,	
Beddoes, Thomas Lovell	V, 584
Browning, Robert	VI, 685
Byron, George Gordon Lord	IV, 757
Campbell, Thomas	V, 442
Carlyle, Thomas	VII, 261
Daniel, Samuel	I, 616
DeQuincey, Thomas	VI, 124
Peacock, Thomas Love	VI, 475
Procter, Bryan Waller	VI, 744, 747
Shelley, Percy Bysshe	V, 705
Spenser, Edmund	I, 392, 395
White, Henry Kirke	IV, 487

BEECHER, CHARLES,
  Beecher, Lyman......VI, 339

BEECHER, HENRY WARD,
Authors and Authorship	VIII, 5
Lincoln, Abraham	VI, 412
Phillips, Wendell	VII, 553
Spencer, Herbert	VIII, 482

BEECHER, LYMAN,
  Dwight, Timothy......IV, 626

BEECHER, WILLIAM C., AND SCOVILLE, SAMUEL,
  Beecher, Henry Ward......VII, 606
  Beecher, Lyman......VI, 340

BEECHING, H. C.,
Bunyan, John	II, 405
Church, Richard William	VII, 730
Gray, Thomas	III, 563
Morris, William	VIII, 338
Newman, John Henry	VII, 744, 755
Tennyson, Alfred Lord	VIII, 97, 110
Vaughan, Henry	II, 445

BEECHEY, HENRY,
  Reynolds, Sir Joshua......IV, 139

BEER, GEORGE L.,
  Fiske, John......VIII, 458

BEERBOHM, MAX,
  Stevenson, Robert Louis......VIII, 253

BEERS, HENRY A.,
Akenside, Mark	III, 543
Bacon, Delia	VI, 202
Beattie, James	IV, 433
Beecher, Henry Ward	VII, 609
Brainard, John Gardiner Calkins	V, 85
Brown, Charles Brockden	IV, 557
Cary, Alice	VI, 639
Chatterton, Thomas	III, 533, 540
Collins, William	III, 422
Edwards, Jonathan	III, 394
Freneau, Philip	V, 188
Gray, Thomas	III, 557, 560
Griswold, Rufus Wilmot	VI, 76
Hawthorne, Nathaniel	VI, 361
Hopkinson, Thomas	IV, 133
Johnson, Samuel	III, 764
Langland, William	I, 116
Lanier, Sidney	VII, 330
Layamon	I, 64
Lewis, Matthew Gregory	IV, 633, 634
Livingston, William	IV, 110
Longfellow, Henry Wadsworth	VII, 395, 399
Mallet, David	III, 497
Map, Walter	I, 61
Mason, William	IV, 326

550 INDEX TO CRITICISMS

Vol. and Page

Mather, Cotton............II, 731
Milton, John..............II, 298
Morgan, Lady Sydney Owenson ....VI, 192
Morris, William........VIII, 338
Motley, John Lothrop....VII, 95
Newman, John Henry.....VII, 750
O'Shaughnessy, Arthur Wm.
 Edgar................VII, 324
Overbury, Sir Thomas......I, 441
Paine, Thomas............IV, 539
Percy, Thomas............IV, 565
Poe, Edgar Allan..........V, 545
Pope, Alexander..........III, 174
Prentice, George Denison..VI, 601
Radcliffe, Ann Ward......IV, 721
Read, Thomas Buchanan..VI, 678
Reeve, Clara.............IV, 512
Rossetti, Gabriel Charles
 Dante................VII, 447
Saxe, John Godfrey......VII, 616
Scott, Sir Walter..........V, 147
Sewall, Samuel...........III, 19
Simms, William Gilmore...VI, 600
Smith, John..............I, 700
Spenser, Edmund..........I, 387
Steevens, George.........IV, 408
Sylvester, Joshua..........I, 608
Taylor, Bayard..........VII, 136
Taylor, William...........V, 320
Tennyson, Alfred Lord...VIII, 96
Thackeray, William Makepeace ....VI, 322
Ticknor, George..........VI, 614
Thomson, James..........III, 261
Tusser, Thomas............I, 310
Vaux, Thomas Lord........I, 276
Walpole, Horace..........IV, 317
Warton, Thomas..........IV, 75
Watson, Thomas...........I, 337
Webster, Daniel...........V, 727
White, Henry Kirke.......IV, 487
Willis, Nathaniel Parker...
 ....VI, 488, 492
Wilson, John..........V, 749, 751
Winthrop, John...........II, 109
Winthrop, Theodore......VI, 267
BEETON, SAMUEL ORCHART,
 Mackay, Charles.........VII, 764
 Moir, David Macbeth......V, 704
 Warner, William..........I, 436
BEGBIE, WARBURTON,
 De Quincey, Thomas......VI, 119
BEHN, APHRA,
 Waller, Edmund..........II, 380
BELFIELD, HENRY H.,
 DeQuincey, Thomas......VI, 128
BELL, HENRY GLASSFORD,
 Gray, David.............VI, 261
 Hogg, James..............V, 265
BELL, J. M.,
 Lytton, Sir Edward George
  Bulwer...............VI, 691
BELL, MACKENZIE,
 Arnold, Sir Edwin.......VIII, 504
 Aytoun, William Edmondstoune ....VI, 446
 De Vere, Aubrey Thomas.VIII, 464
 Hemans, Felicia Dorothea..V, 261
 Ingelow, Jean...........VIII, 377
 Oliphant, Carolina.......V, 479

Vol and Page

Rossetti, Christina Georgina..
 ....VIII, 274
BELL, ROBERT,
 Canning, George...........V, 64
 Cartwright, William.......II, 72
 Chaucer, Geoffrey......I, 138, 143
 Dekker, Thomas..........II, 60
 Dryden John........II, 465, 502
 Fletcher, Phineas.........II, 115
 Grimoald, Nicholas........II, 284
 Heywood, Thomas........II, 126
 Shadwell, Thomas........II, 434
 Shirley, James...........II, 191
 Surrey Earl of............I, 257
 Thomson, James.........III, 268
BELL, THOMAS,
 White, Gilbert...........IV, 148
BELL, W. A.,
 Mann Horace...........VI, 200
BELLEW, J. C. M.,
 Dibdin, Charles..........IV, 586
 Southwell, Robert........I, 361
BELLOC, BESSIE RAYNER,
 Eliot, George...........VII, 191
 Fullerton, Georgiana Charlotte
  Lady ....VII, 566
 Jameson, Anna...........VI, 214
 Manning, Henry Edward VIII, 165
 Priestley, Joseph........IV, 448
 Procter, Adelaide Anne. VI, 394,396
BELLOWS, HENRY WHITNEY,
 Bryant, William Cullen....VII, 111
 Channing, William Ellery..V, 371
 Dewey, Orville..........VII, 496
BELOE, WILLIAM,
 Bruce, James............IV, 205
 Cumberland, Richard.....IV, 560
 Fielding, Henry.........III, 352
 Gascoigne, George........I, 308
 Greene, Robert ....I, 344
 Harvey, Gabriel..........I, 696
 Ireland, William Henry....V, 290
 Jenyns, Soame ....IV, 31, 33
 Porson, Richard.........IV, 521
 Taylor, Jeremy...........II, 207
 Wakefield, Gilbert.......IV, 415
 Walpole, Horace.........IV, 311
 Wilkes, John............IV, 333
 Williams, Helen Maria.....V, 74
BELOW, IDA COMSTOCK,
 Field, Eugene..........VIII, 316
BELSHAM, WILLIAM,
 Locke, John.............II, 532
 Smollett, Tobias George...III, 581
 Pope, Alexander.........III, 175
BENDALL, CECIL,
 Mürlle, Friedrich Max...VIII, 439
BENEDIX, RODERICH,
 Shakespeare, William......I, 506
BENHAM, WILLIAM,
 Cowper, William......IV, 379, 383
BENJAMIN MARCUS,
 Proctor, Richard Anthony.VII, 661
BENJAMIN, PARK,
 Hawthorne, Nathaniel....VI, 363
 Knowles, James Sheridan..VI, 286
BENJAMIN, S. G. W.,
 Franklin, Benjamin.......IV, 90
 Longfellow, Henry Wadsworth ....VII, 407
 Webster, Daniel..........V, 723

Vol. and Page

BENLOWES, W,
 Fletcher, Phineas.........II, 115
BENN, ALFRED W.,
 Buckle, Henry T.........VI, 283
 Gray, Asa...............VII, 670
 Maine, Sir Henry James Sumner ....VII, 652
 Owen, Sir Richard......VIII, 174
BENNETT, JAMES RISDON,
 Harvey, William..........II 157
BENNETT, LEIGH,
 Sternhold, Thomas........I, 262
 Toplady, Augustus Montague.
  ....III, 682
 Watts, Isaac............III, 251
BENNET, WILLIAM,
 Jones, Sir William.......IV, 197
BENSON, ARTHUR CHRISTOPHER,
 Blake, William...........V, 62
 Brontë, Charlotte.........VI, 31
 Browning, Elizabeth Barrett.....VI, 240, 242, 242, 247
 Browning, Robert.......VII, 714
 Earle, John..............II, 184
 Gray, Thomas........III, 556,573
 Hales, John.............II, 150
 Keble, John.............VI, 465
 Lamb, Charles............V, 244
 Laud, William............II, 92
 Lytton, Edward Robert Bulwer Earl.............VIII, 49
 Marvell, Andrew......II, 315, 319
 Milton, John............II, 275
 More, Henry........III, 373, 375
 Rossetti, Christina Georgina..
  ....VIII, 273
 Rossetti, Gabriel Charles Dante
  ....VII, 439
 White, Henry Kirke.....IV, 490
 Wilson, John.............V, 753
BENSON, EUGENE,
 Curtis, George William...VIII, 189
 Hamerton, Philip Gilbert.VIII, 281
 Poe, Edgar Allan.........V, 554
BENTHAM, JEREMY,
 Blackstone, Sir William...III, 703
BENTLEY, RICHARD,
 Bentley, Richard........III, 119
 Pearson, John...........II, 369
BENTON, JOEL,
 Emerson, Ralph Waldo...VII, 379
 Greeley, Horace.........VI, 669
 Poe, Edgar Allan......V, 549, 552
 Thoreau, Henry David...VI, 274
 Webster, Noah...........V, 429
BENTON, THOMAS HART,
 Adams, John Quincy......V, 516
 Marshall, John...........V, 283
BENTZON, TH. (MME. BLANC),
 Browning, Elizabeth Barrett..
  ....VI, 234
 Browning, Robert.......VII, 682
BERDMORE, S.,
 Thackeray, William Makepeace ....VI, 315
BERDOE, EDWARD,
 Browning, Robert.......VII, 712
BERINGTON, JOSEPH,
 Bede ....I, 27
 Dunstan ....I, 43

INDEX TO CRITICISMS 551

	Vol. and Page
Grosseteste, Robert	I, 73
Paris, Matthew	I, 75
BERKELEY, GEORGE,	
Addison, Joseph	II, 647, 654
Books,	III, 6
Newton, Sir Isaac	II, 721
BERKELEY, GEORGE MONCK,	
Berkeley, George	III, 320, 322
Swift, Jonathan	III, 208
BERKELEY, JOHN R. P.,	
Borrow, George Henry	VII, 307
BERKENHEAD, J.,	
Beaumont and Fletcher	I, 579
Butler, Samuel	II, 330
BERKENHOUT, JOHN,	
Lyly, John	I, 421
BERNARD, BAYLE,	
Banim, John	V, 391
Griffin, Gerald	V, 354
Lever, Charles James	VI, 653
Lover, Samuel	VI, 543, 545
Maturin, Charles Robert	IV, 768
Morgan, Sydney Owenson Lady	VI, 195
BERNARD, JOHN,	
Macklin, Charles	IV, 343
BERRY, MARY,	
Baillie, Joanna	V, 691
Brougham, Henry Lord	VI, 522
Burney, Frances	V, 344
Edgeworth, Maria	V, 562
Gibbon, Edward	IV, 173
Godwin, William	V, 300
Walpole, Horace	IV, 312
BERTHELETTE, THOMAS,	
Gower, John	I, 172
BESANT, WALTER,	
Addison, Joseph	II, 660
Alfred the Great	I, 41
Bunyan, John	II, 397
Calverley, Charles Stuart	VII, 543
Chatterton, Thomas	III, 533
D'Urfey, Thomas	II, 687, 688
Eliot, George	VII, 194
Hawthorne, Nathaniel	VI, 369
Jefferies, Richard	VII, 618, 619
Johnson, Samuel	III, 766
Kingsley, Charles	VII, 32
Pope, Alexander	III, 174
Reade, Charles	VII, 529, 531, 534
Scott, Sir Walter	V, 144
Tennyson, Alfred Lord	VIII, 105
BEST, H. D.,	
Johnson, Samuel	III, 728
BETHAN-EDWARDS, M.,	
Edwards, Amelia Blandford	VIII, 177
Young, Arthur	IV, 655
BETHUNE, GEORGE WASHINGTON,	
Browning, Elizabeth Barrett	VI, 244
Coleridge, Sara	V, 734
Hemans, Felicia Dorothea	V, 259
Kemble, Frances Ann	VIII, 215
Landon, Letitia Elizabeth	V, 309
Mitford, Mary Russell	VI, 44
Robinson, Mary	IV, 412
Smith, Charlotte	IV, 498
Tighe, Mary	IV, 551
Walton, Isaac	II, 347
Williams, Helen Maria	V, 75

	Vol. and Page
BETTANY, G. T.,	
Darwin, Charles Robert	VII, 420
Hunter, John	IV, 166
Hutton, James	IV, 338, 340
BEVAN, CHARLES DACRES.	
Beddoes, Thomas Lovell	V, 585
BEYLE, HENRI (COUNT DE STENDHAL),	
Byron, George Gordon Lord	IV, 733
BIAGI, GUIDO,	
Shelley, Mary Wollstonecraft	V, 701
BICKERSTETH, EDWARD,	
Clarke, Adam	V, 185
Doddridge, Philip	III, 303
Fuller, Thomas	II, 170
Hall, Joseph	II, 146, 147
Henry, Matthew	II, 585
Heylin, Peter	II, 175
Hooker, Richard	I, 407
Horne, George	IV, 144
Horsley, Samuel	IV, 496
Howe, John	II, 546
Jewell, John	I, 294
Jortin, John	III, 552
Lardner, Nathaniel	III, 523
Latimer, Hugh	I, 269
Leighton, Robert	II, 359
Leland, John	III, 500
Leslie, Charles	II, 680
Locke, John	II, 523, 532
Mather, Cotton	II, 730
Neal, Daniel	III, 140
Owen, John	II, 352
Rutherford, Samuel	II, 167
Sanderson, Robert	II, 179
Secker, Thomas	III, 522
Sherlock, William	II, 561
Taylor, Jeremy	II, 209
Tillotson, John Robert	II, 440
Toplady, Augustus Montague	III, 681
Usher, James	II, 154
Warburton, William	III, 691
Waterland, Daniel	III, 103
Watts, Isaac	III, 250
BICKNELL, PERCY FAVOR,	
Church, Richard William	VII, 731
Merivale Charles	VIII, 217
Sewall, Samuel	III, 19
BIDWELL, W. H.,	
Strickland, Agnes	VI, 768
BIGELOW, JACOB,	
Ticknor, George	VI, 614
BIGELOW, JOHN,	
Browning, Elizabeth Barrett	VI, 233
Bryant, William Cullen	VII, 113, 117, 119, 125
Fox, Charles James	IV, 501
Franklin, Benjamin	IV, 97, 98, 105
Milnes, Richard Monckton	VII, 561
Sumner, Charles	VI, 753
BIGELOW, WALTER STORRS,	
Browning, Robert	VII, 710
BINNEY, HORACE,	
Marshall, John	V, 281
Wilson, Alexander	IV, 582
BIRCH, THOMAS,	
Boyle, Robert	II, 417
Buchanan, George	I, 315
Chaucer, Geoffrey	I, 126

	Vol. and Page
Cockburn, Catherine	III, 276
Hale, Sir Matthew	II, 306
Milton, John	II, 244
Raleigh, Sir Walter	I, 594
BIRCHENOUGH, MABEL C.,	
Ingelow, Jean	VIII, 378
BIRD, FREDERICK MAYER,	
Beaumont, Joseph	II, 461
Southwell, Robert	I, 360
Waterland, Daniel	III, 102
Wesley, Charles	IV, 37, 39
Whiston, William	III, 304
BIRDWOOD, GEORGE,	
Livingstone, David	VI, 730
BIRRELL, AUGUSTINE,	
Arnold, Matthew	VII, 629, 632 638
Authors and Authorship	VIII, 9
Bagehot, Walter	VII, 100
Books,	III, 10
Borrow, George Henry	VII, 310, 313
Brontë, Charlotte	VI, 21, 25, 27, 30,
Browning, Robert	VII, 681, 688, 705
Burke, Edmund	IV, 307
Carlyle, Thomas	VII, 254, 268
Cowper, William	IV, 393
Crabbe, George	V, 175
Cumberland, Richard	IV, 561
DeQuincey, Thomas	VI, 129
Disraeli, Benjamin	VII, 285
Emerson, Ralph Waldo	VII, 375
Froude, James Anthony	VIII, 255, 265
Gay, John	III, 56, 60
Gibbon, Edward	IV, 192
Hallam, Henry	VI, 178
Hazlitt, William	V, 101, 107
History	VI, 9
Jeffrey, Francis Lord	V, 656
Johnson, Samuel	III, 737 753, 768
Lamb, Charles	V, 235, 238, 243
Landor, Walter Savage	VI, 390
Locker-Lampson, Frederick	VIII, 312, 314
Lowell, James Russell	VIII, 40
Macaulay, Thomas Babington Lord	VI, 113
Milton John	II, 249, 280, 283
More, Hannah	V, 195
Morris, William	VIII, 336
Newman, John Henry	VII, 749, 753
Pope, Alexander	III, 152, 169
Pye, Henry James	IV, 581
Richardson, Samuel	III, 435, 442, 452
Rossetti, Gabriel Charles Dante	VII, 453
Saint-John, Henry	III, 290, 297
Scott, Sir Walter	V, 161
Shakespeare, William	I, 570
Sheridan, Richard Brinsley	IV, 608
Smart, Christopher	III, 594
Southey, Robert	V, 413
Stanhope, Philip Dormer	III, 607
Stephen, Sir Leslie	VIII, 510
Sterne, Laurence	III, 509
Stevenson, Robert Louis	VIII, 240
Swift, Jonathan	III, 226, 236
Tennyson, Alfred Lord	VIII, 105
Thackeray, William Makepeace	VI, 309
Vanbrugh, Sir John	II, 703, 708

INDEX TO CRITICISMS

Wesley, John .... IV, 117, 129
Whitehead, William .... IV, 23
BISBEE, R. E.,
  Robertson, Frederick William
  .... V, 740
BISMARCK, OTTO EDWARD LEOPARD PRINCE VON,
  Motley, John Lothrop ... VII, 86, 87
BISSELL, EDWIN CONE,
  Coverdale, Miles .... I, 292
  Wyclif, John .... I, 103
BISSET, ANDREW,
  Bacon, Francis .... I, 645
  Hume, David .... III, 659
  Mill, James .... V, 308
BISSET, ROBERT,
  Addison, Joseph .... II, 644
  Budgell, Eustace .... III, 92
  Hughes, John .... II, 667
BISSY, COMTE DE,
  Young, Edward .... III, 486
BLACHFORD, LORD,
  Mill, John Stuart .... VI, 703
  Mozley, James Bowling ... VII, 147
BLACK, CLEMENTINA,
  Fielding, Sarah .... III, 518
BLACK JEREMIAHS,
  Ingersoll, Robert Green. VIII, 402
  Seward, William Henry .... VI, 674
BLACK, J. SUTHERLAND,
  Gibbon, Edward .... IV, 178
BLACK, MARGARET MOYES,
  Stevenson, Robert Louis .....
  .... VIII, 238, 243
BLACK, WILLIAM,
  Boswell, James .... IV, 218
  Carlyle, Thomas .... VII, 238
  Goldsmith, Oliver ....
  .... III, 620, 624, 628, 631
  Johnson, Samuel .... III, 762
  Pope, Alexander .... III, 177
  Ramsay, Allan ...... III, 403, 407
BLACK, DR.,
  Hume, David .... III, 648
BLACKBURN, VERNON,
  Hooker, Richard .... I, 409
BLACKBURNE, GERTRUDE M. IRELAND,
  Sidney, Algernon .... II, 354
BLACKER, B. H.,
  Johnstone, Charles .... IV, 413
BLACKIE, JOHN STUART,
  Baillie, Joanna .... V, 695
  Burns, Robert ....
  .... IV, 233, 243, 264
  Byron, George Gordon Lord
  .... IV, 742
  Carlyle, Thomas ...... VII, 231, 269
  Dobell, Sidney Thompson ... VI, 759
  Guthrie, Thomas .... VI, 737
  Hogg, James .... V, 268
  Landor, Walter Savage .... VI, 390
  Macleod, Norman .... VI, 663
  Oliphant, Carolina .... V, 477
  Scott, Sir Walter .... V, 137, 158
  Shelley, Percy Bysshe ...... IV, 711
  Tannahill, Robert .... IV, 548
  Tennyson, Alfred Lord .. VIII, 68
  Thackeray, William Makepeace ...
  .... VI, 316
  Wordsworth, William .... V, 643

BLACKLOCK, DR. ARCHIBALD,
  Burns, Robert .... IV, 228, 248
BLACKMORE, SIR RICHARD,
  Dryden, John .... II, 495
  Milton, John .... II, 258
  Swift, Jonathan .... III 198
  Watts, Isaac .... III, 252
BLACKSHAW, RANDALL,
  Henley, William Ernest .. VIII, 494
BLACKWELL, THOMAS,
  Berkeley, George .... III, 319
BLACKWOOD, JOHN,
  Eliot, George .... VII, 180
  Kinglake, Alexander William .
  .... VIII, 51
BLACKWOOD, WILLIAM,
  Aytoun, William Edmondstoune,
  .... VI, 444
  Byron, George Gordon Lord. IV, 751
  Ferrier, Susan Edmonstone ...
  .... V, 763, 763
  Irving, Washington .... VI, 148
  Maginn, William .... V, 385
  Scott, Sir Walter .... V, 141
BLADES, WILLIAM,
  Berners, Juliana .... I, 191
  Caxton, William .... I, 199
  Chaucer Geoffrey .... I, 139
BLAIKIE, WILLIAM GARDEN,
  Blackie, John Stuart ..... VIII, 305
  Chalmers, Thomas ..... V, 495, 496
  Clarke, Adam .... V. 186
  Guthrie, Thomas .... VI, 737
  Livingstone, David .... VI, 728
BLAINE, JAMES G.,
  Adams, John Quincy .... V. 520
BLAIR, HUGH,
  Addison, Joseph .... II, 655
  Akenside, Mark .... III, 542
  Arbuthnot, John .... III, 84
  Armstrong, John .... III, 698
  Barrow, Isaac .... II, 311
  Blair, Hugh .... IV, 405
  Clarke, Samuel .... II, 748
  Congreve, William .... II, 737
  Cooper, Anthony Ashley ... II, 578
  Cowley, Abraham .... II, 199
  Critic, The .... II, 6
  Farquhar, George .... II, 558
  Fielding, Henry . III, 351. 357, 371
  Hooker, Richard .... I, 405
  Hyde, Edward, Earl of Clarendon,
  .... II. 302
  Lee, Nathaniel .... II, 432
  Locke John .... II, 532
  Macpherson, James ... IV, 272, 274
  Milton, John .... II, 259, 274
  Montagu, Lady Mary Wortley,
  .... III, 465
  More, Henry .... II, 373
  Parnell, Thomas .... II, 616
  Pope, Alexander ....
  .... III, 156, 165. 175, 178
  Ramsay, Allan .... III, 405
  Richardson, Samuel .. III, 447, 455
  Rowe, Nicholas .... II. 622
  Saint-John, Henry .... III, 293
  Shakespeare, William .... I, 553
  Shenstone, William .... III, 472
  Swift, Jonathan .... III, 228
  Temple, Sir Wiliam .... II, 457

Thomson James ..... III. 274, 257
Tillotson John Robert ..... II, 439
Vanbrugh, Sir John .... II, 707
Young, Edward ...... III, 487. 491
BLAKE, H. G. O.,
  Thoreau, Henry David ..... VI, 275
BLAKE, WILLIAM,
  Blair, Robert .... III, 242
  Chaucer, Geoffrey .... I, 142
BLAKESLEY, J. W.,
  Thirlwall, Connop .... VII. 45
BLAKEY, ROBERT,
  Cobbett. William .... V, 269
  Cunningham, Allan .... V, 383
  Defoe, Daniel .... III, 47
  Godwin, William .... V, 297
  Hamilton, Sir William ..... VI, 51
  Montgomery, Robert ...... VI, 47
  Newman, John Henry. VII, 739, 750
  Priestley, Joseph .... IV, 454
  Pusey, Edward Bouverie .. VII, 468
  Taylor, Thomas .... V, 291
  Watts, Isaac .... III, 250
  Wilson, John .... V, 745
BLAKISTON, HERBERT E. D.,
  Warton, Thomas .... IV, 79
BLANC, MME,
  Lanier, Sidney .... VII, 331
BLANCHARD, LAYMAN,
  Jerrold, Douglas William ... VI, 66
  Landon, Letitia Elizabeth ... V, 323
BLANDEN, CHARLES G.,
  Keats, John .... IV, 666
BLENNERHASSETT, SIR ROWLAND,
  Newman, John Henry ..... VII, 743
BLESSINGTON. MARGUERITE COUNTESS.
  Byron George Gordon Lord. IV 733
  Forester, John .... VI, 65
  Landon, Letitia Elizabeth ... V. 323
  Landor. Walter Savage .... VI, 373
  Moore, Thomas .... V, 706
  Rogers. Samuel .... VI, 33
  Shelley, Percy Bysshe ..... IV, 690
BLIND, KARL,
  Bright. John .... VII, 721
  Müller. Friedrich Max .. VIII, 436
BLIND, MATHILDE,
  Brontë, Charlotte .... VI, 30
  Eliot, George . VII, 175, 182, 184
  185. 186. 191, 199.
BLISS, W. D. P.,
  Mill, John Stuart .... VI, 709
BLOCK, LOUIS J.,
  Field, Eugene .... VIII, 317
BLOOD, HENRY AMES,
  Webster Daniel .... V, 726
BLOOMFIELD C. J.,
  Bentley. Richard .... III, 121
  Parr, Samuel .... V. 20
BLOOMFIELD ROBERT,
  Bloomfield, Robert .... IV, 724
  Burns, Robert .... IV. 250
BLOUNT, EDWARD,
  Lyly, John .... I 424
BLOUNT, MRS.,
  Pope, Alexander .... III, 146
BLOWITZ, HENRI GEORGES ADOLPHE OPPERDE,
  Oliphant, Laurence .... VII, 656

INDEX TO CRITICISMS

	Vol. and Page
BLUNT, EDWARD,	
Marlowe, Christopher	I, 353
BLUNT, JOHN HENRY,	
Colet, John	I, 211
Tyndale, William	I, 248
BLUNT, J. J.,	
Butler, Joseph	III, 309
Hall, Robert	V, 111
Paley, William	IV, 471, 473, 475
Parr, Samuel	V, 20
BLUNT, WILFRED SCAWEN,	
Lytton, Edward Robert Bulwer Earl	VIII, 47, 48
BOADEN, JAMES,	
Erskine, Thomas	IV, 729
Garrick, David	III, 697
Glover, Richard	IV, 19
Godwin, William	V, 303
Hayley, William	IV, 653
Inchbald, Elizabeth	IV, 687
Lillo, George	III, 101
Malone, Edmond	IV, 577
Mason, William	IV, 324
BOAS, FREDERICK S.,	
Brooke Arthur	I, 284
Chaucer, Geoffrey	I, 136
Greene, Robert	I, 344
Heywood, John	I 306
Kyd, Thomas	I, 359
Lyly, John	I, 425
Marlowe, Christopher	I, 350, 352, 357
Peele, George	I, 367
Rowe, Nicholas	II, 621
Sackville, Thomas	I, 434
Whetstone, George	I, 334
BOASE, CHARLES WILLIAM,	
Finlay, George	VII, 49
BOASE, GEORGE CLEMENT,	
Gore, Catherine Grace	VI, 264
Haliburton, William Chandler	VI, 456
Helps, Sir Arthur	VII, 41
Lawrence, George Alfred	VII, 84
BOCCACCIO, BIOVANNI,	
Scott, Michael	I, 68
BODENSTED, FRIEDRICH,	
Shakespeare, William	I, 505
BOERNE, L.,	
Shakespeare, William	I, 503
BOGUE, DAVID, AND BENNETT, JAMES,	
Howe, John	II, 545
Owen, John	II, 352
Priestley, Joseph	453
BOHN, HENRY G.,	
Butler, Samuel	II, 332
BÖHRINGER, FREDERICK,	
Wyclif, John	I, 101
BOHUN, EDMUND,	
Ascham, Roger	I, 290
BOILEAU, ABBE,	
Swift,Jonathan	III, 228
BOK, EDWARD W.,	
Authors and Authorship	VIII, 10
BOKER, GEORGE HENRY,	
Taylor, Bayard	VII, 135
BOLINGBROKE, HENRY ST. JOHN LORD,	
Bacon, Francis	I, 655, 658
Pope, Alexander	III, 158

	Vol. and Page
Prior, Matthew	II, 673
Saint-John, Henry	III, 283, 284 284
Warburton, William	III, 689
BOLINBROKE, LADY F.,	
Saint-John, Henry	III, 282
BOLTON, EDMUND,	
Constable, Henry	I, 444
Daniel, Samuel	I, 615
Drayton, Michael	I, 703
Gascoigne, George	I, 307
Greville, Sir Fulke	I, 690
Jonson, Ben	I, 728, 759
Puttenham, George	I, 401
Raleigh, Sir Walter	I, 599
Sackville, Thomas	I, 435
Southwell, Robert	I, 361
Spenser, Edmund	I, 389
Surrey, Earl of	I, 256
BOLTON, HENRY CARRINGTON,	
Priestley, Joseph	IV, 448
BOLTON, SARAH KNOWLES,	
Kane, Elisha Kent	VI, 83
BOMPAS, GEORGE C.,	
Buckland, Francis Trevelyan	VII, 212
BONAPARTE, PRINCE LUCIEN,	
Shakespeare, William	I, 555
BONAPARTE, CHARLES LUCIEN,	
Wilson, Alexander	IV, 583
BONAR, JAMES,	
Butler, Joseph	III, 317
Cobbett, William	V, 275
Godwin, William	V, 303
Mackintosh, Sir James	V, 183
Malthus, Thomas Robert	V, 251
Paley, William	IV, 474
Price, Richard	IV, 136
Priestley, Joseph	IV, 455
Smith, Adam	IV, 53, 68
BOND, R. WARWICK,	
Ruskin, John	VIII, 408, 423
BONER, JOHN H.,	
Poe, Edgar Allan	V, 548
BONIAM, R. AND WALLEY, H.,	
Shakespeare, William	I, 523
BONNEY, THOMAS GEORGE,	
Lyell, Sir Charles	VII, 37, 38
Murchison, Sir Roderick Impey	VI, 631
BORROW, GEORGE,	
Fielding, Henry	III, 342
BOSTON GAZETTE,	
Edwards, Jonathan	III, 381
BOSWELL, ALEXANDER,	
Boswell, James	IV, 212
BOSWELL, JAMES,	
Akenside Mark	III, 541
Birch, Thomas	III, 499
Boswell, James	IV, 213, 214
Buchanan, George	I, 316
Burney, Charles	IV, 589
Chatterton, Thomas	III, 534, 535
Fielding, Henry	III, 351, 357
Gibbon, Edward	IV, 178
Goldsmith, Oliver	III, 615, 623, 635
Granger, James	III, 670
Hamilton, William	III, 336
Hawksworth, John	III, 609
Henry, Robert	IV, 107
Hume, David	III, 648, 649

	Vol. and Page
Jenyns, Soame	IV, 30
Johnson, Samuel	III, 725, 739, 743, 745, 747, 748
Kenrick, William	III, 702
Montagu, Elizabeth	IV, 402
Murray, William	IV, 170
Priestley, Joseph	IV, 452
Richardson, Samuel	III, 432
Sheridan, Thomas	IV, 46
Spence, Joseph	III, 519
Stanhope, Philip Dormer	III, 600
Walton, Isaac	II, 348
Whitefield, George	III, 547
Williams, Helen Maria	V, 74
Young, Edward	III, 485, 487
BOTTA, AMELIA,	
Hawthorne, Nathaniel	VI, 364
BOTTA, ANNE C. LYNCH,	
Baillie, Joanna	V, 694
Browne, Sir Thomas	II, 343
Burnet, Gilbert	II, 592
Calhoun, John Caldwell	V, 676
Campbell, Thomas	V, 444
Donne, John	I, 713
Ford, John	II, 32
Hamilton, Sir William	V, 54
Hawthorne, Nathaniel	VI, 365
Hillhouse, James Abraham	V, 365
Reid, Thomas	IV, 286
Thomson, James	III, 269
Trumbull, John	V, 121
Tuckerman, Henry Theodore	VI, 643
Washington, George	IV, 368
Willis, Nathaniel Parker	VI, 491
BOUCHER, LEON,	
Tennyson, Alfred Lord	VIII, 98
BOUCICAULT, DION,	
Drama, The	VII, 8
BOUGE, DAVID, AND BENNETT, JAMES,	
Pope, Alexander	III, 184
BOUGHTON, WILLIS,	
Whitman, Walt	VIII, 136
BOULGER, G. S.,	
Ray, John	II, 544
BOURCHIER, THOMAS,	
Pecock, Reginald	I, 189
BOURNE, EDWARD GAYLORD,	
Froude, James Anthony	VIII, 265
Gibbon, Edward	IV, 177
Parkman, Francis	VIII, 224
BOURNE, H. R. FOX,	
Bacon Francis	I, 662
Harvey, Gabriel	I, 697
Locke, John	II, 522, 527
Sidney, Sir Philip	I, 331
Spenser, Edmund	I, 372
BOUTWELL, GEORGE,	
Choate, Rufus	VI, 196
Sumner, Charles	VI, 755
Webster, Daniel	V, 729
BOWEN, FRANCIS,	
Buckle, Henry Thomas	VII, 281
Cooper, James Fenimore	V, 683
Darwin, Charles Robert	VII, 427
Emerson, Ralph Waldo	VI, 361
Hallam, Henry	VI, 177, 184
Hildreth, Richard	VI, 453
Holmes Oliver Wendell	VIII, 289

INDEX TO CRITICISMS

Longfellow, Henry Wadsworth ...... VII, 402
Lowell, James Russell.... VIII, 27
Lyell, Sir Charles......... VII, 37
Mann, Horace............. VI, 200
Motley, John Lothrop..... VII, 88
Otis, James.............. III, 717
Pattison, Mark........... VII, 540
Schoolcraft Henry Rowe.. VI, 403
Sedgwick, Catharine Maria. VI, 508
Smith, Adam............. IV, 63
Wayland, Francis......... VI, 449
Whipple, Edwin Percy.... VII, 595
Wilkison, Sir John Gardner.... ....VII, 51, 52
BOWEN, ROBERT ADGER,
Timrod, Henry........... VI, 511
BOWER, GEORGE SPENCER,
Hartley, David....... III, 377, 379
Mill, James............. V, 309
BOWKER, ALFRED,
Alfred, the Great .... I, 39
BOWKER, RICHARD ROGERS,
Browning, Robert........ VII, 679
Collins, William Wilkie... VII, 725
Craik, Dinah Maria Mulock
.... VII, 623
Edwards, Amelia Blandford
.... VIII, 175
Eliot, George............ VII, 172
Manning, Henry Edward VIII, 163
Reade, Charles.......... VII, 536
Ruskin, John....... VIII, 406, 420
Stevenson, Robert Louis VIII, 240
Tupper, Martin Farquhar. VII, 732
BOWLES, CAROLINE A.,
Barton, Bernard.......... V, 596
Beckford, William......... V, 450
Hayley, William......... IV, 651
Hemans, Felicia Dorothea.. V, 257
Smith, Horace............ V, 598
BOWLES, EMILY,
Fullerton, Georgiana Charlotte
Lady .... VII, 566, 567
BOWLES, WILLIAM LISLE,
Burke, Edmund......... IV, 289
Cowper, William......... IV, 383
Ken, Thomas............. II, 568
Pope, Alexander...........
..... III, 154, 156, 159, 159, 185
Sandys, George............ II, 83
Walton, Isaac............. II, 346
BOWMAN, ISA,
Dodgson, Charles Lutwige
.... VIII, 397
BOWRING, SIR JOHN,
Bentham, Jeremy......... V, 167
Blackstone, Sir William.... III, 703
Brougham, Henry Lord.... VI, 526
Cobden, Richard......... VI, 441
Erskine, Thomas........ IV, 729
Opie, Amelia............. V, 741
Tennyson, Alfred Lord... VIII, 77
Williams, Helen Maria..... V, 74
Wolcot, John............ IV, 649
BOWRING, LEWIN B.,
Bowring, Sir John........ VI, 664
BOYD, ANDREW K. H.,
Campbell, John Lord...... VI, 258
Carlyle, Thomas.......... VII, 243
Church, Richard William.. VII, 729

Guthrie, Thomas.......... VI, 737
Helps, Sir Arthur......... VII, 40
Holmes, Oliver Wendell.. VIII, 292
Kingsley, Charles......... VII, 20
Lewes, George Henry..... VII, 139
Liddon, Henry Parry..... VII, 761
Macleod, Norman..... VI, 661, 662
Maurice, John Frederick Denison .... VI, 645
Oliphant, Margaret O. W.....
.... VIII, 367, 368
Stanley, Arthur Penrhyn.. VII, 300
Stevenson, Robert Louis, VIII, 241
Taylor, Sir Henry........ VII, 581
Trollope, Anthony........ VII, 457
BOYD, CARL EVANS,
Bright, John............. VII, 723
BOYD, JAMES ROBERT,
Thomson, James.......... III, 259
BOYD, MARY STUART,
Harte, Francis Bret..... VIII, 467
BOYER, ABEL,
Centlivre, Susannah........ II, 684
Defoe, Daniel............. III, 45
L'Estrange, Sir Roger...... II, 538
BOYES, HECTOR,
James I. of Scotland........ I, 179
BOYESEN, HJALMAR HJORTH,
Brown, Charles Brockden.. IV, 557
Holland, Josiah Gilbert.... VII, 333
Holmes, Oliver Wendell. VIII, 298
Roe, Edward Payson..... VII, 677
Scott, Sir Walter.......... V, 146
Taylor, Bayard.......... VII, 130
Thackeray, William Makepeace .... VI, 320
BOYLE, CHARLES,
Bentley, Richard......... III, 114
BOYLE, G. D.,
Coleridge, Samuel Taylor... V, 215
BOYLE, JOHN (LORD ORRERY),
Arbuthnot, John......... III, 82
Bacon, Francis............. I, 665
Carte, Thomas........... III, 337
Pope, Alexander.......... III, 146
Sidney, Algernon.......... II, 354
Sprat, Thomas............ II, 573
Swift, Jonathan..... III, 198, 208
BOYLE, ROBERT,
Bacon, Francis............. I, 657
Massinger, Phillip......... II, 52
BOYNTON, HENRY WALCOTT,
Henley, William Ernest. VIII, 493
Irving, Washington....... VI, 137
Tennyson, Alfred Lord.. VIII, 85
BOYNTON, JULIA P.,
Craik, Dinah Maria Mulock
.... VII, 624
BRABOURNE, EDWARD LORD,
Austen, Jane............ IV, 621
BRACE, CHARLES LORING,
Darwin, Charles Robert... VII, 416
Mill, John Stuart...... VI, 702, 714
BRADDOCK, GEN. EDWARD,
Washington, George....... IV, 354
BRADDON, MARY E.,
Lytton, Sir Edward George Bulwer .... VI, 685, 692
BRADFIELD, THOMAS,
Arnold, Matthew........ VII, 638
Bryant, William Cullen... VII, 126

Hawthorne, Nathaniel. VI, 355, 361
BRADFORD, ARMORY H.,
Bunyan, John............ II, 405
BRADFORD, GAMALIEL, JR.,
Dryden, John............ II, 506
Emerson, Ralph Waldo... VII, 376
Macaulay, Thomas Babington Lord............... VI, 100
Pater, Walter Horatio... VIII, 277
Trollope, Anthony....... VII, 466
Very, Jones............. VII, 227
BRADLEY, ANDREW CECIL,
Browning, Robert........ VII, 696
Fletcher, John............ I, 629
Marlowe, Christopher... I, 349, 353
Seeley, Sir John Robert. VIII, 309
Tennyson, Alfred Lord.... VIII, 90
BRADLEY, A. E.,
Parkman, Francis....... VIII, 223
BRADLEY, A. G.,
Henry, Patrick........... IV, 351
BRADLEY, GEORGE GRANVILLE
Stanley, Arthur Penrhyn.....
.... VII, 300, 304
BRADLEY, HENRY,
Barnes, William.......... VII, 586
BRADLEY, JOSHUA,
Hopkins, Samuel......... IV, 438
BRADSHAW, JOHN,
Stanhope, Philip Dormer.. III, 607
BRADSTREET, ANNE,
Bradstreet, Anne......... II, 228
Sidney, Sir Philip.......... I, 331
BRADY, CYRUS TOWNSEND,
Brooks, Phillips......... VIII, 232
BRADY, NICHOLAS,
Shadwell, Thomas........ II, 433
BRAE, ANDREW EDMUND,
Chaucer, Geoffrey......... I, 140
BRAITHWAITE, RICHARD,
Chaucer, Geoffrey.......... I, 155
BRAINARD, CHARLES H.,
Thackeray, William Makepeace
.... VI, 296, 309
BRANDES, GEORGE,
Bacon, Francis............ I, 649
Beaumont, Francis......... I, 588
Brooke, Arthur........... I, 285
Chapman, George...... I, 731, 734
Disraeli, Benjamin.. VII, 289, 290
Jonson, Ben............. I, 750
Marlowe, Christopher..... I, 348
Mill, John Stuart.... VI, 704, 711
Shakespeare, William.. I, 453, 455,
456, 459, 464, 470, 476, 477, 480,
484, 489, 495, 499, 507, 509, 510,
514, 519, 523, 526, 527, 531, 532,
533, 536, 538, 542, 546, 577.
BRANDL, ALOIS,
Bowles, William Lisle....... V, 663
Coleridge, Samuel Taylor.....
.... V, 218, 220
Hartley, David........... III, 380
BRANN, HENRY A.,
Ingersoll, Robert Green... VIII, 403
BRAY, ANNA ELIZA,
Defoe, Daniel............ III, 40
Gifford, William........... V, 33
Landon, Letitia Elizabeth... V, 325
Opie, Amelia............. V, 743
Scott, Sir Walter.......... V, 132

INDEX TO CRITICISMS

	Vol. and Page
Southey, Robert	V, 402
BRAY, CHARLES,	
Eliot, George	VII, 176
Newton, Sir Isaac	II, 725
BRAY, WILLIAM,	
Evelyn, John	II, 548
BRECK, SAMUEL,	
Audubon, John James	V, 696
Barlow, Joel	IV, 573
Hamilton, Alexander	IV, 459
BREMER, FREDERIKA,	
Emerson, Ralph Waldo	VII, 345
Lowell, James Russell	VIII, 18
Whittier, John Greenleaf	VIII, 111
BRENAN, GERALD,	
Dickens, Charles	VI, 594
BRERETON, AUSTIN,	
Dibden, Charles	IV, 587
BRETON, NICHOLAS,	
Spenser, Edmund	I, 393
BRETT, REGINALD B.,	
Disraeli, Benjamin	VII, 280
BREWER, E. COBHAM,	
Dunstan,	I, 45
BREWER, JOHN SHERREN,	
Green, John Richard	VII, 508
More, Sir Thomas	I, 237
Shakespeare, William	I, 451, 566
BREWER THOMAS M.,	
Audubon, John James	V, 697
BREWSTER, SIR DAVID,	
Bacon, Francis	I, 654, 659
Darwin, Charles Robert	VII, 423
Ferguson, James	III, 669
Flamsteed, John	II, 662
Junius	IV, 641
Macaulay, Thomas Babington Lord	VI, 98
Napier, Sir John	I, 589
Newton, Sir Isaac	II, 717, 720
Whewell, William	VI, 472
Young, Thomas	V, 88
BRIDGE, HORATIO,	
Bacon, Delia	VI, 204
Hawthorne, Nathaniel	VI, 347, 349
Longfellow, Henry Wadsworth	VII, 385
BRIDGES, J. H.,	
Harvey, William	II, 156
BRIDGES, ROBERT,	
Keats, John	IV, 673, 681
McCosh, James	VIII, 301
Milton, John	II, 272
Stevenson, Robert Louis	VIII, 250
BRIDGES, SIR SAMUEL,	
Swift, Jonathan	III, 221
Thomson, James	III, 259
BRIDGETT, T. E.,	
More, Sir Thomas	I, 239
Richard Rolé of Hampole	I, 92
Wiseman, Nicholas Patrick	VI, 438
BRIGGS, CHARLES F.,	
Lowell, James Russell	VIII, 17
Thoreau, Henry David	VI, 271
BRIGHAM, A ,	
Shakespeare, William	I, 521
BRIGHAM, NICHOLAS,	
Chaucer, Geoffrey	I, 125
BRIGHT, HENRY,	
Hawthorne, Nathaniel	VI, 342, 359

	Vol. and Page
BRIGHT, JAMES W.,	
Ælfric	I, 46
BRIGHT, JOHN,	
Gladstone, William Ewart	VIII, 388
Whittier, John Greenleaf	VIII, 118, 123
BRIGHTWELL, CECILIA LUCY,	
Ferguson, James	III, 669
Opie, Amelia	V, 742
BRIMLEY, GEORGE,	
Carlyle, Thomas	VII, 254
Dickens, Charles	VI, 575, 582
Kingsley, Charles	VII, 26
Lytton, Sir Edward Bulwer	VI, 693
Patmore, Coventry George	VIII, 340
Tennyson, Alfred Lord	VIII, 79
Thackeray William Makepeace	VI, 306, 313
Wordsworth, William	V, 635
BRINE, MARY PUSEY,	
Pusey, Edward Bouverie	VII, 470
BRINTON, DANIEL G.,	
Browning, Robert	VII, 709
Whitman, Walt	VIII, 146
BRISBANE, THOMAS,	
Smith, Alexander	VI, 516, 517
BRISSOT DE WARVILLE, JEAN P.,	
Adams, Samuel	IV, 440
BRISTED, CHARLES ASTOR,	
Map, Walter	I, 61
Whewell, William	VI, 467
BRODERIP, FRANCES FREELING (HOOD),	
Hood, Thomas	V, 459
BRODIE, GEORGE,	
Wyclif, John	I, 105
BRODRIBB, A. A.,	
Barbauld, Anna Lætitia	V, 23
Wakefield, Gilbert	IV, 417
BRODRICK, GEORGE C.,	
Huxley, Thomas Henry	VIII, 321
Wyclif, John	I, 110
BROME, ALEXANDER,	
Beaumont and Fletcher	I, 579
BRONSON, WALTER C.,	
Ames, Fisher	IV, 529
Barlow, Joel	IV, 576
Beecher, Henry Ward	VII, 610
Brown, Charles Brockden	IV, 557
Cary, Alice	VI, 640
Cooper, James Fenimore	V, 679
Dana, Richard Henry	VII, 157
Dwight, Timothy	IV, 628
Edwards, Jonathan	III, 394
Franklin, Benjamin	IV, 106
Freneau, Philip	V, 189
Hamilton, Alexander	IV, 466
Henry, Patrick	IV, 353
Lanier, Sidney	VII, 331
Lincoln, Abraham	VI, 421
Livingston, William	IV, 110
Mather, Cotton	II, 732
Parsons, Thomas William	VIII, 194
Penn, William	II, 631
Prince, Thomas	III, 492
Sewall, Samuel	III, 19
Sigourney, Lydia Huntley	VI, 452
Sumner, Charles	VI, 758
Thoreau, Henry David	VI, 278

	Vol. and Page
Very, Jones	VII, 228
Webster, Noah	V, 429
Whipple, Edwin Percy	VII, 597
Wilson, Alexander	IV, 583
BRONTË, ANNE,	
Cowper, William	IV, 387
BRONTË, CHARLOTTE,	
Arnold, Matthew	VII, 628
Austen, Jane	VI, 614, 617
Borrow George Henry	VII, 312
Brontë, Charlotte	VI, 19, 22
Burns, Robert	IV, 255
Carlyle, Thomas	VII, 262
Dickens, Charles	VI, 572
Dobell, Sidney Thompson	VI, 762
Emerson, Ralph Waldo	VII, 362
Fielding, Henry	III, 359
Hunt, James Henry Leigh	VI, 168
Lytton, Sir Edward George Bulwer	VI, 696
Martineau, Harriet	VII, 56
Scott, Sir Walter	V, 154
Southey, Robert	V, 399
Tennyson, Alfred Lord	VIII, 87
Thackeray, William Makepeace	VI, 302, 312
Wiseman, Nicholas Patrick	VI, 435
BRONTË, EMILY,	
Brontë, Emily	V, 521
BROOK, BENJAMIN,	
Foxe, John	I, 335
BROOKE, CHRISTOPHER,	
Shakespere, William	I, 477
BROOKE, RALPH,	
Camden, William	I, 620
BROOKE, STOPFORD A.,	
Ælfric	I, 46
Alcuin	I, 33
Alfred the Great	I, 41
Asser	I, 43
Bacon, Francis	I 669
Beowulf	I, 17, 20
Blair, Robert	III, 244
Blake, William	V, 62
Browning, Robert	VII, 682, 712, 719
Bruce, James	IV, 208
Bunyan, John	II, 399
Burns, Robert	IV, 267
Cædmon	I, 23
Chapman, George	I, 734
Chaucer, Geoffrey	I, 164
Coleridge, Samuel Taylor	V, 215
Collins, William	III, 421
Congreve, William	II, 745, 758
Cooper, Anthony Ashley	II, 580
Cowper, William	IV, 390, 394
Cynewulf	I, 31
Daniel, Samuel	I, 617
De Quincey, Thomas	VI, 124
Douglas, Gawin	I, 214
Dryden, John	II, 489, 506
Ford, John	II, 33
Gay, John	III, 62
Gray, Thomas	III, 563
Hallam, Henry	VI, 179
Hooker, Richard	I, 410
Hume, David	III, 660
Keats, John	IV, 671
Keble, John	VI, 463
Lamb, Charles	V, 244

INDEX TO CRITICISMS

Vol. and Page
Macaulay, Thomas Babington
  Lord ....VI, 107
MacCarthy, Dennis Florence..
  ....,...VII, 490
Martineau, James ......VIII, 429
Massinger, Philip..........II, 52
Milton, John..II, 252, 255, 266, 282
Moore, Thomas............V, 718
Pope, Alexander..III, 163, 167, 190
Prynne, William...........II, 226
Robertson, Frederick William
  ....V, 738, 739
Rowe, Nicholas...........II, 623
Ruskin, John..........VIII, 413
Scott, Sir Walter..........V, 136
Shakespeare, William......I, 574
Shelley, Percy Bysshe....IV, 700
Smart, Christopher.......III, 594
Smith, Adam.............IV, 70
Smollett, Tobias George...III, 590
South, Robert............II, 610
Sterne, Laurence........III, 509
Swift, Jonathan..........III, 237
Taylor, Jeremy...........II, 211
Tennyson Alfred Lord, VIII, 85, 95
Thomson, James.........III, 259
Turner, Charles Tennyson.VII, 163
Vaughan, Henry..........II, 446
Warton, Thomas.........IV, 79
White, Gilbert...........IV, 151
Wordsworth, William......V, 638
BROOKS, ARTHUR,
  Brooks, Phillips........VIII, 228
BROOKS, CHARLES T.
  Channing, William Ellery...V, 373
BROOKS, CHARLES WILLIAM
  SHIRLEY,
  Browning, Elizabeth Barrett..
  ....VI, 245
BROOKS, JOHN COTTON,
  Brooks, Phillips........VIII, 229
BROOKS, JOHN GRAHAM,
  Fiske, John............VIII, 457
BROOKS, NOAH,
  Benton, Thomas Hart.....VI, 87
  Harte, Francis Bret..VIII, 467, 469
  Lincoln, Abraham......IV, 413
  Stevenson, Robert Louis..VIII, 242
BROOKS, PHILLIPS,
  Agassiz, Louis Jean Rudolph..
  ....VI, 725
  Beecher, Henry Ward....VII, 606
  Books ....III, 10
  Dryden, John...........II, 506
  Franklin, Benjamin......IV, 98
  Gibbon, Edward........IV, 192
  Johnson, Samuel........III, 764
  Milton, John...........II, 281
  Phillips, Wendell........VII, 553
  Stanley, Arthur Penrhyn.....
  ....VII, 298, 303
BROOKS, SARAH WARNER,
  Burns, Robert..........IV, 245
  Pollok, Robert...........V, 73
BROOKS, SHIRLEY,
  Thackeray, William Makepeace,
  ....VI, 292
BROOKS, WILLIAM KEITH,
  Agassiz, Louis Jean Rudolph...
  ....,...VI, 726
  Huxley, Thomas Henry..VIII, 327

Vol. and Page
BROOME, WILLIAM,
  Fenton, Elijah...........III, 20
  Pope, Alexander.....III, 165, 170
BROUGHAM, HENRY LORD,
  Bentham, Jeremy..........V, 166
  Black, Joseph........IV, 345, 345
  Burke, Edmund..........IV, 303
  Butler, Joseph..........III 311
  Byron, George Gordon Lord..
  ....IV, 739, 747
  Campbell John Lord......VI, 258
  Canning, George..........V, 66
  Channing, William Ellery...V, 371
  Davy, Sir Humphry........V, 94
  Defoe, Daniel............III, 36
  Franklin, Benjamin........IV, 86
  Gibbon, Edward.....IV, 185, 194
  Hume, David........III, 653, 658
  Hutcheson Francis......III, 245
  Jefferson, Thomas........V, 45
  Jeffrey, Francis Lord......V, 655
  Johnson, Samuel..III, 737, 741, 745
  Junius, ...IV 539, 645
  Knight, Charles..........VI, 743
  Locke, John........II, 523, 531
  Macaulay, Thomas Babington
    Lord ....VI, 92
  Mill, James...........V, 305, 310
  Milton, John............II, 289
  Mitford, William..........V, 70
  More, Sir Thomas.........I, 235
  Murray, William........IV, 171
  Newton, Sir Isaac......II, 714, 719
  Paley, William..........IV, 472
  Park, Mungo............IV, 485
  Pitt, William............IV, 510
  Priestley, Joseph.I.V, 448, 449, 454
  Ricardo, David........IV, 726, 726
  Robertson, William........
  ....IV, 155, 156, 161
  Rogers, Samuel..........VI, 39
  Romilly, Sir Samuel......IV, 635
  Roscoe, William..........V, 117
  Rumford, Count.........IV, 592
  Sheridan, Richard Brinsley.IV, 600
  Sidney, Algernon.........II, 355
  Smith, Adam..........IV, 59, 63
  South, Robert...........II 608
  Stanhope, Philip Dormer...III, 605
  Stuart, Gilbert...........IV, 27
  Swift, Jonathan.........III 221
  Taylor, Jeremy..........II, 209
  Tillotson, John Robert....II, 440
  Tooke, John Horne.......IV, 572
  Walpole, Horace.........IV, 312
  Wilberforce, William.......V, 201
  Wyclif, John..............I, 106
BROWN, CALVIN S.
  Tennyson, Alfred Lord...VIII, 109
BROWN, CHARLES ARMITAGE,
  Keats, John............IV, 663
  Shakespeare, William........
  ....I, 467, 471, 500
BROWN, CRUM,
  Black, Joseph...........IV, 344
BROWN, HORATIO,
  Symonds, John Addington....
  ....VIII, 202
BROWN, J.,
  Whitefield George........III, 551
  Wesley, John............IV, 125

Vol. and Page
BROWN, JAMES.
  Cartwright, William........II. 70
BROWN, J. HENRY,
  Bailey, Philip James.....VIII, 459
BROWN, J. M.
  Greene, Robert............I, 342
BROWN, JOHN,
  Bailey, Philip James.....VIII 461
  Berkeley, George.........III, 328
  Bunyan, John.....II, 390, 392, 404
  Chalmers, Thomas.........V, 491
  Clive, Caroline...........VI, 740
  Coleridge, Samuel Taylor....V, 211
  Cooper, Anthony Ashley....II, 577
  Hallam, Arthur Henry......V, 198
  Herbert, George............I, 722
  Jeffrey, Francis Lord.......V, 651
  Leighton, Robert..........II, 359
  Scott, Sir Walter...........V, 132
  Thackeray, William Makepeace
  ....VI, 292. 300, 302, 311
  Tennyson, Alfred Lord...VIII. 87
  Vaughan, Henry..........II. 443
BROWN, JOHN CROMBIE,
  Eliot, George............VII. 201
BROWN, J. TAYLOR,
  Brown, John..........VII, 478, 481
BROWN, J. T. T.,
  James I. of Scotland.........I. 182
BROWN, J. WOOD,
  Scott, Michael.............I, 69
BROWN, MADOX,
  Rossetti, Gabriel Charles Dante,
  ....VII, 435
BROWN, P. HUME,
  Froude James Anthony..VIII, 268
  Gardiner, Samuel Rawson VIII, 466
  Knox, John................I, 302
BROWN, ROBERT,
  Brewster, Sir David......VI, 547
  Buckland, Francis Trevelyan..
  ....VII, 213
  Davy, Sir Humphry........V, 92
  Faraday, Michael.........VI, 514
  Herschel, Sir John Frederick
    William............VI, 624, 626
  Taylor, Bayard..........VII, 134
BROWN, SAMUEL GILMAN,
  Ames, Fisher............IV, 527
  Choate, Rufus...........VI, 197
  Dana, Richard Henry.....VII, 156
BROWN, THOMAS,
  Chatterton, Thomas......III, 536
  Dryden, John...........II, 484
  Newton, Sir Isaac..........II, 723
  Robertson, William.......IV, 162
  Smith, Adam............IV, 58
  Stewart, Dugald..........V. 79
BROWN, THOMAS EDWARD,
  Arnold, Matthew.........VII, 639
  Cowper, William.........IV, 393
  Crabbe, George............V, 176
  Defoe, Daniel............III, 40
  Du Maurier, George.....VIII, 344
  Jonson, Ben...........I, 750, 752
  Jowett, Benjamin........VIII, 207
  Law, William............III, 426
  Martineau, Harriet.......VII, 58
  Pusey, Edward Bouverie..VII, 469
  Swift, Jonathan..........III, 215
  Tyndall, John...........VIII, 195

INDEX TO CRITICISMS

	Vol. and Page
Wordsworth, William	V, 624
BROWNE, FRANCIS FISHER,	
Arnold Sir Edwin	VIII, 504
Bryant, William Cullen	VII, 111
Lanier, Sidney	VII, 327
Whitman, Walt	VIII, 142
BROWNE, G. F.,	
Bede	I, 30
BROWNE, H. L.,	
Green, John Richard	VII, 504
BROWNE, IRVING,	
Bacon, Francis	I, 647
Kent, James	V, 503
Murray, William	IV, 172
Prescott, William Hickling	VI, 137
Romilly, Sir Samuel	IV, 636
Story, Joseph	V, 483, 485
BROWNE JAMES P.,	
Fielding, Henry	III, 343
Sterne, Laurence	III, 508
BROWNE, JUNIUS HENRI,	
Greeley, Horace	VI, 668, 671
Simms, George Denison	VI, 603
BROWNE, MATTHEW,	
Chaucer, Geoffrey	I, 127, 163
Dickens, Charles	VI, 580
Wyclif, John	I, 107
BROWNE, SIR THOMAS	
Bacon, Roger	I, 77
BROWNE, WILLIAM,	
Chapman, George	I, 728
Drayton, Michael	I, 706
Daniel, Samuel	I, 615
Davies, Sir John	I, 634
Jonson, Ben	I, 758
Occleve, Thomas	I, 187
Overbury, Sir Thomas	I, 442
Sidney, Sir Philip	I, 322
Spenser, Edmund	I, 378, 393
BROWNE, WILLIAM HAND,	
Halley, Edmund	III, 107
BROWNELL, WILLIAM CRARY,	
Arnold, Sir Edwin	VIII, 503
Arnold, Matthew	VII, 641, 648
Carlyle, Thomas	VII, 252, 254, 260
Dickens, Charles	VI, 580
Eliot, George	VII, 186, 188, 190, 191, 209
Ruskin, John	VIII, 410 423
Southey, Robert	V, 416
Thackeray, William Makepeace	VI, 308, 310, 322
BROWNING, ELIZABETH BARRETT	
Austen, Jane	IV, 619
Blair, Robert	III, 242
Books,	III, 9
Brontë, Charlotte	VI, 27
Browning, Elizabeth Barrett	VI, 228, 229, 343
Browning, Robert	VII, 697
Burns Robert	IV, 255
Butler, Samuel	II, 334
Byron, George Gordon Lord	IV, 758
Carlyle, Thomas	VII, 232
Chaucer, Geoffrey	I, 160,161
Coleridge, Samuel Tayler	V, 214
Cowper, William	IV, 373
Darwin, Erasmus	IV, 425
De Quincey, Thomas	VI, 125

	Vol. and Page
Dickens, Charles	VI, 581
Disraeli, Benjamin	VII, 288
Donne, John	I, 715
Drummond, William	II, 105
Dryden, John	II, 493
Ford John	II, 29
Gaskell, Elizabeth Cleghorn.	VI. 430
Greville, Sir Fulke	I, 691
Gower, John	I, 175
Hemans, Felicia Dorothea	V, 255
Herbert, George	I, 720
Herrick, Robert	II, 238
Horne, Richard Hengist	VII, 547
Hunt, James Henry Leigh	VI, 168
James, George Paine Rainsford	VI, 218
Johnson, Samuel	III, 750
Jonson, Ben	I, 764
Keats, John	IV, 664, 677
Kinglake, Alexander William	VIII, 50
Kingsley, Charles	VII 18
Knowledge	V, 8
Landon, Letitia Elizabeth	V, 327
Landor, Walter Savage	VI, 373, 381, 388
Langland, William	I, 119
Lever, Charles James	VI, 651
Lowell, James Russell	VIII, 36
Lydgate, John	I, 185
Lytton Sir Edward George Bulwer	VI, 696
Macaulay, Thomas Babington Lord	VI, 101
Macpherson, James	IV, 276
Martineau, Harriet	VII, 55
Massinger, Philip	II, 49
Milton, John	II, 290
Mitford, Mary Russell	VI, 41, 44
Montgomery Robert	VI, 46
Poe, Edgar Allan	V, 551, 556
Poets and Poetry	IV, 8
Pomfret John	II, 511
Pope, Alexander	III, 187
Rogers, Samuel	VI, 33
Shakespeare, William	I, 560, 561
Shelley, Percy Bysshe	IV, 706
Shenstone William	III, 474
Shirley, James	II, 191, 200
Smith Alexander	VI, 517
Spenser, Edmund	I, 383
Surrey, Earl of	I, 257
Tennyson, Alfred Lord	VIII, 100
Thackeray, William Makepeace	VI, 311
Trollope, Frances Milton	VI, 331
Waller, Edmund	II, 381
Wither, George	II, 214
Wordsworth, William	V, 633
Young, Edward	III, 493
BROWNING, OSCAR,	
Bacon, Francis	I, 662
Eliot, George	VII, 177, 186, 188, 191, 196
Locke, John	II, 530
BROWNING, ROBERT,	
Beddoes,Thomas Lovell	V, 586, 587
Browning, Elizabeth Barrett	VI, 231, 232, 245
Browning, Robert	VII, 699
Byron, George Gordon Lord	IV, 759

	Vol. and Page
Donne, John	I, 717
FitzGerald, Edward	VII, 515
Knowledge	V, 7
Macpherson, James	IV, 276
Mahoney, Francis	VII, 483
Mandeville, Bernard	III, 71
Poets and Poetry	IV, 8
Quarles, Francis	II, 77
Rossetti, Gabriel Charles Dante	VII, 435
Shakespeare, William	I, 570
Shelley, Mary Wollstonecraft	V, 703
Shelley, Percy Bysshe	IV, 705, 707
Sidney, Sir Philip	I, 331
Smart, Christopher	III, 593
Tennyson, Alfred Lord	VIII, 70
Wordsworth, William	V, 610
BROWNSON, HENRY F.,	
Brownson, Orestes Augustus	VII, 75
BROWNSON, ORESTES AUGUSTUS,	
Beecher, Henry Ward	VII, 607
Brownson, Orestes Augustus	VII, 73
Clarke, James Freeman	VII, 673
Draper, John William	VII, 502
Fullerton, Georgiana Charlotte Lady	VII, 568, 568
Manning, Henry Edward	VIII, 167
Mansel, Henry Longueville	VI, 627
Newman, John Henry	VII, 745
BRUCE, H. A.,	
Napier, Gen. Sir William Francis Patrick	VI, 221
BRUCE, JAMES,	
Bruce, James	IV, 206
BRUCE, JAMES MANNING,	
Ruskin, John	VIII, 407
BRUCE, WALLACE,	
Burns, Robert	IV, 263
Phillips, Wendell	VII, 558
BRUCHHAUSEN, CASPAR,	
Penn, William	II, 631
BRUCKER, JOHANN JAKOB,	
Locke, John	II, 524
BRUNNE, ROBERT DE,	
Thomas of Erceldoune	I, 83
BRUNTON, MARY,	
Fielding, Henry	III, 352
BRYANT, JACOB,	
Gray, Thomas	III, 554
Steevens, George	IV, 409
BRYANT, WILLIAM CULLEN,	
Barlow, Joel	IV, 575
Bryant, William Cullen	VII, 114
Burns, Robert	IV, 258
Byron, George Gordon Lord	IV, 760
Chaucer, Geoffrey	I, 164
Cobden, Richard	VI, 439
Coleridge, Samuel Taylor	V, 215
Cooper, James Fenimore	V, 680, 682, 683
Dana, Richard Henry	VII, 153, 155
Dickens, Charles	VI, 580
Disraeli, Benjamin	VII, 286
Dryden, John	II, 503
Dwight, Timothy	IV, 627
Franklin, Benjamin	IV, 101
Halleck, Fitz-Greene	VI, 494, 498

INDEX TO CRITICISMS

Vol. and Page
Hillhouse, James Abraham.. V. 363
Irving, Washington..........
..........VI, 134, 139, 147, 147
Keats, John..............IV, 677
Kingsley, Charles........VII, 20
Knowledge ....V, 8
Lockhart, John Gibson......V, 756
Longfellow, Henry Wadsworth
..............VII, 390, 398, 403
Martineau, Harriet....VII, 55, 60
Mickle, William Julius.....IV, 42
Moore, Thomas............V, 717
Motley, John Lothrop....VII, 95
Oldham, John............II, 350
Paulding, James Kirke.....VI, 227
Percival, James Gates......VI, 60
Pierpont, John...........VI, 480
Poe, Edgar Allan..........V, 539
Pope, Alexander..........III, 189
Rogers, Samuel............VI, 34
Scott, Sir Walter..........V, 136
Sedgwick, Catharine Maria....
..................VI, 506, 507
Shakespeare, William...I, 543, 567
Sheridan, Richard Brinsley.IV, 595
Southey, Robert..........V, 405
Thomson, James.........III, 269
Trumbull, John............V, 121
Watts, Isaac.............III, 252
Whittier, John Greenleaf.VIII, 112
Wordsworth, William......V, 636
BRYCE, JAMES,
Bright, John............VII, 724
Brooks, Phillips........VIII, 227
Disraeli, Benjamin...........
.........VII, 281, 284, 286, 294
Fawcett, Henry..........VII, 551
Freeman, Edward Augustus..
.... VIII, 162
Gladstone, William Ewart....
.... VIII, 388, 392
Green, John Richard...VII, 505, 508
Hamilton, Alexander......IV, 464
Manning, Henry Edward.VIII, 169
Milnes, Richard Monckton.VII, 562
Stanley, Arthur Penrhyn..VII, 306
Tennyson, Alfred Lord..VIII, 99
Trollope, Anthony.......VII, 459
Washington, George......IV, 363
Wilberforce, Samuel......VI, 734
BRYDGES, SIR SAMUEL EGERTON,
Addison, Joseph...........II, 656
Bloomfield, Robert.......IV, 723
Breton, Nicholas...........I, 678
Brydges, Sir Samuel Egerton, V, 320
Burke, Edmund..........IV, 301
Burns, Robert............IV, 250
Byron, George Gordon Lord..
........................IV, 738
Campbell, Thomas ....V, 440
Carter, Elizabeth.........IV, 492
Canning, George...........V, 66
Chapone, Hester.........IV, 418
Cibber, Theophilus.......III, 396
Collins, William......III, 418, 419
Cowper, William.........IV, 386
Cumberland, Richard......IV, 559
Edwards, Richard..........I, 288
Erskine, Thomas.........IV, 730
Fox, Charles James........IV, 507

Vol. and Page
Gibbon, Edward..........IV, 195
Gifford, William............V, 32
Goldsmith, Oliver.........III, 630
Gray, Thomas....III, 554, 558, 566
Habington, William........II, 135
Hayley, William..........IV, 653
Horner, Francis...........IV, 629
Howell, James............II, 187
Hurd, Richard...........IV, 519
Irving, Washington........VI, 133
Johnson, Samuel.........III, 736
Jones, Sir William.........IV, 198
Oldys, William...........III, 457
Percy, Thomas...........IV, 563
Pope, Alexander..........III, 186
Porson, Richard..........IV, 522
Raleigh, Sir Walter.........I, 599
Ritson, Joseph...........IV, 436
Romilly, Sir Samuel......IV, 635
Sackville, Thomas..........I, 432
Seward, Anna........IV, 541, 543
Shelley, PercyBysshe.....IV, 75
Smith, Charlotte..........IV, 497
Sylvester, Joshua..........I, 609
Warton, Joseph......IV, 396, 397
Warton, Thomas......IV, 72, 76
Watson, Thomas...........I, 337
White, Henry Kirke.......IV, 488
Wither, George...........II, 213
Wood, Anthony..........II, 448
BRYNE, MRS. WILLIAM PITT,
Wiseman, Nicholas Patrick.VI, 436
BRYSKETT, LODOWICK,
Sidney, Sir Philip..........I, 321
BUCHAN, LORD,
Johnson, Samuel........III, 754
Thomson, James.........III, 267
BUCHANAN, GEORGE,
Ascham, Roger............I, 288
Douglas, Gawin............I, 213
BUCHANAN, JAMES,
Choate, Rufus............VI, 195
BUCHANAN, ROBERT,
Arnold, Matthew........VII, 638
Besant, Sir Walter......VIII, 449
Browning, Robert........VII, 693
Burns, Robert............IV, 234
Carlyle, Thomas..VII, 234, 243, 257
Chatterton, Thomas......III, 537
Dickens, Charles.........VI, 591
Dobell, Sidney Thompson....
.... VI, 760, 765
Eliot, George............VII, 176
Gray, David........VI, 260, 261
Hawthorne, Nathaniel.....VI, 354
Keats, John.............IV, 677
Lewes, George Henry.....VII, 138
Moore, Thomas...........V, 718
Peacock, Thomas Love,......
.................VI, 473, 475
Poets and Poetry.........IV, 8
Reade, Charles...VII, 528, 529, 534
Rossetti, Gabriel Charles Dante
.... VII, 437, 444, 450
Scott, Sir Walter..........V, 160
Tennyson, Alfred Lord.......
.... VIII, 69,107
Taylor, Tom.............VII, 215
Whitman, Walt....VIII, 131, 143
BUCKE, CHARLES,
Akenside, Mark..........III, 543

Vol. and Page
BUCKE, RICHARD MAURICE,
Whitman, Walt.........VIII, 133
BUCKINGHAM, EDGAR,
Phillips, Wendell.........VII, 553
BUCKLAND, ANNA,
Sidney, Sir Philip..........I, 326
BUCKLAND, A. R.,
Spurgeon, Charles Haddon.VIII,182
BUCKLAND, A. W.,
Darwin, Charles Robert...VII, 429
BUCKLAND, FRANK,
Hunter, John............IV, 165
BUCKLAND, MRS. WILLIAM,
Buckland, Francis Trevelyan
.......................VII, 210
BUCKLE, HENRY THOMAS,
Barrow, Isaac............II, 312
Berkeley, George........III, 331
Black, Joseph...........IV, 345
Boyle, Robert...........II, 419
Brown, Thomas..........IV 658
Browne, Sir Thomas......II, 342
Buckle, Henry Thomas.....VI, 279
Burke, Edmund.........IV, 304
Campbell, John Lord......VI, 257
Chillingworth, William.....II, 86
Cudworth, Ralph.........II, 385
Faraday, Michael........VI, 513
Gibbon, Edward.........IV, 186
Hume, David...........III, 662
Hunter, John............IV, 167
Hutcheson, Francis......III, 246
Knox, John................I, 297
Leslie, Sir John...........V, 189
Laud, William............II, 92
Macaulay, Thomas Babington
Lord ....VI, 106
Porson, Richard.........IV, 525
Reid, Thomas...........IV, 286
Robertson, William......IV,158
Shelley, Percy Bysshe....IV, 709
Smith, Adam.........IV, 64, 70
Spencer, Herbert........VIII, 479
Stewart, Dugald..........V, 80
Wesley, John............IV, 123
Whewell, William........VI, 470
BUCKLEY, JAMES M.,
Wesley Charles..........IV, 38
Wesley, John............IV, 122
Whitefield, George........III, 549
BUCKNILL, JOHN CHARLES,
Shakespeare, William...I, 517, 530
Swift, Jonathan.....III, 205, 210
BUDDENSIEG, RUDOLF,
Wyclif, John...............I, 109
BUDDLE, JOHN,
Davy, Sir Humphrey........V, 90
BUDGELL, EUSTACE,
Addison, Joseph..........II, 633
BUEL, CLARENCE CLOUGH,
Greeley, Horace..........VI, 672
Stockton, Francis Richard
.... VIII, 473, 474
BULBRING, KARL D.,
Defoe, Daniel............III, 49
BULKLEY, L.,
Eliot, George............VII, 183
BULLEIN, WILLIAM,
Barclay, Alexander.........I, 264
Chaucer, Geoffrey.........I, 153
Gower, John..............I, 174

INDEX TO CRITICISMS

	Vol. and Page
Lydgate, John	I, 183
Skelton, John	I, 219

BULLEN, A. H.,
Armstrong, John	III, 699, 699
Barnes, Barnabe	I, 440
Barnes, Joshua	II, 572
Barton, Bernard	V, 597
Beattie, James	IV, 430
Bloomfield, Robert	IV, 723
Brown, Thomas	II, 540, 541
Browne, Sir Thomas	II, 342
Browne, William	II, 76
Burton, Robert	II, 40
Chamberlayne, William	II, 406, 406
Capman, George	I, 728, 730
Cibber, Theophilus	III, 396
Cotton, Charles	II, 371, 372
Dekker, Thomas	II, 58, 61
Drayton, Michael	I, 708
Dryden, John	II, 506
Dyer, Sir Edward	II, 428
Fletcher, John	I, 631
Ford, John	II, 26, 26
Gifford, William	V, 35
Greene, Robert	I, 340
Habington, William	II, 135
Herrick, Robert	II, 240
Horne, Richard Hengist	VII, 545, 547
Jenyns, Soame	IV, 33
King, Henry	II, 223
Marlowe, Christopher	I, 349, 352, 356
Marston, John	I, 739
Middleton, Thomas	I, 682, 682, 684, 686
Oldmixon, John	III, 125
Peele, George	I, 364, 365, 367
Sedley, Sir Charles	II, 510
Shakespeare, William	I, 463

BULLINGER, J. BASS,
Whiston, William	III, 306

BULWER, SIR HENRY LYTTON,
Canning, George	V, 65
Cobbett, William	V, 271

BUNGAY, GEORGE W.,
Greeley, Horace	VI, 670
Lowell, James Russell	VIII, 28
Mackintosh, Sir James	V, 180
Seward, William Henry	VI, 676
Simms, William Gilmore	VI, 598
Sumner, Charles	VI, 757
Whittier, John Greenleaf	VIII, 112

BUNNER, HENRY CUYLER,
Longfellow, Henry Wadsworth	VII, 382
Stevenson, Robert Louis	VIII, 243
Thackeray, William Makepeace	VI, 298

BUNSEN, CHRISTIAN KARL JOSIAS BARON,
Arnold, Thomas	V, 376
Channing, William Ellery	V, 373
Kingsley, Charles	VII, 24
Schoolcraft, Henry Rowe	VI, 403

BUNSEN, GEORGE VON,
Milnes, Richard Monckton	VII, 565

BUNYAN, JOHN,
Bunyan, John	II, 392

BURDER, GEORGE,
Watts, Isaac	III, 249

	Vol. and Page
BURDER, SAMUEL,	
Rowe, Elizabeth	III, 96

BURDETTE, ROBERT J.,
Penn, William	II, 629

BURGES, SIR JAMES BLAND,
Gibbon, Edward	IV, 174

BURGON, J. W.,
Mansel, Henry Longueville	VI, 627

BURGOYNE, GEN. JOHN,
Robinson, Mary	IV, 411

BURIAL-REGISTER,
Lee, Nathaniel	II, 430
Marlowe, Christopher	I, 346

BURKE, EDMUND,
Authors and Authorship	VIII, 6
Bacon, Francis	I, 665
Bede	I, 28
Blacklock, Thomas	IV, 130
Burney, Frances	V, 343
Coke, Sir Edward	I, 740
Critic, The	II, 5
Goldsmith, Oliver	III, 630
History	VI, 7
Juinus	IV, 643
Paine, Thomas	IV, 537
Pitt, William	III, 678
Reynolds, Sir Joshua	IV, 138
Robertson, William	IV, 160
Saint-John, Henry	III, 292
Smith, Adam	IV, 58
Stanhope, Philip Dormer	III, 603

BURKE, MRS. EDMUND,
Burke, Edmund	IV, 290

BURKE, JAMES,
Burke, Edmund	IV, 303

BURKE, S. HUBERT,
Camden, William	I, 622
Colet, John	I, 212
Fisher, John	I, 231
Surrey, Earl of	I, 256

BURKHARDT, JOHN LEWIS
Defoe Daniel	III, 33

BURLINGAME, EDWARD L.,
Browning, Robert	VII, 685, 717
Eliot, George	VII, 200

BURNABY, ANDREW,
Berkeley, George	III, 320

BURNET, GILBERT,
Boyle, Robert	II, 417
Buchanan, George	I, 315
Cheke, Sir John	I, 277
Colet John	I, 211
Collier, Jeremy	II, 702
Cranmer, Thomas	I, 271
Cudworth, Ralph	II, 384
Dryden, John	II, 463
Earle, John	II, 183
Evelyn, John	II 550
Fletcher, Andrew	II, 610
Foxe, John	I, 335
Hobbes, Thomas	II, 324
Ken, Thomas	II, 567
Leighton, Robert	II, 358
L'Estrange, Sir Roger	II, 538
Mackenzie, Sir George	II, 429
More, Henry	II, 373
More, Sir Thomas	I, 241
Pearson, John	II, 368
Penn, William	II, 626
Pole, Reginald	I, 280
Prior, Matthew	II, 673

	Vol. and Page
Ridley, Nicholas	I, 266
Savile, George	II, 449
Sedley, Sir Charles	II, 508
Selden, John	II, 142
Sherlock, William	II, 561
Sidney, Algernon	II, 353
Somers, John Lord	II, 612
Sprat, Thomas	II, 573
Stillingfleet, Edward	II, 454, 454
Tillotson, John Robert	II, 437
Tyndale, William	I, 246
Villiers, George	II, 376
Wilkins, John	II, 227
Wilmot, John	II 336

BURNET, THOMAS,
Burnet, Gilbert	II, 591

BURNETT, GEORGE,
Bacon, Francis	I, 666

BURNETT, JAMES (LORD MONBODDO),
Burnett, James, Lord Monboddo	IV, 346

BURNEY, CHARLES,
Dryden, John	II, 481
Johnson, Samuel	III, 723
Rogers, Samuel	VI, 32

BURNEY, CHARLOTTE ANN,
Chapone, Hester	IV 417
Garrick, David	III, 695
Warton, Thomas	IV, 72

BURNEY, FRANCES,
Burney, Frances	V, 345
Colman, George	IV, 201
Goldsmith, Oliver	III, 625
Johnson, Samuel	III, 721, 745
Pope, Alexander	III, 146
Rowe, Elizabeth	III, 96
Smart, Christopher	III, 592
Smollett, Tobias George	III, 581
Stanhope, Philip Dormer	III, 603
Sterne, Laurence	III, 510

BURNHAM, RICHARD,
Henry, Matthew	II, 584

BURNS, GILBERT,
Burns, Robert	IV, 224

BURNS, ROBERT,
Beattie, James	IV, 431
Blacklock, Thomas	IV, 129
Blair, Hugh	IV, 403
Burns, Robert	IV, 221, 221, 237, 241, 248,
Cowper, William	IV, 378
Ferguson, Robert	III, 639
Gray, Thomas	III, 564
Henry the Minstrel	I, 201
Milton, John	II, 286
Ramsay, Allan	III, 409
Thomson, James	III, 258
Williams, Helen Maria	V, 74

BURROUGHS, JOHN,
Arnold, Matthew	VII, 644, 647
Audubon, John James	V, 699
Browne, Sir Thomas	II, 341
Browning, Robert	VII, 702
Bryant, William Cullen	VII, 124
Carlyle, Thomas	VII, 244, 255, 268
Cowley, Abraham	II, 197
Darwin, Charles Robert	VII 430
Dickens, Charles	VI, 577, 592
Emerson, Ralph Waldo	VII, 355, 359, 370

560 INDEX TO CRITICISMS

Vol. and Page

Gibbon, Edward..........IV, 189
Holmes, Oliver Wendell.VIII, 299
Johnson, Samuel........III, 733
Poe, Edgar Allan..........V, 548
Ruskin, John............VIII, 416
Shelley, Percy Bysshe.....IV, 710
Spencer, Herbert....:...VIII, 482
Tennyson, Alfred Lord..VIII, 103
Thoreau, Henry David......
.... VI, 270, 275
White, Gilbert............IV, 150
Whitman, Walt....VIII, 133, 150
Whittier, John Greenleaf VIII, 118
Wordsworth, William......V, 641
BURROWS, MONTAGU,
 Wyclif, John..........I, 108, 110
BURT, MARY E.,
 Field, Eugene..........VIII, 317
BURTON, EDMUND,
 Murray, William..........IV, 169
BURTON, JOHN HILL,
 Addison, Joseph...........II, 638
 Bentham, Jeremy..........V, 167
 Bentley, Richard.........III, 116
 Boece, Hector.............I, 243
 Defoe, Daniel.........III, 29, 48
 DeQuincey, Thomas.......VI, 118
 Gay, John...............III, 56
 Hume, David........III, 650, 659
 Knox, John............I, 299, 302
 Lyndsay, Sir David........I, 275
 Owens, Robert...........VI, 84
 Pope, Alexander........III, 166
 Sacheverell, Henry........II, 696
 Saint-John, Henry........III, 289
 Swift, Jonathan..........III, 264
 Thomas of Erceldoune......I, 84
 Tooke, John Horne.......IV, 572
 Tucker, Josiah...........IV, 370
 Walpole, Horace..........IV, 322
 Wyntoun, Andrew..........I, 178
BURTON, MRS. JOHN HILL,
 Burton, John Hill........VII, 315
BURTON, RICHARD,
 Browning, Robert........VII, 717
 Cædmon..................I, 24
 Dickens, Charles.........VI, 595
 Holmes, Oliver Wendell VIII, 300
 Irving, Washington.......VI, 153
 Lanier, Sidney..........VII, 330
 Lowell, James Russell....VIII, 42
 Nashe, Thomas...........I, 415
 Stevenson, Robert Louis.....
 ....VIII, 244, 246
 Stowe, Harriet Beecher......
 ....VIII, 354, 356
 Trollope, Anthony.......VII, 465
 Whittier, John Greenleaf....
 ....VIII, 111, 119
BURTON, SIR RICHARD,
 Gibbon, Edward..........IV, 176
 Murchison, Sir Roderick Impey
 ....VI, 630
BURTON, ROBERT,
 Books...................III 5
BURY, JOHN,
 Browning, Robert.......VII, 703
BURY, RICHARD DE,
 Books...................III, 5
BUSCHIUS, HERMAN,
 Tyndale, William..........I, 244

Vol. and Page

BUSHEL, THOMAS,
 Bacon, Francis............I, 641
BUSHNELL, HORACE,
 Beecher, Henry Ward....VII, 604
 Channing, William Ellery..V, 372
 Longfellow, Henry Wadsworth................VII, 400
BUTLER, ARTHUR JOHN,
 Knight, Charles..........VI, 743
BUTLER, CHARLES,
 Burke, Edmund..........IV, 290
 Fox, Charles James......IV, 504
 Junius...................IV, 640
 Littleton, Sir Thomas......I, 196
 Murray, William..........IV, 171
BUTLER, F. H.,
 Priestley, Joseph..........IV, 451
BUTLER, JOSEPH,
 Butler, Joseph.......III, 308, 310
BUTLER, SAMUEL,
 Beaumont and Fletcher.....I, 580
 Darwin, Erasmus.........IV, 424
 Knowledge...............V, 5
 Poets and Poetry.........IV, 5
BUTLER, PROF.,
 Goldsmith, Oliver.........III, 623
BUTTERWORTH, HEZEKIAH,
 Seward, Anna...........IV, 542
 Whittier, John Greenleaf.VIII, 124
BUXTON, SYDNEY,
 Gladstone, William Ewart.....
 ....VIII, 392
 Manning, Henry Edward.....
 ....VIII, 166
BUXTON, TRAVERS,
 Marvell, Andrew..........II, 319
BYRNE, JAMES,
 Spenser, Edmund..........I, 383
BYRNE, MRS. WILLIAM PITT,
 Lever, Charles James......VI, 652
 Whatley, Richard.........VI, 325
BYROM, JOHN,
 Gibbon, Edward..........IV, 173
 Wesley, Charles..........IV, 35
BYRON, LADY A. I. NOEL,
 Byron, George Gordon Lord..
 ....IV, 744
 Jameson, Anna...........VI, 213
BYRON, GEORGE GORDON
 LORD,
 Authors and Authorship.VIII, 7
 Bacon, Francis............I, 666
 Barlow, Joel.............IV, 574
 Barton, Bernard..........V, 565
 Beckford, William.........V, 447
 Berkeley, George.........III, 329
 Blackstone, Sir William...III, 703
 Books...................III, 7
 Bowles, William Lisle..V, 658, 659
 Brougham, Henry Lord....VI, 531
 Burns, Robert ....IV, 247
 Burton, Robert............II, 38
 Butler, Samuel............II, 331
 Byron, George Gordon Lord..
 ....IV, 743, 747, 750, 756
 Campbell, Thomas.V, 440, 440, 441
 Chaucer, Geoffrey.........I, 157
 Churchill, Charles.........III, 476
 Coleridge, Samuel Taylor.....
 ....V, 207, 219, 222
 Colman, George..........V, 316

Vol. and Page

Cowper, William..........IV, 386
Crabbe, George........V, 172, 172
Disraeli, Isaac.............V, 512
Edgeworth, Maria.....V, 562, 568
Erskine, Thomas ....IV, 729
Fielding, Henry..........III, 358
Fox, Charles James...IV, 499, 503
Galt, John............V, 334, 335
Gibbon, Edward..........IV, 173
Grahame, James..........IV, 567
Gray, Thomas............III, 558
Hallam, Henry............VI, 173
Hayley, William..........IV, 653
Hazlitt, William............V, 103
Hemans, Felicia Dorothea...V, 257
History ....VI, 7
Hogg, James..............V, 262
Holcroft, Thomas.........IV, 545
Horner, Francis..........IV, 629
Hunt, James Henry Leigh....
 ....VI, 155, 167
Jeffrey, Francis Lord.......V, 653
Johnson, Samuel....III, 739, 755
Junius ....IV, 640
Keats, John......IV, 663, 672, 675
Knowledge ....V, 7
Lamb, Lady Caroline.......V, 83
Lewis, Matthew Gregory.....
 ....IV, 631, 633, 635
Mackintosh, Sir James......V, 178
Maturin, Charles Robert...IV, 766
Milton, John..........II, 260, 287
Mitford, William...........V, 70
Montagu, Lady Mary Wortley.
 ....III, 464
Montgomery, James........V, 766
Moore, John.............IV, 426
Moore, Thomas........V, 706, 715
Parr, Samuel..............V, 18
Pope, Alexander.........III, 185
Porson, Richard.........IV, 521
Procter, Bryan Waller.....VI, 747
Pye, Henry James.........IV, 580
Richardson, Samuel.......III, 436
Robertson, William.......IV, 159
Rogers, Samuel......VI, 32, 32, 39
Romilly, Sir Samuel......IV, 634
Scott, Sir Walter............
 ....V, 139, 140, 141, 157
Shakespeare, William...I, 473, 555
Sheridan, Richard Brinsley....
 ....IV, 594, 600, 605
Smith, Horace............V, 598
Smith, Sydney............V, 467
Southey, Robert...V, 403, 411, 411
Spenser, Edmund...........I, 395
Stanhope, Philip Dormer..III, 607
Swift, Jonathan..........III, 229
Walpole, Horace.....IV, 318, 318
Washington, George.......IV, 358
White, Henry Kirke...IV, 487, 488
Wilson, John.............V, 751
Wordsworth, William...V, 622, 629

CABELL, ISA CARRINGTON,
 Disraeli, Benjamin ......
 ....VI, 287, 287
CABLE, LUCY LEFFINGWELL,
 Goldsmith, Oliver........III, 622
CABLE, GEORGE WASHINGTON,
 Field, Eugene ....VIII, 316

INDEX TO CRITICISMS

	Vol. and Page
Holmes, Oliver Wendell	VIII, 297
CABOT, JAMES ELLIOT,	
Emerson, Ralph Waldo	VII, 350
CAINE, HALL,	
Arnold, Sir Edwin	VIII, 504
Brontë, Anne	V, 599
Buchanan, Robert	VIII, 448
Byron, George Gordon Lord	IV, 742
Coleridge, Samuel Taylor	V, 212, 218
Drummond, William	II, 103
Hunt, James Henry Leigh	VI, 160, 166, 170
Longfellow, Henry Wadsworth	VII, 408
Keats, John	IV, 679
Milton, John	II, 273
Rossetti, Gabriel Charles Dante	VII, 436, 446, 447, 453
Shelley, Percy Bysshe	IV, 695
Sheridan, Richard Brinsley	IV, 597
Southey, Robert	V, 402, 405, 417
Sterne, Laurence	III, 511
CAINE, LILY HALL,	
Rossetti, Gabriel Charles Dante	VII, 438
CAIRD, EDWARD,	
Berkeley, George	III, 334
Carlyle, Thomas	VII, 259
Hume, David	III, 664
Jowett Bénjamin	VIII, 210, 212
Wordsworth, William	V, 626
CAIRD, JOHN,	
Bacon, Francis	I, 645, 651
CAIRNES, J. E.,	
Mill, John Stuart	VI, 714
CAIRNES, JOHN,	
Gibbon, Edward	IV, 188
Hamilton, Sir William	VI, 52
Hume, David	III, 664
Mill, John Stuart	VI, 716
Tindal, Matthew	III, 73
Woolston, Thomas	III, 74
CAIRNES, WILLIAM B.	
Franklin, Benjamin	IV, 105
CALAMY, EDMUND,	
Echard, Laurence	III, 22
Howe, John	II, 544
CALDECOTT, ALFRED,	
Martineau, James	VIII, 429
CALDERWOOD, HENRY,	
Hume, David	III, 651, 653
Spencer, Herbert	VIII, 481
CALDWELL, CHARLES,	
Ames, Fisher	IV, 528
CALDWELL, WILLIAM,	
Smith, Adam	IV, 71
CALL, W. M. W.,	
Eliot, George	VII, 183, 189
CALLENDER, J. T.,	
Hamilton, Alexander	IV, 456
COLLOWAY, MORGAN, JR.,	
Lanier, Sidney	VII, 330
CALVERLEY, CHARLES STUART	
Lytton, Sir Edward George Bulwer	VI, 697
CALVERT, GEORGE HENRY,	
Coleridge, Samuel Taylor	V, 220
Goldsmith, Oliver	III, 627

	Vol. and Page
Keats, John	IV, 673, 678
Longfellow, Henry Wadsworth	VII, 399
Robertson Frederick William	V, 740
Shelley, Percy Bysshe	IV, 710
Tennyson, Alfred Lord	VIII, 103
Washington, George	IV, 360
Wordsworth, William	V, 638
CAMBRIDGE GESTA BOOK,	
Dennis, John	III, 75
CAMDEN, WILLIAM,	
Bacon, Francis	I, 639
Littleton, Sir Thomas	I, 196
Puttenham, George	I, 401
Spenser, Edmund	I, 368, 368
CAMERON, MRS CHARLES HAY,	
Tennyson, Alfred Lord	VIII, 68
CAMERON, V. LOVETT,	
Burton, Sir Richard Francis	VII, 758
CAMPAN, JEANNE LOUISE HENRIETTE,	
Franklin, Benjamin	IV, 85
CAMPBELL, DR.,	
Hume, David	III, 647
CAMPBELL, ARCHIBALD,	
Black, William	VIII, 394
CAMPBELL, DOUGLAS,	
Foxe, John	I, 336
CAMPBELL, G. W.	
Somerville, William	III, 127
CAMPBELL HELEN,	
Bradstreet, Anne	II, 230
CAMPBELL JAMES DYKES,	
Bowles, William Lisle	V, 663
Coleridge, Samuel Taylor	V, 213
Coleridge, Sara	V, 734
CAMPBELL, J. F.,	
Macpherson, James	IV, 277
CAMPBELL, J. McLEOD,	
Edwards, Jonathan	III, 390
CAMPBELL, JOHN,	
Alfred the Great	I, 39
Bury, Richard de	I, 89
Geoffrey of Monmouth	I, 55
Oldys, William	III, 457
Raleigh, Sir Walter	I, 593
CAMPBELL, JOHN LORD,	
Bacon, Francis I, 644, 650, 655 660	
Brougham, Henry Lord	VI, 526,532
Erskine, Thomas	IV, 730
Hyde, Edward, Earl of Clarendon	II, 303
Junius	IV 645
Macaulay, Thomas Lord Babington	VI, 104
More, Sir Thomas	I, 237, 238
Murray, John	IV, 171
North, Roger	III, 80
Pope, Alexander	III, 187
CAMPBELL, LEWIS, AND GARNETT, WILLIAM,	
Maxwell, James Clerk	VII, 168
CAMPBELL, LORD,	
Norton, Caroline Elizabeth Sheridan	VII,101
CAMPBELL, THOMAS,	
Akenside, Mark	III, 544
Alexander, Sir William	II, 35
Anstey, Christopher	IV, 480

	Vol and Page
Armstrong, John	III. 698. 699
Baillie, Joanna	V, 693
Barclay, Alexander	I, 264
Beaumont and Fletcher	I, 581
Beaumont, Sir John	I. 580
Blacklock, Thomas	IV. 130
Blair, Robert	III. 242
Bowles, William Lisle	V, 660
Breton, Nicholas	I, 678
Brooke, Henry	III, 713, 714
Browne, William	II. 75
Burns, Robert	IV. 251
Bryon, George Gordon Lord	IV, 744
Carew, Thomas	II, 22
Chamberlayne, William	II, 406
Chapman, George	I, 732
Chatterton, Thomas	III, 536
Chaucer, Geoffrey	I, 142, 150
Churchill, Charles	III, 479
Collins, William	III, 416
Corbet, Richard	I, 743
Cotton, Charles	II, 371
Cowley, Abraham	II, 200
Cowper, William	IV, 385
Crabbe, George	V, 170
Crashaw, Richard	II, 111
Daniel, Samuel	I, 616
D'Avenant, Sir William	II, 218
Davies, Sir John	I. 633
Dekker, Thomas	II. 55
Dodsley, Robert	III. 483
Donne, John	I, 711, 715
Drayton, Michael	I, 704, 706
Drummond, William	II. 105
Dryden, John	II. 498
Dwight, Timothy	IV. 626
Dyer, John	III, 399
Etheredge, Sir George	II, 415
Fairfax, Edward	I, 742
Falconer, William	III, 525
Fanshawe, Sir Richard	II. 185
Fenton, Elijah	III, 20
Fletcher, Giles	I, 623
Fletcher, Phineas	II, 116
Ford, John	II. 89
Garth, Sir Samuel	II, 665
Gay, John	III, 55
Gloucester, Robert of	I. 82
Glover, Richard	IV. 17, 18, 21, 22
Goldsmith, Oliver	III 633
Gower, John	I, 175
Grahame, James	IV. 566
Grainger, James	III, 498
Gray, Thomas	III. 565
Green, Matthew	III, 94
Greene, Robert	I. 344
Habington, William	II, 136
Hall, Joseph	II. 145
Hamilton, William	III. 336
Harding, John	I. 194
Hawes, Stephen	I. 217
Heywood, Thomas	II, 125
Johnson, Samuel	III, 721
Jones, Sir William	IV, 199
Jonson, Ben	I, 753, 758,763
Kyd, Thomas	I 359
Langhorne, John	III, 700
Langland, William	I. 118
Lee, Nathaniel	II, 432
Lillo, George	III, 102
Logan John	IV, 43

INDEX TO CRITICISMS

Mackintosh, Sir James.....V, 178
Mannying, Robert.........I, 87
Marlowe, Christopher.......I, 354
Marryat, Frederick........V, 531
Marston, John.............I, 737
Marvell, Andrew..........II, 316
Mason, William......IV, 323, 324
Massinger, Philip.......II, 41, 47
May, Thomas..............II, 120
Mickle, William Julius.....IV, 42
Milton, John..............II, 260
Minot, Lawrence...........I, 93
More, Henry...............II, 373
Occleve, Thomas...........I, 187
Oway, Thomas ....II, 366
Overbury, Sir Thomas......I, 442
Parnell, Thomas..........II, 616
Peele, George ....I, 365
Philips, John............II, 564
Philips, Katherine........II, 180
Pomfret, John............II, 511
Pope, Alexander..........III, 184
Prior, Matthew...........II, 677
Quarles, Francis.........II, 78
Ramsay, Allan......III, 403, 406
Randolph, Thomas.........I, 744
Rolle, Richard............I, 92
Rowe, Nicholas...........II, 622
Rowley, William..........II, 68
Sackville, Charles.......II, 553
Sackville, Thomas........I, 432
Sedley, Sir Charles......II, 508
Shakespeare, William...I, 458,
469, 474, 478, 540, 559, 490,
...............516, 537
Shenstone, William.......III, 473
Shirley, James...........II, 190
Sidney, Sir Phillip......I, 323
Skelton, John............I, 220
Smart, Christopher......III, 594
Smollett, Tobias George......
...............III, 577, 585, 592
Spenser, Edmund..........I, 395
Sternhold, Thomas,.......I, 262
Stevenson, John Hall.....IV, 34
Sylvester, Joshua........I, 609
Thomson, James......III, 258, 263
Vaughan, Henry.......... II, 443
Walsh, William...........II, 560
Warner, William..........I, 437
Warton, Joseph...........IV, 397
Warton, Thomas...........IV, 77
Watts, Isaac............III, 253
Webster, John.............I, 674
Whitehead, William.......IV, 32
Wither, George...........II, 214
Wyatt, Sir Thomas........I, 251
Young, Edward...........III, 487
CANNING, GEORGE,
  Horner, Francis........IV, 629
CANNING, STRATFORD,
  Porson, Richard........IV, 521
CAPGAVE, JOHN,
  Wyclif, John............I, 99
CAR, THOMAS,
  Crashaw, Richard........II, 110
CAREW, THOMAS,
  Donne, John ....I 714
  Jonson Ben..............I, 759
  May, Thomas............II, 120
  Sandys George..........II, 83

CAREY, CHARLES STOKES,
  Stanhope, Philip Dormer..III, 606
CAREY, HENRY,
  Carey, Henry...........III, 139
  Philips, Ambrose........III, 274
CAREY, HENRY C.,
  Ricardo, David.........IV, 727
  Smith, Adam............IV, 64
CARGILL, ALEXANDER,
  Walton, Isaac..........II, 348
CARLETON, SIR DUDLEY,
  Bacon, Francis.........I, 639
CARLETON, WILLIAM
  Carleton, William......VI, 549
  Fielding, Henry........III, 353
CARLETON, WILL,
  Burns, Robert.........IV, 232, 266
  Payne, John Howard.....V, 736
CARLISLE, EARL OF
  Austen, Jane...........IV, 619
  Fox, Charles James.....IV, 499
  Macaulay, Thomas Babington
    Lord.................VI, 103
  Pope Alexander.........III, 155
  Ticknor, George........VI, 616
CARLISLE, H.,
  Newman, John Henry......
  ....VII, 747, 754
CARLISLE, HARVEY,
  Whewell, William....VI, 469, 472
CARLYLE, ALEXANDER,
  Blair, Hugh............IV, 403
  Blair, Robert..........III, 241
  Dodd, William..........III, 675
  Ferguson, Adam......IV, 610, 611
  Franklin, Benjamin......III, 80
  Home, John.............IV 513
  Hume, David............III, 647
  Hutcheson, Francis.....III, 244
  Macpherson, James......IV, 272
  Shenstone, William.....III, 471
  Smith, Adam............IV, 53
  Smollett, Tobias George....III, 573
  Thomson, James.........III, 265
  Wilkes, John...........IV, 332
CARLYLE, E. IRVING,
  Doyle Sir Francis Hastings
    Charles ....VII, 650
  Savage Richard.........III, 134
  Sheffield, John, Third Earl of
    Mulgrave ....II, 672
  Taylor Brook...........III, 52
  Thomson, William.......III, 501
  Tyndale, William........I, 249
CARLYLE JANE WELSH,
  Colenso, John William.VII, 522,523
  Darwin, Charles Robert...VII, 423
  Forster, John..........VII, 65
  Lewes, George Henry....VII 142
  Maurice, John Frederick Denison
    ....VI, 644
  Strickland, Agnes......VI, 767
  Tennyson, Alfred Lord..VIII, 65
  Thackeray, William Makepeace
    ....VI, 302
  Trollope, Anthony.....VII, 459
  Tyndall, John.........VIII, 195
CARLYLE, THOMAS,
  Addison, Joseph........II, 656
  Airy, Sir George Biddell......
    ....VIII, 183

Akenside Mark..........III, 544
Aclott, Amos Bronson.. VII, 662
Alison, Archibald.........V, 341
Ascham Roger............I, 220
Bacon, Delia.........VI, 203, 206
Bacon, Francis.......I, 644,. 649
Bentham, Jeremy..........V, 165
Books ....III, 7
Boswell James..IV, 210, 216, 216
Bowring, Sir John........VI, 664
Bright, John............VII, 720
Brougham, Henry Lord...VI 524
Bunyan John............II, 394
Burns, Robert............
.........IV, 227, 244, 246, 253
Byron, George Gordon Lord..
...................IV, 734, 757
Campbell, Thomas....V, 434, 442
Carlyle, Thomas....VII, 230, 245
Chalmers, Thomas........V, 492
Channing, William Ellery..V, 370
Child, Lydia Maria.....VII, 221
Clough, Arthur Hugh......VI, 252
Coleridge, Samuel Taylor....
...................V, 210, 222
Cooper, James Fenimore...V, 683
Cunningham, Allan........V, 382
DeQuincey, Thomas........
.............VI, 116, 119, 125
Dickens, Charles......VI, 551, 560
Disraeli, Benjamin......VII, 278
Disraeli, Isaac...........V, 512
Drummond, William.......II, 105
Elliott, Ebenezer.........V, 580
Emerson, Ralph Waldo......
.................VII, 343, 361
Faraday, Michael........VI, 512
Ferguson, Robert........III, 640
Ferrier, James Frederick....
.....................VI, 410
Fielding, Henry.........III, 358
Fox, George............II, 420
Franklin, Benjamin......IV, 88
Fuller, Sarah Margaret..V, 664, 670
Gibbon, Edward.IV, 181, 184, 187
Gilfillan, George........VII, 150
Gladstone, William Ewart....
....................VIII, 384
Godwin, Mary Woolstonecraft
....................IV, 327
Godwin, William......V, 293, 302
Goldsmith, Oliver.....III, 617, 626
Gray, Thomas...........III, 566
Hamilton, Sir William.....VI, 52
Hazlitt, William .... V, 98
Heylin, Peter...........II, 174
Hogg, James............V, 263
Home, Henry...........III, 713
Hume, David....III, 653, 657, 665
Hunt, James Henry Leigh....
..............VI, 155, 164, 168
Hyde, Edward, Earl of Clarendon
..................II, 300
Irving, Edward.......V, 247, 248
Irving, Washington......VI, 133
Jeffrey, Francis Lord......V, 651
Jonson, Ben.............I, 748
Johnson, Samuel..........
..............III, 729, 744, 757
Knox, John.........I, 297, 301
Lamb, Charles........V, 229, 230

INDEX TO CRITICISMS 563

	Vol. and Page
Landor, Walter Savage	VI. 373, 387
Laud, William	II. 91
Locke, John	II, 533
Lockhart, John Gibson	V, 754, 755
Lytton, Sir Edward George Bulwer	VI, 679
Macaulay, Thomas Babington Lord	VI, 92, 98
Malthus, Thomas Robert	V. 252
Martineau, Harriet	VII, 55
Maurice, John Frederick Denison	VI, 644
Mill, John Stuart	VI, 701, 712
Milnes, Richard Monckton	VII. 560
Milton, John	II, 261, 289
Moore, John	IV, 427, 429
Moore, Thomas	V, 712
Newman, Francis William	VIII, 370
Owen, Sir Richard	VIII, 170
Paine, Thomas	IV, 535
Paley, William	IV, 476
Park, Mungo	IV, 485, 485
Poets and Poetry	IV, 7
Pope, Alexander	III, 167, 187
Porter, Jane	V, 673
Procter, Bryan Waller	VI, 744, 745
Pusey, Edward Bouverie	VII, 471
Robertson, William	IV, 162, 163
Rogers, Samuel	VI, 33
Russell, John Earl	VII, 145
Scott, Sir Walter	V, 130, 142, 148
Shakespeare, William	I, 450,560
Smollett, Tobias George	III, 576
Southey, Robert	V, 401, 414
Sterling, John	V, 452
Sterne, Laurence	III, 512
Stewart, Dugald	V, 79
Sumner, Charles	VI, 751
Swift, Jonathan	III, 230
Taylor, Sir Henry	VII, 579
Taylor, William	V, 319
Tennyson, Alfred Lord	VIII, 65, 83, 93
Thackeray, William Makepeace	VI, 291
Thirlwall, Connop	VII, 42
Thoreau, Henry David	VI, 272
Washington, George	IV, 359
Webster, Daniel	V, 719
Whitefield, George	III, 547
Wilberforce, Samuel	VI, 732
Williams, Sir Charles Hanbury	III, 413
Wilson, John	V, 744, 752
Wordsworth, William	V, 613, 631
CARMAN, BLISS, Authors and Authorship	VIII, 10
CARNARVON, EARL, Mansel, Henry Longueville	VI, 626, 628
CARNEGIE, ANDREW, Scott, Sir Walter	V, 132
CARPENTER, FRANK B., Lincoln, Abraham	VI, 413
CARPENTER, FRANK D. Y., Payne, John Howard	V, 737
CARPENTER, FRANK G., Stanley, Sir Henry Morton	VIII, 506

	Vol. and Page
CARPENTER, FREDERIC IVES, Breton, Nicholas	I, 679
Browne, William	II, 77
Chapman, George	I, 734
Crashaw, Richard	II. 114
Daniel, Samuel	I, 617
Donne, John	I, 718
Drayton, Michael	I, 709
Drummond, William	II, 107
Greene, Robert	I, 345
Herrick, Robert	II. 241
Jonson, Ben	I. 767
Milton, John	II. 298
Peele. George	I. 367
Sidney, Sir Philip	I, 332
Spenser, Edmund	I, 400
Vaughan, Henry	II. 446
Webster, John	I, 674, 677
CARPENTER, GEORGE RICE, Brown, Charles Brockden	IV, 552
DeQuincey, Thomas	VI, 124
CARPENTER, H. BERNARD, Browning, Robert	VII, 703
CARPENTER, MATTHEW H., Choate, Rufus	VI, 196
CARPENTER, NATHANIEL, Browne, William	II. 74
CARPENTER, WILLIAM BOYD, Browning, Robert	VII, 718
Coleridge, Samuel Taylor	V, 219
Darwin, Charles Robert	VII, 417
Spurgeon, Charles Haddon	VIII, 178, 180
Tennyson, Alfred Lord	VIII, 90, 108
CARR, J. A. Usher, James	II, 153
CARR, J. COMYNS, Blake, William	V, 61
Reynolds, Sir Joshua	IV, 141
Rossetti, Gabriel Charles Dante	VII, 441
CARR, WILLIAM, Park, Mungo	IV, 486
Wolcot, John	IV, 649
CARROLL, CHARLES, Tyndall, John	VIII, 195
CARRUTHERS, ROBERT, Pope, Alexander	III, 149, 171, 188
Scott, Alexander	I, 319
Waller, Edmund	II, 382
Wilson, John	V, 751
CARTER, ELIZABETH, Fielding, Henry	III, 355
Richardson, Samuel	III, 432
CARTER, FRANKLIN, Butler Joseph	III, 310
Hopkins, Mark	VII 614, 615
CARTERET, LORD, Swift, Jonathan	III, 198
CARTWRIGHT, JULIA (MRS. HENRY ADY), Temple, Sir William	II, 457
Waller, Edmund	II, 379
CARTWRIGHT, WILLIAM, Fletcher, John	I, 629
Shakespeare, William	I, 549
CARY, EDWARD, Curtis, George William	VIII. 187, 188, 188, 189
Fiske, John	VIII, 458

	Vol and Page
CARY, ELISABETH LUTHER. Browning, Robert	VII 683,696
Morris, William	VIII, 332
Rossetti, Gabriel Charles Dante	VII, 455
Tennyson, Alfred Lord	VIII, 97
CARY, HENRY FRANCIS. Anstey, Christopher	IV, 481
Beattie, James	IV, 430, 433
Chatterton, Thomas	III, 536
Coleridge, Samuel Taylor	V. 214
Darwin, Erasmus	IV. 422
Day, Thomas	IV, 50
Gray, Thomas	III, 566
Hayley, William	IV, 653
Johnson, Samuel	III, 739, 749
Jones, Sir William	IV, 199
Logan, John	IV, 44
Mickle, William Julius	IV, 41, 42
Scott, Sir Walter	V, 135
Shakespeare, William	I. 524
Smollett, Tobias George	III. 577, 585
Warton, Joseph	IV, 398
Warton, Thomas	IV, 72, 78
White, Henry Kirke	IV, 488
CARY, PHŒBE, Dickens, Charles	VI, 585
CASSERLY, D. A., Habington, William	II, 134, 136
CASTELAR, EMILIO, Byron, George Gordon Lord	IV, 751, 761
CATES, WILLIAM L. R., Douglas, Gawin	I, 212
Hill, John	III, 644
Holinshed, Raphael	I, 311
Grosseteste, Robert	I, 72
Jewell, John	I, 293
John of Salisbury	I, 59
Johnston, Arthur	II, 54
Leland, John	I, 262
Rowe, Elizabeth	III, 96
Sheridan, Thomas	IV, 46
William of Occam	I, 90
CATHCART, GEORGE R., Agassiz, Jean Louis Rudolphe	VI, 723
Bancroft, George	VIII, 58
Disraeli, Benjamin	VII, 293
Froude James Anthony	VIII. 263
Greeley, Horace	VI, 671
Hawthorne, Nathaniel	VI, 366
Helps Sir Arthur	VII, 40
Johnson, Samuel	III, 760
Merivale, Charles	VIII, 218
Motley, John Lothrop	VII, 94
Simms, William Gilmore	VI 599
Sumner, Charles	VI, 757
Whittier John Greenleaf	VIII, 121
CATTERMOLE, RICHARD, Jewell, John	I, 294
CAVENDISH MARGARET (DUTCHESS OF NEWCASTLE), Cavendish, Margaret	II, 231
Shakespeare, William	I, 549
CAWTHORN, THOMAS, Fielding, Henry	III, 356
CAXTON, WILLIAM, Caxton, William	I, 197
Chaucer, Geoffrey	I, 124, 137, 141

564 INDEX TO CRITICISMS

	Vol. and Page
Malory, Sir Thomas	I, 203
Skelton, John	I 219
CAYLEY, ARTHUR,	
More, Sir Thomas	I, 236
CAZALÉS, M.,	
Burke, Edmund	IV, 290
CECIL, RICHARD,	
Butler, Joseph	III, 313
Latimer, Hugh	I, 268
CECIL, SIR WILLIAM,	
Jewell, John	I, 293
CERVANTES,	
History	VI 5
CECYLL, ROBERT,	
Raleigh, Sir Walter	I, 590
Knox, John	I, 295
CHADWICK, JOHN WHITE,	
Beecher, Henry Ward	VII, 600, 608
Brooks, Phillips	VIII 232
Bryant William Cullen	VII, 114
Clarke, James Freeman	VII 673
Church, Richard William	VII 730
Curtis, George William	VIII, 186, 191
Drummond, Henry	VIII, 365
Emerson, Ralph Waldo	VII, 353
Holmes, Oliver Wendell	VIII, 292, 298
Lecky, William E. H.	VIII, 489
Lowell, James Russell	VIII 34, 35, 42
Mann, Horace	VI, 202
Newman Francis William	VII, 370, 371
McCosh, James	VIII, 302
Parker, Theodore	VI, 209, 212
Pusey, Edward Bouverie	VII, 477
Stephen, Sir Leslie	VIII, 512
Stoddard Richard Henry	VIII, 496
Stowe Harriet Beecher	VIII, 355, 357
CHADWICK, WILLIAM,	
Defoe, Daniel	III, 28, 43
CHALMERS, ALEXANDER,	
Berkeley, George	III, 329
Chatterton, Thomas	III, 530
Cowper, William	IV, 371
Hawkesworth, John	III, 609
Johnson, Samuel	III, 727
Moore, Edward	III, 376
Smollett, Tobias George	III 587
Steele, Sir Richard	II, 757, 762
Swift, Jonathan	III, 229
Tickell, Thomas	III, 106
Warton, Thomas	IV, 72
CHALMERS, GEORGE,	
Defoe, Daniel	III, 33, 45
Lyndsay, Sir David	I, 274
Ramsay, Allan	III, 406
Spenser, Edmund	I, 370
CHALMERS, THOMAS,	
Butler, Joseph	III, 313
Irving, Edward	V, 246
Stewart, Dugald	V, 76
CHAMBERLAIN, JOHN,	
Gladstone, William Ewart	VIII, 389
Spenser, Edmund	I, 368
CHAMBERLAIN, MELLEN,	
Adams, John	V, 52
Webster, Daniel	V, 729

	Vol. and Page
CHAMBERLAIN, N. H.,	
Sewall, Samuel	III, 19
CHAMBERLAIN, ROBERT,	
Shakespeare, William	I, 549
CHAMBERLEN, PAUL,	
Sacheverell, Henry	II, 695
CHAMBERLIN, NICHOLAS,	
Bacon, Francis	I, 649
Middleton, Thomas	I, 681
CHAMBERS, EDMUND KERCHEVER,	
Arnold, Sir Edwin	VIII, 505
Basse, William	II, 131
Cooper, Anthony Ashley	II, 580
Gay, John	III, 55
Leighton, Robert	II, 360
Marvell, Andrew	II, 318
May, Thomas	II, 119
More, Henry	II, 375
Newton, Sir Isaac	II, 726
Palgrave, Francis Turner	VIII 372
Pope, Alexander	III, 158
Rossetti, Christina Georgina	VIII, 272
Spenser, Edmund	I, 377
Usher, James	II, 154
CHAMBERS, ROBERT,	
Addison, Joseph	II, 658
Ainsworth, William Harrison	VII, 487
Akenside, Mark	III, 542
Alison, Archibald	V, 342
Allingham, William	VII, 735
Armstrong, Robert	III, 699
Bage, Robert	IV, 419
Barclay, Robert	II, 412
Barham, Richard Harris	V,476
Beckford, William	V,449
Birch, Thomas	III, 499
Blacklock, Thomas	IV, 131
Blair, Robert	III, 242
Brewster, Sir David	VI, 547
Brown, Charles Brockden	IV, 556
Browning, Elizabeth Barrett	VI, 236, 246
Bruce, James	IV, 206, 208
Bryant, William Cullen	VII,123
Buckland, Francis Trevelyan	VII, 211
Budgell, Eustace	III, 92, 92
Burns, Robert	IV, 237, 242
Burton, John Hill	VII, 316
Carleton, William	VI, 549
Chamberlayne, William	II, 407
Clarke, Samuel	II, 750
Colman, George	V, 317
Cotton, Sir Robert	I, 709
Cowper, William	IV, 374
Cudworth, Ralph	II, 387
Cunningham, Allan	V, 384
Dillon, Wentworth	III, 361
Disraeli, Benjamin	VII, 286, 290
Dobell, Sidney Thompson	VII, 549
Doddridge, Philip	III, 303
Donne, John	I, 716
Dryden, John	II, 488
Edwards, Jonathan	III, 392
Eliot, George	VII, 187
Erskine, Thomas	IV, 731
Fergusson, Robert	III, 640
Ferrier, Susan Edmonstone	V, 764

	Vol. and Page
Fletcher, Giles	I, 623
Foster, John	V, 426
Freeman, Edward Augustus	VIII, 158
Gaskell, Elizabeth Cleghorn	VI, 433
Gilfillan, George	VI., 152
Glovers, Richard	IV, 19
Gore, Catherine Grace	VI, 264
Grant, Anne	V, 330
Greg, William Rathbone	VII, 320
Guthrie, Thomas	VI, 738
Hale, Sir Matthew	II, 307
Haliburton, William Chandler	VI 456
Hallam, Henry	VI 179
Hamilton, Thomas	V, 395
Hamilton, William	III, 336
Harris, James	III, 710
Herschel, Sir John Frederick William	VI, 625
Heylin, Peter	II, 175
Hill, Aaron	III, 278
Hoadley, Benjamin	III, 424
Horsley, Samuel	IV, 496
Ireland, William Henry	V, 290
Irving, Washington	VI,142
Jameson, Anna	VI, 216
Johnstone, Charles	IV, 413
Lamb, Lady Caroline	V, 83
Langhorne, John	III, 701
Leland, John	III, 500
Leslie, Charles	II, 680
L'Estrange, Sir Roger	II, 539
Lever, Charles James	VI, 654
Lockhart, John Gibson	V, 757
Longfellow, Henry Wadsworth	VII, 405
Lowth, William	III, 63
Mackay, Charles	VII,764
Marryat, Frederick	V, 533
Mason, William	IV, 325
Mathias, Thomas James	V, 289
Mickle, William Julius	IV, 40
Middleton, Conyers	III, 280
Motherwell, William	V, 277
Moore, Edward	III, 376
Paley, William	IV, 471, 477
Palgrave, Sir Francis	VI, 265
Park, Mungo	IV, 486
Payne, John Howard	V, 737
Pearson, John	II, 369
Phillips, Ambrose	III, 275
Piozzi, Hester Lynch	IV, 686
Poe, Edgar Allan	V, 541
Pomfret, John	II, 511
Prideaux, Humphrey	II, 697
Pusey, Edward Bouverie	VII, 472
Raleigh, Sir Walter	I, 604
Richardson, Samuel	III, 445
Sadler, Michael Thomas	V, 287
Scott, Michael	V, 279
Scott, Sir Walter	V, 129, 149, 156
Somerville, Mary	VI, 659
Sotheby, William	V, 204
Spedding, James	VII, 319
Speed, John	I, 695
Spelman, Sir Henry	II, 54
Steevens, George	IV, 411
Stillingfleet, Edward	II, 455
Swift, Jonathan	III 225
Tannahill, Robert	IV 549

INDEX TO CRITICISMS

	Vol. and Page
Taylor, John	II, 132
Temple, Sir William	II, 456
Tennant, William	V, 528
Tennyson, Alfred Lord	VIII, 79
Toland, John	II, 682
Trollope, Anthony	VII, 460
Turner, Sharon	V, 499
Vaughan, Henry	II, 444
Webster, Daniel	V, 725
West, Gilbert	III, 368
Whatley, Richard	VI, 327
Whiston, William	III, 305
Wilkie, William	III, 595
Willis, Nathaniel Parker	VI, 491
Wilson, Arthur	II, 128
Wolcot, John	IV, 650

CHAMBERS, WILLIAM,
Chambers, Robert	VI, 619, 621
Hogg, James	V, 265
Mitford, Mary Russell	VI, 42

CHAMPLIN, JOHN DENISON,
| Carey, Henry | III, 137 |

CHAMPNEYS, BASIL,
| Patmore, Coventry K. D. | VIII, 343 |

CHANDLER, BESSIE,
| Carlyle, Thomas | VII, 239 |

CHANDLER MISS
| Miller, Hugh | VI, 64 |

CHANDLER, SAMUEL,
| Watts, Isaac | III, 248 |

CHANNING, ALBERT S. G.,
| Dickens, Charles | V, 587 |

CHANNING, EDWARD,
Hildreth, Richard	VI, 455
Jefferson, Thomas	V, 46
Washington, George	IV, 367

CHANNING, EDWARD T.,
Dana, Richard Henry, Jr.	VII, 500
Goldsmith Oliver	III, 636
Scott, Sir Walter	V, 150
Stanhope, Philip Dormer	III, 604

CHANNING, WILLIAM ELLERY,
Books	III, 8
Brougham, Henry Lord	VI, 531
Carlyle, Thomas	VII, 246
Channing, William Ellery	VI, 366
Fuller, Sarah Margaret	V, 665
Hallam, Henry	VI, 177
Hawthorne, Nathaniel	V, 359
Hopkins, Samuel	IV, 438, 439
Jameson, Anna	VI, 214
Johnson, Samuel	III, 749
Lover, Samuel	VI, 545
Lytton, Sir Edward George Bulwer	VI, 694
Martineau, Harriet	VII, 61
Milman, Henry Hart	VI, 537
Milton, John	II, 251, 275, 288
Mitford, Mary Russell	VI, 43
Steele, Sir Richard	II, 762
Taylor, Sir Henry	VI, 580
Thoreau, Henry David	VI, 269, 273
Trollope, Frances Milton	VI, 331
Wordsworth, William	V, 632

CHANNING, WILLIAM HENRY,
Allston, Washington	V, 419
Bailey, Philip James	VIII, 460
Brontë, Charlotte	VI, 18
Butler, Joseph	III, 309
Channing, William Ellery	V, 367
Hutcheson, Francis	III, 246

	Vol. and Page
Ripley, George	VII, 224, 225

CHAPMAN, EDWARD MORTIMER
| Lecky, William E. H. | VIII, 487, 490 |

CHAPMAN, GEORGE,
| Marlowe, Christopher | I, 353 |

CHAPMAN, JOHN JAY,
Browning, Robert	VII, 683
Emerson, Ralph Waldo	VII, 360, 378
Stevenson, Robert Louis	VIII, 240, 251
Whitman, Walt	VIII, 151

CHAPMAN, MARIA WESTON,
| Channing, William Ellery | V, 368 |
| Martineau, Harriet | VII, 56 |

CHAPPELL, WILLIAM,
Burney, Charles	IV, 589
Carey, William	III, 138
D'Urfey, Thomas	II, 688
Thomson, James	III, 264

CHAPUYS EUSTACE,
| More, Sir Thomas | I, 233 |

CHARLEMONT, LORD,
Burke, Edmund	IV, 289
Hume, David	III, 647
Reynolds, Sir Joshua	IV, 138
Stanhope, Philip Dormer	III, 603
Warton, Joseph	V, 396

CHARLES, ELIZABETH RUNDLE,
| More, Hannah | V, 195 |

CHARLES I.,
| Graham, James | II, 121 |

CHARLES II.,
| Ken, Thomas | II, 567 |
| South, Robert | II, 607 |

CHARLES V. OF FRANCE,
| Fisher, John | I, 230 |
| More, Sir Thomas | I, 234 |

CHARLETT, A.,
| Wood, Anthony | II, 447 |

CHARLTON, LINOEL,
| Cædmon | I, 22 |

CHASE, LUCEIN B.,
| Bancroft, George | VIII, 55 |

CHASE, SALMON PORTLAND,
| Houghton, Henry Lord | VI, 531 |

CHASLES, VICTOR EUPHÉMION PHILARÈTE,
Audubon, John James	V, 697
Bryant, William Cullen	VII, 122
Carlyle, Thomas	VI, 246
Emerson, Ralph Waldo	VII, 363
Franklin, Benjamin	IV, 100
Haliburton, William Chandler	VI, 456
Longfellow, Henry Wadsworth	VII, 403
Melville, Herman	VIII, 62
Shakespeare, William	I, 474, 505, 559

CHATEAUBRIAND, FRANÇOIS RENÉ VICOMTE DE,
Blair, Hugh	IV, 406
Burnet, Gilbert	II, 592
Byron, George Gordon Lord	IV, 758
Chaucer, Geoffrey	I, 159
Gray, Thomas	III, 561, 567
Hyde, Edward, Earl of Clarendon	II, 303
Locke, John	II, 534
Macpherson, James	IV, 275

	Vol. and Page
Milton, John	II, 246, 261, 270, 271, 284
Pitt, William	IV, 510
Raleigh, Sir Walter	I, 603
Richardson, Samuel	III, 448
Scott, Sir Walter	V, 158
Shakespeare, William	I, 472, 504, 554
Sidney, Algernon	II, 355
Spenser, Edmund	I, 382, 391
Swift, Jonathan	III, 230
Tillotson, John Robert	II, 439
Temple, Sir William	II, 459
Young, Edward	III, 493

CHATFIELD–TAYLOR, H. C.,
| Irving, Washington | VI, 146 |

CHATTERTON, THOMAS,
Chatterton, Thomas	III, 527
Collins, William	III, 418
Goldsmith, Oliver	III, 635

CHAUCER, GEOFFREY,
Chaucer, Geoffrey	I, 124, 130, 135
Gower, John	I, 174
Literature	I, 7
Poets and Poetry	IV, 5

CHEETHAM, JAMES,
| Paine, Thomas | IV, 532, 535 |

CHEETHAM, S.
| Mozley, James Bowling | VII, 149 |

CHEEVER, GEORGE BARRELL,
Bunyan, John	II, 394
Cowper, William	IV, 372
Longfellow, Henry Wadsworth	VII, 401
Lowth, Robert	IV, 28, 29

CHENEY, EDNAH D.,
| Alcott, Louisa May | VII, 668 |
| Emerson, Ralph Waldo | VII, 349 |

CHENEY, JOHN VANCE,
Arnold, Matthew	VII, 645
Browning, Robert	VII, 712
Carlyle, Thomas	VII, 271
Coleridge, Samuel Taylor	V, 216
Cowper, William	IV, 393
Hawthorne, Nathaniel	VI, 369
Keats, John	IV, 680

CHENEY, MARY BUSHNELL,
| Bushnell, Horace | VII, 69 |

CHENEY, WARREN,
| Harte, Francis Bret | VIII, 470 |

CHÉNIER, MARIE ANDRÉ,
| Richardson, Samuel | III, 444 |

CHERBULIEZ, VICTOR,
| Carlyle, Thomas | VII, 267 |

CHESEBOROUGH, A. S.,
| Bushnell, Horace | VII, 71 |

CHESTERFIELD, PHILIP DORMER STANHOPE EARL,
Arbuthnot, John	III, 82
Bentley, Richard	III, 121
Berkeley, George	III, 328
Saint–John, Henry	III, 292
Chaucer, Geoffrey	I, 156
Drama, The	VII, 5
History	VI, 6
Johnson, Samuel	III, 743
Richardson, Samuel	III, 443
Saint–John, Henry	III, 285
Stanhope, Philip Dormer	III, 607

CHESTERTON, G. K.,
| Carlyle, Thomas | VII, 276 |

INDEX TO CRITICISMS

Vol. and Page

Harte, Francis Bret..... VIII, 472
Morris. William......... VIII, 338
Stevenson, Robert Louis. VIII, 252
Tennyson, Alfred Lord.. VIII, 110
CHETTLE, HENRY,
   Daniel, Samuel.............. I, 615
   Dekker, Thomas........... II, 58
   Greene, Robert............. I, 339
   Jonson, Ben................ I, 758
   Shakespeare, William....... I, 447
CHEYNE, T. K.,
   Colenso, John William.... VII, 526
CHEYNELL, FRANCIS,
   Chillingworth, William..... II, 84
CHILD, FRANCIS JAMES,
   Mallet, David............. III, 496
   Spenser, Edmund........... I, 396
   Thomson, James...... III, 263, 264
CHILD, LYDIA MARIA,
   Browning, Elizabeth Barrett..
   .... VI, 238
   Child, Lydia Maria....... VII, 221
CHINNOCK, DR. H. S.,
   Colman, George............ V, 316
CHISHOLM, J. A.,
   Haliburton, William Chandler
   .... VI, 455
CHITTENDEN, N. W.,
   Newton, Sir Isaac....... II, 717, 724
CHOATE, JOSEPH H.,
   Choate, Rufus............. VI, 197
   Lincoln, Abraham......... VI, 416
CHOATE, RUFUS,
   Webster, Daniel........... V, 721
CHORLEY, G. F.,
   Austen, Jane.............. IV, 620
CHORLEY, HENRY FOTHERGILL,
   Blessington, Countess of. V, 592, 593
   Browning, Elizabeth Barrett..
   .... VI, 233, 242
   Campbell, Thomas......... V, 435
   Disraeli, Isaac............. V, 510
   Grote, George............. VI, 607
   Hawthorne, Nathaniel. VI, 345, 362
   Hemans, Felicia Dorothea....
   .... V, 255, 258
   Hood, Thomas............. V, 458
   Lamb, Charles............ VI, 231
   Landon, Letitia Elizabeth... V, 325
   Landor, Walter Savage.... VI, 372
   Longfellow, Henry Wadsworth
   .... VII, 401
   Lytton, Sir Edward George
   Bulwer........ VI, 680, 684, 687
   Mitford, Mary Russell... VI, 40, 42
   Moore, Thomas............ V, 710
   Morgan, Sydney Owenson Lady
   .... VI, 193
   Patmore, Coventry...... VIII, 340
   Ruskin, John........... VIII, 409
   Sedgwick, Catharine Maria....
   .... VI, 505, 507
   Smith, Sydney............ VI, 469
   Southey, Robert....... V, 401, 404
   Talfourd, Sir Thomas Noon.. V, 761
   Willis, Nathaniel Parker.... VI, 486
CHRANCH, CHRISTOPHER P.,
   Fuller, Sarah Margaret..... V, 667
CHRISTIE, MARY ELIZABETH,
   Burney, Frances........... V, 348

Vol. and Page

Wordsworth, William...... V, 640
CHRISTIE, RICHARD COPLEY,
   Pattison, Mark...... VII, 539, 541
CHRISTIE, W. D.,
   Dryden, John......... II, 466, 503
CHRISTOPHERS, SAMUEL WOOLCOCK,
   Fuller, Thomas............ II, 169
CHURCH, ALFRED,
   Hutton, Richard Holt... VIII, 374
CHURCH, EDWARD A.
   Du Maurier, George..... VIII, 345
CHURCH, FRANCIS P.,
   White, Richard Grant.... VII, 577
CHURCH, MARY C.,
   Church, Richard William. VII, 729
CHURCH, RICHARD WILLIAM,
   Anselm.................... I, 50
   Arnold, Sir Edwin....... VIII, 503
   Arnold, Thomas............ V, 376
   Bacon, Francis............
   .... I, 647, 651, 653, 662, 668
   Browning, Robert.... VII, 689, 710
   Carlyle, Thomas......... VII, 252
   Coke, Sir Edward.......... I, 741
   Darwin, Charles Robert... VII, 420
   Gray, Asa............... VII, 671
   Harvey, Gabriel............ I, 697
   Helps, Sir Arthur........ VII, 40
   Keble, John......... VI, 460, 467
   Lecky, William E. H..... VIII, 488
   Lowell, James Russell... VIII, 31
   Maurice, John Frederick Denison.................. VI, 646, 648
   Milman, Henry Hart.. VI, 538, 541
   Mozley, James Bowling... VI, 148
   Newman, John Henry. VII, 739, 747
   Pattison, Mark........... VII, 540
   Pusey, Edward Bouverie.....
   .... VII, 469, 471
   Robertson, Frederick William. V, 738
   Sackville, Thomas.......... I, 435
   Shakespeare, William......... I, 545
   Spenser, Edmund.. I, 385, 389, 398
   Stanley, Arthur Penrhyn.. VII, 297
   Tyndall, John.......... VIII, 195
   Ward, William George.... VII, 482
   Wilberforce, Samuel...... VI, 732
   Wordsworth, William...... V, 639
CHURCH, SAMUEL HARDEN,
   Knox, John................ I, 302
   Milton, John.............. II, 279
CHURCHILL, CHARLES,
   Armstrong, John......... III, 699
   Churchill, Charles........ III, 475
   Dodington, George Bubb.. III, 458
   Dryden, John............. II, 496
   Foote, Samuel............ III, 671
   Garrick, David........... III, 694
   Hill, John................ III, 645
   Home, John.............. IV, 515
   Jonson, Ben............... I, 761
   Macklin, Charles......... IV, 342
   Macpherson, James....... IV, 272
   Marvell, Andrew........... II, 316
   Murphy, Arthur.......... IV, 481
   Poets and Poetry.......... IV, 6
   Pope, Alexander.......... III, 182
   Shakespeare, William....... I, 552
   Sheridan, Thomas........ IV, 46
   Smollett, Tobias George... III, 573

Vol. and Page

Spenser, Edmund............ I, 394
Sterne, Laurence........... III, 511
Waller, Edmund............ II, 380
Warburton, William....... III, 683
Whitehead, William....... IV, 22
Wilkes, John.............. IV, 333
CHURCHILL, RANDOLPH S.
LORD,
   Disraeli, Benjamin....... VII, 285
CHURCHILL, WILLIAM,
   Stevenson, Robert Louis.. VIII, 236
CIBBER, COLLEY,
   Addison, Joseph.......... II, 648
   Burnet, Gilbert........... II, 595
   Butler, Samuel. .... II, 330
   Collier, Jeremy........... II, 700
   Dryden, John........ II, 464, 496
   Fielding, Henry.......... III, 339
   Gay, John............... III, 56
   Lee, Nathaniel....... II, 430, 431
   Vanbrugh, Sir John.... II, 704, 707
CIBBER, THEOPHILUS,
   Addison, Joseph.......... II, 634
   Behn, Aphra............. II, 409
   Blacklock, Thomas....... IV, 130
   Brown, Thomas........... II, 540
   Budgell, Eustace.......... III, 92
   Churchyard, Thomas....... I, 417
   Cockburn, Catherine..... III, 275
   Congreve, William........ II, 734
   D'Avenant, Sir William.... II, 219
   Defoe, Daniel............ III, 45
   Dennis, John............. III, 77
   Drummond, William... II, 100, 104
   Dryden, John............. II, 496
   Echard, Laurence......... III, 22
   Etheredge, Sir George..... II, 414
   Farquhar, George...... II, 555, 558
   Fenton, Elijah............ III, 20
   Garth, Sir Samuel........ II, 666
   Gay, John............... III, 60
   Granville, George......... III, 87
   Hall, Joseph............. II, 144
   Hamilton, William........ III, 336
   Harding, John............ I, 193
   Harrington, Sir John........ I, 441
   Hill, Aaron.............. III, 277
   Hobbes, Thomas.......... II, 321
   Howell, James........... II, 188
   Lee, Nathaniel........... II, 432
   L'Estrange, Sir Roger.. II, 537, 538
   Lillo, George............. III, 99
   Lydgate, John............. I, 183
   Manley, Mary de la Rivvere. II, 693
   Mason, William.......... IV, 324
   Milton, John............. II, 258
   Montagu, Charles........ III, 587
   Nabbes, Thomas.......... II, 94
   Oldmixon, John.......... III, 124
   Overbury, Sir Thomas...... I, 442
   Philips, Ambrose......... III, 274
   Philips, John............ III, 563
   Philips, Katherine........ II, 179
   Pitt, Christopher......... III, 254
   Pomfret, John........... II, 511
   Pope, Alexander..........
   .... III, 155, 161, 172, 182
   Prior, Matthew....... II, 673, 674
   Rowe, Elizabeth.......... III, 96
   Rowe, Nicholas....... II, 619, 621
   Sackville, Charles........ II, 553

INDEX TO CRITICISMS

	Vol. and Page
Sandys, George	II, 81, 81
Savage, Richard	III, 132
Sedley, Sir Charles	II, 509
Settle, Elkanah	II, 691, 691
Shakespeare, William	I, 552
Southerne, Thomas	III, 239, 240
Spenser, Edmund	I, 380, 394
Sprat, Thomas	II, 574
Steele, Sir Richard	II, 752, 760
Tate, Nahum	II, 589
Thomson, James	III, 257
Tickell, Thomas	III, 106
Vanbrugh, Sir John	II, 707
Walsh, William	II, 567
Wyatt, Sir Thomas	I, 250

CLAFLIN, MARY B.,
Whittier, John Greenleaf . VIII, 114
CLAGHORN, KATE HOLLADAY,
Burke, Edmund .... IV, 308
CLAREMONT, LORD,
Dryden, John .... II, 492
CLARENDON, GEORGE WILLIAM FREDERICK VILLIERS LORD,
Kinglake, Alexander William
.... VIII, 51
CLARENDON, LORD (EDWARD HYDE),
Carew, Thomas .... II, 20, 21
Cotton, Charles .... II, 370
Earle, John .... II, 183
Gauden, John .... II, 176
Graham, James .... II, 121
Hales, John .... II, 149
Hyde, Eward, Earl of Clarendon,
.... II, 299
Jonson Ben .... I, 747
L'Estrange, Sir Roger ..... II, 537
Laud, Willam .... II, 89
May, Thomas .... II, 118
Selden, John .... II, 137, 142
CLARK, ANDREW,
Aubrey, John .... II, 452, 453
Wood, Anthony .... II, 447
CLARK, EDWARD GORDAN.
George, Henry .... VIII, 379
CLARK, J. SCOTT,
DeQuincey, Thomas ...... VI, 132
CLARK, JOSEPH S.,
Mather, Increase .... II, 690
CLARK, LEWIS GAYLORD,
Webster, Noah .... V, 428
CLARK, W. G.,
Whewell, William ..... VI, 468, 471
CLARKE, ADAM,
Priestley, Joseph .... IV, 453
Wesley, Charles .... IV, 35
CLARKE, CHARLES COWDEN,
Addison, Joseph .... II, 651
Butler, Samuel .... II, 333
Beaumont and Fletcher, I, 579, 583
Chaucer, Geoffrey ..... I, 143, 151
Congreve, William . II, 736, 739, 743
Farquhar, George ..... II, 556, 557
Fielding, Henry .... III, 360
Fletcher, John .... I, 631
Foote, Samuel .... III, 674
Garrick, David .... III, 696
Hazlitt, William .... V, 100
Hood, Thomas .... V, 459
Jonson, Ben .... I, 755, 758, 765

	Vol. and Page
Keats, John	IV, 665
O'Keeffe, John	V, 197
Procter, Bryan Waller	VI, 746
Shakespeare, William,	I, 467, 469, 483, 491, 493, 498, 565
Shelley, Percy Bysshe	IV, 695
Smollett, Tobias George	
	III, 580, 589
Steele, Sir Richard	II, 763
Sterne, Laurence	III, 515
Swift, Jonathan	III, 233
Vanbrugh, Sir John	
	II, 703, 704, 705
Wycherley, William	
	II, 600, 601, 602

CLARKE, CHARLES AND MARY COWDEN,
Chambers, Robert .... VI, 619
Coleridge, Samuel Taylor ... V, 212
Jerrold, Douglas William. VI, 68, 70
Lamb, Mary Ann .... V, 508
CLARKE, E. D.,
Burke, Edmund .... IV, 294
CLARKE, ELIZA,
Wesley, John .... IV, 124
Wesley, Samuel .... III, 87
CLARKE, F. A.,
Ken, Thomas .... II, 569
CLARKE, GRACE JULIAN,
McCosh, James .... VIII, 301
CLARKE, HELEN F.,
Watts, Isaac .... III, 249
CLARKE, HENRY V.,
Miller, Cincinnatus Hiner....
.... VIII, 499
CLARKE, JAMES FREEMAN,
Anselm .... I, 50
Brownson, Orestes Augustus..
.... VII, 74
Channing, William Ellery... V, 368
Emerson, Ralph Waldo .. VII, 364
Fuller, Sarah Margaret ..... V, 665
Hall, Robert .... V, 111
Parker, Theodore ..... VI, 207, 209
Scott, Sir Walter .... V, 144
Shakespeare, William ...... I, 545
Simms, George Denison ... VI, 602
Tyndall, John .... VIII, 197
CLARKE, J. B. B.,
Clarke, Adam .... V, 185
Austen, Jane .... IV, 616
Falconer, William .... III, 525
CLARKE, JOSEPH,
Waterland, Daniel .... III, 102
CLARKE, MARY COWDEN,
Blessington, Countess of ... V, 592
Dickens, Charles .... VI, 561
Fields, James Thomas ... VII, 342
Hazlitt, William .... V, 101
Hunt, James Henry Leigh. VI, 160
Lamb, Charles .... V, 234
Shelley, Mary Wollstonecraft
.... V, 701
CLARKE, R. H.,
Bancroft, George .... VIII, 59
CLARKE, SARAH,
Allston, Washington .... V, 421
CLARKE, WILLIAM,
Daniel, Samuel .... I, 615
Freeman, Edward Augustus
.... VIII, 154, 158

	Vol. and Page
Morris, William	VIII, 330
Whitman, Walt	VIII, 146

CLARKSON, THOMAS,
Penn, William .... II, 626
CLAY, T. L.,
Wood, Anthony .... II, 447
CLAYDEN, P. W.,
Price, Richard .... IV, 135
Rogers, Samuel .... VI, 36
Shakespeare, William ...... I, 518
CLEMENS, SAMUEL LANGHORN (MARK TWAIN).
Cooper, James Fenimore ... V, 687
Drama, The .... VII, 9
Harte, Francis Bret ..... VII, 471
Godwin, William ..... V, 296, 304
Shelley, Percy Bysshe. IV, 698, 716
CLEMENS, WILL M.,
Browne, Charles Farrier ... VI, 503
CLÉMENT DE GENÈVE,
Lillo, George .... III, 99
CLEMM, MRS. MARIA,
Poe, Edgar Allan .... V, 536
CLEMENT, CLARA ERSKINE, AND HUTTON, LAURENCE,
Allston, Washington .... V, 418
Read, Thomas Buchanan .. VI, 676
CLERK, ARCHIBALD,
Macpherson, James .... IV, 277
CLERKE, MISS AGNES MARY,
Airy, Sir George Biddell .. VIII, 184
Black, Joseph .... IV, 345
Boyle, Robert .... II, 418
Ferguson, James .... III, 669
Flamsteed, John .... II, 663
Halley, Edmund ..... III, 107, 108
Herschel, Sir John Frederick
.... William, VI, 626
Wallis, John .... II, 517
CLERKE, MISS E. M.,
Maccarthy, Dennis Florence
.... VII, 489, 490
Proctor, Richard Anthony VII, 660
Somervile, Mary .... VI, 659
CLEVELAND, CHARLES DEXTER
Addison, Joseph .... II, 657
Akenside, Mark .... III, 543
Arnold, Thomas .... V, 381
Baillie, Joanna .... V, 694
Barbauld, Anna Lætitia ... IV, 25
Barrow, Isaac .... II, 312
Barton, Bernard .... V, 597
Bayly, Thomas Haynes .... V, 340
Beecher, Henry Ward ... VII, 604
Beecher, Lyman .... VI, 340
Berkeley, George .... III, 325
Brown, Charles Brockden . IV, 553
Brydges, Sir Samuel Egerton
.... V, 321
Bushnell, Horace .... VII, 70
Campbell, Thomas .... V, 444
Carter, Elizabeth .... IV, 493
Chapone, Hester .... IV, 418
Cowper, William .... IV, 388
Croly, George .... VI, 225
Cunningham, Allan .... V, 384
Curtis, George William .. VIII, 184
Drake, Joseph Rodman ... IV, 661
Dwight, Timothy .... IV, 625, 626
Feltham, Owen .... II, 309
Gay, John .... III, 56

INDEX TO CRITICISMS

	Vol. and Page
Griswold, Rufus Wilmot	VI, 80
Halleck, Fitz-Greene	VI, 497
Holland, Josiah Gilbert	VII, 334
Hopkins, Mark	VII, 615
Hopkinson, Thomas	IV, 132
Jeffrey, Francis Lord	V, 654
Longfellow Henry Wadsworth	-.VII, 397
Lowth, Robert	IV, 29
Mackay, Charles	VII, 764
Moore, Thomas	V, 705
Murray, Lindley	V, 55
Palfrey, John Gorham	VII, 338
Park, Mungo	IV, 486
Penn, William	II, 630
Percival, James Grant	VI, 60
Pierpont, John	VI, 481
Pitt, William	III, 630
Poe, Edgar Allan	V, 553
Quincy, Josiah	VI, 404
Silliman, Benjamin	VI, 407
Somerville, William	III, 126
Smollett, Tobias George	III, 586
South, Robert	II, 608
Southey, Caroline Anne Bowles	V, 762
Story, Joseph	V, 484
Tickell, Thomas	III, 106
Tighe, Mary	IV, 552
Tuckerman, Henry Theodore	VI, 642
Vaughan, Henry	II, 443
Waller, Edmund	II, 381
Warton, Joseph	IV, 398, 402, 406
Warren, Samuel	VII, 108
Watts, Isaac	III, 251
Wayland, Francis	VI, 450
Webster, Noah	V, 431
White, Henry Kirke	IV, 488
Willis, Nathaniel Parker	VI, 490
Wilson, John	V, 749
Wolcot, John	IV, 650
CLEVELAND, GROVER,	
Washington, George	IV, 364
CLEVELAND, JOHN,	
Jonson, Ben	I, 759
CLEVELAND, PAUL R.,	
Roe, Edward Payson	VII, 675
CLEVELAND, ROSE ELIZABETH,	
Eliot, George	VII, 197
CLIFFORD, MARTIN,	
Dryden, John	II, 473, 494
CLIFFTON, WILLIAM,	
Gifford, Wiliam	V, 33
CLIFT, WILLIAM,	
Hunter, John	IV, 164
CLINE, HENRY,	
Hunter, John	IV, 166
CLINTON, GEORGE,	
Byron, George Gordon Lord	IV, 757
CLITHEROW, J.,	
Blackmore, Sir William	III, 702
CLIVE, ARTHUR,	
Boswell, James	IV, 220
Whitman, Walt	VIII, 138
CLODD, EDWARD,	
Arnold, Matthew	VII, 636
Darwin, Charles Robert	VII, 421
FitzGerald, Edward	VII, 515
Hobbes, Thomas	II, 323

	Vol. and Page
Huxley, Thomas Henry	VIII, 328
Proctor. Richard Anthony	VII, 659
CLOUGH. ANNA JEMIMA,	
Clough, Arthur Hugh	VI, 248
CLOUGH. ARTHUR HUGH,	
Burns, Robert	IV, 256
Dryden, John	II, 493
Emerson, Ralph Waldo	VII, 344
Gladstone, William Ewart	VIII, 391
Hume, David	III, 666
Longfellow, Henry Wadsworth	VII, 395
Smith, Alexander	VI, 517
CLOUGH, MRS. ARTHUR HUGH,	
Clough, Arthur Hugh	VI, 249
CLYMER, W. B. SHUBRICK,	
Austen, Jane	VII, 618
Cooper, James Fenimore	V, 688
Landor, Walter Savage	VI, 391
COAN TITUS MUNSON,	
Melville, Herman	VIII, 62, 63
Ruskin, John	VIII, 411
Stoddard, Richard Henry	VIII, 496
COATES, FLORENCE EARL,	
Arnold, Matthew	VII, 629
COBBE, FRANCES POWER,	
Borrow, George Henry	VII, 308
Browning, Elizabeth Barrett	VI, 234
Browning, Robert	VII, 682
Byron,George Gordon Lord	IV, 741
Carlyle, Thomas	VII, 238
Colenso, John William	VII, 522, 525
Darwin, Charles Robert	VII, 427
Helps, Sir Arthur	VII, 41
Landor, Walter Savage	V, 378
Longfellow, Henry Wadsworth	VII, 385
Lyell, Sir Charles	VII, 35, 36
Mill, John Stuart	VI, 715
Parker, Theodore	V, 206, 209
Somerville, Mary	VI, 659
COBBETT, WILLIAM,	
Paine, Thomas	IV, 532
Swift, Jonathan	III, 214
COCKBURN, CATHERINE,	
Butler, Joseph	III, 313
COCKBURN, HENRY LORD,	
Ferguson, Adam	IV, 610
Horner, Francis	IV, 630
Grahame, James	IV, 567
Grant, Anne	V, 329
Guthrie, Thomas	VI, 736
Hen y, Robert	IV, 108
Jeffrey, Francis Lord	V, 651
Macknight, James	IV, 407
Mackenzie, Henry	V, 113
Robertson, William	IV, 155
Stewart, Dugald	V, 76
Wilson, John	V, 748
COFFIN, ROBERT BARRY (BARRY GRAY),	
Davidson, Lucretia Maria	V, 27
COGHILL, ANNIE L.,	
Oliphant, Margaret O. W.	VIII, 368

	Vol. and Page
COGSWELL JOSEPH G.,	
Halleck, Fitz-Greene	VI, 499
COHEN, MARY M.,	
Lazarus, Emma	VII, 611
COKE, SIR EDWARD,	
Littleton. Sir Thomas	I, 196
Raleigh, Sir Walter	I, 591
COKE, LADY MARY,	
Sterne, Laurence	III, 502
COLBY, FRANK MOORE,	
Besant, Sir Walter	VIII, 449
DeVere, Aubrey Thomas	VIII, 462
Elyot, Sir Thomas	I, 253
COLE, CHARLES NELSON,	
Jenyns, Soame	IV, 31
COLE, GRENVILLE A. J.,	
Lyell, Sir Charles	VII, 36
COLERIDGE, CHRISTABEL,	
Gaskell, Elizabeth Cleghorn	VI, 432
COLERIDGE, DERWENT,	
Coleridge, Hartley	V, 574, 576
Kingsley, Charles	VII, 19
Praed, Winthrop Mackworth	V, 331
COLERIDGE, ERNEST HARTLEY	
Byron, George Gordon Lord	IV, 749
Coleridge, Samuel Taylor	V, 228
COLERIDGE, HARTLEY,	
Arnold, Thomas	V, 378
Aschem, Roger	I, 289
Baillie, Joanna	V, 693
Bentley, Richard	III, 111, 117
Browne, William	II, 75
Churchill, Charles	III, 480
Clive, Caroline	VI, 740
Coleridge, Samuel Taylor	V, 207
Congreve, William	II, 741
Dodsley, Robert	III, 483
Donne, John	I, 715
Drayton, Michael	I, 707
Dryden, John	II, 501
Fisher, John	I, 231
Ford, John	II, 30, 31
Goldsmith, Oliver	III, 637
Grainger, James	III, 498
Gray, Thomas	III, 567
Marvell, Andrew	II, 314, 316
Mason, William	IV, 324
Massinger, Philip	II, 41, 49
Parnell, Thomas	II, 616
Roscoe, William	V, 118
Shakespeare, William	I, 469, 492, 538,558
Smart, Christopher	III, 594
Swift, Jonathan	III, 212
Tennyson, Alfred Lord	VII, 65
Wordsworth, William	V, 632
COLERIDGE, HENRY NELSON,	
Coleridge, Samuel Taylor	V, 208
Keats, John	IV, 670
Norton, Caroline E. S.	VII, 104
West, Gilbert	III, 269
COLERIDGE, JOHN DUKE LORD,	
Arnold, Matthew	VII, 629, 644
Wordsworth, William	V, 637
COLERIDGE, SIR JOHN TAYLOR,	
Arnold, Thomas	V, 376
Keble, John	VI, 458, 463

INDEX TO CRITICISMS

Talfourd, Sir Thomas Noon.... V, 760
COLERIDGE, SAMUEL TAYLOR,
Addison, Joseph............II, 645
Alfred the Great............I, 38
Allston, Washington.......V, 420
Asgill, John..............III, 97
Baxter, Richard............II, 426
Beaumont and Fletcher.....I, 581
Berkeley, George..........III, 330
Bowles, William Lisle........
.... V, 659, 660, 661
Brougham, Henry Lord...VI, 523
Browne, Sir Thomas...II, 340, 342
Bunyan, John.............II, 391
Burke, Edmund.............
.... IV, 289, 298, 300, 302
Burnet, Gilbert............II, 594
Butler, Samuel............II, 331
Byron, George Gordon Lord..
.... IV, 732, 752, 756
Canning, George...........V, 66
Chapman, George...........I, 729
Chatterton, Thomas......III, 529
Chaucer, Geoffrey......I, 126, 159
Cobbett, William..........V, 272
Coleridge, Hartley.........V, 572
Coleridge, Samuel Taylor...V, 206
Cotton, Charles............II, 371
Cowley, Abraham..........II, 200
Cowper, William.........IV, 385
Crabbe, George............V, 173
Crashaw, Richard..........II, 111
Daniel, Samuel.........I, 613, 616
Darwin, Erasmus..... IV, 424, 424
Davy, Sir Humphry........V, 93
Defoe, Daniel............III, 34
Donne, John..............I, 714
Drayton, Michael..........I, 706
Dryden, John.....II, 490, 498, 500
Etheredge, Sir George......II, 415
Falconer, William........III, 525
Fielding, Henry..III, 348, 352, 358
Fox, George..............II, 421
Fuller, Thomas...........II, 171
Gay, John................III, 57
Gibbon, Edward..........IV, 183
Gifford, William...........V, 34
Glover, Richard..........IV, 19
Godwin, William......V, 293, 303
Goldsmith, Oliver........III, 636
Gray, Thomas............III, 566
Hall, Robert.............V, 110
Hartley, David......III, 377, 378
Hazlitt, William..........V, 103
Herbert, George..........I, 721
Hervey, James............III, 397
Holcroft, Thomas........IV, 654
Hooker, Richard..........I, 406
Horner, Francis..........IV, 630
Irving, Edward...........V, 246
Johnson, Samuel............
.... III, 730, 741, 755, 755
Jonson, Ben..I, 753, 754, 754, 762
Junius ....IV, 644
Lamb, Charles........V, 229, 229
Landor, Walter Savage......
.... VI, 381, 384
Lardner, Nathaniel.......III, 523
Leighton, Robert..........II, 359
Lyell, Sir Charles........VII, 35

Mackintosh, Sir James......V. 178
Malone, Edmond.........IV 578
Marryat, Frederick........V, 531
Mason, William..........IV, 325
Massinger, Philip..... II. 42, 46. 47
Maturin, Charles Robert...IV, 767
Milton, John..II, 259, 261, 269, 286
Moore, Thomas............V, 711
Napier, Gen. Sir Wm. Francis
Patrick ....VI, 22
Newton, Sir Isaac..........II, 723
North, Roger.............III, 79
Paley, William..........IV, 475
Poets and Poetry.........IV, 7
Pope, Alexander......III, 165, 186
Priestly, Joseph........IV, 446, 453
Richardson, Samuel......III, 448
Robinson, Mary..........IV, 411
Scott, Sir Walter..........V, 142
Selden, John.............II. 141
Shakespeare, William.......I,
465, 466, 477, 495, 503, 508, 509,
512, 515, 520, 524, 526, 532.
Sheridan, Richard Brinsley....
.... IV, 594
Smollett, Tobias George...III, 587
Southey, Robert..V, 406, 412, 414
Spenser, Edmund...........I,395
Sterne, Laurence.........III, 512
Swift, Jonathan......III, 221, 230
Taylor, Jeremy.......IV, 204, 207
Taylor, Sir Henry.......VII, 579
Tennyson, Alfred Lord..VIII, 78
Tooke, John Horne..IV, 570, 572
Turner, Charles Tennyson VII, 162
Walpole, Horace.........IV, 318
Warton, Thomas..........IV, 77
West, Gilbert,...........III, 369
White, Joseph Blanco....V, 361
Wordsworth, William..........
...........V, 617, 619, 625, 629
Young, Edward...........III, 493
COLERIDGE, SARA,
Arnold, Thomas............V, 381
Austen, Jane.............IV, 619
Baillie Joanna............V, 690
Brown, Thomas...........II, 541
Browning, Elizabeth Barrett,
.... VI, 229, 244
Carlyle, Thomas......VII, 250, 254
Coleridge, Samuel Taylor...V, 208
Cotton, Charles...........II, 371
Cowper, William..........IV, 381
Crashaw, Richard..........II, 111
Dickens, Charles......VI, 566. 570
Hervey, James...........III, 397
Lamb, Mary Ann.........V, 508
L'Estrange, Sir Roger......II, 539
Longfellow, Henry Wadsworth
.... VII, 387, 390
More, Hannah............V, 191
Pusey, Edward Bouverie.VII, 467
Richardson, Samuel......III, 449
Spedding, James........VII, 318
Tennyson, Alfred Lord..VIII, 86
White, Joseph Blanco....V, 360
Whitehead, William......IV, 23
Wordsworth, William......V, 634
Young, Edward..........III, 488
COLFAX, SCHUYLER,
Lincoln, Abraham.........VI, 412

COLLET. S D.
Hutton. Richard Holt...VIII. 374
COLLET STEPHEN.
Burns. Robert............IV, 252
Shenstone, William.......III, 473
Wilmot. John.............II 337
COLLIER. JEREMY,
Collier. Jeremy...........II, 699
More Sir Thomas..........I, 234
COLLIER. JOHN PAYNE.
Bale, John................I, 285
Churchyard, Thomas......I, 418
Constable, Henry..........I, 444
Daniel, Samuel............I, 616
Dekker, Thomas..........II, 55
Edwards, Richard..........I. 288
Greene. Robert............I 341
Heywood, John...........II. 305
Heywood, Thomas...II 123. 124
Jonson, Ben..............I, 763
Kyd, Thomas.............I. 359
Lodge, Thomas........I, 625. 626
Lyly, John...............I. 426
Marlowe, Christopher......I, 348
Nashe, Thomas...........I, 413
Peele, George.........I. 364, 366
Raleigh, Sir Walter........I, 600
Shakespeare, William......I, 561
Spenser, Edmund......I. 376, 392
Still, John................I, 430
Sylvester, Joshua..........I, 610
Taylor, John.............II, 133
Udall, Nicholas...........I, 278
COLLIER, WILLIAM FRANCIS,
Bacon, Francis............ I,654
Borrow, George Henry...VII, 310
Burnet, Thomas..........II, 596
Caxton, William..........I, 197
Congreve, William........II, 742
Cowper, William.........IV, 389
Cranmer, Thomas.........I, 273
Darwin, Erasmus.........IV, 425
Defoe Daniel............ III, 31
Dickens, Charles.......VI, 583
Disraeli, Benjamin....... VII, 293
Dryden, John............II, 487
Edwards, Jonathan......III. 386
Hazlitt, William..........V, 104
Hume, David...........III. 658
James, George Paine Rainsford
....................VI, 219
Johnson, Samuel.........III, 758
Macpherson, James......IV, 271
Milton, John.............II, 283
Occleve, Thomas..........I, 188
Poe, Edgar Allan.........V. 557
Raleigh, Sir Walter........I, 604
Ramsay, Allan..........III, 407
Robertson, William......IV, 158
Sackville, Thomas.........I, 433
Scott, Sir Walter..........V, 157
Sidney, Sir Philiip........I, 329
Smollett, Tobias George...III, 584
Steele, Sir Richard........II, 763
Surrey, Earl of..............I, 255
Thomson, James........III, 264
COLLINGWOOD, STUART DODGSON,
Dodgson,Charles Lutwige,VIII. 397
COLLINGWOOD, W. G.,
Ruskin, John..........VIII 419

INDEX TO CRITICISMS

COLLINS, CHARLES ALLSTON
Sterne, Laurence........ III. 503
COLLINS, F. HOWARD,
Spencer, Herbert. .....VIII. 485
COLLINS, JOHN CHURTON,
Arbuthnot, John.........III, 85
Atterbury, Francis.......III. 68
Bacon, Francis............I, 654
Bentley, Richard.........III, 120
Browning, Robert.......VII, 716
Butler, Samuel............II, 335
Capgrave, John............I, 193
Chaucer, Geoffrey.........I, 170
Cibber, Colley............III, 375
Cowley, Abraham.........II, 202
Cranmer, Thomas ....I, 273
Dickens, Charles.........VI, 566
Dryden, John II. 467, 469, 471 477,
479, 480, 482, 483, 484, 488, 491,
491, 492, 504.
Forster, John...........VII, 68
Gay, John................III, 62
Greene, Robert........I, 343, 345
Hawes, Stephen.............I, 218
Herbert, Edward Lord.....II. 98
Hervey, John Lord.......III, 129
Kyd, Thomas...............I, 360
Lodge, Thomas.............I, 627
Lyly, John................I, 425
Mallet, David...........III, 495
Marlowe, Christopher...I, 353, 357
Nashe, Thomas...........I, 415
Palgrave, Francis Turner, VIII, 373
Parnell, Thomas..........II, 617
Peele, George.........I, 365, 367
Pope, Alexander.....III, 171, 193
Porson, Richard..........IV, 526
Raleigh, Sir Walter.........I, 608
Saint-John, Henry,..III, 289,
..................291, 296
Settle, Elkanah..........II, 692
Skelton, John.............I, 223
Shadwell, Thomas.........II. 435
Sprat, Thomas............II, 573
Stanhope, Philip Dormer, III, 608
Stevenson, Robert Louis....
..................VIII, 245
Surrey, Earl of............I, 259
Swift, Jonathan, III, 205, 211, 216
217, 218, 219, 227, 235.
Symonds, John Addington....
....................VIII, 205
Tennyson, Alfred Lord..VIII, 106
Theobald, Lewis.III, 141, 142, 143
Thomson, James..III, 262, 265, 271
Tourneur, Cyril...........I, 688
Waller, Edmund..........II. 383
Warburton, William......III. 687
Wyatt, Sir Thomas........I, 252
Young, Edward..........III, 486
COLLINS, MORTIMER,
Herrick, Robert..........II, 234
Landor, Walter Savage.VI, 382, 385
Praed, Winthrop Mackworth..
.................V, 332
COLLINS, WILLIAM,
Jonson, Ben..............I, 761
Otway, Thomas...........II, 362
Thomson, James.........III, 255
COLLINS, WILLIAM WILKIE,
Jerrold, Douglas William...V, 68

COLLINS. W. LUCAS,
Butler, Joseph.......III, 308, 316
COLLYER, ROBERT.
Fields. James Thomas....VII, 341
COLMAN. GEORGE,
Coleman. George, IV, 201, 202 202
Foote. Samuel..........III, 672
Garrick. David........ ..III, 695
Gibbon, Edward.........IV, 174
Goldsmith. Oliver........III, 617
Lillo, George.............III, 101
COLTON. ARTHUR W.,
Map, Walter...............I, 62
Whitehead. William......IV, 22
COLTON. CHARLES CALEB,
Authors and Authorship.VIII, 7
History, ...VI, 7
COLVIN, SIDNEY,
Browning, Robert.......VII, 700
Eliot, George............VII, 201
Forster, John...........VII, 67
Keats, John, IV, 668, 671, 673, 680
Landor, Walter Savage..VI, 376,
.........380, 383, 384, 390.
Rossetti, Dante Gabriel Charles
....................VII, 442
Shelley, Percy Bysshe.....IV, 704
Stevenson, Robert Louis VIII.
.... 245, 251
COLWELL, STEPHEN,
Smith, Adam............IV, 64
COMBE, GEORGE,
Burns, Robert. ....IV, 228
COMMITTEE OF ROYAL SOCIETY
Newton, Isaac............II, 716
CONANT, SAMUEL STILLMAN,
Austen, Jane.............IV, 620
Coleridge, Sara............V. 734
Curtis, George William ..VIII, 187
Mitford, Mary Russell.....VI, 44
CONDER. G. W.,
Burnet, Gilbert............II, 596
CONDORCET, MARIE JEAN MARQUIS DE,
Franklin, Benjamin........IV, 83
Priestley. Joseph.........IV, 445
CONE, HELEN GRAY,
Cary, Alice..............VI, 639
Fuller, Sarah Margaret.....V, 672
Jackson, Helen Hunt.....VII, 573
Longfellow, Henry Wadsworth
.....................VII, 409
Sigourney, Lydia Huntly..VI, 451
Stowe, Harriet Beecher..VIII, 358
CONE, HELEN GRAY, AND GILDER, JEANETTE L.,
Austen, Jane.............IV. 612
Baillie. Joanna..........V, 689
Blessington, Countess of....V. 589
Godwin, Mary Wollstonecraft.
....................IV, 328
Lamb, Mary Ann..........V, 509
Shelley, Mary Wollstonecraft
......................V, 701
CONFUCIUS,
Knowledge...............V, 5
CONGDON, CHARLES T.,
Emerson, Ralph Waldo...VII, 345
CONGREVE, WILLIAM,
Collier, Jeremy............II. 699
Congreve, William.....,II, 733, 736

Dryden, John.........II. 464 495
Montagu Charles..........II 587
Rowe. Nicholas............II 621
Swift, Jonathan ....III, 213
Wycherley. William........II. 602
CONINGTON. JOHN,
Dryden. John.............II, 487
Pope, Alexander..........III. 150
Tickell. Thomas..........III, 105
CONNELL. RICHARD E.,
O'Reilly, John Boyle.....VII. 768
CONNERY, THOMAS B..
Stanley, Sir Henry Morton....
....................VIII, 506
CONSTABLE, A. G.,
Brougham, Henry Lord....VI. 527
Jeffrey. Francis Lord.......V, 652
Scott, Sir Walter............V, 132
Stewart. Dugald..........V, 76
CONTEMPORARY NEWSPAPER.
Dryden, John.............II. 463
CONVOCATION OF OXFORD,
Wyclif, John................I. 102
CONWAY, KATHERINE E..
O'Reilly, John Boyle.VII. 767. 768
CONWAY, MONCURE. D.
Bacon, Delia..............VI. 204
Barnes, William.........VII. 585
Blake. William............V, 60
Browning. Robert....VII. 679, 709
Bunyan, John.............II, 397
Byron, George Gordon Lord IV. 741
Carlyle Thomas..........VII, 234
Chaucer, Geoffrey..........I 127
Churchill. Charles........III. 477
Coleridge. Hartley........V. 575
DeQuincey. Thomas........VI, 120
Dickens. Charles. VI 561. 569. 589
Emerson. Ralph Waldo.....
..................VII, 346, 367
Fawcett. Henry.........VII, 549
Froude, James Anthony..VIII. 265
Greeley, Horace .....VI. 667, 671
Hawthorne. Nathaniel.VI. 347. 361
Hemans. Felicia Dorothea....V. 260
Hunt. James Henry Leigh .VI. 166
Huxley. Thomas Henry..VIII 326
Kingsley. Charles.........VII 21
Lincoln. Abraham........VI. 415
Martineau. Harriet......VII. 58
Mill, John Stuart......VI 704. 711
Müller, Friedrich Max....VIII 435
Paine, Thomas.............
......IV. 534. 535. 536 539 540
Parker, Theodore ....VI 208
Phillips, Wendell........VII 555
Scott, Sir Walter..........V, 151
Taylor, Bayard..........VII. 130
Tennyson. Alfred Lord..VIII. 69
Thoreau, Henry David.....VI. 268
Whitman. Walt..... VIII. 130. 134
Wilkes, John..............IV, 336
Wilson, John..............V. 747
CONYBREARE, JOHN JOSIAS,
Beowulf..................I, 17
COOK, CLARENCE,
Irving. Washington......VI. 137
COOK, DUTTON,
Addison, Joseph..........II. 650
Dickens. Charles.........VI. 588
Hazlitt William ....V. 101

INDEX TO CRITICISMS

	Vol. and Page
Robinson, Mary	IV, 412
Wilkes, John	IV, 337

COOK, EDWARD T.,
- Ruskin, John .... VIII, 406

COOK, KENINGALE,
- Asgill, John .... III, 98

COOKE, MISS A. M.,
- Peacock, Reginald .... I, 190

COOKE, GEORGE WILLIS,
- Browning, Robert .... VII, 706
- Curtis, George William .... VIII, 186, 191
- Eliot, George .... VII, 175, 197, 203
- Emerson, Ralph Waldo .... VII, 355, 367
- Parkman, Francis .... VIII, 221
- Ruskin, John .... VIII, 406
- Tennyson, Alfred Lord ... VIII, 79

COOKE, GEORGE WINGROVE,
- Pope, Alexander .... III, 148
- Saint–John, Henry ... III, 286, 294

COOKE, JANE GROSVENOR,
- Trollope, Anthony .... VII, 464

COOKE, JOHN ESTEN,
- Browning, Robert .... VII, 706
- Jefferson, Thomas .... V, 43
- Marshall, John .... V, 286
- Thackeray, William Makepeace .... VI, 295

COOKE, PHILIP P.,
- Poe, Edgar Allan .... V, 553

COOKE, THOMAS,
- Pope, Alexander .... III, 181

COOKE, WILLIAM,
- Foote, Samuel .... III, 673
- Goldsmith, Oliver .... III, 616
- Macklin, Charles .... IV, 344

COOLBRITH, INA D.,
- Poets and Poetry .... IV, 10

COOLEY, JAMES A.,
- Agassiz, Louis Jean Rudolphe .... VI, 725

COOLEY, WILLIAM DESBOROUGH,
- Livingstone, David ... VI, 728, 730

COOLIDGE, A. C.,
- Burton, Sir Richard Francis .... VII, 758

COOLIDGE, SUSAN,
- Jackson, Helen Hunt .. VII, 572, 574
- Johnson, Samuel .... III, 334

COOPER, ANTHONY ASHLEY (LORD SHAFTESBURY),
- Cudworth, Ralph .... II, 384, 386
- Locke, John .... II, 524

COOPER, ELIZABETH,
- Barclay, Alexander .... I, 264
- Daniel, Samuel .... I, 615
- Davies, Sir John .... I, 634
- Fairfax Edward .... I, 742
- Greville, Sir Fulke .... I, 690
- Harrington, Sir John .... I, 441
- Nashe, Thomas .... I, 413
- Sackville, Thomas .... I, 432
- Spenser, Edmund .... I, 394
- Warner, William .... I, 436

COOPER, THOMPSON,
- Challoner, Richard .... III, 710
- Cheke, Sir John .... I, 278
- Faber, Frederick William .... VI, 335
- Farmer, Richard .... IV, 340

	Vol. and Page
Granger, James	III, 671
Oldys, William	III, 456

COOPER, WILLIAM DURRANT,
- Udall, Nicholas .... I, 279

COOTE, CHARLES,
- Junius .... IV, 644

COPE, SIR WALTER,
- Shakespeare, William .... I, 464

COPE, SIR WILLIAM H.,
- Kingsley, Charles .... VII, 19

COPELAND, CHARLES TOWNSEND,
- Carlyle, Thomas .... VII, 259

COPLESTON, EDWARD,
- Tyrwhitt, Thomas .... IV, 26

COPNER, JAMES,
- Brewster, Sir David .... VI, 547
- Brown, Thomas .... IV, 659
- Butler, Joseph .... III, 316
- More, Hannah .... V, 192
- Newton, Sir Isaac .... II, 715

COPPÉE, HENRY,
- Akenside, Mark .... III, 543
- Aubrey, John .... II, 452
- Blair, Hugh .... IV, 406
- Colman, George .... IV, 203
- Hallam, Henry .... VI, 179
- Johnson, Samuel .... III, 759
- Smollett, Tobias George ..... III, 577
- Steele, Sir Richard .... II, 764
- Strickland Agnes .... VI, 767
- Tupper, Martin Farquhar .... VII, 733
- Turner, Sharon .... V, 498

COPPING, EDWARD,
- Jerrold, Douglas William ... VI, 70

CORBET, RICHARD,
- Beaumont, Francis .... I, 587
- Shakespere, William .... I, 477

CORKRAN, HENRIETTE,
- Blackie, John Stuart .... VIII, 305

CORNER STONE, PHILADELPHIA LIBRARY,
- Franklin, Benjamin .... IV, 82

CORNEY BOLTON,
- Stowe, John .... I, 420
- Thomson, James .... III, 268

CORNISH, F WARE,
- Hunt, James Henry Leigh ... VI, 164, 171

CORSON, HIRAM,
- Alfred the Great .... I, 40
- Browning, Robert ...... VII, 679, 692, 695
- Byron, George Gordon Lord .. IV, 748, 753
- Chaucer, Geoffrey .... I, 149, 171
- Cowper, William .... IV, 392
- DeQuincey, Thomas .... VI, 129
- Dryden, John .... II, 493
- Fairfax Edward .... I, 742
- Gower, John .... I, 173
- Grimoald Nicholas .... I, 284
- Keats, John .... IV, 680
- Literature .... I, 10
- Lowell, James Russell .... VIII, 41
- Marlowe, Christopher .... I, 357
- Milton, John .... II, 268, 279, 296
- Shelley, Percy Bysshe .... IV, 700
- Southey, Robert .... V, 409
- Spenser, Edmund .... I, 386, 400

	Vol. and Page
Tennyson Alfred Lord	VIII, 88
Wordsworth, William	V, 626, 628, 645

COSSA, LUIGI,
- Locke, John .... II, 520, 532, 536
- Malthus, Thomas Robert ..... V, 253
- Ricardo, David .... IV, 727

COSTELLO, LOUISA STUART,
- Montagu, Lady Mary Wortley .... III, 462

COTTERELL, GEORGE,
- Buchanan, Robert .... VIII, 447
- Cowper, William .... IV, 377
- Lytton, Edward Robert Bulwer Earl .... VIII, 49

COTTLE, AMOS,
- Davy, Sir Humphry .... V, 92
- Southey, Robert .... V, 398

COTTLE, JOSEPH,
- Coleridge, Samuel Taylor .... V, 210

COTTON, CHARLES,
- Behn, Aphra .... II, 409

COTTON, JAMES SOUTHERLAND,
- Burton, Sir Richard Francis .... VII, 759, 760
- Edwards, Amelia Blandford .... VIII, 175
- Freeman, Edward Augustus .... VIII, 159
- Jowett, Benjamin ... VIII, 208, 210
- Symonds, John Addington .... VIII, 204

COUDERT, FREDERICK R.,
- Ingersoll, Robert Green .. VIII, 403

COUES, ELLIOTT,
- Darwin, Charles Robert ..... VII, 430
- Emerson, Ralph Waldo ... VII, 371

COUNTERNAY, THOMAS PEREGRINE,
- Shakespeare, William .... I, 480, 517, 526

COURDAVEAUX, V.,
- Shakespeare, William .... I, 505

COURTHOPE, WILLIAM JOHN,
- Addison, Joseph .... II, 639, 640, 642, 660
- Arnold, Matthew .... VII, 644
- Browning, Robert .... VII, 704
- Bowles, William Lisle .... V, 661
- Broome, William .... III, 239
- Byron, George Gordon Lord .... IV, 762
- Carlyle, Thomas .... VII, 269
- Chapman, George ...... I, 728, 731
- Chaucer, Geoffrey .... I, 132, 135, 152, 170
- Churchyard, Thomas .... I, 418
- Constable, Henry .... I, 445
- Crabbe, George .... V, 175
- Cynewulf .... I, 31
- Douglas, Gawin .... I, 215
- Dryden, John .... II, 494
- Dunbar, William .... I, 227
- Dyer, Sir Edward .... I, 428
- Fenton, Elijah .... III, 21
- Gascoigne, George .... I, 309
- Hawes, Stephen .... I, 219
- Henryson, Robert .... I, 210
- Johnson, Samuel ...... III, 738, 762
- Keats, John .... IV, 673, 680
- Kyd, Thomas .... I, 359 |

INDEX TO CRITICISMS

	Vol. and Page
Layamon	I, 66
Lodge, Thomas	I, 627
Lydgate, John	I, 186
Lyly, John	I, 427
Lytton, Edward Robert Bulwer Earl	VIII, 47
Mannying, Robert	I, 88
Marlowe, Christopher	I, 351
Milton, John	II, 267
Montagu, Lady Mary Wortley	III, 468
Nicholas of Guilford	I, 76
Pater, Walter Horatio	VIII, 277
Peele, George	I, 367
Percy, Thomas	IV, 565
Pope, Alexander	III, 151, 159, 160, 162, 166, 170, 191.
Raleigh, Sir Walter	I, 601
Ritson, Joseph	IV, 437
Robert of Gloucester	I, 82
Sackville, Thomas	I, 435
Scott, Sir Walter	V, 140
Shelley, Percy Bysshe	IV, 700, 713
Spenser, Edmund	I, 390, 392, 400
Steele, Sir Richard	II, 759
Surrey, Earl of	I, 259
Swift, Jonathan	III, 222
Theobald, Lewis	III, 143
Thomas of Erceldoune	I, 84
Wace Robert	I, 60
Walpole, Horace	IV, 322
Warburton, William	III, 689
Warton, Thomas	IV, 74
White, Gilbert	V, 153
Wordsworth, William	V, 624
Wyatt, Sir Thomas	I, 253
COURTNEY, JOHN,	
Jenyns, Soame,	IV, 33
Johnson, Samuel	III, 753
COURTNEY, WILLIAM LEONARD	
Bacon, Rogers	I, 80
Browning, Robert	VII, 690 704
Drama The	VII, 10
Emerson, Ralph Waldo	VII, 358
Hawthorne, Nathaniel	VI, 369
Mill, John Stuart	VI, 706, 708, 710
Reade, Charles	VII, 535
COURTNEY, W. P.,	
Arbuthnot, John	III, 83
Birch, Thomas	III, 499
Hearne, Thomas	III, 89
Mathias, Thomas James	V, 288
Sprat, Thomas	II, 573
Stuart, Gilbert	IV, 27
Tyrwhitt, Thomas	IV, 25
COUSIN, VICTOR,	
Duns Scotus	I, 85
Hamilton, Sir William	VI, 53
Hartley, David	III, 378
Locke, John	II, 525, 533
More, Henry	II, 374
Price, Richard	IV, 136
Reid, Thomas	IV, 284
COWAN, REV. W.,	
Grosseteste, Robert	I, 74
COWLEY, ABRAHAM,	
Bacon, Francis	I, 657
Books	III, 6
Cowley, Abraham	II, 193, 196

	Vol. and Page
Crashaw, Richard	II 110
D'Avenant, Sir William	II, 217
Evelyn, John	II, 547
Harvey, William	II, 156
Philips, Katherine	II, 180
Spenser, Edmund	I, 378
Wotton, Sir Henry	II, 17
COWPER, J. M.,	
More, Sir Thomas	I, 237
COWPER, WILLIAM,	
Addison, Joseph	II, 655
Barclay, John	I, 618
Beattie, James	IV, 430-431
Bentley, Richard	III, 121
Books	III, 7
Boswell, James	IV, 213
Burns, Robert	IV, 249
Bunyan, John	II, 393
Chaucer, Geoffrey	I, 157
Churchill, Charles	III, 478, 478
Collins, William	III, 415
Colman, George	IV, 201
Cowley, Abraham	II, 199
Cowper, William	IV, 371, 375, 377
Dennis, John	III, 77
Dryden, John	II, 497
Dwight, Timothy	IV, 626
Franklin, Benjamin	IV, 99
Gibbon, Edward	IV, 195
Gray, Thomas	III, 563
Hale, Sir Matthew	II, 306
Hume, David	III, 653
Johnson, Samuel	III, 753
Knowledge	V, 6
Milton, John	II, 259, 286
Montagu, Elizabeth	IV, 401
More, Hannah	V, 194
Wilberforce, William	V, 200
Philips, John	II, 563
Poets and Poetry	IV, 6
Pope, Alexander	III, 179, 183, 183
Prior, Matthew	II, 675, 676
Sidney, Sir Philip	I, 324
Stanhope, Philip Dormer	III, 603
Swift, Jonathan	III, 229
Thomson, James	III, 267
Watts, Isaac	III, 251
Wesley, John	IV, 113
COWPER, WILLIAM, (LORD MOUNTTEMPLE),	
Gladstone, William Ewart	VIII, 386
COX, SIR G. W.,	
Colenso, John William	VII, 523, 526
COX, KENYON,	
Allston Washington	V, 422
Hamerton, Philip Gilbert	VIII, 282
Symonds, John Addington	VIII, 205
COX, SAMUEL SULLIVAN,	
Browne, Charles Farrier	VI, 502
Franklin, Benjamin	IV, 101
Harte, Francis Bret	VIII, 469
Irving, Washington	VI, 149
COXE, ARTHUR CLEVELAND,	
Hawthorne, Nathaniel	VI, 352, 364
Keble, John	VI, 457
Laud, William	II, 91
COXE, WILLIAM,	
Atterbury, Francis	III, 65

	Vol and Page
Porson. Richard	IV. 522
Saint-John. Henry	III. 294
William, Sir Charles Hanbury	III, 412
COYLE, HENRY,	
Wilson, Alexander	IV, 585
CRABBE, GEORGE.	
Books	III, 7
Crabbe, George	V, 170, 171
Knowledge	V, 6
Poets and Poetry	IV, 7
Scott, Sir Walter	V, 126
Spenser. Edmund	I, 395
CRACROFT, BERNARD,	
Bacon, Francis	I, 645, 667
CRADOCK, JOSEPH,	
Goldsmith, Oliver	III, 617
Hurd, Richard	IV, 517
Johnson, Samuel	III, 728
CRAIG, JOHN,	
Newton, Sir Isaac	II, 721
CRAIG, W. H.,	
Johnson, Samuel	III, 736
CRAGIE, W. A.,	
Barbour, John	I, 116
Henry the Minstrel	I, 202
CRAIG-KNOX, ISA,	
Poets and Poetry	IV, 8
CRAIK, DINAH MARIA MULOCK,	
Dobell, Sidney Thompson	VI, 759, 764
Fletcher, Phineas	II, 116
Marston, Philip Bourke	VII, 626
CRAIK, GEORGE L.,	
Akenside, Mark	III, 544
Aldhelm,	I, 25
Andrews, Lancelot	I, 636
Anstey, Christopher	IV, 480
Armstrong, John	III, 699
Atterbury, Francis	III, 68
Ayton, Sir Robert	I, 768
Barbour, John	I, 114
Beattie, James	IV, 432
Beaumont and Fletcher	I, 582
Blair, Robert	III, 242
Brougham, Henry Lord	VI, 532
Browne, Sir Thomas	II, 344
Browne, William	II, 75
Burke, Edmund	IV, 304
Burnet, Thomas	II, 597
Burton, Robert	II, 39
Butler, Samuel	II, 332
Campbell, Thomas	V, 444
Carew, Thomas	II, 22
Carlyle Thomas	VII, 263
Chaucer, Geoffrey	I, 130, 144, 162
Chillingworth, William	II, 86
Churchill, Charles	III, 480
Cibber, Colley	III, 374
Cleveland, John	II, 159
Collins, William	III, 418
Congreve, William	II, 742
Corbet, Richard	I, 743
Cowley, Abraham	II, 201
Cowper, William	IV, 382, 389
Crabbe, George	V, 174
Cranmer, Thomas	I, 273
Crashaw, Richard	II, 112
Croly George	VI, 225
Cudworth, Ralph	II, 385
Cumberland, Richard	IV, 561

INDEX TO CRITICISMS 573

Name	Vol and Page
Daniel, Samuel	I. 616
Darwin, Erasmus	IV, 423
Denham, Sir John	II, 221
Donne, John	I, 715
Drayton, Michael	I, 707
Dryden, John	II, 501
Dunbar, William	I, 225
Dyer, John	III, 399
Eadmer	I, 52
Edwards, Richard	I, 288
Evelyn, John	II, 551
Fanshawe, Sir Richard	II, 185
Farquhar, George	II, 559
Ferguson, James	III, 668
Fletcher, Phineas	II, 116
Ford, John	II, 32
Fuller, Thomas	II, 172
Garth, Sir Samuel	II, 666
Glover, Richard	IV, 18
Green, Matthew	III, 94
Hall, Joseph	II, 148
Harrington, James	III, 308
Harrington, Sir John	I, 441
Henry of Huntingdon	I, 59
Henry, Robert	IV, 108
Herbert, George	I, 723
Heywood, Thomas	II, 126
Hill, Aaron	III, 278
Hobbes, Thomas	II, 323
Hooker, Richard	I, 407
Hoveden, Roger de	I, 63
Hume, David	III, 658
Hunt, James Henry Leigh	VI, 163
Hyde, Edward, Earl of Clarendon	II, 304
John of Salisbury	I, 60
Johnson, Samuel	III, 758
Jones, Sir William	IV, 200
Jonson, Ben	I, 758
Kelly, Hugh	III, 678
Knowledge	V, 9
Latimer, Hugh	I, 269
Layamon	III, 65
Lydgate, John	I, 185
Lyndsay, Sir David	I, 274
Lyttleton, George Lord	III, 612
Mackenzie, Sir George	II, 430
Mackenzie, Henry	V, 115
Macpherson, James	IV, 277
Mandeville, Bernard	III, 69
Mannying, Robert	I, 87
Marston, John	I, 737
Massinger, Philip	II, 482
Mathias, Thomas James	V, 288
Middleton, Thomas	I, 683
Napier, Sir John	I, 589
Nashe, Thomas	I, 414
Norris, John	II, 570
Norton, Thomas	I, 318
Orme, Robert	IV, 415
Ornin	I, 70
Parnell, Thomas	II, 617
Percy, Thomas	IV, 564
Philips, John	II, 564
Prior, Matthew	II, 678
Quarries, Francis	II, 266
Raleigh, Sir Walter	I, 604
Randolph, Thomas	I, 744
Ridley, Nicolas	I, 266
Rowe, Nicholas	II, 622
Rowley, William	II, 68

Name	Vol. and Page
Savage, Richard	III. 136
Savile, Sir Henry	I. 620
Seward, Anna	IV, 544
Shakespeare, William	I, 564
Smollett, Tobias George	III, 588
Speed, John	II, 695
Spenser, Edmund	I, 376, 383, 390
Sprat, Thomas	II, 574
Sterne Laurence	III, 514
Stuart, Gilbert	IV, 27
Suckling, Sir John	II, 65
Surrey, Earl of	I, 257, 258
Swift, Jonathan	III, 232
Tennyson, Alfred Lord	VIII, 102
Thomson, James	III, 264, 269
Tickell, Thomas	III, 106
Tighe, Mary	IV, 551
Tillotson, John Robert	II, 440
Vanbrugh, Sir John	II, 708
Waller, Edmund	II, 382
Wallis, John	II, 517
Warner, William	I, 437
West, Gilbert	III, 369
Whiston, William	III, 305
Wilkie, John	IV, 335
William of Malmesbury	I, 54
Wilmot, John	II, 338
Wither, George	II, 214
Wyntoun, Andrew	I, 178
Young, Edward	III, 493
CRAIK, SIR HENRY,	
Arbuthnot, John	III, 82, 84
Atterbury, Francis	III 66, 68
Bentham, Jeremy	V, 169
Beattie, James	IV, 430
Berkeley, George	III, 335
Berners, Lord	I, 228
Boswell, James	III, 219
Brougham, Henry Lord	VI, 528
Burke, Edmund	IV, 307
Burnett, James	III, 347
Burney, Frances	V, 350
Burns, Robert	IV, 270
Butler, Joseph	III, 317
Camden, William	I, 620
Carlyle, Thomas	VII, 274
Caxton, William	I, 199
Chalmers, Thomas	V, 495
Cobbett, William	V, 275
Cudworth, Ralph	III, 384
Defoe, Daniel	III, 49
DeQuincey, Thomas	VI, 131
Digby, Sir Kenelm	II, 182, 182
Disraeli, Benjamin	VII, 295
Disraeli, Isaac	V, 514
Dryden, John	II, 494
Edgeworth, Maria	V, 571
Eliot, George	VII, 182, 207
Evelyn, John	II, 551
Fabyan, Robert	I, 207
Ferguson, Adam	IV, 610, 612
Fielding, Henry	III, 364
Fisher, John	I, 231
Gibbon, Edward	IV, 196
Hall, Joseph	II, 149
Hamilton, Sir William	VI, 57
Heylin, Peter	II, 175
Home, Henry	III, 712, 713
Home, John	IV, 515
Horner, Francis	IV, 630
Horsley, Samuel	IV, 496

Name	Vol and Page
Hume, David	III 651 653
Hutcheson, Francis	III 245
Hyde, Edward, Earl of Clarendon	II. 305
Jeffrey, Francis Lord	V. 652
Johnson, Samuel	III. 748. 767
Lamb, Charles	V. 244
Law, William	III, 430
Locke, John	II, 536
Mackenzie, Sir George	II, 428
May, Thomas	II, 118
Middleton, Conyers	III, 281
Miller, Hugh	VI, 65
Milton, John	II. 279
More, Henry	II, 372
Peacock, Reginald	I, 190
Pitt, William	III. 680
Ramsay, Allan	III, 411
Reid, Thomas	IV, 283
Richardson, Samuel	III, 452
Robertson, William	IV, 164
Rutherford, Samuel	II, 166
Saint-John, Henry	III, 298
Savile, George	II, 448
Scott, Sir Walter	V, 135 152, 161
Smith, Adam	IV, 57
Stanhope, Philip Dormer	III, 606
Sterne, Laurence	III, 516
Stewart Dugald	V, 77, 80
Swift, Jonathan	III, 210, 213, 215, 236
Taylor, Jeremy	II, 211
Temple, Sir William	II, 459
Tillotson, John Robert	II, 441
Walpole, Horace	IV, 321
Walton, Isaac	II, 345
Warburton, William	III, 692
Warton, Thomas	IV, 75, 79
Wesley, John	IV, 128
White, Gilbert	IV, 153
Wilkins, John	II, 227
Wilson, John	V, 748
Wyclif, John	I, 111
CRAMER, FRANK,	
Darwin, Charles Robert	VII, 433
CRANCH, CHRISTOPHER PEARSE,	
Dryden, John	II, 488
Emerson, Ralph Waldo	VII, 359
Taylor, Bayard	VII, 130
CRANDALL, CHARLES H.,	
Browning, Robert	VII, 711
Rossetti, Gabriel Charles Dante	VII, 449
CRANE, T. F.,	
Maccarthy, Denis Florence	VII, 490
CRANE, WALTER,	
Morris, William	VIII, 331, 333
CRANMER, THOMAS,	
Pole, Reginald	I, 281
CRANSTOUN, JAMES,	
Scott, Alexander	I, 319
CRASHAW, RICHARD,	
Ford, John	II, 30
Sidney, Sir Philip	I, 331
CRASHAW, W. H.,	
Dryden, John	II, 507
CRAWFORD, MARION,	
Byron, George Gordon Lord	IV, 763

574 INDEX TO CRITICISMS

	Vol. and Page
Johnson, Samuel	III, 766
Landor, Walter Savage	VI, 391
Sheridan, Richard Brinsley	IV, 608
Wordsworth, William	V, 645

CRAWFORD, VIRGINIA M.,
Patmore, Coventry K. D. .... VIII, 341

CRAWFURD, OSWALD,
Addison, Joseph	II, 652
Beaumont and Fletcher	I, 584
Cibber, Colley	III, 373
Congreve, William	II, 743
Cumberland, Richard	IV, 561
Dibden, Charles	IV, 587
Donne, John	I, 718
Farquhar, George	II, 559
Gay, John	III, 58
Goldsmith, Oliver	III, 633
Gray, Thomas	III, 560
Habington, William	II, 136
Johnson, Samuel	III, 737
Jonson, Ben	I, 766
Mickle, William Juluis	IV, 41
Milton, John	II, 256
Prior, Matthew	II, 679
Sheridan, Richard Brinsley	IV, 603, 607
Vanbrugh, Sir John	II, 708
Wycherley, William	II, 606

CREAST, SIR EDWARD S.,
Mandeville, Sir John .... I, 96

CREASY, SIR EDWARD,
Antsey, Christopher	IV, 480
Boyle, Robert	II, 417
Fielding, Henry	III, 345
Fortescue, Sir John	I, 195
Frere, John Hookham	V, 487
Gray, Thomas	III, 555, 568
Hales, John	II, 150
Hall Edward	I, 260
Hallam, Henry	VI, 176, 179
Langland, William	I, 120
Lewis, Sir George Cornewall	VI, 338
Lyttleton, George Lord	III, 612
Mallory, Sir Thomas	I, 204
Occleve, Thomas	I, 188
Pearson, John	II, 369
Saint-John, Henry	III, 294
Tusser, Thomas	I, 310
Waller, Edmund	II, 382
Williams, Sir Charles Hanbury	III, 413
Wotton, Sir Henry	II, 18
Wyclif, John	I, 107

CREIGHTON, LOUISE,
Chaucer, Geoffrey	I, 134
Raleigh, Sir Walter	I, 604

CREIGHTON, MANDELL,
Bale, John	I, 287
Blamire, Susanna	IV, 204, 205
Cavendish, George	I, 282
Chillingworth, William	II, 87
Green, John Richard	VII, 510
Hall, Edward	I, 260
Harrington, Sir John	I, 441
Spenser, Edmund	I, 385

CRELL, SAMUEL,
Newton, Sir Isaac .... II, 712

CRISP THOMAS S.,
Foster, John .... V, 424

	Vol. and Page
CROCKETT, SAMUEL RUTHERFORD,	
Carlyle, Thomas	VII, 274
Stevenson, Robert Louis	VIII, 248

CROESE, GERARD,
Penn, William .... II, 626

CROFT, SIR HERBERT,
Chatterton, Thomas ...... III, 534

CROFT, HERBERT, JR.,
Young, Edward .... III, 485

CROFTON F. BLAKE,
Haliburton, Thomas Chandler .... VI, 456

CROKER, JOHN WILSON,
Boswell, James	IV, 210, 215
Bowles, William Lisle	V, 660
Brougham, Henry Lord	VI, 531
Burke, Edmund	IV, 302
Burney, Frances	V, 349
Dickens, Charles	VI, 562
Fox, Charles James	IV, 507
Galt, John	V, 335
Hervey, John Lord	III, 129
Junius	IV, 640
Lyttleton, George Lord	III, 613
Macaulay, Catherine	IV, 134
Macaulay, Catherine	IV, 134
Macaulay, Thomas Babington Lord	VI, 97, 99, 105
Mackintosh, Sir James	V, 182
Montagu, Lady Mary Wortley	III, 466
Morgan, Lady Sydney Owenson	VI, 192, 194
Pitt, William	IV, 511
Pope, Alexander	III, 180
Priestley, Joseph	IV, 449
Romilly, Sir Samuel	IV, 635
Sheridan, Richard Brinsley	IV, 600, 606
Smith, Sydney	V, 471
Stevenson, John Hall	IV, 24
Swift, Jonathan	III, 217
Walpole, Horace	IV, 318
Wilberforce, William	V, 201, 202
Williams, Sir Charles Hanbury	III, 412

CROLY, GEORGE,
Burke, Edmund .... IV, 303

CROLY, JENNY C.,
Cary, Phœbe .... VI, 640

CROMEK, R. H.,
Burns, Robert .... IV, 250

CROMWELL, OLIVER,
Raleigh, Sir Walter	I, 601
Spenser, Edmund	I, 369

CROSBY, MARGARET,
Lazarus, Emma .... VII, 613

CROSLAND, MRS. NEWTON (CAMILLA TOULMIN),
Aguilar, Grace	V, 505, 505
Burney, Frances	V, 348
Craik, Dinah Maria Mulock	VII, 624
Fuller, Sarah Margaret	V, 669
Hawthorne, Nathaniel	IV, 348
Stowe, Harriet Beecher	VIII, 350
Taylor, Bayard	VII, 131

CROSS, ALLEN EASTMAN,
Browning, Elizabeth Barrett .... VI, 242

	Vol. and Page
Lazarus, Emma	VII, 612

CROSS, ELWIN,
Chatterton, Thomas ...... III, 527

CROSS, JOHN W.,
Eliot, George	VII, 175
Lewes, George Henry	VII, 138, 142

CROSS, WILBUR L.,
Addison, Joseph	II, 646
Austen, Jane	IV, 624
Barclay, John	I, 619
Beckford, William	V, 450
Behn, Aphra	II, 409
Borrow, George Henry	VII, 314
Brontë, Emily	V, 525
Bunyan, John	II, 400
Dickens, Charles	VI, 564
Edgeworth, Maria	V, 572
Eliot, George	VII, 209
Fielding, Henry	III, 354
Fielding, Sarah	III, 519
Gaskell, Elizabeth Cleghorn	VI, 431
Goldsmith, Oliver	III, 629
Gore, Catherine Grace	VI, 264
Hawthorne, Nathaniel	VII, 371
Inchbald, Mrs. Elizabeth	IV, 688
Kingsley, Charles	VII, 26
Lytton, Sir Edward George Bulwer	VI, 688
Mackenzie, Henry	V, 114
Maturin, Charles Robert	IV, 768
Porter, Jane	V, 674
Radcliffe, Ann Ward	IV, 721
Richardson, Samuel	III, 454
Smollett, Tobias George	III, 591
Sterne, Laurence	III, 517
Thackeray, William Makepeace	VI, 306
Trollope, Anthony	VII, 464

CROSSE, MRS. ANDREW,
Bowles, William Lisle	V, 659
Moore, Thomas	V, 710

CROSSLEY, JAMES,
Fuller, Thomas .... II, 171, 171

CROW, MARTHA FOOTE,
Fletcher, Giles	I, 624
Lodge Thomas	I, 627
Langland, William	I, 117

CROZIER, JOHN BEATTIE,
Beecher, Henry Ward	VII, 609
Dickens, Charles	VI, 594
Emerson, Ralph Waldo	VII, 367

CRUGER, JULIA GRINNELL (JULIEN GORDON),
Eliot, George .... VII, 180

CRUIKSHANK, BRODIE,
Landon, Letitia Elizabeth ..V, 324

CRUTTWELL, CLEMENT,
Wilson, Thomas .... III, 366

CUDWORTH, WARREN H.,
Poe, Edgar Allan .... V, 541

CUMBERLAND, RICHARD,
Bentley, Richard	III, 111
Boswell, James	IV, 209
Burke, Edmund	IV, 299
Cumberland, Richard	IV, 559
Dodington, George Bubb	III, 458
Garrick, David	III, 695
Goldsmith, Oliver	III, 616, 632, 634
Gray, Thomas	III, 564
Jenyns, Soame	IV, 31

INDEX TO CRITICISMS 575

	Vol. and Page
Johnson, Samuel	III, 727, 741
Murray, William	IV, 170
Rogers, Samuel	VI, 38
Smollett, Tobias George	III, 586
Turner, Sharon	V, 498
Walpole, Horace	IV, 321

CUMING, WILLIAM,
  Warburton, William......III, 690
CUMMINGS, C. A.,
  Pierpont, John......VI, 480, 482
CUMPSTON, ELLEN,
  Reade, Charles..........VII, 537
CUNNINGHAM, ALLAN,
  Burney, Frances..........V, 350
  Burns, Robert............IV, 226
  Chalmers, George..........V, 29
  Crabbe, George............V, 173
  Croker, John Wilson...... V, 75
  Croly, George............VI, 224
  Ferrier, Susan Edmondstone.V, 764
  Galt, John...............V, 336
  Gifford, William...........V, 34
  Godwin, William..V, 299, 301, 302
  Gore, Catherine Grace.....VI, 263
  Hallam, Henry...........VI, 174
  Hemans, Felicia Dorothea..V, 258
  Hogg, James..............V, 266
  Hood, Thomas............V, 461
  Hook, Theodore Edward....V, 357
  Hunt, James Henry Leigh.VI, 168
  James, George Paine Rainsford
  .... VI, 218
  Knowles, James Sheridan..VI, 288
  Lamb, Charles............V, 236
  Landon, Letitia Elizabeth..V, 327
  Lockhart, John Gibson......
  .... V, 755, 756,756
  Lytton, Sir Edward George
  Bulwer................ VI, 694
  Mackenzie, Henry..V. 113, 114
  Maturin, Charles Robert...IV, 767
  Moore, Thomas............V, 710
  Morgan, Sydney Owenson
  Lady ....VI, 194
  Motherwell, William.......V, 277
  Napier, Gen. Sir Wm. Francis
  Patrick ....VI, 222, 224
  Radcliffe, Ann Ward......IV, 719
  Reynolds, Sir Joshua......IV, 141
  Roscoe, William...........V, 119
  Scott, Sir Walter..........V, 135
  Southey, Robert..........V, 415
  Tennant, William..........V, 528
  Tennyson, Alfred Lord..VIII, 78
  Vanbrugh, Sir John........II, 707
  Wilson, John..........V, 750, 751
  Wordsworth, William..V, 623, 632
CUNNINGHAM, G. G.,
  Bentley, Richard.........III, 122
  Clarke, Samuel...........II, 749
  Wotton, William..........II, 710
CUNNINGHAM, LT. COL.
  FRANCIS,
  Chapman, George ....I, 728
  Hazlitt, Willam...........V, 104
  Marlowe, Christopher........
  .... I, 347, 350,351
CUNNINGHAM, PETER,
  Dryden, John.............II, 465
  Goldsmith, Oliver........III, 633
  Gray, Thomas............III, 568

	Vol. and Page
Johnson, Samuel	III, 751
Walpole, Horace	IV, 313
Williams, Sir Charles Hanbury	III, 413

CURLL, EDMUND,
  Pope, Alexander..........III, 145
CURRIE, JAMES,
  Burns, Robert...IV, 223, 241, 243
CURTIS, GEORGE TICKNOR,
  Child, Lydia Maria.......VII, 220
  Hamilton, Alexander..IV, 463, 466
  Madison, James...........V, 314
  Washington, George......IV, 362
  Webster, Daniel..........V, 721
  Willis, Nathaniel Parker...VI, 489
CURTIS, GEORGE WILLIAM,
  Adams, John Quincy.......V, 518
  Austen, Jane.............IV, 621
  Brontë, Charlotte.........VI, 28
  Browning, Elizabeth Barrett
  .... VI, 243
  Browning, Robert.......VII, 680
  Bryant, William Cullen......
  ....VII, 111, 116, 118
  Burns, Robert...........IV, 231
  Channing, William Ellery...V, 369
  Clough, Arthur Hugh......VI, 252
  Darwin, Charles Robert..VII, 429
  Dickens, Charles.........VI, 560
  Emerson, Ralph Waldo......
  .... VII, 345, 363
  Fuller, Sarah Margaret.....V 668
  Gaskell, Elizabeth Cleghorn..
  .... VI, 430
  Hawthorne, Nathaniel......
  .... VI, 342, 353, 360, 365
  Holmes, Oliver Wendell......
  .... VIII, 286, 292
  Irving, Washington......VI, 151
  Johnson, Samuel........III, 758
  Lamb, Charles...........V, 234
  Longfellow, Henry Wadsworth
  .... VII, 408
  Lowell, James Russell......
  .... VIII, 22, 29
  Milton, John.............II, 291
  Phillips, Wendell........VII, 553
  Smith, Alexander........VI, 518
  Sumner, Charles.........VI, 754
  Thackeray, William Makepeace
  .... VI, 291, 314
  Thoreau, Henry David...VI, 268
  Washington, George......IV, 363
  Winthrop, Theodore......VI 266
CURTIS, GEORGINA P.,
  Burton, Sir Richard Francis..
  .... VII, 759
CURTIS, JESSIE KINGSLEY,
  Hawthorne, Nathaniel.....VI, 361
CURTIS, WILLIAM ELEROY,
  Jefferson, Thomas.....V, 40, 45
CURTIS, WILLIAM O'LEARY,
  Whitman, Walt........VIII, 146
CURWEN, HENRY,
  Chambers, Robert........VI, 622
  Disraeli, Benjamin.......VII, 290
  Johnson, Samuel........III, 738
  Knight, Charles..........VI, 742
  Macaulay, Thomas Babington
  Lord.............99, 102, 107
  Milton, John............II, 264

	Vol. and Page
Moore, Thomas	V 714
Murray, Lindley	V 55
Richardson, Samuel	III 450
Robertson, William	IV 159
Scott, Sir Walter	V 148
Tannahill, Robert	IV 548

CUTLER, E. J.
  Longfellow, Henry Wadsworth
  .... VII 404
CUTLER, MANASSEH
  Franklin, Benjamin......IV 82
CUVIER, GEORGE BARON AND
  THOUARS, AUBERT DUPETIT,
  Ray, John................II 543
  Rumford, Count..........VI, 590
CUYLER, THEODORE L,
  Carlyle, Thomas......... VII 239
  Whittier, John Greenleaf.VIII 116

D ABNEY, J. P.
  Tyndale, William......I 246
DAILY ADVERTISER
  Carey, Henry............III 137
DALE, R. W.,
  Bright, Thomas......... VII 721
D'ALEMBERT, JEAN LE ROND
  Locke, John.............II 524
DALL, CAROLINE H.
  Barlow, Joel.............IV 573
  Child, Lydia Maria.......VII, 219
  Fuller, Sarah Margaret ....V 671
  Shakespeare, William...... I, 455
DALLAWAY, J.,
  Montagu, Lady Mary Wortley
  .... III, 464
DALLAS, E. S.,
  Porson, Richard.........IV, 525
  Theobald, Lewis........ III 142
  Thackeray, William Makepeace..................VI 315
DALLAS, R. C.
  Byron, George Gordon Lord,IV 748
D'ALVIELLA COUNT GOBLET
  Emerson, Ralph Waldo...VII 371
DAM, HENRY J. W.,
  Harte, Francis Bret.....VIII, 467
DANA, CHARLES ANDERSON
  Authors and Authorship .VII 9
  Lazarus, Emma.........VII, 610
  Lincoln, Abraham........VI, 416
DANA, JAMES D.,
  Gray, Asa..............VII, 671
DANA, RICHARD HENRY
  Allston, Washington ...V, 418, 423
  Brown, Charles Brockden ...
  ....IV 552, 555
  Dickens, Charles........VI, 552
  Greeley, Horace......... VI, 666
  Hazlitt, William..........V, 102
  Irving, Washington... VI, 137, 138
  Neal, John..............VII, 77
  Pollok, Robert...........V, 73
  Quincy, Josiah..........VI 404
  Radcliffe, Ann Ward......VI, 719
  Sedgwick, Catherine, Maria.VI 507
  Ticknor, George.........VI 617
  Wilson, John............V 752
  Wordsworth, William.......V, 632
DANA, RICHARD HENRY JR
  Allston, Washington......V, 419

INDEX TO CRITICISMS

DANA, WILLIAM F.,
  Emerson, Ralph Waldo...VII, 371
DANIEL, GEORGE,
  Cleveland, John...........II, 159
  Donne, John...............I, 714
  Drayton, Michael..........I, 706
  Hawkins, Sir John........IV, 51
  Overbury, Sir Thomas......I, 442
  Shakespeare, William......I, 549
  Waller, Edmund...........II, 379
DANIEL, J. W.,
  Horsley, Samuel..........IV, 494
DANIEL, SAMUEL,
  Chapman, George...........I, 728
  Chaucer, Geoffrey.........I, 154
  Daniel, Samuel............I, 615
  Knowledge................V, 5
  More, Sir Thomas..........I, 241
  Sidney, Sir Philip........I, 321
  Spenser, Edmund...........I, 378
  Sylvester Joshua..........I, 609
DANIELS, J. H.,
  Arnold, Matthew.........VII, 633
DANTE, ALIGHIERI,
  Knowledge................V, 5
  Scott, Michael............I, 68
D'ARBLAY, MADAME (FANNY BURNEY),
  Beattie, James...........IV, 428
  Burke, Edmund...........IV, 289
  Burney, Charles..........IV, 588
  Chapone, Hester..........IV, 418
  Gibbon, Edward..........IV, 173
  Hurd, Richard...........IV, 517
  Lennox, Charlotte.......IV, 469
  Montagu, Elizabeth......IV, 400
  Piozzi, Hester Lynch....IV, 685
  Sheridan, Richard Brinsley IV, 594
DARLEY, GEORGE,
  Beaumont and Fletcher....I, 578
  Beddoes, Thomas Lovell...V, 586
  Fletcher, John............I, 629
DARMESTETER, JAMES,
  Browning, Robert........VII, 703
  Eliot, George...........VII, 203
  Lewes, George Henry....VII, 138
  Macpherson, James.......IV, 280
DARMESTETER, MARY,
  Holinshed, Raphael........I, 312
DART, JOHN,
  Chaucer, Geoffrey.........I, 126
  Pole, Reginald............I, 280
DARTMOUTH, EARL,
  Burnet, Gilbert.......II, 591, 593
DARWIN, CHARLES ROBERT,
  Agassiz, Louis Jean Rudolphe.
  ....VI, 722
  Darwin, Charles Robert...VII, 416
  Darwin, Erasmus......IV, 421, 424
  Lyell, Sir Charles......VII, 34, 38
  Malthus, Thomas Robert....V, 252
  Paley, William..........IV, 475
DARWIN, FRANCIS,
  Darwin, Charles Robert......
  ....VII, 419, 420, 431
  Huxley, Thomas Henry.......
  ....VIII, 324
DASENT, SIR G. W.,
  Lytton, Sir Edward George Bulwer..............VI, 687
  Wilberforce, Samuel......VI, 734

D'AUBIGNE, J. H. MERLE,
  Anselm....................I, 49
  Erigena, John Scotus......I, 35
  Tyndale, William..........I, 245
DAUBRÉE, GABRIEL AUGUSTE,
  Hutton, James............IV, 338
DAVENANT, SIR WILLIAM,
  Books,....................III, 5
  Knowledge.................V, 5
DAVENPORT, R. A.,
  Churchill, Charles.......III, 479
  Falconer, William........III, 525
  Thompson, William.......III, 501
DAVEY, SAMUEL,
  Carlyle, Thomas.........VII, 266
  DeQuincey, Thomas.......IV, 127
  Dickens, Charles.........VI, 586
DAVIDS, J. C.,
  Dickens, Charles.........VI, 551
DAVIDSON, JAMES,
  Burns, Robert...........IV, 268
DAVIDSON, JAMES WOOD.
  Hayne, Paul Hamilton....VII, 592
  Lanier, Sidney.........VII, 327
  Ryan, Abram Joseph.....VII, 598
  Simms, William Gilmore...VI, 598
DAVIDSON, JOHN,
  Brontë, Emily.............V, 523
  Burney, Frances...........V, 351
  Carlyle, Thomas.........VII, 238
  Hazlitt, William..........V, 106
  Keats, John..............IV, 418
  Ruskin, John...........VIII, 420
  Smollett, Tobias George...III, 586
  Tennyson, Alfred Lord.. VIII, 95
DAVIDSON, J. MORRISON,
  Freeman, Edward Augustus..
  ....VIII, 159
  Spurgeon, Charles Haddon....
  ....VIII, 180
DAVIDSON, THOMAS,
  Longfellow, Henry Wadsworth
  ....VII, 383, 388, 401, 410
  Tennyson, Alfred Lord...VIII, 88
DAVIES, JAMES,
  Frere, John Hookham......V, 488
  Godwin, William..........V, 299
  Grote, George............VI, 610
  Lewis, Sir George Cornewall VI, 337
  Lytton, Edward Robert Bulwer Earl.............VIII, 46
  Peacock, Thomas Love.....VI, 475
  Porter, Jane..............V, 674
DAVIES, J. LLEWELYN,
  Arnold, Matthew........VII, 631
  Hughes, Thomas....VIII, 347, 348
DAVIES, JOHN,
  Browne, William..........II, 73
  Dyer, Sir Edward..........I, 428
  Shakespeare, William.........
  ....I, 447, 454, 547
DAVIES, SAMUEL,
  Doddridge, Samuel.......III, 299
  Saint-John, Henry.......III, 293
DAVIES, THOMAS,
  Churchill, Charles.......III, 478
  Cibber, Colley..........III, 370
  Congreve, William........II, 73
  Cumberland, Richard.....IV, 558
  Dryden, John............II, 476
  Foote, Samuel...........III, 673

Goldsmith Oliver.........III, 615
Hill, Aaron.............III, 277, 278
Jonson, Ben............I, 751, 754
Kelly, Hugh.............III, 677
Mallett, David..........III, 495
Otway, Thomas..........II, 363
Saint-John, Henry......III, 293
Shakesphere, William..
  ....I 476, 483, 489, 540
Tate, Nahum............II, 588
DAVIS, JEFFERSON,
  Calhoun, John Caldwell.....V, 675
DAVIS, JOHN,
  Chatterton, Thomas......III, 529
  Washington, George.......IV, 367
DAVIS, THOMAS,
  Carleton, William........VI, 548
DAVIS, THOMAS T.,
  Everett, Edward.........VI, 423
DAVY, SIR HUMPHREY,
  Faraday, Michael.........VI, 51
DAVY, JOHN,
  Davy, Sir Humphry........V, 91
DAVYS, SIR JOHN,
  Chaucer, Geoffrey.........I, 154
  Heywood, John............I, 305
DAWES, ANNA LAURENS,
  Sumner, Charles.........VI, 754
DAWES, HENRY L.,
  Lincoln, Abraham........VI, 419
DAWES, RUFUS,
  Emerson, Ralph Waldo...VII, 344
DAWKINS, C. E.,
  Jefferies, Richard......VII, 619
DAWSON, GEORGE
  Bunyan, John............II, 404
  Defoe, Daniel...........III, 48
  Knowledge................V, 9
DAWSON, HENRY B.,
  Drake, Joseph Rodman....IV, 660
DAWSON, J. W.,
  Huxley, Thomas Henry..VIII, 324
DAWSON, S. E.,
  Tennyson, Alfred Lord..VIII, 84
DAWSON, THOMAS,
  Eliot, George..........VII, 188
DAWSON, WILLIAM J.,
  Arnold, Matthew........VII, 638
  Browning, Robert.......VII, 712
  Carlyle, Thomas........VII, 272
  Coleridge, Samuel Taylor...V, 216
  Dickens, Charles........VI, 589
  Eliot, George..........VII, 206
  Longfellow, Henry Wadsworth
  ....VII, 396, 413
  Poe, Edgar Allan.........V, 559
  Pope, Alexander.........III, 192
  Rossetti, Gabriel Charles Dante
  ....VII, 445
  Ruskin, John..........VIII, 421
  Shelley, Percy Bysshe..IV, 697, 714
  Tennyson, Alfred Lord......
  ....VIII, 89
  Thomson, James.........VII, 445
  Wordsworth, William......V, 645
DAY, GEORGE,
  Kingsley, Charles......VII, 22
DAY, HENRY N.,
  Cowper, William.........IV, 381
DAY, JUDGE,
  Goldsmith, Oliver.......III, 616

INDEX TO CRITICISMS

	Vol. and Page
DAY, LEWIS F.,	
Morris, William	VIII, 332
DEARING, SIR EDWARD,	
Laud, William	II, 89
DEARMER, PERCY,	
Defoe, Daniel	III, 29
Law, William	III, 430
Swift, Jonathan	III, 238
DEBS, EUGENE V.,	
Ingersoll, Robert Green.	VIII, 403
DE BURY, RICHARD,	
de Bury, Richard	I, 89
DE CANDOLLE, AUGUSTIN-PYRAMUS,	
Rumford, Count	IV, 591
DECIUS,	
Adams, Samuel	IV, 440
DECKER, THOMAS,	
Nashe, Thomas	I, 412
DECOSTA, BENJAMIN FRANKLIN,	
Bancroft, George	VIII, 59
DEFOE, DANIEL,	
Defoe, Daniel	III, 24, 32, 42
Hoadley, Benjamin	III, 423
Sacheverell, Henry	II, 696
Swift, Jonathan	III, 197
DEKAY, CHARLES,	
Lazarus, Emma	VII, 611
DEKKER, THOMAS,	
Chettle, Henry	I, 429
Neshe, Thomas	I, 413
Spenser, Edmund	I, 378
DE KOVEN, ANNA FARWELL,	
Story, William Wetmore.	VIII, 319
DELANY, MRS. (MARY GRANVILLE),	
Atterbury, Francis	III, 67
Berkeley, George	III, 319
Burney, Frances	V, 348
Smollett,Tobias George.	III, 579, 580
DELANY, PATRICK,	
Pope, Alexander	III, 171
Swift, Jonathan	III, 198
DELESSERT, BENJAMIN,	
Rumford, Count	IV, 590
DELILLE, EDWARD,	
Holmes, Oliver Wendell	VIII, 294
DELPLACE, L.,	
Wyclif, John	I, 109
DEMAUS, ROBERT,	
Tyndale, William	I, 247
DE MORGAN, AUGUSTUS,	
Bacon, Francis	I, 667
Brewster, Sir David	VI, 547
DeMorgan, Augustus	VI, 632
Junius	IV, 642
Manley, Mrs. Mary de la Riviere	II, 693
Montagu, Charles	II, 587
Moore, John	IV, 426
Newton, Sir Isaac	II, 713, 714
Whewell, William	VI, 468
Whiston, William	III, 304
Wordsworth, William	V, 614
DE MORGAN, SOPHIA ELIZABETH,	
DeMorgan, Augustus	VI, 63
DENHAM, SIR JOHN,	
Chaucer, Geoffrey	I, 155
Cowley, Abraham	II, 198

	Vol. and Page
Fletcher, John	I, 630
Spenser, Edmund	I, 393
Waller, Edmund	II, 379
DENMAN, LORD,	
Dickens, Charles	VI, 575
DENNETT, J. R.,	
Dickens, Charles	VI, 560
Eggleston, Edward	VIII, 476
Harte, Francis Bret	VIII, 468
Lowell, James Russell	VIII, 36
Miller, Cincinnatus Hiner	VIII, 500
Paulding, James Kirke	VI, 227
Praed, Winthrop Mackworth	V, 332
Reade, Charles	VII, 533
Rossetti, Christina Georgina	VIII, 270
Rossetti, Gabriel Charles Dante	VII, 446, 450
Stowe, Harriet Beecher	VIII, 358
Timrod, Henry	VI, 509
DENNIS, JOHN,	
Addison, Joseph	II, 648, 660
Akenside, Mark	III, 545
Arbuthnot, John	III, 83
Armstrong, John	III, 699
Atterbury, Francis	III, 68
Beattie, James	IV, 434
Berkeley, George	III, 326, 335
Blair Robert	III, 244
Broome, William	III, 239
Browne, William	II, 76
Butler, Joseph	III, 310
Butler, Samuel	II, 334
Byrom, John	III, 470
Campbell, Thomas	V, 439
Cibber, Colley	III, 373
Cooper, Anthony Ashley	III, 580
Cowley, Abraham	II, 198, 201
Defoe, Daniel	III, 26
DeQuincey, Thomas	VI, 122, 128
Dryden, John	II, 483, 493, 506
Dyer, John	III, 400
Glover, Richard	IV, 18
Herrick, Robert	II, 239
Hill, Aaron	III, 278
Lamb, Charles	V, 241
Law, William	III, 426, 428
Lillo, George	III, 102
Mallet, David	III, 495
Mandeville, Bernard	III, 70
Milton, John	II, 258, 294
Otway, Thomas	II, 362
Parnell, Thomas	II, 617
Pope, Alexander III, 144, 158, 163, 164, 167, 177, 179, 193	
Ramsay, Allan	III, 408
Rogers, Samuel	VI, 37
Rowe, Nicholas	II, 623
Sackville, Charles	II, 552
Sandys, George	II, 83
Scott, Sir Walter	V, 149
Settle, Elkanah	II, 592
Shadwell, Thomas	II, 434
Shakespeare, William	I, 491
Skelton, John	I, 223
Somerville, William	III, 127
Southey, Robert	V, 405, 412, 417
Spence, Joseph	III, 521
Steele, Sir Richard	II, 752, 756, 767
Swift, Jonathan	III, 224, 236

	Vol. and Page
Theobald, Lewis	III, 141
Thomson, James	III, 260
Tickell, Thomas	III, 106
Warburton, William	III, 686, 692
Wordsworth, William	V, 626
Wycherley, William	II, 599
DENNIS, G. RAVENSCROFT,	
Swift, Jonathan	III, 223
DENTON, REV. W.,	
Bacon, Roger	I, 80
DEPEW, CHAUNCEY M.,	
Lincoln, Abraham	VI, 420
DEPRESSENSE, FRANCIS,	
Manning, Henry Edward	VIII, 166
DE QUINCEY, THOMAS,	
Addison, Joseph	II, 642, 650, 652
Barbauld, Anna Lætitia	V, 24
Bentley, Richard	III, 112, 120, 121
Berkeley, George	III, 320, 327
Books	III, 7
Browne, Sir Thomas	III, 343
Burke, Edmund	IV, 304
Burns, Robert,	IV, 228
Chaucer, Geoffrey	I, 160
Clare, John	VI, 398
Coleridge, Samuel Taylor	V, 208
Cunningham, Allan	V, 383
Davy, Sir Humphry	V, 92
De Quincey, Thomas	VI, 116
Dickens, Charles	VI, 566
Foster, John	V, 425
Fox, Charles James	IV, 504
Gibbon, Edward	IV, 175
Godwin, William	V, 294, 297
Goldsmith, Oliver	III, 618
Hamilton, Sir William	VI, 51
Hazlitt, William	V, 99
Horsley, Samuel	IV, 495
Jameson, George Paine Rainsford	VI, 218
Johnson, Samuel	III, 731, 751
Junius	IV, 646
Keats, John	670, 672, 676
Lamb, Charles	V, 232
Landor, Walter Savage	VI, 379, 388
Literature	I, 8
Mackintosh, Sir James	V, 182
Malthus, Thomas Robert	IV, 251
Maturin, Charles Robert	IV, 768
Middleton, Conyers	III, 280
Milton, John	II, 261, 288
Mitford, William	V, 72
More, Hannah	V, 191, 194
Paley, William	IV, 472
Parr, Samuel	V, 18, 20
Pope, Alexander III, 148, 159, 161, 176, 188	
Porson, Richard	IV, 525
Priestly, Joseph	IV, 447
Ricardo, David	IV, 725
Ritson, Joseph	IV, 436
Roscoe, William	V, 119
Saint-John, Henry	III, 287
Shakespeare, Wiliam	I, 515, 534, 557, 559
Shelley, Percy Bysshe	IV, 691
Smith, Adam	IV, 63
Southey, Robert	V, 400
Sprat, Thomas	II, 574
Steele, Sir Richard	II, 763
Talfourd Sir Thomas Noon	V, 759

INDEX TO CRITICISMS

	Vol. and Page
Tate, Nahum	II, 589
Taylor, Jeremy	II, 208
Warburton, William	III, 688
Webster, Noah	V, 430
Whatley, Richard	VI, 326
Whiston, William	III, 304
Wilson, John	V, 745
Woolman, John	III, 598
Wordsworth, William, V, 609, 633	
DERBY, JAMES CEPHAS, •	
Griswold, Rufus Wilmot	VI, 78
Prentice, George Denison	VI, 602
Seward, William Henry	VI, 676
DERHAM, WILLIAM,	
Ray, John	II, 542
DERIANO, EMILIA GAYANGOS,	
Lowell, James Russell	VIII, 25
DERRICK, SAMUEL,	
Dryden, John	II, 490
DESCARTES, RENÉ,	
Bacon, Francis	I, 657
DESCHAMPS, EUSTACHE,	
Chaucer, Geoffrey	I, 130, 152
DESHLER, CHARLES D.,	
Allston, Washington	V, 423
Barton, Bernard	V, 597
Bowles, William Lisle	V, 599
Bryant, William Cullen	VII, 124
Cowper, William	IV, 382
Dana, Richard Henry	VII, 154
Dobell, Sidney Thompson	VI, 765
Goldsmith, Oliver	III, 638
Latimer, Hugh	I, 268
Longfellow, Henry Wadsworth	VII, 400
Smith, Charlotte	IV, 497
Talfourd, Sir Thomas Noon	V, 761
Warton, Thomas	IV, 78
White, Henry Kirke	IV, 489
Whittier, John Greenleaf, VIII, 123	
DE TABLEY, LORD JOHN,	
Suckling, Sir John	II, 64
DE VERE, AUBREY THOMAS,	
Bede	I, 30
Browning, Robert	VII, 710
Burns, Robert	IV, 238, 263
Chaucer, Geoffrey	I, 165
Coleridge, Hartley	V, 576, 576
Coleridge, Sara	IV, 734, 734
Coleridge, Samuel Taylor	V, 215, 223
Cowper, William	IV, 392
DeVere, Aubrey Thomas,VIII, 465	
Griffin, Gerald	V, 353, 355
Hunt, James Henry Leigh	VI, 167
Keats, John	IV, 678
Landor, Walter Savage	VI, 382
Manning, Henry Edward, VIII, 167	
Milnes, Richard Monckton, III, 565	
Milton, John	II, 267
Newman, John Henry, VII, 743,749	
Poets and Poetry	IV, 10
Pusey, Edward Bouverie	VII, 467
Scott, Sir Walter	V, 162
Shelley, Percy Bysshe	IV, 708
Spenser, Edmund I, 386, 389, 399	
Taylor, Sir Henry	VII, 580, 582, 583
Tennyson, Alfred Lord	VIII, 74, 101
Thirlwall, Connop	VII, 45
Whatley, Richard	VI, 323
Whewell, William	VI, 469, 467

	Vol. and Page
Wordsworth, William, V, 617, 641	
DE VERE, M. SCHELE,	
Langland, William	I, 120, 120
Tooke, John Horne	IV, 572
DEVEREAUX, G. H.,	
Lytton, Sir Edward George Bulwer	VI, 688
DEVEY, LOUISA,	
Lytton, Sir Edward George Bulwer	VI, 684
DEVINNE, THEODORE L.,	
Morris, William	VIII, 331
DEWAR, GEORGE A. B.,	
Cowper, William	IV, 395
D'EWES, SIR SYMONDS,	
Laud, William	II, 89
DEWEY, MARY E.,	
Dewey, Orville	VII, 497
Sedgwick, Catharine Maria	VI, 506
DEWEY, ORVILLE,	
Channing, William Ellery	V, 366
Choate, Rufus	VI, 198
Kane, Elisha Kent	VI, 82
Martineau, Harriet	VII, 55
Prescott, William Hickling	VI, 187
Reade, Charles	VII, 533
Scott, Sir Walter	V, 143
Thackeray, William Makepeace	VI, 296
DE WITT, CORNÉLIS,	
Jefferson, Thomas	V, 42
DEXTER, F.,	
Pierpont, John	VI, 483, 481
DHARMAPALA, ANAGARIKA,	
Müller, Friedrich Max	VIII, 436
D'HOLBACH, BARON,	
Robertson, William	IV, 157
DIBDIN, CHARLES,	
Beaumont and Fletcher	I, 580
Camden, William	I, 621
Dekker, Thomas	II, 59
Dryden, John	II, 476
Ford, John	II, 26
Heywood, Thomas	II, 125
Jonson, Ben	I, 756, 757
Macklin, Charles	IV, 342
Marston, John	I, 736
Massinger, Philip	II, 45, 46
Peele, George	I, 366
Shakespeare, William, 454, 462, 470 472, 476, 495, 507, 511, 520, 528 532, 542, 542.	
Steele, Sir Richard	II, 756
DIBDIN, EDWARD RIMBAULT,	
Dibden, Charles	IV, 586
DIBDIN,THOMAS,	
Dibden, Charles	IV, 586
DIBDIN, THOMAS FROGNALL,	
Addison, Joseph	II, 656
Akenside, Mark	III, 543
Ascham,Roger	I, 290
Barbour, John	I, 113
Barrow, Isaac	II, 312
Baxter, Richard	II, 426
Beattie, James	IV, 432
Berners, Lord	I, 229
Blake, William	V, 58
Boswell, James	IV, 215
Brougham, Henry Lord	VI, 529
Bruce, James	IV, 207
Buchanan, George	I, 317

	Vol. and Page
Bull, George	II, 565
Burnet, Gilbert	II, 595
Burns, Robert	IV, 252
Burton, Robert	II, 39
Byron, George Gordon Lord	IV, 752
Campbell, Thomas	V, 438
Carte, Thomas	III, 338
Caxton, William	I, 198
Chalmers, George	V, 29
Churchyard, Thomas	I, 418
Coleridge, Samuel Taylor	V, 209
Collins, William	III, 417
Cowper, William, IV, 372, 384, 386	
Crabbe, George	V, 172
DeBury, Richard	I, 89
Defoe, Daniel	III, 46
Dekker, Thomas	II, 59
Doddridge, Philip	III, 301
Eadmer,	I, 52
Evelyn, John	II, 548
Farmer, Richard	IV, 341
Foster, John	V, 425
Fox, Charles James	IV, 506
Foxe, John	I, 335
Fuller, Thomas	II, 171
Gibbon, Edward	IV, 192
Goldsmith, Oliver	III, 636
Granger, James	III, 670
Gray, Thomas	III, 562
Greene, Robert	I, 344
Hakluyt, Richard	I, 446
Hall, Joseph	II, 146
Hallam, Henry	VI, 174
Hawes, Stephen	I, 217
Hearne, Thomas	III, 90
Henry, Robert	IV, 108
Holinshed, Raphael	I, 311
Hooker, Richard	I, 406
Howell, James	II, 187
Hume, David	III, 656, 665
Hurd, Richard	IV, 519
Hyde, Edward, Earl of Clarendon	II, 302
Johnson, Samuel	III, 749, 756
Jones, Sir William	IV, 199
Jortin, John	III, 552
Latimer, Hugh	I, 268
Lardner, Nathaniel	III, 524
Leland, John	I, 263
Leslie, Charles	II, 680
Lewis, Matthew Gregory	IV, 633
Lowth, Robert	IV, 29
Lydgate, John	I, 184
Macknight, James	IV, 408
Malmesbury, William of	II, 53
Malone, Edmond	IV, 578
Marlowe, Christopher	I, 354
Middleton, Conyers	III, 279
Milman, Henry Hart	VI, 540
Montgomery, James	V, 767
Moore, Thomas	V, 712
Oldys, William	III, 457
Otway, Thomas	II, 365
Paley, William	IV, 473
Parker, Matthew	I, 303
Pearson, John	II, 369
Penn, William	II, 630
Percy, Thomas	IV, 563
Pope, Alexander	III, 136
Prior, Matthew	II, 677

INDEX TO CRITICISMS 579

	Vol. and Page
Purchas, Samuel	I, 693
Ritson, Joseph	IV, 436
Robertson, William	IV, 157
Rogers, Samuel	VI, 37
Roscoe, William	V, 118
Skelton, John	I, 220
Southey, Robert	V, 404
Steele, Sir Richard	II, 762
Stowe, John	I, 420
Strype, John	III, 93
Surrey, Earl of	I, 257
Taylor, Jeremy	II, 208
Temple, Sir William	II, 458
Wakefield, Gilbert	IV, 416
Warton, Thomas	IV, 73
Watts, Isaac	III, 253
Wilson, Sir Thomas	I, 312
Wordsworth, William	V, 630
DICEY, A. V.,	
Bagehot, Walter	VII, 99
Bentham, Jeremy	V, 168
Bright, John	VII, 724
Buckle, Henry Thomas	VI, 282
Burke, Edmund	IV, 300, 306
Crocker, John Wilson	VI, 72
Fawcett, Henry	VII, 551
Ferrier, Susan Edmonstone	V, 764
Freeman, Edward Augustus	VIII, 158
Green, John Richard	VII, 511
Greg, William Rathbone	VII, 321
Grote, George	VI, 610
Helps, Sir Arthur	VII, 40
Lecky, William E. H.	VIII, 490
Mill, James	V, 306
Motley, John Lothrop	VII, 92
Pattison, Mark	VII, 541
Sheridan, Richard Brinsley	IV, 601
Stephen, Sir Leslie	VIII, 510, 511
Thirlwall, Connop	VII, 45
Trollope, Anthony	VII, 460
DICKENS, CHARLES,	
Alfred the Great	I, 38
Beecher, Henry Ward	VII, 600
Browning, Robert	VII, 690
Bryant, William Cullen	VII, 110
Buckle, Henry Thomas	VI, 284
Dana, Richard Henry, Jr.,	VII, 501
Dickens, Charles	VI, 553, 572
Eliot, George	VII, 181
Hone, William	V, 392
Hood, Thomas	V, 458
Hunt, James Henry Leigh	VI, 157
Irving, Washington	VI, 133, 144, 146, 148
Jeffrey, Francis Lord	V, 650
Jerrold, Douglas William,	VI, 67, 69
Landor, Walter Savage	VI, 375, 385
Procter, Adelaide, Anne	VII, 394
Longfellow, Henry Wadsworth	VII, 381
Lytton, Sir Edward George Bulwer	VI, 681, 698
Prescott, William Hickling	VI, 186
Rogers, Samuel	VI, 34
Smollett, Tobias George	III, 588
Thackeray, William Makepeace	VI, 293
Wilson, John	V, 745
DICKENS, CHARLES, JR.,	
Dickens, Charles	VI, 558, 591

	Vol. and Page
DICKENS, MAMIE,	
Dickens, Charles	VI, 557
DICKENS, MAMIE, AND HOGARTH, GEORGINA,	
Dickens, Charles	VI, 555
DICKINSON, EMILY,	
Eliot, George	VII, 176
Hawthorne, Nathaniel	VI, 367
Jackson, Helen Hunt	VII, 574, 576
Parker, Theodore	VI, 209
DIDEROT, DENIS,	
Richardson, Samuel	III, 438, 446
DIDIER, EUGENE L.,	
Dickens, Charles	VI, 580
Poe, Edgar Allan	V, 544
DIGBY, KENELM,	
Whewell, William	VI, 468
DIGBY, SIR KENELM,	
Browne, Sir Thomas	II, 340
DIGGES, LEONARD,	
Shakespeare, William	I, 509
DILKE, SIR CHARLES WENTWORTH,	
Burke, Edmund	IV, 291
Johnson, Samuel	III, 751
Junius	IV, 641
Montagu, Lady Mary Wortley	III, 463
Pope, Alexander	III, 150, 189
Wilkes, John	IV, 334
DIMAN, J. L.,	
Mozley, James Bowling	VII, 148
DISRAELI, BENJAMIN (EARL OF BEACONSFIELD),	
Brougham, Henry Lord	VI, 527
Cobden, Richard	VI, 440
Disraeli, Isaac	V, 511, 512
Gladstone, William Ewart	VIII, 387, 389
History	VI, 8
Lamb, Lady Caroline	V, 81
Landon, Letitia Elizabeth	V, 322
Lytton, Edward Robert Bulwer Earl	VIII, 43
Macaulay, Thomas Babington Lord	VI, 109
Milnes, Richard Monckton	VII, 559
Russell, John Earl	VII, 143
Saint-John, Henry	III, 287
Toland, John	II, 681
DISRAELI, ISAAC,	
Addison, Joseph	II, 635
Ascham, Roger	I, 289, 290
Aubrey, John	II, 452
Authors and Authorship	VIII, 6
Bacon, Francis	I, 643, 665
Barclay, Alexander	I, 265
Barnes, Joshua	II, 571
Beowulf	I, 17
Bede	I, 29
Bentley, Richard	III, 115, 119
Birch, Thomas	III, 499
Bruce, James	IV, 207
Bunyan, John	II, 402
Burnet, Gilbert	II, 595
Cædmon	I, 22
Camden, William	I, 621
Carey, Henry	III, 137, 139
Cartwright, Thomas	I, 412
Caxton, William	I, 199
Chapman, George	I, 729

	Vol. and Page
Chatterton, Thomas	III, 535
Chaucer, Geoffrey	I, 159
Cheke, Sir John	I, 278
Churchill, Charles	III, 479
Churchyard, Thomas	I, 418
Cibber, Colley	III, 370
Coke, Sir Edward	I, 740
Collins, William	III, 416
Cowley, Abraham	II, 199
Cudworth, Ralph	II, 385
D'Avenant, Sir William	II, 218
Defoe, Daniel	III, 33
Dekker, Thomas	II, 55, 59
Dennis, John	III, 76, 77
Dibdin, Thomas Frognall	V, 506
Dodsley, Robert	III, 483
Drayton, Michael	I, 707
Elyot, Sir Thomas	I, 253
Evelyn, John	II, 549
Farmer, Richard	IV, 341
Gibbon, Edward	IV, 173, 181
Gower, John	I, 172
Gray, Thomas	III, 554, 567
Hakluyt, Richard	I, 446
Harvey, Gabriel	I, 696
Henry, Robert	IV, 107
Heylin, Peter	II, 175
Heywood, John	I, 305
Hill, Aaron	III, 277
Hill, John	III, 646
Hobbes, Thomas	II, 322, 324
Hooker, Richard	I, 407
Horne, George	IV, 144
Hume, David	III, 650
Hunter, John	IV, 666
Hurd, Richard	IV, 519
Hyde, Edward, Earl of Clarendon	II, 303
Jonson, Ben	I, 764
Kenrick, William	III, 702
Knowledge	V, 7
Knox, John	I, 301
Lamb, Charles	V, 239
Langland, William	I, 119, 123
Leland, John	I, 263
L'Estrange, Sir Roger	II, 538
Logan, John	IV, 43, 44
Lydgate, John	I, 185
Macaulay, Catherine	IV, 134
Mallet, David	III, 495
Marvell, Andrew	II, 316
Mickle, Julius William	IV, 41
Milton, John	II, 283
Montagu, Elizabeth	IV, 402
Montagu, Lady Mary Wortley	III, 465
More, Henry	II, 373
More, Sir Thomas	I, 241
Nashe, Thomas	I, 413
Neal, Daniel	III, 140
Ockley, Simon	II, 669
Oldmixon, John	III, 125
Oldys, William	III, 456, 457
Occleve, Thomas	I, 187
Parr, Samuel	V, 19
Poets and Poetry	IV, 6
Pope, Alexander	III, 147, 170
Prior, Matthew	II, 677
Prynne, William	II, 224
Puttenham, George	I, 401
Raleigh, Sir Walter	I, 594

INDEX TO CRITICISMS

	Vol. and Page
Richardson, Samuel	III, 433, 447
Ritson, Joseph	IV, 436
Rymer, Thomas	II, 583
Sale, George	III, 90
Shakespeare, William	I, 460
Shenstone, William	III, 472, 473
Mandeville, Sir John	I, 95
Skelton, John	I, 221
Smollett, Tobias George	III, 575
Southey, Robert	V, 415
Spence, Joseph	III, 520
Spenser, Edmund	I, 371, 391
Steele, Sir Richard	II, 753
Steevens, George	IV, 409, 409
Still, John	I, 430
Stowe, John	I, 420
Stuart, Gilbert	IV, 27
Taylor, Brook	III, 51
Theobald, Lewis	III, 142
Toland, John	II, 681
Tyrwhitt, Thomas	IV, 25
Vanbrugh, Sir John	II, 705
Wakefield, Gilbert	IV, 416
Walpole, Horace	IV, 311, 322
Warburton, William	III, 687, 690
Wilson, Sir Thomas	I, 313
Wood, Anthony	II, 448
Wyatt, Sir Thomas	I, 251
Young, Edward	III, 485, 495
DITCHFIELD, P. H.,	
Bacon, Roger	I, 79
Pole, Reginald	I, 282
Selden, John	II, 139
DIX, JOHN,	
Chatterton, Thomas	III, 530
DIX, JOHN ROSS,	
Morris, George Pope	VI, 400
Willis, Nathaniel Parker	VI, 486
DIXON, RICHARD WATSON,	
Rossetti, Gabriel Charles Dante	VII, 436
DIXON, WILLIAM HEPWORTH,	
Bacon, Francis	I, 644
Campbell, John Lord	VI, 259
Fisher, John	I, 231
Jerrold, Douglas William	VI, 67
Penn, William	II, 628, 630
Raleigh, Sir Walter	I, 596
Spedding, James	VII, 318
DIXON, W. MACNEILE,	
Burke, Edmund	IV, 307
Grote, George	VI, 613
Hallam, Henry	VI, 180
Landor, Walter Savage	VI, 392
Milman, Henry Hart	VI, 539, 542
Palgrave, Francis Turner	VIII, 373
Tennyson, Alfred Lord	VIII, 92
Warburton, William	III, 687
DOANE, WILLIAM CROSWELL,	
Brooks, Phillips	VIII, 228
DOBELL, SIDNEY,	
Brontë, Charlotte	VI, 23, 29
Carlyle, Thomas	VII, 231
Chaucer, Geoffrey	I, 162
Dobell, Sidney Thompson	VI, 761
Lytton, Sir Edward George Bulwer	I, 696
Shakespeare, William	I, 562
Tennyson, Alfred Lord	VIII, 66
DOBSON, AUSTIN,	
Addison, Joseph	II, 644

	Vol. and Page
Anstey, Christopher	IV, 481
Austen, Jane	IV, 614, 615, 618
Basse, William	II, 131
Boswell, James	IV, 219
Bowles, William Lisle	V, 662
Cibber, Colley	III, 375
Congreve, William	II, 743
Dryden, John	II, 503
Fielding, Henry	III, 344, 346, 348, 354, 363
Frere, John Hookham	V, 488
Garrick, David	III, 696
Gay, John	III, 54, 55
Goldsmith, Oliver	III, 628, 630, 635, 638
Green, Matthew	III, 95
Hawkins, Sir John	IV, 53
Herrick, Robert	II, 239
Hervey, John Lord	III, 129
Hood, Thomas	V, 464
Hurd, Richard	IV, 519
Locker-Lampson, Frederick	VIII, 314
Longfellow, Henry Wadsworth	VII, 410
Pope, Alexander	III, 162, 178
Praed, Winthrop Mackworth	V, 333
Prior, Matthew	II, 675, 675, 679
Richardson, Samuel	III, 437, 452
Smollett, Tobias George	III, 585
Steele, Sir Richard	II, 755, 756, 756, 767
Stevenson, Robert Louis	VIII, 238
Swift, Jonathan	III, 205
Walpole, Horace	IV, 314, 315, 320
DODD, HENRY PHILIP,	
Chatterton, Thomas	III, 532
DODD, WILLIAM,	
Dodd, William	III, 676
DODDRIDGE, PHILIP,	
Baxter, Richard	II, 426
Doddridge, Philip	III, 303
Pope, Alexander	III, 164
DODDS, JAMES,	
Chalmers, Thomas	V, 492
DODDS, JAMES MILLER,	
Coverdale, Miles	I, 293
Foxe, John	I, 336
Froude, James Anthony	VIII, 259, 266
Knox, John	I, 299, 302
Leland, John	I, 264
Rutherford, Samuel	II, 167
Spotiswood, John	II, 25
DODGE, MARY ABIGAIL (GAIL HAMILTON),	
Authors and Authorship	VIII, 8
Blake, William	V, 60
Curtis, George William	VIII, 184
Spencer, Herbert	VIII, 483
Whittier, John Greenleaf	VIII, 113
DODGE, RICHARD,	
Stubbs, William	VIII, 453
DODGSON, CHARLES LUTWIDGE	
Tennyson, Alfred Lord	VIII, 67
Thackeray, William Makepeace	VI, 291
DODS, MARCUS,	
Browning, Robert	VII, 708

	Vol. and Page
Drummond, Henry	VIII, 363
Faber, Frederick William	VI, 534
DODSLEY, RICHARD,	
Shenstone, William	III, 471
DODSLEY, ROBERT,	
Gray, Thomas	III, 558
DOE, CHARLES,	
Bunyan, John	II, 389
DOLBY, GEORGE,	
Dickens, Charles	VI, 561
DOLE, NATHAN HASKEL,	
FitzGerald, Edward	VII, 518
DOMETT, ALFRED,	
Milton, John	II, 293
DONALDSON, AUG. B.,	
Church, Richard William	VII, 729
Keble, John	VI, 460
Liddon, Henry Parry	VII, 761
Newman, John Henry	VII, 743, 756
Pusey, Edward Bouverie	VII, 470
DONALDSON, JOHN,	
Cobbett, William	V, 273
Darwin, Erasmus	IV, 422
Davy, Sir Humphry	V, 94
Grahame, James	IV, 568
Tusser, Thomas	I, 310
Young, Arthur	IV, 655
DONNE, JOHN,	
Donne, John	I, 713
DONNE, WILLIAM BODHAM,	
Fletcher, John	I, 631
Gay, John	III, 58
Sheridan, Richard Brinsley	IV, 602
DONNELLY, IGNATIUS,	
Bacon, Delia	VI, 205
Hawthorne, Nathaniel	VI, 347
Shakespeare, William	I, 545
DORAN, JOHN,	
Centlivre, Susannah	II, 684, 685
Cibber, Colley	III, 371
Cockburn, Catherine	III, 276
Cowper, William	IV, 388
Dodd, William	III, 676
Farquhar, George	III, 555
Foote, Samuel	III, 673
Macklin, Charles	IV, 343
Manley, Mrs. Mary de la Riviere	II, 693
Montagu, Elizabeth	IV, 400
Otway, Thomas	II, 362
Robinson, Mary	IV, 412, 412
Settle, Elkanah	III, 691
Southerne, Thomas	III, 240
Vanbrugh, Sir John	II, 703
Young, Edward	III, 488
DORLING, WILLIAM,	
Garrison, William Lloyd	VII, 160
DORNER, AUGUST,	
Duns, Scotus	I, 85
DORNER, J. A.,	
Duns Scotus	I, 86
DORR, JULIA C. R.,	
Dickens, Charles	VI, 570
Eliot, George	VII, 178
Grey, Thomas	III, 557
Jackson, Helen Hunt	VII, 572
Jerrold, Douglas William	VI, 70
DORSEY, ANNA VERNON,	
Norton, Caroline E. S.	VII, 105

INDEX TO CRITICISMS

	Vol. and Page
DOUCE, FRANCIS,	
Shakespeare, William	I, 520, 524, 531
DOUGHERTY, J. J.,	
Bede	I, 26
DOUGLAS, CHARLES,	
Mill, John Stuart	VI, 718
DOUGLAS, SIR GEORGE,	
Blackie, John Stuart	VIII, 306
Ferrier, Susan Edmonstone	V, 764
Galt, John	V, 335, 337
Hamilton, Thomas	V, 395
Moir, David Macbeth	V, 704, 705
Scott, Michael	V, 279, 280
Stevenson, Robert Louis	VIII, 244
Thomson, James	VII, 475
Wilson, John	V, 747, 752
DOUGLAS, J.,	
Blackie, John Stuart	VIII, 305
DOUGLAS, JAMES,	
Bailey, Philip James	VIII, 460
DOUGLAS, MRS. STAIR,	
Whewell, William	VI, 468
DOUGLASS, FREDERICK,	
Phillips, Wendell	VII, 556
DOUGLASS, WILLIAM,	
Berkeley, George	III, 327
DOVER, LORD,	
Walpole, Horace	IV, 314, 318
DOW, JOHN G.,	
Steele, Sir Richard	II, 766
DOWDEN, EDWARD,	
Addison, Joseph	II, 661
Akenside, Mark	III, 545
Arnold, Matthew	VII, 633, 639
Bacon, Francis	I, 661
Barnes, Barnabe	I, 439
Browning, Robert	VII, 687
Burke, Edmund	IV, 308
Burns, Robert	IV, 268
Byron, George Gordon Lord	IV, 765
Carlyle, Thomas	VII, 266
Coleridge, Hartley	V, 577
Coleridge, Samuel Taylor	V, 213
Daniel, Samuel	I, 612
Donne, John	I, 717
Drummond, William	II, 103
Dyer, John	III, 400
Eliot, George	VII, 193, 200
Elliott, Ebenezer	V, 583
Falconer, William	III, 526
Fielding, Henry	III, 353
FitzGerald, Edward	VII, 514, 519
Forster, John	VII, 67
Gibbon, Edward	VI, 188
Glover, Richard	IV, 20
Goldwin, William	V, 298, 300
Goldsmith, Oliver	III, 630, 632
Gray, Thomas	III, 556
Hallam, Henry	VI, 178
Hooker, Richard	I, 410
Hunt, James Henry Leigh	VI, 166, 172
Irving, Washington	VI, 149
Lamb, Charles	V, 237
Landor, Walter Savage	IV, 393
Lewis, Matthew Gregory	IV, 634
Locke, John	II, 522

	Vol. and Page
Longfellow, Henry Wadsworth	VII, 405
Maurice, John Frederick Denison	VI, 648
Milton, John	II, 250
Poe, Edgar Allan	V, 555
Rossetti, Gabriel Charles Dante	VII, 448
Ruskin, John	VIII, 418
Shakespeare, William	I, 457, 458, 463, 467, 479, 481, 483, 493, 494, 510, 522, 528
Shelley, Percy Bysshe	IV, 696, 712
Skelton, John	I, 223
Sidney, Sir Philip	I, 332
South, Robert	II, 608
Southey, Robert	V, 401, 407, 413, 413, 416
Spenser, Edmund	I, 386, 399
Swift, Jonathan	III, 204, 234
Taylor, Sir Henry	VII, 579
Taylor, William	V, 319
Tennyson, Alfred Lord	VIII, 77, 98
Thackeray, William Makepeace	VI, 318
Webster, John	I, 677
White, Henry Kirke	IV, 489
Whitman, Walt	VIII, 141
Wordsworth, William	V, 617, 646
DOWDEN, JOHN,	
Bentley, Richard	III, 124
Cartwright, William	II, 72
Chillingworth, William	II, 88
Clough, Arthur Hugh	VI, 253
Hales, John	II, 151
Jewell, John	I, 294
Laud, William	II, 93
Pearson, John	II, 370
DOWNES, JOHN,	
Granville, George	III, 88
Otway, Thomas	II, 362
DOWNS, ANNIE,	
Eliot, George	VII, 172
DOYLE, J. A.,	
Smith, John	I, 699
DOYLE, CONAN,	
Stevenson, Robert Louis	VIII, 241, 242, 247
DOYLE, SIR FRANCIS HASTINGS,	
Arnold, Matthew	VII, 643
Austen, Jane	IV, 622
Barnes, William	VII, 586
Carlyle, Thomas	VII, 269
Chalmers, Thomas	V, 494
Hallam, Arthur Henry	V, 198, 198
Keble, John	VI, 462
Lewis, Sir George Cornewall	VI, 338
Lytton, Sir Edward George Bulwer	VI, 684
Macaulay, Thomas Babington Lord	VI, 102
Manning, Henry Edward	VIII, 163
Milton, John	II, 255
Newman, John Henry	VII, 741, 748
Pusey, Edward Bouverie	VII, 469
Ruskin, John	VIII, 413
Smith, Sydney	V, 470

	Vol. and Page
Taylor, Sir Henry	VII, 580
Turner, Charles Tennyson	VII, 163
Warren, Samuel	VII, 107
Wordsworth, William	V, 615
DRAKE, NATHAN,	
Addison, Joseph	II, 643, 643, 645, 655
Bacon, Francis	I, 649, 655, 665
Berkeley, George	III, 326, 329
Bloomfield, Robert	IV, 723
Browne, William	II, 75
Budgell, Eustace	III, 92
Burns, Robert	IV, 249
Carter, Elizabeth	IV, 491, 493
Cartwright, William	II, 71
Chapone, Hester	IV, 418
Collins, William	III, 416, 417, 419
Colman, George	IV, 202
Cowper, William	IV, 378, 381
Crashaw, Richard	II, 111
Cumberland, Richard	IV, 560
Daniel, Samuel	I, 614
Dekker, Thomas	II, 59
Donne, John	I, 714
Drayton, Michael	I, 705, 706
Dryden, John	II, 498
Dunbar, William	I, 224
Dyer, John	III, 398, 399
Earle, John	II, 183
Fairfax, Edward	I, 742
Fletcher, Phineas	II, 117
Ford, John	II, 31
Goldsmith, Oliver	III, 635
Greene, Robert	I, 344
Gray, Thomas	III, 558, 561
Hall, Joseph	II, 145
Hawkesworth, John	III, 609
Hayley, William	IV, 653
Herrick, Robert	II, 237
Heywood, Thomas	II, 125
Hill, John	III, 646
Hillhouse, James Abraham	V, 363
Hooker, Richard	I, 405
Hughes, John	II, 667
Hurd, Richard	IV, 519
Jenyns, Soame	IV, 33
Johnson, Samuel	III, 739, 748
Jones, Sir William	IV, 198
Lyly, John	I, 421
Mackenzie, Henry	V, 115
Macpherson, James	IV, 274
Massinger, Philip	II, 47
May, Thomas	II, 120
Mickle, William Julius	IV, 41
Middleton, Thomas	I, 683, 684
Milton, John	II, 251, 272
Moore, Edward	III, 376
Munday, Anthony	I, 726
Murphy, Arthur	IV, 482
Overbury, Sir Thomas	I, 442
Peele, George	I, 366
Philips, Ambrose	III, 275
Pope, Alexander	III, 178, 183
Purchas, Samuel	I, 693
Puttenham, George	I, 401
Radcliffe, Ann Ward	IV, 718
Raleigh, Sir Walter	I, 599, 602, 606
Rogers, Samuel	VI, 36
Rowe, Nicholas	II, 622
Rowley, William	II, 68

INDEX TO CRITICISMS

Shakespeare, William............ I, 466, 468, 478, 531
Sidney, Sir Philip............ I, 331
Smollett, Tobias George..... III, 580
Sotheby, William............ V, 204
Southey, Robert............ V, 406
Southwell, Robert............ I, 361
Speed, John............ I, 695
Spenser, Edmund............ I, 376
Sprat, Thomas............ II, 574
Steele, Sir Richard............ II, 762
Still, John............ I, 430
Surrey, Earl of............ I, 257
Swift, Jonathan............ III, 214, 220
Sylvester, Joshua............ I, 609
Tickell, Thomas............ III, 104
Tuberville, George............ I, 439
Tusser, Thomas............ I, 310
Vaux, Thomas Lord............ I, 277
Waller, Edmund............ II, 381
Walpole, Horace............ IV, 318
Warner, William............ I, 437
Warton, Joseph............ IV, 397
Warton, Thomas............ IV, 76
Watson, Thomas............ I, 337
Watts, Isaac............ III, 252
Webster, John............ I, 674
Whitehead, William............ IV, 22
Wilson, Sir Thomas............ I, 312
Wither, George............ II, 213
Wotton, Sir Henry............ II, 19
Wotton, William............ II, 709
Young, Edward............ III, 487, 491

DRAKE, SAMUEL G.,
Prince, Thomas............ III, 400
Raleigh, Sir Walter............ I, 604

DRANT, THOMAS,
More, Sir Thomas............ I, 241

DRAPER, JOHN WILLIAM,
Bacon, Francis............ I, 660
Franklin, Benjamin............ IV, 102
Hobbes, Thomas............ II, 325
Newton, Sir Isaac............ II, 720, 725
Shakespeare, William............ I, 564

DRAYTON, MICHAEL,
Alexander, Sir William............ II, 34
Beaumont, Sir John............ I, 679
Browne, William............ II, 73
Chapman, George............ I, 732
Chaucer, Geoffrey............ I, 154
Daniel, Samuel............ I, 612, 615
Drayton, Michael............ I, 703
Drummond, William............ II, 100
Gascoigne, George............ I, 307
Jonson, Ben............ I, 759
Lodge, Thomas............ I, 625
Marlowe, Christopher............ I, 354
Nashe, Thomas............ I, 413
Poets and Poetry............ IV, 5
Sandys, George............ II, 81
Shakespeare, William............ I, 456, 548
Sidney, Sir Philip............ I, 330
Spenser, Edmund............ I, 375, 378, 392, 393
Sylvester, Joshua............ I, 609
Warner, William............ I, 436

DREW, G. S.,
Bushnell, Horace............ VII, 71

DRUMMOND, HENRY,
Darwin, Charles Robert..VII, 426

DRUMMOND, JAMES,
Martineau, Harriet............ VII, 59
Martineau, James............ VIII, 427

DRUMMOND, WILLIAM,
Alexander, Sir William..II, 34, 35
Beaumont, Francis............ I, 586
Daniel, Samuel............ I, 611, 613
Dekker, Thomas............ II, 55
Donne, John............ I, 714
Drayton, Michael............ I, 701, 703
Drummond, William............ II, 104
Harrington, Sir John............ I, 440
Jonson, Ben............ I, 745, 754
Marston, John............ I, 735, 736
Overbury, Sir Thomas............ I, 442
Raleigh, Sir Walter............ I, 601, 609
Selden, John............ II, 139
Shakespeare, William............ I, 538
Sidney, Sir Philip............ I, 330
Southwell, Robert............ I, 361
Spenser, Edmund............ I, 368, 393
Sylvester, Joshua............ I, 609
Wotton, Sir Henry............ II, 19

DRURY, G. THORN,
Waller, Edmund............ II, 383

DRYDEN, JOHN,
Addison, Joseph............ II, 654
Beaumont, Francis............ I, 587
Beaumont and Fletcher............ I, 579
Behn, Aphra............ II, 409
Blackmore, Sir Richard...II, 746
Books............ III, 6
Burnet, Gilbert............ II, 590
Butler, Samuel............ II, 330
Chaucer, Geoffrey............ I, 141 155
Chapman, George............ I, 732
Collier, Jeremy............ II, 698, 799
Congreve, William...II, 736, 740
Cowley, Abraham............ II, 198
Cudworth, Ralph............ II, 384
D'Avenant, Sir William...II, 219
Dillon, Wentworth............ II, 360
Donne, John............ I, 714
Drama, The............ VII, 5
Dryden, John............
  II, 463, 463, 472, 473, 485, 490
Etheredge, Sir George............ II, 414
Fairfax, Edward............ I, 742
Fletcher, John............ I, 630
Garth, Sir Samuel............ II, 664
Granville, George............ III, 87
Jonson, Ben............ I, 755, 760
Lee, Nathaniel............ II, 430, 431
Milton, John.....II, 257, 257, 284
Oldham, John............ II, 350
Otway, Thomas............ II, 364
Poets and Poetry............ IV, 5
Rymer, Thomas............ II, 583
Sackville, Charles............ II, 552
Sandys, George............ II, 82
Savile, George............ II, 449
Sedley, Sir Charles............ II, 508
Settle, Elkana............ II, 691
Shadwell, Thomas .... II, 434
Shakespeare, William............
  ...I, 472, 523, 533, 550, 550
Shirley, James............ II, 190
Spenser, Edmund..I, 375, 378, 394
Villiers, George............ II, 376
Walsh, William............ II, 560
Wycherley, William...II, 599, 603

DUDLEY, EARL OF,
Byron, George Gordon Lord... .... IV, 749
Edgeworth, Maria............ V, 568
Tooke, John Horne............ IV, 571

DUDLEY, T. U.,
Hood, Thomas............ V, 465

DUER, JOHN,
Kent, James............ V, 501, 502, 502

DUFF, LADY A. J. GRANT,
Oliphant, Laurence..VII, 655, 657

DUFF, HENRY,
Edgeworth, Maria............ V, 571

DUFF, SIR MOUNTSTUART E. GRANT,
Bagehot, Walter............ VII, 97
Gibbon, Edward............ IV, 176
Hutton, Richard Holt...VIII, 376
Maine, Sir Henry James Sumner .... VII, 651, 653
Manning, Henry Edward....
  .... VIII, 166
Maurice, John Frederick Denison .... VI, 644
Motley, John Lothrop....VII, 85
Peacock, Thomas Love....VI, 473

DUFFERIN, MARQUESS OF,
Sheridan, Richard Brinsley..
  .... IV, 598
Stanley, Arthur Penrhyn.VII, 303

DUFFIELD, PITTS,
Smollett, Tobias George.....
  .... III, 579

DUFFIELD, SAMUEL WILLOUGHBY,
Bowring, Sir John............ VI, 665
Bryant, William Cullen...VII, 125
Doddridge, Philip............ III, 303
Faber, Frederick William..VI, 333
Havergal, Frances Ridley....
  .... VII, 166, 167
Heber, Reginald............ V, 38
Ken, Thomas............ II, 567
Knox, William............ V, 31
Parker, Theodore............ VI, 211
Vaughan, Henry..... II, 442, 444
Wesley, Charles............ IV, 38

DUFFY, SIR CHARLES GAVAN,
Carlyle, Thomas............ VII, 237
Maccarthy, Dennis Florence..
  .... VII, 489, 490
Mangan, James Clarence....V, 602

DUGANNE, AUGUSTUS, J. H.,
Taylor, Bayard............ VII, 134
Willis, Nathaniel Parker...VI, 491

DUILLIER, NICHOLAS FACIO,
Newton, Sir Isaac............ II, 715

DUMONT, PIERRE ÉTIENNE LOUIS,
Romilly, Sir Samuel............ IV, 636

DUNBAR, CHARLES F.,
Franklin, Benjamin............ IV, 102
Hamilton, Alexander............ IV, 467

DUNBAR, NEWELL,
Brooks, Phillips............ VIII, 230

DUNBAR, WILLIAM,
Chaucer, Geoffrey............ I, 152
Henryson, Robert............ I, 208

DUNCAN, P. MARTIN,
Hutton, James............ IV 339
Lyell, Sir Charles............ VII, 38

INDEX TO CRITICISMS

Vol. and Page
Murchison, Sir Roderick...VI, 632
Ray, John.... ....II, 542
DUNCAN, ROBERT,
  Carlyle, Thomas.......V,II, 273
DUNCOMBE, JOHN,
  Cockburn, Catherine......III, 276
DUNCOMBE, WILLIAM,
  Berkeley, George.........III, 327
DUNHAM, S. ASTLEY,
  Centlivre, Susannah......II, 684
  Cibber, Colley...........III, 374
  Congreve, William........II, 741
  Murphy, Arthur..........IV, 482
  Vanbrugh, Sir John.......II, 704
  Wycherley, William...II, 600, 601
DUNLAP, WILLIAM,
  Brown, Charles Brokden.....
    ....IV, 552, 553
  Godwin, William..........V, 303
DUNLOP, FRANCES ANNE,
  Burns, Robert...........IV, 243
  Falconer, William.......III, 525
DUNLOP, JOHN,
  Berkeley, George........III, 326
  Defoe, Daniel............III, 34
  Fielding, Henry.........III, 352
  Godwin, William......V, 298, 300
  Lodge, Thomas.............I, 626
  Lyly, John................I, 421
  Radcliffe, Ann Ward......IV, 718
  Reeve, Clara.............IV, 512
  Richardson, Samuel......III, 439
  Sidney, Sir Philip.........I, 325
  Smollett, Tobias George...III, 584
  Swift, Jonathan.........III, 220
DUNSTER, CHARLES,
  Milton, John.............II, 260
DUNTON, JOHN,
  Norris, John.............II, 570
  Sheffield, John, Third Earl of
    Mulgrave...............II, 670
D'URFEY, THOMAS,
  Oldham, John............II, 350
DURIVAGE, F. A.,
  Inchbald, Mrs. Elizabeth..IV, 688
DUTT, WILLIAM A.
  Borrow, George Henry...VII, 314
DUYCKINCK, EVERT A.,
  Bailey, Philip James.....VIII, 461
  Benton, Thomas Hart.....VI, 87
  Bradstreet, Anne.........II, 229
  Dwight, Timothy.........IV, 627
  Franklin, Benjamin.......IV, 101
  Gilfillan, George........VII, 151
  Goldsmith, Oliver........III, 624
  Halleck, Fitz-Greene......VI, 499
  Johnson, Samuel.........III, 742
  Kane, Elisha Kent.........VI, 82
  Paulding, James Kirk......VI, 227
  Sedgwick, Catharine Maria..VI, 508
  Young, Edward..........III, 489
DUYCKINCK, EVERT A., AND GEORGE L.,
  Allston, Washington......V, 423
  Ames, Fisher............IV, 529
  Brown, Charles Brockden...IV, 553
  Bradford, William......III, 157
  Brainard, John Gardiner Calkins................V, 84, 85
  Brownson, Orestes Augustus..
    ....VII, 74

Vol. and Page
Clay, Henry..............V, 733
Eliot, John..............II, 413
Franklin, Benjamin.......IV, 98
Freneau, Philip...........V, 187
Hamilton, Alexander......IV, 466
Hillhouse, James Abraham......
    ....V, 364
Jay, John.................V, 96
Kennedy, John Pendleton....
    ....VI, 606
Kent, James..............V, 502
Madison, James...........V, 314
Mather, Cotton............II, 728
Morris, George Pope......VI, 402
Murray, Lindley...........V, 55
Neal, John...............VII, 78
Osgood, Frances Sargent....V, 678
Pinkney, Edward Coate.....V, 86
Poe, Edgar Allan..........V, 554
Prince, Thomas...........III, 401
Robertson, William.......IV, 161
Story, Joseph............V, 484
Thoreau, Henry David.....VI, 271
Wilde, Richard Henry......V, 504
Winthrop Theodore........VI, 266
Ward, Nathaniel..........II, 130
Ware, Henry, Jr..........V, 433
Washington, George.......IV, 368
Webster, Daniel..........V, 727
Webster, Noah............V, 431
Williams, Roger..........II, 357
Wilson, Alexander........IV, 582
DWIGHT, SERENO EDWARDS,
  Edwards, Jonathan......III, 382
DWIGHT, THOMAS,
  Holmes, Oliver Wendell...VIII, 287
DWIGHT, TIMOTHY,
  Edwards, Jonathan......III, 389
DYCE, ALEXANDER,
  Akenside, Mark......III, 541, 542
  Beattie, James..........IV, 432
  Bentley, Richard........III, 115
  Breton, Nicholas..........I, 678
  Cavendish, Alexander.....II, 232
  Coleridge, Hartley........V, 574
  Greene, Robert...........I, 341
  Harvey, Gabriel,.........I, 697
  Peele, George............I, 366
  Pope, Alexander........III, 186
  Seward, Anna............IV, 543
  Shakespeare, William....I, 457
  Shirley, James..........II, 191
  Skelton, John............I, 221
  Webster, John.......I, 670, 675
DYE, CHARITY,
  Austen, Jane............IV, 614
DYER, GEORGE,
  Douglas, Gawin..........I, 213
  Dunbar, William..........I, 227
  James I, of Scotland.......I, 180
  Parr, Samuel.............V, 17
DYER, JOHN,
  Savage, Richard.........III, 135
DYER, L.,
  Jowett, Benjamin......VIII, 211
  Romanes, George John...VIII, 285
DYER, OLIVER,
  Bancroft, George.......VIII, 60
  Clay, Henry.............V, 731
DYER, W. T. THISELTON,
  Darwin, Charles Robert...VII, 428

Vol. and Page
EADIE, JOHN,
  Young, Edward......III, 489
EALAND, F.,
  Browning, Robert.........VII, 712
EARDLEY-WILMOT, SIR JOHN E.,
  Brougham, Henry Lord.....VI, 527
EARLE, ALICE MORSE,
  Sewall, Samuel..........III, 18
EARLE, JOHN,
  Aldhelm..................I, 25
  Asser....................I, 43
  Bacon, Francis..........I, 651
  Beaumont, Francis.......I, 587
  Beowulf...................I, 19
  Cædmon...................I, 21
  Cynewulf..................I, 30
  Fuller, Thomas..........II, 173
  Hooker, Richard.........I, 409
  Lyly, John..............I, 423
  Tyndale, William.........I, 248
EARLE, JOHN CHARLES,
  Canning, George..........V, 65
  Fox, Charles James......IV, 500
  Newman, John Henry.....VII, 752
EARLE, MARY TRACY,
  Alcott, Louisa May......VII, 669
EASTLAKE, CHARLES LOCK,
  Walpole, Horace.........IV, 315
EASTLAKE, ELIZABETH LADY,
  Borrow, George Henry....VII, 307
  Burns, Robert............IV, 254
  Grote, George...........VI, 608
  Jameson, Anna...........VI, 215
  Lytton, Sir Edward George Bulwer..................VI, 680
  Motley, John Lothrop....VII, 95
  Norton, Caroline, E. S....VII, 102
  Rossetti, Gabriel Charles Dante
    ....VII, 441
  Strickland, Agnes........VI, 766
  Wiseman, Nicholas Patrick..VI, 435
EATON, WYATT,
  Bryant, William Cullen....VII, 114
  Emerson, Ralph Waldo....VII, 355
  Holmes, Oliver Wendell...VIII, 289
  Longfellow, Henry Wadsworth.
    ....VII, 386
  Whittier, John Greenleaf..VIII, 116
EATWELL, SURGEON-MAJOR, W. C. B.,
  DeQuincey, Thomas.......VI, 120
EBSWORTH, J. W.
  Dibdin, Charles..........IV, 586
  D'Urfey, Thomas.........II, 688
  Gilfillan, George........VII, 150
ECHARD, LAURENCE,
  Milton, John............II, 285
ECKERMANN, JOHN PETER,
  Byron, George Gordon Lord.IV, 754
  Shakespeare, William......
    ....I, 516, 524, 557
EDGEWORTH, F. Y.,
  Jevons, William Stanley......
    ....VII, 491, 491
EDGEWORTH, MARIA,
  Alison, Archibald.........V, 341
  Austen, Jane........IV, 616, 618
  Barbauld, Anna Lætitia....V, 24
  Bowles, William Lisle.....V, 658
  Byron, George Gordon Lord.
    ....IV, 732, 750

INDEX TO CRITICISMS

Vol. and Page

Campbell, Thomas.........V, 441
Cooper, James Fenimore........V, 681
Darwin, Erasmus.........IV, 421
Disraeli, Benjamin.........VII, 286
Godwin, William.........V, 303
Hawkins, Sir John.........IV, 53
Herschel, Sir John Frederick William.........VI, 623
Macaulay, Thomas Babington Lord.........VI, 99, 104
More, Hannah.........V, 193
Roscoe, William.........V, 116
Scott, Sir Walter..V, 127, 140, 147
Smith, Sydney..........V, 468
Stewart, Dugald.........V, 76
Whewel, William.........VI, 471
Wordsworth, William.........V, 608
EDGEWORTH, RICHARD LOVELL,
 Darwin, Erasmus.........IV, 420
 Morgan, Sydney Owenson Lady.........VI, 194
EDMUNDSON, GEORGE,
 Milton, John.........II, 271
EDWARDS, AMELIA B.,
 Beddoes, Thomas Lovell.........V, 587
 Edwards, Amelia Blandford.
  ....VIII, 175
 Landor, Walter Savage.........VI, 382
 Longfellow, Henry Wadsworth
  ....VII, 406
 Rossetti, Gabriel Charles Dante
  ....VII, 445
 Wilkinson, Sir John Gardner.
  ....VII, 51
EDWARDS, EDWARD,
 Hume, David.........III, 658
 Raleigh, Sir Walter.........I, 607
 Spenser, Edmund.........I, 372
EDWARDS, HENRY SUTHERLAND,
 Gay, John.........III, 58
 Sheridan, Richard Brinsley..IV, 603
EDWARDS, JONATHAN,
 Edwards, Jonathan.........III, 381
EDWARDS, MATILDA BETHAM,
 Carter, Elizabeth.........IV, 493
 Mill, John Stuart.........VI, 707
EDWARDS, THOMAS,
 Warburton, William.
  ....III, 682, 685, 689
EGAN, MAURICE FRANCIS,
 Arnold, Matthew.........VII, 644
 Austen, Jane.........IV, 622
 Browning, Elizabeth Barrett
  ....VI, 246
 Crashaw, Richard.........II, 113
 DeVere, Aubrey Thomas.VIII, 464
 Douglas, Gawin.........I, 215
 Eliot, George.........VII, 194
 Fullerton, Georgiana Charlotte Lady.........VII, 566, 568
 Habington, William.......II, 135, 137
 Henryson, Robert.........I, 209
 Longfellow, Henry Wadsworth
  ....VII, 413
 Mitford, Mary Russell.........IV, 46
 Southwell, Robert.........I, 363
 Thackeray, Willam Makepeace.
  ....VI, 307
 Wyclif, John.........I, 110

Vol. and Page

EGERTON, HUGH E.,
 Cobbett, William.........V, 274
EGGLESTON, EDWARD,
 Chalmers, Thomas.........V, 497
 Edgeworth, Maria.........V, 570
 Eggleston, Edward.........VIII, 476
 Eliot, George.........VII, 202
 Franklin, Benjamin.........IV, 103
 Holland, Josiah Gilbert.........
  ....VII, 333, 335
 Lamb, Charles.........V, 243
 Lazarus, Emma.........VII, 611
 Lowell, James Russell.........VIII, 39
EGGLESTON, N. H.,
 Edwards, Jonathan.........III, 383
ELDER, WILLIAM,
 Kane, Elisha Kent.........VI, 81, 82
ELIOT, CHARLES W.,
 Whittier, John Greenleaf..VIII, 122
ELIOT, GEORGE,
 Brontë, Charlotte.....VI, 18, 22, 28
 Brown, John.........VII, 479
 Browning, Elizabeth Barrett.
  ....VI, 237, 238
 Carlyle, Thomas.........VII, 242
 Cowper, William.........IV, 379
 Critic, The.........II, 8
 Darwin, Charles Robert.....VII, 422
 Dickens, Charles.........VI, 582
 Disraeli, Benjamin.........VII, 288
 Eliot, George.......VII, 178, 182, 187
 Emerson, Ralph Waldo.........
  ....VII, 344, 364
 Gaskell, Elizabeth Cleghorn.VI, 429
 Hawthorne, Nathaniel.......VII, 364
 Helps, Sir Arthur.........VII, 39
 Knowledge.........V, 9
 Lecky, William E. H.......VIII, 488
 Lewes, George Henry.........VII, 137
 Lowell, James Russell.........VIII, 37
 Martineau, Harriet.........VII, 59
 More, Hannah.........V, 192
 Newman, Francis William.VIII, 371
 Poets and Poetry.........IV, 9
 Ruskin, John.........VIII, 413
 Spencer, Herbert.........VIII, 477
 Sterling, John.........V, 454
 Whitman, Walt.........VIII, 139
 Wordsworth, William.........V, 632
 Young, Edward.......III, 486, 491
ELIOT, SIR JOHN,
 Raleigh, Sir Walter.........I, 592
ELIOT, SAMUEL A.,
 Brooks, Phillips.........VIII, 233
ELIZABETH, QUEEN,
 Ascham, Roger.........I, 288
ELLIOT, ARTHUR D.,
 Russell, John Lord.........VII, 144
ELLIOT, SIR GILBERT,
 Burke, Edmund.........IV, 294
 Robertson, William.........IV, 156
 Sheridan, Richard Brinsley..IV, 599
ELLIOTT, EBENEZER,
 Baillie, Joanna.........IV, 692
 Bentham, Jeremy.........V, 164
 Burns, Robert.........IV, 253
 Byron, George Gordon Lord.IV, 758
 Campbell, Thomas.........V, 442
 Cobbett, William.........V, 270
 Coleridge, Samuel Taylor......V, 214
 Cowper, William.........IV, 387

Vol. and Page

Crabbe, George.........V, 172
Elliott, Ebenezer.........V, 579
Lytton, Sir Edward George Bulwer.........VI, 687
Milton, John.........II, 261
Moore, Thomas.........V, 716
Wordsworth, William.........V, 631
ELLIS, ANNIE RAINE,
 Burney, Charles.........IV, 588, 589
 Burney, Frances.........V, 349
ELLIS, GEORGE,
 Barclay, Alexander.........I, 264
 Berners, Juliana.........I, 191
 Constable, Henry.........I, 444
 Daniel, Samuel.........I, 615
 Davies, Sir John.........I, 632
 Douglas, Gawin.........I, 213
 Drayton, Michael.........I, 704
 Dunbar, William.........I, 224
 Dyer, Sir Edward.........I, 428
 Gascoigne, George.........I, 307
 Gloucester, Robert of.....I, 81, 157
 Harding, John.........I, 194
 Harrington, Sir John.........I, 441
 Hawes, Stephen.........I, 217
 Henry the Minstrel.........I, 201
 James I of Scotland.........I, 180
 Langland, William.........I, 118
 Layamon.........I, 64
 Lydgate, John.........I, 184
 Lyndsay, Sir David.........I, 274
 Occleve, Thomas.........I, 187
 Spenser, Edmund.........I, 381
 Sternhold, Thomas.........I, 262
 Suckling, Sir John.........II, 65
 Warner, William.........I, 437
 Wyntoun, Andrew.........I, 178
ELLIS, GEORGE EDWARD,
 Berkeley, George.........III, 333
 Emerson, Ralph Waldo......VII, 368
 Longfellow, Henry Wadsworth.
  ....VII, 407
 Palfrey, John Gorham.........VII, 338
 Penn, William.........II, 627
 Rumford, Count.........IV, 591
 Sewall, Samuel.........III, 18
 Sparks, Jared.........VII, 478
ELLIS, GRACE A.,
 Barbauld, Anna Lætitia...V, 22, 25
ELLIS, G. A.,
 Wesley, John.........IV, 121
ELLIS, HAVELOCK,
 Darwin, Charles Robert.....VII, 432
 Marlowe, Christopher...I, 347, 351
 Thoreau, Henry David.........VI, 275
ELLIS, HERCULES,
 Mangan, James Clarence.........V, 601
ELLIS, JAMES J.,
 Spurgeon, Charles Haddon...
  ....VIII, 180
ELLIS, JOHN HARVARD,
 Bradstreet, Anne.........II, 228
ELLIS, ROBERT LESLIE,
 Bacon, Francis.........I, 660
ELLIS, SARAH STICKNEY,
 Watts, Isaac.........III, 249
ELLISON, HENRY,
 Wordsworth, William.........V, 633
ELLWANGER, GEORGE H.,
 Jefferies, Richard.....VII, 619, 622
 Thoreau, Henry David.........VI, 276

INDEX TO CRITICISMS

White, Gilbert .... IV, 151
ELLWOOD, THOMAS,
  Milton, John .... II, 244, 269
ELSDALE, HENRY,
  Tennyson, Alfred Lord..... VIII, 94
ELTON, CHARLES ISAAC, AND MARY AUGUSTA,
  Parker, Matthew .... I, 304
ELTON, OLIVER,
  Whitman, Walt .... VIII, 145
ELWIN, WHITWELL,
  Borrow, George Henry..... VII, 312
  Bowles, William Lisle .... V, 661
  Dodington, George Bubb... III, 459
  Gay, John .... III, 58
  Granville, George .... III, 88
  Hearne, Thomas .... III, 89
  Roscoe, William .... V, 118
  Saint-John, Henry .... III, 296
  Southerne, Thomas .... III, 241
  Sterne, Laurence .... III, 513
  Swift, Jonathan .... III, 222
  Warburton, William .... III, 689, 691
  Warton, Joseph .... IV, 396
  West, Gilbert .... III, 369
ELWIN, WHITWELL AND COURTHOPE, WILLIAM JOHN,
  Bentley, Richard .... III, 120
  Hervey, John Lord .... III, 130
  Pope, Alexander .... III, 154, 157, 160, 180
ELWOOD, MRS. A. K.,
  Godwin, Mary Wollstonecraft. .... IV, 327
  Inchbald, Mrs. Elizabeth..... IV, 687
ELY, RICHARD T.,
  George, Henry .... VIII, 379
  Mill, John Stuart .. VI, 708, 709, 712
  Smith, Adam .... IV, 60, 69
ELZE, KARL,
  Byron, George Gordon Lord. .... IV, 748, 754, 760
  D'Avenant, Sir William... .II, 218
  Nashe, Thomas .... I, 414
  Shakespeare, William .... I, 505
  Stowe, Harriet Beecher... VIII, 357
EMERSON, EDWARD WALDO,
  Carlyle, Thomas .... VII, 255
  Emerson, Ralph Waldo .... VII, 351
EMERSON, RALPH WALDO,
  Alcott, Amos Bronson. VII, 662, 663
  Bacon, Delia .... VI, 203
  Bacon, Francis .... I, 650, 660
  Books .... III, 9
  Bryant, William Cullen .... VII, 122
  Burns, Robert .... IV, 256
  Carlyle, Thomas ..... VII, 229, 255
  Channing, William Ellery. ... V, 369
  Chaucer, Geoffrey .... I, 160
  Clough, Arthur Hugh .. VI, 248, 251
  Coleridge, Samuel Taylor ...... V, 224
  Critic, The .... II, 7
  Dickens, Charles .... VI, 582
  Everett, Edward .... VI, 421
  Emerson, Ralph Waldo ...... VII, 343
  Faraday, Michael .... VI, 514
  Fuller, Sarah Margaret .... V, 665
  Garrison, William Lloyd .... VII, 157
  Gibbon, Edward .... IV, 196
  Hallam, Henry .... VI, 177

Hawthorne, Nathaniel ..... VI, 352
Herbert, George .... I, 724
Hume, David .... III, 662, 665
Jackson, Helen Hunt .... VII, 574
Johnson, Samuel .... III, 758
Jonson, Ben .... I, 766
Landor, Walter Savage .... VI, 373, 384, 387
Lincoln, Abraham .... VI, 415
Literature .... I, 9
Longfellow, Henry Wadsworth. .... VII, 395
Lytton, Sir Edward George Bulwer .... VI, 697
Macaulay, Thomas Babington Lord .... VI, 110, 117
Milton, John .. II, 246, 283, 289, 291
Parker, Theodore .... VI, 207
Poets and Poetry .... IV, 8
Pope, Alexander .... III, 189
Scott, Sir Walter .... V, 135
Shakespeare, William .... I, 461, 541, 561
Sterling, John .... V, 453
Swift, Jonathan .... III, 231
Taylor, Jeremy .... II, 209
Taylor, Thomas .... V, 291
Tennyson, Alfred Lord .... VIII, 66, 92, 100
Thackeray, William Makepeace .... VI, 313
Thoreau, Henry David .... VI, 267
Very, John .... VII, 226
Webster, Daniel .... V, 719
Whitman, Walt .... VIII, 134
Wordsworth, William .... V, 611, 620, 636
EMERY, FRED PARKER,
  Cowley, Abraham .... II, 202
  Goldsmith, Oliver .... III, 633
  Mannying, Robert .... I, 88
  Robertson, William .... IV, 161
  Saxon Chronicle .... I, 57
  Steele, Sir Richard .... II, 756
  Taylor, Jeremy .... II, 204
EMLYN, S.,
  Hale, Sir Matthew .... II, 306
EMMONS, NATHANIEL,
  Jefferson, Thomas .... V, 40
ENFIELD, WILLIAM,
  Burnet, Thomas .... II, 597
ENGEL, EDWARD,
  Browning, Robert ...... VII, 690, 719
  Buckle, Henry Thomas..... VI, 284
  Collins, William Wilkie ..... VII, 728
  Craik, Dinah Maria Mulock. VII, 625
  Dickens, Charles ..... VI, 576, 595
  Disraeli, Benjamin .... VII, 296
  Eliot, George .... VII, 186, 187
  Freeman, Edward Augustus.. .... VIII, 162
  Grote, George .... VI, 612
  Hallam, Henry .... VI, 181
  Lytton, Sir Edward George Bulwer .... VI, 700
  Macaulay, Thomas Babington Lord .... VI, 115
  Morris, William .... VIII, 334
  Procter, Bryan Waller .... VI, 750
  Rossetti, Gabriel Charles Dante .... VII, 455

Ruskin, John .... VIII, 424
Spencer, Herbert .... VIII, 486
Tennyson, Alfred Lord ... VIII, 90
Thackeray, William Makepeace .... VI, 304
Trollope, Anthony .... VII, 465
ENGLISH, THOMAS DUNN,
  Poe, Edgar Allan .... V, 535
ENTRY AT STATIONERS' HALL,
  Milton, John .... II, 257
ERASMUS, DESIDERIUS,
  Colet, John .... I, 210
  More, Sir Thomas .... I, 233
ERCELDOUNE, THOMAS OF,
  Thomas of Erceldoune .... I, 83
ERDMANN, JOHANN EDUARD
  Bacon, Francis .... I, 661
  Bacon, Roger .... I, 78
  Scotus, Duns .... I, 86
  William of Occam .... I, 91
ERNST, C. W.,
  Darwin, Charles Robert ..... VII, 425
ERSKINE, JOHN,
  Edwards, Jonathan .... III, 381
  Robertson, William .... IV, 154
ERSKINE, THOMAS,
  Irving, Edward .... V, 246
  Keble, John .... VI, 459, 460
ERSKINE, THOMAS LORD,
  Fox, Charles James .... IV, 504
  Hale, Sir Matthew .... II, 306
  Moore, Thomas .... V, 710
ESCOTT, T. H. S.,
  Bright, John .... VII, 722
  Lytton, Sir Edward George Bulwer .... VI, 682, 693
  Milnes, Richard Monckton... .... VII, 564
  Pater, Walter Horatio .... VIII, 275
  Robertson, Frederick William .... V, 738
ESPINASSE, FRANCIS,
  Carlyle, Thomas ..... VII, 237, 240
  Eliot, George .... VII, 179
  Emerson, Ralph Waldo ..... VII, 352
  Forster, John .... VII, 66
  Fletcher, Andrew .... II, 612
  Gilfillan, George .... VII, 152
  Hunt, James Henry Leigh.... VII, 161
  Lewes, George Henry .. VII, 139, 142
  Lytton, Sir Edward George Bulwer .... VI, 683
  Mahoney, Francis .... VI, 484
  Mill, John Stuart .... VI, 706
  Smith, Alexander .... VI, 518
ESSEX, EARL OF,
  Bacon, Francis .... I, 638
ETHELWERD, FABIUS,
  Alfred the Great .... I, 36
ETHEREDGE, SIR GEORGE,
  Dryden, John .... II, 484
  Etheredge, Sir George .... II, 413
  Sedley, Sir Charles .... II, 508
EVANS, ABEL,
  Vanbrugh, Sir John .... II, 703
EVANS, A. J.,
  Freeman, Edward Augustus. .... VIII, 154
EVANS, HERBERT ARTHUR,
  Jonson, Ben .... I, 767
  Shakespeare, William .... I, 537

586 INDEX TO CRITICISMS

Vol. and Page
EVANS, JOHN AMPHLETT,
   Dryden John.............II, 469. 505
   Milton, John...............II, 296
   Tennyson, Alfred Lord ...VIII,* 88
EVANS, M. A. B.,
   Lamb, Charles...............V, 243
EVANS, WILLIAM DAVID,
   Home, Henry...............III, 712
EVARTS, WILLIAM H.,
   Seward. William Henry.......VI, 673
   Webster, Daniel............V. 728
EVELYN, JOHN,
   Bacon, Francis..............I, 658
   Bentley, Richard..........III, 113
   Boyle, Robert..............II, 417
   Cavendish, Margaret........II, 231
   Cowley, Abraham............II, 194
   Dryden, John...............II, 481
   Howell, James..............II, 187
   Hyde, Edward, Earl of Clarendon.....................II,'301
   L'Estrange, Sir Roger ......II, 537
   Pepys, Samuel..............II, 512
   Shakespeare, William...........I, 500
   Sidney, Algernon...........II, 353
   Usher, James...............II, 152
   Villiers, George............II, 377
   Wilmot, John...............II. 335
   Wotton, William............II, 709
EVEREST, CHARLES W.,
   Barlow, Joel...............IV, 573
   Brainard, John Gardiner Calkins.....................V, 84
   Percival, James Gates.......VI, 60
   Sigourney, Lydia Huntley ..VI, 451
   Simms, George Denison......VI, 602
   Trumbull, John ....V, 120
EVERETT, ALEXANDER HILL,
   Carlyle, Thomas..........VII, 242
   Channing, William Ellery....V, 370
   Clay, Henry................V, 730
   Hamilton, Thomas..........V, 394
   Henry, Patrick........IV, 350, 351
   Irving, Washington....VI, 138, 145
   Jefferson, Thomas. ....V, 48
   Kennedy, John Pendleton....VI, 605
   Locke, John................II, 525
   Sedgwick, Catharine Maria..VI, 507
   Smith, Adam...............IV, 62
   Stewart, Dugald.............V, 79
   Washington, George........IV, 368
EVERETT, CHARLES CARROLL,
   Brooks, Phillips...... ...VIII, 230
   Browning, Elizabeth Barrett.
   ....VI, 238
   Browning, Robert..........VII, 713
   Emerson, Ralph Waldo......VII, 358
   Longfellow, Henry Wadsworth.
   ....VII, 407
   Martineau, James.........VIII, 429
   Spencer, Herbert.........VIII, 487
   Tennyson, Alfred Lord.....VIII, 92
EVERETT, EDWARD,
   Adams, John................V, 53
   Bancroft, George..........VIII, 57
   Bentley, Richard..........III, 122
   Choate, Rufus..............VI, 198
   Edgeworth, Maria...........V, 568
   Eliot, John................II, 412
   Franklin, Benjamin........IV, 87
   Hall, Basil.. ....V, 457

Vol. and Page
   Irving, Washington..........
   ......VI, 137, 138, 139, 141, 144, 146
   Jefferson, Thomas.............V, 47
   Johnson, Samuel..........III, 756
   Mann, Horace..............VI, 200
   Milton, John...............II, 262
   Motley, John Lothrop......VII, 89
   Percival, James Gates......VI, 59
   Prescott, William Hickling....
   ....VI, 184, 190
   Sparks, Jared..............VI, 477
   Story, Joseph...............V, 483
   Trollope,Frances Milton .....VI, 330
   Washington, George ....IV, 368
   Webster, Daniel.............V, 727
EVERETT, WILLIAM,
   Adams, John Quincy.........V, 520
   Dana, Richard Henry, Jr.....
   ....VII, 500, 502
EVERSHED, HENRY,
   Kingsley, Charles.........VII, 21
EWALD, ALEXANDER CHARLES,
   Hervey, John Lord....III, 128, 130
   Pitt, William..............IV, 509
   Raleigh, Sir Walter..........II, 597
   Savile, George............II, 449
   Sidney, Algernon............II, 355
EWING, ALEXANDER,
   Law, William.............III, 429
EYRE-TODD, GEORGE,
   Alexander, Sir William......II, 36
   Barbour, John..............I, 115
   Beattie, James.............IV, 429
   Blamire, Susanna..........IV, 205
   Burns, Robert.............IV, 267
   Douglas, Gawin.............I, 215
   Drummond, William.......II, 106
   Dunbar, William............I, 227
   Falconer, William.........III, 527
   Fergusson, Robert........III, 642
   Graham, James............II, 122
   Hamilton, William........III, 336
   Henryson, Robert..........I, 209
   James I of Scotland.........I, 181
   Logan, John...............IV, 45
   Oliphant, Carolina.........V, 480
   Ramsay, Allan ......III, 404, 411
   Ross, Alexander..........III, 719
   Smollett, Tobias George...III, 590
   Thomas of Erceldoune........I, 84
   Thomson, James..........III, 260
   Wilkie, William..........III, 596
   Wilson, Alexander........IV, 853
   Wyntoun, Andrew...........I, 178

FAIRBAIRN, A. M.,
   Edwards, Jonathan...III, 394
   Jowett, Benjamin..VIII, 209, 212
   Manning, Henry Edward VIII, 169
   Newman, John Henry......
   ....VII, 744, 755
   Spencer, Herbert ... ..VIII, 481
FAIRBAIRN, EVELINA,
   Oliphant, Laurence........VII, 658
FAIRFAX, BRIAN,
   Villiers, George...........II, 376
FAIRFIELD, FRANCIS GERRY,
   Poe, Edgar Allan.V, 541, 550, 553
FALCKENBERG, RICHARD,
   Cudworth, Ralph...........II, 386
   Hobbes, Thomas...........II. 327

Vol. and Page
   Hume. David..............III. 664
   Newton, Sir Isaac.........II. 725
FALCONER. W. L.,
   Stevenson. Robert Louis.VIII. 246
FALKINER, C. LITTON.
   DeVere, Aubrey Thomas.VIII. 465
   Wolfe, Charles............IV, 722
FALKLAND, LORD,
   Sandys, George............II. 83
FAMILY BIBLE,
   Washington, George......IV. 353
FARADAY, MICHAEL,
   Davy, Sir Humphry.........V, 93
   Somerville, Mary..........VI, 658
FARINGTON, JOSEPH,
   Boswell, James............IV, 209
   Reynolds, Sir Joshua......IV, 139
FARLOW, WILLIAM G..
   Gray, Asa..........VII, 669, 670
FARMER, RICHARD,
   Hume, David.............III. 656
FARNHAM, CHARLES HAIGHT.
   Parkman, Francis......VIII, 219
FARQUHAR, GEORGE,
   Dryden, John..............II. 463
   Farquhar, George..........
   .... II, 555, 556, 556, 556
FARRAR, ADAM STOREY,
   Buckle, Henry Thomas....VI, 281
   Butler, Joseph.........III, 309. 311
   Gibbon, Edward.......IV, 187. 187
   Hobbes, Thomas.........II, 325
   Hume, David.............III, 662
   Peacock, Reginald..........I, 190
   Ray, John.................II, 543
   Saint-John, Henry.........III, 295
   Tindal, Matthew..........III, 72
   Wesley, John.............IV, 123
   Woolston, Thomas........III. 74
FARRAR, ELIZA WARE,
   Bacon, Delia..............VI, 203
   Baillie, Joanna............V, 690
   Edgeworth, Maria.........V, 563
FARRAR, FREDERIC WILLIAM.
   Arnold, Sir Edwin......VIII, 505
   Arnold, Thomas.........VIII, 28
   Bacon, Francis.............I, 668
   Brooks, Phillips........VIII, 228
   Browning, Robert........VII, 705
   Chaucer, Geoffrey.........I, 166
   Colenso, John William...VII, 523
   Coleridge, Samuel Taylor...V, 226
   Cowper, William.....IV, 382, 391
   Dickens, Charles..........VI, 593
   Jowett, Benjamin...VIII, 209, 210
   Ken, Thomas..............II, 569
   Kingsley, Charles........VII, 22
   Longfellow, Henry Wadsworth,
   ....VII, 385
   Lowell, James Russell........
   .... VIII, 27, 40
   Lytton, Edward Robert Bulwer, Earl............VIII. 45
   Maurice, John Frederick Denison ....VI, 646, 649
   Milton, John..........II, 272, 279
   Montgomery, Robert......VI, 48
   Newman, John Henry....VII. 747
   Raleigh, Sir Walter.........I, 596
   Ruskin, John............VIII, 410
   Southey, Robert...........V. 417

INDEX TO CRITICISMS

	Vol. and Page
Stanley, Arthur Penrhyn	VII, 299, 303
Tennyson, Alfred Lord	VIII, 105
Tupper, Martin Farquhar	VII, 732
Wesley, John	IV, 117
Whewell, William	VI, 469
Whittier, John Greenleaf	VIII, 125
Wordsworth, William	V, 641
FARRAR, MRS. JOHN,	
Chalmers, Thomas	V, 492
Opie, Amelia	V, 742
FARRER, J. A.,	
Smith, Adam	IV, 60
FARRER, THOMAS HENRY LORD,	
Cobden, Richard	VI, 443
FAUCIT, HELENA (LADY MARTIN),	
Browning, Robert	VII, 691
FAULCON, FELIX,	
Washington, George	IV, 356
FAUST, A. J.,	
Payne, John Howard	V, 737
FAVRE, ERNEST,	
Agassiz, Louis Jean Rudolphe	VI, 723
FAWCETT, EDGAR,	
Browning, Robert	VII, 688
Critic, The	II, 8
Dickens, Charles	VI, 587
Hayne, Paul Hamilton	VII, 592
Keats, John	IV, 678
Longfellow, Henry Wadsworth	VII, 384
Poe, Edgar Allan	V, 558
Spencer, Herbert	VIII, 480
Thackeray, William Makepeace	VI, 316
Whittier, John Greenleaf	VIII, 122
FAWCETT, HENRY,	
Smith, Adam	IV, 64
FAWCETT, MILLICENT GARRETT,	
Brontë, Charlotte	VI, 20
Browning, Elizabeth Barrett	VI, 239
Edgeworth, Maria	V, 564, 571
Martineau, Harriet	VII, 63
Somerville, Mary	VI, 658
FEALTY, DANIEL,	
Fletcher, Phineas	II, 115
FELL, JOHN,	
Locke, John	II, 519
FELTHAM, OWEN,	
Jonson, Ben	I, 759
FELTON, CORNELIUS CONWAY,	
Blessington, Countess of	V, 594
Bryant, William Cullen	VII, 120
Child, Lydia Maria	VII, 221
Dana, Richard Henry	VII, 153
Everett, Edward	VI, 425
Haliburton, William Chandler	VI, 456
Irving, Washington	VI, 134, 149
Longfellow, Henry Wadsworth	VII, 387, 391
Lowell, James Russell	VIII, 35
Prescott, William Hickling	VI, 190
Simms, William Gilmore	VI, 598

	Vol. and Page
Talfourd, Sir Thomas Noon	V, 760
Willis, Nathaniel Parker	VI, 489, 490, 491
Woolsey, Theodore Dwight	VII, 737
FELTON, HENRY,	
Hyde, Edward, Earl of Clarendon	II, 302
Raleigh, Sir Walter	I, 602
Sprat, Thomas	II, 573
FENNOR, WILLIAM,	
Dekker, Thomas	V, 58
FENTON, ELIJAH,	
Chaucer, Geoffrey	I, 156
Pope, Alexander	III, 178
FENWICK, ELIZA,	
Godwin, Mary Wollstonecraft	IV, 327
FERGUSON, ADAM,	
Reid, Thomas	IV, 283
FERGUSON, JAMES,	
Ferguson, James	III, 668
FERRIAR, JOHN,	
Sterne, Laurence	III, 507, 511
FERRIER, JAMES FREDERICK,	
Berkeley, George	III, 330
Hogg, James	V, 264, 266
Hume, David	III, 661, 661
Reid, Thomas	IV, 285
Wilson, John	V, 748
FERRIS, W. M.,	
Maxwell, James Clerk	VII, 169
FIDDES, RICHARD,	
Cooper, Ahthony Ashley	II, 577
FIELD, BARON,	
Herrick, Robert	II, 233
Heywood, Thomas	II, 126
FIELD, EUGENE,	
Bunyan, John	II, 399
Defoe, Daniel	III, 39
DeQuincey, Thomas	VI, 122
Johnson, Samuel	III, 736
Lowell, James Russell	VIII, 21
Porson, Richard	IV, 524
Ritson, Joseph	IV, 435, 437
Stoddard, Richard Henry	VIII, 495
Walton, Isaac	II, 348
Warburton, William	III, 660
Wilson, John	V, 747
Wordsworth, William	V, 616
FIELD, MRS. E. M.,	
Bunyan, John	II, 398
Defoe, Daniel	III, 38
Kingsley, Charles	VII, 28
FIELD, HENRY M.,	
Cary, Alice	VI, 637
Ingersoll, Robert Green	VIII, 402
FIELD, MRS. HENRY M.,	
Eliot, George	VII, 172
FIELD, JOHN,	
Knox, John	I, 300
FIELD, KATE,	
Browning, Elizabeth Barrett	VI, 231
Dickens, Charles	VI, 554
Eliot, George	VII, 171
Landor, Walter Savage	VI, 375, 384

	Vol. and Page
FIELD, LILIAN F.,	
Dekker, Thomas	II, 62
Spenser, Edmund	I, 387
FIELD, MAUNSELL B.,	
Cooper, James Fenimore	V, 681
Everett, Edward	VI, 423
Greeley, Horace	VI, 668
Halleck, Fitz-Greene	VI, 495
Hawthorne, Nathaniel	VI, 346
James, George Paine Rainsford	VI, 217
Poe, Edgar Allan	V, 538
Willis, Nathaniel Parker	VI, 487
FIELD, MICHAEL,	
Arnold, Matthew	VII, 637
Browning, Robert	VII, 679
Fawcet, Henry	VII, 551
Pater, Walter Horatio	VII, 277
FIELD, NATHANIEL,	
Jonson, Ben	I, 757
FIELD, ROSWELL MARTIN,	
Field, Eugene	VIII, 315
FIELD, WILLIAM,	
Bentham, Jeremy	V, 165
Parr, Samuel	V, 18
FIELDING, HENRY,	
Behn, Aphra	II, 409
Books	III, 6
Lillo, George	III, 99
Poets and Poetry	IV, 6
Pope, Alexander	III, 172
Richardson, Samuel	III, 438
Saint-John, Henry	III, 292
Steele, Sir Richard	II, 760
FIELDS, ANNE,	
Brown, John	VII, 478
DeQuincey, Thomas	VI, 121
Eliot, George	VII, 177
Holmes, Oliver Wendell	VIII, 287
Hunt, James Henry Leigh	VI, 161
Longfellow, Henry Wadsworth	VII, 384
Mitford, Mary Russell	VI, 44
Procter, Bryan Waller	VII, 746
Reade, Charles	VII, 535
Stowe, Harriet Beecher	VII, 351
Tennyson, Alfred Lord	VIII, 73
Thackeray, William Makepeace	VI, 298
Whittier, John Greenleaf	VIII, 114
Wilson, John	V, 747
FIELDS, JAMES T.,	
Agassiz, Louis Jean Rudolphe	VI, 720
Blessington, Countess of	V, 592
Browning, Robert	VII, 701
Campbell, Thomas	V, 445
DeQuincey, Thomas	VII, 117
Dickens, Charles	VI, 554, 575
Hawthorne, Nathaniel	VI, 345
Hood, Thomas	V, 460, 464
Hunt, James Henry Leigh	VI, 157, 164, 170
Lamb, Charles	V, 242
Landor, Walter Savage	VI, 376
Mahoney, Francis	VI, 483
Mitford, Mary Russell	VI, 45
Pope, Alexander	III, 151
Procter, Bryan Waller	VI, 745, 749

588 INDEX TO CRITICISMS

Vol. and Page
Rogers, Samuel............VI, 35
Scott, Sir Walter...........V, 144
Taylor, Bayard.......VII, 129, 134
Tennyson, Alfred Lord..VIII, 69
Thackeray, William Makepeace ....VI, 294, 302, 307
Willis, Nathaniel Parker...VI, 487
Wordsworth, William......V, 613
FIENNES, GERARD,
Thackeray, William Makepeace ....VI, 300
FILMER, EDWARD,
Collier, Jeremy............II, 699
FILON, AUGUSTIN,
Knowles, James Sheridan..VI, 287
Lytton, Sir Edward George
Bulwer........ VI, 691, 700
Shakespeare, William......I, 576
FINCK, HENRY T.,
Shakespeare, William......I, 571
FINDLATER, JANE H.,
Borrow, George Henry......
................VII, 310, 311
FINDLAY, J. J.,
Arnold, Thomas............V, 380
FINDLAY, JOHN RITCHIE,
DeQuincey, Thomas..VI, 121, 127
FINLAY, GEORGE,
Byron, George Gordon Lord
.... IV, 735
FINLAY, JOHN,
Thomas of Erceldoune......I, 83
FIRTH, C. H.,
Hyde, Edward, Earl of Clarendon ....II, 301
Marvell, Andrew..........II, 318
May, Thomas..............II, 119
Pepys, Samuel............II, 514
Prynne, William..........II, 226
Sidney, Algernon..........II, 355
Villiers, George............II, 377
Wilson, Arthur............II, 129
FISH, HAMILTON,
Calhoun, John Caldwell....V, 675
Motley, John Lothrop....VII, 94
FISH, HENRY C.,
Beecher, Lyman..........VI, 340
Edwards, Jonathan.......III, 383
Foster, John..............V, 426
Guthrie, Thomas.....VI, 736, 738
Wayland, Francis ....VI, 447, 450
Whatley, Richard........VI, 327
FISHER, ARABELLA BUCKLEY,
Lyell, Sir Charles........VII, 34
FISHER, CHARLES,
Arnold, Matthew........VII, 647
Jefferies, Richard........VII, 622
FISHER, GEORGE PARK,
Anselm, ...I, 51
Berkeley, George........III, 326
Channing, Wiliam Ellery ...V, 375
Edwards, Jonathan...III, 384, 395
Erigena ....I, 35
Hume, David............III, 665
John of Salisbury...........I, 60
Paley, William...........IV, 478
Pusey, Edward Bouverie.VII, 473
Scotus, Duns..............I, 87
Silliman, Benjamin......VII, 407
Wayland, Francis.........VI, 448
Wesley, John............IV, 125

Vol. and Page
Whatley, Richard........VI, 328
William of Occam..........I, 91
Woolsey, Theodore Dwight..
................VII, 736, 737
FISHER, HERBERT A. L.,
Seeley, Sir John Robert......
.......VIII, 308, 309, 310, 311
FISHER, PAYNE,
Howell, James............II, 188
FISHER, SYDNEY GEORGE,
Fox, George..............II, 422
Franklin, Benjamin..IV, 93, 106
Penn, William........II, 629, 631
Stowe, Harriet Beecher..VIII, 352
FISK, FRANKLIN W.,
Brooks, Phillips........VIII, 230
FISKE, JOHN,
Adams, Samuel..........IV, 444
Agassiz, Louis Jean Rudolphe.
.... VI, 722
Buckle, Henry Thomas....VI, 282
Darwin, Charles Robert......
................VII, 417, 429
Freeman, Edward Augustus..
............VIII, 155, 158, 159
Huxley, Thomas Henry.....
..................VIII, 323
Madison, James...........V, 314
Parkman, Francis......VIII, 222
Raleigh, Sir Walter......I, 599, 605
Spencer, Herbert.......VIII, 479
Tyndall, John..........VIII, 198
Washington, George......IV, 366
FITCH, E. T.,
Whitefield, George........III, 548
FITCH, SIR JOSHUA,
Arnold, Matthew........VII, 640
Arnold, Thomas......V, 378, 380
Stanley, Arthur Penrhyn.VII, 302
FITZGERALD, EDWARD,
Austen, Jane.............IV, 620
Bagehot, Walter........VII, 99
Barton, Bernard.....V, 595, 596
Browning, Elizabeth Barrett
.... VI, 245
Browning, Robert......VII, 700
Brydges, Sir Samuel Egerton..
.... V, 321
Burke, Edmund.........IV, 303
Burns, Robert.......... IV, 259
Carlyle, Thomas............
..VII, 233, 239, 246, 250, 254
Crabbe, George..........V, 175
Dickens, Charles.....VI, 578, 586
Edgeworth, Maria.........V, 563
Emerson, Ralph Waldo..VII, 363
Fawcett, Henry........VII, 549
Forster, John............VII, 66
Gray, Thomas............III, 569
Hare, Julius Charles......VI, 50
Hawthorne, Nathaniel...VI, 366
Helps, Sir Arthur........VII, 41
Keats, John.............IV, 676
Lamb, Charles...........V, 234
Lowell, James Russell......
.... VIII, 31, 37
Martineau, Harriet......VII, 60
Merivale, Charles......VIII, 217
Milton, John...........II, 265
Richardson, Samuel......III, 450
Rogers, Samuel ....VI, 35

Vol. and Page
Scott, Sir Walter..........
.... V, 151, 154, 155, 155
Southey, Robert.......V, 413, 417
Spedding, James.VII, 317, 318, 319
Taylor, Jeremy............II, 209
Tennyson, Alfred Lord......
.... VIII, 80, 83, 86
Thackeray, William Makepeace ....VI, 293, 306, 315
Trench, Richard Chenevix..
.... VII, 589
Trollope, Anthony.......VII, 459
Turner, Charles Tennyson.VII, 162
Wesley, John............IV, 127
Wordsworth, William........
.... V, 614, 626, 638
FITZGERALD, LORD EDWARD,
Paine, Thomas...........IV, 531
FITZGERALD, PERCY,
Boswell, James...........IV, 211
Burns, Robert............IV, 240
Cibber, Colley...........III, 371
Collier, Jeremy...........II, 702
Croker, John Wilson...... VI, 75
Dennis, John............III, 76
Dickens, Charles......VI, 556, 563
Dodd, William..........III, 676
Farquhar, George........II, 557
Forster, John...........VII, 68
Gibbon, Edward.........IV, 176
Goldsmith, Oliver........III, 634
Johnson, Samuel.........III, 733
Lamb, Charles............V, 233
Lytton, Sir Edward George
Bulwer ....VI, 689
Norton, Caroline E. S.,...VII, 105
Ruskin, John........VIII, 410, 410
Sheridan, Richard Brinsley..
.... IV, 599
Sterne, Laurence.III, 503, 510, 517
Tooke, John Horne......IV, 573
Wilkes, John............ IV, 337
Wycherley, William........II, 602
FITZGERALD, S. J. ADAIR,
Carey, Henry ....III, 139
Gay, John................III, 62
Moore, Thomas...........V, 711
FITZGERALD, WILLIAM,
Mangan, James Clarence...V, 603
FITZGIBBON, H. MACAULAY,
Dunbar, William..........I, 226
Minot, Lawrence..........I, 94
Scott, Alexander..........I, 320
FITZPATRICK, RICHARD,
Canning, George..........V, 66
FITZPATRICK, W. J.,
Lever, Charles James......VI, 651
O'Keeffe, John............V, 197
Smollett, Tobias George...III, 589
FITZROY, A. I.,
Clarke, Samuel..........II, 750
Cudworth, Ralph........II, 387
Cumberland, Richard......II, 625
Fox, George............II, 422
Hoadly, Benjamin........III, 424
Penn, William...........II, 531
FLAGG, JARED B.,
Allston, Washington.......V 424
FLAMSTEED, JOHN,
Halley, Edmund.........III, 107
Newton, Sir Isaac.....II, 711, 721

INDEX TO CRITICISMS

FLANAGAN, THOMAS,
  Cranmer, Thomas..........I, 272
FLANDERS, HENRY,
  Jay, John.................V, 95
  Marshall, John..............V, 282
FLATMAN, THOMAS,
  Wilmot, John..............II, 336
FLEAY, FREDERICK GARD,
  Browning, Robert........VII, 707
  Massinger, Philip..........II, 51
  Shakespeare, William...I, 463, 530
FLECKNOE, RICHARD,
  Jonson, Ben...............I, 760
  Suckling, Sir John.........II, 65
FLEMING, ABRAHAM,
  Heywood, John.............I, 305
FLEMING, WILLIAM H.,
  Shakespeare, William.......I, 490
FLETCHER, C. R. L.,
  Bacon, Francis.............I, 668
  Dryden, John..............II, 493
  Goldsmith, Oliver.........III, 638
  Herbert, Edward Lord......II, 97
  Johnson, Samuel..........III, 763
  More, Sir Thomas...........I, 242
FLETCHER, ELIZA,
  Wordsworth, William........V, 610
FLETCHER, GEORGE,
  Shakespeare, William.......I, 517
FLETCHER, JOHN,
  Beaumont, Francis..........I, 587
  Jonson, Ben................I, 757
  Literature...................I, 7
FLETCHER, J. AND SHAKESPEARE, W.
  Chaucer, Geoffrey..........I, 135
FLETCHER, PHINEAS,
  Spenser, Edmund............I, 369
FLETCHER, WILLIAM,
  Byron, George Gordon Lord.IV, 735
FLINT, R.,
  Buckle, Henry Thomas......VI, 282
FLINT, ROBERT,
  Macleod, Norman......VI, 661, 662
FLINT, TIMOTHY,
  Marshall, John.............V, 285
  Quincy, Josiah.............VI, 405
FLOOD, HENRY,
  Burke, Edmund.............IV, 294
  Johnson, Samuel..........III, 754
FLORENCE OF WORCESTER,
  Alfred the Great............I, 36
  Lanfranc....................I, 47
  Young, Thomas..............V, 87
FLOWER, BENJAMIN ORANGE,
  Darwin, Charles Robert....VII, 432
  Miller, Cincinnatus Hiner.VIII, 501
  More, Sir Thomas...........I, 238
  Whittier, John Greenleaf..VIII, 115
FLOWER, SIR WILLIAM H.,
  Owen, Sir Richard........VIII, 172
FLUKE, WILLIAM,
  Coverdale, Miles............I, 291
FLYING POST,
  Steele, Sir Richard........II, 751
FOLEY, P. K.,
  Whittier, John Greenleaf..VIII, 127
FONBLANQUE, ALBANY WILLIAM,
  Mill, James................V, 305
  Montgomery, Robert........VI, 47

FONTENELLE, BERNARD LE BOVYER,
  Newton, Isaac.............II, 716
FOOT, JESSE,
  Hunter, John..............IV, 166
FOOTE, SAMUEL,
  Cibber, Colley...........III, 370
  Dodd, William............III, 675
FORBES, J. D.,
  Whewell, William..........VI, 470
FORBES, SIR WILLIAM,
  Beattie, James.......IV, 428, 432
  Boswell, James............IV, 215
  Dalrymple, Sir David......IV, 146
  Gray, Thomas.............III, 562
  Hume, David..............III, 649
  Priestley, Joseph.........IV, 453
FORD, EDWARD,
  Burnett, James............IV, 347
FORD, EMILY ELLSWORTH,
  Davidson, Lucretia Maria...V, 28
  Osgood, Frances Sargent....V, 679
FORD, JOHN,
  Jonson, Ben...............I, 759
  Raleigh, Sir Walter........I, 592
  Webster, John..............I, 671
FORD, PAUL LEICESTER,
  Franklin, Benjamin........IV, 106
  Jefferson, Thomas..........V, 44
  Washington, George........IV, 365
FORD, RICHARD,
  Borrow, George Henry.VII, 309, 311
  Prescott, William Hickling..VI, 183
FORD, ROBERT,
  Burns, Robert.............IV, 264
FORMAN, EMILY S.,
  Harte, Francis Bret......VIII, 468
FORMAN, HENRY BUXTON,
  Arnold, Matthew..........VII, 635
  Browning, Robert.........VII, 688
  Horne, Richard Hengist......
    ....VII, 545, 548
  Keats, John..........IV, 667, 670
  Morris, William.........VIII, 334
  O'Shaughnessy, Arthur William Edgar...........VII, 322
  Richardson, Samuel.......III, 441
  Rossetti, Gabriel Charles Dante
    ....VII, 445
  Rossetti, Christina Georgina.
    ....VIII, 271
  Story, William Wetmore..VIII, 319
  Shelley, Percy Bysshe.....IV, 698
  Wells, Charles Jeremiah..VII, 165
  Whitman, Walt..........VIII, 143
FORNEY, JOHN W.,
  Bancroft, George........VIII, 55
  Dickens, Charles..........VI, 585
  Everett, Edward...........VI, 424
  Halleck, Fitz-Greene......VI, 495
  Madison, James.............V, 311
FORSTER, H. O. ARNOLD,
  Burke, Edmund............IV, 308
FORSTER, JOHN,
  Anstey, Christopher.......IV, 480
  Beddoes, Thomas Lovell....V, 586
  Blessington, Countess of...V, 592
  Boswell, James............IV, 216
  Browning, Robert.........VII, 685
  Carlyle, Thomas..........VII, 247
  Churchill, Charles...III, 476, 480

Defoe, Daniel.III, 28, 35, 42, 43, 46
  Dickens, Charles........VI, 555, 569
  Fielding, Henry.......III, 347, 360
  Foote, Samuel........III, 672, 673
  Goldsmith, Oliver......III, 617, 627
  Griffin, Gerald.............V, 353
  Hawkins, Sir John..........IV, 51
  Hunt, James Henry Leigh...VI, 159
  Jerrold, Douglas William....VI, 69
  Johnson, Samuel..........III, 731
  Kelly, Hugh..............III, 677
  Lamb, Charles..............V, 230
  Landor, Walter Savage.VI, 374, 379
  Lennox, Charlotte..........IV, 470
  Reynolds, Sir Joshua......IV, 139
  Smollett, Tobias George.....
    ....III, 582, 583
  Southey, Robert............V, 405
  Steele, Sir Richard........
    ....II, 753, 756, 758, 760
  Swift, Jonathan..........III, 212
  Wilkes, John.............IV, 334
FORSTER, JOSEPH,
  Browning, Robert.........VII, 690
  Burns, Robert............IV, 270
  Coleridge, Samuel Taylor...V, 213
  Emerson, Ralph Waldo.....VII, 377
FORSTER, NATHANIEL,
  Butler, Joseph...........III, 306
FORSYTH, P. T.,
  Rossetti, Gabriel Charles Dante
    ....VII, 443
FORSYTH, WILLIAM,
  Behn, Aphra..............II, 408
  Brooke, Henry...........III, 715
  Brougham, Henry Lord......VI, 529
  Cibber, Colley...........III, 375
  Defoe, Daniel.............III, 40
  Fielding, Henry..........III, 355
  Goldsmith, Oliver........III, 638
  Mackenzie, Henry...........V, 114
  Manley, Mrs. Mary de la Riviere..................II, 694
  Richardson, Samuel.......III, 442
  Smollett, Tobias George..III, 588
  Swift, Jonathan..........III, 202
  Walpole, Horace..........IV, 319
  Wesley, John..............IV, 114
FOSCOLO, UGO,
  Pope, Alexander..........III, 184
FOSDICK, WILLIAM W.,
  Simms, George Denison.....VI, 602
FOSS, EDWARD,
  Blackstone, William......III, 705
  Fortescue, Sir John........I, 194
  Murray, William...........IV, 171
  Somers, John Lord.........II, 613
FOSTER, AUGUSTUS J.,
  Trollope, Frances Milton..VI, 330
FOSTER, FRANK H.,
  Hopkins, Samuel.....IV, 438, 440
FOSTER, JOHN,
  Beattie, James...........IV, 433
  Blair, Hugh..............IV, 405
  Chatterton, Thomas.......III, 530
  Coleridge, Samuel Taylor...V, 221
  Edgeworth, Maria..........IV, 567
  Fox, Charles James........IV, 503
  Franklin, Benjamin........IV, 99
  Gibbon, Edward...........IV, 181
  Hall, Robert..............V, 108

INDEX TO CRITICISMS

	Vol. and Page
Hervey, James	III, 397
Johnson, Samuel	III, 748
Junius	IV, 644
Paley, William	IV, 473, 476
Park, Mungo	IV, 485
Smith, Sydney	V, 470
Southey, Robert	V. 408, 414
Tooke, John Horne	IV, 569
Whitefield, George	III, 549

FOSTER, MICHAEL, and LANKESTER, E. RAY.
Huxley, Thomas Henry ...VIII, 327

FOTHERINGHAM, JAMES,
Browning, Robert.......VII, 683, 693

FOULKES, EDMUND S.,
Newman, John Henry.....VII, 751

FOWLER, ROBERT,
Beecher, Henry Ward....VII, 603
Dewey, Orrville..........VII, 496

FOWLER, J. H.,
DeQuincey, Thomas......VI, 131
Macaulay, Thomas Babington Lord..................VI, 115
Thackeray, William Makepeace ....VI, 311

FOWLER, THOMAS,
Bacon, Francis...........I, 646, 668
Butler, Joseph............III, 316
Cooper, Anthony Ashley...... ....II, 576, 580
Hobbes, Thomas..........II, 327
Hutcheson, Francis.......III, 247
Locke, John, II, 523, 528, 530, 532

FOWLER, WILLIAM J.,
Tennyson, Alfred Lord..VIII, 89
Whittier, John Greenleaf, VIII, 126

FOWLER, W. WARDE,
White, Gilbert...........IV, 151

FOX, CAROLINE.
Borrow, George Henry....VII, 307
Bowring, Sir John........VI, 664
Brontë, Charlotte........VI, 18
Campbell, Thomas.......V, 435
Carlyle, Thomas....VII, 230, 260
Cobden, Richard..........VI, 439
Coleridge, Hartley........V, 573
Coleridge, Samuel Taylor...V, 209
Coleridge, Sara..........V, 734
Emerson, Ralph Waldo...VII, 361
Fox, George..............II, 421
Froude, James Anthony.VIII, 257
Hallam, Henry...........VI, 173
Hare, Julius Charles....VI, 49, 50
Jeffrey, Francis Lord.......V, 650
Johnson, Samuel..........III, 730
Kinglake, Alexander William, ...VIII, 50
Kingsley, Charles........VII, 23
Livingstone, David......VI, 726
Mill, John Stuart......VI, 702, 710
Moore, Thomas...........V, 707
Murchison, Sir Roderick Impey ....VI, 630
Opie, Amelia............V, 741
Stanley, Arhur Penrhyn...VII, 303
Tennyson, Alfred Lord.. ....VIII, 67, 93, 100
Thackeray, William Makepeace ....VI, 290
Trench, Richard Chenevix, VII, 588
Tupper, Martin Farquhar..VII, 731

	Vol. and Page
Whately, Richard	VI, 324
Whewell, William	VI, 467
Wordsworth, William	V, 609

FOX, CHARLES JAMES,
Blackstone. William......III, 704
Burke, Edmund..........IV, 289
Sidney, Algernon..........II, 353
Washington, George......IV, 355

FOX, NORMAN,
Fox, George...............II, 422

FOX. SAMUEL,
Alfred the Great............I, 40

FOX, W. J.,
Bentham, Jeremy.........V, 164
Browning, Robert.......VII, 684
Cobbett, William..........V, 270
Elliott, Ebenezer..........V, 581

FOXE, JOHN,
Chaucer, Geoffrey..........I, 149
Cranmer, Thomas..........I, 271
Ridley, Nicholas...........I, 266
Tyndale,William..........I, 244

FOXCROFT, H. C.,
Savile, George.............II, 450

FRANCILLON, R. E.
Eliot, George............VII, 192

FRANCIS, JOHN W.,
Payne John Howard......V, 735

FRANCIS, LADY,
Francis, Sir Philip........IV, 638

FRANCIS, SIR PHILIP,
Burke, Edmund..........IV, 298

FRANCK, RICHARD,
Walton, Isaac.............II, 346

FRANCKLIN, THOMAS,
Bentley, Richard..........III, 115

FRANK, ELIZABETH,
Murray, Lindley...........V, 54

FRANKLIN, BENJAMIN,
Adams, John................V, 52
Cowper, William..........IV, 384
Defoe, Daniel............III, 28
Edwards, Jonathan........III, 389
Fox, Charles James.......IV, 499
Franklin, Benjamin......... ....IV, 80, 82, 94, 98
Home, Henry............III, 712
Mather, Cotton...........III, 727
Paine, Thomas.......IV, 530, 535
Washington, George......IV, 355
Whitefield, George........III, 547

FRASER, ALEXANDER CAMPBELL.
Berkeley, George ....III, 325, 327, 328, 332, 333
Edwards, Jonathan........III, 393
Ferrier, James Frederick..... ....VI, 410, 411
Hume, David............III, 663
Locke, John, II, 523, 528, 531, 536

FRASER, DONALD,
Chalmers, Thomas.........V, 494

FRASER, J.,
Hood, Thomas............V, 463

FRASER, JOHN,
Chaucer, Geoffrey..........I, 167
Proctor, Richard Anthony, VII, 660
Shakespeare, William......I, 545

FRASER, SIR WILLIAM,
Disraeli, Benjamin........VII, 280
Gray, Thomas............III, 557

	Vol. and Page
Swift, Jonathan	III, 226

FREEMAN. EDWARD AUGUSTUS.
Alfred the Great............I, 40
Anslem...................I, 51
Browning, Robert......VII, 678
Butler, Joseph......III, 301, 309
Carlyle, Thomas........VII, 261
Eliot, George...........VII, 203
Finlay, George.......VII, 48, 49
Freeman, Edward Augustus ....VIII, 154
Froude, James Anthony..VIII, 254
Gibbon, Edward..........IV, 189
Gladstone, William Ewart.VII, 391
Green, John Richard, VII, 505, 512
Lanfranc..................I, 48
Layamon..................I, 65
Macaulay, Thomas Babington Lord............. VI, 103, 111
Ormin....................I, 71
Palgrave, Sir Francis......VI, 265
Trollope, Anthony......VII, 461
Wace, Robert..............I, 60
William of Malmesbury.....I, 54

FREEMAN, THOMAS,
Shakespeare, William.......I, 456

FREILIGRATH, FERDINAND,
Harte, Francis Bret......VIII, 468
Shakespeare, William.......I, 504

FREMANTLE, WILLIAM HENRY,
Alford, Henry........VI, 636, 637
Wyclif, John..............I, 111

FRENCH, GEORGE RUSSELL,
Shakespeare, William.......I, 487

FRERE, SIR BARTLE,
Frere, John Hookham......V, 486
Livingstone, David...VI, 728, 730

FREY, ALBERT R.,
Boswell, James...........IV, 211
Brougham, Henry Lord...VI, 528
Burns, Robert............IV, 233
Byron, George Gordon Lord, ...IV, 742
Carlyle, Thomas.........VII, 237
Clay, Henry...............V, 731
Cleveland, John..........II, 159
Croker, John Wilson.......VI, 73
Dryden, John............II, 468
Farquhar, George........II, 556
Garth, Sir Samuel........II, 665
Johnson, Samuel.........III, 734
Junius..................VI, 638
Lytton, Sir Edward George Bulwer....... ....VI, 683
Maginn, William..........V, 387
Marshall, John...........V, 284
More, Henry.............II, 374
Pope, Alexander..........III, 152
Rossetti, Gabriel Charles Dante ....VII, 438
Scott, Sir Walter..........V, 133
Shakespeare, William......I, 488
Shelley, Percy Bysshe....IV, 696
South, Robert............II, 610
Southey, Robert...........V, 402
Spence, Joseph..........III, 520
Swift, Jonathan..........III, 204
Walpole, Horace.........IV, 313
Warburton, William......III, 685
Washington, George......IV, 363 |

INDEX TO CRITICISMS 591

	Vol. and Page
Wilberforce, Samuel	VI, 734
Wilmot, John	II, 337
Wood, Anthony	II, 448
Wordsworth, William	V, 615

FREYTAG, GUSTAV,
Drama, The..............VII, 7
Shakespeare, William.......I, 564

FRIEDMANN, PAUL,
Cranmer, Thomas............I, 272

FRISWELL, JAMES HAIN,
Addison, Joseph...........II, 657
Ainsworth, William Harrison, ...VII, 486
Barbour, John..............I, 114
Butler, Samuel............II, 333
Byron, George Gordon Lord ....IV, 752
Chaucer, Geoffrey...........I, 163
Coleridge, Samuel Taylor...V, 215
Dickens, Charles..........VI, 562
Fuller, Thomas............II, 172
Grote, George.............VI, 612
Hood, Thomas.............V, 463
Hyde, Edward, Earl of Clarendon......................II, 304
Kingsley, Charles..VII, 18, 23, 27
Lever, Charles James......VI, 653
Lytton, Sir George Edward Bulwer................V, 681, 691
Macaulay, Thomas Babington, Lord........................VI, 107
Massinger, Philip.........II, 50
Overbury, Sir Thomas......I, 443
Procter, Bryan Waller.....VI, 748
Reade, Charles..........VII, 533
Richardson, Samuel.......III, 441
Scott, Sir Walter..........V, 136
Steele, Sir Richard.........II, 763
Strickland, Agnes.........VI, 767
Swift, Jonathan..........III, 233
Taylor Jeremy............II, 210
Tennyson, Alfred Lord......
..................VIII, 69, 91
Trollope, Anthony.......VII, 459
Walpole, Horace..........IV, 317
Wither, George............II, 215
Wordsworth, William......V, 620

FRITH, W. P.,
Blessington, Countess of....V, 593
Dickens, Charles..........VI, 558
Edwards, Amelia Blandford..
.....................VIII, 176
Pope, Alexander.........III, 154

FROST, T. GOLD,
Drummond, Henry.....VIII, 365

FROTHINGHAM, OCTAVIUS BROOKS,
Alcott, Amos Bronson....VII, 663
Brownson, Orestes Augustus
.....................VII, 75
Cary, Alice...............VI, 638
Child, Lydia Maria.......VII, 222
Dewey, Orville..........VII, 497
Emerson, Ralph Waldo......
..................VII, 352, 383
Gibbon, Edward...........IV, 187
Greeley, Horace..........VI, 671
Hawthorne, Nathaniel....VI, 347
Longfellow, Henry Wadsworth.
..................VII, 383, 410
Paine, Thomas............IV, 538

	Vol. and Page
Parker, Theodore	VI, 209
Ripley, George	VII, 223, 225
Robertson, Frederick William.	
.....................V, 739	

FROTHINGHAM, RICHARD,
King, Thomas Starr.........VI, 409

FROUDE, JAMES ANTHONY,
Bale, John..................I, 286
Buckle, Henry Thomas.....VI, 279
Bunyan, John...............
......II, 390, 396, 400, 401
Carlyle, Thomas............
.....VII, 234, 241, 243, 253, 258
Clough, Arthur Hugh....VI, 250, 253
Colenso, John William......VII, 523
Disraeli, Benjamin......VII, 288, 292
Eliot, George..............VII, 181
Freeman, Edward Augustus.
.....................VIII, 154
Hakluyt, Richard...........I, 446
History....................VI, 9
Jeffrey, Francis Lord..........V, 652
Keble John............VI, 459, 462
Knox, John..................I, 301
Knowledge..................V, 9
Macaulay, Thomas Babington Lord................VI, 95, 112
Milman, Henry Hart........VII, 537
Milnes, Richard Monckton.VII, 560
Milton, John..............II, 294
More, Sir Thomas............I, 235
Motley, John Lothrop......VII, 89
Newman, John Henry.........
..................VII, 740, 745, 748
Shelley, Percy Bysshe......IV,696
Stanley, Arthur Penrhyn...VII, 300
Surrey, Earl of...............255
Tennyson, Alfred Lord......
.....................VIII, 98, 104
Thirlwall, Connop.........VII, 43
Tyndale, William............I, 246
Wyclif, John................I, 106

FRUIT, JOHN PHELPS,
Poe, Edgar Allan............V. 550

FRY, SIR EDWARD,
Selden, John...........II, 139, 140

FULLER, HIRAM,
Hunt, James Henry Leigh....VI, 157

FULLER, MELVILLE W.,
Benton, Thomas Hart......VI, 88
Disraeli, Benjamin........VII, 292
Marshall, John............V, 283

FULLER, THOMAS,
Abbot, George..............I, 725
Alcuin.....................I, 32
Alfred the Great............I, 37
Andrews, Lancelot...........I, 635
Ascham, Roger..............I, 290
Bacon, Francis........I, 640, 664
Bacon, Roger...............I, 77
Bale John...................I, 286
Beaumont and Fletcher......I, 578
Bede................I, 26, 27
Burton, Robert...........II, 38
Chaucer, Geoffrey......I, 154, 172
Chillingworth, William......II, 85
Churchyard, Thomas.........I, 417
Coke, Sir Edward...........I, 739
Daniel, Samuel......I, 611, 614
Donne, John................I, 711
Drayton, Michael...........I, 701

	Vol. and Page
Elyot, Sir Thomas	I, 253
Fabyan, Robert	I, 206
Fletcher, John	I. 628
Foxe, John	I. 335
Fuller, Thomas	II, 169
Geoffery of Monmouth	I. 55
Gower, John	I, 174
Grosseteste, Robert	I, 73
Hakluyt, Richard	I, 445
Hales, Alexander	I, 72
Hall, Joseph	II, 144, 147
Harding, John	I, 193
Herbert, Edward Lord	II, 99
Herbert, George	I, 720
Heylin, Peter	II, 175
Hooker, Richard	I, 403, 405
Hoveden, Roger de	I, 63
Jewell, John	I, 293
Jonson, Ben	I, 746, 760
Knox, John	I, 301
Langland, William	I, 117
May, Thomas	II, 118
More, Sir Thomas	I, 236, 240
Overbury, Sir Thomas	I, 442
Paris, Matthew	I, 74
Parker, Matthew	I, 303
Peacock, Reginald	I, 189
Pole, Reginald	I, 281
Quarles, Francis	II, 78
Raleigh, Sir Walter	I, 593
Richard, Rolle of Hampole	I, 91
Sandys, George	II, 80, 81
Savile, Sir Henry	I, 619
Scotus, Duns	I, 85
Shakespeare, William	I, 448, 489
Smith, John	I, 698
Southwell, Robert	I, 361
Speed, John	I, 694
Spenser, Edmund	I, 369, 393
Sternhold, Thomas	I, 261
Still, John	I, 429
Stowe, John	I, 419
Tusser, Thomas	I, 310
Tyndale, William	I, 245
Ward, Nathaniel	II, 129
William of Malmesbury	I, 53
William of Occam	I, 90
Wyclif, John	I, 99

FURNESS, HORACE HOWARD,
Shakespeare, William........
........I, 470, 506, 535, 572

FURNESS, WILLIAM HENRY,
Channing, William Ellery.....
.....................V. 367, 372
Emerson, Ralph Waldo....VII, 350

FURNIVALL, FREDERICK JAMES,
Browning, Elizabeth Barrett.
.....................VI, 246
Browning, Robert..........VII, 703
Chaucer, Geoffrey......II, 128, 164
Shakespeare, William ......
I, 458, 463, 471, 480, 481, 484
490, 522, 525, 527, 538

FYFE, J. HAMILTON,
Butler, Joseph............III, 315
Lewis, Sir George Cornewall.
....................VI, 336, 337

FYVIE, JOHN,
Landor, Walter Savage.....VI, 378
Wither, George...........II, 213

GAIRDNER, JAMES,

Name	Vol. and Page
Asser	I, 42
Bede	I, 28
Eadmer	I, 52
Geoffery of Monmouth	I, 56
Hales, Alexander	I, 72
Hall, Edward	I, 260
Henry of Huntingdon	I, 59
More, Sir Thomas	I, 240
Paris, Matthew	I, 74
Pole, Reginald	I, 282
Saxon Chronicle	I, 58

GALT, JOHN,

Byron, George Gordon Lord.
.... IV, 738
Campbell, Thomas ..... V, 442
Moore, Thomas .... V, 715

GALTON, ARTHUR,

Browning, Robert	VII, 695, 705
Chaucer, Geoffrey	I, 167
Manning, Henry Edward	VIII, 168
Pattison, Mark	VII, 540
Tennyson, Alfred Lord	VIII, 85

GALTON, FRANCIS,

Bacon, Francis .... I, 645

GAMAGE, WILLIAM,

Jonson, Ben .... I, 758

GAMBA, COUNT PIETRO,

Byron, George Gordon Lord. IV, 735

GAMMELL, WILLIAM,

Williams, Roger .... II, 357

GANS, EDUARD,

Shakespeare, William ...... I, 503

GARAT, M.,

Gibbon, Edward .... IV, 174

GARBETT, EDWARD,

Lever, Charles James .... VI, 656
Maurice, John Frederick Denison .... VI, 647

GARDEN, FRANCIS,

Smollett, Tobias George ..... III, 583

GARDEN, MRS.,

Hogg, James .... V, 265

GARDINER, H. NORMAN,

Edwards, Jonathan .... III, 385

GARDINER, J. S. J.,

Ames, Fisher .... IV, 527

GARDINER, SAMUEL RAWSON,

Alfred the Great	I, 38
Bacon, Francis	I, 646, 654, 656
Baxter, Richard	II, 425
Browning, Robert	VII, 686
Carlyle, Thomas	VII, 271
Chillingworth, William	II, 87
Drummond, William	II, 101
Forster, John	VII, 67
Fox, George	II, 422
Graham, James	II, 121
Green, John Richard	VII, 511
Hales, John	II, 150
Hall, Joseph	II, 144
Howell, James	II, 187
Langland, William	I, 122
Massinger, Philip	II, 50
Milton, John	II, 253
Motley, John Lothrop	VII, 91, 92
Prynne, William	II, 226
Raleigh, Sir Walter	I, 597
Spedding, James	VII, 319
Stanhope Philip Henry, Earl.	
.... VII, 48	

Name	Vol. and Page
Suckling, Sir John	II, 64

GARDINER AND MULLINGER,

Rymer, Thomas .... II, 582

GARDINER, W. H.,

Cooper, James Fenimore ..... V, 683

GARDNER, DORSEY,

Wilson, Alexander ...... IV, 582, 584

GARFIELD, JAMES ABRAM,

History .... VI, 8
Lincoln, Abraham .... VI, 418

GARLAND, HAMLIN,

Field, Eugene	VIII, 315
George, Henry	VIII, 382
Holmes, Oliver Wendell	VIII, 297
Whitman, Walt	VIII, 133

GARMAN, S.,

Buckland, Francis Trevelyan.
.... VII, 211

GARNETT, RICHARD,

Adams, Sarah Fowler	V, 529, 530
Allingham, William	VII, 735
Arnold, Matthew	VII, 637, 648
Ashmole, Elias	II, 436
Aubrey, John	II, 452, 453
Barclay, John	I, 618
Barclay, Robert	II, 412
Barham, Richard Harris	
.... V, 475, 475	
Barnes, William	VII, 587
Beckford, William	V, 449, 451
Beddoes, Thomas Lovell	V, 588
Behn, Aphra	II, 408
Black, William	VIII, 395
Boyle, Robert	II, 420
Brontë, Emily	V, 522, 526
Browning, Robert	VII, 708
Bruce, James	IV, 208
Buckle, Henry Thomas	VI, 283
Bunyan, John	II, 392, 401
Burnet, Gilbert	II, 594
Burnet, Thomas	II, 597
Burton, John Hill	VII, 316
Carlyle, Thomas	
... VII, 241, 248, 250, 250, 272	
Cary, Henry Francis	V, 456
Coleridge, Hartley	V, 578
Coleridge, Sara	V, 735
Collier, Jeremy	II, 701
Congreve, William	II, 745
Creighton, Mandell	VIII, 454
Croly, George	VI, 225
Cudworth, Ralph	II, 387
Cumberland, Richard	II, 625
Disraeli, Benjamin	VII, 287, 291
Dillon, Wentworth	II, 361
Dobell, Sidney Thompson	
.... VI, 760, 761, 763, 766	
Dryden, John	II, 468, 483, 489
D'Urfey, Thomas	II, 688
Edwards, Jonathan	III, 387
Eliot, George	VII, 191, 199
Emerson, Ralph Waldo	
.... VII, 351, 359, 372	
Etheredge, Sir George	II, 416
Evelyn, John	II, 550
Fenton, Elijah	III, 21
Finlay, George	VII, 49, 50
Freeman, Edward Augustus	
.... VIII, 158	
Gardiner, Samuel Rawson	
.... VIII, 465	

Name	Vol. and Page
Green, John Richard	VII, 512
Greg, William Rathbone	VII, 321
Hamerton, Philip Gilbert	VIII, 283
Hood, Thomas	V, 465
Hook, Theodore Edward	V, 359
Hunt, James Henry Leigh	
.... VI, 169	
Jameson, Anna	VI, 216
Kinglake, Alexander William	
.... VIII, 53	
Landon, Letitia Elizabeth	
.... V, 326, 328	
Lee, Nathaniel	II, 432
L'Estrange, Sir Roger	II, 539
Locke, John	II, 530
Lytton, Edward Robert Bulwer	
.... VIII, 44	
Maginn, William	V, 387, 388
Martineau, James	VIII, 428
Milton, John	II, 279
Montgomery, James	V, 768
Moore, Thomas	V, 711, 714
Morris, William	VIII, 336
North, Roger	III, 80
Norton, Caroline E. S.,	
.... VII, 106	
Oldham, John	II, 351
Oliphant, Margaret O. W.,	
.... VIII, 369	
O'Shaughnessy, Arthur Wm.	
Edgar	VII, 324
Otway, Thomas	II, 363, 366
Patmore, Coventry	
.... VIII, 340, 341, 341	
Peacock, Thomas Love	
.... VI, 474, 476	
Pepys, Samuel	II, 516
Radcliffe, Ann Ward	IV, 718
Ray, John	II, 544
Robertson, Frederick William	
.... V, 738	
Rogers, Samuel	VI, 39
Rossetti, Gabriel Charles Dante	
.... VII, 439, 443, 453, 462	
Rossetti, Christiana Georgina	
.... VIII, 271	
Ruskin, John	VIII, 417
Rymer, Thomas	II, 582
Sackville, Charles	II, 554
Saville, George	II, 450
Settle, Elkanah	II, 692
Sidney, Algernon	II, 355
Shadewell, Thomas	II, 435
Shakespeare, William	I, 535
Sheffield, John, Third Eearl of Mulgrave	II, 671
Shelley, Mary Wollstonecraft	
.... V, 704	
Shelley, Percy Bysshe	
.... IV, 695, 717	
Sherlock, William	II, 562
Smith, Horace	V, 598
Smith, James	V, 339
South, Robert	II, 607
Southey, Caroline Anne Bowles	V, 762
Southey, Robert	V, 403, 417
Spence, Joseph	III, 520, 521
Sprat, Thomas	II, 573
Sterling, John	V, 455
Swift, Jonathan	III, 212, 215

INDEX TO CRITICISMS 593

Symonds, John Addington.... VIII, 202
Temple, Sir William........II, 460
Thackeray, William Makepeace,
.... VI, 317
Thirlwall, Connop.......VII, 44
Tillotson, John Robert.....II, 438
Trollope, Frances Milton....
.................VI, 330, 332
Vaughan, Henry..........II, 446
Villiers, George............I, 377
Wells, Charles Jeremiah..VII, 166
Wycherley, William........II, 606
GARNETT, JAMES M.,
Beowulf ....I, 19
GARNETT, WILLIAM,
Maxwell, James Clerk....VII, 168
GARNETT, W. J.,
Beckford, William.........V, 450
GARRETT, A. C.,
Chaucer, Geoffrey..........I, 138
GARRICK, DAVID,
Churchill, Charles........ III, 475
Colman, George..........IV, 201
Garrick, David...........III, 694
Goldsmith, Oliver........III, 614
Hill, John...............III, 646
Johnson, Samuel.........III, 743
Robertson, William.......IV, 157
Saint-John, Henry........III, 292
Shakespeare, William.......I, 449
Sheridan, Richard Brinsley.IV, 603
Sterne, Laurence........III, 502
GARRICK, MRS. DAVID,
Burnett, James..........IV, 347
GARRISON, FANNY LLOYD,
Garrison, William Lloyd.VII, 159
GARRISON, WILLIAM H.,
Whitman, Walt........VIII, 132
GARRISON, WILLIAM LLOYD,
Parker, Theodore........VI, 207
GARRISON, WENDALL PHILLIPS,
Child, Lydia Maria......VII, 219
FitzGerald, Edward.....VII, 520
Garrison, William Lloyd..VII, 158
Trollope, Frances Milton..VI, 330
Woolman, John.........III, 597
GARTH, SIR SAMUEL,
Atterbury, Frances........III, 64
Blackmore, Sir Richard....II, 746
Congreve, William........II, 740
Dryden, John............II, 495
Gay, John...............III, 60
Sackville, Charles.........II, 553
Wycherley, William......II, 603
GARVIN, LOUIS,
Patmore, Coventry K. D.....
.... VIII, 342
GASCOIGNE, GEORGE,
Chaucer, Geoffrey..........I, 153
GASKELL, CHARLES MILNES,
Cobbett, William..........V, 274
GASKELL, ELIZABETH CLEGHORN,
Brontë, Emily........V, 521, 526
GASSENDI, PIERRE,
Bacon, Francis.............I, 657
GATES, LEWIS E.,
Brontë, Charlotte........VI, 31
Carlyle, Thomas ......VII, 275

Newman, John Henry....VII, 754
Poe, Edgar Allan..........V, 554
Tennyson, Alfred Lord......
...................VIII, 79, 97
GATES, MERRILL EDWARDS,
Lanier, Sidney..........VII, 327
GATTY, ALFRED,
Tennyson, Alfred Lord..VIII, 88
GAY, JOHN,
Addison, Joseph..........II, 641
Authors and Authorship..VIII, 5
Books ....III, 6
Congrave, William........II, 740
Defoe, Daniel............ III, 29
Garth, Sir Samuel.........II, 666
Gay, John................III, 53
Granville, George........III, 88
Montagu, Lady Mary Wortley
.....................III, 460
Pope, Alexander......III, 164, 181
Sheffield, John, Third Earl of
Mulgrave............II, 671, 676
Steele, Sir Richard........II, 757
Swift, Jonathan.........III, 219
Waller, Edmund..........II, 380
GAY, SYDNEY HOWARD,
Irving Washington.......VI, 151
Madison, James...........V, 313
GAY, WILLIAM,
Whitman, Walt........VIII, 148
GAYLEY, CHARLES MILLS,
Goldsmith, Oliver........III, 622
GAYLEY, CHARLES MILLS, AND SCOTT, FRED NEWTON,
Arnold, Matthew........VII, 648
Critic, The................II, 10
Hallam, Henry..........VI, 178
Pope, Alexander.........III, 195
GAZETTE OF AMIENS,
Franklin, Benjamin......IV, 81
GEDDES, ALEXANDER,
Tyndale, William............I, 246
GEIKIE SIR ARCHIBALD,
Burns, Robert...........IV, 269
Campbell, George J. D..VIII, 435
Cowper, William.........IV, 394
Darwin, Charles Robert..VII, 428
Hutton, James..........IV, 339
Lyell, Sir Charles....VII, 36, 37
Macpherson, James......IV, 281
Miller, Hugh..........VI, 63, 65
Murchison, Sir Roderick Impey...........VI, 630, 631
Thomson, James........III, 272
GEIKIE, JOHN CUNNINGHAM,
Latimer, Hugh............I, 269
Tyndale, William...........I, 248
Wyclif, John..............I, 108
GELL, PHILIP LYTTLETON,
Green, John Richard.....VII, 505
GELL, SIR WILLIAM,
Mathias, Thomas James...V, 288
Scott, Sir Walter.........V, 128
GENERAL ADVERTISER,
Hill, Aaron..............III, 277
GENEST, P.,
Cibber, Theophilus........III, 395
Collier, Jeremy..........II, 700
Glover, Richard..........IV, 19
Manley, Mrs. Mary de la
Riviere................II, 694

GENNADIUS, J.,
Johnson, Samuel.........III, 768
GENTLEMAN, FRANCIS,
Shakespeare, William.......I, 496
GENTNER, PHILIP,
Chapman, George..........I, 731
Pope, Alexander..........III, 167
GENUNG, JOHN FRANKLIN,
Stevenson, Robert Louis.VIII, 253
Tennyson, Alfred Lord..VIII, 88
GEOGHEGAN, MARY,
Jefferies, Richard........VII, 620
GEORGE II,
Stanhope, Philip Dormer..III, 599
GEORGE, ANDREW J.,
Addison, Joseph..........II, 661
Arnold, Matthew........VII, 647
Bacon, Francis.............I, 652
Blake, William............V, 63
Bowles, William Lisle......V, 660
Browning, Robert...VII, 686, 717
Bunyan, John............II, 399
Burke, Edmund..........IV, 309
Burns, Robert........IV, 221, 269
Byron, George Gordon Lord..
.... IV, 765
Carlyle, Thomas....VII, 229, 241
Coleridge, Samuel Taylor....
.... V, 205, 227
Critic, The................II, 9
DeQuincey, Thomas.......VI, 132
Dickens, Charles........VI, 594
Goldsmith, Oliver........III, 639
Macaulay, Thomas Babington
Lord ....VI, 100
Marlowe, Christopher.......I, 358
Milton, John............II, 298
Newman, John Henry...VII, 756
Tennyson, Alfred Lord..VIII, 85
Webster, Daniel..........V, 726
Wordsworth, William......V, 619
GEORGE, HENRY,
Smith, Adam............IV, 66
Spencer, Herbert.......VIII, 483
GERARD, FATHER,
Southwell, Robert..........I, 361
GERARD, FRANCES A.,
Blessington, Countess of....V, 595
Morgan, Sydney Owenson Lady
.... V, 195
Norton, Caroline E. S....VII, 103
GERVINUS, G. G.,
Bacon, Francis............I, 666
Lyly, John...............I, 424
Shakespeare, William........
..............I, 474, 477,
479, 481, 490, 494, 496, 498, 504
GESTA GRAYORUM,
Shakespeare, William.......I, 466
GIBB, JOHN,
Anslem ....I, 51
Liddon, Henry Parry....VII. 762
Mozley, James Bowling..VII, 149
GIBBINS, HENRY DE BELTGENS
Carlyle, Thomas....VII, 251, 272
Langland, William ....I, 122
Owens, Robert...........VI, 85
Wesley, John............IV, 125
GIBBON, EDWARD,
Books ....III, 7
Boswell, James...........IV, 214

INDEX TO CRITICISMS

	Vol. and Page
Burke, Edmund	IV, 298, 299, 301
Caxton, William	I, 198
Chillingworth, William	II, 87
Dodwell, Henry	II, 566
Fielding, Henry	III, 351
Fox, Charles James	IV, 499
Gibbon, Edward	IV, 178, 180, 180
Hayley, William	IV, 652
Hearne, Thomas	III, 89
History	VI, 6
Hoadly, Benjamin	III, 423
Hume, David	III, 655, 665
Hurd, Richard	IV, 519
Law, William	III, 427, 428
Lowth, William	III, 63
Mallet, David	III, 496
Middleton, Conyers	III, 280
Montagu, Lady Mary Wortley	III, 465
Parker, Matthew	I, 303
Pitt, William	IV, 510
Pope, Alexander	III, 165
Porson, Richard	IV, 524
Priestley, Joseph	IV, 452
Richardson, Samuel	III, 444
Robertson, William	IV, 160, 162
Saint-John, Henry	III, 291
Sale, George	III, 90
Sandys, George	II, 81
Selden, John	II, 139
Sheridan, Richard Brinsley	IV, 599
Spenser, Edmund	I, 381
Stanhope, Philip Dormer	III, 603
Usher, James	II, 153
Walpole, Horace	IV, 321
Warburton, William	III, 690
Warton, Thomas	IV, 73
West, Gilbert	III, 368
Whiston, William	III, 305
Wilkes, John	IV, 333
Wood, Anthony	II, 448
Wotton, William	II, 709
GIBBONS, THOMAS,	
Watts, Isaac	III, 249
GIBBS, H. J.,	
Milnes, Richard Monckton	VII, 565
Palgrave, Francis Turner	VIII, 372
Procter, Adelaide Anne	VI, 396
Sterling, John	V, 454
Trench, Richard Chenevix	VII, 590
GIBSON CHARLES B.,	
Wolfe, Charles	IV, 722
GIBSON, WILLIAM HAMILTON,	
Roe, Edward Payson	VII, 675
GIFFEN, ROBERT,	
Bagehot, Walter	VII, 98
GIFFORD, JOHN,	
Pitt, William	IV, 510
GIFFORD, WILLIAM,	
Aubrey, John	II, 452
Cowley, Abraham	II, 199
Crabbe, George	V, 172
Drummond, William	II, 100
Edgeworth, Maria	V, 567
Ford, John	II, 25, 27, 28, 29, 31
Jonson, Ben	I, 748, 762
Keats, John	IV, 669

	Vol. and Page
Knowledge	V, 7
Lyly, John	I, 422
Marston, John	I, 737
Mitford, Mary Russell	VI, 43, 45
Piozzi, Hester Lynch	IV, 685
Poets and Poetry	IV, 6
Scott, Sir Walter	V, 149, 149
Shakespeare, William	I, 554
Skelton, John	I, 220
Steevens, George	IV, 409, 409
Wolcot, John	IV, 648
GILES, J. A.	
Alfred the Great	I, 39
Ascham, Roger	I, 289
Asser	I, 42
Bede	I, 27
Geoffery of Monmouth	I, 55
Paris, Matthew	I, 74
William of Malmesbury	I, 54
GILBERT, HENRY,	
Creighton, Mandell	VIII, 455
Fiske, John	VIII, 455
Gardiner, Samuel Rawson	VIII, 465
Harte, Francis Bret	VIII, 466
Henley, William Ernest	VIII, 492, 494
Lecky, William E. H.	VIII, 487
Spencer Herbert	VIII, 487
Stockton, Francis Richard	VIII, 475
Stubbs, William	VIII, 451, 452
GILBERT, J. T.,	
Brooke, Henry	III, 714
GILCHRIST, ALEXANDER,	
Blake, William	V, 57, 63
Cunningham, Allan	V, 384
Hayley, William	IV, 652
GILCHRIST, ANNE,	
Lamb, Mary Ann	V, 510, 509
Whitman, Walt	VIII, 138
GILCHRIST, GRACE,	
Whitman, Walt	VIII, 134
GILCHRIST, HERBERT H.,	
Rossetti, Gabriel Charles Dante	VII, 440
GILDEA, WILLIAM L.,	
Brownson, Orestes Augustus	VII, 76
GILDER, JEANNETTE L.,	
Dodgson, Charles Lutwige	VIII, 398
Franklin, Benjamin	IV, 99
Hamerton, Philip Gilbert	VIII, 282
Parkman, Francis	VIII, 220
GILDER, JOSEPH B.,	
Stoddard, Richard Henry	VIII, 494, 498
GILDER, RICHARD WATSON,	
Brontë, Charlotte	VI, 19
Emerson, Ralph Waldo	VII, 356
Holland, Josiah Gilbert	VII, 333
Jackson, Helen Hunt	VII, 575
Keats, John	IV, 666
Lazarus, Emma	VII, 610
Tennyson, Alfred Lord	VIII, 107
GILDON, CHARLES,	
Behn, Aphra	II, 407
Defoe, Daniel	III, 32

	Vol. and Page
GILES, HENRY,	
Chatterton, Thomas	III, 537
Goldsmith, Oliver	III, 632
Griffin, Gerald	V, 353
Hood, Thomas	V, 462
Savage, Richard	III, 133, 135
GILFILLAN, GEORGE,	
Addison, Joseph	II, 637, 642, 643
Akenside, Mark	III, 542
Barbour, John	I, 114
Beattie, James	IV, 434
Beaumont and Fletcher	I, 582
Blair, Robert	III, 242
Blamire, Susanna	IV, 204
Brougham, Henry Lord	VI, 529
Browne, William	II, 74
Browning, Elizabeth Barrett	VI, 236, 244
Browning, Robert	VII, 699
Burke, Edmund	IV, 300
Burns, Robert	IV, 229
Burton, Robert	II, 39
Butler, Samuel	II, 332
Carew, Thomas	II, 22
Carlyle, Thomas	VII, 254, 263
Chalmers, Thomas	V, 495
Churchill, Charles	III, 477
Coleridge, Samuel Taylor	V, 224
Collins, William	III, 417
Cowper, William	IV, 373
Crabbe, George	V, 171, 174
Crashaw, Richard	II, 110
DeQuincey, Thomas	VI, 117
Disraeli, Benjamin	VII, 287, 292
Dobell, Sidney Thompson	VI, 762, 763
Donne, John	I, 715
Drayton, Michael	I, 707
Douglas, Gawin	I, 214
Dunbar, William	I, 225
Dryden, John	II, 487, 491, 501
Dyer, John	III, 398, 399
Edwards, Jonathan	III, 382, 382
Emerson, Ralph Waldo	VII, 363
Fielding, Henry	III, 347
Foster, John	V, 426
Fuller, Thomas	II, 172
Gifford, William	V, 35
Goldsmith, Oliver	III, 632
Green, Matthew	III, 95
Hall, Robert	V, 109
Hallam, Henry	VI, 178
Hazlitt, William	V, 104
Hemans, Felicia Dorothea	V, 259
Herbert, George	I, 721
Hood, Thomas	V, 461
Irving, Edward	V, 249
Jeffrey, Francis Lord	V, 655
Johnson, Samuel	III, 751
Landor, Walter Savage	VI, 389
Langhorne, John	III, 700
Lewis, Matthew Gregory	IV, 632
Longfellow, Henry Wadsworth	VII, 388, 391
Lydgate, John	I, 185
Lytton, Sir Edward George Bulwer	VI, 690
Moir, David Macbeth	V, 704, 705
Parnell, Thomas	II, 615, 616
Percy, Thomas	IV, 565
Poe, Edgar Allan	V, 537, 557

INDEX TO CRITICISMS

	Vol. and Page
Quarles, Francis	II, 79
Shelley, Percy Bysshe	IV, 702
Shenstone, William	III, 472
Skelton, John	I, 221
Smith, Alexander	VI, 516
Smollett, Tobias George	III, 583
Somerville, William	III, 126
Southwell, Robert	I, 362
Steele, Sir Richard	II, 753
Sterling, John	V, 452
Sterne, Laurence	III, 513
Surrey, Earl of	I, 257
Swift, Jonathan	III, 214, 231
Tennyson, Alfred Lord	VIII, 83
Thackeray, William Makepeace	VI, 308
Thomson, James	III, 264, 268
Warton, Thomas	IV, 78
White, Henry Kirke	IV, 489
Wilson, John	V, 748, 750
Wyatt, Sir Thomas	I, 250, 251
Young, Edward	III, 488
GILL, THEODORE,	
Huxley, Thomas Henry	VIII, 326
GILL, WILLIAM FEARING,	
Poe, Edgar Allan	V, 545, 551, 551
GILLIES, ROBERT PIERCE,	
Beattie, James	IV, 429
Chalmers, Thomas	V, 491
DeQuincey, Thomas	VI, 118
Hogg, James	V, 264
Scott, Sir Walter	V, 130, 131
Southey, Robert	V, 400
Wordsworth, William	V, 611
GILLMAN, JAMES,	
Coleridge, Samuel Taylor	V, 209
GILMAN, ARTHUR,	
Cranmer, Thomas	I, 273
GILMAN, DANIEL COIT,	
Agassiz, Louis Jean Rudolphe	VI, 719
Hamilton, Alexander	IV, 468
Monroe, James	V, 123
GILMAN, D. G.,	
Percival, James Gates	VI, 59
GILMAN, NICHOLAS P.,	
Swift, Jonathan	III, 234
GILMAN, S.,	
Brown, Thomas	IV, 657, 658
GILMAN, PECK, and COLBY,	
Browne, Charles Farrar	VI, 501
Brownson, Orestes Augustus	VII, 72
Bushnell, Horace	VII, 69
Church, Richard William	VII, 728
Clarke, James Freeman	VII, 672
Dewey, Orville	VII, 495
Draper, John William	VII, 503
Fawcett, Henry	VII, 551
Hamerton, Philip Gilbert	VIII, 280
Hopkins, Mark	VII, 613
Ingersoll, Robert Green	VIII, 401
Warner, Charles Dudley	VIII, 440
GILMORE, JOSEPH HENRY,	
Layamon	I, 66
Lowell, James Russell	VIII, 30
Minot, Lawrence	I, 93
GILPIN, WILLIAM,	
Latimer, Hugh	I, 267
Vanbrugh, Sir John	II, 705

	Vol. and Page
GIRARDIN, SAINT-MARC,	
Shakespeare, William	I, 475
GISSING, GEORGE,	
Dickens, Charles	VI, 567, 575, 577, 579
GLADDEN, WASHINGTON,	
Brooks, Phillips	VIII, 234
Eggleston, Edward	VIII, 475, 476
Holland, Josiah Gilbert	VII, 333, 335
Ruskin, John	VIII, 411
GLADSTONE, WILLIAM EWART,	
Bagehot, Walter	VII, 100
Buckle, Henry Thomas	VI, 284
Butler, Joseph	III, 317
Chalmers, Thomas	V, 493
Gladstone, William Ewart	VIII, 390
Hallam, Arthur Henry	V, 198
Keble John	VI, 458
Macaulay, Thomas Babington Lord	VI, 95, 112
Mill, John Stuart	VI, 706
Newman, John Henry	VII, 747
Romanes, George John	VIII, 283
Sheridan, Richard Brinsley	IV, 598
Stanhope, Philip Dormer	III, 602
Tennyson, Alfred Lord	VIII, 87, 91, 97
Warburton, William	III, 685
White, Joseph Blanco	V, 360
Wilberforce, Samuel	VI, 733
Wordsworth, William	V, 615
GLAISHER, J. W. L.,	
Napier, Sir John	I, 589
GLAZEBROOK, MRS. M. G.,	
Browning, Robert	VII, 708
GLEZEBROOK, R. T.,	
Maxwell, James Clerk	VII, 169, 170
Newton, Sir Isaac	II, 715, 726
GLENNIE, J. S. S.,	
Buckle, Henry Thomas	VI, 279
GLOUCESTER, DUKE OF,	
Gibbon, Edward	IV, 179
GLYDE, JOHN,	
FitzGerald, Edward	VII, 516
GODKIN, EDWIN LAURENCE,	
Burke, Edmund	IV, 293
Carlyle, Thomas	VII, 264
Critic, The	II, 10
Greeley, Horace	VI, 667
Huxley, Thomas Henry	VIII, 324
Mill, John Stuart	VI, 717
Parkman, Francis	VII, 220
Stanley, Sir Henry Morton	VIII, 507
GODWIN, FRANCIS,	
de Bury, Richard	I, 89
GODWIN, MARY WOLLSTONECRAFT,	
Chapone, Hester	IV, 418
Godwin, Mary Wollstonecraft	IV, 326
Macaulay, Catherine	IV, 134
GODWIN, PARKE,	
Audubon, John James	V, 699
Bryant, William Cullen	VII, 118
Curtis, George William	VIII, 185, 187
Harte, Francis Bret	VIII, 468
Langhorne, John	III, 700
Prynne, William	II, 223

	Vol. and Page
Shakespeare, William	I, 459
Smith, Adam	IV, 65
GODWIN, WILLIAM,	
Addison, Joseph	II, 655
Chaucer, Geoffrey	I, 142, 149, 151
Dennis, John	III, 77
Fox, Charles James	IV, 503
Gower, John	I, 175
Gibbon, Edward	IV, 191
Godwin, Mary Wollstonecraft	IV, 327, 329
Godwin, William	V, 296
Henryson, Robert	I, 208
Hooker, Richard	I, 405
Hyde, Edward, Earl of Clarendon	II, 302
Irving, Washington	VI, 140
Johnson, Samuel	III, 755
Literature	I, 7
Locke, John	II, 532
Lytton, Sir Edward Bulwer Lord	VI, 686
Milton, John	II, 260, 281, 286
Pitt, William	IV, 508
Raleigh, Sir Walter	I, 606
Richardson, Samuel	III, 447
Saint-John, Henry	III, 286
Shakespeare, William	I, 524, 554
Sherlock, Thomas	III, 455
Shelley, Mary Wolstonecraft	V, 702
Shelley, Percy Bysshe	IV, 703
Sidney, Sir Phillip	I, 324
Smollett, Tobias George	III, 581, 586
Swift, Jonathan	III, 213, 220
Tillotson, John Robert	II, 439
Warton, Thomas	IV, 73
GODOLPHIN, SIDNEY,	
Sandys, George	II, 83
GOETHE, JOHANN WOLFGANG,	
Byron, George Gordon Lord	IV, 751, 753, 757
Carlyle, Thomas	VII, 260
Darwin, Erasmus	IV, 421
Goldsmith, Oliver	III, 625, 626, 630
History	IV, 7
Macpherson, James	IV, 273
Milton, John	II, 271
Richardson, Samuel	III, 444
Scott, Sir Walter	V, 141, 148, 156, 157
Shakespeare, William	I, 501
Thomas, James	III, 263
GOLDSCHMIDT, JENNY (NÉE LIND),	
Stowe, Harriet E. B.	VIII, 351
GOLDSMITH, OLIVER,	
Addison, Joseph	II, 640, 654
Authors and Authorship	VIII, 6
Burke, Edmund	IV, 288
Collins, William	III, 414, 416
Cooper, Anthony Ashley	II, 578
Cowley, Abraham	II, 198
Critic, The	II, 5
Cumberland, Richard	IV, 560
Denham, Sir John	II, 221
Drayton, Michael	I, 706
Dryden, John	II, 486, 492, 496
Garrick, David	III, 694
Garth, Sir Samuel	II, 665
Gay, John	III, 54

596 INDEX TO CRITICISMS

Vol. and Page

Goldsmith, Oliver.......... III. 614, 614, 624, 632
Gray, Thomas......III, 558. 561
Johnson, Samuel........III, 738
Knowledge......V, 6
Leslie, Charles.........II, 679
L'Estrange, Sir Roger......II. 538
Locke. John.......II, 532
Milton, John......II, 274
Moore, Edward.......III, 375, 376
Otway Thomas......II, 366
Parnell, Thomas... II, 615, 616
Philips, Ambrose......III, 275
Philips, John......II, 563
Pope, Alexander..........
.........III, 146, 161, 168. 179
Prior, Matthew......II, 676
Reynolds, Sir Joshua......IV, 137
Saint-John, Henry....III, 285, 293
Savage, Richard......III, 135
Sheffield, John, Third Earl of Mulgrave......II, 671
Shenstone, William......III, 472
Sidney, Sir Philip......I, 329
Smollett, Tobias George......II, 585
Spenser, Edmund......I, 394
Steele, Sir Richard......II, 762
Sterne, Laurence......III, 506
Swift, Jonathan......III, 227
Thomson, James......III, 266
Tickell, Thomas......III, 105, 106
Tillotson, John Robert ......
......II, 439, 457
Waller, Edmund......II, 380
Wilkie, William......III, 595
Young, Edward......III, 491
GOLLANCZ, ISRAEL,
Cynewulf......I, 31
Dryden, John......II, 477
Shakespeare, William........
....I, 457, 461, 467, 476, 529, 539
GONNER, E. C. K.,
Ricardo, David......IV, 727
GOOD, JOHN MASON,
Junius....................IV, 644
GOODALE, G. L.,
Gray, Asa......VII, 671
GOODFELLOW, HENRY,
Kane, Elisha Kent......VI, 81
GOODRICH, CHAUNCY A.,
Burke, Edmund......IV, 295
Pitt, William......III, 680
Webster, Noah......V, 428, 431
GOODRICH, SAMUEL GRISWOLD,
Barbauld, Anna Laetitia......V, 24
Cooper, James Fenimore......V, 680
Hawthorne,Nathaniel......VI, 343
Percival, James Gates......VI, 58
Sigourney, Lydia Huntley...VI, 451
Trumbull, John......V, 121
Webster, Daniel......V, 721
GOODWIN, GORDON,
Browne, William......II, 76
Grainger, James......II, 498
Kelly, Hugh......III, 677
Kenrick, William......III, 702
Strype, John......III, 93
Taylor, John......II, 133, 134
GOOGE, BARNABE,
Bale, John......I, 286
Edwards, Richard......I, 287

Vol. and Page

GORDON, ALEXANDER,
Doddridge, Philip..........
......III, 301, 302, 302, 303
Fergusson, Robert......III, 642
Fox, George ....II, 422
Hales, John......II, 151
Hall, Robert......V, 110
Henry, Matthew......II, 585
Horsley, Samuel......IV, 494
Howe, John......II, 546
Johnston, Arthur......II, 54
Jortin, John......III, 552
Lardner, Nathaniel......III, 523, 524
Newman, Francis William.....
......VIII, 370
Prideaux, Humphrey......II, 697
Priestley, Joseph......IV, 448, 455
South, Robert......II, 607
Taylor, Jeremy......II, 206
Taylor, William......V, 318, 319, 320
Tillotson, John Robert ......II, 438
Usher, James......II, 154
Wesley, Charles......IV, 35, 39
Wesley, John......IV, 125
Wesley, Samuel......III, 86
Whitefield, George......III, 549
Woolston, Thomas......III, 74
GORDON, GEORGE A.,
Brooks, Phillips......VIII, 227
Edwards, Jonathan......III, 394
GORDON, J. T.,
Grant, Anne......V, 330
GORDON, MARGARET MARIA,
Brewster, Sir David......VI, 546
GORDON, MARY,
Channing, William Ellery...V, 368
Coleridge, Hartley......V, 575
DeQuincey, Thomas ......VI, 118
Wilson, John......V, 746
GORDON, PRYSE LOCKHART,
Porson, Richard......IV, 522
GORDON, WALTER,
Knowles, James Sheridan...VI, 288
GORDON, WALTER,
Lytton, Sir Edward George Bulwer......VI, 690
GORRIE, P. DOUGLASS,
Wesley, Charles......IV, 34
GOSSE, EDMUND,
Addison, Joseph......II, 641, 659
Akenside, Mark..III, 542, 542, 545
Amory, Thomas......IV, 47, 48
Arbuthnot, John......III, 85
Armstrong, John......III, 699
Arnold, Matthew......VII, 645
Ascham, Roger......I, 291
Austen, Jane......IV, 624
Ayton, Sir Robert......I, 768
Bacon, Francis......I, 652, 653, 669
Bailey, Philip James......VIII, 462
Barbour, John......I, 116
Barclay, Alexander......I, 265
Barnes, Barnabe......II, 440
Barrow, Isaac......II, 312
Basse, William......II, 131
Baxter, Richard......II, 68
Beattie, James......IV, 433
Beaumont, and Fletcher......I, 585
Beaumont, Joseph......II, 46
Beaumont, Sir John......I, 680
Beddoes, Thomas Lovell......V, 585

Vol. and Page

Behn, Aphra......II, 408, 410
Berkeley, George......III, 326
Blackstone, Sir William......III, 706
Blair, Robert......III, 243
Boswell, James....IV, 211, 213. 219
Boyle, Robert......II, 419
Breton, Nicholas......I, 679
Brontë Charlotte......VI, 26
Brontë, Emily......V, 521, 525
Brooke. Henry......III, 714
Broome, William......III, 239
Browne, Sir Thomas...II, 345, 349
Browne, William......II, 74
Browning, Elizabeth Barrett..
......VI, 247
Browning, Robert......
VII, 684, 684, 689, 690, 691, 719
Bryant, William Cullen....VII, 125
Bunyan, John......II, 400
Burke, Edmund......IV, 307
Burnet, Thomas......II, 597
Burney, Frances......V, 346, 351
Butler, Joseph......III, 313
Butler, Samuel......II, 334
Byrom, John......III, 468
Byron, George Gordon Lord.IV, 763
Camden, William ......I, 622
Campbell, Thomas......V, 446
Carew, Thomas......II, 22
Carlyle, Thomas......VII, 257
Caxton, William......I, 200
Chapman, George......I, 734
Chatterton, Thomas......III, 539
Chaucer, Geoffrey......I, 135, 171
Chillingworth, William......II, 88
Churchill, Charles......III, 482
Cibber, Colley......III, 373
Collier, Jeremy......II, 701
Collins, William......III, 418, 421
Colman George ......IV, 203
Congreve, William..........
......II, 736, 737, 738, 739, 745
Cooper, Anthony Ashley......II, 581
Cowley, Abraham...II, 195, 197, 202
Crashaw, Richard......II, 111, 113
Creighton, Mandell......VIII, 453
Dana, Richard Henry......VII, 154
Daniel, Samuel......I, 617
Darwin, Charles Robert......VII, 434
Darwin, Erasmus......IV, 425
D'Avenant, Sir William......II, 219
Davies, Sir John......I, 634
Defoe, Daniel......III, 39
Dekker, Thomas......II, 61
Denham, Sir John......II, 222
Dennis, John......III, 78
DeQuincey, Thomas......VI, 131
Dickens, Charles......VI, 565, 593
Dillon, Wentworth......II, 361
Disraeli, Isaac......V, 514
Donne, John......I, 712, 717
Drake, Joseph Rodman......IV, 661
Drayton, Michael..I, 705, 705, 708
Drummond, William......II, 106
Dryden, John......II, 471, 481, 505
Dunbar, William......I, 228
D'Urfey, Thomas......II, 688
Dyer, John......III, 400
Eliot, George......VII, 208
Emerson Ralph Waldo......VI, 358
Etheredge, Sir George....II, 414, 415

INDEX TO CRITICISMS

	Vol. and Page
Evelyn, John	II, 551
Farquhar, George	II, 555, 559
Fielding, Henry	III, 348, 349, 365
Fielding, Sarah	III, 518
Finch, Anne, Countess of Winchilsea	II, 668
FitzGerald, Edward	VII, 516, 519, 521
Fletcher, Giles	I, 624
Fletcher, Phineas	II, 118
Foote, Samuel	III, 674
Ford, John	II, 33
Fortescue, Sir John	I, 195
Franklin, Benjamin	IV, 103
Freeman, Edward Augustus	VIII, 161
Froude, James Anthony	VIII, 256
Fuller, Thomas	II, 173
Garth, Sir Samuel	II, 666
Gaskell, Elizabeth Cleghorn	VI, 433
Gibbon, Edward	IV, 190
Glover, Richard	IV, 20
Godwin, William	V, 298
Goldsmith, Oliver	III, 639
Gower, John	I, 177
Grainger, James	III, 498
Gray, Thomas	III, 556, 560, 570, 571
Green, John Richard	VII, 513
Green, Matthew	III, 95
Greene, Robert	I, 344, 345
Greville, Sir Fulke	I, 692
Hall, Edward	I, 261
Hallam, Henry	VI, 180
Hartley, David	III, 380
Herbert, George	I, 725
Herrick, Robert	II, 236, 239
Heywood, Thomas	II, 123, 127
Hoadly, Benjamin	III, 424
Holmes, Oliver Wendell	VIII, 298
Home, Henry	III, 713
Hooker, Richard	I, 410
Horne, Richard Hengist	VII, 545, 548
Howell, James	II, 188
Hume, David	III, 661, 667
Hunt, James Henry Leigh	VI, 170
Hurd, Richard	IV, 520
Hyde, Edward, Earl of Clarendon	II, 305
Irving, Washington	VI, 143
James I of Scotland	I, 182
Johnson, Samuel	III, 738, 752, 768
Johnstone, Charles	IV, 414
Jonson, Ben	I, 754, 756, 757, 767
Jortin, John	III, 552
Junius	IV, 647
Keats, John	IV, 681
Kingsley, Charles	VII, 33
Kyd, Thomas	I, 359
Landor, Walter Savage	VI, 387
Langland, William	I, 122
Lanier, Sidney	VII, 328
Law, William	III, 430
Lee, Nathaniel	II, 432
Lever, Charles James	VI, 653
Lillo, George	III, 102
Locke, John	II, 536
Lockhart, John Gibson	V, 756
Lodge, Thomas	I, 626

	Vol. and Page
Longfellow, Henry Wadsworth	VII, 412
Lovelace, Richard	II, 162
Lowell, James Russell	VIII, 21, 38
Lydgate, John	I, 186
Lyly, John	I, 424
Lyndsay, Sir David	I, 276
Lyttelton, George Lord	III, 613
Lytton, Sir Edward George Bulwer	VI, 700
Macaulay, Thomas Babington Lord	VI, 100
Mackenzie, Henry	V, 115
Macpherson, James	IV, 271, 279
Mandeville, Bernard	III, 71
Manley, Mrs. Mary de la Riviere	II, 694
Marlowe, Christopher	I, 356
Marvell, Andrew	II, 318
Mason, William	IV, 325
Massinger, Philip	II, 46, 52
Middleton, Conyers	III, 281
Middleton, Thomas	I, 686
Milton, John	II, 270, 274
Montagu, Lady Mary Wortley	III, 465
Moore, Thomas	V, 711, 712
More, Sir Thomas	I, 242
Newman, John Henry	VII, 742, 755
Norton, Caroline E. S.	VII, 105
Occleve, Thomas	I, 188
Oldham, John	II, 350
Oldmixon, John	III, 124
O'Shaughnessy, Arthur Wm. Edgar	VII, 323
Otway, Thomas	II, 363, 366
Overbury, Sir Thomas	I, 443
Paley, William	IV, 478
Parnell, Thomas	II, 617
Pater, Walter Horatio	VIII, 275, 277
Patmore, Coventry K. D.	VIII, 340, 342
Peacock, Reginald	I, 190
Peacock, Thomas Love	VI, 474
Pearson, John	II, 370
Pepys, Samuel	II, 515
Philips, Katherine	II, 179, 180
Philips, John	II, 563
Poe, Edgar Allan	V, 547
Pope, Alexander	III, 192, 195
Porter, Jane	V, 674
Prior, Matthew	II, 675
Raleigh, Sir Walter	I, 597, 601, 605, 607, 608
Ramsay, Allan	III, 410
Randolph, Thomas	I, 744
Reid, Thomas	IV, 287
Reynolds, Sir Joshua	IV, 142
Richardson, Samuel	III, 442, 453
Ritson, Joseph	IV, 437
Robertson, William	IV, 159
Roe, Edward Payson	VI, 676
Rogers, Samuel	VI, 38
Ross, Alexander	III, 719
Rossetti, Christina Georgina	VIII, 272
Rossetti, Gabriel Charles Dante	VII, 435, 452

	Vol. and Page
Rowley, William	II, 69
Ruskin, John	VIII, 421
Sackville, Charles	II, 554
Sackville, Thomas	I, 435
Saint-John, Henry	III, 291
Savage, Richard	III, 136
Savile, George	II, 450
Scott, Sir Walter	V, 146
Sedley, Sir Charles	II, 510
Settle, Elkanah	II, 692
Shadwell, Thomas	II, 435
Shakespeare, William	I, 495, 575
Sheffield, John, Third Earl of Mulgrave	II, 671
Shelley, Percy Bysshe	IV, 714
Sheridan, Richard Brinsley	IV, 604
Sherlock, William	II, 561
Sidney, Algernon	II, 355
Sidney, Sir Philip	I, 320, 323
Smart, Christopher	III, 594
Smith, Adams	IV, 68
Smollett, Tobias George	III, 578, 583, 590
Somerville, William	III, 126
South, Robert	II, 609
Southerne, Thomas	III, 241
Southey, Robert	V, 406
Southwell, Robert	I, 363
Spencer, Herbert	VIII, 483
Spenser, Edmund	I, 387
Sprat, Thomas	II, 574
Steele, Sir Richard	II, 766
Sterne, Laurence	III, 517
Stevenson, Robert Louis	VIII, 243, 237
Suckling, Sir John	II, 64, 66
Swift, Jonathan	III, 215, 222, 237
Sylvester, Joshua	I, 610
Taylor, Jeremy	II, 205
Temple, Sir William	II, 459
Tennyson, Alfred Lord	VIII, 106
Thackeray, William Makepeace	VI, 321
Thomson, James	III, 271
Tickell, Thomas	III, 106
Tourneur, Cyril	I, 689
Tyndall, John	VIII, 201
Vanbrugh, Sir John	II, 708
Vaughan, Henry	II, 446
Waller, Edmund	II, 383
Walpole, Horace	IV, 318
Walsh, William	III, 560
Warburton, William	III, 675
Webster, John	I, 670, 671, 673, 674, 677
Wells, Charles Jeremiah	VII, 165
Whitman, Walt	VIII, 149
Whittier, John Greenleaf	VIII, 116, 128
Wilkins, John	II, 227
Williams, Sir Charles Hanbury	III, 413
Wilmot, John	II, 338
Wither, George	II, 215
Wolfe, Charles	IV, 722
Wordsworth, William	V, 620
Wycherley, Thomas	II, 603
Wyclif, John	I, 104
Young, Edward	III, 486, 494

598 INDEX TO CRITICISMS

Vol. and Page
GOULBURN, EDWARD MEYRICK,
  Ward, William George...VII, 481
GOULD, ALICE BACHE,
  Agassiz, Louis Jean Rudolphe
    ....VI, 726
GOULD, ELIZABETH PORTER,
  Adams, Hannah..........V, 125
  Horne, Richard Hengist..VII, 547
GOULD, GEORGE M.,
  Huxley, Thomas Henry.VIII, 323
GOULD, ROBERT,
  Shirley, James............II, 190
GOSTWICK, JOSEPH,
  Carlyle, Thomas.........VII, 256
GOWER, JOHN,
  Chaucer, Geoffrey...........I, 124
  Gower, John...............I, 172
GOWER, LORD RONALD,
  Longfellow, Henry Wadsworth
    ....VII, 382
  Thackeray, William Makepeace
    ....VI, 296
GOWING, EMILIA AYLMER,
  Burton, Sir Richard Francis..
    ....VII, 759
GRAEVIUS, JOHN GEORGE,
  Bentley, Richard..........IV, 120
GRAFTON, RICHARD,
  Hall, Edward..........I, 260, 419
GRAHAM, HENRY GREY,
  Beattie, James............IV, 434
  Blacklock, Thomas........IV, 129
  Blair, Hugh...............IV, 403
  Boswell, James............IV, 212
  Burnett, James............IV, 347
  Burns, Robert........IV, 236, 243
  Dalrymple, Sir David..IV, 146, 147
  Ferguson, Adam..........IV, 610
  Henry, Robert............IV, 107
  Home, John.....IV, 513, 515, 516
  Macknight, James.........IV, 407
  Macpherson, James......IV, 272
  Oliphant, Carolina.........V, 478
  Reid, Thomas............IV, 282
  Robertson, William.......IV, 156
  Smith, Adam............IV, 57
GRAHAM, J. H.,
  Beddoes, Thomas Lovell....V, 587
GRAHAM, JOHN A.,
  Tooke, John Horne.......IV, 570
GRAHAM, P. ANDERSON,
  Jefferies, Richard........VII, 621
  Thoreau, Henry David....VI, 276
GRAHAM, RICHARD D.,
  Arnold, Matthew........VII, 634
  Bailey Philip James....VIII, 462
  Besant, Sir Walter......VIII, 451
  Black, William.........VIII, 395
  Blackmore, Richard D...VIII, 431
  Brontë, Emily............V, 527
  Brown, John.............VIII, 481
  Browning, Elizabeth Barrett..
    ....VI, 260
  Buchanan, Robert......VIII, 448
  Buckle, Henry Thomas....VI, 284
  Collins, William Wilkie...VII, 728
  Darwin, Charles Robert..VII, 434
  Disraeli, Benjamin....VII, 288
  Dobell, Sidney Thompson..VI, 766
  Eliot, George......VII, 185 195

Vol. and Page
Freeman, Edward Augustus
    ....VIII, 161
Froude, James Anthony.VIII, 259
Gardiner, Samuel Rawson..
    ....VIII, 466
Gaskell, Elizabeth Cleghorn..
    ....VI, 430
Green, John Richard.....VII, 509
Ingelow, Jean..........VIII, 378
Kinglake, Alexander William
    ....VIII, 54
Kingsley, Charles........VIII, 27
Lewes, George Henry....VII, 140
Morris, William........VIII, 333
Patmore, Coventry K. D....
    ....VIII, 342
Oliphant, Margaret O. W.....
    ....VIII, 369
Owen, Sir Richard.....VIII, 174
Reade, Charles..........VII, 531
Romanes, George John..VIII, 285
Rossetti, Christina Georgina
    ....VIII, 274
Rossetti, Gabriel Charles Dante
    ....VII, 449
Spencer. Herbert......VIII, 484
Stevenson, Robert Louis.VIII, 250
Stubbs, William........VIII, 452
Thackeray, William Makepeace
    ....VI, 304
Trollope, Anthony.......VII, 464
Tyndall, John..........VIII, 200
GRAHAM, WILLIAM,
  Byron, George Gordon Lord
    ....IV, 743
  Shelley, Percy Bysshe.....IV, 698
GRAMMONT, COUNT,
  Villiers, George............II, 375
GRANGE, JOHN,
  Skelton, John..............I, 220
GRANGER, JAMES,
  Ashmole, Elias............II, 436
  Aubrey, John.............II, 451
  Barrow, Isaac.............II, 311
  Baxter, Richard..........II, 424
  Beaumont, Joseph........II, 461
  Behn, Aphra..............II, 409
  Boyle, Robert............II, 417
  Bunyan, John.............II, 402
  Burton, Robert............II, 38
  Butler, Samuel............II, 331
  Cavendish, Margaret......II, 232
  Chillingworth, William....II, 87
  Cleveland, John...........II, 159
  Cotton, Charles...........II, 371
  Cowley, Abraham.........II, 195
  Cudworth, Ralph..........II, 386
  D'Avenant, Sir William....
    ....II, 217, 218
  Digby, Sir Kenelm........II, 182
  Drummond, William......II, 104
  Dryden, John.............VII, 496
  Evelyn, John..............II, 551
  Fanshawe, Sir Richard....II, 184
  Gauden, John.............II, 176
  Goldsmith, Oliver........III, 625
  Granger, James.........III, 670
  Hale, Sir Matthew........II, 306
  Hall, Joseph.............II, 144
  Harvey, William..........II, 155
  Harrington, James.......II, 308

Vol. and Page
Herbert, Edward Lord....
    ....II, 96, 97
Herrick, Robert...........II, 237
Heylin, Peter.............II, 175
Hobbes, Thomas..........II, 324
Howe, John...............II, 545
Howell, James............II, 188
Hyde, Edward, Earl of Clarendon ....II, 302
Jonson, Ben...............I, 761
Ken, Thomas.............II, 567
Leighton, Robert..........II, 358
L'Estrange, Sir Roger.....II, 538
Marvell, Andrew..........II, 316
Milton, John..............II, 259
Newton, Sir Isaac.........II, 719
Oldham, John............II, 350
Pearson, John............II, 369
Pepys, Samuel............II, 513
Philips, Katherine........II, 180
Purchas, Samuel...........I, 693
Quarles, Francis...........II, 77
Sanderson, Robert........II, 179
Selden, John..............II, 142
Shirley, James............II, 190
Speed, John ....I, 695
Spelman, Sir Henry.......II, 54
Spotiswood, John..........II, 24
Sprat, Thomas............II, 574
Suckling, Sir John.........II, 63
Taylor, Jeremy...........II, 205
Taylor, John..............II, 133
Waller, Edmund..........II, 380
Wither, George...........II, 213
Wilkins, John.............II, 227
Wotton, Sir Henry........II, 19
Wycherley, William......II, 604
GRANT, ALEXANDER H.,
  Keble, John..............VI, 462
GRANT, ANNE,
  Baillie, Joanna.............V, 692
  Brown, Thomas..........IV, 657
  Burke, Edmund..........IV, 291
  Burns, Robert............IV, 249
  Byron George Gordon Lord
    ....IV, 743
  Carter, Elizabeth........IV, 492
  Chalmers, Thomas........V, 490
  Coleridge, Samuel Taylor...V, 222
  Cowper, William.....IV, 375, 383
  DeQuincey, Thomas......VI, 123
  Edgeworth, Maria....V, 565, 565
  Ferrier, Susan Edmonstone.V, 764
  Godwin, Mary Wollstonecraft
    ....IV, 329
  Goldsmith, Oliver........III, 625
  Grahame, James.........IV, 567
  Hall, Basil................V, 456
  Hamilton, Sir William.....VI, 50
  Hamilton, Thomas.......IV, 394
  Hayley, William..........IV, 653
  Heber, Reginald..........V, 37
  Hemans, Felicia Dorothea....
    ....V, 254
  Irving, Edward..........IV, 246
  Jameson, Anna..........VI, 214
  Johnson, Samuel........III, 756
  Kemble, Frances Ann...VIII, 216
  Landon, Letitia Elizabeth..V, 326
  Macpherson, James......IV, 271
  Maturin, Charles Robert...IV, 766

INDEX TO CRITICISMS

	Vol. and Page
Morgan, Sydney Owenson Lady	VI, 194
Paley, William	IV, 475
Richardson, Samuel	III, 440
Scott, Sir Walter	V, 127, 156
Seward, Anna	IV, 543
Wolcot, John	IV, 649

GRANT, FREDERICK RICHARD CHARLES,
Johnson, Samuel	III, 740, 764

GRANT, JAMES,
Campbell, John Lord	VI, 257
Campbell, Thomas	V, 435
Cobbett, William	V, 270
Disraeli, Benjamin	VII, 281
Jeffrey, Francis Lord	V, 650
Macaulay, Thomas Babington Lord	VI, 97

GRANT, JOHN CAMERON,
Mandeville, Sir John	I, 98

GRANT, JOHNSON,
Horne, George	IV, 144

GRANT, ROBERT,
Halley, Edmund	III, 108

GRANT-DUFF, M. E.,
Stanhope, Philip Dormer	III, 606

GRANVILLE, GEORGE (LORD LANSDOWNE),
Pope, Alexander	III, 156, 164

GRANVILLE, HARIET COUNTESS,
Brougham, Henry Lord	VI, 523
Milman, Henry Hart	VI, 539
Smith, Sydney	V, 467

GRANVILLE, MARY (MRS. DELANY),
Mason, William	IV, 324

GRATTAN, HENRY,
Junius	IV, 639

GRATTAN, J. C.,
Adams, John Quincy	V, 515

GRATTAN, THOMAS COOLEY,
Prescott, William Hickling	VI, 181
Story, Joseph	V, 482
Wordsworth, William	V, 612

GRAVES, ALFRED PERCIVAL,
Tennyson, Alfred Lord	VIII, 75

GRAVES, RICHARD,
Shenstone, William	III, 472

GRAVES-SAWLE, ROSE C.,
Landor, Walter Savage	VI, 378

GRAY, ALEXANDER HILL,
Buckle, Henry Thomas	VI, 280

GRAY, ASA,
Agassiz, Louis Jean Rudolph	VI, 724
Bacon, Francis	I, 647
Darwin, Charles Robert	VII, 423, 429
Faraday, Michael	VI, 511
Lyell, Sir Charles	VII, 36, 37
Maxwell, James Clerk	VII, 170

GRAY, DAVID,
Gray, David	VI, 260, 260

GRAY, J. C.

Child, Lydia Maria | VII, 220 |

GRAY, J. M.,
Brown, John	VII, 479
Burns, Robert	IV, 235

	Vol. and Page
GRAY, THOMAS,	
Anstey, Christopher	IV, 479
Boswell, James	IV, 212
Cibber, Colley	III, 374
Colman, George	IV, 202
Cooper, Anthony Ashley	II, 577
Dryden, John	II, 464, 496, 496
Dyer, John	III, 399
Fielding, Henry	III, 346
Grey, Thomas	III, 557, 561
Green, Matthew	III, 95
Hall, Joseph	II, 144
Hurd, Richard	IV, 516
Jenyns, Soame	IV, 32
Johnson, Samuel	III, 738
Knowledge	V, 6
Lydgate, John	I, 183
Lyttelton, George Lord	III, 612
Mason, William	IV, 323
Middleton, Conyers	III, 279
Milton, John	II, 258, 285
Montagu, Lady Mary Wortley	III, 460, 464
Pope, Alexander	III, 146
Shakespeare, William	I, 552
Shenstone, William	III, 471, 472
Sidney, Sir Philip	I, 331
Smart, Christopher	III, 592
Southerne, Thomas	III, 239
Sterne, Laurence	III, 502, 506, 510
Tickell, Thomas	III, 106
Walpole, Horace	IV, 310

GOWER, JOHN,
Chaucer, Geoffrey	I, 124
Gower, John	I, 172

GOWING, EMILIA AYLMER,
Spurgeon, Charles Haddon	VIII, 179

GRAEVIUS, JOHN GEORGE,
Bentley, Richard	III, 120

GRAFTON, RICHARD,
Hall, Edward	I, 260
Stowe, John	I, 419

GRAHAM, GEORGE R.,
Poe, Edgar Allan	V, 537

GRAHAM, HENRY GREY,
Beattie, James	IV, 434
Blacklock, Thomas	IV, 29
Blair, Hugh	IV, 403, 406
Boswell, James	IV, 212
Burnett, James	IV, 347
Burns, Robert	IV, 236, 243
Dalrymple, Sir David	IV, 146, 147
Ferguson, Adam	IV, 610
Macknight, James	IV, 407
Warton, Joseph	IV, 397
West, Gilbert	III, 368

GREELEY, ADOLPHUS WASHINGTON,
Kane, Elisha Kent	VI, 81
Stanley, Sir Henry Morton	VIII, 508

GREELEY, HORACE,
Cary, Alice	VI, 639
Cary, Phœbe	VI, 641
Clay, Henry	V, 731
Cooper, James Fenimore	V, 681
Franklin, Benjamin	V, 88
Fuller, Sarah Margaret	V, 666
Greeley, Horace	VI, 666, 673

	Vol. and Page
Lincoln, Abraham	VI, 414
Poe, Edgar Allan	V, 538
Taylor, Bayard	VII, 134

GREEN, ALICE STOPFORD,
Green, John Richard	VII, 510

GREEN, HENRY,
Barclay, Alexander	I, 265

GREEN, J. B.,
Guthrie, Thomas	VI, 737

GREENE, JOHN RICHARD,
Addison, Joseph	II, 659
Alfred the Great	I, 40
Bacon, Francis	I, 652, 654
Bede	I, 30
Burke, Edmund	IV, 295
Butler, Samuel	II, 333
Bunyan, John	II, 395
Cartwright, Thomas	I, 417
Chaucer, Geoffrey	I, 145
Daniel, Samuel	I, 615
DeQuincey, Thomas	VI, 118
Dryden, John	II, 466
Gauden, John	II, 177
Green, John Richard	VII, 504
Greene, Robert	I, 341
Jonson, Ben	I, 765
Junius	IV, 646
More, Hannah	V, 195
Motley, John Lothrop	VII, 95
Pitt, William	III, 679
Pope, Alexanders	III, 191
Hobbes, Thomas	II, 326
Langland, William	I, 120
Lyly, John	I, 422
Map, Walter	I, 62
Paris, Matthew	I, 75
Saxon Chronicle	I, 58
Sedley, Sir Charles	II, 508
Shakespeare, William	I, 486
Sidney, Sir Philip	I, 323
Spenser, Edmund	I, 384
Smith, Adam	IV, 65
Stanley, Arthur Penrhyn	VII, 297
Steele, Sir Richard	II, 765
Thackeray, William Makepeace	VI, 293
Wesley, Charles	IV, 37
Wesley, John	IV, 115
William of Malmesbury	I, 54
Wycherley, William	II, 605

GREEN, S. G.,
Smart, Christopher	III, 593

GREEN, SAMUEL SWEET,
Bancroft, George	VIII, 56

GREEN, THOMAS,
Burke, Edmund	IV, 290
Gibbon, Edward	IV, 179
Gray, Thomas	III, 562
Hawkesworth, John	III, 609
Jenyns, Soame	IV, 33
Johnson, Samuel	III, 736, 753
Jortin, John	III, 552
Mackintosh, Sir James	V, 181
Mandeville, Bernard	III, 69
Milton, John	II, 254
Mitford, William	V, 70
Moore, John	IV, 426
Paley, William	IV, 473
Parr, Samuel	IV, 19
Piozzi, Hester, Lynch	IV, 685
Pope, Alexander	III, 179

INDEX TO CRITICISMS

	Vol. and Page
Richardson, Samuel	III, 438
Robertson, William	IV, 158
Temple, Sir William	II, 457
Tucker, Abram	III, 643
Wakefield, Gilbert	IV, 419
Walpole, Horace	IV, 316
Warton, Thomas	IV, 73
Watts, Isaac	III, 250
Young, Edward	III, 487

GREENBAUM, SAMUEL,
Lazarus, Emma ..... VII, 612

GREENE, GEORGE WASHINGTON,
Adams, Samuel	IV, 443
Bancroft, George	VIII, 55
Grote, George	VI, 608
Longfellow, Henry Wadsworth	VII, 399

GREENE, HERBERT EVELETH
Swift, Jonathan ..... III, 215

GREENE, JOHN,
Young, Edward ..... III, 488

GREENE, J. REAY,
Carlyle, Thomas ..... VII, 271

GREENE, ROBERT,
Bacon, Roger	I, 77
Chaucer, Geoffrey	I, 125
Lodge, Thomas	I, 625
Marlowe, Christopher	I, 348
Nashe, Thomas	I, 412
Peele, George	I, 364
Shakespeare, William	I, 447

GREENE, SAMUEL A.,
Franklin, Benjamin ..... IV, 98

GREENHILL, W. A.
Mozley, James Bowling .... VII, 150

GREENOUGH, HORATIO,
Allston, Washington ..... V, 421

GREENSLET, FERRIS,
Pater, Walter Horatio .... VII, 276, 280
Stephen, Sir Leslie ..... VIII, 511

GREENWELL, DORA,
Bacon, Francis ..... I, 654
Browning, Elizabeth Barrett ..... VI, 231
Bunyan, John ..... II, 400
Hawthorne, Nathaniel ..... VI, 364
Hunt, James Henry Leigh .... VI, 169
Stowe, Harriet E. B ..... VIII, 352

GREENWOOD, FREDERICK,
Disraeli, Benjamin ..... VII, 280

GREENWOOD, F. W. P.,
Dewey, Orville ..... VII, 497
Heber, Reginald ..... V, 39
Hillhouse, James Abraham ..... V, 363

GREENWOOD, GEORGE G.,
Huxley, Thomas Henry .... VIII, 325

GREENWOOD, P. W. B.,
Sedgwick, Catharine Maria .. VI, 507

GREG, WILLIAM RATHBONE,
Arnold, Matthew	VII, 632
Arnold, Thomas	V, 379
Carlyle, Thomas	VII, 254
Disraeli, Benjamin	VII, 288
Kingsley, Charles	VII, 25, 27, 30
Martineau, Harriet	VII, 59
Newman, Francis William	VIII, 371
Shelley, Percy Bysshe	IV, 694

GREGORY XI,
Wyclif, John ..... I, 99

	Vol. and Page
GREGORY, AUGUSTA,	
Kinglake, Alexander William	VIII, 49, 51
GREGORY, GEORGE,	
Chatterton, Thomas	III, 528
GREGORY, JAMES,	
Beattie, James	IV, 428
GREGORY, JOHN,	
Home, Henry	III, 712
GREGORY, JOHN WALTER,	
Tyndall, John	VIII, 198
GREGORY, OLINTHUS,	
Hall, Robert	V, 108
GREGORY, WARREN FENNO,	
Dryden, John	II, 488, 506
Goldsmith, Oliver	III, 631

GREGO, JOSEPH,
Dickens, Charles ..... VI, 563

GREGORY-FLESHER, HELEN E.,
Miller, Cincinnatus Hiner ..... VIII, 499

GREVILLE CHARLES C. F.,
Blessington, Countess of	V, 593
Bowring, Sir John	VI, 664
Brougham, Henry Lord	VI, 525
Buckle, Henry Thomas	VI, 279
Burke, Edmund	IV, 302
Croker, John Wilson	VI, 72
Fullerton, Georgiana Charlotte Lady	VII, 567
Lewis, Sir George Cornewall	VI, 335
Macaulay, Thomas Babington Lord	VI, 91, 106
Scott, Sir Walter	V, 127
Smith, Sydney	V, 468
Walpole, Horace	IV, 319
Whatley, Richard	VI, 324
Wordsworth, William	V, 608

GREVILLE, HENRY,
Byron, George Gordon Lord	IV, 738
Cobden, Richard	VI, 441
Disraeli, Benjamin	VII, 282
Gaskell, Elizabeth Cleghorn	VI, 428
Hallam, Henry	VI, 176
Kemble, Frances Ann	VIII, 214
Macaulay, Thomas Babington Lord	VI, 104, 106
Scott, Sir Walter	V, 128
Stowe, Harriet Beecher	VIII, 349, 356

GREY, CHARLES EDWARD,
Junius ..... IV, 640

GREY, ROWLAND,
Austen, Jane ..... IV, 615

GREVILLE, FULKE,
Sidney, Sir Philip ... I, 320, 322, 324

GRENVILLE, LORD,
Pitt, William ..... III, 680

GRIFFIN, GERALD,
Griffin, Gerald ..... V, 351

GRIFFIN, EDMUND DORR,
Chalmers, Thomas	V, 490
Lockhart, John Gibson	V, 753
Mackenzie, Henry	V, 113
Scott, Sir Walter	V, 128
Southey, Robert	V, 397

GRIFFIN, G. W.,
Beckford, William ..... V, 449
Prentice, George Dennison ... VI, 601

GRIFFIS, WILLIAM ELLIOT,
Lecky, William E. H. .. VIII, 488, 491

	Vol. and Page
GRIMM, HERMAN,	
Emerson, Ralph Waldo	VII, 350, 371
Newton, Sir Isaac	II, 725
Richardson, Samuel	III, 445
Shakespeare, William	I, 506
GRIMM, FRIEDRICH MELCHIOR,	
Macpherson, James	IV, 272
Walpole, Horace	IV, 316
Young, Edward	III, 487
GRISCOM, JOHN,	
Chalmers, Thomas	V, 490

GRISWOLD, HATTIE TYNG,
Bryant, William Cullen	VII, 113
Dickens, Charles	VI, 567
Fuller, Sarah Margaret	V, 670
Lowell, James Russell	VIII, 19
Poe, Edgar Allan	V, 543

GRISWOLD, RUFUS WILMOT,
Alford, Henry	VI, 636
Allston, Washington	V, 423
Baillie, Joanna	V, 693
Barlow, Joel	IV, 575
Barton, Bernard	V, 596
Bayly, Thomas Haynes	V, 340
Brainard, John Gardiner Calkins	V, 85
Brown, Charles Brockden	IV, 555
Brownson, Orestes Augustus	VII, 73
Bryant, William Cullen	VII, 120
Campbell, Thomas	V, 438, 443
Cary, Alice	VI, 638
Cary, Phœbe	VI, 641
Child, Lydia Maria	III, 221
Croly, George	VI, 225
Dana, Richard Henry	VII, 155
Dewey, Orville	VII, 498
Dwight, Timothy	IV, 626
Edwards, Jonathan	III, 390
Elliott Ebenezer	V, 581
Fields, James Thomas	VII, 341
Freneau, Philip	V, 186
Fuller, Sarah Margaret	V, 671
Halleck, Fitz-Greene	VI, 498
Hamilton, Alexander	IV, 466
Hawthorne, Nathaniel	VI, 352, 357, 364
Hillhouse, James Abraham	V, 364
Heber, Reginald	V, 39
Holmes, Oliver Wendell	VIII, 289
Hunt, James Henry Leigh	VI, 165
Keats, John	IV, 671
Kemble, Frances Ann	VIII, 215
Kennedy, John Pendleton	VI, 605
Lamb, Charles	V, 237
Landon, Letitia Elizabeth	V, 327
Landor, Walter Savage	VI, 387
Longfellow, Henry Wadsworth	VII, 402
Lowell, James Russell	VIII, 31
Lytton, Sir Edward George Bulwer	VI, 595
Marsh, George Perkins	VII, 494
Marshall, John	V, 285
Montgomery, James	V, 767
Motherwell, William	V, 77
Neal, John	VII, 77
Norton, Caroline E. S.	VII, 104
Osgood, Francis Sargent	V, 677, 678
Paulding, James Kirke	VI, 221

INDEX TO CRITICISMS

	Vol. and Page
Percival, James Gates	VI, 60
Pierpont, John	VI, 481
Pinkney, Edward Coate	V, 85
Poe, Edgar Allan	V, 535, 546
Pollok, Robert	V, 73
Prescott, William Hickling	VI, 186
Schoolcraft, Henry Rowe	VI, 403, 405
Sigourney, Lydia Huntley	VI, 452
Simms, William Gilmore	VI, 598
Smith, Horace	V, 598
Sotheby, William	V, 200
Southey, Caroline Anne Bowles	V, 762
Sprague, Charles	VII, 53
Sterling, John	V, 453
Taylor, Sir Henry	VII, 583
Tennyson, Alfred Lord	VIII, 100
Trumbull, John	V, 120
Tuckerman, Theodore Henry	VI, 642
Very, Jones	VII, 227
Ware, Henry, Jr	V, 433
Wayland, Francis	VI, 449
White, Henry Kirke	IV, 484
Whittier, John Greenleaf	VIII, 120
Wilde, Richard Henry	V, 503
Willis, Nathaniel Parker	VI, 489
Wilson, John	V, 750
GROOME, F. H.,	
FitzGerald, Edward	VII, 514
GROSART, ALEXANDER B.,	
Alexander, Sir William	II, 36
Anstey, Christopher	IV, 479
Audubon, John James	V, 699
Ayton, Sir Robert	I, 768
Baxter, Richard	II, 428
Beaumont, Francis	I, 588
Beaumont, Sir John	I, 680
Burns, Robert	IV, 269
Butler, Joseph	III, 307
Campbell, Thomas	V, 441
Clive, Caroline	VI, 740
Cowper, William	IV, 389
Crashaw, Richard	II, 112
Daniel, Samuel	I, 613
Davies, Sir John	I, 634
Dekker, Thomas	II, 56
Edwards, Jonathan	III, 391
Fergusson, Robert	III, 640, 642
Fletcher, Giles	I, 623
Fletcher, Phineas	II, 115, 117
Greene, Robert	I, 345
Harvey, Gabriel	I, 697
Herbert, George	I, 720, 724
Logan, John	IV 44
Marvell, Andrew	II, 317
Nashe, Thomas	I, 412, 414
Rutherford, Samuel	II, 167
Shakespeare, William	I, 461
Sidney, Sir Philip	I, 328
Southwell, Robert	I, 362
Spenser, Edmund	I, 398
Turner, Charles Tennyson	VII, 162
Vaughan, Henry	II, 441, 444
Wilson, Alexander	IV, 582
Wordsworth, William	V, 638
GROSE, FRANCIS,	
Oldys, William	III, 456
GROSER, HORACE G.,	
Coleridge, Samuel Taylor	V, 218

	Vol. and Page
Kingsley, Charles	VII, 28, 29
GROSER, WILLIAM H.,	
Clarke, Adam	V, 185
GROSS, S. D.,	
Hunter, John	IV, 167
GROTE, GEORGE,	
Mill, James	V, 305
Thirlwall, Connop	VII, 43
GROVE, SIR GEORGE,	
Carey, Henry	III, 138
Stanley, Arthur Penrhyn	VII, 299
GRUNDY, FRANCIS H.,	
Gaskell, Eizabeth Cleghorn	VI, 431
Hunt, James Henry Leigh	VI, 159
Lewes, George Henry	VII, 138
Martineau, James	VIII, 425
GRUTER, ISAAC,	
Bacon, Francis	I, 663
GUDEMAN, ALFRED,	
Dodwell, Henry	II, 565
Middleton, Conyers	III, 279
GUERNSEY, ALFRED H.,	
Beecher, Lyman	VI, 339
Carlyle, Thomas	VII, 233
Emerson, Ralph Waldo	VII, 355
Landor, Walter Savage	VI, 390
Wesley, John	IV, 127
GUEST, EDWIN,	
Aldhelm	I, 24
Alfred the Great	I, 39
Cædmon	I, 22
Chatterton, Thomas	III, 536
Chaucer, Geoffrey	I, 143, 159
Douglas, Gawin	I, 213
Langland, William	I, 118
Map, Walter	I, 61
Milton, John	II, 254, 271, 289
Nicholas of Guilford	I, 76
Ormin	I, 71
Prior, Matthew	II, 677
Robert of Gloucester	I, 82
Spenser, Edmund	I, 382
Surrey, Earl of	I, 256
Warton, Thomas	IV, 74
Wyntoun, Andrew	I, 178
GUICCOLI, COUNTESS,	
Byron, George Gordon Lord	IV, 745
GUILD, CURTIS,	
Sedgwick, Catharine Maria	VI, 508
Sumner, Charles	VI, 753
GUILPIN, EDWARD,	
Marston, John	I, 736
GUINEY, LOUISE,	
Farquhar, George	II, 559
Hazlitt, William	V, 100, 105
Herbert, George	I, 724
Hunt, James Henry Leigh	VI, 170
Keats, John	IV, 683
Johnson, Samuel	III, 735
Lovelace, Richard	II, 163
Palgrave, Francis Turner	VIII, 373
Parsons, Thomas William	VIII, 192, 193
Vanbrugh, Sir John	II, 708
Vaughan, Henry	II, 442, 445
Walton, Isaac	II, 349

	Vol. and Page
GUIZOT, FRANÇOIS PIERRE GUILLAUME,	
Alcuin	I, 32
Gibbon, Edward	IV, 182
Hamilton, Alexander	IV, 463
Jefferson, Thomas	V, 46
Laud, William	II, 90
Motley, John Lothrop	VII, 93
Prescott, William Hickling	VI, 188
Shakespeare, William	I, 454, 457, 462, 473, 477, 492, 494 503, 512, 531, 534, 540
Washington, George	IV, 360
GUMMERE, FRANCIS B.,	
Chaucer, Geoffrey	I, 146
GUNSAULUS, FRANK W.,	
Arnold, Sir Edwin	VIII, 505
Gray, David	VI, 260
GUNTON, GEORGE,	
George, Henry	VIII, 380
GURNEY, ARCHER,	
Eliot, George	VII, 180
GURNEY, HUDSON,	
Young, Thomas	V, 86, 87
GURNEY, J. HAMPDEN,	
Wyclif, John	I, 101
GURNEY, JOSEPH JOHN,	
Wilberforce, William	V, 201
GUTHRIE, DAVID K., AND CHARLES L.,	
Guthrie, Thomas	VI, 737
GUTHRIE, THOMAS,	
Brewster, Sir David	VI, 546
Miller, Hugh	VI, 63
GYUOT, ARNOLD,	
Agassiz, Louise Jean Rudolphe	VI, 720, 724
GWYNN, STEPHEN,	
Ferrier, Susan Edmondstone	V, 765
Stevenson, Robert Louis	VIII, 241

H

HABBERTON, JOHN,
Addison, Joseph......II, 659
Alcott, Louise May.....VII, 666
Steele, Sir Richard......II, 765
Washington, George......IV, 362
HABINGTON, WILLIAM,
Chapman, George..........I, 727
Habington, William......II, 134
Jonson, Ben...............I, 759
HACKET, JOHN,
Andrews, Lancelot......I, 635
Donne, John..............I, 711
Laud, William............II, 89
Milton, John............III, 282
HADDEN, J. CUTHBERT,
Browning, Robert.......VII, 685
Burns, Robert..........IV, 236
Campbell, Thomas.V, 439, 440, 446
Defoe, Daniel..........III, 40
Dibdin, Charles........IV, 586
Hogg, James.............V, 266
Wilson, John...........V, 752
HADLEY, ARTHUR TWINING,
Smith, Adam............IV, 69
Woolsey, Theodore Dwight..VII, 737
HADLEY, JAMES,
Tennyson, Alfred Lord.VIII, 83

INDEX TO CRITICISMS

HAECKEL, ERNST HEINRICH,
Darwin, Charles Robert..VII, 429
Huxley, Thomas Henry.VIII, 324
HAGENBACH, KARL RUDOLPH,
Young, Edward..........III. 489
HAGGARD, H. RIDER,
Defoe, Daniel............III, 37
Lytton, Sir Edward George
Bulwer ....VI, 693, 694
HAGUE, JAMES D.,
Darwin, Charles Robert..VII, 418
HAGUE, WILLIAM,
Garrison, William Lloyd..VII, 160
Emerson, Ralph Waldo..VII, 369
HAILES, LORD,
Thomas of Erceldoune......I, 83
HAKE, A. EGMONT,
Borrow, George Henry......
.... VII, 307, 313
HAKE, EDWARD,
Sackville, Thomas..........I, 432
HAKE, GORDON,
Coleridge, Samuel Taylor...V, 216
Milnes Richard Monckton..
.....................VII, 565
Poets and Poetry.........IV, 10
Rossetti, Gabriel Charles Dante
.... VII, 438, 446
Thackeray, William Makepeace ....VI, 297
Wordsworth, William......V, 645
HALDANE, R. B.,
Smith, Adam,............IV, 67
HALE, CHARLES,
Buckle, Henry Thomes....VI, 279
HALE, EDWARD EVERETT,
Arnold, Matthew........VII, 641
Austen, Jane............IV, 622
Aytoun, William Edmonstone
.... VI, 445
Bailey, Philip James....VIII, 462
Barbauld, Anna Lætitia ...V, 26
Brontë, Charlotte........VI, 25
Burns, Robert...........IV, 235
Carlyle, Thomas........VII, 270
Clarke, James Freeman....
.... VII, 672, 673
Colenso, John William...VII, 524
Defoe, Daniel............III, 39
Edgeworth, Maria........V, 570
Emerson, Ralph Waldo......
.... VII, 352, 374
Everett, Edward.....VI, 424, 426
Fuller, Sarah Margaret.....V, 670
Holmes, Oliver Wendell.VIII, 296
King, Thomas Star.......VI, 409
Longfellow, Henry Wadsworth
.... VII, 384
Lowell, James Russell......
.... VIII, 25, 41
Martineau, James.....VIII, 426
Mather, Cotton............II, 731
Mill, John Stuart.........VI, 712
Phillips, Wendell........VII, 554
Pope, Alexander.........III, 159
Ruskin, John...........VIII, 417
Scott, Sir Walter..........V, 137
Stanley, Arthur Penrhyn...
.... VII, 301
Sumner, Charles.........VI, 757
Tennyson, Alfred Lord..VIII, 105

HALE, EDWARD EVERETT, JR.,
Edwards, Jonathan.......III, 394
Franklin, Benjamin.......IV, 105
Herrick, Robert..........II, 241
Pater, Walter Horatio...VIII, 278
HALE, EDWARD EVERETT, AND HALE, EDWARD EVERETT, JR.,
Franklin, Benjamin.......IV, 90
HALE, HORATIO,
Tyndall, John..........VIII, 198
HALE, SARAH JOSEPHA,
Aguilar, Grace........V, 505, 505
Cary, Phœbe...........VI, 641
Carter, Elizabeth........IV, 492
Child, Lydia Maria......VII,222
Craik, Dinah Maria Mulock
.... VII, 625
Davidson, Lucretia Maria..V, 27
Gore, Catherine Grace.....VI, 264
Lamb, Mary Ann..........V, 507
Montagu, Lady Mary Wortley
.... III, 463
Osgood, Francis Sargent....V, 678
Rowe, Elizabeth.........III, 96
Williams, Helen Maria.....V, 74
HALE, SUSAN,
Lennox, Charlotte........IV, 470
Steele, Sir Richard........II, 758
HALES, JOHN OF ETON,
Shakespeare, William.......I, 549
HALES, JOHN W.,
Austen, Jane............IV, 620
Chaucer, Geoffrey..........
.... I, 128, 132, 139, 164
Davies, Sir John............I, 633
Defoe, Daniel ....III, 49
Dickens, Charles........VI, 586
Donne, John..............I, 717
Fletcher, Giles............I, 623
Gascoigne, George..........I, 308
Goldsmith, Oliver........III, 627
Gray, Thomas............III, 572
Hall, Joseph............II, 148
Jonson, Ben..............I, 765
Malory, Sir Thomas.... ....I, 205
Massinger, Philip..........II, 50
Mill, John Stuart.........VI, 717
Milton, John.............II, 275
Percy, Thomas...........IV, 564
Pope, Alexander.........III, 190
Scott, Sir Walter..........V, 143
Shakespeare, William.......I, 522
Southwell, Robert..........I, 361
Spenser, Edmund............
............I, 372, 387, 391
Trollope, Anthony......VII, 462
Wotton, Sir Henry.........II, 19
Wyatt, Sir Thomas........ , 252
HALIBURTON, HUGH,
Thomson, James,........III, 270
HALIFAX, CHARLES MONTAGU, EARL,
Burnet, Gilbert...........II, 590
Sackville, Charles.........II, 552
South, Robert...........II, 607
HALIFAX, SAMUEL,
Butler Joseph..........III, 313
HALL, CAPTAIN BASIL,
Barnard, Lady Anne.......V, 28
Lyell, Sir Charles........VII, 35

HALL, CHARLES E.,
Collins, Mortimer....VII, 81, 82
HALL, GRANVILLE STANLEY,
Locke, John..............II, 530
HALL, HUBERT,
Sidney Sir Philip..........I, 328
HALL, JOSEPH,
Hall, Joseph..............II, 143
Raleigh, Sir Walter.........I, 601
Skelton, John..............I, 220
Spenser, Edmund..........I, 392
Usher, James.............II,153
HALL, NEWMAN,
Beecher, Henry Ward....VII, 600
Spurgeon, Charles Haddon..
.... VIII, 179
HALL, RICHARD.
Fisher, John..............I, 230
HALL, BOBERT,
Blackstone, William......III, 704
Burke, Edmund..........IV, 299
Edwards, Jonathan.......III, 389
Foster, John.............V, 425
Henry, Matthew..........II, 584
Horsley, Samuel.........IV, 495
Hume, David............III, 661
Macknight, James........IV, 408
Paley, William..........IV, 473
Price, Richard..........IV, 136
Priestley, Joseph........IV, 451
Sterne, Laurence........III, 511
HALL, SAMUEL CARTER,
Aguilar, Grace...........V, 505
Ainsworth, William Harrison
.... VII, 486
Barton, Bernard..........V, 595
Bayly, Thomas Haynes....V, 340
Bentham, Jeremy....V, 164, 171
Blanchard, Samuel Laman..V, 481
Blessington, Countess of....V, 593
Bowles, William Lisle......V, 659
Bowring, Sir John........VI, 665
Burns, Robert...........IV, 232
Carleton, William........VI, 548
Cary, Henry Francis......V, 455
Clare, John.............VI, 397
Clarke, Adam............V, 185
Cobbett, William.........V, 272
Cooper, James Fennimore..V, 681
Croly, George...........VI, 224
Cunningham, Allan........V, 383
Dickens, Charles........VI, 557
Disraeli, Benjamin ......VII, 279
Edgeworth, Maria........V, 564
Elliott, Ebenezer........V, 580
Froude, James Anthony.VIII, 260
Godwin, William.........V, 295
Griffin, Gerald..........V, 352
Hall, Robert............V, 110
Hawthorne, Nathaniel......
............VI, 346, 360, 377
Hazlitt, William.........V, 100
Hemans, Felicia Dorothea..V, 256
Hone, William..........V, 392
Hood, Thomas...........V, 460
Hunt, James Henry Leigh.VI, 160
Irving, Edward..........V, 247
Irving, Washington......VI, 136
Jerrold, Douglas William..VI, 69
Knowles, James Sheridan..V, 286
Lamb, Charles............V, 235

INDEX TO CRITICISMS

	Vol. and Page
Landon, Letitia Elizabeth	V, 325
Longfellow, Henry Wadsworth	VII, 411
Lover, Samuel	VI, 544
Lytton, Sir Edward George Bulwer	VI, 682
Maccarthy, Denis Florence	VII, 489
Macaulay, Thomas, Babington Lord	VI, 98
Mackintosh, Sir James	V, 180
Maginn, William	V, 386
Mahoney, Francis	VI, 484
Martineau, Harriet	VII, 58
Mitford, Mary Russell	VI, 43
Montgomery, James	V, 766
Montgomery, Robert	VI, 47
Moore, Thomas	V, 709
More, Hannah	V, 192
Morgan, Sydney Owenson Lady	VI, 193
Norton, Caroline E. S.	VII, 103
Opie, Amelia	V, 742
Procter, Bryan Waller	VI, 746
Quarles, Francis	II, 78
Rogers, Samuel	VI, 36
Russell, John Earl	VII, 144
Sigourney, Lydia Huntley	VI, 451, 451
Southey, Robert	V, 401
Wilberforce, William	V, 202
Wordsworth, William	V, 615
HALL, MRS. SAMUEL CARTER,	
Edgeworth, Maria	V, 564
Marvell, Andrew	II, 317
HALLAM, ARTHUR HENRY,	
Tennyson, Alfred Lord	VIII, 77
HALLAM, HENRY,	
Alcuin,	I, 33
Andrews, Lancelot	I, 635
Ascham, Roger	I, 291
Bacon, Francis	I, 650, 659
Bacon, Roger	I, 79
Barclay, John	I, 618
Beaumont and Fletcher	I, 581
Beaumont, Sir John	I, 680
Barrow, Isaac	II, 312
Bede	I, 29
Bentley, Richard	III, 116, 122
Boyle, Robert	II, 418
Browne, Sir Thomas	341, 341, 343
Browne, William	II, 75
Buchanan, George	I, 316
Bull, George	II, 565
Bunyan, John	II, 394
Burnet, Gilbert	II, 592
Burton Robert	II, 39
Cartwright, Thomas	I, 416
Chapman, George	I, 732
Chatterton, Thomas	III, 536
Chaucer, Geoffrey	I, 143, 158
Chillingworth, William	II, 85
Coke, Sir Edward	I, 740
Congreve, William	II, 736, 737, 737, 739
Cowley, Abraham	II, 196, 200
Cudworth, Ralph	II, 386
Cumberland, Richard	II, 624
Daniel, Samuel	I, 614, 614
Davies, Sir John	I, 633
DeBury, Richard	I, 89
Denham, Sir John	II, 221
Dillon, Wentworth	II, 361
Donne, John	I, 712, 715
Douglas, Gawin	I, 213
Drayton, Michael	I, 702, 704
Dryden, John	II, 480, 482, 485, 487, 488, 490, 492, 500
Earle, John	II, 184
Evelyn, John	II, 551
Fairfax, Edward	I, 742
Feltham, Owen	II, 309
Fletcher, Andrew	II, 611
Fletcher, Giles	I, 623
Fletcher, John	I, 629, 630
Fletcher, Phineas	II, 116
Ford, John	II, 29 31
Garth, Sir Samuel	II, 665
Gascoigne, George	I, 308
Gauden, John	II, 177
Gower, John	I, 175
Gray, Thomas	III, 561
Greene, Robert	I, 341
Greville, Sir Fulke	I, 691
Habington, William	II, 135
Hall, Joseph	II, 145, 146, 147
Hallam, Arthur Henry	V, 197
Harrington, James	II, 308
Hartley, David	III, 378
Harvey, William	II, 156
Hawes, Stephen	I, 217
Herbert, Edward Lord	II, 97, 99
Henry, Robert	IV, 108
Herrick, Robert	II, 237
Herschel, Sir John Frederick William	VI, 624
Heywood, Thomas	II, 123, 124, 126
Hooker, Richard	I, 406
Howell, James	II, 186
Hurd, Richard	IV, 519
Hyde, Edward, Earl of Clarendon	II, 303
Jameson, Anna	VI, 214
Jewell, John	I, 294
John of Salisbury	I, 60
Johnson, Samuel	III, 746
Johnston, Arthur	II, 54
Jonson, Ben	I, 751
Lanfranc	I 48
Latimer, Hugh	I, 269
Layamon	I, 65
Lee, Nathaniel	II, 432
Leslie, Charles	II, 680
L'Estrange, Sir Roger	II, 538
Locke, John	II, 526, 529, 531
Lockhart, John Gibson	V, 756
Lodge, Thomas	I, 626
Lovelace, Richard	II, 162
Lydgate, John	I, 185
Lyndsay, Sir David	I, 274
Macaulay, Catherine	IV, 134
Marlowe, Christopher	I, 349, 351, 352
Marston, John	I, 737
Marvel, Andrew	II, 318
Massinger, Philip	II, 42, 43, 43, 48
May, Thomas	II, 119, 120
Mickle, William Julius	IV, 42
Middleton, Thomas	I, 684
Milton, John	II, 261, 269, 274, 281
Montagu, Elizabeth	IV, 402
Moore, Thomas	V, 714
More, Henry	II, 374
More, Sir Thomas	I, 235, 237
Malone, Edmond	IV, 578
Napier, Sir John	I, 589
Neal, Daniel	III, 140
Norris, John	II, 570
Occleve, Thomas	I, 187
Oldham, John	II, 350
Otway, Thomas	II, 364, 365
Paley, William	IV, 472
Palgrave, Sir Francis	VI, 265
Peacock, Reginald	I, 189
Pearson, John	II, 369
Peele, George	I, 366
Percy, Thomas	IV, 564
Pomfret, John	II, 511
Pope, Alexander	III, 166, 179
Prynne, William	II, 225
Purchas, Samuel	I, 693
Puttenham, George	I, 401
Raleigh, Sir Walter	I, 603, 606
Ray, John	II, 543
Reid, Thomas	IV, 285
Robertson, William	IV, 159
Rogers, Samuel	VI, 38
Rowley, William	II, 68
Saint-John, Henry	III, 294
Sackville, Thomas	I, 432
Sanderson, Robert	II, 179
Savile, Sir Henry	I, 620
Selden, John	II, 140, 141
Shakespeare, William	I, 450, 458, 462, 465, 468, 471, 474, 485, 492, 497, 508, 532, 541
Sheffield, John, Third Earl of Mulgrave	II, 671
Shirley, James	II, 191
Sidney, Algernon	II, 354
Sidney, Sir Philip	I, 327, 329
Skelton, John	I, 221
South, Robert	II, 607
Southerne, Thomas	III, 240
Southwell, Robert	I, 361
Spenser, Edmund	I, 376, 382, 389, 391
Steele, Sir Richard	II, 753, 760
Stewart, Dugald	V, 78
Still, John	I, 430
Stillingfleet, Edward	II, 454
Strype, John	II, 93
Suckling, Sir John	II, 65
Swift, Jonathan	III, 214
Taylor, Brook	III, 52
Taylor, Jeremy	II, 204, 205
Temple, Sir William	II, 458
Tennyson, Alfred Lord	VIII, 86
Theobald, Lewis	III, 142
Ticknor, George	VI, 616
Tillotson, John Robert	II, 439
Usher, James	II, 154
Vanbrugh, Sir John	II, 703, 704
Waller, Edmund	II, 381
Warburton, William	III, 687
Warton, Thomas	IV, 74
Warner, William	I, 437
Webster, John	I, 675
Whiston, William	III, 305
Wilkins, John	II, 227
Wilson, John	V, 751

604 INDEX TO CRITICISMS

Vol. and Page
Wilson, Sir Thomas..........I, 313
Wither, George............II, 214
Wotton, William...........II, 710
HALLECK, FITZ-GREENE,
  Bryant, William Cullen....VII, 119
  Burns, Robert.............IV, 252
  Campbell, Thomas..........V, 442
  Cooper, James Fenimore........V, 685
  Dickens, Charles........VI, 552, 580
  Drake, Joseph Rodman......
  ....IV, 659 659, 660
  Halleck, Fitz-Greene........VI, 496
  Hillhouse, James Abraham....V, 363
HALLECK, REUBEN POST,
  Bacon, Francis..............I, 669
  Bunyan, John..............II, 405
  Donne, John................I, 719
  Johnson, Samuel...........III, 768
  Literature.................I, 10
  Pope, Alexander...........III, 163
  Poor, Richard...............I, 70
  Steele, Sir Richard.........II, 768
  Walton, Isaac..............II, 347
HALLIWELL-PHILLIPS, JAMES
    ORCHARD,
  Mandeville, Sir John........I, 95
  Shakespeare, William...I, 461, 465
HALPINE, C. D.,
  Tennyson, Alfred Lord.....VIII, 91
HALPINE, C. G.,
  Spenser, Edmund............I, 371
HALSEY, FRANCIS WHITING,
  Alcott, Louisa May........VII, 667
  Carlyle, Thomas..........VII, 260
  Gibbon, Edward............IV, 194
  Holmes, Oliver Wendell...VIII, 300
  Lowell, James Russell......VIII, 42
  Müller, Friedrich Max......VIII, 440
  Oliphant, Margaret O. W..VIII, 367
  Palgrave, Francis Turner..VIII, 374
  Parkman, Francis........VIII, 225
  Sparks, Jared..............VI, 479
  Stanley, Sir Henry Morton....
  ....VIII, 509
  Willis, Nathaniel Parker.....VI, 493
HALSTEAD, GEORGE BRUCE,
  DeMorgan, Augustus........VI, 634
HALSTED, MURAT,
  Greeley, Horace...........VI, 670
  Prentice, George Denison ...VI, 604
HAMERIK, ASGER,
  Lanier, Sidney............VII, 326
HAMERTON, PHILIP GILBERT,
  Byron, George Gordon Lord.IV, 763
  Carlyle, Thomas..........VII, 270
  Dickens, Charles...........VI, 589
  Eliot, George............VII, 205
  Emerson, Ralph Waldo....VII, 372
  Hamerton, Philip Gilbert.VIII, 281
  Huxley, Thomas Henry....VIII, 325
  Mill, John Stuart..........VI, 194
  Ruskin, John............VIII, 417
  Scott, Sir Walter..........V, 159
  Shakespeare, William.......I, 571
  Shelley, Percy Bysshe......IV, 712
  Stevenson, Robert Louis......
  ....VIII, 246
  Tennyson, Alfred Lord...VIII, 105
  Thackeray, William Makepeace
  ....VI, 317
  Wordsworth, William......V, 643

Vol. and Page
HAMERTON, MRS. PHILIP GIL-
    BERT,
  Craik, Dinah Maria Mulock
  ....VII, 624
  Hamerton, Philip Gilbert.VIII, 281
HAMILTON, ALEXANDER,
  Hamilton, Alexander........IV, 456
  Washington, George........IV, 366
HAMILTON, ARCHIBALD,
  Knox, John..................I, 295
HAMILTON, CATHARINE J.,
  Austen, Jane...............IV, 613
  Baillie, Joanna.............V, 691
  Edgeworth, Maria...........V, 571
  Inchbald, Elizabeth........IV, 688
  More, Hannah........V, 193, 195
  Morgan, Sydney Owenson Lady.
  ....VI, 193
  Radcliffe, Ann Ward........IV, 720
HAMILTON, MISS E.,
  Hamilton, Sir William.......VI, 52
HAMILTON, SIR EDWARD, W.,
  Gladstone, William Ewart......
  ....VIII, 387
HAMILTON, J.,
  Doddridge, Philip.........III, 300
HAMILTON, JAMES,
  Owen, John................II, 352
HAMILTON, J. A.,
  Erskine, Thomas...........IV, 729
  James, George Paine Rains-
    ford...................VI, 219
  Jerrold, Douglas William....VI, 70
  Morgan, Sydney Owenson
    Lady..................VI, 195
HAMILTON, R. W.,
  Prescott, William Hickling..VI, 184
HAMILTON, THOMAS,
  Macleod, Norman...........VI, 662
HAMILTON, WALTER,
  Cibber, Colley............III, 375
  Dryden, John..............II, 467
  Pye, Henry James...........VI, 580
  Rossetti, Gabriel Charles Dante
  ....VI, 435
  Rowe, Nicholas........II, 620, 623
  Shadwell, Thomas..........II, 435
  Skelton, John..............II, 222
  Southey, Robert.......V, 410, 411
  Tate, Nahum...............II, 589
  Tennyson, Alfred Lord.....VIII, 99
  Whitehead, William....IV, 22, 23
HAMILTON, WILLIAM,
  Ramsay, Allan.............III, 409
HAMILTON, SIR WILLIAM,
  Faraday, Michael..........VI, 511
  Harris, James............III, 709
  Hume, David..............III, 661
  Locke, John...............II, 534
  Parr, Samuel................V, 21
  Reid, Thomas..............IV, 284
  Wallis, John...............II, 517
  Watts, Isaac..............III, 250
HAMILTON, SIR WILLIAM
    ROWAN,
  Airy, Sir George Biddell...VIII, 182
  Berkeley, George..........III, 331
  Brewster, Sir David........VI, 546
  Burns, Robert.............IV, 230
HAMMOND, WILLIAM G.
  Blackstone, William.......III, 705

Vol. and Page
HAMPSON, JOHN,
  Wesley, John.........IV, 112, 119
HANCOCK, ALBERT ELMER,
  Byron, George Gordon Lord.IV, 755
  Shelley, Percy Bysshe,......IV, 717
HANMER, SIR THOMAS,
  Shakespeare, William........I, 500
HANNA, WILLIAM,
  Chalmers, Thomas..........V, 491
HANNAH, JOHN,
  Raleigh, Sir Walter.....I, 600, 604
HANNAY, DAVID,
  Akenside, Mark...........III, 542
  Daniel, Samuel.............I, 617
  Donne, John................I, 719
  Lyly, John.................I, 427
  Marlowe, Christopher.......I, 358
  Marston, John..............I, 739
  Napier, Sir Wm. Francis Pat-
    rick...................VI, 223
  Nashe, Thomas..............I, 415
  Rossetti, Gabriel Charles Dante,
  ....VII, 442
  Smollett, Tobias George......
  ....III, 580, 586, 590
  Spenser, Edmund............I, 377
  Udall, Nicholas............I, 279
  Warner, William...........I, 438
HANNAY, JAMES,
  Aytoun, William Edmondstoune
  ....VI, 445
  Boswell, James............IV, 216
  Buchanan, George...........I, 317
  Burns, Robert.............IV, 256
  Butler, Samuel............II, 332
  Churchill, Charles......III, 477, 480
  Dryden, John..............II, 489
  Gifford, William............V, 35
  Jerrold, Douglas William...VI, 69
  Lyndsay, Sir David.........I, 274
  Mahoney, Francis......VI, 483, 484
  Marryat, Frederick........V, 533
  Marvell, Andrew...........II, 317
  Peacock, Thomas Love......VI, 475
  Poe, Edgar Allan...........V, 537
  Pope, Alexander......III, 149, 188
  Selden, John...............II, 141
  Skelton, John..............I, 221
  Swift, Jonathan...........III, 233
  Thackeray, William Makepeace
  ....VI, 293
  Tupper, Martin Farquhar...VII, 732
  Wilkes, John..............IV, 334
HANNIGAN, D. F.,
  Arnold, Matthew..........VII, 646
  Milnes, Richard Monckton.VII, 562
  Morris, William..........VIII, 337
  Scott, Sir Walter......V, 146, 152
HARBERT, SIR WILLIAM,
  Sidney, Sir Philip..........I, 321
  Spenser, Edmund............I, 393
HARCOURT, LADY,
  Motley, John Lothrop......VII, 87
HARDCASTLE, MARY SCARLETT,
  Campbell, John Lord......VI, 258
HARDING, EDWARD J.,
  Arnold, Matthew..........VII, 637
  Chatterton, Thomas........III, 539
HARDWICKE, HENRY,
  Ames, Fisher..............IV, 528
  Erskine, Thomas...........IV, 730

INDEX TO CRITICISMS

	Vol. and Page
Everett, Edward	VI, 425
Henry, Patrick	IV, 352
Otis, James	III, 717
Saint-John, Henry	III, 290
HARDWICKE, LORD,	
Somers, John Lord	II, 614
HARDY, ARTHUR SHERBURNE,	
Critic, The	II, 9
Hawthorne, Nathaniel	VI, 361
HARDY, FRANCIS,	
Hume, David	III, 649
HARDY, THOMAS,	
Barnes, William	VII, 585, 587
HARDY, THOMAS DUFFUS,	
Rymer, Thomas	II, 582
HARE, AUGUSTUS J. C.,	
Alford, Henry	VI, 636
Dickens, Charles	VI, 565
Edgeworth, Maria	V, 564, 565, 566
Hare, Julius Charles	VI, 49
Hunt, James Henry Leigh	VI, 162
Morgan, Sydney Lady Owenson	VI, 194
Saint-John, Henry	III, 288
Stanley, Arthur Penrhyn	VII, 300, 302
Thirlwall, Connop	VII, 43
HARE, A. W.,	
South, Robert	II, 608
HARE, A. W. AND J. C.,	
Drama, The	VII, 6
Knowledge	V, 7
Milton, John	II, 288
Shakespeare William	I, 478
HARE, JULIUS CHARLES,	
Coleridge, Samuel Taylor	V, 223
Sterling, John	V, 451
HARINGTON, H.,	
Carey, Henry	III, 137
HARNED, THOMAS B.,	
Whitman, Walt	VIII, 133
HARNESS, WILLIAM,	
Byron, George Gordon Lord	VI, 740
HARPER, GEORGE McLEAN,	
Burns, Robert	IV, 242
HARPER, JANET,	
Austen, Jane	IV, 625
Rossetti, Gabriel Charles Dante	VII, 455
HARPSFIELD, NICHOLAS,	
More, Sir Thomas	I, 234
HARRINGTON, H. F.,	
Poe, Edgar Allan	V, 543
HARRINGTON, SIR JOHN,	
Heywood, John	I, 305
Puttenham, George	I, 401
Raleigh, Sir Walter	I, 591
Sidney, Sir Philip	I, 330
Still, John	I, 429
HARRIS, C. ALEXANDER,	
Sewall, Samuel	III, 17
HARRIS, GEORGE,	
Bushnell, Horace	VII, 72
HARRIS, JAMES,	
Fielding, Henry	III, 344
Johnson, Samuel	III, 743
HARRIS, JOHN,	
Hakluyt, Richard	I, 446
HARRIS, WILLIAM TORREY,	
Alcott, Amos Bronson	VII, 604

	Vol. and Page
Carlyle, Thomas	VII, 270
Dickens, Charles	VI, 595
Emerson, Ralph Waldo	VII, 368
George, Henry	VIII, 380
Franklin, Benjamin	IV, 90
Mann, Horace	VI, 201
HARRISON, CONSTANCE CARY,	
Kemble, Frances Ann	VIII, 217
HARRISON, FREDERIC,	
Alfred the Great	I, 38
Arnold, Matthew	VII, 640
Books	III, 9
Bright, John	VII, 721
Brontë, Charlotte	VI, 26, 30
Brontë, Emily	V, 526
Browning, Robert	VII, 683
Carlyle, Thomas	VII, 238, 244, 248, 249, 253, 257, 269
Cowper, William	IV, 392
Darwin, Charles Robert	VII, 422
Defoe, Daniel	III, 36
Dickens, Charles	VI, 563, 587
Disraeli, Benjamin	VII, 290, 295
Eliot, George	VII, 177, 184, 186, 188, 190, 196, 198, 204
Fielding, Henry	III, 361
FitzGerald, Edward	VII, 516
Freeman, Edward Augustus	VIII, 161
Froude, James Anthony	VIII, 261, 267
Gibbon, Edward	IV, 176, 189, 194
Gladstone, William Ewart	VIII, 385
Gray, Thomas	III, 560
Grote, George	VI, 613
Hallam, Henry	VI, 175
Hawthorne, Nathaniel	VI, 357
History	VI, 10
Hume, David	III, 660
Huxley, Thomas Henry	VIII, 323
Keats, John	IV, 683
Kingsley, Charles	VII, 24, 29
Lamb, Charles	V, 241
Lewes, George Henry	VII, 141
Lytton, Sir Edward George Bulwer	VII, 699
Macaulay, Sir Thomas Babington Lord	VI, 96, 114
Malory, Sir Thomas	I, 204
Hill, John Stuart	VI, 707, 711
Milman, Henry Hart	VI, 538
Milton, John	II, 266
Priestley, Joseph	IV, 455
Ruskin, John	VIII, 409, 412, 413, 414
Scott, Sir Walter	V, 159
Shakespeare, William	I, 569
Shelley, Percy Bysshe	IV, 702
Sheridan, Richard Brinsley	IV, 604
Smith, Adam	IV, 70
Spencer, Herbert	VIII, 479
Stephen, Sir Leslie	VIII, 510
Symonds, John Addington	VIII, 206
Tennyson, Alfred Lord	VIII, 94
Thackeray, William Makepeace	VI, 320
Trollope, Anthony	VII, 458, 463
HARRISON, GABRIEL,	
Payne, John Howard	V, 736

	Vol. and Page
HARRISON, JAMES ALBERT,	
Beowulf	I, 19
Byron, George Gordon Lord	IV, 755
Longfellow, Henry Wadsworth	VII, 409
HARRISON, J. O.,	
Clay, Henry	V, 731
HARRISON, WILLIAM,	
Chaucer, Geoffrey	I, 156
Heywood, John	I, 305
HARROP. ROBERT,	
Saint-John, Henry	III, 289, 291
Swift, Jonathan	III, 216
HARSHA, D. A.,	
Doddridge, Philip	III, 300
HART, ALBERT BUSHNELL,	
Fiske, John	VIII, 456, 458
Madison, James	V, 315
Seward, William Henry	VI, 676
Woolman, John	III, 597
HART, CHARLES HENRY,	
Franklin, Benjamin	IV, 90
HART, JOHN S.,	
Adams, Hannah	V, 125
Ames, Fisher	IV, 529
Audubon, John James	V, 698
Baker, Sir Richard	II, 94
Beecher, Lyman	VI, 341
Beaumont and Fletcher	I, 583
Benton, Thomas Hart	VI, 8
Brewster, Sir David	VI, 547
Byrom, John	III, 470
Cavendish, George	I, 282
Challoner, Richard	III, 710
Croly, George	VI, 225
Dibdin, Thomas Frognall	V, 506
Dodd, William	III, 675
Dodsley, Robert	III, 482
Faraday, Michael	VI, 511
Gilfillan, George	VII, 152
Hale, Sir Matthew	II, 305
Harrington, James	I, 307
Herbert, George	I, 723
Heylin, Peter	II, 174
Hillhouse, James Abraham	V, 365
Holland, Josiah Gilbert	VII, 335
Hone, William	V, 391
Kane, Elisha Kent	VI, 83
Kent, James	V, 503
Leland, John	III, 500
Lever, Charles James	VI, 653
Livingstone, David	VI, 730
Macaulay, Catherine	IV, 133
Macknight, James	IV, 408
Marsh, George Perkins	VII, 494
Merivale, Charles	VIII, 218
Otis, James	III, 716
Owen. John	II, 353
Poor, Richard	I, 69
Porter, Jane	V, 673
Raleigh, Sir Walter	I, 604
Read, Thomas Buchanan	VI, 677
Saxe, John Godfrey	VII, 617
Schoolcraft, Henry Rowe	VII, 403
Silliman, Benjamin	VI, 406
Somers, John Lord	II, 612
Sparks, Jared	VI, 478
Stanhope, Philip Henry Earl	VII, 46, 47
Story, Joseph	V, 435

INDEX TO CRITICISMS

	Vol. and Page		Vol. and Page		Vol and Page
Strickland, Agnes	VI, 768	HATTON, JOSEPH,		Hawthorne, Nathaniel	VI, 347
Taylor, Thomas	V, 291	Black, William	VIII, 393	Lytton, Sir Edward George	
Thomson, James	III, 270	Reade, Charles	VII, 533	Bulwer	VI, 686, 693, 694 699
Usher, James	II, 154	HAVEN, S. F.,		Roe, Edward Payson	VII. 674
Wakefield, Gilbert	IV, 417	Mather, Cotton	II, 727	Trollope Anthony	VII 457
Warren, Samuel	VII, 107	HAVERS, G.,		HAWTHORNE. JULIAN, AND	
Whiston, William	III, 305	Bacon, Francis	I. 657	LEMMON, LEONARD.	
Wilkison, Sir John Gardner		HAWEIS, HUGH REGINALD.		Adams, John	V. 54
	VII, 52	Beecher, Henry Ward	VII 600	Alcott. Amos Bronson	VII, 664
Wilson, Alexander	IV, 584	Bunyan, John	II, 399	Allston, Washington	V. 423
Wiseman, Nicholas Patrick		Green, John Richard	VII, 506	Ames, Fisher	IV. 528
	VI, 438	Holmes, Oliver Wendell	VIII, 291	Audubon, John James	V, 109
Winthrop John	II, 109	Irving, Washington	VI. 150	Brown, Charles Brockden	IV, 553
Winthrop, Theodore	V, 266	Longfellow, Henry Wadsworth		Browne, Charles Farrier	VI, 504
Young, Thomas	V, 88		VII, 405	Cooper, James Fenimore	V, 687
HART, JOSEPH C.,		Lowell, James Russell	VIII, 37	Dana, Richard Henry	VII, 157
Shakespeare, William	I, 543	Maurice, John Frederick Denison		Dana, Richard Henry, Jr.	VII, 501
HARTE, WALTER,			VI, 646, 649	Everett, Edward	VI, 427
Chaucer, Geoffrey	, 156	Spurgeon, Charles Haddon		Franklin, Benjamin	IV, 104
HARTE, FRANCIS BRET,			VIII, 178	Freneau, Philip	V, 188
Dickens, Charles	VI, 566	Tennyson, Alfred Lord	VIII, 77	Fuller, Sarah Margaret	V, 672
King, Thomas Starr	VI, 408	Whitman, Walt	VIII, 142	Hamilton, Alexander	IV, 465
Lowell, James Russell		HAWES, DR. WILLIAM,		Harte, Francis Bret	VIII, 471
	VIII, 29, 38	Goldsmith, Oliver	III, 615	Henry, Patrick	IV, 352
HARTLEY, DAVID,		HAWES, SIDAY,		Irving, Washington	VI. 151
Hartley, David	III, 377, 377	Porson, Richard	IV, 525	Jackson, Helen Hunt	VII, 573, 576
HARTOG, P. J.,		HAWES, STEPHEN,		Jay, John	V, 97
Priestley, Joseph	IV, 451	Chaucer, Geoffrey	I, 141	Jefferson, Thomas	V, 49
HARVEY, GABRIEL,		Gower, John	I, 174	Lazarus, Emma	VII, 613
Cartwright, Thomas	I, 416	Hawes, Stephen	I, 216	Lincoln, Abraham	VI, 420
Chaucer, Geoffrey	I, 141, 154	Lydgate, John	I, 183	Madison, James	V, 315
Cheke, Sir John	I, 277	HAWKINS, ANTHONY HOPE,		Mather, Increase	II, 690
Greene, Robert	I, 339	Austen, Jane	IV, 617	Otis, James	III, 718
Sidney, Sir Philip	I, 324	Byron, George Gordon Lord	IV, 753	Paine, Thomas	IV, 538
Skelton, John	I, 220	Sterne, Laurence	III, 510	Paulding, James Kirke	VI. 228
HARVEY, PETER,		Stevenson, Robert Louis	VIII, 250	Sewall, Samuel	III, 18
Webster, Daniel	V, 722	HAWKINS, F. W.,		Simms, William Gilmore	VI, 600
HARVEY, WILLIAM,		Payne, John Howard	V, 736	Stoddard, Richard Henry	VIII, 497
Harvey, William	II, 156	HAWKINS, SIR JOHN		Ticknor, George	VI, 617
HARWOOD, EDWARD,		Addison, Joseph	II, 643	Very, Jones	VII, 228
Warton, Thomas	IV, 76	Akenside, Mark	III, 540	Warner, Charles Dudley	VIII. 444
HASELWOOD, JOSEPH,		Birch, Thomas	III, 499	Whipple, Edwin Percy	VII. 597
Puttenham, George	I, 401	Carey, Henry	III, 137, 139	White, Richard Grant	VII. 579
HASKINS, DAVID GREENE,		D'Urfey, Thomas	II, 687	Winthrop. Theodore	VI, 267
Emerson, Ralph Waldo	VII, 351	Fielding, Henry	III, 351	HAWTHORNE, NATHANIEL,	
HASSALL, ARTHUR,		Gay, John	III, 56	Bacon, Delia	VI, 203, 204
Saint-John, Henry	III, 297	Goldsmith, Oliver	III, 615	Bailey, Philip James	VIII. 459
HASSARD, JNO. R. G.,		Hawkesworth, John	III, 608	Books	III. 8
Brontë, Charlotte	VI, 29	Hill, John	III, 645	Bowring, Sir John	VI, 664
Disraeli, Benjamin	VII, 290	Johnson, Samuel	III, 725, 745	Browning, Elizabeth Barrett	
Fiske, John	VIII, 456	Lennox, Charlotte	IV, 469		VI, 230, 230
Thackeray, William Makepeace		Mandeville, Bernard	III, 69	Browning, Robert	VII, 678
	VI, 315	Philips, Ambrose	III, 273	Burns, Robert	IV, 230
HASWELL, CHARLES H.,		Richardson, Samuel	III, 432, 447	Bryant, William Cullen	VII, 110
Cooper. James Fenimore	V, 687	Savage, Richard	III, 133	Carlyle, Thomas	VII, 232
Dickens, Charles	VI, 559	Stanhope, Philip Dormer	III, 600	Dickens, Charles	VI, 552
Trollope, Frances Milton	VI, 330	HAWKINS, LETITIA MATILDA,		Disraeli. Benjamin	VII, 277
HATFIELD, EDWIN F.,		Walpole, Horace	IV, 311	Eliot. George	VII, 171
Bowring, Sir John	VI, 665	Johnson, Samuel	III, 728	Eliot, John	II, 412
Cowper, William	IV, 377	HAWKINS, THOMAS,		Franklin, Benjamin	IV, 96
Doddridge, Philip	III, 303	Peele, George	I, 365	Fuller, Sarah Margaret	V, 667
Lyte, Henry Francis	V, 499	HAWKS, FRANCIS L.,		Hawthorne. Nathaniel	
Toplady, Augustus Montague		Coke, Sir Edward	I, 741		VI, 341, 351, 353, 356, 359
	III, 681	Hume, David	III, 658	Helps, Sir Arthur	VII, 39
Wesley, John	IV, 128	HAWTHORNE, ELIZABETH,		Hunt, James Henry Leigh	VI, 158
Williams, Helen Maria	V, 75	Hawthorne, Nathaniel	VI, 344	Jameson, Anna	VI, 213
HATFIELD, JAMES TAFT,		HAWTHORNE, JULIAN,		Jerrold, Douglas William	VI, 96
Whitney, William Dwight		Borrow, George Henry	VII, 313	Johnson, Samuel	III, 732
	VIII, 303, 303	Defoe, Daniel	III, 37	Longfellow, Henry Wadsworth	
HATTON, CHARLES,		Emerson, Ralph Waldo			VII, 389, 401
Hobbes, Thomas	II, 321		VII, 347, 356, 369	Lover, Samuel	VI, 543

INDEX TO CRITICISMS

	Vol. and Page
Macaulay, Thomas Babington Lord	VI, 93
Martineau, Harriet	VII, 56
Mather, Cotton	II, 728
Melville Herman	VIII, 62
Mitford, Mary Russell	VI, 42
Patmore, Coventry K. D.	VIII, 339, 341
Procter, Bryan Waller	VI, 745
Reade, Charles	VII, 527
Reynolds, Sir Joshua	IV, 141
Russell, John Earl	VII, 143
Scott, Sir Walter	V, 131
Southey, Robert	V, 416
Taylor, Tom	VII, 213
Tennyson, Alfred Lord	VIII, 67
Thackeray, William Makepeace	VI, 291
Ticknor, George	VI, 614
Warren, Samuel	VII, 107
Washington, George	IV, 360
HAWTHORNE, SOPHIA A., Hawthorne, Nathaniel.	VI, 343, 356
HAY, JOHN, FitzGerald, Edward	VII, 518
Lazarus, Emma	VII, 611
HAY, T. W. LITTLETON, Collins, Mortimer	VII, 82
HAYDON, BENJAMIN ROBERT, Burke, Edmund	IV, 291
Byron, George Gordon Lord	IV, 756
Hazlitt, William	V, 101
Hunt, James Henry Leigh	VI, 155
Jeffrey, Francis Lord	V, 649
Keats, John	IV, 663
Lamb, Charles	V, 231
Moore, Thomas	V, 716
Procter, Bryan Waller	VI, 747
Reynolds, Sir Joshua	IV, 140
Richardson, Samuel	III, 439
Sheridan, Richard Brinsley	IV, 595
Wordsworth, William	V, 629
HAYES, RUTHERFORD B., Lowell, James Russell	VIII, 18
HAYLEY, WILLIAM, Butler, Samuel	II, 331
Chatterton, Thomas	III, 528
Chaucer, Geoffrey	I, 157
Cowper, William	IV, 371, 371, 378
Dryden, John	II, 497
Pope, Alexander	III, 161
Swift, Jonathan	III, 229
Warton, Joseph	IV, 396
HAYLEY, WILLIAM, AND SARGENT, JOHN, Collins, William	III, 414
HAYNE, PAUL HAMILTON, Lanier, Sidney	VII, 326
Poe, Edgar Allan	V, 551
Simms, William Gilmore	VI, 596, 597, 599
Stanley, Arthur Penrhyn	VII, 298
Taylor, Bayard	VII, 131, 135
Timrod, Henry	VI, 509
Whittier, John Greenleaf	VIII, 112
HAYNE, WILLIAM HAMILTON, Hayne, Paul Hamilton	VII, 591
Lanier, Sidney	VII, 325
Marston, Philip Bourke	VII, 627

	Vol. and Page
HAYS, FRANCES, Fullerton, Georgiana Charlotte Lady	VII, 566
HAYWARD, ABRAHAM, Canning, George	V, 67
Edgeworth, Maria	V, 569
Everett, Edward	VI, 422
Junius	IV, 642
Piozzi, Hester Lynch	IV, 686
Rogers, Samuel	VI, 35
Smith, Sydney	V, 469
Stanhope, Philip Dormer	III, 605
Sumner, Charles	VI, 751
Tennyson, Alfred Lord	VIII, 84
Thackeray, William Makepeace	VI, 299
Walpole, Horace	IV, 319
HAYWARD, EDWARD, F., Locker-Lampson, Frederick	VIII, 313
HAYWARD, SIR JOHN, Pole, Reginald	I, 280
HAZELTINE, MAYO WILLIAMSON, Reade, Charles	VII, 534
HAZEWELL, C. C., Monroe, James	V, 123
HAZLITT, WILLIAM, Addison, Joseph	II, 649, 652
Akenside, Mark	III, 543
Amory, Thomas	IV, 47
Arbuthnot, John	III, 85
Bacon, Francis	I, 652, 666
Baillie, Joanna	V, 692
Barbauld, Anna Lætitia	V, 24
Beaumont and Fletcher	I, 581
Bentham, Jeremy	V, 163, 165
Books	III, 7
Boswell, James	IV, 215
Brougham, Henry Lord	VI, 528
Browne, Sir Thomas	II, 342, 346
Browne, William	II, 74
Burke, Edmund	IV, 302
Burney, Frances	V, 349
Burns, Robert	IV, 225, 244, 247
Campbell, Thomas	V, 440, 442
Carew, Thomas	II, 22
Centlivre, Susannah	II, 683, 684, 685
Chalmers, Thomas	V, 490
Chapman, George	I, 732
Chatterton, Thomas	III, 535
Chaucer, Geoffrey	I, 158
Churchill, Charles	III, 479
Cibber, Colley	III, 372
Cobbett, William	V, 272
Coleridge, Samuel Taylor	V, 207, 217, 222
Collier, Jeremy	II, 700
Collins, William	III, 419
Congreve, William	II, 737, 738, 741
Cowper, William	IV, 378, 385
Crabbe, George	V, 172
Crashaw, Richard	II, 111
D'Avenant, Sir William	II, 218
Defoe, Daniel	III, 28, 35, 41
Dekker, Thomas	II, 57
Drayton, Michael	I, 707
Drummond, William	II, 102
Dryden, John	II, 468, 469, 482, 488, 498

	Vol. and Page
Etheredge, Sir George	II, 415
Farquhar, George	II, 556, 557, 558
Fletcher, John	I, 629
Fielding, Henry	III, 345, 346, 352, 357
Ford, John	II, 26, 29, 31
Gay, John	III, 55, 57
Gifford, William	V, 33
Godwin, William	V, 293, 296, 302
Goldsmith, Oliver	III, 622, 626
Gray, Thomas	III, 558, 561, 562
Greville, Sir Fulke	I, 691
Herrick, Robert	II, 237
Heywood, Thomas	II, 123, 126
Holcroft, Thomas	IV, 544, 546
Hunt, James Henry Leigh	VI, 155, 163
Inchbald, Elizabeth	IV, 688
Irving, Edward	V, 248
Irving, Washington	VI, 141
Jeffrey, Francis Lord	V, 649
Johnson, Samuel	III, 727, 741, 755
Jonson, Ben	I, 762
Keats, John	IV, 676
Knowledge	V, 7
Knowles, James Sheridan	VI, 288
Lamb, Charles	V, 229, 235, 236, 238, 239
Lyly, John	I, 424
Mackintosh, Sir James	V, 179, 181
Mackenzie, Henry	V, 114
Malthus, Thomas Robert	V, 251
Marlowe, Christopher	I, 350, 351
Marston, John	I, 737
Massinger, Philip	II, 42, 43, 48
Middleton, Thomas	I, 682
Milton, John	II, 254, 276, 287
Moore, Thomas	V, 712, 715
Murphy, Arthur	IV, 482
Murray, Lindley	V, 55
O'Keeffe, John	V, 196
Otway, Thomas	II, 363
Pope, Alexander	III, 159, 161, 168, 175, 184
Prior, Matthew	II, 677
Radcliffe, Ann Ward	IV, 718
Raleigh, Sir Walter	I, 599
Reynolds, Sir Joshua	IV, 142
Richardson, Samuel	III, 435, 439, 444, 448
Rogers, Samuel	VI, 37
Sackville, Thomas	I, 434
Saint-John, Henry	III, 294
Scott, Sir Walter	V, 135, 141
Shadwell, Thomas	II, 434
Shakespeare, William	I, 456, 465, 467, 468, 471, 478, 485, 490, 492, 495, 496, 498, 499, 503, 515, 520, 524, 528, 529, 534, 537, 540, 556
Shelley, Percy Bysshe	IV, 690, 701, 704
Shenstone, William	III, 473
Sheridan, Richard Brinsley	IV, 602, 603
Sidney, Sir Philip	I, 325
Smollett, Tobias George	III, 587
Southey, Robert	V, 397, 403, 408, 414
Spenser, Edmund	I, 381
Spence, Joseph	III, 520

608 INDEX TO CRITICISMS

	Vol. and Page
Steele, Sir Richard	II, 757
Sterne, Laurence	III, 512
Swift, Jonathan	III, 220, 225
Taylor, Jeremy	II, 204, 208
Thomas, James	III, 262, 267
Tooke, John Horne	IV, 569, 571
Tucker, Abraham	II, 643
Vanbrugh, Sir John	II, 707
Walpole, Horace	IV, 317
Warton, Thomas	IV, 77
Webster, John	I, 674
Wilberforce, William	V, 200
Wordsworth, William	V, 607, 619, 623, 630
Wycherley, William	II, 600, 601, 603
Young, Edward	III, 491, 493

HAZLITT, WILLIAM CAREW,
Carew, Thomas	II, 20
Forster, John	VII, 66
Gascoigne, George	I, 308
Hazlitt, William	V, 99, 107
Herrick, Robert	II, 233, 235
Horne, Richard Hengist	VII, 545, 546
Hunt, James Henry Leigh	VI, 162, 167
Lamb, Charles	V, 237
Lamb, Mary Ann	V, 509
Lewes, George Henry	VII, 139
Locker-Lampson, Frederick	VIII, 312
Lytton, Sir Edward George Bulwer	VI, 683
Procter, Bryan Waller	VI, 747, 750
Suckling, Sir John	II, 64

HEAD, SIR F. B.,
Bruce, James	IV, 206, 207

HEADLEY, HENRY,
Carew, Thomas	II, 21
Daniel, Samuel	I, 615
Drayton, Michael	I, 704
Drummond, William	II, 102
Fletcher, Phineas	II, 116, 117
Fletcher, Giles	I, 623
Gascoigne, George	I, 308
Habington, William	II, 136
Herbert, George	I, 722
King, Henry	II, 223
Lovelace, Richard	II, 161
Mason, William	IV, 324
May, Thomas	II, 120
Warner, William	I, 437

HEALY, GEORGE P. A.,
Audubon, John James	V, 697

HEARNE, THOMAS,
Addison, Joseph	II, 633, 640
Atterbury, Francis	III, 68
Bale, John	I, 286
Barnes, Joshua	II, 571
Baxter, Richard	II, 424
Bentley, Richard	III, 110
Blackmore, Sir Richard	II, 747
Bunyan, John	II, 389
Burnet, Gilbert	II, 592
Burton, Robert	II, 37, 37, 38
Chaucer, Geoffrey	I, 125
Collier, Jeremy	II, 702
Conybeare, John	III, 365
Cowley, Abraham	II, 194
Dodwell, Henry	II, 566

	Vol. and Page
Dryden, John	II, 463, 463
Echard, Laurence	III, 22
Flamsteed, John	II, 662
Hall, Edward	I, 260
Halley, Edmund	III, 107
Hobbes, Thomas	II, 321
Holinshed, Raphael	I, 311
Latimer, Hugh	I, 268
Laud, William	II, 90
Law, William	III, 425
Middleton, Conyers	III, 280
Milton, John	II, 284
Newton, Sir Isaac	II, 712
Parnell, Thomas	II, 615
Pope, Alexander	III, 144, 145
Prideaux, Humphrey	II, 697
Prynne, William	II, 225
Robert of Gloucester	I, 81
Rowe, Nicholas	II, 618
Sacheverell, Henry	II, 695
Selden, John	II, 142
Speed, John	I, 694
Spenser, Edmund	I, 370
Steele, Sir Richard	II, 752, 759
Stillingfleet, Edward	II, 454
Theobald, Lewis	III, 141
Tindal, Matthew	III, 72
Vanburgh, Sir John	II, 737
Wallis, John	II, 517
Wood, Anthony	II, 447
Wotton, William	II, 709
Wyclif, John	I, 104

HEATH, H. FRANK,
Chaucer, Geoffrey	I, 131, 132
Gower, John	I, 177
Henry of Huntington	I, 59
Henryson, Robert	I, 209
Lyndsay, Sir David	I, 276
Mannyng, Robert	I, 88
Nicholas of Guilford	I, 76
Paris, Matthew	I, 75
William of Malmesbury	I, 54

HEATH, RICHARD,
Bunyan, John	II, 401

HEATHCOTE, RALPH,
Ockley, Simon	II, 669

HEBER, REGINALD,
Byron, George Gordon Lord	IV, 753
Cowper, William	IV, 383
Milman, Henry Hart	VI, 540
Southey, Robert	V, 412
Taylor, Jeremy	II, 204, 205, 206, 208
Wesley, John	IV, 123, 127

HEBLER, C.,
Shakespeare, William	I, 505

HECKER, I. T.,
Arnold, Matthew	VII, 643
Brownson, Orestes Augustus	VII, 73
Emerson, Ralph Waldo	VII, 373

HECTOR, ANNIE ALEXANDER,
Norton, Caroline. E. S.	VII, 106

HEDGE, FREDERIC H.,
Emerson, Ralph Waldo	VII, 368
Fuller, Sarah Margaret	V, 671

HEGEL, GEORGE WILLIAM FREDERICH,
Bacon, Roger	I, 79

HEINE, HEINRICH,
Hazlitt William	V, 103

	Vol. and Page
Johnson, Samuel	II, 746
Shakespeare, William	I, 482, 485, 540, 559

HELPS, SIR ARTHUR,
Byron, George Gordon Lord	IV, 759
Dickens, Charles	VI, 554
Emerson, Ralph Waldo	VII, 363
Kingsley, Charles	VII, 19
Milton, John	II, 280
Pepys, Samuel	II, 515
Stowe, Harriet Beecher	VIII, 351

HEMANS, FELICIA DOROTHEA,
Borrow, George Henry	VII, 307
Coleridge, Samuel Taylor	V, 222
Heber, Reginald	V, 37
Milman, Henry Hart	VI, 540
Scott, Sir Walter	V, 127
Taylor, Sir Henry	VII, 580
Tighe, Mary	IV, 550

HEMINGE, JOHN, AND CONDELL HENRIE,
Shakespeare, William	I, 548

HENDERSON, T. F.,
Bradford, William	II, 158
Hall, Robert	V, 110
Henry, Robert	IV, 108
Hooker, Richard	I, 408
Jeffrey, Francis Lord	V, 656
Mackenzie, Sir George	II, 429
Maitland, Sir Richard	I, 333

HENLEY, WILLIAM ERNEST,
Arnold, Matthew	VII, 637
Borrow, George Henry	VII, 311
Boswell, James	IV, 219
Browning, Robert	VII, 710
Burns, Robert	IV, 238, 240, 241, 268
Butler, Samuel	II, 329, 333
Byron, George Gordon Lord	IV, 763
Congreve, William	II, 744
Corker, John Wilson	VII, 74
Dickens, Charles	VI, 590
Disraeli, Benjamin	VII, 294
Fielding, Henry	III, 363
Gay, John	III, 61
Henryson, Robert	I, 208
Herrick, Robert	II, 240
Hood, Thomas	V, 464
Jefferies, Richard	VII, 620
Kingsley, Charles	VII, 29
Landor, Walter Savage	VI, 391
Lever, Charles James	VI, 655
Locker-Lampson, Frederick	VIII, 313
Longfellow, Henry Wadsworth	VII, 413
Macaulay, Thomas Babington Lord	VI, 103
Richardson, Samuel	III, 451
Sidney, Sir Philip	I, 332
Stevenson, Robert Louis	VIII, 234, 239, 246
Tennyson, Alfred Lord	VIII, 106
Thackeray, William Makepeace	VI, 319
Tourneur, Cyril	I, 689
Walton, Isaac	II, 349

HENLEY, WILLIAM ERNEST, AND HENDERSON, THOS. F.,
Burns, Robert	IV, 244, 246
Chambers, Robert	VI, 622

	Vol. and Page
Gilfillan, George	VII, 152
Hogg, James	V, 269

HENNELL, MISS S. S.,
Butler, Joseph ... III, 311

HENRY VIII,
Colet, John ... I, 210

HENRY OF HUNTINGDON,
Alfred the Great ... I, 37

HENRY, ROBERT,
Barbour, John ... I, 113
Giraldus, Cambrensis ... I, 67
Hoveden, Roger de ... I, 63
Langland, William ... I, 117
William of Malmesbury ... I, 53

HENRY, WILLIAM,
Davy, Sir Humphry ... V, 93

HENRY, WILLIAM WIRT,
Henry, Patrick ... IV, 350

HENRYSON, ROBERT,
Chaucer, Geoffrey ... I, 136

HENSLOWE, PHILIP,
Heywood, Thomas ... II, 122, 123
Jonson, Ben ... I, 745

HERAUD, JOHN A.,
Bowles, William Lisle ... V, 662
Dryden, John ... II, 502
Shakespeare, William ... I, 451, 469, 497

HERBERT, DAVID,
Smollett, Tobias George ... III, 579

HERBERT, GEORGE,
Herbert, George ... I, 721
Knowledge ... V, 5
Poets and Poetry ... IV, 5

HERBERT, SIR HENRY,
Shirley, James ... II, 190

HERDER, JOHAN GOTTFRIED,
Alfred the Great ... I, 37
Shakespeare, William ... I, 502

HERFORD, BROOKE,
Wyclif, John ... I, 107

HERFORD, CHARLES HAROLD,
Alison, Archibald ... V, 343
Baillie, Joanna ... V, 695
Bale, John ... I, 285
Bowles, William Lisle ... V, 663
Brown, Thomas ... IV, 659
Byron, George Gordon Lord ... IV, 747
Campbell, Thomas ... V, 439, 446
Carlyle, Thomas ... VII, 274
Chalmers, Thomas ... V, 497
Clough, Arthur Hugh ... VI, 256
Cobbett, William ... V, 276
Coleridge, Samuel Taylor ... V, 221, 228
Colman, George ... V, 318
Coverdale, Miles ... I, 292
DeQuincey, Thomas ... VI, 131
Frere, John Hookham ... V, 489
Galt, John ... V, 336
Gascoigne, George ... I, 308
Gifford, William ... V, 36
Godwin, William ... V, 304
Grimoald, Nicholas ... I, 284
Hall, Robert ... V, 112
Hazlitt, William ... V, 107
Hemans, Felicia Dorothea ... V, 262
Heywood, John ... I, 306
Heywood, Thomas ... II, 127
Hogg, James ... V, 269

	Vol. and Page
Hunt, James Henry Leigh	VI, 167, 172, 180

Inchbald, Elizabeth ... IV, 688, 701
Irving, Edward ... V, 249
Jeffrey, Francis Lord ... V, 657
Lamb, Charles ... V, 238, 244
Landor, Walter Savage ... VI, 383
Lewis, Matthew Gregory ... IV, 634
Mackintosh, Sir James ... V, 184
Maturin, Charles Robert ... IV, 767
Middleton, Thomas ... I, 683, 686
Mill, James ... V, 308
Milman, Henry Hart ... VI, 542
Minot, Lawrence ... I, 94
Mitford, William ... V, 72
More, Sir Thomas ... I, 242
Napier, Gen. Sir Wm. Francis Patrick ... VI, 224
Paine, Thomas ... IV, 539
Paley, William ... IV, 478
Roscoe, William ... V, 119
Scott, Sir Walter ... V, 138
Shelley, Mary Wollstonecraft ... V, 704
Smith, Sydney ... V, 474
Stewart, Dugald ... V, 80
Tannahill, Robert ... IV, 549
Turner, Sharon ... V, 499
Wilson, John ... V, 749

HERNDON, WILLIAM H.,
Lincoln, Abraham ... VI, 416

HERNE, JAMES A.,
Drama, The ... VII, 9

HERON-ALLEN, EDWARD,
FitzGerald, Edward ... VII, 518

HERON, ROBERT,
Burns, Robert ... IV, 249

HERRICK, J. R.,
Mansel, Henry Longueville ... VI, 628

HERRICK, ROBERT,
Denham, Sir John ... II, 222
Fletcher, John ... I, 630
Herrick, Robert ... II, 235
Jonson, Ben ... I, 746

HERRICK, S. E.,
Colet, John ... I, 212
Wesley, John ... IV, 115
Wyclif, John ... I, 104

HERRING, THOMAS,
Berkeley, George ... III, 327
Burton, Robert ... II, 38
Hoadly, Benjamin ... III, 423

HERSCHEL, SIR J. F. W.,
Whewell, William ... VI, 470

HERSCHEL, SIR JOHN,
Books ... III, 7
Young, Thomas ... V, 87

HERSEY, HELOISE E.,
Browning, Robert ... VII, 706

HERTFORD, COUNTESS,
Thomson, James ... III, 263

HERTFORD, LADY (DUCHESS OF SOMERSET),
Fielding, Henry ... III, 349
Hervey, James ... III, 397
Montagu, Lady Mary Wortley ... III, 460

HERTZ, JOSEPH H.,
Martineau, James ... VIII, 428

HERVEY, JAMES,
Secker, Thomas ... III, 521

	Vol. and Page

HERVEY, JOHN LORD,
Blackmore, Sir Richard ... II, 746
Gay, John ... III, 59
Hervey, John Lord ... III, 128
Lyttelton, George Lord ... III, 610
Pope, Alexander ... III, 146
Saint-John, Henry ... III, 283
Stanhope, Philip Dormer ... III, 599

HEWIT, A. F.,
Faber, Frederick William ... VI, 333, 334

HEWLETT, HENRY G.,
Blake, William ... V, 60
Locker-Lampson, Frederick ... VIII, 312
Morris, William ... VIII, 335
Pared, Winthrop Mackworth ... V, 331
Prior, Matthew ... II, 678
Procter, Bryan Waller ... VI, 749
Taylor, Sir Henry ... VII, 583
Turner, Charles Tennyson ... VII, 160

HEY, JOHN,
Lardner, Nathaniel ... III, 524

HEYLIN, PETER,
Bacon, Francis ... I, 640
Fuller, Thomas ... II, 169
Hall, Joseph ... II, 146
Laud, William ... II, 89
Sidney, Sir Philip ... I, 324
Wilson, Arthur ... II, 129

HEYWOOD, ELIZA,
Shakespeare, William ... I, 552

HEYWOOD, THOMAS,
Beaumont, Francis ... I, 586
Jonson, Ben ... I, 746
Marlowe, Christopher ... I, 347
Shakespeare, William ... I, 448, 460
Watson, Thomas ... I, 337

HIBBEN, JOHN GRIER,
Tyndall, John ... VIII, 200

HIBBERT, HENRY GEORGE,
Holcroft, Thomas ... IV, 546

HICKES, GEORGE,
Pepys, Samuel ... II, 512

HIGGINSON, JOHN,
Mather, Cotton ... II, 729

HIGGINSON, THOMAS WENTWORTH,
Austen, Jane ... IV, 622
Bancroft, George ... VIII, 56, 60
Brown, Charles Brockden ... IV, 557
Browning, Robert ... VII, 717
Cary, Alice ... VI, 638
Child, Lydia Maria ... VII, 222
Cooper, James Fenimore ... V, 688
Dana, Richard Henry, Jr. ... VII, 500
Emerson, Ralph Waldo ... VII, 354, 379
Fields, James Thomas ... VII, 340
Fuller, Sarah Margaret ... V, 669, 670
Garrison, William Lloyd ... VII, 158
Hawthorne, Nathaniel ... VII, 349, 362, 367, 368
Hayne, Paul Hamilton ... VII, 592
Hemans, Felicia Dorothea ... V, 261
Holmes, Oliver Wendell ... VIII, 288, 295
Jackson, Helen Hunt ... VII, 574, 576
Lanier, Sidney ... VII, 331
Literature ... I, 8

INDEX TO CRITICISMS

Vol. and Page

Longfellow, Henry Wadsworth
........VII, 387, 399, 400, 414
Lowell, James Russell........
...............VIII, 20, 34, 41
Martineau, Harriet.......VII, 63
Parker, Theodore.........VI, 206
Parkman, Francis........VIII, 219
Phillips, Wendell.....VII, 555, 558
Poe, Edgar Allan...V, 542, 553, 560
Radcliffe, Ann Ward.......IV, 720
Roe, Edward Payson......VII, 676
Shakespeare, William.......I, 575
Sparks, Jared............VI, 478
Stowe, Harriet Beecher.......
................VIII, 354, 358
Sumner, Charles...........VI, 755
Tennyson, Alfred Lord...VIII, 71
Thoreau, Henry David.VI, 270, 277
Warner, Charles Dudley..VIII, 443
Whipple, Edwin Percy.......
................VII, 594, 596
Whitman, Walt.........VIII, 151
Whittier, John Greenleaf.....
................VIII, 116, 129
Willis, Nathaniel Parker....VI, 491
HIGGINSON, THOMAS WENT-
  WORTH, AND BOYNTON,
  HENRY WALCOTT,
Longfellow, Henry Wadsworth
.....................VII, 389
HIGGS, HENRY,
  Young, Arthur........IV, 655, 656
HILDEBURN, CHARLES R.,
  Hopkinson, Thomas.......IV, 133
HILDESLEY, BISHOP,
  Young, Edward..........III, 484
HILDRETH, RICHARD,
  Hamilton, Alexander......IV, 458
  Hopkins, Samuel..........IV, 439
  Mather, Cotton............II, 728
HILL, AARON,
  Dennis, John.............III, 76
  Fielding, Henry..........III, 350
  Mallet, David............III, 495
  Pope, Alexander..III, 145, 146, 182
  Richardson, Samuel.......III, 435
  Savage, Richard......III, 131, 131
  Thomson, James......III, 262, 266
HILL, ABRAHAM,
  Barrow, Isaac............II, 310
HILL, ADAMS SHERMAN,
  Lamb, Charles............V, 234
  Swift, Jonathan.........III, 218
HILL, ALSAGER HAY,
  Gray, David.............VI, 261
HILL, ASTRÆA AND MINERVA,
  Fielding, Henry.........III, 349
HILL, DAVID J.,
  Bryant, William Cullen........
  ....VII, 109, 115
  Irving, Washington.......VI, 150
HILL, FRANK H.,
  Canning, George...........V, 69
HILL, GEORGE BIRKBECK,
  Allingham, William.......VII, 734
  Boswell, James..........IV, 218
  Browning, Robert........VII, 683
  Croker, John Wilson......VI, 74
  Gibbon, Edward..........IV, 193
  Hurd, Richard...........IV, 520
  Johnson, Samuel........III, 746

Vol. and Page

Macaulay, Thomas Babington
  Lord ....VI, 100
Parr, Samuel..............V, 21
Pomfret, John............II, 511
Rossetti, Gabriel Charles Dante
  ....VII, 455
Stanhope, Philip Dormer...III, 606
Stewart, Dugald...........V, 80
Wordsworth, William......V, 646
HILL, HON. LADY,
  Hill, John ....III, 646
HILL, O'DELL TRAVERS,
  Dunstan.................I, 45
  Wyclif, John............I, 101
HILL, ROWLAND,
  Wesley, John...........IV, 111
HILL, THOMAS,
  Darwin, Erasmus........IV, 423
HILLARD, GEORGE STILLMAN,
  Browning, Elizabeth Barrett..
  ....VI, 228, 230, 243
  Browning, Robert.......VII, 678
  Bryant, William Cullen....VII, 121
  Coleridge, Hartley.........V, 573
  Doyle, Sir Francis Hastings
    Charles..............VII, 650
  Everett, Edward.........VI, 425
  Hawthorne, Nathaniel........
  ....VI, 345, 358, 363
  Holmes, Oliver Wendell..VII, 290
  Kemble, Frances Ann....VIII, 216
  Landor, Walter Savage....VI, 383
  Lowell, James Russell...VIII, 30
  Marshall, John...........V, 283
  Milnes, Richard Monckton.VII, 563
  Moore, John.............IV, 427
  Prescott, William Hickling....
  ....VI, 182, 184, 185
  Reynolds, Sir Joshua.......IV, 142
  Rogers, Samuel...........VI, 38
  Smith, John..............I, 698
  Smollett, Tobias George....III,583
  Sterling, John...........V, 453
  Ticknor, George..........VI, 617
  Wayland, Francis.........VI, 450
  Whittier, John Greenleaf.VIII, 121
HILLARD, KATE,
  Beddoes, Thomas Lovell.V, 585, 587
HILLER, ARTHUR CECIL,
  Wilson, John.............V, 753
HILLIARD, HENRY W.,
  Webster, Daniel..........V, 728
HILLIARD, W.,
  Sedgwick, Catharine Maria..VI, 507
HILLIS, NEWELL DWIGHT,
  Carlyle, Thomas.........VII, 275
  Drummond, Henry..VIII, 363, 366
  Emerson, Ralph Waldo....VII, 379
  Gladstone, William Ewart....
  ....VIII, 385
  Livingstone, David.......VI, 729
  Ruskin, John...........VIII, 421
  Tennyson, Alfred Lord........
  ....VIII, 75, 96
HIMES, JOHN A.,
  Milton, John.........II, 269, 298
HINCKS, EDWARD Y.,
  Browning, Elizabeth Barrett..
  ....VI, 235
HINDS, ALLEN B.,
  Foxe, John...............I, 337

Vol. and Page

HINGSTON, EDWARD P.,
  Browne, Charles Farrar.....VI, 502
HINSDALE, B. A.,
  Mann, Horace............VI, 201
  Mill, John Stuart..........VI, 703
HINTON, RICHARD J.,
  Bright, John............VII, 721
  Phillips, Wendell........VII, 554
HIPPISLEY, J. H.,
  Chaucer, Geoffrey............I, 137
  Drayton, Michael...........I, 707
  Hall, Joseph..............II, 147
  Hawes, Stephen............I, 217
  Minot, Lawrence............I, 93
  Sidney, Sir Philip..........I, 331
HIRSCH, EMIL G.,
  Arnold, Sir Edwin.......VIII, 504
HIRSCH, WILLIAM,
  Shakespeare, William........I, 574
HITCHCOCK, E. A.,
  Sperser, Edmund..........I, 389
HITCHCOCK, RIPLEY
  Stoddard, Richard Henry.....
  ....VIII, 496, 498
HITCHCOCK, THOMAS,
  Carlyle, Thomas.........VII, 240
HITCHMAN, FRANCIS,
  Disraeli, Benjamin.......VII, 291
  Johnson, Samuel.........III, 734
HOADLY, BENJAMIN,
  Clarke, Samuel............II, 748
  Defoe, Daniel............III, 32
HOADLY, JOHN,
  Fielding, Sarah..........III, 518
  Goldsmith, Oliver........III, 633
HOAR, GEORGE F.,
  Sumner, Charles.........VI, 755
HOARE, W. H.,
  Hobbes, Thomas..........II, 322
HOARE, SIR RICHARD COLT,
  Giraldus, Cambrensis........I, 67
HOBART, LORD,
  Cobden, Richard.........VI, 442
HOBSON, J. A.,
  George, Henry.........VIII, 382
  Ruskin, John...........VIII, 421
HODDER, GEORGE,
  Coleridge, Samuel Taylor....V, 211
  Dickens, Charles........VII, 571
  Hunt, James Henry Leigh..VI, 159
  Jerrold, Douglas William....VI, 68
  Thackeray, William Makepeace
  ....VI, 294
HODGES, THOMAS,
  Alcuin ....I, 34
  Fox, George..............II, 421
HODGSON, SHADWORTH H.,
  DeQuincey, Thomas.......VI, 129
HODGSON, WILLIAM,
  Jonson, Ben...............I, 759
HOEY, FRANCIS CASHEL,
  Carleton, William........VI, 548
HOFFMAN, DAVID,
  Gibbon, Edward..........IV, 581
  Kent, James...............V, 502
HOGARTH, GEORGE,
  Gay, John................III, 57
  Sheridan, Richard Brinsley....
  ....IV, 602
HOGARTH, GEORGINA,
  Reade, Charles..........VII, 527

INDEX TO CRITICISMS 611

HOGG, JAMES,
Byron, George Gordon Lord.IV, 757
Burns, Robert............IV, 253
Cunningham, Allan.........V, 384
DeQuincey, Thomas.......VI, 123
Galt, John.................V, 334
Hogg, James...............V, 262
Lockhart, John Gibson......V, 753
Logan, John..............IV, 44
Moir, David Macbeth........V, 704
Scott, Sir Walter.......V, 128, 157
Southey, Robert.......V, 397, 409
Wilson, John..............V, 751
Wordsworth, William ..V, 608, 631
HOGG, THOMAS,
Cunningham, Allan.........V, 382
HOGG, THOMAS JEFFERSON,
Godwin, William...........V, 291
Shelley, Percy Bysshe......IV, 693
Southey, Robert...........V, 400
HOLBEACH, HENRY,
Helps, Sir Arthur........VII, 40
HOLCROFT, THOMAS,
Godwin, William...........V, 300
Macklin, Charles..........IV, 343
HOLDEN, EDWARD S.,
Herschel, Sir John Frederick
William................VI, 625
HOLDEN, GEORGE H.,
Hawthorne, Nathaniel.....VI, 367
HOLDEN, R.,
Gibbon, Edward..........IV, 177
HOLDER, CHARLES FREDERICK,
Agassiz, Louis Jean Rudolphe.
......................VI, 725
Darwin, Charles Robert...VII, 421
HOLE, SAMUEL REYNOLDS,
Brown, John.............VII, 478
Dickens, Charles......VI, 558, 591
Lyte, Henry Francis........V, 499
Newman, John Henry.....VII, 742
Pusey, Edward Bouverie..VII, 469
Thackeray, William Makepeace
....................VI, 298, 310
HOLLAND, BERNARD,
Manning, Henry Edward.VIII, 168
HOLLAND, FREDERIC MAY,
Bacon, Roger..............I, 78
Browning, Robert ....VII, 703
Langland, William..........I, 121
Peacock, Reginald..........I, 190
Wyclif, John................I, 109
HOLLAND, F. W.,
Borrow, George Henry....VII, 310
HOLLAND, HENRY SCOTT,
Liddon, Henry Parry.VII, 761, 761
Ruskin, John...........VIII, 422
HOLLAND, HUGH,
Shakespeare, William.......I, 548
HOLLAND, JOSIAH GILBERT,
Beecher, Henry Ward....VII, 607
Browning, Elizabeth Barrett..
......................VI, 239
Bryant, William Cullen....VII, 112
Critic, The................II, 8
Dodge, Mary Abigal.....VIII, 361
Eliot, George............VII, 187
Willis, Nathaniel Parker....VI, 491
HOLLAND, LADY,
Smith, Sydney........V, 468, 471

HOLLAND, SIR HENRY,
Baillie, Joanna.............V, 691
Burney, Frances..........V, 344
Byron, George Gordon Lord.IV, 741
Canning, George...........V, 65
Cobden, Richard..........VI, 440
Coleridge, Samuel Taylor....V, 211
Erskine, Thomas..........IV, 729
Faraday, Michael..........VI, 512
Frere, John Hookham...V, 486, 487
Hallam, Henry............VI, 174
Herschel, Sir John Frederick
William................VI, 625
Lincoln, Abraham.........VI, 414
Macaulay, Thomas Babington
Lord...................VI, 94
Mackintosh, Sir James......V, 180
Malthus, Thomas Robert....V, 250
Milman, Henry Hart......VI, 542
Moore, Thomas............V, 708
Ricardo, David..........IV, 726
Smith, Sydney.............V, 472
Somerville, Mary..........VI, 659
Taylor, Sir Henry........VII, 581
Webster, Daniel...........V, 722
White, Joseph Blanco.......V, 362
Wordsworth, William.......V, 614
HOLLANDER, BERNARD,
Spencer, Herbert........VIII, 483
HOLLOWAY, LAURA C.,
Brontë, Charlotte..........VI, 24
HOLME, STANFORD,
Spurgeon, Charles Haddon....
....................VIII, 180
HOLMES, ABEL,
Sandys, George............II, 82
HOLMES, NATHANIEL,
Bacon, Francis............I, 645
Shakespeare, William.......I, 545
HOLMES, OLIVER WENDELL,
Adams, Hannah...........V, 124
Agassiz, Louis Jean Rodolphe
......................VI, 719
Allston, Washington.......V, 420
Arnold, Sir Edwin......VIII, 503
Authors and Authorship..VIII, 8
Beecher, Henry Ward... .VII, 602
Books ....III, 9
Burns, Robert............IV, 257
Carlyle, Thomas.........VII, 236
Clarke, James Freeman...VII, 672
Coleridge, Samuel Taylor....V, 214
Edwards, Jonathan...III, 385, 387
Emerson, Ralph Waldo.......
............VII, 348, 356, 370
Everett, Edward.........VI, 426
Fields, James Thomas....VII, 340
Gladstone, William Ewart....
....................VIII, 384
Goldsmith, Oliver........III, 621
Griswold, Rufus W.......VI, 78
Halleck, Fitz-Greene......VI, 495
Hawthorne, Nathaniel........
..................VI, 344, 356
Irving, Washington....VI, 133, 151
Knowledge ....V, 8
Lincoln, Abraham........VI, 417
Longfellow, Henry Wadsworth
..................VII, 384, 407
Lowell, James Russell....VIII, 19
Moore, Thomas............V, 717

Motley, John Lothrop........
......VII, 87, 88, 90, 92, 93, 93
Poe, Edgar Allan..........V, 557
Poets and Poetry..........IV, 8
Shakespeare, William ....I, 565
Shelley, Percy Bysshe.....IV, 707
Spenser, Edmund...........I, 397
Sumner, Charles..........VI, 752
Tennyson, Alfred Lord...VIII, 70
Webster, Daniel...........V, 721
Whittier, John Greenleaf.....
................VIII, 114, 126
Willis, Nathaniel Parker.....V, 488
HOLMES, T. R. E.,
Napier, Gen. Sir William Francis Patrick..............VI, 223
HOLROYD, MARIA JOSEPHA,
Gibbon, Edward..........IV, 191
HOLST, DR. H. VON,
Calhoun, John Caldwell.....V, 675
HOLT, JOHN,
Shakespeare, William ....I, 533
HOLT-WHITE, RASHLEIGH,
White, Gilbert...........IV, 149
HOLYOAKE, GEORGE JACOB,
Beecher, Henry Ward....VII, 607
Emerson, Ralph Waldo...VII, 346
Whitefield, George.......III, 548
HOMPES, MAT,
Gaskell, Elizabeth Cleghorn..
.............VI, 428, 430, 430
HONE, PHILIP,
Adams, John Quincy........V, 516
Dickens, Charles......VI, 552, 570
Jay, John.................V, 95
Martineau, Harriet........VI, 55
Monroe, James............V, 122
Prescott, William Hickling..VI, 181
Seward, William Henry....VI, 676
HOOD, EDWIN PAXTON,
Carlyle, Thomas.........VII, 266
Clare, John...........VI, 397, 398
Cobbett, William..........V, 274
Faraday, Michael.........VI, 513
Hogg, James..............V, 267
Milton, John.............II, 290
Smith, Sydney.............V, 473
HOOD, THOMAS,
Coleridge, Samuel Taylor....V, 209
Defoe, Daniel.............III, 42
Dickens, Charles.........VI, 568
Hall, Robert..............V, 110
Hood, Thomas.............V, 459
Lamb, Charles............V, 232
Shakespeare, William ......I, 558
Taylor, Jeremy........II, 206, 210
HOOK, THEODORE,
Colman, George...........V, 317
Motley, John Lothrop....VII, 88
Moore, Thomas...........V, 706
Shelley, Percy Bysshe....IV, 701
HOOK, WALTER FARQUHAR,
Keble, John.............VI, 457
Martineau, Harriet.......VII, 60
Pusey, Edward Bouverie.VII, 467
Ridley, Nicholas...........I, 266
Wyclif, John..............I, 106
HOOKER, SIR JOSEPH DALTON,
Darwin, Charles Robert......
..................VII, 421, 422
Gray, Asa...............VII, 671

INDEX TO CRITICISMS

HOOKER, RICHARD
   Hooker, Richard............I, 405
   Jewell, John ....I, 293
HOOLE, JOHN,
   Johnson, Samuel.........III, 722
HOOPER, JAMES,
   Borrow, George Henry.....VII, 309
HOOPER, RICHARD,
   Sandys, George............II, 83
HOOPER, WILLIAM R.,
   Woolman, John ....III, 597
HOPE, E. R.,
   Havergal, Frances Ridley..VII, 167
HOPE, EVA,
   Cowper, William..........IV, 380
HOPE-SCOTT, J. R.,
   Gladstone, William Ewart...
   ....VIII, 390
HOPKINS, MARK,
   Campbell, George J. D....VIII, 434
   Lowell, James Russell....VIII, 19
HOPKINS, SAMUEL,
   Edwards, Jonathan.......III, 382
HOPKINS, W.,
   Müller, Friedrich Max ...VIII, 439
HOPPIN, J. H.,
   Beecher, Henry Ward.....VII, 605
HORN, FRANZ,
   Shakespeare, William ...I, 512, 557
HORNBROOKE, FRANCIS B.,
   Newman, John Henry.....VII, 752
HORNE, GEORGE,
   Johnson, Samuel ....III, 725
HORNE, HENRY,
   James I of Scotland.........I, 182
HORNE, HERBERT P.,
   Morris, William..........VIII, 337
HORNE, RICHARD HENGIST,
   Ainsworth, William Harrison..
   ....VII, 487
   Bacon, Roger..............I, 78
   Banim, John..............V, 390
   Beaumont and Fletcher......I, 582
   Browning, Elizabeth Barrett..
   ....VI, 229
   Browning, Robert.........
   ....VII, 685, 686, 687
   Carleton, William.........VI, 548
   Chaucer, Geoffrey..........I, 160
   Coleridge, Hartley.........V, 576
   Dickens, Charles......VI, 564, 581
   Forster, John.........VII, 65, 67
   Gore, Catherine Grace.....VI, 263
   Hood, Thomas.............V, 461
   Hook, Theodore Edward...V, 358
   Hunt, James Henry Leigh...
   ....VI, 165, 168
   Jameson, Anna...........VI, 215
   James, George Payne Rainsford ....VI, 217
   Jerrold, Douglas William...VI, 69
   Knowles, James Sheridan...VI, 287
   Landor, Walter Savage....VI, 387
   Lever, Charles James......VI, 653
   Lover, Samuel............VI, 545
   Lytton, Sir Edward George Bulwer..........VI, 687, 688, 689
   Macaulay, Thomas Babington Lord ....VI, 101
   Marryat, Frederick........V 532
   Middleton, Thomas.........I. 681

   Milnes, Richard Monckton.VII, 563
   Milton, John..............II, 290
   Montgomery, Robert.......VI, 48
   Norton, Caroline E. S.....VII, 104
   Poe, Edgar Allan..........V, 558
   Pusey, Edward Bouverie..VII, 471
   Shelley, Mary Wollstonecraft.V, 703
   Smith, Sydney............V, 471
   Talfourd, Sir Thomas Noon..V, 760
   Taylor, Sir Henry........VII, 581
   Tennyson, Alfred Lord......
   ....VIII, 65, 81, 82
   Trollope, Frances Milton...VI, 331
   Wells, Charles Jeremiah...VII, 164
   Wordsworth, William.......V, 633
HORNE, RICHARD HENGIST,
(BROWNING, ELIZABETH
BARRETT),
   Carlyle, Thomas..VII, 242, 249, 251
HORNE, THOMAS HARTWELL,
   Clarke, Adam.............V, 185
   Hurd, Richard............IV, 519
   Lardner, Nathaniel ....III, 524
   Lowth, Robert............IV, 29
   Macknight, James.........IV, 407
   Newton, Sir Isaac.........II, 723
   Wakefield, Gilbert........IV, 416
   Wayland, Francis.........VI, 450
   West, Gilbert ....III, 369
   Wiseman, Nicholas Patrick...
   ....VI, 437
HORNER, FRANCIS,
   Alison, Archibald......V, 341, 342
   Bacon, Francis............I, 665
   Campbell, Thomas.....V, 434, 439
   Cowley, Abraham.........II, 197
   Crabbe, George............V, 172
   Davy, Sir Humphry........V, 90
   Erskine, Thomas ....IV, 729
   Jeffrey, Francis Lord.......V, 648
   Mackintosh, Sir James.....V, 178
   Malthus, Thomas Robert...V, 250
   Romilly, Sir Samuel.......IV, 636
   Sheridan, Richard Brinsley.IV, 594
   Smith, Adam.............IV, 61
   Stewart, Dugald...........V, 79
   Wordsworth, William......V, 628
HORSLEY, SAMUEL,
   Priestley, Joseph..........IV, 415
   Warburton, William .....III, 685
HORSTSMANN, CARL,
   Richard Rolle of Hampole....I, 92
HORTON, ROBERT F.,
   Howe, John..............II, 545
   Law, William............III, 430
HOSMER, JAMES KENDALL,
   Adams, Samuel........IV, 441, 443
   Hutchinson, Thomas......III, 707
   Otis, James.. ....III, 716
HOTCHKISS, WILLIAM H.,
   Hamilton, Alexander......IV, 461
HOTTEN, JOHN CAMDEN, (THEODORE TAYLOR),
   Thackeray, William Makepeace
   ....VI, 293, 306
HOUGHTON, LOUISE SEYMOUR,
   Arnold, Matthew........VII, 633
HOUSE, E. H.,
   Reade, Charles..........VII, 528
HOUSTON, ARTHUR,
   Sackville, Thomas ....I, 434

HOVEY, RICHARD,
   Parsons, Thomas William.VIII, 193
HOWARD, ABRAHAM,
   Campbell, John Lord.......VI, 258
HOWARD, EDWARD,
   Blackmore, Sir Richard.....II, 746
   Dryden, John.............II, 486
HOWARD, HENRY, LORD,
   Raleigh, Sir Walter..........I, 590
HOWARD, JOHN R.,
   Stowe, Harriet Beecher.......
   ....VIII, 351, 356
HOWE, HENRY,
   Ferguson, James..........III, 669
HOWE, JOHN A., JR.,
   Saxe, John Godfrey......VII, 616
HOWE, JULIA WARD,
   Clarke, James Freeman....VII, 672
   Clough, Arthur Hugh......VI, 250
   Combe, George...........VI, 90
   Disraeli, Benjamin........VII, 294
   Emerson, Ralph Waldo......
   ....VII, 353, 360
   Fuller, Sarah Margaret......V. 668
   Garrison, William Lloyd...VII, 159
   Grote, George............VI, 609
   Hawthorne, Nathaniel.....VI, 346
   Jameson, Anna...........VI, 214
   Longfellow, Henry Wadsworth
   ....VII, 388
   Norton, Caroline E. S.....VII, 103
   Parker, Theodore.........VI, 209
   Phillips, Wendell.........VII, 552
HOWE, M. A. DEWOLFE,
   Brooks, Phillips..........VIII, 226
   Browne, Charles Farrar ....VI, 504
   Bryant, William Cullen....VII, 127
   Cooper, James Fenimore....V, 687
   Emerson, Ralph Waldo....VII, 353
   Hawthorne, Nathaniel.....VII, 349
   Holmes, Oliver Wendell......
   ....VIII, 268, 299
   Irving, Washington........VI, 137
   Lowell, James Russell....VIII, 25
   Morris, William.........VIII, 333
   Prescott, William Hickling..VI, 183
   Willis, Nathaniel Parker....VI, 492
   Whitman, Walt ....VIII, 151
   Whittier, John Greenleaf.....
   ....VIII, 128
HOWE, SAMUEL G.,
   Byron, George Gordon Lord.IV, 737
HOWELL, JAMES,
   Fletcher, Phineas..........II, 115
   Jonson, Ben...............I, 746
   King, Henry.............II, 223
   Raleigh, Sir Walter ....I, 592
HOWELL, WILLIAM,
   Raleigh, Sir Walter ....I, 601
HOWELLS, WILLIAM DEAN,
   Agassiz, Louis Jean Rudolphe.
   ....VI, 722
   Austen, Jane.............IV, 623
   Black, William..........VIII, 396
   Bloomfield, Robert........IV, 725
   Brontë, Charlotte.........VI, 27
   Brontë, Emily............V, 525
   Browning, Robert........VII, 695
   Burke, Edmund..........IV, 298
   Chaucer, Geoffrey..........I, 170
   Critic, The................II, 9

INDEX TO CRITICISMS

	Vol. and Page
Curtis, George William	VIII, 187, 188, 188, 189
DeQuincey, Thomas	VI, 130
Dickens, Charles	VI, 566, 567, 570, 571, 590
DuMaurier, George	VIII, 345
Eliot, George	VII, 184, 186, 188
Ellwood, Thomas	II, 575
Emerson, Ralph Waldo	VII, 376
Gibbon, Edward	IV, 187
Goldsmith, Oliver	III, 629
Hazlitt, William	V, 105
Hawthorne, Nathaniel	VI, 350, 355, 358, 370
Harte, Francis Bret	VIII, 472
Herbert Edward Lord	II, 97
Holmes, Oliver Wendell	VIII, 288, 293, 294
Irving, Washington	VI, 146
Kingsley, Charles	VII, 23, 26
Longfellow, Henry Wadsworth	VII, 389, 398, 415
Lowell, James Russell	VIII, 26, 33
Lytton, Sir Edward George Bulwer	VI, 686, 688, 699
Milton, John	II, 268, 270
Palfrey, John Gorham	VII, 337
Parkman, Francis	VIII, 220
Poe, Edgar Allan	V, 556
Pope, Alexander	III, 153, 157
Reade, Charles	VII, 537
Scott, Sir Walter	V, 137, 145
Shakespeare, William	I, 475, 490, 574
Smith, Alexander	VI, 519
Stockton, Francis Richard	VIII, 474
Stowe, Harriet Beecher	VIII, 354
Thackeray, William Makepeace	VI, 300, 304, 305, 308, 322
Thoreau, Henry David	VI, 272
Trollope, Anthony	VII 463
Whittier, John Greenleaf	VIII, 127
Wordsworth, William	V, 624
HOWITT, MARY,	
Baillie, Joanna	V, 693
Barton, Bernard	V, 595
Besant, Sir Walter	VIII, 450
Cobbett, William	V, 273
Dobell, Sidney Thompson	VI, 760
Hawthorne, Nathaniel	VI, 365
Hemans, Felicia Dorothea	V, 258
Landon, Letitia Elizabeth	V, 322
Martineau, Harriet	VII, 61
Read, Thomas Buchanan	VI, 677
Rossetti, Christina Georgina	VIII, 271
Stowe, Harriet Beecher	VIII, 349
Tennyson, Alfred Lord	VIII, 66
HOWITT. WILLIAM,	
Addison, Joseph	II, 635
Baillie. Joanna	V, 691, 693
Burns. Robert	IV, 229
Campbell, Thomas	V, 435
Chatterton. Thomas	III, 530
Chaucer, Geoffrey	I, 143
Coleridge. Samuel Taylor	V, 210
Cowper, William	IV, 373
Crabbe, George	V, 174
Dickens, Charles	VI, 581
Dryden, John	II, 465

	Vol. and Page
Elliott, Ebenezer	V, 579, 581
Fox, George	II, 421
Goldsmith, Oliver	III, 617
Gay, John	III, 54
Gray, Thomas	III, 555
Hemans, Felicia Dorothea	V, 256
Hogg, James	V, 264
Hunt, James Henry Leigh	VI, 165
Keats, John	IV, 671
Landon, Letitia Elizabeth	V, 327
Landor, Walter Savage	VI, 381, 388
Martineau, Harriet	VII, 61
Milton, John	II, 247
Montgomery, James	V, 768
Moore, Thomas	V, 707
Pope, Alexander	III, 149
Procter, Bryan Waller	VI, 748
Rogers, Samuel	VI, 37, 38
Scott, Sir Walter	V, 130
Shelley, Percy Bysshe	IV, 692, 706
Shenstone, William	III, 472
Southey, Robert	V, 398
Spenser, Edmund	I, 371
Swift, Jonathan	III, 201
Tennyson, Alfred Lord	VIII, 66, 82
Thomson, James	III, 256
Tighe, Mary	IV, 550
Wilson, John	V, 745
Wordsworth, William	V, 610, 623
HOWLAND, FRANCES LOUISE, (KENYON WEST),	
D'Avenant, Sir William	II, 219
Pye, Henry James	IV, 581
Rowe, Nicholas	II, 623
Shadwell, Thomas	II, 435
Southey, Robert	V, 411
Tate, Nahum	II, 588, 589
Warton, Thomas	IV, 79
Whitehead, William	IV, 22
HOWSE, EDWARD S.,	
De Morgan, Augustus	VI, 634
HUBBARD, ELBERT,	
Adams, John Quincy	V, 519
Adams, Samuel	IV, 442
Austen, Jane	IV, 613
Eliot, George	VII, 184
Franklin, Benjamin	IV, 93
Goldsmith, Oliver	III, 621
Lowell, James Russell	VIII, 24
Martineau, Harriet	VII, 64
Morris, William	VII, 331
Rossetti, Christina Georgina	VIII, 270, 274
Shelley, Mary Wollstonecraft	V, 702
Swift, Jonathan	III, 206, 237
Whiteman, Walt	VIII, 150
HUBBARD, SARA A.,	
Owen, Sir Richard	VIII, 172
Ruskin, John	VIII, 416
White, Gilbert	IV, 153
HUBBELL, GEORGE ALLEN,	
Mann, Horace	VI, 202
HUBERT, PHILIP G., JR.,	
Franklin, Benjamin	IV, 91
Thoreau, Henry David	VI, 275
HUBNER, CHARLES W.,	
Emerson, Ralph Waldo	VII, 360
HUDSON, ALFRED SERENO,	
Child, Lydia Maria	VII, 220

	Vol. and Page
HUDSON, HENRY NORMAN,	
Bailey, Philip James	VIII, 460
Shakespeare, William	I, 463, 479, 481, 487, 497, 569
Webster, Daniel	V, 728
Wordsworth, William	V, 625, 641
HUDSON, WILLIAM HENRY,	
Addison, Joseph	II, 640, 647
Behn, Aphra	II, 411
Clough, Arthur Hugh	VI, 255
Goldsmith, Oliver	III, 629
Manley, Mrs. Mary de la Riviere	II, 694
Pepys, Samuel	II, 514
Spencer, Herbert	VIII, 483
Steele, Sir Richard	II, 755 768
HUEFFER, FORD MADOX,	
Rossetti, Gabriel Charles Dante	VII, 435, 439, 444, 447
HÜGEL, FRIEDERICH VON,	
Ward, William George	VII, 484
HUGHES, ARTHUR,	
Allingham, William	VII, 734
Rossetti, Gabriel Charles Dante	VII, 439
HUGHES, C. E.,	
Blackmore, Richard D.	VIII, 430
Campbell, George J. D.	VIII, 433
Creighton, Mandell	VIII, 453
Hutton, Richard Holt	VIII, 374
Newman, Francis William	VIII, 370
Romanes, George John	VIII, 283
HUGHES, HUGH PRICE,	
Wesley, John	IV, 121
HUGHES, JAMES L.,	
Dickens, Charles	VI, 595
HUGHES, JOHN,	
Barham, Richard Harris	V, 474, 475
Boyle, Robert	II, 418
Spenser, Edmund	I, 375, 379, 390
HUGHES, R.,	
Blake, William	V, 64
Reynolds, Sir Joshua	IV, 141
HUGHES, THOMAS,	
Alfred the Great	I, 38
Arnold, Thomas	V, 380
Franklin, Benjamin	IV, 89
Kingsley, Charles	VII, 21
Livingstone, David	VI, 729
Martineau, Harriet	VII, 59, 62
Maurice, John Frederick Denison	VI, 648
Stanley, Arthur Penrhyn	VII, 297
Taylor, Tom	VII, 214, 215
Thoreau, Henry David	VI, 273
HUGHES, T. S.,	
Sherlock, Thomas	III, 455
HUGHES, MRS.,	
Hemans, Felicia Dorothea	V, 255
HUGO, VICTOR,	
Jonson, Ben	I, 765
Malone, Edmond	IV, 579
Shakespeare, William	I, 451, 504, 513, 535, 566
Tate, Nahum	II, 588
HULBERT, HENRY W.,	
Irving, Washington	VI, 136
HULL, CHARLES H.,	
Parkman, Francis	VIII, 225
HULLAH, JOHN,	
Helps, Sir Arthur	VII, 39

INDEX TO CRITICISMS

HUMBOLDT, FRIEDRICH HEINRICH ALEXANDER,
  Robertson, William.......IV, 161
HUME, DAVID,
  Alfred the Great............I, 37
  Bacon, Francis.........I, 641, 665
  Berkeley, George.........III, 328
  Blacklock, Thomas........IV, 129
  Camden, William...........I, 621
  Cowley, Abraham..........II, 199
  Denham, Sir John..........II, 221
  Douglas, Gawin............I, 213
  Fairfax, Edward............I, 742
  Franklin, Benjamin.......IV, 99
  Gauden, John..............II, 176
  Gibbon, Edward..........IV, 179
  Harrington, James........II, 308
  Harvey, William..........II, 156
  Henry, Robert............IV, 107
  Hobbes, Thomas..........II, 324
  Home, John........IV, 514, 514
  Hume, David....III, 648, 652, 655
  Hurd, Richard............IV, 518
  Hyde, Edward, Earl of Clarendon....................II 302
  Jonson, Ben................I, 761
  Knox, John............I, 296, 299
  Macpherson, James......IV, 273
  Milton, John.........II, 276, 285
  More, Sir Thomas...........I, 234
  Newton, Sir Isaac.........II, 723
  Parnell, Thomas..........II, 616
  Pepys, Samuel............II, 513
  Pole, Reginald.............I, 280
  Raleigh, Sir Walter.....I, 593, 602
  Robertson, William...IV, 157, 158
  Shakespeare, William.......I, 552
  Smith, Adam...........IV, 58, 61
  Spenser, Edmund...........I, 380
  Stowe, John...............I, 419
  Temple, Sir William......II, 457
  Waller, Edmund..........II, 380
  Wilkie, William..........III, 595
  William of Malmesbury......I, 53
  Wilmot, John.............II, 338
  Wycherley, William........II, 604
  Wyclif, John...............I, 104
HUME, HAMILTON,
  Tennyson, Alfred Lord...VIII, 76
HUME, MARTIN A. S.,
  Raleigh, Sir Walter..I, 598, 601, 608
HUMPHREYS, ARTHUR L.,
  Johnson, Samuel.........III, 735
  Montgomery, Robert......VI, 48
  Tupper, Martin Farquhar.VII, 732
HUMPHREYS, JENNETT,
  Pope, Alexander.........III, 155
HUMPHRY, OZIAS,
  Johnson, Samuel.........III, 720
HUNNEWELL, JAMES F.,
  Scott, Sir Walter..........V, 151
HUNT, EPHRAIM,
  Hawthorne, Nathaniel.....VI, 366
  Whittier, John Greenleaf.VIII, 121
HUNT, JAMES HENRY LEIGH,
  Addison, Joseph.......II, 636, 646
  Alfred the Great............I, 37
  Amory, Thomas..........IV, 47
  Armstrong, John........III, 697
  Bacon, Francis.............I, 667
  Barnard, Lady Anne........V, 29

Beaumont and Fletcher......I, 581
Behn, Aphra..............II, 410
Berners, Juliana............I, 191
Blessington, Countess of....V, 590
Brougham, Henry Lord....VI, 523
Browne, William..........II, 75
Browning, Elizabeth Barrett..
  ....VI, 238, 243, 244
Burns, Robert............IV, 255
Butler, Samuel...........II, 335
Byron, George Gordon Lord...
  ....IV, 737, 743, 755
Campbell, Thomas.....V, 435, 441
Carlyle, Thomas.....VII, 231, 262
Carter, Elizabeth.........IV, 492
Cavendish, Margaret.....III, 231
Centlivre, Susannah.......II, 683
Chaucer, Geoffrey..........I, 159
Churchill, Charles........III, 480
Colenso, John William....VII, 526
Coleridge, Samuel Taylor....
  ....V, 210, 214
Collins, William..........III, 419
Colman, George...........V, 317
Congreve, William.........
  ..II, 735, 736, 737, 737, 739, 741
Cowley, Abraham......II, 195, 200
Cowper, William..........IV, 385
Crabbe, George............V, 172
Defoe, Daniel..........II, 35, 47
Dekker, Thomas...........II, 59
Dickens, Charles.........VI, 582
Doddridge, Philip........III, 300
Drummond, William......III, 102
Dryden, John........II, 465, 501
Evelyn, John.............III, 548
Farquhar, George.....II, 556, 557
Garrick, David..........III, 696
Garth, Sir Samuel.........II, 664
Gifford, William......V, 32, 35
Goldsmith, Oliver........III, 637
Gore, Catherine Grace......VI, 263
Gray, Thomas........III, 562, 568
Green, Matthew..........III, 94
Hazlitt, William...........V, 98
Hood, Thomas............V, 463
Hunt, James Henry Leigh...
  ....VI, 156, 164
James, George Paine Rainsford
  ....VI, 219
Johnson, Samuel.........III, 732
Jonson, Ben..............I, 763
Keats, John..IV, 663, 664, 671, 676
Knowles, James Sheridan..III 288
Lamb, Charles............V, 232
Landor, Walter Savage VI, 372, 379
Lovelace, Richard.........II, 161
Martineau, Harriet.......VII, 61
Marvell, Andrew..........II, 317
Middleton, Thomas........I, 685
Milton, John........II, 262, 290
Mitford, Mary Russell.....VI, 40
Montagu, Lady Mary Wortley
  ....III, 462
Moore, Thomas...........V, 706
More, Hannah............V, 195
Morgan, Sydney Owenson Lady
  ....VI, 194
Newton, Sir Isaac........II, 724
Norton, Caroline E. S....VII. 104
O'Keefe, John.............V, 196

Otway, Thomas........:...II, 367
Park, Mungo.............IV, 485
Parnell, Thomas..........II, 616
Pepys, Samuel...... ..II, 513
Philips John.............II, 563
Philips, Katherine.........II, 180
Poets and Poetry.........IV, 8
Pope, Alexander..........
  .....III, 153, 155, 161, 184, 187
Procter, Bryan Waller.....VI, 748
Radcliffe, Ann Ward...IV, 718, 719
Raleigh, Sir Walter........I, 600
Ramsay, Allan........III, 403, 407
Richardson, Samuel.......III, 434
Rossetti, Gabriel Charles Dante
  ....VII, 450
Sackville, Thomas..........I, 433
Seward, Anna.........IV, 544
Shakespeare, William......I, 558
Shelley, Percy Bysshe..IV, 692, 706
Shenstone, William......III, 474
Sheridan, Richard Brinsley...
  ....IV, 594, 605
Smith, Charlotte.........IV, 497
Smith, Horace.............V, 597
Smith, James............V, 338
Smollett, Tobias George....III, 586
Southerne, Thomas......III, 240
Southey, Robert...... .V, 405
Spenser, Edmund......I, 388, 395
Steele, Sir Richard.....II, 753, 763
Sterne, Laurence.........III, 507
Suckling, Sir John..........II, 64
Swift, Jonathan..........III, 231
Thomson, James......III, 267, 268
Tighe, Mary.............IV, 551
Tucker, Abraham........III, 644
Vanbrugh, Sir John........II, 703
Waller, Edmund..........II, 382
Walpole, Horace..........IV, 313
Warton, Thomas..........IV, 78
Wiseman, Nicholas Patrick.VI, 438
Wolcot, John.............IV, 650
Wordsworth, William........
  ....V, 610, 629, 634
Wycherley, William.........
  ....II, 600, 602, 603, 604
HUNT, JOHN,
  Butler, Joseph...........III, 311
  Cooper, Anthony Ashley...II, 579
  Hume, David............III, 654
  Tindal, Matthew..........III, 72
  Warburton, William......III, 691
  Woolston, Thomas........VII, 74
HUNT, LEIGH, AND LEE, S. ADAMS,
  Williams, Helen Maria......V, 75
HUNT, ROBERT,
  Davy, Sir Humphry........V, 94
HUNT, THEODORE W.,
  Addison, Joseph..........II, 659
  Ælfric....................I, 46
  Browning, Elizabeth Barrett..
  ....VI, 247
  Burke, Edmund..........IV, 296
  Dickens, Charles.........VI, 589
  Everett, Edward........VI, 427
  Fortescue, Sir John ....I, 195
  Hooker, Richard..........II, 409
  Johnson, Samuel........III, 765
  Landor, Walter Savage.....VI, 386

INDEX TO CRITICISMS

	Vol. and Page
Longfellow, Henry Wadsworth	VII, 412
Macaulay, Thomas Babington Lord	VI, 113
Milton, John	II, 278
Swift, Jonathan	III, 224
Whitman, Walt	VIII, 144
HUNT, THORNTON,	
Byron, George Gordon Lord	IV, 740
Hunt, James Henry Leigh	VI, 158
Shelley, Percy Bysshe	IV, 694, 703
HUNT, WILLIAM,	
Burke, Edmund	IV, 296
Collier, Jeremy	II, 702
Fox, Charles James	IV, 502, 505
Freeman, Edward Augustus	VIII, 157
Ken, Thomas	II, 568, 569
Lanfranc	I, 48
Lowth, Robert	IV, 28
Paris, Matthew	I, 75
Sacheverell, Henry	II, 696
HUNT, WILLIAM HOLMAN,	
Rossetti, Gabriel Charles Dante	VII, 443
Ruskin, John	VIII, 409
HUNTINGTON, E. B.,	
Sigourney, Lydia Huntley	VI, 451, 452
HUNTINGTON, GEORGE,	
Thirlwall, Connop	VII, 43
Wilberforce, Samuel	VI, 734
HUNTINGTON, H. A.,	
Centlivre, Susannah	II, 683, 684
Cibber, Colley	III, 373
Farquhar, George	II, 558
HUNTER, JOSEPH,	
Cavendish, George	I, 282
Shakespeare, William	I, 450, 517
HUNTER, SIR WILLIAM WILSON	
Arnold, Sir Edwin	VIII, 505
Thackeray, William Makepeace	VI, 298
HURD, FAYETTE,	
Milton, John	II, 277
HURD, RICHARD,	
Addison, Joseph	II, 644, 652
Ascham, Roger	I, 290
Barrow, Isaac	II, 312
Beattie, James	IV, 433
Boswell, James	IV, 215
Buchanan, George	I, 314
Burnet, Gilbert	II, 593
Clarke, Samuel	II, 748
Cowley, Abraham	II, 199
Dalrymple, Sir David	IV, 145
Fielding, Henry	III, 340
Gibbon, Edward	IV, 181
Horne, George	IV, 144
Jonson, Ben	I, 752, 761
Locke, John	II, 533
Lowth, William	III, 63
Malone, Edmund	IV, 579
Mason, William	IV, 325
Middleton, Conyers	III, 279
Otway, Thomas	II, 363
Roscoe, William	V, 118
Taylor, Jeremy	II, 205
Warburton, William	III, 684, 686, 687, 690

	Vol. and Page
HURDIS, JAMES,	
Akenside, Mark	III, 544
Dillon, Wentworth	II, 361
Dryden, John	II, 498
Kingsley, Charles	VII, 26
HURLL, ESTELLE M.,	
Reynolds, Sir Joshua	IV, 142
HURST, JOHN FLETCHER,	
Colet, John	I, 212
Cranmer, Thomas	I, 273
Knox, John	I, 303
Landor, Walter Savage	VI, 377
Rutherford, Samuel	II, 167
HUSBAND, MARY GILLILAND,	
DuMaurier, George	VIII, 345
HUSK, WILLIAM H.,	
Carey, Henry	III, 139
Hawkins, Sir John	IV, 52
HUTCHINSON, BENJAMIN,	
Akenside, Mark	III, 542
HUTCHINSON, LUCY,	
May, Thomas	II, 119
HUTCHINSON, PETER ORLANDO,	
Hutchinson, Thomas	III, 707
HUTCHINSON, THOMAS,	
Locker-Lampson, Frederick	VIII, 313
Lockhart, John Gibson	V, 757
Macpherson, James	IV, 280
HUTCHINSON, WILLIAM,	
Butler, Joseph	III, 307
HUTH, ALFRED HENRY,	
Buckle, Henry Thomas	VI, 280
HUTSON, CHARLES WOODWARD,	
Hawes, Stephen	I, 219
Mandeville, Sir John	I, 98
Skelton, John	I, 223
Steele, Sir Richard	II, 755
HUTTON, ARTHUR WOLLASTON,	
Manning, Henry Edward	VIII, 164
HUTTON, CATHERINE,	
Bage, Robert	IV, 418
HUTTON, FREDERICK WOLLASTON,	
Darwin, Charles Robert	VII, 425
HUTTON, LAURENCE,	
Boswell, James	IV, 219
Brontë, Charlotte	V, 12
Bunner, Henry Cuyler	VIII, 359
Butler, Samuel	II, 330
Centlivre, Susannah	II, 683
Dodgson, Charles Lutwige	VIII, 398
Drayton, Michael	I, 640
Dickens, Charles	VI, 571, 594
Drummond, William	II, 101
Fergusson, Robert	III, 640
Fiske, John	VIII, 456
Fletcher, John	I, 628
Freeman, Edward Augustus	VIII, 157
Gladstone, William Ewart	VIII, 386
Granger, James	III, 670
Green, John Richard	VII, 507
Grote, George	VI, 609
Home, John	IV, 513
Hood, Thomas	V, 461
Johnson, Samuel	III, 733
Jowett, Benjamin	VIII, 210

	Vol. and Page
Kingsley, Henry	VII, 79
Knowles, James Sheridan	VI, 287
Lamb, Charles	V, 235
Landor, Walter Savage	VI, 378
Lee, Nathaniel	II, 431
Lovelace, Richard	II, 161
Lover, Samuel	VI, 544
Mackenzie, Henry	V, 113
Milton, John	II, 249
Otway, Thomas	II, 362
Pater, Walter Horatio	VIII, 276
Payne, John Howard	V, 736
Ramsay, Allan	III, 403
Richardson, Samuel	III, 435
Scott, Sir Walter	V, 133
Smith, Adam	IV, 68
Sterne, Laurence	III, 504
Tennyson, Alfred Lord	VIII, 76
Walton, Isaac	II, 346
Wolcot, John	IV, 649
HUTTON, RICHARD HOLT,	
Arnold, Matthew	VII, 636
Bagehot, Walter	VII, 97, 97
Baillie, Joanna	V, 694
Burns, Robert	IV, 246
Clough, Arthur Hugh	VI, 253
De Morgan, Augustus	VI, 633
Eliot, George	VII, 183, 185
Emerson, Ralph Waldo	VII, 356, 370
Longfellow, Henry Wadsworth	VII, 396, 409
Greg, William Rathbone	VII, 320
Hawthorne, Nathaniel	VI, 360, 366
Hogg, James	V, 268
Huxley, Thomas Henry	VII, 325
Johnson, Samuel	III, 761
Lamb, Charles	V, 242
Maurice, John Frederick Denison	VI, 645
Milnes, Richard Monckton	VII, 564
Sharp, John Campbell	VII, 570
Newman, John Henry	VII, 741
Poe, Edgar Allan	V, 539, 547
Scott, Sir Walter	V, 132, 136, 140
Stanley, Arthur Penrhyn	VII, 298, 304
Tennyson, Alfred Lord	VIII, 88
Ward, William George	VII, 483
Wordsworth, William	V, 641
HUTTON, WILLIAM,	
Priestley, Joseph	IV, 446
HUTTON, WILLIAM HOLDEN,	
Andrews, Lancelot	I, 637
Barrow, Isaac	II, 311
Baxter, Richard	II, 425, 426
Bull, George	II, 565
Chillingworth, William	II, 86
Church, Richard William	VII, 729
Freeman, Edward Augustus	VIII, 156
Fuller, Thomas	II, 170
Gauden, John	II, 177
Gardiner, Samuel Rawson	VIII, 465
Herbert, George	I, 721
Hooker, Richard	I, 410
Kingsley, Charles	VII, 33
Laud, William	II, 92
Milton, John	II, 282, 283
More, Sir Thomas	I, 239, 240
Robert of Gloucester	I, 82

INDEX TO CRITICISMS

	Vol. and Page
Sherlock, Thomas	III, 455
South, Robert	II, 607
Stillingfleet, Edward	II, 455
Stubbs, William	VIII, 453
Taylor, Jeremy	II, 211
Usher, James	II, 152
HUXLEY, THOMAS HENRY,	
Berkeley, George	III, 322, 325
Carlyle, Thomas	VII, 267
Darwin, Charles Robert	
	VII, 418, 425, 428
Eliot, George	VII, 173
George, Henry	VIII, 380
Harvey, William	II, 157
Hume, David	III, 650
Huxley, Thomas Henry	
	VIII, 321, 322
Literature	I, 9
Lyell, Sir Charles	VII, 35
Mansel, Henry Longueville	VI, 627
Owen, Sir Richard	VIII, 173
Priestley, Joseph	IV, 450
Tyndall, John	VIII, 196
Ward, William George	VII, 483
HYDE, LORD,	
Saint-John, Henry	III, 291
HYDE, THOMAS ALEXANDER,	
Brooks, Phillips,	VIII, 227
HYNDMAN, H. M.,	
George, Henry	VIII, 379
IDDESLEIGH, EARL OF,	
Austen, Jane	IV, 625
INCHBALD, ELIZABETH,	
Colman, George	IV, 202
Cumberland, Richard	IV, 560
Dryden, John	II, 477
Farquhar, George	II, 557
Godwin, William	V, 303
Holcroft, Thomas	IV, 546
Lillo, George	IIII, 100
Shakespeare, William	I, 538
Sheridan, Richard Brinsley	IV, 640
Southerne, Thomas	III, 240
INGELOW, JEAN,	
Knowledge	V, 9
Poets and Poetry	IV, 9
INGERSOLL, CHARLES JARED,	
Calhoun, John Caldwell	V, 676
INGERSOLL, ERNEST,	
Gray, Asa	VII, 670
INGERSOL, ROBERT GREEN,	
Lincoln, Abraham	VI, 415
Paine, Thomas	IV, 533, 535, 537
Whitman, Walt	VIII, 144
INGLEBY, CLEMENT MANSFIELD,	
Milton, John	II, 249
Shakespeare, William	I, 544
INGLISS, BERT,	
Poets and Poetry	IV, 10
INGRAM, JOHN H.,	
Browning, Elizabeth Barrett	
	VI, 234, 236, 246
Chatterton, Thomas	III, 538
Dickens, Charles	VI, 565
Griswold, Rufus Wilmot	VI, 78
Holmes, Oliver Wendell	VIII, 291
Mangan, James Clarence	V, 603
Motherwell, William	V, 278
Poe, Edgar Allan	V, 534, 541

	Vol. and Page
INGRAM, JOHN KELLS,	
Mill, John Stuart	VI, 717
Ricardo, David	IV, 727
Smith, Adam	IV, 67
Tucker, Josiah	IV, 370
Young, Arthur	IV, 656
INNES, ALEXANDER TAYLOR,	
Knox, John	I, 302
Mackenzie, Sir George	II, 429
INNES, C.,	
Boece, Hector	I, 243
INSCRIPTION ON CENOTAPH,	
Anstey, Christopher	IV, 479
Montagu, Lady Mary Wortley	
	III, 460
INSCRIPTION ON GRAVE, TABLET, OR TOMB,	
Adams, John Quincy	V, 515
Bacon, Francis Lord	I, 638
Baxter, Richard	II, 423
Brown, Thomas	II, 540
Browne, Sir Thomas	II, 339
Bruce, James	IV, 205
Burns, Robert	IV, 225
Butler, Samuel	II, 329
Caxton, William	I, 197
Daniel, Samuel	I, 611
Darwin, Erasmus	IV, 420
Davy, Sir Humphrey	V, 91
Day, Thomas	IV, 49
Defoe, Daniel	III, 23
Dibdin, Charles	IV, 585
Donne, John	I, 710
Edwards, Jonathan	III, 381
Ferguson, James	III, 668
Fielding, Henry	III, 339
Gray, David	VI, 260
Hamilton, Alexander	IV, 557
Hamilton, Sir William	VI, 51
Hazlitt, William	V, 98
Hooker, Richard	I, 403
Hume, David	III, 649
Hunter, John	IV, 165
Inchbald, Elizabeth	IV, 687
Johnson, Samuel	III, 723
Landon, Letitia Elizabeth	V, 323
Livingstone, David	VI, 727
Marvell, Andrew	II, 313
Newton, Sir Isaac	II, 713
Pitt, William	IV, 508
Shakespeare, William	I, 447, 448
Sheridan, Richard Brinsley	IV, 594
Smollett, Tobias George	III, 574
Spenser, Edmund	I, 370
Tennyson, Alfred Lord	VIII, 73
Walton, Isaac	II, 345
Warton, Joseph	IV, 396
Wesley, John	IV, 112
White, Gilbert	IV, 147
Wilson, Alexander	IV, 581
INSCRIPTION ON PORTRAIT,	
Tyndale, William	I, 245
IRELAND, ALEXANDER,	
Emerson, Ralph Waldo	VII, 367
Hunt, James Henry Leigh	
	VI, 164, 164, 171
IRELAND, MRS. ALEXANDER,	
Froude, James Anthony	VIII, 256
IRELAND, ANNIE E.,	
Browning, Robert	VII, 710
Carlyle, Thomas	VII, 239

	Vol. and Page
Irving, Edward	V, 248
IRELAND, S. W. H.,	
Macklin, Charles	IV, 344
Mathias, Thomas James	V, 288
IRELAND, WILLIAM HENRY,	
Chatterton, Thomas	III, 529
Ireland, William Henry	V, 290
Malone, Edmond	IV, 579
Steevens, George	IV, 410
IRVING, DAVID,	
Alexander, Sir William	II, 35
Ayton, Sir Robert	I, 768
Barbour, John	I, 113
Barclay, Alexander	I, 265
Blacklock, Thomas	IV, 131
Buchanan, George	I, 316
Burns, Robert	IV, 224
Douglas, Gawin	I, 214
Drummond, William	II, 101
Dunbar, William	I, 224
Henryson, Robert	I, 208
James I of Scotland	I, 182
Lyndsay, Sir David	I, 275
Macpherson, James	IV, 276
Maitland, Sir Richard	I, 333
Scott Alexander	I, 319
Stuart, Gilbert	IV, 27
Taylor, Jeremy	II, 209
Thomas of Erceldoune	I, 84
Urquhart, Sir Thomas	II, 165
Warton, Thomas	IV, 78
Wyntoun, Andrew	I, 178
IRVING, HENRY,	
Drama, The	VII, 8
IRVING, JOHN W.,	
Thackeray, William Makepeace	
	VI, 315
IRVING, PIERRE M.,	
Irving, Washington	VI, 135
IRVING, WALTER,	
Dickens, Charles	VI, 586
IRVING, WASHINGTON,	
Allston, Washington	V, 420
Audubon, John James	V, 697
Boswell, James	IV, 216
Bryant, William Cullen	VII, 120
Byron, George Gordon Lord	IV, 739
Campbell, Thomas	V, 436, 443
Cooper, James Fenimore	V, 684
Goldsmith, Oliver	
	III, 618, 627, 632, 632, 637
Hamilton, Alexander	IV, 458
Hawkins, Sir John	IV, 51
Hawthorne, Nathaniel	IV, 357
Irving, Washington	VI, 139
James I of Scotland	I, 180
Jay, John	V, 95
Kenrick, William	III, 702
Lyly, John	I, 426
Mandeville, Sir John	I, 95
Moore, Thomas	V, 716
Prescott, William Hickling	VI, 185
Roscoe, William	V, 116
Scott, Sir Walter	V, 128
Shakespeare, William	I, 449
Sidney, Sir Philip	I, 325
Sparks, Jared	VI, 467
Ticknor, George	VI, 616
Tuckerman, Henry Theodore	
	VI, 642
Washington, George	IV, 360

INDEX TO CRITICISMS

	Vol. and Page
Willis, Nathaniel Parker	VI, 486

IVIMEY, JOSEPH,
Bunyan, John .... II, 393

JACK, ADOLPHUS ALFRED,
Scott, Sir Walter .... V, 149, 150
JACKSON, A. V. WILLIAMS,
Müller, Friedrich Max..VIII, 440
JACKSON, A. W.,
Martineau, James...VIII, 425, 428
Taylor, William .... V, 320
JACKSON, HELEN HUNT,
Burns, Robert .... IV, 232
Poets and Poetry .... IV, 9
JACKSON, SAMUEL MACAULEY,
Dunstan .... I, 43
Giraldus Cambrensis ...... I, 67
Guthrie, Thomas .... VI, 735
Sherlock, Thomas .... III, 454
Woolston, Thomas .... III, 73
JACKSON, THOMAS,
Wesley, Charles .... IV, 36
Wesley, John .... IV, 119
JACKSON, ZACHARIAH,
Shakespeare, William ..... I, 556
JACOBS, JOSEPH,
Browning, Robert .... VII, 695, 709
Eliot, George .... VII, 193
Howell, James .... II, 188
Martineau, James .... VIII, 429
Newman, John Henry .... VII, 753
Seeley, Sir John Robert......
.... VIII, 308, 309, 310
Stevenson, Robert Louis..VIII, 248
Tennyson, Alfred Lord...VIII, 107
JACOBUS, RUSSELL P.,
Pater, Walter Horatio....VIII, 279
JACOX, FRANCIS,
Beckford, William .... V, 449
Chalmers, Thomas .... V, 495
Cowper, William .... IV, 373
DeQuincey, Thomas .. VI, 122, 126
Dibdin, Charles .... IV, 585
Dunbar, William .... I, 225
Goldsmith, Oliver .... III, 638
Hallam, Henry .... VI, 199
Horsley, Samuel .... IV, 495
Jerrold, Douglas William...VI, 68
Johnson, Samuel .... III, 151
Pope, Alexander .... III, 151
Southey, Robert .... V, 401
Thackeray, William Makepeace
.... VI, 316
JAGO, RICHARD,
Shenstone, William .... III, 473
JAMES, HENRY,
Alcott, Louisa May .... VII, 667
Arnold, Matthew .... VII, 642
Browning, Robert .... VII, 697
Carlyle, Thomas .... VII, 258
Critic, The .... II, 9
Du Maurier, George ..... VIII, 346
Eliot, George ....
.... VII, 183, 185, 186, 196
Emerson, Ralph Waldo....VII, 366
Fuller, Sarah Margaret...... 667
Hamilton, Sir William ..... VI, 54
Hawthorne, Nathaniel......
..VI, 354, 358, 359, 362, 363, 370
Kemble, Frances Ann ......
.... VIII, 213, 216

	Vol. and Page
Kingsley, Charles	VII, 21
Livingstone, David	VI, 730
Lockhart, John Gibson	V, 756
Lowell, James Russell	VIII, 22, 41
Morris, William	VIII, 333
Poe, Edgar Allan	V, 555
Stevenson, Robert Louis	
....	VIII, 244, 246
Story, William Wetmore	VIII, 318
Taylor, Bayard	VII, 132
Thoreau, Henry David	VI, 273
Trollope, Anthony	VII, 461
Whitman, Walt	VIII, 137

JAMES, HENRY, SR.,
Carlyle, Thomas .... VII, 235
Emerson, Ralph Waldo....VII, 348
JAMES I.,
Books .... III, 5
Gower, John .... I, 174
James I .... I, 180
JAMES VI. OF SCOTLAND,
Buchanan, George .... I, 316
JAMESON, ANNA BROWNELL,
Allston, Washington .... V, 421
Blake, William .... V, 58
Browning, Elizabeth Barrett..
.... VI, 229
Burns, Robert .... IV, 237
Carew, Thomas .... II, 20
Channing, William Ellery...V, 366
Chaucer, Geoffrey .... I, 159
Collins, William .... III, 416
Daniel, Samuel .... I, 621
Donne, John .... I, 711
Drayton, Michael .... I, 701
Drummond, William ...... II, 100
Dryden, John .... II, 499
Goldsmith, Oliver .... III, 617
Gray, Thomas .... III, 555
Habington, William .... II, 135
Knowledge .... V, 8
Pope, Alexander .... III, 154
Prior, Matthew .... II, 674
Scott, Sir Walter .... V, 127
Shakespeare, William......
I, 473, 482, 483, 495, 496,
499, 503, 513, 516, 521, 526,
528, 534, 537, 538, 558
Shenstone, William ...... III, 472
Sidney, Sir Philip .... I, 327
Spenser, Edmund ...... I, 370, 388
Surrey, Earl of .... I, 255
Swift, Jonathan .... III, 212
Thackeray, William Makepeace
.... VI, 308
Waller, Edmund .... II, 378
JAMESON, JOHN FRANKLIN,
Hildreth, Richard .... VI, 454
Irving, Washington ...VI, 140, 145
Lowell, James Russell....VIII, 19
Motley, John Lothrop.......
.... VII, 91, 93, 95
Palfrey, John Gorham ..... VII, 339
Parkman, Francis .... VIII, 221
JAMIESON, T. H.,
Barclay, Alexander .... I, 265
JANNEY, SAMUEL N. (JOSIAH MARSH),
Fox, George .... II, 420
JAPP, ALEXANDER HAY,
Blanchard, Samuel Laman...V, 482

	Vol. and Page
DeQuincey, Thomas	VI, 123, 124
Kemble, Frances Ann	VIII, 216
Kingsley, Charles	VII, 30
Lamb, Charles	V, 241
Hallam, Arthur Henry	V, 199
Smith, Alexander	VI, 518
Taylor, Sir Henry	VII, 582, 584
Tennyson, Frederick	VIII, 400
Thoreau, Henry David	VI, 273
Turner, Charles Tennyson	
....	VII, 162, 163

JARDINE, DAVID,
Raleigh, Sir Walter .... I, 595
JARDINE, SIR WILLIAM,
Wilson, Alexander .... IV, 583
JAY, JOHN,
Motley, John Lothrop.....VII, 86
JAY, W. M. L.,
Brooks, Phillips .... VIII, 231
JAY, WILLIAM,
Jay, John .... V, 95
JEAFFRESON, JOHN CORDY,
Akenside, Mark .... III, 541
Byron, George Gordon Lord...
.... IV, 742, 762
Dickens, Charles .... VI, 583
Eliot, George .... VII, 179
Garth, Sir Samuel .... II, 665
Godwin, Mary Wollstonecraft.
.... IV, 331
Reeve, Clara .... IV, 512
Shelley, Percy Bysshe .... IV, 696
Thackeray, William Makepeace
.... VI, 314
JEANS, GEORGE EDWARD,
Trollope, Anthony .... VII, 460
JEANS, WILLIAM T.,
Tyndall, John .... VIII, 198
JEBB, JOHN,
Boyle, Robert .... II, 418
JEBB, RICHARD CLAVERHOUSE,
Bentley, Richard..........
..III, 111, 112, 114, 116, 118, 123
Macaulay, Thomas Babington
Lord .... VI, 94, 109
Porson, Richard ...... IV, 524 526
Swift, Jonathan .... III, 213
Tennyson, Alfred Lord...VIII, 89
JEFFERSON, JOSEPH,
Irving, Washington .... VI, 143
JEFFERSON, THOMAS,
Adams, Samuel .... IV, 441
Burke, Edmond .... IV, 299
Franklin, Benjamin .... IV, 85
Jefferson, Thomas .... V, 41
Madison, James .... V, 312
Marshall, John .... V, 284
Paine, Thomas .... IV, 536
Priestley, Joseph ..... IV, 446, 453
Saint-John, Henry .... IV, 294
Washington, George...IV, 358, 366
JEFFERY, EDWARD,
William, Sir Charles Hanbury.
.... III, 412
JEFFREY, FRANCIS LORD,
Addison, Joseph ...... II, 650, 656
Akenside, Mark .... III, 544
Alison, Archibald .... V, 342
Baillie, Joanna .... V, 692
Barbauld, Anna Lætitia ..... V, 23
Barlow, Joel .... IV, 574

INDEX TO CRITICISMS

Name	Vol. and Page
Barton, Bernard	V, 595
Beattie, James	IV, 430
Burns, Robert	IV, 241, 247, 250
Byron, George Gordon Lord	VI, 750, 754, 756
Campbell, Thomas	V, 439, 440, 441, 442
Cobbett, William	V, 272
Combe, George	VI, 89
Cowper, William	IV, 381, 386
Crabbe, George	V, 173
Cumberland, Richard	IV, 560
Dickens, Charles	VI, 551, 568, 571
Dryden, John	II, 469, 499
Edgeworth, Maria	V, 567
Ford, John	II, 30
Franklin, Benjamin	IV, 84, 99
Galt, John	V, 335
Goldsmith, Oliver	III, 636
Grahame, James	IV, 567
Grant, Anne	V, 329
Gray, Thomas	III, 565
Hazlitt, William	V, 102
Heber, Reginald	V, 37, 38
Hemans, Felicia Dorothea	V, 258
Hogg, James	V, 266
Holcroft, Thomas	IV, 546
Horner, Francis	IV, 629
Hume David	III, 656
Irving, Washington	VI, 141, 144, 144
Jeffrey, Francis Lord	V, 654
Johnson, Samuel	III, 740
Jones, Sir William	IV, 197
Keats, John	IV, 671, 672, 675
Locke, John	II, 533
Lockhart, John Gibson	V, 755, 756
Macaulay, Thomas Babington Lord	VI, 103
Mackintosh, Sir James	V, 179, 182
Montagu, Elizabeth	IV, 402
Montagu, Lady Mary Wortley	III, 466
Montgomery, James	V, 766
Moore, Thomas	V, 711, 714
Oliphant, Margaret O. W.	VIII, 367
Opie, Amelia	V, 743
Otway, Thomas	II, 367
Paley, William	IV, 474, 475
Pepys, Samuel	II, 514
Pope, Alexander	III, 184
Prescott, William Hickling	VI, 186
Priestley, Joseph	IV, 447, 449, 453
Prior, Matthew	II, 676
Procter, Bryan Waller	VI, 747
Raleigh, Sir Walter	I, 595
Reid, Thomas	IV, 284
Richardson, Samuel	III, 433, 447, 448
Rogers, Samuel	VI, 38, 53
Rowe, Nicholas	II, 622
Scott, Sir Walter	V, 138, 140, 149, 150, 54, 155, 155
Shakespeare, William	I, 555
Sheridan, Richard Brinsley	IV, 606
Southey, Robert	V, 403, 407, 407, 409, 411
Sotheby, William	V, 204
Stewart, Dugald	V, 77
Swift, Jonathan	III, 200, 217, 227, 230
Taylor, Jeremy	II, 207
Tennant, William	V, 527
Thomson, James	III, 265, 267
Warburton, William	III, 685, 686, 690
Wilkes, John	IV, 335
Wilson, John	V, 749, 750
Wordsworth, William	V, 621, 622, 629
Young, Edward	III, 492
JEFFREYS, GEORGE LORD,	
Baxter, Richard	II, 423
JENKINS, EDWARD,	
Cavendish, Margaret	II, 232
JENKINS, JOHN S.,	
Calhoun, John Caldwell	V, 675
JENKINS, O. L.,	
Addison, Joseph	II, 641
Brownson, Orestes Augustus	VII, 74
Challoner, Richard	III, 710
Gaskell, Elizabeth Cleghorn	VI, 431
Hooker, Richard	I, 408
Hume, David	III, 659
Lanfranc	I, 48
Longfellow, Henry Wadsworth	VI, 405
Motley, John Lothrop	VII, 94
Ryan, Abram Joseph	VII, 598
Sandys, George	II, 81
Wiseman, Nicholas Patrick	VI, 438
Young, Edward	III, 489
JENNINGS, HENRY J.,	
Newman, John Henry	VII, 744
Tennyson, Alfred Lord	VIII, 71
JENNINGS, LOUIS J.,	
Croker, John Wilson	VI, 72
Disraeli, Benjamin	VII, 277
Oliphant, Laurence	VII, 656
JENYNS, SOAME,	
Johnson, Samuel	III, 725
JEPHSON, HENRY,	
Burke, Edmund	IV, 296
Fox, Charles James	IV, 505
JERDAN, WILLIAM,	
Campbell, Thomas	V, 437
Coleridge, Samuel Taylor	V, 211
Hogg, James	V, 264
Rogers, Samuel	VI, 35
Wordsworth, William	V, 612
JEROME, JEROME K.,	
Dickens, Charles	VI, 574, 594
JERROLD, BLANCHARD,	
Ainsworth, William Harrison	VII, 488
Dickens, Charles	VI, 555
Forster, John	VII, 65
Godwin, William	V, 294
Mahoney, Francis	VI, 483
JERROLD, DOUGLAS,	
Hunt, James Henry Leigh	V, 169
Knowles, James Sheridan	VI, 287
JERROLD, WALTER,	
Foote, Samuel	III, 672
Hook, Theodore Edward	V, 357
Jerrold, Douglas William	VI, 66, 69
Sheridan, Richard Brinsley	IV, 608
JERROLD, WILLIAM BLANCHARD,	
Jerrold, Douglas William	VI, 68
Thackeray, William Makepeace	VI, 295
JERSEY,	
Tate, Natham	II, 588
JESSE, EDWARD,	
White, Gilbert	IV, 152
JESSE, JOHN HENEAGE,	
Chatterton, Thomas	III, 531
Etheredge, Sir George	II, 413
Herbert, Edward Lord	II, 96
Hyde, Edward, Earl of Clarendon	II, 300
Saint-John, Henry	III, 294
Sedley, Sir Charles	II, 508
Sheffield, John, Third Earl of Mulgrave	II, 670
Suckling, Sir John	II, 63
JESSOPP, AUGUSTUS,	
Borrow, George Henry	VII, 308
Carew, Thomas	II, 21
Coleridge, Samuel Taylor	V, 221
Donne, John	I, 712, 713
Hooker, Richard	I, 411
Lamb, Charles	V, 243
Lowell, James Russell	III, 29
North, Roger	III, 79, 80
Ruskin, John	VIII, 410
Shelley, Percy Bysshe	IV, 713
Southey, Robert	V, 406
JEVONS, W. STANLEY,	
Mill, John Stuart	VI, 716
JEWETT, SOPHIE,	
Lanier, Sidney	VII, 327
JEWSBURY, GERALDINE ENDSOR,	
Morgan, Sydney Owenson Lady	VI, 192, 193
JEWSBURY, MARIA JANE (MRS. FLETCHER,)	
Hemans, Felicia Dorothea	V, 254
JOHNES, ARTHUR JAMES,	
Kent, James	V, 502
JOHNS, B. G.,	
Aubrey, John	II, 453
JOHNSON, ALFRED SIDNEY,	
Davidson, Lucretia Maria	V, 26
JOHNSON, ARNOLD BURGES,	
Sumner, Charles	VI, 752
JOHNSON, BRADLEY T.,	
Washington, George	IV, 365
JOHNSON, CHARLES FREDERICK,	
Addison, Joseph	II, 661
Browne, Charles Farriar	VI, 505
Browne, Sir Thomas	II, 345
Bunyan, John	II, 400
Byron, George Gordon Lord	IV, 766
Chaucer, Geoffrey	I, 171
Coleridge, Samuel Taylor	V, 225
Congreve, William	II, 745
Cowley, Abraham	II, 202
Defoe, Daniel	III, 50
Dickens, Charles	VI, 594
Dryden, John	II, 507
Du Maurier, George	VIII, 345
Emerson, Ralph Waldo	VII, 371
Froude, James Anthony	VIII, 266

INDEX TO CRITICISMS

	Vol. and Page
Hawthorne, Nathaniel.	VI, 354, 370
Hunt, James Henry Leigh.	II, 172
Johnson, Samuel.	III, 768
Keats, John.	IV, 674
Knowledge.	V, 10
Longfellow, Henry Wadsworth	VII, 386, 393, 399, 411
Lytton, Sir Edward George...	
Bulwer.	VI, 691
Malory, Sir Thomas	I, 206
Pater, Walter Horatio.	VIII, 276
Rossetti, Gabriel Charles Dante	VII, 455
Shelley, Percy Bysshe.	IV, 699
Steele, Sir Richard.	II, 768
Trollope, Anthony.	VII, 464
Whittier, John Greenleaf.	VIII, 128
Wordsworth, William.	V, 627

JOHNSON, E. G.,
Burton, Sir Richard Francis.. .... VII, 760
Dodgson, Charles Lutwige.... .... VIII, 398, 399

JOHNSON, FLORENCE K.,
Dodge, Mary Abigail..... VIII, 362
Du Maurier, George ..... VIII, 343

JOHNSON, GEORGE W.,
Selden, John .... II, 140

JOHNSON, H. H.,
Livingstone, David........ VI, 729

JOHNSON, J. WESLEY.,
Wesley, John.............. IV, 126

JOHNSON, JOHN,
Hayley, William.......... IV, 651
Shakespeare, William .... I, 549

JOHNSON, LIONEL,
Arnold, Matthew......... VII, 638
Blake, William............. V, 58
Byron, George Gordon Lord... .... IV, 742, 765
Mangan, James Clarence. V, 602, 604
Manning, Henry Edward..... .... VIII, 165, 168
Morris, William......... VIII, 336
Pater, Walter Horatio.... VIII, 277
Rossetti, Christina Georgina.. .... VIII, 273
Thackeray, William Makepeace .... VI, 319

JOHNSON, REGINALD BRIMLEY,
DeQuincey, Thomas....... VI, 130
Hunt, James Henry Leigh.... .... VI, 164, 167, 171
Lytton, Edward Robert Bulwer. .... VIII, 47
Martineau, Harriet....... VII, 64
Mitford, Mary Russell... VI, 45, 46
More, Hannah............. V, 196
Reynolds, Sir Joshua...... IV, 143

JOHNSON, ROBERT W.,
Emerson, Ralph Waldo.... VII, 367

JOHNSON, ROSSITER,
Barnes, William......... VII, 586
Clough, Arthur Hugh..... VI, 248
Dibdin, Charles........... IV, 585
Griffin, Gerald............. V, 351
Halleck, Fritz-Greene..... VI, 494
Hawthorne, Nathaniel..... VI, 366
Lovelace, Richard......... II, 160
Lowell, James Russell... VIII, 31
Mackenzie, Henry......... V, 112

	Vol. and Page
Mangan, James Clarence.	V, 600
Motherwell, William.	V, 276, 277
Pierpont, John.	VI, 480
Pinkney, Edward Coate.	V, 85
Southey, Caroline Anne Bowles	V, 762
Vaughan, Henry.	II, 441
White, Joseph Blanco.	V, 359
Wilde, Richard Henry.	V, 503, 504

JOHNSON, SAMUEL,
Addison, Joseph............ II, 634, 640, 641, 643, 646, 649, 654
Akenside, Mark....... III, 542, 543
Arbuthnot, John... III, 82, 83, 84
Ascham, Roger........ I, 288, 289
Atterbury, Francis....... III, 67
Authors and Authorship.. VIII, 6
Barbauld, Anna Lætitia..... V, 22
Bentley, Richard..... III, 117, 119
Berkeley, George.......... III, 328
Blacklock, Thomas........ IV, 130
Blair, Hugh.............. IV, 404
Boece, Hector............. I, 242
Broome, William......... III, 239
Brown, Thomas........... II, 540
Browne, Sir Thomas........ .... II, 341, 341, 342
Budgell, Eustace....... III, 91, 92
Bunyan, John............. II, 393
Burke, Edmund.......... IV, 289
Burnet, Gilbert........... III, 593
Burney, Frances........... V, 345
Burton, Robert............ II, 38
Butler, Samuel.... II, 330, 331, 334
Carte, Thomas .... III, 337
Chaucer, Geoffrey.......... I, 156
Chatterton, Thomas....... III, 534
Churchill, Charles........ III, 478
Cibber, Colley........ III, 370, 374
Cibber, Theophilus....... III, 395
Collier, Jeremy........... II, 700
Collins, William....... III, 414, 419
Congreve, William........... .... II, 735, 735, 740, 747
Cowley, Abraham.......... .... II, 195, 196, 199
Crabbe, George............ V, 172
Dalrymple, Sir David...... IV, 146
Defoe, Daniel.......... III, 33, 44
Denham, Sir John...... II, 221, 222
Dennis, John.............. III, 77
Dillion, Wentworth....... III, 360
Dodd, William............ III, 675
Dodsley, Robert.......... III, 482
Dryden, John............... ....II, 464, 470, 476, 480, 482, 483, 486, 490, 491, 492, 497
Dyer, John....... III, 398, 398, 399
Fenton, Elijah .... III, 20, 20
Fielding, Henry.......... III, 356
Foote, Samuel........ III, 671, 673
Fox, Charles James........ IV, 499
Garrick, David............ III, 694
Garth, Sir Samuel......... II, 665
Gay, John............. III, 55, 60
Goldsmith, Oliver .... III, 614, 615, 623, 624, 635
Gower, John............... I, 175
Grainger, James.......... III, 498
Granville, George......... III, 88

	Vol. and Page
Gray, Thomas............. III, 554, 558, 561, 564
Hawkins, Sir John........	IV, 50
Hervey, James..........	III, 397
Hill, John	III, 645
History	VI, 6
Hughes, John...........	II, 667
Hume, David.......	III, 648, 665
Hurd, Richard........	IV, 516
Jenyns, Soame..........	IV, 32
Johnston, Arthur........	II, 54
Johnson, Samuel........	III, 721
Jonson, Ben	I, 761
Jortin, John.............	III, 552
Junius	IV, 638, 643
Kelly, Hugh........	III, 677, 677
Knowledge	V, 6
Law, William..........	III, 427
Lennox, Charlotte........	VI, 469
Leslie, Charles...........	II, 679
Literature...............	I, 7
Locke, John.............	II, 529
Lyttelton, George Lord.	II, 611, 612
Macaulay, Catherine.....	IV, 133
Macpherson, James...	IV, 270, 274
Mallet, David.......	III, 494, 497
Mandeville, Bernard	III, 69
Milton, John............... II, 245, 251, 254, 259, 269, 271, 272, 276, 286
Montagu, Charles.........	II, 587
Montagu, Elizabeth.......	IV, 401
More, Hannah...........	V, 194
Newton, Sir Isaac.......	II, 723
Otway, Thomas..	II, 362, 363, 364
Parnell, Thomas......	II, 615, 616
Parr, Samuel............	V, 17
Percy, Thomas...........	IV, 562
Philips, Ambrose.........	III, 273
Philips, John........	II, 562, 564
Piozzi, Hester Lynch	IV, 684
Pitt, Christopher......	III, 254, 254
Poets and Poetry.........	IV, 6
Pomfret, John...........	II, 511
Pope, Alexander........... III, 147, 158, 161, 168, 170, 174, 179
Prior, Matthew........... .... II, 675, 675, 676, 676
Raleigh, Sir Walter	I, 602
Ramsay, Allan..........	III, 405
Reynolds, Sir Joshua.....	IV, 137
Richardson, Samuel........ .... III, 432, 438, 447
Robertson, William.......	IV, 161
Rowe, Nicholas..	II, 620, 621, 622
Rymer, Thomas.........	II, 583
Sackville, Charles........	II, 553
Saint-John, Henry........	III, 285
Savage, Richard.......... .... III, 132, 134, 135, 135
Settle, Elkanah...........	II, 691
Shakespeare, William ...... I, 461, 464, 468, 470, 476, 478, 482, 483, 491, 492, 496, 499, 501, 507, 509, 511, 514, 528, 529, 533, 536, 553
Sheffield, John, Third Earl of Mulgrave...........	II, 670, 672
Shenstone, William...	III, 471, 473
Sherlock, Thomas........	III, 455

INDEX TO CRITICISMS

	Vol. and Page
Smart, Christopher	III, 592
Smith, Adam	IV, 54
Somerville, William	III, 126
Spence, Joseph	III, 520
Spenser, Edmund	I, 380
Sprat, Thomas	II, 573, 574
Stanhope, Philip Dormer	III, 600
Steele, Sir Richard	II, 752, 760
Sterne, Laurence	III, 502, 506
Swift, Jonathan	III, 199, 213, 229
Temple, Sir William	II, 457
Theobald, Lewis	III, 142
Thomson, James	III, 256, 262, 266
Tickell, Thomas	III, 104, 105
Tillotson, John Robert	II, 439
Usher, James	II, 152
Waller, Edmund	II, 378, 380
Walsh, William	II, 560
Warburton, William	III, 683, 685, 689
Warton, Thomas	IV, 76
Watts, Isaac	III, 248, 252
Wesley, John	IV, 111
West, Gilbert	III, 368, 368
Whitefield, George	III, 547, 549
Wilkes, John	IV, 333
Williams, Sir Charles Hanbury	III, 412
Wilmot, John	II, 336
Wycherley, William	II, 600
Young, Edward	III, 492
JOHNSON, W. G.,	
FitzGerald, Edward	VII, 520
JOHNSON, W. H.,	
Arnold, Matthew	VII, 648
JOHNSON, WILLIAM,	
Kent, James	V, 502
JOHNSTON, CHARLES,	
Müller, Friedrich Max	VIII, 439
Wilkes, John	IV, 332
JOHNSTON, HENRY P.,	
Jay, John	V, 96
JOHNSTON, RICHARD MALCOM,	
Thackeray, William Makepeace	VI, 303
JOHNSTON, RICHARD MALCOM, AND BROWNE, WILLIAM HAND,	
Browning, Elizabeth Barrett	VI, 245
Johnson, Samuel	III, 760
JOHNSTONE, JOHN,	
Parr, Samuel	V, 18
JOLLY, EMILY,	
Dobell, Sidney Thompson	VI, 759
JOLLY, WILLIAM,	
Burns, Robert	IV, 237, 246
JONES, ADAM LEROY,	
Edwards, Jonathan	III, 394
JONES, BENCE,	
Davy, Sir Humphry	V, 92
Faraday, Michael	VI, 512, 514
JONES, CHARLES H.,	
Dickens, Charles	VI, 566
Macaulay, Thomas Babington Lord	VI, 112
JONES, JENKIN LLOYD,	
Mann, Horace	VI, 201
JONES, DR. JOHN,	
Franklin, Benjamin	IV, 82

	Vol. and Page
JONES, SIR WILLIAM,	
Milton, John	II, 286
JONES, W. A.,	
Dana, Richard Henry	VII, 155
JONES, WILLIAM,	
Brougham Henry Lord	VI, 524
Law, William	III, 428
JONES, WILLIAM C.,	
Gray, Thomas	III, 560
JONSON, BEN,	
Bacon, Francis	I, 639, 639
Beaumont, Francis	I, 587
Beaumont, Sir John	I, 679
Breton, Nicholas	I, 678
Browne, William	II, 73
Chapman, George	I, 728
Constable, Henry	I, 444
Digby, Sir Kenelm	II, 181
Donne, John	I, 714
Drayton, Michael	I, 701
Fletcher, John	I, 628
Jonson, Ben	I, 746, 752
Kyd, Thomas	I, 359
Lyly, John	I, 421
Marlowe, Christopher	I, 348, 354
Raleigh, Sir Walter	I, 606
Selden, John	I, 141
Shakespeare, William	I, 448, 461, 533, 547, 548
Sidney, Sir Philip	I, 330
Taylor, John	II, 133
JORDAN, DAVID STARR,	
Agassiz, Louis Jean Rodolphe	VI, 725
Darwin, Charles Robert	VII, 431
JORTIN, JOHN,	
Warburton, William	III, 683
JOUFFROY, THEODORE SIMON,	
Hutcheson, Francis	III, 245
JOWETT, BENJAMIN,	
Bentley, Richard	III, 123
Browning, Robert	VII, 678
Bunyan, John	II, 403, 428
Johnson, Samuel	III, 759
Tennyson, Alfred Lord	VIII, 72, 91
Wesley, John	VI, 124
Wyclif, John	I, 109
JOY, H. H.,	
Story, Joseph	V, 484
JOY, JAMES RICHARD,	
Gladstone, William Ewart	VIII, 389
JOYCE, JEREMIAH,	
Paley, William	IV, 475
JOYCE, ROBERT DWYER,	
Emerson, Ralph Waldo	VII, 366
Holmes, Oliver Wendell	VIII, 295
Longfellow, Henry Wadsworth	VII, 405
Lowell, James Russell	VIII, 32
Smollett, Tobias George	III, 579
Whittier, John Greenleaf	VIII, 122
JOYCE, THOMAS,	
Macaulay, Thomas Babington Lord	VI, 96
JULIAN, GEORGE W.,	
Benton, Thomas Hart	VI, 86
Greeley, Horace	VI, 669
JUNIUS,	
Blackstone, Sir William	III, 702

	Vol. and Page
Junius	IV, 643
Murray, William	IV, 170
JUSSERAND, J. J.,	
Barbour, John	I, 116
Bede	I, 28
Beowulf	I, 20
Blake, William	V, 62
Cavendish Margaret	II, 233
Chaucer, Geoffrey	I, 136, 148
Cynewulf	I, 31
Dekker, Thomas	II, 61
Drama, The	VII, 8
Dunbar, William	I, 228
Ford, John	II, 33
Greene, Robert	I, 340
James I of Scotland	I, 180
Langland, William	I, 122
Lodge, Thomas	I, 627
Lydgate, John	I, 186
Lyly, John	I, 423
Malory, Sir Thomas	I, 205
Mandeville, Sir John	I, 97
Map, Walter	I, 62
More, Sir Thomas	I, 238
Nashe, Thomas	I, 414
Philips, Katherine	II, 180
Rolle, Richard	I, 92
Sidney, Sir Philip	I, 326
Wyclif, John	I, 111

KABAOOSA AND WABUNOSA,
Longfellow, Henry Wadsworth .... VII, 397
KALISCH, LUDWIG,
Jerrold, Douglas William ... VI, 66
KAMES, HENRY HOME LORD,
Critic The .... II, 5
Franklin, Benjamin .... IV, 81
KANT, IMMANUEL,
Critic, The .... II, 6
KASSON, FRANK H.,
Hopkins, Mark ...... VII, 614, 615
Mann, Horace .... VI, 200
KAUFMAN, MORITZ,
Carlyle, Thomas .... VII, 237
Eliot, George .... VII, 206
Kingsley, Charles ..... VII, 23, 31
KAUFMANN, M.,
Ruskin, John .... VIII, 411
Smith, Adam .... IV, 67
KAVANAGH, JULIA,
Opie, Amelia .... V, 742
KEAN, CHARLES,
Cibber, Colley .... III, 372
KEATS, JOHN,
Audubon, John James ...... V, 696
Burns, Robert .... IV, 225
Chapman, George .... I, 729
Chatterton, Thomas ...... III, 530, 536, 536
Chaucer, Geoffrey .... I, 158
Hazlitt, William .... V, 102
Hunt, James Henry Leigh .... VI, 154, 163, 165, 167
Keats, John .... IV, 669
Lamb, Charles .... V, 229
Milton, John .... II, 260, 287
Poets and Poetry .... IV, 7
Smollett, Tobias George .. III, 587
Spenser, Edmund ...... I, 382, 395
Washington, George ..... IV, 359

INDEX TO CRITICISMS

Vol. and Page
Wordsworth William........V, 629
KEBBEL, THOMAS EDWARD,
  Austen, Jane..............IV, 616
  Canning, George............V, 67
  Cooper, James Fenimore....V, 688
  Crabbe, George............V, 176
  Croker, John Wilson.......VI, 72
  Disraeli, Benjamin....VII, 279, 288
  Lytton, Sir Edward George Bulwer....................VI, 698
  Macaulay, Thomas Babington Lord..................VI, 106
KEBLE, JOHN,
  Cowper, William..........IV, 387
  Hooker, Richard............I, 406
  Spenser, Edmund...........I, 390
  Hunt, James Henry Leigh..VI, 168
  Ken, Thomas.............II, 568
  Montgomery, James........V, 767
  Wilson, Thomas..........III, 367
  Wordsworth, William......V, 611
KEDDIE, HENRIETTA, (SARAH TYTLER),
  Austen, Jane..............IV, 613
KEDDIE, WILLIAM,
  Faraday, Michael..........VI, 513
  Goldsmith, Oliver........III, 632
KEEGAN, P. Q.,
  Montagu, Lady Mary Wortley. .... III, 467
KEELING, CAPTAIN,
  Shakespeare, William.......I, 500
KEENE, H. G.,
  Sir John Mandeville.........I, 98
KEIGHTLEY, THOMAS,
  Fielding, Henry......III, 343, 348
  Knox, John..............I, 297
  Milton, John..........II, 247, 276
  Pole, Reginald.............I, 281
  Shakespeare, William.......I, 471
KEILL, JOHN,
  Flamsteed, John...........II, 663
KEIR, JAMES,
  Darwin, Erasmus..........IV, 420
  Day, Thomas..............IV, 50
KELLOGG, DAY OTIS,
  Percival, James Gates......VI, 58
KELSALL, THOMAS FORBES,
  Beddoes, Thomas Lovell.V, 586, 587
KELTIE, JOHN SCOTT,
  Beaumont and Fletcher......I, 583
  Green, John Richard......VII, 512
KELTY, MARY ANN,
  Law, William............III, 429
KEMBLE, FRANCES ANN,
  Austen, Jane..............IV, 619
  Baillie, Joanna............V, 694
  Beecher, Henry Ward.....VII, 602
  Browning, Robert........VII, 702
  Byron, George Gordon Lord.IV, 757
  Channing, William Ellery....V, 365
  Corly, George.............VI, 224
  Davy, Sir Humphry.........V, 91
  Dickens, Charles....VI, 551, 567
  FitzGerald, Edward......VII, 515
  Hemans, Felicia Dorothea...V, 254
  Hook, Theodore Edward....V, 356
  Inchbald, Mrs. Elizabeth...IV, 688
  Irving, Washington.......VI, 133
  Jameson, Anna............VI, 213
  Knowles, James Sheridan...VI, 287

Vol. and Page
Lamb, Lady Caroline........V, 82
Longfellow, Henry Wadsworth ....VII, 385
Macaulay, Thomas Babington Lord ....VI, 96
Martineau, Harriet.......VII, 61
Massinger, Philip.......II, 44, 45
Milnes, Richard Monckton.VII, 560
Mitford, Mary Russell......VI, 43
Norton, Caroline E. S......VII, 102
Otway, Thomas...........II, 365
Procter, Adelaide Anne.....VI, 393
Rogers, Samuel............VI, 36
Scott, Sir Walter............V, 154
Sedgwick, Catharine Maria..VI, 506
Shakespeare, William ...I, 486, 544
Shelley, Percy Bysshe......IV, 705
Smith, James..............V, 338
Smith, Sydney............V, 470
Sterling, John.............V, 452
Stowe, Harriet Beecher...VIII, 356
Tennyson, Alfred Lord..... ....VIII, 65, 78
Thackeray, William Makepeace ....VI, 290
KENDRICK, ASAHEL CLARK,
  Willis, Nathaniel Parker....VI, 491
KENEALY, EDWARD VAUGHAN HYDE,
  Maginn, William......V, 386, 387
KENNEDY, HOWARD ANGUS,
  Blackie, John Stuart.....VIII, 306
KENNEDY, CAPTAIN H. A.,
  Buckle, Henry Thomas....VI, 280
KENNEDY, D. JAMES,
  Byron, George Gordon Lord.IV, 736
KENNEDY, JOHN PENDLETON,
  Poe, Edgar Allan...........V 535
KENNEDY, WALKER,
  Whitman, Walt........VIII, 142
KENNEDY, WILLIAM SLOANE,
  Longfellow, Henry Wadsworth ....VII, 409
  Ruskin, John.......VIII, 406, 412
  Whittier, John Greenleaf..VIII, 124
  Whitman, Walt.....VIII, 133, 137
KENNETT, WHITE,
  Pope, Alexander..........III, 164
  Swift, Jonathan..........III, 197
KENDRICK, WILLIAM,
  Goldsmith, Oliver........III, 635
KENT, ARMINE T.,
  Hunt, James Henry Leigh..VI, 166
KENT, CHARLES,
  Chatterton, Thomas......III, 532
  Dickens, Charles.........VI, 561
  Forster, John............VII, 66
  Hunt, James Henry Leigh..VII, 170
  Reade, Charles......VII, 529, 530
  Taylor, Tom............VII, 215
  Wiseman, Nicholas Patrick.VI, 437
KENT, CHARLES W.,
  Cynewulf..................I, 31
KENT, C. B. ROYLANCE,
  Bright, John............VII, 721
  Mill, John Stuart.........VI, 718
KENT, JAMES,
  Hamilton, Alexander..IV, 458, 466
  Irving, Washington....VI, 145, 148
  Marshall, John............V, 285
  Middleton, Conyers.......III,280

Vol. and Page
Murphy, Arthur..........IV, 483
Murray, William..........IV, 171
Story, Joseph..........V, 482, 484
Sumner, Charles..........VI, 751
Turner, Sharon.............V, 499
Webster, Daniel........V, 720, 725
KENT, WILLIAM,
  Kent, James...............V, 501
KENYON, FREDERIC G.,
  Browning, Elizabeth Barrett.. ....VI, 235, 242
KENYON, JAMES B.,
  Spenser, Edmund...........I, 400
KEPPEL, FREDERICK,
  Goldsmith, Oliver........III, 628
  Reynolds, Sir Joshua......IV, 140
KER, WILLIAM PATON,
  Ælfric....................I, 46
  Beowulf..................I, 20
  Chaucer, Geoffrey..I, 137, 147, 149
  Coleridge, Samuel Taylor....V, 228
  Cowper, William.........IV, 384
  Dryden, John............II, 494
  Ellwood, Thomas.........II, 576
  Hakluyt, Richard..........I, 446
  Herbert, Edward Lord..II, 97, 98
  Latimer, Hugh.............I, 269
  Lyly, John................I, 427
  Macaulay, Thomas Babington Lord ....VI, 115
  Malory, Sir Thomas........I, 205
  Marvell, Andrew..........II, 319
  Pepys, Samuel...........II, 516
  Rymer, Thomas..........II, 584
  Tyndale, William..........I, 249
  Walpole, Horace..........IV, 323
KERNAHAN, COULSON,
  Locker-Lampson, Frederick... ....VIII, 312, 313
KERR, ROBERT,
  Sandys, George............II, 81
KETTELL, SAMUEL,
  Bryant, William Cullen....VII, 119
  Dana, Richard Henry.....VII, 153
  Longfellow, Henry Wadsworth ....VII, 381
  Neal, John...............VII, 77
  Whittier, John Greenleaf..... ....VIII, 119
KEYES, GEN. E. D.,
  Channing, William Ellery....V, 370
  Everett, Edward..........VI, 424
  Greeley, Horace..........VI, 669
  Webster, Daniel...........V, 723
KEYSOR, JENNIE ELLIS,
  Cary, Alice...............VI, 639
KIDDLE, AND SCHEM,
  Ascham, Roger.............I, 288
KILVERT, FRANCIS,
  Hurd, Richard...........IV, 517
KING, CHARLES,
  Holmes, Oliver Wendell..VIII, 297
KING, HENRY,
  Donne, John..............I, 710
KING, LIEUT. COLONEL COOPER,
  Washington, George.......IV, 364
  Raleigh, Sir Walter ....I, 593
  Sandys, George............II, 82
KING, JOHN M.,
  Tennyson, Alfred Lord...VIII, 90

INDEX TO CRITICISMS

KING, LORD,
    Locke, John............II, 521
    Stillingfleet, Edward......II, 454
KING, RICHARD ASHE,
    Swift, Jonathan......III, 216, 219
KING, THOMAS STAR,
    DeQuincey, Thomas......VI, 126
    Longfellow, Henry Wadsworth.
    ....VII, 393
    Martineau, James........VIII, 428
    Tennyson, Alfred Lord...VIII, 93
KING, WILLIAM,
    Bentley, Richard.........III, 115
    Johnson, Samuel..........III, 755
    Pope, Alexander..........III, 146
KINGLAKE, ALEXANDER WILLIAM,
    Gladstone, William Ewart....
    ....VIII, 388
    Oliphant, Margaret O. W .VIII, 367
KINGSLAND, WILLIAM G.,
    Browning, Robert........VII, 707
KINGSFORD, C. L.,
    Guilford, Nicholas..........I, 76
    Map, Walter................I, 62
KINGSLEY, CHARLES,
    Brontë, Charlotte..........VI, 27
    Brooke, Henry......III, 714, 715
    Buchanan, George..........I, 315
    Burns, Robert............IV, 265
    Byron, George Gordon Lord.IV, 759
    Carlyle, Thomas.........VII, 262
    Cartwright, William........II, 71
    Darwin, Charles Robert...VII, 427
    Elliott, Ebenezer............V, 582
    Gaskell, Elizabeth Cleghorn...
    ....VI, 429, 431
    Gibbon, Edward..........IV, 195
    Helps, Sir Arthur.........VII, 40
    History....................VI, 8
    Hughes, Thomas........VIII, 347
    Jameson, Anna............VI, 215
    Lyly, John..................I, 422
    Massinger, Philip..........II, 42
    Maurice, John Frederick Denison................VI, 645, 647
    Milton, John..............II, 291
    Mitford, Mary Russell.....VI, 42
    Pope, Alexander......III, 149, 188
    Raleigh, Sir Walter..........I, 595
    Shelley, Percy Bysshe.....IV, 707
    Smith, Alexander.........VI, 517
    Smith, Sydney.............V, 468
    Taylor, Tom.............VII, 213
    Tennyson, Alfred Lord.......
    ....VIII, 82, 83
    Thackeray, William Makepeace
    ....VI, 302
    Webster, John..............I, 672
    Whewell, William.........VI, 467
KINGSLEY, MRS. CHARLES,
    Kingsley, Charles.........VII, 20
KINGSLEY, J. L.,
    Webster, Noah............V, 430
KINGSLEY, ROSE G.,
    Eliot, George............VII, 176
KINNEY, ELIZABETH C.,
    Browning, Elizabeth Barrett.
    ....VI, 233
KIPPIS, ANDREW,
    Bentley, Richard.........III, 110

Doddridge, Philip.........III, 301
Lardner, Nathaniel.......III, 523
KIRBY, GEORGIANA BRUCE,
    Curtis, George William...VIII, 185
KIRK, JOHN FOSTER,
    Clive, Caroline............VI, 739
    Lawrence, George Alfred..VII, 84
    Thackeray, William Makepeace
    ....VI, 301
KIRK, SOPHIA,
    Stevenson, Robert Louis.VIII, 240
KIRKE, EDWARD,
    Gascoigne, George..........I, 307
    Harvey, Gabriel............I, 695
    Spenser, Edmund...........I, 374
KIRKLAND, CAROLINE MATILDA,
    Bryant, William Cullen...VII, 110
    Goldsmith, Oliver.........III, 631
    Washington, George.......IV, 361
KIRKLAND, ELIZABETH STANBURY,
    Chaucer, Geoffrey...........I, 147
    Ferrier, Susan Edmonstone..V, 765
    Knight, Charles...........VI, 743
KIRKLAND, JOHN THORNTON,
    Ames, Fisher.............IV, 527
KIRKLAND, JOSEPH,
    Blackmore, Richard D...VIII, 431
    Reade, Charles......VII, 529, 536
KIRKMAN, REV. J.,
    Browning, Robert........VII, 702
KIRKMAN, JAMES THOMAS,
    Macklin, Charles..........IV, 343
KIRKPATRICK, JAMES,
    Drayton, Michael...........I, 704
KIRKUP, SEYMOUR,
    Blake, William..............V, 57
KIRKUP, T.,
    George, Henry..........VIII, 381
KIRWAN, RICHARD,
    Young, Arthur............IV, 655
KITCHIN, G. W.,
    Spenser, Edmund...........I, 373
KITTON, FREDERIC G.,
    Dickens, Charles.......
    ....VI, 560, 571, 577, 578
KITTREDGE, GEORGE LYMAN,
    Byron, George Gordon Lord.IV, 766
    Chaucer, Geoffrey......I, 131, 147
KLEIN, L.,
    Shakespeare, William.......I, 504
KLOPSTOCK, MADAME FRIEDRICH GOTTLIEB,
    Richardson, Samuel.......III, 443
KNAPP, SAMUEL L.,
    Lydgate, John..............I, 184
    Otis, James..............III, 717
    Winthrop, John............II, 109
KNAPP, WILLIAM I.,
    Borrow, George Henry....VII, 314
KNAUFFT, ERNEST,
    Du Maurier, George......VIII, 344
KNIGHT CHARLES,
    Brougham, Henry Lord....VI, 532
    Carlyle, Thomas.........VII, 233
    Caxton, William............I, 197
    Coleridge, Samuel Taylor....V, 223
    Dennis, John.............III, 78
    DeQuincey, Thomas...VI, 119, 124
    Dodsley, Robert..........III, 482

Farmer, Richard..........IV, 341
Greene, Robert.............I, 341
Hallam, Henry............VI, 174
Johnson, Samuel..........III, 747
Knight, Charles..........VI, 742
Lodge, Thomas.............I, 626
Lyly, John..................I, 422
Maginn, William............V, 386
Malone, Edmond..........IV, 578
Marlowe, Christopher........I, 355
North, Roger.............III, 80
Peele, George..............I, 366
Pope, Alexander..........III, 170
Praed, Winthrop Mackworth...................V, 331
Richardson, Samuel......III, 434
Rowe, Nicholas............II, 621
Shakespeare, William........
  I, 462, 469, 477, 494, 498, 530, 532
Steveens, George.........IV, 410
Tannahill, Robert........IV, 547
Tate, Nahum.............II, 589
Thackeray, William Makepeace..................VI, 292
Theobald, Lewis..........III, 142
Wallis, John..............II, 517
Warburton, William......III, 687
Webster, John..............I, 675
White, Gilbert............IV, 149
Wilson, Alexander..........V, 584
Wilson, John...............V, 751
KNIGHT, HELEN C.,
    Montgomery, James........V, 766
KNIGHT, JOSEPH,
    Boucicault, Dion........VII, 763
    Centlivre, Susannah......II, 685
    Cibber, Colley...........III, 375
    Colman, George..........IV, 203
    Colman, George, Jr.........V, 317
    Foote, Samuel...........III, 674
    Garrick, David......III, 696, 697
    Murphy, Arthur..........IV, 483
    Robinson, Mary..........IV, 412
    Rossetti, Gabriel Charles Dante
    ....VII, 446, 449, 453
KNIGHT, THOMAS,
    Tusser, Thomas............I, 310
KNIGHT, WILLIAM,
    Arnold, Matthew........VII, 641
    Grote, George............VI, 612
    Hume, David......III, 650, 654, 660
    Tennyson, Alfred Lord...VIII, 74
    Wordsworth, William...V, 618, 639
KNIGHTON, HENRY,
    Wyclif, John..............,I, 102
KNOLLYS, FRANCIS,
    Adams, Sarah Flower.......V, 530
KNORTZ, KARL,
    Whitman, Walt.........VIII, 136
KNOWLES, JAMES,
    Tennyson, Alfred Lord...VIII, 73
KNOWLES, JOHN,
    Godwin, Mary Wollstonecraft
    ....IV, 327
KNOX, ALEXANDER,
    Wesley, John.............IV, 111
KNOX, ISA CRAIG,
    Burns, Robert............IV, 257
KNOX, JOHN,
    Buchanan, George..........I, 316
    Knox, John................I, 300

INDEX TO CRITICISMS

Vol. and Page

KNOX, KATHLEEN,
Addison, Joseph............II, 645
KNOX, VICESIMUS,
Fielding, Henry..........III, 357
Chatterton, Thomas......III, 528
Jortin, John..............III, 552
Watts, Isaac............III, 249
KOOPMAN, HARRY LYMAN,
Arnold Matthew.........VII, 646
Milton, John..............II 295
Shakespeare, William.......I, 575
KRAUSE, ERNST,
Darwin, Erasmus.....IV, 421, 425
KREYSSIG, F.,
Shakespeare, William........
...........I, 486, 504, 518, 521
KYNASTON, SIR FRANCIS,
Henryson, Robert..........I, 208

LABOULAYE, EDOUARD RENE,
Everett, Edward..........VI, 425
Franklin, Benjamin.......IV, 89
LACROIX, ALBERT,
Shakespeare, William.......I, 562
LA FARGE, JOHN,
Ruskin, John............VIII, 423
LAING, DAVID,
Lodge, Thomas.............I, 626
Lyndsay, Sir David.........I, 275
LAING, MALCOLM,
Alexander, Sir William.....II, 35
Burnet, Gilbert...........II, 595
Drummond, William.......II, 104
Gauden, John.............II, 177
Hume, David.............III, 656
Macpherson, James........IV, 274
Spotiswood, John..........II, 24
LAING, S.,
Carlyle, Thomas..........VII, 271
Drummond, Henry.......VIII, 364
LAKE, WILLIAM CHARLES,
Arnold, Matthew.........VII, 630
Church, Richard William..VII, 729
Froude, James Anthony..VIII, 261
Keble, Charles...........II, 461
Liddon, Henry Parry.....VII, 761
Mozley, James Bowling...VII, 150
Newman, John Henry VII, 742, 747
Pattison, Mark...........VII, 539
Stanley, Arthur Penrhyn.....
...................VII, 301, 302
Ward, William George....VII, 483
LAMAR, LUCIUS Q. C.,
Sumner, Charles..........VI, 754
LAMARTINE, ALPHONSE MARIE LOUIS DE,
Byron, George Gordon Lord IV, 733
Milton, John..........II, 247, 263
Shakespeare, William...I, 475, 518
LAMB, CHARLES,
Barton, Bernard..........V, 596
Beaumont and Fletcher.....I, 580
Blake, William............V, 56
Bloomfield, Robert........IV, 724
Books....................III, 7
Browne, Sir Thomas........II, 342
Bunyan, John.............II, 393
Burnet, Gilbert..........II, 593
Burns, Robert............IV, 251
Burton, Robert...........II, 39

Vol. and Page

Cavendish, Margaret.......II, 232
Chapman, George.......I, 729, 732
Coleridge, Samuel Taylor ...V, 207
Congreve, William.........II, 738
Cotton, Charles...........II, 371
Cowley, Abraham..........II, 197
Cowper, William..........IV, 385
Defoe, Daniel.........III, 43, 46
Dekker, Thomas........II, 56, 57
Dennis, John.............III, 78
DeQuincey, Thomas.......VI, 124
Dryden, John.............II, 472
Fanshawe, Sir Richard.....II, 185
Farquhar, George.........II, 559
Fletcher, John..........I, 628, 630
Ford, John..........II, 26, 26, 29
Fox, George..............II, 421
Fuller, Thomas...........II, 171
Gibbon, Edward..........IV, 195
Glover, Richard..........IV, 18
Godwin, William..........V, 301
Greville, Sir Fulke..........I, 691
Hazlitt, William............V, 98
Heywood, Thomas. II, 123, 124, 125
Holcroft, Thomas.........IV, 545
Hone, William............V, 393
Hunt, James Henry Leigh..IV, 155
Irving, Edward............V, 245
Jonson, Ben............I, 752, 756
Knowledge.................V, 7
Knowles, James Sheridan....
..................VI, 286, 287
Lamb, Charles............V, 229
Lamb, Mary Ann......V, 507, 509
Landor, Walter Savage....VI, 381
Mackintosh, Sir James......V, 178
Marlowe, Christopher........
...............I, 349, 350, 358
Massinger, Philip..II, 42, 44, 46, 46
Middleton, Thomas....I, 682, 683
More, Hannah.............V, 193
Norton, Thomas...........I, 318
Payne, John Howard.......V, 735
Peele, George.............I, 365
Pope, Alexander.........III, 148
Priestley, Joseph.....IV, 446, 453
Prior, Matthew...........II, 677
Procter, Bryan Waller. VI, 744, 746
Richardson, Samuel...III, 436, 439
Ritson, Joseph...........IV, 435
Robertson, William.......IV, 162
Sackville, Thomas.........I, 434
Shakespeare, William........
...........I, 502, 510, 513, 520
Shelley, Percy, Bysshe.....IV, 704
Sheridan, Richard Brinsley.IV, 603
Shirley, James............II, 190
Sidney, Sir Philip,...I, 323, 325, 327
Southey, Robert......V, 396, 406
Talfourd, Sir Thomas Noon..V, 761
Tate, Nahum.............II, 588
Taylor, Jeremy...........II, 207
Temple, Sir William......II, 458
Thackeray, William Makepeace
....................VI, 295
Tourneur, Cyril...........I, 687
Walton, Isaac........II, 344, 345
Webster, John........I, 670, 672
Wither, George..........II, 212
Woolman, John.........III, 598
Wordsworth, William......V, 622

Vol. and Page

Wycherley, William........II, 604
LAMB, LADY CAROLINE,
Lytton, Sir Edward George
Bulwer...............VI, 679
LAMB, MARTHA J.,
Beecher, Henry Ward....VII, 608
Brougham, Henry Lord....VI, 533
Bryant, William Cullen....VII, 126
Livingston, William.......IV, 109
Murchison, Sir Roderick Impey
....................VI, 632
Porter, Jane..............V, 674
LAMB, MARY ANN,
Lamb, Mary Ann..........V, 509
LAMB, WILLIAM,
Lamb, Lady Caroline.......V, 81
LAMBERT, AGNES,
Seeley, Sir John Robert..VIII, 310
LAMBERT, JOHN,
Marshall, John............V, 284
LANCASTER, HENRY H.,
Burton, John Hill........VII, 316
Eliot, George............VII, 199
Macaulay, Thomas Babington
Lord.................VI, 98
Motley, John Lothrop....VII, 91
LANDON, LETITIA ELIZABETH,
Hemans, Felicia Dorothea...V, 258
LANDON, MELVILLE D. (ELI PERKINS),
Browne Charles Farrar.....VI, 501
LANDOR, ROBERT,
Landor, Walter Savage....VI, 374
LANDOR, WALTER SAVAGE,
Addison, Joseph..........II, 635
Beddoes, Thomas Lovell....V, 586
Bentley, Richard........III, 121
Blessington, Countess of...V, 592
Books...................III, 7
Brougham, Henry Lord........
...............VI, 526, 531
Browning, Elizabeth Barrett
....................VI, 238
Browning, Robert........VII, 697
Burns, Robert.............253
Butler, Samuel..........II, 332
Byron, George Gordon Lord..
................IV, 739, 759
Campbell, Thomas.........V, 443
Carlyle, Thomas.........VII, 263
Chaucer, Geoffrey.....I, 161, 161
Coleridge, Samuel Taylor...V, 222
Cowper, William.........IV, 388
Defoe, Daniel...........III, 24
De Vere, Aubrey........VIII, 463
Dickens, Charles......VI, 553, 584
Donne, John..............I, 715
Dryden, John.............II, 500
Elliott, Ebenezer..........V, 582
Fuller, Sarah Margaret......V, 666
Fullerton, Georgiana Charlotte
....................VII, 567
Gibbon, Edward..........IV, 187
Goldsmith, Oliver........III, 619
Gray, Thomas............III, 559
Grote, George............VI, 609
Hemans, Felicia Dorothea...V, 260
Hume, David............III, 661
Irving, Washington...VI, 149, 149
James, George Payne Rainsford
..................VI, 218

624 INDEX TO CRITICISMS

	Vol. and Page
Junius	IV, 644
Keats, John	IV, 677
Knowledge	V, 7
Lamb, Charles	V, 230, 239
Lamb, Mary Ann	V, 509
Landon, Letitia Elizabeth	V, 323
Landor, Walter Savage	VI, 374, 380, 387
Macaulay, Thomas Babington Lord	VI, 93, 102
Mason, William	IV, 325
Milton, John	II, 272
Mitford, Mary Russell	VI, 41
Moore, Thomas	V, 717
Napier, Gen. Sir Francis Patrick	VI, 222
Porson, Richard	IV, 524
Procter, Bryan Waller	VI, 748
Shelley, Percy Bysshe	IV, 692, 708
South, Robert	II, 608
Southey, Robert	V, 399, 404, 408
Spenser, Edmund	I, 383
Stanhope, Philip Dormer	III, 601
Steele, Sir Richard	II, 763
Swift, Jonathan	III, 232
Tennyson, Alfred Lord	VIII, 66, 91
Wesley, John	IV, 123
Wordsworth, William	V, 626, 636
Young, Edward	III, 489, 493
LANE, JOHN,	
Spenser, Edmund	I, 368
LANE, MRS. JOHN,	
White, Gilbert	IV, 148
LANG, ANDREW,	
Arnold, Matthew	VII, 633, 637, 642
Austen, Jane	IV, 622
Bayle, Thomas Haynes	V, 340
Black, William	VIII, 394
Brontë, Charlotte	VI, 25, 27, 29, 30
Brown, John	VII, 478, 480
Browne, Charles Farrar	VI, 504
Browning, Robert	VII, 689, 693
Bunyan, John	II, 398
Burns, Robert	IV, 262
Carlyle, Thomas	VII, 234
Chapman, George	I, 730, 733
Chatterton, Thomas	III, 539
Coleridge, Samuel Taylor	V, 227
Collins, William Wilkie	VII, 727
Constable, Henry	I, 444
Critic, The	II, 9
Dickens, Charles	VI, 559, 574, 578, 579, 588
Douglas, Gawin	I, 214
Ferguson, Robert	III, 641
Fielding, Henry	III, 363
Forster, John	VII, 66
Freeman, Edward Augustus	VIII, 155
Harte, Francis Bret	VIII, 470
Hawthorne, Nathaniel	VI, 369
Herrick, Robert	II, 240
Huxley, Thomas Henry	VIII, 325
Ireland, William Henry	V, 290
Keats, John	IV, 666
Kingsley, Charles	VII, 27, 29
Lever, Charles James	VI, 652, 655, 656
Lockhart, John Gibson	V, 754, 757

	Vol. and Page
Longfellow, Henry Wadsworth	VII, 396, 413
Lowell, James Russell	VIII, 20
Macpherson, James	IV, 279
Mandeville, Sir John	I, 97
Morris, William	VIII, 333
Pepys, Samuel	II, 515
Poe, Edgar Allan	V, 547, 559
Pope, Alexander	III, 163, 166, 192
Prior, Matthew	II, 679
Radcliffe, Ann Ward	IV, 721
Roe, Edward Payson	VII, 676
Scott, Sir Walter	V, 133, 147, 150, 153
Shelley, Percy Bysshe	IV, 711
Smith, Sydney	V, 473
Stevenson, Robert Louis	VIII, 237, 241
Tennyson, Alfred Lord	VIII, 90, 95, 105
Thackeray, William Makepeace	VI, 297, 318
Walton, Isaac	II, 346, 347
LANG, MRS. ANDREW,	
Richardson, Samuel	III, 451
LANG, PHILIP A.,	
Hamilton, Alexander	IV, 467
LANGBAINE, GERARD,	
Alexander, Sir William	II, 35
Beaumont and Fletcher	I, 580
Behn, Aphra	II, 409
Cavendish, Margaret	II, 231
Chapman, George	II, 732
Chamberlayne, William	II, 406
Cartwright, William	II, 70
Daniel, Samuel	I, 614
D'Avenant, Sir William	II, 219
Dekker, Thomas	II, 59
Denham, Sir John	II, 220
Dryden, John	II, 478, 478, 484, 495
Etheredge, Sir George	II, 414
Fanshawe, Sir Richard	II, 184
Ford, John	II, 25
Greville, Sir Fulke	I, 690
Heywood, Thomas	II, 122, 125
Jonson, Ben	I, 747
Kyd, Thomas	I, 359
Lee, Nathaniel	II, 431
May, Thomas	II, 120
Middleton, Thomas	I, 684
Milton, John	II, 243
Nabbes, Thomas	II, 94
Otway, Thomas	II, 362
Rowley, William	II, 68
Sandys, George	II, 83
Sedley, Sir Charles	II, 509
Selden, John	II, 142
Settle, Elkanah	II, 691
Shadwell, Thomas	II, 434
Shakespeare, William	I, 468, 489
Shirley, James	II, 190
Southerne, Thomas	III, 239
Suckling, Sir John	I, 63
Webster, John	I, 674
Wycherley, William	II, 603
LANGFORD, JOHN ALFRED,	
Bunyan, John	II, 395
Dodd, William	III, 676
Hunt, James Henry Leigh	VI, 166
Lovelace, Richard	II, 162
Raleigh, Sir Walter	I, 606

	Vol. and Page
Southwell, Robert	I, 361
LANGHORN, WILLIAM,	
Collins, William	III, 418
LANGHORNE, JOHN,	
Collins, William	III, 414
Dunbar, William	I, 224
James I. of Scotland	I, 182
LANGLOIS AND SEIGNOBOS,	
History	VI, 10
LANGTON, BENNET,	
Young, Edward	III, 485
LANGUET, HUBERT,	
Dyer, Sir Edward	I, 428
LANIER, CHARLES D.,	
Hughes, Thomas	VII, 348
Stevenson, Robert Louis	VIII, 236
Whitman, Walt	VIII, 147
LANIER, CLIFFORD,	
Lanier, Sidney	VII, 326
LANIER, SIDNEY,	
Barbour, John	I, 115
Chaucer, Geoffrey	I, 146, 166
Daniel, Samuel	I, 612
Darwin, Erasmus	IV, 423
Drummond, William	II, 103
Eliot, George	VII, 174, 178, 181, 183, 189, 194
Emerson, Ralph Waldo	VII, 366
Goldsmith, Oliver	III, 628
Hayne, Paul Hamilton	VII, 592
Keats, John	IV, 673
Langland, William	I, 121
Lanier, Sidney	VII, 325
Lytton, Sir Edward George Bulwer	VI, 698
Morris, William	VIII, 335
Richardson, Samuel	III, 436
Scott, Sir Walter	V, 144
Smollett, Tobias George	III, 585
Sterne, Laurence	III, 508
Taylor, Bayard	VII, 129
Tennyson, Alfred Lord	VIII, 103
Thackeray, William Makepeace	VI, 317
Whitman, Walt	VIII, 134, 140
LANKESTER, EDWIN RAY,	
Darwin, Charles Robert	VII, 433
Ray, John	II, 543
Romanes, John James	VIII, 284
LANMAN, CHARLES,	
Kane, Elisha Kent	VI, 83
Marsh, George Perkins	VII, 492
Payne, John Howard	V, 736
Schoolcraft, Henry Rowe	VI, 404
Tupper, Martin Farquhar	VII, 733
Webster, Daniel	V, 720
LANMAN, CHARLES ROCKWELL,	
Whitney, William Dwight	VIII, 304
LAPLACE, PIERRE SIMON,	
Napier, Sir John	I, 588
Newton, Sir Isaac	II, 719
LAPPENBERG, JOHANN MARTIN,	
Alfred the Great	I, 38
Dunstan	I, 44
LARCOM, LUCY,	
Emerson, Ralph Waldo	VII, 366
Holmes, Oliver Wendell	VIII, 290
Lowell, James Russell	VIII, 39
Whittier, John Greenleaf	VIII, 112

INDEX TO CRITICISMS

	Vol. and Page
LARKIN, HENRY,	
Carlyle, Thomas	VII, 250
LARMINIE, WILLIAM,	
Carlyle, Thomas	VII, 275
LARREMORE, WILBUR,	
Emerson, Ralph Waldo	VII, 373
LATHROP, GEORGE PARSONS,	
Agassiz, Louis Jean Rodolphe.	
	VI, 720
Boker, George Henry.	VII, 765, 766
Browning, Robert	VII, 706
Brownson, Orestes Augustus.	
	VII, 76
Bryant, William Cullen	VII, 127
Curtis, George William	VIII, 184
DeQuincey, Thomas	VI, 127
Eliot, George	VII, 190, 200
Emerson, Ralph Waldo	VII, 365
Fielding, Henry	III, 361
Gray, Thomas	III, 560
Halleck, Fitz-Greene	VI, 497, 497
Hawthorne, Nathaniel	
	VI, 346, 352, 359, 363, 367
Holmes, Oliver Wendell	VIII, 290
Irving, Washington	VI, 142
O'Reilly, John Boyle	VII, 767, 768
Paulding, James Kirke	VI, 227
Stoddard, Richard Henry.	VIII, 477
Ticknor, George	VI, 615
White, Richard Grant	VII, 578
Whitman, Walt	VIII, 143
LATHROP, ROSE HAWTHORNE,	
Alcott, Amos Bronson	VII, 663
Hawthorne, Nathaniel	VI, 349
Thoreau, Henry David	VI, 271
LATIMER, HUGH,	
Colet, John	I, 211
LATROBE, JOHN H. B.,	
Poe, Edgar Allan	V, 539, 558
LATTO, THOMAS C.,	
Burns, Robert	IV, 257
LAUD, WILLIAM,	
Laud, William	II, 89
LAUGEL, A.,	
Disraeli, Benjamin	VII, 278
LAUGHLIN, J. LAURENCE,	
Mill, John Stuart	VI, 709
LAUGHTON, J. K.,	
Marryat, Frederick	V, 533
Purchas, Samuel	I, 693
Williams, Helen Maria	V, 75
LAUGHTON, J. K. and LEE, SIDNEY.	
Raleigh, Sir Walter	I, 605, 606
LAURENCE, FRENCH,	
Burke, Edmund	IV, 290
LAW, ALICE,	
Cowper, William	IV, 394
Rossetti, Christina Georgina.	
	VIII, 273
White, Henry Kirke	IV, 489
LAW, WILLIAM,	
Wesley, John	IV, 111
LAW, ERNEST,	
Pope, Alexander	III, 163
LAWES, HENRY,	
Milton, John	II, 250
LAWRENCE, ARTHUR,	
Bryant, William Cullen	VII, 114
LAWRENCE EUGENE,	
Addison, Joseph	II, 658

	Vol. and Page
Brown, Charles Brockden	IV, 556
Browning, Robert	VII, 686
Burnet, Gilbert	II, 595
Carte, Thomas	III, 337
Echard, Laurence	III, 22
Edwards, Jonathan	III, 392
Fox, Charles James	IV, 507
Franklin, Benjamin	IV, 102
Geoffrey of Monmouth	I, 56
Gibbon, Edward	IV, 195
Habington, William	II, 136
Hamilton, Alexander	IV, 467
Hawthorne, Nathaniel	VI, 368
Hildreth, Richard	VI, 453
Hume, David	III, 658
Landor, Walter Savage	VI, 385
Lyttelton, George Lord	
	III, 612, 613
Macaulay, Catherine	IV, 134
Macpherson, James	IV, 281
Mather, Cotton	II, 729
Oldmixon, John	III, 125
Orme, Robert	IV, 414
Otis, James	III, 718
Peele, George	I, 366
Raleigh, Sir Walter	I, 607
Robertson, William	IV, 158
Sedgwick, Catharine Maria	VI, 508
Sumner, Charles	VI, 756
Temple, Sir William	II, 456
Ticknor, George	VI, 617
Trumbull, John	V, 121
Wesley, Charles	V, 37
Wesley, John	IV, 127
LAWRENCE, FREDERICK,	
Cibber, Colley	III, 371
Fielding, Henry	III, 342, 347
Hill, John	III, 645
Lillo, George	III, 99, 101
Richardson, Samuel	III, 436
Stanhope, Philip Dormer	III, 607
LAWRENCE, WILLIAM,	
Brooks, Phillips	VIII, 230, 233
LAWSON, JAMES,	
Drake, Joseph Rodman	IV, 660
LAWTON, WILLIAM CRANSTON,	
Bancroft, George	VIII, 61
Boker, George Henry	VII, 766
Brooks, Phillips	VIII, 233
Curtis, George William	VIII, 187
Browning, Robert	VII, 715, 716
Child, Lydia Maria	VII, 223
Emerson, Ralph Waldo	
	VII, 360, 378, 380
Field, Eugene	VIII, 318
Fiske, John	VIII, 459
Harte, Francis Bret	VIII, 472
Hawthorne, Nathaniel. VI. 356, 361
Hayne, Paul Hamilton	VII, 594
Holmes, Oliver Wendell	VIII, 299
Irving, Washington	VI, 153
Lanier, Sidney	VII, 332
Longfellow, Henry Wadsworth	
	VII, 394, 415
Lowell, James Russell. VIII, 30, 34
Miller, Cincinnatus Hiner. VII, 501
Parkman. Francis	VIII. 225
Stockton, Francis Richard	
	VIII. 474
Stowe Harriet Beecher	VIII. 355
Warner. Charles Dudley	VIII. 445

	Vol. and Page
Whitman, Walt	VIII, 152
Whittier, John Greenleaf.	VIII, 129
LAYARD, AUSTEN HENRY,	
Wilkinson, Sir John Gardner.	
	VI, 51
LAYARD, GEORGE SOMES,	
Thackeray, William Makepeace	
	VI, 300
LAZARUS, EMMA,	
Emerson, Ralph Waldo	
	VII, 347, 368
Morris, William	VIII, 330
LAZARUS, JOSEPHINE,	
Alcott, Louisa May	VII, 666, 668
Fuller, Sarah Margaret	V, 669
LEACH, ANNA,	
Thackeray, William Makepeace	
	VI, 321
LEADAM, I. S.,	
Bright, John	VII, 721
LEAKE, FREDERIC,	
Wyclif, John	I, 104
LEASK, W. KEATH,	
Boswell, James	IV, 211, 213, 214
Miller, Hugh	VI, 64, 65
LE BAS, CHARLES WEBB,	
Peacock, Reginald	I, 189
Wyclif, John	I, 101, 105
LEBERT, HERMANN,	
Agassiz, Louis Jean Rodolphe.	
	VI, 720
LEBRUN, MADAME VIGÉE,	
Franklin, Benjamin	IV, 86
LA BRUGERE, JEAN DE,	
Authors and Authorship	VIII, 5
LECHLER, GOTTHARD,	
Grosseteste, Robert	I, 74
Langland, William	I, 121
Wyclif, John	I, 108
LECKY, WILLIAM EDWARD HARTPOLE,	
Adams, John	I, 52
Atterbury, Francis	III, 66
Bacon, Francis	I, 661
Bacon, Roger	I, 79
Bethham, Jeremy	V, 168
Berkeley, George	III, 332
Buchanan, George	I, 315
Buckle, Henry Thomas	VI, 283
Burke, Edmund	IV, 292
Burnet, Gilbert	I, 592
Butler, Joseph	III, 309
Carlyle, Thomas	VII, 271
Cooper, Anthony Ashley	II, 579
Darwin, Charles Robert	VII, 433
Defoe, Daniel	III, 48
Edwards, Jonathan	III, 388
Fox, Charles James	IV, 501, 507
Franklin, Benjamin	IV, 102
Gibbon, Edward.	IV, 177, 191, 192
Gladstone, William Ewart	
	VIII, 387
Godwin, Mary Wollstonecraft.	
	IV, 330
Harrington, James	II, 308
Hobbes, Thomas	II, 325
Hoadly, Benjamin	III, 424
Hooker, Richard	I, 408
Hume, David	III, 654
Junius	IV, 642, 647
Locke, John	II, 535

INDEX TO CRITICISMS

	Vol. and Page
Macaulay, Catherine	IV, 135
Milman, Henry Hart	VI, 534
Milton, John	II, 281
Paine, Thomas	IV, 535
Paley, William	IV, 472
Saint-John, Henry	III, 296
Smith, Adam	IV, 66
Swift, Jonathan	III, 214, 232
Taylor, Jeremy	II, 209
Tennyson, Alfred Lord	VIII, 74
Tillotson, John Robert	II, 438
Tooke, John Horne	IV, 571
Tucker, Josiah	IV, 370
Warburton, William	III, 685
Washington, George	IV, 362
Wesley, John	IV, 115
Whatley, Richard	VI, 328
Whitefield, George	III, 548, 551
Wilkie, John	IV, 335
LE CLERC,	
Locke, John	II, 520
LECONTE, JOSEPH,	
Agassiz, Louis Jean Rodolphe.	IV, 725
Darwin, Charles Robert	VII, 431
Fiske, John	VIII, 457
LEE, ARTHUR,	
Burke, Edmund	IV, 288
LEE, ELIZABETH,	
Ingelow, Jean	VIII, 378
Opie, Amelia	V, 744
Procter, Adelaide Anne	VI 396
Seward, Anna	IV, 544
Tighe, Mary	IV, 552
Smith, Charlotte	IV, 498
Strickland, Agnes	VI, 767, 768
LEE, FRANCIS WATTS,	
Morris, William	VIII, 336
LEE, FREDERICK GEORGE,	
Foxe, John	I, 336
Latimer, Hugh	I, 268
Pole, Reginald	I, 281
Wyclif, John	I, 110
LEE, GERALD STANLEY,	
Stowe, Harriet Beecher	VIII, 354, 358
LEE, HARRIET,	
Godwin, William	V, 292
LEE, HENRY,	
Kemble, Frances Ann	VIII, 214, 216
LEE, MAJOR GENERAL HENRY,	
Washington, George	IV, 355
LEE, H. F.,	
Cranmer, Thomas	II, 272
LEE, NATHANIEL,	
Drama, The	VII, 5
Dryden, John	II, 475
Lee, Nathaniel	II, 431
LEE, RUDOLPH,	
Wilson, John	V, 752
LEE, SIDNEY,	
Aguilar, Grace	V, 505
Baker, Sir Richard	II, 94
Basse, William	II, 131
Berners, Lord	I, 229
Blanchard, Samuel Laman.	V, 481
Breton, Nicholas	I, 678
Brooke, Arthur	I, 284
Colet, John	I, 212
Constable, Henry	I, 444

	Vol. and Page
Corbet, Richard	I, 743
Cotton, Sir Robert	I, 709
Crashaw, Richard	II, 113
Daniel, Samuel	I, 613, 613, 614, 614
Disraeli, Isaac	V, 513
Drummond, William	II, 106
Elgot, Sir Thomas	I, 254
Fanshawe, Sir Richard	II, 185
Fletcher, Giles	I, 624
Fletcher, Phineas	II, 117
Gower, John	I 176
Greville, Sir Fulke	I, 692
Harding, John	I, 194
Herbert, Edward Lord	II, 98, 99
Holinshed, Raphael	I, 311
Howell, James	II, 188
Hutton, Richard Holt	VIII, 376
Lee, Nathaniel	II, 432
Leland, John	I, 263
L'Estrange, Sir Roger	II, 537
Mahoney, Francis	VI, 485
Malone, Edmond	IV, 579
Malory, Sir Thomas	I, 205
Montagu, Elizabeth	IV, 401
Nabbes, Thomas	II, 95
Norton, Thomas	I, 318
Otway, Thomas	II, 368
Overbury, Sir Thomas	I, 443
Pope, Alexander	III, 171
Puttenham, George	I, 402
Pye, Henry James	IV, 580
Quarles, Francis	II, 79
Randolph, Thomas	I, 744
Ritson, Joseph	IV, 435
Rowe, Elizabeth	III, 97
Rowe, Nicholas	II, 621
Rymer, Thomas	II, 582
Sackville, Thomas	I, 432
Sandys, George	II, 82
Shakespeare, William	1, 452, 457, 459, 507, 546, 577
Sotheby, William	V, 205
Southwell, Robert	I, 363
Stanhope, Philip Dormer	III, 602
Steevens, George	IV, 409, 410
Sterne, Laurence	III, 505, 510
Stevenson, John Hall,	IV, 24
Still, John	I, 340
Theobald, Lewis	III, 141
Udall, Nicholas	I, 279
Vaux, Thomas Lord	I, 277
Warton, Joseph	IV, 396, 398
Warton, Thomas	IV, 75
Watson, Thomas	I, 338
Webster, John	I, 671, 678
Whetstone, George	I, 334
White, Henry Kirke	IV, 490
Wilmot, John	II, 339
Wither, George	II, 215
Wotton, Sir Henry	II, 19
Wyatt, Sir Thomas	I, 253
LEE, VERNON,	
Ford, John	II, 27
Hamerton, Philip Gilbert	VIII, 281
LEE, WILLIAM,	
Defoe, Daniel	III, 30, 41, 43, 44
LEE-HAMILTON, EUGENE,	
Milton, John	II, 256
LEECHMAN, WILLIAM,	
Hutcheson Francis	III, 244

	Vol. and Page
LEES, C. H.,	
Young, Thomas	V, 89
LE GALLIENNE, RICHARD,	
Arnold, Sir Edwin	VIII, 504
Arnold, Matthew	VII, 637
Basse, William	II, 130, 131
Carew, Thomas	II, 23
Drayton, Michael	I, 705, 708
Drummond, William	I, 102
Herrick, Robert	II, 240
Lanier, Sidney	VII, 327, 332
Marston, Philip Bourke	VII, 626
O'Shaughnessy, Arthur Wm. Edgar	VII, 324
Rossetti, Christina Georgina	VIII, 272
Stevenson, Robert Louis	VIII, 237, 249
Symonds, John Addington	VIII, 205
Tennyson, Alfred Lord	VIII, 71, 95
LEGARÉ, HUGH SWINTON,	
Bentham, Jeremy	V, 166
LEGGE, FRANCIS,	
Wilberforce, Samuel	VI, 735
LEGGETT, WILLIAM,	
Halleck, Fitz-Greene	VI, 497
Pinkney, Edward Coate	V, 85
LEGLER, HENRY E.,	
Percival, James Gates	VI, 59
LEGOUIS, ÉMILE,	
Wordsworth, William	V, 617, 626
LEICESTER, COUNTESS OF,	
Sidney, Algernon	II, 353
LEIGH, JAMES EDWARD AUSTIN,	
Richardson, Samuel	III, 450
Austen, Jane	IV, 612
LEIGH, JOHN,	
Cartwright, William	II, 71
LEIGHTON, SIR FREDERICK,	
Gray, Thomas	III, 569
Rossetti, Gabriel Charles Dante	VII, 440
LEIGHTON, ROBERT,	
Shakespeare, William	I, 451
LEISCHING, LOUIS,	
Oliphant, Laurence	VII, 656
LELAND, CHARLES GODFREY,	
Boker, George Henry	VII, 765
Borrow, George Henry	VII, 308
Browne, Charles Farrar	VI, 502
Carlyle, Thomas	VII, 237, 244
Eliot, George	VII, 177, 194
Griswold, Rufus Wilmot	VI, 77, 79
Hawthorne, Nathaniel	VI, 347
Lincoln, Abraham	VI, 420
Lytton, Sir Edward George Bulwer	VI, 683
Norton, Caroline E. S.	VII, 103
Whitman, Walt	VIII, 149
Willis, Nathaniel Parker	VI, 489
LELAND, FRANCIS,	
Lytton, Edward Robert Bulwer Earl	VIII, 43
LELAND, JOHN,	
Chaucer, Geoffrey	I, 153
De Hoveden, Roger	I, 63
Gower, John	I, 174
Herbert, Edward Lord	II, 99
Hume, David	III, 665

INDEX TO CRITICISMS

	Vol. and Page
Lardner, Nathaniel	III, 523
Lyttelton, George Lord	III, 611
West, Gilbert	III, 368
Woolston, Thomas	III, 73
LE NEVE, PHILIP,	
Drummond, William	II, 104
LENNOX, CHARLOTTE,	
Shakespeare, William	I, 519, 538
LENNOX, CUTHBERT,	
Drummond, Henry	VIII, 363
LENTON, FRANCIS,	
Jonson, Ben	I, 759
LEO, F. A.,	
Shakespeare, William	I, 519
LEONARD, JOHN W.,	
Eggleston, Edward	VIII, 475
Miller, Cincinnatus Hiner	VIII, 498
Stockton, Francis Richard	VIII, 472
Stoddard, Richard Henry	VIII, 494
LESLIE, CHARLES,	
Penn, William	II, 630
Reynolds, Sir Joshua	IV, 141
LESLIE, CHARLES ROBERT,	
Allston, Washington	V, 421
Coleridge, Samuel Taylor	V, 211
Lamb, Charles	V, 233
Rogers, Samuel	VI, 35
Scott, Sir Walter	V, 126
Smith, Sydney	V, 469, 472
Sterne, Laurence	III, 507
Wilson, Alexander	IV, 582, 584
LESLIE, CHARLES ROBERT, AND TAYLOR, TOM,	
Beattie, James	IV, 429
Beckford, William	V, 448, 448
Burney, Francis	V, 346
Montagu, Elizabeth	IV, 400
Reynolds, Sir Joshua	IV, 139
LESLIE, JOHN,	
James I. of Scotland	I, 179
LESLIE, SIR JOHN,	
Newton, Sir Isaac	II, 719
Taylor, Brook	III, 52
Young, Thomas	V, 87
LESLIE, T. E. CLIFFE,	
Smith, Adam	IV, 70
LESSING, GOTTHOLD EPHRAIM,	
Pope, Alexander	III, 182
LESTER, JOHN W.,	
Dobell, Sidney Thompson	VI, 761
L'ESTRANGE, A. G.,	
Carleton, William	VI, 549
Mitford, Mary Russell	VI, 42
Scott, Sir Walter	V, 131
LETOURNEUR, PIERRE,	
Young, Edward	III, 486
LETTSOM, JOHN COAKLEY,	
Johnson, Samuel	III, 724
LEVER, CHARLES,	
Kinglake, Alexander William	VIII, 52
LEVERT, OCTAVIA WALTON,	
Brougham, Henry Lord	VI, 526
Browning, Elizabeth Barrett	VI, 230
Browning, Robert	VII, 678
Byron, George Gordon Lord	IV, 760
Campbell, George J. D.	VIII, 433
Campbell, John Lord	VI, 257
Disraeli, Benjamin	VII, 277, 282

	Vol. and Page
Mackay, Charles	VII, 764
Milnes, Richard Monckton	VII, 560
Raleigh, Sir Walter	I, 595
Read, Thomas Buchanan	VI, 677
Strickland, Agnes	VI, 767
LEVY, AMY,	
Poets and Poetry	IV, 10
LEWES, GEORGE HENRY,	
Austen, Jane	IV, 619
Authors and Authorship	VIII, 7
Bacon, Francis	I, 659
Berkeley, George	III, 321, 330
Boswell, James	IV, 217
Brontë, Charlotte	VI, 23
Buchanan, Robert	VIII, 446
Darwin, Charles Robert	VII, 424
Darwin, Erasmus	IV, 425
Dickens, Charles	V, 586
Drama, The	VII, 7
Eliot, George	VII, 180
Hartley, David	III, 377, 378
Hume, David	III, 662
Knowledge	V, 8
Locke, John	II, 526, 534
Marlowe, Christopher	I, 351
Owen, Sir Richard	VIII, 172
Reid, Thomas	IV, 285
Spencer, Herbert	VIII, 477
Sterling, John	V, 453
Tennyson, Alfred Lord	VIII, 99
LEWIN, WALTER,	
Alcott, Amos Bronson	VII, 664
Alcott, Louisa May	VII, 667
Beecher, Henry Ward	VII, 608
Carlyle, Thomas	VII, 259, 271
Clarke, James Freeman	VII, 672
Curtis, George William	VIII, 190
Dickens, Charles	VI, 590
Eliot, George	VII, 206
Fielding, Henry	III, 363
Harte, Francis Bret	VIII, 471
Hawthorne, Nathaniel	V, 362
Holmes, Oliver Wendell	VIII, 297
Martineau, James	VIII, 430
Oliphant, Laurence	VII, 656
Richardson, Samuel	III, 437
Ruskin, John	VIII, 419
Stowe, Harriet Beecher	VIII, 358
Taylor, Bayard	VII, 132
Thoreau, Henry David	V, 274
Whitman, Walt	VIII, 135
Whittier, John Greenleaf	VIII, 125
LEWIS, CHARLTON T.,	
Bryant, William Cullen	VII, 118
LEWIS, EDWIN HERBERT,	
Addison, Joseph	II, 660
Ælfric	I, 46
Arnold, Matthew	VII, 645
Ascham, Roger	I, 290
Blair, Hugh	IV, 407
Bunyan, John	II, 398
Burke, Edmund	IV, 297
Butler, Joseph	III, 313
Carlyle, Thomas	VII, 272
Channing, William Ellery	V, 375
Coleridge, Samuel Taylor	V, 227
Defoe, Daniel	III, 50
DeQuincey, Thomas	VI, 129
Dickens, Charles	VI, 592
Eliot, George	VII, 206
Emerson, Ralph Waldo	VII, 376

	Vol. and Page
Gibbon, Edward	IV, 196
Goldsmith, Oliver	III, 638
Green, John Richard	VII, 513
Green, Robert	I, 345
Hume, David	III, 667
Irving, Washington	VI, 152
Jeffrey, Francis Lord	V, 657
Johnson, Samuel	III, 766
Lamb, Charles	V, 243
Landor, Walter Savage	VI, 392
Lincoln, Abraham	VI, 420
Lowell, James Russell	VIII, 40
Macaulay, Thomas Babington Lord	VI, 114
Newman, John Henry	VII, 754
Paley, William	IV, 478
Pater, Walter Horatio	VIII, 278
Poor, Richard	I, 70
Raleigh, Sir Walter	I, 608
Ruskin, John	VIII, 420
Saint-John, Henry	III, 298
Scott, Sir Walter	V, 161
Spencer, Herbert	VIII, 484
Sterne, Laurence	III, 515
Swift, Johnathan	III, 237
LEWIS, ERASMUS,	
Arbuthnot, John	III, 82
Prior, Matthew	II, 673
LEWIS, SIR GEORGE CORNE- WALL,	
Berkeley, George	III, 327
Gladstone, William Ewart	VIII, 391
Hallam, Henry	VI, 176, 177
Mill, James	V, 307
Thirlwall, Connop	VII, 43
Wilkinson, Sir John Gardner	VII, 52
LEWIS, SIR GILBERT FRANK- LAND,	
Grote, George	VI, 607
Lewis, Sir George Cornewall	VI, 337
LEWIS, JOHN,	
Caxton, William	I, 197
LEWIS, MARY A.,	
Browning, Robert	VII, 703
LEWIS, S. D.,	
Poe, Edgar Allan	V, 540
LEWIS, WALTER,	
Black, William	VIII, 394
LEY, W. CLEMENT,	
Ruskin, John	VIII, 416
LEYDEN, JOHN,	
Drummond, William	II, 105
LEYLAND, FRANCIS A.,	
Brontë, Emily	V, 524
LIDDELL, MARK H.,	
Chaucer, Geoffrey	I, 132, 140
LIDDON, HENRY PARRY,	
Keble, John	VI, 464
Pusey, Edward Bouverie	VII, 468, 472
White, Joseph Blanco	V, 362
LIEBER, FRANCIS,	
Kent, James	V, 500
Motley, John Lothrop	VII, 89
Prescott, William Hickling	VI, 184
Smith, Adam	IV, 64
Webster, Daniel	V, 725
Woolsey, Theodore Dwight	VII, 736

628   INDEX TO CRITICISMS

LIGHTFOOT, JOSEPH BARBER,
- Donne, John............I, 711
- Pearson, John............II, 369
- Whewell, William.....VI, 468, 472

LILLIE, MRS. JOHN,
- Eliot, George............VII, 175

LILLIE, LUCY C.,
- Alcott, Louisa May...VII, 666, 667
- Griffin, Gerald............V, 353

LILLO. GEORGE,
- Shakespeare, William......I, 531

LILLY, WILLIAM SAMUEL,
- Carlyle, Thomas.VII, 249, 253, 257
- Dickens, Charles......VI, 579, 592
- Froude, James Anthony..VIII, 266
- History................VI, 10
- Manning, Henry Edward.VIII, 167
- Newman, John Henry.....VII, 741
- Pope, Alexander.........III, 193
- Symonds, John Addington....
- ....VIII, 203
- Tennyson, Alfred Lord...VIII, 109
- Thackeray, William Makepeace
- ....VI, 300, 301
- Wiseman, Nicholas Patrick.VI, 439

LILY, WILLIAM,
- Skelton, John..............I, 219

LINCOLN, ROBERT T.,
- Lowell, James Russell....VIII, 25

LINCOLN, ROBERT W.,
- Hopkinson, Thomas.......IV, 132

LINGARD, JOHN,
- Aldhelm ....I, 25
- Bacon, Francis............I, 642
- Bede ....I, 29
- Dunstan ....I, 44
- Gauden, John............II, 177
- Hyde, Edward, Earl of Clarendon ....II, 299
- Laud, William............II, 90
- Raleigh, Sir Walter ....I, 602
- Wyclife, John.............I, 102

LINK, SAMUEL ALBERT,
- Hayne, Paul Hamilton....VII, 593
- Poe, Edgar Allan..........V, 560
- Simms, William Gilmore...VI, 600

LINN, WILLIAM,
- Washington, George......IV, 357

LINTON, ELIZABETH LYNN,
- Drummond, Henry......VIII, 364
- Eliot, George....VII, 188, 189, 195
- Landor, Walter Savage....VI, 375
- Lewes, George Henry.....VII, 138

LINTON, WILLIAM JAMES,
- Adamt, Sarah Flower.......V, 529
- Alcott, Amos Bronson......VII, 663
- Bowring, Sir John........VI, 665
- Craik, Dinah Maria Mulock...
- ....VII, 624
- Dickens. Charles ....VI, 558
- Emerson, Ralph Waldo...VII, 352
- Herrick, Robert..........II, 236
- Hood, Thomas............V, 461
- Horne, Richard Hengist......
- ....VII, 545, 547
- Hunt, James Henry Leigh..VI, 162
- Landor. Walter Savage.....VI, 378
- Lover, Samuel............VI, 544
- Martineau, Harriet.......VII, 58
- Montgomery. Robert......VI. 47
- Newman, Francis William.VIII, 370

Owen, Robert. ....VI, 84
Rossetti, Gabriel Charles Dante
....VII, 439
Ruskin, John .. ..VIII, 407
Spencer, Herbert... ....VIII, 478
Stoddard, Richard Henry.VIII, 497
Suckling, Sir J hn ....II, 67
Tupper, Martin Farquhar..VII, 732
Wells, Charles Jeremiah ..VII, 164
Whitman, Walt.........VIII, 133
Whittier, John Greenleaf.VIII, 117

LINTOT, BERNARD,
- Gay, John...............III, 53

LIPPINCOTT, SARAH JANE, (GRACE GREENWOOD),
- Eliot, George...........VII 174

LIPPMANN, JULIE M.,
- Stockton, Francis Richard....
- ....VIII, 474

LISTER, T. H.,
- Fanshawe, Sir Richard .....II, 184
- Hyde Edward, Earl of Clarendon ....II, 300

LITTLE, JAMES STANLEY,
- Buchanan, Robert.......VIII, 447

LITTLE, MARION,
- Browning, Robert ....VII, 718

LITTLEDALE, RICHARD F.,
- Kingsley, Henry..........VII, 80
- Collins, Mortimer..........VII, 82
- Reade, Charles...........VII, 535
- Trollope, Anthony........VII, 461

LIVINGSTON, LUTHER S.,
- Browning, Robert........VII, 685
- Holmes, Oliver Wendell. .VIII, 292
- Whittier, John Greenleaf.VIII, 128

LLANOVER, LADY,
- Burney, Frances...........V, 344

LLOYD, CHARLES,
- Lamb, Charles............V, 239

LLOYD, DAVID,
- Suckling, Sir John........II, 65
- Cartwright, William.......II, 71

LLOYD, D. D.,
- Macaulay, Thomas Babington Lord ....VI, 96

LLOYD, ROBERT,
- Chaucer, Geoffrey..........I, 156
- Gray, Thomas............III, 563

LOBBAN, J. H.,
- Defoe, Daniel............III, 30
- Fielding, Henry..........III, 365
- Goldsmith, Oliver.........III, 638
- Hazlitt, William...........V, 106
- Hunt, James Henry Leigh..VI, 172
- Johnson, Samuel..........III, 742
- Lamb, Charles............V, 244
- Mackenzie, Henry.........V, 115
- Pope, Alexander..........III, 194
- Steele, Sir Richard........II, 767
- Swift, Jonathan..........III, 237

LOCK, WALTER,
- Keble, John.............VI, 463

LOCKE, JOHN,
- Chillingworth, William.....II, 85
- Knowledge................V, 5
- Locke, John......II, 519, 523
- Newton, Sir Isaac.........II, 711
- Poets and Poetry.........IV, 6
- Selden, John............II, 139
- Spelman, Sir Henry.......II, 54

Tillotson, John Robert.....II, 438
Toland, John ....II, 681

LOCKER-LAMPSON ,FREDERICK,
- Addison, Joseph. ....II, 660
- Boswell, James. ....IV, 211
- Browning, Elizabeth Barrett.
- .. ..VI, 234
- Burns. Robert........ .. .IV, 267
- Campbell Thomas. ......V, 437
- Cowper, William.........IV, 394
- Eliot, George. ....VII, 179
- Gore, Catherine Grace.....VI, 264
- Hood, Thomas............V, 465
- Hunt, James Henry Leigh..VI, 162
- Landor, Walter Savage. ...VI, 378
- Lewes, George Henry.....VII, 139
- Milnes Richard Monckton.VII, 561
- Pope, Alexander......... III, 192
- Praed, Winthrop Mackworth.V, 334
- Rossetti, Gabriel Charles Dante
- ....VII, 454
- Spedding, James.........VII, 318
- Spenser, Edmund.........I, 400
- Stanley, Arthur Penrhyn..VII, 300
- Sterne, Laurence ....III, 509
- Suckling, Sir John ....II, 67
- Thackeray, William Makepeace
- ....VI, 298, 312, 320
- Trollope, Anthony...VII, 458, 463
- Wordsworth, William......V, 645

LOCKHART, C. S. M.,
- Scott, Sir Walter..........V, 159

LOCKHART, JOHN GIBSON,
- Alison, Sir Archibald..VI, 520, 520
- Brougham, Henry Lord....V, 529
- Beckford, William......V, 448, 450
- Borrow, George Henry....VII, 309
- Brontë, Charlotte......VI, 17, 22
- Burns, Robert..............
- .....IV, 227, 241, 244, 253
- Carlyle, Thomas.........VII, 251
- Chalmers, Thomas.........V, 489
- Coleridge, Samuel Taylor.....
- ....V. 207, 219, 222
- Crabbe, George.........V, 171, 173
- Croker, John Wilson.......VI, 72
- Defoe, Daniel............III, 44
- Disraeli, Benjamin.......VII, 288
- Edgeworth, Maria.........V, 563
- Galt, John................V, 336
- Hall, Basil................V, 457
- Hogg, James..............V, 263
- Hook, Edward Theodore...
- ....V, 356, 358
- Jeffrey, Francis Lord...V, 648, 653
- Keats, John..............IV, 675
- Kemble, Frances Ann...VIII, 215
- Langhorne, John.........III, 700
- Lewis, Matthew Gregory.....
- ....IV, 632, 633
- Lockhart, John Gibson....V, 755
- Lytton, Sir Edward George Bulwer ....VI, 678

Macaulay, Thomas Babington Lord ....VI, 104
- Maginn, William............V, 385
- Marryat, Frederick........V, 531
- Mickle, William Julius......IV, 42
- Murchison, Sir Roderick Impey ....VI, 630

INDEX TO CRITICISMS

	Vol. and Page
Norton, Caroline E. S.	VII, 104
Park, Mungo	IV, 484
Ritson, Joseph	IV, 435
Scott, Sir Walter	V, 129, 153
Seward, Anna	IV, 543
Southey, Robert	V, 396
Taylor, Sir Henry	VII, 580
Tennyson, Alfred Lord	VIII, 78, 79
Trollope, Frances Milton	VI, 330
Willis, Nathaniel Parker	VI, 489, 490
Wilson, John	V, 744
Wordsworth, William	V, 606

LOCKHART, ROBERT M.,
Burns, Robert	IV, 240

LOCKHART, WILLIAM,
Manning, Henry Edward	VIII, 165

LOCKIER, DR. DEAN OF PETERBOROUGH,
Etheredge, Sir George	II, 413
Harrington, James	II, 307
Lee, Nathaniel	II, 430
Newton, Isaac	II, 713
Settle, Elkanah	II, 691
Villiers, George	II, 337

LOCKWOOD, M.,
Day, Thomas	IV, 49

LODGE, EDMUND,
Abbot, George	I, 726
Burnet, Gilbert	II, 591
Fisher, John	I, 231
Fox, Charles James	IV, 507
Selden, John	II, 138
Wotton, Sir Henry	II, 18
Wyatt, Sir Thomas	I, 251

LODGE, HENRY CABOT,
Adams, John Quincy	V, 519
Butler, Samuel	II, 333
Chatterton, Thomas	III, 538
Choate, Rufus	VI, 198
Cobbettt, William	V, 272, 274
Cooper, James Fenimore	V, 686
Fox, Charles James	IV, 501
Hamilton, Alexander	IV, 460, 468
Hawthorne, Nathaniel	VI, 369
Holmes, Oliver Wendell	VIII, 294, 297
Keats, John	IV, 674
Madison, James	V, 313
Marshall, John	V, 284
Mather, Cotton	II, 732
Parkman, Francis	VIII, 223
Penn, William	II, 631
Sewall, Samuel	III, 17, 19
Seward, William Henry	VI, 674
Shelley, Percy Bysshe	IV, 699
Washington, George	V, 363
Webster, Daniel	V, 723, 725, 729

LODGE, OLIVER,
Bacon, Roger	I, 79
Halley, Edmund	III, 108
Newton, Sir Isaac	II, 715

LODGE, RICHARD,
Green, John Richard	VII, 513

LODGE, THOMAS,
Daniel, Samuel	I, 612
Lyly, John	I, 426
Spenser, Edmund	I, 392

LOFTIE, WILLIAM JOHN,
Cowper, William	IV, 374

	Vol. and Page
Green, John Richard	VII, 506
More, Sir Thomas	I, 236

LONDON CHRONICLE
Priestley, Joseph	IV, 445

LONDON GAZETTE,
Defoe, Daniel	III, 23, 28
Dryden, John	II, 463

LONDON MAGAZINE,
Wesley, John	IV, 118

LONDON PUBLIC ADVERTURER,
Wilkes, John	IV, 333

LONG, JOHN DAVIS,
Longfellow, Henry Wadsworth	VII, 406
Phillips, Wendell	VII, 556

LONGFELLOW, ALICE M.,
Longfellow, Henry Wadsworth	VII, 397

LONGFELLOW, HENRY WADSWORTH,
Agassiz, Louis Jean Rodolphe	VI, 719
Allston, Washington	V, 418
Arnold, Matthew	VII, 634
Beowulf	I, 17
Burns, Robert	IV, 260
Chaucer, Geoffrey	I, 127, 145
Clough, Arthur Hugh	VI, 248
Curtis, George William	VIII, 188
Dana, Richard Henry	VII, 153
Dickens, Charles	VI, 567
Disraeli, Benjamin	VII, 286
Eliot, George	VII, 199
Gray, Thomas	III, 561
Hawthorne, Nathaniel	VI, 344, 351, 363
History	VI, 8
Irving, Washington	VI, 134, 142
Jameson, Anna	VI, 215
Keats, John	IV, 665
Kemble, Frances Ann	VIII, 214
Kingsley, Charles	VII, 22, 27
Knowledge	V, 8
Lewes, George Henry	VII, 140
Lowell, James Russell	VIII, 27
Lytton, Sir Edward George Bulwer	VI, 692
Milton, John	II, 293
Poe, Edgar Allan	V, 552, 554
Poets and Poetry	IV, 8
Prescott, William Hickling	VI, 181
Procter, Bryan Waller	VII, 748
Schoolcraft, Henry Rowe	VI, 403
Shakespeare, William	I, 567
Sumner, Charles	VI, 751, 751
Taylor, Bayard	VII, 129, 133
Tennyson, Alfred Lord	VIII, 83, 93, 103
Whittier, John Greenleaf	VIII, 112
Wordsworth, William	V, 625, 631

LONGFELLOW, WILLIAM P. P.,
Ruskin, John	VIII, 408

LONGMANN, WILLIAM,
Wyclif, John	I, 106

LONSDALE, EARL OF,
Young, Arthur	IV, 655

LORD, ALICE E.,
Coleridge, Samuel Taylor	V, 213
Lamb, Charles	V, 236
Wordsworth, William	V, 616

	Vol. and Page
LORD, ELIOT	
Mather, Cotton	II, 732
LORD, JOHN.	
Anslem	I, 51
Burke, Edmund	IV, 306
Gladstone, William Ewart	VIII, 390
Hamilton, Alexander	IV, 464
More, Hannah	V, 192, 195
LORD, WALTER FREWEN.	
Disraeli, Benjamin	VII, 286, 288, 289
Lytton, Sir Edward George Bulwer	VI, 700
Thackeray, William Makepeace	VI, 322
Trollope, Anthony	VII, 465

LORING, CHARLES G.,
Choate, Rufus	VI, 197

LORING, W.,
Milman, Henry Hart	VI, 540

LORKINS, THOMAS,
Shakespeare, William	I, 539

LOSSING, BENSON J.,
Allston, Washington	V, 423
Audubon, John James	V, 696
Calhoun, John Caldwell	V, 676
Hamilton, Alexander	IV, 458
Hopkins, Samuel	IV, 439, 443
Hopkinson, Thomas	IV, 133
Mather, Increase	II, 689
Moore, Thomas	V, 709
Morris, George Pope	VI, 401
Otis, James	III, 716
Schoolcraft, Henry Rowe	VI, 403
Webster, Noah	V, 431

LOTHROP, THORNTON KIRKLAND,
Dana, Richard Henry, Jr.	VII, 500
Seward, William Henry	VI, 678

LOUNSBURY, THOMAS R.,
Browning, Robert	VII, 692
Carter, Elizabeth	IV, 494
Chaucer, Geoffrey	I, 129, 131, 134, 146, 168
Congreve, William	II, 735
Cooper, James Fenimore	V, 685
Dennis, John	III, 78
Dryden, John	II, 470, 485, 506
Fielding, Henry	III, 343
Godwin, William	V, 301
Gower, John	I, 173
Gray, Thomas	III, 570
Hawes, Stephen	I, 218
Johnson, Samuel	III, 752, 766
Lydgate, John	I, 186
Lyndsay, Sir David	I, 275
Mason, William	IV, 325
Milton, John	II, 274
Müller, Friedrich Max	VIII, 438
Piozzi, Hester Lynch	IV, 685
Shakespeare, William	I, 573
Southey, Robert	V, 413
Spenser, Edmund	I, 300
Stanhope, Philip Dormer	III, 607
Tennyson, Alfred Lord	VIII, 82, 97
Tyrwhitt, Thomas	IV, 25, 26
Warton, Thomas	IV, 74
Wyclif, John	I, 103

INDEX TO CRITICISMS

Vol. and Page
LOVEJOY, B. G.,
 Bancroft, George........I, 709
LOVELACE, RICHARD.
 Cotton, Charles............II, 370
LOW, SIDNEY.
 Cobden, Richard......VI, 441, 443
 Henley, William Ernest.....
  ....VIII, 491, 493
 Lowell, James Russell.VIII, 33, 39
LOW, SIDNEY JAMES, AND PULLING, F. S.,
 Cotton, Sir Robert..........I, 709
 Eadmer..................I, 52
 Fabyan, Robert ....I, 206
 Fletcher, Andrew..........II, 610
 Fortescue, Sir John.........I, 194
 Hervey, John..............III, 127
 Spelman, Sir Henry........II, 53
LOWE, CHARLES,
 Blackie, John Stuart......VIII, 304
LOWE, FRANCES H.,
 Gaskell, Elizabeth Cleghorn.VI, 434
LOWE, MARTHA PERRY,
 Dobell, Sidney Thompson...VI, 760
 Martineau, Harriet........VII, 56
LOWELL, JAMES RUSSELL,
 Agassiz, Louis Jean Rodolphe.
  ....VI, 720
 Akenside, Mark............III, 544
 Alcott, Amos Bronson.VII, 662, 664
 Allston, Washington....V, 419, 420
 Arnold, Matthew.........VII, 635
 Barbour, John..............VI, 8
 Beattie, James............IV, 432
 Beaumont and Fletcher......I, 585
 Books ....III, 9
 Boswell, James...........IV 211
 Brontë, Charlotte..........VI, 223
 Brown, John ....VII, 479
 Browning, Elizabeth Barrett..
  ....VI, 239
 Browning, Robert........VII, 697
 Brownson, Orestes Augustus..
  ....VII, 74
 Bryant, William Cullen......
  ....VII, 121, 122
 Bunner, Henry Cuyler...VIII, 359
 Bunyan John..............II, 404
 Burke, Edmund...........IV 295
 Burns, Robert............IV, 256
 Carlyle, Thomas............
  ....VII, 239, 255, 261, 263
 Channing, William Ellery....V, 366
 Chapman, George........I, 729, 732
 Chatterton, Thomas.......III, 536
 Chaucer, Geoffrey..........
  ....I, 127, 145, 150, 164
 Child, Lydia Maria........VII, 218
 Churchill, Charles........III, 480
 Clough, Arthur Hugh.VI, 249, 251
 Coleridge, Samuel Taylor....
  ....V, 215, 218, 220
 Cooper, James Fenimore....V, 684
 Cowper, William.........IV, 389
 Crabbe, George............V, 174
 Curtis, George William...VIII, 184
 Dana, Richard Henry.....VII, 156
 Daniel, Samuel.......I, 614, 616
 Darwin, Charles Robert...VII, 427
 Dennis, John............III, 78
 DeQuincey, Thomas......VI, 128

Vol. and Page
 Dickens, Charles......VI, 574, 578
 Disraeli, Benjamin...VII, 289, 292
 Douglas, Gawin............I, 214
 Drayton, Michael......I, 705, 708
 Drummond, William.......II, 101
 Dryden, John...............
  ......II, 469, 482, 485, 493, 502
 Dunbar, William...........I, 225
 Edwards, Jonathan.......III. 392
 Elliott, Ebenezer...........V, 581
 Emerson, Ralph Waldo.....
  ....VII, 345, 356, 365
 Fielding, Henry............
  ....III, 343, 346, 362, 364
 FitzGerald, Edward..VII, 516, 519
 Fletcher, Phineas..........II, 117
 Ford, John..............II, 29, 33
 Franklin, Benjamin.......IV, 87
 Froude, James Anthony..VIII, 260
 Fuller, Sarah Margaret......V, 664
 Garrison, William Lloyd.....
  ....VII, 158, 159
 Gladstone, William Ewart....
  ....VIII, 389
 Gower, John...............I, 176
 Gray, Asa................VII, 669
 Gray, Thomas....III, 562, 568, 570
 Griswold, Rufus Wilmot....IV, 79
 Halleck, Fitz-Greene........VI, 498
 Harvey, Gabriel............I, 697
 Hawthorne, Nathaniel.......
  ....VI, 342, 356, 360, 366, 377
 History..................VI, 8
 Holland, Josiah Gilbert....VII,334
 Holmes, Oliver Wendell.....
  ....VIII, 290, 296
 Hood, Thomas............V, 458
 Hughes, Thomas.........VIII, 347
 Hunt, James Henry Leigh..VI, 170
 Irving, Washington........VI, 148
 Johnson, Samuel.....III, 751, 759
 Jonson, Ben................I, 765
 Keats, John............IV, 676, 677
 Landor, Walter Savage....VI, 386
 Langland, William.........I, 120
 Lincoln, Abraham.........VI, 419
 Longfellow, Henry Wadsworth
  ......VII, 381, 390, 393 398, 404
 Lovelace, Richard........II, 162
 Lowell, James Russell....VIII, 31
 Lyly, John................I, 425
 Lytton, Sir Edward George
  Bulwer..................VI, 691
 Lytton, Edward Robert Bulwer Earl..............VIII, 43
 Marlowe, Christopher.......I, 355
 Marsh, George Perkins....VII, 494
 Marston, John..............I, 737
 Marvell, Andrew..........II, 315
 Massinger, Philip......II, 46, 51
 Mather, Cotton...........II, 732
 Mill, John Stuart..........VI, 713
 Milton, John..........II, 271, 296
 Nashe, Thomas...........I, 414
 Neal, John...............VII, 77
 Newman, John Henry VII, 740, 749
 Overbury, Sir Thomas......I, 443
 Palfrey, John Gorham VII, 337, 338
 Parker, Theodore..........VI, 206
 Pepys, Samuel...........II, 515
 Percival, James Gates....VI, 59, 61

Vol. and Page
 Philips, Ambrose........III, 274
 Phillips, Wendell........VII, 552
 Poe, Edgar Allan......V. 552, 557
 Pope, Alexander............
  ......III, 151, 161, 173. 177, 190
 Quincy, Josiah...........VI, 405
 Raleigh, Sir Walter........I, 596
 Ritson, Joseph...........IV, 437
 Shakespeare, William......I, 535
 Sidney, Sir Philip..........I, 332
 Skelton, John.............I, 222
 Smollett, Tobias George...III, 588
 South, Robert............II, 608
 Southey, Robert..........V, 417
 Southwell, Robert..........I, 362
 Spenser, Edmund..........
  I, 373, 377, 385, 389, 390, 391
  397.
 Stanley, Arthur Penrhyn..VII, 299
 Steele, Sir Richard.........II, 754
 Stephen, Sir Leslie......VIII, 510
 Sterne, Laurence.........III, 507
 Still, John................I, 430
 Surrey, Earl of............I, 259
 Swift, Jonathan......III, 225, 232
 Taylor, Jeremy...........II, 210
 Tennyson, Alfred Lord......
  ....VIII, 91, 94, 103
 Thackeray, William Makepeace
  ....VI, 313
 Thomson, James.........III, 269
 Thoreau, Henry David....VI, 272
 Tupper, Martin Farquhar..VII, 733
 Vaughan, Henry..........II, 444
 Walton, Isaac............II, 347
 Warton, Thomas.........IV, 78
 Washington, George......IV, 362
 Webster, John............II, 675
 White, Gilbert.......IV, 148, 150
 White, Henry Kirke......IV, 488
 Whittier, John Greenleaf...
  ....VIII, 113, 117, 120
 Willis, Nathaniel Parker....VI, 491
 Wither, George..........II, 214
 Wordsworth, William...V, 623, 636
LOWELL, R. T. S.,
 Hearne, Thomas..........III, 89
LOWNDES, WILLIAM THOMAS,
 Berners, Juliana............I, 191
 Edwards, Jonathan.......III, 390
 Hall, Robert..............V, 111
 Hooker, Richard..........I, 406
 Horne, George...........IV, 144
 Ken, Thomas............II, 568
 Macknight, James.......IV, 408
 Whiston, William........III, 305
LOWTH, ROBERT,
 Hooker, Richard..........I, 405
 Lowth, Robert...........IV, 28
 Pope, Alexander.........III, 172
 Shakespeare, William......I, 511
 Spence, Joseph..........III, 519
 Warburton, William.....III, 683
LUARD, HENRY RICHARD,
 Dibdin, Thomas Frognall...V, 506
 Grosseteste, Robert........I, 73
 Hearne, Thomas..........III, 90
 Porson, Richard.........IV, 526
LUBBOCK, SIR JOHN,
 Malory, Sir Thomas........I, 204
 Richardson, Samuel......III, 437

INDEX TO CRITICISMS

	Vol. and Page
LUCAS, E. V.,	
Dodgson, Charles Lutwige....	VIII, 397
LUCE, MORTON,	
Tennyson, Alfred Lord.	VIII, 82, 97
LUCY, HENRY W.,	
Disraeli, Benjamin...	VII, 279, 284
Gladstone, William Ewart....	VIII, 385
LÜDERS, CHARLES HENRY,	
Fielding, Henry............	III, 363
LUDLOW, FITZ-HUGH,	
King, Thomas Starr........	VI, 408
LUDLOW, JAMES MEEKER,	
Holmes, Oliver Wendell..	VIII, 293
Hughes, Thomas....	VIII, 347, 348
LUDWIG, OTTO,	
Shakespeare, William.......	I, 505
LUMSDEN, LIEUT.-COL. H. W.,	
Beowulf..................	I, 19
LUSHINGTON, HENRY,	
Cobbett, William...........	V, 271
LUTTRELL, HENRY,	
Rogers, Samuel	VI, 38
LYALL, SIR ALFRED,	
Maine, Sir Henry James Sumner...............	VII, 651
Tennyson, Alfred Lord..	VIII, 75, 92
LYDGATE, JOHN	
Chaucer, Geoffrey.......	I, 139, 152
LYELL, SIR CHARLES,	
Darwin, Charles Robert...	VII, 422
Hutton, James.............	IV, 338
LYLY, JOHN,	
Authors and Authorship..	VIII, 5
Knowledge................	V, 5
LYMAN, THEODORE,	
Agassiz, Louis Jean Rodolphe	VI, 720, 723
LYNCH, ARTHUR,	
Whitman, Walt.........	VIII, 145
LYON, H. THOMSON,	
Sale George..............	III, 91
LYTE, H. F.,	
Vaughan, Henry...........	II, 443
LYTTELTON, GEORGE LORD,	
Berkeley, George.........	III, 329
Map, Walter................	I, 61
Thomson, James......	III, 255, 266
LYTTELTON, THOMAS,	
Lyttelton, George Lord....	III, 611
LYTTLETON, EDITH,	
Gibbon, Edward..........	IV, 178
LYTTLETON, LORD,	
Beattie, James............	IV, 431
Robertson, William.......	IV, 158
LYTTON, SIR EDWARD GEORGE BULWER LORD,	
Addison, Joseph...........	II, 657
Authors and Authorship .	VIII, 7
Bacon Francis.............	I, 643
Bentham, Jeremy	V, 163
Blanchard, Samuel Laman...	V, 480, 481
Browne, Sir Thomas...	II, 340, 341, 343
Burke, Edmund..........	IV, 305
Brydges Sir Samuel Egerton	V, 321
Campbell Thomas.........	V, 437
Edgeworth Maria........	V, 569
Eliot George	VII, 183

	Vol. and Page
Fox, Charles James........	IV, 500
Goldsmith, Oliver.....	III, 618, 637
Gray, Thomas....	III, 555, 558, 567
Hazlitt, William...........	V, 103
Hume, David............	III, 662
Hunt, James Henry Leigh..	VI, 169
Irving, Washington.......	VI, 149
Johnson, Samuel..........	III, 758
Knowledge................	V, 9
Lamb, Lady Caroline.......	V, 82
Lamb, Charles............	IV, 240
Landon, Letitia Elizabeth..	V, 322
Macaulay, Thomas Babington Lord....................	VI, 97
Milnes, Richard Monckton	VII, 562
Montgomery, Robert......	VI, 48
Patmore, Coventry......	VIII, 341
Pitt, William.............	IV, 508
Praed, Winthrop Mackworth	V, 381
Richardson, Samuel.......	III, 449
Sadler, Michael Thomas.....	V, 287
Saint-John, Henry....	III, 288, 296
Scott, Sir Walter..........	V, 152
Shakespeare, William.......	I, 563
Sheridan, Richard Brinsley...	IV, 604, 607
Southey, Robert..........	V, 415
Sterne, Laurence.........	III, 514
Swift, Jonathan..........	III, 221
Taylor, Jeremy...........	II, 209
Tennyson, Alfred Lord......	VIII, 76, 97, 100
Waller, Edmund..........	II, 382
Walpole, Horace..........	IV, 322
LYTTON, EDWARD ROBERT BULWER (OWEN EARL MEREDITH),	
Knowledge................	V, 9
Lytton, Sir Edward George Bulwer Lord....	VI, 683, 687, 698
LYTTON ROSINA BULWER LADY,	
Forster, John.............	VII, 65
Lytton, Sir Edward George Bulwer Lord..........	VI, 680

MABIE, HAMILTON WRIGHT,
Addison, Joseph...

	Vol. and Page
....	II, 640, 643, 645
Blackmore, Richard D...	VIII, 432
Browning, Robert...	VII, 692, 713
Bryant, William Cullen...	VII, 126
Burns, Robert...........	IV, 264
Burton, Robert...........	II, 40
Carlyle, Thomas.........	VII, 273
Clough, Arthur Hugh.....	VI, 254
Critic, The...............	II, 9
Curtis, George William...	VIII, 186
Dickens, Charles.........	VI, 574
Drummond, Henry......	VIII, 363
Eliot, George............	VII, 194
Emerson, Ralph Waldo.....	VII, 353, 375
Fiske, John..............	VIII, 457
Franklin, Benjamin........	IV, 104
Gray, Thomas............	III, 571
Hawthorne, Nathaniel.	VI, 354, 370
Hopkins, Mark...........	VII, 614
Jackson Helen Hunt.	VII, 572, 574
Johnson Samuel..........	III, 735
Jonson Ben...............	I, 751

	Vol. and Page
Keats, John......	IV, 666, 671, 680
Landor, Walter Savage.....	VI, 391
Lincoln, Abraham........	VI, 421
Longfellow, Henry Wadsworth	VII, 413
Lowell, James Russell..	VIII, 33, 35
Marlowe, Christopher.......	I, 357
Milton, John.............	II, 268
Pater, Walter Horatio....	VIII, 279
Poe, Edgar Allan.......	V, 556, 560
Rossetti, Gabriel Charles Dante	VII, 445, 448
Scott, Sir Walter.......	V, 146, 149
Shakespeare, William.....	I, 453, 455, 470, 510, 577
Spenser, Edmund.........	I, 400
Stockton, Francis Richard...	VIII, 474
Tennyson, Alfred Lord......	VIII, 89, 109
Thackeray, William Makepeace	VI, 320
Warner, Charles Dudley.....	VIII, 442, 444
White, Gilbert............	IV, 153
Whitman, Walt.........	VIII, 147
Whittier, John Greenleaf.	VIII, 126
Willis, Nathaniel Parker...	VI, 492
Woolman, John..........	III, 598
Wordsworth, William.......	V, 645
MACAULAY, CATHERINE,	
Bacon, Francis............	I, 655
Rymer, Thomas..........	II, 583
Sacheverell, Henry........	II, 695
MACAULAY, G. C.,	
Beaumont, Francis........	I, 588
Whitman, Walt........	VIII, 141
MACAULAY, THOMAS BABINGTON LORD,	
Addison, Joseph...	II, 635, 650, 656
Akenside, Mark..........	III, 544
Atterbury, Francis........	III, 67
Austen, Jane..........	IV, 616, 619
Authors and Authorship..	VIII, 7
Bacon, Francis.....	I, 643, 650, 666
Baxter, Richard..........	II, 427
Bentley, Richard.....	III, 111, 122
Blair, Hugh............	IV, 406
Boswell, James...	IV, 210, 216, 220
Brougham, Henry Lord.....	VI, 524, 526
Buckle, Henry Thomas....	VI, 280
Bunyan, John.....	II, 395, 400, 402
Burke, Edmund..........	IV, 303
Burnet, Gilbert.........	II, 591, 595
Burney, Charles..........	IV, 588
Burney, Frances.........	V, 346, 348, 350, 358
Butler, Samuel..........	II, 334
Byron, George Gordon Lord..	IV, 737, 744, 752, 755
Campbell, Thomas........	V, 443
Carlyle, Thomas.........	VII, 261
Cary, Henry Francis......	V, 456
Coke, Sir Edward........	I, 740
Collier, Jeremy.........	II, 699, 700
Congreve, William........	II, 742
Cowley, Abraham........	II, 200
Cowper, William......	IV, 379, 387
Crabbe, George...........	V, 173

INDEX TO CRITICISMS

	Vol. and Page
Cranmer, Thomas	I, 271
Croker, John Wilson	VI, 74
D'Avenant, Sir William	II, 218
Defoe, Daniel	III, 34
Dickens, Charles	VI, 568, 576
Dodwell, Henry	II, 566
Drama, The	VII, 6
Dryden, John	II, 469, 482, 499
D'Urfey, Thomas	II, 688
Emerson, Ralph Waldo	VII, 362
Fletcher, Andrew	II, 611
Fox, Charles James	IV, 506
Fox, George	II, 421
Garrick, David	III, 695
Gauden, John	II, 177
Gay, John	III, 53
Gibbon, Edward	IV, 174, 184
Gifford, William	V, 34
Gladstone, William Ewart	VIII, 384, 390
Goldsmith, Oliver	III, 617, 636
Hallam, Henry	VI, 175, 178
Hickes, George	II, 598
History	VI, 7
Hobbes, Thomas	II, 325
Hume, David	III, 656
Hunt, James Henry Leigh	VI, 157, 168
Hyde, Edward, Earl of Clarendon	II, 300, 303
Jeffrey, Francis Lord	V, 650, 653
Johnson, Samuel	III, 729, 738, 744, 747, 750, 756
Junius	IV, 641
Ken, Thomas	II, 568
Latimer, Hugh	I, 269
Laud, William	II, 91
Law, William	III, 429
Lennox, Charlotte	IV, 470
Leslie, Charles	II, 680
L'Estrange, Sir Roger	II, 539
Lewis, Matthew Gregory	IV, 632
Locke, John	II, 521, 531
Lyttelton, George Lord	III, 610
Lytton, Sir Edward George Bulwer	VI, 679
Macaulay, Thomas Babington Lord	VI, 98
Mackintosh, Sir James	V, 179
Macpherson, James	IV, 276
Mandeville, Bernard	III, 69
Middleton, Conyers	III, 279
Mill, James	V, 310
Milman, Henry Hart	VI, 538
Milton, John	II, 246, 251, 269, 271, 272, 277, 281, 287
Mitford, William	V, 70
Montagu, Charles	II, 587, 587
Montgomery, Robert	VI, 47, 47
Moore, Thomas	V, 713, 760
More, Hannah	V, 191
Napier, Gen. Sir Wm. Francis Patrick	VI, 222
Newton, Sir Isaac	II, 717, 724
Oldmixon, John	III, 125
Orme, Robert	IV, 414
Owen, Sir Richard	VIII, 171
Paley, William	IV, 477
Parr, Samuel	V, 21
Peacock, Thomas Love	VI, 473

	Vol. and Page
Penn, William	II, 627, 628
Pitt, William, Earl of Chatham	III, 679
Pitt, William	IV, 510
Poets and Poetry	IV, 7
Pope, Alexander	III, 148
Porson, Richard	IV, 525
Prescott, William Hickling	VI, 188. 190
Raleigh, Sir Walter	I. 594
Richardson, Samuel	III, 440
Robertson, William	IV, 159
Rogers, Samuel	VI, 32, 39
Sackville, Charles	II, 554
Sadler, Michael Thomas	V. 287
Savage, Richard	III, 133
Savile, George	II, 449
Scott, Sir Walter	V, 129
Sedley, Sir Charles	II, 508
Shakespeare, William	I, 512, 557
Sheffield, John, Third Earl of Mulgrave	II, 670, 672
Shelley, Percy Bysshe	IV, 705
Sheridan, Richard Brinsley	IV, 600, 606
Sherlock, William	II, 561
Smith, Sydney	V, 467
Somers, John Lord	II, 613, 614
Sotheby, William	V, 205
Southey, Robert	V, 404, 411, 412, 413, 414
Spenser, Edmund	I, 382
Sprat, Thomas	II, 574
Stanhope, Philip Dormer	III, 601, 604, 604
Stanhope, Philip Henry Earl	VII, 46
Steele, Sir Richard	II, 753, 763
Steevens, George	IV, 409
Swift, Jonathan	III, 201, 201, 209, 230
Temple, Sir William	II, 458
Tennyson, Alfred Lord	VIII, 92
Tickell, Thomas	III, 106
Tillotson, John Robert	II, 438, 440
Waller, Edmund	II, 381
Walpole, Horace. IV, 312, 318, 322
Whiston, William	III, 305
Whitehead, William	IV, 23
Wilberforce, William	V, 201
Wilkes, John	IV, 333
Williams, Sir Charles Hanbury	III, 413
Wordsworth, William	V, 625, 631
Wycherley, William	II, 600, 602, 605
Wyclif, John	I, 105
MACCALL, WILLIAM, Hamilton, Sir William	VI, 55
Mill, John Stuart	VI, 713
MACHETTA, BLANCHE ROOSEVELT, Longfellow, Henry Wadsworth	VII, 383
MACCLINTOCK, PORTER LANDER, Scott, Sir Walter	V, 125, 153
MACCOLL, MALCOLM, Church, Richard William	VII, 729
Disraeli, Benjamin	VII, 278

	Vol. and Page
MACCULLOCH, J. A., Stevenson, Robert Louis	VIII, 240, 251
Whitman, Walt	VIII, 152
MACCUNN, FLORENCE, Chaucer, Geoffrey	I, 130
Knox, John	I, 299
MACDIARMID, JOHN, Hyde, Edward, Earl of Clarendon	II, 299
More, Sir Thomas	I, 234
MACDONALD, GEORGE, Bacon, Francis	I, 668
Browning, Robert	VII, 698
Byrom, John	III, 470
Davies, Sir John	I, 633
Dekker, Thomas	II, 60
Donne, John	I, 716
Drummond, William	II, 105
Fletcher, Phineas	II, 116
Greville, Sir Fulke	I. 691
Herbert, George	I, 723
Herrick, Robert	II, 238
Knowledge	V, 10
Marlowe, Christopher	I, 355
Milman, Henry Hart	VI, 540
Milton, John	II, 275, 292
Pope, Alexander	III. 160
Quarles, Francis	II, 73
Raleigh, Sir Walter	I, 605, 606
Shakespeare, William	I, 565
Shelley, Percy Bysshe	IV, 698, 702
Sidney, Sir Philip	I, 332
Southwell, Robert	I, 361
Spenser, Edmund	I, 372
Surrey, Earl of	I, 256
Tennyson, Alfred Lord	VIII, 87, 102
Thomson, James	III, 269
Vaughan, Henry	II, 443
Watts, Isaac	III, 252
Wesley, Charles	IV, 37
Wither, George	II, 214
Wordsworth, William	V, 621
MACDONALD, JAMES, Sterne, Laurence	III, 502
MACDONALD, J. R., Fletcher, Andrew	II, 611
Scott, Michael	V, 280
MACDONALD, W. RAE, Napier, Sir John	I, 589
MACDONELL, G. P., Blackstone, Sir William	III, 703, 705
Campbell, John Lord	VI, 260
Coke, Sir Edward	I, 741
Fawcett, Henry	VII, 551
Fortescue, Sir John	I, 195
Malthus, Thomas Robert	V, 253
MACDONELL, JOHN, Bentham Jeremy	V, 168
MACFARLAND, JOHN, Burns, Robert	IV, 264
MAGGILLIVRAY, W., Ray, John	II, 542, 543
MACGREGOR, D. H., Macaulay, Thomas Babington Lord	VI, 115
MACH, ERNST, Newton, Sir Isaac	II, 725
MACHAR, AGNES MAULE, Burns, Robert	VI, 261

INDEX TO CRITICISMS 633

	Vol. and Page
Rutherford, Samuel	II 167
MACILWAIN, GEORGE,	
Hunter, John	IV, 167
Owen, Sir Richard	VIII, 171
MACKAIL, J. W.,	
Fanshawe, Sir Richard	II, 185
Morris, William	VIII, 331
Palgrave, Francis Turner	
	VIII, 372, 373
Stevenson, Robert Louis	VIII, 244
MACKAY, ÆNEAS,	
Barnard, Lady Anne	V, 29
Boece, Hector	I 243
Buchanan, George	I, 314
Chalmers, George	V. 30
Dalrymple, Sir David	IV. 145, 146
Henry the Minstrel	I, 202
Lyndsay, Sir David	I, 275
MACKAY, ANGUS M.,	
Brontë, Anne	V, 600
Brontë, Charlotte	VI, 31
Brontë, Emily	V, 526
MACKAY, CHARLES,	
Adams, John	V, 53
Ainsworth, William Harrison	
	VII, 486
Burns, Robert	IV, 262
Disraeli, Benjamin	VII, 294
Emerson, Ralph Waldo	VII, 351
Jefferson, Thomas	V, 47
Jerrold, Douglas William	VI, 69, 70
Johnson Samuel	III, 744
Miller, Hugh	VI, 63
Procter, Bryan Waller	VI, 750
Ramsay, Allan	III, 405, 410
Rogers, Samuel	VI, 36
Shakespeare, William	I, 562
Thackeray, William Makepeace	
	VI, 297
Washington, George	IV, 362
MACKAY, ERIC,	
Shakespeare, William	I, 570
MACKENZIE, ALEXANDER SLIDELL,	
Franklin, Benjamin	IV, 96
MACKENZIE HENRY,	
Blacklock, Thomas	IV, 129
Burns, Robert	IV, 248
Home, John	IV 513
Wilkie, William	III, 596
MACKENZIE, R. SHELTON.	
DeQuincey, Thomas	VI. 124, 126
Dibdin, Thomas Frognall	V, 506
Dickens, Charles	VI. 554
Holmes, Oliver Wendell	VIII, 292
Jeffrey, Francis Lord	V, 651
Lockhart, John Gibson	V, 754, 757
Maginn, William	V, 386
Moore, Thomas	V, 708
Ramsay, Allan	III. 407
Sadler, Michael Thomas	V, 286, 287
Scott, Sir Walter	V, 132, 150, 155
Sterne, Laurence	III. 503
Wilson, John	V 750
Wordsworth, William	V, 613
MACKINTOSH, SIR JAMES,	
Bacon, Francis	I, 643, 666
Barbauld, Anna Lætitia	V, 23
Berkeley, George	III. 320
Blackstone, William	III, 704
Brown, Thomas	IV, 658

	Vol. and Page
Butler, Joseph	III. 308
Campbell, Thomas	V 441
Cooper, Anthony Ashley	II 578
Defoe, Daniel	III 462
Edgeworth, Maria	V. 562, 567
Edwards, Jonathan	III. 390
Ferguson, Adam	IV, 611
Fielding, Henry	III, 357
Franklin, Benjamin	IV, 84
Godwin, William	V, 298
Goldsmith, Oliver	III, 635
Gray, Thomas	III, 564
Hall, Robert	V, 108
Hartley, David	III, 378
Herschel, Sir John Frederick William	VI, 624
Hobbes, Thomas	II, 325
Horner, Francis	IV, 629
Hume, David	III, 650, 656
Hutcheson, Francis	III, 245
Johnson, Samuel	III, 756
Latimer, Hugh	I, 268
Locke, John	II, 523, 525, 533
Mackenzie, Henry	V, 115
Massinger, Philip	II, 42, 43
Milton, John	II, 288
Montagu, Elizabeth	IV, 402
Montagu, Lady Mary Wortley	
	III, 466
More, Sir Thomas	I, 235, 240
Opie, Amelia	V, 743
Paley, William	IV, 475, 476
Penn, William	II. 629
Pope, Alexander	III, 183
Priestley, Joseph	IV, 447
Reid, Thomas	IV, 284
Reynolds, Sir Joshua	IV, 140
Richardson, Samuel	III, 439, 448
Robertson, William	IV, 156, 157
Rogers, Samuel	VI, 36
Romilly, Sir Samuel	IV, 636
Rowe, Nicholas	II. 621
Scott, Sir Walter	V, 138
Sheridan, Richard Brinsley	
	IV, 600, 605
Smith, Adam	IV. 62
Spenser, Edmund	I. 381
Sterne, Laurence	III, 501
Stewart, Dugald	V, 78, 79
Swift, Jonathan	III, 224, 229
Temple, Sir William	II. 457
Tighe, Mary	IV, 551
Tooke, John Horne	IV 571
Tucker, Abraham	III. 643
Whately, Richard	VI, 326
Wilberforce, William	V, 200
Wordsworth, William	V. 628
Wyclif, John	I, 112
MACKINTOSH, JOHN,	
Barbour, John	I, 115
Blair, Hugh	IV. 404
Buchanan, George	I, 316
Burnet, Gilbert	II 596
Drummond, William	II 106
Fergusson, Robert	III. 641
Henryson, Robert	I, 208
Hume, David	III. 652
James I. of Scotland	I, 179
Macknight, James	IV, 408
Smith, Adam	IV, 60
Smollett, Tobias George	III, 578

	Vol and Page
MACKINTOSH ROBERT	
Darwin Charles Robert	VII 434
Spencer Herbert	VIII 486
Stephen, Sir Leslie	VIII, 511
MACKINTOSH ROBERT JAMES	
Mackintosh. Sir James	V 179
MACKINTOSH, WALLACE AND BELL,	
Atterbury, Francis	III, 65
MACKNIGHT, THOMAS,	
Burke, Edmund	IV. 292, 304
Pope, Alexander	III, 150
Saint-John, Henry	III, 288, 295
Swift, Jonathan	III, 223
Warburton, William	III, 684
MACKY, JOHN,	
Fletcher, Andrew	II, 610
MACLACHLAN, T. BANKS,	
Livingstone, David	VI, 729
MACLAURIN, COLIN,	
Newton, Sir Isaac	II, 722
MACLAY, WILLIAM,	
Hamilton, Alexander	IV. 456
MACLEANE, WALTER,	
Collins, Mortimer	VII, 82
MACLEOD, DONALD,	
Chalmers, Thomas	V, 494
Macleod, Norman	VI. 661
Scott, Sir Walter	V. 130
Shairp, John Campbell	
	VII. 569, 570
Trollope, Anthony	VII. 457, 462
MACLEOD, HENRY DUNNING,	
Smith, Adam	IV, 69
MACMAHON, ELLA,	
Kemble, Frances Ann	VIII, 214
MACMECHAN, ARCHIBALD,	
Carlyle, Thomas	VII. 244
MACMILLAN, DANIEL,	
Borrow, George Henry	VII, 311
Green, John Richard	VII, 511
MACPHERSON, DAVID.	
Wyntoun, Andrew	I, 178
MACPHERSON, HECTOR C.,	
Carlyle, Thomas	VII, 254
Smith, Adam	IV. 57, 61. 70
Spencer, Herbert	VIII, 478, 486
Whewell, William	VI, 472
MACPHERSON JAMES,	
Macpherson, James	IV. 272
MACQUEARY, HOWARD.	
Proctor, Richard Anthony	
	VII. 659, 661
MACQUOID, KATHARINE SARAH,	
Edwards, Amelia Blandford	
	VIII, 178
MACRAY, W. D.,	
Cruden, Alexander	III, 546
Hickes, George	II, 598
MACREADY, WILLIAM CHARLES	
Austen, Jane	IV, 616, 617
Baillie, Joanna	V 693
Browning, Robert	VII 678 686
Carlyle, Thomas	VII 230
Dickens, Charles	VI 565
Dryden, John	II 500
Emerson Ralph Waldo	VII 344
Fielding, Henry	III, 359
Gifford, William	V 34
Knowles, James Sheridan	
	VI. 287 288

INDEX TO CRITICISMS

	Vol. and Page
Lytton, Sir Edward George Bulwer	VI, 689
Macklin, Charles	IV, 342
Martineau, Harriet	VII, 55
Maurice, John Frederick Denison	VI, 644
Massinger, Philip	II, 44
Mathias, Thomas James	V, 288
Piozzi, Hester Lynch	IV, 684
Rogers, Samuel	VI, 33
Scott, Sir Walter	V, 150, 150
Story, Joseph	V, 482
Taylor, Sir Henry	VII, 579

MADDEN, RICHARD ROBERT,
Blessington, Countess of	V, 591
Brougham, Henry Lord	VI, 529
Burns, Robert	IV, 227
Byron, George Gordon Lord	IV, 738
Campbell, Thomas	V, 436
Cowper, William	IV, 372
Disraeli, Benjamin	VII, 277
Forster, John	VII, 65, 66
Hook, Theodore Edward	V, 356
Johnson, Samuel	III, 730
Landon, Letitia Elizabeth	V, 325, 328
Landor, Walter Savage	VI, 373
Lytton, Sir Edward George Bulwer	V, 696
Marryat, Frederick	V, 532
Pope, Alexander	III, 148
Procter, Bryan Waller	VI, 748
Shelley, Percy Bysshe	IV, 690
Talfourd, Sir Thomas Noon	V, 760
Willis, Nathaniel Parker	VI, 487

MADDEN, SIR FREDERICK,
| Bale, John | I, 286 |
| Layamon | I, 64 |

MADDYN, DANIEL OWEN,
| Croker, John Wilson | V, 75 |
| Macaulay, Thomas Babington Lord | VI, 99 |

MADISON, JAMES.
Adams, John	V, 52
Franklin, Benjamin	IV, 83
Hamilton, Alexander	IV, 458, 463
Penn, William	II, 629

MAETERLINCK, MAURICE,
| Emerson, Ralph Waldo | VII, 378 |

MAGINN, WILLIAM,
Byron, George Gordon Lord	IV, 754
Gifford, William	V, 32
Keats, John	IV, 663
Sadler, Michael Thomas	V, 286
Scott, Sir Walter	V, 157
Smith, James	V, 337
Shakespeare, William	I, 474

MAGNUS, LAURIE.
| Wordsworth, William | V, 618, 620 |

MAGOON, E. L.,
Adams, Samuel	IV, 442
Ames, Fisher	IV, 528
Henry, Patrick	IV, 351
Otis, James	III, 718

MAGOUN, GEORGE F.,
Butler, Joseph	III, 316
Cumberland, Richard	II, 624
Edwards, Jonathan	III, 391

MAGRUDDER, ALLAN B.,
| Marshall, John | V, 286 |

	Vol. and Page
MAHAFFY, JOHN PENTLAND,	
Mahoney, Francis	VI, 484

MAHANY, ROWLAND B.,
| Jenyns, Soame | IV, 32 |

MAHLY, JACOB,
| Bentley, Richard | III, 123 |

MAHONY, FRANCIS,
| Dickens, Charles | VI, 580 |

MAIN, ALEXANDER,
| Johnson, Samuel | III, 732 |

MAIN, DAVID M.,
Barnes, Barnabe	I, 439
Browning, Elizabeth Barrett	VI, 241
Lodge Thomas	I, 626
Smith, Charlotte	IV, 497
Spenser, Edmund	I, 388
Tighe, Mary	IV, 552

MAIR, JOHN,
| Henry the Minstrel | I, 201 |

MAIRAN, M.,
| Halley, Edmund | III, 108 |

MAISTRE, JOSEPH,
| Locke, John | II, 525 |

MAITLAND, F. W.,
| Stubbs, William | VIII, 452 |

MAITLAND, SAMUEL ROFFEY,
| Chatterton, Thomas | III, 531 |
| Strype, John | III, 93 |

MAJOR, JOHN,
| Jame I. of Scotland | I, 179 |

MALDEN, MRS. CHARLES,
| Austen, Jane | IV, 615 |

MALET, SIR ALEXANDER,
| Wace, Robert | I, 60 |

MALLET, DAVID,
Bentley, Richard	III, 120
Pope, Alexander	III, 145
Warburton, William	III, 688

MALLET, SIR LOUIS,
| Cobden, Richard | VI, 442 |

MALLOCH, DAVID,
| Mallet, David | III, 495 |

MALLOCK MISS M. M.,
| Kingsley, Charles | VII, 32 |

MALLOCK, WILLIAM HURREL,
Arnold, Matthew	VII, 635
Browning, Robert	VII, 702
Byron, George Gordon Lord	IV, 761
Dickens, Charles	VI, 591
Eliot, George	VII, 201
Lytton, Edward Robert Bulwer Earl	VIII, 44
Scott, Sir Walter	V, 160
Spencer, Herbert	VIII, 486
Tennyson, Alfred Lord	VIII, 103
Thackeray, William Makepeace	VI, 319
Wordsworth, William	V, 639

MALLORY, DANIEL.
| Clay, Henry | V, 730 |

MALLORY, R. DEWITT,
| Hawthorne, Nathaniel | VI, 350 |

MALMESBURY, EARL.
| Harris, James | III, 709 |

MALONE, EDMUND,
Addison, Joseph	II, 634
Bacon, Francis	I, 649
Backstone Sir William	III, 703
Boswell, James	IV, 215
Burke, Edmund	IV, 298

	Vol. and Page
Chatterton, Thomas	III, 534
Dryden, John	II, 472
Dyer, John	III, 398
Gibbon, Edward	IV, 173
Hawkesworth, John	III, 609
Hawkins, Sir John	IV, 50
Hume, David	III, 649, 655
Jenyns, Soame	IV, 30
Johnson, Samuel	III, 722
Junius	IV, 639
Montagu, Lady Mary Wortley	III, 461
Pope, Alexander	III, 147, 154, 175
Reynolds, Sir Joshua	IV, 138
Richardson Samuel	III, 433
Saint-John, Henry	III, 286
Shenstone, William	III, 471
Stanhope, Philip Dormer	III, 600
Sterne, Laurence	III, 502
Thomson, James	III, 256
Walpole, Horace	IV, 310
Warburton, William	III, 684, 688
Wolcot, John	IV, 648

MALORY, SIR THOMAS,
| Malory, Sir Thomas | I, 203 |

MALTBY, WILLIAM,
Burke, Edmund	IV, 295
Mackintosh, Sir James	V, 180
Porson, Richard	IV, 522
Southey, Robert	V, 407
Wakefield, Gilbert	IV, 416

MANCHESTER, DUKE OF,
Addison, Joseph	II, 643
Davies, Sir John	I, 632
Vanbrugh, Sir John	II, 706
Waller, Edmund	II, 379

MANDEVILLE, BERNARD DE,
| Cooper, Anthony Ashley | II, 577 |

MANDEVILLE, SIR JOHN,
| Mandeville, Sir John | I, 95 |

MANGAN, JAMES CLARENCE,
| Mangan, James Clarence | V, 600 |

MANGIN, EDWARD,
| Richardson, Samuel | III, 444 |

MANLEY, MRS. MARY DE LA RIVIÈRE,
Arbuthnot, John	III, 84
Congreve, William	II, 733
Montagu, Charles	II, 586
Steele, Sir Richard	II, 752, 762

MANLY, JOHN MATTHEWS,
| Chaucer, Geoffrey | I, 133 |

MANLY, LOUISE,
Audubon, John James	V, 699
Benton, Thomas Hart	VI, 88
Kennedy, John Pendleton	VI, 606

MANN, HORACE.
| Knowledge | V, 8 |

MANN, MARY,
| Mann, Horace | VI, 200 |

MANN, W. J.,
| Penn, William | II, 631 |

MANNING, ANNE,
| Mitford, Mary Russell | VI, 44 |

MANNING, HENRY EDWARD,
| Newman, John Henry | VII, 753 |
| Ward, William George | VII, 484 |

MANNING, J. M.,
| Prince, Thomas | III, 401 |

MANNING, WILLIAM OKE,
| Kent, James | V, 502 |

INDEX TO CRITICISMS 635

	Vol. and Page
MANNINGHAM, JOHN,	
Shakespeare, William	I, 498
Spenser, Edmund	I, 368, 393
MANSEL, HENRY LONGUEVILLE,	
Berkeley, George	III, 333
DeMorgan, Augustus	VI, 634
MANSFIELD, E. D.,	
Adams, John Quincy	V, 517
Beecher, Lyman	VI, 340
Pierpont, John	VI, 482
MANSFIELD, RICHARD,	
Drama, The	VII, 8
MANSON, EDWARD,	
Inchbald, Mrs. Elizabeth	IV, 688
Prior, Matthew	II, 674
MANT, RICHARD,	
Warton, Thomas	IV, 76
MANTELL, GIDEON ALGERNON,	
Miller, Hugh	VI, 64
MARCH, FRANCIS ANDREW,	
Marsh, George Perkins	VII, 493, 495
Whitney, William Dwight	VIII, 303
MARCOU, JULES,	
Agassiz, Louis Jean Rodolphe	VI, 721
MARILLIER, H. C.,	
Rossetti, Gabriel Charles Dante	VII, 444
MARKHAM, CHARLES EDWIN,	
Poets and Poetry	IV, 10
MARKHAM, W.,	
Burke, Edmund	IV, 288
MARKS, ALFRED,	
Dodd, William	III, 677
MARLBOROUGH, DUKE OF,	
Montagu, Charles	II, 586
MARLBOROUGH HENRIETTA, DUCHESS OF,	
Congreve, William	II, 734
MARLBOROUGH, SARAH JENNINGS, DUCHESS OF,	
Hervey, John Lord	III, 127
Pope, Alexander	III, 178
Sacheverell, Henry	II, 695
Vanbrugh, Sir John	II, 703
MARLOWE, CHRISTOPHER,	
Marlowe Christopher	I, 348
MARMONTEL, JEAN FRANCOIS,	
Pope, Alexander	III, 175
Richardson, Samuel	III, 438, 444
MARRIOTT, J. A. R.,	
Kingsley, Charles	VII, 25, 27
MARRYAT, FLORENCE,	
Marryat, Frederick	V, 531, 532
MARRYAT, FREDERICK,	
Willis, Nathaniel Parker	VI, 486
MARSH, A. R.,	
Mandeville, Bernard	III, 68
MARSH, CAROLINE C.,	
Marsh, George Perkins	VII, 493
MARSH, GEORGE PERKINS,	
Bacon, Francis	I, 650
Beowulf	I, 18
Berners, Lord	I, 229
Caxton, William	I, 199
Chaucer, Geoffrey	I, 150, 162
Cheke, Sir John	I, 278
Choate, Rufus	VI, 196
Coleridge, Samuel Taylor	V, 224
Gower, John	I, 176

	Vol. and Page
Fuller Thomas	II, 172
Holinshed, Raphael	I, 311
Hooker, Richard	I, 407
James I. of Seotland	I, 180
Keats, John	IV, 677
Langland, William	I, 120
Layamon	I, 65
Lever, Charles James	VI, 652
Lyly, John	I, 422
Mandeville, Sir John	I, 96
Mannyng, Robert	I, 88
More, Sir Thomas	I, 239
Nicholas of Guilford	I, 76
Occleve, Thomas	I, 188
Ormin	I, 71
Peacock, Reginald	I, 189
Poor, Richard	I, 70
Puttenham, George	I, 402
Robert of Gloucester	I, 82
Saxon Chronicle	I, 57
Shakespeare, William	I, 564
Shenstone, William	III, 472
Sidney, Sir Philip	I, 329
Skelton, John	I, 222
Spenser, Edmund	I, 397
Sylvester, Joshua	I, 609
Trench, Richard Chenevix	VII, 589
Tyndale, William	II, 246
Walton, Isaac	II, 349
Wilde, Richard Henry	V, 504
Wyclif, John	I, 103
MARSH, HERBERT,	
Usher, James	II, 153
MARSH, O. C.,	
Huxley, Thomas Henry	VIII, 321
MARSHALL, A. F.,	
Fawcett, Henry	VII, 550
MARSHALL, JAMES,	
Godwin, William	V, 298
MARSHALL, JOHN,	
Washington, George	IV, 357
MARSHALL, MRS. JULIAN,	
Godwin, William	V, 296
Shelley, Mary Wollstonecraft	V, 701, 703
Shelley, Percy Bysshe	IV, 697
MARSHALL, S. E.,	
Marshall, John	V, 283
MARSTON, EDWARD,	
Stanley, Sir Henry Morton	VIII, 509
MARSTON, JOHN,	
Marston, John	I, 735
MARSTON, JOHN WESTLAND,	
Dobell, Sidney Thompson	VI, 761
Knowles, James Sheridan	VI, 286
MARSTON, PHILIP BOURKE,	
Fawcett, Henry	VII, 551
Hayne, Paul Hamilton	VII, 591
O'Shaughnessy, Arthur Wm. Edgar	VII, 322
Rossetti, Gabriel Charles Dante	VII, 435
Swift, Jonathan	III, 204
Thomson, James	VII, 474, 475
MARTEL, CHARLES,	
Montagu, Lady Mary Wortley	III, 466
MARTIN, A. S.,	
Browning, Robert	VII, 716

	Vol and Page
MARTIN, BENJAMIN ELLIS	
Dickens, Charles	VI, 556
Kingsley, Henry	VII, 79
Lamb, Charles	V, 235
MARTIN, B. N.,	
Dewey, Orville	VII, 498
MARTIN, DR. E B.,	
Coleridge, Samuel Taylor	V, 212
MARTIN, E. S.,	
Marshall, John	V, 283
MARTIN, FRANCES,	
Craik, Dinah Maria Mulock	VII, 625
MARTIN, LADY (HELENA FAUCIT),	
Shakespeare, William	I, 475, 486, 498
MARTIN, MARY E.,	
Wakefield, Gilbert	IV, 415
MARTIN, SIR THEODORE,	
Aytoun, William Edmondstoune	VI, 444, 445, 446
Browning, Robert	VII, 680
Campbell, Thomas	V, 443
Croker, John Wilson	VI, 73, 74
Kingsley, Charles	VII, 23
Wordsworth, William	V, 620
MARTINEAU, HARRIET,	
Arnold, Thomas	V, 379
Baillie, Joanna	V, 690
Bancroft, George	VIII, 58
Barbauld, Anna Lætitia	V, 25
Beckford, William	V, 448
Brontë, Charlotte	VI, 18
Brougham, Henry Lord	VI, 526, 527
Browning, Elizabeth Barrett	VI, 245
Browning, Robert	VII, 685
Byron, George Gordon Lord	IV, 745
Campbell, John Lord	VI, 257, 259
Campbell, Thomas	V, 436
Canning, George	V, 65
Carlyle, Thomas	VII, 232
Combe, George	VI, 89, 89
Croker, John Wilson	VI, 72
De Quincey, Thomas	VI, 118
Dickens, Charles	VI, 552, 562, 582
Everett, Edward	VI, 423
Foster, John	V, 426
Fuller, Sarah Margaret	V, 666
Garrison, William Loyd	VII, 160
Godwin, William	V, 303
Hallam, Henry	VI, 173
Hemans, Felicia Dorothea	V, 259
Hogg, James	V, 267
Hunt, James Henry Leigh	VI, 156
Jameson, Anna	VI, 214, 216
Jerrold, Douglas William	III, 66
Landon, Letitia Elizabeth	V, 324
Landor, Walter Savage	VI, 374, 385
Lockhart, John Gibson	V, 756, 758
Lytton, Sir Edward George Bulwer	VI, 680, 696
Macaulay, Thomas Babington Lord	VI, 92, 105
Malthus, Thomas Robert	V, 250, 252, 253
Marshall, John	V, 281
Mill, James	V, 307
Milnes, Richard Monckton	VII, 560

INDEX TO CRITICISMS

	Vol. and Page
Mitford, Mary Russell	VI, 41, 45, 46
Napier, Gen. Sir William Francis Patrick	VI, 221, 222
Opie, Amelia	V, 741
Owen, Robert	VI, 83, 85
Park, Mungo	IV, 486
Pitt, William	IV, 511
Rogers, Samuel	VI, 34
Sedwick, Catharine Maria	VI, 505
Smyth, Sydney	V, 468
Somerville, Mary	VI, 657
Southey, Robert	V, 398
Taylor, William	V, 318
Tennyson, Alfred Lord	VIII, 101
Thackeray, William Makepeace	VI, 291, 302, 306
Trollope, Frances Milton	VI, 330
Whately, Richard	VI, 324, 327
Willis, Nathaniel Parker	VI, 487
Wilson, John	V, 746
Wordsworth, William	V, 611
MARTINEAU, JAMES,	
Butler, Joseph	III, 311, 316
Carlyle, Thomas	VII, 262
Channing, William Ellery	V, 372
Clarke, Samuel	II, 750
Colenso, John William	VII, 523
Coleridge, Samuel Taylor	V, 224
Cooper, Anthony Ashley	II, 580
Cudworth, Ralph	II, 387
Eliot, George	VII, 181
Emerson, Ralph Waldo	VII, 348, 375
Greg, William Rathbone	VII, 321
Grote, George	VI, 612
Hamilton, Sir William	V, 54
History	VI, 8
Hutcheson, Francis	III, 244
Kingsley, Charles	VII, 29
Lyell, Sir Charles	VII, 34
Mansel, Henry Longueville	VI, 627
Martineau, Harriet	VII, 57
Maurice, John Frederick Denison	VI, 646
Mill, John Stuart	VI, 713
Newman, Francis William	VIII, 370
Parker, Theodore	VI 209
Priestley, Joseph	IV, 447, 454
Whewell, William	VI, 471
MARTYN, CARLOS,	
Phillips, Wendell	VII, 553
MARVELL, ANDREW,	
Dryden, John	II, 495
May, Thomas	II, 118
Milton, John	II, 257, 282
MARVIN, ABIJAH P.	
Mather, Cotton	II 729
MARZIALS, FRANK T.,	
Collins, William Wilkie	VII, 727
Thackeray, William Makepeace	VI, 300, 305, 310
MASHAM, LADY ESTHER,	
Locke, John	II, 520
Swift, Jonathan	III, 197
MASKELL, J.	
Hickes, George	II, 598
MASON, ARTHUR JAMES,	
Cranmer, Thomas	I, 272
MASON, CAROLINA A.,	
Poe, Edgar Allan	V 541

	Vol. and Page
MASON, EDWARD T.,	
Chalmers, Thomas	V, 494
Hazlitt, William	V, 97
Hood, Thomas	V, 460
Procter, Bryan Waller	VI, 744
Southey, Robert	V, 395
MASON, F.,	
Taylor, John	II, 133
MASON, GEORGE,	
Henry, Patrick	IV, 351
MASON, JOHN MONCK,	
Hamilton, Alexander	IV, 457
Massinger, Philip	II, 46
MASON, SIR JOHN,	
Pole, Reginald	I, 280
MASON, WILLIAM	
Gray, Thomas	III, 554
Hume, David	III, 665
Pope, Alexander	III, 168
Warton, Thomas	IV, 73
MASON, WILLIAM MONCK,	
Swift, Jonathan	III, 208
MASSEY, GERALD,	
Burns, Robert	IV, 257
Lamb, Charles	V, 240
Lamb, Mary Ann	V, 508
Shakespeare, William	I, 463
MASSEY, WILLIAM,	
Franklin, Benjamin	IV, 95
Smollett, Tobias George	III, 588
Tooke, John Horne	IV, 570
MASSINGER, PHILIP,	
Massinger, Philip	II, 45
MASSINGHAM, H. W.,	
Johnson, Samuel	III, 765
MASSON, DAVID,	
Alexander, Sir William	II, 34
Aubrey, John	II, 452
Austen, Jane	IV, 619
Aytoun, William Edmondstoune	VI, 446
Brown, John	VII, 478, 479
Browne, William	II, 74
Buckle, Henry Thomas	VI, 281
Bunyan, John	II, 395
Burton, John Hill	VII, 316
Burton, Robert	II, 39
Carew, Thomas	II, 22
Carlyle, Thomas	VII, 236
Chatterton, Thomas	III, 531, 537
Clough, Arthur Hugh	VI, 249, 251
Crashaw, Richard	II, 111
Defoe, Daniel	III, 47
DeQuincey, Thomas	V, 122
Dickens, Charles	VI, 583
Drummond, William	II, 101, 104, 105
Fletcher, Phineas	II, 116, 117
Ford, John	II, 32
Froude, James Anthony	VIII, 261
Gifford, William	V, 35
Godwin, William	V, 303
Goldsmith, Oliver	III, 619, 622
Habington, William	II, 136
Hales, John	II, 150
Hall, Joseph	II, 145, 147
Hamilton, Sir William	IV, 54
Herbert, Edward Lord	II, 99
Herrick, Robert	II, 241
Hobbes, Thomas	II, 327
Hood, Thomas	V, 462

	Vol and Page
Jerrold, Douglas William	VI 67
Johnson, Samuel	III. 746
Johnston, Arthur	II. 54
Keats, John	IV. 666
Kingsley, Charles	VII. 30
Laud, William	II. 92
Malory, Sir Thomas	I, 204
Massinger, Philip	II, 49
May, Thomas	II, 118
Mill, John Stuart	VI, 713
Miller, Hugh	VI, 63
Milton, John	II. 249, 252. 265
Oliphant, Carolina	V, 478
Prynne, William	II, 225. 226
Radcliffe, Ann Ward	IV, 719
Richardson, Samuel	III. 449
Scott, Sir Walter	V, 143, 160
Selden, John	II. 142
Shelley, Percy Bysshe	IV, 708
Shirley, James	II. 191
Sidney, Sir Philip	I. 325
Smollett, Tobias George	III. 576
Sterne, Laurence	III. 503. 513
Suckling, Sir John	II. 65
Swift, Jonathan	III, 222, 231
Taylor, John	II 133
Thackeray, William Makepeace	VI, 314
Usher, James	II, 154
Vaughan, Henry	II. 444
Walpole, Horace	IV, 317
Wilson, John	V, 752
Wither, George	II, 214
Wood, Anthony	II, 447
Wordsworth, William	V, 635
Wotton, Sir Henry	II, 18
MASSON, ROSALINE ORME,	
Aytoun, William Edmondstoune	VI, 444, 446
Martineau, Harriet	VII, 63
Norton, Caroline E. S.	VII. 105
MASTERMAN, J. HOWARD B.,	
Beaumont, Joseph	II, 461
Browne, Sir Thomas	II, 341, 342
Carew, Thomas	II, 24
Cartwright, William	II, 72
Chamberlayne, William	II, 406
Chillingworth, William	II, 86
Cleveland, John	II, 160
Cowley, Abraham	II, 202
Crashaw, Richard	II, 114
D'Avenant, Sir William	II, 220
Denham, Sir John	II, 222, 222
Digby, Sir Kenelm	II, 183
Ford, John	II, 28, 30, 33
Fuller, Thomas	II, 173
Habington, William	II, 136
Harrington, James	II, 309
Herbert, George	I, 724
Herrick, Robert	II, 241
Hobbes, Thomas	II, 328
Howell, James	II, 188
Lovelace, Richard	II, 163
Massinger, Philip	II, 46, 52
May, Thomas	II, 119, 120
Milton, John	II, 253, 256, 268, 270, 272, 276, 282
Prynne, William	II, 226
Quarles, Francis	II, 78
Selden, John	II, 141

INDEX TO CRITICISMS 637

	Vol. and Page
Shirley, James	II, 192
Suckling, Sir John	II, 67
Sylvester, Joshua	I, 610
Taylor, Jeremy	II, 205
Vaughan, Henry	II, 446
Waller, Edmund	II, 384
Wilkins, John	II, 227
Wilson, Arthur	II, 129
MATHER, COTTON,	
Bradstreet, Anne	II, 229
Mather, Increase	II, 689
Ward, Nathaniel	II, 130
Winthrop, John	II, 108
MATHER, FRANK JEWETT, JR.,	
Chaucer, Geoffrey	I, 140
Lecky, William E. H.	VIII, 490
MATHEWS, WILLIAM,	
Bacon, Francis	I, 668
Beecher, Henry Ward	VII, 605
Brougham, Henry Lord	VI, 530
Browne, Sir Thomas	II, 344
Burke, Edmund	IV, 295
Canning, George	V, 67
Chalmers, Thomas	V, 492
Chaucer, Geoffrey	I, 166
Clay, Henry	V, 732
DeQuincey, Thomas	VI, 127
Disraeli, Benjamin	VII, 283
Erskine, Thomas	IV, 731
Everett, Edward	VI, 426
Fawcett, Henry	VII, 550
Guthrie, Thomas	VI, 738
Hall, Robert	V, 109
Hume, David	III, 659
Jefferson, Thomas	V, 43
Jenyns, Soame	IV, 52
Knox, John	I, 299
Lamb, Charles	V, 241
Lincoln, Abraham	VI, 419
Lytton, Sir Edward George Bulwer	VI, 687, 699
Newman, Francis William	VIII, 371
Paley, William	IV, 478
Pitt, William	III, 680
Porson, Richard	IV, 523
Smith, Adam	IV, 56
South, Robert	II, 609
Sterne, Laurence	III, 503
Tennyson, Alfred Lord	VIII, 79
Webster, Daniel	V, 725
Whitefield, George	III, 548
Wilkes, John	IV, 335
MATHIAS, THOMAS JAMES,	
Burke, Edmund	IV, 301
Burns, Robert	IV, 249
Burnett, James	IV, 148
Butler, Joseph	III, 310
Cowper, William	IV, 385
Dryden, John	II, 489
Erskine, Thomas	IV, 728
Fox, Charles James	IV, 503
Gifford, William	V, 33
Gray, Thomas	III, 565
Hawkins, Sir John	IV, 52
Horsley, Samuel	IV, 495
Hurd, Richard	IV, 519
Jones, Sir William	IV, 198
Lewis, Matthew Gregory	IV, 632
Lyttelton, George Lord	III, 611
Malone, Edmond	IV, 578

	Vol. and Page
Mason, William	IV, 323
Mickle, William Julius	IV, 41
Paine, Thomas	IV, 531
Parr, Samuel	V, 19
Pope, Alexander	III, 183
Porson, Richard	IV, 524
Priestley, Joseph	IV, 453
Radcliffe, Ann Ward	IV, 718
Ritson, Joseph	IV, 436
Roscoe, William	V, 117
Rumford, Count	IV, 592
Secker, Thomas	III, 522
Smollett, Tobias George	III, 586
Southey, Robert	V, 406
Sterne, Laurence	III, 511
Taylor, Thomas	V, 291
Tyrwhitt, Thomas	IV, 26
Wakefield, Gilbert	IV, 416
Wilberforce, William	V, 202
Wolcot, John	IV, 649
MATTHEW, F. D.,	
Wyclif, John	I, 108
MATTHEW OF WESTMINSTER,	
Lanfranc	I, 48
MATTHEWS, BRANDER,	
Arnold, Matthew	VII, 644
Bagehot, Walter	VII, 100
Books	III, 10
Boucicault, Dion	VII, 763
Bunner, Henry Cuyler	VIII, 359, 359
Burton, John Hill	VII, 317
Bryant, William Cullen	VII, 115
Cibber, Colley	III, 374
Cooper, James Fenimore	V, 682, 687
Curtis, George William	VIII, 190
Defoe, Daniel	III, 50
Dickens, Charles	VI, 592
Drake, Joseph Rodman	IV, 661
Drama, The	VII, 10
DuMaurier, George	VIII, 344
Edwards, Jonathan	III, 388
Emerson, Ralph Waldo	VII, 376
Franklin, Benjamin	IV, 91
Gay, John	III, 58
Hamilton, Alexander	IV, 466
Hawthorne, Nathaniel	VI, 351, 369
Irving, Washington	VI, 152
Lamb, Charles	V, 242
Lincoln, Abraham	VI, 420
Locker-Lampson, Frederick	VIII, 312, 313
Longfellow, Henry Wadsworth	VII, 414
Lowell, James Russell	VIII, 27, 29
Poe, Edgar Allan	V, 548, 553
Praed, Winthrop Mackworth	V, 333
Reade, Charles	VII, 536
Saxe, John Godfrey	VII, 617
Scott, Sir Walter	V, 146
Sheridan, Richard Brinsley	IV, 599, 602, 604
Sheridan, Thomas	IV, 47
Simms William Gilmore	VI, 600
Smith, John	I, 700
Stevenson, Robert Louis	VIII, 241, 244
Stowe, Harriet Beecher	VIII, 353
Thackeray, William Makepeace	VI, 301, 305

	Vol. and Page
Thoreau Henry David	VI, 276
Trollope Anthony	VII, 462
MATTHEWS, JAMES NEWTON,	
Burns, Robert	IV, 261
Shakespeare William	I, 570
MATY HENRY,	
Chatterton Thomas	III, 534
MATZ, B. W,	
Dickens Charles	VI, 563
MAURICE, ARTHUR BARTLETT,	
Blackmore, Richard D.	VIII, 432
MAURICE, FREDERICK DENISON,	
Addison, Joseph	II, 657
Bacon, Francis	I, 654, 667
Bentham Jeremy	V, 167
Bentley, Richard	III, 123
Berkeley George	III, 330
Burke, Edmund	IV, 292, 297
Burns, Robert	IV, 257
Butler, Joseph	III, 315
Carlyle, Thomas	VI, 261, 263
Chaucer, Geoffrey	I, 162
Coleridge, Samuel Taylor	V, 224
Cowper. William	IV, 389
Cudworth. Ralph	II, 386
Dryden. John	II, 501
Edwards. Jonathan	III, 386
Fuller. Thomas	II, 172
Gibbon, Edward	IV, 186
Gladstone, William Ewart	VIII, 390
Goldsmith, Oliver	III, 637
Greg. William Rathbone	VII, 320
Hare. Julius Charles	VI, 49
Hartley. David	III, 379
Hooker. Richard	I, 407
Hughes, Thomas	VIII, 347
Jonson. Ben	I, 764
Kingsley, Charles	VII, 22
Landor, Walter Savage	VI, 389
Macaulay, Thomas Babington Lord	VI, 98, 99
Milton, John	II, 291
Maurice, John Frederick Denison	VI, 645
More, Sir Thomas	I, 241
Newman, John Henry	VII, 745
Paley. William	IV, 474
Pope, Alexander	III, 176
Robertson, William	IV, 163
Saint-John. Henry	III, 295
Scotus, Duns	I, 85
Smith, Adam	IV, 59
Spenser, Edmund	I, 383
Sterling, John	V, 451
Swift, Jonathan	III, 231
Tennyson, Alfred Lord	VIII, 101
Thirlwall, Connop	VII, 43, 44
Walton, Isaac	II, 347
William of Occam	I, 90
Wyclif, John	I, 103
MAURICE, JACQUES,	
Blackstone, William	III, 705
MAURICE, RALPH,	
Cranmer, Thomas	I, 270
MAXWELL HERBERT,	
Bacon, Roger	I, 80
MAXWELL, PATRICK,	
Blamire, Susanna	IV, 204

INDEX TO CRITICISMS

	Vol. and Page
MAXWELL, WILLIAM,	
Priestley, Joseph	IV, 451
MAY, SAMUEL J.,	
Whittier, John Greenleaf	VIII, 121
MAY, THOMAS,	
Laud, William	II, 89
MAYER, BRANTZ,	
Sparks, Jared	VI, 479
MAYER, GERTRUDE TOWNSHEND,	
Cavendish, Margaret	II, 23
Inchbald, Mrs. Elizabeth	IV, 688
Mitford, Mary Russell	VI, 45
Montagu, Lady Mary Wortley.	
	III, 467
Opie, Amelia	V, 742
MAYER, S. R. TOWNSHEND,	
Browning, Elizabeth Barrett.	
	VI, 242
Lamb, Lady Caroline	V, 83
Procter, Bryan Waller	VI, 745
MAYO, A. D.,	
King, Thomas Starr	VI, 410
MAYOR, JOHN E. B.,	
Fisher, John	I, 231
MAYOR, J. B.,	
Pope, Alexander	III, 176
MAZZINI, JOSEPH,	
Byron, George Gordon Lord.	
	IV, 738, 758
Carlyle, Thomas	VII, 246
History	VI, 8
McALLISTER, WARD,	
Webster, Daniel	V, 724
McCABE, JAMES, D. JR.,	
Longfellow, Henry Wadsworth,	
	VII, 382
McCABE, W. GORDON,	
Arnold, Matthew	VII, 631
Tennyson, Alfred Lord	VIII, 76
McCARTHY, DENIS FLORENCE,	
Crashaw, Richard	II, 112
Moore, Thomas	V, 708
McCARTHY, JUSTIN,	
Addison, Joseph	II, 638
Arnold, Matthew	VII, 635
Atterbury, Francis	III, 66
Black, William	VIII, 394, 394
Blackmore, Richard D.	VIII, 431
Borrow, George Henry	VII, 309
Bowring, Sir John	VI, 664
Brewster, Sir David	VI, 547
Bright, John	VII, 723
Brontë, Charlotte	VI, 29
Brougham, Henry Lord	
	VI, 528, 530
Browning, Robert	VII, 702
Buchanan, Robert	VIII, 446
Campbell, George J. D.	
	VIII, 433, 434
Campbell, John Lord	VI, 258
Collins, William Wilkie	VII, 726
Darwin, Charles Robert	VII, 424
Defoe, Daniel	III, 38
DeVere, Aubrey	VIII, 464
Dickens, Charles	VI, 556, 585
Eliot, George	
	VII, 171, 189, 201
Faraday, Michael	VII, 513
Freeman, Edward Augustus.	
	VIII, 156

	Vol. and Page
Froude, James Anthony	
	VIII, 256, 258, 263
Gay, John	III, 60
Gladstone, William Ewart	
	VIII, 385, 391
Grote, George	VI, 612
Herschel, Sir John Frederick	
William	VI, 625
Hervey, John Lord	III, 128, 130
Huxley, Thomas Henry	VIII, 324
Kinglake, Alexander William.	
	VIII, 52
Kingsley, Charles	VII, 18, 23, 30
Lecky, William E. H.	VIII, 488
Lewes, George Henry	VII, 140, 142
Longfellow, Henry Wadsworth.	
	VII, 405
Lytton, Sir Edward George Bulwer	VI, 682, 689, 690
Lytton, Edward Robert Bulwer	VIII, 48
Maurice, John Frederick Denison	VI, 647, 654
Macaulay, Thomas Babington	
Lord	VI, 108
Manning, Henry Edward	VIII, 163
Mill, John Stuart	VI, 707
Miller, Hugh	VI, 65
Morris, William	VIII, 335
Müller, Friedrich Max	VIII, 438
Newman, Francis William	
	VIII, 370, 371
Newman, John Henry	
	VII, 739, 744, 748
Paine, Thomas	IV, 540
Penn, William	II, 630
Pope, Alexander	III, 166, 193
Reade, Charles	VII, 527, 533
Rossetti, Gabriel Charles Dante	
	VII, 451
Rowe, Nicholas	II, 623
Ruskin, John	VIII, 414
Russell, John Earl	VII, 144, 145
Saint-John, Henry	III, 290
Somerville, Mary	VI, 660
Spencer, Herbert	VIII, 477, 481
Spurgeon, Charles Haddon	
	VIII, 179
Stanley, Arthur Penrhyn	
	VII, 301, 303
Sumner, Charles	VI, 753
Swift, Jonathan	III, 210
Thackeray, William Makepeace	
	VI, 316
Trollope, Anthony	VII, 458, 460
Tyndall, John	VIII, 197
Wiseman, Nicholas Patrick	VI, 435
McCARTHY, JUSTIN HUNTLY,	
DuMaurier, George	VIII, 345
Mangan, James Clarence	V, 602
McCORMACK, T. J.,	
Müller, Friedrich Max	VIII, 436
McCOSH, JAMES,	
Alison, Archibald	V, 342
Beattie, James	IV, 434
Brown, Thomas	IV, 657, 658
Burnett, James	IV, 348
Chalmers, Thomas	V, 496
Ferguson, Adam	IV, 611
Guthrie, Thomas	VI, 737
Hamilton, Sir William	VI, 56

	Vol. and Page
Hume, David	III, 650, 652, 663
Hutcheson, Francis	III, 247
Hutton, James	IV, 339
Huxley, Thomas Henry	VIII, 324
Mackintosh, Sir James	V, 183
Mill, James	V, 308
Mill, John Stuart	VI, 715
Reid, Thomas	IV, 286
Smith, Adam	IV, 56, 59
Stewart, Dugald	V, 78
McCRAY, FLORINE THAYER,	
Stowe, Harriet Beecher	VIII, 353
McCULLOCH, HUGH,	
Adams, John Quincy	V, 518
Beecher, Henry Ward	VII, 606
Beecher, Lyman	VI, 340
Everett, Edward	VI, 424
Sumner, Charles	VI, 753
Webster, Daniel	V, 724
McCULLOCH, JOHN RAMSAY,	
Defoe, Daniel	III, 46
DeQuincey, Thomas	VI, 125
Hobbes, Thomas	II, 325
Hume, David	III, 654
Locke, John	II, 531
Mandeville, Bernard	III, 69
Malthus, Thomas Robert	V, 252
Mill, James	V, 310
Ricardo, David	IV, 726
Sadler, Michael Thomas	V, 287
Smith, Adam	IV, 62
Young, Arthur	IV, 655
McDERMOT, GEORGE,	
Burke, Edmund	IV, 308
McDONOUGH, A. R.,	
Stoddard, Richard Henry	
	VIII, 496
McEWEN, ARTHUR,	
George, Henry	VIII, 379
McGEE, JAMES E.,	
Wiseman, Nicholas Patrick	VI, 435
McGEE, J. G.,	
Griffin, Gerald	V, 352, 354
McGILCHRIST, JOHN,	
Cobden, Richard	VI, 440
McGILL, ANNA BLANCHE,	
Arnold, Matthew	VII, 631
McKINLEY, CARL,	
Timrod, Henry	VI, 509
McKINLEY, WILLIAM,	
Lincoln, Abraham	VI, 419
McLAREN, CHARLES,	
Bright, John	VII, 723
McLAUGHLIN, EDWARD T.,	
Addison, Joseph	II, 653
DeQuincey, Thomas	VI, 129
Dryden, John	II, 493
Lowell, James Russell	VIII, 40
Sidney, Sir Philip	I, 330
McLEAN, MRS. C. F.,	
George, Henry	VIII, 379
McLINTOCK, JOHN, AND STRONG, JAMES,	
Croly, George	VI, 224
Cumberland, Richard	II, 624
Sternhold, Thomas	I, 261
Tindal, Matthew	III, 72
Tucker, Abraham	III, 643
Whewell, William	II, 466
McCLURE, A. K.,	
Lincoln, Abraham	VI, 418

INDEX TO CRITICISMS

Vol. and Page

McMASTER, JOHN BACH,
- Adams, John.............V, 52
- Adams, Samuel......IV, 441, 460
- Barlow, Joel.............IV, 574
- Franklin, Benjamin.....IV, 89, 103
- Henry, Patrick..........IV, 352
- Macaulay, Thomas Babington Lord................VI, 108

McCORMICK, W. S.,
- Drummond, William......II, 102
- Selden, John.............II, 143

M'CRIE, THOMAS,
- Knox, John..............I, 296
- Lyndsay, Sir Thomas......I, 274

M'DERMOT, MARTIN,
- Cowper, William.........IV, 386
- Goldsmith, Oliver........III, 636
- Gray, Thomas............III, 566
- Pope, Alexander.........III, 169

M'DONNELL, A. C.,
- Scott, Sir Walter..........V, 139

MEAD, EDWIN DOAK,
- Arnold, Thomas...........V, 378
- Emerson, Ralph Waldo....VII, 373
- Keble, John..............VI, 459
- Phillips, Wendell........VII, 558

MEAD, MARIAN,
- Symonds, John Addington.....................VIII, 204

MEAD, WILLIAM EDWARD,
- Lytton, Sir Edward George Bulwer................VI, 692
- Malory, Sir Thomas........I, 206
- Morris, William.........VIII, 334
- Tennyson, Alfred Lord....VIII, 95

MEADE, WILLIAM,
- Marshall, John............V, 282

MEADLEY, GEORGE WILSON,
- Paley, William...........IV, 471

MEANS, D. McG.,
- Malthus, Thomas Robert....V, 251

MEDWIN, THOMAS,
- Byron, George Gordon Lord.IV, 736
- Hemans, Felicia Dorothea...V, 259
- Shelley, Percy Bysshe....IV, 692

MEIKLEJOHN, J. M. D.,
- Arnold, Matthew.........VII, 637
- Browning, Elizabeth Barrett.................... VI, 246
- Browning, Robert........VII, 707
- Byron, George Gordon Lord.IV, 763
- De Quincey, Thomas......VI, 128
- Dickens, Charles..........VI, 589
- Eliot, George............VII, 205
- Longfellow, Henry Wadsworth ....VII, 412
- Macaulay, Thomas Babington Lord...............VI, 113
- Morris, William.........VIII, 336
- Ruskin, John,..........VIII, 417
- Scott, Sir Walter..........V, 136
- Tennyson, Alfred Lord..VIII, 105

MELBORNE, LORD,
- Norton, Caroline Elizabeth Sheridan..............VII, 101

MELLEN, G.,
- Child, Lydia Maria.......VII, 220

MELLONE, SYDNEY HERBERT,
- Browning, Robert...VII, 696, 720
- Martineau, James......VIII, 430
- Newman, John Henry.VII, 746, 757

Vol. and Page

MELMOTH, WILLIAM,
- Addison, Joseph..........II, 634
- Tillotson, John Robert.....II, 439

MELVILLE, HERMAN,
- Hawthorne, Nathaniel.....VI, 356

MELVILLE, JAMES,
- Buchanan, George..........I, 314
- Knox, John...............I, 296

MELVILLE, LEWIS,
- Thackeray, William Makepeace ....VI, 299, 300, 301, 322

MEMES, JOHN,
- Cowper, William..........IV, 387

MEMES, JOHN S.,
- Jenyns, Soame............IV, 32

MENDES, PEREIRA,
- Lazarus, Emma..........VII, 612

MERCIER, MRS. JEROME,
- Burney, Frances..........V, 346

MERCIER, SEBASTIEN,
- Richardson, Samuel.......III, 444

MEREDITH, GEORGE,
- Byron, George Gordon Lord .... IV, 765
- Chaucer, Geoffrey..........I, 161
- Coleridge, Samuel Taylor....V, 224
- Congreve, William.........II, 745
- Drama, The..............VII, 9
- Jonson, Ben..............I, 767
- Keats, John..............IV, 676
- Lamb, Charles............V, 244
- Lytton, Edward Robert Bulwer Earl..............VIII, 47
- Milton, John.............VI, 291
- Shakespeare, William........I, 575
- Shelley, Percy Bysshe.....IV, 707
- Southey, Robert...........V, 404
- Spenser, Edmund..........I, 396
- Stephen, Sir Leslie.......VIII, 512
- Wordsworth, William......V, 635
- Wycherley, William........II, 602

MERES, FRANCIS,
- Chaucer, Geoffrey..........I, 154
- Daniel, Samuel......I, 612, 613
- Drayton, Michael...I, 701, 703, 706
- Greene, Robert............I, 339
- Marlowe, Christopher......I, 346
- Nashe, Thomas............I, 412
- Peele, George.............I, 364
- Shakespeare, William......I, 547
- Sidney, Sir Philip.........I, 324
- Spenser, Edmund......I, 375, 378
- Warner, William..........I, 436
- Wilson, Sir Thomas........I, 312

MERIMEE, PROSPER,
- Cobden, Richard..........VI, 439

MERIVALE, HERMAN,
- Arnold, Matthew.........VII, 643
- Carlyle, Thomas.........VII, 260
- Dickens, Charles.........VII, 590
- Thackeray, William Makepeace .... VI, 297, 318

MERRIAM, C. H.,
- Audubon, John James.....V, 699

MERRIAM, GEORGE S.,
- Arnold, Matthew.........VII 641
- Greeley, Horace.....VI 669, 671
- Holland, Josiah Gilbert .... VII 336 373
- Stowe, Harriet Beecher........ ....VIII 356

Vol. and Page

MERWIN, HENRY CHILDS,
- Sterne Laurence..........III, 504
- Whitman, Walt..........VIII, 150

MERZ, JOHN THEODORE,
- Bacon, Francis............I, 663
- Bentley, Richard.........III, 124
- Gibbon, Edward..........IV, 190
- Newton, Sir Isaac......II, 720, 726
- Young, Thomas...........V, 89

METCALFE, FREDERICK,
- Ormin ....I, 71

MEYNELL, ALICE,
- Dickens, Charles.........VI, 579
- Patmore, Coventry......VIII 341
- Rossetti, Christina Georgina ....VIII, 272
- Rossetti, Gabriel Charles Dante................VII, 452
- Ruskin, John...........VIII, 422

MEYNELL, WILFRED,
- Manning, Henry Edward.VIII 164

MÉZIÈRES ALFRED,
- Shakespeare, William..I, 475, 517

MICHAUD, GUSTAVE,
- Spencer, Herbert....VIII 479, 486

MICKLE, WILLIAM JULIUS,
- Mickle, William Julius.....IV, 41

MIDDLETON, CONYERS,
- Bentley, Richard.........III, 112
- Caxton,William...........I, 198

MIDDLETON, ERASMUS,
- Doddridge, Philip...,.....III, 303

MIDDLETON, THOMAS,
- Nashe, Thomas............I, 412

MIFFLIN, LLOYD,
- Longfellow, Henry Wadsworth .... VII 414

MIKKELSEN, M. A.,
- Hume, David............III 652

MILBURN, WILLIAM HENRY,
- Carlyle, Thomas.........VII, 242
- Young, Thomas........V 87, 89

MILES, ALFRED H.,
- Alford, Henry............VI 637
- Barton, Bernard...........V 597
- Bayle,Thomas Haynes.....V 341
- Blackie John Stuart.....VIII 307
- Bloomfield, Robert.......VI 725
- Bowles, William Lisle.....V 660
- Bowring, Sir John......VI 665
- Campbell, Thomas........V 445
- Clough, Arthur Hugh.....VI 254
- Colman, George..........V 317
- Crabbe, George...........V 176
- Craik, Dinah Maria Mulock..................VII 626
- Croly, George............VI 225
- De Vere, Aubrey, Thomas VIII 465
- Eliot, George............VII 198
- Elliott, Ebenezer.........V. 583
- Faber, Frederick William VI 334
- Havergal, Frances Ridley VII 168
- Heber, Reginald..........V 40
- Hogg, James............V 267
- Hood Thomas............V 465
- Keble John............VI 466
- Knowles, James Sheridan..VI 289
- Lever, Charles James......VI 656
- Longfellow, Henry Wadsworth .... VII 386
- Lyte, Henry Francis..V 499, 500

INDEX TO CRITICISMS

	Vol. and Page
Macaulay, Thomas Babington Lord	VI, 103
Mackay, Charles	VII, 764
Macleod, Norman	VI, 663
Milman, Henry Hart	VI, 541
Montgomery, James	V, 768
Newman, John Henry	VII, 750
Norton, Caroline E. S.	VII, 105
Pollok, Robert	V, 72
Procter, Adelaide Anne	VI, 396
Rogers, Samuel	VI, 39
Southey, Caroline Anne Bowles	V, 763
Southey, Robert	V, 407 409
Stanley, Arthur Penrhyn	VII, 306
Talfourd, Sir Thomas Noon	V, 761
Tennant, William	V, 528
White, Henry Kirke	IV, 490
White, Joseph Blanco	V, 362

MILINE, J. G.,
Froude, James Anthony	VIII, 262
Southwell, Robert	I, 362

MILL, JOHN,
Disraeli, Benjamin	VII, 282, 287, 287

MILL, JOHN STUART,
Bentham, Jeremy	V, 166
Berkeley, George	III, 324, 333
Carlyle, Thomas	VII, 245, 265
Coleridge, Samuel Taylor	V, 223
Gibbon, Edward	IV, 183
Grote, George	VI, 607
Hamilton, Sir William	IV, 54
Hume, David	III, 661
Locke, John	II, 526
Macaulay, Thomas Babington Lord	VI, 101
Maurice, John Frederick Denison	VI, 648
Mill, James	V, 306
Mill, John Stuart	VI, 710
Motley, John Lothrop	VII, 85
Ricardo, David	IV, 726
Spencer, Herbert	VIII, 479
Tennyson, Alfred Lord	VIII, 99
Whately, Richard	VI, 326
Whewell, William	VI, 471
Wordsworth, William	V, 637

MILLAR, A. H.,
Blackie, John Stuart	VIII, 307

MILLAR, J. H.,
Aytoun, William Edmondstoune	VI, 446
Brougham, Henry Lord	VI, 533
Chalmers, Thomas	V, 497
Galt, John	V, 336
Hamilton, Sir William	VI, 57
Hume, David	III, 667
Irving, Washington	VI, 152
Jeffrey, Francis Lord	V, 657
L'Estrange, Sir Roger	II, 539
Mansel, John Longueville	VI, 629
Mill, John Stuart	VI, 718
Richardson, Samuel	III, 452
Smith, Adam	IV, 54

MILLEN, F F.,
Stanley, Sir Henry Morton	VIII, 508

MILLER, MRS. E. FENNICK,
Martineau, Harriet	VII, 58

	Vol. and Page
MILLER, HUGH,	
Akenside, Mark	III, 544
Brewster, Sir David	VI, 547
Burns, Robert	IV, 229
Defoe, Daniel	III, 36
Dickens, Charles	VI, 581
Goldsmith, Oliver	III, 623
Hume, David	III, 662
Jeffrey, Francis Lord	V, 654
Johnson, Samuel	III, 731
Keats, John	IV, 672
Miller, Hugh	VI 62 63
Montgomery, James	V, 766
Scott, Sir Walter	V, 130
Shenstone, William	III, 474
Southey, Robert	V, 415
Tannahill, Robert	IV, 549
Thompson, James	III, 268
Trench, Richard Chenevix	VII, 588
Urquhart, Sir Thomas	II, 164

MILLER, JOAQUIN,
Burns, Robert	IV, 259
Byron, George Gordon Lord	IV, 741
Fields, James Thomas	VII, 340

MILLER, JOSIAH,
Doddridge, Philip	III, 302
Wesley, Charles	IV, 37
Horne, George	IV, 143
Trench, Richard Chenevix	VII, 589
Watts, Isaac	III, 250

MILLER, SAMUEL,
Edwards, Jonathan	III, 382

MILLES, JEREMIAH,
Chatterton, Thomas	III, 534

MILLINGEN, JULIUS,
Byron, George Gordon Lord	IV, 738

MILLS, ABRAHAM,
Bacon, Francis	I, 667
Birch, Thomas	III, 499
Blair, Robert	III, 242
Hamilton, William	III, 336
Hoadly, Benjamin	III, 423
Lowth, William	III, 63
Mandeville, Bernard	III, 70
Spotiswood, John	II, 25
Strype, John	III, 93
Webster, John	I, 672
Whitehead, William	IV, 23

MILMAN, ARTHUR,
Milman, Henry Hart	VI 534 539

MILMAN, HENRY HART.
Cædmon	I, 23
Bede	I, 29
Colenso, John William	VII, 525
Gibbon, Edward	IV, 183, 184
Grosseteste, Robert	I, 73
Keble, John	VI, 458
Langland, William	I, 119
Macaulay, Thomas Babington Lord	VI, 110
Paris, Matthew	I, 75
Prescott, William Hickling	VI, 182, 185
Scotus, Duns	I, 85
Selden, John	II, 139
Warburton, William	III, 686, 691
White, Joseph Blanco	V, 359
William of Occam	I, 90
William of Malmesbury	I, 54

MILNER, JOSEPH,
Wyclif, John	I, 100

	Vol. and Page
MILNES-GASKELL, JAMES,	
Gladstone, William Ewart	VIII, 383
MILNES, RICHARD MONCKTON (LORD HOUGHTON).	
Disraeli, Benjamin	VII, 292
Gladstone, William Ewart	VIII, 383
Gray, David	VI, 261
Gray, Thomas	III, 569
Hunt, James Henry Leigh	VI, 159
Keats, John	IV, 665, 670
Ken, Thomas	II, 567
Knowledge	V, 8
Landor, Walter Savage	VI, 375, 382, 389
Macaulay, Thomas Babington Lord	VI, 104
Russell, John Earl	VII, 146
Scott, Sir Walter	V, 136
Smith, Sydney	V, 469
Tennyson, Alfred Lord	VIII, 81, 82
Thackeray, William Makepeace	VI, 295, 314
Whately, Richard	VI, 327
Wilberforce, Samuel	VI, 733
Wiseman, Nicholas Patrick	VI, 435, 438

MILSAND, J.
Browning, Robert	VII, 698

MILSAND, M J.,
Carlyle, Thomas	VII, 262

MILTON, JOHN.
Books	III, 5
Chaucer, Geoffrey	I, 154
Cheke, Sir John	I, 277
Dunstan	I, 43
History	VI, 5
Jonson, Ben	I, 759
Knowledge	V, 5
Knox, John	I, 300
Literature	I, 7
Marvell, Andrew	II, 313
Milton, John	II, 242
Poets and Poetry	IV, 5
Prynne, William	II, 225
Raleigh, Sir Walter	I, 606
Selden, John	II, 140
Shakespeare, William	I, 468, 549
Spenser, Edmund	I, 393
William of Malmesbury	I, 53
Wyclif, John	I, 104

MILWARD, RICHARD,
Selden, John	II, 140

MINTO, WILLIAM,
Alison, Archibald	V, 342
Alison, Sir Archibald	VI, 521
Andrews, Lancelot	I, 637
Arbuthnot, John	II, 85
Austen, Jane	IV, 623
Atterbury, Francis	II, 68
Bacon, Francis	I, 655, 668
Bagehot, Walter	VII, 98
Baker, Sir Richard	II, 94
Bale, John	I, 287
Barbour, John	I, 114
Barrow, Isaac	II, 312
Beattie, James	IV, 434
Berkeley, George	III, 325
Birch, Thomas	III, 499
Blair, Hugh	IV, 406
Boswell, James	IV, 220
Browne, Sir Thomas	II, 344

INDEX TO CRITICISMS 641

	Vol. and Page
Budgell, Eustace	III, 92
Bunyan, John	II, 403
Burke, Edmund	IV, 297
Burnet, Gilbert	II, 594
Burnett, James	IV, 348
Burney, Frances	V, 347
Burns, Robert	IV, 265
Butler, Joseph	III, 311
Byron, George Gordon Lord	IV, 746, 749
Campbell, Thomas	V, 445
Carlyle, Thomas	VII, 265
Cartwright, Thomas	I, 416
Chalmers, Thomas	V, 496
Chapman, George	I, 733
Chaucer, Geoffrey	I, 128, 151
Chettle, Henry	I, 429
Churchyard, Thomas	I, 418
Clarke, Samuel	II, 750
Cobbett, William	V, 273
Coleridge, Samuel Taylor	V 216,220
Collins, William	III, 418
Constable, Henry	I, 444
Cooper, Anthony Ashley	II, 579
Cowley, Abraham	II, 197
Cowper, William	IV, 376, 393
Cudworth, Ralph	II, 387
Cumberland, Richard	II, 624
Daniel, Samuel	I, 612
Defoe, Daniel	III 25, 28, 36
Dekker, Thomas	II, 57, 60
DeQuincey, Thomas	VI, 126
Dickens, Charles	VI, 587
Digby, Sir Kenelm	II, 182
Disraeli, Isaac	V, 513
Donne, John	I, 711, 713
Drayton, Michael	I, 702, 705, 705
Dryden, John	II, 431, 503
Dunbar, William	I, 225
Edgeworth, Maria	V, 565, 565
Edwards, Jonathan	III, 391
Feltham, Owen	II, 309
Fielding, Henry	III, 345, 364
Ford, John	II, 25, 27, 32
Foster, John	V, 46
Fox, George	II, 422
Franklin, Benjamin	IV, 101
Gaskell, Elizabeth Cleghorn	VI, 428, 433
Gibbon, Edward	IV, 196
Glover, Richard	IV, 20
Gower, John	I, 176
Gray, Thomas	III, 562
Green, Matthew	III, 96
Greene, Robert	I, 342
Hall, Edward	I, 260
Hall, Joseph	II, 144
Hall, Robert	V, 112
Hallam, Henry	VI, 179
Hamilton, Sir William	VI, 55
Hazlitt, William	V, 104
Henry the Minstrel	I, 202
Hoadley, Benjamin	III, 424
Hobbes, Thomas	II, 326
Hogg, James	V, 268
Home, Henry	III, 713
Hooker, Richard	I, 408
Horsley, Samuel	IV 496
Hunt, James Henry Leigh	VI 164
Hutcheson, Francis	III, 246

	Vol. and Page
James I. of Scotland	I, 180
Jeffrey, Francis Lord	V, 655
Johnson, Samuel	III, 748, 760
Jonson, Ben	I, 749, 758, 765
Keats, John	IV, 681
Kyd, Thomas	I, 358
Lamb, Charles	V, 240
Landor, Walter Savage	VI, 389
Lardner, Nathaniel	III, 523
Leland, John	III, 500
Lennox, Charlotte	IV, 470
L'Estrange, Sir Roger	II, 539
Lockhart, John Gibson	V, 758
Lodge, Thomas	I, 626
Lyly, John	I, 427
Lytton, Sir Edward George Bulwer	VI, 693, 694, 698
Lytton, Edward Robert Bulwer	VIII, 46
Macaulay, Thomas Babington Lord	VI, 111
Malory, Sir Thomas	I, 204
Mandeville, Bernard	III, 69
Marlowe, Christopher	I, 353
Marston, John	I, 738
Massinger, Philip	II, 50
Maturin, Charles Robert	IV, 768
Middleton, Thomas	I, 684, 685
Mill, John Stuart	VI, 715
Milton, John	II, 277
Mitford, Mary Russell	VI, 44
Mitford, William	V, 71
Moore, Thomas	V, 710, 714
More, Sir Thomas	I, 240
Motherwell, William	V, 277
Munday, Anthony	I, 726
Occleve, Thomas	I, 188
Oliphant, Carolina	V, 478
Paley, William	IV, 477
Parr, Samuel	V, 21
Pearson, John	III, 369
Penn, William	II, 630
Poe, Edgar Allan	V, 542
Pope, Alexander	III, 152, 174
Price, Richard	IV, 136
Priestley, Joseph	IV, 454
Radcliffe, Ann Ward	IV, 720
Raleigh, Sir Walter	I, 604, 607
Ramsay, Allan	III, 408, 410
Reid, Thomas	IV, 286
Richardson, Samuel	III, 452
Rymer, Thomas	II, 582
Sacheverell, Henry	II, 697
Sackville, Thomas	I, 433
Scott, Sir Walter	V, 139, 156
Selden, John	II, 143
Shakespeare, William	I, 499, 527, 568
Shelley, Percy Bysshe	IV, 715
Sheridan, Richard Brinsley	IV, 597, 605
Sherlock, William	II, 561
Shirley, James	II, 191
Skelton, John	I, 222
Smith, Adam	IV, 55
Smith, Sydney	V, 472
Smollett, Tobias George	III, 578, 582, 583
South, Robert	II, 609
Spenser, Edmund	I 373
Sprat, Thomas	II 574

	Vol. and Page
Steele, Sir Richard	II, 756, 764
Stewart, Dugald	V, 80
Stillingfleet, Edward	II, 454
Strype, John	III, 93
Surrey, Earl of	I, 258
Swift, Jonathan	III, 233
Temple, Sir William	II, 456, 459
Tennant, William	V, 528
Thomson, James	III, 260, 271
Tillotson, John Robert	II, 441
Toland, John	II, 682
Tooke, John Horne	IV, 572
Tourneur, Cyril	I, 687
Tucker, Abraham	III, 644
Udall, Nicholas	I, 279
Warburton, William	III, 692
Watson, Thomas	I, 338
Whitefield, George	III, 550
Wilson, John	V, 752
Wordsworth, William	V, 619, 645
MIRABEAU, HONORÉ GABRIEL RIQUETI COMTE DE, Franklin, Benjamin	IV, 83
MITCHEL, JOHN, Mangan, James Clarence	V, 601, 603
Stanhope, Philip Dormer	III, 602
MITCHELL, DONALD G., Addison, Joseph	II, 646
Alcott, Amos Bronson	VII, 664
Aldhelm	I, 25
Asham, Roger	I, 289
Austen, Jane	IV, 624
Bacon, Francis	I, 648
Bacon, Roger	I, 80
Bancroft, George	VIII, 61
Beaumont and Fletcher	I, 584
Beckford, William	V, 449
Bentley, Richard	III, 112, 123
Black, William	VIII, 395
Boswell, James	IV, 214
Brougham, Henry Lord	VI, 528
Browne, Sir Thomas	II 345
Brownson, Orestes Augustus	VII, 76
Bunyan, John	II, 391
Burney, Frances	V, 347
Burton, Robert	II, 40
Bushnell, Horace	VII, 72
Butler, Samuel	II, 334
Byron, George Gordon Lord	IV, 749
Campbell, Thomas	V, 446
Chapman, George	I, 731
Child, Lydia Maria	VII, 221, 223
Coleridge, Samuel Taylor	V, 213
Collins, William	III, 421
Congreve, William	II, 744
Cooper, James Fenimore	V, 682
Cowper, William	IV, 382
Crabbe, George	V, 176
Croker, John Wilson	VI, 76
Defoe, Daniel	III, 38, 48
Dekker, Thomas	II, 61
DeQuincey, Thomas	VI, 131
Dickens, Charles	VI, 585
Disraeli, Isaac	V 514
Dryden, John	II, 505
Edgeworth, Maria	V 571
Emerson, Ralph Waldo	VII, 378
Fielding, Henry	III 365
Ford, John	II, 33

INDEX TO CRITICISMS

	Vol. and Page
Fox, Charles James	IV, 502
Franklin, Benjamin	IV, 97
Freneau, Philip	V, 188
Froude, James Anthony	VIII, 258
Fuller, Thomas	II, 169
Gibbon, Edward	IV, 189
Goldsmith, Oliver	III, 621
Gray, Thomas	III, 560
Gower, John	I, 173
Hallam, Henry	VI, 180
Hawthorne, Nathaniel	VI, 349, 358
Hazlitt, William	V, 107
Herbert, George	I, 721
Herrick, Robert	II, 234, 240
Holinshed, Raphael	I, 311
Hopkinson, Thomas	IV, 133
Hooker, Richard	I, 409
Howell, James	II, 188
Hume, David	III, 660
Hunt, James Henry Leigh	VI, 163, 167, 172
Irving, Washington	VI, 136, 147
James, George Payne Rainsford	VI, 218, 220
Jeffrey, Francis Lord	V, 657
Johnson, Samuel	III, 736, 745, 746
Jonson, Ben	I, 750, 767
Keats, John	IV, 683
Kingsley, Charles	VII, 27
Lamb, Charles	V, 237, 243
Landor, Walter Savage	VI, 336
Langland, William	I, 121
Locke, John	II, 522
Lockhart, John Gibson	V, 756, 758
Longfellow, Henry Wadsworth	VII, 393, 395, 396
Lyly, John	I, 423
Lytton, Sir Edward George Bulwer	VI, 699
Mackintosh, Sir James	V, 184
Macpherson, James	IV, 271
Malory, Sir Thomas	I, 204
Mandeville, Sir John	I, 97
Marryat, Frederick	V, 534
Marsh, George Perkins	VII, 494, 495
Marvell, Andrew	II, 318
Milton, John	II, 268, 296
Montagu, Lady Mary Wortley	III, 464
Moore, Thomas	V, 713
More, Hannah	V, 193
More, Sir Thomas	I, 242
Paine, Thomas	IV, 541
Parker, Theodore	VI, 212
Pepys, Samuel	II, 515
Pitt, William	IV, 511
Poe, Edgar Allan	V, 545, 552
Pope, Alexander	III, 163, 194
Porter, Jane	V, 674
Prynne, William	II, 225
Raleigh, Sir Walter	I, 598, 635
Richardson, Samuel	III, 452
Ripley, George	VII, 263
Savage, Richard	III, 134
Shakespeare, William	I, 572
Sidney, Sir Philip	I, 324
Simms, William Gilmore	VI, 601
Skelton, John	I, 223
Smith, Adam	IV, 69
Southey, Robert	V, 413

	Vol. and Page
Spenser, Edmund	I, 386, 389
Steele, Sir Richard	II, 754, 756, 760
Sterne, Laurence	I, 516
Swift, Jonathan	III, 206, 215
Taylor, Jeremy	II, 211
Temple, Sir William	II, 456
Thomson, James	III, 260
Thoreau, Henry David	VI, 277
Trumbull, John	V, 121, 161
Walpole, Horace	IV, 315
Waller, Edmund	II, 383
Walton, Isaac	II, 347
Watts, Isaac	III, 251
Webster, John	I, 677
White, Gilbert	IV, 149
Willis, Nathaniel Parker	VI, 492
Wilmot, John	II, 337
Wilson, Alexander	IV, 583
Wilson, John	V, 750, 752
Wordsworth, William	V, 617, 646
Young, Arthur	IV, 656
Young, Edward	III, 490
MITCHELL, MARIA,	
Airy, Sir George Biddell	VIII, 183
Alcott, Amos Bronson	VII, 662
Arnold Matthew	VII, 629
Emerson, Ralph Waldo	VII, 345, 346
Hawthorne, Nathaniel	VI, 343
Hemans, Felicia Dorothea	V, 260
Herschel, Sir John Frederick William	VI, 624
Johnson, Samuel	III, 732
Martineau, James	VIII, 425
Newton, Sir Isaac	II, 714
Somerville, Mary	VI, 657
Whewell, William	VI, 467, 472
MITCHELL, P. CHALMERS,	
Huxley, Thomas Henry	VIII, 322, 328
Tyndall, John	VIII, 199
MITCHELL, S. WEIR,	
Brooks, Phillips	VIII, 229
Coleridge, Samuel Taylor	V, 226
Keats, John	IV, 680
Lincoln, Abraham	VI, 418
MITFORD, JOHN,	
Butler, Samuel	II, 332
Dryden, John	II, 475, 479, 500
Elliott, Ebenezer	V, 581
Falconer, William	III, 525
Goldsmith, Oliver	III, 633
Gray, Thomas	III, 554
Milton, John	II, 247, 276
Swift, Jonathan	III, 227
MITFORD, MARY RUSSELL,	
Anstey, Christopher	IV, 480
Austen, Jane	IV, 612, 619
Baillie, Joanna	V, 693
Banim, John	V, 391
Bowles, William Lisle	V, 658
Browning, Elizabeth Barrett	VI, 229
Browning, Robert	VII, 698
Burns, Robert	IV, 244, 251
Byron, George Gordon Lord	IV, 736
Campbell, Thomas	V, 434
Carlyle, Thomas	VII, 262
Chatterton, Thomas	III, 531
Chaucer, Geoffrey	I, 158

	Vol. and Page
Cibber, Colley	III, 371
Clare, John	VI, 398
Clive, Caroline	VI, 740, 740
Coleridge, Samuel Taylor	V, 210
Cowley, Abraham	II, 197, 198
Dickens, Charles	VI, 582
Frere, John Hookham	V, 487
Griffin, Gerald	V, 352
Hawthorne, Nathaniel	VI, 353
Herrick, Robert	II, 238
Holcroft, Thomas	IV, 546
Holmes, Oliver Wendell	VIII, 290
Hunt, James Henry Leigh	VI, 163
Irving, Washington	VI, 149
Jonson, Ben	I, 764
Kingsley, Charles	VII, 18
Landor, Walter Savage	VI, 382
Lever, Charles James	VI, 651
Lockhart, John Gibson	V, 757
Longfellow, Henry Wadsworth	VII, 403
Lovelace, Richard	II, 161
Marvell, Andrew	II, 317
Mitford, Mary Russell	VI, 40
Moore, Thomas	V, 707
Motherwell, William	V, 277
Opie, Amelia	V, 742
Owen, Robert	VI, 83
Percy, Thomas	IV, 564
Praed, Winthrop Mackworth	V, 331, 332
Richardson, Samuel	III, 445
Scott, Sir Walter	V, 147
Seward, Anna	IV, 543
Shelley, Percy Bysshe	IV, 707
Smith, Charlotte	IV, 498
Southey, Robert	V, 399
Taylor, Tom	VII, 213
Thackeray, William Makepeace	VI, 313
Tupper, Martin Farquhar	VII, 733
Walpole, Horace	IV, 319
Walton, Isaac	II, 348
Webster, Daniel	V, 720
Whittier, John Greenleaf	VIII, 121
MIVART, ST. GEORGE,	
Darwin, Charles Robert	VII, 432
Huxley, Thomas Henry	VIII, 322
Owen, Sir Richard	VIII, 173
Romanes, George John	VIII, 284
Spencer, Herbert	VIII, 484
Wiseman, Nicholas Patrick	VI, 436, 438
M'KIE, JAMES,	
Burns, Robert	IV, 257
M'LEHOSE, WILLIAM C.,	
Burns, Robert	IV, 240
M'NEIL, G. P.,	
Thomas of Erceldoune	I, 84
MOBERLEY, GEORGE,	
Keble, John	VI, 461
MODEN, J.,	
Parker, Theodore	VI, 211
MOFFETT, CLEVELAND,	
Field, Eugene	VIII, 315
MOIR, DAVID MACBETH,	
Aytoun, William Edmondstoune	VI, 444
Bailey, Philip James	VIII, 461
Bayly, Thomas Haynes	V, 340
Burns, Robert	IV, 255

INDEX TO CRITICISMS

	Vol. and Page
Bloomfield, Robert	IV, 724
Bowles, William Lisle	V, 662
Browning, Elizabeth Barrett	VI, 245
Campbell, Thomas	V, 438, 440
Crabbe, George	V, 174
Croly, George	VI, 225
Elliott, Ebenezer	V, 582
Grahame, James	IV, 568
Grant, Anne	V, 330
Heber, Reginald	V, 38
Hemans, Felicia Dorothea	V, 259
Hogg, James	V, 266
Hood, Thomas	V, 462
Hook, Theodore Edward	V, 358
Hunt, James Henry Leigh	VI, 165
Lamb, Charles	V, 237
Landon, Letitia Elizabeth	V, 328
Landor, Walter Savage	VI, 382
Lewis, Matthew Gregory	IV, 634
Lockhart, John Gibson	V, 757
Lytton, Sir Edward George Bulwer	VI, 696
Macaulay, Thomas Babington Lord	VI, 102
Milman, Henry Hart	VI, 540
Mitford, Mary Russell	VI, 45
Montgomery, James	V, 768
Moore, Thomas	V, 710, 712
Motherwell, William	V, 277
Norton, Caroline E. S.	VII, 105
Pollok, Robert	V, 73
Procter, Bryan Waller	VI, 748
Rogers, Samuel	VI, 37, 38
Seward, Anna	IV, 544
Shelley, Percy Bysshe	IV, 707
Southey, Caroline Anne Bowles	V, 762
Southey, Robert	V, 404
Sotheby, William	V, 205
Sterling, John	V, 454
Tennant, William	V, 528
Thomson, James	III, 259
Tighe, Mary	IV, 551
Trench, Richard Chenevix	VII, 589
White, Henry Kirke	IV, 489
Wilson, John	V, 750
Wolfe, Charles	IV, 722
Wordsworth, William	V, 635
MOIR, GEORGE,	
Hamilton, Thomas	V, 394, 394
Montgomery, James	V, 767
MOLLOY, J. FITZGERALD,	
Burney, Frances	V, 349
Dryden, John	II, 468
Foote, Samuel	III, 672
Hervey, John Lord	III, 131
Lamb, Lady Caroline	V, 82
Sheridan, Thomas	IV, 46
MOLMENTI, POMPEO,	
Browning, Elizabeth Barrett	VI, 247
MOLYNEUX, WILLIAM,	
Flamsteed, John	II, 662
Locke, John	II, 524
MONBODDO, LORD (JAMES BURNET),	
Fielding, Henry	III, 350
MONCK, W. H. S.,	
Fullerton, Georgiana Charlotte Lady	VII, 567

	Vol. and Page
Hamilton, Sir William	VI, 53, 56
Jeffrey, Francis Lord	V, 650
Russell, John Earl	VII, 145
MONK, JAMES HENRY,	
Arbuthnot, John	III, 85
Atterbury, Francis	III, 67
Bentley, Richard	III, 111, 113, 113, 117, 118
Middleton, Conyers	III, 280
Wotton, William	II, 710
MONKHOUSE, COSMO,	
Allingham, William	VII, 735
Collins, Mortimer	VII, 82
Hunt, James Henry Leigh	VI, 161
Maginn, William	V, 388
Reynolds, Sir Joshua	IV, 140
Rossetti, Gabriel Charles Dante	VII, 441
Stevenson, Robert Louis	VIII, 244
Tennyson, Alfred Lord	VIII, 93
MOMBERT, J. ISIDOR,	
Alcuin	I, 33
Tyndale, William	I, 248
MONMOUTH, HUMPHERY,	
Tyndale, William	I, 244
MONROE, HARRIET,	
Shelley, Percy Bysshe	IV, 713
MONROE, JAMES,	
Paine, Thomas	IV, 531
MONSON, J. H.,	
Martineau, James	VIII, 427
MONTAGU, BASIL,	
Bacon, Francis. I, 642, 650, 653, 666	
Coke, Sir Edward	I, 740
South, Robert	II, 608
MONTAGU, MRS. BASIL,	
Coleridge, Hartley	V, 574
MONTAGU, ELIZABETH,	
Anstey, Christopher	IV, 479
Beattie, James	IV, 431
Burke, Edmund	IV, 288
Carter, Elizabeth	IV, 491
Fielding, Henry	III, 356
Fox, Charles James	IV, 499
Gray, Thomas	III, 554
Home, Henry	III, 711
Lyttelton, George Lord	III, 612
Macpherson, James	IV, 272
Montagu, Lady Mary Wortley	III, 461
Pitt, William	III, 678
Shakespeare, William	I, 489
Young, Edward	III, 484
MONTAGU, EDWARD WORTLEY,	
Addison, Joseph	II, 634
Congreve, William	II, 734
Montagu, Lady Mary Wortley	III, 461
Pope, Alexander	III, 147
MONTAGU, LADY MARY WORTLEY,	
Addison, Joseph	II, 634, 634
Congreve, William	II, 734
Fielding, Henry	III, 340
Gay, John	III, 60
Johnson, Samuel	III, 740
Knowledge	V, 6
Montagu, Lady Mary Wortley	III, 460
Pope, Alexander	III, 158, 178, 179, 182

	Vol. and Page
Prior, Matthew	II, 676
Richardson, Samuel	III, 438, 444
Saint-John, Henry	III, 283, 285, 292
Smollett, Tobias George	III, 577, 581
Steele, Sir Richard	II, 752, 752
Swift, Jonathan	III, 219, 228
Walpole, Horace	IV, 310
Williams, Sir Charles Hanbury	III, 412
MONTAGU, MATTHEW,	
Sandys, George	II, 80
MONTAGU, RICHARD,	
Savile, Sir Henry	I, 619
MONTAGU, R. W.,	
Johnson, Samuel	III, 752
Maginn, William	V, 388
MONTAGUE, F. C.,	
Bentham, Jeremy	V, 169
Burnet, Gilbert	II, 594
Swift, Jonathan	III, 235
MONTALEMBERT, CHARLES FORBES,	
Anselm	I, 49
Bede	I, 29
MONTEAGLE, LORD,	
Horner, Francis	IV, 630
MONTEGUT, ÉMILE,	
Carlyle, Thomas	VII, 242, 247, 250
Emerson, Ralph Waldo	VII, 361
Hawthorne, Nathaniel	VI, 345, 351
Shakespeare,William	I, 538
MONTGOMERY, HENRY R.,	
Addison, Joseph	II, 657
Congreve, William	II, 742
Dennis, John	III, 78
Parnell, Thomas	II, 617
Savage, Richard	III, 136
MONTGOMERY, JAMES,	
Barlow, Joel	IV, 575
Bloomfield, Robert	IV, 724
Bunyan, John	II, 394
Burns, Robert	IV, 244, 252
Byron, George Gordon Lord	IV, 758
Chatterton, Thomas	III, 529
Cowper, William	IV, 378
Darwin, Erasmus	IV, 424
Drayton,Michael	I, 704
Dryden, John	II, 486
Goldsmith, Oliver	III, 630
Grahame, James	IV, 568
Gray, Thomas	III, 566
Landon, Letitia Elizabeth	V, 327
Milton, John	II, 262, 271, 272, 277, 288
Pope, Alexander	III, 186
Spenser, Edmund	I, 382
Taylor, Jeremy	II, 209
Thomson, James	III 263
Watts, Isaac	III, 250
Wesley, Charles	IV, 36
Wordsworth, William	V, 632
MOODY, WILLIAM VAUGHN,	
Milton, John	II, 250, 256, 270, 275, 276
MOODY, WILLIAM VAUGHN, AND LOVETT, ROBERT MORSS,	
Arnold, Matthew	VII, 649
Brontë, Charlotte	VI, 31

INDEX TO CRITICISMS

	Vol and Page
Browning, Elizabeth Barrett	VI, 247
Browning, Robert	VII, 686
Carlyle, Thomas	VII, 245
DeQuincey, Thomas	VI, 132
Eliot, George	VII, 195
Landor, Walter Savage	VI, 380
Lytton, Sir Edward George Bulwer	VI, 701
Morris, William	VIII, 334
Newman, John Henry	VII, 757
Reade, Charles	VII, 531
Rossetti, Gabriel Charles Dante	VII, 445, 448
Ruskin, John	VIII, 411, 424
Stevenson, Robert Louis	VIII, 254
Thackeray, William Makepeace	VI, 323
Trollope, Anthony	VII, 465
MOOR, JOHN FREWEN,	
Keble, John	VI, 458
MOORE, CHARLES H.,	
Ruskin, John	VIII, 410
MOORE, CHARLES LEONARD,	
Arnold, Matthew	VII, 638
Browning, Robert	VII, 714
Tennyson, Alfred Lord	VIII, 108
MOORE, HELEN,	
Shelley, Mary Woolstonecraft	V, 703
MOORE, HENRY,	
Wesley, John	IV, 114, 119
MOORE, JACOB,	
Winthrop, John	II, 108
MOORE, JOHN,	
Burns, Robert	IV, 248
Smollett, Tobias George	III, 574, 579
MOORE, NORMAN,	
Garth, Sir Samuel	II, 665, 666
Harvey, William	II, 157
Moore, John	IV, 426
White, Gilbert	IV, 153
Wotton, William	II, 709, 710
MOORE, THOMAS,	
Addison, Joseph	II, 635
Barrow, Isaac	II, 312
Blackmore, Sir Richard	II, 746
Blessington, Countess of	V, 590
Bowles, William Lisle	V, 658
Burns, Robert	IV, 225
Bryon, George Gordon Lord	IV, 737, 748
Campbell, Thomas	V, 443, 450
Chaucer, Geoffrey	I, 158
Crabbe, George	V, 171
Davy, Sir Humphry	V, 91
Edgeworth, Maria	V, 562
Gifford, William	V, 32, 33
Gray, Thomas	III, 566
Jefferson, Thomas	V, 45
Jeffrey, Francis Lord	V, 648
Lewis, Matthew Gregory	IV, 631
Macaulay, Thomas Babington Lord	VI, 92
Mathias, Thomas James	V, 289
Mill, James	V, 307
Milton, John	II, 260
Pitt, William	IV, 510
Porson, Richard	IV, 522
Prior, Matthew	II, 677

	Vol. and Page
Sheridan, Richard Brinsley	IV, 595, 602, 604
Smith, Sydney	V, 467
Somerville, Mary	VI, 657
Southey, Robert	V, 403, 412
Stevenson, John Hall	IV, 24
Taylor, Sir Henry	VII, 579
Tighe, Mary	IV, 551
Wordsworth, William	V, 607, 621
MORAN, JOHN,	
Ryan, Abram Joseph	VII, 598, 598
MORAN, DR. JOHN J.	
Poe, Edgar Allan	V, 542
MORE, CRESACRE,	
More, Sir Thomas	I, 234
MORE, HANNAH,	
Beattie, James	IV, 431
Boswell, James	IV, 214
Burke, Edmund	IV, 289
Burnett, James	IV, 346
Carter, Elizabeth	IV, 491
Colman, George	IV, 202
Cowper, William	IV, 381, 384
Fielding, Henry	III, 351
Freeman, Edward Augustus	VIII, 153
Gibbon, Edward	IV, 195
Glover, Richard	IV, 17
Johnson, Samuel	III, 722, 752
Macaulay, Thomas Babington Lord	VI, 91
Montagu, Elizabeth	IV, 399
More, Hannah	V, 194
Otway, Thomas	II, 366
Seward, Anna	IV, 542
Walpole, Horace	IV, 310
MORE, PAUL ELMER,	
Byron, George Gordon Lord	IV, 754, 765
Crabbe, George	V, 177
Franklin, Benjamin	IV, 94
Hawthorne, Nathaniel	VI, 355, 371
Thoreau, Henry David	VI, 278
MORE, SIR THOMAS,	
Colet, John	I, 211
Fisher, John	I, 240
More, Sir Thomas	I, 232
Tyndale, William	I, 248
MOREL, LEON,	
Thomson, James	III, 262
MORELL, J. D.,	
Brown, Thomas	IV, 658
Harris, James	III, 709
Hartley, David	III, 379
Hume, David	III, 652
Price, Edward	IV, 136
Priestley, Joseph	IV, 454
Reid, Thomas	IV, 285
MORFORD, HENRY,	
Griswold, Rufus Wilmot	VI, 77
Osgood, Francis Sargent	V, 678
Simms, William Gilmore	VI, 597
Tuckerman, Henry Theodore	VI, 642
White, Richard Grant	VII, 577
Willis, Nathaniel Parker	VI, 488
MORGAN, APPLETON,	
Poe, Edgar Allan	V, 545
Shakespeare, William	I, 455
MORGAN, C. LLOYD,	
Romanes, George John	VIII, 284

	Vol and Page
MORGAN, FORREST.	
Bagehot, Walter	VII, 99
MORGAN, SYDNEY OWENSON LADY,	
Gifford, William	V, 32
Lamb, Lady Caroline	V, 81
Morgan, Sydney Owenson, Lady	VI, 192
MORGANN MAURICE,	
Shakespeare, William	I, 480, 489
MORIARTY, GERALD P.,	
Swift, Jonathan	III, 211, 228
MORISON, JAMES COTTER,	
Carlyle, Thomas	VII, 268
Cobden, Richard	VI, 441
Gibbon, Edward	IV, 175, 187
Hume, David	III, 666
Macaulay, Thomas Babington Lord	VI, 100
Pattison, Mark	VII, 540
Robertson, William	IV, 163
Stephen, Sir Leslie	VIII, 510
MORISON, J. H.,	
Dewey, Orville	VII, 499
MORISON, SIR RICHARD,	
Latimer, Hugh	I, 267
MORLEY, GEORGE,	
Eliot, George	VII, 182
MORLEY, HENRY,	
Addison, Joseph	II, 653
Ainsworthy, William Harrison	VII, 488
Akenside, Mark	III, 540
Alison, Sir Archibald	VI, 521
Arnold, Thomas	V, 380
Austen, Jane	IV, 621
Bacon, Francis	I, 651
Bacon, Roger	I, 78
Beddoes, Thomas Lovell	V, 586
Bede	I, 26
Berners, Lord	I, 229
Blackmore, Sir Richard	II, 746
Boyle, Robert	II, 419
Broome, William	III, 238
Browning, Elizabeth Barrett	VI, 246
Browning, Robert	VII, 702
Buchanan, George	I, 314, 316
Butler, Joseph	III, 312
Butler, Samuel	II, 333
Cædmon	I, 23
Carlyle, Thomas	VII, 256
Cartwright, Thomas	I, 417
Cartwright, William	I, 70
Cavendish, George	I, 283
Chambers, Robert	VI, 622
Chaucer, Geoffrey	I, 128, 133, 146, 150, 151, 166
Churchyard, Thomas	I, 418
Cobbett, William	V, 275
Collins, William Wilkie	VII, 726
Croker, John Wilson	VI, 74
Cynewulf	I, 30
Daniel, Samuel	I, 617
Davies, Sir John	I, 633
Defoe, Daniel	III, 29, 48
DeMorgan, Augustus	VI, 634
Dennis, John	III, 75
Digby, Sir Kenelm	II, 181
Dillon, Wentworth	II, 360
Drayton, Michael	I, 703

INDEX TO CRITICISMS 645

	Vol and Page
Dunbar, William	I 227
D'Urfey, Thomas	II 686
Eliot, George	VII 202
Ellwood, Thomas	II, 575
Erigena	I 35
Fairfax, Edward	I 742
Fielding, Henry	III 353
Forster, John	VII 66
Foxe, John	I 336
Gascoigne, George	I. 309
Gay, John	III. 55
Geoffery of Monmouth	I, 57
Giraldus, Cambrensis	I, 68
Goldsmith, Oliver	III, 622
Gower, John	I, 173
Green, Matthew	III, 94
Hall, Edward	I, 260
Harrington, Sir John	I, 441
Harvey, Gabriel	I, 697
Hawes Stephen	I. 218
Henryson, Robert	I, 209
Herrick, Robert	II. 236
Heywood, John	I, 304
Hooker, Richard	I, 404
Hoveden, Roger de	I, 63
Hughes, John	II, 667
James I of Scotland	I, 181
Johnson, Samuel	III, 763
Keble, John	VI, 462
Knowles, James Sheridan	VI, 289
Knox, John	I, 299
Langland, William	I, 121
Layamon	I. 66
Lee, Nathaniel	II. 430
L'Estrange, Sir Roger	II 537
Lillo, George	III 102
Literature	I, 9
Locke, John	II, 535
Lodge, Thomas	I, 625
Lovelace, Richard	II. 162
Lydgate, John	I. 185
Lyndsay, Sir David	I, 275
Lytton, Sir Edward George Bulwer	VI, 689
Macaulay, Thomas Babington Lord	VI, 103
Malory, Sir Thomas	I 204
Mandeville, Bernard	III 69
Mandeville, Sir John	I, 97
Milton, John	II. 292
Minot, Lawrence	I 94
Moore, Thomas	V 713
More, Sir Thomas	I, 236
Morris, William	VIII. 335
Nashe, Thomas	I. 415
Newton, Sir Isaac	II. 715
Occleve, Thomas	I. 187
Parker, Matthew	I, 303
Parnell, Thomas	II 614
Peacock, Thomas Love	VI, 476
Peele, George	I. 365
Penn, William	II, 625
Philips, John	II. 563
Planché, James Robinson.	VII. 217
Praed, Winthrop Mackworth V, 333
Ray John	II 541
Rogers, Samuel	VI, 37
Shairp, John Campbell	VII, 570
Shakespeare William	I 463, 493
Sherlock, William	II 561
Sidney Sir Philip	I 327
Smollett Tobias George	III 579

	Vol. and Page
Southey Robert	V 413
Spelman Sir Henry	II 53
Spenser Edmund	I 384 399
Spotiswood John	II. 25
Sprat, Thomas	II 572
Steele, Sir Richard	II 765
Still, John	I 430
Stowe, John	I. 420
Tate, Nahum	II 588
Taylor, Tom	VII 214
Thackeray, William Makepeace	VI, 316
Theobald Lewis	III 140
Trollope Frances Milton	VI 331
Tuberville, George	I 438
Tusser, Thomas	I 310
Wace Robert	I, 60 62
Warner, William	I, 438
Warren, Samuel	VII, 109
Whiston, William	III, 304
Wordsworth, William	V 623
Wyatt, Sir Thomas	I 251
MORLEY HENRY and GRIFFIN W. HALL,	
Bacon, Francis	I, 649
Dekker, Thomas	II, 62
Drayton, Michael	I. 705
Jonson, Ben	II, 753
Shakespeare, William	I, 527, 538
MORLEY, HENRY, AND TYLER MOSES COIT,	
Grosseteste, Robert	I, 73
Hall, Edward	I, 259
Robert of Gloucester	I, 82
MORLEY, JOHN,	
Arnold, Matthew	VII, 630, 646
Bacon, Francis	I, 651
Bagehot, Walter	VII. 97
Browning, Robert	VII, 694
Burke, Edmund	IV 297, 298, 305
Byron, George Gordon Lord	IV, 752, 753. 760
Carlyle, Thomas	VII. 264
Cobden, Richard	VI, 441, 443
Eliot George	VII 176 188, 195, 204
Emerson, Ralph Waldo	VII. 357, 370
FitzGerald, Edward	VII. 520
Gladstone, William Ewart	VIII, 392
Greg, William Rathbone	VII, 320, 321
Lewes George Henry	VII 138
Literature	I, 10
Macaulay, Thomas Babington Lord	VI, 99, 121
Maine, Sir Henry James Sumner	VII. 652
Mill James	V 307
Newman John Henry	VII. 753
Overbury Sir Thomas	I 443
Pattison, Mark	VII. 538
Saint-John Henry	III. 297
Shelley Percy Bysshe	V. 709
Woolston Thomas	III. 74
Wordsworth, William	V 621, 624, 643
Young, Arthur	IV, 656
MORRELL, REV. T.	
Doddridge, Philip	III, 303
MORRILL, JUSTIN S.,	
Erskine Thomas	IV, 729

	Vol. and Page
Herrick, Robert	II, 234
Hume David	III. 651
Jefferson Thomas	V. 43
Johnson, Samuel	III. 765
Saxe, John Godfrey	VII, 616
Tupper Martin Farquhar	VII, 732
Webster, Daniel	V. 724
Whitman Walt	VIII. 131
MORRIS, CHARLES,	
Franklin, Benjamin	IV, 105
MORRIS EDWARD E.,	
Steele, Sir Richard	II, 756
MORRIS, GEORGE P.,	
Knowles, James Sheridan	VI. 288
MORRIS. GEORGE S.	
Bacon, Francis	I. 651
Bacon, Roger	I, 79
Berkeley, George	III 322 334
Davies Sir John	I, 633
Hamilton, Sir William	VI. 56
Hobbes Thomas	II, 327
Hume David	III 664
John of Salisbury	I. 60
Locke John	II 530
Mill, John Stuart	VI. 704 716
Spencer Herbert	VIII, 481
MORRIS, GOUVERNEUR.	
Hamilton Alexander	IV 457, 462
Washington, George	IV 356
MORRIS HARRISON S.,	
Browning, Robert	VII, 709
Whitman, Walt	VIII, 135
MORRIS, SIR LEWIS,	
Tennyson Alfred Lord	VIII, 107
Vaughan, Henry	II, 442
MORRIS, MOWBRAY.	
Dickens, Charles	VI. 573
Scott. Michael	V, 279, 279
Scott, Sir Walter	V. 151
Trollope, Anthony	VII, 461
MORRIS, RICHARD,	
Chaucer, Geoffrey	I, 133
MORRIS, ROBERT. LIVINGSTONE, ROBERT, AND WASHINGTON GEORGE,	
Paine, Thomas	IV, 530
MORRIS WILLIAM,	
Browning, Robert	VII, 699
Rossetti Gabriel, Charles Dante	VII, 448, 450
MORRISON, A. H.,	
Chaucer, Geoffrey	I, 163
DeQuincey, Thomas	VI, 127
Macaulay Thomas Babington Lord	VI 113
Timrod, Henry	VI 510
Willis, Nathaniel Parker	VI 492
MORRISON, JEANIE,	
Browning, Robert	VII, 688
MORSE, CHARLES A. L.	
Arnold, Matthew	VII, 646
MORSE, EDWIN W.,	
Irving, Washington	VI, 148, 153
MORSE, JAMES HERBERT.	
Brown, Charles Brockden	VI, 553
Cooper, James Fenimore	V 686
Dana, Richard Henry	VII 157
Harte, Francis Bret	VII 187
Hawthorne, Nathaniel	VI 368
Irving, Washington	VI 140
Kennedy, John Pendleton	VI 606

646 INDEX TO CRITICISMS

Vol. and Page
Lowell, James Russell....VIII, 32
Neal, John...............VII, 78
Patmore, Coventry......VIII, 342
Poe, Edgar Allan...........V, 547
Simms, William Gilmore....VI. 599
Stowe, Harriet Beecher......
....................VIII, 353. 356
Taylor, Bayard..........VII. 135
Whittier, John Greenleaf.VIII, 124
MORSE, JOHN T., JR.,
Adams, John...............V. 51
Adams, John Quincy....V, 518, 520
Dickens, Charles..........VI, 587
Franklin, Benjamin...IV. 90, 95, 96
Hamilton, Alexander......IV, 459
Holmes, Oliver Wendell......
....................VIII, 287, 294
Jefferson, Thomas........V, 43, 49
Lincoln, Abraham.........VI, 419
MORSE, SAMUEL F.,
Davidson, Lucretia Maria....V, 26
MORSHEAD, E. D. A.,
Lytton, Edward Robert Bulwer................VIII, 48
Tennyson, Frederick.....VIII, 399
MORTON, E. J. C.,
Flamsteed, John..........II, 663
Newton, Sir Isaac..........II, 715
MORTON, JAMES,
Poor, Richard..............I, 70
MOSELEY, HUMPHREY,
Milton, John..............II, 234
Suckling, Sir John..........Ii, 65
MOTHERWELL, WILLIAM,
Motherwell, William........V, 276
MOTLEY, JOHN LOTHROP,
Bright, John............VII, 720
Carlyle, Thomas.......VII, 232, 263
Collins, William Wilkie....VII, 725
Disraeli, Benjamin.......VII, 277
Grote, George............VI, 607
Hallam, Henry...........VI, 173
Hawthorne, Nathaniel....VI, 360
Holmes, Oliver Wendell......
....................VIII, 293
Hughes, Thomas........VIII, 346
Kinglake, Alexander William
....................VIII, 49
Kingsley, Charles.........VII, 18
Longfellow, Henry Wadsworth
.....:................VII, 389
Lowell, James Russell....VIII, 28
Lytton, Sir Edward George
Bulwer................VI, 682
Lytton, Edward Robert Bulwer Earl............VIII, 43
Macaulay, Thomas Babington
Lord..................VI, 93
Milman, Henry Hart......VI, 534
Mill, John Stuart.........VII, 713
Milnes, Richard Monckton VII, 560
Owen, Sir Richard......VIII, 171
Prescott, William Hickling..VI, 190
Sidney, Sir Philip...........I, 331
Stanhope, Philip Henry Earl..
....................VII, 46
Sumner, Charles..........VI, 754
Thackeray, William Makepeace
....................VI, 292
Ticknor, George..........VI, 616
Wilberforce, Samuel......VI. 732

Vol. and Page
MOULE, C. W.,
Barnes, William..........VII, 585
MOULTON, CHARLES WELLS,
Adams, Hannah............V, 124
Alcott, Louisa May......VII, 665
Anselm....................I, 49
Bede,......................I, 25
Browne, William...........II, 72
Chaucer, Geoffrey..........I, 124
Child, Lydia Maria......VII, 218
Echard, Laurence.........III, 22
Edwards, Jonathan.......III, 380
Fisher, John...............I, 230
Fuller, Sarah Margaret.....V, 663
Hoveden. Roger de.........I, 63
Jackson, Helen Hunt.....VII, 571
Lydgate, John..............I. 183
Malory, Sir Thomas........I, 203
Pitt, Christopher.........III. 254
Poor, Richard..............I, 69
Sigourney, Lydia Huntley...VI, 450
Smith, Charlotte.........IV. 496
Stanhope. Philip Dormer...III, 598
Stevenson, John Hall......IV, 24
Stuart, Gilbert...........IV, 27
Walsh, William...........II, 560
MOULTON, LOUISE CHANDLER,
Alcott, Louisa May......VII, 666
Arnold. Sir Edwin......VIII, 505
Carlyle, Thomas.....VII, 241, 258
Emerson, Ralph Waldo..VII, 374
Lytton, Edward Robert Bulwer................VIII, 47
Marston, Philip Bourke...VII, 627
Morris, William.....VIII. 330, 336
O'Shaughnessy, Arthur Wm.
Edgar............VII, 322, 324
Stevenson, Robert Louis.VIII, 247
Tennyson, Alfred Lord...VII, 107
Whittier, John Greenleaf.VIII, 113
MOULTON, RICHARD GREEN,
Collier, Jeremy..........II, 701
Critic, The................II. 8
Eliot, George............VII, 194
Kingsley,Charles.........VII, 27
Walsh, William...........II, 561
MOUNTSTUART, E. GRANT,
Arnold, Matthew........VII, 644
Kinglake, Alexander William
.... VIII, 50
MOXON, EDWARD,
Lamb, Charles.............V, 231
MOZLEY, ANNE,
Mozley, James Bowling...VII, 148
Whately, Richard........VI, 325
MOZLEY, JAMES,
Newman, John Henry....VII, 746
MOZLEY, JAMES BOWLING,
Arnold, Thomas...........V, 379
Carlyle, Thomas........VII, 249
Faber, Frederick William..VI, 332
Heylin, Peter.............I, 174
Keble, John..............VI, 457
Kingsley, Charles.........VII, 18
Laud, William...........II, 91
Pussey, Edward Bouverie. VII, 467
White, Joseph Blanco..V, 360, 361
Wiseman, Nicholas Patrick.VI 437
MOZLEY, THOMAS,
Froude, James Anthony......
.... VIII. 255. 264

Vol. and Page
Keble, John..............VI. 459
Stowe, Harriet Beecher.......
.... VII, 349, 352
Whately Richard.........VI. 327
White, Joseph Blanco.......V 361
MUIR, M. M. PATTISON,
Priestley, Joseph.........IV, 451
MUIR, PEARSON M'ADAM,
Rutherford, Samuel........II, 166
MUIRHEAD, J. H.,
Stevenson, Robert Louis..VIII, 253
MULFORD, ELISHA,
Maurice, John Frederick Denison ....VI, 647
MULLANY, PATRICK FRANCIS
(BROTHER AZARIAS),
Brownson, Orestes Augustus..
.... VII. 75
Eliot, George............VII. 184
Froude, James Anthony..VIII, 264
Newman, John Henry...VII, 744
Ruskin, John...........VIII, 418
Tennyson, Alfred Lord...VIII, 89
Thackeray, William Makepeace
.... VI, 319
MÜLLER, FRIEDRICH MAX,
Arnold, Matthew........VII, 631
Browning, Robert........VII, 717
Carlyle, Thomas........VII, 234
Clough, Arthur Hugh......VI. 256
Darwin, Charles Robert...VII, 417
Dickens, Charles.........VI, 594
Emerson, Ralph Waldo......
.... VII, 346. 377
Froude, James Anthony......
........VII. 255, 257, 257, 267
George, Henry..........VIII, 381
Gladstone. William Ewart....
.... VIII, 391
Kingsley. Charles..VII, 22, 25, 33
Lytton. Sir Edward George
Bulwer ....VI, 693
Mansel, Henry Longueville ...
.... VI, 628
Newman. John Henry....VI, 756
Palgrave, Francis Turner.VIII. 372
Pattison, Mark.........VII. 538
Pusey, Edward Bouverie. VII. 468
Ruskin John..........VIII, 407
Stanley. Arthur Penrhyn.VII, 297
Tennyson, Alfred Lord......
.... VIII, 75, 86
Thackeray. William Makepeace
.... VI, 321
MÜLLER. MRS. FRIEDRICH
MAX,
Müller. Friedrich Max...VIII, 436
MULLINGER, J. BASS,
Alcuin, I..................I 33
Ascham, Roger............I, 290
Asser ....I, 41
Cartwright, Thomas.......I, 417
Harvey, Gabriel..........I, 697
Milton, John..............II 297
Neal, Daniel............III 140
Parker, Matthew.........I 304
Peacock, Reginald.........I 190
Spenser, Edmund..........I 400
William of Malmesbury.....I. 54
MULSO. JOHN.
White. Gilbert..........IV 147

INDEX TO CRITICISMS

MUMBY, ARTHUR,
  Blackmore, Richard D..VIII, 431
MUNGER, THEODORE THORNTON,
  Bushnell, Horace........VII 72
  Holmes, Oliver Wendell......
    ....VIII, 292, 298
  Scott, Sir Walter..........V, 133
MUNRO, ARCHIBALD,
  Burns, Robert...........IV, 39
MUNTZ, IRVING,
  Jefferies, Richard........VII, 621
MURCHISON, SIR RODERICK IMPEY,
  Kane Elisha Kent........VI, 82
  Miller, Hugh.............VI, 64
  Owen, Sir Richard......VIII, 171
  Whewell, William........VI, 467
MURDOCH, ALEXANDER G.,
  Blackie, John Stuart....VIII, 306
  Buchanan, Robert......VIII, 448
  Burns, Robert..........IV, 265
MURDOCH, JOHN,
  Burns, Robert..........IV 222
MURDOCH, PATRICK,
  Thomson, James.........III, 256
MURPHY, ARTHUR,
  Churchill, Charles........III, 475
  Fielding, Henry..III, 340, 344, 355
  Hawkesworth, John.......III, 699
  Johnson Samuel...........
    ....III, 726, 739, 740
  Otway, Thomas..........II, 365
MURRAY, CHARLES AUGUSTUS,
  Marshall, John............V, 282
MURRAY, DAVID CHRISTIE,
  Dickens, Charles..........VI, 593
MURRAY, SIR GEORGE,
  Napier, Gen. Sir Wm. Francis Patrick................VI, 222
MURRAY, GRENVILLE,
  Macaulay, Thomas Babington Lord ....VI, 96
MURRAY, HENRY,
  Buchanan, Robert......VIII, 445
  Carlyle, Thomas........VII, 275
MURRAY, HUGH,
  Park, Mungo............IV, 485
MURRAY, J. CLARK,
  Berkeley, George.........III, 323
  Mandeville, Bernard......III, 70
MURRAY, JAMES D.,
  Freneau, Philip..........V, 187
  Wayland Francis.VI, 448, 449, 450
MURRAY, JOHN,
  Borrow, George Henry...VII, 398
  Byron, George Gordon Lord,
    ....IV, 756
  Leslie, Sir John..........V 189
MURRAY, JOHN O'KANE,
  Alcuin,................I 33
  Banim, John..............V 391
  Challoner, Richard .....III, 710
  Mangan, James Clarence....V 603
  Southwell, Robert........I, 363
MURRAY, J. ROSS,
  Greene, Robert............I 341
  Skelton, John............I 223
MURRAY, LINDLEY,
  Murray, Lindley.........V 55

MURRAY, PATRICK A.,
  Carleton, William.........VI, 549
MURRAY, PATRICK JOSEPH,
  Banim, John..............V, 390
MURRAY-NAIRNE, CHARLES,
  Locke, John..........II, 522, 527
MUSKAU, PUECKLER,
  Morgan, Lady Sydney Owenson ....VI, 192
MUZZEY, A. B.,
  Channing, William Ellery..V, 369
  Emerson, Ralph Waldo...VII, 347
MYALL, WILLIAM,
  Ingersoll, Robert Green.VIII, 402
  Whitefield, George........III, 551
MYERS, ERNEST,
  Milton, John..............II, 293
MYERS, FREDERIC WILLIAM HENRY,
  Arnold, Matthew........VII, 643
  Darwin, Charles Robert..VII, 431
  Eliot, George...........VII, 175
  Poe, Edgar Allan..........V, 549
  Rossetti, Gabriel Charles Dante
    ....VII, 442
  Seeley, Sir John Robert..VIII, 309
  Shelley, Percy Bysshe.....IV, 711
  Stanley, Arthur Penrhyn....
    .... VII, 299, 304
  Tennyson, Alfred Lord..VIII, 108
  Thomson, James.........III, 270
  Trench, Richard Chenevix..
    .... VII, 589
  Wordsworth, William........
    .... V, 615, 619, 624, 640

NADAL, EHRMAN SYME,
  Arnold, Matthew...VII, 642
  Bagehot, Walter........VII, 98
  Browne, Charles Farrar...VI, 503
  Bryant, William Cullen...III, 111
  Collins, William..........III, 420
  Disraeli, Benjamin........VII, 293
  Harte, Francis Bret.....VIII, 469
  Lowell, James Russell .VIII, 23, 29
  Milto , John..............II, 265
  Thackeray, William Makepeace
    ....VI, 296, 307
  White, Gilbert............IV, 153
NAPIER, MACVEY,
  Bacon, Francis............I 659
  Leslie, Sir John...........V, 189
  Newton, Sir Isaac..........II, 724
  Raleigh, Sir Walter...I, 595, 603
  Roscoe, William...........V, 119
  Southey, Robert..........V, 415
  Stewart, Dugald...........V, 77
NARES, EDWARD,
  Cheke, Sir John...........I, 278
NASHE, THOMAS,
  Chaucer, Geoffrey........I 154
  Cheke, Sir John...........I, 277
  Daniel, Samuel...........I 613
  Gascoigne, George.........I 307
  Greene, Robert.......I, 339 344
  Harvey Gabriel............I 696
  Lyly, John...............I 426
  Marlowe Christopher......I 348
  Nashe, Thomas...........I 412
  Peele George.............I 364
  Sidney, Sir Philip..........I 321

Spenser, Edmund..........I, 378
Watson, Thomas..........I, 337
NASH, TREADWAY RUSSEL,
  Butler, Samuel...........II, 331
NAUNTON, SIR ROBERT,
  Greville, Sir Fulke.........I, 690
  Raleigh, Sir Walter........I, 592
  Sackville, Thomas.........I, 431
  Sidney, Sir Philip..........I, 322
NEAL, JOHN,
  Bentham, Jeremy.........V, 163
  Irving, Washington.........
    ....VI, 137, 139, 141, 144
  Longfellow, Henry Wadsworth
    .... VII, 401
  Neal, John............. VII, 77
  Paulding, James Kirke....VI, 226
  Pierpont, John......VI, 480, 481
  Poe, Edgar Allan..........V, 540
  Sedgwick, Catharine Maria..
    .... VI, 506
  Silliman, Benjamin.......VI, 407
  Sparks, Jared............VI, 477
  Sprague, Charles........VII 52
  Trumbull, John...........V, 120
  Wilson, Alexander........IV, 583
NEANDER, AUGUSTUS,
  Anselm ....I, 49
  Bacon, Roger..............I, 79
  Wyclif, John..............I, 105
NEELE, HENRY,
  Browne, William.........II, 74
  Butler, Samuel...........II, 332
  Chamberlayne, William....II, 406
  Collins, William.........III, 419
  Congreve, William........II, 741
  Cowley, Abraham........II, 196
  Cowper, William.........IV, 387
  Cumberland, Richard....IV, 561
  Dryden, John............II, 489
  Goldsmith, Oliver........III, 633
  Gray, Thomas...........III, 566
  Hall, Joseph............II, 145
  Herbet, George...........I, 723
  Jonson, Ben..............I, 763
  Massinger, Philip......II, 43, 48
  Milton, John............II, 261
  Otway, Thomas..........II, 364
  Pope, Alexander.........III, 186
  Rowe, Nicholas...........II, 622
  Sheridan, Richard Brinsley..
    .... IV, 606
  Thomson, James.........III, 268
  Vanbrugh, Sir John.......II, 707
  Young, Edward..........III, 491
NEGREPONTE, MARY,
  Whittier, John Greenleaf....
    .... VIII, 126
NEGRI, GAETANO,
  Eliot, George..VII, 184, 191, 206
NEIL, SAMUEL,
  Bacon, Roger..............I, 79
  Shakespeare, William......I, 563
NEILSON, JOSEPH,
  Choate Rufus...........VI, 199
NEILSON, WILLIAM ALLAN,
  Longfellow Henry Wadsworth
    .... VII, 415
NETTLETON GEORGE HENRY
  Dickens Charles..........VI, 578
  Lever Charles James......VI, 656

INDEX TO CRITICISMS

Vol. and Page

Poe, Edgar Allan..........V, 554
Thackeray, William Makepeace
..............................VI, 322
NETTLESHIP, HENRY,
Mill, John Stuart..........VI, 710
Pattison, Mark..........VII, 539
Ruskin, John..........VIII, 417
NETTLESHIP, JOHN T.,
Browning, Robert.......VII, 709
Rossetti, Gabriel Charles
Dante ....VII, 443
NEVE, PETER LE,
D'Urfey, Thomas..........II, 686
NEVINSON, H. W.,
Hare, Julius Charles......VI, 50
NEW ENGLAND WEEKLY
COURIER,
Berkeley, George.........III, 319
NEWCOME, ALPHONSO G.,
Poe, Edgar Allan..........V, 554
NEWCOMBE, GEORGE,
Trollope, Frances Milton...VI, 329
NEWELL, E. J.,
Blackmore, Richard D..VIII, 432
NEWELL, PETER,
Dodgson, Charles Lutwige....
...............VIII, 398, 399
NEWELL, WILLIAM WELLS,
Geoffery of Monmouth......I, 57
Malory, Sir Thomas........I, 206
Tennyson, Alfred Lord..VIII, 95
NEWMAN, FRANCIS W.,
Arnold, Matthew........VII, 632
Newman, John Henry........
.... VII, 742, 753
NEWMAN, JOHN HENRY,
Arnold, Thomas...........V, 377
Books ....III, 7
Butler, Joseph..........III, 311
Byron, George Gordon Lord..
..............................IV, 750
Carlyle, Thomas........VII, 246
Colerinage, Samuel Taylor...V, 208
Dryden, John...........II, 486
Keble, John.............VI, 461
Laud, William...........II, 91
Milman, Henry Hart......VI, 536
Milton, John.............II, 288
Moore, Thomas...........V, 716
Pusey, Edward Bouverie.VII, 466
Whately, Richard........VI, 324
White, Joseph Blanco......V, 361
NEWTON, ALFRED,
White, Gilbert...........IV, 151
NEWTON, HUMPHREY,
Newton, Sir Isaac........II, 712
NEWTON, SIR ISAAC,
Locke, John..............II, 519
Newton, Sir Isaac.....II, 711, 718
NEWTON, JOHN,
Cowper, William..........IV, 381
NEWTON-ROBINSON, JANETTA,
Burton, Sir Richard Francis..
..................VII, 760
Stevenson, Robert Louis....
.... VIII 240, 247, 248
NEWTON, SIR CHARLES T.,
Finlay, George.......VII, 48, 49
NEWTON, THOMAS,
Milton, John.............II, 245
Warburton, William......III, 684

Vol. and Page

NICHOL, JOHN,
Adams, John Quincy.......V, 520
Bacon, Delia.............VI, 205
Bacon, Francis.....I, 648, 662, 669
Bacon, Roger..............I, 80
Bancroft, George.......VIII, 59
Brown, Charles Brockden..IV, 554
Browne, Charles Farrar....VI, 503
Burns, Robert............IV, 259
Byron, George Gordon Lord..
..............................IV, 761
Carlyle, Thomas.... VII. 253, 272
Channing, William Ellery..V, 373
Chaucer, Geoffrey..........I, 167
Coke, Sir Edward..........I, 741
Cooper, James Fenimore...V, 685
Dana, Richard Henr ....VII, 156
Dobell, Sydney Thompson....
.... VI, 759, 761, 763, 765
Dunbar, William..........I, 226
Dwight, Timothy..........IV, 627
Everett, Edward..........VI, 426
Freneau, Philip..........V, 187
Hamilton, Alexander......IV, 464
Hawthorne, Nathaniel. VI, 354, 363
Hillhouse, James Abraham..V, 365
Irving, Washington.......VI, 150
Jefferson, Thomas..........V, 49
Longfellow, Henry Wadsworth
..................VII, 389, 409
Lyndsay Sir David.........II, 275
Madison, James...........V, 314
Motley, John Lothrop.VII, 90, 95
Parker, Theodore.........VI, 210
Poe, Edgar Allan..........V, 558
Prescott, William Hickling..
.... VI 185, 187, 188
Raleigh, Sir Walter........I, 606
Spedding, James........VII, 319
Swift, Jonathan.........III, 226
Trumbull, John...........V, 121
Washington, George.....IV, 369
Webster, Daniel..........V, 728
Whitman, Walt........VIII, 138
Whittier, John Greenleaf.VIII, 123
Winthrop, Theodore......VI, 267
NICHOL, JOHN PRINGLE,
Hales, Alexander..........I, 71
Stewart, Dugald..........V, 78
NICHOLL, JOHN,
Graham, James..........II, 121
NICHOLS, JOHN,
Hurd, Richard...........IV, 517
Steele, Sir Richard......II, 760
NICHOLS, J. G.,
Walpole, Horace.........IV, 316
NICHOLS, THOMAS L.,
Halleck, Fitz-Greene......VI, 494
NICHOLSON, E. B. and YULE H.,
Mandeville, Sir John......I, 96
NICHOLSON, JOHN,
Burns, Robert............IV, 252
NICHOLSON, J. SHIELD,
Mill, John Stuart.........VI, 709
Smith, Adam.............IV, 68
NICOLAS, SIR HARRIS NICHO-
LAS,
Chaucer, Geoffrey..........I, 127
Collins, William......III, 44, 616
Junius ....IV, 641
Rymer, Thomas..........II, 582

Vol. and Page

Thomson, James..III, 256, 259, 262
Walton, Isaac............II, 347
White Henry Kirke.......IV. 488
NICOLAY, J. G.,
Jefferson, Thomas..........V. 43
Lincoln, Abraham....VI, 415, 420
NICOLL, HENRY J.,
Arbuthnot, John..........III, 85
Bacon, Francis............I, 646
Browning, Elizabeth Barrett..
..............................VI, 246
Carlyle, Thomas......VII, 234, 257
Chambers, Robert.....VI, 621, 622
Cobden, Richard..........VI, 443
Collier, Jeremy............II, 701
DeQuincey, Thomas.......VI, 127
Dunbar, William..........I, 226
Fielding, Henry..III, 343, 355, 362
Gray, Thomas............III, 569
Grote, George............VI, 610
Hallam, Henry............VI, 180
James I. of Scotland........I, 181
Kingsley, Charles........VII, 31
Knight, Charles..........VI, 742
Landor, Walter Savage.....VI, 385
Latimer, Hugh............I, 269
Lever, Charles James......VI, 655
Lytton, Sir Edward George Bul-
wer ....VI, 698
Mackintosh, Sir James.....V, 183
Richardson, Samuel.......III, 442
Romilly, Sir Samuel.......IV, 637
Saint-John, Henry.......III, 296
Sheridan, Richard Brinsley.IV, 607
Smollett, Tobias George......
..................III, 580, 581
Steele, Sir Richard........II, 766
Temple, Sir William.......II, 459
Thackeray, William Make-
peace ....VI, 307
Wilberforce, William......V, 203
Wyatt, Sir Thomas.........I, 252
Young, Edward..........III, 486
NICOLL, WILLIAM ROBERTSON
(WALTER E. WACE),
Drummond, Henry..VIII, 365, 365
Oliphant, Margaret O. W.VIII, 368
Stevenson, Robert Louis..VIII, 242
Tennyson, Alfred Lord...VIII, 77
NICOLL, W. ROBERTSON, AND
WISE, THOMAS J.,
Patmore, Coventry K. D..VIII, 339
NICOLLS, REV.,
Sherlock, Thomas........III, 454
NICOLSON, ALEXANDER,
Smith, Alexander....VI, 516, 517
NICOLSON, WILLIAM,
Bacon, Francis............I, 655
Barnes, Joshua...........II, 571
Boece, Hector ....I, 242
Camden, William..........I, 621
Caxton, William..........I, 198
Drayton, Michael..........I, 704
Evelyn, John............II, 550
Fabyan, Robert...........I, 206
Fuller, Thomas......II, 170, 170
Hall, Edward............I, 260
Herbert, Edward Lord.....II, 96
Hickes, George..........II, 598
Malory, Sir Thomas.......I, 203
Raleigh, Sir Walter ......I, 606

INDEX TO CRITICISMS

	Vol. and Page
Rymer, Thomas	II, 582
Selden, John	II, 139, 139
Speed, John	I, 694
Spotiswood, John	II, 24
Stillingfleet, Edward	II, 454
Stowe, John	I, 419
Usher, James	II, 153
Wood, Anthony	II, 447

NIEBUHR, BERTHOLD GEORGE,
| Canning, George | V, 68 |
| Grote, George | VI, 609 |

NIGHTINGALE, FLORENCE,
| Livingstone, David | VI, 727 |
| Milnes, Richard Monckton | VII, 561 |

NISARD, JEAN MARIE NAPO-LÉON DÉSIRÉ,
| Critic, The | II, 6 |

NIVEN, W. D.,
| Maxwell, James Clerk | VII, 169 |

NOBLE, CHARLES,
Alcott, Amos Bronson	VII, 665
Alcott, Louisa May	VII, 668
Beecher, Henry Ward	VII, 609
Cary, Phœbe	VI, 641
Kennedy, Charles	VI, 606
Sewall, Samuel	III, 19
Simms, William Gilmore	VI, 600
Sumner, Charles	VI, 758

NOBLE, JAMES ASHCROFT,
Arnold, Matthew	VII, 636
Austen, Jane	IV, 623
Bowles, William Lisle	V, 660
Brontë, Charlotte	VI, 24
Brontë, Emily	V, 522
Browning, Elizabeth Barrett	VI, 239, 241
Browning, Robert	VII, 714
Buchanan, Robert	VIII, 447
Coleridge, Hartley	V, 576
DeVere, Aubrey Thomas	VIII, 464
Dickens, Charles	VI, 588
Drummond, William	II, 102
Fielding, Henry	III, 354, 363
Godwin, Mary Wollstonecraft	IV, 328
Gray, David	VI, 262
Hunt, James Henry Leigh	VI, 166, 170
Ingelow, Jean	VIII, 377
Keats, John	IV, 680
Kingsley, Charles	VII, 31
Milton, John	II, 273
Pope, Alexander	III, 177
Richardson, Samuel	III, 451
Rossetti, Gabriel Charles Dante	VII, 448
Stephen, Sir Leslie	VIII, 511
Tupper, Martin Farquhar	VII, 732

NOBLE, MARK,
Arbuthnot, John	III, 84
Barnes, Joshua	II, 572
Brown, Thomas	II, 541
Centlivre, Susannah	II, 683
Clarke, Samuel	II, 748
Collier, Jeremy	II, 702
Congreve, William	II, 740
Defoe, Daniel	III, 24
Dennis, John	III, 77
D'Urfey, Thomas	II, 688
Echard Laurence	III, 22
Flamsteed, John	II, 663

	Vol. and Page
Garth, Sir Samuel	II, 664
Hill, Aaron	III, 277
Leslie, Charles	II, 680
Mather, Increase	II, 689
Montagu, Charles	II, 586
Prideaux, Humphrey	II, 697
Rowe, Elizabeth	III, 96
Sacheverell, Henry	II, 696
Wycherley, William	II, 604

NOBLE, WILLIAM,
| Proctor, Richard Anthony | VII, 660 |

NOEL, RODEN,
Berkeley, George	III, 333
Browning, Robert	VII 690, 692
Buchanan, Robert	VIII, 446
Byron, George Gordon Lord	IV, 747, 750, 763
Chatterton, Thomas	III, 538
Clare, John	VI, 400
Dobell, Sydney Thompson	VI, 764
Horne, Richard Hengist	VII, 547
Keats, John	IV, 673
Rossetti, Gabriel Charles Dante	VII, 449
Symonds, John Addington	VIII, 204
Tennyson, Alfred Lord	VIII 77, 80
Thomson, James	VII, 474, 476
Walpole, Horace	IV, 313
Wordsworth, William	V, 642

NORDAU, MAX,
Milton, John	II, 268
Morris, William	VIII, 336
Rossetti, Gabriel Charles Dante	VII, 445, 454
Ruskin, John	VIII, 420
Tennyson, Alfred Lord	VIII, 108
Whitman, Walt	VIII, 149

NORDHOFF, CHARLES,
| Winthrop, Theodore | VI, 266 |

NORFOLK, DUKE OF,
| More, Sir Thomas | I, 233 |

NORGATE KATE,
| Wace, Robert | I, 61 |

NORMAN, HENRY,
| Emerson, Ralph Waldo | VII, 348 |
| Longfellow, Henry Wadsworth | VII, 392, 411 |

NORRIS, MARY HARRIOTT,
| Eliot, George | VII, 186 |

NORTH, ERNEST D.,
| Lamb, Charles | V, 228 |

NORTH, J. W.,
| Jefferies, Richard | VII, 618 |

NORTH, MARIANNE,
| Gray, Asa | VII, 670 |
| Green, John Richard | VII, 507 |

NORTH, ROGER,
| Littleton, Sir Thomas | I, 196 |

NORTH, SIR THOMAS,
| Shakespeare, William | I, 528 |

NORTHCOTE, HENRY STAFFORD, EARL OF IDDESLEIGH,
Chaucer, Geoffrey	I, 167
Drayton, Michael	I, 705
Gladstone, William Ewart	VIII, 388
Jonson, Ben	I, 766

	Vol. and Page
NORTHCOTE, JAMES,	
Colman, George	IV, 201
Fielding, Henry	III, 358
Goldsmith, Oliver	III, 616
Reynolds, Sir Joshua	IV, 138, 140
Richardson, Samuel	III, 440
Watts, Isaac	III, 253

NORTHCROFT, GEORGE J. H.,
| Browne, Charles Farrar | VI, 504 |

NORTON, ANDREWS,
| Grant, Anne | V, 330 |

NORTON, CHARLES ELIOT,
Blake, William	V, 63
Clough, Arthur Hugh	VI, 250, 256
Coleridge, Sara	V, 734
Dickens, Charles	VI, 584
Emerson, Ralph Waldo	VII, 362
FitzGerald, Edward	VII, 516
Frere, John Hookham	V, 487
Irving, Edward	V, 248
Lincoln, Abraham	VI, 417
Longfellow, Henry Wadsworth	VII, 385, 398
Lowell, James Russell	VIII, 22
Morris, William	VIII, 333
Piozzi, Hester Lynch	IV, 686
Ruskin, John	VIII, 424
Shelley, Percy Bysshe	IV, 694
Ticknor, George	VI, 615, 618
Tyndale, William	I, 248
Very, Jones	VII, 227

NORTON, HON. CAROLINE E. S.,
| Dickens, Charles | VI, 581 |
| Sheridan, Richard Brinsley | IV, 596 |

NORTON, JOHN N.,
| Franklin, Benjamin | IV, 88 |
| Laud, William | II, 92 |

NORTON, MINERVA B.,
| Stanley, Sir Henry Morton | VIII, 507, 509 |

NORTHUP, CLARK SUTHERLAND,
| Stoddard, Richard Henry | VIII, 496 |

NOTT, GEORGE FREDERICK,
Barbour, John	I, 113
Dunbar, William	I, 224
Surrey, Earl of	I, 256
Wyatt, Sir Thomas	I, 251

NOTTINGHAM,
| Defoe, Daniel | III, 23 |

NOURSE, ROBERT,
| Craik, Dinah Maria Mulock | VII, 624 |

NOYES, G. R.,
| Dryden, John | II, 507 |

NUSSEY, ELLEN,
| Brontë, Emily | V, 521 |

OAKESHOTT, B. N.,
| Arnold, Matthew | VII, 648 |

OAKEY, S. W.,
Channing, William Ellery	V, 369
Sumner, Charles	VI, 752
Webster, Daniel	V, 722

OATES, JAMES,
| Tennyson, Alfred Lord | VIII, 83 |

O'BRIEN, FITZ-JAMES,
| Kane, Elisha Kent | VI, 81 |
| Melville, Herman | VIII, 62 |

OCCLEVE, THOMAS,
| Chaucer, Geoffrey | I, 124, **152** |

650 INDEX TO CRITICISMS

O'CONNELL, DANIEL,
 Disraeli, Benjamin........VII, 276
O'CONNOR, JOSEPH,
 Browning, Robert........VII, 689
 Emerson, Ralph Waldo....VII, 366
O'CONNOR, J. V.,
 Taylor, Bayard..........VII, 135
O'CONNOR, THOMAS POWER,
 Blessington, Countess of.....V, 592
 Carlyle, Thomas......VII, 240, 259
 Disraeli, Benjamin....VII, 284. 290
 Fawcett, Henry..........VII, 549
 Hazlitt, William...........V, 101
 MacCarthy, Dennis Florence..
 ....VII, 490
O'CONNOR, V. C. SCOTT,
 Tennyson, Alfred Lord...VIII, 74
O'CONNOR, WILLIAM DOUGLAS,
 Whitman, Walt.........VIII, 130
ODELL, JONATHAN,
 Washington, George......IV, 354
O'DELL, STACKPOOL E.,
 Dickens, Charles..........VI, 570
O'DONOGHUE, D. J.,
 Banim, John..............V, 391
 Carleton, William.....VI, 548, 549
 Lover, Samuel............VI, 546
 Mangan, James Clarence....V, 694
 Swift, Jonathan..........III, 237
OFFOR, GEORGE,
 Bunyan, John............II, 89
OGDEN, R.,
 Fiske, John............VIII, 458
OGLE, GEORGE,
 Chaucer, Geoffrey..........I, 141
O'HAGAN, LORD,
 Moore, Thomas...........V, 709
O'KEEFFE, HENRY E.,
 Newman, John Henry.....VII, 756
 Patmore, Coventry......VIII, 343
O'KEEFE, JOHN,
 Macklin, Charles..........IV, 343
OLDCASTLE, JOHN,
 Taylor, Tom........VII, 214, 215
OLDENBURG, HENRY,
 Bacon, Francis.............I, 657
OLDHAM, JOHN,
 Butler, Samuel............II, 329
 Denham, Sir John..........II, 221
 Milton, John.............II, 257
 Philips, Katherine.........II, 180
 Wilmot, John............II, 336
OLDYS, WILLIAM,
 Lee, Nathaniel............II, 430
 Lyly, John.................I, 421
 Otway, Thomas...........II, 362
 Puttenham, George........I, 401
 Raleigh, Sir Walter ....I, 602
 Shadwell, Thomas........II, 433
 Southerne, Thomas.......III, 240
OLDMIXON, JOHN,
 Defoe, Daniel............III, 45
 Pope, Alexander..........III, 158
 Sacheverell, Henry.........II, 695
OLIPHANT, F. R.,
 Dunbar, William ....I, 227
 Henryson, Robert ....I, 209
OLIPHANT, JAMES,
 Brontë, Charlotte..........VI, 26
 Austen, Jane.............IV, 615
 Dickens, Charles......VI, 564, 578

OLIPHANT, MARGARET O. W.,
 Addison, Joseph........I, 646, 660
 Ainsworth, William Harrison..
 ....VII, 488
 Airy, Sir George Biddell..VIII, 183
 Alford, Henry............VI, 637
 Alison. Sir Archibald......VI, 522
 Austen, Jane.....IV, 614, 616, 617
 Bage, Robert............IV, 419
 Baillie, Joanna........V, 691, 695
 Barbauld, Anna Lætitia ....V, 26
 Beddoes, Thomas Lovell.....V, 586
 Bentham, Jeremy..........V, 168
 Berkeley, George.....III, 321, 323
 Blake, William............V, 61
 Black, William..........VIII, 394
 Blacklock, Thomas........IV, 131
 Blessington, Countess of....V,594
 Bowring, Sir John.........VI, 665
 Brontë, Charlotte..........VI, 28
 Brontë, Emily.............V, 527
 Brewster, Sir David.......VI, 547
 Brown, John...........VII, 480
 Browning, Elizabeth Barrett..
 ....VI, 240, 242
 Browning, Robert........VII, 693
 Buchanan, George..........I, 317
 Buckle, Henry Thomas....VI, 283
 Burke, Edmund..........IV, 306
 Burns, Robert............IV, 233
 Burton, John Hill........VII, 317
 Byron, George Gordon Lord...
 ....IV, 750, 751
 Calverley, Charles Stuart..VII, 543
 Campbell, John Lord......VI, 259
 Campbell, Thomas.....V, 437, 444
 Canning, George...........V, 69
 Carlyle, Thomas..VII, 249, 254, 259
 Chalmers Thomas.. .....V, 495
 Chambers, Robert.........VI, 620
 Clough, Arthur Hugh .....VI, 252
 Cobbett, William..........V, 274
 Collins, Mortimer.........VII, 82
 Collins, William Wilkie.......
 ....VII, 726, 727
 Cowper, William......IV, 376, 391
 Craik, Dinah Maria Mulock...
 ....VII, 623, 625
 Croker, John Wilson....VI, 73, 76
 Croly, George.............VI, 225
 Cunningham, Allan.........V, 384
 Defoe, Daniel............III, 26
 DeQuincey, Thomas.........
 ....VI, 123, 124, 127
 Dickens, Charles..VI, 562, 576, 578
 Disraeli. Isaac........V, 512, 513
 Dunbar, William ....I, 226
 Edgeworth, Maria..........V, 565
 Eliot, George....VII, 182, 189, 194
 Elliott, Ebenezer ....V, 583
 Faraday, Michael..........VI, 514
 Ferrier, James Frederick..VI, 411
 Ferrier, Susan Edmondstone...
 ....V, 765
 Finlay, George..........VII, 50
 Forster, John...........VII, 68
 Foster, John.............V, 426
 Froude, James Anthony..VIII, 258
 Freeman, Edward Augustus..
 ....VIII, 160
 Galt, John..........V, 335, 337

Gardiner, Samuel Rawson....
 ....VIII, 465
 Gaskell. Elizabeth Cleghorn VI, 432
 Godwin, Mary Wollstonecraft
 ....IV, 329
 Gore, Catherine Grace.....VI, 264
 Grahame, James..........IV, 568
 Creen, John Richard......VII, 512
 Greg, William Rathbone...VII, 322
 Griffin, Gerald............V, 354
 Grote, George............VI, 611
 Guthrie, Thomas.........VI, 739
 Hall, Robert..............V, 112
 Hallam, Arthur Henry......V, 199
 Hallam, Henry...........VI, 175
 Hare, Julius Charles.......VI, 49
 Hazlitt, William..........V, 105
 Heber, Reginald..........V, 39
 Helps, Sir Arthur.........VII, 41
 Hemans, Felicia Dorothea...V, 260
 Hogg, James..............V, 267
 Hood, Thomas...........V, 465
 Hook, Theodore Edward....V, 359
 Hughes, Thomas ....VIII, 347
 Hume, David............III, 666
 Hunt, James Henry Leigh....
 ....VI, 164, 166, 172
 Inchbald, Mrs. Elizabeth...IV, 688
 Irving, Edward........V, 246, 249
 James I. of Scotland.........I, 182
 James, George Payne Rains-
 ford....................VI, 219
 Jameson, Anna..........VI, 216
 Jefferies, Richard........VII, 621
 Jeffrey, Francis Lord........V, 656
 Jerrold, Douglas William....VI, 71
 Kinglake, Alexander William.
 ....VIII, 51, 53
 Kingsley, Henry.........VII, 80
 Knox, John............I, 298, 302
 Lamb, Charles..............V, 241
 Landor, Walter Savage....VI, 381
 Lewes, George Henry.....VII, 140
 Lewis, Matthew Gregory.....
 ....IV, 632, 633
 Lewis, Sir George Cornewall.VI, 338
 Lockhart, John Gibson..V, 755, 758
 Lyell, Sir Charles.........VII, 36
 Lytton, Edward Robert Bul-
 wer....................VIII, 46
 Lytton, Sir Ed ard George
 Bulwer....VI, 685, 692, 693, 697
 Macaulay, Thomas Babington
 Lord.................VI, 110
 Mackenzie, Henry..........V, 114
 Maginn, William.......V, 387, 388
 Mahoney, Francis.........VI, 483
 Maine, Sir Henry James Sum-
 ner....................VII, 653
 Mansel, Henry Longueville.VI, 628
 Marryat, Frederick.........V, 533
 Martineau, Harriet.......VII, 62
 Maturin, Charles Robert....IV, 768
 Maurice, John Frederick Deni-
 son................VI, 649, 655
 Mill, James...............V, 306
 Mill, John Stuart..........VI, 705
 Miller, Hugh..............VI, 65
 Milman, Henry Hart...VI, 538, 541
 Montagu, Lady Mary Wortley
 ....III, 468

INDEX TO CRITICISMS

	Vol. and Page
Montgomery, James	V, 768
Moore, Thomas	V, 717
Mozley, James Bowling	VII, 150
Murchison Sir Roderick Impey	VI, 631, 632
Oliphant, Laurence	VII, 655, 657
Paley, William	IV, 478
Palgrave, Sir Francis	VI, 265
Peacock, Thomas Love	VI, 475
Pollock, Robert	V, 73
Procter, Bryan Waller	VI, 749
Pye, Henry James	IV, 580
Radcliffe, Ann Ward	IV, 720
Ramsay, Allan	III, 408
Reade, Charles	VII, 530, 532, 534
Richardson, Samuel	III, 441, 450
Ritson, Joseph	IV, 435
Robertson, Frederick William	V, 740
Rossetti, Gabriel Charles Dante	VII, 445, 447
Ruskin, John	VIII, 413
Scott, Sir Walter	V, 148
Seeley, Sir John Robert	VIII, 308
Shelley, Mary Wollstonecraft	V, 702
Shelley, Percy Bysshe	IV, 699
Sheridan, Richard Brinsley	IV, 597, 605, 607
Smith, Alexander	VI, 517
Southey, Caroline Anne Bowles	V, 763
Southey, Robert	V, 408
Stanhope, Philip Dormer	III, 605
Stanley, Arthur Penrhyn	VII, 301
Sterling, John	V, 455
Stewart, Dugald	V, 80
Swift, Jonathan	III, 236
Taylor, Sir Henry	VII, 583
Tennyson, Alfred Lord	VIII, 73
Thackeray, William Makepeace	VI, 307
Thirlwall, Connop	VII, 44
Thomson, James	VII, 415
Tighe, Mary	IV, 552
Tooke, John Horne	IV, 572
Trollope, Anthony	VII, 462
Tupper, Martin Farquhar	VII, 734
Warren, Samuel	VII, 107, 108, 109
Whewell, William	VI, 469
Wilberforce, William	V, 203
Wilson, John	V, 748, 749
Wolcot, John	IV, 650
OLIPHANT, ROSAMOND,	
Oliphant, Laurence	VII, 655
OLIPHANT, T. L. KINGTON,	
Johnson, Samuel	III, 761
Mannying, Robert	I, 88
OLIVER, GRACE A.,	
Barbauld, Anna Lætitia	V, 23
Edgeworth, Maria	V, 564, 566
Parker, Theodore	VI, 211
Stanley, Arthur Penrhyn	VII 304
OLLIER, CHARLES,	
Ramsay, Allan	III, 410
OLLIER, C. AND J.,	
Keats, John	IV, 675
OLLIER, EDMUND (?)	
Hunt, James Henry Leigh	VI, 157
OLNEY, HENRY,	
Sidney, Sir Philip	I, 329

	Vol. and Page
OLNEY, RICHARD,	
Marshall, John	V, 284
OMOND, G. W. T.,	
Fletcher, Andrew	II, 612
Stevenson, Robert Louis	VIII, 252
ONDERDONK, JAMES L.,	
Boker, George Henry	VII 766
Bryant, William Cullen	VII, 127, 137
Dana, Richard Henry	VII, 154
Hayne, Paul Hamilton	VII, 594
Holland, Josiah Gilbert	VII, 336
Longfellow, Henry Wadsworth	VII, 393, 395, 397
Holmes, Oliver Wendell	VIII, 299
Lowell, James Russell	VIII, 30, 34
Parsons, Thomas William	VIII, 194
Percival, James Gates	VI, 61
Pierpont, John	VII, 482
Poe, Edgar Allan	V, 550
Read, Thomas Buchanan	VI, 678
Sigourney, Lydia Huntley	VI 452
Simms, William Gilmore	VI, 601
Sprague, Charles	VII, 54
Stoddard, Richard Henry	VIII, 498
Story, William Wetmore	VIII, 320
Timrod, Henry	VI, 510
Very, Jones	VII, 228
Whittier, John Greenleaf	VIII, 128
Wilde, Richard Henry	V 504
Willis, Nathaniel Parker	VI, 492, 501
ONSLOW, ARTHUR,	
Saint-John, Henry	III, 285
Stanhope, Philip Dormer	III, 599
ORD, GEORGE,	
Wilson, Alexander	IV, 581
ORDER FOR ARREST,	
Bunyan, John	II 389
ORDER-BOOK OF THE COUNCIL OF STATE,	
Milton, John	II, 282
ORDERICUS, VITALIS,	
Bede	I, 28
Lanfranc	I, 47
ORDISH, T. FAIRMAN,	
Stowe, John	I, 420
O'REILLY, JOHN BOYLE.	
Phillips, Wendell	VII, 558
ORME, ROBERT	
Dwight, Timothy	IV, 627
ORME, WILLIAM,	
Baxter, Richard	II, 424, 426
Burnet, Thomas	II, 597
Clarke, Adam	V, 185
Clarke, Samuel	II, 749
Cruden, Alexander	III, 546
Cudworth, Ralph	II, 385
Cumberland, Richard	II, 624
Dalrymple, Sir David	IV, 146
Doddridge, Philip	III, 301
Dodwell, Henry	II, 566
Edwards, Jonathan	III, 389
Fuller, Thomas	II, 169
Hales, John	II, 150
Hall, Joseph	II, 146
Henry, Matthew	II, 584
Hobbes, Thomas	II, 323
Horne, George	IV, 144
Howe, John	II, 546
Jenyns, Soame	IV, 32

	Vol. and Page
Lardner, Nathaniel	III, 523
Leighton, Robert	II, 359
Locke, John	II, 532
Lowth, Robert	IV, 28, 29
Lowth, William	III, 63
Lyttelton, George Lord	III, 611
Macknight, James	IV, 408
Owen, John	II, 352
Paley, William	IV, 473
Pearson, John	II, 369
Ray, John	II, 542
Selden, John	II, 139
Usher, James	II, 153
Wakefield, Gilbert	IV, 416
Warburton, William	III, 686, 691
Wesley, Samuel	III, 86
West, Gilbert	III, 369
Whiston, William	III, 305
ORMOND, ALEXAN R T.,	
Edwards, Jonathan	III, 385
ORR, MRS. SOUTHERLAND,	
Browning, Robert	VII, 682, 694
ORTON, JOB,	
Baxter, Richard	II, 426
Doddridge, Philip	III, 300
OSBORN, FRANCIS,	
Bacon, Francis	I, 640
OSBORN, H. F.,	
Owen, Sir Richard	VIII, 173
OSBORN, R D.,	
Doyle, Sir Francis Hastings Charles	VII, 649, 650
OSBOURNE, LLOYD,	
Stevenson, Robert Louis	VIII, 236
OSGOOD, FRANCES SARGENT,	
Poe, Edgar Allan	V, 536
OSGOOD, SAMUEL,	
Bryant, William Cullen	VII, 123
Griswold, Rufus Wilmot	VI, 79
O'SHAUGHNESSY, ARTHUR,	
Poets and Poetry	IV, 9
O'SHEA, JOHN AUGUSTUS,	
Mahoney, Francis	VI, 485
OSSOLI, MARGARET FULLER,	
Allston, Washington	V, 420
Brown, Charles Brockden	IV, 555
Browning, Elizabeth Barrett	VI, 235
Browning, Robert	VII, 690, 697
Carlyle, Thomas	VII, 230
Channing, William Ellery	V, 372
Coleridge, Samuel Taylor	V, 214
Cooper, James Fenimore	V, 684
Crabbe, George	V, 174
Emerson, Ralph Waldo	VII, 363
Fuller, Sarah Margaret	V, 670
Herbert, Edward Lord	II, 96
Longfellow, Henry Wadsworth	VII, 403
Lowell, James Russell	VIII, 31
Mackintosh, Sir James	V, 182
Milton, John	II, 290
Prescott, William Hickling	VI, 189
Scott, Sir Walter	V, 139
Shelley, Percy Bysshe	IV, 706
Southey, Robert	V, 409
Sterling, John	V, 454
Taylor, Sir Henry	VII, 581
Tennyson, Alfred Lord	VIII, 81
Wesley, Charles	IV, 36
Wesley, John	IV, 114

INDEX TO CRITICISMS

	Vol. and Page
Wordsworth, William	V, 634
OSWALD, FELIX L.,	
George, Henry	VIII, 381
OTLEY, DREWRY,	
Hunter, John	IV, 164, 167
OTWAY, THOMAS,	
Shakespeare, William	I, 550
OVERTON, JOHN HENRY,	
Andrews, Lancelot	I, 637
Arnold, Thomas	V, 382
Atterbury, Francis	III, 66, 68
Barrow, Isaac	II, 311
Baxter, Richard	II, 428
Bede	I, 28
Berkeley, George	III, 326
Bull, George	II, 565
Butler, Joseph	III, 313
Byrom, John	III, 470
Cædmon	I, 24
Clarke, Adam	V, 186
Conybeare, John	III, 366
Cowper, William	IV, 392
Dodwell, Henry	II, 566
Hervey, James	III, 396
Horne, George	IV, 144
Horsley, Samuel	IV, 496
Keble, John	VI, 463
Ken, Thomas	II, 569
Kingsley, Charles	VII, 22
Law, William	III, 425, 426, 426, 426, 428, 430
Milman, Henry Hart	VI, 536
More, Henry	II, 375
Ridley, Nicholas	I, 266
Secker, Thomas	III, 522
Stillingfleet, Edward	II, 455
Taylor, Jeremy	II, 211
Waterland, Daniel	III, 103
Wesley, John	IV, 116, 128
Wesley, Samuel	III, 86
Whatley, Richard	VI, 328
OWEN, ARTHUR,	
White, Henry Kirke	IV, 488
OWEN, HENRY,	
Secker, Thomas	III, 521
OWEN, JOHN,	
Oliphant, Laurence	VII, 657
OWEN, RICHARD,	
Hunter, John	IV, 165
Livingstone, David	VI, 729, 731
Whewell, William	VI, 470
OWEN, REV. RICHARD,	
Chambers, Robert	VI, 621
OWEN, SIR RICHARD,	
Owen, Sir Richard	VIII, 172
OWEN, ROBERT DALE,	
Bentham, Jeremy	V, 164
Godwin, William	V, 295
Irving, Edward	V, 247
Owens, Robert	VI, 85
Richardson, Samuel	III, 445
Scott, Sir Walter	V, 144
Shelley, Mary Wollstonecraft	V, 700
OXENDEN, ASHTON,	
Manning, Henry Edward	VIII, 163

PACE, RICHARD,
More, Sir Thomas ... I, 233
PACK, RICHARDSON,
Raleigh, Sir Walter .... I, 593

	Vol. and Page
PACKARD, FREDERICK A.,	
Owen, Robert	VI, 84
PACKARD, GEORGE THOMAS,	
Hawthorne, Nathaniel	VI, 346
PAGE, S. FLOOD,	
Bright, John	VII, 724
PAGET, FRANCIS,	
Romanes, George John	VIII, 283
PAGET, JOHN,	
Macaulay, Thomas Babington Lord	VI, 106
PAGET, STEPHEN,	
Hunter, John	IV, 168
PAINE, ELIZABETH,	
Paine, Thomas	IV, 531
PAINE, H. G.,	
Bunner, Henry Cuyler	VIII, 360
PAINE, ROBERT TREAT JR.	
Washington, George	IV, 357
PAINE, THOMAS,	
Washington, George	IV, 356
PAINTER, FRANKLIN V. N.,	
Addison, Joseph	II, 661
Bunyan, John	II, 405
Cowley, Abraham	II, 202
Dryden, John	II, 507
Edwards, Jonathan	III, 384
Hamilton, Alexander	IV, 466
Mather, Cotton	II, 732
Milton, John	II, 275
Pope, Alexander	III, 195
PALEY, WILLIAM,	
Tucker, Abraham	III, 643
PALFREY, C.,	
Wayland, Francis	VI, 450
PALFREY, JOHN GORHAM,	
Dewey, Orville	VII, 498
Hillhouse, James Abraham	V, 364
Holmes, Oliver Wendell	VIII, 289
Martineau, Harriet	VII, 61
Mather, Cotton	II, 727
Pierpont, John	VI, 481
Prescott, William Hickling	VI, 183
Sedgwick, Catharine Maria	VI, 507
Stanhope, Philip Henry Earl	VII, 46, 47
Winthrop, John	II, 108
PALGRAVE, FRANCIS,	
Cædmon	I, 22
Chaucer, Geoffrey	I, 150, 167
Dunstan	I, 44
Hazlitt, William	V, 103
PALGRAVE, FRANCIS TURNER,	
Arnold, Matthew	VII, 640
Barnes, William	VII, 587
Blake, William	V, 63
Browne, William	II, 77
Browning, Robert	VII, 684, 715
Byron, George Gordon Lord	IV, 764
Byrom, John	III, 470
Church, Richard William	VII, 728
Clare, John	VI, 400
Clough, Arthur Hugh	VI, 248, 252
Coleridge, Samuel Taylor	V, 217
Collins, William	III, 422
Cowley, Abraham	II, 202
Taylor, Jeremy	II, 211
Cowper, William	IV, 380, 382, 382
Crabbe, George	V, 177
Crashaw, Richard	II, 114
Dibdin, Charles	V, 586, 586

	Vol. and Page
Doyle, Sir Francis Hastings Charles	VII, 650
Donne, John	I, 717
Douglas, Gawin	I, 216
Drayton, Michael	I, 708
Drummond, William	II, 107
Dunbar, William	I, 226
Dyer, John	III, 399
Elliott, Ebenezer	V, 584
Goldsmith, Oliver	III, 638
Gray, Thomas	III, 559, 573
Hallam, Henry	VI, 180
Heber, Reginald	V, 40
Herrick, Robert	II, 238
Keats, John	IV, 674, 682
Keble, John	VI, 465
Ken, Thomas	III, 569
Lyte, Henry Francis	V, 500
Marvell, Andrew	II, 319
Milton, John	II, 297
O'Shaughnessy, Arthur William Edgar	VII, 324
Ramsay, Allan	III, 408
Scott, Sir Walter	V, 137, 158
Shairp, John Campbell	VII, 571
Shakespeare, William	I, 458, 567
Shelley, Percy Bysshe	IV, 716
Sidney, Sir Philip	I, 327
Smart, Christopher	III, 592
Southey Robert	V, 405
Spenser, Edmund	I, 389, 400
Tennyson, Alfred Lord	VIII, 82, 92
Thomson, James	III, 261
Toplady, Augustus Montague	III, 681
Trench, Richard Chenevix	VII, 590
Turner, Charles Tennyson	VII, 163
Vaughan, Henry	II, 445
Watson, Thomas	I, 338
Watts, Isaac	III, 252
Wordsworth, William	V, 634
PALMER, H. P.,	
White, Gilbert	IV, 148
PALMER, JAMES F.,	
Hunter, John	IV, 167
PALMER, RAY,	
Holmes, Oliver Wendell	VIII, 295
Longfellow, Henry Wadsworth	VII, 392
PALMER, SAMUEL,	
Blake, William	V, 57
PALMER, ROUNDELL (EARL OF SELBORNE),	
Disraeli, Benjamin	VII, 281
Faber, Frederick William	VI, 333
Keble, John	VI, 460
Maurice, John Frederick Denison	VI, 643
Pusey, Edward Bouverie	VII, 470
Watts, Isaac	III, 250
PANCOAST, HENRY S.,	
Bradstreet, Anne	II, 230
Brown, Charles Brockden	IV, 554
Browning, Robert	VII, 718
Cooper, James Fenimore	IV, 682
Eliot, George	VII, 206
Freneau, Philip	V, 188
Herrick, Robert	II, 241
Johnson, Samuel	III, 766
Kingsley, Charles	VII, 33

INDEX TO CRITICISMS 653

	Vol. and Page
Longfellow, Henry Wadsworth	VII, 389
Motley, John Lothrop	VII, 96
Pinkney, Edward Coate	V, 86
Prescott, William Hickling	VI, 191
Read, Thomas Buchanan	VI, 678
Simms, William Gilmore	VI, 600
Smith, John	I, 700
Spenser, Edmund	I, 400

PAOLI, PASCAL,
Boswell, James.......... IV, 212

PARIS, MATTHEW.
Grossetestet Robert........ I, 73

PARISH, REGISTER.
Massinger, Philip.......... II, 41
Warner, William.......... I, 436

PARK, MUNGO,
Park, Mungo............ IV, 483

PARK, THOMAS,
Cooper, Anthony Ashley ..II, 578
Dodington, George Bubb..III, 458
Oldys, William.......... III 457
Walpole, Horace .... IV, 316

PARKE, JOHN,
Franklin, Benjamin........ IV 82

PARKER, BENJAMIN S.,
Hayne, Paul Hamilton...VII, 592

PARKER, FRANCIS W,
Mann, Horace........ VI, 201, 202

PARKER, GILBERT,
Henley, William Ernest..VIII, 492

PARKER, JOHN,
Morris, William.......... VIII, 334

PARKER, JOSEPH,
Beecher, Henry Ward....VII, 605
Dickens, Charles.......... VI, 559
Gladstone, William Ewart... VIII, 385 392

PARKER, THEODORE,
Adams, John............ V, 50
Beecher, Henry Ward....VII, 604
Buckle, Henry Thomas....VI, 281
Emerson, Ralph Waldo...... VII, 343, 361
More, Henry.............. II, 373
Parker, Theodore......... VI, 205
Parkman, Francis....... VIII, 220
Ware, Henry, Jr.......... V, 432
Washington, George...... IV, 361

PARKES, J. AND MERIVALE, H.,
Junius.............. IV, 646

PARKES, KINETON,
Blake, William.......... V, 64
Hamerton, Philip Gilbert.... VIII, 282
Rossetti, Gabriel Charles Dante .... VII, 454

PARKMAN, F.,
Brown, Thomas.......... IV, 658
Palfrey, John Gorham....VII, 339
Whitefield, George........ III, 548

PARKMAN, FRANCIS,
Cooper, James Fenimore....V, 684
Lowell, James Russell...III, 38
Whittier, John Greenleaf... VIII, 122

PARNELL, ARTHUR,
Defoe, Daniel............ III, 44
Macpherson, James...... IV, 282

PARNELL, THOMAS,
Pope, Alexander.......... III, 160

	Vol. and Page
Saint-John, Henry	III, 282
Swift, Jonathan	III, 228

PARR, LOUISA,
Craik, Dinah Maria, Mulock.. VII, 625, 626

PARR, RICHARD,
Usher, James............ II, 152

PARR, SAMUEL,
Farmer, Richard.......... IV, 341
Fox, Charles James...... IV, 499
Hartley, David .... III, 377
Horner, Francis.......... IV, 629
Hurd, Richard.......... IV, 518
Johnson, Samuel.......... III, 754
Jortin, John............ III, 552
Middleton, Conyers...... III, 280
Porson, Richard.......... IV, 524
Priestley, Joseph.... IV, 446, 452
Roscoe, William.......... V, 117
Stewart, Dugald.......... V, 79
Warburton, William...... III, 690

PARROTT, THOMAS MARC,
Macaulay, Thomas, Babington Lord.............. VI, 101

PARSONS, EUGENE,
Tennyson, Frederick....VIII, 400

PARSONS, THOMAS WILLIAM,
Burns, Robert.......... IV, 256
Emerson, Ralph Waldo...VII, 363
Everett, Edward........ VI, 423
Webster, Daniel.......... V, 721

PARSONS, THEOPHILUS,
Prescott, William Hickling. VI, 182

PARTON, JAMES,
Beecher, Henry Ward....VII, 604
Calhoun, John Caldwell.... V, 675
Defoe, Daniel.......... III, 28
Edwards, Jonathan...... III, 383
Franklin, Benjamin. IV, 89, 96, 98
Gibbon, Edward.......... IV, 175
Greeley, Horace.......... VI, 667
Hamilton, Alexander...... IV, 459
Henry, Patrick.......... IV, 350
Jefferson, Thomas........ V, 42
Paine, Thomas...... IV, 533, 538
Thackeray, William Makepeace .... VI, 311
Washington, George...... IV, 369
Williams, Sir Charles Hanbury .... III 413
Willis, Nathaniel Parker..VI, 492
Wolcot, John.......... IV, 650

PASCAL, BLAISE,
History.............. VI, 5

PASTON, GEORGE,
Cumberland, Richard..IV, 559, 561

PATER, WALTER,
Browne, Sir Thomas...... II, 344
Coleridge, Samuel Taylor... V, 215, 218, 225
Lamb, Charles.......... IV, 241
Mansel, Henry Longueville.VI, 628
Milton, John............ II, 256
Rossetti, Gabriel Charles Dante .... VII, 447
Shakespeare, William..I, 466, 508
Smith, Adam.......... IV, 64
Thackeray, William Makepeace .... VI, 307
Webster, John.......... I, 676
Wordsworth, William..... V, 637

	Vol. and Page
PATIN, GUY,	
Browne, Sir Thomas	II, 340
PATMORE, COVENTRY,	
Allingham, William	VII, 734
Barnes, William	VII, 586
Blake, William	V, 59, 61
Clough, Arthur Hugh..VI, 251, 254
Coleridge, Samuel Taylor...V, 216
Emerson, Ralph Waldo...VII, 374
Gilfillan, George	VII, 151
Keats, John	IV, 680
Lamb, Charles	V, 234
Procter, Adelaide Anne....VI, 395
Procter, Bryan Waller....VI, 746
Rossetti, Gabriel Charles Dante .... VII, 453
Shelley, Percy Bysshe....IV, 697

PATMORE, PETER GEORGE,
Blanchard, Samuel Laman.... V, 480, 481
Blessington Countess of....V, 591
Campbell, Thomas........ V, 436
Hazlitt, William.......... V, 99
Lamb, Charles.......... V, 232
Rogers, Samuel.......... VI, 33
Shelley, Percy Bysshe.....IV, 692
Smith, James............ V, 338

PATRICK, DAVID,
Hearne Thomas.......... III, 88
Hervey, James.......... III, 396

PATRICK, DAVID, AND GROOME, FRANCIS HINDES,
Abbot, George............ I, 726
Agassiz, Louis Jean Rodolphe .... VI, 719
Alcuin .... I, 32
Alexander, Sir William..... II, 34
Alison, Archibald........ V, 341
Alison, Sir Archibald...... VI, 519
Amory, Thomas.......... IV, 47
Armstrong, John.......... III, 697
Asgill, John.............. III, 97
Atterbury, Francis........ III, 97
Aytoun, Sir Robert........ I, 768
Barbour, John............ I, 113
Barclay, John............ I, 618
Barclay, Robert.......... II, 411
Barton, Bernard.......... V, 594
Bayly, Thomas Haynes.....V, 339
Blacklock, Thomas........ IV, 129
Blackmore, Sir Richard.....II, 746
Blair, Hugh.............. IV, 403
Bowles, William Lisle......V, 658
Boyle, Robert............ II, 416
Breton, Nicholas.......... I, 678
Bright, John............ VII, 720
Brooke, Henry.......... III, 713
Brown, Thomas.......... II, 540
Buckland, Francis Trevelyan.. VII, 210
Buckle, Henry Thomas....VI, 278
Bull, George............ II, 564
Burton, John Hill........ VII, 315
Calhoun, John Caldwell....V, 674
Campbell, John Lord...... VI, 257
Capgrave, John.......... I, 192
Carlyle, Thomas........ VII, 238
Cavendish, George........ I, 282
Chalmers, George........ V, 29
Chalmers, Thomas........ V, 489
Channing, William Ellery..V, 365

INDEX TO CRITICISMS

	Vol. and Page
Chapone, Hester	IV, 417
Cheke, Sir John	I, 277
Chillingworth, William	II, 84
Clare, John	VI, 396
Colenso, John William	VII, 522
Combe, George	VI, 88
Corbet, Richard	I, 743
Crashaw, Richard	II, 110
Cruden, Alexander	III, 545
Dalrymple, Sir David	IV, 145
De Burry, Richard	I, 88
Dibdin, Thomas Frognall	V, 506
Dyer, John	III, 398
Elliott, Ebenezer	V, 579
Ellwood, Thomas	II, 575
Everett, Edward	VI, 421
Fairfax, Edward	I, 741
Ferguson, Adams	IV, 609
Fergusson, Robert	III, 639
Ferrier, James Frederick	VI, 410
Ferrier, Susan Edmondstone	V, 763
Flamsteed, John	II, 662
Fox, Charles James	IV, 498
Foxe, John	I, 334
Francis, Sir Philip	IV, 637
Frerè, John Hookham	V, 485
Galt, John	V, 334
Garrison, William Lloyd	VII, 157
Grant, Anne	V, 328
Greeley, Horace	VI, 666
Greg, William Rathbone	VII, 320
Habington, William	II, 134
Haliburton, William Chandler	VI, 455
Hall, Basil	V, 456
Hall, Joseph	II, 143
Hamilton, Sir William	VI, 50
Hamilton, William	III, 335
Harding, John	III, 193
Harrington, James	II, 307
Harrington, Sir John	I, 440
Harris, James	III, 709
Henry the Minstrel	I, 201
Herschel, Sir John Frederick William	VI, 623
Hickes, George	II, 598
Hoadley, Benjamin	III, 422
Home, Henry	III, 711
Horner, Francis	IV, 628
Howe, John	III, 544
Hurd, Richard	IV, 516
Hutton, James	IV, 337
Ireland, William Henry	V, 289
Irving, Edward	V, 245
Jay, John	V, 94
Jevons, William Stanley	VII, 491
Knight, Charles	VI, 741
Kyd, Thomas	I, 358
Lanfranc	I, 47
Law, William	III, 425
Leslie, Sir John	V, 189
Lewis, Sir George Cornewall	VI, 335
Liddon, Henry Parry	VII, 761
Lowth, Robert	IV, 28
Lyell, Sir Charles	VII, 33
Lyttelton, George Lord	III, 610
Macleod, Norman	VII, 660
Maginn, William	V, 385
Maine, Sir Henry James Sumner	VII, 651
Mallet, David	III, 494
Manning, Henry Edward	VIII, 162
Mannyng, Robert	I, 87
Mansel, Henry Longueville	VI, 626
Martineau, James	VIII, 425
Maurice John Frederick Denison	VI, 643
Maxwell, James Clerk	VII, 168
Mickle, William Julius	IV, 40
Montagu, Charles	II, 586
Montgomery, Robert	VI, 46
Moore, John	IV, 426
Müller, Friedrich Max	VIII, 435
Murchison, Sir Roderick Impey	VI, 630
Occleve, Thomas	I, 187
Oldys, William	III, 456
Oliphant, Carolina	V, 476
Oliphant, Margaret O. W.	VIII, 366
Owen, John	II, 351
Owen, Sir Richard	VIII, 170
Owen, Robert	VI, 83
Paulding, James Kirke	226
Peacock, Reginald	I, 189
Pearson, John	II, 368
Priestley, Joseph	IV, 444
Procter, Bryan Waller	VI, 744
Proctor, Richard Anthony	VII, 659
Purchas, Samuel	I, 693
Reeve, Clara	IV, 511
Ritson, Joseph	IV, 435
Robertson, Frederick William	V, 737
Rolle, Richard	I, 91
Roscoe, William	V, 116
Rymer, Thomas	II, 582
Sackville, Charles	II, 552
Sanderson, Robert	II, 178
Saville, Sir Henry	I, 619
Schoolcraft, Henry Rowe	VI, 402
Scott, Michael	I, 68
Settle, Elkanah	II, 690
Seward, Anna	IV, 541
Sheffield, John, Third Earl of Mulgrave	II, 670
Shenstone, William	III, 471
South, Robert	II, 606
Spence, Joseph	III, 519
Stewart, Dugald	V, 76
Stillingfleet, Edward	II, 453
Stowe, John	I, 419
Suckling, Sir John	II, 62
Taylor, Thomas	V, 290
Taylor, William	V, 318
Thomson, James	III, 254
Tillotson, John Robert	II, 437
Toplady, Augustus Montague	III, 681
Tourneur, Cyril	I, 687
Trollope, Frances Milton	V, 329
Udall, Nicholas	I, 278
Urquhart, Sir Thomas	II, 163
Wallis, John	II, 517
Warton, Joseph	IV, 395
Wilberforce, Samuel	VI, 731
Wilberforce, William	V, 199
William of Malmesbury	I, 53
Wilmot, John	II, 335
Wilson, Thomas	III, 366

	Vol. and Page
Young, Arthur	IV, 654
Young, Thomas	V, 86
PATTEE, FRED LEWIS,	
Adams, John	V, 54
Adams, John Quincy	V, 520
Adams, Samuel	IV, 444
Allston, Washington	V, 424
Bancroft. George	VIII, 61
Barlow, Joel	IV, 576
Bradstreet, Anne	II, 228
Brown, Charles Brockden	IV, 557
Cary, Alice	VI, 640
Channing, William Ellery	V, 375
Curtis, George William	III, 188
Dewey, Orville	VII, 499
Dwight, Timothy	VII, 628
Eliot, John	II, 413
Fuller, Sarah Margaret	V, 672
Garrison, William Lloyd	VII, 160
Harte, Francis Bret	VIII, 471
Hayne, aul Hamilton	VII, 594
Henry, Patrick	IV, 353
Holland, Josiah Gilbert	VII, 336
Hutchinson, Thomas	III, 708
Irving, Washington	VI, 148
Jackson, Helen	VII, 575
Lincoln, Abraham	VI, 420
Longfellow, Henry Wadsworth	VIII, 394
Lowell, James Russell	VIII, 33
Mather, Cotton	II, 732
Morris, George Pope	VI, 401
Parkman, Francis	VIII, 224
Parsons, Thomas William	VIII, 194
Paulding, James Kirke	VI, 228
Percival, James Gates	VI, 61
Phillips, Wendell	VII, 558
Pierpont, John	VI, 482
Prescott, William Hickling	VI, 191
Ripley, George	VII, 224
Roe, Edward Payton	VII, 677
Sedgwick, Catharine Maria	VI, 508
Sewall, Samuel	III, 19
Smith, John	I, 699
Sprague, Charles	VII, 54
Stoddard, Richard Henry	VIII, 498
Sumner, Charles	VI, 757
Thoreau, Henry David	VII, 271
Washington, George	IV, 369
Webster, Daniel	V, 729
Winthrop, John	II, 109
PATTEN, SIMON N.,	
Mill, John Stuart	VI, 709
Ricardo, David	IV, 728
PATTERSON, R. H.,	
Wilson, John	V, 747
PATTISON, MARK,	
Bede	I, 27
Bentley, Richard	III, 113, 118
Berkeley, George	III, 331
Bowles, William Lisle	V, 661
Buckle, Henry Thomas	VI, 280
Butler, Joseph	III, 313, 314
Byron, George Gordon Lord	IV, 748
Croker, John Wilson	VI, 75
Hervey, John Lord	III, 130
Hurd, Richard	IV, 517
Jortin, John	III, 552

INDEX TO CRITICISMS 655

	Vol. and Page
Lowth, Robert	III, 29, 30
Milton, John	
	II, 248, 255, 266, 270, 278, 280, 281, 282.
Newman, John Henry	VII, 751
Paley William	IV, 477
Pattison, Mark	VII, 538
Pope, Alexander	
	III, 159, 160, 162, 176, 190
Roscoe, William	V, 118
Ruskin, John	VIII, 415
Smollett, Tobias George	III, 577
Taylor, Jeremy	II, 209
Walpole, Horace	IV, 319
Warburton, William	
	III, 684, 686, 691
Warton, Joseph	IV, 396, 398
PATTON, FRANCIS LANDEY,	
Newman, John Henry	VII, 745
PATTON, J. H.,	
Edwards, Jonathan	III, 387
Hawthorne, Nathaniel	VI, 367
Whittier, John Greenleaf	VIII, 123
PAUL, C. KEGAN,	
Eliot, George	VII, 174
Freeman, Edward Augustus	
	VIII, 156
Godwin, Mary Wollstonecraft	
	IV, 329
Godwin, William	
	V, 295, 297, 299, 301
Keble, John	VI, 459, 461
Kingsley, Charles	VII, 20
Lytton, Sir Edward George Bulwer	VI, 682
Manning, Henry Edward	
	VIII, 163
Newman, John Henry	
	VII, 740, 748
Procter, Bryan Waller	VI, 749
Pusey, Edward Bouverie	VII, 469
PAUL, HERBERT,	
Arnold, Matthew	VII, 647
Creighton, Mandell	VIII, 454, 454
Dickens, Charles	VI, 578, 593
Eliot, George	VII, 189, 192, 199
Gibbon, Edward	IV, 194
Gladstone, William Ewart	
	VIII, 386, 392
Lytton, Sir Edward George Bulwer	VI, 692
Macaulay, Thomas Babington Lord	VI, 109
Savile, George	II, 450
Sterne, Laurence	III, 509
Swift, Jonathan	III, 219, 238
Tennyson, Alfred Lord	
	VIII, 72, 108
PAUL, HOWARD,	
Poe, Edgar Allan	V, 543
PAULDING, JAMES KIRK,	
Barton, Bernard	V, 596
Franklin, Benjamin	IV, 85
Moore, Thomas	V, 715
Washington, George	IV, 359
PAULDING, WILLIAM J.,	
Paulding, James Kirke	VI, 227
PAULI, GEORG REINOLD,	
Alfred the Great	I, 38
Asser	I, 42
Chaucer, Geoffrey	I, 130

	Vol. and Page
Gower, John	I, 173
Henry of Huntingdon	I, 58
William of Malmesbury	I, 54
Wyclif, John	I, 101
PAYN, JAMES,	
Calverley, Charles Stuart	VII, 542
Chambers, Robert	VI, 619, 622
DeQuincey, Thomas	VI, 120
Hunt, James Henry Leigh	VI, 170
Macaulay, Thomas Babington Lord	VI, 112
Martineau, Harriet	VII, 62
Mitford, Mary Russell	VI, 43
Reade, Charles	VII, 528
Smith, Alexander	VI, 516
Spenser, Edmund	I, 385
Whewell, William	VI, 469
PAYNE, E. J.	
Churchill, Charles	III, 481
Saint-John, Henry	III 292
PAYNE, JOHN HOWARD,	
Payne, John Howard	V, 735
PAYNE, WILLIAM MORTON,	
Arnold, Matthew	VII, 636
Black, William	VIII, 396
Buchanan, Robert	VIII, 448
Darwin, Charles Robert	VII, 426
Green, John Richard	VII, 507
Holmes, Oliver Wendell	VIII, 292
Lowell, James Russell	VIII, 41
Morris, William	VIII, 338
Müller, Friedrich Max	VIII, 440
Rossetti, Christina Georgina	
	VIII, 273
Rossetti, Gabriel Charles Dante	
	VII, 449, 455
Ruskin, John	VIII, 424
Shelley, Percy Bysshe	IV, 704
Stevenson, Robert Louis	VIII, 253
Symonds, John Addington	
	VIII 206
Tyndall, John	VIII, 200
Whitman, Walt	VIII, 149
PEABODY, ANDREW PRESTON,	
Barbauld, Anna Lætitia	V, 26
Carlyle, Thomas	VII, 243
Chambers, Thomas	V, 497
Channing, William Ellery	V, 375
Dewey, Orville	VII, 498
Dickens, Charles	VI, 589
Edgeworth, Maria	V, 565
Foster, John	V, 425, 426
Griswold, Rufus Wilmot	VI, 77
Hall, Robert	VII, 111
Hawthorne, Nathaniel	VI, 358
Longfellow, Henry Wadsworth	
	VII, 397
Morris, George Pope	VI, 402
Palfrey, John Gorham	VII, 337
Park, Mungo	IV, 486
Prescott, William Hickling	VI, 188
Quincy, Josiah	VI, 405, 405
Scott Sir Walter	V, 144
Sparks, Jared	VI, 479
Story, Joseph	V, 483
Thackeray, William Makepeace	VI, 309
Thoreau, Henry David	VI, 271
Trench, Richard Chenevix	VII, 120
Trumbull, John	V, 120
Very, Jones	VII, 227

	Vol. and Page
Ware, Henry. Jr	V, 432, 433
Washington. George	IV, 368
Wayland, Francis	VI, 450
Whittier, John Greenleaf	VIII, 120
Wilkinson, Sir John Gardner	
	VII, 52
Wordsworth, William	V, 647
PEABODY, CHARLES,	
Macaulay, Thomas Babington Lord	VI, 94
PEABODY, E.,	
Hopkins, Mark	VII, 615
PEABODY, ELIZABETH PALMER,	
Channing, William Ellery	V, 373
PEABODY, FRANCIS G.,	
Brooks, Phillips	VIII, 229
PEABODY, WILLIAM B. O.	
Addison, Joseph	II, 636
Brougham, Henry Lord	VI, 531
Chaucer, Geoffrey	I, 159
Cowper, William	IV, 387
Edgeworth, Maria	V, 566
Gibbon, Edward	IV, 185
Johnson, Samuel	III, 750
Locke, John	II, 521
Longfellow, Henry Wadsworth	
	VII, 387
Mather, Cotton	II, 730
Robertson, William	IV, 155
Sigourney, Lydia Huntley	VI, 451
Smith, Adam	IV, 55
Sparks, Jared	VI, 477
Sprague, Charles	VII, 53
Stanhope, Philip Henry Earl	
	VII, 46
Taylor, Bayard	VII, 133
Wilson, Alexander	IV, 584
PEACHAM, HENRY,	
Buchanan, George	I, 314
Chaucer, Geoffrey	I, 154
Gower, John	I, 174
PEACOCK, EDWARD,	
Milnes, Richard Monckton	VII, 562
PEACOCK, GEORGE,	
Davy, Sir Humphr	V, 94
Young, Thomas	V, 88
PEACOCK, THOMAS LOVE,	
Bacon, Roger	I, 78
Cowper, William	IV, 386
Shelley, Percy Bysshe	IV, 693
Wordsworth, William	V, 630
PEAKE, RICHARD BRINSLEY,	
Colman, George	IV, 203
Colman, George, Jr	V, 316
Foote, Samuel	III, 672
PEALE, REMBRANDT,	
Washington, George	IV, 359
PEARSON, CHARLES H.,	
Anselm	I, 50
Bede	I, 28
Cædmon	I, 23
Geoffery of Monmouth	I, 56
Map, Walter	I, 62
PEARSON, JOHN,	
Hales, John	II, 149
PEARSON, KARL,	
Wyclif, John	I, 109
PEBODY, CHARLES,	
Jeffrey, Francis Lord	V, 652
PECAUT, FELIX,	
Mann, Horace	VI 202

INDEX TO CRITICISMS

PECK, FRANCIS,
  Milton, John............II, 285
PECK, G. W.,
  Longfellow, Henry Wadsworth
    ....VII, 390
  Melville, Herman.......VIII, 62
PECK, HARRY THURSTON,
  Burnett, James..........IV, 346
  Carew, Thomas...........II, 20
  Caxton, William..........I, 197
  Hutcheson, Francis......III, 244
  Ingersoll, Robert Green.VIII, 404
  Mann, Horace............VI, 199
  Murphy, Arthur..........IV, 481
  Murray, William.........IV, 169
  Oldham, John............II, 349
  Sandys, George...........II, 80
  Simms, William Gilmore...VI, 596
  Trollope, Anthony...VII, 458, 464
  Tucker, Josiah..........IV, 369
  Warner, Charles Dudley.VIII, 441
PECK, SAMUEL MINTURN,
  Holmes, Oliver Wendell.VIII, 297
PEDRICK, J. GALE,
  Scott, Sir Walter.........V, 138
PEGGE, SAMUEL,
  Hall, Edward............I, 260
PEEL, SIR ROBERT,
  Airy, Sir George Biddell.VIII, 183
  Morgan, Lady Sydney Owenson
    ....VI, 192
  Murchison, Sir Roderick Impey
    ....VI, 630
PEELE, GEORGE,
  Chaucer, Geoffrey.........I, 135
  Daniel, Samuel...........I, 613
  Harrington, Sir John......I, 440
  Marlowe, Christopher......I, 354
  Sidney, Sir Philip........I, 330
  Spenser, Edmund..........I, 392
  Watson, Thomas..........I, 337
PELLEW, GEORGE,
  Jay, John................V, 96
PELLISSIER, GEORGES,
  Bacon, Francis...........I, 663
  Chatterton, Thomas......III, 533
PEMBERTON, HENRY,
  Newton, Sir Isaac.........II, 713
PENDARVES, MRS. M.,
  Gay, John..............III, 59
  Swift, Jonathan.........III, 198
PENN, WILLIAM,
  Penn, William...........II, 629
PENNELL, ELIZABETH ROBINS,
  Godwin, Mary Wollstonecraft
    ....IV, 330, 331
PENNIMAN, JOSIAH H.,
  Jonson, Ben..............I, 753
PENNINGTON, MONTAGU,
  Carter, Elizabeth........IV, 491
PENNSYLVANIA JOURNAL,
  Paine, Thomas...........IV, 535
PEPPER, WILLIAM,
  Franklin, Benjamin......IV, 103
PEPYS, SAMUEL,
  Bentley, Richard.....III, 112, 113
  Butler, Samuel..........II, 330
  Cavendish, Margaret......II, 231
  D'Avenant, Sir William...II, 216
  Dryden, John............
    ..II, 470, 471, 471, 471, 473, 482

Evelyn, John............II, 547
Ford, John..............II, 26
Fuller, Thomas..........II, 170
Greville, Sir Fulke......I, 690
Hobbes, Thomas.........II, 323
L'Estrange, Sir Roger....II, 537
Penn, William..........II, 626
Prynne, William........II, 223
Sackville, Charles......II, 552
Sedley, Sir Charles.....II, 508
Shakespeare, William...
  1, 468, 472, 487, 489, 498,
  500, 511, 514, 533, 540
Stillingfleet, Edward....II, 453
Taylor, Jeremy.........II, 206
Webster, John..........I, 670
Wilmot, John...........II, 335
PERCIVAL, C. S.,
  Saxe, John Godfrey.....VII, 616
PERCIVAL, JOHN,
  Arnold, Thomas..........V, 380
PERCIVAL, SIR JOHN,
  Berkeley, George.......III, 324
PERCY, THOMAS,
  Carew, Thomas...........II, 21
  Goldsmith, Oliver......III, 616
  Langland, William.......I, 117
  Percy, Thomas..........IV, 563
  Priestley, Joseph.......IV, 451
  Tyrwhitt, Thomas.......IV, 25
  Warner, William.........I, 436
  Wither, George..........II, 213
PERKINS, F. B.,
  Dickens, Charles.....VI, 567, 577
PERLEY, SIDNEY,
  Garrison, William Lloyd..VII, 160
PEROWNE, J. J. STEWART,
  Pusey, Edward Bouverie..VII, 471
  Thirlwall, Connop.....VII, 42, 44
PERRY, BLISS,
  Scott, Sir Walter........V, 153
PERRY, GEORGE G.,
  Andrews, Lancelot.......I, 636
  Bale, John..............I, 287
  Browne, Sir Thomas......II, 344
  Bull, George...........II, 565
  Burnet, Gilbert.........II, 592
  Butler, Joseph.........III, 315
  Dodwell, Henry.........II, 566
  Hales, John............II, 151
  Hall, Joseph...........II, 148
  Hoadly, Benjamin.......III, 424
  Horne, George..........IV, 145
  Horsley, Samuel........IV, 496
  Hurd, Richard..........IV, 518
  Law, William..........III, 429
  Paine, Thomas..........IV, 538
  Quarles, Francis........II, 77
  Stillingfleet, Edward...II, 454
  Tillotson, John Robert...II, 438
  Wesley, John...........IV, 124
PERRY, JENNETTE BARBOUR,
  Whitman, Walt.........VIII, 150
PERRY, NORA,
  Whitman, Walt.........VIII, 139
  Whittier, John Greenleaf.VIII, 113
PERRY, S. S.,
  Eliot, George..........VII, 100
PERRY, THOMAS SERGEANT,
  Addison, Joseph......II, 640, 645
  Beattie, James.........IV, 434

Burns, Robert..........IV, 261
Carlyle, Thomas.......VII, 266
Clough, Arthur Hugh....VI, 251
Collins, William......III, 421
Cowper, William.......IV, 392
Defoe, Daniel.........III, 37
Dryden, John..........II, 504
Goldsmith, Oliver......III, 624
Gray, Thomas..........III, 559
Lillo, George.........III, 100
Milton, John..........II, 278
Otway, Thomas.........II, 367
Percy, Thomas.........IV, 565
Pope, Alexander.......III, 162
Ramsay, Allan.........III, 408
Swift, Jonathan.......III, 234
Ticknor, George.......VI, 615
Walpole, Horace.......IV, 317
PERRY, W. S.,
  Andrews, Lancelot.......I, 635
  Latimer, Hugh...........I, 267
PETER, WILLIAM,
  Romilly, Sir Samuel....IV, 634
PETERBOROUGH, LORD,
  Burnet, Gilbert.........II, 592
PETERBOROUGH, BISHOP OF,
  Jewell, John............I, 294
PETERKIN, ALEXANDER,
  Burns, Robert......IV, 225, 251
PETERSON, JAMES B.,
  Hume, David...........III, 665
PETHERICK, EDWARD A.,
  Hall, Joseph...........II, 147
PETOWE, HENRY,
  Marlowe, Christopher....I, 353
PFLEIDERER, OTTO,
  Coleridge, Samuel Taylor...V, 226
  Whately, Richard......VI, 328
PHELPS, AUSTIN,
  Burke, Edmund.........IV, 306
  Bushnell, Horace.......VII, 69
  Edwards, Jonathan......III, 387
PHELPS, WILLIAM LYON,
  Akenside, Mark........III, 543
  Finch, Anne, Countess of Winchilsea
    ....II, 668
  Gray, Thomas..........III, 571
  Hamilton, William......III, 337
  Hurd, Richard.........IV, 520
  Lowth, Robert.......IV, 29, 30
  Macpherson, James.....IV, 279
  Mallet, David.........III, 496
  Mason, William........IV, 326
  Parnell, Thomas.......II, 617
  Percy, Thomas.........IV, 565
  Pope, Alexander.......III, 170
  Ramsay, Allan.........III, 411
  Thompson, William.....III, 501
  Warton, Joseph........IV, 398
PHILIP, FRANKLIN,
  Dickens, Charles.......VI, 553
PHILIP, ROBERT,
  Bunyan, John..........II, 394
PHILIP, W.,
  Cooper, James Fenimore....V, 682
PHILIPPEAUX, ABBÉ OF BLOIS
  Addison, Joseph........II, 633
PHILIPS, G. S.,
  Jerrold, Douglas William..VI, 70
PHILIPS, JOHN,
  Philips, John..........II, 563

INDEX TO CRITICISMS 657

	Vol. and Page
Saint-John, Henry	III, 282
PHILIPSON, DAVID,	
Dickens, Charles	VI, 564, 578
PHILLIMORE, ROBERT,	
Lyttelton, George Lord	III, 611
PHILLIPPS, CHARLES,	
Prescott, William Hickling	VI, 186
PHILLIPS, CLAUDE,	
Reynolds, Sir Joshua	IV, 143
PHILLIPS, EDWARD,	
Bradstreet, Anne	II, 229
Breton, Nicholas	I, 678
Chapman, George	I, 732
Daniel, Samuel	I, 614
Davies, Sir John	I, 632
Dekker, Thomas	II, 59
Drayton, Michael	I, 706
Drummond, William	II, 104, 104
Dyer, Sir Edward	I, 428
Etheredge, Sir George	II, 414
Fairfax, Edward	I, 742
Fletcher, John	I, 630
Habington, William	II, 135
Harrington, Sir John	I, 440
Jonson, Ben	I, 760
Kyd, Thomas	I, 359
Lydgate, John	I, 183
Lyly, John	I, 424
Marlowe, Christopher	I, 350, 353
Marston, John	I, 736
Milton, John	II, 243
More, Sir Thomas	I, 236
Occleve, Thomas	I, 187
Raleigh, Sir Walter	I, 599
Shakespeare, William	I, 550
Skelton, John	I, 220
Sternhold, Thomas	I, 261
Surrey, Earl of	I, 257
Sylvester, Joshua	I, 609
Warner, William	I, 436
Wither, George	II, 213
PHILLIPS, JANET (BERYL),	
Oliphant, Margaret O. W.	VIII, 368
PHILLIPS, THOMAS,	
Pole, Reginald	I, 280
Reynolds, Sir Joshua	IV, 141
PHILLIPS, W.,	
Godwin, William	V, 302
Lytton, Sir Edward George Bulwer	VI, 685
PHILLIPS, WENDELL,	
Child, Lydia Maria	VII, 218
Garrison, William Lloyd	VII, 158
Lincoln, Abraham	VI, 417
Martineau, Harriet	VII, 63
Parker, Theodore	VI, 206
PHILLIPS, WILLARD,	
Bryant, William Cullen	VII 117
PHILLPOTTS, EDEN,	
Blackmore, Richard D.	VIII, 432
PIATT, DONN,	
Seward, William Henry	VI, 674
PIATT, JOHN JAMES,	
Prentice, George Denison	VI, 603
PIATT, SARAH M. B.,	
Knowledge	V, 10
PICCIOTTO, JAMES,	
Eliot, George	VII, 192
PICKARD, SAMUEL T.,	
Prentice, George Denison	VI, 604
Whittier, John Greenleaf	VIII, 115

	Vol. and Page
PICKERING, JOHN,	
Prescott, William Hickling	VI, 183
PICKFORD, J.,	
Percy, Thomas	IV, 562
PICTET, MARC-AUGUSTE,	
Edgeworth, Maria	V, 561
PICTON, J ALLANSON,	
Fawcett, Henry	VII, 550, 551
Steele, Sir Richard	II, 767
PIERCE, EDWARD L.,	
Mann, Horace	VI, 202
Sumner, Charles	VI, 752, 758
PIERCE, FRANKLIN,	
Hawthorne, Nathaniel	VI, 343
PIERCE, GILBERT A.,	
Dickens, Charles	VI, 586
PIERCE, WILLIAM,	
Madison, James	V, 312
PIERSON, ARTHUR TAPPAN,	
Hume, David	III, 667
PIGOU, ARTHUR CECIL,	
Browning, Robert	VII, 719
PINCKNEY, CHARLES COTESWORTH,	
Calhoun, John Caldwell	V, 676
PINERO, ARTHUR WING,	
Stevenson, Robert Louis	VIII, 254
PINKERTON, JOHN (ROBERT HERON),	
Barbour, John	I, 113
Colman, George	IV, 202
Dryden John	II, 486
Goldsmith, Oliver	III, 633
Gray, Thomas	III, 564
Hume, David	III, 655
Pope, Alexander	III, 183
Thomson, James	III 258
Walpole, Horace	IV, 310
PIOZZI, HESTER LYNCH (MRS. TRALE),	
Baillie, Joanna	V, 692
Burney, Charles	IV, 588
Carter, Elizabeth	IV, 493
Franklin, Benjamin	IV, 85
Goldsmith Oliver	III, 614
Johnson, Samuel	III, 724
Murphy, Arthur	VI, 481
Reynolds, Sir Joshua	IV, 137
Scott, Sir Walter	V, 141
Shelley, Mary Wollstonecraft	V, 702
Thomson, James	III, 256
PITMAN, BENJAMIN H.,	
Hopkins, Samuel	IV, 438
PITMAN, ROBERT C.,	
Browning, Elizabeth Barrett	VI, 246
Coleridge, Samuel Taylor	V, 226
Robertson, Frederick William	V, 740
Stanley, Arthur Penrhyn	VII, 305
PITT, CHRISTOPHER,	
Secker, Thomas	III, 521
Spence, Joseph	III, 519
PITT, WILLIAM,	
Smith, Adam	IV, 61
PLANCHE, JAMES ROBINSON,	
Croly, George	IV, 224
Hood, Thomas	V, 459
Irving, Washington	V, 137
Knowles, James Sheridan	VI, 286
Lover, Samuel	VI, 543

	Vol. and Page
Thackeray, William Makepeace	VI, 294
PLARR, VICTOR.	
White, Gilbert	IV, 148
PLATTS, CHARLES,	
Leslie, Sir John	V, 189
PLAYFAIR, JOHN,	
Hutton, James	IV, 337, 338
Napier, Sir John	I, 588
Newton, Sir Isaac	II, 723
Taylor, Brooks	III, 51
Wallis, John	II, 517
PLAYFAIR, SIR R. LAMBERT,	
Bruce, James	IV, 208
PLAYFAIR, WILLIAM,	
Smith, Adam	IV, 55
PLINY, THE YOUNGER,	
History	VI, 5
PLUMER, JOHN,	
Clare, John	VI, 397
PLUMPTRE, EDWARD HAYES,	
Bacon, Roger	I, 79
Ken, Thomas	II, 567
Müller, Friedrich Max	VIII, 437
Newman, John Henry	VII, 752
PLUNKETT, MRS. H. M.,	
Holland, Josiah Gilbert	VII, 334
POE, EDGAR ALLAN,	
Allston, Washington	V, 418
Bancroft, George	VIII, 58
Boucicault, Dion	VII, 763
Brainard, John Gardiner Calkins	V, 84
Browning, Elizabeth Barrett	VI, 235, 236, 237, 243
Brownson, Orestes Augustus	VII, 73
Bryant, William Cullen	VII, 110, 116, 117, 121
Carlyle, Thomas	VII, 261
Channing, William Ellery	V, 371
Child, Lydia Maria	VII, 218, 221
Coleridge, Samuel Taylor	V, 219
Dana, Richard Henry	VII, 155
Davidson, Lucretia Maria	V, 27
Defoe, Daniel	III, 35
Dickens, Charles	VI, 565, 566
Drake, Joseph Rodman	VI, 660
Emerson, Ralph Waldo	VII, 361
Everett, Edward	VI, 422
Fuller, Sarah Margaret	V, 664, 670, 670
Fullerton, Georgiana Charlotte Lady	VII, 567
Gibbon, Edward	IV, 184
Greeley, Horace	VI, 666
Griswold, Rufus Wilmot	VI, 77, 79
Halleck, Fitz-Greene	VI, 494, 496, 497, 498
Hawthorne, Nathaniel	VI, 351, 364
Heber, Reginald	V, 39
Holmes, Oliver Wendell	VII, 286
Hood, Thomas	V, 462
Horne, Richard Hengist	VII, 546, 546
Irving, Washington	VI, 148
James George Payne Rainsford	VI, 218
Lever, Charles James	VI, 652
Longfellow, Henry Wadsworth	VII, 389, 389, 402, 402

INDEX TO CRITICISMS

	Vol. and Page
Lowell, James Russell	VIII, 27, 30
Lytton, Sir Edward George Bulwer	VI, 695
Macaulay, Thomas Babington Lord	VI, 109
Marryat, Frederick	V, 531
Moore, Thomas	V, 712, 716
Morris, George Pope	VI, 401
Neal, John	VII, 78
Osgood, Francis Sargent	V, 677, 678, 680
Palfrey, John Gorham	VII, 339
Paulding, James Kirke	VI, 226
Pierpont, John	VI, 481
Pinkney, Edward Coate	V, 86
Poe Edgar Allan	V, 535, 551
Sedgwick Catharine Maria	VI, 505, 508
Shelley, Percy Bysshe	IV, 706
Sigourney, Lydia Huntley	VI, 451
Simms, William Gilmore	III, 598
Southey, Robert	V, 413
Sparks, Jared	VI, 476
Sprague, Charles	VII, 53
Taylor, Bayard	VII, 131
Tennyson, Alfred Lord	VIII, 101
Tuckerman, Henry Theodore	VI, 642
Whipple, Edwin Percy	VII, 595
Whittier, John Greenleaf	VIII, 119
Wilde, Richard Henry	V, 503
Willis, Nathaniel Parker	VI, 486, 489, 491, 494, 496
POLE, REGINALD,	
Fisher, John	I, 230
POLLARD, A. F.,	
Burke, Edmund	IV, 309
Froude, James Anthony	VIII, 260
Junius	IV, 647
Swift, Jonathan	III, 217
Wilson, Sir Thomas	I, 313
POLLARD, ALFRED W.,	
Chaucer, Geoffrey	I, 130, 136, 139, 147, 169
Herrick, Robert	II, 234
POLLOCK, SIR FREDERICK,	
Lewes, George Henry	VII, 141
Maine, Sir Henry James Sumner	VII, 652
Milton, John	II, 295
Tennyson, Alfred Lord	VIII, 68
POLLOCK, LADY,	
Disraeli, Benjamin	VII, 282
POLLOCK, W. F.,	
Austen, Jane	IV, 620
POLLOCK, WALTER HERRIES,	
Austen, Jane	IV, 625
Edgeworth, Maria	V, 572
Thackeray, William Makepeace	VI, 305, 312
Trollope, Anthony	VII, 456, 461
POLLOK, ROBERT,	
Byron, George Gordon Lord	IV, 757
Pollok, Robert	V, 72
POND, ENOCH,	
Hopkins, Samuel	IV, 439
Mather, Increase	II, 690
POND, JAMES BURTON,	
Arnold, Sir Edwin	VIII, 502
Arnold, Matthew	VII, 631
Beecher, Henry Ward	VII, 602

	Vol. and Page
Curtis, George William	VIII, 186
Emerson, Ralph Waldo	VII, 354
Garrison, William Lloyd	VII, 159
Ingersoll, Robert Green	VIII, 402
O'Reilly, John Boyle	VII, 768
Phillips, Wendell	VII, 557
Stanley, Sir Henry Morton	VIII, 507
PONSONBY, MARY E.,	
Eliot, George	VII, 180, 209
POOLE, R. L.,	
Bacon, Roger	I, 81
Erigena	I, 35
Scotus, Duns	I, 87
William of Occam	I, 91
POOLE, REGINALD STUART,	
Edwards, Amelia Ann Blandford	VIII, 176
Lane, Edward William	VII, 83
POOLE, STANLEY LANE,	
Addison, Joseph	II, 661
Arnold, Sir Edwin	VIII, 503
Lane, Edward William	VII, 84, 84
Ockley, Simon	II, 669
Steele, Sir Richard	II, 761
Swift, Jonathan	III, 207, 215, 216, 234
POOLE, W. F.,	
Henry, Patrick	IV, 350
POOR, HENRY V.,	
Smith, Adam	IV, 66
POORE, LAURA ELIZABETH,	
Gray, Thomas	III, 562
Pope, Alexander	III, 160
Shakespeare, William	I, 569
POORE, BEN: PERLEY,	
Adams, John Quincey	V, 518
Benton, Thomas Hart	VI, 87
Everett, Edward	VI, 424
POPE, ALEXANDER,	
Addison, Joseph	II, 632, 633, 644, 647
Arbuthnot, John	III, 81, 83
Atterbury, Francis	III, 64
Bacon, Francis	I, 641, 665
Beaumont, Sir John	I, 680
Behn, Aphra	II, 409
Bentley, Richard	III, 119, 119, 121
Berkeley, George	III, 319
Blackmore, Sir Richard	II, 746
Broome, William	III, 238, 239
Budgell, Eustace	III, 91
Butler, Samuel	II, 331
Chapman, George	II, 728
Chaucer, Geoffrey	I, 156, 156
Cibber, Colley	III, 370, 374, 374
Congreve, William	II, 734
Cowley, Abraham	II, 194, 194, 198, 198
Crashaw, Richard	II, 111
Critic, The	II, 5
Daniel, Samuel	I, 613
D'Avenant, Sir William	II, 217, 218
Defoe, Daniel	II, 45
Dennis, John	III, 75, 75, 77
Dillon, Wentworth	II, 360
Drama, The	VII, 5
Dryden, John	II, 464, 468, 487, 496, 496
D'Urfey, Thomas	II, 687
Farquhar, George	II, 558

	Vol. and Page
Fenton, Elijah	III, 20, 20
Garth, Sir Samuel	II, 664
Gay, John	III, 53, 53, 56
Gower, John	I, 175
Granville, George	III, 88
Hearne, Thomas	III, 89
Hervey, John	III, 127
Hill, Aaron	III, 278
Hughes, John	II, 667
James I. of Scotland	I, 182
Jonson, Ben	I, 747
Manley, Mrs. Mary de la Riviere	II, 693
Milton, John	II, 258, 285
Montagu, Charles	II, 586
Montagu, Lady Mary Wortley	III, 460, 464
Murray, William	IV, 169
Newton, Sir Isaac	II, 713, 713, 721
Oldham, John	II, 350
Otway, Thomas	II, 366
Oldmixon, John	III, 124
Parnell, Thomas	II, 615
Philips, Ambrose	III, 273, 273, 274, 275
Philips, John	II, 563
Poets and Poetry	IV, 6
Pope, Alexander	III, 144, 160, 163, 164, 165, 167, 168, 172, 174
Prior, Matthew	II, 673, 676
Quarles, Francis	II, 77
Raleigh, Sir Walter	I, 606
Rowe, Nicholas	II, 618, 621
Rymer, Thomas	II, 583
Sacksville Charles	II, 552, 555
Saint-John, Henry	III, 283, 292
Savage, Richard	III, 132, 132
Secker, Thomas	III, 521
Sedley, Sir Charles	II, 509
Shadwell, Thomas	II, 434
Shakespeare, William	I, 551
Sheffield, John, Third Earl of Mulgrave	II, 670, 671, 671
Sidney, Sir Philip	I, 331
Skelton, John	I, 220
Southerne, Thomas	III, 239
Sprat, Thomas	II, 573
Spenser, Edmund	I, 375, 380, 394
Suckling, Sir John	II, 63
Surrey, Earl of	I, 257
Swift, Jonathan	III, 197, 217
Tate, Nahum	II, 589
Temple, Sir William	II, 457
Theobald, Lewis	III, 141
Tickell, Thomas	III, 104
Vanbrugh, Sir John	II, 706
Waller, Edmund	II, 380
Walsh, William	II, 560, 560
Warburton, William	III, 689
Wilmot, John	II, 336, 338
Wither, George	II, 213
Wycherley, William	II, 599, 604
PORSON, RICHARD,	
Gibbon, Edward	IV, 180, 195
Hawkins, Sir John	IV, 52
Taylor, Thomas	V, 291
PORTER, CHARLOTTE,	
Browning, Robert	VII, 687

INDEX TO CRITICISMS

PORTER, CHARLOTTE, AND CLARKE, HELEN A.,
Browning, Robert........VII, 715
PORTER, DELIA LYMAN,
Eliot, George............VII, 206
Green, John Richard.....VII, 507
PORTER, MRS. GERALD,
Oliphant, Margaret O. W. VIII, 367
PORTER, JANE,
Chatterton, Thomas......III, 536
PORTER, MARIA S.,
Alcott, Louisa May......VII, 668
Parsons, Thomas William VIII, 192
PORTER, MRS. MARY,
Kinglake, Alexander William..
..................VIII, 54
PORTER, NOAH,
Bacon, Francis............I, 651
Burnet, Gilbert...........II, 594
Bushnell, Horace.........VII, 70
Butler, Joseph...........III, 315
Chaucer, Geoffrey.........I, 163
Dickens, Charles.........VI, 585
Edwards, Jonathan.......III, 392
Eliot, George............VII, 183
Hamilton, Sir William....VI, 55
Hartley, David..........III, 379
Hawthorne, Nathaniel....VI, 366
Hutcheson, Frances......III, 246
Huxley, Thomas Henry..VIII, 9
Lewes, George Henry....VII, 139
Literature...............I, 9
Mill, John Stuart........VI, 715
Milman, Henry Hart.........
................VI, 535, 538
Pope, Alexander.........III, 189
Sidney, Sir Philip..........I, 329
Silliman, Benjamin......VI, 407
Smith, Adam.............IV, 59
South, Robert............II, 608
Stanhope, Philip Henry Earl..
..................VII, 47
Ticknor, George..........VI, 617
Tyndall, John...........VIII, 197
Whately, Richard........VI, 327
PORTEUS, BIELBY,
Beattie, James...........IV, 430
Paine, Thomas...........IV, 536
Paley, William...........IV, 473
Secker, Thomas..........III, 522
POSNETT, HUTCHESON MACAULAY,
Milton, John.............II, 295
Wordsworth, William.....V, 642
POSTBOY,
Dryden, John............II, 463
POSTE, BEALE,
Geoffery of Monmouth.....I, 55
POTT, ALFRED,
Liddon, Henry Parry....VII, 761
POTTER, HELEN,
Drama, The.............VII, 10
POTTER, HENRY C.,
Holland, Josiah Gilbert..VII, 335
POTTS, WILLIAM,
Wesley, Charles..........IV, 35
POULTON, EDWARD B.,
Darwin, Charles Robert..VII, 426
Huxley, Thomas Henry..VIII, 327
POWELL, B.,
Newton, Sir Isaac........II, 713

POWELL, E. P.,
Franklin, Benjamin.......IV, 91
Hamilton, Alexander.....IV, 465
Paine, Thomas...........IV, 536
POWELL, G. H.,
Calverley, Charles Stuart..VII, 544
Dodgson, Charles Lutwige..
..................VIII, 399
Smith, Horace............V, 598
POWELL, THOMAS,
Browning, Robert.......VII, 687
Bryant, William Cullen...VII, 117
Cooper, James Fenimore...V, 684
Dana, Richard Henry....VII, 156
Emerson, Ralph Waldo......
.................VII, 362, 389
Fuller, Sarah Margaret.....V, 671
Halleck, Fitz-Greene......VI, 499
Longfellow, He..ry Wadsworth
..................VII, 391
Osgood, Francis Sargent....V, 678
Poe, Edgar Allan........V, 537, 557
Prescott, William Hickling.VI, 186
Sparks, Jared...........VII, 477
Tennyson, Alfred Lord..VIII, 80
Willis, Nathaniel Parker....
................VI, 489, 491
POWER, D'ARCY,
Hunter, John............IV, 168
POWER, HENRY,
Bacon, Francis............I 657
POWER, J. O'CONNOR
Burke, Edmund..........IV, 301
POWER, MISS,
Blessington, Countess of....V, 591
POWERS, FRED PERRY,
Lecky, William E. H....VIII, 489
POWERS, HORATIO NELSON,
Arnold, Matthew........VII, 642
Bryant, William Cullen...VII, 114
Burns, Robert............IV, 263
Emerson, Ralph Waldo...VII, 346
Hamerton. Philip Gilbert....
................VIII, 280, 281
Pater, Walter Horatio...VIII, 276
POYNTER, EDWARD J.
Ruskin, John...........VIII, 415
PRAED, WINTHROP MACKWORTH,
Keble, John............VI, 461
PRENTICE, GEORGE DENISON,
Clay, Henry..............V, 730
PRESCOTT, J. E.,
Faber, Frederick William..VI, 333
Watts, Isaac ....III, 251
Wesley, Charles..........IV, 38
PRESCOTT, WILLIAM HICKLING,
Addison, Joseph..........II, 650
Bailie, Joanna............V, 693
Bancroft, Ceorge........VIII, 58
Brown, Charles Brockden..
.................IV, 554, 555
Bryant, William Cullen...VII, 119
Burns, Robert............IV, 253
Byron, George Gordon Lord
..................IV, 758
Channing, William Ellery...V, 371
Cooper, James Fenimore...V, 683
Cunningham, Allan........V, 383
Edgeworth, Maria........V, 569

Fairfax, Edward..........I, 742
Gibbon, Edward.........IV, 182
Hall, Basil..............V, 458
Hallam, Henry........VI, 175, 177
Halleck, Fitz-Greene......VI, 496
Irving, Washington...VI, 146, 147
Johnson, Samuel..III, 750, 750, 757
Lockhart, John Gibson......
.............V, 755, 756, 757
Mathias, Thomas James....V, 289
Milman, Henry Hart......VI 537
Milton, John......II, 246, 262, 281
Mitford, William..........V, 71
Motley, John Lothrop......
..................VII, 89, 91
Pole, Reginald............I, 281
Pope, Alexander.........III, 185
Prescott, William Hickling..
..................VI, 188
Radcliffe, Ann Ward......IV, 719
Ramsay, Allan...........III, 410
Robertson, William......IV, 163
Roscoe, William..........V, 118
Scott, Sir Walter......V, 142, 158
Strickland, Agnes........VI, 768
Ticknor, George.........VI, 616
Wordsworth, William.....VI, 631
PRESIDENT AND FELLOWS OF HARVARD COLLEGE,
Berkeley, George ....III, 319
PRESSENSÉ, DE FRANCIS,
Carlyle, Thomas.........VII, 273
Robertson, Frederick William
................V, 738, 740
PRESTON, COL. J. T. L.,
Poe, Edgar Allan........V, 539
PRESTON, HARRIET WATERS,
Arnold, Matthew........VII, 636
Browning, Robert.......VII, 686
Ingelow, Jean..........VIII, 370
James I of Scotland........I, 181
Lovelace, Richard........II, 161
Oliphant, Margaret O. W.,..
...................VIII, 369
Suckling, Sir John.........II, 66
Wotton, Sir Henry........II, 19
PRESTON, LORD,
Fletcher, Andrew........II, 610
PRESTON, MARGARET J,
Hayne, Paul Hamilton...VII, 591
Hawthorne, Nathaniel....VI, 369
Keats, John.............IV, 674
Rossetti, Gabriel Charles
Dante ....VII, 453
PRESTON-THOMAS, H.,
Helps, Sir Arthur........VII, 39
PREVOST, ABBE,
Lillo, George............III, 99
Richardson, Samuel......III, 438
PREVOST, F. C. BLAGDON F.
Moore, John............IV, 427
PRICE, CHARLOTTE A.,
Burns, Robert...........IV, 240
PRICE, JAMES,
Mangan, James Clarence.....
...................V, 601
PRICE, WARWICK JAMES,
Pope, Alexander.........III, 167
PRIDEAUX, HUMPHREY,
Echard, Laurence........III, 22
Locke, John.............II, 518

660 INDEX TO CRITICISMS

PRIESTLEY, JOSEPH,
  Gibbon, Edward..........IV, 179
  Geoffery of Monmouth.......I, 55
  Hartley, David............III, 378
  Hume, David.............III, 655
  Paine, Thomas............IV, 537
  Priestley, Joseph.....IV, 445, 447
PRINCE, THOMAS,
  Mather, Cotton............II, 727
  Prince, Thomas...........III, 401
PRINGLE, G. O. S.,
  Mill, John Stuart.........VI, 707
PRINGLE, SIR JOHN,
  Priestley, Joseph.........IV, 449
PRIOR, SIR JAMES,
  Boswell, James.......IV, 211. 217
  Burke, Edmund......IV, 291, 300
  Gifford, William............V, 32
  Johnson, Samuel..........III, 728
  Malone, Edmond..........IV, 579
  Paine, Thomas............IV, 537
  Shakespeare, William......I, 543
  Steevens, George.........IV, 409
  Swift, Jonathan..........III, 02
PRIOR, MATTHEW,
  Atterbury, Francis........III, 67
  Bentley, Richard..........III, 110
  Butler, Samuel............II, 334
  Knowledge ....V, 6
  Milton, John..............II, 284
  Pope, Alexander..........III, 168
  Prior, Matthew............II, 673
  Sackville, Charles.........II, 553
  Spenser, Edmund..........I, 379
PRITCHARD, CHARLES,
  Faraday, Michael.........VI, 512
PROCLAMATION IN GAZETTE,
  Carte, Thomas............III, 337
PROCTER, BRYAN WALLER (BARRY CORNWALL),
  Beddoes, Thomas Lovell....V, 585
  Blessington, Countess of...V, 591
  Books ....III, 9
  Bowles, William Lisle......V, 659
  Brontë, Charlotte..........VI, 28
  Browning, Elizabeth Barrett..
  ....VI, 238
  Byron, George Gordon Lord..
  ....IV, 753
  Campbell, Thomas.........V, 437
  Carlyle, Thomas..........VII, 266
  Coleridge, Samuel Taylor...V, 212
  Cooper, James Fenimore....V, 679
  Crabbe, George............V, 171
  Croly, George............VI, 224
  DeQuincey, Thomas..VI, 119, 127
  Godwin, William..........V, 295
  Hawthorne, Nathaniel.....VI, 353
  Hazlitt, William.......V, 100, 104
  Hood, Thomas............V, 460
  Hunt, James Henry Leigh....
  ....VI, 159
  Irving, Edward............V, 247
  Keats, John...............IV, 677
  Lamb, Charles............V, 233
  Lamb, Mary Ann..........V, 508
  Moore, Thomas......V, 709, 717
  Rogers, Samuel...........VI, 59
  Scott, Sir Walter.........V, 143
  Shakespeare, William......I, 559
  Wordsworth, William..V, 614, 637

PROCTER, MRS. BRYAN WALLER,
  Milnes, Richard Monckton..
  ....VII, 560
PROCTER, L. J.,
  Livingstone, David.......VI, 726
PROCTOR, L. B.,
  Kent, James..............V, 501
PROCTOR, RICHARD A.,
  Darwin, Charles Robert..VII, 426
  Dickens, Cha les.........VI, 573
  Flamsteed, John..........II, 663
  Herschel, Sir John Frederick William ....VI, 625
  Somerville, Mary.........VI, 659
PROTHERO, GEORGE WALTER,
  Creighton, Mandell....VIII, 454
  Freeman, Edward Augustus..
  ....VIII, 160
  Grosseteste, Robert.........I, 73
  Seeley, Sir John Robert....
  ....VIII, 308, 310
PROTHERO, ROWLAND EDMUND,
  Byron, George Gordon Lord
  ....IV, 765
  Gibbon, Edward........IV, 194
  Holmes, Oliver Wendell.....
  ....VIII, 286, 296
  Kingsley, Charles........VII, 26
  Mallet, David............III, 496
  Stanley, Arthur Penrhyn....
  ....VII, 300, 302, 303
  Wesley, John.............IV, 125
  Whittier, John Greenleaf....
  ....VIII, 124
PROWSE, W. J.,
  Smollett, Tobias George...III, 584
PRYME, ABRAHAM DE LA,
  Newton, Sir Isaac.........II, 710
PUBLICK ADVERTISER,
  Sterne, Laurence.........III, 505
PUFFENDORF, SAMUEL,
  Bacon, Francis.............I, 657
PULLING, F. S.,
  Reynolds, Sir Joshua......IV, 142
PULTENEY, RICHARD,
  Ray, John.................II, 542
PUNCH,
  Blackie, John Stuart....VIII, 304
PUNSHON, WILLIAM MORLEY,
  Knowledge ....V, 80
  Macaulay, Thomas Babington Lord ....VI, 110
PURCELL, E.,
  Buchanan, Robert......VIII, 447
  Jefferies, Richard........VII, 621
  Oliphant, Laurence......VII, 657
  Pattison, Mark...........VII, 541
PURCELL, EDMUND SHERIDAN,
  Manning, Henry Edward....
  ....VIII, 165, 167
  Newman, John Henry....VII, 742
PURCHAS, SAMUEL,
  Purchas, Samuel...........I, 693
PURNELL, THOMAS,
  Steele, Sir Richard........II, 754
PURVES, D. LAING,
  Swift, Jonathan..........III, 202
PURVES, JAMES,
  Boswell, James............IV, 218

Fletcher, Andrew..........II, 611
Overbury, Sir Thomas.......I, 443
Thoreau, Henry David....VI, 273
PUSEY, EDWARD BOUVERIE,
  Keble, John..............VI, 462
  Pusey, Edward Bouverie.VII, 466
PUTNAM, ALFRED P.,
  Clarke, James Freeman...VII, 673
  Parker, Theodore.........VI, 210
  Pierpont, John...........VI, 482
  Very, Jones.............VII, 227
  Williams, Helen Maria......V, 75
PUTNAM, GEORGE P.,
  Irving, Washington.......VI, 135
PUTNAM, JAMES O.,
  Kingsley, Charles........VII, 21
  Martineau, Harriet......VII, 57
  Washington, George......IV, 361
PUTTENHAM, GEORGE,
  Chaucer, Geoffrey.....II, 141, 154
  Dyer, Sir Edward..........I, 428
  Gascoigne, George..........I, 307
  Gower, John...............I, 174
  Harding, John.............I, 193
  Heywood, John............I, 305
  Langland, William.........I, 117
  Lydgate, John.............I, 183
  Raleigh, Sir Walter........I, 599
  Skelton, John.............I, 220
  Sternhold, Thomas........I, 261
  Vaux, Thomas Lord.......I, 276
  Wyatt, Sir Thomas........I, 250
PYE, HENRY JAMES,
  Chatterton, Thomas......III, 529
  Shakespeare, William..I, 484, 555
  Warton, Thomas..........IV, 76
PYM, JOHN,
  Raleigh, Sir Walter.........I, 592
PYNCHON, THOMAS RUGGLES,
  Butler, Joseph...........III, 317

QUARLES, FRANCIS,
  Fletcher, Giles..........I, 623
  Fletcher, Phineas........II, 115
  Ridley, Nicholas...........I, 266
QUAYLE, WILLIAM A.,
  Bancroft, George........VIII, 60
  Tennyson, Alfred Lord..VIII, 110
QUEENSBERRY, CATHERINE HYDE, DUCHESS,
  Gay, John.............III, 53, 59
QUICK, ROBERT HERBERT,
  Ascham, Roger...........II, 290
  Literature................I, 8
  Locke, John..............II, 529
  Milton, John.............II, 280
  Spencer, Herbert.......VIII, 479
QUILLER-COUCH, ARTHUR THOMAS,
  Browne, William..........II, 77
  Burns, Robert...........IV, 266
  Calverley, Charles Stuart.VII, 543
  Carlyle, Thomas........VII, 272
  Chaucer, Geoffrey........I, 169
  Coleridge, Samuel Taylor...V, 213
  Daniel, Samuel...........I, 612
  Hazlitt, William..........V, 105
  Jefferies, Richard........VII, 621
  Kinglake, Alexander William..
  ....VIII, 50, 53
  Kingsley, Charles........VII, 32

INDEX TO CRITICISMS

	Vol. and Page
Kingsley, Henry	VII, 81
Milton, John	II, 274
Reade, Charles	VII, 530
Scott, Sir Walter	V, 133
Shakespeare, William	I, 460
Spenser, Edmund	I, 400
Sterne, Laurence	III, 511
Stevenson, Robert Louis	VIII, 235
Swift, Jonathan	III, 205
Tennyson, Alfred Lord	VIII, 108
Thackeray, William Makepeace	VI, 309, 319
Wordsworth, William	V, 628
Wotton, Sir Henry	II, 19

QUILLINAN, EDWARD,
Clough, Arthur Hugh	VI, 251

QUILTER, HARRY.
Collins, William Wilkie	VII, 726
Rossetti, Gabriel Charles Dante	VII, 442
Stanley, Sir Henry Morton	VIII, 509

QUINCY, EDMUND,
Adams, John	V, 53
Ames, Fischer	IV, 528
Barbauld, Anna Lætitia	V, 25
Disraeli, Benjamin	VII, 289
Parker, Theodore	VI, 210
Rumford, Count	IV, 593
Sprague, Charles	VII, 53

QUINCY, JOSIAH,
Adams, Hannah	V, 124
Adams, John Quincy	V, 517
Channing, William Ellery	V, 369
Everett, Edward	VI, 424
Hillhouse, James Abraham	V, 363
Marshall John	V, 282
Mather, Cotton	II, 728
Story, Joseph	V, 483
Ticknor, George	VI, 614
Webster, Daniel	V, 722

QUINCY, JOSIAH, JR.
Macaulay, Catherine	IV, 134

QUINT, WILDER D.,
Fiske, John	VIII, 455

QUINTON, AMELIA STONE,
Jackson, Helen Hunt	VII, 573

RADCLIFF, EBENEZER.
Lardner, Nathaniel	III, 522

RAE, WILLIAM FRASER,
Campbell, Thomas	V, 439
Cowper, William	IV, 374
Crabbe, George	V, 176
Eliot, George	VII, 202
Fox, Charles James	IV, 504
Francis, Sir Philip	IV, 638
Junius	IV, 643
Lewes, George Henry	VII, 138
Moore, Thomas	V, 714
Oliphant, Laurence	VII, 656
Pitt, William	IV, 511
Russell, John Earl	VII, 146
Sheridan, Richard Brinsley	IV, 598, 609
Sheridan, Thomas	IV, 46
Walpole, Horace	IV, 313
Wilkes, John	IV, 336

RAE, JOHN.
Logan, John	IV, 45
Smith, Adam	IV, 56

	Vol. and Page
RAFFETY, FRANK W.,	
Bacon, Francis	I, 652
Green, John Richard	VII, 509
RAGSDALE, JOHN,	
Collins, William	III, 415
RAIKES, E.,	
Thackeray, William Makepeace	VI, 308
RAINSFORD, WILLIAM STEPHEN,	
Brooks, Phillips	VIII, 228
RALEIGH, WALTER,	
Austen, Jane	IV, 623
Beckford, William	V, 449
Behn, Aphra	II, 408
Bentham, Jeremy	V, 169
Brontë, Charlotte	VI, 30
Brooke, Henry	III, 715
Burney, Frances	V, 347
Bunyan, John	II, 405
Burns, Robert	IV, 269
Cobbett, William	V, 275
D'Avenant, Sir William	II, 219
Defoe, Daniel	III, 38
Fielding, Henry	III, 349, 354
Fielding, Sarah	III, 519
Goldsmith, Oliver	III, 628
Godwin, William	V, 300, 302
Green, Robert	I, 340
Hawkesworth, John	III, 610
Inchbald, Mrs. Elizabeth	IV, 689
Johnson, Samuel	III, 746, 766
Jonson, Ben	I, 767
Lewis, Matthew Gregory	IV, 633
Mackenzie, Sir George	II, 430
Malory, Sir Thomas	I, 205
Milton, John	II, 298, 298
Moore, John	IV, 427
Radcliffe, Ann Ward	IV, 721
Richardson, Samuel	III, 443, 446
Shelley, Percy Bysshe	IV, 715
Sidney, Sir Philip	I, 327
Smollett, Tobias George	III, 580, 583
Sprat, Thomas	II, 574
Sterne, Laurence	III, 515, 519
Stevenson, Robert Louis	VIII, 241, 242, 249
Swift, Jonathan	III, 222
Walpole, Horace	IV, 317
RALEIGH, SIR WALTER,	
Gascoigne, George	I, 307
History	VI, 5
Raleigh, Sir Walter	I, 591
Sidney, Sir Philip	I, 321
Spenser, Edmund	I, 378
RALPH, J.,	
Garrick, David	III, 693
RAMÉE, LOUISE DE LA,	
Shelley, Percy Bysshe	IV, 697, 714
RAMSAY, ALLAN,	
Pope, Alexander	III, 165
Prior, Matthew	II, 676
Somerville, William	III, 127
RAMSAY, CHEVALIER,	
Newton, Sir Isaac	II, 713, 721
Pope, Alexander	III, 181
Saint-John, Henry	III, 283
RAMSAY, H.,	
Jonson, Ben	I, 759

	Vol. and Page
RAMSAY, SIR JAMES H.,	
Ælfric	I, 45
Wyclif, John	I, 109
RAMSAY, PHILIP A.,	
Tannahill, Robert	IV, 547
RAND, BENJAMIN,	
Cooper, Anthony Ashley	II, 577, 581
RANDALL, HENRY STEPHENS,	
Henry, Patrick	IV, 352
Sparks, Jared	VI, 478
RANDOLPH, HENRY FITZ,	
Alford, Henry	VI, 635
Aytoun, William Edmondstoune	VI, 444
Faber, Frederick William	VI, 332
Gray, David	VI, 260
Keble, John	VI, 457
Maccarthy, Denis Florence	VII, 489
Mahoney, Francis	VI, 483
Procter, Adelaide Anne	VI, 393
Rossetti, Gabriel Charles Dante	VII, 434
Swift, Jonathan	III, 224
RANDOLPH, JOHN,	
Adams, Samuel	IV, 441
Jewell, John	I, 293
RANDOLPH, SARAH N.,	
Jefferson, Thomas	V, 42
RANDOLPH, THOMAS,	
Feltham, Owen	II, 309
RANDOLPH, THOMAS JEFFERSON,	
Jefferson, Thomas	V, 48
RANDS, WILLIAM BRIGHTY MATTHEW (BROWNE),	
Chaucer, Geoffrey	I, 127, 163
Eliot, George	VII, 196
Wyclif, John	I, 107
RANKE, LEOPOLD VON,	
Alfred the Great	I, 40
Bacon, Francis	I, 651
Bede	I, 30
Coke, Sir Edward	I, 741
Hobbes, Thomas	II, 322
Hyde, Edward, Earl of Clarendon	II, 304
Macaulay, Thomas Babington Lord	VI, 107
Penn, William	II, 631
Raleigh, Sir Walter	I, 596, 604
Saint-John, Henry	III, 288
Savile George	II, 450
RANKIN, ISAAC OGDEN,	
Brooks, Philips	VIII, 233
RANKIN, J. E.,	
Burns, Robert	IV, 230
RANKINE, W. J. M.,	
Young, Thomas	V, 88
RANYARD, ARTHUR C.,	
De Morgan, Augustus	VI, 634
RAPP, MORITZ,	
Shakespeare, William	I, 521
RAUSCHENBUSCH-CLOUGH, EMMA,	
Godwin, Mary Wollstonecraft	IV, 331
RAVENSCROFT, EDWARD,	
Dryden, John	II, 474
Shakespeare, William	I, 461

INDEX TO CRITICISMS

RAWLEY, WILLIAM,
  Bacon, Francis..........I, 640, 664
RAWNSLEY, H. D.,
  Bright, John.............VII, 724
  Coleridge, Hartley..........V, 575
  Ruskin, John............VIII, 408
  Southey, Robert...........V, 402
  Tennyson, Alfred Lord...VIII, 75
  Wordsworth, William.......V, 616
RAY, JOHN,
  Ray, John................II, 542
RAYLEIGH, LORD.
  Tyndall, John..........VIII, 197
RAYMOND, GEORGE LANSING,
  Tennyson, Alfred Lord...VIII, 88
RAYMOND, HENRY J.,
  Lincoln, Abraham ....VI, 417
RAYNER, B. L.,
  Jefferson, Thomas..........V, 48
READ, W. B.,
  Paine, Thomas...........IV, 537
READE, CHARLES,
  Reade, Charles..........VII, 527
READE, CHARLES L., AND REV. COMPTON,
  Boucicault, Dion........VII, 763
  Collins, William Wilkie....VII, 726
  Eliot, George...........VII, 205
  Lytton, Sir Edward George Bulwer................VI, 683
  Reade, Charles..........VII, 536
  Warren, Samuel..........VII, 107
READE, COMPTON,
  Reade, Charles..........VII, 528
READING, POST,
  Newton, Sir Isaac..........II, 712
RECORDS, UNIVERSITY OF OXFORD,
  Shelley, Percy Bysshe......IV, 698
REDCLIFFE, STRATFORD DE,
  Canning, George...........V, 67
REDDING, CYRUS,
  Beckford, William........V, 447
  Campbell, Thomas.....V, 437, 438
  Hunt, James Henry Leigh..VI, 163
  Morgan, Sydney Owenson Lady................VI, 193, 195
  Napier, Gen. Sir William Francis Patrick.............VI, 221
  Talfourd, Thomas Noon.....V, 760
  White, Joseph Blanco.......V, 361
  Wolcot, John............IV, 649
REED, E. J.,
  Longfellow, Henry Wadsworth ....VII, 394
REED, HELEN LEAH,
  Warner, Charles Dudley..VIII, 441
REED, HENRY,
  Addison, Joseph..........II, 645
  Berkeley, George.........III, 321
  Books..................III, 8
  Byron, George Gordon Lord.IV, 750
  Chaucer, Geoffrey......I, 144, 150
  Cowper, William.........IV, 383
  Dryden John............II, 501
  Fuller, Thomas...........II, 170
  Hallam, Henry..........VI, 178
  Irving, Washington....VI, 138, 149
  Johnson, Samuel........III, 744
  Literature................I, 8
  Milton, John..........II, 252, 274

Pope, Alexander..........III, 189
  Shelley, Percy Bysshe......IV, 704
  Stanhope, Philip Dormer...III, 605
  Stanhope, Philip Henry Earl.. ....VII, 47
  Swift, Jonathan..........III, 228
  Walton, Isaac............II, 347
  Wordsworth, William......V, 620
REED, ISAAC,
  Dodsley, Robert.....III, 482, 483
  Farmer, Richard..........IV, 341
  Johnson, Samuel.........III, 746
  Villiers, George............II, 377
REED, WILLIAM BRADFORD,
  Kane, Elisha Kent.........VI, 80
  Stanhope, Philip Henry Earl.. ....VII, 47
  Thackeray, William Makepeace ....VI, 293
REES, THOMAS,
  Hook, Theodore Edward....V, 356
  Hone, William.........V, 392, 393
REESE, LIZETTE WOODWORTH,
  Lamb, Charles...........V, 236
  Lanier, Sidney..........VII, 328
  Stevenson, Robert Louis..... ....VIII, 250
  Timrod, Henry..........VI, 510
REEVE, CLARA,
  Barclay, John............I, 618
REEVE, HENRY,
  Brougham, Henry Lord....VI, 532
REEVE, LOVELL,
  Wilkinson, Sir John Gardner.. ....VII, 51
REHAN, ADA,
  Tennyson, Alfred Lord...VIII, 99
REICHEL, H. R.,
  Fortescue, Sir John.........I, 195
  More, Sir Thomas......I, 239, 240
REID, ANDREW,
  Ferguson, James.........III, 668
REID, CAPTAIN MAYNE,
  Poe, Edgar Allan..........V, 538
REID, STUART J.,
  Blackmore, Richard D.,...... ....VIII, 431, 433
  Russell, John Earl........VII, 146
  Smith, Sydney............V, 470
REID, THOMAS WEMYSS,
  Brontë, Charlotte.VI, 19, 21, 24, 28
  Brontë, Emily............V, 521
  Gladstone, William Ewart.... ....VIII, 389, 390
  Milnes, Richard Monckton III, 561
  Russell, John Earl........VII, 143
  Tennyson, Alfred Lord..VIII, 71
REID, THOMAS,
  Hume, David...........III, 648
  Reid, Thomas...........IV, 283
RENFREW, CARRIE,
  Havergal, Frances Ridley..VII, 167
RENAN, JOSEPH ERNEST,
  Critic, The...............II, 7
RENAN, N.,
  Parker, Theodore.........VI, 212
RENWICK, JAMES,
  Rumford, Count..........IV, 591
REPORT OF GRAND JURY OF CORK, IRELAND,
  Wesley, Charles..........IV. 34

REPPLIER, AGNES.
  Austen, Jane.............IV, 613
  Beddoes, Thomas Lovell.....V, 588
  Black, William.........VIII, 395
  Borrow, George Henry.....VII, 313
  Browning Elizabeth Barrett.. ....VI, 247
  Burney, Frances..........V, 345
  Carew, Thomas............II, 23
  Cowper, William..........IV, 384
  Day, Thomas............IV, 49
  Defoe, Daniel............III, 38
  Edgeworth, Maria.........V, 564
  FitzGerald, Edward.....VII, 519
  Habington, William......II, 135
  Herrick, Robert..........II, 234
  Lamb, Charles............V, 238
  Landor, Walter Savage.....VI, 392
  Lockhart, John Gibson.....V, 754
  Lovelace, Richard.........II. 163
  Mitford, Mary Russell......VI, 43
  Pater Walter Horatio....VIII, 278
  Peacock, Thomas Love....VII, 475
  Richardson, Samuel......III, 453
  Sedley, Sir Charles........II, 510
  Sewall, Samuel..........III, 19
  Thackeray, William Makepeace ....VI, 318
  Walpole, Horace.........IV, 313
RERESBY, SIR JOHN,
  Villiers, George...........II, 376
RESOLUTION OF CONGRESS,
  Paine, Thomas..........IV, 539
  Wilkes, John...........IV, 335
RESOLUTION BY THE PRESBYTERY OF GLASGOW,
  Home, John............IV, 513
REYNALL, RICHARD,
  Wordsworth, William......V, 605
REYNOLD, E. DUBOIS,
  Darwin, Charles Robert...VII, 430
REYNOLDS JOHN HAMILTON,
  Byron, George Gordon Lord.. ....IV, 756
  Keats, John.............IV, 675
  Montagu, Lady Mary Wortley ....III, 462
REYNOLDS, SIR JOSHUA.
  Johnson, Samuel......III, 725, 754
REYNOLDS, MYRA,
  Langhorne, John.........III, 701
  Logan, John.............IV, 45
  Thomson, James.........III, 260
  Warton, Thomas.........IV, 79
  Whitehead, William......IV, 23
RHODES, W. G.,
  Maxwell, James Clerk.....VII, 170
  Tyndall, John..........VIII, 201
RHYS, EARNEST,
  Burns, Robert............IV, 265
  Byron, George Gordon Lord IV, 747
  Chatterton, Thomas......III, 533
  Herrick, Robert..........II, 239
  Hunt, James Henry Leigh.... ....VI, 167, 172
  Marlowe, Christopher.......I, 357
  Swift, Jonathan.........III, 238
  Whitman, Walt........VIII, 131
  Wordsworth, William......V, 645
RHYS, JOHN,
  Malory, Sir Thomas........I, 205

INDEX TO CRITICISMS

	Vol. and Page
RIBOT, THEODULE,	
History	VI, 9
Lewes, George Henry	VII, 140
Mill, John Stuart	VI, 715
Mill, James	V, 309
Spencer, Herbert	VIII, 480
RICARDO, DAVID,	
Smith, Adam	IV, 62
RICE, A. T.,	
Locke, John	II, 528
RICE, G. E.,	
Waller, Edmund	II, 382
RICE, WALLACE,	
Dodge, Mary Abigail	VIII, 361
RICH, BARNABE,	
Greene, Robert	I, 344
RICHARD, HENRY,	
Cobden, Richard	VI, 442
RICHARDS, C. A. L.,	
Arbuthnot, John	III, 85
Brooks, Phillips	VIII, 232
Church, Richard William	VII, 730
Jowett, Benjamin	VIII, 209
Shairp, John Campbell	VII, 570
Ward, William George	VII, 484
Wiseman, Nicholas Patrick	VI, 439
RICHARDSON, ABBY SAGE,	
Chaucer, Geoffrey	I, 146
Farquhar, George	II, 555
Godwin, Mary Wollstonecraft	IV, 331
Hazlitt, William	V, 102
Johnson, Samuel	III, 762
Opie, Amelia	V, 743
Shenstone, William	III, 473
Steele, Sir Richard	II, 754
Swift, Jonathan	III, 204
RICHARDSON, BENJAMIN W.,	
Harvey, William	II, 155
RICHARDSON, CHARLES FRANCIS,	
Adams, Hannah	V, 125
Adams, John	V, 53
Adams John Quincy	V, 520
Adams, Samuel	IV, 443
Ames, Fisher	IV, 529
Beecher, Lyman	VI, 341
Boker, George Henry	VII, 766
Books	III, 10
Bradford, William	II, 158
Brainard, John Gardiner Calkins	V, 85
Brown, Charles Brockden	IV, 557
Browne, Charles Farrar	VI, 503
Bryant, William Cullen	VII, 116, 125
Bushnell, Horace	VII, 71
Calhoun, John Caldwell	V, 677
Channing, William Ellery	V, 375
Clarke, James Freeman	VII, 673
Curtis, George William	VIII, 190
Dewey, Orville	VII, 499
Drake, Joseph Rodman	IV, 661
Draper John William	VII, 503
Edwards, Jonathan	III, 393
Emerson, Ralph Waldo	VII, 359
Franklin, Benjamin	III, 103
Freneau, Philip	V, 187
Fuller, Sarah Margaret	V, 672
Hamilton, Alexander	IV, 468
Hayne, Paul Hamilton	VII, 593

	Vol. and Page
Henry, Patrick	IV, 352
Hildreth, Richard	VI, 454
Holland, Josiah Gilbert	VII, 336
Holmes, Oliver Wendell	VIII, 291
Hopkins, Mark	VII, 615
Hutchinson, Thomas	III, 708
Irving, Washington	VI, 138, 143, 144, 147
Jackson, Helen Hunt	VII, 575
Kent, James	V, 503
Lanier, Sidney	VII, 328
Lincoln, Abraham	VI, 420
Longfellow, Henry Wadsworth	VII, 388, 394, 401, 412
Lowell, James Russell	VIII, 27, 32
Madison, James	V, 315
Mann, Horace	VI, 202
Mather, Cotton	II, 731
Mather, Increase	II, 690
Melville, Herman	VII, 63
Miller, Cincinnatus Hiner	VIII, 500
Motley, John Lothrop	VII, 88
Otis, James	III, 716
Paine, Thomas	IV, 538
Palfrey, John Gorham	VII, 338
Parker, Theodore	VI, 211
Parsons, Thomas William	VIII, 193
Poe, Edgar Allan	V, 555
Prince, Thomas	III, 402
Ripley, George	VII, 225
Sewall, Samuel	III, 18
Seward, William Henry	VI, 676
Simms, William Gilmore	VII, 599
Smith, John	I, 700
Sparks, Jared	VI, 478
Stoddard, Richard Henry	VIII, 497
Story, William Wetmore	VIII, 319
Stowe, Harriet Beecher	VIII, 353
Sumner, Charles	VI, 756
Taylor, Bayard	VII, 136
Thoreau, Henry David	VI, 274
Timrod, Henry	VI, 510
Very, Jones	VII, 228
Ward, Nathaniel	II, 130
Warner, Charles Dudley	VIII, 443
Washington, George	IV, 369
Webster, Daniel	V, 726
Whipple, Edwin Percy	VII, 597
White, Richard Grant	VII, 578
Whitman, Walt	VIII, 144
Whittier, John Greenleaf	VIII, 125
Williams, Rogers	II, 357
Winthrop, John	VII, 110
Woolman, John	III, 597
RICHARDSON, HENRY S.,	
Martineau, Harriet	VI, 63
RICHARDSON, JONATHAN,	
Milton, John	II, 244
RICHARDSON, SAMUEL,	
Fielding, Henry	III, 350, 355
Fielding, Sarah	III, 518
Hill, Aaron	III, 278
Johnson, Samuel	III, 740
Richardson, Samuel	III, 431, 435
Swift, Jonathan	III, 212
RICHARDSON, WILLIAM,	
Shakespeare, William	I, 502

	Vol. and Page
RICHMOND, JOHN.	
Chatterton, Thomas	III, 539
RICHTER, JEAN PAUL FRIEDRICH,	
History	VI, 7
RICKABY, JOSEPH,	
Pusey, Edward Bouverie	VII, 473
RICKMAN, THOMAS C.,	
Paine, Thomas	IV, 532
RIDDELL, HENRY SCOTT,	
Hogg, James	V, 265
RIDDELL, MARIA,	
Burns, Robert	IV, 222
RIDEING, WILLIAM H.,	
Buckland, Francis Trevelyan	VII, 212
Lowell, James Russell	VIII, 19
Thackeray, William Makepeace	VI, 296, 303
Whittier, John Greenleaf	VIII, 113
RIETHMÜLLER, CHRISTOPHER JAMES,	
Hamilton, Alexander	IV, 464
Jefferson, Thomas	V, 46
RIGBY, ELIZABETH,	
Brontë, Charlotte	VI, 22
RIGG, JAMES HARRISON,	
Wesley, John	IV, 115, 121
RIGG, J. M.,	
Anselm	I, 51
Burns, Robert	VI, 245
Hale, Sir Matthew	II, 306
Leslie, Charles	II, 630
Littleton, Sir Thomas	I, 196
McCosh, James	VIII, 302
Moore, Edward	III, 176
Murray, William	IV, 171
Owen, John	II, 353
Penn, William	II, 631
Romilly, Sir Samuel	IV, 636
Somers, John Lord	II, 613
Taylor, Thomas	V, 291
Ward, William George	VII, 485
Waterland, Daniel	III, 103
Whately, Richard	VI, 326, 328
Wilkes, John	IV, 335
RIGGS, JAMES GILBERT,	
Goldsmith, Oliver	III, 629
RILEY, JAMES WHITCOMB,	
Burns, Robert	IV, 233
Chaucer, Geoffrey	I, 169
Field, Eugene	VIII, 317
Longfellow, Henry Wadsworth	VII, 413
Stevenson, Robert Louis	VIII, 238
Tennyson, Alfred Lord	VIII, 107
RIMBAULT, EDWARD F.,	
Burney, Charles	IV, 589
D'Urfey, Thomas	II, 686
Overbury, Sir Thomas	I, 442
RIMMER, ALFRED,	
Dickens, Charles	VI, 564
RIO, APOLLONIA,	
Wiseman, Nicholas Patrick	VI, 437
RIPLEY, GEORGE,	
Bancroft, George	VIII, 58
Bryant, William Cullen	VII, 112
Emerson, Ralph Waldo	VII, 365
Irving, Washington	VI, 146
Mackintosh, Sir James	V, 181

664 INDEX TO CRITICISMS

Martineau, James......VIII, 427
RITCHIE, ANNE ISABELLA THACKERAY,
  Austen, Jane..............IV, 621
  Barbauld, Anna Lætitia.....V, 26
  Brontë, Charlotte.....VI, 20, 25
  Browning, Elizabeth Barrett
    ....VI, 233, 241
  Edgeworth, Maria......... , 569
  Gaskell, Elizabeth Cleghorn..
    ....VI, 428, 429, 430
  Hemans, Felicia Dorothea..V, 257
  Hunt, James Henry Leigh..VI, 162
  Kemble, Frances Ann...VIII, 213
  Opie, Amelia..............V, 743
  Ruskin, John......VIII, 406, 412
  Tennyson, Alfred Lord..VIII, 84
  Thackeray, William Makepeace ....VI, 304, 306, 310
RITCHIE, DAVID G.,
  Buchanan, George.........I, 315
  Spencer, Herbert........VIII, 483
RITCHIE, J. EWING,
  Lewis, Sir George Cornewall..
    ....VI, 336
  Mill, John Stuart........VI, 702
RITSO, FREDERICK,
  Blackstone, William......III, 704
RITSON, JOSEPH,
  Bale, John................I, 286
  Burns, Robert............IV 249
  Chaucer, Geoffrey.........II, 157
  Fergusson, Robert.......III, 640
  Godwin, William..........V, 303
  Holcroft, Thomas........IV, 545
  Home, John..............IV, 515
  Lydgate, John.............I, 184
  Malone, Edmond....IV, 577, 578
  Ramsay, Allan..........III, 409
  Spenser, Edmund.........I, 395
RITTENHOUSE, JESSIE B.,
  FitzGerald, Edward......VII, 519
RIVES, WILLIAM CABELL,
  Madison, James..........V, 313
ROBBINS, ALFRED F.,
  Disraeli, Benjamin......VII, 295
  Murchison, Sir Roderick Impey
    ....VI, 630
ROBBINS, THOMAS,
  Mather, Cotton..........II, 730
ROBERTS, CHARLES G. D.,
  Bryant, William Cullen...VII, 125
  Horne, Richard Hengist..VII, 546
  Lanier, Sidney..........VII, 328
  Miller, Cincinnatus Hiner....
    ....VIII, 500
  O'Reilly, John Boyle.....VII, 768
  Shelley, Percy Bysshe....IV, 715
  Stoddard, Richard Henry..
    ....VIII, 497
  Whitman, Walt........VIII, 144
ROBERTS, EDWARD,
  Roe, Edward Payson.....VII, 674
ROBERTS, GEORGE,
  Fielding, Henry.........III, 342
ROBERTS, L. M.,
  Burns, Robert...........IV, 242
ROBERTS, WILLIAM,
  Dennis, John............III, 76
  Goldsmith, Oliver.......III, 629
  Gray, Thomas...........III, 560

Langhorne, John.........III, 700
More, Hannah............V, 191
Prior, Matthew..........II, 679
Rymer, Thomas..........II, 583
ROBERTSON, ERIC S.,
  Baillie, Joanna...........V, 695
  Barbauld, Anna Lætitia...V, 23
  Barnard, Lady Anne......V, 29
  Behn, Aphra............II, 410
  Brontë, Emily...........V, 525
  Cavendish, Margaret....II, 232
  Eliot, George..........VII, 197
  Hemans, Felicia Dorothea..V, 261
  Longfellow, Henry Wadsworth
    ....VII, 394, 394, 396, 412
  Montagu, Lady Mary Wortley.
    ....III, 465
  Opie, Amelia............V, 743
  Philips, Katherine.......II, 181
  Piozzi, Hester Lynch....IV, 686
  Poe, Edgar Allan........V, 559
  Procter, Adelaide Anne..VI, 395
  Rossetti, Christina Georgina..
    ....VIII, 271
  Seward, Anna..........IV, 542
  Southey, Caroline Anne Bowles
    ....V, 762
  Southwell, Robert........I, 363
  Vaughan, Henry........II, 445
ROBERTSON, FREDERICK LOCKHART,
  Robertson, William......IV, 163
ROBERTSON, FREDERICK WILLIAM
  Channing, William Ellery...V, 367
  Tennyson, Alfred Lord..VIII, 83
ROBERTSON, GEORGE CROOM,
  Bacon, Francis..........I, 662
  Grote, George..........VI, 609
ROBERTSON, J. B.,
  Burke, Edmund.........IV, 292
ROBERTSON, JAMES CRAIGIE,
  Alcuin..................I, 33
  Grosseteste, Robert......I, 73
ROBERTSON, J. FORBES,
  Aytoun, William Edmondstoune.................VI, 445
ROBERTSON, J. LOGIE,
  Browning, Robert.......VII, 714
  Carew, Thomas..........II, 23
  Clarke, Samuel.........II, 750
  Darwin, Charles Robert...VII, 433
  Faraday, Michael........VI, 514
  Hawthorne, Nathaniel...VI, 370
  Jeffrey, Francis Lord....VI, 656
  Johnson, Samuel.......III, 767
  Lyndsay, Sir David......I, 276
  Marvell, Andrew.......II, 319
  Ramsay, Allan....III, 303, 410
  Reid, Thomas...........IV, 287
  Robertson, William....IV, 160, 161
  Smollett, Tobias George...III, 590
  Steele, Sir Richard......II, 767
  Tyndall, John..........III, 199
  Whitman, Walt.......VIII, 149
ROBERTSON, JOHN,
  Whitman, Walt.......VIII, 142
ROBERTSON, WILLIAM,
  Buchanan, George........I, 315
  Gibbon, Edward.........IV, 179
  Hagley William.........IV, 652

Knox, John...............I, 296
Walpole, Horace.........IV, 321
ROBIN, CLAUDE C.,
  Washington, George.....IV, 354
ROBINS, EDWARD, JR.,
  Addison, Joseph.........II, 651
  Cibber, Colley..........III, 374
  Farquhar, George.......II, 556
  Franklin, Benjamin......IV, 97
  Vanbrugh, Sir John.....II, 704
ROBINSON, A. MARY F. (MME. DARMESTETER),
  Baillie, Joanna..........V, 694
  Barbauld, Anna Lætitia....V, 25
  Brontë, Charlotte........VI, 30
  Brontë, Emily...........V, 522
  Hemans, Felicia Dorothea..V, 260
  Rossetti, Gabriel Charles Dante
    ....VII, 440
ROBINSON, CHARLES J.,
  Trench, Richard Chenevix..
    ....VII, 590
ROBINSON, G.,
  Chamberlayne, William....II, 406
ROBINSON, HENRY CRABB,
  Allston, Washington......V, 418
  Baillie, Joanna..........V, 689
  Barbauld, Anna Lætitia....V, 22
  Bentham, Jeremy........V, 165
  Blake, William..........V, 56
  Blessington, Countess of...V, 590
  Brougham, Henry Lord...VI, 525
  Browning, Elizabeth Barrett..
    ....VI, 230
  Carlyle, Thomas........VII, 229
  Coleridge, Hartley.......V, 573
  Coleridge, Samuel Taylor...V, 207
  Crabbe, George..........V, 173
  Croly, George...........VI, 224
  De Quincey, Thomas.....VI, 116
  Dryden, John...........II, 483
  Edgeworth, Maria........V, 567
  Emerson, Ralph Waldo...VII, 344
  Faber, Frederick William..VI, 332
  Faraday, Michael.......VI, 512
  Gibbon, Edward........IV, 181
  Godwin, William........V, 297
  Hall, Robert...........V, 109
  Hare, Julius Charles....VI, 49
  Hazlitt, William.........V, 97
  Hone, William..........V, 392
  Hunt, James Henry Leigh..VI, 167
  Lamb, Charles.........V, 229
  Lamb, Mary Ann........V, 507
  Landor, Walter Savage....VI, 372
  Lytton, Edward Robert Bulwer Earl..............VIII, 49
  Macaulay, Thomas Babington Lord..................VI, 91
  Martineau, Harriet......VII, 56
  Morgan, Lady Sydney Owenson ....VI, 192
  Norton, Caroline Elizabeth Sheridan ....VII, 102
  Payne, John Howard.....V, 735
  Porter, Jane............V, 673
  Rogers, Samuel.........VI, 33
  Shelley, Percy Bysshe....IV, 689
  Southey, Robert...V, 396, 407, 408
  Spenser, Edmund........I, 375
  Stillingfleet, Edward.....II, 454

INDEX TO CRITICISMS 665

	Vol. and Page
Talfourd, Sir Thomas Noon..	V, 759
Tennyson, Alfred Lord..	VIII, 65
Wakefield, Gilbert........	IV, 415
Wesley, John.............	IV, 121
Whewell, William.........	VI, 466
Wilkinson, Sir John Gardner..	VII, 50, 51
Wolcot, John.............	IV, 648
Woolman, John...........	III, 597
Wordsworth, William.......	V, 605, 620, 622
Young, Thomas...........	V, 86

ROBINSON, N.,
Lever, Charles James..VI, 652, 654

ROBINSON, PHIL.,
Emerson, Ralph Waldo...VII, 356

ROBINSON, RALPH,
More, Sir Thomas..........I, 236

ROBINSON, R. T.,
Watts, Isaac............III, 251
Wesley Charles..........IV, 37

ROBINSON, W. CLARKE,
Cynewulf ....I, 31

ROBISON, JOHN,
Black, Joseph............IV, 345

ROCHE, JAMES JEFFREY,
Lowell, James Russell...VIII, 29
O'Reilly John Boyle..VII, 767, 768

ROCHESTER, JOHN WILMOT, EARL,
Dryden, John.............II, 495
Etheredge, Sir George......II, 414
Lee, Nathaniel............II, 431
Otway, Thomas............II, 363
Sedley, Sir Charles..........II, 509
Shadwell, Thomas..........II, 434
Waller, Edmund...........II, 379
Wilmot, John.............II, 335
Wycherley, William........II, 603

ROE, ALFRED S.,
Budgell, Eustace..........III, 91

ROE, EDWARD PAYSON,
Hawthorne, Nathaniel.....VI, 369
Roe, Edward Payson.....VII, 765

ROEBUCK, JOHN ARTHUR,
Bentham, Jeremy..........V, 167
Brougham, Henry Lord....VI, 525
Carlyle, Thomas.........VII, 230
Grote, George............VI, 607
Mill, John Stuart..........VI, 704

ROGERS, ARTHUR,
Kingsley, Charles........VII, 28
Maurice, John Frederick Denison ....VI, 646
Pusey, Edward Bouverie..VII, 470

ROGERS, CHARLES,
Barnard, Lady Anne......V, 28
Burns, Robert............IV, 230
Knox, William...........V, 31
Oliphant, Carolina........V, 477
Tannahill, Robert........IV, 548

ROGERS, HENRY,
Butler, Joseph............III 314
Edwards, Jonathan.......III, 390
Fuller, Thomas........II, 168, 172
Gibbon, Edward..........IV, 178
Howe, John..............II, 546
Locke, John..........II, 527, 535
Marvell, Andrew......II, 314, 316
Newton, Sir Isaac.........II, 717

	Vol. and Page
South, Robert.............	II, 608
Whately, Richard.........	VI, 327
Whitefield, George........	III, 550

ROGERS, JAMES E. THOROLD,
Bright, John.............VII, 723
Cobbett, William........V, 271, 273
Laud, William............II, 92
Saint-John, Henry........III, 288
Selden, John............. II, 138
Smith, Adam.............IV, 65
Spelman, Sir Henry........II, 53

ROGERS, ROBERT CAMERON,
Thackeray, William Makepeace ....VI 320

ROGERS, SAMUEL,
Barbauld, Anna Lætitia.....V, 25
Blair, Hugh...............IV 403
Burke, Edmund..........IV, 295
Burnet, Gilbert...........II, 596
Coleridge, Samuel Taylor....V, 211
Crabbe, George...........V, 171
Cumberland, Richard......IV, 559
Darwin, Erasmus..........IV, 423
Dryden, John.............II, 487
Erskine, Thomas..........IV, 729
Fox, Charles James...IV, 500, 507
Gibbon, Edward..........IV, 186
Hayley, William..........IV, 654
Junius...................IV, 642
Lamb, Lady Caroline.......V, 81
Lewis, Matthew Gregory...IV, 632
Mackintosh, Sir James......V, 180
Massinger, Philip..........II, 49
Milton, John.............II, 246
Mitford William...........V, 70
Murphy, Arthur..........IV, 482
Parr, Samuel.............V, 18
Piozzi, Hester Lynch......IV, 685
Porson, Richard..........IV, 523
Priestley, Joseph..........IV, 448
Shelley, Percy Bysshe......IV, 693
Smith, Adam.............IV, 55
Spenser, Edmund..........I, 306
Surrey, Earl of............I, 255
Warton, Joseph..........IV, 396
Wesley, John.............IV, 114
Wilkes, John.............IV, 334
Williams, Henry Maria.....V, 74
Wolcot, John.............IV, 650
Young, Edward..........III, 489

ROGERS, SHERMAN S.,
Curtis, George William...VIII, 185

ROLPH, JOHN F.,
Fawcett, Henry.........VII 549
Milnes, Richard Moncton VII, 562

ROLFE, WILLIAM J.,
Macaulay, Thomas Babington Lord...................VI, 103
Shakespeare, William........ ....I, 458, 461, 463, 532
Tennyson, Alfred Lord...VIII, 79

ROLLESTON, T. W.,
Whitman, Walt.........VIII, 148
Wolfe, Charles............IV, 722

ROLLINS, ALICE WELLINGTON,
Craik, Dinah Maria Mulock.VII, 624
Holmes, Oliver Wendell..VIII, 296
Jackson, Helen Hunt.....VII, 571

ROMANES, GEORGE JOHN,
Darwin, Charles Robert...... ....VII, 417, 417, 432

	Vol. and Page
Huxley, Thomas Henry..	VIII, 325

ROMANES, MRS. GEORGE JOHN,
Romanes, George John...VIII, 284

ROMILLY, SIR SAMUEL,
Bentham, Jeremy..........V, 162
Brougham, Henry Lord....VI 523
Erskine, Thomas..........IV, 728
Franklin, Benjamin........IV, 82
Mitford, William............V, 70
Smith Adam..............IV, 54

ROOPER, GEORGE,
Buckland, Francis Trevelyan.. ....VII, 212

ROOSE, PAULINE W.,
Whitman, Walt.........VIII, 147

ROOSEVELT, THEODORE,
Benton, Thomas Hart......IV, 87
Bunyan, John..............II, 405
Lowell, James Russell...VIII, 32

ROOT, OREN,
Hamilton, Alexander......IV, 461

ROPES, ARTHUR R.,
Montagu, Lady Mary Wortley ....III, 463

ROSCOE, HENRY,
Blackstone, Sir William...... ....III, 703, 706
Erskine, Thomas..........IV, 730
Jones, Sir William.........IV, 200
Murray, William..........IV, 170
North, Roger............III, 80
Somers, John Lord..........II, 614
Romilly, Sir Samuel........IV, 635
Roscoe, William...........V, 116

ROSCOE, THOMAS,
Fielding, Henry..III, 345, 346, 353
Smollett, Tobias George...III, 587
Swift, Jonathan........ III, 214

ROSCOE, WILLIAM,
Chaucer, Geoffrey..........I, 137
Pope, Alexander......III, 164, 174
Ramsay, Allan..........III, 406
Spenser, Edmund..........I, 375
Swift, Jonathan.........III. 230

ROSCOMMON, EARL OF,
Poets and Poetry..........IV, 5

ROSE, SIR GEORGE,
Warren, Samuel..........VII, 108

ROSE, J. HOLLAND,
Bentham, Jeremy..........V, 169
Owens, Robert...........VI, 85

ROSEBERRY, ARCHIBALD PHILIP PRIMROSE LORD,
Burke, Edmund..........IV, 292
Burns, Robert........IV, 235, 267
Fox, Charles James........IV, 505
Gladstone, William Ewart VIII, 387
Pitt, William.............IV, 510
Stevenson, Robert Louis..... ....VIII, 242, 249

ROSENTHAL, LEWIS,
Franklin, Benjamin........IV, 89

ROSS, D. M.,
Drummond, Henry......VIII, 362

ROSS, J.,
Aytoun, Sir Robert........I, 768
Logan, John..............IV, 44
Ross, Alexander..........IV, 719
Maitland, Sir Richard......I, 333
Scott, Alexander..........I, 319
Tannahill, Robert.........IV, 549

ROSS, JOHN D.,
  Motherwell, William........V, 278
ROSS, JOHN MERRY,
  Barbour, John..............I, 115
  Beowulf....................I, 19
  Boece, Hector..............I, 243
  Burns, Robert.............IV, 245
  Chaucer, Geoffrey..........I, 138
  Douglas, Gawin.............I, 215
  Henry the Minstrel.........I, 202
  James I. of Scotland.......I, 181
  Lyndsay, Sir David.........I, 275
  Saxon Chronicle............I, 58
  Scott, Michael.............I, 69
  Thomas of Erceldoune.......I, 84
  Wyntoun, Andrew............I, 177
ROSSETTI, CHRISTINA
  GEORGINA,
  Keats, John...............IV, 676
  Newman, John Henry.....VII, 741
  Rossetti, Gabriel Charles Dante
  ....VII, 440
ROSSETTI, DANTE GABRIEL,
  Blake, Michael.........V, 58, 59
  Brontë, Emily.............V, 523
  Browning, Elizabeth Barrett..
  ....VI, 230, 238
  Browning, Robert,VII, 678, 692, 693
  Burns, Robert.............IV, 230
  Chatterton, Thomas......III, 532
  Coleridge, Samuel Taylor...V, 212
  Crabbe, George.............V, 147
  Dobell, Sydney Thompson.VI, 764
  Hunt, James Henry Leigh..VI, 160
  James I. of Scotland.......I, 181
  Keats, John...............IV, 679
  Lytton, Edward Robert Bul-
    wer Earl................VIII, 43
  Morris, William.....VIII, 330, 334
  Patmore, Coventry..VIII, 340, 341
  Rossetti, Gabriel Charles Dante
  ....VII, 446
  Shelley, Percy Bysshe.....IV, 711
  Tennyson, Alfred Lord...VIII, 66
  Tupper, Martin Farquhar..VII, 733
  Warren, Samuel...........VII, 108
  Wells, Charles Jeremiah..VII, 164
  Whitman, Walt...........VIII, 134
  Wordsworth, William........V, 636
ROSSETTI, LUCY MADOX,
  Shelley, Mary Wollstonecraft V, 703
ROSSETTI, WILLIAM MICHAEL,
  Browning, Robert.........VII, 680
  Burns, Robert.............IV, 231
  Butler, Samuel......II, 330, 335
  Byron, George Gordon Lord..
  ....IV, 753, 761
  Campbell, Thomas..........V, 444
  Chaucer, Geoffrey..I, 130, 136, 146
  Churchill, Charles.......III, 481
  Cowley, Abraham...........II, 201
  Cowper, William......IV, 384, 390
  Dryden, John....II, 467, 469, 493
  Goldsmith, Oliver.......III, 620
  Gray, Thomas......III, 559, 563
  Hemans, Felicia Dorothea...
  ....V, 256, 260
  Herrick, Robert..........II, 238
  Hood, Thomas..............V, 464
  Keats, John..............
  ..IV, 666, 669, 671, 672, 674, 678

Landor, Walter Savage.....VI, 376
Langland, William..........I, 121
Longfellow, Henry Wadsworth
  ....VII, 396, 405
Marvell, Andrew...........II, 317
Miller, Cincinnatus Hiner VIII, 499
Milton, John........II, 255, 294
Moore, Thomas..............V, 717
Philips, Katherine........II, 180
Poe, Edgar Allan.....V, 548, 552
Pope, Alexander..........III, 191
Rossetti, Christina Georgina..
  ....VIII, 269
Rossetti, Gabriel Charles Dante
  ....VII, 438
Scott, Sir Walter..........V, 136
Shelley, Percy Bysshe........
  ....IV, 699, 700, 710
Spenser, Edmund..I, 374, 385, 391
Thomson, James......III, 265, 270
Vaughan, Henry...........II, 444
Whitman, Walt.....VIII, 137, 140
Wordsworth, William.......V, 639
ROSSLYN, EARL,
  Browning, Elizabeth Barrett..
  ....VI, 232
ROSSMAN, VINCENT D.,
  Walpole, Horace..........IV, 321
ROTHERTON, MARY,
  Tennyson, Alfred Lord...VIII, 111
ROUND, J. H.,
  Freeman, Edward Augustus..
  ....VIII, 159
ROUSSEAU, JEAN-JACQUES,
  Defoe, Daniel............III, 32
  Gibbon, Edward...........IV, 178
  Lillo, George............III, 100
  Pope, Alexander..........III, 174
  Richardson, Samuel......III, 444
ROWE, F. J., AND WEBB, W. T.,
  Tennyson, Alfred Lord...VIII, 108
ROWE, NICHOLAS,
  Asgill, John.............III, 97
  Shakespeare, William....,I, 449 484
ROWLAND, P. F.,
  Defoe, Daniel............III, 41
ROWLANDS, SAMUEL,
  Chettle, Henry...........I, 429
ROWLEY, WILLIAM,
  Webster, John.............I, 672
ROWTON, FREDERIC,
  Berners, Juliana...........I, 191
  Blamire, Susanna.........IV, 204
  Browning, Elizabeth Barrett..
  ....VI, 235, 244
  Carter, Elizabeth........IV, 493
  Cockburn, Catherine......III 276
  Grant, Anne...............V, 330
  Kemble, Frances Ann....VIII, 215
  Landon, Letitia Elizabeth...V, 327
  Opie, Amelia.............IV, 743
  Philips, Katherine........II, 180
  Robinson, Mary...........IV, 412
  Southey, Caroline Anne Bowles
  ....V, 762
  Tighe, Mary..............IV, 551
ROYCE, JOSIAH,
  Browning, Robert.......VII, 715
  Bunyan, John.............II, 391
  Byron, George Gordon Lord
  ....IV, 753

Darwin, Charles Robert...VII, 432
Hume David..............III, 664
Locke, John..............II, 528
Martineau, James.......VIII, 428
Tennyson, Alfred Lord...VIII, 98
ROYDON, MATTHEW,
  Sidney, Sir Philip.........I, 321
RUDD, F. A.,
  De Vere, Aubrey Thomas.....
  ....VIII, 463
  Procter, Adelaide Anne....VI, 395
  Rossetti, Christina Georgina..
  ....VIII, 270
RUDIERDE, EDMOND,
  Marlowe, Christopher......I, 347
RUFFHEAD, OWEN,
  Rowe, Nicholas...........II, 619
  Young, Edward..........III, 484
RUGGLES, HENRY J.,
  Shakespeare, William......I, 525
RUGGLES, JOHN,
  Sprague, Charles.........VII, 53
RUHNKEN, DAVID,
  Bentley, Richard........III, 113
RUMFORD, COUNT,
  Rumford, Count..........IV, 590
RUNKLE, LUCIA GILBERT,
  Hood, Thomas.............V, 465
RUNNINGTON, CHARLES,
  Hale, Sir Matthew........II. 306
RUSH, BENJAMIN,
  Franklin, Benjamin.......IV, 81
RUSHWORTH, JOHN,
  Bacon, Francis............I, 640
RUSKIN, JOHN,
  Bacon, Francis............I, 643
  Browning, Robert........VII, 699
  Burns, Robert...........IV, 262
  Byron, George Gordon Lord..
  ....IV, 762
  Carlyle, Thomas........VII, 257
  Dickens, Charles....VI, 576, 583
  Emerson, Ralph Waldo...VII, 369
  Gibbon, Edward..........IV, 196
  Jameson, Anna............VI, 216
  Johnson, Samuel.........III, 763
  Keats, John.......IV, 673, 677
  Longfellow, Henry Wadsworth
  ....VII, 394
  Pope, Alexander..........III, 189
  Reynolds Sir Joshua......IV, 141
  Richardson, Samuel......III, 445
  Ruskin, John...........VIII, 405
  Scott, Sir Walter......V, 156, 160
  Shakespeare, William......I, 560
  Shelley, Percy Bysshe....IV, 708
  Sidney, Sir Philip.........I, 328
  Southey, Robert...........V, 397
  Tennyson, Alfred Lord.....
  ....VIII, 93, 101
  Whitman, Walt..........VIII, 140
  Wordsworth, William.......V, 636
RUSSEL, J. FULLER,
  Lamb, Charles.............V, 235
RUSSEL, PATRICK,
  Bruce, James.............IV, 207
RUSSELL, A. P.,
  Burns, Robert............IV, 264
  Foote, Samuel...........III, 672
RUSSELL, CHARLES E.,
  Chatterton, Thomas......III, 540

INDEX TO CRITICISMS

	Vol. and Page
RUSSELL, EARL,	
Fox, Charles James	IV, 504
RUSSELL, GEORGE W E.,	
Arnold, Matthew	VII, 630, 649
Calverley, Charles Stuart	VII, 542
Eliot, George	VII, 185, 198
Russell, John Earl	VII, 144
RUSSELL HENRY,	
Clay, Henry	V, 732
Morris, George Pope	VI, 400
RUSSELL, JOHN EARL.	
Brougham, Henry Lord	VI, 530
Burke, Edmund	IV, 305
Canning, George	V, 67
Fox, Charles James	IV, 505
Moore, Thomas	V, 708, 717
Scott, Sir Walter	V, 142
Sheridan, Richard Brinsley	IV, 601
Smith, Sydney	V, 468
RUSSELL, J. SCOTT,	
Faraday, Michael	VI, 512
RUSSELL, PERCY,	
Ainsworth, William Harrison	VII, 488
Alcott, Louisa May	VII, 668
Carleton, William	VI, 549
Gaskell, Elizabeth Cleghorn	VI, 432
Gore, Catherine Grace	VI, 264
Hawthorne, Nathaniel	VI, 370
Reade, Charles	VII, 537
Scott, Michael	V, 279
Smollett, Tobias George	III, 590
RUSSELL, TOM,	
Savage, Richard	III, 134
RUSSELL, WILLIAM,	
Franklin, Benjamin	IV, 87
Montagu, Lady Mary Wortley	III, 463
RUSSELL, WILLIAM CLARK,	
Addison, Joseph	II, 638, 658
Bowles, William Lisle	V, 661
Brontë, Emily	V, 526
Dana, Richard Henry, Jr.	VII, 501
Gay, John	III, 54
Goldsmith, Oliver	III, 620, 623
Hervey, John Lord	III, 131
Philips, Ambrose	III, 273
RUST, GEORGE,	
Taylor, Jeremy	II, 203
RUTHERFORD, MILDRED,	
Craik, Dinah Maria Mulock	VII, 624
Havergal, Francis Ridley	VII, 166
Porter, Jane	V, 674
RUTHRAUFF, C. C.,	
Browne, Charles Farrar	VI, 501
RUTT, JOHN TOWILL,	
Priestley, Joseph	IV, 454
RYAN, RICHARD,	
Clare, John	VI, 398
Hogg, James	V, 267
Landon, Letitia Elizabeth	V, 322
Maturin Charles Robert	IV, 767
Raleigh, Sir Walter	I, 599
Tannahill, Robert	IV, 547
RYDER, ELIOT,	
Berners, Juliana	I, 191
Mangan, James Clarence	VI, 603
RYLAND, JOHN,	
Owen, John	II, 352
Waterland, Daniel	III, 103

	Vol. and Page
RYLE, J. C.,	
Whitefield, George	III, 550
Wesley, John	IV, 127
RYMER, THOMAS,	
Chaucer, Geoffrey	I, 155
D'Avenant, Sir William	II, 217
Milton, John	II, 257
Sackville, Charles	II, 553
Sackville, Thomas	I, 433
Shakespeare, William	I, 509, 511
Spenser, Edmund	I, 394
Waller, Edmund	II, 379

SABIN, JOHN F.,
Bancroft, George....VIII, 57
SACHS, JULIUS VON.
Ray, John | II. 543
SACKVILLE-WEST, REGINALD W.,
Sackville, Thomas | I, 432
SADLER, MICHAEL E.,
Sadler, Michael Thomas | V, 287
SAINTE-BEUVE, CHARLES AGUSTINE,
Cowper, William | IV, 383
Dryden, John | II, 502
Franklin, Benjamin | IV, 100
Gibbon, Edward | IV, 175
Milton, John | II, 292
Pope, Alexander | III, 189
Stanhope, Philip Dormer | III, 607
ST. JOHN, HENRY (VISCOUNT BOLINGBROKE),
History | VI, 6
ST. JOHN, JAMES AUGUSTUS,
Montagu, Lady Mary Wortley | III, 466
Park, Mungo | IV, 484
SAINTSBURY, GEORGE,
Addison, Joseph | II, 643, 661
Ainsworth, William Harrison | VII, 489
Akenside, Mark | III, 545
Alexander, Sir William | II, 36
Alison, Sir Archibald | VI, 522
Amory, Thomas | IV, 48
Armstrong, John | III, 699, 700
Arnold, Matthew | VII, 640
Arnold, Thomas | V, 381
Ascham, Roger | I, 291
Atterbury, Francis | III, 68
Austen, Jane | IV, 624
Aytoun, William Edmonstoune | VI, 445
Bacon, Francis | I, 657, 663
Bage, Robert | IV, 419
Baillie, Joanna | V, 695
Bale, John | I, 286
Barbauld, Anna Lætitia | V, 26
Barclay, Alexander | I, 265
Barham, Richard Harris | V, 476
Barnes, Barnabe | I, 440
Barton, Bernard | V, 597
Basse, William | II, 131
Beattie, James | IV, 433, 434
Beaumont, Joseph | II, 102
Beaumont and Fletcher | I, 584
Beckford, William | V, 450
Beddoes, Thomas Lovell | V, 589
Behn, Aphra | II, 410
Bentham, Jeremy | V, 169

	Vol. and Page
Beowulf	I, 21
Berkeley, George	III, 335
Blackmore, Richard D.	VIII, 432
Blackmore, Sir Richard	II, 747
Blair, Robert	III, 242
Blake, William	V, 63
Bloomfield, Robert	IV, 725
Borrow, George Henry	VII, 312
Boswell, James	IV, 218, 247
Breton, Nicholas	I, 678
Brontë, Charlotte	VI, 25
Brooke, Henry	III, 714
Browne, Sir Thomas	II, 345
Browne, William	II, 76
Browning, Robert	VII, 687, 715
Bryant, William Cullen	VII, 123
Buckle, Henry Thomas	VI, 284
Burke, Edmund	IV, 307
Burnet, Gilbert	II, 595, 596
Burnet, Thomas	II, 598
Burns, Robert	IV, 266
Burton, John Hill	VII, 317
Burton, Robert	II, 40
Butler, Joseph	III, 316
Butler, Samuel	II, 334
Byrom, John	III, 469, 470
Byron, George Gordon Lord	IV, 764
Campbell, Thomas	V, 445
Carew, Thomas	II, 23
Carlyle, Thomas	VII, 236, 240, 248, 250, 251
Cary, Henry Francis	V, 456
Caxton, William	I, 200
Centilivre, Susannah	II, 685
Chalmers, Thomas	V, 497
Chambers, Robert	VI, 621
Chapman, George	I, 731, 734
Chatterton, Thomas	III, 539
Chaucer, Geoffrey	I, 139, 171
Churchill, Charles	III, 482
Churchyard, Thomas	I, 418
Cibber, Colley	III, 373
Clive, Caroline	VI, 741
Clough, Arthur Hugh	VI, 255
Cobbett, William	V, 275
Coleridge, Hartley	V, 578
Coleridge, Samuel Taylor	V, 226
Collier, Jeremy	II, 702
Collins, Mortimer	VII, 83
Collins, William	III, 422
Congreve, William	II, 745
Constable, Henry	I, 444
Corbet, Richard	I, 743
Cotton, Charles	II, 372
Cowper, William	IV, 375, 384, 394
Crabbe, George	V, 177
Crashaw, Richard	II, 113
Cumberland, Richard	IV, 561
Cunningham, Allan	V, 385
Daniel, Samuel	I, 617
Darwin, Charles Robert	VII, 433
Davies, Sir John	I, 634
Davy, Sir Humphry	V, 94
Defoe Daniel	III, 27, 28, 29, 30, 41, 43
Dekker Thomas	II, 56, 58, 61
DeQuincey, Thomas	V, 128
Dickens, Charles	VI, 592, 611
Disraeli, Benjamin	VII, 287, 294
Disraeli, Isaac	V, 514

INDEX TO CRITICISMS

	Vol. and Page
Dobell, Sydney Thompson	VI, 766
Donne, John	I, 718
Douglas, Gawin	I, 216
Doyle, Sir Francis Hastings Charles	VII, 650
Drayton, Michael	I, 702, 705, 705, 708
Dryden, John	II, 467. 470, 470, 471, 472, 473, 473, 474 475, 476, 476, 478, 479, 481, 482, 484, 485, 489. 490, 506
Dyer, Sir Edward	I, 428
Edgeworth, Maria	V, 565
Eliot, George	VII, 186, 188, 198, 207
Elliott, Ebenezer	V, 584
Elyot, Sir Thomas	I, 254
Evelyn, John	II, 551
Felthan, Owen	II, 309
Fergusson, Robert	III, 642
Ferrier, James Frederick	VI, 411
Ferrier, Susan Edmonstone	V, 764
Fielding, Henry	III, 364
Finch, Anne, Countess of Winchilsea	II, 669
Fisher, John	I, 231
FitzGerald, Edward	VII, 517
Fletcher, Andrew	II, 611
Ford, John	II, 26, 27
Forster, John	VII, 68
Freeman, Edward Augustus	VIII, 160
Froude, James Anthony	VIII, 266
Fuller, Thomas	II, 173
Galt, John	V, 336
Garth, Sir Samuel	II, 666
Gascoigne, George	II, 309
Gay, John	II, 54
Gibbon, Edward	IV, 190, 193, 196
Gifford, William	V, 36
Godwin, Mary Wollstonecraft	IV, 328, 330
Godwin, William	V, 304
Goldsmith, Oliver	III, 622, 638
Gower, John	I, 177
Gray, Thomas	III, 572
Green, John Richard	VII, 509
Greene, Robert	I, 340, 343
Greville, Sir Fulke	I, 692
Habington, William	II, 135
Hall, Joseph	II, 145
Hallam, Arthur Henry	V, 199
Hallam, Henry	V, 180
Harrington, James	II, 308
Harvey, Gabriel	I, 697
Hawes, Stephen	I, 216
Hawkesworth, John	III, 610
Hayley, William	IV, 654
Hazlitt, William	V, 106
Heber, Reginald	V, 38
Helps, Sir Arthur	VII, 41
Henry the Minstrel	I, 202
Herbert, Edward Lord	II, 96, 97
Herbert, George	I, 724
Herrick, Robert	II. 236, 237, 240
Heywood, Thomas	II. 122, 123, 127
Hobbes, Thomas	II, 324, 328
Holcroft, Thomas	IV, 547
Home, John	IV, 515
Hooker, Richard	I, 411
Horne. Richard Hengist	VII, 546

	Vol. and Page
Howell, James	II, 186, 189
Hume, David	III, 660, 667
Hunt, James Henry Leigh	VI, 172
Huxley, Thomas Henry	VIII, 326
Hyde, Edward, Earl of Clarendon	II, 304
Irving, Edward	V, 249
James, George Payne Rainsford	VI, 220
Jefferies, Richard	VII, 622
Jeffrey, Francis Lord	V, 656
Jerrold, Douglas William	VI, 71
Johnson, Samuel	III, 736, 737, 742, 752
Jonson, Ben	I, 750, 756, 766
Jowett, Benjamin	VIII, 211
Junius	IV, 647
Keats, John	IV, 683
Keble, John	VI, 465
Kinglake, Alexander William	VIII, 53
Kingsley, Charles	VII, 28, 29, 32
Kingsley, Henry	VII, 80
Knowles, James Sheridan	VI, 289
Kyd, Thomas	I, 360
Lamb, Charles	V, 242
Landon, Letitia Elizabeth	V, 328
Landor, Walter Savage	VI, 392
Langhorne, John	III, 701
Langland, William	I, 122
Latimer, Hugh	I, 270
Lawrence, George Alfred	VII, 85
Leland, John	I, 264
Lever, Charles James	VI, 651, 656
Lewes, George Henry	VII, 140
Lewis, Sir George Cornewall	VI, 339
Locke, John	II, 536
Locker-Lampson, Frederick	VIII, 314
Lockhart, John Gibson	V, 758
Lodge, Thomas	I, 627
Logan, John	IV, 45
Lovelace, Richard	II, 163
Lyly, John	I, 424, 426
Lytton, Edward Robert Bulwer	VIII 47, 49
Lytton, Sir Edward George Bulwer	VI, 686
Macaulay, Thomas Babington Lord	VI, 103, 113, 122
Mackintosh, Sir James	V, 184
Macpherson, James	III, 281
Maginn, William	V, 389
Maine, Sir Henry James Sumner	VII, 653
Mallet, David	III, 497
Mandeville, Bernard	III, 71
Mandeville, Sir John	I, 98
Mansel, Henry Longueville	VI, 629
Marlowe, Christopher	I, 347, 352, 356
Marryat, Frederick	V, 533
Marston, John	I, 736 738
Martineau, Harriet	VII 54
Marvell, Andrew	II, 318
Massinger, Philip	II. 43. 44, 51
Mathias, Thomas James	IV, 289
Maturin, Charles Robert	IV, 767
Maurice, John Frederick Denison	VI 650

	Vol. and Page
Middleton, Conyers	III. 281
Middleton, Thomas	I, 686, 688
Mill, John Stuart	VI. 717
Milman, Henry Hart	VI. 539
Milnes, Richard Monckton	VII, 565
Minot, Lawrence	I, 94
Mitford, Mary Russell	VI. 44
Mitford, William	V, 71
Milton, John	II, 249, 253, 256, 275, 276, 278, 297.
Montagu, Lady Mary Wortley	III. 464. 467
Montgomery, James	V. 768
Moore, Edward	III 376
Moore, John	IV, 427
Moore, Thomas	V, 713, 718
More, Hannah	V. 196
More, Henry	II. 374
More, Sir Thomas	I, 241
Morris, William	VIII 336
Motherwell, William	V, 278
Nabbes, Thomas	II, 95
Napier, Gen. Sir Wm. Francis Patrick	VI, 223
Nashe, Thomas	I, 414
Newman, John Henry	VII, 755
Nicholas of Guilford	I, 77
North, Roger	III, 79, 81
Norton, Caroline E. S.	VII, 106
O'Keeffe. John	V, 197
O'Shaughnessy, Arthur Wm. Edgar	VII, 324
Paine, Thomas	IV, 541
Paley, William	IV, 474, 478
Parnell, Thomas	II, 618
Pater, Walter Horatio	VIII, 279
Pattison, Mark	VII, 541
Peacock, Reginald	I. 190
Peacock, Thomas Love	VI. 476
Peele, George	I, 365, 366
Philips, John	II. 564
Planché, James Robinson	VII 217
Poor, Richard	I, 70
Pope, Alexander	III, 194
Porson, Richard	IV, 526
Praed, Winthrop Mackworth	V. 333
Price, Richard	IV. 136
Prior, Matthew	II, 675
Procter, Bryan Waller	VI, 750
Pusey, Edward Bouverie	VII, 473
Puttenham, George	I, 402
Quarles, Francis	II, 79
Radcliffe, Ann Ward	IV, 721, 722
Raleigh, Sir Walter	I, 605
Randolph, Thomas	I, 744
Richardson, Samuel	III, 453
Robert of Gloucester	I, 82
Robertson, Frederick William	V, 741
Robertson. William	IV, 163
Rolle, Richard	I, 93
Rossetti, Christina Georgina	VIII, 274
Ruskin, John	VIII, 419
Sackville Thomas	I, 433
Saint-John Henry	III, 298
Savile. George	III. 450
Saxon Chronicle	I. 58
Scott Michael	V, 280

INDEX TO CRITICISMS

	Vol. and Page
Scott, Sir Walter	V, 137, 144, 153, 162
Selden, John	II, 138
Settle, Elkanah	II, 692
Shakespeare, William	I, 455, 459, 493, 498, 509, 532, 536, 542, 571.
Sheffield, John, Third Earl of Mulgrave	II, 672
Shelley, Percy Bysshe	IV, 716
Shenstone, William	474
Sheridan, Richard Brinsley	IV, 601
Sherlock, Thomas	III, 455
Sherlock, William	II, 562
Shirley, James	II, 192
Sidney, Sir Philip	I, 328
Smart, Christopher	III, 594
Smith, Adam	IV, 60, 67
Smith, Sydney	V, 473
Smollett, Tobias George	III, 590
Somerville, Mary	VI, 660
South, Robert	II, 610
Southerne, Thomas	III, 241
Southey, Caroline Anne Bowles	V, 763
Southey, Robert	V, 402, 408, 417
Spenser, Edmund	I, 386, 388, 390, 399
Stanhope, Philip Dormer	III, 608
Stanhope, Philip Henry Earl	VII, 48
Steele, Sir Richard	II, 756, 766, 768
Sterne, Laurence	III, 515
Stevenson, Robert Louis	VIII, 240, 249
Suckling, Sir John	II, 67
Surrey, Earl of	I, 259
Swift, Jonathan	III, 237
Sylvester, Joshua	I, 610
Symonds, John Addington	VIII, 206
Taylor, Jeremy	II, 205, 210
Taylor, Sir Henry	VII, 584
Temple, Sir William	II, 460
Tennyson, Alfred Lord	VIII, 86, 109
Thackeray, William Makepeace	VI, 303, 308, 311, 317
Thirlwall, Connop	VII, 43, 44
Thomson, James	III, 263, 264, 270
Thomson, James	VII, 476
Tickell, Thomas	III, 106
Ticknor, George	VI, 617, 618
Trench, Richard Chenevix	VII, 590
Trollope, Anthony	VII, 463
Trollope, Frances Milton	VI, 331
Tuberville, George	I, 439
Tucker, Abraham	III, 644
Tupper, Martin Farquhar	VII, 733
Tusser, Thomas	I, 311
Udall, Nicholas	I, 279
Urqurhant, Sir William	II, 165
Vaughan, Henry	II, 445
Wakefield, Gilbert	IV, 417
Walpole, Horace	IV, 321
Walton, Isaac	II, 349
Warburton, William	III, 687, 692
Ward, William George	VII, 485
Warner, William	I, 438
Warton, Thomas	IV, 75

	Vol. and Page
Watson, Thomas	I, 338
Webster, John	I, 671, 673
Whately, Richard	VI, 328
Whewell, William	VI, 472
White, Henry Kirke	IV, 490
Wilberforce, Samuel	VI, 735
Williams, Helen Maria	V, 75
Wilson, John	V, 748
Wither, George	II, 213
Wolcot, John	IV, 650
Wyatt, Sir Thomas	I, 252
Young, Arthur	IV, 656
Young, Edward	III, 490, 494
SAINT-VICTOR, PAUL DE,	
Swift, Jonathan	III, 233
SALA, GEORGE AUGUSTUS,	
Ainsworth, William Harrison	VII, 489
Brougham, Henry Lord	VI, 527
Bayly, Thomas Haynes	V, 340
Dickens, Charles	VI, 592
Taylor, Tom	VII, 215
SALMON, ARTHUR L.,	
Brontë, Emily	V, 524
SALT, HENRY S.,	
Jefferies, Richard	VII, 618, 620
Melville, Herman	VIII, 62, 64
Shelley, Percy Bysshe	IV, 716
Thomson, James	VII, 474, 477
Thoreau, Henry David	VI, 271
SALVINI, TOMMASO,	
Shakespeare, William	I, 506
SAMPSON, GEORGE,	
Berkeley George	III, 326, 328
SANBORN, FRANKLIN BENJAMIN,	
Alcott, Amos Bronson	VII, 664
Bailey, Philip James	VIII, 461
Emerson, Ralph Waldo	VII, 355, 357
Edwards, Jonathan	III, 393
Gray, Thomas	III, 569
Thoreau, Henry David	VI, 267, 273
SANBORN, KATE A.,	
Austen, Jane	IV, 622
Behn, Aphra	II, 410
Burney, Frances	V, 350
Fuller, Sarah Margaret	V, 668
More, Hannah	V, 192
Morgan, Sydney Owensen Lady	VI, 193
Sigourney, Lydia Huntley	VI, 452
SAND, GEORGE,	
Stowe, Harriet Beecher	VIII, 351
SANDAY, W.,	
Church, Richard William	VII, 728
SANDERS, H. M.,	
Herrick, Robert	II, 235
Otway, Thomas	I, 363, 364
SANDERS, LLOYD C.,	
Aguilar, Grace	V, 504
Barnard, Lady Anne	V, 28
Coleridge, Sara	V, 733
DeMorgan, Augustus	VI, 632
Gilfillan, George	VII, 150
Hall, Robert	V, 108
Hone, William	V, 393
Hutchinson, Thomas	III, 707
Kane, Elisha Kent	VI, 80

	Vol. and Page
Landon, Letitia Elizabeth	V, 322
Madison, James	V, 311
Murchison, Sir Roderick Impey	VI, 631
Opie, Amelia	V, 741
Palgrave, Sir Francis	VI, 265
Phillips, Wendell	VII, 552
Ripley, George	VII, 223
Scott, Michael	V, 278
Smith, James	V, 337
Somerville, Mary	VI, 657
Spedding, James	VII, 317
Story, Joseph	V, 482
Strickland, Agnes	VI, 766
Stubbs, William	VIII, 452
Tennant, William	V, 527
Ward, William George	VII, 481
Whately, Richard	VI, 323
Wilkinson, Sir John Gardner	VII, 50
Wiseman, Nicholas Patrick	VI, 434
SANDERS, REV. FRANCIS,	
Pearson, John	II, 368
SANDERSON, EDGAR,	
Bacon, Francis	I, 652
Chaucer, Geoffrey	I, 147
Hooker, Richard	I, 410
Howe, John	II, 546
Wyclif, John	I, 110
SANDERSON, JOHN,	
Adams, Samuel	IV, 442
Franklin, Benjamin	IV, 85
SANDFORD, SIR DANIEL KEYTE,	
Richardson, Samuel	III, 449
Sterne, Laurence	III, 513
SANDHAM, HENRY,	
Jackson, Helen Hunt	VII, 574
SANDRAS, E. G,	
Chaucer, Geoffrey	I, 162
SANDYS, GEORGE,	
Bacon, Francis	I, 663
Sandys, George	II, 81
SANDYS, J. E.,	
Bentley, Richard	III, 117, 118
Thirlwall, Connop	VII, 44
SANTAYANA, GEORGE,	
Browning, Robert	VII, 718
Emerson, Ralph Waldo	VII, 379
Shakespeare, William	I, 577
Whitman, Walt	VIII, 152
SARGANT, WILLIAM LUCAS,	
Owen, Robert	VI, 84
SARGENT EPES,	
Adams, Sarah Flower	V, 529
Browne, William	II, 76
Clay, Henry	V, 730
Collins, Mortimer	VII, 81
Dyer, Sir Edward	I, 427
Fields, James Thomas	VII, 341
Green, Matthew	III, 95
King, Henry	II, 223
Longfellow, Henry Wadsworth	VII, 406
Mickle, William Julius	IV, 40
Smith, James	V, 339
Sprague, Charles	VII, 52
Tuckerman, Henry Theodore	VI, 643
SARGENT, MRS. JOHN T.,	
Emerson, Ralph Waldo	VII, 367

INDEX TO CRITICISMS

	Vol. and Page
SARGENT, W.,	
Smollett, Tobias George	III. 576
SARGEAUNT, JOHN,	
Johnson, Samuel	III, 748
SARRAZIN, GABRIEL,	
Whitman, Walt	VII, 136
SAUNDERS, CHARLES,	
Marlowe, Christopher	I, 348
SAUNDERS, FREDERICK,	
Audubon, John James	V. 699
Bryant, William Cullen	VII, 126
Byrom, John	III. 470
Chalmers, Thomas	V. 495
Chaucer, Geoffrey	I. 167
Cowper, William	IV. 377, 392
Doddridge, Philip	III, 302
Drake, Joseph Rodman	IV. 661
Evelyn, John	II, 550
Havergal, Frances Ridley	VII, 167
Heber, Reginald	V. 38
Hood, Thomas	V, 463
Jameson, Anna	VI, 216
Johnson, Samuel	III, 765
Longfellow, Henry Wadsworth.	
	VII. 413
Montgomery, James	V. 768
Smollett, Tobias George	III, 578
Toplady, Augustus Montague.	
	III, 681
Vaughan, Henry	II, 445
Wesley, Charles	IV, 38
White, Henry Kirke	IV, 489
Young, Edward	III, 490
SAUNDERS, DR. RICHARD,	
Franklin, Benjamin	IV, 96
SAUNDERS, T. BAILEY,	
Knowles, James Sheridan	VI, 289
Macpherson, James	IV, 272
Porson, Richard	IV, 521
SAVAGE, MINOT JUDSON,	
Brooks, Phillips	VIII, 227
Emerson, Ralph Waldo	VII, 368
Holmes, Oliver Wendell	VII, 287
Lowell, James Russell	VIII, 24
Spencer, Herbert	VIII, 478, 482
Whitman, Walt	VIII, 149
SAVAGE, RICHARD,.	
Dennis, John	III, 76
Fenton, Elijah	III, 20
Hill, Aaron	III, 278
Hutchinson, Thomas	III, 708
Montagu, Lady Mary Wortley.	
	III, 460
Pope, Alexander	III, 145, 171
Savage, Richard	III, 131
Thomson, James	III, 266
SAVAGE, W. H.,	
Longfellow, Henry Wadsworth.	
	VII, 413
Whittier, John Greenleaf	VIII, 127
SAVILE, BOURCHIER WREY,	
Pusey, Edward Bouverie	VII, 472
SAXE, JOHN GODFREY,	
Burns, Robert	IV, 258
Poe, Edgar Allan	V, 557
SAXON CHRONICLE,	
Ælfric	I, 46
SAY, JEAN-BAPTISTE,	
Smith, Adam	IV, 62
SAYCE, A. H.,	
Whitney, William Dwight	VIII, 303

	Vol. and Page
SAYLE, CHARLES,	
Barnes, William	VII, 587
SCANLON, THOMAS,	
George, Henry	VIII. 382
SCHAFF, D. S.,	
Hooker, Richard	I, 409
SCHAFF PHILIP,	
Beecher, Henry Ward	VII. 601
Wiseman, Nicholas Patrick	VI, 435
SCHAFF, PHILIP, AND GILMAN, ARTHUR,	
Whittier, John Greenleaf	VIII, 123
SCHAFF, PHILIP, AND HERZOG, JOHANN JAKOB,	
Colet, John	I, 210
Doddridge, Philip	III, 299
Henry, Matthew	II, 585
Horsley, Samuel	IV, 494
Lowth, William	III, 62
Spotiswood, John	II, 24
Wakefield, Gilbert	IV, 415
SCHEFFIELD, LORD,	
Bruce, James	IV, 206
SCHELLING, FELIX E.,	
Ascham, Roger	I, 291
Breton, Nicholas	I, 679
Chapman, George	I, 734
Daniel, Samuel	I, 614
Donne, John	I, 718
Gascoigne, George	I, 309
Greville, Sir Fulke	I, 692
Heywood, Thomas	II, 128
Middleton, Thomas	I, 686
Munday, Anthony	I, 726
Nashe, Thomas	I, 415
Puttenham, George	I, 402
Watson, Thomas	I, 338
Wither, George	II, 215
Wyatt, Sir Thomas	I, 252
SCHERER, EDMOND,	
Byron, George Gordon Lord	IV, 740, 760
Carlyle, Thomas	VII. 268
Disraeli, Benjamin	VII, 278, 291
Eliot, George	VII, 183, 186, 194
Gladstone, William Ewart	VIII, 384
Keats, John	IV, 678
Mill, John Stuart	VI, 708, 710
Milton, John	II, 264, 277
Shelley, Percy Bysshe	IV, 709
Sterne, Laurence	III, 514
Tennyson, Alfred Lord	
	VIII, 102, 103
Wordsworth, William	V, 627, 640
SCHERER, WILHELM,	
Alcuin	I, 33
Aldhelm	I, 25
Defoe, Daniel	III, 36
Macpherson, James	IV, 278
Milton, John	II, 267
Richardson, Samuel	III, 451
Sterne, Laurence	III, 509
SCHERMERHORN, MARTIN K.,	
Paine, Thomas	IV, 540
SCHERR, J.,	
Addison, Joseph	II, 651
Bacon, Francis	I, 661
Brown, Charles Brockden	IV, 553
Browning, Elizabeth Barrett	
	VI, 236

	Vol. and Page
Browning, Robert	VII. 701
Bryant, William Cullen	VII. 123
Bunyan, John	II, 392
Burns, Robert	IV, 259
Byron, George Gordon Lord	IV, 754
Chatterton, Thomas	III, 538
Congreve, William	II, 743
Cowley, Abraham	II, 196
Cowper, William	IV, 380
Dana, Richard Henry	VII, 156
Dickens, Charles	VI, 570, 573
Draper, John William	VII, 503
Eliot, George	VII, 183, 191
Emerson, Ralph Waldo	VII, 365
Grote, George	VI, 610
Halleck, Fitz-Greene	VI, 499
Hazlitt, William	V, 104
Hume, David	III, 659
Johnson, Samuel	III, 760
Knowles, James Sheridan	VI, 289
Longfellow, Henry Wadsworth.	
	VII, 395
Marlowe, Christopher	I, 355
Otway, Thomas	II, 365
Percy, Thomas	IV, 564
Poe, Edgar Allan	V, 551
Pope, Alexander	III, 177
Prescott, William Hickling	VI, 191
Raleigh, Sir Walter	I, 604
Richardson, Samuel	III, 450
Shelley, Percy Bysshe	IV, 699
Shakespeare, William	I, 568
Smollett, Tobias George	III, 589
Stanhope, Philip Dormer	III, 606
Thackeray, William Makepeace	
	VI, 310, 316
Waller, Edmund	II, 383
SCHICK, J.,	
Kyd, Thomas	I, 360
SCHILLER JOHANN CHRISTOPH FRIEDERICH,	
Darwin, Erasmus	IV, 422
SCHILLER, F. C. S.,	
Darwin, Charles Robert	VII, 433
SCHIMMELPENNICK, MARY ANNE,	
Darwin, Erasmus	IV, 421
Priestley, Joseph	IV, 448
SCHLEGEL, AUGUSTUS WILIAM,	
Addison, Joseph	II, 649
Beaumont and Fletcher	I. 580
D'Avenant, Sir William	II, 219
Drama, The	VII, 6
Dryden, John	II, 498
Garrick, David	III. 695
Johnson, Samuel	III. 746
Jonson, Ben	I. 762
Lillo, George	III, 100
Locke, John	I, 533
Lyly, John	I. 424
Marlowe, Christopher	I. 349
Massinger, Philip	II, 47
Otway, Thomas	II, 364
Pope, Alexander	III. 170
Rowe, Nicholas	II. 622
Sackville, Thomas	I, 434
Shakespeare, William	
	I, 464, 472, 485. 502, 507, 515. 520
SCHLEGEL, FREDERICK,	
Bacon, Francis	I, 658
Byron, George Gordon Lord	IV, 755

INDEX TO CRITICISMS

	Vol. and Page
Chaucer, Geoffrey	I, 158
Gibbon, Edward	IV, 181
Hobbes, Thomas	II, 325
Hume, David	III, 656, 661
Jones, Sir William	IV, 198
Locke, John	II, 525, 533
Macpherson, James	IV, 275
Milton, John	II, 260
Newton, Sir Isaac	II, 723
Richardson, Samuel	III, 448
Robertson, William	IV, 162
Scott, Sir Walter	V, 135
Shakespeare, William	I, 556
Spenser, Edmund	I, 395

SCHLOSSER, FRDEERICK CHRISTOPH,

Fielding, Henry	III, 358
Franklin, Benjamin	IV, 85
Gibbon, Edward	IV, 182
Hume, David	III, 656
Mandeville, Bernard	III, 69
Montagu, Elizabeth	IV, 400
Steele, Sir Richard	II, 756, 758

SCHMID, FANNY,

Lover, Samuel	VI, 545

SCHMIDT, RUDOLF,

Whitman, Walt	VIII, 148

SCHMITZ, LEONHARDT,

Chaucer, Geoffrey	I, 126

SCHOOLCRAFT, HENRY R.,

Longfellow, Henry Wadsworth ...... VII, 395

SCHOPENHAUER, ARTHUR,

Critic, The	II, 6

SCHOULER, JAMES,

Jefferson, Thomas	V, 49
Parkman, Francis	VIII, 219, 222

SCHULZE-GAEVERNITZ, GERHART VON,

Carlyle, Thomas	VII, 271

SCHURZ, CARL,

Clay, Henry	V, 733
Lincoln, Abraham	VI, 418
Webster, Daniel	V, 724, 729

SCHUYLER, EUGENE,

Browning, Elizabeth Barrett	VI, 234, 241
Dickens, Charles	VI, 590
Hawthorne, Nathaniel	VI, 360
Landor, Walter Savage	VI, 386
Longfellow, Henry Wadsworth	VII, 399
Rogers, Samuel	VI, 36
Shelley, Percy Bysshe	IV, 697
Smollett, Tobias George	III, 585

SCHUYLER, MONTGOMERY,

Keats, John	IV, 682
Stevenson, Robert Louis	VIII, 251

SCHWEGLER, ALBERT,

Hume, David	III, 662
Locke, John	II 526

SCOLLARD, CLINTON,

Cleveland, John	II, 159, 160
Hayne, Paul Hamilton	VII, 592
Keats, John	IV, 666

SCOLOKER, ANTHONY,

Shakespeare, William	I, 500

SCOONES, W. BAPTISTE,

Herrick, Robert	II, 239
Howell, James	II, 187
Montagu, Elizabeth	IV, 402

	Vol. and Page
Sidney, Algernon	II, 355
Temple, Sir William	II, 459
Waller, Edmund	II, 382
Walpole, Horace	IV, 319

SCOTT, ADAM,

Scott, Sir Walter	V, 134

SCOTT, CLEMENT,

Arnold, Sir Edwin	VIII, 502
Planché, James Robinson	VII, 215, 216
Taylor, Tom	VII, 215

SCOTT, DAVID.

Blake, William	V, 58
Sterne, Laurence	III, 510

SCOTT, FRED N.,

Johnson, Samuel	III, 720

SCOTT, HENRY W.,

Choate, Rufus	VI, 197

SCOTT, JOHN,

Scott, Sir Walter	V, 141

SCOTT, ROBERT,

Wiseman, Nicholas Patrick. VI, 435

SCOTT, SIR WALTER,

Addison, Joseph	II, 635
Ainsworth, William Harrison	VII, 487
Anstey, Christopher	IV, 480
Austen, Jane	IV, 614, 617, 619
Bage, Robert	IV, 419
Baillie, Joanna	V, 692
Beaumont and Fletcher	I, 580
Behn, Aphra	II, 409
Bentley, Richard	III,121
Berkeley, George	III, 320
Boswell, James	IV, 210, 215
Brougham, Henry Lord	VI, 523
Bunyan, John	II, 389, 393
Burke, Edmund	IV, 291
Burney, Frances	V, 344
Burns, Robert	IV, 226
Butler, Samuel	II, 331
Byron, George Gordon Lord	IV, 742, 747, 748, 752
Campbell, Thomas	V, 442
Canning, George	V, 66
Chambers, Robert	VI, 621
Chatterton, Thomas	III, 535
Chaucer, Geoffrey	I, 150
Churchill, Charles	III, 479
Coleridge, Samuel Taylor	V, 214
Collier, Jeremy	II, 700
Collins William	III, 419
Congreve, William	II, 740
Cooper, James Fenimore	V 679
Cumberland, Richard	IV, 559, 561
Cunningham, Allan	V, 382, 383
D'Avenant, Sir William	II, 218
Davy, Sir Humphry	V, 93
Defoe. Daniel	III, 30, 34, 42, 45
Douglas, Gawin	I, 213
Drama, The	VII 6
Dryden, John	II, 464, 470, 471, 471, 472, 473, 475, 475, 475, 477, 478, 478, 479, 479, 479, 480, 480, 480, 481, 481, 482, 484, 484, 486, 487, 491, 492, 492
Edgeworth, Maria	V, 562, 568
Evelyn, John	II, 549
Ferrier, Susan Edmondstone	V, 763
Fielding, Henry	III, 346, 352, 358

	Vol. and Page
Foote, Samuel	III. 673
Fox Charles James	IV, 500
Frere, John Hookham	V, 486
Galt, John	V, 335
Gifford, William	V, 32, 34
Godwin, William	V, 299, 301, 302, 303
Goldsmith, Oliver	III, 626, 633, 636
Grahame, James	IV, 566, 567
Grant, Anne	V, 329
Heber, Reginald	V, 37
Hemans, Felicia Dorothea	V, 257
Home, John	IV, 514
Irving, Edward	V, 246
Irving, Washington	VI, 138
Jeffrey, Francis Lord	V, 653
Johnson, Samuel	III, 739, 755
Johnstone, Charles	IV, 413
Jonson, Ben	I, 761
Junius	IV, 640
Knox, William	V, 30, 31
Langhorne, John	III, 700
Lewis, Matthew Gregory	IV, 632
Lillo, George	III, 101
Lockhart, John Gibson	V, 755
Lyly, John	I, 422
Lyndsay, Sir David	I, 274
Lytton, Sir Ewdard George Bulwer	VI, 685
Mackenzie, Henry	V, 113. 115
Macpherson, James	IV, 275
Malory, Sir Thomas	I, 204
Massinger, Philip	II, 46
Maturin, Charles Robert	IV, 767, 768
Milton, John	II, 251
Moore, Thomas	V, 706
Morgan, Sydney Owenson Lady	VI, 194
Napier, Sir William Francis Patrick	VI, 221
Otway, Thomas	II, 366
Parr, Samuel	V, 17
Pepys, Samuel	II, 514
Percy, Thomas	IV, 563
Poets and Poetry	IV, 6
Pope, Alexander	III, 147
Prior, Matthew	II, 677
Radcliffe, Ann Ward	IV, 718, 719
Ramsay, Allan	III, 405, 409
Reeve, Clara	IV, 512
Richardson, Samuel	III, 434, 436, 439, 448
Ritson, Joseph	IV, 435, 436
Rogers, Samuel	VI, 32
Rowe, Nicholas	II, 620
Savage, Richard	III, 135
Settle, Elkanah	II, 692
Seward, Anna	IV, 541, 542
Scott, Sir Walter	V, 139
Shadwell, Thomas	II, 434
Shakespeare, William	I, 515, 555
Sheffield, John, Third Earl of Mulgrave	II, 671
Shelley, Mary Wollstonecraft	V, 702
Sheridan, Richard Brinsley	IV, 606
Smith, Charlotte	IV, 497
Smollett, Tobias George	III, 575, 581, 583, 584, 587
Southey, Robert	V, 412
Spenser, Edmund	I 381, 395

INDEX TO CRITICISMS

	Vol. and Page
Sterne, Laurence	III, 502, 507, 512
Stevenson, John Hill	IV, 24
Surrey, Earl of	I, 255
Swift, Jonathan	III, 200, 208, 220, 223, 225
Tate, Nahum	II, 589
Thomas of Erceldoune	I, 83
Thomson, James	III, 267
Tusser, Thomas	I, 310
Villiers, George	II, 376
Walpole, Horace	IV, 317, 318
Warton, Thomas	IV, 73
Webster, John	I, 675
Wesley, John	IV, 121
White, Henry Kirke	IV, 487
Wilson, John	V, 744
Wolcot, John	IV, 650
Wordsworth, William	V, 630
Young, Edward	III, 491
SCOTT, WILLIAM,	
Laud, William	II, 92
Law, William	III, 427
SCOTT, WILLIAM BELL,	
Burns, Robert	IV, 230
Keats, John	IV, 678
Motherwell, William	V, 276
SCOTT, W. J.,	
Wesley, John	IV, 122
SCOVEL, JAMES MATLACK,	
Arnold, Sir Edwin	VIII, 502
Seward, William Henry	VI, 673
SCRIBNER, WILLIAM,	
Faber, Frederick William	VI, 334
SCRYMGEOUR, DANIEL,	
Lockhart, John Gibson	V, 757
SCUDDER, HORACE E.,	
Blake, William	V, 58
Browning, Robert	VII, 703
Bunyan, John	II, 398
Holmes, Oliver Wendell	III, 298
Johnson, Samuel	III, 744
Keats, John	IV, 684
Landor, Walter Savage	V, 385
Longfellow, Henry Wadsworth	VII, 400, 412
Lowell, James Russell	VIII, 26
Ruskin, John	VIII, 415
Webster, Noah	V, 428, 429, 431
Whittier, John Greenleaf	VIII, 119
SCUDDER, VIDA D.,	
Arnold, Matthew	VII, 639
Austen, Jane	IV, 624
Browning, Robert	VII, 714
Bunyan, John	II, 400
Byron, George Gordon Lord	IV, 763
Chaucer, Geoffrey	I, 169
Clough, Arthur Hugh	VI, 254
Eliot, George	VII, 195, 208
Langland, William	I, 123
Macaulay, Thomas Babington Lord	VI, 114
Milton, John	II, 268, 298
More, Sir Thomas	I, 238
Morris, William	VIII, 337
Newman, John Henry	VII, 749
Rossetti, Gabriel Charles Dante	VII, 454
Scott, Sir Walter	V, 146
Shelley, Percy Bysshe	IV, 702
Spenser, Edmund	I, 400
Swift, Jonathan	III, 206

	Vol. and Page
Tennyson, Alfred Lord	VIII, 89
Wordsworth, William	V, 646
SCULL, W. DELAPLAINE,	
Du Maurier, George	VIII, 344
SEARGILL, W. P.,	
Cudworth, Ralph	II, 385
SEARLE, W. S.,	
Beecher, Henry Ward	VII, 601
SEARS, EDWARD I.,	
Boyle, Robert	II, 417
SEARS, LORENZO,	
Adams, Samuel	IV, 444
Bede	I, 26
Calhoun, John Caldwell	V, 676
Clay, Henry	V, 733
Otis, James	III, 717
Pitt, William	III, 680
Sheridan, Richard Brinsley	IV, 601
Sumner, Charles	VI, 756
SEATON, R. C.,	
Shelley, Percy Bysshe	IV, 703
SECCOMBE, THOMAS,	
Lovelace Richard	II, 163
Montgomery, Robert	VI, 48
Munday, Anthony	I, 726
Pitt, Christopher	III, 254
Pomfret, John	II, 511
Robertson, William	IV, 155, 158, 161
Rowley, William	II, 69
Settle, Elkanah	II, 692
Smart, Christopher	III, 592, 594
Smollett, Tobias George	III, 577, 580, 591
Sylvester, Joshua	I, 610
Temple, Sir William	II, 460
Thomson, James	III, 266, 272
Tourneur, Cyril	I, 689
Tuberville, George	I, 439
Urqurhart, Sir Thomas	II, 165
Vanbrugh, Sir John	II, 704, 706
Warren, Samuel	VII, 107, 108
Williams, Roger	II, 357
Williams, Sir Charles Hanbury	III, 413
Winthrop, John	II, 109
SEDLEY, SIR CHARLES,	
Shakespeare, William	I, 551
SEDGWICK, ADAM,	
Chambers, Robert	VI, 620
Darwin, Charles Robert	VII, 422
Lyell, Sir Charles	VII, 37
SEDGWICK, ARTHUR GEORGE,	
Darwin, Erasmus	IV, 425
Disraeli, Benjamin	VII, 283, 291, 293
Eliot, George	VII, 199
Fields, James Thomas	VII, 341
Hamilton, Alexander	IV, 464
Irving, Washington	VI, 151
Kent, James	V, 501
Lever, Charles James	VI, 654
Reade, Charles	VII, 535
Ruskin, John	VIII, 415
SEDGWICK, CATHARINE M.,	
Brontë, Charlotte	VI, 28
Bronte, Emily	V, 523
Brooke, Henry	III, 715
Channing, William Ellery	V, 365
Cooper, James Fenimore	V, 680
Davidson, Lucretia Maria	V, 27

	Vol. and Page
Eliot, George	VII, 185
Fuller, Sarah Margaret	V, 666
Hemans, Felicia Dorothea	V, 255
Jameson, Anna	VI, 213
Jeffrey, Francis Lord	V, 651
Kemble, Frances Ann	VIII, 214
Marshall, John	V, 281
Martineau, Harriet	VII, 55
Mitford, Mary Russell	VI, 41
Opie, Amelia	V, 741
Scott, Sir Walter	V, 154
Thackeray, William Makepeace	VI, 313
Ware, Henry, Jr	V, 432
SEDGWICK, ELLERY,	
Paine, Thomas	IV, 534
SEDGWICK, HENRY DWIGHT,	
Bryant, William Cullen	VII, 114
James, George Payne Rainsford	VI, 217
Jameson, Anna	VI, 214
Martineau, Harriet	VII, 59
SEDGWICK, HENRY D., JR.,	
Bryant, William Cullen	VII, 127
Thackeray, William Makepeace	VI, 321
SEDGWICK, THEODORE,	
Livingston, William	IV, 109
SEEBOHM, FREDERIC,	
Colet, John	I, 211
SEELEY, JOHN ROBERT,	
Milton, John	II, 293
SEELEY, L. B.	
Burney, Frances	V, 350
Walpole, Horace	IV, 320
SEITZ, DON C.,	
Browne, Charles Farrar	VI, 502
SELBORNE, LORD,	
Wordsworth, William	V, 642
SELBY, THOMAS G.,	
Eliot, George	VII, 207
Hawthorne, Nathaniel	VI, 355, 357
SELBY-BIGGE, L. A.,	
Mandeville, Bernard	III, 71
Smith, Adam	IV, 60
SELDEN, JOHN,	
Browne, William	II, 73
Langland, William	I, 117
SELIGMAN, EDWIN R. A.,	
Owens, Robert	VI, 85
SELLARS, WILLIAM YOUNG,	
Shairp, John Campbell	VII, 569
SELWYN, GEORGE,	
Whitman, Walt	VIII, 131, 142
SENDALL, WALTER J.,	
Calverley, Charles Stuart	VII, 542, 543
SENIOR, A. W.,	
Scott, Sir Walter	V, 151, 151, 154
SENIOR, WILLIAM NASSAU,	
Scott, Sir Walter	V, 143
SERGEANT, ADELINE,	
Clive, Caroline	VI, 741
SERGEANT, LEWIS,	
Knox, John	I, 298
Pitt, William	IV, 509
Wyclif, John	I, 102, 110
SERVICE, JOHN,	
Burns, Robert	IV, 246, 260
Ferguson, Robert	III, 641
Stanley, Arthur Penrhyn	VII, 297

INDEX TO CRITICISMS 673

SETH ANDREW
 Hamilton Sir William.....VI, 57
 Huxley Thomas Henry..VIII, 327
 Paley William.......IV, 474, 478
 Reid. Thomas ....IV, 287
 Stewart Dugald...........V, 76
SETON GEORGE.
 Montagu, Lady Mary Wortley
 ....III, 467
 Thackeray. William Makepeace
 ....VI, 294
 Lytton. Edward Robert Bulwer..............VIII, 43, 45
SETOUN, GABRIFJ.
 Burns, Robert........IV, 241, 243
SEVERON, JOSEPH,
 Keats, John......IV. 662, 664, 668
SEWALL, FRANK,
 Symonds, John Addington....
 ....VIII, 205
SEWARD, ANNA,
 Darwin, Erasmus......IV, 420, 423
 Johnson, Samuel..........III, 722
 Reeve, Clara.............IV, 512
 Scott, Sir Walter...........V, 126
 Walpole, Horace..........IV, 310
SEWARD, WILLIAM H.,
 Adams, John Quincy........V, 517
 Clay, Henry..............V, 730
SEWARD, WILLIAM,
 Somers, John Lord.........II, 614
SEWALL, SAMUEL,
 Mather, Cotton............II, 727
SEWEL, WILLIAM,
 Barclay, Robert...........II, 411
SEWELL, GEORGE,
 Philips, John.............II, 56
SEWELL, HENRY,
 Spencer, Herbert........VIII, 482
SEWELL, WILLIAM,
 Carlyle, Thomas..........VII, 247
SEYMOUR. CHARLES C. B.,
 Jones, Sir William.........IV, 198
SEYMOUR, E. H.,
 Shakespeare, William.......I, 531
SEYMOUR, F. H.,
 Dryden, John.............II, 476
SEYMOUR, THOMAS DAY,
 Whitney, William Dwight....
 ....VIII, 302, 303
SHADWELL, CHARLES L.,
 Pater, Walter Horatio....VIII, 278
SHADWELL, THOMAS,
 Dryden, John............II, 489
 Fletcher, John............I 628
 Sedley, Sir Charles........II, 509
 Shakespeare, William.......I, 529
SHADWICK, WILLIAM,
 Defoe Daniel............III, 25
SHAFTESBURY, ANTHONY ASHLEY COOPER EARL,
 Books..................III, 6
 Cooper, Anthony Ashley....II, 577
 Shakespeare, William.......I, 551
 Taylor, Jeremy............II 206
SHAIRP, JOHN CAMPBELL,
 Blair, Hugh..............IV, 406
 Burns, Robert....IV, 231, 245, 259
 Byron, George Gordon Lord IV, 762
 Carlyle, Thomas......VII, 248, 268
 Chaucer, Geoffrey..........I, 165
43 G

Coleridge, Samuel Taylor....
 ....V, 216, 220
Collins, William..........III, 418
Cowper, William..........IV, 380
Fergusson, Robert.........III, 641
Goldsmith, Oliver.........III, 631
Gray, Thomas.............III, 568
Keats, John..............IV, 679
Keble, John..........VI, 458, 462
Macpherson, James........IV, 278
Milton, John..........II, 265, 293
Mozley, James Bowling......
 ....VII, 147, 149
Newman, John Henry VII, 746, 751
Ramsay, Allan.......III, 407, 410
Rossetti, Gabriel Charles Dante
 ....VII, 451
Scott, Sir Walter........V, 136, 159
Shakespeare, William......I, 568
Shelley, Percy Bysshe......IV, 702
Stewart, Dugald...........V, 80
Tennyson, Alfred Lord......
 ....VIII, 79, 104
Thomson, James..........III, 260
Wordsworth, William...V, 622, 625
SHAKESPEARE, WILLIAM,
 Authors and Authorship..VIII, 5
 Books..................III, 5
 Chaucer, Geoffrey..........I, 139
 Drama, The..............VII, 5
 Gower, John..............I, 174
 Knowledge................V, 5
 More, Sir Thomas..........I, 234
 Poets and Poetry..........IV, 5
 Shakespeare, William.......
 ....I, 454, 456, 457, 472
 Spenser, Edmund.......I, 368, 393
SHALER, N. S.,
 Huxley, Thomas Henry..VIII, 328
SHANKS, CHARLES G.,
 Prentice, George Denison...VI, 601
 Simms, George Denison....VI, 603
SHARP, ELIZABETH A.,
 Baillie, Joanna............V 695
 Browning, Elizabeth Barrett..
 ....VI, 239
 Hemans, Felicia Dorothea...V, 261
 Oliphant, Carolina........V, 478
SHARP, JOHN,
 Gray, Thomas...........III, 553
SHARP, R. FARQUHARSON,
 Addison, Joseph..........II, 632
 Ainsworth, William Harrison..
 ....VII, 485
 Arbuthnot, John..........III, 81
 Arnold, Matthew.........VII, 627
 Arnold, Sir Edwin......VIII, 501
 Arnold, Thomas..........IV, 376
 Bacon, Francis............I, 638
 Bagehot, Walter..........VII, 96
 Bailey, Philip James.....VIII, 459
 Banim, John.............V, 389
 Barbauld, Anna Lætitia.....V, 22
 Barham, Richard Harris....V, 474
 Barnes, William..........VII, 584
 Baxter, Richard..........II, 423
 Beaumont and Fletcher.....I, 578
 Beaumont, Francis........I, 586
 Beattie, James...........IV, 428
 Beckford, William........V, 446
 Beddoes, Thomas Lovell....V, 584

Behn, Aphra.............II, 407
Bentham, Jeremy.........V, 162
Bentley, Richard.........III, 109
Berkeley, George.........III, 378
Black, William.........VIII, 393
Blake, William............V, 56
Borrow, George Henry....VII, 306
Boswell, James...........IV, 209
Brontë, Charlotte.........VI, 17
Brown. John............VII, 477
Browne, Sir Thomas.......II 339
Browning, Elizabeth Barrett..
 ....VI, 228
Browning, Robert........VII, 677
Bruce, James............IV, 265
Buchanan, George.........I, 313
Bunyan, John............II 388
Burke, Edmund..........IV, 287
Burnet, Gilbert...........II, 590
Burney, Charles..........IV, 265
Burney, Frances..........V, 343
Burton, Sir Richard Francis..
 ....VII, 757
Butler, Joseph....... III, 306, 318
Byron, George Gordon Lord.IV, 731
Calverley, Charles Stuart..VII, 541
Campbell, Thomas........V, 433
Carleton, William........VI, 548
Carey, Henry Francis......V, 455
Centlivre, Susannah.......II, 682
Chambers, Robert........VI, 618
Chapman, George..........I, 727
Chatterton, Thomas......III, 527
Churchill, Charles.......III, 475
Cibber, Colley..........III, 369
Coleridge, Hartley.........V, 572
Coleridge, Samuel Taylor....V, 205
Collier, Jeremy...........II, 698
Collins, William.........III, 414
Collins, William Wilkie...VII, 725
Colman, George..........IV, 200
Colman, George, Jr........V, 315
Congreve, William........II, 733
Cooper, Anthony Ashley....II, 576
Cowley, Abraham.........II, 193
Cowper, William..........IV, 370
Crabbe, George...........V, 170
Craik, Dinah Maria Mulock..
 ....VII, 623
Croker, John Wilson......VI, 71
Cumberland, Richard.....IV, 558
Cunningham, Allan........V, 622
Daniel, Samuel............I, 611
Darwin, Charles Robert...VII, 415
Darwin, Erasmus.........IV, 420
D'Avenant, Sir William....II, 216
Day, Thomas............IV, 49
Defoe, Daniel............III, 23
Dekker, Thomas..........II, 55
Denham, Sir John........II, 220
DeQuincey, Thomas......VI, 116
Dickens, Charles.........VI, 550
Disraeli, Benjamin.......VII, 276
Disraeli, Isaac...........V, 510
Dobell, Sydney Thompson..VII, 758
Dodgson, Charles Lutwige....
 ....VIII, 396
Donne, John..............I, 710
Doyle, Sir Francis Hastings
 Charles ....VII, 649

INDEX TO CRITICISMS

Name	Vol. and Page
Drayton Michael	I 701
Drummond William	II 100
Dryden, John	II, 462
Edgeworth, Maria	V 561
Edwards Amelia Blandford	VIII 174
Emerson, Ralph Waldo	VII. 342
Etheredge Sir George	II, 413
Evelyn, John	II, 546
Falconer, William	III, 524
Farquhar, George	II, 554
Fawcett, Henry	VII. 548
Fielding, Henry	III, 338
Fi'zGerald, Edward	VII, 514
Fletcher, Giles	I, 623
Fletcher, John	I. 628
Foote, Samuel	III, 671
Forster, John	VII, 64
Foster, John	V. 424
Freeman, Edward Augustus	VIII, 153
Froude, James Anthony	VIII, 254
Fuller, Thomas	II, 168
Garrick, David	III, 693
Garth, Sir Samuel	II, 664
Gascoigne, George	I, 307
Gaskell, Elizabeth Cleghorn	VI, 427
Gay, John	III, 52
Gibbon, Edward	IV, 172
Gifford, William	V, 31
Gladstone, William Ewart	VIII, 383
Godwin, Mary Wollstonecraft	IV, 326
Godwin, William	V, 292
Goldsmith, Oliver	III, 613
Gore, Catherine Grace	VI, 263
Gray, Thomas	III, 553
Green, John Richard	VII, 504
Greville, Sir Fulke	I, 689
Grote, George	VI, 606
Hakluy, Richard	I, 445
Hales, John	II, 149
Hallam, Arthur Henry	V, 197
Hallam, Henry	VI, 173
Hartley, David	III, 376
Hawes, Stephen	I, 216
Hawkins, Sir John	IV, 50
Hawthorne, Nathaniel	VI, 341
Heber, Reginald	V, 36
Helps, Sir Arthur	VII, 38
Hemans, Felicia Dorothea	V, 254
Herbert, George	I, 720
Herrick, Robert	II, 233
Heywood, John	I, 304
Heywood, Thomas	II, 122
Hobbes, Thomas	II, 320
Hogg, James	V, 262
Holmes, Oliver Wendell	VIII, 285
Home, John	IV, 512
Hood, Thomas	V, 458
Hook, Theodore Edward	V, 355
Hooker, Richard	I, 402
Horne, Richard Hengist	VII, 544
Hughes, Thomas	VIII, 346
Hume, David	III, 646
Hunt, James Henry Leigh	VI, 153
Huxley, Thomas Henry	VIII, 320
Inchbald, Mrs. Elizabeth	IV, 686
Ingelow, Jean	VIII, 376
Irving, Washington	VI, 132

Name	Vol. and Page
James, George Payne Rainsford	VI, 216
Jameson, Anna	VI, 213
Jefferies, Richard	VII 618
Jeffrey, Francis Lord	V, 647
Jones, Sir William	IV, 197
Jonson, Ben	I, 745
Jowett, Benjamin	VIII, 207
Keats, John	IV, 662
Kemble Frances Ann	VIII, 213
Ken, Thomas	II, 566
Kinglake, Alexander William	VIII 49
Kingsley, Charles	VII, 17
Knowles, James Sheridan	VI, 285
Knox, John	I, 295
Landor, Walter Savage	VI, 372
Lennox, Charlotte	IV, 469
L'Estrange, Sir Roger	II, 537
Lever, Charles James	VI, 650
Lewes, George Henry	VII, 137
Lewis, Matthew Gregory	IV, 631
Lillo, George	III, 99
Livingstone, David	VI, 726
Locke, John	II, 518
Locker-Lampson, Frederick	VIII, 311
Lockhart, John Gibson	V, 753
Lodge, Thomas	I, 624
Longfellow, Henry Wadsworth	VII, 381
Lover, Samuel	VI, 542
Lowell, James Russell	VIII, 17
Lyly, John	I, 420
Lytton, Edward Robert Bulwer Earl	VIII, 43
Lytton, Sir Edward George Bulwer	VI, 679
Macaulay, Thomas Babington Lord	V, I91
Mackintosh, Sir James	V, 177
Macklin, Charles	IV, 342
Macpherson, Jamef	IV, 270
Malone, Edmond	IV, 577
Malthus, Thomas Robert	V, 249
Mandeville, Sir John	I, 94
Marlowe, Christopher	I, 346
Marryat, Frederick	V, 530
Marston, John	I, 735
Martineau, Harriet	VII, 54
Marvell, Andrew	II, 313
Massinger, Philip	II, 41
Maturin, Charles Robert	IV, 766
Melville, Herman	VIII, 62
Merivale, Charles	VIII, 217
Middleton, Thomas	I, 680
Milford, Mary Russell	VI, 40
Mill, James	V, 304
Mill, John Stuart	VI, 701
Miller, Hugh	VI, 62
Milman, Henry Hart	VI, 533
Milnes, Richard Monckton	VII, 559
Milton, John	II, 242
Moore, Thomas	V, 705
Montagu, Lady Mary Wortley	III, 459
Montgomery, James	V, 55
More, Hannah	V, 190
More, Sir Thomas	I, 232
Morris, William	VIII, 329

Name	Vol. and Page
Motherwell, William	V, 276
Motley, John Lothrop	VII. 85
Mozley, James Bowling	VII. 147
Murray, Lindley	V. 54
Napier Geo. Sir William Francis Patrick	VI. 220
Nashe, Thomas	I. 411
Newman, John Henry	VII, 738
Newton, Sir Isaac	II, 710
Norton, Caroline Elizabeth Sheridan	VII. 101
Oliphant, Laurence	VII, 654
O'Shaughnessy, Arthur Wm. Edgar	VII. 322
Otway, Thomas	II, 361
Paine, Thomas	IV, 529
Paley, William	IV, 470
Palgrave, Francis Turner	VIII, 371
Parr, Samuel	V, 17
Pater, Walter Horatio	VIII, 275
Patmore, Coventry K. D.	VIII, 339
Pattison, Mark	VII, 538
Peacock, Thomas Love	VI, 472
Peele, George	I, 363
Pepys, Samuel	II, 512
Percy, Thomas	IV, 562
Philips, Ambrose	III, 272
Philips, Katherine	II, 179
Piozzi, Hester Lynch	IV, 684
Planché, James Robinson	VII, 216
Porson, Richard	IV, 520
Porter, Jane	V, 673
Praed, Winthrop Mackworth	V, 330
Prescott, William Hickling	VI, 181
Prior, Matthew	II, 672
Pye, Henry James	IV, 580
Radcliffe, Ann Ward	IV, 717
Ramsay, Allan	III, 402
Reade, Charles	VII, 526
Reid, Thomas	IV, 282
Ricardo, David	IV, 725
Richardson, Samuel	III, 431
Robertson, William	IV, 154
Rogers, Samuel	VI, 32
Rowe, Nicholas	II, 618
Rowley, William	II, 68
Ruskin, John	VIII, 404
Sackville, Thomas	I, 431
Saint-John, Henry	III, 282
Savage, Richard	III, 131
Sedley, Sir Charles	II, 508
Seeley, Sir John Robert	VIII, 307
Shadwell, Thomas	II, 433
Shairp, John Campbell	VII, 568
Shakespeare, William	I, 447
Shelley, Mary Wollstonecraft	V, 700
Shelley, Percy Bysshe	IV, 689
Sheridan, Richard Brinsley	IV, 594
Shirley, James	II, 189
Sidney, Sir Philip	I, 320
Smart, Christopher	III, 591
Smith, Alexander	VI, 515
Smith, Horace	V, 597
Smith, Sydney	V, 466
Smollett, Tobias George	III, 573
Spencer, Herbert	VIII, 477

INDEX TO CRITICISMS

	Vol. and Page
Spenser, Edmund	I, 368
Stanhope, Philip Henry Earl	VII, 46
Stanley, Arthur Penrhyn	VII, 296
Steele, Sir Richard	II, 751
Stephen, Sir Leslie	VIII, 510
Sterne, Laurence	III, 501
Stevenson, Robert Louis	VIII, 234
Stowe, Harriet Beecher	VIII, 349
Swift, Jonathan	III, 196
Symonds, John Addington	VIII, 201
Talfourd, Sir Thomas Noon	V, 759
Taylor, Jeremy	II, 203
Taylor, Sir Henry	VII, 579
Taylor, Tom	VII, 213
Temple, Sir William	II, 455
Tennyson, Alfred Lord	VIII, 64
Tennyson, Frederick	VIII, 399
Thackeray, William Makepeace	VI, 290
Thirlwall, Connop	VII, 42
Thomson, James	VII, 473
Tickell, Thomas	III, 103
Tooke, John Horne	IV, 569
Trench, Richard Chenevix	VII, 588
Trollope, Anthony	VII, 456
Tupper, Martin Farquhar	VII, 731
Turner, Charles Tennyson	VII, 161
Tyndale, William	I, 244
Tyndall, John	VIII, 194
Tyrwhitt, Thomas	IV, 25
Vanbrugh, Sir John	II, 703
Waller, Edmund	II, 378
Walpole, Horace	IV, 309
Warburton, William	III, 682
Warren, Samuel	VII, 106
Warton, Thomas	IV, 71
Watts, Isaac	III, 248
Webster, John	I, 670
Wesley, Charles	IV, 34
White, Gilbert	IV, 147
Whitehead, William	IV, 21
Whitman, Walt	VIII, 129
Wilkes, John	IV, 332
Wilson, John	V, 744
Wither, George	II, 212
Wolcot, John	IV, 647
Wolfe, Charles	IV, 722
Wordsworth, William	V, 605
Wotton Sir Henry	II, 17
Wyatt, Sir Thomas	I, 249
Wycherley, William	II, 599
Wyclif, John	I, 99
Young, Edward	III, 484
SHARP, WILLIAM,	
Bowles, William Lisle	V, 660
Browning, Elizabeth Barrett	VI, 241
Browning, Robert	VII, 681, 686, 711
Brydges, Sir Samuel Egerton	V, 321
Buchanan, Robert	VIII, 447
Byron, George Gordon Lord	IV, 763
Clare, John	VI, 399
Coleridge, Hartley	V, 576
Coleridge, Samuel Taylor	V, 216

	Vol. and Page
Coleridge, Sara	V, 735
Disraeli, Benjamin	VII, 294
Dobell, Sydney Thompson	VI, 760
Drummond, William	II, 103
Elliott, Ebenezer	V, 583
Emerson, Ralph Waldo	VII, 359
Hayne, Paul Hamilton	VII, 593
Holmes, Oliver Wendell	VIII, 296
Horne, Richard Hengist	VII, 545
Jackson, Helen Hunt	VII, 575
Keats, John	IV, 674
Lanier, Sidney	VII, 328
Lazarus, Emma	VII, 612
Lecky, William E. H.	VIII, 489
Longfellow, Henry Wadsworth	VII, 401
Lowell, James Russell	VIII, 33
Marston, Philip Bourke	VII, 627
Morris, William	VIII, 330
Pater, Walter Horatio	VIII, 275, 277
Rossetti, Christina Georgina	VIII, 268
Rossetti, Gabriel Charles Dante	VII, 436, 447, 449
Shakespeare, William	I, 459
Shelley, Percy Bysshe	IV, 712
Stevenson, Robert Louis	VIII, 239, 243
Symonds, John Addington	VIII, 202, 203
Taylor, Bayard	VII, 136
Thomson, James	VII, 476
Thoreau, Henry David	VI, 274
Turner, Charles Tennyson	VII, 163
White, Joseph Blanco	V, 362
Whitman, Walt	VIII, 144
Wordsworth, William	V, 627
SHARPE, JOHN,	
William of Malmesbury	I, 53
SHARPE, R. BOWDLER,	
White, Gilbert	IV, 152
SHARPE, SAMUEL,	
Rogers, Samuel	VI, 35
SHARSWOOD, GEORGE,	
Marshall, John	V, 283
SHAW, CUTHBERT,	
Johnson, Samuel	III, 721
Kenrick, William	III, 701
Mallet, David	III, 497
Smollett, Tobias George	III, 586
SHAW, PETER,	
Boyle, Robert	II, 418
SHAW, THOMAS BUDD,	
Addison, Joseph	II, 653
Ainsworth, William Harrison	VII, 487
Beaumont and Fletcher	I, 582
Beckford, William	V, 448
Blackstone, William	III, 704
Bunyan, John	II, 402
Byron, George Gordon Lord	IV, 748
Chatterton, Thomas	III, 536
Chaucer, Geoffrey	I, 161
Coleridge, Samuel Taylor	V, 218
Collins, William	III, 420
Cowper, William	IV, 373, 388
Defoe, Daniel	III, 35
Dekker, Thomas	II, 60
Dickens, Charles	VI, 562, 564, 570

	Vol. and Page
Dryden, John	II, 491
Edgeworth, Maria	V, 569
Fortescue, Sir John	I, 194
Galt, John	V, 336
Gifford, William	V, 35
Godwin, William	V, 299
Goldsmith, Oliver	III, 623
Gray, Thomas	III, 559
Hood, Thomas	V, 461
Hume, David	III, 666
Hunt, James Henry Leigh	VI, 163
James, George Payne Rainsford	I, 219
Johnson, Samuel	III, 757
Jonson, Ben	I, 748, 764
Locke, John	II, 534
Lyly, John	I, 424
Lytton, Sir Edward George Bulwer	VI, 688, 688
Marlowe, Christopher	I, 355
Marryat, Frederick	V, 532
Marston, John	I, 737
Massinger, Philip	II, 49
Milton, John	II, 290
Mitford, Mary Russell	VI, 43
Moore, Thomas	V, 710
Pope, Alexander	III, 173
Radcliffe, Ann Ward	IV, 719
Ramsay, Allan	III, 407
Richardson, Samuel	III, 449
Scott, Sir Walter	V, 151
Shelley, Percy Bysshe	IV, 701
Shenstone, William	III, 473
Sheridan, Richard Brinsley	IV, 604
Shirley, James	II, 191
Smollett Tobias George	III, 581
Southey, Robert	V, 411
Swift, Jonathan	III, 221, 231
Theobald, Lewis	III, 143
Thomson, James	III, 259, 264
Warren, Samuel	VII, 107, 108
Webster, John	I, 675
Young, Edward	III, 493
SHEA, GEORGE,	
Hamilton, Alexander	IV, 460
SHEA, J. G.,	
Froude, James Anthony	VIII, 263
SHEARMAN, THOMAS G.,	
George, Henry	VIII, 381
SHEDD, WILLIAM G. T.,	
Alcuin	I, 33
Anselm	I, 50
Erigena	I, 35
SHEFFIELD, JOHN,	
Books	III, 6
Congreve, William	II, 734
Gibbon, Edward	IV, 191, 192, 193
Knowledge	V, 5
Pope, Alexander	III, 144
Wilmot, John	II, 338
SHELLEY, HENRY C.,	
Burns, Robert	IV, 235
Drummond, Henry	VII, 362
Gray, Thomas	III, 557
Hood, Thomas	V, 466
Shelley, Percy Bysshe	IV, 694
SHELLEY, LADY,	
Shelley, Percy Bysshe	IV, 694
SHELLEY, MARY WOLLSTONECRAFT,	
Godwin, Mary Wollstonecraft	IV, 327

676 INDEX TO CRITICISMS

Vol. and Page
Godwin, William...........V, 294
Holcroft, Thomas.........IV. 545
Inchbald, Elizabeth...IV, 687, 704
Shelley, Percy Bysshe......
..............IV, 690, 690, 706
SHELLEY, PERCY BYSSHE,
Byron, George Gordon Lord..
.... IV, 756
Coleridge, Samuel Taylor....
.... V, 214, 222
Godwin, Mary Wollstonecraft
......................VI, 327
Godwin, William......V, 293, 303
Hunt, James Henry Leigh..
.................VI, 155, 155
Keats, John......IV, 663, 672, 676
Lamb, Charles.............V, 238
Milton, John..............II, 287
Moore, Thomas...........V, 715
Peacock, Thomas Love...VI, 474
Poets and Poetry.........IV, 7
Shakespeare, William......
.... I, 457, 521, 556
Shelley, Mary Wollstonecraft..
.......................V, 700
Shelley, Percy Bysshe.....
.................IV, 690, 700
Sidney, Sir Philip...........I, 323
Smith, Horace...........V, 598
Wordsworth, William..V, 620, 630
SHELLEY, SIR TIMOTHY,
Shelley, Mary Wollstonecraft..
.... V, 700
SHENSTONE, WILLIAM,
Butler, Samuel............II, 331
Johnson, Samuel........III, 740
Percy, Thomas.........IV, 563
Pope, Alexander........III, 183
Somerville, William......III, 126
Thomson, James......III, 255, 266
SHEPARD, CHARLES U.,
Percival, James Gates.....VI, 58
SHERARD, ROBERT H.,
Du Maurier, George.... VIII, 343
SHEPHERD, HENRY A.,
Lanier, Sidney..........VII, 332
SHEPHERD, H. E,
Bentley, Richard........III, 123
Evelyn, John.............II, 551
SHEPHERD, RICHARD HERNE,
Carlyle, Thomas.........VII, 247
Lamb, Charles............V, 240
Tennyson, Alfred Lord.VIII, 80, 91
SHEPPARD, JOHN,
Foster, John............V, 425
SHEPPARD, NATHAN,
Eliot, George...........VII, 203
SHEPPARD, SAMUEL,
Shakespeare, William......I, 531
SHERBORN, G. DAVIES,
Owen, Sir Richard.....VIII, 173
SHERIDAN, RICHARD BRINSLAY,
Cumberland, Richard......IV, 559
Johnson, Samuel......... III, 753
Savage, Richard..........III, 133
Sheridan, Richard Brinsley.IV, 594
SHERIDAN, THOMAS,
Swift, Jonathan..........III, 199
SHERMAN, ELLEN BURNS,
Miller, Cincinnatus Hiner VIII, 501

Vol. and Page
SHERMAN, FRANK DEMPSTER.
Bunner, Henry Cuyler...VIII, 360
SHERMAN, L. A.,
Browning, Robert........VII, 713
Carlyle, Thomas........VII, 249
Chaucer, Geoffrey..........I, 134
Milton, John.............II, 296
SHERWOOD, MARY E. W.,
Agassiz, Louis Jean Rodolphe
.......................VI, 722
Bancroft, George.......VIII, 57
Boker, George Henry....VIII, 765
Browning, Robert.......VII, 683
Carlyle, Thomas........VII 238
Dickens, Charles.........VI, 559
Eliot, George............VII, 180
Emerson, Ralph Waldo...VII, 634
Fuller, Sarah Margaret......V, 669
Harte, Francis Bret.....VIII, 467
Longfellow, Henry Wadsworth
.......................VII. 386
Lowell, James Russell...VIII, 25
Prescott, William Hickling .VI, 182
Ripley, George..........VII, 224
Story, William Wetmore..VIII, 318
Sumner, Charles..........VI, 757
Thackeray, William Makepeace
......................VI, 299
Tuckerman, Henry Theodore..
.....................VI, 642
Webster, Daniel..........V, 724
SHIELDS, CHARLES W.,
Kane, Elisha Kent....VI, 81, 83
SHIPPEN, WILLIAM,
Montagu, Charles........II, 586
Somers, John Lord........II, 612
SHIRLEY, JAMES,
Beaumont and Fletcher.....I. 579
Chaucer, Geoffrey......I, 133, 140
Fletcher, John............I, 629
Ford, John...............II, 30
Johnson, Ben............I, 759
SHIRLEY, WALTER WADDINGTON,
Wyclif, John.............I, 106
SHOLL, ANNA McCLURE,
Pater, Walter Horatio...VIII, 280
SHORTER, CLEMENT,
Arnold, Matthew........VII, 641
Brontë, Anne............V 599
Brontë, Charlotte........VI, 21
Brontë, Emily........V, 525, 526
Carlyle, Thomas........VII, 274
Dickens, Charles.........VI, 592
Eliot, George............VII, 207
Freeman, Edward Augustus..
.....................VIII, 161
Gaskell, Elizabeth Cleghorn VI, 432
Grote, George...........VI 611
Helps, Sir Arthur........VII, 41
Ingelow, Jean..........VIII, 377
Kingsley, Henry.........VII. 79
Lewes, George Henry....VII, 141
Marryat, Frederick......V, 534
Mill, John Stuart.....VI 706, 718
Patmore, Coventry.....VIII, 342
Scott, Sir Walter.........V, 153
Southey, Robert..........V, 411
Spencer, Herbert......VIII, 485
Stevenson, Robert Louis.VII, 250
Stubbs, William........VIII, 452

Vol and Page
Tennyson Alfred Lord VIII. 92
SHORTHOUSE, J. HERNY
Maurice John Frederick Denison ....VI 649
Wordsworth William .....V. 640
SHUCKBURGH. E. S.,
Burney Frances ....V. 349
Carte Thomas...........III 338
SIBLEY. N. W.,
Burke. Edmund..........IV, 293
SICHEL. WALTER.
Arbuthnot, John.........III. 85
Boswell, James..........IV, 220
Byron, George Gordon Lord IV, 743
Defoe, Daniel............III. 50
Disraeli, Benjamin....VII, 285, 293
Evelyn, John.............II, 550
Manley, Mary de la Riviere..II, 694
Pepys Samuel ....II, 516
Saint-John, Henry........III, 290
Steele, Sir Richard.....II, 755, 759
Swift Jonathan...... III, 207, 224
SIDDONS, SARAH,
Shakespeare, William....I, 483, 516
SIDGWICK, HENRY,
Bentham, Jeremy.........V, 168
Mill, John Stuart.........VI, 714
Smith, Adam............IV, 66
Spencer, Herbert......VIII, 487
Ward, William George....VII, 483
SIDNEY, EDWIN,
Whitefield George.......III, 547
SIDNEY, SIR PHILIP,
Chaucer, Geoffrey..........I, 135
Knowledge..............V, 5
Poets and Poetry.........IV. 5
Sackville, Thomas.........I, 432
Spenser, Edmund........I, 375
Surrey, Earl of...........I, 257
SIDNEY. WILLIAM CONNOR.
Johnson, Samuel........III 744
SIGERSON, GEORGE,
Griffin, Gerald...........V, 355
SIGORGNE, PIERRE,
Newton, Sir Isaac........II, 722
SIGOURNEY, LYDIA HUNTLEY,
Edgeworth Maria.........V, 563
Hemans, Felicia Dorothea...V, 258
SIGWART, CHRISTIAN,
Jewell, John............I, 294
SILLARD, P. A.,
Boswell, James........IV, 212, 220
Croker, John Wilson.....VI, 73, 74
SIMCOX, EDITH,
Eliot, George...........VII, 174
Lytton, Sir Edward George
Bulwer................VI, 694
Mill, John Stuart......VI, 703, 714
SIMCOX, GEORGE AUGUSTUS.
Bryant, William Cullen....VI, 123
Buckle, Henry Thomas...VI, 282
Church, Richard William..VII, 730
Clive, Caroline..........VI, 740
Crashaw, Richard........II, 112
Helps, Sir Arthur........VII, 41
Herbert, George..........I, 722
Keble, John.............VI, 465
Kingsley, Charles...VII. 24, 28, 31
Manning, Henry Edward.VIII, 165
Martineau, Harriet.......VII, 60
Mozley, James Bowling....VII, 148

INDEX TO CRITICISMS 677

	Vol. and Page
Procter, Bryan Waller	VI, 749
Sandys, George	II, 83
Vaughan, Henry	II, 444
Ward, William George	VII, 482
Wilberforce, Samuel	VI, 735

SIMCOX, WILLIAM HENRY,
Mozley, James Bowling ... VII, 148

SIME, JAMES,
Bruce, Robert .... IV, 263

SIMMONS, BARTHOLOMEW,
Hood, Thomas .... V, 458

SIMMS, WILLIAM GILMORE
Cooper, James Fenimore. V, 680, 681
Halleck, Fitz-Greene ...... VI, 494
Prescott, William Hickling..VI, 186
Simms, William Gilmore......
.... VI, 509, 596

SIMON OF DURHAM,
Alfred the Great .... I, 37

SIMON, T. COLLYNS,
Berkeley, George .... III, 332

SIMONDS, ARTHUR B.,
Cary, Alice .... VI, 639
Halleck, Fitz-Greene ...... VI, 500
Hayne, Paul Hamilton .... VII, 593
Lanier, Sidney .... VII, 329
Longfellow, Henry Wadsworth
.... VII, 396
Morris, George Pope ...... VI, 402
Osgood, Francis Sargent ... VII, 678
Poe, Edgar Allan .... V, 548
Saxe, John Godfrey ...... VII, 617
Very, Jones .... VII, 228
Whitman, Walt .... VIII, 149

SIMONDS, WILLIAM EDWARD,
Addison, Joseph .... II, 647
Beckford, William .... V, 449
Bunyan, John .... II, 398
Chaucer, Geoffrey .... I, 136
Defoe, Daniel .... III, 50
Eliot, George .... VII, 207
Fielding, Henry .... III, 364
Lewis, Matthew Gregory .. IV, 634
Lytton, Sir Edward George
Bulwer .... VI, 699
Mackenzie, Henry .... V, 114
Marryat, Frederick .... V, 533
Richardson, Samuel ..... III, 437
Sterne, Laurence .... III, 515
Swift, Jonathan .... III, 223

SIMPKINSON, C. H.,
Laud, William .... II, 92

SIMPSON, EVA BLANTYRE,
Stevenson, Robert Louis..VIII, 235

SIMPSON, JAMES Y.,
Drummond, Henry..VIII, 365, 366

SIMPSON, J. PALGRAVE,
Planché, James Robinson....
.... VII, 216, 216

SIMPSON, MATTHEW,
Wesley, Samuel .... III, 86

SIMPSON, RICHARD,
Shakespeare, William...I, 479, 568

SINCLAIR, JOHN,
Chalmers, Thomas .... V, 492

SINCLAIR, WILLIAM MACDONALD,
Cowper, William .... IV, 377

SINGER, SAMUEL WELLER,
Herrick, Robert .... II, 238
Johnson, Samuel .... III, 737

	Vol. and Page
Mason, William	IV, 323
Selden, John	II, 142
Spence, Joseph	III, 520

SINGLETON, ESTHER,
Alcott, Louisa May ...... VII, 668

SINGLETON, ROY,
Blackstone, Sir William....III, 705

SIZERANNE, ROBERT DE LA,
Ruskin, John .... VIII, 422

SKEAT, WALTER W.,
Chatterton, Thomas ...... III, 538
Chaucer, Geoffrey.........
I, 130, 134, 138, 140, 148, 149, 150
150, 152.
Dunbar, William .... I, 224
Langland, William ..... I, 120, 123
Lyndsay, Sir David .... I, 273
Tyrwhitt, Thomas .... IV, 26

SKELTON, JOHN,
Chaucer, Geoffrey .... I, 152
Lydgate, John .... I, 183

SKELTON, SIR JOHN (SHIRLEY),
Addison, Joseph .... II, 638
Arnold, Matthew .... VII, 634
Brontë, Charlotte .... VI, 27
Brown, John .... VII, 479
Browne, Sir Thomas ...... II, 341
Browning, Robert .... VII, 699
Burton, John Hill .... VII, 315
Disraeli, Benjamin..........
.... VII, 282, 285, 290
Dryden, John ..... II, 465, 485, 502
Eliot, George ...... VII, 187, 198
Froude, James Anthony.....
.... VIII, 256, 261, 265
Keats, John .... IV, 674
Knox, John .... I, 298
Macaulay, Thomas Babington
Lord .... VI, 113
Maitland, Sir Richard ..... I, 333
Morris, William .... VIII, 335
Pope, Alexander .... III, 152
Saint-John, Henry ...... III, 289
Smith, Alexander .... VI, 516
Thackeray, William Makepeace
.... VI, 314, 320
Tyndall, John .... VIII, 196

SKENE, F. M. F.,
Scott, Sir Walter .... V, 134

SKINNER, STEPHEN,
Chaucer, Geoffrey .... I, 155

SKIPSEY, JOSEPH,
Blake, William .... V, 61

SKOTTOWE, AUGUSTINE,
Shakespeare, William......
.... I, 465, 485, 499

SLADEN, DOUGLAS,
Buchanan, Robert ...... VIII, 445
Hayne, Paul Hamilton .... VII, 593
Jackson, Helen Hunt .... VII, 575
Lanier, Sidney .... VII, 329
Ryan, Abram Joseph .... VII, 598
Smith, Adam .... IV, 68

SLATER, GERTRUDE,
Oliphant, Margaret O. W.....
.... VIII, 368

SLATER, J. H.,
Burns, Robert .... IV, 265
Lever, Charles James .... VI, 656

SLICER, THOMAS R.,
Curtis, George William...VIII, 190

	Vol. and Page

SLOANE, WILLIAM M.,
Bancroft, George ...... VIII, 56, 60
McCosh, James .... VIII, 301

SMALLEY, GEORGE W.,
Browning, Robert....VII, 680, 711
Curtis, George William...VIII, 191
Darwin, Charles Robert...VII, 416
Disraeli, Benjamin ...... VII, 283
Eliot, George .... VII, 173
Fawcett, Henry .... VI, 549
Froude, James Anthony.....
.... VIII, 255, 264
Holmes, Oliver Wendell..VIII, 286
Huxley, Thomas Henry..VIII, 321
Jowett, Benjamin ...... VII, 208
Lewes, Henry George..... VII, 138
Lowell, James Russell...VIII, 24
Lytton, Edward Robert Bulwer
.... VIII, 44
Mill, John Stuart .... VI, 703
Newman, John Henry ....VII, 753
Phillips, Wendell ...... VII, 557
Spurgeon, Charles Haddon....
.... VIII, 179
Stanley, Sir Henry Morton....
.... VIII, 506
Taylor, Bayard .... VII, 129
Tennyson, Alfred Lord...VIII, 72
Tyndall, John ...... VIII, 195, 198

SMART, CHRISTOPHER,
Fielding, Henry .... III, 356
Hill, John .... III, 645

SMEATON, OLIPHANT,
Douglas, Gawin .... I, 216
Dunbar, William .... I, 228
Guthrie, Thomas ..... VI, 738, 739
Ramsay, Allan ..... III, 404, 408
Smollett, Tobias George....
.... III, 576, 578, 582
Spencer, Herbert ...... VIII, 486

SMELLIE, W.,
Smith, Adam .... IV, 54

SMILES, ROBERT,
Livingstone, David ...... VI, 728

SMILES, SAMUEL
Arnold, Thomas .... V, 377
Audubon, John James ..... V, 698
Authors and Authorship..VIII, 5
Baillie, Joanna .... V, 694
Borrow, George Henry......
.... VII, 308, 310, 311
Browning, Elizabeth Barrett..
.... VI, 231, 237, 237
Browning, Robert ...... VII, 699
Carlyle, Thomas .... VII, 232
Clare, John .... VI, 399
Cobden, Richard .... VI, 439
Coleridge, Hartley .... V, 577
Elliott, Ebenezer .... V, 582
Fuller, Sarah Margaret ... V, 667
Gladstone, William Ewart....
.... VIII, 387
Hawthorne, Nathaniel.VI, 353, 360
Hunt, James Henry Leigh..VI, 169
Lytton, Sir Edward George
Bulwer .... VI, 681, 697
Martineau, Harriet ..... VII, 62
Miller, Hugh .... VI, 62
Napier, Gen. Sir Wm. Francis
Patrick .... VI, 223
Newton, Sir Isaac .... II, 715

INDEX TO CRITICISMS

	Vol. and Page
Poe, Edgar Allan	V, 538, 551
Sterling, John	V, 454
SMITH, ADAM,	
Gibbon, Edward	IV, 180
Gray, Thomas	III, 561
Hume, David	III, 648
Hutcheson, Francis	III, 245
Logan, John	IV, 43
Pope, Alexander	III, 172
Smith, Adam	IV, 61
SMITH, A. L.,	
Smith, Adam	IV, 68
SMITH, ALEXANDER,	
Aytoun, William Edmondstoune	VI, 445
Bacon, Francis	I, 650
Boswell, James	IV, 217
Bunyan, John	II, 401, 403
Burns, Robert	IV, 230, 238, 246
Byron, George Gordon Lord	IV, 760
Carlyle, Thomas	VII, 233
Chaucer, Geoffrey	I, 127, 144, 150, 162
Dickens, Charles	VI, 566, 584
Dobell, Sydney Thompson	VI, 762, 764
Dunbar, William	I, 225
Elliott, Ebenezer	V, 580, 583
Emerson Ralph Waldo	VII, 364
Goldsmith, Oliver	III, 638
Hawthorne, Nathaniel	VI, 351, 365
Lamb, Charles	V, 240
Poets and Poetry	IV, 8
Shakespeare, William	I, 565
Spenser, Edmund	I, 372
SMITH, MRS. BAIRD,	
DeQuincey, Thomas	VI, 120
SMITH, BENJAMIN E.,	
Abbot, George	I, 725
Adams, John	V, 50
Adams, John Quincy	V, 514
Alfred the Great	I, 36
Ames, Fisher	IV, 527
Audubon, John James	V, 695
Bage, Robert	IV, 418
Baker, Sir Richard	II, 93
Bancroft, George	VIII, 54
Barlow, Joel	IV, 573
Barnes, Joshua	II, 571
Barrow, Isaac	III, 310
Beecher, Henry Ward	VII, 599
Blackstone, Sir William	III, 702
Blanchard, Samuel Laman	V, 480
Brontë, Anne	V, 599
Brown, Thomas	IV, 657
Challoner, Richard	III, 710
Choate, Rufus	VI, 195
Churchyard, Thomas	I, 417
Clarke, Samuel	II, 747
Clay, Henry	V, 730
Cobbett, William	V, 269
Cobden, Richard	VI, 439
Coke, Sir Edward	I, 739
Cole, Reginald	I, 279
Constable, Henry	I, 444
Cotton, Charles	II, 370
Cranmer, Thomas	I, 270
Curtis, George William	VIII, 184
Cynewulf	I, 30
Davies, Sir John	I, 632
Davy, Sir Humphry	V, 90
Dodington, George Bubb	III, 458
Erigena, John Scotus	I, 34
Ford, John	II, 25
Fox, George	II, 420
Franklin, Benjamin	IV, 79
Gauden, John	II, 176
Glover, Richard	IV, 17
Gower, John	I, 172
Graham, James	II, 121
Grainger, James	III, 498
Granger, James	III, 670
Grimoald, Nicholas	I, 283
Hamilton, Thomas	V, 394
Hare, Julius Charles	VI, 49
Harvey, William	II, 155
Henry, Matthew	II, 584
Henryson, Robert	I, 207
Hyde, Edward, Earl of Clarendon	II, 299
Jenyns, Soame	IV, 30
Lamb, Lady Caroline	V, 81
Lincoln, Abraham	VI, 411
Leslie, Charles	II, 679
Marshall, John	V, 281
Mathias, Thomas James	V, 287
Montagu, Elizabeth	IV, 398
Moore, Edward	III, 375
Morris, George Pope	VI, 400
Napier, Sir John	I, 588
Neal, Daniel	III, 140
North, Roger	III, 79
Norton, Thomas	I, 318
Oldmixon, John	III, 124
Osgood, Francis Sargent	V, 677
Parker, Matthew	I, 303
Parker, Theodore	VI, 205
Parkman, Francis	VIII, 218
Payne, John Howard	V, 735
Philips, John	II, 562
Pitt, William	III, 678
Pusey, Edward Bouverie	VII, 466
Puttenham, George	I, 401
Quincy, Josiah	VI, 404
Randolph, Thomas	I, 744
Reynolds, Sir Joshua	IV, 137
Ricardo, David	IV, 728
Romilly, Sir Samuel	IV, 634
Ross, Alexander	III, 718
Rumford, Count	IV, 589
Russell, John Earl	VII, 143
Sacheverell, Henry	II, 695
Selden, John	II, 137
Seward, William Henry	VI, 672
Sidney, Algernon	II, 353
Skelton, John	I, 219
Smith, John	I, 698
Sparks, Jared	VI, 476
Spurgeon, Charles Haddon	VIII, 178
Sterling, John	V, 451
Still, John	I, 429
Sumner, Charles	VI, 750
Surrey, Earl of	I, 255
Taylor, Bayard	VII, 128
Thoreau, Henry David	VI, 267
Washington, George	IV, 353
Webster, Daniel	V, 719
Webster, Noah	V, 427
Whipple, Edwin Percy	VII, 594
Whitefield, George	III, 546
Wilson, Alexander	IV, 581
Winthrop, Theodore	VI, 266
Wood, Anthony	II, 446
Woolsey, Theodore Dwight	VII, 736
Wotton, William	II, 709
SMITH, C. C.,	
Disraeli, Isaac	V, 513
Hallam, Henry	VI, 178
Saxe, John Godfrey	VII, 617
Somerville, Mary	VI, 658, 659
Whipple, Edwin Percy	VII, 595
SMITH, MISS C. FELL,	
Murray, Lindley	V, 55, 55
SMITH, CHARLES,	
Spenser, Edmund	I, 370
SMITH, EDMUND,	
Philips, John	II, 563
SMITH, EDWARD,	
Burke, Edmund	IV, 300
Cobbett, William	V, 271
SMITH, MRS. E. V.,	
Reade, Charles	VII, 532
SMITH, FREDERICK M.,	
Thoreau, Henry David	VI, 277
SMITH, GEORGE,	
Heber, Reginald	V, 38
SMITH, GEORGE ADAM,	
Drummond, Henry	VIII, 363
SMITH, GEORGE BARNETT,	
Austen, Jane	IV, 621
Bage, Robert	IV, 419, 419
Bagehot, Walter	VII, 97
Bancroft, George	VIII, 60
Banim, John	V, 391
Bayley, Thomas Haynes	V, 340
Bright, John	VII, 722
Brontë, Charlotte	VI, 27, 28
Brontë, Emily	V, 523
Brown, Charles Brockden	IV, 553, 553, 556
Browning, Elizabeth Barrett	VI, 237, 239, 241, 245
Browning, Robert	VII, 688, 690
Buchanan, Robert	VIII, 446
Bunyan, John	II, 404
Byron, George Gordon Lord	IV, 741
Campbell, Thomas	V, 444
Carleton, William	VI, 550
Cobden, Richard	VI, 443
Cowley, Abraham	II, 201
Cumberland, Richard	IV, 561
Defoe, Daniel	III, 48
Dickens, Charles	VI, 586
Disraeli, Benjamin	VII, 285
Eliot, George	VII, 200
Emerson, Ralph Waldo	VII, 365
Fielding, Henry	III, 345, 348, 361
Frere, John Hookham	V, 486, 488
Graham, James	II, 121
Hawthorne, Nathaniel	VI, 354, 359, 360
Herrick, Robert	II, 238
Johnson, Samuel	III, 761
Lamb, Lady Caroline	V, 83
Landor, Walter Savage	VI, 382
Locker-Lampson, Frederick	VIII, 312
Lowell, James Russell	VIII, 32
Lytton, Edward Robert Bulwer	VIII, 46

INDEX TO CRITICISMS

	Vol. and Page
Milnes, Richard Monckton...	VII, 563
Peacock, Thomas Love	VI, 474, 475
Poe, Edgar Allan	V, 551
Praed, Winthrop Mackworth	VI, 332
Prior, Matthew	II, 678
Raleigh, Sir Walter	I, 600
Richardson, Samuel	III, 451
Russell, John Earl	VII, 144
Shelley, Percy Bysshe	IV, 710
Smollett, Tobias George	III, 584, 589
Stanhope, Philip Dormer	III, 607
Steele, Sir Richard	II, 754
Suckling, Sir John	II, 64, 66
Swift, Jonathan	III, 203, 225, 233
Tennyson, Alfred Lord	VIII, 103
Thackeray, William Makepeace	VI, 307, 310, 311
Tyndale, William	I, 245
Villiers, George	II, 78
Waller, Edmund	II, 383

SMITH, SIR GEORGE MURRAY,
Brontë, Charlotte	VI, 21, 26, 29
Hunt, James Henry Leigh	VI, 162
Procter, Adelaide Anne	VI, 394
Thackeray, William Makepeace	VI, 299

SMITH, G. GREGORY.
Freeman, Edward Augustus	VIII, 161
Green, John Richard	VII, 513
Mallet, David	III, 497
Moir, David Macbeth	V, 705
Tennyson, Frederick	VIII, 400

SMITH, GOLDWIN,
Adams, John	V, 51
Adams, John Quincy	V, 519
Austen, Jane	IV, 620, 623
Bunyan, John	II, 397
Burke, Edmund	IV, 301, 308
Canning, George	V, 68
Clay, Henry	V, 732
Cowper, William	IV, 374, 380, 381
Edgeworth, Maria	V, 569
Fox, Charles James	IV, 502
Franklin, Benjamin	VI, 91
Froude, James Anthony	VIII, 257, 259, 265
Garrison, William Lloyd	VII, 160
Hayley, William	IV, 652
Jefferson, Thomas	V, 48
Junius	IV, 642
Lincoln, Abraham	VI, 412, 419
Madison, James	V, 314
Marvell, Andrew	II, 315, 318
Mather, Cotton	II, 729
Milton, John	II, 278
Mitford, Mary Russell	VI, 46
Paine, Thomas	IV, 536
Scott, Sir Walter	V, 139, 140
Stanley, Arthur Penrhyn	VII, 305
Washington, George	IV, 364
Webster, Daniel	V, 726

SMITH, HENRY J. S.,
| Maxwell, James Clerk | VII, 169 |

SMITH, HORACE,
| Campbell, Thomas | V, 443 |

	Vol. and Page
SMITH, JAMES,	
Colman, George	V, 317

SMITH, JOHN PYE,
| Miller, Hugh | VI, 64 |

SMITH, JOHN TALBOT,
Manning, Henry Edward	VIII, 168
Newman, John Henry	VII, 743
Ryan, Abram Joseph	VII, 599

SMITH, JOHN THOMAS,
| Blake, William | V, 57 |

SMITH, JOSIAH RENICK,
| Defoe, Daniel | III, 42 |

SMITH, M. W.,
| Raleigh, Sir Walter | I, 605 |

SMITH, NINA LARRE,
| Scott, Sir Walter | V, 134 |

SMITH, ROSWELL.
| Holland, Josiah Gilbert | VII, 333 |

SMITH, SYDNEY,
Airy, Sir George Biddell	VIII, 182
Bentham, Jeremy	V, 165
Blair, Hugh	IV, 404
Brown, Thomas	IV, 658
Byron, George Gordon Lord	IV, 743, 747
Campbell, Thomas	V, 434
Canning, George	V, 68
Channing, William Ellery	V, 371
Dickens, Charles	VI, 565
Edgeworth, Maria	V, 563
Everett, Edward	VI, 422
Fox, Charles James	IV, 507
Galt, John	V, 336
Godwin, William	V, 296
Grote, George	VI, 607
Horner, Francis	IV, 630
Jeffrey, Francis Lord	V, 649, 653
Kemble, Frances Ann	VIII, 216
Macaulay, Thomas Babington Lord	VI, 92
Mackintosh, Sir James	V, 178
Malthus, Thomas Robert	V, 250
Milnes, Richard Monckton	VII, 559
More, Hannah	V, 193
Murchison, Sir Roderick Impey	VI, 631
Napier, Gen. Sir William Francis Patrick	VI, 221
Parr, Samuel	V, 19
Rogers, Samuel	VI, 32
Scott, Sir Walter	V, 147, 154, 156
Stewart, Dugald	V, 76, 78
Walpole, Horace	IV, 318
Wordsworth, William	V, 629

SMITH, SIDNEY AND BROUGHAM, HENRY LORD,
| Ritson, Joseph | IV, 436 |

SMITH, SYDNEY C.,
| Prescott, William Hickling | VI, 181 |

SMITH, WALTER C.,
Brown, John	VII, 477, 479
Browning, Robert	VII, 707
Bunyan, John	II, 400
Campbell, John Lord	VI, 258

SMITH, WALTER C.,
| Carlyle, Thomas | VII, 248 |

	Vol. and Page
Coleridge, Samuel Taylor	V, 221
Macleod, Norman	VI, 661, 662
Shelley, Percy Bysshe	IV, 712

SMITH, WILLIAM,
| Spenser, Edmund | I, 392 |

SMITH, WILLIAM,
| Southey, Robert | V, 409 |

SMITH, WILLIAM,
| Greg, William Rathbone | VII, 320 |

SMITH, WILLIAM JAMES,
| Junius | IV, 641 |

SMITHES, SIR THOMAS,
| Jonson, Ben | I, 758 |
| Sidney, Sir Philip | I, 330 |

SMOLLETT, TOBIAS GEORGE,
Fielding, Henry	III, 340
Hume, David	III, 648
Johnson, Samuel	III, 720
Montagu, Lady Mary Wortley	III, 465
Murray, William	IV, 169
Parnell Thomas	II, 616
Pope, Alexander	III, 182
Prior, Matthew	II, 676
Rowe, Nicholas	II, 622
Smollett, Tobias George	III, 574
Stanhope, Philip Dormer	III, 607
Steele, Sir Richard	II, 762
Swift, Jonathan	III, 224
Thomson, James	III, 256

SMYTH, ALBERT H.,
| Hawthorne, Nathaniel | VI, 362, 371 |
| Taylor, Bayard | VII, 131, 134, 136 |

SMYTH, EGBERT C.,
| Edwards, Jonathan | III, 380, 386 |

SMYTH, JAMES MOORE,
| Arbuthnot, John | III, 84 |

SMYTH, WILLIAM,
Blackstone, Sir William	III, 706
Burnet, Gilbert	II, 592, 594
Chalmers George	V, 30
Dodington, George Bubb	III, 459
Gibbon, Edward	IV, 184
Hakluyt, Richard	I, 446
Hallam, Henry	VI, 174, 176
Henry, Robert	IV, 108
Home, John	IV, 515
Hume, David	III, 657
Jenyns, Soame	IV, 33
Locke, John	II, 534
Lyttelton, George Lord	III, 612
Macaulay, Catherine	IV, 134
Mackintosh, Sir James	V, 182
Malthus, Thomas Robert	V, 252
Milton, John	II, 289
ckley, Simon	II, 669
Paine, Thomas	IV, 535
Paley, William	IV, 476
Prideaux, Humphrey	II, 697
Robertson, William	II, 163
Smith, Ad m	IV, 63
Stuart, Gilbert	IV, 27
Turner, Sharon	V, 498
Walpole, Horace	IV, 322
Washington, George	IV, 359, 367

SNEATH, E. HERSHEY,
| Tennyson, Alfred Lord | VIII, 110 |

SNELL, F. J.,
| Chaucer, Geoffrey | I, 134, 139, 139 |
| Gower, John | I, 173 |

INDEX TO CRITICISMS

Vol. and Page

Mannyng, Robert...........I, 88
Minot, Lawrence ....I, 94
Wesley, Charles...........IV, 39
Wesley, John........IV, 118, 120
Wyclif, John...............I, 112
SNELLING, JOSEPH,
  Halleck, Fitz-Greene......VI, 497
SNELLING, W. J.
  Bryant, William Cullen...VII, 120
SNIDER, DENTON JAQUES,
  Shakespeare, William........
  ....I, 486, 488, 500, 513, 530, 537
SOAME, SIR WALTER,
  Waller, Edmund..........II, 380
SOAMES, HENRY,
  Ælfric.....................I, 46
SOMBART, WERNER,
  Owens, Robert...........VI, 86
SOME, THOMAS,
  Latimer, Hugh.............I, 267
SOMERSET, DUCHESS OF,
  Doddridge Philip........III, 302
SOMERVILLE, MARTHA,
  Somerville, Mary.........VI, 658
SOMERVILLE, MARY,
  Edgeworth, Maria.........V, 564
SOMERVILLE, THOMAS,
  Butler, Joseph...........III, 310
SOMERVILLE, WILLIAM,
  Addison, Joseph..........II, 644
  Pope, Alexander.........III, 174
  Ramsay, Alan...........III, 409
SOMMER, H. OSKAR,
  Spenser, Edmund..........I, 377
SOMMERS, THOMAS,
  Fergusson, Robert.......III, 639
SONNECK, O. G.,
  Franklin, Benjamin.......IV, 93
SORBIERE, SAMUEL,
  Wallis, John.............II, 517
SOTHEBY, SAMUEL LEIGH,
  Milton, John.............II, 292
SOTHERAN, CHARLES,
  Greeley, Horace..........VI, 671
SOUTHERN, HENRY C. B.,
  Burnet, Thomas..........II, 597
  Defoe, Daniel............III, 42
  Jenyns, Soame............IV, 33
  Urquhart, Sir Thomas....II, 165
  Vaughan, Henry..........II, 443
SOUTHERNE, THOMAS,
  Behn, Aphra.............II, 408
  Congreve, William........II, 735
SOUTHEY, CHARLES CUTHBERT,
  Southey, Robert...........V, 399
SOUTHEY, ROBERT,
  Allston, Washington......V, 423
  Asgill, John..............III, 98
  Bacon, Roger..............I, 79
  Barbauld, Anna Lætitia....V, 24
  Beattie, James...........IV, 432
  Bede......................I, 29
  Berkeley, George........III, 326
  Bloomfield, Robert......IV, 723
  Bowles, William Lisle....V, 662
  Brontë, Charlotte.........VI, 17
  Bunyan, John............II, 393
  Burke, Edmund..........IV, 302
  Butler, Joseph..........III, 307
  Byrom, John............III, 469

Vol. and Page

Byron, George Gordon Lord..
  ....IV, 733, 751, 756
Chamberlayne, William.....II, 406
Chatterton, Thomas...III, 530, 535
Chaucer, Geoffrey......I, 158, 159
Churchill, Charles........III, 476
Clare, John..............IV, 376
Coleridge, Hartley.........V, 572
Coleridge, Samuel Taylor....V, 206
Collins, William........ III, 420
Cowper, William......IV, 379, 383
Cranmer, Thomas..........I, 271
Daniel, Samuel.............I, 616
Davidson, Lucretia Maria....V, 27
DeQuincey, Thomas......VI, 116
Disraeli, Isaac............V, 512
Donne, John...............I, 715
Drayton, Michael..........I, 707
Dwight, Timothy.........IV, 627
Evelyn, John.........II, 548, 549
Fielding, Henry..........III, 358
Frere, John Hookham......V, 486
Gilbert, Burnet...........II, 593
Glover, Richard.......IV, 18, 18
Godwin, Mary Wollstonecraft,
  ....IV, 326
Godwin, William...........V, 296
Grahame, James..........IV, 567
Grainger, James.........III, 498
Gray, Thomas,.......III, 558, 565
Hallam, Henry...........IV, 176
Hayley, William.....IV, 652, 653
Heber, Reginald............V, 39
Herrick, Robert..........II, 237
Hone, William............V, 393
Hyde, Edward, Earl of Clarendon...................II, 303
Jeffrey, Francis Lord.......V, 653
Johnson, Samuel.........III, 749
Lamb, Charles......V, 231, 239
Landor, Walter Savage........
  ....VI, 372, 379, 380, 381
Law, William............III, 428
Logan, John...............IV, 44
Lyttelton, George Lord....III, 612
Malthus, Thomas Robert....V, 250
Mason, William..........IV, 325
Mather, Cotton..........II, 730
Mickle, William Julius...IV, 40, 41
Milman, Henry Hart......IV, 539
Milton, John......II, 251, 254, 287
Montgomery, James.......V, 767
Moore, Thomas..........IV, 713
More, Hannah............V, 191
Neal, Daniel.............III, 140
Penn, William...........II, 629
Pomfret, John...........II, 511
Pope, Alexander........III, 165
Priestley, Joseph........IV, 446
Prior, Matthew..........II, 677
Pye, Henry James........IV, 580
Raleigh, Sir Walter ....I, 606
Ritson, Joseph..........IV, 436
Robertson, William......IV, 160
Sackville, Thomas..........I, 435
Sadler, Michael Thomas..V, 286, 287
Seward, Anna...........IV, 543
Shadwell, Thomas........II, 434
Shakespeare, William......I, 558
Sidney, Sir Philip......I, 323, 331
Silliman, Benjamin......VI, 407

Vol. and Page

Skelton, John...............I, 221
Smart, Christopher........III, 593
Smith, Horace..............V, 598
Spenser, Edmund......I, 381, 388
Southey, Robert............V, 410
Stanhope, Philip Dormer..III, 604
Taylor, Jeremy............II, 208
Taylor, John..........II, 132, 133
Taylor, Sir Henry........VII, 582
Thompson, William......III, 500
Turner, Sharon............V, 498
Tusser, Thomas............I, 310
Warburton, William......III, 684
Watts, Isaac........III, 249, 253
Wesley, John........IV, 13, 123
Wesley, Samuel..........III, 86
West, Gilbert..........III, 368
White, Henry Kirke....IV, 487, 488
Whitefield, George.......III, 547
Williams, Roger.........II, 356
Wordsworth, William........
  ....V, 606, 622, 628
SOUTHWELL, ROBERT,
  Shakespeare, William......I, 454
SOUTHWORTH, GEORGE C. S.,
  Gascoigne, George........I, 309
SPALDING, DOUGLAS A.,
  Lewes, George Henry.....VII, 141
SPALDING, JOHN LANCASTER,
  Froude, James Anthony..VIII, 263
  Mill, John Stuart.........VI, 712
  Whittier, John Greenleaf.VIII, 122
SPALDING, MARTIN JOHN,
  Faber, Frederick William..VI, 333
  Webster, Daniel...........V, 725
SPALDING, WILLIAM,
  Akenside, Mark........III, 543
  Andrews, Lancelot........I, 636
  Ascham, Roger...........I, 291
  Bale, John..............I, 286
  Barbour, John...........I, 113
  Barrow, Isaac...........II, 311
  Boece, Hector...........I, 243
  Bryant, William Cullen...VII, 121
  Collins, William........III, 420
  Cowper, William.........IV, 389
  Cranmer, Thomas..........I, 272
  Darwin, Erasmus........IV, 422
  Defoe, Daniel............III, 47
  Drayton, Michael..........I, 704
  Ferguson, Adam.........IV, 611
  Fletcher, Phineas........II, 116
  Glover, Richard..........IV, 19
  Hall, Robert.............V, 111
  Helps, Sir Arthur.......VII, 39
  Henry, Matthew.........II, 585
  Hutcheson, Francis......III, 246
  Jameson, Anna.........VI, 215
  Lardner, Nathaniel......III, 524
  Leighton, Robert........II, 360
  Lever, Charles James....VI, 653
  Livingstone, David......VI, 731
  Lydgate, John...........I, 185
  Lytton, Sir Edward George
  Bulwer................VI, 691
  May, Thomas...........II, 119
  Middleton, Thomas.......I, 685
  Palgrave, Sir Francis....VI, 265
  Pitt, William..........III, 680
  Pollok, Robert...........V, 73
  Reid, Thomas..........IV, 285

INDEX TO CRITICISMS

	Vol. and Page
Sandys, George	II, 83
Scott, Michael	I, 69
Shakespeare, William	I, 532
Southerne, Thomas	III, 240
Sternhold, Thomas	I, 262
Turner, Sharon	V, 499
Warner, William	I, 437
Warton, Thomas	IV, 74

SPARKS, JARED,
Brainard, John Gardiner Calkins	V, 84
Franklin, Benjamin	IV, 100
Hall, Basil	V, 457
Henry, Patrick	IV, 351
Marshall, John	V, 285
Prescott, William Hickling	VI, 190
Washington, George	IV, 367
Wayland, Francis	VI, 449
Webster, Noah	V. 429
Wilson, Alexander	IV, 585

SPAROWE, PHILLIP,
Chaucer, Geoffrey	I, 152

SPEDDING, JAMES,
Bacon, Francis	I, 645, 656
Coleridge, Hartley	V, 577
Dickens, Charles	VI, 568
Raleigh, Sir Walter	I, 596
Shakespeare, William	I, 540
Tennyson, Alfred Lord	VIII 81
Turner, Charles Tennyson	VII, 161

SPEED, JOHN GILMER,
Keats, John	IV, 668

SPEGHT, THOMAS,
Chaucer, Geoffrey	I, 154

SPENCE, JOSEPH,
Newton, Sir Isaac	II, 713
Pope, Alexander	III, 161
Wesley, John	IV, 129

SPENCER, CARL,
Poets and Poetry	IV, 10

SPENCER, HERBERT,
Carlyle, Thomas	VII, 273
Critic, The	II, 7
Mill, John Stuart	VI, 701, 713
Tyndall, John	VIII, 196, 199

SPENCER, JESSE AMES,
Treach, Richard Chenevix	VII, 588

SPENCER, O. M.,
Browning, Elizabeth Barrett	VI, 233
Parker, Theodore	VI, 208

SPENDER, A. EDMUND,
Cowper, William	IV, 395

SPENDER, HAROLD,
Tennyson, Alfred Lord	VIII, 109

SPENSER, EDMUND,
Books	III, 5
Camden, William	I, 620
Chaucer, Geoffrey	I, 134, 152, 154
Churchyard, Thomas	I, 417
Daniel, Samuel	I, 615
Harvey, Gabriel	I, 695
Knowledge	V, 5
Peele, George	I, 365
Poets and Poetry	IV, 5
Raleigh, Sir Walter	I, 599, 606
Sackville, Thomas	I, 435
Shakespeare, William	I, 547
Sidney Sir Philip	I, 320, 330
Spenser, Edmund	I, 374, 377
Watson, Thomas	I, 337

	Vol. and Page
SPIELMANN, MARION H.,	
Ruskin, John	VIII, 407, 422
Thackeray, William Makepeace	VI, 321

SPINGARN, JOEL ELIAS,
Ascham, Roger	I, 291
Sidney, Sir Philip	I, 330

SPOFFORD, HARRIET PRESCOTT,
Alcott Amos Bronson	VII, 662
Alcott, Louisa May	VII, 666
Dodge, Mary Abigail	VIII, 360
Goldsmith, Oliver	III, 621
Ingelow, Jean	III, 376
Miller, Cincinnatus Hiner	VIII, 499
Milton, John	II, 295
Reade, Charles	VII, 532
Whittier, John Greenleaf	VIII, 114, 123
Wordsworth, William	V, 628

SPOTISWOOD, JOHN,
Buchanan, George	I, 315
Douglas, Gawin	I, 213
Lyndsay, Sir David	I, 273
Thomas of Erceldoune	I, 83

SPRAGUE, HOMER B.,
Bunyan, John	II, 396
Shakespeare, William	I, 567

SPRAGUE, WILLIAM B.,
Dwight, Timothy	IV, 626
Hall, Robert	V, 109

SPRAT, THOMAS,
Bacon, Francis	I, 641, 657
Cowley, Abraham	II, 194, 196

SPRIGGE, S. SQUIRE,
Besant, Sir Walter	VIII, 450, 451

SPROTT, G. W.,
Leighton, Robert	II, 359
Logan, John	IV, 44
Rutherford, Samuel	II, 166

SPURGEON, MRS. CHARLES HADDON.
Spurgeon, Charles Haddon	II, 180, 182

SQUIRE, W. BARCLAY,
Burney, Charles	IV, 589

STACKHOUSE, THOMAS,
Atterbury, Francis	III, 65

STAËL, ANNE LOUISE GERMAINE NECKER MADAME DE,
Fielding, Henry	III, 351
Knowledge	V, 7
Shakespeare, William	I, 534, 554
Thomson, James	III, 258
Young, Edward	III, 492

STAFFORD, ANTHONY,
Sidney, Sir Philip	I, 321

STAFFORD WENDELL PHILLIPS,
Phillips, Wendell	VII, 554

STAIR, LORD,
Saint-John, Henry	III, 283

STALKER, JAMES,
Spurgeon, Charles Haddon	VIII, 181

STANDEN, SIR ANTHONY,
Raleigh, Sir Walter	I, 590

STANDING, PERCY CROSS,
Brontë, Anne	V, 599

	Vol. and Page
STANHOPE, EUGENIA,	
Stanhope, Philip Dormer	III, 603

STANHOPE, H.,
Pope, Alexander	III, 181

STANHOPE, PHILIP DORMER,
Murray, William	IV, 169

STANHOPE PHILIP HENRY (LORD MAHON),
Addison, Joseph	II, 657
Grey, Thomas	III, 567
Hume, David	III, 657
Johnson, Samuel	III, 730
Junius	IV, 640
Paine, Thomas	IV, 532
Pitt, William	IV, 508
Pope, Alexander	III, 186
Sacheverell, Henry	II, 696
Saint-John, Henry	III, 286, 294
Smith, Adam	IV, 63
Stanhope, Philip Dormer	III, 601, 604, 605
Steele, Sir Richard	II, 759
Swift, Jonathan	III, 218, 221

STANLEY, ARTHUR PENRHYN,
Addison, Joseph	II, 637
Alford, Henry	VI, 636
Andrewes, Lancelot	I, 637
Arnold, Thomas	V, 377
Baxter, Richard	II, 424
Blair, Hugh	IV, 404
Bunyan, John	II, 390, 396
Campbell, Thomas	V, 437
Chaucer, Geoffrey	I, 144
Colenso, John William	VII, 525
Dickens, Charles	VI, 555
Drayton, Michael	I, 701
Dryden, John	II, 465
Gay, John	III, 54
Gladstone, William Ewart	VIII, 383
Goldsmith, Oliver	III, 619
Grote, George	VI, 609
Hooker, Richard	I, 404
Jonson, Ben	I, 749
Keble, John	IV, 464
Kingsley, Charles	VII, 19, 25
Knox, John	I, 297
Leighton, Robert	II, 358
Lyell, Sir Charles	VII, 34
Macaulay, Thomas Babington Lord	VI, 94
Macleod, Norman	VI. 660, 662
Maurice, John Frederick Denison	VI, 647
Milman, Henry Hart	VI, 534, 535, 538, 541, 541
Motley, John Lothrop	VII. 86, 95
Newton, Sir Isaac	II, 714
Pope, Alexander	III, 151
Pusey, Edward Bouverie	VII, 467
Robertson, Frederick William	V. 740
Sheridan, Richard Brinsley	IV. 596
Skelton, John	I 222
Spenser, Edmund	I, 372
Thackeray, William Makepeace	VI, 294
Thirlwall, Connop	VII. 45
Wesley, Charles	IV 37
Wesley, John	IV, 128
Wordsworth, William	V, 613

INDEX TO CRITICISMS

	Vol. and Page
STANLEY, SIR HENRY MORTON,	
Livingstone, David	VI, 727
STANLEY, HIRAM M.	
Austen, Jane	IV, 688
Spenser, Edmund	I, 388
Wordsworth, William	V, 646
STANLEY, THOMAS,	
Suckling, Sir John	II, 62
STANTON, ELIZABETH CADY,	
Browning, Robert	VII, 683
Brownson, Orestes Augustus.	
	VII, 73
Garrison, William Lloyd	VII, 159
Whittier, John Greenleaf.	VIII, 116
STANTON, ELIZABETH CADY, ANTHONY, SUSAN B., AND GAGE, MATILDA J.,	
Fuller, Sarah Margaret	V, 670
STANTON, FRANK L.,	
Holmes, Oliver Wendell	VIII, 297
STANTON, HENRY B.,	
Simms, George Denison	VI, 602
STANTON, THEODORE,	
Parker, Theodore	VI, 208
STAPFER, PAUL,	
Sackville, Thomas	I, 434
Sidney, Sir Philip	I, 329
Shakespeare, William	
	I, 455, 463, 467, 510, 525, 527, 529
STAPLETON, AUGUSTUS GRANVILLE,	
Canning, George	V, 65
STATHAM, F. REGINALD,	
Clough, Arthur Hugh	VI, 256
STEAD, WILLIAM THOMAS,	
Adams, Sarah Flower	V, 530
Browning, Elizabeth Barrett	
	VI, 239
Cowper, William	IV, 377
Heber, Reginald	V, 38
Keble, John	VI, 463
Ken, Thomas	II, 570
Lowell, James Russell	VIII, 28, 38
Lyte, Henry Francis	V, 500
Manning, Henry Edward	
	VIII, 164
Newman, John Henry	VII, 750
Shakespeare, William	I, 571
Spurgeon, Charles Haddon	
	VIII, 181
Toplady, Augustus Montague.	
	III, 681
Wesley, Charles	V, 38
Wesley, John	IV, 116, 120, 128
White, Henry Kirke	IV, 490
STEARNS, FRANK PRESTON,	
Emerson, Ralph Waldo	VII, 353
Froude, James Anthony	V, II, 267
Hawthorne, Nathaniel	VI, 349
Macaulay, Thomas Babington Lord	VI, 100
Müller, Friedrich Max	VIII, 439
Philips, Wendell	VI, 225
Whittier, John Greenleaf.	VIII, 115
STEARNS, O. S.	
Colenso, John William	VII, 524
STEBBING, WILLIAM,	
Prior, Matthew	II, 674
Raleigh, Sir Walter	I, 598, 601
Saint-John, Henry	III, 290
Smollett, Tobias George	III, 582

	Vol. and Page
STEDMAN, ARTHUR,	
Mather, Increase	II, 689
Melville, Herman	VIII, 63
Winthrop, John	II, 107
STEDMAN, EDMUND CLARENCE,	
Adams, Sarah Flower	V, 529
Alford, Henry	VI, 637
Allingham, William	VII, 735
Arnold, Sir Edwin	VIII, 505
Arnold, Matthew	VII, 635
Blake, William	V, 59
Boker, George Henry	VII, 764
Bradstreet, Anne	II, 228
Browning, Elizabeth Barrett	
	VI, 236, 237, 239, 240, 245
Browning, Robert	
	VII, 685, 691, 693, 694, 697, 701
Bryant, William Cullen	
	VII, 112, 118, 124
Calverley, Charles Stuart	VII, 543
Chaucer, Geoffrey	I, 165
Clough, Arthur Hugh	VI, 251
Critic, The	II, 8
Drake, Joseph Rodman	
	IV, 661, 673
Eliot, George	VII, 196
Emerson, Ralph Waldo	VII, 357
Gray, David	VI, 262
Greeley, Horace	VI, 667
Griswold, Rufus Wilmot	VI, 78
Halleck, Fitz-Greene	VI, 500
Harte, Francis Bret	VIII, 470
Hawthorne, Nathaniel	VI, 367, 380
Hayne, Paul Hamilton	
	VII, 590, 592
Holland, Josiah Gilbert	VII, 333
Hood, Thomas	V, 463
Horne, Richard Hengist	VII, 547
Ingelow, Jean	VIII, 377
Jackson, Helen Hunt	VII, 575
Jonson, Ben	I, 767
Keats, John	IV, 680
Kingsley, Charles	VII, 28
Landor, Walter Savage	
	VI, 382, 383, 385, 390
Lanier, Sidney	VII, 329
Lazarus, Emma	VII, 611, 613
Lincoln, Abraham	VI, 417
Longfellow, Henry Wadsworth	
	VII, 389, 392, 394, 397
Lowell, James Russell	VIII, 28, 37
Lytton, Edward Robert Bulwer	VIII, 45, 48
Lytton, Sir Edward George Bulwer	VI, 699
Macaulay, Thomas Babington Lord	VI, 102
Marston, Philip Bourke	
	VII, 626, 627
Mill, John Stuart	VI, 712
Miller, Cincinnatus Hiner	
	VIII, 500
Milnes, Richard Monckton	
	VII, 563
Milton, John	II, 246
Morris, William	VIII, 333
O'Reilly, John Boyle	VII, 767
O'Shaughnessy, Arthur Wm. Edgar	VII, 322, 323
Palgrave, Francis Turner	
	VIII, 372

	Vol. and Page
Parsons, Thomas William	
	VIII, 193
Patmore, Coventry	VIII, 341
Poe, Edgar Allan	
	V, 541, 550, 552, 556, 558
Pope, Alexander	III, 193
Procter, Adelaide Anne	VI, 395
Procter, Bryan Waller	VI, 749
Rossetti, Christina Georgina	
	VIII, 268, 271
Rossetti, Gabriel Charles Dante	VII, 451
Saxe, John Godfrey	VII, 617
Shakespeare, William	I, 536, 573
Shelley, Percy Bysshe	IV, 715
Sidney, Sir Philip	I, 330
Southey, Robert	V, 405
Stevenson, Robert Louis	
	VIII, 243
Stoddard, Richard Henry	
	VIII, 497
Taylor, Bayard	VIII, 130, 133, 135
Taylor, Sir Henry	VII, 583
Tennyson, Alfred Lord	
	VIII, 79, 81, 82, 84, 96, 99
Thomson, James	VII, 474, 475
Timrod, Henry	VI, 508, 509
Trumbull, John	V, 121
Very, Jones	VII, 226
Warner, Charles Dudley	VIII, 442
Webster, John	I, 673
Wells, Charles Jeremiah	VII, 164
Whitman, Walt	
	VIII, 132, 135, 140
Whittier, John Greenleaf	
	VIII, 117, 118, 126
Willis, Nathaniel Parker	VI, 485
STEELE, MARY DAVIES,	
Evelyn, John	II, 549
STEELE, RICHARD,	
Addison, Joseph	
	II, 633, 648, 652
Atterbury, Francis	III, 64
Authors and Authorship	VIII, 5
Burnet, Thomas	II, 596
Centlivre, Susannah	II, 683
Congreve, William	II, 733
Dennis, John	III, 75
D'Urfey, Thomas	I, 687
Garth, Sir Samuel	II, 664
Hoadly, Benjamin	III, 423
Hughes, John	II, 667
Mandeville, Sir John	I, 95
Montagu, Charles	II, 586
Spenser, Edmund	I, 379
Steele, Sir Richard	II, 757
Wycherley, William	II, 601
STEERE, EDWARD,	
Butler, Joseph	III, 311
STEEVENS, GEORGE,	
Johnson, Samuel	III, 724
Mallet, David	III, 495
Shakespeare, William	I, 502
STEPHEN, SIR JAMES,	
Baxter, Richard	II, 427
Taylor, Sir Henry	VII, 582
Tucker, Abraham	III, 643
Whitefield, George	III, 548, 556
STEPHEN, SIR JAMES FITZJAMES,	
Chillingworth, William	II, 88

INDEX TO CRITICISMS 683

Hyde, Edward, Earl of Clarendon .... II 301
Laud, William .... II 88
Taylor, Jeremy .... II, 205, 211
STEPHEN, JAMES KENNETH,
Calverley, Charles Stuart. VII, 543
Lowell, James Russell .... VIII, 20
STEPHEN, SIR LESLIE,
Addison, Joseph ... II, 639, 642, 651
Akenside, Mark .... III, 545
Alison, Sir Archibald ..... VI, 520
Amory, Thomas .... IV, 48
Arbuthnot, John ...... III, 83, 83
Arnold, Matthew .... VIII, 629, 645
Asgill, John .... III, 98
Atterbury, Francis .... III, 67
Authors and Authorship .. VIII, 7
Bagehot, Walter .... VII, 100
Barclay, Robert .... II, 412
Bentham, Jeremy .... V, 168
Bentley, Richard .... III, 123
Berkeley, George ..... III, 326, 334
Blair, Hugh .... IV, 404, 406
Boswell, James ... IV, 211, 218, 220
Brontë, Charlotte .... VI, 29
Brooke, Henry .... III, 715
Broome, William .... III, 238
Browne, Sir Thomas ...... II, 340
Buckle, Henry Thomas .... VI, 283
Budgell, Eustace .... III, 92
Burke, Edmund .... IV, 305
Burnett, James .... IV, 348
Burns, Robert .... IV, 261
Butler, Joseph .... III, 312, 315
Byrom, John .... III, 469
Carey, Henry .... III, 138
Carlyle, Thomas ..... VII, 251, 270
Chatterton, Thomas ...... III, 538
Churchill, Charles .... III, 477
Clare, John .... VI, 399
Clarke, Samuel .... II, 748, 750
Clough, Arthur Hugh ..... VI, 254
Collins, Mortimer .... VII, 82
Combe, George .... VI, 89, 90
Congreve, William ..... II, 735, 744
Conybeare, John .... III, 366
Cooper, Anthony Ashley ... . II, 576, 579
Cowley, Abraham .... II, 202
Cowper, William ...... IV, 384, 390
Crabbe, George .... V, 172, 175
Cudworth, Ralph .... II, 387
Cumberland, Richard .. II, 624, 624
Cumberland, Richard ..... VI, 559
Darwin, Erasmus .... IV, 426
Day, Thomas .... IV, 49
D.foe, Daniel .... III, 26, 36
DeMorgan, Augustus ..... VI, 633
DeQuincey, Thomas ...... VI, 128
Donne, John .... I, 719
Dryden, John .... II, 468, 505
Dyer, John .... III, 400
Edgeworth, Maria .... V, 290
Edwards, Jonathan .... III, 383, 387, 391
Eliot, George .... VII, 187, 189, 190, 195
Emerson, Ralph Waldo .... VII, 354, 380
Etheredge, Sir George ..... II, 416

Evelyn, John .... II, 548
Falconer, William .... III, 526
Farquhar, George .... II, 559
Fawcett, Henry ..... VII, 550, 551
Ferguson, Adam ..... IV, 611, 613
Ferrier, James Frederick ... VI, 410
Ferrier, Susan Edmonstone .. .. V, 765
Fielding, Henry .... III, 344, 347, 349, 361
Fielding, Sarah .... III, 518
Francis, Sir Philip .... IV, 638
Franklin, Benjamin ...... IV, 101
Froude, James Anthony ... . VIII, 256, 262, 268
Fuller, Thomas ...... II, 169, 172
Gay, John .... III, 55
Gibbon, Edward .. IV, 179, 189, 192
Gifford, William .... V, 35
Godwin, Mary Wollstonecraft. .... IV, 328
Godwin, William .. V, 296, 297, 300
Goldsmith, Oliver ..... III, 621, 624
Gray, Thomas .... III, 563, 571
Green, John Richard . VII, 507, 509
Green, Matthew .... III, 95
Hallam, Henry .... VI, 175, 177
Hamilton, Alexander .. IV, 466, 472
Hamilton, Sir William .. VI, 53, 57
Hartley, David .... III, 379
Hawkins, Sir John ...... IV, 51, 52
Hawthorne, Nathaniel. VI, 366, 377
Hayley, William .... IV, 652
Hazlitt, William .... V, 105
Hervey, James .... III, 397
Hill, Aaron .... III, 277
Hoadly, Benjamin ... III, 422, 424
Hobbes, Thomas .... II, 328
Holmes, Oliver Wendell .... VIII, 293, 294, 299
Hume, David ... III, 651, 654, 660
Hurd, Richard .... IV, 518
Hutcheson, Francis ...... III, 247
Huxley, Thomas Henry ... VIII, 328
Johnson, Samuel .... III, 734, 738, 739, 742, 744, ... 752, 761
Jowett, Benjamin .... VIII, 211
Kinglake, Alexander William. .... VIII, 53
Kingsley, Charles .... VII, 23, 24, 27, 31, 32
Kingsley, Henry .... VII, 79
Lamb, Charles .... V, 240
Law, William .... III, 425, 427, 430
Leland, John .... III, 500
Leslie, Charles .... II, 680
Lewes, George Henry ..... VII, 139
Locke, John ...... II, 523, 528, 536
Macaulay, Thomas Babington, Lord .... VI, 114
Mackenzie, Henry .... V, 113
Mackintosh, Sir James ..... V, 183
Macpherson, James ...... IV, 278
Maine, Sir Henry James Sumner .... VII, 651
Malthus, Thomas Robert ... V, 253
Mandeville, Bernard ... III, 70, 70
Martineau, Harriet .... VII, 64
Mason, William .... IV, 326
Massinger, Philip. II, 43, 44, 45, 50

Maurice, John Frederick Denison .... VI, 646, 648
Middleton, Conyers .... III, 281
Mill, James .... V, 308, 309
Milton, John .... II, 250, 282
More, Hannah .... V, 196
Newman, John Henry ..... VII, 751
Newton, Sir Isaac .... II, 725
Norris, John .... II, 571
Oliphant, Laurence ... VII, 656, 658
Owen, Robert .... VI, 84
Paine, Thomas .... IV, 535, 540
Paley, William .... IV, 471, 478
Parr, Samuel .... V, 21
Pepys, Samuel .... II, 516
Piozzi, Hester Lynch ..... IV, 685
Pitt, William .... III, 679
Poe, Edgar Allan .... V, 571
Pope, Alexander ....
III, 155, 157, 162, 163, 167,
.... 168, 169, 177, 180, 191
Praed, Winthrop Mackworth. V, 334
Price, Richard .... IV, 136
Priestley, Joseph .... IV, 455
Reid, Thomas .... IV, 282, 287
Riccardo, David .... IV, 726
Richardson, Samuel ...... III, 450
Ruskin, John ...... VIII, 412, 414
Saint-John, Henry .... III, 291, 299
Savage, Richard .... III, 136
Scott, Sir Walter .. V, 134, 152, 153
Shelley, Percy Bysshe ..... IV, 751
Smith, Adam ...... IV, 60, 65, 71
Smith, Sydney .... V, 474
Spedding, James .... VII, 319
Spenser, Edmund .... I, 398
Swift, Jonathan ....
III, 204, 212, 213, 222, 223,
.... 226, 234
Sterne, Laurence .... III, 508
Stevenson, Robert Louis .... VIII, 253
Stewart, Dugald .... V, 80
Tennyson, Alfred Lord ... VIII, 92
Thackeray, William Makepeace .... VI, 301, 308
Thomson, James .... III, 263
Tickell, Thomas .... III, 105
Tindal, Matthew .... III, 73
Toland, John .... II, 681, 682
Tooke, John Horne ...... IV, 572
Trollope, Anthony .... VII, 459, 465
Tucker, Abraham .... III, 644
Tucker, Josiah ...... IV, 370, 384
Wakefield, Gilbert .... IV, 417
Warburton, William .... III, 685, 688, 692
Waterland, Daniel .... III, 103
Watts, Isaac .... III, 253
Wesley, John .... IV, 127, 131
Whewell, William .... VI, 470
Whiston, William ..... III, 304, 305
Whitefield, George ...... III, 550
Wilberforce, William ... V, 202, 202
Wilson, Thomas .... III, 367
Woolston, Thomas .... III, 74
Wordsworth, William ..... V, 638
Young, Arthur .... VII, 654
Young, Edward ..... III, 489, 492
STEPHENS, ALEXANDER,
Tooke, John Horne .... IV, 569

INDEX TO CRITICISMS

STEPHENS, FREDERIC GEORGE,
  Rossetti, Gabriel Charles Dante.
    ....443, 454
STEPHENS, H. MORSE,
  Jones, Sir William..........IV, 200
STEPHENS, ROBERT,
  Bacon, Francis..............I, 641
STEPHENS, WILLIAM R. W.,
  Anslem ....I, 51
  Colet, John.................I, 211
  Freeman, Edward Augustus..
    ....VIII, 155, 160
  More, Hannah..............V, 193
  More, Sir Thomas...........I, 235
STERLING, JOHN,
  Carlyle, Thomas......VII, 242, 246
  Coleridge, Samuel Taylor.....
    ....V, 214, 219
  Law, William..............III, 426
  Milton, John...............II, 288
  Shakespeare, William........I, 560
  Tennyson, Alfred Lord...VIII, 80
  Wordsworth, William.......V, 607
  Wyclif, John................I, 105
STERNE, LAURENCE,
  Books ....III, 6
  Bunyan, John..............II, 392
  Garrick, David............III, 694
  Sterne, Laurence ....III, 505
STEVENS, ABEL,
  Wesley, John.........IV, 119, 123
STEVENS JOHN AUSTIN,
  Livingston, William........IV, 109
STEVENSON, ARTHUR,
  Knox, John.................I, 297
STEVENSON, JOSEPH,
  Bede.......................I, 27
STEVENSON, ROBERT LOUIS,
  Besant, Sir Walter.......VIII, 450
  Browning, Robert........VII, 694
  Burns, Robert....IV, 232, 238, 261
  Bunyan, John..............II, 397
  Dickens, Charles...........VI, 574
  Fergusson, Robert.........III, 640
  Fielding, Henry..III, 354, 356, 362
  Lytton, Edward Robert Bulwer Earl ....VIII, 45
  Pepys, Samuel.............II, 513
  Richardson, Samuel.......III, 446
  Scott, Sir Walter...........V, 140
  Shakespeare, William ....I, 571
  Spencer, Herbert........VIII, 482
  Thackeray, William Makepeace
    ....VI, 318
  Thoreau, Henry David.VI, 270, 273
  Whitman, Walt.VIII, 131, 135, 141
  Wordsworth, William.......V, 643
STEVINS, WALTER,
  Chaucer, Geoffrey..........I, 140
STEWART, DUGALD,
  Akenside, Mark...........III, 541
  Bacon, Francis.........I, 649, 658
  Beattie, James............IV, 428
  Berkeley, George..........III, 329
  Boyle, Rober ....II, 418
  Buchanan, George..........I, 314
  Burns Robert.............IV, 222
  Clarke, Samuel............II, 749
  Edwards, Jonathan........III, 389
  Harrington, James.........II, 308
  Hartley, David............III, 378

Hobbes, Thomas...........II, 325
Home, Henry..............III, 712
Home, John................IV 514
Hume, David ....III, 652
Hutcheson, Francis........III, 245
Priestley, Joseph..........IV, 454
Pope, Alexander...........III, 175
Reid, Thomas.............IV, 283
Robertson, William..........
    ....IV, 154, 156, 159, 160
Smith, Adam..............IV, 54
Tucker, Abraham..........III, 643
STEWART, GEORGE,
  Longfellow, Henry Wadsworth.
    ....VII, 406
  Parkman, Francis.......VIII, 224
STEWART, J. A.,
  Mill, John Stuart..........VI, 717
STEWART, J. L.,
  Lever, Charles James.......VI, 654
STILES, EZRA,
  Edwards, Jonathan........III, 389
  Washington, George.......IV, 354
STILLÉ, CHARLES J.,
  Wilde, Richard Henry......V, 504
STILLINGFLEET, BENJAMIN,
  Ray, John.................II, 542
STILLINGFLEET, JAMES,
  Law, William.............III, 427
STILLMAN, M. S.,
  Piozzi, Hester Lynch......IV, 686
STILLMAN, WILLIAM JAMES,
  Agassiz, Louis Jean Rodolphe.
    ....VI, 722
  Alcott, Amos Bronson.....VII, 663
  Browning, Robert........VII, 684
  Bryant, William Cullen......
    ....VII, 115, 127
  Buchanan, Robert.......VIII, 445
  Disraeli, Benjamin.........VII, 281
  Emerson, Ralph Waldo....VII, 376
  Froude, James Anthony..VIII, 256
  Gladstone, William Ewart....
    ....VIII, 386
  Holmes, Oliver Wendell..VIII, 289
  Longfellow, Henry Wadsworth.
    ....VII, 386
  Lowell, James Russell....VII, 26
  Marsh, George Perkins...VII, 493
  Morris, William..........VIII, 338
  Owen, Sir Richard........VIII, 172
  Rossetti, Christina Georgina...
    ....VIII, 270
  Rossetti, Gabriel Charles Dante
    ....VII, 440
  Ruskin, John............VIII, 408
  Warner, Charles Dudley..VIII, 442
STIMSON. HENRY A.,
  Müller, Friedrich Max....VIII, 435
STINSON, F. J.,
  Ruskin, John............VIII, 417
STIRLING, JAMES HUTCHISON,
  Berkeley, George..........III, 333
  Hamilton, Sir William.....VI, 55
  Macaulay, Thomas Babington
    Lord ....VI, 110
STIRLING, JAMES,
  Mill, John Stuart..........VI, 713
STIRLING, WILLIAM,
  Prescott, William Hickling....
    ....VI, 184, 187, 189

STIRLING-MAXWELL, SIR WILLIAM,
  Knox, John.................I, 302
  Prescott, William Hickling..VI, 188
STOCKDALE, PERCIVAL,
  Milton, John..............II, 286
  Waller, Edmund...........II, 380
  Williams, Helen Maria......V. 74
STOKES, FRE ERICK A.,
  Suckling, Sir John.........II, 67
STOKES, LOUIS,
  Thirwall, Connop.........VII, 42
STOKES, ADMIRAL LORD,
  Darwin, Charles Robert...VII, 418
STOCKNEY, ALBERT,
  Choate, Rufus............VI, 198
STOCKS, EDWARD VAZEILLE,
  Wesley, John..............IV, 120
STOCKTON, FRANK R.,
  Defoe, Daniel.............III, 39
  Dickens, Charles......VI, 579, 592
  Lowell, James Russell....VIII, 21
  Poe, Edgar Allan..........V, 561
STODDARD, CHARLES WARREN,
  Harte, Francis Bret......VIII, 471
  Stevenson, Robert Louis..VIII, 239
STODDARD, ELIZABETH,
  Locker-Lampson, Frederick..
    ....VIII, 314
  Scott, Sir Walter...........V, 160
STODDARD, FRANCIS HOVEY,
  Austen, Jane.............IV, 615
  Brontë, Charlotte.........VI, 26
  Goldsmith, Oliver.....III, 629, 639
  Hawthorne, Nathaniel.....VI, 355
  Kingsley, Charles.........VII, 33
  Reade, Charles...........VII, 538
  Scott, Sir Walter...........V. 147
STODDARD, RICHARD HENRY,
  Addison, Joseph...........II, 660
  Arnold, Sir Edwin...VIII, 504, 504
  Barham, Richard Harris.....V. 475
  Beddoes, Thomas Lovell.V. 586, 588
  Blake, William.............V, 62
  Bloomfield, Robert....IV. 723, 724
  Boker, George Henry.VII, 765, 766
  Bradstreet, Anne.........II, 230
  Browning, Elizabeth Barrett...
    ....VI, 234, 241, 246, 247
  Browning, Robert........VII, 700
  Bryant, William Cullen......
    ....VII, 117, 123
  Buchanan, Robert........VII, 446
  Burns, Robert............IV, 266
  Byron, George Gordon Lord.IV. 762
  Campbell, Thomas.....V, 439, 445
  Chaucer, Geoffrey..........I, 166
  Clare, John...............VI. 399
  Coleridge, Hartley.....V, 576, 578
  Constable, Henry ....I, 444
  Dana, Richard Henry.....VII, 156
  Elliott, Ebenezer..........V, 584
  Daniel, Samuel............I, 613
  Disraeli, Benjamin........VII, 294
  Drake, Joseph Rodman ...IV. 661
  Drayton, Michael..........I, 708
  Drummond, William......II, 103
  FitzGerald, Edward......VII, 522
  Gifford, William..........V, 33
  Gower, John..............I, 176
  Gray, David ....VI, 261

INDEX TO CRITICISMS

	Vol. and Page
Gray, Thomas	III, 555
Hall, Joseph	II, 145
Halleck, Fitz-Greene	VI, 495, 497, 500
Hawthorne, Nathaniel	VI, 367
Hazlitt, William	V, 100, 105
Hogg, James	V, 266, 269
Johnson, Samuel	III, 761
Keats, John	IV, 668, 679
Lincoln, Abraham	VI, 413
Longfellow, Henry Wadsworth	VII, 387, 392, 405
Lowell, James Russell	VIII, 33
Marlowe, Christopher	I, 347, 356
Melville, Herman	VIII, 63
Milnes, Richard Monckton	VII, 562, 564
Milton, John	II, 273, 275, 294
Moore, Thomas	V, 718
Motherwell, William	V, 278
Peacock, Thomas Love	VI, 474, 476
Poe, Edgar Allan	V, 540, 547, 550, 553, 556, 559
Pope, Alexander	III, 192
Read, Thomas Buchanan	VI, 678
Shelley, Percy Bysshe	IV, 695
Stevenson, Robert Louis	VIII, 246
Taylor, Bayard	VII, 134, 136
Tennyson, Alfred Lord	VIII, 98
Thackeray, William Makepeace	VI, 295, 303, 307
White, Richard Grant	VII, 577, 578
Whittier, John Greenleaf	VIII, 117, 123
Willis, Nathaniel Parker	VI, 490
Wordsworth, William	V, 618, 627
STODDART, ANNA M.,	
Blackie, John Stuart	VIII, 306
Guthrie, Thomas	VI, 737
Knox, John	I, 298
STONE, ELIZABETH,	
Walpole, Horace	IV, 314
STONE, LUCY,	
Garrison, William Lloyd	VII, 160
STONE, WILLIAM L.,	
Wayland, Francis	VI, 448, 448, 452
STORY, MOORFIELD,	
Sumner, Charles	VI, 757
STORRS, R. S.,	
Choate, Rufus	VI, 195
STOROJENKO, NICHOLAS.	
Greene, Robert	I, 342
STORY, ALFRED T.,	
Blake, William	V, 59, 62
Penn, William	II, 628
STORY, JOSEPH,	
Adams, John	V, 52
Adams, John Quincy	V, 514
Everett, Edward	VI, 422
Hamilton, Alexander	IV, 457
Irving, Washington	VI, 145
Jones, Sir William	IV, 199
Kent, James	V, 501
Lowell, James Russell	VIII, 58
Madison, James	V, 313
Marshall, John	V, 281, 284
Monroe, James	V, 122
Quincy, Josiah	VI, 404
Southey, Robert	V, 403
Washington, George	IV, 356

	Vol. and Page
STORY, WILLIAM WETMORE,	
Allston, Washington	V, 422
Barlow, Joel	IV, 576
Barnes, William	VII, 587
Byron, George Gordon Lord	IV, 747
Canning, George	V, 69
Chaucer, Geoffrey	I, 168
Landor, Walter Savage	VI, 386
Lowell, James Russell	VIII, 21
Scott, Sir Walter	IV, 157
Seward Anna	IV, 544
Shakespeare, William	I, 546
Shelley, Percy Bysshe	IV, 714
Story, Joseph	V, 483
Story, William Wetmore	VI, 405
Sumner, Charles	VI, 751
Webster, Daniel	V, 727
STOUGHTON, JOHN,	
Butler, Joseph	III, 309
Doddridge, Philip	III, 302, 303
Wilberforce, William	V, 203
STOWE, HARRIET BEECHER,	
Beecher, Henry Ward	VII, 603
Byron, George Gordon Lord	IV, 746, 752
Edwards, Jonathan	III, 391
Eliot, George	VII, 192
Fields, James Thomas	VII, 340
Gaskell, Elizabeth Cleghorn	VI, 428
Greeley, Horace	VI, 670
Kingsley, Charles	VII, 18
Moore, Thomas	V, 713
Phillips, Wendell	VII, 552
Whittier, John Greenleaf	VIII, 122
STOWE, JOHN,	
Latimer, Hugh	I, 267
STOWELL, HUGH,	
Wilson, Thomas	III, 366
STRACHEY, SIR EDWARD,	
Peacock, Thomas Love	VI, 473
STRACHEY, SIR JOHN,	
Maine, Sir Henry James Sumner	VII, 652
STRACHEY, ST. LOE,	
Gay, John	III, 61
STRAHAN, ALEXANDER,	
Knight, Charles	VI, 742, 743
Macleod, Norman	VI, 660, 662
STRAHAN, ANDREW,	
Robertson, William	IV, 157
STREET, G. S.,	
Boyle, Robert	II, 419
Byron, George Gordon Lord	IV, 743
Hervey, John Lord	III, 131
Sheridan, Richard Brinsley	IV, 609
Trollope, Anthony	VII, 465
Walpole, Horace	IV, 321
STRICKLAND, AGNES,	
Ken, Thomas	II, 568
STRICKLAND, JANE MARGARET,	
Strickland, Agnes	VI, 767
STRONG, AUGUSTUS HOPKINS,	
Browning, Robert	VII, 696, 716
Milton, John	II, 253, 270, 298
Shakespeare, William	I, 576
Tennyson, Alfred Lord	VIII, 90
Wordsworth, William	V, 617, 626
STRONG, ISABEL,	
Stevenson, Robert Louis	VIII, 234

	Vol. and Page
STRUNK, WILLIAM, JR.,	
Dryden, John	II, 494
STRYKER, W. WOOLSEY,	
Hamilton, Alexander	IV, 465
STRYPE, JOHN,	
Churchyard, Thomas	I, 417
Cranmer, Thomas	I, 271
Elyot, Sir Thomas	I, 253
Foxe, John	I, 335
Latimer, Hugh	I, 267
STUART, ESMÉ,	
Lytton, Sir Edward George Bulwer	VI, 694
Poe, Edgar Allan	V, 559
STUART, GILBERT.	
Henry, Robert	IV, 107, 107
Stuart, Gilbert	IV, 27
STUART, JAMES MONTGOMERY,	
Carlyle, Thomas	VII, 257
STUART, LADY LOUISA,	
Fielding, Henry	III, 341
Lillo, George	III, 100
Montagu, Lady Mary Wortley	III, 466
Walpole, Horace	IV, 312
STUART, MOSES,	
Gilfillan, George	VII, 151
STUART-GLENNIE, J. S.,	
Macpherson, James	IV, 278
STUBBE, HENRY,	
Bacon, Francis	I, 664
Sprat, Thomas	II, 573
STUBBES, PHILIP	
Foxe, John	I, 335
STUBBS, CHARLES WILLIAM,	
Kingsley, Charles	VII, 33
Maurice, John Frederick Denison	VI, 650
STUBBS, WILLIAM,	
Carlyle, Thomas	VII, 257
Green, John Richard	VII, 506
Heber, Reginald	V, 38
Peacock, Reginald	I, 190
William of Malmesbury	I, 54
Wyclif, John	I, 107
STUCKENBERG, J. H. W.,	
Newton, Sir Isaac	II, 725
STUCLEY, SIR LEWIS,	
Raleigh, Sir Walter	I, 591
STURGIS, RUSSELL,	
Hamerton, Philip Gilbert	VIII, 283
Ruskin, John	VIII, 411, 413
STURROCK, R. W.,	
Percy, Thomas	IV, 562
SUARD, M.,	
Gibbon, Edward	IV, 178
SUCKLING, ALFRED,	
Suckling, Sir John	II, 63
SUCKLING, SIR JOHN,	
Carew, Thomas	II, 21
D'Avenant, Sir William	II, 216, 219
Hales, John	II, 149
Jonson, Ben	I, 746
Suckling, Sir John	II, 62
SULLIVAN, MARGARET F.,	
Raleigh, Sir Walter	I, 597
SULLIVAN, WILLIAM,	
Hamilton, Alexander	IV, 458
SULLY, JAMES,	
Lewes, George Henry	VII, 141, 142

686 INDEX TO CRITICISMS

Vol. and Page

SULZBERGER, CYRUS L.,
  Lazarus, Emma..........VII, 612
SUMNER, CHARLES,
  Allston, Washington........V, 418
  Brougham, Henry Lord....VI, 525
  Carlyle, Thomas..........VII, 230
  Channing, William Ellery......
    ....V, 366, 371
  Cobden, Richard..........VI, 440
  DeQuincey, Thomas.......VI, 116
  Emerson, Ralph Waldo....VII, 343
  Gladstone, William Ewart....
    ....VIII, 388
  Hawthorne, Nathaniel.VI, 342, 365
  Hunt, James Henry Leigh..VI, 156
  Longfellow, Henry Wadsworth
    ....VII, 381, 402
  Lytton, Sir Edward George Bul-
    wer ....VI, 680
  Macaulay, Thomas Babington
    Lord ....VI, 92
  Milnes, Richard Monckton.VII, 559
  Norton, Caroline Elizabeth
    Sheridan ....VII, 102
  Penn, William.............II, 630
  Prescott, William Hickling..VI, 182
  Procter, Bryan Waller......VI, 744
  Selden, John..............II, 143
  Story, Joseph...............V, 482
  Tennyson, Alfred Lord...VIII, 81
SUMNER, WILLIAM GRAHAM,
  Berkeley, George..........III, 332
  Hamilton, Alexander......IV, 464
  Spencer, Herbert........VIII, 482
SUNDERLAND, ROBERT SPEN-
  CER EARL,
  Locke, John...............II, 519
  Somers, John Lord.........II, 612
SUNDT, ELLERT,
  Borrow, George Henry....VII, 312
SURREY, EARL OF,
  Wyatt, Sir Thomas..........I, 249
SURTEES, ROBERT,
  Butler, Joseph............III, 307
SUSSEX, DUKE OF,
  Herschel, Sir John Frederick
    William................VI, 623
SUTTON, C. W.,
  Hemans, Felicia Dorothea...V, 261
SWAEN, A. E. H.,
  Vanbrugh, Sir John........II, 708
SWANWICK, ANNA,
  Dryden, John..............II, 505
SWEET, HENRY,
  Ormin ....I, 71
  Poor, Richard..............I, 70
SWEETSER, M. F.,
  Allston, Washington ......V, 421
SWIFT, DEANE,
  Swift, Jonathan......III, 199, 208
SWIFT, EDMUND LENTHALL,
  Swift, Jonathan..........III, 210
SWIFT, JONATHAN,
  Addison, Joseph..........II, 613
  Arbuthnot, John..........III, 81
  Atterbury, Francis ....III, 64
  Bentley, Richard....III, 110, 115
  Berkeley, George.....III, 319, 323
  Books ....III, 6
  Bunyan, John.............II, 392
  Burnet, Gilbert...........II, 592

Vol. and Page

Congreve, William.....II, 733, 740
Defoe, Daniel ....III, 23
Dryden, John....II, 486, 492, 496
Fletcher, Andrew..........II, 610
Gay, John............III, 53, 60
Hoadly, Benjamin.........III, 422
Hughes, John.............II, 667
Knowledge ....V, 6
Manley, Mrs. Mary de la Ri-
  viere ....II, 693
Marvell, Andrew..........II, 316
Milton, John..............II, 258
Montagu, Charles.........II, 586
More, Sir Thomas ....I, 234
Newton, Sir Isaac.........II, 721
Penn, William............II, 626
Philips, Ambrose ....III, 273
Poets and Poetry.........IV, 6
Pope, Alexander............
  ....III, 145, 163, 164, 181
Sacheverell, Henry........II, 695
Saint-John, Henry........III, 282
Somers, John Lord........II, 613
South, Robert............II, 607
Steele, Sir Richard.....II, 751, 762
Swift, Jonathan..III, 197, 207, 227
Tate, Nahum..............II, 588
Temple, Sir William.......II, 455
Vanbrugh, Sir John.......II, 705
Young, Edward ....III, 484
SWIFT, LINDSAY,
  Bancroft, George........VIII, 61
  Boker, George Henry.....VII, 765
  Brownson, Orestes Augustus..
    ....VII, 76
  Everett, Edward..........VI, 427
  Greeley, Horace..........VI, 670
  Ripley, George..........VII, 224
SWIGGETT GLEN LEVIN,
  Lanier, Sidney..........VII, 332
SWINBURNE, ALGERNON
  CHARLES,
  Arnold, Matthew........VII, 634
  Beaumont and Fletcher..I, 579, 585
  Beaumont, Francis.........I, 587
  Behn, Aphra........II, 408, 411
  Blake, William............V, 60
  Brontë, Anne..............V, 599
  Brontë, Charlotte..VI, 19, 21, 24,29
  Brontë, Emily............V, 524
  Browning, Elizabeth Barrett..
    ....VI, 240
  Browning, Robert...VII, 701, 709
  Burns, Robert............IV, 268
  Burton, Sir Richard Francis..
    ....VII, 759
  Byron, George Gordon Lord..
    ....IV, 748, 753, 763
  Calverley, Charles Stuart.....
    ....VII, 543
  Carlyle, Thomas.....VII, 258, 269
  Chapman, George..........I, 733
  Chaucer, Geoffrey......I, 167, 167
  Chettle, Henry............I, 429
  Clough, Arthur Hugh......VI, 254
  Coleridge, Samuel Taylor.....
    ....V, 215, 218, 220, 227
  Collins, William..III, 417, 418, 421
  Collins, William Wilkie..VII, 727
  Congreve, William....II, 739, 743
  Croker, John Wilson......VI, 76

Vol. and Page

Dekker, Thomas............
  ....II, 56, 56, 57, 58 60
Dickens, Charles............
  ......VI, 575, 575, 579, 588, 595
Dryden, John.............II, 469
Eliot, George........VII, 185, 205
FitzGerald, Edward......VII, 517
Fletcher, John.............I, 631
Ford, John........II, 27, 28, 30, 32
Heywood, Thomas.II, 124, 125, 128
Jonson, Ben................
  I, 751, 752, 752, 753, 754, 755,
              756. 766
Jowett, Benjamin...VIII, 208, 211
Keats, John..IV, 669, 672, 673, 679
Lamb, Charles.........V, 240, 242
Landor, Walter Savage.......
  ....VI, 376, 381, 390
Lodge, Thomas.............I, 627
Marlowe, Christopher.......I, 355
Marston, John.........I, 736, 738
Marston, Philip Bourke...VII, 626
Massinger, Philip..........II, 51
Middleton, Thomas..........
  ....I, 682, 683, 683, 684, 685
Montagu, Lady Mary Wortley
  ....III, 463
Morris, William.........VIII, 332
Peacock, Thomas Love....VI, 474
Poe, Edgar Allan...V, 546, 556, 558
Peele, George..............I, 366
Poets and Poetry..........IV, 9
Pope, Alexander............
  ....III, 152, 162, 174, 192
Procter, Bryan Waller.....VI, 748
Randolph, Thomas..........I, 744
Reade, Charles.. VII, 530, 531, 534
Rossetti, Christina Georgina..
  ....VIII, 269
Rossetti, Gabriel Charles Dante
  ....VII, 444, 448
Rowley, William..........II, 69
Sedley, Sir Charles........II, 510
Shakespeare, William........
  I, 445, 457, 460, 466, 469, 472
  475, 480, 488, 493, 496, 497, 506,
  508, 522, 529, 539 539, 541, 542,
  542, 542, 543, 570.
Shelley, Percy Bysshe........
  ....IV, 703, 709, 715
Shirley, James............II, 192
Sidney, Sir Philip..........I, 332
Spenser, Edmund...........I, 385
Suckling, Sir John..........II, 67
Taylor, Sir Henry........VII, 580
Tennyson Alfred Lord........
  ....VIII, 87, 94, 104
Thackeray, William Makepeace
  ....VI, 312
Tourneur, Cyril............I, 688
Trollope, Anthony........VII, 463
Webster, John.............
  ....I, 671, 673, 673, 674, 676
Wells, Charles Jeremiah....VII, 164
Whitman, Walt........VIII, 143
Wilmot, John.............II, 338
Wordsworth, William........
  ....V, 618, 621, 642
SWINBURNE, LOUIS,
  Jackson, Helen Hunt.......
  ....VII, 572, 576

INDEX TO CRITICISMS

	Vol. and Page
SWING, DAVID	
Literature	I, 10
SWINTON, WILLIAM,	
Bryant, William Cullen	VII, 112
SYDENHAM, THOMAS,	
Locke, John	II, 518
SYLE, L. DUPONT,	
Dryden, John	II, 506
Goldsmith, Oliver	III, 632
SYMINGTON, ANDREW JAMES,	
Carlyle, Thomas	VII, 235
Lover, Samuel	VI, 544, 545
Moore, Thomas	V, 718
Taylor, Sir Henry	VII, 583
Turner, Charles Tennyson	VII, 162
Wordsworth, William	V, 640
SYMONDS JOHN ADDINGTON,	
Beaumont and Fletcher	I, 584
Browning, Robert	
	VII, 694, 696, 711
Byron, George Gordon Lord	
	IV, 749
Chapman, George	I, 734
Clough, Arthur Hugh	VI, 254
Critic, The	II, 8
Daniel, Samuel	I, 617
Dekker, Thomas	II, 61
Edwards, Amelia Ann Blandford	VIII, 176
Eliot, George	VII, 200
FitzGerald, Edward	VII, 520
Ford, John	II, 27
Gladstone, William Ewart	VIII, 384
Godwin, William	V, 295
Greene, Robert	I, 340, 343
Hawthorne, Nathaniel	V, 367
Heywood, John	I, 305
Heywood, Thomas	II, 127
Jonson, Ben	
	I 751, 752, 754, 757, 758
Jowett, Benjamin	VIII, 207
Keats, John	IV, 665, 630
Lyly, John	I, 422
Marlowe, Christopher	I, 355
Marston, John	I, 738
Milton, John	II, 278
Nashe, Thomas	I, 414
Pater, Walter Horatio	VIII, 276
Peele, George	I, 366
Richardson, Samuel	III, 441
Rossetti, Gabriel Charles Dante	
	VII, 448, 452
Scott, Sir Walter	V, 152, 160
Shakespeare, William	I, 459, 570
Shelley, Percy Bysshe	
	IV, 699, 703, 704, 710
Shirley, James	II, 192
Sidney, Sir Philip	I, 323
Stevenson, Robert Louis	VIII, 240
Still, John	I, 429
Tennyson, Alfred Lord	
	VIII, 69, 105
Thomson, James	VII, 476
Udall, Nicholas	I, 279
Webster, John	I, 677
Wells, Charles Jeremiah	VII, 165
Whitman, Walt	VIII, 133, 145
Wordsworth, illiam	V, 644
SYMONS, ARTHUR,	
Beddoes, Thomas Lovell	V, 588
Browning Robert	VII 690, 693
Buchanan, Robert	VIII, 448
Donne, John	I, 719
Henley, William Ernest	VIII, 492
Ingelow, Jean	VIII, 377
Jefferies, Richard	VII, 622
Morris, William	VIII, 334, 337
Pater, Walter Horatio	VIII, 280
Rossetti, Christina Georgina	
	VIII, 274
Stephen, Sir Leslie	VIII, 511
Stevenson, Robert Louis	VIII, 250
Shakespeare, William	I. 539. 541
Wordsworth, William	V, 628, 647
SYMONS, CHARLES,	
Bentley, Richard	III, 120
Milton, John	II, 246
SZOLD, HENRIETTA,	
Aguilar Grace	V, 505
TABB, JOHN B.,	
Keats, John	IV, 681
Lanier, Sidney	VII, 329
Milton, John	II, 297
Poe, Edgar Allan	V, 559
Shelley, Percy Bysshe	IV, 698
TAINE, HIPPOLYTE ADOLPHE,	
Addison, Joseph	
	II, 637, 642, 653, 658
Akenside, Mark	III, 544
Alfred the Great	I, 40
Bacon, Francis	I, 668
Barrow, Isaac	II, 311, 326
Beattie, James	IV, 434
Beowulf	I, 18
Browning, Elizabeth Barrett	
	VI, 239
Bunyan, John	II, 395
Burke, Edmund	IV, 305
Burns, Robert	IV, 258
Burton, Robert	II, 39
Butler, Samuel	II, 333
Bryon, George Gordon Lord	
	IV, 749, 751, 752, 760
Carlyle, Thomas	VII, 247, 252, 265
Chaucer, Geoffrey	I, 164
Chillingworth, William	II, 87
Clarke, Samuel	II, 749
Cowley, Abraham	II, 197, 201
Cowper, William	IV, 373, 379
Defoe, Daniel	III, 47
Denham, Sir John	II, 222
Dickens, Charles	VI, 572, 585
Donne, John	I, 716
Dryden, John	II. 477, 486, 503
Etheredge, Sir George	II, 415
Fielding, Henry	III, 343, 360
Fox, Charles James	IV, 500
Gay, John	III, 61
Goldsmith, Oliver	III, 622
Gower, John	I, 176
Gray, Thomas	III, 555
Greene, Robert	I, 345
Hales, John	II, 151
Herbert, Edward Lord	II, 99
Hooker, Richard	I, 408
Johnson, Samuel	III, 759
Jonson, Ben	I, 749, 765
Lamb, Charles	V, 240
Latimer, Hugh	I, 268
Layamon	I, 65
Literature	I, 9
Locke, John	II, 535
Lydgate, John	I, 185
Lyly, John	I, 427
Macaulay, Thomas Babington Lord	VI, 107, 110, 111
Macpherson, James	IV, 277
Mandeville, Sir John	I, 96
Marlowe, Christopher	I, 355
May, Thomas	II, 119
Mill John Stuart	VI, 713
Milton, John	II, 264, 283, 293
Montagu, Lady Mary Wortley	
	III, 468
Moore, Thomas	V, 717
Nashe, Thomas	I, 412
Otway, Thomas	II, 367
Pope, Alexander	
	III, 161, 169, 173, 176, 190
Prior, Matthew	II, 674, 678
Prynne, William	II, 226
Richardson, Samuel	
	III, 435, 436, 442, 450
Sackville, Charles	II, 554
Saint-John, Henry	III, 288
Scott, Sir Walter	V, 159
Sedley, Sir Charles	II, 509
Shakespeare, William	
	I, 451, 490, 497, 505, 567
Shelley, Percy Bysshe	IV, 709
Sheridan, Richard Brinsley	
	IV, 596, 607
Sidney, Sir Philip	I, 326
Skelton, John	I, 222
Smollett, Tobias George	
	III, 579, 588
South, Robert	II, 609
Southey, Robert	V, 416
Spenser, Edmund	
	I, 373, 377, 384, 390, 397
Sterne, Laurence	III, 507
Suckling, Sir John	II, 65
Surrey, Earl of	I, 258
Swift, Jonathan	
	III, 202, 210, 225, 227, 233
Taylor, Jeremy	II, 210
Temple, Sir William	II, 455, 459
Tennyson, Alfred Lord	
	VIII, 87, 93, 102
Thackeray, William Makepeace	
	VI, 307, 315
Thomson, James	III, 269
Till tson John Robert	II, 440
Ty dale, William	I, 247
Waller, Edmund	II, 382
Webster, John	I, 676
Wesley, John	IV, 115
Wilmot, John	II, 337
Wordsworth, William	V, 637
Wycherley, William	II, 600, 605
Young, Edward	III, 494
TAIT, ARCHIBALD CAMPBELL,	
Alford, Henry	VI, 635
TAIT, JOHN R.,	
Read, Thomas Buchanan	
	VI, 677, 677
TALBOT, CATHERINE,	
Butler, Joseph	III, 306
TALBOT, MISS,	
Richardson, Samuel	III, 431
TALFOURD, SIR THOMAS NOON,	
Brooke, Henry	III, 714

688 INDEX TO CRITICISMS

	Vol. and Page
Cibber, Colley	III, 374
Coleridge, Samuel Taylor	V, 209
Defoe, Daniel	III, 32
Dennis, John	III, 78
Dickens, Charles	VI, 563
Fielding, Henry	III, 353, 359
Godwin, William	V, 299, 301, 302, 302
Goldsmith, Oliver	III, 629
Hall, Robert	V, 110
Hazlitt, William	V, 99, 103
Lamb, Charles	V, 231, 239
Lamb, Mary Ann	V, 508
Mackenzie, Henry	V, 113, 114, 115
Maturin, Charles Robert	IV, 768
North, Roger	III, 80
Radcliffe, Ann Ward	IV, 719
Richardson, Samuel	III, 440
Rymer, Thomas	II, 583
Scott, Sir Walter	V, 142
Shelley, Mary Wollstonecraft	V, 702
Smollett, Tobias George	III, 577
Southey, Robert	V, 404
Sterne, Laurence	III, 512
Taylor, Jeremy	II, 209
Wordsworth, William	V, 630
TALLACK, WILLIAM,	
Fox, George	II, 421
TALLENTYRE, S. G.,	
Montagu, Lady Mary Wortley	III, 467
Stanhope, Philip Dormer	III, 606
TANISH, EDWARD CAMPBELL,	
Tennyson, Alfred Lord	VIII, 83, 91
TANNAHILL, ROBERT,	
Burns, Robert	IV, 250
TANNER, J. R.,	
Russell, John Earl	VII, 144
Seeley, Sir John Robert	VIII, 307, 310
TARBELL, IDA M.,	
Lincoln, Abraham	VI, 416
TARBOX, INCREASE N.,	
Edwards, Jonathan	III, 384
Raleigh, Sir Walter	I, 597
TARVER, J. C.,	
Cowper, William	IV, 375
TATE, JAMES,	
Bentley, Richard	III, 122
TATE, NAHUM,	
L'Estrange, Sir Roger	II, 538
Shakespeare, William	I, 519, 550
TATHAM, JOHN,	
Ford, John	II, 29
Shakespeare, William	I, 531
TAYLER, C. B.,	
Wyclif, John	I, 101
TAYLER, JOHN JAMES,	
Channing, William Ellery	V, 371
TAYLOR, ARNOLD,	
Taylor, Tom	VII, 215
TAYLOR, BAYARD,	
Arnold, Matthew	VII, 628
Boker, George Henry	VII, 765, 766
Browning, Elizabeth Barrett	VI, 232
Browning, Robert	VII, 687, 697, 701
Bryant, William Cullen	VII, 124
Carlyle, Thomas	VII, 243
Dana, Richard Henry	VII, 316

	Vol. and Page
Eliot, George	VII, 187, 192, 201
Greeley, Horace	VI, 669
Halleck, Fitz-Greene	VI, 495, 500
Hawthorne, Nathaniel	VI, 350
Knowledge	V, 8
Lanier, Sidney	VII, 325
Literature	I, 9
Longfellow, Henry Wadsworth	VII, 394
Lowell, James Russell	VIII, 31
Milnes, Richard Monckton	VII, 563
Mitford, Mary Russell	VI, 42
Prentice, George Denison	VI, 603
Procter, Bryan Waller	VI, 745
Seward, William Henry	VI, 672
Shakespeare, William	I, 567
Taylor, Tom	VII, 214
Tennyson, Alfred Lord	VIII, 66, 83, 86
Thackeray, William Makepeace	VI, 292
Whittier, John Greenleaf	VIII, 112, 121
Willis, Nathaniel Parker	VI, 486
TAYLOR, E. B.,	
Müller, Friedrich Max	VIII, 437
TAYLOR, EMILY,	
Adams, Sarah Flower	V, 529
Elliott, Ebenezer	V, 583
Opie, Amelia	V, 743
Procter, Adelaide Anne	VI, 395
TAYLOR, HANNIS,	
More, Sir Thomas	I, 237
TAYLOR, HELEN,	
Buckle, Henry Thomas	VI, 284
TAYLOR, SIR HENRY,	
Bacon, Francis	I, 669
Burns, Robert	IV, 255
Campbell, Thomas	V, 441
Carlyle, Thomas	VII, 231
Coleridge Samuel Taylor	V, 225
Crabbe, George	V, 175
De Vere, Aubrey Thomas	VIII, 463
Dunstan	I, 44
Gifford, William	V, 33
Godwin, William	V, 304
Herschel, Sir John Frederick William	VI, 624
Lewis, Sir George Cornewall	VI, 337
Lytton, Edward Robert Bulwer	VIII, 48
Manning, Henry Edward	VIII, 163
Martineau, Harriet	VII, 60
Mill, John Stuart	VI, 705
Milnes, Richard Monckton	VII, 561
Moore, Thomas	V, 718
Rogers, Samuel	VI, 37
Scott, Sir Walter	V, 156
Southey, Robert	V, 402, 416
Spedding, James	VII, 319
Tennyson, Alfred Lord	VIII, 67, 86, 101
Turner, Charles Tennyson	VII, 162
Whately, Sir Richard	VI, 325
Wilberforce, Samuel	VI, 732
Wordsworth, William	V, 615
TAYLOR, H. M.,	
Newton, Sir Isaac	II, 725
TAYLOR, I. A.,	
De Vere, Aubrey Thomas	VIII, 463

	Vol. and Page
Jowett, Benjamin	VIII, 209
TAYLOR, ISAAC.	
Chalmers, Thomas	V, 491, 495
Landor, Walter Savage	VI, 388
Oliphant, Laurence	VII, 657
TAYLOR, JOHN,	
Jonson, Ben	I, 745
Shakespeare, William	I, 468
TAYLOR, MARIE HANSEN,	
Taylor, Bayard	VII, 132
TAYLOR, MARIE HANSEN, AND SCUDDER, HORACE E.,	
Taylor, Bayard	VII, 130, 133
TAYLOR, ROBERT,	
Shakespeare, William	I, 531
TAYLOR, SAMUEL,	
Shakespeare, William	I, 473
TAYLOR, SEDLEY,	
De Morgan, Augustus	VI, 633
TAYLOR, TOM,	
Hunter, John	IV, 167
Jerrold, Douglas William	VI, 69
TAYLOR, W. C.,	
Disraeli, Isaac	V, 511, 513
Hume, David	III, 666
TAYLOR, WILLIAM,	
Churchill, Charles	III, 479
TAYLOR, WILLIAM M.,	
Beecher, Henry Ward	VII, 599
Blair, Hugh	IV, 404
Chalmers, Thomas	V, 494, 496
Guthrie, Thomas	VI, 738
Irving, Edward	V, 249
Knox, John	I, 297, 299
Leighton, Robert	II, 360
Macleod, Norman	VI, 661
Rutherford, Samuel	II, 167
TEAGUE, J. JESSOP,	
Ken, Thomas	II, 569
TEDDER, H. R.,	
Coverdale, Miles	I, 292
Dodsley, Robert	III, 483, 483
Eliot, John	II, 413
Geoffery of Monmouth	I, 57
Hone, William	V, 393
TEFFT, BENJAMIN F.,	
Wesley, John	IV, 116
TEIGNMOUTH, LORD,	
Jones, Sir William	IV, 197
TEMPLE, SIR WILLIAM,	
Bentley, Richard	III, 114
Books	III, 6
Gray, Thomas	III, 554
Shakespeare, William	I, 550
Sidney, Sir Philip	I, 330
Spenser, Edmund	I, 394
Swift, Jonathan	III, 197
Waller, Edmund	II, 379
TEN BRINK, BERNHARD	
Ælfric	I, 46
Aldhelm	I, 25
Barbour, John	I, 115
Barclay, Alexander	I, 265
Beowulf	I, 19
Berners, Lord	I, 229
Cædmon	I, 23
Capgrave, John	I, 192
Chaucer, Geoffrey	I, 131, 132, 133, 138, 147, 169
Cynewulf	I, 30
Douglas, Gawin	I, 215

INDEX TO CRITICISMS

	Vol. and Page
Dunbar, William	I, 227
Elyot, Sir Thomas	I, 254
Fortescue, Sir John	I, 195
Geoffery of Monmouth	I, 56
Gower, John	I, 177
Hall, Edward	I, 260
Hawes, Stephen	I, 218
Heywood, John	I, 306
Langland, William	I, 121
Layamon	I, 65
Lydgate, John	I, 186
Malory, Sir Thomas	I, 205
Mannyng, Robert	I, 88
Minot, Lawrence	I, 93
More, Sir Thomas	I, 238, 239
Occleve, Thomas	I, 188
Peacock, Reginald	I, 190
Robert of Gloucester	I, 82
Rolle, Richard	I, 92
Shakespeare, William	I, 470, 487, 514, 519, 523, 525, 573
Skelton, John	I, 223
Tyndale, William	I, 248
Wyatt, Sir Thomas	I, 252
Wyclif, John	I, 102

TENISON, THOMAS,
Bacon, Francis	I, 657

TENNEMANN, WILHELM GOTTLIEB,
Anselm	I, 49
Clarke, Samuel	II, 748
Coleridge, Samuel Taylor	V, 222
Hobbes, Thomas	II, 324
Hume, David	III, 661
Locke, John	II, 524
Price, Richard	IV, 136
Priestley, Joseph	IV, 453
Reid, Thomas	IV, 284
William of Occam	I, 90

TENNYSON, ALFRED LORD,
Alfred the Great	I, 38
Allingham, William	VII, 735
Books	III, 8
Browning, Robert	VII, 678
Byron, George Gordon Lord	IV, 741, 762
Campbell, George J. D.	VIII, 434
Caxton, William	I, 199
Chaucer, Geoffrey	I, 139
Crabbe, George	V, 175
FitzGerald, Edward	VII, 514, 519
Gray, Thomas	III, 569
Hallam, Arthur Henry	V, 198
Ingelow, Jean	VIII, 376
Johnson, Samuel	III, 739
Kane, Elisha Kent	VI, 82
Keats, John	IV, 679
Kingsley, Charles	VII, 24
Knowledge	V, 8
Longfellow, Henry Wadsworth	VII, 382
Lytton, Sir Edward George Bulwer	VI, 680
Macaulay, Thomas Babington Lord	VI, 94
Maurice, John Frederick Denison	VI, 644
Milton, John	II, 292, 294
Poe, Edgar Allan	V, 559
Poets and Poetry	IV, 8
Pope Alexander	III, 169, 192

44 G

	Vol. and Page
Rossetti, Gabriel Charles Dante	VII, 437
Scott, Sir Walter	V, 150
Skakespeare, William	I, 476, 482, 484, 507, 513, 519, 523, 541
Shelley, Percy Bysshe	IV, 711
Tennyson, Alfred Lord	VIII, 84, 90
Turner, Charles Tennyson	VII, 161
Wilson, John	V, 751
Wordsworth, William	V, 635, 636

TENNYSON, HALLAM,
Carlyle, Thomas	VII, 238
Chaucer, Geoffrey	I, 171
Coleridge, Hartley	V, 575
Eliot, George	VII, 171
Gladstone, William Ewart	VIII, 384
Turner, Charles Tennyson	VII, 161
Ward, William George	VII, 482

TERHUNE, MARY VIRGINIA,
Keats, John	IV, 668

TEXTE, JOSEPH,
Defoe, Daniel	III, 39
Gray, Thomas	III, 572
Lillo, George	III, 101
Macpherson, James	IV, 280
Pope, Alexander	III, 178, 194
Richardson, Samuel	III, 443, 453
Sterne, Laurence	III, 516
Thomson, James	III, 271
Young, Edward	III, 490

T. F. (THE REV. PRES. OF CORPUS CHRISTI COLLEGE, OXFORD),
Price, Richard	IV, 136

THACHER, THOMAS,
Adams, Samuel	IV, 440

THACKERAY, WILLIAM MAKEPEACE,
Addison, Joseph	II, 636, 642
Blanchard, Samuel Laman	V, 480, 481
Brontë, Charlotte	VI, 18, 23
Carlyle, Thomas	VII, 246
Congreve, William	II, 742
Dickens, Charles	VI, 569, 572
Fielding, Henry	III, 342, 347, 359
Gay, John	III, 54, 61
Gibbon, Edward	IV, 195
Goldsmith, Oliver	III, 619, 627
Hood, Thomas	V, 459, 462
Howell, James	II, 187
Irving, Washington	VI, 135
Johnson, Samuel	III, 750
Lytton, Sir Edward George Bulwer	VII, 695
Macaulay, Thomas Babington Lord	VI, 94, 110
Orme, Robert	IV, 414
Peacock, Thomas Love	IV, 473
Philips, Ambrose	III, 275
Pope, Alexander	III, 173, 179, 188
Prior, Matthew	II, 677
Reynolds, Sir Joshua	IV, 139
Richardson, Samuel	III, 434, 440
Scott, Sir Walter	V, 131
Smith, John	I, 699
Smollett, Tobias George	III, 575, 584
Southey, Robert	V, 400

	Vol. and Page
Steele, Sir Richard	II, 763
Sterne, Laurence	III, 511, 513
Swift, Jonathan	III, 201, 209, 218, 221, 231
Walpole, Horace	IV, 319
Wesley, John	IV, 123

THANET, OCTAVE,
Longfellow, Henry Wadsworth	VII, 398
Walpole, Horace	IV, 320

THAYER, JOSEPH HENRY,
Woolsey, Theodore Dwight	VII, 736, 737

THAYER, STEPHEN HENRY,
Smith, Alexander	VI, 516

THAYER, WILLIAM ROSCOE,
Bryant, William Cullen	VII, 126
Carlyle, Thomas	VII, 273
Emerson Ralph, Waldo	VII, 372
Lanier, Sidney	VII, 331

THAYER, W. S.,
Lowell, James Russell	VIII, 36
Whittier, John Greenleaf	VIII, 120

THAXTER, CELIA,
Brontë, Charlotte	VI, 29
Kane, Elisha Kent	VI, 82

THEOBALD, LEWIS,
Pope, Alexander	III, 165

THICKNESSE, PHILIP,
Robertson, William	IV, 159

THIRLWALL, CONNOP,
Cowper, William	IV, 378
Eliot, George	VII, 190, 198
Froude, James Anthony	VIII, 257
Grote, George	VI, 609
Irving, Edward	V, 245
Lyell, Sir Charles	VII, 37
Lytton, Sir Edward George Bulwer	VI, 691, 698
Mill, John Stuart	VI, 712
Newman, John Henry	VII, 751
Pusey, Edward Bouverie	VII, 468, 471
Robertson, Frederick William	V, 739

THOM, JOHN HAMILTON,
White, Joseph Blanco	V, 359

THOMAS, EARNEST C.,
De Bury, Richard	I, 89

THOMAS, EDITH M.,
Browning, Elizabeth Barrett	VI, 240
Jackson, Helen Hunt	VII, 572
Lowell, James Russell	VII, 32
Tennyson, Alfred Lord	VIII, 96

THOMAS, F. W.,
Pinkney, Edward Coate	V, 85

THOMAS, JOSEPH,
Hildreth, Richard	VI, 453

THOMAS, OWEN P.,
Dickens, Charles	VI, 555

THOMAS, STEVENS,
Stanley, Sir Henry Morton	VIII, 507

THOMAS, W. MOY,
Collins, William	III, 416, 417
Montagu, Lady Mary Wortley	III, 468
Pope, Alexander	III, 153
Savage, Richard	III, 133

THOMPSON, DANIEL GREENLEAF,
Spencer, Herbert.......VIII, 478

THOMPSON, EDWARD,
Oldham, John.............II, 350

THOMPSON, E. MUNDIE,
Camden, William............I, 622
Capgrave, John.............I, 192

THOMPSON, FRANCIS,
Browning, Robert.......VII, 716
Burns, Robert............IV, 268
Carlyle, Thomas.........VII, 244
Coleridge, Samuel Taylor....V, 217
Crashaw, Richard..........II, 114
Henley, William Ernest..VIII, 493
Landor, Walter Savage.....VI, 393
Pope, Alexander..........III, 195
Tennyson, Alfred Lord...VIII, 74

THOMPSON, HENRY,
More, Hannah..............V, 191

THOMPSON, JAMES,
Macaulay, Thomas Babington Lord..................VI, 111

THOMPSON, JOSEPH,
Edwards, Jonathan.......III, 390

THOMPSON, J. P.,
Dickens, Charles..........VI, 568

THOMPSON, MAURICE,
Browning, Robert........VII, 711
Byron, George Gordon Lord IV, 763
Eliot, George............VII, 206
Hayne, Paul Hamilton.......
..................VII, 591, 593
Lincoln, Abraham.........VI, 416
Lowell, James Russell...VIII, 38
Poets and Poetry.........IV, 10
Scott, Sir Walter..........V, 145
Shelley, Percy Bysshe....IV, 697
Whitman, Walt.........VIII, 148
Wordsworth William.......V, 645

THOMPSON, RICHARD W.,
Adams, John...............V, 53
Jefferson, Thomas.........V, 44
Madison, James...........V, 312
Monroe, James............V, 123

THOMPSON, SIDNEY R.,
Southey, Robert..........V, 409

THOMPSON, SLASON,
Field, Eugene......VIII, 316, 317

THOMPSON, T. P.,
Morgan, Sydney Owenson Lady..................VI, 194

THOMS, W. I.,
Oldys, William..........III, 457

THOMSON, DR. ANTHONY TODD,
Landon, Letitia Elizabeth....V, 325

THOMSON, CLARA LINKLATER,
Carter, Elizabeth........IV, 492
Fielding, Henry.........III, 356
Fielding, Sarah.........III, 519
Hill, Aaron.............III, 278
Mackenzie, Henry.........V, 114
Richardson, Samuel.........
...........III, 437, 443, 454

THOMSON, JAMES,
Armstrong, John........III, 697
Chaucer, Geoffrey.........I, 156
Congreve, William........II, 740
Knowledge..................V, 6
Milton, John.............II, 285
Newton, Sir Isaac........II, 712

Rowe, Nicholas...........II, 621
Shakespeare, William......I, 552
Sidney, Sir Philip........I, 331
Spenser, Edmund...........I, 380
Swift, Jonathan.........III, 223
Thomson, James..........III, 255

THOMSON, JAMES (B. V.),
Blake, William............V, 57
Browning, Elizabeth Barrett..
....................VI 232, 245
Browning, Robert........VII, 699
Emerson, Ralph Waldo...VII, 364
Shelley, Percy Bysshe....IV, 708
Tennyson, Alfred Lord...VIII, 102

THOMSON, J. ARTHUR,
Huxley, Thomas Henry..VIII, 329

THOMSON, KATHERINE (GRACE WHARTON),
Addison, Joseph..........II, 637
Beattie, James...........IV, 429
Burney, Frances...........V, 348
Carter, Elizabeth....IV, 492, 493
Cibber, Colley..........III, 371
Dillon, Wentworth........II, 361
Evelyn, John............II, 548
Galt, John................V, 334
Gay, John...............III, 58
Hervey, John Lord.......III, 129
Howell, James...........II, 186
Landon, Letitia Elizabeth...V, 324
Maginn, William..........V, 388
Montagu, Elizabeth......IV, 400
Montagu, Lady Mary Wortley
......................III, 466
Pepys, Samuel...........II, 514
Raleigh, Sir Walter.......I, 606
Richardson, Samuel......III, 441
Saint-John, Henry.......III, 288
Sedley, Sir Charles......II, 509
Seward, Anna............IV, 542
Smith, Sydney............V, 469
Smollett, Tobias George..III, 576
Stanhope, Philip Dormer..III, 605
Steele, Sir Richard......II, 760
Sterne, Laurence........III, 507
Swift, Jonathan.........III, 209
Vanbrugh, Sir John......II, 705
Walpole, Horace.........IV, 319
Wyatt, Sir Thomas.........I, 250

THOMSON, KATHERINE AND J. C. (GRACE AND PHILIP WHARTON),
Congreve, William.......II, 742
Hervey, John Lord.......III, 128
Hook, Theodore Edward...V, 357
Sackville, Charles......II, 552
Sheridan, Richard Brinsley.IV, 595
Wilmot, John............II, 337

THOMSON, T.,
Darwin, Erasmus.........IV, 412

THOMSON, THOMAS,
Boyle, Robert..........II, 418
Rumford, Count.........IV, 592

THOREAU, HENRY DAVID,
Alcott, Amos Bronson....VII, 662
Carlyle, Thomas........VII, 261
Hawthorne, Nathaniel....VI, 342
Quarles, Francis.........II, 78
Shakespeare, William......I, 561

THORESBY, RALPH,
Ashmole, Elias..........II, 436

THORNBURY, GEORGE WALTER
Blake, William............V, 59
Jonson, Ben...............I, 748
Otway, Thomas............II, 362
Reynolds, Sir Joshua.....IV, 139
Shakespeare, William......I, 562

THORNE, JAMES,
Cowley, Abraham.........II. 195
Gray, Thomas...........III, 556
Walpole, Horace.........IV 315

THORNE, WILLIAM, HENRY,
Eliot, George..........VII, 179

THORNTON, PERCY M.,
Canning, George..........V, 66

THOROWGOOD, T.,
Eliot, John.............II, 412

THORPE, BENJAMIN,
Ælfric....................I, 46
Beowulf..................I, 18
Cædmon...................I, 21

THORPE, FRANCIS NEWTON,
Adams, John..............V, 51
Franklin, Benjamin......VI, 105
Jefferson, Thomas........V, 46
Prescott, William Hickling..VI, 191
Smith, Adam.............IV, 68

THORPE, THOMAS E.,
Davy, Sir Humphry........V, 93
Faraday, Michael........VI, 515
Priestley, Joseph.......VII, 450

THRALE, HESTER LYNCH (MRS. PIOZZI),
Burney, Frances.....V, 343, 348
Montagu, Elizabeth......IV, 399

THRASHER, MAX BENNETT,
Dodge, Mary Abigail....VIII, 360

THURBER, C. H.,
Mann, Horace...........VI, 201

THURSFIELD, J. R.,
Bright, John...........VII, 723

THURSTON, CHARLES RAWSON,
Channing, William Ellery....V. 370

THWING, CHARLES F.,
Brooks, Phillips.......VIII, 231
Emerson, Ralph Waldo...VII, 377
Mozley, James Bowling..VII, 150

THYENNE, FRANCIS,
Chaucer, Geoffrey......I. 125. 154

TICKELL, THOMAS,
Addison, Joseph...II. 633 644 648
Philips, Ambrose......III. 274 274
Philips, John...........II 563
Tickell, Thomas........III. 104

TICKNOR, GEORGE,
Baillie, Joanna..........V, 690
Brougham, Henry Lord...VI, 523
Buckle, Henry Thomas....VI, 280
Byron, George Gordon Lord.IV 732
Campbell, Thomas........V, 434
Carlyle, Thomas.......VII, 230
Chambers, Robert.......VI, 620
Channing, William Ellery....
.................V, 366. 370
Chaucer, Geoffrey........I. 161
Davy, Sir Humphry........V. 90
Edgeworth, Maria.........V. 562
Frere, John Hookham...V 486 487
Gladstone, William Ewart....
.....................VIII. 386
Godwin, William.........V. 293
Grant, Anne.............V 329

INDEX TO CRITICISMS 691

	Vol. and Page
Hallam, Henry	VI, 173
Hamilton, Alexander	IV, 462
Hazlitt, William	V, 97
Herschel, Sir John Frederick William	VI, 623
Jefferson, Thomas	V, 41
Kent, James	V, 500
L'Estrange, Sir Roger	II, 539
Lewis, Sir George Cornewall	VI, 336
Lockhart, John Gibson	V, 754, 756
Longfellow, Henry Wadsworth	VII, 398
Maccarthy, Denis Florence	VII, 489
Macaulay, Thomas Babington Lord	VI, 93
Mackintosh, Sir James	V, 178
Madison, James	V, 311
Malthus, Thomas Robert	V, 250
Mitford, Mary Russell	VI, 40
Prescott, William Hickling	VI, 187, 190
Roscoe, William	V, 116
Scott, Sir Walter	V, 126
Sidney, Sir Philip	I, 325
Smith, Sydney	V, 467
Somerville, Mary	VI, 657
Southey, Robert	V, 396
Stanhope, Philip Henry Earl	VII, 47
Talfourd, Sir Thomas Noon	V, 759
Thackeray, William Makepeace	VI, 311
Whately, Richard	VI, 343
Wilberforce, William	V, 200
Wordsworth, William	V, 606
TIECK, JOHANN LUDWIG,	
Shakespeare, William	I, 473
Ticknor, George	VI, 616
TIFFANY, FRANCIS,	
Morris, William	VIII, 332
TIFFANY, O.,	
Beckford William	V, 447
TIGHE, RICHARD,	
Law, William	III, 425
TILLEY, ARTHUR,	
William of Occam	I, 91
TILLINGHAST, C. B.,	
Scott, Sir Walter	V, 145
TILLOTSON, JOHN,	
Wilkins, John	II, 227
TILTON, THEODORE,	
Beecher, Lyman	V, 340
Browning, Elizabeth Barrett	VI, 232, 242
Irving, Washington	VI, 147
TIMBS, JOHN,	
Beckford William	V, 448
Bentham, Jeremy	V, 164
Lytton, Sir Edward George Bulwer	VII, 681
Mackintosh, Sir James	V, 180
Maginn, William	V, 388
Porson, Richard	IV, 523
Spenser, Edmund	I, 372
Tooke, John Horne	IV, 570
Whately, Richard	VII, 324
TIMPERLEY, C. H.,	
Saint-John, Henry	III, 287
TIREBUCK, WILLIAM,	
Bowles, William Lisle	V, 662

	Vol. and Page
Coleridge, Hartley	V, 578
Lamb, Charles	V, 237
Rossetti, Gabriel Charles Dante	VII, 441
TITHERINGTON, R. H.,	
Beecher, Henry Ward	VII, 606
TITLE PAGE OF FIRST EDITION,	
Barclay, Robert	II, 411
Carew, Thomas	II, 21
Defoe, Daniel	III, 32
Eliot, John	II, 412
Fletcher, Phineas	II, 115
Goldsmith, Oliver	III, 624
Lamb, Charles	V, 238
Marlowe, Christopher	I, 348, 349
Marston, John	I, 735
Milton, John	II, 257
Peele, George	I, 364 364, 365
Pope, Alexander	III, 160, 163
Prynne, William	II, 224
Selden, John	II, 140
Shakespeare, William	I, 454, 456, 457, 460, 461, 464, 468, 472, 476, 477, 484, 489, 491, 491, 494, 495, 500, 511, 519, 523, 531, 532
Shelley, Percy Bysshe	IV, 701, 703, 704
Vaughan, Henry	II, 442
Villiers, George	II, 377
Waller, Edmund	II, 379
Ward, Nathaniel	II, 129
Webster, John	I, 670, 671, 673
White, Gilbert	IV, 149, 152
TOCQUEVILLE, ALEXIS DE,	
Blackstone, William	III, 704
Smith, John	I, 699
TODD, CHARLES BURR,	
Barlow, Joel	IV, 574, 577
TODD, HENRY JOHN,	
Chaucer, Geoffrey	I, 150
Milton, John	II, 245
Spenser, Edmund	I, 375
TODHUNTER, ISAAC,	
Whewell, William	VI, 468
TODHUNTER, JOHN A.,	
Shelley, Percy Bysshe	IV, 711
TODHUNTER, MAURICE,	
FitzGerald, Edward	VII, 517, 520
Seeley, Sir John Robert	VIII, 311
TOFTE, ROBERT,	
Shakespeare, William	I, 464
Tuberville, George	I, 439
TOLAND, JOHN,	
Toland, John	II, 681
TOLLEMACHE, LIONEL A.,	
Calverley, Charles Stuart	VII, 542
Grote, George	VI, 610
Jowett, Benjamin	VIII, 209
Owen, Sir Richard	VIII, 171, 173
TOLMAN, ALBERT H.,	
Lanier, Sidney	VII, 328
TOLSTOI, LEO,	
George, Henry	VIII, 382
TOMB, LINES ON,	
Lamb, Charles	V, 236
Lyttelton, George Lord	III, 610
TOMES, ROBERT,	
Chalmers, Thomas	V, 493
Jeffrey, Francis Lord	V, 652

	Vol. and Page
TOMKINS, W. EARP,	
Dibden, Charles	IV, 586
TOMLINE, GEORGE,	
Pitt, William	IV, 510
TONSON, JACOB,	
Dryden, John	II, 486, 488
Pope, Alexander	III, 156
Tate, Nahum	II, 589
TOOKE, JOHN HORNE,	
Dryden, John	II 498
Locke, John	II, 524
Wilkes, John	IV, 333
TOOKE, WILLIAM,	
Churchill, Charles	III, 476
TOOKER, L. FRANK,	
Timrod, Henry	VI, 509, 510
TORRENS, W. M.,	
Lamb, Lady Caroline	V, 83
TORREY, BRADFORD,	
FitzGerald, Edward	VII, 520
Hawthorne, Nathaniel	VI, 371
Thoreau, Henry David	VI, 271, 278
TORREY, JOHN,	
Gray, Asa	VII, 669
TOUNSON, REV. ROBERT,	
Raleigh, Sir Walter	I, 592
TOURGÉE, ALBION WINEGAR,	
Jackson, Helen Hunt	VII, 573
TOUT, T. F.,	
Brougham, Henry Lord	VI, 533
Burnet, Gilbert	II, 596
Lewis, Sir George Cornewall	VI, 338
Tillotson, John Robert	II, 438
TOVEY, DUNCAN C.,	
Arnold, Matthew	VII, 647
Burton, Robert	II, 40
Chaucer, Geoffrey	I, 171
Fuller, Thomas	II, 173
Gay, John	III, 58
Gray, Thomas	III, 571
Lyly, John	I, 427
Macpherson, James	IV, 281, 281
Patmore, Coventry	VIII, 342
Sandys, George	II, 84
Sidney, Sir Philip	I, 332
Stanhope, Philip Dormer	III, 608
Thomson, James	III, 261
Waller, Edmund	III, 384
TOWLE, GEORGE MAKEPEACE,	
Bright, John	VII, 722
Campbell, George J. D.	VIII, 434
Disraeli, Benjamin	VII, 284, 286
Goldsmith Oliver	III, 620, 634
Grote, George	VI, 612
Lowell, James Russell	VIII, 21
Lyell, Sir Charles	VII, 37
Reade, Charles	VII, 533
TOWNE, E. C.,	
Alcott, Amos Bronson	VII, 662
TOWNLEY, MR.,	
Garth, Sir Samuel	II, 664
TOWNSEND, GEORGE H.,	
Brewster, Sir David	VI, 546
Feltham, Owen	II, 309
Howell, James	II, 186
Mitford, William	V, 69
Raleigh, Sir Walter	I, 590
Ridley, Nicholas	I, 266
Secker, Thomas	III, 521
Turner, Sharon	V, 498

692   INDEX TO CRITICISMS

TOWNSEND, JOHN K.,
  Wilson, Alexander........IV, 584
TOWNSEND, J. W.,
  Alcuin ....I, 33
  Duns, Scotus..............I, 86
  Erigena ....I, 35
  Hales, Alexander..........I, 72
TOWNSEND, M. E.,
  Dickens, Charles..........VI, 574
TOWNSEND, MEREDITH,
  Oliphant, Margaret O. W.VIII, 369
TOWNSEND, WILLIAM C.,
  Erskine, Thomas..........IV, 730
TOWNSHEND, CHAUNCEY HARE,
  Coleridge, Hartley.........V, 574
TOYNBEE, ARNOLD,
  Carlyle, Thomas..........VII, 251
TOZER, H. F.,
  Byron, George Gordon Lord.IV, 726
TRAFTON, ADELINE,
  Brontë, Charlotte..........VI, 19
TRAILL, HENRY DUFF,
  Arnold, Matthew......VII, 632, 641
  Blake, William............V, 62
  Brontë, Charlotte.........VI, 26
  Browning, Elizabeth Barrett..
    ....VI, 247
  Browning, Robert.........VII, 711
  Burke, Edmund..........IV, 308
  Burney, Frances.......V, 345, 347
  Carlyle, Thomas..........VII, 274
  Chaucer, Geoffrey..........I, 148
  Cobbett, William..........V, 276
  Coleridge, Samuel Taylor...V, 216
  Congreve, William.........II, 745
  Cowper, William..........IV, 380
  DeQuincey, Thomas.......VI, 131
  Dickens, Charles..........VI, 593
  Gaskill, Elizabeth Cleghorn.VI, 429
  Gibbon, Edward..........IV, 190
  Gifford, William............V, 36
  Grote, George.............VI, 611
  Hayley, William..........IV, 654
  James, George Payne Rainsford
    ....VI, 220
  Jeffrey, Francis Lord........V, 657
  Jefferies, Richard.........VII, 619
  Kingsley, Henry..........VII, 81
  Knowles, Henry Sheridan..VI, 289
  Landor, Walter Savage.....VI, 393
  Layamon ....I, 66
  Longfellow, Henry Wadsworth
    ....VII, 411
  Lowell, James Russell.VIII, 18, 28
  Mackintosh, Sir James.......V, 183
  Moore, Thomas............V, 711
  Pope, Alexander..........III, 169
  Richardson, Samuel ..III, 437, 445
  Ruskin, John............VIII, 421
  Scott, Sir Walter...........V, 138
  Shelley, Percy Bysshe......IV, 699
  Smith, Alexander.........VI, 519
  Southey, Robert...........V, 417
  Sterne, Laurence .III, 503, 510, 516
  Stevenson, Robert Louis..VIII, 250
  Symonds, John Addington....
    ....VIII, 205
  Tennyson, Alfred Lord...VIII, 92
  Thackeray, William Makepeace
    ....VI. 320

Trollope, Anthony........VII, 464
Tupper, Martin Farquhar..VII, 733
Wilson, John..............V, 749
Wordsworth, William......V, 646
TRAUBEL, HORACE L.,
  Whitman, Walt.........VIII, 136
TREE, HERBERT BEERBOHM,
  Drama, The.............VII, 9
TRELAWNY, EDWARD JOHN,
  Byron, George Gordon Lord...
    ....VI, 739, 745
  Hunt, James Henry Leigh..VI, 156
  Moore, Thomas............V, 713
  Shelley, Mary Woolstonecraft..
    ....V, 700
  Shelley, Percy Bysshe......IV, 693
  Stowe, Harriet Beecher...VIII, 357
TRENCH, MARY,
  Pusey, Edward Bouverie..VII, 470
TRENCH, RICHARD CHENEVIX,
  Baxter, Richard.......... II, 426
  Chatterton, Thomas......III, 537
  Donne, John..............I, 716
  Marvell, Andrew...........II, 315
  Milton, John.............II, 272
  Shakespeare, William .....I, 565
  Tennyson, Alfred Lord...VIII, 102
  Tooke, John Horne........IV, 572
  Wyclif, John...............I, 107
TRENCH, F. H.,
  Wil on, Sir Thomas.........I, 313
  Wood, Anthony...........II, 448
TRENT, WILLIAM PETERFIELD,
  Alcott, Amos Bronson.....VII, 665
  Bancroft, George........VIII, 61
  Browne, Charles Farrar...VI, 505
  Calhoun, John Caldwell ....V, 677
  Emerson, Ralph Waldo....VII, 360
  Franklin, Benjamin........IV, 92
  Hayne, Paul Hamilton....VII, 591
  Holmes, Oliver Wendell..VIII, 300
  Jefferson, Thomas..........V, 49
  Lowell, James Russell.VIII, 34, 42
  Melville, Herman.......VIII, 64
  Milton, John.......II, 250, 256, 298
  Parkman, Francis.......VIII, 225
  Parsons, Thomas William VIII, 194
  Saxe John Godfrey.......VII, 617
  Shelley, Percy Bysshe......IV, 717
  Simms, William Gilmore....
    ....VI, 597, 600
  Stephen, Sir Leslie......VIII, 512
  Stowe, Harriet Beecher......
    ....VIII, 355, 357
  Tennyson, Alfred Lord...VIII, 109
  Timrod, Henry...........VII, 510
  Washington, George.......IV, 365
  Whipple, Edwin Percy....VI, 597
  Whitman, Walt.....VIII, 137, 152
  Whittier, John Greenleaf.VIII, 119
TREVELYAN, GEORGE MACAULAY,
  Carlyle, Thomas..........VII, 252
  Wyclif, John..............I, 112
TREVELYAN, GEORGE OTTO,
  Churchill, Charles........III, 481
  Fox, James Charles.......IV, 501
  Macaulay, Thomas Babington
    Lord..............VI, 94, 99, 107
  Richardson, Samuel......III, 442
  Tooke, John Horne .....IV, 571

Wilkes, John..............IV, 337
Wordsworth, William......V, 625
TRICOUPI, M. SPIRIDION,
  Byron, George Gordon Lord IV, 734
TRIGGS, OSCAR LOVELL,
  Carlyle, Thomas.........VII, 276
TROLLOPE, ANTHONY,
  Congreve, William........II, 743
  Dickens, Charles..VI, 553, 561, 587
  Eliot, George............VII, 202
  Fielding, Henry..........III, 353
  Forster, John............VII, 68
  Hawthorne, Nathaniel.VI, 354, 357
  Horne, Richard Hengist...VII, 546
  Lever Charles James......VI, 652
  Lewes, George Henry........
    ....VII, 137, 140, 142
  Longfellow, Henry Wadsworth
    ....VII, 392, 406
  Lever, Charles James......VI, 655
  Lytton, Sir Edward George Bulwer
    ....VI, 685
  Scott, Sir W lter...........V, 153
  Steele, Sir Richard........II, 754
  Swift, Jonathan..........III, 203
  Taylor, Sir Henry........VII, 581
  Thackeray, William Makepeace
    VI, 296, 300, 303, 304, 306,
                  311, 316
  Trollope, Frances Milton.....
    ....VI, 329, 330
TROLLOPE, FRANCES MILTON,
  Hall, Basil................V 457
TROLLOPE, THOMAS ADOLPHUS,
  Browning, Elizabeth Barrett..
    ....VI, 234
  Browning, Robert........VII, 679
  Dickens, Charles.........VI, 558
  Eliot, George............VII, 161
  Radcliffe, Ann Ward......IV, 720
  Richardson, Samuel......III, 436
  Sidney, Sir Philip..........I, 326
  Smith, Charlotte.........IV, 498
  Smollett, Tobias George...III, 579
  Sterne, Laurence.........III, 508
  Thackeray, William Makepeace
    ....VI, 317
  Trollope, Anthony........VII, 462
TROTTER, JOHN BERNARD,
  Fox, Charles James .. IV, 500, 506
TROTTER, SPENCER,
  Wilson, Alexander........IV, 585
TROWBRIDGE, JOHN TOWNSEND,
  Holmes, Oliver Wendell......
    ....VIII, 289, 300
  Moore, Thomas...........V 718
  Longfellow, Henry Wadsworth
    ....VII, 384, 396
  Poe, Edgar Allan..........V 560
TRUMAN, BEN C.,
  Benton, Thomas Hart..... VI 86
  Fox, Charles James......IV 502
  Hamilton, Alexander......IV, 460
  Jeffrey, Francis Lord......V 652
TRUMBULL, HENRY CLAY,
  Bushnell, Horace........VII. 70
TRUMBULL, JOHN,
  Trumbull, John...........V 120
  Webster, Noah..........V, **427**

INDEX TO CRITICISMS

TRUMBULL M. M.,
  Cobden, Richard..........VI, 441
TRUMBULL. SIR WILLIAM,
  Pope, Alexander..........III, 163
TUBERVILLE GEORGE,
  Brooke, Arthur.............I, 284
  Jefferson. Thomas..........V, 49
  Spenser, Edmund..........I, 368
TUCKERMAN, CHARLES KEATING,
  Airy, Sir George Biddell..VIII, 183
  Arnold, Matthew.........VII, 630
  Bancroft, George........VIII, 57
  Beecher, Lyman..........VI, 340
  Bowring, Sir John..........VI, 665
  Everett, Edward.........VI, 425
  Milnes, Richard Monckton VII, 562
  Pierpont, John.............VI, 480
  Spurgeon, Charles Haddon...
    ....VIII, 179
  Stanley, Sir Henry Morton....
    ....VIII. 506
  Trollope, Anthony........VII 458
TUCKERMAN, HENRY THEODORE,
  Addison, Joseph...........II, 636
TUCKERMAN, HENRY T.,
  Akenside, Mark...........III, 544
  Allston, Washington....V, 419, 421
  Audubon, John James......V, 696
  Berkeley, George.....III, 321, 327
  Brown, Charles Brockden...IV, 556
  Browne, Sir Thomas........II, 343
  Burke, Edmund..........IV, 303
  Campbell, Thomas..........V, 444
  Channing, William Ellery...V, 732
  Clay, Henry................V,733
  Defoe, Daniel..............III, 25
  Dickens, Charles...........VI, 569
  Digby, Sir Kenelm..........II, 182
  Everett, Edward..........VI, 422
  Franklin, Benjamin........IV, 101
  Freneau, Philip............V, 187
  Gibbon, Edward...........IV, 185
  Goldsmith, Oliver........III. 631
  Halleck, Fitz-Greene......VI, 499
  Hamilton, Alexander......IV, 459
  Hawthorne, Nathaniel......
    ....VI, 353, 357, 364
  Hazlitt, William.............V, 104
  Hillhouse, James Abraham..V, 364
  Holmes, Oliver Wendell..VIII, 290
  Hunt, James Henry Leigh..VI, 165
  Irving, Washington....VI, 133, 139
  Jeffrey, Francis Lord........V, 655
  Kennedy, John Pendleton..VI, 606
  Lamb, Charles..............V, 239
  Longfellow, Henry Wadsworth
    ....VII, 403
  Lowell, James Russell...VIII, 31
  Macaulay, Thomas Babington
    Lord....................VI, 109
  Morris, George Pope.......VI, 401
  Neal, John................VII, 77
  Percival, James Gates......VI, 60
  Pierpont, John.............VI, 481
  Poe, Edgar Allan...........V, 553
  Pope, Alexander...........III, 163
  Prescott, William Hickling..VI, 189
  Roscoe, William............V, 117
  Savage, Richard.....III, 135, 136

  Shenstone, William......III, 474
  Smith, Sidney............V. 469
  Sprague, Charles........VII 53
  Southey, Robert......V 411, 416
  Stanhope, Philip Dormer...III 605
  Sterling, John.............V. 454
  Sterne, Laurence.....III. 503. 511
  Ticknor, George..........VI. 616
  Webster, Daniel...........V. 727
  Whittier, John Greenleaf.VIII. 120
  Williams, Roger..........II, 357
TUCKERMAN, BAYARD,
  Beckford, William..........V, 449
  Cavendish, Margaret.......II, 232
  Chaucer, Geoffrey..........I, 146
  Cumberland, Richard......IV, 561
  Defoe, Daniel..............III, 48
  Fielding, Henry...........III, 362
  Goldsmith, Oliver.........III, 628
  Johnstone, Charles........IV, 413
  Lodge, Thomas..............I, 625
  Lytton, Sir Edward George
    Bulwer...............VI, 689, 698
  Mackenzie, Henry..........V, 113
  Haliburton, William Chandler
    ....VI, 455
  Landor, Walter Savage VI, 375, 384
  Lewes, George Henry.....VII, 139
  Marsh, George Perkins....
    ....VII, 493, 495
  Newman, John Henry....VII, 740
  Smith, Sydney............V, 470
  Trollope, Anthony.......VII, 457
  Trollope, Frances Milton...VI, 329
  Whately, Richard.........VI, 324
  Wordsworth, William......V, 616
TUCKWELL, W.,
  Buckland, Francis Trevelyan.
    ....VII, 211
  Kinglake, Alexander William.
    ....VIII, 50, 51, 54
  Pattison, Mark..........VII, 539
  Newman, John Henry....VII, 756
TUDOR, WILLIAM,
  Adams, Samuel...........IV, 441
  Hunt, James Henry Leigh..VI, 163
  Mather, Cotton...........II, 730
  Otis, James.............III, 716
  Silliman, Benjamin........VI, 407
  Ward, Nathaniel..........II, 130
TULLOCH, JOHN,
  Arnold, Matthew.........VII, 629
  Arnold, Thomas............V, 382
  Aubrey, John.............II, 453
  Baxter, Richard......II, 424, 427
  Bentham, Jeremy.........V, 168
  Brooks, Phillips........VIII, 226
  Browne, Sir Thomas........II, 344
  Bunyan, John............II, 403
  Carlyle, Thomas..........VI, 269
  Chalmers, Thomas..........V, 496
  Chillingworth, William....II, 87
  Coleridge, Samuel Taylor...V, 225
  Combe, George............VI, 90
  Cudworth, Ralph....II, 384, 386
  Dickens, Charles..........III, 553
  Digby, Sir Kenelm.........II, 182
  Eliot, George............VII, 204
  Emerson, Ralph Waldo....VI, 345
  Grote, George............VI, 613
  Hales, John...........II, 150, 151

  Hall, Robert...............V 112
  Hare. Julius Charles.......VI, 50
  Harte, Francis Bret.....VIII, 467
  Hobbes. Thomas..........II. 326
  Holmes, Oliver Wendell..VIII. 286
  Hooker, Richard............I, 408
  Howe, John...............II, 545
  Keble. John..............VI, 462
  Kingsley. Charles........VII, 31
  Lewes. George Henry........
    ....VII, 140, 142
  Maurice, John Frederick Denison
    ....VI, 645
  Mill, James................V, 309
  Mill, John Stuart.........VI, 710
  Milman. Henry Hart........
    ....VI, 535, 541, 542
  Milton, John..............II, 277
  More, Henry.........II, 373, 374
  Newman, John Henry VII, 741, 752
  Pusey, Edward Bouverie..VII, 472
  Robertson, Frederick William
    ....V, 740
  Rutherford, Samuel........II, 167
  Scott, Sir Walter..........V. 136
  Stanley, Arthur Penrhyn..VII, 304
  Sterling, John.............V 454
  Stillingfleet, Edward.......II, 454
  Suckling, Sir John..........II, 66
  Taylor, Jeremy........II, 204, 210
  Tyndall, John...........VIII, 197
  Waller, Edmund............II 379
  Whatley, Richard.........VI, 327
  White. Joseph Blanco......V, 362
  Wordsworth, William......V, 641
TULLOCH, W. W.,
  Ramsay, Allan............III, 408
TUPPER, CHARLES LEWIS,
  Maine, Sir Henry James Sumner
    ....VII, 653
TUPPER, MARTIN FARQUHAR,
  Tennyson, Alfred Lord..VIII, 70
  Tupper, Martin Farquhar.VII, 731
TURK, MILTON HAIGHT,
  Alfred the Great............I, 41
TURNBULL, FRANCES L..
  Lanier, Sidney...........VII, 326
TURNBULL, ROBERT,
  Chalmers, Thomas.........V, 490
TURNBULL, WILLIAM B.,
  Crashaw, Richard.........II, 112
TURNER, SHARON,
  Bede.......................I. 29
  Chaucer, Geoffrey..........I. 158
  Colet, John................I. 211
  Fisher, John...............I. 231
  Gower, John...............I. 175
  Layamon...................I. 64
  Lydgate, John.............I. 184
  More, Sir Thomas..........I. 235
  Occleve, Thomas..........I. 187
  Wyclif, John..............I. 105
TURTON, THOMAS,
  Person, Richard..........IV, 622
TUSSER, THOMAS,
  Udall, Nicholas............I, 278
TUTIN, J. R.,
  Crashaw, Richard.........II, 113
TWICHELL, JOSEPH HOPKINS,
  Lamb, Charles............V, 234
  Stowe, Harriet Beecher..VIII, 349

INDEX TO CRITICISMS

Warner, Charles Dudley......
..........VIII, 442, 443
Winthrop, John...........II, 108
TYERMAN, L.,
  Wesley, John.........IV, 114, 119
TYERS, THOMAS,
  Johnson, Samuel............III, 723
TYLER, JAMES ENDELL,
  Hume, David.............III, 657
  Shakespeare, William.......I, 490
TYLER, JOHN,
  Henry, Patrick............IV, 349
TYLER, MOSES COIT,
  Adams, Samuel...........IV, 444
  Barlow, Joel..............IV, 576
  Berkeley, George.....III, 324, 334
  Bradford, William.........II, 158
  Bradstreet, Anne..........II, 228
  Dwight, Timothy......IV, 626, 628
  Edwards, Jonathan...III, 384, 392
  Franklin, Benjamin....IV, 92, 105
  Freneau, Philip........V, 186, 188
  Hamilton, Alexander......IV, 468
  Henry, Patrick............IV, 350
  Hopkinson, Thomas.......IV, 132
  Hutchinson, Thomas......III, 709
  Jefferson, Thomas..........V, 48
  Livingston, William......IV, 109
  Mather, Cotton...........II, 731
  Mather, Increase.........II, 690
  Mill, John Stuart..........VI, 702
  Milton, John.............II, 266
  Otis, James.............III, 718
  Prince, Thomas......III, 401, 402
  Sandys, George..........II, 82
  Sewall, Samuel..........III, 17
  Smith, John...........I, 699, 699
  Trumbull, John.......V, 120, 120
  Ward, Nathaniel..........II, 130
  Washington, George......IV, 369
  Williams, Roger..........II, 356
  Winthrop, John......II, 108, 109
  Woolman, John..........III, 598
TYLER, ROYALL,
  Paine, Thomas...........IV, 531
TYLOR, E. B.,
  Huxley, Thomas Henry..VIII, 326
  Müller, Friedrich Max....VIII, 437
TYNDALE, WILLIAM,
  More, Sir Thomas...........I, 241
  Tyndale, William..........I, 245
TYNDALL, JOHN,
  Brougham, Henry Lord....VI, 532
  Carlyle, Thomas.....VII, 237, 251
  Darwin, Charles Robert...VII, 427
  Emerson, Ralph Waldo...VII, 352
  Faraday, Michael.........VI, 513
  Rumford, Count......IV, 592, 593
  Tennyson, Alfred Lord...VIII, 82
  Young, Thomas............V, 89
TYRWHITT, THOMAS,
  Chatterton, Thomas......III, 534
  Chaucer, Geoffrey.......
    ....I, 141, 150, 151, 157
  Tyrwhitt, Thomas........IV, 25
TYTLER, ALEXANDER FRASER,
  Blair, Hugh..............IV, 405
  Burnett, James......IV, 347, 348
  Dalrymple, Sir David....IV, 146
  Hamilton, William........III, 336
  Home, Henry............III, 711

Hume, David...........III, 656
Ramsay, Allan......III, 404, 406
Smollett, Tobias George....III, 581
Wilkie, William.........III, 596
TYTLER, PATRICK FRASER,
  Barbour, John.............I, 113
  Buchanan, George..........I, 317
  Douglas, Gawin............I, 213
  Dunbar, William...........I, 224
  Henry the Minstrel.........I, 201
  Lyndsay, Sir David........I, 274
  Raleigh, Sir Walter........I, 603
  Scott, Michael.............I, 68
  Spenser, Edmund...........I, 391
  Wyntoun, Andrew..........I, 178
TYTLER, SARAH, AND WATSON
  J. L.,
  Baillie, Joanna............V, 691
  Blamire, Susanna.....IV, 204, 204
  Oliphant, Carolina.........V, 477
TYTLER, WILLIAM,
  James First of Scotland......I, 180

U
EBERWEG, FREDERICH,
  Bacon, Francis.........I, 661
  Clarke, Samuel............II, 749
  Davies, Sir John...........I, 633
  Duns Scotus................I, 86
  Grote, George.............VI, 612
  Hooker, Richard...........I, 408
  Hume, David.............III, 663
  Locke, John..............II, 527
  Newton, Sir Isaac........II, 718
ULRICI, HERMANN,
  Greene, Robert............I, 342
  Heywood, John............I, 305
  Jonson, Ben...............I, 763
  Lyly, John................I, 426
  Marlowe, Christopher......I, 354
  Peele, George.............I, 364
  Shakespeare, William......
    I, 462, 467, 471, 486, 487, 504,
    ....508, 513, 530
  Still, John................I, 430
  Udall, Nicholas............I, 279
UNDERHILL, GEORGE F.,
  Greene, Robert............I, 345
  Longfellow, Henry Wadsworth
    ....VII, 412
  Raleigh, Sir Walter ....I, 601
UNDERHILL, JOHN,
  Besant, Sir Walter...VIII, 449, 450
  Gay, John...........III, 60, 62
UNDERWOOD, FRANCIS H.,
  Adams, John...............V, 53
  Ames, Fisher..............IV, 528
  Ascham, Roger.............I, 290
  Audubon, John James.......V, 698
  Bancroft, George........VIII, 58
  Brownson, Orestes Augustus..
    ....VII, 74
  Bryant, William Cullen...VII, 116
  Bushnell, Horace.........VII, 70
  Cary, Alice..............VI, 639
  Channing, William Ellery....V, 374
  Child, Lydia Maria.......VII, 222
  Clough, Arthur Hugh......VI, 249
  Craik, Dinah Maria Mulock...
    ....VII, 625
  Curtis, George William...VIII, 189
  Dewey, Orville..........VII, 498

Draper, John William.....VII, 503
Edwards, Jonathan........III, 388
Emerson, Ralph Waldo....VII, 366
Fields, James Thomas.....VII, 341
Franklin, Benjamin........IV, 99
Fuller, Sarah Margaret......V, 671
Hamilton, Alexander......IV, 456
Hawthorne, Nathaniel......VI, 346
Holland, Josiah Gilbert....VII, 335
Holmes, Oliver Wendell..VIII, 286
Hughes, Thomas........VIII, 347
Hume, David.............III, 666
Kennedy, John Pendleton..VI, 606
Longfellow Henry Wadsworth.
  ....VII, 383, 404
Lowell, James Russell........
  ....:VIII, 18, 28, 37
Mann, Horace............VI, 202
Marsh, George Perkins....VII, 495
Motley, John Lothrop.....VII, 91
Palfrey, John Gorham.....VII, 339
Parker, Theodore..........VI, 210
Parkman, Francis........VIII, 221
Paulding, James Kirke....VI, 227
Percival, James Gates.....VI, 61
Phillips, Wendell........VII, 558
Saxe, John Godfrey......VII, 617
Sigourney, Lydia Huntley..VI, 452
Simms, William Gilmore...VI, 599
Story, Joseph.............V, 485
Sumner, Charles.........VI, 755
Taylor, Bayard..........VII, 134
Thackeray, William Makepeace
  ....VI, 310
Thoreau, Henry David....VI, 274
Tuckerman, Henry Theodore..
  ....VI, 643
Warner, Charles Dudley...
  ....VIII, 441, 444
Wayland, Francis........VI, 450
Whipple, Edwin Percy.VII, 595, 596
Whitman, Walt.........VIII, 138
Whittier, John Greenleaf.....
  ....VIII, 113, 117
Woolsey, Theodore Dwight...
  ....VII, 737
UNDERWOOD, SARA A.,
  Oliphant, Laurence......VII, 658
UNIVERSITY GRACE BOOK,
  Bentley, Richard.........III, 118
UPCOTT AND SHOBERL,
  Mathias, Thomas James....V, 288
UPHAM, C. W.,
  Prescott, William Hickling..VI, 188
UPHAM, THOMAS COGSWELL,
  Watts, Isaac............III, 250
UPSON, ANSON J.,
  Kemble, Frances Ann....VIII, 214
UPTON, C. B.,
  Hamilton Sir William.....VI, 57
URLIN, R. DENNY,
  Southey, Robert..........V, 412
  Wesley, John............IV, 114
URQUHART, SIR THOMAS,
  Alexander, Sir William....II, 34
URRY, JOHN,
  Chaucer, Geoffrey.........I, 125
URWICK, W.,
  Howe, John.............II, 546
UTTERSON, E. V.
  Berners, Lord............I, 229

INDEX TO CRITICISMS

V

VALENTINE, EDWARD A. UFFINGTON,
Whitman, Walt.........VIII, 151
VAN CLEEF, AUGUSTUS,
Poe, Edgar Allan...........V, 543
VAN CLEVE, JOHN,
McCosh, James......VIII, 301, 302
VANDAM, ALBERT D.,
DuMaurier, George......VIII, 344
Swift, Jonathan..........III, 203
VAN DYKE, HENRY,
Keats, John..........IV, 672, 682
Keble, John.............VI, 466
Milton, John.........II, 267, 280
Tennyson, Alfred Lord.......
............VIII, 72, 89, 92, 95
VAN DYKE, HENRY J., JR.
Johnson, Samuel...........III, 764
AN DYKE, JOHN C.,
Reynolds, Sir Joshua......IV, 140
Ruskin, John.........VIII, 410
VAN LAUN, HENRI,
Chaucer, Geoffrey...........I, 131
Macpherson, James........IV, 278
VAN MILDE T, WILLIAM,
Waterland, Daniel........III, 103
VAN PRINSTERER, M. GROËN,
Motley, John Lothrop.....VII, 94
VAN RENESSELAER, GRATZ,
Scott, Sir Walter...........V, 153
VAN RENSSELAER M. G.,
Allston, Washington........V, 422
Arnold, Matthew.........VII, 632
Stevenson, Robert Louis.....
.............VIII, 237, 250
VAN RENSSELAER, MRS. SCHUYLER,
Fiske, John...............VIII, 458
VAN SANTVOORD, GEORGE,
Jay, John..................V, 95
Marshall, John..........V, 283
Sidney, Algernon..........II, 354
VAUGHAN, CHARLES EDWYN,
Carlyle, Thomas..........VII, 273
Chaucer, Geoffrey...........I, 170
Dryden, John............II, 494
Hazlitt, William..........V, 106
Johnson, Samuel..........III, 767
Pater, Walter Horatio....VIII, 279
Shelley, Percy Bysshe......IV, 715
VAUGHAN, EDWARD T.,
Alford, Henry............VI, 635
Keble, John..........VI, 458, 464
Newman, John Henry.....VII, 746
VAUGHAN, HENRY,
Books ....III, 6
Cartwright, William........II, 71
D'Avenant, Sir William.....II, 217
Herbert, George...........I, 722
Vaughan, Henry..........II, 442
VAUGHAN, HENRY HALFORD,
Shakespeare, William......I, 482
VAUGHAN, HERBERT CRADINAL,
Manning, Henry Edward.....
..............VIII, 166, 169
Wiseman, Nicholas Patrick.VI, 438
VAUGHAN, ROBERT,
Lanfranc................I, 48
Locke, John.............II, 534
Wyclif, John............I, 100

VAUGHAN, ROBERT ALFRED,
Coleridge, Samuel Taylor....V, 224
Emerson, Ralph Waldo....VII, 363
Law, William............III, 429
Smith, Sydney............V, 472
VAUGHAN, SIR WILLIAM,
Marlowe, Christopher........I, 346
VEDDER, HENRY C.,
Harte, Francis Bret......VIII, 471
Hawthorne, Nathaniel.....VI, 370
Miller, Cincinnatus Hiner.VIII, 501
Parkman, Francis.......VIII, 224
Stoddard, Richard Henry.....
................VIII, 495, 497
Stockton, Francis Richard....
....................VIII, 474
VEITCH, JOHN,
Fergusson, Robert........III, 641
Hamilton, Thomas.........V, 394
Hamilton, Sir William..VI, 52, 56
Hamilton, William......III, 336
Hogg, James.........V, 265, 268
Lockhart, John Gibson......V, 758
Thomas of Erceldoune......I, 84
Thomson, James..........III, 270
Wordsworth, William......V, 644
VENABLE, WILLIAM HENRY,
Defoe, Daniel............III, 26
VENABLES, EDMUND,
Bunyan, John.II, 391, 392, 402, 404
Freeman, Edward Augustus..
................VIII, 155
Lowth, William..........III, 63
VENABLES, GEORGE,
Thackeray, William Makepeace
.....................VI, 295
VENABLES, GEORGE STOVIN,
Carlyle, Thomas..........VII, 256
Cobbett, William...........V, 273
Spedding, James.....VII, 318, 319
VERITY, A. W.,
Marlowe, Christopher........I, 350
VERPLANCK, GULIAN CROMMELIN,
Brown, Charles Brockden...IV, 555
Bryant, William Cullen...VII, 119
Congreve, William........II, 742
Irving, Washington....VI, 138, 140
Shakespeare, William........
I, 462, 465, 469, 471, 478, 480,
487, 491, 492, 508, 513, 524,
526, 535
VERSTEGAN, RICHARD,
Chaucer, Geoffrey..........I, 154
VETCH, R. H.
Napier, Gen. Sir William Francis Patrick ....VI, 221, 223
VICTOR, BENJAMIN,
Steele, Sir Richard........II, 753
VICTOR, ORVILLE J.,
Cary, Alice.............VI, 637
VICTORIA, QUEEN,
Hogg, James.............V, 266
Macleod, Norman..........VI, 660
Tennyson, Alfred Lord...VIII, 70
VIGNOLES, O. J.,
Darwin, Charles Robert...VII, 432
VIGNY, ALFRED DE,
Richardson, Samuel......III, 440
VILLEMAIN, ABEL FRANÇOIS,
Richardson, Samuel......III, 449

Thomson, James..........III, 259
VILLIERS, CHARLES PELHAM,
Bright, John............VII, 724
VILLIERS, GEORGE (DUKE OF BUCKINGHAM),
Dryden, John............II, 474
VINCE, C. A.,
Bright, John............VII, 725
VINCENT, DR., DEAN OF WESTMINSTER,
Cumberland, Richard ......IV, 55
VINCENT, LEON H.,
Browning, Robert....VII, 681, 689
Keats, John............IV, 681
VIRGINIA GAZETTE,
Henry, Patrick..........IV, 349
VOLTAIRE, FRANÇOIS MARIE AROULET,
Addison, Joseph..........II, 648
Bacon, Francis............I, 653
Congreve, William.....II, 734, 740
Locke, John.............II, 532
Milton, John............II, 258
Newton, Sir Isaac........II, 722
Penn, William...........II, 629
Pope, Alexander.........III, 181
Richardson, Samuel .....III, 444
Robertson, William......IV, 158
Saint-John, Henry.......III, 283
Shakespeare, William .....I, 501
Sterne, Laurence........III, 506
Swift, Jonathan ....III, 228
Thomson, James.....III, 256, 265
Vanbrugh, Sir John......II, 706
Wycherley, William......II, 603
Young, Edward ....III, 486
VOMHOMRIGH, ESTHER,
Swift, Jonathan..........III, 211
VON GAUPP, OTTO,
Spencer, Herbert....VIII, 478, 485
VON HOLST, DR. H.,
Madison, James...........V, 313
VON SCHEEL, ALBERT,
Hamilton, Sir William.....VI, 51
VON ZITTEL, KARL ALFRED,
Huxley, Thomas Henry..VIII, 327

W

WACE, WALTER E.,
Tennyson, Alfred Lord,
....................VIII, 80
WACKERBARTH, A. DIEDRICH,
Beowulf ....I, 18
WADDELL, HATELY,
Burns, Robert...........IV, 247
WADDELL, JAMES D.,
Benton, Thomas Hart.....VI, 88
WADDINGTON, SAMUEL,
Clough, Arthur Hugh......VI, 253
Coleridge, Hartley.........V, 578
Hood, Thomas............V, 464
Smith, Charlotte........IV, 497
WAILLY, LEON DE,
Burns, Robert...........IV, 254
WAITE, ARTHUR E.,
Lovelace, Richard........II, 161
WAITE, MORRISON R.,
Marshall, John...........V, 284
WAKEFIELD, GILBERT,
Horsley, Samuel.........VI, 495
Porson, Richard.........IV, 520
Wakefield, Gilbert........IV, 415

INDEX TO CRITICISMS

WAKEMAN, HENRY OFFLEY,
  Dunstan .... I, 45
WALDEGRAVE, LORD,
  Lyttelton, George Lord.... III, 610
  Murray, William........... VI, 169
WALDO, S. PUTNAM,
  Monroe, James............. V, 123
WALDSTEIN, CHARLES,
  Eliot, George............. VII, 208
  Ruskin, John............ VIII, 419
WALFORD, EDWARD,
  Newton, Sir Isaac .... II, 714
  Stanhope, Philip Dormer... III, 602
WALFORD, LUCY BETHIA,
  Brontë, Charlotte .... VI, 20
  Carter, Elizabeth......... IV, 492
WALKER, ALBERT PERRY,
  Milton, John............. II, 274
WALKER, E. D.,
  Roe, Edward Payson.........
  .... VII, 675, 676
WALKER, FRANCIS A.,
  Malthus, Thomas Robert.... V, 252
  Smith, Adam............. IV, 68
WALKER, HENRY L.,
  Burns, Rober .... IV, 265
WALKER, HUGH,
  Adams, Sarah Flower....... V, 530
  Alexander, Sir William..... II, 36
  Alison, Sir Archibald...... VI, 522
  Allingham, William....... VII, 735
  Armstrong, John .... III, 699
  Arnold, Matthew.......... VII, 633
  Arnold, Thomas........... V, 381
  Bailey, Philip James...... VII, 462
  Barham, Richard Harris.... V, 476
  Barnes, William......... VII, 587
  Beattie, James........ IV, 433, 434
  Blacklock, Thomas........ IV, 131
  Blair, Robert............. III, 243
  Blanchard, Samuel Laman... V, 482
  Brontë, Anne............. V, 600
  Brontë, Charlotte .... VI, 31
  Brontë, Emily............. V, 527
  Brown, John............ VII, 481
  Browning, Robert.... VII, 684, 690
  Buchanan, George.......... I, 317
  Buckle, Henry Thomas..... VII, 284
  Burns, Robert........ IV, 234, 246
  Burton, John Hill........ VII, 316
  Calverly, Charles Stuart... VII, 544
  Carleton, William .... VI, 550
  Carlyle, Thomas..... VI, 249, 253
  Chambers, Robert.... VI, 621, 623
  Colenso, John William.... VII, 526
  Coleridge, Hartley......... V, 579
  Coleridge, Sara........... V, 735
  Collins, Mortimer........ VII, 83
  De Morgan, Augustus ..... VII, 634
  Dickens, Charles....... VI, 566, 579
  Disraeli, Benjamin....... VII, 295
  Dobell, Sidney Thompson....
  .... VI, 763, 766
  Doyle, Sir Francis Hastings
    Charles .... VII, 650
  Drummond, William....... II, 103
  Falconer, William........ III, 526
  Fergusson, Robert........ III, 641
  Ferrier, James Frederick.....
  .... VI, 411
  Forster, John........... VII, 69

Froude, James Anthony......
  .... VIII, 259
Gaskell, Elizabeth Cleghorn. VI, 433
Gray, David............. VI, 262
Grote, George........... VI, 611
Hamilton, Sir William..... VI, 57
Hamilton, William........ III, 336
Hemans, Felicia Dorothea... V, 261
Home, John......... IV, 514, 516
Hood, Thomas............ V, 466
Horne, Richard Hengist... VII, 546
Hutton, Richard Holt.... VIII, 375
James, George Payne Rains-
  ford .... VI, 220
Jameson, Anna.......... VI, 216
Keble, John............. VI, 466
Kinglake, Alexander William.
  .... V'II, 53
Kingsley, Charles....... VII, 26, 28
Kingsley, Henry......... VII, 81
Knowles, James Sheridan... VI, 289
Knox, John.......... I, 299, 300
Landor, Walter Savage..... VII, 487
Lewis, Sir George Cornewall. VI, 339
Lockhart, John Gibson.. V, 755, 757
Logan, John............ IV, 45
Lover, Samuel........... VI, 545
Lyell, Sir Charles....... VII, 36
Lyndsay, Sir David......... I, 276
Lytton, Sir Edward George Bul-
  wer............ VI, 690, 692, 699
Macpherson, James....... IV, 279
Maginn, William.......... V, 389
Maine, Sir Henry James Sum-
  ner .... VII, 653
Mallett, David....... III, 495, 497
Mangan, James Clarence.... V, 604
Mansel, Henry Longueville...
  .... VI, 629
Marryat, Frederick........ V, 534
Martineau, Harriet....... VII, 64
Maurice, John Frederick Den-
  ison. .... VI, 650
Merivale, Charles....... VIII, 218
Mickle, William Julius...... IV, 43
Mill, John Stuart.. VI, 709, 712, 718
Miller, Hugh............. VI, 65
Milman, Henry Hart..... VI, 539
Milnes, Richard Monckton..
  .... VII, 565
Motherwell, William...... V, 278
Newman, John Henry..... VII, 749
Norton, Caroline E. S..... VII, 106
Praed, Winthrop Mackworth..
  .... V, 334
Procter, Adelaide Anne.... VI, 396
Pusey, Edward Bouverie. VII, 473
Ramsay, Allan ...... III, 404, 411
Robertson, Frederick William
  .... V, 741
Ross, Alexander.......... III, 719
Scott, Michael........... V, 280
Scott, Sir Walter......... V, 140
Smith, Alexander........ VII, 519
Spencer, Herbert........ VIII, 485
Stanhope, Philip Henry Earl..
  .... VII, 48
Stanley, Arthur Penrhyn. VII, 306
Talfourd, Sir Thomas Noon. V, 761
Taylor, Sir Henry... VII, 582, 584
Tennyson, Alfred Lord.. VIII, 79

Thackeray, William Make-
  peace .... VI, 309
Thirlwall, Connop....... VII, 45
Thomson, James.. III, 264, 266, 271
Trench, Richard Chenevix...
  .... VII, 590
Turner, Charles Tennyson..
  .... II, 163
Ward, William George... VII, 485
Whewell, William....... VI, 472
Wilberforce, Samuel...... VI, 735
Wilkie, William......... III, 596
Wordsworth, William...... V, 643
WALKER, JOHN BRISBEN,
  George, Henry......... VIII, 382
WALKER, J.,
  Palfrey, John Gorham... VII, 339
  White, Joseph Blanco...... V, 362
WALKER, J. L.,
  Parkman, Francis.. VIII, 218, 222
WALKER, JOSIAH,
  Burns, Robert........... IV, 224
WALKLEY, A. B.,
  Defoe, Daniel........... III, 49
WALKLEY, THOMAS,
  Shakespeare, William...... I, 511
WALL, ANNIE,
  Browning, Robert....... VII, 688
WALLACE, AFLRED RUSSEL,
  Darwin, Charles Robert....
  .... VII, 427, 430
WALLACE, HORACE BINNEY,
  Griswold, Rufus Wilmot... IV, 79
  Irving, Washington....... VI, 149
  Morris, George Pope...... VI, 401
WALLACE, SUSAN E.,
  Story, William Wetmore. VIII, 318
WALLACE, WILLIAM,
  Alison, Sir Archibald..... VI, 521
  Burns, Robert...... IV, 242, 266
  Chillingworth, William.... II, 86
  Fletcher, Andrew......... II, 612
  Hales, John............. II, 151
  Hutton, Richard Holt.... VIII, 375
  Robertson, William...... IV, 163
WALLACE, LESTER,
  Lover, Samuel........... VI, 544
  Thackeray, William Makepeace
  .... VI, 297
WALLER, EDMUND,
  Chaucer, Geoffrey......... I, 155
  Davenant, Sir William.... II, 217
  Drama, The............. VII, 5
  Jonson, Ben.............. I, 759
  Poets and Poetry......... IV, 5
  Sandys, George........... II, 82
  Sidney, Sir Philip........ I, 331
WALLER, JOHN FRANCIS,
  Burke, Edmund.......... IV, 292
  Chaucer, Geoffrey......... I, 145
  Collins, William......... III, 417
  Cowper, William......... IV, 391
  Fielding, Henry......... III, 359
  Spenser, Edmund.......... I, 384
  Sterne, Laurence........ III, 514
  Swift, Jonathan..... III, 210, 232
  Wordsworth, William..... V, 612
WALLIS, C. J.,
  Barnes, William........ VII, 585
WALMSLEY, GILBERT,
  Johnson, Samuel........ III, 720

INDEX TO CRITICISMS

WALPOLE, HORACE,
Addison, Joseph......II, 634, 654
Anstey, Christopher..IV, 479, 480
Bacon, Francis............I, 665
Barbauld, Anna Lætitia....V, 23
Berkeley, George........III, 327
Birch, Thomas...........III, 499
Boswell, James......IV, 209, 214
Burke, Edmund......IV, 299, 301
Burney, Frances..........V, 348
Butler, Joseph...........III, 310
Cavendish, Margaret....II, 232
Chatterton, Thomas.........
...........III, 528, 534, 535
Chaucer, Geoffrey........I, 157
Churchill, Charles.......III, 475
Cooper, Anthony Ashley..II, 578
Cowley, Abraham........II, 199
Dodd, William..........III, 675
Dodington, George Bubb..III, 459
Dryden, John........II, 481, 496
Evelyn, John............II, 547
Fielding, Henry.........III, 340
Garrick, David..........III, 693
Gibbon, Edward...IV, 179, 180
Glover, Richard......IV, 17, 22
Godwin, Mary Wollstonecraf:.
.....................IV, 326
Goldsmith, Oliver........III, 634
Granville George........III, 88
Gray, Thomas......III, 553, 562
Greville, Sir Fulke........I, 691
Hawkins, Sir John.....IV, 51, 52
Hayley, William..........IV, 652
Herbert, Edward Lord......
................II, 95, 97, 97
Hervey, John Lord......III, 128
Hurd, Richard......IV, 517, 518
Hyde, Edward, Earl of Clarendon..............II, 302
Jenyns, Soame............IV, 32
Johnson, Samuel........III, 754
Lennox, Charlotte.......IV, 469
Lyttelton, George Lord..III, 610
Macaulay, Catherine.....IV, 134
Macpherson, James......IV, 273
Malone, Edmond........IV, 578
Mason, William..........IV, 325
Milton, John........II, 285, 286
Montagu, Elizabeth......IV, 399
Montagu, Lady Mary Wortley.
.............III, 460, 461
More, Hannah...........V, 194
North, Roger............III, 79
Paine, Thomas..........IV, 530
Parr, Samuel............V, 19
Percy, Thomas.........IV, 562
Piozzi, Hester Lynch....IV, 685
Pope, Alexander, III, 161, 173, 179
Quarles, Francis.........II, 78
Radcliffe, Ann Ward.....IV, 718
Reeve, Clara............IV, 511
Richardson, Samuel....III, 447
Robertson, William........
...........IV, 157, 161, 162
Robinson, Mary.........IV, 411
Roscoe, William.........V, 117
Sackville, Charles.......II, 552
Saint-John, Henry......III, 293
Savile, George..........II, 449
Secker, Thomas........III, 522

Seward, Anna...........IV, 542
Shakespeare, William..I, 484, 553
Sheffield, John, Third Earl of Mulgrave........II, 670, 672
Shens one, William......III, 473
Sheridan, Richard Brinsley..
...........IV, 599, 599, 603, 605
Sidney, Sir Philip......I, 322, 329
Smollet, Tobias George......
..................III, 574, 584
Somers, John Lord........II, 613
Spence, Joseph.........III, 520
Spenser, Edmund.....I, 388, 394
Stanhope, Philip Dormer....
..................III, 599, 603
Sterne, Laurence.....III, 506, 510
Swift, Jonathan......III, 199, 229
Taylor, Thomas...........V, 291
Thompson, James....III, 265, 267
Vanbrugh, Sir John......II, 705
Villiers, George..........II, 378
Waller, Edmund........II, 381
Walpole, Horace....IV, 310, 316
Warton, Thomas........IV, 72
Washington, George......IV, 354
Wesley, John.......IV, 111, 120
West, Gilbert...........III, 368
Wilkes, John..........IV, 333
Wilkins, John..........II, 227
Williams, Sir Charles Hanbury
.....................III, 412
Wilmot, John...........II, 338
Young, Edward.........III, 492
WALPOLE, SIR ROBERT,
Saint-John, Henry......III, 283
WALPOLE, SPENCER,
Austen, Jane...........IV, 621
Bentham, Jeremy........V, 168
Brougham, Henry Lord...VI, 532
Buckland, Francis Trevelyan..
..................VII, 210, 212
Burns, Robert..........IV, 260
Byron, George Gordon Lord.IV, 760
Campbell, Thomas........V, 444
Cobbett, William........IV, 274
Coleridge, Samuel Taylor....V, 216
Edgeworth, Maria........V, 569
Hallam, Henry..........VI, 179
Jeffrey, Francis Lord.....V, 656
Mackintosh, Sir James.....V, 183
Mitford, William..........V, 71
Moore, Thomas..........V, 717
Paley, William..........IV, 477
Russell, John Earl......VII, 146
Shelley, Percy Bysshe....IV, 700
Smith, Adam............IV, 66
Smith, Sydney..........V, 473
Southey, Robert.........V, 411
WALROND, THEODORE,
Arnold, Thomas..........V, 378
WALSH, WILLIAM,
Pope, Alexander........III, 156
WALSH, WILLIAM PAKENHAM,
Carleton, William........VI, 549
WALSH, WILLIAM SHEPARD,
Hook, Theodore Edward....V, 359
Lytton, Sir Edward George Bulwer...........V, 684
Roe, Edward Payson....VII, 676
Stevenson, Robert Louis..VIII, 247
Tennyson, Alfred Lord...VIII, 70

WALSINGHAM, SIR FRANCIS,
Sidney, Sir Philip..........I, 320
WALSINGHAM, THOMAS,
Wyclif, John..............I, 99
WALTERS, J. CUMING,
Tennyson, Alfred Lord...VIII, 85
WALTON, ISAAC,
Basse, William..........II, 131
Carew, Thomas..........II, 20
Donne, John.........I, 710, 712
Herbert, George......I, 720, 721
Hooker, Richard.........I, 403
King, Henry............II, 223
Marlowe, Christopher....I, 354
Nashe, Thomas..........I, 413
Sanderson, Robert......II, 178
Walton, Isaac..........II, 346
Wiseman, Nicholas Patrick.VI, 436
Wotton, Sir Henry.......II, 17
WARBURTON, ELIOT,
Chatterton, Thomas......III, 531
Gray, Thomas..........III, 555
Kinglake, Alexander William
.....................VIII, 50
More, Hannah...........V, 195
Walpole, Horace.........IV, 314
Williams, Sir Charles Hanbury
.....................III, 413
WARBURTON, WILLIAM,
Bentley, Richard........III, 115
Butler, Samuel..........II, 334
Byrom, John...........II, 469
Cooper, Anthony Ashley....II, 577
Cudworth, Ralph........II, 385
Fuller, Thomas..........II, 170
Garrick, David..........III, 697
Hume, David......III, 653, 655
Hurd, Richard..........IV, 518
Johnson, Samuel........III, 753
Mallet, David..........III, 494
Pope, Alexander.....III, 170, 172
Robertson, William......IV, 157
Saint-John, Henry......III, 284
Shakespeare, William.....I, 533
Smollett, Tobias George...III, 581
Sterne, Laurence.....III, 502, 506
Taylor, Jeremy..........II, 206
Theobald, Lewis........III, 141
Tillotson, John Robert....II, 437
Tindal, Matthew........III, 72
Walpole, Horace........IV, 421
Warton, Thomas........IV, 72
Young, Edward.........III, 492
WARD, ADOLPHUS WILLIAM,
Addison, Joseph........II, 651
Alexander, Sir William....II, 36
Barclay, Alexander......I, 265
Beaumont and Fletcher...I, 584
Beaumont, Francis......I, 586
Bowles, William Lisle....V, 660
Cartwright, William.....II, 72
Centlivre, Susannah.....II, 685
Chapman, George...I, 727, 730, 733
Chaucer, Geoffrey....I, 132, 165
Cibber, Colley.........III, 372
Collier, Jeremy.........II, 701
Congreve, William.........
.....II, 736, 738, 739, 743
Cowley, Abraham.....II, 196, 197
D'Avenant, Sir William....II, 219
Dekker, Thomas......II, 57, 58, **60**

INDEX TO CRITICISMS

	Vol. and Page
Denham, Sir John	II, 220
Dennis, John	III, 78
Dickens, Charles	VI, 565, 569, 570, 571, 576, 576, 588
Dodington, George Bubb	III, 458
Dryden, John	II, 471, 472, 474, 474, 475, 477, 478, 478, 480, 481, 483, 484, 491, 492, 504
D'Urfey, Thomas	II, 688
Earle, John	II, 184
Etheredge, Sir George	II, 415
Farquhar, George	II, 555, 557
Fenton, Elijah	III, 21
Fletcher, Phineas	II, 117
Ford, John	II, 27, 28, 29, 30
Gaskell, Elizabeth Cleghorn	VI, 429, 431, 432, 433
Granville, George	III, 87, 88
Greene, Robert	I, 341
Greville, Sir Fulke	I, 692
Heywood, Thomas	II, 126
Hill, Aaron	III, 278
Home, John	IV, 514
Jevons, William Stanley	VII, 491, 492
Jonson Ben	I, 750, 752, 754, 755, 757, 757, 758
Kyd, Thomas	I, 360
Langland, William	I, 121
Lee, Nathaniel	II, 432
Lillo, George	III, 99, 101
Lyly, John	I, 425
Manley, Mrs. Mary Riviere	II, 694
Marlowe, Christopher	I, 352
Marston, John	I, 735, 738
Massinger, Philip	II, 42, 43, 43, 44, 44, 46, 46
May, Thomas	II, 119, 120
Middleton, Thomas	I, 681, 681, 682, 685
Milton, John	II, 252, 271, 279, 282, 284, 294
Minot, Lawrence	I, 93
Montagu, Lady Mary Wortley	III, 467
Nashe, Thomas	I, 414
Oldham, John	II, 351
Otway, Thomas	II, 367
Peele, George	I, 367
Philips, Ambrose	III, 275
Pope, Alexander	III, 144, 159, 161, 164, 189
Prynne, William	II, 225
Quarles, Francis	II, 79
Ramsay, Allan	III, 408
Rowe, Nicholas	II, 619, 620, 620, 622
Rowley, William	II, 68
Saint-John Henry	III, 296
Sedley, Sir Charles	II, 509
Settle, Elkanah	II, 692
Shadwell, Thomas	II, 435
Shakespeare, William	I, 469, 479, 506, 541
Sheffield, John, Third Earl of Mulgrave	II, 671, 672
Shelley, Percy Bysshe	IV, 703
Shirley, James	II, 192
Sidney, Sir Philip	I, 326
Southerne, Thomas	III, 241
Spenser, Edmund	I, 398
Steele, Sir Richard	II, 765
Suckling, Sir John	II, 66
Tourneur, Cyril	I, 687
Tyrwhitt, Thomas	IV, 26
Vanbrugh, Sir John	II, 705, 708
Walsh, William	II, 561
Webster, John	I, 670, 673, 674, 676
Whetstone, George	I, 334
Wotton, Sir Henry	II, 19
Wycherley, William	II, 601, 601, 603, 606
Young, Edward	III, 492
WARD, CHARLES A.,	
Cruden, Alexander	III, 546
WARD, EDWARD,	
Pope, Alexander	III, 181
WARD, ELIZABETH STUART PHELPS,	
Brooks, Phillips	VIII, 229
Browning, Elizabeth Barrett	VI, 240
Child, Lydia Maria	VII, 220
Fields, James Thomas	VII, 341
Holmes, Oliver Wendell	VIII, 288
Longfellow, Henry Wadsworth	VII, 386
Stowe, Harriet Beecher	VIII, 350, 358
Whittier, John Greenleaf	VIII, 115
WARD, REV. JOHN,	
Leland, John	I, 263
WARD, REV. JOHN,	
Shakespeare, William	I, 448
WARD, JULIUS HAMMOND,	
Brooks, Phillips	VIII, 230
Dana, Richard Henry	VII, 152
Emerson, Ralp Waldo	VII, 372
Parkman, Francis	VIII, 218, 222
Percival, James Gates	VI, 58
Stowe, Harriet Beecher	VIII, 356
Very, Jones	VII, 227
Whipple, Edwin Percy	VII, 596
WARD, MARY AUGUSTA,	
Brontë, Charlotte	VI, 26
Davies, Sir John	I, 634, 634
Dyer, Sir Edward	I, 428
Newman, John Henry	VII, 753
Sidney, Sir Philip	I, 328
WARD, MAY ALDEN,	
Carlyle, Thomas	VII, 244
Mather, Cotton	II, 729
Ruskin, John	VIII, 408
WARD, NATHANIEL,	
Bradstreet, Anne	II, 229
WARD, RICHARD,	
More, Henry	II, 372
WARD, R. PLUMER,	
Gore, Catherine Grace	VI, 263
WARD, THOMAS HUMPHRY,	
Bacon, Francis	I, 662
Brontë, Emily	V, 521
Browne, William	II, 72
Chaucer, Geoffrey	I, 131
Clough, Arthur Hugh	VI, 253
Collins, Mortimer	VII, 81
Cowley, Abraham	II, 196, 196, 201
Cowper, William	IV, 390
Drummond, William	II, 106
Finch, Anne	II, 668
James I of Scotland	I, 179
Smart, Christopher	III, 593
Warton, Thomas	IV, 78
Watson, Thomas	I, 338
Whitehead, William	IV, 23, 24
WARD, WILFRID,	
Faber, Frederick William	VI, 333
Hutton, Richard Holt	VIII, 375
Huxley, Thomas Henry	VIII, 321
Mill, John Stuart	VI, 706
Newman, John Henry	VII, 757
Ward, William George	VII, 485
Wiseman, Nicholas Patrick	VI, 436, 437
WARD, WILLIAM C.,	
Defoe, Daniel	III, 49
Richardson, Samuel	III, 451
Vanbrugh, Sir John	II, 706
WARD, WILLIAM G.,	
Spencer, Herbert	VIII, 480
Tennyson, Alfred Lord	VIII, 90, 110
WARD, WILLIAM HAYES,	
Ingersoll, Robert Green	VIII, 403
Lanier, Sidney	VII, 326, 327
WARE, HENRY,	
Milnes, Richard Monckton	VII, 562
Parr, Samuel	V, 20
Percival, James Gates	VI, 59
Southey, Robert	V, 407, 410
Spencer, Herbert	VIII, 481
Taylor, Sir Henry	VII, 581
WARE, SIR JAMES,	
Spencer, Edmund	I, 369
WARE, JOHN,	
Ware, Henry, Jr.	V, 432
WARE, WILLIAM,	
Allston, Washington	V, 420
Longfellow, Henry Wadsworth	VII, 402
WARNER, BEVERLEY E.,	
Shakespeare, William	I, 574
WARNER, CHARLES DUDLEY,	
Airy, Sir George Biddell	VIII, 182
Alcott, Amos Bronson	VII, 662
Allingham, William	VII, 734
Bacon, Roger	I, 77
Bale, John	I, 285
Barclay, Alexander	I, 264
Blackie, John Stuart	VIII, 304
Boucicault, Dion	VII, 762
Bowring, Sir John	VI, 663
Bunner, Henry Cuyler	VIII, 359
Cary, Alice	VI, 637
Cary, Phœbe	VI, 640
Cooper, James Fenimore	V, 686
Dana, Richard Henry	VII, 152
Dana, Richard Henry, Jr.	VII, 499
Dibden, Charles	IV, 587
Dodge, Mary Abigail	VIII, 360
Draper, John William	VIII, 502
Drummond, Henry	VIII, 362
Du Maurier, George	VIII, 343
Fenton, Elijah	III, 20
Field, Eugene	VIII, 314
Fields, James Thomas	VII, 339
Finlay, George	VI, 48
Froude, James Anthony	VIII, 263
George, Henry	VIII, 378
Gray, Asa	VII, 669
Havergal, Frances Ridley	VII, 166

INDEX TO CRITICISMS

	Vol. and Page
Henry, Patrick	IV, 349
Hildreth, Richard	VI, 454
Holland, Josiah Gilbert	VII, 333
Irving, Washington	
...	VI, 136, 140, 142, 145, 146, 150
Jackson, Helen Hunt	VII, 573
Lane, Edward William	VII, 83
Lanier, Sidney	VII, 325
Lazarus, Emma	VII, 610, 610
Lover, Samuel	VI, 545
Mackay, Charles	VII, 764
Marsh, George Perkins	VII, 492
McCosh, James	VIII, 300
Newton, Sir Isaac	II, 726
Quarles, Francis	II, 77
Roe, Edward Payson	VII, 674
Ryan, Abram Joseph	VII, 598
Shelley, Percy Bysshe	IV, 712
Smith, John	I, 700
Stanley, Sir Henry Morton	
	VIII, 506
White, Richard Grant	VII, 576
Whitney, William Dwight	
	VIII, 302

WARNER, G. B. LEE,
Alford, Henry ... VI, 635

WARNER, G F.,
Mandeville, Sir John ... I, 94

WARREN, F. M.,
Lodge, Thomas ... I, 625
Lyly, John ... I, 424

WARREN, INA RUSSELLE
Byron, George Gordon Lord IV, 764
Dickens, Charles ... IV, 591
Thoreau, Henry David ... VI, 270
Wordsworth, William ... V, 646

WARREN, SAMUEL,
Blackstone, William ... III, 704
Gibbon, Edward ... IV, 183
Herschel, Sir John Frederick William ... VI, 624
Paley, William ... IV, 473
Scott, Sir Walter ... V, 131
Stanhope, Philip Henry Earl ... VII, 46
Story, Joseph ... V, 484
Stowe, Harriet Beecher ... VIII, 349, 352
Wilson, John ... V, 746

WARTON, JOSEPH,
Addison, Joseph ... II, 641, 649
Akenside, Mark ... III, 540
Armstrong, John ... III, 698
Collins, William ... III, 416
Dyer, John ... III, 398
Fielding, Henry ... III, 340
Gay, John ... III, 53
Granville, George ... III, 88
Mallet, David ... III, 497
Middleton, Conyers ... III, 279
Milton, John ... II, 285
Pope, Alexander ... III, 156, 159, 182
Rowe, Nicholas ... II, 621
Sheffield, John, Third Earl of Mulgrave ... II, 671
Sherlock, Thomas ... III, 455
Spence, Joseph ... III, 520
Swift, Jonathan ... III, 524
Temple, Sir William ... II, 457
Thomson, James ... III, 265, 266
Warburton, William ... III, 688

WARTON, THOMAS,
Addison, Joseph ... II, 654
Bale, John ... I, 286
Barbour, John ... I, 113
Barclay, Alexander ... I, 264
Berners, Juliana ... I, 191
Browne, William ... II, 74
Burton, Robert ... II, 38
Chapman, George ... I, 728
Chatterton, Thomas ... III, 534
Chaucer, Geoffrey ...
... I, 126, 130, 137, 156, 157
Collins, William ... III, 415
Dunbar, William ... I, 224
Edwards, Richards ... I, 288
Fabyan, Robert ... I, 207
Gascoigne, George ... I, 307
Goldsmith, Oliver ... III, 614
Gower, John ... I, 172, 175
Gray, Thomas ... III, 563
Grimoald, Nicholas ... I, 283
Hall, Joseph ... II, 144, 146, 147
Harding, John ... I, 193
Harrington, Sir John ... I, 441
Hawes, Stephen ... I, 217
Heywood, John ... I, 305, 305
Howell, James ... II, 187
Langland, William ... I, 118
Lydgate, John ... I, 184
Mannyng, Robert ... I, 87
Marlowe, Christopher ... I, 354
Marston, John ... I, 736
Milton, John ... II, 251, 254
Montagu, Elizabeth ... IV, 401
Norton, Thomas ... I, 318
Occleve, Thomas ... I, 187
Robert of Gloucester ... I, 81
Rolle, Richard ... I, 92
Sackville, Thomas ... I, 433
Skelton, John ... I, 220
Spenser, Edmund ... I, 380,381
Sternhold, Thomas ... I, 262
Still, John ... I, 430
Surrey, Earl of ... I, 257
Tusser, Thomas ... I, 310
Vaux, Thomas Lord ... I, 276
Warton, Thomas ... IV, 72
Wilson, Sir Thomas ... I, 312
Wyatt, Sir Thomas ... I, 251

WASHBURN, EMELYN W.,
Bacon, Francis ... I, 651
Beowulf ... I, 19
Browne, Sir Thomas ... II, 344
Chaucer, Geoffrey ... I, 167
Douglas, Gawin ... I, 215
Geoffery of Monmouth ... I, 57
Hooker, Richard ... I, 409
Hyde, Edward, Earl of Clarendon ... II, 304
Marston, John ... I, 738
Occleve, Thomas ... I, 188
Spenser, Edmund ... I, 385

WASHBURN, EMORY,
Hutchinson, Thomas ... III, 707

WASHBURNE, E. B.,
Paine, Thomas ... IV, 534

WASHINGTON, GEORGE,
Franklin, Benjamin ... IV, 82
Hamilton, Alexander ... IV, 456
Hopkinson, Thomas ... IV, 132
Paine, Thomas ... IV, 530

	Vol. and Page
Washington, George	IV, 366

WASHINGTON, BUSHROD C.,
Washington, George ... IV, 367

WASSON, DAVID ATWOOD,
Whittier, John Greenleaf ... VIII, 117, 121

WATERLOO, STANLEY,
Field, Eugene ... VIII, 316

WATERS, ROBERT,
Shakespeare, William ... I, 571

WATERS, W. G.,
Collins, Mortimer ... VII, 83

WATERSON, ROBERT C.,
Very, Jones ... VII, 226

WATKINS, CHARLES,
Blackstone, William ... III, 704

WATKINS, JOHN,
Elliott, Ebenezer ... V, 582

WATKINS, REV. M. G.,
Berners, Juliana ... I, 192

WATKINS, M. G ,
Buckland, Francis Trevelyan ... VII, 211, 213
White, Gilbert ... IV, 148

WATKINS, MILDRED CABELL,
Franklin, Benjamin ... IV, 97
Mather, Cotton ... II, 731

WATROUS, GEORGE A.,
Burns, Robert ... IV, 244
Dryden, John ... II, 483

WATSON, AARON,
Milnes, Richard Monckton ... VII, 564

WATSON, ELKANAH,
Franklin, Benjamin ... IV, 81
Paine, Thomas ... IV, 533, 535

WATSON, E. R.,
Monroe, James ... V, 122

WATSON, FOSTER,
Wotton, Sir Henry ... II, 18

WATSON, HENRY BRERETON MARRIOTT,
Henley, William Ernest ... VIII, 491, 493

WATSON, JOHN (IAN MACLAREN),
Drummond, Henry ... VIII, 362
Stevenson, Robert Louis ... VIII, 248

WATSON, JOHN FANNING,
Smith, Adam ... IV, 62

WATSON, JOHN SELBY,
Bentley, Richard ... III, 122
Cobbett, William ... V, 273
Parr, Samuel ... V, 21
Pope, Alexander ... III, 189
Porson, Richard ... IV, 523
Warburton, William ... III, 691
Wilkes, John ... IV, 336

WATSON, RICHARD,
Hartley, David ... III, 377
Wesley, John ... IV, 123, 127
Wesley, Samuel ... III, 86

WATSON, ROBERT SPENCE,
Cædmon ... I, 23

WATSON, ROSAMUND MARRIOTT,
Henley, William Ernest ... VIII, 491

WATSON, THOMAS,
Spenser, Edmund ... I, 392

WATSON, WILLIAM,
Arnold, Matthew ... VII, 645
Browning, Robert ... VII, 713

INDEX TO CRITICISMS

Burns, Robert .... IV, 264
Coleridge, Samuel Taylor .....
.... V, 220, 227
Critic, The .... II, 10
Ford, John .... II, 28
Hunt, James Henry Leigh .. VI, 171
Keats, John .... IV, 667, 680
Lamb, Charles .... V, 236
Landor, Walter Savage .... VI, 383
Longfellow, Henry Wadsworth
.... VII, 406
Lowell, James Russell .. VIII, 40
Macaulay, Thomas Babington
Lord .... VI, 114
Marlowe, Christopher ...... I, 357
Milton, John .... II, 297
Shakespeare, William ...... I, 570
Shelley, Percy Bysshe .... IV, 714
Symonds, John Addington ....
.... VIII, 203
Tennyson, Alfred Lord. VIII, 99
Webster, John .... I, 677
Wordsworth, William .... V, 644
WATT, FRANCIS,
Chambers, Robert .... VI, 622
Elliott, Ebenezer .... V, 580
WATT, JAMES CRABB,
Dickens, Charles .... VI, 556
WATTERSON, HENRY,
Jefferson, Thomas .... V, 46
Prentice, George Denison .. VI, 601
WATTS, ALARIC A.,
Disraeli, Benjamin ...... VII, 286
WATTS, ISAAC,
Doddridge, Philip .... III, 302
Newton, Sir Isaac .... II, 722
Rowe, Elizabeth .... III, 96
WATTS–DUNSTON, THEODORE,
Borrow, George Henry .... VII, 312
Chatterton, Thomas ...... III, 538
Coleridge, Samuel Taylor ... V, 216
FitzGerald, Edward ...... VII, 515
Rossetti, Christina Georgina ..
.... VIII, 269
Rossetti, Gabriel Charles Dante
.... VII, 437, 441
Shelley, Percy Bysshe ..... IV, 714
Whitman, Walt .... VIII, 146
WAUCHOPE, GEORGE ARMSTRONG,
DeQuincey, Thomas .... VI, 131
Eliot, George .. VII, 170, 186, 209
WAUGH, ARTHUR,
Browning, Robert .... VII, 718
Tennyson, Alfred Lord.VIII, 85, 98
WAY, W. IRVING,
Symonds,John Addington.VIII, 204
WAYLAND, D. S.,
Sherlock, Thomas .... III, 455
WAYLAND, FRANCIS, AND H. L.,
Wayland, Francis .... VI, 447
WEBB, DANIEL,
Hooker, Richard .... I, 405
WEBBE, WILLIAM,
Chaucer, Geoffrey .... I, 153
Gascoigne, George .... I, 307
Gower, John .... I, 174
Harvey, Gabriel .... I, 696
Langland, William .... I, 117
Lydgate, John .... I, 183
Lyly, John .... I, 421

Munday, Anthony .... I, 726
Skelton, John .... I, 220
Spenser, Edmund ..... I, 374, 392
Whetstone, George .... I, 334
WEBER, ALFRED,
Bacon, Francis .... I, 663
Bacon, Roger .... I, 80
Berkeley, George .... III, 334
Erigena .... I, 35
Hobbes, Thomas .... II, 328
WEBSTER, DANIEL,
Byron, George Gordon, Lord ..
.... IV, 745
Calhoun, John Caldwell .... V, 676
Hamilton, Alexander ...... IV, 463
Jay, John .... V, 95
Jefferson, Thomas .... V, 47
Knowledge .... V, 8
Lowth, Robert .... IV, 29
Poets and Poetry .... IV, 7
Story, Joseph .... V, 484
Washington, George ...... IV, 366
WEBSTER, JOHN,
Chapman, George .... I, 731
History .... VI, 5
Jonson, Ben .... I, 758
Webster, John .... I, 670
WEBSTER, NOAH,
Johnson, Samuel .... III, 744
Spelman, Sir Henry .... II, 54
Webster, Noah .. V, 427, 427, 429
WEBSTER, WENTWORTH,
Herbert, George .... I, 724
WEDDERBURN, ALEXANDER (LORD LOUGHBOROUGH),
Franklin, Benjamin .... IV, 94
Mallet, David .... III, 494
WEDMORE, FREDERICK,
Du Maurier, George ..... VIII, 346
Hamerton, Philip Gilbert.VIII, 282
Lewes, George Henry ..... VII, 142
WEDGWOOD, JULIA,
Froude, James Anthony . VIII, 260
Hutton, Richard Holt .... VIII, 375
Law, William .... III, 428
Ruskin, John .... VIII, 423
Stanley, Arthur Penrhyn .. VII, 298
Wesley, John .... IV, 124
WEED, THURLOW,
Greeley, Horace .... VI, 668
Junius .... IV, 642
WEEMS, MASON L.,
Franklin, Benjamin .... V, 86
Penn, William .... II, 630
Washington, George ...... IV, 358
WEEVER, JOHN,
Drayton, Michael .... I, 706
Marston, John .... I, 736
Middleton, Thomas .... I, 684
Shakespeare, William ... I, 509, 547
Spenser, Edmund .... I, 391
WEISS, JOHN,
Browning, Robert ..... VII, 691, 698
Parker, Theodore .... VI, 207
Shakespeare, William ... I, 469, 506
WEISS, SUSAN A. T.,
Poe, Edgar Allan .... V, 541
WEITENKAMPF, FRANK,
Story, William Wetmore.VIII, 318
WELCH, ROBERT GILBERT,
Harrick, Robert .... II, 236

WELDON, W. F. R.,
Huxley, Thomas Henry .. VIII, 323
WELLES, GIDEON,
Lincoln, Abraham .... VI, 415
Seward, William Henry ... VI, 674
WELLS, BENJAMIN W.,
Warner, Charles Dudley ... III, 444
WELLS, CAROLYN,
Dodgson, Charles Lutwige ....
.... VIII, 399
WELLS, DAVID A.,
Smith, Adam .... IV, 65
WELLS, H. G.,
Morris, William .... VIII, 337
WELLS, J.,
Bacon, Roger .... I, 81
Pole, Reginald .... I, 281
WELLSLEY, LORD,
Pitt, William .... IV, 508
WELLWOOD, SIR HENRY MONCREIFF,
Edwards, Jonathan .... III, 386
WELWOOD, JAMES,
Rowe, Nicholas .... II, 619
WELLWOOD, JOHN,
Macleod, Norman .... VI, 663
WELSBY, W. N.,
Murray, William .... IV, 170
WELSFORD, HENRY,
Jones, Sir Willliam .... IV, 200
WELSH, ALFRED H.,
Addison, Joseph .... II, 638
Akenside, Mark .... III, 545
Barrow, Isaac .... II, 311
Browning,Elizabeth Barrett.VI, 246
Browning, Robert .... VII, 704
Burns, Robert .... IV, 261
Campbell, Thomas .... V, 439
Channing, William Ellery .. V, 374
Congreve, William .... II, 744
Cooper, James Fenimore .. V, 386
Cowper, William .... IV, 382
Dekker, Thomas .... II, 60
Donne, John .... I, 717
Dryden, John .... II, 504
Draper, John William .... VII, 503
Eliot, George .... VII, 184, 191
Fabyan, Robert .... I, 207
Fielding, Henry .... III, 362
Halleck, Fitz-Greene ..... VI, 500
Hawthorne, Nathaniel ..... VI, 68
Hume, David .... III, 666
Hunter, John .... IV, 168
Irving, Washington .... VI, 142
Johnson, Samuel .... III, 763
Lytton, Sir Edward George
Bulwer .... VI, 698
Mandeville, Sir John ...... I, 96
Occeve, Thomas .... I, 188
Paley, William .... IV, 475
Poe, Edgar Allan .... V, 550
Pope, Alexander .... III, 177
Prescott, William Hickling.VI, 191
Raleigh, Sir Walter .... I, 607
Sackville, Thomas .... I, 434
Shakespeare, William ...... I, 518
Shirley, James .... II, 192
Steele, Sir Richard .... II, 766
Swift, Jonathan .... III, 235
Thoreau, Henry David .... VI, 274
Webster, John .... I, 677

INDEX TO CRITICISMS

	Vol. and Page
Young, Edward	III, 509

WELSH, DAVID,
Brown, Thomas	IV, 657
Whately, Richard	VI, 326

WELSH, JANE,
Byron, George Gordon Lord.	IV, 734

WENDELL, BARRETT,
Alcott, Amos Bronson	VII, 665
Bancroft, George	VIII, 61
Barlow, Joel	IV, 576
Brooks, Phillips	VIII, 231
Brown, Charles Brockden	IV, 554
Browning, Robert	VII, 712
Bryant, William Cullen	VII, 114, 126
Cooper, James Fenimore.	V, 683, 689
Dickens, Charles	VI, 595
Drake, Joseph Rodman	IV, 662
Dryden, John	II, 494
Dwight, Timothy	IV, 628
Edwards, Jonathan	III, 393
Emerson, Ralph Waldo	VII, 360, 379
Everett, Edward	VI, 427
Fiske, John	VIII, 457
Franklin, Benjamin	IV, 104
Freneau, Philip	V, 189
Godwin, William	V, 304
Hamilton, Alexander	IV, 486
Hawthorne, Nathaniel	VI, 370
Irving, Washington	VI, 153
Lowell, James Russell	VIII, 62
Mather, Cotton	II, 729, 731
Motley, John Lothrop	VII, 96
Parker, Theodore	VI, 212
Parkman, Francis	VIII, 224
Phillips, Wendell	VII, 556, 559
Poe, Edgar Allan	V, 544, 561
Prescott, William Hickling	VI, 191
Raleigh, Sir Walter	I, 598
Sparks, Jared	VI, 479
Thoreau, Henry David	VI, 278
Ticknor, George	VI, 615, 617
Trumbull, John	V, 121
Whitman, Walt	VIII, 148
Whittier, John Greenleaf	VIII, 127
Willis, Nathaniel Parker	VI, 493

WENDELL, WINIFRED LEE,
Symonds, John Addington	VIII, 207

WENTWORTH, LORD,
Byron, George Gordon Lord.	IV, 746

WESLEY, CHARLES,
Wesley, Charles	IV, 34

WESLEY, JOHN,
Brooke, Henry	III, 714
Byrom, John	III, 469
Law, William	III, 427
Sterne, Laurence	III, 511
Toplady, Augustus Montague	III, 681
Wesley, Charles	IV, 35
Wesley, John	IV, 110, 111
Wilberforce, William	V, 199

WESLEY, SAMUEL,
Atterbury, Francis	III, 65
Wesley, John	IV, 110, 122

WEST, SIR ALGERNON,
Gladstone, William Ewart.	VIII, 385

WEST, ANDREW FLEMMING,
Alcuin	I, 34

	Vol. and Page
WESTCOTT, BROOKE FOSS,	
Tyndale, William	I, 247
WESTCHESTER, DAVID,	
Warner, Charles Dudley.	VIII, 441

WESTLAKE, J.,
Colenso, John William	VII, 523

WESTWOOD, THOMAS,
Lamb, Charles	V, 233

WETZEL, W. A.,
Franklin Benjamin	IV, 104

WHALLEY, PETER,
Jonson, Ben	I, 747
Lyly, John	I, 44

WHARTON, DUKE OF,
Atterbury, Francis	III, 65

WHARTON, THOMAS,
Gray, Thomas	III, 561

WHARTON, THOMAS I.,
Hopkinson, Thomas	IV, 132

WHATELY, RICHARD,
Austen, Jane	IV, 618
Authors and Authorship	VIII, 8
Butler, Joseph	III, 313
Gibbon, Edward	IV, 195
Shakespeare, William	I, 562, 576
Smith, Adam	IV, 62
Tucker, Josiah	IV, 369

WHEATLEY, HENRY B.,
Burns, Robert	IV, 269
Butler, Samuel	II, 335
Caxton, William	I, 200
Chaucer, Geoffrey	I, 129, 149
Defoe, Daniel	III, 40
Fabyan, Robert	I, 207
Fuller, Thomas	II, 170
Goldsmith, Oliver	III, 629
Drummond, William	II, 107
Fox, John	I, 337
Hakluyt, Richard	I, 446
Howell, James	II, 187
Johnson, Samuel	III, 736
Knight, Charles	VI, 743
Lodge, Thomas	I, 625
Milton, John	II, 269
Pepys, Samuel	II, 513, 516
Percy, Thomas	IV, 562, 565
Raleigh, Sir Walter	I, 598
Scott, Sir Walter	V, 133
Shelley, Percy Bysshe	IV, 717
Smollett, Tobias George	III, 582
Southey, Robert	V, 402
Walpole, Horace	IV, 316
Walton, Isaac	II, 348
Wordsworth, William	V, 624

WHEATLEY, HENRY B., AND CUNNINGHAM, PETER,
Addison, Joseph	II, 639

WHEATLEY, THOMAS,
Shakespeare, William	I, 514

WHEATON, HENRY,
Beowulf	I, 17

WHEELER, A C,
Boucicault, Dion	VII, 763

WHELDON, JAMES,
Hobbes, Thomas	II, 321

WHETSTONE, GEORGE,
Gascoigne, George	I, 307
Spenser, Edmund	I, 375

WHEWELL, WILLIAM
Franklin, Benjamin	IV, 100

	Vol. and Page
Longfellow Henry Wadsworth	VII, 390
Lyell, Sir Charles	VII, 35
Newton, Sir Isaac	II, 723

WHIBLEY, CHARLES,
Burns, Robert	IV, 246
Sterne, Laurence	III, 509
Urquhart, Sir Thomas	II, 164

WHIPPLE, EDWIN PERCY.
Addison, Joseph	II, 635
Agassiz, Louis Jean Rodolphe	VI, 721, 722, 724
Alcott, Amos Bronson	VII, 664
Alcott, Louisa May	VII, 667
Allston, Washington	V, 423
Arnold, Matthew	VII, 643
Bacon, Francis	I, 648
Bailey, Philip James	VIII, 460
Bancroft, George	VIII, 59
Barlow, Joel	IV, 575
Beaumont and Fletcher	I, 582
Beaumont, Francis	I, 587
Beecher, Henry Ward	VII, 607
Brontë, Charlotte	VI, 22
Brown, Charles Brockden	IV, 556
Browning, Elizabeth Barrett	VI, 243
Burke, Edmund	IV, 303
Bryant, William Cullen	VII, 116, 116, 121
Bunyan, John	II, 402
Byron, George Gordon Lord	IV, 739, 755, 759
Campbell, Thomas	V, 443
Carlyle, Thomas	VII, 252
Channing, William Ellery	V, 374
Chapman, George	I, 729, 732
Chaucer, Geoffrey	I, 163
Choate, Rufus	VI, 198
Coke, Sir Edward	I, 740
Coleridge, Samuel Taylor	V, 223
Congreve, William	III, 742
Cooper, James Fenimore	V, 686
Critic, The	II, 6
Curtis, George William	VIII, 190
Dana, Richard Henry	VII, 154, 155
Dana, Richard Henry, Jr	VII, 501
Daniel, Samuel	I, 616
Davies Sir John	I, 634
Dekker, Thomas	II, 55, 59
Dewey, Orville	VII, 499
Dickens, Charles	VI, 576, 581
Dodge, Mary Abigail	VIII, 361
Donne, John	I, 712, 715
Drayton, Michael	I, 705, 707
Dwight, Timothy	IV, 628
Eliot, George	VII, 193, 205
Elliott, Ebenezer	V, 581
Emerson, Ralph Waldo	VII, 365
Everett, Edward	V, 423
Fielding, Henry	III, 353, 355, 359
Fields, James Thomas	VII, 340
Fiske, John	VIII, 456
Fletcher, Giles	I, 623
Fletcher, John	I, 629, 631
Ford, John	II, 32
Franklin, Benjamin	IV, 102
Freneau, Philip	V, 187
Fullerton, Georgina Charlotte Lady	VII, 567
Gibbon, Edward	IV, 186

Vol. and Page
Gifford, William . . . . V, 34
Goldsmith, Oliver. . . . . III, 626
Griswold, Rufus Wilmot . . . VI, 77
Hall, Joseph . . . . II, 146
Hall, Robert . . . . V, 109
Halleck, Fitz-Greene . . . . . . VI, 499
Hamilton, Alexander . . . . . . IV, 464
Hamilton, Sir William. . . . . VI, 54
Harte, Francis Bret . . . . . VIII, 469
Hawthorne, Nathaniel . . . .
. . . . VI, 352, 353, 359
Hayne, Paul Hamilton . . . VII, 592
Hazlitt, William . . . . V, 103
Herbert, George . . . . I, 721
Heywood, Thomas . . . II, 124, 126
Holmes, Oliver Wendell . . . . . .
. . . . VIII, 289, 295
Hooker, Richard. . . . . I, 404
Hopkins, Samuel . . . . IV, 439
Hopkinson, Thomas. . . . . . . IV, 133
Hunt, James Henry Leigh. . VI, 168
Irving, Washington . . . . VI, 141
Jackson, Helen Hunt . . . . . VII, 574
James, George Payne Rainsford . . . . VI, 218
Jameson, Anna. . . . . VI, 215
Jeffrey, Francis Lord . . . . V, 654
Johnson, Samuel. . . . . III, 731
Jonson, Ben. . . . . I, 748, 753, 764
King, Thomas Starr . . . VI, 409, 409
King ley, Charles . . . . VII, 21
Lamb, Charles . . . . V, 240
Literature . . . . I, 7
Lo gfellow, Henry Wadsworth.
. . . . VII, 402
Lovelace, Richard . . . . II, 161
Lowell, James Russell . . . VIII, 37
Lytton, Sir Edward George Bulwer . . . . VI, 685
Macaulay, Thomas Babington Lord . . . . VI, 102, 109
Mackintosh, Sir James. . . . . . V, 182
Madison, James . . . . V, 315
Mann, Horace . . . . VI, 202
Marlowe, Christopher. . . . I, 349, 354
Marston, John. . . . . I, 735, 737
Massinger, Philip . . . . II, 49
Middleton, Thomas. I, 682, 682, 685
Milton, John . . . . . . II, 248, 263, 290
Moore, Thomas. . . . . V, 716
Motley, John Lothrop . . . .
. . . . VII, 87, 88, 93, 94
Neal; Daniel . . . . III, 140
Neal, John. . . . . VII, 77
Paine, Thomas . . . . IV, 538
Palfrey, John Gorham. VII, 338, 339
Percival, James Gates . . . . . . IV, 61
Parker, Theodore . . . . VI, 210
Parkman, Francis . . . . VIII, 221
Par -, Samuel. . . . . V, 18
Paulding, James Kirke . . . . . VI, 228
Pope, Alexander. . . . . III, 187
Prescott William Hickling . . . .
. . . . VI, 184, 186, 189
Procter, Bryan Waller. . VI, 747, 749
Raleigh, Sir Walter . . . . I, 603
Reade, Charles . . . . VII, 536
Rogers, Samuel. . . . . VI, 39
Sackville, Thomas . . . . I, 435
Saxe, John Godfrey . . . . VII, 617
Scott, Sir Walter. . . . . V, 135
Sedley, Sir Charles . . . . II. 509
Shakespeare, William . . . .
. . . . I, 451, 545, 563
Shelley, Percy Bysshe. . IV, 691, 706
Sheridan, Richard Brinsley. IV, 606
Sidney, Sir Philip . . . . I, 326
Sigourney, Lydia Huntley . . . .
. . . . VI, 452, 453, 453
Smith, Sydney . . . . V, 471
South, Robert. . . . . II, 608
Southey, Robert. . . . . V, 415
Sparks, Jared . . . . VI, 478
Spenser, Edmund . . I, 371, 376, 383
Sprague, Charles . . . . VII, 53
Sterne, Laurence . . . . III, 5 3
Stoddard Richard Henry. VIII, 496
Stowe, Harriet Beecher . . VIII, 352
Sumner, Charles . . . . VI, 752, 758
Talfourd, Sir Thomas Noon . . V, 761
Taylor, Bayard. . . . . VII, 132
Tennyson, Alfred Lord . . . VIII, 100
Thackery, William Makepeace.
. . . . VI, 302, 304, 309, 317
Thoreau, Henry David. VI, 270, 273
Ticknor, George . . . . VI, 617, 618
Timrod, Henry . . . . VI, 509
Trollope, Anthony . . . . VII, 462
Trumbull, John . . . . V, 121
Tuckerman, Henry Theodore . .
. . . . VI, 643
Walpole, Horace. . . . . IV, 322
Walton, Isaac . . . . II, 348
Warner, Charles Dudley . . VIII, 443
Warner, William. . . . . I, 437
Washington, George. . . . . IV, 360
Webster, John. . . . . I, 676
White, Richard Grant . . . . . VII, 578
Whitman, Walt . . . . VIII, 139
Whittier, John Greenleaf. VIII, 119
Willis, Nathaniel Parker . . . . VI, 492
Wordsworth, William . . . . V, 633
WHISHAW, JOHN,
Park, Mungo . . . . IV, 484, 485
WHISTLER, J. M'NEILL,
Ruskin, John . . . . VIII, 415
Taylor, Tom . . . . VII, 214
WHISTON, WILLIAM,
Berkeley, George . . . . III, 324
Clarke, Samuel . . . . II, 748
Newton, Sir Isaac. . . . . II, 719
WHITAKER, JOHN,
Buchanan, George. . . . . I, 316
Knox, John. . . . . I, 296
Robertson, William . . . . IV, 162
WHITAKER, THOMAS DUNHAM,
Gibbon, Edmard . . . . IV, 193
Hurd, Richard . . . . IV, 519
Langland, William. . . . . I, 116
Warburton, William . . III, 685, 686
WHITBY, OLIVER,
Chillingworth, William . . . . . II, 84
WHITE, ANDREW DICKSON,
Milman, Henry Hart . . VI, 536, 539
Scott, Sir Walter . . . . V, 144
Silliman, Benjamin . . . . VI, 408
WHITE, CAROLINA LOUISA,
Ælfric . . . . I, 45, 47
WHITE, GILBERT,
Collins, William . . . . III, 414
Johnson, Samuel. . . . . III, 747
Ray John . . . . II, 542
White, Gilbert . . . . IV, 147
WHITE, GLEESON.
Lamb, Charles . . . . V, 243
WHITE, GREENOUGH,
Arnold, Matthew . . . . VII, 641
Caxton, William. . . . . I, 200
Clough, Arthur Hugh . . . . . . VI, 256
Cynewulf . . . . I, 31
Freneau, Philip. . . . . V, 188
Gower, John . . . . I, 177
Hawes, Stephen . . . . I, 218
Irving, Washington . . . . VI, 151
James I. of Scotland. . . . . I, 181
Jay, John. . . . . V, 97
Lanier, Sidney . . . . VII, 329
Layamon . . . . I, 66
Lyndsay, Sir David . . . . I, 276
Morris, William . . . . VIII, 332
Poe, Edgar Allan . . . . V, 548
Wyclif, John . . . . I, 111
WHITE, HENRY KIRKE,
Bloomfield, Robert . . . . IV, 724
Butler, Joseph. . . . . III, 310
Donne, John . . . . I, 714
Drummond, William . . . . II, 105
Knowledge . . . . V, 7
Moore, Thomas . . . . V, 714
Otway, Thomas . . . . II, 366
Sidney, Sir Philip . . . . I, 327
Southey, Robert . . . . V, 403
Tillotson, John Robert. . . . . . II, 439
Warton, Thomas . . . . VI, 76
White, Henry Kirke . . . . IV, 487
WHITE, HORACE,
Lincoln, Abraham . . . . VI, 416
WHITE, REV. JAMES,
Thackeray, William Makepeace.
. . . . VI, 290
WHITE, RICHARD GRANT,
Browning, Robert . . . . VII, 704
Chaucer, Geoffrey. . . . . I, 163
Dickens, Charles. . . . . . . VI, 562, 577
Disraeli, Benjamin . . . . VII, 289
Dryden, John . . . . II, 486
Johnson, Samuel. . . . . III, 747
Layamon . . . . I, 66
Lyly, John. . . . . I, 425
Malone, Edmond . . . . IV, 578
Müller, Friedrich Max . . . . VIII, 438
Ormin . . . . I, 71
Peale, George . . . . I, 366
Pope, Alexander. . . . . III. 171
Seward, William Henry. . . . . VI, 672
Shakespeare, William . . . .
. . . . I, 525, 535, 566
Sheridan, Richard Brinsley. . IV, 607
Steevens, George . . . . IV, 410
Theobald, Lewis . . . . III, 142
Tooke, John Horne . . . . IV, 572
Warburton, William . . . . . . III, 687
Washington, George . . . . IV, 360
Whipple, Edwin Percy . . . . VII, 596
WHITE, ROBERT MEADOWS,
Ormin . . . . I, 70
WHITE, SALLIE JOY,
Edwards, Amelia Blandford . .
. . . . VIII, 175, 176
WHITE, THOMAS,
White, Gilbert . . . . IV, 149
WHITE, WILLIAM,
Johnson, Samuel. . . . . III, 727

Vol. and Page	**Vol. and Page**	**Vol. and Page**
WHITEFIELD, GEORGE,	Milton, John..............II, 295	Tannahill, Robert.........IV, 549
Edwards, Jonathan.......III, 380	Price, Richard...........IV, 135	Thackeray, William Makepeace
Law, William............III, 427	Reid, Thomas............IV, 287	....................VI, 312
Wesley, John.............IV, 111	Shelley, Percy Bysshe.....IV, 712	WHYTE, WILLIAM,
WHITEFOOT, REV. JOHN,	WHITTIER, ELIZABETH H.,	Lytton, Edward Robert Bulwer
Browne, Sir Thomas.......II 339	Adams, John Quincy ....V, 516	....................VIII, 48
WHITEFOOTE, JOHN,	Kane, Elisha Kent.........VI, 80	WICKES, W. K.,
Hall Joseph..............II, 144	WHITTIER, JOHN GREENLEAF,	Carlyle, Thomas.........VII, 241
WHITEHEAD, CHARLES,	Adams, John Quincy........V, 519	Lanier, Sidney...........VII, 330
Marryat, Frederick.........V, 532	Agassiz, Louis Jean Rodolphe.	WICKINS, NICOLAS,
WHITEHEAD, JOHN,	....................VI, 723	Newton, Sir Isaac.........II, 712
Wesley, Charles..........IV, 34	Baxter, Richard......II, 424, 427	WICKSTEED, CHARLES,
Wesley, John.IV, 113, 119, 121, 126	Beecher, Henry Ward.VII, 600, 602	Martineau, James.......VIII, 425
WHITEHEAD, WILLIAM,	Browning, Robert.......VII, 693	WIFFEN BROTHERS,
Whitehead, William.......III, 21	Bryant, William Cullen...VII, 119	Wordsworth, William.......V, 606
WHITELAW, ALEXANDER,	Bunyan, John.............II, 395	WIGHT, O. W.,
Fergusson, Robert........III, 640	Burns, Robert............IV, 265	Hamilton, Sir William.....VI, 54
WHITELOCK, WILLIAM,	Cary, Alice...........VI, 638, 639	WIKOFF, HENRY,
Jay, John..................V, 96	Cary, Phœbe.............VI, 640	Willis, Nathaniel Parker...VI, 488
WHITING, CHARLES G.,	Channing, William Ellery....	WILBERFORCE, REGINALD G.,
Longfellow, Henry Wadsworth	.... V, 368, 373	Manning, Henry Edward....
....................VII, 408	Child, Lydia Maria.......VII, 219	.... VIII, 169
WHITING H.,	Dana, Richar Henry.....VII, 154	WILBERFORCE, ROBERT ISAAC,
Schoolcraft, Henry Rowe...VI, 403	Dodge, Mary Abigail....VIII, 361	AND SAMUEL,
WHITING, LILIAN,	Elliott, Ebenezer..........V, 582	Wilberforce, William........V, 201
Alcott, Louisa May.......VII, 668	Ellwood, Thomas..........II, 575	WILBERFORCE, SAMUEL,
Browning, Elizabeth Barrett..	Fields, James Thomas.....VII, 340	Darwin, Charles Robert....VII, 423
....................VI, 237, 247	Garrison, William Lloyd...VII, 157	Keble, John......VI, 457, 457, 464
WHITING, MARGARET CHRIS-	Halleck, Fitz-Gerald,......VI, 500	Newman, John Henry....VII, 744
TINE,	Holland, Josiah Gilbert...VII, 335	WILBERFORCE, WILF ID,
Pepys, Samuel ....II, 513	Holmes, Oliver Wendell.....	Newman, John Henry....VII, 754
WHITMAN, C. M.,	.... VIII, 291, 295	Ward, William George....VII, 483
Beecher, Henry Ward.....VII, 605	Hopkins, Samuel.........IV, 439	WILBERFORCE, WILLIAM,
Calhoun, John Caldwell .....V, 677	King, Thomas Starr.......VI, 408	Franklin, Benjamin.......IV, 84
Henry, Patrick...........IV, 352	Kingsley, Charles.........VII, 20	Irving, Edward...........V, 245
Phillips, Wendell ....VII, 555	Knowledge ....V, 9	Paine, Thomas...........IV, 537
Webster, Daniel............V, 729	Lazarus, Emma..........VII, 611	Scott, Sir Walter..........V, 155
WHITMAN, SARAH HELEN,	Longfellow, Henry Wadsworth	WILDE, SIR WILLIAM R.,
Poe, Edgar Allan.......V, 537, 546	.... VII, 405	Swift, Jonathan..........III, 201
WHITMAN, WALT,	Lowell, James Russell...VIII, 29	WILDER, B. G.,
Bryant, William Cullen.......	Marvell, Andrew......II, 314, 315	Combe, George...........VI, 89
...............VII, 111, 124	Milton, John.............II, 249	WILFORD, JOHN,
Burns, Robert............IV, 262	Poe, Edgar Allan..........V, 557	Sanderson, Robert.........II, 179
Carlyle, Thomas..........VII, 267	Sewall, Samuel...........III, 17	Tillotson, John Robert......II, 437
Emerson, Ralph Waldo...III, 355	Stowe, Harriet Beecher...VIII, 352	WILKES, GEORGE,
Lincoln, Abraham.........VI, 413	Sumner, Charles.....VI, 751, 753	Shakespeare, William......I, 544
Longfellow, Henry Wadsworth.	Taylor, Bayard......VII, 128, 135	WILKES, JOHN,
....................VII, 410	Walton, Isaac............II, 346	Churchill, Charles.........III, 478
Poe, Edgar Allan..........V, 542	Whipple, Edwin Percy....VII, 596	Johnson, Samuel.........III, 720
Shakespeare, William ......I, 572	Whittier, John Greenleaf..VIII, 112	WILKIN, SIMON,
Tennyson, Alfred Lord......	Woolman, John..........III, 598	Browne, Sir Thomas.......II, 340
...............VIII, 70, 95	Wordsworth, William......V, 636	WILKINSON, WILLIAM
Whitman, Walt ....VIII, 135	WHYTE, ALEXANDER,	CLEAVER,
Whittier, John Greenleaf.VIII, 123	Newman, John Henry.....VII, 748	Eliot, George..VII, 181, 191, 200
WHITMORE, W. H.,	WHYTE, WALT R,	Lowell, James Russell...VIII, 37
Hutchinson, Thomas......III, 707	Aytoun, Willia Edmondstoune	Martineau, James.......VIII, 426
Praed, Winthrop Mackworth.V, 332	.... VI, 446	Webster, Daniel...........V, 722
Prince, Thomas..........III, 401	Baillie, Joanna............V, 695	WILLARD, CHARLOTTE R.,
Sewall, Samuel...........III, 18	Barham, Richard Harris....V, 476	Proctor, Richard Anthony....
WHITNEY, ERNEST,	Blackie, John Stuart.....VIII, 306	.... VII, 660, 661
Barlow, Joel.............IV, 576	Calverley, Charles Stuart....	WILLARD, FRANCES E.,
WHITNEY, WILLIAM DWIGHT,	.... VII, 542, 544	Stowe, Harriet Beecher..VIII, 350
Müller, Friedrich Max....VIII, 437	Canning, George..........V, 69	WILLARD, MABEL CALDWELL,
WHITTAKER, THOMAS,	Frere, John Hookham.......V, 488	Lowell, James Russell...VIII, 33
Bentham, Jeremy..........V, 169	Hogg, James..............V, 269	WILLARD, S.,
Buckle, Henry Thomas....VI, 284	Landor, Walter Savage.VI, 380, 383	Adams, Hannah...........V, 125
Butler, Joseph............III, 318	Lytton, Sir Edward George	Dwight, Timothy.........IV, 627
Harvey, William...........II, 167	Bulwer ....VI, 690, 692	WILLETT, B. W.,
Hobbes, Thomas..........II, 328	Planché, James Robinson..VII, 217	Gaskell, Elizabeth Cleghorn.VI, 432
Jevons, William Stanley...VII, 492	Smith, Horace............V, 598	WILLIAM OF MALMESBURY,
Locke, John..............II, 529	Smith, James.............V, 339	Alcuin ....I, 32

INDEX TO CRITICISMS

Vol. and Page	Vol. and Page	Vol. and Page
Bede.....................I, 28	Bryant, William Cullen....VII,122	Baillie, Joanna.........V, 690, 692
Erigena, John Scotus........I, 34	Disraeli, Benjamin.........VII, 276	Bowles, William Lislie......V, 661
Lanfranc ....I, 48	Emerson, Ralph Waldo....VII, 344	Brougham, Henry Lord....VI, 524
WILLIAM OF NEWBURY,	Halleck, Fitz-Greene......VI, 494	Bryant, William Cullen............
Geoffrey of Monmouth......I, 55	Lamb, Mary Ann..........V, 507	..................VII, 116, 120
WILLIAMS, ALFRED M.,	Lover, Samuel.......VI, 543, 545	Bunyan, John.............II, 389
Banim, John..............V, 391	Lytton, Sir Edward George	Burns, Robert..IV, 238, 244, 254
Brontë, Emily.............V, 524	Bulwer ....VI, 679	Byron, George Gordon Lord.IV, 744
Griffin, Gerald............V, 354	Moore, Thomas............V, 707	Campbell, Thomas..........V, 434
Maccarthy, Denis Florence.VII, 490	Morris, George Pope.......VI, 401	Chaucer, Geoffrey........I, 138, 143
Mahony, Francis.........VI, 484	Norton, Caroline Elizabeth	Churchill, Charles........III, 479
Mangan, James Clarence.....V, 603	Sheridan ....VII, 101	Clare, John...............VI, 398
Oliphant, Carolina....V, 477, 479	Poe, Edgar Allan.....V, 536, 551	Cowper, William..........IV, 387
Pope, Alexander..........III, 194	Procter, Adelaide Anne....VI, 394	Crabbe, George............V, 172
WILLIAMS, EDWARD,	Wordsworth, William......V, 608	Croker, John Wilson......VI, 75
Baxter, Richard..........II. 426	WILLMOTT, ROBERT ARIS,	Cunningham, Allan.........V, 384
Cruden, Alexander.......III, 546	Bowles, William Lisle......V, 658	Davy, Sir Humphry.........V, 93
Edwards, Jonathan.......III, 389	Herbert, George............I, 723	Dickens, Charles..........VI, 551
Hopkins, Samuel..........IV, 439	Pope, Alexander..........III, 187	Dryden, John...II, 472, 476, 500
Horne, George............IV, 144	WILMER, L. A.,	Elliott, Ebenezer...........V, 580
Horsley, Samuel..........IV, 495	Poe, Edgar Allan..........V, 535	Frere, John Hookham......V, 486
Howe, John...............II, 545	WILSON, ARTHUR,	Galt, John................V, 336
Hume, David............III, 661	Bacon, Francis.............I,640	Gay, John................III, 61
Leighton, Robert..........II, 359	WILSON, DANIEL,	Grahame, James......IV, 566, 567
Leland, John.............III, 500	Chambers, Robert........VI, 619	Hazlitt, William..........V, 102
Lowth, Robert............IV, 28	Chatterton, Thomas...III, 532, 537	Heber, Reginald............V, 37
Secker, Thomas..........III, 522	Drummond, William.......II, 101	Hemans, Felicia Dorothea...V, 257
Taylor, Jeremy...........II, 207	Ramsay, Allan...........III, 403	Hogg, James..............V, 266
Tillotson, John Robert......II, 439	WILSON, DAVID,	Home, John..........IV, 514, 515
Toplady, Augustus Montague..	Carlyle, Thomas.........VII,259	Hood, Thomas............V, 461
.... III, 681	Froude, James Anthony..VIII, 267	Hook, Theodore Edward....V, 357
Wilberforce, William........V, 202	WILSON, FRANCIS,	James, George Payne Rains-
WILLIAMS, FOLKESTONE,	Field, Eugene..........VIII, 315	ford ....VI, 218
Anselm ....I, 50	WILSON, H. SCHÜTZ,	Jameson, Anna.......VI, 213, 214
Atterbury, Francis........III, 65	Massinger, Philip......II, 45, 53	Jeffrey, Francis Lord..V, 649, 653
Pope, Alexander..........III, 173	WILSON, JAMES GRANT,	Johnson, Samuel..III, 738, 745, 749
WILLIAMS, FRANCIS HOWARD,	Adams, John..............V, 53	Lamb, Charles.............V, 239
Whitman, Walt.. .....VIII, 144	Audubon, John James......V, 698	Landon, Letitia Elizabeth...V, 327
WILLIAMS, GILLY,	Barbour, John.............I, 115	Lowell, James Russell....VIII, 36
Walpole, Horace..........IV, 316	Bryant, William Cullen... VII, 113	Lytton, Sir Edward George
WILLIAMS, HENRY SMITH,	Carlyle, Thomas.........VII, 233	Bulwer ....VI, 694
Faraday, Michael..........VI, 515	Chambers, Robert,VI, 620, 621, 621	Macaulay, Thomas Babington
Lyell, Sir Charles.........VII, 38	Cooper, James Fenimore......	Lord.........VI, 97, 101, 109
WILLIAMS, HOWARD,	.... V, 681, 686	Mackenzie, Sir George.....II, 429
Dennis, John........ III, 78	Drake, Joseph Rodman....IV, 660	Mackenzie, Henry....V, 115, 115
WILLIAMS, ISAAC	Halleck, Fitz-Greene.........	Macpherson, James.......IV, 276
Pusey, Edward Bouverie...VII, 467	.... VI, 495, 496, 497	Marryat, Frederick.........V, 531
WILLIAMS, JANE,	Hillhouse, James Abraham...V, 363	Milman, Henry Hart......VI, 540
Behn, Aphra..............II, 410	Hogg, James .... V, 265, 267	Milton, John..............II, 270
Carter, Elizabeth..........IV, 493	Irving, Washington......VI, 136	Mitford, Mary Russell..VI, 45, 47
Cockburn, Catherine...... III, 276	James I. of Scotland ....I, 181	Moir, David Macbeth.....IV, 705
Manley, Mrs. Mary de la	Knox, William..............V, 31	Montgomery, James........V, 767
Riviere ....II, 694	Longfellow, Henry Wadsworth	Moore, Thomas......V, 710, 715
Rowe, Elizabeth..........III, 96	.... VII, 412	Motherwell, William........V, 277
Smith, Charlotte..........IV, 498	Maitland, Sir Richard........I, 333	Napier, Sir William Francis
WILLIAMS, ROWLAND,	Mickle, William Julius..... IV, 42	Patrick .... VI, 222
Hare, Julius Charles.......VI 49	Morris, George Pope.......VI, 402	Norton, Caroline E. S.....VII, 103
Keble, John..............VI, 458	Paulding, James Kirke....VI 226	Parr, Samuel...............V, 19
Seeley, Sir John Robert..VIII, 308	Pierpont, John...........VI, 482	Pollok, Robert.............V, 72
Whately, Richard........VI, 324	Poe, Edgar Allan..........V, 538	Pope, Alexander..III, 155, 159, 176
WILLIAMS, W. MATHEW,	Ramsay, Allan...........III, 403	Procter, Bryan Waller.....VI, 747
Rumford, Count..........IV, 593	Simms, William Gilmore..VII, 597	Ramsay, Allan...........III, 406
WILLIAMS, W.,	Smollett, Tobias George....III, 589	Reynolds, Sir Joshua......IV, 142
Spurgeon, Charles Haddon,..	Tannahill, Robert.....IV, 548, 549	Scott, Michael.............V, 279
.... VIII, 181	Taylor, Bayard.........VII, 131	Scott, Sir Walter..........V, 153
WILLIAMSON, HUGH,	Watts, Isaac............III, 253	Shakespeare, William......I, 556
Franklin, Benjamin.......IV, 80	White, Richard Grant....VII, 577	Shelley, Percy Bysshe.....IV, 705
WILLIS, NATHANIEL PARKER,	Willis, Nathaniel Parker...VI, 488	Smith, Sidney............V, 467
Adams, John Quincy.......V, 515	WILSON, JOHN,	Southey, Robert...........V, 404
Benton, Thomas Fart.....VI. 86	Addison, Joseph..........II, 650	Spenser, Edmund.I, 376, 388, 391
Blessington, Countess of....V, 590	Audubon, John James......V, 696	Tennyson, Alfred Lord...VIII, 77

INDEX TO CRITICISMS

	Vol. and Page
Thomson, James	III, 259
Tucker, Abraham	III, 643
Tupper, Martin Farquhar	VII, 733
Warton, Thomas	IV, 74, 78
Wordsworth, William	V, 608, 621, 623, 631

WILSON, RICHARD GRANT,
Dana, Richard Henry.....VII, 153

WILSON, ROBERT BURNS,
Keats, Jon................IV, 680
Poe, Edgar Allan..........V, 546

WILSON, S. LAW,
Carlyle, Thomas.........VII, 244
Clough, Arthur Hugh......VI, 256
Eliot, George............VII, 208
Emerson, Ralph Waldo...VII, 378

WILSON, THOMAS,
Law, William.............III, 426

WILSON WALTER,
Defoe, Daniel....III, 24, 29, 41, 42

WILSON, WOODROW,
Authors and Authorship..VIII, 9
Bagehot, Walter.........VII, 100
Burke, Edmund...........IV, 293
Carlyle, Thomas.........VII, 274
Franklin Benjamin........IV, 92
Gibbon, Edward...........IV, 190
Hamilton, Alexander.....IV, 465
Jefferson, Thomas.........V, 49
Lowell, James Russell...VIII, 40
Macaulay, Thomas Babington Lord ....VI, 108
Maine, Sir Henry James Sumner ....VII, 651, 654
Smith, Adam..........IV, 56, 57
Washington George......IV, 365

WILTON, RICHARD,
Turner, Charles Tennyson.VII, 161

WINCHESTER, CALEB THOMAS,
Addison, Joseph.........II, 661
Burns, Robert...........IV, 270
Byron, George Gordon Lord.IV, 766
Literature ....I, 10
Lowell, James Russell...VIII, 38
Pope, Alexander........III, 195
Swift, Jonathan........III, 238
Tennyson, Alfred Lord..VIII, 86
Wordsworth, William......V, 647

WINDHAM, WILLIAM,
Johnson, Samuel.........III, 722
Montagu, Elizabeth......IV, 402
Paley, William..........IV, 476

WINKS, WILLIAM EDWARD,
Bloomfield, Robert......IV, 724
Gifford, William..........V, 35
Whittier, John Greenleaf.VIII, 113

WINNECKE, A.,
Airy, Sir George Biddell..VIII, 183

WINSHIP, ALBERT EDWARD,
Hopkins, Mark......VII, 614, 616
Mann, Horace............VI, 202

WINSLOW, WILLIAM C.,
Edwards, Amelia Blandford..
.... VIII, 176, 177

WINSOR, JUSTIN,
Mather, Cotton..........II, 731
Parkman, Francis.......VIII, 223

WINSTANLEY, WILLIAM,
Fuller, Thomas..........III, 171
Herrick, Robert.........II, 237
L'Estrange, Sir Roger....II, 538

	Vol. and Page
Milton, John	II, 284

WINTER, WILLIAM,
Curtis, George William..........
.................VIII, 185, 191
Holmes, Oliver Wendell..VIII, 291
Irving, Washington.......VI, 142
Longfellow, Henry Wadsworth...
..................VII, 382, 408
Lytton, Sir Edward George Bulwer ....VI, 690
Poe, Edgar Allan..........V, 557
Shakespeare, William......I, 470
Sheridan, Richard Brinsley.IV, 608

WINTHROP, ROBERT C.,
Adams, John..............V, 51
Adams, John Quincy....V, 515, 520
Bryant, William Cullen....VII, 111
Choate, Rufus............VI, 196
Everett, Edward ....VI, 424
Franklin, Benjamin....IV, 95, 101
Jefferson, Thomas.........V, 43
Kennedy, John Pendleton..VI, 605
Longfellow, Henry Wadsworth.
..................VII 382
Mather, Cotton ....II, 730
Prescott, William Hickling..VI, 191
Quincy, Josiah..........VI, 405
Raleigh, Sir Walter ....I, 596
Rumford, Count ....IV, 592
Seward, William Henry ...VI, 673
Sparks, Jared...........IV, 478
Sumner, Charles.........VI, 757
Webster, Daniel......V, 726, 728
Winthrop, John ....II, 109

WINTHROP, W.,
Tennyson, Frederick.....VIII, 401

WIRT, WILLIAM,
Henry, Patrick...........IV, 349
Jefferson, Thomas.........V, 41
Marshall, John...........V, 281
Monroe, James...........V, 122

WISEMAN, NICHOLAS PATRICK STEPHEN,
Longfellow, Henry Wadsworth.
...................VII, 404
Shakespeare, William .....I, 505

WITHER, GEORGE,
Browne, William ....II, 73

WITHROW, W. H.,
Wesley, John............IV, 118

WODROW, ROBERT,
Fletcher, Ahdrew........II, 610

WOLCOT, JOHN (PETER PINDAR),
Boswell, James..........IV, 213
Bruce, James...........IV, 207
Hawkins, Sir John........IV, 50
Johnson, Samuel........III, 171
Knowledge...............V, 7
Robinson, Mary.........IV, 411
Rumford, Count ....IV, 590

WOLF, FRIED. AUGUST,
Bentley, Richard........III, 121

WOLFE, THEODORE F.,
Brontë, Charlotte........VI, 19
Burns, Robert...........IV, 239
Cary, Alice............VI, 638
Curtis, George William...VIII, 186
Drake, Joseph Rodman ....IV, 660
Hawthorne, Nathaniel....VI, 348
Lowell, James Russell....III, 23

	Vol. and Page
Poe, Edgar Allan	V, 545
Sterne, Laurence	III, 504
Stockton, Francis Richard	
	VIII, 473
Thoreau, Henry David	VI, 270
Ticknor, George	VI, 615

WOOD, ANTHONY,
Abbot, George ....I, 726
Ashmole, Elias............II, 436
Baker, Sir Richard......II, 93, 93
Beaumont, Sir John........I, 680
Browne, William.......II, 72, 74
Burton, Robert........II, 37, 38
Butler, Samuel..........II, 330
Carew, Thomas......II, 20, 21
Cartwright, William.......II, 70
Chapman, George......I, 727, 728
Chillingworth, William.....II, 85
Churchyard, Thomas......I, 417
Colet, John.............I, 211
Corbet, Richard.........I, 743
Daniel, Samuel..........I, 611
D'Avenant, Sir William...II, 217
Denham, Sir John........II, 220
Edwards, Richard.......I, 287
Fletcher, Giles...........I, 623
Greene, Robert..........I, 344
Habington, William......II, 136
Hales, John............II, 149
Hawes, Stephen.........I, 216
Herbert, Edward Lord.....II, 95
Herrick, Robert.........II, 237
Heylin, Peter..........II, 174
Jewell, John...........I, 293
King, Henry...........II, 223
Laud, William..........II, 89
Locke, John...........II, 519
Lovelace, Richard ....
.................II, 160, 161
Lyly, John.............I, 426
Massinger, Philip.......II, 41
Nashe, Thomas.........II, 413
Owen, John............II, 352
Peele, George..........I, 365
Prynne, William........II, 224
Purchas, Samuel.........I, 693
Sackville, Charles.......II, 553
Sanderson, Robert......II, 179
Sandys, George.........II, 81
Savile, Sir Henry ....I, 620
Sprat, Thomas.........II, 573
Sternhold, Thomas.......I, 261
Sylvester, Joshua........I, 609
Taylor, Jeremy ....
................II, 203, 206
Vaughan, Henry.........II, 441
Wilkins, John..........II, 227
Wilmot, John..........II, 338
Wilson, Arthur.........II, 129
Wotton, Sir Henry......II, 17

WOOD, ESTHER,
Rossetti, Gabriel Charles Dante
...............VII, 445, 447

WOOD, HENRY,
Beddoes, Thomas Lovell.....V, 588

WOOD, JOHN,
Pepys, Samuel ....II, 512

WOOD, J. G.,
White, Gilbert..........IV, 147

WOODALL, EDWARD,
Darwin, Charles Robert...VII, 419

	Vol. and Page		Vol. and Page		Vol. and Page
WOODBERRY, GEORGE EDWARD,		Wordsworth, William	V, 610	Flamsteed, John	II, 663
		WORDSWORTH, DOROTHY.		Tillotson, John Robert	II, 439
Addison, Joseph	II, 639	Burns, Robert	IV, 223	Usher, James	II, 153
Arnold, Matthew	VII, 645	Coleridge, Samuel Taylor	V, 206	WRAXALL, SIR NATHANIEL WILLIAM,	
Browning, Robert	VII, 689	Scott, Sir Walter	V, 126		
Bunyan, John	II, 398	Wordsworth, William	V, 605	Fielding, Henry	III, 341
Channing, William Ellery	V, 370, 375	WORDSWORTH, ELIZABETH,		Francis, Sir Philip	IV, 637
		Wordsworth, William	V, 644	Johnson, Samuel	III, 723
Coleridge, Samuel Taylor	V, 217	WORDSWORTH, WILLIAM,		Montagu, Elizabeth	IV, 399
Congreve, William	II, 735, 744	Alfred the Great	I, 38	Sheridan, Richard Brinsley	IV, 599
Cowper, William	IV, 384, 393	Beaumont, Francis	I, 586	WRIGHT, C.,	
Crabbe, George	V, 176	Bentley, Richard	III, 116	McCosh, James	VIII, 301
Darwin, Charles Robert	VII, 420	Books	III, 8	WRIGHT, CHAUNCEY,	
Dobell, Sydney Thompson	VI, 765	Burns, Robert	IV, 250, 251	Mansel, Henry Longueville,	VI, 628
FitzGerald, Edward	VII, 517, 521	Byron, George Gordon Lord	IV, 757		
Griswold, Rufus Wilmot	VI, 77, 79	Chaucer, Geoffrey	I, 158	Mill, John Stuart	VI, 708, 715
Hawthorne, Nathaniel	VI, 350, 352, 356	Chatterton, Thomas	III, 529	WRIGHT, G. FREDERICK,	
		Coleridge, Hartley	V, 572	Gray, Asa	VII, 671
Lamb, Charles	V, 244	Coleridge, Samuel Taylor	V 206	WRIGHT, G. N.,	
Landor, Walter Savage	VI, 383, 391	Coleridge, Sara	V, 733	Berkeley, George	III, 330
Longfellow, Henry Wadsworht.	VII 411	Collins, William	III, 415	WRIGHT, J. C.,	
		Cotton, Charles	II, 371	Tate, Nahum	II, 590
Lowell, James Russell	VIII, 19, 39	Cranmer, Thomas	I, 271	Whitehead, William	IV, 23
Miller, Cincinnatus Hiner	VIII, 500	Dryden, John	II, 487, 498	WRIGHT, J. M. F.,	
Poe, Edgar Allan	V, 544, 555	Dunstan	I, 43	Newton, Sir Isaac	II, 719
Shelley, Percy Bysshe	IV, 699, 703, 704, 715	Dyer, John	III, 399	WRIGHT, O. W.,	
		Finch, Anne Countess of Winchilsea	II, 668	DeQuincey, Thomas	VI, 121
Stevenson, Robert Louis	VIII, 247			WRIGHT, SAMUEL,	
Symonds, John Addington	VIII 203	Gray, Thomas	III, 565	Defoe, Daniel	III, 31
Walpole, Horace	IV, 320	Hemans, Felicia Dorothea	V, 255, 256	WRIGHT, THOMAS,	
Whittier, John Greenleaf	VIII, 118, 125			Ælfric	I, 46
		Hogg, James	V, 263	Alcuin	I, 33
WOODBURY, CHARLES J.,		Jewell, John	I, 293	Aldhelm	I, 24
Emerson, Ralph Waldo	VII, 352, 374	Lamb, Charles	V, 230	Anselm	I, 49
		Laud, William	II 90	Arbuthnot, John	III, 83
WOODFALL, WILLIAM,		Macpherson, James	IV, 274, 275, 276	Asser	I, 42
Wesley, John	IV, 113			Cædmon	I, 22
WOODHOUSE, RICHARD		Milton, John	II, 245 272, 286	Cambrensis	I, 67
DeQuincey, Thomas	VI, 116	Percy, Thomas	IV, 565	Chaucer, Geoffrey	I, 143
WOODHOUSELEE, LORD,		Poets and Poetry	IV, 8	Cowper, William	IV, 374, 376
Tennant, William	V, 527	Pope, Alexander	III 165, 186	Defoe, Daniel	III, 27, 31, 42
WOODMAN H.,		Ridley, Nicholas	I, 266	Dunbar, William	I, 224
Choate, Rufus	VI, 198	Sacheverell, Henry	II, 696	Dunstan	I, 44
WOODS, GEORGE BRYANT,		Scott, Sir Walter	V, 128, 135, 157	Eadmer	I, 52
Philips, Wendell	VII, 555	Shakespeare, William	I, 457, 511	Geoffrey of Monmouth	I, 56
WOODWARD, A. SMITH,		Shelley, Percy Bysshe	IV, 705	Hawes, Stephen	I, 218
Huxley, Thomas Henry	VIII, 326	Smith, Charlotte	IV, 497	Henry of Huntingdon	I, 58
WOOLL, JOHN,		Southey, Robert	V, 398	History	VI, 8
Warton, Joseph	IV, 395, 397	Spenser, Edmund	I, 395	Hoveden, Roger De	I, 63
WOOLSEY, SARAH CHAUNCEY,		Tennyson, Alfred Lord	VIII, 65	John of Salisbury	I, 59
Burney, Frances	V, 344	Thomson, James	III, 267	Langland, William	I, 119, 123
WOOLSEY, THEODORE DWIGHT,		Walpole, Horace	IV, 312	Mandeville, Sir John	I, 96
Silliman, Benjamin	VI, 406	Walton, Isaac	II, 348	Map, Walter	I, 61
WOOLSON, ABBA GOOLD,		Wordsworth, William	V, 618, 628	Tyrwhitt, Thomas	IV, 25
Eliot, George	VII, 204	Wyclif, John	I, 100	William of Malmesbury	I, 53
WOOLSON, CONSTANCE FENIMORE,		WORMAN, J. H.,		WRIGHT, WILLIAM,	
		Macknight, James	IV, 407	Brontë, Charlotte	VI, 19
Cooper, James Fenimore	V, 685	WORSFOLD, W. BASIL,		WRIGHT, WILLIAM ALDIS,	
WORDE, WYNKYN DE,		Addison, Joseph	II, 653	Fitz-Gerald, Edward	VII, 514
Chaucer, Geoffrey	I, 134	Arnold, Matthew	VII, 641	Robert of Gloucester	I, 81
Mandeville, Sir John	I, 95	Critic, The	II, 10	WROTH, WARWICK,	
WORDSWORTH, CHARLES,		Rossetti, Gabriel Charles Dante	VII, 454	Orme, Robert	IV, 414
Andrews, Lancelot	I, 637			Palgrave, Sir Francis	VI, 265
Doyle, Sir Francis Hastings Charles	VII, 649	WORTLEY-STUART, JANE,		WYATT AND LOW,	
		Besant, Sir Walter	VIII, 450	Capgrave, John	I, 193
Shakespeare, William	I, 566	WOTTON, SIR HENRY,		Wilson, Sir Thomas	I, 313
Tennyson, Alfred Lord	VIII, 77	Bacon, Francis	I, 638, 653	WYCHERLEY, WILLIAM,	
Trench, Richard Chevenix	VII, 589	Milton, John	II, 251	Pope, Alexander	III, 156
WORDSWORTH, CHRISTOPHER,		Shakespeare, William	I, 539	Steele, Sir Richard	II, 757
Foxe, John	I, 365	WOTTON, WILLIAM,		WYLE, JAMES HAMILTON,	
		Evelyn, John	II, 549	Wyclif John	I, 109

INDEX TO CRITICISMS

WYLIE, LAURA JOHNSON.
Coleridge, Samuel Taylor....V, 226
Pope, Alexander..........III, 194
Sidney, Sir Philip...........I, 330
WYLIE, WILLIAM HOWIE,
Carlyle, Thomas..........VII, 256
WYNDHAM, HENRY PENRUD-DOCKE,
Dodington, George Bubb..III, 459
WYNDHAM, GEORGE,
Ruskin, John...........VIII, 424
Shakespeare, William........I, 457
WYNNE, JAMES,
Bancroft, George........VIII, 55
Edwards, Jonathan........III, 390
Kennedy, John Pendleton....
....................VI, 605, 605
Marshall, John............V, 285
Silliman, Benjamin........VI, 406
WYNTOUN, ANDREW,
Wyntoun, Andrew..........I, 178
WYON, FREDERICK WILLIAM,
Atterbury, Francis......III, 66
Burnet, Gilbert............II, 596
Defoe, Daniel............III, 48
Oldmixon, John..........III, 125
Manley, Mrs. Mary de la Riviere.................II, 694
Swift, Jonathan..........III, 216

YARNALL, ELLIS,
Wordsworth, William..V, 611
YATES, EDMUND,
Dickens, Charles..........VI, 557
Thackeray, William Makepeace
.............VI, 291, 311, 314
YEATMAN, JOHN PYM,
Asser...................I, 42
Saxon Chronicle............I, 57
YEATS, WILLIAM BUTLER,
Allingham, William......VII, 735
Blake, William.............V, 63
Morris, William........VIII, 339
YEOWELL, JAMES,
Wyatt, Sir Thomas.........I, 250
YONGE, CHARLES DUKE,
Burns, Robert............IV, 244
Cooper, James Fenimore....V, 684
Dickens, Charles..........VI, 586
Dryden, John........II, 485, 488
Goldsmith, Oliver.........III, 623
Grote, George............VI, 609
Hume, David............III, 659
Lamb, Charles............V, 240
Milman, Henry Hart.......VI, 538
Napier, Gen. Sir William Francis Patr'ck............VI, 222
Prescott, William Hickling...
....VI, 184

Sheridan, Richard Brinsley.IV, 604
Thackeray, William Makepeace
..................VI, 302, 309
YONGE, CHARLOTTE M.,
Austen, Jane............IV, 618
Fullerton, Georgiana Charlotte
Lady............VII, 567, 568
Heber, Reginald..........V, 39
More, Hannah.............V, 192
YORKE, CHARLES,
Swift, Jonathan..........III, 198
YOUMANS, EDWARD LIVINGSTON,
Spencer, Herbert........VIII, 480
YOUMANS, ELIZA ANN,
Combe, George............VI, 90
Tyndall, John..........VIII, 200
YOUMANS, WILLIAM JAY,
Franklin, Benjamin.......IV, 104
Schoolcraft, Henry Rowe..VI, 402
Wilson, Alexander........IV, 585
YOUNG, ALEXANDER,
O'Reilly, John Boyle....VII, 768
Parkman, Francis......VIII, 218
Stephen, Sir Leslie......VIII, 510
YOUNG, ARCHIBALD,
Buckland, Francis Trevelyan..
....................VII, 210, 212
YOUNG, ARTHUR,
Boswell, James..........IV, 209
Burke, Edmund..........IV, 300
Burney, Charles..........IV, 588
Gibbon, Edward ....IV, 193
Priestley, Joseph........IV, 445
YOUNG, CHARLES MAYNE,
Wordsworth, William......V, 607
YOUNG, DAVID,
Law, William...........III, 429
YOUNG, EDWARD,
Addison, Joseph......II, 648, 654
Authors and Authorship......
....................VIII, 6
Congreve, William........II, 734
Dryden, John...........II, 496
Knowledge................V, 6
Philips, Ambrose.........III, 273
Pope, Alexander.........III, 182
Shakespeare, William......I, 551
Swift, Jonathan.........III, 199
Thomson, James.........III, 254
Tickell, Thomas.........III, 104
Young, Edward..........III, 486
YOUNG, GERTRUDE JULIAN,
Scott, Sir Walter......V, 150, 151
YOUNG, SIR GEORGE,
Praed, Winthrop Mackworth V, 333
YOUNG, JAMES ANTHONY,
Froude, James Anthony.....
....................VIII, 262

YOUNG, JOHN RUSSELL.
Dickens, Charles..........VI, 560
Greeley, Horace..........VI, 672
Prentice, George Denison..VI, 604
Whitman, Walt.........VIII, 132
YOUNG, MATTHEW,
Macpherson, James........IV, 274
YULE, H.,
Mandeville, Sir John.........I, 97

ZABRISKIE, FRANCIS NICOLL,
Greeley, Horace..........VI, 671
ZANGWILL, ISAAC,
Du Maurier, George.....VIII, 345
ZIMMERN, HELEN,
Edgeworth, Maria..V, 566, 566, 570
ZOLNAY, GEORGE JULIAN,
Poe, Edgar Allen..........V, 546
ZOUCH, THOMAS,
Boyle, Robert............II, 417
Hakluyt, Richard..........I, 446
Sidney, Sir Philip..........I, 325
Walton, Isaac............II, 348
ZUMBINI, BONAVENTURA,
Bunyan, John............II, 396
ANONYMOUS.
Bryant, William Cullen...VII, 116
Burns, Robert............IV, 235
Butler, Joseph...........III, 307
Chaucer, Geoffrey..........I, 135
Churchyard, Thomas........I, 417
Cibber, Theophilus.......III, 396
Cobbett, William..........V, 270
Constable, Henry..........I, 444
Daniel, Samuel...........I, 615
Davies, Sir John..........I, 634
Drayton, Michael..........I, 706
Dryden, John............II, 463
D'Urfey, Thomas..........II, 686
Fielding, Henry.........III, 339
Granger, James..........III, 498
Green, John Richard.....VII, 506
Hearne, Thomas...........II, 89
Henley, William Ernest..VIII, 491
Herrick, Robert......II, 235, 235
Hill, John..............III, 645
Johnson, Samuel.........III, 753
Jonson, Ben..............I, 758
Lodge, Thomas............I, 626
Marlowe, Christopher......I, 346
Marston, John............I, 736
Nashe, Thomas............I, 413
Otway, Thomas...........II, 366
Pope, Alexander.........III, 145
Shadwell, Thomas........II, 434
Shakespeare, William...I, 454, 523
Shelley, Percy Bysshe........
..............IV, 701, 701, 704